CAME TO US

From the first disciples
the Word of God began to
spread throughout the
Roman Empire

GREEK

The first translation
from the Hebrew
was the Septuagint

New Testament Writings

LATIN

3rd—6th CENTURIES

The first Christian
missionaries came to
England bringing the
Bible in Latin.
In the Dark Ages the
monasteries remained
centres of learning

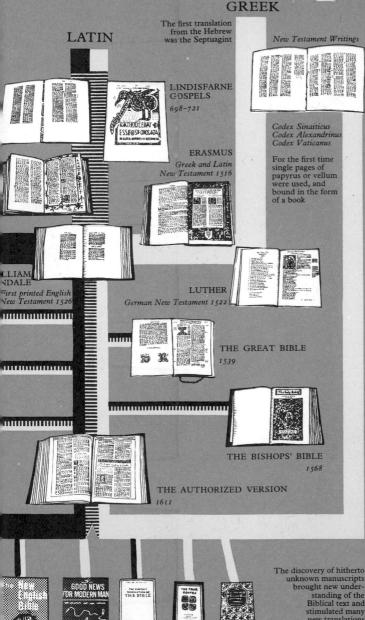

LINDISFARNE
GOSPELS
698-721

Codex Sinaiticus
Codex Alexandrinus
Codex Vaticanus

For the first time
single pages of
papyrus or vellum
were used, and
bound in the form
of a book

12th—15th CENTURIES

In the parish churches and
great cathedrals Biblical
truths were conveyed to
an illiterate age in
stained glass,
paintings and sculpture

ERASMUS
Greek and Latin
New Testament 1516

15th CENTURY

Scholars fleeing from
Constantinople in 1453
brought the Greek text
of the Bible to the West

LUTHER
German New Testament 1522

WILLIAM
TYNDALE
First printed English
New Testament 1526

16th CENTURY

From the Elizabethan era
the Bible belonged
to the English home

THE GREAT BIBLE
1539

17th CENTURY

King James the First
commissioned scholars
to translate the
Authorized Version

THE BISHOPS' BIBLE
1568

THE AUTHORIZED VERSION
1611

18th & 19th CENTURIES

The influence of the Bible
led to social reform,
by Wilberforce, Fry,
Shaftesbury and others.
Popular education and
the spread of literacy
throughout the world
created a new urgency
for books

The discovery of hitherto
unknown manuscripts
brought new under-
standing of the
Biblical text and
stimulated many
new translations

New English Bible 1970

20th CENTURY

Modern technology and
science are being
applied to the
new discoveries of
Biblical sources

New
English
Bible

GOOD NEWS
FOR MODERN MAN

THE MOFFATT
TRANSLATION OF
THE BIBLE

THE FOUR
GOSPELS

This Bible

is for

Garry Menzel

to use at school

and when he leaves

THE NEW
ENGLISH BIBLE

THE BIBLE

A NEW ENGLISH TRANSLATION

Directed by Representatives of

THE BAPTIST UNION OF GREAT BRITAIN AND IRELAND

THE CHURCH OF ENGLAND

THE CHURCH OF SCOTLAND

THE COUNCIL OF CHURCHES FOR WALES

THE IRISH COUNCIL OF CHURCHES

THE LONDON YEARLY MEETING OF
THE SOCIETY OF FRIENDS

THE METHODIST CHURCH OF GREAT BRITAIN

THE ROMAN CATHOLIC CHURCH IN
ENGLAND AND WALES

THE ROMAN CATHOLIC CHURCH IN IRELAND

THE ROMAN CATHOLIC CHURCH
IN SCOTLAND

THE UNITED REFORMED CHURCH

THE BRITISH AND FOREIGN BIBLE SOCIETY

THE NATIONAL BIBLE SOCIETY OF SCOTLAND

THE NEW ENGLISH BIBLE

WITH ILLUSTRATIONS .BY
HORACE KNOWLES

THE BIBLE SOCIETIES
in association with
OXFORD UNIVERSITY PRESS
CAMBRIDGE UNIVERSITY PRESS

Text and notes of The New English Bible
©
THE DELEGATES OF THE OXFORD UNIVERSITY PRESS
AND
THE SYNDICS OF THE CAMBRIDGE UNIVERSITY PRESS
1961, 1970

The New Testament
First edition 1961
Second edition 1970

The Old Testament
First published 1970

This edition first published 1972
Editorial arrangement, section headings
and illustrations
© *The British and Foreign Bible Society* 1972
Fourth Impression 1974

The British and Foreign Bible Society
146 Queen Victoria Street, London EC4V 4BX

The National Bible Society of Scotland
5 St. Andrew Square, Edinburgh EH2 2BL

PRINTED IN GREAT BRITAIN
AT THE UNIVERSITY PRESS, OXFORD
BY VIVIAN RIDLER
PRINTER TO THE UNIVERSITY

BFBS-1974-100M-BN53P   ISBN 0 564 00201 1

PREFACE

TO THE NEW ENGLISH BIBLE

In May 1946 the General Assembly of the Church of Scotland received an overture from the Presbytery of Stirling and Dunblane, where it had been initiated by the Reverend G. S. Hendry, recommending that a translation of the Bible be made in the language of the present day, inasmuch as the language of the Authorized Version, already archaic when it was made, had now become even more definitely archaic and less generally understood. The General Assembly resolved to make an approach to other Churches, and, as a result, delegates of the Church of England, the Church of Scotland, and the Methodist, Baptist, and Congregational Churches met in conference in October. They recommended that the work should be undertaken; that a completely new translation should be made, rather than a revision, such as had earlier been contemplated by the University Presses of Oxford and Cambridge; and that the translators should be free to employ a contemporary idiom rather than reproduce the traditional 'biblical' English.

In January 1947 a second conference, held like the first in the Central Hall, Westminster, included representatives of the University Presses. At the request of this conference, the Churches named above appointed representatives to form the Joint Committee on the New Translation of the Bible. This Committee met for the first time in July of the same year. By January 1948, when its third meeting was held, invitations to be represented had been sent to the Presbyterian Church of England, the Society of Friends, the Churches in Wales, the Churches in Ireland, the British and Foreign Bible Society, and the National Bible Society of Scotland: these invitations were accepted. At a much later stage the hierarchies of the Roman Catholic Church in England and Scotland accepted an invitation to appoint representatives, and these attended as observers.

The Joint Committee provided for the actual work of translation from the original tongues by appointing three panels, to deal, respectively, with the Old Testament, the Apocrypha, and the New Testament. Their members were scholars drawn from various British universities, whom the Committee believed to be representative of competent biblical scholarship at the present time. Apprehending, however, that sound scholarship does not necessarily carry with it a delicate sense of English style, the Committee appointed a fourth panel, of trusted literary advisers, to whom all the work of the translating panels was to be submitted for scrutiny. It should be said that denominational considerations played no part in the appointment of the panels.

The Joint Committee issued general directions to the panels, in pursuance of the aims which the enterprise had in view. The translating panels adopted the following procedure. An individual was invited to submit a draft translation of a particular book, or group of books. Normally he would be a member of the panel concerned. Very occasionally a draft translation was invited from a scholar outside the panel, who was known to have worked specially on the book in question. The draft was circulated in typescript to members of the panel for their consideration. They then met together and discussed the draft round a table, verse by verse, sentence by sentence. Each member brought his view about the meaning of the original to the judgement of his fellows, and discussion went on until they reached a common mind. There are passages where, in the present state of our knowledge, no one could say with certainty which of two (or even more) possible meanings is intended. In such cases, after careful discussion, alternative meanings have been recorded in footnotes, but only where they seemed of sufficient importance. There is probably no member of a panel who has not found himself obliged to give up, perhaps with lingering regret, a cherished view about the meaning of this or that difficult passage, but in the end the panel accepted corporate responsibility for the interpretation set forth in the translation adopted.

The resultant draft was now remitted to the panel of literary advisers. They scrutinized it, once again, verse by verse, sentence by sentence, and took pains to secure, as best they could, the tone and level of language appropriate to the different kinds of writing to be found in the Bible, whether narrative, familiar discourse, argument, law, rhetoric or poetry. The translation thus amended was returned to the translating panel, who examined it to make sure that the meaning intended had not been in any way misunderstood. Passages of peculiar difficulty might on occasion pass repeatedly between the panels. The final form of the version was reached by agreement between the translators concerned and the literary advisers. It was then ready for submission to the Joint Committee.

Since January 1948 the Joint Committee has met regularly twice a year in the Jerusalem Chamber, Westminster Abbey, with four exceptions during 1954-5 when the Langham Room in the precincts of the Abbey was kindly made available. At these meetings the Committee has received reports on the progress of the work from the Conveners of the four panels, and its members have had in their hands typescripts of the books so far translated and revised. They have made such comments and given such advice or decisions as they judged to be necessary, and from time to time they have met members of the panels in conference.

Of the original members of the panels most have happily been able to stay with the work all through, though some have been lost, through death or otherwise, and their places have been filled by fresh appointments.

The Committee has warmly appreciated the courteous hospitality of the Dean of Westminster and of the Trustees of the Central Hall. We owe a great debt to the support and the experienced counsel of the University Presses of Oxford and Cambridge. We recognize gratefully the service rendered to the enterprise by the Reverend Dr. G. S. Hendry and the Reverend Professor J. K. S. Reid, who have successively held the office of Secretary to the Committee. To those who have borne special responsibility, as Chairmen of the Joint Committee, we owe more than could readily be told. Dr. J. W. Hunkin, Bishop of Truro, our first Chairman, brought to the work an exuberant vigour and initiative without which the formidable project might hardly have got off the ground at all. On his lamented death in 1950 he was succeeded by Dr. A. T. P. Williams, then Bishop of Durham and subsequently Bishop of Winchester, who for eighteen years guided our enterprise with judicious wisdom, tact, and benign firmness, but who to our sorrow died when the end of the task was in sight. To both of these we would put on record the gratitude of the Committee and of all engaged in the enterprise.

If we embarked on mentioning the names of those who have served on the various committees and panels, the list would be a long one; and if we mentioned some and not others, the selection would be an invidious one. There are, nevertheless, three names the omission of which would be utterly wrong. As Vice-Chairman and Director, Dr. C. H. Dodd has from start to finish given outstanding leadership and guidance to the project, bringing to the work scholarship, sensitivity, and an ever watchful eye. Professor Sir Godfrey Driver, Joint Director since 1965, has also brought to the work a wealth of knowledge and wisdom; to his enthusiasm, tenacity of purpose, and unflagging devotion the whole enterprise is greatly indebted. Professor W. D. McHardy, Deputy Director since 1968, has made an invaluable contribution particularly, but by no means exclusively, in the sphere of the Apocrypha. It is right that the names of these three scholars should always be associated with The New English Bible. Our debt to them is incalculably great.

DONALD EBOR:
Chairman of the Joint Committee

1970

CONTENTS

CONTENTS

THE NEW TESTAMENT

INTRODUCTION
TO THIS EDITION

THE Bible consists of a collection of books which were written over a very long period of time, in Hebrew, Aramaic, and Greek. The earliest parts of the Old Testament go back more than three thousand years, while the latest portions of it were written a thousand years later, some centuries before the New Testament.

The Bible here appears in a new translation, the New English Bible, which, as the Preface to this volume explains, is not a revision of any previous version, but was made direct from the original languages into contemporary English.

The two basic questions facing the translators were: 'What do we translate?' and 'How do we translate it?' In the first place, an attempt must be made to ensure that what is translated is what was intended by the first writer, in spite of the centuries of copying by hand that have intervened between his own time and the invention of printing.

The Old Testament

In the Old Testament the translators have used as the basis for their work the Hebrew text printed in the 1937 edition of R. Kittel's *Biblia Hebraica*. This is a standard printed edition of the Hebrew Scriptures regularly used by scholars in all countries. It reproduces the text of a Hebrew manuscript dated A.D. 1008, now in Leningrad, which is the earliest complete dated manuscript of the Hebrew Bible extant. A few undated manuscripts of portions of the Old Testament are a century or so older, and there are many fragments that are older still; but until modern times these were thought to be the oldest manuscripts of the Hebrew Bible in existence. In and since 1947, however, much older Hebrew manuscripts have been found in caves at Qumran, near the Dead Sea; they are commonly called the Dead Sea Scrolls. They include two copies of Isaiah and parts of all the other books of the Old Testament except Esther. Some of these Scrolls are up to two thousand years old, and so are much older than the Hebrew texts on which earlier translations of the Old Testament have been based. This recently discovered material has been referred to constantly in preparing the present translation.

At first, Hebrew was written with consonants only, but in course of time dots and strokes were added to indicate the pronunciation of the vowels. There are no such vowel-signs in the Dead Sea Scrolls, as the system was a later development. In this translation, and in most English Bibles, God is frequently referred to as 'the LORD'. This title (when printed thus in capitals) stands for the four Hebrew consonants YHWH which represent the name of the God of Israel. This name was considered too sacred to be pronounced, and the expression 'my Lord' was substituted for it in reading, though the consonants still had to be written. Along with these consonants the vowels for 'my Lord' were inserted. The mixture of the vowels of one word (which had to be read) and the consonants of another (which had to be written, but could not be read out) produced the word 'Jehovah'. This has been used in six places in Exodus, where a name for God, rather than a title, seems most appropriate and there is a footnote explaining why it occurs. It is also used in some footnotes and in combination with other words in some proper names. Elsewhere 'the LORD' is used, as in other English Bibles.

Even before the Scrolls were first copied out, the work of translating the Old Testament from Hebrew into other languages had already started. The Greek translation, known as the Septuagint, was begun in the third century B.C., for the benefit of Greek-speaking Jews in Egypt. Manuscripts of this translation still exist which are much earlier than any Hebrew manuscripts other than the Dead Sea Scrolls. The Greek translation was the first of many such 'ancient versions', which included the Old Latin, the Aramaic Targums, the Syriac (known as the Peshitta), and the Latin Vulgate. These versions provide the modern translator with hints which may help him to recover the early form of the Hebrew text from which the versions were made.

Sometimes, however, both Hebrew text and ancient versions are so obscure that the translators had to put what they supposed, to the best of their judgement, was originally written. Places where this occurs are indicated in the footnotes of this edition by the abbreviation 'Prob. rdg.' standing for 'Probable reading', but in all such cases the literal meaning of the Hebrew text is also given. Since footnotes in this edition are kept to a minimum, there is no indication of a departure from the traditional Hebrew text if the translators' reading has the support of a Dead Sea Scroll or of an ancient version, or if it involves an alteration only of the vowels of the Hebrew (which, as we have seen, were supplied later) but not the consonants. Here and there, the order of the verses has been changed, but the numbering of the verses will make it clear where such changes have taken place, and wherever necessary a footnote is given.

The headings of the Psalms, although forming part of the traditional text of the Old Testament and commonly printed in English Bibles, have been omitted; they are almost certainly not original. On the other hand, as a footnote explains, the identity of the speakers in the Song of Songs has been indicated.

The New Testament

The translators of the New Testament faced a complex situation with regard to the Greek original. No text today commands the same degree of general acceptance as did that underlying the Revised Version at the time of its appearance in 1881. The translators have assessed the evidence coming from three sources, (a) ancient manuscripts of the New Testament in Greek, (b) manuscripts of early translations into other languages, and (c) quotations from the New Testament by early Christian writers, and have in each passage selected for translation the reading which in their judgement seemed most likely to represent what the author wrote. In the footnotes they have recorded other readings which seemed to deserve consideration, referring to the three sources of evidence as 'witnesses'. The Greek text which they followed has since been published in *The Greek New Testament*, edited by R. V. G. Tasker (Oxford and Cambridge University Presses, 1964).

Since the revision of 1881 our knowledge of the Greek used in the New Testament has been greatly enriched by the discovery of many thousands of papyrus documents in popular Greek of the New Testament period. These have given a better appreciation of the finer shades of idiom, which sometimes clarifies the meaning of passages in the New Testament.

The New Testament of the New English Bible was first published in 1961. In this second edition, embodied in the complete Bible in 1970, a number of modifications have been introduced, mostly in minor details. Old Testament passages quoted in the New have been harmonized with the present version of the Old Testament where this seemed desirable and practicable; but where the Greek is not an exact equivalent of the Hebrew, the translators have rendered the Greek that was before them.

The English of the N.E.B.

The second basic question facing the translators was how to express in English the meaning of the text. The translators of the New English Bible were under no such restrictions as earlier revisers had been in their choice of language. They were instructed to replace constructions and idioms of the biblical languages by those of contemporary English. It was not enough to substitute for Hebrew or Greek words English words more or less equivalent. Each word has its own area of meaning, and in different languages these rarely coincide exactly. Instead of trying to render the

same word of the original everywhere by the same English word, the present translators were free to exploit a wide range of English words covering a similar area of
meaning in order to carry over the meaning of the sentence as a whole. They have
sought to say in their own native idiom what they believed the author to be saying
in his, and to use the natural English of the present day, avoiding archaism, jargon,
and stilted or slipshod speech.

The Present Edition

This particular edition of the New English Bible is designed to help readers to
understand a little of the background of the Bible. There are maps, often illustrating
particular journeys, and milestones to mark distances. There are sketches of people,
animals, plants, and different kinds of country-side and of various objects like
altars and temples, houses and ships, books and tools. Some drawings, like that of
the Book of the Law, are repeated to emphasize the unity and coherence of the
sixty-six books which make up our Bible. Often no caption is needed for a picture,
as the verses next to it both explain it and are illustrated by it.

While the text used is that of the New English Bible, without change and with the
footnotes of the Standard Edition, one new feature is the inclusion of more frequent
section headings, to aid the reader in following the main themes and in finding some
particular passage he may be looking for.

Another feature of this edition is the use of two different sizes of type in the text
of some books of the Old Testament. Considerable passages are made up of historical and legal documents, lists of names, genealogies and the like; these are a
real part of God's revelation in the Bible, but they are often of interest to the special-
ist rather than to the general reader. Such passages have been put in smaller type,
but the main narrative and message of the Book continue throughout in larger type.

1972

LIST OF MAPS AND PLANS

THE OLD TESTAMENT

LIST OF MAPS AND PLANS

THE NEW TESTAMENT

THE
OLD TESTAMENT

GUIDE TO THE NOTES

THE footnotes in this edition of the Old Testament serve (*a*) to give cross-references to parallel passages, chiefly in the historical books, (*b*) to indicate where verses or parts of verses have been transposed, (*c*) to give the meaning of proper names where it appears to be reflected in the context, (*d*) to give an alternative interpretation where the Hebrew is capable of such, and (*e*) to indicate places where the translators have adopted what seemed to them the most probable correction of the text where the Hebrew and the ancient versions cannot be convincingly translated as they stand.

Unless otherwise indicated by its wording, a note refers to the single word against which the reference is placed.

ABBREVIATIONS, ETC.

I. GENERAL

Aram.	Aramaic (text or word)
ch(*s*).	chapter(s)
cp.	compare
Heb.	Hebrew (text or word)
mng.	meaning
MS(*S*).	manuscript(s)
om.	omit(s)
or	indicating an alternative interpretation
poss.	possible
prob.	probable
rdg.	reading
Sept.	Septuagint (Greek version of the Old Testament)

[. . .]	In the text itself square brackets are used to indicate words that are probably late additions to the Hebrew text.

II. BOOKS OF THE OLD TESTAMENT

Gen.	Genesis	*1 Sam.*	1 Samuel
Exod.	Exodus	*2 Sam.*	2 Samuel
Lev.	Leviticus	*1 Kgs.*	1 Kings
Num.	Numbers	*2 Kgs.*	2 Kings
Deut.	Deuteronomy	*1 Chr.*	1 Chronicles
Josh.	Joshua	*2 Chr.*	2 Chronicles
Judg.	Judges	*Ezra*	Ezra
Ruth	Ruth	*Neh.*	Nehemiah

Esther	Esther	*Joel*	Joel
Job	Job	*Amos*	Amos
Ps(s).	Psalm(s)	*Obad.*	Obadiah
Prov.	Proverbs	*Jonah*	Jonah
Eccles.	Ecclesiastes	*Mic.*	Micah
S. of S.	Song of Songs	*Nahum*	Nahum
Isa.	Isaiah	*Hab.*	Habakkuk
Jer.	Jeremiah	*Zeph.*	Zephaniah
Lam.	Lamentations	*Hag.*	Haggai
Ezek.	Ezekiel	*Zech.*	Zechariah
Dan.	Daniel	*Mal.*	Malachi
Hos.	Hosea		

MARGINAL NUMBERS

THE conventional verse divisions in the Old Testament are based on those in Hebrew manuscripts. Nevertheless any system of division into numbered verses is foreign to the spirit of this translation, which is intended to convey the meaning in natural English—the prose in paragraphs, the poetic passages in lines corresponding to the structure of the Hebrew.

For purposes of reference, and of comparison with other translations, verse numbers are placed in the margin opposite the line in which the first word belonging to the verse in question appears. Sometimes, however, successive verses are combined in a continuous translation, so that the precise point where a new verse begins cannot be fixed; in these cases the verse numbers, joined by a hyphen, are placed at the point where the passage begins.

HK

GENESIS

God creates the world

1 IN THE BEGINNING of creation,
2 when God made heaven and earth,*a* the
earth was without form and void, with darkness over the face of the abyss, and a mighty
wind that swept*b* over the surface of the
3 waters. God said, 'Let there be light', and
4 there was light; and God saw that the light
was good, and he separated light from dark-
5 ness. He called the light day, and the darkness night. So evening came, and morning
came, the first day.
6   God said, 'Let there be a vault between
the waters, to separate water from water.'
7 So God made the vault, and separated the
water under the vault from the water above
8 it, and so it was; and God called the vault
heaven. Evening came, and morning came,
a second day.
9   God said, 'Let the waters under heaven
be gathered into one place, so that dry land
10 may appear'; and so it was. God called the
dry land earth, and the gathering of the
waters he called seas; and God saw that it
11 was good. Then God said, 'Let the earth
produce fresh growth, let there be on the
earth plants bearing seed, fruit-trees bearing
fruit each with seed according to its kind.'
12 So it was; the earth yielded fresh growth,
plants bearing seed according to their kind
and trees bearing fruit each with seed according to its kind; and God saw that it was good.
13 Evening came, and morning came, a third
day.

God said, 'Let there be lights in the vault 14
of heaven to separate day from night, and
let them serve as signs both for festivals and
for seasons and years. Let them also shine 15
in the vault of heaven to give light on earth.'
So it was; God made the two great lights, 16
the greater to govern the day and the lesser
to govern the night; and with them he made
the stars. God put these lights in the vault 17
of heaven to give light on earth, to govern 18
day and night, and to separate light from
darkness; and God saw that it was good.
Evening came, and morning came, a fourth 19
day.
God said, 'Let the waters teem with count- 20
less living creatures, and let birds fly above
the earth across the vault of heaven.' God 21
then created the great sea-monsters and all
living creatures that move and swarm in the
waters, according to their kind, and every
kind of bird; and God saw that it was good.
So he blessed them and said, 'Be fruitful and 22
increase, fill the waters of the seas; and let
the birds increase on land.' Evening came, 23
and morning came, a fifth day.
God said, 'Let the earth bring forth living 24
creatures, according to their kind: cattle,
reptiles, and wild animals, all according to
their kind.' So it was; God made wild ani- 25
mals, cattle, and all reptiles, each according
to its kind; and he saw that it was good.
Then God said, 'Let us make man in our 26
image and likeness to rule the fish in the sea,
the birds of heaven, the cattle, all wild animals on earth, and all reptiles that crawl

a Or In the beginning God created heaven and earth.   *b Or* and the spirit of God hovering.

I

27 upon the earth.' So God created man in his own image; in the image of God he created
28 him; male and female he created them. God blessed them and said to them, 'Be fruitful and increase, fill the earth and subdue it, rule over the fish in the sea, the birds of heaven, and every living thing that moves
29 upon the earth.' God also said, 'I give you all plants that bear seed everywhere on earth, and every tree bearing fruit which
30 yields seed: they shall be yours for food. All green plants I give for food to the wild animals, to all the birds of heaven, and to all reptiles on earth, every living creature.'
31 So it was; and God saw all that he had made, and it was very good. Evening came, and morning came, a sixth day.

2 Thus heaven and earth were completed
2 with all their mighty throng. On the sixth day God completed all the work he had been doing, and on the seventh day he ceased
3 from all his work. God blessed the seventh day and made it holy, because on that day he ceased from all the work he had set himself to do.
4 This is the story of the making of heaven and earth when they were created.

Garden of Eden

When the LORD God made earth and heaven,
5 there was neither shrub nor plant growing wild upon the earth, because the LORD God had sent no rain on the earth; nor was there
6 any man to till the ground. A flood*c* used to rise out of the earth and water all the sur-
7 face of the ground. Then the LORD God formed a man*d* from the dust of the ground*e* and breathed into his nostrils the breath of life. Thus the man became a living creature.
8 Then the LORD God planted a garden in Eden away to the east, and there he put the
9 man whom he had formed. The LORD God made trees spring from the ground, all trees pleasant to look at and good for food; and in the middle of the garden he set the tree of life and the tree of the knowledge of good and evil.
10 There was a river flowing from Eden to water the garden, and when it left the garden
11 it branched into four streams. The name of the first is Pishon; that is the river which encircles all the land of Havilah, where the
12 gold*f* is. The gold*f* of that land is good; bdellium*g* and cornelians are also to be
13 found there. The name of the second river is Gihon; this is the one which encircles all
14 the land of Cush. The name of the third is Tigris; this is the river which runs east of Asshur. The fourth river is the Euphrates.
15 The LORD God took the man and put him in the garden of Eden to till it and care

for it. He told the man, 'You may eat from 16 every tree in the garden, but not from the 17 tree of the knowledge of good and evil; for on the day that you eat from it, you will certainly die.' Then the LORD God said, 'It 18 is not good for the man to be alone. I will provide a partner for him.' So God formed 19 out of the ground all the wild animals and all the birds of heaven. He brought them to the man to see what he would call them, and whatever the man called each living creature, that was its name. Thus the man 20 gave names to all cattle, to the birds of heaven, and to every wild animal; but for the man himself no partner had yet been found. And so the LORD God put the man 21 into a trance, and while he slept, he took one of his ribs and closed the flesh over the place. The LORD God then built up the rib, 22 which he had taken out of the man, into a woman. He brought her to the man, and 23 the man said:

'Now this, at last—
bone from my bones,
flesh from my flesh!—
this shall be called woman,*h*
for from man*i* was this taken.'

That is why a man leaves his father and 24 mother and is united to his wife, and the two become one flesh. Now they were both 25 naked, the man and his wife, but they had no feeling of shame towards one another.

Man's disobedience

The serpent was more crafty than any wild **3** creature that the LORD God had made. He said to the woman, 'Is it true that God has forbidden you to eat from any tree in the garden?' The woman answered the serpent, 2 'We may eat the fruit of any tree in the garden, except for the tree in the middle of the garden; God has forbidden us either to eat or to touch the fruit of that; if we do, we shall die.' The serpent said, 'Of course you 4 will not die. God knows that as soon as you 5 eat it, your eyes will be opened and you will be like gods*j* knowing both good and evil.' When the woman saw that the fruit of the 6 tree was good to eat, and that it was pleasing

---

c Or mist.   *d Heb.* adam.   *e Heb.* adamah.   *f Or* frankincense.   *g Or* gum resin.
h Heb. ishshah.   *i Heb.* ish.   *j Or* God.

to the eye and tempting to contemplate, she took some and ate it. She also gave her hus-
7 band some and he ate it. Then the eyes of both of them were opened and they dis-covered that they were naked; so they stitched fig-leaves together and made them-selves loincloths.

8 The man and his wife heard the sound of the LORD God walking in the garden at the time of the evening breeze and hid from the LORD God among the trees of the garden.
9 But the LORD God called to the man and
10 said to him, 'Where are you?' He replied, 'I heard the sound as you were walking in the garden, and I was afraid because I was
11 naked, and I hid myself.' God answered, 'Who told you that you were naked? Have you eaten from the tree which I forbade
12 you?' The man said, 'The woman you gave me for a companion, she gave me fruit from
13 the tree and I ate it.' Then the LORD God said to the woman, 'What is this that you have done?' The woman said, 'The serpent
14 tricked me, and I ate.' Then the LORD God said to the serpent:

'Because you have done this you are accursed more than all cattle and all wild creatures.
On your belly you shall crawl, and dust you shall eat
all the days of your life.
15 I will put enmity between you and the woman,
between your brood and hers.
They shall strike at your head,
and you shall strike at their heel.'

16 To the woman he said:

'I will increase your labour and your groan-ing,
and in labour you shall bear children.
You shall be eager[k] for your husband,
and he shall be your master.'

17 And to the man he said:

'Because you have listened to your wife
and have eaten from the tree which I forbade you,
accursed shall be the ground on your account.
With labour you shall win your food from it all the days of your life.
18 It will grow thorns and thistles for you,
none but wild plants for you to eat.

You shall gain your bread by the sweat of 19
your brow
until you return to the ground;
for from it you were taken.
Dust you are, to dust you shall return.'

The man called his wife Eve[l] because she 20 was the mother of all who live. The LORD 21 God made tunics of skins for Adam and his wife and clothed them. He said, 'The man 22 has become like one of us, knowing good and evil; what if he now reaches out his hand and takes fruit from the tree of life also, eats it and lives for ever?' So the LORD 23 God drove him out of the garden of Eden to till the ground from which he had been taken. He cast him out, and to the east of 24 the garden of Eden he stationed the cherubim and a sword whirling and flashing to guard the way to the tree of life.

Cain and Abel

The man lay with his wife Eve, and she con- 4 ceived and gave birth to Cain. She said, 'With the help of the LORD I have brought a man into being.' Afterwards she had an- 2 other child, his brother Abel. Abel was a shepherd and Cain a tiller of the soil. The 3 day came when Cain brought some of the produce of the soil as a gift to the LORD; and Abel brought some of the first-born of 4 his flock, the fat portions of them.[m] The LORD received Abel and his gift with favour; but Cain and his gift he did not receive. Cain 5 was very angry and his face fell. Then the 6 LORD said to Cain, 'Why are you so angry and cast down?

If you do well, you are accepted;[n] 7
if not, sin is a demon crouching at the door.
It shall be eager for you, and you will be mastered by it.'[o]

Cain said to his brother Abel, 'Let us 8 go into the open country.' While they were there, Cain attacked his brother Abel and murdered him. Then the LORD said 9 to Cain, 'Where is your brother Abel?' Cain answered, 'I do not know. Am I my brother's keeper?' The LORD said, 'What 10 have you done? Hark! your brother's blood that has been shed is crying out to me from the ground. Now you are accursed, and ban- 11 ished from[p] the ground which has opened its mouth wide to receive your brother's

k *Or* feel an urge.   l *That is* Life.   m *Or* some of the first-born, that is the sucklings, of his flock.
n *Or* you hold your head up.   o *Or* but you must master it.   p and banished from: *or* more than
(*cp.* 3. 17).

12 blood, which you have shed. When you till the ground, it will no longer yield you its wealth. You shall be a vagrant and a wan-
13 derer on earth.' Cain said to the LORD, 'My punishment is heavier than I can bear;
14 and thou hast driven me today from the ground, and I must hide myself from thy presence. I shall be a vagrant and a wanderer on earth,
15 and anyone who meets me can kill me.' The LORD answered him, 'No: if anyone kills Cain, Cain shall be avenged sevenfold.' So the LORD put a mark on Cain, in order that anyone meeting him should not kill him.
16 Then Cain went out from the LORD's presence and settled in the land of Nod[qr] to the east of Eden.

Cain's descendants

17 Then Cain lay with his wife; and she conceived and bore Enoch. Cain was then building a city, which he named Enoch
18 after his son. Enoch begot Irad; Irad begot Mehujael; Mehujael begot Methushael; Methushael begot Lamech.

19 Lamech married two wives, one named
20 Adah and the other Zillah. Adah bore Jabal who was the ancestor of herdsmen who live
21 in tents; and his brother's name was Jubal; he was the ancestor of those who play the
22 harp and pipe. Zillah, the other wife, bore Tubal-cain, the master of all coppersmiths and blacksmiths, and Tubal-cain's sister
23 was Naamah. Lamech said to his wives:

'Adah and Zillah, listen to me;
wives of Lamech, mark what I say:
I kill a man for wounding me,
a young man for a blow.
Cain may be avenged seven times,　24
but Lamech seventy-seven.'

Seth

25 Adam lay with his wife again. She bore a son, and named him Seth,[s] 'for', she said, 'God has granted me another son in place
26 of Abel, because Cain killed him.' Seth too had a son, whom he named Enosh. At that time men began to invoke the LORD[t] by name.

Adam's descendants

5 This is the record of the descendants of Adam. On the day when God created man he made him in
2 the likeness of God. He created them male and female, and on the day when he created them, he blessed them and called them
3 man. Adam was one hundred and thirty years old when he begot a son in his likeness and image, and
4 named him Seth. After the birth of Seth he lived eight hundred years, and had other sons and
5 daughters. He lived nine hundred and thirty years, and then he died.
6 Seth was one hundred and five years old when he begot Enosh.
7 After the birth of Enosh he lived eight hundred and seven years, and
8 had other sons and daughters. He lived nine hundred and twelve years, and then he died.
9[u] Enosh was ninety years old when
10 he begot Kenan. After the birth of Kenan he lived eight hundred and

11 fifteen years, and had other sons and daughters. He lived nine hundred and five years, and then he
12 died. Kenan was seventy years old
13 when he begot Mahalalel. After the birth of Mahalalel he lived eight hundred and forty years, and
14 had other sons and daughters. He lived nine hundred and ten years, and then he died.
15 Mahalalel was sixty-five years
16 old when he begot Jared. After the birth of Jared he lived eight hundred and thirty years, and had
17 other sons and daughters. He lived eight hundred and ninety-five years, and then he died.
18 Jared was one hundred and sixty-
19 two years old when he begot Enoch. After the birth of Enoch he lived eight hundred years, and had other
20 sons and daughters. He lived nine hundred and sixty-two years, and then he died.
21 Enoch was sixty-five years old
22 when he begot Methuselah. After the birth of Methuselah, Enoch walked with God for three hundred

years, and had other sons and
23 daughters. He lived three hundred
24 and sixty-five years. Having walked with God, Enoch was seen no more, because God had taken him away.
25 Methuselah was one hundred and eighty-seven years old when
26 he begot Lamech. After the birth of Lamech he lived for seven hundred and eighty-two years, and
27 had other sons and daughters. He lived nine hundred and sixty-nine years, and then he died.
28 Lamech was one hundred and eighty-two years old when he be-
29 got a son. He named him Noah, saying, 'This boy will bring us relief from our work, and from the hard labour that has come upon us because of the LORD's curse
30 upon the ground.' After the birth of Noah, he lived for five hundred and ninety-five years, and had
31 other sons and daughters. Lamech lived seven hundred and seventy-
32 seven years, and then he died. Noah was five hundred years old when he begot Shem, Ham and Japheth.

Man's wickedness

6 When mankind began to increase and to spread all over the earth and daughters
2 were born to them, the sons of the gods saw that the daughters of men were beautiful; so they took for themselves such women as
3 they chose. But the LORD said, 'My life-giving spirit shall not remain in man for

---

q *That is* Wandering.　　　r *and settled . . . Nod: or and he lived as a wanderer in the land.*　　　s *That
is* Granted.　　t *This represents the Hebrew consonants* YHWH, *probably pronounced* Yahweh, *but traditionally read as* Jehovah.　　u *Verses 9–32: cp. 1 Chr. 1. 2–4.*

ever; he for his part is mortal flesh: he shall live for a hundred and twenty years.'

4 In those days,[v] when the sons of the gods had intercourse with the daughters of men and got children by them, the Nephilim[w] were on earth. They were the heroes of old, men of renown.

5 When the LORD saw that man had done much evil on earth and that his thoughts 6 and inclinations were always evil, he was sorry that he had made man on earth, and 7 he was grieved at heart. He said, 'This race of men whom I have created, I will wipe them off the face of the earth—man and beast, reptiles and birds. I am sorry that 8 I ever made them.' But Noah had won the LORD's favour.

Noah builds an ark

9 This is the story of Noah. Noah was a righteous man, the one blameless man of 10 his time; he walked with God. He had three 11 sons, Shem, Ham and Japheth. Now God saw that the whole world was corrupt[x] and 12 full of violence. In his sight the world had become corrupted, for all men had lived cor-13 rupt lives on earth. God said to Noah, 'The loathsomeness[y] of all mankind has become plain to me, for through them the earth is full of violence. I intend to destroy them, 14 and the earth with them. Make yourself an ark with ribs of cypress; cover it with reeds 15 and coat it inside and out with pitch. This is to be its plan: the length of the ark shall be three hundred cubits, its breadth fifty 16 cubits, and its height thirty cubits. You shall make a roof for the ark, giving it a fall of one cubit when complete; and put a door in the side of the ark, and build three decks, 17 upper, middle, and lower. I intend to bring the waters of the flood over the earth to destroy every human being under heaven that has the spirit of life; everything on 18 earth shall perish. But with you I will make a covenant, and you shall go into the ark, you and your sons, your wife and your sons' 19 wives with you. And you shall bring living creatures of every kind into the ark to keep them alive with you, two of each kind, a 20 male and a female; two of every kind of bird, beast, and reptile, shall come to you 21 to be kept alive. See that you take and store every kind of food that can be eaten; this 22 shall be food for you and for them.' Exactly as God had commanded him, so Noah did.

The flood

7 The LORD said to Noah, 'Go into the ark, you and all your household; for I have seen that you alone are righteous before me 2 in this generation. Take with you seven pairs, male and female, of all beasts that are ritually clean, and one pair, male and female, of all beasts that are not clean; also 3 seven pairs, male and female, of every bird —to ensure that life continues on earth. In 4 seven days' time I will send rain over the earth for forty days and forty nights, and I will wipe off the face of the earth every living thing that I have made.' Noah did all 5 that the LORD had commanded him. He was 6 six hundred years old when the waters of the flood came upon the earth.

And so, to escape the waters of the flood, 7 Noah went into the ark with his sons, his wife, and his sons' wives. And into the ark 8-9 with Noah went one pair, male and female, of all beasts, clean and unclean, of birds and of everything that crawls on the ground, two by two, as God had commanded. Towards 10 the end of seven days the waters of the flood came upon the earth. In the year when 11 Noah was six hundred years old, on the seventeenth day of the second month, on that very day, all the springs of the great abyss broke through, the windows of the sky were opened, and rain fell on the earth 12 for forty days and forty nights. On that very 13 day Noah entered the ark with his sons, Shem, Ham and Japheth, his own wife, and his three sons' wives. Wild animals of every 14 kind, cattle of every kind, reptiles of every kind that move upon the ground, and birds of every kind—all came to Noah in the ark, 15 two by two of all creatures that had life in them. Those which came were one male and 16 one female of all living things; they came in as God had commanded Noah, and the LORD closed the door on him. The flood 17 continued upon the earth for forty days, and the waters swelled and lifted up the ark so that it rose high above the ground. They 18 swelled and increased over the earth, and the ark floated on the surface of the waters. More and more the waters increased over 19 the earth until they covered all the high mountains everywhere under heaven. The 20 waters increased and the mountains were covered to a depth of fifteen cubits. Every 21 living creature that moves on earth perished, birds, cattle, wild animals, all reptiles, and all mankind. Everything died that had the 22 breath of life in its nostrils, everything on dry land. God wiped out every living thing 23 that existed on earth, man and beast, reptile and bird; they were all wiped out over the whole earth, and only Noah and his company in the ark survived.

After the flood

When the waters had increased over the 24 earth for a hundred and fifty days, God 8

---

v Prob. rdg.; Heb. adds and also afterwards (*cp. Num. 13. 33*).   *w Or* giants.   *x Or* ripe for destruction.   *y Or* end.

thought of Noah and all the wild animals and the cattle with him in the ark, and he made a wind pass over the earth, and the 2 waters began to subside. The springs of the abyss were stopped up, and so were the windows of the sky; the downpour from the 3 skies was checked. The water gradually receded from the earth, and by the end of a hundred and fifty days it had disappeared. 4 On the seventeenth day of the seventh month the ark grounded on a mountain in Ararat. 5 The water continued to recede until the tenth month, and on the first day of the tenth month the tops of the mountains could be seen.

6 After forty days Noah opened the trap- 7 door that he had made in the ark, and released a raven to see whether the water had subsided, but the bird continued flying to and fro until the water on the earth had 8 dried up. Noah waited for seven days,*z* and then he released a dove from the ark to see whether the water on the earth had subsided 9 further. But the dove found no place where she could settle, and so she came back to him in the ark, because there was water over the whole surface of the earth. Noah stretched out his hand, caught her and took 10 her into the ark. He waited another seven days and again released the dove from the 11 ark. She came back to him towards evening with a newly plucked olive leaf in her beak. Then Noah knew for certain that the water 12 on the earth had subsided still further. He waited yet another seven days and released 13 the dove, but she never came back. And so it came about that, on the first day of the first month of his six hundred and first year, the water had dried up on the earth, and Noah removed the hatch and looked out of the ark. The surface of the ground was dry. 14 By the twenty-seventh day of the second 15 month the whole earth was dry. And God 16 said to Noah, 'Come out of the ark, you and your wife, your sons and their wives. 17 Bring out every living creature that is with you, live things of every kind, bird and beast and every reptile that moves on the ground, and let them swarm over the earth 18 and be fruitful and increase there.' So Noah came out with his sons, his wife, and his 19 sons' wives. Every wild animal, all cattle, every bird, and every reptile that moves on

the ground, came out of the ark by families. Then Noah built an altar to the LORD. He 20 took ritually clean beasts and birds of every kind, and offered whole-offerings on the altar. When the LORD smelt the soothing 21 odour, he said within himself, 'Never again will I curse the ground because of man, however evil his inclinations may be from his youth upwards. I will never again kill every living creature, as I have just done.

> While the earth lasts   22
> seedtime and harvest, cold and heat,
> summer and winter, day and night,
> shall never cease.'

God's covenant with Noah

God blessed Noah and his sons and said to **9** them, 'Be fruitful and increase, and fill the earth. The fear and dread of you shall fall 2 upon all wild animals on earth, on all birds of heaven, on everything that moves upon the ground and all fish in the sea; they are given into your hands. Every creature that 3 lives and moves shall be food for you; I give you them all, as once I gave you all green plants. But you must not eat the flesh 4 with the life, which is the blood, still in it. And further, for your life-blood I will 5 demand satisfaction; from every animal I will require it, and from a man also I will require satisfaction for the death of his fellow-man.

> He that sheds the blood of a man,   6
> for that man his blood shall be shed;
> for in the image of God
> has God made man.

But you must be fruitful and increase, 7 swarm throughout the earth and rule*a* over it.'

God spoke to Noah and to his sons with 8 him: 'I now make my covenant with you 9 and with your descendants after you, and 10 with every living creature that is with you, all birds and cattle, all the wild animals with you on earth, all that have come out of the ark. I will make my covenant with you: 11 never again shall all living creatures be destroyed by the waters of the flood, never again shall there be a flood to lay waste the earth.'

God said, 'This is the sign of the covenant 12 which I establish between myself and you

---

z Noah . . . days: *prob. rdg., cp. verse 10; Heb. om.*   *a* Prob. rdg., cp. 1. 28; Heb. increase.

and every living creature with you, to endless generations:

13   My bow I set in the cloud,
      sign of the covenant
      between myself and earth.
14   When I cloud the sky over the earth,
      the bow shall be seen in the cloud.

15 Then will I remember the covenant which I have made between myself and you and living things of every kind. Never again 16 shall the waters become a flood to destroy all living creatures. The bow shall be in the cloud; when I see it, it will remind me of the everlasting covenant between God and 17 living things on earth of every kind.' God said to Noah, 'This is the sign of the covenant which I make between myself and all that lives on earth.'

Noah and his sons

18 The sons of Noah who came out of the ark were Shem, Ham and Japheth; Ham was 19 the father of Canaan. These three were the sons of Noah, and their descendants spread over the whole earth.

20   Noah, a man of the soil, began the plant-21 ing of vineyards. He drank some of the wine, became drunk and lay naked inside his tent. 22 When Ham, father of Canaan, saw his father 23 naked, he told his two brothers outside. So Shem and Japheth took a cloak, put it on their shoulders and walked backwards, and so covered their father's naked body; their faces were turned the other way, so that 24 they did not see their father naked. When Noah woke from his drunken sleep, he learnt what his youngest son had done to 25 him, and said:

    'Cursed be Canaan,
      slave of slaves
      shall he be to his brothers.'

26 And he continued:

    'Bless, O LORD,
      the tents of Shem;*b*
      may Canaan be his slave.
27   May God extend*c* Japheth's bounds,
      let him dwell in the tents of Shem,
      may Canaan be their slave.'

28 After the flood Noah lived for three hun-29 dred and fifty years, and he was nine hundred and fifty years old when he died.

Noah's descendants

10 These are the descendants of the sons of Noah, Shem, Ham and Japheth, the sons born to them after the flood.

2*d*   The sons of Japheth: Gomer, Magog, Madai, Javan,*e* Tubal, Meshech and Tiras.

The sons of Gomer: Ashkenaz, Riphath and 3 Togarmah. The sons of Javan: Elishah, 4 Tarshish, Kittim*f* and Rodanim. From these 5 the peoples of the coasts and islands separated into their own countries, each with their own language, family by family, nation by nation.

The sons of Ham: Cush, Mizraim,*g* Put 6*h* and Canaan. The sons of Cush: Seba, Havil- 7 ah, Sabtah, Raamah and Sabtecha'. The sons of Raamah: Sheba and Dedan. Cush 8 was the father of Nimrod, who began to show himself a man of might on earth; and 9 he was a mighty hunter before the LORD, as the saying goes, 'Like Nimrod, a mighty hunter before the LORD.' His kingdom in 10 the beginning consisted of Babel, Erech, and Accad, all of them in the land of Shinar. From that land he migrated to Asshur 11 and built Nineveh, Rehoboth-Ir, Calah, and 12 Resen, a great city between Nineveh and Calah. From Mizraim sprang the Lydians, 13*i* Anamites, Lehabites, Naphtuhites, Pathrus- 14 ites, Casluhites, and the Caphtorites, from whom the Philistines were descended.

Canaan was the father of Sidon, who was 15 his eldest son, and Heth,*j* the Jebusites, the 16 Amorites, the Girgashites, the Hivites, the 17 Arkites, the Sinites, the Arvadites, the Zem- 18 arites, and the Hamathites. Later the Canaanites spread, and then the Canaanite border 19 ran from Sidon towards Gerar all the way to Gaza; then all the way to Sodom and Gomorrah, Admah and Zeboyim as far as Lasha. These were the sons of Ham, by 20 families and languages with their countries and nations.

Sons were born also to Shem, elder 21 brother of Japheth, the ancestor of all the sons of Eber. The sons of Shem: Elam, 22*k* Asshur, Arphaxad, Lud*l* and Aram. The 23 sons of Aram: Uz, Hul, Gether and Mash. Arphaxad was the father of Shelah, and 24 Shelah the father of Eber. Eber had two 25 sons: one was named Peleg,*m* because in his time the earth was divided; and his brother's name was Joktan. Joktan was the father 26 of Almodad, Sheleph, Hazarmoth, Jerah, Hadoram, Uzal, Diklah, Obal, Abimael, 27 28 Sheba, Ophir, Havilah and Jobab. All these 29 were sons of Joktan. They lived in the eastern 30 hill-country, from Mesha all the way to Sephar. These were the sons of Shem, by 31 families and languages with their countries and nations.

These were the families of the sons of 32 Noah according to their genealogies, nation by nation; and from them came the separate nations on earth after the flood.

---

b Bless . . . Shem: prob. rdg.; Heb. Blessed is the LORD the God of Shem.   *c Heb. japht.*   *d Verses 2–4: cp. 1 Chr. 1. 5–7.*   *e Or Greece.*   *f Or Tarshish of the Kittians.*   *g Or Egypt.*   *h Verses 6–8: cp. 1 Chr. 1. 8–10.*   *i Verses 13–18: cp. 1 Chr. 1. 11–16.*   *j Or the Hittites.*   *k Verses 22–29: cp. 1 Chr. 1. 17–23.*   *l Or the Lydians.*   *m That is Division.*

The tower of Babel

11 Once upon a time all the world spoke a single language and used the same*n* words. ² As men journeyed in the east, they came upon a plain in the land of Shinar and settled ³ there. They said to one another, 'Come, let us make bricks and bake them hard'; they used bricks for stone and bitumen for mortar. 'Come,' they said, 'let us build our- ⁴ selves a city and a tower with its top in the heavens, and make a name for ourselves; or we shall be dispersed all over the earth.' Then the LORD came down to see the city ⁵ and tower which mortal men had built, and ⁶ he said, 'Here they are, one people with a single language, and now they have started to do this; henceforward nothing they have a mind to do will be beyond their reach. Come, let us go down there and confuse ⁷ their speech, so that they will not understand what they say to one another.' So the ⁸ LORD dispersed them from there all over the earth, and they left off building the city. That is why it is called Babel,*o* because the ⁹ LORD there made a babble of the language of all the world; from that place the LORD scattered men all over the face of the earth.

Shem's descendants

10 *p* This is the table of the descendants of Shem. Shem was a hundred years old when he begot Arphaxad, 11 two years after the flood. After the birth of Arphaxad he lived five hundred years, and had other sons 12 and daughters. Arphaxad was thirty-five years old when he begot 13 Shelah. After the birth of Shelah he lived four hundred and three years, and had other sons and daughters.
14 Shelah was thirty years old when 15 he begot Eber. After the birth of Eber he lived four hundred and three years, and had other sons and daughters.
16 Eber was thirty-four years old 17 when he begot Peleg. After the birth of Peleg he lived four hundred and thirty years, and had other sons and daughters.

18 Peleg was thirty years old when 19 he begot Reu. After the birth of Reu he lived two hundred and nine years, and had other sons and daughters.
20 Reu was thirty-two years old 21 when he begot Serug. After the birth of Serug he lived two hundred and seven years, and had other sons and daughters.
22 Serug was thirty years old when 23 he begot Nahor. After the birth of Nahor he lived two hundred years, and had other sons and daughters.
24 Nahor was twenty-nine years old 25 when he begot Terah. After the birth of Terah he lived a hundred and nineteen years, and had other sons and daughters.
26 Terah was seventy years old when he begot Abram, Nahor and Haran.

Terah's descendants

This is the table of the descendants 27 of Terah. Terah was the father of Abram, Nahor and Haran. Haran was the father of Lot. Haran died 28 in the presence of his father in the land of his birth, Ur of the Chaldees. Abram and Nahor married 29 wives; Abram's wife was called Sarai, and Nahor's Milcah. She was Haran's daughter; and he was also the father of Milcah and of Iscah. Sarai was barren; she had 30 no child. Terah took his son 31 Abram, his grandson Lot the son of Haran, and his daughter-in-law Sarai Abram's wife, and they set out from Ur of the Chaldees for the land of Canaan. But when they reached Harran, they settled there. Terah was two hundred and 32 five years old when he died in Harran.

The LORD calls Abram

12 The LORD said to Abram, 'Leave your own country, your kinsmen, and your father's house, and go to a country that I will show you. I will make you into a great nation, I ² will bless you and make your name so great that it shall be used in blessings:

n Or used few.　　*o That is Babylon.*　　*p Verses 10–26: cp. 1 Chr. 1. 24–27.*

3 Those that bless you I will bless,
  those that curse you, I will execrate.
  All the families on earth
  will pray to be blessed as you are blessed.'

4 And so Abram set out as the LORD had bidden him, and Lot went with him. Abram was seventy-five years old when he left
5 Harran. He took his wife Sarai, his nephew Lot, all the property they had collected, and all the dependants they had acquired in Harran, and they started on their journey to
6 Canaan. When they arrived, Abram passed through the country to the sanctuary at Shechem, the terebinth-tree of Moreh. At that time the Canaanites lived in this land.
7 There the LORD appeared to Abram and said, 'I give this land to your descendants.' So Abram built an altar there to the LORD
8 who had appeared to him. Thence he went on to the hill-country east of Bethel and pitched his tent between Bethel on the west and Ai on the east. There he built an altar to the LORD and invoked the LORD by name.
9 Thus Abram journeyed by stages towards the Negeb.

Abram in Egypt

10 There came a famine in the land, so severe that Abram went down to Egypt to live
11 there for a while. When he was approaching Egypt, he said to his wife Sarai, 'I know very well that you are a beautiful woman,
12 and that when the Egyptians see you, they will say, "She is his wife"; then they will
13 kill me but let you live. Tell them that you are my sister, so that all may go well with me because of you and my life may be spared
14 on your account.' When Abram arrived in Egypt, the Egyptians saw that she was in-
15 deed very beautiful. Pharaoh's courtiers saw her and praised her to Pharaoh, and she was taken into Pharaoh's household.
16 He treated Abram well because of her, and Abram came to possess sheep and cattle and asses, male and female slaves, she-asses,
17 and camels. But the LORD struck Pharaoh and his household with grave diseases on
18 account of Abram's wife Sarai. Pharaoh summoned Abram and said to him, 'Why have you treated me like this? Why did you
19 not tell me that she is your wife? Why did you say that she was your sister, so that I took her as a wife? Here she is: take her and
20 be gone.' Then Pharaoh gave his men orders, and they sent Abram away with his wife and all that he had.

Abram and Lot part company

13 Abram went up from Egypt into the Negeb, he and his wife and all that he had, and Lot
2 went with him. Abram was now very rich
3 in cattle and in silver and gold. From the

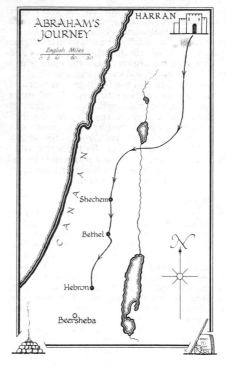

ABRAHAM'S JOURNEY

English Miles

HARRAN

Shechem
Bethel
Hebron
Beersheba

Negeb he journeyed by stages to Bethel, to the place between Bethel and Ai where he had pitched his tent in the beginning, where 4 he had set up an altar on the first occasion and had invoked the LORD by name. Now 5 Lot was travelling with Abram, and he too possessed sheep and cattle and tents. The 6 land could not support them both together; for their livestock were so numerous that they could not settle in the same district, and there were quarrels between Abram's 7 herdsmen and Lot's. The Canaanites and the Perizzites were then living in the land. So Abram said to Lot, 'Let there be no 8 quarrelling between us, between my herdsmen and yours; for we are close kinsmen. The whole country is there in front of you; 9 let us part company. If you go left, I will go right; if you go right, I will go left.' Lot 10 looked up and saw how well-watered the whole Plain of the Jordan was; all the way to Zoar it was like the Garden of the LORD, like the land of Egypt. This was before the LORD had destroyed Sodom and Gomorrah. So Lot chose all the Plain of the Jordan and 11 took the road on the east side. Thus they parted company. Abram settled in the land 12 of Canaan; but Lot settled among the cities

of the Plain and pitched his tents near
13 Sodom. Now the men of Sodom were
wicked, great sinners against the LORD.
14 After Lot and Abram had parted, the
LORD said to Abram, 'Raise your eyes and
look into the distance from the place where
15 you are, north and south, east and west. All
the land you can see I will give to you and
16 to your descendants for ever. I will make
your descendants countless as the dust of
the earth; if anyone could count the dust
upon the ground, then he could count your
17 descendants. Now go through the length
and breadth of the land, for I give it to you.'
18 So Abram moved his tent and settled by the
terebinths of Mamre at Hebron; and there
he built an altar to the LORD.

Abram rescues Lot

14 It was in the time of Amraphel king of
Shinar, Arioch king of Ellasar, Kedorlaomer king of Elam, and Tidal king of
2 Goyim. They went to war against Bera king
of Sodom, Birsha king of Gomorrah, Shinab
king of Admah, Shemeber king of Zeboyim,
3 and the king of Bela, that is Zoar. These
kings joined forces in the valley of Siddim,
4 which is now the Dead Sea. They had been
subject to Kedorlaomer for twelve years,
5 but in the thirteenth year they rebelled. Then
in the fourteenth year Kedorlaomer and his
confederate kings came and defeated the
Rephaim in Ashteroth-karnaim, the Zuzim
in Ham, the Emim in Shaveh-kiriathaim,
6 and the Horites in the hill-country from
Seir*q* as far as El-paran on the edge of the
7 wilderness. On their way back they came to
En-mishpat, which is now Kadesh, and laid
waste all the country of the Amalekites and
also that of the Amorites who lived in
8 Hazazon-tamar. Then the kings of Sodom,
Gomorrah, Admah, Zeboyim, and Bela,
which is now Zoar, marched out and drew
up their forces against them in the valley of
9 Siddim, against Kedorlaomer king of Elam,
Tidal king of Goyim, Amraphel king of
Shinar, and Arioch king of Ellasar, four
10 kings against five. Now the valley of Siddim
was full of bitumen pits; and when the kings
of Sodom and Gomorrah fled, they fell into
them, but the rest escaped to the hill-
11 country. The four kings captured all the
flocks and herds of Sodom and Gomorrah
and all their provisions, and went away.
12 They also carried off Lot, Abram's nephew,
who was living in Sodom, and with him his
13 flocks and herds. But a fugitive came and
told Abram the Hebrew, who at that time
was dwelling by the terebinths of Mamre
the Amorite. This Mamre was the brother
of Eshcol and Aner, who were allies of

Abram. When Abram heard that his kins- 14
man had been taken prisoner, he mustered
his retainers, men born in his household,
three hundred and eighteen of them, and
pursued as far as Dan. Abram and his 15
followers surrounded the enemy by night,
attacked them and pursued them as far as
Hobah, north of Damascus; he then brought 16
back all the flocks and herds and also his
kinsman Lot with his flocks and herds, together with the women and the other captives. On his return from this defeat of 17
Kedorlaomer and his confederate kings, the
king of Sodom came out to meet him in the
valley of Shaveh, which is now the King's
Valley.

Melchizedek blesses Abram

Then Melchizedek king of Salem brought 18
food and wine. He was priest of God Most
High, and he pronounced this blessing on 19
Abram:

'Blessed be Abram
by God Most High,
creator*r* of heaven and earth.
And blessed be God Most High,   20
who has delivered your enemies into your
   power.'
Abram gave him a tithe of all the booty.

The king of Sodom said to Abram, 'Give 21
me the people, and you can take the property'; but Abram said to the king of Sodom, 22
'I lift my hand and swear by the LORD, God
Most High, creator of heaven and earth:
not a thread or a shoe-string will I accept of 23
anything that is yours. You shall never say,
"I made Abram rich." I will accept nothing 24
but what the young men have eaten and
the share of the men who went with me.
Aner, Eshcol, and Mamre shall have their
share.'

The LORD's covenant with Abram

After this the word of the LORD came to **15**
Abram in a vision. He said, 'Do not be
afraid, Abram, I am giving you a very great
reward.'*s* Abram replied, 'Lord GOD, what 2
canst thou give me? I have no standing
among men, for the heir to my household
is Eliezer of Damascus.' Abram continued, 3
'Thou hast given me no children, and so
my heir must be a slave born in my house.'
Then came the word of the LORD to him: 4
'This man shall not be your heir; your heir
shall be a child of your own body.' He took 5
Abram outside and said, 'Look up into the
sky, and count the stars if you can. So
many', he said, 'shall your descendants be.'
Abram put his faith in the LORD, and the 6
LORD counted that faith to him as righteous-

---

q Prob. rdg.; Heb. in their hill-country, Seir.   *r Or* owner.   *s* I am giving . . . reward: *or* I am your
shield, your very great reward.

7 ness; he said to him, 'I am the LORD who brought you out from Ur of the Chaldees
8 to give you this land to occupy.' Abram said, 'O Lord GOD, how can I be sure that
9 I shall occupy it?' The LORD answered, 'Bring me a heifer three years old, a she-goat three years old, a ram three years old,
10 a turtle-dove, and a fledgling.' He brought him all these, halved the animals down the middle and placed each piece opposite its corresponding piece, but he did not halve
11 the birds. When the birds of prey swooped down on the carcasses, Abram scared them
12 away. Then, as the sun was going down, a trance came over Abram and great fear came
13 upon him. The LORD said to Abram, 'Know this for certain, that your descendants will be aliens living in a land that is not theirs; they will be slaves, and will be held in oppres-
14 sion there for four hundred years. But I will punish that nation whose slaves they are, and after that they shall come out with great
15 possessions. You yourself shall join your fathers in peace and be buried in a good old
16 age; and the fourth generation shall return here, for the Amorites will not be ripe for
17 punishment till then.' The sun went down and it was dusk, and there appeared a smok-ing brazier and a flaming torch passing be-
18 tween the divided pieces. That very day the LORD made a covenant with Abram, and he said, 'To your descendants I give this land from the River of Egypt to the Great
19 River, the river Euphrates, the territory of
20 the Kenites, Kenizzites, Kadmonites, Hit-
21 tites, Perizzites, Rephaim, Amorites, Cana-anites, Girgashites, Hivites, and Jebusites.'

Hagar and Ishmael

16 Abram's wife Sarai had borne him no chil-dren. Now she had an Egyptian slave-girl
2 whose name was Hagar, and she said to Abram, 'You see that the LORD has not allowed me to bear a child. Take my slave-girl; perhaps I shall found a family through her.' Abram agreed to what his wife said;
3 so Sarai, Abram's wife, brought her slave-girl, Hagar the Egyptian, and gave her to her husband Abram as a wife.ʳ When this happened Abram had been in Canaan for
4 ten years. He lay with Hagar and she con-ceived; and when she knew that she was
5 with child, she despised her mistress. Sarai said to Abram, 'I have been wronged and you must answer for it. It was I who gave my slave-girl into your arms, but since she has known that she is with child, she has despised me. May the LORD see justice done
6 between you and me.' Abram replied to Sarai, 'Your slave-girl is in your hands;

deal with her as you will.' So Sarai ill-treated her and she ran away.

The angel of the LORD found her by a 7 spring of water in the wilderness on the way to Shur, and he said, 'Hagar, Sarai's slave- 8 girl, where have you come from and where are you going?' She answered, 'I am running away from Sarai my mistress.' The angel of 9 the LORD said to her, 'Go back to your mis-tress and submit to her ill-treatment.' The 10 angel also said, 'I will make your descendants too many to be counted.' And the angel of 11 the LORD said to her:

'You are with child and will bear a son.
You shall name him Ishmael,ᵘ
because the LORD has heard of your ill-treatment.
He shall be a man like the wild ass, 12
his hand against every man
and every man's hand against him;
and he shall live at odds withᵛ all his kins-men.'

She called the LORD who was speaking to 13 her by the name El-Roi,ʷ for she said, 'Have I indeed seen God and still liveˣ after that vision?' That is why men call the well Beer- 14 lahai-roi;ʸ it lies between Kadesh and Bered. Hagar bore Abram a son, and he named 15 the child she bore him Ishmael. Abram 16 was eighty-six years old when Hagar bore Ishmael.

Abram's new name

When Abram was ninety-nine years old, the **17** LORD appeared to him and said, 'I am God Almighty. Live always in my presence and be perfect, so that I may set my covenant 2 between myself and you and multiply your descendants.' Abram threw himself down 3 on his face, and God spoke with him and said, 'I make this covenant, and I make it 4 with you: you shall be the father of a host of nations. Your name shall no longer be 5 Abram,ᶻ your name shall be Abraham,ᵃ for I make you father of a host of nations. I will 6 make you exceedingly fruitful; I will make nations out of you, and kings shall spring from you. I will fulfil my covenant between 7 myself and you and your descendants after you, generation after generation, an ever-lasting covenant, to be your God, yours and your descendants' after you. As an ever- 8 lasting possession I will give you and your descendants after you the land in which you now are aliens, all the land of Canaan, and I will be God to your descendants.'

God said to Abraham, 'For your part, 9 you must keep my covenant, you and your descendants after you, generation by

_t Or_ concubine.   _u That is_ God heard.   _v Or_ live to the east of . . .   _w That is_ God of a vision.
_x_ God and still live: _prob. rdg.; Heb._ hither.   _y That is_ the Well of the Living One of Vision.   _z That is_ High Father.   _a That is_ Father of a Multitude.

10 generation. This is how you shall keep my covenant between myself and you and your descendants after you: circumcise yourselves,
11 every male among you. You shall circumcise the flesh of your foreskin, and it shall be the
12 sign of the covenant between us. Every male among you in every generation shall be circumcised on the eighth day, both those born in your house and any foreigner, not of your blood but bought with your money.
13 Circumcise both those born in your house and those bought with your money; thus shall my covenant be marked in your flesh
14 as an everlasting covenant. Every uncircumcised male, everyone who has not had the flesh of his foreskin circumcised, shall be cut off from the kin of his father. He has broken my covenant.'

Isaac's birth foretold

15 God said to Abraham, 'As for Sarai your wife; you shall call her not Sarai,*b* but Sarah.*c*
16 I will bless her and give you a son by her, I will bless her and she shall be the mother of nations; the kings of many people shall
17 spring from her.' Abraham threw himself down on his face; he laughed and said to himself, 'Can a son be born to a man who is a hundred years old? Can Sarah bear a
18 son when she is ninety?' He said to God, 'If only Ishmael might live under thy special
19 care!' But God replied, 'No. Your wife Sarah shall bear you a son, and you shall call him Isaac.*d* With him I will fulfil my covenant, an everlasting covenant with his
20 descendants after him. I have heard your prayer for Ishmael. I have blessed him and will make him fruitful. I will multiply his descendants; he shall be father of twelve princes, and I will raise a great nation from
21 him. But my covenant I will fulfil with

b *That is* Mockery.   c *That is* Princess.
d *That is* He laughed.

Isaac, whom Sarah will bear to you at this season next year.' When he had finished 22 talking with Abraham, God ascended and left him.

Then Abraham took Ishmael his son, 23 everyone who had been born in his household and everyone bought with money, every male in his household, and he circumcised them that very same day in the flesh of their foreskins as God had told him to do. Abraham was ninety-nine years old 24 when he circumcised the flesh of his foreskin. Ishmael was thirteen years old when 25 he was circumcised in the flesh of his foreskin. Both Abraham and Ishmael were 26 circumcised on the same day, and all the 27 men of his household, born in the house or bought with money from foreigners, were circumcised with him.

The LORD appeared to Abraham by the **18** terebinths of Mamre. As Abraham was sitting at the opening of his tent in the heat of the day, he looked up and saw three men 2 standing in front of him. When he saw them, he ran from the opening of his tent to meet them and bowed low to the ground. 'Sirs,' 3 he said, 'if I have deserved your favour, do not pass by my humble self without a visit. Let me send for some water so that you may 4 wash your feet and rest under a tree; and 5 let me fetch a little food so that you may refresh yourselves. Afterwards you may continue the journey which has brought you my way.' They said, 'Do by all means as

A family encampment

6 you say.' So Abraham hurried into the tent to Sarah and said, 'Take three measures of flour quickly, knead it and make some cakes.'
7 Then Abraham ran to the cattle, chose a fine tender calf and gave it to a servant, who
8 hurriedly prepared it. He took curds and milk and the calf he had prepared, set it before them, and waited on them himself
9 under the tree while they ate. They asked him where Sarah his wife was, and he said,
10 'There, in the tent.' The stranger said, 'About this time next year I will be sure to come back to you, and Sarah your wife shall have a son.' Now Sarah was listening at the opening of the tent, and he was close beside it.
11 Both Abraham and Sarah had grown very old, and Sarah was past the age of child-
12 bearing. So Sarah laughed to herself and said, 'I am past bearing children now that I am out of my time, and my husband is
13 old.' The LORD said to Abraham, 'Why did Sarah laugh and say, "Shall I indeed bear
14 a child when I am old?" Is anything impossible for the LORD? In due season I will come back to you, about this time next year,
15 and Sarah shall have a son.' Sarah lied because she was frightened, and denied that she had laughed; but he said, 'Yes, you did laugh.'

Abraham pleads for Sodom

16 The men set out and looked down towards Sodom, and Abraham went with them to
17 start them on their way. The LORD thought to himself, 'Shall I conceal from Abraham
18 what I intend to do? He will become a great and powerful nation, and all nations on earth will pray to be blessed as he is blessed.
19 I have taken care of him on purpose that he may charge his sons and family after him to conform to the way of the LORD and to do what is right and just; thus I shall fulfil
20 all that I have promised for him.' So the LORD said, 'There is a great outcry over Sodom and Gomorrah; their sin is very
21 grave. I must go down and see whether their deeds warrant the outcry which has reached
22 me. I am resolved to know the truth.' When the men turned and went towards Sodom, Abraham remained standing before the
23 LORD. Abraham drew near him and said, 'Wilt thou really sweep away good and bad
24 together? Suppose there are fifty good men in the city; wilt thou really sweep it away, and not pardon the place because of the
25 fifty good men? Far be it from thee to do this—to kill good and bad together; for then the good would suffer with the bad. Far be it from thee. Shall not the judge of
26 all the earth do what is just?' The LORD said, 'If I find in the city of Sodom fifty good men, I will pardon the whole place
27 for their sake.' Abraham replied, 'May I

presume to speak to the Lord, dust and ashes that I am: suppose there are five short 28 of the fifty good men? Wilt thou destroy the whole city for a mere five men?' He said, 'If I find forty-five there I will not destroy it.' Abraham spoke again, 'Suppose forty 29 can be found there?'; and he said, 'For the sake of the forty I will not do it.' Then 30 Abraham said, 'Please do not be angry, O Lord, if I speak again: suppose thirty can be found there?' He answered, 'If I find thirty there I will not do it.' Abraham con- 31 tinued, 'May I presume to speak to the Lord: suppose twenty can be found there?' He replied, 'For the sake of the twenty I will not destroy it.' Abraham said, 'I pray 32 thee not to be angry, O Lord, if I speak just once more: suppose ten can be found there?' He said, 'For the sake of the ten I will not destroy it.' When the LORD had finished 33 talking with Abraham, he left him, and Abraham returned home.

Destruction of Sodom and Gomorrah

The two angels came to Sodom in the even- 19 ing, and Lot was sitting in the gateway of the city. When he saw them he rose to meet them and bowed low with his face to the ground. He said, 'I pray you, sirs, turn aside 2 to my humble home, spend the night there and wash your feet; you can rise early and continue your journey.' 'No,' they answered, 'we will spend the night in the street.' But 3 Lot was so insistent that they did turn aside and enter his house. He prepared a meal for them, baking unleavened cakes, and they ate them. Before they lay down to sleep, the 4 men of Sodom, both young and old, surrounded the house—everyone without exception. They called to Lot and asked him where 5 the men were who had entered his house that night. 'Bring them out', they shouted, 'so that we can have intercourse with them.'

Lot went out into the doorway to them, 6 closed the door behind him and said, 'No, 7 my friends, do not be so wicked. Look, I 8 have two daughters, both virgins; let me bring them out to you, and you can do what you like with them; but do not touch these men, because they have come under the shelter of my roof.' They said, 'Out of our 9 way! This man has come and settled here as an alien, and does he now take it upon himself to judge us? We will treat you worse than them.' They crowded in on the man Lot and pressed close to smash in the door. But the two men inside reached out, pulled 10 Lot in, and closed the door. Then they 11 struck the men in the doorway with blindness, both small and great, so that they could not find the door.

The two men said to Lot, 'Have you 12 anyone else here, sons-in-law, sons, or

daughters, or any who belong to you in the
13 city? Get them out of this place, because we
are going to destroy it. The outcry against it
has been so great that the LORD has sent us
14 to destroy it.' So Lot went out and spoke to
his intended sons-in-law.ᵉ He said, 'Be
quick and leave this place; the LORD is
going to destroy the city.' But they did not
take him seriously.

15   As soon as it was dawn, the angels urged
Lot to go, saying, 'Be quick, take your wife
and your two daughters who are here, or you
will be swept away when the city is pun-
16 ished.' When he lingered, they took him by
the hand, with his wife and his daughters,
and, because the LORD had spared him, led
17 him on until he was outside the city. When
they had brought them out, they said, 'Flee
for your lives; do not look back and do not
stop anywhere in the Plain. Flee to the hills
18 or you will be swept away.' Lot replied,
19 'No, sirs. You have shown your servant
favour and you have added to your unfailing
care for me by saving my life, but I cannot
escape to the hills; I shall be overtaken by
20 the disaster, and die. Look, here is a town,
only a small place, near enough for me to
reach quickly. Let me escape to it—it is
21 very small—and save my life.' He said to
him, 'I grant your request: I will not over-
22 throw this town you speak of. But flee there
quickly, because I can do nothing until you
are there.' That is why the place was called
23 Zoar.ᶠ The sun had risen over the land as
24 Lot entered Zoar; and then the LORD rained
down fire and brimstone from the skies on
25 Sodom and Gomorrah. He overthrew those
cities and destroyed all the Plain, with everyone living there and everything growing in
26 the ground. But Lot's wife, behind him,
looked back, and she turned into a pillar
of salt.

27   Next morning Abraham rose early and
went to the place where he had stood in the
28 presence of the LORD. He looked down towards Sodom and Gomorrah and all the
wide extent of the Plain, and there he saw
thick smoke rising high from the earth like
29 the smoke of a lime-kiln. Thus, when God
destroyed the cities of the Plain, he thought
of Abraham and rescued Lot from the
disaster, the overthrow of the cities where
he had been living.

Origin of Moab and Ammon

30 Lot went up from Zoar and settled in the
hill-country with his two daughters, because he was afraid to stay in Zoar; he lived
31 with his two daughters in a cave. The elder
daughter said to the younger, 'Our father
is old and there is not a man in the country
32 to come to us in the usual way. Come now,

let us make our father drink wine and then
lie with him and in this way keep the family
alive through our father.' So that night they 33
gave him wine to drink, and the elder
daughter came and lay with him, and he
did not know when she lay down and when
she got up. Next day the elder said to the 34
younger, 'Last night I lay with my father.
Let us give him wine to drink again tonight;
then you go in and lie with him. So we shall
keep the family alive through our father.'
So they gave their father wine to drink again 35
that night, and the younger daughter went
and lay with him, and he did not know when
she lay down and when she got up. In this 36
way both Lot's daughters came to be with
child by their father. The elder daughter bore 37
a son and called him Moab; he was the
ancestor of the present Moabites. The youn- 38
ger also bore a son, whom she called Ben-
ammi; he was the ancestor of the present
Ammonites.

Abraham and Abimelech

Abraham journeyed by stages from there **20**
into the Negeb, and settled between Kadesh
and Shur, living as an alien in Gerar. He 2
said that Sarah his wife was his sister, and
Abimelech king of Gerar sent and took her.
But God came to Abimelech in a dream by 3
night and said, 'You shall die because of
this woman whom you have taken. She is a
married woman.' Now Abimelech had not 4
gone near her; and he said, 'Lord, wilt thou
destroy an innocent people? Did he not tell 5
me himself that she was his sister, and she
herself said that he was her brother. It was
with a clear conscience and in all innocence
that I did this.' God said to him in the dream, 6
'Yes: I know that you acted with a clear
conscience. Moreover, it was I who held
you back from committing a sin against me:
that is why I did not let you touch her. Send 7
back the man's wife now; he is a prophet,
and he will intercede on your behalf, and
you shall live. But if you do not send her
back, I tell you that you are doomed to die,
you and all that is yours.' So Abimelech 8
rose early in the morning, summoned all
his servants and told them the whole story;
the men were terrified. Abimelech then 9
summoned Abraham and said to him, 'Why
have you treated us like this? What harm
have I done to you that you should bring
this great sin on me and my kingdom? You
have done a thing that ought not to be done.'
And he asked Abraham, 'What was your 10
purpose in doing this?' Abraham answered, 11
'I said to myself, There can be no fear of
God in this place, and they will kill me for
the sake of my wife. She is in fact my sister, 12
she is my father's daughter though not by

ᵉ Or his sons-in-law, who had married his daughters.   ᶠ That is Small.

the same mother; and she became my wife.
13 When God set me wandering from my father's house, I said to her, "There is a duty towards me which you must loyally fulfil: wherever we go, you must say that
14 I am your brother." ' Then Abimelech took sheep and cattle, and male and female slaves, gave them to Abraham, and returned
15 his wife Sarah to him. Abimelech said, 'My country lies before you; settle wherever you
16 please.' To Sarah he said, 'I have given your brother a thousand pieces of silver, so that your own people may turn a blind eye on it all, and you will be completely vindicated.'
17 Then Abraham interceded with God, and God healed Abimelech, his wife, and his
18 slave-girls, and they bore children; for the LORD had made every woman in Abimelech's household barren on account of Abraham's wife Sarah.

The birth of Isaac

21 The LORD showed favour to Sarah as he had promised, and made good what he had
2 said about her. She conceived and bore a son to Abraham for his old age, at the time
3 which God had appointed. The son whom Sarah bore to him, Abraham named Isaac.*g*
4 When Isaac was eight days old Abraham circumcised him, as God had commanded.
5 Abraham was a hundred years old when his
6 son Isaac was born. Sarah said, 'God has given me good reason to laugh, and every-
7 body who hears will laugh with me.' She said, 'Whoever would have told Abraham that Sarah would suckle children? Yet I have borne him a son for his old age.'

Hagar and Ishmael sent away

8 The boy grew and was weaned, and on the day of his weaning Abraham gave a feast.
9 Sarah saw the son whom Hagar the Egyptian
10 had borne to Abraham laughing at him, and she said to Abraham, 'Drive out this slave-girl and her son; I will not have this slave-girl's son sharing the inheritance with my
11 son Isaac.' Abraham was vexed at this on
12 his son Ishmael's account, but God said to him, 'Do not be vexed on account of the boy and the slave-girl. Do what Sarah says, because you shall have descendants through
13 Isaac. I will make a great nation of the slave-girl's son too, because he is your own child.'
14 Abraham rose early in the morning, took some food and a waterskin full of water and gave it to Hagar; he set the child on her shoulder and sent her away, and she went and wandered in the wilderness of Beer-
15 sheba. When the water in the skin was finished, she thrust the child under a bush,

and went and sat down some way off, about 16 two bowshots away, for she said, 'How can I watch the child die?' So she sat some way off, weeping bitterly. God heard the child 17 crying, and the*h* angel of God called from heaven to Hagar, 'What is the matter, Hagar? Do not be afraid: God has heard the child crying where you laid him. Get to 18 your feet, lift the child up and hold him in your arms, because I will make of him a great nation.' Then God opened her eyes 19 and she saw a well full of water; she went

to it, filled her waterskin and gave the child a drink. God was with the child, and he 20-21 grew up and lived in the wilderness of Paran. He became an archer, and his mother found him a wife from Egypt.

The pact between Abraham and Abimelech

Now about that time Abimelech, with Phicol 22 the commander of his army, addressed Abraham in these terms: 'God is with you in all that you do. Now swear an oath to me in 23 the name of God, that you will not break faith with me, my offspring, or my descendants. As I have kept faith with you, so shall you keep faith with me and with the country where you have come to live as an alien.' Abraham said, 'I swear.' It happened that 24 25 Abraham had a complaint against Abimelech about a well which Abimelech's men had seized. Abimelech said, 'I do not know 26 who did this. You never told me, and I have heard nothing about it till now.' So Abra- 27 ham took sheep and cattle and gave them to Abimelech; and the two of them made a pact. Abraham set seven ewe-lambs apart, 28 and when Abimelech asked him why he had 29 set these lambs apart, he said, 'Accept these 30 from me in token that I dug this well.' There- 31 fore that place was called Beersheba,*i* because there the two of them swore an oath. When they had made the pact at Beersheba, 32 Abimelech and Phicol the commander of his army returned at once to the country of the Philistines, and Abraham planted a strip of 33 ground*j* at Beersheba. There he invoked the LORD, the everlasting God, by name, and 34 he lived as an alien in the country of the Philistines for many a year.

g That is He laughed.   *h Or* an.   *i That is* Well of Seven *and* Well of an Oath.   *j Or* planted a tamarisk.

God tests Abraham

22 The time came when God put Abraham to the test. 'Abraham', he called, and Abraham 2 replied, 'Here I am.' God said, 'Take your son Isaac, your only son, whom you love, and go to the land of Moriah. There you shall offer him as a sacrifice on one of the 3 hills which I will show you.' So Abraham rose early in the morning and saddled his ass, and he took with him two of his men and his son Isaac; and he split the firewood for the sacrifice, and set out for the place 4 of which God had spoken. On the third day Abraham looked up and saw the place in 5 the distance. He said to his men, 'Stay here with the ass while I and the boy go over there; and when we have worshipped we 6 will come back to you.' So Abraham took the wood for the sacrifice and laid it on his son Isaac's shoulder; he himself carried the fire and the knife, and the two of them went 7 on together. Isaac said to Abraham, 'Father', and he answered, 'What is it, my son?' Isaac said, 'Here are the fire and the wood, but where is the young beast for the sacri- 8 fice?' Abraham answered, 'God will provide himself with a young beast for a sacrifice, my son.' And the two of them went on to- 9 gether and came to the place of which God had spoken. There Abraham built an altar and arranged the wood. He bound his son Isaac and laid him on the altar on top of the 10 wood. Then he stretched out his hand and 11 took the knife to kill his son; but the angel of the LORD called to him from heaven, 'Abraham, Abraham.' He answered, 'Here 12 I am.' The angel of the LORD said, 'Do not raise your hand against the boy; do not touch him. Now I know that you are a God-fearing man. You have not withheld from 13 me your son, your only son.' Abraham looked up, and there he saw a ram caught by its horns in a thicket. So he went and took the ram and offered it as a sacrifice instead 14 of his son. Abraham named that place Jehovah-jireh;[k] and to this day the saying

k *That is* the LORD will provide.

is: 'In the mountain of the LORD it was pro-vided.' Then the angel of the LORD called 15 from heaven a second time to Abraham, 'This is the word of the LORD: By my own 16 self I swear: inasmuch as you have done this and have not withheld your son, your only son, I will bless you abundantly and greatly 17 multiply your descendants until they are as numerous as the stars in the sky and the grains of sand on the sea-shore. Your de-scendants shall possess the cities of their enemies. All nations on earth shall pray to 18 be blessed as your descendants are blessed, and this because you have obeyed me.'

Abraham went back to his men, and to- 19 gether they returned to Beersheba; and there Abraham remained.

Nahor's descendants

After this Abraham was told, 'Milcah has 20 borne sons to your brother Nahor: Uz his 21 first-born, then his brother Buz, and Kemuel father of Aram, and Kesed, Hazo, Pildash, 22 Jidlaph and Bethuel; and a daughter, Re- 23 becca, has been born to Bethuel.' These eight Milcah bore to Abraham's brother Nahor. His concubine, whose name was 24 Reumah, also bore him sons: Tebah, Gaham, Tahash and Maacah.

The death and burial of Sarah

Sarah lived for a hundred and twenty-seven **23** years, and died in Kiriath-arba, which is 2 Hebron, in Canaan. Abraham went in to mourn over Sarah and to weep for her. At 3 last he rose and left the presence of the dead. He said to the Hittites, 'I am an alien and a 4 settler among you. Give me land enough for a burial-place, so that I can give my dead proper burial.' The Hittites answered Abra- 5 ham, 'Do, pray, listen to what we have to 6 say, sir. You are a mighty prince among us. Bury your dead in the best grave we have. There is not one of us who will deny you his grave or hinder you from burying your dead.' Abraham stood up and then bowed 7 low to the Hittites, the people of that country. He said to them, 'If you are willing 8 to let me give my dead proper burial, then listen to me and speak for me to Ephron son of Zohar, asking him to give me the 9 cave that belongs to him at Machpelah, at the far end of his land. Let him give it to me for the full price, so that I may take posses-sion of it as a burial-place within your territory.' Ephron the Hittite was sitting 10 with the others, and he gave Abraham this answer in the hearing of everyone as they came into the city gate: 'No, sir; hear what 11 I have to say. I will make you a gift of the land and I will also give you the cave which is on it. In the presence of all my kinsmen

12 I give it to you; so bury your dead.' Abraham bowed low before the people of the country 13 and said to Ephron in their hearing, 'If you really mean it—but do listen to me! I give you the price of the land: take it and I will 14 bury my dead there.' And Ephron answered, 15 'Do listen to me, sir: the land is worth four hundred shekels of silver. But what is that between you and me? There you may bury 16 your dead.' Abraham came to an agreement with him and weighed out the amount that Ephron had named in the hearing of the Hittites, four hundred shekels of the stan-17 dard recognized by merchants. Thus the plot of land belonging to Ephron at Mach-pelah to the east of Mamre, the plot, the cave that is on it, every tree on the plot, 18 within the whole area, became the legal possession of Abraham, in the presence of all the Hittites as they came into the city 19 gate. After this Abraham buried his wife Sarah in the cave on the plot of land at Machpelah to the east of Mamre, which is 20 Hebron, in Canaan. Thus the plot and the cave on it became Abraham's possession as a burial-place, by purchase from the Hittites.

A wife for Isaac

24 By this time Abraham had become a very old man, and the LORD had blessed him in 2 all that he did. Abraham said to his servant, who had been long in his service and was in charge of all his possessions, 'Put your hand 3 under my thigh: I want you to swear by the LORD, the God of heaven and earth, that you will not take a wife for my son from the women of the Canaanites in whose land I 4 dwell; you must go to my own country and to my own kindred to find a wife for my son 5 Isaac.' The servant said to him, 'What if the woman is unwilling to come with me to this country? Must I in that event take your son back to the land from which you came?' 6 Abraham said to him, 'On no account are 7 you to take my son back there. The LORD the God of heaven who took me from my father's house and the land of my birth, the LORD who swore to me that he would give this land to my descendants—he will send his angel before you, and from there you 8 shall take a wife for my son. If the woman is unwilling to come with you, then you will be released from your oath to me; but you 9 must not take my son back there.' So the servant put his hand under his master Abra-ham's thigh and swore an oath in those terms.

10 The servant took ten camels from his master's herds, and also all kinds of gifts from his master; he set out for Aram-naharaim[1] and arrived at the city where 11 Nahor lived. Towards evening, the time

when the women come out to draw water, he made the camels kneel down by the well outside the city. He said, 'O LORD God of 12 my master Abraham, give me good fortune this day; keep faith with my master Abra-ham. Here I stand by the spring, and the 13 women of the city are coming out to draw water. Let it be like this: I shall say to a girl, 14 "Please lower your jar so that I may drink"; and if she answers, "Drink, and I will water your camels also", that will be the girl whom thou dost intend for thy servant Isaac. In this way I shall know that thou hast kept faith with my master.'

Before he had finished praying silently, 15 he saw Rebecca coming out with her water-jug on her shoulder. She was the daughter of Bethuel son of Milcah, the wife of Abra-ham's brother Nahor. The girl was very 16 beautiful, a virgin, who had had no inter-course with a man. She went down to the spring, filled her jar and came up again. Abraham's servant hurried to meet her and 17 said, 'Give me a sip of water from your jar.' 'Drink, sir', she answered, and at once 18 lowered her jar on to her hand to let him drink. When she had finished giving him a 19 drink, she said, 'Now I will draw water for your camels until they have had enough.' So she quickly emptied her jar into the 20 water-trough, hurried again to the well to draw water and watered all the camels. The 21 man was watching quietly to see whether or not the LORD had made his journey suc-cessful. When the camels had finished drink-22 ing, the man took a gold nose-ring weighing half a shekel, and two bracelets for her wrists weighing ten shekels, also of gold, and said, 'Tell me, please, whose daughter 23 you are. Is there room in your father's house for us to spend the night?' She answered, 24 'I am the daughter of Bethuel, the son of Nahor and Milcah; and we have plenty of 25 straw and fodder and also room for you to spend the night.' So the man bowed down 26 and prostrated himself to the LORD. He 27 said, 'Blessed be the LORD the God of my master Abraham, who has not failed to keep faith and truth with my master; for I have been guided by the LORD to the house of my master's kinsman.'

The girl ran to her mother's house and 28 told them what had happened. Now Rebecca 29-30 had a brother named Laban; and, when he saw the nose-ring, and also the bracelets on his sister's wrists, and heard his sister Rebecca tell what the man had said to her, he ran out to the man at the spring. When he came to him and found him still stand-ing there by the camels, he said, 'Come in, 31 sir, whom the LORD has blessed. Why stay outside? I have prepared the house, and

l That is Aram of Two Rivers.

there is room for the camels.' So he brought 32 the man into the house, unloaded the camels and provided straw and fodder for them, and water for him and all his men to wash 33 their feet. Food was set before him, but he said, 'I will not eat until I have delivered my 34 message.' Laban said, 'Let us hear it.' He answered, 'I am the servant of Abraham. 35 The LORD has greatly blessed my master, and he has become a man of power. The LORD has given him flocks and herds, silver and gold, male and female slaves, camels 36 and asses. My master's wife Sarah in her old age bore him a son, to whom he has 37 given all that he has. So my master made me swear an oath, saying, "You shall not 38 take a wife for my son from the women of the Canaanites in whose land I dwell; but 39 you shall go to my father's house and to my family to find a wife for him." So I said to my master, "What if the woman will not 40 come with me?" He answered, "The LORD, in whose presence I have lived, will send his angel with you and will make your journey successful. You shall take a wife for my son from my family and from my father's house; 41 then you shall be released from the charge I have laid upon you. But if, when you come to my family, they will not give her to you, you shall still be released from the charge." 42 So I came to the spring today, and I said, "O LORD God of my master Abraham, if 43 thou wilt make my journey successful, let it be like this. Here I stand by the spring. When a young woman comes out to draw water, I shall say to her, 'Give me a little 44 water to drink from your jar.' If she answers, 'Yes, do drink, and I will draw water for your camels as well', she is the woman whom 45 the LORD intends for my master's son." Before I had finished praying silently, I saw Rebecca coming out with her water-jar on her shoulder. She went down to the spring and drew some water, and I said to her, 46 "Please give me a drink." She quickly lowered her jar from her shoulder and said, "Drink; and I will water your camels as well." So I drank, and she also gave my 47 camels water. I asked her whose daughter she was, and she said, "I am the daughter of Bethuel, the son of Nahor and Milcah." Then I put the ring in her nose and the brace- 48 lets on her wrists, and I bowed low and prostrated myself before the LORD. I blessed the LORD the God of my master Abraham, who had led me by the right road to take 49 my master's niece for his son. Now tell me if you will keep faith and truth with my master. If not, say so, and I will turn else-where.' 50 Laban and Bethuel answered, 'This is from

the LORD; we can say nothing for or against. Here is Rebecca herself; take her and go. 51 She shall be the wife of your master's son, as the LORD has decreed.' When Abraham's 52 servant heard what they said, he prostrated himself on the ground before the LORD. Then he brought out gold and silver orna- 53 ments, and robes, and gave them to Rebecca, and he gave costly gifts to her brother and her mother. He and his men then ate and 54 drank and spent the night there. When they rose in the morning, he said, 'Give me leave to go back to my master.' Her brother and 55 her mother said, 'Let the girl stay with us for a few days, say ten days, and then she shall go.' But he said to them, 'Do not de- 56 tain me, for the LORD has granted me suc-cess. Give me leave to return to my master.' They said, 'Let us call the girl and see what 57 she says.' They called Rebecca and asked 58 her if she would go with the man, and she said, 'Yes, I will go.' So they let their sister 59 Rebecca and her nurse go with Abraham's servant and his men. They blessed Rebecca 60 and said to her:

'You are our sister, may you be the mother
　　of myriads;
may your sons possess the cities of their
　　enemies.'

Then Rebecca and her companions mounted 61 their camels at once and followed the man. So the servant took Rebecca and went his way.

Isaac meanwhile had moved on as far as 62 Beer-lahai-roi and was living in the Negeb. One evening when he had gone out into the 63 open country hoping to meet them,[m] he looked up and saw camels approaching. When Rebecca raised her eyes and saw 64 Isaac, she slipped hastily from her camel, saying to the servant, 'Who is that man 65 walking across the open towards us?' The servant answered, 'It is my master.' So she took her veil and covered herself. The ser- 66 vant related to Isaac all that had happened. Isaac conducted her into the tent[n] and took 67 her as his wife. So she became his wife, and he loved her and was consoled for the death of his mother.

Descendants of Abraham and Keturah

Abraham married another wife, whose name **25** was Keturah. She bore him Zimran, Jok- 2 shan, Medan, Midian, Ishbak and Shuah. Jokshan became the father of Sheba and 3 Dedan. The sons of Dedan were Asshurim, Letushim and Leummim, and the sons of 4 Midian were Ephah, Epher, Enoch, Abida and Eldaah. All these were descendants of Keturah.

m hoping . . . them: *or* to relieve himself.
1–4: cp. 1 *Chr.* 1. 32, 33.

n Prob. rdg.; Heb. adds Sarah his mother.　　　*o Verses*

The death of Abraham

5 Abraham had given all that he had to Isaac;
6 and he had already in his lifetime given presents to the sons of his concubines, and had sent them away eastwards, to a land of
7 the east, out of his son Isaac's way. Abraham had lived for a hundred and seventy-five
8 years when he breathed his last. He died at a good old age, after a very long life, and
9 was gathered to his father's kin. His sons, Isaac and Ishmael, buried him in the cave at Machpelah, on the land of Ephron son
10 of Zohar the Hittite, east of Mamre, the plot which Abraham had bought from the Hittites. There Abraham was buried with his
11 wife Sarah. After the death of Abraham, God blessed his son Isaac, who settled close by Beer-lahai-roi.

Ishmael's descendants

12 This is the table of the descendants of Abraham's son Ishmael, whom Hagar the Egyp-
13ᵖ tian, Sarah's slave-girl, bore to him. These are the names of the sons of Ishmael named in order of their birth: Nebaioth, Ishmael's eldest son, then Kedar, Adbeel, Mibsam,
15 Mishma, Dumah, Massa, Hadad, Teman,
16 Jetur, Naphish and Kedemah. These are the sons of Ishmael, after whom their hamlets and encampments were named, twelve princes according to their tribal groups.
17 Ishmael had lived for a hundred and thirty-seven years when he breathed his last. So he died and was gathered to his father's kin.
18 Ishmael's sons inhabited the land from Havilah to Shur, which is east of Egypt on the way to Asshur, having settled to the east of his brothers.

The birth of Esau and Jacob

19 This is the table of the descendants of Abraham's son Isaac. Isaac's father was
20 Abraham. When Isaac was forty years old he married Rebecca the daughter of Bethuel the Aramaean from Paddan-aram, the
21 sister of Laban the Aramaean. Isaac appealed to the LORD on behalf of his wife because she was barren; the LORD yielded to his
22 entreaty, and Rebecca conceived. The children pressed hard on each other in her womb, and she said, 'If this is how it is with me, what does it mean?' So she went to seek
23 guidance of the LORD. The LORD said to her:

'Two nations in your womb,
two peoples, going their own ways from birth!
One shall be stronger than the other;
the older shall be servant to the younger.'

24 When her time had come, there were indeed
25 twins in her womb. The first came out red,

hairy all over like a hair-cloak, and they named him Esau. q Immediately afterwards 26 his brother was born with his hand grasping Esau's heel, and they called him Jacob.ʳ Isaac was sixty years old when they were born.

Esau sells his birthright

The boys grew up; and Esau became skilful 27 in hunting, a man of the open plains, but Jacob led a settled life and stayed among the tents. Isaac favoured Esau because he 28 kept him supplied with venison, but Rebecca favoured Jacob. One day Jacob prepared a 29 broth and when Esau came in from the country, exhausted, he said to Jacob, 'I am 30 exhausted; let me swallow some of that red broth': this is why he was called Edom.ˢ Jacob said, 'Not till you sell me your rights 31 as the first-born.' Esau replied, 'I am at 32 death's door; what use is my birthright to me?' Jacob said, 'Not till you swear!'; so 33 he swore an oath and sold his birthright to Jacob. Then Jacob gave Esau bread and the 34 lentil broth, and he ate and drank and went away without more ado. Thus Esau showed how little he valued his birthright.

Isaac at Gerar and Beersheba

There came a famine in the land—not the **26** earlier famine in Abraham's time—and Isaac went to Abimelech the Philistine king at Gerar. The LORD appeared to Isaac and 2 said, 'Do not go down to Egypt, but stay in this country as I bid you. Stay in this 3 country and I will be with you and bless you, for to you and to your descendants I will give all these lands. Thus shall I fulfil the oath which I swore to your father Abraham. I will make your descendants as many as 4 the stars in the sky; I will give them all these lands, and all the nations of the earth will pray to be blessed as they are blessed—all 5 because Abraham obeyed me and kept my charge, my commandments, my statutes, and my laws.' So Isaac lived in Gerar. 6

When the men of the place asked him 7 about his wife, he told them that she was his sister; he was afraid to say that Rebecca was his wife, in case they killed him because of her; for she was very beautiful. When 8 they had been there for some considerable time, Abimelech the Philistine king looked down from his window and saw Isaac and his wife Rebecca laughing together. He sum- 9 moned Isaac and said, 'So she is your wife, is she? What made you say she was your sister?' Isaac answered, 'I thought I should be killed because of her.' Abimelech said, 10 'Why have you treated us like this? One of the people might easily have gone to bed with your wife, and then you would have

11 made us liable to retribution.' So Abimelech warned all the people, threatening that whoever touched this man or his wife would be put to death.

12 Isaac sowed seed in that land, and that year he reaped a hundredfold, and the LORD 13 blessed him. He became more and more powerful, until he was very powerful indeed. 14 He had flocks and herds and many slaves, so that the Philistines were envious of him. 15 They had stopped up all the wells dug by the slaves in the days of Isaac's father Abra-18 ham, and filled them with earth. Isaac dug them again, all those wells dug in his father Abraham's time, and stopped up by the Philistines after his death, and he called them by the names which his father had given them.

16 Then Abimelech said to him, 'Go away 17 from here; you are too strong for us.' So Isaac left that place and encamped in the 19ᵗ valley of Gerar, and stayed there. Then Isaac's slaves dug in the valley and found 20 a spring of running water, but the shepherds of Gerar quarrelled with Isaac's shepherds, claiming the water as theirs. He called the well Esek,ᵘ because they made difficulties 21 for him. His men then dug another well, but the others quarrelled with him over that 22 also, so he called it Sitnah.ᵛ He moved on from there and dug another well, but there was no quarrel over that one, so he called

it Rehoboth,ʷ saying, 'Now the LORD has given us plenty of room and we shall be fruitful in the land.'

23 Isaac went up country from there to Beer-24 sheba. That same night the LORD appeared to him there and said, 'I am the God of your father Abraham. Fear nothing, for I am with you. I will bless you and give you many descendants for the sake of Abraham my servant.' So Isaac built an altar there and 25

invoked the LORD by name. Then he pitched his tent there, and there also his slaves dug a well. Abimelech came to him from Gerar 26 with Ahuzzath his friend and Phicol the commander of his army. Isaac said to them, 27 'Why have you come here? You hate me and you sent me away.' They answered, 'We 28 have seen plainly that the LORD is with you, so we thought, "Let the two of us put each other to the oath and make a treaty that will bind us." We have not attacked you, 29 we have done you nothing but good, and we let you go away peaceably. Swear that you will do us no harm, now that the LORD has blessed you.' So Isaac gave a feast and 30 they ate and drank. They rose early in 31 the morning and exchanged oaths. Then Isaac bade them farewell, and they parted from him in peace. The same day Isaac's 32 slaves came and told him about a well that they had dug: 'We have found water', they said. He named the well Shibah.ˣ 33 This is why the city is called Beershebaʸ to this day.

When Esau was forty years old he married 34 Judith daughter of Beeri the Hittite, and Basemath daughter of Elon the Hittite; this 35 was a bitter grief to Isaac and Rebecca.

---

t *Verse 18 transposed to follow 15.*   u *That is* Difficulty.   v *That is* Enmity.   w *That is* Plenty
of room.   x *That is* Oath.   y *That is* Well of an Oath.

Jacob obtains Isaac's blessing

27 When Isaac grew old and his eyes became so dim that he could not see, he called his elder son Esau and said to him, 'My son', 2 and he answered, 'Here I am.' Isaac said, 'Listen now: I am old and I do not know 3 when I may die. Take your hunting gear, your quiver and your bow, and go out into 4 the country and get me some venison. Then make me a savoury dish of the kind I like, and bring it to me to eat so that I may give 5 you my blessing before I die.' Now Rebecca was listening as Isaac talked to his son Esau. When Esau went off into the country to 6 find some venison and bring it home, she said to her son Jacob, 'I heard your father talking to your brother Esau, and he said, 7 "Bring me some venison and make it into a savoury dish so that I may eat it and bless you in the presence of the LORD before I 8 die." Listen to me, my son, and do what I 9 tell you. Go to the flock and pick me out two fine young kids, and I will make them

into a savoury dish for your father, of the kind 10 he likes. Then take them in to your father, and he will eat them so that he may bless 11 you before he dies.' Jacob said to his mother Rebecca, 'But my brother Esau is a hairy 12 man, and my skin is smooth. Suppose my father feels me, he will know I am tricking him and I shall bring a curse upon myself 13 instead of a blessing.' His mother answered him, 'Let the curse fall on me, my son, but 14 do as I say; go and bring me the kids.' So Jacob fetched them and brought them to his mother, who made them into a savoury 15 dish of the kind that his father liked. Then Rebecca took her elder son's clothes, Esau's best clothes which she kept by her in the house, and put them on her younger son 16 Jacob. She put the goatskins on his hands 17 and on the smooth nape of his neck; and she handed her son Jacob the savoury dish 18 and the bread she had made. He came to his

father and said, 'Father.' He answered, 'Yes, my son; who are you?' Jacob answered his 19 father, 'I am Esau, your elder son. I have done as you told me. Come, sit up and eat some of my venison, so that you may give me your blessing.' Isaac said to his son, 20 'What is this that you found so quickly?', and Jacob answered, 'It is what the LORD your God put in my way.' Isaac then said to 21 Jacob, 'Come close and let me feel you, my son, to see whether you are really my son Esau.' When Jacob came close to his father, 22 Isaac felt him and said, 'The voice is Jacob's voice, but the hands are the hands of Esau.' He did not recognize him because his hands 23 were hairy like Esau's, and that is why he blessed him. He said, 'Are you really my son 24 Esau?', and he answered, 'Yes.' Then Isaac 25 said, 'Bring me some of your venison to eat, my son, so that I may give you my blessing.' Then Jacob brought it to him, and he ate it; he brought wine also, and he drank it. Then his father Isaac said to him, 'Come 26 near, my son, and kiss me.' So he came near 27 and kissed him, and when Isaac smelt the smell of his clothes, he blessed him and said:

'Ah! The smell of my son is like the smell of
    open country
    blessed by the LORD.
God give you dew from heaven   28
and the richness of the earth,
corn and new wine in plenty!
Peoples shall serve you,   29
nations bow down to you.
  Be lord over your brothers;
may your mother's sons bow down to you.
A curse upon those who curse you;
a blessing on those who bless you!'

Isaac finished blessing Jacob; and Jacob 30 had scarcely left his father Isaac's presence, when his brother Esau came in from his hunting. He too made a savoury dish and 31 brought it to his father. He said, 'Come, father, and eat some of my venison, so that you may give me your blessing.' His father 32 Isaac said, 'Who are you?' He said, 'I am Esau, your elder son.' Then Isaac became 33 greatly agitated[z] and said, 'Then who was it that hunted and brought me venison? I ate it all before you came in and I blessed him, and the blessing will stand.' When 34 Esau heard what his father said, he gave a loud and bitter cry and said, 'Bless me too, father.' But Isaac said, 'Your brother came 35 treacherously and took away your blessing.' Esau said, 'He is rightly called Jacob.[a] This 36 is the second time he has supplanted me. He took away my right as the first-born and now he has taken away my blessing. Have you kept back any blessing for me?'

---

z *Or* incensed.   a *That is* He supplanted.

37 Isaac answered, 'I have made him lord over you, and I have given him all his brothers as slaves. I have bestowed upon him corn and new wine for his sustenance. What is there left that I can do for you, my son?'
38 Esau asked his father, 'Had you then only one blessing, father? Bless me too, my
39 father.' And Esau cried bitterly. Then his father Isaac answered:

'Your dwelling shall be far from the richness of the earth,
  far from the dew of heaven above.
40 By your sword shall you live,
  and you shall serve your brother;
  but the time will come when you grow restive
  and break off his yoke from your neck.'

Jacob escapes to Harran

41 Esau bore a grudge against Jacob because of the blessing which his father had given him, and he said to himself, 'The time of mourning for my father will soon be here;
42 then I will kill my brother Jacob.' When Rebecca was told what her elder son Esau was saying, she called her younger son Jacob, and she said to him, 'Esau your
43 brother is threatening to kill you. Now, my son, listen to me. Slip away at once to my
44 brother Laban in Harran. Stay with him for a while until your brother's anger cools.
45 When it has subsided and he forgets what you have done to him, I will send and fetch you back. Why should I lose you both in one day?'
46 Rebecca said to Isaac, 'I am weary to death of Hittite women! If Jacob marries a Hittite woman like those who live here,
28 my life will not be worth living.' Isaac called Jacob, blessed him and gave him instructions. He said, 'You must not marry one of
2 these women of Canaan. Go at once to the house of Bethuel, your mother's father, in Paddan-aram, and there find a wife, one of the daughters of Laban, your mother's
3 brother. God Almighty bless you, make you fruitful and increase your descendants until
4 they become a host of nations. May he bestow on you and your offspring the blessing of Abraham, and may you thus possess the country where you are now living, the land
5 which God gave to Abraham!' So Isaac sent Jacob away, and he went to Paddan-aram to Laban, son of Bethuel the Aramaean, and brother to Rebecca the mother of
6 Jacob and Esau. Esau discovered that Isaac had given Jacob his blessing and had sent him away to Paddan-aram to find a wife there; and that when he blessed him he had forbidden him to marry a woman of Canaan,
7 and that Jacob had obeyed his father and

mother and gone to Paddan-aram. Then 8 Esau, seeing that his father disliked the women of Canaan, went to Ishmael, and, 9 in addition to his other wives, he married Mahalath sister of Nebaioth and daughter of Abraham's son Ishmael.

Jacob's dream at Bethel

Jacob set out from Beersheba and went on 10 his way towards Harran. He came to a cer- 11 tain place and stopped there for the night, because the sun had set; and, taking one of the stones there, he made it a pillow for his head and lay down to sleep. He dreamt that 12 he saw a ladder, which rested on the ground with its top reaching to heaven, and angels of God were going up and down upon it. The LORD was standing beside him[b] and 13 said, 'I am the LORD, the God of your father Abraham and the God of Isaac. This land on which you are lying I will give to you and your descendants. They shall be 14 countless as the dust upon the earth, and you shall spread far and wide, to north and south, to east and west. All the families of the earth shall pray to be blessed as you and your descendants are blessed. I will be with 15 you, and I will protect you wherever you go and will bring you back to this land; for I will not leave you until I have done all that I have promised.' Jacob woke from his sleep 16 and said, 'Truly the LORD is in this place, and I did not know it.' Then he was afraid 17 and said, 'How fearsome is this place! This is no other than the house of God, this is the gate of heaven.' Jacob rose early in the 18 morning, took the stone on which he had laid his head, set it up as a sacred pillar and poured oil on the top of it. He named that 19 place Beth-El;[c] but the earlier name of the city was Luz.

Thereupon Jacob made this vow: 'If God 20 will be with me, if he will protect me on my journey and give me food to eat and clothes to wear, and I come back safely to my father's 21 house, then the LORD shall be my God, and 22 this stone which I have set up as a sacred pillar shall be a house of God. And of all that thou givest me, I will without fail allot a tenth part to thee.'

Jacob, Rachel, and Leah

Jacob continued his journey and came to the **29** land of the eastern tribes. There he saw a 2 well in the open country and three flocks of sheep lying beside it, because the flocks were watered from that well. Over its mouth was a huge stone, and all the herdsmen used to 3 gather there and roll it off the mouth of the well and water the flocks; then they would put it back in its place over the well. Jacob 4 said to them, 'Where are you from, my

b Or on it or by it.   c That is House of God.

friends?' 'We are from Harran', they replied.
5 He asked them if they knew Laban the grandson of Nahor. They answered, 'Yes, we do.'
6 'Is he well?' Jacob asked; and they answered, 'Yes, he is well, and here is his daughter
7 Rachel coming with the flock.' Jacob said, 'The sun is still high, and the time for folding the sheep has not yet come. Water the
8 flocks and then go and graze them.' But they replied, 'We cannot, until all the herdsmen have gathered together and the stone is rolled away from the mouth of the well; then
9 we can water our flocks.' While he was talking to them, Rachel came up with her father's flock, for she was a shepherdess.
10 When Jacob saw Rachel, the daughter of Laban his mother's brother, with Laban's flock, he stepped forward, rolled the stone off the mouth of the well and watered
11 Laban's sheep. He kissed Rachel, and was
12 moved to tears. He told her that he was her father's kinsman and Rebecca's son; so she
13 ran and told her father. When Laban heard the news of his sister's son Jacob, he ran to meet him, embraced him, kissed him warmly and welcomed him to his home. Jacob told
14 Laban everything, and Laban said, 'Yes, you are my own flesh and blood.' So Jacob stayed with him for a whole month.
15 Laban said to Jacob, 'Why should you work for me for nothing simply because you are my kinsman? Tell me what your
16 wages ought to be.' Now Laban had two daughters: the elder was called Leah, and
17 the younger Rachel. Leah was dull-eyed, but Rachel was graceful and beautiful.

Jacob had fallen in love with Rachel and 18 he said, 'I will work seven years for your younger daughter Rachel.' Laban replied, 19 'It is better that I should give her to you than to anyone else; stay with me.' So Jacob 20 worked seven years for Rachel, and they seemed like a few days because he loved her. Then Jacob said to Laban, 'I have served 21 my time. Give me my wife so that we may sleep together.' So Laban gathered all the 22 men of the place together and gave a feast. In the evening he took his daughter Leah 23 and brought her to Jacob, and Jacob slept with her. At the same time Laban gave his 24 slave-girl Zilpah to his daughter Leah. But 25 when morning came, Jacob saw that it was Leah and said to Laban, 'What have you done to me? Did I not work for Rachel? Why have you deceived me?' Laban an- 26 swered, 'In our country it is not right to give the younger sister in marriage before the elder. Go through with the seven days' 27 feast for the elder, and the younger shall be given you in return for a further seven years' work.' Jacob agreed, and completed the 28 seven days for Leah.

Jacob's children

Then Laban gave Jacob his daughter Rachel as wife; and he gave his slave-girl Bilhah to 29 serve his daughter Rachel. Jacob slept with 30 Rachel also; he loved her rather than Leah, and he worked for Laban for a further seven years. When the LORD saw that Leah was 31 not loved, he granted her a child; but Rachel was childless. Leah conceived and bore a 32

HK

Bethel

son; and she called him Reuben,[d] for she said, 'The LORD has seen my humiliation; 33 now my husband will love me.' Again she conceived and bore a son and said, 'The LORD, hearing that I am not loved, has given me this child also'; and she called him 34 Simeon.[e] She conceived again and bore a son; and she said, 'Now that I have borne him three sons my husband and I will surely 35 be united.' So she called him Levi.[f] Once more she conceived and bore a son; and she said, 'Now I will praise the LORD'; therefore she named him Judah.[g] Then for a while she bore no more children.

30 When Rachel found that she bore Jacob no children, she became jealous of her sister and said to Jacob, 'Give me sons, or I shall 2 die.' Jacob said angrily to Rachel, 'Can I take the place of God, who has denied you 3 children?' She said, 'Here is my slave-girl Bilhah. Lie with her, so that she may bear sons to be laid upon my knees, and through 4 her I too may build up a family.' So she gave him her slave-girl Bilhah as a wife, and 5 Jacob lay with her. Bilhah conceived and 6 bore Jacob a son. Then Rachel said, 'God has given judgement for me; he has indeed heard me and given me a son', so she named 7 him Dan.[h] Rachel's slave-girl Bilhah again conceived and bore Jacob another son. 8 Rachel said, 'I have played a fine trick on my sister, and it has succeeded'; so she 9 named him Naphtali.[i] When Leah found that she was bearing no more children, she took her slave-girl Zilpah and gave her to 10 Jacob as a wife, and Zilpah bore Jacob a 11 son. Leah said, 'Good fortune has come', 12 and she named him Gad.[j] Zilpah, Leah's 13 slave-girl, bore Jacob another son, and Leah said, 'Happiness has come, for young women will call me happy.' So she named him Asher.[k]

14   In the time of wheat-harvest Reuben went out and found some mandrakes in the open country and brought them to his mother Leah. Then Rachel asked Leah for some of 15 her son's mandrakes, but Leah said, 'Is it so small a thing to have taken away my husband, that you should take my son's mandrakes as well?' But Rachel said, 'Very well, let him sleep with you tonight in exchange 16 for your son's mandrakes.' So when Jacob came in from the country in the evening, Leah went out to meet him and said, 'You are to sleep with me tonight; I have hired you with my son's mandrakes.' That night 17 he slept with her, and God heard Leah's prayer, and she conceived and bore a fifth 18 son. Leah said, 'God has rewarded me, be-

cause I gave my slave-girl to my husband.' So she named him Issachar.[l] Leah again 19 conceived and bore a sixth son. She said, 20 'God has endowed me with a noble dowry. Now my husband will treat me in princely style, because I have borne him six sons.' So she named him Zebulun.[m] Later she 21 bore a daughter and named her Dinah. Then God thought of Rachel; he heard her 22 prayer and gave her a child; so she con- 23 ceived and bore a son and said, 'God has taken away my humiliation.' She named him 24 Joseph,[n] saying, 'May the LORD add another son!'

Jacob's bargain with Laban

When Rachel had given birth to Joseph, 25 Jacob said to Laban, 'Let me go, for I wish to return to my own home and country. Give me my wives and my children for 26 whom I have served you, and I will go; for you know what service I have done for you.' Laban said to him, 'Let me have my say, 27 if you please. I have become prosperous and the LORD has blessed me for your sake. So 28 now tell me what I owe you in wages, and I will give it you.' Jacob answered, 'You 29 must know how I have served you, and how your herds have prospered under my care. You had only a few when I came, but now 30 they have increased beyond measure, and the LORD brought blessings to you wherever I went. But is it not time for me to provide for my family?' Laban said, 'Then what 31 shall I give you?', but Jacob answered, 'Give me nothing; I will mind your flocks[o] as before, if you will do what I suggest. Today 32 I will go over your flocks and pick out from them every black lamb, and all the brindled and the spotted goats, and they shall be my wages. This is a fair offer, and it will be to 33 my own disadvantage later on, when we come to settling my wages: every goat amongst mine that is not spotted or brindled and every lamb that is not black will have been stolen.' Laban said, 'Agreed; let it be 34 as you have said.' But that day he removed 35 the he-goats that were striped and brindled and all the spotted and brindled she-goats, all that had any white on them, and every ram that was black, and he handed them over to his own sons. Then he put a distance 36 of three days' journey between himself and Jacob, while Jacob was left tending those of Laban's flocks that remained. Thereupon 37 Jacob took fresh rods of white poplar, almond, and plane tree, and peeled off strips of bark, exposing the white of the rods. Then he fixed the peeled rods upright 38

---

d *That is* See, a son.   e *That is* Hearing.   f *That is* Union.   g *That is* Praise.   h *That is* He has given judgement.   i *That is* Trickery.   j *That is* Good Fortune.   k *That is* Happy.
l *That is* Reward.   m *That is* Prince.   n *The name may mean either* He takes away *or* May he add.   o *Prob. rdg.; Heb. adds* I will watch.

in the troughs at the watering-places where
the flocks came to drink; they faced the she-
goats that were on heat when they came to
39 drink. They felt a longing for the rods and
they gave birth to young that were striped
40 and spotted and brindled. As for the rams,
Jacob divided them, and let the ewes run
only with such of the rams in Laban's flock
as were striped and black; and thus he bred
separate flocks for himself, which he did
41 not add to Laban's sheep. As for the goats,
whenever the more vigorous were on heat,
he put the rods in front of them at the troughs
42 so that they would long for the rods; he
did not put them there for the weaker goats.
Thus the weaker came to be Laban's and
43 the stronger Jacob's. So Jacob increased in
wealth more and more until he possessed
great flocks, male and female slaves, camels,
and asses.

Jacob runs away from Laban

31 Jacob learnt that Laban's sons were saying,
'Jacob has taken everything that was our
father's, and all his wealth has come from
2 our father's property.' He also noticed that
Laban was not so well disposed to him as
3 he had once been. Then the LORD said to
Jacob, 'Go back to the land of your fathers
4 and to your kindred. I will be with you.' So
Jacob sent to fetch Rachel and Leah to his
5 flocks out in the country and said to them,
'I see that your father is not as well disposed
to me as once he was; yet the God of my
6 father has been with me. You know how I
have served your father to the best of my
7 power, but he has cheated me and changed
my wages ten times over. Yet God did not
8 let him do me any harm. If Laban said, "The
spotted ones shall be your wages", then all
the flock bore spotted young; and if he
9 said, "The striped ones shall be your wages",
then all the flock bore striped young. God
has taken away your father's property and
10 has given it to me. In the season when the
flocks were on heat, I had a dream: I looked
up and saw that the he-goats mounting the
flock were striped and spotted and dappled.
11 The angel of God said to me in my dream,
12 "Jacob", and I replied, "Here I am", and
he said, "Look up and see: all the he-goats
mounting the flock are striped and spotted
and dappled. I have seen all that Laban is
13 doing to you. I am the God who appeared
to you at Bethel where you anointed a
sacred pillar and where you made your vow.
Now leave this country at once and return
14 to the land of your birth."' Rachel and
Leah answered him, 'We no longer have
15 any part or lot in our father's house. Does
he not look on us as foreigners, now that
he has sold us and spent on himself the
16 whole of the money paid for us? But all

the wealth which God has saved from our
father's clutches is ours and our children's.
Now do everything that God has said.'
17 Jacob at once set his sons and his wives
18 on camels, and drove off all the herds
and livestock which he had acquired in
Paddan-aram, to go to his father Isaac in
Canaan.

19 When Laban the Aramaean had gone to
shear his sheep, Rachel stole her father's
20 household gods, and Jacob deceived Laban,
21 keeping his departure secret. So Jacob ran
away with all that he had, crossed the River
and made for the hill-country of Gilead.
22 Three days later, when Laban heard that
23 Jacob had run away, he took his kinsmen
with him, pursued Jacob for seven days
and caught up with him in the hill-country
24 of Gilead. But God came to Laban in a
dream by night and said to him, 'Be careful to say nothing to Jacob, either good or
bad.'

Laban overtakes Jacob

25 When Laban overtook him, Jacob had
pitched his tent in the hill-country of Gilead,
and Laban pitched his in the company of

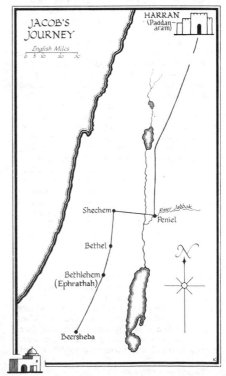

JACOB'S
JOURNEY

English Miles
0 5 10   20   30

HARRAN
(Paddan-
aram)

Shechem

River Jabbok
Peniel

Bethel

Bethlehem
(Ephrathah)

Beersheba

N

26 his kinsmen in the same hill-country. Laban said to Jacob, 'What have you done? You have deceived me and carried off my daughters as though they were captives taken in
27 war. Why did you slip away secretly without telling me? I would have set you on your way with songs and the music of tambourines
28 and harps. You did not even let me kiss my daughters and their children. In this you
29 were at fault. It is in my power to do you an injury, but yesterday the God of your father spoke to me; he told me to be careful to say
30 nothing to you, either good or bad. I know that you went away because you were homesick and pining for your father's house, but why did you steal my gods?'
31 Jacob answered, 'I was afraid; I thought you would take your daughters from me by
32 force. Whoever is found in possession of your gods shall die for it. Let our kinsmen here be witnesses: point out anything I have that is yours, and take it back.' Jacob did not know that Rachel had stolen the gods.
33 So Laban went into Jacob's tent and Leah's tent and that of the two slave-girls, but he found nothing. When he came out of Leah's
34 tent he went into Rachel's. Now she had taken the household gods and put them in the camel-bag and was sitting on them. Laban went through everything in the tent
35 and found nothing. Rachel said to her father, 'Do not take it amiss, sir, that I cannot rise in your presence: the common lot of woman is upon me.' So for all his search Laban did not find his household gods.
36 Jacob was angry, and he expostulated with Laban, exclaiming, 'What have I done wrong? What is my offence, that you have
37 come after me in hot pursuit and gone through all my possessions? Have you found anything belonging to your household? If so, set it here in front of my kinsmen and yours, and let them judge between
38 the two of us. In all the twenty years I have been with you, your ewes and she-goats have never miscarried; I have not eaten the
39 rams of your flocks; I have never brought to you the body of any animal mangled by wild beasts, but I bore the loss myself; you claimed compensation from me for anything
40 stolen by day or by night. This was the way of it: by day the heat consumed me and the
41 frost by night, and sleep deserted me. For twenty years I have been in your household. I worked for you fourteen years to win your two daughters and six years for your flocks, and you changed my wages ten times over.
42 If the God of my father, the God of Abraham and the Fear of Isaac, had not been with me, you would have sent me away empty-handed. But God saw my labour and my hardships, and last night he rebuked you.'

The agreement between Jacob and Laban

43 Laban answered Jacob, 'The daughters are my daughters, the children are my children, the flocks are my flocks; all that you see is mine. But as for my daughters, what can I do today about them and the children they
44 have borne? Come now, we will make an agreement, you and I, and let it stand as a
45 witness between us.' So Jacob chose a great stone and set it upright as a sacred pillar.
46 Then he told his kinsmen to gather stones, and they took them and built a cairn, and there beside the cairn they ate together.
47 Laban called it Jegar-sahadutha,*p* and Jacob
48 called it Gal-ed.*q* Laban said, 'This cairn is witness today between you and me.' For
49 this reason it was named Gal-ed; it was also named Mizpah,*r* for Laban said, 'May the LORD watch between you and me, when we
50 are parted from each other's sight. If you ill-treat my daughters or take other wives beside them when no one is there to see, then God be witness between us.' Laban said
51 further to Jacob, 'Here is this cairn, and here the pillar which I have set up between us. This cairn is witness and the pillar is
52 witness: I for my part will not pass beyond this cairn to your side, and you for your part shall not pass beyond this cairn and this
53 pillar to my side to do an injury, otherwise the God of Abraham and the God of Nahor will judge between us.' And Jacob swore this oath in the name of the Fear of Isaac
54 his father. He slaughtered an animal for sacrifice, there in the hill-country, and summoned his kinsmen to the feast. So they ate together and spent the night there.
55 Laban rose early in the morning, kissed his daughters and their children, blessed them and went home again. Then Jacob
32 continued his journey and was met by angels
2 of God. When he saw them, Jacob said, 'This is the company of God', and he called that place Mahanaim.*s*

Jacob prepares to meet Esau

3 Jacob sent messengers on ahead to his
4 brother Esau to the district of Seir in the Edomite country, and this is what he told them to say to Esau, 'My lord, your servant Jacob says, I have been living with Laban
5 and have stayed there till now. I have oxen, asses, and sheep, and male and female slaves, and I have sent to tell you this, my
6 lord, so that I may win your favour.' The messengers returned to Jacob and said, 'We met your brother Esau already on the way
7 to meet you with four hundred men.' Jacob,

p Aramaic for Cairn of Witness.   *q Hebrew for* Cairn of Witness.   *r That is* Watch-tower.
s That is Two Companies.

much afraid and distressed, divided the
people with him, as well as the sheep, cattle,
8 and camels, into two companies, thinking
that, if Esau should come upon one company and destroy it, the other company
9 would survive. Jacob said, 'O God of my
father Abraham, God of my father Isaac,
O LORD at whose bidding I came back to
my own country and to my kindred, and
10 who didst promise me prosperity, I am not
worthy of all the true and steadfast love
which thou hast shown to me thy servant.
When I crossed the Jordan, I had nothing
but the staff in my hand; now I have two
11 companies. Save me, I pray, from my
brother Esau, for I am afraid that he may
come and destroy me, sparing neither
12 mother nor child. But thou didst say, I will
prosper you and will make your descendants
like the sand of the sea, which is beyond all
counting.'
13   Jacob spent that night there; and as a
present for his brother Esau he chose from
14 the herds he had with him two hundred she-
goats, twenty he-goats, two hundred ewes
15 and twenty rams, thirty milch-camels with
their young, forty cows and ten young bulls,
16 twenty she-asses and ten he-asses. He put
each herd separately into the care of a servant and said to each, 'Go on ahead of me,
17 and leave gaps between the herds.' Then he
gave these instructions to the first: 'When
my brother Esau meets you and asks you
to whom you belong and where you are
going and who owns these beasts you are
18 driving, you are to say, "They belong to
your servant Jacob; he sends them as a
present to my lord Esau, and he is behind

us."' He gave the same instructions to the 19
second, to the third, and all the drovers,
telling them to say the same thing to Esau
when they met him. And they were to add, 20
'Your servant Jacob is behind us'; for he
thought, 'I will appease him with the present
that I have sent on ahead, and afterwards,
when I come into his presence, he will perhaps receive me kindly.' So Jacob's present 21
went on ahead of him, but he himself spent
that night at Mahaneh.

Jacob wrestles at Peniel

During the night Jacob rose, took his two 22
wives, his two slave-girls, and his eleven
sons, and crossed the ford of Jabbok. He 23
took them and sent them across the gorge
with all that he had. So Jacob was left alone, 24
and a man wrestled with him there till[t] daybreak. When the man saw that he could not 25
throw Jacob, he struck him in the hollow
of his thigh, so that Jacob's hip was dis-
located as they wrestled. The man said, 'Let 26
me go, for day is breaking', but Jacob replied, 'I will not let you go unless you bless
me.' He said to Jacob, 'What is your name?', 27
and he answered, 'Jacob.' The man said, 28
'Your name shall no longer be Jacob, but
Israel,[u] because you strove with God and
with men, and prevailed.' Jacob said, 'Tell 29
me, I pray, your name.' He replied, 'Why
do you ask my name?', but he gave him his
blessing there. Jacob called the place Peniel,[v] 30
'because', he said, 'I have seen God face to
face and my life is spared.' The sun rose as 31
Jacob passed through Penuel, limping because of his hip. This is why the Israelites to 32
this day do not eat the sinew of the nerve
that runs in the hollow of the thigh; for the
man had struck Jacob on that nerve in the
hollow of the thigh.

Jacob and Esau reconciled

Jacob raised his eyes and saw Esau coming **33**
towards him with four hundred men; so
he divided the children between Leah and
Rachel and the two slave-girls. He put the 2
slave-girls with their children in front, Leah
with her children next, and Rachel with
Joseph last. He then went on ahead of them, 3
bowing low to the ground seven times as he
approached his brother. Esau ran to meet 4
him and embraced him; he threw his arms
round him and kissed him, and they wept.
When Esau looked up and saw the women 5
and children, he said, 'Who are these with
you?' Jacob replied, 'The children whom
God has graciously given to your servant.'
The slave-girls came near, each with her 6
children, and they bowed low. Then Leah 7

*t Or at.   u That is God strove.   v That is
Face of God (elsewhere Penuel).*

with her children came near and bowed low, and afterwards Joseph and Rachel came 8 near and bowed low also. Esau said, 'What was all that company of yours that I met?' And he answered, 'It was meant to win 9 favour with you, my lord.' Esau answered, 'I have more than enough. Keep what is 10 yours, my brother.' But Jacob said, 'On no account: if I have won your favour, then, I pray, accept this gift from me; for, you see, I come into your presence as into that of a 11 god, and you receive me favourably. Accept this gift which I bring you; for God has been gracious to me, and I have all I want.' So he urged him, and he accepted it.
12   Then Esau said, 'Let us set out, and I will 13 go at your pace.' But Jacob answered him, 'You must know, my lord, that the children are small; the flocks and herds are suckling their young and I am concerned for them, and if the men overdrive them for a single 14 day, all my beasts will die. I beg you, my lord, to go on ahead, and I will go by easy stages at the pace of the children and of the livestock that I am driving, until I come to 15 my lord in Seir.' Esau said, 'Let me detail some of my own men to escort you', but he replied, 'Why should my lord be so kind to 16 me?' That day Esau turned back towards 17 Seir, but Jacob set out for Succoth; and there he built himself a house and made shelters for his cattle. Therefore he named that place Succoth.[w]
18   On his journey from Paddan-aram, Jacob came safely to the city of Shechem in Canaan 19 and pitched his tent to the east of it. The strip of country where he had pitched his tent he bought from the sons of Hamor father of Shechem for a hundred sheep.[x] 20 There he set up an altar and called it El-Elohey-Israel.[y]

Dinah's dishonour avenged

34 Dinah, the daughter whom Leah had borne to Jacob, went out to visit the women of the 2 country, and Shechem, son of Hamor the Hivite the local prince, saw her; he took her, 3 lay with her and dishonoured her. But he remained true to Jacob's daughter Dinah; 4 he loved the girl and comforted her. So Shechem said to his father Hamor, 'Get me 5 this girl for a wife.' When Jacob heard that Shechem had violated his daughter Dinah, his sons were with the herds in the open country, so he said nothing until they came 6 home. Meanwhile Shechem's father Hamor came out to Jacob to discuss it with him. 7 When Jacob's sons came in from the country and heard, they were grieved and angry, because in lying with Jacob's daughter he had done what the Israelites held to be an out-

rage, an intolerable thing. Hamor appealed 8 to them in these terms: 'My son Shechem is in love with this girl; I beg you to let him have her as his wife. Let us ally ourselves in 9 marriage; you shall give us your daughters, and you shall take ours in exchange. You 10 must settle among us. The country is open to you; make your home in it, move about freely and acquire land of your own.' And 11 Shechem said to the girl's father and brothers, 'I am eager to win your favour and I will give whatever you ask. Fix the bride- 12 price and the gift as high as you like, and I will give whatever you ask; but you must give me the girl in marriage.'
     Jacob's sons gave a dishonest reply to 13 Shechem and his father Hamor, laying a trap for them because Shechem had violated their sister Dinah: 'We cannot do this,' they 14 said; 'we cannot give our sister to a man who is uncircumcised; for we look on that as a disgrace. There is one condition on 15 which we will consent: if you will follow our example and have every male among you circumcised, we will give you our 16 daughters and take yours for ourselves. Then we can live among you, and we shall all become one people. But if you refuse to 17 listen to us and be circumcised, we will take the girl and go away.' Their proposal pleased 18 Hamor and his son Shechem; and the young 19 man, who was held in respect above anyone in his father's house, did not hesitate to do what they had said, because his heart was taken by Jacob's daughter.
     So Hamor and Shechem went back to the 20 city gate and addressed their fellow-citizens: 'These men are friendly to us; let them live 21 in our country and move freely in it. The land has room enough for them. Let us marry their daughters and give them ours. But these men will agree to live with us and 22 become one people on this one condition only: every male among us must be circumcised as they have been. Will not their herds, 23 their livestock, and all their chattels then be ours? We need only consent to their condition, and then they are free to live with us.' All the able-bodied men agreed with Hamor 24 and Shechem, and every single one of them was circumcised, every able-bodied male. Then two days later, while they were still in 25 great pain, Jacob's two sons Simeon and Levi, full brothers to Dinah, armed themselves with swords, boldly entered the city and killed every male. They cut down Hamor 26 and his son Shechem and took Dinah from Shechem's house and went off with her. Then 27 Jacob's other sons came in over the dead bodies and plundered the city, to avenge their sister's dishonour. They seized flocks, 28

<hr>

[w] *That is* Shelters.
God of Israel.
     [x] *Or* pieces of money (*cp. Josh. 24. 32; Job 42. 11*).   [y] *That is* God the

29 cattle, asses, and everything, both inside the city and outside in the open country; they also carried off all their possessions, their dependants, and their women, and plundered everything in the houses.

30 Jacob said to Simeon and Levi, 'You have brought trouble on me, you have made my name stink among the people of the country, the Canaanites and the Perizzites. My numbers are few; if they muster against me and attack me, I shall be destroyed, I and my 31 household with me.' They answered, 'Is our sister to be treated as a common whore?'

God blesses Jacob at Bethel

35 God said to Jacob, 'Go up to Bethel and settle there; build an altar there to the God who appeared to you when you were running 2 away from your brother Esau.' So Jacob said to his household and to all who were with him, 'Rid yourselves of the foreign gods which you have among you, purify yourselves, and see your clothes are mended.[z] 3 We are going to Bethel, so that I can set up an altar there to the God who answered me in the day of my distress, and who has been 4 with me all the way that I have come.' So they handed over to Jacob all the foreign gods in their possession and the rings from their ears, and he buried them under the 5 terebinth-tree near Shechem. Then they set out, and the cities round about were panic-stricken, and the inhabitants dared not pur-6 sue the sons of Jacob. Jacob and all the people with him came to Luz, that is Bethel, 7 in Canaan. There he built an altar, and he called the place El-bethel, because it was there that God had revealed himself to him when he was running away from his brother. 8 Rebecca's nurse Deborah died and was buried under the oak below Bethel, and he named it Allon-bakuth.[a]

9 God appeared again to Jacob when he 10 came back from Paddan-aram and blessed him. God said to him:

'Jacob is your name,
but your name shall no longer be Jacob:
Israel shall be your name.'

11 So he named him Israel. And God said to him:

'I am God Almighty.
Be fruitful and increase as a nation;

a host of nations shall come from you,
and kings shall spring from your body.
The land which I gave to Abraham and 12
Isaac I give to you;
and to your descendants after you I give this
land.'

God then left him, and Jacob erected a 13 14 sacred pillar in the place where God had spoken with him, a pillar of stone, and he offered a drink-offering over it and poured oil on it. Jacob called the place where God 15 had spoken with him Bethel.

The death of Rachel

They set out from Bethel, and when there 16 was still some distance to go to Ephrathah, Rachel was in labour and her pains were severe. While her pains were upon her, the 17 midwife said, 'Do not be afraid, this is another son for you.' Then with her last 18 breath, as she was dying, she named him Ben-oni,[b] but his father called him Benjamin.[c] So Rachel died and was buried by 19 the side of the road to Ephrathah, that is Bethlehem. Jacob set up a sacred pillar over 20 her grave; it is known to this day as the Pillar of Rachel's Grave. Then Israel jour-21 neyed on and pitched his tent on the other side of Migdal-eder. While Israel was living 22 in that district, Reuben went and lay with his father's concubine Bilhah, and Israel came to hear of it.

Jacob's sons

The sons of Jacob were twelve. The sons of 23 Leah: Jacob's first-born Reuben, then Simeon, Levi, Judah, Issachar and Zebulun. The sons of Rachel: Joseph and Benjamin. 24 The sons of Rachel's slave-girl Bilhah: Dan 25 and Naphtali. The sons of Leah's slave-girl 26 Zilpah: Gad and Asher. These were Jacob's sons, born to him in Paddan-aram.

The death of Isaac

Jacob came to his father Isaac at Mamre by 27 Kiriath-arba, that is Hebron, where Abraham and Isaac had dwelt. Isaac had lived 28 for a hundred and eighty years when he breathed his last. He died and was gathered 29 to his father's kin at a very great age, and his sons Esau and Jacob buried him.

Esau's descendants

36 This is the table of the descendants 2 of Esau: that is Edom. Esau took Canaanite women in marriage, Adah daughter of Elon the Hittite and Oholibamah daughter of Anah

3 son of Zibeon the Horite,[d] and Basemath, Ishmael's daughter, sister of Nebaioth.
4[e] Adah bore Eliphaz to Esau; Ba-5 semath bore Reuel, and Oholibamah bore Jeush, Jalam and Korah. These were Esau's sons, born to

him in Canaan. Esau took his 6 wives, his sons and daughters and everyone in his household, his herds, his cattle, and all the chattels that he had acquired in Canaan, and went to the district of Seir out of the way of his brother Jacob,

z Or change your clothes.   a That is Oak of Weeping.   b That is Son of my ill luck.
c That is Son of good luck or Son of the right hand.   d Prob. rdg. (cp. verses 20, 21); Heb. Hivite.
e Verses 4, 5, 9–13: cp. 1 Chr. 1. 35–37.

7 because they had so much stock that they could not live together; the land where they were staying could not support them because 8 of their herds. So Esau lived in the hill-country of Seir. Esau is Edom.
9 This is the table of the descendants of Esau father of the Edomites in the hill-country of Seir.
10 These are the names of the sons of Esau: Eliphaz was the son of Esau's wife Adah. Reuel was the 11 son of Esau's wife Basemath. The sons of Eliphaz were Teman, Omar, 12 Zepho, Gatam and Kenaz. Timna was concubine to Esau's son Eliphaz, and she bore him Amalek to him. These are the descendants of Esau's 13 wife Adah. These are the sons of Reuel: Nahath, Zerah, Shammah and Mizzah. These were the descendants of Esau's wife Basemath.
14 These were the sons of Esau's wife Oholibamah daughter of Anah son of Zibeon. She bore him Jeush, Jalam and Korah.
15 These are the chiefs descended from Esau. The sons of Esau's eldest son Eliphaz: chief Teman, chief Omar, chief Zepho, chief 16 Kenaz, chief Korah, chief Gatam, chief Amalek. These are the chiefs descended from Eliphaz in Edom. These are the descendants of Adah.
17 These are the sons of Esau's son Reuel: chief Nahath, chief Zerah, chief Shammah, chief Mizzah. These are the chiefs descended from Reuel in Edom. These are the descendants of Esau's wife Basemath.

18 These are the sons of Esau's wife Oholibamah: chief Jeush, chief Jalam, chief Korah. These are the chiefs born to Oholibamah daughter of Anah wife of Esau.
19 These are the sons of Esau, that is Edom, and these are their chiefs.

Seir's descendants

20 f These are the sons of Seir the Horite, the original inhabitants of the land: Lotan, Shobal, Zibeon, 21 Anah, Dishon, Ezer and Dishan. These are the chiefs of the Horites, 22 the sons of Seir in Edom. The sons of Lotan were Hori and Hemam, and Lotan had a sister named Timna.
23 These are the sons of Shobal: Alvan, Manahath, Ebal, Shepho and Onam.
24 These are the sons of Zibeon: Aiah and Anah. This is the Anah who found some mules in the wilderness while he was tending the asses of his father Zibeon.
25 These are the children of Anah: Dishon and Oholibamah daughter of Anah.
26 These are the children of Dishon: Hemdan, Eshban, Ithran 27 and Cheran. These are the sons of Ezer: Bilhan, Zavan and Akan. 28 These are the sons of Dishan: Uz and Aran.
29 These are the chiefs descended from the Horites: chief Lotan, chief Shobal, chief Zibeon, chief Anah, 30 chief Dishon, chief Ezer, chief Dishan. These are the chiefs that

were descended from the Horites according to their clans in the district of Seir.

The kings of Edom

These are the kings who ruled over 31 g Edom before there were kings in Israel: Bela son of Beor became 32 king in Edom, and his city was named Dinhabah; when he died, 33 he was succeeded by Jobab son of Zerah of Bozrah. When Jobab died, 34 he was succeeded by Husham of Teman. When Husham died, he 35 was succeeded by Hadad son of Bedad, who defeated Midian in Moabite country. His city was named Avith. When Hadad died, 36 he was succeeded by Samlah of Masrekah. When Samlah died, he 37 was succeeded by Saul of Rehoboth on the River. When Saul 38 died, he was succeeded by Baalhanan son of Akbor. When Baal- 39 hanan died, he was succeeded by Hadar. h His city was named Pau; his wife's name was Mehetabel daughter of Matred a woman of Me-zahab. i

These are the names of the chiefs 40 descended from Esau, according to their families, their places, by name: chief Timna, chief Alvah, chief Jetheth, chief Oholibamah, chief 41 Elah, chief Pinon, chief Kenaz, 42 chief Teman, chief Mibzar, chief 43 Magdiel, and chief Iram: all chiefs of Edom according to their settlements in the land which they possessed. (Esau is the father of the Edomites.)

Joseph and his brothers

37 So Jacob lived in Canaan, the country in 2 which his father had settled. And this is the story of the descendants of Jacob.

When Joseph was a boy of seventeen, he used to accompany his brothers, the sons of Bilhah and Zilpah, his father's wives, when they were in charge of the flock; and he brought their father a bad report of them.
3 Now Israel loved Joseph more than any other of his sons, because he was a child of his old age, and he made him a long, sleeved robe.
4 When his brothers saw that their father loved him more than any of them, they hated him and could not say a kind word to him.
5 Joseph had a dream; and when he told it to his brothers, they hated him still more.
6 He said to them, 'Listen to this dream I have 7 had. We were in the field binding sheaves, and my sheaf rose on end and stood upright, and your sheaves gathered round and bowed 8 low before my sheaf.' His brothers answered him, 'Do you think you will one day be a king and lord it over us?' and they hated him still more because of his dreams and 9 what he said. He had another dream, which

he told to his father and his brothers. He said, 'Listen: I have had another dream. The sun and moon and eleven stars were bowing down to me.' When he told it to his 10 father and his brothers, his father took him to task: 'What is this dream of yours?' he said. 'Must we come and bow low to the ground before you, I and your mother and your brothers?' His brothers were jealous of 11 him, but his father did not forget.

Joseph sold into Egypt

Joseph's brothers went to mind their father's 12 flocks in Shechem. Israel said to him, 'Your 13 brothers are minding the flocks in Shechem; come, I will send you to them', and he said, 'I am ready.' He said to him, 'Go and see if 14 all is well with your brothers and the sheep, and bring me back word.' So he sent off Joseph from the vale of Hebron and he came to Shechem. A man met him wander- 15 ing in the open country and asked him what he was looking for. He replied, 'I am look- 16 ing for my brothers. Tell me, please, where they are minding the flocks.' The man said, 17 'They have gone away from here; I heard

f Verses 20–28: cp. 1 Chr. 1. 38–42.　　g Verses 31–43: cp. 1 Chr. 1. 43–54.　　h Or Hadad;
cp. 1 Chr. 1. 50.　　i Or daughter of Mezahab.

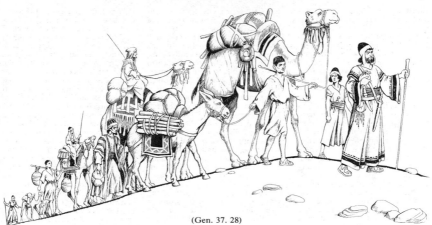

(Gen. 37. 28)

them speak of going to Dothan.' So Joseph followed his brothers and he found them in
18 Dothan. They saw him in the distance, and before he reached them, they plotted to kill
19 him. They said to each other, 'Here comes
20 that dreamer. Now is our chance; let us kill him and throw him into one of these pits and say that a wild beast has devoured him. Then we shall see what will come of his
21 dreams.' When Reuben heard, he came to his rescue, urging them not to take his life.
22 'Let us have no bloodshed', he said. 'Throw him into this pit in the wilderness, but do him no bodily harm.' He meant to save him from them so as to restore him to his father.
23 When Joseph came up to his brothers, they stripped him of the long, sleeved robe which
24 he was wearing, took him and threw him into the pit. The pit was empty and had no water in it.
25 Then they sat down to eat some food and, looking up, they saw an Ishmaelite caravan coming in from Gilead on the way down to Egypt, with camels carrying gum tragacanth
26 and balm and myrrh. Judah said to his brothers, 'What shall we gain by killing our
27 brother and concealing his death? Why not sell him to the Ishmaelites? Let us do him

no harm, for he is our brother, our own flesh and blood'; and his brothers agreed with him. Meanwhile some Midianite merchants 28 passed by and drew Joseph up out of the pit. They sold him for twenty pieces of silver to the Ishmaelites, and they brought Joseph to Egypt. When Reuben went back to the 29 pit, Joseph was not there. He rent his clothes and went back to his brothers and said, 'The 30 boy is not there. Where can I go?'

Joseph's brothers took his robe, killed a 31 goat and dipped it in the goat's blood. Then 32 they tore the robe, the long, sleeved robe, brought it to their father and said, 'Look what we have found. Do you recognize it? Is this your son's robe or not?' Jacob did 33 recognize it, and he replied, 'It is my son's robe. A wild beast has devoured him. Joseph has been torn to pieces.' Jacob rent his 34 clothes, put on sackcloth and mourned his son for a long time. His sons and daughters 35 all tried to comfort him, but he refused to be comforted. He said, 'I will go to my grave mourning for my son.' Thus Joseph's father wept for him. Meanwhile the Midianites 36 had sold Joseph in Egypt to Potiphar, one of Pharaoh's eunuchs, the captain of the guard.[j]

Judah and Tamar

38 About that time Judah left his brothers and went south and pitched his tent in company with an Adul-
2 lamite named Hirah. There he saw Bathshua the daughter of a Canaanite and married her. He slept
3 with her, and she conceived and bore a son, whom she called Er.
4 She conceived again and bore a
5 son whom she called Onan. Once more she conceived and bore a son

whom she called Shelah, and she ceased to bear children[k] when she
6 had given birth to him. Judah found a wife for his eldest son Er;
7 her name was Tamar. But Judah's eldest son Er was wicked in the LORD's sight, and the LORD took
8 his life. Then Judah told Onan to sleep with his brother's wife, to do his duty as the husband's brother and raise up issue for his brother.
9 But Onan knew that the issue would not be his; so whenever he slept

with his brother's wife, he spilled his seed on the ground so as not to raise up issue for his brother. What he did was wicked in the 10 LORD's sight, and the LORD took his life. Judah said to his daughter- 11 in-law Tamar, 'Remain as a widow in your father's house until my son Shelah grows up'; for he was afraid that he too would die like his brothers. So Tamar went and stayed in her father's house.

Time passed, and Judah's wife 12

j Or executioner.　　*k* ceased . . . children: *or* was at Kezib.

Bathshua died. When he had finished mourning, he and his friend Hirah the Adullamite went up to 13 Timnath at sheep-shearing. When Tamar was told that her father-in-law was on his way to shear his 14 sheep at Timnath, she took off her widow's weeds, veiled her face, perfumed herself and sat where the road forks in two directions on the way to Timnath. She did this because she knew that Shelah had grown up and she had not been 15 given to him as a wife. When Judah saw her, he thought she was a prostitute, although she had veiled 16 her face. He turned to her where she sat by the roadside and said, 'Let me lie with you', not knowing that she was his daughter-in-law. She said 'What will you give me to 17 lie with me?' He answered, 'I will send you a kid from my flock', but she said, 'Will you give me a pledge 18 until you send it?' He asked what pledge he should give her, and she replied, 'Your seal and its cord, and

the staff which you hold in your hand.' So he gave them to her and lay with her, and she conceived. 19 She then rose and went home, took off her veil and resumed her widow's 20 weeds. Judah sent the kid by his friend the Adullamite in order to 21 but he could not find her. He asked the men of that place, 'Where is that temple-prostitute, the one who was sitting where the road forks?', but they answered, 'There is no 22 temple-prostitute here.' So he went back to Judah and told him that he had not found her and that the men of the place had said there was 23 no such prostitute there. Judah said, 'Let her keep my pledge, or we shall get a bad name. I did send a kid, but you could not find her.' 24 About three months later Judah was told that his daughter-in-law Tamar had behaved like a common prostitute and through her wanton conduct was with child. Judah said, 'Bring her out so that she may be

burnt.' But when she was brought 25 out, she sent to her father-in-law and said, 'The father of my child is the man to whom these things belong. See if you recognize whose they are, the engraving on the seal, the pattern of the cord, and the staff.' Judah recognized them and 26 said, 'She is more in the right than I am, because I did not give her to my son Shelah.' He did not have intercourse with her again. When 27 her time was come, there were twins in her womb, and while she 28 was in labour one of them put out a hand. The midwife took a scarlet thread and fastened it round the wrist, saying, 'This one appeared first.' No sooner had he drawn back 29 his hand, than his brother came out and the midwife said, 'What! you have broken out first!' So he was named Perez.[l] Soon afterwards his 30 brother was born with the scarlet thread on his wrist, and he was named Zerah.[m]

Joseph and Potiphar's wife

39 When Joseph was taken down to Egypt, he was bought by Potiphar, one of Pharaoh's eunuchs, the captain of the guard, an Egyptian. Potiphar bought him from the Ishmae- 2 lites who had brought him there. The LORD was with Joseph and he prospered. He lived 3 in the house of his Egyptian master, who saw that the LORD was with him and was

giving him success in all that he undertook. Thus Joseph found favour with his master, 4 and he became his personal servant. Indeed, his master put him in charge of his household and entrusted him with all that he had. From the time that he put him in charge 5 of his household and all his property, the LORD blessed the Egyptian's household for Joseph's sake. The blessing of the LORD was on all that was his in house and field. He 6

l That is Breaking out.   *m That is* Redness.

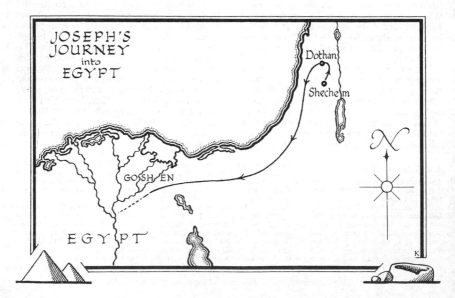

JOSEPH'S JOURNEY into EGYPT

Dothan

Shechem

GOSHEN

EGYPT

left everything he possessed in Joseph's care, and concerned himself with nothing but the food he ate.

7 Now Joseph was handsome and good-looking, and a time came when his master's wife took notice of him and said, 'Come and 8 lie with me.' But he refused and said to her, 'Think of my master. He does not know as much as I do about his own house, and he 9 has entrusted me with all he has. He has given me authority in this house second only to his own, and has withheld nothing from me except you, because you are his wife. How can I do anything so wicked, and sin 10 against God?' She kept asking Joseph day after day, but he refused to lie with her and 11 be in her company. One day he came into the house as usual to do his work, when none of the men of the household were there 12 indoors. She caught him by his cloak, saying, 'Come and lie with me', but he left the cloak in her hands and ran out of the house. 13 When she saw that he had left his cloak in 14 her hands and had run out of the house, she called out to the men of the household, 'Look at this! My husband has brought in a Hebrew to make a mockery of us. He came in here to lie with me, but I gave a loud 15 scream. When he heard me scream and call out, he left his cloak in my hand and ran 16 off.' She kept his cloak with her until his 17 master came home, and then she repeated her tale. She said, 'That Hebrew slave whom you brought in to make a mockery of me, 18 has been here with me. But when I screamed for help and called out, he left his cloak in 19 my hands and ran off.' When Joseph's master heard his wife's story of what his 20 slave had done to her, he was furious. He took Joseph and put him in the Round Tower, where the king's prisoners were kept; and there he stayed in the Round Tower. 21 But the LORD was with Joseph and kept faith with him, so that he won the favour 22 of the governor of the Round Tower. He put Joseph in charge of all the prisoners in 23 the tower and of all their work. He ceased to concern himself with anything entrusted to Joseph, because the LORD was with Joseph and gave him success in everything.

Joseph interprets the prisoners' dreams

40 It happened later that the king's butler and his baker offended their master the king of 2 Egypt. Pharaoh was angry with these two eunuchs, the chief butler and the chief baker, 3 and he put them in custody in the house of the captain of the guard, in the Round 4 Tower where Joseph was imprisoned. The captain of the guard appointed Joseph as 5 their attendant, and he waited on them. One night, when they had been in prison for some

time, they both had dreams, each needing its own interpretation—the king of Egypt's butler and his baker who were imprisoned in the Round Tower. When Joseph came to 6 them in the morning, he saw that they looked dejected. So he asked these eunuchs, who 7 were in custody with him in his master's house, why they were so downcast that day. They replied, 'We have each had a dream 8 and there is no one to interpret it for us.' Joseph said to them, 'Does not interpretation belong to God? Tell me your dreams.' So the chief butler told Joseph his dream: 9 'In my dream', he said, 'there was a vine in front of me. On the vine there were three 10 branches, and as soon as it budded, it blossomed and its clusters ripened into grapes. Now I had Pharaoh's cup in my hand, and 11 I plucked the grapes, crushed them into Pharaoh's cup and put the cup into Pharaoh's hand.' Joseph said to him, 'This is the 12 interpretation. The three branches are three days: within three days Pharaoh will raise 13 you and restore you to your post, and then you will put the cup into Pharaoh's hand as you used to do when you were his butler. But when things go well with you, if you 14 think of me, keep faith with me and bring my case to Pharaoh's notice and help me to get out of this house. By force I was carried 15 off[n] from the land of the Hebrews, and I have done nothing here to deserve being put in this dungeon.'

When the chief baker saw that Joseph 16 had given a favourable interpretation, he said to him, 'I too had a dream, and in my dream there were three baskets of white bread on my head. In the top basket there 17 was every kind of food which the baker prepares for Pharaoh, and the birds were eating out of the top basket on my head.' Joseph 18 answered, 'This is the interpretation. The three baskets are three days: within three 19 days Pharaoh will raise you and hang you up on a tree, and the birds of the air will eat your flesh.'

The third day was Pharaoh's birthday and 20 he gave a feast for all his servants. He raised the chief butler and the chief baker in the presence of his court. He restored the chief 21 butler to his post, and the butler put the cup into Pharaoh's hand; but he hanged the 22 chief baker. All went as Joseph had said in interpreting the dreams for them. Even so 23 the chief butler did not remember Joseph, but forgot him.

Joseph interprets Pharaoh's dreams

Nearly two years later Pharaoh had a dream: **41** he was standing by the Nile, and there came 2 up from the river seven cows, sleek and fat, and they grazed on the reeds. After them 3

n Or stolen.

seven other cows came up from the river,
gaunt and lean, and stood on the river-bank
4 beside the first cows. The cows that were
gaunt and lean devoured the cows that were
5 sleek and fat. Then Pharaoh woke up. He
fell asleep again and had a second dream:
he saw seven ears of corn, full and ripe, grow-
6 ing on one stalk. Growing up after them
were seven other ears, thin and shrivelled
7 by the east wind. The thin ears swallowed
up the ears that were full and ripe. Then
Pharaoh woke up and knew that it was a
8 dream. When morning came, Pharaoh was
troubled in mind; so he summoned all the
magicians and sages of Egypt. He told them
his dreams, but there was no one who could
9 interpret them for him. Then Pharaoh's
chief butler spoke up and said, 'It is time for
10 me to recall my faults. Once Pharaoh was
angry with his servants, and he imprisoned
me and the chief baker in the house of the
11 captain of the guard. One night we both had
dreams, each needing its own interpretation.
12 We had with us a young Hebrew, a slave of
the captain of the guard, and we told him
our dreams and he interpreted them for us,
giving each man's dream its own interpreta-
13 tion. Each dream came true as it had been
interpreted to us: I was restored to my position, and he was hanged.'
14   Pharaoh thereupon sent for Joseph, and
they hurriedly brought him out of the dungeon. He shaved and changed his clothes,
15 and came in to Pharaoh. Pharaoh said to
him, 'I have had a dream, and no one can
interpret it to me. I have heard it said that
you can understand and interpret dreams.'
16 Joseph answered, 'Not I, but God, will
17 answer for Pharaoh's welfare.' Then Pharaoh said to Joseph, 'In my dream I was
18 standing on the bank of the Nile, and there
came up from the river seven cows, fat and
19 sleek, and they grazed on the reeds. After
them seven other cows came up that were
poor, very gaunt and lean; I have never seen
20 such gaunt creatures in all Egypt. These lean,
gaunt cows devoured the first cows, the fat
21 ones. They were swallowed up, but no one
could have guessed that they were in the
bellies of the others, which looked as gaunt
22 as before. Then I woke up. After I had fallen

asleep again, I saw in a dream seven ears of
corn, full and ripe, growing on one stalk.
Growing up after them were seven other 23
ears, shrivelled, thin, and blighted by the east
wind. The thin ears swallowed up the seven 24
ripe ears. When I told all this to the magicians, no one could explain it to me.'
     Joseph said to Pharaoh, 'Pharaoh's dreams 25
are one dream. God has told Pharaoh what
he is going to do. The seven good cows are 26
seven years, and the seven good ears of corn
are seven years. It is all one dream. The seven 27
lean and gaunt cows that came up after them
are seven years, and the empty ears of corn
blighted by the east wind will be seven
years of famine. It is as I have said to 28
Pharaoh: God has let Pharaoh see what he
is going to do. There are to be seven years 29
of great plenty throughout the land. After 30
them will come seven years of famine;
all the years of plenty in Egypt will be
forgotten, and the famine will ruin the
country. The good years will not be remem- 31
bered in the land because of the famine that
follows; for it will be very severe. The 32
doubling of Pharaoh's dream means that
God is already resolved to do this, and he
will very soon put it into effect. Pharaoh 33
should now look for a shrewd and intelligent
man, and put him in charge of the country.
This is what Pharaoh should do: appoint 34
controllers over the land, and take one fifth
of the produce of Egypt during the seven
years of plenty. They should collect all this 35
food produced in the good years that are
coming and put the corn under Pharaoh's
control in store in the cities, and keep it
under guard. This food will be a reserve for 36
the country against the seven years of famine
which will come upon Egypt. Thus the
country will not be devastated by the famine.'

Joseph made ruler over Egypt

The plan pleased Pharaoh and all his cour- 37
tiers, and he said to them, 'Can we find a 38
man like this man, one who has the spirit
of a god[o] in him?' He said to Joseph, 'Since 39
a god[p] has made all this known to you, there
is no one so shrewd and intelligent as you.
You shall be in charge of my household, and 40
all my people will depend on your every

o Or of God.   *p Or* God.

word. Only my royal throne shall make me
41 greater than you.' Pharaoh said to Joseph,
'I hereby give you authority over the whole
42 land of Egypt.' He took off his signet-ring
and put it on Joseph's finger, he had him
dressed in fine linen, and hung a gold chain
43 round his neck. He mounted him in his
viceroy's chariot and men cried 'Make way!'
before him. Thus Pharaoh made him ruler
44 over all Egypt and said to him, 'I am the
Pharaoh. Without your consent no man
shall lift hand or foot throughout Egypt.'
45 Pharaoh named him Zaphenath-paneah, and
he gave him as wife Asenath the daughter
of Potiphera priest of On. And Joseph's
authority extended over the whole of Egypt.
46 Joseph was thirty years old when he
entered the service of Pharaoh king of
Egypt. When he took his leave of the king,
he made a tour of inspection through the
47 country. During the seven years of plenty
48 there were abundant harvests, and Joseph
gathered all the food produced in Egypt
during those years and stored it in the cities,
putting in each the food from the surround-
49 ing country. He stored the grain in huge
quantities; it was like the sand of the sea,
so much that he stopped measuring: it was
beyond all measure.
50 Before the years of famine came, two sons
were born to Joseph by Asenath the daugh-
51 ter of Potiphera priest of On. He named the
elder Manasseh,*q* 'for', he said, 'God has
caused me to forget all my troubles and
52 my father's family.' He named the second
Ephraim,*r* 'for', he said, 'God has made me
53 fruitful in the land of my hardships.' When
the seven years of plenty in Egypt came to
54 an end, seven years of famine began, as
Joseph had foretold. There was famine in
every country, but throughout Egypt there
55 was bread. So when the famine spread
through all Egypt, the people appealed to
Pharaoh for bread, and he ordered them to
56 go to Joseph and do as he told them. In
every region there was famine, and Joseph
opened all the granaries and sold corn to
the Egyptians, for the famine was severe.
57 The whole world came to Egypt to buy corn
from Joseph, so severe was the famine
everywhere.

Joseph's brothers come to Egypt for corn

When Jacob saw that there was corn in **42**
Egypt, he said to his sons, 'Why do you
stand staring at each other? I have heard 2
that there is corn in Egypt. Go down and
buy some so that we may keep ourselves
alive and not starve.' So Joseph's brothers, 3
ten of them, went down to buy grain from
Egypt, but Jacob did not let Joseph's brother 4
Benjamin go with them, for fear that he
might come to harm.

So the sons of Israel came down with 5
everyone else to buy corn, because of the
famine in Canaan. Now Joseph was governor 6
of all Egypt, and it was he who sold the corn
to all the people of the land. Joseph's
brothers came and bowed to the ground
before him, and when he saw his brothers, 7
he recognized them but pretended not to
know them and spoke harshly to them.
'Where do you come from?' he asked. 'From
Canaan,' they answered, 'to buy food.' Al- 8
though Joseph had recognized his brothers,
they did not recognize him. He remem- 9
bered also the dreams he had had about
them; so he said to them, 'You are spies;
you have come to spy out the weak points
in our defences.' They answered, 'No, sir: 10
your servants have come to buy food. We 11
are all sons of one man. Your humble servants are honest men, we are not spies.'
'No,' he insisted, 'it is to spy out our weak- 12
nesses that you have come.' They answered 13
him, 'Sir, there are twelve of us, all brothers,
sons of one man in Canaan. The youngest
is still with our father, and one has disappeared.' But Joseph said again to them, 14
'No, as I said before, you are spies. This is 15
how you shall be put to the proof: unless
your youngest brother comes here, by the life
of Pharaoh, you shall not leave this place.
Send one of your number to bring your 16
brother; the rest will be kept in prison. Thus
your story will be tested, and we shall see
whether you are telling the truth. If not, then,
by the life of Pharaoh, you must be spies.'
So he kept them in prison for three days. 17

Joseph's brothers go back to Canaan

On the third day Joseph said to the brothers, 18
'Do what I say and your lives will be spared;

q That is Causing to forget.   *r That is* Fruit.

19 for I am a God-fearing man: if you are honest men, your brother there shall be kept in prison, and the rest of you shall take corn 20 for your hungry households and bring your youngest brother to me; thus your words will be proved true, and you will not die.'ˢ 21 They said to one another, 'No doubt we deserve to be punished because of our brother, whose suffering we saw; for when he pleaded with us we refused to listen. That is why these sufferings have come upon us.' 22 But Reuben said, 'Did I not tell you not to do the boy a wrong? But you would not listen, and his blood is on our heads, and 23 we must pay.' They did not know that Joseph understood, because he had used an 24 interpreter. Joseph turned away from them and wept. Then, turning back, he played a trick on them. First he took Simeon and 25 bound him before their eyes; then he gave orders to fill their bags with grain, to return each man's silver, putting it in his sack, and to give them supplies for the journey. All 26 this was done; and they loaded the corn on 27 to their asses and went away. When they stopped for the night, one of them opened his sack to give fodder to his ass, and there 28 he saw his silver at the top of the pack. He said to his brothers, 'My silver has been returned to me, and here it is in my pack.' Bewildered and trembling, they said to each other, 'What is this that God has done to us?' 29 When they came to their father Jacob in Canaan, they told him all that had happened 30 to them. They said, 'The man who is lord of the country spoke harshly to us and made 31 out that we were spies. We said to him, "We 32 are honest men, we are not spies. There are twelve of us, all brothers, sons of one father. One has disappeared, and the youngest is 33 with our father in Canaan." This man, the lord of the country, said to us, "This is how I shall find out if you are honest men. Leave one of your brothers with me, take food for 34 your hungry households and go. Bring your youngest brother to me, and I shall know that you are not spies, but honest men. Then I will restore your brother to you, and you 35 can move about the country freely."' But on emptying their sacks, each of them found his silver inside, and when they and their father saw the bundles of silver, they were 36 afraid. Their father Jacob said to them, 'You have robbed me of my children. Joseph has disappeared; Simeon has disappeared; and now you are taking Benjamin. Everything is 37 against me.' Reuben said to his father, 'You may kill both my sons if I do not bring him back to you. Put him in my charge, and I 38 shall bring him back.' But Jacob said, 'My son shall not go with you, for his brother is

dead and he alone is left. If he comes to any harm on the journey, you will bring down my grey hairs in sorrow to the grave.'

Joseph's brothers return with Benjamin

The famine was still severe in the country. **43** When they had used up the corn they had 2 brought from Egypt, their father said to them, 'Go back and buy a little more corn for us to eat.' But Judah replied, 'The man 3 plainly warned us that we must not go into his presence unless our brother was with us. If you let our brother go with us, we will go 4 down and buy food for you. But if you will 5 not let him, we will not go; for the man said to us, "You shall not come into my presence, unless your brother is with you."' Israel said, 6 'Why have you treated me so badly? Why did you tell the man that you had yet another brother?' They answered, 'He questioned us 7 closely about ourselves and our family: "Is your father still alive?" he asked, "Have you a brother?", and we answered his questions. How could we possibly know that he would tell us to bring our brother to Egypt?' Judah 8 said to his father Israel, 'Send the boy with me; then we can start at once. By doing this we shall save our lives, ours, yours, and our dependants', and none of us will starve. I 9 will go surety for him and you may hold me responsible. If I do not bring him back and restore him to you, you shall hold me guilty all my life. If we had not wasted all this time, 10 by now we could have gone back twice over.'

Their father Israel said to them, 'If it 11 must be so, then do this: take in your baggage, as a gift for the man, some of the produce for which our country is famous: a little balsam, a little honey, gum tragacanth, myrrh, pistachio nuts, and almonds. Take 12 double the amount of silver and restore what was returned to you in your packs; perhaps it was a mistake. Take your brother with 13 you and go straight back to the man. May 14 God Almighty make him kindly disposed to you, and may he send back the one whom you left behind, and Benjamin too. As for me, if I am bereaved, then I am bereaved.' So they took the gift and double the amount 15 of silver, and with Benjamin they started at once for Egypt, where they presented themselves to Joseph.

When Joseph saw Benjamin with them, 16 he said to his steward, 'Bring these men indoors, kill a beast and make dinner ready, for they will eat with me at noon.' He did as 17 Joseph told him and brought the men into the house. When they came in they were 18 afraid, for they thought, 'We have been brought in here because of that affair of the silver which was replaced in our packs the first time. He means to trump up some

s Prob. rdg.; Heb. adds and they did so.

charge against us and victimize us, seize our
19 asses and make us his slaves.' So they
approached Joseph's steward and spoke to
20 him at the door of the house. They said,
'Please listen, my lord. After our first visit
21 to buy food, when we reached the place
where we were to spend the night, we opened
our packs and each of us found his silver in
full weight at the top of his pack. We have
22 brought it back with us, and have added
other silver to buy food. We do not know
23 who put the silver in our packs.' He answered,
'Set your minds at rest; do not be afraid. It
was your God, the God of your father, who
hid treasure for you in your packs. I did
receive the silver.' Then he brought Simeon
out to them.

24 The steward brought them into Joseph's
house and gave them water to wash their
feet, and provided fodder for their asses.
25 They had their gifts ready when Joseph
arrived at noon, for they had heard that
26 they were to eat there. When Joseph came
into the house, they presented him with the
gifts which they had brought, bowing to the
27 ground before him. He asked them how
they were and said, 'Is your father well, the
old man of whom you spoke? Is he still
28 alive?' They answered, 'Yes, my lord, our
father is still alive and well.' And they bowed
29 low and prostrated themselves. Joseph
looked and saw his own mother's son, his
brother Benjamin, and asked, 'Is this your
youngest brother, of whom you told me?',
and to Benjamin he said, 'May God be
30 gracious to you, my son!' Joseph was overcome; his feelings for his brother mastered
him, and he was near to tears. So he went
31 into the inner room and wept. Then he
washed his face and came out; and, holding
back his feelings, he ordered the meal to be
32 served. They served him by himself, and the
brothers by themselves, and the Egyptians
who were at dinner were also served separately; for Egyptians hold it an abomination
33 to eat with Hebrews. The brothers were
seated in his presence, the eldest first according to his age and so on down to the youngest:
they looked at one another in astonishment.
34 Joseph sent them each a portion from what
was before him, but Benjamin's was five
times larger than any of the other portions.
Thus they drank with him and all grew
merry.

The missing goblet

44 Joseph gave his steward this order: 'Fill the
men's packs with as much food as they can
carry and put each man's silver at the top
2 of his pack. And put my goblet, my silver
goblet, at the top of the youngest brother's
pack with the silver for the corn.' He did as
3 Joseph said. At daybreak the brothers were

allowed to take their asses and go on their
journey; but before they had gone very far 4
from the city, Joseph said to his steward,
'Go after those men at once, and when you
catch up with them, say, "Why have you
repaid good with evil? Why have you stolen 5
the silver goblet? It is the one from which
my lord drinks, and which he uses for
divination. You have done a wicked thing." '
When he caught up with them, he repeated 6
all this to them, but they replied, 'My lord, 7
how can you say such things? No, sir, God
forbid that we should do any such thing!
You remember the silver we found at the 8
top of our packs? We brought it back to you
from Canaan. Why should we steal silver
or gold from your master's house? If any 9
one of us is found with the goblet, he shall
die; and, what is more, my lord, we will all
become your slaves.' He said, 'Very well, 10
then; I accept what you say. The man in
whose possession it is found shall be my
slave, but the rest of you shall go free.' Each 11
man quickly lowered his pack to the ground
and opened it. The steward searched them, 12
beginning with the eldest and finishing with
the youngest, and the goblet was found in
Benjamin's pack.

At this they rent their clothes; then each 13
man loaded his ass and they returned to the
city. Joseph was still in the house when 14
Judah and his brothers came in. They threw
themselves on the ground before him, and 15
Joseph said, 'What have you done? You
might have known that a man like myself
would practise divination.' Judah said, 'What 16
shall we say, my lord? What can we say to
prove our innocence? God has found out
our sin. Here we are, my lord, ready to be
made your slaves, we ourselves as well as
the one who was found with the goblet.'
Joseph answered, 'God forbid that I should 17
do such a thing! The one who was found
with the goblet shall become my slave, but
the rest of you can go home to your father
in peace.'

Judah pleads for Benjamin

Then Judah went up to him and said, 'Please 18
listen, my lord. Let me say a word to your
lordship, I beg. Do not be angry with me, for
you are as great as Pharaoh. You, my lord, 19
asked us whether we had a father or a
brother. We answered, "We have an aged 20
father, and he has a young son born in his
old age; this boy's full brother is dead and
he alone is left of his mother's children, he
alone, and his father loves him." Your lord- 21
ship answered, "Bring him down to me so
that I may set eyes on him." We told you, 22
my lord, that the boy could not leave his
father, and that his father would die if he
left him. But you answered, "Unless your 23

24 youngest brother comes here with you, you shall not enter my presence again." We went
25 back to your servant our father, and told him what your lordship had said. When our
26 father told us to go and buy food, we answered, "We cannot go down; for without our youngest brother we cannot enter the man's presence; but if our brother is
27 with us, we will go." Our father, my lord, then said to us, "You know that my wife
28 bore me two sons. One left me, and I said, 'He must have been torn to pieces.' I have
29 not seen him to this day. If you take this one from me as well, and he comes to any harm, then you will bring down my grey
30 hairs in trouble to the grave." Now, my lord, when I return to my father without the boy—and remember, his life is bound up
31 with the boy's—what will happen is this: he will see that the boy is not with us and will die, and your servants will have brought down our father's grey hairs in sorrow to the
32 grave. Indeed, my lord, it was I who went surety for the boy to my father. I said, "If I do not bring him back to you, then you
33 shall hold me guilty all my life." Now, my lord, let me remain in place of the boy as your lordship's slave, and let him go with
34 his brothers. How can I return to my father without the boy? I could not bear to see the misery which my father would suffer.'

Joseph makes himself known to his brothers

45 Joseph could no longer control his feelings in front of his attendants, and he called out, 'Let everyone leave my presence.' So there was nobody present when Joseph made
2 himself known to his brothers, but so loudly did he weep that the Egyptians and Pharaoh's
3 household heard him. Joseph said to his brothers, 'I am Joseph; can my father be still alive?' His brothers were so dumbfounded at finding themselves face to face with Joseph that they could not answer.
4 Then Joseph said to his brothers, 'Come closer', and so they came close. He said, 'I am your brother Joseph whom you sold into
5 Egypt. Now do not be distressed or take it amiss that you sold me into slavery here; it was God who sent me ahead of you to
6 save men's lives. For there have now been two years of famine in the country, and there will be another five years with neither
7 ploughing nor harvest. God sent me ahead of you to ensure that you will have descendants on earth, and to preserve you all, a
8 great band of survivors. So it was not you who sent me here, but God, and he has made me a father*t* to Pharaoh, and lord over all
9 his household and ruler of all Egypt. Make haste and go back to my father and give him this message from his son Joseph: "God has

made me lord of all Egypt. Come down to
10 me; do not delay. You shall live in the land of Goshen and be near me, you, your sons and your grandsons, your flocks and herds
11 and all that you have. I will take care of you there, you and your household and all that you have, and see that you are not reduced to poverty; there are still five years of famine
12 to come." You can see for yourselves, and so can my brother Benjamin, that it is Joseph himself who is speaking to you. Tell
13 my father of all the honour which I enjoy in Egypt, tell him all you have seen, and make haste to bring him down here.' Then
14 he threw his arms round his brother Benjamin and wept, and Benjamin too embraced
15 him weeping. He kissed all his brothers and wept over them, and afterwards his brothers talked with him.
16 When the report that Joseph's brothers had come reached Pharaoh's house, he and all his courtiers were pleased. Pharaoh said
17 to Joseph, 'Say to your brothers: "This is what you are to do. Load your beasts and go to Canaan. Fetch your father and your
18 households and bring them to me. I will give you the best that there is in Egypt, and you shall enjoy the fat of the land." You
19 shall also tell them: "Take wagons from Egypt for your dependants and your wives and fetch your father and come. Have no
20 regrets at leaving your possessions, for all the best that there is in Egypt is yours." '
21 The sons of Israel did as they were told, and Joseph gave them wagons, according to Pharaoh's orders, and food for the journey.
22 He provided each of them with a change of clothing, but to Benjamin he gave three hundred pieces of silver and five changes of
23 clothing. Moreover he sent his father ten asses carrying the best that there was in Egypt, and ten she-asses loaded with grain,
24 bread, and provisions for his journey. So he dismissed his brothers, telling them not to quarrel among themselves on the road,
25 and they set out. Thus they went up from Egypt and came to their father Jacob in
26 Canaan. There they gave him the news that Joseph was still alive and that he was ruler of all Egypt. He was stunned and could not
27 believe it, but they told him all that Joseph had said; and when he saw the wagons which Joseph had sent to take him away, his spirit
28 revived. Israel said, 'It is enough. Joseph my son is still alive; I will go and see him before I die.'

Jacob and his family journey to Egypt

46 So Israel set out with all that he had and came to Beersheba where he offered sacri-
2 fices to the God of his father Isaac. God said to Israel in a vision by night, 'Jacob, Jacob',

---

t Or counsellor.

and he answered, 'I am here.' God said, 'I am God, the God of your father. Do not be afraid to go down to Egypt, for there I will make you a great nation. I will go down with you to Egypt, and I myself will bring you back again without fail; and Joseph shall close your eyes.' So Jacob set out from Beersheba. Israel's sons conveyed their father Jacob, their dependants, and their wives in the wagons which Pharaoh had sent to carry them. They took the herds and 6 the stock which they had acquired in Canaan and came to Egypt, Jacob and all his descendants with him, his sons and their sons, 7 his daughters and his sons' daughters: he brought all his descendants to Egypt.

Israelites who entered Egypt

These are the names of the Israelites who entered Egypt: Jacob and his sons, as follows: Reuben, Jacob's eldest son. The sons of Reuben: Enoch, Pallu, Hezron and Carmi. The sons of Simeon: Jemuel, Jamin, Ohad, Jachin, Zohar, and Saul, who was the son of a Canaanite woman. The sons of Levi: Gershon, Kohath and Merari. The sons of Judah: Er, Onan, Shelah, Perez and Zerah; of these Er and Onan died in Canaan. The sons of Perez were Hezron and Hamul. The sons of Issachar: Tola, Pua, Iob and Shimron. The sons of Zebulun: Sered, Elon and Jahleel. These are the sons of Leah whom she bore to Jacob in Paddan-aram, and there was also his daughter Dinah. His sons and daughters numbered thirty-three in all.

16 The sons of Gad: Ziphion, Haggi, Shuni, Ezbon, Eri, Arodi 17 and Areli. The sons of Asher: Imnah, Ishvah, Ishvi, Beriah, and their sister Serah. The sons of Beriah: Heber and Malchiel. 18 These are the descendants of Zilpah whom Laban gave to his daughter Leah; sixteen in all, born to Jacob.

19 The sons of Jacob's wife Rachel: 20 Joseph and Benjamin. Manasseh and Ephraim were born to Joseph in Egypt. Asenath daughter of Potiphera priest of On bore them to 21 him. The sons of Benjamin: Bela, Becher and Ashbel; and the sons of Bela: Gera, Naaman, Ehi, Rosh, Muppim, Huppim and Ard. These 22 are the descendants of Rachel; fourteen in all, born to Jacob.

The son[v] of Dan: Hushim. The 23 24 sons of Naphtali: Jahzeel, Guni, Jezer and Shillem. These are the 25 descendants of Bilhah whom Laban gave to his daughter Rachel; seven in all, born to Jacob.

The persons belonging to Jacob 26 who came to Egypt, all his direct descendants, not counting the wives of his sons, were sixty-six in all. Two sons were born to Joseph in 27 Egypt. Thus the house of Jacob numbered seventy when it entered Egypt.

Jacob and his family in Egypt

Judah was sent ahead that he might appear before Joseph in Goshen, and so they entered Goshen. Joseph had his chariot made ready and went up to meet his father Israel in Goshen. When they met, he threw his arms round him and wept, and embraced him for a long time, weeping. Israel said to Joseph, 'I have seen your face again, and you are still alive. Now I am ready to die.' Joseph said to his brothers and to his father's household, 'I will go and tell Pharaoh; I will say to him, "My brothers and my father's household who were in Canaan have come to me."' Now his brothers were shepherds, men with their own flocks and herds, and they had brought them with them, their flocks and herds and all that they possessed. So Joseph said, 'When Pharaoh summons you and asks you what your occupation is, you must say, "My lord, we have been herdsmen all our lives, as our fathers were before us." You must say this if you are to settle in the land of Goshen, because all shepherds are an abomination to the Egyptians.'

Joseph came and told Pharaoh, 'My **47** father and my brothers have arrived from Canaan, with their flocks and their cattle and all that they have, and they are now in Goshen.' Then he chose five of his brothers 2 and presented them to Pharaoh, who asked 3 them what their occupation was, and they answered, 'My lord, we are shepherds, we and our fathers before us, and we have come 4 to stay in this land; for there is no pasture

u Verses 8–25: cp. Exod. 6. 14–16; Num. 26. 5–50; 1 Chr. 4. 1, 24; 5. 3; 6. 1; 7. 1, 6, 13, 30; 8. 1–5.
v Prob. rdg.; Heb. sons.

in Canaan for our sheep, because the famine
there is so severe. We beg you, my lord, to
5 let us settle now in Goshen.' Pharaoh said
to Joseph, 'So your father and your brothers
6 have come to you. The land of Egypt is
yours; settle them in the best part of it. Let
them live in Goshen, and if you know of any
capable men among them, make them chief
herdsmen over my cattle.'
7 Then Joseph brought his father in and
presented him to Pharaoh, and Jacob gave
8 Pharaoh his blessing. Pharaoh asked Jacob
9 his age, and he answered, 'The years of my
earthly sojourn are one hundred and thirty;
hard years they have been and few, not equal
to the years that my fathers lived in their
10 time.' Jacob then blessed Pharaoh and went
11 out from his presence. So Joseph settled his
father and his brothers, and gave them lands
in Egypt, in the best part of the country, in
the district of Rameses, as Pharaoh had
12 ordered. He supported his father, his brothers, and all his father's household with all
the food they needed.

Joseph's administration

13 There was no bread in the whole country,
so very severe was the famine, and Egypt
14 and Canaan were laid low by it. Joseph collected all the silver in Egypt and Canaan in
return for the corn which the people bought,
15 and deposited it in Pharaoh's treasury. When
all the silver in Egypt and Canaan had been
used up, the Egyptians came to Joseph and
said, 'Give us bread, or we shall die before
16 your eyes. Our silver is all spent.' Joseph
said, 'If your silver is spent, give me your
herds and I will give you bread in return.'
17 So they brought their herds to Joseph, who
gave them bread in exchange for their
horses, their flocks of sheep and herds of
cattle, and their asses. He maintained them
that year with bread in exchange for their
18 herds. The year came to an end, and the
following year they came to him again and
said, 'My lord, we cannot conceal it from
you: our silver is all gone and our herds of
cattle are yours. Nothing is left for your
19 lordship but our bodies and our lands. Why
should we perish before your eyes, we and
our land as well? Take us and our land in
payment for bread, and we and our land
alike will be in bondage to Pharaoh. Give
us seed-corn to keep us alive, or we shall die
20 and our land will become desert.' So Joseph
bought all the land in Egypt for Pharaoh,
because the Egyptians sold all their fields,
so severe was the famine; the land became
21 Pharaoh's. As for the people, Pharaoh set
them to work as slaves from one end of the
22 territory of Egypt to the other. But Joseph
did not buy the land which belonged to the
priests; they had a fixed allowance from

Pharaoh and lived on this, so that they had
no need to sell their land.
Joseph said to the people, 'Listen; I have 2
today bought you and your land for Pharaoh.
Here is seed-corn for you. Sow the land, and 2
give one fifth of the crop to Pharaoh. Four
fifths shall be yours to provide seed for your
fields and food for yourselves, your households, and your dependants.' The people 2
said, 'You have saved our lives. If it please
your lordship, we will be Pharaoh's slaves.'
Joseph established it as a law in Egypt that 2
one fifth should belong to Pharaoh, and this
is still in force. It was only the priests' land
that did not pass into Pharaoh's hands.

Jacob's last will

Thus Israel settled in Egypt, in Goshen; 2
there they acquired land, and were fruitful
and increased greatly. Jacob stayed in Egypt 2
for seventeen years and lived to be a hundred
and forty-seven years old. When the time 2
of his death drew near, he summoned his
son Joseph and said to him, 'If I may now
claim this favour from you, put your hand
under my thigh and swear by the LORD that
you will deal loyally and truly with me and
not bury me in Egypt. When I die like my 3
forefathers, you shall carry me from Egypt
and bury me in their grave.' He answered,
'I will do as you say'; but Jacob said, 'Swear 3
it.' So he swore the oath, and Israel sank
down over the end of the bed.

Jacob blesses Ephraim and Manasseh

The time came when Joseph was told that 4
his father was ill, so he took with him his
two sons, Manasseh and Ephraim. Jacob 2
heard that his son Joseph was coming to
him, and he summoned his strength and sat
up on the bed. Jacob said to Joseph, 'God 3
Almighty appeared to me at Luz in Canaan
and blessed me. He said to me, "I will make 4
you fruitful and increase your descendants
until they become a host of nations. I will
give this land to your descendants after you
as a perpetual possession." Now, your two 5
sons, who were born to you in Egypt before
I came here, shall be counted as my sons;
Ephraim and Manasseh shall be mine as
Reuben and Simeon are. Any children born 6
to you after them shall be counted as yours,
but in respect of their tribal territory they
shall be reckoned under their elder brothers'
names. As I was coming from Paddan-aram 7
I was bereaved of Rachel your mother on
the way, in Canaan, whilst there was still
some distance to go to Ephrath, and I buried
her there by the road to Ephrath, that is
Bethlehem.'
When Israel saw Joseph's sons, he said, 8
'Who are these?' Joseph replied to his father, 9
'They are my sons whom God has given me

here.' Israel said, 'Bring them to me, I beg you, so that I may take them on my knees.'[w]

10 Now Israel's eyes were dim with age, and he could not see; so Joseph brought the boys close to his father, and he kissed them

11 and embraced them. He said to Joseph, 'I had not expected to see your face again, and now God has granted me to see your sons

12 also.' Joseph took them from his father's

13 knees and bowed to the ground. Then he took the two of them, Ephraim on his right at Israel's left and Manasseh on his left at Israel's right, and brought them close to

14 him. Israel stretched out his right hand and laid it on Ephraim's head, although he was the younger, and, crossing his hands, laid his left hand on Manasseh's head; but

15 Manasseh was the elder. He blessed Joseph and said:

'The God in whose presence my forefathers lived,
my forefathers Abraham and Isaac,
the God who has been my shepherd all my life until this day,
16 the angel who ransomed me from all misfortune,
may he bless these boys;
they shall be called by my name,
and by that of my forefathers, Abraham and Isaac;
may they grow into a great people on earth.'

17 When Joseph saw that his father was laying his right hand on Ephraim's head, he was displeased; so he took hold of his father's

hand to move it from Ephraim's head to

18 Manasseh's. He said, 'That is not right, my father. This is the elder; lay your right hand on his head.' But his father refused; he said,

19 'I know, my son, I know. He too shall become a people; he too shall become great, but his younger brother shall be greater than he, and his descendants shall be a whole

20 nation in themselves.' That day he blessed them and said:

'When a blessing is pronounced in Israel,
men shall use your names and say,
God make you like Ephraim and Manasseh',

thus setting Ephraim before Manasseh.

21 Then Israel said to Joseph, 'I am dying. God will be with you and will bring you back to

22 the land of your fathers. I give you one ridge of land more than your brothers: I took it from the Amorites with my sword and my bow.'

Jacob's prophecy concerning his sons

49 Jacob summoned his sons and said, 'Come near, and I will tell you what will happen to you in days to come.

2 Gather round me and listen, you sons of Jacob;
listen to Israel your father.
3 Reuben, you are my first-born,
my strength and the first fruit of my vigour,
excelling in pride, excelling in might,
4 turbulent as a flood, you shall not excel;
because you climbed into your father's bed;
then you defiled his concubine's couch.

w Or may bless them.

(Gen. 49. 9)

5 Simeon and Levi are brothers,
     their spades became weapons of violence.
6 My soul shall not enter their council,
     my heart shall not join their company;
     for in their anger they killed men,
     wantonly they hamstrung oxen.
7 A curse be on their anger because it was
     fierce;
     a curse on their wrath because it was
     ruthless!
     I will scatter them in Jacob,
     I will disperse them in Israel.
8 Judah, your brothers shall praise you,
     your hand is on the neck of your enemies.
     Your father's sons shall do you homage.
9 Judah, you lion's whelp,
     you have returned from the kill, my son,
     and crouch and stretch like a lion;
     and, like a lion,[x] who dare rouse you?
10 The sceptre shall not pass from Judah,
     nor the staff from his descendants,
     so long as tribute is brought to him
     and the obedience of the nations is his.
11 To the vine he tethers his ass,
     and the colt of his ass to the red vine;
     he washes his cloak in wine,
     his robes in the blood of grapes.
12 Darker than wine are his eyes,
     his teeth whiter than milk.
13 Zebulun dwells by the sea-shore,
     his shore is a haven for ships,
     and his frontier rests on Sidon.
14 Issachar, a gelded ass
     lying down in the cattle-pens,
15 saw that a settled home was good
     and that the land was pleasant,
     so he bent his back to the burden
     and submitted to perpetual forced labour.
16 Dan—how insignificant his people,
     lowly as any tribe in Israel![y]
17 Let Dan be a viper on the road,
     a horned snake on the path,
     who bites the horse's fetlock
     so that the rider tumbles backwards.

For thy salvation I wait in hope, O Lord. 18

19 Gad is raided by raiders,
     and he raids them from the rear.
20 Asher shall have rich food as daily fare,
     and provide dishes fit for a king.
21 Naphtali is a spreading terebinth
     putting forth lovely boughs.
22 Joseph is a fruitful tree[z] by a spring
     with branches climbing over the wall.
23 The archers savagely attacked him,
     they shot at him and pressed him hard,
24 but their bow was splintered by the
     Eternal
     and the sinews of their arms were torn
     apart
     by the power of the Strong One of Jacob,
     by the name of the Shepherd[a] of Israel,
25 by the God of your father—so may he help
     you,
     by God Almighty—so may he bless you
     with the blessings of heaven above,
     the blessings of the deep that lurks below.
     The blessings of breast and womb
26 and the blessings of your father are
     stronger
     than the blessings of the everlasting pools[b]
     and the bounty of the eternal hills.
     They shall be on the head of Joseph,
     on the brow of the prince among[c] his
     brothers.
27 Benjamin is a ravening wolf:
     in the morning he devours the prey,
     in the evening he snatches a share of the
     spoil.'

The death and burial of Jacob

28 These, then, are the twelve tribes of Israel,
and this is what their father Jacob said to
them, when he blessed them each in turn.
29 He gave them his last charge and said, 'I
shall soon be gathered to my father's kin;
bury me with my forefathers in the cave on
the plot of land which belonged to Ephron

x Or lioness.   y Or Dan shall judge his people as one of the tribes of Israel.   z Or a fruitful ben-tree.
a Prob. rdg.; Heb. adds stone.   b Or hills.   c the prince among: or the one cursed by.

(Gen. 49. 27)

the Hittite, that is the cave on the plot of land at Machpelah east of Mamre in Canaan, the field which Abraham bought from Ephron the Hittite for a burial-place. There Abraham was buried with his wife Sarah; there Isaac and his wife Rebecca were buried; and there I buried Leah. The land and the cave on it were bought from the Hittites.' When Jacob had finished giving his last charge to his sons, he drew his feet up on to the bed, breathed his last, and was gathered to his father's kin.

Then Joseph threw himself upon his father, weeping and kissing his face. He ordered the physicians in his service to embalm his father Israel, and they did so, finishing the task in forty days, which was the usual time for embalming. The Egyptians mourned him for seventy days; and then, when the days of mourning for Israel were over, Joseph approached members of Pharaoh's household and said, 'If I can count on your goodwill, then speak for me to Pharaoh; tell him that my father made me take an oath, saying, "I am dying. Bury me in the grave that I bought*d* for myself in Canaan." Ask him to let me go up and bury my father, and afterwards I will return.' Pharaoh answered, 'Go and bury your father, as he has made you swear to do.' So Joseph went to bury his father, accompanied by all Pharaoh's courtiers, the elders of his household, and all the elders of Egypt, together with all Joseph's own household, his brothers, and his father's household; only their dependants, with the flocks and herds, were left in Goshen. He took with him chariots and horsemen; they were a very great company. When they came to the threshing-floor of Atad beside the river Jordan, they raised a loud and bitter lament; and there Joseph observed seven days' mourning for his father. When the Canaanites who lived there saw this mourning at the threshing-floor of Atad, they said, 'How bitterly the Egyptians are mourning!'; accordingly they named the place beside the Jordan Abel-mizraim.*e*

Thus Jacob's sons did what he had told them to do. They took him to Canaan and buried him in the cave on the plot of land at Machpelah, the land which Abraham had bought as a burial-place from Ephron the Hittite, to the east of Mamre. Then, after he had buried his father, Joseph returned to Egypt with his brothers and all who had gone up with him.

Joseph reassures his brothers

When their father was dead Joseph's brothers were afraid and said, 'What if Joseph should bear a grudge against us and pay us out for all the harm that we did to him?' They therefore approached Joseph with these words: 'In his last words to us before he died, your father gave us this message for you: "I ask you to forgive your brothers' crime and wickedness; I know they did you harm." So now forgive our crime, we beg; for we are servants of your father's God.' When they said this to him, Joseph wept. His brothers also wept*f* and prostrated themselves before him; they said, 'You see, we are your slaves.' But Joseph said to them, 'Do not be afraid. Am I in the place of God? You meant to do me harm; but God meant to bring good out of it by preserving the lives of many people, as we see today. Do not be afraid. I will provide for you and your dependants.' Thus he comforted them and set their minds at rest.

The death of Joseph

Joseph remained in Egypt, he and his father's household. He lived there to be a hundred and ten years old and saw Ephraim's children to the third generation; he also recognized as his the children of Manasseh's son Machir. He said to his brothers, 'I am dying; but God will not fail to come to your aid and take you from here to the land which he promised on oath to Abraham, Isaac and Jacob.' He made the sons of Israel take an oath, saying, 'When God thus comes to your aid, you must take my bones with you from here.' So Joseph died at the age of a hundred and ten. He was embalmed and laid in a coffin in Egypt.

---

d Or dug.   *e* That is Mourning (or Meadow) of Egypt.   *f* Prob. rdg.; Heb. came.

EXODUS

The suffering of the Israelites

1 THESE ARE THE NAMES of the Israelites who entered Egypt with Jacob,
2 each with his household: Reuben, Simeon,
3 Levi and Judah; Issachar, Zebulun and Ben-
4 jamin; Dan and Naphtali, Gad and Asher.
5 There were seventy of them all told, all direct descendants of Jacob. Joseph was already in Egypt.

6 In course of time Joseph died, he and all
7 his brothers and that whole generation. Now the Israelites were fruitful and prolific; they increased in numbers and became very powerful,*a* so that the country was overrun
8 by them. Then a new king ascended the throne of Egypt, one who knew nothing of
9 Joseph. He said to his people, 'These Israelites have become too many and too strong
10 for us. We must take precautions to see that they do not increase any further; or we shall find that, if war breaks out, they will join the enemy and fight against us, and they will
11 become masters of the country.' So they were made to work in gangs with officers set over them, to break their spirit with heavy labour. This is how Pharaoh's store-
12 cities, Pithom and Rameses, were built. But the more harshly they were treated, the more their numbers increased beyond all bounds, until the Egyptians came to loathe
13 the sight of them. So they treated their
14 Israelite slaves with ruthless severity, and made life bitter for them with cruel servitude, setting them to work on clay and brick-

making, and all sorts of work in the fields. In short they made ruthless use of them as slaves in every kind of hard labour.

Then the king of Egypt spoke to the 15 Hebrew midwives, whose names were Shiphrah and Puah. 'When you are attending the 16 Hebrew women in childbirth,' he told them, 'watch as the child is delivered and if it is a boy, kill him; if it is a girl, let her live.' But they were God-fearing women. They 17 did not do what the king of Egypt had told them to do, but let the boys live. So he sum 18 moned those Hebrew midwives and asked them why they had done this and let the boys live. They told Pharaoh that Hebrew 19 women were not like Egyptian women. When they were in labour they gave birth before the midwife could get to them. So 20 God made the midwives prosper, and the people increased in numbers and in strength. God gave the midwives homes and families 21 of their own, because they feared him. Pharaoh then ordered all his people to 22 throw every new-born Hebrew boy into the Nile, but to let the girls live.

The birth of Moses

A descendant of Levi married a Levite 2 woman who conceived and bore a son. 2 When she saw what a fine child he was, she hid him for three months, but she could 3 conceal him no longer. So she got a rush basket for him, made it watertight with clay and tar, laid him in it, and put it among the reeds by the bank of the Nile. The child's 4

---

a Or numerous.

sister took her stand at a distance to see
5 what would happen to him. Pharaoh's
daughter came down to bathe in the river,
while her ladies-in-waiting walked along
the bank. She noticed the basket among the
reeds and sent her slave-girl for it. She took
6 it from her and when she opened it, she saw
the child. It was crying, and she was filled
with pity for it. 'Why,' she said, 'it is a little
7 Hebrew boy.' Thereupon the sister said to
Pharaoh's daughter, 'Shall I go and fetch
one of the Hebrew women as a wet-nurse to
8 suckle the child for you?' Pharaoh's daughter
told her to go; so the girl went and called
9 the baby's mother. Then Pharaoh's daughter
said to her, 'Here is the child, suckle him for
me, and I will pay you for it myself.' So the
woman took the child and suckled him.
10 When the child was old enough, she brought
him to Pharaoh's daughter, who adopted
him and called him Moses,*b* 'because', she
said, 'I drew*c* him out of the water.'

Moses escapes to Midian

1 One day when Moses was grown up, he
went out to his own kinsmen and saw them
at their heavy labour. He saw an Egyptian
2 strike one of his fellow-Hebrews. He looked
this way and that, and, seeing there was no
one about, he struck the Egyptian down and
3 hid his body in the sand. When he went out
next day, two Hebrews were fighting to-
4 gether. He asked the man who was in the
wrong, 'Why are you striking him?' 'Who
set you up as an officer and judge over us?'
the man replied. 'Do you mean to murder
me as you murdered the Egyptian?' Moses
was alarmed. 'The thing must have become
5 known', he said to himself. When Pharaoh
heard of it, he tried to put Moses to death,
but Moses made good his escape and settled
in the land of Midian.
6   Now the priest of Midian had seven
daughters. One day as Moses sat by a well,
they came to draw water and filled the
7 troughs to water their father's sheep. Some
shepherds came and drove them away;
but Moses got up, took the girls' part and
8 watered their sheep himself. When the girls
came back to their father Reuel, he asked,
'How is it that you are back so quickly
9 today?' 'An Egyptian rescued us from the
shepherds,' they answered; 'and he even
drew the water for us and watered the sheep.'
10 'But where is he then?' he said to his daughters. 'Why did you leave him behind? Go
11 and invite him to eat with us.' So it came
about that Moses agreed to live with the
man, and he gave Moses his daughter Zip-
12 porah in marriage. She bore him a son, and
Moses called him Gershom, 'because', he

said, 'I have become an alien*d* living in a
foreign land.'

Years passed, and the king of Egypt died, 23
but the Israelites still groaned in slavery.
They cried out, and their appeal for rescue
from their slavery rose up to God. He heard 24
their groaning, and remembered his covenant with Abraham, Isaac and Jacob; he 25
saw the plight of Israel, and he took heed
of it.

The call of Moses

Moses was minding the flock of his father- 3
in-law Jethro, priest of Midian. He led the
flock along the side of the wilderness and
came to Horeb, the mountain of God.
There the angel of the LORD appeared to 2
him in the flame of a burning bush. Moses
noticed that, although the bush was on fire,
it was not being burnt up; so he said to 3
himself, 'I must go across to see this wonderful sight. Why does not the bush burn away?'
When the LORD saw that Moses had turned 4
aside to look, he called to him out of the
bush, 'Moses, Moses.' And Moses answered,
'Yes, I am here.' God said, 'Come no nearer; 5
take off your sandals; the place where you
are standing is holy ground.' Then he said, 6
'I am the God of your forefathers, the God
of Abraham, the God of Isaac, the God of
Jacob.' Moses covered his face, for he was
afraid to gaze on God.
    The LORD said, 'I have indeed seen the 7
misery of my people in Egypt. I have heard
their outcry against their slave-masters. I
have taken heed of their sufferings, and have 8
come down to rescue them from the power
of Egypt, and to bring them up out of that
country into a fine, broad land; it is a land
flowing with milk and honey, the home of
Canaanites, Hittites, Amorites, Perizzites,
Hivites, and Jebusites. The outcry of the 9
Israelites has now reached me; yes, I have
seen the brutality of the Egyptians towards
them. Come now; I will send you to Pharaoh 10
and you shall bring my people Israel out of
Egypt.' 'But who am I,' Moses said to God, 11
'that I should go to Pharaoh, and that I
should bring the Israelites out of Egypt?'
God answered, 'I am*e* with you. This shall 12
be the proof that it is I who have sent you:
when you have brought the people out of
Egypt, you shall all worship God here on
this mountain.'
    Then Moses said to God, 'If I go to the 13
Israelites and tell them that the God of their
forefathers has sent me to them, and they
ask me his name, what shall I say?' God 14
answered, 'I AM; that is who I am.'*f* Tell
them that I AM has sent you to them.' And 15

b Heb. Mosheh.   *c Heb. verb* mashah.   *d Heb.* ger.   *e Or* I will be; *Heb.* ehyeh.   *f* I AM . . .
I am: *or* I will be what I will be.

God said further, 'You must tell the Israelites this, that it is JEHOVAH*g* the God of their forefathers, the God of Abraham, the God of Isaac, the God of Jacob, who has sent you to them. This is my name for ever; this 16 is my title in every generation. Go and assemble the elders of Israel and tell them that JEHOVAH the God of their forefathers, the God of Abraham, Isaac and Jacob, has appeared to you and has said, "I have indeed turned my eyes towards you; I have marked all that has been done to you in 17 Egypt, and I am resolved to bring you up out of your misery in Egypt, into the country of the Canaanites, Hittites, Amorites, Perizzites, Hivites, and Jebusites, a land flowing 18 with milk and honey." They will listen to you, and then you and the elders of Israel must go to the king of Egypt. Tell him, "It has happened that the LORD the God of the Hebrews met us. So now give us leave to go a three days' journey into the wilderness 19 to offer sacrifice to the LORD our God." I know well that the king of Egypt will not 20 give you leave unless he is compelled. I shall then stretch out my hand and assail the Egyptians with all the miracles I shall work among them. After that he will send you 21 away. Further, I will bring this people into such favour with the Egyptians that, when you go, you will not go empty-handed. 22 Every woman shall ask her neighbour or any woman who lives in her house for jewellery of silver and gold and for clothing. Load your sons and daughters with them, and plunder Egypt.'

4 Moses answered, 'But they will never believe me or listen to me; they will say, "The 2 LORD did not appear to you."' The LORD said, 'What have you there in your hand?' 3 'A staff', Moses answered. The LORD said, 'Throw it on the ground.' Moses threw it down and it turned into a snake. He ran 4 away from it, but the LORD said, 'Put your hand out and seize it by the tail.' He did so and gripped it firmly, and it turned back 5 into a staff in his hand. 'This is to convince the people that the LORD the God of their forefathers, the God of Abraham, the God of Isaac, the God of Jacob, has appeared to 6 you.' Then the LORD said, 'Put your hand inside the fold of your cloak.' He did so, and when he drew it out the skin was diseased, 7 white as snow. The LORD said, 'Put it back again', and he did so. When he drew it out this time it was as healthy as the rest of his 8 body. 'Now,' said the LORD, 'if they do not believe you and do not accept the evidence of the first sign, they may accept the evidence 9 of the second. But if they are not convinced even by these two signs, and will not accept

what you say, then fetch some water from the Nile and pour it out on the dry ground, and the water you take from the Nile will turn to blood on the ground.'

But Moses said, 'O LORD, I have never been a man of ready speech, never in my life, not even now that thou hast spoken to me; I am slow and hesitant of speech.' The LORD said to him, 'Who is it that gives man speech? Who makes him dumb or deaf? Who makes him clear-sighted or blind? Is it not I, the LORD? Go now; I will help your speech and tell you what to say.' But Moses still protested, 'No, Lord, send whom thou wilt.' At this the LORD grew angry with Moses and said, 'Have you not a brother, Aaron the Levite? He, I know, will do all the speaking. He is already on his way out to meet you, and he will be glad indeed to see you. You shall speak to him and put the words in his mouth; I will help both of you to speak and tell you both what to do. He will do all the speaking to the people for you, he will be the mouthpiece, and you will be the god he speaks for. But take this staff, for with it you are to work the signs.'

At length Moses went back to Jethro his father-in-law and said, 'Let me return to my kinsfolk in Egypt and see if they are still alive.' Jethro told him to go and wished him well.

Moses returns to Egypt

The LORD spoke to Moses in Midian and said to him, 'Go back to Egypt, for all those who wished to kill you are dead.' So Moses took his wife and children, mounted them on an ass and set out for Egypt with the staff of God in his hand. The LORD said to Moses, 'While you are on your way back to Egypt, keep in mind all the portents I have given you power to show. You shall display these before Pharaoh, but I will make him obstinate and he will not let the people go. Then tell Pharaoh that these are the words of the LORD: "Israel is my first-born son. I have told you to let my son go, so that he may worship me. You have refused to let him go, so I will kill your first-born son."'

During the journey, while they were encamped for the night, the LORD met Moses, meaning to kill him, but Zipporah picked up a sharp flint, cut off her son's foreskin, and touched him with it, saying, 'You are my blood-bridegroom.' So the LORD let Moses alone. Then she said,*h* 'Blood-bridegroom by circumcision.'

Meanwhile the LORD had ordered Aaron to go and meet Moses in the wilderness. Aaron went and met him at the mountain of God, and he kissed him. Then Moses told

---

g The Hebrew consonants are YHWH, *probably pronounced* Yahweh, *but traditionally read* Jehovah.
h Or Therefore women say.

Aaron everything, the words the LORD had
sent him to say and the signs he had com-
9 manded him to perform. Moses and Aaron
went and assembled all the elders of Israel.
10 Aaron told them everything that the LORD
had said to Moses; he performed the signs
31 before the people, and they were convinced.
They heard that the LORD had shown his
concern for the Israelites and seen their
misery; and they bowed themselves to the
ground in worship.

Pharaoh's disobedience

5 After this, Moses and Aaron came to Pharaoh and said, 'These are the words of the
LORD the God of Israel: "Let my people go
so that they may keep my pilgrim-feast in
2 the wilderness."' 'Who is the LORD,' asked
Pharaoh, 'that I should obey him and let
Israel go? I care nothing for the LORD: and
3 I tell you I will not let Israel go.' They replied,
'It has happened that the God of the Hebrews
met us. So let us go three days' journey into
the wilderness to offer sacrifice to the LORD
our God, or else he will attack us with pesti-
4 lence or sword.' But the king of Egypt said,
'Moses and Aaron, what do you mean by
distracting the people from their work?
5 Back to your labours! Your people already
outnumber the native Egyptians; yet you
would have them stop working!'
6 That very day Pharaoh ordered the
7 people's overseers and their foremen not
to supply the people with the straw used in
making bricks, as they had done hitherto.
8 'Let them go and collect their own straw, but
see that they produce the same tally of
bricks as before. On no account reduce it.
They are a lazy people, and that is why they
are clamouring to go and offer sacrifice to
9 their god. Keep the men hard at work; let
them attend to that and take no notice of
10 a pack of lies.' The overseers and foremen
went out and said to the people, 'Pharaoh's
orders are that no more straw is to be sup-
11 plied. Go and get it for yourselves wherever
you can find it; but there will be no reduction
12 in your daily task.' So the people scattered all
13 over Egypt to gather stubble for straw, while
the overseers kept urging them on, bidding
them complete, day after day, the same quan-
14 tity as when straw was supplied. Then the
Israelite foremen were flogged because they
were held responsible by Pharaoh's overseers, who asked them, 'Why did you not
complete the usual number of bricks yester-
15 day or today?' So the foremen came and
appealed to Pharaoh: 'Why do you treat
16 your servants like this?' they said. 'We are
given no straw, yet they keep on telling us to
make bricks. Here are we being flogged, but
17 it is your people's fault.' But Pharaoh re-

plied, 'You are lazy, you are lazy. That is
why you talk about going to offer sacrifice
to the LORD. Now go; get on with your work. 18
You will be given no straw, but you must
produce the tally of bricks.' When they were 19
told that they must not let the daily tally of
bricks fall short, the Israelite foremen saw
that they were in trouble. As they came out 20
from Pharaoh's presence they found Moses
and Aaron waiting to meet them, and said, 21
'May this bring the LORD's judgement down
upon you: you have made us stink in the
nostrils of Pharaoh and his subjects; you
have put a sword in their hands to kill us.'

Egyptian gods

The call of Moses repeated

Moses went back to the LORD, and said, 22
'Why, O Lord, hast thou brought misfortune on this people? And why didst thou
ever send me? Since I first went to Pharaoh 23
to speak in thy name he has heaped misfortune on thy people, and thou hast done
nothing at all to rescue them.' The LORD 6
answered, 'Now you shall see what I will
do to Pharaoh. In the end Pharaoh will let
them go with a strong hand, nay, will drive
them from his country with an outstretched
arm.'

God spoke to Moses and said, 'I am the 2
LORD. I appeared to Abraham, Isaac, and 3
Jacob as God Almighty. But I did not let
myself be known to them by my name
JEHOVAH.*i* Moreover, I made a covenant 4
with them to give them Canaan, the land
where they settled for a time as foreigners.

i See note on 3. 15.

B

5 And now I have heard the groaning of the Israelites, enslaved by the Egyptians, and I 6 have called my covenant to mind. Say therefore to the Israelites, "I am the LORD. I will release you from your labours in Egypt. I will rescue you from slavery there. I will redeem you with arm outstretched and with 7 mighty acts of judgement. I will adopt you as my people, and I will become your God. You shall know that I, the LORD, am your God, the God who releases you from your 8 labours in Egypt. I will lead you to the land which I swore with uplifted hand to give to Abraham, to Isaac and to Jacob. I will give it you for your possession. I am the LORD."'

Moses repeated these words to the Israel- 9 ites, but they did not listen to him; they had become impatient because of their cruel slavery.

Then the LORD spoke to Moses and said, 10 'Go and tell Pharaoh king of Egypt to set 11 the Israelites free to leave his country.' Moses 12 made answer in the presence of the LORD, 'If the Israelites do not listen to me, how will Pharaoh listen to such a halting speaker as I am?'

Thus the LORD spoke to Moses and Aaron 13 and gave them their commission to the Israelites and to Pharaoh, namely that they should bring the Israelites out of Egypt.

Genealogy of Moses and Aaron

14 j These were the heads of fathers' families:

Sons of Reuben, Israel's eldest son: Enoch, Pallu, Hezron and Carmi; these were the families of Reuben.

15 Sons of Simeon: Jemuel, Jamin, Ohad, Jachin, Zohar, and Saul, who was the son of a Canaanite woman; these were the families of Simeon.

16 These were the names of the sons of Levi in order of seniority: Gershon, Kohath and Merari. Levi lived to be a hundred and thirty-seven.

17 Sons of Gershon, family by family: Libni and Shimei.

18 Sons of Kohath: Amram, Izhar, Hebron and Uzziel. Kohath lived to be a hundred and thirty-three.

19 Sons of Merari: Mahli and Mushi.

These were the families of Levi 20 in order of seniority. Amram married his father's sister Jochebed, and she bore him Aaron and Moses. Amram lived to be a hundred and thirty-seven.

21 Sons of Izhar: Korah, Nepheg and Zichri.

22 Sons of Uzziel: Mishael, Elzaphan and Sithri.

23 Aaron married Elisheba, who was the daughter of Amminadab

and the sister of Nahshon, and she bore him Nadab, Abihu, Eleazar and Ithamar.

Sons of Korah: Assir, Elkanah 24 and Abiasaph; these were the Korahite families.

Eleazar son of Aaron married 25 one of the daughters of Putiel, and she bore him Phinehas. These were the heads of the Levite families, family by family.

It was this Aaron, together with 26 Moses, to whom the LORD said, 'Bring the Israelites out of Egypt, mustered in their tribal hosts.' These were the men who told 27 Pharaoh king of Egypt to let the Israelites leave Egypt. It was this same Moses and Aaron.

The LORD promises deliverance

28 29 When the LORD spoke to Moses in Egypt he said, 'I am the LORD. Tell Pharaoh king of 30 Egypt all that I say to you.' Moses made answer in the presence of the LORD, 'I am a halting speaker; how will Pharaoh listen to 7 me?' The LORD answered Moses, 'See now, I have made you like a god for Pharaoh, with your brother Aaron as your spokesman. 2 You must tell your brother Aaron all I bid you say, and he will tell Pharaoh, and Pharaoh will let the Israelites go out of his 3 country; but I will make him stubborn. Then will I show sign after sign and portent after 4 portent in the land of Egypt. But Pharaoh will not listen to you, so I will assert my power in Egypt, and with mighty acts of judgement I will bring my people, the Israelites, out of Egypt in their tribal hosts. 5 When I put forth my power against the Egyptians and bring the Israelites out from them, then Egypt will know that I am the 6 LORD.' So Moses and Aaron did exactly as 7 the LORD had commanded. At the time when they spoke to Pharaoh, Moses was eighty years old and Aaron eighty-three.

Aaron's staff

The LORD said to Moses and Aaron, 'If 8 Pharaoh demands some portent from you, then you, Moses, must say to Aaron, "Take your staff and throw it down in front of Pharaoh, and it will turn into a serpent."' When Moses and Aaron came to Pharaoh, 10 they did as the LORD had told them. Aaron threw down his staff in front of Pharaoh and his courtiers, and it turned into a serpent. At this, Pharaoh summoned the wise men 11 and the sorcerers, and the Egyptian magicians too did the same thing by their spells. Every man threw his staff down, and each 12 staff turned into a serpent; but Aaron's staff swallowed up theirs. Pharaoh, how- 13 ever, was obstinate; as the LORD had foretold, he would not listen to Moses and Aaron.

The plague of blood

Then the LORD said to Moses, 'Pharaoh is 14 obdurate: he has refused to set the people free. Go to him in the morning on his way 15 out to the river. Stand and wait on the bank of the Nile to meet him, and take with you

j Verses 14–16: cp. Gen. 46. 8–11; Num. 26. 5, 6, 12, 13.

6 the staff that turned into a snake. Say this to him: "The LORD the God of the Hebrews sent me to bid you let his people go in order to worship him in the wilderness. So far 7 you have not listened to his words; so now the LORD says, 'By this you shall know that I am the LORD.' With this rod that I have in my hand, I shall now strike the water in the Nile and it will be changed into blood. 8 The fish will die and the river will stink, and the Egyptians will be unable to drink water 9 from the Nile." ' The LORD then told Moses to say to Aaron, 'Take your staff and stretch your hand out over the waters of Egypt, its rivers and its streams, and over every pool and cistern, to turn them into blood. There shall be blood throughout the whole of Egypt, blood even in their wooden bowls 0 and jars of stone.' So Moses and Aaron did as the LORD had commanded. He lifted up his staff and struck the water of the Nile in the sight of Pharaoh and his courtiers, and 1 all the water was changed into blood. The fish died and the river stank, and the Egyptians could not drink water from the Nile. 2 There was blood everywhere in Egypt. But the Egyptian magicians did the same thing by their spells; and still Pharaoh remained obstinate, as the LORD had foretold, and did 3 not listen to Moses and Aaron. He turned away, went into his house and dismissed 4 the matter from his mind. Then the Egyptians all dug for drinking water round about the river, because they could not drink from 5 the waters of the Nile itself. This lasted for seven days from the time when the LORD struck the Nile.

The plague of frogs

3 The LORD then told Moses to go into Pharaoh's presence and say to him, 'These are the words of the LORD: "Let my people 2 go in order to worship me. If you refuse to let them go, I will plague the whole of your 3 territory with frogs. The Nile shall swarm with them. They shall come up from the river into your house, into your bedroom and on to your bed, into the houses of your courtiers and your people, into your ovens 4 and your kneading-troughs. The frogs shall clamber over you, your people, and your 5 courtiers." ' Then the LORD told Moses to

say to Aaron, 'Take your staff in your hand and stretch it out over the rivers, streams, and pools, to bring up frogs upon the land of Egypt.' So Aaron stretched out his hand 6 over the waters of Egypt, and the frogs came up and covered all the land. The magicians 7 did the same thing by their spells: they too brought up frogs upon the land of Egypt. Then Pharaoh summoned Moses and Aaron. 8 'Pray to the LORD', he said, 'to take the frogs away from me and my people, and I will let the people go to sacrifice to the LORD.' Moses said, 'Of your royal favour, appoint a 9 time when I may intercede for you and your courtiers and people, so that you and your houses may be rid of the frogs, and none be left except in the Nile.' 'Tomorrow', Phar- 10 aoh said. 'It shall be as you say,' replied Moses, 'so that you may know there is no one like our God, the LORD. The frogs shall 11 depart from you, from your houses, your courtiers, and your people: none shall be left except in the Nile.' Moses and Aaron 12 left Pharaoh's presence, and Moses appealed to the LORD to remove the frogs which he had brought on Pharaoh. The LORD did as 13 Moses had asked, and in house and court-yard and in the open the frogs all perished. They piled them into countless heaps and 14 the land stank; but when Pharaoh found 15 that he was given relief he became obdurate; as the LORD had foretold, he did not listen to Moses and Aaron.

The plague of maggots

The LORD then told Moses to say to Aaron, 16 'Stretch out your staff and strike the dust on the ground, and it will turn into maggots throughout the land of Egypt', and they 17 obeyed. Aaron stretched out his staff and struck the dust, and it turned into maggots on man and beast. All the dust turned into maggots throughout the land of Egypt. The 18 magicians tried to produce maggots in the same way by their spells, but they failed. The maggots were everywhere, on man 19 and beast. 'It is the finger of God', said the magicians to Pharaoh, but Pharaoh remained obstinate; as the LORD had foretold, he did not listen to them.

The plague of flies

20 The LORD told Moses to rise early in the morning and stand in Pharaoh's path as he went out to the river and to say to him, 'These are the words of the LORD: "Let my people 21 go in order to worship me. If you do not let my people go, I will send swarms of flies upon you, your courtiers, your people, and your houses. The houses of the Egyptians shall be filled with the swarms and so shall all the 22 land they live in, but on that day I will make an exception of Goshen, the land where my people live: there shall be no swarms there. Thus you shall know that I, the LORD, am 23 here in the land. I will make a distinction between my people and yours. Tomorrow 24 this sign shall appear."' The LORD did this; dense swarms of flies infested Pharaoh's house and those of his courtiers; throughout Egypt the land was threatened with ruin by 25 the swarms. Pharaoh summoned Moses and Aaron and said to them, 'Go and sacrifice 26 to your God, but in this country.' 'That we cannot do,' replied Moses, 'because the victim we shall sacrifice to the LORD our God is an abomination to the Egyptians. If the Egyptians see us offer such an animal, will they not stone us to death? 27 We must go a three days' journey into the wilderness to sacrifice to the LORD our 28 God, as he commands us.' 'I will let you go,' said Pharaoh, 'and you shall sacrifice to your God in the wilderness; only do 29 not go far. Now intercede for me.' Moses answered, 'As soon as I leave you I will intercede with the LORD. Tomorrow the swarms will depart from Pharaoh, his courtiers, and his people. Only let not Pharaoh trifle any more with the people by preventing them from going to sacrifice to the LORD.' 30 Then Moses left Pharaoh and interceded 31 with the LORD. The LORD did as Moses had said; he removed the swarms from Pharaoh, his courtiers, and his people; not one was 32 left. But once again Pharaoh became obdurate and did not let the people go.

The plague on the cattle

9 The LORD said to Moses, 'Go into Pharaoh's presence and say to him, "These are the words of the LORD the God of the Hebrews: 'Let my people go in order to worship 2 me.' If you refuse to let them go and still 3 keep your hold on them, the LORD will strike your grazing herds, your horses and asses, your camels, cattle, and sheep with a terrible pestilence. But the LORD will make a 4 distinction between Israel's herds and those of the Egyptians. Of all that belong to Israel not a single one shall die."' The LORD fixed 5 a time and said, 'Tomorrow I will do this throughout the land.' The next day the LORD 6 struck. All the herds of Egypt died, but from the herds of the Israelites not one single beast died. Pharaoh inquired and was told 7 that not a beast from the herds of Israel had died; and yet he remained obdurate and did not let the people go.

The plague of boils

The LORD said to Moses and Aaron, 'Take 8 handfuls of soot from a kiln. Moses shall toss it into the air in Pharaoh's sight, and it will 9 turn into a fine dust over the whole of Egypt. All over Egypt it will become festering boils on man and beast.' They took the soot from 10 the kiln and stood before Pharaoh. Moses tossed it into the air and it produced festering boils on man and beast. The magicians 11 were no match for Moses because of the boils, which attacked them and all the Egyptians. But the LORD made Pharaoh 12 obstinate; as the LORD had foretold to Moses, he did not listen to Moses and Aaron.

The plague of hail

The LORD then told Moses to rise early in 13 the morning, present himself before Pharaoh, and say to him, 'These are the words of the LORD the God of the Hebrews: "Let my people go in order to worship me. This time 14 I will strike home with all my plagues against you, your courtiers, and your people, so that you may know that there is none like me in all the earth. By now I could have stretched 15 out my hand, and struck you and your people with pestilence, and you would have vanished from the earth. I have let you live 16 only to show you my power and to spread my fame throughout the land. Since you 17 still obstruct my people and will not let them go, tomorrow at this time I will send 18 a violent hailstorm, such as has never been in Egypt from its first beginnings until now. Send now and bring your herds under cover, 19 and everything you have out in the open field. If anything, whether man or beast, which happens to be in the open, is not brought in, the hail will fall on it, and it will die."' Those 20 of Pharaoh's subjects who feared the word of the LORD hurried their slaves and cattle into their houses. But those who did not take 21 to heart the word of the LORD left their slaves and cattle in the open.

The LORD said to Moses, 'Stretch out your 22 hand towards the sky to bring down hail on the whole land of Egypt, on man and beast and every growing thing throughout the

23 land.' Moses stretched out his staff towards the sky, and the LORD sent thunder and hail, with fire flashing down to the ground. The LORD rained down hail on the land of 24 Egypt, hail and fiery flashes through the hail, so heavy that there had been nothing like it in all Egypt from the time that Egypt be- 25 came a nation. Throughout Egypt the hail struck everything in the fields, both man and beast; it beat down every growing thing and 26 shattered every tree. Only in the land of Goshen, where the Israelites lived, was there no hail.

27 Pharaoh sent and summoned Moses and Aaron. 'This time I have sinned,' he said; 'the LORD is in the right; I and my people 28 are in the wrong. Intercede with the LORD, for we can bear no more of this thunder and hail. I will let you go; you need wait no 29 longer.' Moses said, 'When I leave the city I will spread out my hands in prayer to the LORD. The thunder shall cease, and there shall be no more hail, so that you may know 30 that the earth is the LORD's. But you and your subjects—I know that you do not yet 31 fear the LORD God.' (The flax and barley were destroyed because the barley was in 32 the ear and the flax in bud, but the wheat and spelt were not destroyed because they come 33 later.) Moses left Pharaoh's presence, went out of the city and lifted up his hands to the LORD in prayer: the thunder and hail ceased, 34 and no more rain fell. When Pharaoh saw that the downpour, the hail, and the thunder had ceased, he sinned again, he and his 35 courtiers, and became obdurate. So Pharaoh remained obstinate; as the LORD had foretold through Moses, he did not let the people go.

The plague of locusts

10 Then the LORD said to Moses, 'Go into Pharaoh's presence. I have made him and his courtiers obdurate, so that I may show 2 these my signs among them, and so that you can tell your children and grandchildren the story: how I made sport of the Egyptians, and what signs I showed among them. Thus 3 you will know that I am the LORD.' Moses and Aaron went in to Pharaoh and said to him, 'These are the words of the LORD the God of the Hebrews: "How long will you refuse to humble yourself before me? Let my people go in order to worship me. 4 If you refuse to let my people go, tomorrow I will bring locusts into your country. 5 They shall cover the face of the land so that it cannot be seen. They shall eat up the last remnant left you by the hail. They shall devour every tree that grows in your 6 country-side. Your houses and your courtiers' houses, every house in Egypt, shall

be full of them; your fathers never saw the like nor their fathers before them; such a thing has not happened from their time until now."' He turned and left Pharaoh's pres- 7 ence. Pharaoh's courtiers said to him, 'How long must we be caught in this man's toils? Let their menfolk go and worship the LORD their God. Do you not know by now that Egypt is ruined?' So Moses and Aaron were 8 brought back to Pharaoh, and he said to them, 'You may go and worship the LORD your God; but who exactly is to go?' 'All,' 9 said Moses, 'young and old, boys and girls, sheep and cattle; for we have to keep the LORD's pilgrim-feast.' Pharaoh replied, 'Very 10 well then; take your dependants with you when you go; and the LORD be with you. But beware, there is trouble in store for you. No, your menfolk may go and worship 11 the LORD, for that is all you asked.' So they were driven out from Pharaoh's presence.

Then the LORD said to Moses, 'Stretch 12 out your hand over Egypt so that the locusts may come and invade the land and devour all the vegetation in it, everything the hail has left.' Moses stretched out his staff over 13 the land of Egypt, and the LORD sent a wind roaring in from the east all that day and all that night. When morning came, the east wind had brought the locusts. They invaded 14 the whole land of Egypt, and settled on all its territory in swarms so dense that the like of them had never been seen before, nor ever will be again. They covered the surface 15 of the whole land till it was black with them. They devoured all the vegetation and all the fruit of the trees that the hail had spared. There was no green left on tree or plant throughout all Egypt. Pharaoh hastily sum- 16 moned Moses and Aaron. 'I have sinned against the LORD your God and against you', he said. 'Forgive my sin, I pray, just this 17 once. Intercede with the LORD your God and beg him only to remove this deadly plague from me.' Moses left Pharaoh and inter- 18 ceded with the LORD. The LORD changed 19 the wind into a westerly gale, which carried the locusts away and swept them into the Red Sea.[k] There was not a single locust left in all the territory of Egypt. But the LORD 20 made Pharaoh obstinate, and he did not let the Israelites go.

The plague of darkness

Then the LORD said to Moses, 'Stretch out 21 your hand towards the sky so that there may be darkness over the land of Egypt, darkness that can be felt.' Moses stretched out his 22 hand towards the sky, and it became pitch dark throughout the land of Egypt for three days. Men could not see one another; for 23 three days no one stirred from where he was.

k Or the Sea of Reeds.

But there was no darkness wherever the
24 Israelites lived. Pharaoh summoned Moses.
'Go', he said, 'and worship the LORD. Your
dependants may go with you; but your
25 flocks and herds must be left with us.' But
Moses said, 'No, you must yourself supply
us with animals for sacrifice and whole-
26 offering to the LORD our God; and our own
flocks must go with us too—not a hoof must
be left behind. We may need animals from
our own flocks to worship the LORD our
God; we ourselves cannot tell until we are
there how we are to worship the LORD.'
27 The LORD made Pharaoh obstinate, and he
28 refused to let them go. 'Out! Pester me no
more!' he said to Moses. 'Take care you do
not see my face again, for on the day you
29 do, you die.' 'You are right,' said Moses;
'I shall never see your face again.'

Death of the first-born foretold

11 Then the LORD said to Moses, 'One last
plague I will bring upon Pharaoh and Egypt.
After that he will let you go; he will send
you packing, as a man dismisses a rejected
2 bride. Let the people be told that men and
women alike should ask their neighbours for
3 jewellery of silver and gold.' The LORD made
the Egyptians well-disposed towards them,
and, moreover, Moses was a very great man
in Egypt in the eyes of Pharaoh's courtiers
and of the people.
4 Moses then said, 'These are the words of
the LORD: "At midnight I will go out among
5 the Egyptians. Every first-born creature
in the land of Egypt shall die: the first-born
of Pharaoh who sits on his throne, the first-
born of the slave-girl at the handmill, and
6 all the first-born of the cattle. All Egypt will
send up a great cry of anguish, a cry like
of which has never been heard before, nor
7 ever will be again. But among all Israel not
a dog's tongue shall be so much as scratched,
no man or beast be hurt." Thus you shall
know that the LORD does make a distinc-
8 tion between Egypt and Israel. Then all these
courtiers of yours will come down to me,
prostrate themselves and cry, "Go away,
you and all the people who follow at your
heels." After that I will go away.' Then
Moses left Pharaoh's presence hot with
anger.
9 The LORD said to Moses, 'Pharaoh will
not listen to you; I will therefore show still
10 more portents in the land of Egypt.' All
these portents had Moses and Aaron shown
in the presence of Pharaoh, and yet the LORD
made him obstinate, and he did not let the
Israelites leave the country.

Institution of the Passover

12 The LORD said to Moses and Aaron in
2 Egypt: This month is for you the first of
months; you shall make it the first month
of the year. Speak to the whole com- 3
munity of Israel and say to them: On
the tenth day of this month let each man
take a lamb or a kid for his family, one for
each household, but if a household is too 4
small for one lamb or one kid, then the man
and his nearest neighbour may take one
between them. They shall share the cost,
taking into account both the number of
persons and the amount each of them eats.
Your lamb or kid must be without blemish, 5
a yearling male. You may take equally a
sheep or a goat. You must have it in safe 6
keeping until the fourteenth day of this
month, and then all the assembled community of Israel shall slaughter the victim
between dusk and dark. They must take 7
some of the blood and smear it on the two
door-posts and on the lintel of every house

Door-posts and lintel

in which they eat the lamb. On that night 8
they shall eat the flesh roast on the fire;
they shall eat it with unleavened cakes and
bitter herbs. You are not to eat any of it 9
raw or even boiled in water, but roasted,
head, shins, and entrails. You shall not 10
leave any of it till morning; if anything
is left over until morning, it must be destroyed by fire.
This is the way in which you must eat it: 11
you shall have your belt fastened, your
sandals on your feet and your staff in your
hand, and you must eat in urgent haste. It
is the LORD's Passover. On that night I shall 12
pass through the land of Egypt and kill
every first-born of man and beast. Thus will
I execute judgement, I the LORD, against all
the gods of Egypt. And as for you, the blood 13
will be a sign on the houses in which you are:

when I see the blood I will pass over[l] you; the mortal blow shall not touch you, when I strike the land of Egypt.

14 You shall keep this day as a day of remembrance, and make it a pilgrim-feast, a festival of the LORD; you shall keep it generation after generation as a rule for all 15 time. For seven days you shall eat unleavened cakes. On the very first day you shall rid your houses of leaven; from the first day to the seventh anyone who eats leavened bread 16 shall be outlawed from Israel. On the first day there shall be a sacred assembly and on the seventh day there shall be a sacred assembly: on these days no work shall be done, except what must be done to provide food for everyone; and that will be allowed. 17 You shall observe these commandments because this was the very day on which I brought you out of Egypt in your tribal hosts. You shall observe this day from generation to generation as a rule for all time. 18 You shall eat unleavened cakes in the first month from the evening which begins the fourteenth day until the evening which 19 begins the twenty-first day. For seven days no leaven may be found in your houses, for anyone who eats anything fermented shall be outlawed from the community of Israel, 20 be he foreigner or native. You must eat nothing fermented. Wherever you live you must eat your cakes unleavened. 21 Moses summoned all the elders of Israel and said to them, 'Go at once and get sheep for your families and slaughter the Passover. 22 Then take a bunch of marjoram,[m] dip it in

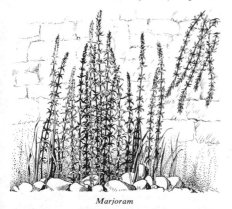

Marjoram

the blood in the basin[n] and smear some blood from the basin[o] on the lintel and the two door-posts. Nobody may go out through 23 the door of his house till morning. The LORD will go through Egypt and strike it, but when

he sees the blood on the lintel and the two door-posts, he will pass over that door and will not let the destroyer enter your houses to strike you. You shall keep this as a rule 24 for you and your children for all time. When 25 you enter the land which the LORD will give you as he promised, you shall observe this rite. Then, when your children ask you, 26 "What is the meaning of this rite?" you shall 27 say, "It is the LORD's Passover, for he passed over the houses of the Israelites in Egypt when he struck the Egyptians but spared our houses."' The people bowed down and prostrated themselves.

The death of the first-born

The Israelites went and did all that the LORD 28 had commanded Moses and Aaron; and by 29 midnight the LORD had struck down every first-born in Egypt, from the first-born of Pharaoh on his throne to the first-born of the captive in the dungeon, and the first-born of cattle. Before night was over 30 Pharaoh rose, he and all his courtiers and all the Egyptians, and a great cry of anguish went up, because not a house in Egypt was without its dead. Pharaoh summoned Moses 31 and Aaron while it was still night and said, 'Up with you! Be off, and leave my people, you and your Israelites. Go and worship the LORD, as you ask; take your sheep and 32 cattle, and go; and ask God's blessing on me also.' The Egyptians urged on the people 33 and hurried them out of the country, 'or else', they said, 'we shall all be dead.' The 34 people picked up their dough before it was leavened, wrapped their kneading-troughs in their cloaks, and slung them on their shoulders. Meanwhile the Israelites had done 35 as Moses had told them, asking the Egyptians for jewellery of silver and gold and for clothing. As the LORD had made the Egyp- 36 tians well-disposed towards them, they let them have what they asked; in this way they plundered the Egyptians.

The exodus from Egypt

The Israelites set out from Rameses on the 37 way to Succoth, about six hundred thousand men on foot, not counting dependants. And 38 with them too went a large company of every kind, and cattle in great numbers, both flocks and herds. The dough they had 39 brought from Egypt they baked into un-leavened cakes, because there was no leaven; for they had been driven out of Egypt and allowed no time even to get food ready for themselves.

The Israelites had been settled in Egypt 40 for four hundred and thirty years. At the 41

l Or stand guard over.   *m Or* hyssop.   *n Or* on the threshold.   *o Or* from the threshold.

42 end of four hundred and thirty years, on this very day, all the tribes of the LORD came out of Egypt. This was a night of vigil as the LORD waited to bring them out of Egypt. It is the LORD's night; all Israelites keep their vigil generation after generation.

Rules for the Passover

43 The LORD said to Moses and Aaron: These are the rules for the Passover. No foreigner may par-
44 take of it; any bought slave may eat it if you have circumcised him;
45 no stranger or hired man may eat
46 it. Each lamb must be eaten inside the one house, and you must not take any of the flesh outside the house. You must not break a single
47 bone of it. The whole community
48 of Israel shall keep this feast. If there are aliens living with you and they are to keep the Passover to the LORD, every male of them must be circumcised, and then he can take part; he shall rank as native-born. No one who is uncircumcised
49 may eat of it. The same law shall apply both to the native-born and to the alien who is living among you.
50   The Israelites did all that the LORD had commanded Moses and
51 Aaron; and on this very day the LORD brought the Israelites out of Egypt mustered in their tribal hosts.

Dedication of the first-born

13 The LORD spoke to Moses and
2 said, 'Every first-born, the first birth of every womb among the Israelites, you must dedicate to me, both man and beast; it is mine.'

Pilgrim-feast of unleavened bread

3 Then Moses said to the people, 'Remember this day, the day on which you have come out of Egypt, the land of slavery, because the LORD by the strength of his hand has brought you out. No leaven
4 may be eaten this day, for today, in the month of Abib, is the day of
5 your exodus; and when the LORD has brought you into the country of the Canaanites, Hittites, Amorites, Hivites, and Jebusites, the land which he swore to your forefathers to give you, a land flowing with milk and honey, then you must observe this rite in this same
6 month. For seven days you shall eat unleavened cakes, and on the seventh day there shall be a pilgrim-
7 feast of the LORD. Only unleavened cakes shall be eaten during the seven days; nothing fermented and no leaven shall be seen throughout
8 your territory. On that day you shall tell your son, "This commemorates what the LORD did for me when I came out of Egypt."
9 You shall have the record of it as a sign upon your hand, and upon your forehead as a reminder, to make sure that the law of the LORD is always on your lips, because the LORD with a strong hand brought
10 you out of Egypt. This is a rule, and you shall keep it at the appointed time from year to year.

First-born belong to the LORD

11 'When the LORD has brought you into the land of the Canaanites as he swore to you and to your fore-
12 fathers, and given it to you, you shall surrender to the LORD the first birth of every womb; and of all first-born offspring of your cattle the males belong to the
13 LORD. Every first-born male ass you may redeem with a kid or lamb, but if you do not redeem it, you must break its neck. Every first-born among your sons you
14 must redeem. When in time to come your son asks you what this means, you shall say to him, "By the strength of his hand the LORD brought us out of Egypt, out of
15 the land of slavery. When Pharaoh proved stubborn and refused to let us go, the LORD killed all the first-born in Egypt both man and beast. That is why I sacrifice to the LORD the first birth of every womb if it is a male and redeem every first-
16 born of my sons. You shall have the record of it as a sign upon your hand, and upon your forehead as a phylactery, because by the strength of his hand the LORD brought us out of Egypt." '

The cloud and the fire

17 Now when Pharaoh let the people go, God did not guide them by the road towards the Philistines, although that was the shortest; for he said, 'The people may change their minds when they see war before them, and
18 turn back to Egypt.' So God made them go round by way of the wilderness towards the Red Sea; and the fifth generation of Israelites departed from Egypt.
19   Moses took the bones of Joseph with him, because Joseph had exacted an oath from the Israelites: 'Some day', he said, 'God will show his care for you, and then, as you go, you must take my bones with you.'
20   They set out from Succoth and encamped
21 at Etham on the edge of the wilderness. And all the time the LORD went before them, by day a pillar of cloud to guide them on their journey, by night a pillar of fire to give them light, so that they could travel night and day.
22 The pillar of cloud never left its place in front of the people by day, nor the pillar of fire by night.

Crossing the Red Sea

14 The LORD spoke to Moses and said, 'Speak
1 to the Israelites: they are to turn back and encamp before Pi-hahiroth,[p] between Migdol and the sea to the east of Baal-zephon; your camp shall be opposite, by the sea.
3 Pharaoh will then think that the Israelites are finding themselves in difficult country,
4 and are hemmed in by the wilderness. I will make Pharaoh obstinate, and he will pursue them, so that I may win glory for myself at the expense of Pharaoh and all his army; and the Egyptians shall know that I am the LORD.' The Israelites did as they were bidden.
5   When the king of Egypt was told that the Israelites had slipped away, he and his courtiers changed their minds completely, and said, 'What have we done? We have let
6 our Israelite slaves go free!' So Pharaoh put horses to his chariot, and took his troops
7 with him. He took six hundred picked chariots and all the other chariots of Egypt, with
8 a commander in each. Then Pharaoh king

p Or where the desert tracks begin.

of Egypt, made obstinate by the LORD, pursued the Israelites as they marched defiantly
9 away. The Egyptians, all Pharaoh's chariots and horses, cavalry and infantry, pursued them and overtook them encamped beside the sea by Pi-hahiroth to the east of Baal-
10 zephon. Pharaoh was almost upon them when the Israelites looked up and saw the Egyptians close behind. In their terror they
11 clamoured to the LORD for help and said to Moses, 'Were there no graves in Egypt, that you should have brought us here to die in the wilderness? See what you have done to
12 us by bringing us out of Egypt! Is not this just what we meant when we said in Egypt, "Leave us alone; let us be slaves to the Egyptians"? We would rather be slaves to the Egyptians than die here in the wilder-
13 ness.' 'Have no fear,' Moses answered; 'stand firm and see the deliverance that the LORD will bring you this day; for as sure as you see the Egyptians now, you will never see
14 them again. The LORD will fight for you; so hold your peace.'
15   The LORD said to Moses, 'What is the meaning of this clamour? Tell the Israelites
16 to strike camp. And you shall raise high your staff, stretch out your hand over the sea and cleave it in two, so that the Israelites
17 can pass through the sea on dry ground. For my part I will make the Egyptians obstinate and they will come after you; thus will I win glory for myself at the expense of Pharaoh and his army, chariots and cavalry
18 all together. The Egyptians will know that I am the LORD when I win glory for myself at the expense of their Pharaoh, his chariots and cavalry.'
19   The angel of God, who had kept in front of the Israelites, moved away to the rear. The pillar of cloud moved from the front
20 and took its place behind them and so came between the Egyptians and the Israelites. And the cloud brought on darkness and early nightfall, so that contact was lost throughout the night.
21   Then Moses stretched out his hand over the sea, and the LORD drove the sea away all night with a strong east wind and turned the sea-bed into dry land. The waters were
22 torn apart, and the Israelites went through the sea on the dry ground, while the waters made a wall for them to right and to left.
23 The Egyptians went in pursuit of them far into the sea, all Pharaoh's horse, his chariots,
24 and his cavalry. In the morning watch the LORD looked down on the Egyptian army through the pillar of fire and cloud, and he
25 threw them into a panic. He clogged their chariot wheels and made them lumber along heavily, so that the Egyptians said, 'It is the LORD fighting for Israel against Egypt; let us
26 flee.' Then the LORD said to Moses, 'Stretch out your hand over the sea, and let the water flow back over the Egyptians, their chariots and their cavalry.' So Moses stretched 27 out his hand over the sea, and at daybreak the water returned to its accustomed place; but the Egyptians were in flight as it advanced, and the LORD swept them out into the sea. The water flowed back and 28 covered all Pharaoh's army, the chariots and the cavalry, which had pressed the pursuit into the sea. Not one man was left alive. Meanwhile the Israelites had passed 29 along the dry ground through the sea, with the water making a wall for them to right and to left. That day the LORD saved Israel 30 from the power of Egypt, and the Israelites saw the Egyptians lying dead on the sea-shore. When Israel saw the great power 31 which the LORD had put forth against Egypt, all the people feared the LORD, and they put their faith in him and in Moses his servant.

The song of Moses

Then Moses and the Israelites sang this song **15** to the LORD:
I will sing to the LORD, for he has risen up
    in triumph;
the horse and his rider he has hurled into
    the sea.
    The LORD is my refuge and my defence, 2
    he has shown himself my deliverer.
    He is my God, and I will glorify him;
    he is my father's God, and I will exalt
    him.
    The LORD is a warrior: the LORD is his 3
    name.
    The chariots of Pharaoh and his army 4
    he has cast into the sea;
    the flower of his officers
    are engulfed in the Red Sea.
    The watery abyss has covered them, 5
    they sank into the depths like a stone.
Thy right hand, O LORD, is majestic in 6
    strength:
thy right hand, O LORD, shattered the enemy.
    In the fullness of thy triumph 7
    thou didst cast the rebels down:
    thou didst let loose thy fury;
    it consumed them like chaff.
At the blast of thy anger the sea piled up: 8
    the waters stood up like a bank:
    out at sea the great deep congealed.
The enemy said, 'I will pursue, I will over- 9
    take;
    I will divide the spoil,
    I will glut my appetite upon them;
    I will draw my sword,
    I will rid myself of them.'
Thou didst blow with thy blast; the sea 10
    covered them.
They sank like lead in the swelling waves.

11 Who is like thee, O Lord, among the
gods[q]?
Who is like thee, majestic in holiness,
worthy of awe and praise, who workest
wonders?
12 Thou didst stretch out thy right hand,
earth engulfed them.
13 In thy constant love thou hast led the people
whom thou didst ransom:
thou hast guided them by thy strength
to thy holy dwelling-place.
14 Nations heard and trembled;
agony seized the dwellers in Philistia.
15 Then the chieftains of Edom were dismayed,
trembling seized the leaders of Moab,
all the inhabitants of Canaan were in turmoil;
16 terror and dread fell upon them:
through the might of thy arm they stayed
stone-still,
while thy people passed, O Lord,
while the people whom thou madest thy
own[r] passed by.
17 Thou broughtest them in and didst plant
them
in the mount that is thy possession,
the dwelling-place, O Lord, of thy own
making,
the sanctuary, O Lord, which thy own hands
prepared.
18 The Lord shall reign for ever and for
ever.

19 For Pharaoh's horse, both chariots and
cavalry, went into the sea, and the Lord
brought back the waters over them, but
Israel had passed through the sea on dry
20 ground. And Miriam the prophetess, Aaron's
sister, took up her tambourine, and all the
women followed her, dancing to the sound
21 of tambourines; and Miriam sang them this
refrain:

Sing to the Lord, for he has risen up in
triumph;
the horse and his rider he has hurled into the
sea.

Bitter water at Marah

22 Moses led Israel from the Red Sea out into
the wilderness of Shur. For three days they
travelled through the wilderness without
23 finding water. They came to Marah, but
could not drink the Marah water because it
was bitter; that is why the place was called
24 Marah. The people complained to Moses
25 and asked, 'What are we to drink?' Moses
cried to the Lord, and the Lord showed him
a log which he threw into the water, and then
the water became sweet.
It was there that the Lord laid down a

precept and rule of life; there he put them
to the test. He said, 'If only you will obey 26
the Lord your God, if you will do what is
right in his eyes, if you will listen to his commands and keep all his statutes, then I will
never bring upon you any of the sufferings
which I brought on the Egyptians; for I the
Lord am your healer.'
They came to Elim, where there were 27
twelve springs and seventy palm-trees, and
there they encamped beside the water.

The Lord gives manna

The whole community of the Israelites set 16
out from Elim and came into the wilderness
of Sin, which lies between Elim and Sinai.
This was on the fifteenth day of the second
month after they had left Egypt.
The Israelites complained to Moses and 2
Aaron in the wilderness and said, 'If only 3
we had died at the Lord's hand in Egypt,
where we sat round the fleshpots and had
plenty of bread to eat! But you have brought
us out into this wilderness to let this whole
assembly starve to death.' The Lord said 4
to Moses, 'I will rain down bread from
heaven for you. Each day the people shall
go out and gather a day's supply, so that I
can put them to the test and see whether
they will follow my instructions or not. But 5
on the sixth day, when they prepare what
they bring in, it shall be twice as much as
they have gathered on other days.' Moses 6
and Aaron then said to all the Israelites, 'In
the evening you will know that it was the
Lord who brought you out of Egypt,
and in the morning you will see the glory 7
of the Lord, because he has heeded your
complaints against him; it is not against
us that you bring your complaints; we
are nothing.' 'You shall know this', Moses 8
said, 'when the Lord, in answer to your
complaints, gives you flesh to eat in the
evening, and in the morning bread in
plenty. What are we? It is against the Lord
that you bring your complaints, and not
against us.'
Moses told Aaron to say to the whole 9
community of Israel, 'Come into the presence of the Lord, for he has heeded your
complaints.' While Aaron was speaking to 10
the community of the Israelites, they looked
towards the wilderness, and there was the
glory of the Lord appearing in the cloud.
The Lord spoke to Moses and said, 'I have 11
heard the complaints of the Israelites. Say
to them, "Between dusk and dark you will
have flesh to eat and in the morning bread
in plenty. You shall know that I the Lord
am your God." '

q Or in might.   r madest thy own: or didst create.

That evening a flock of quails flew in and settled all over the camp, and in the morning a fall of dew lay all around it. When the dew was gone, there in the wilderness, fine flakes appeared, fine as hoar-frost on the ground. When the Israelites saw it, they said to one another, 'What is that?',⁵ because they did not know what it was. Moses said to them, 'That is the bread which the LORD has given you to eat. This is the command the LORD has given: "Each of you is to gather as much as he can eat: let every man take an omer a head for every person in his tent."' The Israelites did this, and they gathered, some more, some less, but when they measured it by the omer, those who had gathered more had not too much, and those who had gathered less had not too little. Each had just as much as he could eat. Moses said, 'No one may keep any of it till morning.' Some, however, did not listen to Moses; they kept part of it till morning, and it became full of maggots and stank, and Moses was angry with them. Each morning every man gathered as much as he could eat, and when the sun grew hot, it melted away. On the sixth day they gathered twice as much food, two omers each. All the chiefs of the community came and told Moses. 'This', he answered, 'is what the LORD has said: "Tomorrow is a day of sacred rest, a sabbath holy to the LORD." So bake what you want to bake now, and boil what you want to boil; put aside what remains over and keep it safe till morning.' So they put it aside till morning as Moses had commanded, and it did not stink, nor did maggots appear in it. 'Eat it today,' said Moses, 'because today is a sabbath of the LORD. Today you will find none outside. For six days you may gather it, but on the seventh day, the sabbath, there will be none.' Some of the people did go out to gather it on the seventh day, but they found none. The LORD said to Moses, 'How long will you refuse to obey my commands and instructions? The LORD has given you the sabbath, and so he gives you two days' food every sixth day. Let each man stay where he is; no one may stir from his home on the seventh day.' And the people kept the sabbath on the seventh day.

Israel called the food manna; it was white, like coriander seed, and it tasted like a wafer made with honey. 'This', said Moses, 'is the command which the LORD has given: "Take a full omer of it to be kept for future generations, so that they may see the bread with which I fed you in the wilderness when I brought you out of Egypt."' So Moses said to Aaron, 'Take a jar and fill it with an omer of manna, and store it in the presence of the LORD to be kept for future generations.' Aaron did as the LORD had commanded Moses, and stored it before the Testimony for safe keeping. The Israelites ate the manna for forty years until they came to a land where they could settle; they ate it until they came to the border of Canaan. (An omer is one tenth of an ephah.)

Coriander seed (Exod. 16. 31)

Water from the rock

The whole community of Israel set out from **17** the wilderness of Sin and travelled by stages as the LORD told them. They encamped at Rephidim, where there was no water for the people to drink, and a dispute arose between them and Moses. When they said, 'Give us water to drink', Moses said, 'Why do you dispute with me? Why do you challenge the LORD?' There the people became so thirsty that they raised an outcry against Moses: 'Why have you brought us out of Egypt with our children and our herds to let us all die of thirst?' Moses cried to the LORD, 'What shall I do with these people? In a moment they will be stoning me.' The LORD answered, 'Go forward ahead of the

s *Heb.* man-hu (*cp. verse 31*).

people; take with you some of the elders of Israel and the staff with which you struck
6 the Nile, and go. You will find me waiting for you there, by a rock in Horeb. Strike the rock; water will pour out of it, and the people shall drink.' Moses did this in the sight of
7 the elders of Israel. He named the place Massah[t] and Meribah,[u] because the Israelites had disputed with him and challenged the LORD with their question, 'Is the LORD in our midst or not?'

War with Amalek

8 The Amalekites came and attacked Israel
9 at Rephidim. Moses said to Joshua, 'Pick your men, and march out tomorrow to fight for us against Amalek; and I will take my stand on the hill-top with the staff of
10 God in my hand.' Joshua carried out his orders and fought against Amalek while Moses, Aaron and Hur climbed to the top
11 of the hill. Whenever Moses raised his hands Israel had the advantage, and when he lowered his hands Amalek had the advan-
12 tage. But when his arms grew heavy they took a stone and put it under him and, as he sat, Aaron and Hur held up his hands, one on each side, so that his hands remained
13 steady till sunset. Thus Joshua defeated Amalek and put its people to the sword.
14 The LORD said to Moses, 'Record this in writing, and tell it to Joshua in these words: "I am resolved to blot out all memory of
15 Amalek from under heaven."' Moses built
16 an altar, and named it Jehovah-nissi and said, 'My oath upon it: the LORD is at war with Amalek generation after generation.'

Jethro visits Moses

18 Jethro priest of Midian, father-in-law of Moses, heard all that God had done for Moses and Israel his people, and how the LORD had brought Israel out of Egypt.
2 When Moses had dismissed his wife Zipporah, Jethro his father-in-law had received
3 her and her two sons. The name of the one was Gershom, 'for', said Moses, 'I have become an alien[v] living in a foreign land';
4 the other's name was Eliezer,[w] 'for', he said, 'the God of my father was my help and saved me from Pharaoh's sword.'
5 Jethro, Moses' father-in-law, now came to him with his sons and his wife, to the wilderness where he was encamped at the
6 mountain of God. Moses was told, 'Here is Jethro, your father-in-law, coming to you
7 with your wife and her two sons.' Moses went out to meet his father-in-law, bowed low to him and kissed him, and they greeted one another. When they came into the tent
8 Moses told him all that the LORD had done to Pharaoh and to Egypt for Israel's sake,

and about all their hardships on the journey, and how the LORD had saved them. Jethro 9 rejoiced at all the good the LORD had done for Israel in saving them from the power of Egypt. He said, 'Blessed be the LORD who 10 has saved you from the power of Egypt and of Pharaoh. Now I know that the LORD is the greatest of all gods, because he has delivered the people from the power of the Egyptians who dealt so arrogantly with them.' Jethro, 11 Moses' father-in-law, brought a whole-offering and sacrifices for God; and Aaron and all the elders of Israel came and shared the meal with Jethro in the presence of God.

Moses sets up a court of law

The next day Moses took his seat to settle 13 disputes among the people, and they were standing round him from morning till evening. When Jethro saw all that he was doing 14 for the people, he said, 'What are you doing for all these people? Why do you sit alone with all of them standing round you from morning till evening?' 'The people come to 15 me', Moses answered, 'to seek God's guidance. Whenever there is a dispute among 16 them, they come to me, and I decide between man and man. I declare the statutes and laws of God.' But his father-in-law said to 17 Moses, 'This is not the best way to do it. You will only wear yourself out and wear 18 out all the people who are here. The task is too heavy for you; you cannot do it by yourself. Now listen to me: take my advice, 19 and God be with you. It is for you to be the people's representative before God, and bring their disputes to him. You must in- 20 struct them in the statutes and laws, and teach them how they must behave and what they must do. But you must yourself search 21 for capable, God-fearing men among all the people, honest and incorruptible men, and appoint them over the people as officers over units of a thousand, of a hundred, of fifty or of ten. They shall sit as a permanent 22 court for the people; they must refer difficult cases to you but decide simple cases themselves. In this way your burden will be lightened, and they will share it with you. If you do this, God will give you strength, 23 and you will be able to go on. And, moreover, this whole people will here and now regain peace and harmony.' Moses listened 24 to his father-in-law and did all he had suggested. He chose capable men from all Israel and appointed them leaders of the people, officers over units of a thousand, of 25 a hundred, of fifty or of ten. They sat as a permanent court, bringing the difficult cases 26 to Moses but deciding simple cases themselves. Moses set his father-in-law on his 27 way, and he went back to his own country.

---

[t] *That is* Challenge.   [u] *That is* Dispute.   [v] Cp. 2. 22.   [w] *That is* God my help.

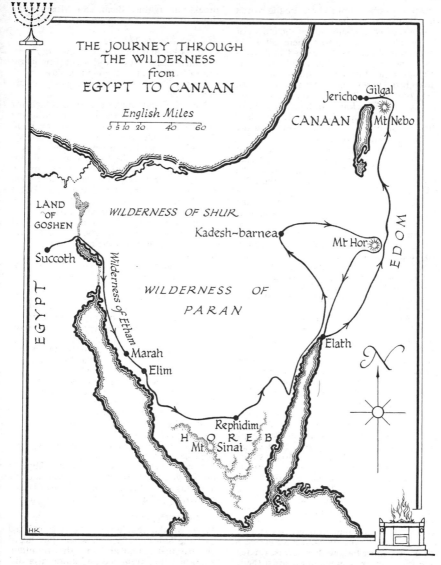

THE JOURNEY THROUGH
THE WILDERNESS
from
EGYPT TO CANAAN

English Miles
5 5 10 20   40   60

CANAAN

Jericho Gilgal
Mt Nebo

LAND
OF
GOSHEN

WILDERNESS OF SHUR

Kadesh-barnea

Mt Hor

EDOM

Succoth

EGYPT

Wilderness of Etham

WILDERNESS OF
PARAN

Marah
Elim

Elath

Rephidim
Mt Sinai

H O R E B

HK

Israel at Mount Sinai

19 In the third month after Israel had left Egypt,[x] they came to the wilderness of Sinai.
2 They set out from Rephidim and entered the wilderness of Sinai, where they encamped, pitching their tents opposite the
3 mountain. Moses went up the mountain of God, and the Lord called to him from the mountain and said, 'Speak thus to the house of Jacob, and tell this to the sons of Israel:
You have seen with your own eyes what I 4 did to Egypt, and how I have carried you on eagles' wings and brought you here to me.
If only you will now listen to me and keep 5 my covenant, then out of all peoples you shall become my special possession; for the whole earth is mine. You shall be my kingdom of 6

x Prob. rdg.; Heb. adds on this day.

priests, my holy nation. These are the words you shall speak to the Israelites.'

7 Moses came and summoned the elders of the people and set before them all these commands which the LORD had laid upon 8 him. The people all answered together, 'Whatever the LORD has said we will do.' Moses brought this answer back to the LORD. 9 The LORD said to Moses, 'I am now coming to you in a thick cloud, so that I may speak to you in the hearing of the people, and their faith in you may never fail.' Moses told the 10 LORD what the people had said, and the LORD said to him, 'Go to the people and hallow them today and tomorrow and make 11 them wash their clothes. They must be ready by the third day, because on the third day the LORD will descend upon Mount 12 Sinai in the sight of all the people. You must put barriers round the mountain and say, "Take care not to go up the mountain or even to touch the edge of it." Any man who touches the mountain must be put to death. 13 No hand shall touch him;[y] he shall be stoned or shot dead:[z] neither man nor beast may live. But when the ram's horn sounds, they 14 may go up the mountain.' Moses came down from the mountain to the people. He hallowed them and they washed their clothes. 15 He said to the people, 'Be ready by the third 16 day; do not go near a woman.' On the third day, when morning came, there were peals of thunder and flashes of lightning, dense cloud on the mountain and a loud trumpet blast; the people in the camp were all terrified. 17 Moses brought the people out from the camp to meet God, and they took their 18 stand at the foot of the mountain. Mount Sinai was all smoking because the LORD had come down upon it in fire; the smoke went up like the smoke of a kiln; all the people 19 were terrified, and the sound of the trumpet grew ever louder. Whenever Moses spoke, God answered him in a peal of thunder.[a] 20 The LORD came down upon the top of Mount Sinai and summoned Moses to the mountain- 21 top, and Moses went up. The LORD said to Moses, 'Go down; warn the people solemnly that they must not force their way through to the LORD to see him, or many of them will 22 perish. Even the priests, who have access to the LORD, must hallow themselves, for fear that the LORD may break out against them.' 23 Moses answered the LORD, 'The people cannot come up Mount Sinai, because thou thyself didst solemnly warn us to set a barrier to the mountain and so to keep it holy.' 24 The LORD therefore said to him, 'Go down; then come up and bring Aaron with you, but let neither priests nor people force their way up to the LORD, for fear that he may

break out against them.' So Moses went 25 down to the people and spoke to them.

The Ten Commandments

God spoke, and these were his words: **20**

I am the LORD your God who brought you 2 out of Egypt, out of the land of slavery.

You shall have no other god[b] to set 3 against me.

You shall not make a carved image for 4 yourself nor the likeness of anything in the heavens above, or on the earth below, or in the waters under the earth.

You shall not bow down to them or wor- 5 ship[c] them; for I, the LORD your God, am a jealous god. I punish the children for the sins of the fathers to the third and fourth generations of those who hate me. But I 6 keep faith with thousands, with[d] those who love me and keep my commandments.

You shall not make wrong use of the 7 name of the LORD your God; the LORD will not leave unpunished the man who misuses his name.

Remember to keep the sabbath day holy. 8 You have six days to labour and do all your 9 work. But the seventh day is a sabbath of 10 the LORD your God; that day you shall not do any work, you, your son or your daughter, your slave or your slave-girl, your cattle or the alien within your gates; for in six days 11 the LORD made heaven and earth, the sea, and all that is in them, and on the seventh day he rested. Therefore the LORD blessed the sabbath day and declared it holy.

Honour your father and your mother, 12 that you may live long in the land which the LORD your God is giving you.

You shall not commit murder.   13

You shall not commit adultery.   14

You shall not steal.   15

You shall not give false evidence against 16 your neighbour.

You shall not covet your neighbour's 17 house; you shall not covet your neighbour's wife, his slave, his slave-girl, his ox, his ass, or anything that belongs to him.

God tests the people

When all the people saw how it thundered 18 and the lightning flashed, when they heard the trumpet sound and saw the mountain smoking, they trembled and stood at a distance. 'Speak to us yourself,' they said to 19 Moses, 'and we will listen; but if God speaks to us we shall die.' Moses answered, 'Do 20 not be afraid. God has come only to test you, so that the fear of him may remain with you and keep you from sin.' So the people stood 21 at a distance, while Moses approached the dark cloud where God was.

---

y Or it.   *z Or* hurled to his death.   *a* in ... thunder: *or* by voice.   *b Or* gods.   *c Or* or be led to worship.   *d* with ... with: *or* for a thousand generations with ...

Laws concerning altars

22 The LORD said to Moses, Say this
to the Israelites: You know now
that I have spoken to you from
23 heaven. You shall not make gods
of silver to be worshipped as well
as me, nor shall you make your-
24 selves gods of gold. You shall make
an altar of earth for me, and you
shall sacrifice on it both your whole-
offerings and your shared-offerings,
your sheep and your cattle. Wherever I cause my name to be invoked, I will come to you and bless
25 you. If you make an altar of stones
for me, you must not build it of
hewn stones, for if you use a chisel
26 on it, you will profane it. You must
not mount up to my altar by steps,
in case your private parts be exposed on it.

Laws concerning slaves

1 These are the laws you shall set
before them:
2　When you buy a Hebrew slave,
he shall be your slave for six years,
but in the seventh year he shall go
free and pay nothing.
3　If he comes to you alone, he
shall go away alone; but if he is
married, his wife shall go away with
him.
4　If his master gives him a wife,
and she bears him sons or daughters, the woman and her children
shall belong to her master, and the
5 man shall go away alone. But if the
slave should say, 'I love my master,
my wife, and my children; I will
6 not go free', then his master shall
bring him to God: he shall bring
him to the door or the door-post,
and his master shall pierce his ear
with an awl, and the man shall be
his slave for life.
7　When a man sells his daughter
into slavery, she shall not go free
8 as a male slave may. If her master
has not had intercourse with her
and she does not please him, he
shall let her be ransomed. He has
treated her unfairly and therefore
has no right to sell her to strangers.
9 If he assigns her to his son, he shall
allow her the rights of a daughter.
10 If he takes another woman, he shall
not deprive the first of meat,
11 clothes, and conjugal rights. If he
does not provide her with these
three things, she shall go free without any payment.

Laws concerning acts of violence

2 Whoever strikes another man and
3 kills him shall be put to death. But
if he did not act with intent, but
they met by act of God, the slayer
may flee to a place which I will
4 appoint for you. But if a man has
the presumption to kill another by
treachery, you shall take him even
from my altar to be put to death.

15　Whoever strikes his father or
mother shall be put to death.
16　Whoever kidnaps a man shall be
put to death, whether he has sold
him, or the man is found in his
possession.
17　Whoever reviles his father or
mother shall be put to death.
18　When men quarrel and one hits
another with a stone or with a
spade,[e] and the man is not killed
19 but takes to his bed; if he recovers
so as to walk about outside with a
stick, then the one who struck him
has no liability, except that he shall
pay for loss of time and shall see
that he is cured.
20　When a man strikes his slave or
his slave-girl with a stick and the
slave dies on the spot, he must be
21 punished. But he shall not be
punished if the slave survives for
one day or two, because he is
worth money to his master.
22　When, in the course of a brawl,
a man knocks against a pregnant
woman so that she has a miscarriage but suffers no further hurt,
then the offender must pay whatever fine the woman's husband demands after assessment.
23　Wherever hurt is done, you shall
24 give life for life, eye for eye, tooth
for tooth, hand for hand, foot for
25 foot, burn for burn, bruise for
bruise, wound for wound.
26　When a man strikes his slave or
slave-girl in the eye and destroys
it, he shall let the slave go free in
27 compensation for the eye. When
he knocks out the tooth of a slave
or a slave-girl, he shall let the slave
go free in compensation for the
tooth.

Owners' liability

28　When an ox gores a man or a
woman to death, the ox shall be
stoned, and its flesh may not be
eaten; the owner of the ox shall
29 be free from liability. If, however,
the ox has for some time past been
a vicious animal, and the owner has
been duly warned but has not kept
it under control, and the ox kills
a man or a woman, then the ox
30 shall be stoned, and the owner shall
be put to death as well. If, however, the penalty is commuted for
a money payment, he shall pay in
redemption of his life whatever is
31 imposed upon him. If the ox gores
a son or a daughter, the same rule
32 shall apply. If the ox gores a slave
or slave-girl, its owner shall pay
thirty shekels of silver to their
master, and the ox shall be stoned.
33　When a man removes the cover
of a well[f] or digs a well[f] and leaves
it uncovered, then if an ox or an
34 ass falls into it, the owner of the
well shall make good the loss. He
shall repay the owner of the beast
in silver, and the dead beast shall
be his.

When one man's ox butts an- 35
other's and kills it, they shall sell
the live ox, share the price and also
share the dead beast. But if it is 36
known that the ox has for some
time past been vicious and the
owner has not kept it under control, he shall make good the loss,
ox for ox, but the dead beast is his.

Laws concerning restitution

When a man steals an ox or a **22**
sheep and slaughters or sells it, he
shall repay five beasts for the ox
and four sheep for the sheep. He 2–4[g]
shall pay in full; if he has no means,
he shall be sold to pay for the theft.
But if the animal is found alive in
his possession, be it ox, ass, or
sheep, he shall repay two.
If a burglar is caught in the act
and is fatally injured, it is not murder; but if he breaks in after sunrise and is fatally injured, then it
is murder.
When a man burns off a field or 5
a vineyard and lets the fire spread
so that it burns another man's
field,[h] he shall make restitution
from his own field according to
the yield expected; and if the whole
field is laid waste, he shall make
restitution from the best part of
his own field or vineyard.
When a fire starts and spreads 6
to a heap of brushwood, so that
sheaves, or standing corn, or a
whole field is destroyed, he who
started the fire shall make full
restitution.
When one man gives another 7
silver or chattels for safe keeping,
and they are stolen from that man's
house, the thief, if he is found, shall
restore twofold. But if the thief is 8
not found, the owner of the house
shall appear before God, to make a
declaration that he has not touched
his neighbour's property. In every 9
case of law-breaking involving an
ox, an ass, or a sheep, a cloak, or
any lost property which may be
claimed, each party shall bring his
case before God; he whom God
declares to be in the wrong shall
restore twofold to his neighbour.
When a man gives an ass, an ox, 10
a sheep or any beast into his neighbour's keeping, and it dies or is
injured or is carried off, there being
no witness, the neighbour shall 11
swear by the LORD that he has not
touched the man's property. The
owner shall accept this, and no
restitution shall be made. If it has 12
been stolen from him, he shall
make restitution to the owner. If 13
it has been mauled by a wild beast,
he shall bring it in as evidence; he
shall not make restitution for what
has been mauled.
When a man borrows a beast 14
from his neighbour and it is injured or dies while its owner is not

<hr>

e Or fist.　　f Or cistern.　　g Verses 2–4 rearranged thus: 3b, 4, 2, 3a.　　h Or When a man uses
his field or vineyard for grazing, and lets his beast loose, and it feeds in another man's field.

15 with it, the borrower shall make full restitution; but if the owner is with it, the borrower shall not make restitution. If it was hired, only the hire shall be due.

Various laws

16 When a man seduces a virgin who is not yet betrothed, he shall pay the bride-price for her to be his 17 wife. If her father refuses to give her to him, the seducer shall pay in silver a sum equal to the bride-price for virgins.

18 You shall not allow a witch to live.

19 Whoever has unnatural connection with a beast shall be put to death.

20 Whoever sacrifices to any god but the LORD shall be put to death under solemn ban.

21 You shall not wrong an alien, or be hard upon him; you were your-22 selves aliens in Egypt. You shall not ill-treat any widow or father-23 less child. If you do, be sure that I will listen if they appeal to me; 24 my anger will be roused and I will kill you with the sword; your own wives shall become widows and your children fatherless.

25 If you advance money to any poor man amongst my people, you shall not act like a money-lender: you must not exact interest in advance from him.

26 If you take your neighbour's cloak in pawn, you shall return it 27 to him by sunset, because it is his only covering. It is the cloak in which he wraps his body; in what else can he sleep? If he appeals to me, I will listen, for I am full of compassion.

28 You shall not revile God, nor curse a chief of your own people.

29 You shall not hold back the first of your harvest, whether corn or wine. You shall give me your first-30 born sons. You shall do the same with your oxen and your sheep. They shall stay with the mother for seven days; on the eighth day you shall give them to me.

31 You shall be holy to me: you shall not eat the flesh of anything in the open country killed by beasts, but you shall throw it to the dogs.

Justice and equity

23 You shall not spread a baseless rumour. You shall not make common cause with a wicked man by giving malicious evidence.

2 You shall not be led into wrong-doing by the majority, nor when you give evidence in a lawsuit, shall you side with the majority to per-3 vert justice; nor shall you favour the poor man in his suit.

4 When you come upon your enemy's ox or ass straying, you 5 shall take it back to him. When you see the ass of someone who hates you lying helpless under its load, however unwilling you may be to help it, you must give him a hand with it.

6 You shall not deprive the poor 7 man of justice in his suit. Avoid all lies, and do not cause the death of the innocent and the guiltless; for I the LORD will never acquit 8 the guilty. You shall not accept a bribe, for bribery makes the discerning man blind and the just man give a crooked answer.

9 You shall not oppress the alien, for you know how it feels to be an alien; you were aliens yourselves in Egypt.

Sabbath years and days

10 For six years you may sow your 11 land and gather its produce; but in the seventh year you shall let it lie fallow and leave it alone. It shall provide food for the poor of your people, and what they leave the wild animals may eat. You shall do likewise with your vineyard and your olive-grove.

12 For six days you may do your work, but on the seventh day you shall abstain from work, so that your ox and your ass may rest, and your home-born slave and the alien may refresh themselves.

13 Be attentive to every word of mine. You shall not invoke other gods: your lips shall not speak their names.

Three pilgrim-feasts

14 Three times a year you shall keep 15 a pilgrim-feast to me. You shall celebrate the pilgrim-feast of Unleavened Bread for seven days; you shall eat unleavened cakes as I have commanded you, at the appointed time in the month of Abib, for in that month you came out of Egypt.

16 No one shall come into my presence empty-handed. You shall celebrate the pilgrim-feast of Harvest, with the firstfruits of your work in sowing the land, and the pilgrim-feast of Ingathering at the end[i] of the year, when you bring 17 in the fruits of all your work on the land. These three times a year shall all your males come into the presence of the Lord GOD.

18 You shall not offer the blood of my sacrifice at the same time as anything leavened.

The fat of my festal offering shall not remain overnight till morning.

19 You shall bring the choicest firstfruits of your soil to the house of the LORD your God.

You shall not boil a kid in its mother's milk.

The LORD promises success

20 And now I send an angel before you to guard you on your way and to bring you to the place I have prepared. Take heed of him and 21 listen to his voice. Do not defy him; he will not pardon your rebelliousness, for my authority rests in him. If you will only listen to his 22 voice and do all I tell you, then I will be an enemy to your enemies, and I will harass those who harass you. My angel will go before you 23 and bring you to the Amorites, the Hittites, the Perizzites, the Canaanites, the Hivites, and the Jebusites, and I will make an end of them. You are not to bow down to their 24 gods, nor worship them, nor observe their rites, but you shall tear down all their images and smash their sacred pillars. Worship the 25 LORD your God, and he will bless your bread and your water. I will take away all sickness out of your midst. None shall miscarry or be 26 barren in your land. I will grant you a full span of life.

I will send my terror before you 27 and throw into confusion all the peoples whom you find in your path. I will make all your enemies turn their backs. I will spread panic 28 before you to drive out in front of you the Hivites, the Canaanites and the Hittites. I will not drive them 29 out all in one year, or the land would become waste and the wild beasts too many for you. I will 30 drive them out little by little until your numbers have grown enough to take possession of the whole country. I will establish your fron-31 tiers from the Red Sea to the sea of the Philistines, and from the wilderness to the River. I will give the inhabitants of the country into your power, and you shall drive them out before you. You shall 32 make no covenant with them and their gods. They shall not stay in 33 your land for fear they make you sin against me; for then you would worship their gods, and in this way you would be ensnared.

Moses on Mount Sinai

24 Then he said to Moses, 'Come up to the LORD, you and Aaron, Nadab and Abihu, and seventy of the elders of Israel. While you are still at a distance, you are to bow down; and then Moses shall approach the 2 LORD by himself, but not the others. The people may not go up with him at all.'

i Or beginning.

3 Moses came and told the people all the words of the LORD, all his laws. The whole people answered with one voice and said, 'We will do all that the LORD has told us.'
4 Moses wrote down all the words of the LORD. He rose early in the morning and built an altar at the foot of the mountain, and put up twelve sacred pillars, one for each of the
5 twelve tribes of Israel. He then sent the young men of Israel and they sacrificed bulls to the LORD as whole-offerings and shared-
6 offerings. Moses took half the blood and put it in basins and the other half he flung
7 against^j the altar. Then he took the book of the covenant and read it aloud for all the people to hear. They said, 'We will obey,
8 and do all that the LORD has said.' Moses then took the blood and flung it over the people, saying, 'This is the blood of the covenant which the LORD has made with you on the terms of this book.'
9 Moses went up with Aaron, Nadab and Abihu, and seventy of the elders of Israel,
10 and they saw^k the God of Israel. Under his feet there was, as it were, a pavement of
11 sapphire,^{l} clear blue as the very heavens; but the LORD did not stretch out his hand towards the leaders of Israel. They stayed there be-
12 fore God;^{m} they ate and they drank. The LORD said to Moses, 'Come up to me on the mountain, stay there and let me give you the tablets of stone, the law and the command-ment, which I have written down that you

may teach them.' Moses arose with Joshua 13 his assistant and went up the mountain of God; he said to the elders, 'Wait for us here 14 until we come back to you. You have Aaron and Hur; if anyone has a dispute, let him go to them.' So Moses went up the mountain 15 and a cloud covered it. The glory of the 16 LORD rested upon Mount Sinai, and the cloud covered the mountain for six days; on the seventh day he called to Moses out of the cloud. The glory of the LORD looked 17 to the Israelites like a devouring fire on the mountain-top. Moses entered the cloud and 18 went up the mountain; there he stayed forty days and forty nights.

Contributions for the sanctuary

25
1 2 The LORD spoke to Moses and said: Tell the Israelites to set aside a contribution for me; you shall accept whatever contribution each man shall freely offer. This is what you shall 3 accept: gold, silver, copper; violet, purple, 4 and scarlet yarn; fine linen and goats' hair; tanned rams' skins, porpoise^n-hides, and 5 acacia-wood; oil for the lamp, balsam for 6 the anointing oil and for the fragrant in-cense; cornelian and other stones ready for 7 setting in the ephod and the breast-piece.^{o} Make me a sanctuary, and I will dwell 8 among them. Make it exactly according to 9 the design I show you, the design for the Tabernacle and for all its furniture. This is how you must make it:

The Ark of the Tokens

1 Make an Ark, a chest of acacia-wood, two and a half cubits long, one cubit and a half wide, and one cubit and a half high. Overlay it with pure gold both inside and out, and put a band of gold all round it.
2 Cast four gold rings for it, and fasten them to its four feet, two rings on each side. Make poles of acacia-wood and plate them with
3 gold, and insert the poles in the rings at the sides of the Ark to lift
4 it. The poles shall remain in the rings of the Ark and never be re-
5 moved. Put into the Ark the Tokens of the Covenant,^{p} which I shall give
6 you. Make a cover of pure gold, two and a half cubits long and one
7 cubit and a half wide. Make two gold cherubim of beaten work at
8 the ends of the cover, one at each end; make each cherub of one
9 piece with the cover. They shall be made with wings outspread and pointing upwards, and shall screen the cover with their wings. They shall be face to face, looking in-
10 wards over the cover. Put the cover above the Ark, and put into the

Ark the Tokens that I shall give
22 you. It is there that I shall meet you, and from above the cover, be-tween the two cherubim over the Ark of the Tokens, I shall deliver to you all my commands for the Israelites.

The table for the Bread

23 Make a table of acacia-wood, two cubits long, one cubit wide, and
24 one cubit and a half high. Overlay it with pure gold, and put a band
25 of gold all round it. Make a rim round it a hand's breadth wide, and
26 a gold band round the rim. Make four gold rings for the table, and put the rings at the four corners by
27 the legs. The rings, which are to receive the poles for carrying the table, must be adjacent to the rim.
28 Make the poles of acacia-wood and plate them with gold; they are to be used for carrying the table.
29 Make its dishes and saucers, and its flagons and bowls from which drink-offerings may be poured:
30 make them of pure gold. Put the Bread of the Presence^q on the table, to be always before me.

The golden lamp-stand

Make a lamp-stand of pure gold. 31 The lamp-stand, stem and bran-ches, shall be of beaten work, its cups, both calyxes and petals, shall be of one piece with it. There are 32 to be six branches springing from its sides; three branches of the lamp-stand shall spring from the

j Or upon.　　k Or they were afraid of . . .　　l Or lapis lazuli.　　m Or They saw God; and . . .
n Strictly sea-cow.　　o Or pouch.　　p Tokens of the Covenant: or Testimony.　　q Or Shewbread.

B*

33 one side and three branches from the other side. There shall be three cups shaped like almond blossoms, with calyx and petals, on the first branch, three cups shaped like almond blossoms, with calyx and petals, on the next branch, and similarly for all six branches spring-
34 ing from the lamp-stand. On the main stem of the lamp-stand there are to be four cups shaped like almond blossoms, with calyx and
35 petals, and there shall be calyxes of one piece with it under the six branches which spring from the lamp-stand, a single calyx under
36 each pair of branches. The calyxes and the branches are to be of one piece with it, all a single piece of
37 beaten work of pure gold. Make seven lamps for this and mount them to shed light over the space
38 in front of it. Its tongs and firepans
39 shall be of pure gold. The lamp-stand and all these fittings shall be made from one talent of pure gold.
40 See that you work to the design which you were shown on the mountain.

The Tabernacle

26 Make the Tabernacle of ten hang-ings of finely woven linen, and vio-let, purple, and scarlet yarn, with cherubim worked on them, all
2 made by a seamster. The length of each hanging shall be twenty-eight cubits and the breadth four cubits;
3 all are to be of the same size. Five of the hangings shall be joined to-gether, and similarly the other five.
4 Make violet loops along the edge of the last hanging in each set,
5 fifty for each set; they must be
6 opposite one another. Make fifty gold fasteners, join the hangings one to another with them, and the Tabernacle will be a single whole.
7 Make hangings of goats' hair, eleven in all, to form a tent over
8 the Tabernacle; each hanging is to be thirty cubits long and four wide; all eleven are to be of the same size.
9 Join five of the hangings together, and similarly the other six; then fold the sixth hanging double at
10 the front of the tent. Make fifty loops on the edge of the last hang-ing in the first set and make fifty loops on the joining edge of the
11 second set. Make fifty bronze[r] fasteners, insert them into the loops and join up the tent to make it a
12 single whole. The additional length of the tent hanging[s] is to fall over
13 the back of the Tabernacle. On each side there will be an addi-tional cubit in the length of the tent hangings; this shall fall over the two sides of the Tabernacle to
14 cover it. Make for the tent a cover of tanned rams' skins and an outer covering of porpoise-hides.
15 Make for the Tabernacle planks

16 of acacia-wood as uprights, each plank ten cubits long and a cubit
17 and a half wide, and two tenons for each plank joined to each other. You shall do the same for all the
18 planks of the Tabernacle. Arrange the planks thus: twenty planks for the south side, facing southwards,
19 with forty silver sockets under them, two sockets under each plank
20 for its two tenons; and for the second or northern side of the
21 Tabernacle, twenty planks, with forty silver sockets, two under
22 each plank. Make six planks for the far end of the Tabernacle on
23 the west. Make two planks for the corners of the Tabernacle at the
24 far end; at the bottom they shall be alike, and at the top, both alike, they shall fit into a single ring. Do
25 the same for both of them; they shall be for the two corners. There shall be eight planks with their silver sockets, sixteen sockets in all, two sockets under each plank severally.
26 Make bars of acacia-wood: five for the planks on the one side of
27 the Tabernacle, five for the planks on the other side and five for the planks on the far end of the Taber-
28 nacle on the west. The middle bar is to run along from end to end
29 half-way up the planks. Overlay the planks with gold, make rings of gold on them to hold the bars,
30 and plate the bars with gold. Set up the Tabernacle according to the design you were shown on the mountain.
31 Make a Veil of finely woven linen and violet, purple, and scar-let yarn, with cherubim worked on
32 it, all made by a seamster. Fasten it with hooks of gold to four posts of acacia-wood overlaid with gold, standing in four silver sockets.
33 Hang the Veil below the fasteners and bring the Ark of the Tokens inside the Veil. Thus the Veil will make a clear separation for you between the Holy Place and the
34 Holy of Holies. Place the cover over the Ark of the Tokens in the
35 Holy of Holies. Put the table out-side the Veil and the lamp-stand at the south side of the Tabernacle, opposite the table which you shall
36 put at the north side. For the entrance of the tent make a screen of finely woven linen, embroidered with violet, purple, and scarlet.
37 Make five posts of acacia-wood for the screen and overlay them with gold; make golden hooks for them and cast five bronze sockets for them.

The altar

27 Make the altar of acacia-wood; it shall be square, five cubits long by
2 five cubits broad and three cubits high. Let its horns at the four

corners be of one piece with it, and overlay it with bronze. Make for
3 it pots to take away the fat and the ashes, with shovels, tossing bowls, forks, and firepans, all of bronze.
4 Make a grating for it of bronze network, and fit four bronze rings on the network at its four corners.
5 Put it below the ledge of the altar, so that the network comes half-
6 way up the altar. Make poles of acacia-wood for the altar and over-
7 lay them with bronze. They shall be inserted in the rings at both sides of the altar to carry it. Leave
8 the altar a hollow shell. As you were shown on the mountain, so shall it be made.

Court of the Tabernacle

9 Make the court of the Tabernacle. For the one side, the south side facing southwards, the court shall have hangings of finely woven linen a hundred cubits long, with
10 twenty posts and twenty sockets of bronze; the hooks and bands on the posts shall be of silver. Simi-
11 larly all along the north side there shall be hangings a hundred cubits long, with twenty posts and twenty sockets of bronze; the hooks and bands on the posts shall be of
12 silver. For the breadth of the court, on the west side, there shall be hangings fifty cubits long, with ten
13 posts and ten sockets. On the east side, towards the sunrise, which was
14 fifty cubits, hangings shall extend fifteen cubits from one corner, with three posts and three sockets, and
15 hangings shall extend fifteen cubits from the other corner, with three posts and three sockets. At the
16 gateway of the court, there shall be a screen twenty cubits long of finely woven linen embroidered with vio-let, purple, and scarlet, with four
17 posts and four sockets. The posts all round the court shall have bands of silver, with hooks of silver, and sockets of bronze. The length of
18 the court shall be a hundred cubits, and the breadth fifty, and the height five cubits, with finely woven linen and bronze sockets through-
19 out. All the equipment needed for serving the Tabernacle, all its pegs and those of the court, shall be of bronze.

Tending the lamp

20 You yourself are to command the Israelites to bring you pure oil of pounded olives ready for the regu-
21 lar mounting of the lamp. In the Tent of the Presence[t] outside the Veil that hides the Tokens, Aaron and his sons shall keep the lamp in trim from dusk to dawn before the LORD. This is a rule binding on their descendants among the Israel-ites for all time.

r Or copper *and so throughout the description of the Tabernacle.*   *s Prob. rdg.; Heb. adds* half the hanging
which remains over.   *t Or* Tent of Meeting.

The priests' vestments

You yourself are to summon to your presence your brother Aaron and his sons out of all the Israelites to serve as my priests: Aaron and his sons Nadab and Abihu, Eleazar and Ithamar. For your brother Aaron make sacred vestments, to give him dignity and grandeur. Tell all the craftsmen whom I have endowed with skill to make the vestments for the consecration of Aaron as my priest. These are the vestments they shall make: a breast-piece, an ephod, a mantle, a chequered tunic, a turban, and a sash. They shall make sacred vestments for Aaron your brother and his sons to wear when they serve as my priests, using gold; violet, purple, and scarlet yarn; and fine linen.

The ephod shall be made of gold, and with violet, purple, and scarlet yarn, and with finely woven linen worked by a seamster. It shall have two shoulder-pieces joined back and front. The waist-band on it shall be of the same workmanship and material as the fabric of the ephod, and shall be of gold, with violet, purple, and scarlet yarn, and finely woven linen. You shall take two cornelians and engrave on them the names of the sons of Israel: six of their names on the one stone, and the six other names on the second, all in order of seniority. With the skill of a craftsman, a seal-cutter, you shall engrave the two stones with the names of the sons of Israel; you shall set them in gold rosettes, and fasten them on the shoulders of the ephod, as reminders of the sons of Israel. Aaron shall bear their names on his two shoulders as a reminder before the LORD.

Make gold rosettes and two chains of pure gold worked into the form of ropes, and fix them on the rosettes. Make the breast-piece of judgement; it shall be made, like the ephod, by a seamster in gold, with violet, purple, and scarlet yarn, and finely woven linen. It shall be a square folded, a span long and a span wide. Set in it four rows of precious stones: the first row, sardin, chrysolite and green felspar; the second row, purple garnet, lapis lazuli and jade; the third row, turquoise, agate and jasper; the fourth row, topaz, cornelian and green jasper, all set in gold rosettes. The stones shall correspond to the twelve sons of Israel name by name; each stone shall bear the name of one of the twelve tribes engraved as on a seal.

Make for the breast-piece chains of pure gold worked into a rope. Make two gold rings, and fix them on the two upper corners of the breast-piece. Fasten the two gold

ropes to the two rings at those 25 corners of the breast-piece, and the other ends of the ropes to the two rosettes, thus binding the breast-piece to the shoulder-pieces 26 on the front of the ephod. Make two gold rings and put them at the two lower corners of the breast-piece on the inner side next to the 27 ephod. Make two gold rings and fix them on the two shoulder-pieces of the ephod, low down in front, along its seam above the 28 waist-band of the ephod. Then the breast-piece shall be bound by its rings to the rings of the ephod with violet braid, just above the waist-band of the ephod, so that the breast-piece will not be detached 29 from the ephod. Thus, when Aaron enters the Holy Place, he shall carry over his heart in the breast-piece of judgement the names of the sons of Israel, as a constant reminder before the LORD.

30 Finally, put the Urim and the Thummim into the breast-piece of judgement, and they will be over Aaron's heart when he enters the presence of the LORD. So shall Aaron bear these symbols of judgement upon the sons of Israel over his heart constantly before the LORD.

31 Make the mantle of the ephod a 32 single piece of violet stuff. There shall be a hole for the head in the middle of it. All round the hole there shall be a hem of woven work, with an oversewn edge, so that it 33 cannot be torn. All round its skirts make pomegranates of violet, purple, and scarlet stuff, with golden 34 bells between them, a golden bell and a pomegranate alternately the whole way round the skirts of the 35 mantle. Aaron shall wear it when he ministers, and the sound of it shall be heard when he enters the Holy Place before the LORD and when he comes out; and so he shall not die.

Turban and breast-piece

Make a rosette of pure gold and 36 engrave on it as on a seal, 'Holy to the LORD'.[u] Fasten it on a violet 37 braid and set it on the very front of the turban. It shall be on Aaron's 38 forehead; he has to bear the blame for shortcomings in the rites with which the Israelites offer their sacred gifts, and the rosette shall be always on his forehead so that they may be acceptable to the LORD.

Make the chequered tunic and 39 the turban of fine linen, but the sash of embroidered work. For 40 Aaron's sons make tunics and sashes; and make tall head-dresses to give them dignity and grandeur. With these invest your brother 41 Aaron and his sons, anoint them, install them and consecrate them; so shall they serve me as priests. Make for them linen drawers reach- 42 ing to the thighs to cover their private parts; and Aaron and his 43 sons shall wear them when they enter the Tent of the Presence or approach the altar to minister in the Holy Place. Thus they will not incur guilt and die. This is a rule binding on him and his descendants for all time.

Consecration of the priests

In consecrating them to be my **29** priests this is the rite to be observed. Take a young bull and two rams without blemish. Take unleavened 2 loaves, unleavened cakes mixed with oil, and unleavened wafers smeared with oil, all made of wheaten flour; put them in a 3 single basket and bring them in it. Bring also the bull and the two rams. Bring Aaron and his sons to 4 the entrance of the Tent of the Presence, and wash them with water. Take the vestments and 5 invest Aaron with the tunic, the mantle of the ephod, the ephod itself and the breast-piece, and fasten the ephod to him with its waist-band. Set the turban on his head, 6 and the symbol of holy dedication on the turban. Take the anointing 7 oil, pour it on his head and anoint him. Then bring his sons forward, 8 invest them with tunics, gird them 9 with the sashes and tie their tall head-dresses on them. They shall hold the priesthood by a rule binding for all time.

Next you shall install Aaron and his sons. Bring the bull to the front 10 of the Tent of the Presence, and they shall lay their hands on its head. Slaughter the bull before the 11 LORD at the entrance to the Tent of the Presence. Take some of its 12 blood, and put it with your finger on the horns of the altar. Pour all the rest of it at the base of the altar. Then take the fat covering the en- 13 trails, the long lobe of the liver, and the two kidneys with the fat upon

---

u as . . . LORD: *or* 'JEHOVAH' as on a seal in sacred characters.

14 them, and burn it on the altar; but the flesh of the bull, and its skin and offal, you shall destroy by fire outside the camp. It is a sin-offering.

15 Take one of the rams, and Aaron and his sons shall lay their hands

16 on its head. Then slaughter it, take its blood and fling it against the

17 sides of the altar. Cut the ram up; wash its entrails and its shins, lay them with the pieces and the head,

18 and burn the whole ram on the altar: it is a whole-offering to the LORD; it is a soothing odour, a food-offering to the LORD.

19 Take the second ram, and let Aaron and his sons lay their hands

20 on its head. Then slaughter it, take some of its blood, and put it on the lobes of the right ears of Aaron and his sons, and on their right thumbs and big toes. Fling the rest of the blood against the sides of the altar.

21 Take some of the blood which is on the altar and some of the anointing oil, and sprinkle it on Aaron and his vestments, and on his sons and their vestments. So shall he and his vestments, and his sons and their vestments become holy.

22 Take the fat from the ram, the fat-tail, the fat covering the entrails, the long lobe of the liver, the two kidneys with the fat upon them, and the right leg: for it is a ram of

23 installation. Take also one round loaf of bread, one cake cooked with oil, and one wafer from the basket of unleavened bread that is before

24 the LORD. Set all these on the hands of Aaron and of his sons and present them as a special gift before

25 the LORD. Then take them out of their hands, and burn them on the altar with the whole-offering for a soothing odour to the LORD: it is

26 a food-offering to the LORD. Take the breast of Aaron's ram of installation, present it as a special gift before the LORD, and it shall be your perquisite.

27 Hallow the breast of the special gift and the leg of the contribution, that which is presented and that which is set aside from the ram of installation, that which is for Aaron

28 and that which is for his sons; and they shall belong to Aaron and his sons, by a rule binding for all time, as a gift from the Israelites, for it is a contribution, set aside from their shared-offerings, their contribution to the LORD.

29 Aaron's sacred vestments shall be kept for the anointing and instal-

30 lation of his sons after him. The priest appointed in his stead from among his sons, the one who entersᵛ the Tent of the Presence to minister in the Holy Place, shall wear them for seven days.

31 Take the ram of installation, and boil its flesh in a sacred place;

32 Aaron and his sons shall eat the ram's flesh and the bread left in the basket, at the entrance to the Tent

33 of the Presence. They shall eat the things with which expiation was made at their installation and their consecration. No unqualified person may eat them, for they are holy.

34 If any of the flesh of the installation, or any of the bread, is left over till morning, you shall destroy it by fire; it shall not be eaten, for it is holy.

35 Do this with Aaron and his sons as I have commanded you, spending seven days over their installation.

36 Offer a bull daily, a sin-offering as expiation for sin; offer the sin-offering on the altar when you make expiation for it, and consecrate it

37 by anointing. For seven days you shall make expiation for the altar, and consecrate it, and it shall be most holy. Whatever touches the altar shall be forfeit as sacred.

Daily sacrifices

38 This is what you shall offer on the altar: two yearling rams regularly

39 every day. You shall offer the one ram at dawn, and the second be-

40 tween dusk and dark, a tenth of an ephah of flour mixed with a quarter of a hin of pure oil of pounded olives, and a drink-offering of a quarter of a hin of wine for the

41 first ram. You shall offer the second ram between dusk and dark, and with it the same grain-offering and drink-offering as at dawn, for a soothing odour: it is a food-offering

42 to the LORD, a regular whole-offering in every generation; you shall make the offering at the entrance to the Tent of the Pre-

43 sence before the LORD, where I meet you and speak to you. I shall meet the Israelites there, and the place will be hallowed by my glory.

44 I shall hallow the Tent of the Presence and the altar; and Aaron and his sons I shall consecrate to

45 serve me as priests. I shall dwell in the midst of the Israelites, I shall

46 become their God, and by my dwelling among them they will know that I am the LORD their God who brought them out of Egypt. I am the LORD their God.

Altar of incense

30 Make an altar on which to burn incense; make it of acacia-wood.

2 It shall be square, a cubit long by a cubit broad and two cubits high; the horns of one piece with it.

3 Overlay it with pure gold, the top, the sides all round, and the horns; and put round it a band of gold.

4 Make pairs of gold rings for it; put them under the band at the two corners on both sides to receive the poles by which it is to be

5 carried. Make the poles of acacia-wood and overlay them with gold.

6 Put it before the Veil in front of the Ark of the Tokens where I will

meet you. On it Aaron shall burn fragrant incense; every morning when he tends the lamps he shall burn the incense, and when he mounts the lamps between dusk and dark, he shall burn the incense; so there shall be a regular burning of incense before the LORD for all time. You shall not offer on it any unauthorized incense, nor any whole-offering or grain-offering; and you shall not pour a drink-offering over it. Aaron shall make expiation with blood on its horns once a year; with blood from the sin-offering of the yearly Expia-tionʷ he shall do this for all time. It is most holy to the LORD.

Expiation money

The LORD spoke to Moses and said: When you number the Israelites for the purpose of registration, each man shall give a ransom for his life to the LORD, to avert plague among them during the registration. As each man crosses over to those already counted he shall give half a shekel by the sacred standard (twenty gerahs to the shekel) as a contribution to the LORD. Everyone from twenty years old and upwards who has crossed over to those already counted shall give a contribution to the LORD. The rich man shall give no more than the half-shekel, and the poor man shall give no less, when you give the contribution to the LORD to make expiation for your lives. The money received from the Israelites for expiation you shall apply to the service of the Tent of the Presence. The expiation for your lives shall be a reminder of the Israelites to the LORD.

The bronze basin

The LORD spoke to Moses and said: Make a bronze basin for ablution with its stand of bronze; put it between the Tent of the Presence and the altar, and fill it with water with which Aaron and his sons shall wash their hands and feet. When they enter the Tent of the Presence they shall wash with water, lest they die. So also when they approach the altar to minister, to burn a food-offering to the LORD, they shall wash their hands and feet, lest they die. It shall be a rule for all time binding on him and his descendants in every generation.

The anointing oil and the incense

The LORD spoke to Moses and said: You yourself shall take spices as follows: five hundred shekels of sticks of myrrh, half that amount (two hundred and fifty shekels) of fragrant cinnamon, two hundred and fifty shekels of aromatic cane, five hundred shekels of cassia by the sacred standard, and a hin of

---

v Or when he enters.   *w Or Atonement.*

5 olive oil. From these prepare sacred anointing oil, a perfume compounded by the perfumer's art. This shall be the sacred anointing 6 oil. Anoint with it the Tent of the Presence and the Ark of the Tokens, 7 the table and all its vessels, the lamp-stand and its fittings, the 8 altar of incense, the altar of whole-offering and all its vessels, the basin 9 and its stand. You shall consecrate them, and they shall be most holy; whatever touches them shall be 10 forfeit as sacred. Anoint Aaron and his sons, and consecrate them 1 to be my priests. Speak to the Israelites and say: This shall be the holy anointing oil for my ser- 2 vice in every generation. It shall not be used for anointing the human body, and you must not prepare any oil like it after the same prescription. It is holy, and 3 you shall treat it as holy. The man who compounds perfume like it, or who puts any of it on any unqualified person, shall be cut off from his father's kin.

4 The LORD said to Moses, Take fragrant spices: gum resin,ˣ aromatic shell, galbanum; add pure frankincense to the spices in equal 5 proportions. Make it into incense, perfume made by the perfumer's craft, salted and pure, a holy thing. 6 Pound some of it into fine powder, and put it in front of the Tokens in the Tent of the Presence, where I

shall meet you; you shall treat it as 37 most holy. The incense prepared according to this prescription you shall not make for your own use. You shall treat it as holy to the 38 LORD. The man who makes any like it for his own pleasure shall be cut off from his father's kin.

The master craftsmen

31 The LORD spoke to Moses and 2 said, Mark this: I have specially chosen Bezalel son of Uri, son of 3 Hur, of the tribe of Judah. I have filled him with divine spirit, making him skilful and ingenious, expert in 4 every craft, and a master of design, 5 whether in gold, silver, copper, or cutting stones to be set, or carving wood, for workmanship of every 6 kind. Further, I have appointed Aholiabʸ son of Ahisamach of the tribe of Dan to help him, and I have endowed every skilled craftsman with the skill which he has. They 7 shall make everything that I have commanded you: the Tent of the Presence, the Ark for the Tokens, the cover over it, and all the fur- 8 nishings of the tent; the table and its vessels, the pure lamp-stand and all its fittings, the altar of incense, 9 the altar of whole-offering and all its vessels, the basin and its stand; 10 the stitched vestments, that is the sacred vestments for Aaron the priest and the vestments for his sons when they minister as priests,

the anointing oil and the fragrant 11 incense for the Holy Place. They shall carry out all I have commanded you.

Sabbath observance

The LORD spoke to Moses and said, 12 Speak to the Israelites, you your- 13 self, and say to them: Above all you shall observe my sabbaths, for the sabbath is a sign between me and you in every generation that you may know that I am the LORD who hallows you. You shall keep 14 the sabbath, because it is a holy day for you. If anyone profanes it he must be put to death. Anyone who does work on it shall be cut off from his father's kin. Work may 15 be done on six days, but on the seventh day there is a sabbath of sacred rest, holy to the LORD. Whoever does work on the sabbath day must be put to death. The Israelites 16 shall keep the sabbath, they shall keep it in every generation as a covenant for ever. It is a sign for 17 ever between me and the Israelites, for in six days the LORD made the heavens and the earth, but on the seventh day he ceased work and refreshed himself.

When he had finished speaking 18 with Moses on Mount Sinai, the LORD gave him the two tablets of the Tokens, tablets of stone written with the finger of God.

The golden calf

2 When the people saw that Moses was so long in coming down from the mountain, they confronted Aaron and said to him, 'Come, make us gods to go ahead of us. As for this fellow Moses, who brought us up 2 from Egypt, we do not know what has become of him.' Aaron answered them, 'Strip 3 the gold rings from the ears of your wives and daughters, and bring them to me.' So all the people stripped themselves of their gold earrings and brought them to Aaron. 4 He took them out of their hands, cast the metal in a mould, and made it into the image of a bull-calf. 'These', he said, 'are your gods, O Israel, that brought you up from 5 Egypt.' Then Aaron was afraid and built an altar in front of it and issued this proclamation, 'Tomorrow there is to be 6 a pilgrim-feast to the LORD.' Next day the people rose early, offered whole-offerings, and brought shared-offerings. After this they sat down to eat and drink and then 7 gave themselves up to revelry. But the LORD said to Moses, 'Go down at once, for your people, the people you brought up from 8 Egypt, have done a disgraceful thing; so quickly have they turned aside from the way

I commanded them. They have made themselves an image of a bull-calf, they have prostrated themselves before it, sacrificed to it and said, "These are your gods, O Israel, that brought you up from Egypt."' So the 9 LORD said to Moses, 'I have considered this people, and I see that they are a stubborn people. Now, let me alone to vent my anger 10 upon them, so that I may put an end to them and make a great nation spring from you.' But Moses set himself to placate the LORD 11 his God: 'O LORD,' he said, 'why shouldst thou vent thy anger upon thy people, whom thou didst bring out of Egypt with great power and a strong hand? Why let the 12 Egyptians say, "So he meant evil when he took them out, to kill them in the mountains and wipe them off the face of the earth"? Turn from thy anger, and think better of the evil thou dost intend against thy people. Remember Abraham, Isaac and Israel, thy 13 servants, to whom thou didst swear by thy own self: "I will make your posterity countless as the stars in the sky, and all this land, of which I have spoken, I will give to them, and they shall possess it for ever."' So the LORD relented, and spared his people 14 the evil with which he had threatened them.

ˣ Or mastic.   ʸ Or Oholiab.

15 Moses turned and went down the mountain with the two tablets of the Tokens in his hands, inscribed on both sides; on the front and on the back they were inscribed.
16 The tablets were the handiwork of God, and the writing was God's writing, engraved on
17 the tablets. Joshua, hearing the uproar the people were making, said to Moses, 'Listen!
18 There is fighting in the camp.' Moses replied,

'This is not the clamour of warriors,
nor the clamour of a defeated people;
it is the sound of singing that I hear.'

19 As he approached the camp, Moses saw the bull-calf and the dancing, and he was angry; he flung the tablets down, and they were shattered to pieces at the foot of the mount-
20 ain. Then he took the calf they had made and burnt it; he ground it to powder, sprinkled it on water, and made the Israelites
21 drink it. He demanded of Aaron, 'What did this people do to you that you should have
22 brought such great guilt upon them?' Aaron replied, 'Do not be angry, sir. The people were deeply troubled; that you well know.
23 And they said to me, "Make us gods to go ahead of us, because, as for this fellow Moses, who brought us up from Egypt, we do not
24 know what has become of him." So I said to them, "Those of you who have any gold, strip it off." They gave it me, I threw it in
25 the fire, and out came this bull-calf.' Moses saw that the people were out of control and that Aaron had laid them open to the secret
26 malice of their enemies. He took his place at the gate of the camp and said, 'Who is on the LORD's side? Come here to me'; and the
27 Levites all rallied to him. He said to them, 'These are the words of the LORD the God of Israel: "Arm yourselves, each of you, with his sword. Go through the camp from gate to gate and back again. Each of you kill his
28 brother, his friend, his neighbour."' The Levites obeyed, and about three thousand
29 of the people died that day. Moses then said, 'Today you have consecrated yourselves to the LORD completely, because you have turned each against his own son and his own brother and so have this day brought a blessing upon yourselves.'
30 The next day Moses said to the people, 'You have committed a great sin. I shall now go up to the LORD; perhaps I may be
31 able to secure pardon for your sin.' So Moses returned to the LORD and said, 'O hear me! This people has committed a great sin: they have made themselves gods of gold.
32 If thou wilt forgive them, forgive. But if not, blot out my name, I pray, from thy book
33 which thou hast written.' The LORD answered Moses, 'It is the man who has sinned against
34 me that I will blot out from my book. But

go now, lead the people to the place which I have told you of. My angel shall go ahead of you, but a day will come when I shall punish them for their sin.' And the LORD 35 smote the people for worshipping the bull-calf which Aaron had made.

Onwards to Canaan

The LORD spoke to Moses: 'Come, go up 33 from here, you and the people you have brought up from Egypt, to the land which I swore to Abraham, Isaac, and Jacob that I would give to their posterity. I will send 2 an angel ahead of you, and will drive out the Canaanites, the Amorites and the Hittites and the Perizzites, the Hivites and the Jebusites. I will bring you to a land flowing with 3 milk and honey, but I will not journey in your company, for fear that I annihilate you on the way; for you are a stubborn people.' When the people heard this harsh sentence 4 they went about like mourners, and no man put on his ornaments. The LORD said 5 to Moses, 'Tell the Israelites, "You are a stubborn people: at any moment, if I journey in your company, I may annihilate you. Put away your ornaments now, and I will determine what to do to you."' And so the 6 Israelites stripped off their ornaments, and wore them no more from Mount Horeb onwards.

The Tent of the Presence

Moses used to take a*z* tent and pitch it at a 7 distance outside the camp. He called it the Tent of the Presence, and everyone who sought the LORD would go out to the Tent of the Presence outside the camp. Whenever 8 Moses went out to the tent, all the people would rise and stand, each at the entrance to his tent, and follow Moses with their eyes until he entered the tent. When Moses 9 entered it, the pillar of cloud came down, and stayed at the entrance to the tent while the LORD spoke with Moses. As soon as the 10 people saw the pillar of cloud standing at the entrance to the tent, they would all prostrate themselves, every man at the entrance to his tent. The LORD would speak 11 with Moses face to face, as one man speaks to another. Then Moses would return to the camp, but his young assistant, Joshua son of Nun, never moved from inside the tent.

The LORD's promise

Moses said to the LORD, 'Thou bidst me 12 lead this people up, but thou hast not told me whom thou wilt send with me. Thou hast said to me, "I know you by name, and, further, you have found favour with me." If I have indeed won thy favour, then teach 13 me to know thy way, so that I can know

z *Or* the.

thee and continue in favour with thee, for this nation is thy own people.' The LORD answered, 'I will go with you in person and set your mind at rest.' Moses said to him, 'Indeed if thou dost not go in person, do not send us up from here; for how can it ever be known that I and thy people have found favour with thee, except by thy going with us? So shall we be distinct, I and thy people, from all the peoples on earth.' The LORD said to Moses, 'I will do this thing that you have asked, because you have found favour with me, and I know you by name.'

And Moses prayed, 'Show me thy glory.' The LORD answered, 'I will· make all my goodness^a pass before you, and I will pronounce in your hearing the Name JEHOVAH.^b I will be gracious to whom I will be gracious, and I will have compassion on whom I will have compassion.' But he added, 'My face you cannot see, for no mortal man may see me and live.' The LORD said, 'Here is a place beside me. Take your stand on the rock and when my glory passes by, I will put you in a crevice of the rock and cover you with my hand until I have passed by. Then I will take away my hand, and you shall see my back, but my face shall not be seen.'

The Covenant

The LORD said to Moses, 'Cut two stone tablets like the first, and I will write on the tablets the words which were on the first tablets, which you broke in pieces. Be ready by morning. Then in the morning go up Mount Sinai; stand and wait for me there on the top. No man shall go up with you, no man shall even be seen anywhere on the mountain, nor shall flocks or herds graze within sight of that mountain.' So Moses cut two stone tablets like the first, and he rose early in the morning and went up Mount Sinai as the LORD had commanded him, taking the two stone tablets in his hands. And the LORD came down in the cloud and took his place beside him and pronounced the Name JEHOVAH. Then the LORD passed in front of him and called aloud, 'JEHOVAH, the LORD, a god compassionate and gracious, long-suffering, ever constant and true, maintaining constancy to thousands, forgiving iniquity, rebellion, and sin, and not sweeping the guilty clean away; but one who punishes sons and grandsons to the third and fourth generation for the iniquity of their fathers!' Moses made haste, bowed to the ground and prostrated himself. He said, 'If I have indeed won thy favour, O Lord, then may the Lord go in our company.

However stubborn a people they are, forgive our iniquity and our sin and take us as thy own possession.'

The LORD said, Here and now I make a 10 covenant. In full view of all your people I will do such miracles as have never been performed in all the world or in any nation. All the surrounding peoples shall see the work of the LORD, for fearful is that which I will do for you.^c Observe all I command 11 you this day; and I for my part will drive out before you the Amorites and the Canaanites and the Hittites and the Perizzites and the Hivites and the Jebusites. Be careful not 12 to make a covenant with the natives of the land against which you are going, or they will prove a snare in your midst. No: you 13 shall demolish their altars, smash their sacred pillars and cut down their sacred poles. You shall not prostrate yourselves to 14 any other god. For the LORD's name is the Jealous God, and a jealous god he is. Be 15 careful not to make a covenant with the natives of the land, or, when they go wantonly after their gods and sacrifice to them, you may be invited, any one of you, to partake of their sacrifices, and marry your 16 sons to their daughters, and when their daughters go wantonly after their gods, they may lead your sons astray too.

You shall not make yourselves gods of 17 cast metal.

You shall observe the pilgrim-feast of 18 Unleavened Bread: for seven days, as I have commanded you, you shall eat unleavened cakes at the appointed time, in the month of Abib, because in the month of Abib you went out from Egypt.

Every first birth of the womb belongs to 19 me, and the males of all your herds, both cattle and sheep. You may buy back the 20 first birth of an ass by giving a sheep instead, but if you do not buy it, you must break its neck. You shall buy back all the first-born of your sons, and no one shall come into my presence empty-handed.

For six days you shall work, but on the 21 seventh day you shall cease work; even at ploughing time and harvest you shall cease work.

You shall observe the pilgrim-feast of 22 Weeks, the firstfruits of the wheat harvest,

a Or character.   *b See note on* 3. 15.   *c* for fearful . . . for you: *or* (for he is to be feared) which
I will do for you.

and the pilgrim-feast of Ingathering at the
23 turn of the year. Three times a year all your
males shall come into the presence of the
24 Lord, the LORD the God of Israel; for after
I have driven out the nations before you and
extended your frontiers, there will be no
danger from covetous neighbours when you
go up these three times to enter the presence
of the LORD your God.
25   You shall not offer the blood of my
sacrifice at the same time as anything
leavened, nor shall any portion of the
victim of the pilgrim-feast of Passover
remain overnight till morning.
26   You shall bring the choicest firstfruits of
your soil to the house of the LORD your God.
    You shall not boil a kid in its mother's
milk.

Moses descends from Mount Sinai

27 The LORD said to Moses, 'Write these words
down, because the covenant I make with
28 you and with Israel is in these words.' So
Moses stayed there with the LORD forty days
and forty nights, neither eating nor drinking,
and wrote down the words of the covenant,
the Ten Words,[d] on the tablets. At length
Moses came down from Mount Sinai with
the two stone tablets of the Tokens in his
hands, and when he descended, he did not
know that the skin of his face shone because
he had been speaking with the LORD. When
Aaron and the Israelites saw how the skin
of Moses' face shone, they were afraid to
approach him. He called out to them, and
Aaron and all the chiefs in the congregation
turned towards him. Moses spoke to them,
and afterwards all the Israelites drew near.
He gave them all the commands with which
the LORD had charged him on Mount Sinai,
and finished what he had to say.
    Then Moses put a veil over his face, and
whenever he went in before the LORD to
speak with him, he removed the veil until
he came out. Then he would go out and tell
the Israelites all the commands he had
received. Whenever the skin of Moses' face
shone in the sight of the Israelites, he would
put the veil back over his face until he went
in again to speak with the LORD.

Commands for the sabbath

35 Moses called the whole community
of Israelites together and thus
addressed them: These are the
2 LORD's commands to you: On six
days you may work, but the seventh
you are to keep as a sabbath of
sacred rest, holy to the LORD. Whoever works on that day shall be put
3 to death. You are not even to light
your fire at home on the sabbath
day.

Commands for the Tabernacle

4 These words Moses spoke to all
the community of Israelites: This
is the command the LORD has
5 given: Each of you set aside a contribution to the LORD. Let all who
6 wish, bring a contribution to the
LORD: gold, silver, copper; violet,
purple, and scarlet yarn; fine linen
7 and goats' hair; tanned rams' skins,
porpoise-hides, and acacia-wood;
8 oil for the lamp, perfume for the
anointing oil and for the fragrant
9 incense; cornelians and other
stones ready for setting in the
10 ephod and the breast-piece. Let
every craftsman among you come
and make everything the LORD has
11 commanded. The Tabernacle, its
tent and covering, fasteners, planks,
12 bars, posts, and sockets, the Ark
and its poles, the cover and the
13 Veil of the screen, the table, its
poles, and all its vessels, the
14 Bread of the Presence, the lamp-
stand for the light, its fittings, lamps
15 and the lamp oil; the altar of incense and its poles, the anointing
oil, the fragrant incense, and the
screen for the entrance of the

16 Tabernacle, the altar of whole-
offering, its bronze grating, poles,
and all appurtenances, the basin
17 and its stand; the hangings of the
court, its posts and sockets, and
the screen for the gateway of the
18 court; the pegs of the Tabernacle
19 and court and their cords, the
stitched vestments for ministering
in the Holy Place, that is the sacred
vestments for Aaron the priest and
the vestments for his sons when
they minister as priests.

The people bring their offerings

20 The whole community of the Israelites went out from Moses' pres-
21 ence, and everyone who was so
minded brought of his own free
will a contribution to the LORD
for the making of the Tent of the
Presence and all its service, and
22 for the sacred vestments. Men and
women alike came and freely
brought clasps, earrings, fingerrings, and pendants, gold ornaments of every kind, every one of
them presenting a special gift of
23 gold to the LORD. And every man
brought what he possessed of violet, purple, and scarlet yarn, fine
linen and goats' hair, tanned rams'
24 skins and porpoise-hides. Every
man, setting aside a contribution of
silver or copper, brought it as a
contribution to the LORD, and all
who had acacia-wood suitable for
any part of the work brought it.
25 Every woman with the skill spun
and brought the violet, purple, and
26 scarlet yarn, and fine linen. All the
women whose skill moved them

spun the goats' hair. The chiefs
brought cornelians and other stones
ready for setting in the ephod and
the breast-piece, the perfume and
oil for the light, for the anointing
oil, and for the fragrant incense.
Every Israelite man and woman
who was minded to bring offerings
to the LORD for all the work which
he had commanded through Moses
did so freely.

The craftsmen receive the contributions

Moses said to the Israelites, 'Mark
this: the LORD has specially chosen
Bezalel son of Uri, son of Hur, of
the tribe of Judah. He has filled
him with divine spirit, making him
skilful and ingenious, expert in
every craft, and a master of design,
whether in gold, silver, and copper,
or cutting precious stones for setting, or carving wood, in every kind
of design. He has inspired both him
and Aholiab son of Ahisamach of
the tribe of Dan to instruct workers
and designers of every kind, en-
gravers, seamsters, embroiderers in
violet, purple, and scarlet yarn and
fine linen, and weavers, fully en-
dowing them with skill to execute
all kinds of work. Bezalel and
Aholiab shall work exactly as the
LORD has commanded, and so also
shall every craftsman whom the
LORD has made skilful and ingenious in these matters, to know
how to execute every kind of work
for the service of the sanctuary.'
    Moses summoned Bezalel, Aho-
liab, and every craftsman to whom

---

d Or Ten Commandments.

the LORD had given skill and who was willing, to come forward and
3 set to work. They received from Moses every contribution which the Israelites had brought for the work of the service of the sanctuary, but the people still brought freewill offerings morning after
4 morning, so that the craftsmen at work on the sanctuary left what they were doing, every one of them,
5 and came to Moses and said, 'The people are bringing much more than we need for doing the work which the LORD has commanded.'
6 So Moses sent word round the camp that no man or woman should prepare anything more as a contribution for the sanctuary. So the
7 people stopped bringing gifts; what was there already was more than enough for all the work they had to do.

Making the Tabernacle

8 Then all the craftsmen among the workers made the Tabernacle of ten hangings of finely woven linen, and violet, purple, and scarlet yarn, with cherubim worked on them, all
9 made by a seamster. The length of each hanging was twenty-eight cubits and the breadth four cubits,
10 all of the same size. They joined five of the hangings together, and
11 similarly the other five. They made violet loops on the outer edge of the one set of hangings and they did the same for the outer edge of
12 the other set of hangings. They made fifty loops for each hanging; they made also fifty loops for the end hanging in the second set, the loops being opposite each other.
13 They made fifty gold fasteners, with which they joined the hangings one to another, and the Tabernacle became a single whole.
14 They made hangings of goats'
15 hair, eleven in all, to form a tent over the Tabernacle; each hanging was thirty cubits long and four cubits wide, all eleven of the same
16 size. They joined five of the hangings together, and similarly the
17 other six. They made fifty loops on the edge of the outer hanging in the first set and fifty loops on the
18 joining edge of the second set, and fifty bronze fasteners to join up the tent and make it a single whole.
19 They made for the tent a cover of tanned rams' skins and an outer covering of porpoise-hides.
20 They made for the Tabernacle planks of acacia-wood as uprights,
21 each plank ten cubits long and a
22 cubit and a half wide, and two tenons for each plank joined to each other. They did the same for all the planks of the Tabernacle.
23 They arranged the planks thus: twenty planks for the south side,
24 facing southwards, with forty silver sockets under them, two sockets under each plank for its two ten-
25 ons; and for the second or north-

*The table
for the Bread
of the Presence*

ern side of the Tabernacle twenty
26 planks with forty silver sockets,
27 two under each plank. They made six planks for the far end of the
28 Tabernacle on the west. They made two planks for the corners of the
29 Tabernacle at the far end; at the bottom they were alike, and at the top, both alike, they fitted into a single ring. They did the same for both of them at the two corners.
30 There were eight planks with their silver sockets, sixteen sockets in all, two sockets under each plank.
31 They made bars of acacia-wood: five for the planks on the one side
32 of the Tabernacle, five bars for the planks on the second side of the Tabernacle, and five bars for the planks on the far end of the Taber-
33 nacle on the west. They made the middle bar to run along from end to end half-way up the frames.
34 They overlaid the frames with gold, made rings of gold on them to hold the bars and plated the bars with gold.
35 They made the Veil of finely woven linen and violet, purple, and scarlet yarn, with cherubim worked on it, all made by a seam-
36 ster. And they made for it four posts of acacia-wood overlaid with gold, with gold hooks, and cast
37 four silver sockets for them. For the entrance of the tent a screen of finely woven linen was made, em-
38 broidered with violet, purple, and scarlet, and five posts of acacia-wood with their hooks. They overlaid the tops of the posts and the bands round them with gold; the five sockets for them were of bronze.

Making the Ark

37 Bezalel then made the Ark, a chest of acacia-wood, two and a half cubits long, one cubit and a half wide, and one cubit and a half high.
2 He overlaid it with pure gold, both

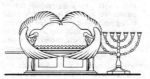

inside and out, and put a band of gold all round it. He cast four 3 gold rings to be on its four feet, two rings on each side of it. He made 4 poles of acacia-wood and plated them with gold, and inserted the 5 poles in the rings at the sides of the Ark to lift it. He made a cover of 6 pure gold, two and a half cubits long and one cubit and a half wide. He made two gold cherubim of 7 beaten work, one at each end; he made 8 each cherub of one piece with the cover. They had wings outspread 9 and pointing upwards, screening the cover with their wings; they stood face to face, looking inwards over the cover.

Making the table

He made the table of acacia-wood, 10 two cubits long, one cubit wide, and one cubit and a half high. He 11 overlaid it with pure gold and put a band of gold all round it. He 12 made a rim round it a hand's breadth wide, and a gold band round the rim. He cast four gold 13 rings for it, and put the rings at the four corners by the four legs. The rings, which were to receive 14 the poles for carrying the table, were close to the rim. These 15 carrying-poles he made of acacia-wood and plated them with gold. He made the vessels for the table, 16 its dishes and saucers, and its flagons and bowls from which drink-offerings were to be poured; he made them of pure gold.

Making the lamp-stand

He made the lamp-stand of pure 17 gold. The lamp-stand, stem, and branches, were of beaten work, its cups, both calyxes and petals, were of one piece with it. There were six 18 branches springing from its sides; three branches of the lamp-stand sprang from one side and three branches from the other side. There 19 were three cups shaped like almond blossoms, with calyx and petals, on the first branch, three cups shaped like almond blossoms, with calyx and petals, on the next branch, and similarly for all six branches springing from the lamp-stand. On the main stem of the 20 lamp-stand there were four cups

*The altar
of incense*

shaped like almond blossoms, with
21 calyx and petals, and there were
calyxes of one piece with it under
the six branches which sprang
from the lamp-stand, a single calyx
22 under each pair of branches. The
calyxes and the branches were of
one piece with it, all a single piece
23 of beaten work of pure gold. He
made its seven lamps, its tongs and
24 firepans of pure gold. The lamp-
stand and all these fittings were
made from one talent of pure gold.

Making the altar of incense

25 He made the altar of incense of
acacia-wood, square, a cubit long
by a cubit broad and two cubits
high, the horns of one piece with it.
26 He overlaid it with pure gold, the
top, the sides all round, and the
horns, and he put round it a band
27 of gold. He made pairs of gold rings
for it; he put them under the band
at the two corners on both sides to
receive the poles by which it was to
28 be carried. He made the poles of
acacia-wood and overlaid them
with gold.

Making the anointing oil and
the incense

29 He prepared the sacred anointing
oil and the fragrant incense, pure,
compounded by the perfumer's art.

Making the altar of whole-
offering

38 He made the altar of whole-offering
of acacia-wood, square, five cubits
long by five cubits broad and three
2 cubits high. Its horns at the four
corners were of one piece with it,
3 and he overlaid it with bronze. He

made all the vessels for the altar,
its pots, shovels, tossing bowls,
forks, and firepans, all of bronze.
4 He made for the altar a grating of
bronze network under the ledge,
5 coming half-way up. He cast four
rings for the four corners of the
bronze grating to receive the poles,
6 and he made the poles of acacia-
wood and overlaid them with
7 bronze. He inserted the poles in
the rings at the sides of the altar
to carry it. He left the altar a
hollow shell.

Making the bronze basin

8 The basin and its stand of bronze
he made out of the bronze mirrors
of the women who were on duty at
the entrance to the Tent of the
Presence.

Court of the Tabernacle

9 He made the court. For the south
side facing southwards the hangings of the court were of finely
woven linen a hundred cubits long,
10 with twenty posts and twenty
sockets of bronze; the hooks and
bands on the posts were of silver.
11 Along the north side there were
hangings of a hundred cubits, with
twenty posts and twenty sockets of
bronze; the hooks and bands on
12 the posts were of silver. On the
west side there were hangings fifty
cubits long, with ten posts and ten
13 sockets; the hooks and bands on
the posts were of silver. On the
east side, towards the sunrise,
14 fifty cubits, there were hangings
15 on either side of the gateway of
the court; they extended fifteen
cubits to one corner, with their
three posts and their three sockets,
and fifteen cubits to the second
16 corner, with their three posts and
their three sockets. The hangings
of the court all round were of finely
17 woven linen. The sockets for the
posts were of bronze, the hooks

and bands on the posts of silver,
the tops of them overlaid with
silver, and all the posts of the court
were bound with silver. The screen 18
at the gateway of the court was of
finely woven linen, embroidered
with violet, purple, and scarlet,
twenty cubits long and five cubits
high to correspond to the hangings
of the court, with four posts and 19
four sockets of bronze, their hooks
of silver, and the tops of them and
their bands overlaid with silver. All 20
the pegs for the Tabernacle and
those for the court were of bronze.

These were the appointments of 21
the Tabernacle, that is the Tabernacle of the Tokens which was
assigned by Moses to the charge
of the Levites under Ithamar son
of Aaron the priest. Bezalel son of 22
Uri, son of Hur, of the tribe of
Judah made everything the LORD
had commanded Moses. He was 23
assisted by Aholiab son of Ahisamach of the tribe of Dan, an
engraver, a seamster, and an em-
broiderer in fine linen with violet,
purple, and scarlet yarn.

Metals for the sanctuary

The gold of the special gift used for 24
the work of the sanctuary amounted
in all to twenty-nine talents seven
hundred and thirty shekels, by
the sacred standard. The silver 25
contributed by the community
when registered was one hundred
talents one thousand seven hundred and seventy-five shekels, by
the sacred standard.

This amounted to a beka a head, 26
that is half a shekel by the sacred
standard, for every man from
twenty years old and upwards,
who had been registered, a total of
six hundred and three thousand
five hundred and fifty men. The 27
hundred talents of silver were for
casting the sockets for the sanctuary and for the Veil, a hundred
sockets to a hundred talents, a
talent to a socket. With the one 28
thousand seven hundred and
seventy-five shekels he made hooks
for the posts, overlaid the tops of
the posts and put bands round
them. The bronze of the special 29
gift came to seventy talents two
thousand four hundred shekels;
with this he made sockets for the 30
entrance to the Tent of the Presence, the bronze altar and its
bronze grating, all the vessels for
the altar, the sockets all round the 31
court, the sockets for the posts at
the gateway of the court, all the
pegs for the Tabernacle, and the
pegs all round the court.

Making the priests' vestments

They used violet, purple, and scar- **39**
let yarn in making the stitched
vestments for ministering in the
sanctuary and in making the sacred
vestments for Aaron, as the LORD
had commanded Moses.

2 They made the ephod of gold, with violet, purple, and scarlet 3 yarn, and finely woven linen. The gold was beaten into thin plates, cut and twisted into braid to be worked in by a seamster with the violet, purple, and scarlet yarn, 4 and fine linen. They made shoulder-pieces for it, joined back and front. 5 The waist-band on it was of the same workmanship and material as the fabric of the ephod; it was gold, with violet, purple, and scarlet yarn, and finely woven linen, as the LORD commanded Moses.

6 They prepared the cornelians, fixed in gold rosettes, engraved by the art of a seal-cutter with the 7 names of the sons of Israel, and fastened them on the shoulders of the ephod as reminders of the sons of Israel, as the LORD had commanded Moses.

8 They made the breast-piece; it was worked like the ephod by a seamster, in gold, with violet, purple, and scarlet yarn, and finely 9 woven linen. They made the breast-piece square, folded, a span long 10 and a span wide. They set in it four rows of precious stones: the first row, sardin, chrysolite and green 11 felspar; the second row, purple 12 garnet, lapis lazuli and jade; the third row, turquoise, agate and 13 jasper; the fourth row, topaz, cornelian and green jasper, all set 14 in gold rosettes. The stones corresponded to the twelve sons of Israel, name by name, each bearing the name of one of the twelve 15 tribes engraved as on a seal. They made for the breast-piece twisted 16 cords of pure gold worked into a rope. They made two gold rosettes and two gold rings, and they fixed 17 the two rings on the two corners of the breast-piece. They fastened the two gold ropes to the two rings at those corners of the breast-piece, 18 and the other ends of the two ropes to the two rosettes, thus binding them to the shoulder-pieces on the 19 front of the ephod. They made two gold rings and put them at the two corners of the breast-piece on the 20 inner side next to the ephod. They made two gold rings and fixed them on the two shoulder-pieces of the ephod, low down and in front, close to its seam above the waist-21 band on the ephod. They bound the breast-piece by its rings to the rings of the ephod with a violet braid, just above the waist-band on the ephod, so that the breast-piece would not become detached from the ephod; so the LORD had

commanded Moses. They made 22 the mantle of the ephod a single piece of woven violet stuff, with a 23 hole in the middle of it which had a hem round it, with an oversewn edge so that it could not be torn. All round its skirts they made 24 pomegranates of violet, purple, and scarlet stuff, and finely woven linen. They made bells of pure gold 25 and put them all round the skirts of the mantle between the pomegranates, a bell and a pomegranate 26 alternately the whole way round the skirts of the mantle, to be worn when ministering, as the LORD commanded Moses.

They made the tunics of fine 27 linen, woven work, for Aaron and his sons, the turban of fine linen, 28 the tall head-dresses and their bands all of fine linen, the drawers of finely woven linen, and the sash 29 of finely woven linen, embroidered in violet, purple, and scarlet, as the LORD had commanded Moses.

They made a rosette of pure 30 gold as the symbol of their holy dedication and inscribed on it as the engraving on a seal, 'Holy to the LORD',^e and they fastened on 31 it a violet braid to fix it on the turban at the top, as the LORD had commanded Moses.

The Tabernacle completed

32 Thus all the work of the Tabernacle of the Tent of the Presence was completed, and the Israelites did everything exactly as the 33 LORD had commanded Moses. They brought the Tabernacle to Moses, the tent and all its furnishings, its fasteners, planks, bars, posts 34 and sockets, the covering of tanned rams' skins, and the outer covering of porpoise-35 hides, the Veil of the screen, the Ark of the 36 Tokens and its poles, the cover, the table and its vessels, and the Bread of the Presence, 37 the pure lamp-stand with its lamps in a row 38 and all its fittings, and the lamp oil, the gold altar, the anointing oil, the fragrant incense, and the screen at the entrance of the tent, 39 the bronze altar, the bronze grating attached to it, its poles and all its furnishings, the 40 basin and its stand, the hangings of the court, its posts and sockets, the screen for the gateway of the court, its cords and pegs, and all the equipment for the service of the Tabernacle for the Tent of the Presence, 41 the stitched vestments for ministering in the sanctuary, that is the sacred vestments for Aaron the priest and the vestments for his 42 sons when they minister as priests. As the LORD had commanded Moses, so the Israel-43 ites carried out the whole work. Moses inspected all the work, and saw that they had carried it out according to the command of the LORD; and he blessed them.

The Tabernacle consecrated

The LORD spoke to Moses and said: On the **40** first day of the first month you shall set up 1 2 the Tabernacle, the Tent of the Presence. You shall put the Ark of the Tokens in it 3 and screen the Ark with the Veil. You shall 4 bring in the table and lay it; then you shall bring in the lamp-stand and mount its lamps. You shall then set the gold altar of incense 5 in front of the Ark of the Tokens and put the screen of the entrance of the Tabernacle in place. You shall put the altar of 6 whole-offering in front of the entrance of the Tabernacle, the Tent of the Presence. You shall put the basin between the Tent 7 of the Presence and the altar and put water in it. You shall set up the court all round 8 and put in place the screen of the gateway of the court. You shall take the anointing 9 oil and anoint the Tabernacle and everything in it; thus you shall consecrate it and all its furnishings, and it shall be holy. You 10 shall anoint the altar of whole-offering and all its vessels; thus shall you consecrate it, and it shall be most holy. You shall anoint 11 the basin and its stand and consecrate it. You shall bring Aaron and his sons to the 12 entrance of the Tent of the Presence and wash them with the water. Then you shall 13 clothe Aaron with the sacred vestments, anoint him and consecrate him; so shall he be my priest. You shall then bring forward 14

_e_ on it ... LORD: _or_ 'JEHOVAH' on it in sacred characters as engraved on a seal.

15 his sons, clothe them in tunics, anoint them as you anointed their father, and they shall be my priests. Their anointing shall inaugurate a hereditary priesthood for all time.

16 Exactly as the LORD had commanded him,
17 so Moses did. In the first month of the second year, on the first day of that month, the Tabernacle was set up.

18 Moses set up the Tabernacle. He put the sockets in place, inserted the planks, fixed
19 the crossbars and set up the posts. He spread the tent over the Tabernacle and fixed the covering of the tent above it, as the LORD
20 had commanded him. He took the Tokens and put them in the Ark, inserted the poles in the Ark, and put the cover over the top
21 of the Ark. He brought the Ark into the Tabernacle, set up the Veil of the screen and so screened the Ark of the Tokens, as
22 the LORD had commanded him. He put the table in the Tent of the Presence on the north side of the Tabernacle outside the
23 Veil and arranged bread on it before the LORD, as the LORD had commanded him.
24 He set the lamp-stand in the Tent of the Presence opposite the table at the south side
25 of the Tabernacle and mounted the lamps before the LORD, as the LORD had com-
26 manded him. He set up the gold altar in the
27 Tent of the Presence in front of the Veil and burnt fragrant incense on it, as the LORD

had commanded him. He set up the screen 28 at the entrance of the Tabernacle, fixed the 29 altar of whole-offering at the entrance of the Tabernacle, the Tent of the Presence, and offered on it whole-offerings and grain-offerings, as the LORD had commanded him. He set up the basin between the Tent of the 30 Presence and the altar and put water there for washing, and Moses and Aaron and his 31 sons used to wash their hands and feet when 32 they entered the Tent of the Presence or approached the altar, as the LORD had commanded Moses. He set up the court all 33 round the Tabernacle and the altar, and put a screen at the gateway of the court.

The cloud over the Tabernacle

Thus Moses completed the work, and the 34 cloud covered the Tent of the Presence, and the glory of the LORD filled the Tabernacle. Moses was unable to enter the Tent of the 35 Presence, because the cloud had settled on it and the glory of the LORD filled the Tabernacle. At every stage of their journey, when 36 the cloud lifted from the Tabernacle, the Israelites broke camp; but if the cloud did 37 not lift from the Tabernacle, they did not break camp until the day it lifted. For the 38 cloud of the LORD hovered over the Tabernacle by day, and there was fire in the cloud by night, and the Israelites could see it at every stage of their journey.

LEVITICUS

Whole-offerings

1 The LORD summoned Moses and spoke to him from the Tent of the 2 Presence, and said, Say this to the Israelites: When any man among you presents an animal as an offering to the LORD, the offering may be presented either from the herd or from the flock.

3 If his offering is a whole-offering from the cattle, he shall present a male without blemish; he shall present it at the entrance to the Tent of the Presence before the LORD 4 self. He shall lay his hand on the head of the victim and it will be accepted on his behalf[a] to make 5 expiation for him. He shall slaughter the bull before the LORD, and the Aaronite priests shall present the blood and fling it against the altar all round at the entrance of 6 the Tent of the Presence. He shall then flay the victim and cut it up. 7 The sons of Aaron the priest shall kindle a fire on the altar and 8 arrange wood on the fire. The Aaronite priests shall arrange the pieces, including the head and the suet, on the wood on the altar-fire, 9 the entrails and shins shall be washed in water, and the priest shall burn it all on the altar as a whole-offering, a food-offering of soothing odour to the LORD.

10 If the man's whole-offering is from the flock, either from the rams or from the goats, he shall 11 present a male without blemish. He shall slaughter it before the LORD at the north side of the altar, and the Aaronite priests shall fling the blood against the altar all 12 round. He shall cut it up, and the priest shall arrange the pieces, to-gether with the head and the suet, 13 on the wood on the altar-fire, the entrails and shins shall be washed in water, and the priest shall pre-sent and burn it all on the altar: it is a whole-offering, a food-offering of soothing odour to the LORD.

14 If a man's offering to the LORD is a whole-offering of birds, he 15 pigeons as his offering. The priest shall present turtle-doves or young shall present it at the altar, and shall wrench off the head and burn it on the altar; and the blood shall 16 be drained out against the side of the altar. He shall take away the crop and its contents in one piece, and throw it to the east side of the 17 altar where the ashes are. He shall tear it by its wings without sever-ing them completely, and shall burn it on the altar, on top of the wood of the altar-fire: it is a whole-offering, a food-offering of sooth-ing odour to the LORD.

Grain-offerings

2 When any person presents a grain-offering to the LORD, his offering shall be of flour. He shall pour oil on it and add frankincense to it. 2 He shall bring it to the Aaronite priests, one of whom shall scoop up a handful of the flour and oil with all the frankincense. The priest shall burn this as a token on the altar, a food-offering of 3 soothing odour to the LORD. The remainder of the grain-offering belongs to Aaron and his sons: it is most sacred, it is taken from the food-offerings of the LORD.

4 When you present as a grain-offering something baked in an oven, it shall consist of unleavened cakes of flour mixed with oil and unleavened wafers smeared with oil. If your offering is a grain- 5 offering cooked on a griddle, it shall be an unleavened cake of flour mixed with oil. Crumble it in 6 pieces and pour oil on it. This is a grain-offering.

If your offering is a grain-offering 7 cooked in a pan, it shall be made of flour with oil. Bring an offering 8 made up in this way to the LORD and present it to the priest, who shall bring it to the altar; then he 9 shall set aside part of the grain-offering as a token and burn it on the altar, a food-offering of soothing odour to the LORD. The 10 remainder of the grain-offering belongs to Aaron and his sons: it is most sacred, it is taken from the food-offerings of the LORD.

No grain-offering which you pre- 11 sent to the LORD shall be made of anything that ferments; you shall not burn any leaven or any honey as a food-offering to the LORD. As 12 for your offering of firstfruits, you shall present them to the LORD, but they shall not be offered up at the altar as a soothing odour. Every 13 offering of yours which is a grain-offering shall be salted; you shall not fail to put the salt of your cove-nant with God on your grain-offering. Salt shall accompany all offerings.

If you present to the LORD a 14 grain-offering of first-ripe grain, you must present fresh corn roa-sted, crushed meal from fully ri-pened corn. You shall add oil to it 15 and put frankincense upon it. This is a grain-offering. The priest shall 16 burn as its token some of the crushed meal, some of the oil, and all the frankincense as a food-offering to the LORD.

a Or by him (*the* LORD).

75

Shared-offerings

3 If a man's offering is a shared-offering from the cattle, male or female, he shall present it without 2 blemish before the LORD. He shall lay his hand on the head of the victim and slaughter it at the entrance to the Tent of the Presence. The Aaronite priests shall fling the blood against the altar 3 all round. One of them shall present part of the shared-offering as a food-offering to the LORD: he shall remove the fat covering the entrails and all the fat upon the en-4 trails, the two kidneys with the fat on them beside the haunches, and the long lobe of the liver with 5 the kidneys. The Aaronites shall burn it on the altar on top of the whole-offering which is upon the wood on the fire, a food-offering of soothing odour to the LORD.

6   If a man's offering as a shared-offering to the LORD is from the flock, male or female, he shall pre-7 sent it without blemish. If he is presenting a ram as his offering, he shall present it before the LORD, 8 lay his hand on the head of the victim and slaughter it in front of the Tent of the Presence. The Aaronites shall then fling its blood 9 against the altar all round. He shall present part of the shared-offering as a food-offering to the LORD; he shall remove its fat, the entire fat-tail cut off close by the spine, the fat covering the entrails and all the 10 fat upon the entrails, the two kidneys with the fat on them beside the haunches, and the long lobe of 11 the liver with the kidneys. The priest shall burn it at the altar, as food offered to the LORD.

12   If the man's offering is a goat, he 13 shall present it before the LORD, lay his hand on its head and slaughter it in front of the Tent of the Presence. The Aaronites shall then 14 fling its blood against the altar all round. He shall present part of the victim as a food-offering to the LORD; he shall remove the fat 15 covering the entrails and all the fat upon the entrails, the two kidneys with the fat on them beside the haunches, and the long lobe of 16 the liver with the kidneys. The priest shall burn this at the altar, as a food-offering of soothing odour. All fat belongs to the LORD. 17 This is a rule for all time from generation to generation wherever you live: you shall not eat any fat or any blood.

Sin-offerings

4 The LORD spoke to Moses and said, 2 Say this to the Israelites: These are the rules for any man who inadvertently transgresses any of the commandments of the LORD and does anything prohibited by them: 3   If the anointed priest sins so as to bring guilt on the people, for the

sin he has committed he shall present to the LORD a young bull with-4 out blemish as a sin-offering. He shall bring the bull to the entrance of the Tent of the Presence before the LORD, lay his hand on its head and slaughter it before the LORD. 5 The anointed priest shall then take some of its blood and bring it to 6 the Tent of the Presence. He shall dip his finger in the blood and sprinkle some of the blood in front of the sacred Veil seven times before 7 the LORD. The priest shall then put some of the blood before the LORD in the Tent of the Presence on the horns of the altar where fragrant incense is burnt, and he shall pour the rest of the bull's blood at the base of the altar of whole-offering at the entrance of the Tent of the 8 Presence. He shall set aside all the fat from the bull of the sin-offering; he shall set aside the fat covering the entrails and all the fat upon the 9 entrails, the two kidneys with the fat on them beside the haunches, and the long lobe of the liver with 10 the kidneys. It shall be set aside as the fat from the ox at the shared-offering is set aside. The priest shall burn the pieces of fat on the altar 11 of whole-offering. But the skin of the bull and all its flesh, including head and shins, its entrails and 12 offal, the whole of it, he shall take away outside the camp to a place ritually clean, where the ash-heap is, and destroy it on a wood-fire on top of the ash-heap.

13   If the whole community of Israel sins inadvertently and the matter is not known to the assembly, if they do what is forbidden in any commandment of the LORD and so in-14 cur guilt, then, when the sin they have committed is notified to them, the assembly shall present a young bull as a sin-offering and shall bring it in front of the Tent of the Pres-15 ence. The elders of the community shall lay their hands on the victim's head before the LORD, and it shall be slaughtered before the LORD. 16 The anointed priest shall then bring some of the blood to the Tent of 17 the Presence, dip his finger in it and sprinkle it in front of the Veil 18 seven times before the LORD. He shall put some of the blood on the horns of the altar before the LORD in the Tent of the Presence and pour all the rest at the base of the altar of whole-offering at the entrance of the Tent of the Presence. 19 He shall then set aside all the fat 20 from the bull and burn it on the altar. He shall deal with this bull as he deals with the bull of the sin-offering, and in this way the priest 21 shall make expiation for their guilt and they shall be forgiven. He shall take the bull outside the camp and burn it as the other bull was burnt. This is a sin-offering for the assembly.

22   When a man of standing sins by

doing inadvertently what is forbidden in any commandment of the LORD his God, thereby incurring guilt, and the sin he has committed 23 is made known to him, he shall bring as his offering a he-goat without blemish. He shall lay his hand 24 on the goat's head and shall slaughter it before the LORD in the place where the whole-offering is slaughtered. It is a sin-offering. The priest 25 shall then take some of the blood of the victim with his finger and put it on the horns of the altar of whole-offering. He shall pour out the rest of the blood at the base of the altar of whole-offering. He shall burn all 26 the fat at the altar in the same way as the fat of the shared-offering. Thus the priest shall make expiation for that man's sin, and it shall be forgiven him.

If any person among the common 27 people sins inadvertently and does what is forbidden in any commandment of the LORD, thereby incurring guilt, and the sin he has 28 committed is made known to him, he shall bring as his offering for the sin which he has committed a she-goat without blemish. He shall lay 29 his hand on the head of the victim and slaughter it in the place where the whole-offering is slaughtered. The priest shall then take some of 30 its blood with his finger and put it on the horns of the altar of whole-offering. All the rest of the blood he shall pour at the base of the altar. He shall remove all its fat as 31 the fat of the shared-offering is removed, and the priest shall burn it on the altar as a soothing odour to the LORD. So the priest shall make expiation for that person's guilt, and it shall be forgiven him.

If the man brings a sheep as his 32 offering for sin, it shall be a ewe without blemish. He shall lay his 33 hand on the head of the victim and slaughter it as a sin-offering in the place where the whole-offering is slaughtered. The priest shall then 34 take some of the blood of the victim with his finger and put it on the horns of the altar of whole-offering. All the rest of the blood he shall pour out at the base of the altar. He shall remove all the fat, as the 35 fat of the sheep is removed from the shared-offering. The priest shall burn the pieces of fat at the altar on top of the food-offerings to the LORD, and shall make expiation for the sin that the man has committed, and it shall be forgiven him.

If a person hears a solemn **5** adjuration to give evidence as a witness to something he has seen or heard and does not declare what he knows, he commits a sin and must accept responsibility.

If a person touches anything un- 2 clean, such as the dead body of an unclean animal, whether wild or domestic, or of an unclean reptile, or if he touches anything unclean in 3 a man, whatever that uncleanness may be, and it is concealed by him although he is aware of it, he shall 4 incur guilt. Or if a person rashly utters an oath to do something evil or good, in any matter in which such a man may swear a rash oath, and it is concealed by him although he is aware of it, he shall in either 5 case incur guilt. Whenever a man incurs guilt in any of these cases and confesses how he has sinned 6 therein, he shall bring to the LORD, as his penalty for the sin that he has committed, a female of the flock, either a ewe or a she-goat, as a sin-offering, and the priest shall make expiation for him on account of his sin which he has committed, and he shall be pardoned.

7 But if he cannot afford as much as a young animal, he shall bring to the LORD for the sin he has committed two turtle-doves or two young pigeons, one for a sin-offering and the other for a whole-8 offering. He shall bring them to the priest, and present first the one intended for the sin-offering. He shall wrench its head back without 9 severing it. He shall sprinkle some of the blood of the victim against the side of the altar, and what is left of the blood shall be drained out at the base of the altar: it is a 0 sin-offering. He shall deal with the second bird as a whole-offering according to custom, and the priest shall make expiation for the sin the man has committed, and it shall be forgiven him.

1 If the man cannot afford two turtle-doves or two young pigeons, for his sin he shall bring as his offering a tenth of an ephah of flour, as a sin-offering. He shall add no oil to it nor put frank-incense on it, because it is a sin-2 offering. He shall bring it to the priest, who shall scoop up a hand-ful from it as a token and burn it on the altar on the food-offerings to the LORD: it is a sin-offering. 3 The priest shall make expiation for the sin the man has committed in any one of these cases, and it shall be forgiven him. The remainder belongs to the priest, as with the grain-offering.

Guilt-offerings

4 The LORD spoke to Moses and 5 said: When any person commits an offence by inadvertently defaulting in dues sacred to the LORD, he shall bring as his guilt-offering to the LORD a ram without blemish from the flock, the value to be determined by you in silver shekels according to the sacred standard, 6 for a guilt-offering; he shall make good his default in sacred dues, adding one fifth. He shall give it to the priest, who shall make

expiation for his sin with the ram of the guilt-offering, and it shall be forgiven him.

17 If and when any person sins un-wittingly and does what is for-bidden by any commandment of the LORD, thereby incurring guilt, 18 he must accept responsibility. He shall bring to the priest as a guilt-offering a ram without blemish from the flock, valued by you, and the priest shall make expiation for the error into which he has un-wittingly fallen, and it shall be 19 forgiven him. It is a guilt-offering; he has been guilty of an offence against the LORD.

6 The LORD spoke to Moses and 2 said: When any person sins and commits a grievous fault against the LORD, whether he lies to a fellow-countryman about a deposit or contract, or a theft, or wrongs 3 him by extortion, or finds lost property and then lies about it, and swears a false oath in regard to any sin of this sort that he com-4 mits—if he does this, thereby in-curring guilt, he shall restore what he has stolen or gained by extor-tion, or the deposit left with him or the lost property which he 5 found, or anything at all concern-ing which he swore a false oath. He shall make full restitution, adding one fifth to it, and give it back to the aggrieved party on the day when he offers his guilt-6 offering. He shall bring to the LORD as his guilt-offering a ram without blemish from the flock, valued by you, as a guilt-offering. 7 The priest shall make expiation for his guilt before the LORD, and he shall be forgiven for any act which has brought guilt upon him.

Further laws concerning offerings

8 The LORD spoke to Moses and 9 said, Give this command to Aaron and his sons: This is the law of the whole-offering. The whole-offering shall remain on the altar-hearth all night till morning, and the altar-fire shall be kept burning there. 10 Then the priest, having donned his linen robe and put on linen drawers to cover himself, shall remove the ashes to which the fire reduces the whole-offering on the altar and put 11 them beside the altar. He shall then change into other garments and take the ashes outside the camp to 12 a ritually clean place. The fire shall be kept burning on the altar; it shall never go out. Every morning the priest shall have fresh wood burning thereon, arrange the whole-offering on it, and on top burn the 13 fat from the shared-offerings. Fire shall always be kept burning on the altar; it shall not go out.

14 This is the law of the grain-offering. The Aaronites shall pre-

sent it before the LORD in front of the altar. The priest shall set aside 15 a handful of the flour from it, with the oil of the grain-offering, and all the frankincense on it. He shall burn this token of it on the altar as a soothing odour to the LORD. The 16 remainder Aaron and his sons shall eat. It shall be eaten in the form of unleavened cakes and in a holy place. They shall eat it in the court of the Tent of the Presence. It shall 17 not be baked with leaven. I have allotted this to them as their share of my food-offerings. Like the sin-offering and the guilt-offering, it is most sacred. Any male descendant 18 of Aaron may eat it, as a due from the food-offerings to the LORD, for generation after generation for all time. Whatever touches them is to be forfeit as sacred.

The LORD spoke to Moses and 19 said: This is the offering which 20 Aaron and his sons shall present to the LORD:[b] one tenth of an ephah of flour, the usual grain-offering, half of it in the morning and half in the evening. It shall be cooked 21 with oil on a griddle; you shall bring it well-mixed, and so present it crumbled in small pieces as a grain-offering, a soothing odour to the LORD. The anointed priest in 22 the line of Aaron shall offer it. This is a rule binding for all time. It shall be burnt in sacrifice to the LORD as a complete offering. Every grain-23 offering of a priest shall be a com-plete offering; it shall not be eaten.

The LORD spoke to Moses and 24 said, Speak to Aaron and his sons 25 in these words: This is the law of the sin-offering. The sin-offering shall be slaughtered before the LORD in the place where the whole-offering is slaughtered; it is most sacred. The priest who officiates 26 shall eat of the flesh; it shall be eaten in a sacred place, in the court of the Tent of the Presence. What-27 ever touches its flesh is to be for-feit as sacred. If any of the blood is splashed on a garment, that shall be washed in a sacred place. An 28 earthenware vessel in which the sin-offering is boiled shall be smashed. If it has been boiled in a copper vessel, that shall be scoured and rinsed with water. Any male of 29 priestly family may eat of this offering; it is most sacred. If, how-30 ever, part of the blood is brought to the Tent of the Presence to make expiation in the holy place, the sin-offering shall not be eaten; it shall be destroyed by fire.

This is the law of the guilt- **7** offering: it is most sacred. The 2 guilt-offering shall be slaughtered in the place where the whole-offering is slaughtered, and its blood shall be flung against the altar all round. The priest shall set 3 aside and present all the fat from

---

b Prob. rdg.; Heb. adds on the day when he is anointed.

it: the fat-tail and the fat covering
4 the entrails, the two kidneys with
the fat on them beside the haunches,
and the long lobe of the liver with
5 the kidneys. The priest shall burn
these pieces on the altar as a food-
offering to the LORD; it is a guilt-
6 offering. Any male of priestly
family may eat it. It shall be eaten
in a sacred place; it is most sacred.
7 There is one law for both sin-
offering and guilt-offering: they
shall belong to the priest who per-
8 forms the rite of expiation. The skin
of any man's whole-offering shall
belong to the priest who presents
9 it. Every grain-offering baked in an
oven and everything that is cooked
in a pan or on a griddle shall belong
10 to the priest who presents it. Every
grain-offering, whether mixed with
oil or dry, shall be shared equally
among all the Aaronites.
11   This is the law of the shared-
12 offering presented to the LORD. If
a man presents it as a thank-
offering, then, in addition to the
thank-offering, he shall present unleavened cakes mixed with oil,
wafers of unleavened flour smeared
with oil, and well-mixed flour and
13 flat cakes mixed with oil. He shall
present flat cakes of leavened bread
in addition to his shared thank-
14 offering. One part of every offering
he shall present as a contribution
for the LORD: it shall belong to the
priest who flings the blood of the
shared-offering against the altar.
15 The flesh shall be eaten on the day
of its presentation; none of it shall
be put aside till morning.
16   If a man's sacrifice is a votive
offering or a freewill offering, it
17 may be eaten on the day it is presented or on the next day. Any
flesh left over on the third day shall
18 be destroyed by fire. If any flesh
of his shared-offering is eaten on
the third day, the man who has
presented it shall not be accepted.
It will not be counted to his credit,
it shall be reckoned as tainted and
the person who eats any of it
19 shall accept responsibility. No flesh
which comes into contact with anything unclean shall be eaten; it
shall be destroyed by fire.
    The flesh may be eaten by any-
20 one who is clean, but the person
who, while unclean, eats flesh from
a shared-offering presented to the
LORD shall be cut off from his
21 father's kin. When any person is
contaminated by contact with anything unclean, be it man, beast, or
reptile, and then eats any of the
flesh from the shared-offerings presented to the LORD, that person
shall be cut off from his father's
kin.
22   The LORD spoke to Moses and
23 said, Speak to the Israelites in these
words: You shall not eat the fat of
24 any ox, sheep, or goat. The fat of

an animal that has died a natural
death or has been mauled by wild
beasts may be put to any other use,
25 but you shall not eat it. Every man
who eats fat from a beast of which
he has presented any part as a food-
offering to the LORD shall be cut off
from his father's kin.
26   You shall eat none of the blood,
whether of bird or of beast, wher-
27 ever you may live. Every person
who eats any of the blood shall be
cut off from his father's kin.
28   The LORD spoke to Moses and
29 said, Speak to the Israelites in these
words: Whoever comes to present
a shared-offering shall set aside
part of it as an offering to the LORD.
30 With his own hands he shall bring
the food-offerings to the LORD. He
shall also bring the fat together
with the breast which is to be presented as a special gift before the
31 LORD; the priest shall burn the fat
on the altar, but the breast shall
belong to Aaron and his descen-
32 dants. You shall give the right hind-
leg of your shared-offerings as a
33 contribution for the priest; it shall
be the perquisite of the Aaronite
who presents the blood and the fat
34 of the shared-offering. I have taken
from the Israelites the breast of the
special gift and the leg of the contribution made out of the shared-
offerings, and have given them as
a due from the Israelites to Aaron
the priest and his descendants
35 for all time. This is the portion
prescribed for Aaron and his descendants out of the LORD's food-
offerings, appointed on the day
when they were presented as priests
36 to the LORD; and on the day when
they were anointed, the LORD commanded that these prescribed portions should be given to them by
the Israelites. This is a rule binding on their descendants for all
time.
37   This, then, is the law of the
whole-offering, the grain-offering,
the sin-offering, the guilt-offering,
the installation-offerings, and the
38 shared-offerings, with which the
LORD charged Moses on Mount
Sinai on the day when he commanded the Israelites to present
their offerings to the LORD in the
wilderness of Sinai.

Consecrating the priests

8 The LORD spoke to Moses and said,
2 'Take Aaron and his sons with him,
the vestments, the anointing oil,
the ox for a sin-offering, the two
rams, and the basket of unleavened
3 cakes, and assemble all the community at the entrance to the Tent
4 of the Presence.' Moses did as the
LORD had commanded him, and
the community assembled at the
entrance to the Tent of the Pres-
5 ence. He told the community that

this was what the LORD had commanded. He presented Aaron and 6
his sons and washed them in water.
He invested Aaron with the tunic, 7
girded him with the sash, robed
him with the mantle, put the ephod
on him, tied it with its waist-band
and fastened the ephod to him with
the band. He put the breast-piece[c] 8
on him and set the Urim and
Thummim in it. He then put the 9
turban upon his head and set the
gold rosette as a symbol of holy
dedication on the front of the turban, as the LORD had commanded
him. Moses then took the anoint- 10
ing oil, anointed the Tabernacle
and all that was within it and consecrated them. He sprinkled some 11
of the oil seven times on the altar,
anointing the altar, all its vessels,
the basin and its stand, to consecrate them. He poured some of 12
the anointing oil on Aaron's head
and so consecrated him. Moses 13
then brought the sons of Aaron
forward, invested them with tunics,
girded them with sashes and tied
their tall head-dresses on them,
as the LORD had commanded
him.
    He then brought up the ox for 14
the sin-offering; Aaron and his
sons laid their hands on its head,
and he slaughtered it. Moses took 15
some of the blood and put it with
his finger on the horns round the
altar. Thus he purified the altar,
and when he had poured out the
rest of the blood at the base of the
altar, he consecrated it by making
expiation for it. He took all the fat 16
upon the entrails, the long lobe of
the liver, and the two kidneys with
their fat, and burnt them on the
altar, but the ox, its skin, its flesh, 17
and its offal, he destroyed by fire

c Or pouch.

outside the camp, as the LORD had commanded him.

18 Moses then brought forward the ram of the whole-offering; Aaron and his sons laid their hands on the
19 ram's head, and he slaughtered it. Moses flung its blood against the
20 altar all round. He cut the ram up and burnt the head, the pieces, and
21 the suet. He washed the entrails and the shins in water and burnt the whole on the altar. This was a whole-offering, a food-offering of soothing odour to the LORD, as the LORD had commanded Moses.
22 Moses then brought forward the second ram, the ram for the installation of priests. Aaron and his sons laid their hands upon its head,
23 and he slaughtered it. Moses took some of its blood and put it on the lobe of Aaron's right ear, on his right thumb, and on the big toe of
24 his right foot. He then brought forward the sons of Aaron, put some of the blood on the lobes of their right ears, on their right thumbs, and on the big toes of their right feet. He flung the rest of the blood against the altar all
25 round; he took the fat, the fat-tail, the fat covering the entrails, the long lobe of the liver, the two kidneys with their fat, and the
26 right leg. Then from the basket of unleavened cakes before the LORD he took one unleavened cake, one cake of bread made with oil, and
27 one wafer, and laid them on the fatty parts and the right leg. He put the whole on the hands of Aaron and of his sons, and he presented it as a special gift before the LORD.
28 He took it from their hands and burnt it on the altar on top of the whole-offering. This was an installation-offering, it was a food-offering of soothing odour to the LORD.
29 Moses then took the breast and presented it as a special gift before the LORD; it was his portion of the ram of installation, as the LORD
30 had commanded him. Moses took some of the anointing oil and some of the blood on the altar and sprinkled it on Aaron and his vestments, and on his sons and their vestments with him. Thus he consecrated Aaron and his vestments, and with him his sons and their vestments.
31 Moses said to Aaron and his sons, 'Boil the flesh of the ram at the entrance to the Tent of the Presence, and eat it there, together with the bread in the installation-basket, in accordance with the command: "Aaron and his sons
32 shall eat it." The remainder of the flesh and bread you shall destroy
33 by fire. You shall not leave the entrance to the Tent of the Presence for seven days, until the day which completes the period of your installation, for it lasts seven days.
34 What was done this day followed

the LORD's command to make ex-
35 piation for you. You shall stay at the entrance to the Tent of the Presence day and night for seven days, keeping vigil to the LORD, so that you do not die, for so I was commanded.'
36 Aaron and his sons did everything that the LORD had commanded through Moses.

Aaron offers sacrifices

9 On the eighth day Moses summoned Aaron and his sons and
2 the Israelite elders. He said to Aaron, 'Take for yourself a bull-calf for a sin-offering and a ram for a whole-offering, both without
3 blemish, and present them before the LORD. Then bid the Israelites take a he-goat for a sin-offering, a calf and a lamb, both yearlings without blemish, for a whole-
4 offering, and a bull and a ram for shared-offerings to be sacrificed before the LORD, together with a grain-offering mixed with oil. This day the LORD will appear to you.'
5 They brought what Moses had commanded to the front of the Tent of the Presence, and all the community approached and stood
6 before the LORD. Moses said, 'This is what the LORD has commanded you to do, so that the glory of the
7 LORD may appear to you. Come near to the altar,' he said to Aaron; 'prepare your sin-offering and your whole-offering and make expiation for yourself and for your household. Then prepare the offering of the people and make expiation for them, as the LORD has commanded.'
8 So Aaron came near to the altar and slaughtered the calf, which was
9 his sin-offering. The sons of Aaron presented the blood to him, and he dipped his finger in the blood and put it on the horns of the altar. The rest of the blood he poured out at
10 the base of the altar. Part of the sin-offering, the fat, the kidneys, and the long lobe of the liver, he burnt on the altar as the LORD had
11 commanded Moses, but the flesh and the skin he destroyed by fire
12 outside the camp. Then he slaughtered the whole-offering; his sons handed him the blood, and he flung it against the altar all round.
13 They handed him the pieces of the whole-offering and the head, and
14 he burnt them on the altar. He washed the entrails and the shins and burnt them on the altar, on top of the whole-offering.
15 He then brought forward the offering of the people. He took the he-goat, the people's sin-offering, slaughtered it and performed the rite of the sin-offering as he had
16 previously done for himself. He presented the whole-offering and prepared it in the manner pre-
17 scribed. He brought forward the grain-offering, took a handful of it and burnt it on the altar, in

addition to the morning whole-offering. He slaughtered the bull 18 and the ram, the shared-offerings of the people. His sons handed him the blood, and he flung it against the altar all round. But the fatty 19 parts of the bull, the fat-tail of the ram, the fat covering the entrails, and the two kidneys with the fat upon them, and the long lobe of the liver, all this fat they first put 20 on the breasts of the animals and then burnt it on the altar. Aaron 21 presented the breasts and the right leg as a special gift before the LORD, as Moses had commanded.

Then Aaron lifted up his hands 22 towards the people and pronounced the blessing over them. He came down from performing the rites of the sin-offering, the whole-offering, and the shared-offerings. Moses 23 and Aaron entered the Tent of the Presence, and when they came out, they blessed the people, and the glory of the LORD appeared to all the people. Fire came out from be- 24 fore the LORD and consumed the whole-offering and the fatty parts on the altar. All the people saw, and they shouted and fell on their faces.

The sin of Nadab and Abihu

Now Nadab and Abihu, sons of 10 Aaron, took their firepans, put fire in them, threw incense on the fire and presented before the LORD illicit fire which he had not commanded. Fire came out from before 2 the LORD and destroyed them; and so they died in the presence of the LORD. Then Moses said to Aaron, 3 'This is what the LORD meant when he said: Among those who approach me, I must be treated as holy; in the presence of all the people I must be given honour.' Aaron was dumbfounded. Moses 4 sent for Mishael and Elzaphan, the sons of Aaron's uncle Uzziel, and said to them, 'Come and carry your cousins outside the camp away from the holy place.' They came 5 and carried them away in their tunics outside the camp, as Moses had told them. Moses then said to 6 Aaron and to his sons Eleazar and Ithamar, 'You shall not leave your hair dishevelled or tear your clothes in mourning, lest you die and the LORD be angry with the whole community. Your kinsmen, all the house of Israel, shall weep for the destruction by fire which the LORD has kindled. You shall not leave 7 the entrance to the Tent of the Presence lest you die, because the LORD's anointing oil is on you.' They did as Moses had said.

Laws concerning priests

The LORD spoke to Aaron and said: 8 You and your sons with you shall 9 not drink wine or strong drink when you are to enter the Tent of the Presence, lest you die. This is

a rule binding on your descendants
10 for all time, to make a distinction
between sacred and profane, be-
11 tween clean and unclean, and to
teach the Israelites all the decrees
which the LORD has spoken to them
through Moses.

12 Moses said to Aaron and his
surviving sons Eleazar and Ithamar, 'Take what is left over of the
grain-offering out of the food-
offerings of the LORD, and eat it
without leaven beside the altar; it
13 is most sacred. You shall eat it in
a sacred place; it is your due and
that of your sons out of the LORD's
food-offerings, for so I was com-
14 manded. You shall eat the breast
of the special gift and the leg of the
contribution in a clean place, you
and your sons and daughters; for
they have been given to you and
your children as your due out of
the shared-offerings of the Israel-
15 ites. The leg of the contribution
and the breast of the special gift
shall be brought, along with the
food-offerings of fat, to be presented as a special gift before the
LORD, and it shall belong to you
and your children together, a due
for all time; for so the LORD has
commanded.'

16 Moses made searching inquiry
about the goat of the sin-offering
and found that it had been burnt.
He was angry with Eleazar and
Ithamar, Aaron's surviving sons,
17 and said, 'Why did you not eat the
sin-offering in the sacred place? It
is most sacred. It was given to you
to take away the guilt of the community by making expiation for
18 them before the LORD. If the blood
is not brought within the sacred
precincts, you shall eat the sin-
offering there as I was commanded.'
19 But Aaron replied to Moses, 'See,
they have today presented their sin-
offering and their whole-offering
before the LORD, and this is what
has befallen me; if I eat a sin-
offering today, will it be right in the
20 eyes of the LORD?' When Moses
heard this, he deemed it right.

Clean and unclean creatures

11 The LORD spoke to Moses and
2 Aaron and said, Speak to the
Israelites in these words: Of all
animals on land these are the
3 creatures you may eat: you may
eat any animal which has a parted
foot or a cloven hoof and also chews
4 the cud; those which have only a
cloven hoof or only chew the cud
you may not eat. These are: the
camel, because it chews the cud
but has not a cloven hoof; you shall
5 regard it as unclean; the rock-
badger,ᵈ because it chews the cud
but has not a parted foot; you shall
6 regard it as unclean; the hare, because it chews the cud but has not
a parted foot; you shall regard it as
7 unclean; the pig, because it has a
parted foot and a cloven hoof but
does not chew the cud; you shall
8 regard it as unclean. You shall not
eat their flesh or even touch their
dead bodies; you shall regard them
as unclean.
9 Of creatures that live in water
these you may eat: all those that
have fins and scales, whether in
10 salt water or fresh; but all that have
neither fins nor scales, whether in
salt or fresh water, including both
small creatures in shoals and larger
creatures, you shall regard as ver-
11 min. They shall be vermin to you;
you shall not eat their flesh, and
their dead bodies you shall treat as
12 those of vermin. Every creature in
the water that has neither fins nor
scales shall be vermin to you.
13 These are the birds you shall regard as vermin, and for this reason
they shall not be eaten: the griffon-
vulture,ᵉ the black vulture, and the
14 bearded vulture;ᶠ the kite and
15 every kind of falcon; every kind of
16 crow,ᵍ the desert-owl, the short-
eared owl, the long-eared owl, and
17 every kind of hawk; the tawny owl,
the fisher-owl, and the screech-owl;
18 the little owl, the horned owl, the
19 osprey, the stork,ʰ every kind of
cormorant, the hoopoe, and the
bat.
20 All teeming winged creatures
that go on four legs shall be
21 vermin to you, except those which
have legs jointed above their feet
for leaping on the ground. Of 22
these you may eat every kind of
great locust, every kind of long-
headed locust, every kind of green
locust, and every kind of desert
locust. Every other teeming winged 23
creature that has four legs you
shall regard as vermin; you would 24
make yourselves unclean with
them: whoeverⁱ touches their dead
bodies shall be unclean till evening.
Whoever picks up their dead bodies 25
shall wash his clothes but remain
unclean till evening.

You shall regard as unclean 26
every animal which has a parted
foot but has not a cloven hoof and
does not chew the cud: whoeverⁱ
touches them shall be unclean. You 27
shall regard as unclean all four-
footed wild animals that go on flat
paws; whoeverⁱ touches their dead
bodies shall be unclean till evening.
Whoever takes up their dead bodies 28
shall wash his clothes but remain
unclean till evening. You shall regard them as unclean.

You shall regard these as unclean 29
among creatures that teem on the
ground: the mole-rat,ʲ the jerboa,
and every kind of thorn-tailed lizard; the gecko, the sand-gecko, the 30
wall-gecko, the great lizard, and the
chameleon. You shall regard these 31
as unclean among teeming creatures; whoeverⁱ touches them when
they are dead shall be unclean till
evening. Anything on which any of 32
them falls when they are dead shall
be unclean, any article of wood or
garment or skin or sacking, any
article in regular use; it shall be
plunged into water but shall remain unclean till evening, when it
shall be clean. If any of these falls 33
into an earthenware vessel, its contents shall be unclean and it shall
be smashed. Any food on which 34
water from such a vessel is poured
shall be unclean, and any drink in
such a vessel shall be unclean. Any- 35
thing on which the dead body of
such a creature falls shall be unclean; an oven or a stove shall be
broken, for they are unclean and

d Or rock-rabbit.   e Or eagle.
f Or ossifrage.   g Or raven.
h Or heron.   i Or whatever.
j Or weasel.

Pigs, camel, rock badger, and hares

Bats and hoopoe (Lev. 11. 19)

36 you shall treat them as such; but a spring or a cistern where water collects shall remain clean, though whatever[k] touches the dead body
37 shall be unclean. When any of their dead bodies falls on seed intended for sowing, it remains
38 clean; but if the seed has been soaked in water and any dead body falls on it, you shall treat it as unclean.
39 When any animal allowed as food dies, all that touch the carcass shall be unclean till evening.
40 Whoever eats any of the carcass shall wash his clothes but remain unclean till evening; whoever takes up the carcass shall wash his clothes and be unclean till evening.
41 All creatures that teem on the ground are vermin; they shall not
42 be eaten. All creatures that teem on the ground, crawl on their bellies, go on all fours or have many legs, you shall not eat, because they are
43 vermin which contaminate. You shall not contaminate yourselves through any teeming creature. You shall not defile yourselves with them and make yourselves unclean
44 by them. For I am the LORD your God; you shall make yourselves holy and keep yourselves holy, because I am holy. You shall not defile yourselves with any teeming creature that creeps on the ground.
45 I am the LORD who brought you up from Egypt to become your God. You shall keep yourselves holy, because I am holy.
46 This, then, is the law concerning beast and bird, every living creature that swims in the water and every living creature that teems on
47 the land. It is to make a distinction between the unclean and the clean, between living creatures that may be eaten and living creatures that may not be eaten.

Purification after childbirth

12 The LORD spoke to Moses and
2 said, Speak to the Israelites in these words: When a woman conceives and bears a male child, she shall be unclean for seven days, as in the period of her impurity through

3 menstruation. On the eighth day, the child shall have the flesh of his
4 foreskin circumcised. The woman shall wait for thirty-three days because her blood requires purification; she shall touch nothing that is holy, and shall not enter the sanctuary till her days of purifica-
5 tion are completed. If she bears a female child, she shall be unclean for fourteen days as for her menstruation and shall wait for sixty-six days because her blood requires
6 purification. When her days of purification are completed for a son or a daughter, she shall bring a yearling ram for a whole-offering and a young pigeon or a turtle-dove for a sin-offering to the priest at the entrance to the Tent of the
7 Presence. He shall present it before the LORD and make expiation for her, and she shall be clean from the issue of her blood. This is the law for the woman who bears a
8 child, whether male or female. If she cannot afford a ram, she shall bring two turtle-doves or two young pigeons, one for a whole-offering and the other for a sin-offering. The priest shall make expiation for her and she shall be clean.

Laws concerning ritual uncleanness

13 The LORD spoke to Moses and
2 Aaron and said: When any man has a discoloration on the skin of his body, a pustule or inflammation, and it may develop into the sores of a malignant skin-disease, he shall be brought to the priest, either to Aaron or to one of his
3 sons. The priest shall examine the sore on the skin; if the hairs on the sore have turned white and it appears to be deeper than the skin, it shall be considered the sore of a malignant skin-disease, and the priest, after examination, shall pro-
4 nounce him ritually unclean. But if the inflammation on his skin is white and seems no deeper than the skin, and the hairs have not turned white, the priest shall isolate the affected person for seven days.
5 If, when he examines him on the seventh day, the sore remains as it

was and has not spread in the skin, he shall keep him in isolation for another seven days. When the 6 priest examines him again on the seventh day, if the sore has faded and has not spread in the skin, the priest shall pronounce him ritually clean. It is only a scab; the man shall wash his clothes and so be clean. But if the scab spreads on 7 the skin after he has been to the priest to be pronounced ritually clean, the man shall show himself a second time to the priest. The 8 priest shall examine him again, and if it continues to spread, he shall pronounce him ritually unclean; it is a malignant skin-disease.
When anyone has the sores of a 9 malignant skin-disease, he shall be brought to the priest, and the priest 10 shall examine him. If there is a white mark on the skin, turning the hairs white, and an ulceration appears in the mark, it is a chronic 11 skin-disease on the body, and the priest shall pronounce him ritually unclean; there is no need for isolation because he is unclean already. If the skin-disease breaks out and 12 covers the affected person from head to foot as far as the priest can see, the priest shall examine him, 13 and if he finds the condition spread all over the body, he shall pronounce him ritually clean. It has all gone white; he is clean. But 14 from the moment when raw flesh appears, the man shall be considered unclean. When the priest 15 sees it, he shall pronounce him unclean. Raw flesh is to be considered unclean; it is a malignant skin-disease. On the other hand, when 16 the raw flesh heals and turns white, the man shall go to the priest, who 17 shall examine him, and if the sores have gone white, he shall pronounce him clean. He is ritually clean.
When a fester appears on the 18 skin and heals up, but is followed 19 by a white mark or reddish-white

k Or whoever.

inflammation on the site of the fester, the man shall show himself
20 to the priest. The priest shall examine him; if it seems to be beneath the skin and the hairs have turned white, the priest shall pronounce him ritually unclean. It is a malignant skin-disease which has broken out on the site of the fester.
21 But if the priest on examination finds that it has no white hairs, is not beneath the skin and has faded, he shall isolate him for seven days.
22 If the affection has spread at all in the skin, then the priest shall pronounce him unclean; for it is a
23 malignant skin-disease. But if the inflammation is no worse and has not spread, it is only the scar of the fester, and the priest shall pronounce him ritually clean.
24 Again, in the case of a burn on the skin, if the raw spot left by the burn becomes a reddish-white or
25 white inflammation, the priest shall examine it. If the hairs on the inflammation have turned white and it is deeper than the skin, it is a malignant skin-disease which has broken out at the site of the burn. The priest shall pronounce the man ritually unclean; it is a malignant
26 skin-disease. But if the priest on examination finds that there is no white hair on the inflammation and it is not beneath the skin and has faded, he shall keep him in isola-
27 tion for seven days. When the priest examines him on the seventh day, if the inflammation has spread at all in the skin, the priest shall pronounce him unclean; it is a
28 malignant skin-disease. But if the inflammation is no worse, has not spread and has faded, it is only a mark from the burn. The priest shall pronounce him ritually clean because it is the scar of the burn.
29 When a man, or woman, has a
30 sore on the head or chin, the priest shall examine it; and if it seems deeper than the skin and the hair is yellow and sparse, the priest shall pronounce him ritually unclean; it is a scurf, a malignant skin-disease of the head or chin.
31 But when the priest sees the sore, if it appears to be no deeper than the skin and yet there is no yellow hair on the place, the priest shall isolate the affected person for seven

(Lev. 11. 29, 30)

32 days. He shall examine the sore on the seventh day: if the scurf has not spread and there are no yellow hairs on it and it seems no deeper
33 than the skin, the man shall get himself shaved except for the scurfy part, and the priest shall keep him in isolation for another seven days.
34 The priest shall examine it again on the seventh day, and if the scurf has not spread on the skin and appears to be no deeper than the skin, the priest shall pronounce him clean. The man shall wash his clothes and so be ritually clean.
35 But if the scurf spreads at all in the skin after the man has been
36 pronounced clean, the priest shall examine him again. If it has spread in the skin, the priest need not even look for yellow hair; the man is
37 unclean. If, however, the scurf remains as it was but black hair has begun to grow on it, it has healed. The man is ritually clean and the priest shall pronounce him so.
38 When a man, or woman, has inflamed patches on the skin and
39 they are white, the priest shall examine them. If they are white and fading, it is dull-white leprosy that has broken out on the skin. The man is ritually clean.
40 When a man's hair falls out from his head, he is bald behind but not
41 ritually unclean. If the hair falls out from the front of the scalp, he is bald on the forehead but clean.
42 But if on the bald patch behind or on the forehead there is a reddish-white sore, it is a malignant skin-disease breaking out on those parts.
43 The priest shall examine him, and if the discoloured sore on the bald patch behind or on the forehead is reddish-white, similar in appearance to a malignant skin-disease on
44 the body, the man is suffering from such a disease; he is ritually unclean and the priest must not fail

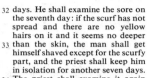

Chameleon and lizard
(Lev. 11. 30)

to pronounce him so. The symptoms are in this case on his head.
45 One who suffers from a malignant skin-disease shall wear his clothes torn, leave his hair dishevelled, conceal his upper lip, and
46 cry, 'Unclean, unclean.' So long as the sore persists, he shall be considered ritually unclean. The man is unclean: he shall live apart and must stay outside the settlement.
47 When there is a stain of mould,
48 whether in a garment of wool or linen, or in the warp or weft of linen or wool, or in a skin or any-
49 thing made of skin; if the stain is greenish or reddish in the garment or skin, or in the warp or weft, or in anything made of skin, it is a stain of mould which must be
50 shown to the priest. The priest shall examine it and put the stained material aside for seven days. On
51 the seventh day he shall examine it again. If the stain has spread in the garment, warp, weft, or skin, whatever the use of the skin, the stain is a rotting mould: it is ritually un-
52 clean. He shall burn the garment or the warp or weft, whether wool or linen, or anything of skin which is stained; because it is a rotting mould, it must be destroyed by fire.
53 But if the priest sees that the stain has not spread in the garment, warp or weft, or anything made of
54 skin, he shall give orders for the stained material to be washed, and then he shall put it aside for an-
55 other seven days. After it has been washed the priest shall examine the stain; if it has not changed its appearance, although it has not spread, it is unclean and you shall destroy it by fire, whether the rot
56 is on the right side or the wrong. If the priest examines it and finds the stain faded after being washed, he shall tear it out of the garment, skin, warp, or weft. If, however,
57 the stain reappears in the garment,

warp or weft, or in anything of skin, it is breaking out afresh and you shall destroy by fire whatever is 58 stained. If you wash the garment, warp, weft, or anything of skin and the stain disappears, it shall be washed a second time and then it shall be ritually clean.

59 This is the law concerning stain of mould in a garment of wool or linen, in warp or weft, or in anything made of skin; by it they shall be pronounced clean or unclean.

14 The LORD spoke to Moses and 2 said: This is the law concerning a man suffering from a malignant skin-disease. On the day when he is to be cleansed he shall be brought 3 to the priest. The priest shall go outside the camp and examine him. If the man is healed of his disease, 4 then the priest shall order two clean small birds to be brought alive for the man who is to be cleansed, together with cedar-wood, scarlet 5 thread, and marjoram.[l] He shall order one of the birds to be killed over an earthenware bowl contain- 6 ing fresh water. He shall then take the living bird and the cedar-wood, scarlet thread, and marjoram and dip them and the living bird in the blood of the bird that has been 7 killed over the fresh water. He shall sprinkle the blood seven times on the man who is to be cleansed from his skin-disease and so cleanse him; the living bird he shall release to fly away over the open country. 8 The man to be cleansed shall wash his clothes, shave off all his hair, bathe in water and so be ritually clean. He may then enter the camp but must stay outside his tent for 9 seven days. On the seventh day he shall shave off all the hair on his head, his beard, and his eyebrows, and then shave the rest of his hair, wash his clothes and bathe in water; then he shall be ritually clean.

10 On the eighth day he shall bring two yearling rams and one yearling ewe, all three without blemish, a grain-offering of three tenths of an ephah of flour mixed with oil, 11 and one log of oil. The officiating priest shall place the man to be cleansed and his offerings before the LORD at the entrance to the 12 Tent of the Presence. He shall then take one of the rams and offer it with the log of oil as a guilt-offering, presenting them as a 13 special gift before the LORD. The ram shall be slaughtered where the sin-offerings and the whole-offerings are slaughtered, within the sacred precincts, because the guilt-offering, like the sin-offering, belongs to the priest. It is most 14 sacred. The priest shall then take some of the blood of the guilt-offering and put it on the lobe of the right ear of the man to be

cleansed, and on his right thumb and the big toe of his right foot. 15 He shall next take the log of oil and pour some of it on the palm 16 of his own left hand, dip his right forefinger into the oil on his left palm and sprinkle some of it with his finger seven times before the 17 LORD. He shall then put some of the oil remaining on his palm on the lobe of the right ear of the man to be cleansed, on his right thumb and on the big toe of his right foot, on top of the blood of the guilt- 18 offering. The remainder of the oil on the priest's palm shall be put upon the head of the man to be cleansed, and thus the priest shall make expiation for him before the 19 LORD. The priest shall then perform the sin-offering and make expiation for the uncleanness of the man who is to be cleansed. After this he shall slaughter the 20 whole-offering and offer it and the grain-offering on the altar. Thus the priest shall make expiation for him, and then he shall be clean.

21 If the man is poor and cannot afford these offerings, he shall bring one young ram as a guilt-offering to be a special gift making expiation for him, and a grain-offering 22 of a tenth of an ephah of flour mixed with oil, and a log of oil, also two turtle-doves or two young pigeons, whichever he can afford, one for a sin-offering and the other 23 for a whole-offering. He shall bring them to the priest for his cleansing on the eighth day, at the entrance to the Tent of the Presence before 24 the LORD. The priest shall take the ram for the guilt-offering and the log of oil, and shall present them as a special gift before the LORD. 25 The ram for the guilt-offering shall then be slaughtered, and the priest shall take some of the blood of the guilt-offering, and put it on the lobe of the right ear of the man to be cleansed and on his right thumb and on the big toe of his right foot. 26 He shall pour some of the oil on 27 the palm of his own left hand and sprinkle some of it with his right forefinger seven times before the 28 LORD. He shall then put some of the oil remaining on his palm on the lobe of the right ear of the man to be cleansed, and on his right thumb and on the big toe of his right foot exactly where the blood 29 of the guilt-offering was put. The remainder of the oil on the priest's palm shall be put upon the head of the man to be cleansed to make expiation for him before the LORD. 30 Of the birds which the man has been able to afford, turtle-doves or young pigeons, whichever it may 31 be, the priest shall deal with one as a sin-offering and with the other as a whole-offering and shall make the grain-offering with them. Thus the priest shall make expiation

l Or hyssop.   *m* Or mud.

before the LORD for the man who is to be cleansed. This is the law 32 for the man with a malignant skin-disease who cannot afford the regular offering for his cleansing.

The LORD spoke to Moses and 33 Aaron and said: When you have 34 entered the land of Canaan which I give you to occupy, if I inflict a fungous infection upon a house in the land you have occupied, its 35 owner shall come and report to the priest that there appears to him to be a patch of infection in his house. The priest shall order the 36 house to be cleared before he goes in to examine the infection, or everything in it will become unclean. After this the priest shall go 37 in to inspect the house. If on inspection he finds the patch on the walls consists of greenish or reddish depressions, apparently going deeper than the surface, he shall go out 38 of the house and, standing at the entrance, shall put it in quarantine for seven days. On the seventh day 39 he shall come back and inspect the house, and if the patch has spread in the walls, he shall order the in- 40 fected stones to be pulled out and thrown away outside the city in an unclean place. He shall then have 41 the house scraped inside throughout, and all the daub[m] they have scraped off shall be tipped outside the city in an unclean place. They 42 shall take fresh stones to replace the others and replaster the house with fresh daub.

If the infection reappears in the 43 house and spreads after the stones have been pulled out and the house scraped and redaubed, the priest 44 shall come and inspect it. If the infection has spread in the house, it is a corrosive growth; the house is unclean. The house shall be 45 demolished, stones, timber, and daub, and it shall all be taken away outside the city to an unclean place. Anyone who has entered the house 46 during the time it has been in quarantine shall be unclean till evening. Anyone who has slept or 47 eaten a meal in the house shall wash his clothes. But if, when the 48 priest goes into the house and inspects it, he finds that the infection has not spread after the redaubing, then he shall pronounce the house ritually clean, because the infection has been cured.

In order to rid the house of im- 49 purity, he shall take two small birds, cedar-wood, scarlet thread, and marjoram. He shall kill one of the 50 birds over an earthenware bowl containing fresh water. He shall 51 then take the cedar-wood, marjoram, and scarlet thread, together with the living bird, dip them in the blood of the bird that has been killed and in the fresh water, and sprinkle the house seven times. Thus he shall purify the house, 52 using the blood of the bird, the fresh water, the living bird, the cedar-wood, the marjoram, and 53 the scarlet thread. He shall set the living bird free outside the city to fly away over the open country, and make expiation for the house; and then it shall be clean.

54 This is the law for all malignant 55 skin-diseases, and for scurf, for mould in clothes and fungus in 56 houses, for a discoloration of the 57 skin, scab, and inflammation, to declare when these are pronounced unclean and when clean. This is the law for skin-disease, mould, and fungus.

15 The LORD spoke to Moses and 2 Aaron and said, Speak to the Israelites and say to them: When any man has a discharge from his body, the 3 discharge is ritually unclean. This is the law concerning the uncleanness due to his discharge whether it continues or has been stopped; in either case he is unclean.

4 Every bed on which the man with a discharge lies down shall be ritually unclean, and everything on which he sits shall be unclean. 5 Any man who touches the bed shall wash his clothes, bathe in water and remain unclean till even- 6 ing. Whoever sits on anything on which the man with a discharge has sat shall wash his clothes, bathe in water and remain unclean till even- 7 ing. Whoever touches the body of the man with a discharge shall wash his clothes, bathe in water and re- 8 main unclean till evening. If the man spits on one who is ritually clean, the latter shall wash his clothes, bathe in water and remain 9 unclean till evening. Everything on which the man sits when riding shall 10 be unclean. Whoever touches anything that has been under him shall be unclean till evening, and whoever handles such things shall wash his clothes, bathe in water and 11 remain unclean till evening. Anyone whom the man with a discharge touches without having rinsed his hands in water shall wash his clothes, bathe in water and remain 12 unclean till evening. Any earthenware bowl touched by the man shall be smashed, and every wooden bowl shall be rinsed with water.

13 When the man is cleansed from his discharge, he shall reckon seven days to his cleansing, wash his clothes, bathe his body in fresh 14 water and be ritually clean. On the eighth day he shall obtain two turtle-doves or two young pigeons and, coming before the LORD at the entrance to the Tent of the 15 Presence, shall give them to the priest. The priest shall deal with one as a sin-offering and the other as a whole-offering, and shall make for him before the LORD the expiation required by the discharge.

16 When a man has emitted semen, he shall bathe his whole body in water and be unclean till evening. 17 Every piece of clothing or skin on which there is any semen shall be washed and remain unclean till 18 evening. This applies also to the woman with whom a man has had intercourse; they shall both bathe themselves in water and remain unclean till evening.

19 When a woman has a discharge of blood, her impurity shall last for seven days; anyone who touches her shall be unclean till evening. 20 Everything on which she lies or 21 sits during her impurity shall be unclean. Anyone who touches her bed shall wash his clothes, bathe in water and remain unclean till even- 22 ing. Whoever touches anything on which she sits shall wash his clothes, bathe in water and remain unclean 23 till evening. If he is on the bed or seat where she is sitting, by touching it he shall become unclean till 24 evening. If a man goes so far as to have intercourse with her and any of her discharge gets on to him, then he shall be unclean for seven days, and every bed on which he lies down shall be unclean.

25 When a woman has a prolonged discharge of blood not at the time of her menstruation, or when her discharge continues beyond the period of menstruation, her impurity shall last all the time of her discharge; she shall be unclean as during the period of her menstrua- 26 tion. Any bed on which she lies during the time of her discharge shall be like that which she used during menstruation, and everything on which she sits shall be unclean as in her menstrual 27 uncleanness. Every person who touches them shall be unclean; he shall wash his clothes, bathe in water and remain unclean till even- 28 ing. If she is cleansed from her discharge, she shall reckon seven days and after that she shall be ritually 29 clean. On the eighth day she shall obtain two turtle-doves or two young pigeons and bring them to the priest at the entrance to the 30 Tent of the Presence. The priest shall deal with one as a sin-offering and with the other as a whole-offering, and make for her before the LORD the expiation required 31 by her unclean discharge.

In this way you shall warn the Israelites against uncleanness, in order that they may not bring uncleanness upon the Tabernacle where I dwell among them, and 32 so die. This is the law for the man who has a discharge, or who has an emission of semen and is thereby 33 unclean, and for the woman who is suffering her menstruation—for everyone, male or female, who has a discharge, and for the man who

n Or for Azazel.

has intercourse with a woman who is unclean.

The Day of Atonement

The LORD spoke to Moses after **16** the death of Aaron's two sons, who died when they offered illicit fire before the LORD. He said to 2 him: Tell your brother Aaron that he must not enter the sanctuary within the Veil, in front of the cover over the Ark, except at the appointed time, on pain of death; for I appear in the cloud above the cover. When Aaron enters the 3 sanctuary, this is what he shall do. He shall bring a young bull for a sin-offering and a ram for a whole-offering. He shall wear a sacred 4 linen tunic and linen drawers to cover himself, and he shall put a linen sash round his waist and wind a linen turban round his head; all these are sacred vestments, and he shall bathe in water before putting them on. He shall take from the 5 community of the Israelites two he-goats for a sin-offering and a ram for a whole-offering. He shall 6 present the bull as a sin-offering and make expiation for himself and his household. Then he shall take 7 the two he-goats and set them before the LORD at the entrance to the Tent of the Presence. He shall 8 cast lots over the two goats, one to be for the LORD and the other for the Precipice.[n] He shall present 9 the goat on which the lot for the LORD has fallen and deal with it as a sin-offering; but the goat on 10 which the lot for the Precipice has fallen shall be made to stand alive before the LORD, for expiation to be made over it before it is driven away into the wilderness to the Precipice.

Aaron shall present his bull as 11 a sin-offering, making expiation for himself and his household, and then slaughter the bull as a sin-offering. He shall take a firepan 12 full of glowing embers from the altar before the LORD, and two handfuls of powdered fragrant incense, and bring them within the Veil. He shall put the incense on 13 the fire before the LORD, and the cloud of incense will hide the cover over the Tokens so that he shall not die. He shall take some of the 14 bull's blood and sprinkle it with his finger both on the surface of the cover, eastwards, and seven times in front of the cover.

He shall then slaughter the peo- 15 ple's goat as a sin-offering, bring its blood within the Veil and do with its blood as he did with the bull's blood, sprinkling it on the cover and in front of it. He shall 16 make for the sanctuary the expiation required by the ritual uncleanness of the Israelites and their acts of rebellion, that is by all their sins; and he shall do the same for the

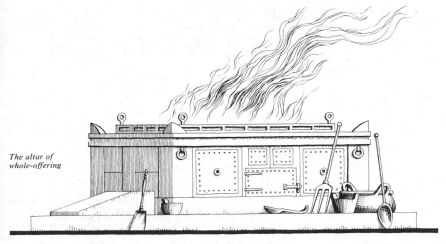

The altar of whole-offering

Tent of the Presence, which dwells among them in the midst of all their uncleanness. No other man shall be within the Tent of the Presence from the time when he enters the sanctuary to make expiation until he comes out, and he shall make expiation for himself, his household, and the whole assembly of Israel.

He shall then come out to the altar which is before the LORD and make expiation for it. He shall take some of the bull's blood and some of the goat's blood and put it all over the horns of the altar; he shall sprinkle some of the blood on the altar with his finger seven times. So he shall purify it from all the uncleanness of the Israelites and hallow it.

When Aaron has finished making expiation for the sanctuary, for the Tent of the Presence, and for the altar, he shall bring forward the live goat. He shall lay both his hands on its head and confess over it all the iniquities of the Israelites and all their acts of rebellion, that is all their sins; he shall lay them on the head of the goat and send it away into the wilderness in charge of a man who is waiting ready. The goat shall carry all their iniquities upon itself into some barren waste and the man shall let it go, there in the wilderness.

Aaron shall then enter the Tent of the Presence, take off the linen clothes which he had put on when he entered the sanctuary, and leave them there. He shall bathe in water in a consecrated place and put on his vestments; then he shall go out and perform his own whole-offering and that of the people, thus making expiation for himself and for the people. He shall burn the fat of

the sin-offering upon the altar. The man who drove the goat away to the Precipice shall wash his clothes and bathe in water, and not till then may he enter the camp. The two sin-offerings, the bull and the goat, the blood of which was brought within the Veil to make expiation in the sanctuary, shall be taken outside the camp and destroyed by fire—skin, flesh, and offal. The man who burns them shall wash his clothes and bathe in water, and not till then may he enter the camp.

This shall become a rule binding on you for all time. On the tenth day of the seventh month you shall mortify yourselves; you shall do no work, whether native Israelite or alien settler, because on this day expiation shall be made on your behalf to cleanse you, and so make you clean before the LORD from all your sins. This is a sabbath of sacred rest for you, and you shall mortify yourselves; it is a rule binding for all time. Expiation shall be made by the priest duly anointed and installed to serve in succession to his father; he shall put on the sacred linen clothes and shall make expiation for the holy sanctuary, the Tent of the Presence, and the altar, on behalf of the priests and the whole assembly of the people. This shall become a rule binding on you for all time, to make for the Israelites once a year the expiation required by all their sins.

And Moses carried out the LORD's commands.

The one place of sacrifice

17 The LORD spoke to Moses and said, Speak to Aaron, his sons, and all the Israelites in these words:

o Or satyrs.

This is what the LORD has commanded. Any Israelite who slaughters an ox, a sheep, or a goat, either inside or outside the camp, and does not bring it to the entrance of the Tent of the Presence to present it as an offering to the LORD before the Tabernacle of the LORD shall be held guilty of bloodshed: that man has shed blood and shall be cut off from his people. The purpose is that the Israelites should bring to the LORD the animals which they slaughter in the open country; they shall bring them to the priest at the entrance to the Tent of the Presence and sacrifice them as shared-offerings to the LORD. The priest shall fling the blood against the altar of the LORD at the entrance to the Tent of the Presence, and burn the fat as a soothing odour to the LORD. They shall no longer sacrifice their slaughtered beasts to the demons° whom they wantonly follow. This shall be a rule binding on them and their descendants for all time.

You shall say to them: Any Israelite or alien settled in Israel who offers a whole-offering or a sacrifice and does not bring it to the entrance of the Tent of the Presence to sacrifice it to the LORD shall be cut off from his father's kin.

Eating blood forbidden

If any Israelite or alien settled in Israel eats any blood, I will set my face against the eater and cut him off from his people, because the life of a creature is the blood, and I appoint it to make expiation on the altar for yourselves: it is the blood, that is the life, that makes expiation. Therefore I have told the Israelites that neither you, nor any alien settled among you, shall eat blood.

13 Any Israelite or alien settled in Israel who hunts beasts or birds that may lawfully be eaten shall drain out the blood and cover it 14 with earth, because the life of every living creature is the blood, and I have forbidden the Israelites to eat the blood of any creature, because the life of every creature is its blood: every man who eats it shall be cut off.

15 Every person, native or alien, who eats that which has died a natural death or has been mauled by wild beasts shall wash his clothes and bathe in water, and remain ritually unclean till evening; 16 then he shall be clean. If he does not wash his clothes and bathe his body, he must accept responsibility.

Immorality forbidden

18 The LORD spoke to Moses and 2 said, Speak to the Israelites in these words: I am the LORD your 3 God. You shall not do as they do in Egypt where you once dwelt, nor shall you do as they do in the land of Canaan to which I am bringing you; you shall not conform to their 4 institutions. You must keep my laws and conform to my institutions without fail: I am the LORD 5 your God. You shall observe my institutions and my laws: the man who keeps them shall have life through them. I am the LORD.

6 No man shall approach a blood-relation for intercourse. I am the 7 LORD. You shall not bring shame on your father by intercourse with your mother: she is your mother; you shall not bring shame upon 8 her. You shall not have intercourse with your father's wife: that is to 9 bring shame upon your father. You shall not have intercourse with your sister, your father's daughter, or your mother's daughter, whether brought up in the family or in another home; you shall not bring 10 shame upon them. You shall not have intercourse with your son's daughter or your daughter's daughter: that is to bring shame upon 11 yourself. You shall not have intercourse with a daughter of your father's wife, begotten by your father: she is your sister, and you shall not bring shame upon her. 12 You shall not have intercourse with your father's sister: she is a 13 blood-relation of your father. You shall not have intercourse with your mother's sister: she is a blood-14 relation of your mother. You shall not bring shame upon your father's brother by approaching his wife: 15 she is your aunt. You shall not have intercourse with your daughter-in-law: she is your son's wife; you shall not bring shame upon her. 16 You shall not have intercourse with your brother's wife: that is

17 to bring shame upon him. You shall not have intercourse with both a woman and her daughter, nor shall you take her son's daughter or her daughter's daughter to have intercourse with them: they are her blood-relations, and such 18 conduct is lewdness. You shall not take a woman who is your wife's sister to make her a rival-wife, and to have intercourse with her during her sister's lifetime.

19 You shall not approach a woman to have intercourse with her during 20 her period of menstruation. You shall not have sexual intercourse with the wife of your fellow-countryman and so make yourself 21 unclean with her. You shall not surrender any of your children to Molech and thus profane the name 22 of your God: I am the LORD. You shall not lie with a man as with a woman: that is an abomination. 23 You shall not have sexual intercourse with any beast to make yourself unclean with it, nor shall a woman submit herself to intercourse with a beast: that is a viola-24 tion of nature. You shall not make yourselves unclean in any of these ways; for in these ways the heathen, whom I am driving out before you, 25 made themselves unclean. This is how the land became unclean, and I punished it for its iniquity so that 26 it spewed out its inhabitants. You, unlike them, shall keep my laws and my rules: none of you, whether natives or aliens settled among you, shall do any of these abominable 27 things. The people who were there before you did these abominable things and the land became un-28 clean. So the land will not spew you out for making it unclean as it 29 spewed them out; for anyone who does any of these abominable things shall be cut off from his people. 30 Observe my charge, therefore, and follow none of the abominable institutions customary before your time; do not make yourselves unclean with them. I am the LORD your God.

Rules about conduct

19 The LORD spoke to Moses and 2 said, Speak to all the community of the Israelites in these words: You shall be holy, because I, the LORD 3 your God, am holy. You shall revere, every man of you, his mother and his father. You shall keep my sabbaths. I am the LORD 4 your God. Do not resort to idols; you shall not make gods of cast metal for yourselves. I am the LORD your God.

5 When you sacrifice a shared-offering to the LORD, you shall slaughter it so as to win acceptance 6 for yourselves. It must be eaten on the day of your sacrifice or the next day. Whatever is left over till the third day shall be destroyed by

fire; it is tainted, and if any of it 7 is eaten on the third day, it will not be acceptable. He who eats it must 8 accept responsibility, because he has profaned the holy-gift to the LORD: that person shall be cut off from his father's kin.

When you reap the harvest of 9 your land, you shall not reap right into the edges of your field; neither shall you glean the loose ears of your crop; you shall not completely 10 strip your vineyard nor glean the fallen grapes. You shall leave them for the poor and the alien. I am the LORD your God.

You shall not steal; you shall 11 not cheat or deceive a fellow-countryman. You shall not swear 12 in my name with intent to deceive and thus profane the name of your God. I am the LORD. You shall not 13 oppress your neighbour, nor rob him. You shall not keep back a hired man's wages till next morning. You shall not treat the deaf 14 with contempt, nor put an obstruction in the way of the blind. You shall fear your God. I am the LORD.

You shall not pervert justice, 15 either by favouring the poor or by subservience to the great. You shall judge your fellow-countryman with strict justice. You shall not go 16 about spreading slander among your father's kin, nor take sides against your neighbour on a capital charge. I am the LORD. You shall 17 not nurse hatred against your brother. You shall reprove your fellow-countryman frankly and so you will have no share in his guilt.ᵖ You 18 shall not seek revenge, or cherish anger towards your kinsfolk; you shall love your neighbour as a man like yourself. I am the LORD.

You shall keep my rules. You 19 shall not allow two different kinds of beast to mate together. You shall not plant your field with two kinds of seed. You shall not put on a garment woven with two kinds of yarn.

When a man has intercourse with 20 a slave-girl who has been assigned to another man and neither ransomed nor given her freedom, inquiry shall be made. They shall not be put to death, because she has not been freed. The man shall 21 bring his guilt-offering, a ram, to the LORD to the entrance of the Tent of the Presence, and with it 22 the priest shall make expiation for him before the LORD for his sin, and he shall be forgiven the sin he has committed.

When you enter the land, and 23 plant any kind of tree for food, you shall treat it as bearing forbidden fruit. For three years it shall be forbidden and may not be eaten. In the fourth year all its 24 fruit shall be a holy-gift to the LORD, and this releases it for use. In the fifth year you may eat its 25

p Or and for that you will incur no blame.

fruit, and thus the yield it gives you shall be increased. I am the LORD your God.

26 You shall not eat meat with the blood in it. You shall not practise
27 divination or soothsaying. You shall not round off your hair from side to side, and you shall not shave
28 the edge of your beards. You shall not gash yourselves in mourning for the dead; you shall not tattoo yourselves. I am the LORD.

29 Do not prostitute your daughter and so make her a whore; thus the land shall not play the prostitute
30 and be full of lewdness. You shall keep my sabbaths, and revere my sanctuary. I am the LORD.

31 Do not resort to ghosts and spirits, nor make yourselves unclean by seeking them out. I am the LORD your God.

32 You shall rise in the presence of grey hairs, give honour to the aged, and fear your God. I am the LORD.

33 When an alien settles with you in your land, you shall not oppress
34 him. He shall be treated as a native born among you, and you shall love him as a man like yourself, because you were aliens in Egypt. I am the LORD your God.

35 You shall not pervert justice in measurement of length, weight, or
36 quantity. You shall have true scales, true weights, true measures dry and liquid. I am the LORD your God who brought you out of
37 Egypt. You shall observe all my rules and laws and carry them out. I am the LORD.

Penalties for disobedience

20 The LORD spoke to Moses and
2 said, Say to the Israelites: Any Israelite or alien settled in Israel who gives any of his children to Molech shall be put to death: the common people shall stone him.
3 I, for my part, set my face against that man and cut him off from his people, because he has given a child of his to Molech, thus making my sanctuary unclean and profan-
4 ing my holy name. If the common people connive at it when a man has given a child of his to Molech
5 and do not put him to death, I will set my face against man and family, and both him and all who follow him in his wanton following after Molech,*q* I will cut off from their people.
6 I will set my face against the man who wantonly resorts to ghosts and spirits, and I will cut that person off
7 from his people. Hallow yourselves and be holy, because I the LORD
8 your God am holy. You shall keep my rules and obey them: I am the LORD who hallows you.
9 When any man reviles his father and his mother, he shall be put to death. He has reviled his father and his mother; his blood shall be on
10 his own head. If a man commits

adultery with his neighbour's wife, both adulterer and adulteress shall
11 be put to death. The man who has intercourse with his father's wife has brought shame on his father. They shall both be put to death; their blood shall be on their own
12 heads. If a man has intercourse with his daughter-in-law, they shall both be put to death. Their deed is a violation of nature; their blood
13 shall be on their own heads. If a man has intercourse with a man as with a woman, they both commit an abomination. They shall be put to death; their blood shall be on
14 their own heads. If a man takes both a woman and her mother, that is lewdness. Both he and they shall be burnt; thus there shall be no
15 lewdness in your midst. A man who has sexual intercourse with any beast shall be put to death, and
16 you shall kill the beast. If a woman approaches any animal to have intercourse with it, you shall kill both woman and beast. They shall be put to death; their blood shall
17 be on their own heads. If a man takes his sister, his father's daughter or his mother's daughter, and they see one another naked, it is a scandalous disgrace. They shall be cut off in the presence of their people. The man has had inter-
18 course with his sister and he shall accept responsibility. If a man lies with a woman during her monthly period and brings shame upon her, he has exposed her discharge and she has uncovered the source of her discharge; they shall both be
19 cut off from their people. You shall not have intercourse with your mother's sister or your father's sister: it is the exposure of a blood-relation. They shall accept respon-
20 sibility. A man who has intercourse with his uncle's wife has brought shame upon his uncle. They shall accept responsibility for their sin and shall be proscribed and put to
21 death. If a man takes his brother's wife, it is impurity. He has brought shame upon his brother; they shall be proscribed.
22 You shall keep all my rules and my laws and carry them out, that the land into which I am bringing you to live may not spew you out.
23 You shall not conform to the institutions of the nations whom I am driving out before you: they did all these things and I abhorred
24 them, and I told you that you should occupy their land, and I would give you possession of it, a land flowing with milk and honey. I am the LORD your God: I have made a clear separation between
25 you and the nations, and you shall make a clear separation between clean beasts and unclean beasts and between unclean and clean birds. You shall not make yourselves vile through beast or bird or anything

that creeps on the ground, for I have made a clear separation between them and you, declaring them unclean. You shall be holy 26 to me, because I the LORD am holy. I have made a clear separation between you and the heathen, that you may belong to me. Any man 27 or woman among you who calls up ghosts or spirits shall be put to death. The people shall stone them; their blood shall be on their own heads.

Holiness of the priests

The LORD said to Moses, Say to **21** the priests, the sons of Aaron: A priest shall not render himself unclean for the death of any of his kin except for a near blood-relation, 2 that is for mother, father, son, daughter, brother, or full sister 3 who is unmarried and a virgin; nor shall he make himself unclean 4 for any married woman*r* among his father's kin, and so profane himself.

Priests shall not make bald 5 patches on their heads as a sign of mourning, nor cut the edges of their beards, nor gash their bodies. They shall be holy to their God, 6 and they shall not profane the name of their God, because they present the food-offerings of the LORD, the food of their God, and they shall be holy. A priest shall 7 not marry a prostitute or a girl who has lost her virginity, nor shall he marry a woman divorced from her husband; for he is holy to his God. You shall keep him holy because 8 he presents the food of your God; you shall regard him as holy because I the LORD, who hallow them, am holy. When a priest's 9 daughter profanes herself by becoming a prostitute, she profanes her father. She shall be burnt to death.

The high priest, the one among 10 his fellows who has had the anointing oil poured on his head and has been consecrated to wear the vestments, shall neither leave his hair dishevelled nor tear his clothes. He 11 shall not enter the place where any man's dead body lies; not even for his father or his mother shall he render himself unclean. He shall 12 not go out of the sanctuary for fear that he dishonour the sanctuary of his God, because the consecration of the anointing oil of his God is upon him. I am the LORD. He shall 13 marry a woman who is still a virgin. He shall not marry a widow, a 14 divorced woman, a woman who has lost her virginity, or a prostitute, but only a virgin from his father's kin; he shall not dis- 15 honour his descendants among his father's kin, for I am the LORD who hallows him.

The LORD spoke to Moses and 16 said, Speak to Aaron in these 17

q Or in his lusting after human sacrifice. *r for any married woman: prob. rdg.; Heb. husband.*

words: No man among your descendants for all time who has any physical defect shall come and present the food of his God. No man with a defect shall come, whether a blind man, a lame man, a man stunted or overgrown, a man deformed in foot or hand, or with mis-shapen brows or a film over his eye or a discharge from it, a man who has a scab or eruption or has had a testicle ruptured. No descendant of Aaron the priest who has any defect in his body shall approach to present the food-offerings of the LORD; because he has a defect he shall not approach to present the food of his God. He may eat the bread of God both from the holy-gifts and from the holiest of holy-gifts, but he shall not come up to the Veil nor approach the altar, because he has a defect in his body. Thus he shall not profane my sanctuaries, because I am the LORD who hallows them. Thus did Moses speak to Aaron and his sons and to all the Israelites.

Holiness of offerings

22 The LORD spoke to Moses and said, Tell Aaron and his sons that they must be careful in the handling of the holy-gifts of the Israelites which they hallow to me, lest they profane my holy name. I am the LORD. Say to them: Any man of your descent for all time who while unclean approaches the holy-gifts which the Israelites hallow to the LORD shall be cut off from my presence. I am the LORD. No man descended from Aaron who suffers from a malignant skin-disease, or has a discharge, shall eat of the holy-gifts until he is cleansed. A man who touches anything which makes him unclean or who has an emission of semen, a man who touches any vermin which makes him unclean or any human being who makes him unclean: any person who touches such a thing shall be unclean till sunset and unless he washes his body shall not eat of the holy-gifts. When the sun goes down, he shall be clean, and after that he may eat from the holy-gifts, because they are his food. He shall not eat an animal that has died a natural death or has been mauled by wild beasts, thereby making himself unclean. I am the LORD. The priests shall observe my charge, lest they make themselves guilty and die for profaning my name. I am the LORD who hallows them. No unqualified person may eat any holy-gift; nor may a stranger lodging with a priest or a hired man eat a holy-gift. A slave bought by a priest with his own money may do so, and slaves born in his household may also share his food. When a priest's daughter marries

an unqualified person, she shall not eat any of the contributions of holy-gifts; but if she is widowed or divorced and is childless and comes back to her father's house as in her childhood, she shall share her father's food. No unqualified person may eat any of it. When a man inadvertently eats a holy-gift, he shall make good the holy-gift to the priest, adding a fifth to its value. The priests shall not profane the holy-gifts of the Israelites which they set aside for the LORD; they shall not let men eat their holy-gifts and so incur guilt and its penalty, because I am the LORD who hallows them. The LORD spoke to Moses and said, Speak to Aaron and his sons and to all the Israelites in these words: When any man of the house of Israel or any alien in Israel presents, whether in fulfilment of a vow or for a freewill offering, such an offering as is presented to the LORD for a whole-offering so as to win acceptance for yourselves, it shall be a male without defect, of cattle, sheep, or goats. You shall not present anything which is defective, because it will not be acceptable on your behalf. When a man presents a shared-offering to the LORD, whether cattle or sheep, to fulfil a special⁵ vow or as a freewill offering, if it is to be acceptable it must be perfect; there shall be no defect in it. You shall present to the LORD nothing blind, disabled, mutilated, with running sore, scab, or eruption, nor set any such creature on the altar as a food-offering to the LORD. If a bull or a sheep is overgrown or stunted, you may make of it a freewill offering, but it will not be acceptable in fulfilment of a vow. If its testicles have been crushed or bruised, torn or cut, you shall not present it to the LORD; this is forbidden in your land. You shall not procure any such creature from a foreigner and present it as food for your God. Their deformity is inherent in them, a permanent defect, and they will not be acceptable on your behalf. The LORD spoke to Moses and said: When a calf, a lamb, or a kid is born, it must not be taken from its mother for seven days. From the eighth day onwards it will be acceptable when offered as a food-offering to the LORD. You shall not slaughter a cow or sheep at the same time as its young. When you make a thank-offering to the LORD, you shall sacrifice it so as to win acceptance for yourselves; it shall be eaten that same day, and none be left till morning. I am the LORD. You shall observe my commandments and perform them. I am the LORD. You shall not profane my

holy name; I will be hallowed among the Israelites. I am the LORD who hallows you, who brought you out of Egypt to become your God. I am the LORD.

The appointed seasons

23 The LORD spoke to Moses and said, Speak to the Israelites in these words: These are the appointed seasons of the LORD, and you shall proclaim them as sacred assemblies; these are my appointed seasons. On six days work may be done, but every seventh day is a sabbath of sacred rest, a day of sacred assembly, on which you shall do no work. Wherever you live, it is the LORD's sabbath.

These are the appointed seasons of the LORD, the sacred assemblies which you shall proclaim in their appointed order. In the first month on the fourteenth day between dusk and dark is the LORD's Passover. On the fifteenth day of this month begins the LORD's pilgrim-feast of Unleavened Bread; for seven days you shall eat unleavened cakes. On the first day there shall be a sacred assembly; you shall not do your daily work. For seven days you shall present your food-offerings to the LORD. On the seventh day also there shall be a sacred assembly; you shall not do your daily work.

The LORD spoke to Moses and said, Speak to the Israelites in these words: When you enter the land which I give you, and you reap its harvest, you shall bring the first sheaf of your harvest to the priest. He shall present the sheaf as a special gift before the LORD onᵗ the day after the sabbath, so as to gain acceptance for yourselves. On the day you present the sheaf, you shall prepare a perfect yearling ram for a whole-offering to the LORD, with the proper grain-offering, two tenths of an ephah of flour mixed with oil, as a food-offering to the LORD, of soothing odour, and also with the proper drink-offering, a quarter of a hin of wine. You shall eat neither bread, nor grain, parched or fully ripened, during that day, the day on which you bring your God his offering; this is a rule binding on your descendants for all time wherever you live.

From the day after the sabbath, the day on which you bring your sheaf as a special gift, you shall count seven full weeks. The day after the seventh sabbath will make fifty days, and then you shall present to the LORD a grain-offering from the new crop. You shall bring from your homes two loaves as a special gift; they shall contain two tenths of an ephah of flour and shall be baked with leaven. They are the LORD's firstfruits. In addition to the bread you shall present seven perfect yearling sheep, one young bull, and two rams. They shall be a whole-offering to the LORD with the proper grain-offering and the proper drink-offering, a food-offering of soothing odour to the LORD.

19 You shall also prepare one he-goat for a sin-offering and two yearling sheep for a shared-offering,

20 and the priest shall present them in addition to the bread of the first-fruits as a special gift before the LORD. They shall be a holy-gift to

21 the LORD for the priest. On that same day you shall proclaim a sacred assembly for yourselves; you shall not do your daily work. This is a rule binding on your descendants for all time wherever you live.

22 When you reap the harvest in your land, you shall not reap right into the edges of your field, neither shall you glean the fallen ears. You shall leave them for the poor and for the alien. I am the LORD your God.

23 The LORD spoke to Moses and

24 said, Speak to the Israelites in these words: In the seventh month you shall keep the first day as a sacred rest, a day of remembrance and acclamation, a day of sacred assem-

25 bly. You shall not do your daily work; you shall present a food-offering to the LORD.

26 The LORD spoke to Moses and

27 said: Further, the tenth day of this seventh month is the Day of Atonement. There shall be a sacred assembly; you shall mortify yourselves and present a food-offering

28 to the LORD. On that same day you shall do no work because it is a day of expiation, to make expiation for you before the LORD your God.

29 Therefore every person who does not mortify himself on that day shall be cut off from his father's

30 kin. I will extirpate any person who

31 does any work on that day. You shall do no work; it is a rule binding on your descendants for all

32 time wherever you live. It is for you a sabbath of sacred rest, and you shall mortify yourselves. From the evening of the ninth day to the following evening you shall keep your sabbath-rest.

33 The LORD spoke to Moses and

34 said, Speak to the Israelites in these words: On the fifteenth day of this seventh month the LORD's pilgrim-feast of Tabernacles[u] begins, and

35 it lasts for seven days. On the first day there shall be a sacred assembly; you shall not do your daily

36 work. For seven days you shall present a food-offering to the LORD; and on the eighth day there shall be a sacred assembly, and you shall present a food-offering to the LORD. It is the closing ceremony; you shall not do your daily work.

37 These are the appointed seasons of the LORD which you shall proclaim as sacred assemblies for presenting food-offerings to the LORD, whole-offerings and grain-offerings, shared-offerings and drink-offerings, each on its day,

38 besides the LORD's sabbaths and all your gifts, your vows, and your freewill offerings to the LORD.

39 Further, from the fifteenth day of the seventh month, when the harvest has been gathered, you shall keep the LORD's pilgrim-feast for seven days. The first day is a sacred rest and so is the eighth day.

40 On the first day you shall take the fruit of citrus-trees, palm fronds, and leafy branches, and willows[v] from the riverside, and you shall rejoice before the LORD your God

41 for seven days. You shall keep this as a pilgrim-feast in the LORD's honour for seven days every year. It is a rule binding for all time on your descendants; in the seventh month you shall hold this pilgrim-

42 feast. You shall live in arbours for seven days, all who are native

43 Israelites, so that your descendants may be reminded how I made the Israelites live in arbours when I brought them out of Egypt. I am the LORD your God.

44 Thus Moses announced to the Israelites the appointed seasons of the LORD.

Tending the lamps

24 The LORD spoke to Moses and

2 said: Command the Israelites to take pure oil of pounded olives ready for the regular mounting of

3 the lamp outside the Veil of the Tokens in the Tent of the Presence. Aaron shall keep the lamp in trim regularly from dusk to dawn before the LORD: this is a rule binding on your descendants

4 for all time. The lamps on the lamp-stand, ritually clean, shall be regularly kept in trim by him before the LORD.

Bread of the Presence

5 You shall take flour and bake it into twelve loaves, two tenths of

6 an ephah to each. You shall arrange them in two rows, six to a row on the table, ritually clean, before the

7 LORD. You shall sprinkle pure frankincense on the rows, and this shall be a token of the bread, offered to the LORD as a food-

8 offering. Sabbath after sabbath he shall arrange it regularly before the LORD as a gift from the Israelites.

9 This is a covenant for ever; it is the privilege of Aaron and his sons, and they shall eat the bread in a holy place, because it is the holiest of holy-gifts. It is his due out of the food-offerings of the LORD for all time.

Various penalties

10-11 Now there was in the Israelite camp a man whose mother was an Israelite and his father an Egyptian; his mother's name was Shelomith daughter of Dibri of the tribe of Dan; and he went out and became involved in a brawl with an Israelite of pure descent. He uttered the Holy Name in blasphemy, so

12 they brought him to Moses; and they kept him in custody until the LORD's will should be clearly made known to them.

13 The LORD spoke to Moses and

14 said, Take the man who blasphemed out of the camp. Everyone who heard him shall put a hand[w] on his head, and then all the community shall stone him to death.

15 You shall say to the Israelites: When any man whatever blasphemes his God, he shall accept

16 responsibility for his sin. Whoever utters the Name of the LORD shall be put to death: all the community shall stone him; alien or native, if he utters the Name, he shall be put to death.

17 When one man strikes another and kills him, he shall be put to

18 death. Whoever strikes a beast and kills it shall make restitution, life

19 for life. When one man injures and disfigures his fellow-countryman, it shall be done to him as he has done;

20 fracture for fracture, eye for eye, tooth for tooth; the injury and disfigurement that he has inflicted upon another shall in turn be inflicted upon him.

21 Whoever strikes a beast and kills it shall make restitution, but whoever strikes a man and kills him

22 shall be put to death. You shall have one penalty for alien and native alike. For I am the LORD your God.

23 Thus did Moses speak to the Israelites, and they took the man who blasphemed out of the camp and stoned him to death. The Israelites did as the LORD had commanded Moses.

Sabbath years and the year of jubilee

25 The LORD spoke to Moses on Mount Sinai and said, Speak to

2 the Israelites in these words: When you enter the land which I give you, the land shall keep sabbaths

3 to the LORD. For six years you may sow your fields and for six years prune your vineyards and gather

4 the harvest, but in the seventh year the land shall keep a sabbath of sacred rest, a sabbath to the LORD. You shall not sow your

5 field nor prune your vineyard. You shall not harvest the crop that grows from fallen grain, nor gather in the grapes from the unpruned vines. It shall be a year of sacred

6 rest for the land. Yet what the land

u Or Booths or Arbours.   _v Or poplars._   _w Or their hands._

itself produces in the sabbath year shall be food for you, for your male and female slaves, for your hired man, and for the stranger

7 lodging under your roof, for your cattle and for the wild animals in your country. Everything it produces may be used for food.

8 　You shall count seven sabbaths of years, that is seven times seven

9 years, forty-nine years, and in the seventh month on the tenth day of the month, on the Day of Atonement, you shall send the ram's horn round. You shall send it through

10 all your land to sound a blast, and so you shall hallow the fiftieth year and proclaim liberation in the land for all its inhabitants. You shall make this your year of jubilee. Every man of you shall return to his patrimony, every man to his

11 family. The fiftieth year shall be your jubilee. You shall not sow, and you shall not harvest the self-sown crop, nor shall you gather in the grapes from the unpruned vines,

12 because it is a jubilee, to be kept holy by you. You shall eat the produce direct from the land.

13 　In this year of jubilee you shall

14 return, every one of you, to his patrimony. When you sell or buy land amongst yourselves, neither party shall drive a hard bargain.

15 You shall pay your fellow-countryman according to the number of years since the jubilee, and he shall sell to you according to the num-

16 ber of annual crops. The more years there are to run, the higher the price, the fewer the years, the lower, because he is selling you a

17 series of crops. You must not victimize one another, but you shall fear your God, because I am

18 the LORD your God. Observe my statutes, keep my judgements and carry them out; and you shall live

19 in the land in security. The land shall yield its harvest; you shall eat your fill and live there secure.

20 If you ask what you are to eat during the seventh year, seeing that you will neither sow nor gather the

21 harvest, I will ordain my blessing for you in the sixth year and the land shall produce a crop to carry

22 over three years. When you sow in the eighth year, you will still be eating from the earlier crop; you shall eat the old until the new crop is gathered in the ninth year.

23 　No land shall be sold outright, because the land is mine, and you

24 are coming into it as aliens and settlers. Throughout the whole land of your patrimony, you shall allow land which has been sold to be

25 redeemed.
　When one of you is reduced to poverty and sells part of his patrimony, his next-of-kin who has the duty of redemption shall come and redeem what his kinsman has sold.

26 When a man has no such next-of-kin and himself becomes able to

27 afford its redemption, he shall take into account the years since the sale and pay the purchaser the balance up to the jubilee. Then he

28 may return to his patrimony. But if the man cannot afford to buy back the property, it shall remain in the hands of the purchaser till the year of jubilee. It shall then revert to the original owner, and he shall return to his patrimony.

29 　When a man sells a dwelling-house in a walled town, he shall retain the right of redemption till the end of the year of the sale; for a time he shall have the right of

30 redemption. If it is not redeemed before a full year is out, the house in the walled town shall vest in perpetuity in the buyer and his descendants; it shall not revert at

31 the jubilee. Houses in unwalled hamlets shall be treated as property in the open country: the right of redemption shall hold good, and in any case the house

32 shall revert at the jubilee. Levites shall have the perpetual right to redeem houses of their own patrimony in towns belonging to them.

33 If one of the Levites does not redeem his house in such a town, then it shall still revert to him at the jubilee, because the houses in Levite towns are their patrimony in

34 Israel. The common land surrounding their towns shall not be sold, because it is their property in perpetuity.

35 　When your brother-Israelite is reduced to poverty and cannot support himself in the community, you shall assist him as you would an alien or a stranger, and he shall

36 live with you. You shall not charge him interest on a loan, either by deducting it in advance from the capital sum, or by adding it on repayment. You shall fear your God, and your brother shall live

37 with you; you shall not deduct interest when advancing him money nor add interest to the payment due for food supplied on credit.

38 I am the LORD your God who brought you out of Egypt to give you the land of Canaan and to become your God.

39 　When your brother is reduced to poverty and sells himself to you, you shall not use him to work for

40 you as a slave. His status shall be that of a hired man or a stranger lodging with you; he shall work for you until the year of jubilee.

41 He shall then leave your service, with his children, and go back to his family and to his ancestral pro-

42 perty: because they are my slaves whom I brought out of Egypt, they shall not be sold as slaves are sold.

43 You shall not drive him with ruthless severity, but you shall fear

44 your God. Such slaves as you have, male or female, shall come from the nations round about you; from

45 them you may buy slaves. You may

also buy the children of those who have settled and lodge with you and such of their family as are born in the land. These may become your property, and you may 46 leave them to your sons after you; you may use them as slaves permanently. But your fellow-Israelites you shall not drive with ruthless severity.

　When an alien or a stranger living 47 with you becomes rich, and your brother becomes poor and sells himself to the alien or stranger or to a member of some alien family, he shall have the right of redemp- 48 tion after he has sold himself. One of his brothers may redeem him, or his uncle, his cousin, or any 49 blood-relation of his family, or, if he can afford it, he may redeem himself. He and his purchaser to- 50 gether shall reckon from the year when he sold himself to the year of jubilee, and the price shall be adjusted to the number of years. His period of service with his owner shall be reckoned at the rate of a hired man. If there are still many 51 years to run to the year of jubilee, he must repay for his redemption a proportionate amount of the sum for which he sold himself; if there 52 are few, he shall reckon and repay accordingly. He shall have the 53 status of a labourer hired from year to year, and you shall not let him be driven with ruthless severity by his owner. If the man is not re- 54 deemed in the intervening years, he and his children shall be released in the year of jubilee; for it is to 55 me that the Israelites are slaves, my slaves whom I brought out of Egypt. I am the LORD your God.

Blessings for obedience

You shall not make idols for your- **26** selves; you shall not erect a carved image or a sacred pillar; you shall not put a figured stone on your land to prostrate yourselves upon, because I am the LORD your God. You shall keep my sabbaths and 2 revere my sanctuary. I am the LORD.

　If you conform to my statutes, if 3 you observe my commandments and carry them out, I will give you 4 rain at the proper time; the land shall yield its produce and the trees of the country-side their fruit. Threshing shall last till vintage and 5 vintage till sowing; you shall eat your fill and live secure in your land. I will give peace in the land, and 6 you shall lie down to sleep with no one to terrify you. I will rid your land of dangerous beasts and it shall not be ravaged by war. You 7 shall put your enemies to flight and they shall fall in battle before you. Five of you shall pursue a hundred 8 and a hundred of you ten thousand; so shall your enemies fall in battle before you. I will look upon 9 you with favour, I will make you fruitful and increase your numbers: I will give my covenant with you 10 its full effect. Your old harvest shall last you in store until you have to clear out the old to make 11 room for the new. I will establish my Tabernacle among you and will not 12 spurn you. I will walk to and fro among you; I will become your God and you shall become my people. 13 I am the LORD your God who brought you out of Egypt and let you be their slaves no longer; I broke the bars of your yoke and enabled you to walk upright.

Punishments for disobedience

14 But if you do not listen to me, if you fail to keep all these command- 15 ments of mine, if you reject my sta- tutes, if you spurn my judgements, and do not obey all my command- 16 ments, but break my covenant, then be sure that this is what I will do: I will bring upon you sudden terror, wasting disease, recurrent fever, and plagues that dim the sight and cause the appetite to fail. You shall sow your seed to no purpose, for 17 your enemies shall eat the crop. I will set my face against you, and you shall be routed by your enemies. Those that hate you shall hound you on until you run when there is no pursuit. 18 If after all this you do not listen to me, I will go on to punish you 19 seven times over for your sins. I will break down your stubborn pride. I will make the sky above you like iron and the earth beneath 20 you like bronze. Your strength shall be spent in vain; your land shall not yield its produce nor the trees of the land their fruit. 21 If you still defy me and refuse to listen, I will multiply your calami- ties seven times, as your sins de- 22 serve. I will send wild beasts among you; they shall tear your children from you, destroy your cattle and bring your numbers low; and your 23 roads shall be deserted. If after all this you have not learnt discipline 24 but still defy me, I in turn will defy you and scourge you seven times 25 over for your sins. I will bring war in vengeance upon you, vengeance irrevocable under covenant; you shall be herded into your cities, I will send pestilence among you, and you shall be given over to the 26 enemy. I will cut short your daily bread until ten women can bake your bread in a single oven; they shall dole it out by weight, and though you eat, you shall not be satisfied. 27 If in spite of this you do not listen 28 to me and still defy me, I will defy you in anger, and I myself will pun- ish you seven times over for your 29 sins. Instead of meat you shall eat 30 your sons and your daughters. I will destroy your hill-shrines and demolish your incense-altars. I will

pile your rotting carcasses on the rotting logs^x that were your idols, 31 and I will spurn you. I will make your cities desolate and destroy your sanctuaries; the soothing odour of your offerings I will not accept. 32 I will destroy your land, and the enemies who occupy it shall be 33 appalled. I will scatter you among the heathen, and I will pursue you with the naked sword; your land shall be desolate and your cities 34 heaps of rubble. Then, all the time that it lies desolate, while you are in exile in the land of your enemies, your land shall enjoy its sabbaths 35 to the full. All the time of its desola- tion it shall have the sabbath rest which it did not have when you 36 lived there. And I will make those of you who are left in the land of your enemies so ridden with fear that, when a leaf flutters behind them in the wind, they shall run as if it were the sword behind them; they shall fall with no one in pur- 37 suit. Though no one pursues them they shall stumble over one an- other, as if the sword were behind them, and there shall be no stand 38 made against the enemy. You shall meet your end among the heathen, and your enemies' land shall swal- 39 low you up. Those who are left shall pine away in an enemy land under their own iniquities; and with their fathers' iniquities upon them too, they shall pine away as they did. 40 But though they confess their iniquity, their own and their fa- thers', their treachery, and even 41 their defiance of me, I will defy them in my turn and carry them off into their enemies' land. Yet if then their stubborn spirit is broken and they 42 accept their punishment in full, I will remember my covenant with Jacob and my covenant with Isaac, yes, and my covenant with Abra- ham, and I will remember the land. 43 The land shall be rid of its people and enjoy in full its sabbaths while it lies desolate, and they shall pay in full the penalty because they re- jected my judgements and spurned 44 my statutes. Yet even then, in their enemies' land, I shall not have re- jected nor spurned them, bringing them to an end and so breaking my covenant with them, because I 45 am the LORD their God. I will re- member on their behalf the cove- nant with the men of former times whom I brought out of Egypt in full sight of all the nations, that I might be their God. I am the LORD. 46 These are the statutes, the judge- ments, and the laws which the LORD established between himself and the Israelites on Mount Sinai through Moses.

Laws concerning dedications

27 The LORD spoke to Moses and 2 said, Speak to the Israelites in

these words: When a man makes a special^y vow to the LORD which requires your valuation of living persons, a male between twenty 3 and sixty years old shall be valued at fifty silver shekels, that is shekels by the sacred standard. If it is a 4 female, she shall be valued at thirty shekels. If the person is between 5 five years old and twenty, the valua- tion shall be twenty shekels for a male and ten for a female. If the 6 person is between a month and five years old, the valuation shall be five shekels for a male and three for a female. If the person is over sixty 7 and a male, the valuation shall be fifteen shekels, but if a female, ten shekels. If the man is too poor to 8 pay the amount of your valuation, the person shall be set before the priest, and the priest shall value him according to the sum which the man who makes the vow can afford: the priest shall make the valuation.

If the vow concerns a beast such 9 as may be offered as an offering to the LORD, then every gift shall be holy to the LORD. He shall not 10 change it for another, or substitute good for bad or bad for good. But if a substitution is in fact made of one beast for another, then both the original beast and its substitute shall be holy to the LORD. If the 11 vow concerns any unclean beast such as may not be offered as an offering to the LORD, then the animal shall be brought before the priest, and he shall value it whether 12 good or bad. The priest's valuation shall be decisive; in case of redemp- 13 tion the payment shall be increased by one fifth.

When a man dedicates his house 14 as holy to the LORD, the priest shall value it whether good or bad, and the priest's valuation shall be decisive. If the donor re- 15 deems his house, he shall pay the amount of the valuation increased by one fifth, and the house shall be his.

If a man dedicates to the LORD 16 part of his ancestral land, you shall value it according to the amount of seed-corn it can carry, at the rate of fifty shekels of silver for a homer of barley seed. If he dedicates his 17 land from the year of jubilee, it shall stand at your valuation; but 18 if he dedicates it after the year of jubilee, the priest shall estimate the price in silver according to the number of years remaining till the next year of jubilee, and this shall be deducted from your valuation. If the man who dedicates his field 19 should redeem it, he shall pay the amount of your valuation in silver, increased by one fifth, and it shall be his. If he does not redeem it 20 but sells the land to another man, it shall no longer be redeemable; when the land reverts at the year 21

x rotting logs: *or* effigies.   y makes a special: *or* discharges a . . .

of jubilee, it shall be like land that has been devoted, holy to the LORD. It shall belong to the priest as his patrimony.

22 If a man dedicates to the LORD land which he has bought, land which is not part of his ancestral 23 land, the priest shall estimate the amount of the value for the period until the year of jubilee, and the man shall give the amount fixed as at that day; it is holy to the 24 LORD. At the year of jubilee the land shall revert to the man from whom he bought it, whose patri- 25 mony it is. Every valuation you make shall be made by the sacred standard (twenty gerahs to the shekel).

26 Notwithstanding, no man may dedicate to the LORD the first-born of a beast which in any case has to be offered as a first-born, whether an ox or a sheep. It is the LORD's. 27 If it is any unclean beast, he may redeem it at your valuation and shall add one fifth; but if it is not redeemed, it shall be sold at your 28 valuation. Notwithstanding, no-thing which a man devotes to the LORD irredeemably from his own property, whether man or beast or ancestral land, may be sold or redeemed. Everything so devoted 29 is most holy to the LORD. No human being thus devoted may be redeemed, but he shall be put to death.

30 Every tithe on land, whether from grain or from the fruit of a tree, belongs to the LORD; it is holy to the LORD. If a man wishes 31 to redeem any of his tithe, he shall pay its value increased by one fifth. Every tenth creature that 32 passes under the counting rod shall be holy to the LORD; this applies to all tithes of cattle and sheep. There 33 shall be no inquiry whether it is good or bad, and no substitution. If any substitution is made, then both the tithe-animal and its sub-stitute shall be forfeit as holy; it shall not be redeemed.

34 These are the commandments which the LORD gave Moses for the Israelites on Mount Sinai.

NUMBERS

Numbering Israel at Sinai

1 On the first day of the second month in the second year after the Israelites came out of Egypt, the LORD spoke to Moses at the Tent of the Presence in the wilderness 2 of Sinai in these words: 'Number the whole community of Israel by families in the father's line, recording the name of every male person 3 aged twenty years and upwards fit for military service. You and Aaron are to make a detailed list of them 4 by their tribal hosts, and you shall have to assist you one head of 5 family from each tribe. These are their names:

of Reuben, Elizur son of Shedeur;
6 of Simeon, Shelumiel son of Zur-ishaddai;
7 of Judah, Nahshon son of Amminadab;
8 of Issachar, Nethaneel son of Zuar;
9 of Zebulun, Eliab son of Helon;
10 of Joseph: of Ephraim, Elishama son of Ammihud;
of Manasseh, Gamaliel son of Pedahzur;
11 of Benjamin, Abidan son of Gideoni;
12 of Dan, Ahiezer son of Ammishaddai;
13 of Asher, Pagiel son of Ocran;
14 of Gad, Eliasaph son of Reuel;
15 of Naphtali, Ahira son of Enan.'

16 These were the conveners of the whole community, chiefs of their fathers' tribes and heads of Israel-17 ite clans. So Moses and Aaron took these men who had been indicated 18 by name. They summoned the whole community on the first day of the second month, and they registered their descent by families in the father's line, recording every male person aged twenty years and 19 upwards, as the LORD had told Moses to do. Thus it was that he drew up the detailed lists in the wilderness of Sinai:

20 The tribal list of Reuben, Israel's eldest son, by families in the father's line, with the name of every male person aged twenty years and up-21 wards fit for service, the number in the list of the tribe of Reuben being forty-six thousand five hundred.

22 The tribal list of Simeon, by families in the father's line, with the name of every male person aged twenty years and upwards fit for 23 service, the number in the list of the tribe of Simeon being fifty-nine thousand three hundred.

24 The tribal list of Gad, by families in the father's line, with the names of all men aged twenty years and 25 upwards fit for service, the number in the list of the tribe of Gad being forty-five thousand six hundred and fifty.

26 The tribal list of Judah, by families in the father's line, with the names of all men aged twenty years and upwards fit for service, 27 the number in the list of the tribe of Judah being seventy-four thousand six hundred.

The tribal list of Issachar, by 28 families in the father's line, with the names of all men aged twenty years and upwards fit for service, the number in the list of the tribe 29 of Issachar being fifty-four thousand four hundred.

The tribal list of Zebulun, by 30 families in the father's line, with the names of all men aged twenty years and upwards fit for service, the number in the list of the tribe 31 of Zebulun being fifty-seven thousand four hundred.

The tribal lists of Joseph: that 32 of Ephraim, by families in the father's line, with the names of all men aged twenty years and up-wards fit for service, the number 33 in the list of the tribe of Ephraim being forty thousand five hundred; that of Manasseh, by families in 34 the father's line, with the names of all men aged twenty years and up-wards fit for service, the number 35 in the list of the tribe of Manasseh being thirty-two thousand two hundred.

The tribal list of Benjamin, by 36 families in the father's line, with the names of all men aged twenty years and upwards fit for service, the number in the list of the tribe 37 of Benjamin being thirty-five thousand four hundred.

The tribal list of Dan, by fami-38 lies in the father's line, with the

names of all men aged twenty years and upwards fit for service,
39 the number in the list of the tribe of Dan being sixty-two thousand seven hundred.
40 The tribal list of Asher, by families in the father's line, with the names of all men aged twenty years
41 and upwards fit for service, the number in the list of the tribe of Asher being forty-one thousand five hundred.
42 The tribal list of Naphtali, by families in the father's line, with the names of all men aged twenty years and upwards fit for service,
43 the number in the list of the tribe of Naphtali being fifty-three thousand four hundred.
44 These were the numbers recorded in the detailed lists by Moses and Aaron and the twelve chiefs of Israel, each representing one tribe
45 and being the head of a family. The total number of Israelites aged twenty years and upwards fit for service, recorded in the lists of
46 fathers' families, was six hundred and three thousand five hundred
47 and fifty. A list of the Levites by their fathers' families was not made.

The Levites appointed over the Tabernacle

48 The LORD spoke to Moses and
49 said, 'You shall not record the total number of the Levites or make a detailed list of them among the
50 Israelites. You shall put the Levites in charge of the Tabernacle of the Tokens, with its equipment and everything in it. They shall carry the Tabernacle and all its equipment; they alone shall be its attendants and shall pitch their tents
51 round it. The Levites shall take the Tabernacle down when it is due to move and shall put it up when it halts; any unqualified person who comes near it shall be put to
52 death. All other Israelites shall pitch their tents, each tribal host in its proper camp and under its
53 own standard. But the Levites shall encamp round the Tabernacle of the Tokens, so that divine wrath may not follow the whole community of Israel; the Tabernacle of the Tokens shall be in their keeping.'
54 The Israelites did exactly as the LORD had told Moses to do.

Plan of the camp

2 The LORD spoke to Moses and
2 Aaron and said, 'The Israelites shall encamp each under his own standard by the emblems of his father's family; they shall pitch their tents round the Tent of the Presence, facing it.
3 'In front of it, on the east, the division of Judah shall be stationed under the standard of its camp by tribal hosts. The chief of

Judah shall be Nahshon son of
4 Amminadab. His host, with its members as detailed, numbers seventy-four thousand six hundred
5 men. Next to Judah the tribe of Issachar shall be stationed. Its chief shall be Nethaneel son of
6 Zuar; his host, with its members as detailed, numbers fifty-four
7 thousand four hundred. Then the tribe of Zebulun: its chief shall be
8 Eliab son of Helon; his host, with its members as detailed, numbers fifty-seven thousand four hundred.
9 The number listed in the camp of Judah, by hosts, is one hundred and eighty-six thousand four hundred. They shall be the first to march.
10 'To the south the division of Reuben shall be stationed under the standard of its camp by tribal hosts. The chief of Reuben shall be
11 Elizur son of Shedeur; his host, with its members as detailed, numbers forty-six thousand five hun-
12 dred. Next to him the tribe of Simeon shall be stationed. Its chief shall be Shelumiel son of Zurishad-
13 dai; his host, with its members as detailed, numbers fifty-nine thou-
14 sand three hundred. Then the tribe of Gad: its chief shall be Eliasaph
15 son of Reuel; his host, with its members as detailed, numbers forty-five thousand six hundred
16 and fifty. The number listed in the camp of Reuben, by hosts, is one hundred and fifty-one thousand four hundred and fifty. They shall
17 be the second to march.
'When the Tent of the Presence moves, the camp of the Levites shall keep its station in the centre of the other camps; they shall all move in the order of their encamping, each man in his proper place under his standard.
18 'To the west the division of Ephraim shall be stationed under the standard of its camp by tribal hosts. The chief of Ephraim shall
19 be Elishama son of Ammihud; his host, with its members as detailed, numbers forty thousand five hun-
20 dred. Next to him the tribe of Manasseh shall be stationed. Its chief shall be Gamaliel son of
21 Pedahzur; his host, with its members as detailed, numbers thirty-
22 two thousand two hundred. Then the tribe of Benjamin: its chief shall
23 be Abidan son of Gideoni; his host, with its members as detailed, numbers thirty-five thousand four
24 hundred. The number listed in the camp of Ephraim, by hosts, is one hundred and eight thousand one hundred. They shall be the third to march.
25 'To the north the division of Dan shall be stationed under the standard of its camp by tribal hosts. The chief of Dan shall be Ahiezer
26 son of Ammishaddai; his host, with its members as detailed, numbers sixty-two thousand seven hundred.

Next to him the tribe of Asher shall 27 be stationed. Its chief shall be Pagiel son of Ocran; his host, with 28 its members as detailed, numbers forty-one thousand five hundred. Then the tribe of Naphtali: its 29 chief shall be Ahira son of Enan; his host, with its members as de- 30 tailed, numbers fifty-three thousand four hundred. The number 31 listed in the camp of Dan is a hundred and fifty-seven thousand six hundred. They shall march, under their standards, last.'
These were the Israelites listed 32 by their fathers' families. The total number in the camp, recorded by tribal hosts, was six hundred and three thousand five hundred and fifty.
The Levites were not included 33 in the detailed lists with their fellow-Israelites, for so the LORD had commanded Moses. The Israelites 34 did exactly as the LORD had commanded Moses, pitching and breaking camp standard by standard, each man according to his family in his father's line.

Concerning the Levites

These were the descendants of 3 Aaron and Moses at the time when the LORD spoke to Moses on Mount Sinai. The names of the sons of 2 Aaron were Nadab the eldest, Abihu, Eleazar and Ithamar. These were the names of Aaron's sons, the anointed priests who had been installed in the priestly office. Nadab and Abihu fell dead before 4 the LORD because they had presented illicit fire before the LORD in the wilderness of Sinai. They left no sons; Eleazar and Ithamar continued to perform the priestly office in their father's presence.
The LORD spoke to Moses and 5 said, 'Bring forward the tribe of 6 Levi and appoint them to serve Aaron the priest and to minister to him. They shall be in attendance 7 on him and on the whole community before the Tent of the Presence, undertaking the service of the Tabernacle. They shall be 8 in charge of all the equipment in the Tent of the Presence, and be in attendance on the Israelites, undertaking the service of the Tabernacle. You shall assign the 9 Levites to Aaron and his sons as especially dedicated to him out of all the Israelites. To Aaron and his 10 line you shall commit the priestly office and they shall perform its duties; any unqualified person who intrudes upon it shall be put to death.'
The LORD spoke to Moses and 11 said, 'I take the Levites for myself out of all the Israelites as a substitute for the eldest male child of every woman; the Levites shall be mine. For every eldest child, 13 if a boy, became mine when I destroyed all the eldest sons in Egypt.

So I have consecrated to myself all the first-born in Israel, both man and beast. They shall be mine. I am the LORD.'

14 The LORD spoke to Moses in the
15 wilderness of Sinai and said, 'Make a detailed list of all the Levites by their families in the father's line, every male from the age of one month and upwards.'

16 Moses made a detailed list of them in accordance with the com-
17 mand given him by the LORD. Now these were the names of the sons of Levi:

Gershon, Kohath and Merari.
18 Descendants of Gershon, by families: Libni and Shimei.
19 Descendants of Kohath, by families: Amram, Izhar, Hebron and Uzziel.
20 Descendants of Merari, by families: Mahli and Mushi.

These were the families of Levi, by fathers' families:
21 Gershon: the family of Libni and the family of Shimei. These
22 were the families of Gershon, and the number of males in their list as detailed, from the age of one month and upwards, was seven
23 thousand five hundred. The families of Gershon were stationed on the west, behind the Tabernacle.
24 Their chief was Eliasaph son of
25 Lael, and in the service of the Tent of the Presence they were in charge of the Tabernacle and its coverings, of the screen at the entrance to
26 the Tent of the Presence, the hangings of the court, the screen at the entrance to the court all round the Tabernacle and the altar, and of all else needed for its maintenance.
27 Kohath: the family of Amram, the family of Izhar, the family of Hebron, the family of Uzziel. These
28 were the families of Kohath, and the number of males, from the age of one month and upwards, was eight thousand six hundred. They
29 were the guardians of the holy things. The families of Kohath were stationed on the south, at the
30 side of the Tabernacle. Their chief
31 was Elizaphan son of Uzziel; they were in charge of the Ark, the table, the lamp-stands and the altars, together with the sacred vessels used in their service, and the screen with everything needed for its main-
32 tenance. The chief over all the chiefs of the Levites was Eleazar son of Aaron the priest, who was appointed overseer of those in
33 charge of the sanctuary.
33 Merari: the family of Mahli, the family of Mushi. These were the
34 families of Merari, and the number of males in their list as detailed from the age of one month and
35 upwards was six thousand two hundred. Their chief was Zuriel son of Abihail; they were stationed on the north, at the side of the

36 Tabernacle. The Merarites were in charge of the planks, bars, posts, and sockets of the Tabernacle, together with its vessels and all the equipment needed for its mainten-
37 ance, the posts, sockets, pegs, and cords of the surrounding court.
38 In front of the Tabernacle on the east, Moses was stationed, with Aaron and his sons, in front of the Tent of the Presence eastwards. They were in charge of the sanctuary on behalf of the Israelites; any unqualified person who came near would be put to death.
39 The number of Levites recorded by Moses on the detailed list by families at the command of the LORD was twenty-two thousand males aged one month and upwards.

Ransoming the first-born

40 The LORD said to Moses, 'Make a detailed list of all the male first-born in Israel aged one month and upwards, and count the number
41 of persons. You shall reserve the Levites for me—I am the LORD—in substitution for the eldest sons of the Israelites, and in the same way the Levites' cattle in substitution for the first-born cattle of the
42 Israelites.' As the LORD had told him to do, Moses made a list of all
43 the eldest sons of the Israelites, and the total number of first-born males recorded by name in the register, aged one month and upwards, was twenty-two thousand two hundred and seventy-three.
44 The LORD spoke to Moses and
45 said, 'Take the Levites as a substitute for all the eldest sons in Israel and the cattle of the Levites as a substitute for their cattle. The Levites shall be mine. I am the
46 LORD. The eldest sons in Israel will
47 outnumber the Levites by two hundred and seventy-three. This remainder must be ransomed, and you shall accept five shekels for each of them, taking the sacred shekel and reckoning twenty gerahs
48 to the shekel; you shall give the money with which they are ran-
49 somed to Aaron and his sons.'
49 Moses took the money paid as ransom for those who remained over when the substitution of Le-
50 vites was complete. The amount received was one thousand three hundred and sixty-five shekels of
51 silver by the sacred standard. In accordance with what the LORD had said, he gave the money to Aaron and his sons, doing what the LORD had told him to do.

a Strictly hide of sea-cow.

The Levites' duties

The LORD spoke to Moses and **4** Aaron and said, 'Among the Le- 2 vites, make a count of the descendants of Kohath between the ages 3 of thirty and fifty, by families in the father's line, comprising everyone who comes to take duty in the service of the Tent of the Presence.
4 'This is the service to be rendered by the Kohathites in the Tent of the Presence; it is most sacred. When the camp is due to 5 move, Aaron and his sons shall come and take down the Veil of the screen and cover the Ark of the Tokens with it; over this they shall 6 put a covering of porpoise-hide*a* and over that again a violet cloth all of one piece; they shall then put its poles in place. Over the Table 7 of the Presence they shall spread a violet cloth and lay on it the dishes, saucers, and flagons, and the bowls for drink-offerings; the Bread regularly presented shall also lie upon it; then they shall spread over them 8 a scarlet cloth and over that a covering of porpoise-hide, and put the poles in place. They shall take 9 a violet cloth and cover the lampstand, its lamps, tongs, firepans, and all the containers for the oil used in its service; they shall put 10 it with all its equipment in a sheet of porpoise-hide slung from a pole. Over the gold altar they shall spread 11 a violet cloth, cover it with a porpoise-hide covering, and put its poles in place. They shall take all 12 the articles used for the service of the sanctuary, put them on a violet cloth, cover them with a porpoise-hide covering, and sling them from a pole. They shall clear 13 the altar of the fat and ashes, spread a purple cloth over it, and then lay 14 on it all the equipment used in its service, the firepans, forks, shovels, tossing-bowls, and all the equipment of the altar, spread a covering of porpoise-hide over it and put the poles in place. Once Aaron and his 15 sons have finished covering the sanctuary and all the sacred equipment, when the camp is due to move, the Kohathites shall come to carry it; they must not touch it on pain of death. All these things are the load to be carried by the Kohathites, the things connected with the Tent of the Presence. Eleazar son of Aaron the priest 16 shall have charge of the lamp-oil, the fragrant incense, the regular grain-offering, and the anointing oil, with the general oversight of

the whole Tabernacle and its contents, the sanctuary and its equipment.'

17 The LORD spoke to Moses and
18 Aaron and said, 'You must not let the families of Kohath be extirpated, and lost to the tribe of Levi.
19 If they are to live and not die when they approach the most holy things, this is what you must do: Aaron and his sons shall come and set each man to his appointed task
20 and to his load, and the Kohathites themselves shall not enter to cast even a passing glance on the sanctuary, on pain of death.'
21 The LORD spoke to Moses and
22 said, 'Number the Gershonites too,
23 families in the father's line. Make a detailed list of all those between the ages of thirty and fifty who come on duty to perform service in the Tent of the Presence.
24 'This is the service to be rendered by the Gershonite families, comprising their general duty and
25 their loads. They shall carry the hangings of the Tabernacle, the Tent of the Presence, its covering, that is the covering of porpoise-hide which is over it, the screen at the entrance to the Tent of the
26 Presence, the hangings of the court, the screen at the entrance to the court surrounding the Tabernacle and the altar, their cords and all the equipment for their service; and they shall perform all the tasks connected with them. These are the acts of service they shall render.
27 All the service of the Gershonites, their loads and their other duties, shall be directed by Aaron and his sons; you shall assign them the loads for which they shall be
28 responsible. This is the service assigned to the Gershonite families in connection with the Tent of the Presence; Ithamar son of Aaron shall be in charge of them.
29 'You shall make a detailed list
30 of the Merarites by families in the father's line, all those between the ages of thirty and fifty, who come on duty to perform service in the Tent of the Presence.
31 'These are the loads for which they shall be responsible in virtue of their service in the Tent of the Presence: the planks of the Tabernacle with its bars, posts, and
32 sockets, the posts of the surrounding court with their sockets, pegs, and cords, and all that is needed for the maintenance of them; you shall assign to each man by name the load for which he is responsible.
33 These are the duties of the Merarite families in virtue of their service in the Tent of the Presence. Ithamar son of Aaron the priest shall be in charge of them.'
34 Moses and Aaron and the chiefs of the community made a detailed list of the Kohathites by families
35 in the father's line, taking all

36 between the ages of thirty and fifty who came on duty to perform service in the Tent of the Presence.
36 The number recorded by families in the detailed lists was two thou-
37 sand seven hundred and fifty. This was the total number in the detailed lists of the Kohathite families who did duty in the Tent of the Presence; they were recorded by Moses and Aaron as the LORD had told them to do through Moses.
38-39 The Gershonites between the ages of thirty and fifty, who came on duty for service in the Tent of the Presence, were recorded in detailed lists by families in the
40 father's line. Their number, by families in the father's line, was two thousand six hundred and
41 thirty. This was the total recorded in the lists of the Gershonite families who came on duty in the Tent of the Presence, and were recorded by Moses and Aaron as the LORD had told them to do.
42-43 The families of Merari, between the ages of thirty and fifty, who came on duty to perform service in the Tent of the Presence, were recorded in detailed lists by fami-
44 lies in the father's line. Their number by families was three thousand
45 two hundred. These were recorded in the Merarite families by Moses and Aaron as the LORD had told them to do through Moses.
46 Thus Moses and Aaron and the chiefs of Israel made a detailed list of all the Levites by families in the
47 father's line, between the ages of thirty and fifty years; these were all who came to perform their various duties and carry their loads in the service of the Tent of the
48 Presence. Their number was eight thousand five hundred and eighty.
49 They were recorded one by one by Moses at the command of the LORD, according to their general duty and the loads they carried.[b] For so the LORD had told Moses to do.

Safeguard against defilement

5 The LORD spoke to Moses and
2 said: Command the Israelites to expel from the camp everyone who suffers from a malignant skin-disease or a discharge, and every-one ritually unclean from contact
3 with a corpse. You shall put them outside the camp, both male and female, so that they will not defile your camps in which I dwell among
4 you. The Israelites did this: they put them outside the camp. As the LORD had said when he spoke to Moses, so the Israelites did.

Law of restitution

5 The LORD spoke to Moses and
6 said, Say to the Israelites: When anyone, man or woman, wrongs another and thereby breaks faith with the LORD, that person has

incurred guilt which demands reparation. He shall confess the sin 7 he has committed, make restitution in full with the addition of one fifth, and give it to the man to whom compensation is due. If there 8 is no next-of-kin to whom compensation can be paid, the compensation payable in that case shall be the LORD's, for the use of the priest, in addition to the ram of expiation with which the priest makes expiation for him.

Every contribution made by way 9 of holy-gift which the Israelites bring to the priest shall be the priest's. The priest shall have the 10 holy-gifts which a man gives; whatever is given to him shall be his.

Law concerning jealousy

The LORD spoke to Moses and 11 said, Speak to the Israelites in these 12 words: When a married woman goes astray, is unfaithful to her husband, and has sexual inter- 13 course with another man, and this happens without the husband's knowledge, and the crime is undetected, because, though she has been defiled, there is no direct evidence against her and she was not caught in the act, but when in such 14 a case a fit of jealousy comes over the husband which causes him to suspect his wife, she being in fact defiled; or when, on the other hand, a fit of jealousy comes over a husband which causes him to suspect his wife, when she is not in fact defiled; then in either case, the 15 husband shall bring his wife to the priest together with the prescribed offering for her, a tenth of an ephah of barley meal. He shall not pour oil on it nor put frankincense on it, because it is a grain-offering for jealousy, a grain-offering of protestation conveying an imputation of guilt. The priest shall bring her 16 forward and set her before the LORD. He shall take clean[c] water 17 in an earthenware vessel, and shall take dust from the floor of the Tabernacle and add it to the water. He shall set the woman before the 18 LORD, uncover her head, and place the grain-offering of protestation in her hands; it is a grain-offering for jealousy. The priest shall hold in his own hand the water of contention which brings out the truth. He 19 shall then put the woman on oath and say to her, 'If no man has had intercourse with you, if you have not gone astray and let yourself become defiled while owing obedience to your husband, then may your innocence be established by the water of contention which brings out the truth. But if, while 20 owing him obedience, you have gone astray and let yourself become defiled, if any man other than your husband has had intercourse with you' (the priest shall here put 21

---

b Prob. rdg.; Heb. adds and his registered ones.   c Or holy.

the woman on oath with an adjuration, and shall continue), 'may the LORD make an example of you among your people in adjurations and in swearing of oaths by bringing upon you miscarriage and un-22 timely birth; and this water that brings out the truth shall enter your body, bringing upon you miscarriage and untimely birth.' The woman shall respond, 'Amen,
23 Amen.' The priest shall write these curses on a scroll and wash them off into the water of contention;
24 he shall make the woman drink the water that brings out the truth, and the water shall enter her body.
25 The priest shall take the grain-offering for jealousy from the woman's hand, present it as a special gift before the LORD, and
26 offer it at the altar. He shall take a handful from the grain-offering by way of token, and burn it at the altar; after this he shall make the
27 woman drink the water. If she has let herself become defiled and has been unfaithful to her husband, then when the priest makes her drink the water that brings out the truth and the water has entered her body, she will suffer a miscarriage or untimely birth, and her name will become an example in adjura-28 tion among her kin. But if the woman has not let herself become defiled and is pure, then her innocence is established and she will bear her child.
29 Such is the law for cases of jealousy, where a woman, owing obedience to her husband, goes astray and lets herself become
30 defiled, or where a fit of jealousy comes over a man which causes him to suspect his wife. He shall set her before the LORD, and the priest shall deal with her as this law pre-31 scribes. No guilt will attach to the husband, but the woman shall bear the penalty of her guilt.

Law for the Nazirite

6 The LORD spoke to Moses and
2 said, Speak to the Israelites in these words: When anyone, man or woman, makes a special[d] vow dedicating himself to the LORD as
3 a Nazirite,[e] he shall abstain from wine and strong drink. These he shall not drink, nor anything made from the juice of grapes; nor shall
4 he eat grapes, fresh or dried. During the whole term of his vow he

shall eat nothing that comes from the vine, nothing whatever, shoot
5 or berry. During the whole term of his vow no razor shall touch his head; he shall let his hair grow long and plait it until he has completed the term of his dedication: he shall
6 keep himself holy to the LORD. During the whole term of his vow he
7 shall not go near a corpse, not even when his father or mother, brother or sister, dies; he shall not make himself ritually unclean for them, because the Nazirite vow to his God
8 is on his head. He shall keep himself holy to the LORD during the whole term of his Nazirite vow.
9 If someone suddenly falls dead by his side touching him and thereby making his hair, which has been dedicated, ritually unclean, he shall shave his head seven days later, on the day appointed for his ritual
10 cleansing. On the eighth day he shall bring two turtle-doves or two young pigeons to the priest at the entrance to the Tent of the Pres-11 ence. The priest shall offer one as a sin-offering and the other as a whole-offering and shall make expiation for him for the sin he has incurred through contact with the dead body; and he shall consecrate
12 his head afresh on that day. The man shall re-dedicate himself to the LORD for the term of his vow and bring a yearling ram as a guilt-offering. The previous period shall not be reckoned, because the hair which he dedicated became unclean.
13 The law for the Nazirite, when the term of his dedication is completed, shall be this. He shall be brought to the entrance to the Tent
14 of the Presence and shall present his offering to the LORD: one yearling ram without blemish as a whole-offering, one yearling ewe without blemish as a sin-offering, one ram without blemish as a
15 shared-offering, and a basket of cakes made of flour mixed with oil, and of wafers smeared with oil, both unleavened, together with the proper grain-offerings and drink-16 offerings. The priest shall present all these before the LORD and offer the man's sin-offering and whole-17 offering; the ram he shall offer as a shared-offering to the LORD, together with the basket of unleavened cakes and the proper grain-offering and drink-offering.

The Nazirite shall shave his head 18 at the entrance to the Tent of the Presence, take the hair which had been dedicated and put it on the fire where the shared-offering is burning. The priest shall take the 19 shoulder of the ram, after boiling it, and take also one unleavened cake from the basket and one unleavened wafer, and put them on the palms of the Nazirite's hands, his hair which had been dedicated having been shaved. The priest 20 shall then present them as a special gift before the LORD; these, together with the breast of the special gift and the leg of the contribution, are holy and belong to the priest. When this has been done, the Nazirite is again free to drink wine.
Such is the law for the Nazirite 21 who has made his vow. Such is the offering he must make to the LORD for his dedication, apart from anything else that he can afford. He must carry out his vow in full according to the law governing his dedication.

The priests' blessing

The LORD spoke to Moses and 22 said, Speak to Aaron and his sons 23 in these words: These are the words with which you shall bless the Israelites:

The LORD bless you and watch over 24
   you;
the LORD make his face shine upon[f] 25
   you
   and be gracious to you;
the LORD look kindly on you and 26
   give you peace.

They shall pronounce my name 27 over the Israelites, and I will bless them.

Offerings for the dedication of the altar

On the day that Moses completed **7** the setting up of the Tabernacle, he anointed and consecrated it; he also anointed and consecrated its equipment, and the altar and its vessels. The chief men of Israel, 2 heads of families—that is the chiefs of the tribes, who had assisted in preparing the detailed lists—came forward and brought their offer- 3 ing before the LORD, six covered wagons and twelve oxen, one wagon from every two chiefs and from each one an ox.[g] These they

d makes a special: or performs a . . .   e That is separated one or dedicated one.   f Or to.   g Or a bull.

brought forward before the Taber-
4 nacle; and the LORD spoke to
5 Moses and said, 'Accept these from
them: they shall be used for the
service of the Tent of the Presence.
Assign them to the Levites as their
several duties require.' `
6 So Moses accepted the wagons
and oxen and assigned them to the
7 Levites. He gave two wagons and
four oxen to the Gershonites as
8 required for their service; four
wagons and eight oxen to the
Merarites as required for their
service, in charge of Ithamar the
9 son of Aaron the priest. He gave
none to the Kohathites because the
service laid upon them was that of
the holy things: these they had to
carry themselves on their shoulders.
10 When the altar was anointed,
the chiefs brought their gift for
its dedication and presented their
11 offering before it. The LORD said
to Moses, 'Let the chiefs present
their offering for the dedication of
the altar one by one, on con-
secutive days.'
12 The chief who presented his
offering on the first day was Nah-
13 shon son of Amminadab of the
tribe of Judah. His offering was one
silver dish weighing a hundred and
thirty shekels by the sacred standard and one silver tossing-bowl
weighing seventy, both full of flour
mixed with oil as a grain-offering;
14 one saucer weighing ten gold
15 shekels, full of incense; one young
bull, one full-grown ram, and one
yearling ram, as a whole-offering;
16 17 one he-goat as a sin-offering; and
two bulls, five full-grown rams,
he-goats, and five yearling rams,
as a shared-offering. This was the
offering of Nahshon son of Amminadab.
18 On the second day Nethaneel son
of Zuar, chief of Issachar, brought
19 his offering. He brought one silver
dish weighing a hundred and thirty
shekels by the sacred standard and
one silver tossing-bowl weighing
seventy, both full of flour mixed
20 with oil as a grain-offering; one
saucer weighing ten gold shekels,
21 full of incense; one young bull, one
full-grown ram, and one yearling
22 ram, as a whole-offering; one he-
23 goat as a sin-offering; and two
bulls, five full-grown rams, five he-
goats, and five yearling rams, as a
shared-offering. This was the offering of Nethaneel son of Zuar.
24 On the third day the chief of the
Zebulunites, Eliab son of Helon,
25 came. His offering was one silver
dish weighing a hundred and thirty
shekels by the sacred standard and
one silver tossing-bowl weighing
seventy, both full of flour mixed
26 with oil as a grain-offering; one
saucer weighing ten gold shekels,
27 full of incense; one young bull, one
full-grown ram, and one yearling
28 ram, as a whole-offering; one he-
29 goat as a sin-offering; and two

bulls, five full-grown rams, five
he-goats, and five yearling rams,
as a shared-offering. This was the
offering of Eliab son of Helon.
30 On the fourth day the chief of
the Reubenites, Elizur son of She-
31 deur, came. His offering was one
silver dish weighing a hundred and
thirty shekels by the sacred standard and one silver tossing-bowl
weighing seventy, both full of flour
mixed with oil as a grain-offering;
32 one saucer weighing ten gold
33 shekels, full of incense; one young
bull, one full-grown ram, and one
yearling ram, as a whole-offering;
34 35 one he-goat as a sin-offering; and
two bulls, five full-grown rams, five
he-goats, and five yearling rams,
as a shared-offering. This was the
offering of Elizur son of Shedeur.
36 On the fifth day the chief of the
Simeonites, Shelumiel son of Zur-
37 ishaddai, came. His offering was
one silver dish weighing a hundred
and thirty shekels by the sacred
standard and one silver tossing-
bowl weighing seventy, both full
of flour mixed with oil as a grain-
38 offering; one saucer weighing ten
39 gold shekels, full of incense; one
young bull, one full-grown ram,
40 and one yearling ram, as a
41 whole-offering; one he-goat as a
sin-offering; and two bulls, five
full-grown rams, five he-goats, and
five yearling rams, as a shared-
offering. This was the offering of
Shelumiel son of Zurishaddai.
42 On the sixth day the chief of the
Gadites, Eliasaph son of Reuel,
43 came. His offering was one silver
dish weighing a hundred and thirty
shekels by the sacred standard and
one silver tossing-bowl weighing
seventy, both full of flour mixed
44 with oil as a grain-offering; one
saucer weighing ten gold shekels,
45 full of incense; one young bull, one
full-grown ram, and one yearling
46 ram, as a whole-offering; one he-
47 goat as a sin-offering; and two
bulls, five full-grown rams, five
he-goats, and five yearling rams,
as a shared-offering. This was the
offering of Eliasaph son of Reuel.
48 On the seventh day the chief of
the Ephraimites, Elishama son of
49 Ammihud, came. His offering was
one silver dish weighing a hundred
and thirty shekels by the sacred
standard and one silver tossing-
bowl weighing seventy, both full
of flour mixed with oil as a grain-
50 offering; one saucer weighing ten
51 gold shekels, full of incense; one
young bull, one full-grown ram,
and one yearling ram, as a
52 whole-offering; one he-goat as a
53 sin-offering; and two bulls, five
full-grown rams, five he-goats, and
five yearling rams, as a shared-
offering. This was the offering of
Elishama son of Ammihud.
54 On the eighth day the chief of
the Manassites, Gamaliel son of
55 Pedahzur, came. His offering was

one silver dish weighing a hundred
and thirty shekels by the sacred
standard and one silver tossing-
bowl weighing seventy, both full
of flour mixed with oil as a grain-
offering; one saucer weighing ten 56
gold shekels, full of incense; one 57
young bull, one full-grown ram,
and one yearling ram, as a
whole-offering; one he-goat as a 58
sin-offering; and two bulls, five 59
full-grown rams, five he-goats, and
five yearling rams, as a shared-
offering. This was the offering of
Gamaliel son of Pedahzur.
On the ninth day the chief of the 60
Benjamites, Abidan son of Gideoni,
came. His offering was one silver 61
dish weighing a hundred and thirty
shekels by the sacred standard and
one silver tossing-bowl weighing
seventy, both full of flour mixed
with oil as a grain-offering; one 62
saucer weighing ten gold shekels, 63
full of incense; one young bull, one
full-grown ram, and one yearling
ram, as a whole-offering; one he- 64
goat as a sin-offering; and two 65
bulls, five full-grown rams, five he-
goats, and five yearling rams, as a
shared-offering. This was the offering of Abidan son of Gideoni.
On the tenth day the chief of the 66
Danites, Ahiezer son of Ammishaddai, came. His offering was one 67
silver dish weighing a hundred and
thirty shekels by the sacred standard and one silver tossing-bowl
weighing seventy, both full of flour
mixed with oil as a grain-offering;
one saucer weighing ten gold 68
shekels, full of incense; one young 69
bull, one full-grown ram, and one
yearling ram, as a whole-offering;
one he-goat as a sin-offering; and 70
two bulls, five full-grown rams,
five he-goats, and five yearling
rams, as a shared-offering. This
was the offering of Ahiezer son of
Ammishaddai.
On the eleventh day the chief of 72
the Asherites, Pagiel son of Ocran,
came. His offering was one silver 73
dish weighing a hundred and thirty
shekels by the sacred standard and
one silver tossing-bowl weighing
seventy, both full of flour mixed
with oil as a grain-offering; one 74
saucer weighing ten gold shekels, 75
full of incense; one young bull, one
full-grown ram, and one yearling
ram, as a whole-offering; one he- 76
goat as a sin-offering; and two 77
bulls, five full-grown rams, five
he-goats, and five yearling rams,
as a shared-offering. This was the
offering of Pagiel son of Ocran.
On the twelfth day the chief of 78
the Naphtalites, Ahira son of Enan,
came. His offering was one silver 79
dish weighing a hundred and thirty
shekels by the sacred standard and
one silver tossing-bowl weighing
seventy, both full of flour mixed
with oil as a grain-offering; one 80
saucer weighing ten gold shekels,
full of incense; one young bull, one 81

full-grown ram, and one yearling
82 ram, as a whole-offering; one he-
83 goat as a sin-offering; and two
bulls, five full-grown rams, five he-
goats, and five yearling rams, as a
shared-offering. This was the offering of Ahira son of Enan.
84 This was the gift from the chiefs
of Israel for the dedication of the
altar when it was anointed: twelve
silver dishes, twelve silver tossing-
bowls, and twelve golden saucers;
85 each silver dish weighed a hundred
and thirty shekels, each silver
tossing-bowl seventy shekels. The
total weight of the silver vessels
was two thousand four hundred
shekels by the sacred standard.
86 There were twelve golden saucers
full of incense, ten shekels each
by the sacred standard: the total
weight of the gold of the saucers
was a hundred and twenty shekels.
87 The number of beasts for the
whole-offering was twelve bulls,
twelve full-grown rams, and twelve
yearling rams, with the prescribed
grain-offerings, and twelve he-goats
88 for the sin-offering. The number of
beasts for the shared-offering was
twenty-four bulls, sixty full-grown
rams, sixty he-goats, and sixty
yearling rams. This was the gift for
the dedication of the altar when it
89 was anointed. And when Moses
entered the Tent of the Presence
to speak with God, he heard the
Voice speaking from above the
cover over the Ark of the Tokens
from between the two cherubim:
the Voice spoke to him.

Aaron sets up the lamps

8 The LORD spoke to Moses and
2 said, 'Speak to Aaron in these
words: "When you mount the
seven lamps, see that they shed
their light forwards in front of the
3 lamp-stand."' Aaron did this: he
mounted the lamps, so as to shed
light forwards in front of the
4 lamp-stand, as the LORD had instructed Moses. The lamp-stand
was made of beaten-work in gold,
as well as the stem and the petals.
Moses made it to match the pattern
which the LORD had shown him.

Levites belong to the LORD

5 The LORD spoke to Moses and
6 said: Take the Levites apart from
the rest of the Israelites and cleanse
7 them ritually. This is what you
shall do to cleanse them. Sprinkle
lustral water over them; they shall
then shave their whole bodies,
wash their clothes, and so be
8 cleansed. Next, they shall take a
young bull as a whole-offering[h]

h *as a whole-offering: prob.*
rdg.; Heb. om.

with its prescribed grain-offering,
flour mixed with oil; and you shall
9 offering. Bring the Levites before
the Tent of the Presence and call
the whole community of Israelites
10 together. Bring the Levites before
the LORD, and let the Israelites lay
11 their hands on their heads. Aaron
shall present the Levites before the
LORD as a special gift from the
Israelites, and they shall be dedicated to the service of the LORD.
12 The Levites shall lay their hands
on the heads of the bulls; one bull
shall be offered as a sin-offering
and the other as a whole-offering
to the LORD, to make expiation
13 for the Levites. Then you shall set
the Levites before Aaron and his
sons, presenting them to the LORD
14 as a special gift. You shall thus
separate the Levites from the rest
of the Israelites, and they shall be
mine.
15 After this, the Levites shall enter
the Tent of the Presence to serve in
it, ritually cleansed and presented
16 as a special gift; for they are given
and dedicated to me, out of all the
Israelites. I have accepted them as
mine in place of all that comes first
from the womb, every first child
17 among the Israelites; for every
first-born male creature, man or
beast, among the Israelites is mine.
On the day when I struck down
every first-born creature in Egypt,
18 I hallowed all the first-born of the
Israelites to myself, and I have
accepted the Levites in their place.
19 I have given the Levites to Aaron
and his sons, dedicated among the
Israelites to perform the service of
the Israelites in the Tent of the
Presence and to make expiation for
them, and then no calamity will
befall them when they come close
to the sanctuary.
20 Moses and Aaron and the whole
community of Israelites carried out
all the commands the LORD had
given to Moses for the dedication

of the Levites. The Levites purified 21
themselves of sin and washed their
clothes, and Aaron presented them
as a special gift before the LORD
and made expiation for them, to
cleanse them. Then at last they 22
went in to perform their service in
the Tent of the Presence, before
Aaron and his sons. Thus the commands the LORD had given to Moses
concerning the Levites were all
carried out.

The Levites' periods of service

The LORD spoke to Moses and 23
said: Touching the Levites: they 24
shall begin their active work in the
service of the Tent of the Presence
at the age of twenty-five. At the 25
age of fifty a Levite shall retire
from regular service and shall serve
no longer. He may continue to 26
assist his colleagues in attendance
in the Tent of the Presence but
shall perform no regular service.
This is how you shall arrange the
attendance of the Levites.

Keeping the Passover

In the first month of the second **9**
year after they came out of Egypt,
the LORD spoke to Moses in the
wilderness of Sinai and said, 'Let 2
the Israelites prepare the Passover
at the time appointed for it. This 3
shall be between dusk and dark on
the fourteenth day of this month,
and you shall keep it at this
appointed time, observing every
rule and custom proper to it.' So 4
Moses told the Israelites to prepare
the Passover, and they prepared it 5
on the fourteenth day of the first
month, between dusk and dark, in
the wilderness of Sinai. The Israelites did exactly as the LORD had
instructed Moses.
It happened that some men were 6
ritually unclean through contact
with a corpse and so could not keep
the Passover on the right day. They
came before Moses and Aaron that
same day and said, 'We are unclean 7
through contact with a corpse.
Must we therefore be debarred
from presenting the LORD's offering at its appointed time with
the rest of the Israelites?' Moses 8
answered, 'Wait, and let me hear
what commands the LORD has
for you.'
The LORD spoke to Moses and 9
said, Tell the Israelites: If any one 10
of you or of your descendants is
ritually unclean through contact
with a corpse, or if he is away on
a long journey, he shall keep a

(Num. 8. 2)

Passover to the LORD none the less.
11 But in that case he shall prepare the victim in the second month, between dusk and dark on the fourteenth day. It shall be eaten with unleavened cakes and bitter herbs;
12 nothing shall be left over till morning, and no bone of it shall be broken. The Passover shall be kept
13 exactly as the law prescribes. The man who, being ritually clean and not absent on a journey, neglects to keep the Passover, shall be cut off from his father's kin, because he has not presented the LORD's offering at its appointed time. That man shall accept responsibility for his sin.

When an alien is settled among 14 you, he also shall keep the Passover to the LORD, observing every rule and custom proper to it. The same law is binding on you all, alien and native alike.

The cloud over the Tabernacle

15 On the day when they set up the Tabernacle, that is the Tent of the Tokens, cloud covered it, and in the evening a brightness like fire
16 appeared over it till morning. So it continued: the cloud covered it by day and a
17 brightness like fire by night. Whenever the cloud lifted from the tent, the Israelites struck camp, and at the place where the cloud settled, there they pitched their camp.
18 At the command of the LORD they struck camp, and at the command of the LORD they encamped again, and continued in camp as long as the cloud rested over the Tabernacle.
19 When the cloud stayed long over the Tabernacle, the Israelites remained in attendance
20 on the LORD and did not move on; and it was the same when the cloud continued over the Tabernacle only a few days: at the command of the LORD they remained in camp, and at the command of the LORD they struck
21 camp. There were also times when the cloud continued only from evening till morning, and in the morning, when the cloud lifted, they moved on. Whether by day or by night, they moved as soon as the cloud lifted.
22 Whether it was for a day or two, for a month or a year, whenever the cloud stayed long over the Tabernacle, the Israelites remained where they were and did not move on; they
23 did so only when the cloud lifted. At the command of the LORD they encamped, and at his command they struck camp. At the LORD's command, given through Moses, they remained in attendance on the LORD.

The silver trumpets

10
1 2 The LORD spoke to Moses and said: Make two trumpets of beaten silver and use them for summoning the community and for
3 breaking camp. When both are sounded, the whole community shall muster before you at the entrance to the Tent of the Presence.
4 If a single trumpet is sounded, the chiefs who are heads of the Israelite clans shall
5 muster. When you give the signal for a shout, those encamped on the east side are to move
6 off. When the signal is given for a second shout those encamped to the south are to move off. A signal to shout is the signal to
7 move off. When you convene the assembly, you shall sound a trumpet but not raise a
8 shout. This sounding of the trumpets is the duty of the Aaronite priests and shall be a rule binding for all time on your descendants.

When you go into battle against an invader 9 and you are hard pressed by him, you shall raise a cheer when the trumpets sound, and this will serve as a reminder of you before the LORD your God and you will be delivered from your enemies. On your festal days and 10 at your appointed seasons and on the first day of every month, you shall sound the trumpets over your whole-offerings and your shared-offerings, and the trumpets shall be a reminder on your behalf before the LORD your God. I am the LORD your God.

The Israelites depart from Sinai

In the second year, on the twentieth day of 11 the second month, the cloud lifted from the Tabernacle of the Tokens, and the Israelites 12 moved by stages from the wilderness of Sinai, until the cloud came to rest in the wilderness of Paran. The first time that they 13 broke camp at the command of the LORD given through Moses, the standard of the 14 division of Judah moved off first with its tribal hosts: the host of Judah under Nahshon son of Amminadab, the host of 15 Issachar under Nethaneel son of Zuar, and 16 the host of Zebulun under Eliab son of Helon. Then the Tabernacle was taken down, 17 and its bearers, the sons of Gershon and Merari, moved off.

Secondly, the standard of the division of 18 Reuben moved off with its tribal hosts: the host of Reuben under Elizur son of Shedeur, the host of Simeon under Shelumiel son of 19 Zurishaddai, and the host of Gad under 20 Eliasaph son of Reuel. The Kohathites, the 21 bearers of the holy things, moved off next, and on their arrival found the Tabernacle set up.

Thirdly, the standard of the division of 22 Ephraim moved off with its tribal hosts: the host of Ephraim under Elishama son of Ammihud, the host of Manasseh under 23 Gamaliel son of Pedahzur, and the host of 24 Benjamin under Abidan son of Gideoni.

Lastly, the standard of the division of 25 Dan, the rearguard of all the divisions, moved off with its tribal hosts: the host of Dan under Ahiezer son of Ammishaddai, the host of Asher under Pagiel son of Ocran, 26 and the host of Naphtali under Ahira son 27 of Enan.

8 This was the order of march for the Israelites, mustered in their hosts, and in this order they broke camp.

9 And Moses said to Hobab son of Reuel the Midianite, his brother-in-law, 'We are setting out for the place which the LORD promised to give us. Come with us, and we will deal generously with you, for the LORD has given an assurance of good fortune for

30 Israel.' But he replied, 'No, I will not; I would rather go to my own country and my

31 own people.' Moses said, 'Do not desert us, I beg you; for you know where we ought to camp in the wilderness, and you will be our

32 guide. If you will go with us, then all the good fortune with which the LORD favours us we will share with you.'

33 Then they moved off from the mountain of the LORD and journeyed for three days, and the Ark of the Covenant of the LORD kept a day's journey ahead of them to find

34 them a place to rest. The cloud of the LORD hung over them by day when they moved

35 camp. Whenever the Ark began to move, Moses said,

'Up, LORD, and may thy enemies be scattered and those that hate thee flee before thee.'

36 When it halted, he said,

'Rest, LORD of the countless thousands of Israel.'

The people cry for meat

1 There came a time when the people complained to the LORD of their hardships. When he heard, he became angry and fire from the LORD broke out among them, and was raging

2 at one end of the camp, when the people appealed to Moses. He interceded with the

3 LORD, and the fire died down. Then they named that place Taberah,*i* because the fire of the LORD had burned among them there.

4 Now there was a mixed company of strangers who had joined the Israelites. These people began to be greedy for better things, and the Israelites themselves wept once again and cried, 'Will no one give us

5 meat? Think of it! In Egypt we had fish for the asking, cucumbers and water-melons,

6 leeks and onions and garlic. Now our throats are parched; there is nothing wherever we

7 look except this manna.' (The manna looked like coriander seed, the colour of gum resin.

8 The people went about collecting it, ground it up in hand-mills or pounded it in mortars, then boiled it in the pot and made it into

9 cakes. It tasted like butter-cakes. When dew fell on the camp at night, the manna fell with

10 it.) Moses heard the people wailing, all of them in their families at the opening of their tents. Then the LORD became very angry,

and Moses was troubled. He said to the 11 LORD, 'Why hast thou brought trouble on thy servant? How have I displeased the LORD that I am burdened with the care of this whole people? Am I their mother? Have I 12 brought them into the world, and am I called upon to carry them in my bosom, like a nurse with her babies, to the land promised by thee on oath to their fathers? Where am 13 I to find meat to give them all? They pester me with their wailing and their "Give us meat to eat." This whole people is a burden 14 too heavy for me; I cannot carry it alone. If that is thy purpose for me, then kill me 15 outright. But if I have won thy favour, let me suffer this trouble at thy hands*j* no longer.'

The LORD answered Moses, 'Assemble 16 seventy elders from Israel, men known to you as elders and officers in the community; bring them to me at the Tent of the Presence, and there let them take their stand with you. I will come down and speak with you there. 17 I will take back part of that same spirit which has been conferred on you and confer it on them, and they will share with you the burden of taking care for the people; then you will not have to bear it alone. And to the 18 people you shall say this: "Hallow yourselves in readiness for tomorrow; you shall have meat to eat. You wailed in the LORD's hearing; you said, 'Will no one give us meat? In Egypt we lived well.' The LORD will give you meat and you shall eat it. Not for one 19 day only, nor for two days, nor five, nor ten, nor twenty, but for a whole month you shall 20 eat it until it comes out at your nostrils and makes you sick; because you have rejected the LORD who dwells in your midst, wailing in his presence and saying, 'Why did we ever come out of Egypt?'"'

Moses replied, 'Here am I with six hun- 21 dred thousand men on the march around me, and thou dost promise them meat to eat for a whole month. How can the sheep 22 and oxen be slaughtered that would be enough for them? If all the fish in the sea could be caught, would they be enough?' The LORD said to Moses, 'Is there a limit to 23 the power of the LORD? You will see this very day whether or not my words come true.'

The elders prophesy

Moses came out and told the people what 24 the LORD had said. He assembled seventy men from the elders of the people and stationed them round the Tent. Then the LORD 25 descended in the cloud and spoke to him. He took back part of that same spirit which he had conferred on Moses and conferred it on the seventy elders; as the spirit alighted

i That is Burning.   *j* this trouble . . . hands: *prob. original rdg., altered in Heb. to* my trouble.

on them, they fell into a prophetic ecstasy, for the first and only time.

26 Now two men named Eldad and Medad, who had been enrolled with the seventy, were left behind in the camp. But, though they had not gone out to the Tent, the spirit alighted on them none the less, and they fell 27 into an ecstasy there in the camp. A young man ran and told Moses that Eldad and Medad were in an ecstasy in the camp, 28 whereupon Joshua son of Nun, who had served with Moses since he was a boy, broke 29 in, 'My lord Moses, stop them!' But Moses said to him, 'Are you jealous on my account? I wish that all the LORD's people were prophets and that the LORD would confer his 30 spirit on them all!' And Moses rejoined the camp with the elders of Israel.

The LORD sends quails

31 Then a wind from the LORD sprang up; it drove quails in from the west, and they were flying all round the camp for the distance of a day's journey, three feet above the ground. 32 The people were busy gathering quails all that day, all night, and all next day, and even the man who got least gathered ten homers. They spread them out to dry all 33 about the camp. But the meat was scarcely between their teeth, and they had not so much as bitten it, when the LORD's anger broke out against the people and he struck 34 them with a deadly plague. That place was called Kibroth-hattaavah[k] because there they buried the people who had been greedy for meat.

Miriam and Aaron speak against Moses

35 From Kibroth-hattaavah the Israelites went on to Hazeroth, and while they were at 12 Hazeroth, Miriam and Aaron began to speak against Moses. They blamed him for his Cushite wife (for he had married a 2 Cushite woman), and they said, 'Is Moses the only one with[l] whom the LORD has spoken? Has he not spoken with[l] us as 3 well?' Moses was in fact a man of great humility, the most humble man on earth. 4 But the LORD heard them and suddenly he said to Moses, Aaron and Miriam, 'Go out all three of you to the Tent of the Presence.' 5 So the three went out, and the LORD descended in a pillar of cloud; he stood at the entrance to the tent and summoned Aaron and Miriam. The two of them went forward, 6 and he said,

'Listen to my words.
If he[m] were your prophet and nothing more,
I would make myself known to him in a vision,
I would speak with him in a dream.

But my servant Moses is not such a prophet; 7 he alone is faithful[n] of all my household.
With him I speak face to face, 8
openly and not in riddles.
He shall see the very form of the LORD.
How do you dare speak against my servant Moses?'

9 Thus the anger of the LORD was roused against them, and he left them; and as the 10 cloud moved from the tent, there was Miriam, her skin diseased and white as snow. Aaron turned towards her and saw her skin diseased. Then he said to Moses, 'Pray, my 11 lord, do not make us pay the penalty of sin, foolish and wicked though we have been. Let her not be like something still-born, 12 whose flesh is half eaten away when it comes from the womb.' So Moses cried, 'Not this, 13 O LORD! Heal her, I pray.' The LORD re- 14 plied, 'Suppose her father had spat in her face, would she not have to remain in disgrace for seven days? Let her be kept for seven days in confinement outside the camp and then be brought back.' So Miriam was 15 kept outside for seven days, and the people did not strike camp until she was brought back. After this they set out from Hazeroth 16 and pitched camp in the wilderness of Paran.

The spies report on Canaan

The LORD spoke to Moses and said, 'Send men 13 out to explore the land of Canaan which I am 1 2 giving to the Israelites; from each of their fathers' tribes send one man, and let him be a man of high rank.' So Moses sent them 3 from the wilderness of Paran at the command of the LORD, all of them leading men among the Israelites. These were their names: 4

from the tribe of Reuben, Shammua son of Zaccur;
from the tribe of Simeon, Shaphat son of 5 Hori;
from the tribe of Judah, Caleb son of 6 Jephunneh;
from the tribe of Issachar, Igal son of 7 Joseph;
from the tribe of Ephraim, Hoshea son of 8 Nun;
from the tribe of Benjamin, Palti son of 9 Raphu;
from the tribe of Zebulun, Gaddiel son of 10 Sodi;
from the tribe of Joseph (that is from the 11 tribe of Manasseh), Gaddi son of Susi;
from the tribe of Dan, Ammiel son of 12 Gemalli;
from the tribe of Asher, Sethur son of 13 Michael;
from the tribe of Naphtali, Nahbi son of 14 Vophsi;
from the tribe of Gad, Geuel son of Machi. 15

---

k That is the Graves of Greed.   *l Or* by.   *m Prob. rdg.; Heb.* the LORD.   *n Or* to be trusted.

16 These are the names of the men whom Moses
sent to explore the land. But Moses called
the son of Nun Joshua, not Hoshea.
17 When Moses sent them to explore the land
of Canaan, he said to them, 'Make your way
up by the Negeb, and go on into the hill-
18 country. See what the land is like, and
whether the people who live there are strong
19 or weak, few or many. See whether it is easy
or difficult country in which they live, and
whether the cities in which they live are weak-
20 ly defended or well fortified; is the land fertile
or barren, and does it grow trees or not? Go
boldly in and take some of its fruit.' It was
the season when the first grapes were ripe.
21 They went up and explored the country
from the wilderness of Zin as far as Rehob
22 by Lebo-hamath. They went up by the
Negeb and came to Hebron, where Ahiman,
Sheshai and Talmai, the descendants of
Anak,[o] were living. (Hebron was built seven
23 years before Zoan in Egypt.) They came to
the gorge of Eshcol,[p] and there they cut a
branch with a single bunch of grapes, and
they carried it on a pole two at a time; they
24 also picked pomegranates and figs. It was
from the bunch of grapes which the Israelites cut there that that place was named the
25 gorge of Eshcol. After forty days they re-
26 turned from exploring the country, and came
back to Moses and Aaron and the whole
community of Israelites at Kadesh in the
wilderness of Paran. They made their report
to them and to the whole community, and
27 showed them the fruit of the country. And
this was the story they told Moses: 'We made
our way into the land to which you sent us.
It is flowing with milk and honey, and here
28 is the fruit it grows; but its inhabitants are
sturdy, and the cities are very strongly fortified; indeed, we saw there the descendants
29 of Anak. We also saw the Amalekites who
live in the Negeb, Hittites, Jebusites, and
Amorites who live in the hill-country, and
the Canaanites who live by the sea and along
the Jordan.'
30 Then Caleb called for silence before Moses
and said, 'Let us go up at once and occupy
the country; we are well able to conquer it.'
31 But the men who had gone with him said,
'No, we cannot attack these people; they are
32 stronger than we are.' Thus their report to
the Israelites about the land which they had
explored was discouraging: 'The country we
explored', they said, 'will swallow up any
who go to live in it. All the people we saw
33 there are men of gigantic size. When we set
eyes on the Nephilim[q] (the sons of Anak[r]
belong to the Nephilim) we felt no bigger
than grasshoppers; and that is how we
looked to them.'

The people rebel against the LORD

Then the whole Israelite community cried **14**
out in dismay; all night long they wept. One 2
and all they made complaints against Moses
and Aaron: 'If only we had died in Egypt
or in the wilderness!' they said. 'Far happier
if we had! Why should the LORD bring us 3
to this land, to die in battle and leave our
wives and our dependants to become the
spoils of war? To go back to Egypt would be
better than this.' And they began to talk of 4
choosing someone to lead them back.
Then Moses and Aaron flung themselves 5
on the ground before the assembled community of the Israelites, and two of those 6
who had explored the land, Joshua son of
Nun and Caleb son of Jephunneh, rent their
clothes and addressed the whole community: 7
'The country we penetrated and explored',
they said, 'is very good land indeed. If the 8
LORD is pleased with us, he will bring us into
this land which flows with milk and honey,
and give it to us. But you must not rebel 9
against the LORD. You need not fear the
people of the land; for there we shall find
food. They have lost the protection that they
had: the LORD is with us. You have nothing
to fear from them.' But by way of answer 10
the assembled Israelites threatened to stone
them, when suddenly the glory of the LORD
appeared to them all in the Tent of the
Presence.
Then the LORD said to Moses, 'How much 11
longer will this people treat me with contempt? How much longer will they refuse to
trust me in spite of all the signs I have shown
among them? I will strike them with pesti- 12
lence. I will deny them their heritage, and
you and your descendants I will make into
a nation greater and more numerous than
they.' But Moses answered the LORD, 'What 13
if the Egyptians hear of it? It was thou who
didst bring this people out of Egypt by thy
strength. What if they tell the inhabitants of 14
this land? They too have heard of thee,
LORD, that thou art with this people, and
art seen face to face, that thy cloud stays
over them, and thou goest before them in a
pillar of cloud by day and in a pillar of fire
by night. If then thou dost put them all to 15
death at one blow, the nations who have
heard these tales of thee will say, "The LORD 16
could not bring this people into the land
which he promised them by oath; and so
he destroyed them in the wilderness."
'Now let the LORD's might be shown in its 17
greatness, true to thy proclamation of thyself—"The LORD, long-suffering, ever con- 18
stant, who forgives iniquity and rebellion,
and punishes sons to the third and fourth

o descendants of Anak: *or* tall men. *p* Eshcol: *that is* Bunch of Grapes. *q* *Or* giants. *r* sons of Anak: *or* tall men.

generation for the iniquity of their fathers, though he does not sweep them clean away."

19 Thou hast borne with this people from Egypt all the way here; forgive their iniquity, I beseech thee, as befits thy great and constant love.'

The LORD pronounces punishment

20 The LORD said, 'Your prayer is answered;
21 I pardon them. But as I live, in very truth
22-23 the glory of the LORD shall fill the earth. Not one of all those who have seen my glory and the signs which I wrought in Egypt and in the wilderness shall see the country which I promised on oath to their fathers. Ten times they have challenged me and not obeyed my voice. None of those who have flouted me
24-25 shall see this land. But my servant Caleb showed a different spirit: he followed me with his whole heart. Because of this, I will bring him into the land in which he has already set foot, the territory of the Amalekites and the Canaanites who dwell in the Vale, and put his descendants in possession of it. Tomorrow you must turn back and set out for the wilderness by way of the Red Sea.'ˢ

26 The LORD spoke to Moses and Aaron and
27 said, 'How long must I tolerateᵗ the complaints of this wicked community? I have heard the Israelites making complaints
28 against me. Tell them that this is the very word of the LORD: As I live, I will bring home to you the words I have heard you
29 utter. Here in this wilderness your bones shall lie, every man of you on the register from twenty years old and upwards, because you have made these complaints against me.
30 Not one of you shall enter the land which I swore with uplifted hand should be your home, except only Caleb son of Jephunneh
31 and Joshua son of Nun. As for your dependants, those dependants who, you said, would become the spoils of war, I will bring them in to the land you have rejected, and
32 they shall enjoy it. But as for the rest of you,

your bones shall lie in this wilderness; your 33 sons shall be wanderers in the wilderness forty years, paying the penalty of your wanton disloyalty till the last man of you dies there. Forty days you spent exploring 34 the country, and forty years you shall spend —a year for each day—paying the penalty of your iniquities. You shall know what it means to have me against you.ᵘ I, the LORD, 35 have spoken. This I swear to do to all this wicked community who have combined against me. There shall be an end of them here in this wilderness; here they shall die.' But the men whom Moses had sent to ex- 36 plore the land, and who came back and by their report set all the community complaining against him, died of the plague before the 37 LORD; they died of the plague because they had made a bad report. Of those who went 38 to explore the land, Joshua son of Nun and Caleb son of Jephunneh alone remained alive.

Israel defeated at Hormah

When Moses reported the LORD's words to 39 all the Israelites, the people were plunged in grief. They set out early next morning and 40 made for the heights of the hill-country, saying, 'Look, we are on our way up to the place the LORD spoke of. We admit that we have been wrong.' But Moses replied, 'Must 41 you persist in disobeying the LORD's command? No good will come of this. Go no 42 further; you will not have the LORD with you, and your enemies will defeat you. For 43 in front of you are the Amalekites and Canaanites, and you will die by the sword, because you have ceased to follow the LORD, and he will no longer be with you.' But they 44 went recklessly on their way towards the heights of the hill-country, though neither the Ark of the Covenant of the LORD nor Moses moved with them out of the camp; and the Amalekites and Canaanites from 45 those hills came down and fell upon them, and crushed them at Hormah.

Laws concerning offerings

15 The LORD spoke to Moses and
2 said, Speak to the Israelites in these words: When you enter the land where you are to live, the land
3 I am giving you, you will make food-offerings to the LORD; they may be whole-offerings or any sacrifice made in fulfilment of a specialᵛ vow or by way of freewill offering or at one of the appointed seasons. When you thus make an offering of soothing odour from herd or flock to the LORD,
4 the man who offers, in presenting it, shall add a grain-offering of a

tenth of an ephah of flour mixed
5 with a quarter of a hin of oil. You shall also add to the whole-offering or shared-offering a quarter of a hin of wine as a drink-offering with each lamb sacrificed.
6 If the animal is a ram, the grain-offering shall be two tenths of an ephah of flour mixed with a third
7 of a hin of oil, and the wine for the drink-offering shall be a third of a hin; in this way you will make an offering of soothing odour to the LORD.
8 When you offer to the LORD a young bull, whether as a whole-offering or as a sacrifice to fulfil

a specialʷ vow, or as a shared-offering, you shall add a grain-offering of three tenths of an ephah 9 of flour mixed with half a hin of oil, and for the drink-offering, half 10 a hin of wine; the whole will thus be a food-offering of soothing odour to the LORD. This is what 11 must be done in each case, for every bull or ram, lamb or kid, whatever the number of each that 12 you offer. Every native Israelite 13 shall observe these rules in each case when he offers a food-offering of soothing odour to the LORD.

When an alien residing with you 14 or permanently settled among you

---

s Or the Sea of Reeds.   t must I tolerate: prob. rdg.; Heb. for.   u Or to thwart me.   v in fulfilment of a special: or to discharge a . . .   w fulfil a special: or discharge a . . .

offers a food-offering of soothing odour to the LORD, he shall do as 5 you do. There is one and the same rule for you and for the resident alien, a rule binding for all time on your descendants; you and the alien are alike before the LORD. 6 There shall be one law and one custom for you and for the alien residing with you.

7 The LORD spoke to Moses and 8 said, Speak to the Israelites in these words: After you have entered the land into which I am bring- 9 ing you, whenever you eat the bread of the country, you shall set aside a contribution for the 10 LORD. You shall set aside a cake made of your first kneading of dough, as you set aside the contribution from the threshing-floor. 11 You must give a contribution to the LORD from your first kneading of dough; this rule is binding on your descendants.

12 When through inadvertence you omit to carry out any of these com- 13 mands which the LORD gave to Moses—any command whatever that the LORD gave you through Moses on that first day and there- 14 after and made binding on your descendants—if it be done inadvertently, unnoticed by the community, then the whole community shall offer one young bull as a whole-offering, a soothing odour

to the LORD, with its proper grain-offering and drink-offering accord- 25 ing to custom; and they shall add one he-goat as a sin-offering. The priest shall make expiation for the whole community of Israelites, and they shall be forgiven. The omission was inadvertent; and they have brought their offering, a food-offering to the LORD; they have made their sin-offering before the 26 LORD for their inadvertence; the whole community of Israelites and the aliens residing among you shall be forgiven. The inadvertence was shared by the whole people.

27 If any individual sins inadvertently, he shall present a yearling 28 she-goat as a sin-offering, and the priest shall make expiation before the LORD for the said individual, 29 and he shall be forgiven. For anyone who sins inadvertently, there shall be one law for all, whether native Israelite or resident alien. 30 But the person who sins presumptuously, native or alien, insults the LORD. He shall be cut 31 off from his people, because he has brought the word of the LORD into contempt and violated his command. That person shall be wholly cut off; the guilt shall be on his head alone.

A sabbath-breaker stoned

32 During the time that the Israelites

were in the wilderness, a man was found gathering sticks on the sabbath day. Those who had caught 33 him in the act brought him to Moses and Aaron and all the community, and they kept him in cus- 34 tody, because it was not clearly known what was to be done with him. The LORD said to Moses, 'The 35 man must be put to death; he must be stoned by all the community outside the camp.' So they 36 took him outside the camp and all stoned him to death, as the LORD had commanded Moses.

Tassels on garments

The LORD spoke to Moses and 37 said, Speak to the Israelites in 38 these words: You must make tassels like flowers on the corners of your garments, you and your children's children. Into this tassel you shall work a violet thread, and 39 whenever you see this in the tassel, you shall remember all the LORD's commands and obey them, and not go your own wanton ways, led astray by your own eyes and hearts. This token is to ensure that you 40 remember all my commands and obey them, and keep yourselves holy, consecrated to your God.

I am the LORD your God who 41 brought you out of Egypt to become your God. I am the LORD your God.

The authority of Moses challenged

16 Now Korah son of Izhar, son of Kohath, son of Levi, with the Reubenites Dathan and Abiram sons of Eliab and On son of Peleth, 2 challenged the authority of Moses. With them in their revolt were two hundred and fifty Israelites, all men of rank in the community, conveners of assembly and men of 3 good standing. They confronted Moses and Aaron and said to them, 'You take too much upon yourselves. Every member of the community is holy and the LORD is among them all. Why do you set yourselves up 4 above the assembly of the LORD?' When Moses heard this, he prostrated himself, 5 and he said to Korah and all his company, 'Tomorrow morning the LORD shall declare who is his, who is holy and may present offerings to him. The man whom the LORD 6 chooses shall present them. This is what you must do, you, Korah, and all your 7 company: you must take censers and put fire in them, and then place incense on them before the LORD tomorrow. The man whom the LORD then chooses is the man who is holy. You take too much upon yourselves, you sons of Levi.'

8 Moses said to Korah, 'Now listen, you 9 sons of Levi. Is it not enough for you that

the God of Israel has set you apart from the community of Israel, bringing you near him to maintain the service of the Tabernacle of the LORD and to stand before the community as their ministers? He has brought you near 10 him and your brother Levites with you; now you seek the priesthood as well. That is why 11 you and all your company have combined together against the LORD. What is Aaron that you should make these complaints against him?'

Moses sent to fetch Dathan and Abiram 12 sons of Eliab, but they answered, 'We are not coming. Is it a small thing that you have 13 brought us away from a land flowing with milk and honey to let us die in the wilderness? Must you also set yourself up as prince over us? What is more, you have not brought 14 us into a land flowing with milk and honey, nor have you given us fields and vineyards to inherit. Do you think you can hoodwink men like us? We are not coming.' This 15 answer made Moses very angry, and he said to the LORD, 'Take no notice of their murmuring. I have not taken from them so much as a single ass; I have done no wrong to any of them.'

Moses said to Korah, 'Present yourselves 16 before the LORD tomorrow, you and all your company, you and they and Aaron.

(Num. 16. 17)

17 Each man of you is to take his censer and put incense on it. Then you shall present them before the LORD with their two hundred and fifty censers, and you and Aaron
18 shall also bring your censers.' So each man took his censer and put fire in it and placed incense on it; Moses and Aaron took their stand at the entrance to the Tent of the
19 Presence, and Korah gathered his whole company together and faced them at the entrance to the Tent of the Presence. Then the glory of the LORD appeared to
20 the whole community. And the LORD spoke
21 to Moses and Aaron and said, 'Stand apart from this company, so that I may make an
22 end of them in a single instant.' But they prostrated themselves and said, 'O God, God of the spirits of all mankind, if one man sins, wilt thou be angry with the whole
23 community?' But the LORD said to Moses,
24 'Tell them to stand back from the dwellings of Korah, Dathan and Abiram.'
25 So Moses rose and went to Dathan and Abiram, and the elders of Israel followed
26 him. He said to the whole community, 'Stand well away from the tents of these wicked men; touch nothing of theirs, or you will be
27 swept away because of all their sins.' So they moved away from the places occupied by Korah, Dathan and Abiram. Now Dathan and Abiram, holding themselves erect, had come out to the entrance of their tents with their wives, their sons, and their dependants.
28 Then Moses said, 'This shall prove to you that it is the LORD who sent me to do all these things, and it was not my own heart
29 that prompted me. If these men die a natural death and share the common fate of man,
30 then the LORD has not sent me; but if the LORD makes a great chasm, and the ground opens its mouth and swallows them and all that is theirs, and they go down alive to Sheol, then you will know that these men have held the LORD in contempt.'
31 Hardly had Moses spoken when the
32 ground beneath them split; the earth opened

its mouth and swallowed them and their homes—all the followers of Korah and all their property. They went down alive into 33 Sheol with all that they had; the earth closed over them, and they vanished from the assembly. At their cries all the Israelites 34 round them fled, shouting, 'Look to yourselves! the earth will swallow us up.' Meanwhile fire had come out from the LORD and 35 burnt up the two hundred and fifty men who were presenting the incense.

Then the LORD spoke to Moses and said, 36 'Bid Eleazar son of Aaron the priest set 37 aside the censers from the burnt remains, and scatter the fire from them far and wide, because they are holy. And the censers of 38 these men who sinned at the cost of their lives you shall make into beaten plates to cover the altar; they are holy, because they have been presented before the LORD. Let them be a sign to the Israelites.' So Eleazar 39 the priest took the bronze[x] censers which the victims of the fire had presented, and they were beaten into plates to make a covering for the altar, as a reminder to the 40 Israelites that no person unqualified, not descended from Aaron, should come forward to burn incense before the LORD, or his fate would be that of Korah and his company. All this was done as the LORD commanded Eleazar through Moses.

Next day all the community of the 41 Israelites raised complaints against Moses and Aaron and taxed them with causing the death of some of the LORD's people. As 42 they gathered against Moses and Aaron, they turned towards the Tent of the Presence and saw that the cloud covered it, and the glory of the LORD appeared. Moses and 43 Aaron came to the front of the Tent of the Presence, and the LORD spoke to Moses and 44 Aaron and said, 'Stand well clear of this 45 community, so that in a single instant I may make an end of them.' Then they prostrated themselves, and Moses said to Aaron, 'Take 46 your censer, put fire from the altar in it, set incense on it, and go with it quickly to the assembled community to make expiation for them. Wrath has gone forth already from the presence of the LORD. The plague has begun.' So Aaron took his censer, as Moses 47 had said, ran into the midst of the assembly and found that the plague had begun among the people. He put incense on the censer and made expiation for the people, standing 48 between the dead and the living, and the plague stopped. Fourteen thousand seven 49 hundred died of it, in addition to those who had died for the offence of Korah. When 50 Aaron came back to Moses at the entrance to the Tent of the Presence, the plague had stopped.

x *Or* copper.

Aaron's staff

7 The LORD spoke to Moses and said, 'Speak
2 to the Israelites and tell them to give you
a staff for each tribe, one from every tribal
chief, twelve in all, and write each man's
3 name on his staff. On Levi's staff write the
name of Aaron, for there shall be one staff
4 for each head of a tribe. You shall put them
all in the Tent of the Presence before the
5 Tokens, where I meet you, and the staff of
the man I choose shall sprout. I will rid myself of the complaints of these Israelites, who
keep on complaining against you.'
6 Moses thereupon spoke to the Israelites,
and each of their chiefs handed him a staff,
each of them one for his tribe, twelve in all,
7 and Aaron's staff among them. Moses put
them before the LORD in the Tent of the
Tokens, and next day when he entered the **8**
tent, he found that Aaron's staff, the staff
for the tribe of Levi, had sprouted. Indeed,
it had sprouted, blossomed, and produced
ripe almonds. Moses then brought out the **9**
staffs from before the LORD and showed
them to all the Israelites; they saw for themselves, and each man took his own staff.
The LORD said to Moses, 'Put back Aaron's **10**
staff in front of the Tokens to be kept as a
warning to all rebels, so that you may rid
me once and for all of their complaints,
and then they shall not die.' Moses did **11**
this; as the LORD had commanded him, so
he did.
The Israelites said to Moses, 'This is the **12**
end of us! We perish, one and all! Every **13**
single person who goes near the Tabernacle
of the LORD dies. Is this to be our final end?'

Priests and Levites

8 The LORD said to Aaron: You and
your sons, together with the members of your father's tribe, shall be **11**
fully answerable for the sanctuary.
You and your sons alone shall be
answerable for your priestly office;
2 but you shall admit your kinsmen
of Levi, your father's tribe, to be
attached to you and assist you
while you and your sons are before
3 the Tent of the Tokens. They shall
be in attendance on you and fulfil
all the duties of the Tent, but shall
not go near the holy vessels and
the altar, or they will die and you
4 with them. They shall be attached
to you and be responsible for the
maintenance of the Tent of the
Presence in every detail; no unqualified person shall come near
5 you. You yourselves shall be responsible for the sanctuary and the
altar, so that wrath may no more
6 fall on the Israelites. I have myself
taken the Levites your kinsmen out
of all the Israelites as a gift for you,
given to the LORD for the maintenance of the Tent of the Presence.
7 But only you and your sons may
fulfil the duties of your priestly
office that concern the altar or lie
within the Veil. This duty is yours;
I bestow on you this gift of priestly
service. The unqualified person
who intrudes on it shall be put to
death.
8 The LORD said to Aaron: I, the
LORD, commit to your control the
contributions made to me, that is
all the holy-gifts of the Israelites.
I give them to you and to your sons
for your allotted portion due to you
9 in perpetuity. Out of the most holy
gifts kept back from the altar-fire
this part shall belong to you: every
offering, whether grain-offering,
sin-offering, or guilt-offering, rendered to me as a most holy gift,
belongs to you and to your sons.
10 You shall eat it as befits most holy
gifts; every male may eat it. You
shall regard it as holy.
11 This also is yours: the contribution from all such of their gifts as
are presented as special gifts by
the Israelites. I give them to you
and to your sons and daughters
with you as a due in perpetuity.
Every person in your household
who is ritually clean may eat them.
12 I give you all the choicest of the
oil, the choicest of the new wine
and the corn, the firstfruits which
13 are given to the LORD. The first-
ripe fruits of all produce in the
land which are brought to the
LORD shall be yours. Everyone in
your household who is clean may
eat them.
14 Everything in Israel which has
been devoted to God shall be yours.
15 All the first-born of man or beast
which are brought to the LORD
shall be yours. Notwithstanding,
you must accept payment in redemption of any first-born of man
16 and of unclean beasts: at the end
of one month you shall redeem it
at the fixed price of five shekels
of silver by the sacred standard
17 (twenty gerahs to the shekel). You
must not, however, allow the redemption of the first-born of a
cow, sheep, or goat; they are holy.
You shall fling their blood against
the altar and burn their fat in sacrifice as a food-offering of soothing
18 odour to the LORD; their flesh shall
be yours, as are the breast of the
special gift and the right leg.
19 All the contributions from holy-
gifts, which the Israelites set aside
for the LORD, I give to you and to
your sons and daughters with you
as a due in perpetuity. This is a
perpetual covenant of salt before
the LORD with you and your
descendants also.
The LORD said to Aaron: You **20**
shall have no patrimony in the
land of Israel, no holding among
them; I am your holding in Israel,
I am your patrimony.
To the Levites I give every tithe **21**
in Israel to be their patrimony, in
return for the service they render
in maintaining the Tent of the
Presence. In order that the Israel- **22**
ites may not henceforth approach
the Tent and thus incur the penalty
of death, the Levites alone shall **23**
perform the service of the Tent,
and they shall accept the full responsibility for it. This rule is
binding on your descendants for
all time. They shall have no patrimony among the Israelites, because **24**
I give them as their patrimony the
tithe which the Israelites set aside
as a contribution to the LORD.
Therefore I say to them: You shall
have no patrimony among the
Israelites.
The LORD spoke to Moses and **25**
said, Speak to the Levites in these **26**
words: When you receive from the
Israelites the tithe which I give you
from them as your patrimony, you
shall set aside from it the contribution to the LORD, a tithe of the
tithe. Your contribution shall count **27**
for you as if it were corn from the
threshing-floor and juice from the
vat. In this way you too shall set **28**
aside the contribution due to the
LORD out of all tithes which you
receive from the Israelites and
shall give the LORD's contribution
to Aaron the priest. Out of all the **29**
gifts you receive you shall set aside
the contribution due to the LORD;
and the gift which you hallow[y]
must be taken from the choicest of
them.
You shall say to the Levites: **30**
When you have set aside the
choicest part of your portion, the
remainder shall count for you as

y you hallow: prob. rdg.; Heb. obscure.

the produce of the threshing-floor 31 and the winepress, and you may eat it anywhere, you and your households. It is your payment for service in the Tent of the Presence.

32 When you have set aside its choicest part, you will incur no penalty in respect of it, and you will not be profaning the holy-gifts of the Israelites; so you will not die.

Purification from uncleanness

19 The LORD spoke to Moses and 2 Aaron and said: This is a law and a statute which the LORD has ordained. Tell the Israelites to bring you a red cow without 3 blemish or defect, which has never borne the yoke. You shall give it to Eleazar the priest, and it shall be taken outside the camp and slaughtered*z* to the east of it. 4 Eleazar the priest shall take some of the blood on his finger and sprinkle it seven times towards the front of the Tent of the Presence. 5 The cow shall be burnt in his sight, skin, flesh, and blood, together 6 with the offal. The priest shall then take cedar-wood, marjoram, and scarlet thread, and throw them into the heart of the fire in which the 7 cow is burning. He shall wash his clothes and bathe his body in water; after which he may enter the camp, but he remains ritually 8 unclean till sunset. The man who burnt the cow shall wash his

clothes and bathe his body in water, but he also remains unclean 9 till sunset. Then a man who is clean shall collect the ashes of the cow and deposit them outside the camp in a clean place. They shall be reserved for use by the Israelite community in the water of ritual purification; for the cow is a sin-10 offering. The man who collected the ashes of the cow shall wash his clothes, but he remains unclean till sunset. This rule shall be binding for all time on the Israelites and on the alien who is living with them. 11 Whoever touches a corpse shall be ritually unclean for seven days. 12 He shall get himself purified with the water of ritual purification on the third day and on the seventh day, and then he shall be clean. If he is not purified both on the third day and on the seventh, he shall 13 not be clean. Everyone who touches a corpse, that is the body of a man who has died, and does not purify himself, defiles the Tabernacle of the LORD. That person shall be cut off from Israel. The water of purification has not been flung over him; he remains unclean, and his impurity is still upon him. 14 When a man dies in a tent, this is the law: everyone who goes into the tent and everyone who was in-15 side the tent shall be ritually unclean for seven days, and every open vessel which has no covering tied over it shall also be unclean.

In the open, anyone who touches a 16 man killed with a weapon or one who has died naturally, or who touches a human bone or a grave, shall be unclean for seven days. For such uncleanness, they shall 17 take some of the ash from the burnt mass of the sin-offering and add fresh water to it in a vessel. Then 18 a man who is clean shall take marjoram, dip it in the water, and sprinkle the tent with all the vessels in it and all the people who were there, or the man who has touched a human bone, a corpse (whether the man was killed or died naturally), or a grave. The man who is 19 clean shall sprinkle the unclean man on the third day and on the seventh; on the seventh day he shall purify him; then the man shall wash his clothes and bathe in water, and at sunset he shall be clean. If a man who is unclean does 20 not get himself purified, that person shall be cut off from the assembly, because he has defiled the sanctuary of the LORD. The water of purification has not been flung over him: he is unclean. This 21 rule shall be binding on you for all time. The man who sprinkles the water of purification shall also wash his clothes, and whoever touches the water shall be unclean till sunset. Whatever the unclean man 22 touches shall be unclean, and any person who touches that shall be unclean till sunset.

Water from the rock

20 In the first month the whole community of Israel reached the wilderness of Zin and stayed some time at Kadesh; there Miriam died and was buried.

2 There was no water for the community; so they gathered against Moses and Aaron. 3 The people disputed with Moses and said, 'If only we had perished when our brothers 4 perished in the presence of the LORD! Why have you brought the assembly of the LORD into this wilderness for us and our beasts to 5 die here? Why did you fetch us up from Egypt to bring us to this vile place, where nothing will grow, neither corn nor figs, vines nor pomegranates? There is not even 6 any water to drink.' Moses and Aaron came forward in front of the assembly to the entrance of the Tent of the Presence. There they fell prostrate, and the glory of the LORD appeared to them. 7 8 The LORD spoke to Moses and said, 'Take a*a* staff, and then with Aaron your brother assemble all the community, and, in front of them all, speak to the rock and it will yield its water. Thus you will produce water for the community out of the rock, for them 9 and their beasts to drink.' Moses left the

presence of the LORD with the staff, as he had commanded him. Then he and Aaron 10 gathered the assembly together in front of the rock, and he said to them, 'Listen to me, you rebels. Must we get water out of this rock for you?' Moses raised his hand and 11 struck the rock twice with his staff. Water gushed out in abundance and they all drank, men and beasts. But the LORD said to Moses 12 and Aaron, 'You did not trust me so far as to uphold my holiness in the sight of the Israelites; therefore you shall not lead this assembly into the land which I promised to give them.' Such were the waters of Me-13 ribah,*b* where the people disputed with the LORD and through which his holiness was upheld.

The Edomites refuse passage to Israel

From Kadesh Moses sent envoys to the 14 king of Edom: 'This is a message from your brother Israel. You know all the hardships we have encountered, how our fathers went 15 down to Egypt, and we lived there for many years. The Egyptians ill-treated us and our fathers before us, and we cried to the LORD 16 for help. He listened to us and sent an angel, and he brought us out of Egypt; and now

---

z Or he shall take it outside the camp and slaughter it . . .   *a Or* the.   *b That is* Dispute.

we are here at Kadesh, a town on your frontier. Grant us passage through your country.
We will not trespass on field or vineyard, or
drink from your wells. We will keep to the
king's highway; we will not turn off to right
or left until we have crossed your territory.'
But the Edomites answered, 'You shall not
cross our land. If you do, we will march out
and attack you in force.' The Israelites said,
'But we will keep to the main road. If we
and our flocks drink your water, we will pay
you for it; we will simply cross your land on
foot.' But the Edomites said, 'No, you shall
not', and took the field against them with
a large army in full strength. Thus the Edomites refused to allow Israel to cross their
frontier, and Israel went a different way to
avoid a conflict.

The death of Aaron

The whole community of Israel set out from
Kadesh and came to Mount Hor. At Mount
Hor, near the frontier of Edom, the LORD
said to Moses and Aaron, 'Aaron shall be
gathered to his father's kin. He shall not
enter the land which I promised to give the
Israelites, because over the waters of Meribah you rebelled against my command.
Take Aaron and his son Eleazar, and go up
Mount Hor. Strip Aaron of his robes and
invest Eleazar his son with them, for Aaron
shall be taken from you: he shall die there.'
Moses did as the LORD had commanded him:
they went up Mount Hor in sight of the
whole community, and Moses stripped
Aaron of his robes and invested his son
Eleazar with them. There Aaron died on the
mountain-top, and Moses and Eleazar came
down from the mountain. So the whole
community saw that Aaron had died, and
all Israel mourned him for thirty days.

The Canaanites attack Israel

1 When the Canaanite king of Arad who lived
in the Negeb heard that the Israelites were
coming by way of Atharim, he attacked them
2 and took some of them prisoners. Israel
thereupon made a vow to the LORD and said,
'If thou wilt deliver this people into my
3 power, I will destroy their cities.' The LORD
listened to Israel and delivered the Canaanites into their power. Israel destroyed them
and their cities and called the place Hormah.*c*

A plague of snakes

4 Then they left Mount Hor by way of the
Red Sea to march round the flank of Edom.
5 But on the way they grew impatient and
spoke against God and Moses. 'Why have
you brought us up from Egypt', they said,
'to die in the desert where there is neither
food nor water? We are heartily sick of this
miserable fare.' Then the LORD sent poison- 6
ous snakes among the people, and they bit
the Israelites so that many of them died.
The people came to Moses and said, 'We 7
sinned when we spoke against the LORD and
you. Plead with the LORD to rid us of the
snakes.' Moses therefore pleaded with the
LORD for the people; and the LORD told 8
Moses to make a serpent*d* of bronze and
erect it as a standard, so that anyone who
had been bitten could look at it and recover.
So Moses made a bronze serpent and erected 9
it as a standard, so that when a snake had
bitten a man, he could look at the bronze
serpent and recover.

The Israelites journey around Moab

The Israelites went on and encamped at 10
Oboth. They moved on from Oboth and 11
encamped at Iye-abarim in the wilderness on
the eastern frontier of Moab. From there 12
they moved and encamped by the gorge of
the Zared. They moved on from the Zared 13
and encamped by the farther side of the
Arnon in the wilderness which extends into
Amorite territory, for the Arnon was the
Moabite frontier; it lies between Moab and
the Amorites. That is why the Book of the 14
Wars of the LORD speaks of Vaheb*e* in
Suphah and the gorges:

Arnon and the watershed of the gorges　15
that falls away towards the dwellings at Ar
and slopes towards the frontier of Moab.

From there they moved on to Beer:*f* this is 16
the water-hole where the LORD said to
Moses, 'Gather the people together and I
will give them water.' It was then that Israel 17
sang this song:

Well up, spring water! Greet it with song,
the spring unearthed by the princes, 18
laid open by the leaders of the people
with sceptre and with mace,
a gift from the wilderness.

And they proceeded from Beer*g* to Nahaliel, 19
and from Nahaliel to Bamoth; then from 20
Bamoth to the valley in the Moabite country
below the summit of Pisgah overlooking the
desert.

Israel conquers Sihon

Then Israel sent envoys to the Amorite king 21
Sihon and said, 'Grant us passage through 22
your country. We will not trespass on field
or vineyard, nor will we drink from your
wells. We will travel by the king's highway
till we have crossed your territory.' But 23
Sihon would not grant Israel passage
through his territory; he mustered all his

c That is Destruction.　　*d Or* snake.　　*e Name meaning* Watershed.　　*f Name meaning* Water-hole.
g Prob. rdg.; Heb. from a gift.

people and came out against Israel in the wilderness. 24 He advanced as far as Jahaz and attacked Israel, but Israel put them to the sword, giving no quarter, and occupied their land from the Arnon to the Jabbok, the territory of the Ammonites, where the 25 country became difficult. So Israel took all these Amorite cities and settled in them, that is in Heshbon and all its dependent 26 villages. Heshbon was the capital of the Amorite king Sihon, who had fought against the former king of Moab and taken from him all his territory as far as the Arnon. 27 Therefore the bards say:

Come to Heshbon, come!
Let us see the city of Sihon rebuilt and restored!
28 For fire blazed out from Heshbon,
and flames from Sihon's city.
It devoured Ar of Moab,
and swept the high ground at Arnon head.
29 Woe to you, Moab;
it is the end of you, you people of Kemosh.
He has made his sons fugitives
and his daughters the prisoners of Sihon the Amorite king.
30 From Heshbon to Dibon their very embers are burnt out
and they are extinct,
while the fire spreads onward to Medeba.
31 Thus Israel occupied the territory of the Amorites.

Israel conquers Og

32 Moses then sent men to explore Jazer; the Israelites captured it together with its dependent villages and drove out the Amorites 33 living there. Then they turned and advanced along the road to Bashan. Og king of Bashan, with all his people, took the field against 34 them at Edrei. The LORD said to Moses, 'Do not be afraid of him. I have delivered him into your hands, with all his people and his land. Deal with him as you dealt with Sihon the Amorite king who lived in Hesh-35 bon.' So they put him to the sword with his sons and all his people, until there was no survivor left, and they occupied his land.

Balak sends for Balaam

22 The Israelites went forward and encamped in the lowlands of Moab on the farther side of the Jordan from Jericho. 2 Balak son of Zippor saw what Israel had 3 done to the Amorites, and Moab was in terror of the people because there were so many of them. The Moabites were sick with 4 fear at the sight of them; and they said to the elders of Midian, 'This horde will soon lick up everything round us as a bull crops the

spring grass.' Balak son of Zippor was at that time king of Moab. He sent a deputation 5 to summon Balaam son of Beor, who was at Pethor by the Euphrates in the land of the Amavites, with this message, 'Look, an entire nation has come out of Egypt; they cover the face of the country and are settling at my very door. Come at once and lay a 6 curse on them, because they are too many for me; then I may be able to defeat them and drive them from the country. I know that those whom you bless are blessed, and those whom you curse are cursed.'

The elders of Moab and Midian took the 7 fees for augury with them, and they came to Balaam and told him what Balak had said. 'Spend this night here,' he said, 'and 8 I will give you whatever answer the LORD gives to me.' So the Moabite chiefs stayed with Balaam. God came to Balaam and 9 asked him, 'Who are these men with you?' Balaam replied, 'Balak son of Zippor king 10 of Moab has sent them to me and he says, "Look, a people newly come out of Egypt 11 is covering the face of the country. Come at once and denounce them for me; then I may be able to fight them and drive them away."' God said to Balaam, 'You are not to go with 12 them or curse the people, because they are to be blessed.'[h] So Balaam rose in the morn-13 ing and said to Balak's chiefs, 'Go back to your own country; the LORD has refused to let me go with you.' Then the Moabite chiefs 14 took their leave and went back to Balak, and told him that Balaam had refused to come with them; whereupon Balak sent a 15 second and larger embassy of higher rank than the first. They came to Balaam and 16 told him, 'This is the message from Balak son of Zippor: "Let nothing stand in the way of your coming. I will confer great 17 honour upon you; I will do whatever you ask me. But you must come and denounce this people for me."' Balaam gave this 18 answer to Balak's messengers: 'Even if Balak were to give me all the silver and gold in his house, I could not disobey the command of the LORD my God in anything, small or great. But stay here for this night, 19 as the others did, that I may learn what more the LORD has to say to me.' During the night 20 God came to Balaam and said to him, 'If these men have come to summon you, then rise and go with them, but do only what I tell you.' So in the morning Balaam rose, 21 saddled his ass and went with the Moabite chiefs.

Balaam's ass

But God was angry because Balaam was 22 going, and as he came riding on his ass,

h Or are blessed.

accompanied by his two servants, the angel of the LORD took his stand in the road to 3 bar his way. When the ass saw the angel standing in the road with his sword drawn, she turned off the road into the fields, and Balaam beat the ass to bring her back on to 4 the road. Then the angel of the LORD stood where the road ran through a hollow, with 5 fenced vineyards on either side. The ass saw the angel and, crushing herself against the wall, crushed Balaam's foot against it, and 6 he beat her again. The angel of the LORD moved on further and stood in a narrow place where there was no room to turn either 7 to right or left. When the ass saw the angel, she lay down under Balaam. At that Balaam lost his temper and beat the ass with his 8 stick. The LORD then made the ass speak, and she said to Balaam, 'What have I done? This is the third time you have beaten me.' 9 Balaam answered the ass, 'You have been making a fool of me. If I had had a sword here, I should have killed you on the spot.' 10 But the ass answered, 'Am I not still the ass which you have ridden all your life? Have I ever taken such a liberty with you before?' 11 He said, 'No.' Then the LORD opened Balaam's eyes: he saw the angel of the LORD standing in the road with his sword drawn, and he bowed down and fell flat on his face 12 before him. The angel said to him, 'What do you mean by beating your ass three times 13 like this? I came out to bar your way but you made straight for me, and three times your ass saw me and turned aside. If she had not turned aside, I should by now have 14 killed you and spared her.' Balaam replied to the angel of the LORD, 'I have done wrong. I did not know that you stood in the road confronting me. But now, if my journey displeases you, I am ready to go back.' 15 The angel of the LORD said to Balaam, 'Go on with these men; but say only what I tell you.' So Balaam went on with Balak's chiefs.

Balaam and Balak

When Balak heard that Balaam was coming, 36 he came out to meet him as far as Ar of Moab by the Arnon on his frontier. Balak 37 said to Balaam, 'Did I not send time and again to summon you? Why did you not come? Did you think that I could not do you honour?' Balaam replied, 'I have come, as 38 you see. But now that I am here, what power have I of myself to say anything? Whatever the word God puts into my mouth, that is what I will say.' So Balaam went with Balak 39 till they came to Kiriath-huzoth, and Balak 40 slaughtered cattle and sheep and sent them to Balaam and to the chiefs who were with him.

In the morning Balak took Balaam and 41 led him up to the Heights of Baal, from where he could see the full extent of the Israelite host. Then Balaam said to Balak, 'Build me **23** here seven altars and prepare for me seven bulls and seven rams.' Balak did as he asked 2 and offered a bull and a ram on each altar. Then he said to him, 'I have prepared the 3-4 seven altars, and I have offered the bull and the ram on each altar.' Balaam said to Balak, 'Take your stand beside your sacrifice, and let me go off by myself. It may happen that the LORD will meet me. Whatever he reveals to me, I will tell you.' So he went forthwith, and God met him. The LORD put words into 5 Balaam's mouth and said, 'Go back to Balak, and speak as I tell you.' So he went 6 back, and found Balak standing by his sacrifice, and with him all the Moabite chiefs. And Balaam uttered his oracle: 7

From Aram,*[i]* from the mountains of the east,
Balak king of Moab has brought me:
'Come, lay a curse for me on Jacob,
come, execrate Israel.'
How can I denounce whom God has not 8
    denounced?
How can I execrate whom the LORD has not
    execrated?
From the rocky heights I see them,   9
I watch them from the rounded hills.
I see a people that dwells alone,
that has not made itself one with the nations.
Who can count the host*[j]* of Jacob   10
or number the hordes*[k]* of Israel?
Let me die as men die who are righteous,
grant that my end may be as theirs!

Then Balak said to Balaam, 'What is this 11 you have done? I sent for you to denounce my enemies, and what you have done is to bless them.' But he replied, 'Must I not keep 12 to the words that the LORD puts into my mouth?'

Balak then said to him, 'Come with me 13 now to another place from which you will see them, though not the full extent of them;

i Or Syria.   *j Or* dust.   *k Or* quarter *or* sands.

you will not see them all. Denounce them for
14 me from there.' So he took him to the Field
of the Watchers[l] on the summit of Pisgah,
where he built seven altars and offered a
15 bull and a ram on each altar. Balaam said to
Balak, 'Take your stand beside your sacri-
16 fice, and I will meet God over there.' The
LORD met Balaam and put words into his
mouth, and said, 'Go back to Balak, and
17 speak as I tell you.' So he went back, and
found him standing beside his sacrifice, with
the Moabite chiefs. Balak asked what the
18 LORD had said, and Balaam uttered his
oracle:

Up, Balak, and listen:
hear what I am charged to say, son of Zippor.
19 God is not a mortal that he should lie,
not a man that he should change his mind.[m]
Has he not spoken, and will he not make it
good?
What he has proclaimed, he will surely fulfil.
20 I have received command to bless;
I will bless and I cannot gainsay it.
21 He has discovered no iniquity in Jacob
and has seen no mischief in Israel.[n]
The LORD their God is with them,
acclaimed among them as king.[o]
22 What its curving horns are to the wild ox,
God is to them, who brought them out of
Egypt.
23 Surely there is no divination in[p] Jacob,
and no augury in[p] Israel;
now is the time to say of Jacob
and of Israel, 'See what God has wrought!'
24 Behold a people rearing up like a lioness,
rampant like a lion;
he will not couch till he devours the prey
and drinks the blood of the slain.

25 Then Balak said to Balaam, 'You will not
denounce them; then at least do not bless
26 them'; and he answered, 'Did I not warn
you that I must do all the LORD tells me?'
27 Balak replied, 'Come, let me take you to
another place; perhaps God will be pleased
to let you denounce them for me from there.'
28 So he took Balaam to the summit of Peor
29 overlooking Jeshimon, and Balaam told him
to build seven altars for him there and pre-
30 pare seven bulls and seven rams. Balak did
as Balaam had said, and he offered a bull
and a ram on each altar.

24 But now that Balaam knew that the LORD
wished him to bless Israel, he did not go and
resort to divination as before. He turned
2 towards the desert; and as he looked, he
saw Israel encamped tribe by tribe. The spirit
3 of God came upon him, and he uttered his
oracle:

The very word of Balaam son of Beor,
the very word of the man whose sight is clear,

the very word of him who hears the words of 4
God,
who with staring eyes sees in a trance
the vision from the Almighty:
how goodly are your tents, O Jacob,   5
your dwelling-places, Israel,
like long rows of palms,   6
like gardens by a river,
like lign-aloes planted by the LORD,
like cedars beside the water!
The water in his vessels shall overflow,   7
and his seed shall be like great waters
so that his king may be taller than Agag,
and his kingdom lifted high.
What its curving horns are to the wild ox,   8
God is to him, who brought him out of
Egypt;
he shall devour his adversaries the nations,
crunch their bones, and smash their limbs in
pieces.
When he reclines he couches like a lion,   9
like a lioness, and no one dares rouse him.
Blessed be they that bless you,
and they that curse you be accursed!

Balaam's oracle

At that Balak was very angry with Balaam, 1
beat his hands together and said, 'I summoned you to denounce my enemies, and
three times you have persisted in blessing
them. Off with you to your own place! 1
I promised to confer great honour upon you,
but now the LORD has kept this honour from
you.' Balaam answered, 'But I told your 1
own messengers whom you sent: "If Balak 1
gives me all the silver and gold in his house,
I cannot disobey the command of the LORD
by doing anything of my own will, good or
bad. What the LORD speaks to me, that is
what I will say." Now I am going to my own 1
people; but first, I will warn you what this
people will do to yours in the days to come.'
So he uttered his oracle: 1

The very word of Balaam son of Beor,
the very word of the man whose sight is clear,
the very word of him who hears the words of 1
God,
who shares the knowledge of the Most High,
who with staring eyes sees in a trance
the vision from the Almighty:
I see him, but not now;   1
I behold him, but not near:
a star shall come forth out of Jacob,
a comet arise from Israel.
He shall smite the squadrons[q] of Moab,
and beat down all the sons of strife.
Edom shall be his by conquest
and Seir, his enemy, shall be his.
Israel shall do valiant deeds;
Jacob shall trample them down,   1
the last survivor from Ar shall he destroy.

l Or Field of Zophim.   *m Or* feel regret.   *n Or* None can discover calamity in Jacob nor see trouble
in Israel.   *o Or* royal care is bestowed on them.   *p Or* against.   *q Or* heads.

He saw Amalek and uttered his oracle:

First of all the nations was Amalek,
but his end shall be utter destruction.

He saw the Kenites and uttered his oracle:

Your refuge, though it seems secure,
your nest, though set on the mountain crag,
is doomed to burning, O Cain.
How long must you dwell there in my sight?

He uttered his oracle:

Ah, who are these assembling in the north,
invaders from the region of Kittim?
They will lay waste Assyria; they will lay
Eber waste:
he too shall perish utterly.

Then Balaam arose and returned home, and
Balak also went on his way.

Israel worships the Baal of Peor

When the Israelites were in Shittim, the
people began to have intercourse with Moabite women, who invited them to the sacrifices offered to their gods; and they ate the
sacrificial food and prostrated themselves
before the gods of Moab. The Israelites
joined in the worship of the Baal of Peor, and
the LORD was angry with them. He said to
Moses, 'Take all the leaders of the people
and hurl them down to their death before
the LORD in the full light of day, that the
fury of his anger may turn away from Israel.'
So Moses said to the judges of Israel, 'Put
to death, each one of you, those of his tribe
who have joined in the worship of the Baal
of Peor.'

One of the Israelites brought a Midianite
woman into his family in open defiance of
Moses and all the community of Israel, while
they were weeping by the entrance of the
Tent of the Presence. Phinehas son of 7
Eleazar, son of Aaron the priest, saw him.
He stepped out from the crowd and took
up a spear, and he went into the inner room 8
after the Israelite and transfixed the two of
them, the Israelite and the woman, pinning
them together. Thus the plague which had
attacked the Israelites was brought to a
stop; but twenty-four thousand had already 9
died.

The LORD spoke to Moses and said, 10
'Phinehas son of Eleazar, son of Aaron the 11
priest, has turned my wrath away from
the Israelites; he displayed among them
the same jealous anger that moved me, and
therefore in my jealousy I did not exterminate the Israelites. Tell him that I hereby 12
grant him my covenant of security of tenure.
He and his descendants after him shall enjoy 13
the priesthood under a covenant for all time,
because he showed his zeal for his God and
made expiation for the Israelites.' The name 14
of the Israelite struck down with the Midianite woman was Zimri son of Salu, a chief
in a Simeonite family, and the Midianite 15
woman's name was Cozbi daughter of Zur,
who was the head of a group of fathers'
families in Midian.

The LORD spoke to Moses and said, 16
'Make the Midianites suffer as they made 17–18
you suffer with their crafty tricks, and strike
them down; their craftiness was your undoing at Peor and in the affair of Cozbi their
sister, the daughter of a Midianite chief, who
was struck down at the time of the plague
that followed Peor.'

The numbering of Israel

After the plague the LORD said to
Moses and Eleazar the priest, son
of Aaron, 'Number the whole community of Israel by fathers' families, recording everyone in Israel
aged twenty years and upwards fit
for military service.' Moses and
Eleazar collected them in the lowlands of Moab by the Jordan near
Jericho,[r] all who were twenty years
of age and upwards, as the LORD
had commanded Moses.

These were the Israelites who
came out of Egypt:

Reubenites (Reuben was Israel's
eldest son): Enoch, the Enochite
family; Pallu, the Palluite family;
Hezron, the Hezronite family;
Carmi, the Carmite family. These
were the Reubenite families; the
number in their detailed list was
forty-three thousand seven hundred and thirty. Son of Pallu: Eliab.
Sons of Eliab: Nemuel, Dathan

and Abiram. These were the same
Dathan and Abiram, conveners of
the community, who defied Moses
and Aaron and joined the company of Korah in defying the LORD.
Then the earth opened its mouth 10
and swallowed them up with
Korah, and so their company died,
while fire burnt up the two hundred
and fifty men, and they became a
warning sign. The Korahites, how- 11
ever, did not die.

Simeonites, by their families: 12
Nemuel, the Nemuelite family;
Jamin, the Jaminite family; Jachin,
the Jachinite family; Zerah, the 13
Zarhite family; Saul, the Saulite
family. These were the Simeonite 14
families; the number in their detailed list was twenty-two thousand
two hundred.

Gadites, by their families: 15
Zephon, the Zephonite family;
Haggi, the Haggite family; Shuni,
the Shunite family; Ozni, the Oz- 16
nite family; Eri, the Erite family;

Arod, the Arodite family; Areli, 17
the Arelite family. These were the 18
Gadite families; the number in
their detailed list was forty thousand five hundred.

The sons of Judah were Er, Onan, 19
Shelah, Perez and Zerah; Er and
Onan died in Canaan. Judahites, 20
by their families: Shelah, the
Shelanite family; Perez, the Perez-
ite family; Zerah, the Zarhite
family. Perezites: Hezron, the Hez- 21
ronite family; Hamul, the Hamul-
ite family. These were the families 22
of Judah; the number in their detailed list was seventy-six thousand
five hundred.

Issacharites, by their families: 23
Tola, the Tolaite family; Pua, the
Puite family; Jashub, the Jashubite 24
family; Shimron, the Shimronite
family. These were the families of 25
Issachar; the number in their detailed list was sixty-four thousand
three hundred.

Zebulunites, by their families: 26

r *Prob. rdg.; Heb. adds* saying.

s *Verses 5–50: cp.* Gen. 46. 8–25; Exod. 6. 14, 15; 1 Chr. chs. 4–8.

Sered, the Sardite family; Elon, the Elonite family; Jahleel, the
27 Jahleelite family. These were the Zebulunite families; the number in their detailed list was sixty thousand five hundred.
28 Josephites, by their families:
29 Manasseh and Ephraim. Manassites: Machir, the Machirite family. Machir was the father of Gilead:
30 Gilead, the Gileadite family. Gileadites: Jeezer, the Jeezerite fami-
31 ly; Helek, the Helekite family; Asriel, the Asrielite family; Shechem,
32 the Shechemite family; Shemida, the Shemidaite family; Hepher, the
33 Hepherite family. Zelophehad son of Hepher had no sons, only daughters; their names were Mahlah, Noah, Hoglah, Milcah and Tir-
34 zah. These were the families of Manasseh; the number in their detailed list was fifty-two thousand seven hundred.
35 Ephraimites, by their families: Shuthelah, the Shuthalhite family; Becher, the Bachrite family; Tahan,
36 the Tahanite family. Shuthalhites:
37 Eran, the Eranite family. These were the Ephraimite families; the number in their detailed list was thirty-two thousand five hundred. These were the Josephites, by families.
38 Benjamites, by their families: Bela, the Belaite family; Ashbel, the Ashbelite family; Ahiram, the
39 Ahiramite family; Shupham, the Shuphamite family; Hupham,
40 the Huphamite family. Belaites: Ard and Naaman. Ard, the Ardite family; Naaman, the Naamite
41 family. These were the Benjamite families; the number in their detailed list was forty-five thousand six hundred.
42 Danites, by their families: Shuham, the Shuhamite family. These were the families of Dan by their
43 families; the number in the detailed list of the Shuhamite family was sixty-four thousand four hundred.
44 Asherites, by their families: Imna, the Imnite family; Ishvi, the Ishvite family; Beriah, the Beriite
45 family. Beriite families: Heber, the Heberite family; Malchiel, the
46 Malchielite family. The daughter
47 of Asher was named Serah. These were the Asherite families; the

number in their detailed list was fifty-three thousand four hundred.
48 Naphtalites, by their families: Jahzeel, the Jahzeelite family;
49 Guni, the Gunite family; Jezer, the Jezerite family; Shillem, the
50 Shillemite family. These were the Naphtalite families by their families; the number in their detailed list was forty-five thousand four hundred.
51 The total in the Israelite lists was six hundred and one thousand seven hundred and thirty.

The land to be apportioned by lot

52 The LORD spoke to Moses and said,
53 'The land shall be apportioned among these tribes according to
54 the number of names recorded. To the larger group you shall give a larger property and to the smaller a smaller; a property shall be given to each in proportion to its size as
55 shown in the detailed lists. The land, however, shall be apportioned by lot; the lots shall be cast for the properties by families in
56 the father's line. Properties shall be apportioned by lot between the larger families and the smaller.'

The tribe of Levi

57 The detailed lists of Levi, by families: Gershon, the Gershonite family; Kohath, the Kohathite family; Merari, the Merarite family.
58 These were the families of Levi: the Libnite, Hebronite, Mahlite, Mushite, and Korahite families. Kohath was the father of Am-
59 ram; Amram's wife was named Jochebed daughter of Levi, born to him in Egypt. She bore to Amram Aaron, Moses, and their sister
60 Miriam. Aaron's sons were Nadab, Abihu, Eleazar and Ithamar.
61 Nadab and Abihu died because they presented illicit fire before the LORD.
62 In the detailed lists of Levi the number of males, aged one month and upwards, was twenty-three thousand. They were recorded separately from the other Israelites because no property was allotted to them among the Israelites.

Caleb and Joshua

These were the detailed lists prepared by Moses and Eleazar the priest when they numbered the Israelites in the lowlands of Moab by the Jordan near Jericho. Among them there was not a single one of the Israelites whom Moses and Aaron the priest had recorded in the wilderness of Sinai; for the LORD had said they should all die in the wilderness. None of them was still living except Caleb son of Jephunneh and Joshua son of Nun.

When daughters inherit

A claim was presented by the daughters of Zelophehad son of Hepher, son of Gilead, son of Machir, son of Manasseh, son of Joseph. Their names were Mahlah, Noah, Hoglah, Milcah and Tirzah. They appeared at the entrance of the Tent of the Presence before Moses, Eleazar the priest, the chiefs, and all the community, and spoke as follows: 'Our father died in the wilderness. He was not among the company of Korah which combined together against the LORD; he died for his own sin and left no sons. Is it right that, because he had no son, our father's name should disappear from his family? Give us our property on the same footing as our father's brothers.'

So Moses brought their case before the LORD, and the LORD spoke to Moses and said, 'The claim of the daughters of Zelophehad is good. You must allow them to inherit on the same footing as their father's brothers. Let their father's patrimony pass to them. Then say this to the Israelites: "When a man dies leaving no son, his patrimony shall pass to his daughter. If he has no daughter, you shall give it to his brothers. If he has no brothers, you shall give it to his father's brothers. If his father had no brothers, then you shall give possession to the nearest survivor in his family, and he shall inherit. This shall be a legal precedent for the Israelites, as the LORD has commanded Moses."'

The wilderness

Joshua succeeds Moses

The LORD said to Moses, 'Go up this mountain, Mount Abarim, and look out over the land which I have given to the Israelites. Then, when you have looked out over it, you shall be gathered to your father's kin like your brother Aaron; for you and Aaron disobeyed my command when the community disputed with me in the wilderness of Zin: you did not uphold my holiness before them at the waters.' These were the waters of Meribah-by-Kadesh in the wilderness of Zin.

Then Moses said, 'Let the LORD, the God of the spirits of all mankind, appoint a man over the community to go out and come in at their head, to lead them out and bring them home, so that the community of the LORD may not be like sheep without a shepherd.' The LORD answered Moses, 'Take 18 Joshua son of Nun, a man endowed with spirit; lay your hand on him and set him 19 before Eleazar the priest and all the community. Give him his commission in their presence, and delegate some of your author- 20 ity to him, so that all the community of the Israelites may obey him. He must appear 21 before Eleazar the priest, who will obtain a decision for him by consulting the Urim before the LORD; at his word they shall go out and shall come home, both Joshua and the whole community of the Israelites.'

Moses did as the LORD had commanded 22 him. He took Joshua, presented him to Eleazar the priest and the whole community, laid his hands on him and gave him his com- 23 mission, as the LORD had instructed him.

Daily sacrifices

The LORD spoke to Moses and said, Give this command to the Israelites: See that you present my offerings, the food for the food-offering of soothing odour, to me at the appointed time.

Tell them: This is the food-offering which you shall present to the LORD: the regular daily whole-offering of two yearling rams without blemish. One you shall sacrifice in the morning and the second between dusk and dark. The grain-offering shall be a tenth of an ephah of flour mixed with a quarter of a hin of oil of pounded olives. (This was the regular whole-offering made at Mount Sinai, a soothing odour, a food-offering to the LORD.) The wine for the proper drink-offering shall be a quarter of a hin to each ram; you are to pour out this strong drink in the holy place as an offering to the LORD. You shall sacrifice the second ram between dusk and dark, with the same grain-offering as at the morning sacrifice and with the proper drink-offering; it is a food-offering of soothing odour to the LORD.

The sabbath, and monthly offerings

For the sabbath day: two yearling rams without blemish, a grain-offering of two tenths of an ephah of flour mixed with oil, and the proper drink-offering. This whole-offering, presented each sabbath, is in addition to the regular whole-offering and the proper drink-offering.

On the first day of every month you shall present a whole-offering to the LORD, consisting of two young bulls, one ram and seven yearling rams without blemish. The grain-offering shall be three tenths of flour mixed with oil for each bull, two tenths of flour mixed with oil 13 for the full-grown ram, and one tenth of flour mixed with oil for each young ram. This is a whole-offering, a food-offering of soothing 14 odour to the LORD. The proper drink-offering shall be half a hin of wine for each bull, a third for the full-grown ram and a quarter for each young ram. This is the whole-offering to be made, month by 15 month, throughout the year. Further, one he-goat shall be sacrificed as a sin-offering to the LORD, in addition to the regular whole-offering and the proper drink-offering.

Sacrifices at the appointed seasons

16 The Passover of the LORD shall be held on the fourteenth day of the
17 first month, and on the fifteenth day there shall be a pilgrim-feast; for seven days you must eat only
18 unleavened cakes. On the first day there shall be a sacred assembly; you shall not do your daily work.
19 As a food-offering, a whole-offering to the LORD, you shall present two young bulls, one ram, and seven yearling rams, all without blemish.
20 You shall offer the proper grain-offerings of flour mixed with oil, three tenths for each bull, two
21 tenths for the ram, and one tenth for each of the seven young rams;
22 and as a sin-offering, one he-goat
23 to make expiation for you. All these you shall offer in addition to the morning whole-offering, which is
24 the regular sacrifice. You shall repeat this daily till the seventh day, presenting food as a food-offering of soothing odour to the LORD, in addition to the regular whole-offering and the proper
25 drink-offering. On the seventh day there shall be a sacred assembly; you shall not do your daily work.
26 On the day of Firstfruits, when you bring to the LORD your grain-offering from the new crop at your Feast of Weeks, there shall be a sacred assembly; you shall not do your daily work. You shall bring 27 a whole-offering as a soothing odour to the LORD: two young bulls, one full-grown ram, and seven yearling rams. The proper 28 grain-offering shall be of flour mixed with oil, three tenths for each bull, two tenths for the one 29 ram, and a tenth for each of the 30 seven young rams, and there shall be one he-goat as a sin-offering to 31 make expiation for you; they shall all be without blemish. All these you shall offer in addition to the regular whole-offering with the proper grain-offering and drink-offering.

On the first day of the seventh 29 month there shall be a sacred assembly; you shall not do your daily work. It shall be a day of acclamation. You shall sacrifice a 2 whole-offering as a soothing odour to the LORD: one young bull, one full-grown ram, and seven yearling rams, without blemish. Their pro- 3 per grain-offering shall be of flour mixed with oil, three tenths for the bull, two tenths for the one ram, and one tenth for each of the 4 seven young rams, and there shall 5 be one he-goat as a sin-offering to make expiation for you. This 6 is in addition to the monthly whole-offering and the regular whole-offering with their proper grain-offerings and drink-offerings according to custom; it is a food-offering of soothing odour to the LORD.

On the tenth day of this seventh 7 month there shall be a sacred assembly, and you shall mortify yourselves; you shall not do any work. You shall bring a whole- 8 offering to the LORD as a soothing odour: one young bull, one full-grown ram, and seven yearling rams; they shall all be without

9 blemish. The proper grain-offering shall be of flour mixed with oil, three tenths for the bull, two tenths
10 for the one ram, and one tenth for
11 each of the seven young rams, and there shall be one he-goat as a sin-offering, in addition to the expiatory sin-offering and the regular whole-offering, with the proper grain-offering and drink-offering.
12 On the fifteenth day of the seventh month there shall be a sacred assembly. You shall not do your daily work, but shall keep a pilgrim-feast to the LORD for seven
13 days. As a whole-offering, a food-offering of soothing odour to the LORD, you shall bring thirteen young bulls, two full-grown rams, and fourteen yearling rams; they
14 shall all be without blemish. The proper grain-offering shall be of flour mixed with oil, three tenths for each of the thirteen bulls, two
15 tenths for each of the two rams,
16 and one tenth for each of the fourteen young rams, and there shall be one he-goat as a sin-offering, in addition to the regular whole-offering with the proper grain-offering and drink-offering.
17 On the second day: twelve young bulls, two full-grown rams, and fourteen yearling rams, without
18 blemish, together with the proper grain-offerings and drink-offerings for bulls, full-grown rams, and young rams, as prescribed accord-
19 ing to their number, and there shall be one he-goat as a sin-offering, in addition to the regular whole-offering with the proper grain-offering and drink-offering.
20 On the third day: eleven bulls, two full-grown rams, and fourteen yearling rams, without blemish,
21 together with the proper grain-offerings and drink-offerings for bulls, full-grown rams, and young rams, as prescribed according to
22 their number, and there shall be one he-goat as a sin-offering, in addition to the regular whole-offering, with the proper grain-offering and drink-offering.
23 On the fourth day: ten bulls,
24 two full-grown rams, and fourteen yearling rams, without blemish, together with the proper grain-offerings and drink-offerings for bulls, full-grown rams, and young rams, as prescribed according to their
25 number, and there shall be one he-goat as a sin-offering, in addition to the regular whole-offering with the proper grain-offering and drink-offering.
26 On the fifth day: nine bulls, two full-grown rams, and fourteen yearling rams, without blemish,
27 together with the proper grain-offerings and drink-offerings for bulls, full-grown rams, and young rams, as prescribed according to
28 their number, and there shall be one he-goat as a sin-offering, in addition to the regular whole-

offering with the proper grain-offering and drink-offering.
29 On the sixth day: eight bulls, two full-grown rams, and fourteen yearling rams, without blemish,
30 together with the proper grain-offerings and drink-offerings for bulls, full-grown rams, and young rams, as prescribed according to
31 their number, and there shall be one he-goat as a sin-offering, in addition to the regular whole-offering with the proper grain-offering and drink-offering.
32 On the seventh day: seven bulls, two full-grown rams, and fourteen yearling rams, without blemish,
33 together with the proper grain-offerings and drink-offerings for bulls, full-grown rams, and young rams, as prescribed according to
34 their number, and there shall be one he-goat as a sin-offering, in addition to the regular whole-offering with the proper grain-offering and drink-offering.
35 The eighth day you shall keep as a closing ceremony; you shall
36 not do your daily work. As a whole-offering, a food-offering of soothing odour to the LORD, you shall bring one bull, one full-grown ram, and seven yearling rams, with-
37 out blemish, together with the proper grain-offerings and drink-offerings for bulls, full-grown rams, and young rams, as prescribed
38 according to their number, and there shall be one he-goat as a sin-offering, in addition to the regular whole-offering with the proper grain-offering and drink-offering.
39 These are the sacrifices which you shall offer to the LORD at the appointed seasons, in addition to the votive offerings, the freewill offerings, the whole-offerings, the grain-offerings, the drink-offerings, and the shared-offerings.
40 Moses told the Israelites exactly what the LORD had commanded him.

Decrees concerning women's vows

30 Then Moses spoke to the heads of the Israelite tribes and said, This
2 is the LORD's command: When a man makes a vow to the LORD or swears an oath and so puts himself under a binding obligation, he must not break his word. Every word he has spoken, he must make
3 good. When a woman, still young and living in her father's house, makes a vow to the LORD or puts herself under a binding obligation,
4 if her father hears of it and keeps silence, then any such vow or
5 obligation shall be valid. But if her father disallows it when he hears of it, none of her vows or obligations shall be valid; the LORD will
6 absolve her, because her father has disallowed it. If the woman is married when she is under a vow or a binding obligation rashly uttered,

then if her husband hears of it and keeps silence when he hears, her vow or obligation by which she has bound herself shall be valid. If, however, her husband disallows it when he hears of it and repudiates the vow which she has taken upon herself or the rash utterance with which she has bound herself, then the LORD will absolve her. Every vow by which a widow or a divorced woman has bound herself shall be valid. But if it is in her husband's house that a woman makes a vow or puts herself under a binding obligation by an oath, and her husband, hearing of it, keeps silence and does not disallow it, then every vow and obligation under which she has put herself shall be valid; but if her husband clearly repudiates them when he hears of them, then nothing that she has uttered, whether vow or obligation, shall be valid. Her husband has repudiated them, and the LORD will absolve her.

The husband can confirm or repudiate any vow or oath by which a woman binds herself to mortification. If he maintains silence day after day, he thereby confirms every vow or obligation under which she has put herself: he confirms them, because he kept silence at the time when he heard them. If he repudiates them some time after he has heard them, he shall be responsible for her default.

Such are the decrees which the LORD gave to Moses concerning a husband and his wife and a father and his daughter, still young and living in her father's house.

Vengeance on the Midianites

The LORD spoke to Moses and said, 'You are to exact vengeance for Israel on the Midianites and then you will be gathered to your father's kin.'

Then Moses spoke to the people in these words: 'Let some men among you be drafted for active service. They shall fall upon Midian and exact vengeance in the LORD's name. You shall send out a thousand men from each of the tribes of Israel.' So the men were called up from the clans of Israel, a thousand from each tribe, twelve thousand in all, drafted for active service. Moses sent out this force, a thousand from each tribe, with Phinehas son of Eleazar the priest, who was in charge of the holy vessels and of the trumpets to give the signal for the battle-cry. They made war on Midian as the LORD had commanded Moses, and slew all the men. In addition to those slain in battle they killed the kings of Midian—Evi, Rekem, Zur, Hur, and Reba, the five kings of Midian—and they put to death also Balaam son of Beor. The Israelites took captive the Midianite women and their dependants, and carried off all their beasts, their flocks, and their property. They burnt all their cities, in which they had settled, and all their encampments. They took all the spoil and plunder, both man and beast, and brought them —captives, plunder, and spoil—to Moses and Eleazar the priest and to all the community of the Israelites, to the camp in the lowlands of Moab by the Jordan at Jericho.

Purifying the spoil

Moses and Eleazar the priest and all the leaders of the community went to meet them outside the camp. Moses spoke angrily to the officers of the army, the commanders of units of a thousand and of a hundred, who were returning from the campaign: 'Have you spared all the women?' he said. 'Remember, it was they who, on Balaam's departure, set about seducing the Israelites into disloyalty to the LORD that day at Peor, so that the plague struck the community of the LORD. Now kill every male dependant, and kill every woman who has had intercourse with a man, but spare for yourselves every woman among them who has not had intercourse. You yourselves, every one of you who has taken life and every one who has touched the dead, must remain outside the camp for seven days. Purify yourselves and your captives on the third day and on the seventh day, and purify also every piece of clothing, every article made of skin, everything woven of goat's hair, and everything made of wood.' Eleazar the priest said to the soldiers returning from battle, 'This is a law and statute which the LORD has ordained through Moses. Anything which will stand fire, whether gold, silver, copper, iron, tin, or lead, you shall pass through fire and then it will be clean. Other things shall be purified by the water of ritual purification; whatever cannot stand fire shall be passed through the water. On the seventh day you shall wash your clothes, and then be clean; after this you may re-enter the camp.'

Dividing the spoil

25 The LORD spoke to Moses and 26 said, 'Count all that has been captured, man or beast, you and Eleazar the priest and the heads 27 of families in the community, and divide it equally between the fighting men who went on the campaign and the whole community. 28 You shall levy a tax for the LORD: from the combatants it shall be one out of every five hundred, whether men, cattle, asses, or sheep, 29 to be taken out of their share and given to Eleazar the priest as a 30 contribution for the LORD. Out of the share of the Israelites it shall be one out of every fifty taken, whether man or beast, cattle, asses, or sheep, to be given to the Levites who are in charge of the LORD's Tabernacle.'

31 Moses and Eleazar the priest did as the LORD had commanded 32 Moses. These were the spoils, over and above the plunder taken by the fighting men: six hundred 33 and seventy-five thousand sheep, 34 seventy-two thousand cattle, sixty-35 one thousand asses; and of persons, thirty-two thousand girls who had had no intercourse with a man.

36 The half-share of those who took part in the campaign was thus three hundred and thirty-seven thousand 37 five hundred sheep, the tax for the LORD from these being six hundred 38 and seventy-five; thirty-six thousand cattle, the tax being seventy-39 two; thirty thousand five hundred 40 asses, the tax being sixty-one; and sixteen thousand persons, the tax 41 being thirty-two. Moses gave Eleazar the priest the tax levied for the LORD, as the LORD had commanded him.

42– The share of the community, 43 being the half-share for the Israelites which Moses divided off from that of the combatants, was three hundred and thirty-seven thousand 44 five hundred sheep, thirty-six thou-45 sand cattle, thirty thousand five 46 hundred asses, and sixteen thou-47 sand persons. Moses took one out of every fifty, whether man or beast, from the half-share of the Israelites, and gave it to the Levites

who were in charge of the LORD's Tabernacle, as the LORD had commanded him.

Then the officers who had commanded the forces on the campaign, the commanders of units of a thousand and of a hundred, came to Moses and said to him, 'Sir, we have checked the roll of the fighting men who were under our command, and not one of them is missing. So we have brought the gold ornaments, the armlets, bracelets, fingerrings, earrings, and pendants that each man has found, to offer them before the LORD as a ransom for our lives.' 48 49 50

Moses and Eleazar the priest 51 received this gold from the commanders of units of a thousand and of a hundred, all of it craftsman's work, and the gold thus 52 levied as a contribution to the LORD weighed sixteen thousand seven hundred and fifty shekels; for every man in the army had 53 taken plunder. So Moses and Elea-54 zar the priest received the gold from the commanders of units of a thousand and of a hundred, and brought it to the Tent of the Presence that the LORD might remember Israel.

The tribes east of Jordan

Now the Reubenites and the Gad-**32** ites had large and very numerous flocks, and when they saw that the land of Jazer and Gilead was good grazing country, they came and 2 said to Moses and Eleazar the priest and to the leaders of the community, 'Ataroth, Dibon, Jazer, 3 Nimrah, Heshbon, Elealeh, Sebam, Nebo, and Beon, the region which 4 the LORD has subdued before the advance of the Israelite community, is grazing country, and our flocks are our livelihood. If', they said, 5 'we have found favour with you, sir, then let this country be given to us as our possession, and do not make us cross the Jordan.' Moses 6 replied to the Gadites and the Reubenites, 'Are your kinsmen to go into battle while you stay here? How dare you discourage the 7 Israelites from crossing over to the land which the LORD has given

(Num. 32. 6)

8 them? This is what your fathers did when I sent them out from Kadesh-barnea to view the land.
9 They went up as far as the gorge of Eshcol and viewed the land, and on their return so discouraged the Israelites that they would not enter the land which the LORD had given
10 them. The LORD became angry that
11 day, and he solemnly swore: "Because they have not followed me with their whole heart, none of the men who came out of Egypt, from twenty years old and upwards, shall see the land which I promised on oath to Abraham, Isaac and
12 Jacob." This meant all except Caleb son of Jephunneh the Kenizzite and Joshua son of Nun, who followed the LORD with their whole
13 heart. The LORD became angry with Israel, and he made them wander in the wilderness for forty years until that whole generation was dead which had done what was
14 wrong in his eyes. And now you are following in your fathers' footsteps, a fresh brood of sinful men to fire the LORD's anger once more
15 against Israel; for if you refuse to follow him, he will again abandon this whole people in the wilderness and you will be the cause of their destruction.'
16 Presently they came forward with this offer: 'We will build folds for our sheep here and towns for our
17 dependants. Then we can be drafted as a fighting force to go at the head of the Israelites until we have brought them to the lands that will be theirs. Meanwhile our dependants can live in the walled towns, safe from the people of the country.
18 We will not return until every Israelite is settled in possession of
19 his patrimony; we will claim no share of the land with them over the Jordan and beyond, because our patrimony has already been allotted to us east of the Jordan.'
20 Moses answered, 'If you stand by your promise, if in the presence of the LORD you are drafted for battle,
21 and the whole draft crosses the Jordan in front of the LORD and remains there until the LORD has
22 driven out his enemies, and the land falls before him, then you may come back and be quit of your obligation to the LORD and to Israel; and this land shall be your possession in the sight of the
23 LORD. But I warn you, if you fail to do all this, you will have sinned against the LORD, and your sin
24 will find you out. So build towns for your dependants and folds for your sheep; but carry out your promise.'
25 The Gadites and Reubenites answered Moses, 'Sir, we are your servants and will do as you com-
26 mand. Our dependants and wives, our flocks and all our beasts shall

remain here in the cities of Gilead;
27 but we, all who have been drafted for active service with the LORD, will cross the river and fight, according to your command.'
28 Accordingly Moses gave these instructions to Eleazar the priest and Joshua son of Nun and to the heads of the families in the Israelite
29 tribes: 'If the Gadites and Reubenites, all who have been drafted for battle before the LORD, cross the Jordan with you, and if the land falls into your hands, then you
30 shall give them Gilead for their possession. But if, thus drafted, they fail to cross with you, then they shall acquire land alongside
31 you in Canaan.' The Gadites and Reubenites said in response, 'Sir, the LORD has spoken, and we will
32 obey. Once we have been drafted, we will cross over before the LORD into Canaan; then we shall have our patrimony here beyond the Jordan.'
33 So to the Gadites, the Reubenites, and half the tribe of Manasseh son of Joseph, Moses gave the kingdoms of Sihon king of the Amorites and Og king of Bashan, the whole land with its towns and the country
34 round them. The Gadites built
35 Dibon, Ataroth, Aroer, Atroth-
36 shophan, Jazer, Jogbehah, Bethnimrah, and Beth-haran, all of them walled towns with folds for
37 their sheep. The Reubenites built Heshbon, Elealeh, Kiriathaim,
38 Nebo, Baal-meon (whose name was changed), and Sibmah; these
39 were the names they gave to the towns they built. The sons of Machir son of Manasseh invaded Gilead, took it and drove out the
40 Amorite inhabitants; Moses then assigned Gilead to Machir son of Manasseh, and he made his home
41 there. Jair son of Manasseh attacked and took the tent-villages of Ham*t* and called them Havvoth-
42 jair.*u* Nobah attacked and took Kenath and its villages and gave it his own name, Nobah.

The stages of Israel's journey

33 These are the stages in the journey of the Israelites, when they were led by Moses and Aaron in their
2 tribal hosts out of Egypt. Moses recorded their starting-points stage by stage as the LORD commanded him. These are their stages from one starting-point to the next:
3 The Israelites left Rameses on the fifteenth day of the first month, the day after the Passover; they marched out defiantly in full view
4 of all the Egyptians, while the Egyptians were burying all the first-born struck down by the LORD as a judgement on their gods.
5 The Israelites left Rameses and encamped at Succoth.
6 They left Succoth and encamped

at Etham on the edge of the wilderness.
They left Etham, turned back near Pi-hahiroth*v* on the east of Baal-zephon, and encamped before Migdol.
They left Pi-hahiroth, passed through the Sea into the wilderness, marched for three days through the wilderness of Etham, and encamped at Marah.
They left Marah and came to Elim, where there were twelve springs of water and seventy palm-trees, and encamped there.
They left Elim and encamped by the Red Sea.
They left the Red Sea and encamped in the wilderness of Sin.
They left the wilderness of Sin and encamped at Dophkah.
They left Dophkah and encamped at Alush.
They left Alush and encamped at Rephidim, where there was no water for the people to drink.
They left Rephidim and encamped in the wilderness of Sinai.
They left the wilderness of Sinai and encamped at Kibroth-hattaavah.
They left Kibroth-hattaavah and encamped at Hazeroth.
They left Hazeroth and encamped at Rithmah.
They left Rithmah and encamped at Rimmon-parez.
They left Rimmon-parez and encamped at Libnah.
They left Libnah and encamped at Rissah.
They left Rissah and encamped at Kehelathah.
They left Kehelathah and encamped at Mount Shapher.
They left Mount Shapher and encamped at Haradah.
They left Haradah and encamped at Makheloth.
They left Makheloth and encamped at Tahath.
They left Tahath and encamped at Tarah.
They left Tarah and encamped at Mithcah.
They left Mithcah and encamped at Hashmonah.
They left Hashmonah and encamped at Moseroth.
They left Moseroth and encamped at Bene-jaakan.
They left Bene-jaakan and encamped at Hor-haggidgad.
They left Hor-haggidgad and encamped at Jotbathah.
They left Jotbathah and encamped at Ebronah.*w*
They left Ebronah and encamped at Ezion-geber.
They left Ezion-geber and encamped in the wilderness of Zin, that is of Kadesh.
They left Kadesh and encamped on Mount Hor on the frontier of Edom.

t Prob. rdg.; Heb. their tent-villages.
w Or Abronah.

u That is Tent-villages of Jair.

v See Exod. 14. 2.

8 Aaron the priest went up Mount Hor at the command of the LORD and there he died, on the first day of the fifth month in the fortieth year after the Israelites came out 9 of Egypt; he was a hundred and twenty-three years old when he died there.

10 The Canaanite king of Arad, who lived in the Canaanite Negeb, heard that the Israelites were coming.

11 They left Mount Hor and encamped at Zalmonah.

12 They left Zalmonah and encamped at Punon.

13 They left Punon and encamped at Oboth.

14 They left Oboth and encamped at Iye-abarim on the frontier of Moab.

15 They left Iyim and encamped at Dibon-gad.

16 They left Dibon-gad and encamped at Almon-diblathaim.

17 They left Almon-diblathaim and encamped in the mountains of Abarim east of Nebo.

Canaan's frontiers and territories

48 They left the mountains of Abarim and encamped in the lowlands of Moab by the Jordan near Jericho. 49 Their camp beside the Jordan extended from Beth-jeshimoth to Abel-shittim in the lowlands of 50 Moab. In the lowlands of Moab by the Jordan near Jericho the LORD spoke to Moses and said, 51 Speak to the Israelites in these words: You will soon be crossing 52 the Jordan to enter Canaan. You must drive out all its inhabitants as you advance, destroy all their carved figures and their images of cast metal, and lay their hill-shrines 53 in ruins. You must take possession of the land and settle there, for to you I have given the land to occupy. 54 You must divide it by lot among your families, each taking its own territory, the large family a large territory and the small family a small. It shall be assigned to them according to the fall of the lot, each tribe and family taking its 55 own territory. If you do not drive out the inhabitants of the land as you advance, any whom you leave in possession will become like a barbed hook in your eye and a thorn in your side. They shall continually dispute your possession of 56 the land, and what I meant to do to them I will do to you.

34 The LORD spoke to Moses and 2 said, Give these instructions to the Israelites: Soon you will be entering Canaan. This is the land assigned to you as a perpetual patrimony, the land of Canaan thus 3 defined by its frontiers. Your southern border shall start from the wilderness of Zin, where it marches with Edom, and run southwards from the end of the Dead Sea on 4 its eastern side. It shall then turn

from the south up the ascent of Akrabbim and pass by Zin, and its southern limit shall be Kadesh-barnea. It shall proceed by Hazar-5 addar to Azmon and from Azmon turn towards the Torrent of Egypt, 6 and its limit shall be the sea. Your western frontier shall be the Great Sea and the seaboard; this shall 7 be your frontier to the west. This shall be your northern frontier: you shall draw a line from the Great 8 Sea to Mount Hor and from Mount Hor to Lebo-hamath, and the limit 9 of the frontier shall be Zedad. From there it shall run to Ziphron, and its limit shall be Hazar-enan; this shall be your frontier to the north. 10 To the east you shall draw a line 11 from Hazar-enan to Shepham; it shall run down from Shepham to Riblah east of Ain, continuing until it strikes the ridge east of the 12 sea of Kinnereth. The frontier shall then run down to the Jordan and its limit shall be the Dead Sea. The land defined by these frontiers shall be your land.

13 Moses gave these instructions to the Israelites: This is the land which you shall assign by lot, each taking your own territory; it is the land which the LORD has ordered to be given to nine tribes and a half tribe. 14 For the Reubenites, the Gadites, and the half tribe of Manasseh have already occupied their terri-15 tories, family by family. These two and a half tribes have received their territory here beyond the Jordan, east of Jericho, towards the sunrise.

16 The LORD spoke to Moses and 17 said, These are the men who shall assign the land for you: Eleazar the 18 priest and Joshua son of Nun. You shall also take one chief from each 19 tribe to assign the land. These are their names:

20 from the tribe of Judah: Caleb son of Jephunneh;

20 from the tribe of Simeon: Samuel son of Ammihud;

21 from the tribe of Benjamin: Elidad son of Kislon;

22 from the tribe of Dan: the chief Bukki son of Jogli;

23 from the Josephites: from Manasseh, the chief Hanniel son of 24 Ephod; and from Ephraim, the chief Kemuel son of Shiphtan;

25 from Zebulun: the chief Elizaphan son of Parnach;

26 from Issachar: the chief Paltiel son of Azzan;

27 from Asher: the chief Ahihud son of Shelomi;

28 from Naphtali: the chief Pedahel son of Ammihud.

29 These were the men whom the LORD appointed to assign the territories in the land of Canaan.

The Levites' towns

35 The LORD spoke to Moses in the lowlands of Moab by the Jordan 2 near Jericho and said: Tell the Israelites to set aside towns in

their patrimony as homes for the Levites, and give them also the common land surrounding the towns. They shall live in the towns, and 3 keep their beasts, their herds, and all their livestock on the common land. The land of the towns which 4 you give the Levites shall extend from the centre of the town outwards for a thousand cubits in each direction. Starting from the town 5 the eastern boundary shall measure two thousand cubits, the southern two thousand, the western two thousand, and the northern two thousand, with the town in the centre. They shall have this as the common land adjoining their towns.

When you give the Levites their 6 towns, six of them shall be cities of refuge, in which the homicide may take sanctuary; and you shall give them forty-two other towns. The 7 total number of towns to be given to the Levites, each with its common land, is forty-eight. When you 8 set aside these towns out of the territory of the Israelites, you shall allot more from the larger tribe and less from the smaller; each tribe shall give towns to the Levites in proportion to the patrimony assigned to it.

Cities of refuge

The LORD spoke to Moses and 9 said, Speak to the Israelites in these 10 words: You are crossing the Jordan to the land of Canaan. You 11 shall designate certain cities to be places of refuge, in which the homicide who has killed a man by accident may take sanctuary. These 12 cities shall be places of refuge from the vengeance of the dead man's next-of-kin, so that the homicide shall not be put to death without standing his trial before the community. The cities appointed as 13 places of refuge shall be six in number, three east of the Jordan 14 and three in Canaan. These six 15 cities shall be places of refuge, so that any man who has taken life inadvertently, whether he be Israelite, resident alien, or temporary settler, may take sanctuary in one of them.

If the man strikes his victim with 16 anything made of iron and he dies, then he is a murderer: the murderer must be put to death. If a man has 17 a stone in his hand capable of causing death and strikes another man and he dies, he is a murderer: the murderer must be put to death. If 18 a man has a wooden thing in his hand capable of causing death, and strikes another man and he dies, he is a murderer: the murderer must be put to death. The dead man's 19 next-of-kin shall put the murderer to death; he shall put him to death because he had attacked his victim. If the homicide sets upon a man 20 openly of malice aforethought or

21 aims a missile at him of set purpose and he dies, or if in enmity he falls upon him with his bare hands and he dies, then the assailant must be put to death; he is a murderer. His next-of-kin shall put the murderer to death because he had attacked his victim.

22 If he attacks a man on the spur of the moment, not being his enemy, or hurls a missile at him not of set 23 purpose, or if without looking he throws a stone capable of causing death and it hits a man, then if the man dies, provided he was not the man's enemy and was not harming 24 him of set purpose, the community shall judge between the striker and the next-of-kin according to these 25 rules. The community shall protect the homicide from the vengeance of the kinsman and take him back to the city of refuge where he had taken sanctuary. He must stay there till the death of the duly 26 anointed high priest. If the homicide ever goes beyond the boundaries of the city where he has 27 taken sanctuary, and the next-of-kin finds him outside and kills him, then the next-of-kin shall not be 28 guilty of murder. The homicide must remain in the city of refuge till the death of the high priest; after the death of the high priest he 29 may go back to his property. These shall be legal precedents for you for all time wherever you live.

Laws concerning homicide

30 The homicide shall be put to death as a murderer only on the testimony of witnesses; the testimony of a single witness shall not be enough to bring him to his death. 31 You shall not accept payment for the life of a homicide guilty of a capital offence; he must be put to 32 death. You shall not accept a payment from a man who has taken sanctuary in a city of refuge, allowing him to go back before the death of the high priest and live at large. 33 You shall not defile your land by bloodshed. Blood defiles the land, and expiation cannot be made on behalf of the land for blood shed on it except by the blood of the 34 man that shed it. You shall not make the land which you inhabit unclean, the land in which I dwell; for I, the LORD, dwell among the Israelites.

Law concerning marriage of heiresses

36 The heads of the fathers' families of Gilead son of Machir, son of Manasseh, one of the families of the sons of Joseph, approached Moses and the chiefs, heads of families in Israel, and addressed 2 them. 'Sir,' they said, 'the LORD commanded you to distribute the land by lot to the Israelites, and you were also commanded to give the patrimony of our brother Zelo- 3 phehad to his daughters. Now if any of them shall be married to a husband from another Israelite tribe, her patrimony will be lost to the patrimony of our fathers and be added to that of the tribe into which she is married, and so part of our allotted patrimony will be lost. Then, when the jubilee year 4 comes round in Israel, her patrimony would be added to the patrimony of the tribe into which she is married, and it would be permanently lost to the patrimony of our fathers' tribe.'

So Moses, instructed by the 5 LORD, gave the Israelites this ruling: 'The tribe of the sons of Joseph is right. This is the LORD's 6 command for the daughters of Zelophehad: They may marry whom they please, but only within a family of their father's tribe. No 7 patrimony in Israel shall pass from tribe to tribe, but every Israelite shall retain his father's patrimony. Any woman of an Israelite tribe 8 who is an heiress may marry a man from any family in her father's tribe. Thus the Israelites shall retain each one the patrimony of his forefathers. No patrimony shall 9 pass from one tribe to another, but every tribe in Israel shall retain its own patrimony.'

The daughters of Zelophehad 10 acted in accordance with the LORD's command to Moses; Mahlah, Tir- 11 zah, Hoglah, Milcah and Noah, the daughters of Zelophehad, married sons of their father's brothers. They married within the families 12 of the sons of Manasseh son of Joseph, and their patrimony remained with the tribe of their father's family.

These are the commandments 13 and the decrees which the LORD issued to the Israelites through Moses in the lowlands of Moab by the Jordan near Jericho.

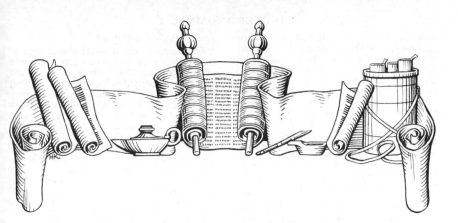

DEUTERONOMY

Moses explains the law

THESE ARE THE WORDS that Moses
spoke to all Israel in Transjordan, in the
wilderness, that is to say in the Arabah
opposite Suph, between Paran on the one
side and Tophel, Laban, Hazeroth, and
Dizahab on the other. (The journey from
Horeb through the hill-country of Seir to
Kadesh-barnea takes eleven days.)

On the first day of the eleventh month of
the fortieth year, after the defeat of Sihon
king of the Amorites who ruled in Heshbon,
and the defeat at Edrei of Og king of Bashan
who ruled in Ashtaroth, Moses repeated to
the Israelites all the commands that the
LORD had given him for them. It was in
Transjordan, in Moab, that Moses resolved
to promulgate this law. These were his words:
The LORD our God spoke to us at Horeb and
said, 'You have stayed on this mountain long
enough; go now, make for the hill-country
of the Amorites, and pass on to all their
neighbours in the Arabah, in the hill-
country, in the Shephelah, in the Negeb, and
on the coast, in short, all Canaan and the
Lebanon as far as the great river, the
Euphrates. I have laid the land open before
you; go in and occupy it, the land which
the LORD swore to give to your forefathers
Abraham, Isaac and Jacob, and to their
descendants after them.'

The court of law

At that time I said to you, 'You are a burden
too heavy for me to carry unaided. The LORD
your God has increased you so that today
you are as numerous as the stars in the sky.
May the LORD the God of your fathers increase your number a thousand times and
may he bless you as he promised. How can
I bear unaided the heavy burden you are
to me, and put up with your complaints?
Choose men of wisdom, understanding, and
repute for each of your tribes, and I will set
them in authority over you.' Your answer
was, 'What you have told us to do is right.'
So I took men of wisdom and repute and
set them in authority over you, some as
commanders over units of a thousand, of a
hundred, of fifty or of ten, and others as
officers, for each of your tribes. And at that
time I gave your judges this command: 'You
are to hear the cases that arise among your
kinsmen and judge fairly between man and
man, whether fellow-countryman or resident
alien. You must be impartial and listen to
high and low alike: have no fear of man, for
judgement belongs to God. If any case is too
difficult for you, bring it before me and I will
hear it.' At the same time I instructed you in
all these duties.

Spies sent out

Then we set out from Horeb, in obedience
to the orders of the LORD our God, and
marched through that vast and terrible
wilderness, as you found it to be, on the
way to the hill-country of the Amorites; and
so we came to Kadesh-barnea. Then I said
to you, 'You have reached the hill-country
of the Amorites which the LORD our God
is giving us. The LORD your God has indeed now laid the land open before you. Go

forward and occupy it in fulfilment of the promise which the LORD the God of your fathers made you; do not be discouraged or

22 afraid.' But you all came to me and said, 'Let us send men ahead to spy out the country and report back to us about the route we should take and the cities we shall

23 find.' I approved this plan and picked twelve

24 of you, one from each tribe. They set out and made their way up into the hill-country as far as the gorge of Eshcol, which they

25 explored. They took samples of the fruit of the country and brought them back to us, and made their report: 'It is a rich land that the LORD our God is giving us.'

26 But you refused to go up and rebelled against the command of the LORD your God.

27 You muttered treason in your tents and said, 'It was because the LORD hated us that he brought us out of Egypt to hand us over to

28 the Amorites to be wiped out. What shall we find up there? Our kinsmen have discouraged us by their report of a people bigger and taller than we are, and of great cities with fortifications towering to the sky. And they told us they saw there the descendants of the Anakim.'[a]

29 Then I said to you, 'You must not dread

30 them nor be afraid of them. The LORD your God who goes at your head will fight for you and he will do again what you saw him

31 do for you in Egypt and in the wilderness. You saw there how the LORD your God carried you all the way to this place, as a father

32 carries his son.' In spite of this you did not

33 trust the LORD your God, who went ahead on the journey to find a place for your camp. He went in fire by night to show you the way you should take, and in a cloud by day.

Caleb and Joshua rewarded

34 When the LORD heard your complaints, he

35 was indignant and solemnly swore: 'Not one of these men, this wicked generation, shall see the rich land which I swore to give

36 your forefathers, except Caleb son of Jephunneh. He shall see it, and to him and his descendants I will give the land on which he has set foot, because he followed the

37 LORD with his whole heart.' On your account the LORD was angry with me also and said, 'You yourself shall never enter it,

38 but Joshua son of Nun, who is in attendance on you, shall enter it. Encourage him, for he shall put Israel in possession of that land.

39 Your dependants who, you thought, would become spoils of war, and your children who do not yet know good and evil, they shall enter; I will give it to them, and they

40 shall occupy it. You must turn back and set out for the wilderness by way of the Red Sea.'[b]

Israel defeated at Hormah

4 You answered me, 'We have sinned against the LORD; we will now go up and attack just as the LORD our God commanded us.' And each of you fastened on his weapons, thinking it an easy thing to invade the hill-country.

4 But the LORD said to me, 'Tell them not to go up and not to fight; for I will not be with them, and their enemies will defeat them.'

4 And I told you this, but you did not listen; you rebelled against the LORD's command and defiantly went up to the hill-country.

4 The Amorites living in the hills came out against you and like bees they chased you; they crushed you at Hormah in Seir. Then

4 you came back and wept before the LORD, but he would not hear you or listen to you.

4 That is why you remained in Kadesh as long as you did.

The years in the wilderness

2 So we turned and set out for the wilderness by way of the Red Sea as the LORD had told me we must do, and we spent many days marching round the hill-country of Seir.

2 Then the LORD said to me, 'You have been long enough marching round these hills;

4 turn towards the north. And give the people this charge: "You are about to go through the territory of your kinsmen the descendants of Esau who live in Seir. Although they

5 are afraid of you, be on your guard and do not provoke them; for I shall not give you any of their land, not so much as a foot's-breadth: I have given the hill-country

6 of Seir to Esau as a possession. You may purchase food from them for silver, and eat it, and you may buy[c] water to drink."' The

7 LORD your God has blessed you in everything you have undertaken; he has watched your journey through this great wilderness; these forty years the LORD your God has been with you and you have gone short of

8 nothing. So we went on past our kinsmen, the descendants of Esau who live in Seir, and along the road of the Arabah which comes from Elath and Ezion-geber, and we turned and followed the road to the wilderness of Moab. There the LORD said to me,

9 'Do not harass the Moabites nor provoke them to battle, for I will not give you any of their land as a possession. I have given Ar to the descendants of Lot as a possession.'

10 (The Emim once lived there—a great and numerous people, as tall as the Anakim.

11 The Rephaim also were reckoned as Anakim; but the Moabites called them Emim. The

12 Horites lived in Seir at one time, but the descendants of Esau occupied their territory: they destroyed them as they advanced and then settled in the land instead of them,

---

a the descendants . . . Anakim: or the tall men.   b Or the Sea of Reeds.   c Or dig for.

just as Israel did in their own territory which
13 the LORD gave them.) 'Come now, cross the
14 gorge of the Zared.' So we went across. The
journey from Kadesh-barnea to the crossing
of the Zared took us thirty-eight years, until
the whole generation of fighting men had
passed away as the LORD had sworn that
15 they would. The LORD's hand was raised
against them, and he rooted them out of
the camp to the last man.
16   When the last of the fighting men among
17 the people had died, the LORD spoke to me,
18 'Today', he said, 'you are to cross by Ar[d]
19 which lies on the frontier of Moab, and
when you reach the territory of the Ammonites, you must not harass them or provoke
them to battle, for I will not give you any
Ammonite land as a possession; I have
20 assigned it to the descendants of Lot.' (This
also is reckoned as the territory of the
Rephaim, who lived there at one time; but
the Ammonites called them Zamzummim.
21 They were a great and numerous people, as
tall as the Anakim, but the LORD destroyed
them as the Ammonites advanced and
occupied their territory instead of them,
22 just as he had done for the descendants of
Esau who lived in Seir. As they advanced,
he destroyed the Horites so that they occupied their territory and took possession in-
23 stead of them: so it is to this day. It was
Caphtorites from Caphtor who destroyed
the Avvim who lived in the hamlets near
Gaza, and settled in the land instead of
24 them.) 'Come, set out on your journey and
cross the gorge of the Arnon, for I have put
Sihon the Amorite, king of Heshbon, and
his territory into your hands. Begin to
25 occupy it and provoke him to battle. Today
I will begin to put the fear and dread of you
upon all the peoples under heaven; if they
so much as hear a rumour of you, they will
quake and tremble before you.'

Israel conquers Sihon

26 Then I sent messengers from the wilderness
of Kedemoth to Sihon king of Heshbon with
27 these peaceful overtures: 'Grant us passage
through your country by the highway: we
will keep to the highway, trespassing neither
28 to right nor to left, and we will pay you the
full price for the food we eat and the water
29 we drink. The descendants of Esau who live
in Seir granted us passage, and so did the
Moabites who live in Ar. We will simply
pass through your land on foot, until we
cross the Jordan to the land which the LORD
30 our God is giving us.' But Sihon king of
Heshbon refused to grant us passage; for
the LORD your God had made him stubborn and obstinate, in order that he and his
land might become subject to you, as it still

is. So the LORD said to me, 'Come, I have 31
begun to deliver Sihon and his territory into
your hands. Begin now to occupy his land.'
Then Sihon with all his people came out to 32
meet us in battle at Jahaz, and the LORD our 33
God delivered him into our hands; we killed
him with his sons and all his people. We 34
captured all his cities at that time and put
to death everyone in the cities, men, women,
and dependants; we left no survivor. We 35
took the cattle as booty and plundered the
cities we captured. From Aroer on the edge 36
of the gorge of the Arnon and the level land
of the gorge, as far as Gilead, no city walls
were too lofty for us; the LORD our God laid
them all open to us. But you avoided the 37
territory of the Ammonites, both the parts
along the gorge of the Jabbok and their
cities in the hills, thus fulfilling all that the
LORD our God had commanded.

Israel conquers Og

Next we turned and advanced along the road 3
to Bashan. Og king of Bashan, with all his
people, came out against us at Edrei. The 2
LORD said to me, 'Do not be afraid of him,
for I have delivered him into your hands,
with all his people and his land. Deal with
him as you dealt with Sihon the king of the
Amorites who lived in Heshbon.' So the 3
LORD our God also delivered Og king of
Bashan into our hands, with all his people.
We slaughtered them and left no survivor,
and at the same time we captured all his 4
cities; there was not a single town that we
did not take from them. In all we took sixty
cities, the whole region of Argob, the kingdom of Og in Bashan; all these were fortified 5
cities with high walls, gates, and bars, apart
from a great many open settlements. Thus 6
we put to death all the men, women, and
dependants in every city, as we did to Sihon
king of Heshbon. All the cattle and the spoil 7
from the cities we took as booty for ourselves.
At that time we took from these two Amor- 8
ite kings in Transjordan the territory that
runs from the gorge of the Arnon to Mount
Hermon (the mountain that the Sidonians 9
call Sirion and the Amorites Senir), all the 10
cities of the tableland, and the whole of
Gilead and Bashan as far as Salcah and
Edrei, cities in the kingdom of Og in Bashan.
(Only Og king of Bashan remained as the 11
sole survivor of the Rephaim. His sarcopha-
gus of basalt[e] was nearly fourteen feet long
and six feet wide, and it may still be seen in
the Ammonite city of Rabbah.)

The tribes east of Jordan

At that time, when we occupied this terri- 12
tory, I assigned to the Reubenites and Gadites the land beyond Aroer on the gorge

d by Ar: or the gully.   *e Or iron.*

of the Arnon and half the hill-country of
13 Gilead with its towns. The rest of Gilead
and the whole of Bashan the kingdom of Og,
all the region of Argob, I assigned to half the
tribe of Manasseh. (All Bashan used to be
14 called the land of the Rephaim. Jair son of
Manasseh took all the region of Argob as
far as the Geshurite and Maacathite border.
There are tent-villages in Bashan still called
15 by his name, Havvoth-jair.*f*) To Machir I
16 assigned Gilead, and to the Reubenites and
the Gadites I assigned land from Gilead to
the gorge of the Arnon, that is to the middle
of the gorge; and its territory ran*gh* to the
gorge of the Jabbok, the Ammonite fron-
17 tier, and included the Arabah, with the
Jordan and adjacent land, from Kinnereth
to the Sea of the Arabah, that is the Dead
Sea, below the watershed of Pisgah on the
18 east. At that time I gave you this command:
'The LORD your God has given you this land
to occupy; let all your fighting men be
drafted and cross at the head of their fellow-
19 Israelites. Only your wives and dependants
and your livestock—I know you have much
livestock—shall stay in the towns I have
20 given you. This you shall do until the LORD
gives your kinsmen security as he has given
it to you, and until they too occupy the land
which the LORD your God is giving them on
the other side of the Jordan; then you may
return to the possession which I have given
you, every man to his own.'
21   At that time also I gave Joshua this charge:
'You have seen with your own eyes all that
the LORD your God has done to these two
kings; he will do the same to all the kingdoms

into which you will cross over. Do not be 22
afraid of them, for the LORD your God himself will fight for you.'

Moses not to enter Canaan

At that same time I pleaded with the LORD, 23
'O Lord GOD, thou hast begun to show to 24
thy servant thy greatness and thy strong
hand: what god is there in heaven or on
earth who can match thy works and mighty
deeds? Let me cross over and see that rich 25
land which lies beyond the Jordan, and the
fine hill-country and the Lebanon.' But be- 26
cause of you the LORD brushed me aside and
would not listen. 'Enough!' he answered.
'Say no more about this. Go to the top of 27
Pisgah and look west and north, south and
east; look well at what you see, for you shall
not cross this river Jordan. Give Joshua his 28
commission, encourage him and strengthen
him; for he will lead this people across, and
he will put them in possession of the land
you see before you.'

So we remained in the valley opposite 29
Beth-peor.

Moses exhorts Israel to obey

Now, Israel, listen to the statutes and laws **4**
which I am teaching you, and obey them;
then you will live, and go in and occupy
the land which the LORD the God of your
fathers is giving you. You must not add 2
anything to my charge, nor take anything
away from it. You must carry out all the
commandments of the LORD your God which
I lay upon you.

   You saw with your own eyes what the 3

---

f That is Tent-villages of Jair.   *g that is . . . ran: or* including the bed of the gorge and the adjacent strip
of land . . .   *h* and its territory ran: *prob. rdg.; Heb.* and territory and . . .

The Sea of the Arabah, the Dead Sea (Deut. 3. 17)

LORD did at Baal-peor; the LORD your God destroyed among you every man who went 4 over to the Baal of Peor, but you who held fast to the LORD your God are all alive today. 5 I have taught you statutes and laws, as the LORD my God commanded me; these you must duly keep when you enter the land 6 and occupy it. You must observe them carefully, and thereby you will display your wisdom and understanding to other peoples. When they hear about these statutes, they will say, 'What a wise and understanding 7 people this great nation is!' What great nation has a god*i* close at hand as the LORD our God is close to us whenever we call to 8 him? What great nation is there whose statutes and laws are just, as is all this law 9 which I am setting before you today? But take good care: be on the watch not to forget the things that you have seen with your own eyes, and do not let them pass from your minds as long as you live, but teach them to 0 your sons and to your sons' sons. You must never forget that day when you stood before the LORD your God at Horeb, and the LORD said to me, 'Assemble the people before me; I will make them hear my words and they shall learn to fear me all their lives on earth, and they shall teach their sons to do so.' 1 Then you came near and stood at the foot of the mountain. The mountain was ablaze with fire to the very skies: there was darkness, 2 cloud, and thick mist. When the LORD spoke to you from the fire you heard a voice speaking, but you saw no figure; there was only a 3 voice. He announced the terms of his covenant to you, bidding you observe the Ten Words,*j* and he wrote them on two tablets 4 of stone. At that time the LORD charged me to teach you statutes and laws which you should observe in the land into which you are passing to occupy it.

Warning against idolatry

5 On the day when the LORD spoke to you out of the fire on Horeb, you saw no figure of 6 any kind; so take good care not to fall into the degrading practice of making figures carved in relief, in the form of a man or a 7 woman, or of any animal on earth or bird 8 that flies in the air, or of any reptile on the ground or fish in the waters under the earth. 9 Nor must you raise your eyes to the heavens and look up to the sun, the moon, and the stars, all the host of heaven, and be led on to bow down to them and worship them; the LORD your God assigned these for the worship of*k* the various peoples under heaven. 0 But you are the people whom the LORD brought out of Egypt, from the smelting-furnace, and took for his own possession, 1 as you are to this day. The LORD was angry

with me on your account and swore that I should not cross the Jordan nor enter the rich land which the LORD your God is giving you for your possession. I shall die in this 22 country; I shall not cross the Jordan, but you are about to cross and occupy that rich land. Be careful not to forget the covenant 23 which the LORD your God made with you, and do not make yourselves a carved figure of anything which the LORD your God has forbidden. For the LORD your God is a 24 devouring fire, a jealous god.

When you have children and grand- 25 children and grow old in the land, if you then fall into the degrading practice of making any kind of carved figure, doing what is wrong in the eyes of the LORD your God and provoking him to anger, I sum- 26 mon heaven and earth to witness against you this day: you will soon vanish from the land which you are to occupy after crossing the Jordan. You will not live long in it; you will be swept away. The LORD 27 will disperse you among the peoples, and you will be left few in number among the nations to which the LORD will lead you. There you will worship gods made by human 28 hands out of wood and stone, gods that can neither see nor hear, neither eat nor smell. But if from there you seek the LORD your 29 God, you will find him, if indeed you search with all your heart and soul. When you are 30 in distress and all these things come upon you, you will in days to come turn back to the LORD your God and obey him. The 31 LORD your God is a merciful god; he will never fail you nor destroy you, nor will he forget the covenant guaranteed by oath with your forefathers.

Search into days gone by, long before 32 your time, beginning at the day when God created man on earth; search from one end of heaven to the other, and ask if any deed as mighty as this has been seen or heard. Did any people ever hear the voice of God 33 speaking out of the fire, as you heard it, and remain alive? Or did ever a god attempt to 34 come and take a nation for himself away from another nation, with a challenge, and with signs, portents, and wars, with a strong hand and an outstretched arm, and with great deeds of terror, as the LORD your God did for you in Egypt in the sight of you all? You have had sure proof that the LORD is 35 God; there is no other. From heaven he let 36 you hear his voice for your instruction, and on earth he let you see his great fire, and out of the fire you heard his words. Because he 37 loved your fathers and chose their children after them, he in his own person brought you out of Egypt by his great strength, so 38 that he might drive out before you nations

i Or gods.   j Or Ten Commandments.

k assigned . . . worship of: or created these for.

greater and more powerful than you and bring you in to give you their land in posses-
39 sion as it is today. This day, then, be sure and take to heart that the LORD is God in heaven above and on earth below; there is
40 no other. You shall keep his statutes and his commandments which I give you today; then all will be well with you and with your children after you, and you will live long in the land which the LORD your God is giving you for all time.

Some cities of refuge

41 Then Moses set apart three cities in the east,
42 in Transjordan, to be places of refuge for the homicide who kills a man without intent, with no previous enmity between them. If he takes sanctuary in one of these cities his
43 life shall be safe. The cities were: Bezer-in-the-Wilderness on the tableland for the Reubenites, Ramoth in Gilead for the Gadites, and Golan in Bashan for the Manassites.

Introduction to the Commandments

44 This is the law which Moses laid down for
45 the Israelites. These are the precepts, the statutes, and the laws which Moses proclaimed to the Israelites, when they came
46 out of Egypt and were in Transjordan in the valley opposite Beth-peor in the land of Sihon king of the Amorites who lived in Heshbon. Moses and the Israelites had defeated him when they came out of Egypt
47 and had occupied his territory and the territory of Og king of Bashan, the two Amorite kings in the east, in Transjordan.
48 The territory ran from Aroer on the gorge of the Arnon to Mount Sirion, that is
49 Hermon; and all the Arabah on the east, in Transjordan, as far as the Sea of the Arabah below the watershed of Pisgah.

5 Moses summoned all Israel and said to them: Listen, O Israel, to the statutes and the laws which I proclaim in your hearing today. Learn them and be careful to observe
2 them. The LORD our God made a covenant
3 with us at Horeb. It was not with our forefathers that the LORD made this covenant, but with us, all of us who are alive and are
4 here this day. The LORD spoke with you face to face on the mountain out of the fire.
5 I stood between the LORD and you at that time to report the words of the LORD; for you were afraid of the fire and did not go up the mountain. And the LORD said:

The Ten Commandments

6 I am the LORD your God who brought you out of Egypt, out of the land of slavery.
7 You shall have no other god*l* to set against me.
8 You shall not make a carved image for

yourself nor the likeness of anything in the heavens above, or on the earth below, or in the waters under the earth.
9 You shall not bow down to them or worship*m* them; for I, the LORD your God, am a jealous god. I punish the children for the sins of the fathers to the third and fourth generations of those who hate me. But I 10 keep faith with thousands, with*n* those who love me and keep my commandments.
11 You shall not make wrong use of the name of the LORD your God; the LORD will not leave unpunished the man who misuses his name.
12 Keep the sabbath day holy as the LORD your God commanded you. You have six 13 days to labour and do all your work. But 14 the seventh day is a sabbath of the LORD your God; that day you shall not do any work, neither you, your son or your daughter, your slave or your slave-girl, your ox, your ass, or any of your cattle, nor the alien within your gates, so that your slaves and slave-girls may rest as you do. Remember 15 that you were slaves in Egypt and the LORD your God brought you out with a strong hand and an outstretched arm, and for that reason the LORD your God commanded you to keep the sabbath day.
16 Honour your father and your mother, as the LORD your God commanded you, so that you may live long, and that it may be well with you in the land which the LORD your God is giving you.
17 You shall not commit murder.
18 You shall not commit adultery.
19 You shall not steal.
20 You shall not give false evidence against your neighbour.
21 You shall not covet your neighbour's wife; you shall not set your heart on your neighbour's house, his land, his slave, his slave-girl, his ox, his ass, or on anything that belongs to him.

The people promise to obey

22 These Commandments the LORD spoke in a great voice to your whole assembly on the mountain out of the fire, the cloud, and the thick mist; then he said no more. He wrote them on two tablets of stone and gave 23 them to me. When you heard the voice out of the darkness, while the mountain was ablaze with fire, all the heads of your tribes and the elders came to me and said, 'The 24 LORD our God has shown us his glory and his greatness, and we have heard his voice out of the fire: today we have seen that God may speak with men and they may still live. Why should we now risk death? for this great 25 fire will devour us. If we hear the voice of the LORD our God again, we shall die. Is there 26

l Or gods.   *m Or* or be led to worship . . .   *n* with . . . with: *or* for a thousand generations with . . .

any mortal man who has heard the voice of the living God speaking out of the fire, as
27 we have, and has lived? You shall go near and listen to all that the LORD our God says, and report to us all that the LORD our God has said to you; we will listen and obey.'
28 When the LORD heard these words which you spoke to me, he said, 'I have heard what this people has said to you; every word they
29 have spoken is right. Would that they always had such a heart to fear me and to observe all my commandments, so that all might be well with them and their children for ever!
30 Go, and tell them to return to their tents,
31 but you yourself stand here beside me, and I will set forth to you all the commandments, the statutes and laws which you shall teach them to observe in the land which I am giving them to occupy.'
32 You shall be careful to do as the LORD your God has commanded you; do not turn
33 from it to right or to left. You must conform to all the LORD your God commands you, if you would live and prosper and remain long in the land you are to occupy.

The greatest commandment

6 These are the commandments, statutes, and laws which the LORD your God commanded me to teach you to observe in the land into which you are passing to occupy it, a land
2 flowing with milk and honey, so that you may fear the LORD your God and keep all his statutes and commandments which I am giving you, both you, your sons, and your descendants all your lives, and so that
3 you may live long. If you listen, O Israel, and are careful to observe them, you will prosper and increase greatly as the LORD the God of your fathers promised you.
4 Hear, O Israel, the LORD*o* is our God, one
5 LORD, and you must love the LORD your God with all your heart and soul and
6 strength. These commandments which I give you this day are to be kept in your heart;
7 you shall repeat them to your sons, and speak of them indoors and out of doors, when you
8 lie down and when you rise. Bind them as a sign on the hand and wear them as a phylac-
9 tery on the forehead; write them up on the door-posts of your houses and on your gates.

Warnings against disobedience

10 The LORD your God will bring you into the land which he swore to your forefathers Abraham, Isaac and Jacob that he would give you, a land of great and fine cities which
11 you did not build, houses full of good things which you did not provide, rock-hewn cisterns which you did not hew, and vine-yards and olive-groves which you did not
12 plant. When you eat your fill there, be care-

o See note on Exod. 3. 15.

A phylactery on the forehead (Deut. 6. 8)

ful not to forget the LORD who brought you out of Egypt, out of the land of slavery. You 13 shall fear the LORD your God, serve him alone and take your oaths in his name. You 14 must not follow other gods, gods of the nations that are around you; if you do, the 15 LORD your God who is in your midst will be angry with you, and he will sweep you away off the face of the earth, for the LORD your God is a jealous god.

You must not challenge the LORD your 16 God as you challenged him at Massah.*p* You 17 must diligently keep the commandments of the LORD your God as well as the precepts and statutes which he gave you. You must 18 do what is right and good in the LORD's eyes so that all may go well with you, and you may enter and occupy the rich land which the LORD promised by oath to your forefathers; then you shall drive out all your 19 enemies before you, as the LORD promised.

When your son asks you in time to come, 20 'What is the meaning of the precepts, statutes, and laws which the LORD our God gave you?', you shall say to him, 'We were 21 Pharaoh's slaves in Egypt, and the LORD brought us out of Egypt with his strong hand, sending great disasters, signs, and portents 22 against the Egyptians and against Pharaoh and all his family, as we saw for ourselves. But he led us out from there to bring us into 23 the land and give it to us as he had promised to our forefathers. The LORD commanded 24 us to observe all these statutes and to fear the LORD our God; it will be for our own

p That is Challenge.

good at all times, and he will continue to
25 preserve our lives. It will be counted to our
credit if we keep all these commandments in
the sight of the LORD our God, as he has
bidden us.'

Israel's relationship with other nations

7 When the LORD your God brings you into
the land which you are entering to occupy
and drives out many nations before you—
Hittites, Girgashites, Amorites, Canaanites,
Perizzites, Hivites, and Jebusites, seven
nations more numerous and powerful than
2 you—when the LORD your God delivers
them into your power and you defeat them,
you must put them to death. You must not
3 make a treaty with them or spare them. You
must not intermarry with them, neither
giving your daughters to their sons nor
4 taking their daughters for your sons; if you
do, they will draw your sons away from the
LORD*q* and make them worship other gods.
Then the LORD will be angry with you and
5 will quickly destroy you. But this is what
you must do to them: pull down their altars,
break their sacred pillars, hack down their
sacred poles and destroy their idols by fire,
6 for you are a people holy to the LORD your
God; the LORD your God chose you out
of all nations on earth to be his special
possession.
7   It was not because you were more numerous than any other nation that the LORD
cared for you and chose you, for you were
8 the smallest of all nations; it was because
the LORD loved you and stood by his oath
to your forefathers, that he brought you
out with his strong hand and redeemed you
from the land of slavery, from the power of
9 Pharaoh king of Egypt. Know then that the
LORD your God is God, the faithful God;
with those who love him and keep his commandments he keeps covenant and faith for
10 a thousand generations, but those who defy
him and show their hatred for him he repays
with destruction: he will not be slow to
requite any who so hate him.
11   You are to observe these commandments,
statutes, and laws which I give you this day,
and keep them.

Blessings for obedience

12 If you listen to these laws and are careful
to observe them, then the LORD your God
will observe the sworn covenant he made
with your forefathers and will keep faith
13 with you. He will love you, bless you and
cause you to increase. He will bless the fruit
of your body and the fruit of your land, your
corn and new wine and oil, the offspring of
your herds, and of your lambing flocks, in
the land which he swore to your forefathers

to give you. You shall be blessed above every 14
other nation; neither among your people nor
among your cattle shall there be impotent
male or barren female. The LORD will take 15
away all sickness from you; he will not bring
upon you any of the foul diseases of Egypt
which you know so well, but will bring them
upon all your enemies. You shall devour all 16
the nations which the LORD your God is
giving over to you. Spare none of them, and
do not worship their gods; that is the snare
which awaits you.
You may say to yourselves, 'These nations 17
outnumber us, how can we drive them out?'
But you need have no fear of them; only 18
remember what the LORD your God did to
Pharaoh and to the whole of Egypt, the great 19
challenge which you yourselves witnessed,
the signs and portents, the strong hand and
the outstretched arm by which the LORD
your God brought you out. He will deal thus
with all the nations of whom you are afraid.
He will also spread panic among them until 20
all who are left or have gone into hiding
perish before you. Be in no dread of them, 21
for the LORD your God is in your midst, a
great and terrible god. He will drive out 22
these nations before you little by little. You
will not be able to exterminate them quickly,
for fear the wild beasts become too numerous for you. The LORD your God will de- 23
liver these nations over to you and will
throw them into great panic in the hour of
their destruction. He will put their kings into 24
your hands, and you shall wipe out their
name from under heaven. When you destroy
them, no man will be able to withstand you.
Their idols you shall destroy by fire; you 25
must not covet the silver and gold on them
and take it for yourselves, or you will be
ensnared by it; for these things are abominable to the LORD your God. You must not 26
introduce any abominable idol into your
houses and thus bring yourselves under
solemn ban along with it. You shall hold it
loathsome and abominable, for it is forbidden under the ban.

A rich land to be possessed

You must carefully observe everything that **8**
I command you this day so that you may live
and increase and may enter and occupy the
land which the LORD promised to your forefathers upon oath. You must remember all 2
that road by which the LORD your God has
led you these forty years in the wilderness
to humble you, to test you and to discover
whether or no it was in your heart to keep
his commandments. He humbled you and 3
made you hungry; then he fed you on manna
which neither you nor your fathers had
known before, to teach you that man

---

q Prob. rdg.; Heb. me.

cannot live on bread alone but lives by every word that comes from the mouth of the 4 LORD. The clothes on your backs did not wear out nor did your feet swell all these 5 forty years. Take this lesson to heart: that the LORD your God was disciplining you as 6 a father disciplines his son; and keep the commandments of the LORD your God, conforming to his ways and fearing him. 7 For the LORD your God is bringing you to a rich land, a land of streams, of springs and underground waters gushing out in hill and 8 valley, a land of wheat and barley, of vines, fig-trees, and pomegranates, a land of olives, 9 oil, and honey. It is a land where you will never live in poverty nor want for anything, a land whose stones are iron-ore and from 10 whose hills you will dig copper. You will have plenty to eat and will bless the LORD your God for the rich land that he has given you.

Warning against forgetting the LORD

11 Take care not to forget the LORD your God and do not fail to keep his commandments, laws, and statutes which I give you this day. 12 When you have plenty to eat and live in 13 fine houses of your own building, when your herds and flocks increase, and your silver and gold and all your possessions increase 14 too, do not become proud and forget the LORD your God who brought you out of 15 Egypt, out of the land of slavery; he led you through the vast and terrible wilderness infested with poisonous snakes and scorpions, a thirsty, waterless land, where he caused water to flow from the hard rock; 16 he fed you in the wilderness on manna which your fathers did not know, to humble you and test you, and in the end to make you 17 prosper. Nor must you say to yourselves, 'My own strength and energy have gained 18 me this wealth', but remember the LORD your God; it is he that gives you strength to become prosperous, so fulfilling the covenant guaranteed by oath with your forefathers, as he is doing now.

19 If you forget the LORD your God and adhere to other gods, worshipping them and bowing down to them, I give you a solemn warning this day that you will certainly be 20 destroyed. You will be destroyed because of your disobedience to the LORD your God, as surely as were the nations whom the LORD destroyed at your coming.

The LORD's promise

9 Listen, O Israel; this day you will cross the Jordan to occupy the territory of nations greater and more powerful than you, and great cities with walls towering to the sky. 2 They are great and tall people, the descendants of the Anakim, of whom you know,

for you have heard it said, 'Who can withstand the sons of Anak?' Know then this 3 day that it is the LORD your God himself who goes at your head as a devouring fire; he will subdue them and destroy them at your approach; you shall drive them out and overwhelm them, as he promised you.

When the LORD your God drives them 4 out before you, do not say to yourselves, 'It is because of my own merit that the LORD has brought me in to occupy this land.' It is 5 not because of your merit or your integrity that you are entering their land to occupy it; it is because of the wickedness of these nations that the LORD your God is driving them out before you, and to fulfil the promise which the LORD made to your forefathers, Abraham, Isaac and Jacob.

Rebellion at Horeb

Know then that it is not because of any merit 6 of yours that the LORD your God is giving you this rich land to occupy; indeed, you are a stubborn people. Remember and never 7 forget, how you angered the LORD your God in the wilderness: from the day when you left Egypt until you came to this place you have defied the LORD. In Horeb you roused 8 the LORD's anger, and the LORD in his wrath was on the point of destroying you. When I went up the mountain to receive the 9 tablets of stone, the tablets of the covenant which the LORD made with you, I remained on the mountain forty days and forty nights without food or drink. Then the LORD gave 10 me the two tablets of stone written with the finger of God, and upon them were all the words the LORD spoke to you out of the fire, upon the mountain on the day of the assembly. At the end of forty days and forty 11 nights the LORD gave me the two tablets of stone, the tablets of the covenant, and said 12 to me, 'Make haste down from the mountain because your people whom you brought out of Egypt have done a disgraceful thing. They have already turned aside from the way which I told them to follow and have cast for themselves an image of metal.'

Then the LORD said to me, 'I have con- 13 sidered this people and I find them a stubborn people. Let me be, and I will destroy 14 them and blot out their name from under heaven; and of you alone I will make a nation more powerful and numerous than they.' So I turned and went down the mount- 15 ain, and it was ablaze; and I had the two tablets of the covenant in my hands. When 16 I saw that you had sinned against the LORD your God and had cast for yourselves an image of a bull-calf, and had already turned aside from the way the LORD had told you to follow, I took the two tablets and flung 17 them down and shattered them in the sight

18 of you all. Then once again I lay prostrate before the Lord, forty days and forty nights without food or drink, on account of all the sins that you had committed, and because you had done what was wrong in the eyes of the Lord and provoked him to 19 anger. I dreaded the Lord's anger and his wrath which threatened to destroy you; and 20 once again the Lord listened to me. The Lord was greatly incensed with Aaron also and would have killed him; so I prayed for 21 him as well at that same time. I took the calf, that sinful thing that you had made, and burnt it and pounded it, grinding it until it was as fine as dust; then I flung its dust into the torrent that flowed down the mount-22 ain. You also roused the Lord's anger at Taberah, and at Massah, and at Kibroth-23 hattaavah. Again, when the Lord sent you from Kadesh-barnea with orders to advance and occupy the land which he was giving you, you defied the Lord your God and did 24 not trust him or obey him. You were defiant from the day that the Lord first 25 knew you. Forty days and forty nights I lay prostrate before the Lord because he had 26 threatened to destroy you, and I prayed to the Lord and said, 'O Lord God, do not destroy thy people, thy own possession, whom thou didst redeem by thy great power and bring out of Egypt by thy strong hand. 27 Remember thy servants, Abraham, Isaac and Jacob, and overlook the stubbornness of this people, their wickedness and their 28 sin; otherwise the people in the land out of which thou didst lead us will say, "It is because the Lord was not able to bring them into the land which he promised them and because he hated them, that he has led them 29 out to kill them in the wilderness." But they are thy people, thy own possession, whom thou didst bring out by thy great strength and by thy outstretched arm.'

The Covenant

10 At that time the Lord said to me, 'Cut two tablets of stone like the first, and make also a wooden chest, an Ark. Come to me on the 2 mountain, and I will write on the tablets the words that were on the first tablets which you broke in pieces, and you shall put them 3 into the Ark.' So I made the Ark of acacia-wood and cut two tablets of stone like the first, and went up the mountain taking the 4 tablets with me. Then in the same writing as before, the Lord wrote down the Ten Words[r] which he had spoken to you out of the fire, upon the mountain on the day of the assem-5 bly, and the Lord gave them to me. I turned and came down the mountain, and I put the tablets in the Ark that I had made, as

the Lord had commanded me, and there they have remained ever since.

6 (The Israelites journeyed by stages from Beeroth-bene-jaakan to Moserah. There Aaron died and was buried; and his son Eleazar succeeded him in the priesthood. 7 From there they came to Gudgodah and from Gudgodah to Jotbathah, a land of 8 many ravines. At that time the Lord set apart the tribe of Levi to carry the Ark of the Covenant of the Lord, to attend on the Lord and minister to him, and to give the blessing in his name, as they have done to 9 this day. That is why the Levites have no holding or patrimony with their kinsmen; the Lord is their patrimony, as he promised them.)

10 I stayed on the mountain forty days and forty nights, as I did before, and once again the Lord listened to me; he consented not 11 to destroy you. The Lord said to me, 'Set out now at the head of the people so that they may enter and occupy the land which I swore to give to their forefathers.'

The Lord demands obedience

12 What then, O Israel, does the Lord your God ask of you? Only to fear the Lord your God, to conform to all his ways, to love him and to serve him with all your heart and 13 soul. This you will do by keeping the commandments of the Lord and his statutes which I give you this day for your good. 14 To the Lord your God belong heaven itself, the highest heaven, the earth and everything 15 in it; yet the Lord cared for your forefathers in his love for them and chose their descendants after them. Out of all nations you were his chosen people as you are this day. 16 So now you must circumcise the foreskin of your hearts and not be stubborn any more, 17 for the Lord your God is God of gods and Lord of lords, the great, mighty, and terrible God. He is no respecter of persons and 18 is not to be bribed; he secures justice for widows and orphans, and loves the alien who lives among you, giving him food and 19 clothing. You too must love the alien, for 20 you once lived as aliens in Egypt. You must fear the Lord your God, serve him, hold fast to him and take your oaths in his name. 21 He is your praise, your God who has done for you these great and terrible things which 22 you have seen with your own eyes. When your forefathers went down into Egypt they were only seventy strong, but now the Lord your God has made you countless as the stars in the sky.

The greatness of the Lord

11 You shall love the Lord your God and keep for all time the charge he laid upon you, the

---

r *Or* Ten Commandments.   s *Verses 6, 7: cp. Num. 33. 31, 32.*

Mount Ebal and Mount Gerizim (Deut. 11. 29)

statutes, the laws, and the commandments.
2 This day you know the discipline of the
LORD, though your children who have
neither known nor experienced it do not;
you know his greatness, his strong hand and
3 outstretched arm, the signs he worked and
his acts in Egypt against Pharaoh the king
4 and his country, and all that he did to the
Egyptian army, its horses and chariots, when
he caused the waters of the Red Sea to flow
over them as they pursued you. In this way
the LORD destroyed them, and so things
5 remain to this day. You know what he did
for you in the wilderness as you journeyed
6 to this place, and what he did to Dathan and
Abiram sons of Eliab, son of Reuben, when
the earth opened its mouth and swallowed
them in the sight of all Israel, together with
their households and their tents and every
7 living thing in their company. With your
own eyes you have seen the mighty work
that the LORD did.

The blessings of the promised land

8 You shall observe all that I command you
this day, so that you may have strength to
enter and occupy the land into which you
9 are crossing, and so that you may live long
in the land which the LORD swore to your
forefathers to give them and their descendants, a land flowing with milk and honey.
10 The land which you are entering to occupy
is not like the land of Egypt from which you
have come, where, after sowing your seed,
you irrigated it by foot like a vegetable
11 garden. But the land into which you are
crossing to occupy is a land of mountains

and valleys watered by the rain of heaven.
It is a land which the LORD your God tends[t] 12
and on which his eye rests from year's end
to year's end. If you pay heed to the com- 13
mandments which I give you this day, and
love the LORD your God and serve him with
all your heart and soul, then I will send rain 14
for your land in season, both autumn and
spring rains, and you will gather your corn
and new wine and oil, and I will provide 15
pasture in the fields for your cattle: you shall
eat your fill. Take good care not to be led 16
astray in your hearts nor to turn aside and
serve other gods and prostrate yourselves
to them, or the LORD will become angry with 17
you: he will shut up the skies and there will
be no rain, your ground will not yield its
harvest, and you will soon vanish from the
rich land which the LORD is giving you. You 18
shall take these words of mine to heart and
keep them in mind; you shall bind them as
a sign on the hand and wear them as a
phylactery on the forehead. Teach them to 19
your children, and speak of them indoors
and out of doors, when you lie down and
when you rise. Write them up on the door- 20
posts of your houses and on your gates.
Then you will live long, you and your chil- 21
dren, in the land which the LORD swore to
your forefathers to give them, for as long as
the heavens are above the earth.

If you diligently keep all these com- 22
mandments that I now charge you to observe,
by loving the LORD your God, by conforming to his ways and by holding fast to
him, the LORD will drive out all these na- 23
tions before you and you shall occupy the

t which . . . tends: *or* whose soil the LORD your God has made firm.

territory of nations greater and more power-
24 ful than you. Every place where you set
the soles of your feet shall be yours. Your
borders shall run from the wilderness to[u]
the Lebanon and from the River, the river
25 Euphrates, to the western sea. No man will
be able to withstand you; the LORD your
God will put the fear and dread of you upon
the whole land on which you set foot, as
26 he promised you. Understand that this day
I offer you the choice of a blessing and a
27 curse. The blessing will come if you listen
to the commandments of the LORD your
28 God which I give you this day, and the curse
if you do not listen to the commandments
of the LORD your God but turn aside from

the way that I command you this day and
follow other gods whom you do not know.
When the LORD your God brings you 29
into the land which you are entering to
occupy, there on Mount Gerizim you shall
pronounce the blessing and on Mount Ebal
the curse. (These mountains are on the other 30
side of the Jordan, close to Gilgal beside
the terebinth of Moreh, beyond the road
to the west which lies in the territory of the
Canaanites of the Arabah.) You are about 31
to cross the Jordan to enter and occupy the
land which the LORD your God is giving you;
you shall occupy it and settle in it, and you 32
shall be careful to observe all the statutes
and laws which I set before you this day.

The one place of worship

12 These are the statutes and laws
that you shall be careful to observe
in the land which the LORD the
God of your fathers is giving you
to occupy as long as you live on
2 earth. You shall demolish all the
sanctuaries where the nations
whose place you are taking worship their gods, on mountain-tops
and hills and under every spreading
3 tree. You shall pull down their
altars and break their sacred pillars,
burn their sacred poles and hack
down the idols of their gods and
thus blot out the name of them
from that place.
4　You shall not follow such practices in the worship of the LORD
5 your God, but you shall resort to
the place which the LORD your God
will choose out of all your tribes to
receive his Name that it may dwell
6 there. There you shall come and
bring your whole-offerings and
sacrifices, your tithes and contributions, your vows and freewill
offerings, and the first-born of your
7 herds and flocks. There you shall
eat before the LORD your God; so
you shall find joy in whatever you
undertake, you and your families,
because the LORD your God has
blessed you.
8　You shall not act as we act here
today, each of us doing what he
9 pleases, for till now you have not
reached the place of rest, the patrimony which the LORD your God
10 is giving you. You shall cross the
Jordan and settle in the land which
the LORD your God allots you as
your patrimony; he will grant you
peace from all your enemies on
every side, and you will live in
11 security. Then you shall bring
everything that I command you to
the place which the LORD your
God will choose as a dwelling for
his Name—your whole-offerings
and sacrifices, your tithes and contributions, and all the choice gifts
that you have vowed to the LORD.
12 You shall rejoice before the LORD
your God with your sons and

daughters, your male and female
slaves, and the Levites who live in
your settlements because they have
no holding or patrimony among
you.
13　See that you do not offer your
whole-offerings in any place at
14 random, but offer them only at the
place which the LORD will choose
in one of your tribes, and there
you must do all I command you.
15 On the other hand, you may freely
kill for food in all your settlements,
as the LORD your God blesses you.
Clean and unclean alike may eat
it, as they would eat the meat of
16 gazelle or buck. But on no account
must you eat the blood; pour it out
17 on the ground like water. In all
your settlements you may not eat
any of the tithe of your corn and
new wine and oil, or any of the first-
born of your cattle and sheep, or
any of the gifts that you vow, or
any of your freewill offerings and
18 contributions; but you shall eat it
before the LORD your God in the
place that the LORD your God will
choose—you, your sons and daughters, your male and female slaves,
and the Levites in your settlements;
so you shall find joy before the
LORD your God in all that you
19 undertake. Be careful not to neglect
the Levites in your land as long as
you live.

When the LORD your God ex- 20
tends your boundaries, as he has
promised you, and you say to
yourselves, 'I would like to eat
meat', because you have a craving
for it, then you may freely eat it.
If the place that the LORD your 21
God will choose to receive his
Name is far away, then you may
slaughter a beast from the herds
or flocks which the LORD has given
you and freely eat it in your own
settlements as I command you.
You may eat it as you would the 22
meat of gazelle or buck; both clean
and unclean alike may eat it. But 23
you must strictly refrain from eating the blood, because the blood is
the life; you must not eat the life
with the flesh. You must not eat it, 24
you must pour it out on the ground
like water. If you do not eat it, all 25
will be well with you and your
children after you; for you will be
doing what is right in the eyes of
the LORD. But such holy-gifts as 26
you may have and the gifts you
have vowed, you must bring to the
place which the LORD will choose.
You must present your whole- 27
offerings, both the flesh and the
blood, on the altar of the LORD
your God; but of your shared-
offerings you shall eat the flesh,
while the blood is to be poured on
the altar of the LORD your God.
See that you listen and do all that 28
I command you, and then it will
go well with you and your children
after you for ever; for you will be
doing what is good and right in
the eyes of the LORD your God.

Warning against idolatry

When the LORD your God exter- 29
minates, as you advance, the
nations whose country you are
entering to occupy, you shall take
their place and settle in their land.
After they have been destroyed, 30
take care that you are not ensnared
into their ways. Do not inquire
about their gods and say, 'How do
these nations worship their gods?

u Prob. rdg.; Heb. and.

31 I too will do the same.' You must not do for the LORD your God what they do, for all that they do for their gods is hateful and abominable to the LORD. As sacrifices for their gods they even burn their sons and their daughters.

32 See that you observe everything I command you: you must not add anything to it, nor take anything away from it.

13 When a prophet or dreamer appears among you and offers you

2 a sign or a portent and calls on you to follow other gods whom you have not known and worship them, even if the sign or portent should

3 come true, do not listen to the words of that prophet or that dreamer. God is testing you through him to discover whether you love the LORD your God with

4 all your heart and soul. You must follow the LORD your God and fear him; you must keep his commandments and obey him, serve

5 him and hold fast to him. That prophet or that dreamer shall be put to death, for he has preached rebellion against the LORD your God who brought you out of Egypt and redeemed you from that land of slavery; he has tried to lead you astray from the path which the LORD your God commanded you to take. You must rid yourselves of this wickedness.

6 If your brother, your father's son or your mother's son, or your son or daughter, or the wife of your bosom or your dearest friend should entice you secretly to go and worship other gods—gods whom neither you nor your fathers

7 have known, gods of the people round about you, near or far, at one end of the land or the other—

8 then you shall not consent or listen. You shall have no pity on him, you shall not spare him nor shield

9 him, you shall put him to death; your own hand shall be the first to be raised against him and then

10 all the people shall follow. You shall stone him to death, because he tried to lead you astray from the LORD your God who brought you out of Egypt, out of the land of

11 slavery. All Israel shall hear of it and be afraid; never again will anything as wicked as this be done among you.

12-13 When you hear that miscreants have appeared in any of the cities which the LORD your God is giving you to occupy, and have led its inhabitants astray by calling on them to serve other gods whom

14 you have not known, then you shall investigate the matter carefully. If, after diligent examination, the report proves to be true and it is shown that this abominable thing

15 has been done among you, you shall put the inhabitants of that city to the sword; you shall lay

the city under solemn ban together

16 with everything in it. You shall gather all its goods into the square and burn both city and goods as a complete offering to the LORD your God; and it shall remain a mound

17 of ruins, never to be rebuilt. Let nothing out of all that has been laid under the ban be found in your possession, so that the LORD may turn from his anger and show you compassion; and in his compassion he will increase you as he

18 swore to your forefathers, provided that you obey the LORD your God and keep all his commandments which I give you this day, doing only what is right in the eyes of the LORD your God.

A forbidden mourning practice

14 You are the sons of the LORD your God: you shall not gash yourselves nor shave your forelocks in mourn-

2 ing for the dead. You are a people holy to the LORD your God, and the LORD has chosen you out of all peoples on earth to be his special possession.

Clean and unclean creatures

3 You shall not eat any abominable

4 thing. These are the animals you

5 may eat: ox, sheep, goat, buck, gazelle, roebuck, wild-goat, white-rumped deer, long-horned ante-

6 lope, and rock-goat. You may eat any animal which has a parted foot or a cloven hoof and also

7 chews the cud; those which only chew the cud or only have a parted or cloven hoof you may not eat. These are: the camel, the hare, and the rock-badger,*v* because they

Rock-badgers

chew the cud but do not have cloven hoofs; you shall regard

8 them as unclean; and the pig, because it has a cloven hoof but does not chew the cud, you shall regard as unclean. You shall not eat their

flesh or even touch their dead carcasses. Of creatures that live in 9 water you may eat all those that have fins and scales, but you may 10 not eat any that have neither fins nor scales; you shall regard them as unclean. You may eat all clean 11 birds. These are the birds you may 12 not eat: the griffon-vulture,*w* the

Griffon-vulture

black vulture, the bearded vulture,*x* the kite, every kind of falcon, every 13 14 kind of crow,*y* the desert-owl, the 15 short-eared owl, the long-eared owl, every kind of hawk, the tawny 16 owl, the screech-owl, the little owl, the horned owl, the osprey, the 17 fisher-owl, the stork,*z* every kind 18 of cormorant, the hoopoe, and the bat.

All teeming winged creatures 19 you shall regard as unclean; they may not be eaten. You may eat 20 every clean insect.

You shall not eat anything that 21 has died a natural death. You shall give it to the aliens who live in your settlements, and they may eat it, or you may sell it to a foreigner; for you are a people holy to the LORD your God.

You shall not boil a kid in its mother's milk.

Law of the tithe

Year by year you shall set aside a 22 tithe of all the produce of your seed, of everything that grows on the land. You shall eat it in the 23 presence of the LORD your God in the place which he will choose as a dwelling for his Name—the tithe of your corn and new wine and oil, and the first-born of your cattle and sheep, so that for all time you may learn to fear the LORD your God. When the LORD your God 24 has blessed you with prosperity, and the place which he will choose

v Or rock-rabbit.　　*w Or* eagle.　　*x Or* ossifrage.　　*y Or* raven.　　*z Or* heron.

Owl and hawk
(Deut. 14. 15–16)

to receive his Name is far from you and the journey too great for you to be able to carry your tithe, 25 You shall tie up the silver and take it with you to the place which the 26 LORD your God will choose. There you shall spend it as you will on cattle or sheep, wine or strong drink, or whatever you desire; you shall consume it there with rejoicing, both you and your family, in the presence of the LORD your 27 God. You must not neglect the Levites who live in your settlements; for they have no holding or patrimony among you. 28 At the end of every third year you shall bring out all the tithe of your produce for that year and 29 leave it in your settlements so that the Levites, who have no holding or patrimony among you, and the aliens, orphans, and widows in your settlements may come and eat their fill. If you do this the LORD your God will bless you in everything to which you set your hand.

The year of remission

15 At the end of every seventh year you shall make a remission of 2 debts. This is how the remission shall be made: everyone who holds a pledge shall remit the pledge of anyone indebted to him. He shall not press a fellow-countryman for repayment, for the LORD's year of 3 remission has been declared.[a] You may press foreigners; but if it is a fellow-countryman that holds anything of yours, you must remit all 4 claim upon it. There will never be 5 any poor among you if only you obey the LORD your God by carefully keeping these commandments which I lay upon you this day; for the LORD your God will bless you with great prosperity in the land which he is giving you to 6 occupy as your patrimony. When the LORD your God blesses you, as he promised, you will lend to men of many nations, but you yourselves will not borrow; you will rule many nations, but they will not rule you. 7 When one of your fellow-countrymen in any of your settlements in the land which the LORD your God is giving you becomes poor, do not be hard-hearted or 8 close-fisted with your countryman in his need. Be open-handed towards him and lend him on pledge 9 as much as he needs. See that you do not harbour iniquitous thoughts when you find that the seventh year, the year of remission, is near, and look askance at your needy countryman and give him nothing. If you do, he will appeal to the 10 LORD against you, and you will be found guilty of sin. Give freely to him and do not begrudge him your bounty, because it is for this very

bounty that the LORD your God will bless you in everything that you do or undertake. The poor will 11 always be with you in the land, and for that reason I command you to be open-handed with your countrymen, both poor and distressed, in your own land.

Treatment of slaves

When a fellow-Hebrew, man or 12 woman, sells himself to you as a slave, he shall serve you for six years and in the seventh year you shall set him free. But when you set 13 him free, do not let him go empty-handed. Give to him lavishly from 14 your flock, from your threshing-floor and your wine-press. Be generous to him, because the LORD your God has blessed you. Do not 18 take it amiss when you have to set him free, for his six years' service to you has been worth twice[b] the wage of a hired man. Then the LORD your God will bless you in everything you do. Remember that 15 you were slaves in Egypt and the LORD your God redeemed you; that is why I am giving you this command today.

If, however, a slave is content to 16 be with you and says, 'I will not leave you, I love you and your family', then you shall take an awl 17 and pierce through his ear to the door, and he will be your slave for life. You shall treat a slave-girl in the same way.

Dedicating the first-born

You shall dedicate to the LORD 19[c] your God every male first-born of your herds and flocks. You shall not plough with the first-born of your cattle, nor shall you shear the first-born of your sheep. Year by 20 year you and your family shall eat them in the presence of the LORD your God, in the place which the LORD will choose. If any animal is 21 defective, if it is lame or blind, or has any other serious defect, you must not sacrifice it to the LORD

a Or has come.   *b worth twice: or equivalent to.*   *c Verse 18 transposed to follow verse 14.*

22 your God. Eat it in your settlements; both clean and unclean alike may eat it as they would the 23 meat of gazelle or buck. But you must not eat the blood; pour it out on the ground like water.

Three pilgrim-feasts

16 Observe the month of Abib and keep the Passover to the LORD your God, for it was in that month that the LORD your God brought you 2 out of Egypt by night. You shall slaughter a lamb, a kid, or a calf as a Passover victim to the LORD your God in the place which he will choose as a dwelling for his 3 Name. You shall eat nothing leavened with it. For seven days you shall eat unleavened cakes, the bread of affliction. In urgent haste you came out of Egypt, and thus as long as you live you shall commemorate the day of your coming 4 out of Egypt. No leaven shall be seen in all your territory for seven days, nor shall any of the flesh which you have slaughtered in the evening of the first day remain 5 overnight till morning. You may not slaughter the Passover victim in any of the settlements which the 6 LORD your God is giving you, but only in the place which he will choose as a dwelling for his Name; you shall slaughter the Passover victim in the evening as the sun goes down, the time of your com- 7 ing out of Egypt. You shall boil it and eat it in the place which the LORD your God will choose, and then next morning you shall turn 8 and go to your tents. For six days you shall eat unleavened cakes, and on the seventh day there shall be a closing ceremony in honour of the LORD your God; you shall do no work.

9 Seven weeks shall be counted: start counting the seven weeks from the time when the sickle is put to 10 the standing corn; then you shall keep the pilgrim-feast of Weeks to the LORD your God and offer a freewill offering in proportion to the blessing that the LORD your 11 God has given you. You shall rejoice before the LORD your God, with your sons and daughters, your male and female slaves, the Levites who live in your settlements, and the aliens, orphans, and widows among you. You shall rejoice in the place which the LORD your God will choose as a dwelling for 12 his Name and remember that you were slaves in Egypt. You shall keep and observe all these statutes.

13 You shall keep the pilgrim-feast of Tabernacles[d] for seven days, when you bring in the produce from your threshing-floor and winepress. 14 You shall rejoice in your feast, with your sons and daughters, your male and female slaves, the Levites,

15 aliens, orphans, and widows who live in your settlements. For seven days you shall keep this feast to the LORD your God in the place which he will choose, when the LORD your God gives you his blessing in all your harvest and in all your work; you shall keep the feast 16 with joy.

Three times a year all your males shall come into the presence of the LORD your God in the place which he will choose: at the pilgrim-feasts of Unleavened Bread, of Weeks, and of Tabernacles. No one shall come into the presence 17 of the LORD empty-handed. Each of you shall bring such a gift as he can in proportion to the blessing which the LORD your God has given you.

Justice

18 You shall appoint for yourselves judges and officers, tribe by tribe, in every settlement which the LORD your God is giving you, and they shall dispense true justice to the 19 people. You shall not pervert the course of justice or show favour, nor shall you accept a bribe; for bribery makes the wise man blind and the just man give a crooked 20 answer. Justice, and justice alone, you shall pursue, so that you may live and occupy the land which the LORD your God is giving you.

21 You shall not plant any kind of tree as a sacred pole beside the altar of the LORD your God which you 22 shall build. You shall not set up a sacred pillar, for the LORD your God hates them.

17 You shall not sacrifice to the LORD your God a bull or sheep that has any defect or serious blemish, for that would be abominable to the LORD your God.

2 If so be that, in any one of the settlements which the LORD your God is giving you, a man or woman is found among you who does what is wrong in the eyes of the LORD your God, by breaking his cove- 3 nant and going to worship other gods and prostrating himself before them or before the sun and moon and all the host of heaven—a thing 4 that I have forbidden—then, if it is reported to you or you hear of it, make thorough inquiry. If the report proves to be true, and it is shown that this abominable thing 5 has been done in Israel, then bring the man or woman who has done this wicked deed to the city gate 6 and stone him to death. Sentence of death shall be carried out on the testimony of two or of three witnesses: no one shall be put to death on the testimony of a single witness. 7 The first stones shall be thrown by the witnesses and then all the people shall follow; thus you shall rid yourselves of this wickedness.

8 When the issue in any lawsuit is beyond your competence, whether it be a case of blood against blood, plea against plea, or blow against blow, that is disputed in your courts, then go up without delay to the place which the LORD your God will choose. There you must 9 go to the levitical priests or to the judge then in office; seek their guidance, and they shall pronounce the sentence. You shall act on the 10 pronouncement which they make from the place which the LORD will choose. See that you carry out all their instructions. Act on the in- 11 struction which they give you, or on the precedent that they cite; do not swerve from what they tell you, either to right or to left. Any- 12 one who presumes to reject the decision either of the priest who ministers there to the LORD your God, or of the judge, shall die; thus you will rid Israel of wickedness. Then all the people will hear 13 of it and be afraid, and will never again show such presumption.

Instructions concerning a king

When you come into the land 14 which the LORD your God is giving you, and occupy it and settle in it, and you then say, 'Let us appoint over us a king, as all the surrounding nations do', you shall appoint 15 as king the man whom the LORD your God will choose. You shall appoint over you a man of your own race; you must not appoint a foreigner, one who is not of your own race. He shall not acquire 16 many horses, nor, to add to his horses, shall he cause the people to go back to Egypt, for this is what the LORD said to you, 'You shall never go back that way.' He shall 17 not acquire many wives and so be led astray; nor shall he acquire great quantities of silver and gold for himself. When he has ascended 18 the throne of the kingdom, he shall make a copy of this law in a book at the dictation of the levitical priests. He shall keep it by him 19 and read from it all his life, so that he may learn to fear the LORD his God and keep all the words of this law and observe these statutes. In 20 this way he shall not become prouder than his fellow-countrymen, nor shall he turn from these commandments to right or to left; then he and his sons will reign long over his kingdom in Israel.

Provision for the priests and Levites

The levitical priests, the whole tribe **18** of Levi, shall have no holding or patrimony in Israel; they shall eat the food-offerings of the LORD, their patrimony. They shall have 2

d Or **Booths** or **Arbours.**

no patrimony among their fellow-countrymen; the LORD is their patrimony, as he promised them.

3 This shall be the customary due of the priests from those of the people who offer sacrifice, whether a bull or a sheep: the shoulders, the cheeks, and the stomach shall 4 be given to the priest. You shall give him also the firstfruits of your corn and new wine and oil, and the first fleeces at the shearing of your 5 flocks. For it was he whom the LORD your God chose from all your tribes to attend on the LORD and to minister in the name of the LORD, both he and his sons for all time.

6 When a Levite comes from any settlement in Israel where he may be lodging to the place which the LORD will choose, if he comes in 7 the eagerness of his heart and ministers in the name of the LORD his God, like all his fellow-Levites 8 who attend on the LORD there, he shall have an equal share of food with them, besides what he may inherit from his father's family.

Against sorcery

9 When you come into the land which the LORD your God is giving you, do not learn to imitate the abominable customs of those 10 other nations. Let no one be found among you who makes his son or daughter pass through fire, no augur or soothsayer or diviner or 11 sorcerer, no one who casts spells or traffics with ghosts and spirits, 12 and no necromancer. Those who do these things are abominable to the LORD, and it is because of these abominable practices that the LORD your God is driving them out before 13 you. You shall be whole-hearted in your service of the LORD your God.

The LORD promises a prophet like Moses

14 These nations whose place you are taking listen to soothsayers and augurs, but the LORD your God 15 does not permit you to do this. The LORD your God will raise up a prophet from among you like myself, and you shall listen to him. 16 All this follows from your request to the LORD your God on Horeb on the day of the assembly. There you said, 'Let us not hear again the voice of the LORD our God, nor see this great fire again, or we shall 17 die.' Then the LORD said to me, 18 'What they have said is right. I will raise up for them a prophet like you, one of their own race, and I will put my words into his mouth. He shall convey all my commands 19 to them, and if anyone does not listen to the words which he will speak in my name I will require 20 satisfaction from him. But the

prophet who presumes to utter in my name what I have not commanded him or who speaks in the name of other gods—that prophet 21 shall die.' If you ask yourselves, 'How shall we recognize a word that the LORD has not uttered?', 22 this is the answer: When the word spoken by the prophet in the name of the LORD is not fulfilled and does not come true, it is not a word spoken by the LORD. The prophet has spoken presumptuously; do not hold him^e in awe.

More cities of refuge

19 When the LORD your God exterminates the nations whose land he is giving you, and you take their place and settle in their cities and 2 houses, you shall set apart three cities in the land which he is giving 3 you to occupy. Divide into three districts the territory which the LORD your God is giving you as patrimony, and determine where each city shall lie. These shall be places in which homicides may take sanctuary.

4 This is the kind of homicide who may take sanctuary there and save his life: the man who strikes another without intent and with no previous enmity between them; 5 for instance, the man who goes into a wood with his mate to fell trees, and, when cutting a tree, he relaxes his grip on the axe,^f the head glances off the tree, hits the other man and kills him. The homicide may take sanctuary in any one of these cities, and his life 6 shall be safe. Otherwise, when the dead man's next-of-kin who had the duty of vengeance pursued him in the heat of passion, he might overtake him if the distance were great, and take his life, although the homicide was not liable to the death-penalty because there had been no previous enmity on his 7 part. That is why I command you to set apart three cities.

8 If the LORD your God extends your boundaries, as he swore to your forefathers, and gives you the whole land which he promised to 9 them, because you keep all the commandments that I am laying down today and carry them out by loving the LORD your God and by conforming to his ways for all time, then you shall add three more cities of refuge to these three. 10 Let no innocent blood be shed in the land which the LORD your God is giving you as your patrimony, or blood-guilt will fall on you.

11 When one man is the enemy of another, and he lies in wait for him, attacks him and strikes him a blow so that he dies, and then takes 12 sanctuary in one of these cities, the elders of his own city shall send to fetch him; they shall hand him over

to the next-of-kin, and he shall die. 13 You shall show him no mercy, but shall rid Israel of the guilt of innocent blood; then all will be well with you.

14 Do not move your neighbour's boundary stone, fixed by the men of former times in the patrimony which you shall occupy in the land the LORD your God gives you for your possession.

Laws concerning witnesses

15 A single witness may not give evidence against a man in the matter of any crime or sin which he commits: a charge must be established on the evidence of two or of three witnesses.

16 When a malicious witness comes forward to give false evidence 17 against a man, and the two disputants stand before the LORD, before the priests and the judges 18 then in office, if, after careful examination by the judges, he be proved to be a false witness giving false evidence against his fellow, 19 you shall treat him as he intended to treat his fellow, and thus rid 20 yourselves of this wickedness. The rest of the people when they hear of it will be afraid: never again will anything as wicked as this be done 21 among you. You shall show no mercy: life for life, eye for eye, tooth for tooth, hand for hand, foot for foot.

Laws concerning warfare

20 When you take the field against an enemy and are faced by horses and chariots and an army greater than yours, do not be afraid of them; for the LORD your God, who brought you out of Egypt, will 2 be with you. When you are about to join battle, the priest shall come 3 forward and address the army in these words: 'Hear, O Israel, this day you are joining battle with the enemy; do not lose heart, or be afraid, or give way to panic in face 4 of them; for the LORD your God will go with you to fight your enemy for you and give you the 5 victory.' Then the officers shall address the army in these words: 'Any man who has built a new house and has not dedicated it shall go back to his house; or he may die in battle and another man 6 dedicate it. Any man who has planted a vineyard and has not begun to use it shall go back home; or he may die in battle and another 7 man use it. Any man who has pledged himself to take a woman in marriage and has not taken her shall go back home; or he may die in battle and another man take her.' 8 The officers shall further address the army: 'Any man who is afraid and has lost heart shall go back home; or his comrades will be

---

^e Or it.   ^f when . . . axe: or as he swings the axe to cut a tree.

9 discouraged as he is.' When these officers have finished addressing the army, commanders shall be appointed to lead it.

10 When you advance on a city to attack it, make an offer of peace.

11 If the city accepts the offer and opens its gates to you, then all the people in it shall be put to forced

12 labour and shall serve you. If it does not make peace with you but offers battle, you shall besiege it,

13 and the LORD your God will deliver it into your hands. You shall put

14 all its males to the sword, but you may take the women, the dependants, and the cattle for yourselves, and plunder everything else in the city. You may enjoy the use of the spoil of your enemies which the

15 LORD your God gives you. That is what you shall do to cities at a great distance, as opposed to those which belong to nations near at

16 hand. In the cities of these nations whose land the LORD your God is giving you as a patrimony, you shall not leave any creature alive.

17 You shall annihilate them—Hittites, Amorites, Canaanites, Perizzites, Hivites, Jebusites—as the LORD your God commanded you,

18 so that they may not teach you to imitate all the abominable things that they have done for their gods and so cause you to sin against the LORD your God.

19 When you are at war, and lay siege to a city for a long time in order to take it, do not destroy its trees by taking the axe to them, for they provide you with food; you shall not cut them down. The trees of the field are not men that you

20 should besiege them. But you may destroy or cut down any trees that you know do not yield food, and use them in siege-works against the city that is at war with you, until it falls.

Undetected murder

21 When a dead body is found lying in open country, in the land which the LORD your God is giving you to occupy, and it is not known who

2 struck the blow, your elders and your judges shall come out and measure the distance to the surrounding towns to find which is

3 nearest. The elders of that town shall take a heifer that has never

4 been mated[g] or worn a yoke, and bring it down to a ravine where there is a stream that never runs dry and the ground is never tilled or sown, and there in the ravine

5 they shall break its neck. The priests, the sons of Levi, shall then come forward; for the LORD your God has chosen them to minister to him and to bless in the name of the LORD, and their voice shall be decisive in all cases of dispute and

6 assault. Then all the elders of the

town nearest to the dead body shall wash their hands over the heifer whose neck has been broken in the

7 ravine. They shall solemnly declare: 'Our hands did not shed this blood, nor did we witness the

8 bloodshed. Accept expiation, O LORD, for thy people Israel whom thou hast redeemed, and do not let the guilt of innocent blood rest upon thy people Israel: let this bloodshed be expiated on their

9 behalf.' Thus, by doing what is right in the eyes of the LORD, you shall rid yourselves of the guilt of innocent blood.

Law concerning women captives

10 When you wage war against your enemy and the LORD your God delivers them into your hands and you take some of them captive,

11 then if you see a comely woman among the captives and take a liking to her, you may marry her.

12 You shall bring her into your house, where she shall shave her head, pare

13 her nails, and discard the clothes which she had when captured. Then she shall stay in your house and mourn for her father and mother for a full month. After that you may have intercourse with her; you shall be her husband and she

14 your wife. But if you no longer find her pleasing, let her go free. You must not sell her, nor treat her harshly, since you have had your will with her.

Law of the first-born

15 When a man has two wives, one loved and the other unloved, if they both bear him sons, and the son of the unloved wife is the elder,

16 then, when the day comes for him to divide his property among his sons, he shall not treat the son of the loved wife as his first-born in contempt of his true first-born, the

17 son of the unloved wife. He shall recognize the rights of his firstborn, the son of the unloved wife, and give him a double share of all that he possesses; for he was the firstfruits of his manhood, and the right of the first-born is his.

Law concerning a disobedient son

18 When a man has a son who is disobedient and out of control, and will not obey his father or his mother, or pay attention when they

19 punish him, then his father and mother shall take hold of him and bring him out to the elders of the

20 town, at the town gate. They shall say to the elders of the town, 'This son of ours is disobedient and out of control; he will not obey us, he

21 is a wastrel and a drunkard.' Then all the men of the town shall stone him to death, and you will thereby

rid yourselves of this wickedness. All Israel will hear of it and be afraid.

Various laws

When a man is convicted of a 22 capital offence and is put to death, you shall hang him on a gibbet; but his body shall not remain on 23 the gibbet overnight; you shall bury it on the same day, for a hanged man is offensive[h] in the sight of God. You shall not pollute the land which the LORD your God is giving you as your patrimony.

When you see a fellow-country- **22** man's ox or sheep straying, do not ignore it but take it back to him. If the owner is not a near neigh- 2 bour and you do not know who he is, take the animal into your own house and keep it with you until he claims it, and then give it back to him. Do the same with his 3 ass or his cloak or anything else that your fellow-countryman has lost, if you find it. You may not ignore it.

When you see your fellow- 4 countryman's ass or ox lying on the road, do not ignore it; you must help him to lift it to its feet again.

No woman shall wear an article 5 of man's clothing, nor shall a man put on woman's dress; for those who do these things are abominable to the LORD your God.

When you come across a bird's 6 nest by the road, in a tree or on the ground, with fledglings or eggs in it and the mother-bird on the nest, do not take both mother and young. Let the mother-bird go free, 7 and take only the young; then you will prosper and live long.

When you build a new house, 8 put a parapet along the roof, or you will bring the guilt of bloodshed on your house if anyone should fall from it.

You shall not sow your vineyard 9 with a second crop, or the full yield will be forfeit, both the yield of the seed you sow and the fruit of the vineyard.

You shall not plough with an ox 10 and an ass yoked together.

You shall not wear clothes woven 11 with two kinds of yarn, wool and flax together.

You shall make twisted tassels 12 on the four corners of your cloaks which you wrap round you.

Laws concerning chastity

When a man takes a wife and after 13 having intercourse with her turns against her and brings trumped-up 14 charges against her, giving her a bad name and saying, 'I took this woman and slept with her and did not find proof of virginity in her', then the girl's father and mother 15

g Prob. rdg.; Heb. put to work.   *h* Or accursed.

'*You shall not plough with an ox and an ass yoked together*' (Deut. 22. 10)

shall take the proof of her virginity to the elders of the town, at the 16 town gate. The girl's father shall say to the elders, 'I gave my daughter in marriage to this man, and 17 he has turned against her. He has trumped up a charge and said, "I have not found proofs of virginity in your daughter." Here are the proofs.' They shall then spread the garment before the elders of 18 the town. The elders shall take the 19 man and punish him: they shall fine him a hundred pieces of silver because he has given a bad name to a virgin of Israel, and hand them to the girl's father. She shall be his 20 wife: he is not free to divorce her all his life long. If, on the other hand, the accusation is true and no proof of the girl's virginity is 21 found, then they shall bring her out to the door of her father's house and the men of her town shall stone her to death. She has committed an outrage in Israel by playing the prostitute in her father's house: you shall rid yourselves of this wickedness.
22   When a man is discovered lying with a married woman, they shall both die, the woman as well as the man who lay with her: you shall rid Israel of this wickedness.
23   When a virgin is pledged in marriage to a man and another man comes upon her in the town and 24 lies with her, you shall bring both of them out to the gate of that town and stone them to death; the girl because, although in the town, she did not cry for help, and the man because he dishonoured another man's wife: you shall rid 25 yourselves of this wickedness. If the man comes upon such a girl in the country and rapes her, then the man alone shall die because he lay 26 with her. You shall do nothing to

the girl, she has done nothing worthy of death: this deed is like that of a man who attacks another 27 and murders him, for the man came upon her in the country and, though the girl cried for help, there was no one to rescue her.
28   When a man comes upon a virgin who is not pledged in marriage and forces her to lie with him, and 29 they are discovered, then the man who lies with her shall give the girl's father fifty pieces of silver, and she shall be his wife because he has dishonoured her. He is not free to divorce her all his life long.
30   A man shall not take his father's wife: he shall not bring shame on his father.

Those excluded from the assembly

23 No man whose testicles have been crushed or whose organ has been severed shall become a member of the assembly of the LORD.
2   No descendant of an irregular union, even down to the tenth generation, shall become a member of the assembly of the LORD.
3   No Ammonite or Moabite, even down to the tenth generation, shall become a member of the assembly of the LORD. They shall never become members of the assembly of 4 the LORD, because they did not meet you with food and water on your way out of Egypt, and because they hired Balaam son of Beor from Pethor in Aram-5 naharaim[i] to revile you. The LORD your God refused to listen to Balaam and turned his denunciation into a blessing, because the 6 LORD your God loved you. You shall never seek their welfare or their good all your life long.
7   You shall not regard an Edomite

i That is Aram of Two Rivers.

as an abomination, for he is your own kin; nor an Egyptian, for you were aliens in his land. The third 8 generation of children born to them may become members of the assembly of the LORD.

Holiness of war camps

When you are encamped against an 9 enemy, you shall be careful to avoid any foulness. When one of your 10 number is unclean because of an emission of seed at night, he must go outside the camp; he may not come within it. Towards evening he 11 shall wash himself in water, and at sunset he may come back into the camp. You shall have a sign out-12 side the camp showing where you can withdraw. With your equip-13 ment you will have a trowel, and when you squat outside, you shall scrape a hole with it and then turn and cover your excrement. For the 14 LORD your God goes about in your camp, to keep you safe and to hand over your enemies as you advance, and your camp must be kept holy for fear that he should see something indecent and go with you no further.

Various laws

You shall not surrender to his 15 master a slave who has taken refuge with you. Let him stay with you 16 anywhere he chooses in any one of your settlements, wherever suits him best; you shall not force him.
No Israelite woman shall be-17 come a temple-prostitute, and no Israelite man shall prostitute himself in this way.
You shall not allow a common 18 prostitute's fee, or the pay of a male prostitute, to be brought into the house of the LORD your God in fulfilment of any vow, for both of

them are abominable to the LORD your God.

19 You shall not charge interest on anything you lend to a fellow-countryman, money or food or anything else on which interest can 20 be charged. You may charge interest on a loan to a foreigner but not on a loan to a fellow-countryman, for then the LORD your God will bless you in all you undertake in the land which you are entering to occupy.

21 When you make a vow to the LORD your God, do not put off its fulfilment; otherwise the LORD your God will require satisfaction of you and you will be guilty of sin. 22 If you choose not to make a vow, 23 you will not be guilty of sin; but if you voluntarily make a vow to the LORD your God, mind what you say and do what you have promised.

24 When you go into another man's vineyard, you may eat as many grapes as you wish to satisfy your hunger, but you may not put any into your basket.

25 When you go into another man's standing corn, you may pluck ears to rub in your hands, but you may not put a sickle to his standing corn.

Law of divorce

4 When a man has married a wife, but she does not win his favour because he finds something shameful in her, and he writes her a note of divorce, gives it to her and dismisses her; and suppose after leaving his house she goes off to become 3 the wife of another man, and this next husband turns against her and writes her a note of divorce which he gives her and dismisses her, or dies after making her his wife—4 then in that case her first husband who dismissed her is not free to take her back to be his wife again after she has become for him unclean. This is abominable to the LORD; you must not bring sin upon the land which the LORD your God is giving you as your patrimony. 5 When a man is newly married, he shall not be liable for military service or any other public duty. He shall remain at home exempt from service for one year and enjoy the wife he has taken.

Various laws

6 No man shall take millstones, or even the upper one alone, in pledge; that would be taking a life in pledge.

7 When a man is found to have kidnapped a fellow-countryman, an Israelite, and to have treated him harshly and sold him, he shall die: you shall rid yourselves of this wickedness.

8 Be careful how you act in all cases of malignant skin-disease; be careful to observe all that the levitical priests tell you; I gave them my commands which you must obey.

9 Remember what the LORD your God did to Miriam, on your way out of Egypt.

10 When you make a loan to another man, do not enter his house 11 to take a pledge from him. Wait outside, and the man whose creditor you are shall bring the pledge 12 out to you. If he is a poor man, you shall not sleep in the cloak he has 13 pledged. Give it back to him at sunset so that he may sleep in it and bless you; then it will be counted to your credit in the sight of the LORD your God.

14 You shall not keep back the wages of a man who is poor and needy, whether a fellow-countryman or an alien living in your country in one of your settlements. 15 Pay him his wages on the same day before sunset, for he is poor and his heart is set on them: he may appeal to the LORD against you, and you will be guilty of sin.

16 Fathers shall not be put to death for their children, nor children for their fathers; a man shall be put to death only for his own sin.

17 You shall not deprive aliens and orphans of justice nor take a 18 widow's cloak in pledge. Remember that you were slaves in Egypt and the LORD your God redeemed you from there; that is why I command you to do this.

19 When you reap the harvest in your field and forget a swathe, do not go back to pick it up; it shall be left for the alien, the orphan, and the widow, in order that the LORD your God may bless you in all that you undertake.

20 When you beat your olive-trees, do not strip them afterwards; what is left shall be for the alien, the orphan, and the widow.

21 When you gather the grapes from your vineyard, do not glean afterwards; what is left shall be for the alien, the orphan, and the widow.

22 Remember that you were slaves in Egypt; that is why I command you to do this.

25 When two men go to law and present themselves for judgement, the judges shall try the case; they shall acquit the innocent and con-2 demn the guilty. If the guilty man is sentenced to be flogged, the judge shall cause him to lie down and be beaten in his presence; the number of strokes shall correspond 3 to the gravity of the offence. They may give him forty strokes, but not more; otherwise, if they go further and exceed this number, your fellow-countryman will have been publicly degraded.

4 You shall not muzzle an ox while it is treading out the corn.

A brother-in-law's duty

5 When brothers live together and one of them dies without leaving a son, his widow shall not marry outside the family. Her husband's

brother shall have intercourse with her; he shall take her in marriage and do his duty by her as her husband's brother. The first son she 6 bears shall perpetuate the dead brother's name so that it may not be blotted out from Israel. But if 7 the man is unwilling to take his brother's wife, she shall go to the elders at the town gate and say, 'My husband's brother refuses to perpetuate his brother's name in Israel; he will not do his duty by me.' At this the elders of the town 8 shall summon him and reason with him. If he still stands his ground and says, 'I will not take her', his 9 brother's widow shall go up to him in the presence of the elders; she shall pull his sandal off his foot and spit in his face and declare: 'Thus we requite the man who will not build up his brother's family.' His family shall be known in 10 Israel as the House of the Unsandalled Man.

Other laws

When two men are fighting and the 11 wife of one of them comes near to drag her husband clear of his opponent, if she puts out her hand and catches hold of the man's genitals, you shall cut off her hand 12 and show her no mercy.

You shall not have unequal 13 weights in your bag, one heavy, the other light. You shall not have 14 unequal measures in your house, one large, the other small. You 15 shall have true and correct weights and true and correct measures, so that you may live long in the land which the LORD your God is giving you. All who commit these 16 offences, all who deal dishonestly, are abominable to the LORD.

The Amalekites to be destroyed

Remember what the Amalekites 17 did to you on your way out of Egypt, how they met you on the 18 road when you were faint and weary and cut off your rear, which was lagging behind exhausted: they showed no fear of God. When the 19 LORD your God gives you peace from your enemies on every side, in the land which he is giving you to occupy as your patrimony, you shall not fail to blot out the memory of the Amalekites from under heaven.

Law of the firstfruits

When you come into the land which 26 the LORD your God is giving you to occupy as your patrimony and settle in it, you shall take the first-2 fruits of all the produce of the soil, which you gather in from the land which the LORD your God is giving you, and put them in a basket. Then you shall go to the place which the LORD your God will choose as a dwelling for his Name and come to 3

the priest, whoever he shall be in those days. You shall say to him, 'I declare this day to the LORD your God that I have entered the land which the LORD swore to our fore-
4 fathers to give us.' The priest shall take the basket from your hand and set it down before the altar of
5 the LORD your God. Then you shall solemnly recite before the LORD your God: 'My father was a homeless[j] Aramaean who went down to Egypt with a small company and lived there until they became a great, powerful, and
6 numerous nation. But the Egyptians ill-treated us, humiliated us and imposed cruel slavery upon
7 us. Then we cried to the LORD the God of our fathers for help, and he listened to us and saw our humiliation, our hardship and dis-
8 tress; and so the LORD brought us out of Egypt with a strong hand and outstretched arm, with terrifying deeds, and with signs and por-
9 tents. He brought us to this place and gave us this land, a land flowing
10 with milk and honey. And now I have brought the firstfruits of the soil which thou, O LORD, hast given me.' You shall then set the basket before the LORD your God and bow down in worship before
11 him. You shall all rejoice, you and the Levites and the aliens living among you, for all the good things which the LORD your God has given to you and to your family.
12 When you have finished taking a tithe of your produce in the third year, the tithe-year, you shall give it to the Levites and to the aliens, the orphans, and the widows. They shall eat it in your settlements and
13 be well fed. Then you shall declare before the LORD your God: 'I have rid my house of the tithe that was holy to thee and given it to the Levites, to the aliens, the orphans, and the widows, according to all the commandments which thou didst lay upon me. I have not
14 broken or forgotten any of thy commandments. I have not eaten any of the tithe while in mourning, nor have I rid myself of it for unclean purposes, nor offered any of it to[k] the dead. I have obeyed the LORD my God: I have done all that thou didst command me. Look 15 down from heaven, thy holy dwelling-place, and bless thy people Israel and the ground which thou hast given to us as thou didst swear to our forefathers, a land flowing with milk and honey.'

A holy people

This day the LORD your God com- 16 mands you to keep these statutes and laws: be careful to observe them with all your heart and soul. You have recognized the LORD this 17 day as your God; you are to conform to his ways, to keep his statutes, his commandments, and his laws, and to obey him. The 18 LORD has recognized you this day as his special possession, as he promised you, and to keep his commandments; he will raise you 19 high above all the nations which he has made, to bring him praise and fame and glory, and to be a people holy to the LORD your God, according to his promise.

Recording the law

27 Moses, with the elders of Israel, gave the people this charge: 'Keep all the command-
2 ments that I lay upon you this day. On the day that you cross the Jordan to the land which the LORD your God is giving you, you shall set up great stones and plaster
3 them over. You shall inscribe on them all the words of this law, when you have crossed over to enter the land which the LORD your God is giving you, a land flowing with milk and honey, as the LORD the God of your
4 fathers promised you. When you have crossed the Jordan you shall set up these stones on Mount Ebal, as I command you
5 this day, and cover them with plaster. You shall build an altar there to the LORD your God: it shall be an altar of stones on which
6 you shall use no tool of iron. You shall build the altar of the LORD your God with blocks of undressed stone, and you shall offer whole-offerings upon it to the LORD
7 your God. You shall slaughter shared-offerings and eat them there, and rejoice
8 before the LORD your God. You shall inscribe on the stones all the words of this law, engraving them with care.'
9 Moses and the levitical priests spoke to all Israel, 'Be silent, Israel, and listen; this day you have become a people belonging
10 to the LORD your God. Obey the LORD your God, and observe his commandments and statutes which I lay upon you this day.'

Curses for disobedience

11 That day Moses gave the people this com-
12 mand: 'Those who shall stand for the

blessing of the people on Mount Gerizim when you have crossed the Jordan are these: Simeon, Levi, Judah, Issachar, Joseph, and Benjamin. Those who shall stand on Mount 13 Ebal for the curse are these: Reuben, Gad, Asher, Zebulun, Dan, and Naphtali.'
The Levites, in the hearing of all Israel, 14 shall intone these words:
'A curse upon the man who carves an 15 idol or casts an image, anything abominable to the LORD that craftsmen make, and sets it up in secret': the people shall all respond and say, 'Amen.'
'A curse upon him who slights his father 16 or his mother': the people shall all say, 'Amen.'
'A curse upon him who moves his neigh- 17 bour's boundary stone': the people shall all say, 'Amen.'
'A curse upon him who misdirects a blind 18 man': the people shall all say, 'Amen.'
'A curse upon him who withholds justice 19 from the alien, the orphan, and the widow': the people shall all say, 'Amen.'
'A curse upon him who lies with his 20 father's wife, for he brings shame upon his father': the people shall all say, 'Amen.'
'A curse upon him who lies with any 21 animal': the people shall all say, 'Amen.'
'A curse upon him who lies with his sister, 22 his father's daughter or his mother's daughter': the people shall all say, 'Amen.'
'A curse upon him who lies with his wife's 23 mother': the people shall all say, 'Amen.'
'A curse upon him who strikes another 24 man in secret': the people shall all say, 'Amen.'

---

j Or wandering.   *k Or* for.

25 'A curse upon him who takes reward to kill a man with whom he has no feud': the people shall all say, 'Amen.'

26 'A curse upon any man who does not fulfil this law by doing all that it prescribes': the people shall all say, 'Amen.'

Blessings for obedience

8 If you will obey the LORD your God by diligently observing all his commandments which I lay upon you this day, then the LORD your God will raise you high above all 2 nations of the earth, and all these blessings shall come to you and light upon you, because you obey the LORD your God:

3 A blessing on you in the city; a blessing on you in the country.

4 A blessing on the fruit of your body, the fruit of your land and of your cattle, the offspring of your herds and of your lambing flocks.

5 A blessing on your basket and your kneading-trough.

6 A blessing on you as you come in; and a blessing on you as you go out.

7 May the LORD deliver up the enemies who attack you and let them be put to rout before you. Though they come out against you by one way, they shall flee before you by seven ways.

8 May the LORD grant you a blessing in your granaries and in all your labours; may the LORD your God bless you in the land which he is giving you.

9 The LORD will set you up as his own holy people, as he swore to you, if you keep the commandments of the LORD your God and 10 conform to his ways. Then all people on earth shall see that the LORD has named you as his very own, and they shall go in 11 fear of you. The LORD will make you prosper greatly in the fruit of your body and of your cattle, and in the fruit of the ground in the land which he swore to your forefathers to 12 give you. May the LORD open the heavens for you, his rich treasure house, to give rain upon your land at the proper time and bless everything to which you turn your hand. You shall lend to many nations, but you 13 shall not borrow; the LORD will make you the head and not the tail: you shall be always at the top and never at the bottom, when you listen to the commandments of the LORD your God, which I give you this day

to keep and to fulfil. You shall turn neither 14 to the right nor to the left from all the things which I command you this day nor shall you follow after and worship other gods.

The consequences of disobedience

But if you do not obey the LORD your God 15 by diligently observing all his commandments and statutes which I lay upon you this day, then all these maledictions shall come to you and light upon you:

A curse upon you in the city; a curse upon 16 you in the country.

A curse upon your basket and your 17 kneading-trough.

A curse upon the fruit of your body, the 18 fruit of your land, the offspring of your herds and of your lambing flocks.

A curse upon you as you come in; and a 19 curse upon you as you go out.

May the LORD send upon you starvation, 20 burning thirst, and dysentery,[1] whatever you are about, until you are destroyed and quickly perish for your evil doings, because you have forsaken me.

May the LORD cause pestilence to haunt 21 you until he has exterminated you out of the land which you are entering to occupy; may the LORD afflict you with wasting 22 disease and recurrent fever, ague and eruptions; with drought, black blight and red; and may these plague you until you perish. May the skies above you be bronze, and the 23 earth beneath you iron. May the LORD turn 24 the rain upon your country into fine sand, and may dust come down upon you from the sky until you are blotted out.

May the LORD put you to rout before the 25 enemy. Though you go out against them by one way, you shall flee before them by seven ways. May you be repugnant to all the kingdoms on earth. May your bodies become 26 food for the birds of the air and the wild beasts, with no man to scare them away.

May the LORD strike you with Egyptian 27 boils and with tumours, scabs, and itches, for which you will find no cure. May the 28 LORD strike you with madness, blindness, and bewilderment; so that you will grope 29 about in broad daylight, just as a blind man gropes in darkness, and you will fail to find your way. You will also be oppressed and robbed, day in, day out, with no one to save you. A woman will be pledged to you, but 30

_1 Or_ cursing, confusion, and rebuke.

another shall ravish her; you will build a house but not live in it; you will plant a
31 vineyard but not enjoy its fruit. Your ox will be slaughtered before your eyes, but you will not eat any of it; and before your eyes your ass will be stolen and will not come back to you; your sheep will be given to the enemy, and there will be no one to recover
32 them. Your sons and daughters will be given to another people while you look on; your eyes will strain after them all day long,
33 and you will be powerless. A nation whom you do not know shall eat the fruit of your land and all your toil, and your lot will be
34 nothing but brutal oppression. The sights
35 you see will drive you mad. May the LORD strike you on knee and leg with malignant boils for which you will find no cure; they will spread from the sole of your foot to
36 the crown of your head. May the LORD give you up, you and the king whom you have appointed, to a nation whom neither you nor your fathers have known, and there you will worship other gods, gods of wood and
37 stone. You will become a horror, a byword, and an object-lesson to all the peoples amongst whom the LORD disperses you.
38 You will carry out seed for your fields in plenty, but you will harvest little; for the
39 locusts will devour it. You will plant vineyards and cultivate them, but you will not drink the wine or gather the grapes; for the
40 grub will eat them. You will have olive-trees all over your territory, but you will not anoint yourselves with their oil; for your
41 olives will drop off. You will bear sons and daughters, but they will not remain yours because they will be taken into captivity.
42 All your trees and the fruit of the ground
43 will be infested with the mole-cricket. The alien who lives with you will raise himself higher and higher, and you will sink lower
44 and lower. He will lend to you but you will not lend to him: he will be the head and you the tail.
45 All these maledictions will come upon you; they will pursue you and overtake you until you are destroyed because you did not obey the LORD your God by keeping the commandments and statutes which he
46 gave you. They shall be a sign and a portent
47 to you and your descendants for ever, because you did not serve the LORD your God with joy and with a glad heart for all your
48 blessings. Then in hunger and thirst, in nakedness and extreme want, you shall serve your enemies whom the LORD will send against you, and they will put a yoke of iron on your neck when they have subdued you.
49 May the LORD raise against you a nation from afar, from the other end of the earth, who will swoop upon you like a vulture, a nation whose language you will not under-
50 stand, a nation of grim aspect with no reverence for age and no pity for the young.
51 They will devour the young of your cattle and the fruit of your land, when you have been subdued. They will leave you neither corn, nor new wine nor oil, neither the off-spring of your herds nor of your lambing
52 flocks, until you are annihilated. They will besiege you in all your cities until they bring down your lofty impregnable walls, those city walls throughout your land in which you trust. They will besiege you within all your cities, throughout the land which the LORD your God has given you. Then you
53 will eat your own children, the flesh of your sons and daughters whom the LORD your God has given you, because of the dire straits to which you will be reduced when your enemy besieges you. The pampered,
54 delicate man will not share with his brother, or the wife of his bosom, or his own remain-
55 ing children, any of the meat which he is eating, the flesh of his own children. He is left with nothing else because of the dire straits to which you will be reduced when your enemy besieges you within your cities. The pampered, delicate woman, the woman
56 who has never even tried to put a foot to the ground, so delicate and pampered she is, will not share with her own husband or her
57 son or her daughter the afterbirth which she expels, or any boy or girl that she may bear. She will herself eat them secretly in her extreme want, because of the dire straits to which you will be reduced when your enemy besieges you within your cities.
58 If you do not observe and fulfil all the law written down in this book, if you do not revere this honoured and dreaded name,
59 this name 'the LORD[m] your God', then the LORD will strike you and your descendants with unimaginable plagues, malignant and persistent, and with sickness, persistent and
60 severe. He will bring upon you once again all the diseases of Egypt which you dread,
61 and they will cling to you. The LORD will bring upon you sickness and plague of every kind not written down in this book of the
62 law, until you are destroyed. Then you who were countless as the stars in the sky will be left few in number, because you did not obey
63 the LORD your God. Just as the LORD took delight in you, prospering and increasing you, so now it will be his delight to destroy and exterminate you, and you will be up-rooted from the land which you are entering
64 to occupy. The LORD will scatter you among all peoples from one end of the earth to the other, and there you will worship other gods whom neither you have known nor your
65 forefathers, gods of wood and stone. Among

m See note on Exod. 3. 15.

those nations you will find no peace, no rest for the sole of your foot. Then the LORD will give you an unquiet mind, dim eyes, and 66 failing appetite. Your life will hang continually in suspense, fear will beset you night and day, and you will find no security all 67 your life long. Every morning you will say, 'Would God it were evening!', and every evening, 'Would God it were morning!', for the fear that lives in your heart and the sights 68 that you see. The LORD will bring you sorrowing back to Egypt by that very road of which I said to you, 'You shall not see that road again'; and there you will offer to sell yourselves to your enemies as slaves and slave-girls, but there will be no buyer.

29 These are the words of the covenant which the LORD commanded Moses to make with the Israelites in Moab, in addition to the covenant which he made with them on Horeb.

The covenant with Israel in Moab

2 Moses summoned all the Israelites and said to them: 'You have seen with your own eyes all that the LORD did in Egypt to Pharaoh, to all his servants, and to the whole land, 3 the great challenge which you yourselves witnessed, those great signs and portents, 4 but to this day the LORD has not given you a mind to learn, or eyes to see, or ears to 5 hear. I led you for forty years in the wilderness; your clothes did not wear out on you, nor did your sandals wear out and fall off 6 your feet; you ate no bread and drank no wine or strong drink, in order that you might learn that I am the LORD your God. 7 You came to this place where Sihon king of Heshbon and Og king of Bashan came to 8 attack us, and we defeated them. We took their land and gave it as patrimony to the Reubenites, the Gadites, and half the tribe 9 of Manasseh. You shall observe the provisions of this covenant and keep them so that you may be successful in all you do.

10 'You all stand here today before the LORD your God, tribal chiefs, elders, and officers, 11 all the men of Israel, with your dependants, your wives, the aliens who live in your camp—all of them, from those who chop 12 wood to those who draw water—and you are ready to accept the oath and enter into the covenant which the LORD your God is 13 making with you today. The covenant is to constitute you his people this day, and he will be your God, as he promised you and as he swore to your forefathers, Abraham, 14 Isaac and Jacob. It is not with you alone that I am making this covenant and this 15 oath, but with all those who stand here with us today before the LORD our God and also with those who are not here with us today. 16 For you know how we lived in Egypt and

how we and you, as we passed through the nations, saw their loathsome idols and the 17 false gods they had, the gods of wood and stone, of silver and gold. If there should be 18 among you a man or woman, family or tribe, who is moved today to turn from the LORD our God and to go worshipping the gods of those nations—if there is among you such a root from which springs gall and wormwood, then when he hears the terms 19 of this oath, he may inwardly flatter himself and think, "All will be well with me even if I follow the promptings of my stubborn heart"; but this will bring everything to ruin. The LORD will not be willing to forgive him; 20 for then his anger and resentment will overwhelm this man, and the denunciations prescribed in this book will fall heavily on him, and the LORD will blot out his name from under heaven. The LORD will single 21 him out from all the tribes of Israel for disaster to fall upon him, according to the oath required by the covenant and prescribed in this book of the law.

'The next generation, your sons who fol- 22 low you and the foreigners who come from distant countries, will see the plagues of this land and the ulcers which the LORD has brought upon its people, the whole land 23 burnt up with brimstone and salt, so that it cannot be sown, or yield herb or green plant. It will be as desolate as were Sodom and Gomorrah, Admah and Zeboyim, when the LORD overthrew them in his anger and rage. Then they, and all the nations with them, 24 will ask, "Why has the LORD so afflicted this land? Why has there been this great outburst of wrath?" The answer will be: 25 "Because they forsook the covenant of the LORD the God of their fathers which he made with them when he brought them out of Egypt. They began to worship other gods 26 and to bow down to them, gods whom they had not known and whom the LORD had not assigned to them. The anger of the LORD 27 was roused against that land, so that he brought upon it all the maledictions written in this book. The LORD uprooted them from 28 their soil in anger, in wrath and great fury, and banished them to another land, where they are to this day."

'There are things hidden, and they belong 29 to the LORD our God, but what is revealed belongs to us and our children for ever; it is for us to observe all that is prescribed in this law.

Choice of life or death

'When these things have befallen you, the **30** blessing and the curse of which I have offered you the choice, if you and your sons take them to heart there in all the countries to which the LORD your God has banished you,

2 if you turn back to him and obey him heart and soul in all that I command you this day, 3 then the LORD your God will show you compassion and restore your fortunes. He will gather you again from all the countries 4 to which he has scattered you. Even though he were to banish you to the four corners of the world, the LORD your God will gather you from there, from there he will fetch you 5 home. The LORD your God will bring you into the land which your forefathers occupied, and you will occupy it again; then he will bring you prosperity and make you more numerous than your forefathers were. 6 The LORD your God will circumcise[n] your hearts and the hearts of your descendants, so that you will love him with all your heart 7 and soul and you will live. Then the LORD your God will turn all these denunciations against your enemies and the foes who per- 8 secute you. You will then again obey the LORD and keep all his commandments which 9-10 I give you this day. The LORD your God will make you more than prosperous in all that you do, in the fruit of your body and of your cattle and in the fruits of the earth; for, when you obey the LORD your God by keeping his commandments and statutes, as they are written in this book of the law, and when you turn back to the LORD your God with all your heart and soul, he will again rejoice over you and be good to you, as he rejoiced over your forefathers.

11 'The commandment that I lay on you this day is not too difficult for you, it is not 12 too remote. It is not in heaven, that you should say, "Who will go up to heaven for us to fetch it and tell it to us, so that we can 13 keep it?" Nor is it beyond the sea, that you should say, "Who will cross the sea for us to fetch it and tell it to us, so that we can 14 keep it?" It is a thing very near to you, upon your lips and in your heart ready to be kept. 15 'Today I offer you the choice of life and 16 good, or death and evil. If you obey the commandments of the LORD your God which I give you this day, by loving the LORD your God, by conforming to his ways and by keeping his commandments, statutes, and laws, then you will live and increase, and the LORD your God will bless you in the 17 land which you are entering to occupy. But if your heart turns away and you do not listen and you are led on to bow down to 18 other gods and worship them, I tell you this day that you will perish; you will not live long in the land which you will enter to 19 occupy after crossing the Jordan. I summon heaven and earth to witness against you this day: I offer you the choice of life or death, blessing or curse. Choose life and then you 20 and your descendants will live; love the

LORD your God, obey him and hold fast to him: that is life for you and length of days in the land which the LORD swore to give to your forefathers, Abraham, Isaac and Jacob.'

Moses addresses Joshua

31 Moses finished speaking these words to all Israel, and then he said, 'I am now a hun- 2 dred and twenty years old, and I can no longer move about as I please; and the LORD has told me that I may not cross the Jordan. The LORD your God will cross over at your 3 head and destroy these nations before your advance, and you shall occupy their lands; and, as he directed, Joshua will lead you across. The LORD will do to these nations 4 as he did to Sihon and Og, kings of the Amorites, and to their lands; he will destroy them. The LORD will deliver them into your 5 power, and you shall do to them as I commanded you. Be strong, be resolute; you 6 must not dread them or be afraid, for the LORD your God himself goes with you; he will not fail you or forsake you.'

Moses summoned Joshua and said to him 7 in the presence of all Israel, 'Be strong, be resolute; for it is you who are to lead this people into the land which the LORD swore to give their forefathers, and you are to bring them into possession of it. The LORD 8 himself goes at your head; he will be with you; he will not fail you or forsake you. Do not be discouraged or afraid.'

The law to be read every seven years

Moses wrote down this law and gave it to 9 the priests, the sons of Levi, who carried the Ark of the Covenant of the LORD, and to all the elders of Israel. Moses gave them this 10 command: 'At the end of every seven years, at the appointed time for the year of remission, at the pilgrim-feast of Tabernacles, when all Israel comes to enter the presence 11 of the LORD your God in the place which he will choose, you shall read this law publicly in the hearing of all Israel. Assemble the 12 people, men, women, and dependants, together with the aliens who live in your settlements, so that they may listen, and learn to fear the LORD your God and observe all these laws with care. Their children, too, 13 who do not know them, shall hear them, and learn to fear the LORD your God all their lives in the land which you will occupy after crossing the Jordan.'

The LORD's last instructions to Moses

The LORD said to Moses, 'The time of your 14 death is drawing near; call Joshua, and then come and stand in the Tent of the Presence so that I may give him his commission.' So

n Or incline.

Moses and Joshua went and took their
15 stand in the Tent of the Presence; and the
LORD appeared in the tent in a pillar of
cloud, and the pillar of cloud stood at the
entrance of the tent.

16 The LORD said to Moses, 'You are about
to die like your forefathers, and this people,
when they come into the land and live among
foreigners, will go wantonly after their gods;
they will abandon me and break the cove-
17 nant which I have made with them. Then
my anger will be roused against them, and
I will abandon them and hide my face from
them. They will be an easy prey, and many
terrible disasters will come upon them. They
will say on that day, "These disasters have
come because our God is not among us."
18 On that day I will hide my face because of all
the evil they have done in turning to other
gods.
19 'Now write down this rule of life*o* and
teach it to the Israelites; make them repeat
it, so that it may be on record against them.
20 When I have brought them into the land
which I swore to give to their forefathers, a
land flowing with milk and honey, and they
have plenty to eat and grow fat, they will
turn to other gods and worship them, they
21 will spurn me and break my covenant; and
many calamities and disasters will follow.
Then this rule of life will confront them as
a record, for it will not be forgotten by their
descendants. For even before I bring them
into the land which I swore to give them,
I know which way their thoughts incline
already.'
22 That day Moses wrote down this rule of
23 life and taught it to the Israelites. The LORD*p*
gave Joshua son of Nun his commission in
these words: 'Be strong, be resolute; for you
shall bring the Israelites into the land which
I swore to give them, and I will be with
you.'
24 When Moses had finished writing down
these laws in a book, from beginning to end,
25 he gave this command to the Levites who
carried the Ark of the Covenant of the
26 LORD: 'Take this book of the law and put
it beside the Ark of the Covenant of the
LORD your God to be a witness against you.
27 For I know how defiant and stubborn you
are; even during my lifetime you have defied
the LORD; how much more, then, will you
28 do so when I am dead? Assemble all the
elders of your tribes and your officers; I will
say all these things in their hearing and will
summon heaven and earth to witness against
29 them. For I know that after my death you
will take to degrading practices and turn
aside from the way which I told you to
follow, and in days to come disaster will
come upon you, because you are doing what

is wrong in the eyes of the LORD and so
provoking him to anger.'

The Song of Moses

Moses recited this song from beginning to 30
end in the hearing of the whole assembly of
Israel:

Give ear to what I say, O heavens, **32**
earth, listen to my words;
my teaching shall fall like drops of rain, 2
my words shall distil like dew,
like fine rain upon the grass
and like the showers on young plants.

When I call aloud the name of the LORD,*q* 3
you shall respond, 'Great is our God,
the creator*r* whose work is perfect, 4
and all his ways are just,
a faithful god, who does no wrong,
righteous and true is He!'

Perverse and crooked generation 5
whose faults have proved you no children of
his,
is this how you repay the LORD, 6
you brutish and stupid people?
Is he not your father who formed you?
Did he not make you and establish you?
Remember the days of old, 7
think of the generations long ago;
ask your father to recount it
and your elders to tell you the tale.

When the Most High parcelled out the 8
nations,
when he dispersed all mankind,
he laid down the boundaries of every people
according to the number of the sons of God;
but the LORD's share was his own people, 9
Jacob was his allotted portion.
He found him in a desert land, 10
in a waste and howling void.
He protected and trained him,
he guarded him as the apple of his eye,
as an eagle watches over its nest, 11
hovers above its young,
spreads its pinions and takes them up,
and carries them upon its wings.
The LORD alone led him, 12
no alien god at his side.
He made him ride on the heights of the 13
earth
and fed him on the harvest of the fields;
he satisfied him with honey from the crags
and oil from the flinty rock,
curds from the cattle, milk from the ewes, 14
the fat of lambs' kidneys,
of rams, the breed of Bashan, and of goats,
with the finest flour of wheat;
and he drank wine from the blood of the
grape.

o rule of life: *or* song.   *p* Prob. rdg.; Heb. He.   *q* Or the name JEHOVAH.   *r* Or rock.

15 Jacob ate and was well fed,
Jeshurun grew fat and unruly,[s]
he grew fat, he grew bloated and sleek.
He forsook God who made him
and dishonoured the Rock of his salvation.
16 They roused his jealousy with foreign gods
and provoked him with abominable practices.
17 They sacrificed to foreign demons that are
no gods,
gods who were strangers to them;
they took up with new gods from their
neighbours,
gods whom your fathers did not acknowledge.
18 You forsook the creator[t] who begot you
and cared nothing for God who brought
you to birth.
19 The LORD saw and spurned them;
his own sons and daughters provoked him.
20 'I will hide my face from them,' he said;
'let me see what their end will be,
for they are a mutinous generation,
sons who are not to be trusted.
21 They roused my jealousy with a god of no
account,
with their false gods they provoked me;
so I will rouse their jealousy with a people of
no account,
with a brutish nation I will provoke them.
22 For fire is kindled by my anger,
it burns to the depths of Sheol;
it devours earth and its harvest
and sets fire to the very roots of the mountains.
23 I will heap on them one disaster after another,
I will use up all my arrows on them:
24 pangs of hunger, ravages of plague,
and bitter pestilence.
I will harry them with the fangs of wild
beasts
and the poison of creatures that crawl in the
dust.
25 The sword will make orphans in the streets
and widows in their own homes;
it will take toll of young man and maid,
of babes in arms and old men.
26 I had resolved to strike them down
and to destroy all memory of them,
27 but I feared that I should be provoked by
their foes,
that their enemies would take the credit
and say, "It was not the LORD,
it was we who raised the hand that did this."'

28 They are a nation that lacks good counsel,
devoid of understanding.
29 If only they had the wisdom to understand
this
and give thought to their end!

30 How could one man pursue a thousand of
them,
how could two put ten thousand to flight,
if their Rock had not sold them to their
enemies,
if the LORD had not handed them over?
31 For the enemy have no Rock like ours,
in themselves they are mere fools.
32 Their vines are vines of Sodom,
grown on the terraces of Gomorrah;
their grapes are poisonous,
the clusters bitter to the taste.
33 Their wine is the venom of serpents,
the cruel poison of asps;
34 all this I have in reserve,
sealed up in my storehouses
35 till the day of punishment and vengeance,
till the moment when they slip and fall;
for the day of their downfall is near,
their doom is fast approaching.
36 The LORD will give his people justice
and have compassion on his servants;
for he will see that their strength is gone:
alone, or defended by his clan, no one is left.

37 He will say, 'Where are your gods,
the rock in which you sought shelter,
38 the gods who ate the fat of your sacrifices
and drank the wine of your drink-offerings?
Let them rise to help you!
Let them give you shelter!
39 See now that I, I am He,
and there is no god beside me:
I put to death and I keep alive,
I wound and I heal;
there is no rescue from my grasp.
40 I lift my hand to heaven
and swear: As I live for ever,
41 when I have whetted my flashing sword,
when I have set my hand to judgement,
then I will punish my adversaries
and take vengeance on my enemies.
42 I will make my arrows drunk with blood,
my sword shall devour flesh,
blood of slain and captives,
the heads of the enemy princes.'
43 Rejoice with him, you heavens,
bow down, all you gods, before him;
for he will avenge the blood of his sons
and take vengeance on his adversaries;
he will punish those who hate him
and make expiation for his people's land.

44 This is the song that Moses came and
recited in the hearing of the people, he and
Joshua son of Nun.
45 Moses finished speaking to all Israel, and
then he said, 'Take to heart all these warnings which I solemnly give you this day:
46 command your children to be careful to
observe all the words of this law. For you
47 they are no empty words; they are your

s *Or* and kicked.   t *Or* rock.

very life, and by them you shall live long in the land which you are to occupy after crossing the Jordan.'

Moses allowed to see Canaan

48 That same day the LORD spoke to Moses
49 and said, 'Go up this mount Abarim, Mount Nebo in Moab, to the east of Jericho, and look out over the land of Canaan that I am giving to the Israelites for their possession.
50 On this mountain you shall die and be gathered to your father's kin, just as Aaron your brother died on Mount Hor and was
51 gathered to his father's kin. This is because both of you were unfaithful to me at the waters of Meribah-by-Kadesh in the wilderness of Zin, when you did not uphold my
52 holiness among the Israelites. You shall see the land from a distance but you may not enter the land I am giving to the Israelites.'

Moses blesses the tribes of Israel

33 This is the blessing that Moses the man of God pronounced upon the Israelites before his death:

2   The LORD came from Sinai
     and shone forth from Seir.
     He showed himself from Mount Paran,
     and with him were myriads of holy ones*u*
     streaming along at his right hand.
3   Truly he loves his people
     and blesses his saints.*v*
     They sit at his feet
     and receive his instruction,
4   the law which Moses laid upon us,
     as a possession for the assembly of Jacob.
5   Then a king arose*w* in Jeshurun,
     when the chiefs of the people were assembled
     together with all the tribes of Israel.

6 Of Reuben he said:*x*

     May Reuben live and not die out,
     but may he be few in number.

7 And of Judah he said this:

     Hear, O LORD, the cry of Judah
     and join him to his people,
     thou whose hands fight for him,
     who art his helper against his foes.

8 Of Levi he said:

     Thou didst give thy Thummim to Levi,
     thy Urim to thy loyal servant
     whom thou didst prove at Massah,
     for whom thou didst plead at the waters of
          Meribah,
9   who said of his parents, I do not know them,
     who did not acknowledge his brothers,
     nor recognize his children.

They observe thy word
and keep thy covenant;
they teach thy precepts to Jacob,   10
thy law to Israel.
They offer thee the smoke of sacrifice
and offerings on thy altar.
Bless all his powers,*y* O LORD,   11
and accept the work of his hands.
Strike his adversaries hip and thigh,
and may his enemies rise no more.

Of Benjamin he said: 12

The LORD's beloved dwells in security,
the High God*z* shields him all the day long,
and he dwells under his protection.

Of Joseph he said: 13

The LORD's blessing is on his land
with precious fruit watered from heaven
     above
and from the deep that lurks below,
with precious fruit ripened by the sun,   14
precious fruit, the produce of the months,
with all good things from the ancient mount- 15
     ains,
the precious fruit of the everlasting hills,

the precious fruits of earth and all its store, 16
by the favour of him who dwells in the burn-
     ing bush.
This shall rest*a* upon the head of Joseph,
on the brow of him who was prince among*b*
     his brothers.
In majesty he shall be like a first-born OX,   17
his horns those of a wild ox
with which he will gore nations
and drive*c* them to the ends of earth.
Such will be the myriads of Ephraim,
and such the thousands of Manasseh.

Of Zebulun he said: 18

Rejoice, Zebulun, when you sally forth,
rejoice in your tents, Issachar.
They shall summon nations to the mountain, 19
there they will offer true sacrifices,
for they shall suck the abundance of the seas
and draw out*d* the hidden wealth of the sand.

---

u and with . . . holy ones: *prob. rdg.; Heb.* and he came from myriads of holiness.
w Or Then there was a king . . .   *x* Of Reuben he said: *prob. rdg.; Heb. om.*   *y Or* skill.   *z* the
High God: *prob. rdg.; Heb.* upon him.   *a Prob. rdg., cp. Gen. 49. 26; Heb.* has an unintelligible form.
b him . . . among: *or* the one cursed by.   *c* and drive: *prob. rdg.; Heb.* together.   *d* draw out: *prob.
rdg.; Heb. obscure.*   *v Or* holy ones.

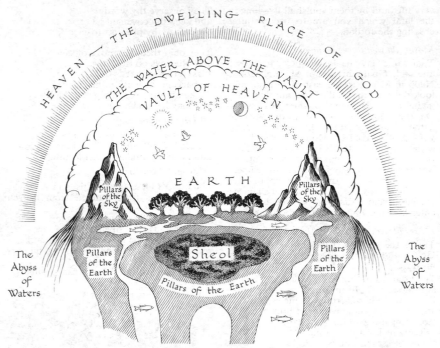

Early conception of the universe

20 Of Gad he said:

Blessed be Gad, in his wide domain;
he couches like a lion
tearing an arm or a scalp.
21 He chose the best for himself,
for to him was allotted a ruler's portion,
when the chiefs of the people were assembled
    together.
He did what the LORD deemed right,
observing his ordinances for Israel.
22 Of Dan he said:

Dan is a lion's cub
springing out from Bashan.

23 Of Naphtali he said:

Naphtali is richly favoured
and full of the blessings of the LORD;
his patrimony stretches to the sea and south-
    ward.
24 Of Asher he said:

Asher is most blest of sons,
may he be the favourite among*e* his brothers
and bathe his feet in oil.
25 May your bolts be of iron and bronze,
and your strength last as long as you live.

There is none like the God of Jeshurun   26
who rides the heavens to your help,
riding the clouds in his glory,
who humbled the gods of old   27
and subdued*f* the ancient powers;
who drove out the enemy before you
and gave the word to destroy.
Israel lives in security,   28
the tribes of Jacob by themselves,
in a land of corn and wine*g*
where the skies drip with dew.
Happy are you, people of Israel, peerless,   29
    set free;
the LORD is the shield that guards you,
the Blessed One is your glorious sword.
Your enemies come cringing to you,
and you shall trample their bodies under
    foot.

The death of Moses

Then Moses went up from the lowlands of **34**
Moab to Mount Nebo, to the top of Pisgah,
eastwards from Jericho, and the LORD
showed him the whole land: Gilead as far
as Dan; the whole of Naphtali; the territory 2
of Ephraim and Manasseh, and all Judah
as far as the western sea; the Negeb and the 3

e Or of.   *f Prob. rdg.; Heb. under.*   *g Or new wine.*

Plain; the valley of Jericho, the Vale of Palm
4 Trees, as far as Zoar. The LORD said to him,
'This is the land which I swore to Abraham,
Isaac and Jacob that I would give to their
descendants. I have let you see it with your
own eyes, but you shall not cross over
into it.'

5 There in the land of Moab Moses the
servant of the LORD died, as the LORD had
6 said. He was buried in a valley in Moab
opposite Beth-peor, but to this day no one
7 knows his burial-place. Moses was a hundred and twenty years old when he died;
his sight was not dimmed nor had his vigour
8 failed. The Israelites wept for Moses in the
lowlands of Moab for thirty days; then the
time of mourning for Moses was ended. And 9
Joshua son of Nun was filled with the spirit
of wisdom, for Moses had laid his hands
on him, and the Israelites listened to him
and did what the LORD had commanded
Moses.

There has never yet risen in Israel a 10
prophet like Moses, whom the LORD knew
face to face: remember all the signs and 11
portents which the LORD sent him to show
in Egypt to Pharaoh and all his servants
and the whole land; remember the strong 12
hand of Moses and the terrible deeds which
he did in the sight of all Israel.

THE BOOK OF
JOSHUA

Israel prepares to occupy Canaan

1 AFTER THE DEATH of Moses the
servant of the LORD, the LORD said to
2 Joshua son of Nun, his assistant, 'My
servant Moses is dead; now it is for you to
cross the Jordan, you and this whole people
of Israel, to the land which I am giving
3 them. Every place where you set foot is
yours: I have given it to you, as I promised
4 Moses. From the desert and the Lebanon
to the great river, the river Euphrates, and
across all the Hittite country westwards to
the Great Sea,*a* all this shall be your land.
5 No one will ever be able to stand against
you: as I was with Moses, so will I be with
6 you; I will not fail you or forsake you. Be
strong, be resolute; it is you who are to put
this people in possession of the land which
7 I swore to give to their fathers. Only be
strong and resolute; observe diligently all
the law which my servant Moses has given
you. You must not turn from it to right or
left, if you would prosper wherever you go.
8 This book of the law must ever be on your
lips; you must keep it in mind day and night
so that you may diligently observe all that
is written in it. Then you will prosper and
9 be successful in all that you do. This is my
command: be strong, be resolute; do not
be fearful or dismayed, for the LORD your
10 God is with you wherever you go.' Then
11 Joshua told the officers to pass through the

camp and give this order to the people: 'Get
food ready to take with you; for within three
days you will be crossing the Jordan to
occupy the country which the LORD your
God is giving you to possess.' To the Reuben- 12
ites, the Gadites, and the half tribe of
Manasseh, Joshua said, 'Remember the 13
command which Moses the servant of the
LORD gave you when he said, "The LORD
your God will grant you security here and
will give you this territory." Your wives 14
and dependants and your herds may stay
east of the Jordan in the territory which
Moses has given you, but for yourselves, all
the warriors among you must cross over as
a fighting force at the head of your kinsmen.
You must help them, until the LORD grants 15
them security like you and they too take
possession of the land which the LORD your
God is giving them. You may then return
to the land which is your own possession,
the territory which Moses the servant of the
LORD has given you east of the Jordan.'
They answered Joshua, 'Whatever you tell 16
us, we will do; wherever you send us, we
will go. As we obeyed Moses, so will we 17
obey you; and may the LORD your God
be with you as he was with Moses! Who- 18
ever rebels against your authority, and
fails to carry out all your orders, shall
be put to death. Only be strong and resolute.'

a Or the Mediterranean Sea.

Rahab and the spies

2 Joshua son of Nun sent two spies out from Shittim secretly with orders to reconnoitre the country. The two men came to Jericho and went to the house of a prostitute named 2 Rahab, and spent the night there. It was reported to the king of Jericho that some Israelites had arrived that night to explore 3 the country. So the king sent to Rahab and said, 'Bring out the men who have come to you and are now in your house; they are 4 here to explore the whole country.' The woman, who had taken the two men and hidden them,*b* replied, 'Yes, the men did come to me, but I did not know where they 5 came from; and when it was time to shut the gate at nightfall, they had gone. I do not know where they were going, but if you hurry after them, you will catch them up.' 6 In fact, she had taken them up on to the roof and concealed them among the stalks of flax which she had laid out there in rows. 7 The messengers went in pursuit of them down the road to the fords of the Jordan, and the gate was closed as soon as they had 8 gone out. The men had not yet settled down, when Rahab came up to them on the roof 9 and said to them, 'I know that the LORD has given this land to you, that terror of you has descended upon us all, and that because of you the whole country is panic-0 stricken. For we have heard how the LORD dried up the water of the Red Sea*c* before you when you came out of Egypt, and what you did to Sihon and Og, the two Amorite kings beyond the Jordan, whom you put to 1 death. When we heard this, our courage failed us; your coming has left no spirit in any of us; for the LORD your God is God 2 in heaven above and on earth below. Swear to me now by the LORD that you will keep faith with my family, as I have kept faith with you. Give me a token of good faith; 3 promise that you will spare the lives of my father and mother, my brothers and sisters and all who belong to them, and save us 4 from death.' The men replied, 'Our lives for yours, so long as you do not betray our business. When the LORD gives us the country, we will deal honestly and faithfully by you.' 5 She then let them down through an opening by a rope; for the house where she lived was 6 on an angle of the wall. 'Take to the hills,' she said, 'or the pursuers will come upon you. Hide yourselves there for three days until they come back, and then go on your 7 way.' The men warned her that they would be released from the oath she had made 8 them take unless she did what they told her. 'When we enter the land,' they said, 'you

must fasten this strand of scarlet cord in the opening through which you have lowered us, and get everybody together here in the house, your father and mother, your brothers and all your family. If anybody goes out of 19 doors into the street, his blood shall be on his own head; we shall be quit of the oath. But if a hand is laid on anyone who stays indoors with you, his blood shall be on our heads. Remember too that, if you betray our 20 business, then we shall be quit of the oath you have made us take.' She replied, 'It shall 21 be as you say', and sent them away. They set off, and she fastened the strand of scarlet cord in the opening. The men made their 22 way into the hills and stayed there three days until the pursuers returned. They had searched all along the road, but had not found them.*d* The two men then turned and 23 came down from the hills, crossed the river and returned to Joshua son of Nun. They told him all that had happened to them and 24 said to him, 'The LORD has put the whole country into our hands, and now all its people are panic-stricken at our approach.'

Israel crosses the Jordan

Joshua rose early in the morning, and he **3** and all the Israelites set out from Shittim and came to the Jordan, where they encamped before crossing the river. At the 2 end of three days the officers passed through the camp, and gave this order to the people: 3 'When you see the Ark of the Covenant of the LORD your God being carried forward by the levitical priests, then you too shall leave your positions and set out. Follow it, but do not go close to it; keep some distance 4 behind, about a thousand yards. This will show you the way you are to go, for you have not travelled this way before.' Joshua 5 then said to the people, 'Hallow yourselves, for tomorrow the LORD will do a great miracle among you.' To the priests he said, 6 'Lift up the Ark of the Covenant and pass in front of the people.' So they lifted up the Ark of the Covenant and went in front of the people. Then the LORD said to Joshua, 7 'Today I will begin to make you stand high in the eyes of all Israel, and they shall know that I will be with you as I was with Moses. Give orders to the priests who carry the Ark 8 of the Covenant, and tell them that when they come to the edge of the waters of the Jordan, they are to take their stand in the river.'

Then Joshua said to the Israelites, 'Come 9 here and listen to the words of the LORD your God. By this you shall know that the 10 living God is among you and that he will drive out before you the Canaanites, the

b Prob. rdg.; Heb. him.   *c Or* the Sea of Reeds.   *d* three days . . . found them: *or* three days while the pursuers scoured the land and searched all along the road, but did not find them.

Hittites, the Hivites, the Perizzites, the Girgashites, the Amorites, and the Jebusites:
11 the Ark of the Covenant of the LORD,*e* the
lord of all the earth, is to cross the Jordan
12 at your head. Choose twelve men from the
tribes of Israel, one man from each tribe.
13 When the priests carrying the Ark of the
LORD, the lord of all the earth, set foot in
the waters of the Jordan, then the waters of
the Jordan will be cut off; the water coming
down from upstream will stand piled up like
14 a bank.' So the people set out from their
tents to cross the Jordan, with the priests in
front of them carrying the Ark of the Cove-
15 nant. Now the Jordan is in full flood in all
its reaches throughout the time of harvest.
When the priests reached the Jordan and
dipped their feet in the water at the edge,
16 the water coming down from upstream was
brought to a standstill; it piled up like a bank
for a long way back, as far as Adam, a town
near Zarethan. The waters coming down to
the Sea of the Arabah, the Dead Sea, were
completely cut off, and the people crossed
17 over opposite Jericho. The priests carrying
the Ark of the Covenant of the LORD stood
firm on the dry bed in the middle of the
Jordan; and all Israel passed over on dry
ground until the whole nation had crossed
the river.

The twelve memorial stones

4 When the whole nation had finished crossing
2 the Jordan, the LORD said to Joshua, 'Take
twelve men from the people, one from each
3 tribe, and order them to lift up twelve stones
from this place, out of the middle of the
Jordan, where the feet of the priests stood
firm. They are to carry them across and set
them down in the camp where you spend the
4 night.' Joshua summoned the twelve men
whom he had chosen out of the Israelites,
5 one man from each tribe, and said to them,
'Cross over in front of the Ark of the LORD
your God as far as the middle of the Jordan,
and let each of you take a stone and hoist
it on his shoulder, one for each of the tribes
6 of Israel. These stones are to stand as a
memorial among you; and in days to come,
when your children ask you what these
7 stones mean, you shall tell them how the
waters of the Jordan were cut off before the
Ark of the Covenant of the LORD when it
crossed the Jordan. Thus these stones will
8 always be a reminder to the Israelites.' The
Israelites did as Joshua had commanded:
they lifted up twelve stones from the middle
of the Jordan, as the LORD had instructed
Joshua, one for each of the tribes of Israel,
carried them across to the camp and set
them down there.
9   Joshua set up twelve stones in the middle

of the Jordan at the place where the priests
stood who carried the Ark of the Covenant,
and there they are to this day. The priests
carrying the Ark remained standing in the
middle of the Jordan until every command
which the LORD had told Joshua to give to
the people was fulfilled, and the people had
made good speed across. When all the
people had finished crossing, then the Ark
of the LORD crossed, and the priests with it.*f*
At the head of the Israelites, there crossed
over the Reubenites, the Gadites, and the
half tribe of Manasseh, as a fighting force,
as Moses had told them to do; about forty
thousand strong, drafted for active service,
they crossed over to the lowlands of Jericho
in the presence of the LORD to do battle.
That day the LORD made Joshua stand
very high in the eyes of all Israel, and the
people revered him, as they had revered
Moses all his life.
The LORD said to Joshua, 'Command the
priests carrying the Ark of the Tokens to
come up from the Jordan.' So Joshua commanded the priests to come up from the
Jordan; and when the priests carrying the
Ark of the Covenant of the LORD came up
from the river-bed, they had no sooner set
foot on dry land than the waters of the
Jordan came back to their place and filled
up all its reaches as before. On the tenth
day of the first month the people came up
out of the Jordan and camped in Gilgal in
the district east of Jericho, and there Joshua
set up the twelve stones which they had
taken from the Jordan. He said to the
Israelites, 'In days to come, when your
descendants ask their fathers what these
stones mean, you shall explain that the
Jordan was dry when Israel crossed over,
and that the LORD your God dried up the
waters of the Jordan in front of you until
you had gone across, just as the LORD your
God did at the Red Sea when he dried it up
for us until we had crossed. Thus all people
on earth will know how strong is the hand
of the LORD; and thus they will stand in awe
of the LORD your God for ever.'

Israel at Gilgal

When all the Amorite kings to the west of
the Jordan and all the Canaanite kings by
the sea-coast heard that the LORD had dried
up the waters before the advance of the
Israelites until they had crossed, their courage melted away and there was no more
spirit left in them for fear of the Israelites.
At that time the LORD said to Joshua,
'Make knives of flint, seat yourself, and
make Israel a circumcised people again.'
Joshua thereupon made knives of flint
and circumcised the Israelites at Gibeath-

---

e of the LORD: *prob. rdg., cp. verse 17; Heb. om.*

f Prob. rdg.; Heb. adds before the people.

4 haaraloth.*g* This is why Joshua circumcised them: all the males who came out of Egypt, all the fighting men, had died in the wilder-
5 ness on the journey from Egypt. The people who came out of Egypt had all been circumcised, but not those who had been born in
6 the wilderness during the journey. For the Israelites travelled in the wilderness for forty years, until the whole nation, all the fighting men among them, had passed away, all who came out of Egypt and had disobeyed the voice of the LORD. The LORD swore that he would not allow any of these to see the land which he had sworn to their fathers to give us, a land flowing with milk
7 and honey. So it was their sons, whom he had raised up in their place, that Joshua circumcised; they were uncircumcised because they had not been circumcised on the
8 journey. When the circumcision of the whole nation was complete, they stayed where they
9 were in camp until they had recovered. The LORD then said to Joshua, 'Today I have rolled away from you the reproaches of the Egyptians.' Therefore the place is called Gilgal*h* to this very day.
10 The Israelites encamped in Gilgal, and at sunset on the fourteenth day of the month they kept the Passover in the lowlands of
11 Jericho. On the day after the Passover, they ate their unleavened cakes and parched grain, and that day it was the produce of
12 the country. It was from that day, when they first ate the produce of the country, that the manna ceased. The Israelites received no more manna; and that year they ate what had grown in the land of Canaan.

The captain of the LORD's army

13 When Joshua came near Jericho he looked up and saw a man standing in front of him with a drawn sword in his hand. Joshua went up to him and said, 'Are you for us or for our enemies?' And the man said to him, 14 'I am here as captain of the army of the LORD.' Joshua fell down before him, face to the ground, and said, 'What have you to say to your servant, my lord?' The captain 15 of the LORD's army said to him, 'Take off your sandals; the place where you are standing is holy'; and Joshua did so.

Destruction of Jericho

Jericho was bolted and barred against the 6 Israelites; no one went out, no one came in. The LORD said to Joshua, 'Look, I have 2 delivered Jericho and her king*i* into your hands. You shall march round the city with 3 all your fighting men, making the circuit of it once, for six days running. Seven priests 4 shall go in front of the Ark carrying seven trumpets made from rams' horns. On the seventh day you shall march round the city seven times and the priests shall blow their trumpets. At the blast of the rams' horns, 5 when you hear the trumpet sound, the whole army shall raise a great shout; and the wall of the city will collapse and the army shall advance, every man straight ahead.' So 6 Joshua son of Nun summoned the priests and gave them their orders: 'Take up the Ark of the Covenant; let seven priests with seven trumpets of ram's horn go in front of the Ark of the LORD.' Then he said to the 7 army, 'March on and make the circuit of the city, and let the men drafted from the two and a half tribes go in front of the Ark of the LORD.' When Joshua had spoken to 8 the army, the seven priests carrying the seven trumpets of ram's horn before the LORD passed on and blew the trumpets, with the Ark of the Covenant of the LORD following

g That is the Hill of Foreskins.   *h That is* Rolling Stones.   *i Prob. rdg.; Heb. adds* the fighting men.

9 them. The drafted men marched in front of the priests who blew the trumpets, and the rearguard followed the Ark, the trum-
10 pets sounding as they marched. But Joshua ordered the army not to shout, or to raise their voices or utter a word, till the day came when he would tell them to shout;
11 then they were to give a loud shout. Thus he caused the Ark of the LORD to go round the city, making the circuit of it once, and then they went back to the camp and spent
12 the night there. Joshua rose early in the morning and the priests took up the Ark
13 of the LORD. The seven priests carrying the seven trumpets of ram's horn went marching in front of the Ark of the LORD, blowing

prostitute's house and bring out her and all who belonged to her, as they had sworn to do. So the young men went and brought 23 out Rahab, her father and mother, her brothers and all who belonged to her. They brought out the whole family and left them outside the Israelite camp. They then set 24 fire to the city and everything in it, except that they deposited the silver and gold and the vessels of copper and iron in the treasury of the LORD's house. Thus Joshua spared 25 the lives of Rahab the prostitute, her household and all who belonged to her, because she had hidden the men whom Joshua had sent to Jericho as spies; she and her family settled permanently among the Israelites.

the trumpets as they went, with the drafted men in front of them and the rearguard following the Ark of the LORD, the trumpets
14 sounding as they marched. They marched round the city once on the second day and returned to the camp; this they did for six
15 days. But on the seventh day they rose at dawn and marched seven times round the city in the same way; that was the only day on which they marched round seven times.
16 The seventh time the priests blew the trumpets and Joshua said to the army, 'Shout!
17 The LORD has given you the city. The city shall be under solemn ban: everything in it belongs to the LORD. No one is to be spared except the prostitute Rahab and everyone who is with her in the house, because she
18 hid the men whom we sent. And you must beware of coveting anything that is forbidden under the ban; you must take none of it for yourselves; this would put the Israelite camp itself under the ban and bring
19 trouble on it. All the silver and gold, all the vessels of copper and iron, shall be holy; they belong to the LORD and they must go
20 into the LORD's treasury.' So they blew the trumpets, and when the army heard the trumpet sound, they raised a great shout, and down fell the walls. The army advanced on the city, every man straight ahead, and
21 took it. Under the ban they destroyed everything in the city; they put everyone to the sword, men and women, young and old, and also cattle, sheep, and asses.
22 But the two men who had been sent out as spies were told by Joshua to go into the

It was then that Joshua laid this curse on 26 Jericho:

May the LORD's curse light on the man who comes forward
    to rebuild this city of Jericho:
the laying of its foundations shall cost him his eldest son,
the setting up of its gates shall cost him his youngest.

Thus the LORD was with Joshua, and his 27 fame spread throughout the country.

Achan's sin

But the Israelites defied the ban: Achan son 7 of Carmi, son of Zabdi, son of Zerah, of the tribe of Judah, took some of the forbidden things, and the LORD was angry with the Israelites.

Joshua sent men from Jericho with orders 2 to go up to Ai, near Beth-aven, east of Bethel, and see how the land lay; so the men went up and explored Ai. They returned to 3 Joshua and reported that there was no need for the whole army to move: 'Let some two

or three thousand men go forward to attack Ai. Do not make the whole army toil up 4 there; the population is small.' And so about three thousand men went up, but they 5 turned tail before the men of Ai, who killed some thirty-six of them; they chased them all the way from the gate to the Quarries*j* and killed them on the pass. At this the courage of the people melted and flowed 6 away like water. Joshua and the elders of Israel rent their clothes and flung themselves face downwards to the ground; they lay before the Ark of the LORD till evening and 7 threw dust on their heads. Joshua said, 'Alas, O Lord GOD, why didst thou bring this people across the Jordan only to hand us over to the Amorites to be destroyed? If only we had been content to settle on the 8 other side of the Jordan! I beseech thee, O Lord; what can I say, now that Israel has 9 been routed by the enemy? When the Canaanites and all the natives of the country hear of this, they will come swarming around us and wipe us off the face of the earth. What wilt thou do then for the honour of thy great name?'

10 The LORD said to Joshua, 'Stand up; why 11 lie prostrate on your face? Israel has sinned: they have broken the covenant which I laid upon them, by taking forbidden things for themselves. They have stolen them, and concealed it by mingling them with their 12 own possessions. That is why the Israelites cannot stand against their enemies: they are put to flight because they have brought themselves under the ban. Unless they destroy every single thing among them that is forbidden under the ban, I will be with them 13 no longer. Stand up; you must hallow the people; tell them they must hallow themselves for tomorrow. Tell them, These are the words of the LORD the God of Israel: You have forbidden things among you, Israel; you cannot stand against your enemies until 14 you have rid yourselves of them. In the morning come forward tribe by tribe, and the tribe which the LORD chooses shall come forward clan by clan; the clan which the LORD chooses shall come forward family by family; and the family which the LORD chooses shall come forward man by man. 15 The man who is chosen as the harbourer of forbidden things shall be burnt, he and all that is his, because he has broken the covenant of the LORD and committed outrage 16 in Israel.' Early in the morning Joshua rose and brought Israel forward tribe by tribe, 17 and the tribe of Judah was chosen. He brought forward the clans of Judah, and the clan of Zerah was chosen; then the clan of Zerah family by family, and the family of 18 Zabdi was chosen. He brought that family

forward man by man, and Achan son of Carmi, son of Zabdi, son of Zerah, of the tribe of Judah, was chosen. Then Joshua 19 said to Achan, 'My son, give honour to the LORD the God of Israel and make your confession to him: tell me what you have done, hide nothing from me.' Achan answered 20 Joshua, 'I confess, I have sinned against the LORD the God of Israel. This is what I did: among the booty I caught sight of a fine 21 mantle from Shinar, two hundred shekels of silver, and a bar of gold weighing fifty shekels. I coveted them and I took them. You will find them hidden in the ground inside my tent, with the silver underneath.' So Joshua 22 sent messengers, who ran to the tent, and there was the stuff*k* hidden in the tent with the silver underneath. They took the things 23 from the tent, brought them to Joshua and all the Israelites, and spread them out before the LORD. Then Joshua took Achan son 24 of Zerah, with the silver, the mantle, and the bar of gold, together with his sons and daughters, his oxen, his asses, and his sheep, his tent, and everything he had, and he and all Israel brought them up to the Vale of Achor.*l* Joshua said, 'What trouble you have 25 brought on us! Now the LORD will bring trouble on you.' Then all the Israelites stoned him to death; and they raised a great pile 26 of stones over him, which remains to this day. So the LORD's anger was abated. That is why to this day that place is called the Vale of Achor.

Destruction of Ai

The LORD said to Joshua, 'Do not be fearful **8** or dismayed; take the whole army and attack Ai. I deliver the king of Ai into your hands, him and his people, his city and his country. Deal with Ai and her king as you dealt with 2 Jericho and her king; but you may keep for yourselves the cattle and any other spoil that you may take. Set an ambush for the city to the west of it.' So Joshua and all the army 3 prepared for the assault on Ai. He chose thirty thousand fighting men and dispatched them by night, with these orders: 'Lie in 4 ambush to the west of the city, not far from it, and all of you hold yourselves in readiness. I myself will approach the city with 5 the rest of the army, and when the enemy come out to meet us as they did last time, we shall take to flight before them. Then 6 they will come out and pursue us until we have drawn them away from the city, thinking that we have taken to flight as we did last time. While we are in flight, come 7 out from your ambush and occupy the city; the LORD your God will deliver it into your hands. When you have taken it, set 8 it on fire. Thus you will do what the LORD

j Or to Shebarim.   k Or the mantle.   l That is Trouble.

9 commands. These are your orders.' So Joshua sent them off, and they went to the place of ambush and waited between Bethel and Ai to the west of Ai, while Joshua spent the night with the army.

10 Early in the morning Joshua rose, mustered the army and marched against Ai, he himself and the elders of Israel at its head.

11 All the armed forces with him marched on until they came within sight of the city. They encamped north of Ai, with the valley be-

12 tween them and the city; but Joshua took some five thousand men and set them in ambush between Bethel and Ai to the west

14 of the city.[m] When the king of Ai saw them, he and the citizens rose with all speed that morning and marched out to do battle against Israel; he did not know that there was an ambush set for him to the west of the

15 city. Joshua and all the Israelites made as if they were routed by them and fled to-

16 wards the wilderness, and all the people in the city were called out in pursuit. So they pursued Joshua and were drawn away from

17 the city. Not a man was left in Ai; they had all gone out in pursuit of the Israelites and during the pursuit had left the city undefended.

18 Then the LORD said to Joshua, 'Point towards Ai with the dagger you are holding, for I will deliver the city into your hands.' So Joshua pointed with his dagger towards

19 Ai. At his signal, the men in ambush rose quickly from their places and, entering the city at a run, took it and promptly set fire to

20 it. The men of Ai looked back and saw the smoke from the city already going up to the sky; they were powerless to make their escape in any direction, and the Israelites who had feigned flight towards the wilder-

21 ness turned on their pursuers. For when Joshua and all the Israelites saw that the ambush had seized the city and that smoke was already going up from it, they turned

22 and fell upon the men of Ai. Those who had come out to meet the Israelites were now hemmed in with Israelites on both sides of them, and the Israelites cut them down until there was not a single survivor, nor had any

23 escaped. The king of Ai was taken alive and

24 brought to Joshua. When the Israelites had

cut down to the last man all the citizens of Ai who were in the open country or in the wilderness to which they had pursued them, and the massacre was complete, they all turned back to Ai and put it to the sword.

25 The number who were killed that day, men and women, was twelve thousand, the whole

26 population of Ai. Joshua held out his dagger and did not draw back his hand until he

27 had put to death all who lived in Ai; but the Israelites kept for themselves the cattle and any other spoil that they took, following the word of the LORD spoken to Joshua. So

28 Joshua burnt Ai to the ground, and left it the desolate ruined mound it remains to this day. He hanged the king of Ai on a tree and

29 left him there till sunset; and when the sun had set, he gave the order and they cut him down and flung down his body at the entrance of the city gate. Over the body they raised a great pile of stones, which is there to this day.

Joshua records the law at Mount Ebal

30 At that time Joshua built an altar to the LORD the God of Israel on Mount Ebal.

31 The altar was of blocks of undressed stone on which no tool of iron had been used, following the commands given to the Israelites by Moses the servant of the LORD, as is described in the book of the law of Moses. At the altar they offered whole-offerings to the LORD, and slaughtered shared-offerings.

32 There in the presence of the Israelites he engraved on blocks[n] of stone a copy of the

33 law of Moses. And all Israel, elders, officers, and judges, took their stand on either side of the Ark, facing the levitical priests who carried the Ark of the Covenant of the LORD —all Israel, native and alien alike. Half of them stood facing Mount Gerizim and half facing Mount Ebal, to fulfil the command of Moses the servant of the LORD that the blessing should be pronounced first. Then

34 Joshua recited the whole of the blessing and the cursing word by word, as they are written in the book of the law. There was not a

35 single word of all that Moses had commanded which he did not read aloud before the whole congregation of Israel, including the women and dependants and the aliens resident in their company.

The Gibeonites' ruse

9 When the news of these happenings reached all the kings west of the Jordan, in the hill-country, the Shephelah, and all the coast of the Great Sea running up to the Lebanon, the kings of the Hittites, Amorites, Canaan-

2 ites, Perizzites, Hivites, and Jebusites agreed

m So Sept.; Heb. adds (13) So the army pitched camp to the north of the city, and the rearguard to the west, while Joshua went that night into the valley.   n Or on the blocks.

to join forces and fight against Joshua and Israel.

3 When the inhabitants of Gibeon heard how Joshua had dealt with Jericho and Ai,
4 they adopted a ruse of their own. They went and disguised themselves, with old sacking for their asses, old wine-skins split and
5 mended, old and patched sandals for their feet, old clothing to wear, and by way of provisions nothing but dry and mouldy
6 bread. They came to Joshua in the camp at Gilgal and said to him and the Israelites, 'We have come from a distant country to
7 ask you now to grant us a treaty.' The Israelites said to the Hivites, 'But maybe you live in our neighbourhood: if so, how
8 can we grant you a treaty?' They said to Joshua, 'We are your slaves.' Joshua asked them who they were and where they came
9 from. 'Sir,' they replied, 'our country is very far away, and we have come because of the renown of the LORD your God. We have heard of his fame, of all that he did to Egypt,
10 and to the two Amorite kings east of the Jordan, Sihon king of Heshbon and Og
11 king of Bashan who lived at Ashtaroth. Our elders and all the people of our country told us to take provisions for the journey and come to meet you, and say, "We are your
12 slaves; please grant us a treaty." Look at our bread; it was hot from the oven when we packed it at home on the day we came
13 away. Now it is dry and mouldy. Look at the wine-skins; they were new when we filled them, and now they are all split; look at our clothes and our sandals, worn out by the
14 long journey.' The chief men of the com-munity accepted some of their provisions, and did not at first seek guidance from the LORD. So Joshua received them peaceably 15 and granted them a treaty, promising to spare their lives, and the chiefs pledged their faith to them on oath.

Within three days of granting them the 16 treaty, the Israelites learnt that they were in fact neighbours and lived near by. So the 17 Israelites set out and on the third day they reached their cities; these were Gibeon, Kephirah, Beeroth, and Kiriath-jearim. The 18 Israelites did not slaughter them, because of the oath which the chief men of the com-munity had sworn to them by the LORD the God of Israel, but the people were all in-dignant with their chiefs. The chiefs all 19 replied to the assembled people, 'But we swore an oath to them by the LORD the God of Israel; we cannot touch them now. What 20 we will do is this: we will spare their lives so that the oath which we swore to them may bring no harm upon us. But though their 21 lives must be spared, they shall be set to chop wood and draw water for the com-munity.' The people agreed to do as their chiefs had said. Joshua summoned the 22 Gibeonites and said, 'Why did you play this trick on us? You told us that you live a long way off, when you are near neighbours. There 23 is a curse upon you for this: for all time you shall provide us with slaves, to chop wood and draw water for the house of my God.' They answered Joshua, 'We were 24 told, sir, that the LORD your God had com-manded Moses his servant to give you the whole country and to exterminate all

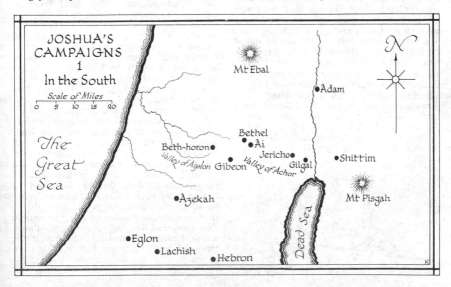

JOSHUA'S
CAMPAIGNS
1
In the South

Scale of Miles
0   5   10   15   20

The
Great
Sea

Mt Ebal

Adam

Bethel
Beth-horon●   ●Ai
Valley of Ajalon   Jericho●   ●Shittim
Gibeon Valley of Achor Gilgal
●Azekah   Mt Pisgah

Dead Sea

●Eglon
●Lachish   ●Hebron

its inhabitants; so because of you we were in terror of our lives, and that is why we
25 did this. We are in your power: do with us
26 whatever you think right and proper.' What he did was this: he saved them from death at the hands of the Israelites, and they did
27 not kill them; but thenceforward he set them to chop wood and draw water for the community and for the altar of the LORD. And to this day they do it at the place which the LORD chose.

Joshua defeats the Amorites in Gibeon

10 When Adoni-zedek king of Jerusalem heard that Joshua had captured Ai and destroyed it (for Joshua had dealt with Ai and her king as he had dealt with Jericho and her king), and that the inhabitants of Gibeon had made their peace with Israel and were living
2 among them, he was greatly alarmed; for Gibeon was a large place, like a royal city: it was larger than Ai, and its men were all
3 good fighters. So Adoni-zedek king of Jerusalem sent to Hoham king of Hebron, Piram king of Jarmuth, Japhia king of Lachish,
4 and Debir king of Eglon, and said, 'Come up and help me, and we will attack the Gibeonites, because they have made their
5 peace with Joshua and the Israelites.' So the five Amorite kings, the kings of Jerusalem, Hebron, Jarmuth, Lachish, and Eglon, joined forces and advanced to take up their
6 positions for the attack on Gibeon. But the men of Gibeon sent this message to Joshua in the camp at Gilgal: 'We are your slaves, do not abandon us, come quickly to our relief. All the Amorite kings in the hill-country have joined forces against us; come
7 and help us.' So Joshua went up from Gilgal with all his forces and all his fighting men.
8 The LORD said to Joshua, 'Do not be afraid of them; I have delivered them into your hands, and not a man will be able to stand
9 against you.' Joshua came upon them suddenly, after marching all night from Gilgal.
10 The LORD threw them into confusion before the Israelites, and Joshua defeated them utterly in Gibeon; he pursued them down the pass of Beth-horon and kept up the slaughter as far as Azekah and Makkedah.
11 As they were fleeing from Israel down the

pass, the LORD hurled great hailstones at them out of the sky all the way to Azekah: more died from the hailstones than the Israelites slew by the sword.

The sun stands still

On that day when the LORD delivered the 12 Amorites into the hands of Israel, Joshua spoke with the LORD, and he said in the presence of Israel:

Stand still, O Sun, in Gibeon;
stand, Moon, in the Vale of Aijalon.

So the sun stood still and the moon halted 13 until a nation had taken vengeance on its enemies, as indeed is written in the Book of Jashar.[o] The sun stayed in mid heaven and made no haste to set for almost a whole day. Never before or since has there been such a 14 day as this day on which the LORD listened to the voice of a man; for the LORD fought for Israel. So Joshua and all the Israelites 15 returned to the camp at Gilgal.

Joshua advances into Canaan

The five kings fled and hid themselves in a 16 cave at Makkedah, and Joshua was told 17 that they had been found hidden in this cave. Joshua replied, 'Roll some great stones to 18 the mouth of the cave and post men there to keep watch over the kings. But you must 19 not stay; keep up the pursuit, attack your enemies from the rear and do not let them reach their cities; the LORD your God has delivered them into your hands.' When 20 Joshua and the Israelites had finished the work of slaughter and all had been put to the sword—except a few survivors who escaped and entered the fortified cities—the 21 whole army rejoined Joshua at Makkedah in peace; not a man of the Israelites suffered so much as a scratch on his tongue. Then 22 Joshua said, 'Open the mouth of the cave, and bring me out those five kings.' They did 23 so; they brought the five kings out of the cave, the kings of Jerusalem, Hebron, Jarmuth, Lachish, and Eglon. When they had 24 brought them to Joshua, he summoned all the Israelites and said to the commanders of the troops who had served with him, 'Come forward and put your feet on the necks of these kings.' So they came forward and put their feet on their necks. Joshua said 25 to them, 'Do not be fearful or dismayed; be strong and resolute; for the LORD will do this to every enemy you fight against.' And 26 he struck down the kings and slew them; then he hung their bodies on five trees, where they remained hanging till evening. At sun- 27 set, on Joshua's orders they took them down from the trees and threw them into the cave in which they had hidden; they piled great

stones against its mouth, and there the stones are to this day.*p*

28 On that same day, Joshua captured Makkedah and put both king and people to the sword, destroying both them and every living thing in the city. He left no survivor, and he dealt with the king of Makkedah as 29 he had dealt with the king of Jericho. Then Joshua and all the Israelites marched on from Makkedah to Libnah and attacked it. 30 The LORD delivered the city and its king to the Israelites, and they put its people and every living thing in it to the sword; they left no survivor there, and dealt with its king as they had dealt with the king of Jericho. 31 From Libnah Joshua and all the Israelites marched on to Lachish, took up their posi- 32 tions and attacked it. The LORD delivered Lachish into their hands; they took it on the second day and put every living thing in it to the sword, as they had done at Libnah. 33 Meanwhile Horam king of Gezer had advanced to the relief of Lachish; but Joshua struck them down, both king and people, and not a man of them survived. 34 Then Joshua and all the Israelites marched on from Lachish to Eglon, took up their 35 positions and attacked it; that same day they captured it and put its inhabitants to the sword, destroying every living thing in 36 it as they had done at Lachish. From Eglon Joshua and all the Israelites advanced to 37 Hebron and attacked it. They captured it and put its king to the sword together with every living thing in it and in all its villages; as at Eglon, he left no survivor, destroying 38 it and every living thing in it. Then Joshua and all the Israelites wheeled round towards 39 Debir and attacked it. They captured the city with its king, and all its villages, put them to the sword and destroyed every living thing; they left no survivor. They dealt with Debir and its king as they had dealt with Hebron and with Libnah and its king. 40 So Joshua massacred the population of the whole region—the hill-country, the Negeb, the Shephelah, the watersheds— and all their kings. He left no survivor, destroying everything that drew breath, as the LORD the God of Israel had commanded. 41 Joshua carried the slaughter from Kadesh-barnea to Gaza, over the whole land of 42 Goshen and as far as Gibeon. All these kings he captured at the same time, and their country with them, for the LORD the 43 God of Israel fought for Israel. And Joshua returned with all the Israelites to the camp at Gilgal.

Joshua defeats Jabin and his allies

11 When Jabin king of Hazor heard of all this, he sent to Jobab king of Madon, to the kings of Shimron and Akshaph, to the northern 2 kings in the hill-country, in the Arabah opposite Kinnereth, in the Shephelah, and in the district of Dor on the west, the Canaan- 3 ites to the east and the west, the Amorites, Hittites, Perizzites, and Jebusites in the hill-country, and the Hivites below Hermon in the land of Mizpah. They took the field with 4 all their forces, a great horde countless as the grains of sand on the sea-shore, among them a great number of horses and chariots. All these kings made common cause, and 5 came and encamped at the waters of Merom to fight against Israel. The LORD said to 6 Joshua, 'Do not be afraid of them, for at this time tomorrow I shall deliver them to Israel all dead men; you shall hamstring their horses and burn their chariots.' So 7 Joshua and his army surprised them by the waters of Merom and fell upon them. The 8 LORD delivered them into the hands of Israel; they struck them down and pursued them as far as Greater Sidon, Misrephoth on the west, and the Vale of Mizpah on the east. They struck them down until not a man was left alive. Joshua dealt with them 9 as the LORD had commanded: he hamstrung their horses and burnt their chariots.

At this point Joshua turned his forces 10 against Hazor, formerly the head of all these kingdoms. He captured the city and put its king to death with the sword. They 11 killed every living thing in it and wiped them all out; they spared nothing that drew breath, and Hazor itself they destroyed by fire. So Joshua captured these kings and 12 their cities and put them to the sword, destroying them all, as Moses the servant of the LORD had commanded. The cities whose 13 ruined mounds are still standing were not burnt by the Israelites; it was Hazor alone that Joshua burnt. The Israelites plundered 14 all these cities and kept for themselves the cattle and any other spoil they took; but they put every living soul to the sword until they had destroyed every one; they did not leave alive any one that drew breath. The 15 LORD laid his commands on his servant Moses, and Moses laid these same commands on Joshua, and Joshua carried them out. Not one of the commands laid on Moses by the LORD did he leave unfulfilled.

Joshua conquers the whole country

And so Joshua took the whole country, the 16 hill-country, all the Negeb, all the land of Goshen, the Shephelah, the Arabah, and the Israelite hill-country with the adjoining lowlands. His conquests extended from the 17 bare mountain which leads up to Seir as far as Baal-gad in the Vale of Lebanon under Mount Hermon. He took prisoner all their

---

p and there . . . day: or on this very day.

kings, struck them down and put them to
18 death. It was a long war that he fought
19 against all these kingdoms. Except for the
Hivites who lived in Gibeon, not one of their
cities came to terms with the Israelites; all
20 were taken by storm. It was the LORD's purpose that they should offer an obstinate
resistance to the Israelites in battle, and that
thus they should be annihilated without
mercy and utterly destroyed,*q* as the LORD
had commanded Moses.
21   It was then that Joshua proceeded to wipe
out the Anakim from the hill-country, from
Hebron, Debir, Anab, all the hill-country
of Judah and all the hill-country of Israel,
destroying both them and their cities. No 22
Anakim were left in the land taken by the
Israelites; they survived only in Gaza, Gath,
and Ashdod.

Thus Joshua took the whole country, 23
fulfilling all the commands that the LORD
had laid on Moses; he assigned it as Israel's
patrimony, allotting to each tribe its share;
and the land was at peace.

Kings defeated by Moses

12 These are the names of the kings
of the land whom the Israelites
slew, and whose territory they
occupied beyond the Jordan towards the sunrise from the gorge
of the Arnon as far as Mount
Hermon and all the Arabah on the
2 east. Sihon the Amorite king who
lived in Heshbon: his rule extended
from Aroer, which is on the edge
of the gorge of the Arnon, along
the middle of the gorge and over
half Gilead as far as the gorge of
the Jabbok, the Ammonite frontier; along the Arabah as far as 3
the eastern side of the Sea of Kinnereth and as far as the eastern
side of the Sea of the Arabah, the
Dead Sea, by the road to Beth-
jeshimoth and from Teman under
the watershed of Pisgah. Og king 4
of Bashan, one of the survivors of
the Rephaim, who lived in Ashtaroth and Edrei: he ruled over 5
Mount Hermon, Salcah, all Bashan
as far as the Geshurite and Maacathite borders, and half Gilead as
far as the boundary of Sihon king
of Heshbon. Moses the servant of 6
the LORD put them to death, he
and the Israelites, and he gave their
land to the Reubenites, the Gadites,
and half the tribe of Manasseh, as
their possession.

Kings defeated by Joshua

These are the names of the kings 7
whom Joshua and the Israelites
put to death beyond the Jordan to
the west, from Baal-gad in the Vale
of Lebanon as far as the bare
mountain that leads up to Seir.
Joshua gave their land to the
Israelite tribes to be their possession according to their allotted
shares, in the hill-country, the 8
Shephelah, the Arabah, the watersheds, the wilderness, and the
Negeb; lands of the Hittites, Amorites, Canaanites, Perizzites, Hivites, and Jebusites. The king of 9
Jericho; the king of Ai which is
beside Bethel; the king of Jeru- 10
salem; the king of Hebron; the 11
king of Jarmuth; the king of Lachish; the king of Eglon; the king 12
of Gezer; the king of Debir; the 13
king of Geder; the king of Hormah; 14
the king of Arad; the king of Lib- 15
nah; the king of Adullam; the 16
king of Makkedah; the king of
Bethel; the king of Tappuah; the 17
king of Hepher; the king of Aphek; 18
the king of Aphek*r*-in-Sharon; the 19
king of Madon; the king of Hazor;
the king of Shimron-meron; the 20
king of Akshaph; the king of 21
Taanach; the king of Megiddo;
the king of Kedesh; the king of 22
Jokneam-in-Carmel; the king of 23
Dor in the district of Dor; the king
of Gaiam-in-Galilee; the king of 24

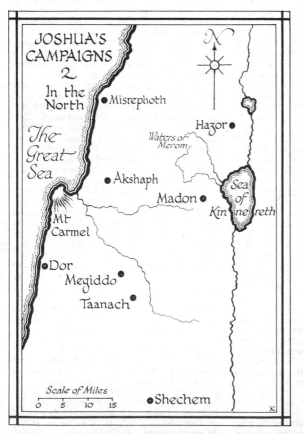

JOSHUA'S CAMPAIGNS 2
In the North

The Great Sea

Misrephoth
Waters of Merom
Hazor
Akshaph
Madon
Sea of Kinnereth
Mt Carmel
Dor
Megiddo
Taanach
Shechem

Scale of Miles
0 5 10 15

---

q offer . . . destroyed: or obstinately engage the Israelites in battle so that they should annihilate them without
mercy, only that he might destroy them . . .   *r of Aphek: prob. rdg.; Heb. om.*

Tirzah: thirty-one kings in all, one of each town.

Districts still to be occupied

13 By this time Joshua had become very old, and the LORD said to him, 'You are now a very old man, and much of the country remains to be 2 occupied. The country which remains is this: all the districts of the Philistines and all the Geshurite 3 country (this is reckoned as Canaanite territory from Shihor to the east of Egypt as far north as Ekron; and it belongs to the five lords of the Philistines, those of Gaza, Ashdod, Ashkelon, Gath, and Ekron); all the districts of the Avvim 4 on the south; all the Canaanite country from the low-lying land which belongs to the Sidonians as far as Aphek, the Amorite frontier; 5 the land of the Gebalites and all the Lebanon to the east from Baal-gad under Mount Hermon as far as 6 Lebo-hamath. I will drive out in favour of the Israelites all the inhabitants of the hill-country from the Lebanon as far as Misrephoth on the west, and all the Sidonians. In the mean time you are to allot all this to the Israelites for their patrimony, as I have commanded 7 you. Distribute this land now to the nine tribes and half the tribe of Manasseh for their patrimony.' 8 For half the tribe of Manasseh and[s] with them the Reubenites and the Gadites had each taken their patrimony which Moses gave them east of the Jordan, as Moses the servant 9 of the LORD had ordained. It started from Aroer which is by the edge of the gorge of the Arnon, and the level land half-way along the gorge, and included all the tableland from 10 Medeba as far as Dibon; all the cities of Sihon, the Amorite king who ruled in Heshbon, as far as 11 the Ammonite frontier; and it also included Gilead and the Geshurite and Maacathite territory, and all Mount Hermon and the whole of 12 Bashan as far as Salcah, all the kingdom of Og which he ruled from both Ashtaroth and Edrei in Bashan. He was a survivor of the remnant of the Rephaim, but Moses put them both to death and occupied 13 their lands. But the Israelites did not drive out the Geshurites and the Maacathites; the Geshurites and the Maacathites live among 14 the Israelites to this day. The tribe of Levi, however, received no patrimony; the LORD the God of Israel is their patrimony, as he promised them.

Territory allotted to the tribes east of Jordan

15 So Moses allotted territory to the tribe of the Reubenites family by 16 family. Their territory started from Aroer which is by the edge of the

gorge of the Arnon, and the level land half-way along the gorge, and included all the tableland as far as 17 Medeba; Heshbon and all its cities on the tableland, Dibon, Bamoth-18 baal, Beth-baal-meon, Jahaz, Kede-19 moth, Mephaath, Kiriathaim, Sibmah, Zereth-shahar on the hill in 20 the Vale, Beth-peor, the watershed 21 of Pisgah, and Beth-jeshimoth, all the cities of the tableland, all the kingdom of Sihon the Amorite king who ruled in Heshbon, whom Moses put to death together with the princes of Midian, Evi, Rekem, Zur, Hur, and Reba, the vassals of Sihon who dwelt in the country. 22 Balaam son of Beor, who practised augury, was among those whom 23 the Israelites put to the sword. The boundary of the Reubenites was the Jordan and the adjacent land: this is the patrimony of the Reuben-

ites family by family, both the cities and their hamlets.

Moses allotted territory to the 24 Gadites family by family. Their 25 territory was Jazer, all the cities of Gilead and half the Ammonite country as far as Aroer which is east of Rabbah. It reached from 26 Heshbon as far as Ramoth-mizpeh and Betonim, and from Mahanaim as far as the boundary of Lo-debar; it included in the valley Beth-27 haram, Beth-nimrah, Succoth, and Zaphon, the rest of the kingdom of Sihon king of Heshbon. The boundary was the Jordan and the adjacent land as far as the end of the Sea of Kinnereth east of the Jordan. This is the patrimony of 28 the Gadites family by family, both the cities and their hamlets.

Moses allotted territory to the 29 half tribe of Manasseh: it was for

s For half . . . Manasseh and: *prob. rdg.*; *Heb. om.*

30 half the tribe of the Manassites family by family. Their territory ran from Mahanaim and included all Bashan, all the kingdom of Og king of Bashan and all Havvoth-
31 jair in Bashan—sixty cities. Half Gilead, and Ashtaroth and Edrei the royal cities of Og in Bashan, belong to the sons of Machir son of Manasseh on behalf of half the Machirites family by family.
32 These are the territories which Moses allotted to the tribes as their patrimonies in the lowlands
33 of Moab east of the Jordan. But to the tribe of Levi he gave no patrimony: the LORD the God of Israel is their patrimony, as he promised them.

Canaan divided by lot

14 Now follow the possessions which the Israelites acquired in the land of Canaan, as Eleazar the priest, Joshua son of Nun, and the heads of the families of the Israelite
2 tribes allotted them. They were assigned by lot, following the LORD's command given through Moses, to the nine and a half
3 tribes. To two and a half tribes Moses had given patrimonies beyond the Jordan; but he gave none to the Levites as he did to the others.
4 The tribe of Joseph formed the two tribes of Manasseh and Ephraim. The Levites were given no share in the land, only cities to dwell in, with their common land
5 for flocks and herds. So the Israelites, following the LORD's command given to Moses, assigned the land.

Joshua gives Hebron to Caleb

6 Now the tribe of Judah had come to Joshua in Gilgal, and Caleb son of Jephunneh the Kenizzite said to him, 'You remember what the LORD said to Moses the man of God concerning you and me at
7 Kadesh-barnea. I was forty years old when Moses the servant of the LORD sent me from there to explore the land, and I brought back an
8 honest report. The others who went with me discouraged the people, but I loyally carried out the purpose of the LORD my God.
9 Moses swore an oath that day and said, "The land on which you have set foot shall be your patrimony and your sons' after you as a possession for ever; for you have loyally carried out the purpose of
10 the LORD my God." Well, the LORD has spared my life as he promised; it is now forty-five years since he made this promise to Moses, at the time when Israel was journeying in the wilderness. Today I am eighty-
11 five years old. I am still as strong as I was on the day when Moses sent me out; I am as fit now for war

as I was then and am ready to take
12 the field again. Give me today this hill-country which the LORD then promised me. You heard on that day that the Anakim were there and their cities were large and well fortified. Perhaps the LORD will be with me and I shall dispossess them
13 as he promised.' Joshua blessed Caleb and gave him Hebron for
14 his patrimony, and that is why Hebron remains to this day in the patrimony of Caleb son of Jephunneh the Kenizzite. It is because he loyally carried out the purpose of
15 the LORD the God of Israel. Formerly the name of Hebron was Kiriath-arba. This Arba was the chief man of the Anakim. And the land was at peace.

Territory allotted to Judah

15 This is the territory allotted to the tribe of the sons of Judah family by family. It started from the Edomite frontier at the wilderness of Zin and ran as far as the Negeb
2 at its southern end, and it had a common border with the Negeb at the end of the Dead Sea, where an inlet of water bends towards the
3 Negeb. It continued from the south by the ascent of Akrabbim, passed by Zin, went up from the south of Kadesh-barnea, passed by Hezron, went on to Addar and turned
4 round to Karka. It then passed along to Azmon, reached the Torrent of Egypt, and its limit was the sea. This was their southern boundary.
5 The eastern boundary is the Dead Sea as far as the mouth of the Jordan and the adjacent land northwards from the inlet of the sea, at the mouth of the Jordan.
6 The boundary goes up to Beth-hoglah; it passes north of Beth-arabah and thence to the stone of
7 Bohan son of Reuben, thence to Debir from the Vale of Achor, and then turns north to the districts[t] in front of the ascent of Adummim south of the gorge. The boundary then passes the waters of En-shemesh and the limit there is
8 En-rogel. It then goes up by the Valley of Ben-hinnom to the southern slope of the Jebusites (that is Jerusalem). Thence it goes up to the top of the hill which faces the Valley of Hinnom on the west; this is at the northern end of the
9 Vale of Rephaim. The boundary then bends round from the top of the hill to the spring of the waters of Nephtoah, runs round to the cities of Mount Ephron and round to Baalah, that is Kiriath-jearim.
10 It then continues westwards from Baalah to Mount Seir, passes on to the north side of the slope of Mount Jearim, that is Kesalon, down to Beth-shemesh and on to
11 Timnah. The boundary then goes

north to the slope of Ekron, bends round to Shikkeron, crosses to Mount Baalah and reaches Jab-
12 neel; its limit is the sea. The western boundary is the Great Sea and the land adjacent. This is the whole circuit of the boundary of the tribe of Judah family by family.

Caleb receives Hebron

13 Caleb son of Jephunneh received his share of the land within the tribe of Judah as the LORD had said to Joshua. It was Kiriath-arba, that is Hebron. This Arba was the
14 ancestor of the Anakim. Caleb drove out the three Anakim: these were Sheshai, Ahiman and Talmai,
15 descendants of Anak. From there he attacked the inhabitants of Debir; the name of Debir was
16 formerly Kiriath-sepher. Caleb announced that whoever should attack Kiriath-sepher and capture it would receive his daughter Ach-
17 sah in marriage. Othniel, son of Caleb's brother Kenaz, captured
18 it, and Caleb gave him his daughter Achsah. When she came to him, he incited her to ask her father for a piece of land. As she sat on the
19 ass, she broke wind, and Caleb asked her, 'What did you mean by that?' She replied, 'I want a favour from you. You have put me in this dry Negeb; you must give me pools of water as well.' So Caleb gave her the upper pool and the lower pool.

The cities of Judah

20 This is the patrimony of the tribe of the sons of Judah family by family. These are the cities belong-
21 ing to the tribe of Judah, the full count. By the Edomite frontier in the Negeb: Kabzeel, Eder, Jagur,
22 Kinah, Dimonah, Ararah,[u] Ke-
24 desh, Hazor, Ithnan, Ziph, Telem,
25 Bealoth, Hazor-hadattah, Kerioth-
26 hezron, Amam, Shema, Moladah,
27 Hazar-gaddah, Heshmon, Beth-
28 pelet, Hazar-shual, Beersheba and
29 its villages, Baalah, Iyim, Ezem,
30 Eltolad, Kesil, Hormah, Ziklag,
32 Madmannah, Sansannah, Lebaoth, Shilhim, Ain, and Rimmon: in all, twenty-nine cities with their hamlets.
33 In the Shephelah: Eshtaol,
34 Zorah, Ashnah, Zanoah, En-
35 gannim, Tappuah, Enam, Jarmuth,
36 Adullam, Socoh, Azekah, Sha-
37 araim, Adithaim, Gederah, namely both parts of Gederah: fourteen cities with their hamlets. Zenan,
38 Hadashah, Migdal-gad, Dilan,
39 Mizpeh, Joktheel, Lachish, Boz-
40 kath, Eglon, Cabbon, Lahmas,
41 Kithlish, Gederoth, Beth-dagon, Naamah, and Makkedah: sixteen cities with their hamlets. Libnah,
42 Ether, Ashan, Jiphtah, Ashnah, Ne-
43 zib, Keilah, Achzib, and Maresh-
44 ah: nine cities with their hamlets.

---

t Prob. rdg., cp. 18. 17; Heb. to Gilgal.   *u Prob. rdg.; Heb. Adadah.*

45 Ekron, with its villages and ham-
46 lets, and from Ekron westwards, all
the cities near Ashdod and their
47 hamlets. Ashdod with its villages
and hamlets, Gaza with its villages
and hamlets as far as the Torrent
of Egypt and the Great Sea and the
land adjacent.
48   In the hill-country: Shamir,
49 Jattir, Socoh, Dannah, Kiriath-
50 sannah, that is Debir, Anab, Esh-
51 temoh, Anim, Goshen, Holon, and
Giloh: eleven cities in all with their
52 hamlets. Arab, Dumah, Eshan,
53 Janim, Beth-tappuah, Aphek,ᵛ
54 Humtah, Kiriath-arba, that is Hebron, and Zior: nine cities in all with
55 their hamlets. Maon, Carmel, Ziph,
56 Juttah, Jezreel, Jokdeam, Zanoah,
57 Cain, Gibeah, and Timnah: ten
cities in all with their hamlets.
59 Halhul, Beth-zur, Gedor, Maarath,
Beth-anoth, and Eltekon: six cities
in all with their hamlets. Tekoa,
Ephrathah, that is Bethlehem, Peor,
Etam, Culom, Tatam, Sores,
Carem, Gallim, Baither, and Ma-
nach: eleven cities in all with
60 their hamlets. Kiriath-baal, that is
Kiriath-jearim, and Rabbah: two
cities with their hamlets.
61   In the wilderness: Beth-arabah,
62 Middin, Secacah, Nibshan, Ir-
melach, and En-gedi: six cities with
their hamlets.
63   At Jerusalem, the men of Judah
were unable to drive out the Jebusites who lived there, and to this
day Jebusites and men of Judah
live together in Jerusalem.

Territory allotted to Ephraim and Manasseh

16 This is the lot that fell to the sons
of Joseph: the boundary runs from
the Jordan at Jericho, east of the
waters of Jericho by the wilderness, and goes up from Jericho into
2 the hill-country to Bethel. It runs
on from Bethel to Luz and crosses
the Archite border at Ataroth.ʷ
3 Westwards it descends to the boundary of the Japhletites as far as the
boundary of Lower Beth-horon
4 and Gezer; its limit is the sea. Here
Manasseh and Ephraim the sons
of Joseph received their patrimony.
5   This was the boundary of the
Ephraimites family by family: their
eastern boundary ran from
Ataroth-addar up to Upper Beth-
6 horon. It continued westwards to
Michmethath on the north, going
round by the east of Taanath-
shiloh and passing by it on the east
7 of Janoah. It descends from Janoah
to Ataroth and Naarath, touches
Jericho and continues to the Jor-
8 dan, and from Tappuah it goes
westwards by the gorge of Kanah;
and its limit is the sea. This is the
patrimony of the tribe of Ephraim
9 family by family. There were also

cities reserved for the Ephraimites
within the patrimony of the Manassites, each of these cities with its
10 hamlets. They did not however
drive out the Canaanites who dwelt
in Gezer; the Canaanites have lived
among the Ephraimites to the present day but have been subject to
forced labour in perpetuity.
17 This is the territory allotted to
the tribe of Manasseh, Joseph's
eldest son. Machir was Manasseh's
eldest son and father of Gilead, a
fighting man; Gilead and Bashan
were allotted to him.
2   The rest of the Manassites family
by family were the sons of Abiezer,
the sons of Helek, the sons of
Asriel, the sons of Shechem, the
sons of Hepher, and the sons of
Shemida; these were the male offspring of Manasseh son of Joseph
family by family.
3   Zelophehad son of Hepher, son
of Gilead, son of Machir, son of
Manasseh, had no sons but only
daughters: their names were Mahlah, Noah, Hoglah, Milcah and
4 Tirzah. They presented themselves
before Eleazar the priest and Joshua
son of Nun, and before the chiefs,
and they said, 'The LORD commanded Moses to allow us to inherit on the same footing as our
kinsmen.' They were therefore
given a patrimony on the same
footing as their father's brothers
according to the commandment of
the LORD.
5   There fell to Manasseh's lot ten
shares, apart from the country of
Gilead and Bashan beyond the
6 Jordan, because Manasseh's daughters had received a patrimony on
the same footing as his sons. The
country of Gilead belonged to the
7 rest of Manasseh's sons. The boundary of Manasseh reached from
Asher as far as Michmethath, which
is to the east of Shechem, and thence
southwards towards Jashub byˣ
8 En-tappuah. The territory of Tappuah belonged to Manasseh, but
Tappuah itself was on the border of
Manasseh and belonged to Eph-
9 raim. The boundary then followed
the gorge of Kanah to the south of
the gorge (these citiesʸ belong to
Ephraim, although they lie among
the cities of Manasseh), the boundary .of Manasseh being on the
north of the gorge; its limit was
10 the sea. The southern side belonged
to Ephraim and the northern to
Manasseh, and their boundary was
the sea. They marched with Asher
on the north and Issachar on the
11 east. But in Issachar and Asher,
Manasseh possessed Beth-shean
and its villages, Ibleam and its
villages, the inhabitants of Dor
and its villages, the inhabitants of
En-dor and its villages, the inhabitants of Taanach and its villages,

and the inhabitants of Megiddo and
its villages. (The third is the district of Dor.ᶻ) The Manassites were 12
unable to occupy these cities; the
Canaanites maintained their hold
on that part of the country. When 13
the Israelites grew stronger, they
put the Canaanites to forced labour,
but they did not drive them out.
    The sons of Joseph appealed to 14
Joshua and said, 'Why have you
given us only one lot and one share
as our patrimony? We are a numerous people; so far the LORD has
blessed us.' Joshua replied, 'If you 15
are so numerous, go up into the
forest in the territory of the Perizzites and the Rephaim and clear it
for yourselves. You are then near
neighboursᵃ in the hill-country of
Ephraim.' The sons of Joseph said, 16
'The hill-country is not enough for
us; besides, all the Canaanites who
inhabit the valley beside Beth-shean
and its villages and also those in the
Vale of Jezreel.' Joshua replied to 17
the tribes of Joseph, that is Ephraim and Manasseh: 'You are a
numerous people with great resources. You shall not have one
lot only. The hill-country is yours. 18
It is forest land; clear it and it shall
be yours to its furthest limits. The
Canaanites may be powerful and
equipped with chariots of iron, but
you will be able to drive them out.'

Division of the land at Shiloh

18 The whole community of the Israelites met together at Shiloh and
established the Tent of the Presence there. The country now lay
subdued at their feet, but there 2
remained seven tribes among the
Israelites who had not yet taken
possession of the patrimonies which
would fall to them. Joshua there- 3
fore said to them, 'How much
longer will you neglect to take
possession of the land which the
LORD the God of your fathers has
given you? Appoint three men 4
from each tribe whom I may send
out to travel through the whole
country. They shall make a register
showing the patrimony suitable for
each tribe, and come back to me,
and then it can be shared out 5
among you in seven portions. Judah
shall retain his boundary in the
south, and the house of Joseph
their boundary in the north. You 6
shall register the land in seven portions, bring the lists here, and I
will cast lots for you in the presence
of the LORD our God. Levi has no 7
share among you, because his share
is the priesthood of the LORD; and
Gad, Reuben, and the half tribe of
Manasseh have already taken possession of their patrimony east of the

---

ᵛ Or Aphekah.   ʷ Ataroth-addar in 16. 5; 18. 13.   ˣ Jashub by: prob. rdg.; Heb. the inhabitants of.
ʸ these cities: prob. rdg.; Heb. obscure.   ᶻ The third . . . Dor: prob. rdg.; Heb. The three districts.
ᵃ You are . . . neighbours: prob. rdg.; Heb. obscure.

Jordan, which Moses the servant of
8 the LORD gave them.' So the men
set out on their journeys. Joshua
ordered the emissaries to survey the
country: 'Go through the whole
country,' he said, 'survey it and
return to me, and I will cast lots
for you here before the LORD in
9 Shiloh.' So the men went and
passed through the country; they
registered it on a scroll, city by
city, in seven portions, and came
to Joshua in the camp at Shiloh.
10 Joshua cast lots for them in Shiloh
before the LORD, and distributed
the land there to the Israelites in
their proper shares.

Territory allotted to Benjamin

11 This is the lot which fell to the tribe
of the Benjamites family by family.
The territory allotted to them lay
between the territory of Judah and
12 Joseph. Their boundary at its northern corner starts from the Jordan;
it goes up the slope on the north
side of Jericho, continuing westwards into the hill-country, and its
limit there is the wilderness of Beth-
13 aven. From there it runs on to Luz,
to the southern slope of Luz, that
is Bethel, and down to Ataroth-
addar over the hill-country south
14 of Lower Beth-horon. The boundary then bends round at the west
corner southwards from the hill-
country above Beth-horon, and its
limit is Kiriath-baal, that is Kiriath-
jearim, a city of Judah. This is the
15 western side. The southern side
starts from the edge of Kiriath-
jearim and ends[b] at the spring of
16 the waters of Nephtoah. It goes
down to the edge of the hill to the
east of the Valley of Ben-hinnom,
north of the Vale of Rephaim,
down the Valley of Hinnom, to the
southern slope of the Jebusites
17 and so to En-rogel. It then bends
round north and comes out at En-
shemesh, goes on to the districts
in front of the ascent of Adummim
and thence down to the Stone of
18 Bohan son of Reuben. It passes to
the northern side of the slope facing
the Arabah and goes down to the
19 Arabah, passing the northern slope
of Beth-hoglah, and its limit is the
northern inlet of the Dead Sea, at
the southern mouth of the Jordan.
This forms the southern boundary.
20 The Jordan is the boundary on the
east side. This is the patrimony of
the Benjamites, the complete circuit
of their boundaries family by family.
21   The cities belonging to the tribe of
the Benjamites family by family are:
Jericho, Beth-hoglah, Emek-keziz,
22 Beth-arabah, Zemaraim, Bethel,
23 24 Avvim, Parah, Ophrah, Kephar-
ammoni, Ophni, and Geba: twelve
cities in all with their hamlets.
25 26 Gibeon, Ramah, Beeroth, Mizpah,

27 Kephirah, Mozah, Rekem, Irpeel,
28 Taralah, Zela, Eleph, Jebus, that is
Jerusalem, Gibeah, and Kiriath-
jearim: fourteen cities in all with
their hamlets. This is the patrimony of the Benjamites family by
family.

Territory allotted to Simeon

19 The second lot cast was for Simeon,
the tribe of the Simeonites family
by family. Their patrimony was
2 included in that of Judah. For their
patrimony they had Beersheba,[c]
3 Moladah, Hazar-shual, Balah,
4 Ezem, Eltolad, Bethul, Hormah,
5 Ziklag, Beth-marcaboth, Hazar-
6 susah, Beth-lebaoth, and Sharu-
hen: in all, thirteen cities and their
7 hamlets. They had Ain, Rimmon,
Ether, and Ashan: four cities and
8 their hamlets, all the hamlets round
these cities as far as Baalath-beer,
Ramath-negeb. This was the patrimony of the tribe of Simeon family
9 by family. The patrimony of the
Simeonites was part of the land
allotted to the men of Judah, because their share was larger than
they needed. The Simeonites therefore had their patrimony within
the territory of Judah.

Territory allotted to Zebulun

10 The third lot fell to the Zebulunites
family by family. The boundary
of their patrimony extended to
11 Shadud.[d] Their boundary went up
westwards as far as Maralah and
touched Dabbesheth and the gorge
12 east of Jokneam. It turned back
from Shadud eastwards towards
the sunrise up to the border of
Kisloth-tabor, on to Daberath and
13 up to Japhia. From there it crossed
eastwards towards the sunrise to
Gath-hepher, to Ittah-kazin, out to
Rimmon, and bent round[e] to Neah.
14 The northern boundary went round
to Hannathon, and its limits were
15 the Valley of Jiphtah-el, Kattath,
Nahalal, Shimron, Idalah, and
Bethlehem: twelve cities in all with
16 their hamlets. These cities and their
hamlets were the patrimony of the
Zebulun family by family.

Territory allotted to Issachar

17 The fourth lot cast was for the sons
18 of Issachar family by family. Their
boundary included Jezreel, Kesul-
19 loth, Shunem, Hapharaim, Shion,
20 Anaharath, Rabbith, Kishion,
21 Ebez, Remeth, En-gannim, En-
22 haddah, and Beth-pazzez. The
boundary touched Tabor, Shaha-
zumah, and Beth-shemesh, and its
limit was the Jordan: sixteen cities
23 with their hamlets. This was the
patrimony of the tribe of the sons
of Issachar family by family, both
cities and hamlets.

Territory allotted to Asher

The fifth lot cast was for the tribe 24
of the Asherites family by family.
Their boundary included Helkath, 25
Hali, Beten, Akshaph, Alam- 26
melech, Amad, and Mishal; it
touched Carmel on the west and
the swamp of Libnath. It then 27
turned back towards the east to
Beth-dagon, touched Zebulun and
the Valley of Jiphtah-el on the
north at Beth-emek and Neiel, and
reached Cabul on its northern side,
and Abdon, Rehob, Hammon, and 28
Kanah as far as Greater Sidon. The 29
boundary turned at Ramah, going
as far as the fortress city of Tyre,
and then back again to Hosah, and
its limits to the west were Mehalbeh, Achzib, Acco,[f] Aphek, and 30
Rehob: twenty-two cities in all
with their hamlets. This was the 31
patrimony of the tribe of Asher
family by family, these cities and
their hamlets.

Territory allotted to Naphtali

The sixth lot cast was for the sons 32
of Naphtali family by family. Their 33
boundary started from Heleph and
from Elon-bezaanannim and ran
past Adami-nekeb and Jabneel as
far as Lakkum, and its limit was
the Jordan. The boundary turned 34
back westwards to Aznoth-tabor
and from there on to Hukok. It
touched Zebulun on the south,
Asher on the west, and the low-
lying land by the Jordan on the
east. Their fortified cities were 35
Ziddim, Zer, Hammath, Rakkath,
Kinnereth, Adamah, Ramah, 36
Hazor, Kedesh, Edrei, En-hazor, 37
Iron, Migdal-el, Horem, Beth- 38
anath, and Beth-shemesh: nineteen cities with their hamlets. This 39
was the patrimony of the tribe of
Naphtali family by family, both
cities and hamlets.

Territory allotted to Dan

The seventh lot cast was for the 40
tribe of the sons of Dan family by
family. The boundary of their 41
patrimony was Zorah, Eshtaol,
Ir-shemesh, Shaalabbin, Aijalon, 42
Jithlah, Elon, Timnah, Ekron, 43
Eltekeh, Gibbethon, Baalath, 44
Jehud, Bene-berak, Gath-rimmon; 45
and on the west Jarkon was the 46
boundary opposite Joppa. But the 47
Danites, when they lost this territory, marched against Leshem,
attacked it and captured it. They
put its people to the sword, occupied it and settled in it; and they
renamed the place Dan after their
ancestor Dan. This was the patri- 48
mony of the tribe of the sons of
Dan family by family, these cities
and their hamlets.

---

b Prob. rdg.; Heb. adds westwards and ends . . .   c Prob. rdg., cp. 1 Chr. 4. 28; Heb. adds and Sheba.
d Prob. rdg.; Heb. Sarid (similarly in verse 12).   e and bent round: prob. rdg.; Heb. which stretched.
f Mehalbeh . . . Acco: prob. rdg.; Heb. from the district of Achzib and Ummah.

Joshua settles in Timnath-serah

49 So the Israelites finished allocating the land and marking out its frontiers; and they gave Joshua son of Nun a patrimony within 50 their territory. They followed the commands of the LORD and gave him the city for which he asked, Timnath-serah in the hill-country of Ephraim, and he rebuilt the city and settled in it.

51 These are the patrimonies which Eleazar the priest and Joshua son of Nun and the heads of families assigned by lot to the Israelite tribes at Shiloh before the LORD at the entrance of the Tent of the Presence. Thus they completed the distribution of the land.

Cities of refuge appointed

20 The LORD spoke to Joshua and 2 commanded him to say this to the Israelites: 'You must now appoint your cities of refuge, of which I 3 spoke to you through Moses. They are to be places where the homicide, the man who kills another inadvertently without intent, may take sanctuary. You shall single them out as cities of refuge from the vengeance of the dead man's 4 next-of-kin. When a man takes sanctuary in one of these cities, he shall halt at the entrance of the city gate and state his case in the hearing of the elders of that city; if they admit him into the city, they shall grant him a place where he may 5 live as one of themselves. When the next-of-kin comes in pursuit, they shall not surrender him: he struck down his fellow without intent and had not previously been at enmity 6 with him. The homicide may stay in that city until he stands trial before the community. On the death of the ruling high priest, he may 7 return to the city and home from which he has fled.' They dedicated Kedesh in Galilee in the hill-country of Naphtali, Shechem in the hill-country of Ephraim, and Kiriath-arba, that is Hebron, in 8 the hill-country of Judah. Across the Jordan eastwards from Jericho they appointed these cities: from the tribe of Reuben, Bezer-in-the-wilderness on the tableland, from the tribe of Gad, Ramoth in Gilead, and from the tribe of Manasseh, 9 Golan in Bashan. These were the appointed cities where any Israelite or any alien residing among them might take sanctuary. They were intended for any man who killed another inadvertently, to ensure

that no one should die at the hand of the next-of-kin until he had stood his trial before the community.

The Levites' cities

21 The heads of the Levite families approached Eleazar the priest and Joshua son of Nun and the heads of the families of the tribes of 2 Israel. They came before them at Shiloh in the land of Canaan and said, 'The LORD gave his command through Moses that we were to receive cities to live in, together 3 to them for our cattle.' The Israelites therefore gave part of their patrimony to the Levites, the following cities with their common land, according to the command of the LORD.

4 This is the territory allotted to the Kohathite family: those Levites who were descended from Aaron the priest received thirteen cities chosen by lot from the tribes of Judah, Simeon, and Benjamin; 5 the rest of the Kohathites were allotted family by family[g] ten cities from the tribes of Ephraim, Dan, and half Manasseh.

6 The Gershonites were allotted family by family thirteen cities from the tribes of Issachar, Asher, Naphtali, and the half tribe of Manasseh in Bashan.

7 The Merarites were allotted family by family twelve cities from the tribes of Reuben, Gad, and Zebulun.

8 So the Israelites gave the Levites these cities with their common land, allocating them by lot as the LORD had commanded through Moses.

9 The Israelites designated the following cities out of the tribes of 10 Judah and Simeon for those sons of Aaron who were of the Kohathite families of the Levites, because 11 their lot came out first. They gave them Kiriath-arba (Arba was the father of Anak), that is Hebron, in the hill-country of Judah, and the 12 common land round it, but they gave the open country near the city, and its hamlets, to Caleb son of Jephunneh as his patrimony.

13[h] To the sons of Aaron the priest they gave Hebron, a city of refuge 14 for the homicide, Libnah, Jattir, 15 Eshtemoa, Holon, Debir, Ashan,[i] 16 Juttah, and Beth-shemesh, each with its common land: nine cities 17 from these two tribes. They also gave cities from the tribe of Benja-18 min, Gibeon, Geba, Anathoth, and Almon, each with its common land: 19 four cities. The number of the cities with their common land given to

the sons of Aaron the priest was thirteen.

20 The cities which the rest of the Kohathite families of the Levites received by lot were from the tribe of Ephraim. They gave them She-21 chem, a city of refuge for the homicide, in the hill-country of Ephraim, Gezer, Kibzaim, and Beth-horon, 22 each with its common land: four cities. From the tribe of Dan, they 23 gave them Eltekeh, Gibbethon, Aijalon, and Gath-rimmon, each 24 with its common land: four cities. From the half tribe of Manasseh, 25 they gave them Taanach and Gath-rimmon, each with its common land: two cities. The number of 26 the cities belonging to the rest of the Kohathite families with their common land was ten.

27 The Gershonite families of the Levites received, out of the share of the half tribe of Manasseh, Golan in Bashan, a city of refuge for the homicide, and Beashtaroth,[j] each with its common land: two cities. From the tribe 28 of Issachar they received Kishon, Daberah, Jarmuth, and En-gannim, 29 each with its common land: four cities. From the tribe of Asher they 30 received Mishal, Abdon, Helkath, 31 and Rehob, each with its common land: four cities. From the tribe of 32 Naphtali they received Kedesh in Galilee, a city of refuge for the homicide, Hammoth-dor, and Kartan, each with its common land: three cities. The number of 33 cities of the Gershonite families with their common land was thirteen.

34 From the tribe of Zebulun the rest of the Merarite families of the Levites received Jokneam, Kartah, Rimmon,[k] and Nahalal, each with 35 its common land: four cities. East 36 of the Jordan at Jericho, from the tribe of Reuben they were given Bezer-in-the-wilderness on the tableland, a city of refuge for the homicide, Jahaz, Kedemoth, and 37 Mephaath, each with its common land: four cities. From the tribe 38 of Gad they received Ramoth in Gilead, a city of refuge for the homicide, Mahanaim, Heshbon, 39 and Jazer, each with its common land: four cities in all. Twelve 40 cities in all fell by lot to the rest of the Merarite families of the Levites.

41 The cities of the Levites within the Israelite patrimonies numbered forty-eight in all, with their common land. Each city had its com-42 mon land round it, and it was the same for all of them.

---

g family by family: *prob. rdg.; Heb.* from the families (*similarly in verse 6*). 6. 57–81.   i *Prob. rdg., cp. 1 Chr. 6. 59; Heb.* Ain.   j *Prob. rdg.; Heb.* Be-ashtarah.   k *Prob. rdg., cp. 19. 13; 1 Chr. 6. 77; Heb.* Dimnah.   h *Verses 13–39: cp. 1 Chr.*

The LORD fulfils his promise

43 Thus the LORD gave Israel all the land which he had sworn to give to their forefathers;
44 they occupied it and settled in it. The LORD gave them security on every side as he had sworn to their forefathers. Of all their enemies not a man could withstand them; the LORD delivered all their enemies into
45 their hands. Not a word of the LORD's promises to the house of Israel went unfulfilled; they all came true.

The altar by the Jordan

22 At that time Joshua summoned the Reubenites, the Gadites, and the half tribe of
2 Manasseh, and said to them, 'You have observed all the commands of Moses the servant of the LORD, and you have obeyed me in all the commands that I too have laid
3 upon you. All this time you have not deserted your brothers; up to this day you have diligently observed the charge laid on you by
4 the LORD your God. And now that the LORD your God has given your brothers security as he promised them, you may turn now and go to your homes in your own land, the land which Moses the servant of the LORD gave
5 you east of the Jordan. But take good care to keep the commands and the law which Moses the servant of the LORD gave you: to love the LORD your God; to conform to his ways; to observe his commandments; to hold fast to him; to serve him with your
6 whole heart and soul.' Joshua blessed them and dismissed them; and they went to their
7-8 homes. He sent them home with his blessing, and with these words: 'Go to your homes richly laden, with great herds, with silver and gold, copper and iron, and with large stores of clothing. See that you share with your kinsmen the spoil you have taken from your enemies.'

Moses had given territory to one half of the tribe of Manasseh in Bashan, and Joshua gave territory to the other half west of the Jordan among their kinsmen.
9 So the Reubenites, the Gadites, and the half tribe of Manasseh left the rest of the Israelites and went from Shiloh in Canaan on their way into Gilead, the land which belonged to them according to the decree of
10 the LORD given through Moses. When these tribes came to Geliloth by the Jordan,[1] they built a great altar there by the river for all
11 to see. The Israelites heard that the Reubenites, the Gadites, and the half tribe of Manasseh had built the altar facing the land of Canaan, at Geliloth by the Jordan oppo-
12 site the Israelite side. When the news reached them, all the community of the Israelites assembled at Shiloh to advance against them

with a display of force. At the same time the 13 Israelites sent Phinehas son of Eleazar the priest into the land of Gilead, to the Reubenites, the Gadites, and the half tribe of Manasseh, and ten leading men with him, 14 one from each of the tribes of Israel, each of them the head of a household among the clans of Israel. They came to the Reubenites, 15 the Gadites, and the half tribe of Manasseh in the land of Gilead, and remonstrated with them in these words: 'We speak for the whole 16 community of the LORD. What is this treachery you have committed against the God of Israel? Are you ceasing to follow the LORD and building your own altar this day in defiance of the LORD? Remember our 17 offence at Peor, for which a plague fell upon the community of the LORD; to this day we have not been purified from it. Was that offence so slight that you dare cease to follow 18 the LORD today? If you defy the LORD today, then tomorrow he will be angry with the whole community of Israel. If the land you 19 have taken is unclean, then cross over to the LORD's own land, where the Tabernacle of the LORD now rests, and take a share of it with us; but do not defy the LORD and involve us in your defiance by building an altar of your own apart from the altar of the LORD our God. Remember the treachery of 20 Achan son of Zerah, who defied the ban and the whole community of Israel suffered for it. He was not the only one who paid for that sin with his life.'

Then the Reubenites, the Gadites, and the 21 half tribe of Manasseh remonstrated with the heads of the clans of Israel: 'The LORD 22 the God of gods, the LORD the God of gods, he knows, and Israel must know: if this had been an act of defiance or treachery against the LORD, you could not save us today. If 23 we had built ourselves an altar meaning to

1 Prob. rdg.; Heb. adds which was in Canaan.

forsake the LORD, or had offered whole-offerings and grain-offerings upon it, or had presented shared-offerings, the LORD him-24 self would exact punishment. The truth is that we have done this for fear that the day may come when your sons will say to ours, "What have you to do with the LORD, the 25 God of Israel? The LORD put the Jordan as a boundary between our sons and your sons. You have no share in the LORD, you men of Reuben and Gad." Thus your sons will prevent our sons from going in awe of the LORD. 26 So we resolved to set ourselves to build an altar, not for whole-offerings and sacrifices, 27 but as a witness between us and you, and between our descendants after us. Thus we shall be able to do service before the LORD, as we do now, with our whole-offerings, our sacrifices, and our shared-offerings; and your sons will never be able to say to our sons that they have no share in the LORD. 28 And we thought, if ever they do say this to us and our descendants, we will point to this copy of the altar of the LORD which we have made, not for whole-offerings and not for sacrifices, but as a witness between us and 29 you. God forbid that we should defy the LORD and forsake him this day by building another altar for whole-offerings, grain-offerings, and sacrifices, in addition to the altar of the LORD our God which stands in front of his Tabernacle.'

30 When Phinehas the priest and the leaders of the community, the heads of the Israelite clans, who were with him, heard what the Reubenites, the Gadites, and the Manas-31 sites said, they were satisfied. Phinehas son of Eleazar the priest said to the Reubenites, Gadites, and Manassites, 'We know now that the LORD is in our midst today; you have not acted treacherously against the LORD, and thus you have preserved all 32 Israel from punishment at his hand.' Then Phinehas son of Eleazar the priest and the leaders left the Reubenites and the Gadites in Gilead and reported to the Israelites in 33 Canaan. The Israelites were satisfied, and they blessed God and thought no more of attacking Reuben and Gad and ravaging 34 their land. The Reubenites and Gadites said, 'The altar is a witness between us that the LORD is God', and they named it 'Witness'.

Joshua exhorts the people to obey the LORD

23 A long time had passed since the LORD had given Israel security from all the enemies who surrounded them, and Joshua was now 2 a very old man. He summoned all Israel, their elders and heads of families, their judges and officers, and said to them, 'I have 3 become a very old man. You have seen for

yourselves all that the LORD our God has done to these peoples for your sake; it was the LORD God himself who fought for you. I have allotted you your patrimony tribe by 4 tribe, the land of all the peoples that I have wiped out and of all these that remain between the Jordan and the Great Sea which lies towards the setting sun. The LORD your 5 God himself drove them out for your sake; he drove them out to make room for you, and you occupied their land, as the LORD your God had promised you. Be resolute 6 therefore: observe and perform everything written in the book of the law of Moses, without swerving to right or to left. You 7 must not associate with the peoples that are left among you; you must not call upon their gods by name, nor*m* swear by them nor prostrate yourselves in worship before them. You must hold fast to the LORD your God 8 as you have done down to this day. For your 9 sake the LORD has driven out great and mighty nations; to this day not a man of them has withstood you. One of you can 10 put to flight a thousand, because the LORD your God fights for you, as he promised. Be 11 on your guard then, love the LORD your God, for*n* if you do turn away and attach your- 12 selves to the peoples that still remain among you, and intermarry with them and associate with them and they with you, then be sure 13 that the LORD will not continue to drive those peoples out to make room for you. They will be snares to entrap you, whips for your backs and barbed hooks in your eyes, until you vanish from the good land which the LORD your God has given you. And now 14 I am going the way of all mankind. You know in your heart of hearts that nothing that the LORD your God has promised you has failed to come true, every word of it. But the same LORD God who has kept his 15 word to you to such good effect can equally bring every kind of evil on you, until he has rooted you out from this good land which he has given you. If you break the covenant 16 which the LORD your God has prescribed and prostrate yourselves in worship before other gods, then the LORD will be angry with you and you will quickly vanish from the good land he has given you.'

Joshua's farewell address

Joshua assembled all the tribes of Israel at 24 Shechem. He summoned the elders of Israel, the heads of families, the judges and officers; and they presented themselves before God. Joshua then said this to all the people: 'This 2 is the word of the LORD the God of Israel: "Long ago your forefathers, Terah and his sons Abraham and Nahor, lived beside the

m you must not call ... nor: *or* the name of their gods shall not be your boast, nor must you ...   *n* Be on ... for: *or* Take very good care to love the LORD your God, but ...

Euphrates, and they worshipped other gods.
3 I took your father Abraham from beside the Euphrates and led him through the length and breadth of Canaan. I gave him
4 many descendants: I gave him Isaac, and to Isaac I gave Jacob and Esau. I put Esau in possession of the hill-country of Seir, but Jacob and his sons went down to Egypt.
5 I sent Moses and Aaron, and I struck the Egyptians with plagues—you know well what I did among them—and after that I
6 brought you out; I brought your fathers out of Egypt and you came to the Red Sea. The Egyptians sent their chariots and cavalry to
7 pursue your fathers to the sea. But when they appealed to the LORD, he put a screen of darkness between you and the Egyptians, and brought the sea down on them and it covered them; you saw for yourselves what I did to Egypt. For a long time you lived
8 in the wilderness. Then I brought you into the land of the Amorites who lived east of the Jordan; they fought against you, but I delivered them into your hands; you took possession of their country and I destroyed
9 them for your sake. The king of Moab, Balak son of Zippor, took the field against Israel. He sent for Balaam son of Beor to
10 lay a curse on you, but I would not listen to him. Instead of that he blessed you; and so
11 I saved you from the power of Balak. Then you crossed the Jordan and came to Jericho. The citizens of Jericho fought against you,[o]
12 but I delivered them into your hands. I spread panic before you, and it was this, not your sword or your bow, that drove out
13 the two kings of the Amorites. I gave you land on which you had not laboured, cities which you had never built; you have lived in those cities and you eat the produce of vineyards and olive-groves which you did not plant."
14 'Hold the LORD in awe then, and worship him in loyalty and truth. Banish the gods whom your fathers worshipped beside the Euphrates and in Egypt, and worship the
15 LORD. But if it does not please you to worship the LORD, choose here and now whom you will worship: the gods whom your fore-fathers worshipped beside the Euphrates, or the gods of the Amorites in whose land you are living. But I and my family, we will wor-
16 ship the LORD.' The people answered, 'God forbid that we should forsake the LORD to
17 worship other gods, for it was the LORD our God who brought us and our fathers up from Egypt, that land of slavery; it was he who displayed those great signs before our eyes and guarded us on all our wanderings

among the many peoples through whose lands we passed. The LORD drove out before 18 us the Amorites and all the peoples who lived in that country. We too will worship the LORD; he is our God.' Joshua answered 19 the people, 'You cannot worship the LORD. He is a holy god, a jealous god, and he will not forgive your rebellion and your sins. If 20 you forsake the LORD and worship foreign gods, he will turn and bring adversity upon you and, although he once brought you prosperity, he will make an end of you.' The people said to Joshua, 'No; we will 21 worship the LORD.' He said to them, 'You 22 are witnesses against yourselves that you have chosen the LORD and will worship him.' 'Yes,' they answered, 'we are witnesses.' He 23 said to them, 'Then here and now banish the foreign gods that are among you, and turn your hearts to the LORD the God of Israel.' The people said to Joshua, 'The 24 LORD our God we will worship and his voice we will obey.' So Joshua made a 25 covenant that day with[p] the people; he drew up a statute and an ordinance for them in Shechem and wrote its terms in the book of 26 the law of God. He took a great stone and set it up there under the terebinth[q] in the sanctuary of the LORD, and said to all the 27 people, 'This stone is a witness against us; for it has heard all the words which the LORD has spoken to us. If you renounce your God, it shall be a witness against you.' Then Joshua dismissed the people, each man 28 to his patrimony.

The death of Joshua

After these things, Joshua son of Nun the 29 servant of the LORD died; he was a hundred and ten years old. They buried him within 30 the border of his own patrimony in Timnath-serah in the hill-country of Ephraim to the north of Mount Gaash. Israel served the 31 LORD during the lifetime of Joshua and of the elders who outlived him and who well knew all that the LORD had done for Israel.

The death of Eleazar

The bones of Joseph, which the Israelites 32 had brought up from Egypt, were buried in Shechem, in the plot of land which Jacob had bought from the sons of Hamor father of Shechem for a hundred sheep;[r] and they passed into the patrimony of the house of Joseph. Eleazar son of Aaron died and was 33 buried in the hill which had been given to Phinehas his son in the hill-country of Ephraim.

---

o *Prob. rdg.; Heb. adds* Amorites, Perizzites, Canaanites, Hittites, Girgashites, Hivites, and Jebusites.　　p *Or* for.
q *Or* pole.　　r *Or* pieces of money (*cp. Gen.* 33. 19; *Job* 42. 11).

THE BOOK OF
JUDGES

Conquests of Judah and Simeon

1 AFTER THE DEATH of Joshua the Israelites inquired of the LORD which tribe 2 should attack the Canaanites first. The LORD answered, 'Judah shall attack. I hereby de-3 liver the country into his power.' Judah said to his brother Simeon, 'Go forward with me into my allotted territory, and let us do battle with the Canaanites; then I in turn will go with you into your territory.' So 4 Simeon went with him; then Judah advanced to the attack, and the LORD delivered the Canaanites and Perizzites into their hands. They slaughtered ten thousand of them at 5 Bezek. There they came upon Adoni-bezek, engaged him in battle and defeated the 6 Canaanites and Perizzites. Adoni-bezek fled, but they pursued him, took him prisoner and 7 cut off his thumbs and his great toes. Adoni-bezek said, 'I once had seventy kings whose thumbs and great toes were cut off picking up the scraps from under my table. What I have done God has done to me.' He was brought to Jerusalem and died there.

8 The men of Judah made an assault on Jerusalem and captured it, put its people to 9 the sword and set fire to the city. Then they turned south to fight the Canaanites of the hill-country, the Negeb, and the Shephelah.

Judah attacked the Canaanites in Hebron, 10 formerly called Kiriath-arba, and defeated Sheshai, Ahiman and Talmai. From there 11 they marched against the inhabitants of Debir, formerly called Kiriath-sepher. Caleb 12 said, 'Whoever attacks Kiriath-sepher and captures it, to him I will give my daughter Achsah in marriage.' Othniel, son of Caleb's 13 younger brother Kenaz, captured it, and Caleb gave him his daughter Achsah. When 14 she came to him, he incited her to ask her father for a piece of land. As she sat on the ass, she broke wind, and Caleb said, 'What did you mean by that?' She replied, 'I want 15 to ask a favour of you. You have put me in this dry Negeb; you must give me pools of water as well.' So Caleb gave her the upper pool and the lower pool.

The descendants of Moses' father-in-law, 16 the Kenite, went up with the men of Judah from the Vale of Palm Trees to the wilderness of Judah which is in the Negeb of Arad and settled among the Amalekites. Judah 17 then accompanied his brother Simeon, attacked the Canaanites in Zephath and destroyed it; hence the city was called Hormah.*a* Judah took Gaza, Ashkelon, and 18 Ekron, and the territory of each. The LORD 19 was with Judah and they occupied the hill-country, but they could not drive out the

a That is Destruction.

inhabitants of the Vale because they had
20 chariots of iron. Hebron was given to Caleb
as Moses had directed, and he drove out the
21 three sons of Anak. But the Benjamites did
not drive out the Jebusites of Jerusalem; and
the Jebusites have lived on in Jerusalem with
the Benjamites till the present day.

Joseph captures Bethel

22 The tribes of Joseph attacked Bethel, and
23 the LORD was with them. They sent spies to
24 Bethel, formerly called Luz. These spies saw
a man coming out of the city and said to
him, 'Show us how to enter the city, and we
25 will see that you come to no harm.' So he
showed them how to enter, and they put the
city to the sword, but let the man and his
26 family go free. He went into Hittite country,
built a city and named it Luz, which is still
its name today.

Conquests of Manasseh and Ephraim

27 Manasseh did not drive out the inhabitants
of Beth-shean with its villages, nor of
Taanach, Dor, Ibleam, and Megiddo, with
the villages of each of them; the Canaanites
28. held their ground in that region. Later, when
Israel became strong, they put them to forced
labour, but they never completely drove
them out.
29 Ephraim did not drive out the Canaanites
who lived in Gezer, but the Canaanites lived
among them there.

Conquests of the other tribes

30 Zebulun did not drive out the inhabitants
of Kitron and Nahalol, but the Canaanites
lived among them and were put to forced
labour.
31 Asher did not drive out the inhabitants of
Acco and Sidon, of Ahlab, Achzib, Helbah,
32 Aphik and Rehob. Thus the Asherites lived
among the Canaanite inhabitants and did
not drive them out.
33 Naphtali did not drive out the inhabitants
of Beth-shemesh and of Beth-anath, but
lived among the Canaanite inhabitants and
put the inhabitants of Beth-shemesh and
Beth-anath to forced labour.
34 The Amorites pressed the Danites back
into the hill-country and did not allow them
35 to come down into the Vale. The Amorites
held their ground in Mount Heres and in
Aijalon and Shaalbim, but the tribes of
Joseph increased their pressure on them until
they reduced them to forced labour.
36 The boundary of the Edomites ran from
the ascent of Akrabbim, upwards from Sela.

The angel of the LORD at Bokim

2 The angel of the LORD came up from Gilgal
to Bokim, and said, 'I brought[b] you up out

of Egypt and into the country which I vowed
I would give to your forefathers. I said, I
will never break my covenant with you, and 2
you in turn must make no covenant with the
inhabitants of the country; you must pull
down their altars. But you did not obey me,
and look what you have done! So I said, I 3
will not drive them out before you; they will
decoy you, and their gods will shut you fast
in the trap.' When the angel of the LORD 4
said this to the Israelites, they all wept and
wailed, and so the place was called Bokim;[c] 5
and they offered sacrifices there to the LORD.

The new generation forsakes the LORD

Joshua dismissed the people, and the Israel- 6
ites went off to occupy the country, each man
to his allotted portion. As long as Joshua was 7
alive and the elders who survived him—
everyone, that is, who had witnessed the
whole great work which the LORD had done
for Israel—the people worshipped the LORD.
At the age of a hundred and ten Joshua son 8
of Nun, the servant of the LORD, died, and 9
they buried him within the border of his own
property in Timnath-heres north of Mount
Gaash in the hill-country of Ephraim. Of 10
that whole generation, all were gathered to
their forefathers, and another generation
followed who did not acknowledge the LORD
and did not know what he had done for Israel. Then the Israelites did what was wrong 11
in the eyes of the LORD, and worshipped
the Baalim.[d] They forsook the LORD, their 12
fathers' God who had brought them out
of Egypt, and went after other gods, gods
of the races whom they lived; they
bowed down before them and provoked
LORD to anger; they forsook the LORD and 13
worshipped the Baal and the Ashtaroth.[e]
The LORD in his anger made them the prey 14
of bands of raiders and plunderers; he sold
them to their enemies all around them, and
they could no longer make a stand. Every 15
time they went out to battle the LORD
brought disaster upon them, as he had said
when he gave them his solemn warning, and
they were in dire straits.

Israel's inconstancy

The LORD set judges over them, who rescued 16
them from the marauding bands. Yet they 17
did not listen to these judges, but turned
wantonly to worship other gods and bowed
down before them; all too soon they abandoned the path of obedience to the LORD's
commands which their forefathers had followed. They did not obey the LORD. When- 18
ever the LORD set up a judge over them, he
was with that judge, and kept them safe from
their enemies so long as he lived. The LORD

---

b Prob. rdg.; Heb. I will bring.   *c That is Weepers.*   *d The Baalim were Canaanite deities.*   *e The*
Ashtaroth *were Canaanite deities.*

would relent as often as he heard them groaning under oppression and ill-treatment.
19 But as soon as the judge was dead, they would relapse into deeper corruption than their forefathers and give their allegiance to other gods, worshipping them and bowing down before them. They gave up none of their evil practices and their wilful ways.
20 And the Lord was angry with Israel and said, 'This nation has broken the covenant which I laid upon their forefathers and has
21 not obeyed me, and now, of all the nations which Joshua left at his death, I will not drive out to make room for them one single man.
22 By their means I will test Israel, to see whether or not they will keep strictly to the way of the
23 Lord as their forefathers did.' So the Lord left those nations alone and made no haste to drive them out or give them into Joshua's hands.

Nations left to test Israel

3 These are the nations which the Lord left as a means of testing all the Israelites who had
2 not taken part in the battles for Canaan, his purpose being to teach succeeding generations of Israel, or those at least who had not learnt in former times, how to make war.
3 These were: the five lords of the Philistines, all the Canaanites, the Sidonians, and the Hivites who lived in Mount Lebanon from Mount Baal-hermon as far as Lebo-hamath.
4 His purpose also was to test whether the Israelites would obey the commands which the Lord had given to their forefathers
5 through Moses. Thus the Israelites lived among the Canaanites, the Hittites, the Amorites, the Perizzites, the Hivites, and the
6 Jebusites. They took their daughters in marriage and gave their own daughters to their sons; and they worshipped their gods.

Othniel delivers Israel from Cushan-rishathaim

7 The Israelites did what was wrong in the eyes of the Lord; they forgot the Lord their God and worshipped the Baalim and the
8 Asheroth.[f] The Lord was angry with Israel and he sold them to Cushan-rishathaim, king of Aram-naharaim,[g] who kept them in sub-
9 jection for eight years. Then the Israelites cried to the Lord for help and he raised up a man to deliver them, Othniel son of Caleb's younger brother Kenaz, and he set
10 them free. The spirit of the Lord came upon him and he became judge over Israel. He took the field, and the Lord delivered Cushan-rishathaim king of Aram into his
11 hands; Othniel was too strong for him. Thus the land was at peace for forty years until Othniel son of Kenaz died.

Ehud delivers Israel from Moab

12 Once again the Israelites did what was wrong in the eyes of the Lord, and because of this he roused Eglon king of Moab
13 against Israel. Eglon mustered the Ammonites and the Amalekites, advanced to attack Israel and took possession of the Vale of
14 Palm Trees. The Israelites were subject to Eglon king of Moab for eighteen years. When
15 they cried to the Lord for help, he raised up a man to deliver them, Ehud son of Gera the Benjamite, who was left-handed. The Israelites sent him to pay their tribute to Eglon king of Moab. Ehud made himself a two-
16 edged sword, only fifteen inches long, which he fastened on his right side under his clothes,
17 and he brought the tribute to Eglon king of Moab. Eglon was a very fat man. When
18 Ehud had finished presenting the tribute, he sent on the men who had carried it, and he
19 himself turned back from the Carved Stones at Gilgal. 'My lord king,' he said, 'I have a word for you in private.' Eglon called for silence and dismissed all his attendants.
20 Ehud then came up to him as he sat in the roof-chamber of his summer palace and said, 'I have a word from God for you.' So
21 Eglon rose from his seat, and Ehud reached with his left hand, drew the sword from his right side and drove it into his belly. The hilt
22 went in after the blade and the fat closed over the blade; he did not draw the sword out but left it protruding behind. Ehud went
23 out to the porch, shut the doors on him and fastened them. When he had gone away,
24 Eglon's servants came and, finding the doors fastened, they said, 'He must be relieving himself in the closet of his summer palace.'
25 They waited until they were ashamed to delay any longer, and still he did not open the doors of the roof-chamber. So they took the key and opened the doors; and there was
26 their master lying on the floor dead. While they had been waiting, Ehud made his escape; he passed the Carved Stones and escaped to Seirah. When he arrived there,
27 he sounded the trumpet in the hill-country of Ephraim, and the Israelites came down from the hills with him at their head. He
28 said to them, 'Follow me, for the Lord has delivered your enemy the Moabites into your hands.' Down they came after him, and they seized the fords of the Jordan against the Moabites and allowed no man to cross.
29 They killed that day some ten thousand Moabites, all of them men of substance and all fighting men; not one escaped.
30 Thus Moab on that day became subject to Israel, and the land was at peace for eighty years.

---

f Plural of Asherah, *the name of a Canaanite goddess.*   *g That is* Aram of Two Rivers.

Shamgar delivers Israel from the Philistines

31 After Ehud there was Shamgar of Beth-anath.[h] He killed six hundred Philistines with an ox-goad, and he too delivered Israel.

Deborah and Barak prepare for battle

4 After Ehud's death the Israelites once again did what was wrong in the eyes of the LORD, 2 so he sold them to Jabin the Canaanite king, who ruled in Hazor. The commander of his forces was Sisera, who lived in Harosheth-3 of-the-Gentiles. The Israelites cried to the LORD for help, because Sisera had nine hundred chariots of iron and had oppressed 4 Israel harshly for twenty years. At that time Deborah wife of Lappidoth,[i] a prophetess,

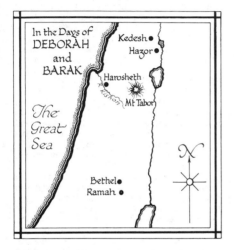

In the Days of
DEBORÀH
and
BARAK

Kedesh●
Hazor● ●

Harosheth

Mt Tabor

The Great Sea

Bethel●
Ramah ●

5 was judge in Israel. It was her custom to sit beneath the Palm-tree of Deborah between Ramah and Bethel in the hill-country of Ephraim, and the Israelites went up to her 6 for justice. She sent for Barak son of Abinoam from Kedesh in Naphtali and said to him, 'These are the commands of the LORD the God of Israel: "Go and draw ten thousand men from Naphtali and Zebulun and bring them with you to Mount Tabor, 7 and I will draw Sisera, Jabin's commander, to the Torrent of Kishon with his chariots and all his rabble, and there I will deliver them 8 into your hands."' Barak answered her, 'If you go with me, I will go; but if you will not 9 go, neither will I.' 'Certainly I will go with you,' she said, 'but this venture will bring you no glory, because the LORD will leave Sisera to fall into the hands of a woman.' So Deborah rose and went with Barak to

Kedesh. Barak summoned Zebulun and 10 Naphtali to Kedesh and marched up with ten thousand men, and Deborah went with him.

Jael kills Sisera

Now Heber the Kenite had parted company 11 with the Kenites, the descendants of Hobab, Moses' brother-in-law, and he had pitched his tent at Elon-bezaanannim near Kedesh.

Word was brought to Sisera that Barak 12 son of Abinoam had gone up to Mount Tabor; so he summoned all his chariots, 13 nine hundred chariots of iron, and his troops, from Harosheth-of-the-Gentiles to the Torrent of Kishon. Then Deborah said to 14 Barak, 'Up! This day the LORD gives Sisera into your hands. Already the LORD has gone out to battle before you.' So Barak came charging down from Mount Tabor with ten thousand men at his back. The 15 LORD put Sisera to rout with all his chariots and his army before Barak's onslaught; but Sisera himself dismounted from his chariot and fled on foot. Barak pursued the chariots 16 and the army as far as Harosheth, and the whole army was put to the sword and perished; not a man was left alive. Mean-17 while Sisera fled on foot to the tent of Jael wife of Heber the Kenite, because Jabin king of Hazor and the household of Heber the Kenite were at peace. Jael came out to meet 18 Sisera and said to him, 'Come in here, my lord, come in; do not be afraid.' So he went into the tent, and she covered him with a rug. He said to her, 'Give me some water to 19 drink; I am thirsty.' She opened a skin full of milk, gave him a drink and covered him up again. He said to her, 'Stand at the tent 20 door, and if anybody comes and asks if someone is here, say No.' But Jael, Heber's 21 wife, took a tent-peg, picked up a hammer, crept up to him, and drove the peg into his skull as he lay sound asleep. His brains oozed out on the ground, his limbs twitched, and he died. When Barak came up in pur-22 suit of Sisera, Jael went out to meet him and said to him, 'Come, I will show you the man you are looking for.' He went in with her, and there was Sisera lying dead with the tent-peg in his skull. That day God gave 23 victory to the Israelites over Jabin king of Canaan, and they pressed home their attacks 24 upon that king of Canaan until they had made an end of him.

The song of Deborah and Barak

That day Deborah and Barak son of Abino-**5** am sang this song:

For the leaders, the leaders[j] in Israel, 2
for the people who answered the call,
bless ye the LORD.

---

h of Beth-anath: or son of Anath. had flowing locks.   i wife of Lappidoth: or a spirited woman.   j Or For those who

3 Hear me, you kings; princes, give ear;
I will sing, I will sing to the LORD.
I will raise a psalm to the LORD the God of
Israel.
4 O LORD, at thy setting forth from Seir,
when thou camest marching out of the plains
of Edom,
earth trembled; heaven quaked;
the clouds streamed down in torrents.
5 Mountains shook in fear before the LORD,
the lord of Sinai,
before the LORD, the God of Israel.
6 In the days of Shamgar of Beth-anath,[k]
in the days of Jael, caravans plied no longer;
men who had followed the high roads
went round by devious paths.
7 Champions there were none,
none left in Israel,
until I,[l] Deborah, arose,
arose, a mother in Israel.
8 They chose new gods,
they consorted with demons.[m]
Not a shield, not a lance was to be seen
in the forty thousand of Israel.
9 Be proud at heart, you marshals of Israel;
you among the people that answered the
call,
bless ye the LORD.
10 You that ride your tawny she-asses,
that sit on saddle-cloths,
and you that take the road afoot,
ponder this well.
11 Hark, the sound of the players striking up
in the places where the women draw water!
It is the victories of the LORD that they commemorate there,
his triumphs as the champion of Israel.
Down to the gates came the LORD's people:
12 'Rouse, rouse yourself, Deborah,
rouse yourself, lead out the host.
Up, Barak! Take prisoners in plenty,
son of Abinoam.'
13 Then down marched the column[n] and its
chieftains,
the people of the LORD marched down[o] like
warriors.
14 The men of Ephraim showed a brave front
in the vale,
crying, 'With you, Benjamin! Your clans-
men are here!'
From Machir down came the marshals,
from Zebulun the bearers of the musterer's
staff.
15 Issachar joined with Deborah in the uprising,[p]
Issachar stood by Barak;
down into the valley they rushed.
But Reuben, he was split into factions,
great were their heart-searchings.
16 What made you linger by the cattle-pens

to listen to the shrill calling of the shepherds?[q]
17 Gilead stayed beyond Jordan;
and Dan, why did he tarry by the ships?
Asher lingered by the sea-shore,
by its creeks he stayed.
18 The people of Zebulun risked their very
lives,
so did Naphtali on the heights of the battlefield.

19 Kings came, they fought;
then fought the kings of Canaan
at Taanach by the waters of Megiddo;
no plunder of silver did they take.
20 The stars fought from heaven,
the stars in their courses fought against
Sisera.
21 The Torrent of Kishon swept him away,
the Torrent barred his flight, the Torrent of
Kishon;
march on in might, my soul!
22 Then hammered the hooves of his horses,
his chargers galloped, galloped away.
23 A curse on Meroz, said the angel of the LORD;
a curse, a curse on its inhabitants,
because they brought no help to the LORD,
no help to the LORD and the fighting men.
24 Blest above women be Jael,
the wife of Heber the Kenite;
blest above all women in the tents.
25 He asked for water: she gave him milk,
she offered him curds in a bowl fit for a
chieftain.
26 She stretched out her hand for the tent-peg,
her right hand to hammer the weary.
With the hammer she struck Sisera, she
crushed his head;
she struck and his brains ebbed out.
27 At her feet he sank down, he fell, he lay;
at her feet he sank down and fell.
Where he sank down, there he fell, done to
death.

28 The mother of Sisera peered through the
lattice,
through the window she peered and shrilly
cried,
'Why are his chariots so long coming?
Why is the clatter of his chariots so long
delayed?'
29 The wisest of her princesses answered her,
yes, she found her own answer:
30 'They must be finding spoil, taking their
shares,
a wench to each man, two wenches,
booty of dyed stuffs for Sisera,
booty of dyed stuffs,
dyed stuff, and striped, two lengths of striped
stuff—
to grace the victor's neck.'

---

k of Beth-anath: or son of Anath.　　　l Or you.　　　m Or satyrs.　　　n Prob. rdg.; Heb. survivor.
o Prob. rdg.; Heb. adds to me.　　　p in the uprising: prob. rdg.; Heb. my officers.　　　q Prob. rdg.; Heb.
adds Reuben was split into factions, great were their heart-searchings.

31 So perish all thine enemies, O LORD;
but let all who love thee be like the sun rising
in strength.

The land was at peace for forty years.

The Midianites conquer Israel

6 The Israelites did what was wrong in the
eyes of the LORD and he delivered them into
2 the hands of Midian for seven years. The
Midianites were too strong for Israel, and
the Israelites were forced to find themselves
hollow places in the mountains, and caves
3 and strongholds. If the Israelites had sown
their seed, the Midianites and the Amalekites and other eastern tribes would come up
4 and attack Israel. They then pitched their
camps in the country and destroyed the
crops as far as the outskirts of Gaza, leaving
nothing to support life in Israel, sheep or ox
5 or ass. They came up with their herds and
their tents, like a swarm of locusts; they and
their camels were past counting. They had
come into the land for its growing crop,*
6 and so the Israelites were brought to desti-
tution by the Midianites, and they cried to
7 the LORD for help. When the Israelites cried
to the LORD because of what they had suf-
8 fered from the Midianites, he sent them a
prophet who said to them, 'These are the
words of the LORD the God of Israel: I
brought you up from Egypt, that land of
9 slavery. I delivered you from the Egyptians
and from all your oppressors. I drove them
out before you and gave you their lands.
10 I said to you, "I am the LORD your God:
do not stand in awe of the gods of the
Amorites in whose country you are settling."
But you did not listen to me.'

The LORD visits Gideon

11 Now the angel of the LORD came and sat
under the terebinth at Ophrah which belonged to Joash the Abiezrite. His son
Gideon was threshing wheat in the winepress, so that he might get it away quickly
12 from the Midianites. The angel of the LORD
showed himself to Gideon and said, 'You
are a brave man, and the LORD is with you.'
13 Gideon said, 'But pray, my lord, if the LORD
really is with us, why has all this happened
to us? What has become of all those wonderful deeds of his, of which we have heard
from our fathers, when they told us how the
LORD brought us out of Egypt? But now the
LORD has cast us off and delivered us into
14 the power of the Midianites.' The LORD
turned to him and said, 'Go and use this
strength of yours, to free Israel from the
power of the Midianites. It is I that send

you.' Gideon said, 'Pray, my lord, how can 15
I save Israel? Look at my clan: it is the
weakest in Manasseh, and I am the least in
my father's family.' The LORD answered, 16
'I will be with you, and you shall lay low all
Midian as one man.' He replied, 'If I stand 17
so well with you, give me a sign that it is
you who speak to me. Please do not leave 18
this place until I come with my gift and lay
it before you.' He answered, 'I will stay until
you come back.' So Gideon went in, pre- 19
pared a kid and made an ephah of flour into
unleavened cakes. He put the meat in a
basket, poured the broth into a pot and
brought it out to him under the terebinth.
As he approached, the angel of God said to 20
him, 'Take the meat and the cakes, and put
them here on the rock and pour out the
broth', and he did so. Then the angel of the 21
LORD reached out the staff in his hand and
touched the meat and the cakes with the tip
of it. Fire sprang up from the rock and consumed the meat and the cakes; and the
angel of the LORD was no more to be seen.
Then Gideon knew that it was the angel of 22
the LORD and said, 'Alas, Lord GOD! Then
it is true: I have seen the angel of the LORD
face to face.' But the LORD said to him, 23
'Peace be with you; do not be afraid, you
shall not die.' So Gideon built an altar there 24
to the LORD and named it Jehovah-shalom.*
It stands to this day at Ophrah-of-the-
Abiezrites.

Gideon tears down the altar of Baal

That night the LORD said to Gideon, 'Take 25
a young bull of your father's, the yearling
bull,* tear down the altar of Baal which belongs to your father and cut down the sacred
pole which stands beside* it. Then build an 26
altar of the proper pattern* to the LORD your
God on the top of this earthwork;* take the
yearling bull and offer it as a whole-offering
with the wood of the sacred pole that you
cut down.' So Gideon took ten of his ser- 27
vants and did as the LORD had told him. He
was afraid of his father's family and his
fellow-citizens, and so he did it by night,
and not by day. When the citizens rose early 28

---

r for its growing crop: *or* and laid it waste.
rdg.; Heb. the second bull, seven years old.
w *Or* stronghold *or* refuge.

s *That is* the LORD is peace.   t the yearling bull: *prob.*
u *Or* on.   v of . . . pattern: *or* with the stones in rows.

in the morning, they found the altar of Baal overturned and the sacred pole which had stood beside it cut down and the yearling bull offered up as a whole-offering on the 29 altar which he had built. They asked each other who had done it, and, after searching inquiries, were told that it was Gideon son 30 of Joash. So the citizens said to Joash, 'Bring out your son. He has overturned the altar of Baal and cut down the sacred pole 31 beside it, and he must die.' But as they crowded round him Joash retorted, 'Are you pleading Baal's cause then? Do you think that it is for you to save him? Whoever pleads his cause shall be put to death at dawn. If Baal is a god, and someone has torn down his altar, let him take up his own 32 cause.' That day Joash named Gideon Jerubbaal,[x] saying, 'Let Baal plead his cause against this man, for he has torn down his altar.'

Gideon's fleece

33 All the Midianites, the Amalekites, and the eastern tribes joined forces, crossed the 34 river and camped in the Vale of Jezreel. Then the spirit of the LORD took possession of Gideon; he sounded the trumpet and the Abiezrites were called out to follow him. 35 He sent messengers all through Manasseh; and they too were called out. He sent messengers to Asher, Zebulun, and Naphtali, 36 and they came up to meet the others. Gideon said to God, 'If thou wilt deliver Israel 37 through me as thou hast promised—now, look, I am putting a fleece of wool on the threshing-floor. If there is dew only on the fleece and all the ground is dry, then I shall be sure that thou wilt deliver Israel through 38 me, as thou hast promised.' And that is what happened. He rose early next day and wrung out the fleece, and he squeezed enough dew 39 from it to fill a bowl with water. Gideon then said to God, 'Do not be angry with me, but give me leave to speak once again. Let me, I pray thee, make one more test with the fleece. This time let the fleece alone be dry, and all the ground be covered with dew.' 40 God let it be so that night: the fleece alone was dry, and on all the ground there was dew.

Gideon selects his army

7 Jerubbaal, that is Gideon, and all the people with him rose early and pitched camp at En-harod;[y] the Midianite camp was in the 2 vale to the north of the hill of Moreh. The LORD said to Gideon, 'The people with you are more than I need to deliver Midian into their hands: Israel will claim the glory for themselves and say that it is their own

GIDEON'S CONQUESTS

The Great Sea

Hill of Moreh
Valley of Jezreel
Abel-meholah •   • Tabbath
                          Succoth
Shechem
                          Penuel
        Ophrah
Bethel •

Scale of Miles
0   10   20   30   40

Dead Sea

strength that has given them the victory. Now make a proclamation for all the people 3 to hear, that anyone who is scared or frightened is to leave Mount Galud[z] at once and go back home.' Twenty-two thousand of them went, and ten thousand were left. The LORD then said to Gideon, 'There are 4 still too many. Bring them down to the water, and I will separate them for you there. When I say to you, "This man shall go with you", he shall go; and if I say, "This man shall not go with you", he shall not go.' So 5 Gideon brought the people down to the water and the LORD said to him, 'Make every man who laps the water with his tongue like a dog stand on one side, and on the other every man who goes down on his knees and drinks.' The number of those who lapped 6 was three hundred, and all the rest went down on their knees to drink, putting their hands to their mouths. The LORD said to 7 Gideon, 'With the three hundred men who lapped I will save you and deliver Midian into your hands, and all the rest may go home.' So Gideon sent all these Israelites 8 home, but he kept the three hundred, and they took with them the jars[a] and the trumpets which the people had. The Midianite camp was below him in the vale.

The Midianites are routed

That night the LORD said to him, 'Go down 9 at once and attack the camp, for I have delivered it into your hands. If you are afraid 10 to do so, then go down first with your servant Purah and listen to what they are saying. 11

---

x That is Let Baal plead.   *y That is* Spring of Fright.   *z Prob. rdg.; Heb.* Mount Gilead.   *a Prob.*
rdg.; Heb. provisions.

D

That will give you courage to go down and attack the camp.' So he and his servant Purah went down to the part of the camp 12 where the fighting men lay. Now the Midianites, the Amalekites, and the eastern tribes were so many that they lay there in the valley like a swarm of locusts; there was no counting their camels; in number they were like 13 grains of sand on the sea-shore. When Gideon came close, there was a man telling his companion a dream. He said, 'I dreamt that I saw a hard, stale barley-cake rolling over and over through the Midianite camp; it came to a tent, hit it*b* and turned it upside down, 14 and the tent collapsed.' The other answered, 'Depend upon it, this is the sword of Gideon son of Joash the Israelite. God has delivered Midian and the whole army into his hands.' 15 When Gideon heard the story of the dream and its interpretation, he prostrated himself. Then he went back to the Israelite camp and said, 'Up! The LORD has delivered the camp 16 of the Midianites into your hands.' He divided the three hundred men into three companies, and gave every man a trumpet 17 and an empty jar with a torch inside it. Then he said to them, 'Watch me: when I come to the edge of the camp, do exactly as I do. 18 When I and my men blow our trumpets, you too all round the camp will blow your trumpets, and shout, "For the LORD and for Gideon!"' 19 Gideon and the hundred men who were with him reached the outskirts of the camp at the beginning of the middle watch; the sentries had just been posted. They blew 20 their trumpets and smashed their jars. The three companies all blew their trumpets and smashed their jars, then grasped the torches in their left hands and the trumpets in their right, and shouted, 'A sword for the LORD 21 and for Gideon!' Every man stood where he was, all round the camp, and the whole 22 camp leapt up in a panic and fled. The three hundred blew their trumpets, and throughout the camp the LORD set every man against his neighbour. The army fled as far as Bethshittah in Zererah, as far as the ridge of 23 Abel-meholah by Tabbath. The Israelites from Naphtali and Asher and all Manasseh were called out and they pursued the Midian-24 ites. Gideon sent men through all the hill-country of Ephraim with this message: 'Come down and cut off the Midianites. Hold the fords of the Jordan against them as far as Beth-barah.' So all the Ephraimites were called out and they held the fords of 25 the Jordan as far as Beth-barah. They captured the two Midianite princes, Oreb and Zeeb. Oreb they killed at the Rock of Oreb, and Zeeb by the Winepress of Zeeb, and they kept up the pursuit of the Midianites;

afterwards they brought the heads of Oreb and Zeeb across the Jordan to Gideon.

The men of Ephraim said to Gideon, 'Why **8** have you treated us like this? Why did you not summon us when you went to fight Midian?'; and they reproached him violently. But he said to them, 'What have I 2 done compared with you? Are not Ephraim's gleanings better than the whole vintage of Abiezer? God has delivered Oreb and Zeeb, 3 the princes of Midian, into your hands. What have I done compared with you?' At these words of his, their anger died down.

Gideon captures the kings of Midian

Gideon came to the Jordan, and he and his 4 three hundred men crossed over to continue the pursuit, weary though they were. He 5 said to the men of Succoth, 'Will you give these men of mine some bread, for they are weary, and I am pursuing Zebah and Zalmunna, the kings of Midian?' But the chief 6 men of Succoth replied, 'Are Zebah and Zalmunna already in your hands, that we should give your army bread?' Gideon said, 7 'For that, when the LORD delivers Zebah and Zalmunna into my hands, I will thresh your bodies with desert thorns and briars.' He went on from there to Penuel and made 8 the same request; the men of Penuel answered like the men of Succoth. He said to 9 the men of Penuel, 'When I return safely, I will pull down your castle.'

Zebah and Zalmunna were in Karkor with 10 their army of fifteen thousand men. These were all that remained of the whole host of the eastern tribes; a hundred and twenty thousand armed men had fallen in battle. Gideon advanced along the track used by 11 the tent-dwellers east of Nobah and Jogbehah, and his attack caught the army when they were off their guard. Zebah and Zal-12 munna fled; but he went in pursuit of these Midianite kings and captured them both; and their whole army melted away.

As Gideon son of Joash was returning 13 from the battle by the Ascent of Heres, he 14 caught a young man from Succoth. He questioned him, and one by one he numbered off the names of the rulers of Succoth and its elders, seventy-seven in all. Gideon 15 then came to the men of Succoth and said, 'Here are Zebah and Zalmunna, about whom you taunted me. "Are Zebah and Zalmunna", you said, "already in your hands, that we should give your weary men bread?"' Then he took the elders of the city 16 and he disciplined those men of Succoth with desert thorns and briars. He also pulled 17 down the castle of Penuel and put the men of the city to death. Then he said to Zebah 18 and Zalmunna, 'What of the men you killed

---

b Prob. rdg.; Heb. adds and it fell.

in Tabor?' They answered, 'They were like you, every one had the look of a king's son.'
19 'They were my brothers,' he said, 'my mother's sons. I swear by the LORD, if you had let them live I would not have killed
20 you'; and he said to his eldest son Jether, 'Up with you, and kill them.' But he was still only a lad, and did not draw his sword,
21 because he was afraid. So Zebah and Zalmunna said, 'Rise up yourself and dispatch us, for you have a man's strength.' So Gideon rose and killed them both, and he took the crescents from the necks of their camels.

Gideon's golden ephod

22 After this the Israelites said to Gideon, 'You have saved us from the Midianites; now you be our ruler, you and your son and your
23 grandson.' Gideon replied, 'I will not rule over you, nor shall my son; the LORD will
24 rule over you.' Then he said, 'I have a request to make: will every one of you give me the earrings from his booty?'—for the enemy wore golden earrings, being Ishmaelites.
25 They said, 'Of course, we will give them.' So a cloak was spread out and every man threw on to it the golden earrings from his
26 booty. The earrings for which he asked weighed seventeen hundred shekels of gold; this was in addition to the crescents and pendants and the purple cloaks worn by the Midianite kings, not counting the chains on
27 the necks of their camels. Gideon made it into an ephod and he set it up in his own city of Ophrah. All the Israelites turned wantonly to its worship, and it became a trap to catch Gideon and his household.

The death of Gideon

28 Thus the Midianites were subdued by the Israelites; they could no longer hold up their
29 heads. For forty years the land was at peace, all the lifetime of Gideon, that is Jerubbaal son of Joash; and he retired to his own home.
30 Gideon had seventy sons, his own offspring,
31 for he had many wives. He had a concubine who lived in Shechem, and she also bore him a son, whom he named Abimelech.
32 Gideon son of Joash died at a ripe old age and was buried in his father's grave at
33 Ophrah-of-the-Abiezrites. After his death, the Israelites again went wantonly to the worship of the Baalim and made Baal-
34 berith their god. They forgot the LORD their God who had delivered them from their
35 enemies on every side, and did not show to the family of Jerubbaal, that is Gideon, the loyalty that was due to them for all the good he had done for Israel.

Abimelech's insurrection

9 Abimelech son of Jerubbaal went to Shechem to his mother's brothers, and spoke with

them and with all the clan of his mother's family. 'I beg you,' he said, 'whisper a word 2 in the ears of the chief citizens of Shechem. Ask them which is better for them: that seventy men, all the sons of Jerubbaal, should rule over them, or one man. Tell them to remember that I am their own flesh and blood.' So his mother's brothers re- 3 peated all this to each of them on his behalf; and they were moved to come over to Abimelech's side, because, as they said, he was their brother. They gave him seventy pieces 4 of silver from the temple of Baal-berith, and with these he hired idle and reckless men, who followed him. He came to his father's 5 house in Ophrah and butchered his seventy brothers, the sons of Jerubbaal, on a single stone block, all but Jotham the youngest, who survived because he had hidden himself. Then all the citizens of Shechem and all 6 Beth-millo came together and made Abimelech king beside the old propped-up terebinth at Shechem.

Jotham's parable

When this was reported to Jotham, he went 7 and stood on the summit of Mount Gerizim. He cried at the top of his voice: 'Listen to me, you citizens of Shechem, and may God listen to you:
'Once upon a time the trees came to 8 anoint a king, and they said to the olive-tree: Be king over us. But the olive-tree 9 answered: What, leave my rich oil by which gods and men are honoured, to come and hold sway over the trees?
'So the trees said to the fig-tree: Then will 10 you come and be king over us? But the fig- 11 tree answered: What, leave my good fruit and all its sweetness, to come and hold sway over the trees?
'So the trees said to the vine: Then will 12 you come and be king over us? But the vine 13 answered: What, leave my new wine which gladdens gods and men, to come and hold sway over the trees?
'Then all the trees said to the thorn-bush: 14 Will you then be king over us? And the 15 thorn said to the trees: If you really mean to anoint me as your king, then come under the protection of my shadow; if not, fire

shall come out of the thorn and burn up the cedars of Lebanon.'

16 Then Jotham said, 'Now, have you acted fairly and honestly in making Abimelech king? Have you done the right thing by Jerubbaal and his household? Have you
17 given my father his due—who fought for you, and threw himself into the forefront of the battle and delivered you from the
18 Midianites? Today you have risen against my father's family, butchered his seventy sons on a single stone block, and made

(Judges 9. 10)

Abimelech, the son of his slave-girl, king over the citizens of Shechem because he is
19 your brother. In this day's work have you acted fairly and honestly by Jerubbaal and his family? If so, I wish you joy in Abimelech
20 and wish him joy in you! If not, may fire come out of Abimelech and burn up the citizens of Shechem and all Beth-millo; may fire also come out from the citizens of Shechem and Beth-millo and burn up Abi-
21 melech.' After which Jotham slipped away and made his escape; he came to Beer, and there he settled out of reach of his brother Abimelech.

Rise and fall of Abimelech

22 After Abimelech had been prince over Israel
23 for three years, God sent an evil spirit to make a breach between Abimelech and the citizens of Shechem, and they played him
24 false. This was done on purpose, so that the violent murder of the seventy sons of Jerubbaal might recoil on their brother Abimelech who did the murder and on the citizens of Shechem who encouraged him
25 to do it. The citizens of Shechem set men to

lie in wait for him on the hill-tops, but they robbed all who passed that way, and so the news reached Abimelech.

Now Gaal son of Ebed came with his 26 kinsmen to Shechem, and the citizens of Shechem transferred their allegiance to him. They went out into the country-side, picked 27 the early grapes in their vineyards, trod them in the winepress and held festival. They went into the temple of their god, where they ate and drank and reviled Abimelech. 'Who is 28 Abimelech,' said Gaal son of Ebed, 'and who are the Shechemites, that we should be his subjects? Have not this son of Jerubbaal and his lieutenant Zebul been subjects of the men of Hamor the father of Shechem? Why indeed should we be subject to him? If only 29 this people were in my charge I should know how to get rid of Abimelech! I would say to him, "Get your men together, and come out and fight." ' When Zebul the 30 governor of the city heard what Gaal son of Ebed said, he was very angry. He resorted 31 to a ruse and sent messengers to Abimelech to say, 'Gaal son of Ebed and his kinsmen have come to Shechem and are turning the city against you. Get up now in the night, 32 you and the people with you, and lie in wait in the open country. Then be up in the morn- 33 ing at sunrise, and advance rapidly against the city. When he and his people come out, do to him what the situation demands.' So 34 Abimelech and his people rose in the night, and lay in wait to attack Shechem, in four companies. Gaal son of Ebed came out and 35 stood in the entrance of the city gate, and Abimelech and his people rose from their hiding-place. Gaal saw them and said to 36 Zebul, 'There are people coming down from the tops of the hills', but Zebul replied, 'What you see is the shadow of the hills, looking like men.' Once more Gaal said, 'There are 37 people coming down from the central ridge of the hills, and one company is coming along the road of the Soothsayers' Tere-

38 binth.' Then Zebul said to him, 'Where are your brave words now? You said, "Who is Abimelech that we should be subject to him?" Are not these the people you despised? 39 Go out and fight him.' Gaal led the citizens of Shechem out and attacked Abimelech, 40 but Abimelech routed him and he fled. The ground was strewn with corpses all the way 41 to the entrance of the gate. Abimelech established himself in Arumah, and Zebul drove away Gaal and his kinsmen and allowed them no place in Shechem.

42 Next day the people came out into the open, and this was reported to Abimelech. 43 He on his side took his supporters, divided them into three companies and lay in wait in the open country; and when he saw the people coming out of the city, he rose and 44 attacked them. Abimelech and the company with him advanced rapidly and took up position at the entrance of the city gate, while the other two companies advanced against all those who were in the open and 45 struck them down. Abimelech kept up the attack on the city all that day and captured it; he killed the people in it, pulled the city 46 down and sowed the site with salt. When the occupants of the castle of Shechem heard of this, they went into the great hall*c* of the 47 temple of El-berith. It was reported to Abimelech that all the occupants of the castle 48 of Shechem had collected together. So he and his people went up Mount Zalmon carrying axes; there he cut brushwood, and took it and hoisted it on his shoulder. He said to his men, 'You see what I am doing; 49 be quick and do the same.' So each man cut brushwood; then they followed Abimelech and laid the brushwood against the hall, and burnt it over their heads. Thus all the occupants of the castle of Shechem died, about a thousand men and women.

50 Abimelech then went to Thebez, be-51 sieged it and took it. There was a strong castle in the middle of the city, and all the citizens, men and women, took refuge there. They shut themselves in and went on to the 52 roof. Abimelech came up to the castle and attacked it. As he approached the entrance 53 to the castle to set fire to it, a woman threw a millstone down on his head and fractured 54 his skull. He called hurriedly to his young armour-bearer and said, 'Draw your sword and dispatch me, or men will say of me: A woman killed him.' So the young man ran 55 him through and he died. When the Israelites saw that Abimelech was dead, they all went 56 back to their homes. It was thus that God requited the crime which Abimelech had committed against his father by the murder 57 of his seventy brothers, and brought all the wickedness of the men of Shechem on their own heads. The curse of Jotham son of Jerubbaal came home to them.

Tola and Jair judge Israel

After Abimelech, Tola son of Pua, son of 10 Dodo, a man of Issachar who lived in Shamir in the hill-country of Ephraim, came in his turn to deliver Israel. He was 2 judge over Israel for twenty-three years, and when he died he was buried in Shamir.

After him came Jair the Gileadite; he 3 was judge over Israel for twenty-two years. He had thirty sons, who rode thirty asses; 4 they had thirty towns in the land of Gilead, which to this day are called Havvoth-jair.*d* When Jair died, he was buried in Kamon. 5

The Ammonites oppress Israel

Once more the Israelites did what was wrong 6 in the eyes of the LORD, worshipping the Baalim and the Ashtaroth, the deities of Aram and of Sidon and of Moab, of the Ammonites and of the Philistines. They forsook the LORD and did not worship him. The LORD was angry with Israel, and he sold 7 them to the Philistines and the Ammonites, who*e* for eighteen years harassed and op- 8 pressed the Israelites who lived beyond the Jordan in the Amorite country in Gilead. Then the Ammonites crossed the Jordan to 9 attack Judah, Benjamin, and Ephraim, so that Israel was in great distress. The Israel- 10 ites cried to the LORD for help and said, 'We have sinned against thee; we have forsaken our God and worshipped the Baalim.' And 11 the LORD said to the Israelites, 'The Egyptians, the Amorites, the Ammonites, the Philistines; the Sidonians too and the 12 Amalekites and the Midianites—all these oppressed you and you cried to me for help; and did not I deliver you? But you forsook 13 me and worshipped other gods; therefore I will deliver you no more. Go and cry for 14 help to the gods you have chosen, and let them save you in the day of your distress.' But the Israelites said to the LORD, 'We have 15 sinned. Deal with us as thou wilt; only save us this day, we implore thee.' They banished 16 the foreign gods and worshipped the LORD; and he could endure no longer to see the plight of Israel.

Then the Ammonites were called to arms, 17 and they encamped in Gilead, while the Israelites assembled and encamped in Mizpah. The people of Gilead and their chief 18 men said to one another, 'If any man will strike the first blow at the Ammonites, he shall be lord over the inhabitants of Gilead.'

Jephthah rules in Gilead

Jephthah the Gileadite was a great warrior; 11 he was the son of Gilead by a prostitute. But 2

c Or vault.   *d That is* Tent-villages of Jair.   *e Prob. rdg.; Heb. adds* in that year.

Gilead had a wife who bore him several sons, and when they grew up they drove Jephthah away; they said to him, 'You have no inheritance in our father's house; you are 3 another woman's son.' So Jephthah, to escape his brothers, went away and settled in the land of Tob, and swept up a number of idle men who followed him.

4 The time came when the Ammonites 5 made war on Israel, and when the fighting began, the elders of Gilead went to fetch 6 Jephthah from the land of Tob. They said to him, 'Come and be our commander so 7 that we can fight the Ammonites.' But Jephthah said to the elders of Gilead, 'You drove me from my father's house in hatred. Why come to me now when you are in 8 trouble?' 'It is because of that', they replied, 'that we have turned to you now. Come with us and fight the Ammonites, and become lord over all the inhabitants of Gilead.' 9 Jephthah said to them, 'If you ask me back to fight the Ammonites and if the LORD delivers them into my hands, then I will be 10 your lord.' The elders of Gilead said again to Jephthah, 'We swear by the LORD, who shall be witness between us, that we will do 11 what you say.' Jephthah then went with the elders of Gilead, and the people made him their lord and commander. And at Mizpah, in the presence of the LORD, Jephthah repeated all that he had said.

Jephthah and the king of Ammon

12 Jephthah sent a mission to the king of Ammon to ask what quarrel he had with them that made him invade their country. 13 The king gave Jephthah's men this answer: 'When the Israelites came up from Egypt, they took our land from the Arnon as far as the Jabbok and the Jordan. Give us back 14 these lands in peace.' Jephthah sent a second 15 mission to the king of Ammon, and they said, 'This is Jephthah's answer: Israel did not take either the Moabite country or the 16 Ammonite country. When they came up from Egypt, the Israelites passed through the wilderness to the Red Sea*f* and came to 17 Kadesh. They then sent envoys to the king of Edom asking him to grant them passage through his country, but the king of Edom would not hear of it. They sent also to the king of Moab, but he was not willing; so 18 Israel remained in Kadesh. They then passed through the wilderness, skirting Edom and Moab, and kept to the east of Moab. They encamped beside the Arnon, but they did not enter Moabite territory, because the 19 Arnon is the frontier of Moab. Israel then sent envoys to the king of the Amorites, Sihon king of Heshbon, asking him to give them free passage through his country to

their destination. But Sihon would not grant 20 Israel free passage through his territory; he mustered all his people, encamped in Jahaz and fought Israel. But the LORD the God of 21 Israel delivered Sihon and all his people into the hands of Israel; they defeated them and occupied all the territory of the Amorites in that region. They took all the Amorite terri- 22 tory from the Arnon to the Jabbok and from the wilderness to the Jordan. The LORD the 23 God of Israel drove out the Amorites for the benefit of his people Israel. And do you now propose to take their place? It is for 24 you to possess whatever Kemosh your god gives you; and all that the LORD our God gave us as we advanced is ours. For that 25 matter, are you any better than Balak son of Zippor, king of Moab? Did he ever quarrel with Israel or attack them? For three hun- 26 dred years Israelites have lived in Heshbon and its dependent villages, in Aroer and its villages, and in all the towns by the Arnon. Why did you not oust*g* them during all that time? We have done you no wrong; it is you 27 who are doing us wrong by attacking us. The LORD who is judge will judge this day between the Israelites and the Ammonites.' But the king of the Ammonites would not 28 listen to the message which Jephthah had sent him.

Jephthah's vow

Then the spirit of the LORD came upon 29 Jephthah and he passed through Gilead and Manasseh, by Mizpeh of Gilead, and from Mizpeh over to the Ammonites. Jephthah 30 made this vow to the LORD: 'If thou wilt deliver the Ammonites into my hands, then 31 the first creature that comes out of the door of my house to meet me when I return from them in peace shall be the LORD's; I will offer that as a whole-offering.' So Jephthah 32 crossed over to attack the Ammonites, and the LORD delivered them into his hands. He 33 routed them with great slaughter all the way from Aroer to Minnith, taking twenty towns, and as far as Abel-keramim. Thus Israel crushed Ammon. But when Jephthah came 34 to his house in Mizpah, who should come out to meet him with tambourines and dances but his daughter, and she his only child; he had no other, neither son nor daughter. When he saw her, he rent his 35 clothes and said, 'Alas, my daughter, you have broken my heart, such trouble you have brought upon me. I have made a vow to the LORD and I cannot go back.' She replied, 36 'Father, you have made a vow to the LORD; do to me what you have solemnly vowed, since the LORD has avenged you on the Ammonites, your enemies. But, father, grant 37 me this one favour. For two months let me

f Or the Sea of Reeds.   *g Or recover.*

be, that I may roam[h] the hills with my companions and mourn that I must die a virgin.'
38 'Go', he said, and he let her depart for two months. She went with her companions and
39 mourned her virginity on the hills. At the end of two months she came back to her father, and he fulfilled the vow he had made;
40 she died a virgin. It became a tradition that the daughters of Israel should go year by year and commemorate the fate of Jephthah's daughter, four days in every year.

The Gileadites defeat Ephraim

12 The Ephraimites mustered their forces and crossed over to Zaphon. They said to Jephthah, 'Why did you march against the Ammonites and not summon us to go with you? We will burn your house over your
2 head.' Jephthah answered, 'I and my people had a feud with the Ammonites, and had I appealed to you for help, you would not
3 have saved us[i] from them. When I saw that we were not to look for help from you, I took my life in my hands and marched against the Ammonites, and the LORD delivered them into my power. Why then do you attack
4 me today?' Jephthah then mustered all the men of Gilead and fought Ephraim, and the
5 Gileadites defeated them. The Gileadites seized the fords of the Jordan and held them against Ephraim. When any Ephraimite who had escaped begged leave to cross, the men of Gilead asked him, 'Are you an Ephraim-
6 ite?', and if he said, 'No', they would retort, 'Say Shibboleth.' He would say 'Sibboleth', and because he could not pronounce the word properly, they seized him and killed him at the fords of the Jordan. At that time forty-two thousand men of Ephraim lost their lives.

Ibzan, Elon, and Abdon judge Israel

7 Jephthah was judge over Israel for six years; when he died he was buried in his own city
8 in Gilead. After him Ibzan of Bethlehem was
9 judge over Israel. He had thirty sons and thirty daughters. He gave away the thirty daughters in marriage and brought in thirty girls for his sons. He was judge over Israel
10 for seven years, and when he died he was buried in Bethlehem.
11 After him Elon the Zebulunite was judge
12 over Israel for ten years. When he died, he was buried in Aijalon in the land of Zebulun.
13 Next Abdon son of Hillel the Pirathonite
14 was judge over Israel. He had forty sons and thirty grandsons, who rode each on his own ass. He was judge over Israel for eight years;
15 and when he died he was buried in Pirathon in the land of Ephraim on the hill of the Amalekite.

SAMSON'S EXPLOITS

DAN
Valley of Sorek
Zorah • Eshtaol
• Lehi
The Great Sea
Ashkelon Timnath
• Gaza
PHILISTINES

The birth of Samson

Once more the Israelites did what was wrong **13** in the eyes of the LORD, and he delivered them into the hands of the Philistines for forty years.
2 There was a man from Zorah of the tribe of Dan whose name was Manoah and whose
3 wife was barren and childless. The angel of the LORD appeared to her and said, 'You are barren and have no child, but you shall
4 conceive and give birth to a son. Now you must do as I say: be careful to drink no wine or strong drink, and to eat no forbidden
5 food; you will conceive and give birth to a son, and no razor shall touch his head, for the boy is to be a Nazirite consecrated to God from the day of his birth. He will strike the first blow to deliver Israel from the power
6 of the Philistines.' The woman went and told her husband; she said to him, 'A man of God came to me; his appearance was that of an[j] angel of God, most terrible to see.
7 I did not ask him where he came from nor did he tell me his name. He said to me, "You shall conceive and give birth to a son. From this time onwards drink no wine or strong drink and eat no forbidden food, for the boy is to be a Nazirite consecrated to God
8 from his birth to the day of his death."' Manoah prayed to the LORD, 'If it please thee, O LORD, let the man of God whom thou didst send come again to tell us what we are to do with the boy who is to be born.'
9 God heard Manoah's prayer, and the angel of God came again to the woman, who was sitting in the fields; her husband was not
10 with her. The woman ran quickly and said to him, 'The man who came to me the other day has appeared to me again.' Manoah
11 went with her at once and approached the man and said, 'Was it you who talked with
12 my wife?' He said, 'Yes, it was I.' 'Now when your words come true,' Manoah said,

---

h Or that I may go down country to . . .   *i and had I . . . saved us: or I did appeal to you for help, but*
you would not save us . . .   *j Or the.*

'what kind of boy will he be and what will he
13 do?' The angel of the LORD answered him,
'Your wife must be careful to do all that I
14 told her: she must not taste anything that
comes from the vine. She must drink no
wine or strong drink, and she must eat no
forbidden food. She must do what I say.'
15 Manoah said to the angel of the LORD, 'May
we urge you to stay? Let us prepare a kid
16 for you.' The angel of the LORD replied,
'Though you urge me to stay, I will not eat
your food; but prepare a whole-offering if
you will, and offer that to the LORD.'
Manoah did not perceive that he was the
17 angel of the LORD and said to him, 'What is
your name? For we shall want to honour
18 you when your words come true.' The angel
of the LORD said to him, 'How can you ask
19 my name? It is a name of wonder.' Manoah
took a kid with the proper grain-offering,
and offered it on the rock to the LORD, to
him whose works are full of wonder. And
while Manoah and his wife were watching,
20 the flame went up from the altar towards
heaven, and the angel of the LORD went up
in the flame; and seeing this, Manoah and
21 his wife fell on their faces. The angel of the
LORD did not appear again to Manoah and
his wife; and Manoah knew that he was the
22 angel of the LORD. He said to his wife, 'We
23 are doomed to die, we have seen God',^k but
she replied, 'If the LORD had wanted to kill
us, he would not have accepted a whole-
offering and a grain-offering at our hands;
he would not now have let us see and hear
24-25 all this.' The woman gave birth to a son and
named him Samson. The boy grew up in
Mahaneh-dan between Zorah and Eshtaol,
and the LORD blessed him, and the spirit of
the LORD began to drive him hard.

Samson's riddle

14 Samson went down to Timnath, and there he
2 saw a woman, one of the Philistines. When
he came back, he told his father and mother
that he had seen a Philistine woman in
Timnath and asked them to get her for him
3 as his wife. His father and mother said to
him, 'Is there no woman among your cousins
or in all our own people? Must you go and
marry one of the uncircumcised Philistines?'
But Samson said to his father, 'Get her for
4 me, because she pleases me.' His father and
mother did not know that the LORD was at
work in this, seeking an opportunity against
the Philistines, who at that time were masters
of Israel.
5 Samson^l went down to Timnath and,
when he reached the vineyards there, a young
6 lion came at him growling. The spirit of the
LORD suddenly seized him and, having no

weapon in his hand, he tore the lion in pieces
as if it were a kid. He did not tell his parents
what he had done. Then he went down and 7
spoke to the woman, and she pleased him.
After a time he went down again to take her 8
to wife; he turned aside to look at the carcass
of the lion, and he saw a swarm of bees in it,
and honey. He scraped the honey into his 9
hands and went on, eating as he went. When
he came to his father and mother, he gave
them some and they ate it; but he did not
tell them that he had scraped the honey out
of the lion's carcass. His father went down 10
to see the woman, and Samson gave a feast
there as the custom of young men was.
When the people saw him, they brought 11
thirty young men to be his escort. Samson 12
said to them, 'Let me ask you a riddle. If
you can guess it during the seven days of the
feast, I will give you thirty lengths of linen
and thirty changes of clothing; but if you 13
cannot guess the answer, then you shall give
me thirty lengths of linen and thirty changes
of clothing.' 'Tell us your riddle,' they said;
'let us hear it.' So he said to them: 14

Out of the eater came something to eat;
out of the strong came something sweet.

At the end of three days they had failed to
guess the riddle. On the fourth day they said 15
to Samson's wife, 'Coax your husband and
make him tell you the riddle, or we shall burn
you and your father's house. Did you invite
us here to beggar us?' So Samson's wife 16
wept over him and said, 'You do not love
me, you only hate me. You have asked my
kinsfolk a riddle and you have not told it to
me.' He said to her, 'I have not told it even
to my father and mother; and am I to tell
you?' But she wept over him every day until 17
the seven feast days were ended, and on the
seventh day, because she pestered him, he
told her, and she told the riddle to her kinsfolk. So that same day the men of the city 18
said to Samson before he entered the bridal
chamber:^m

What is sweeter than honey?
What is stronger than a lion?

and he replied, 'If you had not ploughed
with my heifer, you would not have found
out my riddle.' Then the spirit of the LORD 19
suddenly seized him. He went down to
Ashkelon and there he killed thirty men,
took their belts and gave their clothes to the
men who had answered his riddle; but he
was very angry and went off to his father's
house. And Samson's wife was given in 20
marriage to the friend who had been his
groomsman.

---

k Or a god.   l Prob. rdg.; Heb. adds and his father and mother.   m he entered . . . chamber: prob.
rdg.; Heb. the sun went down.

Samson burns the Philistines' corn

15 After a while, during the time of wheat harvest, Samson went to visit his wife, taking a kid as a present for her. He said, 'I am going to my wife in our bridal chamber', but 2 her father would not let him in. He said, 'I was sure that you hated her, so I gave her in marriage to your groomsman. Her young sister is better than she—take her instead.' 3 But Samson said, 'This time I will settle my score with the Philistines; I will do them 4 some real harm.' So he went and caught three hundred jackals and got some torches; he tied the jackals tail to tail and fastened a 5 torch between each pair of tails. He then set the torches alight and turned the jackals loose in the standing corn of the Philistines. He burnt up standing corn and stooks as 6 well, vineyards and olive groves. The Philistines said, 'Who has done this?' They were told that it was Samson, because the Timnite, his father-in-law, had taken his wife and given her to his groomsman. So the Philistines came and burnt her and her 7 father. Samson said, 'If you do things like this, I swear I will be revenged upon you 8 before I have done.' He smote them hip and thigh with great slaughter; and after that he went down to live in a cave in the Rock of Etam.

PHILISTINES

Samson defeats the Philistines at Lehi

9 The Philistines came up and pitched camp 10 in Judah, and overran Lehi. The men of Judah said, 'Why have you attacked us?' They answered, 'We have come to take Samson prisoner and serve him as he served 11 us.' So three thousand men from Judah went down to the cave in the Rock of Etam. They said to Samson, 'Surely you know that the Philistines are our masters? Now see what you have brought upon us.' He answered, 'I only served them as they had served me.' 12 They said to him, 'We have come down to bind you and hand you over to the Philistines.' 'Then you must swear to me', he said, 'that you will not set upon me your- 13 selves.' They answered, 'No; we will only bind you and hand you over to them, we will not kill you.' So they bound him with two new ropes and brought him up from the cave in the Rock. He came to Lehi, and 14 when they met him, the Philistines shouted in triumph; but the spirit of the LORD suddenly seized him, the ropes on his arms became like burnt tow and his bonds melted away. He found the jaw-bone of an ass, all 15 raw, and picked it up and slew a thousand men. He made this saying: 16

With the jaw-bone of an ass[n] I have flayed
     them like asses;[o]
with the jaw-bone of an ass I have slain a
     thousand men.

When he had said his say, he threw away 17 the jaw-bone; and he called that place Ramath-lehi.[p] He began to feel very thirsty 18 and cried aloud to the LORD, 'Thou hast let me, thy servant, win this great victory, and must I now die of thirst and fall into the hands of the uncircumcised?' God split 19 open the Hollow of Lehi and water came out of it. Samson drank, his strength returned and he revived. This is why the spring in Lehi is called En-hakkore[q] to this day.

Samson was judge over Israel for twenty 20 years in the days of the Philistines.

Samson at Gaza

Samson went to Gaza, and there he saw a **16** prostitute and went in to spend the night with her. The people of Gaza heard that 2 Samson had come, and they surrounded him and lay in wait for him all that night at the city gate. During the night, however, they took no action, saying to themselves, 'When day breaks we shall kill him.' Samson 3 lay in bed till midnight; and when midnight came he rose, seized hold of the doors of the city gate and the two posts, pulled them out, bar and all, hoisted them on to his shoulders and carried them to the top of the hill east of Hebron.

Samson and Delilah

After this Samson fell in love with a woman 4 named Delilah, who lived in the valley of Sorek. The lords of the Philistines went up 5 country to see her and said, 'Coax him and find out what gives him his great strength, and how we can master him, bind him and so hold him captive; then we will each give you eleven hundred pieces of silver.' So 6 Delilah said to Samson, 'Tell me what gives you your great strength, and how you can be bound and held captive.' Samson replied, 7 'If they bind me with seven fresh bowstrings not yet dry, then I shall become as weak as any other man.' So the lords of the Philis- 8 tines brought her seven fresh bowstrings not yet dry, and she bound him with them.

n ass: *Heb.* hamor.   *o* I have . . . asses: *or* I have reddened them blood-red, *or* I have heaped them in heaps; *Heb.* hamor himmartim.   *p* That is Jaw-bone Hill.   *q* That is the Crier's Spring.

9 She had men already hidden in the inner room, and she cried, 'The Philistines are upon you, Samson!' But he snapped the bowstrings as a strand of tow snaps when it feels the fire, and his strength was not tamed.
10 Delilah said to Samson, 'I see you have made a fool of me and told me lies. Tell me this
11 time how you can be bound.' He said to her, 'If you bind me tightly with new ropes that have never been used, then I shall become
12 as weak as any other man.' So Delilah took new ropes and bound him with them. Then she cried, 'The Philistines are upon you, Samson!', while the men waited hidden in the inner room. He snapped the ropes off
13 his arms like pack-thread. Delilah said to him, 'You are still making a fool of me and have told me lies. Tell me: how can you be bound?' He said, 'Take the seven loose locks of my hair and weave them into the warp, and then drive them tight with the beater; and I shall become as weak as any other man.' So she lulled him to sleep, wove the seven loose locks of his hair into the warp,
14 and drove them tight with the beater, and cried, 'The Philistines are upon you, Samson!' He woke from sleep and pulled away
15 the warp and the loom with it.r She said to him, 'How can you say you love me when you do not confide in me? This is the third time you have made a fool of me and have not told me what gives you your great
16 strength.' She so pestered him with these words day after day, pressing him hard and
17 wearying him to death, that he told her his secret. 'No razor has touched my head,' he said, 'because I am a Nazirite, consecrated to God from the day of my birth. If my head were shaved, then my strength would leave me, and I should become as weak as any
18 other man.' Delilah saw that he had told her his secret; so she sent to the lords of the Philistines and said, 'Come up at once, he has told me his secret.' So the lords of the Philistines came up and brought the money
19 with them. She lulled him to sleep on her knees, summoned a man and he shaved the seven locks of his hair for her. She began to take him captive and his strength left him.
20 Then she cried, 'The Philistines are upon you, Samson!' He woke from his sleep and said, 'I will go out as usual and shake my-

self'; he did not know that the LORD had left him. The Philistines seized him, gouged 2 out his eyes and brought him down to Gaza. There they bound him with fetters of bronze, and he was set to grinding corn in the prison. But his hair, after it had been shaved, began 2 to grow again.

The death of Samson

The lords of the Philistines assembled to- 2 gether to offer a great sacrifice to their god Dagon and to rejoice before him. They said, 'Our god has delivered Samson our enemy into our hands.' The people, when they saw 2 him, praised their god, chanting:

Our god has delivered our enemy into our hands,
the scourge of our land who piled it with our dead.

When they grew merry, they said, 'Call 2 Samson, and let him fight to make sport for us.' So they summoned Samson from prison and he made sport before them all. They stood him between the pillars, and Samson 2 said to the boy who held his hand, 'Put me where I can feel the pillars which support the temple, so that I may lean against them.' The temple was full of men and women, and 2 all the lords of the Philistines were there, and there were about three thousand men and women on the roof watching Samson as he fought. Samson called on the LORD 2 and said, 'Remember me, O Lord GOD, re-member me: give me strength only this once, O God, and let me at one stroke be avenged on the Philistines for my two eyes.' He put 2 his arms round the two central pillars which supported the temple, his right arm round one and his left round the other, and braced himself and said, 'Let me die with the 3 Philistines.' Then Samson leaned forward with all his might, and the temple fell on the lords and on all the people who were in it. So the dead whom he killed at his death were more than those he had killed in his life. His brothers and all his father's family 3 came down, carried him up to the grave of his father Manoah between Zorah and Eshtaol and buried him there. He had been judge over Israel for twenty years.

Micah and the Levite

17 There was once a man named Micah from the hill-country of
2 Ephraim. He said to his mother, 'You remember the eleven hundred pieces of silver which were taken from you, and how you called down a curse on the thief in my hearing?

I have the money; I took it and now I will give it back to you.'s His mother said, 'May the LORD
3 bless you, my son.' So he gave the eleven hundred pieces of silver back to his mother, and she said, 'I now solemnly dedicate this money of mine to the LORD for the benefit of my son, to make a

carved idol and a cast image.' He 4 returned the money to his mother, and she took two hundred pieces of silver and handed them to a silversmith, who made them into an idol and an image, which stood in Micah's house.
This man Micah had a shrine, 5 and he made an ephod and tera-

r the warp . . . with it: *prob. rdg.; Heb. adds an unintelligible word.*   s and now . . . you: *transposed from verse 3.*

phim*t* and installed one of his sons to be his priest. In those days there was no king in Israel and every man did what was right in his own eyes.

7 Now there was a young man from Bethlehem in Judah, from the clan of Judah, a Levite named Ben-
8 gershom.*u* He had left the city of Bethlehem to go and find somewhere to live. On his way he came to Micah's house in the hill-
9 country of Ephraim. Micah said to him, 'Where have you come from?' He replied, 'I am a Levite from Bethlehem in Judah, and I am looking for somewhere to live.'
10 Micah said to him, 'Stay with me and be priest and father to me. I will give you ten pieces of silver
11 a year, and provide you with food and clothes.' The Levite agreed to stay with the man and was treated
12 as one of his own sons. Micah installed the Levite, and the young man became his priest and a mem-
13 ber of his household. Micah said, 'Now I know that the LORD will make me prosper, because I have a Levite for my priest.'

The Danites explore Laish

18 In those days there was no king in Israel and the tribe of the Danites was looking for territory to occupy, because they had not so far come into possession of the territory allotted to them among the tribes
2 of Israel. The Danites therefore sent out five fighting men of their clan from Zorah and Eshtaol to

prospect, with instructions to go and explore the land. They came to Micah's house in the hill-country of Ephraim and spent the night
3 there. While they were there, they recognized the speech of the young Levite; they turned there and then and said to him, 'Who brought you here? What are you doing? What
4 is your business here?' He said, 'This is all Micah's doing: he has hired me and I have become his
5 priest.' They said to him, 'Then inquire of God on our behalf whether our mission will be success-
6 ful.' The priest replied, 'Go in peace. Your mission is in the
7 LORD's hands.' The five men went on their way and came to Laish. There they found the inhabitants living a carefree life, in the same way as the Sidonians, a quiet, carefree folk, with no hereditary king to keep the country under his thumb.*v* They were a long way from the Sidonians, and had no contact
8 with the Aramaeans. So the five men went back to Zorah and Eshtaol, and when their kinsmen
9 asked their news, they said, 'Come and attack them. It is an excellent country that we have seen. Will you hang back and do nothing about it? Start off now and take
10 possession of the land. When you get there, you will find a people living a carefree life in a wide expanse of open country. God has delivered it into your hands, a place where there is no lack of anything on earth.'

The Danites steal Micah's gods

And so six hundred armed men 11 from the clan of the Danites set out from Zorah and Eshtaol. They 12 went up country and encamped in Kiriath-jearim in Judah: this is why that place to this day is called Mahaneh-dan;*w* it lies west of Kiriath-jearim. From there they 13 passed on to the hill-country of Ephraim and came to Micah's house. The five men who had been 14 to explore the country round Laish spoke up and said to their kinsmen, 'Do you know that in one of these houses there are now an ephod and teraphim, an idol and an image? Now consider what you had best do.' So they turned aside to Micah's 15 house and greeted him. The six 16 hundred armed Danites took their stand at the entrance of the gate, and the five men who had gone to 17 explore the country went indoors to take the idol and the image, ephod and teraphim, while the priest was standing at the entrance with the six hundred armed men. The five men entered Micah's house 18 and took the idol and the image, ephod and teraphim.*x* The priest asked them what they were doing, but they said to him, 'Be quiet; not 19 a word. Come with us and be our priest and father. Which is better, to be priest in the household of one man or to be priest to a whole tribe and clan in Israel?' This 20 pleased the priest; so he took the

---

t Or household gods.   *u* named Ben-gershom: *prob. rdg., cp. 18. 30; Heb.* he lodged there.   *v* with
no . . . thumb: *prob. rdg.; Heb.* and none humiliating anything in the land with inherited authority.   *w* That
is the Camp of Dan.   *x* *Prob. rdg.; Heb.* the idol of the ephod, and teraphim and image.

Bethlehem

ephod and teraphim, the idol and the image, and joined the com-
21 pany. They turned and went off, putting the dependants, the herds,
22 and the valuables in front. The Danites had gone some distance from Micah's house, when his neighbours were called out in pur-
23 suit and caught up with them. They shouted after them, and the Danites turned round and said to Micah, 'What is the matter with you?
24 Why have you come after us?' He said, 'You have taken my gods which I made for myself, you have taken the priest, and you have gone off and left me nothing. How dare you say, "What is the matter
25 with you?"' The Danites said to him, 'Do not shout at us. We are desperate men and if we fall upon you it will be the death of yourself
26 and your family.' With that the Danites went on their way and Micah, seeing that they were too strong for him, turned and went home.

Destruction of Laish

27 Thus they carried off the priest and the things Micah had made for himself, and attacked Laish, whose people were quiet and carefree. They put them to the sword and
28 set fire to their city. There was no one to save them, for the city was a long way from Sidon and they had no contact with the Aramaeans,^{y} although the city was in the vale near Beth-rehob. They rebuilt the
29 city and settled in it, naming it Dan after the name of their forefather Dan, a son of Israel; but its original
30 name was Laish. The Danites set up the idol, and Jonathan son of Gershom, son of Moses, and his sons were priests to the tribe of Dan until the people went into exile.
31 (They set up for themselves the idol which Micah had made, and it was there as long as the house of God was at Shiloh.)

A Levite and his concubine

19 In those days when no king ruled in Israel, a Levite was living in the heart of the hill-country of Eph-raim. He had taken himself a con-cubine from Bethlehem in Judah.
2 In a fit of anger she had left him and had gone to her father's house in Bethlehem in Judah. When she
3 had been there four months, her husband set out after her with his servant and two asses to appeal to her and bring her back. She brought him in to the house of her father, who welcomed him when he saw
4 him. His father-in-law, the girl's father, pressed him and he stayed with him three days, and they were well entertained during their visit.
5 On the fourth day, they rose early in the morning, and he prepared to

leave, but the girl's father said to his son-in-law, 'Have something to
6 eat first, before you go.' So the two of them sat down and ate and drank together. The girl's father said to the man, 'Why not spend the night
7 and enjoy yourself?' When he rose to go, his father-in-law urged him to stay, and again he stayed for the
8 night. He rose early in the morning on the fifth day to depart, but the girl's father said, 'Have something to eat first.' So they lingered till
9 late afternoon, eating and drinking together. Then the man stood up to go with his concubine and ser-vant, but his father-in-law said, 'See how the day wears on towards sunset. Spend the night here and enjoy yourself, and then rise early tomorrow and set out for home.'
10 But the man would not stay the night; he rose and left. He had reached a point opposite Jebus, that is Jerusalem, with his two
11 laden asses and his concubine, and when they were close to Jebus, the weather grew wild and stormy, and the young man said to his master, 'Come now, let us turn into this Jebusite town and spend the night
12 there.' But his master said to him, 'No, not into a strange town where the people are not Israelites; let us
13 go on to Gibeah. Come, we will go and find some other place, and spend the night in Gibeah or
14 Ramah.' So they went on until sunset overtook them; they were then near Gibeah which belongs to
15 Benjamin. They turned in to spend the night there, and went and sat down in the open street of the town; but nobody took them into his house for the night.
16 Meanwhile an old man was com-ing home in the evening from his work in the fields. He was from the hill-country of Ephraim, but he lived in Gibeah, where the people
17 were Benjamites. He looked up, saw the traveller in the open street of the town, and asked him where he was going and where he came
18 from. He answered, 'We are travel-ling from Bethlehem in Judah to the heart of the hill-country of Ephraim. I come from there; I have been to Bethlehem in Judah and I am going home, but nobody has
19 taken me into his house. I have straw and provender for the asses, food and wine for myself, the girl, and the young man; we have all
20 we need, sir.' The old man said, 'You are welcome, I will supply all your wants; you must not spend
21 the night in the street.' So he took him inside and provided fodder for the asses; they washed their feet,
22 and ate and drank. While they were enjoying themselves, some of the worst scoundrels in the town surrounded the house, hurling themselves against the door and

shouting to the old man who owned the house, 'Bring out the man who has gone into your house, for us to
23 have intercourse with him.' The owner of the house went outside to them and said, 'No, my friends, do nothing so wicked. This man is my guest; do not commit this out-rage. Here is my daughter, a virgin;^{z}
24 let me bring her^a out to you. Rape her^a and do to her^a what you please; but you shall not commit such an outrage against this man.' But the
25 men refused to listen to him, so the Levite took hold of his concubine and thrust her outside for them. They assaulted her and abused her all night till the morning, and when dawn broke, they let her go. The
26 girl came at daybreak and fell down at the entrance of the man's house where her master was, and lay there until it was light. Her
27 master rose in the morning and opened the door of the house to set out on his journey, and there was his concubine lying at the door with her hands on the threshold.
28 He said to her, 'Get up and let us be off'; but there was no answer. So he lifted her on to his ass and set
29 off for home. When he arrived there, he picked up a knife, and he took hold of his concubine and cut her up limb by limb into twelve pieces; and he sent them through the length and breadth of Israel. He told the
30 men he sent with them to say to every Israelite, 'Has the like of this happened or been seen from the time the Israelites came up from Egypt till today? Consider this among yourselves and speak your minds.' So everyone who saw them said, 'No such thing has ever hap-pened or been seen before.'

Preparing to attack Gibeah

20 All the Israelites, the whole com-munity from Dan to Beersheba and out of Gilead also, left their homes as one man and assembled before the LORD at Mizpah. The leaders
2 of the people and all the tribes of Israel presented themselves in the general assembly of the people of God, four hundred thousand foot-soldiers armed with swords; and
3 the Benjamites heard that the Israel-ites had gone up to Mizpah. The Israelites asked how this wicked
4 thing had come about, and the Levite, to whom the murdered woman belonged, answered, 'I and my concubine came to Gibeah in Benjamin to spend the night there.
5 The citizens of Gibeah rose against me that night and surrounded the house where I was, intending to kill me; and they raped my concu-bine and she died. I took her and
6 cut her in pieces, and sent them through the length and breadth of Israel, because of the filthy outrage

---

^{y} *Prob. rdg., cp. verse 7; Heb. men.*
Heb. them.

^{z} *Prob. rdg.; Heb. adds* and his concubine.

^{a} *Prob. rdg.;*

7 they had committed in Israel. Now it is for you, the whole of Israel, to say here and now what you think 8 ought to be done.' All the people rose to their feet as one man and said, 'Not one of us shall go back to his tent, not one shall return 9 home. This is what we will now do to Gibeah. We will draw lots for 10 the attack: and we will take ten men out of every hundred in all the tribes of Israel, a hundred out of every thousand, and a thousand out of every ten thousand, to collect provisions for the people for those who have taken the field against Gibeah in Benjamin to avenge the outrage committed in 11 Israel.' Thus all the Israelites to a man were massed against the town.

Israel defeats the Benjamites

12 The tribes of Israel sent men all through the tribe of Benjamin saying, 'What is this wicked thing which has happened in your midst? 13 Hand over to us those scoundrels in Gibeah, and we will put them to death and purge Israel of this wickedness.' But the Benjamites refused to listen to their fellow-14 Israelites. They flocked from their cities to Gibeah to go to war with 15 the Israelites, and that day they mustered out of their cities twenty-six thousand men armed with swords. There were also seven hundred picked men from Gibeah, 16 left-handed men, who could sling a stone and not miss by a hair's 17 breadth. The Israelites, without Benjamin, numbered four hundred thousand men armed with swords, 18 every one a fighting man. The Israelites at once moved on to Bethel, and there they sought an oracle from God, asking, 'Which of us shall attack Benjamin first?', and the LORD's answer was, 'Judah 19 shall attack first.' So the Israelites set out at dawn and encamped 20 opposite Gibeah. They advanced to do battle with Benjamin and drew up their forces before the 21 town. The Benjamites made a sally from Gibeah and left twenty-two thousand of Israel dead on the 23[b] field that day. The Israelites went up to Bethel,[c] lamented before the LORD until evening and inquired whether they should again attack their brother Benjamin. The LORD 22 said, 'Yes, attack him.' Then the Israelites took fresh courage and again formed up on the same 24 ground as the first day. So the second day they advanced against 25 the Benjamites, who sallied out from Gibeah to meet them and laid another eighteen thousand armed 26 men low. The Israelites, the whole people, went back to Bethel, where they sat before the LORD lamenting and fasting until evening, and they offered whole-offerings and shared-27 offerings before the LORD. In those days the Ark of the Covenant of 28 God was there, and Phinehas son of Eleazar, son of Aaron, served before the LORD.[d] The Israelites inquired of the LORD and said, 'Shall we again march out to battle against Benjamin our brother or shall we desist?' The LORD answered, 'Attack him: tomorrow I will de-liver him into your hands.' Israel 29 then posted men in ambush all round Gibeah.

On the third day the Israelites 30 advanced against the Benjamites and drew up their forces at Gibeah as they had before; and the Ben-31 jamites sallied out to meet the army. They were drawn away from the town and began the attack as before by killing a few Israelites, about thirty,[e] on the highways which led across open country, one to Bethel and the other to Gibeah. They thought they were defeating 32 them once again, but the Israelites had planned a retreat to draw them away from the town out on to the highways. Meanwhile the 33 main body of Israelites left their positions and re-formed in Baal-tamar, while those in ambush, ten thousand picked men all told, burst out from their position in the neighbourhood of Gibeah and 34 came in on the east of the town. There was soon heavy fighting; yet the Benjamites did not suspect the disaster that was threatening them. So the LORD put Benjamin 35 to flight before Israel, and on that day the Israelites killed twenty-five thousand one hundred Ben-jamites, all armed men.

The men of Benjamin now saw 36 that they had been defeated, for all that the Israelites, trusting in the ambush which they had set by Gibeah, had given way before them. The men in ambush made a 37 sudden dash on Gibeah, fell on the town from all sides and put all the inhabitants to the sword. The 38

b *Verses 22 and 23 transposed.*
the Ark.   e *Or about thirty wounded men.*

c to Bethel: *prob. rdg., cp. verses 18, 26; Heb. om.*   d *Or before*

Bethel

agreed signal between the Israelites and those in ambush[f] was to be a column of smoke sent up from the
39 town. The Israelites then faced about in the battle; and Benjamin began to cut down the Israelites, killing about thirty of them,[g] in the belief that they were defeating them as they had done in the first en-
40 counter. As the column of smoke began to go up from the town, the Benjamites looked back and thought the whole town was going
41 up in flames. When the Israelites faced about, the Benjamites saw that disaster had overtaken them
42 and were seized with panic. They turned and fled before the Israelites in the direction of the wilderness, but the fighting caught up with them and soon those from the town were among them, cutting
43 them down. They hemmed in the Benjamites, pursuing them without respite,[h] and overtook them at a
44 point to the east of Gibeah. Eighteen thousand of the Benjamites
45 fell, all of them fighting men. The survivors turned and fled into the wilderness towards the Rock of Rimmon. The Israelites picked off the stragglers on the roads, five thousand of them, and chased them until they had cut down and killed
46 two thousand more. Twenty-five thousand armed men of Benjamin fell in battle that day, all fighting
47 men. The six hundred who survived turned and fled into the wilderness as far as the Rock of Rimmon, and there they remained
48 for four months. The Israelites then turned back to deal with the Benjamites, and put to the sword the people in the towns and the cattle, every creature that they found; they also set fire to every town within their reach.

Wives for the Benjamites

21 In Mizpah the Israelites had bound themselves by oath that none of them would marry his daughter to
2 a Benjamite. The people now came

to Bethel and remained there in God's presence till sunset, raising their voices in loud lamentation.
3 They said, 'O LORD God of Israel, why has it happened in Israel that one tribe should this day be lost to
4 Israel?' Next day the people rose early, built an altar there and offered whole-offerings and shared-
5 offerings. At that the Israelites asked themselves whether among all the tribes of Israel there was anyone who did not go up to the assembly before the LORD; for under the terms of the great oath anyone who had not gone up to the LORD at Mizpah was to be put
6 to death. And the Israelites felt remorse over their brother Benjamin, because, as they said, 'This day Israel has lost one whole tribe.'
7 So they asked, 'What shall we do for wives for those who are left? We have sworn to the LORD not to give any of our daughters to them
8 in marriage. Is there anyone in all the tribes of Israel who did not go up to the LORD at Mizpah?' Now it happened that no one from Jabesh-gilead had come to the
9 camp for the assembly; so when they held a roll-call of the people, they found that no inhabitant of
10 Jabesh-gilead was present. Thereupon the community sent off twelve thousand fighting men with orders to go and put the inhabitants of Jabesh-gilead to the sword, men,
11 women, and dependants. 'This is what you shall do,' they said: 'put to death every male person, and every woman who has had intercourse with a man, but spare any who are virgins.' This they did.
12 Among the inhabitants of Jabesh-gilead they found four hundred young women who were virgins and had not had intercourse with a man, and they brought them to the camp at Shiloh in Canaan.
13 Then the whole community sent messengers to the Benjamites at the Rock of Rimmon to parley with them, and peace was pro-

claimed. At this the Benjamites 14 came back, and were given those of the women of Jabesh-gilead who had been spared; but these were not enough.
The people were still full of re- 15 morse over Benjamin because the LORD had made this gap in the tribes of Israel, and the elders of 16 the community said, 'What shall we do for wives for the rest? All the women in Benjamin have been massacred.' They said, 'Heirs there 17 must be for the remnant of Benjamin who have escaped! Then Israel will not see one of its tribes blotted out. We cannot give them 18 our own daughters in marriage because we have sworn that there shall be a curse on the man who gives a wife to a Benjamite.' Then 19 they bethought themselves of the pilgrimage in honour of the LORD, made every year to Shiloh, the place which lies to the north of Bethel, on the east side of the highway from Bethel to Shechem and to the south of Lebonah. They said 20 to the Benjamites, 'Go and hide in the vineyards and keep watch. 21 When the girls of Shiloh come out to dance, sally out of the vineyards, and each of you seize one of them for his wife; then make your way home to the land of Benjamin. Then, if their fathers or brothers 22 come and complain to us, say to them, "Let us keep them with your approval, for none of us has captured a wife in battle. Had you offered them to us, the guilt would be yours."'
All this the Benjamites did. They 23 carried off as many wives as they needed, snatching them as they danced; then they went their way and returned to their patrimony, rebuilt their cities and settled in them. The Israelites also dispersed by 24 tribes and families, and every man went back to his own patrimony.
In those days there was no king 25 in Israel and every man did what was right in his own eyes.

---

f Prob. rdg.; Heb. adds an unintelligible word.   g to cut . . . them: or to kill about thirty wounded men
among the Israelites.   h without respite: or from Nohah.

RUTH

Naomi and Ruth

1 LONG AGO, in the time of the Judges, there was a famine in the land, and a man from Bethlehem in Judah went to live in the Moabite country with his wife and his ² two sons. The man's name was Elimelech, his wife's name was Naomi, and the names of his two sons Mahlon and Chilion. They were Ephrathites from Bethlehem in Judah. They arrived in the Moabite country and there they stayed. ³ Elimelech Naomi's husband died, so that ⁴ she was left with her two sons. These sons married Moabite women, one of whom was called Orpah and the other Ruth. They had ⁵ lived there about ten years, when both Mahlon and Chilion died, so that the woman was bereaved of her two sons as well as of ⁶ her husband. Thereupon she set out with her two daughters-in-law to return home, because she had heard while still in the Moabite country that the LORD had cared ⁷ for his people and given them food. So with her two daughters-in-law she left the place where she had been living, and took the ⁸ road home to Judah. Then Naomi said to her two daughters-in-law, 'Go back, both of you, to your mothers' homes. May the LORD keep faith with you, as you have kept ⁹ faith with the dead and with me; and may he grant each of you security in the home of a new husband.' She kissed them and they ⁰ wept aloud. Then they said to her, 'We will ¹ return with you to your own people.' But Naomi said, 'Go back, my daughters. Why should you go with me? Am I likely to bear ² any more sons to be husbands for you? Go back, my daughters, go. I am too old to marry again. But even if I could say that I had hope of a child, if I were to marry this ³ night and if I were to bear sons, would you then wait until they grew up? Would you then refrain from marrying? No, no, my

daughters, my lot is more bitter than yours, because the LORD has been against me.' At ¹⁴ this they wept again. Then Orpah kissed her mother-in-law and returned to her people, but Ruth clung to her.

'You see,' said Naomi, 'your sister-in-law ¹⁵ has gone back to her people and her gods;ᵃ go back with her.' 'Do not urge me to go ¹⁶ back and desert you', Ruth answered. 'Where you go, I will go, and where you stay, I will stay. Your people shall be my people, and your God my God. Where you ¹⁷ die, I will die, and there I will be buried. I swear a solemn oath before the LORD your God: nothing butᵇ death shall divide us.' When Naomi saw that Ruth was determined ¹⁸ to go with her, she said no more, and the ¹⁹ two of them went on until they came to Bethlehem. When they arrived in Bethlehem, the whole town was in great excitement about them, and the women said, 'Can this be Naomi?' 'Do not call me Naomi,'ᶜ she ²⁰ said, 'call me Mara,ᵈ for it is a bitter lot that the Almighty has sent me. I went away full, ²¹ and the LORD has brought me back empty. Why do you call me Naomi? The LORD has pronounced against me; the Almighty has brought disaster on me.' This is how ²² Naomi's daughter-in-law, Ruth the Moabitess, returned with her from the Moabite country. The barley harvest was beginning when they arrived in Bethlehem.

Ruth gleans in the field of Boaz

Now Naomi had a kinsman on her husband's **2** side, a well-to-do man of the family of Elimelech; his name was Boaz. Ruth the ² Moabitess said to Naomi, 'May I go out to the cornfields and glean behind anyone who will grant me that favour?' 'Yes, go, my ³ daughter', she replied. So Ruth went gleaning in the fields behind the reapers. As it happened, she was in that strip of the fields which belonged to Boaz of Elimelech's family, and there was Boaz coming out from ⁴ Bethlehem. He greeted the reapers, saying, 'The LORD be with you'; and they replied, 'The LORD bless you.' Then he asked his ⁵ servant in charge of the reapers, 'Whose girl is this?' 'She is a Moabite girl', the servant ⁶ answered, 'who has just come back with Naomi from the Moabite country. She asked ⁷ if she might glean and gather among the swathes behind the reapers. She came and has been on her feet with hardly a moment's restᵉ from daybreak till now.' Then Boaz ⁸

ᵃ Or god. ᵇ I swear ... nothing but: or The LORD your God do so to me and more if ... ᶜ That is Pleasure. ᵈ That is Bitter. ᵉ Prob. rdg.; Heb. adds in the house.

said to Ruth, 'Listen to me, my daughter: do not go and glean in any other field, and do not look any further, but keep close to 9 my girls. Watch where the men reap, and follow the gleaners; I have given them orders not to molest you. If you are thirsty, go and 10 drink from the jars the men have filled.' She fell prostrate before him and said, 'Why are you so kind as to take notice of me when I 11 am only a foreigner?' Boaz answered, 'They have told me all that you have done for your mother-in-law since your husband's death, how you left your father and mother and the land of your birth, and came to a people 12 you did not know before. The LORD reward your deed; may the LORD the God of Israel, under whose wings you have come to take 13 refuge, give you all that you deserve.' 'Indeed, sir,' she said, 'you have eased my mind and spoken kindly to me; may I ask you as a favour not to treat me only as one of your 14 slave-girls?'ᶠ When meal-time came round, Boaz said to her, 'Come here and have something to eat, and dip your bread into the sour wine.' So she sat beside the reapers, and he passed her some roasted grain. She ate all she wanted and still had some left 15 over. When she got up to glean, Boaz gave the men orders. 'She', he said, 'may glean even among the sheaves; do not scold her. 16 Or you may even pull out some corn from the bundles and leave it for her to glean, without reproving her.'

Naomi's advice

17 So Ruth gleaned in the field till evening, and when she beat out what she had gleaned, it 18 came to about a bushel of barley. She took it up and went into the town, and her mother-in-law saw how much she had gleaned. Then Ruth brought out what she had saved from 19 her meal and gave it to her. Her mother-in-law asked her, 'Where did you glean today? Which way did you go? Blessings on the man who kindly took notice of you.' So she told her mother-in-law whom she had been working with. 'The man with whom I worked today', she said, 'is called Boaz.' 20 'Blessings on him from the LORD', said Naomi. 'The LORD has kept faith with the living and the dead. For this man is related 21 to us and is our next-of-kin.' 'And what is more,' said Ruth the Moabitess, 'he told me to stay close to his men until they had 22 finished all his harvest.' 'It is best for you, my daughter,' Naomi answered, 'to go out with his girls; let no one catch you in another 23 field.' So she kept close to his girls, gleaning with them till the end of both barley and wheat harvests; but she lived with her mother-in-law.

Ruth and Boaz at the threshing-floor

One day Ruth's mother-in-law Naomi said 3 to her, 'My daughter, I want to see you happily settled. Now there is our kinsman 2 Boaz; you were with his girls. Tonight he is winnowing barley at his threshing-floor. Wash and anoint yourself, put on your 3 cloak and go down to the threshing-floor, but do not make yourself known to the man until he has finished eating and drinking. But when he lies down, take note of the 4 place where he lies. Then go in, turn back the covering at his feet and lie down. He will tell you what to do.' 'I will do whatever you 5 tell me', Ruth answered. So she went down 6 to the threshing-floor and did exactly as her mother-in-law had told her. When Boaz 7 had eaten and drunk, he felt at peace with the world and went to lie down at the far end of the heap of grain. She came in quietly, turned back the covering at his feet and lay down. About midnight something disturbed 8 the man as he slept; he turned over and, lo and behold, there was a woman lying at his feet. 'Who are you?' he asked. 'I am your 9 servant, Ruth', she replied. 'Now spread your skirt over your servant, because you are my next-of-kin.' He said, 'The LORD 10 has blessed you, my daughter. This last proof of your loyalty is greater than the first; you have not sought after any young man, rich or poor. Set your mind at rest, my daughter. I will do whatever you ask; for, as the whole neighbourhood knows, you are a capable woman. Are you sure that I am the next- 11 of-kin? There is a kinsman even closer than I. Spend the night here and then in the 12 morning, if he is willing to act as your next-of-kin, well and good; but if he is not willing, I will do so; I swear it by the LORD. Now lie down till morning.' So she lay at 13 his feet till morning, but rose before one man could recognize another; and he said, 'It must not be known that a woman has been to the threshing-floor.' Then he said, 'Bring me the cloak you have on, and hold 14 it out.' So she held it out, and he put in six measures of barley and lifted it on her back, and she went to the town. When she 15 came to her mother-in-law, Naomi asked, 'How did things go with you, my daughter?' Ruth told her all that the man had done for her. 'He gave me these six measures 16 of barley,' she said; 'he would not let me come home to my mother-in-law empty-handed.' Naomi answered, 'Wait, my daugh- 17 ter, until you see what will come of it. He will not rest until he has settled the matter today.'

ᶠ *may I . . . slave-girls?: or* if you please, treat me as one of your slave-girls.

Boaz acquires Elimelech's property

4 Now Boaz had gone up to the city gate, and was sitting there; and, after a time, the next-of-kin of whom he had spoken passed by. 'Here,' he cried, calling him by name, 'come 2 and sit down.' He came and sat down. Then Boaz stopped ten elders of the town, and asked them to sit there, and they did so. 3 Then he said to the next-of-kin, 'You will remember the strip of field that belonged to our brother Elimelech. Naomi has returned from the Moabite country and is selling it. 4 I promised to open the matter with you, to ask you to acquire it in the presence of those who sit here, in the presence of the elders of my people. If you are going to do your duty as next-of-kin, then do so, but if not, someone must do it. So tell me, and then I shall know; for I come after you as next-of-kin.' He answered, 'I will act as next-of-kin.' 5 Then Boaz said, 'On the day when you acquire the field from Naomi, you also acquire Ruth the Moabitess, the dead man's wife, so as to perpetuate the name of the 6 dead man with his patrimony.' Thereupon the next-of-kin said, 'I cannot act myself, for I should risk losing my own patrimony. You must therefore do my duty as next-of-kin. I cannot act.' 7 Now in those old days, when property was redeemed or exchanged, it was the custom for a man to pull off his sandal and give it to the other party. This was the form 8 of attestation in Israel. So the next-of-kin said to Boaz, 'Acquire it for yourself', and 9 pulled off his sandal. Then Boaz declared to the elders and all the people, 'You are witnesses today that I have acquired from Naomi all that belonged to Elimelech and all that belonged to Mahlon and Chilion; 0 and, further, that I have myself acquired Ruth the Moabitess, wife of Mahlon, to be my wife, to perpetuate the name of the deceased with his patrimony, so that his name may not be missing among his kindred and at the gate of his native place. You are witnesses this day.' Then the elders and all 11 who were at the gate said, 'We are witnesses. May the LORD make this woman, who has come to your home, like Rachel and Leah, the two who built up the house of Israel. May you do great things in Ephrathah and keep a name alive in Bethlehem. May your 12 house be like the house of Perez, whom Tamar bore to Judah, through the offspring the LORD will give you by this girl.'

Boaz marries Ruth

So Boaz took Ruth and made her his wife. 13 When they came together, the LORD caused her to conceive and she bore Boaz a son. Then the women said to Naomi, 'Blessed 14 be the LORD today, for he has not left you without a next-of-kin. May the dead man's name be kept alive in Israel. The child will 15 give you new life and cherish you in your old age; for your daughter-in-law who loves you, who has proved better to you than seven sons, has borne him.' Naomi took the 16 child and laid him in her lap and became his nurse. Her neighbours gave him a name: 17 'Naomi has a son,' they said; 'we will call him Obed.' He was the father of Jesse, the father of David.

Genealogy from Perez to David

This is the genealogy of Perez: Perez was 18 the father of Hezron, Hezron of Ram, Ram 19 of Amminadab, Amminadab of Nahshon, 20 Nahshon of Salmon, Salmon of Boaz, Boaz 21 of Obed, Obed of Jesse, and Jesse of David. 22

D *

THE FIRST BOOK OF
SAMUEL

The birth of Samuel

1 THERE WAS A MAN from Ramatha-
im, a Zuphite from the hill-country of
Ephraim, named Elkanah son of Jeroham,
son of Elihu, son of Tohu, son of Zuph an
2 Ephraimite; and he had two wives named
Hannah and Peninnah. Peninnah had chil-
3 dren, but Hannah was childless. This man
used to go up from his own town every year
to worship and to offer sacrifice to the LORD
of Hosts in Shiloh. There Eli's two sons,
Hophni and Phinehas, were priests of the

LORD. On the day when Elkanah sacrificed, 4
he gave several shares of the meat to his
wife Peninnah with all her sons and daughters; but, although he loved Hannah, he 5
gave her only one share, because the LORD
had not granted her children. Further, 6
Hannah's rival used to torment her and
humiliate her because she had no children.
Year after year this happened when they 7
went up to the house of the LORD; her rival
used to torment her. Once when she was
in tears and would not eat, her husband 8
Elkanah said to her, 'Hannah, why are you

crying and eating nothing? Why are you so miserable? Am I not more to you than ten sons?' After they had finished eating and drinking at the sacrifice at Shiloh, Hannah rose in deep distress, and stood before the LORD and prayed to him, weeping bitterly. Meanwhile Eli the priest was sitting on his seat beside the door of the temple of the LORD. Hannah made a vow in these words: 'O LORD of Hosts, if thou wilt deign to take notice of my trouble and remember me, if thou wilt not forget me but grant me offspring, then I will give the child to the LORD for his whole life, and no razor shall ever touch his head.' For a long time she went on praying before the LORD, while Eli watched her lips. Hannah was praying silently; but, although her voice could not be heard, her lips were moving and Eli took her for a drunken woman. He said to her, 'Enough of this drunken behaviour! Go away till the wine has worn off.' 'No, sir,' she answered, 'I am a sober person, I have drunk no wine or strong drink, and I have been pouring out my heart before the LORD. Do not think me so degraded, sir; all this time I have been speaking out of the fullness of my grief and misery.' 'Go in peace,' said Eli, 'and may the God of Israel answer the prayer you have made to him.' Hannah said, 'May I be worthy of your kindness.' And she went away and took something to eat, no longer downcast. Next morning they were up early and, after prostrating themselves before the LORD, returned to their own home at Ramah. Elkanah had intercourse with his wife Hannah, and the LORD remembered her. She conceived, and in due time bore a son, whom she named Samuel, 'because', she said, 'I asked the LORD for him.'

Samuel is lent to the LORD

Elkanah, with his whole household, went up to make the annual sacrifice to the LORD and to redeem his vow. Hannah did not go with them, but said to her husband, 'When the child is weaned I will come up with him to enter the presence of the LORD, and he shall[a] stay there always.' Her husband Elkanah said to her, 'Do what you think best; stay at home until you have weaned him. Only, may the LORD indeed see your vow fulfilled.' So the woman stayed and nursed her son until she had weaned him; and when she had weaned him, she took him up with her. She took also a bull three years old, an ephah of meal, and a flagon of wine, and she brought him, child as he was, into the house of the LORD at Shiloh. They slaughtered the bull, and brought the boy

to Eli. Hannah said to him, 'Sir, as sure as you live, I am the woman who stood near you here praying to the LORD. It was this boy that I prayed for and the LORD has given me what I asked. What I asked I have received; and now I lend him to the LORD; for his whole life he is lent to the LORD.' And they prostrated themselves there before the LORD.

The song of Hannah

Then Hannah offered this prayer: **2**

My heart rejoices in the LORD,
in the LORD I now hold my head high;
my mouth is full of derision of my foes,
exultant because thou hast saved me.
    There is none except thee,   2
    none so holy as the LORD,
    no rock like our God.
Cease your proud boasting,   3
let no word of arrogance pass your lips;
for the LORD is a god of all knowledge:
he governs all that men do.

Strong men stand in mute[b] dismay   4
but those who faltered put on new strength.
Those who had plenty sell themselves for a   5
    crust,
and the hungry grow strong again.
The barren woman has seven children,
and the mother of many sons is left to
    languish.

The LORD kills and he gives life,   6
he sends down to Sheol, he can bring the
    dead up again.
The LORD makes a man poor, he makes him   7
    rich,
he brings down and he raises up.
He lifts the weak out of the dust   8
and raises the poor from the dunghill;
to give them a place among the great,
to set them in seats of honour.

For the foundations of the earth are the
    LORD's,
he has built the world upon them.
He will guard the footsteps of his saints,   9
while the wicked sink into silence and gloom;
not by mere strength shall a man prevail.

Those that stand against the LORD will be   10
    terrified
when the High God[c] thunders out of heaven.

---

a come up ... he shall: *or* bring him up, and he shall come into the presence of the LORD and ...   *b* in mute: *prob. rdg.; Heb. obscure.*   *c* the High God: *prob. rdg.; Heb. upon him.*

The LORD is judge even to the ends of the
earth,
he will give strength to his king
and raise high the head of his anointed
prince.

11 Then Elkanah went to Ramah with his
household, but the boy remained behind in
the service of the LORD under Eli the priest.

Wickedness of Eli's sons

12 Now Eli's sons were scoundrels and had no
13 regard for the LORD. The custom of the
priests in their dealings with the people was
this: when a man offered a sacrifice, the
priest's servant would come while the flesh
14 was stewing and would thrust a three-
pronged fork into the cauldron or pan or
kettle or pot; and the priest would take
whatever the fork brought out. This should
have been their practice whenever Israelites
15 came to sacrifice at Shiloh; but now under
Eli's sons, even before the fat was burnt,
the priest's servant came and said to the
man who was sacrificing, 'Give me meat to
roast for the priest; he will not accept what
has been already stewed, only raw meat.'
16 And if the man answered 'Let them burn
the fat first, and then take what you want',
he said, 'No, give it to me now, or I will take
17 it by force.' The young men's sin was very
great in the LORD's sight; for they brought
the LORD's sacrifice into general contempt.
18 Samuel continued in the service of the
LORD, a mere boy with a linen ephod fastened
19 round him. Every year his mother made him
a little cloak and took it to him when she
went up with her husband to offer the annual
20 sacrifice. Eli would give his blessing to
Elkanah and his wife and say, 'The LORD
grant you children by this woman in place
of the one for which you asked him.'*d* Then
they went home again.

21 The LORD showed his care for Hannah,
and she conceived and gave birth to three
sons and two daughters; meanwhile the boy
Samuel grew up in the presence of the LORD.

22 Eli, now a very old man, had heard how
his sons were treating all the Israelites, and
how they lay with the women who were
serving at the entrance to the Tent of the
23 Presence. So he said to them, 'Why do you
do such things? I hear from all the people
24 how wickedly you behave. Have done with
it, my sons; for it is no good report that I
hear spreading among the LORD's people.
25 If a man sins against another man, God will
intervene; but if a man sins against the
LORD, who can intercede for him?' For all
this, they did not listen to their father's
rebuke, for the LORD meant that they should
26 die. But the young Samuel, as he grew up,
commended himself to the LORD and to men.

Eli and his family condemned

Now a man of God came to Eli and said, 27
'This is the word of the LORD: You know
that I revealed myself to your forefather
when he and his family were in Egypt in
slavery in the house of Pharaoh. You know 28
that I chose him from all the tribes of Israel
to be my priest, to mount the steps of my
altar, to burn sacrifices and to carry*e* the
ephod before me; and that I assigned all the
food-offerings of the Israelites to your family.
Why then do you show disrespect for my 29
sacrifices and the offerings which I have
ordained? What makes you resent them?
Why do you honour your sons more than
me by letting them batten on the choicest
offerings of my people Israel? The LORD's 30
word was, "I promise that your house and
your father's house shall serve before me
for all time"; but now his word is, "I will
have no such thing: I will honour those who
honour me, and those who despise me shall
meet with contempt. The time is coming 31
when I will lop off every limb of your own
and of your father's family, so that no man
in your house shall come to old age. You 32
will even resent*f* the prosperity I give to
Israel; never again shall there be an old man
in your house. If I allow any to survive to 33
serve my altar, his eyes will grow dim and
his appetite fail, his issue will be weaklings
and die off. The fate of your two sons shall 34
be a sign to you: Hophni and Phinehas shall
both die on the same day. I will appoint for 35
myself a priest who will be faithful, who will
do what I have in my mind and in my heart.
I will establish his family to serve in perpetual succession before my anointed king.
Any of your family that still live will come 36
and bow humbly before him to beg a fee, a
piece of silver and a loaf, and will ask for a
turn of priestly duty to earn a crust of
bread."'

The LORD calls Samuel

So the child Samuel was in the LORD's **3**
service under his master Eli. Now in those
days the word of the LORD was seldom heard,
and no vision was granted. But one night 2
Eli, whose eyes were dim and his sight failing, was lying down in his usual place, while 3
Samuel slept in the temple of the LORD
where the Ark of God was. Before the lamp
of God had gone out, the LORD called him, 4
and Samuel answered, 'Here I am', and ran 5
to Eli saying, 'You called me: here I am.'
'No, I did not call you,' said Eli; 'lie down
again.' So he went and lay down. The LORD 6
called Samuel again, and he got up and went
to Eli. 'Here I am,' he said; 'surely you called
me.' 'I did not call, my son,' he answered;

d for which . . . him: or which you lent him.   *e Or wear.*   *f You . . . resent: prob. rdg.; Heb. obscure.*

7 'lie down again.' Now Samuel had not yet come to know the LORD, and the word of the LORD had not been disclosed to him.
8 When the LORD called him for the third time, he again went to Eli and said, 'Here I am; you did call me.' Then Eli understood that
9 it was the LORD calling the child; he told Samuel to go and lie down and said, 'If he calls again, say, "Speak, LORD; thy servant hears thee."' So Samuel went and lay down in his place.
10 The LORD came and stood there, and called, 'Samuel, Samuel', as before. Samuel answered, 'Speak; thy servant hears thee.'
11 The LORD said, 'Soon I shall do something in Israel which will ring in the ears of all
12 who hear it. When that day comes I will make good every word I have spoken against Eli and his family from beginning to end.
13 You are to[g] tell him that my judgement on his house shall stand for ever because[h] he knew of his sons' blasphemies against God[i]
14 and did not rebuke them. Therefore I have sworn to the family of Eli that their abuse of sacrifices and offerings shall never be expiated.'
15 Samuel lay down till morning and then opened the doors of the house of the LORD, but he was afraid to tell Eli about the vision.
16 Eli called Samuel: 'Samuel, my son', he
17 said; and he answered, 'Here I am.' Eli asked, 'What did the LORD say to you? Do not hide it from me. God forgive you if you hide one
18 word of all that he said to you.' Then Samuel told him everything and hid nothing. Eli said, 'The LORD must do what is good in his eyes.'
19 As Samuel grew up, the LORD was with him, and none of his words went unfulfilled.
20 From Dan to Beersheba, all Israel recognized that Samuel was confirmed as a pro-
21 phet of the LORD. So the LORD continued to appear in Shiloh, because he had revealed himself there to Samuel.[j]

The Philistines capture the Ark

4 So Samuel's word had authority throughout Israel. And the time came when the Philistines mustered for battle against Israel, and the Israelites went out to meet them. The Israelites encamped at Eben-ezer and the
2 Philistines at Aphek. The Philistines drew up their lines facing the Israelites, and when they joined battle the Israelites were routed by the Philistines, who killed about four
3 thousand men on the field. When the army got back to the camp, the elders of Israel asked, 'Why did the LORD let us be routed today by the Philistines? Let us fetch the Ark of the Covenant of the LORD from Shiloh to go with us and deliver us from the

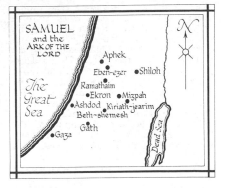

power of our enemies.' So the people sent 4 to Shiloh and fetched the Ark of the Covenant of the LORD of Hosts, who is enthroned upon the cherubim; Eli's two sons, Hophni and Phinehas, were there with the Ark. When the Ark came into the camp all the 5 Israelites greeted it with a great shout, and the earth rang with the shouting. The 6 Philistines heard the noise and asked, 'What is this great shouting in the camp of the Hebrews?' When they knew that the Ark of the LORD had come into the camp, they were 7 afraid and cried, 'A god has come into the camp. We are lost! No such thing has ever happened before. We are utterly lost! Who 8 can deliver us from the power of these mighty gods? These are the very gods who broke the Egyptians and crushed them in the wilderness. Courage, Philistines, and 9 act like men, or you will become slaves to the Hebrews as they were yours. Be men, and fight!' The Philistines then gave battle, 10 and the Israelites were defeated and fled to their homes. It was a great defeat, and thirty thousand Israelite foot-soldiers perished. The Ark of God was taken, and Eli's two 11 sons, Hophni and Phinehas, were killed.

The death of Eli and his sons

A Benjamite ran from the battlefield and 12 reached Shiloh on the same day, his clothes rent and dust on his head. When he arrived 13 Eli was sitting on a seat by the road to Mizpah, for he was deeply troubled about the Ark of God. The man entered the city with his news, and all the people cried out in horror. When Eli heard it, he asked, 'What 14 does this uproar mean?' The man hurried to Eli and told him. Eli was ninety-eight 15 years old and sat staring with sightless eyes; so the man said to him, 'I am the man who 16 has just arrived from the battle; this very day I have escaped from the field.' Eli asked,

---

g Prob. rdg.; Heb. I will. altered in Heb. to to them.   h because: prob. rdg.; Heb. in guilt.   i against God: prob. original reading, j Prob. rdg.; Heb. adds according to the word of the LORD.

17 'What is the news, my son?' The runner answered, 'The Israelites have fled from the Philistines; utter panic has struck the army; your two sons, Hophni and Phinehas, are 18 killed, and the Ark of God is taken.' At the mention of the Ark of God, Eli fell backwards from his seat by the gate and broke his neck, for he was old and heavy. So he died; he had been judge over Israel for 19 forty years. His daughter-in-law, the wife of Phinehas, was with child and near her time, and when she heard of the capture of the Ark and the deaths of her father-in-law and her husband, her labour suddenly began and 20 she crouched down and was delivered. As she lay dying, the women who attended her said, 'Do not be afraid; you have a son.' But she did not answer or heed what they 21 said. Then they named the boy Ichabod,[k] saying, 'Glory has departed from Israel' (in allusion to the capture of the Ark of God and the death of her father-in-law and her 22 husband); 'Glory has departed from Israel,' they said, 'because the Ark of God is taken.'

PHILISTINES

The Ark causes havoc

5 After the Philistines had captured the Ark of God, they brought it from Eben-ezer to 2 Ashdod; and there they carried it into the temple of Dagon and set it beside Dagon 3 himself. When the people of Ashdod rose next morning, there was Dagon fallen face downwards before the Ark of the LORD; so they took him and put him back in his place. 4 Next morning when they rose, Dagon had again fallen face downwards before the Ark of the LORD, with his head and his two hands lying broken off beside his platform; only 5 Dagon's body remained on it. This is why from that day to this the priests of Dagon and all who enter the temple of Dagon at Ashdod do not set foot upon Dagon's platform. 6 Then the LORD laid a heavy hand upon the people of Ashdod; he threw them into distress and plagued them with tumours, and their territory swarmed with rats.[l] There was death and destruction all through the 7 city. When the men of Ashdod saw this, they said, 'The Ark of the God of Israel shall not stay here, for he has laid a heavy hand upon 8 us and upon Dagon our god.' So they sent

and called all the Philistine princes together to ask what should be done with the Ark. They said, 'Let the Ark of the God of Israel be taken across to Gath.' They took it there, and after its arrival the hand of the LORD 9 caused great havoc in the city; he plagued everybody, high and low alike, with the tumours which broke out. Then they sent 10 the Ark of God on to Ekron. When the Ark reached Ekron, the people cried, 'They have brought the Ark of the God of Israel over to us, to kill us and our families.' So they 11 summoned all the Philistine princes and said, 'Send the Ark of the God of Israel away; let it go back to its own place, or it will be the death of us all.' There was death and destruction all through the city; for the hand of God lay heavy upon it. Even those 12 who did not die were plagued with tumours; the cry of the city went up to heaven.

The Philistines return the Ark

When the Ark of the LORD had been in their 6 territory for seven months, the Philistines 2 summoned the priests and soothsayers and asked, 'What shall we do with the Ark of the LORD? Tell us how we ought to send it back to its own place.' They answered, 'If 3 you send the Ark of the God of Israel back, do not let it go without a gift, but send it back with a gift for him by way of indemnity; then you will be healed and restored to favour; there is no reason why his hand should not be lifted from you.' When 4 they were asked, 'What gift shall we send back to him?', they answered, 'Send five tumours modelled in gold and five gold rats, one for each of the Philistine princes, for the same plague afflicted all of you and your princes. Make models of your tumours and 5 of the rats which are ravaging the land, and give honour to the God of Israel; perhaps he will relax the pressure of his hand on you, on your god, and on your land. Why should 6 you be stubborn like Pharaoh and the Egyptians? Remember how this god made sport of them until they let Israel go. Now 7 make a new wagon ready with two milch-cows which have never been yoked; harness the cows to the wagon, and take their calves from them and drive them back to their stalls. Then take the Ark of the LORD and 8 put it on the wagon, place in a casket, beside it, the gold offerings that you are sending to him as an indemnity, and let it go where it will. Watch it: if it goes up towards its own 9 territory to Beth-shemesh, then it is the LORD who has done us this great injury; but if not, then we shall know that his hand has not touched us, but we have been the victims of chance.'

The men did this. They took two milch- 10

k That is No-glory.   l Or mice.

Kiriath-jearim

cows and harnessed them to a wagon, shut-
11 ting up their calves in the stall, and they
placed the Ark of the LORD on the wagon
together with the casket, the gold rats, and
12 the models of their haemorrhoids. Then the
cows went straight in the direction of Beth-
shemesh; they kept to the same road, lowing
as they went and turning neither right nor
left, while the Philistine princes followed
them as far as the territory of Beth-shemesh.
13 Now the people of Beth-shemesh were har-
vesting their wheat in the Vale, and when
they looked up and saw the Ark they re-
14 joiced at the sight of it. The wagon came to
the farm of Joshua of Beth-shemesh and
halted there. Close by stood a great stone;
so they chopped up the wood of the wagon
and offered the cows as a whole-offering to
15 the LORD. Then the Levites lifted down the
Ark of the LORD and the casket containing
the gold offerings, and laid them on the
great stone; and the men of Beth-shemesh
offered whole-offerings and shared-offerings
16 that day to the LORD. The five princes of the
Philistines watched all this, and returned to
Ekron the same day.
17   These golden haemorrhoids which the
Philistines sent back as a gift of indemnity
to the LORD were for Ashdod, Gaza, Ashkelon, Gath, and Ekron, one for each city.
18 The gold rats were for all the towns of the
Philistines governed by the five princes, both
fortified towns and open settlements. The
great stone where they deposited the Ark
of the LORD stands witness on the farm of
Joshua of Beth-shemesh to this very day.
19   But the sons of Jeconiah did not rejoice
with the rest of the men of Beth-shemesh
when they welcomed the Ark of the LORD,
and he struck down seventy of them. The
20 people mourned because the LORD had
struck them so heavy a blow, and the men
of Beth-shemesh said, 'No one is safe in the
presence of the LORD, this holy God. To
21 whom can we send it, to be rid of him?' So
they sent this message to the inhabitants of
Kiriath-jearim: 'The Philistines have re-

turned the Ark of the LORD; come down and
take charge of it.' Then the men of Kiriath- **7**
jearim came and took the Ark of the LORD
away; they brought it into the house of
Abinadab on the hill and consecrated his
son Eleazar as its custodian.

Samuel judges Israel

So for a long while the Ark was housed in 2
Kiriath-jearim; and after some time, twenty
years later, there was a movement throughout Israel to follow the LORD. So Samuel 3
addressed these words to the whole nation:
'If your return to the LORD is whole-hearted,
banish the foreign gods and the Ashtaroth
from your shrines; turn to the LORD with
heart and mind, and worship him alone, and
he will deliver you from the Philistines.' The 4
Israelites then banished the Baalim and the
Ashtaroth, and worshipped the LORD alone.
Samuel summoned all Israel to an assem- 5
bly at Mizpah, so that he might intercede
with the LORD for them. When they had 6
assembled there, they drew water and poured
it out before the LORD and fasted all day,
confessing that they had sinned against the
LORD. It was at Mizpah that Samuel acted
as judge over Israel.
When the Philistines heard that the Israel- 7
ites had assembled at Mizpah, their princes
marched against them. The Israelites heard
that the Philistines were advancing, and they
were afraid. They said to Samuel, 'Do not 8
cease to pray for us to the LORD our God to
save us from the power of the Philistines.'

9 Thereupon Samuel took a sucking lamb, offered it up complete as a whole-offering and prayed aloud to the LORD on behalf of Israel; and the LORD answered his prayer.
10 As Samuel was offering the sacrifice and the Philistines were advancing to battle with the Israelites, the LORD thundered loud and long over the Philistines and threw them into confusion. They fled in panic before the Israelites,
11 who set out from Mizpah in pursuit and kept up the slaughter of the Philistines till they reached a point below Beth-car.
12 There Samuel took a stone and set it up as a monument between Mizpah and Jeshanah,*m* naming it Eben-ezer,*n* 'for to this point',
13 he said, 'the LORD has helped us.' Thus the Philistines were subdued and no longer encroached on the territory of Israel; and the hand of the LORD was against them as long
14 as Samuel lived. The cities they had captured were restored to Israel, and from Ekron to Gath the borderland was freed from their control. Between Israel and the
15 Amorites peace was maintained. Samuel acted as judge in Israel as long as he lived,
16 and every year went on circuit to Bethel and Gilgal and Mizpah; he dispensed justice at
17 all these places, returning always to Ramah. That was his home and the place from which he governed Israel, and there he built an altar to the LORD.

Israel demands a king

8 When Samuel grew old, he appointed his
2 sons to be judges in Israel. The eldest son was named Joel and the second Abiah; they
3 acted as judges in Beersheba. His sons did not follow in their father's footsteps but were intent on their own profit, taking bribes and perverting the course of justice.
4 So all the elders of Israel met, and came to
5 Samuel at Ramah and said to him, 'You are now old and your sons do not follow in your footsteps; appoint us a king to govern us,
6 like other nations.' But their request for a king to govern them displeased Samuel, and
7 he prayed to the LORD. The LORD answered Samuel, 'Listen to the people and all that they are saying; they have not rejected you, it is I whom they have rejected, I whom they
8 will not have to be their king. They are now doing to you just what they have done to me since I brought them up from Egypt: they have forsaken me and worshipped other
9 gods. Hear what they have to say now, but give them a solemn warning and tell them
10 what sort of king will govern them.' Samuel told the people who were asking him for a
11 king all that the LORD had said to him. 'This will be the sort of king who will govern you', he said. 'He will take your sons and make them serve in his chariots and with his

cavalry, and will make them run before his chariot. Some he will appoint officers over 12 units of a thousand and units of fifty. Others will plough his fields and reap his harvest; others again will make weapons of war and equipment for mounted troops. He will take 13 your daughters for perfumers, cooks, and confectioners, and will seize the best of your 14 cornfields, vineyards, and olive-yards, and give them to his lackeys. He will take a tenth 15 of your grain and your vintage to give to his eunuchs and lackeys. Your slaves, both men 16 and women, and the best of your cattle and your asses he will seize and put to his own use. He will take a tenth of your flocks, and 17 you yourselves will become his slaves. When 18 that day comes, you will cry out against the king whom you have chosen; but it will be too late, the LORD will not answer you.' The 19 people refused to listen to Samuel; 'No,' they said, 'we will have a king over us; then 20 we shall be like other nations, with a king to govern us, to lead us out to war and fight our battles.' So Samuel, when he had heard 21 what the people said, told the LORD; and he 22 answered, 'Take them at their word and appoint them a king.' Samuel then dismissed all the men of Israel to their homes.

Saul seeks the lost asses

There was a man from the district of Ben- 9 jamin, whose name was Kish son of Abiel, son of Zeror, son of Bechorath, son of Aphiah a Benjamite. He was a man of substance, and had a son named Saul, a young 2 man in his prime; there was no better man among the Israelites than he. He was a head taller than any of his fellows.

One day some asses belonging to Saul's 3 father Kish had strayed, so he said to his son Saul, 'Take one of the servants with you, and go and look for the asses.' They crossed 4 the hill-country of Ephraim and went through the district of Shalisha but did not find them; they passed through the district of Shaalim but they were not there; they passed through the district of Benjamin but again did not find them. When they had entered the district 5 of Zuph, Saul said to the servant with him, 'Come, we ought to turn back, or my father will stop thinking about the asses and begin to worry about us.' The servant answered, 6 'There is a man of God in the city here, who has a great reputation, because everything he says comes true. Suppose we go there; he may tell us something about this errand of ours.' Saul said, 'If we do go, what shall we 7 offer him? There is no food left in our packs and we have no present for the man of God, nothing at all.' The servant answered him 8 again, 'Wait! I have here a quarter-shekel of silver. I can give that to the man, to tell us

m Prob. rdg. (cp. 2 Chr. 13. 19); Heb. the tooth.   *n That is Stone of Help.*

10 *o* what we should do.' Saul said, 'Good! let us go to him.' So they went to the city where 9 the man of God was. (In days gone by in Israel, when a man wished to consult God, he would say, 'Let us go to the seer.' For what is nowadays called a prophet used to 11 be called a seer.) As they were going up the hill to the city they met some girls coming out to draw water and asked, 'Shall we find 12 the seer there?' 'Yes,' they said, 'the seer is ahead of you now; he has just*p* arrived in the city because there is a feast at the hill-13 shrine today. As you enter the city you will meet him before he goes up to the shrine to eat; the people will not start until he comes, for he has to bless the sacrifice before the company can eat. Go up now, and you will 14 find him at once.' So they went up to the city, and just as they were going in, there was Samuel coming towards them on his way up to the shrine.

Samuel and Saul

15 Now the day before Saul came, the LORD had disclosed his intention to Samuel in 16 these words: 'At this same time tomorrow I will send you a man from the land of Benjamin. Anoint him prince over my people Israel, and then he shall deliver my people from the Philistines. I have seen the sufferings of my people and their cry has reached 17 my ears.' The moment Saul appeared the LORD said to Samuel, 'Here is the man of whom I spoke to you. This man shall rule 18 my people.' Saul came up to Samuel in the gateway and said, 'Would you tell me where 19 the seer lives?' Samuel replied, 'I am the seer. Go on ahead of me to the hill-shrine and you shall eat with me today; in the morning I will set you on your way, after telling you what you have on your mind. 20 Trouble yourself no more about the asses lost three days ago, for they have been found. But what is it that all Israel is wanting? It is you and your ancestral house.' 21 'But I am a Benjamite,' said Saul, 'from the smallest of the tribes of Israel, and my family is the least important of all the families of the tribe of Benjamin. Why do you say this to 22 me?' Samuel then brought Saul and his servant into the dining-hall and gave them a place at the head of the company, which 23 numbered about thirty. Then he said to the cook, 'Bring the portion that I gave you and 24 told you to put on one side.' So the cook took up the whole haunch and leg and put it before Saul; and Samuel said, 'Here is the portion of meat*q* kept for you. Eat it: it has been reserved for you at this feast to which I have invited the people.' So Saul dined 25 with Samuel that day, and when they came

down from the hill-shrine to the city a bed was spread on the roof for Saul, and he 26 stayed there that night. At dawn Samuel called to Saul on the roof, 'Get up, and I will set you on your way.' When Saul rose, he and Samuel went out together into the street. As they came to the end of the town, 27 Samuel said to Saul, 'Tell the boy to go on.' He did so, and then Samuel said, 'Stay here a moment, and I will tell you the word of God.'

Saul is anointed king

Samuel took a flask of oil and poured it over **10** Saul's head, and he kissed him and said, 'The LORD anoints you prince over his people Israel; you shall rule the people of the LORD and deliver them from the enemies round about them. You shall have a sign that the LORD has anointed you prince to govern his inheritance: when you leave me 2 today, you will meet two men by the tomb of Rachel at Zelzah in the territory of Benjamin. They will tell you that the asses you are looking for have been found and that your father is concerned for them no longer; he is anxious about you and says again and again, "What shall I do about my son?" From there go across country as far as the 3 terebinth of Tabor, where three men going up to Bethel to worship God will meet you. One of them will be carrying three kids, the second three loaves, and the third a flagon of wine. They will greet you and will offer 4 you two loaves, which you will accept from them. Then when you reach the Hill of God, 5 where the Philistine governor*r* resides, you will meet a company of prophets coming down from the hill-shrine, led by lute, harp, fife, and drum, and filled with prophetic rapture. Then the spirit of the LORD will 6 suddenly take possession of you, and you too will be rapt like a prophet and become another man. When these signs happen, do 7 whatever the occasion demands; God will be with you. You shall go down to Gilgal 8 ahead of me, and I will come to you to sacrifice whole-offerings and shared-offerings. Wait seven days until I join you; then I will tell you what to do.' As Saul turned to leave 9 Samuel, God gave him a new heart. On that same day all these signs happened. When 10 they reached the Hill there was a company of prophets coming to meet him, and the spirit of God suddenly took possession of him, so that he too was filled with prophetic rapture. When people who had known him 11 previously saw that he was rapt like the prophets, they said to one another, 'What can have happened to the son of Kish? Is Saul also among the prophets?' One of the 12

o Verses 9 and 10 transposed.   p the seer . . . just: prob. rdg.; Heb. he is ahead of you, hurry now, for he has today . . .   q the portion of meat: prob. rdg.; Heb. what is left over.   r Or garrison.

men of that place said, 'And whose sons are they?' Hence the proverb, 'Is Saul also 13 among the prophets?' When the prophetic 14 rapture had passed, he went home.ˢ Saul's uncle said to him and the boy, 'Where have you been?' Saul answered, 'To look for the asses, and when we could not find them, we 15 went to Samuel.' His uncle said, 'Tell me 16 what Samuel said.' 'He told us that the asses had been found', said Saul; but he did not repeat what Samuel had said about his being king.

Samuel presents Saul to Israel

17 Meanwhile Samuel summoned the Israelites 18 to the LORD at Mizpah and said to the people, 'This is the word of the LORD the God of Israel: I brought Israel up from Egypt; I delivered you from the Egyptians and from 19 all the kingdoms that oppressed you; but today you have rejected your God who saved you from all your misery and distress; you have said, "No, set up a king over us." Now therefore take up your positions before the LORD tribe by tribe and clan by clan.' 20 Samuel then presented all the tribes of Israel, and Benjamin was picked by lot. 21 Then he presented the tribe of Benjamin, family by family, and the family of Matri was picked. Then he presented the family of Matri, man by man, and Saul son of Kish was picked; but when they looked for him 22 he could not be found. They went on to ask the LORD, 'Will the man be coming back?' The LORD answered, 'There he is, hiding 23 among the baggage.' So someone ran and fetched him out, and as he took his stand among the people, he was a head taller than 24 anyone else. Samuel said to the people, 'Look at the man whom the LORD has chosen; there is no one like him in this whole nation.' They all acclaimed him, shouting, 'Long 25 live the king!' Samuel then explained to the people the nature of a king, and made a written record of it on a scroll which he deposited before the LORD; he then dis- 26 missed them to their homes. Saul too went

ˢ *Prob. rdg.; Heb.* to the hill-shrine.

home to Gibeah, and with him went some fighting men whose hearts God had moved. But there were scoundrels who said, 'How 27 can this fellow deliver us?' They thought nothing of him and brought him no gifts.

Saul defeats the Ammonites

About a month later Nahash the Ammonite 11 attacked and besieged Jabesh-gilead. The men of Jabesh said to Nahash, 'Come to terms with us and we will be your subjects.' Nahash answered them, 'On one condition 2 only will I come to terms with you: that I gouge out your right eyes and bring dis- grace on Israel.' The elders of Jabesh-gilead 3 then said, 'Give us seven days' respite to send messengers throughout Israel and then, if no one relieves us, we will surrender to you.' When the messengers came to Gibeah, 4 where Saul lived, and delivered their mes- sage, all the people broke into lamentation. Saul was just coming from the field driving 5 in the oxen, and asked why the people were lamenting; and they repeated what the men of Jabesh had said. When Saul heard this, 6 the spirit of God suddenly seized him. In his anger he took a pair of oxen and cut 7 them in pieces, and sent messengers with the pieces all through Israel to proclaim that the same would be done to the oxen of any man who did not follow Saul and Samuel into battle. The fear of the LORD fell upon the people and they came out, to a man. Saul mustered them in Bezek; there were 8 three hundred thousand men from Israel and thirty thousand from Judah. He said 9 to the men who brought the message, 'Tell the men of Jabesh-gilead, "Victory will be yours tomorrow by the time the sun is hot."' The men of Jabesh heard what the mes- sengers reported and took heart; and they 10 said to Nahash, 'Tomorrow we will sur- render to you, and then you may deal with us as you think fit.' Next day Saul drew up 11 his men in three columns; they forced their way right into the enemy camp during the morning watch and massacred the Ammon- ites while the day grew hot, after which the survivors scattered until no two men were left together.

Israel accepts Saul as king

Then the people said to Samuel, 'Who said 12 that Saul should not reign over us? Hand the men over to us to be put to death.' But 13 Saul said, 'No man shall be put to death on a day when the LORD has won such a victory in Israel.' Samuel said to the people, 'Let 14 us now go to Gilgal and there renew our allegiance to the kingdom.' So they all went 15 to Gilgal and invested Saul there as king in the presence of the LORD, sacrificing shared-offerings before the LORD; and Saul and all the Israelites celebrated the occasion with great joy.

Samuel addresses the people

12 Then Samuel thus addressed the assembled Israelites: 'I have listened to your request 2 and installed a king to rule over you. And the king is now your leader, while I am old and white-haired and my sons are with you; but I have been your leader ever since I was 3 a child. Here I am. Lay your complaints against me in the presence of the LORD and of his anointed king. Whose ox have I taken, whose ass have I taken? Whom have I wronged, whom have I oppressed? From whom have I taken a bribe, to turn a blind eye? Tell me, and I will make restitution.' 4 They answered, 'You have not wronged us, you have not oppressed us; you have not 5 taken anything from any man.' Samuel then said to them, 'This day the LORD is witness among you, his anointed king is witness, that you have found my hands empty.' They 6 said, 'He is witness.' Samuel said to the people, 'Yes, the LORD is witness, the LORD who gave you Moses and Aaron and brought 7 your fathers out of Egypt. Now stand up, and here in the presence of the LORD I will put the case against you and recite all the victories which he has won for you and for 8 your fathers. After Jacob and his sons had come down to Egypt and the Egyptians had made them suffer, your fathers cried to the LORD for help, and he sent Moses and Aaron, who brought them out of Egypt and 9 settled them in this place. But they forgot the LORD their God, and he abandoned them to Sisera, commander-in-chief of Jabin king of Hazor, to the Philistines, and to the king of Moab, and they had to fight against them. 10 Then your fathers cried to the LORD for help: "We have sinned, we have forsaken the LORD and we have worshipped the Baalim and the Ashtaroth. But now, if thou wilt deliver us from our enemies, we will 11 worship thee." So the LORD sent Jerubbaal and Barak, Jephthah and Samson, and delivered you from your enemies on every side; and you lived in peace and quiet.

12 'Then, when you saw Nahash king of the Ammonites coming against you, although the LORD your God was your king, you said to me, "No, let us have a king to rule over 13 us." Now, here is the king you asked for; you chose him, and the LORD has set a king 14 over you. If you will revere the LORD and give true and loyal service, if you do not rebel against his commands, and if you and the king who reigns over you are faithful to 15 the LORD your God, well and good; but if you do not obey the LORD, and if you rebel

against his commands, then he will set his face against you and against your king.

16 'Stand still, and see the great wonder 17 which the LORD will do before your eyes. It is now wheat harvest; when I call upon the LORD and he sends thunder and rain, you will see and know how wicked it was in the LORD's eyes for you to ask for a king.' So 18 Samuel called upon the LORD and he sent thunder and rain that day; and all the people were in great fear of the LORD and of Samuel. They said to Samuel, 'Pray for us your 19 servants to the LORD your God, to save us from death; for we have added to all our other sins the great wickedness of asking for a king.' Samuel said to the people, 'Do not 20 be afraid; although you have been so wicked, do not give up the worship of the LORD, but serve him with all your heart. Give up the 21 worship of false gods which can neither help nor save, because they are false. For his 22 name's sake the LORD will not cast you off, because he has resolved to make you his own people. As for me, God forbid that I 23 should sin against the LORD and cease to pray for you. I will show you what is right and good: to revere the LORD and worship 24 him faithfully with all your heart. Consider what great things he has done for you; but 25 if you persist in wickedness, you shall be swept away, you and your king.'

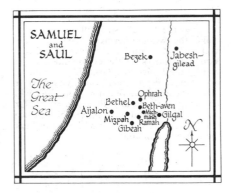

Saul usurps the priest's office

Saul was fifty years[t] old when he became 13 king, and he reigned over Israel for twenty-two[u] years. He picked three thousand men 2 from Israel, two thousand to be with him in Michmash and the hill-country of Bethel and a thousand to be with Jonathan in Gibeah of Benjamin; and he sent the rest of the people home.

Jonathan killed the Philistine governor[v] 3 in Geba, and the news spread among the

---

t fifty years: *prob. rdg.; Heb.* a year.   *u Prob. rdg.; Heb.* two.   *v Or* garrison.

Philistines that the Hebrews were in revolt.[w]
Saul sounded the trumpet all through the
4 land; and when the Israelites all heard that
Saul had killed a Philistine governor and
that the name of Israel stank among the
Philistines, they answered the call to arms
5 and came to join Saul at Gilgal.[x] The Philistines mustered to attack Israel; they had
thirty thousand chariots and six thousand
horse, with infantry as countless as sand on
the sea-shore. They went up and camped at
6 Michmash, to the east of Beth-aven. The
Israelites found themselves in sore straits,
for the army was hard pressed, so they hid
themselves in caves and holes and among
7 the rocks, in pits and cisterns. Some of them
crossed the Jordan into the district of Gad
and Gilead, but Saul remained at Gilgal,
and all the people at his back were in
8 alarm.[y] He waited seven days for his meeting with Samuel, but Samuel did not come
to Gilgal; so the people began to drift away
9 from Saul. He said therefore, 'Bring me the
whole-offering and the shared-offerings', and
10 he offered up the whole-offering. Saul had
just finished the sacrifice, when Samuel
arrived, and he went out to greet him.
11 Samuel said, 'What have you done?', and
Saul answered, 'I saw that the people were
drifting away from me, and you yourself
had not come as you had promised, and the
Philistines were assembling at Michmash;
12 and I thought, "The Philistines will now
move against me at Gilgal, and I have not
placated the LORD"; so I felt compelled to
13 make the whole-offering myself.' Samuel
said to Saul, 'You have behaved foolishly.
You have not kept the command laid on
you by the LORD your God; if you had, he
would have established your dynasty over
14 Israel for all time. But now your line will
not endure; the LORD will seek a man after
his own heart, and will appoint him prince
over his people, because you have not kept
the LORD's command.'

GIBEAH
2½
MILES
JERUSALEM

15   Samuel left Gilgal without more ado and
went on his way. The rest of the people
followed Saul, as he moved from Gilgal
towards the enemy. At Gibeah of Benjamin
he mustered the people who were with him;

they were about six hundred men. Saul and 16
his son Jonathan and the men they had with
them took up their quarters in Gibeah of
Benjamin, while the Philistines were encamped in Michmash. Raiding parties went 17
out from the Philistine camp in three directions. One party turned towards Ophrah in
the district of Shual, another towards Beth- 18
horon, and the third towards the range of
hills overlooking the valley of Zeboim and
the wilderness beyond.

No blacksmith was to be found in the 19
whole of Israel, for the Philistines were
determined to prevent the Hebrews from
making swords and spears. The Israelites 20
had to go down to the Philistines for their
ploughshares, mattocks, axes, and sickles

Mattock

to be sharpened. The charge was two-thirds 21
of a shekel for ploughshares and mattocks,
and one-third of a shekel for sharpening the
axes and setting the goads.[z] So when war 22
broke out none of the followers of Saul and
Jonathan had either sword or spear; only
Saul and Jonathan carried arms.

War with the Philistines

Now the Philistines had posted a force to 23
hold the pass of Michmash; and one day **14**
Saul's son Jonathan said to his armour-
bearer, 'Come, let us go over to the Philistine post beyond that ridge'; but he did not
tell his father. Saul, at the time, had his tent 2
under the pomegranate-tree at Migron on
the outskirts of Gibeah; and he had about
six hundred men with him. The ephod was 3
carried by Ahijah son of Ahitub, Ichabod's
brother, son of Phinehas son of Eli, the
priest of the LORD at Shiloh. Nobody knew
that Jonathan had gone. On either side of 4
the pass through which Jonathan tried to
make his way over to the Philistine post stood
two sharp columns of rock, called Bozez[a]
and Seneh;[b] one of them was on the north 5
towards Michmash, and the other on the
south towards Geba. Jonathan said to his 6
armour-bearer, 'Now we will visit the post
of those uncircumcised rascals. Perhaps the
LORD will take a hand in it, and if he will,
nothing can stop him. He can bring us safe

---

w that . . . revolt: *prob. rdg.; Heb. has* saying, Let the Hebrews hear *after* through the land.   *x* they
answered . . . Gilgal: *or* they were summoned to follow Saul to Gilgal.   *y* but Saul . . . in alarm: *or* but
Saul was still at Gilgal, and all the army joined him there.   *z* one-third . . . the goads: *prob. rdg.; Heb.*
obscure.   *a That is* Shining.   *b That is* Bramble-bush.

7 through, whether we are few or many.' The young man answered, 'Do what you will, go forward; I am with you whatever you do.'
8 'Good!' said Jonathan, 'we will cross over
9 and let them see us. If they say, "Stay where you are till we come to you", then we will stay where we are and not go up to them.
10 But if they say, "Come up to us", we will go up; this will be the sign that the LORD
11 has put them into our power.' So they showed themselves to the Philistines, and the Philistines said, 'Look! Hebrews coming out of the holes where they have been
12 hiding!' And they called across to Jonathan and the young man, 'Come up to us; we have something to show you.' Jonathan said to the young man, 'Come on, the LORD has
13 put them into the power of Israel.' Jonathan climbed up on hands and feet, and the young man followed him. The Philistines fell in front of Jonathan, and the young man, com-
14 ing behind him, dispatched them. In that first attack Jonathan and his armour-bearer killed about twenty of them, like men cut-
15 ting a furrow across a half-acre field. Terror spread through the army in the field and through the whole people; the men at the post and the raiding parties were terrified; the very earth quaked, and there was panic.
16 Saul's men on the watch in Gibeah of Benjamin saw the mob of Philistines surging
17 to and fro in confusion; so he ordered the people to call the roll and find out who was missing; and they called the roll and found that Jonathan and his armour-bearer were
18 absent. Saul said to Ahijah, 'Bring forward the ephod', for it was he who carried the
19 ephod at that time before Israel. But while Saul was still speaking, the confusion in the Philistine camp was increasing more and more, and he said to the priest, 'Hold your
20 hand.' Then Saul and all his men with shouting made for the battlefield, where they found the enemy fighting one another in complete
21 disorder. The Hebrews who up to now had been under the Philistines, and had been with them in camp, changed sides and joined the Israelites under Saul and Jon-
22 athan. All the Israelites in hiding in the hill-country of Ephraim heard that the Philistines were in flight, and they also
23 joined in and set off in hot pursuit. The LORD delivered Israel that day, and the fighting passed on beyond Beth-aven.

Jonathan's life in danger

24 Now the Israelites on that day had been driven to exhaustion. Saul had adjured the people in these words: 'A curse be on the man who eats any food before nightfall until I have taken vengeance on my enemies.'
25 So no one ate any food. Now there was

honeycomb[c] in the country-side; but when 26 his men came upon it, dripping with honey though it was, not one of them put his hand to his mouth for fear of the oath. But Jon- 27 athan had not heard his father lay this solemn prohibition on the people, and he stretched out the stick that was in his hand, dipped the end of it in the honeycomb, put it to his mouth and was refreshed. One of 28 the people said to him, 'Your father solemnly forbade this; he said, "A curse on the man who eats food today!"' Now the men were faint with hunger. Jonathan said, 'My 29 father has done the people nothing but harm; see how I am refreshed by this mere taste of honey. How much better if the 30 people had eaten today whatever they took from their enemies by way of spoil! Then there would indeed have been a great slaughter of Philistines.'

They defeated the Philistines that day, 31 and pursued them from Michmash to Aijalon. But the people were so faint with hunger that they turned to plunder and 32 seized sheep, cattle, and bullocks; they slaughtered them on the bare ground, and ate the meat with the blood in it. Someone 33 told Saul that the people were sinning against the LORD by eating their meat with the blood in it. 'This is treason!' cried Saul. 'Roll a great stone here at once.' He then 34 said, 'Go about among the people and tell them to bring their oxen and sheep, and let each man slaughter his here and eat it; and so they will not sin against the LORD by eating meat with the blood in it.' So as night fell each man came, driving his own ox, and slaughtered it there. Thus Saul came to build 35 an altar to the LORD, and this was the first altar to the LORD that Saul built.

Saul said, 'Let us go down and make a 36 night attack on the Philistines and harry them till daylight; we will not spare a man of them.' The people answered, 'Do what you think best', but the priest said, 'Let us first consult God.' So Saul inquired of God, 37 'Shall I pursue the Philistines? Wilt thou put them into Israel's power?'; but this time he received no answer. So he said, 'Let all 38 the leaders of the people come forward and let us find out where the sin lies this day. As 39 the LORD lives, the deliverer of Israel, even if it lies in my son Jonathan, he shall die.' Not a soul answered him. Then he said to 40 the Israelites, 'All of you stand on one side, and I and my son Jonathan will stand on the other.' The people answered, 'Do what you

c Now . . . honeycomb: *prob. rdg.; Heb.* All the land went into the forest, and there was honey.

41 think best.' Saul said to the LORD the God of Israel, 'Why hast thou not answered thy servant today? If this guilt lie in me or in my son Jonathan, O LORD God of Israel, let the lot be Urim; if it lie in thy people Israel, let it be Thummim.' Jonathan and Saul were
42 taken, and the people were cleared. Then Saul said, 'Cast lots between me and my son Jonathan'; and Jonathan was taken.
43 Saul said to Jonathan, 'Tell me what you have done.' Jonathan told him, 'True, I did taste a little honey on the tip of my stick.
44 Here I am; I am ready to die.' Then Saul swore a great oath that Jonathan should die.
45 But the people said to Saul, 'Shall Jonathan die, Jonathan who has won this great victory in Israel? God forbid! As the LORD lives, not a hair of his head shall fall to the ground, for he has been at work with God today.' So the people ransomed Jonathan and he
46 did not die. Saul broke off the pursuit of the Philistines because they had made their way home.

Saul's conquests, and his descendants

47 When Saul had made his throne secure in Israel, he fought against his enemies on every side, the Moabites, the Ammonites, the Edomites, the king of Zobah, and the Philistines; and wherever he turned he was
48 successful.[d] He displayed his strength by defeating the Amalekites and freeing Israel from hostile raids.
49 Saul's sons were: Jonathan, Ishyo and Malchishua. These were the names of his two daughters: Merab the elder and Michal
50 the younger. His wife was Ahinoam daughter of Ahimaaz, and his commander-in-chief
51 was Abner son of his uncle Ner; Kish, Saul's father, and Ner, Abner's father, were sons[e] of Abiel.
52 There was bitter warfare with the Philistines throughout Saul's lifetime; any strong man and any brave man that he found he took into his own service.

Destruction of the Amalekites

15 Samuel said to Saul, 'The LORD sent me to anoint you king over his people Israel. Now
2 listen to the voice of the LORD. This is the very word of the LORD of Hosts: "I am resolved to punish the Amalekites for what they did to Israel, how they attacked them
3 on their way up from Egypt." Go now and fall upon the Amalekites and destroy them, and put their property under ban. Spare no one; put them all to death, men and women, children and babes in arms, herds and flocks,
4 camels and asses.' Thereupon Saul called out the levy and mustered them in Telaim.

There were two hundred thousand footsoldiers and another ten thousand from Judah.[f] He came to the Amalekite city and 5 halted for a time in the gorge. Meanwhile 6 he sent word to the Kenites to leave the Amalekites and come down, 'or', he said, 'I shall destroy you as well as them; but you were friendly to Israel when they came up from Egypt.' So the Kenites left the Amalekites. Then Saul cut the Amalekites to pieces, 7 all the way from Havilah to Shur on the borders of Egypt. Agag the king of the 8 Amalekites he took alive, but he destroyed all the people, putting them to the sword. Saul and his army spared Agag and the 9 best of the sheep and cattle, the fat beasts and the lambs and everything worth keeping; they were unwilling to destroy them, but anything that was useless and of no value they destroyed.

The LORD rejects Saul

Then the word of the LORD came to Samuel: 10 'I repent of having made Saul king, for he 11 has turned his back on me and has not obeyed my commands.' Samuel was angry; all night he cried aloud to the LORD. Early 12 next morning he went to meet Saul, but was told that he had gone to Carmel; Saul had set up a monument for himself there, and had then turned and gone down to Gilgal. There Samuel found him, and Saul greeted 13 him with the words, 'The LORD's blessing upon you! I have obeyed the LORD's commands.' But Samuel said, 'What then is this 14 bleating of sheep in my ears? Why do I hear the lowing of cattle?' Saul answered, 'The 15 people have taken them from the Amalekites. These are what they spared, the best of the sheep and cattle, to sacrifice to the LORD your God. The rest we completely destroyed.' Samuel said to Saul, 'Let be, and I will tell 16 you what the LORD said to me last night.' 'Tell me', said Saul. So Samuel went on, 17 'Time was when you thought little of yourself, but now you are head of the tribes of Israel, and the LORD has anointed you king over Israel. The LORD sent you with strict 18 instructions to destroy that wicked nation, the Amalekites; you were to fight against them until you had wiped them out. Why 19 then did you not obey the LORD? Why did you pounce upon the spoil and do what was wrong in the eyes of the LORD?' Saul 20 answered Samuel, 'But I did obey the LORD; I went where the LORD sent me, and I have brought back Agag king of the Amalekites. The rest of them I destroyed. Out of the 21 spoil the people took sheep and oxen, the choicest of the animals laid under ban, to

---

d Or he found ample provision. *e Prob. rdg.; Heb.* son. *f Prob. rdg.; Heb.* ten thousand with the
men of Judah.

sacrifice to the Lord your God at Gilgal.'

22 Samuel then said:

Does the Lord desire offerings and sacrifices
as he desires obedience?
Obedience is better than sacrifice,
and to listen to him than the fat of rams.
23 Defiance of him is sinful as witchcraft,
yielding to men^g as evil as ^h idolatry.ⁱ
Because you have rejected the word of the
Lord,
the Lord has rejected you as king.

24 Saul said to Samuel, 'I have sinned. I
have ignored the Lord's command and
your orders: I was afraid of the people and
25 deferred to them. But now forgive my sin,
I implore you, and come back with me, and
I will make my submission before the Lord.'
26 Samuel answered, 'I will not come back with
you; you have rejected the word of the Lord
and therefore the Lord has rejected you as
27 king over Israel.' He turned to go, but Saul
28 caught the edge of his cloak and it tore. And
Samuel said to him, 'The Lord has torn the
kingdom of Israel from your hand today and
will give it to another, a better man than you.
29 God who is the Splendour of Israel does not
deceive or change his mind; he is not a man
30 that he should change his mind.' Saul said,
'I have sinned; but honour me this once
before the elders of my people and before
Israel and come back with me, and I will
make my submission to the Lord your God.'
31 So Samuel went back with Saul, and Saul
32 made his submission to the Lord. Then
Samuel said, 'Bring Agag king of the Amalekites.' So Agag came to him with faltering
step and said, 'Surely the bitterness of death
33 has passed.' Samuel said, 'Your sword has
made women childless, and your mother of
all women shall be childless too.' Then
Samuel hewed Agag in pieces before the
Lord at Gilgal.

34 Saul went to his own home at Gibeah, and
35 Samuel went to Ramah; and he never saw
Saul again to his dying day, but he mourned
for him, because the Lord had repented of
having made him king over Israel.

David anointed king

16 The Lord said to Samuel, 'How long will
you mourn for Saul because I have rejected
him as king over Israel? Fill your horn with
oil and take it with you; I am sending you
to Jesse of Bethlehem; for I have chosen
2 myself a king among his sons.' Samuel
answered, 'How can I go? Saul will hear of it
and kill me.' 'Take a heifer with you,' said
the Lord; 'say you have come to offer a
3 sacrifice to the Lord, and invite Jesse to
the sacrifice; then I will let you know what

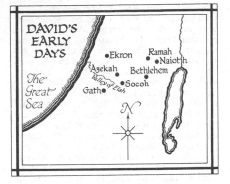

you must do. You shall anoint for me the
man whom I show you.' Samuel did as the 4
Lord had told him, and went to Bethlehem.
The elders of the city came in haste to meet
him, saying, 'Why have you come? Is all
well?' 'All is well,' said Samuel; 'I have 5
come to sacrifice to the Lord. Hallow yourselves and come with me to the sacrifice.'
He himself hallowed Jesse and his sons and
invited them to the sacrifice also. They came, 6
and when Samuel saw Eliab he thought,
'Here, before the Lord, is his anointed king.'
But the Lord said to him, 'Take no account 7
of it if he is handsome and tall; I reject him.
The Lord does not see as man sees; men
judge by appearances but the Lord judges
by the heart.' Then Jesse called Abinadab 8
and made him pass before Samuel, but he
said, 'No, the Lord has not chosen this one.'
Then he presented Shammah, and Samuel 9
said, 'Nor has the Lord chosen him.' Seven 10
of his sons Jesse presented to Samuel, but
he said, 'The Lord has not chosen any of
these.' Then Samuel asked, 'Are these all?' 11
Jesse answered, 'There is still the youngest,
but he is looking after the sheep.' Samuel
said to Jesse, 'Send and fetch him; we will
not sit down until he comes.' So he sent and 12
fetched him. He was handsome, with ruddy
cheeks and bright eyes.^j The Lord said,
'Rise and anoint him: this is the man.'
Samuel took the horn of oil and anointed 13
him in the presence of his brothers. Then
the spirit of the Lord came upon David and
was with him from that day onwards. And
Samuel set out on his way back to Ramah.

David plays the harp for Saul

The spirit of the Lord had forsaken Saul, 14
and at times an evil spirit from the Lord
would seize him suddenly. His servants said 15
to him, 'You see, sir, how an evil spirit from

---

g *yielding to men:* or arrogance *or* obstinacy.   h *as evil as: prob. rdg.; Heb.* evil and . . .   i *Or*
household gods; *Heb.* teraphim.   j *and bright eyes: prob. rdg.; Heb.* obscure.

16 God seizes you; why do you not command your servants here to go and find some man who can play the harp?—then, when an evil spirit from God comes on you, he can 17 play and you will recover.' Saul said to his servants, 'Find me a man who can play well 18 and bring him to me.' One of his attendants said, 'I have seen a son of Jesse of Bethlehem who can play; he is a brave man and a good fighter, wise in speech and handsome, and 19 the LORD is with him.' Saul therefore sent messengers to Jesse and asked him to send him his son David, who was with the sheep. 20 Jesse took a homer of bread, a skin of wine, and a kid, and sent them to Saul by his son 21 David. David came to Saul and entered his service; and Saul loved him dearly, and he 22 became his armour-bearer. So Saul sent word to Jesse: 'Let David stay in my service, 23 for I am pleased with him.' And whenever a spirit from God came upon Saul, David would take his harp and play on it, so that Saul found relief; he recovered and the evil spirit left him alone.

Goliath challenges Israel

17 The Philistines collected their forces for war and massed at Socoh in Judah; they camped between Socoh and Azekah at Ephes-2 dammim. Saul and the Israelites also massed, and camped in the Vale of Elah. They drew 3 up their lines facing the Philistines, the Philistines occupying a position on one hill and the Israelites on another, with a valley 4 between them. A champion came out from the Philistine camp, a man named Goliath, from Gath; he was over nine feet in height. 5 He had a bronze helmet on his head, and he wore plate-armour of bronze, weighing five 6 thousand shekels. On his legs were bronze greaves, and one of his weapons was a 7 dagger of bronze. The shaft of his spear was like a weaver's beam, and its head, which was of iron, weighed six hundred shekels; and his shield-bearer marched ahead of him. 8 The champion stood and shouted to the ranks of Israel, 'Why do you come out to do battle, you slaves of Saul? I am the Philistine champion; choose your man to meet 9 me. If he can kill me in fair fight, we will become your slaves; but if I prove too strong for him and kill him, you shall be our slaves 10 and serve us. Here and now I defy the ranks of Israel. Give me a man,' said the Philis-11 tine, 'and we will fight it out.' When Saul and the Israelites heard what the Philistine said, they were shaken and dismayed.

12 David was the son of an Ephrathite*k* called Jesse, who had eight sons. By Saul's 13 time he had become a feeble old man, and his three eldest sons had followed Saul to the war. The eldest was called Eliab, the next Abinadab, and the third Shammah; David was the youngest. The three eldest 14 followed Saul, while David used to go to 15 Saul's camp and back to Bethlehem to mind his father's flocks.

Morning and evening for forty days the 16 Philistine came forward and took up his position. Then one day Jesse said to his son 17 David, 'Take your brothers an ephah of this parched grain and these ten loaves of bread, and run with them to the camp. These ten 18 cream-cheeses are for you to take to the commanding officer. See if your brothers are well and bring back some token from them.' Saul and the brothers and all the 19 Israelites were in the Vale of Elah, fighting the Philistines. Early next morning David 20 left someone in charge of the sheep, set out on his errand and went as Jesse had told him. He reached the lines just as the army was going out to take up position and was raising the war-cry. The Israelites and the 21 Philistines drew up their ranks opposite each other. David left his things in charge 22 of the quartermaster, ran to the line and went up to his brothers to greet them. While 23 he was talking to them the Philistine champion, Goliath, came out from the Philistine ranks and issued his challenge in the same words as before; and David heard him. When the Israelites saw the man they ran 24 from him in fear. 'Look at this man who 25 comes out day after day to defy Israel', they said. 'The king is to give a rich reward to the man who kills him; he will give him his daughter in marriage too and will exempt his family from service due in Israel.' Then 26 David turned to his neighbours and said, 'What is to be done for the man who kills this Philistine and wipes out our disgrace? And who is he, an uncircumcised Philistine, to defy the army of the living God?' The 27 people told him how the matter stood and what was to be done for the man who killed him. His elder brother Eliab overheard 28 David talking with the men and grew angry. 'What are you doing here?' he asked. 'And who have you left to look after those few sheep in the wilderness? I know you, you impudent young rascal; you have only come to see the fighting.' David answered, 'What 29 have I done now? I only asked a question.' And he turned away from him to someone 30 else and repeated his question, but everybody gave him the same answer.

David kills Goliath

What David had said was overheard and 31 reported to Saul, who sent for him. David 32 said to him, 'Do not lose heart, sir. I will go and fight this Philistine.' Saul answered, 33 'You cannot go and fight with this Philistine;

k Prob. rdg.; Heb. adds Is this the man from Bethlehem in Judah?

(1 Sam. 17. 44)

you are only a lad, and he has been a fighting
34 man all his life.' David said to Saul, 'Sir, I
am my father's shepherd; when a lion or
bear comes and carries off a sheep from the
35 flock, I go after it and attack it and rescue the
victim from its jaws. Then if it turns on me,
I seize it by the beard and batter it to death.
36 Lions I have killed and bears, and this uncircumcised Philistine will fare no better
than they; he has defied the army of the
37 living God. The LORD who saved me from
the lion and the bear will save me from this
Philistine.' 'Go then,' said Saul; 'and the
38 LORD will be with you.' He put his own tunic
on David, placed a bronze helmet on his
head and gave him a coat of mail to wear;
39 he then fastened his sword on David over
his tunic. But David hesitated, because he
had not tried them, and said to Saul, 'I cannot go with these, because I have not tried
40 them.' So he took them off. Then he picked
up his stick, chose five smooth stones from
the brook and put them in a shepherd's bag
which served as his pouch. He walked out to
meet the Philistine with his sling in his hand.
41 The Philistine came on towards David,
42 with his shield-bearer marching ahead; and
he looked David up and down and had
nothing but contempt for this handsome lad
43 with his ruddy cheeks and bright eyes.[l] He
said to David, 'Am I a dog that you come
out against me with sticks?' And he swore
44 at him in the name of his god. 'Come on,'
he said, 'and I will give your flesh to the
45 birds and the beasts.' David answered, 'You
have come against me with sword and spear
and dagger, but I have come against you
in the name of the LORD of Hosts, the God
of the army of Israel which you have defied.
46 The LORD will put you into my power this
day; I will kill you and cut your head off
and leave your carcass and the carcasses of
the Philistines to the birds and the wild
beasts; all the world shall know that there
47 is a God in Israel. All those who are gathered
here shall see that the LORD saves neither by
sword nor spear; the battle is the LORD's,
and he will put you all into our power.'
49 When the Philistine began moving towards him again, David ran quickly to
49 engage him. He put his hand into his bag,
took out a stone, slung it, and struck the
Philistine on the forehead. The stone sank

into his forehead, and he fell flat on his face
on the ground. So David proved the victor 50
with his sling and stone; he struck Goliath
down and gave him a mortal wound, though
he had no sword. Then he ran to the Philis- 51
tine and stood over him, and grasping his
sword, he drew it out of the scabbard, dispatched him and cut off his head. The
Philistines, when they saw that their hero
was dead, turned and ran. The men of Israel 52
and Judah at once raised the war-cry and
hotly pursued them all the way to Gath and
even to the gates of Ekron. The road that
runs to Shaaraim, Gath, and Ekron was
strewn with their dead. On their return from 53
the pursuit of the Philistines, the Israelites
plundered their camp. David took Goliath's 54
head and carried it to Jerusalem, leaving his
weapons in his tent.

Saul promotes David

Saul had said to Abner his commander-in- 55
chief, when he saw David going out against
the Philistine, 'That boy there, Abner, whose
son is he?' 'By your life, your majesty,' said
Abner, 'I do not know.' The king said to 56
Abner, 'Go and find out whose son the lad
is.' When David came back after killing the 57
Philistine, Abner took him and presented
him to Saul with the Philistine's head still
in his hand. Saul asked him, 'Whose son 58
are you, young man?', and David answered,
'I am the son of your servant Jesse of
Bethlehem.'

That same day, when Saul had finished **18**
talking with David, he kept him and would 1-2
not let him return any more to his father's
house, for he saw that Jonathan had given
his heart to David and had grown to love
him as himself. So Jonathan and David 3
made a solemn compact because each loved
the other as dearly as himself. And Jon- 4
athan stripped off the cloak he was wearing
and his tunic, and gave them to David, together with his sword, his bow, and his belt.
David succeeded so well in every venture on 5
which Saul sent him that he was given a
command in the army, and his promotion
pleased the ordinary people, and even
pleased Saul's officers.

Saul becomes jealous of David

At the home-coming of the army when 6
David returned from the slaughter of the
Philistines, the women came out from all
the cities of Israel to look on, and the dancers
came out to meet King Saul with tambourines, singing, and dancing. The women 7
as they made merry sang to one another:

Saul made havoc among thousands
but David among tens of thousands.

l handsome . . . bright eyes: prob. rdg.; Heb. obscure.

8 Saul was furious, and the words rankled.
He said, 'They have given David tens of
thousands and me only thousands; what
9 more can they do but make him king?' From
that day forward Saul kept a jealous eye on
David.
10 Next day an evil spirit from God seized
upon Saul; he fell into a frenzy*m* in the house,
and David played the harp to him as he had
11 before. Saul had his spear in his hand, and
he hurled it at David, meaning to pin him
to the wall; but twice David swerved aside.
12 After this Saul was afraid of David, because
he saw that the LORD had forsaken him and
13 was with David. He therefore removed David
from his household and appointed him to
the command of a thousand men. David led
14 his men into action, and succeeded in everything that he undertook, because the LORD
15 was with him. When Saul saw how successful he was, he was more afraid of him than
16 ever; all Israel and Judah loved him because
he took the field at their head.
17 Saul said to David, 'Here is my elder
daughter Merab; I will give her to you in
marriage, but in return you must serve me
valiantly and fight the LORD's battles.' For
Saul meant David to meet his end at the
hands of the Philistines and not himself.
18 David answered Saul, 'Who am I and what
are my father's people, my kinsfolk, in
Israel, that I should become the king's son-
19 in-law?' However, when the time came for
Saul's daughter Merab to be married to
David, she had already been given to Adriel
20 of Meholah. But Michal, Saul's other daughter, fell in love with David, and when Saul
was told of this, he saw that it suited his
21 plans. He said to himself, 'I will give her to
him; let her be the bait that lures him to his
death at the hands of the Philistines.' So
Saul proposed a second time to make David
22 his son-in-law, and ordered his courtiers to
say to David privately, 'The king is well disposed to you and you are dear to us all; now
is the time for you to marry into the king's
23 family.' When Saul's people spoke in this
way to David, he said to them, 'Do you
think that marrying the king's daughter is a
matter of so little consequence that a poor
man of no consequence, like myself, can do
24 it?' Saul's courtiers reported what David
25 had said, and he replied, 'Tell David this:
all the king wants as the bride-price is the
foreskins of a hundred Philistines, by way
of vengeance on his enemies.' Saul was
counting on David's death at the hands of
26 the Philistines. The courtiers told David

what Saul had said, and marriage with the
king's daughter on these terms pleased him
well. Before the appointed time, David went 27
out with his men and slew two hundred
Philistines; he brought their foreskins and
counted them out to the king in order to be
accepted as his son-in-law. So Saul married
his daughter Michal to David. He saw clearly 28
that the LORD was with David, and knew
that Michal his daughter had fallen in love
with him; and so he grew more and more 29
afraid of David and was his enemy for the
rest of his life.
The Philistine officers used to come out 30
to offer single combat; and whenever they
did, David had more success against them
than all the rest of Saul's men, and he won
a great name for himself.

Saul tries to kill David

Saul spoke to Jonathan his son and all his 19
household about killing David. But Jonathan was devoted to David and told him 2
that his father Saul was looking for an opportunity to kill him. 'Be on your guard tomorrow morning,' he said; 'conceal yourself,
and remain in hiding. Then I will come out 3
and join my father in the open country where
you are and speak to him about you, and if
I discover anything I will tell you.' Jonathan 4
spoke up for David to his father Saul and
said to him, 'Sir, do not wrong your servant
David; he has not wronged you; his conduct
towards you has been beyond reproach. Did 5
he not take his life in his hands when he
killed the Philistine, and the LORD won a
great victory for Israel? You saw it, you
shared in the rejoicing; why should you
wrong an innocent man and put David to
death without cause?' Saul listened to Jon- 6
athan and swore solemnly by the LORD that
David should not be put to death. So Jon- 7
athan called David and told him all this;
then he brought him to Saul, and he was in
attendance on the king as before.
War broke out again, and David attacked 8
the Philistines and dealt them such a blow
that they ran before him.
An evil spirit from the LORD came upon 9
Saul as he was sitting in the house with his
spear in his hand; and David was playing
the harp. Saul tried to pin David to the wall 10
with the spear, but he avoided the king's
thrust so that Saul drove the spear into the
wall. David escaped and got safely away.
That night Saul sent servants to keep watch 11
on David's house, intending to kill him in
the morning, but David's wife Michal

m Or fell into prophetic rapture.

warned him to get away that night, 'or tomorrow', she said, 'you will be a dead man.'
2 She let David down through a window and
3 he slipped away and escaped. Michal took their household gods and put them on the bed; at its head she laid a goat's-hair rug
4 and covered it all with a cloak. When the men arrived to arrest David she told them
5 he was ill. Saul sent them back to see David for themselves. 'Bring him to me, bed and
6 all,' he said, 'and I will kill him.' When they came, there were the household gods on the
7 bed and the goat's-hair rug at its head. Then Saul said to Michal, 'Why have you played this trick on me and let my enemy get safe away?' And Michal answered, 'He said to me, "Help me to escape or I will kill you."'
8 Meanwhile David made good his escape and came to Samuel at Ramah, and told him how Saul had treated him. Then he and Samuel went to Naioth and stayed there.
10 Saul was told that David was there, and he sent a party of men to seize him. When they saw the company of prophets in rapture, with Samuel standing at their head, the spirit of God came upon them and they fell into
11 prophetic rapture. When this was reported to Saul he sent another party. These also fell into a rapture, and when he sent more
12 men a third time, they did the same. Saul himself then set out for Ramah and came to the great cistern in Secu. He asked where Samuel and David were and was told that
13 they were at Naioth in Ramah. On his way there the spirit of God came upon him too and he went on, in a rapture as he went, till
14 he came to Naioth in Ramah. There he too stripped off his clothes and like the rest fell into a rapture before Samuel and lay down naked all that day and all that night. That is why men say, 'Is Saul also among the prophets?'

Friendship of David and Jonathan

20 Then David made his escape from Naioth in Ramah and came to Jonathan. 'What have I done?' he asked. 'What is my offence? What does your father think I have done
2 wrong, that he seeks my life?' Jonathan answered him, 'God forbid! There is no thought of putting you to death. I am sure my father will not do anything whatever without telling me. Why should my father hide such a thing from me? I cannot believe
3 it!' David said, 'I am ready to swear to it: your father has said to himself, "Jonathan must not know this or he will resent it", because he knows that you have a high regard for me. As the LORD lives, your life upon it, there is only a step between me and
4 death.' Jonathan said to David, 'What do
5 you want me to do for you?' David answered,

'It is new moon tomorrow, and I ought to dine with the king. Let me go and lie hidden in the fields until the third evening. If your 6 father happens to miss me, then say, "David asked me for leave to pay a rapid visit to his home in Bethlehem, for it is the annual sacrifice there for the whole family." If he 7 says, "Well and good", that will be a good sign for me; but if he flies into a rage, you will know that he is set on doing me wrong. My lord, keep faith with me; for you and 8 I have entered into a solemn compact before the LORD. Kill me yourself if I am guilty. Why let me fall into your father's hands?' 'God forbid!' cried Jonathan. 'If I find my 9 father set on doing you wrong I will tell you.' David answered Jonathan, 'How will you 10 let me know if he answers harshly?' Jon- 11 athan said, 'Come with me into the fields.' So they went together into the fields, and 12 Jonathan said to David, 'I promise you, David, in the sight of the LORD the God of Israel, this time tomorrow I will sound my father for the third time and, if he is well disposed to you, I will send and let you know. If my father means mischief, the 13 LORD do the same to me and more, if I do not let you know and get you safely away. The LORD be with you as he has been with my father! I know that as long as I live you 14 will show me faithful friendship, as the LORD requires; and if I should die, you will 15 continue loyal to my family for ever. When the LORD rids the earth of all David's enemies, may the LORD call him to account 16 if he and his house are no longer my friends.' Jonathan pledged himself afresh to David 17 because of his love for him, for he loved him as himself. Then he said to him, 'To- 18 morrow is the new moon, and you will be missed when your place is empty. So go down 19 at nightfall for the third time to the place where you hid on the evening of the feast and stay by the mound there. Then I will 20 shoot three arrows towards it, as though I were aiming at a mark. Then I will send my 21 boy to find the arrows. If I say to him, "Look, the arrows are on this side of you, pick them up", then you can come out of hiding. You will be quite safe, I swear it; for there will be nothing amiss. But if I say 22 to the lad, "Look, the arrows are on the other side of you, further on", then the LORD has said that you must go; the LORD stand 23 witness between us for ever to the pledges we have exchanged.'

Jonathan gives David warning

So David hid in the fields. The new moon 24 came, the dinner was prepared, and the king sat down to eat. Saul took his customary 25 seat by the wall, and Abner sat beside him; Jonathan too was present, but David's place

26 was empty. That day Saul said nothing, for
he thought that David was absent by some
chance, perhaps because he was ritually
27 unclean. But on the second day, the day
after the new moon, David's place was still
empty, and Saul said to his son Jonathan,
'Why has not the son of Jesse come to the
28 feast, either yesterday or today?' Jonathan
answered Saul, 'David asked permission to
29 go to Bethlehem. He asked my leave and
said, "Our family is holding a sacrifice in
the town and my brother himself has ordered
me to be there. Now, if you have any regard
for me, let me slip away to see my brothers."
That is why he has not come to dine with
30 the king.' Saul was angry with Jonathan,
'You son of a crooked and unfaithful mother!
You have made friends with the son of Jesse
only to bring shame on yourself and dishonour on your mother; I see how it will be.
31 As long as Jesse's son remains alive on earth,
neither you nor your crown will be safe.
Send at once and fetch him; he deserves to
32 die.' Jonathan answered his father, 'Deserves
33 to die! Why? What has he done?' At that,
Saul picked up his spear and threatened to
kill him; and he knew that his father was
34 bent on David's death. Jonathan left the
table in a rage and ate nothing on the second
day of the festival; for he was indignant on
David's behalf because his father had humiliated him.
35   Next morning, Jonathan went out into
the fields to meet David at the appointed
36 time, taking a young boy with him. He said
to the boy, 'Run and find the arrows; I am
going to shoot.' The boy ran on, and he shot
37 the arrows over his head. When the boy
reached the place where Jonathan's arrows
had fallen, Jonathan called out after him,

38 'Look, the arrows are beyond you. Hurry!
No time to lose! Make haste!' The boy
39 gathered up the arrows and brought them
to his master; but only Jonathan and David
knew what this meant; the boy knew nothing.
40 Jonathan handed his weapons to the boy
and told him to take them back to the city.
41 When the boy had gone, David got up from
behind the mound and bowed humbly three
times. Then they kissed one another and
shed tears together, until David's grief was
42 even greater than Jonathan's. Jonathan
said to David, 'Go in safety; we have
pledged each other in the name of the
LORD who is witness for ever between you
and me and between your descendants and
mine.'

David escapes to the cave of Adullam

David went off at once, while Jonathan returned to the city. David made his way to 2
the priest Ahimelech at Nob, who hurried
out to meet him and said, 'Why have you
come alone and no one with you?' David 2
answered Ahimelech, 'I am under orders
from the king: I was to let no one know
about the mission on which he was sending
me or what these orders were. When I took
leave of my men I told them to meet me in
such and such a place. Now, what have you 3
got by you? Let me have five loaves, or as
many as you can find.' The priest answered 4
David, 'I have no ordinary bread available.
There is only the sacred bread; but have the
young men kept themselves from women?'
David answered the priest, 'Women have 5
been denied us hitherto, when I have been
on campaign, even an ordinary campaign,
and the young men's bodies have remained
holy; and how much more will they be holy
today?' So, as there was no other bread there, 6
the priest gave him the sacred bread, the
Bread of the Presence, which had just been
taken from the presence of the LORD to be
replaced by freshly baked bread on the day
that the old was removed. One of Saul's 7
servants happened to be there that day, detained before the LORD; his name was Doeg
the Edomite, and he was the strongest of all
Saul's herdsmen. David said to Ahimelech, 8
'Have you a spear or sword here at hand?
I have no sword or other weapon with me,
because the king's business was urgent.' The 9
priest answered, 'There is the sword of
Goliath the Philistine whom you slew in the
Vale of Elah; it is wrapped up in a cloak
behind the ephod. If you wish to take that,
take it; there is no other weapon here.'
David said, 'There is no sword like it; give
it to me.'

That day, David went on his way, eluding 10
Saul, and came to Achish king of Gath. The 11
servants of Achish said to him, 'Surely this
is David, the king of his country, the man of
whom they sang as they danced:

Saul made havoc among thousands
but David among tens of thousands.'

These words were not lost on David, and 12
he became very much afraid of Achish
king of Gath. So he altered his behaviour 13
in public and acted like a lunatic in front
of them all, scrabbling on the double doors
of the city gate and dribbling down his
beard. Achish said to his servants, 'The 14
man is mad! Why bring him to me? Am I 15
short of madmen that you bring this one to
plague me? Must I have this fellow in my
house?'

David made his escape and went from 2

there to the cave of Adullam. When his brothers and all his family heard that he was 2 there, they joined him. Men in any kind of distress or in debt or with a grievance gathered round him, about four hundred 3 in number, and he became their chief. From there David went to Mizpeh in Moab and said to the king of Moab, 'Let my father and mother come and take shelter with you 4 until I know what God will do for me.' So he left them at the court of the king of Moab, and they stayed there as long as David was in his stronghold.

Doeg kills the priests of Nob

5 The prophet Gad said to David, 'You must not stay in your stronghold; go at once into Judah.' So David went as far as the forest of 6 Hareth. News that David and his men had been seen reached Saul while he was in Gibeah, sitting under the tamarisk-tree on the hill-top with his spear in his hand and 7 all his retainers standing about him. He said to them, 'Listen to me, you Benjamites: do you expect the son of Jesse to give you all fields and vineyards, or make you all officers 8 over units of a thousand and a hundred? Is that why you have all conspired against me? Not one of you told me when my son made a compact with the son of Jesse; none of you spared a thought for me or told me that my son had set my own servant against me, who is lying in wait for me now.'
9 Then Doeg the Edomite, who was standing with the servants of Saul, spoke: 'I saw the son of Jesse coming to Nob, to Ahimelech son 10 of Ahitub. Ahimelech consulted the LORD on his behalf, then gave him food and handed over to him the sword of Goliath the Philis-11 tine.' The king sent for Ahimelech the priest and his family, who were priests at Nob, and 12 they all came into his presence. Saul said, 'Now listen, you son of Ahitub', and the man 13 answered, 'Yes, my lord?' Then Saul said to him, 'Why have you and the son of Jesse plotted against me? You gave him food and the sword too, and consulted God on his behalf; and now he has risen against me and 14 is at this moment lying in wait for me.' 'And who among all your servants', answered Ahimelech, 'is like David, a man to be trusted, the king's son-in-law, appointed to your staff and holding an honourable place 15 in your household? Have I on this occasion done something profane in consulting God on his behalf? God forbid! I trust that my lord the king will not accuse me or my family; for I know nothing whatever about 16 it.' But the king said, 'Ahimelech, you must 17 die, you and all your family.' He then turned to the bodyguard attending him and said, 'Go and kill the priests of the LORD; for they are in league with David, and, though they

knew that he was a fugitive, they did not tell me.' The king's men, however, were unwilling to raise a hand against the priests of the LORD. The king therefore said to Doeg 18 the Edomite, 'You, Doeg, go and fall upon the priests'; so Doeg went and fell upon the priests, killing that day with his own hand eighty-five men who could carry the ephod. He put to the sword every living thing in 19 Nob, the city of priests: men and women, children and babes in arms, oxen, asses, and sheep. One son of Ahimelech named 20 Abiathar made his escape and joined David. He told David how Saul had killed the 21 priests of the LORD. Then David said to him, 22 'When Doeg the Edomite was there that day, I knew that he would inform Saul. I have gambled with the lives of all your father's family. Stay here with me, have no fear; he 23 who seeks your life seeks mine, and you will be safe with me.'

David in Keilah

The Philistines were fighting against Keilah 23 and plundering the threshing-floors; and when David heard this, he consulted the 2 LORD and asked whether he should go and attack the Philistines. The LORD answered, 'Go, attack them, and relieve Keilah.' But 3 David's men said to him, 'As we are now, we have enough to fear from Judah. How much worse if we challenge the Philistine forces at Keilah!' David consulted the LORD 4 once again and the LORD answered him, 'Go to Keilah; I will give the Philistines into your hands.' So David and his men went to Keilah 5 and fought the Philistines; they carried off their cattle, inflicted a heavy defeat on them and relieved the inhabitants. Abiathar son 6 of Ahimelech made good his escape and joined David at Keilah, bringing the ephod with him. Saul was told that David had 7 entered Keilah, and he said, 'God has put him into my hands; for he has walked into a trap by entering a walled town with gates and bars.' He called out the levy to march 8 on Keilah and besiege David and his men. When David learnt how Saul planned his 9 undoing, he told Abiathar the priest to bring the ephod, and then he prayed, 'O LORD 10 God of Israel, I thy servant have heard news that Saul intends to come to Keilah and destroy the city because of me. Will the 11 citizens of Keilah surrender me to him? Will Saul come as I have heard? O LORD God of Israel, I pray thee, tell thy servant.' The LORD answered, 'He will come.' Then 12 David asked, 'Will the citizens of Keilah surrender me and my men to Saul?', and the LORD answered, 'They will.' Then David 13 left Keilah at once with his men, who numbered about six hundred, and moved about from place to place. When the news reached

A walled town with gates (1 Sam. 23. 7)

Saul that David had escaped from Keilah, he made no further move.

David in the wilderness

14 While David was living in the fastnesses of the wilderness of Ziph, in the hill-country, Saul searched for him day after day, but 15 God did not put him into his power. David well knew that Saul had come out to seek his life; and while he was at Horesh in the 16 wilderness of Ziph, Saul's son Jonathan came to him there and gave him fresh cou- 17 rage in God's name: 'Do not be afraid,' he said; 'my father's hand shall not touch you. You will become king of Israel and I shall hold rank after you; and my father knows 18 it.' The two of them made a solemn com- pact before the LORD; then David remained 19 in Horesh and Jonathan went home. While Saul was at Gibeah the Ziphites brought him this news: 'David, we hear, is in hiding among us in the fastnesses of Horesh on the hill of Hachilah, south of Jeshimon. 20 Come down, your majesty, come whenever you will, and we are able to surrender him 21 to you.' Saul said, 'The LORD has indeed blessed you; you have saved me a world of 22 trouble. Go now and make further inquiry, and find out exactly where he is and who saw him there. They tell me that he by him- 23 self is crafty enough to outwit me. Find out which of his hiding-places he is using; then come back to me at such and such a place, and I will go along with you. So long as he stays in this country, I will hunt him down, if I have to go through all the clans of Judah 24 one by one.' They set out for Ziph without delay, ahead of Saul; David and his men were in the wilderness of Maon in the

Arabah to the south of Jeshimon. Saul set 25 off with his men to look for him; but David got wind of it and went down to a refuge in the rocks, and there he stayed in the wilder- ness of Maon. Hearing of this, Saul went into the wilderness after him; he was on one 26 side of the hill, David and his men on the other. While David and his men were trying desperately to get away and Saul and his followers were closing in for the capture, a 27 runner brought a message to Saul: 'Come at once! the Philistines are harrying the land.' So Saul called off the pursuit and turned back 28 to face the Philistines. This is why that place is called the Dividing Rock. David went up 29 from there and lived in the fastnesses of En-gedi.

David spares Saul at En-gedi

When Saul returned from the pursuit of the **2**4 Philistines, he learnt that David was in the wilderness of En-gedi. So he took three 2 thousand men picked from the whole of Israel and went in search of David and his men to the east of the Rocks of the Wild Goats. There beside the road were some 3 sheepfolds, and near by was a cave, at the far end of which David and his men were sitting concealed. Saul came to the cave and went in to relieve himself. His men said to 4 David, 'The day has come: the LORD has put your enemy into your hands, as he promised he would, and you may do what you please with him.' David said to his men,

n Verses 4–7 are re-arranged thus: 4a, 6, 7a, 4b, 5, 7b.

'God forbid that I should harm my master, the LORD's anointed, or lift a finger against him; he is the LORD's anointed.' So David reproved his men severely and would not let them attack Saul. He himself got up stealthily and cut off a piece of Saul's cloak; but when he had cut it off, his conscience smote him. Saul rose, left the cave and went on his way; whereupon David also came out of the cave and called after Saul, 'My lord the king!' When Saul looked round, David prostrated himself in obeisance and said to him, 'Why do you listen when they say that David is out to do you harm? Today you can see for yourself that the LORD put you into my power in the cave; I had a mind to kill you, but no, I spared your life and said, "I cannot lift a finger against my master, for he is the LORD's anointed." Look, my dear lord, look at this piece of your cloak in my hand. I cut it off, but I did not kill you; this will show you that I have no thought of violence or treachery against you, and that I have done you no wrong; yet you are resolved to take my life. May the LORD judge between us! but though he may take vengeance on you for my sake, I will never lift my hand against you; "One wrong begets another", as the old saying goes, yet I will never lift my hand against you. Who has the king of Israel come out against? What are you pursuing? A dead dog, a mere flea. The LORD will be judge and decide between us; let him look into my cause, he will plead for me and will acquit me.'

When David had finished speaking, Saul said, 'Is that you, David my son?', and he wept. Then he said, 'The right is on your side, not mine; you have treated me so well, I have treated you so badly. Your goodness to me this day has passed all bounds: the LORD put me at your mercy but you did not kill me. Not often does a man find his enemy and let him go safely on his way; so may the LORD reward you well for what you have done for me today! I know now for certain that you will become king, and that the kingdom of Israel will flourish under your rule. Swear to me by the LORD then that you will not exterminate my descendants and blot out my name from my father's house.' David swore an oath to Saul; and Saul went back to his home, while David and his men went up to their fastness.

David greets Nabal

25 Samuel died, and all Israel came together to mourn for him, and he was buried in his house in Ramah. Afterwards David went down to the wilderness of Paran.

There was a man at Carmel in Maon, who

had great influence and owned three thousand sheep and a thousand goats; and he was shearing his flocks in Carmel. His name was Nabal and his wife's name Abigail; she was a beautiful and intelligent woman, but her husband, a Calebite, was surly and mean. David heard in the wilderness that Nabal was shearing his flocks, and sent ten of his men, saying to them, 'Go up to Carmel, find Nabal and give him my greetings. You are to say, "All good wishes for the year ahead! Prosperity to yourself, your household, and all that is yours! I hear that you are shearing. Your shepherds have been with us lately and we did not molest them; nothing of theirs was missing all the time they were in Carmel. Ask your own people and they will tell you. Receive my men kindly, for this is an auspicious day with us, and give what you can to David your son and your servant."' David's servants came and delivered this message to Nabal in David's name. When they paused, Nabal answered, 'Who is David? Who is this son of Jesse? In these days every slave who breaks away from his master sets himself up as a chief.º Am I to take my food and my wine and the meat I have provided for my shearers and give it to men who come from I know not where?' David's men turned and made their way back to him and told him all this. He said to his men, 'Buckle on your swords, all of you.' So they buckled on their swords and followed David, four hundred of them, while two hundred stayed behind with the baggage.

Abigail appeases David

One of the young men said to Abigail, Nabal's wife, 'David sent messengers from the wilderness to ask our master politely for a present, and he flew outᵖ at them. The men have been very good to us and have not molested us, nor did we miss anything all the time we were going about with them in the open country. They were as good as a wall round us, night and day, while we were minding the flocks. Think carefully what you had better do, for it is certain ruin for our master and his whole family; he is such a good-for-nothing that it is no good talking to him.' So Abigail hastily collected two hundred loaves and two skins of wine, five sheep ready dressed, five measures of parched grain, a hundred bunches of raisins, and two hundred cakes of dried figs, and loaded them on asses, but told her husband nothing about it. Then she said to her servants, 'Go on ahead, I will follow you.' As she made her way on her ass, hidden by the hill, there were David and his men coming down towards her, and she met them. David

---

o Or In these days there are many slaves who break away from their master.   *p* flew out: or screamed.

had said, 'It was a waste of time to protect this fellow's property in the wilderness so well that nothing of his was missing. He has 22 repaid me evil for good.' David swore a great oath: 'God do the same to me and more if I leave him a single mother's son alive by morning!'

23 When Abigail saw David she dismounted in haste and prostrated herself before him, 24 bowing low to the ground at his feet, and said, 'Let me take the blame, my lord, but allow me, your humble servant, to speak out 25 and let my lord give me a hearing. How can you take any notice of this good-for-nothing? He is just what his name Nabal means: "Churl" is his name, and churlish his behaviour. I did not myself, sir, see the 26 men you sent. And now, sir, the LORD has restrained you from bloodshed and from giving vent to your anger. As the LORD lives, your life upon it, your enemies and all who want to see you ruined will be like Nabal. 27 Here is the present which I, your humble servant, have brought; give it to the young 28 men under your command. Forgive me, my lord, if I am presuming; for the LORD will establish your family for ever, because you have fought his wars. No calamity shall 29 overtake you as long as you live. If any man sets out to pursue you and take your life, the LORD your God will wrap your life up and put it with his own treasure, but the lives of your enemies he will hurl away like 30 stones from a sling. When the LORD has made good all his promises to you, and has 31 made you ruler of Israel, there will be no reason why you should stumble or your courage falter because you have shed innocent blood or given way to your anger. Then when the LORD makes all you do prosper, you will remember me, your ser-32 vant.' David said to Abigail, 'Blessed is the LORD the God of Israel who has sent you 33 today to meet me. A blessing on your good sense, a blessing on you because you have saved me today from the guilt of bloodshed 34 and from giving way to my anger. For I swear by the life of the LORD the God of Israel who has kept me from doing you wrong: if you had not come at once to meet me, not a man of Nabal's household, not a single mother's son, would have been left 35 alive by morning.' Then David took from her what she had brought him and said, 'Go home in peace, I have listened to you and I grant your request.'

David marries Abigail

36 On her return she found Nabal holding a banquet in his house, a banquet fit for a king. He grew merry and became very drunk, so drunk that his wife said nothing to him, 37 trivial or serious, till daybreak. In the morn-ing, when the wine had worn off, she told him everything, and he had a seizure and lay there like a stone. Ten days later the 38 LORD struck him again and he died. When 39 David heard that Nabal was dead he said, 'Blessed be the LORD, who has himself punished Nabal for his insult, and has kept me his servant from doing wrong. The LORD has made Nabal's wrongdoing recoil on his own head.' David then sent to make proposals that Abigail should become his wife. And his servants came to Abigail at Carmel 40 and said to her, 'David has sent us to fetch you to be his wife.' She rose and prostrated 41 herself with her face to the ground, and said, 'I am his slave to command, I would wash the feet of my lord's servants.' So Abigail 42 made her preparations with all speed and, with her five maids in attendance, accompanied by David's messengers, rode away on an ass; and she became David's wife. David 43 had also married Ahinoam of Jezreel; both these women became his wives. Saul mean-44 while had given his daughter Michal, David's wife, to Palti son of Laish from Gallim.

David spares Saul at Ziph

The Ziphites came to Saul at Gibeah to 26 report that David was in hiding on the hill of Hachilah overlooking Jeshimon. Saul 2 went down at once to the wilderness of Ziph, taking with him three thousand picked men, to search for David there. He encamped 3 beside the road on the hill of Hachilah overlooking Jeshimon, while David was still in the wilderness. As soon as David knew that Saul had come to the wilderness in pursuit of him, he sent out scouts and found that 4 Saul had reached such and such a place. Without delay, he went to the place where 5 Saul had pitched his camp and observed where Saul and Abner son of Ner, the commander-in-chief, were lying. Saul lay within the lines with his troops encamped in a circle round him. David turned to 6 Ahimelech the Hittite and Abishai son of Zeruiah, Joab's brother, and said, 'Who will venture with me into the camp, to go to Saul?' Abishai answered, 'I will.' David and 7 Abishai entered the camp at night and found Saul lying asleep within the lines with his spear thrust into the ground by his head. Abner and the army were lying all round him. Abishai said to David, 'God has put 8 your enemy into your power today; let me strike him and pin him to the ground with one thrust of the spear; I shall not have to strike twice.' David said to him, 'Do him no 9 harm; who has ever lifted a finger against the LORD's anointed and gone unpunished? As the LORD lives,' went on David, 'the 10 LORD will strike him down; either his time will come and he will die, or he will go down to battle and meet his end. God forbid that I should lift a finger against the LORD's anointed! But now let us take the spear which is by his head, and the water-jar, and go.' So David took the spear and the water-jar from beside Saul's head and they went. The whole camp was asleep; no one saw him, no one knew anything, no one even woke up. A heavy sleep sent by the LORD had fallen on them.

Then David crossed over to the other side and stood on the top of a hill a long way off; there was no little distance between them. David shouted across to the army and hailed Abner, 'Answer me, Abner!' He answered, 'Who are you to shout to the king?' David said to Abner, 'Do you call yourself a man? Is there anyone like you in Israel? Why, then, did you not keep watch over your lord the king, when someone came to harm your lord the king? This was not well done. As the LORD lives, you deserve to die, all of you, because you have not kept watch over your master the LORD's anointed. Look! Where are the king's spear and the water-jar that were by his head?'

Saul recognized David's voice and said, 'Is that you, David my son?' 'Yes, sir, it is', said David. 'Why must your majesty pursue me? What have I done? What mischief am I plotting? Listen, my lord, to what I have to say. If it is the LORD who has set you against me, may an offering be acceptable to him; but if it is men, a curse on them in the LORD's name; for they have ousted me today from my share in the LORD's inheritance and have banished me to serve other gods! Do not let my blood be shed on foreign soil, far from the presence of the LORD, just because the king of Israel came out to look for a flea, as one might hunt a partridge over the hills.' Saul answered, 'I have done wrong; come back, David my son. You have held my life precious this day, and I will never harm you again. I have been a fool, I have been sadly in the wrong.' David answered, 'Here is the king's spear; let one of your men come across and fetch it. The LORD who rewards uprightness and loyalty will reward the man into whose power he put you today, when I refused to lift a finger against the LORD's anointed. As I held your life precious today, so may the LORD hold mine precious and deliver me from every distress.' Then Saul said to David, 'A blessing is on you, David my son. You will do great things and be victorious.' So David went on his way and Saul returned home.

David lives among the Philistines

27 David thought, 'One of these days I shall be killed by Saul. The best thing for me to

do will be to escape into Philistine territory; then Saul will lose all further hope of finding me anywhere in Israel, search as he may, and I shall escape his clutches.' So David 2 and his six hundred men crossed the frontier forthwith to Achish son of Maoch king of Gath. David settled in Gath with Achish, 3 taking with him his men and their families and his two wives, Ahinoam of Jezreel and Abigail of Carmel, Nabal's widow. Saul was 4 told that David had escaped to Gath, and he gave up the search. David said to Achish, 5 'If I stand well in your opinion, grant me a place in one of your country towns where I may settle. Why should I remain in the royal city with your majesty?' Achish 6 granted him Ziklag on that day: that is why Ziklag still belongs to the kings of Judah.

David spent a year and four months in 7 Philistine country. He and his men would 8 sally out and raid the Geshurites, the Gizrites, and the Amalekites, for it was they who inhabited the country from Telaim[q] all the way to Shur and Egypt. When David raided 9 the country he left no one alive, man or woman; he took flocks and herds, asses and camels, and clothes too, and then came back again to Achish. When Achish asked, 10 'Where was your raid today?', David would answer, 'The Negeb of Judah' or 'The Negeb of the Jerahmeelites' or 'The Negeb of the Kenites'. Neither man nor woman 11 did David bring back alive to Gath, for fear that they should denounce him and his men for what they had done. This was his practice as long as he remained with the Philistines. Achish trusted David, thinking that he had 12 won such a bad name among his own people the Israelites that he would remain his subject all his life.

q from Telaim: prob. rdg.; Heb. from of old.

28 In those days the Philistines mustered their army for an attack on Israel. Achish said to David, 'You know that you and your men must take the field with me.' David answered Achish, 'Good, you will learn what your servant can do.' And Achish said to David, 'I will make you my bodyguard for life.'

Saul and the medium at En-dor

3 By this time Samuel was dead, and all Israel had mourned for him and buried him in Ramah, his own city; and Saul had banished from the land all who trafficked with ghosts and spirits. The Philistines mustered and encamped at Shunem, and Saul gathered all the Israelites and encamped on Gilboa; and when Saul saw the Philistine force, fear struck him to the heart. He inquired of the LORD, but the LORD did not answer him, whether by dreams or by Urim or by prophets. So he said to his servants, 'Find me a woman who has a familiar spirit, and I will go and inquire through her.' His servants told him that there was such a woman at En-dor. Saul put on different clothes and went in disguise with two of his men. He came to the woman by night and said, 'Tell me my fortunes by consulting the dead, and call up the man I name to you.' But the woman answered, 'Surely you know what Saul has done, how he has made away with those who call up ghosts and spirits; why do you press me to do what will lead to my death?' Saul swore her an oath: 'As the LORD lives, no harm shall come to you for this.' The woman asked whom she should call up, and Saul answered, 'Samuel.' When the woman saw Samuel appear, she shrieked and said to Saul, 'Why have you deceived me? You are Saul!' The king said to her, 'Do not be afraid. What do you see?' The woman answered, 'I see a ghostly form coming up from the earth.' 'What is it like?' he asked; she answered, 'Like an old man coming up, wrapped in a cloak.' Then Saul knew it was Samuel, and he bowed low with his face to the ground, and prostrated himself. Samuel said to Saul, 'Why have you disturbed me and brought me up?' Saul answered, 'I am in great trouble; the Philistines are pressing me and God has turned away; he no longer answers me through prophets or through dreams, and I have summoned you to tell me what I should do.' Samuel said, 'Why do you ask me, now that the LORD has turned from you and become your adversary? He has done what he foretold through me. He has torn the kingdom from your hand and given it to another man, to David. You have not obeyed the LORD, or executed the judgement

of his fury against the Amalekites; that is why he has done this to you today. For the same reason the LORD will let your people Israel fall into the hands of the Philistines and, what is more, tomorrow you and your sons shall be with me. Yes, indeed, the LORD will give the Israelite army into the hands of the Philistines.' Saul was overcome and fell his full length to the ground, terrified by Samuel's words. He had no strength left, for he had eaten nothing all day and all night.

The woman went to Saul and saw that he was much disturbed, and she said to him, 'I listened to what you said and I risked my life to obey you. Now listen to me: let me set before you a little food to give you strength for your journey.' But he refused to eat anything. When his servants joined the woman in pressing him, he yielded, rose from the ground and sat on the couch. The woman had a fatted calf at home, which she quickly slaughtered. She took some meal, kneaded it and baked unleavened cakes, which she set before Saul and his servants. They ate the food and departed that same night.

The Philistines distrust David

The Philistines mustered all their troops at **29** Aphek, while the Israelites encamped at En-harod[r] in Jezreel. The Philistine princes were advancing with their troops in units of a hundred and a thousand; David and his men were in the rear of the column with Achish. The Philistine commanders asked, 'Why are those Hebrews there?' Achish answered, 'This is David, the servant of Saul king of Israel who has been with me now for a year or more. I have had no fault to find in him ever since he came over to me.' The Philistine commanders were indignant and said to Achish, 'Send the man back to the town which you allotted to him. He shall not fight side by side with us, or he may turn traitor in the battle. What better way to buy his master's favour, than at the price of our lives? This is that David of whom they sang, as they danced:

Saul made havoc among thousands
but David among tens of thousands.'

Achish summoned David and said to him, 'As the LORD lives, you are an upright man and your service with my troops has well satisfied me. I have had no fault to find with you ever since you joined me, but the other princes are not willing to accept you. Now go home in peace, and you will then be doing nothing that they can regard as wrong.' David protested, 'What have I done, or what fault have you found in me from the

r Prob. rdg.; Heb. at the spring.

day I first entered your service till now, that I should not come and fight against the
9 enemies of my lord the king?' Achish answered David, 'I agree that you have been as true to me as an angel of God, but the Philistine commanders insist that you shall
10 not fight alongside them. Now rise early in the morning with those of your lord's subjects who have followed you, and go to the town which I allotted to you; harbour no evil thoughts, for I am well satisfied with you. Rise early and start as soon as it is light.'
11 So David and his men rose early to start that morning on their way back to the land of the Philistines, while the Philistines went on to Jezreel.

An Amalekite raid

30 On the third day David and his men reached Ziklag. Now the Amalekites had made a raid into the Negeb, attacked Ziklag and
2 set fire to it; they had carried off all the women, high and low, without putting one of them to death. These they drove with them
3 and continued their march. When David and his men approached the town, they found it destroyed by fire, and their wives, their sons, and their daughters carried off.
4 David and the people with him wept aloud
5 until they could weep no more. David's two

wives, Ahinoam of Jezreel and Abigail widow of Nabal of Carmel, were among the captives. David was in a desperate position 6 because the people, embittered by the loss of their sons and daughters, threatened to stone him. So David sought strength in the LORD his God. He told Abiathar the priest, 7 son of Ahimelech, to bring the ephod. When Abiathar had brought the ephod, David 8 inquired of the LORD, 'Shall I pursue these raiders? and shall I overtake them?' The answer came, 'Pursue them: you will overtake them and rescue everyone.' So David 9 and his six hundred men set out and reached the ravine of Besor.⁵ Two hundred of them 10 who were too weary to cross the ravine stayed behind, and David with four hundred pressed on in pursuit.

In the open country they came across an 11 Egyptian and took him to David. They gave him food to eat and water to drink, also a 12 lump of dried figs and two bunches of raisins. When he had eaten these he revived; for he had had nothing to eat or drink for three days and nights. David asked him, 'Whose slave 13 are you? and where have you come from?' 'I am an Egyptian boy,' he answered, 'the slave of an Amalekite, but my master left me behind because I fell ill three days ago. We had raided the Negeb of the Kerethites, 14 part of Judah, and the Negeb of Caleb; we also set fire to Ziklag.' David asked, 'Can 15 you guide me to this band?' 'Swear to me by God', he answered, 'that you will not put me to death or hand me back to my master, and I will guide you to them.' So he led him down, 16 and there they were scattered everywhere, eating and drinking and celebrating the capture of the great mass of spoil taken from Philistine and Judaean territory.

David rescues the Amalekites' captives

David attacked from dawn till dusk and 17 continued till next day; only four hundred young men mounted on camels made good their escape. David rescued all those whom 18 the Amalekites had taken, including his two wives. No one was missing, high or low, sons 19

s *Prob. rdg.; Heb. adds* those who were left over remained.

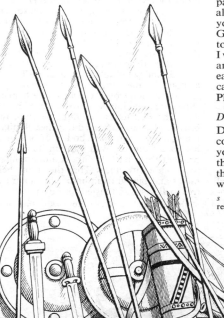

or daughters, and none of the spoil, nor
anything they had taken for themselves:
20 David recovered everything. They took all
the flocks and herds, drove the cattle before
21 him[t] and said, 'This is David's spoil.' When
David returned to the two hundred men who
had been too weak to follow him and whom
he had left behind at the ravine of Besor,
they came forward to meet him and his men.
David greeted them all, inquiring how things
22 were with them. But some of those who had
gone with David, worthless men and scoundrels, broke in and said, 'These men did not
go with us; we will not allot them any of the
spoil that we have retrieved, except that each
of them may take his own wife and children
23 and then go.' 'That you shall never do,' said
David, 'considering what the LORD has given
us, and how he has kept us safe and given
24 the raiding party into our hands. Who could
agree with what you propose? Those who
stayed with the stores shall have the same
share as those who went into battle. They
25 shall share and share alike.' From that time
onwards, this has been the established custom in Israel down to this day.
26   When David reached Ziklag, he sent some
of the spoil to the elders of Judah and to his
friends, with this message: 'This is a present
for you out of the spoil taken from the
27 LORD's enemies.' He sent to those in Beth-
28 uel, in Ramoth-negeb, in Jattir, in Ararah,[u]
29 in Siphmoth, in Eshtemoa, in Rachal, in the
cities of the Jerahmeelites, in the cities of
30 the Kenites, in Hormah, in Borashan, in
31 Athak, in Hebron, and in all the places over
which he and his men had ranged.

The death of Saul and his sons

31 1[v] The Philistines fought a battle against Israel,
and the men of Israel were routed, leaving
2 their dead on Mount Gilboa. The Philistines
hotly pursued Saul and his sons and killed
the three sons, Jonathan, Abinadab and
3 Malchishua. The battle went hard for Saul,
for some archers came upon him and he was
4 wounded in the belly by the archers. So he
said to his armour-bearer, 'Draw your sword
and run me through, so that these un-

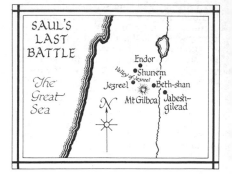

SAUL'S
LAST
BATTLE

*The
Great
Sea*

Endor
Shunem
Valley of Jezreel
Jezreel   Beth-shan
Mt Gilboa   Jabesh-
gilead

circumcised brutes may not come and taunt
me and make sport of me.' But the armour-
bearer refused, he dared not; whereupon
Saul took his own sword and fell on it. When 5
the armour-bearer saw that Saul was dead,
he too fell on his sword and died with him.
Thus they all died together on that day, Saul, 6
his three sons, and his armour-bearer, as
well as his men. And all the Israelites in the 7
district of the Vale and of the Jordan, when
they saw that the other Israelites had fled
and that Saul and his sons had perished, fled
likewise, abandoning their cities, and the
Philistines went in and occupied them.
   Next day, when the Philistines came to strip 8
the slain, they found Saul and his three sons
lying dead on Mount Gilboa. They cut off his 9
head and stripped him of his weapons; then
they sent messengers through the length and
breadth of their land to take the good news
to idols and people alike. They deposited his 10
armour in the temple of Ashtoreth and
nailed his body on the wall of Beth-shan.
When the inhabitants of Jabesh-gilead heard 11
what the Philistines had done to Saul, the 12
bravest of them journeyed together all night
long and recovered the bodies of Saul and
his sons from the wall of Beth-shan; they
brought them back to Jabesh and anointed
them there with spices. Then they took their 13
bones and buried them under the tamarisk-
tree in Jabesh, and fasted for seven days.

t They took . . . before him: *prob. rdg.; Heb.* David took all the flocks and herds; they drove before that cattle.
u *Prob. rdg.; Heb.* Aroer.   v *Verses 1–13: cp. 1 Chr.* 10. *1–12.*

THE SECOND BOOK OF
SAMUEL

David learns of Saul's death

1 WHEN DAVID returned from his victory over the Amalekites, he spent two days 2 in Ziklag. And on the third day after Saul's death a man came from the army with his clothes rent and dust on his head. When he came into David's presence he fell to the 3 ground in obeisance, and David asked him where he had come from. He answered, 'I 4 have escaped from the army of Israel.' And David said to him, 'What news? Tell me.' 'The army has been driven from the field,' he answered, 'and many have fallen in battle. 5 Saul and Jonathan his son are dead.' David said to the young man who brought the news, 'How do you know that Saul and Jonathan 6 are dead?' The man answered, 'It so happened that I was on Mount Gilboa and saw Saul leaning on his spear with the chariots 7 and horsemen closing in upon him. He turned round and, seeing me, called to me. 8 I said, "What is it, sir?" He asked who I was, 9 and I said, "An Amalekite." Then he said to me, "Come and stand over me and dispatch me. I still live, but the throes of death 10 have seized me." So I stood over him and gave him the death-blow; for I knew that, broken as he was, he could not live. Then I took the crown from his head and the armlet from his arm, and I have brought them here 11 to you, sir.' At that David caught at his clothes and rent them, and so did all the 12 men with him. They beat their breasts and wept, because Saul and Jonathan his son and the people of the LORD, the house of Israel, had fallen in battle; and they fasted till evening. David said to the young man who 13 brought the news, 'Where do you come from?', and he answered, 'I am the son of an alien, an Amalekite.' 'How is it', said David, 14 'that you were not afraid to raise your hand to slay the LORD's anointed?' And he sum- 15 moned one of his own young men and ordered him to fall upon the man. So the young man struck him down and killed him; and David said, 'Your blood be on your 16 own head; for out of your own mouth you condemned yourself when you said, "I killed the LORD's anointed."'

David laments over Saul and Jonathan

David made this lament over Saul and Jon- 17 athan his son; and he ordered that this dirge 18 over them should be taught to the people of Judah. It was written down and may be found in the Book of Jashar:[a]

O prince of Israel, laid low in death!   19
  How are the men of war fallen!

Tell it not in Gath,   20
proclaim it not in the streets of Ashkelon,
  lest the Philistine women rejoice,
  lest the daughters of the uncircumcised
    exult.

Hills of Gilboa, let no dew or rain fall on 21
  you,
  no showers on the uplands[b]!
For there the shields of the warriors lie
  tarnished,
  and the shield of Saul, no longer bright
    with oil.

a Or the Book of the Upright.   *b* showers on the uplands: *prob. rdg.; Heb.* fields of offerings.

22 The bow of Jonathan never held back
from the breast of the foeman, from the
blood of the slain;
the sword of Saul never returned
empty to the scabbard.

23 Delightful and dearly loved were Saul and
Jonathan;
in life, in death, they were not parted.
They were swifter than eagles,
stronger than lions.

24 Weep for Saul, O daughters of Israel!
who clothed you in scarlet and rich em-
broideries,
who spangled your dress with jewels of
gold.

25 How are the men of war fallen, fallen on the
field!
O Jonathan, laid low in death!

26 I grieve for you, Jonathan my brother;
dear and delightful you were to me;
your love for me was wonderful,
surpassing the love of women.

27 Fallen, fallen are the men of war;
and their armour left on the field.

David made king of Judah

2 After this David inquired of the LORD,
'Shall I go up into one of the cities of Judah?'
The LORD answered, 'Go.' David asked, 'To
which city?', and the answer came, 'To
2 Hebron.' So David went to Hebron with his
two wives, Ahinoam of Jezreel and Abigail
3 widow of Nabal of Carmel. David also
brought the men who had joined him, with
their families, and they settled in the city^c
4 of Hebron. The men of Judah came, and
there they anointed David king over the
house of Judah.
Word came to David that the men of
5 Jabesh-gilead had buried Saul, and he sent
them this message: 'The LORD bless you
because you kept faith with Saul your lord
6 and buried him. For this may the LORD
keep faith and truth with you, and I for my
part will show you favour too, because you
7 have done this. Be strong, be valiant, now
that Saul your lord is dead, and the people
of Judah have anointed me to be king over
them.'

Abner and Joab in conflict

8 Meanwhile Saul's commander-in-chief,
Abner son of Ner, had taken Saul's son
Ishbosheth, brought him across the Jordan
9 to Mahanaim, and made him king over
Gilead, the Asherites, Jezreel, Ephraim,
10 and Benjamin, and all Israel. Ishbosheth
was forty years old when he became king
over Israel, and he reigned two years. The
tribe of Judah, however, followed David.

David's rule over Judah in Hebron lasted 11
seven years and a half.
Abner son of Ner, with the troops of 12
Saul's son Ishbosheth, marched out from
Mahanaim to Gibeon, and Joab son of 13
Zeruiah marched out with David's troops
from Hebron. They met at the pool of
Gibeon and took up their positions one on
one side of the pool and the other on the
other side. Abner said to Joab, 'Let the 14
young men come forward and join in single
combat before us.' Joab answered, 'Yes, let
them.' So they came up, one by one, and 15
took their places, twelve for Benjamin and
for Ishbosheth and twelve from David's
men. Each man seized his opponent by the 16
head and thrust his sword into his side; and
thus they fell together. That is why that
place, which lies in Gibeon, was called the
Field of Blades.

Abner kills Asahel

There ensued a fierce battle that day, and 17
Abner and the men of Israel were defeated
by David's troops. All three sons of Zerui- 18
ah were there, Joab, Abishai and Asahel.

Asahel, who was swift as a gazelle on the
plains, ran straight after Abner, swerving 19
neither to right nor left in his pursuit.
Abner turned and asked, 'Is it you, Asahel?' 20
Asahel answered, 'It is.' Abner said, 'Turn 21
aside to right or left, tackle one of the young
men and win his belt for yourself.' But
Asahel would not abandon the pursuit.
Abner again urged him to give it up. 'Why 22
should I kill you?' he said. 'How could I
look Joab your brother in the face?' When 23
he still refused to turn aside, Abner struck
him in the belly with a back-thrust of his
spear^d so that the spear came out behind
him, and he fell dead in his tracks. All who
came to the place where Asahel lay dead
stopped there. But Joab and Abishai kept 24
up the pursuit of Abner, until, at sunset, they
reached the hill of Ammah, opposite Giah on
the road leading to the pastures of Gibeon.

c Prob. rdg.; Heb. cities. 　　*d a back-thrust of his spear: prob. rdg.; Heb. obscure.*

The fighting ceases

5 The Benjamites rallied to Abner and, forming themselves into a single company, took up their stand on the top of the hill of 6 Ammah.*e* Abner called to Joab, 'Must the slaughter go on for ever? Can you not see that it will be all the more bitter in the end? Will you never recall the people from the 7 pursuit of their kinsmen?' Joab answered, 'As God lives, if you had not spoken, the people would not have given up the pursuit 8 till morning.' Then Joab sounded the trumpet, and all the people abandoned the pursuit of the men of Israel and the fighting 9 ceased. Abner and his men moved along the Arabah all that night, crossed the Jordan and went on all the morning till they 10 reached Mahanaim. When Joab returned from the pursuit of Abner, he assembled his troops and found that, besides Asahel, nineteen of David's men were missing. 11 David's forces had routed the Benjamites and the followers of Abner, killing three 12 hundred and sixty of them. They took up Asahel and buried him in his father's tomb at Bethlehem. Joab and his men marched all night, and as day broke they reached Hebron.

3 The war between the houses of Saul and David was long drawn out, David growing steadily stronger while the house of Saul became weaker and weaker.

David's sons born at Hebron

2 *f* Sons were born to David at Hebron. His eldest was Amnon, whose mother was 3 Ahinoam of Jezreel; his second Chileab, whose mother was Abigail widow of Nabal of Carmel; the third Absalom, whose mother was Maacah daughter of Talmai king of 4 Geshur; the fourth Adonijah, whose mother was Haggith; the fifth Shephatiah, whose 5 mother was Abital; and the sixth Ithream, whose mother was David's wife Eglah. These were all born to David at Hebron.

Abner plans a covenant with David

6 As the war between the houses of Saul and David went on, Abner made his position 7 gradually stronger in the house of Saul. Now Saul had had a concubine named Rizpah daughter of Aiah. Ishbosheth asked Abner, 'Why have you slept with my father's con-8 cubine?' Abner was very angry at this and exclaimed, 'Am I a baboon in the pay of Judah? Up to now I have been loyal to the house of your father Saul, to his brothers and friends, and I have not betrayed you into David's hands; yet you choose this moment to charge me with disloyalty over 9 this woman. But now, so help me God, I will do all I can to bring about what the

Lord swore to do for David: I will set to 10 work to bring down the house of Saul and to put David on the throne over Israel and Judah from Dan to Beersheba.' Ishbosheth 11 could not say another word; he was too much afraid of Abner. Then Abner, seeking 12 to make friends where he could, instead of going to David himself sent envoys with this message: 'Let us come to terms, and I will do all I can to bring the whole of Israel over to you.' David sent answer: 13 'Good, I will come to terms with you, but on this one condition, that you do not come into my presence without bringing Saul's daughter Michal to me.' David also sent 14 messengers to Saul's son Ishbosheth with the demand: 'Hand over to me my wife Michal to whom I was betrothed at the price of a hundred Philistine foreskins.' There-15 upon Ishbosheth sent and took her away from her husband, Paltiel son of Laish. Paltiel followed her as far as Bahurim, weep-16 ing all the way, until Abner ordered him to go back home, and he went.

Abner now approached the elders of 17 Israel and said, 'For some time past you have wanted David for your king; now is the 18 time to act, for this is the word of the Lord about David: "By the hand of my servant David I will deliver my people Israel from the Philistines and from all their enemies."' Abner spoke also to the Benjamites and then 19 went on to report to David at Hebron all that the Israelites and the Benjamites had agreed. When Abner was admitted to David's 20 presence, there were twenty men with him and David gave a feast for them all. Then 21 Abner said to David, 'I shall now go and bring the whole of Israel over to your majesty, and they shall make a covenant with you. Then you will be king over a realm after your own heart.' David dismissed Abner, granting him safe conduct.

Joab kills Abner

David's men and Joab returned from a raid 22 bringing a great deal of plunder with them, and by this time Abner, after his dismissal, was no longer with David in Hebron. So 23 when Joab and his raiding party arrived, they were greeted with the news that Abner son of Ner had been with the king and had departed under safe conduct. Joab went in to 24 the king and said, 'What have you done? Here you have had Abner with you. How could you let him go? He has got clean away! You know Abner son of Ner: he came mean-25 ing to deceive you, to learn all about your movements and to find out what you are doing.' When he left David's presence, Joab 26 sent messengers after Abner and they brought him back from the Pool of Sirah; but David

Hebron

27 knew nothing of all this. On Abner's return to Hebron, Joab drew him aside in the gateway, as though to speak privately with him, and there, in revenge for his brother Asahel, he stabbed him in the belly, and he died. 28 When David heard the news he said, 'I and my realm are for ever innocent in the sight of the LORD of the blood of Abner son of 29 Ner. May it recoil upon the head of Joab and upon all his family! May the house of Joab never be free from running sore or foul disease, nor lack a son fit only to ply the distaff or doomed to die by the sword or beg 30 his bread!' So Joab and Abishai his brother slew Abner because he had killed their 31 brother Asahel in battle at Gibeon. Then David ordered Joab and all the people with him to rend their clothes, put on sackcloth and beat their breasts for Abner, and the 32 king himself walked behind the bier. They buried Abner in Hebron and the king wept aloud at the tomb, while all the people wept 33 with him. The king made this lament for Abner:

Must Abner die so base a death?
34 Your hands were not bound,
   your feet not thrust into fetters;
you fell as one who falls at a ruffian's hands.

And the people wept for him again.
35   They came to persuade David to eat something; but it was still day and he swore, 'So help me God! I will not touch food of any 36 kind before sunset.' The people took note of this and approved; indeed, everything 37 the king did pleased them. Everyone through-

out Israel knew on that day that the king had had no hand in the murder of Abner son of Ner. The king said to his servants, 38 'Do you not know that a warrior, a great man, has fallen this day in Israel? King 39 though I am, I feel weak and powerless in face of these ruthless sons of Zeruiah; they are too much for me; the LORD will requite the wrongdoer as he deserves.'

The murder of Ishbosheth

When Saul's son Ishbosheth heard that **4** Abner had been killed in Hebron, his courage failed him and all Israel was dismayed. Now Ishbosheth had[g] two officers, 2 who were captains of raiding parties, and whose names were Baanah and Rechab; they were Benjamites, sons of Rimmon of Beeroth, Beeroth being reckoned part of Benjamin; but the Beerothites had fled to 3 Gittaim, where they have lived ever since.

(Saul's son Jonathan had a son lame in 4 both feet. He was five years old when word of the death of Saul and Jonathan came from Jezreel. His nurse had picked him up and fled, but in her hurry to get away he fell and was crippled. His name was Mephibosheth.)

Rechab and Baanah, the sons of Rimmon 5 of Beeroth, came to the house of Ishbosheth in the heat of the day and went in, while he was taking his midday rest. Now the door- 6 keeper had been sifting wheat, but she had grown drowsy and fallen asleep, so Rechab and his brother Baanah crept in, found their 7 way to the room where he was asleep on the bed, and struck him dead. They cut off his

g had: *prob. rdg.; Heb. om.*

head and took it with them, and, making their way along the Arabah all night, came
8 to Hebron. They brought Ishbosheth's head to David at Hebron and said to the king, 'Here is the head of Ishbosheth son of Saul, your enemy, who sought your life. The LORD has avenged your majesty today on Saul and
9 on his family.' David answered Rechab and his brother Baanah, the sons of Rimmon of Beeroth, with an oath: 'As the LORD lives, who has rescued me from all my troubles!
10 I seized the man who brought me word that Saul was dead and thought it good news; I killed him in Ziklag, and that was how I
11 rewarded him for his news. How much more when ruffians have killed an innocent man on his bed in his own house? Am I not to take vengeance on you now for the blood you have shed, and rid the earth of you?'
12 David gave the word, and the young men killed them; they cut off their hands and feet and hung them up beside the pool in Hebron, but the head of Ishbosheth they took and buried in Abner's tomb at Hebron.

David made king of all Israel

1 h Now all the tribes of Israel came to David at Hebron and said to him, 'We are your
2 own flesh and blood. In the past, while Saul was still king over us, you led the forces of Israel to war and you brought them home again. And the LORD said to you, "You shall be shepherd of my people Israel; you shall
3 be their prince."' All the elders of Israel

came to the king at Hebron; there David made a covenant with them before the LORD, and they anointed David king over Israel. David came to the throne at the age of 4 thirty and reigned for forty years. In Hebron 5 he had ruled over Judah for seven years and a half, and for thirty-three years he reigned in Jerusalem over Israel and Judah together.

David captures Zion

The king and his men went to Jerusalem to 6 attack the Jebusites, whose land it was. The Jebusites said to David, 'Never shall you come in here; not till you have disposed of the blind and the lame', meaning that David should never come in. None the less David 7 did capture the stronghold of Zion, and it is now known as the City of David. David 8 said on that day, 'Everyone who would kill a Jebusite, let him use his grappling-iron to reach the lame and the blind, David's bitter enemies.' That is why they say, 'No blind or lame man shall come into the LORD's house.'

David took up his residence in the strong- 9 hold and called it the City of David. He built the city[i] round it, starting at the Millo and working inwards. So David steadily 10 grew stronger, for the LORD the God of Hosts was with him.

Hiram recognizes David's sovereignty

Hiram king of Tyre sent an embassy to 11 j David; he sent cedar logs, and with them carpenters and stonemasons, who built

h Verses 1–3, 6–10: cp. 1 Chr. 11. 1–9.   *i the city: prob. rdg., cp. 1 Chr. 11. 8; Heb. om.*   *j Verses 11–25: cp. 1 Chr. 14. 1–16.*

12 David a house. David knew by now that the LORD had confirmed him as king over Israel and had made his royal power stand higher for the sake of his people Israel.

David's children born at Jerusalem

13 After he had moved from Hebron he took more concubines and wives from Jerusalem; and more sons and daughters were born to 14 k him. These are the names of the children born to him in Jerusalem: Shammua, Shobab, 15 Nathan, Solomon, Ibhar, Elishua, Nepheg, 16 Japhia, Elishama, Eliada and Eliphelet.

David routs the Philistines

17 When the Philistines learnt that David had been anointed king over Israel, they came up in force to seek him out. David, hearing 18 of this, took refuge in the stronghold. The Philistines came and overrun the Vale 19 of Rephaim. So David inquired of the LORD, 'If I attack the Philistines, wilt thou deliver them into my hands?' And the LORD answered, 'Go, I will deliver the Philistines 20 into your hands.' So he went up and attacked them at Baal-perazim and defeated them there. 'The LORD has broken through my enemies' lines,' David said, 'as a river breaks its banks.' That is why the place was named 21 Baal-perazim.l The Philistines left their idols behind them there, and David and his men carried them off.
22 The Philistines made another attack and 23 overran the Vale of Rephaim. David inquired of the LORD, who said, 'Do not attack now but wheel round and take them in the 24 rear opposite the aspens. As soon as you hear a rustling sound in the tree-tops, then act at once; for the LORD will have gone out before you to defeat the Philistine army.' 25 David did as the LORD had commanded, and drove the Philistines in flight all the way from Geba to Gezer.

David removes the Ark

6 After that David again summoned the picked 2 m men of Israel, thirty thousand in all, and went with the whole army to Baalathjudahn to fetch the Ark of God which bears the name of the LORD of Hosts, who is en-3 throned upon the cherubim. They mounted the Ark of God on a new cart and conveyed it from the house of Abinadab on the hill, with Uzzah and Ahio, sons of Abinadab, 4 guiding the cart. They took it with the Ark of God upon it from Abinadab's house on 5 the hill, with Ahio walking in front. David and all Israel danced for joy before the LORD without restraint to the sound of singing,o

of harps and lutes, of tambourines and castanets and cymbals. But when they came to a 6 certain threshing-floor, the oxen stumbled, and Uzzah reached out to the Ark of God and took hold of it. The LORD was angry 7 with Uzzah and struck him down there for his rash act. So he died there beside the Ark of God. David was vexed because the LORD's 8 anger had broken out upon Uzzah, and he called the place Perez-uzzah,p the name it still bears. David was afraid of the LORD 9 that day and said, 'How can I harbour the Ark of the LORD after this?' He felt he could 10 not take the Ark of the LORD with him to the City of David, but turned aside and carried it to the house of Obed-edom the Gittite. Thus the Ark of the LORD remained 11 at Obed-edom's house for three months, and the LORD blessed Obed-edom and all his family.

David brings the Ark to Jerusalem

When they told David that the LORD had 12 q blessed Obed-edom's family and all that was his because of the Ark of God, he went and brought up the Ark of God from the house of Obed-edom to the City of David with much rejoicing. When the bearers of 13 the Ark of the LORD had gone six steps he sacrificed an ox and a buffalo. David, wear-14 ing a linen ephod, danced without restraint before the LORD. He and all the Israelites 15 brought up the Ark of the LORD with shouting and blowing of trumpets. But as the Ark 16 of the LORD was entering the City of David, Saul's daughter Michal looked down through a window and saw King David leaping and capering before the LORD, and she despised him in her heart. When they had brought in 17 the Ark of the LORD, they put it in its place inside the tent that David had pitched for it, and David offered whole-offerings and shared-offerings before the LORD. After 18 David had completed these sacrifices, he blessed the people in the name of the LORD of Hosts and gave food to all the people, a 19 flat loaf of bread, a portion of meat, and a cake of raisins, to every man and woman in the whole gathering of the Israelites. Then all the people went home. When David 20 returned to greet his household, Michal, Saul's daughter, came out to meet him and said, 'What a glorious day for the king of Israel, when he exposed his person in the sight of his servants' slave-girls like any empty-headed fool!' David answered 21 Michal, 'But it was done in the presence of the LORD, who chose me instead of your father and his family and appointed me

k *Verses 14–16: cp. 1 Chr. 3. 5–8; 14. 4–7.*　　l *That is Baal of Break-through.*　　m *Verses 2–11: cp. 1 Chr. 13. 6–14.*　　n *to Baalath-judah: prob. rdg., cp. 1 Chr. 13. 6; Heb. from the lords of Judah.*　　o *without . . . singing: prob. rdg., cp. 1 Chr. 13. 8; Heb. to the beating of batons.*　　p *That is Outbreak on Uzzah.*　　q *Verses 12–19: cp. 1 Chr. 15. 25—16. 3.*

prince over Israel, the people of the LORD.
22 Before the LORD I will dance for joy, yes,
and I will earn yet more disgrace and lower
myself still more in your eyes. But those
girls of whom you speak, they will honour
23 me for it.' Michal, Saul's daughter, had no
child to her dying day.

The LORD's covenant with David

1 r As soon as the king was established in his
house and the LORD had given him security
2 from his enemies on all sides, he said to
Nathan the prophet, 'Here I live in a house
of cedar, while the Ark of God is housed in
3 curtains.' Nathan answered the king, 'Very
well, do whatever you have in mind, for
4 the LORD is with you.' But that night the
5 word of the LORD came to Nathan: 'Go and
say to David my servant, "This is the word
of the LORD: Are you the man to build me
6 a house to dwell in? Down to this day I
have never dwelt in a house since I brought
Israel up from Egypt; I made my journey in
7 a tent and a tabernacle. Wherever I journeyed with Israel, did I ever ask any of the
judges[s] whom I appointed shepherds of my
people Israel why they had not built me a
8 house of cedar?" Then say this to my servant David: "This is the word of the LORD
of Hosts: I took you from the pastures, and
from following the sheep, to be prince over
9 my people Israel. I have been with you
wherever you have gone, and have destroyed
all the enemies in your path. I will make you
a great name among the great ones of the
10 earth. I will assign a place for my people
Israel; there I will plant them, and they shall
dwell in their own land. They shall be disturbed no more, never again shall wicked
men oppress them as they did in the past,
11 ever since the time when I appointed judges
over Israel my people; and I will give you
peace from all your enemies. The LORD has
told you that he would build up your royal
12 house. When your life ends and you rest
with your forefathers, I will set up one of
your family, one of your own children, to
succeed you and I will establish his kingdom.
13 It is he that shall build a house in honour of my
name, and I will establish his royal throne
14 for ever. I will be his father, and he shall be
my son. When he does wrong, I will punish
him as any father might, and not spare the
15 rod. My love will never be withdrawn from
him as I withdrew it from Saul, whom I
16 removed from your path. Your family shall
be established and your kingdom shall stand
for all time in my sight, and your throne
shall be established for ever."'
17   Nathan recounted to David all that had

been said to him and all that had been revealed. Then King David went into the 18
presence of the LORD and took his place
there and said, 'What am I, Lord GOD, and
what is my family, that thou hast brought
me thus far? It was a small thing in thy 19
sight to have planned for thy servant's house
in days long past. But such, O Lord GOD,
is the lot of a man embarked on a high
career.[t] And now what more can I say? for 20
well thou knowest thy servant David, O
Lord GOD. Thou hast made good thy word; 21
it was thy purpose to spread thy servant's
fame, and so thou hast raised me to this
greatness. Great indeed art thou, O Lord 22
GOD; we have never heard of one like thee;
there is no god but thee. And thy people 23
Israel, to whom can they be compared? Is
there any other nation on earth whom thou,
O God, hast set out to redeem from slavery
to be thy people? Any other for whom thou
hast done great and terrible things to win
fame for thyself? Any other whom thou hast
redeemed for thyself from Egypt by driving
out other nations and their gods to make
way for them? Thou hast established thy 24
people Israel as thy own for ever, and thou,
O LORD, hast become their God. But now, 25
LORD God, perform what thou hast promised for thy servant and his house, and
for all time; make good what thou hast said.
May thy fame be great for evermore and let 26
men say, "The LORD of Hosts is God over
Israel." So shall the house of thy servant
David be established before thee. O LORD 27
of Hosts, God of Israel, thou hast shown me
thy purpose, in saying to thy servant, "I will
build up your house"; and therefore I have
made bold to offer this prayer to thee. Thou, 28
O Lord GOD, art God; thou hast made these
noble promises to thy servant, and thy promises come true; be pleased now to bless 29
thy servant's house that it may continue
always before thee; thou, O Lord GOD, hast
promised, and thy blessing shall rest upon
thy servant's house for evermore.'

David extends his kingdom

After this David defeated the Philistines 8 1 u
and conquered them, and took from them
Metheg-ha-ammah. He defeated the Moab- 2
ites, and he made them lie along the ground
and measured them off with a length of
cord; for every two lengths that were to be
put to death one full length was spared. The
Moabites became subject to him and paid
him tribute. David also defeated Hadadezer 3
the Rehobite, king of Zobah, who was on
his way to re-erect his monument of victory
by[v] the river Euphrates. From him David 4

---

r Verses 1–29: cp. 1 Chr. 17. 1–27.   s Prob. rdg., cp. 1 Chr. 17. 6; Heb. tribes.   t embarked on a
high career: prob. rdg., cp. 1 Chr. 17. 17; Heb. om.   u Verses 1–14: cp. 1 Chr. 18. 1–13.   v re-erect . . .
victory by: or recover control of the crossings of . . .

captured seventeen hundred horse and twenty thousand foot; he hamstrung all the chariot-horses, except a hundred which he 5 retained. When the Aramaeans of Damascus came to the help of Hadadezer king of Zobah, David destroyed twenty-two thou- 6 sand of them, and established garrisons among these Aramaeans; they became subject to him and paid him tribute. Thus the LORD gave David victory wherever he went. 7 David took the gold quivers borne by Hadadezer's servants and brought them to 8 Jerusalem; and he also took a great quantity of bronze^w from Hadadezer's cities, Betah and Berothai.

9 When Toi king of Hamath heard that David had defeated the entire army of 10 Hadadezer, he sent his son Joram to King David to greet him and to congratulate him on defeating Hadadezer in battle (for Hadadezer had been at war with Toi); and he brought with him vessels of silver, gold, and 11 copper, which King David dedicated to the LORD. He dedicated also the silver and gold taken from all the nations he had subdued, 12 from Edom and Moab, from the Ammonites, the Philistines, and Amalek, as well as part of the spoil taken from Hadadezer the Rehobite, king of Zobah.

13 David made a great name for himself by the slaughter of eighteen thousand Edomites in the Valley of Salt, and on returning 14 he stationed garrisons throughout Edom, and all the Edomites were subject to him. Thus the LORD gave victory to David wherever he went.

David's officers

15 ^x David ruled over the whole of Israel and 16 maintained law and justice among all his people. Joab son of Zeruiah was in command of the army; Jehoshaphat son of Ahilud was 17 secretary of state; Zadok and Abiathar son of Ahimelech, son of Ahitub,^y were priests; 18 Seraiah was adjutant-general; Benaiah son of Jehoiada commanded the Kerethite and Pelethite guards. David's sons were priests.

David shows kindness to Mephibosheth

9 David asked, 'Is any member of Saul's family left, to whom I can show true kind- 2 ness for Jonathan's sake?' There was a servant of Saul's family named Ziba; and he was summoned to David. The king asked, 'Are you Ziba?', and he answered, 'Your 3 servant, sir.' So the king said, 'Is no member of Saul's family still alive to whom I may show the kindness that God requires?' 'Yes,' said Ziba, 'there is a son of Jonathan still alive; he is a cripple, lame in both feet.'

'Where is he?' said the king, and Ziba 4 answered, 'He is staying with Machir son of Ammiel in Lo-debar.'

So the king sent and fetched him from 5 Lo-debar, from the house of Machir son of Ammiel, and when Mephibosheth, son of 6 Jonathan and Saul's grandson, entered David's presence, he prostrated himself and did obeisance. David said to him, 'Mephibosheth', and he answered, 'Your servant, sir.' Then David said, 'Do not be afraid; 7 I mean to show you kindness for your father Jonathan's sake, and I will give you back the whole estate of your grandfather Saul; you shall have a place for yourself at my table.' So Mephibosheth prostrated himself 8 again and said, 'Who am I that you should spare a thought for a dead dog like me?' Then David summoned Saul's servant Ziba 9 to his presence and said to him, 'I assign to your master's grandson all the property that belonged to Saul and his family. You 10 and your sons and your slaves must cultivate the land and bring in the harvest to provide for your master's household, but Mephibosheth your master's grandson shall have a place at my table.' This man Ziba had fifteen sons and twenty slaves. Then Ziba 11 answered the king, 'I will do all that your majesty commands.' So Mephibosheth took his place in the royal household like one of the king's sons. He had a young son, named 12 Mica; and the members of Ziba's household were all Mephibosheth's servants, while 13 Mephibosheth lived in Jerusalem and had his regular place at the king's table, crippled as he was in both feet.

David defeats the Ammonites and Aramaeans

Some time afterwards the king of the Am- **10** monites died and was succeeded by his son Hanun. David said, 'I must keep up the 2 same loyal friendship with Hanun son of Nahash as his father showed me', and he sent a mission to condole with him on the death of his father. But when David's envoys entered the country of the Ammonites, the Ammonite princes said to Hanun 3 their lord, 'Do you suppose David means to do honour to your father when he sends you his condolences? These men of his are spies whom he has sent to find out how to overthrow the city.' So Hanun took David's 4 servants, and he shaved off half their beards, cut off half their garments up to the buttocks, and dismissed them. When David heard how 5 they had been treated, he sent to meet them, for they were deeply humiliated, and ordered them to wait in Jericho and not to return until their beards had grown again. The 6

---

w Or copper.　　x Verses 15–18: cp. 20. 23–26; 1 Kgs. 4. 2–6; 1 Chr. 18. 14–17.　　y and Abiathar . . .
Ahitub: prob. rdg., cp. 1 Sam. 22. 11, 20; 2 Sam. 20. 25; Heb. son of Ahitub and Ahimelech son of Abiathar.
z Verses 1–19: cp. 1 Chr. 19. 1–19.

House-tops of an Eastern city

Ammonites knew that they had fallen into bad odour with David, so they hired the Aramaeans of Beth-rehob and of Zobah to come to their help with twenty thousand infantry; they also hired the king of Maacah with a thousand men, and twelve thousand

7 men from Tob. When David heard of it, he
8 sent out Joab and all the fighting men. The Ammonites came and took up their position at the entrance to the city, while the Aramaeans of Zobah and of Rehob and the men of Tob and Maacah took up theirs in the

9 open country. When Joab saw that he was threatened both front and rear, he detailed some picked Israelite troops and drew them

10 up facing the Aramaeans. The rest of his forces he put under his brother Abishai, who took up a position facing the Ammonites.

11 'If the Aramaeans prove too strong for me,' he said, 'you must come to my relief; and if the Ammonites prove too strong for you,

12 I will come to yours. Courage! Let us fight bravely for our people and for the cities[a] of

13 our God. And the LORD's will be done.' But when Joab and his men came to close quarters with the Aramaeans, they put them

14 to flight; and when the Ammonites saw them in flight, they too fled before Abishai and entered the city. Then Joab returned from the battle against the Ammonites and

15 came to Jerusalem. The Aramaeans saw that they had been worsted by Israel; but

16 they rallied their forces, and Hadadezer sent to summon other Aramaeans from the Great Bend of the Euphrates, and they advanced to Helam under Shobach, commander of

17 Hadadezer's army. Their movement was reported to David, who immediately mustered all the forces of Israel, crossed the Jordan and advanced to meet them at Helam. There the Aramaeans took up positions facing David and engaged him, but

18 were put to flight by Israel. David slew seven hundred Aramaeans in chariots and forty thousand horsemen, mortally wounding Shobach, who died on the field. When all

19 the vassal kings of Hadadezer saw that they had been worsted by Israel, they sued for peace and submitted to the Israelites. The Aramaeans never dared help the Ammonites again.

David and Bathsheba

11 At the turn of the year, when kings take the field, David sent Joab out with his other officers and all the Israelite forces, and they ravaged Ammon and laid siege to Rabbah,

2 while David remained in Jerusalem. One evening David got up from his couch and, as he walked about on the roof of the palace, he saw from there a woman bathing, and she was very beautiful. He sent to inquire

3 who she was, and the answer came, 'It must be Bathsheba daughter of Eliam and wife of Uriah the Hittite.' So he sent messengers

4 to fetch her, and when she came to him, he had intercourse with her, though she was still being purified after her period, and then she went home. She conceived, and sent

5 word to David that she was pregnant. David

6 ordered Joab to send Uriah the Hittite to him. So Joab sent him to David, and when

7 he arrived, David asked him for news of Joab and the troops and how the campaign was going; and then said to him, 'Go down

8 to your house and wash your feet after your journey.' As he left the palace, a present from the king followed him. But Uriah did

9 not return to his house; he lay down by the palace gate with the king's slaves. David

10 heard that Uriah had not gone home, and said to him, 'You have had a long journey, why did you not go home?' Uriah answered

11 David, 'Israel and Judah are under canvas,[b]

---

a Or altars.   *b* under canvas: *or at* Succoth.

and so is the Ark, and my lord Joab and your majesty's officers are camping in the open; how can I go home to eat and drink and to sleep with my wife? By your life, I 12 cannot do this!' David then said to Uriah, 'Stay here another day, and tomorrow I will let you go.' So Uriah stayed in Jerusalem 13 that day. The next day David invited him to eat and drink with him and made him drunk. But in the evening Uriah went out to lie down in his blanket^c among the king's slaves and did not go home.

David plans Uriah's death

14 The following morning David wrote a letter 15 to Joab and sent Uriah with it. He wrote in the letter, 'Put Uriah opposite the enemy where the fighting is fiercest and then fall 16 back, and leave him to meet his death.' Joab had been watching the city, and he stationed Uriah at a point where he knew they would 17 put up a stout fight. The men of the city sallied out and engaged Joab, and some of David's guards fell; Uriah the Hittite was 18 also killed. Joab sent David a dispatch with 19 all the news of the battle and gave the messenger these instructions: 'When you have 20 finished your report to the king, if he is angry and asks, "Why did you go so near the city during the fight? You must have known there would be shooting from the 21 wall. Remember who killed Abimelech son of Jerubbesheth. It was a woman who threw down an upper millstone on to him from the wall of Thebez and killed him! Why did you go so near the wall?"—if he asks this, then tell him, "Your servant Uriah the Hittite also is dead."'
22   So the messenger set out and, when he came to David, he made his report as Joab had instructed. David was angry with Joab and said to the messenger, 'Why did you go so near the city during the fight? You must have known you would be struck down from the wall. Remember who killed Abimelech son of Jerubbesheth. Was it not a woman who threw down an upper millstone on to him from the wall of Thebez and killed him? 23 Why did you go near the wall?' He answered, 'The enemy massed against us and sallied out into the open; we pressed them back as 24 far as the gateway. There the archers shot down at us from the wall and some of your majesty's men fell; and your servant Uriah 25 the Hittite is dead.' David said to the man, 'Give Joab this message: "Do not let this

c in his blanket: or on his pallet.

distress you—there is no knowing where the sword will strike; press home your attack on the city, and you will take it and raze it to the ground"; and tell him to take heart.'

When Uriah's wife heard that her husband 26 was dead, she mourned for him; and when 27 the period of mourning was over, David sent for her and brought her into his house. She became his wife and bore him a son. But what David had done was wrong in the eyes of the LORD.

Nathan's parable

The LORD sent Nathan the prophet to David, **12** and when he entered his presence, he said to him, 'There were once two men in the same city, one rich and the other poor. The 2 rich man had large flocks and herds, but the 3 poor man had nothing of his own except one little ewe lamb. He reared it himself, and it grew up in his home with his own sons. It ate from his dish, drank from his cup and nestled in his arms; it was like a daughter to him. One day a traveller came to the rich 4 man's house, and he, too mean to take something from his own flocks and herds to serve to his guest, took the poor man's lamb and served up that.' David was very angry, and 5 burst out, 'As the LORD lives, the man who did this deserves to die! He shall pay for 6 the lamb four times over, because he has done this and shown no pity.' Then Nathan 7 said to David, 'You are the man. This is the word of the LORD the God of Israel to you: "I anointed you king over Israel, I rescued you from the power of Saul, I gave you your 8 master's daughter^d and his wives to be your own, I gave you the daughters of Israel and Judah; and, had this not been enough, I would have added other favours as great. Why then have you flouted the word of the 9 LORD by doing what is wrong in my eyes? You have struck down Uriah the Hittite with the sword; the man himself you murdered by the sword of the Ammonites, and you have stolen his wife. Now, therefore, 10 since you have despised me and taken the wife of Uriah the Hittite to be your own wife, your family shall never again have rest from the sword." This is the word of the LORD: 11 "I will bring trouble upon you from within your own family; I will take your wives and give them to another man before your eyes, and he will lie with them in broad daylight. What you did was done in secret; but I will 12 do this in the light of day for all Israel to see."' David said to Nathan, 'I have sinned 13 against the LORD.' Nathan answered him, 'The LORD has laid on another the consequences of your sin: you shall not die, but, 14 because in this you have shown your con-

d Prob. rdg.; Heb. house.

tempt for the LORD,[e] the boy that will be born to you shall die.'

The birth of Solomon

15 When Nathan had gone home, the LORD struck the boy whom Uriah's wife had borne 16 to David, and he was very ill. David prayed to God for the child; he fasted and went in and spent the night fasting, lying on the 17 ground. The older men of his household tried to get him to rise from the ground, but he refused and would eat no food with them. 18 On the seventh day the boy died, and David's servants were afraid to tell him. 'While the boy was alive,' they said, 'we spoke to him, and he did not listen to us; how can we now tell him that the boy is dead? He may do 19 something desperate.' But David saw his servants whispering among themselves and guessed that the boy was dead. He asked, 'Is the boy dead?', and they answered, 'He 20 is dead.' Then David rose from the ground, washed and anointed himself, and put on fresh clothes; he entered the house of the LORD and prostrated himself there. Then he went home, asked for food to be brought, 21 and when it was ready, he ate it. His servants asked him, 'What is this? While the boy lived you fasted and wept for him, but now that 22 he is dead you rise up and eat.' He answered, 'While the boy was still alive I fasted and wept, thinking, "It may be that the LORD will be gracious to me, and the boy may live." 23 But now that he is dead, why should I fast? Can I bring him back again? I shall go to 24 him; he will not come back to me.' David consoled Bathsheba his wife; he went to her and had intercourse with her, and she gave birth to a son and called him Solomon. And 25 because the LORD loved him, he sent word through Nathan the prophet that for the LORD's sake he should be given the name Jedidiah.[f]

David captures Rabbah

6[g] Joab attacked the Ammonite city of Rab-
27 bah and took the King's Pool. He sent messengers to David with this report: 'I have attacked Rabbah and have taken the 28 pool. You had better muster the rest of the army yourself, besiege the city and take it; otherwise I shall take the city and the name 29 to be proclaimed over it will be mine.' David accordingly mustered his whole forces, marched to Rabbah, attacked it and took it. 30 He took the crown from the head of Milcom, which weighed a talent of gold and was set with a precious stone, and this he placed on his own head. He also removed a great 31 quantity of booty from the city; he took its inhabitants and set them to work with saws

and other iron tools, sharp and toothed, and made them work in the brick-kilns. David did this to all the cities of the Ammonites; then he and all his people returned to Jerusalem.

Amnon and Tamar

Now David's son Absalom had a beautiful 13 sister named Tamar, and Amnon, another of David's sons, fell in love with her. Amnon 2 was so distressed that he fell sick with love for his half-sister; for he thought it an impossible thing to approach her since she was a virgin. But he had a friend named 3 Jonadab, son of David's brother Shimeah, who was a very shrewd man. He said to 4 Amnon, 'Why are you so low-spirited morning after morning, my lord? Will you not tell me?' So Amnon told him that he was in love with Tamar, his brother Absalom's sister. Jonadab said to him, 'Take to your 5 bed and pretend to be ill. When your father comes to visit you, say to him, "Please let my sister Tamar come and give me my food. Let her prepare it in front of me, so that I may watch her and then take it from her own hands."' So Amnon lay down and pre- 6 tended to be ill. When the king came to visit him, he said, 'Sir, let my sister Tamar come and make a few cakes in front of me, and serve them to me with her own hands.' So 7 David sent a message to Tamar in the palace: 'Go to your brother Amnon's quarters and prepare a meal for him.' Tamar 8 came to her brother and found him lying down; she took some dough and kneaded it, made the cakes in front of him and baked them. Then she took the pan and turned 9 them out before him. But Amnon refused to eat and ordered everyone out of the room. When they had all left, he said to 10 Tamar, 'Bring the food over to the recess so that I may eat from your own hands.' Tamar took the cakes she had made and brought them to Amnon in the recess. But when she 11 offered them to him, he caught hold of her and said, 'Come to bed with me, sister.' But 12 she answered, 'No, brother, do not dishonour me, we do not do such things in Israel; do not behave like a beast. Where 13 could I go and hide my disgrace?—and you would sink as low as any beast in Israel. Why not speak to the king for me? He will 14 not refuse you leave to marry me.' He would not listen, but overpowered her, dishonoured her and raped her.

Then Amnon was filled with utter hatred 15 for her; his hatred was stronger than the love he had felt, and he said to her, 'Get up and go.' She answered, 'No. It is wicked to 16 send me away. This is harder to bear than

---

[e] the LORD: prob. rdg.; Heb. the enemies of the LORD. 26–31: cp. 1 Chr. 20. 1–3.

[f] That is Beloved of the LORD.   [g] Verses

all you have done to me.' He would not listen
17 to her, but summoned the boy who attended
18 him and said, 'Get rid of this woman, put
her out and bolt the door after her.' She had
on a long, sleeved robe, the usual dress of
unmarried princesses; and the boy turned
19 her out and bolted the door. Tamar threw
ashes over her head, rent the long, sleeved
robe that she was wearing, put her hands on
her head and went away, sobbing as she
20 went. Her brother Absalom asked her, 'Has
your brother Amnon been with you? Keep
this to yourself, he is your brother; do not
take it to heart.' So Tamar remained in her
21 brother Absalom's house, desolate. When
King David heard the whole story he was
very angry; but he would not hurt Amnon
because he was his eldest son and he loved
22 him. Absalom did not speak a single
word to Amnon, friendly or unfriendly; he
hated him for having dishonoured his sister
Tamar.

Absalom avenges Tamar

23 Two years later Absalom invited all the
king's sons to his sheep-shearing at Baal-
24 hazor, near Ephron.*h* He approached the
king and said, 'Sir, I am shearing; will your
25 majesty and your servants come?' The king
answered, 'No, my son, we must not all
come and be a burden to you.' Absalom
pressed him, but David was still unwilling
to go and dismissed him with his blessing.
26 But Absalom said, 'If you cannot, may my
brother Amnon come with us?' 'Why should
27 he go with you?' the king asked; but Absalom pressed him again, so he let Amnon
and all the other princes go with him.
28   Then Absalom prepared a feast fit for a
king. He gave his servants these orders:
'Bide your time, and when Amnon is merry
with wine I shall say to you, "Strike." Then
kill Amnon. You have nothing to fear, these
are my orders; be bold and resolute.'
29 Absalom's servants did as he had told them,
whereupon all the king's sons mounted their
mules in haste and set off for home.
30   While they were on their way, a rumour
reached David that Absalom had murdered
all the royal princes and that not one was
31 left alive. The king stood up and rent his
clothes and then threw himself on the
ground; all his servants were standing round
32 him with their clothes rent. Then Jonadab,
son of David's brother Shimeah, said, 'Your
majesty must not think that they have killed
all the young princes; only Amnon is dead;
Absalom has looked black ever since Amnon
33 ravished his sister Tamar. Your majesty
must not pay attention to a mere rumour
that all the princes are dead; only Amnon
is dead.'

Absalom escapes

Absalom made good his escape. Meanwhile 34
the sentry looked up and saw a crowd of
people coming down the hill from the direction of Horonaim.*i* He came and reported
to the king, 'I see men coming down the hill
from Horonaim.' Then Jonadab said to the 35
king, 'Here come the royal princes, just as
I said they would.' As he finished speaking, 36
the princes came in and broke into loud
lamentations; the king and all his servants
also wept bitterly.
    But Absalom went to take refuge with 37
Talmai son of Ammihur king of Geshur;
and for a long while the king mourned
for Amnon. Absalom, having escaped to 38
Geshur, stayed there for three years; and 39
David's heart went out to him with longing,
for he became reconciled to the death of
Amnon.

Joab plans Absalom's return

Joab son of Zeruiah saw that the king's **14**
heart was set on Absalom, so he sent to 2
Tekoah and fetched a wise woman. He said
to her, 'Pretend to be a mourner; put on
mourning, go without anointing yourself,
and behave like a bereaved woman who has
been long in mourning. Then go to the king 3
and repeat what I tell you.' He then told her
exactly what she was to say.
    When the woman from Tekoah came into 4
the king's presence, she threw herself, face
downwards, on the ground and did obeisance, and cried, 'Help, your majesty!' The 5
king asked, 'What is it?' She answered,
'O sir, I am a widow; my husband is dead.
I had two sons; they came to blows out in 6
the country where there was no one to part
them, and one of them struck the other and
killed him. Now, sir, the kinsmen have risen 7
against me and they all cry, "Hand over the
man who has killed his brother, so that we
can put him to death for taking his brother's
life, and so cut off the succession." If they
do this, they will stamp out my last live
ember and leave my husband no name and
no descendant upon earth.' 'Go home,' 8
said the king to the woman, 'and I will
settle your case.' But the woman continued, 9
'The guilt be on me, your majesty, and on
my father's house; let the king and his
throne be blameless.' The king said, 'If 10
anyone says anything more to you, bring

h Prob. rdg.; Heb. Ephraim.   *i* Prob. rdg.; Heb. from a road behind him.

him to me and he shall never molest you again.' Then the woman went on, 'Let your majesty call upon the LORD your God, to prevent his kinsmen bound to vengeance from doing their worst and destroying my son.' The king swore, 'As the LORD lives, not a hair of your son's head shall fall to the ground.'

The woman then said, 'May I add one word more, your majesty?' 'Say on', said the king. So she continued, 'How then could it enter your head to do this same wrong to God's people? Out of your own mouth, your majesty, you condemn yourself: you have refused to bring back the man you have banished. We shall all die; we shall be like water that is spilt on the ground and lost; but God will spare the man who does not set himself to keep the outlaw in banishment. I came to say this to your majesty because the people have threatened me. I thought, "If I can only speak to the king, perhaps he will attend to my case; for he will listen, and he will save me from the man who is seeking to cut off me and my son together from Israel, God's own possession." I thought too that the words of my lord the king would be a comfort to me; for your majesty is like the angel of God and can decide between right and wrong. The LORD your God be with you!' Then the king said to the woman, 'Tell me no lies: I shall now ask you a question.' 'Speak on, your majesty', she said. So he asked, 'Is the hand of Joab behind you in all this?' 'Your life upon it, sir!' she answered; 'when your majesty asks a question, there is no way round it, right or left. Yes, your servant Joab did prompt me; it was he who put the whole story into my mouth. He did it to give a new turn to this affair. Your majesty is as wise as the angel of God and knows all that goes on in the land.'

The king said to Joab, 'You have my consent; go and fetch back the young man Absalom.' Then Joab humbly prostrated himself, took leave of the king with a blessing and said, 'Now I know that I have found favour with your majesty, because you have granted my humble petition.' Joab went at once to Geshur and brought Absalom to Jerusalem, but the king said, 'Let him go to his own quarters; he shall not come into my presence.' So Absalom went to his own quarters and did not enter the king's presence.

No one in all Israel was so greatly admired for his beauty as Absalom; he was without flaw from the crown of his head to the sole of his foot. His hair, when he cut his hair (as he had to do every year, for he found it heavy), weighed two hundred shekels by the royal standard. Three sons were born to Absalom, and a daughter named Tamar, who was a very beautiful woman.

David receives Absalom

Absalom remained in Jerusalem for two 28 whole years without entering the king's presence. He summoned Joab to send a 29 message by him to the king, but Joab refused to come; he sent for him a second time, but he still refused. Then Absalom 30 said to his servants, 'You know that Joab has a field next to mine with barley growing in it; go and set fire to it.' So Absalom's servants set fire to the field. Joab promptly 31 came to Absalom in his own quarters and said to him, 'Why have your servants set fire to my field?' Absalom answered Joab, 32 'I had sent for you to come here, so that I could ask you to give the king this message from me: "Why did I leave Geshur? It would be better for me if I were still there. Let me now come into your majesty's presence and, if I have done any wrong, put me to death."' When Joab went to the king 33 and told him, he summoned Absalom, who came and prostrated himself humbly before the king; and he greeted Absalom with a kiss.

Absalom's conspiracy

After this, Absalom provided himself with 15 a chariot and horses and an escort of fifty men. He made it a practice to rise early and 2 stand beside the road which runs through the city gate. He would hail every man who had a case to bring before the king for judgement and would ask him what city he came from. When he answered, 'I come, sir, from such and such a tribe of Israel', Absalom 3 would say to him, 'I can see that you have a very good case, but you will get no hearing from the king.' And he would add, 'If only 4 I were appointed judge in the land, it would be my business to see that everyone who brought a suit or a claim got justice from me.' Whenever a man approached to prostrate 5 himself, Absalom would stretch out his hand, take hold of him and kiss him. By behaving 6 like this to every Israelite who sought the king's justice, Absalom stole the affections of the Israelites.

At the end of four years, Absalom said 7 to the king, 'May I have leave now to go to Hebron to fulfil a vow there that I made to the LORD? For when I lived in Geshur, in 8 Aram, I made this vow: "If the LORD brings me back to Jerusalem, I will become a worshipper of the LORD in Hebron."' The king 9 answered, 'Certainly you may go'; so he set off for Hebron at once. Absalom sent 10 runners through all the tribes of Israel with this message: 'As soon as you hear the sound of the trumpet, then say, "Absalom is king in Hebron."' Two hundred men 11

DAVID'S KINGDOM

The Great Sea

When the king departed, all his household followed him except ten concubines, whom he left in charge of the palace. At the Far House the king and all the people who were with him halted. His own servants then stood[j] beside him, while the Kerethite and Pelethite guards and Ittai[k] with the six hundred Gittites under him marched past the king. The king said to Ittai the Gittite, 'Are you here too? Why are you coming with us? Go back and stay with the new king, for you are a foreigner and, what is more, an exile from your own country. You came only yesterday, and today must you be compelled to share my wanderings? I do not know where I am going. Go back home and take your countrymen with you; and may the LORD ever be your steadfast friend.' Ittai swore to the king, 'As the LORD lives, your life upon it, wherever you may be, in life or in death, I, your servant, will be there.' David said to Ittai, 'It is well, march on!' So Ittai the Gittite marched on with his whole company and all the dependants who were with him. The whole country-side re-echoed with their weeping. And the king remained standing[l] while all the people crossed the gorge of the Kidron before him, by way of the olive-tree in the wilderness.[m]

The Ark is taken to Jerusalem

Zadok also was there with all the Levites; they were carrying the Ark of the Covenant of God, which they set down beside Abiathar[n] until all the people had passed out of the city. But the king said to Zadok, 'Take the Ark of God back to the city. If I find favour with the LORD, he will bring me back and will let me see the Ark and its dwelling-place again. But if he says he does not want me, then here I am; let him do what he pleases with me.' The king went on to say to Zadok the priest, 'Can you make good use of your eyes? You may safely go back to the city, you and Abiathar,[o] and take with you the two young men, Ahimaaz your son and Abiathar's son Jonathan. Do not forget: I will linger at the Fords of the Wilderness until you can send word to me.' Then Zadok and Abiathar took the Ark of God back to Jerusalem and stayed there.

David's counterplot

David wept as he went up the slope of the Mount of Olives; he was bare-headed and went bare-foot. The people with him all had their heads uncovered and wept as they went. David had been told that Ahithophel was among the conspirators with Absalom, and

accompanied Absalom from Jerusalem; they were invited and went in all innocence, knowing nothing of the affair. Absalom also sent to summon Ahithophel the Gilonite, David's counsellor, from Giloh his city, where he was offering the customary sacrifices. The conspiracy gathered strength, and Absalom's supporters increased in number.

David prepares his escape

When news reached David that the men of Israel had transferred their allegiance to Absalom, he said to those who were with him in Jerusalem, 'We must get away at once; or there will be no escape from Absalom for any of us. Make haste, or else he will soon be upon us and bring disaster on us, showing no mercy to anyone in the city.' The king's servants said to him, 'As your majesty thinks best; we are ready.'

j Prob. rdg.; Heb. passed.   k and Ittai: prob. rdg.; Heb. om.   l Prob. rdg.; Heb. passing.   m by way . . . wilderness: prob. rdg.; Heb. obscure.   n beside Abiathar: prob. rdg.; Heb. and Abiathar went up.   o you and Abiathar: prob. rdg., cp. verse 29; Heb. om.

he prayed, 'Frustrate, O LORD, the counsel of Ahithophel.'

As David was approaching the top of the ridge where it was the custom to prostrate oneself to God, Hushai the Archite was there to meet him with his tunic rent and earth on his head. David said to him, 'If you come with me you will only be a hindrance; but you can help me to frustrate Ahithophel's plans if you go back to the city and say to Absalom, "I will be your majesty's servant; up to now I have been your father's servant, and now I will be yours." You will have with you, as you know, the priests Zadok and Abiathar; tell them everything that you hear in the king's household. They have with them Zadok's son Ahimaaz and Abiathar's son Jonathan, and through them you may pass on to me everything you hear.' So Hushai, David's friend, came to the city as Absalom was entering Jerusalem.

Ziba's treachery

When David had moved on a little from the top of the ridge, he was met by Ziba the servant of Mephibosheth, who had with him a pair of asses saddled and loaded with two hundred loaves, a hundred clusters of raisins, a hundred bunches of summer fruit, and a flagon of wine. The king said to him, 'What are you doing with these?' Ziba answered, 'The asses are for the king's family to ride on, the bread and the summer fruit are for the servants to eat, and the wine for anyone who becomes exhausted in the wilderness.' The king asked, 'Where is your master's grandson?' 'He is staying in Jerusalem,' said Ziba, 'for he thought that the Israelites might now restore to him his grandfather's throne.' The king said to Ziba, 'You shall have everything that belongs to Mephibosheth.' Ziba said, 'I am your humble servant, sir; may I continue to stand well with you.'

Shimei curses David

As King David approached Bahurim, a man of Saul's family, whose name was Shimei son of Gera, came out, cursing as he came. He showered stones right and left on David and on all the king's servants and on everyone, soldiers and people alike. This is what Shimei said as he cursed him: 'Get out, get out, you scoundrel! you man of blood! The LORD has taken vengeance on you for the blood of the house of Saul whose throne you stole, and he has given the kingdom to your son Absalom. You murderer, see how your crimes have overtaken you!'

Then Abishai son of Zeruiah said to the king, 'Why let this dead dog curse your majesty? I will go across and knock off his head.' But the king said, 'What has this to do with you, you sons of Zeruiah? If he curses and if the LORD has told him to curse David, who can question it?' David said to 11 Abishai and to all his servants, 'If my son, my own son, is out to kill me, who can wonder at this Benjamite? Let him be, let him curse; for the LORD has told him to do it. But perhaps the LORD will mark my suf- 12 ferings and bestow a blessing on me in place of the curse laid on me this day.' David and 13 his men continued on their way, and Shimei moved along the ridge of the hill parallel to David's path, cursing as he went and hurling stones across the valley at him and kicking up the dust. When the king and all the 14 people with him reached the Jordan, they were worn out; and they refreshed themselves there.

Ahithophel advises Absalom

By now Absalom and all his Israelites had 15 reached Jerusalem, and Ahithophel with him. When Hushai the Archite, David's 16 friend, met Absalom he said to him, 'Long live the king! Long live the king!' But 17 Absalom retorted, 'Is this your loyalty to your friend? Why did you not go with him?' Hushai answered Absalom, 'Because I mean 18 to attach myself to the man chosen by the LORD, by this people, and by all the men of Israel, and with him I will remain. After all, 19 whom ought I to serve? Should I not serve the son? I will serve you as I have served your father.' Then Absalom said to Ahitho- 20 phel, 'Give us your advice: how shall we act?' Ahithophel answered, 'Have inter- 21 course with your father's concubines whom he left in charge of the palace. Then all Israel will come to hear that you have given great cause of offence to your father, and this will confirm the resolution of your followers.' So they set up a tent for Absalom 22 on the roof, and he lay with his father's concubines in the sight of all Israel. In those 23 days a man would seek counsel of Ahithophel as readily as he might make an inquiry of the word of God; that was how Ahithophel's counsel was esteemed by David and Absalom.

Ahithophel said to Absalom, 'Let me pick **17** twelve thousand men, and I will pursue David tonight. I shall overtake him when 2 he is tired and dispirited; I will cut him off from his people and they will all scatter; and I shall kill no one but the king. I will bring 3 all the people over to you as a bride is brought to her husband. It is only one man's life that you are seeking; the rest of the people will be unharmed.' Absalom and all 4 the elders of Israel approved of Ahithophel's advice; but Absalom said, 'Summon Hushai 5 the Archite and let us hear what he too has to say.' Hushai came, and Absalom told 6 him all that Ahithophel had said and asked him, 'Shall we do what he says? If not, say what you think.'

Hushai advises Absalom

7 Hushai said to Absalom, 'For once the counsel that Ahithophel has given is not 8 good. You know', he went on, 'that your father and the men with him are hardened warriors and savage as a bear in the wilds robbed of her cubs. Your father is an old campaigner and will not spend the night 9 with the main body; even now he will be lying hidden in a pit or in some such place. Then if any of your men are killed at the outset, anyone who hears the news will say, "Disaster has overtaken the followers of 10 Absalom." The courage of the most resolute and lion-hearted will melt away, for all Israel knows that your father is a man of 11 war and has determined men with him. My advice is this. Wait until the whole of Israel, from Dan to Beersheba, is gathered about you, countless as grains of sand on the sea-shore, and then you shall march with them 12 in person. Then we shall come upon him somewhere, wherever he may be, and descend on him like dew falling on the ground, and not a man of his family or of his followers 13 will be left alive. If he retreats into a city, all Israel will bring ropes to that city, and we will drag it into a ravine until not a stone 14 can be found on the site.' Absalom and all the men of Israel said, 'Hushai the Archite gives us better advice than Ahithophel.' It was the LORD's purpose to frustrate Ahithophel's good advice and so bring disaster upon Absalom.

Leakages of information

15 Hushai told Zadok and Abiathar the priests all the advice that Ahithophel had given to Absalom and the elders of Israel, and also 16 his own. 'Now send quickly to David,' he said, 'and warn him not to spend the night at the Fords of the Wilderness but to cross the river at once, before a blow can be struck 17 at the king and his followers.' Jonathan and Ahimaaz were waiting at En-rogel, and a servant girl would go and tell them what happened and they would pass it on to King David; for they could not risk being seen 18 entering the city. But this time a lad saw them and told Absalom; so the two of them hurried to the house of a man in Bahurim. He had a pit in his courtyard, and they 19 climbed down into it. The man's wife took a covering, spread it over the mouth of the pit and strewed grain over it, and no one 20 was any the wiser. Absalom's servants came to the house and asked the woman, 'Where are Ahimaaz and Jonathan?' She answered,

'They went beyond the pool.' The men searched but could not find them; so they went back to Jerusalem. When they had gone the two climbed out of the pit and went off to report to King David and said, 'Over the water at once, make haste!', and they told him Ahithophel's plan against him. So David and all his company began at once to cross the Jordan; by daybreak there was not one who had not reached the other bank.

Ahithophel takes his life

When Ahithophel saw that his advice had not been taken he saddled his ass, went straight home to his own city, gave his last instructions to his household, and hanged himself. So he died and was buried in his father's grave.

David's men rout the Israelites

By the time that Absalom had crossed the Jordan with the Israelites, David was already at Mahanaim. Absalom had appointed Amasa as commander-in-chief instead of Joab; he was the son of a man named Ithra, an Ishmaelite, by Abigal daughter of Nahash and sister to Joab's mother Zeruiah. The Israelites and Absalom camped in the district of Gilead. When David came to Mahanaim, he was met by Shobi son of Nahash from the Ammonite town Rabbah, Machir son of Ammiel from Lo-debar, and Barzillai the Gileadite from Rogelim, bringing mattresses and blankets, bowls and jugs.[p] They brought also wheat and barley, meal and parched grain, beans and lentils, honey and curds, sheep and fat cattle, and offered them to David and his people to eat, knowing that the people must be hungry and thirsty and weary in the wilderness.

David mustered the people who were with him, and appointed officers over units of a thousand and a hundred. Then he divided the army in three, one division under the command of Joab, one under Joab's brother Abishai son of Zeruiah, and the third under Ittai the Gittite. The king announced to the army that he was coming out himself with them to battle. But they said, 'No, you must not come out; if we turn and run, no one will take any notice, nor will they, even if half of us are killed; but you are worth ten thousand of us, and it would be better now for you to remain in the city in support.' 'I will do what you think best', answered the king; and he then stood beside the gate, and the army marched past in their units of a thousand and a hundred. The king gave orders to Joab, Abishai, and Ittai: 'Deal gently with the young man Absalom for my sake.' The whole army heard the king giving all his officers this order to spare Absalom.

---

p bringing . . . jugs: *prob. rdg.; Heb.* a couch, bowls and a potter's vessel.

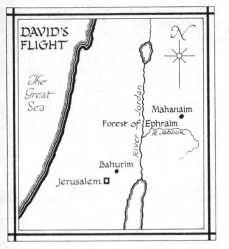

DAVID'S FLIGHT

The Great Sea

River Jordan

Mahanaim

Forest of Ephraim

R. Jabbok

Bahurim

Jerusalem

The army took the field against the Israelites and the battle was fought in the forest of Ephron.*q* There the Israelites were routed before the onslaught of David's men; so great was the rout that twenty thousand men fell that day. The fighting spread over the whole country-side, and the forest took toll of more people that day than the sword.

Joab kills Absalom

Now some of David's men caught sight of Absalom. He was riding a mule and, as it passed beneath a great oak,*r* his head was caught in its boughs; he found himself in mid air and the mule went on from under him. One of the men who saw it went and told Joab, 'I saw Absalom hanging from an oak.' While the man was telling him, Joab broke in, 'You saw him? Why did you not strike him to the ground then and there? I would have given you ten pieces of silver and a belt.' The man answered, 'If you were to put in my hands a thousand pieces of silver, I would not lift a finger against the king's son; for we all heard the king giving orders to you and Abishai and Ittai that whoever finds himself near the young man Absalom must take great care of him. If I had dealt him a treacherous blow, the king would soon have known, and you would have kept well out of it.' 'That is a lie!' said Joab. 'I will make a start and show you.'*s* So he picked up three stout sticks and drove them against Absalom's chest while he was held fast in the tree and still alive. Then ten young men who were Joab's armour-bearers closed in on Absalom, struck at him and killed him. Joab sounded the trumpet, and

q Prob. rdg.; Heb. Ephraim.   *r Or* terebinth.
on you like this.

the army came back from the pursuit of Israel because he had called it off. They took 17 Absalom's body and flung it into a great pit in the forest, and raised over it a huge pile of stones. The Israelites all fled to their homes.

The pillar in the King's Vale had been set 18 up by Absalom in his lifetime, for he said, 'I have no son to carry on my name.' He had named the pillar after himself; and to this day it is called Absalom's Monument.

David grieves over Absalom

Ahimaaz son of Zadok said, 'Let me run 19 and take the news to the king that the LORD has avenged him and delivered him from his enemies.' But Joab replied, 'This is no day 20 for you to be the bearer of news. Another day you may have news to carry, but not today, because the king's son is dead.' Joab 21 told a Cushite to go and report to the king what he had seen. The Cushite bowed low before Joab and set off running. Ahimaaz 22 pleaded again with Joab, 'Come what may,' he said, 'let me run after the Cushite.' 'Why should you, my son?' asked Joab. 'You will get no reward for your news.' 'Come what 23 may,' he said, 'I will run.' 'Go, then', said Joab. So Ahimaaz ran by the road through the Plain of the Jordan and outstripped the Cushite.

David was sitting between the two gates 24 when the watchman went up to the roof of the gatehouse by the wall and, looking out, saw a man running alone. The watchman 25 called to the king and told him. 'If he is alone,' said the king, 'then he has news.' The man came nearer and nearer. Then the 26 watchman saw another man running. He called down to the gate-keeper and said, 'Look, there is another man running alone.' The king said, 'He too brings news.' The 27 watchman said, 'I see by the way he runs that the first runner is Ahimaaz son of Zadok.' The king said, 'He is a good fellow and shall earn the reward for good news.' Ahimaaz called out to the king, 'All is well!' 28 He bowed low before him and said, 'Blessed be the LORD your God who has given into

s I will . . . show you: or I can waste no more time

your hands the men who rebelled against
29 your majesty.' The king asked, 'Is all well
with the young man Absalom?' Ahimaaz
answered, 'Sir, your servant Joab sent me,[t]
I saw a great commotion, but I did not know
30 what had happened.' The king told him to
stand on one side; so he turned aside and
31 stood there. Then the Cushite came in and
said, 'Good news, your majesty! The Lord
has avenged you this day on all those who
32 rebelled against you.' The king said to the
Cushite, 'Is all well with the young man
Absalom?' The Cushite answered, 'May all
the king's enemies and all rebels who would
33 do you harm be as that young man is.' The
king was deeply moved and went up to the
roof-chamber over the gate and wept, crying out as he went, 'O, my son! Absalom
my son, my son Absalom! If only I had died
instead of you! O Absalom, my son, my
son.'

Joab's advice to David

19 Joab was told that the king was weeping
2 and mourning for Absalom; and that day
victory was turned to mourning for the whole
army, because they heard how the king
3 grieved for his son; they stole into the
city like men ashamed to show their faces
4 after a defeat in battle. The king hid his
face and cried aloud, 'My son Absalom;
5 O Absalom, my son, my son.' But Joab
came into the king's quarters and said to
him, 'You have put to shame this day all
your servants, who have saved you and your
sons and daughters, your wives and your
6 concubines. You love those that hate you
and hate those that love you; you have made
us feel, officers and men alike, that we are
nothing to you; for it is plain that if Absalom
were still alive and all of us dead, you would
7 be content. Now go at once and give your
servants some encouragement; if you refuse,
I swear by the Lord that not a man will stay
with you tonight, and that would be a worse
disaster than any you have suffered since
8 your earliest days.' Then the king rose and
took his seat in the gate; and when the army

was told that the king was sitting in the gate,
they all appeared before him.

Judah is reconciled to David

Meanwhile the Israelites had all scattered
to their homes. Throughout all the tribes
of Israel people were discussing it among
themselves and saying, 'The king has saved
us from our enemies and freed us from the
power of the Philistines, and now he has
fled the country because of Absalom. But
Absalom, whom we anointed king, has fallen
in battle; so now why have we no plans for
bringing the king back?'
What all Israel was saying came to the
king's ears.[u] So he sent word to Zadok and
Abiathar the priests: 'Ask the elders of
Judah why they should be the last to bring
the king back to his palace. Tell them, "You
are my brothers, my flesh and my blood;
why are you last to bring me back?" And
tell Amasa, "You are my own flesh and
blood. You shall be my commander-in-
chief, so help me God, for the rest of your
life in place of Joab."' David's message won
all hearts in Judah, and they sent to the king,
urging him to return with all his men.
So the king came back to the Jordan; and
the men of Judah came to Gilgal to meet
him and escort him across the river. Shimei
son of Gera the Benjamite from Bahurim
hastened down among the men of Judah to
meet King David with a thousand men from
Benjamin; Ziba was there too, the servant
of Saul's family, with his fifteen sons and
twenty servants. They rushed into the Jordan under the king's eyes and crossed to and
fro conveying his household in order to win
his favour. Shimei son of Gera, when he had
crossed the river, fell down before the king
and said to him, 'I beg your majesty not to
remember how disgracefully your servant
behaved when your majesty left Jerusalem;
do not hold it against me or take it to heart.
For I humbly acknowledge that I did wrong,
and today I am the first of all the house of
Joseph to come down to meet your majesty.'
But Abishai son of Zeruiah objected, 'Ought

t Sir . . . sent me: *prob. rdg.; Heb.* At the sending of Joab the king's servant and your servant.   *u* What
. . . ears: *prob. rdg.; Heb. has these words after* back to his palace *and adds* to his palace.

not Shimei to be put to death because he cursed the LORD's anointed prince?' David answered, 'What right have you, you sons of Zeruiah, to oppose me today? Why should any man be put to death this day in Israel? I know now that I am king of Israel.' Then the king said to Shimei, 'You shall not die', and confirmed it with an oath.

Mephibosheth and Barzillai greet David

Saul's grandson Mephibosheth also went down to meet the king. He had not dressed his feet, combed his beard or washed his clothes, from the day the king went out until he returned victorious. When he came from Jerusalem to meet the king, David said to him, 'Why did you not go with me, Mephibosheth?' He answered, 'Sir, my servant deceived me; I did intend to harness my ass and ride with the king (for I am lame), but his stories set your majesty against me. Your majesty is like the angel of God; you must do what you think right. My father's whole family, one and all, deserved to die at your majesty's hands, but you gave me, your servant, my place at your table. What further favour can I expect of the king?' The king answered, 'You have said enough. My decision is that you and Ziba are to share the estate.' Mephibosheth said, 'Let him have it all, now that your majesty has come home victorious.'

Barzillai the Gileadite too had come down from Rogelim, and he went as far as the Jordan with the king to send him on his way. Now Barzillai was very old, eighty years of age; it was he who had provided for the king while he was at Mahanaim, for he was a man of high standing. The king said to Barzillai, 'Cross over with me and I will provide for your old age in my household in Jerusalem.' Barzillai answered, 'Your servant is far too old to go up with your majesty to Jerusalem. I am already eighty; and I cannot tell good from bad. I cannot taste what I eat or drink; I cannot hear the voices of men and women singing. Why should I be a burden any longer on your majesty? Your servant will attend the king for a short way across the Jordan; and why should the king reward me so handsomely? Let me go back and end my days in my own city near the grave of my father and mother. Here is my son Kimham; let him cross over with your majesty, and do for him what you think best.' The king answered, 'Kimham shall cross with me and I will do for him whatever you think best; and I will do for you whatever you ask.'

All the people crossed the Jordan while the king waited. The king then kissed Barzillai and gave him his blessing. Barzillai went back to his own home; the king crossed 40 over to Gilgal, Kimham with him. All the people of Judah escorted the king over the river, and so did half the people of Israel.

Further disloyalty in Israel

The men of Israel came to the king in a body 41 and said, 'Why should our brothers of Judah have got possession of the king's person by joining King David's own men and then escorting him and his household across the Jordan?' The men of Judah replied, 'Be- 42 cause his majesty is our near kinsman. Why should you resent it? Have we eaten at the king's expense? Have we received any gifts?' The men of Israel answered, 'We have ten 43 times your interest in the king and, what is more, we are senior to you; why do you disparage us? Were we not the first to speak of bringing the king back?' The men of Judah used language even fiercer than the men of Israel.

There happened to be a man there, a **20** scoundrel named Sheba son of Bichri, a man of Benjamin. He blew the trumpet and cried out:

> What share have we in David?
> We have no lot in the son of Jesse.
> Away to your homes, O Israel.

The men of Israel all left David, to follow 2 Sheba son of Bichri, but the men of Judah stood by their king and followed him from the Jordan to Jerusalem.

When David came home to Jerusalem he 3 took the ten concubines whom he had left in charge of the palace and put them under guard; he maintained them but did not have intercourse with them. They were kept in confinement to the day of their death, widowed in the prime of life.

The end of Sheba's revolt

The king said to Amasa, 'Call up the men of 4 Judah and appear before me again in three days' time.' So Amasa went to call up the 5 men of Judah, but it took longer than the time fixed by the king. David said to Abishai, 6 'Sheba son of Bichri will give us more trouble than Absalom; take the royal bodyguard and follow him closely. If he has occupied some fortified cities, he may escape us.' Abishai was followed by Joab[v] with the 7 Kerethite and Pelethite guards and all the fighting men; they left Jerusalem in pursuit of Sheba son of Bichri. When they reached 8 the great stone in Gibeon, Amasa came towards them. Joab was wearing his tunic and over it a belt supporting a sword in its scabbard. He came forward, concealing his treachery, and said to Amasa, 'I hope you 9 are well, my brother', and with his right

---

v Abishai . . . Joab: prob. rdg.; Heb. Some men of Joab followed him.

hand he grasped Amasa's beard to kiss him.
10 Amasa was not on his guard against the sword in Joab's hand. Joab struck him with it in the belly and his entrails poured out to the ground; he did not strike a second blow, for Amasa was dead. Joab and his brother Abishai went on in pursuit of Sheba son of
11 Bichri. One of Joab's young men stood over Amasa and called out, 'Follow Joab, all
12 who are for Joab and for David!' Amasa's body lay soaked in blood in the middle of the road, and when the man saw how all the people stopped, he rolled him off the road into the field and threw a cloak over him; for everyone who came by saw the
13 body and stopped. When he had been dragged from the road, they all went on after Joab in pursuit of Sheba son of Bichri.
14   Sheba passed through all the tribes of Israel until he came to Abel-beth-maacah,[w] and all the clan of Bichri[x] rallied to him and
15 followed him into the city. Joab's forces came up and besieged him in Abel-beth-maacah, raised a siege-ramp against it and began undermining the wall to bring it down.
16 Then a wise woman stood on the rampart[y] and called from the city, 'Listen, listen! Tell Joab to step forward and let me speak with
17 him.' So he came forward and the woman said, 'Are you Joab?' He answered, 'I am.' 'Listen to what I have to say, sir', she went
18 on, to which he replied, 'I am listening.' 'In the old days', she said, 'there was a saying, "Go to Abel for the answer", and that settled
19 the matter. My city is known to be one of the most peaceable and loyal[z] in Israel; she is like a watchful mother in Israel, and you are seeking to kill her. Would you destroy the
20 LORD's own possession?' Joab answered, 'God forbid, far be it from me to ruin or
21 destroy! That is not our aim; but a man from the hill-country of Ephraim named Sheba son of Bichri has raised a revolt against King David; surrender this one man, and I will retire from the city.' The woman said to Joab, 'His head shall be thrown to you over
22 the wall.' Then the woman withdrew, and her wisdom won over the assembled people; they cut off Sheba's head and threw it to Joab. Then he sounded the trumpet and the whole army left the city and dispersed to their homes, while Joab went back to the king in Jerusalem.

David's officers

23[a] Joab was in command of the army,[b] and Benaiah son of Jehoiada commanded the
24 Kerethite and Pelethite guards. Adoram was in charge of the forced levy, and Jehosh-

aphat son of Ahilud was secretary of state. Sheva was adjutant-general, and Zadok and Abiathar were priests; Ira the Jairite was David's priest.

The Gibeonites avenged

In David's reign there was a famine that lasted year after year for three years. So David consulted the LORD, and he answered, 'Blood-guilt rests on Saul and on his family because he put the Gibeonites to death.' (The Gibeonites were not of Israelite descent; they were a remnant of Amorite stock whom the Israelites had sworn that they would spare. Saul, however, had sought to exterminate them in his zeal for Israel and Judah.) King David summoned the Gibeonites, therefore, and said to them, 'What can be done for you? How can I make expiation, so that you may have cause to bless the LORD's own people?' The Gibeonites answered, 'Our feud with Saul and his family cannot be settled in silver and gold, and there is no one man in Israel whose death would content us.' 'Then what do you want me to do for you?' asked David. They answered, 'Let us make an end of the man who caused our undoing and ruined us, so that he shall never again have his place within the borders of Israel. Hand over to us seven of that man's sons, and we will hurl them down to their death before[c] the LORD in Gibeah of Saul, the LORD's chosen king.' The king agreed to hand them over, but he spared Mephibosheth son of Jonathan, son of Saul, because of the oath that had been taken in the LORD's name by David and Saul's son Jonathan. The king then took the two sons whom Rizpah daughter of Aiah had borne to Saul, Armoni and Mephibosheth, and the five sons whom Merab, Saul's daughter, had borne to Adriel son of Barzillai of Meholah. He handed them over to the Gibeonites, and they flung them down from the mountain before the LORD; the seven of them fell together. They were put to death in the first days of harvest at the beginning of the barley harvest. Rizpah daughter of Aiah took sackcloth and spread it out as a bed for herself on the rock, from the beginning of harvest until the rains came and fell from heaven upon the bodies. She allowed no bird to set upon them by day nor any wild beast by night. When David was told what Rizpah daughter of Aiah the concubine of Saul had done, he went and took the bones of Saul and his son Jonathan from the citizens of Jabesh-gilead, who had stolen them from the public square at Beth-shan, where the

---

w *Prob. rdg., cp. verse 15*; *Heb.* Abel and Beth-maacah.
rampart: *transposed from verse 15*.   z My city . . . loyal: *prob. rdg.*; *Heb.* I am the requited ones of the
loyal ones.   a *Verses 23–26: cp. 8. 16–18; 1 Kgs. 4. 2–6; 1 Chr. 18. 15–17.*   b *Prob. rdg., cp. 8. 16;*
Heb. adds Israel.   c *Or for.*
      x *Prob. rdg.*; *Heb.* Beri.   y stood . . .

Philistines had hung them on the day they
13 defeated Saul at Gilboa. He removed the
bones of Saul and Jonathan from there and
gathered up the bones of the men who had
14 been hurled to death. They buried the bones
of Saul and his son Jonathan in the territory
of Benjamin at Zela, in the grave of his
father Kish. Everything was done as the king
ordered, and thereafter the LORD was willing
to accept prayers offered for the country.

Abishai rescues David

15 Once again war broke out between the
Philistines and Israel. David and his men
went down to the battle, but as he fought
16 with the Philistines he fell exhausted. Then
Benob, one of the race of the Rephaim,
whose bronze spear weighed three hundred
shekels^d and who wore a belt of honour,
took David prisoner and was about to kill
17 him. But Abishai son of Zeruiah came to
David's help, struck the Philistine down and
killed him. Then David's officers took an
oath that he should never again go out with
them to war, for fear that the lamp of Israel
might be extinguished.

More annals of war

18^e Some time later war with the Philistines
broke out again in Gob: it was then that
Sibbechai of Hushah killed Saph, a descen-
19 dant of the Rephaim. In another war with
the Philistines in Gob, Elhanan son of Jair^f
of Bethlehem killed Goliath of Gath, whose
20 spear had a shaft like a weaver's beam. In
yet another war in Gath there appeared a
giant with six fingers on each hand and six
toes on each foot, twenty-four in all. He too
21 was descended from the Rephaim; and,
when he defied Israel, Jonathan son of
22 David's brother Shimeai killed him. These
four giants were the descendants of the
Rephaim in Gath, and they all fell at the
hands of David and his men.

David's song of deliverance

22 These are the words of the song David sang
to the LORD on the day when the LORD
delivered him from the power of all his
enemies and from the power of Saul:

2^g The LORD is my stronghold, my fortress and
my champion,
3 my God, my rock where I find safety;
my shield, my mountain fastness, my strong
tower,
my refuge, my deliverer, who saves me from
violence.
4 I will call on the LORD to whom all praise is
due,
and I shall be delivered from my enemies.
5 When the waves of death swept round me,

and torrents of destruction overtook me,
the bonds of Sheol tightened about me, 6
the snares of death were set to catch me;
then in anguish of heart I cried to the LORD, 7
I called for help to my God;
he heard me from his temple,
and my cry rang in his ears.
The earth heaved and quaked, 8
heaven's foundations shook;
they heaved, because he was angry.
Smoke rose from his nostrils, 9
devouring fire came out of his mouth,
glowing coals and searing heat.
He swept the skies aside as he descended, 10
thick darkness lay under his feet.
He rode on a cherub, he flew through the air; 11
he swooped^h on the wings of the wind.
He curtained himself in darkness 12
and made dense vapour his canopy.
Thick clouds came out of the radiance before 13
him;
glowing coals burned brightly.
The LORD thundered from the heavens 14
and the voice of the Most High spoke out.
He loosed his arrows, he sped them far and 15
wide,
his lightning shafts, and sent them echoing.
The channels of the sea-bed were revealed, 16
the foundations of earth laid bare
at the LORD's rebuke,
at the blast of the breath of his nostrils.
He reached down from the height and took 17
me,
he drew me out of mighty waters,
he rescued me from my enemies, strong as 18
they were,
from my foes when they grew too powerful
for me.
They confronted me in the hour of my peril, 19
but the LORD was my buttress.
He brought me out into an open place, 20
he rescued me because he delighted in me.
The LORD rewarded me as my righteousness 21
deserved;
my hands were clean, and he requited me.
For I have followed the ways of the LORD 22
and have not turned wickedly from my God;
all his laws are before my eyes, 23
I have not failed to follow his decrees.

*d shekels: prob. rdg.; Heb. weight.   e Verses 18–22: cp. 1 Chr. 20. 4–7.   f Jair: prob. rdg., cp. 1 Chr.
20. 5; Heb. Jaare-oregim.   g Verses 2–51: cp. Ps. 18. 2–50.   h Prob. rdg., cp. Ps. 18. 10; Heb. was seen.*

E

24 In his sight I was blameless
and kept myself from wilful sin;
25 the LORD requited me as my righteousness
deserved
and my purity in his eyes.

26 With the loyal thou showest thyself loyal
and with the blameless man blameless.
27 With the savage man thou showest thyself
savage,
and[i] tortuous with the perverse.
28 Thou deliverest humble folk,
thou lookest with contempt upon the proud.
29 Thou, LORD, art my lamp,
and the LORD will lighten my darkness.
30 With thy help I leap over a bank,
by God's aid I spring over a wall.

31 The way of God is perfect,
the LORD's word has stood the test;
he is the shield of all who take refuge in him.
32 What god is there but the LORD?
What rock but our God?—
33 the God who girds me[j] with strength
and makes my way blameless,[k]
34 who makes me swift as a hind
and sets me secure on the mountains;
35 who trains my hands for battle,
and my arms aim an arrow tipped with
bronze.

36 Thou hast given me the shield of thy salvation,
in thy providence thou makest me great.
37 Thou givest me room for my steps,
my feet have not faltered.
38 I pursue my enemies and destroy them,
I do not return until I have made an end of
them.
39 I make an end of them, I strike them down;
they rise no more, they fall beneath my feet.
40 Thou dost arm me with strength for the
battle
and dost subdue my foes before me.
41 Thou settest[l] my foot on my enemies' necks,
and I bring to nothing those that hate me.
42 They cry out[m] and there is no one to help
them,
they cry to the LORD and he does not answer.
43 I will pound them fine as dust on the ground,
like mud in the streets will I trample them.[n]
44 Thou dost deliver me from the clamour of
the people,
and makest me master of the nations.
A people I never knew shall be my subjects.
45 Foreigners shall come cringing to me;
as soon as they hear tell of me, they shall obey
me.

46 Foreigners shall be brought captive to me,
and come limping from their strongholds.
47 The LORD lives, blessed is my rock,
high above all is God my rock and safe
refuge.

48 O God, who grantest me vengeance,
who dost subdue peoples under me,
49 who dost snatch me from my foes and set
me over my enemies,
thou dost deliver me from violent men.
50 Therefore, LORD, I will praise thee among
the nations
and sing psalms to thy name,
51 to one who gives his king great victories
and in all his acts keeps faith with his
anointed king,
with David and his descendants for ever.

David's last words

These are the last words of David: 23

The very word of David son of Jesse,
the very word of the man whom the High
God raised up,
the anointed prince of the God of Jacob,
and the singer of Israel's psalms:
2 the spirit of the LORD has spoken through
me,
and his word is on my lips.
3 The God of Israel spoke,
the Rock of Israel spoke of me:
'He who rules men in justice,
who rules in the fear of God,
4 is like the light of morning at sunrise,
a morning that is cloudless after rain
and makes the grass sparkle from the earth.'

5 Surely, surely my house is true to God;
for he has made a pact with me for all time,
its terms spelled out and faithfully kept,
my whole salvation, all my[o] delight.
6 But the ungodly put forth no shoots,
they are all like briars tossed aside;
7 none dare put out his hand to pick them up,
none touch them but[p] with tool of iron or of
wood;
they are fit only for burning in the fire.[q]

David's heroes

These are the names of David's heroes. First 8[r]
came Ishbosheth the Hachmonite,[s] chief of
the three; it was he who brandished his
spear[t] over eight hundred dead, all slain at
one time. Next to him was Eleazar son of 9
Dodo the Ahohite,[u] one of the heroic three.
He was with David at Pas-dammim where

---

i With the savage . . . savage, and: *or* With the pure thou showest thyself pure, but . . .   *j* who girds me:
prob. rdg., cp. Ps. 18. 32; Heb. my refuge *or* my strength.   *k* and makes . . . blameless: *prob. rdg., cp. Ps.*
18. 32; Heb. unintelligible.   l Prob. rdg., cp. Ps. 18. 40; Heb. unintelligible.   m cry out: *prob. rdg., cp.*
Ps. 18. 41; Heb. look.   *n Prob. rdg., cp. Ps. 18. 42; Heb. adds* will I stamp them down.   *o Prob. rdg.,*
Heb. om.   p but: *prob. rdg.; Heb.* he shall be filled.   *q Prob. rdg.; Heb. adds* in sitting.   *r* Verses
8–39: *cp. 1 Chr. 11. 10–41.   s Prob. rdg.; Heb.* Josheb-basshebeth a Tahchemonite.   *t* who . . . spear:
prob. rdg., cp. 1 Chr. 11. 11; Heb. unintelligible.   u the Ahohite: *prob. rdg., cp. 1 Chr. 11. 12; Heb.* son of Ahohi.

blood of these men who risked their lives for it?' So he would not drink it. Such were the exploits of the heroic three.

Abishai the brother of Joab son of Zeruiah 18 was chief of the thirty. He once brandished his spear over three hundred dead, and he was famous among the thirty. Some think 19 he even surpassed the rest of the thirty*z* in reputation, and he became their captain, but he did not rival the three. Benaiah son 20 of Jehoiada, from Kabzeel, was a hero of many exploits. It was he who smote the two champions of Moab, and who went down into a pit and killed a lion on a snowy day. It was he who also killed the Egyptian, a 21 man of striking appearance armed with a spear: he went to meet him with a club, snatched the spear out of the Egyptian's hand and killed him with his own weapon. Such were the exploits of Benaiah son of 22 Jehoiada, famous among the heroic thirty.*z* He was more famous than the rest of the 23 thirty, but he did not rival the three. David appointed him to his household.

Asahel the brother of Joab was one of 24 the thirty, and Elhanan son of Dodo from Bethlehem; Shammah from Harod, and 25 Elika from Harod; Helez from Beth-pelet,*a* 26 and Ira son of Ikkesh from Tekoa; Abiezer 27 from Anathoth, and Mebunnai from Hushah; Zalmon the Ahohite, and Maharai 28 from Netophah; Heled son of Baanah from 29 Netophah, and Ittai son of Ribai from Gibeah of Benjamin; Benaiah from Pirathon, 30 and Hiddai from the ravines of Gaash; Abi- 31 albon from Beth-arabah,*b* and Azmoth from Bahurim;*c* Eliahba from Shaalbon, and 32 Hashem the Gizonite; Jonathan son of*d* Shammah the Hararite, and Ahiam son of 33 Sharar the Hararite;*e* Eliphelet son of Ahas- 34 bai son of the Maacathite, and Eliam son of Ahithophel the Gilonite; Hezrai from 35 Carmel, and Paarai the Arbite; Igal son 36 of Nathan from Zobah, and Bani the Gadite; Zelek the Ammonite, and Naharai from 37 Beeroth, armour-bearer to Joab son of Zeruiah; Ira the Ithrite, Gareb the Ithrite, 38 and Uriah the Hittite: there were thirty- 39 seven in all.

David numbers Israel and Judah

Once again the Israelites felt the LORD's **24** 1*f* anger, when he incited David against them and gave him orders that Israel and Judah should be counted. So he instructed Joab 2 and the officers of the army*g* with him to go round all the tribes of Israel, from Dan to

the Philistines*v* had gathered for battle.
10 When the Israelites fell back, he stood his ground and rained blows on the Philistines until, from sheer weariness, his hand stuck fast to his sword; and so the LORD brought about a great victory that day. Afterwards the people rallied behind him, but it was
11 only to strip the dead. Next to him was Shammah son of Agee a Hararite. The Philistines had gathered at Lehi, where there was a field with a fine crop of lentils; and, when the Philistines put the people to flight,
12 he stood his ground in the field, saved it*w* and defeated them. So the LORD again brought about a great victory.
13 Three of the thirty went down towards the beginning of harvest to join David at the cave of Adullam, while a band of Philistines was encamped in the Vale of Rephaim.
14 At that time David was in the stronghold and a Philistine garrison held Bethlehem.
15 One day a longing came over David, and he exclaimed, 'If only I could have a drink of water from the well*x* by the gate of
16 Bethlehem!' At this the heroic three made their way through the Philistine lines and drew water from the well by the gate of Bethlehem and brought it to David. But David refused to drink it; he poured it out
17 to the LORD and said, 'God forbid that I should do such a thing! Can I drink*y* the

v He was ... Philistines: *prob. rdg., cp. 1 Chr. 11. 13; Heb.* With David when they taunted them among the Philistines.   w saved it: *or cleared it of the Philistines.*   x *Or cistern.*   y I drink: *prob. rdg., cp. 1 Chr.* 11. 19; *Heb. om.*   z *Prob. rdg.; Heb.* three.   a *Prob. rdg., cp. Josh. 15. 27; Heb.* from Pelet.   b *Prob. rdg., cp. Josh. 18. 22; Heb.* from Arabah.   c *Prob. rdg., cp. 1 Chr. 11. 33; Heb.* from Barhum.   d Hashem ... son of: *prob. rdg., cp. 1 Chr. 11. 34; Heb.* the sons of Jashen, Jonathan.   e *Prob. rdg., cp. 1 Chr.* 11. 35; *Heb.* Ararite.   f *Verses 1–25: cp. 1 Chr. 21. 1–27.*   g Joab ... army: *prob. rdg., cp. 1 Chr.* 21. 2; *Heb.* Joab the officer of the army.

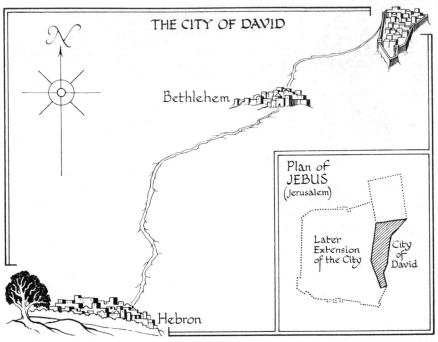

THE CITY OF DAVID

Bethlehem

Plan of
JEBUS
(Jerusalem)

Later
Extension
of the City

City
of
David

Hebron

The city David captured and made the head of his kingdom

Beersheba, and make a record of the people
3 and report the number to him. Joab answered, 'Even if the LORD your God should
increase the people a hundredfold and your
majesty should live to see it, what pleasure
4 would that give your majesty?' But Joab
and the officers were overruled by the king
and they left his presence in order to count
5 the people. They crossed the Jordan and
began at Aroer and the level land of the
gorge, proceeding towards Gad[h] and Jazer.
6 They came to Gilead and to the land of the
Hittites, to Kadesh, and then to Dan and
7 Iyyon[i] and so round towards Sidon. They
went as far as the walled city of Tyre and
all the towns of the Hivites and Canaanites,
and then went on to the Negeb of Judah at
8 Beersheba. They covered the whole country
and arrived back at Jerusalem after nine
9 months and twenty days. Joab reported to
the king the total number of people: the number of able-bodied men, capable of bearing
arms, was eight hundred thousand in Israel
and five hundred thousand in Judah.

David chooses his punishment

10 After he had counted the people David's
conscience smote him, and he said to the
LORD, 'I have done a very wicked thing:
I pray thee, LORD, remove thy servant's
guilt, for I have been very foolish.' He rose 11
next morning, and meanwhile the command
of the LORD had come to the prophet Gad,
David's seer, to go and speak to David: 12
'This is the word of the LORD: I have three
things in store for you; choose one and I
will bring it upon you.' So Gad came to 13
David and repeated this to him and said,
'Is it to be three years of famine in your
land, or three months of flight with the
enemy at your heels, or three days of
pestilence in your land? Consider carefully
what answer I am to take back to him who
sent me.' Thereupon David said to Gad, 'I 14
am in a desperate plight; let us fall into the
hands of the LORD, for his mercy is great;
and let me not fall into the hands of men.'
So the LORD sent a pestilence throughout 15
Israel from morning till the hour of dinner,
and from Dan to Beersheba seventy thousand of the people died. Then the angel 16
stretched out his arm towards Jerusalem to
destroy it; but the LORD repented of the
evil and said to the angel who was destroying the people, 'Enough! Stay your hand.'
At that moment the angel of the LORD was

h began at ... Gad: *prob. rdg.*; *Heb.* encamped in Aroer on the right of the level land of the gorge Gad.   *i Prob. rdg.*, *cp. 1 Kgs. 15. 20*; *Heb.* Yaan.

standing by the threshing-floor of Araunah the Jebusite.

17 When David saw the angel who was striking down the people, he said to the LORD, 'It is I who have done wrong, the sin is mine; but these poor sheep, what have they done? Let thy hand fall upon me and upon 18 my family.' That same day Gad came to David and said to him, 'Go and set up an altar to the LORD on the threshing-floor of 19 Araunah the Jebusite.' David did what Gad told him to do, and went up as the LORD had 20 commanded. When Araunah looked down and saw the king and his servants coming over towards him, he went out, prostrated 21 himself low before the king and said, 'Why has your majesty come to visit his servant?' David answered, 'To buy the threshing-floor from you to build an altar to the LORD,

so that the plague which has attacked the people may be stopped.' Araunah answered 22 David, 'I beg your majesty to take it and sacrifice what you think fit. I have here the oxen for a whole-offering, and their harness and the threshing-sledges for the fuel.' Araunah*j* gave it all to the king for his own 23 use and said to him, 'May the LORD your God accept you.' But the king said to 24 Araunah, 'No, I will buy it from you; I will not offer to the LORD my God whole-offerings that have cost me nothing.' So David bought the threshing-floor and the oxen for fifty shekels of silver. He built an altar to the 25 LORD there and offered whole-offerings and shared-offerings. Then the LORD yielded to his prayer for the land; and the plague in Israel stopped.

j Prob. rdg.; Heb. adds the king.

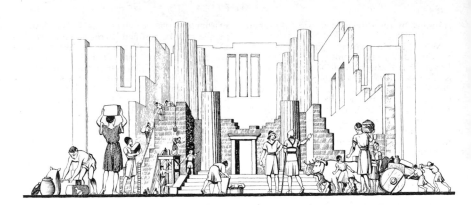

THE FIRST BOOK OF
KINGS

Abishag cares for David

1 KING DAVID was now a very old man
and, though they wrapped clothes round
2 him, he could not keep warm. So his household said to him, 'Let us find a young virgin
for your majesty, to attend you and take
care of you; and let her lie in your bosom,
3 sir, and make you warm.' So they searched
all over Israel for a beautiful maiden and
found Abishag, a Shunammite, and brought
4 her to the king. She was a very beautiful girl,
and she took care of the king and waited on
him, but he had no intercourse with her.

Solomon to succeed David

5 Now Adonijah, whose mother was Haggith,
was boasting that he was to be king; and
he had already provided himself with chariots and horsemen[a] and fifty outrunners.
6 Never in his life had his father corrected
him or asked why he behaved as he did. He
was a very handsome man, too, and was
7 next in age to Absalom. He talked with Joab
son of Zeruiah and with Abiathar the priest,
8 and they gave him their strong support; but
Zadok the priest, Benaiah son of Jehoiada,
Nathan the prophet, Shimei, Rei, and
David's bodyguard of heroes, did not take
9 his side. Adonijah then held a sacrifice of
sheep, oxen, and buffaloes at the stone
Zoheleth beside En-rogel, and he invited all
his royal brothers and all those officers of
the household who were of the tribe of
10 Judah. But he did not invite Nathan the

prophet, Benaiah and the bodyguard, or
Solomon his brother.

Then Nathan said to Bathsheba, the 11
mother of Solomon, 'Have you not heard
that Adonijah son of Haggith has become
king, all unknown to our lord David? Now 12
come, let me advise you what to do for your
own safety and for the safety of your son
Solomon. Go in and see King David and 13
say to him, "Did not your majesty swear to
me, your servant, that my son Solomon
should succeed you as king; that it was he
who should sit on your throne? Why then
has Adonijah become king?" Then while 14
you are still speaking there with the king,
I will follow you in and tell the whole
story.'

So Bathsheba went to the king in his 15
private chamber; he was now very old, and
Abishag the Shunammite was waiting on
him. Bathsheba bowed before the king and 16
prostrated herself. 'What do you want?'
said the king. She answered, 'My lord, you 17
swore to me your servant, by the LORD your
God, that my son Solomon should succeed
you as king, and that he should sit on your
throne. But now, here is Adonijah become 18
king, all unknown to your majesty. He has 19
sacrificed great numbers of oxen, buffaloes,
and sheep, and has invited to the feast all
the king's sons, and Abiathar the priest, and
Joab the commander-in-chief, but he has
not invited your servant Solomon. And now, 20
your majesty, all Israel is looking to you to

a Or a chariot and horses.

244

announce who is to succeed you on the
21 throne. Otherwise, when you, sir, rest with
your forefathers, my son Solomon and I
22 shall be treated as criminals.' She was still
speaking to the king when Nathan the pro-
23 phet arrived. The king was told that Nathan
was there; he came into the king's presence
and prostrated himself with his face to the
24 ground. 'My lord,' he said, 'your majesty
must, I suppose, have declared that Adonijah
should succeed you and that he should sit
25 on your throne. He has today gone down
and sacrificed great numbers of oxen, buffaloes, and sheep, and has invited to the feast
all the king's sons, Joab the commander-in-
chief, and Abiathar the priest; and at this
very moment they are eating and drinking
in his presence and shouting, "Long live
26 King Adonijah!" But he has not invited me
your servant, Zadok the priest, Benaiah son
27 of Jehoiada, or your servant Solomon. Has
this been done by your majesty's authority,
while we[b] your servants have not been told
who should succeed you on the throne?'
28 Thereupon King David said, 'Call Bathsheba', and she came into the king's presence
29 and stood before him. Then the king swore
an oath to her: 'As the LORD lives, who has
30 delivered me from all my troubles: I swore
by the LORD the God of Israel that Solomon
your son should succeed me and that he
should sit on my throne, and this day I give
31 effect to my oath.' Bathsheba bowed low to
the king and prostrated herself; and she
said, 'May my lord King David live for
ever!'

Solomon is anointed king

32 Then King David said, 'Call Zadok the
priest, Nathan the prophet, and Benaiah
son of Jehoiada.' They came into the king's
33 presence and he gave them these orders:
'Take the officers of the household with you;
mount my son Solomon on the king's mule
34 and escort him down to Gihon. There
Zadok the priest and Nathan the prophet
shall anoint him king over Israel. Sound the
trumpet and shout, "Long live King Sol-
35 omon!" Then escort him home again, and he
shall come and sit on my throne and reign
in my place; for he is the man that I have
appointed prince over Israel and Judah.'
36 Benaiah son of Jehoiada answered the king,
'It shall be done. And may the LORD, the
37 God of my lord the king, confirm it! As the
LORD has been with your majesty, so may
he be with Solomon; may he make his throne
even greater than the throne of my lord King
38 David.' So Zadok the priest, Nathan the
prophet, and Benaiah son of Jehoiada, together with the Kerethite and Pelethite
guards, went down and mounted Solomon

on King David's mule and escorted him to
Gihon. Zadok the priest took the horn of 39
oil from the Tent of the LORD and anointed
Solomon; they sounded the trumpet and all
the people shouted, 'Long live King Solomon!' Then all the people escorted him 40
home in procession, with great rejoicing and
playing of pipes, so that the very earth split
with the noise.

Adonijah's plot fails

Adonijah and his guests had finished their 41
banquet when the noise reached their ears.
Joab, hearing the sound of the trumpet, exclaimed, 'What is all this uproar in the city?
What has happened?' While he was still 42
speaking, Jonathan son of Abiathar the
priest arrived. 'Come in', said Adonijah.
'You are an honourable man and bring good
news.' 'Far otherwise,' Jonathan replied; 43
'our lord King David has made Solomon
king and has sent with him Zadok the priest, 44
Nathan the prophet, and Benaiah son of
Jehoiada, together with the Kerethite and
Pelethite guards; they have mounted him on
the king's mule, and Zadok the priest and 45
Nathan the prophet have anointed him king
at Gihon, and they have now escorted him
home rejoicing, and the city is in an uproar.
That was the noise you heard. More than 46
that, Solomon has taken his seat on the royal
throne. Yes, and the officers of the house- 47
hold have been to greet our lord King David
with these words: "May your God make the
name of Solomon your son more famous
than your own and his throne even greater
than yours", and the king bowed upon his
couch. What is more, he said this: "Blessed 48
be the LORD the God of Israel who has set
a successor on my throne this day while I
am still alive to see it."' Then Adonijah's 49
guests all rose in panic and scattered.
Adonijah himself, in fear of Solomon, 50
sprang up and went to the altar and caught
hold of its horns. Then a message was sent 51
to Solomon: 'Adonijah is afraid of King
Solomon; he has taken hold of the horns of
the altar and has said, "Let King Solomon
first swear to me that he will not put his
servant to the sword."' Solomon said, 'If 52
he proves himself a man of worth, not a hair
of his head shall fall to the ground; but if he
is found to be troublesome, he shall die.'
Then King Solomon sent and had him 53
brought down from the altar; he came in
and prostrated himself before the king, and
Solomon ordered him home.

David's last words to Solomon

When the time of David's death drew near, **2**
he gave this last charge to his son Solomon:
'I am going the way of all the earth. Be 2

---

b Has this ... while we: *or* If this has been done by your majesty's authority, then we ...

3 strong and show yourself a man. Fulfil your duty to the LORD your God; conform to his ways, observe his statutes and his commandments, his judgements and his solemn precepts, as they are written in the law of Moses, so that you may prosper in whatever 4 you do and whichever way you turn, and that the LORD may fulfil this promise that he made about me: "If your descendants take care to walk faithfully in my sight with all their heart and with all their soul, you shall never lack a successor on the throne of 5 Israel." You know how Joab son of Zeruiah treated me and what he did to two commanders-in-chief in Israel, Abner son of Ner and Amasa son of Jether. He killed them both, breaking the peace by bloody acts of war; and with that blood he stained the belt about my waist and the sandals on my feet. 6 Do as your wisdom prompts you, and do not let his grey hairs go down to the grave 7 in peace. Show constant friendship to the family of Barzillai of Gilead; let them have their place at your table; they befriended me when I was a fugitive from your brother 8 Absalom. Do not forget Shimei son of Gera, the Benjamite from Bahurim, who cursed me bitterly the day I went to Mahanaim. True, he came down to meet me at the Jordan, and I swore by the LORD that I would 9 not put him to death. But you do not need to let him go unpunished now; you are a wise man and will know how to deal with him; bring down his grey hairs in blood to the grave.'

The death of David

10 So David rested with his forefathers and was
11 buried in the city of David, having reigned over Israel for forty years, seven in Hebron
12 and thirty-three in Jerusalem; and Solomon succeeded his father David as king and was firmly established on the throne.

Solomon puts Adonijah to death

13 Then Adonijah son of Haggith came to Bathsheba, the mother of Solomon. 'Do you come as a friend?' she asked. 'As a
14 friend,' he answered; 'I have something to
15 say to you.' 'Tell me', she said. 'You know', he went on, 'that the throne was mine and that all Israel was looking to me to be king; but I was passed over and the throne has gone to my brother; it was his by the LORD's
16 will. And now I have one request to make of you; do not refuse me.' 'What is it?' she
17 said. He answered, 'Will you ask King Solomon (he will never refuse you) to give me Abishag the Shunammite in marriage?'
18 'Very well,' said Bathsheba, 'I will speak for
19 you to the king.' So Bathsheba went in to King Solomon to speak for Adonijah. The king rose to meet her and kissed her, and

seated himself on his throne. A throne was set for the king's mother and she sat at his right hand. Then she said, 'I have one small 20 request to make of you; do not refuse me.' 'What is it, mother?' he replied; 'I will not refuse you.' 'It is this, that Abishag the 21 Shunammite should be given to your brother Adonijah in marriage.' At that Solomon 22 answered his mother, 'Why do you ask for Abishag the Shunammite as wife for Adonijah? you might as well ask for the throne, for he is my elder brother and has both Abiathar the priest and Joab son of Zeruiah on his side.' Then King Solomon swore by the 23 LORD: 'So help me God, Adonijah shall pay for this with his life. As the LORD lives, who 24 has established me and set me on the throne of David my father and has founded a house for me as he promised, this very day Adonijah shall be put to death!' Thereupon King 25 Solomon gave Benaiah son of Jehoiada his orders, and he struck him down and he died.

Solomon dismisses Abiathar

Abiathar the priest was told by the king to 26 go off to Anathoth to his own estate. 'You deserve to die,' he said, 'but in spite of this day's work I shall not put you to death, for you carried the Ark of the Lord GOD before my father David, and you shared in all the hardships that he endured.' So Solomon dis- 27 missed Abiathar from his office as priest of the LORD, and so fulfilled the sentence that the LORD had pronounced against the house of Eli in Shiloh.

Solomon puts Joab to death

News of all this reached Joab, and he fled 28 to the Tent of the LORD and caught hold of the horns of the altar; for he had sided with Adonijah, though not with Absalom. When 29 King Solomon learnt that Joab had fled to the Tent of the LORD and that he was by the altar, he sent Benaiah son of Jehoiada with orders to strike him down. Benaiah 30 came to the Tent of the LORD and ordered Joab in the king's name to come away; but he said, 'No; I will die here.' Benaiah reported Joab's answer to the king, and the 31 king said, 'Let him have his way; strike him down and bury him, and so rid me and my father's house of the guilt for the blood that he wantonly shed. The LORD will hold him 32 responsible for his own death, because he struck down two innocent men who were better men than he, Abner son of Ner, commander of the army of Israel, and Amasa son of Jether, commander of the army of Judah, and ran them through with the sword, without my father David's knowledge. The 33 guilt of their blood shall recoil on Joab and his descendants for all time; but David and his descendants, his house and his throne,

will enjoy perpetual prosperity from the
34 LORD.' So Benaiah son of Jehoiada went
up to the altar and struck Joab down
and killed him, and he was buried in his
35 house on the edge of the wilderness. Thereafter the king appointed Benaiah son of
Jehoiada to command the army in his place,
and installed Zadok the priest in place of
Abiathar.

Shimei forfeits his life

36 Next the king sent for Shimei and said to
him, 'Build yourself a house in Jerusalem
and stay there; you are not to leave the city
37 for any other place. If ever you leave it and
cross the gorge of the Kidron, you shall die;
make no mistake about that. Your blood
38 will be on your own head.' And Shimei said
to the king, 'I accept your sentence; I will
do as your majesty commands.' So for a
long time Shimei remained in Jerusalem;
39 but three years later two of his slaves ran
away to Achish son of Maacah, king of
Gath. When Shimei heard that his slaves
40 were in Gath, he immediately saddled his
ass and went there to Achish in search of
his slaves; he came to Gath and returned
41 with them. When King Solomon was told
that Shimei had gone from Jerusalem to
42 Gath and back, he sent for him and said,
'Did I not require you to swear by the LORD?
Did I not give you this solemn warning: "If
ever you leave this city for any other place,
you shall die; make no mistake about it"?
43 And you said, "I accept your sentence; I
obey." Why then have you not kept the oath
which you swore by the LORD, and the order
44 which I gave you? Shimei, you know in your
own heart all the mischief you did to my
father David; the LORD is now making
45 that mischief recoil on your own head. But
King Solomon is blessed and the throne
of David will be secure before the LORD
46 for all time.' The king then gave orders to
Benaiah son of Jehoiada, and he went out
and struck Shimei down; and he died. Thus
Solomon's royal power was securely established.

Solomon marries Pharaoh's daughter

3 Solomon allied himself to Pharaoh king of
Egypt by marrying his daughter. He brought
her to the City of David, until he had finished
building his own house and the house of
2 the LORD and the wall round Jerusalem. The
people however continued to sacrifice at the
hill-shrines, for till then no house had been
built in honour of the name of the LORD.
3 Solomon himself loved the LORD, conforming to the precepts laid down by his father
David; but he too slaughtered and burnt
sacrifices at the hill-shrines.

Solomon asks the LORD for wisdom

Now King Solomon went to Gibeon to offer 4
a sacrifice, for that was the chief hill-shrine,
and he used to offer a thousand whole-
offerings on its altar. There that night the 5c
LORD God appeared to him in a dream and
said, 'What shall I give you? Tell me.' And 6
Solomon answered, 'Thou didst show great
and constant love to thy servant David my
father, because he walked before thee in
loyalty, righteousness, and integrity of heart;
and thou hast maintained this great and
constant love towards him and hast now
given him a son to succeed him on the throne.
Now, O LORD my God, thou hast made thy 7
servant king in place of my father David,
though I am a mere child, unskilled in
leadership. And I am here in the midst of 8
thy people, the people of thy choice, too
many to be numbered or counted. Give thy 9
servant, therefore, a heart with skill to
listen, so that he may govern thy people
justly and distinguish good from evil. For
who is equal to the task of governing this
great people of thine?' The Lord was well 10
pleased that Solomon had asked for this,
and he said to him, 'Because you have asked 11
for this, and not for long life for yourself,
or for wealth, or for the lives of your
enemies, but have asked for discernment in
administering justice, I grant your request; 12
I give you a heart so wise and so understanding that there has been none like you
before your time nor will be after you. I give 13
you furthermore those things for which you
did not ask, such wealth and honour[d] as
no king of your time can match. And if you 14
conform to my ways and observe my ordinances and commandments, as your father
David did, I will give you long life.' Then he 15
awoke, and knew it was a dream.

Solomon came to Jerusalem and stood
before the Ark of the Covenant of the
Lord; there he sacrificed whole-offerings
and brought shared-offerings, and gave a
feast to all his household.

Solomon and the two mothers

Then there came into the king's presence 16
two women who were prostitutes and stood
before him. The first said, 'My lord, this 17
woman and I share the same house, and I
gave birth to a child when she was there
with me. On the third day after my baby 18
was born she too gave birth to a child. We
were quite alone; no one else was with us
in the house; only the two of us were there.
During the night this woman's child died 19
because she overlaid it, and she got up in 20
the middle of the night, took my baby from
my side while I, your servant, was asleep,

21 and laid it in her bosom, putting her dead child in mine. When I got up in the morning to feed my baby, I found him dead; but when I looked at him closely, I found that
22 it was not the child that I had borne.' The other woman broke in, 'No; the living child is mine; yours is the dead one', while the first retorted, 'No; the dead child is yours; mine is the living one.' So they went on
23 arguing in the king's presence. The king thought to himself, 'One of them says, "This is my child, the living one; yours is the dead one." The other says, "No; it is your child
24 that is dead and mine that is alive." ' Then he said, 'Fetch me a sword.' They brought
25 in a sword and the king gave the order: 'Cut the living child in two and give half to one
26 and half to the other.' At this the woman who was the mother of the living child, moved with love for her child, said to the king, 'Oh! sir, let her have the baby; whatever you do, do not kill it.' The other said, 'Let neither of us have it; cut it in two.'
27 Thereupon the king gave judgement: 'Give the living baby to the first woman; do not
28 kill it. She is its mother.' When Israel heard the judgement which the king had given, they all stood in awe of him; for they saw that he had the wisdom of God within him to administer justice.

Solomon's officers and governors

4
1 2 King Solomon reigned over Israel. His officers were as follows:

In charge of the calendar:*f* Azariah son of Zadok the priest.
3 Adjutant-general:*g* Ahijah son*h* of Shisha. Secretary of state: Jehoshaphat son of Ahilud.
4 Commander of the army: Benaiah son of Jehoiada.
Priests: Zadok and Abiathar.
5 Superintendent of the regional governors: Azariah son of Nathan.
King's Friend: Zabud son of Nathan.
6 Comptroller of the household: Ahishar. Superintendent of the forced levy: Adoniram son of Abda.

7 Solomon had twelve regional governors over Israel and they supplied the food for the king and the royal household, each being responsible for one month's provision
8 in the year. These were their names:

Ben-hur in the hill-country of Ephraim.
9 Ben-dekar in Makaz, Shaalbim, Beth-shemesh, Elon, and Beth-hanan.
10 Ben-hesed in Aruboth; he had charge also of Socoh and all the land of Hepher.

11 Ben-abinadab, who had married Solomon's daughter Taphath, in all the district of Dor.
12 Baana son of Ahilud in Taanach and Megiddo, all Beth-shean as far as Abel-meholah beside Zartanah, and from Beth-shean below Jezreel as far as Jokmeam.
13 Ben-geber in Ramoth-gilead, including the tent-villages of Jair son of Manasseh in Gilead and the region of Argob in Bashan, sixty large walled cities with gate-bars of bronze.
14 Ahinadab son of Iddo in Mahanaim.
15 Ahimaaz in Naphtali; he also had married a daughter of Solomon, Basmath.
16 Baanah son of Hushai in Asher and Aloth.
17 Jehoshaphat son of Paruah in Issachar.
18 Shimei son of Elah in Benjamin.
19 Geber son of Uri in Gilead, the land of Sihon king of the Amorites and of Og king of Bashan.
In addition, one governor over all the governors*i* in the land.

Solomon's prosperity and wisdom increase

20 The people of Judah and Israel were countless as the sands of the sea; they ate and they
21 drank, and enjoyed life. Solomon ruled over all the kingdoms from the river Euphrates to Philistia and as far as the frontier of Egypt; they paid tribute and were subject to him all his life.
22 Solomon's provision for one day was
23 thirty kor of flour and sixty kor of meal, ten fat oxen and twenty oxen from the pastures and a hundred sheep, as well as stags,
24 gazelles, roebucks, and fattened fowl. For he was paramount over all the land west of the Euphrates from Tiphsah to Gaza, ruling all the kings west of the river; and he enjoyed
25 peace on all sides. All through his reign Judah and Israel continued at peace, every man under his own vine and fig-tree, from Dan to Beersheba.
26 Solomon had forty thousand chariot-horses in his stables and twelve thousand cavalry horses.
27 The regional governors, each for a month in turn, supplied provisions for King Solomon and for all who came to his table; they
28 never fell short in their deliveries. They provided also barley and straw, each according to his duty, for the horses and chariot-horses where it was required.
29 And God gave Solomon depth of wisdom and insight, and understanding as wide as
30 the sand on the sea-shore, so that Solomon's wisdom surpassed that of all the men of the

---

e Verses 2–6: cp. 2 Sam. 8. 16–18; 20. 23–26; 1 Chr. 18. 15–17. Elihoreph.   *g* Prob. rdg., cp. 1 Chr. 18. 16; Heb. Adjutants-general.   *i* over . . . governors: prob. rdg.; Heb. om.

f In . . . calendar: prob. rdg.; Heb.   *h* Prob. rdg.; Heb. sons.

east and of all Egypt. For he was wiser than any man, wiser than Ethan the Ezrahite, and Heman, Kalcol, and Darda, the sons of Mahol; his fame spread among all the surrounding nations. He uttered three thousand proverbs, and his songs numbered a thousand and five. He discoursed of trees, from the cedar of Lebanon down to the marjoram that grows out of the wall, of beasts and birds, of reptiles and fishes. Men of all races came to listen to the wisdom of Solomon, and from all the kings of the earth who had heard of his wisdom he received gifts.

Solomon's alliance with King Hiram

5 When Hiram king of Tyre heard that Solomon had been anointed king in his father's place, he sent envoys to him, because he had always been a friend of David. Solomon sent this answer to Hiram: 'You know that my father David could not build a house in honour of the name of the LORD his God, because he was surrounded by armed nations until the LORD made them subject to him. But now on every side the LORD my God has given me peace; there is no one to oppose me, I fear no attack. So I propose to build a house in honour of the name of the LORD my God, following the promise given by the LORD to my father David: "Your son whom I shall set on the throne in your place will build the house in honour of my name." If therefore you will now give orders that cedars be felled and brought from Lebanon, my men will work with yours, and I will pay you for your men whatever sum you fix; for, as you know, we have none so skilled at felling timber as your Sidonians.' When Hiram received Solomon's message, he was greatly pleased and said,

'Blessed be the LORD today who has given David a wise son to rule over this great people.' And he sent this reply to Solomon: 'I have received your message. In this matter of timber, both cedar and pine, I will do all you wish. My men shall bring down the logs from Lebanon to the sea and I will make them up into rafts to be floated to the place you appoint; I will have them broken up there and you can remove them. You, on your part, will meet my wishes if you provide the food for my household.' So Hiram kept Solomon supplied with all the cedar and pine that he wanted, and Solomon supplied Hiram with twenty thousand kor of wheat as food for his household and twenty kor of oil of pounded olives; Solomon gave this yearly to Hiram. (The LORD had given Solomon wisdom as he had promised him; there was peace between Hiram and Solomon and they concluded an alliance.) King Solomon raised a forced levy from the whole of Israel amounting to thirty thousand men. He sent them to Lebanon in monthly relays of ten thousand, so that the men spent one month in Lebanon and two at home; Adoniram was superintendent of the whole levy. Solomon had also seventy thousand hauliers and eighty thousand quarrymen, apart from the three thousand three hundred foremen in charge of the work who superintended the labourers. By the king's orders they quarried huge, massive blocks for laying the foundation of the LORD's house in hewn stone. Solomon's and Hiram's builders and the Gebalites shaped the blocks and prepared both timber and stone for the building of the house.

It was in the four hundred and eightieth year after the Israelites had come out of Egypt, in the fourth year of Solomon's reign over Israel, in the second month of that year, the month of Ziv, that he began to build the house of the LORD.

Solomon builds the Temple

The house which King Solomon built for the LORD was sixty cubits long by twenty cubits broad, and its height was thirty cubits. The vestibule in front of the sanctuary was twenty cubits long, spanning the whole breadth of the house, while it projected ten cubits in front of the house; and he furnished the house with embrasures.

---

j Verses 2–11: cp. 2 Chr. 2. 3–16.   *k Verses 1–3: cp. 2 Chr. 3. 2–4.*

5 Then he built a terrace against its wall round both the sanctuary and the inner shrine. He made arcades 6 all round: the lowest arcade was five cubits in depth, the middle six, and the highest seven; for he made rebates all round the outside of the main wall so that the bearer beams might not be set into 7 the walls. In the building of the house, only blocks of undressed stone direct from the quarry were used; no hammer or axe or any iron tool whatever was heard in the house while it was being built.

8 The entrance to the lowest arcade was in the right-hand corner of the house; there was access by a spiral stairway from that to the middle arcade, and from the 9-10 middle arcade to the highest. So he built the house and finished it, having constructed the terrace five cubits high against the whole building, braced the house with struts of cedar and roofed it with beams and coffering of cedar.

11 Then the word of the LORD came 12 to Solomon, saying, 'As for this house which you are building, if you are obedient to my ordinances and conform to my precepts and loyally observe all my commands, then I will fulfil my promise to you, the promise I gave to your father 13 David, and I will dwell among the Israelites and never forsake my people Israel.'

14 So Solomon built the LORD's 15 house and finished it. He lined the inner walls of the house with cedar boards, covering the interior from floor to rafters with wood; the floor he laid with boards of pine. 16 In the innermost part of the house he partitioned off a space of twenty cubits with cedar boards from floor to rafters and made of it an inner shrine, to be the Most Holy Place. 17 The sanctuary in front of this was 18 forty cubits long. The cedar inside the house was carved with open flowers and gourds; all was cedar, no stone was left visible.

19 He prepared an inner shrine in the furthest recesses of the house to receive the Ark of the Covenant 20 of the LORD. This inner shrine was twenty cubits square and it stood twenty cubits high; he overlaid it with red gold and made an altar 21 of cedar. And Solomon overlaid the inside of the house with red gold and drew a Veil[l] with golden chains across in front of the inner 22 shrine.[m] The whole house he overlaid with gold until it was all covered; and the whole of the altar by the inner shrine he overlaid with gold.

23[n] In the inner shrine he made two cherubim of wild olive, each ten 24 cubits high. Each wing of the cherubim was five cubits long, and from wing-tip to wing-tip was ten cubits. 25 Similarly the second cherub measured ten cubits; the two cherubim 26 were alike in size and shape, and 27 each ten cubits high. He put the cherubim within the shrine at the furthest recesses and their wings were outspread, so that a wing of the one cherub touched the wall on one side and a wing of the other touched the wall on the other side, and their other wings met in the 28 middle; and he overlaid the cherubim with gold. 29 Round all the walls of the house he carved figures of cherubim, palm-trees, and open flowers, both in the inner chamber and in the 30 outer. The floor of the house he overlaid with gold, both in the inner chamber and in the outer. 31 At the entrance to the inner shrine he made a double door of wild olive; the pilasters and the[o] doorposts were pentagonal. The doors 32 were of wild olive, and he carved cherubim, palms, and open flowers on them, overlaying them with gold and hammering the gold upon the 33 cherubim and the palms. Similarly for the doorway of the sanctuary he made a square frame of wild 34 olive and a double door of pine, each leaf having two swivel-pins. 35 On them he carved cherubim, palms, and open flowers, overlaying them evenly with gold over the carving.

36 He built the inner court with three courses of dressed stone and one course of lengths of cedar. 37 In the fourth year of Solomon's reign the foundation of the house of the LORD was laid, in the month 38 of Ziv; and in the eleventh year, in the month of Bul, the house was finished in all its details according to the specification. It had taken seven years to build.

Solomon's other buildings

7 Solomon had been engaged on his building for thirteen years by the 2 time he had finished it. He built the House of the Forest of Lebanon, a hundred cubits long, fifty broad, and thirty high, constructed of four rows of cedar columns, over which were laid lengths of 3 cedar. It had a cedar roof, extending over the beams, which rested on the columns, fifteen in each row; and the number of the beams was 4 forty-five. There were three rows of window-frames, and the windows corresponded to each other 5 at three levels. All the doorways and the windows had square frames, and window corresponded to window at three levels.

He made also the colonnade, 6 fifty cubits long and thirty broad,[p] with a cornice above.

He built the Hall of Judgement, 7 the hall containing the throne where he was to give judgement; this was panelled in cedar from floor to rafters.

His own house where he was to 8 reside, in a court set back from the colonnade, and the house he made for Pharaoh's daughter whom he had married, were constructed like the hall.

All these were made of heavy 9 blocks of stone, hewn to measure and trimmed with the saw on the inner and outer sides, from foundation to coping and from the court of the house[q] as far as the great court. At the base were heavy 10 stones, massive blocks, some ten and some eight cubits in size, and 11 above were heavy stones dressed to measure, and cedar. The great 12 court had three courses of dressed stone all around and a course of lengths of cedar; so had the inner court of the house of the LORD, and so had the vestibule of the house.

Hiram the craftsman at work in the Temple

King Solomon fetched from Tyre 13 Hiram, the son of a widow of the 14 tribe of Naphtali. His father, a native of Tyre, had been a worker in bronze, and he himself was a man of great skill and ingenuity, versed in every kind of craftsmanship in bronze. Hiram came to King Solomon and executed all his works.

He cast in a mould the two 15 bronze pillars. One stood eighteen cubits high and it took a cord twelve cubits long to go round it; it was hollow, and the metal was four fingers thick.[s] The second pillar was the same. He made two 16 capitals of solid copper to set on the tops of the pillars, each capital five cubits high. He made two bands 17 of ornamental network, in festoons of chain-work, for the capitals on the tops of the pillars, a band of network for each capital. Then he 18 made pomegranates in two rows all round on top of the ornamental network of the one pillar; he did the same with the other capital. (The capitals at the tops of the 19 pillars in the vestibule were shaped like lilies and were four cubits high.) Upon the capitals at the tops of 20 the two pillars, immediately above the cushion, which was beyond the network upwards, were two hundred pomegranates in rows all round on the two capitals.[t] Then 21 he erected the pillars at the vesti-

---

l a Veil: prob. rdg.; Heb. om.   m Prob. rdg.; Heb. adds and overlaid it with gold.   n Verses 23–28: cp. 2 Chr. 3. 10–13.   o and the: prob. rdg.; Heb. om.   p Prob. rdg.; Heb. adds and a colonnade and pillars in front of them.   q Prob. rdg., cp. verse 12; Heb. from outside.   r Verses 15–21: cp. 2 Chr. 3. 15–17.   s it was . . . thick: prob. rdg., cp. Jer. 52. 21; Heb. om.   t the two capitals: prob. rdg.; Heb. the second capital.

bule of the sanctuary. When he had erected the pillar on the right side, he named it Jachin;[u] and when he had erected the one on the left side, he named it Boaz.[v]

22 On the tops of the pillars was lily-work. Thus the work of the pillars was finished.

3w He then made the Sea of cast metal; it was round in shape, the diameter from rim to rim being ten cubits; it stood five cubits high, and it took a line thirty cubits long to go round it. 24 All round the Sea on the outside under its rim, completely surrounding the thirty[x] cubits of its circumference, were two rows of gourds, cast in one piece 25 with the Sea itself. It was mounted on twelve oxen, three facing north, three west, three south, and three east, their hind quarters turned inwards; the Sea rested on top of 26 them. Its thickness was a handbreadth; its rim was made like that of a cup, shaped like the calyx of a lily; it held two thousand bath of water.

27 He also made the ten trolleys of bronze; each trolley was four cubits long, four wide, and three high. 28 This was the construction of the trolleys. They had panels set in 29 frames; on these panels were portrayed lions, oxen, and cherubim, and similarly on the frames. Above and below the lions, oxen, and cherubim[y] were fillets of hammered 30 work of spiral design. Each trolley had four bronze wheels with axles of bronze; it also had four flanges and handles beneath the laver, and

these handles were of cast metal with a spiral design on their sides. 31 The opening for the basin was set within a crown which projected one cubit; the opening was round with a level edge,[z] and it had decorations in relief. (The panels of the trolleys were square, not 32 round.) The four wheels were beneath the panels, and the wheelforks were made in one piece with the trolleys; the height of each 33 wheel was a cubit and a half. The wheels were constructed like those of a chariot, their axles, hubs, spokes, and felloes being all of cast 34 metal. The four handles were at the four corners of each trolley, of 35 one piece with the trolley. At the top of the trolley there was a circular band half a cubit high; the struts and panels on[a] the trolley 36 were of one piece with it. On the plates, that is on the panels,[b] he carved cherubim, lions, and palmtrees, wherever there was a blank space, with spiral work all round it. 37 This is how the ten trolleys were made; all of them were cast alike, having the same size and the same shape.

38 He then made ten bronze basins, each holding forty bath and measuring four cubits; there was a basin for each of the ten trolleys. 39 He put five trolleys on the right side of the house and five on the left side; and he put the Sea in the south-east corner of it.

40c Hiram made also the pots, the shovels, and the tossing-bowls. So he finished all the work which he

had undertaken for King Solomon on the house of the LORD: the two 41 pillars; the two bowl-shaped capitals on the tops of the pillars; the two ornamental networks to cover the two bowl-shaped capitals on 42 the tops of the pillars; the four hundred pomegranates for the two networks, two rows of pomegranates for each network, to cover the bowl-shaped capitals on the two pillars; the ten trolleys 43 and the ten basins on the trolleys; the one Sea and the twelve oxen 44 which supported it; the pots, the 45 shovels, and the tossing-bowls— all these objects in the house of the LORD which Hiram made for King Solomon being of bronze, burnished work. In the Plain of 46 the Jordan the king cast them, in the foundry between Succoth and Zarethan.

Solomon put all these objects in 47 their places; so great was the quantity of bronze used in their making that the weight of it was beyond all reckoning. He made also all 48 the furnishings for the house of the LORD: the golden altar and the golden table upon which was set the Bread of the Presence; the 49 lamp-stands of red gold, five on the right side and five on the left side of the inner shrine; the flowers, lamps, and tongs, of gold; the 50 cups, snuffers, tossing-bowls, saucers, and firepans, of red gold; and the panels for the doors of the inner sanctuary, the Most Holy Place, and for the doors of the house,[d] of gold.

The Ark brought into the Temple

51 When all the work which King Solomon did for the house of the LORD was completed, he brought in the sacred treasures of his father David, the silver, the gold, and the vessels, and deposited them in the storehouses of the house of the LORD.

1e Then Solomon summoned the elders of Israel, all the heads of the tribes who were chiefs of families in Israel, to assemble in Jerusalem, in order to bring up the Ark of the Covenant of the LORD from the City 2 of David, which is called Zion. All the men of Israel assembled in King Solomon's presence at the pilgrim-feast in the month Ethanim, 3 the seventh month. When the elders of Israel had all come, the priests took the Ark of 4 the LORD and carried it up with the Tent of the Presence and all the sacred furnishings of the Tent: it was the priests and the Levites 5 together who carried them up. King Sol-

omon and the whole congregation of Israel, assembled with him before the Ark, sacrificed sheep and oxen in numbers past counting or reckoning. Then the priests brought 6 in the Ark of the Covenant of the LORD to its place, the inner shrine of the house, the Most Holy Place, beneath the wings of the cherubim. The cherubim spread their wings 7 over the place of the Ark; they formed a screen above the Ark and its poles. The poles 8 projected, and their ends could be seen from the Holy Place immediately in front of the inner shrine, but from nowhere else outside; they are there to this day. There was nothing 9 inside the Ark but the two tablets of stone which Moses had deposited there at Horeb, the tablets of the covenant which the LORD made with the Israelites when they left Egypt.

Then the priests came out of the Holy 10 Place, since the cloud was filling the house of the LORD, and they could not continue 11

---

u Or Jachun, meaning It shall stand. v Or Booz, meaning In strength. w Verses 23–26: cp.
2 Chr. 4. 2–5. x Prob. rdg.; Heb. ten. y and cherubim: prob. rdg.; Heb. om. z Prob. rdg.;
Heb. adds a cubit and a half (cp. verse 32). a Prob. rdg.; Heb. adds the head of. b Prob. rdg.;
Heb. adds its struts. c Verses 40–51: cp. 2 Chr. 4. 11—5. 1. d Prob. rdg.; Heb. adds for the temple.
e Verses 1–9: cp. 2 Chr. 5. 2–10.

to minister because of it, for the glory of the
12 *f* LORD filled his house. And Solomon said:

> O LORD who hast set the sun in heaven,
>   but hast chosen to dwell in thick darkness,
> 13 here have I built thee a lofty house,
>   a habitation for thee to occupy for ever.

Solomon blesses the people

14 And as they stood waiting, the king turned
round and blessed all the assembly of Israel
15 in these words: 'Blessed be the LORD the
God of Israel who spoke directly to my
father David and has himself fulfilled his
16 promise. For he said, "From the day when
I brought my people Israel out of Egypt, I
chose no city out of all the tribes of Israel
where I should build a house for my Name
to be there, but I chose David to be over my
17 people Israel." My father David had in
mind to build a house in honour of the name
18 of the LORD the God of Israel, but the LORD
said to him, "You purposed to build a house
in honour of my name; and your purpose
19 was good. Nevertheless, you shall not build
it; but the son who is to be born to you,
he shall build the house in honour of my
20 name." The LORD has now fulfilled his promise: I have succeeded my father David and
taken his place on the throne of Israel, as
the LORD promised; and I have built the
house in honour of the name of the LORD
21 the God of Israel. I have assigned therein a
place for the Ark containing the Covenant
of the LORD, which he made with our forefathers when he brought them out of Egypt.'

Solomon prays to the LORD

22 Then Solomon, standing in front of the altar
of the LORD in the presence of the whole
assembly of Israel, spread out his hands
23 towards heaven and said, 'O LORD God of
Israel, there is no god like thee in heaven
above or on earth beneath, keeping covenant
with thy servants and showing them constant
love while they continue faithful to thee in
24 heart and soul. Thou hast kept thy promise
to thy servant David my father; by thy deeds
this day thou hast fulfilled what thou didst
25 say to him in words. Now therefore, O LORD
God of Israel, keep this promise of thine
to thy servant David my father: "You shall
never want for a man appointed by me to
sit on the throne of Israel, if only your sons
look to their ways and walk before me as
26 you have walked before me." And now,
O God of Israel, let the words which thou
didst speak to thy servant David my father
be confirmed.
27 'But can God indeed dwell on earth?
Heaven itself, the highest heaven, cannot
contain thee; how much less this house that

I have built! Yet attend to the prayer and 28
the supplication of thy servant, O LORD my
God, listen to the cry and the prayer which
thy servant utters this day, that thine eyes 29
may ever be upon this house night and day,
this place of which thou didst say, "My
Name shall be there"; so mayest thou hear
thy servant when he prays towards this
place. Hear the supplication of thy servant 30
and of thy people Israel when they pray
towards this place. Hear thou in heaven thy
dwelling and, when thou hearest, forgive.
'When a man wrongs his neighbour and 31
he is adjured to take an oath, and the adjuration is made before thy altar in this house,
then do thou hear in heaven and act: be thou 32
thy servants' judge, condemning the guilty
man and bringing his deeds upon his own
head, acquitting the innocent and rewarding
him as his innocence may deserve.
'When thy people Israel are defeated by 33
an enemy because they have sinned against
thee, and they turn back to thee, confessing
thy name and making their prayer and supplication to thee in this house, do thou hear 34
in heaven; forgive the sin of thy people
Israel and restore them to the land which
thou gavest to their forefathers.
'When the heavens are shut up and there 35
is no rain because thy servant and thy
people Israel have sinned against thee, and
when they pray towards this place, confessing thy name and forsaking their sin
when they feel thy punishment, do thou hear 36
in heaven and forgive their sin; so mayest
thou teach them the good way which they
should follow; and grant rain to thy land
which thou hast given to thy people as their
own possession.
'If there is famine in the land, or pesti- 37
lence, or black blight or red, or locusts new-
sloughed or fully grown; or if their enemies
besiege them in any of their cities; or if
plague or sickness befall them, then hear the 38
prayer or supplication of every man among
thy people Israel, as each one, prompted
by the remorse of his own heart, spreads out
his hands towards this house: hear it in 39
heaven thy dwelling and forgive, and act.
And, as thou knowest a man's heart, reward
him according to his deeds, for thou alone
knowest the hearts of all men; and so they 40
will fear thee all their lives in the land thou
gavest to our forefathers.
'The foreigner too, the man who does not 41
belong to thy people Israel, but has come
from a distant land because of thy fame (for 42
men shall hear of thy great fame and thy
strong hand and arm outstretched), when
he comes and prays towards this house, hear 43
in heaven thy dwelling and respond to the
call which the foreigner makes to thee, so

f Verses 12–50: cp. 2 Chr. 6. 1–39.

that like thy people Israel all peoples of the earth may know thy fame and fear thee, and learn that this house which I have built bears thy name.

44 'When thy people go to war with an enemy, wherever thou dost send them, when they pray to the LORD, turning towards this city which thou hast chosen and towards this house which I have built in honour of 45 thy name, do thou in heaven hear their prayer and supplication, and grant them justice.

46 'Should they sin against thee (and what man is free from sin?) and shouldst thou in thy anger give them over to an enemy, who carries them captive to his own land, far or 47 near; if in the land of their captivity they learn their lesson and make supplication again to thee in that land and say, "We have sinned and acted perversely and wickedly", 48 if they turn back to thee with heart and soul in the land of their captors, and pray to thee, turning towards their land which thou gavest to their forefathers and towards this city which thou didst choose and this house which I have built in honour of thy name; 49 then in heaven thy dwelling do thou hear their prayer and supplication, and grant 50 them justice. Forgive thy people their sins and transgressions against thee; put pity 51 for them in their captors' hearts. For they are thy possession, thy people whom thou didst bring out of Egypt, from the smelting-52 furnace, and so thine eyes are ever open to the entreaty of thy servant and of thy people Israel, and thou dost hear whenever they 53 call to thee. Thou thyself hast singled them out from all the peoples of the earth to be thy possession; so thou didst promise through thy servant Moses when thou didst bring our forefathers from Egypt, O Lord GOD.'

Solomon again blesses Israel

54 When Solomon had finished this prayer and supplication to the LORD, he rose from before the altar of the LORD, where he had been kneeling with his hands spread out to 55 heaven, stood up and in a loud voice blessed 56 the whole assembly of Israel: 'Blessed be the LORD who has given his people Israel rest, as he promised: not one of the promises he made through his servant Moses has failed. 57 The LORD our God be with us as he was with our forefathers; may he never leave us nor 58 forsake us. May he turn our hearts towards him, that we may conform to all his ways, observing his commandments, statutes, and judgements, as he commanded our fore-59 fathers. And may the words of my supplication to the LORD be with the LORD our God day and night, that, as the need arises day

by day, he may grant justice to his servant and justice to his people Israel. So all the 60 peoples of the earth will know that the LORD is God, he and no other, and you will be 61 perfect in loyalty to the LORD our God as you are this day, conforming to his statutes and observing his commandments.'

Dedicating the Temple

When the king and all Israel came to offer 62 sacrifices before the LORD, Solomon offered 63 as shared-offerings to the LORD twenty-two thousand oxen and a hundred and twenty thousand sheep; thus it was that the king and the Israelites dedicated the house of the LORD. On that day also the king con- 64*g* secrated the centre of the court which lay in front[h] of the house of the LORD; there he offered the whole-offering, the grain-offering, and the fat portions of the shared-offerings, because the bronze altar which stood before the LORD was too small to take them all, the whole-offering, the grain-offering, and the fat portions of the shared-offerings.

So Solomon and all Israel with him, a 65 great assembly from Lebo-hamath to the Torrent of Egypt, celebrated the pilgrim-feast at that time before the LORD our God for seven days. On the eighth day he dis- 66 missed the people; and they blessed the king, and went home happy and glad at heart for all the prosperity granted by the LORD to his servant David and to his people Israel.

The LORD appears again to Solomon

When Solomon had finished the house of **9** 1[i] the LORD and the royal palace and all the plans for building on which he had set his heart, the LORD appeared to him a second 2 time, as he had appeared to him at Gibeon. The LORD said to him, 'I have heard the 3 prayer and supplication which you have offered me; I have consecrated this house which you have built, to receive my Name for all time, and my eyes and my heart shall be fixed on it for ever. And if you, on your 4 part, live in my sight as your father David lived, in integrity and uprightness, doing all I command you and observing my statutes and my judgements, then I will establish 5 your royal throne over Israel for ever, as I promised your father David when I said, "You shall never want for a man upon the throne of Israel." But if you or your sons 6 turn back from following me and do not observe my commandments and my statutes which I have set before you, and if you go and serve other gods and prostrate yourselves before them, then I will cut off Israel 7 from the land which I gave them; I will renounce this house which I have consecrated in honour of my name, and Israel

---

g *Verses 64–66: cp. 2 Chr. 7. 7–10.*   *h* *Or to the east.*   *i* *Verses 1–9: cp. 2 Chr. 7. 11–22.*

shall become a byword and an object lesson
8 among all peoples. And this house will become a ruin; every passer-by will be appalled and gasp at the sight of it; and they will ask, "Why has the LORD so treated this land and
9 this house?" The answer will be, "Because they forsook the LORD their God, who brought their forefathers out of Egypt, and clung to other gods, prostrating themselves before them and serving them; that is why the LORD has brought this great evil on them." '

King Hiram is dissatisfied

10ʲ Solomon had taken twenty years to build the two houses, the house of the LORD and
11 the royal palace. Hiram king of Tyre had supplied him with all the timber, both cedar and pine, and all the gold, that he desired, and King Solomon gave Hiram twenty cities
12 in the land of Galilee. But when Hiram went from Tyre to inspect the cities which Solomon had given him, they did not satisfy him,
13 and he said, 'What kind of cities are these you have given me, my brother?' And so he called them the Land of Cabul,ᵏ the name
14 they still bear. Hiram sent a hundred and twenty talents of gold to the king.

Solomon conscripts labour

15 This is the record of the forced labour which King Solomon conscripted to build the house of the LORD, his own palace, the Millo, the wall of Jerusalem, and Hazor, Megiddo, and
16 Gezer. Gezer had been attacked and captured by Pharaoh king of Egypt, who had burnt it to the ground, put its Canaanite inhabitants to death, and given it as a marriage gift to his daughter, Solomon's wife;
17 and Solomon rebuilt it. He also built Lower
18 Beth-horon, Baalath, and Tamar in the
19 wilderness, as well as all his store-cities, and the towns where he quartered his chariots and horses; and he carried out all his cherished plans for building in Jerusalem, in the Lebanon, and throughout his whole
20 dominion. All the survivors of the Amorites, Hittites, Perizzites, Hivites, and Jebusites,
21 who did not belong to Israel—that is their descendants who survived in the land, wherever the Israelites had been unable to annihilate them—were employed by Solomon on
22 perpetual forced labour, as they still are. But Solomon put none of the Israelites to forced labour; they were his fighting men,ˡ his captains and lieutenants, and the commanders
23 of his chariots and of his cavalry. The number of officers in charge of the foremen over Solomon's work was five hundred and fifty;

these superintended the people engaged on the work.
24 Then Solomon brought Pharaoh's daughter up from the City of David to her own house which he had built for her; later on he built the Millo.
25 Three times a year Solomon used to offer whole-offerings and shared-offerings on the altar which he had built to the LORD, making smoke-offerings before the LORD. So he completed the house.

Solomon's fleet

26 King Solomon built a fleet of ships at Ezion-geber, near Elothᵐ on the shore of the Red Sea,ⁿ in Edom. Hiram sent men of
27 his own to serve with the fleet, experienced
28 seamen, to work with Solomon's men; and they went to Ophir and brought back four hundred and twenty talents of gold, which they delivered to King Solomon.

The queen of Sheba visits Solomon

10 The queen of Sheba heard of Solomon's fameᵖ and came to test him with hard questions.
2 She arrived in Jerusalem with a very large retinue, camels laden with spices, gold in great quantity, and precious stones. When she came to Solomon, she told him every-
3 thing she had in her mind, and Solomon answered all her questions; not one of them was too abstruse for the king to answer.
4 When the queen of Sheba saw all the wisdom of Solomon, the house which he had built,
5 the food on his table, the courtiers sitting round him, and his attendants standing behind in their livery, his cupbearers, and the whole-offerings which he used to offer in the house of the LORD, there was no more
6 spirit left in her. Then she said to the king, 'The report which I heard in my own country
7 about you and your wisdom was true, but I did not believe it until I came and saw for myself. Indeed I was not told half of it; your wisdom and your prosperity go far beyond
8 the report which I had of them. Happy are your wives, happy these courtiers of yours who wait on you every day and hear your
9 wisdom! Blessed be the LORD your God who has delighted in you and has set you on the throne of Israel; because he loves Israel for ever, he has made you their king to main-
10 tain law and justice.' Then she gave the king a hundred and twenty talents of gold, spices in great abundance, and precious stones. Never again came such a quantity of spices as the queen of Sheba gave to King Solomon.

---

j Verses 10–28: cp. 2 Chr. 8. 1–18.　　k That is Sterile Land.　　l Prob. rdg.; Heb. adds and his servants.
m Or Elath.　　n Or the Sea of Reeds.　　o Verses 1–25: cp. 2 Chr. 9. 1–24.　　p Prob. rdg., cp.
2 Chr. 9. 1; Heb. adds to the name of the LORD.

Solomon's wealth

11 Besides all this, Hiram's fleet of ships, which had brought gold from Ophir, brought in also from Ophir cargoes of almug wood and
12 precious stones. The king used the wood to make stools for the house of the LORD and for the royal palace, as well as harps and lutes for the singers. No such almug wood has ever been imported or even seen since that time.
13 And King Solomon gave the queen of Sheba all she desired, whatever she asked, in addition to all that he gave her of his royal bounty. So she departed and returned with her retinue to her own land.
14 Now the weight of gold which Solomon received yearly was six hundred and sixty-
15 six talents, in addition to the tolls levied by the customs officers and profits on foreign trade, and the tribute of*q* the kings of Arabia and the regional governors.
16 King Solomon made two hundred shields of beaten gold, and six hundred shekels of
17 gold went to the making of each one; he also made three hundred bucklers of beaten gold, and three minas of gold went to the making of each buckler. The king put these into the House of the Forest of Lebanon.
18 The king also made a great throne of ivory
19 and overlaid it with fine gold. Six steps led up to the throne; at the back of the throne there was the head of a calf. There were arms

on each side of the seat, with a lion standing beside each of them, and twelve lions stood 20 on the six steps, one at either end of each step. Nothing like it had ever been made for any monarch. All Solomon's drinking 21 vessels were of gold, and all the plate in the House of the Forest of Lebanon was of red gold; no silver was used, for it was reckoned of no value in the days of Solomon. The king 22 had a fleet of merchantmen at sea with Hiram's fleet; once every three years this fleet of merchantmen came home, bringing gold and silver, ivory, apes and monkeys.

Solomon's wisdom and fame

Thus King Solomon outdid all the kings of 23 the earth in wealth and wisdom, and all the 24 world courted him, to hear the wisdom which God had put in his heart. Each brought 25 his gift with him, vessels of silver and gold, garments, perfumes and spices, horses and mules, so much year by year.

And Solomon got together many chariots 26*r* and horses; he had fourteen hundred chariots and twelve thousand horses, and he stabled some in the chariot-towns and kept others at hand in Jerusalem. The king made 27 silver as common in Jerusalem as stones, and cedar as plentiful as sycomore-fig in the Shephelah. Horses were imported from 28 Egypt and Coa for Solomon; the royal merchants obtained them from Coa by

q and the tribute of: prob. rdg.; Heb. and all.

r Verses 26–29: cp. 2 Chr. 1. 14–17; 9. 25–28.

E *

29 purchase. Chariots were imported from Egypt for six hundred silver shekels each, and horses for a hundred and fifty; in the same way the merchants obtained them for export from all the kings of the Hittites and the kings of Aram.

Solomon defects from true worship

11 King Solomon was a lover of women, and besides Pharaoh's daughter he married many foreign women, Moabite, Ammonite, 2 Edomite, Sidonian, and Hittite, from the nations with whom the LORD had forbidden the Israelites to intermarry, 'because', he said, 'they will entice you to serve their gods.' But Solomon was devoted to them and loved 3 them dearly. He had seven hundred wives, who were princesses, and three hundred concubines, and they turned his heart from the 4 truth. When he grew old, his wives turned his heart to follow other gods, and he did not remain wholly loyal to the LORD his 5 God as his father David had been. He followed Ashtoreth, goddess of the Sidonians, and Milcom, the loathsome god of the 6 Ammonites. Thus Solomon did what was wrong in the eyes of the LORD, and was not 7 loyal to the LORD like his father David. He built a hill-shrine for Kemosh, the loathsome god of Moab, on the height to the east of Jerusalem, and for Molech, the loathsome god 8 of the Ammonites. Thus he did for the gods to which all his foreign wives burnt offerings 9 and made sacrifices. The LORD was angry with Solomon because his heart had turned away from the LORD the God of Israel, who 10 had appeared to him twice and had strictly commanded him not to follow other gods; 11 but he disobeyed the LORD's command. The LORD therefore said to Solomon, 'Because you have done this and have not kept my covenant and my statutes as I commanded you, I will tear the kingdom from you and 12 give it to your servant. Nevertheless, for the sake of your father David I will not do this in your day; I will tear it out of your son's 13 hand. Even so not the whole kingdom; I will leave him one tribe for the sake of my servant David and for the sake of Jerusalem, my chosen city.'

Two adversaries of Solomon

14 Then the LORD raised up an adversary for Solomon, Hadad the Edomite, of the royal 15 house of Edom. At the time when David reduced Edom, his commander-in-chief Joab had destroyed every male in the country 16 when he went into it to bury the slain. He and the armies of Israel remained there for six months, until he had destroyed every 17 male in Edom. Then Hadad, who was still

a boy, fled the country with some of his father's Edomite servants, intending to enter Egypt. They set out from Midian, made their 18 way to Paran and, taking some men from there, came to Pharaoh king of Egypt, who assigned Hadad a house and maintenance and made him a grant of land. Hadad found 19 great favour with Pharaoh, who gave him in marriage a sister of Queen Tahpenes his wife. She bore him his son Genubath; 20 Tahpenes weaned the child in Pharaoh's house, and he lived there along with Pharaoh's children. When Hadad heard in Egypt 21 that David rested with his forefathers and that his commander-in-chief Joab was also dead, he said to Pharaoh, 'Let me go so that I may return to my own country.' 'What is 22 it that you find wanting in my country', said Pharaoh, 'that you want to go back to your own?' 'Nothing,' said Hadad, 'but do, pray, let me go.' He remained an adversary for 25 Israel all through Solomon's reign. This is the harm that Hadad caused: he maintained a stranglehold on Israel and became king of Edom.

Then God raised up another adversary 23 against Solomon, Rezon son of Eliada, who had fled from his master Hadadezer king of Zobah. He gathered men about him and 24 became a captain of freebooters, who came to Damascus and occupied it; he became king there.

Ahijah prophesies to Jeroboam

Jeroboam son of Nebat, one of Solomon's 26 courtiers, an Ephrathite from Zeredah, whose widowed mother was named Zeruah, rebelled against the king. And this is the 27 story of his rebellion. Solomon had built the Millo and closed the breach in the wall of the city of his father David. Now this Jer- 28 oboam was a man of great energy; and Solomon, seeing how the young man worked, had put him in charge of all the labour-gangs in the tribal district of Joseph. On one 29 occasion Jeroboam had left Jerusalem, and the prophet Ahijah from Shiloh met him on the road. The prophet was wrapped in a new cloak, and the two of them were alone in the open country. Then Ahijah took hold of the 30 new cloak he was wearing, tore it into twelve pieces and said to Jeroboam, 'Take ten 31 pieces, for this is the word of the LORD God of Israel: "I am going to tear the kingdom from the hand of Solomon and give you ten tribes. But one tribe will remain his, 32 for the sake of my servant David and for the sake of Jerusalem, the city I have chosen out of all the tribes of Israel. I have done this 33 because Solomon has forsaken me; he has prostrated himself before Ashtoreth goddess

s Verse 25 transposed to follow verse 22.

of the Sidonians, Kemosh god of Moab, and Milcom god of the Ammonites, and has not conformed to my ways. He has not done what is right in my eyes or observed my statutes and judgements as David his father
34 did. Nevertheless I will not take the whole kingdom from him, but will maintain his rule as long as he lives, for the sake of my chosen servant David, who did observe my
35 commandments and statutes. But I will take the kingdom, that is the ten tribes, from his
36 son and give it to you. One tribe I will give to his son, that my servant David may always have a flame burning before me in Jerusalem, the city which I chose to receive my Name.
37 But I will appoint you to rule over all that you can desire, and to be king over Israel.
38 If you pay heed to all my commands, if you conform to my ways and do what is right in my eyes, observing my statutes and commandments as my servant David did, then I will be with you. I will establish your family for ever as I did for David; I will give Israel
39 to you, and punish David's descendants as they have deserved, but not for ever." '
40 After this Solomon sought to kill Jeroboam, but he fled to King Shishak in Egypt and remained there till Solomon's death.

The death of Solomon

41ᵗ The other acts and events of Solomon's reign, and all his wisdom, are recorded in
42 the annals of Solomon. The reign of King Solomon in Jerusalem over the whole of
43 Israel lasted forty years. Then he rested with his forefathers and was buried in the city of David his father, and he was succeeded by his son Rehoboam.

Rehoboam's unwise decision

1ᵘ Rehoboam went to Shechem, for all Israel
2 had gone there to make him king. When Jeroboam son of Nebat, who was still in Egypt, heard of it, he remained there, having taken refuge there to escape King Solomon.
3 They now recalled him, and he and all the assembly of Israel came to Rehoboam and
4 said, 'Your father laid a cruel yoke upon us; but if you will now lighten the cruel slavery he imposed on us and the heavy yoke he laid
5 on us, we will serve you.' 'Give me three days,' he said, 'and come back again.' So
6 the people went away. King Rehoboam then consulted the elders who had been in attendance on his father Solomon while he lived: 'What answer do you advise me to give to
7 this people?' And they said, 'If today you are willing to serve this people, show yourself their servant now and speak kindly to

them, and they will be your servants ever after.' But he rejected the advice which the 8 elders gave him. He next consulted those who had grown up with him, the young men in attendance, and asked them, 'What answer 9 do you advise me to give to this people's request that I should lighten the yoke which my father laid on them?' The young men 10 replied, 'Give this answer to the people who say that your father made their yoke heavy and ask you to lighten it; tell them: "My little finger is thicker than my father's loins. My father laid a heavy yoke on you; I will 11 make it heavier. My father used the whip on you; but I will use the lash." ' Jeroboam and 12 the people all came back to Rehoboam on the third day, as the king had ordered. And the king gave them a harsh answer. He 13 rejected the advice which the elders had given him and spoke to the people as the young 14 men had advised: 'My father made your yoke heavy; I will make it heavier. My father used the whip on you; but I will use the lash.' So the king would not listen to the people; 15 for the LORD had given this turn to the affair, in order that the word he had spoken by Ahijah of Shiloh to Jeroboam son of Nebat might be fulfilled.

Israel secedes from Rehoboam

When all Israel saw that the king would not 16 listen to them, they answered:

What share have we in David?
We have no lot in the son of Jesse.
Away to your homes, O Israel;
now see to your own house, David.

So Israel went to their homes, and Re- 17 hoboam ruled over those Israelites who lived in the cities of Judah.

Then King Rehoboam sent out Adoram, 18 the commander of the forced levies, but the Israelites stoned him to death; thereupon King Rehoboam mounted his chariot in haste and fled to Jerusalem. From that 19 day to this, the whole of Israel has been in rebellion against the house of David.

When the men of Israel heard that Jerobo- 20 am had returned, they sent and called him to the assembly and made him king over the whole of Israel. The tribe of Judah alone followed the house of David.

When Rehoboam reached Jerusalem, he 21ᵛ assembled all the house of Judah, the tribe of Benjamin also, a hundred and eighty thousand chosen warriors, to fight against the house of Israel and recover his kingdom. But the word of God came to Shemaiah the 22 man of God: 'Say to Rehoboam son of 23 Solomon, king of Judah, and to the house

THE TWO
KINGDOMS

The Great Sea

ISRAEL
Samaria
Shechem
Bethel

JERUSALEM

JUDAH

of Judah and to Benjamin and the rest of
24 the people, "This is the word of the LORD:
You shall not go up to make war on your
kinsmen the Israelites. Return to your homes,
for this is my will." ' So they listened to the
word of the LORD and returned home, as
the LORD had told them.

ISRAEL

Jeroboam's rival religion

25 Then Jeroboam rebuilt Shechem in the hill-
country of Ephraim and took up residence
there; from there he went out and built
26 Penuel. 'As things now stand,' he said to
himself, 'the kingdom will revert to the house
27 of David. If this people go up to sacrifice in
the house of the LORD in Jerusalem, it will
revive their allegiance to their lord Rehoboam king of Judah, and they will kill me and
28 return to King Rehoboam.' After giving
thought to the matter he made two calves
of gold and said to the people, 'It is too
much trouble for you to go up to Jerusalem;
here are your gods, Israel, that brought you
29 up from Egypt.' One he set up at Bethel and

the other he put at Dan, and this thing be- 30
came a sin in Israel; the people went to
Bethel to worship the one, and all the way
to Dan to worship the other. He set up 31
shrines on the hill-tops also and appointed
priests from every class of the people, who
did not belong to the Levites. He instituted 32
a pilgrim-feast on the fifteenth day of the
eighth month like that in Judah, and he
offered sacrifices upon the altar. This he
did at Bethel, sacrificing to the calves that
he had made and compelling the priests of
the hill-shrines, which he had set up, to serve
at Bethel. So he went up to the altar that he 33
had made at Bethel on the fifteenth day of
the eighth month; there, in a month of his
own choosing, he instituted for the Israelites a pilgrim-feast and himself went up to
the altar to burn the sacrifice.

The LORD shows disapproval

As Jeroboam stood by the altar to burn the **13**
sacrifice, a man of God from Judah, moved
by the word of the LORD, appeared at Bethel.
He inveighed against the altar in the LORD's 2
name, crying out, 'O altar, altar! This is the
word of the LORD: "Listen! A child shall be
born to the house of David, named Josiah.
He will sacrifice upon you the priests of the
hill-shrines who make offerings upon you,
and he will burn human bones upon you." '
He gave a sign the same day: 'This is the 3
sign which the LORD has ordained: This
altar will be rent in pieces and the ashes
upon it will be spilt.' When King Jeroboam 4
heard the sentence which the man of God
pronounced against the altar at Bethel, he
pointed to him from the altar and said,
'Seize that man!' Immediately the hand
which he had pointed at him became paralysed, so that he could not draw it back. The 5
altar too was rent in pieces and the ashes
were spilt, in fulfilment of the sign that the
man of God had given at the LORD's command. The king appealed to the man of God 6
to pacify the LORD his God and pray for
him that his hand might be restored. The
man of God did as he asked; his hand was
restored and became as it had been before.
Then the king said to the man of God, 'Come 7
home and take refreshment at my table, and
let me give you a present.' But the man of 8
God answered, 'If you were to give me half
your house, I would not enter it with you:

SHECHEM
20
MILES
BETHEL

I will eat and drink nothing in this place,
9 for the LORD's command to me was to eat
and drink nothing, and not to go back by
10 the way I came.' So he went back another
way; he did not return by the road he had
taken to Bethel.

The prophet disobeys the LORD

11 At that time there was an aged prophet
living in Bethel. His sons came and recounted to him all that the man of God had
done in Bethel that day; they also told their
12 father what he had said to the king. Their
father said to them, 'Which road did he
take?' They pointed out the road taken by
the man of God who had come from Judah.
13 He said to his sons, 'Saddle an ass for me.'
14 They saddled the ass, and he mounted it and
went after the man of God. He found him
seated under a terebinth and said to him,
'Are you the man of God who came from
15 Judah?' And he said, 'Yes, I am.' 'Come
home and eat with me', said the prophet.
16 'I cannot go back with you or enter your
house,' said the other; 'I can neither eat nor
17 drink with you in this place, for it was told
me by the word of the LORD: "You shall eat
and drink nothing there, nor shall you go
18 back the way you came."' And the old man
said to him, 'I also am a prophet, as you
are; and an angel commanded me by the
word of the LORD to bring you home with
me to eat and drink with me.' He was lying;
19 but the man of Judah went back with him
20 and ate and drank in his house. While they
were still seated at table the word of the
LORD came to the prophet who had brought
21 him back, and he cried out to the man of
God from Judah, 'This is the word of the
LORD: "You have defied the word of the
LORD your God and have not obeyed his
22 command; you have come back to eat and
to drink in the place where he forbade it;
therefore your body shall not be laid in the
grave of your forefathers."'

The prophet's death and burial

23 After they had eaten and drunk, he saddled
an ass for the prophet whom he had brought
24 back. As he went on his way a lion met him
and killed him, and his body was left lying
in the road, with the ass and the lion both

standing beside it. Some passers-by saw the 25
body lying in the road and the lion standing
beside it, and they brought the news to the
city where the old prophet lived. When the 26
prophet who had caused him to break his
journey heard it, he said, 'It is the man of
God who defied the word of the LORD. The
LORD has given him to the lion, and it has
broken his neck and killed him in fulfilment
of the word of the LORD.' He told his sons 27
to saddle an ass and, when they had saddled
it, he set out and found the body lying in 28
the road with the ass and the lion standing
beside it; the lion had neither devoured the
body nor broken the back of the ass. Then 29
the prophet lifted the body of the man of
God, laid it on the ass and brought it back
to his own city to mourn over it and bury it.
He laid the body in his own grave and they 30
mourned for him, saying, 'My brother, my
brother!' After burying him, he said to his 31
sons, 'When I die, bury me in the grave
where the man of God lies buried; lay my
bones beside his; for the sentence which he 32
pronounced at the LORD's command against
the altar in Bethel and all the hill-shrines of
Samaria shall be carried out.'

Ahijah pronounces judgement on Jeroboam

After this Jeroboam still did not abandon 33
his evil ways but went on appointing priests
for the hill-shrines from all classes of the
people; any man who offered himself he
would consecrate to be priest of a hill-
shrine. By doing this he brought guilt upon 34
his own house and doomed it to utter
destruction.

At that time Jeroboam's son Abijah fell **14**
ill, and Jeroboam said to his wife, 'Come 2
now, disguise yourself so that people may
not be able to recognize you as my wife, and
go to Shiloh. Ahijah the prophet is there,
the man who said I was to be king over this
people. Take with you ten loaves, some 3
raisins, and a flask of syrup, and go to him;
he will tell you what will happen to the
child.' Jeroboam's wife did so; she set off 4
at once for Shiloh and came to Ahijah's
house. Now Ahijah could not see, for his
eyes were fixed in the blindness of old age,
and the LORD had said to him, 'The wife of 5
Jeroboam is on her way to consult you about
her son, who is ill; you shall give her such
and such an answer.' When she came in,
concealing who she was, and Ahijah heard 6
her footsteps at the door, he said, 'Come in,
wife of Jeroboam. Why conceal who you
are? I have heavy news for you. Go and tell 7
Jeroboam: "This is the word of the LORD
the God of Israel: I raised you out of the
people and appointed you prince over my
people Israel; I tore away the kingdom from 8

the house of David and gave it to you; but you have not been like my servant David, who kept my commands and followed me with his whole heart, doing only what was
9 right in my eyes. You have outdone all your predecessors in wickedness; you have provoked me to anger by making for yourself other gods and images of cast metal; and
10 you have turned your back on me. For this I will bring disaster on the house of Jeroboam and I will destroy them all, every mother's son, whether still under the protection of the family or not, and I will sweep away the house of Jeroboam in Israel, as a
11 man sweeps up dung until none is left. Those of that house who die in the city shall be food for the dogs, and those who die in the country shall be food for the birds. It is the word of the LORD."
12 'You must go home now; the moment you set foot in the city, the child will die.
13 All Israel will mourn for him and bury him; he alone of all Jeroboam's family will have proper burial, because in him alone could the LORD the God of Israel find anything
14 good. Then the LORD will set up a king over Israel who shall put an end to the house of
15 Jeroboam. This first; and what next? The LORD will strike Israel, till it trembles like a reed in the water; he will uproot its people from this good land which he gave to their forefathers and scatter them beyond the Euphrates, because they have made their sacred poles and provoked the LORD's anger.
16 And he will abandon Israel for the sins that Jeroboam has committed and has led Israel
17 to commit.' Jeroboam's wife went home at once to Tirzah and, as she crossed the
18 threshold of the house, the boy died. They buried him, and all Israel mourned over him; and thus the word of the LORD was fulfilled which he had spoken through his servant Ahijah the prophet.

Other records of Jeroboam's reign
19 The other events of Jeroboam's reign, in war and peace, are recorded in the annals
20 of the kings of Israel. He reigned twenty-two years; then he rested with his forefathers and was succeeded by his son Nadab.

Wickedness in Judah
21 In Judah Rehoboam son of Solomon had become king. He was forty-one years old when he came to the throne, and he reigned for seventeen years in Jerusalem, the city which the LORD had chosen out of all the tribes of Israel to receive his Name. Rehoboam's mother was a woman of Ammon
22 called Naamah. Judah did what was wrong

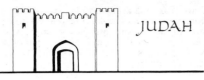

JUDAH

in the eyes of the LORD, rousing his jealous indignation by the sins they committed, beyond anything that their forefathers had done. They erected hill-shrines, sacred 23 pillars, and sacred poles, on every high hill and under every spreading tree. Worse still, 24 all over the country there were male prostitutes attached to the shrines, and the people adopted all the abominable practices of the nations whom the LORD had dispossessed in favour of Israel.

The Temple is plundered
In the fifth year of Rehoboam's reign 25 Shishak king of Egypt attacked Jerusalem. He removed the treasures of the house of 26 the LORD and of the royal palace, and seized everything, including all the shields of gold that Solomon had made. King Rehoboam 27 replaced them with bronze shields and entrusted them to the officers of the escort who guarded the entrance of the royal palace. Whenever the king entered the house of the 28 LORD, the escort carried them; afterwards they returned them to the guard-room.

Other records of Rehoboam's reign
The other acts and events of Rehoboam's 29 reign are recorded in the annals of the kings of Judah. There was continual fighting be- 30 tween him and Jeroboam. He rested with 31 his forefathers and was buried with them in the city of David. (His mother was a woman of Ammon, whose name was Naamah.) He was succeeded by his son Abijam.

Abijam reigns over Judah
In the eighteenth year of the reign of Jer- 15 oboam son of Nebat, Abijam became king of Judah. He reigned in Jerusalem for three 2 years; his mother was Maacah grand-daughter of Abishalom. All the sins that his 3 father had committed before him he committed too, nor was he faithful to the LORD his God as his ancestor David had been. But for David's sake the LORD his God gave 4 him a flame to burn in Jerusalem, by establishing his dynasty and making Jerusalem secure, because David had done what was 5 right in the eyes of the LORD and had not disobeyed any of his commandments all his life, except in the matter of Uriah the Hittite.[y]

w Verses 25–28: cp. 2 Chr. 12. 9–11.　x Verses 29–31: cp. 2 Chr. 12. 13–16.　y Prob. rdg.; Heb. adds
(6) There was war between Rehoboam and Jeroboam all his days (cp. 14. 30).

7 The other acts and events of Abijam's reign are recorded in the annals of the kings of Judah. There was fighting between Abijam 8 and Jeroboam. And Abijam rested with his forefathers and was buried in the city of David; and he was succeeded by his son Asa.

Asa reigns over Judah

9 In the twentieth year of Jeroboam king of 10 Israel, Asa became king of Judah. He reigned in Jerusalem for forty-one years; his grandmother was Maacah granddaughter 11 of Abishalom. Asa did what was right in the eyes of the LORD, like his ancestor David. 12 He expelled from the land the male prostitutes attached to the shrines and did away with all the idols which his predecessors had 13ᶻ made. He even deprived his own grandmother Maacah of her rank as queen mother because she had an obscene object made for the worship of Asherah; Asa cut it down and burnt it in the gorge of the 14 Kidron. Although the hill-shrines were allowed to remain, Asa himself remained 15 faithful to the LORD all his life. He brought into the house of the LORD all his father's votive offerings and his own, gold and silver and sacred vessels.

Asa's alliance with Ben-hadad

16 Asa was at war with Baasha king of Israel 17ᵃ all through their reigns. Baasha king of Israel invaded Judah and fortified Ramah to cut off all access to Asa king of Judah. 18 So Asa took all the gold and silver that remained in the treasuries of the house of the LORD and of the royal palace, and sent his servants with them to Ben-hadad son of Tabrimmon, son of Hezion, king of Aram, whose capital was Damascus, with instruc- 19 tions to say, 'There is an alliance between us, as there was between our fathers. I now send you this present of silver and gold; break off your alliance with Baasha king of Israel, so that he may abandon his campaign 20 against me.' Ben-hadad listened willingly to King Asa; he ordered the commanders of his armies to move against the cities of Israel, and they attacked Iyyon, Dan, Abel-beth-maacah, and that part of Kinnereth which marches with the land of Naphtali. 21 When Baasha heard of it, he stopped fortify- 22 ing Ramah and fell back on Tirzah. Then King Asa issued a proclamation requiring every man in Judah to join in removing the stones of Ramah and the timbers with which Baasha had fortified it; no one was exempted; and he used them to fortify Geba of Benjamin and Mizpah.

Other records of Asa's reign

All the other events of Asa's reign, his ex- 23ᵇ ploits and his achievements, and the cities he built, are recorded in the annals of the kings of Judah. But in his old age his feet were crippled by disease. He rested with his 24 forefathers and was buried with them in the city of his ancestor David; and he was succeeded by his son Jehoshaphat.

ISRAEL

Nadab reigns over Israel

Nadab son of Jeroboam became king of 25 Israel in the second year of Asa king of Judah, and he reigned for two years. He did 26 what was wrong in the eyes of the LORD and followed in his father's footsteps, repeating the sin which he had led Israel to commit. Baasha son of Ahijah, of the house of Is- 27 sachar, conspired against him and attacked him at Gibbethon, a Philistine city, which Nadab was besieging with all his forces. And Baasha slew him and usurped the 28 throne in the third year of Asa king of Judah. As soon as he became king, he struck down 29 all the family of Jeroboam, destroying every living soul and leaving not one survivor. Thus the word of the LORD was fulfilled which he spoke through his servant Ahijah the Shilonite. This happened because of the 30 sins of Jeroboam and the sins which he led Israel to commit, and because he had provoked the anger of the LORD the God of Israel. The other events of Nadab's reign 31 and all his acts are recorded in the annals of the kings of Israel. Asa was at war with 32 Baasha king of Israel all through their reigns.

Baasha reigns over Israel

In the third year of Asa king of Judah, 33 Baasha son of Ahijah became king of all Israel in Tirzah and reigned twenty-four years. He did what was wrong in the eyes 34 of the LORD and followed in Jeroboam's footsteps, repeating the sin which he had led Israel to commit. Then the word of the LORD **16** came to Jehu son of Hanani concerning Baasha: 'I raised you from the dust and 2 made you a prince over my people Israel, but you have followed in the footsteps of Jeroboam and have led my people Israel into

z Verses 13–15: cp. 2 Chr. 15. 16–18. a Verses 17–22: cp. 2 Chr. 16. 1–6. b Verses 23, 24: cp. 2 Chr. 16. 11–14.

sin, and have provoked me to anger with
3 their sins. Therefore I will sweep away
Baasha and his house and will deal with it
as I dealt with the house of Jeroboam son of
4 Nebat. Those of Baasha's family who die
in the city shall be food for the dogs, and
those who die in the country shall be food
5 for the birds.' The other events of Baasha's
reign, his achievements and his exploits,
are recorded in the annals of the kings of
6 Israel. Baasha rested with his forefathers
and was buried in Tirzah; and he was suc-
7 ceeded by his son Elah. Moreover the word
of the LORD concerning Baasha and his
family came through the prophet Jehu son
of Hanani, because of all the wrong that he
had done in the eyes of the LORD, thereby
provoking his anger: because he had not
only sinned like the house of Jeroboam, but
had also brought destruction upon it.

Elah reigns over Israel

8 In the twenty-sixth year of Asa king of
Judah, Elah son of Baasha became king of
Israel and he reigned in Tirzah two years.
9 Zimri, who was in his service commanding
half the chariotry, plotted against him. The
king was in Tirzah drinking himself drunk
in the house of Arza, comptroller of the
10 household there, when Zimri broke in and
attacked him, assassinated him and made
himself king. This took place in the twenty-
11 seventh year of Asa king of Judah. As soon
as he had become king and was enthroned,
he struck down all the family of Baasha and
left not a single mother's son alive, kinsman
12 or friend. He destroyed the whole family of
Baasha, and thus fulfilled the word of the
LORD concerning Baasha, spoken through
13 the prophet Jehu. This was what came of all
the sins which Baasha and his son Elah had
committed and the sins into which they had
led Israel, provoking the anger of the LORD
the God of Israel with their worthless idols.
14 The other events and acts of Elah's reign are
recorded in the annals of the kings of Israel.

Rival factions in Israel

15 In the twenty-seventh year of Asa king of
Judah, Zimri reigned in Tirzah for seven
days. At the time the army was investing
16 the Philistine city of Gibbethon. When the
Israelite troops in the field heard of Zimri's
conspiracy and the murder of the king, there
and then in the camp they made their commander Omri king of Israel by common
17 consent. Then Omri and his whole force
withdrew from Gibbethon and laid siege to
18 Tirzah. Zimri, as soon as he saw that the
city had fallen, retreated to the keep of the
royal palace, set the whole of it on fire over
19 his head and so perished. This was what came
of the sin he had committed by doing what

was wrong in the eyes of the LORD and following in the footsteps of Jeroboam, repeating the sin into which he had led Israel. The 20
other events of Zimri's reign, and his conspiracy, are recorded in the annals of the
kings of Israel.

Thereafter the people of Israel were split 21
into two factions: one supported Tibni son
of Ginath, determined to make him king;
the other supported Omri. Omri's party 22
proved the stronger; Tibni lost his life and
Omri became king.

Omri reigns over Israel

It was in the thirty-first year of Asa king 23
of Judah that Omri became king of Israel
and he reigned twelve years, six of them in
Tirzah. He bought the hill of Samaria from 24
Shemer for two talents of silver and built
a city on it which he named Samaria after
Shemer the owner of the hill. Omri did what 25
was wrong in the eyes of the LORD; he outdid all his predecessors in wickedness. He 26
followed in the footsteps of Jeroboam son
of Nebat, repeating the sins which he had
led Israel to commit, so that they provoked
the anger of the LORD their God with their
worthless idols. The other events of Omri's 27
reign, and his exploits, are recorded in the
annals of the kings of Israel. So Omri rested 28
with his forefathers and was buried in
Samaria; and he was succeeded by his son
Ahab.

Ahab reigns over Israel

Ahab son of Omri became king of Israel in 29
the thirty-eighth year of Asa king of Judah,
and he reigned over Israel in Samaria for
twenty-two years. He did more that was 30
wrong in the eyes of the LORD than all his
predecessors. As if it were not enough for 31
him to follow the sinful ways of Jeroboam
son of Nebat, he contracted a marriage with
Jezebel daughter of Ethbaal king of Sidon,
and went and worshipped Baal; he prostrated
himself before him and erected an altar to 32
him in the temple of Baal which he built in
Samaria. He also set up a sacred pole; indeed 33
he did more to provoke the anger of the
LORD the God of Israel than all the kings of
Israel before him. In his days Hiel of Bethel 34
rebuilt Jericho; laying its foundations cost
him his eldest son Abiram, and the setting
up of its gates cost him Segub his youngest
son. Thus was fulfilled what the LORD had
spoken through Joshua son of Nun.

Food during famine

Elijah the Tishbite, of Tishbe in Gilead, said **17**
to Ahab, 'I swear by the life of the LORD the
God of Israel, whose servant I am, that there
shall be neither dew nor rain these coming

Samaria was a fortified city built on a hill

2 years unless I give the word.' Then the word
3 of the LORD came to him: 'Leave this place
and turn eastwards; and go into hiding in
4 the ravine of Kerith east of the Jordan. You
shall drink from the stream, and I have
commanded the ravens to feed you there.'
5 He did as the LORD had told him: he went
and stayed in the ravine of Kerith east of
6 the Jordan, and the ravens brought him
bread and meat morning and evening, and
7 he drank from the stream. After a while the
stream dried up, for there had been no rain
8 in the land. Then the word of the LORD
9 came to him: 'Go now to Zarephath, a village of Sidon, and stay there; I have com-
10 manded a widow there to feed you.' So he
went off to Zarephath. When he reached the
entrance to the village, he saw a widow
gathering sticks, and he called to her and
said, 'Please bring me a little water in a
11 pitcher to drink.' As she went to fetch it, he
called after her, 'Bring me, please, a piece
12 of bread as well.' But she said, 'As the LORD
your God lives, I have no food to sustain
me except a handful of flour in a jar and a
little oil in a flask. Here I am, gathering two
or three sticks to go and cook something for
13 my son and myself before we die.' 'Never
fear,' said Elijah; 'go and do as you say; but
first make me a small cake from what you
have and bring it out to me; and after that
make something for your son and yourself.
14 For this is the word of the LORD the God of
Israel: "The jar of flour shall not give out

nor the flask of oil fail, until the LORD sends
rain on the land."' She went and did as 15
Elijah had said, and there was food for him
and for her and her family for a long time.
The jar of flour did not give out nor did the 16
flask of oil fail, as the word of the LORD
foretold through Elijah.

Elijah revives the widow's son

Afterwards the son of this woman, the 17
mistress of the house, fell ill and grew worse
and worse, until at last his breathing ceased.
Then she said to Elijah, 'What made you 18
interfere, you man of God? You came here
to bring my sins to light and kill my son!'
'Give me your son,' he said. He took the 19
boy from her arms and carried him up to
the roof-chamber where his lodging was,
and laid him on his own bed. Then he called 20
out to the LORD, 'O LORD my God, is this
thy care for the widow with whom I lodge,
that thou hast been so cruel to her son?'
Then he breathed deeply*c* upon the child three 21
times and called on the LORD, 'O LORD my
God, let the breath of life, I pray, return to
the body of this child.' The LORD listened 22
to Elijah's cry, and the breath of life returned
to the child's body, and he revived; Elijah 23
lifted him up and took him down from the
roof into the house, gave him to his mother
and said, 'Look, your son is alive.' Then she 24
said to Elijah, 'Now I know for certain that
you are a man of God and that the word of
the LORD on your lips is truth.'

c Or stretched himself.

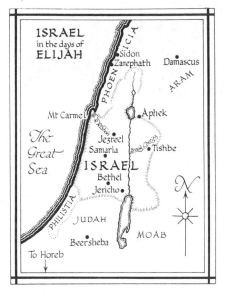

ISRAEL
in the days of
ELIJAH

The
Great
Sea

To Horeb

Ahab searches for fodder

18 Time went by, and in the third year the word
of the LORD came to Elijah: 'Go and show
yourself to Ahab, and I will send rain upon
2 the land.' So he went to show himself to
Ahab. At this time the famine in Samaria
3 was at its height, and Ahab summoned
Obadiah, the comptroller of his household,
4 a devout worshipper of the LORD. When
Jezebel massacred the prophets of the LORD,
he had taken a hundred of them and hidden
them in caves, fifty by fifty, giving them food
5 and drink to keep them alive. Ahab said to
Obadiah, 'Let us go through the land, both
of us, to every spring and gully; if we can
find enough grass we may keep the horses
and mules alive and lose none of our cattle.'
6 They divided the land between them for
their survey, Ahab going one way by himself
and Obadiah another.

Obadiah encounters Elijah

7 As Obadiah was on his way, Elijah met him.
Obadiah recognized him and fell prostrate
before him and said, 'Can it be you, my lord
8 Elijah?' 'Yes,' he said, 'it is I; go and tell
9 your master that Elijah is here.' 'What wrong
have I done?' said Obadiah. 'Why should
you give me into Ahab's hands? He will put
10 me to death. As the LORD your God lives,
there is no nation or kingdom to which my
master has not sent in search of you. If they
said, "He is not here", he made that kingdom or nation swear on oath that they

could not find you. Yet now you say, "Go 11
and tell your master that Elijah is here."
What will happen? As soon as I leave you, 12
the spirit of the LORD will carry you away,
who knows where? I shall go and tell Ahab,
and when he fails to find you, he will kill me.
Yet I have been a worshipper of the LORD
from boyhood. Have you not been told, my 13
lord, what I did when Jezebel put the LORD's
prophets to death, how I hid a hundred of
them in caves, fifty by fifty, and kept them
alive with food and drink? And now you 14
say, "Go and tell your master that Elijah is
here"! He will kill me.' Elijah answered, 'As 15
the LORD of Hosts lives, whose servant I am,
I swear that I will show myself to him this
very day.' So Obadiah went to find Ahab 16
and gave him the message, and Ahab went
to meet Elijah.

Elijah confronts Ahab

As soon as Ahab saw Elijah, he said to him, 17
'Is it you, you troubler of Israel?' 'It is not 18
I who have troubled Israel,' he replied, 'but
you and your father's family, by forsaking
the commandments of the LORD and following Baal. But now, send and summon all 19
Israel to meet me on Mount Carmel, and
the four hundred and fifty prophets of Baal
with them and the four hundred prophets
of the goddess Asherah, who are Jezebel's
pensioners.' So Ahab sent out to all the 20
Israelites and assembled the prophets on
Mount Carmel. Elijah stepped forward and 21
said to the people, 'How long will you sit on
the fence? If the LORD is God, follow him;
but if Baal, then follow him.' Not a word did
they answer. Then Elijah said to the people, 22
'I am the only prophet of the LORD still left,
but there are four hundred and fifty prophets
of Baal. Bring two bulls; let them choose one 23
for themselves, cut it up and lay it on the
wood without setting fire to it, and I will
prepare the other and lay it on the wood
without setting fire to it. You shall invoke 24
your god by name and I will invoke the
LORD by name; and the god who answers
by fire, he is God.' And all the people
shouted their approval.

No answer from Baal

Then Elijah said to the prophets of Baal, 25
'Choose one of the bulls and offer it first,
for there are more of you; invoke your god
by name, but do not set fire to the wood.'
So they took the bull provided for them and 26
offered it, and they invoked Baal by name
from morning until noon, crying, 'Baal,
Baal, answer us'; but there was no sound, no
answer. They danced wildly beside the altar
they had set up. At midday Elijah mocked 27
them: 'Call louder, for he is a god; it may be
he is deep in thought, or engaged, or on a

journey; or he may have gone to sleep and
28 must be woken up.' They cried still louder
and, as was their custom, gashed themselves
with swords and spears until the blood ran.
29 All afternoon they raved and ranted till the
hour of the regular sacrifice, but still there
was no sound, no answer, no sign of
attention.

The LORD answers by fire

30 Then Elijah said to all the people, 'Come
here to me.' They all came, and he repaired
the altar of the LORD which had been torn
31 down. He took twelve stones, one for each
tribe of the sons of Jacob, the man named
32 Israel by the word of the LORD. With these
stones he built an altar in the name of the
LORD; he dug a trench round it big enough
33 to hold two measures of seed; he arranged
the wood, cut up the bull and laid it on the
34 wood. Then he said, 'Fill four jars with water
and pour it on the whole-offering and on the
wood.' They did so, and he said, 'Do it
again.' They did it again, and he said, 'Do
35 it a third time.' They did it a third time, and
the water ran all round the altar and even
36 filled the trench. At the hour of the regular
sacrifice the prophet Elijah came forward
and said, 'LORD God of Abraham, of Isaac,
and of Israel, let it be known today that thou
art God in Israel and that I am thy servant
and have done all these things at thy com-
37 mand. Answer me, O LORD, answer me and
let this people know that thou, LORD, art
God and that it is thou that hast caused
38 them to be back-sliders.'[d] Then the fire
of the LORD fell. It consumed the whole-
offering, the wood, the stones, and the earth,
39 and licked up the water in the trench. When
all the people saw it, they fell prostrate and
cried, 'The LORD is God, the LORD is God.'
40 Then Elijah said to them, 'Seize the prophets of Baal; let not one of them escape.'
They seized them, and Elijah took them
down to the Kishon and slaughtered them
there in the valley.

Elijah prays for rain

41 Elijah said to Ahab, 'Go back now, eat and
drink, for I hear the sound of coming rain.'
42 He did so, while Elijah himself climbed to
the crest of Carmel. There he crouched on
the ground with his face between his knees.
43 He said to his servant, 'Go and look out to
the west.' He went and looked; 'There is
nothing to see', he said. Seven times Elijah
ordered him back, and seven times he went.
44 The seventh time he said, 'I see a cloud no
bigger than a man's hand, coming up from
the west.' 'Now go', said Elijah, 'and tell
Ahab to harness his chariot and be off, or the
45 rain will stop him.' Meanwhile the sky had
grown black with clouds, the wind rose, and
heavy rain began to fall. Ahab mounted his
chariot and set off for Jezreel; but the power
46 of the LORD had come upon Elijah: he
tucked up his robe and ran before Ahab all
the way to Jezreel.

Elijah flies from Ahab

19 Ahab told Jezebel all that Elijah had done
and how he had put all the prophets to death
with the sword. Jezebel then sent a mes-
2 senger to Elijah to say, 'The gods do the
same to me and more, unless by this time
tomorrow I have taken your life as you took
3 theirs.' He was afraid and fled for his life.
When he reached Beersheba in Judah, he
4 left his servant there and himself went a
day's journey into the wilderness. He came
upon a broom-bush, and sat down under it
and prayed for death: 'It is enough,' he said;
'now, LORD, take my life, for I am no better
5 than my fathers before me.' He lay down
under the bush and, while he slept, an angel
6 touched him and said, 'Rise and eat.' He
looked, and there at his head was a cake
baked on hot stones, and a pitcher of water.
7 He ate and drank and lay down again. The
angel of the LORD came again and touched
him a second time, saying, 'Rise and eat;
8 the journey is too much for you.' He rose

---

d Or thou that dost bring them back to their allegiance.

and ate and drank and, sustained by this food, he went on for forty days and forty 9 nights to Horeb, the mount of God. He entered a cave and there he spent the night.

The LORD encourages Elijah

Suddenly the word of the LORD came to 10 him: 'Why are you here, Elijah?' 'Because of my great zeal for the LORD the God of Hosts', he said. 'The people of Israel have forsaken thy covenant, torn down thy altars and put thy prophets to death with the sword. I alone am left, and they seek to take 11 my life.' The answer came: 'Go and stand on the mount before the LORD.' For the LORD was passing by: a great and strong wind came rending mountains and shattering rocks before him, but the LORD was not in the wind; and after the wind there was an earthquake, but the LORD was not in the 12 earthquake; and after the earthquake fire, but the LORD was not in the fire; and after 13 the fire a low murmuring sound. When Elijah heard it, he muffled his face in his cloak and went out and stood at the entrance of the cave. Then there came a voice: 'Why 14 are you here, Elijah?' 'Because of my great zeal for the LORD the God of Hosts', he said. 'The people of Israel have forsaken thy covenant, torn down thy altars and put thy prophets to death with the sword. I alone am left, and they seek to take my life.'

15 The LORD said to him, 'Go back by way of the wilderness of Damascus, enter the city and anoint Hazael to be king of Aram; 16 anoint Jehu son^e of Nimshi to be king of Israel, and Elisha son of Shaphat of Abel-17 meholah to be prophet in your place. Anyone who escapes the sword of Hazael Jehu will slay, and anyone who escapes the sword 18 of Jehu Elisha will slay. But I will leave seven thousand in Israel, all who have not bent the knee to Baal, all whose lips have not kissed him.'

The call of Elisha

19 Elijah departed and found Elisha son of Shaphat ploughing; there were twelve pair of oxen ahead of him, and he himself was with the last of them. As Elijah passed, he 20 threw his cloak over him, and Elisha, leaving his oxen, ran after Elijah and said, 'Let me kiss my father and mother goodbye, and then I will follow you.' 'Go back,' he replied; 21 'what have I done to prevent you?' He followed him no further but went home, took his pair of oxen, slaughtered them and burnt the wooden gear to cook the flesh, which he gave to the people to eat. Then he followed Elijah and became his disciple.

ARAM

Ahab defeats the Aramaeans

Ben-hadad king of Aram, having mustered 20 all his forces, and taking with him thirty-two kings with their horses and chariots, marched against Samaria to take it by siege or assault. He sent envoys into the city to 2 Ahab king of Israel to say, 'Hear what Ben-3 hadad says: Your silver and gold are mine, your wives and your splendid sons are mine.'^{f} The king of Israel answered, 'As you say, 4 my lord king, I am yours and all that I have.' The envoys came again and said, 'Hear what 5 Ben-hadad says: I demand that you hand over your silver and gold, your wives and your sons. This time tomorrow I will send 6 my servants to search your house and your subjects' houses and to take possession of everything you prize, and remove it.' The 7 king of Israel then summoned all the elders of the land and said, 'You see this? The man is plainly picking a quarrel; for I did not demur when he sent to claim my wives and my sons, my silver and gold.' All the elders 8 and all the people answered, 'Do not listen to him; you must not consent.' So he gave 9 this reply to Ben-hadad's envoys: 'Say to my lord the king: I accepted your majesty's demands on the first occasion; but what you now ask I cannot do.' The envoys went away and reported to their master, and Ben-hadad 10 sent back word: 'The gods do the same to me and more, if there is enough dust in Samaria to provide a handful for each of my men.' The king of Israel made reply, 11 'Remind him of the saying: "The lame must not think himself a match for the nimble."' This message reached Ben-hadad while he 12 and the kings were drinking in their quarters.^{g} At once he ordered his men to attack the city, and they did so.

Meanwhile a prophet had come to Ahab 13 king of Israel and said to him, 'This is the word of the LORD: "You see this great rabble? Today I will give it into your hands and you shall know that I am the LORD."' 'Whom will you use for that?' asked Ahab. 14 'The young men who serve the district officers', was the answer. 'Who will draw up the line of battle?' asked the king. 'You', said the prophet. Then Ahab called up these 15 young men, two hundred and thirty-two all told, and behind them the people of Israel,

e Or grandson (cp. 2 Kgs. 9. 2). quarters: or at Succoth.　　　f Or are your wives and your sons any good to me?　　　g in their

6 seven thousand in all. They went out at midday, while Ben-hadad and his allies, those thirty-two kings, were drinking themselves drunk in their quarters.*ʰ* The young 7 men sallied out first, and word was sent to Ben-hadad that a party had come out of Samaria. 'If they have come out for peace,' 8 he said, 'take them alive; if for battle, take them alive.'

19 So out of the city the young men went, 20 and the army behind them; each struck down his man, and the Aramaeans fled. The Israelites pursued them, but Ben-hadad king of Aram escaped on horseback with some 21 of the cavalry. Then the king of Israel advanced and captured the horses and chariots, inflicting a heavy defeat on the Aramaeans.

Ben-hadad prepares another attack

22 Then the prophet came to the king of Israel and said to him, 'Build up your forces; you know what you must do. At the turn of the year the king of Aram will renew the attack.' 23 But the king of Aram's ministers gave him this advice: 'Their gods are gods of the hills; that is why they defeated us. Let us fight them in the plain; and then we shall have the 24 upper hand. What you must do is to relieve the kings of their command and appoint 25 other officers in their place. Raise another army like the one you have lost. Bring your cavalry and chariots up to their former strength, and then let us fight them in the plain, and we shall have the upper hand.' He listened to their advice and acted on it. 26 At the turn of the year Ben-hadad mustered the Aramaeans and advanced to 27 Aphek to attack Israel. The Israelites too were mustered and formed into companies, and then went out to meet them and encamped opposite them. They seemed no better than a pair of new-born kids, while the Aramaeans covered the country-side. 28 The man of God came to the king of Israel and said, 'This is the word of the LORD: The Aramaeans may think that the LORD is a god of the hills and not a god of the valleys; but I will give all this great rabble into your hands and you shall know that I am the LORD.'

Ahab spares Ben-hadad

29 They lay in camp opposite one another for seven days; on the seventh day battle was joined and the Israelites destroyed a hundred thousand of the Aramaean infantry in 30 one day. The survivors fled to Aphek, into the citadel, and the city wall fell upon the twenty-seven thousand men who were left. Ben-hadad took refuge in the citadel, retreat-

ing into an inner room; and his attendants 31 said to him, 'Listen; we have heard that the kings of Israel are men to be trusted. Let us therefore put sackcloth round our waists and wind rough cord round our heads and go out to the king of Israel. It may be that he will spare your life.' So they fastened on 32 the sackcloth and the cord, and went to the king of Israel and said, 'Your servant Ben-hadad pleads for his life.' 'My royal cousin,' he said, 'is he still alive?' The men, taking the 33 word for a favourable omen, caught it up at once and said, 'Your cousin, yes, Ben-hadad.' 'Go and fetch him', he said. Then Ben-hadad came out and Ahab invited him into his chariot. And Ben-hadad said to 34 him, 'I will restore the cities which my father took from your father, and you may establish for yourself a trading quarter in Damascus, as my father did in Samaria.' 'On these terms', said Ahab, 'I will let you go.' So he granted him a treaty and let him go.

The LORD condemns Ahab

One of a company of prophets, at the com- 35 mand of the LORD, ordered a certain man to strike him, but the man refused. 'Because 36 you have not obeyed the LORD,' said the prophet, 'when you leave me, a lion will attack you.' When the man left, a lion did meet him and attacked him. The prophet 37 fell in with another man and ordered him to strike him. He struck and wounded him. Then the prophet went off, with a bandage 38 over his eyes, and thus disguised waited by the wayside for the king. As the king was 39 passing, he called out to him, 'Sir, I went into the thick of the battle, and a soldier came over to me with a prisoner and said, "Take charge of this fellow. If by any chance he gets away, your life shall be forfeit, or 40 you shall pay a talent of silver." As I was busy with one thing and another, sir, he disappeared.' The king of Israel said to him, 'You deserve to die.' And he said to the king of Israel,*ⁱ* 'You have passed sentence on yourself.' Then he tore the bandage from 41 his eyes, and the king of Israel saw that he was one of the prophets. And he said to the 42 king, 'This is the word of the LORD: "Because you let that man go when I had put him under a ban, your life shall be forfeit for his life, your people for his people."' The 43 king of Israel went home sullen and angry and entered Samaria.

Ahab and Naboth's vineyard

Naboth of Jezreel had a vineyard near the **21** palace of Ahab king of Samaria. One day 2 Ahab made a proposal to Naboth: 'Your

---

h in their quarters: *or* at Succoth.   *i* You deserve . . . Israel: *prob. rdg.; Heb. om.*

ISRAEL

vineyard is close to my palace; let me have it for a garden; I will give you a better vineyard in exchange for it or, if you prefer, its
3 value in silver.' But Naboth answered, 'The LORD forbid that I should let you have land
4 which has always been in my family.' So Ahab went home sullen and angry because Naboth would not let him have his ancestral land. He lay down on his bed, covered his
5 face and refused to eat. His wife Jezebel came in to him and said, 'What makes you so
6 sullen and why do you refuse to eat?' He told her, 'I proposed to Naboth of Jezreel that he should let me have his vineyard at its value or, if he liked, in exchange for another; but he would not let me have the vineyard.'
7 'Are you or are you not king in Israel?' said Jezebel. 'Come, eat and take heart; I will make you a gift of the vineyard of
8 Naboth of Jezreel.' So she wrote a letter in Ahab's name, sealed it with his seal and sent it to the elders and notables of Naboth's
9 city, who sat in council with him. She wrote: 'Proclaim a fast and give Naboth the seat of
10 honour among the people. And see that two scoundrels are seated opposite him to charge him with cursing God and the king, then
11 take him out and stone him to death.' So the elders and notables of Naboth's city, who sat with him in council, carried out the instructions Jezebel had sent them in
12 her letter: they proclaimed a fast and gave
13 Naboth the seat of honour, and these two scoundrels came in, sat opposite him and charged him publicly with cursing God and the king. Then they took him outside the
14 city and stoned him, and sent word to Jezebel that Naboth had been stoned to death.

Elijah pronounces judgement on Ahab

15 As soon as Jezebel heard that Naboth had been stoned and was dead, she said to Ahab, 'Get up and take possession of the vineyard which Naboth refused to sell you, for he is no longer alive; Naboth of Jezreel is dead.'
16 When Ahab heard that Naboth was dead, he got up and went to the vineyard to take
17 possession. Then the word of the LORD came
18 to Elijah the Tishbite: 'Go down at once to Ahab king of Israel, who is in Samaria; you will find him in Naboth's vineyard, where
19 he has gone to take possession. Say to him, "This is the word of the LORD: Have you killed your man, and taken his land as well?" Say to him, "This is the word of the LORD:

Where dogs licked the blood of Naboth, there dogs shall lick your blood."' Ahab 20 said to Elijah, 'Have you found me, my enemy?' 'I have found you', he said, 'because you have sold yourself to do what is wrong in the eyes of the LORD. I will bring*j* 21 disaster upon you; I will sweep you away and destroy every mother's son of the house of Ahab in Israel, whether under protection of the family or not. And I will deal with your 22 house as I did with the house of Jeroboam son of Nebat and of Baasha son of Ahijah, because you have provoked my anger and led Israel into sin.' And the LORD went on 23 to say of Jezebel, 'Jezebel shall be eaten by dogs by the rampart of Jezreel. Of the house 24 of Ahab, those who die in the city shall be food for the dogs, and those who die in the country shall be food for the birds.' (Never 25 was a man who sold himself to do what is wrong in the LORD's eyes as Ahab did, and all at the prompting of Jezebel his wife. He committed gross abominations in going 26 after false gods, doing everything that the

j he said, . . . bring: *or* he said, 'Because you . . . LORD, I am bringing . . .

Entrance to a vineyard

Amorites did, whom the LORD had dis-
27 possessed in favour of Israel.) When Ahab
heard this, he rent his clothes, put on sackcloth and fasted; he lay down in his sackcloth and went about muttering to himself.
28 Then the word of the LORD came to Elijah
29 the Tishbite: 'Have you seen how Ahab has
humbled himself before me? Because he
has thus humbled himself, I will not bring
disaster upon his house in his own lifetime,
but in his son's.'

ISRAEL   JUDAH

Jehoshaphat allies himself with Ahab

2 For three years there was no war between
2k the Aramaeans and the Israelites, but in the
third year Jehoshaphat king of Judah went
3 down to visit the king of Israel. The latter
said to his courtiers, 'You know that
Ramoth-gilead belongs to us, and yet we do
nothing to recover it from the king of Aram.'
4 He said to Jehoshaphat, 'Will you join me in
attacking Ramoth-gilead?' Jehoshaphat said
to the king of Israel, 'What is mine is yours:
5 myself, my people, and my horses.' Then
Jehoshaphat said to the king of Israel, 'First
6 let us seek counsel from the LORD.' The king
of Israel assembled the prophets, some four
hundred of them, and asked them, 'Shall
I attack Ramoth-gilead or shall I refrain?'
'Attack,' they answered; 'the Lord will
deliver it into your hands.' Jehoshaphat
7 asked, 'Is there no other prophet of the LORD
here through whom we may seek guidance?'
8 'There is one more', the king of Israel
answered, 'through whom we may seek
guidance of the LORD, but I hate the man,
because he prophesies no good for me; never
anything but evil. His name is Micaiah son
of Imlah.' Jehoshaphat exclaimed, 'My lord
9 king, let no such word pass your lips!' So
the king of Israel called one of his eunuchs
and told him to fetch Micaiah son of Imlah
with all speed.

The prophets promise success

10 The king of Israel and Jehoshaphat king of
Judah were seated on their thrones, in shining
armour, at the entrance to the gate of
Samaria, and all the prophets were prophesy-
11 ing before them. One of them, Zedekiah son
of Kenaanah, made himself horns of iron
and said, 'This is the word of the LORD:
"With horns like these you shall gore the

Aramaeans and make an end of them."' In 12
the same vein all the prophets prophesied,
'Attack Ramoth-gilead and win the day;
the LORD will deliver it into your hands.'
The messenger sent to fetch Micaiah told 13
him that the prophets had with one voice
given the king a favourable answer. 'And
mind you agree with them', he added. 'As 14
the LORD lives,' said Micaiah, 'I will say
only what the LORD tells me to say.'

Micaiah prophesies defeat

When Micaiah came into the king's presence, 15
the king said to him, 'Micaiah, shall we
attack Ramoth-gilead or shall we refrain?'
'Attack and win the day,' he said; 'the LORD
will deliver it into your hands.' 'How often 16
must I adjure you', said the king, 'to tell
me nothing but the truth in the name of
the LORD?' Then Micaiah said, 'I saw all 17
Israel scattered on the mountains, like sheep
without a shepherd; and I heard the LORD
say, "They have no master, let them go home
in peace."' The king of Israel said to 18
Jehoshaphat, 'Did I not tell you that he
never prophesies good for me, nothing but
evil?' Micaiah went on, 'Listen now to the 19
word of the LORD. I saw the LORD seated on
his throne, with all the host of heaven in
attendance on his right and on his left. The 20
LORD said, "Who will entice Ahab to attack
and fall on[l] Ramoth-gilead?" One said one
thing and one said another; then a spirit 21
came forward and stood before the LORD
and said, "I will entice him." "How?" said
the LORD. "I will go out", he said, "and be 22
a lying spirit in the mouth of all his prophets." "You shall entice him," said the
LORD, "and you shall succeed; go and do
it." You see, then, how the LORD has put 23
a lying spirit in the mouth of all these
prophets of yours, because he has decreed
disaster for you.' Then Zedekiah son of 24
Kenaanah came up to Micaiah and struck
him in the face: 'And how did the spirit of
the LORD pass from me to speak to you?' he
said. Micaiah answered, 'That you will find 25
out on the day when you run into an inner
room to hide yourself.' Then the king of 26
Israel ordered Micaiah to be arrested and
committed to the custody of Amon the
governor of the city and Joash the king's
son.[m] 'Lock this fellow up', he said, 'and 27
give him prison diet of bread and water
until I come home in safety.' Micaiah re- 28
torted, 'If you do return in safety, the LORD
has not spoken by me.'

Ahab dies in battle

So the king of Israel and Jehoshaphat king 29
of Judah marched on Ramoth-gilead, and 30

k Verses 2–35: cp. 2 Chr. 18. 2–34.   l Or at.   m son: or deputy.

the king of Israel said to Jehoshaphat, 'I will disguise myself to go into battle, but you shall wear your royal robes.' So he
31 went into battle in disguise. Now the king of Aram had commanded the thirty-two captains of his chariots not to engage all and sundry but the king of Israel alone.
32 When the captains saw Jehoshaphat, they thought he was the king of Israel and turned to attack him. But Jehoshaphat cried out
33 and, when the captains saw that he was not the king of Israel, they broke off the attack
34 on him. But one man drew his bow at random and hit the king of Israel where the breastplate joins the plates of the armour.

So he said to his driver, 'Wheel round and take me out of the line; I am wounded.'
35 When the day's fighting reached its height, the king was facing the Aramaeans propped up in his chariot, and the blood from his wound flowed down upon the floor of the
36 chariot; and in the evening he died. At sunset the herald went through the ranks, crying, 'Every man to his city, every man to his
37 country.' Thus died the king. He was brought
38 to Samaria and they buried him there. The chariot was swilled out at the pool of Samaria, and the dogs licked up the blood, and the prostitutes washed themselves in it, in fulfilment of the word the LORD had spoken.

Other records of Ahab's reign

39 Now the other acts and events of Ahab's reign, the ivory house and all the cities he built, are recorded in the annals of the kings
40 of Israel. So Ahab rested with his forefathers and was succeeded by his son Ahaziah.

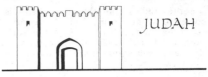

JUDAH

Jehoshaphat reigns over Judah

Jehoshaphat son of Asa had become king of 41 Judah in the fourth year of Ahab king of Israel. He was thirty-five years old when he 42 came to the throne, and he reigned in Jerusalem for twenty-five years; his mother was Azubah daughter of Shilhi. He followed in 43 the footsteps of Asa his father and did not swerve from them; he did what was right in the eyes of the LORD. But the hill-shrines were allowed to remain; the people continued to slaughter and burn sacrifices there. Jehosha- 44 phat remained at peace with the king of Israel. The other events of Jehoshaphat's 45 reign, his exploits and his wars, are recorded in the annals of the kings of Judah. But he 46 did away with such of the male prostitutes attached to the shrines as were still left over from the days of Asa his father.

There was no king in Edom, only^o a 47 viceroy of Jehoshaphat; he built merchant- 48 men to sail to Ophir for gold, but they never made the journey because they were wrecked at Ezion-geber. Ahaziah son of Ahab pro- 49 posed to Jehoshaphat that his own men should go to sea with his; but Jehoshaphat would not consent.

Jehoshaphat rested with his forefathers 50 and was buried with them in the city of David his father, and was succeeded by his son Joram.

ISRAEL

Ahaziah reigns over Israel

Ahaziah son of Ahab became king of Israel 51 in Samaria in the seventeenth year of Jehoshaphat king of Judah, and reigned over Israel for two years. He did what was 52 wrong in the eyes of the LORD, following in the footsteps of his father and mother and in those of Jeroboam son of Nebat, who had led Israel into sin. He served Baal and wor- 53 shipped him, and provoked the anger of the LORD the God of Israel, as his father had done.

---

n Verses 41–43: cp. 2 Chr. 20. 31–33.   *o only: prob. rdg.; Heb. om.*

THE SECOND BOOK OF
KINGS

Elijah foretells Ahaziah's death

1 AFTER AHAB'S DEATH Moab rebelled against Israel.

2 Ahaziah fell through a latticed window in his roof-chamber in Samaria and injured himself; he sent messengers to inquire of Baal-zebub the god of Ekron whether he 3 would recover from his illness. The angel of the LORD ordered Elijah the Tishbite to go and meet the messengers of the king of Samaria and say to them, 'Is there no god in Israel, that you go to inquire of Baal-4 zebub the god of Ekron? This is the word of the LORD to your master: "You shall not rise from the bed where you are lying; you 5 will die."' Then Elijah departed. The messengers went back to the king. When asked 6 why they had returned, they answered that a man had come to meet them and had ordered them to return and say to the king who had sent them, 'This is the word of the LORD: "Is there no god in Israel, that you send to inquire of Baal-zebub the god of Ekron? In consequence, you shall not rise from the bed where you are lying; you will 7 die."' The king asked them what kind of man it was who had met them and said this.

'A hairy man', they answered, 'with a leather 8 apron round his waist.' 'It is Elijah the Tishbite', said the king.

Fire falls from heaven

Then the king sent a captain to him with 9 his company of fifty. He went up and found the prophet sitting on a hill-top and said to him, 'Man of God, the king orders you to come down.' Elijah answered the captain, 10 'If I am a man of God, may fire fall from heaven and consume you and your company!' Fire fell from heaven and consumed the officer and his fifty men. The king sent 11 another captain of fifty with his company, and he went up and said to the prophet, 'Man of God, this is the king's command: Come down at once.' Elijah answered, 'If 12 I am a man of God, may fire fall from heaven and consume you and your company!' God's fire fell from heaven and consumed the man and his company. The king sent 13 the captain of a third company with his fifty men, and this third captain went up the hill to Elijah and knelt down before him and pleaded with him: 'Man of God, consider me and these fifty servants of yours, and

14 set some value on our lives. Fire fell from heaven and consumed the other two captains of fifty and their companies; but let
15 my life have some value in your eyes.' The angel of the LORD said to Elijah, 'Go down with him. Do not be afraid.' So he rose and
16 went down with him to the king, and he said, 'This is the word of the LORD: "You have sent to inquire of Baal-zebub the god of Ekron, and therefore you shall not rise from the bed where you are lying; you will die."'
17 The word of the LORD which Elijah had spoken was fulfilled, and Ahaziah died; and because he had no son, his brother Jehoram succeeded him in the second year of Joram son of Jehoshaphat king of Judah.

Other records of Ahaziah's reign
18 The other events of Ahaziah's reign are recorded in the annals of the kings of Israel.

Elijah is taken up to heaven
2 The time came when the LORD would take Elijah up to heaven in a whirlwind. Elijah
2 and Elisha left Gilgal, and Elijah said to Elisha, 'Stay here; for the LORD has sent me to Bethel.' But Elisha said, 'As the LORD lives, your life upon it, I will not leave you.'
3 So they went down country to Bethel. There a company of prophets came out to Elisha and said to him, 'Do you know that the LORD is going to take your lord and master from you today?' 'I do know,' he replied;
4 'say no more.' Then Elijah said to him, 'Stay here, Elisha; for the LORD has sent me to Jericho.' But he replied, 'As the LORD lives, your life upon it, I will not leave you.' So
5 they went to Jericho. There a company of prophets came up to Elisha and said to him, 'Do you know that the LORD is going to take your lord and master from you today?' 'I do
6 know,' he said; 'say no more.' Then Elijah said to him, 'Stay here; for the LORD has sent me to the Jordan.' The other replied, 'As the LORD lives, your life upon it, I will not leave you.' So the two of them went on.
7 Fifty of the prophets followed them, and stood watching from a distance as the two
8 of them stopped by the Jordan. Elijah took his cloak, rolled it up and struck the water with it. The water divided to right and left, and they both crossed over on dry ground.
9 While they were crossing, Elijah said to Elisha, 'Tell me what I can do for you before I am taken from you.' Elisha said, 'Let me
10 inherit a double share of your spirit.' 'You have asked a hard thing', said Elijah. 'If you see me taken from you, may your wish be granted; if you do not, it shall not be
11 granted.' They went on, talking as they went, and suddenly there appeared chariots of fire and horses of fire, which separated them one from the other, and Elijah was carried

up in the whirlwind to heaven. When Elisha 12 saw it, he cried, 'My father, my father, the chariots and the horsemen of Israel!', and he saw him no more. Then he took hold of his mantle and rent it in two, and he picked 13 up the cloak which had fallen from Elijah, and came back and stood on the bank of the Jordan. There he too struck the water with 14 Elijah's cloak and said, 'Where is the LORD the God of Elijah?' When he struck the water, it was again divided to right and left, and he crossed over. The prophets from 15 Jericho, who were watching, saw him and said, 'The spirit of Elijah has settled on Elisha.' So they came to meet him, and fell on their faces before him and said, 'Your 16 servants have fifty stalwart men. Let them go and search for your master; perhaps the spirit of the LORD has lifted him up and cast him on some mountain or into some valley.' But he said, 'No, you must not send them.' They pressed him, however, until he had not 17 the heart to refuse. So they sent out the fifty men but, though they searched for three days, they did not find him. When they came back 18 to Elisha, who had remained at Jericho, he said to them, 'Did I not tell you not to go?'

Elisha purifies Jericho's water supply
The people of the city said to Elisha, 'You 19 can see how pleasantly our city is situated, but the water is polluted and the country is troubled with miscarriages.' He said, 'Fetch 20 me a new bowl and put some salt in it.' When they had fetched it, he went out to the 21 spring and, throwing the salt into it, he said, 'This is the word of the LORD: "I purify this water. It shall cause no more death or miscarriage."' The water has remained pure 22 till this day, in fulfilment of Elisha's word.

Boys jeer at Elisha
He went up from there to Bethel and, as he 23 was on his way, some small boys came out of the city and jeered at him, saying, 'Get along with you, bald head, get along.' He turned 24 round and looked at them and he cursed them in the name of the LORD; and two she-bears came out of a wood and mauled forty-two of them. From there he went on to 25 Mount Carmel, and thence back to Samaria.

Jehoram reigns over Israel
In the eighteenth year of Jehoshaphat king **3** of Judah, Jehoram son of Ahab became king of Israel in Samaria, and he reigned for twelve years. He did what was wrong in the 2 eyes of the LORD, though not as his father and his mother had done; he did remove the sacred pillar of the Baal which his father had made. Yet he persisted in the sins into which 3 Jeroboam son of Nebat had led Israel, and did not give them up.

MOAB

Elisha provides water for the army

4 Mesha king of Moab was a sheep-breeder, and he used to supply the king of Israel regularly with the wool of a hundred thousand lambs and a hundred thousand rams. 5 When Ahab died, the king of Moab rebelled 6 against the king of Israel. Then King Jehoram came from Samaria and mustered all 7 Israel. He also sent this message to Jehoshaphat king of Judah: 'The king of Moab has rebelled against me. Will you join me in attacking Moab?' 'I will,' he replied; 'what is mine is yours: myself, my people, and my 8 horses.' 'From which direction shall we attack?' Jehoram asked. 'Through the wil-9 derness of Edom', replied the other. So the king of Israel set out with the king of Judah and the king of Edom. When they had been seven days on the march, they had no water 10 left for the army or the pack-animals. Then the king of Israel said, 'Alas, the LORD has brought together three kings, only to put us 11 at the mercy of the Moabites.' But Jehoshaphat said, 'Is there not a prophet of the LORD here through whom we may seek guidance of the LORD?' One of the officers of the king of Israel answered, 'Elisha son of Shaphat is here, the man who poured water 12 on Elijah's hands.' 'The word of the LORD is with him', said Jehoshaphat. So the king of Israel and Jehoshaphat and the king of 13 Edom went down to Elisha. Elisha said to the king of Israel, 'Why do you come to me? Go to the prophets of your father and your mother.' But the king of Israel said to him, 'No; the LORD has called us three kings out 14 to put us at the mercy of the Moabites.' 'As the LORD of Hosts lives, whom I serve,' said Elisha, 'I would not spare a look or a glance for you, if it were not for my regard for 15 Jehoshaphat king of Judah. But now, fetch me a minstrel.' They fetched a minstrel, and while he was playing, the power of the LORD 16 came upon Elisha and he said, 'This is the word of the LORD: "Pools will form all over 17 this ravine." The LORD has decreed that you shall see neither wind nor rain, yet this ravine shall be filled with water for you and your army and your pack-animals to drink. 18 But that is a mere trifle in the sight of the LORD; what he will also do, is to put Moab 19 at your mercy. You will raze to the ground every fortified town and every noble city; you will cut down all their fine trees; you

will stop up all the springs of water; and you will spoil every good piece of land by littering it with stones.' In the morning at 20 the hour of the regular sacrifice they saw water flowing in from the direction of Edom, and the land was flooded.

Destruction of Moab

Meanwhile all Moab had heard that the 21 kings had come up to fight against them, and every man, young and old, who could carry arms, was called out and stationed on the frontier. When they got up next morning 22 and the sun had risen over the water, the Moabites saw the water in front of them red like blood and cried out, 'It is blood. The 23 kings must have quarrelled and attacked one another. Now to the plunder, Moab!' When they came to the Israelite camp, the 24 Israelites turned out and attacked them and drove the Moabites headlong in flight, and themselves entered the land of Moab, de-stroying as they went. They razed the cities 25 to the ground; they littered every good piece of land with stones, each man casting one stone on to it; they stopped up every spring of water; they cut down all their fine trees; and they harried Moab until only in Kir-haresheth were any buildings left standing, and even this city the slingers surrounded and attacked.

When the king of Moab saw that the war 26 had gone against him, he took seven hundred men with him, armed with swords, to cut a way through to the king of Aram, but they failed in the attempt. Then he took his eldest 27 son, who would have succeeded him, and offered him as a whole-offering upon the city wall. The Israelites were filled with such consternation at this sight,[a] that they struck camp and returned to their own land.

Elisha provides oil for a widow

The wife of a member of a company of 4 prophets appealed to Elisha. 'My husband, your servant, has died', she said. 'You know that he was a man who feared the LORD; but a creditor has come to take away my two

a The Israelites . . . sight: or There was such great anger against the Israelites . . .

ISRAEL

2 boys as his slaves.' Elisha said to her, 'How can I help you? Tell me what you have in the house.' 'Nothing at all', she answered,
3 'except a flask of oil.' 'Go out then', he said, 'and borrow vessels from all your neighbours; get as many empty ones as you can.
4 Then, when you come home, shut yourself in with your sons, pour from the flask into all these vessels and, as they are filled, set
5 them aside.' She left him and shut herself in with her sons. As they brought her the
6 vessels she filled them. When they were all full, she said to one of her sons, 'Bring me another.' 'There is not one left', he said.
7 Then the flow of oil ceased. She came out and told the man of God, and he said, 'Go and sell the oil and redeem your boys who are being taken as pledges,[b] and you and they can live on what is left.'

Elisha rewards the Shunammite woman

8 It happened once that Elisha went over to Shunem. There was a great lady there who pressed him to accept her hospitality, and so, whenever he came that way, he stopped
9 to take food there. One day she said to her husband, 'I know that this man who comes
10 here regularly is a holy man of God. Why not build up the wall to make him a little roof-chamber, and put in it a bed, a table, a seat, and a lamp, and let him stay there
11 whenever he comes to us?' Once when he arrived and went to this roof-chamber and
12 lay down to rest, he said to Gehazi, his servant, 'Call this Shunammite woman.' He called her and, when she appeared before
13 the prophet, he said to his servant, 'Say to her, "You have taken all this trouble for us. What can I do for you? Shall I speak for you to the king or to the commander-in-chief?"' But she replied, 'I am content where I am,
14 among my own people.' He said, 'Then what can be done for her?' Gehazi said, 'There is only this: she has no child and her
15 husband is old.' 'Call her back', Elisha said. When she was called, she appeared
16 in the doorway, and he said, 'In due season, this time next year, you shall have a son in your arms.' But she said, 'No, no, my lord, you are a man of God and would not lie
17 to your servant.' Next year in due season the woman conceived and bore a son, as Elisha had foretold.

The Shunammite woman's son dies

18 When the child was old enough, he went out one day to the reapers where his father was.
19 All of a sudden he cried out to his father, 'O my head, my head!' His father told a
20 servant to carry him to his mother. He brought him to his mother; the boy sat on her lap till midday, and then he died. She
21 went up and laid him on the bed of the man of God, shut the door and went out. She
22 called her husband and said, 'Send me one of the servants and a she-ass, I must go to the man of God as fast as I can, and come
23 straight back.' 'Why go to him today?' he asked. 'It is neither new moon nor sabbath.'[c]
24 'Never mind that', she answered. When the ass was saddled, she said to her servant, 'Lead on and do not slacken pace unless I tell
25 you.' So she set out and came to the man of God on Mount Carmel. The man of God spied her in the distance and said to Gehazi, his servant, 'That is the Shunammite woman
26 coming. Run and meet her, and ask, "Is all well with you? Is all well with your husband? Is all well with the boy?"' She answered,
27 'All is well.' When she reached the man of God on the hill, she clutched his feet. Gehazi came forward to push her away, but the man of God said, 'Let her alone; she is in great distress, and the LORD has concealed it from me and not told me.' 'My lord,' she
28 said, 'did I ask for a son? Did I not beg you not to raise my hopes and then dash them?'
29 Then he turned to Gehazi: 'Hitch up your cloak; take my staff with you and run. If you meet anyone on the way, do not stop to greet him; if anyone greets you, do not answer him. Lay my staff on the boy's face.'
30 But the mother cried, 'As the LORD lives, your life upon it, I will not leave you.' So he got up and followed her.[d]

Elisha revives the child

31 Gehazi went on ahead of them and laid the staff on the boy's face, but there was no sound and no sign of life. So he went back to meet Elisha and told him that the boy
32 had not roused. When Elisha entered the house, there was the boy dead, on the bed
33 where he had been laid. He went into the room, shut the door on the two of them and
34 prayed to the LORD. Then, getting on to the bed, he lay upon the child, put his mouth to the child's mouth, his eyes to his eyes and his hands to his hands; and, as he pressed[e] upon him, the child's body grew warm.
35 Elisha got up and walked once up and down the room; then, getting on to the bed again, he pressed[e] upon him and breathed into him[f] seven times; and the boy opened his

b redeem . . . pledges: or pay off your debt.   c Or full moon.   d Or went with her.   e Prob.
rdg.; Heb. crouched.   f and breathed into him: or and the boy sneezed.

36 eyes. The prophet summoned Gehazi and said, 'Call this Shunammite woman.' She answered his call and the prophet said,
37 'Take your child.' She came in and fell prostrate before him. Then she took up her son and went out.

Elisha provides an antidote

38 Elisha returned to Gilgal at a time when there was a famine in the land. One day, when a group of prophets was sitting at his feet, he said to his servant, 'Set the big pot on the fire and prepare some broth for the
39 company.' One of them went out into the fields to gather herbs and found a wild vine, and filled the skirt of his garment with bitter-apples.*g* He came back and sliced them into the pot, not knowing what they were.
40 They poured it out for the men to eat, but, when they tasted it, they cried out, 'Man of God, there is death in the pot', and they
41 could not eat it. The prophet said, 'Fetch some meal.' He threw it into the pot and said, 'Now pour out for the men to eat.' This time there was no harm in the pot.

Elisha provides bread for the people

42 A man came from Baal-shalisha, bringing the man of God some of the new season's bread, twenty barley loaves, and fresh ripe ears of corn.*h* Elisha said, 'Give this to the
43 people to eat.' But his disciple protested, 'I cannot set this before a hundred men.' Still he repeated, 'Give it to the people to eat; for this is the word of the LORD: "They will eat and there will be some left over."'
44 So he set it before them, and they ate and left some over, as the LORD had said.

Elisha cures Naaman

5 Naaman, commander of the king of Aram's army, was a great man highly esteemed by his master, because by his means the LORD had given victory to Aram; but he was a
2 leper.*i* On one of their raids the Aramaeans brought back as a captive from the land of Israel a little girl, who became a servant
3 to Naaman's wife. She said to her mistress, 'If only my master could meet the prophet who lives in Samaria, he would get rid of
4 the disease for him.' Naaman went in and reported to his master word for word what the girl from the land of Israel had said.
5 'Very well, you may go,' said the king of Aram, 'and I will send a letter to the king of Israel.' So Naaman went, taking with him ten talents of silver, six thousand shekels of
6 gold, and ten changes of clothing. He delivered the letter to the king of Israel, which read thus: 'This letter is to inform you that I am sending to you my servant Naaman,

In the Footsteps of ELISHA

The Great Sea

Mt Carmel
Shunem
Jezreel
Dothan
Ramoth-gilead
Abel-meholah
Samaria
Bethel
Jericho
Gilgal

and I beg you to rid him of his disease.'
7 When the king of Israel read the letter, he rent his clothes and said, 'Am I a god*j* to kill and to make alive, that this fellow sends to me to cure a man of his disease? Surely you must see that he is picking a quarrel
8 with me.' When Elisha, the man of God, heard how the king of Israel had rent his clothes, he sent to him saying, 'Why did you rend your clothes? Let the man come to me, and he will know that there is a prophet in
9 Israel.' So Naaman came with his horses and chariots and stood at the entrance to
10 Elisha's house. Elisha sent out a messenger to say to him, 'If you will go and wash seven times in the Jordan, your flesh will be re-
11 stored and you will be clean.' Naaman was furious and went away, saying, 'I thought he would at least have come out and stood, and invoked the LORD his God by name, waved his hand over the place and so rid me
12 of the disease. Are not Abana and Pharpar, rivers of Damascus, better than all the waters of Israel? Can I not wash in them and be clean?' So he turned and went off in a rage.
13 But his servants came up to him and said, 'If the prophet had bidden you do something difficult, would you not do it? How much more then, if he tells you to wash and be
14 clean?' So he went down and dipped himself in the Jordan seven times as the man of God had told him, and his flesh was restored as a little child's, and he was clean.

Naaman promises allegiance to the LORD

15 Then he and his retinue went back to the man of God and stood before him; and he said, 'Now I know that there is no god

---

g Or poisonous wild gourds.   *h* fresh . . . corn: *prob. rdg.; Heb. unintelligible.*   *i* he was a leper: *or* his skin was diseased.   *j Or* Am I God.

anywhere on earth except in Israel. Will you accept a token of gratitude from your ser-
16 vant?' 'As the LORD lives, whom I serve,' said the prophet, 'I will accept nothing.' He
17 was pressed to accept, but he refused. 'Then if you will not,' said Naaman, 'let me, sir, have two mules' load of earth. For I will no longer offer whole-offering or sacrifice to
18 any god but the LORD. In this one matter only may the LORD pardon me: when my master goes to the temple of Rimmon to worship, leaning on my arm, and I worship in the temple of Rimmon when he worships
19 there, for this let the LORD pardon me.' And Elisha bade him farewell.

Naaman had gone only a short distance
20 on his way, when Gehazi, the servant of Elisha the man of God, said to himself, 'What? Has my master let this Aramaean, Naaman, go scot-free, and not accepted what he brought? As the LORD lives, I will run
21 after him and get something from him.' So Gehazi hurried after Naaman. When Naaman saw him running after him, he jumped down from his chariot to meet him and said,
22 'Is anything wrong?' 'Nothing,' said Gehazi, 'but my master sent me to say that two young men of the company of prophets from the hill-country of Ephraim have just arrived. Could you provide them with a talent of
23 silver and two changes of clothing?' Naaman said, 'By all means; take two talents.' He pressed[k] him to take them; so he tied up the two talents of silver in two bags, and the two changes of clothing, and gave them to his two servants, and they walked ahead
24 carrying them. When Gehazi came to the citadel[l] he took them from the two servants, deposited them in the house and dismissed
25 the men; and they departed. When he went in and stood before his master, Elisha said, 'Where have you been, Gehazi?' 'Nowhere',
26 said Gehazi. But he said to him, 'Was I not with you in spirit when the man turned back from his chariot to meet you? Is it not true that you have the money? You may buy gardens with it,[m][n] and olive-trees and vine-yards, sheep and oxen, slaves and slave-
27 girls; but the disease of Naaman will fasten on you and on your descendants for ever.' Gehazi left his presence, his skin diseased, white as snow.

Elisha makes an axehead float

6 A company of prophets said to Elisha, 'You can see that this place where our community is living, under you as its head, is too small
2 for us. Let us go to the Jordan and each fetch a log, and make ourselves a place to live in.'
3 The prophet agreed. Then one of them said, 'Please, sir, come with us.' 'I will', he said,

and he went with them. When they reached 4 the Jordan, they began cutting down trees; but it chanced that, as one man was felling 5 a trunk, the head of his axe flew off into the water. 'Oh, master!' he exclaimed, 'it was a borrowed one.' 'Where did it fall?' asked the 6 man of God. When he was shown the place, he cut off a piece of wood and threw it in and made the iron float. Then he said, 'There 7 you are, lift it out.' So he stretched out his hand and took it.

ARAM

Elisha discloses the king of Aram's plans

Once, when the king of Aram was making 8 war on Israel, he held a conference with his staff at which he said, 'I mean to attack in such and such a direction.' But the man of 9 God warned the king of Israel: 'Take care to avoid this place, for the Aramaeans are going down that way.' So the king of Israel 10 sent to the place about which the man of God had given him this warning; and the king took special precautions every time he found himself near that place. The king of 11 Aram was greatly perturbed at this and, summoning his staff, he said to them, 'Tell me, one of you, who has betrayed us to the king of Israel?' 'None of us, my lord king,' 12 said one of his staff; 'but Elisha, the prophet in Israel, tells the king of Israel the very words you speak in your bedchamber.' 'Go 13 and find out where he is,' said the king, 'and I will send and seize him.' He was told that the prophet was at Dothan, and he sent a 14 strong force there with horses and chariots. They came by night and surrounded the city.

Elisha deceives the Aramaeans

When the disciple of the man of God rose 15 early in the morning and went out, he saw a force with horses and chariots surrounding the city. 'Oh, master,' he said, 'which way are we to turn?' He answered, 'Do not be 16 afraid, for those who are on our side are more than those on theirs.' Then Elisha 17 offered this prayer: 'O LORD, open his eyes and let him see.' And the LORD opened the young man's eyes, and he saw the hills covered with horses and chariots of fire all round Elisha. As they came down towards 18 him, Elisha prayed to the LORD: 'Strike this

---

k Prob. rdg.; Heb. broke out on.   *l Or* hill.   *m* gardens with it: *prob. rdg.; Heb.* garments.
n Is it not . . . with it: *or* Was it a time to get the money and to get garments?

host, I pray thee, with blindness'; and he
19 struck them blind as Elisha had asked. Then
Elisha said to them, 'You are on the wrong
road; this is not the city. Follow me and I
will lead you to the man you are looking for.'
20 And he led them to Samaria. As soon as
they had entered Samaria, Elisha prayed,
'O LORD, open the eyes of these men and let
them see again.' And he opened their eyes
and they saw that they were inside Samaria.
21 When the king of Israel saw them, he said
to Elisha, 'My father, am I to destroy them?'
22 'No, you must not do that', he answered.
'You may destroy*o* those whom you have
taken prisoner with your own sword and
bow, but as for these men, give them food
and water, and let them eat and drink, and
23 then go back to their master.' So he prepared a great feast for them, and they ate
and drank and then went back to their
master. And Aramaean raids on Israel
ceased.

Ben-hadad besieges Samaria

24 But later, Ben-hadad king of Aram called
up his entire army and marched to the siege
25 of Samaria. The city was near starvation,
and they besieged it so closely that a donkey's
head was sold for eighty shekels of silver, and
a quarter of a kab of locust-beans for five
26 shekels. One day, as the king of Israel was
walking along the city wall, a woman called
27 to him, 'Help, my lord king!' He said, 'If the
LORD will not bring you help, where can I
find any for you? From threshing-floor or
28 from winepress? What is your trouble?' She
replied, 'This woman said to me, "Give up
your child for us to eat today, and we will
29 eat mine tomorrow." So we cooked my son
and ate him; but when I said to her the next
day, "Now give up your child for us to eat",
30 she had hidden him.' When he heard the
woman's story, the king rent his clothes. He
was walking along the wall at the time, and
when the people looked, they saw that he
had sackcloth underneath, next to his skin.
31 Then he said, 'The LORD do the same to me
and more, if the head of Elisha son of
Shaphat stays on his shoulders today.'

Elisha promises relief from the famine

32 Elisha was sitting at home, the elders with
him. The king had dispatched one of his
retinue but, before the messenger arrived,
Elisha said to the elders, 'See how this son
of a murderer has sent to behead me! Take
care, when the messenger comes, to shut the
door and hold it fast against him. Can you
not hear his master following on his heels?'
33 While he was still speaking, the king*p*
arrived and said, 'Look at our plight! This

is the LORD's doing. Why should I wait any
longer for him to help us?' But Elisha 7
answered, 'Hear this word of the LORD: By
this time tomorrow a shekel will buy a
measure of flour or two measures of barley
in the gateway of Samaria.' Then the lieu- 2
tenant on whose arm the king leaned said
to the man of God, 'Even if the LORD were
to open windows in the sky, such a thing
could not happen!' He answered, 'You will
see it with your own eyes, but none of it will
you eat.'

The Aramaeans abandon their camp

At the city gate were four lepers.*q* They said 3
to one another, 'Why should we stay here
and wait for death? If we say we will go into 4
the city, there is famine there, and we shall
die; if we say we will stay here, we shall die
just the same. Well then, let us go to the
camp of the Aramaeans and give ourselves
up: if they spare us, we shall live; if they put
us to death, we can but die.' And so in the 5
twilight they set out for the Aramaean camp;
but when they reached the outskirts, they
found no one there; for the Lord had caused 6
the Aramaean army to hear a sound like
that of chariots and horses and of a great
host, so that the word went round: 'The
king of Israel has hired the kings of the
Hittites and the kings of Egypt to attack us.'
They had fled at once in the twilight, aban- 7
doning their tents, their horses and asses,
and leaving the camp as it stood, while they
fled for their lives. When the four men came 8
to the outskirts of the camp, they went into
a tent and ate and drank and looted silver
and gold and clothing, and made off and
hid them. Then they came back, went into
another tent and rifled it, and made off and
hid the loot. Then they said to one another, 9
'What we are doing is not right. This is a
day of good news and we are keeping it to
ourselves. If we wait till morning, we shall
be held to blame. We must go now and give
the news to the king's household.' So they 10
came and called to the watch at the city gate
and described how they had gone to the
Aramaean camp and found not a single man
in it and had heard no sound: nothing but
horses and asses tethered, and the tents left
as they were. Then the watch called out and 11
gave the news to the king's household in the
palace. The king rose in the night and said 12
to his staff, 'I will tell you what the Aramaeans have done. They know that we are
starving, and they have left their camp to
go and hide in the open country, expecting
us to come out, and then they can take us
alive and enter the city.' One of his staff 13
said, 'Send out a party of men with some of

o Prob. rdg.; Heb. Would you destroy.   *p Prob. rdg.; Heb.* messenger.   *q Or* men suffering from skin-disease.

the horses that are left; if they live, they will be as well off as all the other Israelites who are still left; if they die,[r] they will be no worse off than all those who have already perished. Let them go and see what has 14 happened.' So they picked two mounted men, and the king dispatched them in the track of the Aramaean army with the order 15 to go and find out what had happened. They followed as far as the Jordan and found the whole road littered with clothing and equipment which the Aramaeans had flung aside in their haste. The messengers returned and 16 reported this to the king. Then the people went out and plundered the Aramaean camp, and a measure of flour was sold for a shekel and two measures of barley for a shekel, so 17 that the word of the LORD came true. Now the king had appointed the lieutenant on whose arm he leaned to take charge of the gate, and the people trampled him to death there, just as the man of God had foretold 18 when the king visited him. For when the man of God said to the king, 'By this time tomorrow a shekel will buy two measures of barley or one measure of flour in the 19 gateway of Samaria', the lieutenant had answered, 'Even if the LORD were to open windows in the sky, such a thing could not happen!' And the man of God had said, 20 'You will see it with your own eyes, but none of it will you eat.' And this is just what happened to him: the people trampled him to death at the gate.

ISRAEL

The famine, and after

8 Elisha said to the woman whose son he had restored to life, 'Go away at once with your household and find lodging where you can, for the LORD has decreed a seven years' famine and it has already come upon the 2 land.' The woman acted at once on the word of the man of God and went away with her household; and she stayed in the Philistine 3 country for seven years. When she came back at the end of the seven years, she sought an audience of the king to appeal 4 for the return of her house and land. Now the king was questioning Gehazi, the servant of the man of God, about all the great things 5 Elisha had done; and, as he was describing to the king how he had brought the dead to

life, the selfsame woman began appealing to the king for her house and her land. 'My lord king,' said Gehazi, 'this is the very woman, and this is her son whom Elisha brought to life.' The king asked the woman 6 about it, and she told him. Then he entrusted the case to a eunuch and ordered him to restore all her property to her, with all the revenues from her land from the time she left the country till that day.

Hazael succeeds Ben-hadad

Elisha came to Damascus, at a time when 7 Ben-hadad king of Aram was ill; and when he was told that the man of God had arrived, he bade Hazael take a gift with him and go 8 to the man of God and inquire of the LORD through him whether he would recover from his illness. Hazael went, taking with him as 9 a gift all kinds of wares of Damascus, forty camel-loads. When he came into the prophet's presence, he said, 'Your son Ben-hadad king of Aram has sent me to you to ask whether he will recover from his illness.' 'Go and tell him that he will recover,' he 10 answered; 'but the LORD has revealed to me that in fact he will die.' The man of God 11 stood there with set face like a man stunned, until he could bear it no longer; then he wept. 'Why do you weep, my lord?' said 12 Hazael. He answered, 'Because I know the harm you will do to the Israelites: you will set their fortresses on fire and put their young men to the sword; you will dash their children to the ground and you will rip open their pregnant women.' But Hazael said, 13 'But I am a dog, a mere nobody; how can I do this great thing?' Elisha answered, 'The LORD has revealed to me that you will be king of Aram.' Hazael left Elisha and re- 14 turned to his master, who asked him what Elisha had said. 'He told me that you would recover', he replied. But the next day he 15 took a blanket and, after dipping it in water, laid it over the king's face, and he died; and Hazael succeeded him.

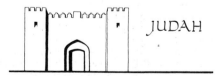

JUDAH

Joram reigns over Judah

In the fifth year of Jehoram son of Ahab 16 king of Israel, Joram son of Jehoshaphat king of Judah became king. He was thirty- 17[s] two years old when he came to the throne, and he reigned in Jerusalem for eight years.

---

r if they live . . . if they die: *prob. rdg.; Heb. obscure.*   *s* Verses 17–22: cp. 2 Chr. 21. 5–10.

8 He followed the practices of the kings of Israel as the house of Ahab had done, for he had married Ahab's daughter; and he did what was wrong in the eyes of the LORD. 9 But for his servant David's sake the LORD was unwilling to destroy Judah, since he had promised to give him and his sons a flame, to burn for all time.

Edom and Libnah revolt

20 During his reign Edom revolted against 21 Judah and set up its own king. Joram crossed over to Zair with all his chariots. He and his chariot-commanders set out by night, but they were surrounded by the Edomites and defeated,*t* whereupon the people fled to their 22 tents. So Edom has remained independent of Judah to this day; Libnah also revolted at 23 the same time. The other acts and events of Joram's reign are recorded in the annals of the 24 kings of Judah. So Joram rested with his fore-fathers and was buried with them in the city of David, and his son Ahaziah succeeded him.

Ahaziah reigns over Judah

25 *u* In the twelfth year of Jehoram son of Ahab king of Israel, Ahaziah son of Joram king 26 of Judah became king. Ahaziah was twenty-two years old when he came to the throne, and he reigned in Jerusalem for one year; his mother was Athaliah granddaughter of 27 Omri king of Israel. He followed the prac-tices of the house of Ahab and did what was wrong in the eyes of the LORD like the house of Ahab, for he was connected with that 28 house by marriage. He allied himself with Jehoram son of Ahab to fight against Hazael king of Aram at Ramoth-gilead; but King Jehoram was wounded by the Aram-29 aeans, and returned to Jezreel to recover from the wounds which were inflicted on him at Ramoth in battle with Hazael king of Aram; and because of his illness Ahaziah son of Joram king of Judah went down to Jezreel to visit him.

ISRAEL

Elisha anoints Jehu king of Israel

9 Elisha the prophet summoned one of the company of prophets and said to him, 'Hitch up your cloak, take this flask of oil 2 with you and go to Ramoth-gilead. When you arrive, you will find Jehu son of Jehosha-phat, son of Nimshi; go in and call him aside

from his fellow-officers, and lead him through to an inner room. Then take the flask and 3 pour the oil on his head and say, "This is the word of the LORD: I anoint you king over Israel"; then open the door and flee for your life.' So the young prophet went to 4 Ramoth-gilead. When he arrived, he found 5 the officers sitting together and said, 'Sir, I have a word for you.' 'For which of us?' asked Jehu. 'For you, sir', he said. He rose 6 and went into the house, and the prophet poured the oil on his head, saying, 'This is the word of the LORD the God of Israel: "I anoint you king over Israel, the people of the LORD. You shall strike down the house 7 of Ahab your master, and I will take ven-geance on Jezebel for the blood of my servants the prophets and for the blood of all the LORD's servants. All the house of 8 Ahab shall perish and I will destroy every mother's son of his house in Israel, whether under the protection of the family or not. And I will make the house of Ahab like the 9 house of Jeroboam son of Nebat and the house of Baasha son of Ahijah. Jezebel shall 10 be devoured by dogs in the plot of ground at Jezreel and no one will bury her."' Then he opened the door and fled. When Jehu 11 rejoined the king's officers, they said to him, 'Is all well? What did this crazy fellow want with you?' 'You know him and the way his thoughts run', he said. 'Nonsense!' they 12 replied; 'tell us what happened.' 'I will tell you exactly what he said: "This is the word of the LORD: I anoint you king over Israel."' They snatched up their cloaks and spread 13 them under him on the stones*v* of the steps, and sounded the trumpet and shouted, 'Jehu is king.'

Jehu kills Jehoram and Ahaziah

Then Jehu son of Jehoshaphat, son of 14 Nimshi, laid his plans against Jehoram, while Jehoram and the Israelites were defend-ing Ramoth-gilead against Hazael king of Aram. King Jehoram had returned to Jez-15 reel to recover from the wounds inflicted on him by the Aramaeans, in the war he fought against Hazael king of Aram. Jehu said to them, 'If you are on my side, see that no one escapes from the city to tell the news in Jezreel.' He mounted his chariot and drove 16 to Jezreel, for Jehoram was laid up there, and Ahaziah king of Judah had gone down to visit him.

The watchman standing on the watch-17 tower in Jezreel saw Jehu and his troop approaching and called out, 'I see a troop of men.' Then Jehoram said, 'Fetch a horse-man and send to find out if they come peaceably.' The horseman went to meet him 18

t and defeated: *prob. rdg.; Heb.* and he defeated Edom. *rdg.; Heb. obscure.*

u Verses 25–29: cp. 2 Chr. 22. 1–6.   *v Prob.*

and said, 'The king asks, "Is it peace?" ' Jehu said, 'Peace? What is peace to you? Fall in behind me.' Thereupon the watchman reported, 'The messenger has met them but he
19 is not coming back.' A second horseman was sent; when he met them, he also said, 'The king asks, "Is it peace?" ' 'Peace?' said Jehu. 'What is peace to you? Fall in behind
20 me.' Then the watchman reported, 'He has met them but he is not coming back. The driving is like the driving of Jehu son*w* of
21 Nimshi, for he drives furiously.' 'Harness my chariot', said Jehoram. They harnessed it, and Jehoram king of Israel and Ahaziah king of Judah went out each in his own chariot to meet Jehu, and met him by the
22 plot of Naboth of Jezreel. When Jehoram saw Jehu, he said, 'Is it peace, Jehu?' But he replied, 'Do you call it peace while your mother Jezebel keeps up her obscene idol-
23 worship and monstrous sorceries?' Jehoram wheeled about and fled, crying out to
24 Ahaziah, 'Treachery, Ahaziah!' Jehu seized his bow and shot Jehoram between the shoulders; the arrow pierced his heart and
25 he sank down in his chariot. Then Jehu said to Bidkar, his lieutenant, 'Pick him up and throw him into the plot of land belonging to Naboth of Jezreel; remember how, when you and I were riding side by side behind Ahab his father, the LORD pronounced this
26 sentence against him: "It is the very word of the LORD: as surely as I saw yesterday the blood of Naboth and the blood of his sons, I will requite you in this plot." So pick him up and throw him into it and thus fulfil the
27 word of the LORD.' When Ahaziah king of Judah saw this, he fled by the road to Beth-haggan. Jehu went after him and said, 'Make sure of him too.' They shot him down in his chariot on the road up the valley*x* near Ibleam, but he escaped to Megiddo and died
28 there. His servants conveyed his body to Jerusalem and buried him in his tomb with his forefathers in the city of David.
29   In the eleventh year of Jehoram son of Ahab, Ahaziah became king over Judah.

The death of Jezebel

30 Jehu came to Jezreel. Now Jezebel had heard what had happened; she had painted her eyes and dressed her hair, and she stood
31 looking down from a window. As Jehu entered the gate, she said, 'Is it peace, you
32 Zimri, you murderer of your master?' He looked up at the window and said, 'Who is on my side, who?' Two or three eunuchs
33 looked out, and he said, 'Throw her down.' They threw her down, and some of her blood splashed on to the wall and the horses,
34 which trampled her underfoot. Then he went in and ate and drank. 'See to this

accursed woman', he said, 'and bury her; for she is a king's daughter.' But when they 35 went to bury her they found nothing of her but the skull, the feet, and the palms of the hands; and they went back and told him. 36 Jehu said, 'It is the word of the LORD which his servant Elijah the Tishbite spoke, when he said, "In the plot of ground at Jezreel the dogs shall devour the flesh of Jezebel, and 37 Jezebel's corpse shall lie like dung upon the ground in the plot at Jezreel so that no one will be able to say: This is Jezebel." '

Jehu destroys the house of Ahab

Now seventy sons of Ahab were left in 10 Samaria. Jehu therefore sent a letter to Samaria, to the elders, the rulers of the city, and to the tutors of Ahab's children, in which he wrote: 'Now, when this letter 2 reaches you, since you have in your care your master's family as well as his chariots and horses, fortified cities and weapons, choose the best and the most suitable of 3 your master's family, set him on his father's throne, and fight for your master's house.' They were panic-stricken and said, 'The two 4 kings could not stand against him; what hope is there that we can?' Therefore the 5 comptroller of the household and the governor of the city, with the elders and the tutors, sent this message to Jehu: 'We are your servants. Whatever you tell us we will do; but we will not make anyone king. Do as you think fit.' Then he wrote them a second 6 letter: 'If you are on my side and will obey my orders, then bring the heads of your master's sons to me at Jezreel by this time tomorrow.' Now the royal princes, seventy in all, were with the nobles of the city who were bringing them up. When the letter 7 reached them, they took the royal princes and killed all seventy; they put their heads in baskets and sent them to Jehu in Jezreel. When the messenger came to him and 8 reported that they had brought the heads of the royal princes, he ordered them to be put in two heaps and left at the entrance of the city gate till morning. In the morning he 9 went out, stood there and said to all the people, 'You are fair judges. If I conspired against my master and killed him, who put all these to death? Be sure then that every 10 word which the LORD has spoken against the house of Ahab shall be fulfilled, and that the LORD has now done what he spoke through his servant Elijah.' So Jehu put to 11 death all who were left of the house of Ahab in Jezreel, as well as all his nobles, his close friends, and his priests, until he had left not one survivor.

    Then he set out for Samaria, and on the 12 way there, when he had reached a shepherds'

¹³ shelter,ʸ he came upon the kinsmen of Ahaziah king of Judah and said, 'Who are you?' 'We are kinsmen of Ahaziah,' they replied; 'and we have come down to greet the families of the king and of the queen ¹⁴ mother.' 'Take them alive', he said. So they took them alive; then they slew them and flung them into the pit that was there, forty-two of them; they did not leave a single survivor.

¹⁵ When he had left that place, he found Jehonadab son of Rechab coming to meet him. He greeted him and said, 'Are you with me heart and soul, as I am with you?' 'I am', said Jehonadab. 'Then if you are,' said Jehu, 'give me your hand.' He gave him his hand and Jehu helped him up into his chariot. ¹⁶ 'Come with me,' he said, 'and you will see my zeal for the LORD.' So he took him with ¹⁷ him in his chariot. When he came to Samaria, he put to death all of Ahab's house who were left there and so blotted it out, in fulfilment of the word which the LORD had spoken to Elijah.

Jehu stamps out Baal-worship

¹⁸ Then Jehu called all the people together and said to them, 'Ahab served the Baal a little; ¹⁹ Jehu will serve him much. Now, summon all the prophets of Baal, all his ministers and priests; not one must be missing. For I am holding a great sacrifice to Baal, and no one who is missing from it shall live.' In this way Jehu outwitted the ministers of Baal in ²⁰ order to destroy them. So Jehu said, 'Let a sacred ceremony for Baal be held.' They did ²¹ so, and Jehu himself sent word throughout Israel, and all the ministers of Baal came; there was not a man left who did not come. They went into the temple of Baal and it was ²² filled from end to end. Then he said to the person who had charge of the wardrobe, 'Bring out robes for all the ministers of ²³ Baal'; and he brought them out. Then Jehu and Jehonadab son of Rechab went into the temple of Baal and said to the ministers of Baal, 'Look carefully and make sure that there are no servants of the LORD here with ²⁴ you, but only the ministers of Baal.' Then they went in to offer sacrifices and whole-offerings. Now Jehu had stationed eighty men outside and said to them, 'I am putting these men in your charge, and any man who lets one escape shall answer for it with his ²⁵ life.' When he had finished offering the whole-offering, Jehu ordered the guards and the lieutenants to go and cut them all down, and let not one of them escape; so they slew them without quarter. The escort and the lieutenants then rushed into the keep of the ²⁶ temple of Baal and brought out the sacred

pole² from the temple of Baal and burnt it; and they pulled down the sacred pillar of ²⁷ the Baal and the temple itself and made a privy of it—as it is today. Thus Jehu stamped ²⁸ out the worship of Baal in Israel. He did ²⁹ not however abandon the sins of Jeroboam son of Nebat who led Israel into sin, but he maintained the worship of the golden calves of Bethel and Dan.

The LORD commends Jehu

Then the LORD said to Jehu, 'You have done ³⁰ well what is right in my eyes and have done to the house of Ahab all that it was in my mind to do. Therefore your sons to the fourth generation shall sit on the throne of Israel.' But Jehu was not careful to follow ³¹ the law of the LORD the God of Israel with all his heart; he did not abandon the sins of Jeroboam who led Israel into sin.

In those days the LORD began to work ³² havoc on Israel, and Hazael struck at them in every corner of their territory eastwards ³³ from the Jordan: all the land of Gilead, Gad, Reuben, and Manasseh, from Aroer which is by the gorge of the Arnon, including Gilead and Bashan.

Other records of Jehu's reign

The other events of Jehu's reign, his achieve- ³⁴ ments and his exploits, are recorded in the annals of the kings of Israel. So Jehu rested ³⁵ with his forefathers and was buried in Samaria; and he was succeeded by his son Jehoahaz. Jehu reigned over Israel in Sa- ³⁶ maria for twenty-eight years.

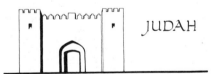

Athaliah seizes the throne

As soon as Athaliah mother of Ahaziah saw **11** ¹ᵃ that her son was dead, she set out to destroy all the royal line. But Jehosheba daughter of ² King Joram, sister of Ahaziah, took Ahaziah's son Joash and stole him away from among the princes who were being murdered; she putᵇ him and his nurse in a bedchamber where he was hidden from Athaliah and was not put to death. He remained con- ³ cealed with her in the house of the LORD for six years, while Athaliah ruled the country. In the seventh year Jehoiada sent for the ⁴ captains of units of a hundred, both of the Carites and of the guards, and he brought them into the house of the LORD; he made

---

ʸ a shepherds' shelter: or Beth-eker of the Shepherds. ᶻ Prob. rdg.; Heb. sacred pillars. ᵃ Verses
1–20: cp. 2 Chr. 22. 10—23. 21.   ᵇ she put: prob. rdg., cp. 2 Chr. 22. 11; Heb. om.

'Bring her outside the precincts and put to the sword anyone in attendance on her'; for the priest said, 'She shall not be put to death in the house of the LORD.' So they laid hands 16 on her and took her out by the entry for horses to the royal palace, and there she was put to death.

Jehoiada puts down idolatry

Then Jehoiada made a covenant between 17 the LORD and the king and people that they should be the LORD's people, and also between the king and the people. And all the 18 people went into the temple of Baal and pulled it down; they smashed to pieces its altars and images, and they slew Mattan the priest of Baal before the altars. Then Jehoiada set a watch over the house of the LORD; he took the captains of units of a 19 hundred, the Carites and the guards and all the people, and they escorted the king from the house of the LORD through the Gate of the Guards to the royal palace, and seated him on the royal throne. The whole 20 people rejoiced and the city was tranquil. That is how Athaliah was put to the sword in the royal palace.

Rebuilding the Temple

Joash was seven years old when he became 21 king. In the seventh year of Jehu, Joash be- **12** came king, and he reigned in Jerusalem for forty years; his mother was Zibiah of Beersheba. He did what was right in the eyes of 2 the LORD all his days, as Jehoiada the priest had taught him. The hill-shrines, however, 3 were allowed to remain; the people still continued to sacrifice and make smoke-offerings there.

Then Joash ordered the priests to take all 4 the silver brought as holy-gifts into the house of the LORD, the silver for which each man was assessed,*g* the silver for the persons assessed under his name, and any silver which any man brought voluntarily to the house of the LORD. He ordered the priests, 5 also, each to make a contribution from his own funds, and to repair the house wherever it was found necessary. But in the twenty- 6 third year of the reign of Joash the priests had still not carried out the repairs to the house. King Joash summoned Jehoiada the 7 priest and the other priests and said to them, 'Why are you not repairing the house? Henceforth you need not contribute from your own funds for the repair of the house.' So the priests agreed neither to receive 8 money from the people nor to undertake the repairs of the house. Then Jehoiada the 9 priest took a chest and bored a hole in the

an agreement with them and put them on their oath in the house of the LORD, and 5 showed them the king's son, and gave them the following orders: 'One third of you who are on duty on the sabbath are to be on guard 6 in the palace; the rest of you are to be on special duty in the house of the LORD, one third at the Sur Gate and the other third at 7 the gate with*c* the outrunners. Your two companies who are off duty on the sabbath shall be on duty for the king in the house of 8 the LORD. So you shall be on guard round the king, each man with his arms at the ready, and anyone who comes near the ranks is to be put to death; you must be with the king wherever he goes.'

Jehoiada anoints Joash king

9 The captains carried out the orders of Jehoiada the priest to the letter. Each took his men, both those who came on duty on the sabbath and those who came off, and 10 came to Jehoiada. The priest handed out to the captains King David's spears and shields, 11 which were in the house of the LORD. Then the guards took up their stations, each man carrying his arms at the ready, from corner to corner of the house to north and south,*d* 12 surrounding the king. Then he brought out the king's son, put the crown on his head, handed him the warrant and anointed him king. The people clapped their hands and 13 shouted, 'Long live the king.' When Athaliah heard the noise made by the guards and the people, she came into the house of the LORD 14 where the people were and found the king standing, as was the custom, on the dais,*e* amidst outbursts of song and fanfares of trumpets in his honour, and all the populace rejoicing and blowing trumpets. Then Athaliah rent her clothes and cried, 'Treason! 15 Treason!' Jehoiada the priest gave orders to the captains in command of the troops:

c Or behind.　　*d Prob. rdg.; Heb. adds* of the altar and the house.　　*e Or* by the pillar.　　*f 11. 21—* 12. 15: cp. 2 Chr. 24. 1–14.　　*g* the silver . . . assessed: *prob. rdg.; Heb. obscure.*

lid and put it beside the altar on the right side going into the house of the LORD, and the priests on duty at the entrance put in it all the money brought into the house of the

10 LORD. And whenever they saw that the chest was well filled, the king's secretary and the high priest came and melted down the silver found in the house of the LORD and weighed

11 it. When it had been checked, they gave the silver to the foremen over the work in the house of the LORD and they paid the carpenters and the builders working on the temple

12 and the masons and the stone-cutters; they used it also to buy timber and hewn stone for the repairs and for all other expenses

13 connected with them. They did not use the silver brought into the house of the LORD to make silver cups, snuffers, tossing-bowls,

14 trumpets, or any gold or silver vessels; but they paid it to the workmen and used it for

15 the repairs. No account was demanded from the foremen to whom the money was given for the payment of the workmen, for they

16 were acting on trust. Money from guilt-offerings and sin-offerings was not brought into the house of the LORD: it belonged to the priests.

Hazael threatens Jerusalem

17 Then Hazael king of Aram came up and attacked Gath and took it; and he moved

18 on against Jerusalem. But Joash king of Judah took all the holy-gifts that Jehoshaphat, Joram, and Ahaziah his forefathers, kings of Judah, had dedicated, and his own holy-gifts, and all the gold that was found in the treasuries of the house of the LORD and in the royal palace, and sent them to Hazael king of Aram; and he withdrew from Jerusalem.

Other records of Joash's reign

19 The other acts and events of the reign of Joash are recorded in the annals of the kings

20*h* of Judah. His servants revolted against him and struck him down in the house of Millo

21 on the descent to Silla. It was his servants Jozachar son of Shimeath and Jehozabad son of Shomer who struck the fatal blow; and he was buried with his forefathers in the city of David. He was succeeded by his son Amaziah.

Jehoahaz reigns over Israel

3 In the twenty-third year of Joash son of Ahaziah king of Judah, Jehoahaz son of Jehu became king over Israel in Samaria

2 and he reigned seventeen years. He did what was wrong in the eyes of the LORD and continued the sinful practices of Jeroboam son of Nebat who led Israel into sin, and did

h Verses 20, 21: cp. 2 Chr. 24. 25–27.

ISRAEL

not give them up. So the LORD was roused 3 to anger against Israel and he made them subject for some years to Hazael king of Aram and Ben-hadad son of Hazael. Then 4 Jehoahaz sought to placate the LORD, and the LORD heard his prayer, for he saw how the king of Aram oppressed Israel. The LORD 5 appointed a deliverer for Israel, who rescued them from the power of Aram, and the Israelites settled down again in their own homes. But they did not give up the sinful 6 practices of the house of Jeroboam who led Israel into sin, but continued in them; the goddess Asherah*i* remained in Samaria. Hazael had left Jehoahaz no armed force 7 except fifty horsemen, ten chariots, and ten thousand infantry; all the rest the king of Aram had destroyed and made like dust under foot.

The other events of the reign of Jehoahaz, 8 and all his achievements and his exploits, are recorded in the annals of the kings of Israel. So Jehoahaz rested with his fore- 9 fathers and was buried in Samaria; and he was succeeded by his son Jehoash.

Jehoash reigns over Israel

In the thirty-ninth year of Joash king of 10 Judah, Jehoash son of Jehoahaz became king over Israel in Samaria and reigned sixteen years. He did what was wrong in the 11 eyes of the LORD; he did not give up any of the sinful practices of Jeroboam son of Nebat who led Israel into sin, but continued in them. The other events of the reign of 12 Jehoash, all his achievements, his exploits and his war with Amaziah king of Judah, are recorded in the annals of the kings of Israel. So Jehoash rested with his forefathers 13 and was buried in Samaria with the kings of Israel, and Jeroboam sat upon his throne.

Elisha's last words

Elisha fell ill and lay on his deathbed, and 14 Jehoash king of Israel went down to him and wept over him and said, 'My father! My father, the chariots and the horsemen of Israel!' 'Take bow and arrows', said Elisha, 15 and he took bow and arrows. 'Put your hand 16 to the bow', said the prophet. He did so, and Elisha laid his hands on those of the king. Then he said, 'Open the window toward the 17 east'; he opened it and Elisha told him to

i the goddess Asherah: or the sacred pole.

shoot, and he shot. Then the prophet said, 'An arrow for the LORD's victory, an arrow for victory over Aram! You will defeat
18 Aram utterly at Aphek'; and he added, 'Now take up your arrows.' When the king had taken them, Elisha said, 'Strike the ground with them.' He struck three times
19 and stopped. The man of God was furious with him and said, 'You should have struck five or six times; then you would have defeated Aram utterly; as it is, you will strike Aram three times and no more.'
20   Then Elisha died and was buried.

A miracle at Elisha's grave
Year by year Moabite raiders used to invade
21 the land. Once some men were burying a dead man when they caught sight of the raiders. They threw the body into the grave of Elisha and made off; when the body touched the prophet's bones, the man came to life and rose to his feet.
22   All through the reign of Jehoahaz, Hazael
23 king of Aram oppressed Israel. But the LORD was gracious and took pity on them; because of his covenant with Abraham, Isaac, and Jacob, he looked on them with favour and was unwilling to destroy them; nor has he even yet banished them from his
24 sight. When Hazael king of Aram died and
25 was succeeded by his son Ben-hadad, Jehoash son of Jehoahaz recaptured the cities which Ben-hadad had taken in war from Jehoahaz his father; three times Jehoash defeated him and recovered the cities of Israel.

JUDAH

Amaziah reigns over Judah
14 1j In the second year of Jehoash son of Jehoahaz king of Israel, Amaziah son of Joash
2 king of Judah succeeded his father. He was twenty-five years old when he came to the throne, and he reigned in Jerusalem for twenty-nine years; his mother was Jehoaddin of Jerusalem. He did what was right in
3 the eyes of the LORD, yet not as his forefather David had done; he followed his father
4 Joash in everything. The hill-shrines were allowed to remain; the people continued to
5 slaughter and burn sacrifices there. When the royal power was firmly in his grasp, he put to death those of his servants who had
6 murdered the king his father; but he spared the murderers' children in obedience to the

LORD's command written in the law of Moses: 'Fathers shall not be put to death for their children, nor children for their fathers; a man shall be put to death only for his own sin.' He defeated ten thousand 7 Edomites in the Valley of Salt and captured Sela; he gave it the name Joktheel, which it still bears.

Judah and Israel in conflict
Then Amaziah sent messengers to Jehoash 8k son of Jehoahaz, son of Jehu, king of Israel, to propose a meeting. But Jehoash king of 9 Israel sent this answer to Amaziah king of Judah: 'A thistle in Lebanon sent to a cedar in Lebanon to say, "Give your daughter in marriage to my son." But a wild beast in Lebanon, passing by, trampled on the thistle. You have defeated Edom, it is true; and it 10 has gone to your head. Stay at home and enjoy your triumph. Why should you involve yourself in disaster and bring yourself to the ground, and Judah with you?'
But Amaziah would not listen; so Jehoash 11 king of Israel marched out, and he and Amaziah king of Judah met one another at Beth-shemesh in Judah. The men of Judah 12 were routed by Israel and fled to their homes. But Jehoash king of Israel captured Amaziah 13 king of Judah, son of Joash, son of Ahaziah, at Beth-shemesh. He went to Jerusalem and broke down the city wall from the Gate of Ephraim to the Corner Gate, a distance of four hundred cubits. He also took all the 14 gold and silver and all the vessels found in the house of the LORD and in the treasuries of the royal palace, as well as hostages, and returned to Samaria.

Other records of Jehoash's reign
The other events of the reign of Jehoash, 15 and all his achievements, his exploits and his wars with Amaziah king of Judah, are recorded in the annals of the kings of Israel. So Jehoash rested with his forefathers and 16 was buried in Samaria with the kings of Israel; and he was succeeded by his son Jeroboam.

The death of Amaziah
Amaziah son of Joash, king of Judah, out- 17 lived Jehoash son of Jehoahaz, king of Israel, by fifteen years. The other events of 18 Amaziah's reign are recorded in the annals of the kings of Judah. A conspiracy was 19 formed against him in Jerusalem and he fled to Lachish; but they sent after him to Lachish and put him to death there. Then his 20 body was conveyed on horseback to Jerusalem, and there he was buried with his forefathers in the city of David. The people of 21 Judah took Azariah, now sixteen years old,

j Verses 1–6: cp. 2 Chr. 25. 1–4.   k Verses 8–14: cp. 2 Chr. 25. 17–24.   l Verses 17–22: cp. 2 Chr. 25. 25—26. 2.

and made him king in succession to his
22 father Amaziah. It was he who built Elath
and restored it to Judah after the king
rested with his forefathers.

ISRAEL

Jeroboam II reigns over Israel

23 In the fifteenth year of Amaziah son of
Joash king of Judah, Jeroboam son of
Jehoash king of Israel became king in
24 Samaria and reigned for forty-one years. He
did what was wrong in the eyes of the LORD;
he did not give up the sinful practices of
Jeroboam son of Nebat who led Israel into
25 sin. He re-established the frontiers of Israel
from Lebo-hamath to the Sea of the Arabah,
in fulfilment of the word of the LORD the
God of Israel spoken by his servant the
prophet Jonah son of Amittai, of Gath-
26 hepher. For the LORD had seen how bitterly
Israel had suffered; no one was safe, whether
under the protection of his family or not,
27 and Israel was left defenceless. But the LORD
had made no threat to blot out the name of
Israel under heaven, and he saved them
28 through Jeroboam son of Jehoash. The
other events of Jeroboam's reign, and all
his achievements, his exploits, the wars he
fought and how he recovered Damascus and
Hamath in Jaudi for[m] Israel, are recorded in
29 the annals of the kings of Israel. So Jeroboam rested with his forefathers the kings
of Israel; and he was succeeded by his son
Zechariah.

JUDAH

Azariah reigns over Judah

5 In the twenty-seventh year of Jeroboam king
of Israel, Azariah[n] son of Amaziah king of
2 Judah became king. He was sixteen years
old when he came to the throne, and he
reigned in Jerusalem for fifty-two years; his
3 mother was Jecoliah of Jerusalem. He did
what was right in the eyes of the LORD, as
4 Amaziah his father had done. But the hill-

shrines were allowed to remain; the people
still continued to slaughter and burn sacrifices there. The LORD struck the king with 5[p]
leprosy,[q] which he had till the day of his
death; he was relieved of all duties and lived
in his own house, while his son Jotham was
comptroller of the household and regent.
The other acts and events of Azariah's 6
reign are recorded in the annals of the kings
of Judah. So he rested with his forefathers 7
and was buried with them in the city of
David; and he was succeeded by his son
Jotham.

ISRAEL

Zechariah reigns over Israel

In the thirty-eighth year of Azariah king of 8
Judah, Zechariah son of Jeroboam became
king over Israel in Samaria and reigned six
months. He did what was wrong in the eyes 9
of the LORD, as his forefathers had done;
he did not give up the sinful practices of
Jeroboam son of Nebat who led Israel into
sin. Shallum son of Jabesh formed a con- 10
spiracy against him, attacked him in Ibleam,
killed him and usurped the throne. The other 11
events of Zechariah's reign are recorded in
the annals of the kings of Israel. Thus the 12
word of the LORD spoken to Jehu was fulfilled: 'Your sons to the fourth generation
shall sit on the throne of Israel.'

Shallum reigns over Israel

Shallum son of Jabesh became king in the 13
thirty-ninth year of Uzziah king of Judah,
and he reigned one full month in Samaria.
Then Menahem son of Gadi came up from 14
Tirzah to Samaria, attacked Shallum son
of Jabesh there, killed him and usurped the
throne. The other events of Shallum's reign 15
and the conspiracy that he formed are recorded in the annals of the kings of Israel.

Menahem reigns over Israel

Then Menahem, starting out from Tirzah, 16
destroyed Tappuah and everything in it and
ravaged its territory; he ravaged it because
it had not opened its gates to him, and he
ripped open all the pregnant women.
    In the thirty-ninth year of Azariah king of 17
Judah, Menahem son of Gadi became king
over Israel and he reigned in Samaria for
ten years. He did what was wrong in the 18

---

m in Jaudi for: *prob. rdg.; Heb.* to Judah in.   *n* Uzziah *in verses* 13, 30, 32, 34.   *o* Verses 2, 3: cp.
2 Chr. 26. 3, 4.   *p* Verses 5–7: cp. 2 Chr. 26. 21–23.   *q* Or a skin-disease.

eyes of the LORD; he did not give up the sinful practices of Jeroboam son of Nebat who
19 led Israel into sin. In his days Pul king of Assyria invaded the country, and Menahem gave him a thousand talents of silver to obtain his help in strengthening his hold on
20 the kingdom. Menahem laid a levy on all the men of wealth in Israel, and each had to give the king of Assyria fifty silver shekels. Then the king of Assyria withdrew without
21 occupying the country. The other acts and events of Menahem's reign are recorded in
22 the annals of the kings of Israel. So Menahem rested with his forefathers; and he was succeeded by his son Pekahiah.

Pekahiah reigns over Israel

23 In the fiftieth year of Azariah king of Judah, Pekahiah son of Menahem became king over Israel in Samaria and reigned for two years.
24 He did what was wrong in the eyes of the LORD; he did not give up the sinful practices of Jeroboam son of Nebat who led Israel
25 into sin. Pekah son of Remaliah, his lieutenant, formed a conspiracy against him and, with the help of fifty Gileadites, attacked him in Samaria in the citadel of the royal palace,[r]
26 killed him and usurped the throne. The other acts and events of Pekahiah's reign are recorded in the annals of the kings of Israel.

Pekah reigns over Israel

27 In the fifty-second year of Azariah king of Judah, Pekah son of Remaliah became king over Israel in Samaria and reigned for
28 twenty years. He did what was wrong in the eyes of the LORD; he did not give up the sinful practices of Jeroboam son of Nebat who
29 led Israel into sin. In the days of Pekah king of Israel, Tiglath-pileser king of Assyria came and seized Iyyon, Abel-beth-maacah, Janoah, Kedesh, Hazor, Gilead, and Galilee, with all the land of Naphtali, and deported
30 the people to Assyria. Then Hoshea son of Elah formed a conspiracy against Pekah son of Remaliah, attacked him, killed him and usurped the throne in the twentieth year of
31 Jotham son of Uzziah. The other acts and events of Pekah's reign are recorded in the annals of the kings of Israel.

Jotham reigns over Judah

32 In the second year of Pekah son of Remaliah king of Israel, Jotham son of Uzziah
33 s king of Judah became king. He was twenty-five years old when he came to the throne, and he reigned in Jerusalem for sixteen years; his mother was Jerusha daughter of
34 Zadok. He did what was right in the eyes of the LORD, as his father Uzziah had done;
35 but the hill-shrines were allowed to remain

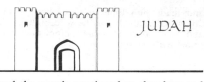

JUDAH

and the people continued to slaughter and burn sacrifices there. It was he who constructed the upper gate of the house of the LORD. The other acts and events of Jotham's 36 reign are recorded in the annals of the kings of Judah. In those days the LORD began to 37 make Rezin king of Aram and Pekah son of Remaliah attack Judah. And Jotham 38 rested with his forefathers and was buried with them in the city of David his forefather; and he was succeeded by his son Ahaz.

Ahaz reigns over Judah

In the seventeenth year of Pekah son of 16 Remaliah, Ahaz son of Jotham king of Judah became king. Ahaz was twenty years 2 t old when he came to the throne, and he reigned in Jerusalem for sixteen years. He did not do what was right in the eyes of the LORD his God like his forefather David, but 3 followed in the footsteps of the kings of Israel; he even passed his son through the fire, adopting the abominable practice of the nations whom the LORD had dispossessed in favour of the Israelites. He slaughtered 4 and burnt sacrifices at the hill-shrines and on the hill-tops and under every spreading tree.

Assyria relieves Judah

Then Rezin king of Aram and Pekah son of 5 Remaliah king of Israel attacked Jerusalem and besieged Ahaz but could not bring him to battle. At that time the king of Edom[u] 6 recovered Elath and drove the Judaeans out of it; so the Edomites entered the city and have occupied it to this day. Ahaz sent mes- 7 sengers to Tiglath-pileser king of Assyria to say, 'I am your servant and your son. Come and save me from the king of Aram and from the king of Israel who are attacking me.' Ahaz took the silver and gold found in the 8 house of the LORD and in the treasuries of the royal palace and sent them to the king of Assyria as a bribe. The king of Assyria 9 listened to him; he advanced on Damascus, captured it, deported its inhabitants to Kir and put Rezin to death.

Ahaz rearranges the Temple

When King Ahaz went to meet Tiglath- 10 pileser king of Assyria at Damascus, he saw there an altar of which he sent a sketch and a detailed plan to Uriah the priest. Accord- 11 ingly, Uriah built an altar, following all the

---

r *Prob. rdg.; Heb. adds* Argob and Arieh.   s *Verses 33–35: cp.* 2 Chr. 27. 1–3.   t *Verses 2–4: cp.*
2 Chr. 28. 1–4.   u *the king of Edom: prob. rdg.; Heb.* Rezin king of Aram.

instructions that the king had sent him from Damascus, and had it ready against the
12 king's return. When the king returned from Damascus, he saw the altar, approached it
13 and mounted the steps; there he burnt his whole-offering and his grain-offering and poured out his drink-offering, and he flung the blood of his shared-offerings against it.
14 The bronze altar that was before the LORD he removed from the front of the house, from between this altar and the house of the LORD, and put it on the north side of this
15 altar. Then King Ahaz gave these instructions to Uriah the priest: 'Burn on the great altar the morning whole-offering and the evening grain-offering, and the king's whole-offering and his grain-offering, and the whole-offering of all the people of the land, their grain-offering and their drink-offerings, and fling against it all the blood of the sacrifices. But the bronze altar shall be mine, to
16 offer morning sacrifice.' Uriah the priest
17 did all that the king told him. Then King Ahaz broke up the trolleys and removed the panels, and he took down the basin and the Sea of bronze from the oxen which
18 supported it and put it on a stone base. In the house of the LORD he turned round the structure they had erected for use on the sabbath, and the outer gate for the king, to
19 *v* satisfy the king of Assyria. The other acts and events of the reign of Ahaz are recorded
20 in the annals of the kings of Judah. So Ahaz rested with his forefathers and was buried with them in the city of David; and he was succeeded by his son Hezekiah.

Samaria's inhabitants deported to Assyria

17 In the twelfth year of Ahaz king of Judah, Hoshea son of Elah became king over Israel
2 in Samaria and reigned nine years. He did what was wrong in the eyes of the LORD, but not as the previous kings of Israel had done.
3 Shalmaneser king of Assyria made war upon him and Hoshea became tributary to him.
4 But when the king of Assyria discovered that Hoshea was being disloyal to him, sending messengers to the king of Egypt at So,*w* and withholding the tribute which he had been

ISRAEL

paying year by year, the king of Assyria arrested him and put him in prison. Then he 5 invaded the whole country and, reaching Samaria, besieged it for three years. In the 6 ninth year of Hoshea he captured Samaria and deported its people to Assyria and settled them in Halah and on the Habor, the river of Gozan, and in the cities of Media.

The reason for the deportation

All this happened to the Israelites because 7 they had sinned against the LORD their God who brought them up from Egypt, from the rule of Pharaoh king of Egypt; they paid homage to other gods and observed the laws 8 and customs of the nations whom the LORD had dispossessed before them and uttered 9 blasphemies against the LORD their God; they built hill-shrines for themselves in all their settlements, from watch-tower to fortified city, and set up sacred pillars and sacred 10 poles on every high hill and under every spreading tree, and burnt sacrifices at all the 11 hill-shrines there, as the nations did whom the LORD had displaced before them. By this wickedness of theirs they provoked the LORD's anger. They worshipped idols, a 12 thing which the LORD had forbidden them to do. Still the LORD solemnly charged 13 Israel and Judah by every prophet and seer, saying, 'Give up your evil ways; keep my commandments and statutes given in the law which I enjoined on your forefathers and delivered to you through my servants the prophets.' They would not listen, how- 14 ever, but were as stubborn and rebellious as their forefathers had been, who refused to put their trust in the LORD their God; they 15 rejected his statutes and the covenant which he had made with their forefathers and the solemn warnings which he had given to them; they followed worthless idols and

v Verses 19, 20: cp. 2 Chr. 28. 26, 27.   *w to the king of Egypt at So: prob. rdg.; Heb. to So king of Egypt.*

became worthless themselves; they imitated the nations round about them, a thing which
16 the LORD had forbidden them to do. Forsaking every commandment of the LORD their God, they made themselves images of cast metal, two calves, and also a sacred pole; they prostrated themselves to all the host of heaven and worshipped the Baal,
17 and they made their sons and daughters pass through the fire. They practised augury and divination; they sold themselves to do what was wrong in the eyes of the LORD and so provoked his anger.
18 Thus it was that the LORD was incensed against Israel and banished them from his presence; only the tribe of Judah was left.
19 Even Judah did not keep the commandments of the LORD their God but followed
20 the practices adopted by Israel; so the LORD rejected the whole race of Israel and punished them and gave them over to plunderers
21 and finally flung them out of his sight. When he tore Israel from the house of David, they made Jeroboam son of Nebat king, who seduced Israel from their allegiance to the
22 LORD and led them into grave sin. The Israelites persisted in all the sins that Jeroboam had committed and did not give
23 them up, until finally the LORD banished the Israelites from his presence, as he had threatened through his servants the prophets, and they were carried into exile from their own land to Assyria; and there they are to this day.

Idolatry in Samaria

24 Then the king of Assyria brought people from Babylon, Cuthah, Avva, Hamath, and Sepharvaim, and settled them in the cities of Samaria in place of the Israelites; so they
25 occupied Samaria and lived in its cities. In the early years of their settlement they did not pay homage to the LORD; and the LORD
26 sent lions among them, and the lions preyed upon them. The king was told that the deported peoples whom he had settled in the cities of Samaria did not know the established usage of the god of the country, and that he had sent lions among them which were preying upon them because they did
27 not know this. The king of Assyria, therefore, gave orders that one of the priests deported from Samaria should be sent back to live there and teach the people the usage of the
28 god of the country. So one of the deported priests came and lived at Bethel, and taught them how they should pay their homage to
29 the LORD. But each of the nations made its own god, and they set them up·within^x the hill-shrines which the Samaritans had made,
30 each nation in its own settlements. Succothbenoth was worshipped by the men of

Babylon, Nergal by the men of Cuth, Ashima by the men of Hamath, Nibhaz and
31 Tartak by the Avvites; and the Sepharvites burnt their children as offerings to Adrammelech and Anammelech, the gods of Sepharvaim. While still paying homage to the
32 LORD, they appointed people from every class to act as priests of the hill-shrines and they resorted to them there. They paid
33 homage to the LORD while at the same time they served their own gods, according to the custom of the nations from which they had been carried into exile.

Israel continues disobedient

They keep up these old practices to this day;
34 they do not pay homage to the LORD, for they do not keep his^y statutes and his^y judgements, the law and commandment, which he enjoined upon the descendants of Jacob whom he named Israel. When the
35 LORD made a covenant with them, he gave them this commandment: 'You shall not pay homage to other gods or bow down to them or serve them or sacrifice to them, but you
36 shall pay homage to the LORD who brought you up from Egypt with great power and with outstretched arm; to him you shall bow down, to him you shall offer sacrifice. You shall faithfully keep the statutes, the
37 judgements, the law, and the commandments which he wrote for you, and you shall not pay homage to other gods. You shall
38 not forget the covenant which I made with you; you shall not pay homage to other gods. But to the LORD your God you shall
39 pay homage, and he will preserve you from all your enemies.' However, they would not
40 listen but continued their former practices. While these nations paid homage to the
41 LORD they continued to serve their images, and their children and their children's children have maintained the practice of their forefathers to this day.

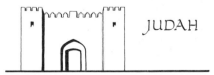

Hezekiah reigns over Judah

In the third year of Hoshea son of Elah **18** king of Israel, Hezekiah son of Ahaz king of Judah became king. He was twenty-five **2** years old when he came to the throne, and he reigned in Jerusalem for twenty-nine years; his mother was Abi daughter of Zechariah. He did what was right in the **3** eyes of the LORD, as David his forefather

---

x Or in niches at.   *y Prob. rdg.; Heb. their.*   *z Verses 1–3: cp. 2 Chr. 29. 1, 2.*

4 had done. It was he who suppressed the hill-shrines, smashed the sacred pillars, cut down every sacred pole and broke up the bronze serpent that Moses had made; for up to that time the Israelites had been burning sacrifices to it; they called it Nehushtan.
5 He put his trust in the LORD the God of Israel; there was nobody like him among all the kings of Judah who succeeded him or
6 among those who had gone before him. He remained loyal to the LORD and did not fail in his allegiance to him, and he kept the commandments which the LORD had given
7 to Moses. So the LORD was with him and he prospered in all that he undertook; he rebelled against the king of Assyria and was
8 no longer subject to him. He conquered the Philistine country as far as Gaza and its boundaries, alike the watch-tower and the fortified city.

ASSYRIA

Shalmaneser captures Samaria

9 In the fourth year of Hezekiah's reign (that was the seventh year of Hoshea son of Elah king of Israel) Shalmaneser king of Assyria
10 made an attack on Samaria, invested it and captured it after a siege of three years; it was in the sixth year of Hezekiah (the ninth year of Hoshea king of Israel) that Samaria
11 was captured. The king of Assyria deported the Israelites to Assyria and settled them in Halah and on the Habor, the river of Gozan,
12 and in the cities of Media, because they did not obey the LORD their God but violated his covenant and every commandment that Moses the servant of the LORD had given them; they would not listen and they would not obey.

Sennacherib invades Judah

13ᵃ In the fourteenth year of the reign of Hezekiah, Sennacherib king of Assyria attacked and took all the fortified cities of Judah.
14 Hezekiah king of Judah sent a message to the king of Assyria at Lachish: 'I have done wrong; withdraw from my land, and I will pay any penalty you impose upon me.' So the king of Assyria laid on Hezekiah king of Judah a penalty of three hundred talents
15 of silver and thirty talents of gold; and Hezekiah gave him all the silver found in

the house of the LORD and in the treasuries of the royal palace. At that time Hezekiah 16 broke up the doors of the temple of the LORD and the door-frames which he himself had plated, and gave them to the king of Assyria.

Sennacherib presses for surrender

From Lachish the king of Assyria sent the 17 commander-in-chief, the chief eunuch, and the chief officerᵇ with a strong force to King Hezekiah at Jerusalem, and they went up and came to Jerusalem and halted by the conduit of the Upper Pool on the causeway which leads to the Fuller's Field. When they 18 called for the king, Eliakim son of Hilkiah, the comptroller of the household, came out to them, with Shebna the adjutant-general and Joah son of Asaph, the secretary of state. The chief officer said to them, 'Tell 19 Hezekiah that this is the message of the Great King, the king of Assyria: "What ground have you for this confidence of yours? Do you think fine words can take 20 the place of skill and numbers? On whom then do you rely for support in your rebellion against me? On Egypt? Egypt is a splintered 21 cane that will run into a man's hand and pierce it if he leans on it. That is what Pharaoh king of Egypt proves to all who rely on him. And if you tell me that you are rely- 22 ing on the LORD your God, is he not the god whose hill-shrines and altars Hezekiah has suppressed, telling Judah and Jerusalem that they must prostrate themselves before this altar in Jerusalem?"

'Now, make a bargain with my master 23 the king of Assyria: I will give you two thousand horses if you can find riders for them. Will you reject the authority of even 24 the least of my master's servants and rely on Egypt for chariots and horsemen? Do you 25 think that I have come to attack this place and destroy it without the consent of the LORD? No; the LORD himself said to me, "Attack this land and destroy it."'

Eliakim son of Hilkiah, Shebna, and Joah 26 said to the chief officer, 'Please speak to us in Aramaic, for we understand it; do not speak Hebrew to us within earshot of the people on the city wall.' The chief officer an- 27 swered, 'Is it to your master and to you that my master has sent me to say this? Is it not to the people sitting on the wall who, like you, will have to eat their own dung and drink their own urine?' Then he stood and 28 shouted in Hebrew, 'Hear the message of the Great King, the king of Assyria. These are 29 the king's words: "Do not be taken in by Hezekiah. He cannot save you from me. Do 30

---

a Verses 13–37: cp. Isa. 36. 1–22; 2 Chr. 32. 1–19.
chief officer: *or* Tartan, Rab-saris, and Rab-shakeh.

b the commander-in-chief, the chief eunuch, and the

not let him persuade you to rely on the LORD, and tell you that the LORD will save you and that this city will never be surrendered to the
31 king of Assyria." Do not listen to Hezekiah; these are the words of the king of Assyria: "Make peace with me. Come out to me, and then you shall each eat the fruit of his own vine and his own fig-tree, and drink the
32 water of his own cistern, until I come and take you to a land like your own, a land of grain and new wine, of corn and vineyards, of olives, fine oil, and honey—life for you all, instead of death. Do not listen to Hezekiah; he will only mislead you by telling you
33 that the LORD will save you. Did the god of any of these nations save his land from the
34 king of Assyria? Where are the gods of Hamath and Arpad? Where are the gods of Sepharvaim, Hena, and Ivvah? Where are the gods of Samaria? Did they save Samaria
35 from me? Among all the gods of the nations is there one who saved his land from me? And how is the LORD to save Jerusalem?"'
36 The people were silent and answered not a word, for the king had given orders that
37 no one was to answer him. Eliakim son of Hilkiah, comptroller of the household, Shebna the adjutant-general, and Joah son of Asaph, secretary of state, came to Hezekiah with their clothes rent and reported what the chief officer had said.

Hezekiah seeks Isaiah's advice

19 1c When King Hezekiah heard their report, he rent his clothes and wrapped himself in sackcloth, and went into the house of the
2 LORD. He sent Eliakim comptroller of the household, Shebna the adjutant-general, and the senior priests, all covered in sackcloth,
3 to the prophet Isaiah son of Amoz, to give him this message from the king: 'This day is a day of trouble for us, a day of reproof and contempt. We are like a woman who has no strength to bear the child that is
4 coming to the birth. It may be that the LORD your God heard all the words of the chief officer whom his master the king of Assyria sent to taunt the living God, and will confute what he, the LORD your God, heard. Offer a prayer for those who still survive.'
5 King Hezekiah's servants came to Isaiah,
6 and he told them to say this to their master: 'This is the word of the LORD: "Do not be alarmed at what you heard when the lackeys
7 of the king of Assyria blasphemed me. I will put a spirit in him and he shall hear a rumour and withdraw to his own country; and there I will make him fall by the sword."'

Hezekiah prays for help

8 So the chief officer withdrew. He heard that the king of Assyria had left Lachish, and he

found him attacking Libnah. But when the 9 king learnt that Tirhakah king of Cush was on the way to make war on him, he sent messengers again to Hezekiah king of Judah, to say to him, 'How can you be 10 deluded by your god on whom you rely when he promises that Jerusalem shall not fall into the hands of the king of Assyria? Surely you have heard what the kings of 11 Assyria have done to all countries, exterminating their people; can you then hope to escape? Did their gods save the nations 12 which my forefathers destroyed, Gozan, Harran, Rezeph, and the people of Betheden living in Telassar? Where are the kings 13 of Hamath, of Arpad, and of Lahir, Sepharvaim, Hena, and Ivvah?'

Hezekiah took the letter from the mes- 14 sengers and read it; then he went up into the house of the LORD, spread it out before the LORD and offered this prayer: 'O LORD 15 God of Israel, enthroned on the cherubim, thou alone art God of all the kingdoms of the earth; thou hast made heaven and earth. Turn thy ear to me, O LORD, and listen; 16 open thine eyes, O LORD, and see; hear the message that Sennacherib has sent to taunt the living God. It is true, O LORD, that the 17 kings of Assyria have ravaged the nations and their lands, that they have consigned 18 their gods to the fire and destroyed them; for they were no gods but the work of men's hands, mere wood and stone. But 19 now, O LORD our God, save us from his power, so that all the kingdoms of the earth may know that thou, O LORD, alone art God.'

The LORD answers Hezekiah

Isaiah son of Amoz sent to Hezekiah and 20 said, 'This is the word of the LORD the God of Israel: I have heard your prayer to me concerning Sennacherib king of Assyria. This is the word which the LORD has spoken 21 concerning him:

The virgin daughter of Zion disdains you,
      she laughs you to scorn;
the daughter of Jerusalem tosses her head
      as you retreat.
Whom have you taunted and blasphemed? 22
      Against whom have you clamoured,
casting haughty glances at the Holy One of
      Israel?
You have sent your messengers to taunt 23
      the Lord,
      and said:
I have mounted my chariot and done mighty
      deeds:
I have gone high up in the mountains,
      into the recesses of Lebanon.

I have cut down its tallest cedars,
the best of its pines,
I have reached its farthest corners,
forest and meadow.
24 I have dug wells
and drunk the waters of a foreign land,
and with the soles of my feet I have dried up
all the streams of Egypt.
25 Have you not heard long ago?
I did it all.
In days gone by I planned it
and now I have brought it about,
making fortified cities tumble down
into heaps of rubble.[d]
26 Their citizens, shorn of strength,
disheartened and ashamed,
were but as plants in the field, as green
herbs,
as grass on the roof-tops blasted before
the east wind.[e]
27 I know your rising up[f] and your sitting
down,
your going out and your coming in.
28 The frenzy of your rage against me[g] and your
arrogance
have come to my ears.
I will put a ring in your nose
and a hook in your lips,
and I will take you back by the road
on which you have come.

29 This shall be the sign for you: this year you
shall eat shed grain and in the second year
what is self-sown; but in the third year sow
and reap, plant vineyards and eat their fruit.
30 The survivors left in Judah shall strike fresh
root under ground and yield fruit above
31 ground, for a remnant shall come out of
Jerusalem and survivors from Mount Zion.
The zeal of the LORD will perform this.
32 'Therefore, this is the word of the LORD
concerning the king of Assyria:

He shall not enter this city
nor shoot an arrow there,
he shall not advance against it with shield
nor cast up a siege-ramp against it.
33 By the way on which he came he shall go
back;
this city he shall not enter.
This is the very word of the LORD.
34 I will shield this city to deliver it,
for my own sake and for the sake of my
servant David.'

The LORD strikes down the Assyrians

35 That night the angel of the LORD went out
and struck down a hundred and eighty-five
thousand men in the Assyrian camp; when
36 morning dawned, they all lay dead. So Sen-

nacherib king of Assyria broke camp, went
back to Nineveh and stayed there. One day, 37
while he was worshipping in the temple of
his god Nisroch, Adrammelech and Sharezer
his sons murdered him and escaped to the
land of Ararat. He was succeeded by his son
Esarhaddon.

Hezekiah falls ill

At this time Hezekiah fell dangerously ill 20 1h
and the prophet Isaiah son of Amoz came
to him and said, 'This is the word of the
LORD: Give your last instructions to your
household, for you are a dying man and will
not recover.' Hezekiah turned his face to the 2
wall and offered this prayer to the LORD:
'O LORD, remember how I have lived before 3
thee, faithful and loyal in thy service, always
doing what was good in thine eyes.' And he
wept bitterly. But before Isaiah had left the 4
citadel, the word of the LORD came to him:
'Go back and say to Hezekiah, the prince of 5
my people: "This is the word of the LORD
the God of your father David: I have heard
your prayer and seen your tears; I will heal
you and on the third day you shall go up to
the house of the LORD. I will add fifteen 6
years to your life and deliver you and this
city from the king of Assyria, and I will
protect this city for my own sake and for my
servant David's sake."' Then Isaiah told 7
them to apply a fig-plaster; so they made
one and applied it to the boil, and he recovered. Then Hezekiah asked Isaiah what 8
sign the LORD would give him that he would
be cured and would go up into the house of
the LORD on the third day. And Isaiah said, 9
'This shall be your sign from the LORD that
he will do what he has promised; shall the
shadow go forward ten steps or back ten
steps?' Hezekiah answered, 'It is an easy 10
thing for the shadow to move forward ten
steps; rather let it go back ten steps.' Isaiah 11
the prophet called to the LORD, and he made
the shadow go back ten steps where it had
advanced down the stairway of Ahaz.

BABYLON

Hezekiah receives Babylonian envoys

At this time Merodach-baladan son of 12i
Baladan king of Babylon sent envoys with
a gift to Hezekiah; for he had heard that he

---

d heaps of rubble: prob. rdg., cp. Isa. 37. 26; Heb. obscure.   e the east wind: prob. rdg., cp. Isa. 37. 27; Heb. it is
mature.   f your rising up: prob. rdg., cp. Isa. 37. 28; Heb. om.   g Prob. rdg., cp. Isa. 37. 29; Heb. repeats the
frenzy of your rage against me.   h Verses 1–11: cp. Isa. 38. 1–8, 21, 22.   i Verses 12–19: cp. Isa. 39. 1–8.

13 had been ill. Hezekiah welcomed them and showed them all his treasury, silver and gold, spices and fragrant oil, his armoury and everything to be found among his treasures; there was nothing in his house and in all his realm that Hezekiah did not show them. 14 Then the prophet Isaiah came to King Hezekiah and asked him, 'What did these men say and where have they come from?' 'They have come from a far-off country,' 15 Hezekiah answered, 'from Babylon.' Then Isaiah asked, 'What did they see in your house?' 'They saw everything,' Hezekiah replied; 'there was nothing among my trea- 16 sures that I did not show them.' Then Isaiah said to Hezekiah, 'Hear the word of the 17 LORD: The time is coming, says the LORD, when everything in your house, and all that your forefathers have amassed till the present day, will be carried away to Babylon; not 18 a thing shall be left. And some of the sons who will be born to you, sons of your own begetting, shall be taken and shall be made eunuchs in the palace of the king of Babylon.' 19 Hezekiah answered, 'The word of the LORD which you have spoken is good'; thinking to himself that peace and security would last out his lifetime.

Other records of Hezekiah's reign

20 The other events of Hezekiah's reign, his exploits, and how he made the pool and the conduit and brought water into the city, are recorded in the annals of the kings of Judah. 21 So Hezekiah rested with his forefathers and was succeeded by his son Manasseh.

Manasseh revives idolatry

21 1 ʲ Manasseh was twelve years old when he came to the throne, and he reigned in Jerusalem for fifty-five years; his mother was 2 Hephzi-bah. He did what was wrong in the eyes of the LORD, in following the abominable practices of the nations which the LORD had dispossessed in favour of the Israelites. 3 He rebuilt the hill-shrines which his father Hezekiah had destroyed, he erected altars to the Baal and made a sacred pole as Ahab king of Israel had done, and prostrated himself before all the host of heaven and wor 4 shipped them. He built altars in the house of the LORD, that house of which the LORD had said, 'Jerusalem shall receive my Name.'

He built altars for all the host of heaven in 5 the two courts of the house of the LORD; he 6 made his son pass through the fire, he practised soothsaying and divination, and dealt with ghosts and spirits. He did much wrong in the eyes of the LORD and provoked his anger; and the image that he had made of 7 the goddess Asherah he put in the house, the place of which the LORD had said to David and Solomon his son, 'This house and Jerusalem, which I chose out of all the tribes of Israel, shall receive my Name for all time. I will not again make Israel outcasts from 8 the land which I gave to their forefathers, if only they will be careful to observe all my commands and all the law that my servant Moses gave them.' But they did not obey, 9 and Manasseh misled them into wickedness far worse than that of the nations which the LORD had exterminated in favour of the Israelites.

The LORD foretells Judah's destruction

Then the LORD spoke through his servants 10 the prophets: 'Because Manasseh king of 11 Judah has done these abominable things, outdoing the Amorites before him in wickedness, and because he has led Judah into sin with his idols, this is the word of the LORD 12 the God of Israel: I will bring disaster on Jerusalem and Judah, disaster which will ring in the ears of all who hear of it. I will 13 mark down every stone of Jerusalem with the plumb-line of Samaria and the plummet of the house of Ahab; I will wipe away Jerusalem as when a man wipes his plate and turns it upside down, and I will cast off 14 what is left of my people, my own possession, and hand them over to their enemies. They shall be plundered and fall a prey to all their enemies; for they have done what is wrong in 15 my eyes and have provoked my anger from the day their forefathers left Egypt up to the present day. And this Manasseh shed 16 so much innocent blood that he filled Jerusalem full to the brim, not to mention the sin into which he led Judah by doing what is wrong in my eyes.' The other events and 17 acts of Manasseh's reign, and the sin that he committed, are recorded in the annals of the kings of Judah. So Manasseh rested with 18 his forefathers and was buried in the garden-tomb of his family, in the garden of Uzza; he was succeeded by his son Amon.

Amon reigns over Judah

Amon was twenty-two years old when he 19ᵏ came to the throne, and he reigned in Jerusalem for two years; his mother was Meshullemeth daughter of Haruz of Jotbah. He did 20 what was wrong in the eyes of the LORD as

---

j Verses 1–9: cp. 2 Chr. 33. 1–9.   *k Verses 19–24: cp. 2 Chr. 33. 21–25.*

21 his father Manasseh had done. He followed in his father's footsteps and served the idols that his father had served and prostrated 22 himself before them. He forsook the LORD the God of his fathers and did not conform 23 to his ways. King Amon's courtiers conspired against him and murdered him in his 24 house; but the people of the land killed all the conspirators and made his son Josiah 25 king in his place. The other events of Amon's reign are recorded in the annals of the kings 26 of Judah. He was buried in his grave in the garden of Uzza; he was succeeded by his son Josiah.

Beginning of Josiah's reign over Judah

1 *l* Josiah was eight years old when he came to the throne, and he reigned in Jerusalem for thirty-one years; his mother was Jedidah 2 daughter of Adaiah of Bozkath. He did what was right in the eyes of the LORD; he followed closely in the footsteps of his forefather David, swerving neither right nor left.

Hilkiah discovers the book of the law

3 *m* In the eighteenth year of his reign Josiah sent Shaphan son of Azaliah, son of Meshullam, the adjutant-general, to the house of the 4 LORD. 'Go to the high priest Hilkiah,' he said, 'and tell him to melt down the silver that has been brought into the house of the LORD, which those on duty at the entrance 5 have received from the people, and to hand it over to the foremen in the house of the LORD, to pay the workmen who are carrying 6 out repairs in it, the carpenters, builders, and masons, and to purchase timber and 7 hewn stones for its repair. They are not to be asked to account for the money that has been given them; they are acting on trust.' 8 The high priest Hilkiah told Shaphan the

adjutant-general that he had discovered the book of the law in the house of the LORD, and he gave it to him, and Shaphan read it. Then Shaphan came to report to the king 9 and told him that his servants had melted down the silver in the house of the LORD and handed it over to the foremen there. Then Shaphan the adjutant-general told the 10 king that the high priest Hilkiah had given him a book, and he read it out in the king's presence. When the king heard what was in 11 the book of the law, he rent his clothes, and 12 ordered the priest Hilkiah, Ahikam son of Shaphan, Akbor son of Micaiah, Shaphan the adjutant-general, and Asaiah the king's attendant, to go and seek guidance of the 13 LORD for himself, for the people, and for all Judah, about what was written in this book that had been discovered. 'Great is the wrath of the LORD', he said, 'that has been kindled against us, because our forefathers did not obey the commands in this book and do all that is laid upon us.'

So Hilkiah the priest, Ahikam, Akbor, 14 Shaphan, and Asaiah went to Huldah the prophetess, wife of Shallum son of Tikvah, son of Harhas, the keeper of the wardrobe, and consulted her at her home in the second quarter of Jerusalem. 'This is the word of the 15 LORD the God of Israel,' she answered: 'Say to the man who sent you to me, "This is the 16 word of the LORD: I am bringing disaster on this place and its inhabitants as foretold in the book which the king of Judah has read, because they have forsaken me and burnt 17 sacrifices to other gods, provoking my anger with all the idols they have made with their own hands; therefore, my wrath is kindled against this place and will not be quenched." This is what you shall say to the king of 18 Judah who sent you to seek guidance of the LORD: "This is the word of the LORD the God of Israel: You have listened to my words and shown a willing heart, you hum- 19 bled yourself before the LORD when you heard me say that this place and its inhabitants would become objects of loathing and scorn, you rent your clothes and wept before me. Because of all this, I for my part have heard you. This is the very word of the LORD. Therefore, I will gather you to your fore- 20 fathers, and you will be gathered to your grave in peace; you will not live to see all the disaster which I am bringing upon this place."' So they brought back word to the king.

Josiah reads the book to the people

Then the king sent and called all the elders **23** of Judah and Jerusalem together, and went 2 up to the house of the LORD; he took with him the men of Judah and the inhabitants of Jerusalem, the priests and the prophets, the whole population, high and low. There he read out to them all the book of the covenant discovered in the house of the LORD; 3 and then, standing on the dais,[o] the king made a covenant before the LORD to obey him and keep his commandments, his testimonies, and his statutes, with all his heart and soul, and so fulfil the terms of the covenant written in this book. And all the people pledged themselves to the covenant.

Josiah puts down idolatrous worship

4 Next, the king ordered the high priest Hilkiah, the deputy high priest,[p] and those on duty at the entrance, to remove from the house of the LORD all the objects made for Baal and Asherah and all the host of heaven; he burnt these outside Jerusalem, in the open country by the Kidron, and carried 5 the ashes to Bethel. He suppressed the heathen priests whom the kings of Judah had appointed to burn sacrifices at the hill-shrines in the cities of Judah and in the neighbourhood of Jerusalem, as well as those who burnt sacrifices to Baal, to the sun and moon and planets and all the host 6 of heaven. He took the symbol of Asherah[q] from the house of the LORD to the gorge of the Kidron outside Jerusalem, burnt it there and pounded it to dust, which was then scattered over the common burial-ground. 7 He also pulled down the houses of the male prostitutes attached to the house of the LORD, where the women wove vestments in honour of Asherah.

8 He brought in all the priests from the cities of Judah and desecrated the hill-shrines where they had burnt sacrifices, from Geba to Beersheba, and dismantled the hill-shrines of the demons[r] in front of the gate of Joshua, the governor of the city, to the left 9 of the city gate. These priests, however, never came up to the altar of the LORD in Jerusalem but used to eat unleavened bread with 10 the priests of their clan. He desecrated Topheth in the Valley of Ben-hinnom, so that no one might make his son or daughter pass through the fire in honour of Molech.[s] 11 He destroyed the horses that the kings of Judah had set up in honour of the sun at the entrance to the house of the LORD, beside the room of Nathan-melek the eunuch in the colonnade, and he burnt the chariots of the 12 sun. He pulled down the altars made by the kings of Judah on the roof by the upper chamber of Ahaz and the altars made by Manasseh in the two courts of the house of

the LORD; he pounded them to dust and threw it into the gorge of the Kidron. Also, 13 on the east of Jerusalem, to the south of the Mount of Olives, the king desecrated the hill-shrines which Solomon the king of Israel had built for Ashtoreth the loathsome goddess of the Sidonians, and for Kemosh the loathsome god of Moab, and for Milcom the abominable god of the Ammonites; he broke down the sacred pillars and 14 cut down the sacred poles and filled the places where they had stood with human bones.

At Bethel he dismantled the altar by[t] the 15 hill-shrine made by Jeroboam son of Nebat who led Israel into sin, together with the hill-shrine itself; he broke its stones in pieces, crushed them to dust and burnt the sacred pole. When Josiah set eyes on the 16 graves which were there on the hill, he sent and took the bones from them and burnt them on the altar to desecrate it, thus fulfilling the word of the LORD announced by the man of God when Jeroboam stood by the altar at the feast. But when he caught sight of the grave of the man of God who had foretold these things, he asked, 'What 17 is that monument I see there?' The people of the city answered, 'The grave of the man of God who came from Judah and foretold all that you have done to the altar at Bethel.' 'Leave it alone,' he said; 'let no one disturb 18 his bones.' So they spared his bones and also those of the prophet who came from Samaria. Further, Josiah suppressed all the hill- 19 shrines in the cities of Samaria, which the kings of Israel had set up and thereby provoked the LORD's anger, and he did to them what he had done at Bethel. He slaughtered 20 on the altars all the priests of the hill-shrines who were there, and he burnt human bones upon them. Then he went back to Jerusalem.

A memorable Passover

The king ordered all the people to keep the 21 Passover to the LORD their God, as this book of the covenant prescribed; no such Pass- 22 over had been kept either when the judges were ruling Israel or during the times of the kings of Israel and Judah. But in the eigh- 23 teenth year of Josiah's reign this Passover was kept to the LORD in Jerusalem. Further, 24 Josiah got rid of all who called up ghosts and spirits, of all household gods and idols and all the loathsome objects seen in the land of Judah and in Jerusalem, so that he might fulfil the requirements of the law written in the book which the priest Hilkiah had discovered in the house of the LORD. No king 25

---

o Or by the pillar.   *p* Prob. rdg.; Heb. priests.   *q* symbol of Asherah: or sacred pole.   *r* Or satyrs.
s in honour of Molech: or for an offering.   *t* Prob. rdg.; Heb. om.

before him had turned to the LORD as he did, with all his heart and soul and strength, following the whole law of Moses; nor did any king like him appear again.

26 Yet the LORD did not abate his fierce anger; it still burned against Judah because of all the provocation which Manasseh had
27 given him. 'Judah also I will banish from my presence', he declared, 'as I banished Israel; and I will cast off this city of Jerusalem which once I chose, and the house where I promised that my Name should be.'

The death of Josiah

28 The other events and acts of Josiah's reign are recorded in the annals of the kings of
29 Judah. It was in his reign that Pharaoh Necho king of Egypt set out for the river Euphrates to help the king of Assyria. King Josiah went to meet him; and when they met at Megiddo,
30 [u] Pharaoh Necho slew him. His attendants conveyed his body in a chariot from Megiddo to Jerusalem and buried him in his own burial place. Then the people of the land took Josiah's son Jehoahaz and anointed him king in place of his father.

Jehoahaz reigns over Judah

31 Jehoahaz was twenty-three years old when he came to the throne, and he reigned in Jerusalem for three months; his mother was Hamutal daughter of Jeremiah of Libnah.
32 He did what was wrong in the eyes of the
33 LORD, as his forefathers had done. Pharaoh Necho removed him from the throne[v] in Jerusalem, and imposed on the land a fine of a hundred talents of silver and one talent
34 of gold. Pharaoh Necho made Josiah's son Eliakim king in place of his father and changed his name to Jehoiakim. He took Jehoahaz and brought him to Egypt, where
35 he died. Jehoiakim paid the silver and gold to Pharaoh, taxing the country to meet Pharaoh's demands; he exacted it from the people, from every man according to his assessment, so that he could pay Pharaoh Necho.

Jehoiakim reigns over Judah

36 Jehoiakim was twenty-five years old when he came to the throne, and he reigned in Jerusalem for eleven years; his mother was
37 Zebidah daughter of Pedaiah of Rumah. He did what was wrong in the eyes of the LORD,
4 as his forefathers had done. During his reign Nebuchadnezzar king of Babylon took the field, and Jehoiakim became his vassal;

BABYLON

but three years later he broke with him and revolted. The LORD launched against him 2 raiding-parties of Chaldaeans, Aramaeans, Moabites, and Ammonites, letting them range through Judah and ravage it, as the LORD had foretold through his servants the prophets. All this happened to Judah in 3 fulfilment of the LORD's purpose to banish them from his presence, because of all the sin that Manasseh had committed and be- 4 cause of the innocent blood that he had shed; he had drenched Jerusalem with innocent blood, and the LORD would not forgive him. The other events and acts of Jehoiakim's 5 reign are recorded in the annals of the kings of Judah. He rested with his forefathers, and 6 was succeeded by his son Jehoiachin. The 7 king of Egypt did not leave his own land again, because the king of Babylon had stripped him of all his possessions, from the Torrent of Egypt to the river Euphrates.

Nebuchadnezzar besieges Jerusalem

Jehoiachin was eighteen years old when he 8 [w] came to the throne, and he reigned in Jerusalem for three months; his mother was Nehushta daughter of Elnathan of Jerusalem. He did what was wrong in the eyes 9 of the LORD, as his father had done. At that 10 time the troops of Nebuchadnezzar king of Babylon advanced on Jerusalem and besieged the city. Nebuchadnezzar arrived 11 while his troops were besieging it, and 12 Jehoiachin king of Judah, his mother, his courtiers, his officers, and his eunuchs, all surrendered to the king of Babylon. The king of Babylon, now in the eighth year of his reign, took him prisoner; and, as the 13 LORD had foretold, he carried off all the treasures of the house of the LORD and of the royal palace and broke up all the vessels of gold which Solomon king of Israel had made for the temple of the LORD. He carried 14 the people of Jerusalem into exile, the officers and the fighting men, ten thousand in number, together with all the craftsmen and smiths; only the weakest class of people were left. He deported Jehoiachin to Babylon; 15 he also took into exile from Jerusalem to Babylon the king's mother and his wives, his eunuchs and the foremost men of the

u Verses 30–34: cp. 2 Chr. 36. 1–4.   v removed . . . throne: prob. rdg., cp. 2 Chr. 36. 3; Heb. bound him
at Riblah in the land of Hamath when he was king . . .   w Verses 8–17: cp. 2 Chr. 36. 9, 10.

16 land. He also deported to Babylon all the men of substance, seven thousand in number, and a thousand craftsmen and smiths, all of them able-bodied men and skilled armourers.

17 He made Mattaniah, uncle of Jehoiachin, king in his place and changed his name to Zedekiah.

Zedekiah reigns over Judah

18 x Zedekiah was twenty-one years old when he came to the throne, and he reigned in Jerusalem for eleven years; his mother was Hamutal daughter of Jeremiah of Libnah.

19 He did what was wrong in the eyes of the

20 LORD, as Jehoiakim had done. Jerusalem and Judah so angered the LORD that in the end he banished them from his sight; and Zedekiah rebelled against the king of Babylon.

Zedekiah is taken captive

25 1 y In the ninth year of his reign, in the tenth month, on the tenth day of the month, Nebuchadnezzar king of Babylon advanced with all his army against Jerusalem, invested it and erected watch-towers against

2 it on every side; the siege lasted till the

3 eleventh year of King Zedekiah. In the fourth month of that year,z on the ninth day of the month, when famine was severe in the city and there was no food for the common

4 people, the city was thrown open. When Zedekiah king of Judah saw this,a he and all his armed escort left the city and fled by night through the gate called Between the Two Walls, near the king's garden. They escaped towards the Arabah, although the

5 Chaldaeans were surrounding the city. But the Chaldaean army pursued the king and overtook him in the lowlands of Jericho;

6 and all his company was dispersed. The king was seized and brought before the king of Babylon at Riblah, where he pleaded his

7 case before him. Zedekiah's sons were slain before his eyes; then his eyes were put out, and he was brought to Babylon in fetters of bronze.

Destruction of Jerusalem

8 In the fifth month, on the seventh day of the month, in the nineteenth year of Nebuchadnezzar king of Babylon, Nebuzaradan, captain of the king's bodyguard, came to

9 Jerusalem and set fire to the house of the LORD and the royal palace; all the houses in the city, including the mansion of Gedaliah,b

10 were burnt down. The Chaldaean forces with the captain of the guard pulled down the walls all round Jerusalem. Nebuzaradan 11 captain of the guard deported the rest of the people left in the city, those who had deserted to the king of Babylon and any remaining artisans.c He left only the weakest class of 12 people to be vine-dressers and labourers.

The Chaldaeans broke up the pillars of 13 bronze in the house of the LORD, the trolleys, and the Sea of bronze, and took the metal to Babylon. They took also the pots, shovels, 14 snuffers, saucers, and all the vessels of bronze used in the service of the temple. The captain 15 of the guard took away the precious metal, whether gold or silver, of which the firepans and the tossing-bowls were made. The bronze 16 of the two pillars, the one Sea, and the trolleys, which Solomon had made for the house of the LORD, was beyond weighing. The one pillar was eighteen cubits high and 17 its capital was bronze; the capital was three cubits high, and a decoration of network and pomegranates ran all round it, wholly of bronze. The other pillar, with its network, was exactly like it.

The captain of the guard took Seraiah the 18 chief priest and Zephaniah the deputy chief priest and the three on duty at the entrance; he took also from the city a eunuch who was 19 in charge of the fighting men, five of those with right of access to the king who were still in the city, the adjutant-generald whose duty was to muster the people for war, and sixty men of the people who were still there. These 20 Nebuzaradan captain of the guard brought to the king of Babylon at Riblah. There, in 21 the land of Hamath, the king of Babylon had them flogged and put to death. So Judah went into exile from their own land.

Gedaliah is murdered

Nebuchadnezzar king of Babylon appointed 22 Gedaliah son of Ahikam, son of Shaphan, governor over the few people whom he had left in Judah. When the captains of the armed 23 bands and their men heard that the king of Babylon had appointed Gedaliah governor, they all came to him at Mizpah: Ishmael son of Nethaniah, Johanan son of Kareah, Seraiah son of Tanhumeth of Netophah, and Jaazaniah of Beth-maacah. Then Gedaliah 24 gave them and their men this assurance: 'Have no fear of the Chaldaean officers. Settle down in the land and serve the king of Babylon; and then all will be well with you.' But in the seventh month Ishmael son of 25 Nethaniah, son of Elishama, who was a member of the royal house, came with ten men and murdered Gedaliah and the Jews

---

x 24. 18—25. 21: cp. Jer. 52. 1–27.   y Verses 1–12: cp. Jer. 39. 1–10; verses 1–17: cp. 2 Chr. 36. 17–20.
z In . . . year: prob. rdg., cp. Jer. 52. 6; Heb. om.   a When . . . this: prob. rdg., cp. Jer. 39. 4; Heb. om.
b Gedaliah: prob. rdg.; Heb. a great man.   c any remaining artisans: prob. rdg., cp. Jer. 52. 15; Heb. the remaining crowd.   d Prob. rdg.; Heb. adds commander-in-chief.

and Chaldaeans who were with him at Miz-
26 pah. Thereupon all the people, high and low,
and the captains of the armed bands, fled to
Egypt for fear of the Chaldaeans.

Jehoiachin released and honoured in Babylon

7ᵉ In the thirty-seventh year of the exile of
Jehoiachin king of Judah, on the twenty-
seventh day of the twelfth month, Evil-
merodachᶠ king of Babylon in the year of
his accession showed favour to Jehoiachin
king of Judah. He brought him out of prison,
treated him kindly and gave him a seat at 28
table above the kings with him in Babylon.
So Jehoiachin discarded his prison clothes 29
and lived as a pensioner of the king for the
rest of his life. For his maintenance, a regu- 30
lar daily allowance was given him by the
king as long as he lived.

e Verses 27–30: cp. Jer. 52. 31–34.   *f Or Ewil-marduk.*

Babylon—the city of exile

THE FIRST BOOK OF THE
CHRONICLES

Genealogies from Adam to Ishmael

1 1 2*a* ADAM, Seth, Enosh, Kenan,
3 Mahalalel, Jared, Enoch, Methu-
4 selah, Lamech, Noah.
The sons of Noah: Shem, Ham
and Japheth.
5*b* The sons of Japheth: Gomer,
Magog, Madai, Javan,*c* Tubal,
6 Meshech and Tiras. The sons of
Gomer: Ashkenaz, Diphath and
7 Togarmah. The sons of Javan:
Elishah, Tarshish, Kittim*d* and
Rodanim.
8*e* The sons of Ham: Cush, Mizra-
9 im,*f* Put and Canaan. The sons
of Cush: Seba, Havilah, Sabta,
Raama and Sabtecha. The sons of
10 Raama: Sheba and Dedan. Cush
was the father of Nimrod, who
began to show himself a man of
11*g* might on earth. From Mizraim
sprang the Lydians, Anamites,
12 Lehabites, Naphtuhites, Pathrus-
ites, Casluhites, and the Caphtorites, from whom the Philistines
were descended.
13 Canaan was the father of Sidon,
who was his eldest son, and Heth,*h*
14 the Jebusites, the Amorites, the
15 Girgashites, the Hivites, the Ark-
16 ites, the Sinites, the Arvadites, the
Zemarites, and the Hamathites.
17*i* The sons of Shem: Elam, Asshur,
Arphaxad, Lud*j* and Aram. The
sons of Aram: Uz, Hul, Gether
18 and Mash. Arphaxad was the father
of Shelah, and Shelah the father of
19 Eber. Eber had two sons: one was
named Peleg,*k* because in his time
the earth was divided, and his

20 brother's name was Joktan. Joktan
was the father of Almodad, She-
21 leph, Hazarmoth, Jerah, Hador-
22 am, Uzal, Diklah, Ebal,*l* Abimael,
23 Sheba, Ophir, Havilah and Jobab.
All these were sons of Joktan.
24*m* The line of*n* Shem: Arphaxad,
25 Shelah, Eber, Peleg, Reu, Serug,
26
27 Nahor, Terah, Abram, also known
28 as Abraham, whose sons were Isaac
and Ishmael.

Abraham's descendants

29*o* The sons of*p* Ishmael in the order
of their birth: Nebaioth the eldest,
then Kedar, Adbeel, Mibsam,
30 Mishma, Dumah, Massa, Hadad,
31 Teman, Jetur, Naphish and Kedemah. These were Ishmael's sons.
32*q* The sons of Keturah, Abraham's
concubine: she bore him Zimran,
Jokshan, Medan, Midian, Ishbak
and Shuah. The sons of Jokshan:
33 Sheba and Dedan. The sons of
Midian: Ephah, Epher, Enoch,
Abida and Eldaah. All these were
descendants of Keturah.

Esau's descendants

34 Abraham was the father of Isaac,
and Isaac's sons were Esau and
35*r* Israel. The sons of Esau: Eliphaz,
Reuel, Jeush, Jalam and Korah.
36 The sons of Eliphaz: Teman, Omar,
Zephi, Gatam, Kenaz, Timna and
37 Amalek. The sons of Reuel:
Nahath, Zerah, Shammah and
Mizzah.

Seir's descendants

The sons of Seir: Lotan, Shobal, 38
Zibeon, Anah, Dishon, Ezer and
Dishan. The sons of Lotan: Hori 39
and Homam; and Lotan had a
sister named Timna. The sons of 40
Shobal: Alvan, Manahath, Ebal,
Shephi and Onam. The sons of
Zibeon: Aiah and Anah. The son*t* 41
of Anah: Dishon. The sons of
Dishon: Amram, Eshban, Ithran
and Cheran. The sons of Ezer: 42
Bilhan, Zavan and Akan. The sons
of Dishan: Uz and Aran.

Kings of Edom

These are the kings who ruled over 43
Edom before there were kings in
Israel: Bela son of Beor, whose city
was named Dinhabah. When he 44
died, he was succeeded by Jobab
son of Zerah of Bozrah. When
Jobab died, he was succeeded by
Husham of Teman. When Husham 46
died, he was succeeded by Hadad
son of Bedad, who defeated Midian
in Moabite country. His city was
named Avith. When Hadad died, 47
he was succeeded by Samlah of
Masrekah. When Samlah died, he 48
was succeeded by Saul of Rehoboth
on the River. When Saul died, he 49
was succeeded by Baal-hanan son
of Akbor. When Baal-hanan died, 50
he was succeeded by Hadad. His
city was named Pai; his wife's
name was Mehetabel daughter of
Matred a woman of Me-zahab.*v*
After Hadad died the chiefs in 51
Edom were: chief Timna, chief

---

a Verses 2–4: cp. Gen. 5. 9–32.   *b Verses 5–7: cp. Gen. 10. 2–4.*   *c Or Greece.*   *d Or Tarshish of the Kittians.*   *e Verses 8–10: cp. Gen. 10. 6–8.*   *f Or Egypt.*   *g Verses 11–16: cp. Gen. 10. 13–18.*   *h Or the Hittites.*   *i Verses 17–23: cp. Gen. 10. 22–29.*   *j Or the Lydians.*   *k That is Division.*   *l Or Obal, cp. Gen. 10. 28.*   *m Verses 24–27: cp. Gen. 11. 10–26.*   *n The line of: prob. rdg.; Heb. om.*   *o Verses 29–31: cp. Gen. 25. 13–16.*   *p The sons of: prob. rdg., cp. Gen. 25. 13; Heb. om.*   *q Verses 32, 33: cp. Gen. 25. 1–4.*   *r Verses 35–37: cp. Gen. 36. 4, 5, 9–13.*   *s Verses 38–42: cp. Gen. 36. 20–28.*   *t Prob. rdg.; Heb. sons; the same correction is made in several other places in chs. 1–9.*   *u Verses 43–54: cp. Gen. 36. 31–43.*   *v Or daughter of Mezahab.*

2 Aliah, chief Jetheth, chief Oholi-
3 bamah, chief Elah, chief Pinon,
4 chief Kenaz, chief Teman, chief
   Mizbar, chief Magdiel and chief
   Iram. These were the chiefs of
   Edom.

Israel's sons

2 These were the sons of Israel:
   Reuben, Simeon, Levi, Judah, Issa-
2 char, Zebulun, Dan, Joseph, Benjamin, Naphtali, Gad and Asher.

Judah's descendants

3 The sons of Judah: Er, Onan and
   Shelah; the mother of these three
   was a Canaanite woman, Bathshua.[w] Er, Judah's eldest son, displeased the LORD and the LORD
4 slew him. Then Tamar, Judah's
   daughter-in-law, bore him Perez
   and Zerah, making in all five sons
5 of Judah. The sons of Perez: Hez-
6 ron and Hamul. The sons of Zerah:
   Zimri, Ethan, Heman, Calcol and
7 Darda, five in all. The son of
   Zimri: Carmi.[x] The son of Carmi:
8 Achar, who troubled Israel by his
   violation of the sacred ban. The
9 son of Ethan: Azariah. The sons
   of Hezron: Jerahmeel, Ram and
10 Caleb. Ram was the father of
   Amminadab, Amminadab father
11 of Nahshon prince of Judah. Nahshon was the father of Salma,
12 Salma father of Boaz, Boaz father
13 of Obed, Obed father of Jesse. The
   eldest son of Jesse was Eliab, the
   second Abinadab, the third Shimea,
14 the fourth Nethaneel, the fifth Rad-
15 dai, the sixth Ozem, the seventh
16 David; their sisters were Zeruiah
   and Abigail. The sons of Zeruiah:
   Abishai, Joab and Asahel, three in
17 all. Abigail was the mother of
   Amasa; his father was Jether the
   Ishmaelite.
18 Caleb son of Hezron had Jerioth
   by Azubah his wife;[y] these were her
   sons: Jesher, Shobab and Ardon.
19 When Azubah died, Caleb married
20 Ephrath, who bore him Hur. Hur
   was the father of Uri, and Uri father
21 of Bezalel. Later, Hezron, then
   sixty years of age, had intercourse
   with the daughter of Machir father
   of Gilead, having married her, and
22 she bore Segub. Segub was the
   father of Jair, who had twenty-
23 three cities in Gilead. Geshur and
   Aram took from them Havvoth-
   jair, and Kenath and its dependent
   villages, a total of sixty towns. All
   these were descendants of Machir
24 father of Gilead. After the death
   of Hezron, Caleb had intercourse
   with Ephrathah and she bore him
   Ashhur the founder of Tekoa.
25 The sons of Jerahmeel eldest son
   of Hezron by[z] Ahijah were Ram
   the eldest, Bunah, Oren and Ozem.

26 Jerahmeel had another wife, whose
   name was Atarah; she was the
27 mother of Onam. The sons of Ram
   eldest son of Jerahmeel: Maaz,
28 Jamin and Eker. The sons of
   Onam: Shammai and Jada. The
29 sons of Shammai: Nadab and
   Abishur. The name of Abishur's
30 wife was Abihail; she bore him
   Ahban and Molid. The sons of
31 Nadab: Seled and Ephraim; Seled
   died without children. Ephraim's
32 son was Ishi, Ishi's son Sheshan,
   Sheshan's son Ahlai. The sons of
   Jada brother of Shammai: Jether
   and Jonathan; Jether died without
33 children. The sons of Jonathan:
   Peleth and Zaza. These were the
   descendants of Jerahmeel.
34 Sheshan had daughters but no
   sons. He had an Egyptian servant
35 named Jarha; he gave his daughter
   in marriage to this Jarha, and she
36 bore him Attai. Attai was the father
   of Nathan, Nathan father of Zabad,
37 Zabad father of Ephlal, Ephlal
38 father of Obed, Obed father of
   Jehu, Jehu father of Azariah,
39 Azariah father of Helez, Helez
40 father of Elasah, Elasah father of
   Sisamai, Sisamai father of Shal-
41 lum, Shallum father of Jekamiah,
   and Jekamiah father of Elishama.
42 The sons of Caleb brother of
   Jerahmeel: Mesha the eldest, founder of Ziph, and[a] Mareshah foun-
43 der of Hebron. The sons of Hebron: Korah, Tappuah, Rekem and
44 Shema. Shema was the father of
   Raham father of Jorkoam, and
   Rekem was the father of Shammai.
45 The son of Shammai was Maon, and
   Maon was the founder of Beth-zur.
46 Ephah, Caleb's concubine, was the
   mother of Haran, Moza and Gazez;
   Haran was the father of Gazez.
47 The sons of Jahdai: Regem,
   Jotham, Geshan, Pelet, Ephah and
48 Shaaph. Maacah, Caleb's concubine, was the mother of Sheber and
49 Tirhanah; she bore also Shaaph
   founder of Madmannah, and Sheva
   founder of Machbenah and Gibea.
   Caleb also had a daughter named
   Achsah.
50 The descendants of Caleb: the
   sons of Hur, the eldest son of
   Ephrathah: Shobal the founder of
51 Kiriath-jearim, Salma the founder
   of Bethlehem, and Hareph the
52 founder of Beth-gader. Shobal the
   founder of Kiriath-jearim was
   the father of Reaiah[b] and the ancestor of half the Manahethites.[c]
53 The clans of Kiriath-jearim: Ith-
   rites, Puhites, Shumathites and
   Mishraites, from whom were descended the Zareathites and the
   Eshtaulites.
54 The descendants of Salma:
   Bethlehem, the Netophathites,

Ataroth, Beth-joab, half the Manahethites, and the Zorites.
The clans of Sophrites[d] living 55
at Jabez: Tirathites, Shimeathites,
and Suchathites. These were Kenites who were connected by marriage with the ancestor of the
Rechabites.

David's descendants

These were the sons of David, born 3 1[e]
at Hebron: the eldest Amnon,
whose mother was Ahinoam of
Jezreel; the second Daniel, whose
mother was Abigail of Carmel;
the third Absalom, whose mother 2
was Maacah daughter of Talmai
king of Geshur; the fourth Adonijah, whose mother was Haggith;
the fifth Shephatiah, whose mother 3
was Abital; the sixth Ithream,
whose mother was David's wife
Eglah. These six were born at 4
Hebron, where David reigned seven
years and six months. In Jerusalem
he reigned thirty-three years, and 5[f]
there the following sons were born
to him: Shimea, Shobab, Nathan
and Solomon; these four were sons
of Bathsheba daughter of Ammiel.
There were nine others: Ibhar, 6
Elishama, Eliphelet, Nogah, Ne- 7
pheg, Japhia, Elishama, Eliada 8
and Eliphelet. These were all the 9
sons of David, with their sister
Tamar, in addition to his sons by
concubines.
Solomon's son was Rehoboam, 10
his son Abia, his son Asa, his son
Jehoshaphat, his son Joram, his 11
son Ahaziah, his son Joash, his son 12
Amaziah, his son Azariah, his son
Jotham, his son Ahaz, his son Hez- 13
ekiah, his son Manasseh, his 14
son Amon, and his son Josiah.
The sons of Josiah: the eldest was 15
Johanan, the second Jehoiakim,
the third Zedekiah, the fourth
Shallum. The sons of Jehoiakim: 16
Jeconiah and Zedekiah. The sons 17
of Jeconiah, a prisoner:[g] Shealtiel,
Malchiram, Pedaiah, Shenazzar, 18
Jekamiah, Hoshama and Ned-
abiah. The sons of Pedaiah: Zerub- 19
babel and Shimei. The sons of
Zerubbabel: Meshullam and Hananiah; they had a sister, Shelomith.
There were five others: Hashubah, 20
Ohel, Berechiah, Hasadiah and
Jushab-hesed. The sons of Han- 21
aniah: Pelatiah and Isaiah; his son
was Rephaiah, his son Arnan, his
son Obadiah, his son Shecaniah.
The sons of Shecaniah: Shemaiah,[h] 22
Hattush, Igeal, Bariah, Neariah
and Shaphat, six in all. The sons 23
of Neariah: Elioenai, Hezekiah
and Azrikam, three in all. The sons 24
of Elioenai: Hodaiah, Eliashib,
Pelaiah, Akkub, Johanan, Dalaiah
and Anani, seven in all.

---

w Bathshua: *or* daughter of Shua.
wife: *prob. rdg.; Heb.* a woman and.
b Prob. rdg., cp. 4. 2; Heb. the seer.
e Verses 1–4: cp. 2 Sam. 3. 2–5.
or Jeconiah: Assir, . . .

x The son . . . Carmi: *prob. rdg. (cp. Josh.* 7. *1, 18); Heb. om.*   *y* his
   z by: prob. rdg.; Heb. om.   *a Prob. rdg.; Heb. adds* the sons of.
   c Prob. rdg., cp. verse 54; Heb. Menuhoth.   *d Or* secretaries.
f Verses 5–8: cp. 14. 4–7; 2 Sam. 5. 14–16.   *g* Jeconiah, a prisoner:
   h Prob. rdg.; Heb. adds and the sons of Shemaiah.

More of Judah's descendants

4 The sons of Judah: Perez, Hezron,
2 Carmi, Hur and Shobal. Reaiah
son of Shobal was the father of
Jahath, Jahath father of Ahumai
and Lahad. These were the clans
of the Zorathites.
3-4 The sons of Etam: Jezreel, Ish-
ma, Idbash, Penuel the founder
of Gedor, and Ezer the founder of
Hushah; they had a sister named
Hazelelponi. These were the sons
of Hur: Ephrathah the eldest, the
founder of Bethlehem.
5 Ashhur the founder of Tekoa
had two wives, Helah and Naarah.
6 Naarah bore him Ahuzam, Hepher,
Temeni and Haahashtari.[i] These
7 were the sons of Naarah. The sons
of Helah: Zereth, Jezoar, Ethnan
8 and Coz. Coz was the father of
Anub and Zobebah and the clans
of Aharhel son of Harum.
9 Jabez ranked higher than his
brothers; his mother called him
Jabez because, as she said, she had
10 borne him in pain. Jabez called
upon the God of Israel and said,
'I pray thee, bless me and grant
me wide territories. May thy hand
be with me, and do me no harm,
I pray thee, and let me be free from
pain'; and God granted his petition.
11 Kelub brother of Shuah was the
father of Mehir the father of Esh-
12 ton. Eshton was the father of Beth-
rapha, Paseah, and Tehinnah father
of Ir-nahash. These were the men
of Rechah.
13 The sons of Kenaz: Othniel and
Seraiah. The sons of Othniel:
Hathath and Meonothai.
14 Meonothai was the father of
Ophrah.
Seraiah was the father of Joab
founder of Ge-harashim,[j] for they
were craftsmen.
15 The sons of Caleb son of Jephunneh: Iru, Elah and Naam. The son
of Elah: Kenaz.
16 The sons of Jehaleleel: Ziph and
Ziphah, Tiria and Asareel.
17-18 The sons of Ezra: Jether, Mered,
Epher and Jalon. These were the
sons of Bithiah daughter of Pharaoh, whom Mered had married;
she conceived and gave birth to[k]
Miriam, Shammai and Ishbah
founder of Eshtemoa. His Jewish
wife was the mother of Jered
founder of Gedor, Heber founder
of Soco, and Jekuthiel founder of
19 Zanoah. The sons of his[l] wife Hodiah sister of Naham were Daliah
father of Keilah the Garmite, and
Eshtemoa the Maacathite.
20 The sons of Shimon: Amnon,
Rinnah, Ben-hanan and Tilon.
The sons of Ishi: Zoheth and
Ben-zoheth.
21 The sons of Shelah son of Judah:

Er founder of Lecah, Laadah founder of Mareshah, the clans of the
guild of linen-workers at Ashbea,
22 Jokim, the men of Kozeba, Joash,
and Saraph who fell out with Moab
and came back to Bethlehem.[m]
23 (The records are ancient.) They
were the potters, and those who
lived at Netaim and Gederah were
there on the king's service.

Simeon's descendants

24 The sons of Simeon: Nemuel,
25 Jamin, Jarib, Zerah, Saul, his son
Shallum, his son Mibsam and his
26 son Mishma. The sons of Mishma:
his son Hamuel, his son Zaccur and
27 his son Shimei. Shimei had sixteen
sons and six daughters, but others
of his family had fewer children,
and the clan as a whole did not
increase as much as the tribe of
28 Judah. They lived at Beersheba,
29 Moladah, Hazar-shual, Bilhah,
30 Ezem, Tolad, Bethuel, Hormah,
31 Ziklag, Beth-marcaboth, Hazar-
susim, Beth-birei, and Shaaraim.
These were their cities until David
32 came to the throne. Their settlements[n] were Etam, Ain, Rimmon, Tochen, and Ashan, five
33 cities in all. They had also hamlets
round these cities as far as Baal.
These were the places where they
lived.
The names on their register were:
34 Meshobab, Jamlech, Joshah son
35 of Amaziah, Joel, Jehu son of
Josibiah, son of Seraiah, son of
36 Asiel, Elioenai, Jaakobah, Jesho-
haiah, Asaiah, Adiel, Jesimiel,
37 Benaiah, Ziza son of Shiphi, son
of Allon, son of Jedaiah, son of
38 Shimri, son of Shemaiah, whose
names are recorded as princes in
their clans, and their families had
39 greatly increased. They then went
from the approaches to Gedor east
of the valley in search of pasture
40 for their flocks. They found rich
and good pasture in a wide stretch
of open country where everything
was quiet and peaceful; before then
it had been occupied by Hamites.
41 During the reign of Hezekiah king
of Judah these whose names are
written above came and destroyed
the tribes of Ham[o] and the Meunites
whom they found there. They
annihilated them so that no trace
of them has remained to this day;
and they occupied the land in their
42 place, for there was pasture for
their flocks. Of their number five
hundred Simeonites invaded the
hill-country of Seir, led by Pelatiah,
Neariah, Rephaiah, and Uzziel, the
43 sons of Ishi. They destroyed all
who were left of the surviving
Amalekites; and they live there
still.

Reuben's descendants

The sons of Reuben, the eldest of **5**
Israel's sons. (He was, in fact, the
first son born, but because he had
committed incest with a wife of
his father's the rank of the eldest
was transferred to the sons of
Joseph, Israel's son, who, however,
could not be registered as the eldest
son. Judah held the leading place 2
among his brothers because he
fathered a ruler, and the rank of
the eldest was his, not[p] Joseph's.)
The sons of Reuben, the eldest of 3
Israel's sons: Enoch, Pallu, Hezron and Carmi. The sons of Joel: 4
his son Shemaiah, his son Gog,
his son Shimei, his son Micah, his 5
son Reaia, his son Baal, his son 6
Beerah, whom Tiglath-pileser king
of Assyria carried away into exile;
he was a prince of the Reubenites.
His kinsmen, family by family, as 7
registered in their tribal lists: Jeiel
the chief, Zechariah, Bela son of 8
Azaz, son of Shema, son of Joel.
They lived in Aroer, and their
lands stretched as far as Nebo and
Baal-meon. Eastwards they occu- 9
pied territory as far as the edge of
the desert which stretches from the
river Euphrates, for they had large
numbers of cattle in Gilead. During 10
Saul's reign they made war on the
Hagarites, whom they conquered,
occupying their encampments over
all the country east of Gilead.

Gad's descendants

Adjoining them were the Gadites, 11
occupying the district of Bashan
as far as Salcah: Joel the chief; 12
second in rank, Shapham; then
Jaanai and Shaphat in Bashan.
Their fellow-tribesmen belonged to 13
the families of Michael, Meshullam, Sheba, Jorai, Jachan, Zia and
Heber, seven in all. These were 14
the sons of Abihail son of Huri,
son of Jaroah, son of Gilead, son
of Michael, son of Jeshishai, son
of Jahdo, son of Buz. Ahi son of 15
Abdiel, son of Guni, was head of
their family; they lived in Gilead, 16
in Bashan and its villages, in all
the common land of Sharon as far
as it stretched. These registers were 17
all compiled in the reigns of Jotham
king of Judah and Jeroboam king
of Israel.

History of the tribes east of Jordan

The sons of Reuben, Gad, and half 18
the tribe of Manasseh: of their
fighting men armed with shield
and sword, their archers and their
battle-trained soldiers, forty-four
thousand seven hundred and sixty
were ready for active service. They 19
made war on the Hagarites, Jetur,

---

i Temeni and Haahashtari: *or* the Temanite and the Ahashtarite.   *j* Or the Valley of Craftsmen.   *k* and
gave birth to: *prob. rdg.; Heb. om.*   *l* his: *prob. rdg.; Heb. om.*   *m* and came . . . Bethlehem: *prob. rdg.;*
Heb. unintelligible.   *n* Prob. rdg.; Heb. hamlets.   *o* the tribes of Ham: *prob. rdg., cp. verse 40; Heb.*
their tribes.   *p* his, not: *prob. rdg.; Heb. om.*

0 Nephish, and Nodab. They were given help against them, for they cried to their God for help in the battle, and because they trusted him he listened to their prayer, and the Hagarites and all their allies 1 surrendered to them.[q] They drove off their cattle, fifty thousand camels, two hundred and fifty thousand sheep, and two thousand 2 asses, and they took a hundred thousand captives. Many had been killed, for the war was of God's making, and they occupied the land instead of them until the exile.

3 Half the tribe of Manasseh lived in the land from Bashan to Baalhermon, Senir, and Mount Hermon, and were numerous also in 4 Lebanon. The heads of their families were: Epher, Ishi, Eliel, Azriel, Jeremiah, Hodaviah, and Jahdiel, all men of ability and repute, heads 5 of their families. But they sinned against the God of their fathers, and turned wantonly to worship the gods of the peoples whom God 6 had destroyed before them. So the God of Israel stirred up Pul king of Assyria, that is Tiglath-pileser king of Assyria, and he carried into exile Reuben, Gad, and half the tribe of Manasseh. He took them to Halah, Habor, Hara, and the river Gozan, where they are to this day.

Levi's descendants

6 The sons of Levi: Gershon,[r] Ko-
2 hath and Merari. The sons of Kohath: Amram, Izhar, Hebron 3 and Uzziel. The children of Amram: Aaron, Moses and Miriam. The sons of Aaron: Nadab, Abihu, 4 Eleazar and Ithamar. Eleazar was the father of Phinehas, Phinehas 5 father of Abishua, Abishua father of Bukki, Bukki father of Uzzi, 6 Uzzi father of Zerahiah, Zerahiah 7 father of Meraioth, Meraioth father of Amariah, Amariah father of 8 Ahitub, Ahitub father of Zadok, 9 Zadok father of Ahimaaz, Ahima-10 az of Johanan, and Johanan father of Azariah, the priest who officiated 11 in the LORD's house which Solomon built at Jerusalem. Azariah 12 was the father of Amariah, Amariah father of Ahitub, Ahitub father of Zadok, Zadok father of Shallum, 13 Shallum father of Hilkiah, Hilkiah 14 father of Azariah, Azariah father of Seraiah, and Seraiah father of 15 Jehozadak. Jehozadak went into exile when the LORD sent Judah and Jerusalem into exile under Nebuchadnezzar.

5[t] The sons of Levi: Gershom,

17 Kohath and Merari. The sons of 18 Gershom: Libni and Shimei. The sons of Kohath: Amram, Izhar, 19 Hebron and Uzziel. The sons of Merari: Mahli and Mushi. The clans of Levi, family by family: 20[u] Gershom: his son Libni, his son 21 Jahath, his son Zimmah, his son Joah, his son Iddo, his son Zerah, 22[v] his son Jeaterai. The sons of Kohath: his son Amminadab, his son 23 Korah, his son Assir, his son Elkanah, his son Ebiasaph, his son 24 Assir, his son Tahath, his son Uriel, his son Uzziah, his son Saul. 25 The sons of Elkanah: Amasai and 26 Ahimoth, his son Elkanah, his 27 son Zophai, his son Nahath, his son Eliab, his son Jeroham, his son 28 Elkanah. The sons of Samuel: Joel the eldest and Abiah the second. 29 The sons of Merari: his son Mahli, his son Libni, his son Shimei, his 30 son Uzza, his son Shimea, his son Haggiah, his son Asaiah.

David's musicians

31 These are the men whom David appointed to take charge of the music in the house of the LORD when the Ark should be deposited 32 there. They performed their musical duties before the Tent of the Presence until Solomon built the house of the LORD in Jerusalem, and took their regular turns of 33 duty there. The following, with their descendants, took this duty. Of the line of Kohath: Heman the musician, son of Joel, son 34 of Samuel, son of Elkanah, son of Jeroham, son of Eliel, son of 35 Toah, son of Zuph, son of Elkanah, son of Mahath, son of Amasai, 36 son of Elkanah, son of Joel, son 37 of Azariah, son of Zephaniah, son of Tahath, son of Assir, son of 38 Ebiasaph, son of Korah, son of Izhar, son of Kohath, son of Levi, 39 son of Israel. Heman's colleague Asaph stood at his right hand. He 40 was the son of Berachiah, son 41[w] of Shimea, son of Michael, son of Baaseiah, son of Malchiah, son of Ethni, son of Zerah, son of Adaiah, 42 son of Ethan, son of Zimmah, son 43 of Shimei, son of Jahath, son of 44 Gershom, son of Levi. On their left stood their colleague of the line of Merari: Ethan son of Kishi, 45 son of Abdi, son of Malluch, son of Hashabiah, son of Amaziah, 46 son of Hilkiah, son of Amzi, son 47 of Bani, son of Shamer, son of Mahli, son of Mushi, son of Merari, 48 son of Levi. Their kinsmen the Levites were dedicated to all the service of the Tabernacle, the house of God.

Aaron's descendants

But it was Aaron and his descen- 49 dants who burnt the sacrifices on the altar of whole-offering and the altar of incense, in fulfilment of all the duties connected with the most sacred gifts, and to make expiation for Israel, exactly as Moses the servant of God had commanded. The sons of Aaron: 50[x] his son Eleazar, his son Phinehas, his son Abishua, his son Bukki, his 51 son Uzzi, his son Zerahiah, his son 52 Meraioth, his son Amariah, his son Ahitub, his son Zadok, his son 53 Ahimaaz.

Cities of the Levites

These are their settlements in en- 54 campments in the districts assigned to the descendants of Aaron, to the clan of Kohath, for it was to them that the lot had fallen: they gave 55 them Hebron in Judah, with the common land round it, but they 56 assigned to Caleb son of Jephunneh the open country belonging to the town and its hamlets. They gave 57[y] to the sons of Aaron: Hebron the city[z] of refuge, Libnah, Jattir, Eshtemoa, Hilen, Debir, Ashan, 58 59 and Beth-shemesh, each with its common land. And from the tribe 60 of Benjamin: Geba, Alemeth, and Anathoth, each with its common land, making thirteen cities in all by their clans.

They gave to the remaining clans 61 of the sons of Kohath ten cities by lot from the half tribe of Manasseh. To the sons of Gershom according 62 to their clans they gave thirteen cities from the tribes of Issachar, Asher, Naphtali, and Manasseh in Bashan. To the sons of Merari 63 according to their clans they gave by lot twelve cities from the tribes of Reuben, Gad, and Zebulun. Israel gave these cities, each with 64 its common land, to the Levites. (The cities mentioned above, from 65 the tribes of Judah, Simeon, and Benjamin, were assigned by lot.) Some of the clans of Kohath had 66 cities allotted[a] to them. They gave 67 them the city[b] of refuge, Shechem in the hill-country of Ephraim, Gezer, Jokmeam, Beth-horon, 68 Aijalon, and Gath-rimmon, each 69 with its common land. From the 70 half tribe of Manasseh, Aner and Bileam, each with its common land, were given to the rest of the clans of Kohath.

To the sons of Gershom they 71 gave from the half tribe of Manasseh: Golan in Bashan, and Ashtaroth, each with its common land. From the tribe of Issachar: Ked- 72 esh, Daberath, Ramoth, and Anem, 73

q They were . . . surrendered to them: or They attacked them boldly, and the Hagarites and all their allies surrendered to them, for they cried . . . to their prayer.   r Gershom in verses 16 and 17.   s Verses 4–8: cp. verses 50–53.   t Verses 16–19: cp. Exod. 6. 16–19.   u Verses 20, 21: cp. verses 41–43.   v Verses 22–28: cp. verses 33–38.   w Verses 41–43: cp. verses 20, 21.   x Verses 50–53: cp. verses 4–8.   y Verses 57–81: cp. Josh. 21. 13–39.   z Prob. rdg., cp. Josh. 21. 13; Heb. cities.   a allotted: prob. rdg., cp. Josh. 21. 20; Heb. of their frontier.   b Prob. rdg., cp. Josh. 21. 21; Heb. cities.

74 each with its common land. From the tribe of Asher: Mashal, Abdon,
75 Hukok, and Rehob, each with its
76 common land. From the tribe of Naphtali: Kedesh in Galilee, Hammon, and Kiriathaim, each with its common land.
77 To the rest of the sons of Merari they gave from the tribe of Zebulun: Rimmon and Tabor, each
78 with its common land. On the east of Jordan, opposite Jericho, from the tribe of Reuben: Bezer-in-the-
79 wilderness, Jahzah, Kedemoth, and Mephaath, each with its common
80 land. From the tribe of Gad: Ramoth in Gilead, Mahanaim,
81 Heshbon, and Jazer, each with its common land.

Issachar's descendants

7 1 c The sons of Issachar: Tola, Pua,
2 Jashub and Shimron, four. The sons of Tola: Uzzi, Rephaiah, Jeriel, Jahmai, Jibsam, and Samuel, all able men and heads of families by paternal descent from Tola according to their tribal lists; their number in David's time was twenty-
3 two thousand six hundred. The son of Uzzi: Izrahiah. The sons of Izrahiah: Michael, Obadiah, Joel and Isshiah, making a total of
4 five, all of them chiefs. In addition there were bands of fighting men recorded by families according to the tribal lists to the number of thirty-six thousand, for they had
5 many wives and children. Their fellow-tribesmen in all the clans of Issachar were able men, eighty-seven thousand; every one of them was registered.

Benjamin's and Dan's descendants

6 The sons of Benjamin: Bela, Becher
7 and Jediael, three. The sons of Bela: Ezbon, Uzzi, Uzziel, Jerimoth and Iri, five. They were heads of their families and able men; the number registered was twenty-two
8 thousand and thirty-four. The sons of Becher: Zemira, Joash, Eliezer, Elioenai, Omri, Jeremoth, Abiah, Anathoth and Alemeth; all these
9 were sons of Becher according to their tribal lists, heads of their families and able men; and the number registered was twenty thou-
10 sand two hundred. The son of Jediael: Bilhan. The sons of Bilhan: Jeush, Benjamin, Ehud, Kenaanah, Zethan, Tarshish and Ahishahar.
11 All these were descendants of Jediael, heads of d families and able men. The number was seventeen thousand two hundred men, fit for active service in war.
12 The sons of Dan: e Hushim and the sons of Aher. f

Naphtali's descendants

13 The sons of Naphtali: Jahziel, Guni, Jezer, Shallum. These were sons of Bilhah.

Manasseh's descendants

14 g The sons of Manasseh, h born of
15 his concubine, an Aramaean: Machir father of Gilead. Machir married a woman whose name was i Maacah. The second son was named Zelophehad, and Zelo-
16 phehad had daughters. Maacah wife of Machir had a son whom she named Peresh. His brother's
17 name was Sheresh, and his sons were Ulam and Rakem. The son of Ulam: Bedan. These were the sons
18 of Gilead son of Machir, son of Manasseh. His sister Hammoleketh was the mother of Ishhod, Abiezer
19 and Mahalah. The sons of Shemida: Ahian, Shechem, Likhi and Aniam.

Ephraim's descendants

20 The sons of Ephraim: Shuthelah, his son Bered, his son Tahath, his
21 son Eladah, his son Tahath, his son Zabad, his son Shuthelah. Ephraim's other sons Ezer and Elead were killed by the native Gittites when they came down to lift their
22 cattle. Their father Ephraim long mourned for them, and his kins-
23 men came to comfort him. Then he had intercourse with his wife; she conceived and had a son whom he named Beriah (because disaster j
24 had come on his family). He had a daughter named Sherah; she built Lower and Upper Beth-
25 horon and Uzzen-sherah. He also had a son named Rephah; his son was Resheph, his son Telah, his
26 son Tahan, his son Laadan, his son Ammihud, his son Elishama,
27 his son Nun, his son Joshua.
28 Their lands and settlements were: Bethel and its dependent villages, to the east Naaran, to the west Gezer, Shechem, and Gaza, with
29 their villages. In the possession of Manasseh were Beth-shean, Taanach, Megiddo, and Dor, with their villages. In all of these lived the descendants of Joseph the son of Israel.

Asher's descendants

30 The sons of Asher: Imnah, Ishvah, Ishvi and Beriah, together with
31 their sister Serah. The sons of Beriah: Heber and Malchiel father
32 of Birzavith. Heber was the father of Japhlet, Shomer, Hotham, and
33 their sister Shua. The sons of Japhlet: Pasach, Bimhal and Ashvath. These were the sons of Japh-
34 let. The sons of Shomer: Ahi,
35 Rohgah, Jehubbah and Aram. The

sons of his brother Hotham: k Zophah, Imna, Shelesh and Amal. The sons of Zophah: Suah, Harnepher, Shual, Beri, Imrah, Bezer, Hod, Shamma, Shilshah, Ithran and Beera. The sons of Jether: Jephunneh, Pispah and Ara. The sons of Ulla: Arah, Haniel and Rezia. All these were descendants of Asher, heads of families, picked men of ability, leading princes. They were enrolled among the fighting troops; the total number was twenty-six thousand men.

Benjamin's descendants

The sons of Benjamin were: the eldest Bela, the second Ashbel, the third Aharah, the fourth Nohah and the fifth Rapha. The sons of Bela: Addar, Gera father of Ehud, l Abishua, Naaman, Ahoah, Gera, Shephuphan and Huram. These were the sons of Ehud, heads of families living in Geba, who were removed to Manahath: Naaman, Ahiah, and Gera—he it was who removed them. He was the father of Uzza and Ahihud. Shaharaim had sons born to him in Moabite country, after putting away his wives Mahasham and Baara. By his wife Hodesh he had Jobab, Zibia, Mesha, Malcham, Jeuz, Shachia and Mirmah. These were his sons, heads of families. By Mahasham he had had Abitub and Elpaal. The sons of Elpaal: Eber, Misham, Shamed who built Ono and Lod with its villages, also Beriah and Shema who were heads of families living in Aijalon, having expelled the inhabitants of Gath. Ahio, Shashak, Jeremoth, Zebadiah, Arad, Ader, Michael, Ispah, and Joha were sons of Beriah; Zebadiah, Meshullam, Hezeki, Heber, Ishmerai, Jezliah, and Jobab were sons of Elpaal; Jakim, Zichri, Zabdi, Elienai, Zilthai, Eliel, Adaiah, Beraiah, and Shimrath were sons of Shimei; Ishpan, Heber, Eliel, Abdon, Zichri, Hanan, Hananiah, Elam, Antothiah, Iphedeiah, and Penuel were sons of Shashak; Shamsherai, Shehariah, Athaliah, Jaresiah, Eliah, and Zichri were sons of Jeroham. These were enrolled in the tribal lists as heads of families, chiefs living in Jerusalem.

Saul's family

Jehiel founder of Gibeon lived at Gibeon; his wife's name was Maacah. His eldest son was Abdon, followed by Zur, Kish, Baal, Nadab, Gedor, Ahio, Zacher and Mikloth. Mikloth was the father of Shimeah; they lived alongside their kinsmen in Jerusalem.

---

c Verses 1, 6, 13, 30 and 8. 1–5: cp. Gen. 46. 13, 17, 21–24.   d Prob. rdg.; Heb. to the heads of.   e The sons of Dan: prob. rdg., cp. Gen. 46. 23; Heb. And Shuppim and Huppim, the sons of Ir.   f Or another. g Verses 14–19: cp. Num. 26. 29–33.   h Prob. rdg.; Heb. adds Asriel.   i whose name was: prob. rdg.; Heb. to Huppim and Shuppim, and his sister's name was . . .   j Heb. beraah.   k Prob. rdg., cp. verse 32; Heb. Helem.   l father of Ehud: prob. rdg., cp. Judg. 3. 15; Heb. Abihud.   m Verses 29–38: cp. 9. 35–44.

33 Ner was the father of Kish, Kish father of Saul, Saul father of Jonathan, Malchishua, Abinadab 34 and Eshbaal. Jonathan's son was Meribbaal, and he was the father 35 of Micah. The sons of Micah: Pithon, Melech, Tarea and Ahaz. 36 Ahaz was the father of Jehoaddah, Jehoaddah father of Alemeth, Azmoth and Zimri. Zimri was the 37 father of Moza, and Moza father of Binea; his son was Raphah, his 38 son Elasah, and his son Azel. Azel had six sons, whose names were Azrikam, Bocheru, Ishmael, Sheariah, Obadiah and Hanan. All these 39 were sons of Azel. The sons of his brother Eshek: the eldest Ulam, the second Jeush, the third Eli- 40 phelet. The sons of Ulam were able men, archers, and had many sons and grandsons, a hundred and fifty. All these were descendants of Benjamin.

Repatriated Israelites

9 So all Israel were registered and recorded in the book of the kings of Israel; but Judah for their sins were carried away to exile in 2[n] Babylon. The first to occupy their ancestral land in their cities were lay Israelites, priests, Levites, and 3 temple-servitors. Jerusalem was occupied partly by Judahites, partly by Benjamites, and partly by men 4 of Ephraim and Manasseh. Judahites:[o] Uthai son of Ammihud, son of Omri, son of Imri, son of Bani, a descendant of Perez son of Judah. 5 Shelanites: Asaiah the eldest and 6 his sons. The sons of Zerah: Jeuel and six hundred and ninety of their 7 kinsmen. Benjamites: Sallu son of Meshullam, son of Hodaviah, son 8 of Hassenuah, Ibneiah son of Jeroham, Elah son of Uzzi, son of Micri, Meshullam son of Shephatiah, son of Reuel, son of Ibniah, 9 and their recorded kinsmen numbering nine hundred and fifty-six, all heads of families. 10 Priests: Jedaiah, Jehoiarib, Ja- 11 chin, Azariah son of Hilkiah, son of Meshullam, son of Zadok, son of Meraioth, son of Ahitub, the officer in charge of the house of 12 God, Adaiah son of Jeroham, son of Pashhur, son of Malchiah, Maasai son of Adiel, son of Jahzerah, son of Meshullam, son of 13 Meshillemith, son of Immer, and their colleagues, heads of families numbering one thousand seven hundred and sixty, men of substance and fit for the work connected with the service of the house of God. 14 Levites: Shemaiah son of Has-

shub, son of Azrikam, son of Ha- shabiah, a descendant of Merari, 15 Bakbakkar, Heresh, Galal, Mattaniah son of Mica, son of Zichri, 16 son of Asaph, Obadiah son of Shemaiah, son of Galal, son of Jeduthun, and Berechiah son of Asa, son of Elkanah, who lived in the hamlets of the Netophathites. 17 The door-keepers were Shallum, Akkub, Talmon, and Ahiman; their brother Shallum was the 18 chief. Until then they had all been door-keepers in the quarters of the Levites at the king's gate, on the 19 east. Shallum son of Kore, son of Ebiasaph, son of Korah, and his kinsmen of the Korahite family were responsible for service as guards of the thresholds of the Tabernacle; their ancestors had performed the duty of guarding the entrances to the camp of the 20 LORD. Phinehas son of Eleazar had been their overseer in the past— 21 the LORD be with him! Zechariah son of Meshelemiah was the door-keeper of the Tent of the Presence. 22 Those picked to be door-keepers numbered two hundred and twelve in all, registered in their hamlets. David and Samuel the seer had installed them because they were 23 trustworthy. They and their sons had charge, by watches, of the gates of the house, the tent-dwelling 24 of the LORD. The door-keepers were to be on four sides, east, west, 25 north, and south. Their kinsmen from their hamlets had to come on duty with them for seven days at a 26 time in turn. The four principal door-keepers were chosen for their trustworthiness; they were Levites and had charge of the rooms and the stores in the house of God. 27 They always slept in the precincts of the house of God (for the watch was their duty) and they had charge of the key for opening the gates 28 every morning. Some of them had charge of the vessels used in the service of the temple, keeping count of them as they were brought in 29 and taken out. Some of them were detailed to take charge of the furniture and all the sacred vessels, the flour, the wine, the oil, the incense, and the spices. 30 Some of the priests compounded 31 the ointment for the spices. Mattithiah the Levite, the eldest son of Shallum the Korahite, was in charge of the preparation of the wafers because he was trustworthy. 32 Some of their Kohathite kinsmen were in charge of setting out the rows of the Bread of the Presence every sabbath.

These, the musicians, heads of 33 Levite families, were lodged in rooms set apart for them, because they were liable for duty by day and by night. These are the heads of Levite 34 families, chiefs according to their tribal lists, living in Jerusalem.

Saul's family

Jehiel founder of Gibeon lived at 35[p] Gibeon; his wife's name was Maacah, and his sons were Abdon 36 the eldest, Zur, Kish, Baal, Ner, Nadab, Gedor, Ahio, Zechariah 37 and Mikloth. Mikloth was the 38 father of Shimeam; they lived alongside their kinsmen in Jerusalem.[q] Ner was the father of Kish, 39 Kish father of Saul, Saul father of Jonathan, Malchishua, Abinadab and Eshbaal. The son of Jonathan 40 was Meribbaal, and Meribbaal was the father of Micah. The sons 41 of Micah: Pithon, Melech, Tahrea and Ahaz. Ahaz was the father of 42 Jarah, Jarah father of Alemeth, Azmoth, and Zimri; Zimri father of Moza, and Moza father of 43 Binea; his son was Rephaiah, his son Elasah, his son Azel. Azel had 44 six sons, whose names were Azrikam, Bocheru, Ishmael, Sheariah, Obadiah and Hanan. These were the sons of Azel.

n Verses 2–22: cp. Neh. 11. 3–22. rdg.; Heb. adds with their kinsmen.

o Prob. rdg.; Heb. om.

p Verses 35–44: cp. 8. 29–38.

q Prob.

F

PHILISTINES

The death of Saul

10 1ᵣ The Philistines fought a battle against Israel, and the men of Israel were routed, 2 leaving their dead on Mount Gilboa. The Philistines hotly pursued Saul and his sons and killed the three sons, Jonathan, Abi- 3 nadab and Malchishua. The battle went hard for Saul, for some archers came upon 4 him and he was wounded by them. So he said to his armour-bearer, 'Draw your sword and run me through, so that these un-circumcised brutes may not come and make sport of me.' But the armour-bearer refused, he dared not; whereupon Saul took his own 5 sword and fell on it. When the armour-bearer saw that Saul was dead, he too fell 6 on his sword and died. Thus Saul died and his three sons; his whole house perished at 7 one and the same time. And all the Israelites in the Vale, when they saw that their army had fled and that Saul and his sons had perished, fled likewise, abandoning their cities, and the Philistines went in and occupied them. 8 Next day, when the Philistines came to strip the slain, they found Saul and his sons 9 lying dead on Mount Gilboa. They stripped him, cut off his head and took away his armour; then they sent messengers through the length and breadth of their land to take the good news to idols and people alike. 10 They deposited his armour in the temple of their god,ˢ and nailed up his skull in the 11 temple of Dagon. When the people of Jabesh-gilead heard all that the Philistines 12 had done to Saul, the bravest of them set out together to recover the bodies of Saul and his sons; they brought them back to Jabesh and buried their bones under the oak-tree there, and fasted for seven days. Thus Saul 13 paid with his life for his unfaithfulness: he had disobeyed the word of the LORD and had resorted to ghosts for guidance. He had 14 not sought guidance of the LORD, who therefore destroyed him and transferred the kingdom to David son of Jesse.

David anointed king over Israel

Then all Israel assembled at Hebron to wait **11** upon David. 'We are your own flesh and blood', they said. 'In the past, while Saul 2 was still king, you led the forces of Israel to war, and you brought them home again. And the LORD your God said to you, "You shall be shepherd of my people Israel, you shall be their prince."' All the elders of 3 Israel came to the king at Hebron; there David made a covenant with them before the LORD, and they anointed David king over Israel, as the LORD had said through the lips of Samuel.

David captures Zion

Then David and all Israel went to Jerusalem 4 (that is Jebus, where the Jebusites, the in-habitants of the land, lived). The people of 5 Jebus said to David, 'Never shall you come in here'; none the less David did capture the stronghold of Zion, and it is now known as the City of David. David said, 'The first man 6 to kill a Jebusite shall become a commander or an officer', and the first man to go up was Joab son of Zeruiah; so he was given the command.

David took up his residence in the strong- 7 hold: that is why they called it the City of David. He built the city round it, starting at 8 the Millo and including its neighbourhood, while Joab reconstructed the rest of the city. So David steadily grew stronger, for the 9 LORD of Hosts was with him.

David's chief men

10ᵘ Of David's heroes these were the chief, men who lent their full strength to his government and, with all Israel, joined in making him king; such was the LORD's 11 decree for Israel. First came Jasho-boam the Hachmonite, chief of the three; he it was who bran-dished his spear over three hun- 12 dred, all slain at one time. Next to him was Eleazar son of Dodo the Ahohite, one of the heroic three. 13 He was with David at Pas-dammim where the Philistines had gathered for battle in a field carrying a good crop of barley; and when the people had fled from the Philistines 14 he stood his ground in the field, saved itᵛ and defeated them. So the LORD brought about a great victory.

15 Three of the thirty chiefs went down to the rock to join David at the cave of Adullam, while the Philistines were encamped in the 16 Vale of Rephaim. At that time David was in the stronghold, and a Philistine garrison held Bethle- 17 hem. One day a longing came over David, and he exclaimed, 'If only I could have a drink of water from the wellʷ by the gate of Bethlehem!' At this the three made their way 18 through the Philistine lines and drew water from the well by the gate of Bethlehem, and brought it to David. But David refused to drink it; he poured it out to the LORD and said, 'God forbid that 19 I should do such a thing! Can I drink the blood of these men? They have brought it at the risk of their lives.' So he would not drink it. Such were the exploits of the heroic three.

Abishai the brother of Joab was 20 chief of the thirty. He once bran-dished his spear over three hundred dead, and he was famous among the

r Verses 1–12: cp. 1 Sam. 31. 1–13.   s Or gods.   t Verses 1–9: cp. 2 Sam. 5. 1–3, 6–10.   u Verses 10–41: cp. 2 Sam. 23. 8–39.   v saved it: or cleared it of the Philistines.   w Or cistern.

21 thirty. He held higher rank than the rest of the thirty and became their captain, but he did not rival 22 the three. Benaiah son of Jehoiada, from Kabzeel, was a hero of many exploits. It was he who smote the two champions of Moab, and who went down into a pit and killed a 23 lion on a snowy day. It was he who also killed the Egyptian, a giant seven and a half feet high armed with a spear as big as the beam of a loom; he went to meet him with a club, snatched the spear out of the Egyptian's hand and killed him 24 with his own weapon. Such were the exploits of Benaiah son of Jehoiada, famous among the heroic 25 thirty.[x] He was more famous than the rest of the thirty, but did not rival the three. David appointed him to his household.

26 These were his valiant heroes: Asahel the brother of Joab, and Elhanan son of Dodo from Beth- 27 lehem; Shammoth from Harod,[y] and Helez from a place unknown; 28 Ira son of Ikkesh from Tekoa, and 29 Abiezer from Anathoth; Sibbecai from Hushah, and Ilai the Ahohite; 30 Maharai from Netophah, and Heled son of Baanah from Net- 31 ophah; Ithai son of Ribai from Gibeah of Benjamin, and Benaiah 32 from Pirathon; Hurai from the ravines of Gaash, and Abiel from 33 Beth-arabah; Azmoth from Bahu- rim, and Eliahba from Shaalbon; 34 Hashem the Gizonite, and Jon- athan son of Shage the Hararite; 35 Ahiam son of Sacar the Hararite, 36 and Eliphal son of Ur; Hepher from Mecherah, and Ahijah from 37 a place unknown; Hezro from Carmel, and Naarai son of Ezbai; 38 Joel the brother of Nathan, and 39 Mibhar the son of Haggeri; Zelek the Ammonite, and Naharai from Beeroth, armour-bearer to Joab 40 son of Zeruiah; Ira the Ithrite, and 41 Gareb the Ithrite; Uriah the Hit- 42 tite, and Zabad son of Ahlai. Adina son of Shiza the Reubenite, a chief of the Reubenites, was over these 43 thirty. Also Hanan son of Maacah, 44 and Joshaphat the Mithnite; Uzzia from Ashtaroth, Shama and Jeiel the sons of Hotham from Aroer; 45 Jediael son of Shimri, and Joha his 46 brother, the Tizite; Eliel the Ma- havite, and Jeribai and Joshaviah sons of Elnaam, and Ithmah the 47 Moabite; Eliel, Obed, and Jasiel, from Zobah.[z]

David builds his army

2 These are the men who joined David at Ziklag while he was banned from the presence of Saul son of Kish. They ranked among 2 the warriors valiant in battle. They carried bows and could sling stones or shoot arrows with the left hand or the right; they were Benjamites, 3 kinsmen of Saul. The foremost were Ahiezer and Joash, the sons of Shemaah the Gibeathite; Jeziel and Pelet, men of Beth-azmoth; Berach- 4 ah and Jehu of Anathoth; Ish- maiah the Gibeonite, a hero among the thirty and a chief among them; Jeremiah, Jahaziel, Johanan, and 5 Josabad of Gederah; Eluzai, Jer- imoth, Bealiah, Shemariah, and 6 Shephatiah the Haruphite; Elka- nah, Isshiah, Azareel, Joezer, 7 Jashobeam, the Korahites; and Joelah and Zebadiah sons of Jero- ham, of Gedor.

8 Some Gadites also joined David at the stronghold in the wilderness, valiant men trained for war, who could handle the heavy shield and spear, grim as lions and swift as 9 gazelles on the hills. Ezer was their chief, Obadiah the second, Eliab 10 the third; Mishmannah the fourth 11 and Jeremiah the fifth; Attai the 12 sixth and Eliel the seventh; Johanan the eighth and Elzabad the ninth; 13 Jeremiah the tenth and Machbanai 14 the eleventh. These were chiefs of the Gadites in the army, the least of them a match for a hundred, the greatest a match for a thousand. 15 These were the men who in the first month crossed the Jordan, which was in full flood in all its reaches, and wrought havoc in the valleys, east and west.

16 Some men of Benjamin and Judah came to David at the strong- 17 hold. David went out to them and said, 'If you come as friends to help me, join me and welcome; but if you come to betray me to my enemies, innocent though I am of any crime of violence, may the God 18 of our fathers see and judge.' At that a spirit took possession of Amasai, the chief of the thirty, and he said:

We are on your side, David!
We are with you, son of Jesse!
Greetings, greetings to you
and greetings to your ally!
For your God is your ally.

So David welcomed them and attached them to the columns of his raiding parties.

19 Some men of Manasseh had deserted to David when he went with the Philistines to war against Saul, though he did not, in fact, fight on the side of the Philistines. Their princes brusquely dismissed him, saying to themselves that he would desert them for his master Saul, and that would cost them 20 their heads. The men of Manasseh who deserted to him when he went to Ziklag were these: Adnah, Jo- zabad, Jediael, Michael, Jozabad,

Elihu, and Zilthai, each command- ing his thousand in Manasseh. It 21 was they who stood valiantly by David against the raiders, for they were all good fighters, and they were given commands in his forces. From day to day men came in to 22 help David, until he had gathered an immense army.

David's army at Hebron

These are the numbers of the armed 23 bands which joined David at He- bron to transfer Saul's sovereignty to him, as the LORD had said: men 24 of Judah, bearing heavy shield and spear, six thousand eight hundred, drafted for active service; of Sim- 25 eon, fighting men drafted for active service, seven thousand one hun- dred; of Levi, four thousand six 26 hundred, together with Jehoiada 27 prince of the house of Aaron and three thousand seven hundred men, and Zadok a valiant fighter, with 28 twenty-two officers of his own clan; of Benjamin, Saul's kinsmen, three 29 thousand, though most of them had hitherto remained loyal to the house of Saul; of Ephraim, twenty thou- 30 sand eight hundred, fighting men, famous in their own clans; of the 31 half tribe of Manasseh, eighteen thousand, who had been nominated to come and make David king; of 32 Issachar, whose tribesmen were skilled in reading the signs of the times to discover what course Israel should follow, two hundred chiefs, with all their kinsmen under their command; of Zebulun, fifty thou- 33 sand troops well-drilled for battle, armed with every kind of weapon, bold and single-minded; of Naph- 34 tali, a thousand officers with thirty- seven thousand men bearing heavy shield and spear; of the Danites, 35 twenty-eight thousand six hundred well-drilled for battle; of Asher, 36 forty thousand troops well-drilled for battle; of the Reubenites and 37 the Gadites and the half tribe of Manasseh east of Jordan, a hun- dred and twenty thousand, armed with every kind of weapon.

All these warriors, bold men in 38 battle, came to Hebron, loyally determined to make David king over the whole of Israel; the rest of Israel, too, had but one thought, to make him king. They spent three 39 days there with David, eating and drinking, for their kinsmen made provision for them. Their neigh- 40 bours also round about, as far away as Issachar, Zebulun, and Naphtali, brought food on asses and camels, on mules and oxen, supplies of meal, fig-cakes, raisin-cakes, wine and oil, oxen and sheep, in plenty; for there was rejoicing in Israel.

---

x Prob. rdg.; Heb. three. Heb. obscure.
y Prob. rdg., cp. 2 Sam. 23. 25; Heb. Haror.
z from Zobah: prob. rdg.;

David's intentions for the Ark

13 David consulted the officers over units of a thousand and a hundred on every matter 2 brought forward. Then he said to the whole assembly of Israel, 'If you approve, and if the LORD our God opens a way, let us^a send to our kinsmen who have stayed behind, in all the districts of Israel, and also to the priests and Levites in the cities where they have common lands, bidding them join us. 3 Let us fetch the Ark of our God, for while 4 Saul lived we never resorted to it.' The whole assembly resolved to do this; the entire nation approved it.

David recovers the Ark

5 So David assembled all Israel from the Shihor in Egypt to Lebo-hamath, in order to fetch the Ark of God from Kiriath-6^b jearim. Then David and all Israel went up to Baalah, to Kiriath-jearim, which belonged to Judah, to fetch the Ark of God, the LORD enthroned upon the cherubim, the 7 Ark which bore his name.^c And they conveyed the Ark of God on a new cart from the house of Abinadab, with Uzza and Ahio 8 guiding the cart. David and all Israel danced for joy before God without restraint to the sound of singing, of harps and lutes, of tambourines, and cymbals and trumpets. 9 But when they came to the threshing-floor of Kidon, the oxen stumbled, and Uzza put 10 out his hand to hold the Ark. The LORD was angry with Uzza and struck him down because he had put out his hand to the Ark. 11 So he died there before God. David was vexed because the LORD's anger had broken out upon Uzza, and he called the place 12 Perez-uzza,^d the name it still bears. David was afraid of God that day and said, 'How can I harbour the Ark of God after this?' 13 So he did not take the Ark with him into the City of David, but turned aside and carried it to the house of Obed-edom the 14 Gittite. Thus the Ark of God remained beside the house of Obed-edom, in its tent,^e for three months, and the LORD blessed the family of Obed-edom and all that he had.

Hiram recognizes David's sovereignty

Hiram king of Tyre sent an embassy to **14** David; he sent cedar logs, and masons and carpenters with them to build him a house. David knew by now that the LORD had con- 2 firmed him as king over Israel and had made his royal power stand higher for the sake of his people Israel.

David's children born at Jerusalem

David married more wives in Jerusalem, 3 and more sons and daughters were born to him. These are the names of the children 4^g born to him in Jerusalem: Shammua, Shobab, Nathan, Solomon, Ibhar, Elishua, 5 Elpelet, Nogah, Nepheg, Japhia, Elishama, 6 7 Beeliada and Eliphelet.

David defeats the Philistines

When the Philistines learnt that David had 8 been anointed king over the whole of Israel, they came up in force to seek him out. David, hearing of this, went out to face them. Now the Philistines had come and 9 raided the Vale of Rephaim. So David in- 10 quired of God, 'If I attack the Philistines, wilt thou deliver them into my hands?' And the LORD answered, 'Go; I will deliver them into your hands.' So he went up and attacked 11 them at Baal-perazim and defeated them there. 'God has used me to break through my enemies' lines,' David said, 'as a river breaks its banks'; that is why the place was named Baal-perazim.^h The Philistines left 12 their gods behind them there, and by David's orders these were burnt.

The Philistines made another raid on the 13 Vale. Again David inquired of God, and 14 God said to him, 'No, you must go up towards their rear; wheel round without making contact andⁱ come upon them opposite the aspens. Then, as soon as you hear a 15 rustling sound in the tree-tops, you shall give battle, for God will have gone out before you to defeat the Philistine army.' David 16 did as God commanded, and they drove the Philistine army in flight all the way from Gibeon to Gezer. So David's fame spread 17 through every land, and the LORD inspired all nations with dread of him.

David brings the Ark to Jerusalem

David built himself quarters in the City of **15** David, and prepared a place for the Ark of God and pitched a tent for it. Then he 2 decreed that only Levites should carry the Ark of God, since they had been chosen by

---

a and if . . . let us: *or* and if it is from the LORD our God, let us seize the opportunity and . . .   *b Verses 6–14: cp. 2 Sam. 6. 2–11.*   *c* which bore his name: *prob. rdg.; Heb. obscure.*   *d That is* Outbreak on Uzza. *e Or* in his tent.   *f Verses 1–16: cp. 2 Sam. 5. 11–25.*   *g Verses 4–7: cp. 3. 5–8.*   *h That is* Baal of Break-through.   *i* No . . . contact and: *or* Do not go up to the attack; withdraw from them and then . . .

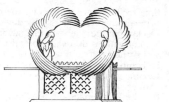

the LORD to carry it and to serve him[j] for
3 ever. Next David assembled all Israel at
Jerusalem, to bring up the Ark of the LORD
4 to the place he had prepared for it. He
gathered together the sons of Aaron and the
5 Levites: of the sons of Kohath, Uriel the
chief with a hundred and twenty of his kins-
6 men; of the sons of Merari, Asaiah the chief
with two hundred and twenty of his kins-
7 men; of the sons of Gershom, Joel the chief
with a hundred and thirty of his kinsmen;
8 of the sons of Elizaphan, Shemaiah the chief
9 with two hundred of his kinsmen; of the sons
of Hebron, Eliel the chief with eighty of
10 his kinsmen; of the sons of Uzziel, Amminadab the chief with a hundred and twelve
11 of his kinsmen. And David summoned
Zadok and Abiathar the priests, together
with the Levites, Uriel, Asaiah, Joel, Shemai-
12 ah, Eliel, and Amminadab, and said to
them, 'You who are heads of families of the
Levites, hallow yourselves, you and your
kinsmen, and bring up the Ark of the LORD
the God of Israel to the place which I have
13 prepared for it. It was because you were not
present the first time, that the LORD our God
broke out upon us. For we had not sought
14 his guidance as we should have done.' So
the priests and the Levites hallowed themselves to bring up the Ark of the LORD the
15 God of Israel, and the Levites carried the
Ark of God, bearing it on their shoulders
with poles as Moses had prescribed at the
command of the LORD.
16 David also ordered the chiefs of the Levites to install as musicians those of their
kinsmen who were players skilled in making
joyful music on their instruments, lutes and
17 harps and cymbals. So the Levites installed

Heman son of Joel and, from his kinsmen,
Asaph son of Berechiah; and from their
kinsmen the Merarites, Ethan son of Kush-
aiah, together with their kinsmen of the 18
second degree, Zechariah, Jaaziel, Shemiramoth, Jehiel, Unni, Eliab, Benaiah, Maaseiah, Mattithiah, Eliphelehu, and Mikneiah, and the door-keepers Obed-edom and
Jeiel. They installed the musicians Heman, 19
Asaph, and Ethan to sound the cymbals of
bronze; Zechariah, Jaaziel, Shemiramoth, 20
Jehiel, Unni, Eliab, Maaseiah, and Benaiah
to play on lutes;[k] Mattithiah, Eliphelehu, 21
Mikneiah, Obed-edom, Jeiel, and Azaziah
to play on harps.[l] Kenaniah, officer of the 22
Levites, was precentor in charge of the music
because of his proficiency. Berechiah and 23
Elkanah were door-keepers for the Ark,
while the priests Shebaniah, Jehoshaphat, 24
Nethaneel, Amasai, Zechariah, Benaiah,
and Eliezer sounded the trumpets before
the Ark of God; and Obed-edom and Jehiah
also were door-keepers for the Ark.

Then David and the elders of Israel and 25[m]
the captains of units of a thousand went to
bring up the Ark of the Covenant of the
LORD with much rejoicing from the house
of Obed-edom. Because God had helped 26
the Levites who carried the Ark of the Covenant of the LORD, they sacrificed seven bulls
and seven rams.

Now David and all the Levites who carried 27
the Ark, and the musicians, and Kenaniah
the precentor,[n] were arrayed in robes of
fine linen; and David had on a linen ephod.
All Israel escorted the Ark of the Covenant 28
of the LORD with shouts of acclamation,
blowing on horns and trumpets, clashing
cymbals and playing on lutes and harps.
But as the Ark of the Covenant of the LORD 29
was entering the city of David, Saul's daughter Michal looked down through a window
and saw King David dancing and making
merry, and she despised him in her heart.

David gives thanks to the LORD

When they had brought in the Ark of God, **16** 1[o]
they put it inside the tent that David had
pitched for it, and they offered whole-
offerings and shared-offerings before God.

j Or it.   *k Prob. rdg.; Heb. adds* al alamoth, *possibly a musical term.*   *l Prob. rdg.; Heb. adds* al
hashsheminith lenasseah, *possibly musical terms.*   *m Verses 25–29: cp. 2 Sam. 6. 12–16.*   *n* the precentor: *prob. rdg.; Heb. obscure.*   *o Verses 1–3: cp. 2 Sam. 6. 17–19.*

2 After David had completed these sacrifices, he blessed the people in the name of the 3 LORD and gave food, a loaf of bread, a portion of meat, and a cake of raisins, to 4 each Israelite, man or woman. He appointed certain Levites to serve before the Ark of the LORD, to repeat the Name, to confess and to praise the LORD the God of Israel. 5 Their leader was Asaph; second to him was Zechariah; then came Jaaziel,[p] Shemiramoth, Jehiel, Mattithiah, Eliab, Benaiah, Obed-edom, and Jeiel, with lutes and harps, 6 Asaph, who sounded the cymbals; and Benaiah and Jahaziel the priests, who blew the trumpets before the Ark of the Covenant 7 of God continuously throughout that day. It was then that David first ordained the offering of thanks to the LORD by Asaph and his kinsmen:

8[q] Give the LORD thanks and invoke him by name,
    make his deeds known in the world around.
9 Pay him honour with song and psalm
    and think upon all his wonders.
10 Exult in his hallowed name;
    let those who seek the LORD be joyful in heart.
11 Turn to the LORD, your strength,[r]
    seek his presence always.
12 Remember the wonders that he has wrought,
    his portents and the judgements he has given,
13 O offspring of Israel his servants, O chosen sons of Jacob.
14 He is the LORD our God;
    his judgements fill the earth.
15 He called to mind his covenant from long ago,[s]
    the promise he extended to a thousand generations—
16 the covenant made with Abraham,
    his oath given to Isaac,
17 the decree by which he bound himself for Jacob,
    his everlasting covenant with Israel:
18 'I will give you the land of Canaan', he said,
    'to be your possession, your patrimony.'
19 A small company it was,
    few in number, strangers in that land,
20 roaming from nation to nation,
    from one kingdom to another;
21 but he let no man ill-treat them,
    for their sake he admonished kings:
22 'Touch not my anointed servants,
    do my prophets no harm.'

Sing to the LORD, all men on earth, 23[t]
    proclaim his triumph day by day.
Declare his glory among the nations, 24
    his marvellous deeds among all peoples.
Great is the LORD and worthy of all praise; 25
    he is more to be feared than all gods.
For the gods of the nations are idols every 26
    one;
    but the LORD made the heavens.
Majesty and splendour attend him, 27
    might and joy are in his dwelling.

Ascribe to the LORD, you families of 28
    nations,
ascribe to the LORD glory and might;
    ascribe to the LORD the glory due to his 29
    name,
bring a gift and come before him.
    Bow down to the LORD in the splendour
    of holiness,[u]
    and dance in his honour, all men on earth. 30
    He has fixed the earth firm, immovable.
Let the heavens rejoice and the earth exult, 31
    let men declare among the nations, 'The
    LORD is king.'
Let the sea roar and all the creatures in it, 32
    let the fields exult and all that is in them;
    then let the trees of the forest shout for joy 33
    before the LORD when he comes to judge
    the earth.

It is good to give thanks to the LORD, 34
    for his love endures for ever.
Cry, 'Deliver us, O God our saviour, 35
    gather us in and save us from the nations
    that we may give thanks to thy holy name
    and make thy praise our pride.'

Blessed be the LORD the God of Israel 36
    from everlasting to everlasting.

And all the people said 'Amen' and 'Praise the LORD.'

After the celebrations

David left Asaph and his kinsmen there be- 37 fore the Ark of the Covenant of the LORD, to perform regular service before the Ark as each day's duty required; as door-keepers 38 he left Obed-edom son of Jeduthun, and Hosah. (Obed-edom and his kinsmen were sixty-eight in number.) He left Zadok the 39 priest and his kinsmen the priests before the Tabernacle of the LORD at the hillshrine in Gibeon, to make offerings there to 40 the LORD upon the altar of whole-offering regularly morning and evening, exactly as it is written in the law enjoined by the LORD upon Israel. With them he left Heman and 41 Jeduthun and the other men chosen and nominated to give thanks to the LORD, 'for

p *Prob. rdg., cp.* 15. 18, 20; *Heb.* Jeiel. symbol of his strength; *lit.* and his strength. 96. 1–13.   u *Or* in holy vestments. 47, 48.

q *Verses 8–22: cp. Ps.* 105, 1–15. s *from long ago: or* for ever. v *Verse 34: cp. Ps.* 107. 1.

r *your strength: or* the t *Verses 23–33: cp. Ps.* w *Verses 35, 36: cp. Ps.* 106.

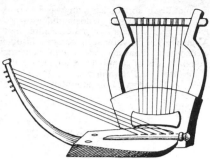

42 his love endures for ever.' They had trumpets and cymbals for the players, and the instruments used for sacred song. The sons of Jeduthun kept the gate.

43 So all the people went home, and David returned to greet his household.

The LORD's promise to David

1ˣ As soon as David was established in his house, he said to Nathan the prophet, 'Here I live in a house of cedar, while the Ark of the Covenant of the LORD is housed in 2 curtains.' Nathan answered David, 'Do whatever you have in mind, for God is with 3 you.' But that night the word of God came 4 to Nathan: 'Go and say to David my servant, "This is the word of the LORD: It is not you 5 who shall build me a house to dwell in. Down to this day I have never dwelt in a house since I brought Israel up from Egypt; I 6 lived in a tent and a tabernacle.ʸ Wherever I journeyed with Israel, did I ever ask any of the judges whom I appointed shepherds of my people why they had not built me a 7 house of cedar?" Then say this to my servant David: "This is the word of the LORD of Hosts: I took you from the pastures, and from following the sheep, to be prince over 8 my people Israel. I have been with you wherever you have gone, and have destroyed all the enemies in your path. I will make you as famous as the great ones of the earth. 9 I will assign a place for my people Israel; there I will plant them, and they shall dwell in their own land. They shall be disturbed no more, never again shall wicked men wear 10 them down as they did from the time when I first appointed judges over Israel my people, and I will subdue all your enemies. But I will make you great and the LORD 11 shall build up your royal house. When your life ends and you go to join your forefathers, I will set up one of your family, one of your own sons, to succeed you, and I will estab- 12 lish his kingdom. It is he shall build me a

house, and I will establish his throne for all time. I will be his father, and he shall be my 13 son. I will never withdraw my love from him as I withdrew it from your predecessor. But 14 I will give him a sure place in my house and kingdom for all time, and his throne shall be established for ever." '

David prays to the LORD

Nathan recounted to David all that had 15 been said to him and all that had been revealed. Then King David went into the 16 presence of the LORD and took his place there and said, 'What am I, LORD God, and what is my family, that thou hast brought me thus far? It was a small thing in thy 17 sight, O God, to have planned for thy servant's house in days long past, and now thou lookest upon me as a man already embarked on a high career, O LORD God. What more can David say to thee of the 18 honour thou hast done thy servant, well though thou knowest him? For the sake of 19 thy servant, LORD, and according to thy purpose, thou hast brought me to all this greatness. O LORD, we have never heard of 20 one like thee; there is no god but thee. And 21 thy people Israel, to whom can they be compared? Is there any other nation on earth whom God has gone out to redeem from slavery, to make them his people? Thou hast won a name for thyself by great and terrible deeds, driving out nations before thy people whom thou didst redeem from Egypt. Thou hast made thy people 22 Israel thy own for ever, and thou, O LORD, hast become their God. But now, LORD, let 23 what thou hast promised for thy servant and his house stand fast for all time; make good what thou hast said. Let it stand fast, 24 that thy fame may be great for ever, and let men say, "The LORD of Hosts, the God of Israel, is Israel's God." So shall the house of thy servant David be established before thee. Thou, my God, hast shown me thy 25

ˣ Verses 1–27: cp. 2 Sam. 7. 1–29.   ʸ I lived . . . tabernacle: *prob. rdg.; Heb.* I have been from tent to tent and from a tabernacle.

purpose to build up thy servant's house; therefore I have been able to pray before 26 thee. Thou, O LORD, art God, and thou hast made these noble promises to thy servant; 27 thou hast been pleased to bless thy servant's house, that it may continue always before thee; thou it is who hast blessed it, and it shall be blessed for ever.'

David extends his kingdom

18 1 After this David defeated the Philistines and conquered them, and took from them Gath 2 with its villages; he defeated the Moabites, and they became subject to him and paid 3 him tribute. He also defeated Hadadezer king of Zobah-hamath, who was on his way to set up a monument of victory by the river 4 Euphrates. From him David captured a thousand chariots, seven thousand horsemen and twenty thousand foot; he hamstrung all the chariot-horses, except a hundred 5 which he retained. When the Aramaeans of Damascus came to the help of Hadadezer king of Zobah, David destroyed 6 twenty-two thousand of them, and established garrisons among these Aramaeans; they became subject to him and paid him tribute. Thus the LORD gave David victory 7 wherever he went. David took the gold quivers borne by Hadadezer's servants and 8 brought them to Jerusalem. He also took a great quantity of bronze[a] from Hadadezer's cities, Tibhath and Kun; from this Solomon made the Sea of bronze,[a] the pillars, and the bronze[a] vessels.

9 When Tou king of Hamath heard that David had defeated the entire army of 10 Hadadezer king of Zobah, he sent his son Hadoram to King David to greet him and to congratulate him on defeating Hadadezer in battle (for Hadadezer had been at war with Tou); and he brought with him vessels 11 of gold, silver, and copper, which King David dedicated to the LORD. He dedicated also the silver and the gold which he had carried away from all the other nations, from Edom and Moab, from the Ammonites and the Philistines, and from Amalek.

12 Edom was defeated by Abishai son of Zeruiah, who destroyed eighteen thousand 13 of them in the Valley of Salt and stationed garrisons in the country. All the Edomites now became subject to David. Thus the LORD gave victory to David wherever he went.

David's government

14b David ruled over the whole of Israel and maintained law and justice among all his people. Joab son of Zeruiah was in com- 15 mand of the army; Jehoshaphat son of Ahilud was secretary of state; Zadok and 16 Abiathar son of Ahimelech, son of Ahitub,[c] were priests; Shavsha was adjutant-general; Benaiah son of Jehoiada commanded the 17 Kerethite and Pelethite guards. The eldest sons of David were in attendance on the king.

ARAM

Joab defeats the Aramaeans and Ammonites

Some time afterwards Nahash king of the **19** Ammonites died and was succeeded by his son. David said, 'I must keep up the same 2 loyal friendship with Hanun son of Nahash as his father showed me', and he sent a mission to condole with him on the death of his father. But when David's envoys entered the country of the Ammonites to condole with Hanun, the Ammonite princes 3 said to Hanun, 'Do you suppose David means to do honour to your father when he sends you his condolences? These men of his are spies whom he has sent to find out how to overthrow the country.' So Hanun 4 took David's servants, and he shaved them, cut off half their garments up to the hips, and dismissed them. When David heard how 5 they had been treated, he sent to meet them, for they were deeply humiliated, and ordered them to wait in Jericho and not to return until their beards had grown again. The 6 Ammonites knew that they had brought themselves into bad odour with David, so Hanun and the Ammonites sent a thousand talents of silver to hire chariots and horse-men from Aram-naharaim,[e] Maacah, and Aram-zobah.[f] They hired thirty-two thou- 7 sand chariots and the king of Maacah and his people, who came and encamped before Medeba, while the Ammonites came from their cities and mustered for battle. When 8 David heard of it, he sent out Joab and all the fighting men. The Ammonites came and 9 took up their position at the entrance to the city, while the allied kings took up theirs in the open country. When Joab saw that 10 he was threatened both front and rear, he detailed some picked Israelite troops and drew them up facing the Aramaeans. The 11 rest of his forces he put under his brother

---

z Verses 1–13: cp. 2 Sam. 8. 1–14.   a Or copper.   b Verses 14–17: cp. 2 Sam. 8. 15–18; 20. 23–26; 1 Kgs. 4. 2–4.   c and Abiathar . . . Ahitub: prob. rdg., cp. 2 Sam. 8. 17; Heb. son of Ahitub and Abimelech son of Abiathar.   d Verses 1–19: cp. 2 Sam. 10. 1–19.   e That is Aram of Two Rivers.
f Maacah, and Aram-zobah: prob. rdg.; Heb. Aram-maacah, and Zobah.

12 Abishai, who took up a position facing the Ammonites. 'If the Aramaeans prove too strong for me,' he said, 'you must come to my relief; and if the Ammonites prove too 13 strong for you, I will relieve you. Courage! Let us fight bravely for our people and for the cities^g of our God. And the LORD's will 14 be done.' But when Joab and his men came to close quarters with the Aramaeans, they 15 put them to flight; and when the Ammonites saw them in flight, they too fled before his brother Abishai and entered the city. Then 16 Joab came to Jerusalem. The Aramaeans saw that they had been worsted by Israel, and they sent messengers to summon other Aramaeans from the Great Bend of the Euphrates under Shophach, commander of 17 Hadadezer's army. Their movement was reported to David, who immediately mustered all the forces of Israel, crossed the Jordan and advanced against them and took up battle positions. The Aramaeans like-wise took up positions facing David and 18 engaged him, but were put to flight by Israel. David slew seven thousand Aramaeans in chariots and forty thousand infantry, killing Shophach the commander 19 of the army. When Hadadezer's men saw that they had been worsted by Israel, they sued for peace and submitted to David. The Aramaeans were never again willing to give support to the Ammonites.

Joab destroys Rabbah

1^h At the turn of the year, when kings take the field, Joab led the army out and ravaged the Ammonite country. He came to Rabbah and laid siege to it, while David remained in Jerusalem; he reduced the city and razed 2 it to the ground. David took the crown from the head of Milcom and found that it weighed a talent of gold and was set with a precious stone, and this he placed on his own head. He also removed a great quantity 3 of booty from the city; he took its inhabitants and set them to work with saws and other iron tools, sharp and toothed. David did this to all the cities of the Ammonites; then he and all his people returned to Jerusalem.

Three more victories

4ⁱ Some time later war with the Philistines broke out in Gezer; it was then that Sib-bechai of Hushah killed Sippai, a descendant of the Rephaim, and the Philistines 5 were reduced to submission. In another war with the Philistines, Elhanan son of Jair killed Lahmi brother of Goliath of Gath, whose spear had a shaft like a weaver's beam. 6 In yet another war in Gath, there appeared

a giant with six fingers on each hand and six toes on each foot, twenty-four in all; he too was descended from the Rephaim, and, 7 when he defied Israel, Jonathan son of David's brother Shimea killed him. These 8 giants were the descendants of the Rephaim in Gath, and they all fell at the hands of David and his men.

David numbers Israel and Judah

Now Satan, setting himself against Israel, 21 1^j incited David to count the people. So he 2 instructed Joab and his public officers to go out and number Israel, from Beersheba to Dan, and to report the number to him. Joab answered, 'Even if the LORD should 3 increase his people a hundredfold, would not your majesty still be king and all the people your slaves? Why should your majesty want to do this? It will only bring guilt on Israel.' But Joab was overruled by the king; he 4 set out and went up and down the whole country. He then came to Jerusalem and 5 reported to David the numbers recorded: those capable of bearing arms were one million one hundred thousand in Israel, and four hundred and seventy thousand in Judah. Levi and Benjamin were not counted 6 by Joab, so deep was his repugnance against the king's order.

David owns his guilt and makes an offering

God was displeased with all this and pro- 7 ceeded to punish Israel. David said to God, 8 'I have done a very wicked thing: I pray thee remove thy servant's guilt, for I have been very foolish.' And the LORD said to Gad, 9 David's seer, 'Go and tell David, "This is 10 the word of the LORD: I have three things to offer you; choose one of them and I will bring it upon you."' So Gad came to David 11 and said to him, 'This is the word of the LORD: "Make your choice: three years of 12 famine, three months of harrying by your foes and close pursuit by the sword of your enemy, or three days of the LORD's own sword, bringing pestilence throughout the country, and the LORD's angel working destruction in all the territory of Israel." Consider now what answer I am to take back to him who sent me.' Thereupon David 13 said to Gad, 'I am in a desperate plight; let me fall into the hands of the LORD, for his mercy is very great; and let me not fall into the hands of man.' So the LORD sent a 14 pestilence throughout Israel, and seventy thousand men of Israel died. And God sent 15 an angel to Jerusalem to destroy it; but, as he was destroying it, the LORD saw and repented of the evil, and said to the destroying angel at the moment when he was

---

g Or altars.   *h Verses 1–3: cp. 2 Sam. 12. 26–31.*
1–27: cp. 2 Sam. 24. 1–25.

i Verses 4–7: cp. 2 Sam. 21. 18–22.   *j Verses*

standing beside the threshing-floor of Ornan the Jebusite, 'Enough! Stay your hand.'

16 When David looked up and saw the angel of the Lord standing between earth and heaven, with his sword drawn in his hand and stretched out over Jerusalem, he and the elders, clothed in sackcloth, fell prostrate 17 to the ground; and David said to God, 'It was I who gave the order to count the people. It was I who sinned, I, the shepherd,[k] who did wrong. But these poor sheep, what have they done? O Lord my God, let thy hand fall upon me and upon my family, but check this plague on the people.'[l]

18 The angel of the Lord, speaking through the lips of Gad, commanded David to go to the threshing-floor of Ornan the Jebusite and to set up there an altar to the Lord. 19 David went up as Gad had bidden him in 20 the Lord's name. Ornan's four sons who were with him hid themselves, but he was busy threshing his wheat when he turned 21 and saw the angel. As David approached, Ornan looked up and, seeing the king, came out from the threshing-floor and prostrated 22 himself before him. David said to Ornan, 'Let me have the site of the threshing-floor that I may build on it an altar to the Lord; sell it me at the full price, that the plague which has attacked my people may be 23 stopped.' Ornan answered David, 'Take it and let your majesty do as he thinks fit; see, here are the oxen for whole-offerings, the threshing-sledges for the fuel, and the wheat for the grain-offering; I give you everything.' 24 But King David said to Ornan, 'No, I will pay the full price; I will not present to the Lord what is yours, or offer a whole- 25 offering which has cost me nothing.' So 26 David gave Ornan six hundred shekels of gold for the site, and built an altar to the Lord there; on this he offered whole-offerings and shared-offerings, and called upon the Lord, who answered him with fire falling from heaven on the altar of whole- 27 offering. Then, at the Lord's command, the angel sheathed his sword.

The site for the Temple

28 It was when David saw that the Lord had answered him at the threshing-floor of Ornan the Jebusite that he offered sacrifice 29 there. The tabernacle of the Lord and the altar of whole-offering which Moses had made in the wilderness were then at the hill- 30 shrine in Gibeon; but David had been unable to go there and seek God's guidance, so shocked and shaken was he at the sight of 22 the angel's sword. Then David said, 'This is to be the house of the Lord God, and this is to be an altar of whole-offering for Israel.'

David prepares for building

David now gave orders to assemble the 2 aliens resident in Israel, and he set them as masons to dress hewn stones and to build the house of God. He laid in a great store 3 of iron to make nails and clamps for the doors, more bronze than could be weighed and cedar-wood without limit; the men of 4 Sidon and Tyre brought David an ample supply of cedar. David said, 'My son Sol- 5 omon is a boy of tender years, and the house that is to be built to the Lord must be exceedingly magnificent, renowned and celebrated in every land; therefore I must make preparations for it myself.' So David made abundant preparation before his death.

He sent for Solomon his son and charged 6 him to build a house for the Lord the God of Israel. 'Solomon, my son,' he said, 'I had 7 intended to build a house in honour of the name of the Lord my God; but the Lord 8 forbade me and said, "You have shed much blood in my sight and waged great wars; for this reason you shall not build a house in honour of my name. But you shall have a 9[m] son who shall be a man of peace; I will give him peace from all his enemies on every side; his name shall be Solomon, 'Man of Peace', and I will grant peace and quiet to Israel in his days. He shall build a house in honour 10 of my name; he shall be my son and I will be a father to him, and I will establish the throne of his sovereignty over Israel for ever." Now, Solomon my son, the Lord be 11 with you! May you prosper and build the house of the Lord your God, as he promised you should. But may the Lord grant you 12 wisdom and discretion, so that when he gives you authority in Israel you may keep the law of the Lord your God. You will 13 prosper only if you are careful to observe the decrees and ordinances which the Lord enjoined upon Moses for Israel; be strong and resolute, neither faint-hearted nor dismayed.

'In spite of all my troubles, I have here 14 ready for the house of the Lord a hundred thousand talents of gold and a million talents of silver, with great quantities of bronze and iron, more than can be weighed; timber and stone, too, I have got ready; and you may add to them. Besides, you have a large force 15 of workmen, masons, sculptors, and carpenters, and countless men skilled in work of every kind, in gold and silver, bronze and 16 iron. So now to work, and the Lord be with you!'

David ordered all the officers of Israel to 17 help Solomon his son: 'Is not the Lord 18 your God with you? Will he not give you

---

k I, the shepherd: prob. rdg.; Heb. doing wrong. not for a plague.   m Verse 9: cp. 1 Kgs. 5. 4.

l check . . . people: prob. rdg.; Heb. among thy people,

peace on every side? For he has given the inhabitants of the land into my power, and they will be subject to the LORD and his 19 people. Devote yourselves, therefore, heart and soul, to seeking guidance of the LORD

your God, and set about building his sanctuary, so that the Ark of the Covenant of the LORD and God's holy vessels may be brought into a house built in honour of his name.'

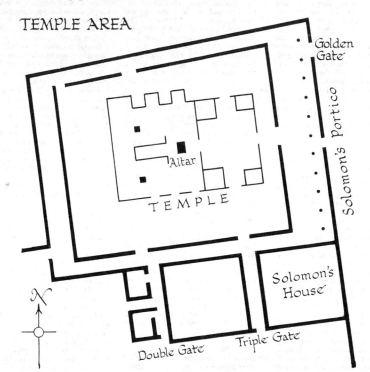

TEMPLE AREA

Golden Gate

Solomon's Portico

Altar

TEMPLE

N

Solomon's House

Double Gate   Triple Gate

Enrolling the Levites

3 David was now an old man, weighed down with years, and he appointed Solomon his son king 2 over Israel. He gathered together all the officers of Israel, the priests, 3 and the Levites. The Levites were enrolled from the age of thirty upwards, their males being thirty-4 eight thousand in all. Of these, twenty-four thousand were to be responsible for the maintenance and service of the house of the LORD, six thousand to act as officers 5 and magistrates, four thousand to be door-keepers, and four thousand to praise the LORD on the musical instruments which David had made for the service of praise. 6 David organized them in divisions, called after Gershon, Kohath, and Merari, the sons of Levi.
7   The sons of Gershon: Laadan

8 and Shimei. The sons of Laadan: Jehiel the chief, Zetham and Joel, 9 three.ⁿ These were the heads of the families grouped under Laadan. 10 The sons of Shimei: Jahath, Ziza, 11 Jeush and Beriah, four. Jahath was the chief and Ziza the second, but Jeush and Beriah, having few children, were reckoned for duty as a single family. 12   The sons of Kohath: Amram, Izhar, Hebron and Uzziel, four. 13 The sons of Amram: Aaron and Moses. Aaron was set apart, he and his sons in perpetuity, to dedicate the most holy gifts,ᵒ to burn sacrifices before the LORD, to serve him, and to give the bless-14 ing in his name for ever, but the sons of Moses, the man of God, were to keep the name of Levite. 15 The sons of Moses: Gershom and 16 Eliezer. The sons of Gershom: 17 Shubael the chief. The sons of

Eliezer: Rehabiah the chief. Eliezer had no other sons, but Rehabiah had very many. The sons of Izhar: 18 Shelomoth the chief. The sons of 19 Hebron: Jeriah the chief, Amariah the second, Jahaziel the third and Jekameam the fourth. The sons of 20 Uzziel: Micah the chief and Isshiah the second.
The sons of Merari: Mahli and 21 Mushi. The sons of Mahli: Eleazar and Kish. When Eleazar died, he 22 left daughters but no sons, and their cousins, the sons of Kish, married them. The sons of Mushi: 23 Mahli, Eder and Jeremoth, three.
Such were the Levites, grouped 24 by families in the father's line whose heads were entered in the detailed list; they performed duties in the service of the house of the LORD. For David said, 'The LORD 25 the God of Israel has given his

n *Prob. rdg.; Heb. adds* The sons of Shimei: Shelomith, Haziel and Haran, three.   o *to dedicate . . . gifts: or* to be hallowed as most holy.

people peace and has made his
26 abode in Jerusalem for ever. The
Levites will no longer have to
27 carry the Tabernacle or any of the
vessels for its service.' By these last
words of David the Levites were
enrolled from the age of twenty
28 upwards. Their duty was to help
the sons of Aaron in the service of
the house of the LORD: they were
responsible for the care of the
courts and the rooms, for the cleansing of all holy things, and the general service of the house of God;
29 for the rows of the Bread of
the Presence, the flour for the
grain-offerings, unleavened wafers,
cakes baked on the griddle, and
pastry, and for the weights and
30 measures. They were to be on duty
continually before the LORD every
morning and evening, giving thanks
31 and praise to him, and at every
offering of whole-offerings to the
LORD, on sabbaths, new moons
and at the appointed seasons,
according to their prescribed num-
32 ber. The Levites were to have
charge of the Tent of the Presence
and of the sanctuary, but the sons
of Aaron their kinsmen were
charged with the service of worship in the house of the LORD.

24 The divisions of the sons of
Aaron: his sons were Nadab and
2 Abihu, Eleazar and Ithamar. Nadab and Abihu died before their
father, leaving no sons; therefore
Eleazar and Ithamar held the office
3 of priest. David, acting with Zadok
of the sons of Eleazar and with
Ahimelech of the sons of Ithamar,
organized them in divisions for the
discharge of the duties of their
4 office. The male heads of families
proved to be more numerous in the
line of Eleazar than in that of Ithamar, so that sixteen heads of families were grouped under the line of
Eleazar and eight under that of
5 Ithamar. He organized them by
drawing lots among them, for there
were sacred officers*p* and officers of
God in the line of Eleazar and
6 in that of Ithamar. Shemaiah the
clerk, a Levite, son of Nethaneel,
wrote down the names in the
presence of the king, the officers,
Zadok the priest, and Ahimelech
son of Abiathar, and of the heads
of the priestly and levitical families,
one priestly family being taken
from the line of Eleazar and one
7 from that of Ithamar. The first lot
fell to Jehoiarib, the second to
8 Jedaiah, the third to Harim, the
9 fourth to Seorim, the fifth to
Malchiah, the sixth to Mijamin,
10 the seventh to Hakkoz, the eighth
11 to Abiah, the ninth to Jeshua, the
12 tenth to Shecaniah, the eleventh to
13 Eliashib, the twelfth to Jakim, the
thirteenth to Huppah, the four-

14 teenth to Jeshebeab, the fifteenth
to Bilgah, the sixteenth to Immer,
15 the seventeenth to Hezir, the eigh-
16 teenth to Aphses, the nineteenth to
Pethahiah, the twentieth to Jehez-
17 ekel, the twenty-first to Jachin,
18 the twenty-second to Gamul, the
twenty-third to Delaiah, and the
19 twenty-fourth to Maaziah. This
was their order of duty for the discharge of their service when they
entered the house of the LORD,
according to the rule prescribed
for them by their ancestor Aaron,
who had received his instructions
from the LORD the God of Israel.
20 Of the remaining Levites: of
the sons of Amram: Shubael. Of
the sons of Shubael: Jehdeiah.
21 Of Rehabiah: Isshiah, the chief
22 of Rehabiah's sons. Of the line of
Izhar: Shelomoth. Of the sons
23 of Shelomoth: Jahath. The sons of
Hebron: Jeriah the chief, Amariah
the second, Jahaziel the third and
24 Jekameam the fourth. The sons of
Uzziel: Micah. Of the sons of
25 Micah: Shamir; Micah's brother:
Isshiah. Of the sons of Isshiah:
26 Zechariah. The sons of Merari:
Mahli and Mushi and also*q* Jaaziah
27 his son. The sons of Merari: of
Jaaziah: Beno, Shoham, Zaccur
28 and Ibri. Of Mahli: Eleazar, who
29 had no sons; of Kish: the sons of
30 Kish: Jerahmeel; and the sons of
Mushi: Mahli, Eder and Jerimoth.
These were the Levites by families.
31 These also, side by side with their
kinsmen the sons of Aaron, cast
lots in the presence of King David,
Zadok, Ahimelech, and the heads
of the priestly and levitical families,
the senior and junior houses casting
lots side by side.

The singers

25 David and his chief officers assigned
special duties to the sons of Asaph,
of Heman, and of Jeduthun, leaders
in inspired prophecy to the accompaniment of harps, lutes, and cymbals; the number of the men who
performed this work in the temple
2 was as follows. Of the sons of
Asaph: Zaccur, Joseph, Nethaniah
and Asarelah; these were under
Asaph, a leader in inspired pro-
3 phecy under the king. Of the sons
of Jeduthun: Gedaliah, Izri,*r* Isaiah,
Shimei, Hashabiah, Mattithiah,
these six under their father Jeduthun, a leader in inspired prophecy
to the accompaniment of the harp,
giving thanks and praise to the
4 LORD. Of the sons of Heman: Bukkiah, Mattaniah, Uzziel, Shubael,
Jerimoth, Hananiah, Hanani,
Eliathah, Giddalti, Romamti-ezer,
Joshbekashah, Mallothi, Hothir,
5 and Mahazioth; all these were sons
of Heman the king's seer, given to
him through the promises of God

for his greater glory. God had
given Heman fourteen sons and
three daughters, and they all served 6
under their father for the singing
in the house of the LORD; they took
part in the service of the house
of God, with cymbals, lutes, and
harps, while Asaph, Jeduthun, and
Heman were under the king. Reck- 7
oned with their kinsmen, trained
singers of the LORD, they brought
the total number of skilled musicians up to two hundred and eighty-
eight. They cast lots for their duties, 8
young and old, master-singer and
apprentice side by side.
The first lot fell*s* to Joseph: he 9
and his brothers and his sons,
twelve.*t* The second to Gedaliah:
he and his brothers and his sons,
twelve. The third to Zaccur: his 10
sons and his brothers, twelve. The 11
fourth to Izri: his sons and his
brothers, twelve. The fifth to 12
Nethaniah: his sons and his brothers, twelve. The sixth to Bukkiah: 13
his sons and his brothers, twelve.
The seventh to Asarelah: his sons 14
and his brothers, twelve. The eighth 15
to Isaiah: his sons and his brothers,
twelve. The ninth to Mattaniah: 16
his sons and his brothers, twelve.
The tenth to Shimei: his sons and 17
his brothers, twelve. The eleventh to 18
Azareel: his sons and his brothers,
twelve. The twelfth to Hashabi- 19
ah: his sons and his brothers,
twelve. The thirteenth to Shubael: 20
his sons and his brothers, twelve.
The fourteenth to Mattithiah: his 21
sons and his brothers, twelve. The 22
fifteenth to Jeremoth: his sons and
his brothers, twelve. The sixteenth 23
to Hananiah: his sons and his
brothers, twelve. The seventeenth 24
to Joshbekashah: his sons and his
brothers, twelve. The eighteenth to 25
Hanani: his sons and his brothers,
twelve. The nineteenth to Mallothi: 26
his sons and his brothers, twelve.
The twentieth to Eliathah: his sons 27
and his brothers, twelve. The 28
twenty-first to Hothir: his sons and
his brothers, twelve. The twenty- 29
second to Giddalti: his sons and
his brothers, twelve. The twenty- 30
third to Mahazioth: his sons and
his brothers, twelve. The twenty- 31
fourth to Romamti-ezer: his sons
and his brothers, twelve.

Door-keepers

The divisions of the door-keepers: **26**
Korahites: Meshelemiah son of
Kore, son of Ebiasaph.*u* Sons of 2
Meshelemiah: Zechariah the eldest,
Jediael the second, Zebediah the
third, Jathniel the fourth, Elam
the fifth, Jehohanan the sixth,
Elioenai the seventh. Sons of Obed- 4
edom: Shemaiah the eldest, Jeho-
zabad the second, Joah the third,
Sacar the fourth, Nethaneel the

---

p sacred officers: or officers of the sanctuary.   q and also: prob. rdg.; Heb. the sons of.   r Prob. rdg.,
cp. verse 11; Heb. Zeri.   s Prob. rdg.; Heb. adds to Asaph.   t he . . . twelve: prob. rdg.; Heb. om.
u son of Ebiasaph: prob. rdg.; Heb. from the sons of Asaph.

5 fifth, Ammiel the sixth, Issachar the seventh, Peulthai the eighth 6 (for God had blessed him). Shemaiah, his son, was the father of sons who had authority in their family, for they were men of great ability.
7 Sons of Shemaiah: Othni, Rephael, Obed, Elzabad and his brothers Elihu and Semachiah, men of 8 ability. All these belonged to the family of Obed-edom; they, their sons and brothers, were men of ability, fit for service in the temple; 9 total: sixty-two. Sons and brothers of Meshelemiah, all men of ability, 10 eighteen. Sons of Hosah, a Merarite: Shimri the chief (he was not the eldest, but his father had made 11 him chief), Hilkiah the second, Tebaliah the third, Zechariah the fourth. Total of Hosah's sons and brothers: thirteen.
12 The male heads of families constituted the divisions of the door-keepers; their duty was to serve in the house of the LORD side by side 13 with their kinsmen. Young and old, family by family, they cast lots 14 for the gates. The lot for the east gate fell to Shelemiah; then lots were cast for his son Zechariah, a prudent counsellor, and he was 15 allotted the north gate. To Obed-edom was allotted the south gate, and the gatehouse to his sons. 16 Hosah*v* was allotted the west gate, together with the Shallecheth gate on the ascending causeway. Guard 17 corresponded to guard. Six Levites were on duty daily on the east side, four on the north and four on the south, and two at each gatehouse; 18 at the western colonnade there were four at the causeway and two 19 at the colonnade itself. These were the divisions of the door-keepers, Korahites and Merarites.

Store-keepers

20 Fellow-Levites were in charge of the stores of the house of God and 21 of the stores of sacred gifts. Of the children of Laadan, descendants of the Gershonite line through Laadan, heads of families in the group of Laadan the Gershonite, 22 Jehiel and*w* his brothers Zetham and Joel were in charge of the stores of the house of the LORD. 23 Of the families of Amram, Izhar, 24 Hebron and Uzziel, Shubael son of Gershom, son of Moses, was 25 overseer of the stores. The line of Eliezer his brother: his son Rehabiah, his son Isaiah, his son Joram, his son Zichri, and his son Shelomoth. 26 This Shelomoth and his kinsmen were in charge of all the stores of the sacred gifts dedicated by David the king, the heads of families, the officers over units of a thousand and a hundred, and other 27 officers of the army. They had dedicated some of the spoils taken in

the wars for the upkeep of the house 28 of the LORD. Everything which Samuel the seer, Saul son of Kish, Abner son of Ner, and Joab son of Zeruiah had dedicated, in short every sacred gift, was under the charge of Shelomoth and his kins-29 men. Of the family of Izhar, Kenaniah and his sons acted as clerks and magistrates in the secular 30 affairs of Israel. Of the family of Hebron, Hashabiah and his kinsmen, men of ability to the number of seventeen hundred, had the oversight of Israel west of the Jordan, both in the work of the LORD and in the service of the king. 31 Also of the family of Hebron, Jeriah was the chief. (In the fortieth year of David's reign search was made in the family histories of the Hebronites, and men of great ability were found among 32 them at Jazer in Gilead.) His kinsmen, all men of ability, two thousand seven hundred of them, heads of families, were charged by King David with the oversight of the Reubenites, the Gadites, and the half tribe of Manasseh, in religious and civil affairs alike.

Officers of the kingdom

27 The number of the Israelites—that is to say, of the heads of families, the officers over units of a thousand and a hundred, and the clerks who had their share in the king's service in the various divisions which took monthly turns of duty throughout the year—was twenty-four thousand in each division.
2 First, Jashobeam son of Zabdiel commanded the division for the first month with twenty-four thou-3 sand in his division; a member of the house of Perez, he was chief officer of the temple staff for the 4 first month. Eleazar son of*x* Dodai the Ahohite commanded the division for the second month with twenty-four thousand in his divi-5 sion. Third, Benaiah son of Jehoiada the chief priest, commander of the army, was the officer for the third month with twenty-four thou-6 sand in his division (he was the Benaiah who was one of the thirty warriors and was a chief among the thirty); but his son Ammizabad 7 commanded his division. Fourth, Asahel, the brother of Joab, was the officer commanding for the fourth month with twenty-four thousand in his division; and his successor was Zebediah his son. 8 Fifth, Shamhuth the Zerahite*y* was the officer commanding for the fifth month with twenty-four thou-9 sand in his division. Sixth, Ira son of Ikkesh, a man of Tekoa, was the officer commanding for the sixth month with twenty-four thou-10 sand in his division. Seventh, Helez

an Ephraimite, from a place unknown, was the officer commanding for the seventh month with twenty-four thousand in his division. Eighth, Sibbecai the Hushathite, 11 of the family of Zerah, was the officer commanding for the eighth month with twenty-four thousand in his division. Ninth, Abiezer, from 12 Anathoth in Benjamin, was the officer commanding for the ninth month with twenty-four thousand in his division. Tenth, Maharai the 13 Netophathite, of the family of Zerah, was the officer commanding for the tenth month with twenty-four thousand in his division. Eleventh, Benaiah the Pirathonite, 14 from Ephraim, was the officer commanding for the eleventh month with twenty-four thousand in his division. Twelfth, Heldai the 15 Netophathite, of the family of Othniel, was the officer commanding for the twelfth month with twenty-four thousand in his division.

The following were the prin-16 cipal officers in charge of the tribes of Israel: of Reuben, Eliezer son of Zichri; of Simeon, Shephatiah son of Maacah; of Levi, 17 Hashabiah son of Kemuel; of Aaron, Zadok; of Judah, Elihu a 18 kinsman of David; of Issachar, Omri son of Michael; of Zebulun, 19 Ishmaiah son of Obadiah; of Naphtali, Jerimoth son of Azriel; of 20 Ephraim, Hoshea son of Azaziah; of the half tribe of Manasseh, Joel son of Pedaiah; of the half 21 of Manasseh in Gilead, Iddo son of Zechariah; of Benjamin, Jaasiel son of Abner; of Dan, Azareel son 22 of Jeroham. These were the officers in charge of the tribes of Israel.

The abandoned census

David took no census of those 23 under twenty years of age, for the LORD had promised to make the Israelites as many as the stars in the heavens. Joab son of Zeruiah 24 did begin to take a census but he did not finish it; this brought harm upon Israel, and the census was not entered in the chronicle of King David's reign.

The king's own officers

Azmoth son of Adiel was in charge 25 of the king's stores; Jonathan son of Uzziah was in charge of the stores in the country, in the cities, in the villages and in the fortresses. Ezri son of Kelub had oversight of 26 the workers on the land; Shimei of 27 Ramah was in charge of the vine-dressers, while Zabdi of Shephem had charge of the produce of the vineyards for the wine-cellars. Baal-28 hanan the Gederite supervised the wild olives and the sycomore-figs in the Shephelah; Joash was in

v Hosah: *prob. rdg.; Heb.* Shuppim and Hosah.   *w* Jehiel and: *prob. rdg.; Heb.* Jehieli. The sons of Jehieli . . .   *x* Eleazar son of: *prob. rdg., cp. 11. 12; Heb. om.*   *y* the Zerahite: *prob. rdg.; Heb.* the Izrah.

29 charge of the oil-stores. Shitrai of Sharon was in charge of the herds grazing in Sharon, Shaphat son of Adlai of the herds in the vales. 30 Obil the Ishmaelite was in charge of the camels, Jehdeiah the Meronothite of the asses. Jaziz the Hagerite was in charge of the flocks. All these were the officers in charge of King David's posses- 32 sions. David's favourite nephew Jonathan, a counsellor, a discreet and learned man, and Jehiel the Hachmonite, were tutors to the king's sons. Ahithophel was a 33 king's counsellor; Hushai the Archite was the King's Friend. Ahitho- 34 phel was succeeded by Jehoiada son of Benaiah, and Abiathar. Joab was commander of the army.

David addresses his people

28 David assembled at Jerusalem all the officers of Israel, the officers over the tribes, over the divisions engaged in the king's service, over the units of a thousand and a hundred, and those in charge of all the property and the cattle of the king and of his sons, as well as the eunuchs, the heroes and all the men of 2 ability. Then King David rose to his feet and said, 'Hear me, kinsmen and people. I had in mind to build a house as a resting-place for the Ark of the Covenant of the LORD which might serve as a footstool for the feet of our God, and I made preparations 3 to build it. But God said to me, "You shall not build a house in honour of my name, for you have been a fighting man and you have 4 shed blood." Nevertheless, the LORD the God of Israel chose me out of all my father's family to be king over Israel in perpetuity; for it was Judah that he chose as ruling tribe, and, out of the house of Judah, my father's family; and among my father's sons it was I whom he was pleased to make king 5 over all Israel. And out of all my sons—for the LORD gave me many sons—he chose Solomon to sit upon the throne of the 6 LORD's sovereignty over Israel; and he said to me, "It is Solomon your son who shall build my house and my courts, for I have chosen him to be a son to me and I will be 7 a father to him. I will establish his sovereignty in perpetuity, if only he steadfastly obeys my commandments and my laws as they are 8 now obeyed." Now therefore, in the presence of all Israel, the assembly of the LORD, and within the hearing of our God, I bid you all study carefully the commandments of the LORD your God, that you may possess this good land and hand it down as an inheritance for all time to your children after 9 you. And you, Solomon my son, acknowledge your father's God and serve him with whole heart and willing mind, for the LORD searches all hearts and discerns every invention of men's thoughts. If you search for him, he will let you find him, but if you forsake him, he will cast you off for ever. 10 Remember, then, that the LORD has chosen you to build a house for a sanctuary: be steadfast and do it.'

David gives the building plans to Solomon

11 David gave Solomon his son the plan of the porch of the temple[z] and its buildings, strong-rooms, roof-chambers and inner courts, and the shrine of expiation;[a] also 12 the plans of all he had in mind for the courts of the house of the LORD and for all the rooms around it, for the stores of God's house and for the stores of the sacred gifts, for the divisions of the priests and the 13 Levites, for all the work connected with the service of the house of the LORD and for all the vessels used in its service. He prescribed 14 the weight of gold for all the gold vessels[b] used in the various services, and the weight of silver[c] for all the silver vessels used in the various services; and the weight of gold for 15 the gold lamp-stands and their lamps; and the weight of silver for the silver lamp-stands, the weight required for each lamp-stand and its lamps according to the use of each; and the weight of gold for each of the 16 tables for the rows of the Bread of the Presence, and of silver for the silver tables. He prescribed also the weight of pure gold 17 for the forks, tossing-bowls and cups, the weight of gold for each of the golden dishes and of silver[c] for each of the silver dishes; the weight also of refined gold for the altar 18 of incense, and of gold for the model of the chariot, that is the cherubim with their wings outspread to screen the Ark of the Covenant of the LORD. 'All this was drafted by the 19 LORD's own hand,' said David; 'my part was to consider the detailed working out of the plan.'

Then David said to Solomon his son, 'Be 20 steadfast and resolute and do it; be neither faint-hearted nor dismayed, for the LORD God, my God, will be with you; he will neither fail you nor forsake you, until you have finished all the work needed for the service of the house of the LORD. Here are 21 the divisions of the priests and the Levites, ready for all the service of the house of God. In all the work you will have the help of every willing craftsman for any task; and the officers and all the people will be entirely at your command.'

The people contribute willingly

King David then said to the whole assembly, **29** 'My son Solomon is the one chosen by God, Solomon alone, a boy of tender years; and this is a great work, for it is a palace not for man but for the LORD God. Now to the best 2

---

z of the temple: *prob. rdg.; Heb. om.*   a the shrine ... expiation: *or* the place for the Ark with its cover.
b for ... vessels: *prob. rdg.; Heb.* for gold.   c of silver: *prob. rdg.; Heb. om.*

of my strength I have made ready for the house of my God gold for the gold work, silver for the silver, bronze for the bronze, iron for the iron, and wood for the woodwork, together with cornelian and other gems for setting, stones for mosaic work, precious stones of every sort, and marble 3 in plenty. Further, because I delight in the house of my God, I give my own private store of gold and silver for the house of my God—over and above all the store which 4 I have collected for the sanctuary—namely three thousand talents of gold, gold from Ophir, and seven thousand talents of fine silver for overlaying the walls of the build- 5 ings, for providing gold for the gold work, silver for the silver, and for any work to be done by skilled craftsmen. Now who is willing to give with open hand to the LORD today?'

6 Then the heads of families, the officers administering the tribes of Israel, the officers over units of a thousand and a hundred, and the officers in charge of the king's service, 7 responded willingly and gave for the work of the house of God five thousand talents of gold, ten thousand darics, ten thousand talents of silver, eighteen thousand talents of bronze, and a hundred thousand talents 8 of iron. Further, those who possessed precious stones gave them to the treasury of the house of the LORD, into the charge of 9 Jehiel the Gershonite. The people rejoiced at this willing response, because in the loyalty of their hearts they had given willingly to the LORD; King David also was full 10 of joy, and he blessed the LORD in the presence of all the assembly and said, 'Blessed art thou, LORD God of our father 11 Israel, from of old and for ever. Thine, O LORD, is the greatness, the power, the glory, the splendour, and the majesty; for everything in heaven and on earth is thine;[d] thine, O LORD, is the sovereignty, and thou art 12 exalted over all as head. Wealth and honour come from thee; thou rulest over all; might and power are of thy disposing; thine it is 13 to give power and strength to all. And now, we give thee thanks, our God, and praise thy glorious name.

14 'But what am I, and what is my people, that we should be able to give willingly like this? For everything comes from thee, and it is only of thy gifts that we give to thee. 15 We are aliens before thee and settlers, as were all our fathers; our days on earth are like a shadow, we have no abiding place. 16 O LORD our God, from thee comes all this wealth that we have laid up to build a house in honour of thy holy name, and everything is thine. I know, O my God, that thou dost 17 test the heart and that plain honesty pleases thee; with an honest heart I have given all these gifts willingly, and have rejoiced now to see thy people here present give willingly to thee. O LORD God of Abraham, Isaac 18 and Israel our fathers, maintain this purpose for ever in thy people's thoughts and direct their hearts toward thyself. Grant that 19 Solomon my son may loyally keep thy commandments, thy solemn charge, and thy statutes, that he may fulfil them all and build the palace for which I have prepared.'

Solomon is installed king

Then, turning to the whole assembly, David 20 said, 'Now bless the LORD your God.' So all the assembly blessed the LORD the God of their fathers, bowing low and prostrating themselves before the LORD and the king. The next day they sacrificed to the LORD 21 and offered whole-offerings to him, a thousand oxen, a thousand rams, a thousand lambs, with the prescribed drink-offerings, and abundant sacrifices for all Israel. So 22 they ate and drank before the LORD that day with great rejoicing. They then appointed Solomon, David's son, king a second time and anointed him as the LORD's prince, and Zadok as priest. So Solomon sat on the 23 LORD's throne as king in place of his father David, and he prospered and all Israel obeyed him. All the officers and the war- 24 riors, as well as all the sons of King David, swore fealty to King Solomon. The LORD 25 made Solomon stand very high in the eyes of all Israel, and bestowed upon him sovereignty such as no king in Israel had had before him.

Other records of David's reign

David son of Jesse had ruled over the whole 26 of Israel, and the length of his reign over 27 Israel was forty years; he ruled for seven years in Hebron, and for thirty-three in Jerusalem. He died in ripe old age, full of 28 years, wealth, and honour; and Solomon his son ruled in his place. The events of 29 King David's reign from first to last are recorded in the books of Samuel the seer, of Nathan the prophet, and of Gad the seer, with a full account of his reign, his 30 prowess, and of the times through which he and Israel and all the kingdoms of the world had passed.

d is thine: *prob. rdg.; Heb. om.*

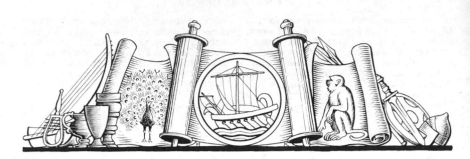

THE SECOND BOOK OF THE
CHRONICLES

Solomon prays for wisdom

1 KING SOLOMON, David's son, strengthened his hold on the kingdom, for the LORD his God was with him and made him very great.

2 Solomon spoke to all Israel, to the officers over units of a thousand and of a hundred, the judges and all the leading men of Israel,
3 the heads of families; and he, together with all the assembled people, went to the hill-shrine at Gibeon; for the Tent of God's Presence, which Moses the LORD's servant
4 had made in the wilderness, was there. (But David had brought up the Ark of God from Kiriath-jearim to the place which he had prepared for it, for he had pitched a tent for
5 it in Jerusalem.) The altar of bronze also, which Bezalel son of Uri, son of Hur, had made, was there in front of the Tabernacle of the LORD; and Solomon and the assembly
6 resorted to it.*a* There Solomon went up to the altar of bronze before the LORD in the Tent of the Presence and offered on it a
7*b* thousand whole-offerings. That night God appeared to Solomon and said, 'What shall
8 I give you? Tell me.' Solomon answered, 'Thou didst show great and constant love to David my father and thou hast made me
9 king in his place. Now, O LORD God, let thy word to David my father be confirmed, for thou hast made me king over a people
10 as numerous as the dust on the earth. Give me now wisdom and knowledge, that I may lead this people; for who is fit to govern
11 this great people of thine?' God answered Solomon, 'Because this is what you desire, because you have not asked for wealth or possessions or honour*c* or the lives of your enemies or even long life for yourself, but have asked for wisdom and knowledge to govern my people over whom I have made you king, wisdom and knowledge are given 12 to you; I shall also give you wealth and possessions and honour*c* such as no king has had before you and none shall have after you.' Then Solomon returned from 13 the hill-shrine at Gibeon, from before the Tent of the Presence, to Jerusalem and ruled over Israel.

Solomon builds up his cavalry

Solomon got together many chariots and 14*e* horses; he had fourteen hundred chariots and twelve thousand horses, and he stabled some in the chariot-towns and kept others at hand in Jerusalem. The king made silver 15 and gold as common in Jerusalem as stones, and cedar as plentiful as sycomore-fig in the Shephelah. Horses were imported from 16 Egypt and Coa for Solomon; the royal merchants obtained them from Coa by purchase. Chariots were imported from 17 Egypt for six hundred silver shekels each, and horses for a hundred and fifty; in the same way the merchants obtained them for export from all the kings of the Hittites and the kings of Aram.

Solomon negotiates with King Huram

Solomon resolved to build a house in honour **2** of the name of the LORD, and a royal palace for himself. He engaged seventy thousand 2 hauliers and eighty thousand quarrymen, and three thousand six hundred men to superintend them. Then Solomon sent this 3*e*

---

a resorted to it: *or* worshipped him.   *b Verses 7–12: cp. 1 Kgs. 3. 5–14.*   *c Or* riches.   *d Verses*
14–17: cp. 9. 25–28; 1 Kgs. 10. 26–29.   *e Verses 3–16: cp. 1 Kgs. 5. 2–11.*

message to Huram king of Tyre: 'You were so good as to send my father David cedar-wood to build his royal residence. Now I am about to build a house in honour of the name of the LORD my God and to consecrate it to him, so that I may burn fragrant incense in it before him, and present the rows of the Bread of the Presence regularly, and whole-offerings morning and evening, on the sabbaths and the new moons and the appointed festivals of the LORD our God; for this is a duty laid upon Israel for ever. 5 The house I am about to build will be a great house, because our God is greater than all 6 gods. But who is able to build him a house when heaven itself, the highest heaven, cannot contain him? And who am I that I should build him a house, except that I may 7 burn sacrifices before him? Send me then a skilled craftsman, a man able to work in gold and silver, copper[f] and iron, and in purple, crimson, and violet yarn, who is also an expert engraver and will work with my skilled workmen in Judah and in Jerusalem who were provided by David my father. 8 Send me also cedar, pine, and algum timber from Lebanon, for I know that your men are expert at felling the trees of Lebanon; my 9 men will work with yours to get an ample supply of timber ready for me, for the house which I shall build will be great and wonder-10 ful. I will supply provisions for your servants, the woodmen who fell the trees: twenty thousand kor of wheat and twenty thousand kor of barley, with twenty thousand bath of wine and twenty thousand bath of oil.'

Huram king of Tyre sent this answer by 11 letter to Solomon: 'It is because of the love which the LORD has for his people that he has made you king over them.' The letter 12 went on to say, 'Blessed is the LORD the God of Israel, maker of heaven and earth, who has given to King David a wise son, endowed with intelligence and understanding, to build a house for the LORD and a royal palace for himself. I now send you a skilful 13 and experienced craftsman, master Huram. He is the son of a Danite woman, his father 14 a Tyrian; he is an experienced worker in gold and silver, copper[f] and iron, stone and wood, as well as in purple, violet, and crimson yarn, and in fine linen; he is also a trained engraver who will be able to work with your own skilled craftsmen and those of my lord David your father, to any design submitted to him. Now then, let my lord 15 send his servants the wheat and the barley, the oil and the wine, which he promised; we will fell all the timber in Lebanon that 16 you need and float it as rafts to the roadstead at Joppa, and you will convey it from there up to Jerusalem.'

Solomon takes a census

Solomon took a census of all the aliens resi- 17 dent in Israel, similar to the census which David his father had taken; these were found to be a hundred and fifty-three thousand six hundred. He made seventy thousand of them 18 hauliers and eighty thousand quarrymen, and three thousand six hundred superintendents to make the people work.

Solomon builds the Temple

3 Then Solomon began to build the house of the LORD in Jerusalem on Mount Moriah, where the LORD had appeared to his father David, on the site which David had prepared on the threshing-floor of Ornan the Jebusite. He began to build 2 in the second month of the fourth 3 year of his reign. These are the foundations which Solomon laid for building the house of God: the length, according to the old standard of measurement, was sixty 4 cubits and the breadth twenty. The vestibule in front of the house[h] was twenty cubits long, spanning the whole breadth of the house, and its height was twenty; on the inside he 5 overlaid it with pure gold. He panelled the large chamber with pine, covered it with fine gold and carved on it palm-trees and chain-work. 6 He adorned the house with precious stones for decoration, and the gold 7 he used was from Parvaim. He

covered the whole house with gold, its rafters and frames, its walls and doors; and he carved cherubim on the walls. 8 He made the Most Holy Place twenty cubits long, corresponding to the breadth of the house, and twenty cubits broad. He covered 9 it all with six hundred talents of fine gold, and the weight of the nails was fifty shekels of gold. He also covered the upper chambers with gold. 10[i] In the Most Holy Place he carved two images of cherubim and over-11 laid them with gold. The total span of the wings of the cherubim was twenty cubits. A wing of the one cherub extended five cubits to reach the wall of the house, while 12 its other wing reached out five cubits to meet a wing of the other cherub. Similarly, a wing of the second cherub extended five cubits to reach the other wall of the house, while its other wing met a wing of 13 the first cherub. The wings of these

cherubim extended twenty cubits; they stood with their feet on the ground, facing the outer chamber. He made the Veil of violet, purple, 14 and crimson yarn, and fine linen, and embroidered cherubim on it.

In front of the house he erected 15[j] two pillars eighteen cubits high, with an architrave five cubits high on top of each. He made chain-16 work like a necklace[k] and set it round the tops of the pillars, and he carved a hundred pomegranates and set them in the chain-work. He 17 erected the two pillars in front of the temple, one on the right and one on the left; the one on the right he named Jachin[l] and the one on the left Boaz.[m]

He then made an altar of bronze, **4** twenty cubits long, twenty cubits broad, and ten cubits high. He also 2[n] made the Sea of cast metal; it was round in shape, the diameter from rim to rim being ten cubits; it stood five cubits high, and it took a line thirty cubits long to go round it.

f Or bronze. *g* Verses 2–4: cp. 1 Kgs. 6. 1–3. *h* house: prob. rdg.; Heb. length. *i* Verses 10–13: cp. 1 Kgs. 6. 23–28. *j* Verses 15–17: cp. 1 Kgs. 7. 15–21. *k* necklace: prob. rdg.; Heb. obscure. *l* Or Jachin, meaning It shall stand. *m* Or Booz, meaning In strength. *n* Verses 2–5: cp. 1 Kgs. 7. 23–26.

F *

3 Under the Sea, on every side, completely surrounding the thirty° cubits of its circumference, were what looked like gourds,^{p} two rows of them, cast in one piece with the
4 Sea itself. It was mounted on twelve oxen, three facing north, three west, three south, and three east, their hind quarters turned inwards; the Sea rested on top of
5 them. Its thickness was a handbreadth; its rim was made like that of a cup, shaped like the calyx of a lily; when full it held three thou-
6 sand bath. He also made ten basins for washing, setting five on the left side and five on the right; in these they rinsed everything used for the whole-offering. The Sea was made for the priests to wash in.
7 He made ten golden lamp-stands in the prescribed manner and set them in the temple, five on the right
8 side and five on the left. He also made ten tables and placed them in the temple, five on the right and five on the left; and he made a
9 hundred golden tossing-bowls. He made the court of the priests and the great precinct and the doors for it, and overlaid the doors of both
10 with copper; he put the Sea at the right side, at the south-east corner of the temple.
11 ^{q} Huram made the pots, the shovels, and the tossing-bowls. So he finished the work which he had undertaken for King Solomon on
12 the house of God. The two pillars; the two bowl-shaped capitals^r on the tops of the pillars; the two ornamental networks to cover the two bowl-shaped capitals on the
13 tops of the pillars; the four hundred pomegranates for the two networks, two rows of pomegranates for each network, to cover the two bowl-shaped capitals on
14 the two^s pillars; the ten^t trolleys and the ten^t basins on the trolleys;
15 the one Sea and the twelve oxen
16 which supported it; the pots, the shovels, and the tossing-bowls^u— all these^v objects master Huram made of bronze, burnished work for King Solomon for the house of the LORD. In the Plain of the Jor-17 dan the king cast them, in the foundry between Succoth and Zeredah. Solomon made great quantities 18 of all these objects; the weight of the copper^w used was beyond reckoning.

Solomon made also all the fur-19 nishings for the house of God: the golden altar, the tables upon which was set the Bread of the Presence, 20 the lamp-stands of red gold whose lamps burned before the inner shrine in the prescribed manner, the flowers and lamps and tongs of 21 solid gold, the snuffers, tossing-22 bowls, saucers, and firepans of red gold, and, at the entrance to the house, the inner doors leading to the Most Holy Place and those leading to the sanctuary, of gold. When all the work which Solomon did for the house of the LORD **5** was completed, he brought in the sacred treasures of his father David, the silver, the gold, and the vessels, and deposited them in the storehouses of the house of God.

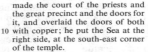

Solomon installs the Ark

2 ^{x} Then Solomon summoned the elders of Israel, and all the heads of the tribes who were chiefs of families in Israel, to assemble in Jerusalem, in order to bring up the Ark of the Covenant of the LORD from the City
3 of David, which is called Zion. All the men of Israel assembled in the king's presence at the pilgrim-feast in the seventh month.
4 When the elders of Israel had all come, the
5 Levites took the Ark and carried it up with the Tent of the Presence and all the sacred furnishings of the Tent: it was the priests and the Levites together who carried them
6 up. King Solomon and the whole congregation of Israel, assembled with him before the Ark, sacrificed sheep and oxen in num-
7 bers past counting or reckoning. Then the priests brought in the Ark of the Covenant of the LORD to its place, the inner shrine of the house, the Most Holy Place, beneath the wings of the cherubim. The cherubim 8 spread their wings over the place of the Ark, and formed a covering above the Ark and its poles. The poles projected, and their ends 9 could be seen from the Holy Place immediately in front of the inner shrine, but from nowhere else outside; they are there to this day. There was nothing inside the Ark but 10 the two tablets which Moses had put there at Horeb, the tablets of the covenant^y which the LORD made with the Israelites when they left Egypt.

Songs of praise

Now when the priests came out of the Holy 11 Place (for all the priests who were present had hallowed themselves without keeping to their divisions), all the levitical singers, 12 Asaph, Heman, and Jeduthun, their sons and their kinsmen, clothed in fine linen, stood with cymbals, lutes, and harps, to the east of the altar, together with a hundred and twenty priests who blew trumpets. Now the 13 trumpeters and the singers joined in unison to sound forth praise and thanksgiving to the LORD, and the song was raised with trumpets, cymbals, and musical instruments, in praise of the LORD, because 'that^z is good, for his love endures for ever'; and the house was filled with the cloud of the glory of the LORD. The priests could not continue to 14 minister because of the cloud, for the glory

o *Prob. rdg.; Heb.* ten.   p *Prob. rdg., cp. 1 Kgs. 7. 24; Heb.* oxen.   q *4. 11—5. 1: cp. 1 Kgs. 7. 40—51.*
r *bowl-shaped capitals: prob. rdg., cp. 1 Kgs. 7. 41; Heb.* the bowls and the capitals.   s *two: prob. rdg., cp. 1 Kgs. 7. 42; Heb.* surface of the.   t *the ten: prob. rdg., cp. 1 Kgs. 7. 43; Heb.* he made the . . .   u *tossing-bowls: prob. rdg., cp. 1 Kgs. 7. 45; Heb.* forks.   v *Prob. rdg., cp. 1 Kgs. 7. 45; Heb.* their.   w *Or* bronze.
x *Verses 2—10: cp. 1 Kgs. 8. 1—9.*   y *the tablets of the covenant: prob. rdg., cp. 1 Kgs. 8. 9; Heb. om.*
z *Or* he.

a of the LORD filled the house of God. Then Solomon said:

O LORD who hast chosen to dwell in thick darkness,

2 here have I built thee a lofty house,
a habitation for thee to occupy for ever.

Solomon blesses Israel

3 And as they stood waiting, the king turned round and blessed all the assembly of Israel 4 in these words: 'Blessed be the LORD the God of Israel who spoke directly to my father David and has himself fulfilled his 5 promise. For he said, "From the day when I brought my people out of Egypt, I chose no city out of all the tribes of Israel where I should build a house for my Name to be there, nor did I choose any man to be prince 6 over my people Israel. But I chose Jerusalem for my Name to be there, and I chose David 7 to be over my people Israel." My father David had in mind to build a house in honour of the name of the LORD the God of Israel, 8 but the LORD said to him, "You purposed to build a house in honour of my name; and 9 your purpose was good. Nevertheless, you shall not build it; but the son who is to be born to you, he shall build the house in 10 honour of my name." The LORD has now fulfilled his promise: I have succeeded my father David and taken his place on the throne of Israel, as the LORD promised; and I have built the house in honour of the name 11 of the LORD the God of Israel. I have installed there the Ark containing the covenant of the LORD which he made with Israel.'

Solomon prays to the LORD

12 Then Solomon, standing in front of the altar of the LORD, in the presence of the whole assembly of Israel, spread out his 13 hands. He had made a bronze*b* platform, five cubits long, five cubits broad, and three cubits high, and had placed it in the centre of the precinct. He mounted it and knelt down in the presence of the assembly, and, spreading out his hands towards heaven, 14 he said, 'O LORD God of Israel, there is no god like thee in heaven or on earth, keeping covenant with thy servants and showing them constant love while they continue faith- 15 ful to thee in heart and soul. Thou hast kept thy promise to thy servant David my father; by thy deeds this day thou hast fulfilled 16 what thou didst say to him in words. Now, therefore, O LORD God of Israel, keep this promise of thine to thy servant David my father: "You shall never want for a man appointed by me to sit on the throne of Israel, if only your sons look to their ways and conform to my law, as you have done

in my sight." And now, O LORD God of 17 Israel, let the word which thou didst speak to thy servant David be confirmed.

'But can God indeed dwell with man on 18 the earth? Heaven itself, the highest heaven, cannot contain thee; how much less this house that I have built! Yet attend to the 19 prayer and the supplication of thy servant, O LORD my God; listen to the cry and the prayer which thy servant utters before thee, that thine eyes may ever be upon this house 20 day and night, this place of which thou didst say, "It shall receive my Name"; so mayest thou hear thy servant when he prays towards this place. Hear thou the supplica- 21 tions of thy servant and of thy people Israel when they pray towards this place. Hear from heaven thy dwelling and, when thou hearest, forgive.

'When a man wrongs his neighbour and 22 he is adjured to take an oath, and the adjuration is made before thy altar in this house, then do thou hear from heaven and act: 23 be thou thy servants' judge, requiting the guilty man and bringing his deeds upon his own head, acquitting the innocent and rewarding him as his innocence may deserve.

'When thy people Israel are defeated by 24 an enemy because they have sinned against thee, and they turn back to thee, confessing thy name and making their prayer and supplication before thee in this house, do 25 thou hear from heaven; forgive the sin of thy people Israel and restore them to the land which thou gavest to them and to their forefathers.

'When the heavens are shut up and there 26 is no rain, because thy servant and thy people Israel have sinned against thee, and when they pray towards this place, confessing thy name and forsaking their sin when they feel thy punishment, do thou hear in 27 heaven and forgive their sin; so mayest thou teach them the good way which they should follow, and grant rain to thy land which thou hast given to thy people as their own possession.

'If there is famine in the land, or pestilence, 28 or black blight or red, or locusts new-sloughed or fully grown, or if their enemies besiege them in any*c* of their cities, or if plague or sickness befall them, then hear the 29 prayer or supplication of every man among thy people Israel, as each one, prompted by his own suffering and misery, spreads out his hands towards this house; hear it from 30 heaven thy dwelling and forgive. And, as thou knowest a man's heart, reward him according to his deeds, for thou alone knowest the hearts of all men; and so they will 31 fear and obey thee all their lives in the land thou gavest to our forefathers.

a Verses 1–39: cp. 1 Kgs. 8. 12–50.   *b Or copper.*   *c in any: prob. rdg.; Heb. in the land.*

32 'The foreigner too, the man who does not belong to thy people Israel, but has come from a distant land because of thy great fame and thy strong hand and arm outstretched, when he comes and prays towards 33 this house, hear from heaven thy dwelling and respond to the call which the foreigner makes to thee, so that like thy people Israel all peoples of the earth may know thy fame and fear thee, and learn that this house which I have built bears thy name.

34 'When thy people go to war with their enemies, wherever thou dost send them, and they pray to thee, turning towards this city which thou hast chosen and towards this house which I have built in honour of thy 35 name, do thou from heaven hear their prayer and supplication, and grant them justice.

36 'Should they sin against thee (and what man is free from sin?) and shouldst thou in thy anger give them over to an enemy, who 37 carries them captive to a land far or near; if in the land of their captivity they learn their lesson and turn back and make supplication to thee in that land and say, "We have sin-38 ned and acted perversely and wickedly", if they turn back to thee with heart and soul in the land of their captivity to which they have been taken, and pray, turning towards their land which thou gavest to their forefathers and towards this city which thou didst choose and this house which I have 39 built in honour of thy name; then from heaven thy dwelling do thou hear their prayer and supplications and grant them justice. Forgive thy people their sins against 40 thee. Now, O my God, let thine eyes be open and thy ears attentive to the prayer made in 41 this place. Arise now, O LORD God, and come to thy place of rest, thou and the Ark of thy might. Let thy priests, O LORD God, be clothed with salvation and thy saints 42 rejoice in prosperity. O LORD God, reject not thy anointed prince; remember thy servant David's loyal service.'[d]

Fire from heaven

7 When Solomon had finished this prayer, fire came down from heaven and consumed the whole-offering and the sacrifices, while 2 the glory of the LORD filled the house. The priests were unable to enter the house of the LORD because the glory of the LORD had 3 filled it. All the Israelites were watching as the fire came down with the glory of the LORD on the house, and where they stood on the paved court they bowed low to the ground and worshipped and gave thanks to the LORD, because 'that[e] is good, for his love endures for ever.'

Celebrations

Then the king and all the people offered 4 sacrifice before the LORD. King Solomon 5 offered a sacrifice of twenty-two thousand oxen and a hundred and twenty thousand sheep; in this way the king and all the people dedicated the house of God. The priests 6 stood at their appointed posts; so too the Levites with their musical instruments for the LORD's service, which King David had made for giving thanks to the LORD—'for his love endures for ever'—whenever he rendered praise with their help; opposite them, the priests sounded their trumpets; and all the Israelites were standing there.

Then Solomon consecrated the centre of 7 the court which lay in front[g] of the house of the LORD; there he offered the wholeofferings and the fat portions of the sharedofferings, because the bronze altar which he had made could not take the wholeoffering, the grain-offering, and the fat portions. So Solomon and all Israel with 8 him, a very great assembly from Lebohamath to the Torrent of Egypt, celebrated the pilgrim-feast at that time for seven days. On the eighth day they held a closing 9 ceremony; for they had celebrated the dedication of the altar for seven days; the pilgrim-feast lasted seven days. On the 1 twenty-third day of the seventh month he sent the people to their homes, happy and glad at heart for all the prosperity granted by the LORD to David and Solomon and to his people Israel.

The LORD appears again to Solomon

When Solomon had finished the house of 1 the LORD and the royal palace and had successfully carried out all that he had planned for the house of the LORD and the palace, the LORD appeared to him by night 1 and said, 'I have heard your prayer and I have chosen this place to be my place of sacrifice. When I shut up the heavens and 1 there is no rain, or command the locusts to consume the land, or send a pestilence against my people, if my people whom I 1 have named my own submit and pray to me and seek me and turn back from their evil ways, I will hear from heaven and forgive their sins and heal their land. Now my eyes 1 will be open and my ears attentive to the prayers which are made in this place. I have chosen and consecrated this house, that my Name may be there for all time and my eyes and my heart be fixed on it for ever. And if 1 you, on your part, live in my sight as your father David lived, doing all I command you, and observing my statutes and my

---

d thy servant . . . service: or thy constant love for David thy servant.   e Or he.   f Verses 7–22:
cp. 1 Kgs. 8. 64—9. 9.   g Or to the east.

18 judgements, then I will establish your royal throne, as I promised by a covenant granted to your father David when I said, "You shall 19 never want for a man to rule over Israel." But if you turn away and forsake my statutes and my commandments which I have set before you, and if you go and serve other gods and 20 prostrate yourselves before them, then I will uproot you from my land which I gave you, I will reject this house which I have consecrated in honour of my name, and make it a byword and an object-lesson among all 21 peoples. And this house will become a ruin; every passer-by will be appalled at the sight of it, and they will ask, "Why has the LORD 22 so treated this land and this house?" The answer will be, "Because they forsook the LORD the God of their fathers, who brought them out of Egypt, and clung to other gods, prostrating themselves before them and serving them; that is why the LORD has brought this great evil on them."'

Solomon consolidates his kingdom

1ʰ Solomon had taken twenty years to build the house of the LORD and his own palace, 2 and he rebuilt the cities which Huram had 3 given him, and settled Israelites in them. He 4 went to Hamath-zobah and seized it, and rebuilt Tadmor in the wilderness and all the store-cities which he had built in Hamath. 5 He also built Upper Beth-horon and Lower Beth-horon as fortified cities with walls and 6 barred gates, and Baalath, as well as all his store-cities, and all the towns where he quartered his chariots and horses; and he carried out all his cherished plans for building in Jerusalem, in the Lebanon, and throughout his whole dominion. All the 7 survivors of the Hittites, Amorites, Perizzites, Hivites, and Jebusites, who did not belong to Israel—that is their descendants 8 who survived in the land, wherever the Israelites had been unable to exterminate them— were employed by Solomon on forced labour, as they still are. He put none of the Israelites 9 to forced labour for his public works; they were his fighting men, his captains and lieutenants, and the commanders of his chariots and of his cavalry. These were King 10 Solomon's officers, two hundred and fifty of them, in charge of the foremen who superintended the people.

Solomon brought Pharaoh's daughter up 11 from the City of David to the house he had built for her, for he said, 'No wife of mine shall live in the house of David king of Israel, because this place which the Ark of the LORD has entered isⁱ holy.'

Solomon completes the Temple

Then Solomon offered whole-offerings to the 12 LORD on the altar which he had built to the east of the vestibule, according to what was 13 required for each day, making offerings according to the law of Moses for the sabbaths, the new moons, and the three annual appointed feasts—the pilgrim-feasts of Unleavened Bread, of Weeks, and of Tabernacles.ʲ Following the practice of his father 14 David, he drew up the roster of service for the priests and that for the Levites for leading the praise and for waiting upon the priests, as each day required, and that for the door-keepers at each gate; for such was the instruction which David the man of God

h Verses 1–18: cp. 1 Kgs. 9. 10–28.
j Or Booths.

i this place which . . . is: prob. rdg.; Heb. those which . . . are.

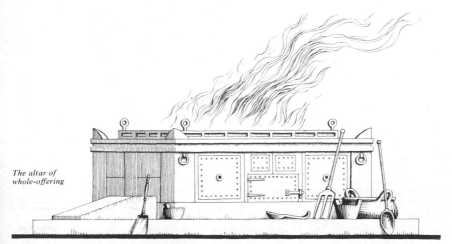

The altar of
whole-offering

15 had given. The instructions which David had given concerning the priests and the Levites and concerning the treasuries were not forgotten.

16 By this time all Solomon's work was achieved, from the foundation of the house of the LORD to its completion; the house of

17 the LORD was perfect. Then Solomon went to Ezion-geber and to Eloth on the coast of

18 Edom, and Huram sent ships under the command of his own officers and manned by crews of experienced seamen; and these, in company with Solomon's servants, went to Ophir and brought back four hundred and fifty talents of gold, which they delivered to King Solomon.

The queen of Sheba visits Solomon

9 1ᵏ The queen of Sheba heard of Solomon's fame and came to test him with hard questions. She arrived in Jerusalem with a very large retinue, camels laden with spices, gold in abundance, and precious stones. When she came to Solomon, she told him every-

2 thing she had in her mind, and Solomon answered all her questions; not one of them

3 was too abstruse for him to answer. When the queen of Sheba saw the wisdom of

4 Solomon, the house which he had built, the food on his table, the courtiers sitting round him, his attendants and his cupbearers in their livery standing behind, and the stairs by which he went up to the house of the LORD, there was no more spirit left in her.

5 Then she said to the king, 'The report which I heard in my own country about you and

6 your wisdom was true, but I did not believe what they told me until I came and saw for myself. Indeed, I was not told half of the greatness of your wisdom; you surpass the

7 report which I had of you. Happy are your wives, happy these courtiers of yours who wait on you every day and hear your wis-

8 dom! Blessed be the LORD your God who has delighted in you and has set you on his throne as his king; because in his love your God has elected Israel to make it endure for ever, he has made you king over it to main-

9 tain law and justice.' Then she gave the king a hundred and twenty talents of gold, spices in great abundance, and precious stones. There had never been any spices to equal those which the queen of Sheba gave to King Solomon.

10 Besides all this, the servants of Huram and of Solomon, who had brought gold from Ophir, brought also cargoes of algum

11 wood and precious stones. The king used the wood to make stands for the house of the LORD and for the royal palace, as well as harps and lutes for the singers. The like

of them had never before been seen in the land of Judah.

12 King Solomon gave the queen of Sheba all she desired, whatever she asked, besides his gifts in return forˡ what she had brought him. Then she departed and returned with her retinue to her own land.

Solomon's wealth and wisdom

13 Now the weight of gold which Solomon received yearly was six hundred and sixty-

14 six talents, in addition to the tolls levied on merchants and on traders who imported goods; all the kings of Arabia and the regional governors alsoᵐ brought gold and silver to the king.

15 King Solomon made two hundred shields of beaten gold, and six hundred shekels of

16 gold went to the making of each one; he also made three hundred bucklers of beaten gold, and three hundred shekels of gold went to the making of each buckler. The king

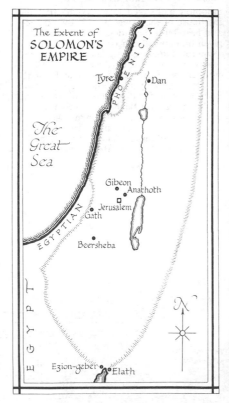

The Extent of
SOLOMON'S
EMPIRE

PHOENICIA

Tyre
•Dan

The Great Sea

Gibeon
• Anathoth
Jerusalem
Gath
EGYPT
Beersheba

EGYPT

Ezion-geber• •Elath

---

k Verses 1–24: cp. 1 Kgs. 10. 1–25.   l his gifts . . . for: prob. rdg.; Heb. om.   m all . . . also: or and on all the kings of Arabia and the regional governors who . . .

put these into the House of the Forest of Lebanon.

17 The king also made a great throne of
18 ivory and overlaid it with pure gold. Six steps and a footstool for the throne were all encased in gold. There were arms on each side of the seat, with a lion standing beside
19 each of them, and twelve lions stood on the six steps, one at either end of each step. Nothing like it had ever been made for any
20 monarch. All Solomon's drinking vessels were of gold, and all the plate in the House of the Forest of Lebanon was of red gold; silver was reckoned of no value in the days
21 of Solomon. The king had a fleet of ships plying to Tarshish with Huram's men; once every three years this fleet of merchantmen came home, bringing gold and silver, ivory, apes, and monkeys.

22 Thus King Solomon outdid all the kings
23 of the earth in wealth and wisdom, and all the kings of the earth courted him, to hear the wisdom which God had put in his heart.
24 Each brought his gift with him, vessels of silver and gold, garments, perfumes and spices, horses and mules, so much year by year.
25 *n* Solomon had standing for four thousand horses and chariots, and twelve thousand cavalry horses, and he stabled some in the chariot-towns and kept others at hand in
26 Jerusalem. He ruled over all the kings from the Euphrates to the land of the Philistines
27 and the border of Egypt. He made silver as common in Jerusalem as stones, and cedar as plentiful as sycomore-fig in the Shephelah.
28 Horses were imported from Egypt and from all countries for Solomon.

Other records of Solomon's reign

29 *o* The rest of the acts of Solomon's reign, from first to last, are recorded in the history of Nathan the prophet, in the prophecy of Ahijah of Shiloh, and in the visions of Iddo the seer concerning Jeroboam son of Nebat.
30 Solomon ruled in Jerusalem over the whole
31 of Israel for forty years. Then he rested with his forefathers and was buried in the city of David his father, and he was succeeded by his son Rehoboam.

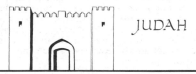

JUDAH

Rehoboam is made king

p Rehoboam went to Shechem, for all Israel
2 had gone there to make him king. When Jeroboam son of Nebat heard of it in Egypt, where he had taken refuge to escape Sol-
3 omon, he returned from Egypt. They now recalled him, and he and all Israel came to
4 Rehoboam and said, 'Your father laid a cruel yoke upon us; but if you will now lighten the cruel slavery he imposed on us and the heavy yoke he laid on us, we will
5 serve you.' 'Give me three days,' he said, 'and come back again.' So the people went
6 away. King Rehoboam then consulted the elders who had been in attendance on his father Solomon while he lived: 'What answer
7 do you advise me to give to this people?' And they said, 'If you show yourself well-disposed to this people and gratify them by speaking kindly to them, they will be your servants
8 ever after.' But he rejected the advice which the elders gave him. He next consulted those who had grown up with him, the young men
9 in attendance, and asked them, 'What answer do you advise me to give to this people's request that I should lighten the yoke which my father laid on them?' The
10 young men replied, 'Give this answer to the people who say that your father made their yoke heavy and ask you to lighten it; tell them: "My little finger is thicker than my
11 father's loins. My father laid a heavy yoke on you; I will make it heavier. My father used the whip on you; but I will use the
12 lash."' Jeroboam and the people all came back to Rehoboam on the third day, as the
13 king had ordered. And the king gave them a harsh answer. He rejected the advice which
14 the elders had given him and spoke to the people as the young men had advised: 'My father made your yoke heavy; I will make it heavier. My father used the whip on you;
15 but I will use the lash.' So the king would not listen to the people; for the LORD had given this turn to the affair, in order that the word he had spoken by Ahijah of Shiloh to Jeroboam son of Nebat might be fulfilled.

Israel rebels against Judah

16 When all Israel saw*q* that the king would not listen to them, they answered:

What share have we in David?
We have no lot in the son of Jesse.
Away to your homes, O Israel;
now see to your own house, David.

17 So all Israel went to their homes, and Rehoboam ruled over those Israelites who lived in the cities of Judah.
18 Then King Rehoboam sent out Hadoram, the commander of the forced levies, but the Israelites stoned him to death; whereupon King Rehoboam mounted his chariot in

n Verses 25–28: cp. 1. 14–17; 1 Kgs. 10. 26–29.   *o Verses 29–31: cp. 1 Kgs. 11. 41–43.*   *p Verses 1–19: cp. 1 Kgs. 12. 1–19.*   *q saw: prob. rdg., cp. 1 Kgs. 12. 16; Heb. om.*

19 haste and fled to Jerusalem. From that day to this, Israel has been in rebellion against the house of David.

Strengthening Judah

11 1ʳ When Rehoboam reached Jerusalem, he assembled the tribes of Judah and Benjamin, a hundred and eighty thousand chosen warriors, to fight against Israel and recover 2 his kingdom. But the word of the LORD came 3 to Shemaiah the man of God: 'Say to Rehoboam son of Solomon, king of Judah, and to all the Israelites in Judah and Benjamin, 4 "This is the word of the LORD: You shall not go up to make war on your kinsmen. Return to your homes, for this is my will."' So they listened to the word of the LORD and abandoned their campaign against Jeroboam.

5 Rehoboam resided in Jerusalem and built up the defences of certain cities in Judah. 6 The cities in Judah and Benjamin which he fortified were Bethlehem, Etam, Tekoa, 7 8 Beth-zur, Soco, Adullam, Gath, Mareshah, 9 10 Ziph, Adoraim, Lachish, Azekah, Zorah, 11 Aijalon, and Hebron. He strengthened the fortifications of these fortified cities, and put governors in them, as well as supplies of 12 food, oil, and wine. Also he stored shields and spears in every one of the cities, and strengthened their fortifications. Thus he retained possession of Judah and Benjamin. 13 Now the priests and the Levites throughout the whole of Israel resorted to Re- 14 hoboam from all their territories; for the Levites had left all their common land and their own patrimony and had gone to Judah and Jerusalem, because Jeroboam and his successors rejected their services as priests 15 of the LORD, and he appointed his own priests for the hill-shrines, for the demons,ˢ and for 16 the calves which he had made. Those, from all the tribes of Israel, who were resolved to seek the LORD the God of Israel followed the Levites to Jerusalem to sacrifice to the LORD 17 the God of their fathers. So they strengthened the kingdom of Judah and for three years made Rehoboam son of Solomon secure, because he followed the example of David and Solomon during that time.

Rehoboam's family

18 Rehoboam married Mahalath, whose father was Jerimoth son of David and whose mother was Abihail daughter of Eliab son 19 of Jesse. His sons by her were: Jeush, 20 Shemariah and Zaham. Next he married Maacah granddaughter of Absalom, who bore him Abijah, Attai, Ziza and Shelomith. 21 Of all his wives and concubines, Rehoboam loved Maacah most; he had in all eighteen

wives and sixty concubines and became the father of twenty-eight sons and sixty daughters. He appointed Abijah son of Maacah 22 chief among his brothers, making him crown prince and planning to make him his successor on the throne. He showed discretion 23 in detailing his sons to take charge of all the fortified cities throughout the whole territory of Judah and Benjamin; he also made generous provision for them and procured themᵗ wives.

Shishak invades Judah

When the kingdom of Rehoboam was on a 12 firm footing and he became strong, he forsook the law of the LORD, he and all Israel with him. In the fifth year of Rehoboam's 2 reign, because of this disloyalty to the LORD, Shishak king of Egypt attacked Jerusalem with twelve hundred chariots and sixty 3 thousand horsemen, and brought with him from Egypt an innumerable following of Libyans, Sukkites, and Cushites.ᵘ He cap- 4 tured the fortified cities of Judah and reached Jerusalem. Then Shemaiah the prophet came 5 to Rehoboam and the leading men of Judah, who had assembled in Jerusalem before the advance of Shishak, and said to them, 'This is the word of the LORD: You have abandoned me; therefore I now abandon you to Shishak.' The princes of Israel and the king 6 submitted and said, 'The LORD is just.' When the LORD saw that they had sub- 7 mitted, there came from him this word to Shemaiah: 'Because they have submitted I will not destroy them, I will let them barely escape; my wrath shall not be poured out on Jerusalem by means of Shishak, but they 8 shall become his servants; then they will know the difference between serving me and serving the rulers of other countries.' Shi- 9ᵛ shak king of Egypt in his attack on Jerusalem removed the treasures of the house of the LORD and of the royal palace. He seized everything, including the shields of gold that Solomon had made. King Re- 10 hoboam replaced them with bronze shields and entrusted them to the officers of the escort who guarded the entrance of the royal palace. Whenever the king entered the house 11 of the LORD, the escort entered, carrying the shields; afterwards they returned them to the guard-room. Because Rehoboam submitted, 12 the LORD's wrath was averted from him, and he was not utterly destroyed; Judah enjoyed prosperity.

A summary of Rehoboam's reign

Thus King Rehoboam increased his power 13 in Jerusalem. He was forty-one years old

---

r Verses 1–4: cp. 1 Kgs. 12. 21–24.   s Or satyrs.   t procured them: prob. rdg.; Heb. asked for a multitude of . . .   u Or Nubians.   v Verses 9–11: cp. 1 Kgs. 14. 25–28.   w Verses 13–16: cp. 1 Kgs. 14. 29–31.

when he came to the throne, and he reigned for seventeen years in Jerusalem, the city which the LORD had chosen out of all the tribes of Israel as the place to receive his Name. Rehoboam's mother was a woman 14 of Ammon called Naamah. He did what was wrong, he did not make a practice of seeking 15 guidance of the LORD. The events of Rehoboam's reign, from first to last, are recorded in the histories of Shemaiah the prophet and Iddo the seer.ˣ There was continual fighting between Rehoboam and Jeroboam. 16 oboam. He rested with his forefathers and was buried in the city of David; and he was succeeded by his son Abijah.

Abijah reigns over Judah

13 In the eighteenth year of King Jeroboam's 2 reign Abijah became king of Judah. He reigned in Jerusalem for three years; his mother was Maacah daughter of Uriel of Gibeah. There was fighting between Abijah 3 and Jeroboam. Abijah drew up his army of four hundred thousand picked troops in order of battle, while Jeroboam formed up against him with eight hundred thousand 4 picked troops. Abijah took up position on the slopes of Mount Zemaraim in the hill-country of Ephraim and called out, 'Hear 5 me, Jeroboam and all Israel: Ought you not to know that the LORD the God of Israel gave the kingship over Israel to David and his descendants in perpetuity by a covenant of 6 salt? Yet Jeroboam son of Nebat, the servant of Solomon son of David, rose in 7 rebellion against his lord, and certain worthless scoundrels gathered round him, who stubbornly opposed Solomon's son Rehoboam when he was young and inexperienced, 8 and he was no match for them. Now you propose to match yourselves against the kingdom of the LORD as ruled by David's sons, you and your mob of supporters and the golden calves which Jeroboam has made to 9 be your gods. Have you not dismissed from office the Aaronites, priests of the LORD, and the Levites, and followed the practice of other lands in appointing priests? Now, if any man comes for consecration with an offering of a young bull and seven rams, you accept him as a priest to a god that is no 10 god. But as for us, the LORD is our God and we have not forsaken him; we have Aaronites as priests ministering to the LORD with the Levites, duly discharging their office. 11 Morning and evening, these burn whole-offerings and fragrant incense to the LORD and offer the Bread of the Presence arranged in rows on a table ritually clean; they also kindle the lamps on the golden lamp-stand every evening. Thus we do indeed keep the charge of the LORD our God, whereas you

have forsaken him. God is with us at our 12 head, and his priests stand there with trumpets to signal the battle-cry against you. Men of Israel, do not fight the LORD the God of your fathers; you will have no success.'

Judah defeats Israel

Jeroboam sent a detachment of his troops 13 to go round and lay an ambush in the rear, so that his main body faced Judah while the ambush lay behind them. The men of Judah 14 turned to find that they were engaged front and rear. Then they cried to the LORD for help. The priests sounded their trumpets, and the men of Judah raised a shout, and 15 when they did so, God put Jeroboam and all Israel to rout before Abijah and Judah. The 16 Israelites fled before the men of Judah, and God delivered them into their power. So 17 Abijah and his men defeated them with very heavy losses, and five hundred thousand picked Israelites fell in the battle. After this, 18 the Israelites were reduced to submission, and Judah prevailed because they relied on the LORD the God of their fathers. Abijah 19 followed up his victory over Jeroboam and captured from him the cities of Bethel, Jeshanah, and Ephron, with their villages. Jeroboam did not regain his power during 20 the days of Abijah; finally the LORD struck him down and he died.

Other records of Abijah's reign

But Abijah established his position; he 21 married fourteen wives and became the father of twenty-two sons and sixteen daughters. The other events of Abijah's reign, both 22 what he said and what he did, are recorded in the story of the prophet Iddo. Abijah **14** rested with his forefathers and was buried in the city of David; and he was succeeded on the throne by his son Asa. In his days the land was at peace for ten years.

Asa reigns over Judah

Asa did what was good and right in the eyes 2 of the LORD his God. He suppressed the 3 foreign altars and the hill-shrines, smashed the sacred pillars and hacked down the sacred poles, and ordered Judah to seek 4 guidance of the LORD the God of their fathers and to keep the law and the commandments. He also suppressed the hill- 5 shrines and the incense-altars in all the cities, and the kingdom was at peace under him. He built fortified cities in Judah, for the land 6 was at peace. He had no war to fight during those years, because the LORD had given him security. He said to the men of Judah, 'Let 7 us build these cities and fortify them, with walls round them, and towers and barred gates. The land still lies open before us.

ˣ *Prob. rdg.; Heb. adds* to be enrolled by genealogy.

Because we have sought guidance of the LORD our God, he has sought us and given us security on every side.' So they built and prospered.

Judah defeats the Cushites

8 Asa had an army equipped with shields and spears; three hundred thousand men came from Judah, and two hundred and eighty thousand from Benjamin, shield-bearers and 9 archers; all were valiant warriors. Zerah the Cushite came out against them with an army a million strong and three hundred chariots. 10 When he reached Mareshah, Asa came out to meet him and they took up position in 11 the valley of Zephathah at Mareshah. Asa called upon the LORD his God and said, 'There is none like thee, O LORD, to help men, whether strong or weak; help us, O LORD our God, for on thee we rely and in thy name we have come out against this horde. O LORD, thou art our God, how can 12 man vie with thee?' So the LORD gave Asa and Judah victory over the Cushites and they 13 fled, and Asa and his men pursued them as far as Gerar. The Cushites broke before the LORD and his army, and many of them fell mortally wounded; and Judah carried off 14 great loads of spoil. They destroyed all the cities around Gerar, for the LORD had struck the people with panic; and they plundered 15 the cities, finding rich spoil in them all. They also killed the herdsmen and seized many sheep and camels, and then they returned to Jerusalem.

Asa seeks the LORD's guidance

15 The spirit of God came upon Azariah son 2 of Oded, and he went out to meet Asa and said to him, 'Hear me, Asa and all Judah and Benjamin. The LORD is with you when you are with him; if you look for him, he will let himself be found; if you forsake him, 3 he will forsake you. For a long time Israel was without the true God, without a priest 4 to interpret the law and without law.[y] But when, in their distress, they turned to the LORD the God of Israel and sought him, he 5 let himself be found by them. At those times there was no safety for people as they went about their business; the inhabitants of every land had their fill of trouble; there was 6 ruin on every side, nation at odds with nation, city with city, for God harassed them with 7 every kind of distress. But now you must be strong and not let your courage fail; for your 8 work will be rewarded.' When Asa heard these words,[z] he resolutely suppressed the loathsome idols in all Judah and Benjamin and in the cities which he had captured in the hill-country of Ephraim; and he repaired

the altar of the LORD which stood before the vestibule of the LORD's house.[a] Then he 9 assembled all Judah and Benjamin and all who had come from Ephraim, Manasseh, and Simeon to reside among them; for great numbers had come over to him from Israel, when they saw that the LORD his God was with him. So they assembled at Jerusalem 10 in the third month of the fifteenth year of Asa's reign, and that day they sacrificed to 11 the LORD seven hundred oxen and seven thousand sheep from the spoil which they had brought. And they entered into a cove- 12 nant to seek guidance of the LORD the God of their fathers with all their heart and soul; all who would not seek the LORD the God of 13 Israel were to be put to death, young and old, men and women alike. Then they bound 14 themselves by an oath to the LORD, with loud shouts of acclamation while trumpets and horns sounded; and all Judah rejoiced at 15 the oath, because they had bound themselves with all their heart and had sought him earnestly, and he had let himself be found by them. So the LORD gave them security on every side. King Asa also deprived Maacah 16[b] his grandmother of her rank as queen mother because she had an obscene object made for the worship of Asherah; Asa cut it down, ground it to powder and burnt it in the gorge of the Kidron. Although the hill- 17 shrines were allowed to remain in Israel, Asa himself remained faithful all his life. He 18 brought into the house of God all his father's votive offerings and his own, gold and silver and sacred vessels. And there was no more 19 war until the thirty-fifth year of Asa's reign.

Asa buys Ben-hadad's assistance

In the thirty-sixth year of the reign of Asa, **16** Baasha king of Israel invaded Judah and fortified Ramah to cut off all access to Asa king of Judah. So Asa brought out silver 2 and gold from the treasuries of the house of the LORD and the royal palace, and sent this request to Ben-hadad king of Aram, whose capital was Damascus: 'There is an alliance 3 between us, as there was between our fathers. I now send you herewith silver and gold; break off your alliance with Baasha king of Israel, so that he may abandon his campaign against me.' Ben-hadad listened willingly to 4 King Asa and ordered the commanders of his armies to move against the cities of Israel, and they attacked Iyyon, Dan, Abel-mayim, and all the store-cities of Naphtali. When Baasha heard of it, he ceased fortify- 5 ing Ramah and stopped all work on it. Then 6 King Asa took with him all the men of Judah and they carried away the stones of Ramah and the timbers with which Baasha had

---

[y] *without law: or* without the law.   [z] *Prob. rdg.; Heb. adds* and the prophecy, Oded the prophet.   [a] house: *prob. rdg.; Heb. om.*   [b] *Verses 16–18: cp. 1 Kgs. 15. 13–15.*   [c] *Verses 1–6: cp. 1 Kgs. 15. 17–22.*

fortified it; and he used them to fortify Geba and Mizpah.

Hanani prophesies to Asa

7 At that time the seer Hanani came to Asa king of Judah and said to him, 'Because you relied on the king of Aram and not on the LORD your God, the army of the king of 8 Israel has escaped. The Cushites and the Libyans, were they not a great army with a vast number of chariots and horsemen? Yet, because you relied on the LORD, he delivered 9 them into your power. The eyes of the LORD range through the whole earth, to bring aid and comfort to those whose hearts are loyal to him. You have acted foolishly in this affair; you will have wars from now on.' 10 Asa was angry with the seer and put him in the stocks; for these words of his had made the king very indignant. At the same time he treated some of the people with great brutality.

Other records of Asa's reign

11*d* The events of Asa's reign, from first to last, are recorded in the annals of the kings of 12 Judah and Israel. In the thirty-ninth year of his reign Asa became gravely affected with gangrene in his feet; he did not seek guidance 13 of the LORD but resorted to physicians. He rested with his forefathers, in the forty-first 14 year of his reign, and was buried in the tomb which he had bought*e* for himself in the city of David, being laid on a bier*f* which had been heaped with all kinds of spices skilfully compounded; and they kindled a great fire in his honour.

Jehoshaphat reigns over Judah

17 Asa was succeeded by his son Jehoshaphat, who determined to resist Israel by force. 2 He posted troops in all the fortified cities of Judah and stationed officers*g* throughout Judah and in the cities of Ephraim which 3 his father Asa had captured. The LORD was with Jehoshaphat, for he followed the example his father had set in his early years 4 and did not resort to the Baalim; he sought guidance of the God of his father and obeyed his commandments and did not fol- 5 low the practices of Israel. So the LORD established the kingdom under his rule, and all Judah brought him gifts, and his wealth 6 and fame*h* became very great. He took pride in the service of the LORD; he also suppressed the hill-shrines and the sacred poles in Judah.

Teaching the people

7 In the third year of his reign he sent his officers, Ben-hayil, Obadiah, Zechariah,

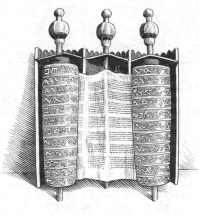

Nethaneel, and Micaiah, to teach in the cities of Judah, together with the Levites, 8 Shemaiah, Nethaniah, Zebadiah, Asahel, Shemiramoth, Jehonathan, Adonijah, Tobiah, and Tob-adonijah,*i* accompanied by the priests Elishama and Jehoram. They taught 9 in Judah, having with them the book of the law of the LORD; they went round the cities of Judah, teaching the people.

Jehoshaphat becomes ever more powerful

So the dread of the LORD fell upon all the 10 rulers of the lands surrounding Judah, and they did not make war on Jehoshaphat. Certain Philistines brought a gift, a great 11 quantity of silver, to Jehoshaphat; the Arabs too brought him seven thousand seven hundred rams and seven thousand seven hundred he-goats. Jehoshaphat became ever 12 more powerful and built fortresses and store-cities in Judah; and he had much work on 13 hand in the cities of Judah. He had regular, seasoned troops in Jerusalem, enrolled 14 according to their clans in this way: of Judah, the officers over units of a thousand: Adnah the commander, together with three hundred thousand seasoned troops; and 15 next to him the commander Johanan, with two hundred and eighty thousand; and next 16 to him Amasiah son of Zichri, who had volunteered for the service of the LORD, with two hundred thousand seasoned troops; and 17 of Benjamin: an experienced soldier Eliada, with two hundred thousand men armed with bows and shields; next to him Jehozabad, 18 with a hundred and eighty thousand fully-armed men. These were the men who served 19 the king, apart from those whom the king had posted in the fortified cities throughout Judah.

d Verses 11–14: cp. 1 Kgs. 15. 23, 24.   e Or dug.   f Or in a niche.   g Or garrisons.
h Or riches.   i Prob. rdg.; Heb. adds the Levites.

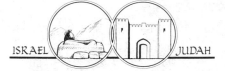

ISRAEL   JUDAH

Jehoshaphat visits Ahab

18 When Jehoshaphat had become very wealthy and famous,*ʲ* he allied himself with Ahab
2*ᵏ* by marriage. Some years afterwards he went down to visit Ahab in Samaria, and Ahab slaughtered many sheep and oxen for him and his retinue, and incited him to attack
3 Ramoth-gilead. What Ahab king of Israel said to Jehoshaphat king of Judah was this: 'Will you join me in attacking Ramoth-gilead?' And he answered, 'What is mine is yours, myself and my people; I will join
4 with you in the war.' Then Jehoshaphat said to the king of Israel, 'First let us seek counsel
5 from the Lord.' The king of Israel assembled the prophets, some four hundred of them, and asked them, 'Shall I attack Ramoth-gilead or shall I refrain?' 'Attack,' they answered; 'God will deliver it into your
6 hands.' Jehoshaphat asked, 'Is there no other prophet of the Lord here through
7 whom we may seek guidance?' 'There is one more', the king of Israel answered, 'through whom we may seek guidance of the Lord, but I hate the man, because he never prophesies any good for me; never anything but evil. His name is Micaiah son of Imla.' Jehoshaphat exclaimed, 'My lord
8 king, let no such word pass your lips!' So the king of Israel called one of his eunuchs and told him to fetch Micaiah son of Imla with all speed.

Conflicting prophecies

9 The king of Israel and Jehoshaphat king of Judah were seated on their thrones, clothed in their royal robes and in shining armour, at the entrance to the gate of Samaria, and all the prophets were prophesying before
10 them. One of them, Zedekiah son of Kenaanah, made himself horns of iron and said, 'This is the word of the Lord: "With horns like these you shall gore the Aramaeans
11 and make an end of them."' In the same vein all the prophets prophesied, 'Attack Ramoth-gilead and win the day; the Lord
12 will deliver it into your hands.' The messenger sent to fetch Micaiah told him that the prophets had with one voice given the king a favourable answer. 'And mind you
13 agree with them', he added. 'As the Lord lives,' said Micaiah, 'I will say only what my God tells me to say.'
14 When Micaiah came into the king's presence, the king said to him, 'Micaiah, shall I attack Ramoth-gilead or shall I refrain?' 'Attack and win the day,' he said, 'and it will fall into your hands.' 'How often
15 must I adjure you', said the king, 'to tell me nothing but the truth in the name of the
16 Lord?' Then Micaiah said, 'I saw all Israel scattered on the mountains, like sheep without a shepherd; and I heard the Lord say, "They have no master; let them go home
17 in peace."' The king of Israel said to Jehoshaphat, 'Did I not tell you that he never prophesies good for me, nothing but evil?'
18 Micaiah went on, 'Listen now to the word of the Lord: I saw the Lord seated on his throne, with all the host of heaven in attendance on his right and on his left. The Lord
19 said, "Who will entice Ahab to attack and fall on*ˡ* Ramoth-gilead?" One said one thing
20 and one said another; then a spirit came forward and stood before the Lord and said, "I will entice him." "How?" said the
21 Lord. "I will go out", he said, "and be a lying spirit in the mouth of all his prophets." "You shall entice him," said the Lord, "and you shall succeed; go and do it." You see,
22 then, how the Lord has put a lying spirit in the mouth of all these prophets of yours, because he has decreed disaster for you.'
23 Then Zedekiah son of Kenaanah came up to Micaiah and struck him in the face: 'And how did the spirit of the Lord pass from me to speak to you?' he said. Micaiah answered,
24 'That you will find out on the day when you run into an inner room to hide yourself.'
25 Then the king of Israel ordered Micaiah to be arrested and committed to the custody of Amon the governor of the city and Joash the king's son.*ᵐ* 'Lock this fellow up', he
26 said, 'and give him prison diet of bread and water until I come home in safety.' Micaiah
27 retorted, 'If you do return in safety, the Lord has not spoken by me.'*ⁿ*

Ahab dies in battle

28 So the king of Israel and Jehoshaphat king
29 of Judah marched on Ramoth-gilead, and the king of Israel said to Jehoshaphat, 'I will disguise myself to go into battle, but you shall wear your royal robes.' So he went
30 into battle in disguise. Now the king of Aram had commanded the captains of his chariots not to engage all and sundry but the king of Israel alone. When the captains
31 saw Jehoshaphat, they thought he was the king of Israel and wheeled to attack him. But Jehoshaphat cried out, and the Lord came to his help; and God drew them away
32 from him. When the captains saw that he was not the king of Israel, they broke off
33 the attack on him. But one man drew his

j Or rich.   *k Verses 2–34: cp. 1 Kgs. 22. 2–35.*
rdg.; Heb. adds and he said, 'Listen, peoples, all together.'
l Or at.   *m son: or* deputy.   *n Prob.*

bow at random and hit the king of Israel where the breastplate joins the plates of the armour. So he said to his driver, 'Wheel round and take me out of the line; I am 34 wounded.' When the day's fighting reached its height, the king of Israel was facing the Aramaeans, propped up in his chariot; he remained so till evening, and at sunset he died.

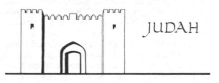

JUDAH

The prophet Jehu rebukes Jehoshaphat

19 As Jehoshaphat king of Judah returned in 2 safety to his home in Jerusalem, Jehu son of Hanani, the seer, went out to meet him and said, 'Do you take delight in helping the wicked and befriending the enemies of the LORD? The LORD will make you suffer for 3 this. Yet there is some good in you, for you have swept away the sacred poles from the land and have made a practice of seeking guidance of God.'

Jehoshaphat appoints judges

4 Jehoshaphat had his residence in Jerusalem, but he went out again among his people from Beersheba to the hill-country of Ephraim and brought them back to the LORD the 5 God of their fathers. He appointed judges throughout the land, one in each of the 6 fortified cities of Judah, and said to them, 'Be careful what you do; you are there as judges, to please not man but the LORD, 7 who is with you when you pass sentence. Let the dread of the LORD be upon you, then; take care what you do, for the LORD our God will not tolerate injustice, partiality, or bribery.'

8 In Jerusalem Jehoshaphat appointed some of the Levites and priests and some heads of families by paternal descent in Israel to administer the law of the LORD and to arbitrate in lawsuits among the inhabitants[o] of 9 the city, and he gave them these instructions: 'You must always act in the fear of the LORD, 10 faithfully and with singleness of mind. In every suit which comes before you from your kinsmen, in whatever city they live, whether cases of bloodshed or offences against the law or the commandments, against statutes or regulations, you shall warn them to commit no offence against the LORD; otherwise you and your kinsmen will suffer for it. If you act thus, you will be free 11 of all offence. Your authority in all matters

which concern the LORD is Amariah the chief priest, and in those which concern the king it is Zebediah son of Ishmael, the prince of the house of Judah; the Levites are your officers. Be strong and resolute, and may the LORD be on the side of the good!'

Invasion from the east

It happened some time afterwards that the **20** Moabites, the Ammonites, and some of the Meunites made war on Jehoshaphat. News 2 was brought to him that a great horde of them was attacking him from beyond the Dead Sea, from Edom, and was already at Hazazon-tamar, which is En-gedi. Jeho- 3 shaphat in his alarm resolved to seek guidance of the LORD and proclaimed a fast for all Judah. Judah gathered together to ask 4 counsel of the LORD; from every city of the land they came to consult him. Jehoshaphat 5 stood up in the assembly of Judah and Jerusalem in the house of the LORD, in front of the New Court, and said, 'O LORD God of 6 our fathers, art not thou God in heaven? Thou rulest over all the kingdoms of the nations; in thy hand are strength and power, and there is none who can withstand thee. Didst not thou, O God our God, dispossess 7 the inhabitants of this land in favour of thy people Israel, and give it for ever to the descendants of Abraham thy friend? So 8 they lived in it and have built a sanctuary in it in honour of thy name and said, "Should 9 evil come upon us, war or flood,[p] pestilence or famine, we will stand before this house and before thee, for in this house is thy Name, and we will cry to thee in our distress and thou wilt hear and save." Thou didst not 10 allow Israel, when they came out of Egypt,

Levite and priest

---

o in . . . inhabitants: *prob. rdg.; Heb. obscure.*   p *Prob. rdg.; Heb.* judgement.

to enter the land of the Ammonites, the Moabites, and the people of the hill-country of Seir, so they turned aside and left them 11 alone and did not destroy them. Now see how these people repay us: they are coming to drive us out of thy possession which 12 thou didst give to us. Judge them, O God our God, for we have no strength to face this great horde which is invading our land; we know not what we ought to do; we lift our eyes to thee.'

Judah's victory is assured

13 So all Judah stood there before the LORD, with their dependants, their wives and their 14 children. Then, in the midst of the assembly, the spirit of the LORD came upon Jahaziel son of Zechariah, son of Benaiah, son of Jeiel, son of Mattaniah, a Levite of the line 15 of Asaph, and he said, 'Attend, all Judah, all inhabitants of Jerusalem, and King Jehoshaphat; this is the word of the LORD to you: "Have no fear; do not be dismayed by this great horde, for the battle is in God's 16 hands, not yours. Go down to meet them tomorrow; they will come up by the Ascent of Ziz. You will find them at the end of the 17 valley, east of the wilderness of Jeruel. It is not you who will fight this battle; stand firm and wait, and you will see the deliverance worked by the LORD: he is on your side, O Judah and Jerusalem. Do not fear or be dismayed; go out tomorrow to face them; 18 for the LORD is on your side." ' Jehoshaphat bowed his face to the ground, and all Judah and the inhabitants of Jerusalem fell down before the LORD to make obeisance to him. 19 Then the Levites of the lines of Kohath and Korah stood up and praised the LORD the God of Israel with a mighty shout.

The LORD deludes the enemy

20 So they rose early in the morning and went out to the wilderness of Tekoa; and, as they were starting, Jehoshaphat took his stand and said, 'Hear me, O Judah and inhabitants of Jerusalem: hold firmly to your faith in the LORD your God and you will be upheld; have faith in his prophets and you will 21 prosper.' After consulting with the people, he appointed men to sing to the LORD and praise the splendour of his holiness*q* as they went before the armed troops, and they sang:

> Give thanks to the LORD,
> for his love endures for ever.

22 As soon as their loud shouts of praise were heard, the LORD deluded the Ammonites and Moabites and the men of the hill-country of Seir, who were invading Judah,

and they were defeated. It turned out that 23 the Ammonites and Moabites had taken up a position against the men of the hill-country of Seir, and set themselves to annihilate and destroy them; and when they had exterminated the men of Seir, they savagely attacked one another. So when Judah came 24 to the watch-tower in the wilderness and looked towards the enemy horde, there they were all lying dead upon the ground; none had escaped. When Jehoshaphat and his 25 men came to collect the booty, they found a large number of cattle, goods, clothing, and precious things, which they plundered until they could carry away no more. They spent three days collecting the booty, there was so much of it. On the fourth day they assem- 26 bled in the Valley of Berakah,*r* the name that it bears to this day because they blessed the LORD there. Then all the men of Judah and 27 Jerusalem, with Jehoshaphat at their head, returned home to the city in triumph; for the LORD had given them cause to triumph over their enemies. They entered Jerusalem 28 with lutes, harps, and trumpets playing, and went into the house of the LORD. So the dread 29 of God fell upon the rulers of every country, when they heard that the LORD had fought against the enemies of Israel; and the realm 30 of Jehoshaphat was at peace, God giving him security on all sides.

Other records of Jehoshaphat's reign

Thus Jehoshaphat reigned over Judah. He 31*s* was thirty-five years old when he came to the throne, and he reigned in Jerusalem for twenty-five years; his mother was Azubah daughter of Shilhi. He followed in the foot- 32 steps of Asa his father and did not swerve from them; he did what was right in the eyes of the LORD. But the hill-shrines were allowed 33 to remain, and the people did not set their hearts upon the God of their fathers. The 34 other events of Jehoshaphat's reign, from first to last, are recorded in the history of Jehu son of Hanani, which is included in the annals of the kings of Israel.

Jehoshaphat's fleet is wrecked

Later Jehoshaphat king of Judah allied him- 35 self with Ahaziah king of Israel; he did wrong in joining with him to build ships for trade 36 with Tarshish; these were built in Eziongeber. But Eliezer son of Dodavahu of 37 Mareshah denounced Jehoshaphat with this prophecy: 'Because you have joined with Ahaziah, the LORD will bring your work to nothing.' So the ships were wrecked and could not make the voyage to Tarshish.

q Or singers in sacred vestments to praise the LORD. cp. *1 Kgs. 22. 41–43.*   *r That is* Valley of Blessing.   *s Verses 31–33:*

A city gate of Jerusalem

Joram reigns over Judah

21 Jehoshaphat rested with his forefathers and was buried with them in the city of David. 2 He was succeeded by his son Joram, whose brothers were Azariah, Jehiel, Zechariah, Azariah, Michael, and Shephatiah, sons of Jehoshaphat. All of them were sons of 3 Jehoshaphat king of Judah, and their father gave them many gifts, silver and gold and other costly things, as well as fortified cities in Judah; but the kingship he gave to Joram because he was the eldest.

4 When Joram was firmly established on his father's throne, he put to the sword all his brothers and also some of the princes of 5ᵗ Israel. He was thirty-two years old when he came to the throne, and he reigned in Jeru- 6 salem for eight years. He followed the practices of the kings of Israel as the house of Ahab had done, for he had married Ahab's daughter; and he did what was wrong in the 7 eyes of the LORD. But for the sake of the covenant which he had made with David, the LORD was unwilling to destroy the house of David, since he had promised to give him and his sons a flame, to burn for all time.

Edom claims independence

8 During his reign Edom revolted against 9 Judah and set up its own king. Joram, with his commanders and all his chariots, advanced into Edom. He and his chariot-commanders set out by night, but they were surrounded by the Edomites and defeated.ᵘ 10 So Edom has remained independent of Judah to this day. Libnah revolted against him at the same time, because he had forsaken the LORD the God of his fathers, 11 and because he had built hill-shrines in the hill-country of Judah and had seduced the inhabitants of Jerusalem into idolatrous practices and corrupted Judah.

The death of Joram

A letter reached Joram from Elijah the 12 prophet, which ran thus: 'This is the word of the LORD the God of David your father: "You have not followed in the footsteps of Jehoshaphat your father and of Asa king of Judah, but have followed the kings of 13 Israel and have seduced Judah and the inhabitants of Jerusalem, as the house of Ahab did; and you have put to death your own brothers, sons of your father's house, men better than yourself. Because of all this, the 14 LORD is about to strike a heavy blow at your people, your children, your wives, and all your possessions, and you yourself will 15 suffer from a chronic disease of the bowels, until they prolapse and become severely ulcerated."' Then the LORD aroused against 16 Joram the anger of the Philistines and of the Arabs who live near the Cushites, and they 17 invaded Judah and made their way right through it, carrying off all the property which they found in the king's palace, as well as his sons and wives; not a son was left to him except the youngest, Jehoahaz. It was after all this that the LORD struck 18 down the king with an incurable disease of the bowels. It continued for some time, and 19 towards the end of the second year the disease caused his bowels to prolapse, and the painful ulceration brought on his death. But his people kindled no fire in his honour as they had done for his fathers. He was 20 thirty-two years old when he became king, and he reigned in Jerusalem for eight years. His passing went unsung, and he was buried in the city of David, but not in the burial-place of the kings.

t Verses 5–10: cp. 2 Kgs. 8. 17–22.   *u and defeated: prob. rdg.; Heb. and he defeated them.*

Ahaziah reigns over Judah

22 ¹ᵛ Then the inhabitants of Jerusalem made Ahaziah, his youngest son, king in his place, for the raiders who had joined the Arabs in the campaign had killed all the elder sons. So Ahaziah son of Joram became king of ² Judah. He was forty-two years old when he came to the throne, and he reigned in Jerusalem for one year; his mother was Athaliah ³ granddaughter of Omri. He too followed the practices of the house of Ahab, for his mother was his counsellor in wickedness. ⁴ He did what was wrong in the eyes of the LORD like the house of Ahab, for they had been his counsellors after his father's death, ⁵ to his undoing. He followed their counsel also in the alliance he made with Jehoram son of Ahab king of Israel, to fight against Hazael king of Aram at Ramoth-gilead. But Jehoram was wounded by the Aramaeans, ⁶ and returned to Jezreel to recover from the wounds which were inflicted on him at Ramoth in battle with Hazael king of Aram.

Jehu kills Ahaziah

Because of Jehoram's illness Ahaziah son of Joram king of Judah went down to Jez-⁷ reel to visit him. It was God's will that the visit of Ahaziah to Jehoram should be the occasion of his downfall. During the visit he went out with Jehoram to meet Jehu son of Nimshi, whom the LORD had anointed ⁸ to bring the house of Ahab to an end. So it came about that Jehu, who was then at variance with the house of Ahab, found the officers of Judah and the kinsmen of Ahaziah who were his attendants, and killed ⁹ them. Then he searched out Ahaziah himself, and his men captured him in Samaria, where he had gone into hiding. They brought him to Jehu and put him to death; they gave him burial, for they said, 'He was a son of Jehoshaphat who sought the guidance of the LORD with his whole heart.' Then the house of Ahaziah had no one strong enough to rule.

Athaliah seizes the throne

¹⁰ʷ As soon as Athaliah mother of Ahaziah saw that her son was dead, she set out to extirpate ¹¹ the royal line of the house of Judah. But Jehosheba daughter of King Joram took Ahaziah's son Joash and stole him away from among the princes who were being murdered; she put him and his nurse in a bedchamber. Thus Jehosheba, daughter of King Joram and wife of Jehoiada the priest, because she was Ahaziah's sister, hid Joash from Athaliah so that she did not put him ¹² to death. He remained concealed with them in the house of God for six years, while Athaliah ruled the country.

Joash is proclaimed king

In the seventh year Jehoiada felt himself **23** strong enough to make an agreement with Azariah son of Jeroham, Ishmael son of Jehohanan, Azariah son of Obed, Maaseiah son of Adaiah, and Elishaphat son of Zichri, all captains of units of a hundred. They went ² all through Judah and gathered to Jerusalem the Levites from the cities of Judah and the heads of clans in Israel, and they came to Jerusalem. All the assembly made a com- ³ pact with the king in the house of God, and Jehoiada said to them, 'Here is the king's son! He shall be king, as the LORD promised that the sons of David should be. This is ⁴ what you must do: a third of you, priests and Levites, as you come on duty on the sabbath, are to be on guard at the threshold gates, another third are to be in the royal ⁵ palace, and another third are to be at the Foundation Gate, while all the people will be in the courts of the house of the LORD. Let no one enter the house of the LORD ⁶ except the priests and the attendant Levites; they may enter, for they are holy, but all the people shall continue to keep the LORD's charge. The Levites shall mount guard ⁷ round the king, each with his weapons at the ready; anyone who tries to enter the house is to be put to death. They shall stay with the king wherever he goes.'

The Levites and all Judah carried out the ⁸ orders of Jehoiada the priest to the letter. Each captain took his men, both those who came on duty on the sabbath and those who came off, for Jehoiada the priest had not released the outgoing divisions. And Jehoi- ⁹ ada the priest handed out to the captains King David's spears, shields, and bucklers, which were in the house of God; and he ¹⁰ posted all the people, each man carrying his weapon at the ready, from corner to corner of the house to north and south,ˣ surrounding the king. Then they brought out the ¹¹ king's son, put the crown on his head, handed him the warrant and proclaimed him king, and Jehoiada and his sons anointed him; and a shout went up: 'Long live the king.' When Athaliah heard the noise of ¹² the people as they ran about cheering for the king, she came into the house of the LORD where the people were and found the king ¹³ standing on the daisʸ at the entrance, amidst outbursts of song and fanfares of trumpets in his honour; all the populace were rejoicing and blowing trumpets, and singers with musical instruments were leading the celebrations. Athaliah rent her clothes and cried,

v Verses 1–6: cp. 2 Kgs. 8. 25–29.　　*w 22. 10—23. 21: cp. 2 Kgs. 11. 1–20.*　　*x Prob. rdg.; Heb. adds of the altar and the house.*　　*y Prob. rdg., cp. 2 Kgs. 11. 14; Heb. by his pillar.*

14 'Treason! Treason!' Jehoiada the priest gave orders to² the captains in command of the troops: 'Bring her outside the precincts and let anyone in attendance on her be put to the sword'; for the priest said, 'Do not kill 15 her in the house of the LORD.' So they laid hands on her and took her to the royal palace and killed her there at the passage to the Horse Gate.

Jehoiada makes a covenant

16 Then Jehoiada made a covenant between the LORD*a* and the whole people and the king, 17 that they should be the LORD's people. And all the people went into the temple of Baal and pulled it down; they smashed its altars and images, and they slew Mattan the priest 18 of Baal before the altars. Then Jehoiada committed the supervision of the house of the LORD to the charge of the priests and the Levites whom David had allocated to the house of the LORD, to offer whole-offerings to the LORD as prescribed in the law of Moses, with the singing and rejoicing as handed 19 down from David. He stationed the door-keepers at the gates of the house of the LORD, to prevent anyone entering who was 20 in any way unclean. Then he took the captains of units of a hundred, the nobles, and the governors of the people, and all the people of the land, and they escorted the king from the house of the LORD through the Upper Gate to the royal palace, and 21 seated him on the royal throne. The whole people rejoiced and the city was tranquil. That is how Athaliah was put to the sword.

Joash repairs the Temple

1*b* Joash was seven years old when he became king, and he reigned in Jerusalem for forty years; his mother was Zibiah of Beersheba. 2 He did what was right in the eyes of the LORD as long as Jehoiada the priest was alive. 3 Jehoiada chose him two wives, and he had a family of sons and daughters.

4 Some time after this, Joash decided to 5 repair the house of the LORD. So he assembled the priests and the Levites and said to them, 'Go through the cities of Judah and collect the annual tax from all the Israelites for the restoration of the house of your God, and do it quickly.' But the Levites did not act 6 quickly. The king then called for Jehoiada the chief priest and said to him, 'Why have you not required the Levites to bring in from Judah and Jerusalem the tax imposed by Moses the servant of the LORD and by the assembly of Israel for the Tent of the 7 Tokens?' For the wicked Athaliah and her adherents had broken into the house of God and had devoted all its holy things to

the service of the Baalim. So the king ordered 8 them to make a chest and to put it outside the gate of the house of the LORD; and pro- 9 clamation was made throughout Judah and Jerusalem that the people should bring to the LORD the tax imposed on Israel in the wilderness by Moses the servant of God. And all the leaders and all the people gladly 10 brought their taxes and cast them into the chest until it was full. Whenever the chest 11 was brought to the king's officers by the Levites and they saw that it was well filled, the king's secretary and the chief priest's officer would come to empty it, after which it was carried back to its place. This they did daily, and they collected a great sum of money. The king and Jehoiada gave it to 12 those responsible for carrying out the work in the house of the LORD, and they hired masons and carpenters to do the repairs, as well as craftsmen in iron and copper*c* to restore the house. So the workmen pro- 13 ceeded with their task and the new work progressed under their hands; they restored the house of God according to its original design and strengthened it. When they had 14 finished, they brought what was left of the money to the king and to Jehoiada, and it was made into vessels for the house of the LORD, both for service and for sacrificing, saucers and other vessels of gold and silver. While Jehoiada lived, whole-offerings were offered in the house of the LORD continually.

The death of Jehoiada

Jehoiada, now old and weighed down with 15 years, died at the age of a hundred and thirty and was buried with the kings in the 16 city of David, because he had done good in Israel and served God and his house.

Joash has Zechariah stoned

After the death of Jehoiada the leading men 17 of Judah came and made obeisance to the king. He listened to them, and they forsook 18 the house of the LORD the God of their fathers and worshipped sacred poles and idols. And Judah and Jerusalem suffered for this wickedness. But the LORD sent pro- 19 phets to bring them back to himself, pro-phets who denounced them and were not heeded. Then the spirit of God took posses- 20 sion of Zechariah son of Jehoiada the priest, and he stood looking down on the people and said to them, 'This is the word of God: "Why do you disobey the commands of the LORD and court disaster? Because you have forsaken the LORD, he has forsaken you."' But they made common cause against him, 21 and on orders from the king they stoned him to death in the court of the house of the

---

z gave orders to: prob. rdg., cp. 2 Kgs. 11. 15; Heb. brought out. 11. 17; Heb. him.   *b Verses 1–14; cp. 2 Kgs. 11. 21—12. 15.*

a the LORD: prob. rdg., cp. 2 Kgs. c Or bronze.

22 LORD. King Joash did not remember the loyalty of Zechariah's father Jehoiada but killed his son, who said as he was dying, 'May the LORD see this and exact the penalty.'

The death of Joash

23 At the turn of the year an Aramaean army advanced against Joash; they invaded Judah and Jerusalem and massacred all the officers, so that the army ceased to exist, and sent all 24 their spoil to the king of Damascus. Although the Aramaeans had invaded with a small force, the LORD delivered a very great army into their hands, because the people had forsaken the LORD the God of their fathers; and Joash suffered just punishment. 25ᵈ When the Aramaeans had withdrawn, leaving the king severely wounded, his servants conspired against him to avenge the death of the son of Jehoiada the priest; and they killed him on his bed. Thus he died and was buried in the city of David, but not in 26 the burial-place of the kings. The conspirators were Zabad son of Shimeath an Ammonite woman and Jehozabad son of Shimrith 27 a Moabite woman. His children, the many oracles about him, and his reconstruction of the house of God are all on record in the story given in the annals of the kings. He was succeeded by his son Amaziah.

Amaziah reigns over Judah

25 1ᵉ Amaziah was twenty-five years old when he came to the throne, and he reigned in Jerusalem for twenty-nine years; his mother was 2 Jehoaddan of Jerusalem. He did what was right in the eyes of the LORD, but not whole-3 heartedly. When the royal power was firmly in his grasp, he put to death those of his servants who had murdered the king his 4 father; but he spared their children, in obedience to the LORD's command written in the law of Moses: 'Fathers shall not die for their children, nor children for their fathers; a man shall die only for his own sin.'

Amaziah's victory in the Valley of Salt

5 Then Amaziah assembled the men of Judah and drew them up by families, all Judah and Benjamin as well, under officers over units of a thousand and a hundred. He mustered those of twenty years old and upwards and found their number to be three hundred thousand, all picked troops ready for service, 6 able to handle spear and shield. He also hired a hundred thousand seasoned troops from Israel for a hundred talents of silver. 7 But a man of God came to him and said, 'My lord king, do not let the Israelite army march with you; the LORD is not with Israel

—all these Ephraimites! For, if you make 8 these peopleᶠ your allies in the war, God will overthrow you in battle; he has power to help or to overthrow.' Then Amaziah said 9 to the man of God, 'What am I to do about the hundred talents which I have spent on the Israelite army?' The man of God answered, 'It is in the LORD's power to give you much more than that.' So Amaziah 10 detached the troops which had come to him from Ephraim and sent them home; that infuriated them against Judah and they went home in a rage.

Then Amaziah took heart and led his 11 men to the Valley of Salt and there killed ten thousand men of Seir. The men of Judah 12 captured another ten thousand men alive, brought them to the top of a cliffᵍ and hurled them over so that they were all dashed to pieces. Meanwhile the troops which Ama- 13 ziah had sent home without allowing them to take part in the battle raided the cities of Judah from Samaria to Beth-horon, massacred three thousand people in them and carried off quantities of booty.

Israel attacks Judah

After Amaziah had returned from the defeat 14 of the Edomites, he brought the gods of the people of Seir and, setting them up as his own gods, worshipped them and burnt sacrifices to them. The LORD was angry with 15 Amaziah for this and sent a prophet who said to him, 'Why have you resorted to gods who could not save their own people from you?' But while he was speaking, the king 16 said to him, 'Have we appointed you counsellor to the king? Stop! Why risk your life?' The prophet did stop, but first he said, 'I know that God has determined to destroy you because you have done this and have not listened to my counsel.'

Then Amaziah king of Judah, after con- 17ʰ sultation, sent messengers to Jehoash son of Jehoahaz, son of Jehu, king of Israel, to propose a meeting. But Jehoash king of 18 Israel sent this answer to Amaziah king of Judah: 'A thistle in Lebanon sent to a cedar in Lebanon to say, "Give your daughter in marriage to my son." But a wild beast in Lebanon, passing by, trampled on the thistle. You have defeated Edom, you say, but it 19 has gone to your head. Enjoy your glory at home and stay there. Why should you involve yourself in disaster and bring yourself to the ground, and Judah with you?' But Amaziah would not listen; and this 20 was God's doing in order to give Judah into the power of Jehoash, because they had resorted to the gods of Edom. So Jehoash 21 king of Israel marched out, and he and

---

d *Verses 25–27: cp.* 2 Kgs. 12. 20, 21. *Heb. obscure.* g *a cliff: or* Sela.

e *Verses 1–4: cp.* 2 Kgs. 14. 1–6. h *Verses 17–24: cp.* 2 Kgs. 14. 8–14.

f *these people: prob. rdg.;*

Amaziah king of Judah met one another at
22 Beth-shemesh in Judah. The men of Judah
were routed by Israel and fled to their homes.
23 But Jehoash king of Israel captured Amaziah
king of Judah, son of Joash, son of Jehoahaz, at Beth-shemesh, and brought him to
Jerusalem. There he broke down the city
wall from the Gate of Ephraim to the
Corner Gate, a distance of four hundred
24 cubits; he also took[i] all the gold and silver
and all the vessels found in the house of God,
in the care of Obed-edom, and the treasures
of the royal palace, as well as hostages, and
returned to Samaria.

Other records of Amaziah's reign

25 Amaziah son of Joash, king of Judah, outlived Jehoash son of Jehoahaz, king of
26 Israel, by fifteen years. The other events of
Amaziah's reign, from first to last, are recorded in the annals of the kings of Judah
27 and Israel. From the time when he turned
away from the LORD, there was conspiracy
against him in Jerusalem and he fled to
Lachish; but they sent after him to Lachish
28 and put him to death there. Then his body
was conveyed on horseback to Jerusalem,
and there he was buried with his forefathers
in the city of David.

Uzziah reigns over Judah

26 All the people of Judah took Uzziah, now
sixteen years old, and made him king in
2 succession to his father Amaziah. It was he
who built Eloth and restored it to Judah
after the king rested with his forefathers.
3 [k] Uzziah was sixteen years old when he
came to the throne, and he reigned in Jerusalem for fifty-two years; his mother was
4 Jecoliah of Jerusalem. He did what was right
in the eyes of the LORD, as Amaziah his
5 father had done. He set himself to seek the
guidance of God in the days of Zechariah,
who instructed him in the fear of God; as
long as he sought guidance of the LORD,
God caused him to prosper.

Uzziah's armaments

6 He took the field against the Philistines and
broke down the walls of Gath, Jabneh, and
Ashdod; and he built cities in the territory
7 of Ashdod and among the Philistines. God
aided him against them, against the Arabs
who lived in Gur-baal, and against the
8 Meunites. The Ammonites brought gifts to
Uzziah and his fame spread to the borders
of Egypt, for he had become very powerful.
9 Besides, he built towers in Jerusalem at the
Corner Gate, at the Valley Gate, and at the
10 escarpment, and fortified them. He built
other towers in the wilderness and dug many

cisterns, for he had large herds of cattle both
in the Shephelah and in the plain. He also
had farmers and vine-dressers in the hill-
country and in the fertile lands, for he loved
the soil.

Uzziah had an army of soldiers trained 11
and ready for service, grouped according
to the census made by Jeiel the adjutant-
general and Maaseiah the clerk under the
direction of Hananiah, one of the king's
commanders. The total number of heads of 12
families which supplied seasoned warriors
was two thousand six hundred. Under their 13
command was an army of three hundred
and seven thousand five hundred, a powerful fighting force to aid the king against his
enemies. Uzziah prepared for the whole 14
army shields, spears, helmets, coats of mail,
bows, and[l] sling-stones. In Jerusalem he had 15
machines designed by engineers for use upon
towers and bastions, made to discharge
arrows and large stones. His fame spread
far and wide, for he was so wonderfully
gifted that he became very powerful.

Uzziah's pride leads to his undoing

But when he grew powerful his pride led to 16
his own undoing:[m] he offended against the
LORD his God by entering the temple of the
LORD to burn incense on the altar of incense.
Azariah the priest and eighty others of the 17
LORD's priests, courageous men, went in
after King Uzziah, confronted him and said, 18
'It is not for you, Uzziah, to burn incense to
the LORD, but for the Aaronite priests who
have been consecrated for that office. Leave
the sanctuary; for you have offended, and
that will certainly bring you no honour from
the LORD God.' The king, who had a censer 19

in his hand ready to burn incense, was indignant; and because of his indignation at
the priests, leprosy broke out on his forehead in the presence of the priests, there in
the house of the LORD, beside the altar of
incense. When Azariah the chief priest and 20

i he also took: *prob. rdg., cp. 2 Kgs. 14. 14; Heb. om.
3, 4: cp. 2 Kgs. 15. 2, 3.   *l* Prob. rdg.; Heb. adds for.
proud that he acted corruptly.

j 25. 25—26. 2: cp. 2 Kgs. 14. 17–22.   *k* Verses
m his pride . . . undoing: or he became so

the other priests looked towards him, they
saw that he had leprosy on his forehead and
they hurried him out of the temple, and indeed he himself hastened to leave, because
the LORD had struck him with the disease.
21[n] And King Uzziah remained a leper till the
day of his death; he lived in his own house
as a leper, relieved of all duties and excluded
from the house of the LORD, while his son
Jotham was comptroller of the household
22 and regent. The other events of Uzziah's
reign, from first to last, are recorded by the
23 prophet Isaiah son of Amoz. So he rested
with his forefathers and was buried in a
burial-ground, but not that of the kings; for
they said, 'He is a leper'; and he was succeeded by his son Jotham.

Jotham reigns over Judah

27 1[o] Jotham was twenty-five years old when he
came to the throne, and he reigned in Jerusalem for sixteen years; his mother was
2 Jerushah daughter of Zadok. He did what
was right in the eyes of the LORD, as his
father Uzziah had done, but unlike him he
did not enter the temple of the LORD; the
people, however, continued their corrupt
3 practices. He constructed the upper gate of
the house of the LORD and built extensively
4 on the wall at Ophel. He built cities in the
hill-country of Judah, and forts and towers
5 on the wooded hills. He made war on the
king of the Ammonites and defeated him;
and that year the Ammonites gave him a
hundred talents of silver, ten thousand kor
of wheat and ten thousand of barley. They
paid him the same tribute in the second and
6 third years. Jotham became very powerful
because he maintained a steady course of
7 obedience to the LORD his God. The other
events of Jotham's reign, all that he did in
war and in peace, are recorded in the annals
8 of the kings of Israel and Judah. He was
twenty-five years old when he came to the
throne, and he reigned in Jerusalem for
9 sixteen years. He rested with his forefathers
and was buried in the city of David; and he
was succeeded by his son Ahaz.

Ahaz reigns over Judah

28 1[p] Ahaz was twenty years old when he came
to the throne, and he reigned in Jerusalem
for sixteen years. He did not do what was
right in the eyes of the LORD like his fore-
2 father David, but followed in the footsteps of the kings of Israel, and cast metal
3 images for the Baalim. He also burnt sacrifices in the Valley of Ben-hinnom; he even
burnt his sons in the fire according to the
abominable practice of the nations whom
the LORD had dispossessed in favour of the
Israelites. He slaughtered and burnt sacri- 4
fices at the hill-shrines and on the hill-tops
and under every spreading tree.

Ahaz suffers defeats

The LORD his God let him suffer at the hands 5
of the king of Aram, and the Aramaeans
defeated him, took many captives and
brought them to Damascus; he was also
made to suffer at the hands of the king of
Israel, who inflicted a severe defeat on him.
This was Pekah son of Remaliah, who killed 6
in one day a hundred and twenty thousand
men of Judah, seasoned troops, because they
had forsaken the LORD the God of their
fathers. And Zichri, an Ephraimite hero, 7
killed Maaseiah the king's son[q] and Azrikam
the comptroller of the household and Elkanah the king's chief minister. The Israel- 8
ites took captive from their kinsmen two
hundred thousand women and children;
they also took a large amount of booty and
brought it to Samaria.

The Israelites surrender their captives

A prophet of the LORD was there, Oded by 9
name; he went out to meet the army as it
returned to Samaria and said to them, 'It is
because the LORD the God of your fathers
is angry with Judah that he has given them
into your power; and you have massacred
them in a rage that has towered up to heaven.
Now you propose to force the people of 10
Judah and Jerusalem, male and female, into
slavery. Are not you also guilty men before
the LORD your God? Now, listen to me. 11
Send back those you have taken captive
from your kinsmen, for the anger of the
LORD is roused against you.' Next, some 12
Ephraimite chiefs, Azariah son of Jehohanan, Berechiah son of Meshillemoth,
Hezekiah[r] son of Shallum, and Amasa son
of Hadlai, met those who were returning
from the war and said to them, 'You must 13
not bring these captives into our country;
what you are proposing would make us
guilty before the LORD and add to our sins
and transgressions. We are guilty enough
already, and there is fierce anger against
Israel.' So the armed men left the captives 14
and the spoil with the officers and the
assembled people. The captives were put in 15
charge of men nominated for this duty, who
found clothes from the spoil for all who were
naked. They clothed them and shod them,
gave them food and drink, and anointed
them; those who were tottering from exhaustion they conveyed on the backs of asses, and
so brought them to their kinsmen in Jericho,
in the Vale of Palm Trees. Then they themselves returned to Samaria.

n Verses 21–23: cp. 2 Kgs. 15. 5–7. *o Verses 1–3: cp. 2 Kgs. 15. 33–35.* *p Verses 1–4: cp. 2 Kgs. 16. 2–4.* *q* son: *or* deputy. *r Or* Jehizkiah.

Ahaz is unfaithful to the LORD

16 At that time King Ahaz sent to the king of
17 Assyria for help. The Edomites had invaded
again and defeated Judah and taken away
18 prisoners; and the Philistines had raided the
cities of the Shephelah and of the Negeb of
Judah and had captured Beth-shemesh,
Aijalon, and Gederoth, as well as Soco,
Timnah, and Gimzo with their villages, and
19 occupied them. The LORD had reduced
Judah to submission because of Ahaz king
of Judah; for his actions in Judah had been
unbridled and he had been grossly unfaithful
20 to the LORD. Then Tiglath-pileser king of
Assyria marched against him and, so far
21 from assisting him, pressed him hard. Ahaz
stripped the house of the LORD, the king's
palace and the houses of his officers, and
gave the plunder to the king of Assyria; but
all to no purpose.

22 This King Ahaz, when hard pressed, became more and more unfaithful to the LORD;
23 he sacrificed to the gods of Damascus who
had defeated him and said, 'The gods of the
kings of Aram helped them; I will sacrifice
to them so that they may help me.' But in
fact they caused his downfall and that of all
24 Israel. Then Ahaz gathered together the
vessels of the house of God and broke them
up, and shut the doors of the house of the
LORD; he made himself altars at every corner
25 in Jerusalem, and at every single city of
Judah he made hill-shrines to burn sacrifices
to other gods and provoked the anger of the
LORD the God of his fathers.

Other records of the reign of Ahaz

26 s The other acts and all the events of his reign,
from first to last, are recorded in the annals
27 of the kings of Judah and Israel. So Ahaz
rested with his forefathers and was buried in
the city of Jerusalem, but was not given
burial with the kings of Judah. He was
succeeded by his son Hezekiah.

Hezekiah calls for repentance

1 t Hezekiah was twenty-five years old when he
came to the throne, and he reigned in Jerusalem for twenty-nine years; his mother was
2 Abijah daughter of Zechariah. He did what
was right in the eyes of the LORD, as David
his forefather had done.
3 In the first year of his reign, in the first
month, he opened the gates of the house of
4 the LORD and repaired them. He brought in
the priests and the Levites and gathered them
5 together in the square on the east side, and
said to them, 'Levites, listen to me. Hallow
yourselves now, hallow the house of the
LORD the God of your fathers, and remove
6 the pollution from the sanctuary. For our

forefathers were unfaithful and did what was
wrong in the eyes of the LORD our God: they
forsook him, they would have nothing to
do with his dwelling-place, they turned their
backs on it. They shut the doors of the porch 7
and extinguished the lamps, they ceased to
burn incense and offer whole-offerings in
the sanctuary to the God of Israel. Therefore 8
the anger of the LORD fell upon Judah and
Jerusalem and he made them repugnant, an
object of horror and derision, as you see for
yourselves. Hence it is that our fathers have 9
fallen by the sword, our sons and daughters
and our wives are in captivity. Now I intend 10
that we should pledge ourselves to the LORD
the God of Israel, in order that his anger may
be averted from us. So, my sons, let no time 11
be lost; for the LORD has chosen you to serve
him and to minister to him, to be his ministers
and to burn sacrifices.'

Worship is restored

Then the Levites set to work—Mahath son 12
of Amasai and Joel son of Azariah of the
family of Kohath; of the family of Merari,
Kish son of Abdi and Azariah son of
Jehalelel; of the family of Gershon, Joah
son of Zimmah and Eden son of Joah; of 13
the family of Elizaphan, Shimri and Jeiel;
of the family of Asaph, Zechariah and
Mattaniah; of the family of Heman, Jehiel 14
and Shimei; and of the family of Jeduthun,
Shemaiah and Uzziel. They assembled their 15
kinsmen and hallowed themselves, and then
went in, as the king had instructed them at
the LORD's command, to purify the house
of the LORD. The priests went inside to 16
purify the house of the LORD; they removed
all the pollution which they found in the
temple into the court of the house of the
LORD, and the Levites took it from them
and carried it outside to the gorge of the
Kidron. They began the rites on the first 17
day of the first month, and on the eighth
day they reached the porch; then for eight
days they consecrated the house of the LORD,
and on the sixteenth day of the first month
they finished. Then they went into the palace 18
and said to King Hezekiah, 'We have purified the whole of the house of the LORD, the
altar of whole-offering with all its vessels,
and the table for the Bread of the Presence
arranged in rows with all its vessels; and we 19
have put in order and consecrated all the
vessels which King Ahaz cast aside during
his reign, when he was unfaithful. They
are now in place before the altar of the
LORD.'

Then King Hezekiah rose early, assembled 20
the officers of the city and went up to the
house of the LORD. They brought seven bulls, 21

---

s Verses 26, 27: cp. 2 Kgs. 16. 19, 20. *t Verses 1, 2: cp. 2 Kgs. 18. 1–3.*

seven rams, and seven lambs for the whole-offering,[u] and seven he-goats as a sin-offering for the kingdom, for the sanctuary, and for Judah; these he commanded the priests of Aaron's line to offer on the altar of the LORD.
22 So the bulls were slaughtered, and the priests took their blood and flung it against the altar; the rams were slaughtered, and their blood was flung against the altar; the lambs were slaughtered, and their blood was
23 flung against the altar. Then the he-goats for the sin-offering were brought before the king and the assembly, who laid their hands
24 on them; and the priests slaughtered them and used their blood as a sin-offering on the altar to make expiation for all Israel. For the king had commanded that the whole-offering and the sin-offering should be made for all Israel.
25 He posted the Levites in the house of the LORD with cymbals, lutes, and harps, according to the rule prescribed by David, by Gad the king's seer and Nathan the prophet; for this rule had come from the LORD through
26 his prophets. The Levites stood ready with the instruments of David, and the priests
27 with the trumpets. Hezekiah gave the order

that the whole-offering should be offered on the altar. At the moment when the whole-offering began, the song to the LORD began too, with the trumpets, led by the instru-
28 ments of David king of Israel. The whole assembly prostrated themselves, the singers sang and the trumpeters sounded; all this continued until the whole-offering was com-
29 plete. When the offering was complete, the king and all his company bowed down and
30 prostrated themselves. And King Hezekiah and his officers commanded the Levites to praise the LORD in the words of David and of Asaph the seer. So they praised him most joyfully and bowed down and prostrated themselves.

The people bring their sacrifices

31 Then Hezekiah said, 'You have now given to the LORD with open hands; approach with your sacrifices and thank-offerings for the house of the LORD.' So the assembly

brought sacrifices and thank-offerings; and every man of willing spirit brought whole-
32 offerings. The number of whole-offerings which the assembly brought was seventy bulls, a hundred rams, and two hundred lambs; all these made a whole-offering to
33 the LORD. And the consecrated offerings were six hundred bulls and three thousand
34 sheep. But the priests were too few and could not flay all the whole-offerings; so their colleagues the Levites helped them until the work was completed and all the priests had hallowed themselves—for the Levites had been more scrupulous than
35 the priests in hallowing themselves. There were indeed whole-offerings in abundance, besides the fat of the shared-offerings and the drink-offerings for the whole-offerings. In this way the service of the house of the
36 LORD was restored; and Hezekiah and all the people rejoiced over what God had done for the people and because it had come about so suddenly.

Hezekiah appeals to Israel to repent

Then Hezekiah sent word to all Israel and **30** Judah, and also wrote letters to Ephraim and Manasseh, inviting them to come to the house of the LORD in Jerusalem to keep the Passover of the LORD the God of Israel. The
2 king and all his officers and all the assembly in Jerusalem had agreed to keep the Passover in the second month, but they had not been
3 able to keep it at that time, because not enough priests had hallowed themselves and the people had not assembled in Jerusalem.
4 The proposal was acceptable to the king and the whole assembly. So they resolved to
5 make a proclamation throughout all Israel, from Beersheba to Dan, that the people should come to Jerusalem to keep the Pass-over of the LORD the God of Israel. Never before had so many kept it according to the prescribed form. Couriers went throughout
6 all Israel and Judah with letters from the king and his officers, proclaiming the royal command: 'Turn back, men of Israel, to the LORD the God of Abraham, Isaac, and Israel, so that he may turn back to those of you who escaped capture by the kings of Assyria. Do not be like your forefathers and
7 your kinsmen, who were unfaithful to the LORD the God of their fathers, so that he made them an object of horror, as you your-selves saw. Do not be stubborn as your fore-
8 fathers were; submit yourselves to the LORD and enter his sanctuary which he has sancti-fied for ever, and worship the LORD your God, so that his anger may be averted from you. For when you turn back to the LORD,
9 your kinsmen and your children will win compassion from their captors and return

u for the whole-offering: *prob. rdg.; Heb. om.*

to this land. The LORD your God is gracious and compassionate, and he will not turn away from you if you turn back to him.'

10 So the couriers passed from city to city through the land of Ephraim and Manasseh and as far as Zebulun, but they were treated 11 with scorn and ridicule. However, a few men of Asher, Manasseh, and Zebulun submitted 12 and came to Jerusalem. Further, the hand of God moved the people in Judah with one accord to carry out what the king and his officers had ordered at the LORD's command.

Great rejoicing in Jerusalem

13 Many people, a very great assembly, came together in Jerusalem to keep the pilgrim-feast of Unleavened Bread in the second 14 month. They began by removing the altars in Jerusalem; they removed the altars for burning sacrifices and threw them into the 15 gorge of the Kidron. They killed the passover lamb on the fourteenth day of the second month; and the priests and the Levites were bitterly ashamed. They hallowed themselves and brought whole-16 offerings to the house of the LORD. They took their accustomed places, according to the direction laid down for them in the law of Moses the man of God; the priests flung against the altar the blood which they re-17 ceived from the Levites. But many in the assembly had not hallowed themselves; therefore the Levites had to kill the passover lamb for every one who was unclean, in 18 order to hallow him to the LORD. For a majority of the people, many from Ephraim, Manasseh, Issachar, and Zebulun, had not kept themselves ritually clean, and therefore kept the Passover irregularly. But Hezekiah prayed for them, saying, 'May the good 19 LORD grant pardon to every one who makes a practice of seeking guidance of God, the LORD the God of his fathers, even if he has not observed the rules for the purification of 20 the sanctuary.' The LORD heard Hezekiah 21 and healed the people. And the Israelites who were present in Jerusalem kept the feast of Unleavened Bread for seven days with great rejoicing, and the Levites and the priests praised the LORD every day with un-22 restrained fervour.*v* Hezekiah spoke encouragingly to all the Levites who had shown true understanding in the service of the LORD.

So they spent the seven days of the festival sacrificing shared-offerings and making confession to*w* the LORD the God of their fathers.

Then the whole assembly agreed to keep 23 the feast for another seven days; so they kept it for another seven days with general rejoicing. For Hezekiah king of Judah set 24 aside for the assembly a thousand bulls and seven thousand sheep, and his officers set aside for the assembly a thousand bulls and ten thousand sheep; and priests hallowed themselves in great numbers. So the whole 25 assembly of Judah, including the priests and the Levites, rejoiced, together with all the assembly which came out of Israel, and the resident aliens from Israel and those who lived in Judah. There was great rejoicing in 26 Jerusalem, the like of which had not been known there since the days of Solomon son of David king of Israel. Then the priests 27 and the Levites stood to bless the people; the LORD listened to their cry, and their prayer came to God's holy dwelling-place in heaven.

The people give willingly

When this was over, all the Israelites present **31** went out to the cities of Judah and smashed the sacred pillars, hacked down the sacred poles and broke up the hill-shrines and the altars throughout Judah and Benjamin, Ephraim and Manasseh, until they had made an end of them. That done, the Israelites returned, each to his own patrimony in his own city.

Then Hezekiah installed the priests and 2 the Levites in office, division by division, allotting to each priest or Levite his own particular duty, for whole-offerings or shared-offerings, to give thanks or to sing praise, or to serve in the gates of the several quarters in the LORD's house.

The king provided from his own resources, 3 as the share due from him, the whole-offerings for both morning and evening, and for sabbaths, new moons, and appointed seasons, as prescribed in the law of the LORD. He ordered the people living in Jeru-4 salem to provide the share due from the priests and the Levites, so that they might devote themselves entirely to the law of the LORD. As soon as the king's order was issued 5 to the Israelites, they gave generously from the firstfruits of their corn and new wine, oil and honey, all the produce of their land; they brought a full tithe of everything. The 6 Israelites and the Judaeans living in the cities of Judah also brought a tithe of cattle and sheep, and a tithe of all produce as offerings dedicated to the LORD their God, and they stacked the produce in heaps. They 7 began to deposit the heaps in the third

---

v with unrestrained fervour: *prob. rdg.; Heb.* with powerful instruments. *w* making confession to: *or* confessing.

month and completed them in the seventh.
8 When Hezekiah and his officers came and saw the heaps, they blessed the LORD and
9 his people Israel. Hezekiah asked the priests
10 and the Levites about these heaps, and Azariah the chief priest, who was of the line of Zadok, answered, 'From the time when the people began to bring their contribution into the house of the LORD, they have had enough to eat, enough and to spare; indeed, the LORD has so greatly blessed them that they have this great store left over.'

Providing for the Levites

11 Then Hezekiah ordered store-rooms to be prepared in the house of the LORD, and this
12 was done; and the people honestly brought in their contributions, the tithe, and their dedicated gifts. The overseer in charge of them was Conaniah the Levite, with Shimei
13 his brother as his deputy; Jehiel, Azaziah, Nahath, Asahel, Jerimoth, Jozabad, Eliel, Ismachiah, Mahath, and Benaiah were appointed by King Hezekiah and Azariah, the chief overseer of the house of God, to assist
14 Conaniah and Shimei his brother. And Kore son of Imnah the Levite, keeper of the East Gate, was in charge of the freewill offerings to God, to apportion the contributions made to the LORD and the most sacred offerings.
15 Eden, Miniamin, Jeshua, Shemaiah, Amariah, and Shecaniah in the priestly cities assisted him in the fair distribution of portions to their kinsmen, young and old[x] alike,
16 by divisions. Irrespective of their registration, shares were distributed to all males three years of age and upwards who entered the house of the LORD to take their daily part in the service, according to their divi-
17 sions, as their office demanded. The priests were registered by families, the Levites from twenty years of age and upwards by their
18 offices in their divisions. They were registered with all their dependants, their wives, their sons, and their daughters, the whole company of them, because in virtue of their permanent standing they had to keep them-
19 selves duly hallowed. As for the priests of Aaron's line in the common lands attached to their cities, in every city men were nominated to distribute portions to every male among the priests and to every one who was registered with the Levites.
20 Such was the action taken by Hezekiah throughout Judah; he did what was good and right and loyal in the sight of the LORD
21 his God. Whatever he undertook in the service of the house of God and in obedience to the law and the commandment to seek guidance of his God, he did with all his heart, and he prospered.

ASSYRIA

Sennacherib invades Judah

After these events and this example of loyal **32** conduct, Sennacherib king of Assyria invaded Judah and encamped against the fortified cities, believing that he could attach them to himself. When Hezekiah saw 2 that he had come and was determined to attack Jerusalem, he consulted his civil and 3 military officers about blocking up the springs outside the city; and they encouraged him. They gathered together a large num- 4 ber of people and blocked up all the springs and the stream which flowed through the land. 'Why', they said, 'should Assyrian kings come here and find plenty of water?' Then the king acted boldly; he made good 5 every breach in the city wall and erected towers on it; he built another wall outside it and strengthened the Millo of the city of David; he also collected a great quantity of weapons and shields. He appointed military 6 commanders over the people and assembled them in the square by the city gate and spoke encouragingly to them in these words: 'Be 7 strong; be brave. Do not let the king of Assyria or the rabble he has brought with him strike terror or panic into your hearts. We have more on our side than he has. He 8 has human strength; but we have the LORD our God to help us and to fight our battles.' So spoke Hezekiah king of Judah, and the people were buoyed up by his words.

Sennacherib presses for surrender

After this, Sennacherib king of Assyria, 9 while he and his high command were at Lachish, sent envoys to Jerusalem to deliver this message to Hezekiah king of Judah and to all the Judaeans in Jerusalem: 'Senna- 10 cherib king of Assyria says, "What gives you confidence to stay in Jerusalem under siege? Hezekiah is misleading you into risk- 11 ing death by famine or thirst where you are, when he tells you that the LORD your God will save you from the grip of the Assyrian king. Was it not Hezekiah himself who sup- 12 pressed the LORD's hill-shrines and altars and told the people of Judah and Jerusalem that they must prostrate themselves before one altar only and burn sacrifices there? You 13 know very well what I and my forefathers have done to all the peoples of the lands. Were the gods of these nations able to save

---

x Or high and low.   *y Verses 1–19: cp. 2 Kgs. 18. 13–37; Isa. 36. 1–22.*

14 their lands from me? Not one of the gods of these nations, which my forefathers exterminated, was able to save his people from me.
15 Much less will your god save you! How, then, can Hezekiah deceive you or mislead you like this? How can you believe him, for no god of any nation or kingdom has been able to save his people from me or my forefathers? Much less will your gods save you!"'
16 The envoys of Sennacherib spoke still more against the LORD God and against his
17 servant Hezekiah. And the king himself wrote a letter to defy the LORD the God of Israel, in these terms: 'Just as the gods of other nations could not save their people from me, so the god of Hezekiah will not
18 save his people from me.' Then they shouted in Hebrew at the top of their voices at the people of Jerusalem on the wall, to strike them with fear and terror, hoping thus to
19 capture the city. They described the god*z* of Jerusalem as being like the gods of the other peoples of the earth—things made by the hands of men.
20 *a* In this plight King Hezekiah and the prophet Isaiah son of Amoz cried to heaven
21 in prayer. So the LORD sent an angel who cut down all the fighting men, as well as the leaders and the commanders, in the camp of the king of Assyria, so that he went home disgraced to his own land. When he entered the temple of his god, certain of his own sons struck him down with their swords.
22 Thus the LORD saved Hezekiah and the inhabitants of Jerusalem from Sennacherib king of Assyria and all their enemies; and
23 he gave them respite on every side. Many people brought to Jerusalem offerings for the LORD and costly gifts for Hezekiah king of Judah. From then on he was held in high honour by all the nations.

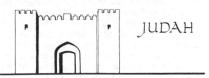

JUDAH

Hezekiah falls ill

24 About this time Hezekiah fell dangerously ill and prayed to the LORD; the LORD said, 'I will heal you',*b* and granted him a sign.
25 But, being a proud man, he was not grateful for the good done to him, and Judah and
26 Jerusalem suffered for it. Then, proud as he was, Hezekiah submitted, and the people of Jerusalem with him, and the LORD's anger did not fall on them again in Hezekiah's time.

Events in Hezekiah's life

Hezekiah enjoyed great wealth and fame.*c*
27 He built for himself treasuries for silver and gold, precious stones and spices, shields and other costly things; and barns for the har-
28 vests of corn, new wine, and oil; and stalls for every kind of cattle, as well as sheepfolds. He amassed*d* a great many flocks and
29 herds; God had indeed given him vast riches. It was this same Hezekiah who
30 blocked the upper outflow of the waters of Gihon and directed them downwards and westwards to the city of David. In fact, Hezekiah was successful in everything he attempted, even in the affair of the envoys
31 sent by the king*e* of Babylon—the envoys who came to inquire about the portent which had been seen in the land at the time when God left him to himself, to test him and to discover all that was in his heart.

The other events of Hezekiah's reign, and
32 his works of piety, are recorded in the vision of the prophet Isaiah son of Amoz and in the annals of the kings of Judah and Israel.
33 So Hezekiah rested with his forefathers and was buried in the uppermost of the graves of David's sons; all Judah and the people of Jerusalem paid him honour when he died, and he was succeeded by his son Manasseh.

Manasseh reigns over Judah

Manasseh was twelve years old when he **33** 1*f*
came to the throne, and he reigned in Jeru-
2 salem for fifty-five years. He did what was wrong in the eyes of the LORD, in following the abominable practices of the nations which the LORD had dispossessed in favour
3 of the Israelites. He rebuilt the hill-shrines which his father Hezekiah had dismantled, he erected altars to the Baalim and made sacred poles, he prostrated himself before all the host of heaven and worshipped them.

---

z Or gods.   *a* Verses 20–22: cp. 2 Kgs. 19. 1–37; Isa. 37. 1–38.   *b* I will heal you: prob. rdg., cp. 2 Kgs. 20. 5; Heb. om.   *c* Or riches.   *d* Prob. rdg.; Heb. adds cities.   *e* Prob. rdg., cp. 2 Kgs. 20. 12; Heb. officers.   *f* Verses 1–9: cp. 2 Kgs. 21. 1–9.

4 He built altars in the house of the LORD, that house of which the LORD had said, 'In 5 Jerusalem shall my Name be for ever.' He built altars for all the host of heaven in the 6 two courts of the house of the LORD; he made his sons pass through the fire in the Valley of Ben-hinnom, he practised soothsaying, divination, and sorcery, and dealt with ghosts and spirits. He did much wrong in the eyes of the LORD and provoked his 7 anger; and the image that he had had carved in relief he put in the house of God, the place of which God had said to David and Solomon his son, 'This house and Jerusalem, which I chose out of all the tribes of Israel, 8 shall receive my Name for all time. I will not again displace Israel from the land which I assigned to their forefathers, if only they will be careful to observe all that I commanded them through Moses, all the law, 9 the statutes, and the rules.' But Manasseh misled Judah and the inhabitants of Jerusalem into wickedness far worse than that of the nations which the LORD had exterminated in favour of the Israelites.

Manasseh repents

10 The LORD spoke to Manasseh and to his 11 people, but they paid no heed. So the LORD brought against them the commanders of the army of the king of Assyria; they captured Manasseh with spiked weapons, and bound him with fetters, and brought him 12 to Babylon. In his distress he prayed to the LORD his God and sought to placate him, and made his humble submission before the 13 God of his fathers. He prayed, and God accepted his petition and heard his supplication. He brought him back to Jerusalem and restored him to the throne; and thus Manasseh learnt that the LORD was God.

14 After this he built an outer wall for the city of David, west of Gihon in the gorge, and extended it to the entrance at the Fish Gate, enclosing Ophel; and he raised it to a great height. He also put military commanders 15 in all the fortified cities of Judah. He removed the foreign gods and the carved image from the house of the LORD and all the altars which he had built on the temple mount and in Jerusalem, and threw them 16 out of the city. Moreover, he repaired the altar of the LORD and sacrificed at it shared-offerings and thank-offerings, and commanded Judah to serve the LORD the God 17 of Israel. But the people still continued to sacrifice at the hill-shrines, though only to the LORD their God.

Other records of Manasseh's reign

18 The rest of the acts of Manasseh, his prayer to his God, and the discourses of the seers who spoke to him in the name of the LORD the God of Israel, are recorded in the chronicles of the kings of Israel. His prayer 19 and the answer he received to it, and all his sin and unfaithfulness, and the places where he built hill-shrines and set up sacred poles and carved idols, before he submitted, are recorded in the chronicles of the seers. So 20 Manasseh rested with his forefathers and was buried in the garden-tomb of*ᵍ* his family; he was succeeded by his son Amon.

Amon reigns over Judah

Amon was twenty-two years old when he 21*ʰ* came to the throne, and he reigned in Jerusalem for two years. He did what was wrong 22 in the eyes of the LORD as his father Manasseh had done. He sacrificed to all the images that his father Manasseh had made, and worshipped them. He was not submissive 23 before the LORD like his father Manasseh; his guilt was much greater. His courtiers 24 conspired against him and murdered him in his house; but the people of the land killed 25 all the conspirators and made his son Josiah king in his place.

Josiah's early reforms

Josiah was eight years old when he came 34 to the throne, and he reigned in Jerusalem for thirty-one years. He did what was right 2 in the eyes of the LORD; he followed in the footsteps of his forefather David, swerving neither right nor left. In the eighth year of 3 his reign, when he was still a boy, he began to seek guidance of the God of his forefather David; and in the twelfth year he began to purge Judah and Jerusalem of the hill-shrines and the sacred poles, and the carved idols and the images of metal. He saw to it 4 that the altars for the Baalim were destroyed and he hacked down the incense-altars which stood above them; he broke in pieces the sacred poles and the carved and metal images, grinding them to powder and scattering it on the graves of those who had sacrificed to them. He also burnt the bones of the 5 priests on their altars and purged Judah and Jerusalem. In the cities of Manasseh, Eph- 6 raim, and Simeon, and as far as Naphtali, he burnt down their houses wherever he found them; he destroyed the altars and the 7 sacred poles, ground the idols to powder, and hacked down the incense-altars throughout the land of Israel. Then he returned to Jerusalem.

Hilkiah discovers the book of the law

In the eighteenth year of his reign, after he 8*ʲ* had purified the land and the house, he sent

g the garden-tomb of: *prob. rdg., cp. 2 Kgs. 21. 18; Heb. om.*   h *Verses 21–25: cp. 2 Kgs. 21. 19–24.*
i *Verses 1, 2: cp. 2 Kgs. 22. 1, 2.*   j *Verses 8–32: cp. 2 Kgs. 22. 3—23. 3.*

Shaphan son of Azaliah and Maaseiah the governor of the city and Joah son of Joahaz the secretary of state to repair the house of 9 the LORD his God. They came to Hilkiah the high priest and gave him the silver that had been brought to the house of God, the silver which the Levites, on duty at the threshold, had gathered from Manasseh, Ephraim, and all the rest of Israel, as well as from Judah and Benjamin and the in-10 habitants of Jerusalem. It was then handed over to the foremen in charge of the work in the house of the LORD, and these men, working in the house, used it for repairing 11 and strengthening the fabric; they gave it also to the carpenters and builders to buy hewn stone, and timber for rafters and beams, for the buildings which the kings of Judah -13 had allowed to fall into ruin. The men did their work honestly under the direction of Jahath and Obadiah, Levites of the line of Merari, and Zechariah and Meshullam, members of the family of Kohath. These also had control of the porters and directed the workmen of every trade. The Levites were all skilled musicians, and some of them were 14 secretaries, clerks, or door-keepers. When they fetched the silver which had been brought to the house of the LORD, the priest Hilkiah discovered the book of the law of

the LORD which had been given through 15 Moses. Then Hilkiah told Shaphan the adjutant-general, 'I have discovered the book of the law in the house of the LORD.' Hilkiah 16 gave the book to Shaphan, and he brought it to the king and reported to him: 'Your servants are doing all that was entrusted to 17 them. They have melted down the silver in the house of the LORD and have handed it over to the foremen and the workmen.' 18 Shaphan the adjutant-general also told the

king that the priest Hilkiah had given him a book; and he read it out in the king's presence. When the king heard what was in 19 the book of the law, he rent his clothes, and 20 ordered Hilkiah, Ahikam son of Shaphan, Abdon son of Micah, Shaphan the adjutant-general, and Asaiah the king's attendant, to 21 go and seek guidance of the LORD, for himself and for all who still remained in Israel and Judah, about the contents of the book that had been discovered. 'Great is the wrath of the LORD,' he said, 'and it has been poured out upon us because our forefathers did not observe the command of the LORD and do all that is written in this book.'

Destruction of Jerusalem foretold

So Hilkiah and those whom the king had 22 instructed went to Huldah the prophetess, wife of Shallum son of Tikvah,^{k} son of Hasrah, the keeper of the wardrobe, and consulted her at her home in the second quarter of Jerusalem. 'This is the word of 23 the LORD the God of Israel,' she answered: 'Say to the man who sent you to me, "This 24 is the word of the LORD: I am bringing disaster on this place and its inhabitants, fulfilling all the imprecations recorded in the book which was read in the presence of the king of Judah, because they have forsaken 25 me and burnt sacrifices to other gods, provoking my anger with all the idols they have made with their own hands; therefore my wrath is poured out upon this place and will not be quenched." This is what you shall say 26 to the king of Judah who sent you to seek guidance of the LORD: "This is the word of the LORD the God of Israel: You have listened to my words and shown a willing 27 heart, you humbled yourself before God when you heard what I said about this place and its inhabitants; you humbled yourself and rent your clothes and wept before me. Because of all this,^{l} I for my part have heard you. This is the very word of the LORD. Therefore, I will gather you to your fore- 28 fathers, and you will be gathered to your grave in peace; you will not live to see all the disaster which I am bringing upon this place and upon its inhabitants." ' So they brought back word to the king.

Josiah reads the book to the people

Then the king sent and called all the elders 29 of Judah and Jerusalem together, and went up to the house of the LORD; he took with 30 him all the men of Judah and the inhabitants of Jerusalem, the priests and the Levites, the whole population, high and low. There he read them the whole book of the covenant discovered in the house of the LORD; and 31 then, standing on the dais, the king made a

k Prob. rdg., cp. 2 Kgs. 22. 14; Heb. Tokhath.   *l Because of all this: prob. rdg.; Heb. om.*

covenant before the LORD to obey him and keep his commandments, his testimonies, and his statutes, with all his heart and soul, and so fulfil the terms of the covenant written 32 in this book. Then he swore an oath with all who were present in Jerusalem to keep the covenant.[m] Thereafter the inhabitants of Jerusalem did obey the covenant of God, 33 the God of their fathers. Josiah removed all abominable things from all the territories of the Israelites, so that everyone living in Israel might serve the LORD his God. As long as he lived they did not fail in their allegiance to the LORD the God of their fathers.

Josiah keeps the Passover

35 Josiah kept a Passover to the LORD in Jerusalem, and the passover lamb was killed on 2 the fourteenth day of the first month. He appointed the priests to their offices and encouraged them to perform the service of 3 the house of the LORD. He said to the Levites, the teachers of Israel, who were dedicated to the LORD, 'Put the holy Ark in the house which Solomon son of David king of Israel built; it is not to be carried about on your shoulders. Now is the time to serve the 4 LORD your God and his people Israel: prepare yourselves by families according to your divisions, following the written instructions of David king of Israel and those 5 of Solomon his son; and stand in the Holy Place as representatives of the family groups of the lay people, your brothers, one division 6 of Levites to each family group. Kill the passover lamb and hallow yourselves and prepare for your brothers to fulfil the word of the LORD given through Moses.'

7 Josiah contributed on behalf of all the lay people present thirty thousand small cattle, that is young rams and goats, for the Passover, in addition to three thousand bulls; all these were from the king's own resources. 8 And his officers contributed willingly for the people, the priests, and the Levites. Hilkiah, Zechariah, and Jehiel, the chief officers of the house of God, gave on behalf of the priests two thousand six hundred small cattle for the Passover, in addition to three 9 hundred bulls. And Conaniah, Shemaiah and Nethaneel his brothers, and Hashabiah, Jeiel, and Jozabad, the chiefs of the Levites, gave on behalf of the Levites for the Passover five thousand small cattle in addition to five hundred bulls.

10 When the service had been arranged, the priests stood in their places and the Levites in their divisions, according to the king's 11 command. They killed the passover victim, and the priests flung the blood against the 12 altar as the Levites flayed the animals. Then they removed the fat flesh,[n] which they allocated to the people by groups of families for them to offer to the LORD, as prescribed in the book of Moses; and so with the bulls. They cooked the passover victim over the 13 fire according to custom, and boiled the holy offerings in pots, cauldrons, and pans, and served them quickly to all the people. After 14 that they made the necessary preparations for themselves and the priests, because the priests of Aaron's line were engaged till nightfall in offering whole-offerings and the fat portions; so the Levites made the necessary preparations for themselves and for the priests of Aaron's line. The singers, 15 the sons of Asaph, were in their places according to the rules laid down by David and by Asaph, Heman, and Jeduthun, the king's seers. The door-keepers stood, each at his gate; there was no need for them to leave their posts, because their kinsmen the Levites had made the preparations for them.

In this manner all the service of the LORD 16 was arranged that day, to keep the Passover and to offer whole-offerings on the altar of the LORD, according to the command of King Josiah. The people of Israel who were 17 present kept the Passover at that time and the pilgrim-feast of Unleavened Bread for seven days. No Passover like it had been 18 kept in Israel since the days of the prophet Samuel; none of the kings of Israel had ever kept such a Passover as Josiah kept, with the priests and Levites and all Judah and Israel who were present and the inhabitants of Jerusalem. In the eighteenth 19 year of Josiah's reign this Passover was kept.

Josiah dies in battle

After Josiah had thus organized all the ser- 20 vice of the house, Necho king of Egypt marched up to attack Carchemish on the Euphrates; and Josiah went out to confront him. But Necho sent envoys to him, saying, 21 'What do you want with me, king of Judah? I have no quarrel with you today, only with those with whom I am at war. God has purposed to speed me on my way, and God is on my side; do not stand in his way, or he will destroy you.' Josiah would not be 22 deflected from his purpose but insisted on fighting; he refused to listen to Necho's words spoken at God's command, and he sallied out to join battle in the vale of Megiddo. The archers shot at him; he was 23 severely wounded and told his bodyguard to carry him off. They lifted him out of his 24 chariot and carried him in his viceroy's chariot to Jerusalem. There he died and was buried among the tombs of his ancestors, and all Judah and Jerusalem mourned for

m to keep the covenant: *prob. rdg., cp. 2 Kgs. 23. 3; Heb.* and Benjamin.　　　　*n* fat flesh: *or* whole-offering.

25 him. Jeremiah also made a lament for Josiah; and to this day the minstrels, both men and women, commemorate Josiah in their lamentations. Such laments have become traditional in Israel, and they are found in the written collections.

Other records of Josiah's reign

26 The other events of Josiah's reign, and his works of piety, all performed in accordance with what is laid down in the law of the LORD, 27 and his acts, from first to last, are recorded in the annals of the kings of Israel and Judah.

Reign and dethronement of Jehoahaz

1ᵒ The people of the land took Josiah's son Jehoahaz and made him king in place of his 2 father in Jerusalem. He was twenty-three years old when he came to the throne, and he reigned in Jerusalem for three months. 3 Then Necho king of Egypt deposed him and fined the country a hundred talents of silver 4 and one talent of gold, and made his brother Eliakim king over Judah and Jerusalem in his place, changing his name to Jehoiakim; he also carried away his brother Jehoahaz to Egypt.

Jehoiakim reigns over Judah

5 Jehoiakim was twenty-five years old when he came to the throne, and he reigned in Jerusalem for eleven years. He did what was 6 wrong in the eyes of the LORD his God. So Nebuchadnezzar king of Babylon marched against him and put him in fetters and took 7 him to Babylon. He also removed to Babylon some of the vessels of the house of the LORD and put them into his own palace 8 there. The other events of Jehoiakim's reign, including the abominations he committed, and everything of which he was held guilty, are recorded in the annals of the kings of Israel and Judah. He was succeeded by his son Jehoiachin.

Nebuchadnezzar takes Jehoiachin captive

9ᵖ Jehoiachin was eight years old when he came to the throne, and he reigned in Jerusalem for three months and ten days. He did what 10 was wrong in the eyes of the LORD. At the

o *Verses 1–4: cp. 2 Kgs. 23. 30–34.*   p *Verses 9, 10: cp. 2 Kgs. 24. 8–17.*

turn of the year King Nebuchadnezzar sent and brought him to Babylon, together with the choicest vessels of the house of the LORD, and made his father's brother Zedekiah king over Judah and Jerusalem.

Zedekiah reigns over Judah

Zedekiah was twenty-one years old when he 11 came to the throne, and he reigned in Jerusalem for eleven years. He did what was 12 wrong in the eyes of the LORD his God; he did not defer to the guidance of the prophet Jeremiah, the spokesman of the LORD. He 13 also rebelled against King Nebuchadnezzar, who had laid on him a solemn oath of allegiance. He was obstinate and stubborn and refused to return to the LORD the God of Israel.

Nebuchadnezzar destroys Jerusalem

All the chiefs of Judah and the priests and 14 the people became more and more unfaithful, following all the abominable practices

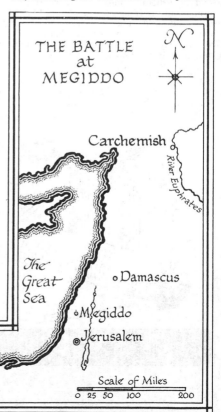

THE BATTLE at MEGIDDO

Carchemish

River Euphrates

The Great Sea

Damascus

Megiddo

Jerusalem

EGYPT

Scale of Miles
0 25 50 100 200

of the other nations; and they defiled the
house of the LORD which he had hallowed
15 in Jerusalem. The LORD God of their fathers
had warned them betimes through his messengers, for he took pity on his people and
16 on his dwelling-place; but they never ceased
to deride his messengers, scorn his words
and scoff at his prophets, until the anger of
the LORD burst out against his people and

BABYLON

17q could not be appeased. So he brought
against them the king of the Chaldaeans,
who put their young men to the sword in
the sanctuary and spared neither young man
nor maiden, neither the old nor the weak;
18 God gave them all into his power. And he
brought all the vessels of the house of God,
great and small, and the treasures of the
house of the LORD and of the king and his
officers—all these he brought to Babylon.
19 And they burnt down the house of God,

razed the city wall of Jerusalem and burnt
down all its stately mansions and all their
precious possessions until everything was
destroyed. Those who escaped the sword he 20
took captive to Babylon, and they became
slaves to him and his sons until the sovereignty passed to the Persians, while the 21
land of Israel ran the full term of its sabbaths.
All the time that it lay desolate it kept the
sabbath rest, to complete seventy years in
fulfilment of the word of the LORD by the
prophet Jeremiah.

Proclamation of Cyrus

Now in the first year of Cyrus king of 22r
Persia, so that the word of the LORD spoken
through Jeremiah might be fulfilled, the
LORD stirred up the heart of Cyrus king of
Persia; and he issued a proclamation
throughout his kingdom, both by word of
mouth and in writing, to this effect:

This is the word of Cyrus king of Persia: 23
The LORD the God of heaven has given
me all the kingdoms of the earth, and he
himself has charged me to build him a
house at Jerusalem in Judah. To every
man of his people now among you I say,
the LORD his God bes with him, and let
him go up.

q *Verses 17–20: cp. 2 Kgs. 25. 1–17.*   r *Verses 22, 23: cp. Ezra 1. 1–3.*   s be: *prob. rdg., cp. Ezra
1. 3; Heb. om.*

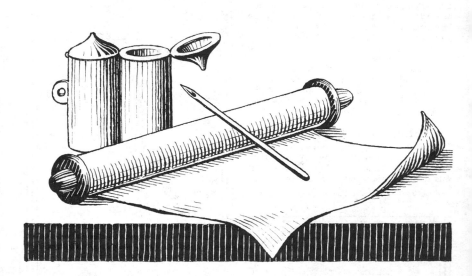

THE BOOK OF
EZRA

Proclamation of Cyrus

1 NOW in the first year of Cyrus king of Persia, so that the word of the LORD spoken through Jeremiah might be fulfilled, the LORD stirred up the heart of Cyrus king of Persia; and he issued a proclamation throughout his kingdom, both by word of mouth and in writing, to this effect:

2   This is the word of Cyrus king of Persia: The LORD the God of heaven has given me all the kingdoms of the earth, and he himself has charged me to build him a house at Jerusalem in Judah.
3 To every man of his people now among you I say, God be with him, and let him go up to Jerusalem in Judah, and rebuild the house of the LORD the God of Israel, the God whose city is Jerusalem.
4 And every remaining Jew, wherever he may be living, may claim aid from his neighbours in that place, silver and gold, goods*a* and cattle, in addition to the voluntary offerings for the house of God in Jerusalem.

Repatriating the Jews

Thereupon the heads of families of Judah 5 and Benjamin, and the priests and the Levites, answered the summons, all whom God had moved to go up to rebuild the house of the LORD in Jerusalem. Their 6 neighbours all assisted them with gifts of every kind, silver*b* and gold, goods*a* and cattle and valuable gifts in abundance,*c* in addition to any voluntary service. Moreover, 7 Cyrus king of Persia produced the vessels of the house of the LORD which Nebuchadnezzar had removed from Jerusalem and placed in the temple of his god; and he handed 8 them over into the charge of Mithredath the treasurer, who made an inventory of them for Sheshbazzar the ruler of Judah. This 9 was the list: thirty gold basins, a thousand silver basins, twenty-nine vessels of various kinds, thirty golden bowls, four hundred and 10 ten silver bowls of various types, and a thousand other vessels. The vessels of gold and 11 silver amounted in all to five thousand four hundred; and Sheshbazzar took them all up to Jerusalem, when the exiles were brought back from Babylon.

The roll of returning exiles

1*d* Of the captives whom Nebuchadnezzar king of Babylon had taken into exile in Babylon, these were the people of the province who returned to Jerusalem and 2 Judah, each to his own city, led by Zerubbabel, Jeshua,*e* Nehemiah, Seraiah, Reelaiah, Mordecai, Bilshan, Mispar, Bigvai, Rehum and Baanah.

a Or pack-animals.   *b* with gifts . . . silver: *prob. rdg., cp. 1 Esdras 2. 9; Heb.* with vessels of silver.   *c* in abundance: *prob. rdg., cp. 1 Esdras 2. 9; Heb.* apart.   *d Verses 1–70: cp. Neh. 7. 6–73.*   *e Or* Joshua (*cp. Hag. 1. 1*).

The roll of the men of the people 3 of Israel: the family of Parosh, two thousand one hundred and seventy- 4 two; the family of Shephatiah, three hundred and seventy-two; 5 the family of Arah, seven hundred 6 and seventy-five; the family of Pahath-moab, namely the families of Jeshua and[f] Joab, two thousand 7 eight hundred and twelve; the family of Elam, one thousand two 8 hundred and fifty-four; the family of Zattu, nine hundred and forty- 9 five; the family of Zaccai, seven 10 hundred and sixty; the family of Bani, six hundred and forty-two; 11 the family of Bebai, six hundred 12 and twenty-three; the family of Azgad, one thousand two hundred 13 and twenty-four; the family of Adonikam, six hundred and sixty- 14 six; the family of Bigvai, two thou- 15 sand and fifty-six; the family of Adin, four hundred and fifty-four; 16 the family of Ater, namely that of 17 Hezekiah, ninety-eight; the family of Bezai, three hundred and twenty- 18 three; the family of Jorah, one 19 hundred and twelve; the family of Hashum, two hundred and twenty- 20 three; the family of Gibbar, ninety- 21 five. The men[g] of Bethlehem, one 22 hundred and twenty-three; the men 23 of Netophah, fifty-six; the men of Anathoth, one hundred and 24 twenty-eight; the men of Beth- 25 azmoth,[h] forty-two; the men of Kiriath-jearim,[i] Kephirah, and Beeroth, seven hundred and forty- 26 three; the men[j] of Ramah and Geba, six hundred and twenty-one; 27 the men of Michmas, one hundred 28 and twenty-two; the men of Bethel and Ai, two hundred and twenty- 29 three; the men[k] of Nebo, fifty-two; 30 the men of Magbish, one hundred 31 and fifty-six; the men of the other Elam, one thousand two hundred 32 and fifty-four; the men of Harim, 33 three hundred and twenty; the men of Lod, Hadid, and Ono, seven 34 hundred and twenty-five; the men of Jericho, three hundred and forty- 35 five; the men of Senaah, three thousand six hundred and thirty.

36 Priests: the family of Jedaiah, of the line of Jeshua, nine hundred 37 and seventy-three; the family of Immer, one thousand and fifty- 38 two; the family of Pashhur, one thousand two hundred and forty- 39 seven; the family of Harim, one thousand and seventeen.

40 Levites: the families of Jeshua and Kadmiel, of the line of Ho- 41 daviah, seventy-four. Singers: the family of Asaph, one hundred and 42 twenty-eight. The guild of door-keepers: the family of Shallum, the family of Ater, the family of Tal-mon, the family of Akkub, the family of Hatita, and the family of Shobai, one hundred and thirty-nine in all.

43 Temple-servitors: the family of Ziha, the family of Hasupha, the 44 family of Tabbaoth, the family of Keros, the family of Siaha, the 45 family of Padon, the family of Lebanah, the family of Hagabah, 46 the family of Akkub, the family of Hagab, the family of Shamlai,[l] 47 family of Hanan, the family of Giddel, the family of Gahar, the 48 family of Reaiah, the family of Rezin, the family of Nekoda, the 49 family of Gazzam, the family of Uzza, the family of Paseah, the 50 family of Besai, the family of Asnah, the family of the Meunim,[m] 51 the family of the Nephusim,[n] the family of Bakbuk, the family of Hakupha, the family of Harhur, 52 the family of Bazluth, the family of Mehida, the family of Harsha, 53 the family of Barkos, the family of 54 Sisera, the family of Temah, the family of Neziah, and the family of Hatipha.

55 Descendants of Solomon's ser-vants: the family of Sotai, the family of Hassophereth, the family 56 of Peruda, the family of Jaalah, the family of Darkon, the family of 57 Giddel, the family of Shephatiah, the family of Hattil, the family of Pochereth-hazzebaim, and the family of Ami.

58 The temple-servitors and the descendants of Solomon's servants

amounted to three hundred and ninety-two in all.

The following were those who 59 returned from Tel-melah, Tel-harsha, Kerub, Addan, and Im-mer, but could not establish their father's family nor whether by descent they belonged to Israel: the family of Delaiah, the family 60 of Tobiah, and the family of Nekoda, six hundred and fifty-two. Also of the priests: the family of 61 Hobaiah, the family of Hakkoz, and the family of Barzillai who had married a daughter of Barzillai the Gileadite and went by his[o] name. These searched for their names 62 among those enrolled in the gene-alogies, but they could not be found; they were disqualified for the priesthood as unclean, and the 63 governor forbade them to partake of the most sacred food until there should be a priest able to consult the Urim and the Thummim.

The whole assembled people 64 numbered forty-two thousand three hundred and sixty, apart 65 from their slaves, male and female, of whom there were seven thou-sand three hundred and thirty-seven; and they had two hundred singers, men and women. Their 66 horses numbered seven hundred and thirty-six, their mules two hundred and forty-five, their camels 67 four hundred and thirty-five, and their asses six thousand seven hun-dred and twenty.

When they came to the house of 68 the Lord in Jerusalem, some of the heads of families volunteered to rebuild the house of God on its original site. According to their 69 resources they gave for the fabric fund a total of sixty-one thousand drachmas of gold, five thousand minas of silver, and one hundred priestly robes.

The priests, the Levites, and some 70 of the people lived in Jerusalem and its suburbs;[p] the singers, the door-keepers, and temple-servitors,[q] and all other Israelites, lived in their own towns.

Building the altar

3 When the seventh month came, the Israel-ites now being settled in their towns, the

people assembled as one man in Jerusalem. Then Jeshua son of Jozadak and his fellow- 2 priests, and Zerubbabel son of Shealtiel and his kinsmen, set to work and built the altar of the God of Israel, in order to offer upon it whole-offerings as prescribed in the law of Moses the man of God. They put the altar 3 in place first, because they lived in fear of the foreign population; and they offered upon it whole-offerings to the Lord, both morning and evening offerings. They kept 4

---

f and: prob. rdg., cp. Neh. 7. 11; Heb. om. cp. Neh. 7. 28; Heb. the family of Azmoth. j Prob. rdg., cp. Neh. 7. 30; Heb. family. Shalmai (cp. Neh. 7. 48).   m Or Meinim. p in Jerusalem and its suburbs: prob. rdg., cp. 1 Esdras 5. 46; Heb. om.

g Prob. rdg., cp. Neh. 7. 26; Heb. family.   h Prob. rdg., i Prob. rdg., cp. Neh. 7. 29; Heb. the family of Kiriath-arim. k Prob. rdg.; Heb. family (also in verses 30–35).   l Or n Or Nephisim.   o Prob. rdg., cp. 1 Esdras 5. 38; Heb. their. q Prob. rdg.; Heb. adds in their towns.

the pilgrim-feast of Tabernacles[r] as ordained, and offered whole-offerings every day in the
5 number prescribed for each day, and, in addition to these, the regular whole-offerings and the offerings for sabbaths,[s] for new moons and for all the sacred seasons appointed by the LORD, and all voluntary
6 offerings brought to the LORD. The offering of whole-offerings began from the first day of the seventh month, although the foundation of the temple of the LORD had not yet been
7 laid. They gave money for the masons and carpenters, and food and drink and oil for the Sidonians and the Tyrians to fetch cedarwood from the Lebanon to the roadstead at Joppa, by licence from Cyrus king of Persia.

Rebuilding the Temple

8 In the second year after their return to the house of God in Jerusalem, and in the second month, Zerubbabel son of Shealtiel and Jeshua son of Jozadak started work, aided by all their fellow-Israelites, the priests and the Levites and all who had returned from captivity to Jerusalem. They appointed Levites from the age of twenty years and upwards to supervise the work of
9 the house of the LORD. Jeshua with his sons and his kinsmen, Kadmiel, Binnui, and Hodaviah,[t] together assumed control of those responsible for the work on the house of God.[u]
10 When the builders had laid the foundation of the temple of the LORD, the priests in their robes took their places with their trumpets, and the Levites, the sons of Asaph, with their cymbals, to praise the LORD in the manner
11 prescribed by David king of Israel; and they chanted praises and thanksgiving to the LORD, singing, 'It is good to give thanks to the LORD,[v] for his love towards Israel endures for ever.' All the people raised a great shout of praise to the LORD because the foundation of the house of the LORD had
12 been laid. But many of the priests and Levites and heads of families, who were old enough to have seen the former house, wept and wailed aloud when they saw the foundation of this house laid, while many others shouted for joy at the top of their voice.

13 The people could not distinguish the sound of the shout of joy from that of the weeping and wailing, so great was the shout which the people were raising, and the sound could be heard a long way off.

Work is halted

4 When the enemies of Judah and Benjamin heard that the returned exiles were building a temple to the LORD the God of Israel, they
2 approached Zerubbabel and Jeshua and the heads of families and said to them, 'Let us join you in building, for like you we seek your God, and we have been sacrificing to him ever since the days of Esarhaddon king of Assyria, who brought us here.' But
3 Zerubbabel and Jeshua and the rest of the heads of families in Israel said to them, 'The house which we are building for our God is no concern of yours. We alone will build it for the LORD the God of Israel, as his majesty Cyrus king of Persia commanded us.'
4 Then the people of the land caused the Jews to lose heart and made them afraid to continue building; and in order to defeat
5 their purpose they bribed officials at court to act against them. This continued throughout the reign of Cyrus and into the reign of Darius king of Persia.
6 At the beginning of the reign of Ahasuerus, the people of the land brought a charge in writing against the inhabitants of Judah and Jerusalem.
7 And in the days of Artaxerxes king of Persia, with the agreement of Mithredath, Tabeel and all his colleagues wrote to him; the letter was written in Aramaic and read aloud in Aramaic.
8[x] Rehum the high commissioner and Shimshai the secretary wrote a letter to King Artaxerxes concerning Jerusalem in the following terms:

9 From Rehum the high commissioner, Shimshai the secretary, and all their colleagues, the judges, the commissioners, the overseers, and chief officers, the men of Erech and Babylon, and the Elamites
10 in Susa, and the other peoples whom the great and renowned Asnappar[y] deported and settled in the city of Samaria and in the rest of the province of Beyond-Euphrates.

11 Here follows the text of their letter:

To King Artaxerxes from his servants, the men of the province of Beyond-Euphrates:
12 Be it known to Your Majesty that the

---

r Or Booths. s for sabbaths: *prob. rdg., cp. 1 Esdras 5. 52*; *Heb. om.* t Binnui, and Hodaviah: *prob. rdg.; Heb. and his sons the family of Judah.* u *Prob. rdg.; Heb. adds* the'family of Henadad, their family and their kinsmen the Levites. v to give thanks to the LORD: *prob. rdg., cp. Ps. 106. 1; Heb. om.* w and Jeshua: *prob. rdg., cp. 1 Esdras 5. 68; Heb. om.* x *From 4. 8 to 6. 18 the text is in Aramaic.* y *Or* Osnappar.

Jews who left you and came to these parts have reached Jerusalem and are rebuilding that wicked and rebellious city; they have surveyed[z] the foundations and are

13 completing the walls. Be it known to Your Majesty that, if their city is rebuilt and the walls are completed, they will pay neither general levy, nor poll-tax, nor land-tax, and in the end[a] they will harm

14 the monarchy. Now, because we eat the king's salt and it is not right that we should witness the king's dishonour, therefore we have sent to inform Your Majesty,

15 in order that search may be made in the annals of your predecessors. You will discover by searching through the annals that this has been a rebellious city, harmful to the monarchy and its provinces, and that sedition has long been rife within its walls. That is why the city was laid waste.

16 We submit to Your Majesty that, if it is rebuilt and its walls are completed, the result will be that you will have no more footing in the province of Beyond-Euphrates.

17 The king sent this answer:

To Rehum the high commissioner, Shimshai the secretary, and all your colleagues resident in Samaria and in the rest of the province of Beyond-Euphrates,

18 greeting. The letter which you sent to me has now been read clearly in my presence.

19 I have given orders and search has been made, and it has been found that the city in question has a long history of revolt against the monarchy, and that rebellion

20 and sedition have been rife in it. Powerful kings have ruled in Jerusalem, exercising authority over the whole province of Beyond-Euphrates, and general levy, poll-tax, and land-tax have been paid to them.

21 Therefore, issue orders that these men must desist. This city is not to be rebuilt until a decree to that effect is issued by

22 me. See that you do not neglect your duty in this matter, lest more damage and harm be done to the monarchy.

23 When the text of the letter from King Artaxerxes was read before Rehum the high commissioner, Shimshai the secretary, and their colleagues, they hurried to Jerusalem and forcibly compelled the Jews to stop

24 work. From then onwards the work on the house of God in Jerusalem stopped; and it remained at a standstill till the second year of the reign of Darius king of Persia.

Work begins again

5 But the prophets Haggai[b] and Zechariah grandson of Iddo upbraided the Jews in Judah and Jerusalem, prophesying in the name of the God of Israel. Then Zerubbabel 2 son of Shealtiel and Jeshua son of Jozadak at once began to rebuild the house of God in Jerusalem, and the prophets of God were with them and supported them. Tattenai, 3 governor of the province of Beyond-Euphrates, Shethar-bozenai, and their colleagues promptly came to them and said, 'Who issued a decree permitting you to rebuild this house and complete its furnishings?' They also asked them for the names 4 of the men engaged in the building. But the 5 elders of the Jews were under God's watchful eye, and they were not prevented from continuing the work, until such time as a report should reach Darius and a royal letter should be received in answer.

A letter to Darius

Here follows the text of the letter sent by 6 Tattenai, governor of the province of Beyond-Euphrates, Shethar-bozenai, and his colleagues, the inspectors in the province of Beyond-Euphrates, to King Darius. This is 7 the written report that they sent:

To King Darius, all greetings. Be it 8 known to Your Majesty that we went to the province of Judah and found the house of the great God being rebuilt by the Jewish elders,[c] with massive stones and timbers laid in the walls. The work was being done thoroughly and was making good progress under their direction. We 9 asked these elders who had issued a decree for the rebuilding of this house and the completion of the furnishings. We 10 also asked them for their names, so that we might make a list of the leaders for your information. This was their reply: 11 'We are the servants of the God of heaven and earth, and we are rebuilding the house originally built many years ago; a great king of Israel built it and completed it. But because our forefathers provoked the 12 anger of the God of heaven, he put them into the power of Nebuchadnezzar the Chaldaean, king of Babylon, who pulled down this house and carried the people captive to Babylon. However, Cyrus 13 of Babylon in the first year of his reign

---

z have surveyed: *prob. rdg.; Aram.* are surveying.   a in the end: *or* certainly.   b *Prob. rdg., cp.*
1 Esdras 6. 1; *Aram. adds* the prophet.   c by ... elders: *prob. rdg., cp.* 1 Esdras 6. 8; *Aram. om.*

14 issued a decree that this house of God should be rebuilt. Moreover, there were gold and silver vessels of the house of God, which Nebuchadnezzar had taken from the temple in Jerusalem and put in the temple in Babylon; and these King Cyrus took out of the temple in Babylon. He gave them to a man named Shesh-15 bazzar, whom he had appointed governor, and said to him, "Take these vessels; go and restore them to the temple in Jeru-salem, and let the house of God there be 16 rebuilt on its original site." Then this Sheshbazzar came and laid the founda-tion of the house of God in Jerusalem; and from that time until now the rebuilding has continued, but it is not yet finished.'
17 Now, therefore, if it please Your Majesty, let search be made in the royal archives in Babylon, to discover whether a decree was issued by King Cyrus for the rebuild-ing of this house of God in Jerusalem. Then let the king send us his wishes in the matter.

Darius replies

6 Then King Darius issued an order, and search was made in the archives where the 2 treasures were deposited in Babylon. But it was in Ecbatana, in the royal residence in the province of Media, that a scroll was found, on which was written the following memo-randum:

3   In the first year of King Cyrus, the king issued this decree concerning the house of God in Jerusalem: Let the house be rebuilt as a place where sacrifices are offered and fire-offerings brought. Its height shall be sixty cubits and its breadth 4   sixty cubits, with three courses of massive stones and one[d] course of timber, the cost to be defrayed from the royal treasury. 5   Also the gold and silver vessels of the house of God, which Nebuchadnezzar took out of the temple in Jerusalem and brought to Babylon, shall be restored; they shall all be taken back to the temple in Jerusalem, and restored each to its place in the house of God.

6 Then King Darius issued this order:[e]

Now, Tattenai, governor of the province of Beyond-Euphrates, Shethar-bozenai,

and your colleagues, the inspectors in the province of Beyond-Euphrates, you are to keep away from the place, and to 7 leave the governor of the Jews and their elders free to rebuild this house of God; let them rebuild it on its original site. I also issue an order prescribing what 8 you are to do for these elders of the Jews, so that the said house of God may be rebuilt. Their expenses are to be de-frayed in full from the royal funds accru-ing from the taxes of the province of Beyond-Euphrates, so that the work may not be brought to a standstill. And let 9 them have daily without fail whatever they want, young bulls, rams, or lambs as whole-offerings for the God of heaven, or wheat, salt, wine, or oil, as the priests in Jerusalem demand, so that they may 10 offer soothing sacrifices to the God of heaven, and pray for the life of the king and his sons. Furthermore, I decree that, 11 if any man tampers with this edict, a beam shall be pulled out of his house and he shall be fastened erect to it and flogged; and, in addition, his house shall be forfeit.[f] And may the God who made 12 that place a dwelling for his Name over-throw any king or people that shall pre-sume to tamper with this edict or to destroy this house of God in Jerusalem. I Darius have issued a decree; it is to be carried out to the letter.

The Temple is completed

Then Tattenai, governor of the province 13 of Beyond-Euphrates, Shethar-bozenai, and their colleagues carried out to the letter the instructions which King Darius had sent them, and the elders of the Jews went on 14 with the rebuilding. As a result of the pro-phecies of Haggai the prophet and Zechariah grandson of Iddo they had good success and finished the rebuilding as commanded by the God of Israel and according to the decrees of Cyrus and Darius;[g] and the house was 15 completed on the twenty-third[h] day of the month Adar, in the sixth year of King Darius. Then the people of Israel, the priests and 16 the Levites and all the other exiles who had returned, celebrated the dedication of the house of God with great rejoicing. For its 17 dedication they offered one hundred bulls, two hundred rams, and four hundred lambs, and as a sin-offering for all Israel twelve he-goats, corresponding to the number of the tribes of Israel. And they re-established the 18 priests in their groups and the Levites in their divisions for the service of God in Jerusalem, as prescribed in the book of Moses.

---

d Prob. rdg., cp. 1 Esdras 6. 25; Aram. a new.   e Then . . . order: prob. rdg., cp. 1 Esdras 6. 27; Aram. om. f Or made into a dunghill (mng. of Aram. word uncertain).   g Prob. rdg.; Aram. adds and Artaxerxes king of Persia.   h Prob. rdg., cp. 1 Esdras 7. 5; Aram. third.

19 On the fourteenth day of the first month the exiles who had returned kept the Pass-
20 over. The priests and the Levites, one and all, had purified themselves; all of them were ritually clean, and they killed the passover lamb for all the exiles who had returned, for
21 their fellow-priests and for themselves. It was eaten by the Israelites who had come back from exile and by all who had separated themselves from the peoples of the land and their uncleanness and sought the
22 LORD the God of Israel. And they kept the pilgrim-feast of Unleavened Bread for seven days with rejoicing; for the LORD had given them cause for joy by changing the disposition of the king of Assyria towards them, so that he encouraged them in the work of the house of God, the God of Israel.

Ezra surveys Jerusalem

7 Now after these events, in the reign of Artaxerxes king of Persia, there came up from Babylon one Ezra son of Seraiah,
2 of Azariah, son of Hilkiah, son of Shallum,
3 son of Zadok, son[i] of Ahitub, son of Amari-
4 ah, son of Azariah, son of Meraioth, son
5 of Zerahiah, son of Uzzi, son of Bukki, son of Abishua, son of Phinehas, son of Eleazar,
6 son of Aaron the chief priest. He was a scribe[j] learned in the law of Moses which the LORD the God of Israel had given them; and the king granted him all that he asked, for the hand of the LORD his God was upon him.
7 In the seventh year of King Artaxerxes, other Israelites, priests, Levites, singers, door-keepers, and temple-servitors went up with
8 him to Jerusalem; and they reached Jeru-salem in the fifth month, in the seventh year
9 of the king. On the first day of the first month Ezra fixed the day for departure from Babylon, and on the first day of the fifth month he arrived at Jerusalem, for the gracious hand of his God was upon him.
10 For Ezra had devoted himself to the study and observance of the law of the LORD and to teaching statute and ordinance in Israel.

Artaxerxes writes to Ezra

11 This is a copy of the royal letter which King Artaxerxes had given to Ezra the priest and scribe, a scribe versed in questions concern-ing the commandments and the statutes of the LORD laid upon Israel:

12[k] Artaxerxes, king of kings, to Ezra the priest and scribe learned in the law of the God of heaven:

13 This is my decision. I hereby issue a decree that any of the people of Israel or of its priests or Levites in my kingdom who volunteer to go to Jerusalem may go with you. You are sent by the king and his 14 seven counsellors to find out how things stand in Judah and Jerusalem with regard to the law of your God with which you are entrusted. You are also to convey the 15 silver and gold which the king and his counsellors have freely offered to the God of Israel whose dwelling is in Jerusalem, together with any silver and gold that you 16 may find throughout the province of Bab-ylon, and the voluntary offerings of the people and of the priests which they freely offer for the house of their God in Jeru-salem. In pursuance of this decree you 17 shall use the money solely for the purchase of bulls, rams, and lambs, and the proper grain-offerings and drink-offerings, to be offered on the altar in the house of your God in Jerusalem. Further, should any 18 silver and gold be left over, you and your colleagues may use it at your discretion according to the will of your God. The 19 vessels which have been given you for the service of the house of your God you shall hand over to the God of Jerusalem; and 20 if anything else should be required for the house of your God, which it may fall to you to provide, you may provide it out of the king's treasury.

And I, King Artaxerxes, issue an order 21 to all treasurers in the province of Beyond-Euphrates that whatever is demanded of you by Ezra the priest, a scribe learned in the law of the God of heaven, is to be sup-plied exactly, up to a hundred talents of 22 silver, a hundred kor of wheat, a hundred bath of wine, a hundred bath of oil, and salt without reckoning. Whatever is de- 23 manded by the God of heaven, let it be diligently carried out for the house of the God of heaven; otherwise wrath may fall upon the realm of the king and his sons. We also make known to you that you 24 have no authority to impose general levy, poll-tax, or land-tax on any of the priests, Levites, musicians, door-keepers, temple-servitors, or other servants of this house of God.

And you, Ezra, in accordance with the 25 wisdom of your God with which you are entrusted, are to appoint arbitrators and judges to judge all your people in the pro-vince of Beyond-Euphrates, all who ac-knowledge the laws of your God;[l] and you and they are to instruct those who do not acknowledge them. Whoever will not obey 26 the law of your God and the law of the king, let judgement be rigorously executed

i Or grandson.   *j Or* doctor of the law.   *k The text of verses 12–26 is in Aramaic.*   *l* to judge ... your God: *or* all of them versed in the laws of your God, to judge all the people in the province of Beyond-Euphrates.

upon him, be it death, banishment, confiscation of property, or imprisonment.

27 Then Ezra said,[m] 'Blessed be the LORD the God of our fathers who has prompted the king thus to add glory to the house of the 28 LORD in Jerusalem, and has made the king and his counsellors and all his high officers well disposed towards me!'

So, knowing that the hand of the LORD my God was upon me, I took courage and assembled leading men out of Israel to go up with me.

Another register

8 These are the heads of families, as registered, family by family, of those who went up with me from Babylon in the reign of King 2 Artaxerxes: of the family of Phinehas, Gershom; of the family of Ithamar, Daniel; of the family of 3 David, Hattush son of[n] Shecaniah; of the family of Parosh, Zechariah, and with him a hundred and fifty 4 males in the register; of the family of Pahath-moab, Elihoenai son of Zerahiah, and with him two hun-5 dred males; of the family of Zattu,[o] Shecaniah son of Jahaziel, and with 6 him three hundred males; of the family of Adin, Ebed son of Jon-7 athan, and with him fifty males; of the family of Elam, Isaiah son of Athaliah, and with him seventy 8 males; of the family of Shephatiah, Zebadiah son of Michael, and with 9 him eighty males; of the family of Joab, Obadiah son of Jehiel, and with him two hundred and eighteen 10 males; of the family of Bani,[p] Shelomith son of Josiphiah, and with him a hundred and sixty males; of the family of Bebai, 11 Zechariah son of Bebai, and with him twenty-eight males; of the 12 family of Azgad, Johanan son of Hakkatan, and with him a hundred and ten males. The last were 13 the family of Adonikam, and these were their names: Eliphelet, Jeiel, and Shemaiah, and with them sixty males; and the family of Bigvai, 14 Uthai and Zabbud, and with them seventy males.

Ezra reviews the people

15 I assembled them by the river which flows toward Ahava; and we encamped there three days. When I reviewed the people and 16 the priests, I found no Levite there. So I sent Eliezer, Ariel, Shemaiah, Elnathan, Jarib, Elnathan, Nathan, Zechariah, and Meshullam, prominent men, and Joiarib and El-17 nathan, men of discretion, with instructions to go to Iddo, the chief man of the settlement at Casiphia; and I gave them a message for him and his kinsmen, the temple-servitors there, asking for servitors for the house of 18 our God to be sent to us. And, because the gracious hand of our God was upon us, they let us have Sherebiah, a man of discretion, of the family of Mahli son of Levi, son of Israel, together with his sons and kinsmen, 19 eighteen men; also Hashabiah, together with Isaiah of the family of Merari, his kinsmen 20 and their sons, twenty men; besides two hundred and twenty temple-servitors (this was an order instituted by David and his officers to assist the Levites). These were all indicated by name.

Returning to Jerusalem

21 Then I proclaimed a fast there by the river Ahava, so that we might mortify ourselves before our God and ask from him a safe journey for ourselves, our dependants, and 22 all our possessions. For I was ashamed to ask the king for an escort of soldiers and horsemen to help us against enemies on the way, because we had said to the king, 'The hand of our God is upon all who seek him, working their good; but his fierce anger is 23 on all who forsake him.' So we fasted and asked our God for a safe journey, and he answered our prayer.

Then I separated twelve of the chiefs of the 24 priests, together with[q] Sherebiah and Hashabiah and ten of their kinsmen, and handed 25 over to them the silver and gold and the vessels which had been set aside by the king, his counsellors and his officers and all the Israelites who were present, as their contribution to the house of our God. I handed 26 over to them six hundred and fifty talents of silver, a hundred silver vessels weighing two talents, a hundred talents of gold, twenty 27 golden bowls worth a thousand drachmas, and two vessels of a fine red copper,[r] precious as gold. And I said to the men, 'You are 28 dedicated to the LORD, and the vessels too are sacred; the silver and gold are a voluntary offering to the LORD the God of your fathers. Watch over them and guard them, 29 until you hand them over in the presence of the chiefs of the priests and the Levites and the heads of families of Israel in Jerusalem, in the rooms of the house of the LORD.'

So the priests and Levites received the 30 consignment of silver and gold and vessels, to be taken to the house of our God in Jerusalem; and on the twelfth day of the first 31 month we left the river Ahava bound for Jerusalem. The hand of our God was upon us, and he saved us from enemy attack and from ambush on the way. When we arrived 32 at Jerusalem, we rested for three days. And 33 on the fourth day the silver and gold and the vessels were deposited in the house of our God in the charge of Meremoth son of Uriah the priest, who had with him Eleazar son of Phinehas, and they had with them the Levites Jozabad son of Jeshua and

---

m Then Ezra said: *prob. rdg., cp. 1 Esdras 8. 25; Heb. om.*
o of Zattu: *prob. rdg., cp. 1 Esdras 8. 32; Heb. om.*
q together with: *prob. rdg., cp. 1 Esdras 8. 54; Heb. om.*
n son of: *prob. rdg.; Heb. of the family of.*
p of Bani: *prob. rdg., cp. 1 Esdras 8. 36; Heb. om.*
r red copper: *or orichalc.*

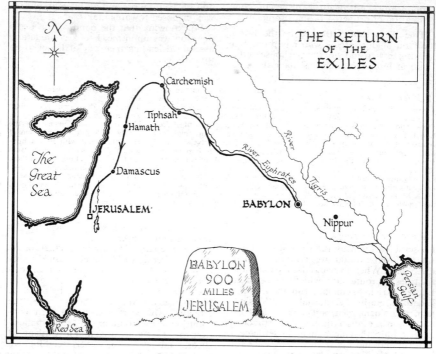

THE RETURN
OF THE
EXILES

Probable route of Ezra's company

34 Noadiah son of Binnui. Everything was checked as it was handed over, and at the same time a written record was made of the 35 whole consignment. Then those who had come home from captivity, the exiles who had returned, offered as whole-offerings to the God of Israel twelve bulls for all Israel, ninety-six rams and seventy-two[s] lambs, with twelve he-goats as a sin-offering; all these were offered as a whole-offering to the LORD.
36 They also delivered the king's commission to the royal satraps and governors in the province of Beyond-Euphrates; and these gave support to the people and the house of God.

Ezra receives bad news

9 When all this had been done, some of the leaders approached me and said, 'The people of Israel, including priests and Levites, have not kept themselves apart from the foreign population and from the abominable practices of the Canaanites, the Hittites, the Perizzites, the Jebusites, the Ammonites, the Moabites, the Egyptians, and the Amor-
2 ites. They have taken women of these nations as wives for themselves and their sons, so that the holy race has become mixed with the foreign population; and the leaders and magistrates have been the chief offenders.' When I heard this news, I rent my robe and 3 mantle, and tore my hair and my beard, and I sat dumbfounded; and all who went in 4 fear of the words of the God of Israel rallied to me because of the offence of these exiles. I sat there dumbfounded till the evening sacrifice.

Ezra pleads for mercy

Then, at the evening sacrifice, I rose from 5 my humiliation and, in my rent robe and mantle, I knelt down and spread out my hands to the LORD my God and said, 'O my 6 God, I am humiliated, I am ashamed to lift my face to thee, my God; for we are sunk in our iniquities, and our guilt is so great that it reaches high heaven. From the days of our 7 fathers down to this present day our guilt has been great. For our iniquities we, our kings, and our priests have been subject to death, captivity, pillage, and shameful humiliation at the hands of foreign kings, and such is our present plight. But now, for a 8 brief moment, the LORD our God has been

s Prob. rdg., cp. 1 Esdras 8. 65; Heb. seventy-seven.

gracious to us, leaving us some survivors and giving us a foothold in this holy place. He has brought light to our eyes again and given us some chance to renew our lives in 9 our slavery. For slaves we are; nevertheless, our God has not forsaken us in our slavery, but has made the kings of Persia so well disposed towards us as to give us the means of renewal, so that we may repair the house of our God and rebuild its ruins, and to give us a wall of defence in' Judah and Jerusalem. 10 Now, O our God, what are we to say after this? For we have neglected the commands 11 which thou gavest through thy servants the prophets, when thou saidst, "The land which you are entering and will possess is a polluted land, polluted by the foreign population with their abominable practices, which have made it unclean from end to end. 12 Therefore, do not give your daughters in marriage to their sons, and do not marry your sons to their daughters, and never seek their welfare or prosperity. Thus you will be strong and enjoy the good things of the land, and pass it on to your children as an ever-13 lasting possession." Now, after all that we have suffered for our evil deeds and for our great guilt—although thou, our God, hast punished us less than our iniquities deserved and hast allowed us to survive as now we 14 do—shall we again disobey thy commands and join in marriage with peoples who indulge in such abominable practices? Would not thy anger against us be unrelenting, 15 until no remnant, no survivor was left? O LORD God of Israel, thou art righteous; now as before, we are only a remnant that has survived. Look upon us, guilty as we are in thy sight; for because of our guilt none of us can stand in thy presence.'

The people repent

10 While Ezra was praying and making confession, prostrate in tears before the house of God, a very great crowd of Israelites assembled round him, men, women, and 2 children, and they all wept bitterly. Then Shecaniah son of Jehiel, one of the family of Elam, spoke up and said to Ezra, 'We have committed an offence against our God in marrying foreign wives, daughters of the foreign population. But in spite of this, there 3 is still hope for Israel. Now, therefore, let us pledge ourselves to our God to dismiss all these women and their brood, according to your advice, my lord, and the advice of those who go in fear of the command of our God; and let us act as the law prescribes.

Up now, the task is yours, and we will sup- 4 port you. Take courage and act.'

Ezra stood up and made the chiefs of the 5 priests, the Levites, and all the Israelites swear to do as had been said; and they took the oath. Then Ezra left his place in front 6 of the house of God and went to the room of Jehohanan grandson of Eliashib and lodged" there; he neither ate bread nor drank water, for he was mourning for the offence committed by the exiles who had returned. Next, there was issued throughout Judah 7 and Jerusalem a proclamation that all the exiles should assemble in Jerusalem, and 8 that if anyone did not arrive within three days, it should be within the discretion of the chief officers and the elders to confiscate all his property and to exclude him from the community of the exiles. So all the men of 9 Judah and Benjamin assembled in Jerusalem within the three days; and on the twentieth day of the ninth month the people all sat in the forecourt of the house of God, trembling with apprehension and shivering in the heavy rain. Ezra the priest stood up 10 and said, 'You have committed an offence in marrying foreign wives and have added to Israel's guilt. Make your confession now 11 to the LORD the God of your fathers and do his will, and separate yourselves from the foreign population and from your foreign wives.' Then all the assembled 12 people shouted in reply, 'Yes; we must do what you say. But there is a great crowd of 13 us here, and it is the rainy season; we cannot go on standing out here in the open. Besides, this business will not be finished in one day or even two, because we have committed so grave an offence in this matter. Let our leading men act for the whole 14 assembly, and let all in our cities who have married foreign women present themselves at appointed times, each man with the elders and judges of his own city, until God's anger against us on this account is averted.' Only Jonathan son of Asahel and 15 Jahzeiah son of Tikvah, supported by Meshullam and Shabbethai the Levite, opposed this.

So the exiles acted as agreed, and Ezra 16 the priest selected' certain men, heads of households representing their families, all of them designated by name. They began their formal inquiry into the matter on the first day of the tenth month, and by the first 17 day of the first month they had finished their inquiry into all the marriages with foreign women.

---

t Or thereby giving us a wall of defence for . . .   *u Prob. rdg., cp. 1 Esdras* 9. 2; *Heb.* went.   *v and*
Ezra the priest selected: *prob. rdg., cp. 1 Esdras* 9. 16; *Heb. obscure.*

A list of the offenders

18 Among the members of priestly families who had married foreign women were found Maaseiah, Eliezer, Jarib, and Gedaliah of the family of Jeshua son of Jozadak 19 and his brothers. They pledged themselves to dismiss their wives, and they brought a ram from the flock as a guilt-offering for their 20 sins. Of the family of Immer: 21 Hanani and Zebadiah. Of the family of Harim: Maaseiah, Elijah, 22 Shemaiah, Jehiel and Uzziah. Of the family of Pashhur: Elioenai, Maaseiah, Ishmael, Nethaneel, Jozabad and Elasah. 23 Of the Levites: Jozabad, Shimei, Kelaiah (that is Kelita), Pethahiah,

24 Judah and Eliezer. Of the singers: Eliashib. Of the door-keepers: Shallum, Telem and Uri. 25 And of Israel: of the family of Parosh: Ramiah, Izziah, Malchiah, Mijamin, Eleazar, Malchiah and 26 Benaiah. Of the family of Elam: Mattaniah, Zechariah, Jehiel, Ab-27 di, Jeremoth and Elijah. Of the family of Zattu: Elioenai, Eliashib, Mattaniah, Jeremoth, Zabad and 28 Aziza. Of the family of Bebai: Jehohanan, Hananiah, Zabbai and 29 Athlai. Of the family of Bani: Meshullam, Malluch, Adaiah, Ja-30 shub, Sheal and Jeremoth. Of the family of Pahath-moab: Adna, Kelal, Benaiah, Maaseiah, Mattaniah, Bezalel, Binnui and Ma-31 hasseh. Of the family of Harim:

Eliezer, Isshijah, Malchiah, Shemaiah, Simeon, Benjamin, Malluch 32 and Shemariah. Of the family of 33 Hashum: Mattenai, Mattattah, Zabad, Eliphelet, Jeremai, Manasseh and Shimei. Of the family of 34 Bani: Maadai, Amram and Uel, Benaiah, Bedeiah and Keluhi, Van-35 iah, Meremoth, Eliashib, Mattan-37 iah, Mattenai and Jaasau. Of the 38 family of[w] Binnui: Shimei, She-39 lemiah, Nathan and Adaiah, Mak-40 nadebai, Shashai and Sharai, Azareel, Shelemiah and Shemariah, 41 Shallum, Amariah and Joseph. Of 42 the family of Nebo: Jeiel, Mattithiah, Zabad, Zebina, Jaddai, Joel and Benaiah. All these had married 44 foreign women, and they dismissed them, together with their children.[x]

THE BOOK OF
NEHEMIAH

Nehemiah prays for Jerusalem

1 THE NARRATIVE of Nehemiah son of Hacaliah.

In the month Kislev in the twentieth year, 2 when I was in Susa the capital city, it happened that one of my brothers, Hanani, arrived with some others from Judah; and I asked them about Jerusalem and about the Jews, the families still remaining of those 3 who survived the captivity. They told me that those still remaining in the province

who had survived the captivity were facing great trouble and reproach; the wall of Jerusalem was broken down and the gates had been destroyed by fire. When I heard 4 this news, I sat down and wept; I mourned for some days, fasting and praying to the God of heaven. This was my prayer: 'O 5 LORD God of heaven, O great and terrible God who faithfully keepest covenant with those who love thee and observe thy commandments, let thy ear be attentive and thine 6 eyes open, to hear my humble prayer which

---

w Of the family of: *prob. rdg.*, *cp. 1 Esdras 9. 34; Heb.* and Bani and.   x and they ... children: *prob. rdg.*, *cp. 1 Esdras 9. 36; Heb.* and some of them were women; and they had borne sons.

I make to thee day and night on behalf of thy servants the sons of Israel. I confess the sins which we Israelites have all committed against thee, and of which I and my father's 7 house are also guilty. We have wronged thee and have not observed the commandments, statutes, and rules which thou didst enjoin 8 upon thy servant Moses. Remember what thou didst impress upon him in these words: "If you are unfaithful, I will disperse you 9 among the nations; but if you return to me and observe my commandments and fulfil them, I will gather your children who have been scattered to the ends of the earth and will bring them home to the place which I have chosen as a dwelling for my Name." 10 They are thy servants and thy people, whom thou hast redeemed with thy great might and 11 thy strong hand. O Lord, let thy ear be attentive to my humble prayer, and to the prayer of thy servants who delight to revere thy name. Grant me good success this day, and put it into this man's heart to show me kindness.'

Nehemiah journeys to Jerusalem

2 Now I was the king's cupbearer, and one day, in the month Nisan, in the twentieth year of King Artaxerxes, when his wine was ready, I took it up and handed it to the king, and as I stood before him I was feeling very 2 unhappy. He said to me, 'Why do you look so unhappy? You are not ill; it can be nothing but unhappiness.' I was much afraid 3 and answered, 'The king will live for ever. But how can I help looking unhappy when the city where my forefathers are buried 4 lies waste and its gates are burnt?' 'What are you asking of me?' said the king. I 5 prayed to the God of heaven, and then I answered, 'If it please your majesty, and if I enjoy your favour, I beg you to send me to Judah, to the city where my forefathers 6 are buried, so that I may rebuild it.' The king, with the queen consort sitting beside him, asked me, 'How long will the journey last, and when will you return?' Then the king approved the request and let me go, 7 and I told him how long I should be. Then I said to the king, 'If it please your majesty, let letters be given me for the governors in the province of Beyond-Euphrates with orders to grant me all the help I need for my 8 journey to Judah. Let me have also a letter for Asaph, the keeper of your royal forests, instructing him to supply me with timber to make beams for the gates of the citadel, which adjoins the palace, and for the city wall, and for the palace which I shall occupy.' The king granted my requests, for the gracious hand of my God was upon me. I came in due course to the governors in 9 the province of Beyond-Euphrates and presented to them the king's letters; the king had given me an escort of army officers with cavalry. But when Sanballat the Horonite 10 and the slave Tobiah, an Ammonite, heard this, they were much vexed that someone should have come to promote the interests of the Israelites.

Nehemiah surveys the walls

When I arrived in Jerusalem, I waited three 11 days. Then I set out by night, taking a few 12 men with me; but I told no one what my God was prompting me to do for Jerusalem. I had no beast with me except the one on which I myself rode. I went out by night 13 through the Valley Gate towards the Dragon Spring and the Dung Gate, and I inspected the places where the walls of Jerusalem had been broken down and her gates burnt. Then I passed on to the Fountain Gate and 14 the King's Pool; but there was no room for me to ride through. I went up the valley in 15 the night and inspected the city wall; then I re-entered the city by the Valley Gate. So I arrived back without the magistrates know- 16 ing where I had been or what I was doing. I had not yet told the Jews, the priests, the nobles, the magistrates, or any of those who would be responsible for the work.

Rebuilding begins

Then I said to them, 'You see our wretched 17 plight. Jerusalem lies in ruins, its gates destroyed by fire. Come, let us rebuild the wall of Jerusalem and be rid of the reproach.' I told them how the gracious hand 18 of my God had been upon me and also what the king had said to me. They replied, 'Let us start the rebuilding.' So they set about the work vigorously and to good purpose. But when Sanballat the Horonite, Tobiah 19 the Ammonite slave, and Geshem the Arab heard of it, they jeered at us, asking contemptuously, 'What is this you are doing? Is this a rebellion against the king?' But I 20 answered them, 'The God of heaven will give us success. We, his servants, are making a start with the rebuilding. You have no stake, or claim, or traditional right in Jerusalem.'

Allocating the work

3 Eliashib the high priest and his fellow-priests started work and re-built the Sheep Gate. They laid its beams^a and set its doors in place; they carried the work as far as the Tower of the Hundred, as far as the Tower of Hananel, and con- 2 secrated it. Next to Eliashib the men of Jericho worked; and next to them Zaccur son of Imri.

The Fish Gate was built by the 3 sons of Hassenaah; they laid its tie-beams and set its doors in place with their bolts and bars. Next to 4 them Meremoth son of Uriah, son of Hakkoz, repaired his section;

_____

a *laid its beams: prob. rdg.; Heb.* consecrated it.

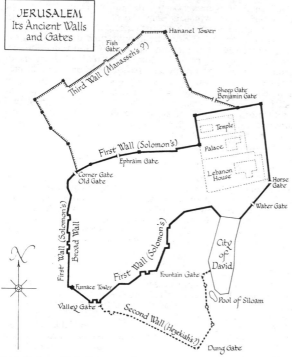

JERUSALEM
Its Ancient Walls
and Gates

buk, ruler of half the district of
Beth-zur, did the repairs as far as
a point opposite the burial-place
of David, as far as the artificial pool
and the House of the Heroes.*
After him the Levites did the re- 17
pairs: Rehum son of Bani and next
to him Hashabiah, ruler of half
the district of Keilah, did the repairs for his district. After him their 18
kinsmen did the repairs: Binnui
son of Henadad, ruler of half the
district of Keilah; next to him 19
Ezer son of Jeshua, ruler of Mizpah, repaired a second section
opposite the point at which the
ascent meets the escarpment; after 20
him Baruch son of Zabbai repaired a second section, from the
escarpment to the door of the
house of Eliashib the high priest.
After him Meremoth son of Uriah, 21
son of Hakkoz, repaired a second
section, from the door of the house
of Eliashib to the end of the house
of Eliashib.

After him the priests of the neigh- 22
bourhood of Jerusalem did the
repairs. Next Benjamin and Has- 23
shub did the repairs opposite their
own house; and next Azariah son
of Maaseiah, son of Ananiah, did
the repairs beside his house. After 24
him Binnui son of Henadad repaired a second section, from the
house of Azariah as far as the
escarpment and the corner. Palal 25
son of Uzai worked opposite the
escarpment and the upper tower
which projects from the king's
house and belongs to the court of
the guard. After him Pedaiah son
of Parosh' worked as far as a 26
point on the east opposite the
Water Gate and the projecting
tower. Next the men of Tekoa re- 27
paired a second section, from a
point opposite the great projecting
tower as far as the wall of Ophel.

Above the Horse Gate the priests 28
did the repairs opposite their own
houses. After them Zadok son of 29
Immer did the repairs opposite his
own house; after him Shemaiah
son of Shecaniah, the keeper of the
East Gate, did the repairs. After 30
him Hananiah son of Shelemiah
and Hanun, sixth son of Zalaph,
repaired a second section. After
him Meshullam son of Berechiah
did the repairs opposite his room.
After him Malchiah, a goldsmith, 31
did the repairs as far as the house
of the temple-servitors and the
merchants, opposite the Mustering Gate, as far as the roof-
chamber at the corner. Between 32
the roof-chamber at the corner and
the Sheep Gate the goldsmiths and
merchants did the repairs.

next to them Meshullam son of
Berechiah, son of Meshezabel; next
to them Zadok son of Baana did
5 the repairs; and next again the men
of Tekoa did the repairs, but their
nobles would not demean themselves to serve their governor.
6 The Jeshanah Gate^b was repaired
by Joiada son of Paseah and Meshullam son of Bosodeiah; they
laid its tie-beams and set its doors
in place with their bolts and bars.
7 Next to them Melatiah the Gibeonite and Jadon the Meronothite, the
men of Gibeon and Mizpah, did
the repairs as far as the seat of
the governor of the province of
8 Beyond-Euphrates. Next to them
Uzziel son of Harhaiah, a goldsmith, did the repairs, and next
Hananiah, a perfumer; they reconstructed Jerusalem as far as
9 the Broad Wall. Next to them
Rephaiah son of Hur, ruler of half
the district of Jerusalem, did the
10 repairs. Next to them Jedaiah son
of Harumaph did the repairs opposite his own house; and next Hat-
11 tush son of Hashabniah. Malchiah

son of Harim and Hasshub son of
Pahath-moab repaired a second
section including the Tower of the
12 Ovens.^{c} Next to them Shallum son
of Hallohesh, ruler of half the district of Jerusalem, did the repairs
with the help of his daughters.
13 The Valley Gate was repaired
by Hanun and the inhabitants of
Zanoah; they rebuilt it and set its
doors in place with their bolts and
bars, and they repaired a thousand
cubits of the wall as far as the Dung
14 Gate. The Dung Gate itself was
repaired by Malchiah son of Rechab, ruler of the district of Beth-
hakkerem; he rebuilt^d it and set its
15 doors in place with their bolts and
bars. The Fountain Gate was repaired by Shallun son of Col-
hozeh, ruler of the district of Mizpah; he rebuilt^d it and roofed it and
set its doors in place with their
bolts and bars; and he built the
wall of the Pool of Shelah next to
the king's garden and onwards as
far as the steps leading down from
the City of David.
16 After him Nehemiah son of Az-

b The Jeshanah Gate: or The gate of the Old City.   c Or Furnaces.   d Prob. rdg.; Heb. he will rebuild.
e Or and the barracks.
f Prob. rdg.; Heb. adds and the temple-servitors lodged on Ophel (cp. 11. 21).

Overcoming opposition

4 When Sanballat heard that we were rebuilding the wall, he was very indignant; in his
2 anger he jeered at the Jews and said in front of his companions and of the garrison in Samaria, 'What do these feeble Jews think they are doing? Do they mean to reconstruct the place? Do they hope to offer sacrifice and finish the work in a day? Can they make stones again out of heaps of rubble, and
3 burnt at that?' Tobiah the Ammonite, who was beside him, said, 'Whatever it is they are building, if a fox climbs up their stone walls, it will break them down.'

4   Hear us, our God, for they treat us with contempt. Turn back their reproach upon their own heads and let them become objects
5 of contempt in a land of captivity. Do not condone their guilt or let their sin be struck off the record, for they have openly provoked the builders.

6   We built up the wall until it was continuous all round up to half its height; and
7 the people worked with a will. But when Sanballat and Tobiah, the Arabs and Ammonites and Ashdodites, heard that the new work on the walls of Jerusalem had made progress and that the filling of the breaches
8 had begun, they were very angry; and they all banded together to come and attack
9 Jerusalem and to create confusion. So we prayed to our God, and posted a guard day and night against them.

10   But the men of Judah said, 'The labourers' strength has failed, and there is too much rubble; we shall never be able to rebuild
11 the wall by ourselves.' And our adversaries said, 'Before they know it or see anything, we shall be upon them and kill them, and
12 so put an end to the work.' When the Jews who lived among them came in to the city, they warned us many times that they would gather from every place where they lived to
13 attack us, and that they would station themselves on the lowest levels below the wall, on patches of open ground. Accordingly I posted my people by families, armed with
14 swords, spears, and bows. Then I surveyed the position and at once addressed the nobles, the magistrates, and all the people. 'Do not be afraid of them', I said. 'Remember the Lord, great and terrible, and fight for your brothers, your sons and daughters,
15 your wives and your homes.' Our enemies

g keeping his right hand on: *prob. rdg.; Heb. obscure.*
they, their sons and daughters were many.

heard that everything was known to us, and that God had frustrated their plans; and we all returned to our work on the wall.

Defending the working party

From that day forward half the men under 16 me were engaged in the actual building, while the other half stood by holding their spears, shields, and bows, and wearing coats of mail; and officers supervised all the people of Judah who were engaged on the 17 wall. The porters carrying the loads had one hand on the load and a weapon in the other. The builders had their swords attached 18 to their belts as they built; the trumpeter was beside me. I addressed the nobles, the 19 magistrates, and all the people: 'The work is great and covers much ground', I said. 'We are isolated on the wall, each man at some distance from his neighbour. Wher- 20 ever the trumpet sounds, rally to us there, and our God will fight for us.' So we con- 21 tinued with the work, half the men holding the spears, from daybreak until the stars came out. At the same time I had said to the 22 people, 'Let every man and his servant pass the night in Jerusalem, to act as a guard for us by night and a working party by day.' So neither I nor my kinsmen nor the men 23 under me nor my bodyguard ever took off our clothes, each keeping his right hand on[g] his weapon.

Nehemiah forbids enslaving fellow-countrymen

There came a time when the common people, **5** both men and women, raised a great outcry against their fellow-Jews. Some complained 2 that they were giving their sons and daughters as pledges[h] for food to keep themselves alive; others that they were mortgaging their 3 fields, vineyards, and houses to buy corn in the famine; others again that they were 4 borrowing money on their fields and vineyards to pay the king's tax. 'But', they said, 5 'our bodily needs are the same as other people's, our children are as good as theirs; yet here we are, forcing our sons and daughters to become slaves. Some of our daughters are already enslaved, and there is nothing we can do, because our fields and vineyards now belong to others.' I was very angry when 6 I heard their outcry and the story they told. I mastered my feelings and reasoned with 7 the nobles and the magistrates. I said to them, 'You are holding your fellow-Jews as pledges for debt.' I rebuked them severely and said, 'As far as we have been able, we 8 have bought back our fellow-Jews who had been sold to other nations; but you are now

h that they . . . as pledges: *prob. rdg.; Heb. that*

selling your own fellow-countrymen, and they will have to be bought back by us!' They were silent and had not a word to say.

9 I went on, 'What you are doing is wrong. You ought to live so much in the fear of God that you are above reproach in the eyes of the nations who are our enemies.

10 Speaking for myself, I and my kinsmen and the men under me are advancing them money and corn. Let us give up this taking

11 of persons as pledges for debt. Give back today to your debtors their fields and vineyards, their olive-groves and houses, as well as the income[i] in money, and in corn, new

12 wine, and oil.' 'We will give them back', they promised, 'and exact nothing more. We will do what you say.' So, summoning the priests, I put the offenders on oath to do as they had

13 promised. Then I shook out the fold of my robe and said, 'So may God shake out from his house and from his property every man who does not fulfil this promise. May he be shaken out like this and emptied!' And all the assembled people said 'Amen' and praised the LORD. And they did as they had promised.

Nehemiah forgoes his allowance

14 Moreover, from the time when I was appointed governor in the land of Judah, from the twentieth to the thirty-second year of King Artaxerxes, a period of twelve years, neither I nor my kinsmen drew the governor's

15 allowance of food. Former governors had laid a heavy burden on the people, exacting from them a daily toll[j] of bread and wine to the value of forty shekels of silver. Further, the men under them had tyrannized over the people; but, for fear of God, I did not be-

16 have like this. I also put all my energy into the work on this wall, and I acquired no land; and all my men were gathered there

17 for the work. Also I had as guests at my table a hundred and fifty Jews, including the magistrates, as well as men who came

18 to us from the surrounding nations. The provision which had to be made each day was an ox and six prime sheep; fowls also were prepared for me, and every ten days skins of wine in abundance. Yet, in spite of all this, I did not draw the governor's allowance, because the people were so heavily

19 burdened. Remember for my good, O God, all that I have done for this people.

Further attempts to weaken Jerusalem

6 When the news came to Sanballat, Tobiah, Geshem the Arab, and the rest of our enemies, that I had rebuilt the wall and that not a single breach remained in it, although I had not yet set up the doors in the gates,

Sanballat and Geshem sent me an invitation 2 to come and confer with them at Hak-kephirim in the plain of Ono; this was a ruse on their part to do me harm. So I sent 3 messengers to them with this reply: 'I have important work on my hands at the moment; I cannot come down. Why should the work be brought to a standstill while I leave it and come down to you?' They sent me a 4 similar invitation four times, and each time I gave them the same answer. On a fifth 5 occasion Sanballat made a similar ap-proach, but this time his messenger came with an open letter. It ran as follows: 'It is 6 reported among the nations—and Gashmu[k] confirms it—that you and the Jews are plotting rebellion, and it is for this reason that you are rebuilding the wall, and—so the report goes—that you yourself want to be king. You are also said to have put up 7 prophets to proclaim in Jerusalem that Judah has a king, meaning yourself. The king will certainly hear of this. So come at once and let us talk the matter over.' Here 8 is the reply I sent: 'No such thing as you allege has taken place; you have made up the whole story.' They were all trying to 9 intimidate us, in the hope that we should then relax our efforts and that the work would never be finished. So I applied myself to it with greater energy.

One day I went to the house of Shemaiah 10 son of Delaiah, son of Mehetabel, for he was confined to his house. He said, 'Let us meet in the house of God, within the sanctuary, and let us shut the doors, for they are com-ing to kill you—they are coming to kill you by night.' But I said, 'Should a man like me 11 run away? And can a man like me go into the sanctuary and survive[l]? I will not go in.' Then it dawned on me: God had not sent 12 him. His prophecy aimed at harming me, and Tobiah and Sanballat had bribed him to utter it. He had been bribed to frighten me 13 into compliance and into committing sin; then they could give me a bad name and discredit me. Remember Tobiah and San- 14 ballat, O God, for what they have done, and also the prophetess Noadiah and all the other prophets who have tried to in-timidate me.

The wall is finished

On the twenty-fifth day of the month Elul 15 the wall was finished; it had taken fifty-two days. When our enemies heard of it, and all 16 the surrounding nations saw it,[m] they thought it a very wonderful achievement,[n] and they recognized that this work had been accom-plished by the help of our God.

---

i Prob. rdg.; Heb. hundredth.   *j* a daily toll: *prob. rdg.; Heb. obscure.*   *k* Geshem *in 2. 19 and*
6. 1, 2.   *l* and survive: *or* to save his life.   *m Or* were afraid.   *n* they thought . . . achievement:
prob. rdg.; Heb. they fell very much in their own eyes.

7 All this time the nobles in Judah were sending many letters to Tobiah, and receiv-
8 ing replies from him. For many in Judah were in league with him, because he was a son-in-law of Shecaniah son of Arah, and his son Jehohanan had married a daughter
9 of Meshullam son of Berechiah. They were always praising[o] him in my presence and repeating to him what I said. Tobiah also wrote to me to intimidate me.

Nehemiah appoints guards for Jerusalem

7 Now when the wall had been rebuilt, and I had set the doors in place and the gate-keepers[p] had been appointed, I gave the 2 charge of Jerusalem to my brother Hanani, and to Hananiah, the governor of the citadel, for he was trustworthy and God-fearing above other men. And I said to them, 'The 3 entrances to Jerusalem are not to be left open during the heat of the day; the gates must be kept shut and barred while the gate-keepers are standing at ease. Appoint guards from among the inhabitants of Jerusalem, some on sentry-duty and others posted in front of their own homes.'

The roll of returning exiles

4 The city was large and spacious; there were few people in it and no 5 houses had yet been rebuilt. Then God prompted me to assemble the nobles, the magistrates, and the people, to be enrolled family by family. And I found the book of the genealogies of those who had been the first to come back. This
6[q] is what I found written in it: Of the captives whom Nebuchadnezzar king of Babylon had taken into exile, these are the people of the province who have returned to Jerusalem and Judah, each to his
7 own town, led by Zerubbabel, Jeshua,[r] Nehemiah, Azariah, Raamiah, Nahamani, Mordecai, Bilshan, Mispereth, Bigvai, Nehum and Baanah.
The roll of the men of the people
8 of Israel: the family of Parosh, two thousand one hundred and seventy-
9 two; the family of Shephatiah, three hundred and seventy-two;
10 the family of Arah, six hundred
11 and fifty-two; the family of Pahath-moab, namely the families of Jeshua and Joab, two thousand eight
12 hundred and eighteen; the family of Elam, one thousand two hun-
13 dred and fifty-four; the family of Zattu, eight hundred and forty-
14 five; the family of Zaccai, seven
15 hundred and sixty; the family of Binnui, six hundred and forty-
16 eight; the family of Bebai, six hun-
17 dred and twenty-eight; the family of Azgad, two thousand three
18 hundred and twenty-two; the family of Adonikam, six hundred and
19 sixty-seven; the family of Bigvai,
20 two thousand and sixty-seven; the family of Adin, six hundred and
21 fifty-five; the family of Ater, namely
22 that of Hezekiah, ninety-eight; the family of Hashum, three hundred
23 and twenty-eight; the family of Bezai, three hundred and twenty-
24 four; the family of Harif, one
25 hundred and twelve; the family of
26 Gibeon, ninety-five. The men of Bethlehem and Netophah, one hun-
27 dred and eighty-eight; the men of Anathoth, one hundred and
28 twenty-eight; the men of Beth-
29 azmoth, forty-two; the men of Kiriath-jearim, Kephirah, and Beeroth, seven hundred and forty-
30 three; the men of Ramah and Geba, six hundred and twenty-
31 one; the men of Michmas, one
32 hundred and twenty-two; the men of Bethel and Ai, one hundred and
33 twenty-three; the men of[s] Nebo,
34 fifty-two; the men[t] of the other Elam, one thousand two hundred
35 and fifty-four; the men of Harim,
36 three hundred and twenty; the men of Jericho, three hundred and
37 forty-five; the men of Lod, Hadid, and Ono, seven hundred and
38 twenty-one; the men of Senaah, three thousand nine hundred and thirty.
39 Priests: the family of Jedaiah, of the line of Jeshua, nine hundred
40 and seventy-three; the family of Immer, one thousand and fifty-
41 two; the family of Pashhur, one thousand two hundred and forty-
42 seven; the family of Harim, one thousand and seventeen.
43 Levites: the families of Jeshua and[u] Kadmiel, of the line of Hod-
44 vah, seventy-four. Singers: the family of Asaph, one hundred
45 and forty-eight. Door-keepers: the family of Shallum, the family of Ater, the family of Talmon, the family of Akkub, the family of Hatita, and the family of Shobai, one hundred and thirty-eight in all.
46 Temple-servitors: the family of Ziha, the family of Hasupha, the
47 family of Tabbaoth, the family of Keros, the family of Sia, the family
48 of Padon, the family of Lebanah, the family of Hagabah, the family
49 of Shalmai, the family of Hanan, the family of Giddel, the family of
50 Gahar, the family of Reaiah, the family of Rezin, the family of
51 Nekoda, the family of Gazzam, the family of Uzza, the family of
52 Paseah, the family of Besai, the family of the Meunim, the family
53 of the Nephishesim,[v] the family of Bakbuk, the family of Hakupha, the family of Harhur, the family 54 of Bazlith,[w] the family of Mehida, the family of Harsha, the family 55 of Barkos, the family of Sisera, the family of Temah, the family of 56 Neziah, and the family of Hatipha.
Descendants of Solomon's ser- 57 vants: the family of Sotai, the family of Sophereth, the family of Perida, the family of Jaalah, the 58 family of Darkon, the family of Giddel, the family of Shephatiah, 59 the family of Hattil, the family of Pochereth-hazzebaim, and the family of Amon.
The temple-servitors and the 60 descendants of Solomon's servants amounted to three hundred and ninety-two in all.
The following were those who 61 returned from Tel-melah, Tel-harsha, Kerub, Addon, and Immer, but could not establish their father's family nor whether by descent they belonged to Israel: the family of Delaiah, the family of 62 Tobiah, the family of Nekoda, six hundred and forty-two. Also of the 63 priests: the family of Hobaiah, the family of Hakkoz, and the family of Barzillai who had married a daughter of Barzillai the Gileadite and went by his[x] name. These 64 searched for their names among those enrolled in the genealogies, but they could not be found; they were disqualified for the priest-hood as unclean, and the governor 65 forbade them to partake of the most sacred food until there should be a priest able to consult the Urim and the Thummim.
The whole assembled people 66 numbered forty-two thousand three hundred and sixty, apart 67 from their slaves, male and female, of whom there were seven thousand three hundred and thirty-seven; and they had two hundred and forty-five singers, men and women. Their horses numbered 68 seven hundred and thirty-six, their mules two hundred and forty-five, their camels four hundred and 69

o Or repeating rumours about ...   p Prob. rdg.; Heb. adds the singers and the Levites.   q Verses 6–73;
cp. Ezra 2. 1–70.   r Or Joshua (cp. Hag. 1. 1).   s Prob. rdg., cp. Ezra 2. 29; Heb. adds the other.
t Prob. rdg.; Heb. family (also in verses 35–38).   u and: prob. rdg., cp. Ezra 2. 40; Heb. to.   v Or
Nephushesim.   w Or Bazluth (cp. Ezra 2. 52).   x Prob. rdg., cp. 1 Esdras 5. 38; Heb. their.

thirty-five, and their asses six thousand seven hundred and twenty. 70 Some of the heads of families gave contributions for the work. The governor gave to the treasury a thousand drachmas of gold, fifty tossing-bowls, and five hundred 71 and thirty priestly robes. Some of the heads of families gave for the fabric fund twenty thousand drachmas of gold and two thousand two 72 hundred minas of silver. What the rest of the people gave was twenty thousand drachmas of gold, two thousand minas of silver, and sixty-seven priestly robes.

The priests, the Levites, and 73 some of the people lived in Jerusalem and its suburbs;[y] the doorkeepers, the singers, the temple-servitors, and all other Israelites, lived in their own towns.

Ezra reads the law to the people

When the seventh month came, and the
8 Israelites were now settled in their towns, the people assembled as one man in the square in front of the Water Gate, and Ezra the scribe[z] was asked to bring the book of the law of Moses, which the LORD had enjoined 2 upon Israel. On the first day of the seventh month, Ezra the priest brought the law before the assembly, every man and woman, and all who were capable of understanding 3 what they heard.[a] He read from it, facing the square in front of the Water Gate, from early morning till noon, in the presence of the men and the women, and those who could understand;[b] all the people listened attentively to the book of the law. Ezra the scribe 4 stood on a wooden platform made for the purpose,[c] and beside him stood Mattithiah, Shema, Anaiah, Uriah, Hilkiah, and Maaseiah on his right hand; and on his left Pedaiah, Mishael, Malchiah, Hashum, Hashbaddanah, Zechariah and Meshullam. 5 Ezra opened the book in the sight of all the people, for he was standing above them; and when he opened it, they all 6 stood. Ezra blessed the LORD, the great God, and all the people raised their hands and answered, 'Amen, Amen'; and they bowed their heads and prostrated themselves humbly before the LORD. Jeshua, Bani, Shere-

biah, Jamin, Akkub, Shabbethai, Hodiah, Maaseiah, Kelita, Azariah, Jozabad, Hanan, Pelaiah, the Levites,[d] expounded the law to the people while they remained in their places. They read from the book of the law 8 of God clearly, made its sense plain and gave instruction in what was read.

Then Nehemiah the governor and Ezra 9 the priest and scribe, and the Levites who instructed the people, said to them all, 'This day is holy to the LORD your God; do not mourn or weep.' For all the people had been weeping while they listened to the words of the law. Then he said to them, 'You may go 10 now; refresh yourselves with rich food and sweet drinks, and send a share to all who cannot provide for themselves; for this day is holy to our Lord. Let there be no sadness, for joy in the LORD is your strength.' The Levites silenced the people, saying, 'Be 11 quiet, for this day is holy; let there be no sadness.' So all the people went away to eat 12 and to drink, to send shares to others and to celebrate the day with great rejoicing, because they had understood what had been explained to them.

Great rejoicing in Jerusalem

On the second day the heads of families of 13 the whole people, with the priests and the Levites, assembled before Ezra the scribe to study the law. And they found written 14 in the law that the LORD had given commandment through Moses that the Israelites should live in arbours[e] during the feast of the seventh month, and that they should 15 make proclamation throughout all their cities and in Jerusalem: 'Go out into the hills and fetch branches of olive and wild olive, myrtle and palm, and other leafy boughs to make arbours, as prescribed.' So 16 the people went out and fetched them and made arbours for themselves, each on his own roof, and in their courts and in the courts of the house of God, and in the square at the Water Gate and the square at the Ephraim Gate. And the whole community 17 of those who had returned from the captivity made arbours and lived in them, a thing that the Israelites had not done from the days of Joshua son of Nun to that day;

y in Jerusalem and its suburbs: *prob. rdg.*, cp. *1 Esdras* 5. 46; Heb. om.　　z Or doctor of the law.　　a were capable . . . heard: *or* would teach them to understand.　　b could understand: *or* were to instruct.　　c Or for the address.　　d *Prob. rdg.*; Heb. and the Levites.　　e Or tabernacles *or* booths.

8 and there was very great rejoicing. And day by day, from the first day to the last, the book of the law of God was read. They kept the feast for seven days, and on the eighth day there was a closing ceremony, according to the rule.

Recounting past mercies

9 On the twenty-fourth day of this month the Israelites assembled for a fast, clothed in sackcloth and with earth on their heads. 2 Those who were of Israelite descent separated themselves from all the foreigners; they took their places and confessed their sins and the iniquities of their forefathers. 3 Then they stood up in their places, and the book of the law of the LORD their God was read for one fourth of the day, and for another fourth they confessed and did obeisance to the LORD their God. Upon the steps 4 assigned to the Levites stood Jeshua, Bani, Kadmiel, Shebaniah, Bunni, Sherebiah, Bani, and Kenani, and they cried aloud to 5 the LORD their God. Then the Levites, Jeshua, Kadmiel, Bani, Hashabniah, Sherebiah, Hodiah, Shebaniah, and Pethahiah, said, 'Stand up and bless the LORD your God, saying: From everlasting to everlasting thy glorious name is blessed*f* and 6 exalted above all blessing and praise. Thou alone art the LORD; thou hast made heaven, the highest heaven with all its host, the earth and all that is on it, the seas and all that is in them. Thou preservest all of them, 7 and the host of heaven worships thee. Thou art the LORD, the God who chose Abram and brought him out of Ur of the Chaldees and named him Abraham. Thou didst 8 find him faithful to thee and didst make a covenant with him to give to him and to his descendants the land of the Canaanites, the Hittites, the Amorites, the Perizzites, the Jebusites, and the Girgashites; and thou didst fulfil thy promise, for thou art just.

9 'And thou didst see the misery of our forefathers in Egypt and didst hear their cry for 10 help at the Red Sea,*g* and didst work signs and portents against Pharaoh, all his courtiers and all the people of his land, knowing how arrogantly they treated our forefathers, and thou didst win for thyself a name that 11 lives on to this day. Thou didst tear the sea apart before them so that they went through the middle of it on dry ground; but thou didst cast their pursuers into the depths, like 12 a stone cast into turbulent waters. Thou didst guide them by a pillar of cloud in the day-time and by a pillar of fire at night to give them light on the road by which they 13 travelled. Thou didst descend upon Mount Sinai and speak with them from heaven, and give them right judgements and true laws, and statutes and commandments which were good, and thou didst make known to them 14 thy holy sabbath and give them commandments, statutes, and laws through thy servant Moses. Thou gavest them bread from heaven 15 to stay their hunger and thou broughtest water out from a rock for them to quench their thirst, and thou didst bid them enter and take possession of the land which thou hadst solemnly sworn to give them. But 16 they, our forefathers, were arrogant and stubborn, and disobeyed thy commandments. They refused to obey and did not 17 remember the miracles which thou didst accomplish among them; they remained stubborn, and they appointed a man to lead them back to slavery in Egypt. But thou art a forgiving god, gracious and compassionate, long-suffering and ever constant, and thou didst not forsake them. Even when 18 they made the image of a bull-calf in metal and said, "This is your god who brought you up from Egypt", and were guilty of great blasphemies, thou in thy great compassion 19 didst not forsake them in the wilderness. The pillar of cloud did not fail to guide them on their journey by day nor the pillar of fire by night to give them light on the road by which they travelled. Thou gavest thy good 20 spirit to instruct them; thy manna thou didst not withhold from them, and thou gavest them water to quench their thirst. Forty years long thou didst sustain them in 21 the wilderness, and they lacked nothing; their clothes did not wear out and their feet were not swollen.

'Thou gavest them kingdoms and peoples, 22 allotting these to them as spoils of war. Thus they took possession of the land of Sihon king of Heshbon and the land of Og king of Bashan. Thou didst multiply their de- 23 scendants so that they became countless as the stars in the sky, bringing them into the land which thou didst promise to give to their forefathers as their possession. When 24 their descendants entered the land and took possession of it, thou didst subdue before them the Canaanites who inhabited it and gavest these, kings and peoples alike, into their hands to do with them whatever they wished. They captured fortified cities and a 25 fertile land and took possession of houses full of all good things, rock-hewn cisterns, vineyards, olive-trees, and fruit-trees in abundance; so they ate and were satisfied and grew fat and found delight in thy great goodness. But they were defiant and rebelled 26 against thee; they turned their backs on thy law and killed thy prophets, who solemnly warned them to return to thee, and they were guilty of great blasphemies. Because of 27

f thy glorious name is blessed: *prob. rdg.; Heb.* and let them bless thy glorious name.   *g Or* the Sea of Reeds.

this thou didst hand them over to their enemies who oppressed them. But when, in the time of their oppression, they cried to thee for help, thou heardest them from heaven and in thy great compassion didst send them saviours to save them from their 28 enemies. But when they had had a respite, they once more did what was wrong in thine eyes; and thou didst abandon them to their enemies who held them in subjection. But again they cried to thee for help, and many times over thou heardest them from heaven 29 and in thy compassion didst save them. Thou didst solemnly warn them to return to thy law, but they grew arrogant and did not heed thy commandments; they sinned against thy ordinances, which bring life to him who keeps them. Stubbornly they turned away in mulish obstinacy and would not obey. 30 Many years thou wast patient with them and didst warn them by thy spirit through thy prophets; but they would not listen. Therefore thou didst hand them over to 31 foreign peoples. Yet in thy great compassion thou didst not make an end of them nor forsake them; for thou art a gracious and compassionate god.

A binding declaration

32 'Now therefore, our God, thou great and mighty and terrible God, who faithfully keepest covenant, do not make light of the hardships that have befallen us—our kings, our princes, our priests, our prophets, our forefathers, and all thy people—from the days of the kings of Assyria to this day. In 33 all that has befallen us thou hast been just, thou hast kept faith, but we have done wrong. Our kings, our princes, our priests, 34 and our forefathers did not keep thy law nor heed thy commandments and the warnings which thou gavest them. Even under 35 their own kings, while they were enjoying the great prosperity which thou gavest them and the broad and fertile land which thou didst bestow upon them, they did not serve thee; they did not abandon their evil ways. Today we are slaves, slaves here in the land 36 which thou gavest to our forefathers so that they might eat its fruits and enjoy its good things. All its produce now goes to the kings 37 whom thou hast set over us because of our sins. They have power over our bodies, and they do as they please with our beasts, while we are in dire distress.

'Because of all this we make a binding 38 declaration in writing, and our princes, our Levites, and our priests witness the sealing.

Ancient seals

The substance of the covenant

10 'Those who witness the sealing are Nehemiah the governor, son of 2 Hacaliah, Zedekiah, Seraiah, Azar-3 iah, Jeremiah, Pashhur, Amariah, 4 Malchiah, Hattush, Shebaniah, 5 Malluch, Harim, Meremoth, Oba-6 diah, Daniel, Ginnethon, Baruch, 7 8 Meshullam, Abiah, Mijamin, Ma-aziah, Bilgai, Shemaiah; these are 9 the priests. The Levites: Jeshua[h] son of Azaniah, Binnui of the fami-10 ly of Henadad, Kadmiel; and their brethren, Shebaniah, Hodiah,[i] Kel-11 ita, Pelaiah, Hanan, Mica, Rehob, 12 Hashabiah, Zaccur, Sherebiah, 13 Shebaniah, Hodiah, Bani, Beninu. 14 The chiefs of the people: Parosh, Pahath-moab, Elam, Zattu, Bani, 15 16 Bunni, Azgad, Bebai, Adonijah, 17 Bigvai, Adin, Ater, Hezekiah, Az-18 zur, Hodiah, Hashum, Bezai, 19 20 Hariph, Anathoth, Nebai,[j] Mag-21 piash, Meshullam, Hezir, Meshe-22 zabel, Zadok, Jaddua, Pelatiah, 23 Hanan, Anaiah, Hoshea, Hanan-24 iah, Hasshub, Hallohesh, Pilha, 25 Shobek, Rehum, Hashabnah, Ma-26 27 aseiah, Ahiah, Hanan, Anan, Mal-luch, Harim, Baanah.

28 'The rest of the people, the priests, the Levites, the door-keepers, the singers, the temple-servitors, with their wives, their sons, and their daughters, all who are capable of understanding, all who for the sake of the law of God have kept themselves apart from 29 the foreign population, join with the leading brethren,[k] when the oath is put to them, in swearing to obey God's law given by Moses the servant of God, and to observe and fulfil all the commandments of the LORD our Lord, his rules and his statutes.

30 'We will not give our daughters in marriage to the foreign population or take their daughters for our 31 sons. If on the sabbath these people bring in merchandise, especially corn, for sale, we will not buy from them on the sabbath or on any holy day. We will forgo the crops of the seventh year and release every person still held as a pledge for debt.

32 'We hereby undertake the duty of giving yearly the third of a shekel for the service of the house 33 of our God, for the Bread of the Presence, the regular grain-offering and whole-offering, the sabbaths, the new moons, the appointed seasons, the holy-gifts, and the sin-offerings to make expiation on behalf of Israel, and for all else that has to be done in the house óf our God. We, the priests, the 34 Levites, and the people, have cast lots for the wood-offering, so that it may be brought into the house of our God by each family in turn, at appointed times, year by year, to burn upon the altar of the LORD our God, as prescribed in the law. We undertake to bring the first-35 fruits of our land and the first-fruits of every fruit-tree, year by year, to the house of the LORD; also 36 to bring to the house of our God, to the priests who minister in the house of our God, the first-born of our sons and of our cattle, as prescribed in the law, and the first-born of our herds and of our flocks; and to bring to the priests the first 37 kneading of our dough, and the first of the fruit of every tree, of the new wine and of the oil, to the store-rooms in the house of our God; and to bring to the Levites the tithes from our land, for it is

h Prob. rdg.; Heb. and Jeshua. *i Or, with Ezra 2. 40,* Hodaviah. *j Or* Nobai. *k* the leading brethren: *prob. rdg.; Heb.* their brethren, their leading men.

38 the Levites who collect the tithes in all our farming villages. The Aaronite priest shall be with the Levites when they collect the tithes; and the Levites shall bring up one tenth of the tithes to the house of our God, to the appropriate rooms 39 in the storehouse. For the Israelites and the Levites shall bring the contribution of corn, new wine, and oil to the rooms where the vessels of the sanctuary are kept, and where the ministering priests, the door-keepers, and the singers are lodged. We will not neglect the house of our God.'

Residents in Jerusalem

11 The leaders of the people settled in Jerusalem; and the rest of the people cast lots to bring one in every ten to live in Jerusalem, the holy city, while the remaining nine 2 lived in other towns. And the people were grateful to all those who volunteered to live in Jerusalem.

3 These are the chiefs of the province who lived in Jerusalem; but, in the towns of Judah, other Israelites, priests, Levites, temple-servitors, and descendants of Solomon's servants lived on their own 4 property, in their own towns. Some members of the tribes of Judah and Benjamin lived in Jerusalem. Of Judah: Athaiah son of Uzziah, son of Zechariah, son of Amariah, son of Shephatiah, son of Mahalalel of 6 the family of Perez, all of whose family, to the number of four hundred and sixty-eight men of sub- 5 stance, lived in Jerusalem; and Maaseiah son of Baruch, son of Col-hozeh, son of Hazaiah, son of Adaiah, son of Joiarib, son of Zechariah of the Shelanite family. 7 These were the Benjamins: Sallu son of Meshullam, son of Joed, son of Pedaiah, son of Kolaiah, son of Maaseiah, son of Ithiel, son of 8 Isaiah, and his kinsmen Gabbai and Sallai, nine hundred and 9 twenty-eight in all. Joel son of Zichri was their overseer, and Judah son of Hassenuah was second over the city.[l]

10 Of the priests: Jedaiah son of 11 Joiarib, son of[m] Seraiah, son of Hilkiah, son of Meshullam, son of Zadok, son of Meraioth, son of Ahitub, supervisor of the house of 12 God, and his[n] brethren responsible for the work in the temple, eight hundred and twenty-two in all; and Adaiah son of Jeroham, son of Pelaliah, son of Amzi, son of Zechariah, son of Pashhur, son of 13 Malchiah, and his brethren, heads

of fathers' houses, two hundred and forty-two in all; and Amasai[o] son of Azarel, son of Ahzai, son of 14 Meshillemoth, son of Immer, and his brethren, men of substance, a hundred and twenty-eight in all; their overseer was Zabdiel son of Haggedolim.

15 And of the Levites: Shemaiah son of Hasshub, son of Azrikam, son of Hashabiah, son of Bunni; 16 and Shabbethai and Jozabad of the chiefs of the Levites, who had charge of the external business of 17 the house of God; and Mattaniah son of Micah, son of Zabdi, son of Asaph, who as precentor led the prayer of thanksgiving, and Bakbukiah who held the second place among his brethren; and Abda son of Shammua, son of 18 Galal, son of Jeduthun. The number of Levites in the holy city was two hundred and eighty-four in all. 19 The gate-keepers who kept guard at the gates were Akkub, Talmon, and their brethren, a hundred and 20 seventy-two. The rest of the Israelites[p] were in all the towns of Judah, each man on his own inherited 21 property. But the temple-servitors lodged on Ophel, and Ziha and Gishpa were in charge of them. 22 The overseer of the Levites in Jerusalem was Uzzi son of Bani, son of Hashabiah, son of Mattaniah, son of Mica, of the family of Asaph the singers, for the supervision of the business of the house 23 of God. For they were under the king's orders, and there was obligatory duty for the singers every 24 day. Pethahiah son of Meshezabel, of the family of Zerah son of Judah, was the king's adviser on all matters affecting the people.

Settlements outside Jerusalem

25 As for the hamlets with their surrounding fields: some of the men of Judah lived in Kiriath-arba and its villages, in Dibon and its villages, and in Jekabzeel and its 26 hamlets, in Jeshua, Moladah, and 27 Bethpelet, in Hazar-shual, and in 28 Beersheba and its villages, in Ziklag and in Meconah and its villages, 29 in Enrimmon, Zorah, and Jarmuth, 30 in Zanoah, Adullam, and their hamlets, in Lachish and its fields and Azekah and its villages. Thus they occupied the country from Beersheba to the Valley of Hinnom. 31 The men of Benjamin lived in[q] Geba, Michmash, Aiah, and Bethel 32 with its villages, in Anathoth, Nob, 33 and Ananiah, in Hazor, Ramah, 34 and Gittaim, in Hadid, Zeboim,

and Neballat, in Lod, Ono, and[r] 35 Ge-harashim.[s] And certain divi- 36 sions of the Levites in Judah were attached to Benjamin.

Priests and Levites

These are the priests and the Levites 12 who came back with Zerubbabel son of Shealtiel, and Jeshua:[t] Sera- iah, Jeremiah, Ezra, Amariah, Mal- 2 luch, Hattush, Shecaniah, Rehum, 3 Meremoth, Iddo, Ginnethon, Ab- 4 iah, Mijamin, Maadiah, Bilgah, 5 Shemaiah, Joiarib, Jedaiah, Sallu, 6 7 Amok, Hilkiah, Jedaiah. These were the chiefs of the priests and of their brethren in the days of Jeshua.

And the Levites: Jeshua, Binnui, 8 Kadmiel, Sherebiah, Judah, and Mattaniah, who with his brethren was in charge of the songs of thanksgiving. And Bakbukiah and 9 Unni their brethren stood opposite them in the service. And Jeshua 10 was the father of Joiakim, Joiakim the father of Eliashib, Eliashib of Joiada, Joiada the father of Jon- 11 athan, and Jonathan the father of Jaddua. And in the days of Joiakim 12 the priests who were heads of families were: of Seraiah, Meraiah; of Jeremiah, Hananiah; of Ezra, Me- 13 shullam; of Amariah, Jehohanan; of Malluch,[u] Jonathan; of Sheban- 14 iah, Joseph; of Harim, Adna; of 15 Meraioth, Helkai; of Iddo, Zecha- 16 riah; of Ginnethon, Meshullam; of 17 Abiah, Zichri; of Miniamin[v]; of Moadiah, Piltai; of Bilgah, Sham- 18 mua; of Shemaiah, Jehonathan; of 19 Joiarib, Mattenai; of Jedaiah, Uzzi; of Sallu,[w] Kallai; of Amok, Eber; 20 of Hilkiah, Hashabiah; of Jedaiah, 21 Nethaneel.

[x]The heads of the priestly fami- 22 lies[y] in the days of Eliashib, Joiada, Johanan, and Jaddua were recorded down to the reign of Darius the Persian. The heads of the levitical 23 families were recorded in the annals only down to the days of Johanan the grandson of Eliashib. And the 24 chiefs of the Levites: Hashabiah, Sherebiah, Jeshua, Binnui,[z] Kad- miel, with their brethren in the other turn of duty, to praise and to give thanks, according to the commandment of David the man of God, turn by turn. Mattaniah, 25 Bakbukiah, Obadiah, Meshullam, Talmon, and Akkub were gate-keepers standing guard at the gate-houses. This was the arrangement 26 in the days of Joiakim son of Jeshua, son of Jozadak, and in the days of Nehemiah the governor and of Ezra the priest and scribe.

---

l second over the city: *or* over the second quarter of the city.   *m* son of: *prob. rdg.; Heb.* obscure.
n *Prob. rdg.; Heb.* their.   *o* *Prob. rdg.; Heb.* Amashsai.   *p* *Prob. rdg.; Heb. adds* the levitical priests.
q *Prob. rdg.; Heb.* from.   *r* and: *prob. rdg.; Heb.* om.   *s* *Or* and the Valley of Woods *or* and the
Valley of Craftsmen.   *t* *Or* Joshua.   *u* *Prob. rdg.; Heb.* Malluchi, *or* Melichu.   *v* *A name is
missing here.*   *w* *Prob. rdg., cp. verse 7; Heb.* Sallai.   *x* *Prob. rdg.; Heb. prefixes* The Levites.
y heads . . . families: *prob. rdg.; Heb.* heads of the families and the priests.   *z* Jeshua, Binnui: *prob.
rdg.; Heb.* and Jeshua son of.

Dedicating the wall

27 At the dedication of the wall of Jerusalem they sought out the Levites in all their settlements, and brought them to Jerusalem to celebrate the dedication with[a] rejoicing, with thanksgiving and song, to the accom-
28 paniment of cymbals, lutes, and harps. And the Levites,[b] the singers, were assembled from the district round Jerusalem and from
29 the hamlets of the Netophathites; also from Beth-gilgal and from the region of Geba and Beth-azmoth;[c] for the singers had built themselves hamlets in the neighbourhood of
30 Jerusalem. The priests and the Levites purified themselves; and they purified the people,
31 the gates, and the wall. Then I brought the leading men of Judah up on to the city wall, and appointed two great choirs to give thanks. One went in procession[d] to the right,
32 going along the wall to the Dung Gate; and after it went Hoshaiah with half the lead-
33 ing men of Judah, and Azariah, Ezra, Me-
34 shullam, Judah, Benjamin, Shemaiah, and
35 Jeremiah; and certain of the priests with trumpets: Zechariah son of Jonathan, son of Shemaiah, son of Mattanaiah, son of Mica-
36 iah, son of Zaccur, son of Asaph, and his kinsmen, Shemaiah, Azarel, Milalai, Gilalai, Maai, Nethaneel, Judah, and Hanani, with the musical instruments of David the man
37 of God; and Ezra the scribe led them. They went past the Fountain Gate and thence straight forward by the steps up to the City of David, by the ascent to the city wall, past the house of David, and on to the Water
38 Gate on the east. The other thanksgiving choir went to the left,[e] and I followed it with half the leading men of[f] the people, continuing along the wall, past the Tower of
39 the Ovens[g] to the Broad Wall, and past the Ephraim Gate, and over the Jeshanah Gate,[h] and over the Fish Gate, taking in the Tower of Hananel and the Tower of the Hundred, as far as the Sheep Gate; and they halted at
40 the Gate of the Guardhouse. So the two thanksgiving choirs took their place in the house of God, and I and half the magis-
41 trates with me; and the priests Eliakim, Maaseiah, Miniamin, Micaiah, Elioenai, Zechariah, and Hananiah, with trumpets;
42 and Maaseiah, Shemaiah, Eleazar, Uzzi, Jehohanan, Malchiah, Elam, and Ezer. The singers, led by Izrahiah, raised their voices.
43 A great sacrifice was celebrated that day, and they all rejoiced because God had given them great cause for rejoicing; the women and children rejoiced with them. And the rejoicing in Jerusalem was heard a long way off.

Providing for the priests and Levites

44 On that day men were appointed to take charge of the store-rooms for the contributions, the firstfruits, and the tithes, to gather in the portions required by the law for the priests and Levites according to the extent of the farmlands round the towns; for all Judah was full of rejoicing at the ministry
45 of the priests and Levites. And they performed the service of their God and the service of purification, as did the singers and the door-keepers, according to the rules laid down by David and his son Solomon.
46 For it was in the days of David that Asaph took the lead as chief of the singers and director[i] of praise and thanksgiving to God.
47 And in the days of Zerubbabel and of Nehemiah all Israel gave the portions for the singers and the door-keepers as each day required; and they set apart the portion for the Levites, and the Levites set apart the portion for the Aaronites.

Nehemiah's reforms

13 On that day at the public reading from the book of Moses, it was found to be laid down that no Ammonite or Moabite should ever
2 enter the assembly of God, because they did not meet the Israelites with food and water but hired Balaam to curse them, though our God turned the curse into a blessing. When
3 the people heard the law, they separated from Israel all who were of mixed blood.

Nehemiah rebukes Eliashib

4 But before this, Eliashib the priest, who was appointed over the store-rooms of the house of our God, and who was connected by marriage with Tobiah, had provided for his
5 use a large room where formerly they had kept the grain-offering, the incense, the temple vessels, the tithes of corn, new wine, and oil prescribed for the Levites, singers, and door-keepers, and the contributions for the priests. All this time I was not in Jeru-
6 salem because, in the thirty-second year of Artaxerxes king of Babylon, I had gone to the king. Some time later, I asked permission from him and returned to Jerusalem.
7 There I discovered the wicked thing that Eliashib had done for Tobiah's sake in

---

a Prob. rdg.; Heb. and.   b the Levites: prob. rdg.; Heb. the sons of.   c Beth-azmoth: prob. rdg., cp. 7. 28; Heb. Azmoth.   d One ... procession: prob. rdg.; Heb. Processions.   e to the left: prob. rdg.; Heb. to the front.   f the leading men of: prob. rdg.; Heb. om.   g Or Furnaces.   h the Jeshanah Gate: or the gate of the Old City.   i Prob. rdg.; Heb. song.

providing him with a room in the courts of
8 the house of God. I was greatly displeased
and threw all Tobiah's belongings out of the
9 room. Then I gave orders that the room
should be purified, and that the vessels of
the house of God, with the grain-offering
and incense, should be put back into it.

Concerning the Levites

10 I also learnt that the Levites had not been
given their portions; both they and the
singers, who were responsible for their
respective duties, had made off to their
11 farms. So I remonstrated with the magistrates and said, 'Why is the house of God
deserted?' And I recalled the men and re-
12 stored them to their places. Then all Judah
brought the tithes of corn, new wine, and
13 oil into the storehouses; and I put in charge
of them Shelemiah the priest, Zadok the
accountant, and Pedaiah a Levite, with
Hanan son of Zaccur, son of Mattaniah, as
their assistant, for they were considered
trustworthy men; their duty was the distribution of their shares to their brethren.
14 Remember this, O God, to my credit, and
do not wipe out of thy memory the devotion
which I have shown in the house of my God
and in his service.

Concerning the sabbath

15 In those days I saw men in Judah treading
winepresses on the sabbath, collecting quantities of produce and piling it on asses—
wine, grapes, figs, and every kind of load,
which they brought into Jerusalem on the
sabbath; and I protested when they about
16 selling food on that day. Tyrians living in
Jerusalem also brought in fish and all kinds
of merchandise and sold them on the sabbath to the people of Judah, even in Jeru-
17 salem. Then I complained to the nobles of
Judah and said to them, 'How dare you pro-
18 fane the sabbath in this wicked way? Is not
this just what your fathers did, so that our
God has brought all this evil on us and on
this city? Now you are bringing more wrath
upon Israel by profaning the sabbath.'
19 When the entrances to Jerusalem had been
cleared in preparation for the sabbath, I
gave orders that the gates should be shut

and not opened until after the sabbath.
And I appointed some of the men under me
to have charge of the gates so that no load
might enter on the sabbath. Then on one or 20
two occasions the merchants and all kinds
of traders camped just outside Jerusalem,
but I cautioned them. 'Why are you camp- 21
ing in front of the city wall?' I asked. 'If you
do it again, I will take action against you.'
After that they did not come on the sabbath
again. And I commanded the Levites who 22
were to purify themselves and take up duty
as guards at the gates, to ensure that the
sabbath was kept holy. Remember this also
to my credit, O God, and spare me in thy
great love.

Concerning mixed marriages

In those days also I saw that some Jews had 23
married women from Ashdod, Ammon, and
Moab. Half their children spoke the language 24
of Ashdod or of the other peoples and could
not speak the language of the Jews. I argued 25
with them and reviled them, I beat them and
tore out their hair; and I made them swear
in the name of God: 'We will not marry our
daughters to their sons, or take any of their
daughters in marriage for our sons or for
ourselves.' 'Was it not for such women', I 26
said, 'that King Solomon of Israel sinned?
Among all the nations there was no king
like him; he was loved by his God, and God
made him king over all Israel; nevertheless
even he was led by foreign women into sin.
Are we then to follow your example and 27
commit this grave offence, breaking faith
with our God by marrying foreign women?'
Now one of the sons of Joiada son of 28
Eliashib the high priest had married a daughter of Sanballat the Horonite; therefore I
drove him out of my presence. Remember, 29
O God, to their shame that they have defiled
the priesthood and the covenant of the
priests*j* and the Levites.
Thus I purified them from everything 30
foreign, and I made the Levites and the
priests resume the duties of their office; I 31
also made provision for the wood-offering,
at appointed times, and for the firstfruits.
Remember me for my good, O God.

j Or priesthood.

ESTHER

A royal banquet

1 THE EVENTS here related happened in the days of Ahasuerus, the Ahasuerus who ruled from India to Ethiopia, a hundred and
2 twenty-seven provinces. At this time he sat on his royal throne in Susa the capital city.
3 In the third year of his reign he gave a banquet for all his officers and his courtiers; and when his army of Persians and Medes, with his nobles and provincial governors,
4 were in attendance, he displayed the wealth of his kingdom and the pomp and splendour of his majesty for many days, a hundred and
5 eighty in all. When these days were over, the king gave a banquet for all the people present in Susa the capital city, both high and low; it was held in the garden court of the royal pavilion and lasted seven days.
6 There were white curtains and violet hangings fastened to silver rings with bands of fine linen and purple;[a] there were alabaster pillars and couches of gold and silver set on a mosaic pavement of malachite and alabaster, of mother-of-pearl and turquoise.
7 Wine was served in golden cups of various patterns: the king's wine flowed freely as
8 befitted a king, and the law of the drinking was that there should be no compulsion, for the king had laid it down that all the stewards of his palace should respect each
9 man's wishes. In addition, Queen Vashti gave a banquet for the women in the royal apartments of King Ahasuerus.

The queen refuses to obey the king

10 On the seventh day, when he was merry with wine, the king ordered Mehuman, Biztha, Harbona, Bigtha, Abagtha, Zethar, and Carcas, the seven eunuchs who were in attendance on the king's person, to bring Queen 11 Vashti before him wearing her royal crown, in order to display her beauty to the people and the officers; for she was indeed a beautiful woman. But Queen Vashti refused to 12 come in answer to the royal command conveyed by the eunuchs. This greatly incensed the king, and he grew hot with anger.

Then the king conferred with his wise men 13 versed in misdemeanours;[b] for it was his royal custom to consult all who were versed in law and religion, those closest to him 14 being Carshena, Shethar, Admatha, Tarshish, Meres, Marsena, and Memucan, the seven princes of Persia and Media who had access to the king and held first place in the kingdom. He asked them, 'What does the 15 law require to be done with Queen Vashti for disobeying the command of King Ahasuerus brought to her by the eunuchs?' Then 16 Memucan made answer before the king and the princes: 'Queen Vashti has done wrong, and not to the king alone, but also to the officers and to all the peoples in all the provinces of King Ahasuerus. Every woman 17 will come to know what the queen has done, and this will make them treat their husbands with contempt; they will say, "King Ahasuerus ordered Queen Vashti to be brought before him and she did not come." The great 18 ladies of Persia and Media, who have heard of the queen's conduct, will tell all the king's officers about this day, and there will be endless disrespect and insolence! If it please 19 your majesty, let a royal decree go out from you and let it be inscribed in the laws of the

a bands . . . purple: *or* white and purple cords. *b* Or times.

PERSIAN
EMPIRE

ARMENIA

MESOPOTAMIA

R. Euphrates

R. Tigris

MEDIA

ELAM

PARTHIA

PERSIA

Babylon

Jerusalem

ARABIA

EGYPT

Persians and Medes, never to be revoked, that Vashti shall not again appear before King Ahasuerus; and let the king give her place as queen to another woman who is
20 more worthy of it than she. Thus when this royal edict is heard through the length and breadth of the kingdom, all women will give honour to their husbands, high and low
21 alike.' Memucan's advice pleased the king and the princes, and the king did as he had
22 proposed. Letters were sent to all the royal provinces, to every province in its own script and to every people in their own language, in order that each man might be master in his own house and control all his own womenfolk.[c]

Esther is taken to the palace
2 Later, when the anger of King Ahasuerus

had died down, he remembered Vashti and what she had done and what had been
2 decreed against her. So the king's attendants said, 'Let beautiful young virgins be
3 sought out for your majesty; and let your majesty appoint commissioners in all the provinces of your kingdom to bring all these beautiful young virgins into the women's quarters in Susa the capital city. Let them be committed to the care of Hegai, the king's eunuch in charge of the women, and let cosmetics be provided for them;
4 and let the one who is most acceptable to the king become queen in place of Vashti.' This idea pleased the king and he acted on it.
5 Now there was in Susa the capital city a Jew named Mordecai son of Jair, son of
6 Shimei, son of Kish, a Benjamite; he had

c *and control . . . womenfolk:* prob. rdg.; Heb. *and speak in his own language.*

been carried into exile from Jerusalem among those whom Nebuchadnezzar king of Babylon had carried away with Jeconiah 7 king of Judah. He had a foster-child Hadassah, that is Esther, his uncle's daughter, who had neither father nor mother. She was a beautiful and charming girl, and after the death of her father and mother Mordecai 8 had adopted her as his own daughter. When the king's order and his edict were published, and many girls were brought to Susa the capital city to be committed to the care of Hegai, Esther too was taken to the king's palace to be entrusted to Hegai, who had 9 charge of the women. She attracted his notice and received his special favour: he readily provided her with her cosmetics and her allowance of food, and also with seven picked maids from the king's palace, and he gave her and her maids privileges in the women's quarters.

10   Esther had not disclosed her race or her family, because Mordecai had forbidden her 11 to do so. Every day Mordecai passed along by the forecourt of the women's quarters to learn how Esther was faring and what was happening to her.

Esther is made queen

12 The full period of preparation prescribed for the women was twelve months, six months with oil and myrrh and six months with perfumes and cosmetics. When the period was complete, each girl's turn came 13 to go to King Ahasuerus, and she was allowed to take with her whatever she asked, when she went from the women's quarters 14 to the king's palace. She went into the palace in the evening and returned in the morning to another part of the women's quarters, to be under the care of Shaashgaz, the king's eunuch in charge of the concubines. She did not again go to the king unless he expressed a wish for her; then she was summoned by name.

15   When the turn came for Esther, daughter of Abihail the uncle of Mordecai her adoptive father, to go to the king, she asked for nothing to take with her except what was advised by Hegai, the king's eunuch in charge of the women; and Esther charmed 16 all who saw her. When she was taken to King Ahasuerus in the royal palace, in the seventh year of his reign, in the tenth month, 17 that is the month Tebeth, the king loved her more than any of his other women and treated her with greater favour and kindness than the rest of the virgins. He put a royal crown on her head and made her queen in 18 place of Vashti. Then the king gave a great banquet for all his officers and courtiers, a banquet in honour of Esther. He also pro-claimed a holiday[d] throughout the provinces and distributed gifts worthy of a king.

Mordecai saves the king's life

19 2 Mordecai was in attendance at court; on his instructions Esther had not disclosed her family or her race, she had done what Mordecai told her, as she did when she was 21 his ward. One day when Mordecai was in attendance at court, Bigthan and Teresh, two of the king's eunuchs, keepers of the threshold, who were disaffected, were plotting to lay hands on King Ahasuerus. This 22 became known to Mordecai, who told Queen Esther; and she told the king, mentioning Mordecai by name. The affair was investi- 23 gated and the report confirmed; the two men were hanged on the gallows. All this was recorded in the royal chronicle in the presence of the king.

Haman's plot against the Jews

3 After this, King Ahasuerus promoted Haman son of Hammedatha the Agagite, advancing him and giving him precedence above all his fellow-officers. So the king's 2 attendants at court all bowed down to Haman and did obeisance, for so the king had commanded; but Mordecai did not bow down to him or do obeisance. Then the 3 attendants at court said to Mordecai, 'Why do you flout his majesty's command?' Day 4 by day they challenged him, but he refused to listen to them; so they informed Haman, in order to discover if Mordecai's refusal would be tolerated, for he had told them that he was a Jew. When Haman saw that 5 Mordecai was not bowing down to him or doing obeisance, he was infuriated. On 6 learning who Mordecai's people were, he scorned to lay hands on him alone, and looked for a way to destroy all the Jews throughout the whole kingdom of Ahasuerus, Mordecai and all his race.

In the twelfth year of King Ahasuerus, in 7 the first month, Nisan, they cast lots, Pur as it is called, in the presence of Haman, taking day by day and month by month, and the lot fell on the thirteenth day of the twelfth month,[e] the month Adar. Then Haman said 8 to King Ahasuerus, 'There is a certain people, dispersed among the many peoples in all the provinces of your kingdom, who keep themselves apart. Their laws are different from those of every other people; they do not keep your majesty's laws. It does not befit your majesty to tolerate them. If it 9 please your majesty, let an order be made in writing for their destruction; and I will pay ten thousand talents of silver to your majesty's officials, to be deposited in the royal treasury.' So the king took the signet-ring 10 from his hand and gave it to Haman son of Hammedatha the Agagite, the enemy of the 11 Jews; and he said to him, 'The money and the people are yours; deal with them as you wish.'

12 On the thirteenth day of the first month the king's secretaries were summoned and, in accordance with Haman's instructions, a writ was issued to the king's satraps and the governor of every province, and to the officers over each separate people: for each province in its own script and for each people in their own language. It was drawn up in the name of King Ahasuerus and 13 sealed with the king's signet. Thus letters were sent by courier to all the king's provinces with orders to destroy, slay, and exterminate all Jews, young and old, women and children, in one day, the thirteenth day of the twelfth month, the month Adar, and 14 to plunder their possessions. A copy of the writ was to be issued as a decree in every province and to be published to all the peoples, so that they might be ready for that 15 day. The couriers were dispatched posthaste at the king's command, and the decree was issued in Susa the capital city. The king and Haman sat down to drink; but the city of Susa was thrown into confusion.

Esther plans to save the Jews

4 When Mordecai learnt all that had been done, he rent his clothes, put on sackcloth and ashes, and went through the city crying 2 loudly and bitterly. He came within sight of the palace gate, because no one clothed with sackcloth was allowed to pass through 3 the gate. In every province reached by the royal command and decree there was great mourning among the Jews, with fasting and weeping and beating of the breast. Most of them made their beds of sackcloth and ashes. 4 When Queen Esther's maids and eunuchs came and told her, she was distraught, and sent garments for Mordecai, so that they might take off the sackcloth and clothe him with them; but he would not accept them. 5 Then Esther summoned Hathach, one of the king's eunuchs who had been appointed to wait upon her, and ordered him to find out from Mordecai what the trouble was and 6 what it meant. Hathach went to Mordecai in the city square in front of the palace gate, 7 and Mordecai told him all that had happened to him and how much money Haman had offered to pay into the royal treasury for 8 the destruction of the Jews. He also gave him a copy of the writ for their destruction issued in Susa, so that he might show it to Esther and tell her about it, bidding her go to the king to plead for his favour and en- 9 treat him for her people. Hathach went and 10 told Esther what Mordecai had said, and

she sent him back with this message: 'All 11 the king's courtiers and the people of the provinces are aware that if any person, man or woman, enters the king's presence in the inner court unbidden, there is one law only: that person shall be put to death, unless the king stretches out to him the golden sceptre; then and then only shall he live. It is now thirty days since I myself was called to go to the king.' But when they told Mordecai 12 what Esther had said, he bade them go back 13 to her and say, 'Do not imagine that you alone of all the Jews will escape because you are in the royal palace. If you remain silent 14 at such a time as this, relief and deliverance for the Jews will appear from another quarter, but you and your father's family will perish. Who knows whether it is not for such a time as this that you have come to royal estate?' Esther gave them this 15 answer to take back to Mordecai: 'Go and 16 assemble all the Jews to be found in Susa and fast for me; take neither food nor drink for three days, night or day, and I and my maids will fast as you do. After that I will go to the king, although it is against the law; and if I perish, I perish.' So Mordecai went 17 away and did exactly as Esther had bidden him.

Esther invites the king and Haman to a banquet

On the third day Esther put on her royal 5 robes and stood in the inner court of the king's palace, facing the palace itself; the king was seated on his royal throne in the palace, facing the entrance. When the king caught 2 sight of Queen Esther standing in the court, she won his favour and he stretched out to her the golden sceptre which he was holding. Thereupon Esther approached and touched the head of the sceptre. Then the 3 king said to her, 'What is it, Queen Esther? Whatever you ask of me, up to half my kingdom, shall be given to you.' 'If it please 4 your majesty,' said Esther, 'will you come today, sire, and Haman with you, to a banquet which I have made ready for you?' The king gave orders that Haman should 5 be fetched quickly, so that Esther's wish might be fulfilled; and the king and Haman went to the banquet which she had prepared. Over the wine the king said to Esther, 6 'Whatever you ask of me shall be given to you. Whatever you request of me, up to half my kingdom, it shall be done.' Esther 7 said in answer, 'What I ask and request of you is this. If I have won your majesty's 8 favour, and if it please you, sire, to give me what I ask and to grant my request, will your majesty and Haman come tomorrow to the banquet which I shall prepare for you both? Tomorrow I will do as your majesty has said.'

Haman sets up gallows for Mordecai

9 So Haman went away that day in good
spirits and well pleased with himself. But
when he saw Mordecai in attendance at
court and how he did not rise nor defer to
10 him, he was filled with rage; but he kept
control of himself and went home. Then he
11 sent for his friends and his wife Zeresh and
held forth to them about the splendour of
his wealth and his many sons, and how the
king had promoted him and advanced him
12 above the other officers and courtiers. 'That
is not all,' said Haman; 'Queen Esther invited no one but myself to accompany the
king to the banquet which she had prepared;
and she has invited me again tomorrow with
13 the king. Yet all this means nothing to me
so long as I see that Jew Mordecai in atten-
14 dance at court.' Then his wife Zeresh and all
his friends said to him, 'Let a gallows seventy-
five feet high be set up, and recommend to
the king in the morning to have Mordecai
hanged upon it. Then go with the king to
the banquet in good spirits.' Haman thought
this an excellent plan, and he set up the
gallows.

The king honours Mordecai

6 That night sleep eluded the king, so he
ordered the chronicle of daily events to be
2 brought; and it was read to him. Therein
was recorded that Mordecai had given information about Bigthana and Teresh, the
two royal eunuchs among the keepers of
the threshold who had plotted to lay hands
3 on King Ahasuerus. Whereupon the king
said, 'What honour or dignity has been conferred on Mordecai for this?' The king's
courtiers who were in attendance told him
that nothing had been done for Mordecai.
4 The king asked, 'Who is that in the court?'
Now Haman had just entered the outer
court of the palace to recommend to the
king that Mordecai should be hanged on

the gallows which he had prepared for him.
The king's servants answered, 'It is Haman 5
standing there'; and the king bade him enter.
He came in, and the king said to him, 'What 6
should be done for the man whom the king
wishes to honour?' Haman said to himself,
'Whom would the king wish to honour more
than me?' And he said to the king, 'For the 7
man whom the king wishes to honour, let 8
there be brought royal robes which the king
himself wears, and a horse which the king
rides, with a royal crown upon its head.
And let the robes and the horse be delivered 9
to one of the king's most honourable officers,
and let him attire the man whom the king
wishes to honour and lead him mounted on
the horse through the city square, calling out
as he goes: "See what is done for the man
whom the king wishes to honour."' Then 10
the king said to Haman, 'Fetch the robes
and the horse at once, as you have said, and
do all this for Mordecai the Jew who is in
attendance at court. Leave nothing undone
of all that you have said.' So Haman took 11
the robes and the horse, attired Mordecai,
and led him mounted through the city
square, calling out as he went: 'See what is
done for the man whom the king wishes to
honour.'

Then Mordecai returned to court and 12
Haman hurried off home mourning, with
head uncovered. He told his wife Zeresh and 13
all his friends everything that had happened
to him. And this was the reply of his friends
and his wife Zeresh: 'If Mordecai, in face of
whom your fortunes begin to fall, belongs to
the Jewish race, you will not get the better of
him; he will see your utter downfall.'

The king executes Haman

While they were still talking with Haman, 14
the king's eunuchs arrived and hurried him
away to the banquet which Esther had
prepared.

7 So the king and Haman went to dine with
2 Queen Esther. Again on that second day,
over the wine, the king said, 'Whatever you
ask of me will be given to you, Queen Esther.
Whatever you request of me, up to half my
3 kingdom, it shall be done.' Queen Esther
answered, 'If I have found favour with your
majesty, and if it please your majesty, my
request and petition is that my own life and
4 the lives of my people may be spared. For
we have been sold, I and my people, to be
destroyed, slain, and exterminated. If it had
been a matter of selling us, men and women
alike, into slavery, I should have kept
silence; for then our plight would not be
5 such as to injure the king's interests.' Then
King Ahasuerus said to Queen Esther, 'Who
is he, and where is he, who has presumed to
6 do such a thing as this?' 'An adversary and
an enemy,' said Esther, 'this wicked Haman.'
At that Haman was dumbfounded in the
7 presence of the king and the queen. The king
rose from the banquet in a rage and went to
the garden of the pavilion, while Haman
remained where he was, to plead for his life
with Queen Esther; for he saw that in the
8 king's mind his fate was determined. When
the king returned from the garden to the
banqueting hall, Haman had flung himself
across the couch on which Esther was reclining. The king exclaimed, 'Will he even
assault the queen here in my presence?' No
sooner had the words left the king's mouth
9 than Haman hid his face in despair.*f* Then
Harbona, one of the eunuchs in attendance
on the king, said, 'At Haman's house stands
the gallows, seventy-five feet high, which he
himself has prepared for Mordecai, who
once served the king well.' 'Hang Haman on
10 it', said the king. So they hanged him on the
gallows that he himself had prepared for
Mordecai. After that the king's rage abated.

Esther pleads for the Jews

8 On that day King Ahasuerus gave Queen
Esther the house of Haman, enemy of the
Jews; and Mordecai came into the king's
presence, for Esther had told him how he
2 was related to her. Then the king took off
his signet-ring, which he had taken back
from Haman, and gave it to Mordecai. And
Esther put Mordecai in charge of Haman's
house.
3 Once again Esther spoke before the king,
falling at his feet in tears and pleading with
him to avert the calamity planned by Haman
the Agagite and to frustrate his plot against
4 the Jews. The king stretched out the golden
sceptre to Esther, and she rose and stood
5 before the king, and said, 'May it please
your majesty: if I have found favour with

you, and if the proposal seems right to your
majesty and I have won your approval, let
a writ be issued to recall the letters which
Haman son of Hammedatha the Agagite
wrote in pursuance of his plan to destroy
the Jews in all the royal provinces. For how 6
can I bear to see the calamity which is coming upon my race? Or how can I bear to see
the destruction of my family?' Then King 7
Ahasuerus said to Queen Esther and to
Mordecai the Jew, 'I have given Haman's
house to Esther, and he has been hanged on
the gallows, because he threatened the lives
of the Jews. Now you shall issue a writ con- 8
cerning the Jews in my name, in whatever
terms you think fit, and seal it with the royal
signet; for an order written in the name of
the king and sealed with the royal signet
cannot be revoked.'

The king issues a favourable decree

And so, on the twenty-third day of the third 9
month, the month Sivan, the king's secretaries were summoned; and a writ was issued
to the Jews, exactly as Mordecai directed,
and to the satraps, the governors, and the
officers in the provinces from India to
Ethiopia, a hundred and twenty-seven provinces, for each province in its own script
and for each people in their own language,
and also for the Jews in their own script and
language. The writ was drawn up in the 10
name of King Ahasuerus and sealed with
the royal signet, and letters were sent by
mounted couriers riding on horses from the
royal stables. By these letters the king granted 11
permission to the Jews in every city to unite
and defend themselves, and to destroy, slay,
and exterminate the whole strength of any
people or province which might attack them,
women and children too, and to plunder
their possessions, throughout all the pro- 12
vinces of King Ahasuerus, in one day, the
thirteenth day of the twelfth month, the
month Adar. A copy of the writ was to be 13
issued as a decree in every province and
published to all peoples, and the Jews were
to be ready for that day, the day of vengeance
on their enemies. So the couriers, mounted 14
on their royal horses, were dispatched posthaste at the king's urgent command; and
the decree was issued also in Susa the capital
city.
Mordecai left the king's presence in royal 15
robes of violet and white, wearing a great
golden crown and a cloak of fine linen and
purple, and all the city of Susa shouted for
joy. For the Jews there was light and joy, 16
gladness and honour. In every province and 17
every city reached by the royal command
and decree, there was joy and gladness for

f Haman . . . despair: *prob. rdg.; Heb.* they covered Haman's face.

the Jews, feasting and holiday. And many of the peoples of the land professed themselves Jews, because fear of the Jews had seized them.

The Jews destroy their enemies

9 On the thirteenth day of the twelfth month, the month Adar, the time came for the king's command and his edict to be carried out. The very day on which the enemies of the Jews had hoped to gain the upper hand over them was to become the day when the Jews should gain the upper hand over those who 2 hated them. On that day the Jews united in their cities in all the provinces of King Ahasuerus to fall upon those who had planned their ruin. No one could resist them, because fear of them had seized all peoples. 3 All the officers of the provinces, the satraps and the governors, and all the royal officials, aided the Jews, because fear of Mordecai 4 had seized them. Mordecai had become a great personage in the royal palace; his fame had spread throughout all the provinces as the power of the man grew steadily greater. 5 So the Jews put their enemies to the sword, with great slaughter and destruction; they worked their will on those who hated them. 6 In Susa, the capital city, the Jews killed five 7 hundred men and destroyed them; and they killed also Parshandatha, Dalphon and 8 Aspatha, Poratha, Adalia and Aridatha, 9 10 Parmashta, Arisai, Aridai and Vaizatha, the ten sons of Haman son of Hammedatha, the enemy of the Jews; but they did not touch the plunder. 11 That day when the number of those killed in Susa the capital city came to the notice 12 of the king, he said to Queen Esther, 'In Susa, the capital city, the Jews have killed and destroyed five hundred men and the ten sons of Haman. What have they done in the rest of the king's provinces? Whatever you ask further will be given to you; what- 13 ever more you seek shall be done.' Esther answered him, 'If it please your majesty, let tomorrow be granted to the Jews in Susa to do according to the edict for today; and let the bodies of Haman's ten sons be hung 14 up on the gallows.' The king gave orders for this to be done; the edict was issued in Susa and Haman's ten sons were hung up on the 15 gallows. The Jews in Susa united again on the fourteenth day of the month Adar and killed three hundred men in Susa; but they did not touch the plunder. 16 The rest of the Jews in the king's provinces had united to defend themselves; they took vengeance on[g] their enemies by killing seventy-five thousand of those who hated them; but they did not touch the plunder. 17 This was on the thirteenth day of the month

Adar, and they rested on the fourteenth day and made that a day of feasting and joy. 18 The Jews in Susa had united on the thirteenth and fourteenth days of the month, and rested on the fifteenth day and made that a 19 day of feasting and joy. This is why isolated Jews who live in remote villages keep the fourteenth day of the month Adar in joy and feasting, as a holiday on which they send presents of food to one another.

The feast of Purim

20 Then Mordecai set these things on record and sent letters to all the Jews in all the provinces of King Ahasuerus, far and near, 21 binding them to keep the fourteenth and fifteenth days of the month Adar, year by 22 year, as the days on which the Jews obtained relief from their enemies and as the month which was changed for them from sorrow into joy, from a time of mourning to a holiday. They were to keep them as days of feasting and joy, days for sending presents of food to one another and gifts to the poor.

23 So the Jews undertook to continue the 24 practice that they had begun in accordance with Mordecai's letter. This they did because Haman son of Hammedatha the Agagite, the enemy of all the Jews, had plotted to destroy the Jews and had cast lots, Pur as it is called, with intent to crush 25 and destroy them. But when the matter came before the king, he issued written orders that the wicked plot which Haman had devised against the Jews should recoil on his own head, and that he and his sons 26 should be hanged on the gallows. Therefore, these days were named Purim after the word Pur. Accordingly, because of all that was written in this letter, because of all they had 27 seen and experienced in this affair, the Jews resolved and undertook, on behalf of themselves, their descendants, and all who should join them, that they would without fail keep these two days as a yearly festival in the prescribed manner and at the appointed 28 time; that these days should be remembered and kept, generation after generation, in every family, province, and city, that the days of Purim should always be observed among the Jews, and that the memory of them should never cease among their descendants.

29 Queen Esther daughter of Abihail gave full authority in writing to[h] Mordecai the Jew, to confirm this second letter about 30 Purim. Letters wishing peace and security were sent to all the Jews in the hundred and twenty-seven provinces of King Ahasuerus, 31 making the observance of these days of Purim at their appointed time binding on

g Prob. rdg.; Heb. got respite from.   h Prob. rdg.; Heb. and.

them, as Mordecai the Jew[i] had prescribed.
In the same way they had prescribed regulations for fasts and lamentations for themselves and their descendants. The command
of Esther confirmed these regulations for
Purim, and the record is preserved in writing.

32

Other records concerning Mordecai

10 King Ahasuerus imposed forced labour on
2 the land and the coasts and islands. All the

king's acts of authority and power, and the
dignities which he conferred on Mordecai,
are written in the annals of the kings of
Media and Persia. For Mordecai the Jew 3
was second only to King Ahasuerus; he was
a great man among the Jews and was popular with the mass of his countrymen, for he
sought the good of his people and promoted
the welfare of all their descendants.[j]

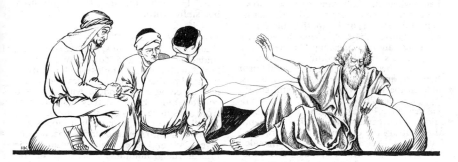

THE BOOK OF

JOB

Prologue

1 THERE LIVED in the land of Uz a man
of blameless and upright life named Job,
who feared God and set his face against
2 wrongdoing. He had seven sons and three
3 daughters; and he owned seven thousand
sheep and three thousand camels, five hundred yoke of oxen and five hundred asses,
with a large number of slaves. Thus Job
was the greatest man in all the East.
4 Now his sons used to foregather and give,
each in turn, a feast in his own house; and
they used to send and invite their three
5 sisters to eat and drink with them. Then,
when a round of feasts was finished, Job
sent for his children and sanctified them,
rising early in the morning and sacrificing
a whole-offering for each of them; for he
thought that they might somehow have

sinned against God and committed blasphemy in their hearts. This he always did.

The court of heaven

The day came when the members of the 6
court of heaven took their places in the
presence of the LORD, and Satan[a] was there
among them. The LORD asked him where 7
he had been. 'Ranging over the earth', he
said, 'from end to end.' Then the LORD 8
asked Satan, 'Have you considered my servant Job? You will find no one like him on
earth, a man of blameless and upright life,
who fears God and sets his face against
wrongdoing.' Satan answered the LORD, 9
'Has not Job good reason to be God-fearing?
Have you not hedged him round on every 10
side with your protection, him and his
family and all his possessions? Whatever he
does you have blessed, and his herds have

---

i Prob. rdg.; Heb. adds and Queen Esther.
a Or the adversary.

j Or and was in friendly relations with all his race.

11 increased beyond measure. But stretch out your hand and touch all that he has, and 12 then he will curse you to your face.' Then the LORD said to Satan, 'So be it. All that he has is in your hands; only Job himself you must not touch.' And Satan left the LORD's presence.

Job's great loss

13 When the day came that Job's sons and daughters were eating and drinking in the 14 eldest brother's house, a messenger came running to Job and said, 'The oxen were ploughing and the asses were grazing near 15 them, when the Sabaeans swooped down and carried them off, after putting the herdsmen to the sword; and I am the only one to 16 escape and tell the tale.' While he was still speaking, another messenger arrived and said, 'God's fire flashed from heaven. It struck the sheep and the shepherds and burnt them up; and I am the only one to escape 17 and tell the tale.' While he was still speaking, another arrived and said, 'The Chaldaeans, three bands of them, have made a raid on the camels and carried them off, after putting the drivers to the sword; and I am the only one to escape and tell the tale.' 18 While this man was speaking, yet another arrived and said, 'Your sons and daughters were eating and drinking in the eldest 19 brother's house, when suddenly a whirlwind swept across from the desert and struck the four corners of the house, and it fell on the 20 young people and killed them; and I am the only one to escape and tell the tale.' At this Job stood up and rent his cloak; then he shaved his head and fell prostrate on the 21 ground, saying:

Naked I came from the womb,
naked I shall return whence I came.
The LORD gives and the LORD takes away;
blessed be the name of the LORD.

22 Throughout all this Job did not sin; he did not charge God with unreason.

Job's personal affliction

2 Once again the day came when the members of the court of heaven took their places in the presence of the LORD, and Satan was 2 there among them. The LORD asked him where he had been. 'Ranging over the earth', 3 he said, 'from end to end.' Then the LORD asked Satan, 'Have you considered my servant Job? You will find no one like him on earth, a man of blameless and upright life, who fears God and sets his face against wrongdoing. You incited me to ruin him without a cause, but his integrity is still 4 unshaken.' Satan answered the LORD, 'Skin for skin! There is nothing the man will 5 grudge to save himself. But stretch out

your hand and touch his bone and his flesh, and see if he will not curse you to your face.'

Then the LORD said to Satan, 'So be it. 6 He is in your hands; but spare his life.' And 7 Satan left the LORD's presence, and he smote Job with running sores from head to foot, so that he took a piece of a broken pot to 8 scratch himself as he sat among the ashes. Then his wife said to him, 'Are you still 9 unshaken in your integrity? Curse God and die!' But he answered, 'You talk as any 10 wicked fool of a woman might talk. If we accept good from God, shall we not accept evil?' Throughout all this, Job did not utter one sinful word.

Job's friends sympathize

When Job's three friends, Eliphaz of Teman, 11 Bildad of Shuah, and Zophar of Naamah, heard of all these calamities which had overtaken him, they left their homes and arranged to come and condole with him and comfort him. But when they first saw him 12 from a distance, they did not recognize him; and they wept aloud, rent their cloaks, and tossed dust into the air over their heads. For 13 seven days and seven nights they sat beside him on the ground, and none of them said a word to him; for they saw that his suffering was very great.

Job bewails his plight

After this Job broke silence and cursed the **3** day of his birth: 1-

Perish the day when I was born 3
and the night which said, 'A man is conceived'!
May that day turn to darkness; may God 4
above not look for it,
nor light of dawn shine on it.
May blackness sully it, and murk and gloom, 5
cloud smother that day, swift darkness
eclipse its sun.
Blind darkness swallow up that night; 6
count it not among the days of the year,
reckon it not in the cycle of the months.
That night, may it be barren for ever, 7
no cry of joy be heard in it.
Cursed be it by those whose magic binds 8
even the monster of the deep,
who are ready to tame Leviathan himself
with spells.
May no star shine out in its twilight; 9
may it wait for a dawn that never comes,
nor ever see the eyelids of the morning,
because it did not shut the doors of the womb 10
that bore me
and keep trouble away from my sight.
Why was I not still-born, 11
why did I not die when I came out of the
womb?

12 Why was I ever laid on my mother's knees
   or put to suck at her breasts?
16 Why was I not hidden like an untimely birth,
   like an infant that has not lived to see the
    light?
13 For then I should be lying in the quiet grave,
   asleep in death, at rest,
14 with kings and their ministers
   who built themselves palaces,
15 with princes rich in gold
   who filled their houses with silver.
17b There the wicked man chafes no more,
   there the tired labourer rests;
18 the captive too finds peace there
   and hears no taskmaster's voice;
19 high and low are there,
   even the slave, free from his master.

20 Why should the sufferer be born to see the
   light?
   Why is life given to men who find it so bitter?
21 They wait for death but it does not come,
   they seek it more eagerly than[c] hidden
    treasure.
22 They are glad when they reach the tomb,
   and when they come to the grave they exult.
23 Why should a man be born to wander blindly,
   hedged in by God on every side?
24 My sighing is all my food,
   and groans pour from me in a torrent.
25 Every terror that haunted me has caught up
   with me,
   and all that I feared has come upon me.
26 There is no peace of mind nor quiet for me;
   I chafe in torment and have no rest.

First speech of Eliphaz

4 Then Eliphaz the Temanite began:

2 If one ventures to speak with you, will you
   lose patience?
   For who could hold his tongue any longer?
3 Think how once you encouraged those who
   faltered,
   how you braced feeble arms,
4 how a word from you upheld the stumblers
   and put strength into weak knees.
5 But now that adversity comes upon you, you
   lose patience;
   it touches you, and you are unmanned.
6 Is your religion no comfort to you?
   Does your blameless life give you no hope?
7 For consider, what innocent man has ever
   perished?
   Where have you seen the upright destroyed?
8 This I know, that those who plough mischief
   and sow trouble
   reap as they have sown;
9 they perish at the blast of God
   and are shrivelled by the breath of his
    nostrils.

The roar of the lion, the whimpering of his 10
   cubs, fall silent;
the teeth of the young lions are broken;
the lion perishes for lack of prey   11
and the whelps of the lioness are abandoned.

A word stole into my ears,   12
and they caught the whisper of it;
in the anxious visions of the night,   13
when a man sinks into deepest sleep,
terror seized me and shuddering;   14
the trembling of my body frightened me.
A wind brushed my face   15
and made the hairs bristle on my flesh;
and a figure stood there whose shape I could 16
   not discern,
an apparition loomed before me,
and I heard the sound of a low voice:
'Can mortal man be more righteous than 17
   God,
or the creature purer than his Maker?
If God mistrusts his own servants   18
and finds his messengers at fault,
how much more those that dwell in houses 19
   whose walls are clay,
whose foundations are dust,
which can be crushed like a bird's nest
or torn down between dawn and dark,   20
how much more shall such men perish outright and unheeded,
[d]die, without ever finding wisdom?'   21

Call if you will; is there any to answer you? **5**
To which of the holy ones will you turn?
The fool is destroyed by his own angry 2
   passions,
and the end of childish resentment is death.
I have seen it for myself: a fool uprooted,   3
his home in sudden ruin about him,[e]
his children past help,   4
browbeaten in court with none to save them.
[f]Their rich possessions are snatched from 5
   them;
what they have harvested others hungrily
   devour;
the stronger man seizes it from the panniers,
panting, thirsting for their wealth.
Mischief does not grow out of the soil   6
nor trouble spring from the earth;
man is born to trouble,   7
as surely as birds fly[g] upwards.

For my part, I would make my petition to 8
   God
and lay my cause before him,
who does great and unsearchable things,   9
marvels without number.
He gives rain to the earth   10
and sends water on the fields;
he raises the lowly to the heights,   11
the mourners are uplifted by victory;

b Verse 16 transposed to follow verse 12.   *c Or* seek it among . . .   *d Prob. rdg.; transposing* Their
rich possessions are snatched from them *to follow 5. 4.*   *e* ruin about him: *prob. rdg.; Heb. obscure.*
f Line transposed from 4. 21.   *g Or* as sparks shoot.

12 he frustrates the plots of the crafty,
and they win no success,
13 he traps the cunning in their craftiness,
and the schemers' plans are thrown into confusion.
14 In the daylight they run into darkness,
and grope at midday as though it were night.
15 He saves the destitute from their greed,
and the needy from the grip of the strong;
16 so the poor hope again,
and the unjust are sickened.

17 Happy the man whom God rebukes!
therefore do not reject the discipline of the Almighty.
18 For, though he wounds, he will bind up;
the hands that smite will heal.
19 You may meet disaster six times, and he will save you;
seven times, and no harm shall touch you.
20 In time of famine he will save you from death,
in battle from the sword.
21 You will be shielded from the lash of slander,[h]
and when violence comes you need not fear.
22 You will laugh at violence and starvation
and have no need to fear wild beasts;
23 for you have a covenant with the stones to spare your fields,
and the weeds have been constrained to leave you at peace.
24 You will know that all is well with your household,
you will look round your home and find nothing amiss;
25 you will know, too, that your descendants will be many
and your offspring like grass, thick upon the earth.
26 You will come in sturdy old age to the grave
as sheaves come in due season to the threshing-floor.

27 We have inquired into all this, and so it is;
this we have heard, and you may know it for the truth.

Job's reply

6 Then Job answered:

2 O that the grounds for my resentment might be weighed,
and my misfortunes set with them on the scales!
3 For they would outweigh the sands of the sea:
what wonder if my words are wild?[i]
4 The arrows of the Almighty find their mark in me,
and their poison soaks into my spirit;
God's onslaughts wear me away.

Does the wild ass bray when he has grass 5
or the ox low when he has fodder?
Can a man eat tasteless food unseasoned with 6
salt,
or find any flavour in the juice of mallows?
Food that should nourish me sticks in my 7
throat,
and my bowels rumble with an echoing sound.

O that I might have my request, 8
that God would grant what I hope for:
that he would be pleased to crush me, 9
to snatch me away with his hand and cut me off!
For that would bring me relief, 10
and in the face of unsparing anguish I would leap for joy.[j]
Have I the strength to wait? 11
What end have I to expect, that I should be patient?
Is my strength the strength of stone, 12
or is my flesh bronze?
Oh how shall I find help within myself? 13
The power to aid myself is put out of my reach.

Devotion is due from his friends 14
to one who despairs and loses faith in the Almighty;
but my brothers have been treacherous as a 15
mountain stream,
like the channels of streams that run dry,
which turn dark with ice 16

or are hidden with piled-up snow;
or they vanish the moment they are in spate, 17
dwindle in the heat and are gone.
Then the caravans, winding hither and 18
thither,
go up into the wilderness and perish;[k]
the caravans of Tema look for their waters, 19
travelling merchants of Sheba hope for them;
but they are disappointed, for all their con- 20
fidence,
they reach them only to be balked.
So treacherous have you now been to me:[l] 21
you felt dismay and were afraid.
Did I ever say, 'Give me this or that; 22
open your purses to save my life;
rescue me from my enemy; 23
ransom me out of the hands of ruthless men'?

Tell me plainly, and I will listen in silence; 24
show me where I have erred.

---

h from . . . slander: or when slander is rife.   *i what . . . wild?: or* therefore words fail me.   *j Prob.*
rdg.; Heb. adds I have not denied the words of the Holy One.   *k Or* and are lost.   *l So . . . to me:*
prob. rdg.; Heb. obscure.

25 How harsh are the words of the upright man!
    What do the arguments of wise men*m* prove?
26 Do you mean to argue about words
    or to sift the utterance of a man past hope?
27 Would you assail an orphan*n*?
    Would you hurl yourselves on a friend?
28 So now, I beg you, turn and look at me:
    am I likely to lie to your faces?
29 Think again, let me have no more injustice;
    think again, for my integrity is in question.
30 Do I ever give voice to injustice?
    Does my sense not warn me when my words
        are wild?

7 Has not man hard service on earth,
    and are not his days like those of a hired
        labourer,
2 like those of a slave longing for the shade
    or a servant kept waiting for his wages?
3 So months of futility are my portion,
    troubled nights are my lot.
4 When I lie down, I think,
    'When will it be day that I may rise?'
    When the evening grows long and I lie down,
    I do nothing but toss till morning twilight.
5 My body is infested with worms,
    and scabs cover my skin.*o*
6 My days are swifter than a shuttle*p*
    and come to an end as the thread runs out.*q*
7 Remember, my life is but a breath of wind;
    I shall never again see good days.
8 Thou wilt behold me no more with a seeing
        eye;
    under thy very eyes I shall disappear.
9 As clouds break up and disperse,
    so he that goes down to Sheol never comes
        back;
10 he never returns home again,
    and his place will know him no more.*r*

11 But I will not hold my peace;
    I will speak out in the distress of my mind
    and complain in the bitterness of my soul.
12 Am I the monster of the deep, am I the sea-
        serpent,
    that thou settest a watch over me?
13 When I think that my bed will comfort me,
    that sleep will relieve my complaining,
14 thou dost terrify me with dreams
    and affright me with visions.
15 I would rather be choked outright;
    I would prefer death to all my sufferings.
16 I am in despair, I would not go on living;
    leave me alone, for my life is but a vapour.
17 What is man that thou makest much of him
    and turnest thy thoughts towards him,
18 only to punish him morning by morning
    or to test him every hour of the day?
19 Wilt thou not look away from me for an
        instant?

Wilt thou not let me be while I swallow my
    spittle?
20 If I have sinned, how do I injure thee,
    thou watcher of the hearts of men?
    Why hast thou made me thy butt,
    and why have I become thy target?
21 Why dost thou not pardon my offence
    and take away my guilt?
    But now I shall lie down in the grave;
    seek me, and I shall not be.

First speech of Bildad
Then Bildad the Shuhite began: 8
    How long will you say such things,   2
    the long-winded ramblings of an old man?
    Does God pervert judgement?   3
    Does the Almighty pervert justice?
    Your sons sinned against him,   4
    so he left them to be victims of their own
        iniquity.
    If only you will seek God betimes   5
    and plead for the favour of the Almighty,
    if you are innocent and upright,   6
    then indeed will he watch over you
    and see your just intent fulfilled.
    Then, though your beginnings were humble,   7
    your end will be great.

    Inquire now of older generations   8
    and consider the experience of their fathers;
    for we ourselves are of yesterday and are   9
        transient;
    our days on earth are a shadow.
    Will not they speak to you and teach you   10
    and pour out the wisdom of their hearts?
    Can rushes grow where there is no marsh?   11
    Can reeds flourish without water?
    While they are still in flower and not ready   12
        to cut,*s*
    they wither earlier than*t* any green plant.
    Such is the fate of all who forget God;   13
    the godless man's life-thread breaks off;
    his confidence is gossamer,   14
    and the ground of his trust a spider's web.
    He leans against his house but it does not   15
        stand;
    he clutches at it but it does not hold firm.
    His is the lush growth of a plant in the sun,   16
    pushing out shoots over the garden;
    but its roots become entangled in a stony   17
        patch
    and run against a bed of rock.
    Then someone uproots it from its place,   18
    which*u* disowns it and says, 'I have never
        known you.'
    That is how its life withers away,   19
    and other plants spring up from the earth.

    Be sure, God will not spurn the blameless   20
        man,

---

m wise men: *prob. rdg.; Heb. unintelligible.*   *n Or* a blameless man.   *o Prob. rdg.; Heb. adds* it is
cracked and discharging.   *p Or* a fleeting odour.   *q* as . . . out: *or* without hope.   *r Or* and he will not
be noticed any more in his place.   *s* and . . . cut: *or* they are surely cut.   *t Or* wither like . . .   *u Or* and.

nor will he grasp the hand of the wrongdoer.

21 He will yet fill your mouth with laughter,
and shouts of joy will be on your lips;

22 your enemies shall be wrapped in confusion,
and the tents of the wicked shall vanish away.

Job's reply

9 Then Job answered:

2 Indeed this I know for the truth,
that no man can win his case against God.

3 If a man chooses to argue with him,
God will not answer one question in a
thousand.*v*

4 He is wise, he is powerful;
what man has stubbornly resisted him and
survived?

5 It is God who moves mountains, giving them
no rest,
turning them over in his wrath;

6 who makes the earth start from its place
so that its pillars are convulsed;

7 who commands the sun's orb not to rise
and shuts up the stars under his seal;

8 who by himself spread out the heavens
and trod on the sea-monster's back;*w*

9 who made Aldebaran and Orion,
the Pleiades and the circle of the southern
stars;

10 who does great and unsearchable things,
marvels without number.

11 He passes by me, and I do not see him;
he moves on his way undiscerned by me;

12 if he hurries on, who can bring him back?
Who will ask him what he does?

13 God does not turn back his wrath;
the partisans of Rahab lie prostrate at his
feet.

14 How much less can I answer him
or find words to dispute with him?

15 Though I am right, I get no answer,
though I plead with my accuser for mercy.

16 If I summoned him to court and he responded,
I do not believe that he would listen to my
plea—

17 for he bears hard upon me for a trifle
and rains blows on me without cause;

18 he leaves me no respite to recover my breath
but fills me with bitter thoughts.

19 If the appeal is to force, see how strong he is;
if to justice, who can compel him to give me
a hearing?

20 Though I am right, he condemns me out of
my own mouth;
though I am blameless, he twists my words.

21 Blameless, I say; of myself
I reck nothing, I hold my life cheap.

22 But it is all one; therefore I say,
'He destroys blameless and wicked alike.'

23 When a sudden flood brings death,
he mocks the plight of the innocent.

24 The land is given over to the power of the
wicked,
and the eyes of its judges are blindfold.*x*

25 My days have been swifter than a runner,
they have slipped away and seen no prosperity;

26 they have raced by like reed-built skiffs,
swift as vultures swooping on carrion.

27 If I think, 'I will forget my griefs,
I will show a cheerful face and smile',

28 I tremble in every nerve;*y*
I know that thou wilt not hold me innocent.

29 If I am to be accounted guilty,
why do I labour in vain?

30 Though I wash myself with soap
or cleanse my hands with lye,

31 thou wilt thrust me into the mud
and my clothes will make me loathsome.

32 He is not a man as I am, that I can answer him
or that we can confront one another in court.

33 If only there were one to arbitrate between us
and impose his authority on us both,

34 so that God might take his rod from my back,
and terror of him might not come on me
suddenly.

35 I would then speak without fear of him;
for I know I am not what I am thought to be.

10
I am sickened of life;
I will give free rein to my griefs,
I will speak out in bitterness of soul.

2 I will say to God, 'Do not condemn me,
but tell me the ground of thy complaint
against me.

3 Dost thou find any advantage in oppression,
in spurning the fruit of all thy labour
and smiling on the policy of wicked men?

4 Hast thou eyes of flesh
or dost thou see as mortal man sees?

5 Are thy days as those of a mortal
or thy years as the life of a man,

6 that thou lookest for guilt in me
and dost seek in me for sin,

7 though thou knowest that I am guiltless
and have none to save me from thee?

8 'Thy hands gave me shape and made me;
and dost thou at once turn and destroy me?

---

v If a man . . . thousand: *or* If God is pleased to argue with him, man cannot answer one question in a thousand.
w Or on the crests of the waves.   *x* Prob. rdg.; Heb. adds if not he, then who?   *y* Or I am afraid
of all that I must suffer.

9 Remember that thou didst knead me like clay;
and wouldst thou turn me back into dust?

10 Didst thou not pour me out like milk
and curdle me like cheese,

11 clothe me with skin and flesh
and knit me together with bones and sinews?

12 Thou hast given me life and continuing favour,
and thy providence has watched over my spirit.

13 Yet this was the secret purpose of thy heart,
and I know that this was thy intent:

14 that, if I sinned, thou wouldst be watching me
and wouldst not acquit me of my guilt.

15 If I indeed am wicked, the worse for me!
If I am righteous, even so I may lift up my head;[z]

16 if I am proud as a lion, thou dost hunt me down
and dost confront me again with marvellous power;

17 thou dost renew thy onslaught upon me,
and with mounting anger against me
bringest fresh forces to the attack.

18 Why didst thou bring me out of the womb?
O that I had ended there and no eye had seen me,

19 that I had been carried from the womb to the grave
and were as though I had not been born.

20 Is not my life short and fleeting?
Let me be, that I may be happy for a moment,

21 before I depart to a land of gloom,
a land of deep darkness, never to return,

22 a land of gathering shadows, of deepening darkness,
lit by no ray of light,[a] dark[b] upon dark.'

First speech of Zophar

11 Then Zophar the Naamathite began:

2 Should this spate of words not be answered?
Must a man of ready tongue be always right?

3 Is your endless talk to reduce men to silence?
Are you to talk nonsense and no one rebuke you?

4 You claim that your opinions are sound;
you say to God, 'I am spotless in thy sight.'

5 But if only he would speak
and open his lips to talk with you,

6 and expound to you the secrets of wisdom,
for wonderful are its effects!
[Know then that God exacts from you less than your sin deserves.]

7 Can you fathom the mystery of God,
can you fathom the perfection of the Almighty?

It is higher than heaven; you can do nothing. 8
It is deeper than Sheol; you can know nothing.

Its measure is longer than the earth 9
and broader than the sea.

If he passes by, he may keep secret his 10
passing;
if he proclaims it, who can turn him back?

He surely knows which men are false, 11
and when he sees iniquity, does he not take note of it?[c]

Can a fool grow wise? 12
can a wild ass's foal be born a man?

If only you had directed your heart rightly 13
and spread out your hands to pray to him!

If you have wrongdoing in hand, thrust it 14
away;
let no iniquity make its home with you.

Then you could hold up your head without 15
fault,
a man of iron, knowing no fear.

Then you will forget your trouble; 16
you will remember it only as flood-waters
that have passed;

life will be lasting, bright as noonday, 17
and darkness will be turned to morning.

You will be confident, because there is hope; 18
sure of protection, you will lie down in confidence;[d]

great men will seek your favour. 19

Blindness will fall on the wicked; 20
the ways of escape are closed to them,
and their hope is despair.

Job's reply

Then Job answered: **12**

No doubt you are perfect men[e] 2
and absolute wisdom is yours!

But I have sense as well as you; 3
in nothing do I fall short of you;
what gifts indeed have you that others have not?

Yet I am a laughing-stock to my friend— 4
a laughing-stock, though I am innocent and blameless,
one that called upon God, and he answered.[f]

Prosperity and ease look down on mis- 5
fortune,
on the blow that fells the man who is already reeling,

while the marauders' tents are left un- 6
disturbed
and those who provoke God live safe and sound.[g]

Go and ask the cattle, 7
ask the birds of the air to inform you,
or tell the creatures that crawl to teach you, 8

---

z *Prob. rdg.; Heb. adds* filled with shame and steeped in my affliction.   a *lit . . . light: or* a place of disorder.
b *Prob. rdg.; Heb. obscure.*   c does . . . of it?: *or* he does not stand aloof.   d *Prob. rdg.; Heb. adds*
and you will lie down unafraid.   e *Prob. rdg.; Heb.* No doubt you are people.   f *Or* and he afflicted
me.   g *Prob. rdg.; Heb. adds* He brings it in full measure to whom he will (*cp. 21. 17*).

G*

and the fishes of the sea to give you instruction.

9 Who cannot learn from all these
that the LORD's own hand has done this?

11ʰ (Does not the ear test what is spoken
as the palate savours food?

12 There is wisdom, remember, in age,
and long life brings understanding.)

10 In God's hand are the souls of all that live,
the spirits of all human kind.

13 Wisdom and might are his,
with him are firmness and understanding.

14 If he pulls down, there is no rebuilding;
if he imprisons, there is no release.

15 If he holds up the waters, there is drought;
if he lets them go, they turn the land upside
down.

16 Strength and success belong to him,
deceived and deceiver are his to use.

17 He makes counsellors behave like idiots
and drives judges mad;

18 he looses the bonds imposed by kings
and removes the girdle of office from their
waists;

19 he makes priests behave like idiots
and overthrows men long in office;

20 those who are trusted he strikes dumb,
he takes away the judgement of old men;

21 he heaps scorn on princes
and abates the arrogance of nobles.

23ⁱ He leads peoples astray and destroys
them,
he lays them low, and there they lie.

24 He takes away their wisdom from the rulers
of the nations
and leaves them wandering in a pathless
wilderness;

25 they grope in the darkness without light
and are left to wander like a drunkard.

22 He uncovers mysteries deep in obscurity
and into thick darkness he brings light.

13 All this I have seen with my own eyes,
with my own ears I have heard it, and understood it.

2 What you know, I also know;
in nothing do I fall short of you.

3 But for my part I would speak with the
Almighty
and am ready to argue with God,

4 while you like fools are smearing truth with
your falsehoods,
stitching a patchwork of lies, one and all.

5 Ah, if you would only be silent
and let silence be your wisdom!

6 Now listen to my arguments
and attend while I put my case.

7 Is it on God's behalf that you speak so
wickedly,

or in his defence that you allege what is
false?

8 Must you take God's part,
or put his case for him?

9 Will all be well when he examines you?
Will you quibble with him as you quibble
with a man?

10 He will most surely expose you
if you take his part by falsely accusing me.

11 Will not God's majesty strike you with dread,
and terror of him overwhelm you?

12 Your pompous talk is dust and ashes,
your defences will crumble like clay.

13 Be silent, leave me to speak my mind,
and let what may come upon me!

14 I will put my neck in the noose
and take my life in my hands.

15 If he would slay me, I should not hesitate;
I should still argue my cause to his face.

16 This at least assures my success,
that no godless man may appear before him.

17 Listen then, listen to my words,
and give a hearing to my exposition.

18 Be sure of this: once I have stated my case
I know that I shall be acquitted.

19 Who is there that can argue so forcibly with
me
that he could reduce me straightway to
silence and death?

20 Grant me these two conditions only,
and then I will not hide myself out of thy
sight:

21 take thy heavy hand clean away from me
and let not the fear of thee strike me with
dread.

22 Then summon me, and I will answer;
or I will speak first, and do thou answer me.

23 How many iniquities and sins are laid to my
charge?
let me know my offences and my sin.

24 Why dost thou hide thy face
and treat me as thy enemy?

25 Wilt thou chase a driven leaf,
wilt thou pursue dry chaff,

26 prescribing punishment for me
and making me heir to the iniquities of my
youth,

27 putting my feet in the stocksʲ
and setting a slave-mark on the arches of
my feet?ᵏ

h Verse 10 transposed to follow verse 12.
adds keeping a close watch on all I do.
transposed to follow 14. 2.

i Verse 22 transposed to follow verse 25.
k Prob. rdg.; Heb. adds verse 28, he is like . . . have eaten, now

j Prob. rdg.; Heb.

14 Man born of woman is short-lived and full of disquiet.

2 He blossoms like a flower and then he withers;
he slips away like a shadow and does not stay;
*l*he is like a wine-skin that perishes
or a garment that moths have eaten.

3 Dost thou fix thine eyes on such a creature, and wilt thou bring him into court to confront thee?*m*

5 The days of his life are determined,
and the number of his months is known to thee;
thou hast laid down a limit, which he cannot pass.

6 Look away from him therefore and leave him alone
counting the hours day by day like a hired labourer.

7 If a tree is cut down,
there is hope that it will sprout again
and fresh shoots will not fail.

8 Though its roots grow old in the earth,
and its stump is dying in the ground,

9 if it scents water it may break into bud
and make new growth like a young plant.

10 But a man dies, and he disappears;*n*
man comes to his end, and where is he?

11 As the waters of a lake dwindle,
or as a river shrinks and runs dry,

12 so mortal man lies down, never to rise
until the very sky splits open.
If a man dies, can he live again?*o*
He shall never be roused from his sleep.

13 If only thou wouldst hide me in Sheol
and conceal me till thy anger turns aside,
if thou wouldst fix a limit for my time there,
and then remember me!

14 *p*Then I would not lose hope, however long my service,
waiting for my relief to come.

15 Thou wouldst summon me, and I would answer thee;
thou wouldst long to see the creature thou hast made.

16 But now thou dost count every step I take,
watching all my course.

17 Every offence of mine is stored in thy bag;
thou dost keep my iniquity under seal.

18 Yet as a falling mountain-side is swept away,
and a rock is dislodged from its place,

19 as water wears away stones,
and a rain-storm scours the soil from the land,
so thou hast wiped out the hope of frail man;

20 thou dost overpower him finally, and he is gone;
his face is changed, and he is banished from thy sight.

22*q* His flesh upon him becomes black,
and his life-blood dries up within him.*r*

21 His sons rise to honour, and he sees nothing of it;
they sink into obscurity, and he knows it not.

Second speech of Eliphaz

Then Eliphaz the Temanite answered: **15**

2 Would a man of sense give vent to such foolish notions
and answer with a bellyful of wind?

3 Would he bandy useless words
and arguments so unprofitable?

4 Why! you even banish the fear of God from your mind,
usurping the sole right to speak in his presence;

5 your iniquity dictates what you say,
and deceit is the language of your choice.

6 You are condemned out of your own mouth, not by me;
your own lips give evidence against you.

7 Were you born first of mankind?
were you brought forth before the hills?

8 Do you listen in God's secret council
or usurp all wisdom for yourself alone?

9 What do you know that we do not know?
What insight have you that we do not share?

10 We have age and white hairs in our company,
men older than your father.

11 Does not the consolation of God suffice you,
a word whispered quietly in your ear?

12 What makes you so bold at heart,
and why do your eyes flash,

13 that you vent your anger on God
and pour out such a torrent of words?

14 What is frail man that he should be innocent,
or any child of woman that he should be justified?

15 If God puts no trust in his holy ones,
and the heavens are not innocent in his sight,

16 how much less so is man, who is loathsome and rotten
and laps up evil like water!

---

*l he is like . . . have eaten: 13. 28 transposed here.
pure out of unclean? No one.*   *n Or and is powerless.*
p See note on verse 12.   *q Verses 21 and 22 transposed.*
maybe, regret him, and his slaves mourn his loss.

m So one Heb. MS.; others add (4) Who can produce
o Line transposed from beginning of verse 14.
r His flesh . . . within him: or His own kin,

17 I will tell you, if only you will listen,
and I will describe what I have seen
18 [what has been handed down by wise men
and was not concealed from them by their
fathers;
19 to them alone the land was given,
and no foreigner settled among them]:
20 the wicked are racked with anxiety all their
days,
the ruthless man for all the years in store for
him.
21 The noise of the hunter's scare rings in his
ears,
and in time of peace the raider falls on him;
22 he cannot hope to escape from dark death;
he is marked down for the sword;
23 he is flung out as food for vultures;
such a man knows that his destruction is
certain.
24 Suddenly a black day comes upon him,
distress and anxiety overwhelm him
[like a king ready for battle];
25 for he has lifted his. hand against God
and is pitting himself against the Almighty,
26 charging him head down,
with the full weight of his bossed shield.

27 Heavy though his jowl is and gross,
and though his sides bulge with fat,
28 the city where he lives will lie in ruins,
his house will be deserted;
it will soon become a heap of rubble.
29 He will no longer be rich, his wealth will not
last,
and he will strike no root in the earth;ˢ
30 scorching heat will shrivel his shoots,
and his blossom will be shaken off by the
wind.
31 He deceives himself, trusting in his high rank,
for all his dealings will come to nothing.
32 His palm-trees will wither unseasonably,
and his branches will not spread;
33 he will be like a vine that sheds its unripe
grapes,
like an olive-tree that drops its blossom.
34 For the godless, one and all, are barren,
and their homes, enriched by bribery, are
destroyed by fire;
35 they conceive mischief and give birth to
trouble,
and the child of their womb is deceit.

Job's reply

16 Then Job answered:

2 I have heard such things often before,
you who make trouble, all of you, with every
breath,
3 saying, 'Will this windbag never have done?
What makes him so stubborn in argument?'
4 If you and I were to change places,
I could talk like you;

how I could harangue you
and wag my head at you!
But no, I would speak words of encourage- 5
ment,
and then my condolences would flow in
streams.
If I speak, my pain is not eased; 6
if I am silent, it does not leave me.
Meanwhile, my friend wearies me with false 7
sympathy;
they tear me to pieces, he and hisʳ fellows. 8
He has come forward to give evidence against
me;
the liar testifies against me to my face,
in his wrath he wears me down, his hatred is 9
plain to see;
he grinds his teeth at me.

My enemies look daggers at me,
they bare their teeth to rend me, 10
they slash my cheeks with knives;
they are all in league against me.
God has left me at the mercy of malefactors 11
and cast me into the clutches of wicked men.
I was at ease, but he set upon me and mauled 12
me,
seized me by the neck and worried me.
He set me up as his target;
his arrows rained upon me from every side; 13
pitiless, he cut deep into my vitals,
he spilt my gall on the ground.
He made breach after breach in my defences; 14
he fell upon me like a fighting man.

I stitched sackcloth together to cover my 15
body
and I buried my forelock in the dust;
my cheeks were flushed with weeping 16
and dark shadows were round my eyes,
yet my hands were free from violence 17
and my prayer was sincere.

O earth, cover not my blood 18
and let my cry for justice find no rest!
For look! my witness is in heaven; 19
there is one on high ready to answer for me.
My appeal will come before God, 20
while my eyes turn again and again to him.
If only there were one to arbitrate between 21
man and God,
as between a man and his neighbour!
For there are but few years to come 22
before I take the road from which I shall not
return.

My mind is distraught, my days are num- **1**ᵗ
bered,
and the grave is waiting for me.
Wherever I turn, men taunt me, 2
and my day is darkened by their sneers.
Be thou my surety with thyself, 3
for who else can pledge himself for me?

---

s Prob. rdg.; Heb. adds he will not escape from darkness.   *t Prob. rdg.; Heb.* my.

4 Thou wilt not let those men triumph,
  whose minds thou hast sunk in ignorance;
5 if such a man denounces his friends to their
  ruin,
  his sons' eyes shall grow dim.

6 I am held up as a byword in every land,
  a portent for all to see;
7 my eyes are dim with grief,
  my limbs wasted to a shadow.
8 Honest men are bewildered at this,
  and the innocent are indignant at my plight.
9 In spite of all, the righteous man maintains
  his course,
  and he whose hands are clean grows strong
  again.

10 But come on, one and all, try again!
   I shall not find a wise man among you.
11 My days die away like an echo;
   my heart-strings[u] are snapped.
12 Day is turned into night,
   and morning[v] light is darkened before me.
13 If I measure Sheol for my house,
   if I spread my couch in the darkness,
14 if I call the grave my father
   and the worm my mother or my sister,
15 where, then, will my hope be,
   and who will take account of my piety?
16 I cannot take them down to Sheol with me,
   nor can they descend with me into the earth.

Second speech of Bildad

18 Then Bildad the Shuhite answered:

2 How soon will you bridle[w] your tongue?
  Do but think, and then we will talk.
3 What do you mean by treating us as cattle?
  Are we nothing but brute beasts to you?[x]
4 Is the earth to be deserted to prove you right,
  or the rocks to be moved from their place?

5 No, it is the wicked whose light is extinguished,
  from whose fire no flame will rekindle;
6 the light fades in his tent,
  and his lamp dies down and fails him.
7 In his iniquity his steps totter,
  and his disobedience trips him up;
8 he rushes headlong into a net
  and steps through the hurdle that covers a
  pit;
9 his heel is caught in a snare,
  the noose grips him tight;
10 a cord lies hidden in the ground for him
   and a trap in the path.
11 The terrors of death suddenly beset him
   and make him piss over his feet.
12 For all his vigour he is paralysed with fear,
   strong as he is, disaster awaits him.

Disease eats away his skin,   13
Death's eldest child devours his limbs.
He is torn from the safety of his home,   14
and Death's terrors escort him to their king.[y]
Magic herbs lie strewn about his tent,   15
and his home is sprinkled with sulphur to
  protect it.
His roots beneath dry up,   16
and above, his branches wither.
His memory vanishes from the face of the   17
  earth
and he leaves no name in the world.
He is driven from light into darkness   18
and banished from the land of the living.
He leaves no issue or offspring among his   19
  people,
no survivor in his earthly home;
in the west men hear of his doom and are   20
  appalled;
in the east they shudder with horror.
Such is the fate of the dwellings of evildoers, 21
and of the homes of those who care nothing
  for God.

Job's reply

Then Job answered: **19**

How long will you exhaust me   2
and pulverize me with words?
Time and time again you have insulted me   3
and shamelessly done me wrong.
If in fact I had erred,   4
the error would still be mine.
But if indeed you lord it over me   5
and try to justify the reproaches levelled at
  me,
I tell you, God himself has put me in the   6
  wrong,
he has drawn the net round me.
If I cry 'Murder!' no one answers;   7
if I appeal for help, I get no justice.
He has walled in my path so that I cannot   8
  break away,
and he has hedged in the road before me.
He has stripped me of all honour   9
and has taken the crown from my head.
On every side he beats me down and I am   10
  gone;
he has pulled up my tent-rope[z] like a tree.
His anger is hot against me   11
and he counts me his enemy.
His raiders gather in force[a]   12
and encamp about my tent.

My brothers hold aloof from me,   13
my friends are utterly estranged from me;
my kinsmen and intimates fall away,   14-15
my retainers have forgotten me;
my slave-girls treat me as a stranger,
I have become an alien in their eyes.

---

u *Prob. rdg.; Heb.* the desires of my heart.   v morning: *prob. rdg.; Heb.* near.   w bridle: *prob. rdg.;*
Heb. unintelligible.   x *Prob. rdg.; Heb. adds* rending himself in his anger.   y *Or and you conduct*
him to the king of terrors.   z *Or* he has uprooted my hope.   a *Prob. rdg.; Heb. adds* they raise an
earthwork against me.

16 I summon my slave, but he does not answer,
    though I entreat him as a favour.
17 My breath is noisome to my wife,
    and I stink in the nostrils of my own family.
18 Mere children despise me
    and, when I rise, turn their backs on me;
19 my intimate companions loathe me,
    and those whom I love have turned against
      me.
20 My bones stick out through my skin,[b]
    and I gnaw my under-lip with my teeth.
21 Pity me, pity me, you that are my friends;
    for the hand of God has touched me.
22 Why do you pursue me as God pursues me?
    Have you not had your teeth in me long
      enough?
23 O that my words might be inscribed,
    O that they might be engraved in an in-
      scription,
24 cut with an iron tool and filled with lead
    to be a witness[c] in hard rock!
25 But in my heart I know that my vindicator
      lives
    and that he will rise last to speak in court;
26 and I shall discern my witness standing at
      my side[d]
    and see my defending counsel, even God
      himself,
27 whom I shall see with my own eyes,
    I myself and no other.
28 My heart failed me when you said,
    'What a train of disaster he has brought on
      himself!
    The root of the trouble lies in him.'
29 Beware of the sword that points at you,
    the sword that sweeps away all iniquity;
    then you will know that there is a judge.[e]

Second speech of Zophar

20 Then Zophar the Naamathite answered:

2 My distress of mind forces me to reply,
    and this is why[f] I hasten to speak:
3 I have heard arguments that are a reproach
      to me,
    a spirit beyond my understanding gives me
      the answers.
4 Surely you know that this has been so since
      time began,
    since man was first set on the earth:
5 the triumph of the wicked is short-lived,
    the glee of the godless lasts but a moment?
6 Though he stands high as heaven,
    and his head touches the clouds,
7 he will be swept utterly away like his own
      dung,
    and all that saw him will say, 'Where is he?'

He will fly away like a dream and be lost,   8
    driven off like a vision of the night;
the eye which glimpsed him shall do so no   9
      more
    and shall never again see him in his place.
The youth and strength which filled his bones 11[g]
    shall lie with him in the dust.
His sons will pay court to the poor,   10
    and their[h] hands will give back his wealth.
Though evil tastes sweet in his mouth,   12
    and he savours it, rolling it round his tongue,
though he lingers over it and will not let it go, 13
    and holds it back on his palate,
yet his food turns in his stomach,   14
    changing to asps' venom within him.
He gulps down wealth, then vomits it up,   15
    or God makes him discharge it.
He sucks the poison of asps,   16
    and the tongue of the viper kills him.
Not for him to swill down rivers of cream[i]   17
    or torrents of honey and curds;
he must give back his gains without swallow- 18
      ing them,
    and spew up his profit undigested;
for he has hounded and harassed the poor,   19
    he has seized houses which he did not build.
Because his appetite gave him no rest,   20
    and he cannot escape his own desires,
nothing is left for him to eat,   21
    and so his well-being does not last;
with every need satisfied his troubles begin, 22
    and the full force of hardship strikes him.
God vents his anger upon him   23
    and rains on him cruel blows.
He is wounded by weapons of iron   24
    and pierced by a bronze-tipped arrow;
out at his back the point comes,   25
    the gleaming tip from his gall-bladder.
Darkness unrelieved awaits him,   26
    a fire that needs no fanning will consume him.
[Woe betide any survivor in his tent!]
The heavens will lay bare his guilt,   27
    and earth will rise up to condemn him.
A flood will sweep away his house,   28
    rushing waters on the day of wrath.
Such is God's reward for the wicked man   29
    and the lot appointed for the rebel[j] by God.

Job's reply

Then Job answered: **21**

Listen to me, do but listen,   2
    and let that be the comfort you offer me.
Bear with me while I have my say;   3
    when I have finished, you may mock.
May not I too voice[k] my thoughts?   4
Have not I as good cause to be impatient?
Look at my plight, and be aghast;   5
    clap your hand to your mouth.

---

b Prob. rdg.; Heb. adds and my flesh.   *c to . . . witness: or* for ever.   *d* my witness . . . side: *prob.
rdg.; Heb. unintelligible.   e Or* judgement.   *f* this is why: *prob. rdg.; Heb. obscure.   g Verses* 10
and 11 *transposed.   h Prob. rdg.; Heb.* his.   *i* rivers of cream: *prob. rdg.; Heb. obscure.   j* the rebel:
prob. rdg.; Heb. his word.   *k* May . . . voice: *prob. rdg.; Heb. obscure.*

6 When I stop to think, I am filled with horror,
and my whole body is convulsed.

7 Why do the wicked enjoy long life,
hale in old age, and great and powerful?

8 They live to see their children settled,
their kinsfolk and descendants flourishing;

9 their families are secure and safe;
the rod of God's justice does not reach them.

10 Their bull mounts and fails not of its purpose;
their cow calves and does not miscarry.

11 Their children like lambs run out to play,
and their little ones skip and dance;

12 they rejoice with tambourine and harp
and make merry to the sound of the flute.

13 Their lives close in prosperity,
and they go down to Sheol in peace.

14 To God they say, 'Leave us alone;
we do not want to know your ways.

15 What is the Almighty that we should worship him,
or what should we gain by seeking his favour?'

16 Is not the prosperity of the wicked in their own hands?
Are not their purposes very different from God's¹?

17 How often is the lamp of the wicked snuffed out,
and how often does their ruin come upon them?
How often does God in his anger deal out suffering,
bringing it in full measure to whom he will?ᵐ

18 How often is that man like a wisp of straw before the wind,
like chaff which the storm-wind whirls away?

19 You say, 'The trouble he has earned, God will keep for his sons';
no, let him be paid for it in full and be punished.

20 Let his own eyes see damnation come upon him,
and the wrath of the Almighty be the cup he drinks.

21 What joy shall he have in his children after him,
if his very months and days are numbered?

22 Can any man teach God,
God who judges even those in heaven above?

23 One man, I tell you, dies crowned with success,
lapped in security and comfort,

24 his loins full of vigour
and the marrow juicy in his bones;

25 another dies in bitterness of soul
and never tastes prosperity;

26 side by side they are laid in earth,
and worms are the shroud of both.

27 I know well what you are thinking
and the arguments you are marshalling against me;

28 I know you will ask, 'Where is the great man's home now,
what has become of the home of the wicked?'

29 Have you never questioned travellers?
Can you not learn from the signs they offer,

30 that the wicked is spared when disaster comes
and conveyed to safety before the day of wrath?

31 No one denounces his conduct to his face,
no one requites him for what he has done.

32-33 When he is carried to the grave,
all the world escorts him, before and behind;
the dust of earth is sweet to him,
and thousands keep watch at his tomb.

34 How futile, then, is the comfort you offer me!
How false your answers ring!

Third speech of Eliphaz

22 Then Eliphaz the Temanite answered:

2 Can man be any benefit to God?
Can even a wise man benefit him?

3 Is it an asset to the Almighty if you are righteous?
Does he gain if your conduct is perfect?

4 Do not think that he reproves you because you are pious,
that on this count he brings you to trial.

5 No: it is because you are a very wicked man,
and your depravity passes all bounds.

6 Without due cause you take a brother in pledge,
you strip men of their clothes and leave them naked.

7 When a man is weary, you give him no water to drink
and you refuse bread to the hungry.

8 Is the earth, then, the preserve of the strong
and a domain for the favoured few?

9 Widows you have sent away empty-handed,
orphans you have struck defenceless.

10 No wonder that there are pitfalls in your path,
that scares are set to fill you with sudden fear.

11 The light is turned into darkness, and you cannot see;
the flood-waters cover you.

12 Surely God is at the zenith of the heavens
and looks down on all the stars, high as they are.

13 But you say, 'What does God know?
Can he see through thick darkness to judge?

14 His eyes cannot pierce the curtain of the clouds
as he walks to and fro on the vault of heaven.'

15 Consider the course of the wicked man,
the path the miscreant treads:

---

l God's: prob. rdg.; Heb. mine.

m Line transposed from 12. 6.

16 see how they are carried off before their time,
their very foundation flowing away like a
river;
17 these men said to God, 'Leave us alone;
what can the Almighty do to us?'
18 Yet it was he that filled their houses with
good things,
although their purposes and his were very
different.
19 The righteous see their fate and exult,
the innocent make game of them;
20 for their riches are swept away,
and the profusion of their wealth is destroyed
by fire.

21 Come to terms with God and you will
prosper;
that is the way to mend your fortune.
22 Take instruction from his mouth
and store his words in your heart.
23 If you come back to the Almighty in true
sincerity,
if you banish wrongdoing from your home,
24 if you treat your precious metal as dust[n]
and the gold of Ophir as stones from the
river-bed,
25 then the Almighty himself will be your
precious metal;
he will be your silver in double measure.
26 Then, with sure trust in[o] the Almighty,
you will raise your face to God;
27 you will pray to him, and he will hear you,
and you will have cause to fulfil your vows.
28 In all your designs you will succeed,
and light will shine on your path;
29 but God brings down the pride of the
haughty[p]
and keeps safe the man of modest looks.
30 He will deliver the innocent,[q]
and you will be delivered, because your
hands are clean.

Job's reply

23 Then Job answered:
2 My thoughts today are resentful,
for God's hand is heavy on me in my trouble.
3 If only I knew how to find him,
how to enter his court,
4 I would state my case before him
and set out my arguments in full;
5 then I should learn what answer he would
give
and find out what he had to say.
6 Would he exert his great power to browbeat
me?
No; God himself would never bring a charge
against me.

There the upright are vindicated before him, 7
and I shall win from my judge an absolute
discharge.
If I go forward,[r] he is not there; 8
if backward,[s] I cannot find him;
when I turn[t] left,[u] I do not descry him; 9
I face right,[v] but I see him not.
But he knows me in action or at rest; 10
when he tests me, I prove to be gold.
My feet have kept to the path he has set me, 11
I have followed his way and not turned
from it.
I do not ignore the commands that come 12
from his lips,
I have stored in my heart what he says.
He decides,[w] and who can turn him from his 13
purpose?
He does what his own heart desires.
What he determines, that he carries out; 14
his mind is full of plans like these.
Therefore I am fearful of meeting him; 15
when I think about him,[x] I am afraid;
it is God who makes me faint-hearted 16
and the Almighty who fills me with fear,
yet I am not reduced to silence by the dark- 17
ness
nor[y] by the mystery which hides him.

[z] The day of reckoning is no secret to the **24**
Almighty,
though those who know him have no hint of
its date.
Wicked men move boundary-stones 2
and carry away flocks and their shepherds.
In the field they reap what is not theirs, 6[a]
and filch the late grapes from the rich[b] man's
vineyard.
They drive off the orphan's ass 3
and lead away the widow's ox with a rope.
They snatch the fatherless infant from the 9
breast
and take the poor man's child in pledge.
They jostle the poor out of the way; 4
the destitute huddle together, hiding from
them.
The poor rise early like the wild ass, 5
when it scours the wilderness for food;
but though they work till nightfall,[c]
their children go hungry.[d]
Naked and bare they pass the night; 7
in the cold they have nothing to cover
them.
They are drenched by rain-storms from the 8
hills
and hug the rock, their only shelter.
Naked and bare they go about their work, 10
and hungry they carry the sheaves;

---

n Prob. rdg.; Heb. if you put your precious metal on dust.   *o* with . . . in: *or* delighting in.   *p* but . . .
haughty: *prob. rdg.; Heb.* obscure.   *q Prob. rdg.; Heb.* the not innocent.   *r Or* east.   *s Or* west.
t Prob. rdg.; Heb. he turns.   *u Or* north.   *v Or* south.   *w* He decides: *prob. rdg.; Heb.* He in one.
x when . . . him: *or* I stand aloof.   *y* yet I am not . . . nor: *or* indeed I am . . . and . . .   *z Prob. rdg.;*
Heb. prefixes Why.   *a* Verses 3–9 re-arranged to restore the natural order.   *b Or* wicked.   *c Prob.*
rdg.; Heb. Arabah.   *d* go hungry: *prob. rdg.; Heb.* to it food.

11 they press the oil in the shade where two
     walls meet,
   they tread the winepress but themselves go
     thirsty.
12 Far from the city, they groan like dying men,
   and like wounded men they cry out;
   but God pays no heed to their prayer.
13 Some there are who rebel against the light of
     day,
   who know nothing of its ways
   and do not linger in the paths of light.
14 The murderer rises before daylight
   to kill some miserable wretch.*e*
15 The seducer watches eagerly for twilight,
   thinking, 'No eye will catch sight of me.'
   The thief prowls*f* by night,*g*
   his face covered with a mask,
16 and in the darkness breaks into houses
   which he has marked down in the day.
   One and all,*h* they are strangers to the day-
     light,
17 but dark night is morning to them;
   and in the welter of night they are at home.
18 Such men are scum on the surface of the
     water;
   their fields have a bad name throughout the
     land,
   and no labourer will go near their vineyards.
19 As drought and heat make away with snow,
   so the waters of Sheol*i* make away with the
     sinner.
20 The womb forgets him, the worm sucks him
     dry;
   he will not be remembered ever after.*j*
21 He may have wronged the barren childless
     woman
   and been no help to the widow;
22 yet God in his strength carries off even the
     mighty;
   they may rise, but they have no firm hope of
     life.
23 He lulls them into security and confidence;
   but his eyes are fixed on their ways.
24 For a moment they rise to the heights, but
     are soon gone;
   iniquity is snapped like a stick.*k*
   They are laid low and wilt like a mallow-
     flower;
   they droop like an ear of corn on the stalk.
25 If this is not so, who will prove me wrong
   and make nonsense of my argument?

Third speech of Bildad

25 Then Bildad the Shuhite answered:
2 Authority and awe rest with him
   who has established peace in his realm on
     high.
3 His squadrons are without number;

at whom will they not spring from ambush?
How then can a man be justified in God's 4
   sight,
or one born of woman be innocent?
If the circling moon is found wanting,   5
and the stars are not innocent in his eyes,
much more so man who is but a maggot,   6
mortal man who is only a worm.

Job's reply

Then Job answered: **26**

What help you have given to the man with- 2
   out resource,
what deliverance you have brought to the
   powerless!
What counsel you offer to a man at his wit's 3
   end,
what sound advice to the foolish!
Who has prompted you to say such things, 4
and whose spirit is expressed in your speech?

In the underworld the shades writhe in fear, 5
the waters and all that live in them are
   struck with terror.*l*
Sheol is laid bare,   6
and Abaddon uncovered before him.
God spreads the canopy of the sky over chaos 7
and suspends earth in the void.
He keeps the waters penned in dense cloud- 8
   masses,

and the clouds do not burst open under their
   weight.
He covers the face of the full moon,*m*   9
unrolling his clouds across it.
He has fixed the horizon on the surface of the 10
   waters
at the farthest limit of light and darkness.
The pillars of heaven quake   11
and are aghast at his rebuke.
With his strong arm he cleft the sea-monster, 12
and struck down the Rahab by his skill.
At his breath the skies are clear,   13
and his hand breaks the twisting*n* sea-serpent.
These are but the fringe of his power;   14
and how faint the whisper that we hear of
   him!
[Who could fathom the thunder of his
   might?]

---

*e See note on verse 15.   f The thief prowls: prob. rdg.; Heb. Let him be like a thief.   g Line transposed
from end of verse 14.   h One and all: transposed from after* but *in next verse.   i snow . . . Sheol: prob.
rdg.; Heb. snow-water, Sheol.   j Prob. rdg.; Heb. here adds* iniquity is snapped like a stick *(see note on
verse 24).   k Line transposed from end of verse 20.   l are struck with terror: prob. rdg.; Heb. om.
m Or He overlays the surface of his throne.   n Or primeval.*

27 Then Job resumed his discourse:

2 I swear by God, who has denied me justice,
and by the Almighty, who has filled me with
bitterness:

3 so long as there is any life left in me
and God's breath is in my nostrils,

4 no untrue word shall pass my lips
and my tongue shall utter no falsehood.

5 God forbid that I should allow you to be
right;
till death, I will not abandon my claim to
innocence.

6 I will maintain the rightness of my cause,
I will never give up;
so long as I live, I will not change.

7 May my enemy meet the fate of the wicked,
and my antagonist the doom of the wrongdoer!

8 What hope has a godless man, when he is
cut off,*o*
when God takes away his life?

9 Will God listen to his cry
when trouble overtakes him?

10 Will he trust himself to the Almighty
and call upon God at all times?

11 I will teach you what is in God's power,
I will not conceal the purpose of the Almighty.

12 If all of you have seen these things,
why then do you talk such empty nonsense?

13 This is the lot prescribed by God for the
wicked,
and the ruthless man's reward from the
Almighty.

14 He may have many sons, but they will fall
by the sword,
and his offspring will go hungry;

15 the survivors will be brought to the grave
by pestilence,
and no widows will weep for them.

16 He may heap up silver like dirt
and get himself piles of clothes;

17 he may get them, but the righteous will wear
them,
and his silver will be shared among the
innocent.

18 The house he builds is flimsy as a bird's nest
or a shelter put up by a watchman.

19 He may lie down rich one day, but never
again;
he opens his eyes and all is gone.

20 Disaster overtakes him like a flood,
and a storm snatches him away in the night;

21 the east wind lifts him up and he is gone;
it whirls him far from home;

22 it flings itself on him without mercy,
and he is battered and buffeted by its force;

23 it snaps its fingers at him
and whistles over him wherever he may be.

God's unfathomable wisdom

28 There are mines for silver
and places where men refine gold;

2 where iron is won from the earth
and copper smelted from the ore;

3 the end of the seam lies in darkness,
and it is followed to its farthest limit.*p*

4 Strangers cut the galleries;*q*
they are forgotten as they drive forward far
from men.*r*

5 While corn is springing from the earth above,
what lies beneath is raked over like a fire,

6 and out of its rocks comes lapis lazuli,
dusted with flecks of gold.

7 No bird of prey knows the way there,
and the falcon's keen eye cannot descry it;

8 proud beasts do not set foot on it,
and no serpent comes that way.

9 Man sets his hand to the granite rock
and lays bare the roots of the mountains;

10 he cuts galleries in the rocks,
and gems of every kind meet his eye;

11 he dams up the sources of the streams
and brings the hidden riches of the earth to
light.

12 But where can wisdom be found?
And where is the source of understanding?

13 No man knows the way to it;
it is not found in the land of living men.

14 The depths of ocean say, 'It is not in us',
and the sea says, 'It is not with me.'

15 Red gold cannot buy it,
nor can its price be weighed out in silver;

16 it cannot be set in the scales against gold of
Ophir,
against precious cornelian or lapis lazuli;

17 gold and crystal are not to be matched with it,
no work in fine gold can be bartered for it;

18 black coral and alabaster are not worth
mention,
and a parcel of wisdom fetches more than
red coral;

19 topaz*s* from Ethiopia is not to be matched
with it,
it cannot be set in the scales against pure gold.

20 Where then does wisdom come from,
and where is the source of understanding?

21 No creature on earth can see it,
and it is hidden from the birds of the air.

22 Destruction and death say,
'We know of it only by report.'

23 But God understands the way to it,
he alone knows its source;

24 for he can see to the ends of the earth
and he surveys everything under heaven.

25 When he made a counterpoise for the wind
and measured out the waters in proportion,

o Or What is a godless man's thread of life when it is cut . . .
and deep darkness.   *q* Strangers . . . galleries: *prob. rdg.; Heb. obscure.*   *r Prob. rdg.; Heb. adds*
languishing without foothold.   *s Or* chrysolite.   *p Prob. rdg.; Heb. adds* stones of darkness

26 when he laid down a limit for the rain
and a path for the thunderstorm,
27 even then he saw wisdom and took stock
of it,
he considered it and fathomed its very
depths.
28 And he said to man:
The fear of the Lord is wisdom,
and to turn from evil is understanding.

Job's final plea

29 Then Job resumed his discourse:
2 If I could only go back to the old days,
to the time when God was watching over me,
3 when his lamp shone above my head,
and by its light I walked through the darkness!
4 If I could be as in the days of my prime,
when God protected my home,
5 while the Almighty was still there at my side,
and my servants stood round me,
6 while my path flowed with milk,
and the rocks streamed oil!
7 If I went through the gate out of the town
to take my seat in the public square,
8 young men saw me and kept out of sight;
old men rose to their feet,
9 men in authority broke off their talk
and put their hands to their lips;
10 the voices of the nobles died away,
and every man held his tongue.
21[t] They listened to me expectantly
and waited in silence for my opinion.
22 When I had spoken, no one spoke again;
my words fell gently on them;
23 they waited for them as for rain
and drank them in like showers in spring.
24 When I smiled on them, they took heart;
when my face lit up, they lost their gloomy
looks.
25 I presided over them, planning their course,
like a king encamped with his troops.[u]

11 Whoever heard of me spoke in my favour,
and those who saw me bore witness to my
merit,
12 how I saved the poor man when he called for
help
and the orphan who had no protector.
13 The man threatened with ruin blessed me,
and I made the widow's heart sing for joy.
14 I put on righteousness as a garment and it
clothed me;
justice, like a cloak or a turban, wrapped me
round.
15 I was eyes to the blind
and feet to the lame;
16 I was a father to the needy,

and I took up the stranger's cause.
I broke the fangs of the miscreant   17
and rescued the prey from his teeth.
I thought, 'I shall die with my powers un-   18
impaired
and my days uncounted as the grains of
sand,[v]
with my roots spreading out to the water   19

and the dew lying on my branches,
with the bow always new in my grasp   20
and the arrow ever ready to my hand.'[w]

But now I am laughed to scorn   **30**
by men of a younger generation,
men whose fathers I would have disdained
to put with the dogs who kept my flock.
What use were their strong arms to me,   2
since their sturdy vigour had wasted away?
They gnawed roots[x] in the desert,   3
gaunt with want and hunger,[y]
they plucked saltwort and wormwood   4
and root of broom[z] for their food.
Driven out from the society of men,[a]   5
pursued like thieves with hue and cry,
they lived in gullies and ravines,   6
holes in the earth and rocky clefts;
they howled like beasts among the bushes,   7
huddled together beneath the scrub,
vile base-born wretches,   8
hounded from the haunts of men.
Now I have become the target of their taunts, 9
my name is a byword among them.
They loathe me, they shrink from me,   10
they dare to spit in my face.
They run wild and savage[b] me;   11
at sight of me they throw off all restraint.
On my right flank they attack in a mob;[c]   12
they raise their siege-ramps against me,
they tear down my crumbling defences to my   13
undoing,
and scramble up against me unhindered;
they burst in through the gaping breach;   14
at the moment of the crash they come rolling in.
Terror upon terror overwhelms me,   15
it sweeps away my resolution like the wind,
and my hope of victory vanishes like a
cloud.
So now my soul is in turmoil within me,   16
and misery has me daily in its grip.

t Verses 21–25 transposed to this point.   u Prob. rdg.; Heb. adds as when one comforts mourners.
v Or as those of the phoenix.   w Verses 21–25 transposed to follow verse 10.   x roots: prob. rdg.;
Heb. om.   y Prob. rdg.; Heb. adds yesterday waste and derelict land.   z root of broom: probably
fungus on broom root.   a the society of men: prob. rdg.; Heb. obscure.   b They run . . . savage:
prob. rdg.; Heb. He runs . . . savages.   c Prob. rdg.; Heb. adds they let loose my feet.

17 By night pain pierces my very bones,
and there is ceaseless throbbing in my veins;
18 my garments are all bespattered with my phlegm,
which chokes me like the collar of a shirt.
19 God himself[d] has flung me down in the mud,
no better than dust or ashes.

20 I call for thy help, but thou dost not answer;
I stand up to plead, but thou sittest aloof;
21 thou hast turned cruelly against me
and with thy strong hand pursuest me in hatred;
22 thou dost snatch me up and set me astride the wind,
and the tempest[e] tosses me up and down.
23 I know that thou wilt hand me over to death,
to the place appointed for all mortal men.

24 Yet no beggar held out his hand
but was relieved[f] by me in his distress.
25 Did I not weep for the man whose life was hard?
Did not my heart grieve for the poor?
26 Evil has come though I expected good;
I looked for light but there came darkness.
27 My bowels are in ferment and know no peace;
days of misery stretch out before me.
28 I go about dejected and friendless;
I rise in the assembly, only to appeal for help.
29 The wolf is now my brother,
the owls of the desert have become my companions.
30 My blackened skin peels off,
and my body is scorched by the heat.
31 My harp has been tuned for a dirge,
my flute to the voice of those who weep.

31 2[g] What is the lot prescribed by God above,
the reward from the Almighty on high?
3 Is not ruin prescribed for the miscreant
and calamity for the wrongdoer?
4 Yet does not God himself see my ways
and count my every step?

5 I swear I have had no dealings with falsehood
and have not embarked on a course of deceit.
1 I have come to terms with my eyes,
never to take notice of a girl.
6 Let God weigh me in the scales of justice,
and he will know that I am innocent!
7 If my steps have wandered from the way,
if my heart has followed my eyes,
or any dirt stuck to my hands,
8 may another eat what I sow,
and may my crops be pulled up by the roots!
9 If my heart has been enticed by a woman
or I have lain in wait at my neighbour's door,
10 may my wife be another man's slave,

and may other men enjoy her.
[But that is a wicked act, an offence before 11 the law;
it would be a consuming and destructive fire, 12
raging[h] among my crops.]
If I have ever rejected the plea of my slave 13
or of my slave-girl, when they brought their complaint to me,
what shall I do if God appears? 14
What shall I answer if he intervenes?
Did not he who made me in the womb make 15 them?
Did not the same God create us in the belly?
If I have withheld their needs from the poor 16
or let the widow's eye grow dim with tears,
if I have eaten my crust alone, 17
and the orphan has not shared it with me—
the orphan who from boyhood honoured 18 me like a father,
whom I guided from the day of his[i] birth—
if I have seen anyone perish for lack of 19 clothing,
or a poor man with nothing to cover him,
if his body had no cause to bless me, 20
because he was not kept warm with a fleece from my flock,
if I have raised[j] my hand against the inno- 21 cent,[k]
knowing that men would side with me in court,
then may my shoulder-blade be torn from 22 my shoulder,
my arm be wrenched out of its socket!
But the terror of God was heavy upon me,[l] 23
and for fear of his majesty I could do none of these things.

If I have put my faith in gold 24
and my trust in the gold of Nubia,
if I have rejoiced in my great wealth 25
and in the increase of riches;
if I ever looked on the sun in splendour 26
or the moon moving in her glory,
and was led astray in my secret heart 27
and raised my hand in homage;
this would have been an offence before the 28 law,
for I should have been unfaithful to God on high.

If my land has cried out in reproach at me, 38
and its furrows have joined in weeping,
if I have eaten its produce without payment 39
and have disappointed my creditors,
may thistles spring up instead of wheat, 40
and weeds instead of barley!

Have I rejoiced at the ruin of the man that 29 hated me
or been filled with malice when trouble overtook him,

---

d *God himself: prob. rdg.; Heb. om.*   e *the tempest: prob. rdg.; Heb. unintelligible.*   f *was relieved: prob. rdg.; Heb. unintelligible.*   g *Verse 1 transposed to follow verse 5.*   h *Prob. rdg.; Heb. uprooting.*
i *Prob. rdg.; Heb. my.*   j *Or waved.*   k *Or orphan.*   l *Prob. rdg.; Heb. A fear towards me is a disaster from God.*   m *Verses 38–40 transposed (but see note p, page 395).*

30 even though I did not allow my tongue to sin
    by demanding his life with a curse?
31 Have the men of my household never said,
    'Let none of us speak ill of him!
32 No stranger has spent the night in the street'?
    For I have kept open house for the traveller.
33 Have I ever concealed my misdeeds as men
        do,
    keeping my guilt to myself,
34 because I feared the gossip of the town
    or dreaded the scorn of my fellow-citizens?
35 Let me but call a witness in my defence!
    Let the Almighty state his case against me!
    If my accuser had written out his indictment,
    I would not keep silence and remain in-
        doors.ⁿ
36 No! I would flaunt it on my shoulder
    and wear it like a crown on my head;
37 I would plead the whole record of my life
    and present that in court as my defence.^o

            Job's speeches are finished.^p

Elihu intervenes

32 So these three men gave up answering Job;
    for he continued to think himself righteous.
2 Then Elihu son of Barakel the Buzite, of the
    family of Ram, grew angry; angry because
3 Job had made himself out more righteous
    than God,^q and angry with the three friends
    because they had found no answer to Job
4 and had let God appear wrong.^r Now Elihu
    had hung back while they were talking with
5 Job because they were older than he; but,
    when he saw that the three had no answer,
6 he could no longer contain his anger. So
    Elihu son of Barakel the Buzite began to
    speak:

    I am young in years,
    and you are old;
    that is why I held back and shrank
    from displaying my knowledge in front of
        you.
7 I said to myself, 'Let age speak,
    and length of years expound wisdom.'
8 But the spirit of God himself is in man,
    and the breath of the Almighty gives him
        understanding;
9 it is not only the old who are wise
    or the aged who understand what is right.
10 Therefore I say: Listen to me;
    I too will display my knowledge.
11 Look, I have been waiting upon your words,
    listening for the conclusions of your thoughts,
    while you sought for phrases;
12 I have been giving thought to your con-
        clusions,
    but not one of you refutes Job or answers his
        arguments.

Take care then not to claim that you have   13
    found wisdom;
God will rebut him, not man.
I will not string^s words together like you^t   14
    or answer him as you have done.

If these men are confounded and no longer   15
    answer,
    if words fail them,
am I to wait because they do not speak,   16
    because they stand there and no longer
        answer?
I, too, have a furrow to plough;   17
I will express my opinion;
for I am bursting with words,   18
a bellyful of wind gripes me.
My stomach is distended as if with wine,   19
    bulging like a blacksmith's bellows;
I must speak to find relief,   20
I must open my mouth and answer;
I will show no favour to anyone,   21
I will flatter no one, God or man;^u   22
for I cannot use flattering titles,
    or my Maker would soon do away with me.

Elihu addresses Job

Come now, Job, listen to my words   33
and attend carefully to everything I say.
Look, I am ready to answer;   2
the words are on the tip of my tongue.
My heart assures me that I speak with   3
    knowledge,
and that my lips speak with sincerity.
For the spirit of God made me,   4
and the breath of the Almighty gave me life.
Answer me if you can,   5
marshal your arguments and confront me.
In God's sight^v I am just what you are;   6
I too am only a handful of clay.
Fear of me need not abash you,   7
nor any pressure from me overawe you.
You have said your say and I heard you;   8
I have listened to the sound of your words:
'I am innocent', you said, 'and free from   9
    offence,
blameless and without guilt.
Yet God finds occasions to put me in the   10
    wrong
and counts me his enemy;
he puts my feet in the stocks   11
and keeps a close watch on all I do.'

Well, this is my answer: You are wrong.   12
God is greater than man;
why then plead your case with him?   13
for no one can answer his arguments.
Indeed, once God has spoken   14
he does not speak a second time to con-
    firm it.
In dreams, in visions of the night,   15

n Line transposed from verse 34.   o Verses 38–40 transposed to follow verse 28 (but see note p).   p The last line of verse 40 retained here.   q Or had justified himself with God.   r Prob. original rdg., altered in Heb. to and had not proved Job wrong.   s Prob. rdg.; Heb. He has not strung.   t Prob. rdg.; Heb. towards me.   u Prob. rdg.; Heb. I will not flatter man.   v In God's sight: or In strength.

when deepest sleep falls upon men,
16 while they sleep on their beds, God makes
them listen,
and his correction strikes them with terror.
17 To turn a man from reckless conduct,
to check the pride[w] of mortal man,
18 at the edge of the pit he holds him back alive
and stops him from crossing the river of
death.
19 Or again, man learns his lesson on a bed of
pain,
tormented by a ceaseless ague in his bones;
20 he turns from his food with loathing
and has no relish for the choicest meats;
21 his flesh hangs loose upon him,
his bones are loosened and out of joint,
22 his soul draws near to the pit,
his life to the ministers of death.
23 Yet if an angel, one of thousands, stands by
him,
a mediator between him and God,
to expound what he has done right
and to secure mortal man his due;[x]
24 if he speaks in the man's favour and says,
'Reprieve him,
let him not go down to the pit, I have the
price of his release';
25 then that man will grow sturdier[y] than he
was in youth,
he will return to the days of his prime.
26 If he entreats God to show him favour,
to let him see his face and shout for joy;[z]
27 if he declares before all men, 'I have sinned,
turned right into wrong and thought nothing
of it';
28 then he saves himself from going down to
the pit,
he lives and sees the light.
29 All these things God may do to a man,
again and yet again,
30 bringing him back from the pit
to enjoy the full light of life.
31 Listen, Job, and attend to me;
be silent, and I myself will speak.
32 If you have any arguments, answer me;
speak, and I would gladly find you proved
right;
33 but if you have none, listen to me:
keep silence, and I will teach you wisdom.

Elihu addresses Job's friends

34 Then Elihu went on to say:
2 Mark my words, you wise men;
you men of long experience, listen to me;
3 for the ear tests what is spoken
as the palate savours food.
4 Let us then examine for ourselves what is
right;
let us together establish the true good.

Job has said, 'I am innocent,   5
but God has deprived me of justice,
he has falsified my case;   6
my state is desperate, yet I have done no
wrong.'
Was there ever a man like Job   7
with his thirst for irreverent talk,
choosing bad company to share his journeys, 8
a fellow-traveller with wicked men?
For he says that it brings a man no profit   9
to find favour with God.
But listen to me, you men of good sense.   10
Far be it from God to do evil
or the Almighty to play false!
For he pays a man according to his work   11
and sees that he gets what his conduct
deserves.
The truth is, God does no wrong,   12
the Almighty does not pervert justice.
Who committed the earth to his keeping?   13
Who but he established the whole world?
If he were to turn his thoughts inwards   14
and recall his life-giving spirit,
all that lives would perish on the instant,   15
and man return again to dust.

Elihu addresses Job

Now Job, if you have the wit, consider this; 16
listen to the words I speak.
Can it be that a hater of justice holds the   17
reins?
Do you disparage a sovereign whose rule is
so fair,
who will say to a prince, 'You scoundrel',   18
and call his magnates blackguards to their
faces;
who does not show special favour to those   19
in office
and thinks no more of rich than of poor?
All alike are God's creatures,
who may die in a moment, in the middle of   20
the night;
at his touch the rich are no more,
and the mighty vanish though no hand is
laid on them.
His eyes are on the ways of men,   21
and he sees every step they take;
there is nowhere so dark, so deep in shadow,   22
that wrongdoers may hide from him.
Therefore he repudiates all that they do;   25
he turns on them in the night, and they are
crushed.
There are no appointed days for men   23
to appear before God for judgement.
He holds no inquiry, but breaks the powerful 24
and sets up others in their place.
For their crimes he strikes them down[a]   26[b]
and makes them disgorge their bloated
wealth,[c]

---

w the pride: *prob. rdg.; Heb. obscure.*   x *Line transposed from verse 26.*   y will grow sturdier: *prob.
rdg.; Heb. unintelligible.*   z *See note on verse 23.*   a he strikes them down: *prob. rdg.; Heb. om.*
b *Verse 25 transposed to follow verse 22.*   c *Or and chastises them where people see.*

27 because they have ceased to obey him
and pay no heed to his ways.
28 Then the cry of the poor reaches his ears,
and he hears the cry of the distressed.
30 [Even if he is silent, who can condemn him?
If he looks away, who can find fault?
What though he makes a godless man king
over a stubborn nation and all its people?]

31 But suppose you were to say to God,
'I have overstepped the mark; I will do no
more[d] mischief.
32 Vile wretch that I am, be thou my guide;
whatever wrong I have done, I will do wrong
no more.'
33 Will he, at these words, condone your rejection of him?
It is for you to decide, not me:
but what can you answer?
34 Men of good sense will say,
any intelligent hearer will tell me,
35 'Job talks with no knowledge,
and there is no sense in what he says.
36 If only Job could be put to the test once and
for all
for answers that are meant to make mischief!
37 He is a sinner and a rebel as well[e]
with his endless ranting against God.'

35 Then Elihu went on to say:

2 Do you think that this is a sound plea
or maintain that you are in the right against
God?—
3 if you say, 'What would be the advantage
to me?
how much should I gain from sinning?'
4 I will bring arguments myself against you,
you and your three friends.
5 Look up at the sky and then consider,
observe the rain-clouds towering above you.
6 How does it touch him if you have
sinned?
However many your misdeeds, what does it
mean to him?
7 If you do right, what good do you bring
him,
or what does he gain from you?
8 Your wickedness touches only men, such as
you are;
the right that you do affects none but mortal
man.

9 Men will cry out beneath the burdens of
oppression
and call for help against the power of the
great;
10 but none of them asks, 'Where is God my
Maker
who gives protection by night,

who grants us more knowledge than the 11
beasts of the earth
and makes us wiser than the birds of the air?'
So, when they cry out, he does not answer, 12
because they are self-willed and proud.
All to no purpose! God does not listen, 13
the Almighty does not see.

The worse for you when you say, 'He does 14
not see me'!
Humble yourself[f] in his presence and wait
for his word.
But now, because God does not grow angry 15
and punish
and because he lets folly pass unheeded,
Job gives vent to windy nonsense 16
and makes a parade of empty words.

Then Elihu went on to say: **36**

Be patient a little longer, and let me en- 2
lighten you;
there is still something more to be said on
God's side.
I will search far and wide to support my 3
conclusions,
as I defend the justice of my Maker.
There are no flaws in my reasoning; 4
before you stands one whose conclusions are
sound.

God,[g] I say, repudiates the high and[h] 5
mighty
and does not let the wicked prosper, 6
but allows the just claims of the poor and
suffering;
he does not deprive the sufferer of his due.[i] 7
Look at kings on their thrones:
when God gives them sovereign power, they
grow arrogant.
Next you may see them loaded with fetters, 8
held fast in captives' chains:
he denounces their conduct to them, 9
showing how insolence and tyranny was their
offence;
his warnings sound in their ears 10
and summon them to turn back from their
evil courses.
If they listen to him, they spend[j] their days 11
in prosperity
and their years in comfort.
But, if they do not listen, they die, their 12
lesson unlearnt,

---

d more: *prob. rdg.; Heb.* obscure.   *e Prob. rdg.; Heb.* adds between us it is enough.   *f* Humble yourself: *prob. rdg.; Heb.* Judge.   *g Prob. rdg.; Heb.* adds a mighty one and not.   *h* and: *prob. rdg.;
Heb. om.*   *i* deprive . . . due: *or* withdraw his gaze from the righteous.   *j Prob. rdg.; Heb.* adds they end.

and cross the river of death.

13 Proud men rage against him
and do not cry to him for help when caught
in his toils;

14 so they die in their prime,
like male prostitutes,[k] worn out.[l]

15 Those who suffer he rescues through suffering
and teaches them by the discipline of affliction.

16 Beware, if you are tempted to exchange hardship for comfort,[m]
for unlimited plenty spread before you, and
a generous table;

17 if you eat your fill of a rich man's fare
when you are occupied with the business of
the law,

18 do not be led astray by lavish gifts of wine
and do not let bribery warp your judgement.

19 Will that wealth of yours, however great,
avail you,
or all the resources of your high position?

21[n] Take care not to turn to mischief;
for that is why you are tried by affliction.

20 Have no fear if in the breathless terrors of
the night
you see nations vanish where they stand.

22 God towers in majesty above us;
who wields such sovereign power as he?

23 Who has prescribed his course for him?
Who has said to him, 'Thou hast done
wrong'?

24 Remember then to sing the praises of his
work,
as men have always sung them.

25 All men stand back from[o] him;
the race of mortals look on from afar.

26 Consider; God is so great that we cannot
know him;
the number of his years is beyond reckoning.

27 He draws up drops of water from the sea[p]
and distils rain from the mist he has made;

28 the rain-clouds pour down in torrents,[q]
they descend in showers on mankind;

31 thus he sustains the nations
and gives them food in plenty.

29 Can any man read the secret of the sailing
clouds,
spread like a carpet under[r] his pavilion?

30 See how he unrolls the mist across the
waters,
and its streamers[s] cover the sea.

32[t] He charges the thunderbolts with flame
and launches them straight[u] at the mark;

in his anger he calls up the tempest, 33
and the thunder is the herald of its coming.[v]

This too makes my heart beat wildly **37**
and start from its place.

Listen, listen to the thunder of God's voice 2
and the rumbling of his utterance.

Under the vault of heaven he lets it roll, 3
and his lightning reaches the ends of the
earth;

there follows a sound of roaring 4
as he thunders with the voice of majesty.[w]

God's voice is marvellous in its working;[x] 5
he does great deeds that pass our knowledge.

For he says to the snow, 'Fall to earth', 6
and to the rainstorms, 'Be fierce.'

And when his voice is heard,
the floods of rain pour down unchecked.[y]

He shuts every man fast indoors,[z] 7
and all men whom he has made must stand
idle;

the beasts withdraw into their lairs 8
and take refuge in their dens.

The hurricane bursts from its prison, 9
and the rain-winds bring bitter cold;

at the breath of God the ice-sheet is formed, 10
and the wide waters are frozen hard as iron.

He gives the dense clouds their load of 11
moisture,
and the clouds spread his mist abroad,

as they travel round in their courses, 12
steered by his guiding hand
to do his bidding
all over the habitable world.[a]

Elihu concludes his argument

Listen, Job, to this argument; 14
stand still, and consider God's wonderful
works.

Do you know how God assigns them their 15
tasks,
how he sends light flashing from his clouds?

Do you know why the clouds hang poised 16
overhead,
a wonderful work of his consummate skill,

sweating there in your stifling clothes, 17
when the earth lies sultry under the south
wind?

Can you beat out the vault of the skies, as 18
he does,
hard as a mirror of cast metal?

Teach us then what to say to him; 19
for all is dark, and we cannot marshal our
thoughts.

Can any man dictate to God when he is[b] to 20
speak?

---

*k Cp. Deut. 23. 17.   l worn out: prob. rdg.; Heb. unintelligible.   m for comfort: prob. rdg.; Heb. om.
n Verses 20 and 21 transposed.   o Or gaze at.   p from the sea: prob. rdg.; Heb. om.   q in torrents: prob. rdg.; Heb. which.   r spread . . . under: prob. rdg.; Heb. crashing noises.   s its streamers:
prob. rdg.; Heb. the roots of.   t Verse 31 transposed to follow verse 28.   u and . . . straight: prob. rdg.;
Heb. and gives orders concerning it.   v in his anger . . . coming: prob. rdg.; Heb. obscure.   w See note on
verse 6.   x Prob. rdg.; Heb. thundering.   y And when . . . unchecked: prob. rdg.; some words in these lines
transposed from verse 4.   z indoors: prob. rdg.; Heb. obscure.   a Prob. rdg.; Heb. adds (13) whether he
makes him attain the rod, or his earth, or constant love.   b Prob. rdg.; Heb. I am.*

or command him to make proclamation?

21 At one moment the light is not seen,
it is overcast with clouds and rain;
then the wind passes by and clears them
away,
22 and a golden glow comes from the north.[c]
23 But the Almighty we cannot find; his power
is beyond our ken,
and his righteousness not slow to do justice.
24 Therefore mortal men pay him reverence,
and all who are wise look to him.

The LORD speaks to Job

38 Then the LORD answered Job out of the
tempest:

2 Who is this whose ignorant words
cloud my design in darkness?
3 Brace yourself and stand up like a man;
I will ask questions, and you shall answer.
4 Where were you when I laid the earth's
foundations?
Tell me, if you know and understand.
5 Who settled its dimensions? Surely you
should know.
Who stretched his measuring-line over it?
6 On what do its supporting pillars rest?
Who set its corner-stone in place,
7 when the morning stars sang together
and all the sons of God shouted aloud?
8 Who watched over the birth of the sea,[d]
when it burst in flood from the womb?—
9 when I wrapped it in a blanket of cloud
and cradled it in fog,
10 when I established its bounds,
fixing its doors and bars in place,
11 and said, 'Thus far shall you come and no
farther,
and here your surging waves shall halt.'[e]
12 In all your life have you ever called up the
dawn
or shown the morning its place?
13 Have you taught it to grasp the fringes of
the earth
and shake the Dog-star from its place;
14 to bring up the horizon in relief as clay under
a seal,
until all things stand out like the folds of a
cloak,
15 when the light of the Dog-star is dimmed
and the stars of the Navigator's Line go out
one by one?
16 Have you descended to the springs of the sea
or walked in the unfathomable deep?
17 Have the gates of death been revealed to you?
Have you ever seen the door-keepers of the
place of darkness?
18 Have you comprehended the vast expanse
of the world?

Come, tell me all this, if you know.
19 Which is the way to the home of light
and where does darkness dwell?
20 And can you then take each to its appointed
bound
and escort it on its homeward path?
21 Doubtless you know all this; for you were
born already,
so long is the span of your life!

22 Have you visited the storehouse of the
snow
or seen the arsenal where hail is stored,
23 which I have kept ready for the day of calamity,
for war and for the hour of battle?
24 By what paths is the heat spread abroad
or the east wind carried far and wide over
the earth?
25 Who has cut channels for the downpour
and cleared a passage for the thunderstorm,
26 for rain to fall on land where no man lives
and on the deserted wilderness,
27 clothing lands waste and derelict with
green
and making grass grow on thirsty ground[f]?
28 Has the rain a father?
Who sired the drops of dew?
29 Whose womb gave birth to the ice,
and who was the mother of the frost from
heaven,
30 which lays a stony cover over the waters
and freezes the expanse of ocean?
31 Can you bind the cluster of the Pleiades
or loose Orion's belt?
32 Can you bring out the signs of the zodiac in
their season
or guide Aldebaran and its train?
33 Did you proclaim the rules that govern the
heavens,
or determine the laws of nature on earth?
34 Can you command the dense clouds
to cover you with their weight of waters?
35 If you bid lightning speed on its way,
will it say to you, 'I am ready'?
36 Who put wisdom in depths of darkness
and veiled understanding in secrecy[g]?
37 Who is wise enough to marshal the rain-
clouds
and empty the cisterns of heaven,
38 when the dusty soil sets hard as iron,
and the clods of earth cling together?
39 Do you hunt her prey for the lioness
and satisfy the hunger of young lions,
40 as they crouch in the lair
or lie in wait in the covert?
41 Who provides the raven with its quarry
when its fledglings croak[h] for lack of food?

---

[c] *Prob. rdg.*; *Heb. adds* this refers to God, terrible in majesty.   [d] Who . . . sea: *prob. rdg.*; *Heb.* And he
held back the sea with two doors.   [e] *Prob. rdg.*; *Heb.* here one shall set on your surging waves.   [f] thirsty
ground: *prob. rdg.*; *Heb.* source.   [g] secrecy: *prob. rdg.*; *Heb.* word unknown.   [h] *Prob. rdg.*; *Heb. adds*
they cry to God.

39 Do you know when the mountain-goats are born
or attend the wild doe when she is in labour?

2 Do you count the months that they carry their young
or know the time of their delivery,

3 when they crouch down to open their wombs
and bring their offspring to the birth,

4 when the fawns grow and thrive in the open forest,
and go forth and do not return?

5 Who has let the wild ass of Syria range at will
and given the wild ass of Arabia its freedom?—

6 whose home I have made in the wilderness
and its lair in the saltings;

7 it disdains the noise of the city
and is deaf to the driver's shouting;

8 it roams the hills as its pasture
and searches for anything green.

9 Does the wild ox consent to serve you,
does it spend the night in your stall?

10 Can you harness its strength[i] with ropes,
or will it harrow the furrows[i] after you?

11 Can you depend on it, strong as it is,
or leave your labour to it?

12 Do you trust it to come back
and bring home your grain to the threshing-floor?

13 The wings of the ostrich are stunted;[j]
[k] her pinions and plumage are so scanty[l]

14 that she abandons her eggs to the ground,
letting them be kept warm by the sand.

15 She forgets that a foot may crush them,
or a wild beast trample on them;

16 she treats her chicks heartlessly as if they were not hers,
not caring if her labour is wasted

17 (for God has denied her wisdom
and left her without sense),

18 while like a cock she struts over the uplands,
scorning both horse and rider.

Did you give the horse his strength? 19
Did you clothe his neck with a mane?
Do you make him quiver like a locust's 20 wings,
when his shrill neighing strikes terror?
He shows his mettle as he paws and prances; 21
he charges the armoured line with all his might.
He scorns alarms and knows no dismay; 22
he does not flinch before the sword.
The quiver rattles at his side, 23
the spear and sabre flash.
Trembling with eagerness, he devours the 24 ground
and cannot be held in when he hears the horn;
at the blast of the horn he cries 'Aha!' 25
and from afar he scents the battle.[m]
Does your skill teach the hawk to use its 26 pinions
and spread its wings towards the south?
Do you instruct the vulture to fly high 27
and build its nest aloft?
It dwells among the rocks and there it 28 lodges;
its station is a crevice in the rock;
from there it searches for food, 29
keenly scanning the distance,
that its brood may be gorged with blood; 30
and where the slain are, there the vulture is.

Can you pull out the whale[n] with a gaff **41**
or can you slip a noose round its tongue?
Can you pass a cord through its nose 2
or put a hook through its jaw?
Will it plead with you for mercy 3
or beg its life with soft words?
Will it enter into an agreement with you 4
to become your slave for life?
Will you toy with it as with a bird 5
or keep it on a string like a song-bird for your maidens?
Do trading-partners haggle over it 6
or merchants share it out?

Then the LORD said to Job: **40**

Is it for a man who disputes with the 2 Almighty to be stubborn?
Should he that argues with God answer back?

Job answers

And Job answered the LORD: 3
What reply can I give thee, I who carry no 4 weight?
I put my finger to my lips.
I have spoken once and now will not answer 5 again;
twice have I spoken, and I will do so no more.

---

i Prob. rdg.; Heb. transposes strength *and* furrows.   *j* are stunted: *prob. rdg.; Heb. unintelligible.*   *k Prob.*
rdg.; Heb. prefixes if.   *l Prob. rdg.; Heb.* godly *or* stork.   *m Prob. rdg.; Heb. adds* the thunder of the
captains and the shouting.   *n Or* Leviathan.   *o 41. 1–6 (in Heb. 40. 25–30) transposed to this point.*

The LORD speaks again

6 Then the LORD answered Job out of the tempest:

7 Brace yourself and stand up like a man;
  I will ask questions, and you shall answer.
8 Dare you deny that I am just
  or put me in the wrong that you may be right?
9 Have you an arm like God's arm,
  can you thunder with a voice like his?
10 Deck yourself out, if you can, in pride and
  dignity,
  array yourself in pomp and splendour;
11 unleash the fury of your wrath,
  look upon the proud man and humble him;
12 look upon every proud man and bring him
  low,
  throw down the wicked where they stand;
13 hide them in the dust together,
  and shroud them in an unknown grave.
14 Then I in my turn will acknowledge
  that your own right hand can save you.

15 Consider the chief of the beasts, the crocodile,^p
  who devours cattle as if they were grass:^q
16 what strength is in his loins!
  what power in the muscles of his belly!
17 His tail is rigid as^r a cedar,
  the sinews of his flanks are closely knit,
18 his bones are tubes of bronze,
  and his limbs like bars of iron.
19 He is the chief of God's works,
  made to be a tyrant over his peers;^s
20 for he takes^t the cattle of the hills for his prey
  and in his jaws he crunches all wild beasts.
21 There under the thorny lotus he lies,
  hidden in the reeds and the marsh;
22 the lotus conceals him in its shadow,
  the poplars of the stream surround him.
23 If the river is in spate, he is not scared,
  he sprawls at his ease though the stream is in
  flood.
24 Can a man blind^u his eyes and take him
  or pierce his nose with the teeth of a trap?
7^v Can you fill his skin with harpoons
  or his head with fish-hooks?

If ever you lift your hand against him, 8
  think of the struggle that awaits you, and
  let be.
No, such a man is in desperate case, 9
  hurled headlong at the very sight of him.
How fierce he is when he is roused! 10
  Who is there to stand up to him?
Who has ever attacked him^w unscathed? 11
  Not a man^x under the wide heaven.
I will not pass over in silence his limbs, 12
  his prowess and the grace of his proportions.
Who has ever undone his outer garment 13
  or penetrated his doublet of hide?
Who has ever opened the portals of his face? 14
  for there is terror in his arching teeth.
His back^y is row upon row of shields, 15
  enclosed in a wall^z of flints;
one presses so close on the other 16
  that air cannot pass between them,
each so firmly clamped to its neighbour 17
  that they hold and cannot spring apart.
His sneezing sends out sprays of light, 18
  and his eyes gleam like the shimmer of dawn.
Firebrands shoot from his mouth, 19
  and sparks come streaming out;
his nostrils pour forth smoke 20
  like a cauldron on a fire blown to full heat.
His breath sets burning coals ablaze, 21
  and flames flash from his mouth.
Strength is lodged in his neck, 22
  and untiring energy dances ahead of him.
Close knit is his underbelly, 23
  no pressure will make it yield.
His heart is firm as a rock, 24
  firm as the nether millstone.
When he raises himself, strong men^a take 25
  fright,
  bewildered at the lashings of his tail.
Sword or spear, dagger or javelin, 26
  if they touch him, they have no effect.
Iron he counts as straw, 27
  and bronze as rotting wood.
No arrow can pierce him, 28
  and for him sling-stones are turned into
  chaff;
to him a club is a mere reed, 29
  and he laughs at the swish of the sabre.
Armoured beneath with jagged sherds, 30
  he sprawls on the mud like a threshing-
  sledge.
He makes the deep water boil like a cauldron, 31
  he whips up the lake like ointment in a
  mixing-bowl.
He leaves a shining trail behind him, 32
  and the great river is like white hair in his
  wake.
He has no equal on earth; 33
  for he is made quite without fear.

p *chief . . . crocodile: prob. rdg.; Heb.* beasts (behemoth) which I have made with you.   q *cattle . . . grass: prob. rdg.; Heb.* grass like cattle.   r *Or* He bends his tail like . . .   s *Prob. rdg.; Heb.* his sword.
t *Prob. rdg.; Heb.* they take.   u Can a man blind: *prob. rdg.; Heb. obscure.*   v *Verses 1–6 transposed to follow* 39. 30.   w *Prob. rdg.; Heb.* me.   x *Prob. rdg.; Heb.* He is mine.   y *Prob. rdg.; Heb.* pride.
z *Prob. rdg.; Heb.* seal.   a strong men: *or* leaders *or* gods.

34 He looks down on all creatures, even the
    highest;
  he is king over all proud beasts.

Job repents

42 Then Job answered the LORD:
2 I know that thou canst do all things
  and that no purpose is beyond thee.
3 But I have spoken of great things which I
    have not understood,
  things too wonderful for me to know.[b]
5 I knew of thee then only by report,
  but now I see thee with my own eyes.
6 Therefore I melt away;[c]
  I repent in dust and ashes.

Epilogue

7 When the LORD had finished speaking to
Job, he said to Eliphaz the Temanite, 'I am
angry with you and your two friends, because
you have not spoken as you ought about me,
8 as my servant Job has done. So now take
seven bulls and seven rams, go to my servant
Job and offer a whole-offering for yourselves,
and he will intercede for you; I will surely
show him favour by not being harsh with
you because you have not spoken as you
9 ought about me, as he has done.' Then Eliphaz the Temanite and Bildad the Shuhite
and Zophar the Naamathite went and carried
out the LORD's command, and the LORD
showed favour to Job when he had interceded for his friends. So the LORD restored 10
Job's fortunes and doubled all his possessions.

Then all Job's brothers and sisters and 11
his former acquaintance came and feasted
with him in his home, and they consoled
and comforted him for all the misfortunes
which the LORD had brought on him; and
each of them gave him a sheep[d] and a gold
ring. Furthermore, the LORD blessed the 12
end of Job's life more than the beginning;
and he had fourteen thousand head of small
cattle and six thousand camels, a thousand
yoke of oxen and as many she-asses. He had 13
seven[e] sons and three daughters; and he 14
named his eldest daughter Jemimah, the
second Keziah and the third Keren-happuch.
There were no women in all the world so 15
beautiful as Job's daughters; and their
father gave them an inheritance with their
brothers.

Thereafter Job lived another hundred and 16
forty years, he saw his sons and his grandsons to four generations, and died at a very 17
great age.

---

b Prob. rdg.; Heb. adds (4) O listen, and let me speak; I will ask questions, and you shall answer.   *c Or*
despise myself.   *d Or* piece of money.   *e Or* fourteen.

PSALMS

BOOK 1

1

The source of happiness

1 Happy is the man
    who does not take the wicked for his guide
    nor walk the road that sinners tread
    nor take his seat among the scornful;
2   the law of the LORD is his delight,
the law his meditation night and day.
3   He is like a tree
    planted beside a watercourse,
    which yields its fruit in season
    and its leaf never withers:
    in all that he does he prospers.
4 Wicked men are not like this;
    they are like chaff driven by the wind.
5 So when judgement comes the wicked shall
        not stand firm,
    nor shall sinners stand in the assembly of
        the righteous.
6   The LORD watches over the way of the
        righteous,
    but the way of the wicked is doomed.

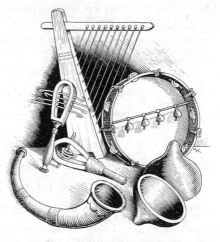

2

The LORD's anointed king

1   Why are the nations in turmoil?
    Why do the peoples hatch their futile
        plots?
2   The kings of the earth stand ready,
    and the rulers conspire together
    against the LORD and his anointed king.
3   'Let us break their fetters,' they cry,
    'let us throw off their chains!'
4   The Lord who sits enthroned in heaven
    laughs them to scorn;
5 then he rebukes them in anger,
    he threatens them in his wrath.
6   Of me he says, 'I have enthroned my king
    on Zion my holy mountain.'
7   I will repeat the LORD's decree:
    'You are my son,' he said;
    'this day I become your father.
8   Ask of me what you will:
    I will give you nations as your inheritance,
    the ends of the earth as your possession.
9   You shall break them with a rod of iron,
    you shall shatter them like a clay pot.'
10   Be mindful then, you kings;
    learn your lesson, rulers of the earth:
11-12   worship the LORD with reverence;
    tremble, and kiss the king,[a]

lest the LORD be angry and you are struck
        down in mid course;
    for his anger flares up in a moment.
    Happy are all who find refuge in him.

3

Confidence in adversity

LORD, how my enemies have multiplied!   1
    Many rise up against me,
    many there are who say of me,   2
    'God will not bring him victory.'
But thou, LORD, art a shield to cover me: 3
    thou art my glory, and thou dost raise my
        head high.
    I cry aloud to the LORD,   4
    and he answers me from his holy moun-
        tain.
    I lie down and sleep,   5
    and I wake again, for the LORD upholds me.
    I will not fear the nations in their myriads   6
    who set on me from all sides.

Rise up, LORD; save me, O my God.   7
    Thou dost strike all my foes across the
        face
    and breakest the teeth of the wicked.
    Thine is the victory, O LORD,   8
    and may[b] thy blessing rest upon thy people.

4

Peace of heart

    Answer me when I call, O God, main-   1
        tainer of my right,

---

a tremble ... king: *prob. rdg.; lit.* tremble and kiss the mighty one; *Heb. obscure.*   *b* Thine ... and may:
or O LORD of salvation, may ...

I was hard pressed, and thou didst set me at large;
  be gracious to me now and hear my prayer.

2 Mortal men, how long will you pay me not honour but dishonour,
or set your heart on trifles and run after lies?

3 Know that the LORD has shown me[c] his marvellous love;
the LORD hears when I call to him.

4 However angry your hearts, do not do wrong;
though you lie abed resentful,[d] do not break silence:

5 pay your due of sacrifice, and trust in the LORD.

6 There are many who say, 'If only we might be prosperous again!
But the light of thy presence has fled from us, O LORD.'

7 Yet in my heart thou hast put more happiness
than they enjoyed when there was corn and wine in plenty.

8 Now I will lie down in peace, and sleep;
for thou alone, O LORD, makest me live unafraid.

5

Prayer for guidance

1 Listen to my words, O LORD,
consider my inmost thoughts;

2 heed my cry for help, my king and my God.

3 In the morning, when I say my prayers,
thou wilt hear me.
I set out my morning sacrifice[e]
and watch for thee, O LORD.

4 For thou art not a God who welcomes wickedness;
evil can be no guest of thine.[f]

5 There is no place for arrogance before thee;
thou hatest evildoers,

6 thou makest an end of all liars.

The LORD detests traitors and men of blood.

7 But I, through thy great love, may come into thy house,
and bow low toward thy holy temple in awe of thee.

8 Lead me, LORD, in thy righteousness,
because my enemies are on the watch;
give me a straight path to follow.

9 There is no trusting what they say,
they are nothing but wind.
Their throats are an open[g] sepulchre;
smooth talk runs off their tongues.

10 Bring ruin on them, O God;
let them fall by their own devices.

Cast them out, after all their rebellions,
for they have defied thee.

11 But let all who take refuge in thee rejoice,
let them for ever break into shouts of joy;
shelter those who love thy name,
that they may exult in thee.

12 For thou, O LORD, wilt bless the righteous;
thou wilt hedge him round with favour as with a shield.

6

Prayer for help in time of trouble

1 O LORD, do not condemn me in thy anger,
do not punish me in thy fury.

2 Be merciful to me, O LORD, for I am weak;
heal me, my very bones are shaken;

3 my soul quivers in dismay.
And thou, O LORD—how long?

4 Come back, O LORD; set my soul free,
deliver me for thy love's sake.

5 None talk of thee among the dead;
who praises thee in Sheol?

6 I am wearied with groaning;
all night long my pillow is wet with tears,
I soak my bed with weeping.

7 Grief dims my eyes;
they are worn out with all my woes.

8 Away from me, all you evildoers,
for the LORD has heard the sound of my weeping.

9 The LORD has heard my entreaty;
the LORD will accept my prayer.

10 All my enemies shall be confounded and dismayed;
they shall turn away in sudden confusion.

7

Prayer for justice

1 O LORD my God, in thee I find refuge;
save me, rescue me from my pursuers,

2 before they tear at my throat like a lion
and carry me off beyond hope of rescue.

3 O LORD my God, if I have done any of these things—
if I have stained my hands with guilt,

4 if I have repaid a friend evil for good
or set free an enemy who attacked me without cause,

5 may my adversary come after me and overtake me,
trample my life to the ground
and lay my honour in the dust!

6 Arise, O LORD, in thy anger,
rouse thyself in wrath against my foes.

7 Awake, my God who hast ordered that justice be done;
let the peoples assemble around thee,
and take thou thy seat on high above them.

---

c Prob. rdg.; Heb. him.   *d* lie abed resentful: *prob. rdg.; Heb.* say on your beds.   *e Or* plea.   *f* who welcomes . . . thine: *or* who protects a wicked man; an evil man cannot be thy guest.   *g Or* inscribed.

8 O Lord, thou who dost pass sentence on
the nations,
O Lord, judge me as my righteousness
deserves,
for I am clearly innocent.

9 Let wicked men do no more harm,
establish the reign of righteousness,[h]
thou who examinest both heart and mind,
thou righteous God.

10 God, the High God, is my shield
who saves men of honest heart.

11 God is a just judge,
every day he requites the raging enemy.

12 He sharpens his sword,
strings his bow and makes it ready.

13 He has prepared his deadly shafts
and tipped his arrows with fire.

14 But the enemy is in labour with iniquity;
he conceives mischief, and his brood is lies.

15 He has made a pit and dug it deep,
and he himself shall fall into the hole that
he has made.

16 His mischief shall recoil upon himself,
and his violence fall on his own head.

17 I will praise the Lord for his righteousness
and sing a psalm to the name of the Lord
Most High.

8

The Lord's glory and man's dignity

1 O Lord our sovereign,
how glorious is thy name in all the earth!
Thy majesty is praised high as the heavens.

2 Out of the mouths of babes, of infants at
the breast,
thou hast rebuked[i] the mighty,
silencing enmity and vengeance to teach thy
foes a lesson.

3 When I look up at thy heavens, the work of
thy fingers,
the moon and the stars set in their place
by thee,

4 what is man that thou shouldst remember
him,
mortal man that thou shouldst care for
him?

5 Yet thou hast made him little less than a
god,
crowning him with glory and honour.

6 Thou makest him master over all thy
creatures;
thou hast put everything under his feet:

7 all sheep and oxen, all the wild beasts,

8 the birds in the air and the fish in the
sea,
and all that moves along the paths of
ocean.

O Lord our sovereign,   9
how glorious is thy name in all the earth!

9–10

Downfall of the godless

I will praise thee, O Lord, with all my   1
heart,
I will tell the story of thy marvellous acts.
I will rejoice and exult in thee,   2
I will praise thy name in psalms, O thou
Most High,
when my enemies turn back,   3
when they fall headlong and perish at thy
appearing;
for thou hast upheld my right and my   4
cause,
seated on thy throne, thou righteous
judge.
Thou hast rebuked the nations and over-   5
whelmed the ungodly,
thou hast blotted out their name for all time.
The strongholds of the enemy are thrown   6
down for evermore;
thou hast laid their cities in ruins, all
memory of them is lost.
The Lord thunders,[j] he sits enthroned for   7
ever:
he has set up his throne, his judgement-
seat.
He it is who will judge the world with justice   8
and try the cause of the peoples fairly.
So may the Lord be a tower of strength for   9
the oppressed,
a tower of strength in time of need,
that those who acknowledge thy name may   10
trust in thee;
for thou, Lord, dost not forsake those
who seek thee.

---

h the reign of righteousness: *or* the cause of the righteous.
prob. rdg.; Heb. unintelligible.

i *Prob. rdg.; Heb.* founded.   j thunders:

11 Sing psalms to the LORD who dwells in
       Zion,
    proclaim his deeds among the nations.
12 For the Avenger of blood has remembered
       men's desire,
    and has not forgotten the cry of the poor.

13 Have pity on me, O LORD; look upon my
       affliction,
    thou who hast lifted me up[k] and caught me
       back from the gates of death,
14 that I may repeat all thy praise
    and exult at this deliverance in the gates of
       Zion's city.

15   The nations have plunged into a pit of
       their own making;
    their own feet are entangled in the net which
       they hid.
16 Now the LORD makes himself known.
    Justice is done:
       the wicked man is trapped in his own
       devices.
17   They rush blindly down to Sheol, the
       wicked,
    all the nations who are heedless of God.
18 But the poor shall not always be unheeded
    nor the hope of the destitute be always
       vain.
19 Arise, LORD, give man no chance to boast
       his strength;
    summon the nations before thee for
       judgement.
20 Strike them with fear, O LORD,
    let the nations know that they are but
       men.
10 Why stand so far off, LORD,
    hiding thyself in time of need?
2   The wicked man in his pride hunts down
       the poor:
    may his crafty schemes be his own un-
       doing!
3   The wicked man is obsessed with his own
       desires,
    and in his greed gives wickedness his
       blessing;
4   arrogant as he is, he scorns the LORD
    and leaves no place for God in all his
       schemes.
5   His ways are always devious;
    thy judgements are beyond his grasp,[l]
    and he scoffs at all restraint.
6   He says to himself, 'I shall never be shaken;
    no misfortune can check my course.'[m]
7   His mouth is full of lies and violence;
    mischief and trouble lurk under his tongue.
8   He lies in ambush in the villages
    and murders innocent men by stealth.
    He is watching[n] intently for some poor
       wretch;

he seizes him and drags him away in his 9
    net;
he crouches stealthily, like a lion in its lair
    crouching to seize its victim;
    the good man[o] is struck down and sinks 10
       to the ground,
    and poor wretches fall into his toils.
He says to himself, 'God has forgotten; 11
he has hidden his face and has seen nothing.'

Arise, LORD, set[p] thy hand to the task; 12
    do not forget the poor, O God.
Why, O God, has the wicked man rejected 13
       thee
    and said to himself that thou dost not
       care?
Thou seest that mischief and trouble are his 14
    companions,
    thou takest the matter into thy own hands.
The poor victim commits himself to thee;
fatherless, he finds in thee his helper.
    Break the power of wickedness and wrong; 15
    hunt out all wickedness until thou canst
       find no more.

The LORD is king for ever and ever; 16
    the nations have vanished from his land.
Thou hast heard the lament of the humble, 17
       O LORD,
    and art attentive to their heart's desire,
    bringing justice to the orphan and the 18
       downtrodden
that fear may never drive men from their
       homes again.

11

A sure refuge

In the LORD I have found my refuge; why 1
    do you say to me,
    'Flee to the mountains like a bird;
see how the wicked string their bows 2
    and fit the arrow to the string,
    to shoot down honest men out of the
       darkness'?
When foundations are undermined, what 3
    can the good man do?
    The LORD is in his holy temple, 4
    the LORD's throne is in heaven.
His eye is upon mankind, he takes their
    measure at a glance.
The LORD weighs just and unjust 5
    and hates with all his soul the lover of
       violence.
    He shall rain down red-hot coals upon the 6
       wicked;
brimstone and scorching winds shall be the
    cup they drink.
For the LORD is just and loves just dealing; 7
    his face is turned towards the upright man.

---

k thou . . . me up: *prob. rdg.; Heb.* from those who hate me.   *l* beyond his grasp: *prob. rdg.; Heb.* on high
before him.   *m* my course: *prob. rdg.; Heb.* which.   *n Prob. rdg.; Heb.* storing up.   *o* the good man:
prob. rdg.; Heb. om.   p Or who settest.

12

When good faith is gone

1 Help, Lord, for loyalty is no more;
  good faith between man and man is over.
2 One man lies to another:
  they talk with smooth lip and double heart.
3 May the Lord make an end of such smooth
    lips
  and the tongue that talks so boastfully!
4 They said, 'Our tongue can win the day.
  Words are our ally; who can master us?'
5 'For the ruin of the poor, for the groans of
    the needy,
  now I will arise,' says the Lord,
    'I will place him in the safety for which he
    longs.'

6 The words of the Lord are pure words:
  silver refined in a crucible,
  gold*q* seven times purified.
7 Do thou, Lord, protect us
  and guard us from a profligate and evil
    generation.*r*
8 The wicked flaunt themselves on every
    side,
  while profligacy stands high among man-
    kind.

13

Prayer of the oppressed

1 How long, O Lord, wilt thou quite forget me?
  How long wilt thou hide thy face from me?
2 How long must I suffer anguish in my soul,
    grief in my heart, day and night?
  How long shall my enemy lord it over me?
3 Look now and answer me, O Lord my God.
  Give light to my eyes lest I sleep the sleep of
    death,
4 lest my adversary say, 'I have overthrown
    him',
  and my enemies rejoice at my downfall.
5 But for my part I trust in thy true love.
  My heart shall rejoice, for thou hast set
    me free.
6 I will sing to the Lord, who has granted all
    my desire.

14

Man's wickedness

1*s* The impious fool says in his heart,
    'There is no God.'
  How vile men are, how depraved and
    loathsome;
  not one does anything good!
2 The Lord looks down from heaven
  on all mankind
  to see if any act wisely,
    if any seek out God.

But all are disloyal, all are rotten to the core; 3
  not one does anything good,
  no, not even one.

Shall they not rue it, 4
  all evildoers who devour my people
  as men devour bread,
  and never call upon the Lord?
There they were in dire alarm; 5
for God was in the brotherhood of the
  godly.
The resistance of their victim was too 6
  much for them,
  because the Lord was his refuge.
If only Israel's deliverance might come out 7
  of Zion!
When the Lord restores his people's
  fortunes,
let Jacob rejoice, let Israel be glad.

15

What the Lord requires

O Lord, who may lodge in thy tabernacle? 1
Who may dwell on thy holy mountain?
The man of blameless life, who does what 2
  is right
and speaks the truth from his heart;
who has no malice on his tongue, 3
who never wrongs a friend
and tells no tales against his neighbour;
the man who shows his scorn for the 4
    worthless
and honours all who fear the Lord;
who swears to his own hurt and does not
    retract;
who does not put his money out to usury 5
and takes no bribe against an innocent
    man.
He who does these things shall never be
    brought low.

16

Security and contentment

Keep me, O God, for in thee have I found 1
  refuge.
I have said to the Lord, 2
  'Thou, Lord, art my felicity.'
The gods whom earth holds sacred are 3
    all worthless,
and cursed are all who make them their
    delight;*t*
those who run after them*u* find trouble with- 4
    out end.
I will not offer them libations of blood
nor take their names upon my lips.
Thou, Lord, my allotted portion, thou 5
    my cup,
thou dost enlarge my boundaries:

---

q gold: *prob. rdg.; Heb.* to the earth.   *r* a profligate and evil generation: *prob. rdg.; Heb.* the generation
which is for ever.   *s Verses 1–7: cp. Ps. 53.* 1–6.   *t* are all worthless . . . delight: *prob. rdg.; Heb.*
obscure.   *u* after them: *prob. rdg.; Heb. obscure.*

6 the lines fall for me in pleasant places,
indeed I am well content with my inheritance.
7 I will bless the LORD who has given me
counsel:
in the night-time wisdom comes to me in
my inward parts.
8 I have set the LORD continually before me:
with him[v] at my right hand I cannot be
shaken.
9 Therefore my heart exults
and my spirit rejoices,
my body too rests unafraid;
10 for thou wilt not abandon me to Sheol
nor suffer thy faithful servant to see the pit.
11 Thou wilt show me the path of life;
in thy presence is the fullness of joy,
in thy right hand pleasures for evermore.

17

Prayer for the LORD's help

1 Hear, LORD, my plea for justice,
give my cry a hearing,
listen to my prayer,
for it is innocent of all deceit.
2 Let judgement in my cause issue from thy
lips,
let thine eyes be fixed on justice.
3 Thou hast tested my heart and watched me
all night long;
thou hast assayed me and found in me no
mind to evil.
4 I will not speak of the deeds of men;
I have taken good note of all thy sayings.
5 I have not strayed from the course of duty;
I have followed thy path and never
stumbled.
6 I call upon thee, O God, for thou wilt
answer me.
Bend down thy ear to me, listen to my words.
7 Show me how marvellous thy true love
can be,
who with thy hand dost save
all who seek sanctuary from their enemies.
8 Keep me like the apple of thine eye;
hide me in the shadow of thy wings
9 from the wicked who obstruct me,
from deadly foes who throng round me.
10 They have stifled all compassion;
their mouths are full of pride;
11 they press me hard,[w] now they hem me in,
on the watch to bring me to the ground.
12 The enemy is like a lion eager for prey,
like a young lion crouching in ambush.
13 Arise, LORD, meet him face to face and bring
him down.
Save my life from the wicked;
14 make an end of them[x] with thy sword.

With thy hand, O LORD, make an end of
them;[x]
thrust them out of this world in the prime
of their life,
gorged as they are with thy good things,
blest with many sons
and leaving their children wealth in plenty.
But my plea is just: I shall see thy face,   15
and be blest with a vision of thee when I
awake.

18

Song of deliverance

I love thee, O LORD my strength.   1
The LORD is my stronghold, my fortress and   2[y]
my champion,
my God, my rock where I find safety,
my shield, my mountain refuge, my strong
tower.
I will call on the LORD to whom all praise is   3
due,
and I shall be delivered from my enemies.
When the bonds of death held me fast,   4
destructive torrents overtook me,
the bonds of Sheol tightened round me,   5
the snares of death were set to catch me;
then in anguish of heart I cried to the LORD,   6
I called for help to my God;
he heard me from his temple,
and my cry reached his ears.
The earth heaved and quaked,   7
the foundations of the mountains shook;
they heaved, because he was angry.
Smoke rose from his nostrils,   8
devouring fire came out of his mouth,
glowing coals and searing heat.
He swept the skies aside as he descended,   9
thick darkness lay under his feet.
He rode on a cherub, he flew through the air;   10
he swooped on the wings of the wind.
He made darkness around him his hiding-   11
place
and dense[z] vapour his canopy.[a]
Thick clouds came out of the radiance before   12
him,
hailstones and glowing coals.
The LORD thundered from the heavens   13
and the voice of the Most High spoke out.[b]
He loosed his arrows, he sped them far and   14
wide,
he shot forth lightning shafts and sent them
echoing.
The channels of the sea-bed were revealed,   15
the foundations of earth laid bare
at the LORD's rebuke,
at the blast of the breath of his[c] nostrils.
He reached down from the height and took   16
me,
he drew me out of mighty waters,

v with him: *prob. rdg.*; *Heb. om.*   *w* they press me hard: *prob. rdg.*; *Heb.* our footsteps.   *x* make
an end of them: *prob. rdg.*; *Heb. unintelligible.*   *y* *Verses 2–50: cp.* 2 Sam. 22. 2–51.   *z* *Prob. rdg.*,
cp. 2 Sam. 22. 12; *Heb.* dark.   *a* *Prob. rdg.*; *Heb. adds* thick clouds.   *b* *Prob. rdg.*; *Heb. adds* hailstones and glowing coals.   *c* *Prob. rdg.*; *Heb.* thy.

17 he rescued me from my enemies, strong as
    they were,
from my foes when they grew too powerful
    for me.
18 They confronted me in the hour of my peril,
but the LORD was my buttress.
19 He brought me out into an open place,
he rescued me because he delighted in me.
20 The LORD rewarded me as my righteousness
    deserved;
my hands were clean, and he requited me.
21 For I have followed the ways of the LORD
and have not turned wickedly from my God;
22 all his laws are before my eyes,
I have not failed to follow his decrees.
23 In his sight I was blameless
and kept myself from wilful sin;
24 the LORD requited me as my righteousness
    deserved
and the purity of my life in his eyes.

25 With the loyal thou showest thyself loyal
and with the blameless man blameless.
26 With the savage man thou showest thyself
    savage,
and[d] tortuous with the perverse.
27 Thou deliverest humble folk,
    and bringest proud
        looks down to
        earth.
28 Thou, LORD, dost
    make my lamp
    burn bright,
and my God will
    lighten my
    darkness.

29 With thy help I leap over a bank,
by God's aid I spring over a wall.

30 The way of God is perfect,
the LORD's word has stood the test;
he is the shield of all who take refuge in him.
31 What god is there but the LORD?
What rock but our God?—
32 the God who girds me with strength
and makes my way blameless,
33 who makes me swift as a hind
and sets me secure on the mountains;
34 who trains my hands for battle,
and my arms aim an arrow tipped with
    bronze.

35 Thou hast given me the shield of thy salva-
    tion,
thy hand sustains me, thy providence makes
    me great.
36 Thou givest me room for my steps,
my feet have not faltered.
37 I pursue my enemies and overtake them,
I do not return until I have made an end of
    them.

I strike them down and they will never rise 38
    again;
they fall beneath my feet.
Thou dost arm me with strength for the 39
    battle
and dost subdue my foes before me.
Thou settest my foot on my enemies' necks, 40
and I bring to nothing those that hate me.
They cry out and there is no one to help 41
    them,
they cry to the LORD and he does not answer.
I will pound them fine as dust before the 42
    wind,
like mud in the streets will I trample them.[e]
Thou dost deliver me from the clamour of 43
    the people,
and makest me master of the nations.
A people I never knew shall be my subjects;
as soon as they hear tell of me, they shall obey 44
    me,
and foreigners shall come cringing to me.
Foreigners shall be brought captive to me, 45
and emerge from their strongholds.

The LORD lives, blessed is my rock, 46
high above all is God who saves me.

O God, who grantest me vengeance, 47
who layest nations prostrate at my feet,
who dost rescue me from my foes and set me 48
    over my enemies,
thou dost deliver me from violent men.
Therefore, LORD, I will praise thee among the 49
    nations
and sing psalms to thy name,
to one who gives his king great victories 50
and in all his acts keeps faith with his
    anointed king,
with David and his descendants for ever.

19

The LORD's works and words

The heavens tell out the glory of God, 1
    the vault of heaven reveals his handiwork.
One day speaks to another, 2
night with night shares its knowledge,
    and this without speech or language 3
    or sound of any voice.
Their music goes out through all the earth, 4
    their words reach to the end of the world.
In them a tent is fixed for the sun,
who comes out like a bridegroom from his 5
    wedding canopy,
rejoicing like a strong man to run his race.
    His rising is at one end of the heavens, 6
    his circuit touches their farthest ends;
    and nothing is hidden from his heat.

The law of the LORD is perfect and revives 7
    the soul.

---

d With the savage ... savage, and: *or* With the pure thou showest thyself pure, but ...
cp. 2 Sam. 22. 43; *Heb.* will I empty them out.   *e Prob. rdg.,*

The LORD's instruction never fails,
and makes the simple wise.
8 The precepts of the LORD are right and rejoice the heart.
The commandment of the LORD shines
clear
and gives light to the eyes.
9 The fear of the LORD is pure and abides
for ever.
The LORD's decrees are true and righteous
every one,
10 more to be desired than gold, pure gold in
plenty,
sweeter than syrup or honey from the
comb.
11 It is these that give thy servant warning,
and he who keeps them wins a great
reward.

12 Who is aware of his unwitting sins?
Cleanse me of any secret fault.
13 Hold back thy servant also from sins of
self-will,
lest they get the better of me.
Then I shall be blameless
and innocent of any great transgression.

14 May all that I say and think be acceptable to
thee,
O LORD, my rock and my redeemer!

20

Victory to the LORD's anointed king

1 May the LORD answer you in the hour of
trouble!
The name of Jacob's God be your tower of
strength,
2 give you help from the sanctuary
and send you support from Zion!
3 May he remember all your offerings
and look with favour on your rich
sacrifices,
4 give you your heart's desire
and grant success to all your plans!
5 Let us sing aloud in praise of your victory,
let us do homage to the name of our God!
The LORD grant all you ask!

6 Now I know
that the LORD has given victory to his
anointed king:
he will answer him from his holy heaven
with the victorious might of his right
hand.
7 Some boast of chariots and some of
horses,
but our boast is the name of the LORD our
God.
8 They totter and fall,
but we rise up and are full of courage.
9 O LORD, save the king,
and answer us in the hour of our calling.

21

Coming victory

The king rejoices in thy might, O LORD: 1
well may he exult in thy victory,
for thou hast given him his heart's desire 2
and hast not refused him what he asked.
Thou dost welcome him with blessings and 3
prosperity
and set a crown of fine gold upon his
head.
He asked of thee life, and thou didst give it 4
him,
length of days for ever and ever.
Thy salvation has brought him great 5
glory;
thou dost invest him with majesty and
honour,
for thou bestowest blessings on him for 6
evermore
and dost make him glad with joy in thy
presence.
The king puts his trust in the LORD; 7
the loving care of the Most High holds
him unshaken.

Your hand shall reach all your enemies: 8
your right hand shall reach those who hate
you;
at your coming you shall plunge them into 9
a fiery furnace;
the LORD in his anger will strike them
down,
and fire shall consume them.
It will exterminate their offspring from 10
the earth
and rid mankind of their posterity.
For they have aimed wicked blows at 11
you,
they have plotted mischief but could not
prevail;
but you will catch them round the 12
shoulders
and will aim with your bow-strings at their
faces.

Be exalted, O LORD, in thy might; 13
we will sing a psalm of praise to thy power.

22

Anguish and praise

My God, my God, why hast thou forsaken 1
me
and art so far from saving me, from heed-
ing my groans?
O my God, I cry in the day-time but thou 2
dost not answer,
in the night I cry but get no respite.
And yet thou art enthroned in holiness, 3
thou art he whose praises Israel sings.
In thee our fathers put their trust; 4
they trusted, and thou didst rescue
them.

5 Unto thee they cried and were delivered;
in thee they trusted and were not put to
shame.

6 But I am a worm, not a man,
abused by all men, scorned by the people.

7 All who see me jeer at me,
make mouths at me and wag their heads:

8 'He threw himself on the LORD for rescue;
let the LORD deliver him, for he holds him
dear!'

9 But thou art he who drew me from the
womb,
who laid me at my mother's breast.

10 Upon thee was I cast at birth;
from my mother's womb thou hast been
my God.

11 Be not far from me,
for trouble is near, and I have no helper.

12 A herd of bulls surrounds me,
great bulls of Bashan beset me.

13 Ravening and roaring lions
open their mouths wide against me.

14 My strength drains away like water
and all my bones are loose.
My heart has turned to wax and melts within
me.

15 My mouth^f is dry as a potsherd,
and my tongue sticks to my jaw;
I am laid^g low in the dust of death.

16 The huntsmen are all about me;
a band of ruffians rings me round,
and they have hacked off^h my hands and
my feet.

17 I tell my tale of misery,
while they look on and gloat.

18 They share out my garments among them
and cast lots for my clothes.

19 But do not remain so far away, O LORD;
O my help, hasten to my aid.

20 Deliver my very self from the sword,
my precious life from the axe.

21 Save me from the lion's mouth,
my poor body^i from the horns of the
wild ox.

22 I will declare thy fame to my brethren;
I will praise thee in the midst of the
assembly.

23 Praise him, you who fear the LORD;
all you sons of Jacob, do him honour;
stand in awe of him, all sons of Israel.

24 For he has not scorned the downtrodden,
nor shrunk in loathing from his plight,
nor hidden his face from him,
but gave heed to him when he cried out.

25 Thou dost inspire my praise in the full
assembly;
and I will pay my vows before all who fear
thee.

26 Let the humble eat and be satisfied.

Let those who seek the LORD praise him
and be in good heart for ever.

Let all the ends of the earth remember and 27
turn again to the LORD;
let all the families of the nations bow down
before him.

For kingly power belongs to the LORD, 28
and dominion over the nations is his.

How can those buried in the earth do him 29
homage,
how can those who go down to the grave
bow before him?

But I shall live for his sake,
my posterity^j shall serve him. 30

This shall be told of the Lord to future
generations;
and they shall justify him, 31
declaring to a people yet unborn
that this was his doing.

23

The LORD my shepherd

The LORD is my shepherd; I shall want 1
nothing.

He makes me lie down in green pastures, 2
and leads me beside the waters of peace;
he renews life within me, 3
and for his name's sake guides me in the
right path.

Even though I walk through a valley dark 4
as death
I fear no evil, for thou art with me,
thy staff and thy crook are my comfort.

Thou spreadest a table for me in the sight of 5
my enemies;
thou hast richly bathed my head with
oil,
and my cup runs over.

Goodness and love unfailing, these will 6
follow me
all the days of my life,
and I shall dwell in the house of the
LORD
my whole life long.

---

f *Prob. rdg.; Heb.* My strength.   g I am laid: *prob. rdg.; Heb.* thou wilt lay me.   h and they have
hacked off: *prob. rdg.; Heb.* like a lion.   i my poor body: *prob. rdg.; Heb.* thou hast answered me.
j But I . . . posterity: *prob. rdg.; Heb. obscure.*

24

Entrance of the king of glory

1 The earth is the LORD's and all that is in it,
the world and those who dwell therein.

2 For it was he who founded it upon the seas
and planted it firm upon the waters
beneath.

3 Who may go up the mountain of the
LORD?
And who may stand in his holy place?

4 He who has clean hands and a pure heart,
who has not set his mind on falsehood,
and has not committed perjury.

5 He shall receive a blessing from the LORD,
and justice from God his saviour.

6 Such is the fortune of those who seek him,
who seek the face of the God of Jacob.

7 Lift up your heads, you gates,
lift yourselves up, you everlasting doors,
that the king of glory may come in.

8 Who is the king of glory?
The LORD strong and mighty,
the LORD mighty in battle.

9 Lift up your heads, you gates,
lift them up, you everlasting doors,
that the king of glory may come in.

10 Who then is the king of glory?
The king of glory is the LORD of Hosts.

25

The source of lasting prosperity

1 Unto thee, O LORD my God, I lift up my
heart.

2 In thee I trust: do not put me to shame,
let not my enemies exult over me.

3 No man who hopes in thee is put to
shame;
but shame comes to all who break faith
without cause.

4 Make thy paths known to me, O LORD;
teach me thy ways.

5 Lead me in thy truth and teach me;
thou art God my saviour.
For thee I have waited all the day long,
for the coming of thy goodness, LORD.*k*

6 Remember, LORD, thy tender care and thy
love unfailing,
shown from ages past.

7 Do not remember the sins and offences
of my youth,
but remember me in thy unfailing love.

8 The LORD is good and upright;
therefore he teaches sinners the way they
should go.

9 He guides the humble man in doing right,
he teaches the humble his ways.

10 All the ways of the LORD are loving and
sure

to men who keep his covenant and his
charge.

11 For the honour of thy name, O LORD,
forgive my wickedness, great as it is.

12 If there is any man who fears the LORD,
he shall be shown the path that he should
choose;

13 he shall enjoy lasting prosperity,
and his children after him shall inherit
the land.

14 The LORD confides his purposes to those
who fear him,
and his covenant is theirs to know.

15 My eyes are ever on the LORD,
who alone can free my feet from the net.

16 Turn to me and show me thy favour,
for I am lonely and oppressed.

17 Relieve the sorrows of my heart
and bring me out of my distress.

18 Look at my misery and my trouble
and forgive me every sin.

19 Look at my enemies, see how many they
are
and how violent their hatred for me.

20 Defend me and deliver me,
do not put me to shame when I take refuge
in thee.

21 Let integrity and uprightness protect
me,
for I have waited for thee, O LORD.

22 O God, redeem Israel from all his sorrows.

26

Prayer for a firm footing

1 Give me justice, O LORD,
for I have lived my life without reproach,
and put unfaltering trust in the LORD.

2 Test me, O LORD, and try me;
put my heart and mind to the proof.

3 For thy constant love is before my eyes,
and I live in thy truth.

4 I have not sat among worthless men,
nor do I mix with hypocrites;

5 I hate the company of evildoers
and will not sit among the ungodly.

6 I wash my hands in innocence
to join in procession round thy altar,
O LORD,

7 singing of thy marvellous acts,
recounting them all with thankful voice.

8 O LORD, I love the beauty of thy house,
the place where thy glory dwells.

9 Do not sweep me away with sinners,
nor cast me out with men who thirst for
blood,

10 whose fingers are active in mischief,
and their hands are full of bribes.

11 But I live my life without reproach;
redeem me, O LORD, and show me thy
favour.

k for the coming . . . LORD: *transposed from end of verse 7.*

12 When once my feet are planted on firm
    ground,
I will bless the LORD in the full assembly.

27

The cure for anxiety

1 The LORD is my light and my salvation;
    whom should I fear?
The LORD is the refuge of my life;
    of whom then should I go in dread?

2 When evildoers close in on me to devour me,
    it is my enemies, my assailants,
    who stumble and fall.

3 If an army should encamp against me,
    my heart would feel no fear;
if armed men should fall upon me,
    even then I should be undismayed.

4 One thing I ask of the LORD,
    one thing I seek:
that I may be constant in the house of the
    LORD
all the days of my life,
to gaze upon the beauty of the LORD
    and to seek him[l] in his temple.

5 For he will keep me safe beneath his roof
    in the day of misfortune;
he will hide me under the cover of his tent;
    he will raise me beyond reach of distress.

6 Now I can raise my head high
    above the enemy all about me;
so will I acclaim him with sacrifice before
    his tent
and sing a psalm of praise to the LORD.

7 Hear, O LORD, when I call aloud;
    show me favour and answer me.

8 'Come,' my heart has said,
    'seek his face.'[m]
I will seek thy face, O LORD;

9   do not hide it from me,
    nor in thy anger turn away thy servant,
    whose help thou hast been;
do not cast me off or forsake me, O God my
    saviour.

10 Though my father and my mother forsake
    me,
    the LORD will take me into his care.

12 Teach me thy way, O LORD;
    do not give me up to the greed of my
    enemies;
lead me by a level path
    to escape my watchful foes;
liars stand up to give evidence against me,
    breathing malice.

13 Well I know that I shall see the goodness
    of the LORD
    in the land of the living.

14 Wait for the LORD; be strong, take courage,
    and wait for the LORD.

28

Prayer for mercy and help

To thee, O LORD, I call;   1
O my Rock, be not deaf to my cry,
lest, if thou answer me with silence,
    I become like those who go down to the
    abyss.

Hear my cry for mercy   2
    when I call to thee for help,
    when I lift my hands to thy holy shrine.

Do not drag me away with the ungodly, with 3
    evildoers,
who speak civilly to neighbours, with malice
    in their hearts.

Reward them for their works, their evil 4
    deeds;
reward them for what their hands have
    done;
give them their deserts.

Because they pay no heed to the works of 5
    the LORD
or to what his hands have done,
may he tear them down and never build
    them up!

Blessed be the LORD,   6
    for he has heard my cry for mercy.
The LORD is my strength, my shield,   7
    in him my heart trusts;
so I am sustained, and my heart leaps for joy,
    and I praise him with my whole body.[n]
The LORD is strength to his people,   8
    a safe refuge for his anointed king.

O save thy people and bless thy own,   9
    shepherd them, carry them for ever.

29

The LORD speaks in the storm

Ascribe to the LORD, you gods,   1
ascribe to the LORD glory and might.
Ascribe to the LORD the glory due to his 2
    name;
bow down to the LORD in the splendour
    of holiness.[o]
The God of glory thunders: 3
    the voice of the LORD echoes over the
    waters,
    the LORD is over the mighty waters.
The voice of the LORD is power.   4
The voice of the LORD is majesty.
The voice of the LORD breaks the cedars, 5
    the LORD splinters the cedars of Lebanon.
He makes Lebanon skip like a calf,   6
Sirion like a young wild ox.
The voice of the LORD makes flames of fire 7
    burst forth,
the voice of the LORD makes the wilderness 8
    writhe in travail;
    the LORD makes the wilderness of Kadesh
    writhe.

l Or and to pay my morning worship.   *m* seek his face: *prob. rdg.; Heb.* seek ye my face.   *n* with my
whole body: *prob. rdg.; Heb.* from my song.   *o* the splendour of holiness: *or* holy vestments.

9 The voice of the LORD makes the hinds
calve
and brings kids early to birth;
and in his temple all cry, 'Glory!'
10 The LORD is king above[p] the flood,
the LORD has taken his royal seat as king for
ever.
11 The LORD will give strength to his people;
the LORD will bless his people with peace.

30

Self-confidence shaken

1 I will exalt thee, O LORD;
thou hast lifted me up
and hast not let my enemies make merry
over me.
2 O LORD my God, I cried to thee and thou
didst heal me.
3 O LORD, thou hast brought me up from Sheol
and saved my life as I was sinking into the
abyss.[q]
4 Sing a psalm to the LORD, all you his loyal
servants,
and give thanks to his holy name.
5 In his anger is disquiet, in his favour there is
life.
Tears may linger at nightfall,
but joy comes in the morning.
6 Carefree as I was, I had said,
'I can never be shaken.'
7 But, LORD, it was thy will to shake my
mountain refuge;
thou didst hide thy face, and I was struck
with dismay.
8 I called unto thee, O LORD,
and I pleaded with thee, Lord, for mercy:
9 'What profit in my death if I go down into
the pit?
Can the dust confess thee or proclaim thy
truth?
10 Hear, O LORD, and be gracious to me;
LORD, be my helper.'
11 Thou hast turned my laments into
dancing;
thou hast stripped off my sackcloth and
clothed me with joy,
12 that my spirit may sing psalms to thee and
never cease.
I will confess thee for ever, O LORD my God.

31

The LORD's unfailing love

1 With thee, O LORD, I have sought shelter,
let me never be put to shame.
Deliver me in thy righteousness;
2 bow down and hear me,
come quickly to my rescue;
be thou my rock of refuge,
a stronghold to keep me safe.

Thou art to me both rock and stronghold; 3
lead me and guide me for the honour of
thy name.
Set me free from the net men have hidden for 4
me;
thou art my refuge,
into thy keeping I commit my spirit. 5
Thou hast redeemed me, O LORD thou God
of truth.
Thou hatest all who worship useless idols, 6
but I put my trust in the LORD.
I will rejoice and be glad in thy unfailing 7
love;
for thou hast seen my affliction
and hast cared for me in my distress.
Thou hast not abandoned me to the power 8
of the enemy
but hast set me free to range at will.
Be gracious to me, O LORD, for I am in 9
distress,
and my eyes are dimmed with grief.[r]
My life is worn away with sorrow 10
and my years with sighing;
strong as I am, I stumble under my load of
misery;
there is disease in all my bones.
I have such enemies that all men scorn 11
me;[s]
my neighbours find me a burden,
my friends shudder at me;
when they see me in the street they turn
quickly away.
I am forgotten, like a dead man out of 12
mind;
I have come to be like something lost.
For I hear many men whispering 13
threats from every side,
in league against me as they are
and plotting to take my life.
But, LORD, I put my trust in thee; 14
I say, 'Thou art my God.'
My fortunes are in thy hand; 15
rescue me from my enemies and those who
persecute me.
Make thy face shine upon thy servant; 16
save me in thy unfailing love.
O LORD, do not put me to shame when I 17
call upon thee;
let the wicked be ashamed, let them sink into
Sheol.
Strike dumb the lying lips 18
which speak with contempt against the
righteous
in pride and arrogance.
How great is thy goodness, 19
stored up for those who fear thee,
made manifest before the eyes of men
for all who turn to thee for shelter.
Thou wilt hide them under the cover of 20
thy presence
from men in league together;

---

p Or since. *q* and saved . . . abyss: *or* and rescued me alive from among those who go down to the abyss.
r Prob. rdg.; Heb. adds my soul and my body. *s* I have . . . scorn me: *or* I am scorned by all my enemies.

thou keepest them beneath thy roof,
safe from contentious men.

21 Blessed be the LORD,
who worked a miracle of unfailing love
for me
when I was in sore straits.[t]
22 In sudden alarm I said,
'I am shut out from thy sight.'
But thou didst hear my cry for mercy
when I called to thee for help.
23 Love the LORD, all you his loyal servants.
The LORD protects the faithful
but pays the arrogant in full.
24 Be strong and take courage,
all you whose hope is in the LORD.

32

Confession, forgiveness and happiness

1 Happy the man whose disobedience is
forgiven,
whose sin is put away!
2 Happy is a man when the LORD lays no guilt
to his account,
and in his spirit there is no deceit.
3 While I refused to speak, my body wasted
away
with moaning all day long.
4 For day and night
thy hand was heavy upon me,
the sap in me dried up as in summer
drought.
5 Then I declared my sin, I did not conceal my
guilt.
I said, 'With sorrow I will confess
my disobedience to the LORD';
then thou didst remit the penalty of my sin.
6 So every faithful heart shall pray to thee
in the hour of anxiety,[u] when great floods
threaten.
Thou art a refuge for me from distress
so that it cannot touch me;[v]
7 thou dost guard me[w] and enfold me in
salvation
beyond all reach of harm.[x]

8 I will teach you, and guide you in the way
you should go.
I will keep you under my eye.
9 Do not behave like horse or mule, unreason-
ing creatures,
whose course must be checked with bit and
bridle.
10 Many are the torments of the ungodly;
but unfailing love enfolds him who trusts in
the LORD.
11 Rejoice in the LORD and be glad, you righteous men,
and sing aloud, all men of upright heart.

33

The LORD omnipotent

1 Shout for joy before the LORD, you who
are righteous;
praise comes well from the upright.
2 Give thanks to the LORD on the harp;
sing him psalms to the ten-stringed lute.
3 Sing to him a new song;
strike up with all your art and shout in
triumph.
4 The word of the LORD holds true,
and all his work endures.
5 The LORD loves righteousness and justice,
his love unfailing fills the earth.
6 The LORD's word made the heavens,
all the host of heaven was made at his
command.
7 He gathered the sea like water in a goat-
skin;
he laid up the deep in his store-chambers.
8 Let the whole world fear the LORD
and all men on earth stand in awe of him.
9 For he spoke, and it was;
he commanded, and it stood firm.
10 The LORD brings the plans of nations to
nothing;
he frustrates the counsel of the peoples.
11 But the LORD's own plans shall stand for
ever,
and his counsel endure for all generations.
12 Happy is the nation whose God is the LORD,
the people he has chosen for his own
possession.
13 The LORD looks out from heaven,
he sees the whole race of men;
14 he surveys from his dwelling-place
all the inhabitants of earth.
15 It is he who fashions the hearts of all men
alike,
who discerns all that they do.
16 A king is not saved by a great army,
nor a warrior delivered by great strength.
17 A man cannot trust his horse to save him,
nor can it deliver him for all its strength.

---

[t] when . . . straits: *prob. rdg.; Heb.* like a city besieged.   [u] of anxiety: *prob. rdg.; Heb. unintelligible.*
[v] *Prob. rdg.; Heb.* him.   [w] *Prob. rdg.; Heb. adds an unintelligible word.*   [x] beyond . . . harm:
transposed from end of verse 9.

18 The LORD's eyes are turned towards those
 who fear him,
 towards those who hope for his unfailing
 love
19 to deliver them from death,
 to keep them alive in famine.
20 We have waited eagerly for the LORD;
 he is our help and our shield.
21 For in him our hearts are glad,
 because we have trusted in his holy name.
22 Let thy unfailing love, O LORD, rest upon us,
 as we have put our hope in thee.

34

The LORD's goodness

1 I will bless the LORD continually;
 his praise shall be always on my lips.
2 In the LORD I will glory;
 the humble shall hear and be glad.
3 O glorify the LORD with me,
 and let us exalt his name together.
4 I sought the LORD's help and he answered
 me;
 he set me free from all my terrors.
5 Look towards him and shine with joy;
 no longer hang your heads in shame.
6 Here was a poor wretch who cried to the
 LORD;
 he heard him and saved him from all his
 troubles.
7 The angel of the LORD is on guard
 round those who fear him, and rescues
 them.
8 Taste, then, and see that the LORD is good.
 Happy the man who finds refuge in him!
9 Fear the LORD, all you his holy people;
 for those who fear him lack nothing.
10 Unbelievers suffer want and go hungry,
 but those who seek the LORD lack no good
 thing.
11 Come, my children, listen to me:
 I will teach you the fear of the LORD.
12 Which of you delights in life
 and desires a long life to enjoy all good
 things?
13 Then keep your tongue from evil
 and your lips from uttering lies;
14 turn from evil and do good,
 seek peace and pursue it.
15 The eyes of the LORD are upon the righteous,
 and his ears are open to their cries.
16 The LORD sets his face against evildoers
 to blot out their memory from the earth.
17 When men cry for help, the LORD hears
 them
 and sets them free from all their troubles.
18 The LORD is close to those whose courage
 is broken
 and he saves those whose spirit is crushed.

19 The good man's misfortunes may be many,
 the LORD delivers him out of them all.
20 He guards every bone of his body,
 and not one of them is broken.
21 Their own misdeeds are death to the
 wicked,
 and those who hate the righteous are
 brought to ruin.

22 The LORD ransoms the lives of his servants,
 and none who seek refuge in him are
 brought to ruin.

35

Prayer for vindication

1 Strive, O LORD, with those who strive
 against me;
 fight against those who fight me.
2 Grasp shield and buckler,
 and rise up to help me.
3 Uncover the spear and bar the way
 against my pursuers.
 Let me hear thee declare,
 'I am your salvation.'
4 Shame and disgrace be on those who seek
 my life;
 and may those who plan to hurt me retreat
 in dismay!
5 May they be like chaff before the wind,
 driven by the angel of the LORD!
6 Let their way be dark and slippery
 as the angel of the LORD pursues them!
7 For unprovoked they have hidden a net[y]
 for me,
 unprovoked they have dug a pit to trap me.
8 May destruction unforeseen come on him;
 may the net which he hid catch him;
 may he crash headlong into it!
9 Then I shall rejoice in the LORD
 and delight in his salvation.
10 My very bones cry out,
 'LORD, who is like thee?—
 thou saviour of the poor from those too
 strong for them,
 the poor and wretched from those who prey
 on them.'
11 Malicious witnesses step forward;
 they question me on matters of which I
 know nothing.
12 They return me evil for good,
 lying in wait[z] to take my life.
13 And yet when they were sick, I put on sackcloth,
 I mortified myself with fasting.
 When my prayer came back unanswered,
14 I walked with head bowed in grief as if for
 a brother;
 as one in sorrow for his mother I lay prostrate in mourning.

---

y Prob. rdg., transposing a pit *from this line to follow* have dug.
bereavement.   *z* lying in wait: *prob. rdg.; Heb.*

15 But when I stumbled, they crowded
        round rejoicing,
    they crowded about me;
    nameless ruffians[a] jeered at me
    and nothing would stop them.

16 When I slipped, brutes who would mock
        even a hunchback
    ground their teeth at me.

17 O Lord, how long wilt thou look on
    at those who hate me for no reason[b]?
    Rescue me out of their cruel grasp,
    save my precious life from the unbelievers.

18 Then I will praise thee before a great
        assembly,
    I will extol thee where many people meet.

19 Let no treacherous enemy gloat over me
    nor leer at me in triumph.[c]

20 No friendly greeting do they give
    to peaceable folk.
    They invent lie upon lie,

21 they open their mouths at me:
    'Hurrah!' they shout in their joy,
    feasting their eyes on me.

22 Thou hast seen all this, O Lord, do not
        keep silence;
    O Lord, be not far from me.

23 Awake, bestir thyself, to do me justice,
    to plead my cause, my Lord and my
        God.

24 Judge me, O Lord my God, as thou art
        true;
    do not let them gloat over me.

25 Do not let them say to themselves, 'Hurrah!
    We have swallowed him up at one gulp.'

26 Let them all be disgraced and dismayed
    who rejoice at my fall;
    let them be covered with shame and dis-
        honour
    who glory over me.

27 But let all who would see me righted shout
        for joy,
    let them cry continually,
    'All glory to the Lord
    who would see his servant thrive!'

28 So shall I talk of thy justice
    and of thy praise all the day long.

36

Man's sin and the LORD's righteousness

1 Deep in his heart, sin whispers to the
        wicked man
    who cherishes no fear of God.

2 For he flatters himself in his own opinion
    and, when he is found out, he does not
        mend his ways.[d]

3 All that he says is mischievous and false;
    he has turned his back on wisdom;

4 in his bed he plots how best to do mischief.
    So set is he on his wrong courses
    that he rejects nothing evil.

But thy unfailing love, O Lord, reaches to 5
        heaven,
    thy faithfulness to the skies.
Thy righteousness is like the lofty moun- 6
        tains,
    thy judgements are like the great abyss;
O Lord, who savest man and beast,
    how precious is thy unfailing love! 7
Gods and men seek refuge in the shadow of
        thy wings.
They are filled with the rich plenty of thy 8
        house,
    and thou givest them water from the flow-
        ing stream of thy delights;
for with thee is the fountain of life, 9
    and in thy light we are bathed with light.
Maintain thy love unfailing over those 10
        who know thee,
    and thy justice toward men of honest
        heart.
Let not the foot of pride come near me, 11
    no wicked hand disturb me.
There they lie, the evildoers, 12
    they are hurled down and cannot rise.

37

Advice of an old man

Do not strive to outdo the evildoers 1
    or emulate those who do wrong.
For like grass they soon wither, 2
    and fade like the green of spring.
Trust in the Lord and do good; 3
settle in the land and find safe pasture.
    Depend upon the Lord, 4
    and he will grant you your heart's desire.
    Commit your life to the Lord; 5
trust in him and he will act.
    He will make your righteousness shine 6
        clear as the day
    and the justice of your cause like the sun
        at noon.
    Wait quietly for the Lord, be patient till 7
        he comes;
    do not strive to outdo the successful
    nor envy him who gains his ends.
Be angry no more, have done with wrath; 8
    strive not to outdo in evildoing.

---

a nameless ruffians: *or* ruffians who give me no rest.   *b* *Line transposed from verse 19.*   *c See note*
on verse 17.   *d* he does . . . ways: *prob. rdg.; Heb. unintelligible.*

9 For evildoers will be destroyed,
but they who hope in the LORD shall possess the land.

10 A little while, and the wicked will be no more;
look well, and you will find their place is empty.

11 But the humble shall possess the land
and enjoy untold prosperity.

12 The wicked mutter against the righteous man
and grind their teeth at the sight of him;

13 the Lord shall laugh at them,
for he sees that their time is coming.

14 The wicked have drawn their swords
and strung their bows
to bring low the poor and needy
and to slaughter honest men.

15 Their swords shall pierce their own hearts
and their bows be broken.

16 Better is the little which the righteous has
than the great wealth of the wicked.

17 For the strong arm of the wicked shall be broken,
but the LORD upholds the righteous.

18 The LORD knows each day of the good man's life,
and his inheritance shall last for ever.

19 When times are bad, he shall not be distressed,
and in days of famine he shall have enough.

20 But the wicked shall perish,
and their children shall beg their bread.*e*
The enemies of the LORD, like fuel in a furnace,*f*
are consumed in smoke.

21 The wicked man borrows and does not pay back,
but the righteous is a generous giver.

22 All whom the LORD has blessed shall possess the land,
and all who are cursed by him shall be destroyed.

23 It is the LORD who directs a man's steps,
he holds him firm and watches over his path.

24 Though he may fall, he will not go headlong,
for the LORD grasps him by the hand.

25 I have been young and am now grown old,
and never have I seen a righteous man forsaken.*g*

26 Day in, day out, he lends generously,
and his children become a blessing.

27 Turn from evil and do good,
and live at peace for ever;

28 for the LORD is a lover of justice
and will not forsake his loyal servants.
The lawless are banished for ever
and the children of the wicked destroyed.

29 The righteous shall possess the land
and shall live there at peace for ever.

30 The righteous man utters words of wisdom
and justice is always on his lips.

31 The law of his God is in his heart,
his steps do not falter.

32 The wicked watch for the righteous man
and seek to take his life;

33 but the LORD will not leave him in their power
nor let him be condemned before his judges.

34 Wait for the LORD and hold to his way;
he will keep you*h* safe from wicked men*i*
and will raise you to be master of the land.
When the wicked are destroyed, you shall be there to see.

35 I have watched a wicked man at his work,
rank as a spreading tree in its native soil.

36 I passed by one day, and he was gone;
I searched for him, but he could not be found.

37 Now look at the good man, watch him who is honest,
for the man of peace leaves descendants;

38 but transgressors are wiped out one and all,
and the descendants of the wicked are destroyed.

39 Deliverance for the righteous comes from the LORD,
their refuge in time of trouble.

40 The LORD will help them and deliver them;*j*
he will save them because they seek shelter with him.

38

Prayer in affliction

1 O LORD, do not rebuke me in thy anger,
nor punish me in thy wrath.

2 For thou hast aimed thy arrows*k* at me,
and thy hand weighs heavy upon me.

3 Thy indignation has left no part of my body unscarred;
there is no health in my whole frame because of my sin.

4 For my iniquities have poured over my head;
they are a load heavier than I can bear.

5 My wounds fester and stink because of my folly.

6 I am bowed down and utterly prostrate.

7 All day long I go about as if in mourning,
for my loins burn with fever,
and there is no wholesome flesh in me.

8 All battered and benumbed,
I groan aloud in my heart's longing.

---

e Line transposed from verse 25.   f like . . . furnace: prob. rdg.; Heb. like the worth of rams.   g See note on verse 20.   h Prob. rdg.; Heb. them.   i he will . . . wicked men: transposed from verse 40. j See note on verse 34.   k thou . . . arrows: prob. rdg.; Heb. thy arrows have come down.

9 O Lord, all my lament lies open before
   thee
   and my sighing is no secret to thee.
10 My heart beats fast, my strength has ebbed
   away,
   and the light has gone out of my eyes.
11 My friends and my companions shun me in
   my sickness,
   and my kinsfolk keep far away.
12 Those who wish me dead defame me,
   those who mean to injure me spread cruel
   gossip
   and mutter slanders all day long.
13 But I am deaf, I do not listen;
   I am like a dumb man who cannot open
   his mouth.
14 I behave like a man who cannot hear
   and whose tongue offers no defence.
15 On thee, O LORD, I fix my hope;
   thou wilt answer, O Lord my God.
16 I said, 'Let them never rejoice over me
   who exult when my foot slips.'
17 I am indeed prone to stumble,
   and suffering is never far away.
18 I make no secret of my iniquity
   and am anxious at the thought of my sin.
19 But many are my enemies, all without
   cause,[l]
   and many those who hate me wrongfully.
20 Those who repay good with evil
   oppose me because my purpose is good.
21 But, LORD, do not thou forsake me;
   keep not far from me, my God.
22 Hasten to my help, O Lord my salvation.

39

The brevity of life

1 I said: I will keep close watch over myself
   that all I say may be free from sin.
   I will keep a muzzle on my mouth,
   so long as wicked men confront me.
2 In dumb silence I held my peace.
   So my agony was quickened,
3 and my heart burned within me.
   My mind wandered as the fever grew,
   and I began to speak:
4 LORD, let me know my end
   and the number of my days;
   tell me how short my life must be.
5 I know thou hast made my days a mere span
   long,
   and my whole life is nothing in thy sight.
   Man, though he stands upright, is but a
   puff of wind,
6 he moves like a phantom;
   the riches[m] he piles up are no more than
   vapour,
   he does not know who will enjoy them.
7 And now, Lord, what do I wait for?
   My hope is in thee.

Deliver me from all who do me wrong,   8
make me no longer the butt of fools.
I am dumb, I will not open my mouth,   9
because it is thy doing.
Plague me no more;   10
I am exhausted by thy blows.
When thou dost rebuke a man to punish his   11
sin,
all his charm festers and drains away;
indeed man is only a puff of wind.
Hear my prayer, O LORD;   12
listen to my cry,
hold not thy peace at my tears;
for I find shelter with thee,
I am thy guest, as all my fathers were.
Frown on me no more and let me smile   13
again,
before I go away and cease to be.

40

Thanksgiving and petition

I waited, waited for the LORD,   1
he bent down to me and heard my cry.
He brought me up out of the muddy pit,   2
out of the mire and the clay;
he set my feet on a rock
and gave me a firm footing;
and on my lips he put a new song,   3
a song of praise to our God.
Many when they see will be filled with awe
and will learn to trust in the LORD:
happy is the man   4
who makes the LORD his trust,
and does not look to brutal and treacherous
men.
Great things thou hast done,   5
O LORD my God;
thy wonderful purposes are all for our
good;
none can compare with thee;
I would proclaim them and speak of them,
but they are more than I can tell.
If thou hadst desired sacrifice and offering   6
thou wouldst have given me ears to hear.
If thou hadst asked for whole-offering and
sin-offering
I would have said, 'Here I am.'[n]   7
My desire is to do thy will, O God,   8
and thy law is in my heart.
In the great assembly I have proclaimed what   9
is right,
I do not hold back my words,
as thou knowest, O LORD.
I have not kept thy goodness hidden in my   10
heart;
I have proclaimed thy faithfulness and
saving power,
and not concealed thy unfailing love and
truth
from the great assembly.

l all . . . cause: *prob. rdg.*; *Heb.* living.   *m* the riches: *prob. rdg.*; *Heb.* they murmur.   *n Prob. rdg.*;
Heb. adds in a scroll of a book it is prescribed for me.

11 Thou, O Lord, dost not withhold
     thy tender care from me;
thy unfailing love and truth for ever guard
     me.

12 For misfortunes beyond counting
     press on me from all sides;
     my iniquities have overtaken me,
     and my sight fails;
     they are more than the hairs of my head,
     and my courage forsakes me.
13*o* Show me favour, O Lord, and save me;
     hasten to help me, O Lord.
14 Let those who seek to take my life
     be put to shame and dismayed one and
     all;
let all who love to hurt me shrink back dis-
     graced;
15 let those who cry 'Hurrah!' at my down-
     fall
     be horrified at their reward of shame.
16 But let all those who seek thee
     be jubilant and rejoice in thee;
and let those who long for thy saving help
     ever cry,
     'All glory to the Lord!'

17 But I am poor and needy;
     O Lord, think of me.*p*
     Thou art my help and my salvation;
     O my God, make no delay.

41

Prayer for healing

1 Happy the man who has a concern for the
     helpless!
     The Lord will save him in time of trouble.
2 The Lord protects him and gives him
     life,
     making him secure in the land;
     the Lord never leaves him*q* to the greed of
     his enemies.
3 He nurses him on his sick-bed;
     he turns his bed when he is ill.

4 But I said, 'Lord, be gracious to me;
heal me, for I have sinned against thee.'
5 'His case is desperate,' my enemies say;
     'when will he die, and his line become
     extinct?'
6 All who visit me speak from an empty heart,
     alert to gather bad news;
     then they go out to spread it abroad.
7 All who hate me whisper together about me
     and love to make the worst of everything:
8   'An evil spell is cast upon him;
he is laid on his bed, and will rise no more.'
9 Even the friend whom I trusted, who ate at
     my table,*r*
     exults over my misfortune.

O Lord, be gracious and restore me,   10
     that I may pay them out to the full.*s*
Then I shall know that thou delightest in   11
     me
     and that my enemy will not triumph over
     me.
But I am upheld by thee because of my   12
     innocence;
     thou keepest me for ever in thy sight.

Blessed be the Lord, the God of Israel,   13
from everlasting to everlasting.

        Amen, Amen.

BOOK 2

42–43

Thirsting for God

As a hind longs for the running streams,   1
so do I long for thee, O God.
With my whole being I thirst for God, the   2
     living God.
When shall I come to God and appear in his
     presence?

Day and night, tears are my food;   3
'Where is your God?' they ask me all day
     long.
As I pour out my soul in distress, I call to   4
     mind
how I marched in the ranks of the great to
     the house of God,
among exultant shouts of praise, the clamour
     of the pilgrims.
     How deep I am sunk in misery,   5
     groaning in my distress;
     yet I will wait for God;
     I will praise him continually,
     my deliverer, my God.

---

*o Verses 13–17: cp. Ps. 70. 1–5   p O Lord . . . me: prob. rdg.; Heb. may the Lord think of me.   q never
leaves him: prob. rdg.; Heb. do thou not give him up . . .   r who . . . table: or slanders me.   s to the
full: transposed from end of verse 9.*

6 I am sunk in misery, therefore will I remember thee,
though from the Hermons and the springs
of Jordan,
and from the hill of Mizar,
7 deep calls to deep in the roar of thy catar-
acts,
and all thy waves, all thy breakers, pass over
me.
8 The LORD makes his unfailing love shine
forth[t]
alike by day and night;
his praise on my lips is a prayer
to the God of my life.
9 I will say to God my rock, 'Why hast thou
forgotten me?'
Why must I go like a mourner because my
foes oppress me?
10 My enemies taunt me, jeering[u] at my misfortunes;
'Where is your God?' they ask me all day
long.
11 How deep I am sunk in misery,
groaning in my distress:
yet I will wait for God;
I will praise him continually,
my deliverer, my God.

43 Plead my cause and give me judgement
against an impious race;
save me from malignant men and liars, O
God.
2 Thou, O God, art my refuge; why hast thou
rejected me?
Why must I go like a mourner because my
foes oppress me?
3 Send forth thy light and thy truth to be my
guide
and lead me to thy holy hill, to thy tabernacle,
4 then shall I come to the altar of God, the
God of my joy,
and praise thee on the harp, O God, thou
God of my delight.
5 How deep I am sunk in misery,
groaning in my distress:
yet I will wait for God;
I will praise him continually,
my deliverer, my God.

44

Perplexity in defeat

1 O God, we have heard for ourselves,
our fathers have told us
all the deeds which thou didst in their
days,
2 all the work of thy hand in days of old.
Thou didst plant them in the land and drive
the nations out,
thou didst make them strike root, breaking
up the peoples;

it was not our fathers' swords won them the 3
land,
nor their arm that gave them the victory,
but thy right hand and thy arm
and the light of thy presence; such was
thy favour to them.
Thou art my king and my God; 4
at thy bidding Jacob is victorious.
By thy help we will throw back our enemies, 5
in thy name we will trample down our
adversaries.
I will not trust in my bow, 6
nor will my sword win me the victory;
for thou dost deliver us from our foes 7
and put all our enemies to shame.
In God have we gloried all day long, 8
and we will praise thy name for ever.
But now thou hast rejected and humbled us 9
and dost no longer lead our armies into
battle.
Thou hast hurled us back before the enemy, 10
and our foes plunder us as they will.
Thou hast given us up to be butchered like 11
sheep
and hast scattered us among the nations.
Thou hast sold thy people for next to nothing 12
and had no profit from the sale.
Thou hast exposed us to the taunts of our 13
neighbours,
to the mockery and contempt of all around.
Thou hast made us a byword among the 14
nations,
and the peoples shake their heads at us;
so my disgrace confronts me all day long, 15
and I am covered with shame
at the shouts of those who taunt and abuse 16
me
as the enemy takes his revenge.
All this has befallen us, but we do not forget 17
thee
and have not betrayed thy covenant;
we have not gone back on our purpose, 18
nor have our feet strayed from thy path.
Yet thou hast crushed us as the sea-serpent 19
was crushed
and covered us with the darkness of death.
If we had forgotten the name of our God 20
and spread our hands in prayer to any other,
would not God find this out, 21
for he knows the secrets of the heart?
Because of thee we are done to death all day 22
long,
and are treated as sheep for slaughter.
Bestir thyself, Lord; why dost thou sleep? 23
Awake, do not reject us for ever.
Why dost thou hide thy face, 24
heedless of our misery and our sufferings?
For we sink down to the dust 25
and lie prone on the earth.
Arise and come to our help; 26
for thy love's sake set us free.

---

t makes . . . forth: *or* entrusts me to his unfailing love.　　　　*u* jeering: *prob. rdg.; Heb. obscure.*

45

Royal wedding song

1 My heart is stirred by a noble theme,
  in a king's honour I utter the song I have
    made,
    and my tongue runs like the pen of an
     expert scribe.

2   You surpass all mankind in beauty,
    your lips are moulded in grace,
  so you are blessed by God for ever.

3 With your sword ready at your side, warrior
    king,

4 your limbs resplendent*ᵛ* in their royal armour,
  ride on to execute true sentence and just
     judgement.
    Your right hand shall show you a scene
     of terror:

5   your sharp arrows flying, nations beneath
     your feet,
    the courage of the king's foes melting
     away!*ʷ*

6 Your throne is like God's throne, eternal,
    your royal sceptre a sceptre of righteous-
     ness.

7 You have loved right and hated wrong;
  so God, your God, has anointed you
    above your fellows with oil, the token of
     joy.

8 Your robes are all fragrant with myrrh and
    powder of aloes,
    and the music of strings greets you
    from a palace panelled with ivory.

Myrrh

A princess takes her place among the noblest 9
  of your women,
  a royal lady at your side in gold of Ophir.

Listen, my daughter, hear my words   10
  and consider them:
  forget your own people and your father's
    house;
  and, when the king desires your beauty,   11
    remember that he is your lord.
Do him obeisance, daughter of Tyre,   12
  and the richest in the land will court you
    with gifts.

In the palace honour awaits her;*ˣ*   13
  she is a king's daughter,
  arrayed in cloth-of-gold richly em- 14
    broidered.
Virgins shall follow her into the presence
    of the king;
  her companions shall be brought to her,
  escorted with the noise of revels and 15
    rejoicing
  as they enter the king's palace.

You shall have sons, O king, in place of 16
    your forefathers
  and will make them rulers over all the
    land.*ʸ*
I will declare your fame to all generations; 17
therefore the nations will praise you for ever
    and ever.

46

The city of God

God is our shelter and our refuge,   1
  a timely help in trouble;
so we are not afraid when the earth heaves 2
    and the mountains are hurled into the sea,
    when its waters seethe in tumult   3
    and the mountains quake before his
     majesty.
There is a river whose streams gladden the 4
    city of God,*ᶻ*
    which the Most High has made his holy
     dwelling;
    God is in that city; she will not be over- 5
     thrown,
    and he will help her at the break of day.
Nations are in tumult, kingdoms hurled 6
    down;
    when he thunders, the earth surges like the
     sea.
The LORD of Hosts is with us,   7
  the God of Jacob our high stronghold.

Come and see what the LORD has done,   8
  the devastation he has brought upon earth,
  from end to end of the earth he stamps out 9
    war:

---

v your limbs resplendent: *prob. rdg.; Heb.* and in your pomp prosper.   *w* the courage . . . away: *prob.*
rdg.; Heb. obscure.   *x* honour awaits her: *prob. rdg.; Heb.* all honoured.   *y* over all the land: *or* in all
the earth.   *z* the city of God: *or* a wondrous city.

he breaks the bow, he snaps the spear
and burns the shield in the fire.

10 Let be then: learn that I am God,
high over the nations, high above earth.

11 The LORD of Hosts is with us,
the God of Jacob our high stronghold.

47

God is king of all

1 Clap your hands, all you nations;
acclaim our God with shouts of joy.

2 How fearful is the LORD Most High,
great sovereign over all the earth!

3 He lays the nations prostrate beneath us,
he lays peoples under our feet;

4 he chose our patrimony for us,
the pride of Jacob whom he loved.

5 God has gone up with shouts of acclamation,
the LORD has gone up with a fanfare of
trumpets.

6 Praise God,*a* praise him with psalms;
praise our king, praise him with psalms.

7 God is king of all the earth;
sing psalms with all your art.

8 God reigns over the nations,
God is seated on his holy throne.

9 The princes of the nations assemble
with the families of Abraham's line;*b*
for the mighty ones of earth belong to
God,
and he is raised above them all.

48

Praise of Zion

1 The LORD is great and worthy of our praise
in the city of our God, upon his holy hill.

2 Fair and lofty, the joy of the whole earth
is Zion's hill, like the farthest reaches of
the north,*c*
the hill of the great King's city.

3 In her palaces God is known for a tower of
strength.

4 See how the kings all gather round her,
marching on in company.

5 They are struck with amazement when they
see her,
they are filled with alarm and panic;

6 they are seized with trembling,
they toss in pain like a woman in labour,

7 like the ships of Tarshish
when an east wind wrecks them.

8 All we had heard we saw with our own eyes
in the city of the LORD of Hosts,
in the city of our God,
the city which God plants firm for evermore.

O God, we re-enact the story of thy true 9
love
within thy temple;
the praise thy name deserves, O God, 10
is heard at earth's farthest bounds.
Thy hand is charged with justice,
and the hill of Zion rejoices, 11
Judah's daughter-cities exult
in thy judgements.

Make the round of Zion in procession, 12
count the number of her towers,
take good note of her ramparts, 13
pass her palaces in review,
that you may tell generations yet to come:
Such is God, 14
our God for ever and ever;
he shall be our guide eternally.

49

The common lot

Hear this, all you nations; 1
listen, all who inhabit this world,
all mankind, every living man, 2
rich and poor alike;
for the words that I speak are wise, 3
my thoughtful heart is full of understanding.

I will set my ear to catch the moral of the 4
story
and tell on the harp how I read the riddle;
why should I be afraid in evil times, 5
beset by the wickedness of treacherous
foes,
who trust in their riches 6
and boast of their great wealth?
Alas! no man can ever ransom himself 7
nor pay God the price of that release;
his ransom would cost too much, 8
for ever beyond his power to pay,
the ransom that would let him live on 9
always
and never see the pit of death.

But remember this:*d* wise men must die; 10
stupid men, brutish men, all perish.*e*
The grave is their eternal home, 11
their dwelling for all time to come;
they may give their own names to estates,
but they must leave their riches to others.*f*
For men are like oxen whose life cannot 12
last,
they are like cattle whose time is short.
Such is the fate of foolish men 13
and of all who seek to please them:
like sheep they run headlong into Sheol, 14
the land of Death;
he is their shepherd and urges them on;
their flesh must rot away*g*

---

a Praise God: *or* Praise, you gods.   *b* the families of Abraham's line: *prob. rdg.; Heb.* the God of Abraham.
c Or of Zaphon.   *d* But remember this: *prob. rdg.; Heb.* But he will remember this.   *e* *Line transposed from
here to follow verse 11.*   *f* *Line transposed from verse 10.*   *g* and urges . . . rot away: *prob. rdg.; Heb. obscure.*

and their bodies be wasted by Sheol,
stripped of all honour.
15 But God will ransom my life,
he will take me from the power of
Sheol.
16 Do not envy a man when he grows
rich,
when the wealth of his family increases;
17 for he will take nothing when he dies,
and his wealth will not go with him.
18 Though in his lifetime he counts himself
happy
and men praise him in his*[h]* prosperity,
19 he*[i]* will go to join the company of his forefathers
who will never again see the light.
20 For men are like oxen whose life cannot
last,
they are like cattle whose time is short.

50

God's basis of judgement

1 God, the LORD God, has spoken
and summoned the world from the rising to
the setting sun.
2 God shines out from Zion, perfect in
beauty.
3 Our God is coming and will not keep
silence:
consuming fire runs before him
and wreathes him closely round.*[j]*
4 He summons heaven on high and earth
to the judgement of his people:
5 'Gather to me my loyal servants,
all who by sacrifice have made a covenant
with me.'
6 The heavens proclaim his justice,
for God himself is the judge.

7 Listen, my people, and I will speak;
I will bear witness against you, O Israel:
I am God, your God,
8 shall I not*[k]* find fault with your sacrifices,
though*[l]* your offerings are before me
always?
9 I need take no young bull from your
house,
no he-goat from your folds;
10 for all the beasts of the forest are mine
and the cattle in thousands on my hills.
11 I know every bird on those hills,
the teeming life of the fields is my care.
12 If I were hungry, I would not tell you,
for the world and all that is in it are
mine.
13 Shall I eat the flesh of your bulls
or drink the blood of he-goats?

14 Offer to God the sacrifice of thanksgiving
and pay your vows to the Most High.
15 If you call upon me in time of trouble,
I will come to your rescue, and you shall
honour me.

16 God's word to the wicked man is this:
What right have you to recite my laws
and make so free with the words of my
covenant,
17 you who hate correction
and turn your back when I am speaking?
18 If you meet a thief, you choose him as your
friend;
you make common cause with adulterers;
19 you charge your mouth with wickedness
and harness your tongue to slander.
20 You are for ever talking against your
brother,
stabbing your own mother's son in the
back.
21 All this you have done, and shall I keep
silence?
You thought that I was another like yourself,
but point by point I will rebuke you to
your face.
22 Think well on this, you who forget God,
or I will tear you in pieces and no one
shall save you.
23 He who offers a sacrifice of thanksgiving
does me due honour,
and to him who follows my way*[m]*
I will show the salvation of God.

51

Prayer for forgiveness

1 Be gracious to me, O God, in thy true
love;
in the fullness of thy mercy blot out my
misdeeds.

2 Wash away all my guilt
and cleanse me from my sin.
3 For well I know my misdeeds,
and my sins confront me all the day
long.
4 Against thee, thee only, I have sinned
and done what displeases thee,
so that thou mayest be proved right in thy
charge
and just in passing sentence.

5 In iniquity I was brought to birth
and my mother conceived me in sin;
6 yet, though thou hast hidden the truth in
darkness,

---

h him . . . his: *prob. rdg.; Heb.* you . . . your.   *i* he: *prob. rdg.; Heb.* you.   *j* and wreathes him closely
round: *or* and rages round him.   *k Or* I will not.   *l Or* for.   *m* him who follows my way: *prob. rdg.;
Heb.* him who puts a way.

through this mystery thou dost teach me wisdom.

7 Take hyssop[n] and sprinkle me, that I may be clean;
wash me, that I may become whiter than snow;

8 let me hear the sounds of joy and gladness,
let the bones dance which thou hast broken.

9 Turn away thy face from my sins
and blot out all my guilt.

Hyssop

0 Create a pure heart in me, O God,
and give me a new and steadfast spirit;

1 do not drive me from thy presence
or take thy holy spirit from me;

2 revive in me the joy of thy deliverance
and grant me a willing spirit to uphold me.

3 I will teach transgressors the ways that lead to thee,
and sinners shall return to thee again.

4 O LORD God, my deliverer, save me from bloodshed,[o]
and I will sing the praises of thy justice.

5 Open my lips, O Lord,
that my mouth may proclaim thy praise.

6 Thou hast no delight in sacrifice;
if I brought thee an offering, thou wouldst not accept it.

7 My sacrifice, O God, is a broken spirit;
a wounded heart, O God, thou wilt not despise.

8 Let it be thy pleasure to do good to Zion,
to build anew the walls of Jerusalem.

9 Then only shalt thou delight in the appointed sacrifices;[p]
then shall young bulls be offered on thy altar.

52

Where wickedness leads

Why make your wickedness your boast, you 1 2
man of might,
forging wild lies all day against God's loyal servant?
Your slanderous tongue is sharp as a razor.
You love evil and not good, 3
falsehood, not speaking the truth;
cruel gossip you love and slanderous talk. 4
So may God[q] pull you down to the ground, 5
sweep you away, leave you ruined and homeless,
uprooted from the land of the living.
The righteous will look on, awestruck, 6
and laugh at his plight:
'This is the man', they say, 7
'who does not make God his refuge,
but trusts in his great wealth
and takes refuge in wild lies.'
But I am like a spreading olive-tree in God's 8
house;
for I trust in God's true love for ever and ever.
I will praise thee for ever for what thou hast 9
done,
and glorify thy name among thy loyal servants;
for that is good.

53

Man's wickedness

The impious fool says in his heart, 1[r]
'There is no God.'
How vile men are, how depraved and loathsome;
not one does anything good!
God looks down from heaven 2
on all mankind
to see if any act wisely,
if any seek out God.
But all are unfaithful, all are rotten to the 3
core;
not one does anything good,
no, not even one.

Shall they not rue it, 4
these evildoers who devour my people
as men devour bread,
and never call upon God?
There they were in dire alarm 5
when God scattered them.
The crimes of the godless were frustrated;[s]
for God had rejected them.
If only Israel's deliverance might come out 6
of Zion!
When God restores his people's fortunes,
let Jacob rejoice, let Israel be glad.

---

n Or marjoram.   *o Or* from punishment by death.   *p Prob. rdg.; Heb. adds* a whole-offering and
one wholly consumed.   *q Or* So God will.   *r Verses 1–6: cp. Ps. 14. 1–7.   *s* The crimes . . .
frustrated: *prob. rdg.; Heb. obscure.*

54

God is my helper

1 Save me, O God, by the power of thy
name,
and vindicate me through thy might.
2 O God, hear my prayer,
listen to my supplication.
3 Insolent men rise to attack me,
ruthless men seek my life;
they give no thought to God.

4 But God is my helper,
the Lord the mainstay of my life.
5 May their own malice recoil on my
watchful foes;
silence them by thy truth, O LORD.
6 I will offer thee a willing sacrifice
and praise thy name, for that is good;
7 God has rescued me from every trouble,
and I look on my enemies' downfall with
delight.

55

A friend's disloyalty

1 Listen, O God, to my pleading,
do not hide thyself when I pray.
2 Hear me and answer,
for my cares give me no peace.
3 I am panic-stricken at the shouts of my
enemies,
at the shrill clamour of the wicked;
for they heap trouble on me
and they revile me in their anger.
4 My heart is torn with anguish
and the terrors of death come upon me.
5 Fear and trembling overwhelm me
and I shudder from head to foot.
6 'Oh that I had the wings of a dove
to fly away and be at rest!
7 I should escape far away
and find a refuge in the wilderness;
8 soon I should find myself a sanctuary
from wind and storm,
9 from the blasts of calumny, O Lord,
from my enemies' contentious tongues.
I have seen violence and strife in the city;
10 day and night they encircle it,
all along its walls;
it is filled with trouble and mischief,
11 alive with rumour and scandal,
and its public square is never free
from violence and spite.
12 It was no enemy that taunted me,
or I should have avoided him;
no adversary that treated me with scorn,
or I should have kept out of his way.
13 It was you, a man of my own sort,
my comrade, my own dear friend,

with whom I kept pleasant company 1
in the house of God.

May death strike them,
and may they*u* perish in confusion,
may they go down alive into Sheol;
for their homes are haunts of evil!

But I will call upon God; 1₆
the LORD will save me.
Evening and morning and at noon 1₇
I nurse my woes, and groan.
He has heard my cry, he rescued me 1₈
and gave me back my peace,
when they beset me like archers,*v*
massing against me,
like Ishmael and the desert tribes 1₉
and those who dwell in the·East,
who have no respect for an oath
nor any fear of God.
Such men do violence to those at peace 2₀
with them
and break their promised word;
their speech is smoother than butter 2₁
but their thoughts are of war;
their words are slippery as oil
but sharp as drawn swords.

Commit your fortunes to the LORD, 2₂
and he will sustain you;
he will never let the righteous be shaken.
Cast them, O God, into the pit of destruc- 2₃
tion;
bloodthirsty and treacherous,
they shall not live out half their days;
but I will put my trust in thee.

56

In God I trust

Be gracious to me, O God, for the enemy 1
persecute me,
my assailants harass me all day long.
All the day long my watchful foes perse- 2
cute me;
countless are those who assail me.
Appear on high*w* in my day of fear; 3
I put my trust in thee.
With God to help me I will shout defiance, 4
in God I trust and shall not be afraid;
what can mortal men do to me?
All day long abuse of me is their only 5
theme,
all their thoughts are hostile.
In malice they are on the look-out, and 6
watch for me,
they dog my footsteps;
but, while they lie in wait for me,
it is they who will not*x* escape. 7
O God, in thy anger bring ruin on the
nations.

---

t Prob. rdg.; Heb. prefixes And I said.   *u Prob. rdg.; Heb.* we.   *v* when . . . archers: *prob. rdg.; Heb.*
obscure.   *w* Appear on high: *prob. rdg.; Heb.* Height.   *x* it is . . . not: *prob. rdg.; Heb.* for iniquity.

8 Enter my lament in thy book,[y]
store every tear in thy flask.[z]
9 Then my enemies will turn back
on the day when I call upon thee;[a]
for this I know, that God is on my side,
10 with God to help me I will shout defiance.[b]
11 In God I trust and shall not be afraid;
what can man do to me?
12 I have bound myself with vows to thee,
O God,
and will redeem them with due thank-
offerings;
13 for thou hast rescued me from death[c]
to walk in thy presence, in the light of life.

57

Prayer for God to show himself

1 Be gracious to me, O God, be gracious;
for I have made thee my refuge.
I will take refuge in the shadow of thy
wings
until the storms are past.
2 I will call upon God Most High,
on God who fulfils his purpose for me.
3 He will send his truth and his love that never
fails,
he will send from heaven and save me.
God himself will frustrate my persecutors;
4 for I lie down among lions, man-eaters,
whose teeth are spears and arrows
and whose tongues are sharp swords.
5 Show thyself, O God, high above the
heavens;
let thy glory shine over all the earth.
6 Men have prepared a net to catch me as
I walk,
but I bow my head to escape from it;
they have dug a pit in my path
but have fallen into it themselves.
7 [d] My heart is steadfast, O God,
my heart is steadfast.
I will sing and raise a psalm;
8 awake, my spirit,
awake, lute and harp,
I will awake at dawn of day.[e]
9 I will confess thee, O Lord, among the
peoples,
among the nations I will raise a psalm to
thee,
10 for thy unfailing love is wide as the heavens
and thy truth reaches to the skies.
11 Show thyself, O God, high above the
heavens;
let thy glory shine over all the earth.

58

The triumph of righteousness

1 Answer, you rulers:[f] are your judgements
just?
Do you decide impartially between man and
man?
2 Never! Your hearts devise all kinds of
wickedness
and survey the violence that you have done
on earth.

3 Wicked men, from birth they have taken
to devious ways;
liars, no sooner born than they go astray,
4 venomous with the venom of serpents,
of the deaf asp which stops its ears
5 and will not listen to the sound of the
charmer,
however skilful his spells may be.

6 O God, break the teeth in their mouths.
Break, O Lord, the jaws of the unbelievers.[g]
7 May they melt, may they vanish like water,
may they wither like trodden grass,[h]
8 like an abortive birth which melts away
or a still-born child which never sees[i] the
sun!
9 All unawares, may they be rooted up like[j] a
thorn-bush,
like weeds which a man angrily[k] clears
away!

10 The righteous shall rejoice that he has seen
vengeance done
and shall wash his feet in the blood of the
wicked,
11 and men shall say,
'There is after all a reward for the righteous;
after all, there is a God that judges on earth.'

59

God my strong tower

1 Rescue me from my enemies, O my God,
be my tower of strength against all who
assail me,
2 rescue me from these evildoers,
deliver me from men of blood.
3 Savage men lie in wait for me,
they lie in ambush ready to attack me;
for no fault or guilt of mine, O Lord,
4-5 innocent as I am, they run to take post
against me.
But thou, Lord God of Hosts, Israel's God,
do thou bestir thyself at my call, and look:
awake, and punish all the nations.

---

y Enter . . . book: *prob. rdg.*; *Heb. obscure*.   z *Prob. rdg.*; *Heb. adds* is it not in thy book?   a Enter
. . . thee: *or* Thou hast entered my lament in thy book, my tears are put in thy flask. Then my enemies turned
back, when I called upon thee.   b *Prob. rdg.*; *Heb. adds* With the Lord to help me I will shout defiance.
c *Prob. rdg.*; *Heb. adds* is it not my feet from stumbling (*cp. Ps. 116. 8*).   d *Verses 7–11: cp. Ps. 108.
1–5.*   e at dawn of day: *or* the dawn.   f *Or* you gods.   g the jaws of the unbelievers: *or* the
lions' fangs.   h like trodden grass: *prob. rdg.*; *Heb. obscure*.   i sees: *prob. rdg.*; *Heb.* they see.
j may they be rooted up like: *prob. rdg.*; *Heb.* your pots.   k angrily: *prob. rdg.*; *Heb.* like anger.

Have no mercy on villains and traitors,

6 who run wild at nightfall like dogs,
snarling and prowling round the city,

15 *l* wandering to and fro in search of food,
and howling if they are not satisfied.

7 From their mouths comes a stream of
nonsense;
'But who will hear?' they murmur.

8 But thou, O LORD, dost laugh at them,
and deride all the nations.

9 O my strength,*m* to thee I turn in the night-
watches;
for thou, O God, art my strong tower.

10 My God, in his true love, shall be my
champion;
with God's help, I shall gloat over my
watchful foes.

11 Wilt thou not kill them, lest my people
forget?
Scatter them by thy might and bring them
to ruin.

12 Deliver them,*n* O Lord, to be destroyed
by their own sinful words;
let what they have spoken entrap them in
their pride.
Let them be cut off for their cursing and
falsehood;

13 bring them to an end in thy wrath,
and they will be no more;
then they will know that God is ruler in
Jacob,
even to earth's farthest limits.*o p*

16 But I will sing of thy strength,
and celebrate thy love when morning
comes;
for thou hast been my strong tower
and a sure retreat in days of trouble.

17 O thou my strength, I will raise a psalm to
thee;
for thou, O God, art my strong tower.

60

Help against enemies

1 O God, thou hast cast us off and broken
us;
thou hast been angry and rebuked us
cruelly.

2 Thou hast made the land quake and torn
it open;
it gives way and crumbles into pieces.

3 Thou hast made thy people drunk with a
bitter draught,
thou hast given us wine that makes us
stagger.

4 But thou hast given a warning to those
who fear thee,
to make their escape before the sentence
falls.

Deliver those that are dear to thee; 5*q*
save them with thy right hand, and
answer.

God has spoken from his sanctuary:*r* 6
'I will go up now and measure out She-
chem;
I will divide the valley of Succoth into
plots;
Gilead and Manasseh are mine; 7
Ephraim is my helmet, Judah my sceptre;
Moab is my wash-bowl, I fling my shoes at 8
Edom;
Philistia is the target of my anger.'

Who can bring me to the fortified city, 9
who can guide me to Edom,
since thou, O God, hast abandoned us 10
and goest not forth with our armies?
Grant us help against the enemy, 11
for deliverance by man is a vain hope.
With God's help we shall do valiantly, 12
and God himself will tread our enemies
under foot.

61

Prayer for support

Hear my cry, O God, listen to my prayer. 1
From the end of the earth I call to thee with 2
fainting heart;
lift me up and set me upon a rock.
For thou hast been my shelter, 3
a tower for refuge from the enemy.
In thy tent will I make my home for ever 4
and find my shelter under the cover of thy
wings.
For thou, O God, hast heard my vows 5
and granted the wish*s* of all who revere thy
name.

To the king's life add length of days, 6
year upon year for many generations;
may he dwell in God's presence for ever, 7
may true and constant love preserve him.

So will I ever sing psalms in honour of thy 8
name
as I fulfil my vows day after day.

62

Dependence on God

Truly my heart waits silently for God; 1
my deliverance comes from him.
In truth he is my rock of deliverance, 2
my tower of strength, so that I stand unshaken.
How long will you assail a man with your 3
threats,
all battering on a leaning wall?

*l Verse transposed.   m Or refuge.   n Deliver them: prob. rdg.; Heb. Our shield.   o Prob.
rdg.; Heb. adds* (14) *who run wild at nightfall like dogs, snarling and prowling round the city (cp. verse 6).
p Verse 15 transposed to follow verse 6.   q Verses 5–12: cp. Ps. 108. 6–13.   r from his sanctuary: or
in his holiness.   s Prob. rdg.; Heb. the inheritance.*

4 In truth men plan to topple him from his
    height,
  and stamp on the fallen stones.[t]
  With their lips they bless him, the hypo-
    crites,
  but revile him in their hearts.

5 Truly my heart waits silently for God;
    my hope of deliverance comes from him.
6 In truth he is my rock of deliverance,
    my tower of strength, so that I am un-
      shaken.
7 My deliverance and my honour depend
    upon God,
  God who is my rock of refuge and my
    shelter.
8 Trust always in God, my people,
    pour out your hearts before him;
  God is our shelter.

9 In very truth men are a puff of wind,
    all men are faithless;
  put them in the balance and they can only
    rise,
  all of them lighter than wind.

10 Put no trust in extortion,
    do not be proud of stolen goods;
  though wealth breeds wealth, set not your
    heart on it.
11 One thing God has spoken,
    two things I have learnt:
  'Power belongs to God'
12 and 'True love, O Lord, is thine';
  thou dost requite a man for his deeds.

63

Remembering God

1 O God, thou art my God, I seek thee early
    with a heart that thirsts for thee
    and a body wasted with longing for thee,
  like a dry and thirsty land that has no water.
2 So longing, I come before thee in the
    sanctuary
    to look upon thy power and glory.
3 Thy true love is better than life;
    therefore I will sing thy praises.
4 And so I bless thee all my life
    and in thy name lift my hands in prayer.

I am satisfied as with a rich and sumptuous 5
    feast
  and wake the echoes with thy praise.
When I call thee to mind upon my bed   6
  and think on thee in the watches of the
    night,
remembering how thou hast been my help 7
  and that I am safe in the shadow of thy
    wings,
  then I humbly follow thee with all my 8
    heart,
  and thy right hand is my support.

Those who seek my life, bent on evil,   9
  shall sink into the depths of the earth;
  they shall be given over to the sword;   10
  they shall be carrion for jackals.

The king shall rejoice in God,   11
  and whoever swears by God's name shall
    exult;
  the voice of falsehood shall be silenced.

64

God overthrows evildoers

Hear me, O God, hear my lament;   1
  keep me safe from the threats of the
    enemy.
Hide me from the factions of the wicked, 2
  from the turbulent mob of evildoers,
who sharpen their tongues like swords   3
  and wing their cruel words like arrows,[u]
to shoot down the innocent from cover,   4
  shooting suddenly, themselves unseen.
They boldly[v] hide their snares,   5
  sure that none will see them;
they hatch their secret plans[w] with skill and 6
    cunning,
with evil[x] purpose and deep design.
  But God with his arrow shoots them down, 7
  and sudden is their overthrow.

They may repeat their wicked tales,[y]   8
  but their mischievous tongues[z] are their
    undoing.
All who see their fate take fright at it,
  every man is afraid;   9
  'This is God's work', they declare;
  they learn their lesson from what he has
    done.
The righteous rejoice and seek refuge in the 10
    LORD
  and all the upright exult.

65

Praise for God's abundant provision

We owe thee praise, O God, in Zion;   1-2
  thou hearest prayer, vows shall be paid to
    thee.

---

t the fallen stones: *transposed from end of verse 3.*
their arrow a cruel word.   v *See first note on verse 8.*
intelligible.   x evil: *prob. rdg.; Heb.* man.   y *They . . . tales: transposed from after* boldly *in verse 5.*
z their mischievous tongues: *prob. rdg.; Heb.* against them their tongues.

u and wing . . . arrows: *prob. rdg.; Heb.* they tread
w their secret plans: *prob. rdg.; Heb.* un-

3 All men shall lay their guilt before thee:
    our sins are too heavy for us;
    only thou canst blot them out.
4 Happy is the man of thy choice, whom thou
    dost bring
    to dwell in thy courts;
    let us enjoy the blessing of thy house,
    thy holy temple.
5 By deeds of terror answer us with victory,
    O God of our deliverance,
    in whom men trust from the ends of the
    earth
    and far-off seas;
6 thou art girded with strength,
  and by thy might dost fix the mountains in
    their place,
7 dost calm the rage of the seas and their
    raging waves.*a*
8 The dwellers at the ends of the earth
    hold thy signs in awe;
    thou makest morning and evening sing
    aloud in triumph.

9 Thou dost visit the earth and give it
    abundance,
    as often as thou dost enrich it
    with the waters of heaven, brimming in
    their channels,
    providing rain*b* for men.
    For this is thy provision for it,
10 watering its furrows, levelling its ridges,
    softening it with showers and blessing its
    growth.
11 Thou dost crown the year with thy good
    gifts
    and the palm-trees drip with sweet juice;
12 the pastures in the wild are rich with
    blessing
    and the hills wreathed in happiness,
13 the meadows are clothed with sheep
    and the valleys mantled in corn,
    so that they shout, they break into song.

66

Answered prayer

Acclaim our God, all men on earth; 1
let psalms declare the glory of his name, 2
make glorious his praise.
Say unto God, 'How fearful are thy works! 3
Thy foes cower before the greatness of thy
    strength.
All men on earth fall prostrate in thy 4
    presence,
and sing to thee, sing psalms in honour of
    thy name.'
Come and see all that God has done, 5
tremendous in his dealings with mankind.
He turned the waters into dry land 6
so that his people passed through the sea
    on foot;
there did we rejoice in him.*c*

He rules for ever by his power, 7
his eye rests on the nations;
let no rebel rise in defiance.

Bless our God, all nations; 8
let his praise be heard far and near.
He set us in the land of the living; 9
he keeps our feet from stumbling.
For thou, O God, hast put us to the proof 10
and refined us like silver.
Thou hast caught us in a net, 11
thou hast bound our bodies fast;
thou hast let men ride over our heads. 12
We went through fire and water,
but thou hast brought us out into liberty.

I will bring sacrifices into thy temple 13
and fulfil my vows to thee,
vows which I made with my own lips 14
and swore with my own mouth when in
    distress.
I will offer thee fat beasts as sacrifices 15
and burn rams as a savoury offering;
I will make ready oxen and he-goats.

a Prob. rdg.; Heb. adds and tumult of people.
we will rejoice in him.

b Or corn.   *c* there . . . him: *or* where we see this,

16 Come, listen, all who fear God,
   and I will tell you all that he has done for
   me;
17 I lifted up my voice in prayer,
   his high praise was on my lips.
18 If I had cherished evil thoughts,
   the Lord would not have heard me;
19 but in truth God has heard
   and given heed to my prayer.
20 Blessed is God
   who has not withdrawn his love and care
   from me.

67

Let all peoples praise thee

1 God be gracious to us and bless us,
  God make his face shine upon us,
2 that his ways may be known on earth
  and his saving power among all the
  nations.
3 Let the peoples praise thee, O God;
  let all peoples praise thee.
4 Let all nations rejoice and shout in
  triumph;
  for thou dost judge the peoples with
  justice
  and guidest the nations of the earth.
5 Let the peoples praise thee, O God;
  let all peoples praise thee.
6 The earth has given its increase
  and God, our God, will bless us.

7 God grant us his blessing,
  that all the ends of the earth may fear him.

68

Song of triumph

1 God arises and his enemies are scattered;
  those who hate him flee before him,
2 driven away like smoke in the wind;
  like wax melting at the fire,
  the wicked perish at the presence of
  God.
3 But the righteous are joyful, they exult before God,
  they are jubilant and shout for joy.

4 Sing the praises of God, raise a psalm to his
  name,
  extol him who rides over the desert plains.*d*
  Be joyful*e* and exult before him,
5 father of the fatherless, the widow's
  champion—
  God in his holy dwelling-place.
6 God gives the friendless a home
  and brings out the prisoner safe and
  sound;
  but rebels must live in the scorching desert.

O God, when thou didst go forth before 7
  thy people,
  marching across the wilderness,
earth trembled, the very heavens quaked   8
before God the lord of Sinai, before God the
  God of Israel.

Of thy bounty, O God, thou dost refresh 9
  with rain
  thy own land in its weariness,
  the land which thou thyself didst provide,
  where thy own people made their home, 10
which thou, O God, in thy goodness pro-
  videst for the poor.

The Lord proclaims good news:*f*   11–13
'Kings with their armies have fled headlong.'
O mighty host, will you linger among the
  sheepfolds
  while the women in your tents divide the
  spoil—
  an image of a dove, its wings sheathed in
  silver
  and its pinions in yellow gold—
  while the Almighty scatters kings far and 14
  wide
  like snowflakes falling on Zalmon?

The hill of Bashan is a hill of God indeed, 15
  a hill of many peaks is Bashan's hill.
But, O hill of many peaks, why gaze in 16
  envy
  at the hill where the LORD delights to
  dwell,
where the LORD himself will live for ever?
Twice ten thousand were God's chariots, 17
  thousands upon thousands,
when the Lord came in holiness from Sinai.*g*
Thou didst go up to thy lofty home with 18
  captives in thy train,
  having received tribute from men;
in the presence of the LORD God no rebel
  could live.

Blessed is the Lord: 19
  he carries us day by day,
  God our salvation.
Our God is a God who saves us,   20
in the LORD God's hand lies escape from
  death.*h*
God himself will smite*i* the head of his 21
  enemies,
  those proud sinners with their flowing
  locks.
The Lord says, 'I will return from the 22
  Dragon,*j*
  I will return from the depths of the sea,
that you may dabble your feet in blood, 23
  while the tongues of your dogs are eager*k*
  for it.'

---

d over the desert plains: *or* on the plains.
f proclaims good news: *or* gives the word, women bearing good news.   *g* came … from Sinai: *prob. rdg.*;
Heb. obscure.   *h* in the LORD God's hand … death: *or* death is expelled by the LORD God.   *i* will
smite: *or* smites.   *j* the Dragon: *or* Bashan.   *k* are eager: *prob. rdg.*; *Heb.* from enemies.
e Be joyful: *prob. rdg.*; *Heb.* In the LORD is his name.

H

24 Thy procession, O God, comes into view,
the procession of my God and King into
the sanctuary:
25 at its head the singers, next come minstrels,
girls among them playing on tambourines.
26 In the great concourse they bless God,
all Israel assembled[l] bless the LORD.
27 There is the little tribe of Benjamin leading
them,
there the company of Judah's princes,
the princes of Zebulun and of Naphtali.

28 O God, in virtue of thy power[m]—
that godlike power which has acted for
us—
29 command kings to bring gifts to thee
for the honour of thy temple in Jerusalem.
30 Rebuke those wild beasts of the reeds, that
herd of bulls,
the bull-calf warriors of the nations;[n]
31 scatter these nations which revel in war;
make them bring tribute from Egypt,
precious stones and silver from Pathros;[o]
let Nubia stretch out[p] her hands to God.

32 All you kingdoms of the world, sing praises
to God,
sing psalms to the Lord,
33 to him who rides on the heavens, the
ancient heavens.
Hark! he speaks in the mighty thunder.
34 Ascribe all might to God, Israel's High God,
Israel's pride and might throned in the
skies.
35 Terrible is God as he comes from his
sanctuary;
he is Israel's own God,
who gives to his people might and abundant
power.

Blessed be God.

69

A cry of distress

1 Save me, O God;
for the waters have risen up to my neck.
2 I sink in muddy depths and have no foothold;
I am swept into deep water, and the flood
carries me away.
3 I am wearied with crying out, my throat is
sore,
my eyes grow dim as I wait for God to help
me.
4 Those who hate me without reason
are more than the hairs of my head;
they outnumber my hairs, those who accuse
me falsely.
How can I give back what I have not stolen?

O God, thou knowest how foolish I am, 5
and my guilty deeds are not hidden from
thee.
Let none of those who look to thee be 6
shamed on my account,
O Lord GOD of Hosts;
let none who seek thee be humbled through
my fault,
O God of Israel.
For in thy service I have suffered re- 7
proach;
I dare not show my face for shame.
I have become a stranger to my brothers, 8
an alien to my own mother's sons;
bitter enemies of thy temple tear me in 9
pieces;[q]
those who reproach thee reproach me.
I have broken my spirit with fasting, 10
only to lay myself open to many reproaches.
I have made sackcloth my clothing 11
and have become a byword among them.
Those who sit by the town gate talk about 12
me;
drunkards sing songs about me in their
cups.
But I lift up this prayer to thee, O LORD: 13
accept me[r] now in thy great love,
answer me with thy sure deliverance,
O God.
Rescue me from the mire, do not let me 14
sink;
let me be rescued from the muddy depths,[s]
so that no flood may carry me away, 15
no abyss swallow me up,
no deep close over me.
Answer me, O LORD, in the goodness of thy 16
unfailing love,
turn towards me in thy great affection.
I am thy servant, do not hide thy face from 17
me.
Make haste to answer me, for I am in
distress.
Come near to me and redeem me; 18
ransom me, for I have many enemies.

Thou knowest what reproaches I bear, 19
all my anguish is seen by thee.
Reproach has broken my heart, 20
my shame and my dishonour[t] are past
hope;
I looked for consolation and received
none,
for comfort and did not find any.
They put poison in my food 21
and gave me vinegar when I was thirsty.
May their own table be a snare to them 22
and their sacred feasts lure them to their
ruin;

l assembled: *prob. rdg.; Heb. obscure.*   *m* O God . . . power: *prob. rdg.; Heb.* Your God your power.
n See first note on verse 31.   *o* precious . . . Pathros: *prob. rdg.,* transposed from verse 30 and slightly
altered.   *p* stretch out: *prob. rdg.; Heb. obscure.*   *q* bitter . . . pieces: *or* zeal for thy temple has eaten me
up (*cp.* John 2. 17).   *r Prob. rdg.; Heb.* acceptance.   *s* from . . . depths: *prob. rdg.; Heb.* from my haters
and from the depths.   *t* my shame and my dishonour: *transposed from after* reproaches *in verse 19.*

23 may their eyes be darkened so that they
     do not see,
   let a continual ague shake their loins.
24 Pour out thine indignation upon them
     and let thy burning anger overtake
     them.
25 May their settlements be desolate,
     and no one living in their tents;
26 for they pursue him whom thou hast
     struck down
   and multiply the torments of those whom
     thou hast wounded.
27 Give them the punishment their sin
     deserves;[u]
   exclude them from thy righteous mercy;
28 let them be blotted out from the book of
     life
   and not be enrolled among the righteous.

29 But by thy saving power, O God, lift me
     high
   above my pain and my distress,
30 then I will praise God's name in song
   and glorify him with thanksgiving;
31 that will please the LORD more than the
     offering of a bull,
   a young bull with horn and cloven hoof.

32 See and rejoice, you humble folk,
   take heart, you seekers after God;
33 for the LORD listens to the poor
   and does not despise those bound to his
     service.
34 Let sky and earth praise him,
   the seas and all that move in them,
36 for God will deliver Zion
   and rebuild the cities of Judah.
   His servants' children shall inherit them;
   they shall dwell there in their own
     possession
   and all who love his name shall live in
     them.

70

Prayer for help

1[v] Show me favour,[w] O God, and save me;
    hasten to help me, O LORD.
2 Let all who seek my life be brought to
     shame and dismay,
   let all who love to hurt me shrink back dis-
     graced;
3 let those who cry 'Hurrah!' at my down-
     fall
   turn back at the shame they incur,
4 but let all who seek thee
   be jubilant and rejoice in thee,
   and let those who long for thy saving help
     ever cry,
   'All glory to God!'

But I am poor and needy;   5
O God, hasten to my aid.
Thou art my help, my salvation;
O LORD, make no delay.

71

Prayer in old age

In thee, O LORD, I have taken refuge;   1
never let me be put to shame.
As thou art righteous rescue me and save   2
  my life;
hear me and set me free,
be a rock of refuge for me,   3
where I may ever find safety at thy call;
for thou art my towering crag and stronghold.
O God, keep my life safe from the wicked,   4
from the clutches of unjust and cruel men.

Thou art my hope, O Lord,   5
my trust, O LORD, since boyhood.
From birth I have leaned upon thee,   6
my protector since I left[x] my mother's
  womb.[y]
To many I seem a solemn warning;   7
but I have thee for my strong refuge.
My mouth shall be full of thy praises,   8
I shall tell of thy splendour all day long.
Do not cast me off when old age comes,   9
nor forsake me when my strength fails,
when my enemies' rancour bursts upon me[z]   10
and those who watch me whisper together,
saying, 'God has forsaken him;   11
after him! seize him; no one will rescue
  him.'
O God, do not stand aloof from me;   12
O my God, hasten to my help.
Let all my traducers be shamed and dis-   13
  honoured,
let all who seek my hurt be covered with
  scorn.
But I will wait in continual hope,   14
I will praise thee again and yet again;
all day long thy righteousness,   15
thy saving acts, shall be upon my lips.
Thou shalt ever be the theme of my praise,[a]
  although I have not the skill of a poet.
I will begin with a tale of great deeds, O Lord 16
  GOD,
and sing of thy righteousness, thine alone.
O God, thou hast taught me from boy-   17
  hood,
all my life I have proclaimed thy marvellous works;
and now that I am old and my hairs are   18
  grey,
forsake me not, O God,
when I extol thy mighty arm to future generations,

---

u Give them . . . deserves: *or* Add punishment to punishment.   *v Verses 1–5: cp. Ps. 40. 13–17.*   *w* Show
me favour: *prob. rdg., cp. Ps. 40. 13; Heb. om.*   *x* my . . . left: *or* who didst bring me out from.   *y See
note on verse 15.*   *z* enemies' . . . me: *prob. rdg.; Heb.* enemies say of me.   *a Line transposed from verse 6.*

19 thy power and righteousness, O God, to
    highest heaven;
    for thou hast done great things.
    Who is like thee, O God?
20 Thou hast made me pass through bitter and
    deep distress,
    yet dost revive me once again
    and lift me again from earth's watery
    depths.
21 Restore me to honour, turn and comfort
    me,
22 then I will praise thee on the lute
    for thy faithfulness, O God;
    I will sing psalms to thee with the harp,
    thou Holy One of Israel;
23 songs of joy shall be on my lips;
    I will sing thee psalms, because thou hast
    redeemed me.
24 All day long my tongue shall tell of thy
    righteousness;
    shame and disgrace await those who seek
    my hurt.

72

Prayer for the king

1 O God, endow the king with thy own justice,
    and give thy righteousness to a king's son,
2 that he may judge thy people rightly
    and deal out justice to the poor and
    suffering.
3 May hills and mountains afford thy people
    peace and prosperity in righteousness.
4 He shall give judgement for the suffering
    and help those of the people that are
    needy;
    he shall crush the oppressor.
5 He shall live as long as the sun endures,
    long as the moon, age after age.
6 He shall be like rain falling on early
    crops,
    like showers watering[b] the earth.
7 In his days righteousness shall flourish,
    prosperity abound until the moon is no
    more.
8 May he hold sway from sea to sea,
    from the River to the ends of the earth.
9 Ethiopians shall crouch low before him;
    his enemies shall lick the dust.
10 The kings of Tarshish and the islands shall
    bring gifts,
    the kings of Sheba and Seba shall present
    their tribute,
11 and all kings shall pay him homage,
    all nations shall serve him.
12 For he shall rescue the needy from their rich
    oppressors,
    the distressed who have no protector.
13 May he have pity on the needy and the
    poor,
    deliver the poor from death;

14 may he redeem them from oppression and
    violence
    and may their blood be precious in his
    eyes.

15 May the king live long
    and receive gifts of gold[c] from Sheba;
    prayer be made for him continually,
    blessings be his all the day long.
16 May there be abundance of corn in the
    land,
    growing in plenty to the tops of the
    hills;
    may the crops flourish like Lebanon,
    and the sheaves[d] be numberless as blades
    of grass.
17 Long may the king's name endure,
    may it live for ever like the sun;
    so shall all peoples pray to be blessed as he
    was,
    all nations tell of his happiness.

18 Blessed be the LORD God, the God of
    Israel,
    who alone does marvellous things;
19 blessed be his glorious name for ever,
    and may his glory fill all the earth.
                    Amen, Amen.

20 Here end the prayers of David son of Jesse.

BOOK 3

73

A true assessment of life

1 How good God is to the upright![e]
    How good to those who are pure in heart!

2 My feet had almost slipped,
    my foothold had all but given way,
3 because the boasts of sinners roused my
    envy
    when I saw how they prosper.
4 No pain, no suffering is theirs;
    they are sleek and sound in limb;
5 they are not plunged in trouble as other
    men are,
    nor do they suffer the torments of mortal
    men.
6 Therefore pride is their collar of jewels
    and violence the robe that wraps them
    round.
7 Their eyes gleam through folds of fat;
    while vain fancies pass through their
    minds.
8 Their talk is all sneers and malice;
    scornfully they spread their calumnies.
9 Their slanders reach up to heaven,
    while their tongues ply to and fro on
    earth.

---

b like showers watering: *prob. rdg.; Heb. unintelligible.*
rdg.; Heb. from a city.   *e* How ... upright: *prob. rdg.; Heb.* How good it is to Israel!   *c Or* frankincense.   *d* the sheaves: *prob.*

10 And so my people follow their lead*f*
and find nothing to blame in them,*g*
11 even though they say, 'What does God
know?
The Most High neither knows nor cares.'
12 So wicked men talk, yet still they prosper,
and rogues*h* amass great wealth.

13 So it was all in vain that I kept my heart
pure
and washed my hands in innocence.
14 For all day long I suffer torment
and am punished every morning.
15 Yet had I let myself talk on in this fashion,
I should have betrayed the family of God.
16 So I set myself to think this out
but I found it too hard for me,

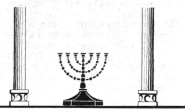

17 until I went into God's sacred courts;
there I saw clearly what their end would
be.
18 How often thou dost set them on slippery
ground
and drive them headlong into ruin!
19 Then in a moment how dreadful their end,
cut off root and branch by death with all
its terrors,
20 like a dream when a man rouses himself,
O Lord,
like images in sleep which are dismissed
on waking!

21 When my heart was embittered
I felt the pangs of envy,
22 I would not understand, so brutish was I,
I was a mere beast in thy sight, O God.
23 Yet I am always with thee,
thou holdest my right hand;
24 thou dost guide me by thy counsel
and afterwards wilt receive me with glory.
25 Whom have I in heaven but thee?
And having thee,*i* I desire nothing else on
earth.
26 Though heart and body fail,
yet God is my possession for ever.
27 They who are far from thee are lost;
thou dost destroy all who wantonly forsake thee.

But my chief good is to be near thee, 28
O God;
I have chosen thee, Lord GOD, to be my
refuge.*j*

74

In time of national humiliation

Why hast thou cast us off, O God? Is it for 1
ever?
Why art thou so stern, so angry with the
sheep of thy flock?
Remember the assembly of thy people,   2
taken long since for thy own,*k*
and Mount Zion, which was thy home.
Now at last*l* restore what was ruined beyond 3
repair,
the wreck that the foe has made of thy
sanctuary.

The shouts of thy enemies filled the holy 4
place,*m*
they planted their standards there as
tokens of victory.
They brought it crashing down,*n*   5
like woodmen plying their axes in the
forest;
they ripped the carvings clean out,   6
they smashed them with hatchet and pick.
They set fire to thy sanctuary,   7
tore down and polluted the shrine sacred
to thy name.
They said to themselves, 'We will sweep them 8
away',
and all over the land they burnt God's holy
places.*o*

We cannot see what lies before us,*p* we have 9
no prophet now;
we have no one who knows how long this
is to last.
How long, O God, will the enemy taunt thee? 10
Will the adversary pour scorn on thy name
for ever?
Why dost thou hold back thy hand,   11
why keep thy right hand within thy
bosom?

But thou, O God, thou king from of old, 12
thou mighty conqueror all the world over,
by thy power thou didst cleave the sea- 13
monster in two
and break the sea-serpent's heads above
the waters;
thou didst crush Leviathan's many heads 14
and throw him to the sharks*q* for food.
Thou didst open channels for spring and 15
torrent;
thou didst dry up rivers never known to
fail.

f their lead: *prob. rdg.*; *Heb.* hither.   *g* and find . . . in them: *prob. rdg.*; *Heb.* obscure.   *h* yet . . .
rogues: *prob. rdg.*; *Heb.* those at ease for ever.   *i* *Or* And compared with thee.   *j* *Prob. rdg.*; *Heb.*
adds to tell all thy works.   *k* *Prob. rdg.*; *Heb.* adds thou didst redeem the tribe of thy possession.
l Now at last: *prob. rdg.*; *Heb.* Thy steps.   *m* the holy place: *or* thy meeting place.   *n* They . . .
down: *prob. rdg.*; *Heb.* unintelligible.   *o* holy places: *or* meeting places.   *p* what . . . us: *prob. rdg.*;
Heb. our signs.   *q* to the sharks: *prob. rdg.*; *Heb.* to a people, desert-dwellers.

16 The day is thine, and the night is thine also,
    thou didst ordain the light of moon and sun;
17   thou hast fixed all the regions of the earth;
    summer and winter, thou didst create them
    both.

18 Remember, O LORD, the taunts of the enemy,
    the scorn a savage nation pours on thy name.
19 Cast not to the beasts the soul that confesses
    thee;
    forget not for ever the sufferings of thy
    servants.
20 Look upon thy creatures:[r] they are filled with
    hatred,
    and earth is the haunt of violence.
21 Let not the oppressed be shamed and
    turned away;
    let the poor and the downtrodden praise thy
    name.
22 Rise up, O God, maintain thy own cause;
    remember how brutal men taunt thee all
    day long.
23 Ignore no longer the cries of thy assailants,
    the mounting clamour of those who defy
    thee.

75

God is judge

1 We give thee thanks, O God, we give thee
    thanks;
    thy name is brought very near to us
    in the story of thy wonderful deeds.

2   I seize the appointed time
    and then I judge mankind with justice.
3   When the earth rocks, with all who live
    on it,
    I make its pillars firm.
4   To the boastful I say, 'Boast no more',
    and to the wicked, 'Do not toss your
    proud horns:
5   toss not your horns against high heaven
    nor speak arrogantly against your
    Creator.'
6   No power from the east nor from the west,
    no power from the wilderness, can raise a
    man up.
7   For God is judge;
    he puts one man down and raises up another.
8   The LORD holds a cup in his hand,
    and the wine foams in it, hot with spice;
    he offers it to every man for drink,
    and all the wicked on earth must drain it to
    the dregs.
9   But I will glorify him for ever;
    I will sing praises to the God of Jacob.

10   I will break off the horns of the wicked,
    but the horns of the righteous shall be
    lifted high.

76

The greatness of Israel's God

    In Judah God is known,   1
    his name is great in Israel;
    his tent is pitched in Salem,   2
    in Zion his battle-quarters are set up.[s]
    He has broken the flashing arrows,   3
    shield and sword and weapons of war.

    Thou art terrible, O Lord, and mighty: 4
    men that lust for plunder stand aghast,   5
    the boldest swoon away,
    and the strongest cannot lift a hand.
    At thy rebuke, O God of Jacob,   6
    rider and horse fall senseless.
    Terrible art thou, O Lord;   7
    who can stand in thy presence when thou
    art angry?
    Thou didst give sentence out of heaven;   8
    the earth was afraid and kept silence.
    O God, at thy rising[t] in judgement   9
    to deliver all humble men on the earth,
    for all her fury Edom shall confess thee,   10
    and the remnant left in Hamath shall
    dance in worship.

    Make vows to the LORD your God, and pay   11
    them duly;
    let the peoples all around him bring their
    tribute;[u]
    for he breaks the spirit of princes,   12
    he is the terror of the kings on earth.

77

Musings on Israel's history

    I cried aloud to God,   1
    I cried to God, and he heard me.
    In the day of my distress I sought the Lord,   2
    and by night I lifted[v] my outspread hands in
    prayer.
    I lay sweating and nothing would cool me;
    I refused all comfort.
    When I called God to mind, I groaned;   3
    as I lay thinking, darkness came over my
    spirit.
    My eyelids were tightly closed;   4
    I was dazed and I could not speak.
    My thoughts went back to times long past,   5
    I remembered forgotten years;
    all night long I was in deep distress,   6
    as I lay thinking, my spirit was sunk in
    despair.

    Will the Lord reject us for evermore   7
    and never again show favour?
    Has his unfailing love now failed us utterly,   8
    must his promise time and again be un-
    fulfilled?
    Has God forgotten to be gracious,   9
    has he in anger withheld his mercies?

---

[r] *thy creatures: prob. rdg.; Heb.* the covenant, because.   [s] *are set up: prob. rdg.; Heb.* thither *(at begin-*
ning of verse 3).   [t] O God . . . *rising: prob. rdg.; Heb.* When God rises.   [u] *Prob. rdg.; Heb. adds*
for the terror *(cp. verse 12).*   [v] I lifted: *prob. rdg.; Heb. om.*

10 'Has his right hand', I said, 'lost its grasp?
    Does it hang powerless,^w the arm of the
    Most High?'

11 But then, O Lord, I call to mind thy deeds;^x
    I recall thy wonderful acts in times gone by.

12   I meditate upon thy works
    and muse on all that thou hast done.

13 O God, thy way is holy;
    what god is so great as our God?

14 Thou art the God who workest miracles;
    thou hast shown the nations thy power.

15 With thy strong arm thou didst redeem thy
    people,
    the sons of Jacob and Joseph.

16   The waters saw thee, O God,
    they saw thee and writhed in anguish;
    the ocean was troubled to its depths.

17 The clouds poured water, the skies thun-
    dered,
    thy arrows flashed hither and thither.

18   The sound of thy thunder was in the
    whirlwind,^y
    thy lightnings lit up the world,
    earth shook and quaked.

19 Thy path was through the sea, thy way
    through mighty waters,
    and no man marked thy footsteps.

20   Thou didst guide thy people like a flock of
    sheep,
    under the hand of Moses and Aaron.

78

Lessons from Israel's history

1   Mark my teaching, O my people,
    listen to the words I am to speak.

2   I will tell you a story with a meaning,
    I will expound the riddle of things past,

3   things that we have heard and know,
    and our fathers have repeated to us.

4   From their sons we will not hide
    the praises of the Lord and his might
    nor the wonderful acts he has performed;
    then they shall repeat them to the next
    generation.

5   He laid on Jacob a solemn charge
    and established a law in Israel,
    which he commanded our fathers
    to teach their sons,

6   that it might be known to a future genera-
    tion,
    to children yet unborn,
    and these would repeat it to their sons in
    turn.

7   He charged them to put their trust in God,
    to hold his great acts ever in mind
    and to keep all his commandments;

8   not to do as their fathers did,
    a disobedient and rebellious race,
    a generation with no firm purpose,
    with hearts not fixed steadfastly on God.

The men of Ephraim, bowmen all and 9
    marksmen,
turned and ran in the hour of battle.

They had not kept God's covenant 10
    and had refused to live by his law;
they forgot all that he had done 11
    and the wonderful acts which he had
    shown them.

He did wonders in their fathers' sight 12
in the land of Egypt, the country of
    Zoan:
he divided the sea and took them 13
    through it,
making the water stand up like banks on
    either side.

He led them with a cloud by day 14
    and all night long with a glowing fire.
He cleft the rock in the wilderness 15
    and gave them water to drink, abundant
    as the sea;
he brought streams out of the cliff 16
    and made water run down like rivers.
But they sinned against him yet again: 17
    in the desert they defied the Most High,
they tried God's patience wilfully, 18
    demanding food to satisfy their hunger.
They vented their grievance against God 19
    and said,
'Can God spread a table in the wilder-
    ness?'

When he struck a rock, water gushed 20
    out
until the gullies overflowed;
they said, 'Can he give bread as well,
    can he provide meat for his people?'

When he heard this, the Lord was filled with 21
    fury:
fire raged against Jacob,
anger blazed up against Israel,
because they put no trust in God 22
    and had no faith in his power to save.
Then he gave orders to the skies above 23
    and threw open heaven's doors,
he rained down manna for them to eat 24
    and gave them the grain of heaven.
So men ate the bread of angels; 25
he sent them food to their heart's desire.
He let loose the east wind from heaven 26
    and drove the south wind by his power;
he rained meat like a dust-storm upon 27
    them,
flying birds like the sand of the sea-
    shore,
which he made settle all over the camp 28
    round the tents where they lived.
So the people ate and were well filled, 29
    for he had given them what they craved.
Yet they did not abandon their com- 30
    plaints.^z
even while the food was in their mouths.

*w lost . . . powerless: prob. rdg.; Heb. unintelligible.
the Lord, for.*   *y Or in the chariot-wheels.*

x Prob. rdg.; Heb. then I call to mind the deeds of

z Or craving.

31 Then the anger of God blazed up against
      them;
   he spread death among their stoutest
      men
   and brought the young men of Israel to
      the ground.

32 In spite of all, they persisted in their
      sin
   and had no faith in his wonderful acts.
33 So in one moment he snuffed out their
      lives
   and ended their years in calamity.
34 When he struck them, they began to seek
      him,
   they would turn and look eagerly for
      God;
35 they remembered that God was their
      Creator,
   that God Most High was their deliverer.
36   But still they beguiled him with words
   and deceived him with fine speeches;
37 they were not loyal to him in their hearts
   nor were they faithful to his covenant.
38 Yet he wiped out their guilt
   and did not smother his own[a] natural
      affection;
   often he restrained his wrath
   and did not rouse his anger to its height.
39 He remembered that they were only mortal
      men,
   who pass by like a wind and never return.

40 How often they rebelled against him in the
      wilderness
   and grieved him in the desert!
41 Again and again they tried God's patience
   and provoked the Holy One of Israel.
42 They did not remember his prowess
   on the day when he saved them from the
      enemy,
43 how he set his signs in Egypt,
   his portents in the land of Zoan.
44 He turned their streams into blood,
   and they could not drink the running
      water.
45 He sent swarms of flies which devoured
      them,
   and frogs which brought devastation;
46   he gave their harvest over to locusts
   and their produce to the grubs;
47 he killed their vines with hailstones
   and their figs with torrents of rain;
48 he abandoned their cattle to the plague
   and their beasts to the arrows of pesti-
      lence.
49 He loosed upon them the violence of his
      anger,
   wrath and enmity and rage,
   launching those messengers of evil
50-51 to open a way for his fury.

He struck down all the first-born in
   Egypt,
the flower of their manhood in the tents of
   Ham,
not shielding their lives from death
but abandoning their bodies to the plague.
But he led out his own people like sheep   52
and guided them like a flock in the wilderness.
He led them in safety and they were not 53
   afraid,
and the sea closed over their enemies.
He brought them to his holy mountain,   54
the hill which his right hand had won;
he drove out nations before them,   55
he allotted their lands to Israel as a possession
and settled his tribes in their dwellings.
Yet they tried God's patience and rebelled 56
   against him;
they did not keep the commands of the Most
   High;
they were renegades, traitors like their 57
   fathers,
they changed, they went slack like a bow.
   They provoked him to anger with their 58
      hill-shrines
   and roused his jealousy with their carved
      images.
When God heard this, he put them out of 59
   mind
and utterly rejected Israel.
   He forsook his home at Shiloh,   60
   the tabernacle in which he dwelt among
      men;
   he surrendered the symbol of his strength 61
      into captivity
   and his pride into enemy hands;
   he gave his people over to the sword   62
      and put his own possession out of
         mind.
Fire devoured his young men,   63
and his maidens could raise no lament for
   them;
his priests fell by the sword,   64
and his widows could not weep.

Then the Lord awoke as a sleeper awakes, 65
like a warrior heated with wine;
he struck his foes in the back parts   66
and brought perpetual shame upon them.
   He despised the clan of Joseph   67
   and did not choose the tribe of Ephraim;
   he chose the tribe of Judah   68
   and Mount Zion which he loved;
he built his sanctuary high as the heavens, 69
founded like the earth to last for ever.
He chose David to be his servant   70
   and took him from the sheepfolds;
   he brought him from minding the ewes   71
   to be the shepherd of his people Jacob;[b]

---

a his own: prob. rdg.; Heb. om.   b Prob. rdg.; Heb. adds and Israel his possession.

72   and he shepherded them in singleness of
      heart
      and guided them with skilful hand.

79

A lament over the destruction of Jerusalem

1 O God, the heathen have set foot in thy
   domain,
      defiled thy holy temple
      and laid Jerusalem in ruins.
2   They have thrown out the dead bodies of
      thy servants
      to feed the birds of the air;
      they have made thy loyal servants carrion
      for wild beasts.
3 Their blood is spilled all round Jerusalem
   like water,
      and there they lie unburied.
4   We suffer the contempt of our neigh-
      bours,
      the gibes and mockery of all around us.
5 How long, O LORD, wilt thou be roused to
   such fury?
      Must thy jealousy rage like a fire?
6 Pour out thy wrath over nations which do
   not know thee
   and over kingdoms which do not invoke
   thee by name;
7 see how they have devoured Jacob and laid
   waste his homesteads.

Do not remember against us the guilt of 8
   past generations
   but let thy compassion come swiftly to
   meet us,
   we have been brought so low.
Help us, O God our saviour, for the honour 9
   of thy name;
   for thy name's sake deliver us and wipe
   out our sins.
Why should the nations ask, 'Where is their 10
   God?'
   Let thy vengeance for the bloody slaughter
   of thy servants
   fall on those nations before our very eyes.
Let the groaning of the captives reach thy 11
   presence
   and in thy great might set free death's
   prisoners.
As for the contempt our neighbours pour 12
   on thee, O Lord,
   turn it back sevenfold on their own heads.
Then we thy people, the flock which thou 13
   dost shepherd,
   will give thee thanks for ever
and repeat thy praise to every generation.

80

The vine: an allegory

   Hear us, O shepherd of Israel,   1
who leadest Joseph like a flock of sheep.

Show thyself, thou that art throned on the cherubim,

2 to Ephraim and to Benjamin.
Rouse thy victorious might from slumber,*c*
come to our rescue.

3 Restore us, O God,
and make thy face shine upon us that we may be saved.

4 O Lord God of Hosts,
how long wilt thou resist thy people's prayer?

5 Thou hast made sorrow their daily bread
and tears of threefold grief their drink.

6 Thou hast humbled us before our neighbours,
and our enemies mock us to their hearts' content.

7 O God of Hosts, restore us;
make thy face shine upon us that we may be saved.

8 Thou didst bring a vine out of Egypt;
thou didst drive out nations and plant it;

9 thou didst clear the ground before it,
so that it made good roots and filled the land.

10 The mountains were covered with its shade,
and its branches were like those of mighty cedars.

11 It put out boughs all the way to the Sea
and its shoots as far as the River.

12 Why hast thou broken down the wall round it
so that every passer-by can pluck its fruit?

13 The wild boar from the thickets gnaws it,
and swarming insects from the fields feed on it.

14 O God of Hosts, once more look down from heaven,
take thought for this vine and tend it,

15 this stock that thy right hand has planted.*d*

16 Let them that set fire to it or cut it down
perish before thy angry face.

17 Let thy hand rest upon the man at thy right side,
the man whom thou hast made strong for thy service.

18 We have not turned back from thee,
so grant us new life, and we will invoke thee by name.

19 Lord God of Hosts, restore us;
make thy face shine upon us that we may be saved.

81

God appeals to Israel

1 Sing out in praise of God our refuge,*e*
acclaim the God of Jacob.

2 Take pipe and tabor,
take tuneful harp and lute.

3 Blow the horn for the new month,
for the full moon on the day of our pilgrim-feast.

4 This is a law for Israel,
an ordinance of the God of Jacob,

5 laid as a solemn charge on Joseph
when he came out of Egypt.*f*

6 When I lifted the load from his shoulders,
his hands let go the builder's basket.

7 When you cried to me in distress, I rescued you;
unseen, I answered you in thunder.
I tested you at the waters of Meribah,
where I opened your mouths and filled them.*g*

16 I fed Israel*h* with the finest wheat-flour
and satisfied him with honey from the rocks.

8 Listen, my people, while I give you a solemn charge—
do but listen to me, O Israel:

9 you shall have no strange god
nor bow down to any foreign god;

10 I am the Lord your God
who brought you up from Egypt.*j*

11 But my people did not listen to my words
and Israel would have none of me;

12 so I sent them off, stubborn as they were,
to follow their own devices.

13 If my people would but listen to me,
if Israel would only conform to my ways,

14 I would soon bring their enemies to their knees
and lay a heavy hand upon their persecutors.

15 Let those who hate them*k* come cringing to them,
and meet with everlasting troubles.*l*

82

In the court of heaven

1 God takes his stand in the court of heaven
to deliver judgement among the gods themselves.

2 How long will you judge unjustly
and show favour to the wicked?

3 You ought to give judgement for the weak and the orphan,
and see right done to the destitute and downtrodden,

4 you ought to rescue the weak and the poor,
and save them from the clutches of wicked men.

5 But you know nothing, you understand nothing,
you walk in the dark
while earth's foundations are giving way.

c from slumber: prob. rdg.; Heb. and Manasseh.
hast made strong for thy service (*cp. verse 17*).   *d Prob. rdg.; Heb. adds* and on the son whom thou
unfamiliar language.   *g Line transposed from end of verse 10.*   *e Or* strength.   *f Prob. rdg.; Heb. adds* I hear an
him.   *i Verse transposed.*   *j See note on verse 7.*   *h* I fed Israel: *prob. rdg.; Heb.* He fed
hate the Lord.   *l Verse 16 transposed to follow verse 7.*   *k* those . . . them: *prob. rdg.; Heb.* those who

6 This is my sentence: Gods you may be,
  sons all of you of a high god,*m*
7 yet you shall die as men die;*n*
  princes fall, every one of them, and so
  shall you.

8 Arise, O God, and judge the earth;
  for thou dost pass all nations through thy
  sieve.

83

Prayer during national distress

1 Rest not, O God;
  O God, be neither silent nor still,
2 for thy enemies are making a tumult,
  and those that hate thee carry their heads
  high.
3 They devise cunning schemes against thy
  people
  and conspire against those thou hast made
  thy treasure:
4 'Come, away with them,' they cry,
  'let them be a nation no longer,
  let Israel's name be remembered no
  more.'
5 With one mind they have agreed together
  to make a league against thee:
6 the families of Edom, the Ishmaelites,
  Moabites and Hagarenes,
7 Gebal, Ammon and Amalek,
  Philistia and the citizens of Tyre,
8 Asshur too their ally,
  all of them lending aid to the descendants
  of Lot.
9 Deal with them as with Sisera,
  as with Jabin by the torrent of Kishon,
10 who fell vanquished as Midian*o* fell at
  En-harod,*p*
  and were spread on the battlefield like
  dung.
11 Make their princes like Oreb and Zeeb,
  make all their nobles like Zebah and
  Zalmunna;
12 for they said, 'We will seize for ourselves
  all the pastures of God's people.'
13 Scatter them, O God, like thistledown,
  like chaff before the wind.
14 Like fire raging through the forest
  or flames which blaze across the hills,
15 hunt them down with thy tempest,
  and dismay them with thy storm-wind.
16 Heap shame upon their heads, O LORD,
  until they confess the greatness of thy
  name.
17 Let them be abashed, and live in perpetual dismay;
  let them feel their shame and perish.
18 So let them learn that thou alone art LORD,
  God Most High over all the earth.

84

Praise of God's house

How dear is thy dwelling-place,   1
  thou LORD of Hosts!
I pine, I faint with longing   2
for the courts of the LORD's temple;
my whole being cries out with joy
to the living God.
Even the sparrow finds a home,   3
and the swallow has her nest,
where she rears her brood beside thy altars,
O LORD of Hosts, my King and my God.
Happy are those who dwell in thy house;   4
they never cease from praising thee.
Happy the men whose refuge is in thee,   5
whose hearts are set on the pilgrim ways*q*!
As they pass through the thirsty valley   6
they find water from a spring;
and the LORD provides even men who lose
  their way
with pools to quench their thirst.*r*
So they pass on from outer wall to inner,   7
and the God of gods shows himself in
  Zion.

O LORD God of Hosts, hear my prayer;   8
listen, O God of Jacob.
O God, look upon our lord the king   9
and accept thy anointed prince with
  favour.

Better one day in thy courts   10
than a thousand days at home;
better to linger by the threshold of God's
  house
than to live in the dwellings of the wicked.
The LORD God is a battlement and a   11
  shield;
grace and honour are his to give.
The LORD will hold back no good thing
from those whose life is blameless.

O LORD of Hosts,   12
happy the man who trusts in thee!

85

Words of peace

LORD, thou hast been gracious to thy   1
  land
and turned the tide of Jacob's fortunes.
Thou hast forgiven the guilt of thy people   2
and put away all their sins.
Thou hast taken back all thy anger   3
and turned from thy bitter wrath.

Turn back to us, O God our saviour,   4
and cancel thy displeasure.
Wilt thou be angry with us for ever?   5
Must thy wrath last for all generations?

---

m Or of the Most High.   *n Or* as Adam died.
p En-harod: *prob. rdg., cp. Judg. 7. 1; Heb.* Endor.
. . . thirst: *prob. rdg.; Heb. obscure.*

o as Midian: *transposed from previous verse.*
q are set . . . ways: *or* high praises fill.   *r* they find

6 Wilt thou not give us new life
   that thy people may rejoice in thee?
7 O Lord, show us thy true love
   and grant us thy deliverance.

8 Let me hear the words of the Lord:
   are they not[s] words of peace,
   peace to his people and his loyal servants
   and to all who turn and trust in him?
9 Deliverance is near to those who worship
   him,
   so that glory may dwell in our land.
10 Love and fidelity have come together;
   justice and peace join hands.
11 Fidelity springs up from earth
   and justice looks down from heaven.
12 The Lord will add prosperity,
   and our land shall yield its harvest.
13 Justice shall go in front of him
   and the path before his feet shall be peace.[t]

86

Prayer for protection and guidance

1 Turn to me, Lord, and answer;
   I am downtrodden and poor.
2 Guard me, for I am constant and true;
   save thy servant who puts his trust in thee.
3 O Lord my God,[u] show me thy favour;
   I call to thee all day long.
4 Fill thy servant's heart with joy, O Lord,
   for I lift up my heart to thee.
5 Thou, O Lord, art kind and forgiving,
   full of true love for all who cry to thee.
6 Listen, O Lord, to my prayer
   and hear my pleading.
7 In the day of my distress I call on thee;
   for thou wilt answer me.

8 Among the gods not one is like thee,
   O Lord,
   no deeds are like thine.
9 All the nations thou hast made, O Lord, will
   come,
   will bow down before thee and honour thy
   name;
10 for thou art great, thy works are wonderful,
   thou alone art God.

11 Guide me, O Lord,
   that I may be true to thee and follow thy
   path;
   let me be one in heart
   with those who revere thy name.
12 I will praise thee, O Lord my God, with all
   my heart
   and honour thy name for ever.

For thy true love stands high above me; 13
thou hast rescued my soul from the depths
   of Sheol.
O God, proud men attack me;   14
   a mob of ruffians seek my life
   and give no thought to thee.
Thou, Lord, art God, compassionate and 15
   gracious,
   forbearing, ever constant and true.
Turn towards me and show me thy favour; 16
   grant thy slave protection
   and rescue thy slave-girl's son.
Give me proof of thy kindness;   17
   let those who hate thee see to their shame
that thou, O Lord, hast been my help and
   comfort.

87[v]

Praise of Zion

The Lord loves the gates of Zion   1-2
more than all the dwellings of Jacob;
her[w] foundations are laid upon holy hills,
and he has made her his home.[x]   4-5
I will count Egypt and Babylon among my
   friends;
Philistine, Tyrian and Nubian shall be[y]
   there;
and Zion shall be called a mother
   in whom men of every race are born.
The Lord shall write against each in the 6
   roll of nations:
'This one was born in her.'
Singers and dancers alike all chant[z] your 7
   praises,
proclaiming glorious things of you, O city 3
   of God.

88

Face to face with death

O Lord, my God, by day I call for help,[a] 1
by night I cry aloud in thy presence.
Let my prayer come before thee,   2
hear my loud lament;
for I have had my fill of woes,   3
and they have brought me to the threshold
   of Sheol.
I am numbered with those who go down 4
   to the abyss
and have become like a man beyond help,
like a man who lies dead[b]   5
or the slain who sleep in the grave,
whom thou rememberest no more
because they are cut off from thy care.
Thou hast plunged me into the lowest 6
   abyss,
in dark places, in the depths.

7 Thy wrath rises against me,
   thou hast turned on me the full force of
      thy anger.[c]
8 Thou hast taken all my friends far from
      me,
   and made me loathsome to them.
   I am in prison and cannot escape;
9 my eyes are failing and dim with anguish.
   I have called upon thee, O LORD, every
      day
   and spread out my hands in prayer to
      thee.

10 Dost thou work wonders for the dead?
    Shall their company rise up and praise
       thee?
11 Will they speak of thy faithful love in the
       grave,
    of thy sure help in the place of Destruc-
       tion?
12 Will thy wonders be known in the dark,
    thy victories in the land of oblivion?

13 But, LORD, I cry to thee,
    my prayer comes before thee in the
       morning.
14 Why hast thou cast me off, O LORD,
    why dost thou hide thy face from me?
15 I have suffered from boyhood and come near
       to death;
    I have borne thy terrors, I cower beneath
       thy blows.
16 Thy burning fury has swept over me,
    thy onslaughts have put me to silence;
17 all the day long they surge round me like
       a flood,
    they engulf me in a moment.
18 Thou hast taken lover and friend far from
       me,
    and parted me from my companions.

89

The LORD's covenant with David

1 I will sing the story of thy love, O LORD, for
    ever;
    I will proclaim thy faithfulness to all genera-
       tions.
2 Thy true love is firm as the ancient earth,[d]
    thy faithfulness fixed as the heavens.
5[e] The heavens praise thy wonders, O LORD,
    and the council of the holy ones exalts thy
       faithfulness.
6 In the skies who is there like the LORD,
    who like the LORD in the court of heaven,
7 like God who is dreaded among the
       assembled holy ones,
    great and terrible above all who stand
       about him?

O LORD God of Hosts, who is like thee?   8
Thy strength[f] and faithfulness, O LORD,
    surround thee.
Thou rulest the surging sea,   9
    calming the turmoil[g] of its waves.
Thou didst crush the monster Rahab with a 10
    mortal blow
    and scatter thy enemies with thy strong
       arm.
Thine are the heavens, the earth is thine also; 11
    the world with all that is in it is of thy
       foundation.
Thou didst create Zaphon and Amanus;[h]   12
Tabor and Hermon echo thy name.
    Strength of arm and valour are thine;   13
    thy hand is mighty, thy right hand lifted
       high;
       thy throne is built upon righteousness and 14
          justice,
    true love and faithfulness herald thy coming.

Happy the people who have learnt to   15
    acclaim thee,
    who walk, O LORD, in the light of thy
       presence!
In thy name they shall rejoice all day long; 16
    thy righteousness shall lift them up.
Thou art thyself the strength in which they 17
    glory;
    through thy favour we hold our heads
       high.
The LORD, he is our shield;   18
    the Holy One of Israel, he is our king.

Then didst thou announce in a vision   19
    and declare to thy faithful servants:
I have made a covenant with him I have   3
    chosen,
I have sworn to my servant David:
'I will establish your posterity for ever,   4
I will make your throne endure for all
    generations.'
I have endowed a warrior with princely
    gifts,
so that the youth I have chosen towers over
    his people.
I have discovered David my servant;   20
I have anointed him with my holy oil.
My hand shall be ready to help him   21
    and my arm to give him strength.
No enemy shall strike at him   22
    and no rebel bring him low;
I will shatter his foes before him   23
    and vanquish those who hate him.
My faithfulness and true love shall be   24
    with him
    and through my name he shall hold his
       head high.
I will extend his rule over the Sea   25
    and his dominion as far as the River.

c anger: *or* waves.   d Thy . . . earth: *prob. rdg.; Heb.* Thou hast said for ever true love shall be made firm.
e *Verses 3 and 4 transposed to follow* servants *in verse 19.*   f Thy strength: *prob. rdg.; Heb. obscure.*
g turmoil: *prob. rdg.; Heb. obscure.*   h Amanus: *prob. rdg.; Heb.* right hand *or* south.

26 He will say to me, 'Thou art my father,
      my God, my rock and my safe refuge.'
27 And I will name him my first-born,
      highest among the kings of the earth.
28 I will maintain my love for him for ever
      and be faithful in my covenant with him.
29 I will establish his posterity for ever
      and his throne as long as the heavens
      endure.
30 If his sons forsake my law
      and do not conform to my judgements,
31 if they renounce my statutes
      and do not observe my commands,
32 I will punish their disobedience with the rod
      and their iniquity with lashes.
33 Yet I will not deprive him of my true love
      nor let my faithfulness prove false;
34 I will not renounce my covenant
      nor change my promised purpose.
35 I have sworn by my holiness once and for
      all,
      I will not break my word to David:
36 his posterity shall continue for ever,
      his throne before me like the sun;
37 it shall be sure for ever as the moon's
      return,
      faithful so long as the skies remain.*i*

38 Yet thou hast rejected thy anointed king,
      thou hast spurned him and raged against
      him,*j*
39 thou hast denounced the covenant with thy
      servant,
      defiled his crown and flung it to the ground.
40 Thou hast breached his walls
      and laid his fortresses in ruin;
41 all who pass by plunder him,
      and he suffers the taunts of his neighbours.
42 Thou hast increased the power of his
      enemies
      and brought joy to all his foes;
43 thou hast let his sharp sword be driven
      back
      and left him without help in the battle.
44 Thou hast put an end to his glorious rule*k*
      and hurled his throne to the ground;
45 thou hast cut short the days of his youth and
      vigour
      and covered him with shame.

46 How long, O LORD, wilt thou hide thyself
      from sight?
      How long must thy wrath blaze like fire?
47 Remember that I shall not live for ever;*l*
      hast thou created man in vain?
48 What man shall live and not see death
      or save himself from the power of Sheol?
49 Where are those former acts of thy love,
      O Lord,
      those faithful promises given to David?

Remember, O Lord, the taunts hurled at 50
      thy servant,
how I have borne in my heart the calumnies
      of the nations;*m*
so have thy enemies taunted us, O LORD, 51
      taunted the successors of thy anointed
      king.

Blessed is the LORD for ever.   52

      Amen, Amen.

BOOK 4

90

The everlasting God and mortal man

Lord, thou hast been our refuge   1
      from generation to generation.
      Before the mountains were brought forth, 2
      or earth and world were born in travail,
from age to age everlasting thou art God.
      Thou turnest man back into dust;   3
      'Turn back,' thou sayest, 'you sons of
      men';
      for in thy sight a thousand years are as 4
      yesterday;
      a night-watch passes, and thou hast cut 5
      them off;
      they are like a dream at daybreak,
      they fade like grass which springs up*n* with 6
      the morning
      but when evening comes is parched and
      withered.
So we are brought to an end by thy anger   7
      and silenced by thy wrath.
      Thou dost lay bare our iniquities before 8
      thee
      and our lusts in the full light of thy
      presence.
      All our days go by under the shadow of 9
      thy wrath;
      our years die away like a murmur.
Seventy years is the span of our life,   10
      eighty if our strength holds;*o*
      the hurrying years are labour and sorrow,
      so quickly they pass and are forgotten.
      Who feels the power of thy anger,   11
      who feels thy wrath like those that fear
      thee?
Teach us to order our days rightly,   12
      that we may enter the gate of wisdom.
      How long, O LORD?   13
      Relent, and take pity on thy servants.
      Satisfy us with thy love when morning 14
      breaks,
      that we may sing for joy and be glad all
      our days.

---

i so long . . . remain: prob. rdg.; Heb. a witness in the skies.
mind.   k his glorious rule: prob. rdg.; Heb. from his purity.
m the calumnies . . . nations: prob. rdg.; Heb. all of many peoples.
away.   o Or eighty at the most.

j raged against him: or put him out of
l live for ever: prob. rdg.; Heb. obscure.
n Prob. rdg.; Heb. adds and passes

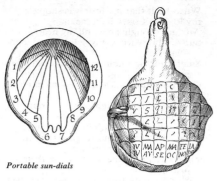

Portable sun-dials

You shall step on asp and cobra, 13
you shall tread safely on snake and serpent.

Because his love is set on me, I will deliver 14
him;
I will lift him beyond danger, for he knows
me by my name.
When he calls upon me, I will answer; 15
I will be with him in time of trouble;
I will rescue him and bring him to honour.
I will satisfy him with long life 16
to enjoy the fullness of my salvation.

15 Repay us days of gladness for our days of
suffering,
for the years thou hast humbled us.
16 Show thy servants thy deeds
and their children thy majesty.
17 May all delightful things be ours, O Lord
our God;
establish firmly all we do.

91

Trust in God

1 You that live in the shelter of the Most
High
and lodge under the shadow of the
Almighty,
2 who say, 'The LORD is my safe retreat,
my God the fastness in which I trust';
3 he himself will snatch you away
from fowler's snare or raging tempest.
4 He will cover you with his pinions,
and you shall find safety beneath his wings;
5 you shall not fear the hunters' trap by
night
or the arrow that flies by day,
6 the pestilence that stalks in darkness
or the plague raging at noonday.
7 A thousand may fall at your side,
ten thousand close at hand,
but you it shall not touch;
his truth[p] will be your shield and your
rampart.[q]
8 With your own eyes you shall see all this;
you shall watch the punishment of the
wicked.
9 For you, the LORD is a[r] safe retreat;
you have made the Most High your refuge.
10 No disaster shall befall you,
no calamity shall come upon your home.
11 For he has charged his angels
to guard you wherever you go,
12 to lift you on their hands
for fear you should strike your foot against
a stone.

92

The LORD's goodness and righteousness

O LORD, it is good to give thee thanks, 1
to sing psalms to thy name, O Most
High,
to declare thy love in the morning 2
and thy constancy every night,
to the music of a ten-stringed lute, 3
to the sounding chords of the harp.
Thy acts, O LORD, fill me with exultation; 4
I shout in triumph at thy mighty deeds.
How great are thy deeds, O LORD! 5
How fathomless thy thoughts!

He who does not know this is a brute, 6
a fool is he who does not understand this:
that though the wicked grow like grass 7
and every evildoer prospers,
they will be destroyed for ever.
While thou, LORD, dost reign on high 8
eternally,
thy foes will surely perish, 9
all evildoers will be scattered.

I lift my head high, like a wild ox tossing its 10
horn;
I am anointed richly with oil.
I gloat over all who speak ill of me, 11
I listen for the downfall of my cruel foes.
The righteous flourish like a palm-tree, 12
they grow tall as a cedar on Lebanon;
planted as they are in the house of the 13
LORD,
they flourish in the courts of our God,
vigorous in old age like trees full of sap, 14
luxuriant, wide-spreading,
eager to declare that the LORD is just, 15
the LORD my rock,[s] in whom there is no
unrighteousness.

93

The LORD is king

The LORD is king; he is clothed in majesty; 1
the LORD clothes himself with might and
fastens on his belt of wrath.

p Or his arm.   *q his truth . . . rampart: transposed from end of verse 4.*   *r Prob. rdg.; Heb. my.*
s Or creator.

Thou hast fixed the earth immovable and
firm,
2 thy throne firm from of old;
from all eternity thou art God.
3 O Lord, the ocean lifts up, the ocean lifts
up its clamour;
the ocean lifts up[t] its pounding waves.
4 The Lord on high is mightier far
than the noise of great waters,
mightier than the breakers of the sea.

5 Thy law stands firm, and holiness is the
beauty of thy temple,
while time shall last, O Lord.

94

The teacher of mankind

1 O Lord, thou God of vengeance,
thou God of vengeance, show thyself.
2 Rise up, judge of the earth;
punish the arrogant as they deserve.
3 How long shall the wicked, O Lord,
how long shall the wicked exult?
4 Evildoers are full of bluster,
boasting and swaggering;
5 they beat down thy people, O Lord,
and oppress thy chosen nation;
6 they murder the widow and the stranger
and do the fatherless to death;
7 they say, 'The Lord does not see,
the God of Jacob pays no heed.'
8 Pay heed yourselves, most brutish of the
people;
you fools, when will you be wise?
9 Does he that planted the ear not hear,
he that moulded the eye not see?
10 Shall not he that instructs the nations
correct them?
The teacher of mankind, has he no[u]
knowledge?
11 The Lord knows the thoughts of man,
that they are but a puff of wind.

12 Happy the man whom thou dost instruct,
O Lord,
and teach out of thy law,
13 giving him respite from adversity
until a pit is dug for the wicked.
14 The Lord will not abandon his people
nor forsake his chosen nation;
15 for righteousness still informs his judgement,[v]
and all upright men follow it.

16 Who is on my side against these sinful
men?
Who will stand up for me against these
evildoers?
17 If the Lord had not been my helper,
I should soon have slept in the silent grave.

When I felt that my foot was slipping, 18
thy love, O Lord, held me up.
Anxious thoughts may fill my heart, 19
but thy presence is my joy and my consolation.
Shall sanctimonious calumny call thee 20
partner,
or he that contrives a mischief under cover
of law?
For they put the righteous on trial[w] for 21
his life
and condemn to death innocent men.
But the Lord has been my strong tower, 22
and God my rock of refuge;
our God requites the wicked for their in- 23
justice,
the Lord puts them to silence for their
misdeeds.

95

Call to worship

Come! Let us raise a joyful song to the 1
Lord,
a shout of triumph to the Rock of our
salvation.
Let us come into his presence with thanks- 2
giving,
and sing him psalms of triumph.
For the Lord is a great God, 3
a great king over all gods;
the farthest places of the earth are in his 4
hands,
and the folds of the hills are his;
the sea is his, he made it; 5
the dry land fashioned by his hands is
his.
Come! Let us throw ourselves at his feet 6
in homage,
let us kneel before the Lord who made
us;
for he is our God, 7
we are his people, we the flock he shepherds.
You shall know[x] his power today
if you will listen to his voice.

Do not grow stubborn, as you were at 8
Meribah,[y]
as at the time of Massah[z] in the wilderness,
when your forefathers challenged me, 9
tested me and saw for themselves all that
I did.
For forty years I was indignant 10
with that generation, and I said:
They are a people whose hearts are astray,
and they will not discern my ways.
As I swore in my anger: 11
They shall never enter my rest.

---

*t the ocean lifts up: or let the ocean lift up.   u no: prob. rdg.; Heb. om.   v for . . . judgement: prob.
rdg.; Heb. for judgement will return as far as righteousness.   w they put . . . trial: prob. rdg.; Heb. they cut
the righteous.   x You shall know: prob. rdg.; Heb. om.   y That is Dispute.   z That is Challenge.*

96

A new song

1[a] Sing a new song to the LORD;
   sing to the LORD, all men on earth.
2 Sing to the LORD and bless his name,
   proclaim his triumph day by day.
3 Declare his glory among the nations,
   his marvellous deeds among all peoples.
4 Great is the LORD and worthy of all praise;
   he is more to be feared than all gods.
5 For the gods of the nations are idols
      every one;
   but the LORD made the heavens.
6 Majesty and splendour attend him,
   might and beauty are in his sanctuary.

7 Ascribe to the LORD, you families of
      nations,
   ascribe to the LORD glory and might;
8 ascribe to the LORD the glory due to his
      name,
   bring a gift and come into his courts.
9 Bow down to the LORD in the splendour
      of holiness,[b]
   and dance in his honour, all men on
      earth.
10 Declare among the nations, 'The LORD is
      king.
   He has fixed the earth firm, immovable;
   he will judge the peoples justly.'
11 Let the heavens rejoice and the earth exult,
   let the sea roar and all the creatures in it,
12 let the fields exult and all that is in
      them;
   then let all the trees of the forest shout for
      joy
13 before the LORD when he comes to judge
      the earth.
   He will judge the earth with righteous-
      ness
   and the peoples in good faith.

97

The LORD is king

1 The LORD is king, let the earth be glad,
   let coasts and islands all rejoice.
2 Cloud and mist enfold him,
   righteousness and justice
   are the foundation of his throne.
3 Fire goes before him
   and burns up his enemies all around.
4 The world is lit up beneath his lightning-
      flash;
   the earth sees it and writhes in pain.
5 The mountains melt like wax as the LORD
      approaches,
   the Lord of all the earth.
6 The heavens proclaim his righteousness,
   and all peoples see his glory.

7 Let all who worship images, who vaunt their
   idols,
   be put to shame;
   bow down, all gods,[c] before him.

8 Zion heard and rejoiced, the cities of Judah
   were glad
   at thy judgements, O LORD.
9 For thou, LORD, art most high over all the
   earth,
   far exalted above all gods.

10 The LORD loves[d] those who hate evil;
   he keeps his loyal servants safe
   and rescues them from the wicked.
11 A harvest of light is sown for the righteous,
   and joy for all good men.
12 You that are righteous, rejoice in the
      LORD
   and praise his holy name.

98

When the LORD comes

1 Sing a new song to the LORD,
   for he has done marvellous deeds;
   his right hand and holy arm have won him
      victory.
2 The LORD has made his victory known;
   he has displayed his righteousness to all
      the nations.
3 He has remembered his constancy,
   his love for the house of Israel.
   All the ends of the earth have seen
      the victory of our God.

4 Acclaim the LORD, all men on earth,
   break into songs of joy, sing psalms.
5 Sing psalms in the LORD's honour with
      the harp,
   with the harp and with the music of the
      psaltery.
6 With trumpet and echoing horn
   acclaim the presence of the LORD our
      king.
7 Let the sea roar and all its creatures,
   the world and those who dwell in it.
8 Let the rivers clap their hands,
   let the hills sing aloud together
9 before the LORD; for he comes
   to judge the earth.
   He will judge the world with righteous-
      ness
   and the peoples in justice.

99

The LORD is king

1 The LORD is king, the peoples are perturbed;
   he is throned on the cherubim, earth quivers.
2 The LORD is great in Zion;
   he is exalted above all the peoples.

---

a Verses 1–13: cp. 1 Chr. 16. 23–33.   *b the splendour of holiness: or holy vestments.*   *c bow . . . gods:*
or all gods bow down . . .   *d The LORD loves: prob. rdg.; Heb. Lovers of the LORD.*

H *

3 They extol his[e] name as great and terrible;
4 he is holy, he is mighty,
   a king who loves justice.

Thou hast established justice and equity;
thou hast dealt righteously in Jacob.
5 Exalt the LORD our God,
   bow down before his footstool;
   he is holy.

6 Moses and Aaron among his priests,
   and Samuel among those who call on his
     name,
   called to the LORD, and he answered.
7 He spoke to them in a pillar of cloud;
   they followed his teaching and kept the
     law he gave them.
8 Thou, O LORD our God, thou didst answer
     them;
   thou wast a God who forgave all their mis-
     deeds
   and held them innocent.
9 Exalt the LORD our God,
   bow down towards his holy hill;
   for the LORD our God is holy.

100

The LORD is God

1 Acclaim the LORD, all men on earth,
2 worship the LORD in gladness;
   enter his presence with songs of exultation.
3 Know that the LORD is God;
   he has made us and we are his own,
   his people, the flock which he shepherds.
4 Enter his gates with thanksgiving
   and his courts with praise.
   Give thanks to him and bless his name;
5 for the LORD is good and his love is ever-
     lasting,
   his constancy endures to all generations.

101

Character of a righteous ruler

1 I sing of loyalty and justice;
   I will raise a psalm to thee, O LORD.[f]

2 I will follow a wise and blameless course,
   whatever may befall me.[g]
   I will go about my house in purity of heart.
3 I will set before myself no sordid aim;
   I will hate disloyalty, I will have none of it.
4 I will reject all crooked thoughts;
   I will have no dealings with evil.
5 I will silence those who spread tales behind
     men's backs,
   I will not sit at table with proud, pompous
     men,
6 I will choose the most loyal for my com-
     panions;
   my servants shall be men whose lives are
     blameless.

No scandal-monger shall live in my house- 7
     hold;
no liar shall set himself up where I can see him.
Morning after morning I will put all wicked 8
     men to silence
and will rid the LORD's city of all evildoers.

102

Prayer for restoration

   LORD, hear my prayer   1
   and let my cry for help reach thee.
   Hide not thy face from me   2
   when I am in distress.
   Listen to my prayer
   and, when I call, answer me soon;
   for my days vanish like smoke,   3
   my body is burnt up as in an oven.
   I am stricken, withered like grass;   4
   I cannot find the strength to eat.
   Wasted away,[h] I groan aloud   5
   and my skin hangs on my bones.
   I am like a desert-owl in the wilderness,   6
   an owl that lives among ruins.

   Thin and meagre, I wail in solitude,   7
   like a bird that flutters on the roof-top.
   My enemies insult me all the day long;   8
   mad with rage, they conspire against me.
   I have eaten ashes for bread   9
   and mingled tears with my drink.
   In thy wrath and fury   10
   thou hast taken me up and flung me aside.
   My days decline as the shadows lengthen, 11
   and like grass I wither away.

But thou, LORD, art enthroned for ever   12
   and thy fame shall be known to all genera-
     tions.
Thou wilt arise and have mercy on Zion;   13
   for the time is come[i] to pity her.
   Her very stones are dear to thy servants,   14
   and even her dust moves them with pity.
Then shall the nations revere thy name,   15
     O LORD,
   and all the kings of the earth thy glory,
   when the LORD builds up Zion again   16
   and shows himself in his glory.

---

e Prob. rdg.; Heb. thy.   *f* I sing ... O LORD: *or* I will follow a course of justice and loyalty; I will hold
thee in awe, O LORD.   *g* whatever may befall me: *prob. rdg.; Heb.* when comest thou to me?   *h* Wasted
away: *transposed from previous verse.*   *i Prob. rdg.; Heb. adds* season.

17 He turns to hear the prayer of the destitute
and does not scorn them when they pray.
18 This shall be written down for future generations,
and a people yet unborn shall praise the
LORD.
19 The LORD looks down from his sanctuary
on high,
from heaven he surveys the earth
20 to listen to the groaning of the prisoners
and set free men under sentence of death;
21 so shall the LORD's name be on men's lips in
Zion
and his praise shall be told in Jerusalem,
22 when peoples are assembled together,
peoples and kingdoms, to serve the LORD.

23 My strength is broken in mid course;
24 the time allotted me is short.
Snatch me not away before half my days
are done,
for thy years last through all generations.
25 Long ago thou didst lay the foundations
of the earth,
and the heavens were thy handiwork.
26 They shall pass away, but thou endurest;
like clothes they shall all grow old;
thou shalt cast them off like a cloak,
and they shall vanish;
27 but thou art the same and thy years shall
have no end;
28 thy servants' children shall continue,
and their posterity shall be established in thy
presence.

103

Meditating on the LORD's goodness

1 Bless the LORD, my soul;
my innermost heart, bless his holy name.
2 Bless the LORD, my soul,
and forget none of his benefits.
3 He pardons all my guilt
and heals all my suffering.
4 He rescues me from the pit of death
and surrounds me with constant love,
with tender affection;
5 he contents me with all good in the prime
of life,
and my youth is ever new like an eagle's.
6 The LORD is righteous in his acts;
he brings justice to all who have been
wronged.
7 He taught Moses to know his way
and showed the Israelites what he could
do.
8 The LORD is compassionate and gracious,
long-suffering and for ever constant;
9 he will not always be the accuser
or nurse his anger for all time.
10 He has not treated us as our sins deserve
or requited us for our misdeeds.

For as the heaven stands high above the 11
earth,
so his strong love stands high over all who
fear him.
Far as east is from west,   12
so far has he put our offences away from us.
As a father has compassion on his children, 13
so has the LORD compassion on all who
fear him.
For he knows how we were made,   14
he knows full well that we are dust.

Man's days are like the grass;   15
he blossoms like the flowers of the field:
a wind passes over them, and they cease 16
to be,
and their place knows them no more.
But the LORD's love never fails those who 17
fear him;
his righteousness never fails their sons and
their grandsons
who listen to his voice^j and keep his 18
covenant,
who remember his commandments and
obey them.

The LORD has established his throne in 19
heaven,
his kingly power over the whole world.
Bless the LORD, all his angels,   20
creatures of might who do his bidding.
Bless the LORD, all his hosts,   21
his ministers who serve his will.
Bless the LORD, all created things,   22
in every place where he has dominion.

Bless the LORD, my soul.

104

Meditating on nature

Bless the LORD, my soul: 1
O LORD my God, thou art great indeed,
clothed in majesty and splendour,
and wrapped in a robe of light.   2
Thou hast spread out the heavens like a
tent
and on their waters laid the beams of thy 3
pavilion;
who takest the clouds for thy chariot,
riding on the wings of the wind;
who makest the winds thy messengers   4
and flames of fire thy servants;
thou didst fix the earth on its foundation 5
so that it never can be shaken;
the deep overspread it like a cloak,   6
and the waters lay above the mountains.
At thy rebuke they ran,   7
at the sound of thy thunder they rushed
away,
flowing over the hills,   8
pouring down into the valleys
to the place appointed for them.

j who listen to his voice: *transposed from end of verse 20.*

9 Thou didst fix a boundary which they might
   not pass;
   they shall not return to cover the earth.

10 Thou dost make springs break out in the
   gullies,
   so that their water runs between the hills.
11 The wild beasts all drink from them,
   the wild asses quench their thirst;
12 the birds of the air nest on their banks
   and sing among the leaves.

13 From thy high pavilion thou dost water
   the hills;
   the earth is enriched by thy provision.
14 Thou makest grass grow for the cattle
   and green things for those who toil for
   man,
   bringing bread out of the earth
15 and wine to gladden men's hearts,
   oil to make their faces shine
   and bread to sustain their strength.
16 The trees of the LORD are green and leafy,
   the cedars of Lebanon which he planted;
17 the birds build their nests in them,
   the stork makes her home in their tops.[k]
18 High hills are the haunt of the mountain-
   goat,
   and boulders a refuge for the rock-
   badger.

19 Thou hast made the moon to measure the
   year
   and taught the sun where to set.

When thou makest darkness and it is night, 20
all the beasts of the forest come forth;
   the young lions roar for prey,   21
   seeking their food from God.
When thou makest the sun rise, they slink 22
   away
   and go to rest in their lairs;
but man comes out to his work   23
   and to his labours until evening.
Countless are the things thou hast made, 24
   O LORD.
Thou hast made all by thy wisdom;
   and the earth is full of thy creatures,
   beasts great and small.   25

Here is the great immeasurable sea,
   in which move creatures beyond number.
Here ships sail to and fro,   26
here is Leviathan whom thou hast made thy
   plaything.[l]

All of them look expectantly to thee   27
   to give them their food at the proper time;
what thou givest them they gather up;   28
   when thou openest thy hand, they eat their
   fill.
Then thou hidest thy face, and they are 29
   restless and troubled;
   when thou takest away their breath, they fail
   [and they return to the dust from which
   they came];
but when thou breathest into them, they 30
   recover;
   thou givest new life to the earth.

k in their tops: prob. rdg.; Heb. the pine-trees.

l thy plaything: or that it may sport in it.

●

31 May the glory of the LORD stand for ever
and may he rejoice in his works!
32 When he looks at the earth, it quakes;
when he touches the hills, they pour forth
smoke.

33 I will sing to the LORD as long as I live,
all my life I will sing psalms to my God.
34 May my meditation please the LORD,
as I show my joy in him!
35 Away with all sinners from the earth
and may the wicked be no more!

Bless the LORD, my soul.

O praise the LORD.

105

How the LORD led Israel

1 *m* Give the LORD thanks and invoke him by
name,
make his deeds known in the world
around.
2 Pay him honour with song and psalm
and think upon all his wonders.
3 Exult in his hallowed name;
let those who seek the LORD be joyful in
heart.
4 Turn to the LORD, your strength,
seek his presence always.
5 Remember the wonders that he has
wrought,
his portents and the judgements he has
given,
6 O offspring of Abraham his servant,
O chosen sons of Jacob.

7 He is the LORD our God;
his judgements fill the earth.
8 He called to mind his covenant from long
ago,*n*
the promise he extended to a thousand
generations—
9 the covenant made with Abraham,
his oath given to Isaac,
10 the decree by which he bound himself for
Jacob,
his everlasting covenant with Israel:
11 'I will give you the land of Canaan', he
said,
'to be your possession, your patrimony.'
12 A small company it was,
few in number, strangers in that land,
13 roaming from nation to nation,
from one kingdom to another;
14 but he let no one ill-treat them,
for their sake he admonished kings:
15 'Touch not my anointed servants,
do my prophets no harm.'

16 He called down famine on the land
and cut short their daily bread.

m Verses 1–15: cp. 1 Chr. 16. 8–22.

But he had sent on a man before them, 17
Joseph, who was sold into slavery;
he was kept a prisoner with fetters on his 18
feet
and an iron collar clamped on his neck.
He was tested by the LORD's command 19
until what he foretold came true.
Then the king sent and set him free, 20
the ruler of nations released him;
he made him master of his household 21
and ruler over all his possessions,
to correct his officers at will 22
and teach his counsellors wisdom.
Then Israel too went down into Egypt 23
and Jacob came to live in the land of
Ham.
There God made his people very fruitful, 24
he made them stronger than their enemies,
whose hearts he turned to hatred of his 25
people
and double-dealing with his servants.
He sent his servant Moses 26
and Aaron whom he had chosen.
They were his mouthpiece to announce 27
his signs,
his portents in the land of Ham.
He sent darkness, and all was dark, 28
but still they resisted his commands.
He turned their waters into blood 29
and killed all their fish.
Their country swarmed with frogs, 30
even their princes' inner chambers.
At his command came swarms of flies 31
and maggots the whole land through.
He changed their rain into hail 32
and flashed fire over their country.
He blasted their vines and their fig-trees 33
and splintered the trees throughout the
land.
At his command came locusts, 34
hoppers past all number,
they consumed every green thing in the 35
land,
consumed all the produce of the soil.
Then he struck down all the first-born in 36
Egypt,
the firstfruits of their manhood;
he led Israel out, laden with silver and 37
gold,
and among all their tribes no man fell.
The Egyptians were glad when they went, 38
for fear of Israel had taken hold of them.
He spread a cloud as a screen, 39
and fire to light up the night.
They asked, and he sent them quails, 40
he gave them bread from heaven in plenty.
He opened a rock and water gushed out, 41
a river flowing in a parched land;
for he had remembered his solemn promise 42
given to his servant Abraham.
So he led out his people rejoicing, 43
his chosen ones in triumph.

n from long ago: or for ever.

44 He gave them the lands of heathen nations
and they took possession where others had
toiled,
45 so that they might keep his statutes
and obey his laws.

O praise the LORD.

106

Israel's persistent disobedience

1 O praise the LORD.

It is good to give thanks to the LORD;
for his love endures for ever.
2 Who will tell of the LORD's mighty acts
and make his praises heard?
3 Happy are they who act justly
and do right at all times!
4 Remember me, LORD, when thou showest
favour to thy people,
look upon me when thou savest them,
5 that I may see the prosperity of thy chosen,
rejoice in thy nation's joy and exult with thy
own people.

6 We have sinned like our forefathers,
we have erred and done wrong.
7 Our fathers in Egypt took no account of thy
marvels,
they did not remember thy many acts of
faithful love,
but in spite of all[o] they rebelled by the
Red Sea.[p]
8 Yet the LORD delivered them for his
name's sake
and so made known his mighty power.
9 He rebuked the Red Sea and it dried up,
he led his people through the deeps as
through the wilderness.
10 So he delivered them from those who hated
them,
and claimed them back from the enemy's
hand.
11 The waters closed over their adversaries,
not one of them survived.
12 Then they believed his promises and sang
praises to him.

13 But they quickly forgot all he had done
and would not wait to hear his counsel;
14 their greed was insatiable in the wilderness,
they tried God's patience in the desert.
15 He gave them what they asked
but sent a wasting sickness among them.[q]

16 They were envious of Moses in the camp,
and of Aaron, who was consecrated to the
LORD.
17 The earth opened and swallowed Dathan,
it closed over the company of Abiram;

fire raged through their company, 18
the wicked perished in flames.

At Horeb they made a calf 19
and bowed down to an image;
they exchanged their Glory[r] 20
for the image of a bull that feeds on grass.
They forgot God their deliverer, 21
who had done great deeds in Egypt,
marvels in the land of Ham, 22
terrible things at the Red Sea.
So his purpose was to destroy them, 23
but Moses, the man he had chosen,
threw himself into the breach
to turn back his wrath lest it destroy them.

They made light of the pleasant land, 24
disbelieving his promise;
they muttered treason in their tents 25
and would not obey the LORD.
So with uplifted hand he swore 26
to strike them down in the wilderness,
to scatter their descendants among the 27
nations
and disperse them throughout the world.

They joined in worshipping the Baal of Peor 28
and ate meat sacrificed to lifeless gods.
Their deeds provoked the LORD to anger, 29
and plague broke out amongst them;
but Phinehas stood up and interceded, 30
so the plague was stopped.
This was counted to him as righteousness 31
throughout all generations for ever.

They roused the LORD to anger at the 32
waters of Meribah,
and Moses suffered because of them;
for they had embittered his spirit 33
and he had spoken rashly.

They did not destroy the peoples round 34
about,
as the LORD had commanded them to do,
but they mingled with the nations, 35
learning their ways;
they worshipped their idols 36
and were ensnared by them.
Their sons and their daughters 37
they sacrificed to foreign demons;
they shed innocent blood, 38
the blood of sons and daughters
offered to the gods of Canaan,
and the land was polluted with blood.
Thus they defiled themselves by their 39
conduct
and they followed their lusts and broke
faith with God.
Then the LORD grew angry with his people 40
and loathed them, his own chosen nation;
so he gave them into the hands of the 41
nations,
and they were ruled by their foes;

---

o in spite of all: prob. rdg.; Heb. obscure.   *p Or the Sea of Reeds.*   *q among them: or in their*
throats.   *r their Glory: or the glory of God (cp. Jer. 2. 11; Romans 1. 23).*

42 their enemies oppressed them
and made them subject to their power.
43 Many times he came to their rescue,
but they were disobedient and rebellious
still.[s]
44 And yet, when he heard them wail and
cry aloud,
he looked with pity on their distress;
45 he called to mind his covenant with
them
and, in his boundless love, relented;
46 he roused compassion for them
in the hearts of all their captors.

47 Deliver us, O LORD our God,
and gather us in from among the nations
that we may give thanks to thy holy name
and make thy praise our pride.

48 Blessed be the LORD the God of Israel
from everlasting to everlasting;
and let all the people say 'Amen.'

O praise the LORD.

BOOK 5
107

The LORD's enduring love

1 It is good to give thanks to the LORD,
for his love endures for ever.
2 So let them say who were redeemed by the
LORD,
redeemed by him from the power of the
enemy
3 and gathered out of every land,
from east and west, from north and south.

4 Some lost their way in desert wastes;
they found no road to a city to live in;
5 hungry and thirsty,
their spirit sank within them.
6 So they cried to the LORD in their trouble,
and he rescued them from their distress;
7 he led them by a straight and easy way
until they came to a city to live in.
8 Let them thank the LORD for his enduring
love
and for the marvellous things he has done
for men:
9 he has satisfied the thirsty
and filled the hungry with good things.

Some sat in darkness, dark as death,   10
prisoners bound fast in iron,
because they had rebelled against God's   11
commands
and flouted the purpose of the Most High.
Their spirit was subdued by hard labour;   12
they stumbled and fell with none to help
them.
So they cried to the LORD in their trouble,   13
and he saved them from their distress;
he brought them out of darkness, dark as   14
death,
and broke their chains.
Let them thank the LORD for his enduring   15
love
and for the marvellous things he has done
for men:
he has shattered doors of bronze,   16
bars of iron he has snapped in two.

Some were fools, they took to rebellious   17
ways,
and for their transgression they suffered
punishment.
They sickened at the sight of food   18
and drew near to the very gates of death.
So they cried to the LORD in their trouble,   19
and he saved them from their distress;
he sent his word to heal them   20
and bring them alive out of the pit of
death.[t]
Let them thank the LORD for his enduring   21
love
and for the marvellous things he has done
for men.
Let them offer sacrifices of thanksgiving   22
and recite his deeds with shouts of joy.

Others there are who go to sea in ships   23
and make their living on the wide waters.
These men have seen the acts of the LORD   24
and his marvellous doings in the deep.
At his command the storm-wind rose   25
and lifted the waves high.
Carried up to heaven, plunged down to the 26
depths,
tossed to and fro in peril,
they reeled and staggered like drunken men, 27
and their seamanship was all in vain.

s *Prob. rdg.; Heb. adds* and were brought low by
their guilt.   t alive *. . . death: prob. rdg.; Heb.*
from their corruption.

28 So they cried to the LORD in their trouble,
and he brought them out of their distress.
29 The storm sank to a murmur
and the waves of the sea were stilled.
30 They were glad then that all was calm,
as he guided them to the harbour they
desired.
31 Let them thank the LORD for his enduring
love
and for the marvellous things he has done
for men.
32 Let them exalt him in the assembly of the
people
and praise him in the council of the elders.

33 He turns rivers into desert
and springs of water into thirsty ground;
34 he turns fruitful land into salt waste,
because the men who dwell there are so
wicked.
35 Desert he changes into standing pools,
and parched land into springs of water.
36 There he gives the hungry a home,
and they build themselves a city to live in;
37 they sow fields and plant vineyards
and reap a fruitful harvest.
38 He blesses them and their numbers increase,
and he does not let their herds lose
strength.
39 Tyrants[u] lose their strength and are brought
low
in the grip of misfortune and sorrow;
40 he brings princes into contempt
and leaves them wandering in a trackless
waste.
41 But the poor man he lifts clear of his troubles
and makes families increase like flocks of
sheep.
42 The upright see it and are glad,
while evildoers are filled with disgust.
43 Let the wise man lay these things to heart,
and ponder the record of the LORD's
enduring love.

108

Prayer for God's help

1[v] My heart is steadfast, O God,
my heart is steadfast.
I will sing and raise a psalm;
awake,[w] my spirit,
2 awake, lute and harp,
I will awake at dawn of day.[x]
3 I will confess thee, O LORD, among the
peoples,
among the nations I will raise a psalm to
thee;
4 for thy unfailing love is wider than the
heavens
and thy truth reaches to the skies.

Show thyself, O God, high above the 5
heavens;
let thy glory shine over all the earth.
Deliver those that are dear to thee; 6[y]
save with thy right hand and answer.

God has spoken from his sanctuary:[z] 7
'I will go up now and measure out
Shechem;
I will divide the valley of Succoth into
plots;
Gilead and Manasseh are mine; 8
Ephraim is my helmet, Judah my sceptre;
Moab is my wash-bowl, I fling my shoes at 9
Edom;
Philistia is the target of my anger.'

Who can bring me to the impregnable city, 10
who can guide me to Edom,
since thou, O God, hast abandoned us 11
and goest not forth with our armies?
Grant us help against the enemy, 12
for deliverance by man is a vain hope.
With God's help we shall do valiantly, 13
and God himself will tread our enemies
under foot.

109

A cry for vengeance

O God of my praise, be silent no longer, 1
for wicked men heap calumnies upon me. 2
They have lied to my face
and ringed me round with words of hate. 3
They have attacked me without a cause[a]
and accused me though I have done 4
nothing unseemly.[b]
They have repaid me evil for good 5
and hatred in return for my love.
They say, 'Put up some rascal to denounce 6
him,
an accuser to stand at his right side.'
But when judgement is given, that rascal 7
will be exposed
and his follies accounted a sin.
May his days be few; 8
may his hoarded wealth[c] fall to another!
May his children be fatherless, 9
his wife a widow!
May his children be vagabonds and 10
beggars,
driven from their homes!
May the money-lender distrain on all his 11
goods
and strangers seize his earnings!
May none remain loyal to him, 12
and none have mercy on his fatherless
children!
May his line be doomed to extinction, 13
may their name be wiped out within a
generation!

u Prob. rdg.; Heb. om.   *v Verses 1–5: cp. Ps. 57. 7–11.*   *w* awake: *prob. rdg.; Heb. also.*   *x* at dawn of day: *or* the dawn.   *y Verses 6–13: cp. Ps. 60. 5–12.*   *z* from his sanctuary: *or* in his holiness.   *a Prob. rdg.; Heb. adds* in return for my love.   *b* though ... unseemly: *prob. rdg.; Heb. obscure.*   *c* hoarded wealth: *or* charge, cp. Acts 1. 20.

14 May the sins of his forefathers be remembered
and his mother's wickedness never be
wiped out!

15 May they remain on record before the
LORD,
but may he extinguish their name from
the earth!

16 For that man never set himself
to be loyal to his friend
but persecuted the downtrodden and the
poor
and hounded the broken-hearted to their
death.

17 Curses he loved: may the curse fall on
him!
He took no pleasure in blessing: may no
blessing be his!

18 He clothed himself in cursing like a
garment:
may it seep into his body like water
and into his bones like oil!

19 May it wrap him round like the clothes
he puts on,
like the belt which he wears every day!

20 May the LORD so requite my accusers
and those who speak evil against me!

21 But thou, O LORD God,
deal with me as befits thy honour;
in the goodness of thy unfailing love
deliver me,

22 for I am downtrodden and poor,
and my heart within me is distracted.

23 I fade like a passing shadow,
I am shaken off like a locust.

24 My knees are weak with fasting
and my flesh wastes away, so meagre is
my fare.

25 I have become the victim of their taunts;
when they see me they toss their heads.

26 Help me, O LORD my God;
save me, by thy unfailing love,

27 that men may know this is thy doing
and thou alone, O LORD, hast done it.

28 They may curse, but thou dost bless;
may my opponents be put to shame,
but may thy servant rejoice!

29 May my accusers be clothed with dishonour,
wrapped in their shame as in a cloak!

30 I will lift up my voice to extol the
LORD,
and before a great company I will praise
him.

31 For he stands at the poor man's right
side
to save him from his adversaries.[d]

110

The LORD's king and priest

The LORD said to my lord,   1
'You shall sit[e] at my right hand
when[f] I make your enemies the footstool
under your feet.'

When the LORD from Zion hands you the 2
sceptre, the symbol of your power,
march forth through the ranks of[g] your
enemies.

At birth[h] you were endowed with princely 3
gifts
and[i] resplendent[j] in holiness.
You have shone with the dew of youth since
your mother bore you.

The LORD has sworn and will not change his 4
purpose:
'You are a priest for ever,
in the succession of Melchizedek.'

The Lord at your right hand   5
has broken kings in the day of his anger.

So the king in his majesty,[k] sovereign of a 6
mighty land,
will punish nations;[l]

he will drink from the torrent beside the 7
path
and therefore will hold his head high.

111

Praise of the LORD's goodness

O praise the LORD.   1

With all my heart will I praise the LORD
in the company of good men, in the whole
congregation.

Great are the doings of the LORD;   2
all men study them for their delight.

His acts are full of majesty and splendour; 3
righteousness is his for ever.

He has won a name by his marvellous 4
deeds;
the LORD is gracious and compassionate.

He gives food to those who fear him,   5
he keeps his covenant always in mind.

He showed his people what his strength 6
could do,
bestowing on them the lands of other
nations.

His works are truth and justice;   7
his precepts all stand on firm foundations,
strongly based to endure for ever,   8
their fabric goodness and truth.

He sent and redeemed his people;   9
he decreed that his covenant should always
endure.
Holy is his name, inspiring awe.

---

d Prob. rdg.; Heb. his judges.   *e* You shall sit: *or* Sit.   *f Or* until *or* while.   *g Or* reign in
the midst of.   *h* At birth: *or* On the day of your power.   *i* you were . . . and: *or* your people
offered themselves willingly; *mng. of Heb. uncertain.*   *j Or* apparelled.   *k* So . . . majesty: *poss.*
rdg.; Heb. full of corpses, he crushed.   *l* So . . . nations: *or* He shall punish the nations—heaps of
corpses, broken heads—over a wide expanse.

10 The fear of the LORD is the beginning[m] of
   wisdom,
and they who live by it grow in understanding.
Praise will be his for ever.

112

Happiness of the God-fearing man

1 O praise the LORD.

Happy is the man who fears the LORD
and finds great joy in his commandments.
2 His descendants shall be the mightiest in the
   land,
a blessed generation of good men.
3 His house shall be full of wealth and riches;
righteousness shall be his for ever.
4 He is gracious, compassionate, good,
a beacon in darkness for honest men.
5 It is right for a man to be gracious in his
   lending,
to order his affairs with judgement.
6 Nothing shall ever shake him;
his goodness shall be remembered for all
   time.
7 Bad news shall have no terrors for him,
because his heart is steadfast, trusting in
   the LORD.
8 His confidence is strongly based, he will have
   no fear;
and in the end he will gloat over his
   enemies.
9 He gives freely to the poor;
righteousness shall be his for ever;
in honour he carries his head high.
10 The wicked man shall see it with rising
   anger
and grind his teeth in despair;
the hopes of wicked men shall come to
   nothing.

113

The LORD's power and goodness

1 O praise the LORD.

Praise the LORD, you that are his servants,
praise the name of the LORD.
2 Blessed be the name of the LORD
now and evermore.
3 From the rising of the sun to its setting
may the LORD's name be praised.
4 High is the LORD above all nations,
his glory above the heavens.
5-6 There is none like the LORD our God
in heaven or on earth,
who sets his throne so high
but deigns to look down so low;
7 who lifts the weak out of the dust
and raises the poor from the dunghill,

giving them a place among princes,   8
among the princes of his people;
who makes the woman in a childless house 9
a happy mother of children.[n]

114

The wonders of the Exodus

O praise the LORD.[o]   1

When Israel came out of Egypt,
Jacob from a people of outlandish speech,
Judah became his sanctuary,   2
Israel his dominion.
The sea looked and ran away;   3
Jordan turned back.
The mountains skipped like rams,   4
the hills like young sheep.
What was it, sea? Why did you run?   5
Jordan, why did you turn back?
Why, mountains, did you skip like rams,   6
and you, hills, like young sheep?
Dance, O earth, at the presence of the   7
Lord,
at the presence of the God of Jacob,
who turned the rock into a pool of water,   8
the granite cliff into a fountain.

115

False gods and God

Not to us, O LORD, not to us,   1
but to thy name ascribe the glory,
for thy true love and for thy constancy.

Why do the nations ask,   2
'Where then is their God?'
Our God is in high heaven;   3
he does whatever pleases him.
Their idols are silver and gold,   4
made by the hands of men.
They have mouths that cannot speak,   5
and eyes that cannot see;
they have ears that cannot hear,   6
nostrils, and cannot smell;
with their hands they cannot feel,   7
with their feet they cannot walk,
and no sound comes from their throats.
Their makers grow to be like them,   8
and so do all who trust in them.

But Israel trusts in the LORD;   9
he is their helper and their shield.
The house of Aaron trusts in the LORD;   10
he is their helper and their shield.
Those who fear the LORD trust in the   11
   LORD;
he is their helper and their shield.
The LORD remembers us, and he will bless   12
   us;
he will bless the house of Israel,
he will bless the house of Aaron.

---

m Or chief part.   *n O praise the LORD transposed to the beginning of Ps. 114.*   *o See note on
Ps. 113. 9.*

13 The LORD will bless all who fear him,
high and low alike.

14 May the LORD give you increase,
both you and your sons.
15 You are blessed by the LORD,
the LORD who made heaven and earth.
16 The heavens, they are the LORD's;
the earth he has given to all mankind.
17 It is not the dead who praise the LORD,
not those who go down into silence;
18 but we, the living, bless the LORD,
now and for evermore.

O praise the LORD.

116

Thanksgiving for deliverance from death

1 I love the LORD, for he has heard me
and listens to my prayer;
2 for he has given me a hearing
whenever I have cried to him.
3 The cords of death bound me,
Sheol held me in its grip.
Anguish and torment held me fast;
4 so I invoked the LORD by name,
'Deliver me, O LORD, I beseech thee;
for I am thy slave.'[p]
5 Gracious is the LORD and righteous,
our God is full of compassion.
6 The LORD preserves the simple-hearted;
I was brought low and he saved me.
7 Be at rest once more, my heart,
for the LORD has showered gifts upon you.
8 He has rescued me from death
and my feet from stumbling.
9 I will walk in the presence of the LORD
in the land of the living.

10 I was sure that I should be swept away,
and my distress was bitter.
11 In panic I cried,
'How faithless all men are!'
12 How can I repay the LORD
for all his gifts to me?
13 I will take in my hands the cup of salvation
and invoke the LORD by name.
14 I will pay my vows to the LORD
in the presence of all his people.
15 A precious thing in the LORD's sight
is the death of those who die faithful to him.
16 [q]I am thy slave, thy slave-girl's son;
thou hast undone the bonds that bound me.
17 To thee will I bring a thank-offering
and invoke the LORD by name.
18 I will pay my vows to the LORD
in the presence of all his people,
19 in the courts of the LORD's house,
in the midst of you, Jerusalem.

O praise the LORD.

117

Call to praise God

1 Praise the LORD, all nations,
extol him, all you peoples;
2 for his love protecting us is strong,
the LORD's constancy is everlasting.

O praise the LORD.

118

His love endures for ever

1 It is good to give thanks to the LORD,
for his love endures for ever.
2 Declare it, house of Israel:
his love endures for ever.
3 Declare it, house of Aaron:
his love endures for ever.
4 Declare it, you that fear the LORD:
his love endures for ever.
5 When in my distress I called to the LORD,
his answer was to set me free.
6 The LORD is on my side, I have no fear;
what can man do to me?
7 The LORD is on my side, he is my helper,
and I shall gloat over my enemies.
8 It is better to find refuge in the LORD
than to trust in men.
9 It is better to find refuge in the LORD
than to trust in princes.
10 All nations surround me,
but in the LORD's name I will drive them away.
11 They surround me on this side and on that,
but in the LORD's name I will drive them away.
12 They surround me like bees at the honey;
they attack me, as fire attacks brushwood,
but in the LORD's name I will drive them away.
13 They thrust hard against me so that I nearly fall;
but the LORD has helped me.
14 The LORD is my refuge and defence,
and he has become my deliverer.
15 Hark! Shouts of deliverance
in the camp of the victors[r]!
With his right hand the LORD does mighty deeds,
16 the right hand of the LORD raises up.
17 I shall not die but live
to proclaim the works of the LORD.
18 The LORD did indeed chasten me,
but he did not surrender me to Death.

p for . . . slave: *transposed from the beginning of verse 16; Heb. adds* O LORD. *q Prob. rdg.; Heb. prefixes* For I am thy slave, O LORD; *see note on verse 4.* *r Or* righteous.

19   Open to me the gates of victory;[s]
     I will enter by them and praise the LORD.
20   This is the gate of the LORD;
     the victors[t] shall make their entry through
     it.
21   I will praise thee, for thou hast answered
     me
     and hast become my deliverer.
22   The stone which the builders rejected
     has become the chief corner-stone.
23   This is the LORD's doing;
     it is marvellous in our eyes.
24   This is the day on which the LORD has
     acted:[u]
     let us exult and rejoice in it.
25   We pray thee, O LORD, deliver us;
     we pray thee, O LORD, send us prosperity.
26   Blessed in the name of the LORD are all
     who come;
     we bless you from the house of the LORD.
27   The LORD is God; he has given light to us,
     the ordered line of pilgrims by the horns
     of the altar.
28   Thou art my God and I will praise thee;
     my God, I will exalt thee.
29   It is good to give thanks to the LORD,
     for his love endures for ever.

119

Meditations on the law of the LORD

1   Happy are they whose life is blameless,
     who conform to the law of the LORD.
2   Happy are they who obey his instruction,
     who set their heart on finding him;
3   who have done no wrong
     and have lived according to his will.
4   Thou, Lord, hast laid down thy precepts
     for men to keep them faithfully.
5   If only I might hold a steady course,
     keeping thy statutes!
6   I shall never be put to shame
     if I fix my eyes on thy commandments.

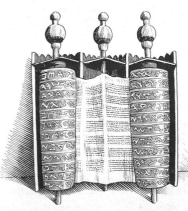

I will praise thee in sincerity of heart   7
as I learn thy just decrees.
Thy statutes will I keep faithfully;   8
O do not leave me forsaken.

How shall a young man steer an honest   9
     course?
By holding to thy word.
With all my heart I strive to find thee;   10
let me not stray from thy commandments.
I treasure thy promise in my heart,   11
for fear that I might sin against thee.
Blessed art thou, O LORD;   12
teach me thy statutes.
I say them over, one by one,   13
the decrees that thou hast proclaimed.
I have found more joy along the path of   14
     thy instruction
than in any kind of wealth.
I will meditate on thy precepts   15
and keep thy paths ever before my eyes.
In thy statutes I find continual delight;   16
I will not forget thy word.

Grant this to me, thy servant: let me live   17
and, living, keep thy word.
Take the veil from my eyes, that I may see   18
the marvels that spring from thy law.
I am but a stranger here on earth,[v]   19
do not hide thy commandments from me.
My heart pines with longing   20
day and night for thy decrees.
The proud have felt thy rebuke;   21
cursed are those who turn from thy
     commandments.
Set me free from scorn and insult,   22
for I have obeyed thy instruction.
The powers that be sit scheming together   23
     against me;
but I, thy servant, will study thy statutes.
Thy instruction is my continual delight;   24
I turn to it for counsel.

I lie prone in the dust;   25
grant me life according to thy word.
I tell thee all I have done and thou dost   26
     answer me;
teach me thy statutes.
Show me the way set out in thy precepts,   27
and I will meditate on thy wonders.
I cannot rest for misery;   28
renew my strength in accordance with thy
     word.
Keep falsehood far from me   29
and grant me the grace of living by thy
     law.
I have chosen the path of truth   30
and have set thy decrees before me.
I hold fast to thy instruction;   31
O LORD, let me not be put to shame.
I will run the course set out in thy com-   32
     mandments,
for they gladden my heart.

s Or righteousness.   *t Or* righteous.   *u Or* which the LORD has made.   *v Or* in the land.

33 Teach me, O LORD, the way set out in thy
statutes,
and in keeping them I shall find my
reward.
34 Give me the insight to obey thy law
and to keep it with all my heart;
35 make me walk in the path of thy commandments,
for that is my desire.
36 Dispose my heart toward thy instruction
and not toward ill-gotten gains;
37 turn away my eyes from all that is vile,
grant me life by thy word.
38 Fulfil thy promise for thy servant,
the promise made to those who fear thee.
39 Turn away the censure which I dread,
for thy decrees are good.
40 How I long for thy precepts!
In thy righteousness grant me life.

41 Thy love never fails; let it light on me,
O LORD,
and thy deliverance, for that was thy
promise;
42 then I shall have my answer to the man
who taunts me,
because I trust in thy word.
43 Rob me not of my power to speak the
truth,
for I put my hope in thy decrees.
44 I will heed thy law continually,
for ever and ever;
45 I walk in freedom wherever I will,
because I have studied thy precepts.
46 I will speak of thy instruction before kings
and will not be ashamed;
47 in thy commandments I find continuing
delight;
I love them with all my heart.
48 I will welcome thy commandments^w
and will meditate on thy statutes.

49 Remember the word spoken to me, thy
servant,
on which thou hast taught me to fix my
hope.
50 In time of trouble my consolation is this,
that thy promise has given me life.
51 Proud men treat me with insolent scorn,
but I do not swerve from thy law.
52 I have cherished thy decrees all my life
long,
and in them I find consolation, O LORD.
53 Gusts of anger seize me as I think of evil
men
who forsake thy law.
54 Thy statutes are the theme of my song^x
wherever I make my home.
55 In the night I remember thy name,
O LORD,
and dwell upon thy law.
56 This is true of me,
that I have kept thy precepts.

57 Thou, LORD, art all I have;
I have promised to keep thy word.
58 With all my heart I have tried to please
thee;
fulfil thy promise and be gracious to
me.
59 I have thought much about the course of
my life
and always turned back to thy instruction;
60 I have never delayed but always made
haste
to keep thy commandments.
61 Bands of evil men close round me,
but I do not forget thy law.
62 At midnight I rise to give thee thanks
for the justice of thy decrees.
63 I keep company with all who fear thee,
with all who follow thy precepts.
64 The earth is full of thy never-failing love;
O LORD, teach me thy statutes.

65 Thou hast shown thy servant much kindness,
fulfilling thy word, O LORD.
66 Give me insight, give me knowledge,
for I put my trust in thy commandments.
67 I went astray before I was punished;
but now I pay heed to thy promise.
68 Thou art good and thou doest good;
teach me thy statutes.
69 Proud men blacken my name with lies,
yet I follow thy precepts with all my heart;
70 their hearts are thick and gross;
but I continually delight in thy law.
71 How good it is for me to have been
punished,
to school me in thy statutes!
72 The law thou hast ordained means more
to me
than a fortune in gold and silver.

73 Thy hands moulded me and made me
what I am;
show me how I may learn thy commandments.
74 Let all who fear thee be glad when they
see me,
because I hope for the fulfilment of thy
word.
75 I know, O LORD, that thy decrees are
just
and even in punishing thou keepest faith
with me.
76 Let thy never-failing love console me,
as thou hast promised me, thy servant.
77 Extend thy compassion to me, that I may
live;
for thy law is my continual delight.
78 Put the proud to shame, for with their lies
they wrong me;
but I will meditate on thy precepts.
79 Let all who fear thee turn to me,
all who cherish thy instruction.

---

w Prob. rdg.; Heb. adds which I love.   *x* the theme of my song: *or* wonderful to me.

80 Let me give my whole heart to thy statutes,
so that I am not put to shame.

81 I long with all my heart for thy deliverance,
hoping for the fulfilment of thy word;
82 my sight grows dim with looking for thy promise
and still I cry, 'When wilt thou comfort me?'
83 Though I shrivel like a wine-skin in the smoke,
I do not forget thy statutes.
84 How long has thy servant to wait
for thee to fulfil thy decree against my persecutors?
85 Proud men who flout thy law
spread tales about me.
86 Help me, for they hound me with their lies,
but thy commandments all stand for ever.
87 They had almost swept me from the earth,
but I did not forsake thy precepts;
88 grant me life, as thy love is unchanging,
that I may follow all thy instruction.

89 Eternal is thy word, O LORD,
planted firm in heaven.
90 Thy promise[y] endures for all time,
stable as the earth which thou hast fixed.
91 This day, as ever, thy decrees stand fast;
for all things serve thee.
92 If thy law had not been my continual delight,
I should have perished in all my troubles;
93 never will I forget thy precepts,
for through them thou hast given me life.
94 I am thine; O save me,
for I have pondered thy precepts.
95 Evil men lie in wait to destroy me;
but I will give thought to thy instruction.
96 I see that all things come to an end,
but thy commandment has no limit.

97 O how I love thy law!
It is my study all day long.
98 Thy commandments are mine for ever;
through them I am wiser than my enemies.
99 I have more insight than all my teachers,
for thy instruction is my study;
100 I have more wisdom than the old,
because I have kept thy precepts.
101 I set no foot on any evil path
in my obedience to thy word;
102 I do not swerve from thy decrees,
for thou thyself hast been my teacher.
103 How sweet is thy promise in my mouth,
sweeter on my tongue than honey!
104 From thy precepts I learn wisdom;
therefore I hate the paths of falsehood.

105 Thy word is a lamp to guide my feet
and a light on my path;
106 I have bound myself by oath and solemn vow
to keep thy just decrees.
107 I am cruelly afflicted;
O LORD, revive me and make good thy word.
108 Accept, O LORD, the willing tribute of my lips
and teach me thy decrees.
109 Every day I take my life in my hands,
yet I never forget thy law.
110 Evil men have set traps for me,
but I do not stray from thy precepts.
111 Thy instruction is my everlasting inheritance;
it is the joy of my heart.
112 I am resolved to fulfil thy statutes;
they are a reward that never fails.

113 I hate men who are not single-minded,
but I love thy law.
114 Thou art my shield and hiding-place;
I hope for the fulfilment of thy word.
115 Go, you evildoers, and leave me to myself,
that I may keep the commandments of my God.
116 Support me as thou hast promised, that I may live;
do not disappoint my hope.
117 Sustain me, that I may see deliverance;
so shall I always be occupied with thy statutes.
118 Thou dost reject those who stray from thy statutes,
for their talk is all malice and lies.
119 In thy sight all the wicked on earth are scum;
therefore I love thy instruction.
120 The dread of thee makes my flesh creep,
and I stand in awe of thy decrees.

121 I have done what is just and right;
thou wilt not abandon me to my oppressors.
122 Stand surety for the welfare of thy servant;
let not the proud oppress me.[z]
123 My sight grows dim with looking for thy deliverance
and waiting for thy righteous promise.
124 In all thy dealings with me, LORD, show thy true love
and teach me thy statutes.
125 I am thy servant; give me insight
to understand thy instruction.
126 It is time to act, O LORD;
for men have broken thy law.
127 Truly I love thy commandments
more than the finest gold.

y *Prob. rdg.; Heb.* Thy constancy.   z oppress me: *or* charge me falsely.

28 It is by thy precepts that I find the right
way;
I hate the paths of falsehood.

29 Thy instruction is wonderful;
therefore I gladly keep it.

30 Thy word is revealed, and all is light;
it gives understanding even to the un-
taught.

31 I pant, I thirst,
longing for thy commandments.

32 Turn to me and be gracious,
as thou hast decreed for those who love
thy name.

33 Make my step firm according to thy
promise,
and let no wrong have the mastery over
me.

34 Set me free from man's oppression,
that I may observe thy precepts.

35 Let thy face shine upon thy servant
and teach me thy statutes.

36 My eyes stream with tears
because men do not heed thy law.

37 How just thou art, O LORD!
How straight and true are thy decrees!

38 How just is the instruction thou givest!
It is fixed firm and sure.

39 I am speechless with resentment,
for my enemies have forgotten thy
words.

40 Thy promise has been tested through and
through,
and thy servant loves it.

41 I may be despised and of little account,
but I do not forget thy precepts.

42 Thy justice is an everlasting justice,
and thy law is truth.

43 Though I am oppressed by trouble and
anxiety,
thy commandments are my continual
delight.

44 Thy instruction is ever just;
give me understanding that I may live.

45 I call with my whole heart; answer me,
LORD.
I will keep thy statutes.

46 I call to thee; O save me
that I may heed thy instruction.

47 I rise before dawn and cry for help;
I hope for the fulfilment of thy word.

48 Before the midnight watch also my eyes
are open
for meditation on thy promise.

49 Hear me, as thy love is unchanging,
and give me life, O LORD, by thy decree.

50 My pursuers in their malice are close
behind me,
but they are far from thy law.

151 Yet thou art near, O LORD,
and all thy commandments are true.

152 I have long known from thy instruction
that thou hast given it eternal foundations.

153 See in what trouble I am and set me
free,
for I do not forget thy law.

154 Be thou my advocate and win release for
me;
true to thy promise, give me life.

155 Such deliverance is beyond the reach of
wicked men,
because they do not ponder thy statutes.

156 Great is thy compassion, O LORD;
grant me life by thy decree.

157 Many are my persecutors and enemies,
but I have not swerved from thy instruction.

158 I was cut to the quick when I saw traitors
who had no regard for thy promise.

159 See how I love thy precepts, O LORD!
Grant me life, as thy love is unchanging.

160 Thy word is founded in truth,
and thy just decrees are everlasting.

161 The powers that be persecute me without
cause,
yet my heart thrills at thy word.

162 I am jubilant over thy promise,
like a man carrying off much booty.

163 Falsehood I detest and loathe,
but I love thy law.

164 Seven times a day I praise thee
for the justice of thy decrees.

165 Peace is the reward of those who love thy
law;
no pitfalls beset their path.

166 I hope for thy deliverance, O LORD,
and I fulfil thy commandments;

167 gladly I heed thy instruction
and love it greatly.

168 I heed thy precepts and thy instruction,
for all my life lies open before thee.

169 Let my cry of joy reach thee, O LORD;
give me understanding of thy word.

170 Let my supplication reach thee;
be true to thy promise and save me.

171 Let thy praise pour from my lips,
because thou teachest me thy statutes;

172 let the music of thy promises be on my
tongue,
for thy commandments are justice itself.

173 Let thy hand be prompt to help me,
for I have chosen thy precepts;

174 I long for thy deliverance, O LORD,
and thy law is my continual delight.

175 Let me live and I will praise thee;
let thy decrees be my support.

176 I have strayed like a lost sheep;
come, search for thy servant,
for I have not forgotten thy commandments.

120

Prayer of an exile

1 I called to the LORD in my distress,
and he answered me.
2 'O LORD,' I cried, 'save me from lying lips
and from the tongue of slander.'
3 What has he in store for you, slanderous
tongue?
What more has he for you?
4 Nothing but a warrior's sharp arrows
or red-hot charcoal.
5 Hard is my lot, exiled in Meshech,
dwelling by the tents of Kedar.
6 All the time that I dwelt
among men who hated peace,
7 I sought peace; but whenever I spoke of it,
they were for war.

121

The only source of help

1 If I lift up my eyes to the hills,
where shall I find help?
2 Help comes only from the LORD,
maker of heaven and earth.
3 How could he let your foot stumble?
How could he, your guardian, sleep?
4 The guardian of Israel
never slumbers, never sleeps.
5 The LORD is your guardian,
your defence at your right hand;
6 the sun will not strike you by day
nor the moon by night.
7 The LORD will guard you against all evil;
he will guard you, body and soul.

8 The LORD will guard your going and your
coming,
now and for evermore.

122

Jerusalem, the city of peace

1 I rejoiced when they said to me,
'Let us go to the house of the LORD.'
2 Now we stand within your gates,
O Jerusalem:
3 Jerusalem that is built to be a city
where people come together in unity;
4 to which the tribes resort, the tribes of the
LORD,
to give thanks to the LORD himself,
the bounden duty of Israel.
5 For in her are set the thrones of justice,
the thrones of the house of David.
6 Pray for the peace of Jerusalem:
'May those who love you prosper;
7 peace be within your ramparts
and prosperity in your palaces.'
8 For the sake of these my brothers and my
friends,
I will say, 'Peace be within you.'
9 For the sake of the house of the LORD our
God
I will pray for your good.

123

Looking to the LORD

1 I lift my eyes to thee
whose throne is in heaven.
2 As the eyes of a slave follow his master's
hand
or the eyes of a slave-girl her mistress,
so our eyes are turned to the LORD our God
waiting for kindness from him.
3 Deal kindly with us, O LORD, deal kindly,
for we have suffered insult enough;
4 too long have we had to suffer
the insults of the wealthy,
the scorn of proud men.

124

A merciful escape

1 If the LORD had not been on our side,
Israel may now say,
2 if the LORD had not been on our side
when they assailed us,
3 they would have swallowed us alive
when their anger was roused against us.
4 The waters would have carried us away
and the torrent swept over us;
5 over us would have swept
the seething waters.
6 Blessed be the LORD, who did not leave us
to be the prey between their teeth.
7 We have escaped like a bird
from the fowler's trap;
the trap broke, and so we escaped.

8 Our help is in the name of the LORD,
maker of heaven and earth.

125

Stability and security

1 Those who trust in the LORD are like
Mount Zion,
which cannot be shaken but stands fast
for ever.
2 As the hills enfold Jerusalem,
so the LORD enfolds his people, now and
evermore.
3 The sceptre of wickedness shall surely find
no home
in the land allotted to the righteous,
so that the righteous shall not set
their hands to injustice.
4 Do good, O LORD, to those who are good
and to those who are upright in heart.
5 But those who turn aside into crooked
ways,
may the LORD destroy them, as he destroys
all evildoers!

Peace be upon Israel!

126

Recalling past blessings

1 When the LORD turned the tide of Zion's
fortune,
we were like men who had found new
health.[a]
2 Our mouths were full of laughter
and our tongues sang aloud for joy.
Then word went round among the nations,
'The LORD has done great things for them.'
3 Great things indeed the LORD then did
for us,
and we rejoiced.

4 Turn once again our fortune, LORD,
as streams return in the dry south.
5 Those who sow in tears
shall reap with songs of joy.
6 A man may go out weeping,
carrying his bag of seed;
but he will come back with songs of joy,
carrying home his sheaves.

127

Success depends on the LORD

1 Unless the LORD builds the house,
its builders will have toiled in vain.
Unless the LORD keeps watch over a city,
in vain the watchman stands on guard.
2 In vain you rise up early
and go late to rest,
toiling for the bread you eat;
he supplies the need of those he loves.[b]

Sons are a gift from the LORD   3
and children a reward from him.
Like arrows in the hand of a fighting man 4
are the sons of a man's youth.
Happy is the man   5
who has his quiver full of them;
such men shall not be put to shame
when they confront their enemies in court.

128

Long life and prosperity

Happy are all who fear the LORD,   1
who live according to his will.
You shall eat the fruit of your own   2
labours,
you shall be happy and you shall prosper.
Your wife shall be like a fruitful vine 3
in the heart of your house;
your sons shall be like olive-shoots
round about your table.
This is the blessing in store for the man 4
who fears the LORD.
May the LORD bless you from Zion;   5
may you share the prosperity of Jerusalem
all the days of your life,
and live to see your children's children! 6

Peace be upon Israel!

129

Prayer against Zion's enemies

Often since I was young have men   1
attacked me—
let Israel now say—
often since I was young have men attacked 2
me,
but never have they prevailed.
They scored my back with scourges,   3
like ploughmen driving long furrows.
Yet the LORD in his justice   4
has cut me loose from the bonds of the
wicked.
Let all enemies of Zion   5
be thrown back in shame;
let them be like grass growing on the roof, 6
which withers before it can shoot,
which will never fill a mower's hand   7
nor yield an armful for the harvester,
so that passers-by will never say to them, 8
'The blessing of the LORD be upon you!
We bless you in the name of the LORD.'

130

Out of the depths

Out of the depths have I called to thee, 1
O LORD;
Lord, hear my cry.   2
Let thy ears be attentive
to my plea for mercy.

---

a like . . . health: *or* like dreamers.   *b* Prob. rdg.; Heb. adds an unintelligible word.

3 If thou, LORD, shouldest keep account of
sins,
who, O Lord, could hold up his head?
4 But in thee is forgiveness,
and therefore thou art revered.
5 I wait for the LORD with all my soul,
I hope for the fulfilment of his word.
6 My soul waits^c for the Lord
more eagerly than watchmen for the
morning.
Like men who watch for the morning,
7 O Israel, look for the LORD.
For in the LORD is love unfailing,
and great is his power to set men free.
8 He alone will set Israel free
from all their sins.

131

Humble submission

1 O LORD, my heart is not proud,
nor are my eyes haughty;
I do not busy myself with great matters
or things too marvellous for me.
2 No; I submit myself, I account myself
lowly,
as a weaned child clinging to its mother.^d
3 O Israel, look for the LORD
now and evermore.

132

The LORD's covenant with David

1 O LORD, remember David
in the time of his adversity,
2 how he swore to the LORD
and made a vow to the Mighty One of
Jacob:
3 'I will not enter my house
nor will I mount my bed,
4 I will not close my eyes in sleep
or my eyelids in slumber,
5 until I find a sanctuary for the LORD,
a dwelling for the Mighty One of Jacob.'
6 We heard of it in Ephrathah;
we came upon it in the region of Jaar.
7 Let us enter his dwelling,
let us fall in worship at his footstool.
8 Arise, O LORD, and come to thy resting-
place,
thou and the ark of thy power.
9 Let thy priests be clothed in righteousness
and let thy loyal servants shout for joy.
10 For thy servant David's sake
reject not thy anointed king.
11 The LORD swore to David
an oath which he will not break:
'A prince of your own line
will I set upon your throne.

12 If your sons keep my covenant
and heed the teaching that I give them,
their sons in turn for all time
shall sit upon your throne.'
13 For the LORD has chosen Zion
and desired it for his home:
14 'This is my resting-place for ever;
here will I make my home, for such is my
desire.
15 I will richly bless her destitute^e
and satisfy her needy with bread.
16 With salvation will I clothe her priests;
her loyal servants shall shout for joy.
17 There will I renew the line of David's
house
and light a lamp for my anointed king;
18 his enemies will I clothe with shame,
but on his head shall be a shining crown.'

133

Blessing on brotherly unity

1 How good it is and how pleasant
for brothers to live^f together!
2 It is fragrant as oil poured upon the head
and falling over the beard,
Aaron's beard, when the oil runs down
over the collar of his vestments.
3 It is like the dew of Hermon falling
upon the hills of Zion.
There the LORD bestows his blessing,
life for evermore.

134

An evening blessing

1 Come, bless the LORD,
all you servants of the LORD,
who stand night after night
in the house of the LORD.
2 Lift up your hands in the sanctuary
and bless the LORD.
3 The LORD, maker of heaven and earth,
bless you from Zion!

135

Extolling the LORD's greatness

1 O praise the LORD.

Praise the name of the LORD;
praise him, you servants of the LORD,
2 who stand in the house of the LORD,
in the temple courts of our God.
3 Praise the LORD, for that is good;
honour his name with psalms, for that is
pleasant.
4 The LORD has chosen Jacob to be his own
and Israel as his special treasure.
5 I know that the LORD is great,
that our Lord is above all gods.

6 Whatever the LORD pleases,
that he does, in heaven and on earth,
in the sea, in the depths of ocean.
7 He brings up the mist from the ends of
the earth,
he opens rifts*g* for the rain,
and brings the wind out of his storehouses.
8 He struck down all the first-born in
Egypt,
both man and beast.
9 In Egypt he sent signs and portents
against Pharaoh and all his subjects.
10 He struck down mighty nations
and slew great kings,
11 Sihon king of the Amorites, Og the king
of Bashan,
and all the princes of Canaan,
12 and gave their land to Israel,
to Israel his people as their patrimony.
13 O LORD, thy name endures for ever;
thy renown, O LORD, shall last for all
generations.
14 The LORD will give his people justice
and have compassion on his servants.
15 The gods of the nations are idols of silver
and gold,
made by the hands of men.
16 They have mouths that cannot speak
and eyes that cannot see;
17 they have ears that do not hear,
and there is no breath in their nostrils.*h*
18 Their makers grow like them,
and so do all who trust in them.
19 O house of Israel, bless the LORD;
O house of Aaron, bless the LORD.
20 O house of Levi, bless the LORD;
you who fear the LORD, bless the LORD.
21 Blessed from Zion be the LORD
who dwells in Jerusalem.

O praise the LORD.

136

His love endures for ever

1 It is good to give thanks to the LORD,
for his love endures for ever.
2 Give thanks to the God of gods;
his love endures for ever.
3 Give thanks to the Lord of lords;
his love endures for ever.
4 Alone he works great marvels;
his love endures for ever.
5 In wisdom he made the heavens;
his love endures for ever.
6 He laid the earth upon the waters;
his love endures for ever.
7 He made the great lights,
his love endures for ever,
8 the sun to rule by day,
his love endures for ever,
9 the moon and the stars to rule by night;
his love endures for ever.

10 He struck down the first-born of the
Egyptians,
his love endures for ever,
11 and brought Israel from among them;
his love endures for ever.
12 With strong hand and outstretched arm,
his love endures for ever,
13 he divided the Red Sea in two,
his love endures for ever,
14 and made Israel pass through it,
his love endures for ever;
15 but Pharaoh and his host he swept into
the sea;
his love endures for ever.
16 He led his people through the wilderness;
his love endures for ever.
17 He struck down great kings;
his love endures for ever.
18 He slew mighty kings,
his love endures for ever,
19 Sihon king of the Amorites,
his love endures for ever,
20 and Og the king of Bashan;
his love endures for ever.
21 He gave their land to Israel,
his love endures for ever,
22 to Israel his servant as their patrimony;
his love endures for ever.
23 He remembered us when we were cast
down,
his love endures for ever,
24 and rescued us from our enemies;
his love endures for ever.
25 He gives food to all his creatures;
his love endures for ever.
26 Give thanks to the God of heaven,
for his love endures for ever.

137

An exile's longings for Jerusalem

1 By the rivers of Babylon we sat down and
wept
when we remembered Zion.
2 There on the willow-trees*i*
we hung up our harps,

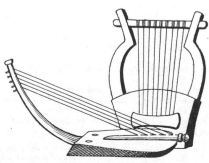

3 for there those who carried us off
   demanded music and singing,
   and our captors called on us to be
     merry:
   'Sing us one of the songs of Zion.'
4 How could we sing the LORD's song
   in a foreign land?

5 If I forget you, O Jerusalem,
   let my right hand wither away;
6 let my tongue cling to the roof of my
     mouth
   if I do not remember you,
   if I do not set Jerusalem
   above my highest joy.
7 Remember, O LORD, against the people of
     Edom
   the day of Jerusalem's fall,
   when they said, 'Down with it, down
     with it,
   down to its very foundations!'
8 O Babylon, Babylon the destroyer,
   happy the man who repays you
   for all that you did to us!
9 Happy is he who shall seize your children
   and dash them against the rock.

138

Confidence in the LORD's purpose

1 I will praise thee, O LORD, with all my
     heart;
   boldly, O God, will I sing psalms to thee.*j*
2 I will bow down towards thy holy temple,
   for thy love and faithfulness I will praise
     thy name;
   for thou hast made thy promise wide as the
     heavens.
3 When I called to thee thou didst answer
     me
   and make me bold and valiant-hearted.
4 Let all the kings of the earth praise*k* thee,
     O LORD,
   when they hear the words thou hast
     spoken;
5 and let them sing of *l* the LORD's ways,
   for great is the glory of the LORD.
6 For the LORD, high as he is, cares for the
     lowly,
   and from afar he humbles the proud.
7 Though I walk among foes thou dost pre-
     serve my life,
   exerting thy power against the rage of my
     enemies,
   and with thy right hand thou savest me.
8 The LORD will accomplish his purpose for
     me.
   Thy true love, O LORD, endures for ever;
   leave not thy work unfinished.

139

God's knowledge of man

LORD, thou hast examined me and knowest 1
  me.
Thou knowest all, whether I sit down or 2
  rise up;
thou hast discerned my thoughts from
  afar.
Thou hast traced my journey and my 3
  resting places,
and art familiar with all my paths.
For there is not a word on my tongue 4
but thou, LORD, knowest them all.*m*
Thou hast kept close guard before me and 5
  behind
and hast spread thy hand over me.
Such knowledge is beyond my under- 6
  standing,
so high that I cannot reach it.
Where can I escape from thy spirit? 7
Where can I flee from thy presence?
If I climb up to heaven, thou art there; 8
if I make my bed in Sheol, again I find
  thee.
If I take my flight to the frontiers of the 9
  morning
or dwell at the limit of the western sea,
even there thy hand will meet me   10
and thy right hand will hold me fast.
If I say, 'Surely darkness will steal over 11
  me,
night will close around me',
darkness is no darkness for thee   12
and night is luminous as day;
to thee both dark and light are one.

Thou it was who didst fashion my inward 13
  parts;
thou didst knit me together in my mother's
  womb.
I will praise thee, for thou dost fill me with 14
  awe;
wonderful thou art, and wonderful thy
  works.
Thou knowest me through and through:
my body is no mystery to thee,   15
how I was secretly kneaded into shape
and patterned in the depths of the earth.
Thou didst see my limbs unformed in the 16
  womb,
and in thy book they are all recorded;
day by day they were fashioned,
not one of them was late in growing.*n*
How deep I find thy thoughts, O God, 17
how inexhaustible their themes!
Can I count them? They outnumber the 18
  grains of sand;
to finish the count, my years must equal
  thine.

j boldly . . . thee: *or* I will sing psalms to thee before the gods.   *k Or* confess.   *l Or* walk in.
m For . . . them all: *or* If there is any offence on my tongue, thou, LORD, knowest it all.   *n* was late in
growing: *prob. rdg.; Heb. om.*

19 O God, if only thou wouldst slay the wicked!
If those men of blood would but leave me in peace—
20 those who provoke thee with deliberate evil
and rise in vicious rebellion against thee!
21 How I hate them, O LORD, that hate thee!
I am cut to the quick when they oppose thee;
22 I hate them with undying hatred;
I hold them all my enemies.
23 Examine me, O God, and know my thoughts;
test me, and understand my misgivings.
24 Watch lest I follow any path that grieves thee;
guide me in the ancient*o* ways.

140

Prayer for the LORD's protection

1 Rescue me, O LORD, from evil men;
keep me safe from violent men,
2 whose heads are full of wicked schemes,
who stir up contention day after day.
3 Their tongues are sharp as serpents' fangs;
on their lips is spiders' poison.
4 Guard me, O LORD, from wicked men;
keep me safe from violent men,
who plan to thrust me out of the way.
5 Arrogant men set hidden traps for me,
rogues spread their nets
and lay snares for me along the path.
6 I said, 'O LORD, thou art my God;
O LORD, hear my plea for mercy.
7 O LORD God, stronghold of my safety,
thou hast shielded my head in the day of battle.
8-9 Frustrate, O LORD, their designs against me;
never let the wicked gain their purpose.
If any of those at my table rise against me,
let their own conspiracies be their undoing.
10 Let burning coals be tipped upon them;
let them be plunged into the miry depths, never to rise again.
11 Slander shall find no home in the land;
evil and violence shall be hounded to destruction.'
12 I know that the LORD will give their due to the needy
and justice to the downtrodden.
13 Righteous men will surely give thanks to thy name;
the upright will worship in thy presence.

141

Prayer for preservation from sin

1 O LORD, I call to thee, come quickly to my aid;
listen to my cry when I call to thee.
2 Let my prayer be like incense duly set before thee
and my raised hands like the evening sacrifice.
3 Set a guard, O LORD, over my mouth;
keep watch at the door of my lips.
4 Turn not my heart to sinful thoughts
nor to any pursuit of evil courses.
The evildoers appal me;*p*
not for me the delights of their table.
5 I would rather be buffeted by the righteous
and reproved by good men.
My head shall not be anointed with the oil of wicked men,
for that would make me a party to their crimes.
6 They shall founder on the rock of justice
and shall learn how acceptable my words are.
7 Their bones shall be scattered at the mouth of Sheol,
like splinters of wood or stone on the ground.
8 But my eyes are fixed on thee, O LORD God;
thou art my refuge; leave me not unprotected.
9 Keep me from the trap which they have set for me,
from the snares of evildoers.
10 Let the wicked fall into their own nets,
whilst I pass in safety, all alone.

142

When no way of escape is in sight

1 I cry aloud to the LORD;
to the LORD I plead aloud for mercy.
2 I pour out my complaint before him
and tell over my troubles in his presence.
3 When my spirit is faint within me,
thou art there to watch over my steps.
In the path that I should take
they have hidden a snare.
4 I look to my right hand,
I find no friend by my side;
no way of escape is in sight,
no one comes to rescue me.
5 I cry to thee, O LORD,
and say, 'Thou art my refuge;
thou art all I have
in the land of the living.
6 Give me a hearing when I cry,
for I am brought very low;
save me from my pursuers,
for they are too strong for me.

o Or everlasting.   *p* appal me: *prob. rdg.*; *Heb.* with men.

7 Set me free from my prison,
so that I may praise thy name.'
The righteous shall crown me with garlands,*q*
when thou givest me my due reward.

143

Prayer for mercy and help

1 LORD, hear my prayer;
be true to thyself, and listen to my pleading;
then in thy righteousness answer me.
2 Bring not thy servant to trial before thee;
against thee no man on earth can be right.
3 An enemy has hunted me down,
has ground my living body under foot
and plunged me into darkness like a man
long dead,
4 so that my spirit fails me
and my heart is dazed with despair.
5 I dwell upon the years long past,
upon the memory of all that thou hast
done;
the wonders of thy creation fill my mind.
6 To thee I lift my outspread hands,
athirst for thee in a thirsty land.
7 LORD, make haste to answer,
for my spirit faints.
Do not hide thy face from me
or I shall be like those who go down to
the abyss.
8 In the morning let me know thy true love;
I have put my trust in thee.
Show me the way that I must take;
to thee I offer all my heart.
9 Deliver me, LORD, from my enemies,
for with thee have I sought refuge.
10 Teach me to do thy will, for thou art my
God;
in thy gracious kindness, show me the
level road.
11 Keep me safe, O LORD, for the honour of
thy name
and, as thou art just, release me from my
distress.
12 In thy love for me, reduce my enemies to
silence
and bring destruction on all who oppress
me;
for I am thy servant.

144

God in nature, history and providence

1 Blessed is the LORD, my rock,'
who trains my hands for war,
my fingers for battle;
2 my help that never fails, my fortress,
my strong tower and my refuge,
my shield in which I trust,
he who puts nations under my feet.

O LORD, what is man that thou carest for 3
him?
What is mankind? Why give a thought to
them?
Man is no more than a puff of wind, 4
his days a passing shadow.
If thou, LORD, but tilt the heavens, down 5
they come;
touch the mountains, and they smoke.
Shoot forth thy lightning flashes, far and 6
wide,
and send thy arrows whistling.
Stretch out thy hands from on high to 7
rescue me
and snatch me from great waters.'

I will sing a new song to thee, O God, 9
psalms to the music of a ten-stringed lute.
O God who gavest victory to kings 10
and deliverance to thy servant David,
rescue me from the cruel sword;
snatch me from the power of foreign foes, 11
whose every word is false
and all their oaths are perjury.

Happy*s* are we whose sons in their early 12
prime
stand like tall towers,
our daughters like sculptured pillars
at the corners of a palace.
Our barns are full and furnish plentiful 13
provision;
our sheep bear lambs in thousands upon
thousands;
the oxen in our fields are fat and sleek; 14
there is no miscarriage or untimely birth,
no cries of distress in our public places.
Happy are the people in such a case as ours; 15
happy the people who have the LORD for
their God.

145

The LORD's unfathomable greatness

I will extol thee, O God my king, 1
and bless thy name for ever and ever.
Every day will I bless thee 2
and praise thy name for ever and ever.
Great is the LORD and worthy of all praise; 3
his greatness is unfathomable.
One generation shall commend thy works 4
to another
and set forth thy mighty deeds.
My theme shall be thy marvellous works, 5
the glorious splendour of thy majesty.
Men shall declare thy mighty acts with 6
awe
and tell of thy great deeds.
They shall recite the story of thy abound- 7
ing goodness
and sing of thy righteousness with joy.

---

q crown me with garlands: or crowd round me.   *r Prob. rdg.; Heb. adds from the power of foreign foes,*
(8) whose every word is false and all their oaths are perjury (cp. verse 11).   *s Prob. rdg.; Heb. Who.*

8 The LORD is gracious and compassionate,
for bearing, and constant in his love.

9 The LORD is good to all men,
and his tender care rests upon all his
creatures.

10 All thy creatures praise thee, LORD,
and thy servants bless thee.

11 They talk of the glory of thy kingdom
and tell of thy might,

12 they proclaim to their fellows how mighty
are thy deeds,
how glorious the majesty of thy kingdom.

13 Thy kingdom is an everlasting kingdom,
and thy dominion stands for all generations.

14 In all his promises the LORD keeps faith,
he is unchanging in all his works;
the LORD holds up those who stumble
and straightens backs which are bent.

15 The eyes of all are lifted to thee in hope,
and thou givest them their food when it is
due;

16 with open and bountiful hand
thou givest what they desire[t] to every
living creature.

17 The LORD is righteous in all his ways,
unchanging in all that he does;

18 very near is the LORD to those who call to
him,
who call to him in singleness of heart.

19 He fulfils their desire if only they fear him;
he hears their cry and saves them.

20 The LORD watches over all who love him
but sends the wicked to their doom.

21 My tongue shall speak out the praises of
the LORD,
and all creatures shall bless his holy name
for ever and ever.

146

The LORD, the only saviour

1 O praise the LORD.

Praise the LORD, my soul.

2 As long as I live I will praise the LORD;
I will sing psalms to my God all my life
long.

3 Put no faith in princes,
in any man, who has no power to save.

4 He breathes his last breath,
he returns to the dust;
and in that same hour all his thinking ends.

5 Happy the man whose helper is the God
of Jacob,
whose hopes are in the LORD his God,

6 maker of heaven and earth,
the sea, and all that is in them;
who serves wrongdoers as he has sworn

7 and deals out justice to the oppressed.

The LORD feeds the hungry
and sets the prisoner free.

8 The LORD restores sight to the blind
and straightens backs which are bent;
the LORD loves the righteous

9 and watches over the stranger;
the LORD gives heart to the orphan and
widow
but turns the course of the wicked to their
ruin.

10 The LORD shall reign for ever,
thy God, O Zion, for all generations.

O praise the LORD.

147

The LORD's care for Israel

1 O praise the LORD.

How good it is to sing psalms to our God!
How pleasant to praise him!

2 The LORD is rebuilding Jerusalem;
he gathers in the scattered sons of Israel.

3 It is he who heals the broken in spirit
and binds up their wounds,

4 he who numbers the stars one by one
and names them one and all.

5 Mighty is our Lord and great his power,
and his wisdom beyond all telling.

6 The LORD gives new heart to the humble
and brings evildoers down to the dust.

7 Sing to the LORD a song of thanksgiving,
sing psalms to the harp in honour of our
God.

8 He veils the sky in clouds
and prepares rain for the earth;
he clothes the hills with grass
and green plants for the use of man.

9 He gives the cattle their food
and the young ravens all that they gather.

10 The LORD sets no store by the strength of
a horse
and takes no pleasure in a runner's legs;

11 his pleasure is in those who fear him,
who wait for his true love.

12 Sing to the LORD, Jerusalem;
O Zion, praise your God,

13 for he has put new bars in your gates;
he has blessed your children within them.

14 He has brought peace to your realm
and given you fine wheat in plenty.

15 He sends his command to the ends of the
earth,
and his word runs swiftly.

16 He showers down snow, white as wool,
and sprinkles hoar-frost thick as ashes;

17 crystals of ice he scatters like bread-
crumbs;
he sends the cold, and the water stands
frozen;

---

t they desire: or thou wilt.

18   he utters his word, and the ice is melted;
     he blows with his wind and the waters
       flow.
19   To Jacob he makes his word known,
     his statutes and decrees to Israel;
20   he has not done this for any other nation,
     nor taught them his decrees.

     O praise the LORD.

148

Praise from the whole creation

1   O praise the LORD.

     Praise the LORD out of heaven;
     praise him in the heights.
2   Praise him, all his angels;
     praise him, all his host.
3   Praise him, sun and moon;
     praise him, all you shining stars;
4   praise him, heaven of heavens,
     and you waters above the heavens.
5   Let them all praise the name of the LORD,
     for he spoke the word and they were
       created;
6   he established them for ever and ever
     by an ordinance which shall never pass
       away.

7   Praise the LORD from the earth,
     you water-spouts and ocean depths;
8   fire and hail, snow and ice,
     gales of wind obeying his voice;
9   all mountains and hills;
     all fruit-trees and all cedars;
10   wild beasts and cattle,
     creeping things and winged birds;
11   kings and all earthly rulers,
     princes and judges over the whole earth;
12   young men and maidens,
     old men and young together.
13   Let all praise the name of the LORD,
     for his name is high above all others,
     and his majesty above earth and heaven;
14   he has exalted his people in the pride of
       power
     and crowned with praise his loyal servants,
     all Israel, the people nearest him.

     O praise the LORD.

149

Israel to praise the LORD

     O praise the LORD.   1

     Sing to the LORD a new song,
     sing his praise in the assembly of the
       faithful;
     let Israel rejoice in his maker   2
     and the sons of Zion exult in their king.
     Let them praise his name in the dance,   3
     and sing him psalms with tambourine and
       harp.
     For the LORD accepts the service of his   4
       people;
     he crowns his humble folk with victory.
     Let his faithful servants exult in triumph;   5
     let them shout for joy as they kneel before
       him.
     Let the high praises of God be on their   6
       lips
     and a two-edged sword in their hand,
     to wreak vengeance on the nations   7
     and to chastise the heathen;
     to load their kings with chains   8
     and put their nobles in irons;
     to execute the judgement decreed against   9
       them—
     this is the glory of all his faithful servants.

     O praise the LORD.

150

Universal praise

     O praise the LORD.   1

     O praise God in his holy place,
     praise him in the vault of heaven, the
       vault of his power;
     praise him for his mighty works,   2
     praise him for his immeasurable greatness.
     Praise him with fanfares on the trumpet,   3
     praise him upon lute and harp;
     praise him with tambourines and dancing,   4
     praise him with flute and strings;
     praise him with the clash of cymbals,   5
     praise him with triumphant cymbals;
     let everything that has breath praise the   6
       LORD!

     O praise the LORD.

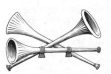

PROVERBS

The value of proverbs

1 The proverbs of Solomon son of David, king of Israel,

2 by which men will come to wisdom and instruction
and will understand words that bring understanding,

3 and by which they will gain a well-instructed intelligence,
righteousness, justice, and probity.

4 The simple will be endowed with shrewdness
and the young with knowledge and prudence.

5 If the wise man listens, he will increase his learning,
and the man of understanding will acquire skill

6 to understand proverbs and parables,
the sayings of wise men and their riddles.

7 The fear of the LORD is the beginning[a] of knowledge,
but fools scorn wisdom and discipline.

8 Attend, my son, to your father's instruction
and do not reject the teaching of your mother;

9 for they are a garland of grace on your head
and a chain of honour round your neck.

Exhortation and warning

11 My son, bad men may tempt you[b] and say,
'Come with us; let us lie in wait for someone's blood;
let us waylay[c] an innocent man who has done us no harm.

12 Like Sheol we will swallow them alive;
though blameless, they shall be like men who go down to the abyss.

13 We shall take rich treasure of every sort
and fill our homes with booty;

14 throw in your lot with us,
and we will have a common purse.'

15 My son, do not go along with them,
keep clear of their ways;

16 they hasten hot-foot into crime,
impatient to shed blood.

In vain is a net spread wide 17
if any bird that flies can see it.
These men lie in wait for their own blood 18
and waylay[c] no one but themselves.
This is the fate[d] of men eager for ill-gotten gain: 19
it robs those who get it of their lives.

Wisdom's appeal

Wisdom cries aloud in the open air, 20
she raises her voice in public places;
she calls at the top of the busy street 21
and proclaims at the open gates of the city:
'Simple fools, how long will you be content with your simplicity?[e] 22
If only you would respond to my reproof, 23
I would give you my counsel
and teach you my precepts.
But because you refused to listen when I called, 24
because no one attended when I stretched out my hand,
because you spurned all my advice 25
and would have nothing to do with my reproof,
I in my turn will laugh at your doom 26
and deride you when terror comes upon you,
when terror comes upon you like a hurricane 27
and your doom descends like a whirlwind.[f]
Insolent men delight in their insolence;
stupid men hate knowledge.[g]
When they call upon me, I will not answer them; 28
when they search for me, they shall not find me.
Because they hate knowledge 29
and have not chosen to fear the LORD,
because they have not accepted my counsel 30
and have spurned all my reproof,
they shall eat the fruits of their behaviour 31
and have a surfeit of their own devices;
for the simpleton turns a deaf ear and comes to grief, 32
and the stupid are ruined by their own complacency.

---

a Or chief part.   *b Prob. rdg.; Heb. adds* do not come, *or, with some MSS.,* do not consent.   *c Prob. rdg.; Heb.* store up.   *d This . . . fate: prob. rdg.; Heb.* Such are the courses.   *e The rest of verse 22 transposed to follow verse 27.*   *f Prob. rdg.; Heb. adds* when anguish and distress come upon you.   *g Insolent . . . knowledge: transposed from end of verse 22.*

33 But whoever listens to me shall live without a care,
undisturbed by fear of misfortune.'

Reward of seeking wisdom

2 My son, if you take my words to heart
and lay up my commands in your mind,
2 giving your attention to wisdom
and your mind to understanding,
3 if you summon discernment to your aid
and invoke understanding,
4 if you seek her out like silver
and dig for her like buried treasure,
5 then you will understand the fear of the LORD
and attain to the knowledge of God;
6 for the LORD bestows wisdom
and teaches knowledge and understanding.
7 Out of his store he endows the upright with ability
as a shield for those who live blameless lives;
8 for he guards the course of justice
and keeps watch over the way of his loyal servants.

9 Then you will understand what is right and just
and keep[h] only to the good man's path;
10 for wisdom will sink into your mind,
and knowledge will be your heart's delight.
11 Prudence will keep watch over you,
understanding will guard you,
12 it will save you from evil ways
and from men whose talk is subversive,
13 who forsake the honest course
to walk in ways of darkness,
14 who rejoice in doing evil
and exult in evil and subversive acts,
15 whose own ways are crooked,
whose tracks are devious.
16 It will save you from the adulteress,
from the loose woman with her seductive words,
17 who forsakes the teaching of her childhood
and has forgotten the covenant of her God;
18 for her path[i] runs downhill towards death,
and her course is set for the land of the dead.
19 No one who resorts to her[j] finds his way back
or regains the path to life.

20 See then that you follow the footsteps of good men
and keep to the course of the righteous;
21 for the upright shall dwell on earth
and blameless men remain there;
22 but the wicked shall be uprooted from it
and traitors weeded out.

Advice to a young man

My son, do not forget my teaching, **3**
but guard my commands in your heart;
for long life and years in plenty 2
will they bring you, and prosperity as well.
Let your good faith and loyalty never 3 fail,
but bind them about your neck.
Thus will you win favour and success 4
in the sight of God and man.

Put all your trust in the LORD 5
and do not rely on your own understanding.
Think of him in all your ways, 6
and he will smooth your path.
Do not think how wise you are, 7
but fear the LORD and turn from evil.
Let that be the medicine to keep you in 8 health,
the liniment for your limbs.
Honour the LORD with your wealth 9
as the first charge on all your earnings;
then your granaries will be filled with 10 corn[k]
and your vats bursting with new wine.
My son, do not spurn the LORD's correc- 11 tion
or take offence at his reproof;
for those whom he loves the LORD re- 12 proves,
and he punishes a favourite son.

Happy he who has found wisdom, 13
and the man who has acquired understanding;
for wisdom is more profitable than silver, 14
and the gain she brings is better than gold.
She is more precious than red coral, 15
and all your jewels are no match for her.
Long life is in her right hand, 16
in her left hand are riches and honour.
Her ways are pleasant ways 17
and all her paths lead to prosperity.
She is a staff of life to all who grasp 18 her,
and those who hold her fast are safe.

In wisdom the LORD founded the earth 19
and by understanding he set the heavens in their place;
by his knowledge the depths burst forth 20
and the clouds dropped dew.

h keep: *prob. rdg.; Heb.* uprightness.   i *Prob. rdg.; Heb.* house.   j resorts to her: *or* takes to them.
k with corn: *or* to overflowing.

21 My son, keep watch over your ability and
    prudence,
    do not let them slip from sight;
22 they shall be a charm hung about your
    neck
    and an ornament on your breast.
23 Then you will go your way without a care,
    and your feet will not stumble.
24 When you sit, you need have no fear;
    when you lie down, your sleep will be
    pleasant.
25 Do not be afraid when fools are frightened
    or when ruin comes upon the wicked;
26 for the LORD will be at your side,
    and he will keep your feet clear of the trap.
27 Refuse no man any favour that you owe
    him
    when it lies in your power to pay it.
28 Do not say to your friend, 'Come back
    again;
    you shall have it tomorrow'—when you
    have it already.
29 Plot no evil against your friend,
    your unsuspecting neighbour.
30 Do not pick a quarrel with a man for no
    reason,
    if he has not done you a bad turn.
31 Do not emulate a lawless man,
    do not choose to follow his footsteps;
32 for one who is not straight is detestable to
    the LORD,
    but upright men are in God's confidence.
33 The LORD's curse rests on the house of the
    evildoer,
    while he blesses the home of the righteous.
34 Though God himself meets the arrogant
    with arrogance,
    yet he bestows his favour on the meek.[l]
35 Wise men are adorned with[m] honour,
    but the coat[n] on a fool's back is contempt.

4 Listen, my sons, to a father's instruction,
    consider attentively how to gain under-
    standing;
2 for it is sound learning I give you;
    so do not forsake my teaching.
3 I too have been a father's son,
    tender in years, my mother's only child.
4 He taught me and said to me:
    Hold fast to my words with all your heart,
    keep my commands and you will have
    life.
5 Do not forget or turn a deaf ear to what
    I say.

7 The first thing[o] is to acquire wisdom;
    gain understanding though it cost you all
    you have.
6 Do not forsake her, and she will keep you
    safe;
    love her, and she will guard you;

cherish her, and she will lift you high;   8
    if only you embrace her, she will bring
    you to honour.
She will set a garland of grace on your   9
    head
    and bestow on you a crown of glory.

Listen, my son, take my words to heart,   10
    and the years of your life shall be multi-
    plied.
I will guide you in the paths of wisdom   11
    and lead you in honest ways.
As you walk you will not slip,   12
    and, if you run, nothing will bring you
    down.
Cling to instruction and never let it go;   13
    observe it well, for it is your life.
Do not take to the course of the wicked   14
    or follow the way of evil men;
    do not set foot on it, but avoid it;   15
    turn aside and go on your way.
For they cannot sleep unless they have   16
    done some wrong;
    unless they have been someone's downfall
    they lose their sleep.
The bread they eat is the fruit of crime   17
    and they drink wine got by violence.
The course of the righteous is like morning   18
    light,
    growing brighter till it is broad day;
    but the ways of the wicked are like dark-   19
    ness at night,
    and they do not know what has been their
    downfall.

My son, attend to my speech,   20
    pay heed to my words;
    do not let them slip out of your mind,   21
    keep them close in your heart;
    for they are life to him who finds them,   22
    and health to his whole body.
Guard your heart more than any treasure,   23
    for it is the source of all life.
Keep your mouth from crooked speech   24
    and your lips from deceitful talk.
Let your eyes look straight before you,   25
    fix your gaze upon what lies ahead.
Look out for the path that your feet must   26
    take,
    and your ways will be secure.
Swerve neither to right nor left,   27
    and keep clear of every evil thing.

l Or wretched.   m are adorned with: prob. rdg.; Heb. shall inherit.   n the coat: prob. rdg.; Heb.
obscure.   o Prob. rdg.; Heb. adds wisdom.

Faithfulness in marriage

5 My son, attend to my wisdom
and listen to my good counsel,
2 so that you may observe proper prudence
and your speech be informed with knowledge.
3 For though the lips of an adulteress drip
honey
and her tongue is smoother than oil,
4 yet in the end she is more bitter than wormwood,
and sharp as a two-edged sword.
5 Her feet go downwards on the path to
death,
her course is set for Sheol.
6 She does not watch for the road that leads
to life;
her course turns this way and that, and
what does she care?[p]

7 Now, my son, listen to me
and do not ignore what I say:
8 keep well away from her
and do not go near the door of her house;
9 or you will lose your dignity in the eyes of
others
and your honour before strangers;
10 strangers will batten on your wealth,
and your hard-won gains pass to another
man's family.
11 The end will be that you will starve,
you will shrink to mere skin and bones.
12 Then you will say, 'Why did I hate correction
and set my heart against reproof?
13 I did not listen to the voice of my teachers
or pay attention to my masters.
14 I soon earned[q] a bad name
and was despised in the public assembly.'

15 Drink water from your own cistern
and running water from your own spring;
16 do not let your[r] well overflow into the road,
your runnels of water pour into the street;
17 let them be yours alone,
not shared with strangers.
18 Let your fountain, the wife of your youth,
be blessed, rejoice in her,
19 a lovely doe, a graceful hind, let her be
your companion;
you will at all times be bathed in her love,
and her love will continually wrap you
round.
Wherever you turn, she will guide you;
when you lie in bed, she will watch over
you,
and when you wake she will talk with
you.[s]
20 Why, my son, are you wrapped up in the
love of an adulteress?
Why do you embrace a loose woman?

21 For a man's ways are always in the LORD's
sight
who watches for every path that he must
take.
22 The wicked man is caught in his own
iniquities
and held fast in the toils of his own sin;
23 he will perish for want of discipline,
wrapped in the shroud of his boundless
folly.

On pledges

6 My son, if you pledge yourself to another
man
and stand surety for a stranger,
2 if you are caught by your promise,
trapped by some promise you have made,
3 do what I now tell you ·
and save yourself, my son:
when you fall into another man's power,
bestir yourself, go and pester the man,
4 give yourself no rest,
allow yourself no sleep.
5 Save yourself like a gazelle from the toils,
like a bird from the grasp of the fowler.

On idleness

6 Go to the ant, you sluggard,
watch her ways and get wisdom.
7 She has no overseer,
no governor or ruler;
8 but in summer she prepares her store of
food
and lays in her supplies at harvest.
9 How long, you sluggard, will you lie abed?
When will you rouse yourself from sleep?
10 A little sleep, a little slumber,
a little folding of the hands in rest,
11 and poverty will come upon you like a
robber,
want like a ruffian.

A troublemaker

12 A scoundrel, a mischievous man, is he
who prowls about with crooked talk—
13 a wink of the eye,
a touch with the foot,
a sign with the fingers.
14 Subversion is the evil that he is plotting,
he stirs up quarrels all the time.
15 Down comes disaster suddenly upon him;
suddenly he is broken beyond all remedy.

What the LORD hates

16 Six things the LORD hates,
seven things are detestable to him:
17 a proud eye, a false tongue,
hands that shed innocent blood,
18 a heart that forges thoughts of mischief,
and feet that run swiftly to do evil,

---

p what . . . care?: *or* she is restless.   q *Or* I almost earned.   r do not let your: *prob. rdg.; Heb.*
shall your.   s Wherever . . . with you: *transposed from ch. 6 (verse 22).*

19 a false witness telling a pack of lies,
and one who stirs up quarrels between
brothers.

Warnings against adultery

20 My son, observe your father's commands
and do not reject the teaching of your
mother;
21 wear them always next your heart
and bind them close about your neck;
23ᵗ for a command is a lamp, and teaching a
light,
reproof and correction point the way of
life,
24 to keep you from the wife of another
man,
from the seductive tongue of the loose
woman.
25 Do not desire her beauty in your heart
or let her glance provoke you;
26 for a prostitute can be had for the price of
a loaf,
but a married woman is out for bigger
game.
27 Can a man kindle fire in his bosom
without burning his clothes?
28 If a man walks on hot coals,
will his feet not be scorched?
29 So is he who sleeps with his neighbour's
wife;
no one can touch such a woman and go
free.
30 Is not a thief contemptible when he steals
to satisfy his appetite, even if he is hungry?
31 And, if he is caught, must he not pay seven
times over
and surrender all that his house contains?
32 So one who commits adultery is a senseless
fool:
he dishonours the woman and ruins himself;
33 he will get nothing but blows and con-
tumely
and will never live down the disgrace;
34 for a husband's anger is a jealous anger
and in the day of vengeance he will show
no mercy;
35 compensation will not buy his forgiveness;ᵘ
no bribe, however large, will purchase his
connivance.

7 My son, keep my words,
store up my commands in your mind.
2 Keep my commands if you would live,
and treasure my teaching as the apple of
your eye.
3 Wear them like a ring on your finger;
write them on the tablet of your memory.

Call Wisdom your sister, 4
greet Understanding as a familiar friend;
then they will save you from the adulteress, 5
from the loose woman with her seductive
words.

I glancedᵛ out of the window of my house, 6
I looked down through the lattice,
and I saw among simple youths, 7
there amongst the boys I noticed
a lad, a foolish lad,
passing along the street, at the corner, 8
stepping out in the direction of her house
at twilight, as the day faded, 9
at dusk as the night grew dark;
suddenly a woman came to meet him, 10
dressed like a prostitute, full of wiles,
flighty and inconstant, 11
a woman never content to stay at home,
lying in wait at every corner, 12
now in the street, now in the public
squares.
She caught hold of him and kissed him; 13
brazenly she accosted him and said,
'I have had a sacrifice, an offering, to make 14
and I have paid my vows today;
that is why I have come out to meet you, 15
to watch for you and find you.
I have spread coverings on my bed 16
of coloured linen from Egypt.
I have sprinkled my bed with myrrh, 17
my clothesʷ with aloes and cassia.
Come! Let us drown ourselves in pleasure, 18
let us spend a whole night of love;
for the man of the house is away, 19
he has gone on a long journey,
he has taken a bag of silver with him; 20
until the moon is full he will not be home.'
Persuasively she led him on, 21
she pressed him with seductive words.
Like a simple fool he followed her, 22
like an ox on its way to the slaughter-
house,
like an antelope bounding into the noose,
like a bird hurrying into the trap; 23
he did not know that he was risking his life
until the arrow pierced his vitals.

But now, my son, listen to me, 24
attend to what I say.
Do not let your heart entice you into her 25
ways,
do not stray down her paths;
many has she pierced and laid low, 26
and her victims are without number.
Her house is the entrance to Sheol, 27
which leads down to the halls of death.

Wisdom and folly contrasted

Hear how Wisdom lifts her voice **8**
and Understanding cries out.

ᵗ *Verse 22 transposed to follow* wrap you round *in 5. 19.*
obscure.   ᵛ I glanced: *prob. rdg.; Heb. om.*
ᵘ compensation . . . forgiveness: *prob. rdg.; Heb.*
ʷ my clothes: *prob. rdg.; Heb. om.*

2 She stands at the cross-roads,
   by the wayside, at the top of the hill;
3 beside the gate, at the entrance to the city,
   at the entry by the open gate she calls
   aloud:
4 'Men, it is to you I call,
   I appeal to every man:
5 understand, you simple fools, what it is
   to be shrewd;
   you stupid people, understand what sense
   means.
6 Listen! For I will speak clearly,
   you will have plain speech from me;
7 for I speak nothing but truth
   and my lips detest wicked talk.
8 All that I say is right,
   not a word is twisted or crooked.
9 All is straightforward to him who can
   understand,
   all is plain to the man who has knowledge.
10 Accept instruction and not silver,
   knowledge rather than pure gold;
11 for wisdom is better than red coral,
   no jewels can match her.
12 I am Wisdom, I bestow shrewdness
   and show the way to knowledge and prudence.
13 ˣPride, presumption, evil courses,
   subversive talk, all these I hate.
14 I have force, I also have ability;
   understanding and power are mine.
15 Through me kings are sovereign
   and governors make just laws.
16 Through me princes act like princes,
   from me all rulers on earth derive their
   nobility.
17 Those who love me I love,
   those who search for me find me.
18 In my hands are riches and honour,
   boundless wealth and the rewards of
   virtue.
19 My harvest is better than gold, fine gold,
   and my revenue better than pure silver.
20 I follow the course of virtue,
   my path is the path of justice;
21 I endow with riches those who love me
   and I will fill their treasuries.

22 'The LORD created me the beginning of
   his works,
   before all else that he made, long ago.
23 Alone, I was fashioned in times long past,
   at the beginning, long before earth itself.
24 When there was yet no ocean I was born,
   no springs brimming with water.
25 Before the mountains were settled in their
   place,
   long before the hills I was born,
26 when as yet he had made neither land nor
   lake
   nor the first clodʸ of earth.

27 When he set the heavens in their place I
   was there,
   when he girdled the ocean with the
   horizon,
28 when he fixed the canopy of clouds overhead
   and set the springs of ocean firm in their
   place,
29 when he prescribed its limits for the seaᶻ
   and knit together earth's foundations.
30 Then I was at his side each day,
   his darling and delight,
   playing in his presence continually,
31 playing on the earth, when he had finished
   it,
   while my delight was in mankind.

32 'Now, my sons, listen to me,
   listen to instruction and grow wise, do not
   reject it.
   Happy is the man who keeps to my ways,
34 happy the man who listens to me,
   watching daily at my threshold
   with his eyes on the doorway;
35 for he who finds me finds life
   and wins favour with the LORD,
36 while he who finds me not, hurts himself,
   and all who hate me are in love with
   death.'

9 Wisdom has built her house,
   she has hewn her seven pillars;
2 she has killed a beast and spiced her wine,
   and she has spread her table.
3 She has sent out her maidens to proclaim
   from the highest part of the town,
4 'Come in, you simpletons.'
   She says also to the fool,
5 'Come, dine with me
   and taste the wine that I have spiced.
6 Cease to be silly, and you will live,
   you will grow in understanding.'

7 Correct an insolent man, and be sneered at
   for your pains;
   correct a bad man, and you will put yourself in the wrong.
8 Do not correct the insolent or they will
   hate you;
   correct a wise man, and he will be your
   friend.
9 Lecture a wise man, and he will grow
   wiser;
   teach a righteous man, and his learning
   will increase.

10 The first step to wisdom is the fear of the
   LORD,
   and knowledge of the Holy One is understanding;
11 for through me your days will be multiplied
   and years will be added to your life.

---

x *Prob. rdg.; Heb. prefixes* The fear of the LORD is to hate evil.   y the first clod: *or* the sum of the clods.
z *Prob. rdg.; Heb. adds* and the water shall not disobey his command.

12 If you are wise, it will be to your own
advantage;
if you are haughty, you alone are to blame.
13 The Lady Stupidity is a flighty creature;
the simpleton, she cares for nothing.
14 She sits at the door of her house,
on a seat in the highest part of the town,
15 to invite the passers-by indoors
as they hurry on their way:
16 'Come in, you simpletons', she says.
She says also to the fool,
17 'Stolen water is sweet
and bread got by stealth tastes good.'
18 Little does he know that death lurks there,
that her guests are in the depths of Sheol.

A collection of wise sayings

10 The proverbs of Solomon:

A wise son brings joy to his father;
a foolish son is his mother's bane.
2 Ill-gotten wealth brings no profit;
uprightness is a safeguard against death.
3 The LORD does not let the righteous go
hungry,[a]
but he disappoints the cravings[b] of the
wicked.
4 Idle hands make a man poor;
busy hands grow rich.
5 A thoughtful son puts by in summer;
a son who sleeps at harvest is a disgrace.
6 Blessings are showered on the righteous;
the wicked are choked by their own
violence.
7 The righteous are remembered in blessings;
the name of the wicked turns rotten.
8 A wise man takes a command to heart;
a foolish talker comes to grief.
9 A blameless life makes for security;
crooked ways bring a man down.
10 To wink at a fault causes trouble;
a frank rebuke leads to peace.
11 The words of good men are a fountain of
life;
the wicked are choked by their own
violence.
12 Hate is always picking a quarrel,
but love turns a blind eye to every fault.
13 The man of understanding has wisdom on
his lips;
a rod is in store for the back of the fool.
14 Wise men lay up knowledge;
when a fool speaks, ruin is near.
15 A rich man's wealth is his strong city,
but poverty is the undoing of the helpless.
16 The good man's labour is his livelihood;
the wicked man's earnings bring him to a
bad end.
17 Correction is the high road to life;
neglect reproof and you miss the way.

18 There is no spite in a just man's talk;
it is the stupid who are fluent with
calumny.
19 When men talk too much, sin is never far
away;
common sense holds its tongue.
20 A good man's tongue is pure silver;
the heart of the wicked is trash.
21 The lips of a good man teach many,
but fools perish for want of sense.
22 The blessing of the LORD brings riches
and he sends no sorrow with them.
23 Lewdness is sport for the stupid;
wisdom a delight to men of understanding.
24 The fears of the wicked will overtake
them;
the desire of the righteous will be granted.
25 When the whirlwind has passed by, the
wicked are gone;
the foundations of the righteous are
eternal.
26 Like vinegar on the teeth or smoke in the
eyes,
so is the lazy servant to his master.
27 The fear of the LORD brings length of days;
the years of the wicked are few.
28 The hope of the righteous blossoms;
the expectation of the wicked withers
away.
29 The way of the LORD gives refuge to the
honest man,
but dismays those who do evil.
30 The righteous man will never be shaken;
the wicked shall not remain on earth.
31 Wisdom flows from the mouth of the
righteous;
the subversive tongue will be rooted out.
32 The righteous man can suit his words to
the occasion;
the wicked know only subversive talk.

11 False scales are the LORD's abomination;
correct weights are dear to his heart.
2 When presumption comes in, in comes
contempt,
but wisdom goes with sagacity.
3 Honesty is a guide to the upright,
but rogues are balked by their own per-
versity.
4 Wealth is worth nothing in the day of
wrath,
but uprightness is a safeguard against
death.
5 By uprightness the blameless keep their
course,
but the wicked are brought down by their
wickedness.
6 Uprightness saves the righteous,
but rogues are trapped in their own greed.
7 When a man dies, his thread of life ends,
and with it ends the hope of affluence.

a Or be afraid.   *b Or* the clamour.

8 A righteous man is rescued from disaster,
and the wicked man plunges into it.

9 By his words a godless man tries to ruin
others,
but they are saved when the righteous
plead for them.

10 A city rejoices in the prosperity of the
righteous;
there is jubilation when the wicked perish.

11 By the blessing of the upright a city is
built up;
the words of the wicked tear it down.

12 A man without sense despises others,
but a man of understanding holds his
peace.

13 A gossip gives away secrets,
but a trusty man keeps his own counsel.

14 For want of skilful strategy an army is lost;
victory is the fruit of long planning.

15 Give a pledge for a stranger and know no
peace;
refuse to stand surety and be safe.

16 Grace in a woman wins honour,
but she who hates virtue makes a home for
dishonour.
Be timid in business and come to beggary;
be bold and make a fortune.

17 Loyalty brings its own reward;
a cruel man makes trouble for his kin.

18 A wicked man earns a fallacious[c] profit;
he who sows goodness reaps a sure
reward.[d]

19 A man set on righteousness finds life,
but the pursuit of evil leads to death.

20 The LORD detests the crooked heart,
but honesty is dear to him.

21 Depend upon it: an evil man shall not
escape punishment;
the righteous and all their offspring shall
go free.

22 Like a gold ring in a pig's snout
is a beautiful woman without good sense.

23 The righteous desire only what is good;
the hope of the wicked comes to nothing.

24 A man may spend freely and yet grow
richer;
another is sparing beyond measure, yet
ends in poverty.

25 A generous man grows fat and prosperous,
and he who refreshes others will himself
be refreshed.

26 He who withholds his grain is cursed by
the people,
but he who sells his corn is blessed.

27 He who eagerly seeks what is good finds
much favour,
but if a man pursues evil it turns upon him.

28 Whoever relies on his wealth is riding for a
fall,
but the righteous flourish like the green leaf.

29 He who brings trouble on his family
inherits the wind,
and a fool becomes slave to a wise man.

30 The fruit of righteousness is a tree of life,
but violence means the taking away of life.

31 If the righteous in the land get their
deserts,
how much more the wicked man and the
sinner!

12 He who loves correction loves knowledge;
he who hates reproof is a mere brute.

2 A good man earns favour from the LORD;
the schemer is condemned.

3 No man can establish himself by wickedness,
but good men have roots that cannot be
dislodged.

4 A capable wife is her husband's crown;
one who disgraces him is like rot in his
bones.

5 The purposes of the righteous are lawful;
the designs of the wicked are full of deceit.

6 The wicked are destroyed[e] by their own
words;
the words of the good man are his salvation.

7 Once the wicked are down, that is the end
of them,
but the good man's line continues.

8 A man is commended for his intelligence,
but a warped mind is despised.

9 It is better to be modest[f] and earn one's
living
than to be conceited[g] and go hungry.

10 A righteous man cares for his beast,
but a wicked man is cruel at heart.

11 He who tills his land has enough to eat,
but to follow idle pursuits is foolishness.

12 The stronghold of the wicked crumbles
like clay,[h]
but the righteous take lasting root.

13 The wicked man is trapped by his own
falsehoods,
but the righteous comes safe through
trouble.

14 One man wins success by his words;
another gets his due reward by the work of
his hands.

15 A fool thinks that he is always right;
wise is the man who listens to advice.

16 A fool shows his ill humour at once;
a clever man slighted conceals his feelings.

---

c Or fraudulent.   d a sure reward: or the reward of honesty.   e Prob. rdg.; Heb. are an ambush
for blood.   f Or scorned.   g Or honoured.   h Prob. rdg.; Heb. A wicked man covets a stronghold of crumbling earth.

17 An honest speaker comes out with the truth,
but the false witness is full of deceit.
18 Gossip can be sharp as a sword,
but the tongue of the wise heals.
19 Truth spoken stands firm for ever,
but lies live only for a moment.
20 Those who plot evil delude themselves,
but there is joy for those who seek the common good.
21 No mischief will befall the righteous,
but wicked men get their fill of adversity.
22 The LORD detests a liar
but delights in the honest man.
23 A clever man conceals his knowledge,
but a stupid man broadcasts his folly.
24 Diligence brings a man to power,
but laziness to forced labour.
25 An anxious heart dispirits a man,
and a kind word fills him with joy.
26 A righteous man recoils from evil,[i]
but the wicked take a path that leads them astray.
27 The lazy hunter puts up no game,
but the industrious man reaps a rich harvest.[j]
28 The way of honesty leads to life,
but there is a well-worn path to death.

13 A wise man sees the reason for his father's correction;
an arrogant man will not listen to rebuke.
2 A good man enjoys the fruit of righteousness,
but violence is meat and drink for the treacherous.
3 He who minds his words preserves his life;
he who talks too much comes to grief.
4 A lazy man is torn by appetite unsatisfied,
but the diligent grow fat and prosperous.
5 The righteous hate falsehood;
the doings of the wicked are foul and deceitful.
6 To do right is the protection of an honest man,
but wickedness brings sinners to grief.[k]
7 One man pretends to be rich, although he has nothing;
another has great wealth but goes in rags.[l]
8 A rich man must buy himself off,
but a poor man is immune from threats.
9 The light of the righteous burns brightly;
the embers of the wicked will be put out.
10 A brainless fool causes strife by his presumption;
wisdom is found among friends in council.
11 Wealth quickly come by dwindles away,
but if it comes little by little, it multiplies.

12 Hope deferred makes the heart sick;
a wish come true is a staff of life.
13 To despise a word of advice is to ask for trouble;
mind what you are told, and you will be rewarded.
14 A wise man's teaching is a fountain of life
for one who would escape the snares of death.
15 Good intelligence wins favour,
but treachery leads to disaster.
16 A clever man is wise and conceals everything,
but the stupid parade their folly.
17 An evil messenger causes trouble,[m]
but a trusty envoy makes all go well again.
18 To refuse correction brings poverty and contempt;
one who takes a reproof to heart comes to honour.
19 Lust indulged sickens a man;[n]
stupid people loathe to mend their ways.
20 Walk with the wise and be wise;
mix with the stupid and be misled.
21 Ill fortune follows the sinner close behind,
but good rewards the righteous.
22 A good man leaves an inheritance to his descendants,
but the sinner's hoard passes to the righteous.
23 Untilled land might yield food enough for the poor,
but even that may be lost through injustice.
24 A father who spares the rod hates his son,
but one who loves him keeps him in order.
25 A righteous man eats his fill,
but the wicked go hungry.

14 The wisest women build up their homes;
the foolish pull them down with their own hands.
2 A straightforward man fears the LORD;
the double-dealer scorns him.
3 The speech of a fool is a rod for his back;[o]
a wise man's words are his safeguard.
4 Where there are no oxen the barn is empty,
but the strength of a great ox ensures rich crops.
5 A truthful witness is no liar;
a false witness tells a pack of lies.
6 A conceited man seeks wisdom, yet finds none;
to one of understanding, knowledge comes easily.
7 Avoid a stupid man,
you will hear not a word of sense from him.

---

i recoils from evil: *prob. rdg.; Heb.* let him spy out his friend.   *j* but . . . harvest: *prob. rdg.; Heb. obscure.*
k brings . . . grief: *or* plays havoc with a man.   *l* One man . . . rags: *or* One man may grow rich though he has nothing; another may grow poor though he has great wealth.   *m* causes trouble: *or* is unsuccessful.
n Lust . . . a man: *or* Desire fulfilled is pleasant to the appetite.   *o* his back: *prob. rdg.; Heb.* pride.

8 A clever man has the wit to find the right way;
the folly of stupid men misleads them.

9 A fool is too arrogant to make amends;
upright men know what reconciliation means.

10 The heart knows its own bitterness,
and a stranger has no part in its joy.

11 The house of the wicked will be torn down,
but the home of the upright flourishes.

12 A road may seem straightforward to a man,
yet may end as the way to death.

13 Even in laughter the heart may grieve,
and mirth may end in sorrow.

14 The renegade reaps the fruit of his conduct,
a good man the fruit of his own achievements.

15 A simple man believes every word he hears;
a clever man understands the need for proof.

16 A wise man is cautious and turns his back on evil;
the stupid is heedless and falls headlong.

17 Impatience runs into folly;
distinction comes by careful thought.*p*

18 The simple wear the trappings of folly;
the clever are crowned with knowledge.

19 Evil men cringe before the good,
wicked men at the righteous man's door.

20 A poor man is odious even to his friend;
the rich have friends in plenty.

21 He who despises a hungry man does wrong,
but he who is generous to the poor is happy.

22 Do not those who intend evil go astray,
while those with good intentions are loyal and faithful?

23 The pains of toil bring gain,
but mere talk brings nothing but poverty.

24 Insight is the crown of the wise;
folly the chief ornament of the stupid.

25 A truthful witness saves life;
the false accuser utters nothing but lies.

26 A strong man who trusts in the fear of the LORD
will be a refuge for his sons.

27 The fear of the LORD is the fountain of life
for the man who would escape the snares of death.

28 Many subjects make a famous king;
with none to rule, a prince is ruined.

29 To be patient shows great understanding;
quick temper is the height of folly.

30 A tranquil mind puts flesh on a man,
but passion rots his bones.

31 He who oppresses*q* the poor insults his Maker;
he who is generous to the needy honours him.

32 An evil man is brought down by his wickedness;
the upright man is secure in his own honesty.

33 Wisdom is at home in a discerning mind,
but is ill at ease in the heart of a fool.

34 Righteousness raises a people to honour;
to do wrong is a disgrace to any nation.

35 A king shows favour to an intelligent servant,
but his displeasure strikes down those who fail him.

15 A soft answer turns away anger,
but a sharp word makes tempers hot.

2 A wise man's tongue spreads knowledge;
stupid men talk nonsense.

3 The eyes of the LORD are everywhere,
surveying evil and good men alike.

4 A soothing word is a staff of life,
but a mischievous tongue breaks the spirit.

5 A fool spurns his father's correction,
but to take a reproof to heart shows good sense.

6 In the righteous man's house there is ample wealth;
the gains of the wicked bring trouble.

7 The lips of a wise man promote knowledge;
the hearts of the stupid are dishonest.

8 The wicked man's sacrifice is abominable to the LORD;
the good man's prayer is his delight.

9 The conduct of the wicked is abominable to the LORD,
but he loves the seeker after righteousness.

10 A man who leaves the main road resents correction,
and he who hates reproof will die.

11 Sheol and Abaddon lie open before the LORD,
how much more the hearts of men!

12 The conceited man does not take kindly to reproof
and he will not consult the wise.

13 A merry heart makes a cheerful face;
heartache crushes the spirit.

14 A discerning mind seeks knowledge,
but the stupid man feeds on folly.

15 In the life of the downtrodden every day is wretched,
but to have a glad heart is a perpetual feast.

16 Better a pittance with the fear of the LORD
than great treasure and trouble in its train.

p distinction . . . thought: *prob. rdg.; Heb.* a man of careful thought is hated.   *q Or* slanders.

17 Better a dish of vegetables if love go
with it
than a fat ox eaten in hatred.

18 Bad temper provokes a quarrel,
but patience heals discords.

19 The path of the sluggard is a tangle of
weeds,
but the road of the diligent is a highway.

20 A wise son brings joy to his father;
a young fool despises his mother.

21 Folly may amuse the empty-headed;
a man of understanding makes straight
for his goal.

22 Schemes lightly made come to nothing,
but with long planning they succeed.

23 A man may be pleased with his own
retort;
how much better is a word in season!

24 For men of intelligence the path of life
leads upwards
and keeps them clear of Sheol below.

25 The LORD pulls down the proud man's
home
but fixes the widow's boundary-stones.

26 A bad man's thoughts are the LORD's
abomination,
but the words of the pure are a delight.*r*

27 A grasping man brings trouble on his
family,
but he who spurns a bribe will enjoy long
life.

28 The righteous think before they answer;
a bad man's ready tongue is full of mischief.

29 The LORD stands aloof from the wicked,
he listens to the righteous man's prayer.

30 A bright look brings joy to the heart,
and good news warms a man's marrow.

31 Whoever listens to wholesome reproof
shall enjoy the society of the wise.

32 He who refuses correction is his own worst
enemy,
but he who listens to reproof learns sense.

33 The fear of the LORD is a training in
wisdom,
and the way to honour is humility.

16 A man may order his thoughts,
but the LORD inspires the words he utters.

2 A man's whole conduct may be pure in his
own eyes,
but the LORD fixes a standard for the spirit
of man.

3 Commit to the LORD all that you do,
and your plans will be fulfilled.

4 The LORD has made each thing for its own
end;
he made even the wicked for a day of
disaster.

Proud men, one and all, are abominable 5
to the LORD;
depend upon it: they will not escape
punishment.

Guilt is wiped out by faith and loyalty, 6
and the fear of the LORD makes men turn
from evil.

When the LORD is pleased with a man and 7
his ways,
he makes even his enemies live at peace
with him.

Better a pittance honestly earned 8
than great gains ill gotten.

Man plans his journey by his own wit, 9
but it is the LORD who guides his steps.

The king's mouth is an oracle, 10
he cannot err when he passes sentence.

Scales*s* and balances*t* are the LORD's 11
concern;
all the weights in the bag are his business.

Wickedness is abhorrent to kings, 12
for a throne rests firm on righteousness.

Honest speech is the desire of kings, 13
they love a man who speaks the truth.

A king's anger is a messenger of death, 14
and a wise man will appease it.

In the light of the king's countenance is 15
life,
his favour is like a rain-cloud in the spring.

How much better than gold it is to gain 16
wisdom,
and to gain discernment is better than pure
silver.

To turn from evil is the highway of the 17
upright;
watch your step and save your life.

Pride comes before disaster, 18
and arrogance before a fall.

Better sit humbly with those in need 19
than divide the spoil with the proud.

The shrewd man of business will succeed 20
well,
but the happy man is he who trusts in the
LORD.

The sensible man seeks advice from the 21
wise,
he drinks it in and increases his knowledge.*u*

Intelligence is a fountain of life to its 22
possessors,
but a fool is punished by his own folly.

The wise man's mind guides his speech, 23
and what his lips impart increases learning.*v*

Kind words are like dripping honey, 24
sweetness on the tongue and health for
the body.

A road may seem straightforward to a 25
man,
yet may end as the way to death.

---

r the words . . . delight: *or* gracious words are pure.   *s Or* Pointer.   *t Prob. rdg.; Heb.* balances of
justice.   *u* he drinks . . . knowledge: *or* and he whose speech is persuasive increases learning.   *v* and
what . . . learning: *or* and increases the learning of his utterance.

26 The labourer's appetite is always plaguing him,
    his hunger spurs him on.

27 A scoundrel repeats evil gossip;
    it is like a scorching fire on his lips.

28 Disaffection stirs up quarrels,
    and tale-bearing breaks up friendship.

29 A man of violence draws others on
    and leads them into lawless ways.

30 The man who narrows his eyes is disaffected at heart,
    and a close-lipped man is bent on mischief.

31 Grey hair is a crown of glory,
    and it is won by a virtuous life.

32 Better be slow to anger than a fighter,
    better govern one's temper than capture a city.

33 The lots may be cast into the lap,
    but the issue depends wholly on the LORD.

17 Better a dry crust and concord with it
    than a house full of feasting and strife.

2 A wise slave may give orders to a disappointing son
    and share the inheritance with the brothers.

3 The melting-pot is for silver and the crucible for gold,
    but it is the LORD who assays the hearts of men.

4 A rogue gives a ready ear to mischievous talk,
    and a liar listens to slander.

5 A man who sneers at the poor insults his Maker,
    and he who gloats over another's ruin will answer for it.

6 Grandchildren are the crown of old age,
    and sons are proud of their fathers.

7 Fine talk is out of place in a boor,
    how much more is falsehood in the noble!

8 He who offers a bribe finds it work like a charm,
    he prospers in all he undertakes.

9 He who conceals another's offence seeks his goodwill,
    but he who harps on something breaks up friendship.

10 A reproof is felt by a man of discernment
    more than a hundred blows by a stupid man.

11 An evil man is set only on disobedience,
    but a messenger without mercy will be sent against him.

12 Better face a she-bear robbed of her cubs
    than a stupid man in his folly.

13 If a man repays evil for good,
    evil will never quit his house.

14 Stealing water starts a quarrel;
    drop a dispute before you bare your teeth.

15 To acquit the wicked and condemn the righteous,
    both are abominable in the LORD's sight.

16 What use is money in the hands of a stupid man?
    Can he buy wisdom if he has no sense?

17 A friend is a loving companion at all times,
    and a brother is born to share troubles.

18 A man is without sense who gives a guarantee
    and surrenders himself to another as surety.

19 He who loves strife loves sin.
    He who builds a lofty entrance invites thieves.

20 A crooked heart will come to no good,
    and a mischievous tongue will end in disaster.

21 A stupid man is the bane of his parent,
    and his father has no joy in a boorish son.

22 A merry heart makes a cheerful countenance,
    but low spirits sap a man's strength.

23 A wicked man accepts a bribe under his cloak
    to pervert the course of justice.

24 Wisdom is never out of sight of a discerning man,
    but a stupid man's eyes are roving everywhere.

25 A stupid son exasperates his father
    and is a bitter sorrow to the mother who bore him.

26 Again, to punish the righteous is not good
    and it is wrong to inflict blows on men of noble mind.

27 Experience uses few words;
    discernment keeps a cool head.

28 Even a fool, if he holds his peace, is thought wise;
    keep your mouth shut and show your good sense.

18 The man who holds aloof seeks every pretext
    to bare his teeth in scorn at competent people.

2 The foolish have no interest in seeking to understand,
    but prefer to display their wit.

3 When wickedness comes in, in comes contempt;
    with loss of honour comes reproach.

4 The words of a man's mouth are a gushing torrent,
    but deep is the water in the well of wisdom.[w]

5 It is not good to show favour to the wicked
    or to deprive the righteous of justice.

---

w The words . . . wisdom: prob. rdg., inverting phrases.

6 When the stupid man talks, contention
follows;
his words provoke blows.

7 The stupid man's tongue is his undoing;
his lips put his life in jeopardy.

8 A gossip's whispers are savoury morsels,
gulped down into the inner man.

9 Again, the lazy worker is own brother
to the man who enjoys destruction.

10 The name of the LORD is a tower of
strength,
where the righteous may run for refuge.

11 A rich man's wealth is his strong city,
a towering wall, so he supposes.

12 Before disaster comes, a man is proud,
but the way to honour is humility.

13 To answer a question before you have
heard it out
is both stupid and insulting.

14 A man's spirit may sustain him in sickness,
but if the spirit is wounded, who can
mend it?

15 Knowledge comes to the discerning mind;
the wise ear listens to get knowledge.

16 A gift opens the door to the giver
and gains access to the great.

17 In a lawsuit the first speaker seems right,
until another steps forward and cross-
questions him.

18 Cast lots, and settle a quarrel,
and so keep litigants apart.

19 A reluctant brother is more unyielding
than a fortress,
and quarrels are stubborn as the bars of a
castle.

20 A man may live by the fruit of his tongue,
his lips may earn him a livelihood.

21 The tongue has power of life and death;
make friends with it and enjoy its fruits.

22 Find a wife, and you find a good thing;
so you will earn the favour of the LORD.

23 The poor man speaks in a tone of entreaty,
and the rich man gives a harsh answer.

24 Some companions are good only for idle
talk,
but a friend may stick closer than a
brother.

19 Better be poor and above reproach
than rich and crooked in speech.

2 Again, desire without knowledge is not
good;
the man in a hurry misses the way.

3 A man's own folly wrecks his life,
and then he bears a grudge against the
LORD.

4 Wealth makes many friends,
but a man without means loses the friend
he has.

5 A false witness will not escape punishment,
and one who utters nothing but lies will
not go free.

6 Many curry favour with the great;
a lavish giver has the world for his
friend.

7 A poor man's brothers all dislike him,
how much more is he shunned by his
friends!
Practice in evil makes the perfect scoundrel;
the man who talks too much meets his
deserts.

8 To learn sense is true self-love;
cherish discernment and make sure of
success.

9 A false witness will not escape punishment,
and one who utters nothing but lies will
perish.

10 A fool at the helm is out of place,
how much worse a slave in command of
men of rank!

11 To be patient shows intelligence;
to overlook faults is a man's glory.

12 A king's rage is like a lion's roar,
his favour like dew on the grass.

13 A stupid son is a calamity to his father;
a nagging wife is like water dripping endlessly.

14 Home and wealth may come down from
ancestors,
but an intelligent wife is a gift from the
LORD.

15 Laziness is the undoing of the worthless;
idlers must starve.

16 To keep the commandments keeps a man
safe,
but scorning the way of the LORD brings
death.

17 He who is generous to the poor lends to
the LORD;
he will repay him in full measure.

18 Chastise your son while there is hope for
him,
but be careful not to flog him to death.

19 A man's ill temper brings its own punishment;
try to save him, and you make matters
worse.

20 Listen to advice and accept instruction,
and you will die a wise man.

21 A man's heart may be full of schemes,
but the LORD's purpose will prevail.

22 Greed is a disgrace to a man;
better be a poor man than a liar.

23 The fear of the LORD is life;
he who is full of it will rest untouched by
evil.

24 The sluggard plunges his hand in the dish
but will not so much as lift it to his
mouth.

25 Strike an arrogant man, and he resents it
like a fool;
reprove an understanding man, and he
understands what you mean.

26 He who talks his father down vexes his
mother;
he is a son to bring shame and disgrace on
them.
27 A son who ceases to accept correction
is sure to turn his back on the teachings of
knowledge.
28 A rascally witness perverts justice,
and the talk of the wicked fosters mischief.
29 There is a rod in pickle for the arrogant,
and blows ready for the stupid man's back.

20 Wine is an insolent fellow, and strong
drink makes an uproar;
no one addicted to their company grows
wise.
2 A king's threat is like a lion's roar;
one who ignores it is his own worst enemy.
3 To draw back from a dispute is honourable;
it is the fool who bares his teeth.
4 The sluggard who does not plough in
autumn
goes begging at harvest and gets nothing.
5 Counsel in another's heart is like deep
water,
but a discerning man will draw it up.
6 Many a man protests his loyalty,
but where will you find one to keep faith?
7 If a man leads a good and upright life,
happy are the sons who come after him!
8 A king seated on the judgement-throne
has an eye to sift all that is evil.
9 Who can say, 'I have a clear conscience;
I am purged from my sin'?
10 A double standard in weights and measures
is an abomination to the LORD.
11 Again, a young man is known by his
actions,
whether his conduct is innocent or guilty.ˣ
12 The ear that hears, the eye that sees,
the LORD made them both.
13 Love sleep, and you will end in poverty;
keep your eyes open, and you will eat your
fill.
14 'A bad bargain!' says the buyer to the
seller,
but off he goes to brag about it.
15 There is gold in plenty and coral too,
but a wise word is a rare jewel.
16 Take a man's garment when he pledges his
word for a stranger
and hold that as a pledge for the unknown
person.
17 Bread got by fraud tastes good,
but afterwards it fills the mouth with grit.
18 Care is the secret of good planning;
wars are won by skilful strategy.
19 A gossip will betray secrets;ʸ
have nothing to do with a tattler.

20 If a man reviles father and mother,
his lamp will go out when darkness comes.
21 If you begin by piling up property in
haste,
it will bring you no blessing in the end.
22 Do not think to repay evil for evil,
wait for the LORD to deliver you.
23 A double standard in weights is an
abomination to the LORD,
and false scales are not good in his sight.
24 It is the LORD who directs a man's steps;
how can mortal man understand the road
he travels?
25 It is dangerous to dedicate a gift rashly
or to make a vow and have second
thoughts.
26 A wise king sifts out the wicked
and turns back for them the wheel of
fortune.
27 The LORD shines into a man's very soul,
searching out his inmost being.
28 A king's guards are loyalty and good faith,
his throne is upheld by righteousness.
29 The glory of young men is their strength,
the dignity of old men their grey hairs.
30 A good beating purges the mind,
and blows chasten the inmost being.

21 The king's heart is under the LORD's
hand;
like runnels of water, he turns it wherever
he will.
2 A man may think that he is always right,
but the LORD fixes a standard for the heart.
3 Do what is right and just;
that is more pleasing to the LORD than
sacrifice.
4 Haughty looks and a proud heart—
these sins mark a wicked man.
5 Forethought and diligence are sure of
profit;
the man in a hurry is as sure of poverty.
6 He who makes a fortune by telling lies
runs needlessly into the toils of death.
7 The wicked are caught up in their own
violence,
because they refuse to do what is just.
8 The criminal's conduct is tortuous;
straight dealing is a sign of integrity.
9 Better to live in a corner of the house-top
than have a nagging wife and a brawling
household.
10 The wicked man is set on evil;
he has no pity to spare for his friend.
11 The simple man is made wise when he
sees the insolent punished,
and learns his lesson when the wise man
prospers.
12 The just Godᶻ makes the wicked man's
home childless;ᵃ
he overturns the wicked and ruins them.

---

x Prob. rdg.; Heb. upright.   y Or He who betrays secrets is a gossip.   z Or The just man.
a makes . . . childless: prob. rdg.; Heb. considers the wicked man's home.

13 If a man shuts his ears to the cry of the helpless,
he will cry for help himself and not be heard.

14 A gift in secret placates an angry man;
a bribe slipped under the cloak pacifies great wrath.

15 When justice is done, all good men rejoice,
but it brings ruin to evildoers.

16 A man who takes leave of common sense comes to rest in the company of the dead.

17 Love pleasure and you will beg your bread;
a man who loves wine and oil will never grow rich.

18 The wicked man serves as a ransom for the righteous,
so does a traitor for the upright.

19 Better to live alone in the desert
than with a nagging and ill-tempered wife.

20 The wise man has his home full of fine and costly treasures;
the stupid man is a mere spendthrift.

21 Persevere in right conduct and loyalty
and you shall find life and honour.

22 A wise man climbs into a city full of armed men
and undermines its strength and its confidence.

23 Keep a guard over your lips and tongue
and keep yourself out of trouble.

24 The conceited man is haughty, his name is insolence;
conceit and impatience are in all he does.

25 The sluggard's cravings will be the death of him,
because his hands refuse to work;

26 all day long his cravings go unsatisfied,
while the righteous man gives without stint.

27 The wicked man's sacrifice is an abomination to the LORD;
how much more when he offers it with vileness at heart!

28 A lying witness will perish,
but he whose words ring true will leave children behind him.

29 A wicked man puts a bold face on it,
whereas the upright man secures his line of retreat.

30 Face to face with the LORD,
wisdom, understanding, counsel go for nothing.

31 A horse may be made ready for the day of battle,
but victory comes from the LORD.

22 A good name is more to be desired than great riches;
esteem is better than silver or gold.

2 Rich and poor have this in common:
the LORD made them both.

3 A shrewd man sees trouble coming and lies low;
the simple walk into it and pay the penalty.

4 The fruit of humility is the fear of God
with riches and honour and life.

5 The crooked man's path is set with snares and pitfalls;
the cautious man will steer clear of them.

6 Start a boy on the right road,
and even in old age he will not leave it.

7 The rich lord it over the poor;
the borrower becomes the lender's slave.

8 The man who sows injustice reaps trouble,
and the end of his work will be the rod.[b]

9 The kindly man will be blessed,
for he shares his food with the poor.

10 Drive out the insolent man, and strife goes with him;
if he sits on the bench, he makes a mockery of justice.

11 The LORD loves a sincere man;
but you will make a king your friend with your fine phrases.

12 The LORD keeps watch over every claim at law,
and overturns the scoundrel's case.

13 The sluggard protests, 'There's a lion outside;
I shall get myself killed in the street.'

14 The words of an adulteress are like a deep pit;
those whom the LORD has cursed will fall into it.

15 Folly is deep-rooted in the heart of a boy;
a good beating will drive it right out of him.

16 Oppression of the poor may bring gain to a man,
but giving to the rich leads only to penury.

Thirty wise sayings

17 The sayings of the wise:
Pay heed and listen to my words,
open your mind to the knowledge I impart;

18 to keep them in your heart will be a pleasure,
and then you will always have them ready on your lips.

19 I would have you trust in the LORD
and so I tell you these things this day for your own good.

20 Here I have written out for you thirty sayings,
full of knowledge and wise advice,

21 to impart to you a knowledge of the truth,
that you may take back a true report[c] to him who sent you.

---

b the rod: or the threshing.   c Prob. rdg.; Heb. adds words of truth.

22 Never rob a helpless man because he is
    helpless,
nor ill-treat a poor wretch in court;
23 for the LORD will take up their cause
and rob him who robs them of their
    livelihood.
24 Never make friends with an angry man
nor keep company with a bad-tempered
    one;
25 be careful not to learn his ways,
or you will find yourself caught in a trap.
26 Never be one to give guarantees,
or to pledge yourself as surety for another;
27 for if you cannot pay, beware:
your bed will be taken from under you.

28 Do not move the ancient boundary-stone
which your forefathers set up.
29 You see a man skilful at his craft:
he will serve kings, he will not serve
    common men.

23 When you sit down to eat with a ruling
    prince,
be sure to keep your mind on what is
    before you,
2 and if you are a greedy man,
cut your throat first.
3 Do not be greedy for his dainties,
for they are not what they seem.
4 Do not slave to get wealth;[d]
be a sensible man, and give up.
5 Before you can look round, it will be gone;
it will surely grow wings
like an eagle, like a bird in the sky.
6 Do not go to dinner with a miser,[e]
do not be greedy for his dainties;
7 for they will stick in your[f] throat like a
    hair.
He will bid you eat and drink,
but his heart is not with you;
8 you will bring up the mouthful you have
    eaten,
and your winning words will have been
    wasted.

9 Hold your tongue in the hearing of a
    stupid man;
for he will despise your words of wisdom.
10 Do not move the ancient boundary-stone
or encroach on the land of orphans:
11 they have a powerful guardian
who will take up their cause against you.
12 Apply your mind to instruction
and open your ears to knowledge when it
    speaks.

13 Do not withhold discipline from a boy;
take the stick to him, and save him from
    death.
14 If you take the stick to him yourself,
you will preserve him from the jaws of
    death.

15 My son, if you are wise at heart,
my heart in its turn will be glad;
16 I shall rejoice with all my soul
when you speak plain truth.

17 Do not try to emulate sinners;
envy only those who fear the LORD day
    by day;
18 do this, and you may look forward to the
    future,
and your thread of life will not be cut
    short.

19 Listen, my son, listen, and become wise;
set your mind on the right course.
20 Do not keep company with drunkards
or those who are greedy for the flesh-
    pots;
21 for drink and greed will end in poverty,
and drunken stupor goes in rags.

22 Listen to your father, who gave you life,
and do not despise your mother when she
    is old.
23 Buy truth, never sell it;
buy wisdom, instruction, and under-
    standing.
24 A good man's father will rejoice
and he who has a wise son will delight in
    him.
25 Give your father and your mother cause
    for delight,
let her who bore you rejoice.

26 My son, mark my words,
and accept my guidance with a will.
27 A prostitute is a deep pit,
a loose woman a narrow well;
28 she lies in wait like a robber
and betrays her husband with man after
    man.

29 Whose is the misery? whose the remorse?
Whose are the quarrels and the anxiety?
Who gets the bruises without knowing
    why?
Whose eyes are bloodshot?
30 Those who linger late over their wine,
those who are always trying some new
    spiced liquor.
31 Do not gulp down the wine, the strong red
    wine,
when the droplets form on the side of the
    cup;[g]
32 in the end it will bite like a snake
and sting like a cobra.

d to get wealth: *or* for an invitation to a feast.   *e Or* a man with an evil eye.   *f Prob. rdg.; Heb.* his.
g Prob. rdg.; Heb. adds it runs smoothly to and fro.

33 Then your eyes see strange sights,
your wits and your speech are confused;
34 you become like a man tossing out at sea,
like one who clings to*ʰ* the top of the
rigging;
35 you say, 'If it lays me flat, what do I care?
If it brings me to the ground, what of it?
As soon as I wake up,
I shall turn to it again.'

24 Do not emulate wicked men
or long to make friends with them;
2 for violence is all they think of,
and all they say means mischief.

3 Wisdom builds the house,
good judgement makes it secure,
4 knowledge furnishes the rooms
with all the precious and pleasant things
that wealth can buy.

5 Wisdom prevails over strength,
knowledge over brute force;
6 for wars are won by skilful strategy,
and victory is the fruit of long planning.

7 Wisdom is too high for a fool;
he dare not open his mouth in court.

8 A man who is bent on mischief
gets a name for intrigue;
9 the intrigues of foolish men misfire,
and the insolent man is odious to his
fellows.

10 If your strength fails on a lucky*ⁱ* day,
how helpless will you be on a day of
disaster!

11 When you see a man being dragged to be
killed, go to his rescue,
and save those being hurried away to their
death.
12 If you say, 'But I do not know this man',
God, who fixes a standard for the heart,
will take note.
God who watches you—be sure he will
know;
he will requite every man for what he does.

13 Eat honey, my son, for it is good,
and the honeycomb so sweet upon the
tongue.
14 Make wisdom too your own;
if you find it, you may look forward to
the future,
and your thread of life will not be cut
short.

15 Do not lie in wait like a felon at the good
man's house,
or raid his farm.

Though the good man may fall seven 16
times, he is soon up again,
but the rascal is brought down by misfortune.
Do not rejoice when your enemy falls,   17
do not gloat when he is brought down;
or the LORD will see and be displeased with 18
you,
and he will cease to be angry with him.

Do not vie with evildoers   19
or emulate the wicked;
for wicked men have no future to look 20
forward to;
their embers will be put out.

My son, fear the LORD and grow rich,   21
but have nothing to do with men of rank,
they will bring about disaster without 22
warning;
who knows what ruin such men may
cause*ʲ*?

More sayings of wise men: 23

Partiality in dispensing justice is not good.
A judge who pronounces a guilty man 24
innocent
is cursed by all nations, all peoples
execrate him;
but for those who convict the guilty all 25
will go well,
they will be blessed with prosperity.
A straightforward answer   26
is as good as a kiss of friendship.

First put all in order out of doors   27
and make everything ready on the land;
then establish your house and home.

Do not be a witness against your neigh- 28
bour without good reason
nor misrepresent him in your evidence.
Do not say,   29
'I will do to him what he has done to
me;
I will requite him for what he has done.'

I passed by the field of an idle man,   30
by the vineyard of a man with no sense.
I looked, and it was all dried up,   31
it was overgrown with thistles
and covered with weeds,
and the stones of its walls had been torn
down.
I saw and I took good note,   32
I considered and learnt the lesson:
a little sleep, a little slumber,   33
a little folding of the hands in rest,
and poverty will come upon you like a 34
robber,
want like a ruffian.

h clings to: *prob. rdg.; Heb.* lies on.   *i* lucky: *prob. rdg.; Heb. om.*   *j* they . . . cause: *or they will
come to sudden disaster; who knows what the ruin of such men will be.*

Proverbs transcribed under Hezekiah

25 More proverbs of Solomon transcribed by the men of Hezekiah king of Judah:

2 The glory of God is to keep things hidden
but the glory of kings is to fathom them.
3 The heavens for height, the earth[k] for depth:
unfathomable is the heart of a king.
4 Rid silver of its impurities,
then it may go to[l] the silversmith;
5 rid the king's presence of wicked men,
and his throne will rest firmly on right-eousness.
6 Do not put yourself forward in the king's presence
or take your place among the great;
7 for it is better that he should say to you, 'Come up here',
than move you down to make room for a nobleman.
8 Be in no hurry to tell everyone what you have seen,
or it will end in bitter reproaches from your friend.
9 Argue your own case with your neighbour,
but do not reveal another man's secrets,
10 or he will reproach you when he hears of it
and your indiscretion will then be beyond recall.
11 Like apples of gold set in silver filigree
is a word spoken in season.
12 Like a golden earring or a necklace of Nubian gold
is a wise man whose reproof finds atten-tive ears.
13 Like the coolness of snow in harvest
is a trusty messenger to those who send him.[m]
14 Like clouds and wind that bring no rain
is the man who boasts of gifts he never gives.
15 A prince may be persuaded by patience,
and a soft tongue may break down solid bone.[n]
16 If you find honey, eat only what you need,
too much of it will make you sick;
17 be sparing in visits to your neighbour's house,
if he sees too much of you, he will dislike you.
18 Like a club or a sword or a sharp arrow
is a false witness who denounces his friend.
19 Like a tooth decayed or a foot limping
is a traitor relied on in the day of trouble.
20 Like one who dresses[o] a wound with vinegar,
so is the sweetest of singers to the heavy-hearted.

21 If your enemy is hungry, give him bread to eat;
if he is thirsty, give him water to drink;
22 so you will heap glowing coals on his head,
and the LORD will reward you.
23 As the north wind holds back the rain,
so an angry glance holds back slander.
24 Better to live in a corner of the house-top
than have a nagging wife and a brawling household.
25 Like cold water to the throat when it is dry
is good news from a distant land.
26 Like a muddied spring or a tainted well
is a righteous man who gives way to a wicked one.
27 A surfeit of honey is bad for a man,
and the quest for honour is burdensome.
28 Like a city that has burst out of its con-fining walls[p]
is a man who cannot control his temper.

26 Like snow in summer or rain at harvest,
honour is unseasonable in a stupid man.
2 Like a fluttering sparrow or a darting swallow,
groundless abuse gets nowhere.
3 The whip for a horse, the bridle for an ass,
the rod for the back of a fool!
4 Do not answer a stupid man in the lan-guage of his folly,
or you will grow like him;
5 answer a stupid man as his folly deserves,
or he will think himself a wise man.
6 He who sends a fool on an errand
cuts his own leg off and displays the stump.
7 A proverb in the mouth of stupid men
dangles helpless as a lame man's legs.
8 Like one who gets the stone caught in his sling
is he who bestows honour on a fool.
9 Like a thorn that pierces a drunkard's hand
is a proverb in a stupid man's mouth.
10 Like an archer who shoots at any passer-by[q]
is one who hires a stupid man or a drun-kard.
11 Like a dog returning to its vomit
is a stupid man who repeats his folly.
12 Do you see that man who thinks himself so wise?
There is more hope for a fool than for him.
13 The sluggard protests, 'There is a lion[r] in the highway,
a lion at large in the streets.'
14 A door turns on its hinges,
a sluggard on his bed.
15 A sluggard plunges his hand in the dish
but is too lazy to lift it to his mouth.

---

k Or the underworld.   *l* then it may go to: *or* and it will come out bright for.   *m Prob. rdg.; Heb. adds* refreshing his master.   *n* solid bone: *or* authority.   *o Prob. rdg.; Heb. adds* a garment on a cold day.   *p Or* that is breached and left unwalled.   *q* passer-by: *transposed from end of verse.*   *r Or* snake.

16 A sluggard is wiser in his own eyes
   than seven men who answer sensibly.
17 Like a man who seizes a passing cur by the
   ears
   is he who meddles in another's quarrel.
19s A man who deceives another
   and then says, 'It was only a joke',
18 is like a madman shooting at random
   his deadly darts and arrows.
20 For lack of fuel a fire dies down
   and for want of a tale-bearer a quarrel
   subsides.
21 Like bellows for the coal and fuel for the
   fire
   is a quarrelsome man for kindling strife.
22 A gossip's whispers are savoury morsels
   gulped down into the inner man.
23 Glib speech that covers a spiteful heart
   is like glaze spread on earthenware.
24 With his lips an enemy may speak you fair
   but inwardly he harbours deceit;
25 when his words are gracious, do not trust
   him,
   for seven abominations fill his heart;
26 he may cloak his enmity in dissimulation,
   but his wickedness is shown up before the
   assembly.
27 If he digs a pit, he will fall into it;
   if he rolls a stone, it will roll back upon
   him.
28 A lying tongue makes innocence seem
   guilty,
   and smooth words conceal their sting.

27 Do not flatter yourself about tomorrow,
   for you never know what a day will bring
   forth.
2 Let flattery come from a stranger, not from
   yourself,
   from the lips of an outsider and not from
   your own.
3 Stone is a burden and sand a dead weight,
   but to be vexed by a fool is more burdensome than either.
4 Wrath is cruel and anger is a deluge;
   but who can stand up to jealousy?
5 Open reproof is better
   than love concealed.
6 The blows a friend gives are well meant,
   but the kisses of an enemy are perfidious.
7 A man full-fed refuses honey,
   but even bitter food tastes sweet to a
   hungry man.
8 Like a bird that strays far from its nest
   is a man far from his home.
9 Oil and perfume bring joy to the heart,
   but cares torment a man's very soul.
10 Do not neglect your own friend or your
   father's;t
   a neighbour at hand is better than a
   brother far away.

11 Be wise, my son, then you will bring joy
   to my heart,
   and I shall be able to forestall my critics.
12 A shrewd man sees trouble coming and
   lies low;
   the simple walk into it and pay the penalty.
13 Take a man's garment when he pledges
   his word for a stranger
   and hold that as a pledge for the unknown
   person.
14 If one man greets another too heartily,
   he may give great offence.
15 Endless dripping on a rainy day—
   that is what a nagging wife is like.
16 As well try to control the wind as to
   control her!
   As well try to pick up oil in one's fingers!
17 As iron sharpens iron,
   so one man sharpens the wits of another.
18 He who guards the fig-tree will eat its fruit,
   and he who watches his master's interests
   will come to honour.
19 As face answers face reflected in the water,
   so one man's heart answers another's.
20 Sheol and Abaddon are insatiable;
   a man's eyes too are never satisfied.
21 The melting-pot is for silver and the
   crucible for gold,
   but praise is the test of character.
22 Pound a fool with pestle and mortar,u
   his folly will never be knocked out of him.

23 Be careful to know your own sheep
   and take good care of your flocks;
24 for possessions do not last for ever,
   nor will a crown endure to endless generations.
25 The grass disappears, new shoots are seen
   and the green growth on the hills is
   gathered in;
26 the lambs clothe you,
   the he-goats are worth the price of a field,
27 while the goats' milk is enough for your
   food
   and nourishment for your maidens.

28 The wicked man runs away with no one in
   pursuit,
   but the righteous is like a young lion in
   repose.
2 It is the fault of a violent man that quarrels
   start,
   but they are settled by a man of discernment.
3 A tyrant oppressing the poor
   is like driving rain which ruins the crop.
4 The lawless praise wicked men;
   the law-abiding contend with them.
5 Bad men do not know what justice is,
   but those who seek the LORD know everything good.

s *Verses 18 and 19 transposed.*   t *Prob. rdg.; Heb. adds* or how should you enter your brother's house
in the day of your ruin?   u *Prob. rdg.; Heb. adds* with groats.

6 Better be poor and above reproach
   than rich and crooked.

7 A discerning son observes the law,
   but one who keeps riotous company
   wounds his father.

8 He who grows rich by lending at discount
   or at interest
   is saving for another who will be generous
   to the poor.

9 If a man turns a deaf ear to the law,
   even his prayers are an abomination.

10 He who tempts the upright into evil
   courses
   will himself fall into the pit he has dug.
   The honest shall inherit a fortune,
   but the wicked shall inherit nothing.

11 The rich man may think himself wise,
   but a poor man of discernment sees
   through him.

12 When the just are in power, there are great
   celebrations,[v]
   but when the wicked come to the top,
   others are downtrodden.

13 Conceal your faults, and you will not
   prosper;
   confess and give them up, and you will
   find mercy.

14 Happy the man who is scrupulous in
   conduct,
   but he who hardens his heart falls into
   misfortune.

15 Like a starving lion or a thirsty bear
   is a wicked man ruling a helpless people.

16 The man who is stupid and grasping will
   perish,
   but he who hates ill-gotten gain will live
   long.

17 A man charged with bloodshed
   will jump into a well to escape arrest.

18 Whoever leads an honest life will be
   safe,
   but a rogue will fail, one way or another.

19 One who cultivates his land has plenty to
   eat;
   idle pursuits lead to poverty.

20 A man of steady character will enjoy
   many blessings,
   but one in a hurry to grow rich will not
   go unpunished.

21 To show favour is not good;
   but men will do wrong for a mere crust of
   bread.

22 The miser[w] is in a hurry to grow rich,
   never dreaming that want will overtake
   him.

23 Take a man to task and in the end win
   more thanks
   than the man with a flattering tongue.

24 To rob your father or mother and say you
   do no wrong
   is no better than wanton destruction.

25 A self-important[x] man provokes quarrels,
   but he who trusts in the LORD grows fat
   and prosperous.

26 It is plain stupidity to trust in one's own
   wits,
   but he who walks the path of wisdom will
   come safely through.

27 He who gives to the poor will never want,
   but he who turns a blind eye gets nothing
   but curses.

28 When the wicked come to the top, others
   are pulled down;[y]
   but, when they perish, the righteous come
   into power.

29 A man who is still stubborn after much
   reproof
   will suddenly be broken past mending.

2 When the righteous are in power the
   people rejoice,
   but they groan when the wicked hold
   office.

3 A lover of wisdom brings joy to his father,
   but one who keeps company with harlots
   squanders his wealth.

4 By just government a king gives his
   country stability,
   but by forced contributions he reduces it
   to ruin.

5 A man who flatters his neighbour
   is spreading a net for his feet.

6 An evil man is ensnared by his sin,[z]
   but a righteous man lives and flourishes.

7 The righteous man is concerned for the
   cause of the helpless,
   but the wicked understand no such concern.

8 Arrogance can inflame a city,
   but wisdom averts the people's anger.

9 If a wise man goes to law with a fool,
   he will meet abuse or derision, but get no
   remedy.

10 Men who have tasted blood hate an honest
   man,
   but the upright set much store by his
   life.

11 A stupid man gives free rein to his
   anger;
   a wise man waits and lets it grow cool.

12 If a prince listens to falsehood,
   all his servants will be wicked.

13 Poor man and oppressor have this in
   common:
   what happiness each has comes from the
   LORD.

14 A king who steadfastly deals out justice
   to the weak
   will be secure for ever on his throne.

15 Rod and reprimand impart wisdom,
   but a boy who runs wild brings shame on
   his mother.

---

v Or there is great pageantry.   w Or The man with the evil eye.   x Or grasping.   y are pulled
down: or hide themselves.   z An evil . . . sin: or When an evil man steps out a trap awaits him.

16 When the wicked are in power, sin is in
power,
but the righteous will gloat over their
downfall.
17 Correct your son, and he will be a comfort
to you
and bring you delights of every kind.
18 Where there is no one in authority,^a the
people break loose,
but a guardian of the law keeps them on
the straight path.
19 Mere words will not keep a slave in order;
he may understand, but he will not respond.
20 When you see someone over-eager to
speak,^b
there will be more hope for a fool than for
him.
21 Pamper a slave from boyhood,
and in the end he will prove ungrateful.
22 A man prone to anger provokes a quarrel
and a hot-head is always doing wrong.
23 Pride will bring a man low;
a man lowly in spirit wins honour.
24 He who goes shares with a thief is his own
enemy:
he hears himself put on oath and dare not
give evidence.
25 A man's fears will prove a snare to him,
but he who trusts in the LORD has a high
tower of refuge.
26 Many seek audience of a prince,
but in every case the LORD decides.
27 The righteous cannot abide an unjust man,
nor the wicked a man whose conduct is
upright.

Sayings of Agur

30 Sayings of Agur son of Jakeh from Massa:^c
This is the great man's very word: I am
weary, O God,
I am weary and worn out;
2 I am a dumb brute, scarcely a man,
without a man's powers of understanding;
3 I have not learnt wisdom
nor have I received knowledge from the
Holy One.
4 Who has ever gone up to heaven and come
down again?
Who has cupped the wind in the hollow
of his hands?
Who has bound up the waters in the fold
of his garment?
Who has fixed the boundaries of the earth?
What is his name or his son's name, if
you know it?
5 God's every promise has stood the test:
he is a shield to all who seek refuge with
him.

Add nothing to his words,   6
or he will expose you for a liar.
Two things I ask of thee;   7
do not withhold them from me before
I die.
Put fraud and lying far from me;   8
give me neither poverty nor wealth,
provide me only with the food I need.
If I have too much, I shall deny thee   9
and say, 'Who is the LORD?'
If I am reduced to poverty, I shall steal
and blacken the name of my God.

Never disparage a slave to his master,   10
or he will speak ill of you, and you will pay
for it.

There is a sort of people who defame their   11
fathers
and do not speak well of their own
mothers;
a sort who are pure in their own eyes   12
and yet are not cleansed of their filth;
a sort—how haughty are their looks,   13
how disdainful their glances!
A sort whose teeth are swords,   14
their jaws are set with knives,
they eat the wretched out of the country
and the needy out of house and home.^d

The leech has two daughters;   15
'Give', says one, and 'Give', says the other.

Three things there are which will never be
satisfied,
four which never say, 'Enough!'
The grave and a barren womb,^e   16
a land thirsty for water
and fire that never says, 'Enough!'

The eye that mocks a father or scorns a   17
mother's old age^f
will be plucked out by magpies
or eaten by the vulture's young.

Three things there are which are too wonder- 18
ful for me,
four which I do not understand:
the way of a vulture in the sky,   19
the way of a serpent on the rock,
the way of a ship out at sea,
and the way of a man with a girl.

The way of an unfaithful wife is this: 20
she eats, then she wipes her mouth
and says, 'I have done no harm.'

At three things the earth shakes,   21
four things it cannot bear:
a slave turned king,   22
a churl gorging himself,
a woman unloved when she is married,   23
and a slave-girl displacing her mistress.

---

a Or no vision.   *b Or* someone hasty in business.   *c from* Massa: *prob. rdg. (cp. 31. 1); Heb.* the oracle.
d house and home: *prob. rdg.; Heb.* man.   *e Or* a woman's desire.   *f* old age: *prob. rdg.; Heb. unintelligible.*

24 Four things there are which are smallest on
     earth
   yet wise beyond the wisest:
25 ants, a people with no strength,
   yet they prepare their store of food in the
     summer;
26 rock-badgers, a feeble folk,
   yet they make their home among the
     rocks;
27 locusts, which have no king,
   yet they all sally forth in detachments;
28 the lizard, which can be grasped in the
     hand,
   yet is found in the palaces of kings.

29 Three things there are which are stately in
     their stride,
   four which are stately as they move:
30 the lion, a hero among beasts,
   which will not turn tail for anyone;
31 the strutting cock and the he-goat;
   and a king going forth to lead his
     army.*g*

32 If you are churlish and arrogant
   and fond of filthy talk, hold your tongue;
33 for wringing out the milk produces curd
   and wringing the nose produces blood,
   so provocation leads to strife.

Sayings of Lemuel

31 Sayings of Lemuel king of Massa, which his
   mother taught him:
2 What, O my son, what shall I say to
     you,
   you, the child of my womb and answer to
     my prayers?
3 Do not give the vigour of your manhood
     to women
   nor consort with those who make eyes at*h*
     kings.
4 It is not for kings, O Lemuel, not for kings
     to drink wine
   nor for princes to crave strong drink;
5 if they drink, they will forget rights and
     customs
   and twist the law against their wretched
     victims.
6 Give strong drink to the desperate
   and wine to the embittered;
7 such men will drink and forget their
     poverty
   and remember their trouble no longer.
8 Open your mouth and speak up for the
     dumb,
   against the suit of any that oppose them;

open your mouth and pronounce just 9
   sentence
and give judgement for the wretched and
   the poor.

A capable wife

Who can find a capable wife? 10
Her worth is far beyond coral.
Her husband's whole trust is in her, 11
and children are not lacking.
She repays him with good, not evil, 12
all her life long.
She chooses wool and flax 13
and toils at her work.
Like a ship laden with merchandise, 14
she brings home food from far off.
She rises while it is still night 15
and sets meat before her household.*i*
After careful thought she buys a field 16
and plants a vineyard out of her earnings.
She sets about her duties with vigour 17
and braces herself for the work.
She sees that her business goes well, 18
and never puts out her lamp at night.
She holds the distaff in her hand, 19
and her fingers grasp the spindle.
She is open-handed to the wretched 20
and generous to the poor.
She has no fear for her household when it 21
   snows,
for they are wrapped in two cloaks.
She makes her own coverings, 22
and clothing of fine linen and purple.
Her husband is well known in the city gate 23
when he takes his seat with the elders of
   the land.
She weaves linen and sells it, 24
and supplies merchants with their sashes.
She is clothed in dignity and power 25
and can afford to laugh at tomorrow.
When she opens her mouth, it is to speak 26
   wisely,
and loyalty is the theme of her teaching.
She keeps her eye on the doings of her 27
   household
and does not eat the bread of idleness.
Her sons with one accord call her happy; 28
her husband too, and he sings her praises:
'Many a woman shows how capable she 29
   is;*j*
but you excel them all.'
Charm is a delusion and beauty fleeting; 30
it is the God-fearing woman who is
   honoured.
Extol her for the fruit of all her toil, 31
and let her labours bring her honour in
   the city gate.

g going forth to lead his army: *prob. rdg.; Heb. unintelligible.*   *h* who make eyes at: *prob. rdg.; Heb.*
unintelligible.   *i Prob. rdg.; Heb. adds* and a prescribed portion for her maidens.   *j Or* Many
daughters show how capable they are.

ECCLESIASTES

Preface

1 THE WORDS of the speaker, the son of David, king in Jerusalem.
2 Emptiness, emptiness, says the Speaker,
3 emptiness, all is empty. What does man gain from all his labour and his toil here under
4 the sun? Generations come and generations go, while the earth endures for ever.
5 The sun rises and the sun goes down; back it returns to its place*a* and rises there again.
6 The wind blows south, the wind blows north, round and round it goes and returns
7 full circle. All streams run into the sea, yet the sea never overflows; back to the place from which the streams ran they return to run again.
8 All things are wearisome;*b* no man can speak of them all. Is not the eye surfeited with seeing, and the ear sated with hearing?
9 What has happened will happen again, and what has been done will be done again, and
10 there is nothing new under the sun. Is there anything of which one can say, 'Look, this is new'? No, it has already existed, long ago
11 before our time. The men of old are not remembered, and those who follow will not be remembered by those who follow them.
12 I, the Speaker, ruled as king over Israel in
13 Jerusalem; and in wisdom I applied my mind to study and explore all that is done under heaven. It is a sorry business that God has
14 given men to busy themselves with. I have seen all the deeds that are done here under the sun; they are all emptiness and chasing
15 the wind. What is crooked cannot become straight; what is not there cannot be counted.
16 I said to myself, 'I have amassed great wisdom, more than all my predecessors on the throne in Jerusalem; I have become familiar
17 with wisdom and knowledge.' So I applied my mind to understand wisdom and knowledge, madness and folly, and I came to see
18 that this too is chasing the wind. For in much wisdom is much vexation, and the more a man knows, the more he has to suffer.

The emptiness of pleasures

2 I said to myself, 'Come, I will plunge into pleasures and enjoy myself'; but this too
2 was emptiness. Of laughter I said, 'It is madness!' And of pleasure, 'What is the
3 good of that?' So I sought to stimulate myself with wine, in the hope of finding out what was good for men to do under heaven

throughout the brief span of their lives. But my mind was guided by wisdom, not blinded by*c* folly.

The emptiness of amassing wealth

I undertook great works; I built myself 4 houses and planted vineyards; I made my- 5 self gardens and parks and planted all kinds of fruit-trees in them; I made myself pools 6 of water to irrigate a grove of growing trees; I bought slaves, male and female, and I 7 had my home-born slaves as well; I had possessions, more cattle and flocks than any of my predecessors in Jerusalem; I amassed 8 silver and gold also, the treasure of kings and provinces; I acquired singers, men and women, and all that man delights in.*d* I was 9 great, greater than all my predecessors in Jerusalem; and my wisdom stood me in good stead. Whatever my eyes coveted, I 10 refused them nothing, nor did I deny myself any pleasure. Yes indeed, I got pleasure from all my labour, and for all my labour this was my reward. Then I turned and reviewed all 11 my handiwork, all my labour and toil, and I saw that everything was emptiness and chasing the wind, of no profit under the sun.

The emptiness of both wisdom and folly

I set myself to look at wisdom and at mad- 12 ness and folly.*e* Then I perceived that wisdom 13 is more profitable than folly, as light is more profitable than darkness: the wise man has 14 eyes in his head, but the fool walks in the

---

a back . . . place: *prob. rdg.; Heb.* to its place panting.   *b Prob. rdg.; Heb.* weary.   *c* not blinded by: *prob. rdg.; Heb.* to grasp.   *d Prob. rdg.; Heb.* adds two unintelligible words.   *e The rest of verse 12 transposed to follow verse 18.*

dark. Yet I saw also that one and the same
15 fate overtakes them both. So I said to myself,
'I too shall suffer the fate of the fool. To
what purpose have I been wise? What*f* is
the profit of it? Even this', I said to myself,
16 'is emptiness. The wise man is remembered
no longer than the fool, for, as the passing
days multiply,*g* all will be forgotten. Alas,
17 wise man and fool die the same death!' So
I came to hate life, since everything that was
done here under the sun was a trouble to
me; for all is emptiness and chasing the
18 wind. So I came to hate all my labour and
toil here under the sun, since I should have
to leave its fruits to my successor. What sort
of a man will he be who succeeds me, who
19 inherits what others have acquired?*h* Who
knows whether he will be a wise man or a
fool? Yet he will be master of all the fruits
of my labour and skill here under the sun.
This too is emptiness.

Despair

20 Then I turned and gave myself up to despair,
reflecting upon all my labour and toil here
21 under the sun. For anyone who toils with
wisdom, knowledge, and skill must leave it
all to a man who has spent no labour on it.
This too is emptiness and utterly wrong.
22 What reward has a man for all his labour,
his scheming, and his toil here under the
23 sun? All his life long his business is pain and
vexation to him; even at night his mind
24 knows no rest. This too is emptiness. There
is nothing better for a man to do than to
eat and drink and enjoy himself in return
for his labours. And yet I saw that this comes
25 from the hand of God. For without him who
can enjoy his food, or who can be anxious?
26 God gives wisdom and knowledge and joy
to the man who pleases him, while to the
sinner is given the trouble of gathering and
amassing wealth only to hand it over to
someone else who pleases God. This too is
emptiness and chasing the wind.

A time for everything

3 For everything its season, and for every
activity under heaven its time:
2 a time to be born and a time to die;
a time to plant and a time to uproot;
3 a time to kill and a time to heal;
a time to pull down and a time to build up;
4 a time to weep and a time to laugh;
a time for mourning and a time for dancing;
5 a time to scatter stones and a time to gather
them;
a time to embrace and a time to refrain from
embracing;

a time to seek and a time to lose; 6
a time to keep and a time to throw away;
a time to tear and a time to mend; 7
a time for silence and a time for speech;
a time to love and a time to hate; 8
a time for war and a time for peace.

What profit does one who works get from 9
all his labour? I have seen the business that 10
God has given men to keep them busy. He 11
has made everything to suit its time; moreover he has given men a sense of time past
and future, but no comprehension of God's
work from beginning to end. I know that 12
there is nothing good for man*i* except to be
happy and live the best life he can while he
is alive. Moreover, that a man should eat 13
and drink and enjoy himself, in return for
all his labours, is a gift of God. I know that 14
whatever God does lasts for ever; to add to
it or subtract from it is impossible. And he
has done it all in such a way that men must
feel awe in his presence. Whatever is has 15
been already,*j* and whatever is to come has
been already, and God summons each event
back in its turn.

Creatures of chance

Moreover I saw here under the sun that, 16
where justice ought to be, there was wickedness, and where righteousness ought to be,
there was wickedness. I said to myself, 'God 17
will judge the just man and the wicked
equally; every activity and*k* every purpose
has its proper time.' I said to myself, 'In 18
dealing with men it is God's purpose*l* to
test them and to see what they truly are.'*m*
For man is a creature of chance and the 19
beasts are creatures of chance, and one mis-
chance awaits them all: death comes to both
alike. They all draw the same breath. Men
have no advantage over beasts; for everything is emptiness. All go to the same place: 20
all came from the dust, and to the dust all
return. Who knows whether the spirit*n* of 21
man goes upward or whether the spirit*n*
of the beast goes downward to the earth?'
So I saw that there is nothing better than 22
that a man should enjoy his work, since that
is his lot. For who can bring him through
to see what will happen next?

On injustice and on human achievement

Again, I considered all the acts of oppres- 4
sion here under the sun; I saw the tears of
the oppressed, and I saw that there was no
one to comfort them. Strength was on the
side of their oppressors, and there was no
one to avenge them. I counted the dead 2

f Prob. rdg.; Heb. Then.   *g* for . . . multiply: *prob. rdg.; Heb.* because already.   *h* What sort . . .
acquired: *see note on verse 12.*   *i* for man: *prob. rdg., cp. 2. 24; Heb.* in them.   *j Or* Whatever has
been already is.   *k Prob. rdg.; Heb.* and upon.   *l* it is God's purpose: *prob. rdg.; Heb.* obscure.
m Prob. rdg.; Heb. adds they to them.   *n Or* breath.

happy because they were dead, happier than
3 the living who are still in life. More fortunate than either I reckoned the man yet
unborn, who had not witnessed the wicked
4 deeds done here under the sun. I considered
all toil and all achievement and saw that it
comes from rivalry between man and man.
This too is emptiness and chasing the wind.
5 The fool folds his arms and wastes away.
6 Better one hand full and peace of mind, than
both fists full and toil that is chasing the
wind.

Rich but lonely

7 Here again, I saw emptiness under the sun:
8 a lonely man without a friend, without son
or brother, toiling endlessly yet never satisfied with his wealth—'For whom', he asks,
'am I toiling and denying myself the good
things of life?' This too is emptiness, a sorry
9 business. Two are better than one; they
10 receive a good reward for their toil, because,
if one falls, the other*o* can help his companion up again; but alas for the man who
falls alone with no partner to help him up.
11 And, if two lie side by side, they keep each
other warm; but how can one keep warm by
12 himself? If a man is alone, an assailant may
overpower him, but two can resist; and a
cord of three strands is not quickly snapped.

The emptiness of greatness

13 Better a young man poor and wise than a
king old and foolish who will listen to advice
14 no longer. A man who leaves prison may
well come to be king, though born a pauper
15 in his future kingdom. But I have studied all
life here under the sun, and I saw his place
16 taken by yet another young man, and no
limit set to the number of the subjects whose
master he became. And he in turn will be
no hero to those who come after him. This
too is emptiness and chasing the wind.

Reverence for God

5 Go carefully when you visit the house of
God. Better draw near in obedience than
offer the sacrifice of fools, who sin without
2 a thought. Do not rush into speech, let
there be no hasty utterance in God's presence. God is in heaven, you are on earth;
3 so let your words be few. The sensible man
has much business on his hands; the fool
4 talks and it is so much chatter. When you
make a vow to God, do not be slow to pay
it, for he has no use for fools; pay whatever
5 you vow. Better not vow at all than vow and
6 fail to pay. Do not let your tongue lead you
into sin, and then say before the angel of

God that it was a mistake; or God will be
angry at your words, and all your achievements will be brought to nothing.*p* You 7
must fear God.

On injustice

If you witness in some province the oppres- 8
sion of the poor and the denial of right and
justice, do not be surprised at what goes on,
for every official has a higher one set over
him, and the highest*q* keeps watch over them
all. The best thing for a country is a king 9
whose*r* own lands are well tilled.

The problems wealth brings

The man who loves money can never have 10
enough, and the man who is in love with
great wealth enjoys no return from it. This
too is emptiness. When riches multiply, so 11
do those who live off them; and what advantage has the owner, except to look at them?
Sweet is the sleep of the labourer whether 12
he eats little or much; but the rich man owns
too much and cannot sleep. There is a 13
singular evil here under the sun which I
have seen: a man hoards wealth to his own
hurt, and then that wealth is lost through 14
an unlucky venture, and the owner's son
left with nothing. As he came from the 15
womb of mother earth, so must he return,
naked as he came; all his toil produces
nothing which he can take away with him.
This too is a singular evil: exactly as he 16
came, so shall he go, and what profit does
he get when his labour is all for the wind?
What is more, all his days are overshadowed; 17
gnawing anxiety and great vexation are his
lot, sickness*s* and resentment. What I have 18
seen is this: that it is good and proper for a
man to eat and drink and enjoy himself in
return for his labours here under the sun,
throughout the brief span of life which God
has allotted him. Moreover, it is a gift of 19
God that every man to whom he has granted
wealth and riches and the power to enjoy
them should accept his lot and rejoice in his
labour. He will not dwell overmuch upon 20
the passing years; for God fills his*t* time with
joy of heart.

Here is an evil under the sun which I have **6**
seen, and it weighs heavy upon men. Con- 2
sider the man to whom God grants wealth,
riches, and substance,*u* and who lacks nothing that he has set his heart on: if God has
not given him the power to enjoy these things,
but a stranger enjoys them instead, that is
emptiness and a grave disorder. A man may 3
have a hundred children and live a long life;
but however many his days may be, if he

---

o if one falls, the other: prob. rdg.; Heb. obscure.
and empty things and many words.
Highest . . .   r whose: prob. rdg.; Heb. for.
prob. rdg.; Heb. om.   u Or honour.

p Prob. rdg.; Heb. adds for in a multitude of dreams
q for every . . . the highest: or though every . . . over him, the
s sickness: prob. rdg.; Heb. and his sickness.   t his:

does not get satisfaction from the good things of life and in the end receives no burial, then I maintain that the still-born 4 child is in better case than he. Its coming is an empty thing, it departs into darkness, and 5 in darkness its name is hidden; it has never seen the sun or known anything,[v] yet its 6 state is better than his. What if a man should live a thousand years twice over, and never prosper? Do not both go to one place?

This brief span

7 The end of all man's toil is but to fill his 8 belly, yet his appetite is never satisfied. What advantage then in facing life has the wise man over the fool, or the poor man for all 9 his experience? It is better to be satisfied with what is before your eyes than give rein to desire; this too is emptiness and chasing 10 the wind. Whatever has already existed has been given a name, its nature is known; a man cannot contend with what is stronger 11 than he. The more words one uses the greater is the emptiness of it all; and where 12 is the advantage to a man? For who can know what is good for a man in this life, this brief span of empty existence through which he passes like a shadow? Who can tell a man what is to happen next here under the sun?

Wisdom and folly compared

7 A good name smells sweeter than the finest ointment, and the day of death is better 2 than the day of birth. Better to visit the house of mourning than the house of feasting; for to be mourned is the lot of every man, and the living should take this to 3 heart. Grief is better than laughter: a sad 4 face may go with a cheerful heart. Wise men's thoughts are at home in the house of mourning, but a fool's thoughts in the house 5 of mirth. It is better to listen to a wise man's 6 rebuke than to the praise of fools. For the laughter of a fool is like the crackling of thorns under a pot. This too is emptiness. 7 Slander drives a wise man crazy and breaks 8 a strong man's[w] spirit. Better the end of anything than its beginning; better patience 9 than pride. Do not be quick to show resent-10 ment; for resentment is nursed by fools. Do not ask why the old days were better than 11 these; for that is a foolish question. Wisdom is better than possessions and an advantage 12 to all who see the sun. Better have wisdom behind you than money; wisdom profits men by giving life to those who know her. 13 Consider God's handiwork; who can 14 straighten what he has made crooked? When

things go well, be glad; but when things go ill, consider this: God has set the one alongside the other in such a way that no one can find out what is to happen next.[x] In my empty existence I have seen it all, 15 from a righteous man perishing in his righteousness to a wicked man growing old in his wickedness. Do not be over-righteous 16 and do not be over-wise. Why make yourself a laughing-stock? Do not be over-wicked 17 and do not be a fool. Why should you die before your time? It is good to hold on to 18 the one thing and not lose hold of the other; for a man who fears God will succeed both ways. Wisdom makes the wise man stronger 19 than the ten rulers of a city. The world 20 contains no man so righteous that he can do right always and never do wrong.[y] Moreover, do not pay attention to every- 21 thing men say, or you may hear your servant disparage you; for you know very well how 22 many times you yourself have disparaged others. All this I have put to the test of 23 wisdom. I said, 'I am resolved to be wise', but wisdom was beyond my grasp—what- 24 ever has happened lies beyond our grasp, deep down, deeper than man can fathom. I went on to reflect, I set my mind[z] to 25 inquire and search for wisdom and for the reason in things, only to discover that it is folly to be wicked and madness to act like a fool. The wiles of a woman I find mightier[a] 26 than death; her heart is a trap to catch you and her arms are fetters. The man who is pleasing to God may escape her, but she will catch a sinner. 'See,' says the Speaker, 27 'this is what I have found, reasoning things out one by one, after searching long without 28 success: I have found one man in a thousand worth the name, but I have not found one woman among them all. This alone I have 29 found, that God, when he made man, made him straightforward, but man invents endless subtleties of his own.'

The unknown future

Who is wise enough for all this? Who knows **8** the meaning of anything? Wisdom lights up a man's face, but grim looks make a man hated.[b] Do as the king commands you, and 2 if you have to swear by God, do not be precipitate. Leave the king's presence and 3 do not persist in a thing which displeases him; he does what he chooses. For the 4 king's word carries authority. Who can question what he does? Whoever obeys a 5 command will come to no harm. A wise man knows in his heart the right time and method for action. There is a time and a 6

---

v Or it.   *w* strong man's: *prob. rdg.; Heb. obscure.*   *x* find out . . . next: *or* hold him responsible.
y can do . . . wrong: *or* prospers without ever making a mistake.   *z Prob. rdg.; Heb. adds* to know and.
a Or more bitter.   *b* make . . . hated: *prob. rdg.; Heb. obscure.*

method for every enterprise, although man 7 is greatly troubled by ignorance of the future; 8 who can tell him what it will bring? It is not in man's power to restrain the wind,[c] and no one has power over the day of death. In war no one can lay aside his arms, no wealth 9 will save its possessor. All this I have seen, having applied my mind to everything done under the sun. There was a time when one man had power over another and could 10 make him suffer. It was then that I saw wicked men approaching and even entering[d] the holy place; and they went about the city priding themselves on having done right. 11 This too is emptiness. It is because sentence upon a wicked act is not promptly carried 12 out that men do evil so boldly. A sinner may do wrong[e] and live to old age, yet I know that it will be well with those who fear God: 13 their fear of him ensures this, but it will not be well with a wicked man nor will he live long; the man who does not fear God is a 14 mere shadow. There is an empty thing found on earth: when the just man gets what is due to the unjust, and the unjust what is due to the just. I maintain that this too is empti-15 ness. So I commend enjoyment, since there is nothing good for a man to do here under the sun but to eat and drink and enjoy himself; this is all that will remain with him to reward his toil throughout the span of life which God grants him here under the sun. 16 I applied my mind to acquire wisdom and to observe the business which goes on upon earth, when man never closes an eye in 17 sleep day or night; and always I perceived that God has so ordered it that man should not be able to discover what is happening here under the sun. However hard a man may try, he will not find out; the wise man may think that he knows, but he will be unable to find the truth of it.

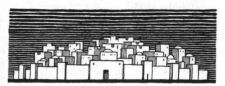

Good man and sinner fare alike

9 I applied my mind to all this, and I understood that the righteous and the wise and all their doings are under God's control; but is it love or hatred? No man knows. Everything that confronts him, everything 2 is empty, since one and the same fate befalls

every one, just and unjust alike, good and bad, clean and unclean, the man who offers sacrifice and the man who does not. Good man and sinner fare alike, the man who can take an oath and the man who dares not. This is what is wrong in all that is done here 3 under the sun: that one and the same fate befalls every man. The hearts of men are full of evil; madness fills their hearts all through their lives, and after that they go down to join the dead. But for a man who is counted 4 among the living there is still hope: remember, a live dog is better than a dead lion. True, the living know that they will die; but 5 the dead know nothing. There are no more rewards for them; they are utterly forgotten. For them love, hate, ambition,[f] all are now 6 over. Never again will they have any part in what is done here under the sun.

Time and chance govern all

Go to it then, eat your food and enjoy it, and 7 drink your wine with a cheerful heart; for already God has accepted what you have done. Always be dressed in white and never 8 fail to anoint your head. Enjoy life with a 9 woman you love all the days of your allotted span here under the sun, empty as they are;[g] for that is your lot while you live and labour here under the sun. Whatever task lies to 10 your hand, do it with all your might; because in Sheol, for which you are bound, there is neither doing nor thinking, neither understanding nor wisdom. One more thing 11 I have observed here under the sun: speed does not win the race nor strength the battle. Bread does not belong to the wise, nor wealth to the intelligent, nor success to the skilful; time and chance govern all. Moreover, no 12 man knows when his hour will come; like fish caught in a net, like a bird taken in a snare, so men are trapped when bad times come suddenly.

Wisdom better than strength

This too is an example of wisdom as I have 13 observed it here under the sun, and notable I find it. There was a small town with few 14 inhabitants, and a great king came to attack it; he besieged it and constructed great siege-works against it. There was in it a 15 poor wise man, and he alone might have saved the town by his wisdom, but no one remembered that poor wise man. 'Surely', 16 I said to myself, 'wisdom is better than strength.' But the poor man's wisdom was despised, and his words went unheeded. A wise man who speaks his mind calmly 17 is more to be heeded than a commander

---

c Or to retain the breath of life.   *d* approaching . . . entering: *prob. rdg.; Heb.* obscure.   *e Prob.*
rdg.; Heb. adds an unintelligible word.   *f Or* passion.   *g Prob. rdg.; Heb.* adds all your days,
empty as they are.

18 shouting orders among fools. Wisdom is better than weapons of war, and one mistake can undo many things done well.

On rulers and subjects

10 Dead flies make the perfumer's sweet ointment turn rancid and ferment; so can a little 2 folly make wisdom lose its worth. The mind of the wise man faces right, but the mind of 3 the fool faces left. Even when he walks along the road, the fool shows no sense and calls 4 everyone else*h* a fool. If your ruler breaks out in anger against you, do not resign your post; submission makes amends for great mis-5 takes. There is an evil that I have observed here under the sun, an error for which a 6 ruler is responsible: the fool given high office, but*i* the great and the rich in humble 7 posts. I have seen slaves on horseback and men of high rank going on foot like slaves. 8 The man who digs a pit may fall into it, and he who pulls down a wall may be bitten by 9 a snake. The man who quarries stones may strain himself, and the woodcutter runs a 10 risk of injury. When the axe is blunt and has not first*j* been sharpened, then one must use more force; the wise man has a better 11 chance of success. If a snake bites before it is charmed, the snake-charmer loses his fee.

12 A wise man's words win him favour, but 13 a fool's tongue is his undoing. He begins by talking nonsense and ends in mischief 14 run mad. The fool talks on and on; but no man knows what is coming, and who can 15 tell him what will come after that? The fool wearies himself to death*k* with all his labour, for he does not know the way to town.

16 Woe betide the land when a slave has become its king, and its princes feast in the 17 morning. Happy the land when its king is nobly born, and its princes feast at the right time of day, with self-control, and not as 18 drunkards. If the owner is negligent the rafters collapse, and if he is idle the house 19 crumbles away. The table has its pleasures, and wine makes a cheerful life; and money 20 is behind it all. Do not speak ill of the king in your ease, or of a rich man in your bedroom; for a bird may carry your voice, and a winged messenger may repeat what you say.

Actions, not speculation

11 Send your grain across the seas, and in time 2 you will get a return. Divide your merchandise among seven ventures, eight maybe, since you do not know what disasters may occur on earth.*l* If the clouds are heavy with 3 rain, they will discharge it on the earth; whether a tree falls south or north, it must lie as it falls. He who watches the wind will 4 never sow, and he who keeps an eye on the clouds will never reap. You do not know 5 how a pregnant woman comes to have a body and a living spirit in her womb; nor do you know how God, the maker of all things, works. In the morning sow your seed 6 betimes, and do not stop work until evening, for you do not know whether this or that sowing will be successful, or whether both alike will do well.

Advice to a young man

The light of day is sweet, and pleasant to the 7 eye is the sight of the sun; if a man lives for 8 many years, he should rejoice in all of them. But let him remember that the days of darkness will be many. Everything that is to come will be emptiness. Delight in your boyhood, 9 young man, make the most of the days of your youth; let your heart and your eyes show you the way; but remember that for all these things God will call you to account. Banish discontent from your mind, and 10 shake off the troubles of the body; boyhood and the prime of life are mere emptiness.

Remember your Creator in the days of **1** your youth, before the time of trouble comes and the years draw near when you will say, 'I see no purpose in them.'*m* Remember him 2 before the sun and the light of day give place to darkness, before the moon and the stars grow dim, and the clouds return with the rain—when the guardians of the house 3 tremble, and the strong men stoop, when the women grinding the meal cease work because they are few, and those who look through the windows look no longer, when 4 the street-doors are shut, when the noise of the mill is low, when the chirping of the sparrow grows faint*n* and the song-birds fall silent;*o* when men are afraid of a steep place 5 and the street is full of terrors, when the blossom whitens on the almond-tree and the locust's paunch is swollen and caperbuds have no more zest. For man goes to his everlasting home, and the mourners go about the streets. Remember him before the 6 silver cord is snapped*p* and the golden bowl is broken, before the pitcher is shattered at the spring and the wheel broken at the well, before the dust returns to the earth as it began and the spirit*q* returns to God who

---

h calls everyone else: *or* tells everyone he is. *i* but: *prob. rdg.; Heb. om.* *j* first: *prob. rdg.; Heb.* face. *k* fool . . . death: *prob. rdg.; Heb. obscure.* *l Or* on land. *m Or* I have no pleasure in them. *n* grows faint: *prob. rdg.; Heb. obscure.* *o Prob. rdg.; Heb.* sink low. *p* is snapped: *prob. rdg.; Heb.* unintelligible. *q Or* breath.

8 gave it. Emptiness, emptiness, says the Speaker, all is empty.

Conclusion

9 So the Speaker, in his wisdom, continued to teach the people what he knew. He turned over many maxims in his mind and sought
10 how best to set them out. He chose his words to give pleasure, but what he wrote was the
11 honest truth. The sayings of the wise are sharp as goads, like nails driven home; they lead the assembled people, for they come from one shepherd. One further warning, 12 my son: the use of books is endless, and much study is wearisome.

13 This is the end of the matter: you have heard it all. Fear God and obey his commands; there is no more to man than this. For God brings everything we do to judge- 14 ment, and every secret, whether good or bad.

THE SONG OF SONGS

Bride[a]

1 I will sing the song of all songs to Solomon
2 that he may[b] smother me with kisses.

Your love is more fragrant than wine,
3 fragrant is[c] the scent of your perfume,
and your name like perfume poured out;[d]
for this the maidens love you.
4 Take me with you, and we will run together;
bring me into your chamber, O king.

Companions

Let us rejoice and be glad for you;
let us praise your love more than wine,
and your caresses more than any song.

Bride

5 I am dark but lovely, daughters of Jerusalem,
like the tents of Kedar
or the tent-curtains of Shalmah.
6 Do not look down on me; a little dark I may be
because I am scorched by the sun.
My mother's sons were displeased with me,
they sent me to watch over the vineyards;
so I did not watch over my own vineyard.
7 Tell me, my true love,
where you mind your flocks,
where you rest them at midday,
that I may not be left picking lice
as I sit among your companions' herds.

Bridegroom

8 If you yourself do not know,
O fairest of women,
go, follow the tracks of the sheep
and mind your kids by the shepherds' huts.
9 I would compare you, my dearest,
to Pharaoh's chariot-horses.

Your cheeks are lovely between plaited 10 tresses,
your neck with its jewelled chains.

Companions

We will make you braided plaits of gold 11 set with beads of silver.

Bride

While the king reclines on his couch, 12 my spikenard gives forth its scent. My beloved is for me a bunch of myrrh 13 as he lies on my breast, my beloved is for me a cluster of henna- 14 blossom from the vineyards of En-gedi.

Bridegroom

How beautiful you are, my dearest, 15 O how beautiful, your eyes are like doves!

Bride

How beautiful you are, O my love, 16 and how pleasant!

Bridegroom

Our couch is shaded with branches; the beams of our house are of cedar, 17 our ceilings are all of fir.

Bride

I am an asphodel in Sharon, **2** a lily growing in the valley.

Bridegroom

No, a lily among thorns 2 is my dearest among girls.

a The Hebrew text implies, by its pronouns, different speakers, but does not indicate them; they are given, however, in two MSS. of Sept.   b I will ... that he may: or The song of all songs which was Solomon's; may he ...
c Or more fragrant than.   d poured out: prob. rdg.; Heb. word uncertain.

Bride

3 Like an apricot-tree among the trees of
   the wood,
   so is my beloved among boys.
   To sit in its shadow was my delight,
   and its fruit was sweet to my taste.
4 He took me into the wine-garden
   and gave me loving glances.
5 He refreshed me with raisins, he revived me
   with apricots;
   for I was faint with love.
6 His left arm was under my head, his right arm
   was round me.

Bridegroom

7 I charge you, daughters of Jerusalem,
   by the spirits and the goddesses*e* of the
   field:
   Do not rouse her, do not disturb my love
   until she is ready.*f*

Bride

8 Hark! My beloved! Here he comes,
   bounding over the mountains, leaping over
   the hills.
9 My beloved is like a gazelle
   or a young wild goat:
   there he stands outside our wall,
   peeping in at the windows, glancing through
   the lattice.
10 My beloved answered, he said to me:
   Rise up, my darling;
   my fairest, come away.
11 For now the winter is past,
   the rains are over and gone;
12 the flowers appear in the country-side;
   the time is coming when the birds will sing,
   and the turtle-dove's cooing will be heard
   in our land;
13 when the green figs will ripen on the fig-
   trees
   and the vines*g* give forth their fragrance.
   Rise up, my darling;
   my fairest, come away.

Bridegroom

14 My dove, that hides in holes in the cliffs
   or in crannies on the high ledges,
   let me see your face, let me hear your voice;
   for your voice is pleasant, your face is
   lovely.

Companions

15 Catch for us the jackals, the little jackals,*h*
   that spoil our vineyards, when the vines
   are in flower.

Bride

16 My beloved is mine and I am his;
   he delights in the lilies.

While the day is cool and the shadows are 17
   dispersing,
turn, my beloved, and show yourself
a gazelle or a young wild goat
on the hills where cinnamon grows.*i*

Night after night on my bed   3
I have sought my true love;
I have sought him but not found him,
I have called him but he has not answered.
I said, 'I will rise and go the rounds of the 2
   city,
through the streets and the squares,
seeking my true love.'
I sought him but I did not find him,
I called him but he did not answer.
The watchmen, going the rounds of the 3
   city, met me,
and I asked, 'Have you seen my true love?'
Scarcely had I left them behind me   4
   when I met my true love.
I seized him and would not let him go
until I had brought him to my mother's
   house,
to the room of her who conceived me.

Bridegroom

I charge you, daughters of Jerusalem,   5
by the spirits and the goddesses*j* of the
   field:
Do not rouse her, do not disturb my love
until she is ready.*k*

Companions

What is this coming up from the wilderness 6
like a column of smoke
from burning myrrh or frankincense,
from all the powdered spices that merchants bring?
Look; it is Solomon carried in his litter;   7
sixty of Israel's chosen warriors
are his escort,
all of them skilled swordsmen,   8
all trained to handle arms,
each with his sword ready at his side
to ward off the demon of the night.

The palanquin which King Solomon had 9
   made for himself
was of wood from Lebanon.
Its poles he had made of silver,   10
its head-rest of gold;
its seat was of purple stuff,
and its lining was of leather.

Come out, daughters of Jerusalem;   11
you daughters of Zion, come out and welcome King Solomon,
wearing the crown with which his mother
   has crowned him,
on his wedding day, on his day of joy.

---

e by . . . goddesses: or by the gazelles and the hinds.   *f until . . . ready: or while she is resting.*   *g Prob.*
rdg.; Heb. adds blossom.   *h Or fruit-bats.*   *i on . . . grows: or on the rugged hills or on the hills of Bether.*
j by . . . goddesses: or by the gazelles and the hinds.   *k until . . . ready: or while she is resting.*

Bridegroom

4 How beautiful you are, my dearest, how
beautiful!
Your eyes behind your veil are like doves,
your hair like a flock of goats streaming
down Mount Gilead.

2 Your teeth are like a flock of ewes just
shorn
which have come up fresh from the dipping;
each ewe has twins and none has cast a
lamb.

3 Your lips are like a scarlet thread,
and your words are delightful;[l]
your parted lips behind your veil
are like a pomegranate cut open.

4 Your neck is like David's tower,
which is built with winding courses;
a thousand bucklers hang upon it,
and all are warriors' shields.

5 Your two breasts are like two fawns,
twin fawns of a gazelle.[m]

6 While the day is cool and the shadows are
dispersing,
I will go to the mountains of myrrh
and to the hills of frankincense.

7 You are beautiful, my dearest,
beautiful without a flaw.

8 Come from Lebanon, my bride;
come with me from Lebanon.
Hurry down from the top of Amana,
from Senir's top and Hermon's,
from the lions' lairs, and the hills the
leopards haunt.

9 You have stolen my heart,[n] my sister,
you have stolen it,[o] my bride,
with one of your eyes, with one jewel of
your necklace.

10 How beautiful are your breasts, my sister,
my bride!
Your love is more fragrant than wine,
and your perfumes sweeter than any
spices.

11 Your lips drop sweetness like the honeycomb, my bride,
syrup and milk are under your tongue,
and your dress has the scent of Lebanon.

3*p* Your two cheeks[q] are an orchard of pomegranates,
an orchard full of rare fruits:[r]

14 spikenard and saffron, sweet-cane and cinnamon
with every incense-bearing tree,
myrrh and aloes
with all the choicest spices.

12 My sister, my bride, is a garden close-locked,
a garden close-locked, a fountain sealed.

Bride

The fountain in my garden[s] is a spring of 15
running water
pouring down from Lebanon.
Awake, north wind, and come, south wind; 16
blow upon my garden that its perfumes may
pour forth,
that my beloved may come to his garden
and enjoy its rare fruits.

Bridegroom

I have come to my garden, my sister and **5**
bride,
and have plucked my myrrh with my
spices;
I have eaten my honey and my syrup,
I have drunk my wine and my milk.
Eat, friends, and drink,
until you are drunk with love.

Bride

I sleep but my heart is awake. 2
Listen! My beloved is knocking:

'Open to me, my sister, my dearest,
my dove, my perfect one;
for my head is drenched with dew,
my locks with the moisture of the night.'

'I have stripped off my dress; must I put it 3
on again?
I have washed my feet; must I soil them
again?'

When my beloved slipped his hand through 4
the latch-hole,
my bowels stirred within me.
When I arose to open for my beloved, 5
my hands dripped with myrrh;
the liquid myrrh from my fingers
ran over the knobs of the bolt.
With my own hands I opened to my love, 6
but my love had turned away and gone by;
my heart sank when he turned his back.
I sought him but I did not find him,
I called him but he did not answer.
The watchmen, going the rounds of the city, 7
met me;
they struck me and wounded me;
the watchmen on the walls took away my
cloak.
I charge you, daughters of Jerusalem, 8
if you find my beloved, will you not tell him[t]
that I am faint with love?

Companions

What is your beloved more than any other, 9
O fairest of women?
What is your beloved more than any other,
that you give us this charge?

---

l Or and your mouth is lovely.   *m Prob. rdg.; Heb. adds* which delight in the lilies.   *n* stolen my heart:
or put heart into me.   *o* stolen it: *or* put heart into me.   *p Verse 12 transposed to follow verse 14.*
q Your two cheeks: *prob. rdg.; Heb.* Your shoots.   *r Prob. rdg.; Heb. adds* henna with spikenard.
s my garden: *prob. rdg.; Heb.* gardens.   *t* will you . . . him: *or* what will you tell him?

Bride

10   My beloved is fair and ruddy,
     a paragon among ten thousand.
11   His head is gold, finest gold;
     his locks are like palm-fronds.[u]
12   His eyes are like doves beside brooks of
     water,
     splashed by the milky water
     as they sit where it is drawn.
13   His cheeks are like beds of spices or chests
     full of perfumes;
     his lips are lilies, and drop liquid myrrh;
14   his hands are golden rods set in topaz;
     his belly a plaque of ivory overlaid with lapis
     lazuli.
15   His legs are pillars of marble in sockets of
     finest gold;
     his aspect is like Lebanon, noble as cedars.
16   His whispers are[v] sweetness itself, wholly
     desirable.
     Such is my beloved, such is my darling,
     daughters of Jerusalem.

Companions

6 Where has your beloved gone,
     O fairest of women?
     Which way did your beloved go,
     that we may help you to seek him?

Bride

2   My beloved has gone down to his garden,
     to the beds where balsam grows,
     to delight in the garden[w] and to pick the
     lilies.
3   I am my beloved's, and my beloved is mine,
     he who delights in the lilies.

Bridegroom

4   You are beautiful, my dearest, as Tirzah,
     lovely as Jerusalem.[x]
5   Turn your eyes away from me;
     they dazzle me.
     Your hair is like a flock of goats streaming
     down Mount Gilead;
6   your teeth are like a flock of ewes come up
     fresh from the dipping,
     each ewe has twins and none has cast a lamb.
7   Your parted lips behind your veil
     are like a pomegranate cut open.
8   There may be sixty princesses,
     eighty concubines, and young women past
     counting,
9   but there is one alone, my dove, my perfect
     one,
     her mother's only child,
     devoted to the mother who bore her;
     young girls see her and call her happy,
     princesses and concubines praise her.

Who is this that looks out like the dawn,   10
beautiful as the moon, bright as the sun,
majestic as the starry heavens?

I went down to a garden of nut-trees   11
to look at the rushes by the stream,
to see if the vine had budded
or the pomegranates were in flower.
I did not know myself;   12
she made me feel more than a prince
reigning over the myriads[y] of his people.

Companions

Come back, come back, Shulammite   13
maiden,
come back, that we may gaze upon you.

Bridegroom

How you love to gaze on the Shulammite
maiden,
as she moves between the lines of dancers!

How beautiful are your sandalled feet,   **7**
O prince's daughter!
The curves of your thighs are like jewels,
the work of a skilled craftsman.
Your navel is a rounded goblet   2
that never shall want for spiced wine.
Your belly is a heap of wheat
fenced in by lilies.
Your two breasts are like two fawns,   3
twin fawns of a gazelle.
Your neck is like a tower of ivory.   4
Your eyes are the pools in Heshbon,
beside the gate of the crowded city.[z]
Your nose is like towering Lebanon
that looks towards Damascus.
You carry your head like Carmel;   5
the flowing hair on your head is lustrous
black,
your tresses are braided with ribbons.
How beautiful, how entrancing you are,   6
my loved one, daughter of delights!
You are stately as a palm-tree,   7
and your breasts are the clusters of dates.
I said, 'I will climb up into the palm   8
to grasp its fronds.'
May I find your breasts like clusters of
grapes on the vine,
the scent of your breath like apricots,
and your whispers like spiced wine   9
flowing smoothly to welcome my caresses,
gliding down through lips and teeth.

Bride

I am my beloved's, his longing is all for me.   10
Come, my beloved, let us go out into the   11
fields
to lie among the henna-bushes;

---

u Prob. rdg.; Heb. adds black as the raven.   *v Or* His nature is.
x Prob. rdg.; Heb. adds majestic as the starry heavens (*see verse 10*).   *w Prob. rdg.; Heb.* gardens.
z Or the gate of Beth-rabbim.   *y Prob. rdg.; Heb.* chariots.

12 let us go early to the vineyards
and see if the vine has budded or its blossom
      opened,
  if the pomegranates are in flower.
  There will I give you my love,
13 when the mandrakes give their perfume,
  and all rare fruits are ready at our door,
  fruits new and old
  which I have in store for you, my love.

8 If only you were my own true brother
  that sucked my mother's breasts!
  Then, if I found you outside, I would kiss
      you,
  and no man would despise me.
2 I would lead you to the room of the mother
      who bore me,
  bring you to her house for you to embrace
      me;*a*
  I would give you mulled wine to drink
  and the fresh juice of pomegranates,
3 your*b* left arm under my head and your*b* right
      arm round me.

Bridegroom

4 I charge you, daughters of Jerusalem:
  Do not rouse her, do not disturb my love
  until she is ready.*c*

Companions

5 Who is this coming up from the wilderness
  leaning on her beloved?

Bridegroom

  Under the apricot-trees I roused you,
  there where your mother was in labour
      with you,
  there where she who bore you was in
      labour.
6 Wear me as a seal upon your heart,
  as a seal upon your arm;
  for love is strong as death,
  passion cruel as the grave;

it blazes up like blazing fire,
fiercer than any flame.
Many waters cannot quench love,   7
  no flood can sweep it away;
  if a man were to offer for love
  the whole wealth of his house,
  it would be utterly scorned.

Companions

  We have a little sister   8
  who has no breasts;
  what shall we do for our sister
  when she is asked in marriage?
  If she is a wall,   9
  we will build on it a silver parapet,
  but*d* if she is a door,
  we will close it up with planks of cedar.

Bride

I am a wall and my breasts are like towers; 10
so in his eyes I am as one who brings content-
      ment.
Solomon has a vineyard at Baal-hamon;   11
  he has let out his vineyard to guardians,
  and each is to bring for its fruit
  a thousand pieces of silver.
But my vineyard is mine to give;   12
  the thousand pieces are yours, O Solomon,
  and the guardians of the fruit shall have
      two hundred.

Bridegroom

  My bride, you who sit in my garden,   13
  what is it that my friends*e* are listening to?
  Let me also hear your voice.

Bride

  Come into the open, my beloved,   14
and show yourself like a gazelle or a young
      wild goat
  on the spice-bearing mountains.

---

a for you to embrace me: *or* to teach me how to love you.   *b Prob. rdg.; Heb.* his.   *c* until ... ready:
or while she is resting.   *d Or* and.   *e* my garden ... friends: *prob. rdg.; Heb.* the gardens, friends.

THE BOOK OF THE PROPHET
ISAIAH

The case against Judah

1 THE VISION received by Isaiah son of Amoz concerning Judah and Jerusalem during the reigns of Uzziah, Jotham, Ahaz, and Hezekiah, kings of Judah.

2 Hark you heavens, and earth give ear,
    for the LORD has spoken:
    I have sons whom I reared and brought up,
    but they have rebelled against me.
3   The ox knows its owner
    and the ass its master's stall;
    but Israel, my own people,
    has no knowledge, no discernment.

4 O sinful nation, people loaded with iniquity,
    race of evildoers, wanton destructive children
    who have deserted the LORD,
    spurned the Holy One of Israel
    and turned your backs on him.
5   Where can you still be struck
    if you will be disloyal still?
    Your head is covered with sores,
    your body diseased;
6 from head to foot there is not a sound spot in you—
    nothing but bruises and weals and raw wounds
    which have not felt compress or bandage
    or soothing oil.
7 Your country is desolate, your cities lie in ashes.
    Strangers devour your land before your eyes;
    it is desolate as Sodom[a] in its overthrow.
8   Only Zion is left,
    like a watchman's shelter in a vineyard,
    a shed in a field of cucumbers,
    a city well guarded.

9 If the LORD of Hosts had not left us a remnant,
    we should soon have been like Sodom,
    no better than Gomorrah.

Empty religious observances

10 Hear the word of the LORD, you rulers of Sodom;
    attend, you people of Gomorrah, to the instruction of our God:
11   Your countless sacrifices, what are they to me?
    says the LORD.
    I am sated with whole-offerings of rams
    and the fat of buffaloes;
    I have no desire for the blood of bulls,
    of sheep and of he-goats.
12–   Whenever you come to enter my presence—
    who asked you for this?
    No more shall you trample my courts.
    The offer of your gifts is useless,
    the reek of sacrifice is abhorrent to me.
    New moons and sabbaths and assemblies,
    sacred seasons and ceremonies, I cannot endure.
14 I cannot tolerate your new moons and your festivals;
    they have become a burden to me,
    and I can put up with them no longer.
15   When you lift your hands outspread in prayer,
    I will hide my eyes from you.
    Though you offer countless prayers,
    I will not listen.
    There is blood on your hands;
16   wash yourselves and be clean.

---

a Sodom: *prob. rdg.; Heb.* strangers.

Put away the evil of your deeds,
away out of my sight.
17 Cease to do evil and learn to do right,
pursue justice and champion the oppressed;
give the orphan his rights, plead the widow's
cause.

The LORD's answer

18 Come now, let us argue it out,
says the LORD.
Though your sins are scarlet,
they may become white as snow;
though they are dyed crimson,
they may yet be like wool.
19 Obey with a will,
and you shall eat the best that earth yields;
20 but, if you refuse and rebel,
locust-beans shall be your only food.[b]
The LORD himself has spoken.

Verdict on social corruption

21 How the faithful city has played the whore,
once the home of justice where righteousness
dwelt—
but now murderers!
22 Your silver has turned into base metal
and your liquor is diluted with water.
23 Your very rulers are rebels, confederate with
thieves;
every man of them loves a bribe
and itches for a gift;
they do not give the orphan his rights,
and the widow's cause never comes before
them.

The LORD will discipline Judah

24 This therefore is the word of the Lord, the
LORD of Hosts, the Mighty One of Israel:
Enough! I will secure a respite from my foes
and take vengeance on my enemies.
25 Once again I will act against you
to refine away your base metal as with
potash
and purge all your impurities;
26 I will again make your judges what once
they were
and your counsellors like those of old.
Then at length you shall be called
the home of righteousness, the faithful city.
27 Justice shall redeem Zion
and righteousness her repentant people.
28 Rebels and sinners shall be broken together
and those who forsake the LORD shall
cease to be.
29 For the sacred oaks in which you delighted
shall fail you,
the garden-shrines of your fancy shall disappoint you.

You shall be like a terebinth whose leaves 30
have withered,
like a garden without water;
the strongest tree[c] shall become like tow, 31
and what is made of it[d] shall go up in
sparks,
and the two shall burst into flames together
with no one to quench them.

Zion's glorious future

This is the word which Isaiah son of Amoz 2
received in a vision concerning Judah and
Jerusalem.

In days to come 2[e]
the mountain of the LORD's house
shall be set over all other mountains,
lifted high above the hills.
All the nations shall come streaming to it,
and many peoples shall come and say, 3
'Come, let us climb up on to the mountain of
the LORD,
to the house of the God of Jacob,
that he may teach us his ways
and we may walk in his paths.'
For instruction issues from Zion,
and out of Jerusalem comes the word of
the LORD;
he will be judge between nations, 4
arbiter among many peoples.
They shall beat their swords into mattocks
and their spears into pruning-knives;[f]
nation shall not lift sword against nation
nor ever again be trained for war.

Worldliness and idolatry

O people of Jacob, come, 5
let us walk in the light of the LORD.
Thou hast abandoned thy people the house 6
of Jacob;
for they are crowded with traders[g]
and barbarians like the Philistines,
and with the children of foreigners everywhere.
Their land is filled with silver and gold, 7
and there is no end to their treasure;
their land is filled with horses,
and there is no end to their chariots;
their land is filled with idols, 8
and they bow down to the work of their
own hands,
to what their fingers have made.
Mankind shall be brought low, 9
all men shall be humbled;
and how can they raise themselves?[h]
Get you into the rocks and hide yourselves in 10
the ground
from the dread of the LORD and the splendour of his majesty.

---

b locust-beans . . . food: or, with Scroll, you shall be eaten by the sword.   c Or the strong man.
d Or what he makes.   e Verses 2–4: cp. Mic. 4. 1–3.   f They shall beat . . . pruning-knives: cp. Joel 3.
9–12.   g Or hawkers.   h Prob. rdg.; Heb. and do not forgive them.

11 Man's proud eyes shall be humbled,
the loftiness of men brought low,
and the LORD alone shall be exalted
on that day.

The day of the LORD

12 For the LORD of Hosts has a day of doom
waiting
for all that is proud and lofty,
for all that is high and lifted up,
13 for all the cedars of Lebanon, lofty and high,
and for all the oaks of Bashan,
14 for all lofty mountains and for all high hills,
15 for every high tower and for every sheer wall,
16 for all ships of Tarshish and all the dhows of
Arabia.
17 Then man's pride shall be brought low,
and the loftiness of man shall be humbled,
and the LORD alone shall be exalted
on that day,
18 while the idols shall pass away utterly.
19 Get you into caves in the rocks
and crevices in the ground
from the dread of the LORD and the splendour of his majesty,
when he rises to inspire the earth with fear.
20 On that day a man shall fling away
his idols of silver and his idols of gold
which he has made for himself to worship;
he shall fling them to the dung-beetles and
the bats,
21 and creep into clefts in the rocks and crannies in the cliffs
from the dread of the LORD and the splendour of his majesty,
when he rises to inspire the earth with
fear.
22 Have no more to do with man, for what is he
worth?
He is no more than the breath in his
nostrils.

The LORD will undermine Judah's stability

3 Be warned: the Lord, the LORD of Hosts,
is stripping Jerusalem and Judah
of every prop and stay,[i]
2 warrior and soldier,
judge and prophet, diviner and elder,
3 captains of companies and men of rank,
counsellor, magician, and cunning en-
chanter.
4 Then I will appoint mere boys to be their
captains,
who shall govern as the fancy takes them;
5 the people shall deal harshly
each man with his fellow and with his neighbour;
children shall break out against their
elders,
and nobodies against men of substance.

If a man takes hold of his brother in his 6
father's house,
saying, 'You have a cloak, you shall be our
chief;
our stricken family shall be under you',
he will cry out that day and say, 7
'I will not be your master;
there is neither bread nor cloak in my
house,
and you shall not make me head of the
clan.'

Disaster on Judah

Jerusalem is stricken and Judah fallen 8
because they have spoken and acted
against the LORD,
rebelling against the glance of his glorious
eye.
The look on their faces testifies against 9
them;
like Sodom they proclaim their sins
and do not conceal them.[j]
Woe upon them! they have earned their own
disaster.
Happy[k] the righteous man! all goes well 10
with him,
for such men enjoy the fruit of their
actions.
Woe betide the wicked! with him all goes ill, 11
for he reaps the reward that he has earned.
Money-lenders strip my people bare, 12
and usurers lord it over them.
O my people! your guides lead you astray
and confuse the path that you should take.
The LORD comes forward to argue his case 13
and stands to judge his people.
The LORD opens the indictment 14
against the elders of his people and their
officers:
You have ravaged the vineyard,
and the spoils of the poor are in your
houses.
Is it nothing to you that you crush my 15
people
and grind the faces of the poor?
This is the very word of the Lord, the LORD
of Hosts.

The fate of the women of Zion

Then the LORD said: 16
Because the women of Zion hold themselves high
and walk with necks outstretched and wanton glances,
moving with mincing gait
and jingling feet,
the Lord will give the women of Zion bald 17
heads,
the LORD will strip the hair from their foreheads,

---

i *Prob. rdg.; Heb. adds* all stay of bread and all stay of water.
of Sodom, denounce them; they do not deny them.

j *like . . . them: or* and their sins, like those
k *Prob. rdg.; Heb.* Say.

18 In that day the Lord will take away all
19 finery: anklets, discs, crescents, pendants,
20 bangles, coronets, head-bands, armlets,
21 necklaces, lockets, charms, signets, nose-
22 rings, fine dresses, mantles, cloaks, flounced
23 skirts, scarves of gauze, kerchiefs of linen,
turbans, and flowing veils.

24 So instead of perfume you shall have the
    stench of decay,
    and a rope in place of a girdle,
    baldness instead of hair elegantly coiled,
    a loin-cloth of sacking instead of a mantle,
    and branding instead of beauty.
25 Your men shall fall by the sword,
    and your warriors in battle;
26 then Zion's gates shall mourn and la-
    ment,
    and she shall sit on the ground stripped
    bare.

4 Then on that day
seven women shall take hold of one man and
    say,
    'We will eat our own bread and wear our
      own clothes
    if only we may be called by your name;
    take away our disgrace.'

The future glory of Zion

2 On that day the plant that the LORD has
    grown
    shall become glorious in its beauty,
    and the fruit of the land shall be
    the pride and splendour
    of the survivors of Israel.

3 Then those who are left in Zion, who
4 remain in Jerusalem, every one enrolled in
the book of life, shall be called holy. If the
Lord washes away the filth of the women
of Zion and cleanses Jerusalem from the
blood that is in it by a spirit of judgement,
5 a consuming spirit, then over every building on Mount Zion and on all her places of
assembly the LORD will create a cloud of
smoke by day and a bright flame of fire by
night; for glory shall be spread over all as
6 a covering and a canopy, a shade from the
heat by day, a refuge and a shelter from
rain and tempest.

The vineyard: an allegory

5 I will sing for my beloved
    my love-song about his vineyard:
    My beloved had a vineyard
    high up on a fertile hill-side.
2 He trenched it and cleared it of stones
    and planted it with red vines;
    he built a watch-tower in the middle
    and then hewed out a winepress in it.

He looked for it to yield grapes,
    but it yielded wild grapes.
Now, you who live in Jerusalem,   3
    and you men of Judah,
    judge between me and my vineyard.
What more could have been done for my   4
    vineyard
    that I did not do in it?
Why, when I looked for it to yield grapes,
    did it yield wild grapes?
Now listen while I tell you   5
    what I will do to my vineyard:
I will take away its fences and let it be burnt,
I will break down its walls and let it be
    trampled underfoot,
    and so I will leave it derelict;   6
    it shall be neither pruned nor hoed,
    but shall grow thorns and briars.
Then I will command the clouds
    to send no more rain upon it.
The vineyard of the LORD of Hosts is Israel,   7
    and the men of Judah are the plant he
    cherished.
He looked for justice and found it denied,
    for righteousness but heard cries of dis-
    tress.

Judah's complacency and hypocrisy

Shame on you! you who add house to house   8
    and join field to field,
    until not an acre remains,
and you are left to dwell alone in the land.
    The LORD of Hosts has sworn[1] in my hear-   9
    ing:
Many houses shall go to ruin,
fine large houses shall be uninhabited.
Five acres of vineyard shall yield only a   10
    gallon,
and ten bushels of seed return only a peck.
    Shame on you! you who rise early in the   11
    morning
    to go in pursuit of liquor
and draw out the evening inflamed with wine,
    at whose feasts there are harp and lute,   12
    tabor and pipe and wine,
    who have no eyes for the work of the LORD,
    and never see the things that he has done.
Therefore my people are dwindling away   13
    all unawares;
    the nobles are starving to death,
    and the common folk die of thirst.

l has sworn: *prob. rdg.*; Heb. *om.*

14 Therefore Sheol gapes with straining throat
and has opened her measureless jaws:
down go nobility and common people,
their noisy bustling mob.*m*
15 Mankind is brought low, men are humbled,
humbled are haughty looks.
16 But the LORD of Hosts sits high in judgement,
and by righteousness the holy God shows
himself holy.
17 Young rams shall feed where fat bullocks
once pastured,
and kids shall graze broad acres where cattle
grew fat.*n*
18 Shame on you! you who drag wickedness
along like a tethered sheep
and sin like a heifer on a rope,
19 who say, 'Let the LORD make haste,
let him speed up his work for us to see it,
let the purpose of the Holy One of Israel
be soon fulfilled, so that we may know it.'
20 Shame on you! you who call evil good and
good evil,
who turn darkness into light and light into
darkness,
who make bitter sweet and sweet bitter.
21 Shame on you! you who are wise in your
own eyes
and prudent in your own esteem.
22 Shame on you! you mighty topers, valiant
mixers of drink,
23 who for a bribe acquit the guilty
and deny justice to those in the right.

Foreign invasion
26*o* So he will hoist a signal to a nation far
away,
he will whistle to call them from the end of
the earth;
and see, they come, speedy and swift;
27 none is weary, not one of them stumbles,
not one slumbers or sleeps.
None has his belt loose about his waist
or a broken thong to his sandals.
28 Their arrows are sharpened and their bows
all strung,
their horses' hooves flash like shooting
stars,
their chariot-wheels are like the whirlwind.
29 Their growling is the growling of a lioness,
they growl like young lions,
which roar as they seize the prey
and carry it beyond reach of rescue.
30 They shall roar over it on that day
like the roaring of the sea.
If a man looks over the earth, behold, darkness closing in,
and the light darkened on the hill-tops*p*!

The call of Isaiah
In the year of King Uzziah's death I saw the 6
Lord seated on a throne, high and exalted,
and the skirt of his robe filled the temple.
About him were attendant seraphim, and 2
each had six wings; one pair covered his face
and one pair his feet, and one pair was spread
in flight. They were calling ceaselessly to one 3
another,

Holy, holy, holy is the LORD of Hosts:
the whole earth is full of his glory.

And, as each one called, the threshold shook 4
to its foundations, while the house was filled
with smoke. Then I cried, 5

Woe is me! I am lost,
for I am a man of unclean lips
and I dwell among a people of unclean lips;
yet with these eyes I have seen the King, the
LORD of Hosts.

Then one of the seraphim flew to me carry- 6
ing in his hand a glowing coal which he had
taken from the altar with a pair of tongs. He 7
touched my mouth with it and said,

See, this has touched your lips;
your iniquity is removed,
and your sin is wiped away.

Then I heard the Lord saying, Whom shall 8
I send? Who will go for me? And I answered,
Here am I; send me. He said, Go and tell this 9
people:

You may listen and listen, but you will not
understand.*q*
You may look and look again, but you
will never know.*r*
This people's wits are dulled, 10
their ears are deafened and their eyes blinded,
so that they cannot see with their eyes
nor listen with their ears
nor understand with their wits,
so that they may turn and be healed.

Then I asked, How long, O Lord? And he 11
answered,

Until cities fall in ruins and are deserted,
houses are left without people,
and the land goes to ruin and lies waste,
until the LORD has sent all mankind far 12
away,
and the whole country is one vast desolation.
Even if a tenth part of its people remain 13
there,
they too will be exterminated
[like an oak or a terebinth,
a sacred pole thrown out from its place in
a hill-shrine*s*].

---

m nobility . . . mob: *or* nobility, common people and noisy mob, and are restless there.   *n* Young . . .
grew fat: *prob. rdg.*; *Heb. unintelligible.*   *o Verses 24 and 25 transposed to follow 10. 4.*   *p* hill-tops:
or clouds.   *q Or* but how will you understand?   *r Or* but how will you know?   *s* a sacred pole
. . . hill-shrine: *prob. rdg.*; *Heb. obscure.*

News of the Aramaean–Ephraimite alliance

7 While Ahaz son of Jotham and grandson of Uzziah was king of Judah, Rezin king of Aram with Pekah son of Remaliah, king of Israel, marched on Jerusalem, but could not 2 force a battle. When the house of David heard that the Aramaeans had come to terms with the Ephraimites, king and people were 3 shaken like forest trees in the wind. Then the LORD said to Isaiah, Go out with your son Shear-jashub[t] to meet Ahaz at the end of the conduit of the Upper Pool by the causeway 4 leading to the Fuller's Field, and say to him, Be on your guard, keep calm; do not be frightened or unmanned by these two smouldering stumps of firewood, because Rezin and his Aramaeans with Remaliah's son are 5 burning with rage. The Aramaeans with Ephraim and Remaliah's son have laid their 6 plans against you, saying, Let us invade Judah and break her spirit;[u] let us make her join with us, and set the son of Tabeal on the 7 throne. Therefore the Lord GOD has said:

This shall not happen now, and never shall,
8   for all that the chief city of Aram is Damascus,
    and Rezin is the chief of Damascus;
    within sixty-five years
    Ephraim shall cease to be a nation,
9   for all that Samaria is the chief city of Ephraim,
    and Remaliah's son the chief of Samaria.
Have firm faith, or you will not stand firm.

The sign Immanuel

10 Once again the LORD spoke to Ahaz and 11 said, Ask the LORD your God for a sign, from your lowest Sheol or from highest heaven. 12 But Ahaz said, No, I will not put the LORD 13 to the test by asking for a sign. Then the answer came: Listen, house of David. Are you not content to wear out men's patience? Must you also wear out the patience of my 14 God? Therefore the Lord himself shall give you a sign: A young woman is with child, and she will bear a son, and will[v] call him 15 Immanuel.[w] By the time that he has learnt to reject evil and choose good, he will be 16 eating curds and honey;[x] before that child has learnt to reject evil and choose good, desolation will come upon the land before 17 whose two kings you cower now. The LORD will bring on you, your people, and your house, a time the like of which has not been seen since Ephraim broke away from Judah.[y]

Assyrian devastation

18 On that day the LORD will whistle for the fly

from the distant streams of Egypt and for the bee from Assyria. They shall all come and 19 settle in the precipitous ravines and in the clefts of the rock; camel-thorn and stink-wood shall be black with them. On that day 20 the Lord shall shave the head and body with a razor hired on the banks of the Euphrates,[z] and it shall remove the beard as well. On that 21 day a man shall save alive a young cow and two ewes; and he shall get so much milk that 22 he eats curds; for all who are left in the land shall eat curds and honey. On that day every 23 place where there used to be a thousand vines worth a thousand pieces of silver shall be given over to thorns and briars. A man shall 24 go there only to hunt with bow and arrows, for thorns and briars cover the whole land; and no one who fears thorns and briars shall 25 set foot on any of those hills once worked with the hoe. Oxen shall be turned loose on them, and sheep shall trample them.

The LORD said to me, Take a large tablet **8** and write on it in common writing,[a] Maher-shalal-hash-baz;[b] and fetch Uriah the priest 2 and Zechariah son of Jeberechiah for me as trustworthy witnesses. Then I lay with the 3 prophetess, and she conceived and bore a son; and the LORD said to me, Call him Maher-shalal-hash-baz. Before the boy can say 4 Father or Mother, the wealth of Damascus and the spoils of Samaria shall be carried off and presented to the king of Assyria.

Once again the LORD said to me: 5

Because this nation has rejected   6
the waters of Shiloah, which run so softly
    and gently,[c]
therefore the Lord will bring up against it   7
    the strong, flooding waters of the Euphrates,
    the king of Assyria and all his glory;
it shall run up all its channels
and overflow all its banks;
it shall sweep through Judah in a flood,   8
pouring over it and rising shoulder-high.
The whole expanse of the land shall be
    filled,
so wide he spreads his wings; for God is
    with us.[d]

Take note, you nations, and be dismayed.   9
Listen, all you distant parts of the earth:
you may arm yourselves but will be dismayed;
you may arm yourselves but will be dismayed.
Make your plans, but they will be foiled,   10
propose what you please, but it shall not
    stand;
for God is with us.[d]

---

t That is A remnant shall return.   *u Or* and parley with her.   *v Or* you will.   *w That is* God is with us.   *x* he will . . . honey: *or* curds and honey will be eaten.   *y Prob. rdg.; Heb. adds* the king of Assyria.   *z Prob. rdg.; Heb. adds* with the king of Assyria.   *a* in common writing: *or* with an ordinary stylus.   *b That is* Speed-spoil-hasten-plunder.   *c Prob. rdg.; Heb. adds* Rezin and the son of Remaliah.   *d* God is with us: *Heb.* Immanuel.

A personal word to Isaiah

11 These were the words of the LORD to me, for his hand was strong upon me; and he warned me not to follow[e] the ways of this people:
12 You shall not say 'too hard' of everything that this people calls hard; you shall neither
13 dread nor fear that which they fear. It is the LORD of Hosts whom you must count 'hard';[f]
14 he it is whom you must fear and dread. He shall become your 'hardship',[f] a boulder and a rock which the two houses of Israel shall run against and over which they shall stumble, a trap and a snare to those who live
15 in Jerusalem; and many shall stumble over them, many shall fall and be broken, many shall be snared and caught.

Apostasy, anarchy and gloom

16   Fasten up the message,
seal the oracle with my teaching;[g]
17   and I will wait for the LORD
    who hides his face from the house of Jacob;
    I will watch for him.
18 See, I and the sons whom the LORD has given me
    are to be signs and portents in Israel,
sent by the LORD of Hosts who dwells on Mount Zion.
19   But men will say to you,
    'Seek guidance of ghosts and familiar spirits
    who squeak and gibber;
    a nation may surely seek guidance of its gods,
    of the dead on behalf of the living,
20   for an oracle or a message?'
    They will surely say some such thing as this;
    but what they say is futile.
21 So despondency and fear will come over them,
    and then, when they are afraid and fearful, they will turn against their king and their gods.
22 Then, whether they turn their gaze upwards or look down,
    everywhere is distress and darkness inescapable,
    constraint and gloom that cannot be avoided;
9 for there is no escape for an oppressed people.

For, while the first invader has dealt lightly with the land of Zebulun and the land of Naphtali, the second has dealt heavily with Galilee of the Nations on the road beyond Jordan to the sea.

The Prince of peace

The people who walked in darkness   2
have seen a great light:
    light has dawned upon them,
    dwellers in a land as dark as death.
Thou hast increased their joy and[h] given   3
    them great gladness;
they rejoice in thy presence as men rejoice at harvest,
or as they are glad when they share out the spoil;
    for thou hast shattered the yoke that   4
    burdened them,
    the collar that lay heavy on their shoulders,
    the driver's goad, as on the day of Midian's defeat.
All the boots of trampling soldiers   5
and the garments fouled with blood
shall become a burning mass, fuel for fire.
For a boy has been born for us, a son given   6
    to us
    to bear the symbol of dominion on his shoulder;
    and he shall be called
    in purpose wonderful, in battle God-like,
    Father for all time,[i] Prince of peace.
Great shall the dominion be,   7
and boundless the peace
bestowed on David's throne and on his kingdom,
to establish it and sustain it
with justice and righteousness
from now and for evermore.
The zeal of the LORD of Hosts shall do this.

Israel's futile efforts at rebuilding

The Lord has sent forth his word against   8
    Jacob
    and it shall fall on Israel;
    all the people shall be humbled,   9
    Ephraim and the dwellers in Samaria,
    though in their pride and arrogance they say,
The bricks are fallen, but we will build in   10
    hewn stone;
    the sycomores are hacked down,
    but we will use cedars instead.
The LORD has raised their foes[j] high against   11
    them
    and spurred on their enemies,

12 Aramaeans from the east and Philistines
   from the west,
   and they have swallowed Israel in one
   mouthful.
   For all this his anger has not turned back,
   and his hand is stretched out still.
13 Yet the people did not come back to him
   who struck them,
   or seek guidance of the LORD of Hosts;
14 therefore on one day the LORD cut off from
   Israel
   head and tail, palm and reed.[k]
16 This people's guides have led them astray;
   those who should have been guided are in
   confusion.
17 Therefore the Lord showed no mercy to their
   young men,
   no tenderness to their orphans and
   widows;
   all were godless and evildoers,
   every one speaking profanity.
   For all this his anger has not turned back,
   and his hand is stretched out still.

Social injustices

18 Wicked men have been set ablaze like a
   fire
   fed with briars and thorns,
   kindled in the forest thickets;
   they are wrapped in a murky pall of smoke.
19 The land is scorched by the fury of the LORD
   of Hosts,
   and the people have become fuel for the
   fire.[l]
20 On the right, one man eats his fill but yet
   is hungry;
   on the left, another devours but is not
   satisfied;
   each feeds on his own children's flesh,
   and neither spares his own brother.[m]
21 [n]For all this his anger has not turned
   back,
   and his hand is stretched out still.

10 Shame on you! you who make unjust laws
   and publish burdensome decrees,
2 depriving the poor of justice,
   robbing the weakest of my people of their
   rights,
   despoiling the widow and plundering the
   orphan.
3 What will you do when called to account,
   when ruin from afar confronts you?
   To whom will you flee for help
   and where will you leave your children,
4 so that they do not cower before the gaoler
   or fall by the executioner's hand?
   For all this his anger has not turned back,
   and his hand is stretched out still.

So, as tongues of fire lick up the stubble   [24[o]]
   and the heat of the flame dies down,
   their root shall moulder away,
   and their shoots vanish like dust;
for they have spurned the instruction of the
   LORD of Hosts
and have rejected the word of the Holy One
   of Israel.
So the anger of the LORD is roused against   [25[o]]
   his people,
he has stretched out his hand against them
   and struck them down;
   the mountains trembled,
   and their corpses lay like offal in the
   streets.
For all this his anger has not turned
   back,
and his hand is stretched out still.

ASSYRIA

How the LORD uses Assyria

The Assyrian! He is the rod that I wield in   5
   my anger,
   and the staff of my wrath is in his
   hand.[p]
I send him against a godless nation,   6
I bid him march against a people who
   rouse my wrath,
to spoil and plunder at will
   and trample them down like mud in the
   streets.
But this man's purpose is lawless,   7
   lawless are the plans in his mind;
   for his thought is only to destroy
   and to wipe out nation after nation.
'Are not my officers all kings?' he says;   8
   'see how Calno has suffered the fate of   9
   Carchemish.
Is not Hamath like Arpad, and Samaria like
   Damascus?
Before now I have found kingdoms full of   10
   idols,
   with more images than Jerusalem and
   Samaria,
and now, what I have done to Samaria and   11
   her worthless gods,
I will do also to Jerusalem and her idols.'

The king of Assyria's fall

When the Lord has finished all that he means 12
to do on Mount Zion and in Jerusalem, he
will punish the king of Assyria for this fruit

---

*k Prob. rdg.; Heb. adds (15) The aged and honoured are the head, and the prophet who gives false instruction is
the tail.   l See note on verse 20.   m and neither . . . brother: transposed from end of verse 19.
n Prob. rdg.; Heb. prefixes Manasseh devours Ephraim, and Ephraim Manasseh; together they are against Judah.
o These are verses 24 and 25 of ch. 5, transposed to this point.   p and . . . hand: prob. rdg.; Heb. obscure.*

of his pride and for his arrogance and vain-
13 glory, because he said:

By my own might I have acted
and in my own wisdom I have laid my
   schemes;
I have removed the frontiers of nations
and plundered their treasures,
like a bull I have trampled on their inhabitants.

14 My hand has found its way to the wealth of
   nations,
and, as a man takes the eggs from a
   deserted nest,
so have I taken every land;
not a wing fluttered,
not a beak gaped, no chirp was heard.

15 Shall the axe set itself up against the hewer,
or the saw claim mastery over the sawyer,
as if a stick were to brandish him who
   wields it,
or a staff of wood to wield one who is not
   wood?

16 Therefore the Lord, the LORD of Hosts, will
   send disease
on his sturdy frame, from head to toe,^{q}
and within his flesh^r a fever like fire shall
   burn.

17 The light of Israel shall become a fire
and his Holy One a flame,
which in one day shall burn up and consume
   his thorns and his briars;

18 the glory of forest and meadow shall be
   destroyed
as when a man falls in a fit;

19 and the remnant of trees in the forest shall
   be so few
that a child may count them one by one.

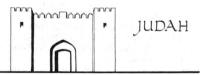
JUDAH

A remnant will repent

20 On that day the remnant of Israel, the survivors of Jacob, shall cease to lean on him
that proved their destroyer, but shall loyally
lean on the LORD, the Holy One of Israel.

21 A remnant shall turn again, a remnant of
   Jacob,
to God their champion.

22 Your people, Israel, may be many as the
   sands of the sea,
but only a remnant shall turn again,

the instrument of final destruction,
justice in full flood;^{s}
for the Lord, the LORD of Hosts, will bring 23
   final destruction
upon all the earth.

Relief from oppression promised

Therefore these are the words of the Lord, 24
the LORD of Hosts: My people who live in
Zion, you must not be afraid of the Assyrians,
though they beat you with their rod and lift
their staff against you as the Egyptians did;
for soon, very soon, my anger will come to an 25
end, and my wrath will all be spent.^{t} Then 26
the LORD of Hosts will brandish his whip
over them as he did when he struck Midian
at the Rock of Oreb, and will lift his staff
against the River as he did against Egypt.

On that day 27
the burden they laid on your shoulder
   shall be removed
and their yoke shall be broken from your
   neck.
An invader from Rimmon^u has come to 28
   Aiath,
has passed by Migron,
and left his baggage-train at Michmash;
he has passed by Maabarah 29
and camped for the night at Geba.
Ramah is anxious, Gibeah of Saul is in panic.
Raise a shrill cry, Bath-gallim; 30
hear it, Laish, and answer her, Anathoth:
'Madmenah is in flight; take refuge, people 31
   of Gebim.'
Today he is due to pitch his camp in Nob; 32
he gives the signal to advance
against the mount of the daughter of Zion,
the hill of Jerusalem.

The LORD's reign of righteousness and peace

Look, the Lord, the LORD of Hosts, 33
cleaves the trees with a flash of lightning,
the tallest are hewn down, the lofty laid low,
the heart of the forest is felled with the 34
   axe,
and Lebanon with its noble trees has fallen.
Then a shoot shall grow from the stock of 11
   Jesse,
and a branch shall spring from his roots.
The spirit of the LORD shall rest upon him, 2
a spirit of wisdom and understanding,
a spirit of counsel^v and power,
a spirit of knowledge and the fear of the
   LORD.^{w}
He shall not judge by what he sees 3
nor decide by what he hears;

q from . . . toe: *transposed from verse 18.*   r within his flesh: *or* in his strong body.   s the instrument . . . flood: *or* wasting with sickness, yet overflowing with righteousness.   t will . . . spent: *prob. rdg.;*
Heb. obscure.   u and their yoke . . . Rimmon: *prob. rdg.; Heb.* and their yoke from upon your neck,
and a yoke shall be broken because of oil. He . . .   v *Or* force.   w *Prob. rdg.; Heb. adds* and his
delight shall be in the fear of the LORD.

4 he shall judge the poor with justice
and defend the humble in the land with
equity;
his mouth shall be a rod to strike down the
ruthless,*
and with a word he shall slay the wicked.
5 Round his waist he shall wear the belt of
justice,
and good faith shall be the girdle round
his body.
6 Then the wolf shall live with the sheep,
and the leopard lie down with the kid;
the calf and the young lion shall grow up
together,
and a little child shall lead them;
7 the cow and the bear shall be friends,
and their young shall lie down together.
The lion shall eat straw like cattle;
8 the infant shall play over the hole of the
cobra,
and the young child dance over the viper's
nest.
9 They shall not hurt or destroy in all my holy
mountain;
for as the waters fill the sea,
so shall the land be filled with the knowledge
of the LORD.

0 On that day a scion from the root of Jesse
shall be set up as a signal to the peoples;
the nations shall rally to it,
and its resting-place shall be glorious.

When Judah and Israel reunite

1 On that day the Lord will make his power
more glorious by recovering the remnant of
his people, those who are still left, from
Assyria and Egypt, from Pathros, from Cush
and Elam, from Shinar, Hamath and the
islands of the sea.

2 Then he will raise a signal to the nations
and gather together those driven out of
Israel;
he will assemble Judah's scattered people
from the four corners of the earth.
3 Ephraim's jealousy shall vanish,
and Judah's enmity shall be done away.
Ephraim shall not be jealous of Judah,
nor Judah the enemy of Ephraim.
4 They shall swoop down on the Philistine
flank in the west
and together they shall plunder the tribes
of the east;

Edom and Moab shall be within their grasp,
and Ammon shall obey them.
The LORD will divide the tongue of the 15
Egyptian sea
and wave his hand over the River
to bring a scorching wind;
he shall split it into seven channels
and let men go across dry-shod.
So there shall be a causeway for the remnant 16
of his people,
for the remnant rescued from Assyria,
as there was for Israel when they came up
out of Egypt.

Songs of praise

You shall say on that day: **12**
I will praise thee, O LORD,
though thou hast been angry with me;
thy anger has turned back,
and thou hast comforted me.
God is indeed my deliverer. 2
I am confident and unafraid;
for the LORD is my refuge and defence
and has shown himself my deliverer.
And so you shall draw water with joy 3
from the springs of deliverance.

You shall all say on that day: 4
Give thanks to the LORD and invoke him by
name,
make his deeds known in the world
around;
declare that his name is supreme.
Sing psalms to the LORD, for he has tri- 5
umphed,
and this must be made known in all the
world.
Cry out, shout aloud, you that dwell in 6
Zion,
for the Holy One of Israel is among you in
majesty.

Destruction of Babylon

Babylon: an oracle which Isaiah son of **13**
Amoz received in a vision.

Raise the standard on a windy height, 2
roar out your summons,
beckon with arm upraised to the advance,
draw your swords, you nobles.
I have given my warriors their orders 3
and summoned my fighting men to launch
my anger;
they are eager for my triumph.

x *Prob. rdg.; Heb.* land.

4 Hark, a tumult in the mountains, the sound
    of a vast multitude;
hark, the roar of kingdoms, of nations
    gathering!
The LORD of Hosts is mustering a host for
    war,
5 men from a far country, from beyond the
    horizon.
It is the LORD with the weapons of his
    wrath
coming to lay the whole land waste.
6 Howl, for the Day of the LORD is at
    hand;
it comes, a mighty blow from Almighty
    God.
7 Thereat shall every hand hang limp,
every man's courage shall melt away,
8 his stomach hollow with fear;
anguish shall grip them, like a woman in
    labour.
One man shall look aghast at another,
and their faces shall burn with shame.
9 The Day of the LORD is coming indeed,
that cruel day of wrath and fury,
to make the land a desolation
and exterminate its wicked people.
10 The stars of heaven in their constellations
    shall give no light,
the sun shall be darkened at its rising,
and the moon refuse to shine.
11 I will bring disaster upon the world
and their due punishment upon the wicked.
I will check the pride of the haughty
and bring low the arrogance of ruthless
    men.
12 I will make men scarcer than fine gold,
rarer than gold of Ophir.
13 Then the heavens shall shudder,[y]
and the earth shall be shaken from its
    place
at the fury of the LORD of Hosts, on the day
    of his anger.
14 Then, like a gazelle before the hunter
or a flock with no man to round it up,
each man will go back to his own people,
every one will flee to his own land.
15 All who are found will be stabbed,
all who are taken will fall by the sword;
16 their infants will be dashed to the ground
    before their eyes,
their houses rifled and their wives ravished.
17 I will stir up against them the Medes,
who care nothing for silver and are not
    tempted by gold,[z]
18 who have no pity on little children
and spare no mother's son;
19 and Babylon, fairest of kingdoms,
proud beauty of the Chaldaeans,
shall be like Sodom and Gomorrah
when God overthrew them.

Never again shall she be inhabited,   20
no man shall dwell in her through all the
    ages;
there no Arab shall pitch his tent,
no shepherds fold their flocks.
There marmots shall have their lairs,   21
and porcupines shall overrun her houses;
there desert owls shall dwell,
and there he-goats shall gambol;
jackals shall occupy her mansions,[a]   22
and wolves her gorgeous palaces.
Her time draws very near,
and her days have not long to run.

When Israel is restored

The LORD will show compassion for Jacob 14
and will once again make Israel his choice.
He will settle them on their own soil, and
strangers will come to join them and attach
themselves to Jacob. Many nations shall 2
escort Israel to her place, and she shall
employ them as slaves and slave-girls on the
land of the LORD; she shall take her captors
captive and rule over her task-masters.

The fall of the king of Babylon

When the LORD gives you relief from your 3
pain and your fears and from the cruel
slavery laid upon you, you will take up this 4
song of derision over the king of Babylon:

See how the oppressor has met his end and
    his frenzy ceased!
The LORD has broken the rod of the wicked, 5
    the sceptre of the ruler
who struck down peoples in his rage   6
with unerring blows,
who crushed nations in anger
and persecuted them unceasingly.
The whole world has rest and is at peace;   7
it breaks into cries of joy.
The pines themselves and the cedars of 8
    Lebanon exult over you:
Since you have been laid low, they say,
no man comes up to fell us.

Sheol below was all astir   9
to meet you at your coming;
she roused the ancient dead to meet you,
all who had been leaders on earth;
she made all who had been kings of the
    nations
rise from their thrones.
One and all they greet you with these words: 10
So you too are as weak as we are,
and have become one of us!
Your pride and all the music of your lutes 11
have been brought down to Sheol;[b]
maggots are the pallet beneath you,
and worms your coverlet.

y *Prob. rdg.; Heb.* Then I will make the heavens shudder.
men to the ground.   a *Prob. rdg.; Heb.* her widows.
Sheol to the crowding throng of your dead.

z *Prob. rdg.; Heb.* adds bows shall dash young
    b *Or* Your pride has been brought down to

12 How you have fallen from heaven, bright
    morning star,
  felled to the earth, sprawling helpless across
    the nations!
13 You thought in your own mind,
    I will scale the heavens;
  I will set my throne high above the stars of
    God,
    I will sit on the mountain where the gods
    meet
    in the far recesses of the north.
14 I will rise high above the cloud-banks
    and make myself like the Most High.
15 Yet you shall be brought down to Sheol,
    to the depths of the abyss.
16 Those who see you will stare at you,
    they will look at you and ponder:
  Is this, they will say, the man who shook the
    earth,
    who made kingdoms quake,
17 who turned the world into a desert
    and laid its cities in ruins,
    who never let his prisoners go free to their
    homes,
18 the kings of every land?
    Now they lie all of them in honour,
    each in his last home.
19 But you have been flung out unburied,
    mere loathsome carrion,
    a companion to the slain pierced by the
    sword
    who have gone down to the stony abyss.
    And you, a corpse trampled underfoot,
20 shall not share burial with them,
  for you have ruined your land and slaugh-
    tered your people.
  Such a brood of evildoers shall never be seen
    again.
21 Make the shambles ready for his sons
    butchered for their fathers' sin;
    they shall not rise up and possess the
    world
    nor cover the face of the earth with cities.

22 I will rise against them, says the LORD of
Hosts; I will destroy the name of Babylon
and what remains of her, her offspring and
23 posterity, says the LORD; I will make her a
haunt of the bustard, a waste of fen, and
sweep her with the besom of destruction.
This is the very word of the LORD of Hosts.

The LORD's plan for the whole earth

24 The LORD of Hosts has sworn:
  In very truth, as I planned, so shall it be;
    as I designed, so shall it fall out:
25 I will break the Assyrian in my own land
    and trample him underfoot upon my
    mountains;
    his yoke shall be lifted from you,
    his burden taken from your shoulders.

This is the plan prepared for the whole earth, 26
this the hand stretched out over all the
    nations.
  For the LORD of Hosts has prepared his plan: 27
  who shall frustrate it?
His is the hand stretched out, and who shall
    turn it back?

PHILISTINES

Philistia

In the year that King Ahaz died this oracle 28
came from God:

  Let none of you rejoice, you Philistines, 29
    because the rod that chastised you is
    broken;
for a viper shall be born of a snake as a plant
    from the root,
    and its fruit shall be a flying serpent.
But the poor shall graze their flocks in my 30
    meadows,
    and the destitute shall lie down in peace;
    but the offspring of your roots I will kill
    by starvation,
    and put the remnant of you to death.
Howl in the gate, cry for help in the city, 31
    let all Philistia be in turmoil;
    for a great enemy is coming from the
    north,
    not a man straying from his ranks.
What answer is there for the envoys of the 32
    nation?
This, that the LORD has fixed Zion in her
    place,
    and the afflicted among his people shall
    take refuge there.

MOAB

Moab

        Moab: an oracle.   **15**
On the night when Ar is sacked, Moab meets
    her doom;
  on the night when Kir is sacked, Moab meets
    her doom.
The people of Dibon go up*c* to the hill-shrines 2
    to weep;
Moab howls over Nebo and over Medeba.
The hair is torn from every head, and every
    beard shaved off.

c The people . . . go up: prob. rdg.; Heb. He has gone up to the house and Dibon.

3 In the streets men go clothed with sackcloth,
   they cry out on the roofs;
   in the public squares every man howls,
   weeping as he goes through them.
4 Heshbon and Elealeh cry for help,
   their voices are heard as far as Jahaz.
   Thus Moab's stoutest warriors become cowards,
   and her courage ebbs away.
5 My heart cries out for Moab,
   whose nobles have fled[d] as far as Zoar.[e]
On the ascent to Luhith men go up weeping;
on the road to Horonaim there are cries of 'Disaster!'
6 The waters of Nimrim are desolate indeed;
   the grass is parched, the herbage dead,
   not a green thing is left;
7 and so the people carry off across the gorge of the Arabim
   their hard-earned wealth and all their savings.
8 The cry for help echoes round the frontiers of Moab,
   their howling reaches Eglaim and Beer-elim.
9 The waters of Dimon already run with blood;
   yet I have more troubles in store for Dimon,
   for I have a vision[f] of the survivors of Moab,
   of the remnant of Admah.

16 The rulers of the country send a present of lambs
   from Sela in the wilderness
   to the hill of the daughter of Zion;
2 the daughters of Moab at the fords of the Arnon
   shall be like fluttering birds, like scattered nestlings.
3 'Take up our cause with all your might;
   let your shadow shield us at high noon, dark as night.
   Shelter the homeless, do not betray the fugitive;
4 let the homeless people of Moab find refuge with you;
   hide them from the despoiler.'

When extortion has done its work and the looting is over,
   when the heel of the oppressor has vanished from the land,
5 a throne shall be set up in mutual trust in David's tent,
   and on it there shall sit a true judge,
one who seeks justice and is swift to do right.

6 We have heard tell of Moab's pride, how great it is,
   we have heard of his pride, his overweening pride;
   his talk is full of lies.

For this all Moab shall howl; 7
   Moab shall howl indeed;
   he[g] shall mourn for the prosperous farmers of Kir-hareseth,
   utterly ruined;
   the orchards of Heshbon, 8
   the vines of Sibmah languish,
though their red grapes once laid low the lords of the nations,
   though they reached as far as Jazer
   and trailed out to the wilderness,
though their branches spread abroad and crossed the sea.
Therefore I will weep for Sibmah's vines as 9
   I weep for Jazer.
I will drench you with my tears, Heshbon and Elealeh;
   for over your summer-fruits and your harvest
   the shouts of the harvesters are ended.
Joy and gladness shall be banished from the 10 meadows,
no more shall men shout and sing in the vineyards,
   no more shall they tread wine in the wine-presses;
   I have silenced the shouting of the harvesters.
Therefore my heart throbs 11
   like a harp for Moab,
   and my very soul for Kir-hareseth.[h]
When Moab comes to worship 12
   and wearies himself at the hill-shrines,
   when he enters his sanctuary to pray,
   he will gain nothing.

These are the words which the LORD spoke 13
long ago about Moab; and now he says, In 14
three years, as a hired labourer counts them
off, the glory of Moab shall become contemptible for all his vast numbers; a handful
shall be left and those of no account.

DAMASCUS

Damascus
     Damascus: an oracle. 17
Damascus shall be a city no longer,
   she shall be but a heap of ruins.
For ever desolate, flocks shall have her for 2
   their own,
   and lie there undisturbed.
No longer shall Ephraim boast a fortified 3
   city,
   or Damascus a kingdom;
the remnant of Aram and the glory of Israel,
   their fate is one.
This is the very word of the LORD of Hosts.

d have fled: *prob. rdg.; Heb. om.*   e *Prob. rdg.; Heb. adds* Eglath Shelishiya.   f I have a vision:
prob. rdg.; Heb. a lion.   g *Prob. rdg.; Heb.* you.   h *Prob. rdg.; Heb.* Kir-hares.

ISRAEL

Israel

4　On that day Jacob's weight shall dwindle
and the fat on his limbs waste away,

5　as when the harvester gathers up the standing
corn
and reaps the ears in armfuls,
or as when a man gleans the ears in the Vale
of Rephaim,

6　or as when one beats an olive-tree
and only gleanings are left on it,
two or three berries on the top of a branch,
four or five on the boughs of the fruiting
tree.
This is the very word of the LORD the God of
Israel.

7　On that day men shall look to their Maker
and turn their eyes to the Holy One of Israel;

8　they shall not look to the altars made by their
own hands nor to anything that their fingers
have made, sacred poles or incense-altars.

9　On that day their strong cities shall be
deserted like the cities of the Hivites and
the Amorites, which they abandoned when
Israel came in; all shall be desolate.

10　For you forgot the God who delivered you,
and did not remember the rock, your
stronghold.
Plant then, if you will, your gardens in
honour of Adonis,
strike your cuttings for a foreign god;

11　protect your gardens on the day you plant
them,
and next day make the seed sprout.
But the crop will be scorched when wasting
disease comes
in the day of incurable pain.

12　Listen! it is the thunder of many peoples,
they thunder with the thunder of the sea.
Listen! it is the roar of nations
roaring with the roar of mighty waters.

13　When he rebukes them, away they fly,
driven like chaff on the hills before the
wind,
like thistledown before the storm.

14　At evening all is confusion,
and before morning they are gone.
Such is the fate of our plunderers,
the lot of those who despoil us.

Cush

8　There is a land of sailing ships,
a land beyond the rivers of Cush

2　which sends its envoys by the Nile,
journeying on the waters in vessels of reed.

Go, swift messengers,
go to a people tall and smooth-skinned,
to a people dreaded near and far,
a nation strong and proud,
whose land is scoured by rivers.
All you who dwell in the world, inhabitants　3
of earth,
shall see when the signal is hoisted on the
mountains
and shall hear when the trumpet sounds.

These were the words of the LORD to me:　4
From my dwelling-place I will look quietly
down
when the heat shimmers in the summer
sun,
when the dew is heavy at harvest time.
Before the vintage, when the budding is　5
over
and the flower ripens into a berry,
the shoots shall be cut down with knives,
the branches struck off and cleared away.
All shall be left to birds of prey on the　6
hills
and to beasts of the earth;
in summer the birds shall make their home
there,
in winter every beast of the earth.

At that time tribute shall be brought to the　7
LORD of Hosts from a people tall and
smooth-skinned, dreaded near and far, a
nation strong and proud, whose land is
scoured by rivers. They shall bring it to
Mount Zion, the place where men invoke
the name of the LORD of Hosts.

EGYPT

Egypt

Egypt: an oracle.　**19**

See how the LORD comes riding swiftly upon
a cloud,
he shall descend upon Egypt;
the idols of Egypt quail before him,
Egypt's courage melts within her.
I will set Egyptian against Egyptian,　2
and they shall fight one against another,
neighbour against neighbour,
city against city and kingdom against kingdom.
Egypt's spirit shall sink within her,　3
and I will throw her counsels into confusion.
They may resort to idols and oracle-
mongers,
to ghosts and spirits,

4 but I will hand Egypt over to a hard master,
  and a cruel king shall rule over them.
  This is the very word of the Lord, the LORD
  of Hosts.

5 The waters of the Nile shall drain away,
  the river shall be parched and run dry;
6 its channels shall stink,
  the streams of Egypt shall be parched and
  dry up;
  reeds and rushes shall wither away;
7 the lotus too beside the Nile[i]
  and all that is sown along the Nile shall
  dry up,
  shall be blown away and vanish.
8 The fishermen shall groan and lament,
  all who cast their hooks into the Nile
  and those who spread nets on the water shall
  lose heart.
9 The flax-dressers shall hang their heads,
  the women carding and the weavers shall
  grow pale,
10 Egypt's spinners shall be downcast,
  and all her artisans sick at heart.

11 Fools that you are, you princes of
  Zoan!
  Wisest of Pharaoh's counsellors you may
  be,
  but stupid counsellors you are.
  How can you say to Pharaoh,
  'I am the heir of wise men and spring from
  ancient kings'?
12 Where are your wise men, Pharaoh,
  to teach you and make known to you
  what the LORD of Hosts has planned for
  Egypt?
13 Zoan's princes are fools, the princes of
  Noph are dupes;
  the chieftains of her clans have led Egypt
  astray.
14 The LORD has infused into them
  a spirit that warps their judgement;
  they make Egypt miss her way in all she
  does,
  as a drunkard will miss his footing as he
  vomits.
15 There shall be nothing in Egypt that any
  man can do,
  head or tail, palm or rush.

16 When that day comes the Egyptians shall
  become weak as women; they shall fear and
  tremble when they see the LORD of Hosts
  raise his hand against them, as raise it he
17 will. The land of Judah shall strike terror
  into Egypt; its very name shall cause dismay,
  because of the plans that the LORD of Hosts
  has laid against them.
18 When that day comes there shall be five
  cities in Egypt speaking the language of

Canaan and swearing allegiance to the LORD
of Hosts, and one of them shall be called the
City of the Sun.[j]

19 When that day comes there shall be an
altar to the LORD in the heart of Egypt, and
a sacred pillar set up for the LORD upon her
20 frontier. It shall stand as a token and a reminder to the LORD of Hosts in Egypt, so
that when they appeal to him against their
oppressors, he may send a deliverer to
champion their cause, and he shall rescue
21 them. The LORD will make himself known to
the Egyptians; on that day they shall acknowledge the LORD and do him service with sacrifice and grain-offering, make vows to him
22 and pay them. The LORD will strike down
Egypt, healing as he strikes; then they will
turn back to him and he will hear their
prayers and heal them.

23 When that day comes there shall be a
highway between Egypt and Assyria; Assyrians shall come to Egypt and Egyptians
to Assyria; then Egyptians shall worship
with[k] Assyrians.
24 When that day comes Israel shall rank
with Egypt and Assyria, those three, and
shall be a blessing in the centre of the world.
25 So the LORD of Hosts will bless them:
A blessing be upon Egypt my people, upon
Assyria the work of my hands, and upon
Israel my possession.

ASSYRIA

Assyria's conquest of Egypt and Cush

20 Sargon King of Assyria sent his commander-
in-chief[l] to Ashdod, and he took it by storm.
2 At that time the LORD said to Isaiah son of
Amoz, Come, strip the sackcloth from your
waist and take your sandals off. He did so,
3 and went about naked and barefoot. The
LORD said, My servant Isaiah has gone
naked and barefoot for three years as a sign
4 and a warning to Egypt and Cush; just so
shall the king of Assyria lead the captives of
Egypt and the exiles of Cush naked and barefoot, their buttocks shamefully exposed,
5 young and old alike. All men shall be dismayed, their hopes in Cush and their pride
6 in Egypt humbled. On that day those who
dwell along this coast will say, So much for
all our hopes on which we relied for help and
deliverance from the king of Assyria; what
escape have we now?

---

i Prob. rdg.; Heb. adds on the mouth of the Nile.
be slaves to.   l Or sent Tartan.

j the City of the Sun: or Heliopolis.   k Or shall

BABYLON

Babylon

21   A wilderness: an oracle.

Rough weather, advancing like a storm in
   the south,
coming from the wilderness, from a land of
   terror!

2   Grim is the vision shown to me:
   the traitor betrayed, the spoiler himself despoiled.
   Up, Elam; up, Medes, to the siege,
      no time for weariness!

3   At this my limbs writhe in anguish,
   I am gripped by pangs like a woman in
      labour.
   I am distraught past hearing, dazed past
      seeing,

4   my mind reels, sudden convulsions seize me.

   The cool twilight I longed for has become a
      terror:

5   the banquet is set out, the rugs are spread;
      they are eating and drinking—
   rise, princes, burnish your shields.

6   For these were the words of the Lord to
      me:
   Go, post a watchman to report what he
      sees.

7   He sees chariots, two-horsed chariots,
   riders on asses, riders on camels.
   He is alert, alert, always on the alert.

8   Then the look-out cried:
   All day long I stand on the Lord's watch-
      tower
   and night after night I keep my station.

See, there come men in a chariot, a two-   9
   horsed chariot.
And a voice calls back:
Fallen, fallen is Babylon,
and all the images of her gods lie shattered
   on the ground.
O my people,   10
once trodden out and winnowed on the
   threshing-floor,
   what I have heard from the LORD of
      Hosts,
   from the God of Israel, I have told you.

Dumah

             Dumah: an oracle.   11

One calls to me from Seir:
Watchman, what is left of the night?
Watchman, what is left?
The watchman answered: 12
Morning comes, and also night.*m*
Ask if you must; then come back again.

THE ARABS

The Arabs

          With the Arabs: an oracle.   13

You caravans of Dedan, that camp in the
   scrub with the Arabs,
   bring water to meet the thirsty.   14
You dwellers in Tema, meet the fugitives
   with food,
for they flee from the sword, the sharp edge 15
   of the sword,
from the bent bow, and from the press of
   battle.

For these are the words of the Lord to me: 16
Within a year, as a hired labourer counts off
the years, all the glory of Kedar shall come
to an end; few shall be the bows left to the 17
warriors of Kedar.
The LORD the God of Israel has spoken.

Jerusalem in ferment

       The Valley of Vision:*n* an oracle.   **22**

Tell me, what is amiss
   that you have all climbed on to the roofs,
O city full of tumult, town in ferment   2
   and filled with uproar,
   whose slain were not slain with the sword
   and did not die in battle?

---

m and also night: *or* and the night is full spent.   *n* *Or* of Calamity.

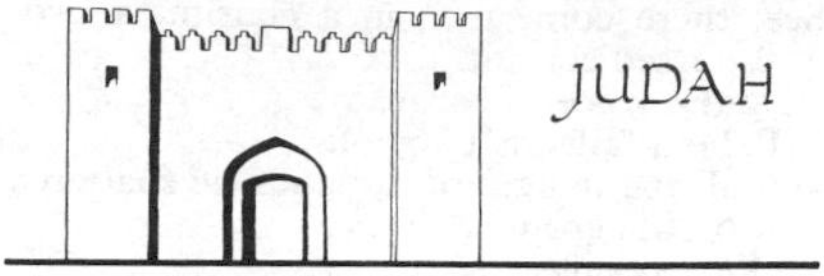

3 Your commanders are all in flight,
huddled together out of bowshot;
all your stoutest warriors are huddled together,
they have taken to their heels.
4 Then I said, Turn your eyes away from me;
leave me to weep in misery.
Do not thrust consolation on me
for the ruin of my own people.

5 For the Lord, the LORD of Hosts, has
ordained a day of tumult, a day of trampling
and turmoil in the Valley of Vision,[n] rousing
cries for help that echo among the mountains.

6 Elam took up his quiver,
horses were harnessed to the chariots of Aram,[o]
Kir took the cover from his shield.
7 Your fairest valleys were overrun by chariots and horsemen,
the gates were hard beset,
8 the heart of Judah's defence was laid open.

On that day you looked to the weapons
9 stored in the House of the Forest; you filled
all the many pools in the City of David,
10 collecting water from the Lower Pool.[p] Then
you surveyed the houses in Jerusalem, tearing some down to make the wall inaccessible,
11 and between the two walls you made a
cistern for the Waters of the Old Pool;
but you did not look to the Maker of it all
or consider him who fashioned it long ago.
12 On that day the Lord, the LORD of Hosts,
called for weeping and beating the breast,
for shaving the head and putting on sackcloth;
13 but instead there was joy and merrymaking,
slaughtering of cattle and killing of sheep,
eating of meat and drinking of wine, as you thought,
Let us eat and drink; for tomorrow we die.

14 The LORD of Hosts has revealed himself to
me; in my hearing he swore:

Your wickedness shall never be purged
until you die.
This is the word of the Lord, the LORD of Hosts.

Words to Shebna the steward

These were the words of the Lord, the LORD 15
of Hosts:
Go to this steward,
to Shebna, comptroller of the household, and say:
What right, what business, have you here, 16
that you have dug yourself a grave here,
cutting out your grave on a height
and carving yourself a resting-place in the rock?
The LORD will shake you out, 17
shake you as a garment[q] is shaken out
to rid it of lice;
then he will bundle you tightly and throw you 18
like a ball into a great wide land.
There you shall die,
and there shall lie your chariot of honour,
an object of contempt to your master's household.
I will remove you from office and drive you 19
from your post.

On that day I will send for my servant 20
Eliakim son of Hilkiah; I will invest him 21
with your robe, gird him with your sash; and
hand over your authority to him. He shall
be a father to the inhabitants of Jerusalem
and the people of Judah. I will lay the key of 22
the house of David on his shoulder; what he
opens no man shall shut, and what he shuts
no man shall open. He shall be a seat of 23
honour for his father's family; I will fasten
him firmly in place like a peg. On him shall 24
hang all the weight of the family, down to
the lowest dregs—all the little vessels, both
bowls and pots. On that day, says the LORD 25
of Hosts, the peg which was firmly fastened
in its place shall be removed; it shall be
hacked out and shall fall, and the load of
things hanging on it shall be destroyed. The
LORD has spoken.

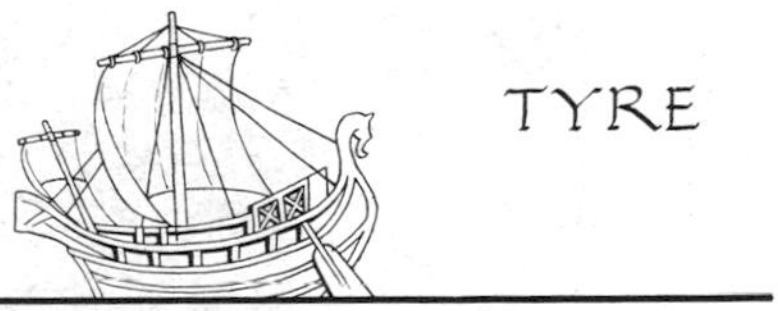

Tyre

Tyre: an oracle. 23

The ships of Tarshish howl, for the harbour is sacked;
the port of entry from Kittim is swept away.
The people of the sea-coast, the merchants 2–3
of Sidon, wail,
people whose agents cross the great waters,
whose harvest[r] is the grain of the Shihor
and their revenue the trade of nations.

n *Or* of Calamity. *o* *Prob. rdg.; Heb.* man. *p* you filled . . . Lower Pool: *or* you took note of the cracks, many as they were, in the wall of the City of David, and you collected water from the Lower Pool.
q *Prob. rdg.; Heb.* man. *r* whose harvest: *prob. rdg.; Heb.* the harvest of the Nile.

4 Sidon, the sea-fortress,ˢ cries in her dis-
    appointment,ᵗ
  I no longer feel the anguish of labour or bear
    children;
  I have no young sons to rear, no daughters
    to bring up.
5   When the news is confirmed in Egypt
    her people sway in anguish at the fate of
    Tyre.
6   Make your way to Tarshish, they say,
    howl, you who dwell by the sea-coast.
7   Is this your busy city, ancient in story,
    on whose voyages you were carried to settle
    far away?

8 Whose plan was this against Tyre, the city of
    battlements,
    whose merchants were princes
    and her traders the most honoured men on
    earth?
9 The LORD of Hosts planned it to prick every
    noble's pride
    and bring all the most honoured men on
    earth into contempt.
10   Take to the tillage of your fields, you
    people of Tarshish;
    for your marketᵘ is lost.
11 The LORD has stretched out his hand over
    the sea
    and shaken kingdoms,
  he has given his command to destroy the
    marts of Canaan;
12 and he has said, You shall busy yourselves
    no more,
    you, the sorely oppressed virgin city of
    Sidon.
    Though you arise and cross over to Kittim,
    even there you shall find no rest.

13   Look at this land, the destined home of
   shipsᵛ! The Chaldeansʷ erected theirˣ siege-
  towers, dismantled its palaces and laid it in
  ruins.

14   Howl, you ships of Tarshish;
    for your haven is sacked.

15   From that day Tyre shall be forgotten for
  seventy years, the span of one king's life. At
  the end of the seventy years her plight shall
  be that of the harlot in the song:

16 Take your harp, go round the city,
    poor forgotten harlot;
  touch the strings sweetly, sing all your songs,
    make men remember you again.

17 At the end of seventy years, the LORD will
  turn again to Tyre; she shall go back to her
  old trade and hire herself out to every king-
18 dom on earth. The profits of her trading will
  be dedicated to the LORD; they shall not be
  hoarded or stored up, but shall be given to

those who worship the LORD, to purchase
food in plenty and fine attire.

The LORD's judgement on the earth

Beware, the LORD will empty the earth,   **24**
split it open and turn it upside down,
    and scatter its inhabitants.
    Then it will be the same for priest and 2
      people,
the same for master and slave, mistress and
    slave-girl,
seller and buyer,
borrower and lender, debtor and creditor.
    The earth is emptied clean away   3
    and stripped clean bare.
For this is the word that the LORD has
    spoken.
    The earth dries up and withers,   4
    the whole world withers and grows sick;
    the earth's high places sicken,
    and earth itself is desecrated by the feet of 5
      those who live in it,
because they have broken the laws, dis-
    obeyed the statutes
    and violated the eternal covenant.
For this a curse has devoured the earth   6
    and its inhabitants stand aghast.
    For this those who inhabit the earth
    dwindle
    and only a few men are left.

    The new wine dries up, the vines sicken, 7
    and all the revellers turn to sorrow.
    Silent the merry beat of tambourines,   8
    hushed the shouts of revelry,
    the merry harp is silent.
    No one shall drink wine to the sound of 9
      song;
    the liquor will be bitter to the man who
    drinks it.
    The city of chaos is a broken city,   10
    every house barred, that no one may enter.
    Men call for wine in the streets;   11
    all revelry is darkened,
    and mirth is banished from the land.

    Desolation alone is left in the city   12
    and the gate is broken into pieces.
So shall it be in all the world, in every nation, 13
    as when an olive-tree is beaten and
    stripped,
    as when the vintage is ended.

Men raise their voices and cry aloud,   14
    they shout in the west,ʸ so great is the
      LORD's majesty.
    Therefore let the LORD be glorified in the 15
    regions of the east,
    and the name of the LORD the God of
    Israel
    in the coasts and islands of the west.

---

s the sea-fortress: *prob. rdg.; Heb.* the sea, sea-fortress, saying.   t in her disappointment: *prob. rdg.; Heb.*
be disappointed.   u *Prob. rdg.; Heb.* girdle.   v *Or* marmots.   w *Prob. rdg.; Heb. adds* this was the
people; it was not Assyria.   x *Prob. rdg.; Heb.* his.   y in the west: *or* more loudly than the sea.

16 From the ends of the earth we have heard
them sing,
How lovely is righteousness!
But I thought, Villainy, villainy!
Woe to the traitors and their treachery!
Traitors double-dyed they are indeed!
17 The hunter's scare, the pit, and the trap
threaten all who dwell in the land;
18 if a man runs from the rattle of the
scare
he will fall into the pit;
if he climbs out of the pit
he will be caught in the trap.
When the windows of heaven above are
opened
and earth's foundations shake,
19 the earth is utterly shattered,
it is convulsed and reels wildly.
20 The earth reels to and fro like a drunken
man
and sways like a watchman's shelter;
the sins of men weigh heavy upon it,
and it falls to rise no more.

21 On that day the LORD will punish
the host of heaven in heaven, and on earth
the kings of the earth,
22 herded together, close packed like prisoners
in a dungeon;
shut up in gaol, after a long time they shall
be punished.
23 The moon shall grow pale and the sun hide
its face in shame;
for the LORD of Hosts has become king
on Mount Zion and in Jerusalem,
and shows his glory before their elders.

A song of thanksgiving

25 O LORD, thou art my God;
I will exalt thee and praise thy name;
for thou hast accomplished a wonderful
purpose,
certain and sure, from of old.
2 For thou hast turned cities into heaps of
ruin,
and fortified towns into rubble;
every mansion in the cities is swept away,
never to be rebuilt.
3 For this a cruel nation holds thee in
honour,
the cities of ruthless nations fear thee.

Truly thou hast been a refuge to the poor, 4
a refuge to the needy in his trouble,
shelter from the tempest and shade from the
heat.
For the blast of the ruthless is like an icy
storm
or a scorching drought; 5
thou subduest the roar of the foe, ᶻ
and the song of the ruthless dies away.

The LORD's care and kindness

On this mountain the LORD of Hosts will 6
prepare
a banquet of rich fare for all the peoples,
a banquet of wines well matured and
richest fare,
well-matured wines strained clear.
On this mountain the LORD will swallow up 7
that veil that shrouds all the peoples,
the pall thrown over all the nations;
he will swallow up death for ever. 8
Then the Lord GOD will wipe away the tears
from every face
and remove the reproach of his people from
the whole earth.
The LORD has spoken.

Deliverance for the oppressed

On that day men will say, 9
See, this is our God
for whom we have waited to deliver us;
this is the LORD for whom we have waited;
let us rejoice and exult in his deliverance.
For the hand of the LORD will rest on this 10
mountain,
but Moab shall be trampled under his feet
as straw is trampled into a midden.
In it Moab shall spread out his hands 11
as a swimmer spreads his hands to swim,
but he shall sink his pride with every stroke
of his hands.
The LORD has thrown down the high 12
defences of your walls,
has levelled them to the earth
and brought them down to the dust.

Jerusalem: a city of righteousness and peace

On that day this song shall be sung in Judah: **26**
We have a strong city
whose walls and ramparts are our deliverance.

z *Prob. rdg.; Heb. adds* heat in the shadow of a cloud.

2 Open the gates to let a righteous nation in,
  a nation that keeps faith.
3 Thou dost keep in peace men of constant
    mind,
  in peace because they trust in thee.
4   Trust in the LORD for ever;
  for the LORD himself is an everlasting
    rock.
5 He has brought low all who dwell high in a
    towering city;
  he levels it to the ground and lays it in the
    dust,
6 that the oppressed and the poor may tread
    it underfoot.
7   The path of the righteous is level,
  and thou markest out the right way for the
    upright.
8 We too look to the path prescribed in thy
    laws, O LORD;
  thy name and thy memory are our heart's
    desire.
9   With all my heart I long for thee in the
    night,
  I seek thee eagerly when dawn breaks;
  for, when thy laws prevail in the land,
  the inhabitants of the world learn justice.
10 The wicked are destroyed, they have never
    learnt justice;
  corrupt in a land of honest ways,
  they do not regard the majesty of the
    LORD.

Death and resurrection

11 O LORD, thy hand is lifted high,
  but the bitter enemies of thy people do
    not see it;[a]
  let the fire of thy enmity destroy them.
12 O LORD, thou wilt bestow prosperity on us;
  for in truth all our works are thy doing.
13   O LORD our God,
  other lords than thou have been our
    masters,
  but thee alone do we invoke by name.
14   The dead will not live again,
  those long in their graves will not rise;
  to this end thou hast punished them and
    destroyed them,
  and made all memory of them perish.
15   Thou hast enlarged the nation, O LORD,
  enlarged it and won thyself honour,
  thou hast extended all the frontiers of the
    land.
16   In our distress, O LORD, we[b] sought thee
    out,
  chastened by the mere whisper of thy
    rebuke.
17   As a woman with child, when her time is
    near,
  is in labour and cries out in her pains,
  so were we in thy presence, O LORD.

18 We have been with child, we have been in
  labour,
  but have brought forth wind.
  We have won no success for the land,
  and no one will be born to inhabit the
    world.
19 But thy dead live, their bodies will rise again.
  They that sleep in the earth will awake and
    shout for joy;
  for thy dew is a dew of sparkling light,
  and the earth will bring those long dead to
    birth again.

The coming judgement

20 Go, my people, enter your rooms
  and shut your doors behind you;
  withdraw for a brief while, until wrath has
    gone by.
21 For see, the LORD is coming from his place
  to punish the inhabitants of the earth for
    their sins;
  then the earth shall uncover her blood-
    stains
  and hide her slain no more.

Allegories of the LORD's judgements

27 On that day the LORD will punish
  with his cruel sword, his mighty and power-
    ful sword,
  Leviathan that twisting[c] sea-serpent,
  that writhing serpent Leviathan,
  and slay the monster of the deep.

2 On that day sing to the pleasant vineyard,
3   I the LORD am its keeper,
  moment by moment I water it for fear its
    green leaves fail.
  Night and day I tend it,
4   but I get no wine;
  I would as soon have briars and thorns,
  then I would wage war upon it and burn it
    all up,
5 unless it grasps me as its refuge and makes
    peace with me—
  unless it makes peace with me.

6 In time to come Jacob's offspring shall
    take root
  and Israel shall bud and blossom,
  and they shall fill the whole earth with
    fruit.

7 Has God struck him down as he struck
    others down?
  Has the slayer been slain as he slew others?
8-10 This then purges Jacob's iniquity,
  this[e] has removed his sin:
  that he grinds all altar stones to powder like
    chalk;
  no sacred poles and incense-altars are left
    standing.

---

a Prob. rdg.; Heb. adds let them see and be ashamed.   *b Prob. rdg.; Heb.* they.   *c Or* primeval.
d Verses 8–10 re-arranged thus: 9, 10a, 8, 10b.   *e Prob. rdg.; Heb. adds* all fruit.

The fortified city is left solitary,
and his quarrel with her ends in brushing
her away,[f]
removing her by a cruel blast when the
east wind blows;
it is a homestead stripped bare, deserted like
a wilderness;
there the calf grazes and there lies down,
and crops every twig.

11 Its boughs snap off when they grow dry,
and women come and light their fires with
them.
For they are a people without sense;
therefore their maker will show them no
mercy,
he who formed them will show them no
favour.

The ingathering of dispersed Israelites

12 On that day the LORD will beat out the
grain,
from the streams of the Euphrates to the
Torrent of Egypt;
but you Israelites will be gleaned
one by one.

13 On that day
a blast shall be blown on a great trumpet,
and those who are lost in Assyria
and those dispersed in Egypt will come in
and worship the LORD on the holy mountain,
in Jerusalem.

ISRAEL   JUDAH

The LORD's purpose for Ephraim

28 Oh, the proud garlands of the drunkards
of Ephraim
and the flowering sprays, so lovely in their
beauty,
on the heads of revellers dripping with perfumes,
overcome with wine!

2 See, the Lord has one at his bidding, mighty
and strong,
whom he sets to work with violence
against the land,
like a sweeping storm of hail, like a destroying tempest,
like a torrent of water in overwhelming flood.

3 The proud garlands of Ephraim's drunkards
shall be trampled underfoot,

and the flowering sprays, so lovely in their 4
beauty
on the heads dripping with perfumes,
shall be like early figs ripe before summer;
he who sees them plucks them,
and their bloom is gone while they lie in
his hand.

On that day the LORD of Hosts shall be a 5
lovely garland,
a beautiful diadem for the remnant of his
people,
a spirit of justice for one who presides in a 6
court of justice,
and of valour for[g] those who repel the enemy
at the gate.

Corruption of priests and prophets

These too are addicted to wine, 7
clamouring in their cups:
priest and prophet are addicted to strong
drink
and bemused with wine;
clamouring in their cups, confirmed topers,[h]
hiccuping in drunken stupor;
every table is covered with vomit, 8
filth that leaves no clean spot.
Who is it that the prophet hopes to teach, 9
to whom will what they hear make sense?
Are they babes newly weaned, just taken
from the breast?
It is all harsh cries and raucous shouts, 10
'A little more here, a little there!'
So it will be with barbarous speech and 11
strange tongue
that this people will hear God speaking,
this people to whom he once said, 12
'This is true rest; let the exhausted have rest.
This is repose', and they refused to listen.
Now to them the word of the LORD will be 13
harsh cries and raucous shouts,
'A little more here, a little there!'—
and so, as they walk, they will stumble backwards,
they will be injured, trapped and caught.
Listen then to the word of the LORD, you 14
arrogant men
who rule this people in Jerusalem.
You say, 'We have made a treaty with Death 15
and signed a pact with Sheol:
so that, when the raging flood sweeps by, it
shall not touch us;
for we have taken refuge in lies
and sheltered behind falsehood.'
These then are the words of the Lord 16
GOD:
Look, I am laying a stone in Zion, a block of
granite,
a precious corner-stone for a firm foundation;
he who has faith shall not waver.

---

f Prob. rdg.; Heb. adds by dismissing her.   *g* for: *prob. rdg.; Heb. om.*   *h* These too ... topers: *or* These
too lose their way through wine and are set wandering by strong drink: priest and prophet lose their way through
strong drink and are fuddled with wine; are set wandering by strong drink, lose their way through tippling.

An eastern threshing-floor

17 I will use justice as a plumb-line
and righteousness as a plummet;
hail shall sweep away your refuge of lies,
and flood-waters carry away your shelter.
18 Then your treaty with Death shall be
annulled
and your pact with Sheol shall not stand;
the raging waters will sweep by,
and you will be like land swept by the
flood.
19 As often as it sweeps by, it will take you;
morning after morning it will sweep by,
day and night.
The very thought of such tidings
will bring nothing but dismay;
20 for 'The bed is too short for a man to
stretch,
and the blanket too narrow to cover him.'
21 But the LORD shall arise as he rose on Mount
Perazim
and storm with rage as he did in the Vale of
Gibeon
to do what he must do—how strange a deed!
to perform his work—how outlandish a
work!
22 But now have done with your arrogance,
lest your bonds grow tighter;
for I have heard destruction decreed
by the Lord GOD of Hosts for the whole land.

The parable of the ploughman

23 Listen and hear what I say,
attend and hear my words.
24 Will the ploughman continually plough for
the sowing,
breaking his ground and harrowing it?
25 Does he not, once he has levelled it,
broadcast the dill and scatter the cummin?
Does he not plant the wheat in rows
with barley[i] and spelt along the edge?

Does not his God instruct him and train him 26
aright?
Dill is not threshed with a sledge, 27
and the cartwheel is not rolled over cummin;
dill is beaten with a rod,
and cummin with a flail.
Corn is crushed, but not to the uttermost, 28
not with a final crushing;
his cartwheels rumble over it and break it
up,
but they do not grind it fine.
This message, too, comes from the LORD of 29
Hosts,
whose purposes are wonderful
and his power great.

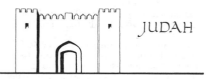

Judgement and mercy for Judah

Alas for Ariel! Ariel, **29**
the city where David encamped.
Add year to year,
let the pilgrim-feasts run their round,
and I will bring Ariel to sore straits, 2
when there shall be moaning and lamentation.
I will make her my Ariel indeed, my fiery
altar.
I will throw my army round you like a wall; 3
I will set a ring of outposts all round you
and erect siege-works against you.

i Prob. rdg.; Heb. adds an unintelligible word.

4 You shall be brought low, you will speak
     out of the ground
   and your words will issue from the earth;
   your voice will come like a ghost's from the
     ground,
   and your words will squeak out of the
     earth.
5 Yet the horde of your enemies shall crumble
     into dust,
   the horde of ruthless foes shall fly like
     chaff.
   Then suddenly, all in an instant,
6 punishment shall come from the LORD of
     Hosts
   with thunder and earthquake and a great
     noise,
   with storm and tempest and a flame of
     devouring fire;
7 and the horde of all the nations warring
     against Ariel,
   all their baggage-trains and siege-works,
   and all her oppressors themselves,
   shall fade as a dream, a vision of the
     night.
8 Like a starving man who dreams
   and thinks that he is eating,
   but wakes up to find himself empty,
   or a thirsty man who dreams
   and thinks that he is drinking,
   but wakes up to find himself thirsty and dry,
   so shall the horde of all the nations be
   that war against Mount Zion.

Judah's religion and politics condemned

9 Loiter and be dazed, enjoy yourselves and be
     blinded,
   be drunk but not with wine, reel but not with
     strong drink;
10 for the LORD has poured upon you a spirit
     of deep stupor;
   he has closed your eyes, the prophets,
   and muffled your heads, the seers.

11 All prophetic vision has become for you
   like a sealed book. Give such a book to one
   who can read and say, 'Come, read this'; he
   will answer, 'I cannot, because it is sealed.
12 Give it to one who cannot read and say,
   'Come, read this'; he will answer, 'I cannot
   read.'
13 Then the Lord said:

   Because this people approach me with their
     mouths
   and honour me with their lips
   while their hearts are far from me,
   and their religion is but a precept of men,
     learnt by rote,
14 therefore I will yet again shock this people,
     adding shock to shock:
   the wisdom of their wise men shall vanish
   and the discernment of the discerning shall
     be lost.

15 Shame upon those who seek to hide their
     purpose
   too deep for the LORD to see,
   and who, when their deeds are done in the
     dark,
   say, 'Who sees us? Who knows of us?'
16 How you turn things upside down,
   as if the potter ranked no higher than the
     clay!
   Shall the thing made say of its maker, 'He
     did not make me'?
   Shall the pot say of the potter, 'He has no
     skill'?
17 The time is but short
   before Lebanon goes back to grassland
   and the grassland is no better than scrub.

Future revival and restoration

18 On that day deaf men shall hear
   when a book is read,
   and the eyes of the blind shall see
   out of impenetrable darkness.
19 The lowly shall once again rejoice in the
     LORD,
   and the poorest of men exult in the Holy
     One of Israel.
20 The ruthless shall be no more, the arrogant
   shall cease to be;
   those who are quick to see mischief,
21 those who charge others with a sin
   or lay traps for him who brings the wrong-
     doer into court
   or by falsehood deny justice to the right-
     eous—
   all these shall be exterminated.

22 Therefore these are the words of the LORD
   the God of the house of Jacob, the God who
   ransomed Abraham:

   This is no time for Jacob to be shamed,
   no time for his face to grow pale;
23 for his descendants will hallow my name
   when they see what I have done in their
     nation.
   They will hallow the Holy One of Jacob
   and hold the God of Israel in awe;
24 those whose minds are confused will gain
     understanding,
   and the obstinate will receive instruction.

Egypt's help is worthless

30 Oh, rebel sons! says the LORD,
   you make plans, but not of my devising,
   you weave schemes, but not inspired by
     me,
   piling sin upon sin;
2 you hurry down to Egypt without consulting
     me,
   to seek protection under Pharaoh's shel-
     ter
   and take refuge under Egypt's wing.

3 Pharaoh's protection will bring you disappointment
and refuge under Egypt's wing humiliation;
4 for, though his officers are at Zoan
and his envoys reach as far as Hanes,
5 all are left in sorry plight by that unprofitable
nation,
no help they find, no profit, only disappointment and disgrace.

6 The Beasts of the South: an oracle.

Through a land of hardship and distress
the tribes of lioness and roaring lion,
sand-viper and venomous flying serpent,
carry their wealth on the backs of asses
and their treasures on camels' humps
to an unprofitable people.
7 Vain and worthless is the help of Egypt;
therefore have I given her this name,
Rahab Quelled.
8 Now come and write it on a tablet,
engrave it as an inscription before their
eyes,
that it may be there in future days,
a testimony for all time.
9 For they are a race of rebels, disloyal sons,
sons who will not listen to the LORD's instruction;
10 they say to the seers, 'You shall not
see',
and to the visionaries, 'You shall have no
true visions;
give us smooth words and seductive visions.
11 Turn aside, leave the straight path,
and rid us for ever of the Holy One of
Israel.'

The LORD is waiting to show his favour

These are the words of the Holy One of 12
Israel:
Because you have rejected this warning
and trust in devious and dishonest practices,
resting on them for support,
therefore you shall find this iniquity will be 13
like a crack running down
a high wall, which bulges
and suddenly, all in an instant, comes crashing down,
as an earthen jar is broken with a crash, 14
mercilessly shattered,
so that not a shard is found among the
fragments
to take fire from the glowing embers,
or to scoop up water from a pool.

These are the words of the Lord GOD the 15
Holy One of Israel:
Come back, keep peace, and you will be
safe;
in stillness and in staying quiet, there lies
your strength.
But you would have none of it; you said, 16
No,
we will take horse and flee;
therefore you shall be put to flight:
We will ride apace;
therefore swift shall be the pace of your
pursuers.
When a thousand flee at the challenge of 17
one,
you shall all flee at the challenge of five, until
you are left
like a pole on a mountain-top, a signal post
on a hill.

K

18 Yet the LORD is waiting to show you his favour,
　　yet he yearns to have pity on you;
　　for the LORD is a God of justice.
　　Happy are all who wait for him!

A future day of blessing promised

19 O people of Zion who dwell in Jerusalem, you shall weep no more. The LORD will show you favour and answer you when he hears
20 your cry for help. The Lord may give you bread of adversity and water of affliction, but he who teaches you shall no longer be hidden out of sight, but with your own eyes
21 you shall see him always. If you stray from the road to right or left you shall hear with your own ears a voice behind you saying,
22 This is the way; follow it. You will reject, as things unclean, your silvered images and your idols sheathed in gold; you will loathe them like a foul discharge and call them
23 ordure.[j] The Lord will give you rain for the seed you sow, and as the produce of your soil he will give you heavy crops of corn in plenty. When that day comes the cattle shall
24 graze in broad pastures; the oxen and asses that work your land shall be fed with well-seasoned fodder, winnowed with shovel and
25 fork. On each high mountain and each lofty hill shall be streams of running water, on the day of massacre when the highest in the
26 land fall. The moon shall shine with a brightness like the sun's, and the sun with seven times his wonted brightness, seven days' light in one, on the day when the LORD binds up the broken limbs of his people and heals their wounds.

The LORD will afflict Assyria

27 　See, the name of the LORD comes from afar,
　　his anger blazing and his doom heavy.
　　His lips are charged with wrath
　　and his tongue is a devouring fire.
28 　His breath is like a torrent in spate,
　　rising neck-high,
　a yoke to force the nations to their ruin,
　a bit in the mouth to guide the peoples astray.
29 　But for you there shall be songs,
　　as on a night of sacred pilgrimage,
　your hearts glad, as the hearts of men who
　　　walk to the sound of the pipe
　on their way to the LORD's hill, to the rock of
　　Israel.
30 　Then the LORD shall make his voice heard
　　in majesty
　and show his arm sweeping down in fierce
　　anger
　　with devouring flames of fire,
　with cloudburst and tempests of rain and
　　hailstones;

for at the voice of the LORD Assyria's 3 heart fails her,
　as she feels the stroke of his rod.
Tambourines and harps and shaking sis- 3 trums
　shall keep time
　with every stroke of his rod,
of the chastisement which the LORD inflicts on her.
Long ago was Topheth made ready,[k] 3
　made deep and broad,
　its fire-pit a blazing mass of logs,
　and the breath of the LORD like a stream of brimstone
　blazing in it.

Deliverance is from the LORD, not Egypt

Shame upon those who go down to Egypt ·
　for help
and rely on horses,
　putting their trust in chariots many in number
and in horsemen in their thousands,
but do not look to the Holy One of Israel
　or seek guidance of the LORD!
Yet the LORD too in his wisdom can bring 2
　about trouble
and he does not take back his words;
he will rise up against the league of evil-doers,
against all who help those who do wrong.
The Egyptians are men, not God,[l] 3
　their horses are flesh, not spirit;
and, when the LORD stretches out his hand,
the helper will stumble and he who is helped
　will fall,
and they will all vanish together.

This is what the LORD has said to me: ·

As a lion or a young lion growls over its prey
when the muster of shepherds is called out against it,
　and is not scared at their noise
　or cowed by their clamour,
so shall the LORD of Hosts come down to do battle
　for Mount Zion and her high summit.
Thus the LORD of Hosts, like a bird hover- ·
　ing over its young,
will be a shield over Jerusalem;
he will shield her and deliver her,
standing over her and delivering her.
O Israel, come back to him whom you have
　so deeply offended,
for on that day when you spurn, one and all,
the idols of silver and the idols of gold
which your own sinful hands have made,

_____

j call them ordure: or say to them, Be off.
l Or gods.

k Prob. rdg.; Heb. adds is that prepared also for the king?

8 Assyria shall fall by the sword, but by no
sword of man;
a sword that no man wields shall devour
him.
He shall flee before the sword,
and his young warriors shall be put to
forced labour,
9 his officers shall be helpless from terror
and his captains too dismayed to flee.
This is the very word of the LORD
whose fire blazes in Zion,
and whose furnace is set up in Jerusalem.

When righteousness prevails

2 Behold, a king shall reign in righteousness
and his rulers rule with justice,
2 and a man shall be a refuge from the wind
and a shelter from the tempest,
or like runnels of water in dry ground,
like the shadow of a great rock in a thirsty
land.
3 The eyes that can see will not be clouded,
and the ears that can hear will listen;
4 the anxious heart will understand and
know,
and the man who stammers will at once
speak plain.
5 The scoundrel will no longer be thought
noble,
nor the villain called a prince;
6 for the scoundrel will speak like a scoundrel
and will hatch evil in his heart;
he is an impostor in all his actions,
and in his words a liar even to the LORD;
he starves the hungry of their food
and refuses drink to the thirsty.
7 The villain's ways are villainous
and he devises infamous plans
to ruin the poor with his lies
and deny justice to the needy.
8 But the man of noble mind forms noble
designs
and stands firm in his nobility.

Times of dearth and times of plenty

9 You women that live at ease, stand up
and hear what I have to say.
You young women without a care, mark my
words.
10 You have no cares now, but when the year
is out, you will tremble,
for the vintage will be over and no produce
gathered in.
11 You who are now at ease, be anxious;
tremble, you who have no cares.
Strip yourselves bare;
put a cloth round your waists
12 and beat your breasts
for the pleasant fields and fruitful vines.

On the soil of my people shall spring up 13
thorns and briars,
in every happy home and in the busy town,
for the palace is forsaken and the crowded 14
streets deserted;
citadel[m] and watch-tower are turned into
open heath,
the joy of wild asses ever after and pasture
for the flocks,
until a spirit from on high is lavished upon us. 15
Then the wilderness will become grassland
and grassland will be cheap as scrub;
then justice shall make its home in the 16
wilderness,
and righteousness dwell in the grassland;
when righteousness shall yield peace 17
and its fruit be quietness and confidence for
ever.
Then my people shall live in a tranquil 18
country,
dwelling in peace, in houses full of ease;
it will be cool on the slopes of the forest 19
then,
and cities shall lie peaceful in the plain.
Happy shall you be, sowing every man by 20
the water-side,
and letting ox and ass run free.

The LORD, the mainstay of the age

Ah! you destroyer, yourself undestroyed, 33
betrayer still unbetrayed,
when you cease to destroy you will be
destroyed,
after all your betrayals, you will be
betrayed yourself.

O LORD, show us thy favour; we hope in thee. 2
Uphold us every morning,
save us when troubles come.
At the roar of the thunder the peoples flee, 3
at thy rumbling nations are scattered;
their spoil is swept up as if young locusts had 4
swept it,
like a swarm of locusts men swarm upon it.

The LORD is supreme, for he dwells on high; 5
if you fill Zion with justice and with righteousness,
then he will be the mainstay of the age:[n] 6
wisdom and knowledge are the assurance of
salvation;
the fear of the LORD is her[o] treasure.

Righteousness amidst moral decay

Hark, how the valiant cry aloud for help, 7
and those sent to sue for peace weep
bitterly!
The highways are deserted, no travellers 8
tread the roads.
Covenants are broken, treaties are flouted;
man is of no account.

m Or hill; Heb. Ophel.   n the age: prob. rdg.; Heb. your times.   o Prob. rdg.; Heb. his.

9 The land is parched and wilting,
Lebanon is eaten away and crumbling;
Sharon has become a desert,
Bashan and Carmel are stripped bare.
10 Now, says the LORD, I will rise up.
Now I will exalt myself, now lift myself up.
11 What you conceive and bring to birth is
chaff and stubble;
a wind like fire shall devour you.
12 Whole nations shall be heaps of white ash,
or like thorns cut down and set on fire.
13 You who dwell far away, hear what I have
done;
acknowledge my might, you who are near.
14 In Zion sinners quake with terror,
the godless are seized with trembling and
ask,
Can any of us live with a devouring fire?
Can any live in endless burning?
15 The man who lives an upright life and speaks
the truth,
who scorns to enrich himself by extortion,
who snaps his fingers at a bribe,
who stops his ears to hear nothing of
bloodshed,
who closes his eyes to the sight of evil—
16 that is the man who shall dwell on the
heights,
his refuge a fastness in the cliffs,
his bread secure and his water never failing.

17 Your eyes shall see a king in his splendour
and will look upon a land of far distances.
18 You will call to mind what once you
feared:
'Where then is he that counted, where is he
that weighed,
where is he that counted the treasures?'
19 You will no longer see that barbarous
people,
that people whose speech was so hard to
catch,
whose stuttering speech you could not
understand.

The LORD our king

20 Look upon Zion, city of our solemn
feasts,
let your eyes rest on Jerusalem,
a land of comfort, a tent that shall never be
shifted,
whose pegs shall never be pulled up,
not one of its ropes cast loose.
21 There we have the LORD's majesty;[p]
it will be a place[q] of rivers and broad
streams;
but[r] no galleys shall be rowed there,
no stately ship sail by.
22 For the LORD our judge, the LORD our law-
giver,
the LORD our king—he himself will save us.

[Men may say, Your rigging is slack; 2
it will not hold the mast firm in its socket,
nor can the sails be spread.]
Then the blind man shall have a full share of
the spoil
and the lame shall take part in the pillage;
no man who dwells there shall say, 'I am 2
sick';
and the sins of the people who live there
shall be pardoned.

Desolation

Approach, you nations, to listen,   3
and attend, you peoples;
let the earth listen and everything in it,
the world and all that it yields;
for the LORD's anger is turned against all 2
the nations
and his wrath against all the host of them:
he gives them over to slaughter and
destruction.
Their slain shall be flung out,   3
the stench shall rise from their corpses,
and the mountains shall stream with their
blood.
All the host of heaven shall crumble into 4
nothing,
the heavens shall be rolled up like a scroll,
and the starry host fade away,
as the leaf withers from the vine
and the ripening fruit from the fig-tree;
for the sword of the LORD[s] appears in 5
heaven.
See how it descends in judgement on
Edom,
on the people whom he dooms[t] to destruction.
The LORD has a sword steeped in blood,   6
it is gorged with fat,
the fat of rams' kidneys, and the blood of
lambs and goats;
for he has a sacrifice in Bozrah,
a great slaughter in Edom.
Wild oxen shall come down and buffaloes[u] 7
with them,
bull and bison together,
and the land shall drink deep of blood
and the soil be sated with fat.
For the LORD has a day of vengeance,   8
the champion of Zion has a year when he
will requite.
Edom's torrents shall be turned into pitch 9
and its soil into brimstone,
and the land shall become blazing pitch,
which night and day shall never be
quenched,
and its smoke shall go up for ever.
From generation to generation it shall lie
waste,
and no man shall pass through it ever
again.

p Or threshing-floor.   *q it . . . place: or instead.*
rdg.; Heb. my sword.   *t Prob. rdg.; Heb. I doom.*

r Or and.   *s the sword of the LORD: prob.*
u and buffaloes: prob. rdg.; Heb. om.

1 Horned owl and bustard shall make their
home in it,
screech-owl and raven shall haunt it.
He has stretched across it a measuring-line
of chaos,
2 and its frontiers shall be a jumble of
stones.
No king shall be acclaimed there,
and all its princes shall come to nought.
3 Thorns shall sprout in its palaces;
nettles and briars shall cover its walled
towns.
It shall be rough land fit for wolves, a haunt
of desert-owls.
4 Marmots shall consort with jackals,
and he-goat shall encounter he-goat.
There too the nightjar shall rest
and find herself a place for repose.
5 There the sand-partridge shall make her
nest,
lay her eggs and hatch them
and gather her brood under her wings;
there shall the kites gather,
one after another.
6 Consult the book of the Lord and read it:
not one of these shall be lacking,
not one miss its fellow,
for with his own mouth he has ordered it
and with his own breath he has brought
them together.
7 He it is who has allotted each its place,
and his hand has measured out their
portions;
they shall occupy it for ever
and dwell there from generation to generation.

Restoration

5 Let the wilderness and the thirsty land be
glad,
let the desert rejoice and burst into flower.
2 Let it flower with fields of asphodel,
let it rejoice and shout for joy.
The glory of Lebanon is given to it,
the splendour too of Carmel and Sharon;
these shall see the glory of the Lord, the
splendour of our God.

Strengthen the feeble arms, 3
steady the tottering knees;
say to the anxious, Be strong and fear not. 4
See, your God comes with vengeance,
with dread retribution he comes to save you.
Then shall blind men's eyes be opened, 5
and the ears of the deaf unstopped.
Then shall the lame man leap like a deer, 6
and the tongue of the dumb shout aloud;
for water springs up in the wilderness,
and torrents flow in dry land.
The mirage becomes a pool, 7
the thirsty land bubbling springs;
instead of reeds and rushes, grass shall grow
in the rough land where wolves now lurk.
And there shall be a causeway there 8
which shall be called the Way of Holiness,
and the unclean shall not pass along it;
it shall become a pilgrim's way,*v*
no fool shall trespass on it.
No lion shall come there, 9
no savage beast climb on to it;
not one shall be found there.
By it those he has ransomed shall return
and the Lord's redeemed come home; 10
they shall enter Zion with shouts of triumph,
crowned with everlasting gladness.
Gladness and joy shall be their escort,
and suffering and weariness shall flee away.

Sennacherib invades Judah

In the fourteenth year of the reign of Heze- **36** 1*w*
kiah, Sennacherib king of Assyria attacked
and took all the fortified cities of Judah.
From Lachish he sent the chief officer*x* with 2
a strong force to King Hezekiah at Jerusalem; and he halted by the conduit of the
Upper Pool on the causeway which leads
to the Fuller's Field. There Eliakim son of 3
Hilkiah, the comptroller of the household,
came out to him, with Shebna the adjutant-
general and Joah son of Asaph, the secretary
of state. The chief officer said to them, 'Tell 4
Hezekiah that this is the message of the
Great King, the king of Assyria: "What
ground have you for this confidence of

v a pilgrim's way: prob. rdg.; Heb. unintelligible.
x Or sent Rab-shakeh.

w Verses 1–22: cp. 2 Kgs. 18. 13–37; 2 Chr. 32. 1–19.

5 yours? Do you think fine words can take the place of skill and numbers? On whom then do you rely for support in your rebel-
6 lion against me? On Egypt? Egypt is a splintered cane that will run into a man's hand and pierce it if he leans on it. That is what Pharaoh king of Egypt proves to all
7 who rely on him. And if you tell me that you are relying on the LORD your God, is he not the god whose hill-shrines and altars Hezekiah has suppressed, telling Judah and Jerusalem that they must prostrate themselves before this altar alone?"'

Sennacherib presses for surrender

8 'Now, make a bargain with my master the king of Assyria: I will give you two thousand
9 horses if you can find riders for them. Will you reject the authority of even the least of my master's servants and rely on Egypt for
10 chariots and horsemen? Do you think that I have come to attack this land and destroy it without the consent of the LORD? No; the LORD himself said to me, "Attack this land and destroy it."'
11 Eliakim, Shebna, and Joah said to the chief officer, 'Please speak to us in Aramaic, for we understand it; do not speak Hebrew to us within earshot of the people on the
12 city wall.' The chief officer answered, 'Is it to your master and to you that my master has sent me to say this? Is it not to the people sitting on the wall who, like you, will have to eat their own dung and drink their own
13 urine?' Then he stood and shouted in Hebrew, 'Hear the message of the Great
14 King, the king of Assyria. These are the king's words: "Do not be taken in by Heze-
15 kiah. He cannot save you. Do not let him persuade you to rely on the LORD, and tell you that the LORD will save you and that this city will never be surrendered to the
16 king of Assyria." Do not listen to Hezekiah; these are the words of the king of Assyria: "Make peace with me. Come out to me, and then you shall each eat the fruit of his own vine and his own fig-tree, and drink the
17 water of his own cistern, until I come and take you to a land like your own, a land of grain and new wine, of corn and vineyards.
18 Beware lest Hezekiah mislead you by telling you that the LORD will save you. Did the god of any of these nations save his land from
19 the king of Assyria? Where are the gods of Hamath and Arpad? Where are the gods of Sepharvaim? Where are the gods of Samaria? Did they save Samaria from me?
20 Among all the gods of these nations is there one who saved his land from me? And how is the LORD to save Jerusalem?"'
21 The people were silent and answered not

y *Verses 1–38: cp. 2 Kgs. 19. 1–37; 2 Chr. 32. 20–22.*
he heard.

a word, for the king had given orders that no one was to answer him. Eliakim son 2 of Hilkiah, comptroller of the household, Shebna the adjutant-general, and Joah son of Asaph, secretary of state, came to Hezekiah with their clothes rent and reported what the chief officer had said.

Hezekiah seeks Isaiah's advice

When King Hezekiah heard their report, he 3 rent his clothes and wrapped himself in sackcloth, and went into the house of the LORD. He sent Eliakim comptroller of the house- 2 hold, Shebna the adjutant-general, and the senior priests, all covered in sackcloth, to the prophet Isaiah son of Amoz, to give him 3 this message from the king: 'This day is a day of trouble for us, a day of reproof and contempt. We are like a woman who has no strength to bear the child that is coming to the birth. It may be that the LORD your 4 God heard the words of the chief officer whom his master the king of Assyria sent to taunt the living God, and will confute what he, the LORD your God, heard. Offer a prayer for those who still survive.' King 5 Hezekiah's servants came to Isaiah, and he 6 told them to say this to their master: 'This is the word of the LORD: "Do not be alarmed at what you heard when the lackeys of the king of Assyria blasphemed me. I will put 7 a spirit in him, and he shall hear a rumour and withdraw to his own country; and there I will make him fall by the sword."'

Hezekiah prays to the LORD

So the chief officer withdrew. He heard that 8 the king of Assyria had left Lachish, and he found him attacking Libnah. But when the 9 king learnt that Tirhakah king of Cush was on the way to make war on him, he sent messengers again[z] to Hezekiah king of 10 Judah, to say to him, 'How can you be deluded by your god on whom you rely when he promises that Jerusalem shall not fall into the hands of the king of Assyria? Surely you have heard what the kings of 11 Assyria have done to all countries, exterminating their people; can you then hope to escape? Did their gods save the nations 12 which my forefathers destroyed, Gozan, Harran, Rezeph, and the people of Beth-eden living in Telassar? Where are the kings 13 of Hamath, of Arpad, and of Lahir, Sepharvaim, Hena, and Ivvah?'

Hezekiah took the letter from the messengers and read it; then he went up into the house of the LORD, spread it out before the LORD and offered this prayer: 'O LORD of Hosts, God of Israel, enthroned on the

z *again: prob. rdg., cp. 2 Kgs. 19. 9; Heb. and*

cherubim, thou alone art God of all the kingdoms of the earth; thou hast made heaven and earth. Turn thy ear to me, O LORD, and listen; open thine eyes, O LORD, and see; hear the message that Sennacherib has sent to taunt the living God. It is true, O LORD, that the kings of Assyria have laid waste every country, that they have consigned their gods to the fire and destroyed them; for they were no gods but the work of men's hands, mere wood and stone. But now, O LORD our God, save us from his power, so that all the kingdoms of the earth may know that thou, O LORD, alone art God.'

The LORD answers Hezekiah

1 Isaiah son of Amoz sent to Hezekiah and said, 'This is the word of the LORD the God of Israel: I have heard your prayer to me concerning Sennacherib king of Assyria. 2 This is the word which the LORD has spoken concerning him:

The virgin daughter of Zion disdains you,
    she laughs you to scorn;
the daughter of Jerusalem tosses her head
    as you retreat.
3   Whom have you taunted and blasphemed?
    Against whom have you clamoured,
casting haughty glances at the Holy One of
    Israel?
4   You have sent your servants to taunt the
    Lord,
    and said:
With my countless chariots I have gone up
    high in the mountains, into the recesses of
    Lebanon.
I have cut down its tallest cedars,
    the best of its pines,
I have reached its highest limit of forest and
    meadow.[a]
5   I have dug wells
    and drunk the waters of a foreign land,
and with the soles of my feet I have dried up
    all the streams of Egypt.

6   Have you not heard long ago?
    I did it all.
    In days gone by I planned it
    and now I have brought it about,
    making fortified cities tumble down
    into heaps of rubble.
7 Their citizens, shorn of strength,
    disheartened and ashamed,
    were but as plants in the field, as green
    herbs,
    as grass on the roof-tops blasted before
    the east wind.
8   I know your rising up and your sitting
    down,
    your going out and your coming in.

a and meadow: prob. rdg.; Heb. its meadow.

The frenzy of your rage against me and your 29
    arrogance
have come to my ears.
I will put a ring in your nose
    and a hook in your lips,
    and I will take you back by the road
    on which you have come.

This shall be the sign for you: this year you 30 shall eat shed grain and in the second year what is self-sown; but in the third year sow and reap, plant vineyards and eat their fruit. The survivors left in Judah shall strike fresh 31 root under ground and yield fruit above ground, for a remnant shall come out of 32 Jerusalem and survivors from Mount Zion. The zeal of the LORD of Hosts will perform this.

'Therefore, this is the word of the LORD 33 concerning the king of Assyria:

He shall not enter this city
    nor shoot an arrow there,
    he shall not advance against it with shield
    nor cast up a siege-ramp against it.
By the way on which he came he shall go 34
    back;
    this city he shall not enter.
    This is the very word of the LORD.
I will shield this city to deliver it,   35
for my own sake and for the sake of my
    servant David.'

The LORD strikes down the Assyrians

The angel of the LORD went out and struck 36 down a hundred and eighty-five thousand men in the Assyrian camp; when morning dawned, they all lay dead. So Sennacherib 37 king of Assyria broke camp, went back to Nineveh and stayed there. One day, while 38 he was worshipping in the temple of his god Nisroch, Adrammelech and Sharezer his sons murdered him and escaped to the land of Ararat. He was succeeded by his son Esarhaddon.

Hezekiah falls ill, and recovers

At this time Hezekiah fell dangerously ill **38** 1[b] and the prophet Isaiah son of Amoz came to him and said, 'This is the word of the LORD: Give your last instructions to your household, for you are a dying man and will not recover.' Hezekiah turned his face to the 2 wall and offered this prayer to the LORD: 'O LORD, remember how I have lived before 3 thee, faithful and loyal in thy service, always doing what was good in thine eyes.' And he wept bitterly. Then the word of the LORD 4 came to Isaiah: 'Go and say to Hezekiah: 5 "This is the word of the LORD the God of your father David: I have heard your prayer and seen your tears; I will add fifteen

b Verses 1–8, 21, 22: cp. 2 Kgs. 20. 1–11.

6 years to your life. I will deliver you and this city from the king of Assyria and will pro-
21c tect this city."' Then Isaiah told them to apply a fig-plaster; so they made one and applied it to the boil, and he recovered.
22 Then Hezekiah said, 'By what sign shall I know that I shall go up into the house of the
7 LORD?' And Isaiah said,d 'This shall be your sign from the LORD that he will do what he
8 has promised. Watch the shadow cast by the sun on the stairway of Ahaz: I will bring backwards ten steps the shadow which has gone down on the stairway.' And the sun went back ten steps on the stairway down which it had gone.

Hezekiah's poem

9 A poem of Hezekiah king of Judah after his recovery from his illness, as it was written down:

10 I thought: In the prime of life I must pass away;
    for the rest of my years I am consigned to the gates of Sheol.
11 I said: I shall no longer see the LORD in the land of the living;
    never again, like those who live in the world,
    shall I look on a man.
12 My dwelling is taken from me,
    pulled up like a shepherd's tent;
    thou hast cut short my life like a weaver who severs the web from the thrum.
    From morning to night thou tormentest me,
13 then I am racked with pain till the morning.
    All my bones are broken, as a lion would break them;
    from morning to night thou tormentest me.
14 I twitter as if I were a swallow,
    I moan like a dove.
    My eyes falter as I look up to the heights;
    O Lord, pay heed, stand surety for me.
15 How can I complain, what can I say to the LORD
    when he himself has done this?
    I wander to and fro all my life long in the bitterness of my soul.
16 Yet, O Lord, my soul shall live with thee;
    do thou give my spirit rest.e
    Restore me and give me life.
17 Bitterness had indeed been my lot in place of prosperity;
    but thou by thy love hast brought me back from the pit of destruction;
    for thou hast cast all my sins behind thee.

Sheol cannot confess thee,   18
Death cannot praise thee,
nor can they who go down to the abyss hope for thy truth.
The living, the living alone can confess 19 thee
    as I do this day,
as a father makes thy truth known, O God, to his sons.
The LORD is at hand to save me;   20
    so let us sound the music of our praises
all our life long in the house of the LORD.f

Hezekiah receives Babylonian envoys

At this time Merodach-baladan son of Baladan king of Babylon sent envoys with a gift to Hezekiah; for he had heard that he had been ill and was well again. Hezekiah 2 welcomed them and showed them all his treasury, silver and gold, spices and fragrant oil, his entire armoury and everything to be found among his treasures; there was nothing in his house and in all his realm that Hezekiah did not show them. Then the prophet Isaiah 3 came to King Hezekiah and asked him,

c *Verses 21, 22 transposed.*   d *And Isaiah said: prob. rdg., cp. 2 Kgs. 20. 9; Heb. om.*   e *Yet . . . rest: prob. rdg.; Heb. unintelligible.*   f *Verses 21, 22 transposed to follow verse 6.*   g *Verses 1–8: cp. 2 Kgs. 20. 12–19.*

(Isa. 40. 11)

'What did these men say and where have they come from?' 'They have come from a far-off country,' Hezekiah answered, 'from 4 Babylon.' Then Isaiah asked, 'What did they see in your house?' 'They saw everything,' Hezekiah replied; 'there was nothing among 5 my treasures that I did not show them.' Then Isaiah said to Hezekiah, 'Hear the word of 6 the LORD of Hosts: The time is coming, says the LORD, when everything in your house, and all that your forefathers have amassed till the present day, will be carried away to 7 Babylon; not a thing shall be left. And some of the sons who will be born to you, sons of your own begetting, shall be taken and shall be made eunuchs in the palace of the king of 8 Babylon.' Hezekiah answered, 'The word of the LORD which you have spoken is good'; thinking to himself that peace and security would last out his lifetime.

Good news for Zion

40 Comfort, comfort my people;[h]
—it is the voice of your God;
2   speak tenderly to Jerusalem[i]
and tell her this,
that she has fulfilled her term of bondage,
that her penalty is paid;
she has received at the LORD's hand
double[j] measure for all her sins.

3   There is a voice that cries:
Prepare a road for the LORD through the wilderness,
clear a highway across the desert for our God.
4   Every valley shall be lifted up,
every mountain and hill brought down;
rugged places shall be made smooth
and mountain-ranges become a plain.

Thus shall the glory of the LORD be 5 revealed,
and all mankind together shall see it;
for the LORD himself has spoken.

A voice says, 'Cry',   6
and another asks, 'What shall I cry?'
'That all mankind is grass,
they last no longer than a flower of the field.
The grass withers, the flower fades,   7
when the breath of[k] the LORD blows upon them;[l]
the grass withers, the flowers fade,   8
but the word of our God endures for evermore.'

You who bring Zion good news,[m] up with 9 you to the mountain-top;
lift up your voice and shout,
you who bring good news to Jerusalem,[n]
lift it up fearlessly;
cry to the cities of Judah, 'Your God is here.'

Here is the Lord GOD coming in might,   10
coming to rule with his right arm.
His recompense comes with him,
he carries his reward before him.
He will tend his flock like a shepherd   11
and gather them together with his arm;
he will carry the lambs in his bosom
and lead the ewes to water.

None can compare with the LORD

Who has gauged the waters in the palm of 12 his hand,
or with its span set limits to the heavens?
Who has held all the soil of earth in a bushel,
or weighed the mountains on a balance
and the hills on a pair of scales?

h Comfort . . . people: *or* Comfort, O my people, comfort.   *i* speak . . . Jerusalem: *or* bid Jerusalem be of good heart.   *j* double: *or* full.   *k* the breath of: *or* a wind from.   *l* Prob. rdg.; *Heb. adds* surely the people are grass.   *m* You . . . news: *or* O Zion, bringer of good news.   *n* you . . . Jerusalem: *or* O Jerusalem, bringer of good news.

13 Who has set limits to the spirit of the LORD?
What counsellor stood at his side to instruct him?
14 With whom did he confer to gain discernment?
Who taught him how to do justice
or gave him lessons in wisdom?
15 Why, to him nations are but drops from a bucket,
no more than moisture on the scales;
coasts and islands weigh as light as specks of dust.
16 All Lebanon does not yield wood enough for fuel
or beasts enough for a sacrifice.
17 All nations dwindle to nothing before him,
he reckons them mere nothings, less than nought.

18 What likeness will you find for God
or what form to resemble his?
19 Is it an image which a craftsman sets up,
and a goldsmith covers with plate
and fits with studs of silver as a costly gift?
20 Or is it mulberry-wood that will not rot
which a man chooses,
seeking out a skilful craftsman for it,
to mount an image that will not fall?

[6[o]] Each workman helps the others,
each man encourages his fellow.
[7[o]] The craftsman urges on the goldsmith,
the gilder urges the man who beats the anvil,
he declares the soldering to be sound;
he fastens the image with nails
so that it will not fall down.

Just cause for confidence in God

21 Do you not know, have you not heard,
were you not told long ago,
have you not perceived ever since the world began,
22 that God sits throned on the vaulted roof of earth,
whose inhabitants are like grasshoppers[p]?
He stretches out the skies like a curtain,
he spreads them out like a tent to live in;
23 he reduces the great to nothing
and makes all earth's princes less than nothing.
24 Scarcely are they planted, scarcely sown,
scarcely have they taken root in the earth,
before he blows upon them and they wither away,
and a whirlwind carries them off like chaff.
25 To whom then will you liken me,
whom set up as my equal?
asks the Holy One.
Lift up your eyes to the heavens; 26
consider who created it all,
led out their host one by one
and called them all by their names;
through his great might, his might and power,
not one is missing.
Why do you complain, O Jacob, 27
and you, Israel, why do you say,
'My plight is hidden from the LORD
and my cause has passed out of God's notice'?
Do you not know, have you not heard? 28
The LORD, the everlasting God, creator of the wide world,
grows neither weary nor faint;
no man can fathom his understanding.
He gives vigour to the weary, 29
new strength to the exhausted.
Young men may grow weary and faint, 30
even in their prime they may stumble and fall;
but those who look to the LORD will win new strength, 31
they will grow wings like eagles;
they will run and not be weary,
they will march on and never grow faint.

The LORD addresses the nations

Keep silence before me, all you coasts and islands; 41
let the peoples come to meet me.[q]
Let them come near, then let them speak;
we will meet at the place of judgement, I and they.
Tell me, who raised up that one from the east, 2
one greeted by victory wherever he goes?
Who is it that puts nations into his power
and makes kings go down before him,[r]
he scatters them with his sword like dust
and with his bow like chaff before the wind;
he puts them to flight and passes on unscathed, 3
swifter than any traveller on foot?
Whose work is this, I ask, who has brought it to pass? 4
Who has summoned the generations from the beginning?
It is I, the LORD, I am the first,
and to the last of them I am He.
Coasts and islands saw it and were afraid, 5
the world trembled from end to end.[s]

The LORD addresses Israel

But you, Israel my servant, 8
you, Jacob whom I have chosen,
race of Abraham my friend,

o These are verses 6 and 7 of ch. 41, transposed to this point. *p Or* locusts. *q* come to meet me: *prob. rdg., transposing, with slight change, from end of verse 5; Heb.* win new strength (*repeated from 40. 31*). *r* before him: *prob. rdg.; Heb. om.* *s See note on verse 1.* *t Verses 6 and 7 transposed to follow 40. 20.*

9 I have taken you up,
  have fetched you from the ends of the
      earth,
  and summoned you from its farthest
      corners,
  I have called you my servant,
  have chosen you and not cast you off:
10 fear nothing, for I am with you;
   be not afraid, for I am your God.
   I strengthen you, I help you,
   I support you with my victorious right
      hand.

11 Now shall all who defy you
   be disappointed and put to shame;
   all who set themselves against you
   shall be as nothing; they shall vanish.
12 You will look for your assailants but not
      find them;
   all who take up arms against you
   shall be as nothing, nothing at all.
13 For I, the LORD your God,
   take you by the right hand;
   I say to you, Do not fear;
   it is I who help you,
14 fear not, Jacob you worm and Israel poor
      louse.
   It is I who help you, says the LORD,
   your ransomer, the Holy One of Israel.
15 See, I will make of you a sharp threshing-
      sledge,
   new and studded with teeth;
   you shall thresh the mountains and crush
      them
   and reduce the hills to chaff;
16 you shall winnow them, the wind shall
      carry them away
   and a great gale shall scatter them.
   Then shall you rejoice in the LORD
   and glory in the Holy One of Israel.

Provision for the wilderness journey

17 The wretched and the poor look for water
      and find none,
   their tongues are parched with thirst;
   but I the LORD will give them an answer,
   I, the God of Israel, will not forsake them.
18 I will open rivers among the sand-dunes
   and wells in the valleys;
   I will turn the wilderness into pools
   and dry land into springs of water;
19 I will plant cedars in the wastes,
   and acacia and myrtle and wild olive;
   the pine shall grow on the barren heath
   side by side with fir and box,
20 that men may see and know,
   may once for all give heed and understand
   that the LORD himself has done this,
   that the Holy One of Israel has per-
      formed it.

A challenge to the idols of the nations

Come, open your plea, says the LORD,   21
present your case, says Jacob's King;
   let them come forward, these idols,   22
   let them foretell the future.
   Let them declare the meaning of past
      events
   that we may give our minds to it;
   let them predict things that are to be
   that we may know their outcome.
   Declare what will happen hereafter;   23
   then we shall know you are gods.
   Do what you can, good or ill,
   anything that may grip us with fear and
      awe.
   You cannot! You are sprung from no-   24
      thing,
   your works are rotten;
   whoever chooses you is vile as you are.
   I roused one from the north, and he   25
      obeyed;
   I called one from the east, summoned him
      in^u my name,
   he marches over viceroys as if they were
      mud,
   like a potter treading his clay.
Tell us, who declared this from the beginning, 26
   that we might know it,
   or told us beforehand so that we could
      say, 'He was right'?
Not one declared, not one foretold,
   not one heard a sound from you.
Here is one who will speak first as advocate 27
   for Zion,
   here I appoint defending counsel for Jeru-
      salem;
but from the other side no advocate steps 28
   forward
   and, when I look, there is no one there.
I ask a question and no one answers;
   see what empty things they are!   29
   Nothing that they do has any worth,
   their effigies are wind, mere nothings.

The LORD's chosen servant

Here is my servant, whom I uphold,   **42**
   my chosen one in whom I delight,
   I have bestowed my spirit upon him,
   and he will make justice shine on the
      nations.
He will not call out or lift his voice high, 2
   or^v make himself heard in the open street.
He will not break a bruised reed,   3
   or snuff out a smouldering wick;
   he will make justice shine on every race,^w
   never faltering, never breaking down,^x   4
   he will plant justice on earth,
   while coasts and islands wait for his
      teaching.

---

u summoned him in: *or* who will call on.   *v* He will not . . . *or*: *or* In very truth he will call out and lift
his voice high, and . . .   *w* on every race: *or* in truth.   *x* never faltering . . . down: *or* he will neither
rebuke nor wound.

5 Thus speaks the LORD who is God,
    he who created the skies and stretched
        them out,
    who fashioned the earth and all that grows
        in it, *
  who gave breath to its people,
    the breath of life to all who walk upon it:
6 I, the LORD, have called you with righteous
      purpose
    and taken you by the hand;
  I have formed you, and appointed you
    to be a light*y* to all peoples,
  a beacon for the nations,
7   to open eyes that are blind,
    to bring captives out of prison,
    out of the dungeons where they lie in
      darkness.
8 I am the LORD; the LORD*z* is my name;
  I will not give my glory to another god,
    nor my praise to any idol.
9 See how the first prophecies have come to
    pass,
    and now I declare new things;
  before they break from the bud I announce
    them to you.

A new song to the LORD

10 Sing a new song to the LORD,
    sing his praise throughout the earth,
    you that sail the sea, and all sea-creatures,
    and you that inhabit the coasts and islands.
11 Let the wilderness and its towns rejoice,
    and the villages of the tribe of Kedar.
  Let those who live in Sela shout for joy
    and cry out from the hill-tops.
12 You coasts and islands, all uplift his
      praises;
  let all ascribe glory to the LORD.
13 The LORD will go forth as a warrior,
  he will rouse the frenzy of battle like a
      hero;
  he will shout, he will raise the battle-cry
    and triumph over his foes.
14 Long have I lain still,
  I kept silence and held myself in check;
  now I will cry like a woman in labour,
    whimpering, panting and gasping.
15 I will lay waste mountains and hills
    and shrivel all their green herbs;
  I will turn rivers into desert wastes*a*
    and dry up all the pools.
16 Then will I lead blind men on their way*b*
  and guide them by paths they do not
      know;
  I will turn darkness into light before them
    and straighten their twisting roads.
  All this I will do and leave nothing undone.
17   Those who trust in an image,
  those who take idols for their gods
  turn tail in bitter shame.

Israel's persistent disobedience

Hear now, you that are deaf;   18
you blind men, look and see:
yet who is blind but my servant,   19
who so deaf as the messenger whom I
  send?
Who so blind as the one who holds my
  commission,
so deaf as the servant of the LORD?
You have seen much but remembered   20
  little,
your ears are wide open but nothing is
  heard.
It pleased the LORD, for the furtherance   21
  of his justice,
to make his law a law of surpassing
  majesty;
yet here is a people plundered and taken   22
  as prey,
all of them ensnared, trapped in holes,
lost to sight in dungeons,
carried off as spoil without hope of rescue,
as plunder with no one to say, 'Give it
  back.'
Hear this, all of you who will,   23
listen henceforward and give me a hearing:
who gave away Jacob for plunder,   24
who gave Israel away for spoil?
Was it not the LORD? They sinned against
  him,
they would not follow his ways
and refused obedience to his law;
so in his anger he poured out upon Jacob   25
his wrath and the fury of battle.
It wrapped him in flames, yet still he did
  not learn the lesson,
scorched him, yet he did not lay it to heart.

Israel ransomed

But now this is the word of the LORD,   **4.**
the word of your creator, O Jacob,
of him who fashioned you, Israel:
Have no fear; for I have paid your ransom;
I have called you by name and you are my
  own.
When you pass through deep waters, I am   2
  with you,
when you pass through rivers,
they will not sweep you away;
walk through fire and you will not be
  scorched,
through flames and they will not burn
  you.
For I am the LORD your God,   3
the Holy One of Israel, your deliverer;
for your ransom I give Egypt,
Nubia and Seba are your price.

---

y Or a covenant.   *z* the LORD: *or* He.
b Prob. rdg.; Heb. adds which they do not know.

a desert wastes: *prob. rdg.; Heb.* coasts and islands.

4 You are more precious to me than the
Assyrians,
you are honoured and I have loved you,
I would give the Edomites in exchange for
you,
and the Leummim for your life.

The LORD's absolute power to redeem

5 Have no fear; for I am with you;
I will bring your children from the east
and gather you all from the west.
6 I will say to the north, 'Give them up',
and to the south, 'Do not hold them back.
Bring my sons and daughters from afar,
bring them from the ends of the earth;
7 bring every one who is called by my name,
all whom I have created, whom I have
formed,
all whom I have made for my glory.'
8 Bring out this people,
a people who have eyes but are blind,
who have ears but are deaf.
9 All the nations are gathered together
and the peoples assembled.
Who amongst them can expound this
thing
and interpret for us all that has gone before?
Let them produce witnesses to prove their
case,
or let them listen and say, 'That is the
truth.'
10 My witnesses, says the LORD, are you, my
servants,
you whom I have chosen
to know me and put your faith in me
and understand that I am He.
Before me there was no god fashioned
nor ever shall be after me.
11 I am the LORD, I myself,
and none but I can deliver.
12 I myself have made it known in full, and
declared it,
I and no alien god amongst you,
and you are my witnesses, says the LORD.
13 I am God; from this very day I am He.
What my hand holds, none can snatch
away;
what I do, none can undo.

14 Thus says the LORD your ransomer, the
Holy One of Israel:
For your sakes I have sent to Babylon;
I will lay the Chaldaeans prostrate as they
flee,
and their cry of triumph will turn to
groaning.
15 I am the LORD, your Holy One,
your creator, Israel, and your King.

The LORD appeals to Israel

16 Thus says the LORD,
who opened a way in the sea
and a path through mighty waters,

who drew on chariot and horse to their 17
destruction,
a whole army, men of valour;
there they lay, never to rise again;
they were crushed, snuffed out like a wick:
Cease to dwell on days gone by 18
and to brood over past history.
Here and now I will do a new thing; 19
this moment it will break from the bud.
Can you not perceive it?
I will make a way even through the wilderness
and paths in the barren desert;
the wild beasts shall do me honour, 20
the wolf and the ostrich;
for I will provide water in the wilderness
and rivers in the barren desert,
where my chosen people may drink.
I have formed this people for myself 21
and they shall proclaim my praises.
Yet you did not call upon me, O Jacob; 22
much less did you weary yourself in my
service, O Israel.
You did not bring me sheep as whole- 23
offerings
or honour me with sacrifices;
I asked you for no burdensome offerings
and wearied you with no demands for
incense.
You did not buy me sweet-cane with your 24
money
or glut me with the fat of your sacrifices;
rather you burdened me with your sins
and wearied me with your iniquities.
I alone, I am He, 25
who for his own sake wipes out your transgressions,
who will remember your sins no more.
Cite me by name, let us argue it out; 26
set forth your pleading and justify yourselves.
Your first father transgressed, 27
your spokesmen rebelled against me,
and your princes profaned my sanctu- 28
ary;
so I sent Jacob to his doom
and left Israel to execration.

Hear me now, Jacob my servant, **44**
hear me, my chosen Israel.
Thus says the LORD your maker, 2
your helper, who fashioned you from
birth:
have no fear, Jacob my servant,
Jeshurun whom I have chosen,
for I will pour down rain on a thirsty 3
land,
showers on the dry ground.
I will pour out my spirit on your offspring
and my blessing on your children.
They shall spring up like a green tamarisk, 4
like poplars by a flowing stream.

5 This man shall say, 'I am the LORD's man',
that one shall call himself a son of Jacob,
another shall write the LORD's name on his
hand
and shall add the name of Israel to his own.

There is no god but the LORD

6 Thus says the LORD, Israel's King,
the LORD of Hosts, his ransomer:
I am the first and I am the last,
and there is no god but me.
7 Who is like me? Let him stand up,
let him declare himself and speak and
show me his evidence,
let him announce beforehand*c* things to
come,
let him*d* declare what is yet to happen.
8 Take heart, do not be afraid.
Did I not foretell this long ago?
I declared it, and you are my witnesses.
Is there any god beside me,
or any creator, even one that I do not
know?
9 Those who make idols are less than nothing;
all their cherished images profit nobody;
their worshippers are blind,
sheer ignorance makes fools of them.
10 If a man makes a god or casts an image,
his labour is wasted.
11 Why! its votaries show their folly;
the craftsmen too are but men.
Let them all gather together and confront
me,
all will be afraid and look the fools they
are.

The foolishness of idolatry

12 The blacksmith sharpens a graving tool and
hammers out his work*e* hot from the coals
and shapes it with his strong arm; when he
grows hungry his strength fails, if he has no
13 water to drink he tires. The woodworker
draws his line taut and marks out a figure
with a scriber; he planes the wood and
measures it with callipers, and he carves it
to the shape of a man, comely as the human
form, to be set up presently in a house.*f*
14 A man plants a cedar and the rain makes
it grow, so that later on he will have cedars
to cut down; or he chooses an ilex or an oak
to raise a stout tree for himself in the forest.
15 It becomes fuel for his fire: some of it he
takes and warms himself, some he kindles
and bakes bread on it, and some he makes
into a god and prostrates himself, shaping
it into an idol and bowing down before it.
16 The one half of it he burns in the fire and on
this he roasts meat, so that he may eat his
roast and be satisfied; he also warms himself at it and he says, 'Good! I can feel the

heat, I am growing warm.' Then what is 17
left of the wood he makes into a god by carving it into shape; he bows down to it and
prostrates himself and prays to it, saying,
'Save me; for thou art my god.' Such people 18
neither know nor understand, their eyes
made too blind to see, their minds too narrow to discern. Such a man will not use his 19
reason, he has neither the wit nor the sense
to say, 'Half of it I have burnt, yes, and used
its embers to bake bread; I have roasted
meat on them too and eaten it; but the rest
of it I turn into this abominable thing and
so I am worshipping a log of wood.' He feeds 20
on ashes indeed! His own deluded mind has
misled him, he cannot recollect himself so
far as to say, 'Why! this thing in my hand is
a sham.'

A reminder to Israel

Remember all this, Jacob, 21
remember, Israel, for you are my servant,
I have fashioned you, and you are to serve
me;
you shall not forget me, Israel.
I have swept away your sins like a dis- 22
solving mist,
and your transgressions are dispersed like
clouds;
turn back to me; for I have ransomed you.
Shout in triumph, you heavens, for it is the 23
LORD's doing;
cry out for joy, you lowest depths of the
earth;
break into songs of triumph, you mountains,
you forest and all your trees;
for the LORD has ransomed Jacob
and made Israel his masterpiece.

The LORD's purpose for Jerusalem

Thus says the LORD, your ransomer, 24
who fashioned you from birth:
I am the LORD who made all things,
by myself I stretched out the skies,
alone I hammered out the floor of the
earth.
I frustrate false prophets and their signs 25
and make fools of diviners;
I reverse what wise men say
and make nonsense of their wisdom.
I make my servants' prophecies come true 26
and give effect to my messengers' designs.
I say of Jerusalem,
'She shall be inhabited once more',
and of the cities of Judah, 'They shall be
rebuilt;
all their ruins I will restore.'
I say to the deep waters, 'Be dried up; 27
I will make your streams run dry.'

*c let him announce beforehand: prob. rdg.; Heb. since my appointing an ancient people and . . . d Prob.
rdg.; Heb. them. e his work: prob. rdg.; Heb. he works. f Or a shrine.*

28   I say to Cyrus, 'You shall be my shepherd
          to carry out all my purpose,
      so that Jerusalem may be rebuilt
      and the foundations of the temple may be
          laid.'

Cyrus used by the LORD

45 Thus says the LORD to Cyrus his anointed,
          Cyrus whom he has taken by the hand
      to subdue nations before him
      and undo the might of kings;
          before whom gates shall be opened
          and no doors be shut:
2   I will go before you
          and level the swelling hills;
      I will break down gates of bronze
      and hack through iron bars.
3   I will give you treasures from dark vaults,
          hoarded in secret places,
          that you may know that I am the LORD,
          Israel's God who calls you by name.
4 For the sake of Jacob my servant and Israel
          my chosen
      I have called you by name
  and given you your title, though you have
          not known me.
5   I am the LORD, there is no other;
          there is no god beside me.
      I will strengthen you though you have not
          known me,
6   so that men from the rising and the setting
          sun
      may know that there is none but I:
      I am the LORD, there is no other;
7   I make the light, I create darkness,
          author alike of prosperity and trouble.
   I, the LORD, do all these things.

8   Rain righteousness, you heavens,
      let the skies above pour down;
      let the earth open to receive it,
          that it may bear the fruit of salvation
          with righteousness in blossom at its side.
      All this I, the LORD, have created.

The LORD answers Israel's objection

9   Will the pot contend[g] with the potter,
          or the earthenware[h] with the hand that
          shapes it?
   Will the clay ask the potter what he is
          making?
      or his[i] handiwork say to him, 'You have
          no skill'?

Will the babe say[j] to his father, 'What are 10
      you begetting?',
   or to his mother, 'What are you bringing
      to birth?'
Thus says the LORD, Israel's Holy One, his 11
      maker:
   Would you dare question me concerning
      my children,
   or instruct me in my handiwork?
   I alone, I made the earth 12
   and created man upon it;
I, with my own hands, stretched out the
      heavens
   and caused all their host to shine.
   I alone have roused this man in righteous- 13
      ness,
   and I will smooth his path before him;
   he shall rebuild my city
   and let my exiles go free—
      not for a price nor for a bribe,
   says the LORD of Hosts.

The nations will acknowledge the LORD

Thus says the LORD: 14
   Toilers of Egypt and Nubian merchants
   and Sabaeans bearing tribute[k]
shall come into your power and be your
      slaves,
shall come and march behind you in chains;
   they shall bow down before you in supplica-
      tion, saying,
'Surely God is among you and there is no
      other,
   no other god.
How then canst thou be a god that hidest 15
      thyself,
   O God of Israel, the deliverer?'

Those who defy him are confounded and 16
      brought to shame,
   those who make idols perish in confusion.
But Israel has been delivered by the LORD, 17
      delivered for all time to come;
   they shall not be confounded or put to shame
      for all eternity.

The only God

Thus says the LORD, the creator of the 18
      heavens,
   he who is God,
   who made the earth and fashioned it
   and himself fixed it fast,
   who created it no empty void,
   but made it for a place to dwell in:
   I am the LORD, there is no other.
I do not speak in secret, in realms of darkness, 19
   I do not say to the sons of Jacob,
   'Look for me in the empty void.'
I the LORD speak what is right, declare what
      is just.

g Will . . . contend: *prob. rdg.*; Heb. Ho! he has contended.   *h Or* shard.   *i Prob. rdg.*; Heb. your.
j Will . . . say: *prob. rdg.*; Heb. Ho! you that say.   k bearing tribute: *or* men of stature.

20 Gather together, come, draw near,
   all you survivors of the nations,
   you fools, who carry your wooden idols in
      procession
   and pray to a god that cannot save you.
21 Come forward and urge your case, consult
      together:
   who foretold this in days of old,
   who stated it long ago?
   Was it not I the LORD?
   There is no god but me;
   there is no god other than I, victorious and
      able to save.
22 Look to me and be saved,
   you peoples from all corners of the earth;
   for I am God, there is no other.
23 By my life I have sworn,
   I have given a promise of victory,
   a promise that will not be broken,
   that to me every knee shall bend
   and by me every tongue shall swear.
24 In the LORD alone, men shall say,
   are victory and might;
   and all who defy him
   shall stand ashamed in his presence,
25 but all the sons of Israel shall stand
      victorious
   and find their glory in the LORD.

The impotence of idols

46 Bel has crouched down, Nebo has stooped
      low:
   their images, once carried in your proces-
      sions,
   have been loaded on to beasts and cattle,
   a burden for the weary creatures;
2 they stoop and they crouch;
   not for them to bring the burden to safety;
   the gods themselves go into captivity.
3 Listen to me, house of Jacob
   and all the remnant of the house of Israel,
   a load on me from your birth, carried by me
      from the womb:
4 till you grow old I am He,
   and when white hairs come, I will carry
      you still;
   I have made you and I will bear the burden,
   I will carry you and bring you to safety.
5 To whom will you liken me? Who is my
      equal?
   With whom can you compare me? Where
      is my like?
6 Those who squander their bags of gold
   and weigh out their silver with a balance
   hire a goldsmith to fashion them into a god;
   then they worship it and fall prostrate
      before it;
7 they hoist it shoulder-high and carry it home;
   they set it down on its base;
   there it must stand, it cannot stir from its
      place.

Let a man cry to it as he will, it never
   answers him;
it cannot deliver him from his troubles.

God will carry out his plan

Remember this, you rebels,   8
consider it well, and abandon hope,
remember all that happened long ago;   9
for I am God, there is no other,
I am God, and there is no one like me;
I reveal the end from the beginning,   10
from ancient times I reveal what is to
   be;
I say, 'My purpose shall take effect,
I will accomplish all that I please.'
I summon a bird of prey[l] from the east,   11
one from a distant land to fulfil my pur-
   pose.
Mark this; I have spoken, and I will bring
   it about,
I have a plan to carry out, and carry it out
   I will.
Listen to me, all you stubborn hearts,   12
for whom victory is far off:
I bring my victory near, it is not far off,   13
and my deliverance shall not be delayed;
I will grant deliverance in Zion
and give my glory to Israel.[m]

BABYLON

Disaster befalling Babylon

Down with you, sit in the dust,   **47**
virgin daughter of Babylon.
Down from your throne, sit on the ground,
daughter of the Chaldaeans;
never again shall men call you
soft-skinned and delicate.
Take up the millstone, grind meal, uncover 2
   your tresses;
strip off your skirt, bare your thighs, wade
   through rivers,
so that your nakedness may be plain to see 3
and your shame exposed.
I will take vengeance, I will treat with none
   of you,
says the Holy One of Israel, our ransomer, 4
whose name is the LORD of Hosts.

Sit silent,   5
be off into the shadows, daughter of the
   Chaldaeans;
for never again shall men call you
queen of many kingdoms.

---

l a bird of prey: *or* a massed host.   *m* and give my glory to Israel: *or* for Israel my glory.

6 When I was angry with my people,
  I dishonoured my own possession
  and gave them into your power.
  You showed them no mercy,
  you made your yoke weigh heavy on the
    aged.
7 You said then, 'I shall reign a queen for
    ever',
  while[n] you gave no thought to this
  and did not consider how it would end.
8 Now therefore listen to this,
  you lover of luxury, carefree on your throne.
  You say to yourself,
  'I am, and who but I?
  No widow's weeds for me, no deaths of
    children.'
9 Yet suddenly, in a single day,
  these two things shall come upon you;
  they shall both come upon you in full
    measure:[o]
  children's deaths and widowhood,
  for all your monstrous sorceries, your
    countless spells.
10 Secure in your wicked ways you thought,
   'No one is looking.'
   Your wisdom betrayed you, omniscient as
     you were,
   and you said to yourself,
   'I am, and who but I?'
11 Therefore evil shall come upon you,
   and you will not know how to master it;
   disaster shall befall you,
   and you will not be able to charm it away;
   ruin all unforeseen
   shall come suddenly upon you.
12 Persist in your spells and your monstrous
     sorceries,[p]
   maybe you can get help from them,
   maybe you will yet inspire awe.
13 But no! in spite of your many wiles you
     are powerless.
   Let your astrologers, your star-gazers
   who foretell your future month by month,
   persist, and save you!
14 But look, they are gone like chaff;
   fire burns them up;
   they cannot snatch themselves from the
     flames;
   this is no glowing coal to warm them,
   no fire for them to sit by.
15 So much for your magicians
   with whom you have trafficked all your
     life:
   they have stumbled off, each his own way,
   and there is no one to save you.

God reveals the future

48 Hear this, you house of Jacob,
   you who are called by the name of Israel,
   you who spring from the seed of Judah;

JUDAH

who swear by the name of the LORD
and boast in the God of Israel,
but not in honesty or sincerity,
although you call yourselves citizens of a 2
  holy city
and lean for support on the God of Israel;
his name is the LORD of Hosts.
Long ago I announced what would first 3
  happen,
I revealed it with my own mouth;
suddenly I acted and it came about.
I knew that you were stubborn, 4
your neck stiff as iron, your brow like
  bronze,
therefore I told you of these things long 5
  ago,
and declared them before they came about,
so that you could not say, 'This was my
  idol's doing;
my image, the god that I fashioned, he
  ordained them.'
You have heard what I said; consider it 6
  well,
and you must admit the truth of it.
Now I show you new things,
hidden things which you did not know
  before.
They were not created long ago, but in this 7
  very hour;
you had never heard of them before today.
You cannot say, 'I know them already.'
You neither heard nor knew, 8
long ago your ears were closed;
for I knew that you were untrustworthy,
  treacherous,
a notorious rebel from your birth.
For the sake of my own name I was 9
  patient,[q]
rather than destroy you I held myself in
  check.
See how I tested you, not as silver is tested, 10
but in the furnace of affliction; there I
  purified you.
For my honour, for my own honour I 11
  did it;
let them disparage my past triumphs[r] if
  they will:
I will not give my glory to any other god.

Hear me, Jacob, 12
and Israel whom I called:
I am He; I am the first,
I am the last also.

---

n for ever', while: *or* of a wide realm, for all time'; but.
rdg.; Heb. adds with which you have trafficked all your life (*cp. verse* 15).
r my past triumphs: *transposed from verse* 9.

o in full measure: *or* at random.   *p* Prob.
q See note on verse 11.

13 With my own hands I founded the earth,
    with my right hand I formed the expanse of
       sky;
    when I summoned them,
       they sprang at once into being.
14 Assemble, all of you, and listen to me;
    which of you has declared what is com-
       ing,
    that he whom I love shall wreak my*s* will on
       Babylon
    and the Chaldaeans shall be scattered?
15 I, I myself, have spoken, I have called him,
    I have made him appear, and wherever he
       goes he shall prosper.
16 Draw near to me and hear this:
       from the beginning I have never spoken in
          secret;
       from the moment of its first happening
          I was there.*t*

'Come out of Babylon'

17 Thus says the LORD your ransomer, the
       Holy One of Israel:
    I am the LORD your God:
    I teach you for your own advantage
    and lead you in the way you must go.
18 If only you had listened to my commands,
    your prosperity would have rolled on like a
       river in flood
    and your just success like the waves of the
       sea;
19 in number your children would have been
       like the sand
    and your descendants countless as its
       grains;
    their name would never be erased or blotted
       from my sight.
20 Come out of Babylon, hasten away from the
       Chaldaeans;
    proclaim it with loud songs of triumph,
       crying the news to the ends of the earth;
    tell them, 'The LORD has ransomed his ser-
       vant Jacob.'
21 Though he led them through desert places
       they suffered no thirst,
    for them he made water run from the rock,
    for them he cleft the rock and streams gushed
       forth.

22   There is no peace for the wicked,
          says the LORD.

The mission of the LORD's servant

49   Listen to me, you coasts and islands,
       pay heed, you peoples far away:
       from birth the LORD called me,
       he named me from my mother's womb.

He made my tongue his sharp sword   2
   and concealed me under cover of his hand;
   he made me a polished arrow
   and hid me out of sight in his quiver.
He said to me, 'You are my servant,   3
   Israel through whom I shall win glory';
   so I rose to honour in the LORD's sight
   and my God became my strength.'*u*
Once I said, 'I have laboured in vain;   4
I have spent my strength for nothing, to no
   purpose';
   yet in truth my cause is with the LORD
   and my reward is in God's hands.
And now the LORD who formed me in the   5
   womb to be his servant,
   to bring Jacob back to him
   that Israel should be gathered to him,*v*
   now the LORD calls me again:*w*
   it is too slight a task for you, as my ser-   6
      vant,
   to restore the tribes of Jacob,
   to bring back the descendants of Israel:
   I will make you a light to the nations,
   to be my salvation*x* to earth's farthest
      bounds.

Thus says the Holy One, the LORD who   7
   ransoms Israel,
   to one who thinks little of himself,
   whom every nation abhors,
   the slave of tyrants:
   When they see you kings shall rise,
   princes shall rise and bow down,
   because of the LORD who is faithful,
   because of the Holy One of Israel who has
      chosen you.

The LORD's care for the returning exiles

Thus says the LORD: 8
In the hour of my favour I answered you,
and I helped you on the day of deliverance,*y*
putting the land to rights
and sharing out afresh its desolate fields;
I said to the prisoners, 'Go free',   9
and to those in darkness, 'Come out and
   be seen.'
They shall find pasture in the desert sands*z*
and grazing on all the dunes.
They shall neither hunger nor thirst,   10
no scorching heat or sun shall distress
   them;
for one who loves them shall lead them
and take them to water at bubbling
   springs.
I will make every hill a path   11
and build embankments for my highways.

---

*s Or his.   t Prob. rdg.; Heb. adds and now the Lord GOD has sent me, and his spirit.   u so I rose
. . . strength: transposed from end of verse 5.   v be gathered to him: or not be swept away.   w See
note on verse 3.   x to be my salvation: or that my salvation may reach.   y Prob. rdg.; Heb. adds
I have formed you, and appointed you to be a light to all peoples (cp. 42. 6).   z desert sands: prob.
rdg.; Heb. ways.*

12 See, they come; some from far away,
these from the north and these from the west
and those from the land of Syene.

13 Shout for joy, you heavens, rejoice, O earth,
you mountains, break into songs of triumph,
for the LORD has comforted his people
and has had pity on his own in their distress.

Zion's vast population

14 But Zion says,
'The LORD has forsaken me; my God has forgotten me.'

15 Can a woman forget the infant at her breast,
or a loving mother the child of her womb?
Even these forget, yet I will not forget you.

16 Your walls are always before my eyes,
I have engraved them on the palms of my hands.

17 Those who are to rebuild you make better speed
than those who pulled you down,
while those who laid you waste depart.

18 Raise your eyes and look around you:
see how they assemble, how they are flocking back to you.
By my life I, the LORD, swear it,
you shall wear them proudly as your jewels,
and adorn yourself with them like a bride;

19 I did indeed make you waste and desolate,
I razed you to the ground,
but your boundaries*a* shall now be too narrow
for your inhabitants—
and those who laid you in ruins are far away.

20 The children born in your bereavement shall yet say in your hearing,
'This place is too narrow; make room for me to live in.'

21 Then you will say to yourself,
'All these children, how did I come by them,
bereaved and barren as I was?
Who reared them
when I was left alone, left by myself;
where did I get them all?'

22 The Lord GOD says,
Now is the time: I will beckon to the nations
and hoist a signal to the peoples,
and they shall bring your sons in their arms
and carry your daughters on their shoulders;

23 kings shall be your foster-fathers
and their princesses shall be your nurses.
They shall bow to the earth before you
and lick the dust from your feet;
and you shall know that I am the LORD
and that none who look to me will be disappointed.

24 Can his prey be taken from the strong man,
or the captive be rescued from the ruthless?
And the LORD answers,

25 The captive shall be taken even from the strong,
and the prey of the ruthless shall be rescued;
I will contend with all who contend against you
and save your children from them.

26 I will force your oppressors to feed on their own flesh
and make them drunk with their own blood as if with fresh wine,
and all mankind shall know
that it is I, the LORD, who save you,
I your ransomer, the Mighty One of Jacob.

Israel's unresponsiveness

50

The LORD says,
Is there anywhere a deed of divorce
by which I have put your mother away?
Was there some creditor of mine
to whom I sold you?
No; it was through your own wickedness
that you were sold
and for your own misconduct that your mother was put away.

2 Why, then, did I find no one when I came?
Why, when I called, did no one answer?
Did you think my arm too short to redeem,
did you think I had no power to save?
Not so. By my rebuke I dried up the sea
and turned rivers into desert;
their fish perished for lack of water
and died on the thirsty ground;

3 I clothed the skies in mourning
and covered them with sackcloth.

The LORD's obedient servant

4 The Lord GOD has given me
the tongue of a teacher
and skill to console the weary
with a word in the morning;
he sharpened my hearing
that I might listen like one who is taught.

5 The Lord GOD opened my ears
and I did not disobey or turn back in defiance.

6 I offered my back to the lash,
and let my beard be plucked from my chin,
I did not hide my face from spitting and insult;

---

a I did . . . boundaries: *or* your wasted and desolate land, your ruined countryside.

7 but the Lord GOD stands by to help me;
  therefore no insult can wound me.
I have set my face like flint,
  for I know that I shall not be put to shame,
8 because one who will clear my name is at
  my side.
Who dare argue against me? Let us confront
  one another.
Who will dispute my cause? Let him come
  forward.
9 The Lord GOD will help me;
  who then can prove me guilty?
They will all wear out like a garment,
  the moths will eat them up.

Torment for the godless

10 Which of you fears the LORD and obeys his
  servant's commands?
The man who walks in dark places with no
  light,
yet trusts in the name of the LORD and leans
  on his God.
11 But you who kindle a fire and set fire-
  brands alight,
  go, walk into your own fire
  and among the fire-brands you have set
  ablaze.
  This is your fate at my hands:
  you shall lie down in torment.

A lesson from history

51 Listen to me, all who follow the right and
  seek the LORD:
  look to the rock from which you were
  hewn,
  to the quarry from which you were dug;
2 look to your father Abraham
  and to Sarah who gave you birth:
when I called him he was but one,
  I blessed him and made him many.
3 The LORD has indeed comforted Zion,
  comforted all her ruined homes,
  turning her wilderness into an Eden,
  her thirsty plains into a garden of the
  LORD.
Joy and gladness shall be found in her,
  thanksgiving and melody.
4 Pay heed to me, my people,
  and hear me, O my nation;
  for my law shall shine forth
  and I will flash the light of my judgement
  over the nations.
5 My victory is near, my deliverance has gone[b]
  forth
  and my arm shall rule the nations;
  for me coasts and islands shall wait
  and they shall look to me for protection.
6 Lift your eyes to the heavens,
  look at the earth beneath:

the heavens grow murky as smoke;
the earth wears into tatters like a garment,
and those who live on it die like maggots;
but my deliverance is everlasting
and my saving power shall never wane.

7 Listen to me, my people who know what
  is right,
you who lay my law to heart:
do not fear the taunts of men,
let no reproaches dismay you;
8 for the grub will devour them like a garment
and the moth as if they were wool,
but my saving power shall last for ever
and my deliverance to all generations.

Encouragement for the exiles

9 Awake, awake, put on your strength, O arm
  of the LORD,
  awake as you did long ago, in days gone
  by.
Was it not you
who hacked the Rahab in pieces and ran the
  dragon through?
10 Was it not you
who dried up the sea, the waters of the great
  abyss,
and made the ocean depths a path for the
  ransomed?
11 So the LORD's people shall come back, set
  free,
  and enter Zion with shouts of triumph,
  crowned with everlasting joy;
  joy and gladness shall overtake them as
  they come,
  and sorrow and sighing shall flee away.
12 I, I myself, am he that comforts you.
Why then fear man, man who must die,
man frail as grass?
13 Why have you forgotten the LORD your
  maker,
who stretched out the skies and founded
  the earth?
Why are you continually afraid, all the
  day long,
why dread the fury of oppressors ready to
  destroy you?
Where is that fury?
14 He that cowers under it shall soon stand upright and not die,
  he shall soon reap the early crop and not
  lack bread.

15 I am the LORD your God, the LORD of
Hosts is my name. I cleft the sea and its
16 waves roared, that I might fix the heavens in
place and form the earth and say to Zion,
'You are my people.' I have put my words in
your mouth and kept you safe under the
shelter of my hand.

b Or shone.

'Awake; rise up, Jerusalem'

17 Awake, awake; rise up, Jerusalem.
You have drunk from the LORD's hand
the cup of his wrath,
drained to its dregs the bowl of drunkenness;
18 of all the sons you have borne there is not
one to guide you,
of all you have reared, not one to take you
by the hand.
19 These two disasters have overtaken you;
who can console you?—
havoc and ruin, famine and the sword;
who can comfort you?
20 Your sons are in stupor, they lie at the
head of every street,
like antelopes caught in the net,
glutted with the wrath of the LORD,
the rebuke of your God.
21 Therefore listen to this, in your affliction,
drunk that you are, but not with wine:
22 thus says the LORD, your Lord and your
God,
who will plead his people's cause:
Look, I take from your hand
the cup of drunkenness;
you shall never again drink from the bowl
of my wrath,
23 I will give it instead to your tormentors
and oppressors,
those who said to you, 'Lie down and we
will walk over you';
and you made your backs like the ground
beneath them,
like a roadway for passers-by.

52 Awake, awake, put on your strength, O Zion,
put on your loveliest garments, holy city of
Jerusalem;
for never shall the uncircumcised and the
unclean enter you again.
2 Rise up, captive Jerusalem, shake off the
dust;
loose your neck from the collar that binds
it,
O captive daughter of Zion.

Good news for Zion

3 The LORD says, You were sold but no price
was paid, and without payment you shall be
4 ransomed. The Lord GOD says, At the beginning my people went down into Egypt to
live there, and at the end it was the Assyrians
5 who oppressed them; but now what do I find
here? says the LORD. My people carried off
and no price paid, their rulers derided, and
my name reviled all day long, says the LORD.
6 But on that day my people shall know my
name; they shall know that it is I who speak;
here I am.

How lovely on the mountains are the feet of 7
the herald
who comes to proclaim prosperity and bring
good news,
the news of deliverance,
calling to Zion, 'Your God is king.'
Hark, your watchmen raise their voices 8
and shout together in triumph;
for with their own eyes they shall see
the LORD returning in pity to Zion.
Break forth together in shouts of triumph, 9
you ruins of Jerusalem;
for the LORD has taken pity on his people
and has ransomed Jerusalem.
The LORD has bared his holy arm 10
in the sight of all nations,
and the whole world from end to end
shall see the deliverance of our God.
Away from Babylon; come out, come out, 11
touch nothing unclean.
Come out from Babylon, keep yourselves
pure,
you who carry the vessels of the LORD.
But you shall not come out in urgent haste 12
nor leave like fugitives;
for the LORD will march at your head,
your rearguard will be Israel's God.

The LORD's suffering servant

Behold, my servant shall prosper, 13
he shall be lifted up, exalted to the heights.

Time was when many[c] were aghast at you, 14
my people;[d]
so now many nations[e] recoil at sight of him, 15
and kings curl their lips in disgust.
For they see what they had never been told
and things unheard before fill their
thoughts.

Who could have believed what we have 53
heard,
and to whom has the power of the LORD been
revealed?

He grew up before the LORD like a young 2
plant
whose roots are in parched ground;
he had no beauty, no majesty to draw our
eyes,
no grace to make us delight in him;
his form, disfigured, lost all the likeness of a
man,
his beauty changed beyond human semblance.[f]
He was despised, he shrank from the sight 3
of men,
tormented and humbled by suffering;
we despised him, we held him of no
account,
a thing from which men turn away their
eyes.

c Or the great.   d See note on 53. 2.   e Or great nations.   f his form . . . semblance: *trans-*
posed from end of 52. 14.

4 Yet on himself he bore our sufferings,
　　our torments he endured,
　　while we counted him smitten by God,
　　struck down by disease and misery;
5 but he was pierced for our transgressions,
　　tortured for our iniquities;
　　the chastisement he bore is health for us
　　and by his scourging we are healed.

6 We had all strayed like sheep,
　　each of us had gone his own way;
　　but the LORD laid upon him
　　the guilt of us all.
7 He was afflicted, he submitted to be
　　struck down
　　and did not open his mouth;
　　he was led like a sheep to the slaughter,
　　like a ewe that is dumb before the shear-
　　ers.*g*
8 Without protection, without justice,*h* he was
　　taken away;
　　and who gave a thought to his fate,
　　how he was cut off from the world of living
　　men,
　　stricken to the death for my people's trans-
　　gression?
9 He was assigned a grave with the wicked,
　　a burial-place among the refuse of man-
　　kind,
　　though he had done no violence
　　and spoken no word of treachery.
10 Yet the LORD took thought for his tor-
　　tured servant
　　and healed him who had made himself*i* a
　　sacrifice for sin;
　　so shall he enjoy long life and see his chil-
　　dren's children,
　　and in his hand the LORD's cause shall
　　prosper.

After all his pains he shall be bathed in 11
　　light,
　　after his disgrace he shall be fully vindi-
　　cated;
　　so shall he, my servant, vindicate many,
　　himself bearing the penalty of their guilt.
Therefore I will allot him a portion with the 12
　　great,
　　and he shall share the spoil with the
　　mighty,
　　because he exposed himself to face death*j*
　　and was reckoned among transgressors,
　　because he bore the sin of many
　　and interceded for their transgressions.

The LORD's affection for Israel

Sing aloud, O barren woman who never 5
　　bore a child,
　　break into cries of joy, you who have never
　　been in labour;
　　for the deserted wife has more sons than
　　she who lives in wedlock,
　　says the LORD.
Enlarge the limits of your home,　　　　　2
　　spread wide the curtains of your tent;
　　let out its ropes to the full
　　and drive the pegs home;
　　for you shall break out of your confines 3
　　right and left,
　　your descendants shall dispossess wide
　　regions,*k*
　　and re-people cities now desolate.
Fear not; you shall not be put to shame, 4
　　you shall suffer no insult, have no cause
　　to blush.
It is time to forget the shame of your
　　younger days
　　and remember no more the reproach of
　　your widowhood;
for your husband is your maker, whose name 5
　　is the LORD of Hosts;
　　your ransomer is the Holy One of Israel
　　who is called God of all the earth.
The LORD has acknowledged you a wife 6
　　again,
　　once deserted and heart-broken,
　　your God has called you a bride still
　　young
　　though once rejected.
On the impulse of a moment I forsook 7
　　you,
　　but with tender affection I will bring you
　　home again.
In sudden anger　　　　　　　　　　　　8
　　I hid my face from you for a moment;
　　but now have I pitied you with a love which
　　never fails,
　　says the LORD who ransoms you.

g Prob. rdg.; Heb. adds and he would not open his mouth.　　*h Without protection, without justice: or*
After arrest and sentence.　　　　*i healed . . . himself: prob. rdg.; Heb.* he made sick, if you make.　　　　*j Or*
because he poured out his life to the death.　　*k wide regions: or* the nations.

9 These days recall for me the days of Noah:
  as I swore that the waters of Noah's flood
  should never again pour over the earth,
  so now I swear to you
  never again to be angry with you or reproach
  you.
10 Though the mountains move and the hills
  shake,
  my love shall be immovable and never
  fail,
  and my covenant of peace shall not be
  shaken.
  So says the LORD who takes pity on you.

The LORD will rebuild Zion

11 O storm-battered city, distressed and dis-
  consolate,
  now I will set your stones in the finest
  mortar
  and your foundations in lapis lazuli;
12 I will make your battlements of red jasper[l]
  and your gates of garnet;[m]
  all your boundary-stones shall be jewels.
13 Your masons shall all be instructed by the
  LORD,
  and your sons shall enjoy great prosperity;
14 and in triumph[n] shall you be restored.
  You shall be free from oppression and have
  no fears,
  free from terror, and it shall not come near
  you;
15 should any attack you, it will not be my
  doing,
  the aggressor, whoever he be, shall perish for
  his attempt.
16 It was I who created the smith
  to fan the coals in the furnace
  and forge weapons each for its purpose,
  and I who created the destroyer to lay
  waste;
17 but now no weapon made to harm you shall
  prevail,
  and you shall rebut every charge brought
  against you.
  Such is the fortune of the servants of the
  LORD;
  their vindication comes from me.
  This is the very word of the LORD.

The LORD's invitation

5 Come, all who are thirsty, come, fetch water;
  come, you who have no food, buy corn and
  eat;
  come and buy, not for money, not for a
  price.[o]
2 Why spend money and get what is not bread,
  why give the price of your labour and go
  unsatisfied?
  Only listen to me and you will have good food
  to eat,
  and you will enjoy the fat of the land.

Come to me and listen to my words,   3
  hear me, and you shall have life:
  I will make a covenant with you, this time
  for ever,
  to love you faithfully as I loved David.
I made him a witness to all races,   4
  a prince and instructor of peoples;
and you in turn shall summon nations you   5
  do not know,
and nations that do not know you shall come
  running to you,
  because the LORD your God,
  the Holy One of Israel, has glorified you.

Inquire of the LORD while he is present,   6
  call upon him when he is close at hand.
Let the wicked abandon their ways   7
  and evil men their thoughts;
let them return to the LORD, who will have
  pity on them,
  return to our God, for he will freely forgive.
For my thoughts are not your thoughts,   8
  and your ways are not my ways.
  This is the very word of the LORD.
For as the heavens are higher than the   9
  earth,
so are my ways higher than your ways
  and my thoughts than your thoughts;
and as the rain and the snow come down   10
  from heaven
and do not return until they have watered
  the earth,
  making it blossom and bear fruit,
and give seed for sowing and bread to eat,
so shall the word which comes from my   11
  mouth prevail;
  it shall not return to me fruitless
without accomplishing my purpose
  or succeeding in the task I gave it.
You shall indeed go out with joy   12
  and be led forth in peace.
Before you mountains and hills shall break
  into cries of joy,
and all the trees of the wild shall clap their
  hands,
  pine-trees shall shoot up in place of camel- 13
  thorn,
  myrtles instead of briars;
  all this shall win the LORD a great name,
  imperishable, a sign for all time.

'A house of prayer for all nations'

These are the words of the LORD: **56**
Maintain justice, do the right;
for my deliverance is close at hand,
  and my righteousness will show itself
  victorious.
Happy is the man who follows these pre-   2
  cepts,
  happy the mortal who holds them fast,
  who keeps the sabbath undefiled,
  who refrains from all wrong-doing!

---

l Or carbuncle.   *m Or* firestone.   *n Or* in righteousness.   *o Prob. rdg.; Heb. adds* wine and milk.

3 The foreigner who has given his allegiance
to the LORD must not say,
'The LORD will keep me separate from his
people for ever';
and the eunuch must not say,
'I am nothing but a barren tree.'
4 For these are the words of the LORD:
The eunuchs who keep my sabbaths,
who choose to do my will and hold fast to
my covenant,
5 shall receive from me something better than
sons and daughters,
a memorial and a name in my own house and
within my walls;
I will give them an everlasting name,
a name imperishable for all time.
6 So too with the foreigners who give their
allegiance to me, the LORD,
to minister to me and love my name
and to become my servants,
all who keep the sabbath undefiled
and hold fast to my covenant:
7 them will I bring to my holy hill
and give them joy in my house of prayer.
Their offerings and sacrifices shall be acceptable on my altar;
for my house shall be called
a house of prayer for all nations.
8 This is the very word of the Lord GOD,
who brings home the outcasts of Israel:
I will yet bring home all that remain to be
brought in.

Failure of Israel's leaders

9 Come, beasts of the plain, beasts of the forest,
come, eat your fill,
10 for Israel's watchmen are blind, all of them
unaware.
They are all dumb dogs who cannot bark,
stretched on the ground, dreaming, lovers
of sleep,
11 greedy dogs that can never have enough.
They are shepherds who understand nothing,
absent each of them on his own pursuits,
each intent on his own gain wherever he
can find it.
12 'Come,' says each of them, 'let me fetch
wine,
strong drink, and we will drain it down;
let us make tomorrow like today,
or greater far!'
57 The righteous perish,
and no one takes it to heart;
men of good faith are swept away, but no
one cares,
the righteous are swept away before the onset
of evil,
2 but they enter into peace;
they have run a straight course
and rest in their last beds.

Immoral religious practices

Come, stand forth, you sons of a sooth- 3
sayer.
You spawn of an adulterer and a harlot,
who is the target of your jests? 4
Against whom do you open your mouths
and wag your tongues,
children of sin that you are, spawn of a
lie,
burning with lust under the terebinths, 5
under every spreading tree,
and sacrificing children in the gorges,
under the rocky clefts?
And you, woman, 6
your place is with the creatures of the
gorge;
that is where you belong.
To them you have dared to pour a libation
and present an offering of grain.[p]
On a high mountain-top 7
you have made your bed;
there too you have gone up to offer sacrifice.
In spite of all this am I to relent?[q]
Beside door and door-post you have put up 8
your sign.
Deserting me, you have stripped and lain
down
on the wide bed which you have made,
and you drove bargains with men
for the pleasure of sleeping together,
and you have committed countless acts of
fornication
in the heat of your lust.
You drenched your tresses in oil 9
blended with many perfumes;
you sent out your procurers far and
wide
even down to the gates of Sheol.
Worn out by your unending excesses, 10
even so you never said, 'I am past hope.'
You earned a livelihood
and so you had no anxiety.
Whom do you fear so much, that you should 11
be false,
that you never remembered me or gave me a
thought?
Did I not hold my peace and seem not to
see
while you showed no fear of me?
Now I will denounce your conduct 12
that you think so righteous.
These idols of yours shall not help when you 13
cry;
no idol shall save you.
The wind shall carry them off, one and
all,
a puff of air shall blow them away;
but he who makes me his refuge shall possess
the earth
and inherit my holy hill.

p See note on verse 7. *q Line transposed from end of verse 6.*

The LORD's care for wilful Israel

14 Then a voice shall be heard:
Build up a highway, build it and clear the track,
  sweep away all that blocks my people's path.

15 Thus speaks the high and exalted one,
  whose name is holy, who lives for ever:
I dwell in a high and holy place
with him who is broken and humble in spirit,
  to revive the spirit of the humble,
  to revive the courage of the broken.

16 I will not be always accusing,
  I will not continually nurse my wrath.
For a breath of life passed out from me,
and by my own act I created living creatures.

17 For a time I was angry at the guilt of Israel;
  I smote him in my anger and withdrew my favour.
But he ran wild and went his wilful way.

18 Then I considered his ways,
  I cured him and gave him relief,
and I brought him comfort in full measure,

19 brought peace to those who mourned for him,
  by the words that issue from my lips,
peace for all men, both near and far,
  and so I cured him, says the LORD.

20 But the wicked are like a troubled sea,
a sea that cannot rest,
whose troubled waters cast up mud and filth.

21 There is no peace for the wicked,
  says the LORD.

True and false fasting

58 Shout aloud without restraint;
  lift up your voice like a trumpet.
Call my people to account for their transgression
and the house of Jacob for their sins,

2 although they ask counsel of me day by day
and say they delight in knowing my ways,
although, like nations which have acted rightly
and not forsaken the just laws of their gods,
they ask me for righteous laws
and say they delight in approaching God.

3 Why do we fast, if thou dost not see it?
Why mortify ourselves, if thou payest no heed?
Since you serve your own interest only on your fast-day
and make all your men work the harder,

4 since your fasting leads only to wrangling and strife
and dealing vicious blows with the fist,
on such a day you are keeping no fast
that will carry your cry to heaven.

Is it a fast like this that I require,   5
  a day of mortification such as this,
that a man should bow his head like a bulrush
and make his bed on sackcloth and ashes?
Is this what you call a fast,
  a day acceptable to the LORD?
Is not this what I require of you as a fast: 6
  to loose the fetters of injustice,
  to untie the knots of the yoke,
  to snap every yoke
and set free those who have been crushed?
Is it not sharing your food with the hungry,   7
taking the homeless poor into your house,
  clothing the naked when you meet them
  and never evading a duty to your kinsfolk?
Then shall your light break forth like the   8
  dawn
and soon you will grow healthy like a wound newly healed;
  your own righteousness shall be your vanguard
  and the glory of the LORD your rearguard.
Then, if you call, the LORD will answer;   9
  if you cry to him, he will say, 'Here I am.'
  If you cease to pervert justice,
to point the accusing finger and lay false charges,
  if you feed the hungry from your own   10
  plenty
and satisfy the needs of the wretched,
then your light will rise like dawn out of darkness
and your dusk be like noonday;
  the LORD will be your guide continually   11
and will satisfy your needs in the shimmering heat;
  he will give you strength of limb;
  you will be like a well-watered garden,
like a spring whose waters never fail.
The ancient ruins will be restored by your   12
  own kindred
and you will build once more on ancestral foundations;
you shall be called Rebuilder of broken walls,
  Restorer of houses in ruins.

The reward for honouring the sabbath

If you cease to tread the sabbath underfoot,   13
  and keep my holy day free from your own affairs,
  if you call the sabbath a day of joy
  and the LORD's holy day a day to be honoured,
  if you honour it by not plying your trade,
  not seeking your own interest
  or attending to your own affairs,
then you shall find your joy in the LORD,   14
and I will set you riding on the heights of the earth,
and your father Jacob's patrimony shall be yours to enjoy;
  the LORD himself has spoken it.

Iniquities—a barrier

59 The LORD's arm is not so short that he cannot save
    nor his ear too dull to hear;
2 it is your iniquities that raise a barrier between you and your God,
    because of your sins he has hidden his face so that he does not hear you.
3 Your hands are stained with blood and your fingers with crime;
    your lips speak lies and your tongues utter injustice.
4 No man sues with just cause, no man goes honestly to law;
    all trust in empty words, all tell lies, conceive mischief and give birth to trouble.
5 They hatch snakes' eggs, they weave cobwebs;
    eat their eggs and you will die, for rotten eggs hatch only rottenness.
6 As for their webs, they will never make cloth,
    no one can use them for clothing; their works breed trouble
    and their hands are busy with deeds of violence.
7 They rush headlong into crime in furious haste to shed innocent blood;
    their schemes are schemes of mischief and leave a trail of ruin and devastation.
8 They do not know the way to peace, no justice guides their steps;
    all the paths they follow are crooked; no one who walks in them enjoys true peace.

Confession of sinfulness

9 Therefore justice is far away from us, right does not reach us;
    we look for light but all is darkness, for the light of dawn, but we walk in deep gloom.
10 We grope like blind men along a wall, feeling our way like men without eyes;
    we stumble at noonday as if it were twilight,
    like dead men in the ghostly underworld.
11 We growl like bears, like doves we moan incessantly,
    waiting for justice, and there is none; for deliverance, but it is still far away.
12 Our acts of rebellion against thee are past counting
    and our sins bear witness against us; we remember our many rebellions, we know well our guilt:
13 we have rebelled and broken faith with the LORD,
    we have relapsed and forsaken our God; we have conceived lies in our hearts and repeated them
    in slanderous and treacherous words.

Justice is rebuffed and flouted   14
while righteousness stands aloof;
    truth stumbles in the market-place and honesty is kept out of court,
    so truth is lost to sight,   15
and whoever shuns evil is thought a madman.

The LORD intervenes

The LORD saw, and in his eyes it was an evil thing,
    that there was no justice;
    he saw that there was no man to help   16
and was outraged that no one intervened;
    so his own arm brought him victory and his own integrity upheld him.
He put on integrity as a coat of mail   17
and the helmet of salvation on his head;
    he put on garments of vengeance and wrapped himself in a cloak of jealous anger.
High God of retribution that he is,   18
he pays in full measure,
wreaking his anger on his foes, retribution on his enemies.
So from the west men shall fear his name,   19
fear his glory from the rising of the sun;
    for it shall come like a shining river, the spirit of the LORD hovering over it,
    come as the ransomer of Zion   20
and of all in Jacob who repent of their rebellion.
This is the very word of the LORD.

This, says the LORD, is my covenant, which 21
I make with them: My spirit which rests on you and my words which I have put into your mouth shall never fail you from generation to generation of your descendants from now onward for ever. The LORD has said it.

Jerusalem's glorious future

Arise, Jerusalem,   **60**
rise clothed in light; your light has come and the glory of the LORD shines over you.
For, though darkness covers the earth   2
and dark night the nations,
    the LORD shall shine upon you and over you shall his glory appear;
    and the nations shall march towards your 3 light
    and their kings to your sunrise.

Lift up your eyes and look all around: 4
    they flock together, all of them, and come to you;
    your sons also shall come from afar, your daughters walking beside them leading the way.
Then shall you see, and shine with joy,   5
    then your heart shall thrill with pride: the riches of the sea shall be lavished upon you
    and you shall possess the wealth of nations.

⁶ Camels in droves shall cover the land,
dromedaries of Midian and Ephah,
all coming from Sheba
laden with golden spice' and frankincense,
heralds of the LORD's praise.

⁷ All Kedar's flocks shall be gathered for you,
rams of Nebaioth shall serve your need,
acceptable offerings on my altar,
and glory shall be added to glory in my
temple.

⁸ Who are these that sail along like clouds,
that fly like doves to their dovecotes?

⁹ They are vessels assembling from the coasts
and islands,
ships from Tarshish leading the convoy;
they bring your sons from afar,
their gold and their silver with them,
to the honour of the LORD your God,
the Holy One of Israel;
for he has made you glorious.

¹⁰ Foreigners shall rebuild your walls
and their kings shall be your servants;
for though in my wrath I struck you down,
now I have shown you pity and favour.

¹¹ Your gates shall be open continually,
they shall never be shut day or night,
that through them may be brought the
wealth of nations
and their kings under escort.

¹² For the nation or kingdom which refuses
to serve you shall perish, and wide regions
shall be laid utterly waste.

¹³ The wealth of Lebanon shall come to you,
pine, fir,ˢ and boxwood,ᵗ all together,
to bring glory to my holy sanctuary,
to honour the place where my feet rest.

¹⁴ The sons of your oppressors shall come forward to do homage,
all who reviled you shall bow low at your
feet;
they shall call you the City of the LORD,
the Zion of the Holy One of Israel.

No longer will you be deserted,   15
a wife hated and unvisited;ᵘ
I will make you an eternal pride
and a never-ending joy.
You shall suck the milk of nations   16
and be suckled at the breasts of kings.
So you shall know that I the LORD am your
deliverer,
your ransomer the Mighty One of Jacob.

For bronzeᵛ I will bring you gold   17
and for iron I will bring silver,
bronzeᵛ for timber and iron for stone;
and I will make your government be peace
and righteousness rule over you.
The sound of violence shall be heard no 18
longer in your land,
or ruin and devastation within your
borders;
but you shall call your walls Deliverance
and your gates Praise.

The sun shall no longer be your light by day, 19
nor the moon shine on you when evening
falls;
the LORD shall be your everlasting light,
your God shall be your glory.
Never again shall your sun set   20
nor your moon withdraw her light;
but the LORD shall be your everlasting light
and the days of your mourning shall be
ended.

Your people shall all be righteous   21
and shall for ever possess the land,
a shoot of my own planting,
a work of my own hands to bring me
glory.
The few shall become ten thousand,   22
the little nation great.
I am the LORD;
soon, in the fullness of time, I will bring this
to pass.

Good news proclaimed

The spirit of the Lord GOD is upon me   **61**
because the LORD has anointed me;
he has sent me to bring good news to the
humble,
to bind up the broken-hearted,
to proclaim liberty to captives
and release to those in prison;
to proclaim a year of the LORD's favour   2
and a day of the vengeance of our God;
to comfort all who mourn,ʷ
to give them garlands instead of ashes,   3
oil of gladness instead of mourners' tears,
a garment of splendour for the heavy heart.
They shall be called Trees of Righteousness,
planted by the LORD for his glory.

r golden spice: or gold.   s Or elm.   t Or cypress.   u Or divorced and unmated.   v Or copper.
w Prob. rdg.; Heb. adds to appoint to Zion's mourners.

4   Ancient ruins shall be rebuilt
     and sites long desolate restored;
     they shall repair the ruined cities
     and restore what has long lain desolate.
5   Foreigners shall serve as shepherds of your
        flocks,
     and aliens shall till your land and tend
        your vines;
6   but you shall be called priests of the LORD
     and be named ministers of our God;
     you shall enjoy the wealth of other nations
     and be furnished[x] with their riches.
7 And so, because shame in double measure
     and jeers and insults[y] have been my
        people's lot,
   they shall receive in their own land a double
        measure of wealth,
     and everlasting joy shall be theirs.
8 For I, the LORD, love justice
     and hate robbery and wrong-doing;
   I will grant them a sure reward
     and make an everlasting covenant with
        them;
9   their posterity will be renowned among
        the nations
     and their offspring among the peoples;
     all who see them will acknowledge in them
   a race whom the LORD has blessed.

A hymn of praise

10   Let me rejoice in the LORD with all my
        heart,
     let me exult in my God;
     for he has robed me in salvation as a gar-
        ment
     and clothed me in integrity as a cloak,
   like a bridegroom with his priestly garland,
     or a bride decked in her jewels.
11   For, as the earth puts forth her blossom
     or bushes in the garden burst into flower,
   so shall the Lord GOD make righteousness
        and praise
     blossom before all the nations.

Prayer for Jerusalem, and its answer

62   For Zion's sake I will not keep silence,
     for Jerusalem's sake I will speak out,
     until her right shines forth like the sun-
        rise,
     her deliverance like a blazing torch,
2   until the nations see the triumph of your
        right
     and all kings see your glory.
     Then you shall be called by a new name
     which the LORD shall pronounce with his
        own lips;
3   you will be a glorious crown in the LORD's
        hand,
     a kingly diadem in the hand of your God.

No more shall men call you Forsaken,   4
no more shall your land be called Deso-
     late,
but you shall be named Hephzi-bah;[z]
     and your land Beulah;[a]
     for the LORD delights in you
     and to him your land is wedded.
   For, as a young man weds a maiden,   5
     so you shall wed him who rebuilds
        you,
     and your God shall rejoice over you
     as a bridegroom rejoices over the bride.
I have posted watchmen on your walls,   6
     Jerusalem,
who shall not keep silence day or night:
     'You who invoke the LORD's name,
take no rest, give him no rest   7
     until he makes Jerusalem
     a theme of endless praise on earth.'

The LORD's proclamation

The LORD has sworn with raised right hand   8
     and mighty arm:
Never again will I give your grain to feed
     your foes
     or let foreigners drink the new wine
     for which you have toiled;
but those who bring in the corn shall eat and   9
     praise the LORD,
and those who gather the grapes shall drink
     in my holy courts.

Go out of the gates, go out,   10
prepare a road for my people;
build a highway, build it up,
clear away the boulders;
raise a signal to the peoples.
This is the LORD's proclamation   11
to earth's farthest bounds:
Tell the daughter of Zion,
Behold, your deliverance has come.
His recompense comes with him;
he carries his reward before him;
and they shall be called a Holy People,   12
the Ransomed of the LORD,
a People long-sought, a City not forsaken.

The LORD's day of vengeance

'Who is this coming from Edom,   **63**
coming from Bozrah, his garments stained
     red?
Under his clothes his muscles stand out,
and he strides, stooping in his might.'
It is I, who announce that right has won
     the day,
I, who am strong to save.
'Why is your clothing all red,   2
like the garments of one who treads grapes
     in the vat?'

---

x be furnished: *prob. rdg.; Heb. unintelligible.*
z *That is* My delight is in her.   *a That is* Wedded.
y and insults: *prob. rdg.; Heb.* they shout in triumph.

3   I have trodden the winepress alone;
no man, no nation was with me.
I trod them down in my rage,
I trampled them in my fury;
and their life-blood spurted over my gar-
    ments
and stained all my clothing.

4   For I resolved on a day of vengeance;
the year for ransoming my own had
    come.

5   I looked for a helper but found no one,
I was amazed that there was no one to
    support me;
yet my own arm brought me victory,
alone my anger supported me.

6   I stamped on nations in my fury,
I pierced them in my rage
and let their life-blood run out upon the
    ground.

Recalling past mercies

7   I will recount the LORD's acts of unfailing
    love
and the LORD's praises as High God,
all that the LORD has done for us
and his great goodness to the house of
    Israel,
all that he has done for them in his tender-
    ness
and by his many acts of love.

8   He said, 'Surely they are my people,
my sons who will not play me false';

9   and he became their deliverer in all their
    troubles.
It was no envoy, no angel, but he himself that
    delivered them;
he himself ransomed them by his love and
    pity,
lifted them up and carried them
through all the years gone by.

10   Yet they rebelled and grieved his holy
    spirit;
only then was he changed into their
    enemy
and himself fought against them.

11   Then men remembered days long past
and him who drew out[b] his people:
Where is he who brought them up from
    the Nile
with the shepherd[c] of his flock?
Where is he who put within him
his holy spirit,

12   who made his glorious power march
at the right hand of Moses,
dividing the waters before them,
to win for himself an everlasting name,

13   causing them to go through the depths
sure-footed as horses in the wilderness,

like cattle moving down into a valley with-   14
    out stumbling,
guided by the spirit of the LORD?
So didst thou lead thy people
to win thyself a glorious name.

Prayer to the LORD as father

Look down from heaven and behold   15
from the heights where thou dwellest holy
    and glorious.
Where is thy zeal, thy valour,
thy burning and tender love?
Stand not aloof;[d] for thou art our father,   16
though Abraham does not know us nor
    Israel acknowledge us.
Thou, LORD, art our father;
thy name is our Ransomer[e] from of old.
Why, LORD, dost thou let us wander from   17
    thy ways
and harden our hearts until we cease to
    fear thee?
turn again for the sake of thy servants,
the tribes of thy patrimony.
Why have wicked men trodden down thy   18
    sanctuary,[f]
why have our enemies trampled on thy
    shrine?
We have long been reckoned as beyond thy   19
    sway,
as if we had not been named thy own.

Why didst thou not rend the heavens and   64
    come down,
and make the mountains shudder before
    thee
as when fire blazes up in brushwood   2
or fire makes water boil?
then would thy name be known to thy
    enemies
and nations tremble at thy coming.
When thou didst terrible things that we did   3
    not look for,
the mountains shuddered before thee.
Never has ear heard[g] or eye seen   4
any other god taking the part of those who
    wait for him.
Thou dost welcome him who rejoices to do   5
    what is right,
who remembers thee in thy ways.
Though thou wast angry, yet we sinned,
in spite of it we have done evil from of
    old,
we all became like a man who is unclean   6
and all our righteous deeds like a filthy
    rag;
we have all withered[h] like leaves
and our iniquities sweep us away like the
    wind.

---

b That is Moses *whose name resembles the Heb. verb meaning* draw out, *cp. Exod.* 2. 10 *and the note there.*
c Or shepherds.   *d* Stand not aloof: *prob. rdg.; Heb. obscure in context.*   *e Or* our Kinsman.
f Why . . . sanctuary: *prob. rdg.; Heb.* For a little while they possessed thy holy people.   *g* Never . . .
heard: *prob. rdg.; Heb.* They have never heard or listened.   *h* have all withered: *or* are all carried away.

7 There is no one who invokes thee by name
   or rouses himself to cling to thee;
   for thou hast hidden thy face from us
   and abandoned us to our iniquities.
8 But now, LORD, thou art our father;
   we are the clay, thou the potter,
   and all of us are thy handiwork.
9 Do not be angry beyond measure, O LORD,
   and do not remember iniquity for ever;
   look on us all, look on thy people.
10 Thy holy cities are a wilderness,
   Zion a wilderness, Jerusalem desolate;
11 our sanctuary, holy and glorious,
   where our fathers praised thee,
   has been burnt to the ground
   and all that we cherish is a ruin.
12 After this, O LORD, wilt thou hold back,
   wilt thou keep silence and punish us
   beyond measure?

The LORD appeals to an unruly people

65 I was there to be sought by a people who did
   not ask,
   to be found by men who did not seek me.
   I said, 'Here am I, here am I',
   to a nation that did not invoke me by name.
2 I spread out my hands all day
   appealing to an unruly people
   who went their evil way,
   following their own devices,
3 a people who provoked me
   continually to my face,
   offering sacrifice in gardens, burning incense
   on brick altars,
4 crouching among graves, keeping vigil all
   night long,
   eating swine's flesh, their cauldrons full of a
   tainted brew.
5 'Stay where you are,' they cry,
   'do not dare touch me; for I am too sacred
   for you.'
   Such people are a smouldering fire,
   smoking in my nostrils all day long.
6 All is on record before me; I will not keep
   silence;
7 I will repay[i] your iniquities,
   yours and your fathers', all at once, says the
   LORD,
   because they burnt incense[j] on the mountains
   and defied me on the hills;
   I will first measure out their reward
   and then pay them in full.

New heavens and a new earth

8 These are the words of the LORD:
   As there is new wine in a cluster of grapes
   and men say, 'Do not destroy it; there is a
   blessing in it',
   so will I do for my servants' sake:
   I will not destroy the whole nation.

I will give Jacob children to come after 9
   him
   and Judah heirs who shall possess my
   mountains;
   my chosen shall inherit them
   and my servants shall live there.
   Flocks shall range over Sharon,   10
   and the Vale of Achor be a pasture for
   cattle;
   they shall belong to my people who seek me.
But you that forsake the LORD and forget my 11
   holy mountain,
   who spread a table for the god of Fate,
   and fill bowls of spiced wine in honour of
   Fortune,
   I will deliver you to your fate, to execution, 12
   and you shall all bend the neck to the
   sword,
   because I called and you did not answer,
   I spoke and you did not listen;
   and you did what was wrong in my eyes
   and you chose what was against my will.
Therefore these are the words of the Lord 13
   GOD:
   My servants shall eat but you shall starve;
   my servants shall drink but you shall go
   thirsty;
   my servants shall rejoice but you shall be
   put to shame;
   my servants shall shout in triumph   14
   in the gladness of their hearts,
   but you shall cry from sorrow
   and wail from anguish of spirit;
   your name shall be used as an oath by my 15
   chosen,
   and the Lord GOD shall give you over to
   death;
   but his servants he shall call by another
   name.
   He who invokes a blessing on himself in 16
   the land
   shall do so by the God whose name is
   Amen,
   and he who utters an oath in the land
   shall do so by the God of Amen;
   the former troubles are forgotten
   and they are hidden from my sight.
   For behold, I create   17
new heavens and a new earth.
   Former things shall no more be remembered
   nor shall they be called to mind.
   Rejoice and be filled with delight,   18
   you boundless realms which I create;
for I create Jerusalem to be a delight
   and her people a joy;
I will take delight in Jerusalem and rejoice 19
   in my people;
   weeping and cries for help
   shall never again be heard in her.
There no child shall ever again die an infant, 20
   no old man fail to live out his life;

---

i Prob. rdg., transposing and then pay *to follow* reward.   *j Or* sacrifices.

every boy shall live his hundred years
    before he dies,
whoever falls short of a hundred shall be
    despised.[k]

21 Men shall build houses and live to inhabit
    them,
    plant vineyards and eat their fruit;
22   they shall not build for others to inhabit
    nor plant for others to eat.
My people shall live the long life of a tree,
    and my chosen shall enjoy the fruit of their
    labour.
23 They shall not toil in vain or raise children
    for misfortune.
    For they are the offspring of the blessed
      of the LORD
    and their issue after them;
24 before they call to me, I will answer,
    and while they are still speaking I will listen.
25 The wolf and the lamb shall feed together
    and the lion shall eat straw like cattle.[l]
They shall not hurt or destroy in all my holy
    mountain,
    says the LORD.

Reverence for the LORD

66 These are the words of the LORD:
Heaven is my throne and earth my footstool.
Where will you build a house for me,
    where shall I my resting-place be?
2   All these are of my own making
    and all these are mine.
    This is the very word of the LORD.

The man I look to is a man down-trodden
    and distressed,
    one who reveres my words.
3 But to sacrifice an ox or to[m] kill a man,
slaughter a sheep or break a dog's neck,
offer grain or offer pigs' blood,
burn incense as a token and worship an
    idol—
all these are the chosen practices of men
    who[n] revel in their own loathsome rites.
4 I too will practise those wanton rites of theirs
    and bring down on them the very things
      they dread;
    for I called and no one answered,
    I spoke and no one listened.
    They did what was wrong in my eyes
    and chose practices not to my liking.

5 Hear the word of the LORD, you who revere
    his word:
    Your fellow-countrymen who hate you,
    who spurn you because you bear my name,
      have said,
    'Let the LORD show his glory,
      then we shall see you rejoice';
    but they shall be put to shame.

That roar from the city, that uproar in the 6
    temple,
is the sound of the LORD dealing retribution
    to his foes.

Jerusalem, a mother of children

Shall a woman bear a child without pains? 7
give birth to a son before the onset of labour?
    Who has heard of anything like this? 8
    Who has seen any such thing?
Shall a country be born after one day's
    labour,
shall a nation be brought to birth all in a
    moment?
But Zion, at the onset of her pangs, bore her
    sons.
    Shall I bring to the point of birth and not 9
      deliver?
    the LORD says;
    shall I who deliver close the womb?
    your God has spoken.

Rejoice with Jerusalem and exult in her, 10
    all you who love her;
    share her joy with all your heart,
    all you who mourn over her.
Then you may suck and be fed from the 11
    breasts that give comfort,
delighting in her plentiful milk.
    For thus says the LORD: 12
I will send peace flowing over her like a river,
and the wealth of nations like a stream in
    flood;
    it shall suckle you,
    and you shall be carried in their arms
    and dandled on their knees.
    As a mother comforts her son, 13
    so will I myself comfort you,
    and you shall find comfort in Jerusalem.
    This you shall see and be glad at heart, 14
    your limbs shall be as fresh as grass in
      spring;
the LORD shall make his power known among
    his servants
    and his indignation felt among his foes.
For see, the LORD is coming in fire, 15
    with his chariots like a whirlwind,
    to strike home with his furious anger
    and with the flaming fire of his reproof.
The LORD will judge by fire, 16
    with fire he will test all living men,
    and many will be slain by the LORD;
    those who hallow and purify themselves 17
      in garden-rites,
    one after another in a magic ring,
those who eat the flesh of pigs and rats[o] and
    all vile vermin,
    shall meet their end, one and all,
    says the LORD,
for I know their deeds and their thoughts. 18

---

[k] Or cursed.   [l] Prob. rdg.; Heb. adds and the food of the snake shall be dust.   [m] to sacrifice an
ox or to: or those who sacrifice an ox and . . .   [n] are the chosen practices of men who: or have chosen
their own devices and . . .   [o] Or jerboas.

Universal praise

Then I myself will come to gather all nations
    and races,
    and they shall come and see my glory;
19   and I will perform a sign among them.
I will spare some of them and send them to
    the nations,
    to Tarshish, Put, and Lud,[p]
    to Meshek, Rosh,[q] Tubal, and Javan,[r]
distant coasts and islands which have never
    yet heard of me
    and have not seen my glory;
    these shall announce that glory among the
    nations.
20   From every nation they shall bring your
    countrymen
    on horses, in chariots and wagons,
    on mules and dromedaries,
    as an offering to the LORD,
    on my holy mountain Jerusalem,
    says the LORD,

as the Israelites bring offerings
    in pure vessels to the LORD's house;
and some of them I will take for priests, for 21
    Levites,
    says the LORD.
For, as the new heavens and the new earth 22
which I am making shall endure in my sight,
    says the LORD,
so shall your race and your name endure;
    and month by month at the new moon, 23
    week by week on the sabbath,
all mankind shall come to bow down before
    me,
    says the LORD;
    and they shall come out and see 24
the dead bodies of those who have rebelled
    against me;
their worm shall not die nor their fire be
    quenched,
    and they shall be abhorred by all man-
    kind.

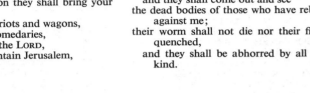

THE BOOK
OF THE PROPHET
JEREMIAH

Jeremiah's call and two visions

1 THE WORDS of Jeremiah son of Hilkiah,
one of the priests at Anathoth in Benjamin.
2 The word of the LORD came to him in the
thirteenth year of the reign of Josiah son of
3 Amon, king of Judah; also during the reign
of Jehoiakim son of Josiah, king of Judah,
until the eleventh year of Zedekiah son of
Josiah, king of Judah, was completed. In the
fifth month the people of Jerusalem were
carried away into exile.

4 5 The word of the LORD came to me: 'Before
I formed you in the womb I knew you for
my own; before you were born I consecrated

you, I appointed you a prophet to the
nations.' 'Ah! Lord GOD,' I answered, 'I do 6
not know how to speak; I am only a child.'
But the LORD said, 'Do not call yourself a 7
child; for you shall go to whatever people
I send you and say whatever I tell you to say.
Fear none of them, for I am with you and 8
will keep you safe.' This was the very word
of the LORD. Then the LORD stretched out 9
his hand and touched my mouth, and said
to me, 'I put my words into your mouth.
This day I give you authority over nations 10
and over kingdoms, to pull down and to
uproot, to destroy and to demolish, to build
and to plant.'

p Or Lydia.   *q* Meshek, Rosh: *prob. rdg.; Heb.* those who draw the bow.   *r Or* Greece.

11 The word of the LORD came to me: 'What is it that you see, Jeremiah?' 'An almond in 12 early bloom',*a* I answered. 'You are right,' said the LORD to me, 'for I am early on the 13 watch*b* to carry out my purpose.' The word of the LORD came to me a second time: 'What is it that you see?' 'A cauldron', I said, 'on a fire, fanned by the wind; it is 14 tilted away from the north.' The LORD said:

From the north disaster shall flare up
   against all who live in this land;
15 for now I summon all peoples and kingdoms
      of the north,
   says the LORD.
Their kings shall come and each shall set up
      his throne
   before the gates of Jerusalem,
   against her walls on every side,
   and against all the cities of Judah.
16 I will state my case against my people
   for all the wrong they have done in for-
      saking me,
   in burning sacrifices to other gods,
   worshipping the work of their own
      hands.
17 Brace yourself, Jeremiah;
   stand up and speak to them.
   Tell them everything I bid you,
do not let your spirit break at sight of
      them,
   or I will break you before their eyes.
18 This day I make you a fortified city,
   a pillar of iron, a wall of bronze,
   to stand fast against the whole land,
against the kings and princes of Judah,
   its priests and its people.
19 They will make war on you but shall not
      overcome you,
   for I am with you and will keep you
      safe.
   This is the very word of the LORD.

When Israel was faithful

2
2 The word of the LORD came to me: Go, make a proclamation that all Jerusalem shall hear: These are the words of the LORD:

I remember the unfailing devotion of your
      youth,
   the love of your bridal days,
when you followed me in the wilderness,
   through a land unsown.
3 Israel then was holy to the LORD,
   the firstfruits of his harvest;
   no one who devoured her went un-
      punished,
   evil always overtook them.
   This is the very word of the LORD.

Israel's apostasy

Listen to the word of the LORD, people of 4 Jacob, families of Israel, one and all. These 5 are the words of the LORD:

What fault did your forefathers find in me,
   that they wandered far from me,
pursuing empty phantoms and themselves
      becoming empty;
that they did not ask, 'Where is the LORD, 6
   who brought us up from Egypt,
   and led us through the wilderness,
   through a country of deserts and shifting
      sands,
   a country barren and ill-omened, where no
      man ever trod,
   no man made his home?'
I brought you into a fruitful land 7
   to enjoy its fruit and the goodness of it;
   but when you entered upon it you defiled it
   and made the home I gave you loath-
      some.
The priests no longer asked, 'Where is the 8
   LORD?'
Those who handled the law had no thought
      of me,
   the shepherds of the people rebelled
      against me;
   the prophets prophesied in the name of
      Baal
   and followed gods powerless to help.
Therefore I will bring a charge against you 9
      once more,
   says the LORD,
   against you and against your descendants.
Cross to the coasts and islands of Kittim 10
      and see,
   send to Kedar and consider well,
   see whether there has been anything like
      this:
has a nation ever changed its gods, 11
   although they were no gods?
But my people have exchanged their Glory
   for a god altogether powerless.
Stand aghast at this, you heavens, 12
   tremble in utter despair,
   says the LORD.
Two sins have my people committed: 13
   they have forsaken me,
   a spring of living water,
and they have hewn out for themselves
      cisterns,
cracked cisterns that can hold no water.

Desperate pursuit of foreign gods

Is Israel a slave? Was he born in slavery? 14
If not, why has he been despoiled?
Why do lions roar and growl at him? 15
Why has his land been laid waste,
   why are his cities razed to the ground and
      abandoned?

a Heb. shaked.   *b Heb.* shoked.

16 Men of Noph and Tahpanhes
    will break your heads.
17 Is it not your desertion of the LORD your
    God
      that brings all this upon you?
18 And now, why should you make off to Egypt
    to drink the waters of the Shihor?
  Or why make off to Assyria
    to drink the waters of the River?
19 It is your own wickedness that will punish
    you,
  your own apostasy that will condemn you.
  See for yourselves how bitter a thing it is and
    how evil,
  to forsake the LORD your God and revere
    me no longer.
    This is the very word of the Lord GOD of
    Hosts.
20 Ages ago you broke your yoke and snapped
    your traces,
  crying, 'I will not be your slave';
  and you sprawled in promiscuous vice
  on all the hill-tops, under every spreading
    tree.
21 I planted you as a choice red vine,
    true stock all of you,
  yet now you are turned into a vine
    debased and worthless!
22 The stain of your sin is still there and I see it,
  though you wash with soda and do not stint
    the soap.
    This is the very word of the Lord GOD.
23 How can you say, 'I am not polluted, not I!
  I have not followed the Baalim'?
  Look how you conducted yourself in the
    valley;
    remember what you have done.
  You have been like a she-camel,
  twisting and turning as she runs,
24   rushing alone into*c* the wilderness,
  snuffing the wind in her lust;
    who can restrain her in her heat?
  No one need tire himself out in pursuit of
    her;
    she is easily found at mating time.
25 Why not save your feet from stony ground
  and your throats from thirst?
  But you said, 'No; I am desperate.
  I love foreign gods and I must go after
    them.'
26 As a thief is ashamed when he is found out,
    so the people of Israel feel ashamed,
  they, their kings, their princes,
    their priests and their prophets;
27 they say 'You are our father' to a block of
    wood
    and cry 'Mother' to a stone.
  But on me they have turned their backs
    and averted their faces from me.
  And now on the day of disaster they say,
    'Rise up and save us.'

Where are they, those gods you made for 28
  yourselves?
Let them come and save you in the day of
  disaster.
For you, Judah, have as many gods as you
  have towns.*d*
  The LORD answers,   29
Why argue your case with me?
You are rebels, every one of you.
In vain I struck down your sons,   30
  the lesson was not learnt;
still your own sword devoured your prophets
  like a ravening lion.
*e*Have I shown myself inhospitable to Israel 31
  like some wilderness or waterless land?
Why do my people say, 'We have broken
  away;
  we will never come back to thee'?

Captivity foretold

Will a girl forget her finery   32
  or a bride her ribbons?
Yet my people have forgotten me
  over and over again.
How well you pick your way in search of 33
  lovers!
Why! even the worst of women can learn
  from you.
Yes, and there is blood on the corners of 34
  your robe—
  the life-blood of the innocent poor.
  You did not get it by housebreaking
  but by your sacrifices under every oak.
You say, 'I am innocent;   35
  surely his anger has passed away.'
But I will challenge your claim
  to have done no sin.
Why do you so lightly change your course? 36
Egypt will fail you as Assyria did;
  you shall go out from here,   37
  each of you with his hands above his
    head,
  for the LORD repudiates those in whom
    you trusted,
  and from them you shall gain nothing.

Israel's adultery

If a man puts away his wife   **3**
  and she leaves him,
  and if she then becomes another's,
  may he go back to her again?
  Is not that woman defiled,
  a forbidden thing?
  You have played the harlot with many
    lovers;
  can you come back to me?
  says the LORD.

---

c rushing alone into: *prob. rdg.; Heb.* a wild-ass taught in.   *d* towns: *or* blood-spattered altars.
e Prob. rdg.; Heb. prefixes You, O generation, see the word of the LORD.

2 Look up to the high bare places and see:
where have you not been ravished?
You sat by the wayside to catch lovers,
like an Arab lurking in the desert,
and defiled the land
with your fornication and your wickedness.
3 Therefore the showers were withheld
and the spring rain failed.
But yours was a harlot's brow,
and you were resolved to show no shame.
4 Not so long since, you called me 'Father,
dear friend of my youth',
5 thinking, 'Will he be angry for ever?
Will he rage eternally?'
This is how you spoke; you have done evil
and gone unchallenged.

The LORD pleads with Israel

6 In the reign of King Josiah, the LORD said
to me, Do you see what apostate Israel did?
She went up to every hill-top and under
every spreading tree, and there she played
7 the whore. Even after she had done all this,
I said to her, Come back to me, but she would
not. That faithless woman, her sister Judah,
8 saw it all; she saw too that I had put apostate
Israel away and given her a note of divorce
because she had committed adultery. Yet
that faithless woman, her sister Judah, was
not afraid; she too has gone and played the
9 whore. She defiled the land with her thoughtless harlotry and her adulterous worship of
10 stone and wood. In spite of all this that faithless woman, her sister Judah, has not come
back to me in good faith, but only in pretence.
This is the very word of the LORD.
11 The LORD said to me, Apostate Israel is
less to blame than that faithless woman
12 Judah. Go and proclaim this message to the
north:

Come back to me, apostate Israel,
says the LORD,
I will no longer frown on you.
For my love is unfailing, says the LORD,
I will not be angry for ever.
13 Only you must acknowledge your wrongdoing,
confess your rebellion against the LORD
your God.
Confess your promiscuous traffic with
foreign gods
under every spreading tree,
confess that you have not obeyed me.
This is the very word of the LORD.

Jerusalem's glorious future

14 Come back to me, apostate children, says
the LORD, for I am patient with you, and I
will take you, one from a city and two from
15 a clan, and bring you to Zion. There will

I give you shepherds after my own heart,
and they shall lead you with knowledge and
understanding. In those days, when you 16
have increased and become fruitful in the
land, says the LORD, men shall speak no
more of the Ark of the Covenant of the LORD;
they shall not think of it nor remember it
nor resort to it; it will be needed no more.
At that time Jerusalem shall be called the 17
Throne of the LORD. All nations shall gather
in Jerusalem to honour the LORD's name;
never again shall they follow the promptings
of their evil and stubborn hearts. In those 18
days Judah shall join Israel, and together
they shall come from a northern land into the
land I gave their fathers as their patrimony.

Repentance

I said, How gladly would I treat you as a son, 19
giving you a pleasant land,
a patrimony fairer than that of any
nation!
I said, You shall call me Father
and never cease to follow me.
But like a woman who is unfaithful to her 20
lover,
so you, Israel, were unfaithful to me.
This is the very word of the LORD.
Hark, a sound of weeping on the bare 21
places,
Israel's people pleading for mercy!
For they have taken to crooked ways
and ignored the LORD their God.
Come back to me, wayward*f* sons; 22
I will heal your apostasy.

O LORD, we come! We come to thee;
for thou art our God.
There is no help in worship on the hill- 23
tops,
no help from clamour on the heights;
truly in the LORD our God
is Israel's only salvation.
From our early days 24
Baal, god of shame, has devoured
the fruits of our fathers' labours,
their flocks and herds, their sons and
daughters.
Let us lie down in shame, wrapped round by 25
our dishonour,
for we have sinned against the LORD our
God,
both we and our fathers,
from our early days till now,
and we have not obeyed the LORD our God.

If you will but come back, O Israel, **4**
if you will but come back to me, says the
LORD,
if you will banish your loathsome idols
from my sight,
and stray no more,

f Or apostate.

2 if you swear by the life of the LORD,
in truth, in justice and uprightness,
then shall the nations pray to be blessed
   like you*g*
and in you*g* shall they boast.

Threat of invasion

3 These are the words of the LORD to the men
of Judah and Jerusalem:

Break up your fallow ground,
do not sow among thorns,
4 circumcise yourselves to the service of the
   LORD,
circumcise your hearts,
men of Judah and dwellers in Jerusalem,
lest the fire of my fury blaze up and burn
   unquenched,
because of your evil doings.
5 Tell this in Judah,
proclaim it in Jerusalem,
blow the trumpet throughout the land,
sound the muster,
give the command, Stand to!—and let us
   fall back
on the fortified cities.
6 Raise the signal—To Zion!
make for safety, lose no time,
for I bring disaster out of the north,
and dire destruction.
7 A lion has come out from his lair,
the destroyer of nations;
he has struck his tents, he has broken
   camp,
to harry your land
and lay your cities waste and unpeopled.
8 Well may you put on sackcloth,
beat the breast and wail,
for the anger of the LORD
is not averted from us.
9 On that day, says the LORD,
the hearts of the king and his officers shall
   fail them,
priests shall be struck with horror and
   prophets dumbfounded.

10 And I said, O Lord GOD, thou surely didst
deceive this people and Jerusalem in saying,
'You shall have peace', while the sword is at
our throats.

The enemy advances

11 At that time this people and Jerusalem shall
be told:

A scorching wind from the high bare places
   in the wilderness
sweeps down upon my people,
no breeze for winnowing or for cleansing;
12 a wind too strong for these
will come at my bidding,
and now I will state my case against them.

Like clouds the enemy advances   13
with a whirlwind of chariots;
his horses are swifter than eagles—
alas, we are overwhelmed!
O Jerusalem, wash the wrongdoing from   14
   your heart
and you may yet be saved;
how long will you cherish
your evil schemes?
Hark, a runner from Dan,   15
tidings of evil from Mount Ephraim!
Tell all this to the nations,   16
proclaim the doom of Jerusalem:
hordes of invaders come from a distant
   land,
howling against the cities of Judah.
Their pickets are closing in all round   17
   her,
because she has rebelled against me.
This is the very word of the LORD.
Your own ways, your own deeds   18
have brought all this upon you;
this is your punishment,
and all this comes of your rebellion.*h*
Oh, the writhing of my bowels   19
and the throbbing of my heart!
I cannot keep silence.
I hear the sound of the trumpet,
the sound of the battle-cry.
Crash upon crash,   20
the land goes down in ruin,
my tents are thrown down,
their coverings torn to shreds.
How long must I see the standard raised   21
and hear the trumpet call?
My people are fools, they know nothing   22
   of me;
silly children, with no understanding,
they are clever only in wrongdoing,
and of doing right they know nothing.

Universal chaos

I saw the earth, and it was without form   23
   and void;
the heavens, and their light was gone.
I saw the mountains, and they reeled;   24
all the hills rocked to and fro.
I saw, and there was no man,   25
and the very birds had taken flight.
I saw, and the farm-land was wilder-   26
   ness,
and the towns all razed to the ground,
before the LORD in his anger.
These are the words of the LORD: 27
The whole land shall be desolate,
though I will not make an end of it.
Therefore the earth will mourn   28
and the heavens above turn black.
For I have made known my purpose;
I will not relent or change my mind.

---

g Prob. rdg.; Heb. him.   *h* your rebellion: *prob. rdg.*; Heb. obscure.

29 At the sound of the horsemen and archers
the whole country is in flight;
they creep into caves, they hide in thickets,
they scramble up the crags.
Every town is forsaken,
no one dwells there.

Zion spurned

30 And you, what are you doing?
When you dress yourself in scarlet,
deck yourself out with golden ornaments,
and make your eyes big with antimony,
you are beautifying yourself to no purpose.
Your lovers spurn you
and are out for your life.
31 I hear a sound as of a woman in labour,
the sharp cry of one bearing her first
child.
It is Zion, gasping for breath,
clenching her fists.
Ah me! I am weary,
weary of slaughter.

Rebellion and false security

5 Go up and down the streets of Jerusalem
and see for yourselves;
search her wide squares:
can you find any man who acts justly,
who seeks the truth,
that I may forgive that city?
2 Men may swear by the life of the LORD,
but they only perjure themselves.
3 O LORD, are thine eyes not set upon the
truth?
Thou didst strike them down,
but they took no heed;
didst pierce them to the heart,
but they refused to learn.
They set their faces harder than flint
and refused to come back.
4 I said, 'After all, these are the poor,
these are stupid folk,
who do not know the way of the LORD,
the ordinances of their God.
5 I will go to the great
and speak with them;
for they will know the way of the LORD,
the ordinances of their God.'
But they too have broken the yoke
and snapped their traces.
6 Therefore a lion out of the scrub shall
strike them down,
a wolf from the plains shall ravage them;
a leopard shall prowl about their cities
and maul any who venture out.
For their rebellious deeds are many,
their apostasies past counting.

How can I forgive you for all this? 7
Your sons have forsaken me and sworn
by gods
that are no gods.
I gave them all they needed, yet they
preferred adultery,
and haunted the brothels;
each neighs after another man's wife, 8
like a well-fed and lusty stallion.
Shall I not punish them for this? 9
the LORD asks.
Shall I not take vengeance
on such a people?
Go along her rows of vines and slash 10
them,
yet do not make an end of them.
Hack away her green branches,
for they are not the LORD's.
Faithless are Israel and Judah, 11
both faithless to me.
This is the very word of the LORD.
They have denied the LORD, 12
saying, 'He does not exist.
No evil shall come upon us;
we shall never see sword or famine.
The prophets will prove mere wind, 13
the word not in them.'

The coming invader

And so, because you talk in this way, these 14
are the words of the LORD the God of Hosts
to me:
I will make my words a fire in your mouth;
and it shall burn up this people like brushwood.

I bring against you, Israel, a nation from 15
afar,
an ancient people established long ago,
says the LORD.
A people whose language you do not
know,
whose speech you will not understand;
they are all mighty warriors, 16
their jaws are a grave, wide open,
to devour your harvest and your bread, 17
to devour your sons and your daughters,
to devour your flocks and your herds,
to devour your vines and your fig-trees.
They shall batter down the cities in which
you trust,[i]
walled though they are.

But in those days, the LORD declares, I 18
will still not make an end of you. When you 19
ask, 'Why has the LORD our God done all
this to us?' I shall answer, 'As you have
forsaken me and served alien gods in your
own land, so shall you serve foreigners[j] in
a land that is not yours.'

---

i Prob. rdg.; Heb. adds with the sword.   *j* Or foreign gods.

Corruption and complacency

20 Tell this to the people of Jacob,
proclaim it in Judah:

21 Listen, you foolish and senseless people,
who have eyes and see nothing,
ears and hear nothing.

22 Have you no fear of me? says the LORD;
will you not shiver before me,
before me, who made the shivering sand
to bound the sea,
a barrier it never can pass?
Its waves heave and toss but they are
powerless;
roar as they may, they cannot pass.

23 But this people has a rebellious and
defiant heart,
rebels they have been and now they are
clean gone.

24 They did not say to themselves,
'Let us fear the LORD our God,
who gives us the rains of autumn
and spring showers in their turn,
who brings us unfailingly
fixed seasons of harvest.'

25 But your wrongdoing has upset nature's
order,
and your sins have kept from you her kindly
gifts.

26 For among my people there are wicked
men,
who lay snares like a fowler's net^k
and set deadly traps to catch men.

27 Their houses are full of fraud,
as a cage is full of birds.
They grow rich and grand,

28 bloated and rancorous;
their thoughts are all of evil,
and they refuse to do justice,
the claims of the orphan they do not put
right
nor do they grant justice to the poor.

29 Shall I not punish them for this?
says the LORD;
shall I not take vengeance
on such a people?

30 An appalling thing, an outrage,
has appeared in this land:

31 prophets prophesy lies and priests go hand
in hand with them,
and my people love to have it so.
How will you fare at the end of it all?

Warning to Jerusalem

6 Save yourselves, men of Benjamin,
come out of Jerusalem,
blow the trumpet in Tekoa,
fire the beacon on Beth-hakkerem,
for calamity looms from the north
and great disaster.

2 Zion, delightful and lovely:
her end is near—

she to whom the shepherds come   3
and bring their flocks with them.
There they pitch their tents all round her,
each grazing his own strip of pasture.
Declare war solemnly against her;   4
come, let us attack her at noon.
Too late! the day declines
and the shadows lengthen.
Come then, let us attack her by night   5
and destroy her palaces.
These are the words of the LORD of Hosts: 6
Cut down the trees of Jerusalem
and raise siege-ramps against her,
the city whose name is Licence,
oppression is rampant in her.
As a well keeps its water fresh,   7
so she keeps her evil fresh.
Violence and outrage echo in her streets;
sickness and wounds stare me in the face.
Learn your lesson, Jerusalem,   8
lest my love for you be torn from my heart,
and I leave you desolate,
a land where no one can live.
These are the words of the LORD of Hosts: 9
Glean the remnant of Israel
like a vine,
pass your hand like a vintager one last time
over the branches.
To whom can I address myself,   10
to whom give solemn warning? Who will
hear me?
Their ears are uncircumcised;
they cannot listen;
they treat the LORD's word as a reproach;
they show no concern with it.
But I am full of the anger of the LORD,   11
I cannot hold it in.
I must pour it out on the children in the
street
and on the young men in their gangs.
Man and wife alike shall be caught in it,
the greybeard and the very old.
Their houses shall be turned over to others, 12
their fields and their women alike.
For I will raise my hand, says the LORD,
against the people of the country.
For all, high and low,   13
are out for ill-gotten gain;
prophets and priests are frauds,
every one of them;
they dress my people's wound, but skin-   14
deep only,
with their saying, 'All is well.'
All well? Nothing is well!
Are they ashamed when they practise their   15
abominations?
Ashamed? Not they!
They can never be put out of countenance.
Therefore they shall fall with a great crash,^l
and be brought to the ground on the day of
my reckoning.
The LORD has said it.

---

k who . . . net: *prob. rdg.; Heb. unintelligible.*   l with a great crash: *or* where they fall *or* among the fallen.

The LORD rejects his people

16 These are the words of the LORD: Stop at the cross-roads; look for the ancient paths; ask, 'Where is the way that leads to what is good?' Then take that way, and you will find rest for yourselves. But they said, 'We 17 will not.' Then I will appoint watchmen to direct you; listen for their trumpet-call. But 18 they said, 'We will not.' Therefore hear, you nations, and take note, all you who witness it, 19 of the plight of this people. Listen, O earth, I bring ruin on them, the harvest of all their scheming; for they have given no thought to my words and have spurned my instruction. 20 What good is it to me if frankincense is brought from Sheba and fragrant spices from distant lands? I will not accept your whole-offerings, your sacrifices do not please me. 21 Therefore these are the words of the LORD:

I will set obstacles before this people
which shall bring them to the ground;
fathers and sons, friends and neighbours
shall all perish together.

Terror let loose

22 These are the words of the LORD:

See, a people is coming from a northern land,
a great nation rouses itself from earth's
farthest corners.
23 They come with bow and sabre, cruel men
and pitiless,
bestriding their horses, they sound like the
thunder of the sea,
they are like men arrayed for battle against
you, Zion.
24 We have heard tell of them
and our hands hang limp,
agony grips us, the anguish of a woman in
labour.
25 Do not go out into the country,
do not walk by the high road;
for the foe, sword in hand,
is a terror let loose.
26 Daughter of my people, wrap yourself in
sackcloth,
sprinkle ashes over yourself, wail bitterly,
as one who mourns an only son;
in an instant shall the marauder be upon us.
27 I have appointed you an assayer of my
people;
you will know how to test them and will
assay their conduct;
28 arch-rebels all of them,
mischief-makers, corrupt to a man.
29 The bellows puff and blow, the furnace
glows;
in vain does the refiner smelt the ore,
lead, copper and iron[m] are not separated out.
30 Call them spurious silver;
for the LORD has spurned them.

Proclamation in the temple

This word came from the LORD to Jeremiah. 7 Stand at the gate of the LORD's house and 2 there make your proclamation: Listen to the words of the LORD, all you men of Judah who come in through these gates to worship him. These are the words of the LORD of Hosts the 3 God of Israel: Mend your ways and your doings, that I may let you live in this place. You keep saying, 'This place[n] is the temple 4 of the LORD, the temple of the LORD, the temple of the LORD!' This catchword of yours is a lie; put no trust in it. Mend your 5 ways and your doings, deal fairly with one another, do not oppress the alien, the orphan, 6 and the widow, shed no innocent blood in this place, do not run after other gods to your own ruin. Then will I let you live in this 7 place, in the land which I gave long ago to your forefathers for all time. You gain no-8 thing by putting your trust in this lie. You 9 steal, you murder, you commit adultery and perjury, you burn sacrifices to Baal, you run after other gods whom you have not known; then you come and stand before me in this 10 house, which bears my name, and say, 'We are safe'; safe, you think, to indulge in all these abominations. Do you think that this 11 house, this house which bears my name, is a robbers' cave? I myself have seen all this, says the LORD. Go to my shrine at Shiloh, 12 which once I made a dwelling for my Name, and see what I did to it because of the wickedness of my people Israel. And now 13 you have done all these things, says the LORD; though I took pains to speak to you, you did not listen, and though I called, you gave no answer. Therefore what I did to 14 Shiloh I will do to this house which bears my name, the house in which you put your trust, the place I gave to you and your fore-fathers; I will fling you away out of my 15 sight, as I flung away all your kinsfolk, the whole brood of Ephraim.

No prayer for Jerusalem

Offer up no prayer, Jeremiah, for this people, 16 raise no plea or prayer on their behalf, and do not intercede with me; for I will not listen to you. Do you not see what is going on in 17 the cities of Judah and in the streets of Jeru-salem? Children are gathering wood, fathers 18 lighting fires, women kneading dough to make crescent-cakes in honour of the queen of heaven; and drink-offerings are poured out to other gods than me—all to provoke and hurt me. But is it I, says the LORD, whom 19 they hurt? No; it is themselves, covering their own selves with shame. Therefore, 20 says the Lord GOD, my anger and my fury

m copper and iron: *transposed from after* mischief-makers *in verse 28.*   n This place: *prob. rdg.; Heb.* Those.

shall fall on this place, on man and beast, on trees and crops, and it shall burn unquenched.

Israel's stubbornness

21 These are the words of the LORD of Hosts the God of Israel: Add whole-offerings to 22 sacrifices and eat the flesh if you will. But when I brought your forefathers out of Egypt, I gave them no commands about whole-offering and sacrifice; I said not a 23 word about them. What I did command them was this: If you obey me, I will be your God and you shall be my people. You must conform to all my commands, if you would 24 prosper. But they did not listen; they paid no heed, and persisted in disobedience with evil and stubborn hearts; they looked back-25 wards and not forwards, from the day when your forefathers left Egypt until now. I took pains to send to them all my servants the 26 prophets; they did not listen to me, they paid no heed, but were obstinate and proved even 27 more wicked than their forefathers. When you tell them this, they will not listen to you; 28 if you call them, they will not answer. Then you shall say to them, This is the nation that did not obey the LORD its God nor accept correction; truth has perished, it is heard no more on their lips.

Idolatrous practices

29 O Jerusalem, cut off your hair,
the symbol of your dedication, and throw it away;
raise up a lament on the high bare places.

For the LORD has spurned the generation which has roused his wrath, and has aban-30 doned them. For the men of Judah have done what is wrong in my eyes, says the LORD. They have defiled with their loathsome idols 31 the house that bears my name, they have built a shrine of Topheth in the Valley of Ben-hinnom, at which to burn their sons and daughters; that was no command of mine, 32 nor did it ever enter my thought. Therefore a time is coming, says the LORD, when it shall no longer be called Topheth or the Valley of Ben-hinnom, but the Valley of Slaughter; for the dead shall be buried in Topheth be-33 cause there is no room elsewhere. So the bodies of this people shall become food for the birds of the air and the wild beasts, and there will be no one to scare them away. 34 From the cities of Judah and the streets of Jerusalem I will banish all sounds of joy and gladness, the voice of the bridegroom and the bride; for the land shall become desert.

At that time, says the LORD, men shall **8** bring out from their graves the bones of the kings of Judah, of the officers, priests, and prophets, and of all who lived in Jerusalem. They shall expose them to the sun, the moon, 2 and all the host of heaven, whom they loved and served and adored, to whom they resorted and bowed in worship. Those bones shall not be gathered up nor buried but shall become dung on the ground. All the sur-3 vivors of this wicked race, wherever I have banished them, would rather die than live. This is the very word of the LORD of Hosts.

Headlong to ruin

You shall say to them, These are the words 4 of the LORD:
If men fall, can they not also rise?
If a man breaks away, can he not return?
Then why are this people so wayward, 5
incurable in their waywardness?
Why have they clung to their treachery
and refused to return to their obedience?
I have listened to them 6
and heard not one word of truth,
not one sinner crying remorsefully,
'Oh, what have I done?'
Each one breaks away*o* in headlong career
as a war-horse plunges in battle.

The stork in the sky 7
knows the time to migrate,
the dove and the swift and the wryneck
know the season of return;
but my people do not know the ordinances
of the LORD.
How can you say, 'We are wise, 8
we have the law of the LORD',
when scribes with their lying pens
have falsified it?
The wise are put to shame, they are dismayed 9
and have lost their wits.
They have spurned the word of the LORD,
and what sort of wisdom is theirs?
Therefore will I give their wives to other men 10
and their lands to new owners.
For all, high and low,
are out for ill-gotten gain;
prophets and priests are frauds,
every one of them;
they dress my people's wound, but skin-11
deep only,
with their saying, 'All is well.'
All well? Nothing is well!
Are they ashamed when they practise their 12
abominations?
Ashamed? Not they!
They can never be put out of countenance.
Therefore they shall fall with a great crash,*p*
and be brought to the ground on the day of
my reckoning.
The LORD has said it.

---

o breaks away: *or* is wayward.   *p* with a great crash: *or* where they fall *or* among the fallen.

13 I would gather their harvest, says the
    LORD,
  but there are no grapes on the vine,
  no figs on the fig-tree;
  even their leaves are withered.
14 Why do we sit idle? Up, all of you together,
    let us go into our walled cities and there meet
    our doom.
  For the LORD our God has struck us down,
  he has given us a draught of bitter poison;
  for we have sinned against the LORD.
15 Can we hope to prosper when nothing
    goes well?
  Can we hope for respite when the terror
    falls suddenly?
16 The snorting of his horses is heard from
    Dan;
  at the neighing of his stallions the whole land
    trembles.
  The enemy come; they devour the land and
    all its store,
  city and citizens alike.
17 Beware, I am sending snakes against you,
  vipers, such as no man can charm,
  and they shall bite you.
  This is the very word of the LORD.

The prophet's lament

18 How can I bear my sorrow?*q*
  I am sick at heart.
19 Hark, the cry of my people
  from a distant land:
  'Is the LORD not in Zion?
  Is her King no longer there?'
  Why do they provoke me with their images
  and foreign gods?
20 Harvest is past, summer is over,
  and we are not saved.
21 I am wounded at the sight of my people's
    wound;
  I go like a mourner, overcome with horror;
22 Is there no balm in Gilead,
  no physician there?
  Why has no new skin grown over their
    wound?

Deceit and disloyalty

9 Would that my head were all water,
  my eyes a fountain of tears,
  that I might weep day and night
  for my people's dead!

2 Oh that I could find in the wilderness a
    shelter by the wayside,
  that I might leave my people and depart!
  Adulterers are they all, a mob of traitors.
3 The tongue is their weapon, a bow ready
    bent.
  Lying, not truth, is master in the land.

They run from one sin to another,
  and for me they care nothing.
  This is the very word of the LORD.

Be on your guard, each man against his 4
    friend;
  put no trust even in a brother.
  Brother supplants brother,*r*
  and friend slanders friend.
  They make game of their friends   5
  but never speak the truth;
  they have trained their tongues to lies;
  deep in their sin, they cannot retrace their
    steps.
Wrong follows wrong, deceit follows deceit; 6
  they refuse to acknowledge me.
  This is the very word of the LORD.
Therefore these are the words of the LORD 7
    of Hosts:
  I am their refiner and will assay them.
  How can I disregard my people?
  Their tongue is a cruel arrow,   8
  their mouths speak lies.
  One speaks amicably to another,
  while inwardly he plans a trap for him.
  Shall I not punish them for this?   9
  says the LORD;
  shall I not take vengeance
  on such a people?

Over the mountains will I raise weeping and 10
    wailing,
  and over the desert pastures will I chant
    a dirge.
  They are scorched and untrodden,
  they hear no lowing of cattle;
  birds of the air and beasts have fled and are
    gone.

Devastation of Judah

I will make Jerusalem a heap of ruins, a 11
    haunt of wolves,
  and the cities of Judah an unpeopled waste.

What man is wise enough to understand 12
this, to understand what the LORD has said
and to proclaim it? Why has the land become
a dead land, scorched like the desert and untrodden? The LORD said, It is because they 13
forsook my law which I set before them;
they neither obeyed me nor conformed to it.
They followed the promptings of their own 14
stubborn hearts, they followed the Baalim
as their forefathers had taught them. There- 15
fore these are the words of the LORD of
Hosts the God of Israel: I will feed this
people with wormwood and give them bitter
poison to drink. I will scatter them among 16
nations whom neither they nor their forefathers have known; I will harry them with
the sword until I have made an end of them.

---

q How . . . sorrow?: prob. rdg.; Heb. unintelligible.
supplanter like Jacob (cp. Gen. 27. 35 and note).

r Brother supplants brother: or Every brother is a

Lamentation in Zion

17 These are the words of the LORD of Hosts:

Summon the wailing women to come,
  send for the women skilled in keening
18 to come quickly and raise a lament for us,
  that our eyes may run with tears
  and our eyelids be wet with weeping.
19 Hark, hark, lamentation is heard in Zion:
  How fearful is our ruin! How great our
    shame!
We have left our lands, our houses have been
    pulled down.
20 Listen, you women, to the words of the
    LORD,
  that your ears may catch what he says.
  Teach your daughters the lament,
  let them teach one another this dirge:
21 Death has climbed in through our win-
    dows,
  it has entered our palaces,
  it sweeps off the children in the open air
  and drives young men from the streets.

22 This is the word of the LORD:

The corpses of men shall fall and lie like
    dung in the fields,
  like swathes behind the reaper, but no one
    shall gather them.

If a man must boast . . .

23 These are the words of the LORD:

Let not the wise man boast of his wis-
    dom
  nor the valiant of his valour;
  let not the rich man boast of his riches;
24 but if any man would boast, let him boast
    of this,
  that he understands and knows me.
For I am the LORD, I show unfailing love,
  I do justice and right upon the earth;
  for on these I have set my heart.
  This is the very word of the LORD.

The time is coming, says the LORD, when 25
I will punish all the circumcised, Egypt and 26
Judah, Edom and Ammon, Moab, and all
who haunt the fringes of the desert;[s] for all
alike, the nations and Israel, are uncircumcised in heart.

Lifeless gods and the living God

Listen, Israel, to this word that the LORD **10**
has spoken against you:

Do not fall into the ways of the nations, 2
  do not be awed by signs in the heavens;
  it is the nations who go in awe of these.
  For the carved images of the nations are 3
    a sham,
  they are nothing but timber cut from the
    forest,
  worked with his chisel by a craftsman;
  he adorns it with silver and gold, 4
fastening them on with hammer and nails
  so that they do not fall apart.
They can no more speak than a scarecrow in 5
    a plot of cucumbers;
  they must be carried, for they cannot walk.
  Do not be afraid of them: they can do no
    harm,
  and they have no power to do good.
  Where can one be found like thee, O LORD? 6
Great thou art and great the might of thy
    name.
Who shall not fear thee, king of the nations? 7
  for fear is thy fitting tribute.
Where among the wisest of the nations and
    all their royalty
  can one be found like thee?
  They are fools and blockheads one and all, 8
  learning their nonsense from a log of
    wood.
The beaten silver is brought from Tarshish 9
  and the gold from Ophir;
  all are the work of craftsmen and gold-
    smiths.
  They are draped in violet and purple,
  all the work of skilled men.

---

s who . . . desert: *or* the dwellers in the desert who clip the hair on their temples.

10 But the LORD is God in truth,
   a living god, an eternal king.
   The earth quakes under his wrath,
   nations cannot endure his fury.

11 [You shall say this to them: The gods who
   did not make heaven and earth shall perish
   from the earth and from under these
   heavens.]

12 *t* God made the earth by his power,
   fixed the world in place by his wisdom,
   unfurled the skies by his understanding.

13 At the thunder of his voice the waters in
      heaven are amazed; *u*
   he brings up the mist from the ends of the
      earth,
   he opens rifts *v* for the rain
   and brings the wind out of his storehouses.

14 All men are brutish and ignorant;
   every goldsmith is discredited by his idol;
   for the figures he casts are a sham,
   there is no breath in them.

15 They are worth nothing, mere mockeries,
   which perish when their day of reckoning
      comes.

16 God, Jacob's creator, is not like these;
   for he is the maker of all.
   Israel is the people he claims as his own;
   the LORD of Hosts is his name.

Exile at hand

17 Put your goods together and carry them
      out of the country,
   living as you are under siege.

18 For these are the words of the LORD:
   This time I will uproot
   the whole population of the land,
   and I will press them hard and squeeze
      them dry.

19 O the pain of my wounds!
   Cruel are the blows I suffer.
   But this is my plight, I said, and I must
      endure it.

20 My home is ruined, my tent-ropes all
      severed,
   my sons have left me and are gone,
   there is no one to pitch my tent again,
   no one to put up its curtains.

21 The shepherds of the people are mere
      brutes;
   they never consult the LORD,
   and so they do not prosper,
   and all their flocks at pasture are scattered.

22 Hark, a rumour comes flying,
      then a mounting uproar from the land of
         the north,
   an army to make Judah's cities desolate, a
      haunt of wolves.

I know, O LORD,   23
   that man's ways are not of his own choos-
      ing;
   nor is it for a man to determine his course
      in life.
Correct us, O LORD, but with justice, not   24
      in anger,
   lest thou bring us almost to nothing.
Pour out thy fury on nations   25
   that have not acknowledged thee,
   on tribes that have not invoked thee by
      name;
   for they have devoured Jacob and made an
      end of him
   and have left his home a waste.

The covenant broken

The word which came to Jeremiah from the **11**
LORD: Listen to the terms of this covenant 2
and repeat them to the men of Judah and the
inhabitants of Jerusalem. Tell them, These 3
are the words of the LORD the God of Israel:
A curse on the man who does not observe
the terms of this covenant by which I bound 4
your forefathers when I brought them out
of Egypt, from the smelting-furnace. I said,
If you obey me and do all that I tell you,
you shall become my people and I will become your God. And I will thus make good 5
the oath I swore to your forefathers, that
I would give them a land flowing with milk
and honey, the land you now possess.
I answered, 'Amen, LORD.' Then the LORD 6
said: Proclaim all these terms in the cities of
Judah and in the streets of Jerusalem. Say,
Listen to the terms of this covenant and
carry them out. I have protested to your 7
forefathers since I brought them out of
Egypt, till this day; I took pains to warn
them: Obey me, I said. But they did not 8
obey; they paid no attention to me, but each
followed the promptings of his own stubborn and wicked heart. So I brought on
them all the penalties laid down in this
covenant by which I had bound them, whose
terms they did not observe.

The LORD said to me, The men of Judah 9
and the inhabitants of Jerusalem have
entered into a conspiracy: they have gone 10
back to the sins of their earliest forefathers
and refused to listen to me. They have
followed other gods and worshipped them;
Israel and Judah have broken the covenant
which I made with their fathers. Therefore 11
these are the words of the LORD: I now bring
on them disaster from which they cannot
escape; though they cry to me for help I will
not listen. The inhabitants of the cities of 12
Judah and of Jerusalem may go and cry for
help to the gods to whom they have burnt

---

t Verses 12–16: cp. 51. 15–19.
tumult of waters in heaven.   *u At the thunder . . . amazed: prob. rdg.; Heb. At the sound of his giving*
                                           v rifts: prob. rdg.; Heb. lightnings.

sacrifices; they will not save them in the
13 hour of disaster. For you, Judah, have as
many gods as you have towns; you have set
up as many altars to burn sacrifices to Baal
14 as there are streets in Jerusalem. So offer
up no prayer for this people; raise no cry or
prayer on their behalf, for I will not listen
when they call to me in the hour of disaster.

15 What right has my beloved in my house
     with her shameless ways?
Can the flesh of fat offerings on the altar
     ward off the disaster that threatens you?
16 Once the LORD called you an olive-tree,
     leafy and fair;
but now with a great roaring noise
     you will feel sharp anguish;*w*
fire sets its leaves alight
     and consumes*x* its branches.

17   The LORD of Hosts who planted you has
threatened you with disaster, because of the
harm Israel and Judah brought on themselves when they provoked me to anger by
burning sacrifices to Baal.

Plots to kill Jeremiah

18 It was the LORD who showed me, and so I
knew; he opened my eyes to what they were
19 doing. I had been like a sheep led obedient
to the slaughter; I did not know that they
were hatching plots against me and saying,
'Let us cut down the tree while the sap is in
it; let us destroy him out of the living, so
that his very name shall be forgotten.'
20 O LORD of Hosts who art a righteous judge,
     testing the heart and mind,
I have committed my cause to thee;
     let me see thy vengeance upon them.

21 Therefore these are the words of the LORD
about the men of Anathoth who seek to take
my life, and say, 'Prophesy no more in the
22 name of the LORD or we will kill you'—these
are his words: I will punish them: their young
men shall die by the sword, their sons and
23 daughters shall die by famine. Not one of
them shall survive; for in the year of their
reckoning I will bring ruin on the men of
Anathoth.

The prophet's problem

12 O LORD, I will dispute with thee, for thou
     art just;
yes, I will plead my case before thee.
Why do the wicked prosper
     and traitors live at ease?
2   Thou hast planted them and their roots
         strike deep,
     they grow up and bear fruit.
     Thou art ever on their lips,
     yet far from their hearts.

But thou knowest me, O LORD, thou seest 3
     me;
thou dost test my devotion to thyself.
Drag them away like sheep to the shambles;
     set them apart for the day of slaughter.

How long must the country lie parched 4
     and its green grass wither?
No birds and beasts are left, because its
     people are so wicked,
because they say, 'God will not see what
     we are doing.'

If you have raced with men and the runners 5
     have worn you down,
how then can you hope to vie with horses?
If you fall headlong in easy country,
     how will you fare in Jordan's dense
     thickets?
All men, your brothers and kinsmen, are 6
     traitors to you,
     they are in full cry after you;
trust them not, for all the fine words they
     give you.

I have forsaken the house of Israel, 7
I have cast off my own people.
I have given my beloved into the power of
     her foes.
My own people have turned on me like a 8
     lion from the scrub,
roaring against me; therefore I hate them.
     Is this land of mine a hyena's lair, 9
     with birds of prey hovering all around it?
Come, you wild beasts; come, all of you,
     flock to the feast.

Many shepherds have ravaged my vineyard 10
     and trampled down my field,
they have made my pleasant field a desolate
     wilderness,
made it a waste land, waste and waterless, 11
     to my sorrow.
The whole land is waste, and no one cares.

Plunderers have swarmed across the high 12
bare places in the wilderness, a sword of the
LORD devouring the land from end to end;
no creature can find peace.

Men sow wheat and reap thistles; 13
     they sift but get no grain.
They are disappointed of their*y* harvest
because of the anger of the LORD.

These are the words of the LORD about 14
all those evil neighbours who are laying
hands on the land which I gave to my people
Israel as their patrimony: I will uproot them
from that*z* soil. Yet, if they will learn the 16*a*
ways of my people, swearing by my name,
'By the life of the LORD', as they taught my
people to swear by the Baal, they shall form
families among my people. But if they will 17

---

w you will feel sharp anguish: *transposed from end of verse 15.*
consume.   *y* *Prob. rdg.; Heb.* your.   *z* *Prob. rdg.; Heb.* their.   *x* consumes: *prob. rdg.; Heb. they*
15 transposed to follow destroy them *in verse 17.*   *a* *The rest of verse 14 and verse*

The wine-jars

You shall say this to them: These are the 12 words of the LORD the God of Israel: Wine-jars should be filled with wine. They will answer, 'We know quite well that wine-jars should be filled with wine.' Then you shall 13 say to them, These are the words of the LORD: I will fill all the inhabitants of this land with wine until they are drunk—kings of David's line who sit on his throne, priests, prophets, and all who live in Jerusalem. I will dash them to pieces one against 14 another, fathers and sons alike, says the LORD, I will show them no compassion or pity or tenderness; nor refrain from destroying them.[d]

The LORD appeals to Judah

Hear and attend. Be not too proud to 15
  listen,
for it is the LORD who speaks.
Ascribe glory to the LORD your God 16
  before the darkness falls,
before your feet stumble
  on the twilit hill-sides,
before he turns the light you look for
  to deep gloom and thick darkness.
If in those depths of gloom you will not 17
  listen,
then for very anguish I can only weep and
  shed tears,[e]
my eyes must stream with tears;
for the LORD's flock is carried away into
  captivity.
Say to the king and the queen mother:[f] 18
Down, take a humble seat,
for your proud crowns are fallen from your
  heads.
Your cities in the Negeb are besieged, 19
and no one can relieve them;
all Judah has been swept into exile,
  swept clean away.
Lift up your eyes and see 20
those who are coming from the north.
Where is the flock that was entrusted to
  you,
the flock you were so proud of?
What will you say when you suffer 21
because your leaders[g] cannot be found,
though it was you who trained them
  to be your head?
Will not pangs seize you,
like the pangs of a woman in labour,
when you wonder, 22
'Why has this come upon me?'
For your many sins your skirts are torn
  off you,
your limbs uncovered.

not listen, I will uproot that people, uproot and destroy them. Also I will uproot Judah 15 from among them; but after I have uprooted them, I will have pity on them again and will bring each man back to his patrimony and his land. This is the very word of the LORD.

The linen girdle

13 These were the words of the LORD to me: Go and buy yourself a linen girdle and put it round your waist, but do not let it come 2 near water. So I bought it as the LORD had 3 told me and put it round my waist. The 4 LORD spoke to me a second time: Take the girdle which you bought and put round your waist; go at once to Perath and hide 5 it in a crevice among the rocks. So I went and hid the girdle at[b] Perath, as the LORD had 6 told me. After a long time the LORD said to me: Go at once to Perath and fetch back the 7 girdle which I told you to hide there. So I went to Perath and looked for the place where I had hidden it, but when I picked it up, I saw that it was spoilt, and no good for 8 9 anything. Again the LORD spoke to me and these were his words: Thus will I spoil the gross pride of Judah, the gross pride of 10 Jerusalem. This wicked nation has refused to listen to my words; they have followed other gods, serving them and bowing down to them. So it shall be[c] like this girdle, no 11 good for anything. For, just as a girdle is bound close to a man's waist, so I bound all Israel and all Judah to myself, says the LORD, so that they should become my people to win a name for me, and praise and glory; but they did not listen.

b Or by.   *c Prob. rdg.; Heb.* And let it be.
e If . . . shed tears: *or* If you will not listen to this, for very anguish I must weep in secret.   *f Or* queen.
d nor refrain . . . them: *or* so corrupt are they.
g leaders: *transposed from next line.*

23   Can the Nubian change his skin,
      or the leopard its spots?
      And you? Can you do good,
      you who are schooled in evil?
24   Therefore I will scatter you^h like chaff
      driven by the desert wind.
25   This is your lot, the portion of the rebel,
      measured out by me, says the LORD,
      because you have forsaken me
      and trusted in false gods.
26   So I myself have stripped off your skirts
      and laid bare your shame.
27   Your adulteries, your lustful neighing,
      your wanton lewdness, are an offence to
      me.^i
      On the hills and in the open country
      I have seen your foul deeds.
      Alas, Jerusalem, unclean that you are!
      How long, how long will you delay?^j

Drought

14 This came to Jeremiah as the word of the
      LORD concerning the drought:

2   Judah droops, her cities languish,
      her men sink to the ground;
      Jerusalem's cry goes up.
3   Their flock-masters send their boys for
      water;
      they come to the pools but find no water
      there.
      Back they go, with empty vessels;
4   the produce^k of the land has failed,
      because there is no rain.
      The farmers' hopes are wrecked,
      they uncover their heads for grief.
5   The hind calves in the open country
      and forsakes her young
      because there is no grass;
6   for lack of herbage, wild asses stand on the
      high bare places
      and snuff the wind for moisture,
      as wolves do, and their eyes begin to fail.
7   Though our sins testify against us,
      yet act,^l O LORD, for thy own name's sake.
      Our disloyalties indeed are many; we have
      sinned against thee.
8   O hope of Israel, their saviour in time of
      trouble,
      must thou be a stranger in the land,
      a traveller pitching his tent for a night?

9   Must thou be like a man suddenly over-
      come,
      like a man powerless to save himself?
      Thou art in our midst, O LORD,
      and thou hast named us thine; do not forsake
      us.

Jeremiah pleads with the LORD

10   The LORD speaks thus of this people: They
love to stray from my ways, they wander
where they will. Therefore he has no more
pleasure in them; he remembers their guilt
now, and punishes their sins. Then the LORD 11
said to me, Do not pray for the well-being
of this people. When they fast, I will not 12
listen to their cry; when they sacrifice whole-
offering and grain-offering, I will not accept
them. I will make an end of them with sword,
with famine and pestilence. But I said, 13
O Lord GOD, the prophets tell them that
they shall see no sword and suffer no famine;
for thou wilt give them lasting prosperity in
this place. The LORD answered me, The 14
prophets are prophesying lies in my name.
I have not sent them; I have given them no
charge; I have not spoken to them. The
prophets offer them false visions, worthless
augury, and their own deluding fancies.
Therefore these are the words of the LORD 15
about the prophets who, though not sent
by me, prophesy in my name and say that
neither sword nor famine shall touch this
land: By sword and by famine shall those
prophets meet their end. The people to 16
whom they prophesy shall be flung out into
the streets of Jerusalem, victims of famine
and sword; they, their wives, their sons, and
their daughters, with no one to bury them:
I will pour down upon them the evil they
deserve.

      So this is what you shall say to them: 17
      Let my eyes stream with tears,
      ceaselessly, day and night.
      For the virgin daughter of my people
      has been broken in pieces,
      struck by a cruel blow.
      If I go out into the country,   18
      I see men slain by the sword;
      if I enter the city, I see the ravages of
      famine;
      prophet and priest alike
      go begging round the land and are never
      at rest.
      Hast thou spurned Judah utterly?   19
      Dost thou loathe Zion?
      Why hast thou wounded us, and there is no
      remedy;
      why let us hope for better days, and we
      find nothing good,
      for a time of healing, and all is disaster?

---

h Prob. rdg.; Heb. them.   *i* an offence to me (*Heb.* you): *transposed from verse 26.*   *j* How . . .
delay?: *prob. rdg.; Heb.* unintelligible.   *k* the produce: *prob. rdg.; Heb.* obscure.   *l Or* turn away.

20 We acknowledge our wickedness,
     the guilt of our forefathers;
   O LORD, we have sinned against thee.
21 Do not despise the place where thy name
     dwells
   nor bring contempt on the throne of thy
     glory.
   Remember thy covenant with us and do
     not make it void.
22 Can any of the false gods of the nations
     give rain?
   Or do the heavens send showers of them-
     selves?
   Art thou not God, O LORD,
   that we may hope in thee?
   It is thou only who doest*m* all these things.

The LORD answers Jeremiah

15 The LORD said to me, Even if Moses and
Samuel stood before me, I would not be
moved to pity this people. Banish them from
2 my presence; let them be gone. When they
ask where they are to go, you shall say to
them, These are the words of the LORD:
     Those who are for death shall go to their
       death,
     and those for the sword to the sword;
     those who are for famine to famine,
     and those for captivity to captivity.
3   Four kinds of doom do I ordain for them,
says the LORD: the sword to kill, dogs to
tear, birds of prey from the skies and beasts
4 from their lairs to devour and destroy. I
will make them repugnant to all the kingdoms of the earth, because of the crimes of
Manasseh son of Hezekiah, king of Judah,
in Jerusalem.
5   Who will take pity on you, Jerusalem,
     who will offer you consolation?
     Who will turn aside to wish you well?
6 You cast me off, says the LORD,
     you turned your backs on me.
   So I stretched out my hand and ruined
     you;
     I was weary of relenting.
7   I winnowed them and scattered them
       through the cities of the land;
     I brought bereavement on them, I de-
       stroyed my people,
     for they would not abandon their ways.
8   I made widows among them more in
       number
     than the sands of the sea;
     I brought upon them a horde of raiders*n*
       to plunder at high noon.
     I made the terror of invasion fall upon
       them
     all in a moment.

The mother of seven sons grew faint,   9
  she sank into a swoon;
her light was quenched while it was yet
  day;
she was left humbled and shamed.
All the remnant I gave to perish by the
  sword
at the hand of their enemies.
This is the very word of the LORD.

The LORD's care for Jeremiah

Alas, alas, my mother, that you ever gave   10
  me birth!
a man doomed to strife, with the whole
  world against me.
I have borrowed from no one, I have lent
  to no one,
yet all men abuse me.

The LORD answered,   11

But I will greatly strengthen you;
in time of distress and in time of disaster
I will bring the enemy to your feet.
Can iron break steel from the north?*o*   12
LORD, thou knowest;   15
remember me, LORD, and come to visit
  me,
take vengeance for me on my persecutors.
Be patient with me and take me not
  away,
see what reproaches I endure for thy sake.
I have to suffer those who despise thy   16
  words,
but thy word is joy and happiness to me,
for thou hast named me thine,
O LORD, God of Hosts.
I have never kept company with any gang   17
  of roisterers,
or made merry with them;
because I felt thy hand upon me I have sat
  alone;
for thou hast filled me with indignation.
Why then is my pain unending,   18
my wound desperate and incurable?
Thou art to me like a brook that is not to be
  trusted,
whose waters fail.

This was the LORD's answer: 19

If you will turn back to me, I will take you
  back
and you shall stand before me.
If you choose noble utterance and reject
  the base,
you shall be my spokesman.
This people will turn again to you,
but you will not turn to them.

---

m Or madest.   *n* I brought . . . raiders: *prob. rdg.; Heb. obscure.*   *o Prob. rdg.; Heb. adds* and
bronze. *Heb. also adds* (13) I will give away your wealth as spoil, and your treasure for no payment, because of
your sin throughout your country. (14) I will make your enemies pass through a land you do not know; for my
anger is a blazing fire and it shall burn for ever (*cp. 17. 3, 4*).

20 To withstand them I will make you impreg-
      nable,
    a wall of bronze.
  They will attack you but they will not prevail,
      for I am with you to deliver you
      and save you, says the LORD;
21   I will deliver you from the wicked,
      I will rescue you from the ruthless.

Exile and after

16 The word of the LORD came to me: You
1 2 shall not marry a wife; you shall have neither
3 son nor daughter in this place. For these are
  the words of the LORD concerning sons and
  daughters born in this place, the mothers
  who bear them and the fathers who beget
4 them in this land: When men die, struck
  down by deadly ulcers, there shall be no
  wailing for them and no burial; they shall
  be like dung lying upon the ground. When
  men perish by sword or famine, their
  corpses shall become food for birds and for
  beasts.
5   For these are the words of the LORD: Enter
  no house where there is a mourning-feast;
  do not go in to wail or to bring comfort,
  for I have withdrawn my peace from this
  people, says the LORD, my love and affec-
6 tion. High and low shall die in this land,
  but there shall be no burial, no wailing for
  them; no one shall gash himself, or shave
7 his head. No one shall give the mourner a
  portion of bread to console him for the
  dead, nor give him the cup of consolation,
8 even for his father or mother. Nor shall you
  enter a house where there is feasting, to sit
9 eating and drinking there. For these are
  the words of the LORD of Hosts, the God of
  Israel: In your own days, in the sight of you
  all, and in this very place, I will silence all
  sounds of joy and gladness, and the voice
  of bridegroom and bride.
10   When you tell this people all these things
  they will ask you, 'Why has the LORD
  decreed that this great disaster is to come
  upon us? What wrong have we done? What
  sin have we committed against the LORD our
11 God?' You shall answer, Because your forefathers forsook me, says the LORD, and followed other gods, serving them and bowing
  down to them. They forsook me and did
12 not keep my law. And you yourselves have
  done worse than your forefathers; for each
  of you follows the promptings of his wicked
  and stubborn heart instead of obeying me.
13 So I will fling you headlong out of this land
  into a country unknown to you and to your
  forefathers; there you can serve other gods
  day and night, for I will show you no favour.
14 Therefore, says the LORD, the time is coming
  when men shall no longer swear, 'By the life

of the LORD who brought the Israelites up
from Egypt', but, 'By the life of the LORD 15
who brought the Israelites back from a
northern land and from all the lands to
which he had dispersed them'; and I will
bring them back to the soil which I gave to
their forefathers.
  I will send for many fishermen, says the 16
LORD, and they shall fish for them. After
that I will send for many hunters, and they
shall hunt them out from every mountain
and hill and from the crevices in the rocks.
For my eyes are on all their ways; they are 17
not hidden from my sight, nor is their
wrongdoing concealed from me. I will first 18
make them pay in full*p* for the wrong they
have done and the sin they have committed
by defiling with the dead lumber of their
idols the land which belongs to me, and by
filling it with their abominations.

  O LORD, my strength and my stronghold, 19
    my refuge in time of trouble,
    to thee shall the nations come
    from the ends of the earth and say,
    Our forefathers inherited only a sham,
    an idol vain and useless.
Can man make gods for himself?   20
    They would be no gods.
    Therefore I am teaching them,   21
    once for all will I teach them
    my power and my might,
    and they shall learn that my name is the
      LORD.

Judah's sin recorded

The sin of Judah is recorded with an iron **17**
tool, engraved on the tablet of their heart
with a point of adamant and carved on the
horns of their altars to bear witness against 2
them.*q* Their altars and their sacred poles
stand by every spreading tree, on the heights

---

p in full: *or* double.   *q* to bear . . . them: *prob. rdg.; Heb.* as their sons remember.

3 and the hills in the mountain country. I will give away your wealth as spoil, and all your treasure for no payment,[r] because of your[s] sin throughout your country. You will lose possession[t] of the patrimony which I gave you. I will make you serve your enemies as slaves in a land you do not know; for my anger is a blazing fire[u] and it shall burn for ever.

A curse and a blessing

5 These are the words of the LORD:

A curse on the man who trusts in man
and leans for support on human kind,
while his heart is far from the LORD!
6 He shall be like a juniper in the desert;
when good comes he shall not see it.
He shall dwell among the rocks in the wilderness,
in a salt land where no man can live.
7 Blessed is the man who trusts in the LORD,
and rests his confidence upon him.
8 He shall be like a tree planted by the waterside,
that stretches its roots along the stream.
When the heat comes it has nothing to fear;
its spreading foliage stays green.
In a year of drought it feels no care,
and does not cease to bear fruit.

The heart is deceitful

9 The heart is the most deceitful of all things,
desperately sick;[v] who can fathom it?
10 I, the LORD, search the mind
and test the heart,
requiting man for his conduct,
and as his deeds deserve.
11 Like a partridge which gathers into its nest
eggs which it has not laid,
so is the man who amasses wealth unjustly.
Before his days are half done he must leave it,
and prove but a fool at the last.

Prayer for deliverance

12 O throne of glory, exalted from the beginning,
the place of our sanctuary,
13 O LORD on whom Israel's hope is fixed,
all who reject thee shall be put to shame;
all in this land who forsake thee shall be humbled,[w]
for they have rejected the fountain of living water.[x]
14 Heal me, O LORD, and I shall be healed,
save me and I shall be saved;
for thou art my praise.

They say to me, 'Where is the word of the 15 LORD?
Let it come if it can!'
It is not the thought of disaster that makes me 16 press after thee;
never did I desire this day of despair.
Thou knowest all that has passed my lips;
it was approved by thee.
Do not become a terror to me; 17
thou art my only refuge on the day of disaster.
May my persecutors be foiled, not I; 18
may they be terrified, not I.
Bring on them the day of disaster;
destroy them, destroy them utterly.

On keeping the sabbath

These were the words of the LORD to me: 19 Go and stand in the Benjamin[y] Gate, through which the kings of Judah go in and out, and in all the gates of Jerusalem. Say, 20 Hear the words of the LORD, you princes of Judah, all you men of Judah, and all you inhabitants of Jerusalem who come in through these gates. These are the words 21 of the LORD: Observe this with care, that you do not carry any load on the sabbath or bring it through the gates of Jerusalem. You shall not bring any load out of your 22 houses or do any work on the sabbath, but you shall keep the sabbath day holy as I commanded your forefathers. Yet they did 23 not obey or pay attention, but obstinately refused to hear or learn their lesson. Now 24 if you will obey me, says the LORD, and refrain from bringing any load through the gates of this city on the sabbath, and keep that day holy by doing no work on it, then 25 kings shall come through the gates of this city, kings[z] who shall sit on David's throne. They shall come riding in chariots or on horseback, escorted by their captains, by the men of Judah and the inhabitants of Jerusalem; and this city shall be inhabited for ever. People shall come from the cities 26 of Judah, the country round Jerusalem, the land of Benjamin, the Shephelah, the hill-country and the Negeb, bringing whole-offerings, sacrifices, grain-offerings, and frankincense, bringing also thank-offerings to the house of the LORD. But if you do not 27 obey me by keeping the sabbath day holy and by not carrying any load as you come through the gates of Jerusalem on the sabbath, then I will set fire to those gates; it shall consume the palaces of Jerusalem and shall not be put out.

r for no payment: *prob. rdg., cp. 15. 13*; *Heb.* your hill-shrines.   s your: *prob. rdg., cp. 15. 13*; *Heb. om.*   t You ... possession: *prob. rdg.*; *Heb. obscure.*   u for ... fire: *prob. rdg., cp. 15. 14*; *Heb.* for you have kindled a fire in my anger.   v the most ... sick: *or* too deceitful for any man.   w humbled: *prob. rdg.*; *Heb.* written.   x *Prob. rdg.*; *Heb. adds* the LORD.   y Benjamin: *prob. rdg.*; *Heb.* sons of the people.   z *Prob. rdg.*; *Heb. adds* and officers.

At the potter's house

18 These are the words which came to Jere-
2 miah from the LORD: Go down at once to
the potter's house, and there I will tell you
3 what I have to say. So I went down to the
potter's house and found him working at
4 the wheel. Now and then a vessel he was
making out of the clay would be spoilt in
his hands, and then he would start again
and mould it into another vessel to his
5 liking. Then the word of the LORD came to
6 me: Can I not deal with you, Israel, says the
LORD, as the potter deals with his clay? You
are clay in my hands like the clay in his,

7 O house of Israel. At any moment I may
threaten to uproot a nation or a kingdom,
8 to pull it down and destroy it. But if the
nation which I have threatened turns back
from its wicked ways, then I shall think
better of the evil I had in mind to bring on
9 it. Or at any moment I may decide to build
10 or to plant a nation or a kingdom. But if
it does evil in my sight and does not obey
me, I shall think better of the good I had in
11 mind for it. Go now and tell the men of
Judah and the inhabitants of Jerusalem that
these are the words of the LORD: I am the
potter; I am preparing evil for you and
perfecting my designs against you. Turn
back, every one of you, from his evil course;
12 mend your ways and your doings. But they
answer, 'Things are past hope. We will do
as we like, and each of us will follow the
promptings of his own wicked and stubborn

heart.' Therefore these are the words of the 13
LORD:

Inquire among the nations: who ever heard
the like of this?
The virgin Israel has done a thing most
horrible.
Will the snow cease to fall on the rocky 14
slopes of Lebanon?
Will the cool rain streaming in torrents ever
fail?
No, but my people have forgotten me; 15
they burn sacrifices to a mere idol,
so they stumble in their paths, the ancient
ways,
and they take to byways and unmade
roads;
their own land they lay waste, 16
and men will jeer at it for ever in contempt.
All who go by will be horror-struck and
shake their heads.
Like a wind from the east 17
I will scatter them before their enemies.
In the hour of their downfall
I will turn my back towards them and not
my face.

Jeremiah prays for vindication

'Come, let us decide what to do with Jere- 18
miah', men say. 'There will still be priests
to guide us, still wise men to advise, still
prophets to proclaim the word. Come, let
us invent some charges against him; let us
pay no attention to his message.'

But do thou, O LORD, pay attention, 19
and hear what my opponents are saying
against me.
Is good to be repaid with evil?[a] 20
Remember how I stood before thee,
pleading on their behalf
to avert thy wrath from them.
Therefore give their sons over to famine, 21
leave them at the mercy of the sword.
Let their women be childless and widowed,
let death carry off their men,
let their young men be cut down in
battle.
Bring raiders upon them without warning, 22
and let screams of terror ring out from
their houses.
For they have dug a pit to catch me
and have hidden snares for my feet.
Well thou knowest, O LORD, 23
all their murderous plots against me.
Do not blot out their wrongdoing
or annul their sin;
when they are brought stumbling into thy
presence,
deal with them on the day of thy anger.

a Prob. rdg.; Heb. adds they have dug a pit for me (*cp. verse 22*).

The broken jar

19 These are the words of the LORD: Go and buy an earthenware jar. Then take with you some of the elders of the people and of the
2 priests, and go out to the Valley of Ben-hinnom, on which the Gate of the Potsherds opens, and there proclaim what I tell you.
3 Say, Hear the word of the LORD, you princes of Judah and inhabitants of Jerusalem. These are the words of the LORD of Hosts the God of Israel: I will bring on this place a disaster which shall ring in the ears of all who hear
4 of it. For they have forsaken me, and treated this place as if it were not mine, burning sacrifices to other gods whom neither they nor their fathers nor the kings of Judah have known, and filling this place with the blood
5 of the innocent. They have built shrines to Baal, where they burn their sons as whole-offerings to Baal. It was no command of mine; I never spoke of it; it never entered
6 my thought. Therefore, says the LORD, the time is coming when this place shall no longer be called Topheth or the Valley of
7 Ben-hinnom, but the Valley of Slaughter. In this place I will shatter the plans of Judah and Jerusalem as a jar is shattered; I will make the people fall by the sword before their enemies, at the hands of those who would kill them, and I will give their corpses
8 to the birds and beasts to devour. I will make this city a scene of horror and contempt, so that every passer-by will be horror-struck and jeer in contempt at the sight of its
9 wounds. I will compel men to eat the flesh of their sons and their daughters; they shall devour one another's flesh in the dire straits to which their enemies and those who would
10 kill them will reduce them in the siege. Then you must shatter the jar before the eyes of
11 the men who have come with you and say to them, These are the words of the LORD of Hosts: Thus will I shatter this people and this city as one shatters an earthen vessel so that it cannot be mended, and the dead shall be buried in Topheth because there is no
12 room elsewhere to bury them. This is what I will do to this place, says the LORD, and to those who live there: I will make this city
13 like Topheth. Because of their defilement, the houses of Jerusalem and those of the kings of Judah shall be like Topheth, every one of the houses on whose roofs men have burnt sacrifices to the host of heaven and poured drink-offerings to other gods.
14 Jeremiah came in from Topheth, where the LORD had sent him to prophesy, and stood in the court of the LORD's house. He
15 said to all the people, These are the words of the LORD of Hosts the God of Israel: I am bringing on this city and on all its

blood-spattered altars every disaster with which I have threatened it, for its people have remained obstinate and refused to listen to me.

Jeremiah arrested and released

When Pashhur son of Immer the priest, the **20** chief officer in the house of the LORD, heard Jeremiah prophesying these things, he had 2 him flogged[b] and put him into the stocks at the Upper Gate of Benjamin, in the house of the LORD. The next morning he released 3 him, and Jeremiah said to him, The LORD has called you not Pashhur but Magor-missabib.[c] For these are the words of the 4 LORD: I will make you a terror to yourself and to all your friends; they shall fall by the sword of the enemy before your very eyes. I will hand over all Judah to the king of Babylon, and he will deport them to Babylon and put them to the sword. I will give all this 5 city's store of wealth and riches and all the treasures of the kings of Judah to their enemies; they shall seize them as spoil and carry them off to Babylon. You, Pashhur, 6 and all your household shall go into captivity and come to Babylon. There shall you die and there shall you be buried, you and all your friends to whom you have been a false prophet.

The prophet's inner conflict

O LORD, thou hast duped me, and I have 7
been thy dupe;
thou hast outwitted me and hast pre-vailed.
I have been made a laughing-stock all the day long,
everyone mocks me.
Whenever I speak I must needs cry out 8
and proclaim violence and destruction.
I am reproached and mocked all the time
for uttering the word of the LORD.
Whenever I said, 'I will call him to mind 9
no more,
nor speak in his name again',
then his word was imprisoned in my body,
like a fire blazing in my heart,
and I was weary with holding it under,
and could endure no more.
For I heard many whispering,[d] 10
'Denounce him! we will denounce him.'
All my friends were on the watch for a false step,
saying, 'Perhaps he may be tricked, then we can catch him
and take our revenge.'

b had him flogged: *or* struck him.   *c That is* Terror let loose.   *d Prob. rdg.; Heb. adds* Terror let loose.

11 But the LORD is on my side, strong and ruthless,
therefore my persecutors shall stumble and
fall powerless.
Bitter shall be their abasement when they
fail,
and their shame shall long be remembered.
12 O LORD of Hosts, thou dost test the
righteous
and search the depths of the heart;
to thee have I committed my cause,
let me see thee take vengeance on them.
13 Sing to the LORD, praise the LORD;
for he rescues the poor from those who
would do them wrong.

14 A curse on the day when I was born!
Be it for ever unblessed,
the day when my mother bore me!
15 A curse on the man who brought word to my
father,
'A child is born to you, a son',
and gladdened his heart!
16 That man shall fare like the cities
which the LORD overthrew without mercy.
He shall hear cries of alarm in the morning
and uproar at noon,
17 because death did not claim me before
birth,
and my mother did not become my grave,
her womb great with me for ever.
18 Why did I come forth from the womb
to know only sorrow and toil,
to end my days in shame?

Life or death

21 The word which came from the LORD to
Jeremiah when King Zedekiah sent to him
Pashhur son of Malchiah and Zephaniah
the priest, son of Maaseiah, with this re-
2 quest: 'Nebuchadrezzar king of Babylon is
making war on us; inquire of the LORD on
our behalf. Perhaps the LORD will perform
a miracle as he has done in past times, so
that Nebuchadrezzar may raise the siege.'
3 But Jeremiah answered them, Tell Zedekiah,
4 these are the words of the LORD the God of
Israel: I will turn back upon you your own
weapons with which you are fighting the
king of Babylon and the Chaldaeans besieging you outside the wall; and I will bring
5 them into the heart of this city. I myself will
fight against you in burning rage and great
fury, with an outstretched hand and a strong
6 arm. I will strike down those who live in
this city, men and cattle alike; they shall die
7 of a great pestilence. After that, says the
LORD, I will take Zedekiah king of Judah,
his courtiers and the people, all in this city
who survive pestilence, sword, and famine,
and hand them over to Nebuchadrezzar the
king of Babylon, to their enemies and those
who would kill them. He shall put them to

the sword and shall show no pity, no mercy
or compassion.
You shall say further to this people, 8
These are the words of the LORD: I offer you
now a choice between the way of life and the
way of death. Whoever remains in this city 9
shall die by sword, by famine, or by pestilence, but whoever goes out to surrender to
the Chaldaeans, who are now besieging you,
shall survive; he shall take home his life, and
nothing more. I have set my face against this 10
city, meaning to do them harm, not good,
says the LORD. It shall be handed over to
the king of Babylon, and he shall burn it to
the ground.

Judah's covenant with the LORD

To the royal house of Judah.
Listen to the word of the LORD: 11
O house of David, these are the words of 12
the LORD:
Administer justice betimes,
rescue the victim from his oppressor,
lest the fire of my fury blaze up and burn unquenched
because of your evil doings.

The LORD says, 13
I am against you who lie in the valley,
you, the rock in the plain,
you who say, 'Who can come down upon
us?
Who can penetrate our lairs?'
I will punish you as you deserve, 14
says the LORD,
I will kindle fire on the heathland around
you,
and it shall consume everything round
about.

These were the words of the LORD: Go **22**
down to the house of the king of Judah and
say this: Listen to the words of the LORD, 2
O king of Judah, you who sit on David's
throne, you and your courtiers and your
people who come in at these gates. These are 3
the words of the LORD: Deal justly and fairly,
rescue the victim from his oppressor, do not
ill-treat or do violence to the alien, the
orphan or the widow, do not shed innocent
blood in this place. If you obey, and only if 4
you obey, kings who sit on David's throne
shall yet come riding through these gates in
chariots and on horses, with their retinue of
courtiers and people. But if you do not 5
listen to my words, then by myself I swear,
says the LORD, this house shall become a
desolate ruin. For these are the words of the 6
LORD about the royal house of Judah:

Though you are dear to me as Gilead
or as the heights of Lebanon,
I swear that I will make you a wilderness,
a land of unpeopled cities.

7   I will dedicate an armed host to fight
against you,
    a ravening horde;
  they shall cut your choicest cedars down
and fling them on the fire.

8   Men of many nations shall pass by this
city and say to one another, 'Why has the
9 LORD done this to such a great city?' The
answer will be, 'Because they forsook their
covenant with the LORD their God; they
worshipped other gods and served them.'

Concerning Shallum

10 Weep not for the dead nor brood over his
    loss.
  Weep rather for him who has gone away,
    for he shall never return,
    never again see the land of his birth.

11   For these are the words of the LORD concerning Shallum son of Josiah, king of
Judah, who succeeded his father on the
throne and has gone away: He shall never
12 return; he shall die in the place of his exile
and never see this land again.

Concerning Jehoiakim

13 Shame on the man who builds his house by
    unjust means
  and completes its roof-chambers by fraud,
  making his countrymen work without
    payment,
  giving them no wage for their labour!
14 Shame on the man who says, 'I will build a
    spacious house
  with airy roof-chambers,
  set windows in it, panel it with cedar
    and paint it with vermilion'!
15   If your cedar is more splendid,
    does that prove you a king?
  Think of your father: he ate and drank,
  dealt justly and fairly; all went well with him.
16   He dispensed justice to the lowly and
    poor;[e]
  did not this show he knew me? says the LORD.
17 But you have no eyes, no thought for any-
    thing but gain,
  set only on the innocent blood you can
    shed,
  on cruel acts of tyranny.

18   Therefore these are the words of the LORD
concerning Jehoiakim son of Josiah, king of
Judah:

  For him no mourner shall say, 'Alas,
    brother, dear brother!'
  no one say, 'Alas, lord and master!'
19 He shall be buried like a dead ass,
    dragged along and flung out
    beyond the gates of Jerusalem.

Concerning Jerusalem

  Get up into Lebanon and cry aloud,   20
  make your voice heard in Bashan,
cry aloud from Abarim, for all who befriend
    you are broken.
I spoke to you in your days of prosperous 21
    ease,
but you said, 'I will not listen.'
This is how you behaved since your youth;
  never have you obeyed me.
The wind shall carry away all your 22
    friends,[f]
  your lovers shall depart into exile.
Then you will be put to shame and
    abashed
  for all your evil deeds.[g]
You dwellers in Lebanon, who make your 23
    nests among the cedars,
  how you will groan when the pains come
    upon you,
  like the pangs of a woman in labour!

Concerning Coniah

By my life, says the LORD, Coniah son of 24
Jehoiakim, king of Judah, shall be the
signet-ring on my right hand no longer. Yes,
Coniah, I will pull you off. I will hand you 25
over to those who seek your life, to those
you fear, to Nebuchadrezzar king of Babylon and to the Chaldaeans. I will fling you 26
headlong, you and the mother who gave
you birth, into another land, a land where
you were not born; and there shall you both
die. They shall never come back to their 27
own land, the land for which they long.

  This man, Coniah, then, is he a mere 28
puppet, contemptible and broken, only a
thing unwanted? Why else are he and his
children flung out headlong and hurled into
a country they do not know?
  O land, land, land, hear the words of the 29
LORD: These are the words of the LORD: 30
Write this man down as stripped of all
honour, one who in his own life shall not
prosper, nor shall he leave descendants to
sit in prosperity on David's throne or rule
again in Judah.

---

e Prob. rdg.; Heb. adds all went well (*repeated from verse 15*).   *f Or* shepherds.   *g Or* calamities.

The remnant returns

23 Shame on the shepherds who let the sheep of my flock scatter and be lost! says the 2 LORD. Therefore these are the words of the LORD the God of Israel about the shepherds who tend my people: You have scattered and dispersed my flock. You have not watched over them; but I am watching you to punish you for your evil doings, says the 3 LORD. I will myself gather the remnant of my sheep from all the lands to which I have dispersed them. I will bring them back to their homes, and they shall be fruitful and 4 increase. I will appoint shepherds to tend them; they shall never again know fear or dismay or punishment. This is the very word of the LORD.

5 The days are now coming, says the LORD,
when I will make a righteous Branch spring
from David's line,
a king who shall rule wisely,
maintaining law and justice in the land.
6 In his days Judah shall be kept safe,
and Israel shall live undisturbed.
This is the name to be given to him:
The LORD is our Righteousness.

7 Therefore the days are coming, says the LORD, when men shall no longer swear, 'By the life of the LORD who brought Israel up 8 from Egypt', but, 'By the life of the LORD who brought the descendants of the Israelites back from a northern land and from all the lands to which he had dispersed them, to live again on their own soil.'

Against the prophets

9 On the prophets.

Deep within me my heart is broken,
there is no strength in my bones;
because of the LORD, because of his dread
words
I have become like a drunken man,
like a man overcome with wine.
10 For the land is full of adulterers,
and because of them the earth lies
parched,
the wild pastures have dried up.
The course that they run is evil,
and their powers are misused.
11 For prophet and priest alike are godless;
I have come upon the evil they are doing
even in my own house.
This is the very word of the LORD.

12 Therefore the path shall turn slippery beneath their feet;
they shall be dispersed in the dark and shall
fall there.
For I will bring disaster on them when their
day of reckoning comes.
This is the very word of the LORD.

I found the prophets of Samaria men of 13 no sense:
they prophesied in Baal's name and led my
people Israel astray.
In the prophets of Jerusalem I see a thing 14
most horrible:
adulterers and hypocrites that they are,
they encourage evildoers,
so that no man turns back from his sin;
to me all her inhabitants are like Sodom and
Gomorrah.

These then are the words of the LORD of 15 Hosts concerning the prophets:

I will give them wormwood to eat
and a bitter poison to drink;
for a godless spirit has spread over all the
land
from the prophets of Jerusalem.

These are the words of the LORD of Hosts: 16

Do not listen to what the prophets say,
who buoy you up with false hopes;
the vision they report springs from their own
imagination,
it is not from the mouth of the LORD.
They say to those who spurn the word of the 17
LORD,
'Prosperity shall be yours';
and to all who follow the promptings of their
own stubborn heart they say,
'No disaster shall befall you.'
But which of them has stood in the council 18
of the LORD,
seen him and heard his word?
Which of them has listened to his word
and obeyed?
See what a scorching wind has gone out 19
from the LORD,
a furious whirlwind;
it whirls round the heads of the wicked.
The LORD's anger is not to be turned 20
aside,
until he has accomplished and fulfilled his
deep designs.
In days to come you will fully understand.
I did not send these prophets, yet they 21
went in haste;
I did not speak to them, yet they prophesied.
If they have stood in my council, 22
let them proclaim my words to my people
and turn them from their evil course and
their evil doings.
Am I a god only near at hand, not far away? 23
Can a man hide in any secret place and I not 24
see him?
Do I not fill heaven and earth?
This is the very word of the LORD.

I have heard what the prophets say, the 25
prophets who speak lies in my name and
cry, 'I have had a dream, a dream!' How long 26
will it be till they change their tune, these

prophets who prophesy lies and give voice
27 to their own inventions? By these dreams
which they tell one another these men think
they will make my people forget my name,
as their fathers forgot my name for the name
28 of[h] Baal. If a prophet has a dream, let him
tell his dream; if he has my word, let him
speak my word in truth. What has chaff to
29 do with grain? says the LORD. Do not my
words scorch[i] like fire? says the LORD. Are
they not like a hammer that splinters rock?
30 I am against the prophets, says the LORD,
who steal my words from one another for
31 their own use. I am against the prophets,
says the LORD, who concoct words of their
own and then say, 'This is his very word.'
32 I am against the prophets, says the LORD,
who dream lies and retail them, misleading
my people with wild and reckless falsehoods.
It was not I who sent them or commissioned
them, and they will do this people no good.
This is the very word of the LORD.

'The LORD's burden'

33 When you are asked by this people or by
a prophet or priest what the burden of the
LORD's message is, you shall answer, You
are his burden, and I shall throw you down,
34 says the LORD. If prophet or priest or lay-
man uses the term 'the LORD's burden',
35 I will punish that man and his family. The
form of words you shall use in speaking
amongst yourselves is: 'What answer has the
LORD given?' or, 'What has the LORD
36 said?' You shall never again mention 'the
burden of the LORD'; that is reserved for the
man to whom he entrusts his message. If
you do, you will make nonsense of the words
of the living God, the LORD of Hosts our
37 God. This is the form you shall use in speaking to a prophet: 'What answer has the
LORD given?' or, 'What has the LORD said?'
38 But to any of you who do say, 'the burden
of the LORD', the LORD speaks thus: Because you say, 'the burden of the LORD',
39 though I sent to tell you not to say it, therefore I myself will carry you like a burden
and throw you down, casting out of my sight
both you and the city which I gave to you and
40 to your forefathers. I will inflict on you endless reproach, endless shame which shall
never be forgotten.

Good and bad figs

24 This is what the LORD showed me: I saw
two baskets of figs set out in front of the
sanctuary of the LORD. This was after
Nebuchadrezzar king of Babylon had deported from Jerusalem Jeconiah son of
Jehoiakim, king of Judah, with the officers
of Judah, the craftsmen and the smiths,[j]

and taken them to Babylon. In one basket the 2
figs were very good, like the figs that are
first ripe; in the other the figs were very bad,
so bad that they were not fit to eat. The 3
LORD said to me, 'What are you looking at,
Jeremiah?' 'Figs,' I answered, 'the good very
good, and the bad so bad that they are not
fit to eat.' Then this word came to me from 4
the LORD: These are the words of the LORD 5
the God of Israel: I count the exiles of Judah
whom I sent away from this place to the land
of the Chaldaeans as good as these good
figs. I will look upon them meaning to do 6
them good, and I will restore them to their
land; I will build them up and not pull them
down, plant them and not uproot them. I 7
will give them the wit to know me, for I am
the LORD; they shall become my people and
I will become their God, for they will come
back to me with all their heart. But Zedekiah 8
king of Judah, his officers and the survivors
of Jerusalem, whether they remain in this
land or live in Egypt—all these I will treat
as bad figs, says the LORD, so bad that they
are not fit to eat. I will make them repugnant 9
to all the kingdoms of the earth, a reproach,
a by-word, an object-lesson and a thing of
ridicule wherever I drive them. I will send 10
against them sword, famine, and pestilence
until they have vanished from the land which
I gave to them and to their forefathers.

The years of Babylonian rule

This came to Jeremiah as the word concern- 25
ing all the people of Judah in the fourth year
of Jehoiakim son of Josiah, king of Judah
(that is the first year of Nebuchadrezzar king

---

h for the name of: or by their worship of.   i scorch: prob. rdg.; Heb. thus.   j the smiths: or the harem.

2 of Babylon). This is what the prophet Jeremiah said to all Judah and all the inhabitants
3 of Jerusalem: For twenty-three years, from the thirteenth year of Josiah son of Amon, king of Judah, to the present day, I have been receiving the words of the LORD and taking pains to speak to you, but you have not
4 listened. The LORD has taken pains to send you his servants the prophets, but you have not listened or shown any inclination to
5 listen. If each of you will turn from his wicked ways and evil courses, he has said, then you shall for ever live on the soil which the LORD gave to you and to your forefathers.
6 You must not follow other gods, serving and worshipping them, nor must you provoke me to anger with the idols your hands have made; then I will not do you harm.
7 But you did not listen to me, says the LORD; you provoked me to anger with the idols your hands had made and so brought harm upon yourselves.
8 Therefore these are the words of the LORD of Hosts: Because you have not listened to
9 my words, I will summon all the tribes of the north, says the LORD: I will send for my servant Nebuchadrezzar king of Babylon. I will bring them against this land and all its inhabitants and all these nations round it; I will exterminate them and make them a thing of horror and derision, a scandal for
10 ever. I will silence all sounds of joy and gladness among them, the voices of bridegroom and bride, and the sound of the handmill; I will quench the light of every lamp.
11 For seventy years this whole country shall be a scandal and a horror; these nations shall be in subjection to the king of Bab-
12 ylon. When those seventy years are completed, I will punish the king of Babylon and his people, says the LORD, for all their misdeeds and make the land of the Chaldaeans
13 a waste for ever. I will bring upon that country all I have said, all that is written in this book, all that Jeremiah has prophesied
14 against these peoples. They will be the victims[k] of mighty nations and great kings, and thus I will repay them for their actions and their deeds.

Punishment for the nations

15 These were the words of the LORD the God of Israel to me: Take from my hand this cup of fiery wine and make all the nations to
16 whom I send you drink it. When they have drunk it they will vomit and go mad; such is the sword which I am sending among them.
17 Then I took the cup from the LORD's hand, gave it to all the nations to whom the LORD sent
18 me and made them drink it: to Jerusalem,

the cities of Judah, its kings and officers, making them a scandal, a thing of horror and derision and an object of ridicule, as they still are: to Pharaoh king of Egypt, his 19 courtiers, his officers, all his people, and all 20 his rabble of followers, all the kings of the land of Uz, all the kings of the Philistines: to Ashkelon, Gaza, Ekron, and the remnant of Ashdod: also to Edom, Moab, and the 21 Ammonites, all the kings of Tyre, all the 22 kings of Sidon, and the kings of the coasts and islands: to Dedan, Tema, Buz, and all 23 who roam the fringes of the desert,[l] all the 24 kings of Arabia living in the wilderness, all 25 the kings of Zamri, all the kings of Elam, and all the kings of the Medes, all the kings 26 of the north, neighbours or far apart, and all the kingdoms on the face of the earth. Last of all the king of Sheshak[m] shall drink. You shall say to them, These are the words 27 of the LORD of Hosts the God of Israel: Drink this, get drunk and be sick; fall, to rise no more, before the sword which I am sending among you. If they refuse to take 28 the cup from you and to drink, say to them, These are the words of the LORD of Hosts: You must and shall drink. I will first punish 29 the city which bears my name; do you think that you can be exempt? No, you cannot be exempt, for I am invoking the sword against all that inhabit the earth. This is the very word of the LORD of Hosts.

Prophesy to them and tell them all I have 30 said:

The LORD roars from Zion on high
  and thunders from his holy dwelling-
    place.
Yes, he roars across the heavens, his home;
an echo comes back like the shout of men
    treading grapes.
The great noise reaches to the ends of the 31
  earth
  and all its inhabitants.
For the LORD brings a charge against the
  nations,
he goes to law with all mankind
  and has handed the wicked over to the
    sword.
This is the very word of the LORD.

These are the words of the LORD of 32
  Hosts:
Ruin spreads from nation to nation,
a mighty tempest is blowing up from the
  ends of the earth.

In that day those whom the LORD has 33 slain shall lie like dung on the ground from one end of the earth to the other; no one shall wail for them, they shall not be taken up and buried.

---

k They . . . victims: *prob. rdg.; Heb.* They were the victims.   *l* who roam . . . desert: *or* who clip the hair on their temples.   *m A name for Babylon.*

The plight of the shepherds

34 Howl, shepherds, cry aloud,
sprinkle yourselves with ashes, you
masters of the flock.
It is your turn to go to the slaughter,
and you shall fall like fine rams.
35 The shepherds shall have nowhere to flee,
the flockmasters no way of escape.
36 Hark, the shepherds cry out, the flock-
masters howl,
for the LORD is ravaging their pasture,
37 and their peaceful homesteads lie in ruins
beneath his anger.
38 They flee like a young lion abandoning his
lair,
for their land has become a waste,
wasted by the cruel sword and by his anger.

Proclamation in the temple

26 At the beginning of the reign of Jehoiakim
son of Josiah, king of Judah, this word came
2 to Jeremiah from the LORD: These are the
words of the LORD: Stand in the court of the
LORD's house and speak to the inhabitants
of all the cities of Judah who come to worship
there. You shall tell them everything that
I command you to say to them, keeping
3 nothing back. Perhaps they may listen, and
every man may turn back from his evil
courses. Then I will relent, and give up my
purpose to bring disaster on them for their
4 evil deeds. You shall say to them, These are
the words of the LORD: If you do not obey
me, if you do not follow the law I have set
5 before you, and listen to the words of my
servants the prophets, the prophets whom
I have taken pains to send to you, but you
6 have never listened to them, then I will make
this house like Shiloh and this city an object
of ridicule to all nations on earth.
7 The priests, the prophets, and all the
people heard Jeremiah say this in the LORD's
8 house and, when he came to the end of what
the LORD had commanded him to say to
them, priests, prophets, and people seized
9 him and threatened him with death. 'Why',
they demanded, 'have you prophesied in the
LORD's name that this house shall become
like Shiloh and this city waste and uninhabited?' The people all gathered against
10 Jeremiah in the LORD's house. The officers
of Judah heard what was happening, and
they went up from the royal palace to the
LORD's house and took their places there at
11 the entrance of the new gate. Then the priests
and the prophets said to the officers and all
the people, 'Condemn this fellow to death.
He has prophesied against this city: you
12 have heard it with your own ears.' Then
Jeremiah said to the officers and the people,
'The LORD sent me to prophesy against this
house and this city all that you have heard.
13 If you now mend your ways and your doings

and obey the LORD your God, then he may
relent and revoke the disaster with which he
has threatened you. But I am in your hands; 14
do with me whatever you think right and
proper. Only you may be certain that, if you 15
put me to death, you and this city and all
who live in it will be guilty of murdering an
innocent man; for in very truth the LORD
has sent me to you to say all this in your
hearing.'

Jeremiah saved from death

Then the officers and all the people said to 16
the priests and the prophets, 'This man
ought not to be condemned to death, for he
has spoken to us in the name of the LORD
our God.' Some of the elders of the land 17
also stood up and said to the assembled
people, 'In the time of Hezekiah king of 18
Judah, Micah of Moresheth was prophesying and said to all the people of Judah:
"These are the words of the LORD of Hosts:

Zion shall become a ploughed field,
Jerusalem a heap of ruins,
and the temple-hill rough heath."

Did King Hezekiah and all Judah put him 19
to death? Did not the king show reverence
for the LORD and seek to placate him? Then
the LORD relented and revoked the disaster
with which he had threatened them. Are we
to bring great disaster on ourselves?'

There was another man who prophesied 20
in the name of the LORD, Uriah son of
Shemaiah, from Kiriath-jearim. He also
prophesied against this city and this land,
just as Jeremiah had done. King Jehoiakim 21
with all his officers and his bodyguard heard
what he said and sought to put him to death.
When Uriah heard of it, he was afraid and
fled to Egypt. King Jehoiakim sent Elnathan 22
son of Akbor with others to fetch Uriah 23
from Egypt, and they brought him to the
king. He had him put to death by the sword,
and his body flung into the burial-place of
the common people. But Ahikam son of 24
Shaphan used his influence on Jeremiah's
behalf to save him from death at the hands
of the people.

The yoke of Babylon

At the beginning of the reign of Zedekiah 27
son of Josiah, king of Judah, this word came
from the LORD to Jeremiah: These are the 2
words of the LORD to me: Take the cords
and bars of a yoke and put them on your
neck. Then send to the kings of Edom, 3
Moab, Ammon, Tyre, and Sidon by the
envoys who have come from them to Zedekiah king of Judah in Jerusalem, and give 4
them the following message for their masters:
These are the words of the LORD of Hosts
the God of Israel: Say to your masters:

5 I made the earth with my great strength and with outstretched arm, I made man and beast on the face of the earth, and I give it 6 to whom I see fit. I now give all these lands to my servant Nebuchadrezzar king of Babylon, and I give him also all the beasts 7 of the field to serve him. All nations shall serve him, and his son and his grandson, until the destined hour of his own land comes, and then mighty nations and great 8 kings shall use him as they please. If any nation or kingdom will not serve Nebuchadrezzar king of Babylon or submit to his yoke, I will punish them with sword, famine, and pestilence, says the LORD, until I leave 9 them entirely in his power. Therefore do not listen to your prophets, your diviners, your wise women, your soothsayers, and your sorcerers when they tell you not to serve the 10 king of Babylon. They are prophesying falsely to you; and so you will be carried far from your own land, and I shall banish you 11 and you will perish. But if any nation submits to the yoke of the king of Babylon and serves him, I will leave them on their own soil, says the LORD; they shall cultivate it and live there.

Judah must submit to Babylon

12 I have said all this to Zedekiah king of Judah: If you will submit to the yoke of the king of Babylon and serve him and his 13 people, then you shall save your lives. Why should you and your people die by sword, famine, and pestilence, the fate with which the LORD has threatened any nation which 14 does not serve the king of Babylon? Do not listen to the prophets who tell you not to become subject to the king of Babylon; they 15 are prophesying falsely to you. I have not sent them, says the LORD; they are prophesying falsely in my name, and so I shall banish you and you will perish, you and these prophets who prophesy to you.

16 I said to the priests and all the people, These are the words of the LORD: Do not listen to your prophets who tell you that the vessels of the LORD's house will very soon be brought back from Babylon; they 17 are only prophesying falsely to you. Do not listen to them; serve the king of Babylon, and save your lives. Why should this city 18 become a ruin? If they are prophets, and if they have the word of the LORD, let them intercede with the LORD of Hosts to grant that the vessels still left in the LORD's house, in the royal palace, and in Jerusalem, may 19 not be carried off to Babylon. For these are the words of the LORD of Hosts concerning the pillars, the sea, the trolleys, and all the 20 other vessels still left in this city, which

Nebuchadrezzar king of Babylon did not take when he deported Jeconiah son of Jehoiakim, king of Judah, from Jerusalem to Babylon, together with all the nobles of Judah and Jerusalem. These indeed are the 21 words of the LORD concerning the vessels still left in the LORD's house, in the royal palace, and in Jerusalem: They shall be taken to Babylon 22 and stay there until I recall them, says the LORD; then I will bring them back and restore them to this place.

Hananiah's false prophecy

That same year,[n] in the fifth month of the 28 first[o] year of the reign of Zedekiah king of Judah, Hananiah son of Azzur, the prophet from Gibeon, said to me in the house of the LORD, in the presence of the priests and all the people, 'These are the words of the LORD 2 of Hosts the God of Israel: I have broken the yoke of the king of Babylon. Within 3 two years I will bring back to this place all the vessels of the LORD's house which Nebuchadrezzar king of Babylon took from here and carried off to Babylon. I will also bring 4 back to this place, says the LORD, Jeconiah son of Jehoiakim, king of Judah, and all the exiles of Judah who went to Babylon; for I will break the yoke of the king of Babylon.' The prophet Jeremiah said to Han- 5 aniah the prophet in the presence of the priests and all the people standing in the LORD's house: 'May it be so! May the LORD 6 indeed do this: may he fulfil all that you have prophesied, by bringing back the vessels of the LORD's house and all the exiles from Babylon to this place! Only hear what 7 I have to say to you and to all the people: the prophets who preceded you and me 8 from earliest times have foretold war, famine, and pestilence for many lands and for great kingdoms. If a prophet foretells pros- 9 perity, when his words come true it will be known that the LORD has sent him.'

Then the prophet Hananiah took the 10 yoke from the neck of the prophet Jeremiah and broke it, saying before all the people, 11 'These are the words of the LORD: Thus will I break the yoke of Nebuchadrezzar king of Babylon; I will break it off the necks of all nations within two years';[p] and the prophet Jeremiah went his way. After Hananiah 12 had broken the yoke which had been on Jeremiah's neck, the word of the LORD came to Jeremiah: Go and say to Hananiah, These 13 are the words of the LORD: You have broken bars of wood; in their place you shall get bars of iron. For these are the words of the 14 LORD of Hosts the God of Israel: I have put a yoke of iron on the necks of all these

n *Prob. rdg.; Heb. adds* at the beginning of the reign. years: *or* while there are still two full years to run.

o *Prob. rdg.; Heb.* fourth.   p *within two*

nations, making them serve Nebuchadrezzar king of Babylon. They shall serve him, and I have given him even the beasts of the field.

15 Then Jeremiah said to Hananiah, 'Listen, Hananiah. The LORD has not sent you, and you have led this nation to trust in false 16 prophecies. Therefore these are the words of the LORD: Beware, I will remove you from the face of the earth; you shall die within the year, because you have preached rebel- 17 lion against the LORD.' The prophet Hananiah died that same year, in the seventh month.

Letter to the exiles

29 Jeremiah sent a letter from Jerusalem to the remaining elders among the exiles, to the priests and prophets, and to all the people whom Nebuchadnezzar had deported from 2 Jerusalem to Babylon, after King Jeconiah had left Jerusalem with the queen mother and the eunuchs, the officers of Judah and Jerusalem, the craftsmen and the smiths.*q* 3 The prophet entrusted the letter to Elasah son of Shaphan and Gemariah son of Hilkiah, whom Zedekiah king of Judah had sent to Babylon to King Nebuchadrezzar. 4 This is what he wrote: These are the words of the LORD of Hosts the God of Israel: To all the exiles whom I have carried off from 5 Jerusalem to Babylon: Build houses and live in them; plant gardens and eat their 6 produce. Marry wives and beget sons and daughters; take wives for your sons and give your daughters to husbands, so that they may bear sons and daughters and you may increase there and not dwindle away. 7 Seek the welfare of any city to which I have carried you off, and pray to the LORD for it; on its welfare your welfare will depend. 8 For these are the words of the LORD of Hosts the God of Israel: Do not be deceived by the prophets or the diviners among you, and do not listen to the wise women whom 9 you set to dream dreams. They prophesy falsely to you in my name; I did not send them. This is the very word of the LORD. 10 These are the words of the LORD: When a full seventy years has passed over Babylon, I will take up your cause and fulfil the promise of good things I made you, by bringing 11 you back to this place. I alone know my purpose for you, says the LORD: prosperity and not misfortune, and a long line of chil- 12 dren after you. If you invoke me and pray 13 to me, I will listen to you: when you seek me, you shall find me; if you search with all 14 your heart, I will let you find me, says the LORD. I will restore your fortunes and gather you again from all the nations and all the places to which I have banished you, says the LORD, and bring you back to the place from which I have carried you into exile.

You say that the LORD has raised up 15 prophets for you in Babylon. These are the 16 words of the LORD concerning the king who sits on the throne of David and all the people who live in this city, your fellow-countrymen who have not gone into exile with you. These are the words of the LORD 17 of Hosts: I bring upon them sword, famine, and pestilence, and make them like rotten figs, too bad to be eaten. I pursue them with 18 sword, famine, and pestilence, and make them repugnant to all the kingdoms of the earth, an object of execration and horror, of derision and reproach, among all the nations to which I have banished them. Just as they did not listen to my words, says 19 the LORD, when I took pains to send them my servants the prophets, so you did not listen, says the LORD. But now, you exiles 20 whom I have sent from Jerusalem to Babylon, listen to the words of the LORD. These 21 are the words of the LORD of Hosts the God of Israel concerning Ahab son of Kolaiah and Zedekiah son of Maaseiah, who prophesy falsely to you in my name. I will hand them over to Nebuchadrezzar king of Babylon, and he will put them to death before your eyes. Their names shall be used by all 22 the exiles of Judah in Babylon when they curse a man; they shall say, May the LORD treat you like Zedekiah and Ahab, whom the king of Babylon roasted in the fire! For 23 their conduct in Israel was an outrage: they committed adultery with other men's wives, and without my authority prophesied in my name, and what they prophesied was false. I know; I can testify. This is the very word of the LORD.

Reaction to Jeremiah's letter

To Shemaiah the Nehelamite.*r* These are 24 25 the words of the LORD of Hosts the God of Israel: You have sent a letter in your own name to Zephaniah son of Maaseiah the priest, in which you say: 'The LORD has 26 appointed you to be priest in place of Jehoiada the priest, and it is your duty, as officer in charge of the LORD's house, to put every madman who sets up as a prophet into the stocks and the pillory. Why, then, 27

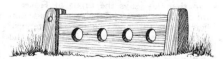

have you not reprimanded Jeremiah of Anathoth, who poses as a prophet before you? On the strength of this he has sent to 28

---

q the smiths: *or* the harem.   *r Prob. rdg.; Heb. adds* you shall say, saying.

us in Babylon and said, "Your exile will be long; build houses and live in them, plant
29 gardens and eat their produce." ' Zephaniah the priest read this letter to Jeremiah the
30 prophet, and the word of the LORD came to
31 Jeremiah: Send and tell all the exiles that these are the words of the LORD concerning Shemaiah the Nehelamite: Because Shemaiah has prophesied to you, though I did not send him, and has led you to trust in
32 false prophecies, these are now the words of the LORD: I will punish Shemaiah and his children. He shall have no one to take his place in this nation and enjoy the prosperity which I will bestow on my people, says the LORD, because he has preached rebellion against me.

Deliverance and restoration

30 The word which came to Jeremiah from
2 the LORD. These are the words of the LORD the God of Israel: Write in a book all that
3 I have said to you, for this is the very word of the LORD: The time is coming when I will restore the fortunes of my people Israel and Judah, says the LORD, and bring them back to the land which I gave to their forefathers; and it shall be their possession.
4   This is what the LORD has said to Israel
5 and Judah. These are the words of the LORD:

You shall hear a cry of terror, of fear without relief.
6 Ask and see: can a man bear a child?
Why then do I see every man
gripping his sides like a woman in labour,
every face changed, all turned pale?
7   Awful is that day:
when has there been its like?
A time of anguish for Jacob,
yet he shall come through it safely.

8   In that day, says the LORD of Hosts, I will break their yoke off their necks and snap their cords; foreigners shall no longer use
9 them as they please; they shall serve the LORD their God and David their king, whom I will raise up for them.
10 And you, Jacob my servant, have no fear; despair not, O Israel, says the LORD.

s Prob. rdg.; Heb. adds one judging your case.
Your sore cannot be healed.

For I will bring you back safe from afar
and your offspring from the land where they are captives;
and Jacob shall be at rest once more,
prosperous and unafraid.
For I am with you and will save you, says 11
the LORD.
I will make an end of all the nations
amongst whom I have scattered you,
but I will not make an end of you;
though I punish you as you deserve,
I will not sweep you clean away.

For these are the words of the LORD to 12
Zion:
Your injury is past healing,
cruel was the blow you suffered.
There can be no^s remedy for your sore, 13
the new skin cannot grow.
All your lovers have forgotten you; 14
they look for you no longer.
I have struck you down
as an enemy strikes, and punished you cruelly;
for your wickedness is great and your sins are many.
Why complain of your injury, 15
that your sore cannot be healed?^{t}
I have done this to you,
because your wickedness is great and your sins are many.

Yet all who devoured you shall themselves 16
be devoured,
all your oppressors shall go into captivity.
Those who plunder you shall be plundered,
and those who despoil you I will give up to be spoiled.
I will cause the new skin to grow 17
and heal your wounds, says the LORD,
although men call you the Outcast,
Zion, nobody's friend.

These are the words of the LORD: 18
Watch; I will restore the fortunes of Jacob's clans
and show my love for all his dwellings.
Every city shall be rebuilt on its mound of ruins,
every mansion shall have its familiar household.
From them praise shall be heard 19
and sounds of merrymaking.
I will increase them, they shall not diminish,
I will raise them to honour, they shall no longer be despised.
Their sons shall be what they once were, 20
and their community shall be established in my sight.
I will punish all their oppressors;

t Why . . . healed?: or Cry not for help in your injury.

21 a ruler shall appear, one of themselves,
a governor shall arise from their own
number.
I will myself bring him[u] near and so he[v]
shall approach me;
for no one ventures of himself to approach
me,
says the LORD.
22 So you shall be my people,
and I will be your God.
23 See what a scorching wind has gone out
from the LORD,
a sweeping whirlwind.
It whirls round the heads of the wicked;
24 the LORD's anger is not to be turned aside,
till he has finished and achieved his heart's
desire.
In days to come you will understand.

The LORD's love for Israel

31 At that time, says the LORD, I will become
God of all the families of Israel, and they
2 shall become my people. These are the words
of the LORD:

A people that survived the sword
found favour in the wilderness;
Israel journeyed to find rest;
3 long ago[w] the LORD appeared to them:
I have dearly loved you from of old,
and still I maintain my unfailing care for
you.
4 I will build you up again, O virgin Israel,
and you shall be rebuilt.
Again you shall adorn yourself with
jingles,
and go forth with the merry throng of
dancers.
5 Again you shall plant vineyards on the hills
of Samaria,
vineyards which those who planted them
defiled;
6 for a day will come when the watchmen on
Ephraim's hills cry out,
Come, let us go up to Zion, to the LORD
our God.

Israel's home-coming

7 For these are the words of the LORD:

Break into shouts of joy for Jacob's sake,
lead the nations, crying loud and clear,
sing out your praises and say,
The LORD has saved his people,
and preserved a remnant of Israel.
8 See how I bring them from the land of the
north;
I will gather them from the ends of the
earth,
their blind and lame among them,
women with child and women in labour,
a great company.

They come home, weeping as they come,   9
but I will comfort them and be their escort.
I will lead them to flowing streams;
they shall not stumble, their path will be so
smooth.
For I have become a father to Israel,
and Ephraim is my eldest son.

Listen to the word of the LORD, you 10
nations,
announce it, make it known to coasts and
islands far away:
He who scattered Israel shall gather them
again
and watch over them as a shepherd
watches his flock.
For the LORD has ransomed Jacob 11
and redeemed him from a foe too strong
for him.
They shall come with shouts of joy to 12
Zion's height,
shining with happiness at the bounty of
the LORD,
the corn, the new wine, and the oil,
the young of flock and herd.
They shall become like a watered garden
and they shall never want again.
Then shall the girl show her joy in the dance, 13
young men and old shall rejoice;
I will turn their mourning into gladness,
I will relent and give them joy to outdo their
sorrow.
I will satisfy the priests with the fat of the 14
land
and fill my people with my bounty.
This is the very word of the LORD.

Israel's repentance

These are the words of the LORD: 15
Hark, lamentation is heard in Ramah, and
bitter weeping,
Rachel weeping for her sons.
She refuses to be comforted: they are no
more.

These are the words of the LORD: 16
Cease your loud weeping,
shed no more tears;
for there shall be a reward for your toil,
they shall return from the land of the
enemy.
You shall leave descendants after you;[x] 17
your sons shall return to their own land.
I listened; Ephraim was rocking in his grief: 18
'Thou hast trained me to the yoke like an
unbroken calf,
and now I am trained;
restore me, let me return,
for thou, LORD, art my God.
Though I broke loose I have repented: 19
now that I am tamed I beat my breast;

u Or them.   v Or they.   w long ago: or from afar.   x You shall . . . you: or There shall be hope
for your posterity.

in shame and remorse
I reproach myself for the sins of my
youth.'

20 Is Ephraim still my dear son,
a child in whom I delight?
As often as I turn my back on him
I still remember him;
and so my heart yearns for him,
I am filled with tenderness towards him.
This is the very word of the LORD.

21 Build cairns to mark your way,
set up sign-posts;
make sure of the road,
the path which you will tread.
Come back, virgin Israel,
come back to your cities.

22 How long will you twist and turn, my wayward child?
For the LORD has created a new thing in the
earth:
a woman turned into a man.

When Judah's fortunes are restored

23 These are the words of the LORD of Hosts
the God of Israel: Once more shall these
words be heard in the land of Judah and in
her cities, when I restore their fortunes:

The LORD bless you,
the LORD, your true goal,[y] your holy
mountain.

24 Ploughmen and shepherds who wander
with their flocks
shall live together there.[z]

25 For I have given deep draughts to the
thirsty,
and satisfied those who were faint with
hunger.

26 Thereupon I woke and looked about me,
and my dream[a] had been pleasant.

27 The time is coming, says the LORD, when
I will sow Israel and Judah with the seed of
28 man and the seed of cattle. As I watched over
them with intent to pull down and to uproot, to demolish and destroy and harm, so
now will I watch over them to build and to
plant. This is the very word of the LORD.

29 In those days it shall no longer be said,

'The fathers have eaten sour grapes
and the children's teeth are set on edge';

30 for a man shall die for his own wrongdoing;
the man who eats sour grapes shall have his
own teeth set on edge.

A new covenant

31 The time is coming, says the LORD, when
I will make a new covenant with Israel and
32 Judah. It will not be like the covenant I
made with their forefathers when I took
them by the hand and led them out of
Egypt. Although they broke my covenant,

I was patient with them, says the LORD. But 33
this is the covenant which I will make with
Israel after those days, says the LORD; I will
set my law within them and write it on their
hearts; I will become their God and they
shall become my people. No longer need 34
they teach one another to know the LORD; all
of them, high and low alike, shall know me,
says the LORD, for I will forgive their wrongdoing and remember their sin no more.

These are the words of the LORD, who 35
gave the sun for a light by day and the moon
and stars for a light by night, who cleft the
sea and its waves roared; the LORD of Hosts
is his name:

If this fixed order could vanish out of my 36
sight,
says the LORD,
then the race of Israel too could cease for
evermore
to be a nation in my sight.

These are the words of the LORD: If any 37
man could measure the heaven above or
fathom the depths of the earth beneath, then
I could spurn the whole race of Israel because of all they have done. This is the very
word of the LORD.

The time is coming, says the LORD, when 38
the city shall be rebuilt in the LORD's honour
from the Tower of Hananel to the Corner
Gate. The measuring line shall then be laid 39
straight out over the hill of Gareb and round
Goath.[b] All the valley and every field as far 40
as the gorge of the Kidron to the corner by
the Horse Gate eastwards shall be holy to
the LORD. It shall never again be pulled
down or demolished.

Jeremiah imprisoned

The word which came to Jeremiah from the 32
LORD in the tenth year of Zedekiah king of
Judah (the eighteenth year of Nebuchadrezzar). At that time the forces of the Bab- 2
ylonian king were besieging Jerusalem, and
the prophet Jeremiah was imprisoned in the
court of the guard-house attached to the
royal palace. Zedekiah king of Judah had 3
imprisoned him after demanding what he
meant by this prophecy: 'These are the
words of the LORD: I will deliver this city
into the hands of the king of Babylon, and
he shall take it. Zedekiah king of Judah will 4
not escape from the Chaldaeans but will be
surrendered to the king of Babylon; he will
speak with him face to face and see him with
his own eyes. Zedekiah will be taken to 5
Babylon and will remain there until I turn
my thoughts to him, says the LORD. However much you fight against the Chaldaeans
you will have no success.'

---

[y] the LORD . . . goal: *or* O home of righteousness.
[a] *Or* sleep.   [b] *Or* Goah.

[z] *Prob. rdg.; Heb. adds* Judah and all his cities.

Jeremiah and the field

6 Jeremiah said, The word of the LORD came
7 to me: Hanamel son of your uncle Shallum
is coming to see you and will say, 'Buy my
field at Anathoth; you have the right of
8 redemption, as next of kin, to buy it.' As
the LORD had foretold, my cousin Hanamel
came to the court of the guard-house and
said, 'Buy my field at Anathoth in Benjamin.
You have the right of redemption and possession as next of kin; buy it.' I knew that this
9 was the LORD's message; so I bought the
field at Anathoth from my cousin Hanamel
and weighed out the price, seventeen shekels
10 of silver. I signed and sealed the deed and
had it witnessed; then I weighed out the
11 money on the scales. I took my copies of
the deed of purchase, both the sealed and
12 the unsealed, and gave them to Baruch son
of Neriah, son of Mahseiah, in the presence
of Hanamel my cousin, of the witnesses
whose names were on the deed of purchase,
and of the Judaeans sitting in the court of
13 the guard-house. In the presence of them all
14 I gave my instructions to Baruch: These are
the words of the LORD of Hosts the God
of Israel: Take these copies of the deed of
purchase, the sealed and the unsealed, and
deposit them in an earthenware jar so that
15 they may be preserved for a long time. For
these are the words of the LORD of Hosts the
God of Israel: The time will come when
houses, fields, and vineyards will again be
16 bought and sold in this land. After I had
given the deed of purchase to Baruch son of
17 Neriah, I prayed to the LORD: O Lord GOD,
thou hast made the heavens and the earth
by thy great strength and with thy outstretched arm; nothing is impossible for
18 thee. Thou keepest faith with thousands and
thou dost requite the sins of fathers on to
the heads of their sons. O great and mighty
God whose name is the LORD of Hosts,
19 great are thy purposes and mighty thy
actions. Thine eyes watch all the ways of
men, and thou rewardest each according to
20 his ways and as his deeds deserve. Thou didst
work signs and portents in Egypt and hast
continued them to this day, both in Israel
and amongst all men, and hast won for thy-
21 self a name that lives on to this day. Thou
didst bring thy people Israel out of Egypt
with signs and portents, with a strong hand
and an outstretched arm, and with terrible
22 power. Thou didst give them this land which
thou didst promise with an oath to their
forefathers, a land flowing with milk and
23 honey. They came and took possession of
it, but they did not obey thee or follow thy
law, they disobeyed all thy commands; and
so thou hast brought this disaster upon
24 them. Look at the siege-ramps, the men who
are advancing to take the city, and the city
given over to its assailants from Chaldaea,
the victim of sword, famine, and pestilence.
The word thou hast spoken is fulfilled and
thou dost see it. And yet thou hast bidden 25
me buy the field, O Lord GOD, and have the
deed witnessed, even though the city is given
to the Chaldaeans.

The LORD's plan for Judah

These are the words of the LORD to Jeremiah: 26
I am the LORD, the God of all flesh; is any- 27
thing impossible for me? Therefore these are 28
the words of the LORD: I will deliver this city
into the hands of the Chaldaeans and of
Nebuchadrezzar king of Babylon, and he
shall take it. The Chaldaeans who are fight- 29
ing against this city will enter it, set it on fire
and burn it down, with the houses on whose
roofs sacrifices have been burnt to Baal and
drink-offerings poured out to other gods, by
which I was provoked to anger.

From their earliest days Israel and Judah 30
have been doing what is wrong in my eyes,
provoking me to anger by their actions, says
the LORD. For this city has so roused my 31
anger and my fury, from the time it was built
down to this day, that I would rid myself of
it. Israel and Judah, their kings, officers, 32
priests, prophets, and everyone living in
Jerusalem and Judah have provoked me to
anger by their wrongdoing. They have turned 33
their backs on me and averted their faces;
though I took pains to teach them, they
would not hear or learn their lesson. They 34
set up their loathsome idols in the house
which bears my name and so defiled it. They 35
built shrines to Baal in the Valley of Ben-
hinnom, to surrender their sons and daughters to Molech. It was no command of mine,
nor did it ever enter my thought to do this
abominable thing and lead Judah into sin.

Now, therefore, these are the words of the 36
LORD the God of Israel to this city of which
you say, 'It is being given over to the king
of Babylon, with sword, famine, and pestilence': I will gather them from all the lands 37
to which I banished them in my anger, rage,
and fury, and I will bring them back to this
place and let them dwell there undisturbed.
They shall become my people and I will be- 38
come their God. I will give them one heart 39
and one way of life so that they shall fear me
at all times, for their own good and the good
of their children after them. I will enter into 40
an eternal covenant with them, to follow
them unfailingly with my bounty; I will fill
their hearts with fear of me, and so they will
not turn away from me. I will rejoice over 41
them, rejoice to do them good, and faithfully
with all my heart and soul I will plant them
in this land. For these are the words of the 42
LORD: As I brought on this people such

great disaster, so will I bring them all the
43 prosperity which I now promise them. Fields
shall again be bought and sold in this land
of which you now say, 'It is desolate, without man or beast; it is given over to the
44 Chaldaeans.' Fields shall be bought and sold,
deeds signed, sealed, and witnessed, in Benjamin, in the neighbourhood of Jerusalem,
in the cities of Judah, of the hill-country, of
the Shephelah, and of the Negeb; for I will
restore their fortunes. This is the very word
of the LORD.

Future blessings

33 The word of the LORD came to Jeremiah a
second time while he was still imprisoned in
2 the court of the guard-house: These are the
words of the LORD who made the earth, who
formed it and established it; the LORD is
3 his name: If you call to me I will answer you,
and tell you great and mysterious things
4 which you do not understand. These are the
words of the LORD the God of Israel concerning the houses in this city and the royal
palace, which are to be razed to the ground,
5 concerning siege-ramp and sword, and at-
tackers^c who fill the houses with the corpses
of those whom he struck down in his furious
rage: I hid my face from this city because of
6 their wicked ways, but now I will bring her
healing; I will heal and cure Judah and Israel,
and will let my people see an age of peace
7 and security. I will restore their fortunes and
8 build them again as once they were. I will
cleanse them of all the wickedness and sin
that they have committed; I will forgive all
the evil deeds they have done in rebellion
9 against me. This city will win me a name^d
and praise and glory before all the nations on
earth, when they hear of all the blessings I
bestow on her; and they shall be moved and
filled with awe because of the blessings and
the peace which I have brought upon her.
10   These are the words of the LORD: You say
of this place, 'It is in ruins, and neither man
nor beast lives in the cities of Judah or in the
streets of Jerusalem. It is all a waste, inhabited by neither man nor beast.' Yet in
11 this place shall be heard once again the
sounds of joy and gladness, the voice of the
bridegroom and the bride; here too shall be
heard voices shouting, 'Praise the LORD of
Hosts, for he is good, for his love endures for
ever', as they offer praise and thanksgiving
in the house of the LORD. For I will restore
the fortunes of the land as once they were.
This is the word of the LORD.
12   These are the words of the LORD of Hosts:
In this place and in all its cities, now ruined
and inhabited by neither man nor beast,
there shall once more be a refuge where
13 shepherds may fold their flocks. In the cities

of the hill-country, of the Shephelah, of the
Negeb, in Benjamin, in the neighbourhood
of Jerusalem and the cities of Judah, flocks
will once more pass under the shepherd's
hand as he counts them. This is the word of
the LORD.

Wait, says the LORD, the days are coming 14
when I will bestow on Israel and Judah all
the blessings I have promised them. In those 15
days, at that time, I will make a righteous
Branch of David spring up; he shall maintain law and justice in the land. In those days 16
Judah shall be kept safe and Jerusalem shall
live undisturbed; and this shall be her name:
The LORD is our Righteousness.

The covenant with David confirmed

For these are the words of the LORD: David 17
will never lack a successor on the throne of
Israel, nor will the levitical priests lack a 18
man who shall come before me continually
to present whole-offerings, to burn grain-
offerings and to make other offerings.
This word came from the LORD to Jere- 19
miah: These are the words of the LORD: If 20
the law that I made for the day and the night
could be annulled so that they fell out of
their proper order, then my covenant with 21
my servant David could be annulled so that
none of his line should sit upon his throne;
so also could my covenant with the levitical
priests who minister to me. Like the in- 22
numerable host of heaven or the countless
sands of the sea, I will increase the descendants of my servant David and the Levites
who minister to me.
The word of the LORD came to Jeremiah: 23
Have you not observed how this people 24
have said, 'It is the two families whom he
chose that the LORD has spurned'? So others
will despise my people and no longer regard
them as a nation. These are the words of the 25
LORD: If I had not made my law for day and
night nor established a fixed order in heaven
and earth, then I would spurn the descen- 26
dants of Jacob and of my servant David,
and would not take any of David's line to
be rulers over the descendants of Abraham,
Isaac and Jacob. But now I will restore their
fortunes and have compassion upon them.

The LORD's word to Zedekiah

The word which came to Jeremiah from the 34
LORD when Nebuchadrezzar king of Babylon and his army, with all his vassal kingdoms and nations, were fighting against
Jerusalem and all her towns: These are the 2
words of the LORD the God of Israel: Go
and say to Zedekiah king of Judah, These
are the words of the LORD: I will give this
city into the hands of the king of Babylon
and he will burn it down. You shall not 3

---

c *Prob. rdg.; Heb. adds* the Chaldaeans.

d *Prob. rdg.; Heb. adds* of joy.

escape, you will be captured and handed over to him. You will see him face to face, and he will speak to you in person; and you 4 shall go to Babylon. But listen to the LORD's word to you, Zedekiah king of Judah. This is his word: You shall not die by the sword; 5 you will die a peaceful death, and they will kindle fires in your honour like the fires kindled in former times for the kings your ancestors who preceded you. 'Alas, my lord!' they will say as they beat their breasts in mourning for you. This I have spoken. This 6 is the very word of the LORD. The prophet Jeremiah repeated all this to Zedekiah king 7 of Judah in Jerusalem when the army of the king of Babylon was attacking Jerusalem and the remaining cities of Judah, namely Lachish and Azekah. These were the only fortified cities left in Judah.

Israel goes back on the covenant

8 The word that came to Jeremiah from the LORD after Zedekiah had made a covenant with all the people in Jerusalem to proclaim 9 an act of freedom for the slaves. All who had Hebrew slaves, male or female, were to set them free; they were not to keep their 10 fellow Judaeans in servitude. All the officers and people, having made this covenant to set free their slaves, both male and female, and not to keep them in servitude any longer, 11 fulfilled its terms and let them go. After-wards, however, they changed their minds and forced back again into slavery the men 12 and women whom they had freed. Then this word came from the LORD to Jeremiah: 13 These are the words of the LORD the God of Israel: I made a covenant with your fore-fathers on the day that I brought them out of Egypt, out of the land of slavery. These 14 were its terms: 'Within seven years each of you shall set free any Hebrew who has sold himself to you as a slave and has served you for six years; you shall set him free.' Your forefathers did not listen to me or obey me. 15 You, on the contrary, recently proclaimed an act of freedom for the slaves and made a covenant in my presence, in the house that bears my name, and so have done what is 16 right in my eyes. But you too have profaned my name. You have all taken back the slaves you had set free and you have forced them, both male and female, to be your slaves 17 again. Therefore these are the words of the LORD: After you had proclaimed an act of freedom, a deliverance for your kinsmen and your neighbours, you did not obey me; so I will proclaim a deliverance for you, says the LORD, a deliverance over to sword, to pestilence, and to famine, and I will make you repugnant to all the kingdoms of the 18 earth. You have disregarded my covenant and have not fulfilled the terms to which you

yourselves had agreed; so I will make you like the calf of the covenant when they cut it into two and passed between the pieces. Those who passed between the pieces of the 19 calf were the officers of Judah and Jerusalem, the eunuchs and priests and all the people of the land. I will give them up to their enemies 20 who seek their lives, and their bodies shall be food for birds of prey and wild beasts. I will deliver Zedekiah king of Judah and 21 his officers to their enemies who seek their lives and to the army of the king of Babylon, which is now raising the siege. I will give 22 the command, says the LORD, and will bring them back to this city. They shall attack it and take it and burn it down, and I will make the cities of Judah desolate and un-peopled.

Jeremiah and the Rechabites

The word which came to Jeremiah from the 35 LORD in the days of Jehoiakim son of Josiah, king of Judah: Go and speak to the Recha- 2 bites, bring them to one of the rooms in the house of the LORD and offer them wine to drink. So I fetched Jaazaniah son of Jere- 3 miah, son of Habaziniah, with his brothers and all his sons and all the family of the Rechabites. I brought them into the house 4 of the LORD to the room of the sons of Hanan son of Igdaliah, the man of God; this adjoins the officers' room above that of Maaseiah son of Shallum, the keeper of the threshold. I set bowls full of wine and drinking-cups 5 before the Rechabites and invited them to drink wine; but they said, 'We will not drink 6 wine, for our forefather Jonadab son of Rechab laid this command on us: "You shall never drink wine, neither you nor your chil-dren. You shall not build houses or sow seed 7 or plant vineyards; you shall have none of these things. Instead, you shall remain tent-dwellers all your lives, so that you may live long in the land where you are sojourners."

L

8 We have honoured all the commands of our forefather Jonadab son of Rechab and have drunk no wine all our lives, neither we nor our wives, nor our sons, nor our daughters.
9 We have not built houses to live in, nor have
10 we possessed vineyards or sown fields. We have lived in tents, obeying and observing all the commands of our forefather Jonadab.
11 But when Nebuchadrezzar king of Babylon invaded the land we said, "Come, let us go to Jerusalem before the advancing Chaldaean and Aramaean armies." And we have stayed in Jerusalem.'
12 Then the word of the LORD came to Jere-
13 miah: These are the words of the LORD of Hosts the God of Israel: Go and say to the men of Judah and the inhabitants of Jerusalem, You must accept correction and obey
14 my words, says the LORD. The command of Jonadab son of Rechab to his descendants not to drink wine has been honoured; they have not drunk wine to this day, for they have obeyed their ancestor's command. But I have taken especial pains to warn you and
15 yet you have not obeyed me. I sent my servants the prophets especially to say to you, 'Turn back every one of you from his evil course, mend your ways and cease to follow other gods and worship them; then you shall remain on the land that I have given to you and to your forefathers.' Yet you did not
16 obey or listen to me. The sons of Jonadab son of Rechab have honoured their ancestor's command laid on them, but this
17 people have not listened to me. Therefore, these are the words of the LORD the God of Hosts, the God of Israel: Because they did not listen when I spoke to them, nor answer when I called them, I will bring upon Judah and upon all the inhabitants of Jerusalem the disaster with which I threatened them.
18 To the Rechabites Jeremiah said, These are the words of the LORD of Hosts the God of Israel: Because you have kept the command of Jonadab your ancestor and obeyed all his instructions and carried out all that
19 he told you to do, therefore these are the words of the LORD of Hosts the God of Israel: Jonadab son of Rechab shall not want a descendant to stand before me for all time.

Jeremiah dictates his message

36 In the fourth year of Jehoiakim son of Josiah, king of Judah, this word came to
2 Jeremiah from the LORD: Take a scroll and write on it every word that I have spoken to you about Jerusalem and Judah and all the nations, from the day that I first spoke to you in the reign of Josiah down to the pre-
3 sent day. Perhaps the house of Judah will be warned of the calamity that I am planning

to bring on them, and every man will abandon his evil course; then I will forgive their wrongdoing and their sin. So Jeremiah called 4 Baruch son of Neriah, and he wrote on the scroll at Jeremiah's dictation all the words which the LORD had spoken to him. He gave 5 Baruch this instruction: 'I am prevented from going to the LORD's house. You must 6 go there in my place on a fast-day and read the words of the LORD in the hearing of the people from the scroll you have written at my dictation. You shall read them in the hearing of all the men of Judah who come in from their cities. Then perhaps they will 7 present a petition to the LORD and every man will abandon his evil course; for the LORD has spoken against this people in great anger and wrath.' Baruch son of Neriah did 8 all that the prophet Jeremiah had told him to do, and read the words of the LORD in the LORD's house out of the book.

The king burns the scroll

In the ninth month of the fifth year of the 9 reign of Jehoiakim son of Josiah, king of Judah, all the people in Jerusalem and all who came there from the cities of Judah proclaimed a fast before the LORD. Then 10 Baruch read Jeremiah's words in the house of the LORD out of the book in the hearing of all the people; he read them from the room of Gemariah son of the adjutant-general Shaphan in the upper court at the entrance to the new gate of the LORD's house. Micaiah son of Gemariah, son of 11 Shaphan, heard all the words of the LORD out of the book and went down to the 12 palace, to the adjutant-general's room where all the officers were gathered—Elishama the adjutant-general, Delaiah son of Shemaiah, Elnathan son of Akbor, Gemariah son of Shaphan, Zedekiah son of Hananiah and all the other officers. There Micaiah repeated 13 all the words he had heard when Baruch read out of the book in the people's hearing. Then the officers sent Jehudi son of Netha- 14 niah, son of Shelemiah, son of Cushi, to Baruch with this message: 'Come here and bring the scroll from which you read in the people's hearing.' So Baruch son of Neriah brought the scroll to them, and they said, 15 'Sit down and*e* read it to us.' When they 16 heard what he read, they turned to each other trembling and said, 'We must report this to the king.' They asked Baruch to tell them how he had come to write all this. He said to them, 'Jeremiah dictated every word of it to me, and I wrote it down in ink in the book.' The officers said to Baruch, 'You and 1 Jeremiah must go into hiding so that no one may know where you are.' When they had 2 deposited the scroll in the room of Elishama

---

e Sit down and: or This time.

the adjutant-general, they went to the court and reported everything to the king.

21 The king sent Jehudi to fetch the scroll. When he had fetched it from the room of Elishama the adjutant-general, he read it to the king and to all the officers in attendance.

22 It was the ninth month of the year, and the king was sitting in his winter apartments with a fire burning in a brazier in front of

23 him. When Jehudi had read three or four columns of the scroll, the king cut them off

with a penknife and threw them into the fire in the brazier. He went on doing so until the whole scroll had been thrown on

24 the fire. Neither the king nor any of his courtiers who heard these words showed

25 any fear or rent their clothes; and though Elnathan, Delaiah, and Gemariah begged the king not to burn the scroll, he would

26 not listen to them. The king then ordered Jerahmeel, a royal prince,[f] Seraiah son of Azriel, and Shelemiah son of Abdeel to fetch the scribe Baruch and the prophet Jeremiah; but the Lord had hidden them.

Another scroll is prepared

27 After the king had burnt the scroll with all that Baruch had written on it at Jeremiah's dictation, the word of the Lord came to

28 Jeremiah: Now take another scroll and write on it all the words that were on the first scroll which Jehoiakim king of Judah burnt.

29 You shall say to Jehoiakim king of Judah, These are the words of the Lord: You burnt this scroll and said, Why have you written here that the king of Babylon shall come and destroy this land and exterminate both

30 men and beasts? Therefore these are the words of the Lord about Jehoiakim king of Judah: He shall have no one to succeed

him on the throne of David, and his dead body shall be exposed to scorching heat by day and frost by night. I will punish him 31 and also his offspring and his courtiers for their wickedness, and I will bring down on them and on the inhabitants of Jerusalem and on the men of Judah all the calamities with which I threatened them, and to which they turned a deaf ear. Then Jeremiah took 32 another scroll and gave it to the scribe Baruch son of Neriah, who wrote on it at Jeremiah's dictation all the words of the book which Jehoiakim king of Judah had burnt; and much else was added to the same effect.

Jerusalem's fate foretold

King Zedekiah son of Josiah was set on the 37 throne of Judah by Nebuchadrezzar king of Babylon, in succession to Coniah son of Jehoiakim. Neither he nor his courtiers nor 2 the people of the land listened to the words which the Lord spoke through the prophet Jeremiah.

King Zedekiah sent Jehucal son of Shele- 3 miah and the priest Zephaniah son of Maaseiah to the prophet Jeremiah to say to him, 'Pray for us to the Lord our God.' At the time Jeremiah was free to come and 4 go among the people; he had not yet been thrown into prison. Meanwhile, Pharaoh's 5 army had marched out of Egypt, and when the Chaldaeans who were besieging Jerusalem heard of it they raised the siege. Then 6 this word came from the Lord to the prophet Jeremiah: These are the words of the Lord 7 the God of Israel: Say to the king of Judah who sent you to consult me, Pharaoh's army which marched out to help you is on its way back to Egypt, its own land, and the Chal- 8 daeans will return to the attack. They will capture this city and burn it to the ground. These are the words of the Lord: Do not 9 deceive yourselves, do not imagine that the Chaldaeans will go away and leave you alone. They will not go; for even if you 10 defeated the whole Chaldaean force with which you are now fighting, and only the wounded were left lying in their tents, they would rise and burn down the city.

Jeremiah imprisoned

When the Chaldaean army had raised the 11 siege of Jerusalem because of the advance of Pharaoh's army, Jeremiah was on the 12 point of leaving Jerusalem to go into Benjamite territory and take possession of his patrimony in the presence of the people there. Irijah son of Shelemiah, son of Hana- 13 niah, the officer of the guard, was in the Benjamin Gate when Jeremiah reached it, and he arrested the prophet, accusing him

---

[f] a royal prince: *or* the king's deputy.

14 of going over to the Chaldaeans. 'It is a lie,' said Jeremiah; 'I am not going over to the Chaldaeans.' Irijah would not listen to him but arrested him and brought him before 15 the officers. The officers were indignant with Jeremiah; they flogged him and imprisoned him in the house of Jonathan the scribe, 16 which they had converted into a prison; for Jeremiah had been put into a vaulted pit beneath the house, and here he remained for a long time.

17 King Zedekiah had Jeremiah brought to him and consulted him privately in the palace, asking him if there was a word from the LORD. 'Indeed there is,' said Jeremiah; 'you shall fall into the hands of the king of 18 Babylon.' Then Jeremiah said to King Zedekiah, 'What wrong have I done to you or your courtiers or this people? Why have 19 you thrown me into prison? Where are your prophets who prophesied that the king of Babylon would not attack you or your 20 country? I pray you now, my lord king, give me a hearing and let my petition be presented: do not send me back to the house of Jonathan the scribe, or I shall die there.' 21 Then King Zedekiah gave the order and Jeremiah was committed to the court of the guard-house and was granted a daily ration of one loaf from the Street of the Bakers, until the bread in the city was all gone. So Jeremiah remained in the court of the guard-house.

Ebed-melech rescues Jeremiah

38 Shephatiah son of Mattan, Gedaliah son of Pashhur, Jucal son of Shelemiah, and Pashhur son of Malchiah heard what Jeremiah 2 was saying to all the people: These are the words of the LORD: Whoever remains in this city shall die by sword, by famine, or by pestilence, but whoever goes out to surrender to the Chaldaeans shall survive; he shall survive, he shall take home his life and nothing 3 more. These are the words of the LORD: This city will fall into the hands of the king of Babylon's army, and they will capture it. 4 Then the officers said to the king, 'The man must be put to death. By talking in this way he is discouraging the soldiers and the rest of the people left in the city. He is pursuing not the people's welfare but their ruin.' 5 King Zedekiah said, 'He is in your hands; 6 the king is powerless against you.' So they took Jeremiah and threw him into the pit,[g] in the court of the guard-house, letting him down with ropes. There was no water in the pit, only mud, and Jeremiah sank in the 7-8 mud. Now Ebed-melech the Cushite, a eunuch, who was in the palace, heard that they had thrown Jeremiah into the pit and

went to tell the king, who was seated in the Benjamin Gate. 'Your majesty,' he said, 9 'these men have shown great wickedness in their treatment of the prophet Jeremiah. They have thrown him into the pit, and when there is no more bread in the city he will die of hunger where he lies.' Thereupon 10 the king told Ebed-melech the Cushite to take three men with him and hoist Jeremiah out of the pit before he died. So Ebed- 11 melech went to the palace with the men and took some tattered, cast-off clothes from the wardrobe[h] and let them down with ropes to Jeremiah in the pit. Ebed-melech the Cush- 12 ite said to Jeremiah, 'Put these old clothes under your armpits to ease the ropes.' Jeremiah did this, and they pulled him up 13 out of the pit with the ropes; and he remained in the court of the guard-house.

Zedekiah's dilemma

King Zedekiah had the prophet Jeremiah 14 brought to him by the third entrance to the LORD's house and said to him, 'I want to ask you something; hide nothing from me.' Jeremiah answered, 'If I speak out, you will 15 certainly put me to death; if I offer you any advice, you will not take it.' But King 16 Zedekiah swore to Jeremiah privately, 'By the life of the LORD who gave us our lives, I will not put you to death, nor will I hand you over to these men who are seeking to take your life.' Jeremiah said to Zedekiah, 17 'These are the words of the LORD the God of Hosts, the God of Israel: If you go out and surrender to the officers of the king of Babylon, you shall live and this city shall not be burnt down; you and your family shall live. But if you do not surrender to the officers 18 of the king of Babylon, the city shall fall into the hands of the Chaldaeans, and they shall burn it down, and you will not escape them.' King Zedekiah said to Jeremiah, 'I am afraid 19 of the Judaeans who have gone over to the enemy. I fear the Chaldaeans will give me up to them and I shall be roughly handled.' Jeremiah answered, 'They will not give you 20 up. If you obey the LORD in everything I tell you, all will be well with you and you shall live. But if you refuse to go out and 21 surrender, this is what the LORD has shown me: all the women left in the king of Judah's 22 palace will be led out to the officers of the king of Babylon and they will say:

Your own friends have misled you
   and have been too strong for you;
they have let your feet sink in the mud
   and have turned away and left you.

All your women and children will be led out 23 to the Chaldaeans, and you will not escape;

---

g *Prob. rdg.; Heb. adds* Malchiah son (*or* deputy) of the king.   h *the wardrobe: prob. rdg.; Heb.* underneath the treasury.

you will be seized by the king of Babylon
24 and this city will be burnt down.' Zedekiah
said to Jeremiah, 'Let no one know about
25 this, and you shall not be put to death. If
the officers hear that I have been speaking
with you and they come to you and say,
"Tell us what you said to the king and what
he said to you; hide nothing from us, and
26 we will not put you to death", then answer,
"I was presenting a petition to the king not
to send me back to the house of Jonathan
27 to die there."' The officers all came to Jeremiah and questioned him, and he said to
them just what the king had told him to say;
so their talk came to an end and they were
28 none the wiser. Jeremiah remained in the
court of the guard-house till the day Jerusalem fell.

Jerusalem taken

1[i] In the tenth month of the ninth year of the
reign of Zedekiah king of Judah, Nebuchadrezzar advanced with all his army
against Jerusalem, and they laid siege to it.
2 In the fourth month of the eleventh year of
Zedekiah, on the ninth day of the month,
3 the city was thrown open. All the officers
of the king of Babylon came in and took
their seats in the middle gate: Nergalsarezer
of Simmagir, Nebusarsekim[j] the chief eunuch,[k] Nergalsarezer the commander of the
frontier troops,[l] and all the other officers of
4 the king of Babylon. When Zedekiah king
of Judah saw them, he and all his armed
escort left the city and fled by night by way
of the king's garden through the gate called
Between the Two Walls. They escaped to-
5 wards the Arabah, but the Chaldaean army
pursued them and overtook Zedekiah in the
lowlands of Jericho. The king was seized and
brought before Nebuchadrezzar king of
Babylon at Riblah in the land of Hamath,
6 and he pleaded his case before him. The king
of Babylon slew Zedekiah's sons before his
eyes at Riblah; he also put to death the
7 nobles of Judah. Then Zedekiah's eyes were
put out, and he was bound in fetters of
8 bronze to be brought to Babylon. The Chaldaeans burnt the royal palace and the house
of the LORD and the houses[m] of the people,
and pulled down the walls of Jerusalem.
9 Nebuzaradan captain of the bodyguard deported to Babylon the rest of the people left
in the city, those who had deserted to him
10 and any remaining artisans.[n] At the same
time the captain of the guard left behind
the weakest class of the people, those who
owned nothing at all, and made them vine-
dressers and labourers.

Jeremiah and Ebed-melech kept safe

Nebuchadrezzar king of Babylon sent orders 11
about Jeremiah to Nebuzaradan captain of
the guard. 'Take him,' he said; 'take special 12
care of him, and do him no harm of any
kind, but do for him whatever he says.' So 13
Nebuzaradan captain of the guard sent
Nebushazban the chief eunuch, Nergalsarezer the commander of the frontier troops,
and all the chief officers of the king of Babylon, and they fetched Jeremiah from the 14
court of the guard-house and handed him
over to Gedaliah son of Ahikam, son of
Shaphan, to take him out to the Residence.
So he stayed with his own people.

The word of the LORD had come to Jere- 15
miah while he was under arrest in the court
of the guard-house: Go and say to Ebed- 16
melech the Cushite, These are the words of
the LORD of Hosts the God of Israel: I will
make good the words I have spoken against
this city, foretelling ruin and not prosperity,
and when that day comes you will be there
to see it. But I will preserve you on that day, 17
says the LORD, and you shall not be handed
over to the men you fear. I will keep you 18
safe and you shall not fall a victim to the
sword; because you trusted in me you shall
escape, you shall take home your life and
nothing more. This is the very word of the
LORD.

Jeremiah stays in Jerusalem

The word which came from the LORD con- **40**
cerning Jeremiah: Nebuzaradan captain of
the guard had taken him in chains to Ramah
along with the other exiles from Jerusalem
and Judah who were being deported to
Babylon; and there he set him free, and took 2
it upon himself to say to Jeremiah, 'The
LORD your God threatened this place with
disaster, and has duly carried out his threat 3
that this should happen to all of you because you have sinned against the LORD and
not obeyed him. But as for you, Jeremiah, 4
today I remove the fetters from your wrists.
Come with me to Babylon if you wish, and
I will take special care of you; but if you
prefer not to come, well and good. The
whole country lies before you; go wherever
you think best.' Jeremiah had not yet 5
answered when Nebuzaradan went on,[o]
'Go back to Gedaliah son of Ahikam,
son of Shaphan, whom the king of Babylon has appointed governor of the cities
of Judah, and stay with him openly; or
else go wherever you choose.' Then the
captain of the guard granted him an allowance of food, and gave him a present, and

---

i Verses 1–10: cp. 52. 4–16 and 2 Kgs. 25. 1–12.   *j* Probably a different form of Nebushazban (verse 13).
k the chief eunuch: or Rab-saris.   *l* the commander . . . troops: or Rab-mag.   *m* of the LORD and
the houses: prob. rdg.; Heb. om.   *n* artisans: prob. rdg., cp. 52. 15; Heb. people who were left.   *o* Jeremiah . . . went on: prob. rdg.; Heb. unintelligible in context.

6 so took leave of him. Jeremiah then came to Gedaliah son of Ahikam at Mizpah and stayed with him among the people left in the land.

Gedaliah made governor

7 When all the captains of the armed bands in the country-side and their men heard that the king of Babylon had appointed Gedaliah son of Ahikam governor of the land, and had put him in charge of the weakest class of the population, men, women, and children, who had not been 8 deported to Babylon, they came to him at Mizpah; Ishmael son of Nethaniah came, and Johanan and Jonathan sons of Kareah, Seraiah son of Tanhumeth, the sons of Ephai*p* from Netophah, and Jezaniah of 9 Beth-maacah, with their men. Gedaliah son of Ahikam, son of Shaphan, gave them all this assurance: 'Have no fear of the Chaldaean officers. Settle down in the land and serve the king of Babylon; and then all will 10 be well with you. I am to stay in Mizpah and attend upon the Chaldaeans whenever they come, and you are to gather in the summer-fruits, wine, and oil, store them in jars, and settle in the towns you have taken over.' 11 The Judaeans also, in Moab, Ammon, Edom and other countries, heard that the king of Babylon had left a remnant in Judah and that he had set over them Gedaliah son 12 of Ahikam, son of Shaphan. The Judaeans, therefore, from all the places where they were scattered, came back to Judah and presented themselves before Gedaliah at Mizpah; and they gathered in a considerable store of fruit and wine.

13 Johanan son of Kareah and all the captains of the armed bands from the country- 14 side came to Gedaliah at Mizpah and said to him, 'Do you know that Baalis king of the Ammonites has sent Ishmael son of Nethaniah to assassinate you?' But Gedaliah 15 son of Ahikam did not believe them. Then Johanan son of Kareah said in private to Gedaliah, 'Let me go, unknown to anyone else, and kill Ishmael son of Nethaniah. Why allow him to assassinate you, and so let all the Judaeans who have rallied round you be scattered and the remnant of Judah 16 lost?' Gedaliah son of Ahikam answered him, 'Do no such thing. Your story about Ishmael is a lie.'

Gedaliah assassinated

41 In the seventh month Ishmael son of Nethaniah, son of Elishama, who was a member of the royal house, came with ten men to Gedaliah son of Ahikam at Mizpah. While 2 they were at table with him there, Ishmael son of Nethaniah and the ten men with him rose to their feet and assassinated Gedaliah son of Ahikam, son of Shaphan, whom the king of Babylon had appointed governor of the land. They also murdered the Judaeans 3 with him in Mizpah and the Chaldaeans who happened to be there. The second day after 4 the murder of Gedaliah, while it was not yet common knowledge, there came eighty men 5 from Shechem, Shiloh, and Samaria. They had shaved off their beards, their clothes were rent and their bodies gashed, and they were carrying grain-offerings and frankincense to take to the house of the LORD. Ishmael son of Nethaniah came out weeping 6 from Mizpah to meet them, and, when he met them, he said, 'Come to Gedaliah son of Ahikam.' But as soon as they reached the 7 centre of the town, Ishmael son of Nethaniah and his men murdered them and threw their bodies into a pit, all except ten of them who 8 said to Ishmael, 'Do not kill us, for we have a secret hoard in the country, wheat and barley, oil and honey.' So he held his hand and did not kill them with the others. The 9 pit into which he threw the bodies of those whose death he had caused by using Gedaliah's name was the pit which King Asa had made when threatened by Baasha king of Israel; and the dead bodies filled it. He 10 rounded up the rest of the people in Mizpah, that is the king's daughters and all who remained in Mizpah when Nebuzaradan captain of the guard appointed Gedaliah son of Ahikam governor; and with these he set out to cross over into Ammon. When Johanan 11 son of Kareah and all the captains of the armed bands heard of the crimes committed by Ishmael son of Nethaniah, they took all 12 the men they had and went to attack him. They found him by the great pool in Gibeon. The people with Ishmael were glad when they 13 saw Johanan son of Kareah and the captains of the armed bands with him; and all whom 14 Ishmael had taken prisoner at Mizpah turned and joined Johanan son of Kareah. But Ishmael son of Nethaniah escaped from 15 Johanan with eight men, and they made their way to the Ammonites.

Johanan's request to Jeremiah

Johanan son of Kareah and all the captains 16 of the armed bands took from Mizpah the survivors whom he had rescued from Ishmael son of Nethaniah after the murder of Gedaliah son of Ahikam—men, armed and unarmed, women, children, and eunuchs, whom he had brought back from Gibeon. They started out and broke their journey at 17 Kimham's holding near Bethlehem, on their way into Egypt to escape the Chaldaeans. 18 They were afraid because Ishmael son of Nethaniah had assassinated Gedaliah son

p Or Ophai.

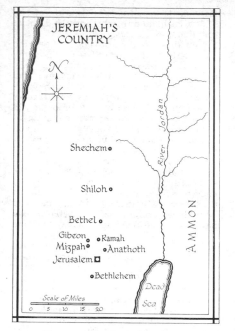

JEREMIAH'S COUNTRY

Shechem●

Shiloh ●

Bethel ●

Gibeon ●   ● Ramah
Mizpah ●   ● Anathoth
Jerusalem ◻

● Bethlehem

AMMON

River Jordan

Dead Sea

Scale of Miles
0   5   10   15   20

of Ahikam, whom the king of Babylon had appointed governor of the country.

42 All the captains of the armed bands, including Johanan son of Kareah and Azariah son of Hoshaiah, together with the people, high and low, came to the prophet Jeremiah 2 and said to him, 'May our petition be acceptable to you: Pray to the LORD your God on our behalf and on behalf of this remnant; for, as you see for yourself, only a few of us 3 remain out of many. Pray that the LORD your God may tell us which way we ought 4 to go and what we ought to do.' Then the prophet Jeremiah said to them, 'I have heard your request and will pray to the LORD your God as you desire, and whatever answer the LORD gives I will tell you; I will 5 keep nothing back.' They said to Jeremiah, 'May the LORD be a true and faithful witness against us if we do not keep our oath! We swear that we will do whatever the LORD 6 your God sends you to tell us. Whether we like it or not, we will obey the LORD our God to whom we send you, in order that it may be well with us; we will obey the LORD our God.'

Warning against settling in Egypt

7 Within ten days the word of the LORD came 8 to Jeremiah; so he summoned Johanan son of Kareah, all the captains of the armed

bands with him, and all the people, both high and low. He said to them, These are 9 the words of the LORD the God of Israel, to whom you sent me to present your petition: If you will stay in this land, then I will build 10 you up and not pull you down, I will plant you and not uproot you; I grieve for the disaster which I have brought upon you. Do not be afraid of the king of Babylon 11 whom you now fear. Do not be afraid of him, says the LORD; for I am with you, to save you and deliver you from his power. I will show you compassion, and he too will 12 have compassion on you; he will let you stay on your own soil. But it may be that 13 you will disobey the LORD your God and say, 'We will not stay in this land. No, we 14 will go to Egypt, where we shall see no sign of war, never hear the sound of the trumpet, and not starve for want of bread; and there we will live.' Then hear the word of the LORD, 15 you remnant of Judah. These are the words of the LORD of Hosts the God of Israel: If you are bent on going to Egypt, if you do settle there, then the sword you fear will 16 overtake you in Egypt, and the famine you dread will still be with you, even in Egypt, and there you will die. All the men who are 17 bent on going to Egypt and settling there will die by sword, by famine, or by pestilence; not one shall escape or survive the calamity which I will bring upon them. These are the 18 words of the LORD of Hosts the God of Israel: As my anger and my wrath were poured out upon the inhabitants of Jerusalem, so will my wrath be poured out upon you when you go to Egypt; you will become an object of execration and horror, of ridicule and reproach; you will never see this place again. To you, then, remnant of Judah, 19 the LORD says, Do not go to Egypt. Make no mistake, I can bear witness against you this day. You deceived yourselves when you 20 sent me to the LORD your God and said, 'Pray for us to the LORD our God; tell us all that the LORD our God says and we will do it.' I have told you everything today; but 21 you have not obeyed the LORD your God in what he sent me to tell you. So now be 22 sure of this: you will die by sword, by famine, and by pestilence in the place where you desire to go and make your home.

Journey to Egypt

When Jeremiah had finished reciting to the **43** people all that the LORD their God had sent him to say, Azariah son of Hoshaiah and 2 Johanan son of Kareah and their party had the effrontery to say to*q* Jeremiah, 'You are lying; the LORD our God has not sent you to forbid us to go and make our home in Egypt. Baruch son of Neriah has incited 3

q to say to: *or* to say: It is being said to.

you against us in order to put us in the power
of the Chaldaeans, so that they may kill us
4 or deport us to Babylon.' Johanan son of
Kareah and the captains of the armed bands
and all the people refused to obey the LORD
5 and stay in Judah. So Johanan son of
Kareah and the captains collected the remnant of Judah, all who had returned from
the countries among which they had been
scattered to make their home in Judah—
6 men, women and children, including the
king's daughters, all the people whom Nebuzaradan captain of the guard had left with
Gedaliah son of Ahikam, son of Shaphan,
as well as the prophet Jeremiah and Baruch
7 son of Neriah; these all went to Egypt and
came to Tahpanhes, disobeying the LORD.

Jeremiah prophesies to the remnant

8 The word of the LORD came to Jeremiah at
9 Tahpanhes: Take some large stones and set
them in cement in the pavement at the
entrance to Pharaoh's palace in Tahpanhes.
10 Let the Judaeans see you do it and say to
them, These are the words of the LORD of
Hosts the God of Israel: I will send for my
servant Nebuchadrezzar king of Babylon,
and he will place his throne on these stones
that I have set there, and spread his canopy
11 over them. He will then proceed to strike
Egypt down, killing those doomed to death,
taking captive those who are for captivity,
and putting to the sword those who are for
12 the sword. He will set fire to the temples of
the Egyptian gods, burning the buildings and
carrying the gods into captivity. He will scour
the land of Egypt as a shepherd scours his
clothes to rid them of lice. He will leave
13 Egypt with his purpose achieved. He will
smash the sacred pillars of Beth-shemesh in
Egypt and burn down the temples of the
Egyptian gods.

44 The word that came to Jeremiah for all
the Judaeans who were living in Egypt, in
Migdol, Tahpanhes, Noph, and the district
2 of Pathros: These are the words of the LORD
of Hosts the God of Israel: You have seen
the calamity that I brought upon Jerusalem
and all the cities of Judah: today they are
3 laid waste and left uninhabited, all because
of the wickedness of those who provoked
me to anger by going after other gods, gods
unknown to them, by burning sacrifices to
them. It was you and your fathers who did
4 this. I took pains to send all my servants the
prophets to you with this warning: 'Do not
do this abominable thing which I hate.'
5 But your fathers would not listen; they paid
no heed. They did not give up their wickedness or cease to burn sacrifices to other gods;
6 so my anger and wrath raged like a fire

through the cities of Judah and the streets
of Jerusalem, and they became the desolate
ruin that they are today.

Now these are the words of the LORD the 7
God of Hosts, the God of Israel: Why bring
so great a disaster upon yourselves? Why
bring destruction upon Judaeans, men and
women, children and babes, and leave yourselves without a survivor? This is what comes 8
of your provoking me by all your idolatry in
burning sacrifices to other gods in Egypt
where you have made your home. You will
destroy yourselves and become an object of
ridicule and reproach to all the nations of
the earth. Have you forgotten all the wicked- 9
ness committed by your forefathers, by the
kings of Judah and their wives, by yourselves
and your wives in the land of Judah and in
the streets of Jerusalem? To this day you 10
have shown no remorse, no reverence; you
have not conformed to the law and the
statutes which I set before you and your forefathers. These, therefore, are the words of 11
the LORD of Hosts the God of Israel: I have
made up my mind to bring calamity upon
you and exterminate the people of Judah.
I will deal with the remnant of Judah who 12
were bent on going to make their home in
Egypt; in Egypt they shall all meet their
end. Some shall fall by the sword, others
will meet their end by famine. High and
low alike will die by sword or by famine
and will be an object of execration and
horror, of ridicule and reproach. I will 13
punish those who live in Egypt as I punished
those in Jerusalem, by sword, famine, and
pestilence. Those who had remained in 14
Judah came to make their home in Egypt,
confident that they would return and live
once more in Judah. But they shall not
return;[r] not one of them shall survive, not
one escape.

Sacrificing to the queen of heaven

Then all the men who knew that their wives 15
were burning sacrifices to other gods and
the crowds of women standing by[s] answered
Jeremiah, 'We will not listen to what you 16
tell us in the name of the LORD. We intend 17
to fulfil all the promises by which we have
bound ourselves: we will burn sacrifices to
the queen of heaven and pour drink-
offerings to her as we used to do, we and
our fathers, our kings and our princes, in
the cities of Judah and in the streets of Jerusalem. We then had food in plenty and were
content; no calamity touched us. But from 18
the time we left off burning sacrifices to the
queen of heaven and pouring drink-offerings
to her, we have been in great want, and in
the end we have fallen victims to sword and

---

r Prob. rdg.; Heb. adds except fugitives.
in Pathros.   *s Prob. rdg.; Heb. adds* and all the people who lived in Egypt,

men of Judah; they shall no longer swear in Egypt, 'By the life of the Lord GOD.' I am 27 on the watch to bring you evil and not good, and all the men of Judah who are in Egypt shall meet their end by sword and by famine until not one is left.[t] It is then that all the 28 survivors of Judah who have made their home in Egypt shall know whose word prevails, theirs or mine.

This is the sign I give you, says the LORD, 29 that I intend to punish you in this place, so that you may learn that my words against you will prevail to bring evil upon you: These are the words of the LORD: I will 30 hand over Pharaoh Hophra king of Egypt to his enemies and to those who seek his life, just as I handed over Zedekiah king of Judah to his enemy Nebuchadrezzar king of Babylon who was seeking to take his life.

The LORD's word to Baruch

The word which the prophet Jeremiah spoke 45 to Baruch son of Neriah when he wrote these words in a book at Jeremiah's dictation in the fourth year of Jehoiakim son of Josiah, king of Judah: These are the words of the 2 LORD the God of Israel concerning you, Baruch: You said, 'Woe is me, for the LORD 3 has added grief to all my trials. I have worn myself out with my labours and have had no respite.' This is what you shall say to 4 Baruch, These are the words of the LORD: What I have built, I demolish; what I have planted, I uproot. So it will be with the whole earth. You seek great things for your- 5 self. Leave off seeking them; for I will bring disaster upon all mankind, says the LORD, and I will let you live wherever you go, but you shall save your life and nothing more.

Against the nations

This came to the prophet Jeremiah as the 46 word of the LORD concerning the nations.

EGYPT

9 famine.' And the women said, 'When we burnt sacrifices to the queen of heaven and poured drink-offerings to her, our husbands knew full well that we were making crescent-cakes marked with her image and pouring 0 drink-offerings to her.' When Jeremiah received this answer from these men and 1 women and all the people, he said, 'The LORD did not forget those sacrifices which you and your fathers, your kings and princes and the people of the land burnt in the cities of Judah and in the streets of Jerusalem, and 2 they mounted up in his mind until he could no longer tolerate them, so wicked were your deeds and so abominable the things you did. Your land became a desolate waste, an object of horror and ridicule, with no in- 3 habitants, as it still is. This calamity has come upon you because you burnt these sacrifices and sinned against the LORD and did not obey the LORD or conform to his laws, statutes, and teachings.'

4 Jeremiah further said to all the people and to the women, Listen to the word of the LORD, all you from Judah who live in Egypt. 5 These are the words of the LORD of Hosts the God of Israel: You women have made your actions match your words. 'We will carry out our vows', you said, 'to burn sacrifices to the queen of heaven and to pour drink-offerings to her.' Well then, fulfil your vows by all means, and make your words good. 5 But listen to the word of the LORD, all you from Judah who live in Egypt. I have sworn by my great name, says the LORD, that my name shall never again be on the lips of the

Egypt

Of Egypt: concerning the army of Pharaoh 2 Necho king of Egypt at Carchemish on the river Euphrates, which Nebuchadrezzar king of Babylon defeated in the fourth year of Jehoiakim son of Josiah, king of Judah.

Hold shield and buckler ready 3
and advance to battle;

t Prob. rdg.; Heb. adds Few will escape the sword in Egypt to return to Judah.

4 harness the horses, let the riders mount;
form up, your helmets on, your lances burnished;
on with your coats of mail!
5 But now, what sight is this?
They are broken and routed,
their warriors beaten down;
they have turned to flight and do not look
behind them.
Terror let loose!
This is the very word of the LORD.

6 Can the swift escape, can the warrior save
himself?
In the north, by the river Euphrates,
they stumble and fall.

7 Who is this rising like the Nile,
like its streams turbulent in flood?
8 Egypt is rising like the Nile,
like its streams turbulent in flood.

He*u* says:

I will rise and cover the earth,
I will destroy both city and people.

9 Charge, horsemen! On, you flashing chariots,
on!
Forward, the warriors,
Cushites and men of Put carrying shields,
Lydians grasping their bent bows!
10 This is the day of the Lord, the GOD of Hosts,
a day of vengeance, vengeance on his
enemies;
the sword shall devour and be sated,
drunk with their blood.
For the GOD of Hosts, the Lord, holds
sacrifice
in a northern land, by the river Euphrates.
11 Go up into Gilead and fetch balm,
O virgin people of Egypt.
You have tried many remedies, all in
vain;
no skin shall grow over your wounds.
12 The nations have heard your cry,
and the earth echoes with your screams;
warrior stumbles against warrior
and both fall together.

13 The word which the LORD spoke to the
prophet Jeremiah when Nebuchadrezzar
king of Babylon was coming to harry the
land of Egypt:

14 Announce it in Egypt, proclaim it in Migdol,
proclaim it in Noph and Tahpanhes.
Say, Stand to! Be ready!
for a sword devours all around you.
15 Why does Apis flee, why does your bull-god
not*v* stand fast?
The LORD has thrust him out.
16 The rabble of Egypt stumbles and falls,
man against man;

each says, 'Quick, back to our people,
to the land of our birth, far from the cruel
sword!'
Give Pharaoh of Egypt the title King Bombast,
the man who missed his moment.
By my life, says the King
whose name is the LORD of Hosts,
one shall come mighty as Tabor among the
hills,
as Carmel by the sea.
Make ready your baggage for exile,
you native people of Egypt;
for Noph shall become a waste,
ruined and unpeopled.

Egypt was a lovely heifer,
but a gadfly from the north descended on
her.
The mercenaries in her land were like stall-
fed calves;
but they too turned and fled,
not one of them stood his ground.
The hour of their downfall has come upon
them,
their day of reckoning.
Hark, she is hissing like a snake,
for the enemy has come in all his force.
They fall upon her with axes
like woodcutters at their work.
They cut down her forest, says the LORD,
and it flaunts itself no more;
for they are many as locusts and past counting.
The Egyptians are put to shame, enslaved
to a northern race.
The LORD of Hosts the God of Israel has
spoken:
I will punish Amon god of No,*w*
Egypt with her gods and her princes,
Pharaoh and all who trust in him.
I will deliver them to those bent on their
destruction,
to Nebuchadrezzar king of Babylon and his
troops;
yet in after time the land shall be peopled as
of old.
This is the very word of the LORD.

Israel

But you, Jacob my servant, have no fear,
despair not, O Israel;
for I will bring you back safe from afar
and your offspring from the land where
they are captives;
and Jacob shall be at rest once more,
prosperous and unafraid.
O Jacob my servant, have no fear,
says the LORD; for I am with you.
I will make an end of all the nations
amongst whom I have banished you;

---

u Or It.   *v* Why does Apis . . . not: *or* Why is your bull-god routed, why does he not . . .   *w Prob.
rdg.; Heb. adds* and Pharaoh.

but I will not make an end of you;
though I punish you as you deserve,
I will not sweep you clean away.

PHILISTINES

The Philistines

47 This came to the prophet Jeremiah as the word of the LORD concerning the Philistines 2 before Pharaoh's harrying of Gaza: The LORD has spoken:

See how waters are rising from the north
and swelling to a torrent in spate,
flooding the land and all that is in it,
cities and all who live in them.
Men shall shriek in alarm
and all who live in the land shall howl.
3   Hark, the pounding of his chargers' hooves,
the rattle of his chariots and their rumbling wheels!
Fathers spare no thought for their children;
their hands hang powerless,
4 because the day is upon them when Philistia
will be despoiled,
and Tyre and Sidon destroyed to the last defender;
for the LORD will despoil the Philistines,
that remnant of the isle of Caphtor.
5 Gaza is shorn bare, Ashkelon ruined.
Poor remnant of their strength,
how long will you gash yourselves and cry:
6   Ah, sword in the hand of the LORD,
how long will it be before you rest?
Sheathe yourself, rest and be quiet.
7 How can it rest? for the LORD has given it
work to do
against Ashkelon and the plain by the sea;
there he has assigned the sword its task.

MOAB

Moab

48 Of Moab. The LORD of Hosts the God of Israel has spoken:

Alas for Nebo! it is laid waste;
Kiriathaim is put to shame and captured,
Misgab reduced to shame and dismay;
2   Moab is renowned no longer.

In Heshbon they plot evil against her:
Come, destroy her, and leave her no
longer a nation.
And you who live in Madmen shall be
struck down,
your people pursued by the sword.
Hark to the cries of anguish from Horonaim: 3
great havoc and disaster!
Moab is broken.   4
Their cries are heard as far as Zoar.
On the ascent of Luhith   5
men go up weeping bitterly;
on the descent of Horonaim
cries of 'Disaster!' are heard.
Flee, flee for your lives   6
like a sand-grouse in the wilderness.
Because you have trusted in your defences 7
and your arsenals,
you too will be captured,
and Kemosh will go into exile,
his priests and his captains with him;
and a spoiler shall descend on every city. 8
No city shall escape,
valley and tableland will be laid waste and
plundered;
the LORD has spoken.

Let a warning flash to Moab,ˣ   9
for she shall be laid in ruinsʸ
and her cities shall become waste places
with no inhabitant.
A curse on him who is slack in doing the 10
LORD's work!
A curse on him who withholds his sword
from bloodshed!

All his life long, Moab has lain undisturbed 11
like wine settled on its lees,
not emptied from vessel to vessel;
he has not gone into exile.
Therefore the taste of him is unaltered,
and the flavour stays unchanged.
Therefore the days are coming, says the 12
LORD,
when I will send men to tilt the jars; they shall
tilt them
and empty his vessels and smash his jars;
and Moab shall be betrayed by Kemosh, 13
as Israel was betrayed by Bethel,
a god in whom he trusted.

How can you say, 'We are warriors   14
and men valiant in battle'?
The spoiler of Moab and her cities has 15
come up,
and the flower of her army goes down to
the slaughter.

This is the very word of the King whose name
is the LORD of Hosts.

The downfall of Moab is near at hand,   16
disaster rushes swiftly upon him.

x Let . . . Moab: or Doom Moab to become saltings.   y laid in ruins: prob. rdg.; Heb. obscure.

17   Grieve for him, all you his neighbours
and all you who acknowledge him,
and say, 'Alas! The commander's staff is
   broken,
broken is the baton of honour.'

18   Come down from your place of honour,
sit on the thirsty ground, you natives of
   Dibon;
for the spoiler of Moab has come upon you
and destroyed your citadels.

19   You that live in Aroer, stand on the roadside
and watch,
ask the fugitives, the man running, the
woman escaping,
ask them, 'What has happened?'

20   Moab is reduced to shame and dismay:
howl and shriek,
proclaim by the Arnon that Moab is despoiled,

21   and that judgement has come to the table-
22   land, to Holon and Jahazah, Mephaath and
23   Dibon, Nebo and Beth-diblathaim and
24   Kiriathaim, Beth-gamul, Beth-meon, Kiri-
oth and Bozrah, and to all the cities of Moab
far and near.

25   Moab's horn is hacked off
and his strong arm is broken,
says the LORD.

26   Make Moab drunk—he has defied the
   LORD—
until he overflows with his vomit
and even he becomes a butt for derision.

27   But was Israel ever your butt?
Was he ever in company with thieves,
that whenever you spoke of him you should
shake your head?

28   Leave your cities, you inhabitants of Moab,
and find a home among the crags;
become like a dove which nests
in the rock-face at the mouth of a cavern.

29   We have heard of Moab's pride, and proud
indeed he is,
proud, presumptuous, overbearing, insolent.

30   I know his arrogance, says the LORD;
his boasting is false, false are his deeds.

31   Therefore I will howl over Moab
and cry in anguish at the fate of every soul
in Moab;
I will moan over the men of Kir-heres.

32   I will weep for you more than I wept for
Jazer,
O vine of Sibmah
whose branches spread out to the sea
and stretch as far as Jazer.
The despoiler has fallen on your fruit and
on your vintage,

33   gladness and joy are taken away
from the meadows of Moab,

and I have stopped the flow of wine from
the vats;
nor shall shout follow shout from the harvesters—not one shout.

Heshbon and[z] Elealeh utter cries of anguish 34
which are heard in Jahaz; the sound carries from Zoar to Horonaim and Eglath-
shelishiyah; for the waters of Nimrim have
become a desolate waste. In Moab I will 35
stop their sacrificing at hill-shrines and burning of offerings to their gods, says the LORD.
Therefore my heart wails for Moab like a 36
reed-pipe, wails like a pipe for the men of
Kir-heres. Their hard-earned wealth has
vanished. Every man's head is shorn in 37
mourning, every beard shaved, every hand
gashed, and every waist girded with sackcloth. On Moab's roofs and in her broad 38
streets nothing is heard but lamentation; for
I have broken Moab like a useless thing.[a]
Moab in her dismay has shamefully turned 39
to flight. Moab has become a butt of derision and a cause of dismay to all her
neighbours.

   For the LORD has spoken: 40

   A vulture shall swoop down
and spread out his wings over Moab.
The towns are captured, the strongholds 41
taken;
on that day the spirit of Moab's warriors
shall fail
like the spirit of a woman in childbirth.
Then Moab shall be destroyed, no more 42
to be a nation;
for he defied the LORD.
The hunter's scare, the pit, and the trap 43
threaten all who dwell in Moab,
says the LORD.
If a man runs from the scare 44
he will fall into the pit;
if he climbs out of the pit
he will be caught in the trap.
All this will I bring on Moab in the year of
their reckoning.
This is the very word of the LORD.

In the shadow of Heshbon the fugitives stand 45
helpless;
for fire has blazed out from Heshbon,
flames have shot out from the palace of
Sihon;
they devour the homeland of Moab
and the country of the sons of tumult.
Alas for you, Moab! the people of Kemosh 46
have vanished,
for your sons are taken into captivity
and your daughters led away captive.
Yet in days to come I will restore Moab's 47
fortunes.
This is the very word of the LORD.

Here ends the sentence on Moab.

---

z and: *prob. rdg., cp. Isa. 15. 4; Heb.* as far as.   *a Prob. rdg.; Heb. adds* says the LORD.

Ammon

9 Of the people of Ammon. Thus says the LORD:

Has Israel no sons? Has he no heir?
Why has Milcom inherited the land of Gad,
   and why do his people live in the cities of
   Gad?
2 Look, therefore, a time is coming,
   says the LORD,
when I will make Rabbath Ammon hear the
   battle-cry,
   when it will become a desolate mound of
   ruins
   and its villages will be burnt to ashes,
   and Israel shall disinherit those who dis-
   inherited him,
   says the LORD.

3 Howl, Heshbon, for Ai is despoiled.
   Cry aloud, you villages round Rabbath
   Ammon,
   put on sackcloth and beat your breast,
   and score your bodies with gashes.
   For Milcom will go into exile,
   and with him his priests and officers.
4 Why do you boast of your resources,
   you whose resources are melting away,
you wayward people who trust in your
   arsenals,
   and say, 'Who will dare attack me?'
5 Beware, I am bringing fear upon you from
   every side,[b]
   and every one of you shall be driven headlong
   with no man to round up the stragglers.
6 Yet after this I will restore the fortunes of
   Ammon.
   This is the very word of the LORD.

Edom

7 Of Edom. The LORD of Hosts has said:

Is wisdom no longer to be found in Teman?
Have her sages no skill in counsel?
Has their wisdom decayed?
8 The people of Dedan have turned and fled
   and taken refuge in remote places;
   for I will bring Esau's calamity upon him
   when his day of reckoning comes.
9 When the vintagers come to you
   they will surely leave gleanings;
   and if thieves raid your early crop in the
   night,
   they will take only as much as they want.
10 But I have ransacked Esau's treasure,
   I have uncovered his hiding-places,
   and he has nowhere to conceal himself;
his children, his kinsfolk and his neighbours
   are despoiled;
   there is no one to help him.

11 What! am I to save alive your fatherless
   children?
   Are your widows to trust in me?

12 For the LORD has spoken: Those who
were not doomed to drink the cup shall drink
it none the less. Are you alone to go unpunished? You shall not go unpunished;
you shall drink it. For by my life, says the
LORD, Bozrah shall become a horror and
reproach, a byword and a thing of ridicule;
and all her towns shall be a byword for
ever.

14 When a herald was sent among the nations,
   crying,
'Gather together and march against her,
rouse yourselves for battle',
I heard this message from the LORD:[d]

15 Look, I make you the least of all nations,
   an object of all men's contempt.
16 Your overbearing arrogance and your insolent heart
   have led you astray,
   you who haunt the crannies among the
   rocks
   and keep your hold on the heights of the
   hills.
   Though you build your nest high as a
   vulture,
   thence I will bring you down.
   This is the very word of the LORD.
17 Edom shall become a scene of horror,
   all who pass that way shall be horror-
   struck
   and shall jeer in derision at the blows she
   has borne,
18 overthrown like Sodom and Gomorrah
   and their neighbours,[e]
   says the LORD.
   No man shall live there,
   no mortal make a home in her.
19 Look, like a lion coming up
   from Jordan's dense thickets to the peren-
   nial pastures,
   in a moment I will chase every one away
   and round up the choicest of[f] her rams.
   For who is like me? Who is my equal?
What shepherd can stand his ground before
me?

20 Therefore listen to the LORD's whole purpose against Edom and all his plans against
the people of Teman:

   The young ones of the flock shall be carried off,
   and their pasture shall be horrified at their
   fate.
21 At the sound of their fall the land quakes;
   it cries out, and the cry is heard at the Red
   Sea.[g]

---

*b Prob. rdg.; Heb. adds says the Lord GOD of Hosts.
14–16: cp. Obad. 1–4.*   *e Or inhabitants.*
g Or the Sea of Reeds.

c Verses 9 and 10: cp. Obad. 5, 6.   *d Verses
f the choicest of: prob. rdg.; Heb. who is chosen?*

22 A vulture shall soar and swoop down
and spread out his wings over Bozrah,
and on that day the spirit of Edom's warriors shall fail
like the spirit of a woman in labour.

DAMASCUS

Damascus

23 Of Damascus.

Hamath and Arpad are in confusion,
for they have heard news of disaster;
they are tossed up and down in anxiety
like the unresting sea.
24 Damascus has lost heart and turns to flight;
trembling has seized her,
the pangs of childbirth have gripped her.
25   How forlorn is the town of joyful song,
the city of gladness!
26 Therefore her young men shall fall in her
streets
and all her warriors lie still in death that day.
This is the very word of the LORD of Hosts.
27 Then will I kindle a fire against the wall of
Damascus
and it shall consume the palaces of Ben-
hadad.

THE ARABS

The Arabs

28 Of Kedar and the royal princes[h] of Hazer
which Nebuchadrezzar king of Babylon subdued. The LORD has said:

Come, attack Kedar,
despoil the Arabs of the east.
29   Carry off their tents and their flocks,
their tent-hangings and all their vessels,
drive off their camels too,
and a cry shall go up: 'Terror let loose!'
30   Flee, flee; make haste,
take refuge in remote places, O people of
Hazer,
for the king of Babylon has laid his plans
and formed a design against you,
says the LORD.
31 Come, let us attack a nation living at peace,
in fancied security,
with neither gates nor bars,
sufficient to themselves.

Their camels shall be carried off as booty,
their vast herds of cattle as plunder;
I will scatter them before the wind to roam
the fringes of the desert,[i]
and bring ruin upon them from every side.
Hazer shall become a haunt of wolves,
for ever desolate;
no man shall live there,
no mortal make a home in her.
This is the very word of the LORD.

Elam

This came to the prophet Jeremiah as the
word of the LORD concerning Elam, at the
beginning of the reign of Zedekiah king of
Judah: Thus says the LORD of Hosts:

Listen, I will break the bow of Elam,
the chief weapon of their might;
I will bring four winds against Elam
from the four quarters of heaven;
I will scatter them before these four winds,
and there shall be no nation
to which the exiles from Elam shall not
come.
I will break Elam before their foes,
before those who are bent on their destruction;
I will vent my anger upon them in disaster;
I will harry them with the sword
until I make an end of them.
Then I will set my throne in Elam,
and there I will destroy the king and his
officers.
This is the very word of the LORD.
Yet in days to come I will restore the fortunes
of Elam.
This is the very word of the LORD.

BABYLON

Babylon

The word which the LORD spoke concerning
Babylon, concerning the land of the Chaldaeans, through the prophet Jeremiah:

Declare and proclaim among the nations,
keep nothing back, spread the news:
Babylon is taken,
Bel is put to shame, Marduk is in despair;
the idols of Babylon are put to shame,
her false gods are in despair.
For a nation out of the north has fallen
upon her;
they will make her land a desolate waste
where neither man nor beast shall live.

h royal princes: or kingdom.   i them . . . desert: or to the wind those who clip the hair on their temples.

4 In those days, at that time, says the LORD, the people of Israel and the people of Judah shall come together and go in tears to seek 5 the LORD their God; they shall ask after Zion, turning their faces towards her, and they shall come and join themselves to the LORD in an everlasting covenant which shall not be forgotten.

6 My people were lost sheep, whose shepherds let them stray and run wild on the mountains; they went from mountain to 7 hill and forgot their fold. Whoever found them devoured them, and their enemies said, 'We incur no guilt, because they have sinned against the LORD, the LORD who is the true goal and the hope of all their fathers.'

8 Flee from Babylon, from the land of the Chaldaeans;
go forth, and be like he-goats leading the flock.

9 For I will stir up a host of mighty nations
and bring them against Babylon,
marshalled against her from a northern land;
and from the north she shall be captured.
Their arrows shall be like a practised warrior
who never comes back empty-handed;
10 the Chaldaeans shall be plundered,
and all who plunder them shall take their fill.
This is the very word of the LORD.

11 You ravaged my patrimony; but though you rejoice and exult,
though you run free like a heifer after threshing,
though you neigh like a stallion,
12 your mother shall be cruelly disgraced,
she who bore you shall be put to shame.
Look at her, the mere rump of the nations,
a wilderness, parched and desert,
13 unpeopled through the wrath of the LORD,
nothing but a desolate waste;
all who pass by Babylon shall be horror-struck
and jeer in derision at the sight of her wounds.

14 Marshal your forces against Babylon, on every side,
you whose bows are ready strung;
shoot at her, spare no arrows.

15 Shout in triumph over her, she has thrown up her hands,
her bastions are down, her walls demolished;
this is the vengeance of the LORD.
Take vengeance on her;
as she has done, so do to her.

16 Destroy every sower in Babylon,
every reaper with his sickle at harvest-time.

Before the cruel sword every man will go back to his people,
every man flee to his own land.

Israel is a scattered flock   17
harried and chased by lions:
as the king of Assyria was the first to feed on him,
so the king of Babylon was the last to gnaw his bones.

Therefore the LORD of Hosts the God of   18
Israel says this:
I will punish the king of Babylon and his country
as I have punished the king of Assyria.
I will bring Israel back to his pasture,   19
and he shall graze on Carmel and Bashan;
in the hills of Ephraim and Gilead he shall eat his fill.

In those days, says the LORD, when that   20
time comes, search shall be made for the iniquity of Israel but there shall be none, and for the sin of Judah but it shall not be found; for those whom I leave as a remnant I will forgive.

Attack the land of Merathaim;   21
attack it and the inhabitants of Pekod;
put all to the sword and destroy them,
and do whatever I bid you.
This is the very word of the LORD.

Hark, the sound of war in the land   22
and great destruction!
See how the hammer of all the earth   23
is hacked and broken in pieces,
how Babylon has become
a horror among the nations.
O Babylon, you have laid a snare to be   24
your own undoing;
you have been trapped, all unawares;
there you are, you are caught,
because you have challenged the LORD.
The LORD has opened his arsenal   25
and brought out the weapons of his wrath;
for this is work for the Lord the GOD of Hosts
in the land of the Chaldaeans.
Her harvest-time has come: 26
throw open her granaries,[j] pile her in heaps;
destroy her, let no survivor be left.
Put all her warriors to the sword;   27
let them be led to the slaughter.
Woe upon them! for their time has come,
their day of reckoning.
I hear the fugitives escaping from the land 28
of Babylon
to proclaim in Zion the vengeance of the LORD our God.

Let your arrows be heard whistling against 29
Babylon,
all you whose bows are ready strung.

j Or cattle-pens.

Pitch your tents all around her
so that no one escapes.
Pay her back for all her misdeeds;
as she has done, so do to her,
for she has insulted the LORD the Holy One
of Israel.
30 Therefore her young men shall fall in her
streets,
and all her warriors shall lie still in death that
day.
This is the very word of the LORD.

31 I am against you, insolent city;
for your time has come, your day of reckoning.
This is the very word of the Lord GOD of
Hosts.
32 Insolence shall stumble and fall
and no one shall lift her up,
and I will kindle fire in the heath around
her
and it shall consume everything round
about.

33 The LORD of Hosts has said this:

The peoples of Israel and Judah together are
oppressed;
their captors hold them firmly and refuse to
release them.
34 But they have a powerful advocate,
whose name is the LORD of Hosts;
he himself will plead their cause,
bringing distress on Babylon and turmoil on
its people.

35 A sword hangs over the Chaldaeans,
over the people of Babylon, her officers and
her wise men,
says the LORD.
36 A sword over the false prophets, and they
are made fools,
a sword over her warriors, and they despair,
37 a sword over her horses and her chariots
and over all the rabble within her,
and they shall become like women;
a sword over her treasures, and they shall
be plundered,
38 a sword over her waters, and they shall
dry up;
for it is a land of idols
that glories in its dreaded gods.*k*

39 Therefore marmots and jackals shall skulk
in it, desert-owls shall haunt it, nevermore
shall it be inhabited by men and no one shall
40 dwell in it through all the ages. As when
God overthrew Sodom and Gomorrah and
their neighbours,*l* says the LORD, no man
shall live there, no mortal make a home in
her.

See, a people is coming from the north, a 41
great nation,
mighty*m* kings rouse themselves from earth's
farthest corners;
armed with bow and sabre, they are cruel 42
and pitiless;
bestriding horses, they sound like the thunder
of the sea;
they are like men arrayed for battle against
you, Babylon.
The king of Babylon has heard news of 43
them
and his hands hang limp;
agony grips him, anguish as of a woman in
labour.
Look, like a lion coming up 44
from Jordan's dense thickets to the peren-
nial pastures,
in a moment I will chase every one away
and round up the choicest of*n* the rams.
For who is like me? Who is my equal?
What shepherd can stand his ground before
me?

Therefore listen to the LORD's whole pur- 45
pose against Babylon and all his plans
against the land of the Chaldaeans:

The young ones of the flock shall be carried
off
and their pasture shall be horrified at their
fate.
At the sound of the capture of Babylon 46
the land quakes and her cry is heard among
the nations.

For thus says the LORD: **5**

I will raise a destroying wind
against Babylon and those who live in
Kambul,*o*
and I will send winnowers to Babylon, 2
who shall winnow her and empty her land;
for they shall assail her on all sides on the
day of disaster.
How shall the archer then string his bow 3
or put on his coat of mail?

Spare none of her young men, destroy all her
host,
and let them fall dead in the land of the 4
Chaldaeans,
pierced through in her streets.
Israel and Judah are not left widowed 5
by their God, by the LORD of Hosts;
but the land of the Chaldaeans is full of
guilt,
condemned by the Holy One of Israel.

Flee out of Babylon, every man for himself, 6
or you will be struck down for her sin;
for this is the LORD's day of vengeance,
and he is paying her full recompense.

k dreaded gods: *or* dire portents.　　*l Or* inhabitants.　　*m Or* many.　　*n* the choicest of: *prob.*
rdg.; Heb. who is chosen?　　*o* Kambul: *prob. rdg.; Heb.* the heart of my opponents.

7 Babylon has been a gold cup in the LORD's
   hand
   to make all the earth drunk;
   the nations have drunk of her wine,
   and that has made them mad.
8 Babylon falls suddenly and is broken.
   Howl over her,
   fetch balm for her wound;
   perhaps she will be healed.
9 We would have healed Babylon, but she
   would not be*p* healed.
   Leave her and let us be off, each to his own
   country;
   for her doom reaches to heaven
   and mounts up to the skies.
10 The LORD has made our innocence plain
   to see;
   come, let us proclaim in Zion
   what the LORD our God has done.

11 Sharpen the arrows, fill the quivers.
   The LORD has roused the spirit of the king
   of the Medes;
   for the LORD's purpose against Babylon
   is to destroy it,
   and his vengeance is the avenging of his
   temple.
12 Raise the standard against Babylon's
   walls,
   mount a strong guard, post a watch, set an
   ambush;
   for the LORD has both planned and carried
   out
   what he threatened to do to the people of
   Babylon.
13 O opulent city, standing beside great waters,
   your end has come, your destiny is certain.
14 The LORD of Hosts has sworn by himself,
   saying,
   Once I filled you with men, countless as
   locusts,
   yet a song of triumph shall be chanted over
   you.

The maker of all

5*q* God made the earth by his power,
   fixed the world in place by his wisdom,
   unfurled the skies by his understanding.
16 At the thunder of his voice the waters in
   heaven are amazed;*r*
   he brings up the mist from the ends of the
   earth,
   he opens rifts*s* for the rain
   and brings the wind out of his storehouses.
17 All men are brutish and ignorant,
   every goldsmith is discredited by his
   idol;
   for the figures he casts are a sham,
   there is no breath in them.

They are worth nothing, mere mockeries, 18
which perish when their day of reckoning
comes.
God, Jacob's creator, is not like these; 19
for he is the maker of all.
Israel is the people he claims as his own;
the LORD of Hosts is his name.

Babylon taken

You are my battle-axe, my weapon of war; 20
with you I will break nations in pieces,
and with you I will destroy kingdoms.
With you I will break horse and rider, 21
with you I will break chariot and rider,
with you I will break man and woman, 22
with you I will break young and old,
with you I will break young man and maiden,
with you I will break shepherd and flock, 23
with you I will break ploughman and team,
with you I will break viceroys and governors.
So will I repay Babylon and the people of 24
Chaldaea
for all the wrong which they did in Zion in
your sight.
This is the very word of the LORD.

I am against you, O destroying mountain,*t* 25
you who destroy the whole earth,
and I will stretch out my hand against you
and send you tumbling from your terraces
and make you a burnt-out mountain.
No stone of yours shall be used as a corner- 26
stone,
no stone for a foundation;
but you shall be desolate, for ever waste.
This is the very word of the LORD.

Raise a standard in the land,*u* 27
blow the trumpet among the nations,
hallow the nations for war against her,
summon the kingdoms of Ararat, Minni, and
Ashkenaz,
appoint a commander-in-chief against her,
bring up the horses like a dark swarm of
locusts;*v*
hallow the nations for war against her, 28
the king of the Medes, his viceroys and
governors,
and all the lands of his realm.
The earth quakes and writhes; 29
for the LORD's designs against Babylon
are fulfilled,
to make the land of Babylon desolate and
unpeopled.
Babylon's warriors have given up the 30
fight,
they skulk in the forts;
their courage has failed, they have become
like women.
Her buildings are set on fire, the bars of her
gates broken.

---

p would not be: *or* was not.   *q* Verses 15–19: *cp. 10. 12–16.*   *r* At the thunder . . . amazed: *prob.*
rdg.; Heb. At the sound of his giving tumult of waters in heaven.   *s* rifts: *prob. rdg.; Heb.* lightnings.
t Or O Mount of the Destroyer.   *u* Or earth.   *v* Or hoppers.

L*

31 Runner speeds to meet runner,
    messenger to meet messenger,
    bringing news to the king of Babylon
    that every quarter of his city is taken,
32   the river-crossings are seized,
    the guard-towers set on fire
    and the garrison stricken with panic.

Judgement on Babylon

33 For the LORD of Hosts the God of Israel has
    spoken:
    Babylon is like a threshing-floor when it is
      trodden;
    soon, very soon, harvest-time will come.

34 'Nebuchadrezzar king of Babylon has
      devoured me
    and sucked me dry,
    he has set me aside like an empty jar.
    Like a dragon he has gulped me down;
    he has filled his maw with my delicate
      flesh
    and spewed me up.
35 On Babylon be the violence done to me,
    the vengeance taken upon me!',
    Zion's people shall say.
    'My blood be upon the Chaldaeans!',
    Jerusalem shall say.

36 Therefore the LORD says:
    I will plead your cause, I will avenge you;
    I will dry up her sea*w* and make her waters
      fail;
37 and Babylon shall become a heap of ruins,
    a haunt of wolves,
    a scene of horror and derision, with no
      inhabitant.

38 Together they roar like young lions,
    they growl like the whelps of a lioness.
39 I will cause their drinking bouts to end in
      fever
    and make them so drunk that they will
      writhe and toss,
    then sink into unending sleep, never to
      wake.
    This is the very word of the LORD.
40 I will bring them like lambs to the
      slaughter,
    rams and he-goats together.
41 Sheshak*x* is captured,
    the pride of the whole earth taken;
    Babylon has become a horror amongst the
      nations!
42 The sea has surged over Babylon,
    she is covered by its roaring waves.
43 Her cities have become waste places,
    a land dried up and desert,
    a land in whose cities no man lives
    and through which no mortal travels.
44 I will punish Bel in Babylon
    and make him bring up what he has
      swallowed;

nations shall never again come streaming to
    him.
The wall of Babylon has fallen;
    come out of her, O my people,   45
    and let every man save himself
    from the anger of the LORD.
Then beware of losing heart,   46
fear no rumours spread abroad in the land,
    as rumour follows rumour,
    each year a new one:
violence on earth and ruler against ruler.
Therefore a time is coming   47
    when I will punish Babylon's idols,
    and all her land shall be put to shame,
    and all her slain shall lie fallen in her midst.
Heaven and earth and all that is in them   48
    shall sing in triumph over Babylon;
for marauders from the north shall overrun
    her.
This is the very word of the LORD.
Babylon must fall for the sake of*y* Israel's   49
    slain,
as the slain of all the world fell for the sake
    of Babylon.
You who have escaped from her sword, off   50
    with you, do not linger.
Remember the LORD from afar
    and call Jerusalem to mind.
We are put to shame by the reproaches we   51
    have heard,
    and our faces are covered with confusion:
strangers have entered the sacred courts of
    the LORD's house.

A time is coming therefore, says the LORD,   52
    when I will punish her idols,
    and all through the land there shall be the
      groaning of the wounded.
Though Babylon should reach to the skies   53
    and make her high towers inaccessible,
I will send marauders to overrun her.
    This is the very word of the LORD.
Hark, cries of agony from Babylon!   54
Sounds of destruction from the land of the
    Chaldaeans!
For the LORD is despoiling Babylon   55
and will silence the hum of the city,
before the advancing wave that booms and
    roars
    like mighty waters.
For marauders march on Babylon herself,   56
    her warriors are captured and their bows are
      broken;
for the LORD, a God of retribution, will repay
    in full.
I will make her princes and her wise men   57
    drunk,
    her viceroys and governors and warriors,
    and they shall sink into unending sleep,
      never to wake.
This is the very word of the King,
    whose name is the LORD of Hosts.

---

w Possibly the Euphrates.   *x A name for Babylon.*   *y for the sake of: prob. rdg.; Heb. om.*

58 The LORD of Hosts says:
The walls of broad Babylon shall be razed
    to the ground,
    her lofty gates shall be set on fire.
Worthless now is the thing for which the
    nations toiled;
    the peoples wore themselves out for a mere
    nothing.

Jeremiah and Seraiah

59 The instructions given by the prophet Jeremiah to the quartermaster Seraiah son of Neriah and grandson of Mahseiah, when he went to Babylon with Zedekiah king of Judah in the fourth year of his reign.
60 Jeremiah, having written down in a^z book^a a full description of the disaster which would
61 come upon Babylon, said to Seraiah, 'When you come to Babylon, look at this, read it
62 all and then say, "Thou, O LORD, hast declared thy purpose to destroy this place and leave it with no one living in it, man or beast; it shall be desolate, for ever waste."
63 When you have finished reading the book, tie a stone to it and throw it into the Eu-
64 phrates, and then say, "So shall Babylon sink, never to rise again after the disaster which I shall bring upon her." '

Thus far are the collected sayings of Jeremiah.

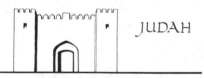

JUDAH

Zedekiah's reign

1^b Zedekiah was twenty-one years old when he came to the throne, and he reigned in Jerusalem for eleven years; his mother was Hamutal daughter of Jeremiah of Libnah.
2 He did what was wrong in the eyes of the
3 LORD, as Jehoiakim had done. Jerusalem and Judah so angered the LORD that in the end he banished them from his sight; and Zedekiah rebelled against the king of Babylon.

Zedekiah taken captive

4 In the ninth year of his reign, in the tenth month, on the tenth day of the month, Nebuchadrezzar king of Babylon advanced with all his army against Jerusalem, invested it and erected watch-towers against it on every
5 side; the siege lasted till the eleventh year of
6 King Zedekiah. In the fourth month of that year, on the ninth day of the month, when famine was severe in the city and there was no food for the common people, the city 7 was thrown open. When Zedekiah king of Judah saw this, he and^c all his armed escort left the city and fled by night through the gate called Between the Two Walls, near the king's garden. They escaped towards the Arabah, although the Chaldaeans were surrounding the city. But the Chaldaean army 8 pursued the king and overtook him in the lowlands of Jericho; and all his company was dispersed. The king was seized and 9 brought before the king of Babylon at Riblah in the land of Hamath, where he pleaded his case before him. The king of Babylon 10 slew Zedekiah's sons before his eyes; he also put to death all the princes of Judah in Riblah. Then the king of Babylon put 11 Zedekiah's eyes out, bound him with fetters of bronze, brought him to Babylon and committed him to prison till the day of his death.

Jerusalem destroyed

In the fifth month, on the tenth day of the 12 month, in the nineteenth year of Nebuchadrezzar king of Babylon, Nebuzaradan, captain of the king's bodyguard,^{d} came to Jerusalem and set fire to the house of the 13 LORD and the royal palace; all the houses in the city, including the mansion of Gedaliah,^{e} were burnt down. The Chaldaean 14 forces with the captain of the guard pulled down the walls all round Jerusalem. ^{f}Nebu- 15 zaradan captain of the guard deported the rest of the people left in the city, those who had deserted to the king of Babylon and any remaining artisans. The captain of the guard 16 left only the weakest class of people to be vine-dressers and labourers.

The Chaldaeans broke up the pillars of 17 bronze in the house of the LORD, the trolleys, and the sea of bronze, and took the metal to Babylon. They took also the pots, shovels, 18 snuffers, tossing-bowls, saucers, and all the vessels of bronze used in the service of the temple. The captain of the guard took away 19 the precious metal, whether gold or silver, of which the cups, firepans, tossing-bowls, pots, lamp-stands, saucers, and flagons were made. The bronze of the two pillars, of the one sea 20 and of the twelve oxen supporting it, which King Solomon had made for the house of the LORD, was beyond weighing. The one 21 pillar was eighteen cubits high and twelve cubits in circumference; it was hollow and the metal was four fingers thick. It had a 22

z Or one.   a Prob. rdg.; Heb. adds all these things which are written concerning Babylon.   b Verses 1–27: cp. 39. 1–10 and 2 Kgs. 24. 18—25. 21.   c When Zedekiah . . . and: prob. rdg., cp. 2 Kgs. 25. 4; Heb. om.   d captain . . . bodyguard: prob. rdg., cp. 2 Kgs. 25. 8; Heb. captain of the bodyguard stood before the king of Babylon.   e Gedaliah: prob. rdg.; Heb. the great man.   f Prob. rdg., cp. 39. 9 and 2 Kgs. 25. 11; Heb. prefixes The weakest class of the people (cp. verse 16).

capital of bronze, five cubits high, and a decoration of network and pomegranates ran all round it, wholly of bronze. The other pillar, with its pomegranates, was exactly
23 like it. Ninety-six pomegranates were exposed to view and there were a hundred in all on the network all round.
24 The captain of the guard took Seraiah the chief priest and Zephaniah the deputy chief priest and the three on duty at the entrance;
25 he took also from the city a eunuch who was in charge of the fighting men, seven of those with right of access to the king who were still in the city, the adjutant-general*g* whose duty was to muster the people for war, and sixty men of the people who were still there.
26 These Nebuzaradan captain of the guard brought to the king of Babylon at Riblah.
27 There, in the land of Hamath, the king of Babylon had them flogged and put to death. So Judah went into exile from their own land.

Total number of exiles
28 These were the people deported by Nebuchadrezzar in the seventeenth*h* year: three
29 thousand and twenty-three Judaeans. In his eighteenth year, eight hundred and thirty-
30 two people from Jerusalem; in his twenty-third year, seven hundred and forty-five

Judaeans were deported by Nebuzaradan the captain of the bodyguard: all together four thousand six hundred people.

Jehoiachin honoured in Babylon
In the thirty-seventh year of the exile of 31 Jehoiachin king of Judah, on the twenty-fifth day of the twelfth month, Evil-merodach king of Babylon in the year of his accession showed favour to Jehoiachin king of Judah. He brought him out of prison, treated him 32 kindly and gave him a seat at table above the kings with him in Babylon. So Jehoiachin 33 discarded his prison clothes and lived as a pensioner of the king for the rest of his life. For his maintenance a regular daily allow- 34 ance was given him by the king of Babylon as long as he lived, to the day of his death.

LAMENTATIONS

Sorrows of captive Zion
1 How solitary lies the city, once so full of people!
Once great among nations, now become a widow;
once queen among provinces, now put to forced labour!
2 Bitterly she weeps in the night,
tears run down her cheeks;
she has no one to bring her comfort
among all that love her;
all her friends turned traitor
and became her enemies.
3 Judah went into the misery of exile
and endless servitude.
Settled among the nations,
she found no resting-place;
all her persecutors fell upon her
in her sore straits.

The paths to Zion mourn, 4
for none attend her sacred feasts;
all her gates are desolate.
Her priests groan and sigh,
her virgins are cruelly treated.
How bitter is her fate!
Her adversaries have become her mas- 5
ters,
her enemies take their ease,
for the LORD has cruelly punished her
because of misdeeds without number;
her young children have gone,
driven away captive by the enemy.
All majesty has vanished 6
from the daughter of Zion.
Her princes have become like deer
that can find no pasture
and run on, their strength all spent,
pursued by the hunter.

g Prob. rdg.; Heb. adds commander-in-chief.
2 Kgs. 25. 27–30.

h Prob. rdg.; Heb. seventh.

i Verses 31–34: cp.

7　Jerusalem has remembered
　　her days of misery and wandering,[a]
　　when her people fell into the power of the
　　　adversary
　　and there was no one to help her.
　　The adversary saw and mocked
　　at her fallen state.

8　Jerusalem had sinned greatly,
　　and so she was treated like a filthy rag;
　　all those who had honoured her held her
　　　cheap,
　　for they had seen her nakedness.
　　What could she do but sigh
　　and turn away?

9　Uncleanness clung to her skirts,
　　and she gave no thought to her fate.
　　Her fall was beyond belief
　　and there was no one to comfort her.
　　Look, LORD, upon her misery,
　　see how the enemy has triumphed.

10　The adversary stretched out his hand
　　to seize all her treasures;
　　then it was that she saw Gentiles
　　entering her sanctuary,
　　Gentiles forbidden by thee to enter
　　the assembly, for it was thine.

11　All her people groaned,
　　they begged for bread;
　　they sold their treasures for food
　　to give them strength again.

　　Look, O LORD, and see
　　how cheap I am accounted.

12　Is it of no concern to you who pass by?
　　If only you would look and see:
　　is there any agony like mine,
　　like these my torments
　　with which the LORD has cruelly punished
　　　me
　　in the day of his anger?

13　He sent down fire from heaven,
　　it ran through my bones;
　　he spread out a net to catch my feet,
　　and turned me back;
　　he made me an example of desolation,
　　racked with sickness all day long.

14　My transgressions were bound[b] upon me,
　　his own hand knotted them round me;
　　his yoke was lifted on to my neck,
　　my strength failed beneath its weight;
　　the Lord abandoned me to its hold,[c]
　　and I could not stand.

15　The Lord treated with scorn
　　all the mighty men within my walls;
　　he marshalled rank on rank against me
　　to crush my young warriors.
　　The Lord trod down, like grapes in the
　　　press,
　　the virgin daughter of Judah.

16　For these things I weep over my plight,[d]
　　my eyes run with tears;

for any to comfort me and renew my
　　strength
are far to seek;
my sons are an example of desolation,
for the enemy is victorious.

Prayer and confession

Zion lifted her hands in prayer,　17
　but there was no one to comfort her;
　the LORD gave Jacob's enemies the order
　to beset him on every side.
Jerusalem became a filthy rag in their midst.

The LORD was in the right;　18
　it was I who rebelled against his com-
　　mands.
Listen, O listen, all you nations,
　and look on my agony:
my virgins and my young men are gone into
　captivity.
I called to my lovers, they broke faith with　19
　me;
my priests and my elders in the city
　went hungry and could find nothing,
although they sought food for themselves
　to renew their strength.
See, LORD, how sorely I am distressed.　20
My bowels writhe in anguish
　and my stomach turns within me,
because I wantonly rebelled.
The sword makes orphans in the streets,
　as plague does within doors.
Hear me when I groan　21
　with no one to comfort me.
All my enemies, when they heard of my
　calamity,
rejoiced at what thou hadst done;
but hasten the day thou hast promised
when they shall become like me.
Let all their evil deeds come before　22
　thee;
torment them in their turn,
　as thou hast tormented me
for all my transgressions;
for my sighs are many and my heart is
　faint.

The LORD punishes Zion

What darkness the Lord in his anger　2
has brought upon the daughter of Zion!
He hurled down from heaven to earth
the glory of Israel,
and did not remember in the day of his
　anger
that Zion was his footstool.
The Lord overwhelmed without pity　2
all the dwellings of Jacob.
In his wrath he tore down
the strongholds of the daughter of Judah;
he levelled with the ground and desecrated
the kingdom and its rulers.

----

a Prob. rdg.; Heb. adds all her treasures which have been from days of old.　　*b bound: prob. rdg.; Heb.
word unknown.　　c its hold: prob. rdg.; Heb. obscure.　　d my plight: prob. rdg.; Heb.* my eye.

3   In his anger he hacked down
the horn of Israel's pride,
he withdrew his helping hand
when the enemy came on;
and he blazed in Jacob like flaming fire
that rages far and wide.

4   In enmity he strung his bow;
he took his stand like an adversary
and with his strong arm he slew
all those who had been his delight;
he poured his fury out like fire
on the tent of the daughter of Zion.

5   The Lord played an enemy's part
and overwhelmed Israel.
He overwhelmed all their towered mansions
and brought down their strongholds in
ruins;
sorrow upon sorrow he brought
to the daughter of Judah.

6   He stripped his tabernacle as a vine is
stripped,
and made the place of assembly a ruin.
In Zion the LORD blotted out all memory
of festal assembly*e* and of sabbath;
king and priest alike he scorned
in the grimness of his anger.

7   The Lord spurned his own altar
and laid a curse upon his sanctuary.
He delivered the walls of her mansions
into the power of the enemy;
in the LORD's very house they raised
shouts of victory
as on a day of festival.

8   The LORD was minded to bring down in
ruins
the walls of the daughter of Zion;
he took their measure with his line
and did not scruple to demolish her;
he made rampart and wall lament,
and both together lay dejected.

9   Her gates are sunk into the earth,
he has shattered and broken their bars;
her king and her rulers are among the
Gentiles,
and there is no law;
her prophets too have received
no vision from the LORD.

10   The elders of the daughter of Zion
sit on the ground and sigh;
they have cast dust on their heads
and clothed themselves in sackcloth;
the virgins of Jerusalem
bow their heads to the ground.

11   My eyes are blinded with tears,
my bowels writhe in anguish.
In my bitterness my bile is spilt on the
earth
because of my people's wound,
when children and infants faint
in the streets of the town

12   and cry to their mothers,
'Where can we get corn and wine?'—
when they faint like wounded things
in the streets of the city,
gasping out their lives
in their mothers' bosom.

13   How can I cheer you? Whose plight is like
yours,
daughter of Jerusalem?
To what can I compare you for your comfort,
virgin daughter of Zion?
For your wound gapes wide as the ocean;
who can heal you?

14   The visions that your prophets saw for
you
were false and painted shams;
they did not bring home to you your guilt
and so reverse your fortunes.
The visions that they saw for you were
delusions,
false and fraudulent.*f*

15   All those who pass by
snap their fingers at you;
they hiss and wag their heads at you,
daughter of Jerusalem:
'Is this the city once called Perfect in beauty,
Joy of the whole earth?'

16   All your enemies
make mouths and jeer at you;
they hiss and grind their teeth,
saying, 'Here we are,
this is the day we have waited for;
we have lived to see it.'

17   The LORD has done what he planned to do,
he has fulfilled his threat,
all that he ordained from days of old.
He has demolished without pity
and let the enemy rejoice over you,
filling your adversaries with pride.

18   Cry with a full heart*g* to the Lord,
O wall of the daughter of Zion;
let your tears run down like a torrent
by day and by night.
Give yourself not a moment's rest,
let your tears never cease.

19   Arise and cry aloud in the night;
at the beginning of every watch
pour out your heart like water
in the Lord's very presence.
Lift up your hands to him
for the lives of your children.*h*

20   Look, LORD, and see:
who is it that thou hast thus tormented?
Must women eat the fruit of their wombs,
the children they have brought safely to
birth?
Shall priest and prophet be slain
in the sanctuary of the Lord?

---

e festal assembly: *or* appointed seasons.   *f* fraudulent: *or* causing banishment.   *g* Cry . . . heart:
prob. rdg.; Heb. Their heart cried.   *h* *Prob. rdg.; Heb. adds* who faint with hunger at every street-corner.

21 There in the streets young men and old
  lie on the ground.
  My virgins and my young men have fallen
  by sword and by famine;
  thou hast slain them in the day of thy
  anger,
  slaughtered them without pity.
22 Thou didst summon my enemies against
  me from every side,
  like men assembling for a festival;
  not a man escaped, not one survived
  in the day of the LORD's anger.
  All whom I brought safely to birth and
  reared
  were destroyed by my enemies.

Despair

3 I am the man who has known affliction,
  I have felt the rod of his wrath.
2 It was I whom he led away and left to walk
  in darkness, where no light is.
3 Against me alone he has turned his hand,
  and so it is all day long.
4 He has wasted away my flesh and my skin
  and broken all my bones;
5 he has built up walls around me,
  behind and before,
6 and has cast me into a place of darkness
  like a man long dead.
7 He has walled me in so that I cannot
  escape,
  and weighed me down with fetters;
8 even when I cry out and call for help,
  he rejects my prayer.
9 He has barred my road with blocks of
  stone
  and tangled up my way.
10 He lies in wait for me like a bear
  or a lion lurking in a covert.
11 He has made my way refractory and
  lamed me
  and left me desolate.
12 He has strung his bow
  and made me the target for his arrows;
13 he has pierced my kidneys with shafts
  drawn from his quiver.
14 I have become a laughing-stock to all
  nations,
  the target of their mocking songs all
  day.
15 He has given me my fill of bitter herbs
  and made me drunk with wormwood.

He has broken my teeth on gravel; 16
  fed on ashes, I am racked with pain;
  peace has gone out of my life, 17
  and I have forgotten what prosperity
  means.
  Then I cry out that my strength has gone 18
  and so has my hope in the LORD.

Hope

The memory of my distress and my 19
  wanderings
  is[i] wormwood and gall.
  Remember, O remember, 20
  and stoop down to me.[j][k]
  All this I take to heart 21
  and therefore I will wait patiently:
  the LORD's true love is surely not spent,[l] 22
  nor has his compassion failed;
  they are new every morning, 23
  so great is his constancy.
  The LORD, I say, is all that I have; 24
  therefore I will wait for him patiently.
  The LORD is good to those who look for 25
  him,
  to all who seek him;
  it is good to wait in patience and sigh 26
  for deliverance by the LORD.
  It is good, too, for a man 27
  to carry the yoke in his youth.
  Let him sit alone and sigh 28
  if it is heavy upon him;
  let him lay his face in the dust, 29
  and there may yet be hope.
  Let him turn his cheek to the smiter 30
  and endure full measure of abuse;
  for the Lord will not cast off 31
  his servants[m] for ever.
  He may punish cruelly, yet he will have 32
  compassion
  in the fullness of his love;
  he does not willingly afflict 33
  or punish any mortal man.

Repentance

To trample underfoot 34
  any prisoner in the land,
  to deprive a man of his rights 35
  in defiance of the Most High,
  to pervert justice in the courts— 36
  such things the Lord has never approved.

Who can command and it is done, 37
  if the Lord has forbidden it?
  Do not both bad and good proceed 38
  from the mouth of the Most High?
  Why should any man living complain, 39
  any mortal who has sinned?
  Let us examine our ways and put them to 40
  the test
  and turn back to the LORD;

---

i The memory . . . is: *or* Remember my distress and my wanderings, the . . .   *j* stoop down to me: *prob.*
original rdg., *altered in Heb. to* I sink down.   *k* Remember . . . me: *or* I remember, I remember them and
sink down.   *l* spent: *prob. rdg.*; *Heb. unintelligible.*   *m* his servants: *prob. rdg.*; *Heb. om.*

41 let us lift up our hearts, not our hands,
to God in heaven.

42 We ourselves have sinned and rebelled,
and thou hast not forgiven.

43 In anger thou hast turned[n] and pursued us
and slain without pity;

44 thou hast hidden thyself behind the clouds
beyond reach of our prayers;

45 thou hast treated us as offscouring and refuse
among the nations.

46 All our enemies make mouths
and jeer at us.

47 Before us lie hunter's scare and pit,
devastation and ruin.

48 My eyes run with streams of water
because of my people's wound.

49 My eyes stream with unceasing tears
and refuse all comfort,

50 while the LORD in heaven looks down
and watches my affliction,[o]

51 while the LORD torments[p] me
with the fate of all the daughters of my city.

Prayer for vindication

52 Those who for no reason were my enemies
drove me cruelly like a bird;

53 they thrust me alive into the silent pit,
and they closed it over me with a stone;

54 the waters rose high above my head,
and I said, 'My end has come.'

55 But I called on thy name, O LORD,
from the depths of the pit;

56 thou heardest my voice; do not turn a deaf ear
when I cry, 'Come to my relief.'

57 Thou wast near when I called to thee;
thou didst say, 'Have no fear.'

58 Lord, thou didst plead my cause
and ransom my life;

59 thou sawest, LORD, the injustice done to me
and gavest judgement in my favour;

60 thou sawest their vengeance,
all their plots against me.

61 Thou didst hear their bitter taunts, O LORD,
their many plots against me,

62 the whispering, the murmurs of my enemies
all the day long.

63 See how, whether they sit or stand,
they taunt me bitterly.

64 Pay them back for their deeds, O LORD,
pay them back what they deserve.

65 Show them how hard thy heart can be,
how little concern thou hast for them.

66 Pursue them in anger and exterminate them
from beneath thy heavens, O LORD.

Zion's wretched condition

4

How dulled is the gold,
how tarnished the fine gold!
The stones of the sanctuary[q] lie strewn
at every street-corner.

2 See Zion's precious sons,
once worth their weight in finest gold,
now counted as pitchers of earthenware
made by any potter's hand.

3 Even whales[r] uncover the teat
and suckle their young;
but the daughters of my people are cruel
as ostriches in the desert.

4 The sucking infant's tongue
cleaves to its palate from thirst;
young children beg for bread
but no one offers them a crumb.

5 Those who once fed delicately
are desolate in the streets,
and those nurtured in purple
now grovel on dunghills.

6 The punishment[s] of my people is worse
than the penalty[t] of Sodom,
which was overthrown in a moment
and no one wrung his hands.

7 Her crowned princes[u] were once purer than snow,
whiter than milk;
they were ruddier than branching coral,[v]
and their limbs were lapis lazuli.

8 But their faces turned blacker than soot,
and no one knew them in the streets;
the skin was drawn tight over their bones,
dry as touchwood.

9 Those who died by the sword were more fortunate
than those who died of hunger;
these wasted away, deprived
of the produce of the field.

10 Tender-hearted women with their own hands
boiled their own children;
their children became their food
in the day of my people's wounding.

11 The LORD glutted his rage
and poured forth his anger;
he kindled a fire in Zion,
and it consumed her foundations.

12 This no one believed, neither the kings of the earth
nor anyone that dwelt in the world:
that enemy or invader would enter
the gates of Jerusalem.

---

n Prob. rdg.; Heb. hidden.   *o* my affliction: *prob. rdg.; Heb.* my eye.   *p* the LORD torments: *prob. rdg.; Heb.* tormenting.   *q* The stones of the sanctuary: *or* Bright gems.   *r Prob. rdg.; Heb.* jackals.   *s Or* iniquity.   *t Or* sin.   *u* crowned princes: *or* Nazirites.   *v* than . . . coral: *prob. rdg.; Heb.* branch than coral.

13 It was for the sins of her prophets
and for the iniquities of her priests,
who shed within her walls
the blood of the righteous.

14 They wandered blindly in the streets,
so stained with blood
that men would not touch
even their garments.

15 'Away, away; unclean!' men cried to
them.
'Away, do not come near.'
They hastened away, they wandered
among the nations,*w*
unable to find any resting-place.

16 The LORD himself scattered them,
he thought of them no more;
he showed no favour to priests,
no pity for elders.

When Zion's punishment is complete

17 Still we strain our eyes,
looking in vain for help.
We have watched and watched
for a nation powerless to save us.

18 When we go out, we take to by-ways
to avoid the public streets;
our days are all but finished,*x*
our end has come.

19 Our pursuers have shown themselves
swifter
than vultures in the sky;
they are hot on our trail over the hills,
they lurk to catch us in the wilderness.

20 The LORD's anointed, the breath of life
to us,
was caught in their machinations;
although we had thought to live
among the nations, safe under his protection.

21 Rejoice and be glad, daughter of Edom,
you who live in the land of Uz.
Yet the cup shall pass to you in your
turn,
and when you are drunk you will expose
yourself to shame.

22 The punishment for your sin, daughter of
Zion, is now complete,
and never again shall you be carried into
exile.
But you, daughter of Edom, your sin shall
be punished,
and your guilt revealed.

Prayer for restoration

Remember, O LORD, what has befallen us; **5**
look, and see how we are scorned.
Our patrimony is turned over to strangers 2
and our homes to foreigners.
We are like orphans, without a father; 3
our mothers are like widows.
We must buy our own water to drink, 4
our own wood can only be had at a price.
The yoke is on our necks, we are over- 5
driven;
we are weary and are given no rest.
We came to terms, now with the Egyptians, 6
now with the Assyrians, to provide us with
food.
Our fathers sinned and are no more, 7
and we bear the burden of their guilt.
Slaves have become our rulers, 8
and there is no one to rescue us from them.
We must bring in our food from the wilder- 9
ness,
risking our lives in the scorching heat.*y*
Our skins are blackened as in a furnace 10
by the ravages of starvation.
Women were raped in Zion, 11
virgins raped in the cities of Judah.
Princes were hung up by their hands, 12
and elders received no honour.
Young men toil to grind corn, 13
and boys stumble under loads of wood.
Elders have left off their sessions in the 14
gate,
and young men no longer pluck the strings.
Joy has fled from our hearts, 15
and our dances are turned to mourning.
The garlands have fallen from our heads; 16
woe betide us, sinners that we are.
For this we are sick at heart, 17
for all this our eyes grow dim:
because Mount Zion is desolate 18
and over it the jackals run wild.

O LORD, thou art enthroned for ever, 19
thy throne endures from one generation
to another.
Why wilt thou quite forget us 20
and forsake us these many days?
O LORD, turn us back to thyself, and we will 21
come back;
renew our days as in times long past.
For if thou hast utterly rejected us, 22
then great indeed has been thy anger
against us.

w Prob. rdg.; Heb. adds they said.   *x* our . . . finished: *prob. rdg.; Heb.* our end has drawn near, our days
are complete.   *y* in the scorching heat: *or* by the sword.

THE BOOK OF THE PROPHET
EZEKIEL

A vision of God

1 ON THE FIFTH DAY of the fourth
month in the thirtieth year, while I was
among the exiles by the river Kebar,*a* the
heavens were opened and I saw a vision of
2 God. On the fifth day of the month in the
fifth year of the exile of King Jehoiachin,
3 the word of the LORD came to Ezekiel son
of Buzi the priest, in Chaldaea, by the river
Kebar, and there the hand of the LORD
came upon him.

4 I saw a storm wind coming from the north,
a vast cloud with flashes of fire and brilliant
light about it; and within was a radiance like
5 brass, glowing in the heart of the flames. In
the fire was the semblance of four living
6 creatures in human form. Each had four
7 faces and each four wings; their legs were
straight, and their hooves were like the
hooves of a calf, glittering like a disc of
8 bronze. Under the wings on each of the four
sides were human hands; all four creatures
9 had faces and wings, and their wings touched
one another. They did not turn as they
moved; each creature went straight for-
10 ward. Their faces were like this: all four had
the face of a man and the face of a lion on the
right, on the left the face of an ox and the
11 face of an eagle. Their wings were spread;
each living creature had one pair touching

its neighbours',*b* while one pair covered its
body. They moved straight forward in what- 12
ever direction the spirit*c* would go; they
never swerved in their course. The appear- 13
ance of the creatures was as if fire from
burning coals or torches were darting to
and fro among them; the fire was radiant,
and out of the fire came lightning.*d*

As I looked at the living creatures, I saw 15
wheels on the ground, one beside each of
the four.*e* The wheels sparkled like topaz, 16
and they were all alike: in form and working
they were like a wheel inside a wheel, and 17
when they moved in any of the four directions they never swerved in their course. All 18
four had hubs and each hub had a projection
which had the power of sight,*f* and the rims
of the wheels were full of eyes all round.
When the living creatures moved, the wheels 19
moved beside them; when the creatures rose
from the ground, the wheels rose; they 20
moved in whatever direction the spirit*c*
would go; and the wheels rose together with
them, for the spirit of the living creatures
was in the wheels. When the one moved, the 2
other moved; when the one halted, the other
halted; when the creatures rose from the
ground, the wheels rose together with them,
for the spirit of the creatures was in the
wheels.

a Or the Kebar canal.   *b its neighbours': prob. rdg.; Heb. unintelligible.*   *c Or wind.*   *d Prob.
rdg., cp. Sept.; Heb. adds (14) and the living creatures went out (prob. rdg.; Heb. obscure) and in like rays of light.*
e one ... four: prob. rdg.; Heb. obscure.   *f the power of sight: prob. rdg.; Heb. fear.*

22 Above the heads of the living creatures was, as it were, a vault glittering like a sheet of ice, awe-inspiring, stretched over their 23 heads above them. Under the vault their wings were spread straight out, touching one another, while one pair covered the body of 24 each. I heard, too, the noise of their wings; when they moved it was like the noise of a great torrent or of a cloud-burst,*g* like the noise of a crowd or of an armed camp; when 25 they halted their wings dropped. A sound was heard above the vault over their heads, 26 as they halted with drooping wings. Above the vault over their heads there appeared, as it were, a sapphire*h* in the shape of a throne, and high above all, upon the throne, 27 a form in human likeness. I saw what might have been brass glowing like fire in a furnace from the waist upwards; and from the waist downwards I saw what looked like fire with 28 encircling radiance. Like a rainbow in the clouds on a rainy day was the sight of that encircling radiance; it was like the appearance of the glory of the LORD.

Mission and message

2 When I saw this I threw myself on my face, and heard a voice speaking to me: Man, he 2 said, stand up, and let me talk with you. As he spoke, a spirit came into me and stood me on my feet, and I listened to him speak-3 ing. He said to me, Man, I am sending you to the Israelites, a nation of rebels who have rebelled against me. Past generations of them have been in revolt against me to this 4 very day, and this generation to which I am sending you is stubborn and obstinate. When you say to them, 'These are the words 5 of the Lord GOD', they will know that they have a prophet among them, whether they listen or whether they refuse to listen, be-6 cause they are rebels. But you, man, must not be afraid of them or of what they say, though they are rebels against you and rene-gades, and you find yourself sitting on scor-pions. There is nothing to fear in what they say, and nothing in their looks to terrify 7 you, rebels though they are. You must speak my words to them, whether they listen or whether they refuse to listen, rebels that they 8 are. But you, man, must listen to what I say and not be rebellious like them. Open your mouth and eat what I give you.

9 Then I saw a hand stretched out to me, 10 holding a scroll. He unrolled it before me, and it was written all over on both sides with **3** dirges and laments and words of woe. Then he said to me, 'Man, eat what is in front of you, eat this scroll; then go and speak to the 2 Israelites.' So I opened my mouth and he 3 gave me the scroll to eat. Then he said, 'Man,

swallow this scroll I give you, and fill your-self full.' So I ate it, and it tasted as sweet as honey.

Man, he said to me, go and tell the Israel-4 ites what I have to say to them. You are sent 5 not to people whose speech is thick and diffi-cult, but to Israelites. No; I am not sending 6 you to great nations whose speech is so thick and so difficult that you cannot make out what they say; if however I had sent you to them they would have listened to you. But 7 the Israelites will refuse to listen to you, for they refuse to listen to me, so brazen are they all and stubborn. But I will make you a 8 match for them. I will make you as brazen as they are and as stubborn as they are. I will 9 make your brow like adamant, harder than flint. Never fear them, never be terrified by them, rebels though they are. And he said 10 to me, Listen carefully, man, to all that I have to say to you, and take it to heart. Go 11 to your fellow-countrymen in exile and speak to them. Whether they listen or refuse to listen, say, 'These are the words of the Lord GOD.'

Then a spirit*i* lifted me up, and I heard 12 behind me a fierce rushing sound as the glory of the LORD rose*j* from his place. I heard the sound of the living creatures' 13 wings brushing against one another, the sound of the wheels beside them, and a fierce rushing sound. A spirit*i* lifted me and 14 carried me along, and I went full of exalta-tion, the hand of the LORD strong upon me. So I came to the exiles at Tel-abib who were 15 settled by the river Kebar. For seven days I stayed with them, dumbfounded.

At the end of seven days the word of the 16 LORD came to me: Man, I have made you 17 a watchman for the Israelites; you will take messages from me and carry my warnings to them. It may be that I pronounce sentence 18 of death on a wicked man:*k* if you do not warn him to give up his wicked ways and so save his life, the guilt is his; because of his wickedness he shall die, but I will hold you answerable for his death. But if you have 19 warned him and he still continues in his wicked and evil ways, he shall die because of his wickedness, but you will have saved your-self. Or it may be that a righteous man turns 20 away and does wrong, and I let that be the cause of his downfall; he will die because you have not warned him. He will die for his sin; the righteous deeds he has done will not be taken into account, and I will hold you answerable for his death. But if· you 21 have warned the righteous man not to sin and he has not sinned, then he will have saved his life because he has been warned, and you will have saved yourself.

g Or of the Almighty.   *h Or lapis lazuli.*
k Prob. rdg.; Heb. adds if you do not warn him.

i Or wind.   *j rose: prob. rdg.; Heb. obscure.*

The LORD speaks to Ezekiel

22 The hand of the LORD came upon me there, and he said to me, Rise up; go out into the 23 plain, and there I will speak to you. So I rose and went out into the plain; the glory of the LORD was there, like the glory which I had seen by the river Kebar, and I threw 24 myself down on my face. Then a spirit came into me and stood me on my feet, and spoke to me: Go, he said, and shut yourself up in 25 your house. You shall be tied and bound with ropes, man, so that you cannot go out 26 among the people. I will fasten your tongue to the roof of your mouth and you will be unable to speak; you will not be the one to 27 rebuke them, rebels though they are. But when I have something to say to you, I will give you back the power of speech. Then you will say to them, 'These are the words of the Lord GOD.' If anyone will listen, he may listen, and, if he refuses to listen, he may refuse; for they are rebels.

The siege of Jerusalem portrayed

4 Man, take a tile and set it before you. Draw 2 a city on it, the city of Jerusalem: lay siege to it, erect watch-towers against it, raise a siege-ramp, put mantelets in position, and bring battering-rams against it all round. 3 Then take an iron griddle, and put it as a wall of iron between you and the city. Keep your face turned towards the city; it will be the besieged and you the besieger. This will be a sign to the Israelites.

4 Now lie on your left side, and I will lay Israel's iniquity on you; you shall bear their iniquity for as many days as you lie on that 5 side. Allowing one day for every year of their iniquity, I ordain that you bear it for one hundred and ninety days; thus you shall bear 6 Israel's iniquity. When you have completed all this, lie down a second time on your right side, and bear Judah's iniquity for forty days; 7 I count one day for every year. Then turn your face towards the siege of Jerusalem and 8 bare your arm, and prophesy against it. See how I tie you with ropes so that you cannot turn over from one side to the other until you complete the days of your distress.

9 Then take wheat and barley, beans and lentils, millet and spelt. Mix them all in one bowl and make your bread out of them. You are to eat it during the one hundred and ninety days you spend lying on your side. And you must weigh out your food; you 10 may eat twenty shekels' weight a day, taking it from time to time. Measure out your 11 drinking water too; you may drink a sixth of a hin a day, taking it from time to time. You are to eat your bread baked like barley 12 cakes, using human dung as fuel, and you must bake it where people can see you. Then 13 the LORD said, 'This is the kind of bread, unclean bread, that the Israelites will eat in the foreign lands into which I shall drive them.' But I said, 'O Lord GOD, I have never 14 been made unclean, never in my life have I eaten what has died naturally or been killed by wild beasts; no tainted meat has ever passed my lips.' So he allowed me to 15 use cow-dung instead of human dung to bake my bread.

Then he said to me, Man, I am cutting 16 short their daily bread in Jerusalem; people will weigh out anxiously the bread they eat, and measure with dismay the water they drink. So their food and their water will run 17 short until they are dismayed at the sight of one another; they will waste away because of their iniquity.

Man, take a sharp sword, take it like a 5 barber's razor and run it over your head and your chin. Then take scales and divide the hair into three. When the siege comes to an 2 end, burn one third of the hair in a fire in the centre of the city; cut up one third with the sword all round the city; scatter one third to the wind, and I will follow it with drawn sword. Take a few of these hairs and 3 tie them up in a fold of your robe. Then take 4 others of them, throw them into the fire and burn them, and out of them fire will come upon all Israel.

The reason for Jerusalem's fall

These are the words of the Lord GOD: This 5 city of Jerusalem I have set among the nations, with other countries around her, and she has rebelled against my laws and 6 my statutes more wickedly than those nations and countries; for her people have rejected my laws and refused to conform to my statutes.

Therefore the Lord GOD says: Since you 7 have been more ungrateful than the nations around you and have not conformed to my statutes and have not kept my laws or even the laws of the nations around you, there- 8 fore, says the Lord GOD, I, in my turn, will be against you; I will execute judgements in your midst for the nations to see, such judge- 9 ments as I have never executed before nor ever will again, so abominable have your offences been. Therefore, O Jerusalem, 10 fathers will eat their children and children their fathers in your midst; I will execute

Ancient weights

judgements on you, and any who are left in
11 you I will scatter to the four winds. As I live,
says the Lord GOD, because you have defiled
my holy place with all your vile and abominable rites, I in my turn will consume you
without pity; I in my turn will not spare you.
12 One third of your people shall die by pestilence and perish by famine in your midst;
one third shall fall by the sword in the
country round about; and one third I will
scatter to the four winds and follow with
13 drawn sword. Then my anger will be spent,
I will abate my fury against them and be
calm; when my fury is spent they will know
that it is I, the LORD, who spoke in jealous
14 passion. I have made you a scandal[l] and a
reproach to the nations around you, and all
15 who pass by will see it. You will be an object
of reproach and abuse, a terrible lesson to
the nations around you, when I pass sentence
on you and do judgement in anger and fury.
16 I, the LORD, have spoken. When I shoot the
deadly arrows of famine against you,[m] arrows
of destruction, I will shoot to destroy you.
I will bring famine upon you and cut short
17 your daily bread; I will unleash famine and
beasts of prey upon you, and they will leave
you childless. Pestilence and slaughter will
sweep through you, and I will bring the
sword upon you. I, the LORD, have spoken.

Israel a desolate waste

6 These were the words of the LORD to me:
2 Man, look towards the mountains of Israel,
3 and prophesy to them: Mountains of Israel,
hear the word of the Lord GOD. This is his
word to mountains and hills, watercourses
and valleys: I am bringing a sword against
you, and I will destroy your hill-shrines.
4 Your altars will be made desolate, your
incense-altars shattered, and I will fling
5 down your slain before your idols. I will
strew the corpses of the Israelites before

their idols, and I will scatter your bones
about your altars. In all your settlements the 6
blood-spattered altars[n] shall be laid waste
and the hill-shrines made desolate. Your
altars will be waste and desolate and your
idols shattered and useless, your incense-
altars hewn down, and all your works wiped
out; with the slain falling about you, you 7
shall know that I am the LORD. But when 8
they fall,[o] I will leave you, among the nations,
some who survive the sword. When you are
scattered in foreign lands, these survivors, 9
in captivity among the nations, will remember how I was grieved because their hearts
had turned wantonly from me and their
eyes had gone roving wantonly after idols.
Then they will loathe themselves for all the
evil they have done with their abominations.
So they will know that I am the LORD, that 10
I was uttering no vain threat when I said
that I would bring this evil upon them.

These are the words of the Lord GOD: 11
Beat your hands together, stamp with your
foot, bemoan your vile abominations, people
of Israel. Men will fall by sword, famine, and
pestilence. Far away they will die by pesti- 12
lence; at home they will fall by the sword; any
who survive or are spared will die by famine,
and so at last my anger will be spent. You 13
will know that I am the LORD when their
slain fall among the idols round their altars,
on every high hill, on all mountain-tops,
under every spreading tree, under every
leafy terebinth, wherever they have brought
offerings of soothing odour for their idols
one and all. So I will stretch out my hand 14

over them and make the land a desolate
waste in all their settlements, more desolate
than the desert of Riblah.[p] They shall know
that I am the LORD.

Impending ruin

The word of the LORD came to me: Man, **7**
                                          1 2

l Or desolation.   *m* *Prob. rdg.; Heb.* them.
n blood-spattered altars: *or* cities.   *o* when
they fall: *prob. rdg.; Heb.* obscure.   *p* *Prob.*
rdg.; Heb. Diblah.

the Lord GOD says this to the land of Israel:
An end is coming, the end is coming upon
3 the four corners of the land.*q* The end is now
upon you; I will unleash my anger against
you; I will call you to account for your doings
and bring your abominations upon your
4 own heads. I will neither pity nor spare you:
I will make you suffer for your doings and
the abominations that continue in your
midst. So you shall know that I am the LORD.
5 These are the words of the Lord GOD:
Behold, it comes, disasters one upon another;
6 7 the end, the end, it comes, it comes.*r* Doom
is coming upon you, dweller in the land; the
time is coming, the day is near, with con-
8 fusion and the crash of thunder.*s* Now, in
an instant, I will vent my rage upon you and
let my anger spend itself. I will call you to
account for your doings and bring your
9 abominations upon your own heads. I will
neither pity nor spare; I will make you
suffer for your doings and the abominations
that continue in your midst. So you shall
know that it is I, the LORD, who strike the
blow.
10 Behold, the day! the doom is here, it has
burst upon them. Injustice buds, insolence
11 blossoms, violence shoots up into injustice
and wickedness. And it is all their fault, the
fault of their turmoil and tumult and all
12 their restless ways. The time has come, the
day has arrived; the buyer has no reason to

Buyer and seller

be glad, and the seller none for regret, for
13 I am angry at all their turmoil. The seller
will never go back on his bargain while
either of them lives; for the bargain will
never be reversed because of the turmoil,
and no man will exert himself, even in his
14 iniquity, as long as he lives. The trumpet
has sounded and all is ready, but no one
goes out to war.

Outside is the sword, inside are pestilence 15
and famine; in the country men will die by
the sword, in the city famine and pestilence
will carry them off. If any escape and take 16
to the mountains, like moaning doves, there
will I slay them, each for his iniquity, while 17
their hands hang limp and their knees run
with urine. They will go in sackcloth, shud- 18
dering from head to foot, with faces downcast and heads close shaved. They shall fling 19
their silver into the streets and cast aside
their gold like filth; their silver and their
gold will be powerless to save them on the
day of the LORD's fury. Their hunger will
not be satisfied nor their bellies filled; for
their iniquity will be the cause of their downfall. They have fed their pride on their 20
beautiful jewels, which they made into vile
and abominable images. Therefore I will
treat their jewels like filth, I will hand them 21
over as plunder to foreigners and as booty
to the most evil people on earth, and these
will defile them. I will turn my face from 22
them and let my treasured land be profaned;
brigands will come in and defile it.
Clench your fists, for the land is full of 23
bloodshed*t* and the city full of violence. I 24
will let in the scum of nations to take possession of their houses; I will quell the pride
of the strong, and their sanctuaries shall be
profaned. Shuddering will come over them, 25
and they will look in vain for peace. Tempest 26
shall follow upon tempest and rumour upon
rumour. Men will go seeking a vision from
a prophet; there will be no more guidance
from a priest, no counsel from elders. The 27
king will mourn, the prince will be clothed
with horror, the hands of the common
people will shake with fright. I will deal with
them as they deserve, and call them to
account for their doings; and so they shall
know that I am the LORD.

Ezekiel's vision of Jerusalem

On the fifth day of the sixth month in the **8**
sixth year, I was sitting at home and the
elders of Judah were with me. Suddenly
the hand of the Lord GOD came upon me,
and I saw what looked like a man. He seemed 2
to be all fire from the waist down and to shine
and glitter like brass from the waist up. He 3
stretched out what seemed a hand and
seized me by the forelock. A spirit*u* lifted me
up between heaven and earth, carried me
to Jerusalem in a vision of God and put
me down at the entrance to the inner gate
facing north, where stands the image of
Lust to rouse lustful passion. The glory of 4
the God of Israel was there, like the vision
I had seen in the plain. The LORD said to 5
me, 'Man, look northwards.' I did so, and

---

q Or earth.   *r Prob. rdg.; Heb. adds* it wakes up, behold it comes.   *s* and the crash of thunder: *prob.*
rdg.; Heb. unintelligible.   *t* bloodshed: *prob. rdg.; Heb.* the judgement of bloodshed.   *u Or* wind.

there to the north of the altar gate, at the
6 entrance, was that image of Lust. 'Man,' he
said, 'do you see what they are doing? The
monstrous abominations which the Israelites practise here are driving me far from my
sanctuary, and you will see even more such
abominations.'
7 Then he brought me to the entrance of the
court, and I looked and found a hole in the
8 wall. 'Man,' he said to me, 'dig through
the wall.' I did so, and it became an opening.
9 'Go in,' he said, 'and see the vile abomina-
10 tions they practise here.' So I went in and
saw figures of reptiles, beasts, and vermin,
and all the idols of the Israelites, carved
11 round the walls. Seventy elders of Israel were
standing in front of them, with Jaazaniah
son of Shaphan in the middle, and each held
a censer from which rose the fragrant smoke
12 of incense. 'Man,' he said to me, 'do you
see what the elders of Israel are doing in
darkness, each at the shrine of his own
carved image? They think that the LORD
does not see them, or that he has forsaken
13 the country. You will see', he said, 'yet
more monstrous abominations which they
practise.'
14 Then he brought me to that gateway of
the LORD's house which faces north; and
there I saw women sitting and wailing for
15 Tammuz. 'Man, do you see that?' he asked
me. 'But you will see abominations more
16 monstrous than these.' So he took me to
the inner court of the LORD's house, and
there, by the entrance to the sanctuary of
the LORD, between porch and altar, were
some twenty-five men with their backs to
the sanctuary and their faces to the east,
17 prostrating themselves to the rising sun. He
said to me, 'Man, do you see that? Is it
because they think these abominations a
trifle, that the Jews have filled the country
with violence? They provoke me further to
anger, even while they seek to appease me;
18 I will turn upon them in my rage; I will
neither pity nor spare. Loudly as they may
cry to me, I will not listen.'

Godfearing Israelites marked

9 A loud voice rang in my ears: 'Here they
come, those appointed to punish the city,
each carrying his weapon of destruction.'
2 Then I saw six men approaching from the
road that leads to the upper northern gate,
each carrying a battle-axe, one man among
them dressed in linen, with pen and ink at
his waist; and they halted by the altar of
3 bronze. Then the glory of the God of Israel
rose from above the cherubim. He came to
the terrace of the temple and called to the
man dressed in linen with pen and ink at his
4 waist. 'Go through the city, through Jeru-

salem,' said the LORD, 'and put a mark on
the foreheads of those who groan and lament
over the abominations practised there.' Then 5
I heard him say to the others, 'Follow him
through the city and kill without pity; spare
no one. Kill and destroy them all, old men 6
and young, girls, little children and women,
but touch no one who bears the mark. Begin
at my sanctuary.' So they began with the
elders in front of the temple. 'Defile the 7
temple,' he said, 'and fill the courts with
dead bodies; then go out into the city and
kill.'

Ezekiel pleads for Jerusalem

While they did their work, I was left alone; 8
and I threw myself upon my face, crying out,
'O Lord GOD, must thou destroy all the
Israelites who are left, pouring out thy
anger on Jerusalem?' He answered, 'The 9
iniquity of Israel and Judah is great indeed;
the land is full of murder, the city is filled
with injustice. They think the LORD has
forsaken this country; they think he sees
nothing. But I will neither pity nor spare 10
them; I will make them answer for all they
have done.' Then the man dressed in linen 11
with pen and ink at his waist came and made
his report: 'I have done what thou hast
commanded.'

The cherubim

Then I saw, above the vault over the heads 10
of the cherubim, as it were a throne of
sapphire[v] visible above them. The LORD 2
said to the man dressed in linen, 'Come in
between the circling wheels under the cherubim, and take a handful of the burning
embers lying among the cherubim; then toss
them over the city.' So he went in before
my eyes.

The cherubim stood on the right side of 3
the temple as a man enters, and a cloud filled
the inner court. The glory of the LORD rose 4
high from above the cherubim and moved
on to the terrace; and the temple was filled
with the cloud, while the radiance of the
glory of the LORD filled the court. The sound 5
of the wings of the cherubim could be heard
as far as the outer court, as loud as if God
Almighty were speaking. Then he told the 6
man dressed in linen to take fire from between the circling wheels and among the
cherubim; the man came and stood by a
wheel, and a cherub from among the cheru- 7
bim put its hand into the fire that lay among
them, and, taking some fire, gave it to the
man dressed in linen; and he received it and
went out.

Under the wings of the cherubim there 8
appeared what seemed a human hand. And 9
I saw four wheels beside the cherubim, one

v Or lapis lazuli.

wheel beside each cherub. They had the
10 sparkle of topaz, and all four were alike,
11 like a wheel inside a wheel. When the chera-
bim moved in any of the four directions,
they never swerved in their course; they
went straight on in the direction in which
their heads were turned, never swerving in
12 their course. Their whole bodies, their backs
and hands and wings, as well as the wheels,
were full of eyes all round the four of them.[w]
13 The whirring of the wheels sounded in my
14 ears. Each had four faces: the first was that
of a cherub, the second that of a man, the
third that of a lion, and the fourth that of
an eagle.

15 Then the cherubim raised themselves up,
those same living creatures I had seen by the
16 river Kebar. When the cherubim moved, the
wheels moved beside them; when the chera-
bim lifted their wings and rose from the
ground, the wheels did not turn away from
17 them. When the one halted, the other
halted; when the one rose, the other rose;
for the spirit of the creatures was in the
18 wheels. Then the glory of the LORD left the
temple terrace and halted above the chera-
19 bim. The cherubim lifted their wings and
raised themselves from the ground; I watched
them go with the wheels beside them. They
halted at the eastern gateway of the LORD's
house, and the glory of the God of Israel
was over them.
20 These were the living creatures I had seen
beneath the God of Israel at the river Kebar;
21 I knew that they were cherubim. Each had
four faces and four wings and the semblance
22 of human hands under their wings. Their
faces were like those I had seen in vision by
the river Kebar;[x] they moved, each one of
them, straight forward.

Judgement on the rulers

11 A spirit[y] lifted me up and brought me to the
eastern gate of the LORD's house, the gate
that faces east. By the doorway were twenty-
five men, and I saw among them two of high
office, Jaazaniah son of Azzur and Pelatiah
2 son of Benaiah. The LORD said to me, Man,
it is these who are planning mischief and
3 plotting trouble in this city, saying to themselves, 'There will be no building of houses
yet awhile; the city is a stewpot and we are
4 the meat in it.' Therefore, said he, prophesy
5 against them, prophesy, O man. Then the
spirit of the LORD came suddenly upon me,
and he told me to say, These are the words
of the LORD: This is what you are saying
to yourselves, you men of Israel; well do I
know the thoughts that rise in your mind.
6 You have killed and killed in this city and
7 heaped the streets with the slain. These,

therefore, are the words of the Lord GOD:
The bodies of the slain that you have put
there, it is they that are the meat. The city
is indeed the stewpot, but I will take you out
of it. It is a sword that you fear, and a sword 8
I will bring upon you, says the Lord GOD.
I will take you out of it; I will give you over 9
to a foreign power; I will bring you to justice.
You too shall fall by the sword when I judge 10
you on the frontier of Israel; thus you shall
know that I am the LORD. So the city will 11
not be your stewpot, nor you the meat in it.
On the frontier of Israel I will judge you;
thus you shall know that I am the LORD. 12
You have not conformed to my statutes nor
kept my laws, but you have followed the
laws of the nations around you.

While I was prophesying, Pelatiah son of 13
Benaiah fell dead; and I threw myself upon
my face, crying aloud, 'O Lord GOD, must
thou make an end of all the Israelites who
are left?'

Promise of restoration and renewal

The word of the LORD came to me: Man, 14
they are your brothers, your brothers and
your kinsmen, this whole people of Israel,
to whom the men who now live in Jerusalem
have said, 'Keep your distance from the
LORD; the land has been made over to us as
our property.' Say therefore, These are the 16
words of the Lord GOD: When I sent them
far away among the nations and scattered
them in many lands, for a while I became
their sanctuary in the countries to which
they had gone. Say therefore, These are the 17
words of the Lord GOD: I will gather them
from among the nations and assemble them
from the countries over which I have scattered them, and I will give them the soil
of Israel. When they come into it, they will 18
do away with all their vile and abominable
practices. I will give them a different heart 19
and put a new spirit into them; I will take
the heart of stone out of their bodies and
give them a heart of flesh. Then they will 20
conform to my statutes and keep my laws.
They will become my people, and I will become their God. But as for those whose 21
heart is set upon[z] their vile and abominable
practices, I will make them answer for all
they have done. This is the very word of the
Lord GOD.

The Glory leaves Jerusalem

Then the cherubim lifted their wings, with 22
the wheels beside them and the glory of the
God of Israel above them. The glory of the 23
LORD rose up and left the city, and halted
on the mountain to the east of it. And a 24
spirit[a] lifted me up and brought me to the

*w Prob. rdg.; Heb. adds their wheels.   x Prob. rdg.; Heb. adds and them.   y Or wind.   z Prob.
rdg.; Heb. adds the heart of.   a Or wind.*

exiles in Chaldaea. All this came in a vision sent by the spirit of God, and then the vision 25 that I had seen left me. I told the exiles all that the LORD had revealed to me.

Ezekiel, a sign

12
1 2 The word of the LORD came to me: Man, you live among a rebellious people. Though they have eyes they will not see, though they have ears they will not hear, because they 3 are a rebellious people. Therefore, man, pack up what you need for a journey into exile, by day before their eyes; then set off on your journey. When you leave home and go off into exile before their eyes, it may be 4 they will see that they are rebels. Bring out your belongings, packed as for exile; do it by day, before their eyes, and then at evening, still before their eyes, leave home, as if 5 you were going into exile. Next, before their eyes, break a hole through the wall, and 6 carry your belongings out through it. When dusk falls, take your pack on your shoulder, before their eyes, and carry it out, with your face covered so that you cannot see the ground. I am making you a warning sign for the Israelites.
7 I did exactly as I had been told. By day

Babylon

I brought out my belongings, packed as for exile, and at evening I broke through the wall with my hands. When dusk fell, I shouldered my pack and carried it out before their eyes.
Next morning, the word of the LORD 8 came to me: Man, he said, have not the 9 Israelites, that rebellious people, asked you what you are doing? Tell them that these 10 are the words of the Lord GOD: This oracle concerns the prince in Jerusalem, and all the Israelites therein.[b] Tell them that you 11 are a sign to warn them; what you have done will be done to them; they will go into exile and captivity. Their prince will shoulder his 12 pack in the dusk and go through a hole made to let him out, with his face covered so that he cannot be seen nor himself see the ground. But I will cast my net over him, and 13 he will be caught in the meshes. I will bring him to Babylon, the land of the Chaldaeans, though he will not see it; and there he will die. I will scatter his bodyguard and drive 14 all his squadrons to the four winds; I will follow them with drawn sword. Then they 15 shall know that I am the LORD, when I disperse them among the nations and scatter them through many lands. But I will leave 16 a few of them who will escape sword, famine, and pestilence, to tell the whole story of their abominations to the peoples among whom they go; and they shall know that I am the LORD.

A warning to the people

And the word of the LORD came to me: Man, 17 18 he said, as you eat you must tremble, and as you drink you must shudder with dread. Say to the common people, These are the 19 words of the Lord GOD about those who live in Jerusalem and about the land of Israel: They will eat with dread and be filled with horror as they drink; the land shall be filled with horror because it is sated with the violence of all who live there. Inhabited 20 cities shall be deserted, and the land shall become a waste. Thus you shall know that I am the LORD.

Mistaken beliefs corrected

The word of the LORD came to me: Man, 21 22 he said, what is this proverb current in the land of Israel: 'Time runs on, visions die away'? Say to them, These are the words 23 of the Lord GOD: I have put an end to this proverb; it shall never be heard in Israel again. Say rather to them, The time, with all the vision means, is near. There will be 24 no more false visions, no specious divination among the Israelites, for I, the LORD, 25 will say what I will, and it shall be done. It shall be put off no longer: in your lifetime,

b therein: *prob. rdg.; Heb.* among them.

you rebellious people, I will speak, I will act. This is the very word of the Lord GOD.

26 27 The word of the LORD came to me: Man, he said, the Israelites say that the vision you now see is not to be fulfilled for many years: 28 you are prophesying of a time far off. Say to them, These are the words of the Lord GOD: No word of mine shall be delayed; even as I speak it shall be done. This is the very word of the Lord GOD.

Condemnation of false prophets

13
1 2 The LORD said to me, Man, prophesy of the prophets of Israel; prophesy, and say to those who prophesy out of their own hearts, 3 Hear what the LORD says: These are the words of the Lord GOD: Oh, the wicked folly of the prophets! Their inspiration comes from themselves; they have seen no vision. 4 Your prophets, Israel, have been like jackals 5 among ruins. They have not gone up into the breach to repair the broken wall round the Israelites, that they may stand firm in 6 battle on the day of the LORD. Oh, false vision and lying divination! Oh, those prophets who say, 'It is the very word of the LORD', when it is not the LORD who has sent them; yet they expect their words to control 7 the event. Is it not a false vision that you prophets have seen? Is not your divination a lie? You call it the very word of the LORD, but it is not I who have spoken.

8 These, then, are the words of the Lord GOD: Because your words are false and your visions a lie, I am against you, says the Lord 9 GOD. I will raise my hand against the prophets whose visions are false, whose divinations are a lie. They shall have no place in the counsels of my people; they shall not be entered in the roll of Israel nor set foot upon its soil. Thus you shall know that I 10 am the Lord GOD. Rightly, for they have misled my people by saying that all is well when all is not well. It is as if they were building a wall and used whitewash for the 11 daubing. Tell these daubers that it will fall; rain will pour down in torrents, and I will send hailstones hard as rock streaming down 12 and I will unleash a stormy wind. When the building falls, men will ask, 'Where is the 13 plaster you should have used?' So these are the words of the Lord GOD: In my rage I will unleash a stormy wind; rain will come in torrents in my anger, hailstones hard as 14 rock in my fury, until all is destroyed. I will demolish the building which you have daubed with whitewash and level it to the ground, so that its foundations are laid bare. It shall fall, and you shall be destroyed within it; thus you shall know that I am the 15 LORD. I will spend my rage on the building and on those who daubed it with wash; and

people[c] will say, 'The building is gone and the men who daubed it are gone, those 16 prophets of Israel who prophesied to Jerusalem, who saw visions of prosperity when there was no prosperity.' This is the very word of the Lord GOD.

Now turn, man, to the women of your 17 people who prophesy out of their own hearts, and prophesy to them. Say to them, 18 These are the words of the Lord GOD: I loathe you, you women who hunt men's lives by sewing magic bands upon the wrists and putting veils over the heads of persons of every age; are you to hunt the lives of my people and keep your own lives safe? You 19 have violated my sanctity before my people with handfuls of barley and scraps of bread. You bring death to those who should not die, and life to those who should not live, by lying to this people of mine who listen to lies. So these are the words of the Lord 20 GOD: I am against your magic bands with which you hunt men's lives for the excitement of it. I will tear them from your arms 21 and set those lives at liberty, lives that you hunt for the excitement of it. I will tear up your long veils and save my people from you; you shall no longer have power to hunt them. Thus you shall know that I am the LORD. You discouraged the righteous 22 man with lies, when I meant him no hurt; you so strengthened the wicked that he would not abandon his evil ways and be saved; and therefore you shall never see your 23 false visions again nor practise your divination any more. I will rescue my people from your power; and thus you shall know that I am the LORD.

Insincerity and hypocrisy cursed

Some of the elders of Israel came to visit **14**
me, and while they sat with me the LORD 2 said to me, Man, these people have set their 3 hearts on their idols and keep their eyes fixed on the sinful things that cause their downfall. Am I to let such men consult me? Speak to them and tell them that these are the 4 words of the Lord GOD: If any Israelite, with his heart set on his idols and his eyes fixed on the sinful things that cause his downfall, comes to a prophet, I, the LORD, in my own person, shall be constrained to answer him, despite his many idols. My 5 answer will grip the hearts of the Israelites, estranged from me as they are, one and all, through their idols. So tell the Israelites that 6 these are the words of the Lord GOD: Turn away, turn away from your idols; turn your backs on all your abominations. If any man, 7 Israelite or alien, renounces me, sets his heart upon idols and fixes his eyes upon the vile thing that is his downfall—if such

c Prob. rdg.; Heb. I.

a man comes to consult me through a prophet, I, the LORD, in my own person, shall 8 be constrained to answer him. I will set my face against that man; I will make him an example and a byword; I will rid my people of him. Thus you shall know that I am the 9 LORD. If a prophet is seduced into making a prophecy, it is I the LORD who have seduced him; I will stretch out my hand and 10 rid my people Israel of him. Both shall be punished; the prophet and the man who 11 consults him alike are guilty. And never again will the Israelites stray from their allegiance, never again defy my will and bring pollution upon themselves; they will become my people, and I will become their God. This is the very word of the Lord GOD.

Righteous survivors

12 These were the words of the LORD to me: 13 Man, when a country sins by breaking faith with me, I will stretch out my hand and cut short its daily bread. I will send famine upon 14 it and destroy both men and cattle. Even if those three men were living there, Noah, Danel[d] and Job, they would save none but themselves by their righteousness. This is 15 the very word of the Lord GOD. If I should turn wild beasts loose in a country to destroy its inhabitants, until it became a waste through which no man would pass for fear 16 of the beasts, then, if those three men were living there, as I live, says the Lord GOD, they would not save even their own sons and daughters; they would save themselves alone, 17 and the country would become a waste. Or if I should bring the sword upon that country and command it to go through the land and 18 should destroy men and cattle, then, if those three men were living there, as I live, says the Lord GOD, they could save neither son nor daughter; they would save themselves 19 alone. Or if I should send pestilence on that land and pour out my fury upon it in blood, 20 to destroy men and cattle, then, if Noah, Danel and Job were living there, as I live, says the Lord GOD, they would save neither son nor daughter; they would save themselves alone by their righteousness.

21 These were the words of the Lord GOD: How much less hope is there for Jerusalem when I inflict on her these four punishments of mine, sword and famine, wild beasts and pestilence, to destroy both men and cattle! 22 Some will be left in her, some survivors to be brought out, both sons and daughters. Look at them as they come out to you, and see how they have behaved and what they have done. This will be some comfort to you for all the harm I have done to Jerusalem 23 and all I have inflicted upon her. It will bring you comfort when you see how they have behaved and what they have done; for you will know that it was not without reason that I dealt thus with her. This is the very word of the Lord GOD.

The useless vine

These were the words of the LORD to me: **15**
Man, how is the vine better than any other 2
  tree,
than a branch from a tree in the forest?
  Is wood got from it   3
  fit to make anything useful?
  Can men make it into a peg
  and hang things on it?
  If it is put on the fire for fuel,   4
  if its two ends are burnt by the fire
  and the middle is charred,
  is it fit for anything useful?
Nothing useful could be made of it even 5
  when whole;
how much less, when it is burnt by the fire
  and charred,
  can it be made into anything useful!
So these are the words of the Lord GOD: 6
I treat the vine, as against forest-trees,
  only as fuel for the fire,
even so I treat the people of Jerusalem;
  I set my face against them.   7
Though they escape from the fire, fire shall
  burn them up.
Thus you shall know that I am the LORD
  when I set my face against them,
  making the land a waste   8
because they have broken faith.
This is the very word of the Lord GOD.

Jerusalem's unfaithfulness

The word of the LORD came to me: Man, **16**
he said, make Jerusalem see her abominable 1 2
conduct. Tell her that these are the words 3
of the Lord GOD to her: Canaan is the land
of your ancestry and there you were born;
an Amorite was your father and a Hittite
your mother. This is how you were treated 4
at birth: when you were born, your navel-
string was not tied, you were not bathed in
water ready for the rubbing, you were not
salted as you should have been nor wrapped
in swaddling clothes. No one cared for you 5
enough to do any of these things or, indeed,
to have any pity for you; you were thrown
out on the bare ground in your own filth
on the day of your birth. Then I came by 6
and saw you kicking helplessly in your own
blood; I spoke to you, there in your blood,
and bade you live. I tended you like an 7
evergreen plant, like something growing in
the fields; you throve and grew. You came
to full womanhood; your breasts became
firm and your hair grew, but still you were
naked and exposed.

d Or, as otherwise read, Daniel.

8 Again I came by and saw that you were ripe for love. I spread the skirt of my robe over you and covered your naked body. Then I plighted my troth and entered into a covenant with you, says the Lord GOD, 9 and you became mine. Then I bathed you in water and washed off the blood and 10 anointed you with oil. I gave you robes of brocade and sandals of stout hide; I fastened a linen girdle round you and dressed you in 11 lawn. For jewellery I put bracelets on your 12 arms and a chain round your neck; I gave you a nose-ring, I put pendants in your ears 13 and a beautiful coronet on your head. You had ornaments of gold and silver, your dresses were of linen, lawn, and brocade. You had flour and honey and olive oil for food, and you grew very beautiful, you grew 14 into a queen. The fame of your beauty went all over the world, for the splendour with which I decked you made it perfect. This is the very word of the Lord GOD.

15 But you trusted to your beauty and prostituted your fame; you committed fornication, offering yourself freely to any passer-by for 16 your beauty to become his. You took some of your clothes and decked a platform for yourself in gay colours and there you committed fornication; you had intercourse with him for your beauty to become his.[e] 17 You took the splendid ornaments of gold and silver which I had given you, and made for yourself male images with which you com- 18 mitted fornication. You covered them with your robes of brocade and offered up my oil 19 and my incense before them. You took the food I had given you, the flour, the oil, and the honey, with which I had fed you, and set it before them as an offering of soothing odour. This is the very word of the Lord GOD.

20 You took the sons and daughters whom you had borne to me, and sacrificed them to these images for their food. Was this of less 21 account than your fornication? No! you slaughtered my children and handed them over, you surrendered them to your images. 22 With all your abominable fornication you forgot those early days when you lay naked and exposed, kicking helplessly in your own blood.

23 After all the evil you had done (Oh! the 24 pity of it, says the Lord GOD), you built yourself a couch and constructed a high- 25 stool in every open place. You built up your high-stools at the top of every street and disgraced your beauty, offering your body to any passer-by in countless acts of fornica- 26 tion. You committed fornication with your gross neighbours, the Egyptians, and provoked me to anger by your countless acts of fornication.

27 I stretched out my hand against you and cut down your portion. Then I gave you up to women who hated you, Philistine women, who were so disgusted by your lewd ways. Not content with this, you committed forni- 28 cation with the Assyrians, led them into fornication and still were not content. You 29 committed countless acts of fornication in Chaldaea, the land of commerce, and even with this you were not content.

30 How you anger me! says the Lord GOD. You have done all this like the imperious whore you are. You have built your couch 31 at the top of every street and constructed your stool in every open place, but, unlike the common prostitute, you have scorned a fee. An adulterous wife who owes obedi- 32 ence to her husband takes a fee from[f] strangers. The prostitute also takes her fee; 33 but you give presents to all your lovers, you bribe them to come from all quarters to commit fornication with you. You are the 34 very opposite of other women in your fornication: no one runs after you, you do not receive a fee, you give it. You are the very opposite.

35 Listen to the words of the LORD, whore that you are. These are the words of the 36 Lord GOD: You have been prodigal in your excesses, you have exposed your naked body in fornication with your lovers. In return for your abominable idols and for the slaughter of the children you have given them, I will gather all those lovers to whom 37 you made advances,[g] all whom you loved and all whom you hated. I will gather them in from all quarters against you; I will strip you naked before them, and they shall see your whole body naked. I will put you on 38 trial for adultery and murder, and I will charge you with[h] blood shed in jealousy and fury. Then I will hand you over to them. 39 They will demolish your couch and pull down your high-stool; they will strip your clothes off, take away your splendid ornaments, and leave you naked and exposed. They will bring up the mob against you and 40 stone you, they will hack you to pieces with their swords. They will burn down your 41 houses and execute judgement on you, and many women shall see it. I will put an end to your fornication, and you shall never again give a fee to your lovers. Then I will 42 abate my fury, and my jealousy will turn away from you. I will be calm and will no longer be provoked to anger. For you had 43 forgotten the days of your youth and exasperated me with all your doings: so I in my turn brought retribution upon you for your deeds. This is the very word of the Lord GOD.

e you had intercourse . . . his: prob. rdg.; Heb. obscure.   f a fee from: prob. rdg.; Heb. om.   g to whom . . . advances: or whom you charmed.   h charge you with: prob. mng.; Heb. give you.

Jerusalem and her sisters

Did you not commit these obscenities, as
44 well as all your other abominations? Dealers
in proverbs will say of you, 'Like mother,
45 like daughter.' You are a true daughter of
a mother who loathed her husband and
children. You are a true sister of your sisters
who loathed their husbands and children.
You are all daughters of a Hittite mother
46 and an Amorite father. Your elder sister
was Samaria, who lived with her daughters
to the north of you; your younger sister,
who lived with her daughters to the south of
47 you, was Sodom. Did you not behave as
they did and commit the same abominations?
You came very near to doing even worse
48 than they. As I live, says the Lord God,
your sister Sodom and her daughters never
behaved as you and your daughters have
49 done. This was the iniquity of your sister
Sodom: she and her daughters had pride of
wealth and food in plenty, comfort and ease,
and yet she never helped the poor and
50 wretched. They grew haughty and did deeds
abominable in my sight, and I made away
51 with them, as you have seen. Samaria was
never half the sinner you have been; you
have committed more abominations than
she, abominations which have made your
52 sister seem innocent. You must bear the
humiliation which you thought your sisters
deserved. Your sins are so much more
abominable than theirs that they appear
innocent in comparison with you; and now
you must bear your shame and humiliation
and make your sisters seem innocent.
53 But I will restore the fortunes of Sodom
and her daughters and of Samaria and her
daughters, and I will restore yours at the
54 same time. Even though you bring them
comfort, you will bear your shame, you will
55 be disgraced for all you have done; but
when your sister Sodom and her daughters
become what they were of old, and when
your sister Samaria and her daughters become what they were of old, then you and
56 your daughters will be restored. Did you
not hear and talk much of your sister
57 Sodom in the days of your pride, before
your wickedness was exposed, in the days
when the daughters of Aram with those
about her were disgraced, and the daughters
of the Philistines round about, who so de-
58 spised you? Now you too must bear the
consequences of your lewd and abominable conduct. This is the very word of the
Lord.
59 These are the words of the Lord God:
I will treat you as you have deserved, because you violated a covenant and made
60 light of a solemn oath. But I will remember

the covenant I made with you when you
were young, and I will establish with you a
covenant which shall last for ever. And you 61
will remember your past ways and feel
ashamed when you receive your sisters, the
elder and the younger. For I will give them
to you as daughters, and they shall not be
outside your covenant.*i* Thus I will establish 62
my covenant with you, and you shall know
that I am the Lord. You will remember, 63
and will be so ashamed and humiliated that
you will never open your mouth again once
I have accepted expiation for all you have
done. This is the very word of the Lord God.

The eagles and the vine

These were the words of the Lord to me: 17
Man, speak to the Israelites in allegory and 2
parable. Tell them that these are the words 3
of the Lord God:

A great eagle
with broad wings and long pinions,
in full plumage, richly patterned,
came to Lebanon.
He took the very top of a cedar-tree,
he plucked its highest twig;   4
he carried it off to a land of commerce,
and planted it in a city of merchants.
Then he took a native seed   5
and put it in nursery-ground;
he set it like a willow,
a shoot beside abundant water.
It sprouted and became a vine,   6
sprawling low along the ground
and bending its trailing boughs towards
him*j*
with its roots growing beneath him.
So it became a vine, it branched out
and put forth shoots.
But there was another great eagle   7
with broad wings and thick plumage;
and this vine gave its roots
a twist towards him;*j*
it pushed out its trailing boughs towards
him,
seeking drink from the bed where it was
planted,
though it had been set   8
in good ground beside abundant water
that it might bear shoots and be fruitful
and become a noble vine.

Tell them that these are the words of the 9
Lord God:

Can such a vine flourish?
Will not its roots be broken off
and its fruit be stripped,
and all its fresh sprouting leaves wither,
until it is uprooted and carried away
with little effort and few hands?

---

i and they . . . covenant: *or* though not on the ground of your covenant.   *j* Or inwards.

10 If it is transplanted, can it flourish?
Will it not be utterly shrivelled,
as though by the touch of the east wind,
    on the bed where it ought to sprout?

The parable explained

11 These were the words of the LORD to me:
12 Say to that rebellious people, Do you not

know what this means? The king of Babylon came to Jerusalem, took its king and its officers and had them brought to him at
13 Babylon. He took a prince of the royal line and made a treaty with him, putting him on his oath. He took away the chief men of the
14 country, so that it should become a humble kingdom unable to raise itself but ready to
15 observe the treaty and keep it in force. But the prince rebelled against him and sent messengers to Egypt, asking for horses and men in plenty. Can such a man prosper? Can he escape destruction if he acts in this way? Can he violate a covenant and escape?
16 As I live, says the Lord GOD, I swear that he shall die in the land of the king who put him on the throne; he made light of his oath and violated the covenant he made with him.
17 He shall die in Babylon. Pharaoh will send no large army, no great host, to protect him in battle; no siege-ramp will be raised, no watch-tower put up, nor will the lives of
18 many men be lost. He has violated a covenant and has made light of his oath. He had submitted, and yet he did all these things; he shall not escape.
19   These then are the words of the Lord GOD: As I live, he has made light of the oath he took by me and has violated the covenant I made with him. I will bring retribution upon
20 him; I will cast my net over him, and he shall be caught in its meshes. I will carry him to Babylon and bring him to judgement there,
21 because he has broken faith with me. In all his squadrons every commander shall fall by the sword; those who are left will be scattered to the four winds. Thus you shall know that it is I, the LORD, who have spoken.

The noble cedar

22 These are the words of the Lord GOD:

  I, too, will take a slip
  from the lofty crown of the cedar
  and set it in the soil;
I will pluck a tender shoot from the topmost
    branch
  and plant it.

I will plant it high on a lofty mountain,   23
  the highest mountain in Israel.
It will put out branches, bear its fruit,
  and become a noble cedar.
Winged birds of every kind will roost under it,
  they will roost in the shelter of its sweeping boughs.
  All the trees of the country-side will know 24
  that it is I, the LORD,
  who bring low the tall tree
  and raise the low tree high,
  who dry up the green tree
  and make the dry tree put forth buds.
I, the LORD, have spoken and will do it.

Personal responsibility

These were the words of the LORD to me: **18**
What do you all mean by repeating this 2
proverb in the land of Israel:

'The fathers have eaten sour grapes,
  and the children's teeth are set on edge'?

As I live, says the Lord GOD, this proverb 3
shall never again be used in Israel. Every 4
living soul belongs to me; father and son
alike are mine. The soul that sins shall die.
   Consider the man who is righteous and 5
does what is just and right. He never feasts 6
at mountain-shrines, never lifts his eyes to
the idols of Israel, never dishonours another man's wife, never approaches a woman

7 during her periods. He oppresses no man, he returns the debtor's pledge, he never robs. He gives bread to the hungry and 8 clothes to those who have none. He never lends either at discount or at interest. He shuns injustice and deals fairly between man 9 and man. He conforms to my statutes and loyally observes my laws. Such a man is righteous: he shall live, says the Lord GOD.

10 He may have a son who is a man of violence and a cut-throat who turns his back on these 11 rules.^k He obeys none of them, he feasts at mountain-shrines, he dishonours another 12 man's wife, he oppresses the unfortunate and the poor, he is a robber, he does not return the debtor's pledge, he lifts his eyes 13 to idols and joins in abominable rites; he lends both at discount and at interest. Such a man shall not live. Because he has committed all these abominations he shall die, and his blood will be on his own head.

14 This man in turn may have a son who sees all his father's sins; he sees, but he commits 15 none of them. He never feasts at mountain-shrines, never lifts his eyes to the idols of Israel, never dishonours another man's wife, 16 He oppresses no man, takes no pledge, does not rob. He gives bread to the hungry and 17 clothes to those who have none. He shuns injustice, he never lends either at discount or at interest. He keeps my laws and conforms to my statutes. Such a man shall not die for his father's wrongdoing; he shall live.

18 His father may have been guilty of oppression and robbery and may have lived an evil life among his kinsfolk, and so has died be-19 cause of his iniquity. You may ask, 'Why is the son not punished for his father's iniquity?' Because he has always done what is just and right and has been careful to obey 20 all my laws, therefore he shall live. It is the soul that sins, and no other, that shall die; a son shall not share a father's guilt, nor a father his son's. The righteous man shall reap the fruit of his own righteousness, and the wicked man the fruit of his own wickedness.

21 It may be that a wicked man gives up his sinful ways and keeps all my laws, doing what is just and right. That man shall live; 22 he shall not die. None of the offences he has committed shall be remembered against him; he shall live because of his righteous deeds. 23 Have I any desire, says the Lord GOD, for the death of a wicked man? Would I not rather that he should mend his ways and live?

24 It may be that a righteous man turns back from his righteous ways and commits every kind of abomination that the wicked practise; shall he do this and live? No, none of

his former righteousness will be remembered in his favour; he has broken his faith, he has sinned, and he shall die. You say that the 25 Lord acts without principle? Listen, you Israelites, it is you who act without principle, not I. If a righteous man turns from his 26 righteousness, takes to evil ways and dies,^l it is because of these evil ways that he dies. Again, if a wicked man turns from his 27 wicked ways and does what is just and right, he will save his life. If he sees his offences as 28 they are and turns his back on them all, then he shall live; he shall not die.

'The Lord acts without principle', say 29 the Israelites. No, Israelites, it is you who act without principle, not I. Therefore, 30 Israelites, says the Lord GOD, I will judge every man of you on his deeds. Turn, turn from your offences, or your iniquity will be your downfall. Throw off the load of your 31 past misdeeds; get yourselves a new heart and a new spirit. Why should you die, you men of Israel? I have no desire for any man's 32 death. This is the very word of the Lord GOD.

The lioness and her cubs

Raise a lament over the princes of Israel **19** and say: 2

> Your mother was a lioness
> among the lions!
> She made her lair among the young lions
> and many were the cubs she bore.
> One of her cubs she raised,   3
> and he grew into a young lion.
> He learnt to tear his prey,
> he devoured men.
> Then the nations shouted at^m him   4
> and he was caught in their pit,
and they dragged him with hooks to the land
> of Egypt.
His case, she saw, was desperate, her hope 5
> was lost;
> so she took another of her cubs
> and made him a young lion.
> He prowled among the lions   6
> and acted like a young lion.
> He learnt to tear his prey,
> he devoured men;
he broke down their palaces, laid their cities 7
> in ruins.
> The land and all that was in it
> was aghast at the noise of his roaring.
> From the provinces all round   8
> the nations raised the hue and cry;
> they cast their net over him
> and he was caught in their pit.
> With hooks they drew him into a cage   9
> and brought him to the king of Babylon,
> who flung him into prison,
that his voice might never again be heard
> on the mountains of Israel.

---

k who turns . . . rules: prob. rdg.; Heb. unintelligible.
m shouted at: or heard a report about.

l Prob. rdg.; Heb. adds because of them.

The vine

10 Your mother was a vine in a vineyard[n]
    planted by the waterside.
    It grew fruitful and luxuriant,
    for there was water in plenty.
11 It had stout branches,
    fit to make sceptres for those who bear rule.
It grew tall, finding its way through the
    foliage,
and conspicuous for its height and many
    trailing boughs.
12 But it was torn up in anger and thrown to the
    ground;
    the east wind blighted it,
    its fruit was blown off,
    its strong branches were blighted,
    and fire burnt it.
13 Now it is replanted in the wilderness,
    in a dry and thirsty land;
14 and fire bursts forth from its own branches
    and burns up its shoots.[o]
    It has no strong branch any more
    to make a sceptre for those who bear rule.
This is the lament and as a lament it passed
into use.

From Egypt to Canaan

20 On the tenth day of the fifth month in the
seventh year, some of the elders of Israel
came to consult the Lord and were sitting
2 with me. Then this word came to me from
3 the Lord: Man, say to the elders of Israel,
This is the word of the Lord God: Do you
come to consult me? As I live, I will not be
consulted by you. This is the very word of
the Lord God.
4 Will you judge them? Will you judge them,
O man? Then tell them of the abominations
5 of their forefathers and say to them, These
are the words of the Lord God: When I chose
Israel, with uplifted hand I bound myself by
oath to the race of Jacob and revealed myself to them in Egypt; I lifted up my hand
6 and declared: I am the Lord your God. On
that day I swore with hand uplifted that I
would bring them out of Egypt into the land
I had sought out for them, a land flowing
7 with milk and honey, fairest of all lands. I
told them, every one, to cast away the loathsome things on which they feasted their eyes
and not to defile themselves with the idols of
Egypt. I am the Lord your God, I said.
8 But they rebelled against me, they refused
to listen to me, and not one of them cast
away the loathsome things on which he
feasted his eyes or forsook the idols of
Egypt. I had thought to pour out my wrath
and exhaust my anger on them in Egypt.
9 I acted for the honour of my name, that it
might not be profaned in the sight of the
nations among whom Israel was living:

I revealed myself to them by bringing Israel
out of Egypt. I brought them out of Egypt 10
and led them into the wilderness. There 11
I gave my statutes to them and taught them
my laws, so that by keeping them men might
have life. Further, I gave them my sabbaths 12
as a sign between us, so that they should
know that I, the Lord, was hallowing them
for myself. But the Israelites rebelled against 13
me in the wilderness; they did not conform
to my statutes, they rejected my laws, though
by keeping them men might have life, and
they utterly desecrated my sabbaths. So
again I thought to pour out my wrath on
them in the wilderness to destroy them.
I acted for the honour of my name, that it 14
might not be profaned in the sight of the
nations who had seen me bring them out.
Further, I swore to them in the wilderness 15
with uplifted hand that I would not bring
them into the land I had given them, that
land flowing with milk and honey, fairest
of all lands. For they had rejected my laws, 16
they would not conform to my statutes and
they desecrated my sabbaths, because they
loved to follow idols of their own. Yet I 17
pitied them too much to destroy them and
did not make an end of them in the wilderness. I commanded their sons in the wilder- 18
ness not to conform to their fathers' statutes,
nor observe their laws, nor defile themselves
with their idols. I said, I am the Lord your 19
God, you must conform to my statutes; you
must observe my laws and act according to
them. You must keep my sabbaths holy, 20
and they will become a sign between us; so
you will know that I am the Lord your God.
But the sons too rebelled against me. They 21
did not conform to my statutes or observe
my laws, though any who had done so would
have had life through them, and they desecrated my sabbaths. Again I thought to
pour out my wrath and exhaust my anger on
them in the wilderness. I acted for the honour 22
of my name, that it might not be profaned
in the sight of the nations who had seen me
bring them out. Yes, and in the wilderness 23
I swore to them with uplifted hand that I
would disperse them among the nations and
scatter them abroad, because they had dis- 24
obeyed my laws, rejected my statutes, desecrated my sabbaths, and turned longing eyes
toward the idols of their forefathers. I did 25
more; I imposed on them statutes that were
not good statutes, and laws by which they
could not win life. I let them defile them- 26
selves with gifts to idols; I made them surrender their eldest sons to them so that I
might fill them with horror. Thus they
would know that I am the Lord.
Speak then, O man, to the Israelites and say 27
to them, These are the words of the Lord

n in a vineyard: prob. rdg.; Heb. obscure in context.   *o Prob. rdg.; Heb. adds its fruit.*

God: Once again your forefathers insulted
28 me and broke faith with me: when I brought
them into the land which I had sworn with
uplifted hand to give them, they marked down
every hill-top and every leafy tree, and there
they offered their sacrifices, they made the
gifts which roused my anger, they set out their
offerings of soothing odour and poured out
29 their drink-offerings. I asked them, What is
this hill-shrine to which you are going up?
And 'hill-shrine' has been its name ever since.

The LORD reasons with Israel

30 So tell the Israelites, These are the words of
the Lord God. Are you defiling yourselves
as your forefathers did? Are you wantonly
giving yourselves to their loathsome gods?
31 When you bring your gifts, when you pass
your sons through the fire, you are still defiling yourselves in the service of your crowd
of idols. How can I let you consult me, men
of Israel? As I live, says the Lord God, I will
32 not be consulted by you. When you say to
yourselves, 'Let us become like the nations
and tribes of other lands and worship wood
and stone', you are thinking of something
33 that can never be. As I live, says the Lord
God, I will reign over you with a strong hand,
with arm outstretched and wrath outpoured.
34 I will bring you out from the peoples and
gather you from the lands over which you
have been scattered by my strong hand,
my outstretched arm and outpoured wrath.

I will bring you into the wilderness of the 35
peoples; there will I confront you, and there
will I state my case against you. Even as I did 36
in the wilderness of Egypt against your forefathers, so will I state my case against you.
This is the very word of the Lord God.

I will pass you under the rod and bring 37
you within the bond*p* of the covenant. I will 38
rid you of those who revolt and rebel against
me. I will take them out of the land where
they are now living, but they shall not set
foot on the soil of Israel. Thus shall you
know that I am the Lord.

Now, men of Israel, these are the words 39
of the Lord God: Go, sweep away your idols,
every man of you. So in days to come you
will never be disobedient to me or desecrate
my holy name with your gifts and your
idolatries. But on my holy hill, the lofty hill 40
of Israel, says the Lord God, there shall
the Israelites serve me in the land, every one
of them. There will I receive them with
favour; there will I demand your contribution and the best of your offerings, with all
your consecrated gifts. I will receive your 41
offerings of soothing odour, when I have
brought you out from the peoples and
gathered you from the lands where you have
been scattered. I, and only I, will have your
worship, for all the nations to see.

You will know that I am the Lord, when 42
I bring you home to the soil of Israel, to the
land which I swore with uplifted hand to give

your forefathers. There you will remember 43
your past ways and all the wanton deeds with
which you have defiled yourselves, and will
loathe yourselves for all the evils you have
done. You will know that I am the Lord, 44
when I have dealt with you, O men of Israel,
not as your wicked ways and your vicious
deeds deserve but for the honour of my name.
This is the very word of the Lord God.

A forest fire

These were the words of the Lord to me: 45
Man, turn and face towards Teman*q* and 46
pour out your words to the south; prophesy
to the rough country of the Negeb. Say to 47
it, Listen to the words of the Lord. These
are the words of the Lord God: I will set
fire to you, and the fire will consume all the

p Or muster.   *q Or* face southward.

wood, green and dry alike. Its fiery flame shall not be put out, but from the Negeb northwards every face will be scorched 48 by it. All men will see that it is I, the LORD, who have set it ablaze; it shall 49 not be put out. 'Ah no! O Lord GOD,' I cried; 'they say of me, "He deals only in parables."'

The sword of slaughter

21 These were the words of the LORD to me: 2 Man, turn and face towards Jerusalem, and pour out your words against her sanctuary;[r] 3 prophesy against the land of Israel. Say to the land of Israel, These are the words of the LORD: I am against you; I will draw my sword from the scabbard and cut off 4 from you both righteous and wicked. It is because I would cut off your righteous and your wicked equally that my sword will be drawn from the scabbard against all men, 5 from the Negeb northwards. All men shall know that I the LORD have drawn my sword; 6 it shall never again be sheathed. Groan in their presence, man, groan bitterly until 7 your lungs are bursting. When they ask you why you are groaning, say to them, 'I groan at the thing I have heard; when it comes, all hearts melt, all courage fails, all hands fall limp, all men's knees run with urine. It is coming. It is here.' This is the very word of the Lord GOD.

8　These were the words of the LORD to me: 9 Prophesy, man, and say, This is the word of the Lord:

A sword, a sword is sharpened and burnished,
10　sharpened to kill and kill again,
　　burnished to flash[s] like lightning.
　　Ah! the club is brandished, my son,
　　to defy all wooden idols!
11　The sword is given to be burnished
　　ready for the hand to grasp.
　　The sword—it is sharpened,
　　it is burnished,
　　ready to be put into the slayer's hand.
12　Cry, man, and howl; for all this falls on my people, it falls on Israel's princes who are delivered over to the sword and are slain with my people. Therefore beat your breast 13 in remorse, for it is the test—and what if it is not in truth the club of defiance? This is the very word of the Lord GOD.
14 But you, man, prophesy and clap your hands together;
　　swing the sword twice, thrice:
　　it is the sword of slaughter,
　　the great sword of slaughter whirling about them.

That their hearts may be troubled and many 15 stumble and fall,
I have set the threat of the sword at all their gates,
　　the threat of the sword[t] made to flash like lightning
　　and drawn to kill.
Be sharpened, turn right; be unsheathed, 16 turn left,
　　wherever your point is aimed.
I, too, will clap my hands together and abate 17 my anger. I, the LORD, have spoken.

The king of Babylon advances

These were the words of the LORD to me: 18 Man, trace out two roads by which the 19 sword of the king of Babylon may come, starting both of them from the same land. Then carve a signpost, carve it at the point where the highway forks. Mark out a road 20 for the sword to come to the Ammonite city of Rabbah, to Judah, and to Jerusalem at the heart of it. For the king of Babylon halts 21 to take the omens at the parting of the ways, where the road divides. He casts lots with arrows, consults teraphim[u] and inspects the livers of beasts. The augur's arrow marked 22 'Jerusalem' falls at his right hand: here, then,[v] he must raise a shout and sound the battle-cry, set battering-rams against the gates, pile siege-ramps and build watch-towers. It may well seem to the people that 23 the auguries are false, whereas they will put me in mind of their wrongdoing, and they will fall into their enemies' hand. These there- 24 fore are the words of the Lord GOD: Be-cause you have kept me mindful of your wrongdoing by your open rebellion, and your sins have been revealed in all your acts, because you have kept yourselves in my mind, you will fall into the enemies' hand by force.

You, too, you impious and wicked prince 25 of Israel, your fate has come upon you in the hour of final punishment. These are the 26 words of the Lord GOD: Put off your diadem, lay aside your crown. All is changed; raise the low and bring down the high. Ruin! 27 Ruin! I will bring about such ruin as never was before, until the rightful sovereign comes. Then I will give him all.

Prophecy to Ammon

Man, prophesy and say, These are the words 28 of the Lord GOD to the Ammonites and to their shameful god:

A sword, a sword drawn for slaughter,
　　burnished for destruction,[w]
　　to flash like lightning!

---

r her sanctuary: *prob. rdg.*; *Heb.* sanctuaries. 　　 *s* to flash: *prob. rdg.*; *Heb.* unintelligible. 　　 *t* the threat of the sword: *prob. rdg.*; *Heb. obscure in context.* 　　 *u Or* household gods. 　　 *v Prob. rdg.*; *Heb.* adds he must set battering-rams. 　　 *w* for destruction: *prob. rdg.*; *Heb. obscure.*

29 Your visions are false, your auguries a lie,
   which bid you bring it^x down
   upon the necks of impious and wicked men,
   whose fate has come upon them
   in the hour of final punishment.
30 Sheathe it again.
   I will judge you in the place where you were
      born,
   the land of your origin.
31 I will pour out my rage upon you;
   I will breathe out my blazing wrath over you.
   I will hand you over to brutal men,
   skilled in destruction.
32 You shall become fuel for fire,
   your blood shall be shed within the land
   and you shall leave no memory behind.
   For I, the LORD, have spoken.

Corruption in Jerusalem

22 These were the words of the LORD to me:
2 Man, will you judge her, will you judge the
murderous city and bring home to her all
3 her abominable deeds? Say to her, These
are the words of the Lord GOD: Alas for
the city that sheds blood within her walls
and brings her fate upon herself, the city
that makes herself idols and is defiled there-
4 by! The guilt is yours for the blood you have
shed, the pollution is on you for the idols
you have made. You have shortened your
days by this and brought the end of your
years nearer. This is why I exposed you to
the contempt of the nations and the mockery
5 of every country. Lands far and near will
taunt you with your infamy and gross dis-
6 order. In you the princes of Israel, one and
all, have used their power to shed blood;
7 men have treated their fathers and mothers
with contempt, they have oppressed the
alien and ill-treated the orphan and the
8 widow. You have disdained what is sacred
9 to me and desecrated my sabbaths. In you,
Jerusalem, informers have worked to procure bloodshed; in you are men who have
feasted at mountain-shrines and have com-
10 mitted lewdness. In you men have exposed
their fathers' nakedness; they have violated
11 women during their periods; they have committed an outrage with their neighbours'
wives and have lewdly defiled their daughters-
in-law; they have ravished their sisters, their
12 own fathers' daughters. In you men have
accepted bribes to shed blood, and they
have exacted discount and interest on their
loans. You have oppressed your fellows for
gain, and you have forgotten me. This is the
very word of the Lord GOD.
13   See, I strike with my clenched fist in anger
at your ill-gotten gains and at the bloodshed
14 within your walls. Will your strength or

courage stand when I deal with you? I, the
LORD, have spoken and I will act. I will dis- 15
perse you among the nations and scatter
you abroad; thus will I rid you altogether
of your defilement. I will sift you^y in the 16
sight of the nations, and you will know that
I am the LORD.

The crucible

These were the words of the LORD to me: 17
Man, to me all Israelites are an alloy, their 18
silver alloyed with copper, tin, iron, and
lead.^z Therefore, these are the words of the 19
Lord GOD: Because you have all become
alloyed, I will gather you together into Jerusalem, as a mass of silver, copper, iron, lead, 20
and tin is gathered into a crucible for the
fire to be blown to full heat to melt them.
So will I gather you in my anger and wrath,
set you there and melt you; I will collect 21
you and blow up the fire of my anger until
you are melted within it. You will be melted 22
as silver is melted in a crucible, and you will
know that I, the LORD, have poured out my
anger upon you.

The whole society corrupt

These were the words of the LORD to me: 23
Man, say to Jerusalem, You are like a land 24
on which no rain has fallen; no shower has
come down upon you^a in the days of indignation. The princes within her are like lions 25
growling as they tear their prey. They have
devoured men, and seized their treasure and
all their wealth; they have widowed many
women within her walls. Her priests have 26
done violence to my law^b and profaned what
is sacred to me. They make no distinction
between sacred and common, and lead men
to see no difference between clean and unclean. They have disregarded my sabbaths,
and I am dishonoured among them. Her 27
officers within her are like wolves tearing
their prey, shedding blood and destroying
men's lives to acquire ill-gotten gain. Her 28
prophets use whitewash instead of plaster;^c
their vision is false and their divination a lie.
They say, 'This is the word of the Lord GOD',
when the LORD has not spoken. The com- 29
mon people are bullies and robbers; they
ill-treat the unfortunate and the poor, they
are unjust and cruel to the alien. I looked 30
for a man among them who could build up
a barricade, who could stand before me in
the breach to defend the land from ruin; but
I found no such man. I poured out my 31
indignation upon them and utterly destroyed
them in the fire of my wrath. Thus I brought
on them the punishment they had deserved.
This is the very word of the Lord GOD.

---

x Prob. rdg.; Heb. you.   *y I will sift you: or You will be profaned.*   *z their silver . . . lead: prob.*
rdg.; Heb. copper, tin, iron, and lead inside a crucible; they are an alloy, silver.   *a Prob. rdg.; Heb. it.*
b Or instruction.   *c Cp. 13. 8–16.*

Two sisters

23 ¹ ² The word of the LORD came to me: Man, he said, there were once two women, ³ daughters of the same mother. They played the whore in Egypt, played the whore while they were still girls; for there they let their breasts be fondled and their virgin bosoms ⁴ pressed. The elder was named Oholah, her sister Oholibah. They became mine and bore me sons and daughters. 'Oholah' is Samaria, ⁵ 'Oholibah' Jerusalem. While she owed me obedience Oholah played the whore and was infatuated with her Assyrian lovers, staff ⁶ officers in blue,*ᵈ* viceroys and governors, handsome young cavaliers all of them, ⁷ riding on horseback. She played the whore with all of them, the flower of the Assyrian youth; and she let herself be defiled with all ⁸ their idols, wherever her lust led her. She never gave up the whorish ways she had learnt in Egypt, where men had lain with her when young, had pressed her virgin bosom and overwhelmed her with their ⁹ fornication. So I abandoned her to her lovers, the Assyrians, with whom she was ¹⁰ infatuated. They ravished her, they took her sons and daughters, and they killed her with the sword. She became a byword among women, and judgement was passed upon her. ¹¹ Oholibah, her sister, had watched her, and she gave herself up to lust and played the ¹² whore worse than her sister. She, too, was infatuated with Assyrians, viceroys, governors and staff officers, all handsome young cavaliers, in full dress, riding on horseback. ¹³ I found that she too had let herself be de- ¹⁴ filed; both had gone the same way; but she carried her fornication to greater lengths: she saw male figures carved on the wall, sculptured forms of Chaldaeans, picked out ¹⁵ in vermilion. Belts were round their waists, and on their heads turbans with dangling ends. All seemed to be high officers and looked like Babylonians, natives of Chal- ¹⁶ daea. As she looked she was infatuated with them, so she sent messengers to Chaldaea ¹⁷ for them. And the Babylonians came to her to share her bed, and defiled her with forni- cation; she was defiled by them until she ¹⁸ was filled with revulsion. She made no secret that she was a whore but let herself be ravished until I was filled with revulsion ¹⁹ against her as I was against her sister. She played the whore again and again, remember- ing how in her youth she had played the ²⁰ whore in Egypt. She was infatuated with their male prostitutes, whose members were like those of asses and whose seed came in ²¹ floods like that of horses. So, Oholibah, you relived the lewdness of your girlhood in Egypt when you let your bosom be pressed and your breasts fondled.*ᵉ*

²² Therefore these are the words of the Lord GOD: I will rouse them against you, Oholi- bah, those lovers of yours who have filled you with revulsion, and bring them upon ²³ you from every side, the Babylonians and all those Chaldaeans, men of Pekod, Shoa, and Koa, and all the Assyrians with them. Handsome young men they are, viceroys and governors, commanders and staff offi- cers,*ᶠ* riding on horseback. They will come ²⁴ against you with war-horses, with chariots and wagons, with a host drawn from the nations, armed with shield, buckler, and helmet; they will beset you on every side. I will give them authority to judge, and they will use that authority to judge you. I will ²⁵ turn my jealous wrath loose on you, and they will make you feel their fury. They will cut off your nose and your ears, and in the end you*ᵍ* will fall by the sword.*ʰ* They will ²⁶ strip you of your clothes and take away all your finery. So I will put a stop to your lewd- ²⁷ ness and the way in which you learnt to play the whore in Egypt. You will never cast longing eyes on such things again, never remember Egypt any more.

²⁸ These are the words of the Lord GOD: I am handing you over to those whom you hate, those who have filled you with revul- ²⁹ sion; and they will make you feel their hatred. They will take all you have earned and leave you naked and exposed; that body with which you have played the whore will be ravished. It is your lewdness and your ³⁰ fornication that have brought this upon you, it is because you have followed alien peoples and played the whore and have allowed yourself to be defiled with their idols. You have followed in your sister's foot- ³¹ steps, and I will put her cup into your hand.

³² These are the words of the Lord GOD:

You shall drink from your sister's cup,
    a cup deep and wide,
charged with mockery and scorn,
    more than ever cup can hold.
It*ⁱ* will be full of drunkenness and grief, ³³
    a cup of ruin and desolation,
the cup of your sister Samaria;
and you shall drink it to the dregs. ³⁴
Then you will chew*ʲ* it in pieces
    and tear out your breasts.
This is my verdict, says the Lord GOD.

³⁵ Therefore, these are the words of the Lord GOD: Because you have forgotten me and flung me behind your back, you must bear the guilt of your lewdness and your fornication.

d Or violet.   *e* fondled: *prob. rdg.; Heb. unintelligible.*   *f* staff officers: *prob. rdg., cp. verses 5 and 12;*
Heb. obscure.   *g* in the end you: *or* your successors.   *h Prob. rdg.; Heb. adds* They will take your
sons and daughters, and in the end you will be burnt.   *i Prob. rdg.; Heb.* You.   *j Or* dash.

36 The LORD said to me, Man, will you judge Oholah and Oholibah? Then tax them with 37 their vile offences. They have committed adultery, and there is blood on their hands. They have committed adultery with their idols and offered my children to them for 38 food, the children they had borne me. This too they have done to me: they have polluted my sanctuary and desecrated my sab- 39 baths. They came into my sanctuary and desecrated it by slaughtering their sons as an offering to their idols; this they did in 40 my own house. They would send for men from a far-off country; and the men came at the messenger's bidding. You bathed your body for these men, you painted your eyes, 41 decked yourself in your finery, you sat yourself upon a bed of state and had a table put ready before it and laid my own incense and 42 my own oil on it. Loud were the voices of the light-hearted crowd; and besides ordinary folk Sabaeans were there, brought from the wilderness; they put bracelets on the women's hands and beautiful garlands on 43 their heads. I thought: Ah that woman, grown old in adultery! Now they will com- 44 mit fornication with her—with her of all women! They resorted to her as a prostitute; 45 they resorted to Oholah and Oholibah, those lewd women. Upright men will condemn them for their adultery and bloodshed; for adulterous they are, and blood is on their 46 hands. These are the words of the Lord GOD: Summon the invading host; abandon them 47 to terror and rapine. Let the host stone them and hack them to pieces with their swords, kill their sons and daughters and burn down 48 their houses. Thus I will put an end to lewdness in the land, and other women shall be 49 taught not to be as lewd as they. You shall pay the penalty for your lewd conduct and be punished for your idolatries, and you will know that I am the Lord GOD.

The corroded cauldron

24 These were the words of the LORD, spoken to me on the tenth day of the tenth month 2 in the ninth year: Man, write down a name for this day, this very day: This is the day 3 the king of Babylon invested Jerusalem. Sing a song of derision to this people of rebels; say to them, These are the words of the Lord GOD:

Set a cauldron on the fire,
    set it on and pour water into it.
4 Into it collect the pieces,
    all the choice pieces,
cram it with leg and shoulder and the best
        of the bones;
5 take the best of the flock.

Pack the logs[k] round it underneath;
seethe the stew
and boil the bones in it.

O city running with blood,   6
O pot green with corrosion,
corrosion that will never be clean!
Therefore these are the words of the Lord
GOD:

Empty it, piece after piece,
    though no lot is cast for any of them.
The city had blood in her midst   7
and she poured it out on the gleaming
        rock,
    not on the ground: she did not pour it
        there
    for the dust to cover it.
But I too have spilt blood on the gleaming   8
        white rock
    so that it cannot be covered,
to make anger flare up and to call down
        vengeance.
Therefore these are the words of the Lord   9
GOD:

O city running with blood,
    I too will make a great fire-pit.
Fill it with logs, light the fire;   10
    make an end of the meat,
pour out all the broth[l] and the bones with it.[m]
Then set the pot empty on the coals   11
    so that its copper may be heated red-hot,
    and then the impurities in it may be melted
    and its corrosion burnt off.
Try as you may,[n]   12
the corrosion is so deep that it will not come
        off;
    only fire will rid it of corrosion for you.
Even so, when I cleansed you in your filthy   13
        lewdness,
    you did not become clean from it,
    and therefore you shall never again be
        clean
    until I have satisfied my anger against
        you.

I, the LORD, have spoken; the time is com- 14 ing, I will act. I will not refrain nor pity nor relent; I will judge you for your conduct and for all that you have done. This is the very word of the Lord GOD.

Ezekiel's wife dies

These were the words of the LORD to me: 15 Man, I am taking from you at one blow the 16 dearest thing you have, but you must not wail or weep or give way to tears. Keep in 17 good heart; be quiet, and make no mourning for the dead; cover your head as usual and put sandals on your feet. You shall not cover your upper lip in mourning nor eat the bread of despair.

---

k Prob. rdg., cp. verse 10; Heb. bones.   l pour . . . broth: prob. rdg.; Heb. mix ointment.   m with it:
prob. rdg.; Heb. will be scorched.   n Try as you may: prob. rdg.; Heb. obscure.

18   I spoke to the people in the morning; and that very evening my wife died. Next morn-
19 ing I did as I was told. The people asked me to say what meaning my behaviour had for
20 them. I answered, These were the words of
21 the Lord to me: Tell the Israelites, This is the word of the Lord God: I will desecrate my sanctuary, which has been the pride of your strength, the delight of your eyes and your heart's desire; and the sons and daughters whom you have left behind shall fall by
22 the sword. But, I said, you shall do as I have done: you shall not cover your upper lip in
23 mourning nor eat the bread of despair. You shall cover your head and put sandals on your feet; you shall not wail nor weep. Because of your wickedness you will pine
24 away and will lament to*o* one another. The Lord says, Ezekiel will be a sign to warn you, and when it happens you will do as he has done, and you will know that I am the Lord God.
25   And now, man, a word for you: I am taking from them that fortress whose beauty so gladdened them, the delight of their eyes, their heart's desire; I am taking their sons
26 and their daughters. Soon fugitives will come and tell you their news by word of mouth.
27 At once you will recover the power of speech and speak with the fugitives; you will no longer be dumb. So will you be a portent to them, and they shall know that I am the Lord.

will make Rabbah a camel-pasture and Ammon a sheep-walk. Thus you shall know that
6 I am the Lord. These are the words of the Lord God: Because you clapped your hands and stamped your feet, and exulted over the
7 land of Israel with single-minded scorn, I will stretch out my hand over you and make you the prey of the nations and cut you off from all other peoples; in every land I will exterminate you and bring you to utter ruin. Thus you shall know that I am the Lord.

Moab

These are the words of the Lord God: Be-
8 cause Moab said, 'Judah is like all the rest',
9 I will expose the flank of Moab and lay open its cities,*p* from one end to the other—the fairest of its cities: Beth-jeshimoth, Baal-
10 meon and Kiriathaim. I will hand over Moab and Ammon together to the tribes of the east to be their possession, so that the Ammonites shall not be remembered among
11 the nations, and so that I may execute judgement upon Moab. Thus they shall know that I am the Lord.

Ammon

25 These were the words of the Lord to me:
2 Man, look towards the Ammonites and
3 prophesy against them. Say to the Ammonites, Listen to the word of the Lord God. These are his words: Because you cried 'Aha!' when you saw my holy place desecrated, the soil of Israel laid waste and the
4 people of Judah sent into exile, I will hand you over as a possession to the tribes of the east. They shall pitch their camps and put up their dwellings among you; they shall eat
5 your crops; they shall drink your milk. I

Edom

These are the words of the Lord God: Be-
12 cause Edom took deliberate revenge on Judah and by so doing incurred lasting guilt, I will stretch my hand out over Edom, says
13 the Lord God, and destroy both man and beast in it, laying waste the land from Teman as far as Dedan; they shall fall by the sword. I will wreak my vengeance upon Edom
14 through my people Israel. They will deal with Edom as my anger and fury demand, and it shall feel my vengeance. This is the very word of the Lord God.

o Or for.   *p and lay . . . cities: prob. rdg.; Heb.* from the cities, from its cities.

PHILISTINES

Philistia

15 These are the words of the Lord GOD: Because the Philistines have taken deliberate revenge and have avenged themselves with single-minded scorn, giving vent to their
16 age-long enmity in destruction, I will stretch out my hand over the Philistines, says the Lord GOD, I will wipe out the Kerethites and destroy all the rest of the dwellers by the sea.
17 I will take fearful vengeance upon them and punish them in my fury. When I take my vengeance, they shall know that I am the LORD.

TYRE

Tyre

26 These were the words of the LORD to me on the first day of the first month in the eleventh
2 year: Man, Tyre has said of Jerusalem,

Aha! she that was the gateway of the nations
is broken,
her gates swing open to me;
I grow rich, she lies in ruins.

3 Therefore these are the words of the Lord GOD:

I am against you, Tyre,
and will bring up many nations against you
as the sea brings up its waves;
4 they will destroy the walls of Tyre and pull
down her towers.
I will scrape the soil off her
and make her a gleaming rock,
5 she shall be an islet where men spread their
nets;
I have spoken, says the Lord GOD.
She shall become the prey of nations,
6 and her daughters*q* shall be slain by the
sword in the open country.

Thus they shall know that I am the LORD.

7 These are the words of the Lord GOD:
I am bringing against Tyre from the north
Nebuchadrezzar king of Babylon, king of
kings. He will come with horses and chariots,
with cavalry and a great army.

Your daughters in the open country   8
he will put to the sword.
He will set up watch-towers against you,
pile up siege-ramps against you
and raise against you a screen of shields.
He will launch his battering-rams on your   9
walls
and break down your towers with his axes.
He will cover you with dust from the thou-   10
sands of his cavalry;
at the thunder of his horses
and of his chariot-wheels
your walls will quake when he enters your
gates
as men enter a city that is breached.
He will trample all your streets   11
with the hooves of his horses
and put your people to the sword,
and your strong pillars will fall to the
ground.
Your wealth will become spoil,   12
your merchandise will be plundered,
your walls levelled,
your pleasant houses pulled down,
your stones, your timber and your rubble
will be dumped into the sea.
So I will silence the clamour of your songs,   13
and the sound of your harps shall be heard
no more.
I will make you a gleaming rock,   14
a place for fishermen to spread their nets,
and you shall never be rebuilt.
I, the LORD, have spoken.
This is the very word of the Lord GOD.

These are the words of the Lord GOD to   15
Tyre: How the coasts and islands will shake
at the sound of your downfall, while the
wounded groan, and the slaughter goes on
in your midst! Then all the sea-kings will   16
come down from their thrones, and lay aside
their cloaks, and strip off their brocaded
robes. They will wear coarse loin-cloths;
they will sit on the ground, shuddering at
every moment, horror-struck at your fate.
Then they will raise this dirge over you: 17

How you are undone, swept from the sea,
O famous city!
You whose strength lay in the sea,
you and your inhabitants,
who spread their terror throughout the
mainland.*r*
Now the coast-lands tremble on the day of   18
your downfall,
and the isles of the sea are appalled at your
passing.

For these are the words of the Lord GOD: 19
When I make you a desolate city, like a city
where no man can live, when I bring up the

q Or daughter-towns.   *r* the mainland: *prob. rdg.; Heb.* her inhabitants.

primeval ocean against you and the great
20 waters cover you, I will thrust you down
with those that descend to the abyss, to the
dead of all the ages. I will make you dwell
in the underworld as in places long desolate,
with those that go down to the abyss. So
you will never again be inhabited or take
21 your place in the land of the living. I will
bring you to a fearful end, and you shall be
no more; men may look for you but will
never find you again. This is the very word
of the Lord GOD.

Dirge over Tyre

27 These were the words of the LORD to me:
2 3 Man, raise a dirge over Tyre and say, Tyre,
throned above your harbours, you who carry
the trade of the nations to many coasts and
islands, these are the words of the Lord GOD:

O Tyre, you said,
'I am perfect in beauty.'
4 Your frontiers are on the high seas,
your builders made your beauty perfect;
5 they fashioned all your timbers
of pine from Senir;
they took a cedar from Lebanon
to raise up a mast over you.
6 They made your oars of oaks from Bashan;
they made your deck strong[s] with boxwood
from the coasts of Kittim.
7 Your canvas was linen,
patterned linen from Egypt
to make your sails;
your awnings were violet and purple
from the coasts of Elishah.
8 Men of Sidon and Arvad became your oarsmen;
you had skilled men within you, O Tyre,
who served as your helmsmen.
9 You had skilled veterans from Gebal
caulking your seams.
You had all sea-going ships and their sailors
to market your wares;
10 men of Pharas,[t] Lud,[u] and Put, served
as warriors in your army;
they hung shield and helmet around
you,
and it was they who gave you your glory.
11 Men of Arvad and Cilicia manned all your
walls,
men of Gammad were posted on your
towers
and hung their shields around your battlements;
it was they who made your beauty perfect.
12 Tarshish was a source of your commerce,
from its abundant resources offering silver
and iron, tin and lead, as your staple wares.
13 Javan,[v] Tubal, and Meshech dealt with you,

offering slaves and vessels of bronze as your
imports. Men from Togarmah offered horses, 14
mares, and mules as your staple wares.
Rhodians dealt with you, great islands were 15
a source of your commerce, paying what was
due to you in ivory and ebony. Edom was a 16
source of your commerce, so many were your
undertakings, and offered purple garnets,
brocade and fine linen, black coral and red
jasper,[w] for your staple wares. Judah and 17
Israel dealt with you, offering wheat from
Minnith, and meal, syrup, oil, and balsam,
as your imports. Damascus was a source of 18
your commerce, so many were your undertakings, from its abundant resources offering wine of Helbon and wool of Suhar, and 19
casks of wine from Izalla,[x] for your staple
wares; wrought iron, cassia, and sweet cane
were among your imports. Dedan dealt 20
with you in coarse woollens for saddle-
cloths. Arabia and all the chiefs of Kedar 21
were the source of your commerce in lambs,
rams, and he-goats; this was your trade
with them. Dealers from Sheba and Raamah 22
dealt with you, offering the choicest spices,
every kind of precious stone and gold, as
your staple wares. Harran, Kanneh, and 23
Eden, dealers from Asshur and all Media,
dealt with you; they were your dealers in 24
gorgeous stuffs, violet cloths and brocades,
in stores of coloured fabric rolled up and
tied with cords; your dealings with them
were in these.

Ships of Tarshish were the caravans for your 25
imports;
you were deeply laden with full cargoes
on the high seas.
Your oarsmen brought you into many 26
waters,
but on the high seas an east wind wrecked
you.
Your wealth, your staple wares, your im- 27
ports,
your sailors and your helmsmen,
your caulkers, your merchants, and your
warriors,
all your ship's company,
all who were with you,
were flung into the sea on the day of your
disaster;
at the cries of your helmsmen the troubled 28
waters tossed.

When all the rowers disembark from their 29
ships,
when the sailors, the helmsmen all together,
go ashore,
they exclaim over your fate, 30
they cry out bitterly;
they throw dust on their heads
and sprinkle themselves with ashes.

---

s strong: prob. rdg.; Heb. ivory.   *t Or Persia.*   *u Or Lydia.*   *v Or Ionia.*   *w Or and*
carbuncles.   *x casks . . . Izalla: prob. rdg.; Heb. obscure.*

31 They tear out their hair at your plight
and put on sackcloth;
they weep bitterly over you,
bitterly wailing.
32 In their lamentation they raise a dirge over
you,
and this is their dirge:
Who was like Tyre,
with her buildings piled[y] off shore?
33 When your wares were unloaded off the
sea
you met the needs of many nations;
with your vast resources and your imports
you enriched the kings of the earth.
34 Now you are broken by the sea
in deep water;
your wares and all your company are gone
overboard.
35 All who dwell on the coasts and islands
are aghast at your fate;
horror is written on the faces of their kings
and their hair stands on end.
36 Among the nations the merchants jeer in
derision at you;
you have come to a fearful end and shall be
no more for ever.

To the prince of Tyre

28 These were the words of the LORD to me:
2 Man, say to the prince of Tyre, This is the
word of the Lord GOD:

In your arrogance you say,
'I am a god;
I sit throned like a god on the high seas.'
Though you are a man and no god,
you try to think the thoughts of a god.
3 What? are you wiser than Danel[z]?
Is no secret too dark for you?
4 Clever and shrewd as you are,
you have amassed wealth for yourself,
you have amassed gold and silver in your
treasuries;
5 by great cleverness in your trading
you have heaped up riches,
and with your riches your arrogance has
grown.

6 Therefore these are the words of the Lord
GOD:

Because you try to think the thoughts of a
god
7 I will bring strangers against you,
the most ruthless of nations,
who will draw their swords against your fine
wisdom
and lay your pride in the dust,
8 sending you down to the pit[a] to die
a death of disgrace on the high seas.

Will you dare to say that you are a god   9
when you face your assailants,
though you are a man and no god
in the hands of those who lay you low?
You will die strengthless   10
at the hands of strangers.

For I have spoken. This is the very word of
the Lord GOD.

Dirge over the king of Tyre

These were the words of the LORD to me: 11
Man, raise this dirge over the king of Tyre, 12
and say to him, This is the word of the Lord
GOD:

You set the seal on perfection;
full of wisdom you were and altogether
beautiful.
You were in an Eden, a garden of God,   13
adorned with gems of every kind:
sardin and chrysolite and jade,
topaz, cornelian and green jasper,
lapis lazuli,[b] purple garnet and green
felspar.
Your jingling beads were of gold,
and the spangles you wore were made for
you
on the day of your birth.
I set you with a towering cherub[c] as   14
guardian;
you were on God's holy hill
and you walked proudly among stones
that flashed with fire.
You were blameless in all your ways   15
from the day of your birth
until your iniquity came to light.
Your commerce grew so great,   16
lawlessness filled your heart and you went
wrong,
so I brought you down in disgrace from the
mountain of God,
and the guardian cherub banished you[d]
from among the stones that flashed like
fire.
Your beauty made you arrogant,   17
you misused your wisdom to increase your
dignity.
I flung you to the ground,
I left you there, a sight for kings to see.
So great was your sin in your wicked trading 18
that you desecrated your sanctuaries.
So I kindled a fire within you,
and it devoured you.
I left you as ashes on the ground
for all to see.
All among the nations who knew you were   19
aghast:
you came to a fearful end and shall be no
more for ever.

---

y with her buildings piled: *prob. rdg.; Heb. obscure.*
a *Or* to destruction.   b *Or* sapphire.   c I set ... cherub: *prob. rdg.; Heb.* You were a towering
cherub whom I set.   d and the ... you: *or* and I parted you, O guardian cherub, ...

z *Or, as otherwise read,* Daniel; *cp.* 14. 14, 20.

Sidon

20 These were the words of the LORD to me:
21 Man, look towards Sidon and prophesy
22 against her. These are the words of the Lord
GOD:

Sidon, I am against you
and I will show my glory in your midst.

Men will know that I am the LORD
when I execute judgement upon her
and thereby prove my holiness.
23 I will let loose pestilence upon her
and bloodshed in her streets;
the slain will fall in her streets,
beset on all sides by the sword;
then men will know that I am the LORD.

24 No longer shall the Israelites suffer from
the scorn of their neighbours, the pricking
of briars and scratching of thorns, and they
shall know that I am the Lord GOD.

When the Israelites return

25 These are the words of the Lord GOD: When
I gather the Israelites from the peoples
among whom they are scattered, I shall
thereby prove my holiness in the sight of all
nations. They shall live on their native soil,
26 which I gave to my servant Jacob. They shall
live there in peace of mind, build houses and
plant vineyards; they shall live there in
peace of mind when I execute judgement on
all their scornful neighbours. Thus they shall
know that I am the LORD their God.

Egypt, Israel and Babylon

29 These were the words of the LORD to me on
the twelfth day of the tenth month in the
2 tenth year: Man, look towards Pharaoh king
of Egypt and prophesy against him and all
3 his country. Say, These are the words of the
Lord GOD:

I am against you,
Pharaoh king of Egypt,
you great monster,
lurking in the streams of the Nile.
You have said, 'My Nile is my own;
it was I who made it.'
4 I will put hooks in your jaws
and make them cling^e to your scales.

I will hoist you out of its streams
with all its fish clinging to your scales.
I will fling you into the wilderness,   5
you and all the fish in your streams;
you will fall on the bare ground
with none to pick you up and bury you;
I will make you food
for beasts and for birds.
So all who live in Egypt will know   6
that I am the LORD,
for the support that you gave to the
Israelites
was no better than a reed,
which splintered in the hand when they   7
grasped you,
and tore their armpits;
when they leaned upon you, you snapped
and their limbs gave way.

This therefore is the word of the Lord   8
GOD: I am bringing a sword upon you to
destroy both man and beast. The land of   9
Egypt shall become a desolate waste, and
they shall know that I am the LORD, because
you said, 'The Nile is mine; it was I who
made it.' I am against you therefore, you   10
and your Nile, and I will make Egypt desolate, wasted by drought, from Migdol to
Syene and up to the very frontier of Cush.
No foot of man shall pass through it, no   11
foot of beast; it shall lie uninhabited for
forty years. I will make the land of Egypt   12
the most desolate of desolate lands; her
cities shall lie derelict among the ruined
cities. For forty years shall they lie derelict,
and I will scatter the Egyptians among the
nations and disperse them among the lands.

These are the words of the Lord GOD: At   13
the end of forty years I will gather the Egyptians from the peoples among whom they
are scattered. I will turn the fortunes of   14
Egypt and bring them back to Pathros, the
land of their origin, where they shall become
a petty kingdom. She shall be the most   15
paltry of kingdoms and never again exalt
herself over the nations, for I will make the
Egyptians too few to rule over them. The   16
Israelites will never trust Egypt again; this
will be a reminder to them of their sin in
turning to Egypt for help. They shall know
that I am the Lord GOD.

These were the words of the LORD to me   17
on the first day of the first month in the
twenty-seventh year: Man, long did Nebu-   18
chadrezzar king of Babylon keep his army
in the field against Tyre, until every head was
rubbed bare and every shoulder chafed. But
neither he nor his army gained anything from
Tyre for their long service against her. This,   19
therefore, is the word of the Lord GOD: I am
giving the land of Egypt to Nebuchadrezzar
king of Babylon. He shall carry off its wealth,

e make them cling: prob. rdg.; Heb. make the fish of your streams cling.

he shall spoil and plunder it, and so his army
20 will be paid. I have given him the land of
Egypt as the wages for his service because
they have disregarded me. This is the very
word of the Lord GOD.
21   At that time I will make Israel put out
fresh shoots, and give you back the power to
speak among them, and they will know that
I am the LORD.

Day of reckoning for the nations

30 These were the words of the LORD to me:
2 Man, prophesy and say, These are the words
of the Lord GOD:

Woe, woe for the day!
3   for a day is near,
    a day of the LORD is near,
    a day of cloud, a day of reckoning for the
        nations.
4   Then a sword will come upon Egypt,
    and there will be anguish in Cush,
    when the slain fall in Egypt,
    when its wealth is taken and its foundations
        are torn up.
5   Cush and Put and Lud,*f*
    all the Arabs and Libyans and the peoples
        of allied lands,
    shall fall with them by the sword.
6 These are the words of the LORD:

    All who support Egypt shall fall
    and her boasted might be brought low;
    from Migdol to Syene men shall fall by the
        sword.
    This is the very word of the Lord GOD.
7   They shall be the most desolate of desolate
lands, and their cities shall lie derelict among
8 the ruined cities. When I set Egypt on fire
and all her helpers are broken, they will
9 know that I am the LORD. When that time
comes messengers shall go out in haste from
my presence to alarm Cush, still without a
care, and anguish shall come upon her in
Egypt's hour. Even now it is on the way.
10   These are the words of the Lord GOD:

    I will make an end of Egypt's hordes
    by the hands of Nebuchadrezzar king of
        Babylon.
11   He and his people with him, the most ruth-
        less of nations,
    will be brought to ravage the land.
    They will draw their swords against Egypt
    and fill the land with the slain.
12   I will make the streams of the Nile dry land
    and sell Egypt to evil men;
    I will lay waste the land and everything in it
        by foreign hands.
    I, the LORD, have spoken.
13 These are the words of the Lord GOD:

    I will make an end of the lordlings*g*
    and wipe out the princelings*h* of Noph;

and never again shall a prince arise in Egypt.
    Then I will put fear in that land,
I will lay Pathros waste and set fire to Zoan 14
    and execute judgement on No.
I will pour out my rage upon Sin, 15
    the bastion of Egypt,
    and destroy the horde of Noph.
I will set Egypt on fire, 16
    and Syene shall writhe in anguish;
    the walls of No shall be breached
    and flood-waters shall burst into it.
The young men of On and Pi-beseth*i* shall 17
    fall by the sword
    and the cities themselves go into cap-
        tivity.
Daylight shall fail in Tahpanhes 18
    when I break the yoke of Egypt there;
    then her boasted might shall be subdued;
    a cloud shall cover her,
    and her daughters*j* shall go into cap-
        tivity.
Thus I will execute judgement on Egypt, 19
    and they shall know that I am the LORD.

    This was the word of the LORD to me on 20
the seventh day of the first month in the
eleventh year: Man, I have broken the arm 21
of Pharaoh king of Egypt. See, it has not
been bound up with dressings and bandage
to give it strength to wield a sword. These, 22
therefore, are the words of the Lord GOD:
I am against Pharaoh king of Egypt; I will
break both his arms, the sound and the
broken, and make the sword drop from his
hand. I will scatter the Egyptians among the 23
nations and disperse them over many lands.
Then I will strengthen the arms of the king 24
of Babylon and put my sword in his hand;
but I will break Pharaoh's arms, and he shall
lie wounded and groaning before him. I will 25
give strength to the arms of the king of
Babylon, but the arms of Pharaoh will fall.
Men will know that I am the LORD, when
I put my sword in the hand of the king of
Babylon, and he stretches it out over the
land of Egypt. I will scatter the Egyptians 26
among the nations and disperse them over
many lands, and they shall know that I am
the LORD.

The great cedar

On the first day of the third month in the **31**
eleventh year this word came to me from the
LORD: Man, say to Pharaoh king of Egypt 2
and all his horde:

    What are you like in your greatness?

Look at Assyria: it was a cedar in Lebanon, 3
    whose fair branches overshadowed the
        forest,
towering high with its crown finding a way
    through the foliage.

f Or Lydia.   *g Or* idols.   *h Or* false gods.   *i Or* Bubastis.   *j Or* daughter-towns.

4 Springs nourished it, underground waters
    gave it height,
their streams washed the soil all round it
and sent forth their rills to every tree in the
    country.
5 So it grew taller than every other tree.
Its boughs were many, its branches spread
    far;
    for water was abundant in the channels.
6 In its boughs all the birds of the air had their
    nests,
under its branches all wild creatures bore
    their young,
and in its shadow all great nations made their
    home.
7   A splendid great tree it was, with its long
    spreading boughs,
for its roots were beside abundant waters.
8   No cedar in God's garden overshadowed
    it,
no fir could compare with its boughs,
and no plane-tree had such branches;
not a tree in God's garden
could rival its beauty.
9   I, the LORD, gave it beauty
with its mass of spreading boughs,
the envy of all the trees in Eden,
the garden of God.

The cedar's fall

10 Therefore these are the words of the Lord
GOD: Because it grew so high and pushed
its crown up through the foliage, and its
11 pride mounted as it grew, therefore I handed
it over to a prince of the nations to deal with
it; I made an example of it as its wickedness
12 deserved. Strangers from the most ruthless
of nations hewed it down and flung it away.
Its sweeping boughs fell on the mountains
and in all the valleys, and its branches lay
broken beside all the streams in the land.
All nations of the earth came out from
13 under its shade and left it. All the birds of
the air settled on its fallen trunk; the wild
14 creatures all stood by its branches. Never
again, therefore, shall the well-watered trees
grow so high or push their crowns up through
the foliage. Nor shall the strongest of them,
well watered though they be, stand erect in
their full height; for all have been given over
to death, to the world below, to share the
common doom and go down to the abyss.
15   These are the words of the Lord GOD:
When he went down to Sheol, I closed the
deep over him as a gate, I dammed its rivers,
the great waters were held back. I put
Lebanon in mourning for him, and all the
16 trees of the country-side wilted. I made
nations shake with the crash of his fall, when
I brought him down to Sheol with those who
go down to the abyss. From this all the trees
of Eden, all the choicest and best of Lebanon,

all the well-watered trees, drew comfort in
the world below. They too like him had gone 17
down to Sheol, to those slain with the sword;
and those who had lived in his shadow were
scattered among the nations. Which among 18
the trees of Eden was like you in glory and
greatness? Yet you will be brought down
with the trees of Eden to the world below;
you will lie with those who have been slain
by the sword, in the company of the strengthless dead. This stands for Pharaoh and all
his horde. This is the very word of the Lord
GOD.

Dirge over Pharaoh

On the first day of the twelfth month in the **32**
twelfth year the word of the LORD came to
me: Man, raise a dirge over Pharaoh king 2
of Egypt and say to him:
  Young lion of the nations, you are undone.
You were like a monster in the waters of the
    Nile
    scattering the water with its snout,[k] [l]
churning the water with its feet
    and fouling the streams.

  These are the words of the Lord GOD: 3
When many nations are gathered together
I will spread my net over you, and you will
be dragged up in its meshes. I will fling you 4
on land, dashing you down on the bare
ground. I will let all the birds of the air
settle upon you and all the wild beasts gorge
themselves on your flesh. Your flesh I will 5
lay on the mountains, and fill the valleys
with the worms that feed on it. I will drench 6
the land with your discharge, drench it with
your blood to the very mountain-tops, and
the watercourses shall be full of you. When 7
I put out your light I will veil the sky and
blacken its stars; I will veil the sun with a
cloud, and the moon shall not give its light.
I will darken all the shining lights of the sky 8
above you and bring darkness over your
land. This is the very word of the Lord GOD.
  I will disquiet many peoples when I bring 9
your broken army among the nations into
lands you have never known. I will appal 10
many peoples with your fate; when I brandish my sword in the faces of their kings,
their hair shall stand on end. In the day of
your downfall each shall tremble for his
own fate from moment to moment. For these 11
are the words of the Lord GOD: The sword
of the king of Babylon shall come upon
you. I will make the whole horde of you fall 12
by the sword of warriors who are of all men
the most ruthless. They shall make havoc of
the pride of Egypt, and all its horde shall be
wiped out. I will destroy all their cattle be- 13
side many waters. No foot of man, no hoof
of beast, shall ever churn them up again.

---

k snout: *prob. rdg.; Heb.* streams.   *l* scattering . . . snout: *or* heaving itself up in the streams.

14 Then will I let their waters settle and their streams run smooth as oil. This is the very
15 word of the Lord GOD. When I have laid Egypt waste, and the whole land is devastated, when I strike down all who dwell there, they shall know that I am the LORD.
16 This is a dirge, and the women of the nations shall sing it as a dirge. They shall sing it as a dirge, as a dirge over Egypt and all its horde. This is the very word of the Lord GOD.

A lesson from history

17 On the fifteenth day of the first month in the twelfth year, the word of the LORD came to me:

18 Man, raise a lament, you and the daughters of the nations,
over the hordes of Egypt and her nobles,
whom I will bring down*m* to the world below
with those that go down to the abyss.

19 Are you better favoured than others?
Go down and be laid to rest with the strengthless dead.

20 A sword stands ready. Those who marched with her, and all her horde, shall fall into the
21 midst of those slain by the sword. Warrior chieftains in Sheol speak to Pharaoh and those who aided him:
The strengthless dead, slain by the sword,
22 have come down and are laid to rest. There is Assyria with all her company, her buried around her, all of them slain and fallen by
23 the sword. Her graves are set in the recesses of the abyss, with her company buried around her, all of them slain, fallen by the sword, men who once filled the land of the
24 living with terror. There is Elam, with all her hordes buried around her, all of them slain, fallen by the sword; they have gone down strengthless to the world below, men who struck terror into the land of the living but now share the disgrace of those that go
25 down to the abyss. In the midst of the slain a resting-place has been made for her, with all her hordes buried around her; all of them strengthless, slain by the sword. For they who once struck terror into the land of the living now share the disgrace of those that go down to the abyss; they are assigned
26 a place in the midst of the slain. There are Meshech and Tubal with all their hordes, with their buried around them, all of them strengthless and slain by the sword, men who once struck terror into the land of the
27 living. Do they not rest with warriors fallen strengthless,*n* who have gone down to Sheol with their weapons, their swords under their heads and their shields over their bones,*o*

though the terror of their prowess once lay on the land of the living? You also, Pharaoh, 28 shall lie broken in the company of the strengthless dead, resting with those slain by the sword. There is Edom, her kings and all 29 her princes, who, for all their prowess, have been lodged with those slain by the sword; they shall rest with the strengthless dead and with those that go down to the abyss. There 30 are all the princes of the North and all the Sidonians, who have gone down in shame with the slain, for all the terror they inspired by their prowess. They rest strengthless with those slain by the sword, and they share the disgrace of those that go down to the abyss.

Pharaoh will see them and will take com- 31 fort for his lost hordes—Pharaoh who, with all his army, is slain by the sword, says the Lord GOD; though he spread*p* terror through- 32 out the land of the living, yet he with all his horde is laid to rest with those that are slain by the sword, in the company of the strengthless dead. This is the very word of the Lord GOD.

A watchman for the people

These were the words of the LORD to me: **33** Man, say to your fellow-countrymen, When 2 I set armies in motion against a land, its people choose one of themselves to be a watchman. When he sees the enemy ap- 3 proaching and blows his trumpet to warn the people, then if anyone does not heed 4 the warning and is overtaken by the enemy, he is responsible for his own fate. He is 5 responsible because, when he heard the alarm, he paid no heed to it; if he had heeded it, he would have escaped. But if the watch- 6 man does not blow his trumpet or warn the people when he sees the enemy approaching, then any man who is killed is caught with all his sins upon him; but I will hold the watchman answerable for his death.

Man, I have appointed you a watchman 7 for the Israelites. You will take messages from me and carry my warnings to them. It may be that I pronounce sentence of 8 death on a man because he is wicked; if you do not warn him to give up his ways, the guilt is his and because of his wickedness he shall die, but I will hold you answerable for his death. But if you have warned him to 9 give up his ways, and he has not given them up, he will die because of his wickedness, but you will have saved yourself.

Man, say to the Israelites, You complain, 10 'We are burdened by our sins and offences; we are pining away because of them; we despair of life.' So tell them: As I live, says 11 the Lord GOD, I have no desire for the death of the wicked. I would rather that a wicked

m her nobles . . . down: *prob. rdg.; Heb. obscure.*   *n Prob. rdg.; Heb.* from strengthless ones.   *o* and
. . . bones: prob. rdg.; Heb. unintelligible.   *p Prob. rdg.; Heb.* I have spread.

man should mend his ways and live. Give up your evil ways, give them up; O Israelites, why should you die?

Personal responsibility

12 Man, say to your fellow-countrymen, When a righteous man goes wrong, his righteousness shall not save him. When a wicked man mends his ways, his former wickedness shall not bring him down. When a righteous man sins, all his righteousness cannot save his 13 life. It may be that, when I tell the righteous man that he will save his life, he presumes on his righteousness and does wrong; then none of his righteous acts will be remembered: he will die for the wrong he has done. 14 It may be that when I pronounce sentence of death on the wicked, he mends his ways 15 and does what is just and right: if he then restores the pledges he has taken, repays what he has stolen, and, doing no more wrong, follows the rules that ensure life, he 16 shall live and not die. None of the sins he has committed shall be remembered against him; he shall live, because he does what is just and right.

17 Your fellow-countrymen are saying, 'The Lord acts without principle', but it is their 18 ways that are unprincipled. When a righteous man gives up his righteousness and does 19 wrong, he shall die because of it; and when a wicked man gives up his wickedness and does what is just and right, he shall live. 20 How, Israel, can you say that the Lord acts without principle, when I judge every man of you on his deeds?

Jerusalem has fallen!

21 On the fifth day of the tenth month in the twelfth year of our captivity, fugitives came to me from Jerusalem and told me that the city had fallen. The evening before they 22 arrived, the hand of the LORD had come upon me, and by the time they reached me in the morning the LORD had given me back my speech. My speech was restored and I was no longer dumb.

Israel's hypocrisy

These were the words of the LORD to me: 23 Man, the inhabitants of these wastes on the 24 soil of Israel say, 'When Abraham took possession of the land he was but one; now we are many, and the land has been granted to us in possession.' Tell them, therefore, 25 that these are the words of the Lord GOD: You eat meat with the blood in it, you lift up your eyes to idols, you shed*q* blood; and yet you expect to possess the land! You 26 trust to the sword, you commit abominations, you defile one another's wives; and you expect to possess the land! Tell them 27 that these are the words of the Lord GOD: As I live, among the ruins they shall fall by the sword; in the open country I will give them for food to beasts; in dens and caves they shall die by pestilence. I will make the 28 land a desolate waste; her boasted might shall be brought to nothing, and the mountains of Israel shall be an untrodden desert. When I make the land a desolate waste be- 29 cause of all the abominations they have committed, they will know that I am the LORD.

Man, your fellow-countrymen gather in 30 groups and talk of you under walls and in doorways and say to one another, 'Let us go and see what message there is from the LORD.' So my people will come crowding in, 31

q Or pour out.

(Ezek. 33. 30)

as people do, and sit down in front of you. They will hear what you have to say, but they will not do it. 'Fine words^r!' they will say, but their hearts are set on selfish gain. 32 You are no more to them than a singer of fine songs^s with a lovely voice, or a clever harpist; they will listen to what you say but 33 will certainly not do it. But when it comes, as come it will, they will know that there has been a prophet in their midst.

Careless shepherds

34 These were the words of the LORD to me: 2 Prophesy, man, against the shepherds of Israel; prophesy and say to them, You shepherds, these are the words of the Lord GOD: How I hate the shepherds of Israel who care only for themselves! Should not 3 the shepherd care for the sheep? You consume the milk, wear the wool, and slaughter the fat beasts, but you do not feed the sheep. 4 You have not encouraged the weary, tended the sick, bandaged the hurt, recovered the straggler, or searched for the lost; and even the strong you have driven with ruthless 5 severity. They are scattered, they have no shepherd, they have become the prey of 6 wild beasts. My sheep go straying over the mountains and on every high hill, my flock is dispersed over the whole country, with no one to ask after them or search for them. 7 Therefore, you shepherds, hear the words 8 of the LORD. As surely as I live, says the Lord GOD, because my sheep are ravaged by wild beasts and have become their prey for lack of a shepherd, because my shepherds have not asked after the sheep but have cared only for themselves and not for the sheep— 9 therefore, you shepherds, hear the words of 10 the LORD. These are the words of the Lord GOD: I am against the shepherds and will demand my sheep from them. I will dismiss those shepherds: they shall care only for themselves no longer; I will rescue my sheep from their jaws, and they shall feed on them no more.

The LORD as shepherd

11 For these are the words of the Lord GOD: Now I myself will ask after my sheep and 12 go in search of them. As a shepherd goes in search of his sheep when his flock is dispersed all around him, so I will go in search of my sheep and rescue them, no matter where they were scattered in dark and 13 cloudy days. I will bring them out from every nation, gather them in from other lands, and lead them home to their own soil. I will graze them on the mountains of Israel, by her streams and in all her green fields. 14 I will feed them on good grazing-ground, and their pasture shall be the high mount-

ains of Israel. There they will rest, there in good pasture, and find rich grazing on the mountains of Israel. I myself will tend my 15 flock, I myself pen them in their fold, says the Lord GOD. I will search for the lost, recover 16 the straggler, bandage the hurt, strengthen the sick, leave the healthy and strong to play, and give them their proper food.

Reign of peace

As for you, my flock, these are the words of 17 the Lord GOD: I will judge between one sheep and another. You rams and he-goats! Are you not satisfied with grazing on good 18 herbage, that you must trample down the rest with your feet? Or with drinking clear water, that you must churn up the rest with your feet? My flock has to eat what you have 19 trampled and drink what you have churned up. These, therefore, are the words of the 20 Lord GOD to them: Now I myself will judge between the fat sheep and the lean. You 21 hustle the weary with flank and shoulder, you butt them with your horns until you have driven them away and scattered them abroad. Therefore I will save my flock, and 22 they shall be ravaged no more; I will judge between one sheep and another. Then I will 23 set over them one shepherd to take care of them, my servant David; he shall care for them and become their shepherd. I, the 24 LORD, will become their God, and my servant David shall be a prince among them. I, the LORD, have spoken. I will make a 25 covenant with them to ensure prosperity; I will rid the land of wild beasts, and men shall live in peace of mind on the open pastures and sleep in the woods. I will 26 settle them in the neighbourhood of my hill and send them rain in due season, blessed rain. Trees in the country-side shall bear 27 their fruit, the land shall yield its produce, and men shall live in peace of mind on their own soil. They shall know that I am the LORD when I break the bars of their yokes and rescue them from those who have enslaved them. They shall never be ravaged 28 by the nations again nor shall wild beasts devour them; they shall live in peace of mind, with no one to alarm them. I will give 29 prosperity to their plantations; they shall never again be victims of famine in the land nor any longer bear the taunts of the nations. They shall know that I, the LORD their God, 30 am with them, and that they are my people Israel, says the Lord GOD. You are my flock, 31 my people, the flock I feed, and I am your God. This is the very word of the Lord GOD.

Prophecy to Seir

These were the words of the LORD to me: **35** Man, look towards the hill-country of Seir 2

r *Fine words*: or *Love songs*.   s *fine songs*: or *love songs*.

3 and prophesy against it. Say, These are the words of the Lord GOD:

O hill-country of Seir, I am against you:
I will stretch out my hand over you
and make you a desolate waste.

4 I will lay your cities in ruins
and you shall be made desolate;
thus you shall know that I am the LORD.

5 For you have maintained an immemorial feud
and handed over the Israelites to the sword
in the hour of their doom,
at the time of their final punishment.

6 Therefore, as I live, says the Lord GOD,
I make blood your destiny, and blood shall pursue you;
you are most surely guilty of blood,
and blood shall pursue you.

7 I will make the hill-country of Seir a desolate waste
and put an end to all in it who pass to and fro;

8 I will fill your hills and your valleys with its slain,
and those slain by the sword shall fall into your streams.

9 I will make you desolate for ever,
and your cities shall not be inhabited;
thus you shall know that I am the LORD.

10 You say, The two nations and the two countries shall be mine and I will take possession of them, though the LORD is^t there. Therefore, as I live, says the Lord GOD, your anger and jealousy shall be requited, for I will do to you what you have done in your hatred against them. I shall be known among you when I judge you; you shall know that I am the LORD. I have heard all your blasphemies; you have said, 'The mountains of Israel are desolate and have been given to us to devour.' You have set yourselves up against me and spoken recklessly against me. I myself have heard you. These are the words of the Lord GOD: I will make you so desolate that the whole world will gloat over you. I will do to you as you did to Israel my own possession when you gloated over its desolation. O hill-country of Seir, you will be desolate, and it will be the end of all Edom. Thus men will know that I am the LORD.

Prophecy to Israel

36 And do you, man, prophesy to the mountains of Israel and say, Mountains of Israel, 2 hear the words of the LORD. These are the words of the Lord GOD: The enemy has said, 'Aha! now the everlasting highlands 3 are ours.' Therefore prophesy and say, These are the words of the Lord GOD: You

mountains of Israel, all round you men gloated over you and trampled you down when you were seized and occupied by the rest of the nations; your name was bandied about in the common talk of men. There- 4 fore, listen to the words of the Lord GOD when he speaks to the mountains and hills, to the streams and valleys, to the desolate palaces and deserted cities, all plundered and despised by the rest of the nations round you. These are the words of the Lord GOD: 5 In the fire of my jealousy I have spoken plainly against the rest of the nations, and against Edom above all. For Edom, swollen with triumphant scorn, seized on my land to hold it up to public contempt. Therefore 6 prophesy over the soil of Israel and say to the mountains and hills, the streams and valleys, These are the words of the Lord GOD: I have spoken my mind in jealousy and anger because you have had to endure the taunts of all nations. Therefore, says the 7 Lord GOD, I have sworn with uplifted hand that the nations round about shall be punished for^u their taunts. But you, moun- 8 tains of Israel, you shall put forth your branches and yield your fruit for my people Israel, for their home-coming is near. See 9 now, I am for you, I will turn to you, and you shall be tilled and sown. I will plant 10 many men upon you—the whole house of Israel. The cities shall again be inhabited and the palaces rebuilt. I will plant many men 11 and beasts upon you; they shall increase and be fruitful. I will make you populous as in days of old and more prosperous than you were at first. Thus you will know that I am the LORD. I will make men—my people 12 Israel—tread your paths again. They shall settle in you, and you shall be their possession; but you shall never again rob them of their children.

These are the words of the Lord GOD: 13 People say that you are a land that devours men and robs your tribes of their children. But you shall never devour men any more 14 nor rob your tribes of their children, says the Lord GOD. I will never let you hear the 15 taunts of the nations again nor shall you have to endure the reproaches of the peoples. This is the very word of the Lord GOD.

His holy name

These were the words of the LORD to me: 16 Man, when the Israelites lived on their own 17 soil they defiled it with their ways and deeds; their ways were foul and disgusting in my sight. I poured out my fury upon them be- 18 cause of the blood they had poured out upon the land, and the idols with which they had defiled it. I scattered them among the 19 nations, and they were dispersed among

t Or has been.   u be punished for: or bear.

different countries; I passed on them the sentence which their ways and deeds de-
20 served. When they came among those nations, they caused my holy name to be profaned wherever they came: men said of them, 'These are the people of the LORD, and it is from his land that they have come.'
21 And I spared them for the sake of my holy name which the Israelites had profaned among the nations to whom they had gone.
22 Therefore tell the Israelites that these are the words of the Lord GOD: It is not for your sake, you Israelites, that I am acting, but for the sake of my holy name, which you have profaned among the peoples where you
23 have gone. I will hallow my great name, which has been profaned among those nations. When they see that I reveal my holiness through you, the nations will know that I am the LORD, says the Lord GOD.
24 I will take you out of the nations and gather you from every land and bring you to your
25 own soil. I will sprinkle clean water over you, and you shall be cleansed from all that defiles you; I will cleanse you from the taint of
26 all your idols. I will give you a new heart and put a new spirit within you; I will take the heart of stone from your body and give you
27 a heart of flesh. I will put my spirit into you and make you conform to my statutes, keep
28 my laws and live by them. You shall live in the land which I gave to your ancestors; you shall become my people, and I will become
29 your God. I will save you from all that defiles you; I will call to the corn and make it plentiful; I will bring no more famine upon
30 you. I will make the trees bear abundant fruit and the ground yield heavy crops, so that you will never again have to bear the
31 reproach of famine among the nations. You will recall your wicked ways and evil deeds, and you will loathe yourselves because of
32 your wickedness and your abominations. It is not for your sake that I am acting; be sure of that, says the Lord GOD. Feel, then, the shame and disgrace of your ways, men of Israel.

Restoring the land

33 These are the words of the Lord GOD: When I cleanse you of all your wickedness, I will re-people the cities, and the palaces shall
34 be rebuilt. The land now desolate shall be tilled, instead of lying waste for every passer-
35 by to see. Men will say that this same land which was waste has become like a garden of Eden, and people will make their homes in the cities once ruined, wasted, and shat-
36 tered, but now well fortified. The nations still left around you will know that it is I, the LORD, who have rebuilt the shattered

cities and planted anew the waste land; I, the LORD, have spoken and will do it.
These are the words of the Lord GOD: 37 Yet again will I let the Israelites ask me to act in their behalf. I will make their men numerous as sheep, like the sheep offered 38 as holy-gifts, like the sheep in Jerusalem at times of festival. So shall their ruined cities be filled with human flocks, and they shall know that I am the LORD.

The dry bones

The hand of the LORD came upon me, and **37** he carried me out by his spirit and put me down in a plain full of bones. He made me 2 go to and fro across them until I had been round them all;*v* they covered the plain, countless numbers of them, and they were very dry. He said to me, 'Man, can these 3 bones live again?' I answered, 'Only thou knowest that, Lord GOD.' He said to me, 4 'Prophesy over these bones and say to them, O dry bones, hear the word of the LORD. This is the word of the Lord GOD to these 5 bones: I will put breath*w* into you, and you shall live. I will fasten sinews on you, bring 6 flesh upon you, overlay you with skin, and put breath in you, and you shall live; and you shall know that I am the LORD.' I began 7 to prophesy as he had bidden me, and as I prophesied there was a rustling sound and the bones fitted themselves together. As I 8 looked, sinews appeared upon them, flesh covered them, and they were overlaid with skin, but there was no breath in them. Then 9 he said to me, 'Prophesy to the wind, pro- phesy, man, and say to it, These are the words of the Lord GOD: Come, O wind, come from every quarter and breathe into these slain, that they may come to life.' I began to prophesy as he had bidden me: 10 breath came into them; they came to life and rose to their feet, a mighty host. He said 11 to me, 'Man, these bones are the whole people of Israel. They say, "Our bones are dry, our thread of life is snapped, our web is severed from the loom."*x* Prophesy, there- 12 fore, and say to them, These are the words of the Lord GOD: O my people, I will open your graves and bring you up from them, and restore you to the land of Israel. You 13 shall know that I am the LORD when I open your graves and bring you up from them, O my people. Then I will put my spirit*y* into 14 you and you shall live, and I will settle you on your own soil, and you shall know that I the LORD have spoken and will act. This is the very word of the LORD.'

The kingdom united

These were the words of the LORD to me: 15

v He made . . . all: *or* He made me pass all round them. *prob. rdg.; Heb.* we are completely cut off.   *y Or* breath.   *w Or* wind *or* spirit.   *x* our web . . . loom:

16 Man, take one leaf of a wooden tablet and write on it, 'Judah and his associates of Israel.' Then take another leaf and write on it, 'Joseph, the leaf of Ephraim and all his 17 associates of Israel.' Now bring the two together to form one tablet; then they will be 18 a folding tablet in your hand. When your fellow-countrymen ask you to tell them 19 what you mean by this, say to them, These are the words of the Lord GOD: I am taking the leaf of Joseph, which belongs to Ephraim and his associate tribes of Israel, and joining*z* to it the leaf of Judah. Thus I shall make them one tablet, and they shall be one in my 20 hand. The leaves on which you write shall be visible in your hand for all to see.

21 Then say to them, These are the words of the Lord GOD: I am gathering up the Israelites from their places of exile among the nations; I will assemble them from every quarter and restore them to their own soil. 22 I will make them one single nation in the land, on the mountains of Israel, and they shall have one king; they shall no longer be two nations or divided into two kingdoms. 23 They shall never again be defiled with their idols, their loathsome ways and all their disloyal acts; I will rescue them from all their sinful backsliding and purify them. Thus they shall become my people, and I 24 will become their God. My servant David shall become king over them, and they shall have one shepherd. They shall conform to my laws, they shall observe and carry out 25 my statutes. They shall live in the land which I gave my servant Jacob, the land where your fathers lived. They and their descendants shall live there for ever, and my servant 26 David shall for ever be their prince. I will make a covenant with them to bring them prosperity; this covenant shall be theirs for ever.*a* I will greatly increase their numbers, and I will put my sanctuary for ever in their 27 midst. They shall live under the shelter of my dwelling; I will become their God and 28 they shall become my people. The nations shall know that I the LORD am keeping Israel sacred to myself, because my sanctuary is in the midst of them for ever.

Gog's plan to attack Israel

38 These were the words of the LORD to me: 2 Man, look towards Gog, the prince of Rosh, Meshech, and Tubal, in the land of Magog, 3 and prophesy against him. Say, These are the words of the Lord GOD: I am against you, Gog, prince of Rosh, Meshech, and 4 Tubal. I will turn you about, I will put hooks in your jaws. I will lead you out, you and your whole army, horses and horsemen, all fully equipped, a great host with shield and buckler, every man wielding a sword, and 5 with them the men of Pharas, Cush, and Put, all with shield and helmet; Gomer and all 6 its squadrons, Beth-togarmah with its squadrons from the far recesses of the north— a great concourse of peoples with you. Be prepared; make ready, you and all the 7 host which has gathered to join you, and hold yourselves in reserve for me.*b* After 8 many days you will be summoned; in years to come you will enter a land restored from ruin, whose people are gathered from many nations upon the mountains of Israel that have been desolate so long. The Israelites, brought out from the nations, will all be living undisturbed; and you will come up, 9 driving in like a hurricane; you will cover the land like a cloud, you and all your squadrons, a great concourse of peoples.

This is the word of the Lord GOD: At 10 that time a thought will enter your head and you will plan evil. You will say, 'I will 11 attack a land of open villages, I will fall upon a people living quiet and undisturbed, undefended by walls, with neither gates nor bars.' You will expect to come plundering, 12 spoiling, and stripping bare the ruins where men now live again, a people gathered out of the nations, a people acquiring cattle and goods, and making their home at the very centre of the world. Sheba and Dedan, the 13 traders of Tarshish and her leading merchants, will say to you, 'Is it for plunder that you have come? Have you gathered your host to get spoil, to carry off silver and gold, to seize cattle and goods, to collect rich spoil?'

Therefore, prophesy, man, and say to 14 Gog, These are the words of the Lord GOD: In that day when my people Israel is living undisturbed, will you not awake and come 15 with many nations from your home in the far recesses of the north, all riding on horses, a great host, a mighty army? You will come 16 up against my people Israel; and in those future days you will be like a cloud covering the earth. I will bring you against my land, that the nations may know me, when they see me prove my holiness at your expense, O Gog.

Universal terror against Gog

This is the word of the Lord GOD: When I 17 spoke in days of old through my servants the prophets, who prophesied in those days unceasingly, it was you whom I threatened to bring against Israel. On that day, when at 18 length Gog comes against the land of Israel, says the Lord GOD, my wrath will boil over. In my jealousy and in the heat of my anger 19 I swear that on that day there shall be a great earthquake throughout the land of Israel.

z Prob. rdg.; Heb. adds them.   *a Prob. rdg.; Heb. adds* and I will put them.   *b* and hold . . . me: *or* and you shall be their rallying-point.

20 The fish in the sea and the birds in the air, the wild animals and all reptiles that move on the ground, all mankind on the face of the earth, all shall be shaken before me. Mountains shall be torn up, the terraced hills collapse, and every wall crash to the
21 ground. I will summon universal terror against Gog, says the Lord GOD, and his men shall turn their swords against one
22 another. I will bring him to judgement with pestilence and bloodshed; I will pour down teeming rain, hailstones hard as rock, and fire and brimstone, upon him, upon his squadrons, upon the whole concourse of
23 peoples with him. Thus will I prove myself great and holy and make myself known to many nations; they shall know that I am the LORD.

Destruction of Gog and his horde

39 And you, man, prophesy against Gog and say, These are the words of the Lord GOD: I am against you, Gog, prince of Rosh,
2 Meshech, and Tubal. I will turn you about and drive you, I will fetch you up from the far recesses of the north and bring you to
3 the mountains of Israel. I will strike the bow from your left hand and dash the arrows
4 from your right hand. There on the mountains of Israel you shall fall, you, all your squadrons, and your allies; I will give you as food to the birds of prey and the wild

dwellers in the cities of Israel shall come out and gather weapons to light their fires, buckler and shield, bow and arrows, throwing-stick and lance, and they shall 10 kindle fires with them for seven years. They shall take no wood from the fields nor cut it from the forests but shall light their fires with the weapons. Thus they will plunder their plunderers and spoil their spoilers. This is the very word of the Lord GOD.

In that day I will give to Gog, instead of*c* 11 a burial-ground in Israel, the valley of Abarim east of the Sea.*d* There they shall bury Gog and all his horde, and all Abarim will be blocked; and they shall call it the Valley of Gog's Horde. For seven months 12 the Israelites shall bury them and purify the land; all the people shall take their share 13 in the burying. The day that I win myself honour shall be a memorable day for them. This is the very word of the Lord GOD. Men 14 shall be picked for the regular duty of going through the country and searching for*e* any left above ground, to purify the land; they shall begin their search at the end of the seven months. They shall go through the 15 country, and whenever one of them sees a human bone he shall put a marker beside it, until it has been buried in the Valley of Gog's Horde. So no more shall be heard of 16 that great horde,*f* and the land will be purified.

The land of Israel

5 beasts. You shall fall on the bare ground, for it is I who have spoken. This is the very word
6 of the Lord GOD. I will send fire on Magog and on those who live undisturbed in the coasts and islands, and they shall know that
7 I am the LORD. My holy name I will make known in the midst of my people Israel and will no longer let it be profaned; the nations shall know that in Israel I, the LORD, am holy.
8 Behold, it comes; it shall be, says the Lord
9 GOD, the day of which I have spoken. The

Israel's fortunes restored

Man, these are the words of the Lord GOD: 17 Cry to every bird that flies and to all the wild beasts: Come, assemble, gather from every side to my sacrifice, the great sacrifice

---

c Prob. rdg.; Heb. adds there. those who are passing through.   *d That is* the Dead Sea.   *e* searching for: *prob. rdg.; Heb.* burying   *f* So ... horde: *prob. rdg.; Heb.* obscure.

18 I am making for you on the mountains of Israel; eat flesh and drink blood, eat the flesh of warriors and drink the blood of princes of the earth; all these are your rams and sheep, he-goats and bulls, and buffaloes 19 of Bashan. You shall cram yourselves with fat and drink yourselves drunk on blood at the sacrifice which I am preparing for you. 20 At my table you shall eat your fill of horses and riders, of warriors and all manner of fighting men. This is the very word of the Lord GOD.

21 I will show my glory among the nations; all shall see the judgement that I execute and the heavy hand that I lay upon them. 22 From that day forwards the Israelites shall 23 know that I am the LORD their God. The nations shall know that the Israelites went into exile for their iniquity, because they were faithless to me. So I hid my face from them and handed them over to their enemies, and they fell, every one of them, by the sword. I dealt with them as they deserved, 24 defiled and rebellious as they were, and hid my face from them.

These, therefore, are the words of the 25 Lord GOD: Now I will restore the fortunes of Jacob and show my affection for all Israel, and I will be jealous for my holy name. They shall forget their shame and all 26 their unfaithfulness to me, when they are at home again on their own soil, undisturbed, with no one to alarm them. When I bring 27 them home out of the nations and gather them from the lands of their enemies, I will make them an example of my holiness, for many nations to see. They will know that 28 I am the LORD their God, because I who sent them into exile among the nations will bring them together again on the soil of their own land and leave none of them behind. No 29 longer will I hide my face from them, I who have poured out my spirit upon Israel. This is the very word of the Lord GOD.

A vision: the temple buildings

40 At the beginning of the year, on the tenth day of the month, in the twenty-fifth year of our exile, that is fourteen years after the destruction of the city, on that very day, the hand of the LORD came upon 2 me and he brought me there. In a vision God brought me to the land of Israel and set me on a very high mountain, where I saw what seemed the buildings of a city facing me. 3 He led me towards it, and I saw a man like a figure of bronze holding a cord of linen thread and a measuring-rod, and standing at 4 the gate. 'Man,' he said to me, 'look closely and listen carefully; mark well all that I show you, for this is why you have been brought here. Tell the Israelites all that you see.'

5 Round the outside of the temple ran a wall. The length of the rod which the man was holding was six cubits, reckoning by the long cubit which was one cubit and a hand's breadth. He measured the thickness and the height of the wall; 6 each was one rod. He came to a gate which faced eastwards, went up its steps and measured the threshold of the gateway; its depth 7 was one rod. Each cell was one rod long and one rod wide; the space between the cells five cubits, and the threshold of the gateway at the end of the vestibule on the 8 side facing the temple one rod. He measured the vestibule of the gate 9 and found it eight cubits, with pilasters two cubits thick; the vestibule of the gateway lay at the end

near the temple. Now the cells of 10 the gateway, looking back eastwards, were three in number on each side; all three of the same size, and their pilasters on each side of 11 the same size also. He measured the entrance into the gateway; it was ten cubits wide, and the gateway itself throughout its length 12 thirteen cubits wide. In front of the cells on each side lay a kerb, one cubit wide; each cell was six cubits 13 by six. He measured the width of the gateway through the cell doors which faced one another, from the back of one cell to the back of the opposite cell; he made it twenty-14 five cubits, and the vestibule twenty cubits, across; the gateway on every side projected into*g* the court. 15 From the front of the entrance-gate to the outer face of the vestibule of the inner gate the distance was 16 fifty cubits. Both cells and pilasters had loopholes all round inside the gateway, and the vestibule had windows all round within and palms carved on each pilaster.

The outer court

17 He brought me to the outer court, and I saw rooms and a pavement all round the court: in all, thirty 18 rooms on the pavement. The pavement ran up to the side of the gateways, as wide as they were long; 19 this was the lower pavement. He measured the width of the court from the front of the lower gateway to the outside of the inner gateway; it was a hundred cubits. 20 He led me round to the north and I saw a gateway facing northwards, belonging to the outer court, and

he measured its length and its breadth. Its cells, three on each 21 side, together with its pilasters and its vestibule, were the same size as those of the first gateway, fifty cubits long by twenty-five wide. So 22 too its windows, and those of*h* its vestibule, and its palms were the same size as those of the gateway which faced east; it was approached by seven steps with its vestibule facing them. A gate like that on the 23 east side led to the inner court opposite the northern gateway; he measured from gateway to gateway, and it was a hundred cubits. Then he led me round to the south, 24 and I found a gateway facing southwards. He measured its cells, its pilasters, and its vestibule, and found it the same size as the others, fifty cubits long by twenty-five 25 wide. Both gateway and vestibule had windows all round like the others. It was approached by seven 26 steps with a vestibule facing them and palms carved on each pilaster. The inner court had a gateway 27 facing southwards, and he measured from gateway to gateway; it was a hundred cubits.

The inner court

He brought me into the inner 28 court through the southern gateway, measured it and found it the same size as the others. So were its 29 cells, pilasters, and vestibule, fifty cubits long by twenty-five wide. It and its vestibule had windows all round.*i* Its vestibule faced the 31 outer court; it had palms carved on its pilasters, and eight steps led up to it.

32 Then he brought me into the inner court, towards the east, and measured the gateway and found
33 it the same size as the others. So too were its cells, pilasters, and vestibule; it and its vestibule had windows all round, and it was fifty
34 cubits long by twenty-five cubits. Its vestibule faced the outer court and had a palm carved on each pilaster;
35 eight steps led up to it. Then he brought me to the north gateway and measured it and found it the
36 same size as the others. So were its cells, pilasters, and vestibule, and it had windows all round; it was fifty cubits long by twenty-five
37 wide. Its vestibule faced the outer court and had palms carved on the pilaster at each side; eight steps led up to it.
38 There was a room opening out from the vestibule of the gateway;[j] here the whole-offerings were
39 washed. In the vestibule of the gateway were two tables on each side, at which to slaughter the whole-offering, the sin-offering,
40 and the guilt-offering. At the corner on the outside, as one goes up to the opening of the northern gateway, stood two tables, and two more at the other corner of the
41 vestibule of the gateway. Another four stood on each side at the corner of the gateway, eight tables in all at which slaughtering was done.
42 Four tables used for the whole-offering were of hewn stone, each a cubit and a half long by a cubit and a half wide and a cubit high; and on them they put the instruments used for the whole-offering
43 and other sacrifices. The flesh of the offerings was on the tables, and ledges a hand's breadth in width were fixed all round facing inwards.
44 Then he brought me right into the inner court, and I saw two rooms in the inner court, one at the corner of the northern gateway, facing south, and one at the corner of the southern gateway,
45 facing north. This room facing south, he told me, is for the priests
46 who have charge of the temple. The room facing north is for the priests who have charge of the altar; these are the sons of Zadok, who alone of the Levites may come near to
47 serve the LORD. He measured the court; it was square, a hundred cubits each way, and the altar lay in front of the temple.
48 Then he brought me into the vestibule of the temple, and measured a pilaster of the vestibule; it was five cubits on each side, the width of the gateway fourteen cubits and that of the corners of the gateway three cubits in each

49 direction. The vestibule was twenty cubits long by twelve wide; ten steps led up to it, and by the pilasters rose pillars, one on each side.

The Holy of Holies

41 Then he brought me into the sanctuary and measured the pilasters; they were six cubits wide on each
2 side. The opening was ten cubits wide and its corners five cubits wide in each direction. He measured its length; it was forty cubits,
3 and its width twenty. He went inside and measured the pilasters at the opening: they were two cubits; the opening itself was six cubits, and the corners of the opening were seven cubits in each direction.
4 Then he measured the room at the far end of the sanctuary; its length and its breadth were each twenty cubits. He said to me, 'This is the Holy of Holies.'

Exterior of the temple

5 He measured the wall of the temple; it was six cubits high, and each arcade all round the house was
6 four cubits wide. The arcades were arranged in three tiers, each tier in thirty sections. In the wall all round the temple there were intakes for the arcades, so that they could be supported without being fastened into the wall of the temple.
7 The higher up the arcades were, the broader they were all round by the addition of the intakes, one above the other all round the temple; the temple itself had a ramp running upwards on a base, and in this way one went up from the lowest to the highest tier by way of the middle tier.
8 Then I saw a raised pavement all round the temple, and the foundations of the arcades were flush with it and measured a full rod, six
9 cubits high. The outer wall of the arcades was five cubits thick. There was an unoccupied area beside the terrace[k] which was adjacent to the
11 [l] temple, and the arcades opened on to this area, one opening facing northwards and one southwards; the unoccupied area was five cubits
10 wide on all sides. There was a free space[m] twenty cubits wide all round
12 the temple. On the western side, at the far end of the free space, stood a building seventy cubits wide; its wall was five cubits thick all round, and its length ninety cubits.
13 He measured the temple; it was a hundred cubits long; and the free space, the building, and its walls,
14 a hundred cubits in all. The eastern front of the temple and the free

space was a hundred cubits wide. He measured the length of the 15 building at the far end of the free space to the west of the temple, and its corridors on each side: a hundred cubits.

Interior of the temple

The sanctuary, the inner shrine and the outer vestibule were panelled; the embrasures all round the three 16 of them were framed with wood all round. From the ground up to the 17 windows and above the door, both in the inner and outer chambers, round all the walls, inside and out, were carved figures,[n] cherubim and 18 palm-trees, a palm between every pair of cherubim. Each cherub had two faces: one the face of a man, 19 looking towards one palm-tree, and the other the face of a lion, looking towards another palm-tree. Such was the carving round the whole of the temple. The cherubim and 20 the palm-trees were carved from the ground up to the top of the doorway and on the wall of the sanctuary. The door-posts of the sanctuary 21 were square.[o]

In front of[p] the Holy Place was 22 what seemed an altar of wood, three cubits high and two cubits long; it was fitted with corner-posts, and its base and sides also were of wood. He told me that this was the table which stood before the LORD. The sanctuary had a 23 double door, and the Holy Place also had a double door: the double 24 doors had swinging leaves, a pair for each door. Cherubim and palm-25 trees like those on the walls were carved on them.[q] Outside there was a wooden cornice over the vestibule; on both sides of the vestibule 26 were loopholes, with palm-trees carved at the corners.[r]

Then he took me to the outer 42 court round by the north and brought me to the rooms facing the free space and facing the buildings to the north. The length along the 2 northern side was a hundred cubits, and the breadth fifty. Facing the 3 free space measuring twenty cubits, which adjoined the inner court, and facing the pavement of the outer court, were corridors at three levels corresponding to each other. In front of the rooms a passage, 4 ten cubits wide and a hundred cubits long, ran towards the inner court; their entrances faced northwards. The upper rooms were 5 shorter than the lower and middle rooms, because the corridors took building space from them. For they 6 were all at three levels and had no pillars as the courts had, so that

---

j the vestibule of the gateway: *prob. rdg.; Heb.* pilasters, the gates.   k beside the terrace: *prob. rdg.; Heb.* between the arcades.   l *Verses 10 and 11 transposed.*   m There . . . space: *prob. rdg.; Heb.* Between the rooms.   n carved figures: *prob. rdg.; Heb.* measures and carving.   o The door-posts . . . square: *prob. rdg.; Heb.* unintelligible.   p In front of: *prob. rdg.; Heb.* The face of.   q *Prob. rdg.; Heb.* adds on the doors of the sanctuary.   r *Prob. rdg.; Heb.* adds and the arcades of the temple and the cornices.

the lower and middle levels were recessed from the ground upwards.
7 An outside wall, fifty cubits long, ran parallel to the rooms and in front of them, on the side of the
8 outer court. The rooms adjacent to the outer court were fifty cubits
9 long, and those facing the sanctuary a hundred cubits. Below these rooms was an entry from the east as one entered them from the
10 outer court where the wall of the court began.[s] On the south side, passing by the free space and the
11 building, were other rooms with a passage in front of them. These rooms corresponded, in length and breadth and in general character, to those facing north, whose exits
12 and entrances were the same as those of the rooms on the south.

As one[t] went eastwards, where the passages began, there was an entrance in the face of the inner[u] wall.
13 Then he said to me, 'The northern and southern rooms facing the free space are the consecrated rooms where the priests who approach the LORD may eat the most sacred offerings. There they shall put these offerings as well as the grain-offering, the sin-offering, and the guilt-offering; for the place is holy.
14 When the priests have entered the Holy Place they shall not go into the outer court again without leaving here the garments they have worn while performing their duties, for these are holy. They shall put on other garments when they approach the place assigned to the people.'

The temple area

When he had finished measuring 15 the inner temple, he brought me out towards the gateway which faces eastwards and measured the whole area. He measured the east 16 side with the measuring-rod, and it was five hundred cubits. He turned 17 and measured the north side with his rod, and it was five hundred cubits. He turned to the south side 18 and measured it with his rod; it was five hundred cubits. He turned 19 to the west and measured it with his rod; it was five hundred cubits. So he measured all four sides; in 20 each direction the surrounding wall measured five hundred cubits. This marked off the sacred area from the profane.

The Glory fills the temple

43 He led me to the gate, the gate facing east-
2 wards, and I beheld the glory of the God of Israel coming from the east. His voice was like the sound of a mighty torrent, and the
3 earth shone with his glory. The form that I saw was the same as that which I had seen when he came to destroy the city, and as that which I had seen by the river Kebar,[v]
4 and I fell on my face. The glory of the LORD came up to the temple towards the gate
5 which faced eastwards. A spirit[w] lifted me up and brought me into the inner court, and
6 the glory of the LORD filled the temple. Then I heard one speaking to me from the temple,
7 and the man was standing at my side. He said, Man, do you see the place of my throne, the place where I set my feet, where I will dwell among the Israelites for ever? Neither they nor their kings shall ever defile my holy name again with their wanton dis-

loyalty, and with the corpses[x] of their kings when they die. They set their threshold by 8 mine and their door-post beside mine, with a wall between me and them, and they defiled my holy name with the abominations they committed, and I destroyed them in my anger. But now they shall abandon their 9 wanton disloyalty and remove the corpses[x] of their kings far from me, and I will dwell among them for ever. So tell the Israelites, 10 man, about this temple, its appearance and proportions, that they may be ashamed of their iniquities. If they are ashamed of all 11 they have done, you shall describe to them the temple and its fittings, its exits and entrances, all the details and particulars of its elevation and plan; explain them and draw them before their eyes, so that they may keep them in mind and carry them out. This is the plan of the temple to be built on 12 the top of the mountain; all its precincts on every side shall be most holy.

Altar and sacrifices

13 These were the dimensions of the altar in cubits (the cubit that is a cubit and a hand's breadth). This was the height of the altar: the base was a cubit high[y] and projected a cubit; on its edge was a rim one
14 span deep. From the base to the cubit-wide ridge of the lower pedestal-block was two cubits, and from this shorter pedestal-block to the cubit-wide ridge of the taller pedestal-block was four cubits.
15 The altar-hearth was four cubits high and was surmounted by four
16 horns a cubit high. The hearth was twelve cubits long and twelve cubits
17 wide, being a perfect square. The upper pedestal-block was fourteen

cubits long and fourteen cubits wide along its four sides, and the rim round it was half a cubit deep. The base of the altar projected a cubit, and there were steps facing eastwards.
18 He said to me, Man, these are the words of the Lord GOD: These are the regulations for the altar when it has been made, for sacrificing whole-offerings on it and
19 flinging the blood against it. The levitical priests of the family of Zadok, and they alone, may come near to me to serve me, says the Lord GOD. You shall assign them
20 a young bull for a sin-offering; you shall take some of the blood and put it on the four horns of the altar, on the four corners of the upper

pedestal and all round the rim, and so purify it and make expiation for it. Then take the bull assigned as 21 the sin-offering, and they shall destroy it by fire in the proper place within the precincts but outside the Holy Place. On the second day 22 you shall present a he-goat without blemish as a sin-offering, and with it they shall purify the altar as they did with the bull. When you have 23 completely purified the altar, you shall present a young bull without blemish and a ram without blemish from the flock. You shall present 24 them before the LORD; the priests shall throw salt on them and sacrifice them as a whole-offering to the LORD. For seven days you shall 25 provide as a daily sin-offering a

---

s began: *prob. rdg.; Heb.* breadth.
v Or the Kebar canal.   *w Or* wind.
base of the cubit.

t Prob. rdg.; Heb. they.

x Or effigies.

u Prob. rdg.; Heb. word unknown.
y the base . . . high: *prob. rdg.; Heb.* the

goat, a young bull, and a ram from the flock; all of them shall be pro-
26 vided free from blemish. For seven days they shall make expiation for the altar, and pronounce it ritually
27 clean, and consecrate it. At the end of that time, on the eighth day and onwards, the priests shall sacrifice on the altar your whole-offerings and your shared-offerings, and I will accept you. This is the very word of the Lord GOD.

The east gate

44 He again brought me round to the outer gate of the sanctuary facing
2 eastwards, and it was shut. The LORD said to me, This gate shall be kept shut; it must not be opened. No man may enter by it, for the LORD the God of Israel has entered
3 by it. It shall be kept shut. The prince, however, when he is here as prince, may sit there to eat food in the presence of the LORD; he shall come in and go out by the vestibule of the gate.

Priests and Levites

4 He brought me round to the nor-thern gate facing the temple, and I saw the glory of the LORD filling the LORD's house, and I fell on my
5 face. The LORD said to me, Mark well, man, look closely, and listen carefully to all that I say to you, to all the rules and regulations for the house of the LORD. Mark well the entrance to the house of the LORD and all the exits from the
6 sanctuary. Say to that rebel people of Israel, These are the words of the Lord GOD: Enough of all these abominations of yours, you Israel-
7 ites! You have added to them by bringing foreigners, uncircumcised in mind and body, to stand in my sanctuary and defile my house when you present my food to me, both fat and blood, and they have made
8 my covenant void. Instead of keeping charge of my holy things yourselves, you have chosen to put these men in charge of my sanctuary.
9 These are the words of the Lord GOD: No foreigner, uncircumcised in mind and body, shall enter my sanctuary, not even a foreigner
10 living among the Israelites. But the Levites, though they deserted me when the Israelites went astray after their idols and had to bear the punishment of their iniquity,
11 shall yet do service in my sanctuary. They shall take charge of the gates of the temple and do service there. They shall slaughter the whole-offering and the sacrifice for the people and shall be in attendance
12 to serve them. Because they served them in the presence of their idols and brought Israel to the ground by their iniquity, says the Lord

GOD, I have sworn with uplifted hand that they shall bear the pun-
13 ishment of their iniquity. They shall not have access to me, to serve me as priests; they shall not come near to my holy things or to the Holy of Holies; they shall bear the shame of the abominable deeds
14 they have done. I will put them in charge of the temple with all the service which must be per-formed there.
15 But the levitical priests of the family of Zadok remained in charge of my sanctuary when the Israelites went astray from me; these shall approach me to serve me. They shall be in attendance on me, pre-senting the fat and the blood, says
16 the Lord GOD. It is they who shall enter my sanctuary and approach my table to serve me and observe
17 my charge. When they come to the gates of the inner court they shall dress in linen; they shall wear no wool when they serve me at the gates of the inner court and within.
18 They shall wear linen turbans, and linen drawers on their loins; they shall not fasten their clothes with
19 a belt so that they sweat. When they go out to the people in the outer court, they shall take off the clothes they have worn while serv-ing, leave them in the sacred rooms and put on other clothes; other-wise they will transmit the sacred influence to the people through their clothing.
20 They shall neither shave their heads nor let their hair grow long;
21 they shall only clip their hair. No priest shall drink wine when he is
22 to enter the inner court. He may not marry a widow or a divorced woman; he may marry a virgin of Israelite birth. He may, however, marry the widow of a priest.
23 They shall teach my people to distinguish the sacred from the pro-
24 fane, and show them the difference between clean and unclean. When disputes break out, they shall take their place in court, and settle the case according to my rules. At all my appointed seasons they shall observe my laws and statutes. They shall keep my sabbaths holy.
25 They shall not defile themselves by contact with any dead person, except² father or mother, son or
26 daughter, brother or unmarried sister. After purification, they shall
27 count seven days and then be clean. When they enter the inner court to serve in the Holy Place, they shall present their sin-offering, says the Lord GOD.
28 They shall own no patrimony in Israel; I am their patrimony. You shall grant them no holding in
29 Israel; I am their holding. The grain-offering, the sin-offering, and the guilt-offering shall be eaten by them, and everything in Israel de-
30 voted to God shall be theirs. The

first of all the firstfruits and all your contributions of every kind shall belong wholly to the priests. You shall give the first lump of your dough to the priests, that a bless-ing may rest upon your home.
31 The priests shall eat no carrion, bird or beast, whether it has died naturally or been killed by a wild animal.

Dividing the land

45 When you divide the land by lot among the tribes for your posses-sion, you shall set apart from it a sacred reserve for the LORD, twenty-five thousand cubits in length and twenty thousand in width; the whole enclosure shall be sacred.
2 Of this a square plot, five hundred cubits each way, shall be devoted to the sanctuary, with fifty cubits of open land round it. From this
3 area you shall measure out a space twenty-five thousand by ten thou-sand cubits, in which the sanctuary, the holiest place of all, shall stand.
4 This space is for the priests who serve in the sanctuary and who come nearest in serving the LORD. It shall include space for their houses and a sacred plot for the
5 sanctuary. An area of twenty-five thousand by ten thousand cubits shall belong to the Levites, the temple servants; on this shall stand
6 the towns in which they live. You shall give to each town an area of five thousand by twenty-five thou-sand cubits alongside the sacred reserve; this shall belong to all
7 Israel. On either side of the sacred reserve and of the city's holding the prince shall have a holding facing the sacred reserve and the city's holding, running westwards on the west and eastwards on the east. It shall run alongside one of the tribal portions, and stretch to the western limit of the land and
8 to the eastern. It shall be his hold-ing in Israel; the princes of Israel shall never oppress my people again but shall give the land to Israel, tribe by tribe.

Fair weights and measures

9 These are the words of the Lord GOD: Enough, princes of Israel! Put an end to lawlessness and rob-bery; maintain law and justice; relieve my people and stop your
10 evictions, says the Lord GOD. Your scales shall be honest, your bushel and your gallon shall be honest.
11 There shall be one standard for each, taking each as the tenth of a homer, and the homer shall have its fixed standard. Your shekel
12 weight shall contain twenty gerahs; your mina shall contain weights of tenᵈ and twenty-five and fifteen shekels.

---

z any ... except: or anyone else's dead, but only their own ...

a Prob. rdg.; Heb. twenty.

Contributions

13 These are the contributions you shall set aside: out of every homer of wheat or of barley, one sixth of

14 an ephah. For oil the rule is[b] one tenth of a bath from every kor (at

15 ten bath to the kor); one sheep in every flock of two hundred is to be reserved by every Israelite clan. For a grain-offering, a whole-offering, and a shared-offering, to make expiation for them, says the

16 Lord GOD, all the people of the land shall bring[c] this contribution

17 to the prince in Israel; and the prince shall be responsible for the whole-offering, the grain-offering, and the drink-offering, at pilgrim-feasts, new moons, sabbaths, and every sacred season observed by Israel. He himself is to provide the sin-offering and the grain-offering, the whole-offering and the shared-offering, needed to make expiation for Israel.

Purifying the sanctuary

18 These are the words of the Lord GOD: On the first day of the first month you shall take a young bull without blemish, and purify the

19 sanctuary. The priest shall take some of the blood from the sin-offering and put it on the door-posts of the temple, on the four corners of the altar pedestal and on the gate-posts of the inner

20 court. You shall do the same on the seventh day of the month;[d] in this way you shall make expiation for the temple.

The Passover

21 On the fourteenth day of the first month you shall hold the Passover, the pilgrim-feast of seven days; bread must be eaten unleavened.

22 On that day the prince shall provide a bull as a sin-offering for himself and for all the people.

23 During the seven days of the feast he shall offer daily as a whole-offering to the LORD seven bulls and seven rams without blemish, and a he-goat as a daily sin-offering.

24 With every bull and ram he shall provide a grain-offering of one ephah, together with a hin of oil

25 for each ephah. He shall do the same thing also on the fifteenth day of the seventh month at the pilgrim-feast; this also shall last

seven days, and he shall provide the same sin-offering and whole-offering and the same quantity of grain and oil.

Rules and regulations

46 These are the words of the Lord GOD: The eastern gate of the inner court shall remain closed for the six working days; it may be opened only on the sabbath and at new

2 moon. When the prince comes through the porch of the gate from the outside, he shall halt at the door-post, and the priests shall sacrifice his whole-offering and shared-offerings. On the terrace he shall bow down at the gate and then go out, but the gate shall not

3 be shut till the evening. On sabbaths and at new moons the people also shall bow down before the LORD at the entrance to that gate.

4 The whole-offering which the prince sacrifices to the LORD shall be as follows: on the sabbath, six sheep without blemish and a ram

5 without blemish; the grain-offering shall be an ephah with the ram and as much as he likes with the sheep, together with a hin of oil for every

6 ephah. At the new moon it shall be a young bull without blemish, six sheep and a ram, all without

7 blemish. He shall provide as the grain-offering to go with the bull one ephah and with the ram one ephah, with the sheep as much as he can afford, adding a hin of oil for every ephah.

8 When the prince comes in, he shall enter through the porch of the gate and come out by the same

9 way. But on festal days when the people come before the LORD, a man who enters by the northern gate to bow down shall leave by the southern gate, and a man who enters by the southern gate shall leave by the northern gate. He shall not turn back and go out through the gate by which he came in but

10 shall go straight on. The prince shall then be among them, going in when they go in and coming out when they come out.

11 At pilgrim-feasts and on festal days the grain-offering shall be an ephah with a bull, an ephah with a ram and as much as he likes with a sheep, together with a hin of oil for every ephah.

12 When the prince provides a whole-offering or shared-offerings

as a voluntary sacrifice to the LORD, the eastern gate shall be opened for him,[e] and he shall make his whole-offering and his shared-offerings as he does on the sabbath; when he goes out the gate shall be closed[f] behind him.

13 You shall provide a yearling sheep without blemish daily as a whole-offering to the LORD; you shall provide it morning by morn-

14 ing. With it every morning you shall provide as a grain-offering one sixth of an ephah with a third of a hin of oil to moisten the flour; the LORD's grain-offering is an observance prescribed for all time.

15 Morning by morning, as a regular whole-offering, they shall offer a sheep with the grain-offering and the oil.

16 These are the words of the Lord GOD: When the prince makes a gift out of his property to any of his sons, it shall belong to his sons, since it is part of the family pro-

17 perty. But when he makes such a gift to one of his slaves, it shall be his only till the year of manu-mission, when it shall revert to the prince; it is the property of his sons and shall belong to them.

18 The prince shall not oppress the people by taking part of their holdings; he shall give his sons an in-heritance from his own holding of land, so that my people may not be scattered and separated from their holdings.

19 Then he brought me through the entrance by the side of the gate to the rooms which face north (the sacred rooms reserved for the priests), and, pointing to a place

20 on their western side, he said to me, 'This is the place where the priests shall boil the guilt-offering and the sin-offering and bake the grain-offering; they shall not take it into the outer court for fear they trans-mit the sacred influence to the

21 people.' Then he brought me into the outer court and took me across to the four corners of the court, at each of which there was a further

22 court. These four courts were vaul-ted and were the same size, forty cubits long by thirty cubits wide.

23 Round each of the four was a row of stones, with fire-places con-structed close up against the rows.

24 He said to me, 'These are the kitchens where the attendants shall boil the people's sacrifices.'

The river of life

47 He brought me back to the gate of the temple, and I saw a spring of water issuing from under the terrace of the temple towards the east; for the temple faced east. The water was running down along the right side, to

the south of the altar. He took me out through the northern gate and brought me round by an outside path to the eastern gate of the court, and water was trickling from the right side. When the man went out east-wards he had a line in his hand. He measured a thousand cubits and made me walk

---

b Prob. rdg.; Heb. adds the bath, the oil.   c All . . . bring: prob. rdg.; Heb. unintelligible.   d Prob. rdg.; Heb. adds This comes from a man who is wrong and foolish. Cp. Lev. 23. 24 ; Num. 29. 1.   e the eastern . . . him: or he shall open the gate facing east.   f the gate . . . closed: or he shall close the gate.

through the water; it came up to my ankles.

4 He measured another thousand and made me walk through the water; it came up to my knees. He measured another thousand and made me walk through the water; it
5 was up to my waist. Another thousand, and it was a torrent I could not cross, for the water had risen and was now deep enough to swim in; it had become a torrent that
6 could not be crossed. 'Mark this, man', he said, and led me back to the bank of the
7 torrent. When we came back to the bank I saw a great number of trees on each side.
8 He said to me, 'This water flows out to the region lying east, and down to the Arabah; at last it will reach that sea whose waters
9 are foul, and they will be sweetened. When any one of the living creatures that swarm

upon the earth comes where the torrent flows, it shall draw life from it. The fish shall be innumerable; for these waters come here so that the others may be sweetened, and where the torrent flows everything shall live. From En-gedi as far as En-eglaim fishermen 10 shall stand on its shores, for nets shall be spread there. Every kind of fish shall be there in shoals, like the fish of the Great Sea; but its swamps and pools shall not have their 11 waters sweetened but shall be left as salt-pans. Beside the torrent on either bank all 12 trees good for food shall spring up. Their leaves shall not wither, their fruit shall not cease; they shall bear early every month. For their water comes from the sanctuary; their fruit is for food and their foliage for enjoyment.'

(Ezek. 47. 10)

Boundary lines

3 These are the words of the Lord GOD: These are the boundary lines within which the twelve tribes of Israel shall enter into possession of the land, Joseph receiving two por-
4 tions. The land which I swore with hand uplifted to give to your fathers you shall divide with each other; it shall be assigned to you by lot as
5 your patrimony. This is the frontier: on its northern side, from the Great Sea through Hethlon, Lebo-
6 hamath, Zedad, Berutha, and Sibraim, which are between the frontiers of Damascus and Hamath, to Hazar-enan, near the fron-

17 tier of Hauran. So the frontier shall run from the sea to Hazar-enan on the frontier of Damascus and northwards; this is its northern side.
18 The eastern side runs alongside the territories of Hauran, Damascus, and Gilead, and alongside the territory of Israel; Jordan sets the boundary to the eastern sea, to Tamar. This is the eastern side.
19 The southern side runs from Tamar to the waters of Meribah-by-Kadesh; the region assigned to you reaches the Great Sea. This is the southern side towards the
20 Negeb. The western side is the Great Sea, which forms a boundary as far as a point opposite

Lebo-hamath. This is the western side. You shall distribute this land 21 among the tribes of Israel and 22 assign it by lot as a patrimony for yourselves and for any aliens living in your midst who leave sons among you. They shall be treated as native-born in Israel and with you shall receive a patrimony by lot among the tribes of Israel. You shall 23 give the alien his patrimony with the tribe in which he is living. This is the very word of the Lord GOD.

Tribal allotments

These are the names of the tribes: **48** In the extreme north, in the direction of Hethlon, to Lebo-hamath

M

and Hazar-enan, with Damascus on the northern frontier in the direction of Hamath, and so from the eastern side to the western, shall be Dan: one portion.

2 Bordering on Dan, from the eastern side to the western, shall be Asher: one portion.

3 Bordering on Asher, from the eastern side to the western, shall be Naphtali: one portion.

4 Bordering on Naphtali, from the eastern side to the western, shall be Manasseh: one portion.

5 Bordering on Manasseh, from the eastern side to the western, shall be Ephraim: one portion.

6 Bordering on Ephraim, from the eastern side to the western, shall be Reuben: one portion.

7 Bordering on Reuben, from the eastern side to the western, shall be Judah: one portion.

8 Bordering on Judah, from the eastern side to the western, shall be the reserve which you shall set apart. Its breadth shall be twenty-five thousand cubits and its length the same as that of the other portions, from the eastern side to the western, and the sanctuary shall be in the middle of it.

9 The reserve which you shall set apart for the LORD shall measure twenty-five thousand cubits by 10 twenty*g* thousand. The reserve shall be apportioned thus: the priests shall have an area measuring twenty-five thousand cubits on the north side, ten thousand on the west, ten thousand on the east, and twenty-five thousand on the south side; the sanctuary of the LORD 11 shall be in the middle of it. It shall be for the consecrated priests, the sons of Zadok, who kept my charge and did not follow the Israelites when they went astray, as the 12 Levites did. The area set apart for the priests from the reserved territory shall be most sacred, reaching the frontier of the Levites.

13 The Levites shall have a portion running parallel to the border of the priests. It shall be twenty-five thousand cubits long by ten thousand wide; altogether, the length shall be twenty-five thousand cubits and the breadth ten thousand.

14 They shall neither sell nor exchange any part of it, nor shall the best of the land be alienated; for it is holy to the LORD.

15 The strip which is left, five thousand cubits in width by twenty-five thousand, is the city's secular land for dwellings and common land, and the city shall be in the middle 16 of it. These shall be its dimensions: on the northern side four thousand five hundred cubits, on the southern side four thousand five hundred cubits, on the eastern side four thousand five hundred cubits, on 17 the western side four thousand five hundred cubits. The common land belonging to the city shall be two hundred and fifty cubits to the north, two hundred and fifty to the south, two hundred and fifty to the east, and two hundred and 18 fifty to the west. What is left parallel to the reserve, ten thousand cubits to the east and ten thousand to the west,*h* shall provide food for those who work in 19 the city. Those who work in the city shall cultivate it; they may be drawn from any of the tribes of Israel.

20 You shall set apart the whole reserve, twenty-five thousand cubits square, as sacred, as far as the hold-21 ing of the city. What is left over on each side of the sacred reserve and the holding of the city shall be assigned to the prince. Eastwards, what lies over against the reserved twenty-five thousand cubits, as far as the eastern side, and westwards, what lies over against the twenty-five thousand cubits to the western side, parallel to the tribal portions, shall be assigned to the prince; the sacred reserve and the sanctuary 22 itself shall be in the centre. The*i*

holding of the Levites and the*i* holding of the city shall be in the middle of that which is assigned to the prince; it shall be between the frontiers of Judah and Benjamin.

The rest of the tribes: from the 23 eastern side to the western shall be Benjamin: one portion.

Bordering on Benjamin, from 24 the eastern side to the western, shall be Simeon: one portion.

Bordering on Simeon, from the 25 eastern side to the western, shall be Issachar: one portion.

Bordering on Issachar, from the 26 eastern side to the western, shall be Zebulun: one portion.

Bordering on Zebulun, from the 27 eastern side to the western, shall be Gad: one portion.

Bordering on Gad, on the side 28 of the Negeb, the border on the south stretches from Tamar to the waters of Meribah-by-Kadesh, to the Brook as far as the Great Sea.

This is the land which you shall 29 allot as a patrimony to the tribes of Israel, and these shall be their lots. This is the very word of the Lord GOD.

The city gates

These are to be the ways out of the 30 city, and they are to be named after the tribes of Israel. The northern side, four thousand five hundred cubits long, shall have three gates, those of Reuben, Judah, and Levi; the eastern side, four thousand five 32 hundred cubits long, three gates, those of Joseph, Benjamin, and Dan; the southern side, four thou-33 sand five hundred cubits long, three gates, those of Simeon, Issachar, and Zebulun; the western side, 34 four thousand five hundred cubits long, three gates, those of Gad, Asher, and Naphtali. The peri-35 meter of the city shall be eighteen thousand cubits, and the city's name for ever after shall be Jehovah-shammah.*j*

---

g Prob. rdg.; Heb. ten. rdg.; *Heb.* Some of the.   *h Prob. rdg.; Heb. adds* and it shall be parallel to the sacred reserve.   *i Prob.*
j That is the LORD is there.

THE BOOK OF

DANIEL

The Jews in Babylon

1 IN THE THIRD YEAR of the reign of Jehoiakim king of Judah, Nebuchadnezzar king of Babylon came to Jerusalem and laid 2 siege to it. The Lord delivered Jehoiakim king of Judah into his power, together with all that was left of the vessels of the house of God; and he carried them off to the land of Shinar, to the temple of his god, where he 3 deposited the vessels in the treasury. Then the king ordered Ashpenaz, his chief eunuch, to take certain of the Israelite exiles, of the 4 blood royal and of the nobility, who were to be young men of good looks and bodily without fault, at home in all branches of knowledge, well-informed, intelligent, and fit for service in the royal court; and he was to instruct them in the literature and lan- 5 guage of the Chaldaeans. The king assigned them a daily allowance of food and wine from the royal table. Their training was to last for three years, and at the end of that time they would*a* enter the royal service.

Four young men refuse the king's food

6 Among them there were certain young men from Judah called Daniel, Hananiah, Mish- 7 ael and Azariah; but the master of the eunuchs gave them new names: Daniel he called Belteshazzar, Hananiah Shadrach, Mishael Meshach and Azariah Abed-nego. 8 Now Daniel determined not to contaminate himself by touching the food and wine

assigned to him by the king, and he begged the master of the eunuchs not to make him do so. God made the master show kindness 9 and goodwill to Daniel, and he said to him, 10 'I am afraid of my lord the king: he has assigned you your food and drink, and if he sees you looking dejected, unlike the other young men of your own age, it will cost me my head.' Then Daniel said to the guard 11 whom the master of the eunuchs had put in charge of Hananiah, Mishael, Azariah and himself, 'Submit us to this test for ten days. 12 Give us only vegetables to eat and water to drink; then compare our looks with those 13 of the young men who have lived on the food assigned by the king, and be guided in your treatment of us by what you see.'*b* The guard 14 listened to what they said and tested them for ten days. At the end of ten days they 15 looked healthier and were better nourished than all the young men who had lived on the food assigned them by the king. So the guard 16 took away the assignment of food and the wine they were to drink, and gave them only the vegetables.

The young men presented to the king

To all four of these young men God had 17 given knowledge and understanding of books and learning of every kind, while Daniel had a gift for interpreting visions and dreams of every kind. The time came which the king 18 had fixed for introducing the young men to court, and the master of the eunuchs brought

---

a at the end . . . would: *or* all of them were to.

b be guided . . . see: *or* treat us as you see fit.

them into the presence of Nebuchadnezzar.
19 The king talked with them and found none of them to compare with Daniel, Hananiah, Mishael and Azariah; so they entered the 20 royal service. Whenever the king consulted them on any matter calling for insight and judgement, he found them ten times better than all the magicians and exorcists in his 21 whole kingdom. Now Daniel was there till the first year of King Cyrus.

Cameo Portrait of Nebuchadnezzar

Nebuchadnezzar's dream

2 In the second year of his reign Nebuchadnezzar had dreams, and his mind was so troubled 2 that he could not sleep. Then the king gave orders to summon the magicians, exorcists, sorcerers, and Chaldaeans to tell him what he had dreamt. They came in and stood in 3 the royal presence, and the king said to them, 'I have had a dream and my mind has been 4 troubled to know what my dream was.' The Chaldaeans, speaking in Aramaic, said, *c*'Long live the king! Tell us what you dreamt 5 and we will tell you the interpretation.' The king answered, 'This is my declared intention. If you do not tell me both dream and interpretation, you shall be torn in pieces 6 and your houses shall be forfeit.*d* But if you can tell me the dream and the interpretation, you will be richly rewarded and loaded with honours. Tell me, therefore, the dream and 7 its interpretation.' They answered a second time, 'Let the king tell his servants the dream, 8 and we will tell him the interpretation.' The king answered, 'It is clear to me that you are trying to gain time, because you see that my 9 intention has been declared. If you do not make known to me the dream, there is one law that applies to you, and one only. What is more, you have agreed among yourselves to tell me a pack of lies to my face in the hope that with time things may alter. Tell me the dream, therefore, and I shall know that you 10 can give me the interpretation.' The Chaldaeans answered in the presence of the king, 'Nobody on earth can tell your majesty what you wish to know; no great king or prince has ever made such a demand of magician, 11 exorcist, or Chaldaean. What your majesty requires of us is too hard; there is no one but the gods, who dwell remote from mortal 12 men, who can give you the answer.' At this the king lost his temper and in a great rage

ordered the death of all the wise men of Babylon. A decree was issued that the wise 13 men were to be executed, and accordingly men were sent to fetch Daniel and his companions for execution.

Daniel before the king

When Arioch, the captain of the king's body- 14 guard, was setting out to execute the wise men of Babylon, Daniel approached him cautiously and with discretion and said, 15 'Sir, you represent the king; why has his majesty issued such a peremptory decree?' Arioch explained everything; so Daniel went 16 in to the king's presence and begged for a certain time by which he would give the king the interpretation. Then Daniel went home 17 and told the whole story to his companions, Hananiah, Mishael and Azariah. They 18 should ask the God of heaven in his mercy, he said, to disclose this secret, so that they and he with the rest of the wise men of Babylon should not be put to death. Then in a 19 vision by night the secret was revealed to Daniel, and he blessed the God of heaven in 20 these words:

Blessed be God's name from age to age,
for all wisdom and power are his.
He changes seasons and times; 21
he deposes kings and sets them up;
he gives wisdom to the wise
and all their store of knowledge to the men
　　who know;
he reveals deep mysteries; 22
he knows what lies in darkness,
and light has its dwelling with him.
To thee, God of my fathers, I give thanks 23
　　and praise,
for thou hast given me wisdom and power;
thou hast now revealed to me what we asked,
and told us what the king is concerned to
　　know.

Daniel therefore went to Arioch who had 24 been charged by the king to put to death the wise men of Babylon and said to him, 'Do not put the wise men of Babylon to death. Take me into the king's presence, and I will now tell him the interpretation of the dream.' Arioch in great trepidation brought Daniel 25 before the king and said to him, 'I have found among the Jewish exiles a man who will make known to your majesty the interpretation of your dream.' Thereupon the 26 king said to Daniel (who was also called Belteshazzar), 'Can you tell me what I saw in my dream and interpret it?' Daniel 27 answered in the king's presence, 'The secret about which your majesty inquires no wise man, exorcist, magician, or diviner can disclose to you. But there is in heaven a god 28

c The Aramaic text begins here and continues to the end of ch. 7. Aram. word uncertain).　　　　*d Or made into a dunghill (mng. of Aram.*

who reveals secrets, and he has told King
Nebuchadnezzar what is to be at the end of
this age. This is the dream and these the
29 visions that came into your head: the
thoughts that came to you, O king, as you
lay on your bed, were thoughts of things to
come, and the revealer of secrets has made
30 known to you what is to be. This secret has
been revealed to me not because I am wise
beyond all living men, but because your
majesty is to know the interpretation and
understand the thoughts which have entered
your mind.'

Daniel interprets the king's dream
31 'As you watched, O king, you saw a great
image. This image, huge and dazzling,
32 towered before you, fearful to behold. The
head of the image was of fine gold, its breast
and arms of silver, its belly and thighs of
33 bronze,*e* its legs of iron, its feet part iron and
34 part clay. While you looked, a stone was
hewn from a mountain, not by human hands;
it struck the image on its feet of iron and clay
35 and shattered them. Then the iron, the clay,
the bronze, the silver, and the gold, were all
shattered to fragments and were swept away
like chaff before the wind from a threshing-
floor in summer, until no trace of them remained. But the stone which struck the image
grew into a great mountain filling the whole
36 earth. That was the dream. We shall now tell
37 your majesty the interpretation. You, O
king, king of kings, to whom the God of
heaven has given the kingdom with all its
38 power, authority, and honour; in whose
hands he has placed men and beasts and
birds of the air, wherever they dwell, granting you sovereignty over them all—you are
39 that head of gold. After you there shall arise
another kingdom, inferior to yours, and yet
a third kingdom, of bronze, which shall have
40 sovereignty over the whole world. And there
shall be a fourth kingdom, strong as iron; as
iron shatters and destroys all things, it shall
41 break and shatter the whole earth.*f* As, in
your vision, the feet and toes were part potter's clay and part iron, it shall be a divided
kingdom. Its core shall be partly of iron just
as you saw iron mixed with the common clay;
42 as the toes were part iron and part clay, the
kingdom shall be partly strong and partly
43 brittle. As, in your vision, the iron was mixed
with common clay, so shall men mix with
each other by intermarriage, but such alli-
ances shall not be stable: iron does not mix
44 with clay. In the period of those kings the
God of heaven will establish a kingdom
which shall never be destroyed; that kingdom
shall never pass to another people; it shall
shatter and make an end of all these kingdoms, while it shall itself endure for ever.

This is the meaning of your vision of the stone 45
being hewn from a mountain, not by human
hands, and then shattering the iron, the
bronze, the clay, the silver, and the gold. The
mighty God has made known to your majesty
what is to be hereafter. The dream is sure and
the interpretation to be trusted.'

Daniel and his friends promoted
Then King Nebuchadnezzar prostrated him- 46
self and worshipped Daniel, and gave orders
that sacrifices and soothing offerings should
be made to him. 'Truly,' he said, 'your god 47
is indeed God of gods and Lord over kings,
a revealer of secrets, since you have been able
to reveal this secret.' Then the king promoted 48
Daniel, bestowed on him many rich gifts,
and made him regent over the whole province of Babylon and chief prefect over all
the wise men of Babylon. Moreover at 49
Daniel's request the king put Shadrach,
Meshach and Abed-nego in charge of the
administration of the province of Babylon.
Daniel himself, however, remained at court.

The golden image
King Nebuchadnezzar made an image of **3**
gold, ninety feet high and nine feet broad.
He had it set up in the plain of Dura in the
province of Babylon. Then he sent out a 2
summons to assemble the satraps, prefects,
viceroys, counsellors, treasurers, judges,
chief constables, and all governors of provinces to attend the dedication of the image
which he had set up. So they assembled— 3
the satraps, prefects, viceroys, counsellors,
treasurers, judges, chief constables, and all
governors of provinces—for the dedication
of the image which King Nebuchadnezzar
had set up; and they stood before the image
which Nebuchadnezzar had set up. Then the 4
herald loudly proclaimed, 'O peoples and
nations of every language, you are commanded, when you hear the sound of horn, 5
pipe, zither, triangle, dulcimer, music, and
singing of every kind, to prostrate yourselves
and worship the golden image which King
Nebuchadnezzar has set up. Whoever does 6
not prostrate himself and worship shall forthwith be thrown into a blazing furnace.'
Accordingly, no sooner did all the peoples 7
hear the sound of horn, pipe, zither, triangle, dulcimer, music, and singing of every
kind, than all the peoples and nations of
every language prostrated themselves and
worshipped the golden image which King
Nebuchadnezzar had set up.

The three Jews refuse to worship the image
It was then that certain Chaldaeans came 8
forward and brought a charge against the
Jews. They said to King Nebuchadnezzar, 9

e Or copper.   *f* the whole earth: *prob. rdg.; Aram.* and like iron which shatters all these.

10 'Long live the king! Your majesty has issued an order that every man who hears the sound of horn, pipe, zither, triangle, dulcimer, music, and singing of every kind shall fall 11 down and worship the image of gold. Whoever does not do so shall be thrown into 12 a blazing furnace. There are certain Jews, Shadrach, Meshach and Abed-nego, whom you have put in charge of the administration of the province of Babylon. These men, your majesty, have taken no notice of your command; they do not serve your god, nor do they worship the golden image which you 13 have set up.' Then in rage and fury Nebuchadnezzar ordered Shadrach, Meshach and Abed-nego to be fetched, and they were 14 brought into the king's presence. Nebuchadnezzar said to them, 'Is it true, Shadrach, Meshach and Abed-nego, that you do not serve my god or worship the golden 15 image which I have set up? If you are ready at once to prostrate yourselves when you hear the sound of horn, pipe, zither, triangle, dulcimer, music, and singing of every kind, and to worship the image that I have set up, well and good. But if you do not worship it, you shall forthwith be thrown into the blazing furnace; and what god is there 16 that can save you from my power?' Shadrach, Meshach and Abed-nego said to King Nebuchadnezzar, 'We have no need to 17 answer you on this matter. If there is a god who is able to save us from the blazing furnace, it is our God whom we serve, and he 18 will save us from your power, O king; but if not, be it known to your majesty that we will neither serve your god nor worship the golden image that you have set up.'

Deliverance from the furnace

19 Then Nebuchadnezzar flew into a rage with Shadrach, Meshach and Abed-nego, and his face was distorted with anger. He gave 20 orders that the furnace should be heated up to seven times its usual heat, and commanded some of the strongest men in his army to bind Shadrach, Meshach and Abednego and throw them into the blazing fur- 21 nace. Then those men in their trousers, their shirts, and their hats and all their other clothes, were bound and thrown into the 22 blazing furnace. Because the king's order was urgent and the furnace exceedingly hot, the men who were carrying Shadrach, Meshach and Abed-nego were killed by the 23 flames that leapt out; and those three men, Shadrach, Meshach and Abed-nego, fell bound into the blazing furnace.
24 Then King Nebuchadnezzar was amazed and sprang to his feet in great trepidation. He said to his courtiers, 'Was it not three men whom we threw bound into the fire?'

They answered the king, 'Assuredly, your majesty.' He answered, 'Yet I see four men 25 walking about in the fire free and unharmed; and the fourth looks like a god.' Nebu- 26 chadnezzar approached the door of the blazing furnace and said to the men, 'Shadrach, Meshach and Abed-nego, servants of the Most High God, come out, come here.' Then Shadrach, Meshach and Abed-nego came out from the fire. And the satraps, 27 prefects, viceroys, and the king's courtiers gathered round and saw how the fire had had no power to harm the bodies of these men; the hair of their heads had not been singed, their trousers were untouched, and no smell of fire lingered about them.

Nebuchadnezzar blesses God

Then Nebuchadnezzar spoke out, 'Blessed 28 is the God of Shadrach, Meshach and Abed-nego. He has sent his angel to save his servants who put their trust in him, who disobeyed the royal command and were willing to yield themselves to the fire rather than to serve or worship any god other than their own God. I therefore issue a decree that 29 any man, to whatever people or nation he belongs, whatever his language, if he speaks blasphemy against the God of Shadrach, Meshach and Abed-nego, shall be torn to pieces and his house shall be forfeit;[g] for there is no other god who can save men in this way.' Then the king advanced the for- 30 tunes of Shadrach, Meshach and Abednego in the province of Babylon.

The king's proclamation

King Nebuchadnezzar to all peoples and **4** nations of every language living in the whole world: May all prosperity be yours! It is my pleasure to recount the signs and 2 marvels which the Most High God has worked for me:

> How great are his signs, 3
> and his marvels overwhelming!
> His kingdom is an everlasting kingdom,
> his sovereignty stands to all generations.

The king's two visions

I, Nebuchadnezzar, was living peacefully at 4 home in the luxury of my palace. As I lay 5 on my bed, I saw a dream which terrified me; and fantasies and visions which came into my head dismayed me. So I issued an order 6 summoning into my presence all the wise men of Babylon to make known to me the interpretation of the dream. Then the magicians, exorcists, Chaldaeans, and diviners came in, and in their presence I related my dream. But they could not interpret it. And 8 yet another came into my presence, Daniel, who is called Belteshazzar after the name

g Or made into a dunghill (mng. of Aram. word uncertain).

of my god, a man possessed by the spirit of
the holy gods. To him, too, I related the
9 dream: 'Belteshazzar, chief of the magicians,
whom I myself know to be possessed by the
spirit of the holy gods, and whom no secret
baffles, listen to the vision I saw in a dream,
and tell me its interpretation.

10   'Here is the vision which came into my
head as I was lying upon my bed:

As I was looking,
I saw a tree of great height at the centre of
the earth;
11   the tree grew and became strong,
reaching with its top to the sky
and visible to earth's farthest bounds.
12   Its foliage was lovely,
and its fruit abundant;
and it yielded food for all.
Beneath it the wild beasts found shelter,
the birds lodged in its branches,
and from it all living creatures fed.

13   'Here is another vision which came into
my head as I was lying upon my bed:

As I was watching, there was a Watcher,
a Holy One coming down from heaven.
14   He cried aloud and said,
"Hew down the tree, lop off the branches,
strip away the foliage, scatter the fruit.
Let the wild beasts flee from its shelter
and the birds from its branches,
15 but leave the stump with its roots in the
ground.
So, tethered with an iron ring,
let him eat his fill of the lush grass;
let him be drenched with the dew of
heaven
and share the lot of the beasts in their
pasture;
16   let his mind cease to be a man's mind,
and let him be given the mind of a beast.
Let seven times pass over him.
17   The issue has been determined by the
Watchers
and the sentence pronounced by the Holy
Ones.

Thereby the living will know that the Most
High is sovereign in the kingdom of men:
he gives the kingdom to whom he will and
he may set over it the humblest of mankind."

Daniel's interpretation

18 'This is the dream which I, King Nebuchadnezzar, have dreamed; now, Belteshazzar, tell me its interpretation; for, though
all the wise men of my kingdom are unable to tell me what it means, you can
tell me, since the spirit of the holy gods is
in you.'
19   Daniel, who was called Belteshazzar, was
dumbfounded for a moment, dismayed by

his thoughts; but the king said, 'Do not let
the dream and its interpretation dismay you.'
Belteshazzar answered, 'My lord, if only the
dream were for those who hate you and its
interpretation for your enemies! The tree 20
which you saw grow and become strong,
reaching with its top to the sky and visible
to earth's farthest bounds, its foliage lovely 21
and its fruit abundant, a tree which yielded
food for all, beneath which the wild beasts
dwelt and in whose branches the birds
lodged, that tree, O king, is you. You have 22
grown and become strong. Your power has
grown and reaches the sky; your sovereignty
stretches to the ends of the earth. Also, O 23
king, you saw a Watcher, a Holy One, coming down from heaven and saying, "Hew
down the tree and destroy it, but leave its
stump with its roots in the ground. So,
tethered with an iron ring, let him eat his
fill of the lush grass; let him be drenched
with the dew of heaven and share the lot of
the beasts until seven times pass over him."
This is the interpretation, O king—it is a 24
decree of the Most High which touches my
lord the king. You will be banished from the 25
society of men; you will have to live with
the wild beasts; you will feed on grass like
oxen and you will be drenched with the dew
of heaven. Seven times will pass over you
until you have learnt that the Most High is
sovereign over the kingdom of men and
gives it to whom he will. The command 26
was given to leave the stump of the tree with
its roots. By this you may know that from
the time you acknowledge the sovereignty
of heaven your rule will endure. Be advised 27
by me, O king: redeem your sins by charity
and your iniquities by generosity to the
wretched. So may you long enjoy peace of
mind.'

Nebuchadnezzar's madness

All this befell King Nebuchadnezzar. At the 28 29
end of twelve months the king was walking
on the roof of the royal palace at Babylon,
and he exclaimed, 'Is not this Babylon the 30
great which I have built as a royal residence
by my own mighty power and for the honour
of my majesty?' The words were still on his 31
lips, when a voice came down from heaven:
'To you, King Nebuchadnezzar, the word is
spoken: the kingdom has passed from you.
You are banished from the society of men 32
and you shall live with the wild beasts; you
shall feed on grass like oxen, and seven times
will pass over you until you have learnt that
the Most High is sovereign over the kingdom of men and gives it to whom he will.' At 33
that very moment this judgement came upon
Nebuchadnezzar. He was banished from the
society of men and ate grass like oxen; his
body was drenched by the dew of heaven,

until his hair grew long like goats' hair and his nails like eagles' talons.[h]

Nebuchadnezzar's sanity restored

34 At the end of the appointed time, I, Nebuchadnezzar, raised my eyes to heaven and I returned to my right mind. I blessed the Most High, praising and glorifying the Ever-living One:

His sovereignty is never-ending
and his rule endures through all generations;
35 all dwellers upon earth count for nothing
and he deals as he wishes with the host of heaven;[i]
no one may lay hand upon him
and ask him what he does.

36 At that very time I returned to my right mind and my majesty and royal splendour were restored to me for the glory of my kingdom. My courtiers and my nobles sought audience of me. I was established in my kingdom and my power was greatly increased. 37 Now I, Nebuchadnezzar, praise and exalt and glorify the King of heaven; for all his acts are right and his ways are just and those whose conduct is arrogant he can bring low.

Belshazzar's feast

5 Belshazzar the king gave a banquet for a thousand of his nobles and was drinking wine in the presence of the thousand. 2 Warmed by the wine, he gave orders to fetch the vessels of gold and silver which his father Nebuchadnezzar had taken from the sanctuary at Jerusalem, that he and his nobles, his concubines and his courtesans, might drink from them. 3 So the vessels of gold and silver from the sanctuary in the house of God at Jerusalem were brought in, and the king and his nobles, his concubines and his courtesans, 4 drank from them. They drank wine and praised the gods of gold and silver, of bronze 5 and iron, and of wood and stone. Suddenly there appeared the fingers of a human hand writing on the plaster of the palace wall opposite the lamp, and the king could see 6 the back of the hand as it wrote. At this the king's mind was filled with dismay and he turned pale, he became limp in every limb 7 and his knees knocked together. He called loudly for the exorcists, Chaldaeans, and diviners to be brought in; then, addressing the wise men of Babylon, he said, 'Whoever can read this writing and tell me its interpretation shall be robed in purple and honoured with a chain of gold round his neck and shall rank as third in the kingdom.' 8 Then all the king's wise men came in, but

they could not read the writing or interpret it to the king. King Belshazzar sat there pale 9 and utterly dismayed, while his nobles were perplexed.

Daniel and the writing on the wall

The king and his nobles were talking when 10 the queen entered the banqueting-hall: 'Long live the king!' she said. 'Why this dismay, and why do you look so pale? There is a 11 man in your kingdom who has in him the spirit of the holy gods, a man who was known in your father's time to have a clear understanding and godlike wisdom. King Nebuchadnezzar, your father, appointed him chief of the magicians, exorcists, Chaldaeans, and diviners. This same Daniel, 12 whom the king named Belteshazzar, is known to have a notable spirit, with knowledge and understanding, and the gift of interpreting dreams, explaining riddles and unbinding spells;[j] let him be summoned now and he will give the interpretation.' Daniel was then brought into the king's 13 presence and the king said to him, 'So you are Daniel, one of the Jewish exiles whom the king my father brought from Judah. I have heard that you possess the spirit of 14 the holy gods and that you are a man of clear understanding and peculiar wisdom. The wise men, the exorcists, have just been 15 brought into my presence to read this writing and tell me its interpretation, and they have been unable to interpret it. But I have heard 16 it said of you that you are able to give interpretations and to unbind spells.[k] So now, if you are able to read the words and tell me what they mean, you shall be robed in purple and honoured with a chain of gold round your neck and shall rank as third in the kingdom.' Then Daniel answered in the 17 king's presence, 'Your gifts you may keep for yourself; or else give your rewards to another. Nevertheless I will read the writing to your majesty and tell you its interpretation. My lord king, the Most High God gave 18 your father Nebuchadnezzar a kingdom and power and glory and majesty; and, because 19 of this power which he gave him, all peoples and nations of every language trembled before him and were afraid. He put to death whom he would and spared whom he would, he promoted them at will and at will degraded them. But, when he became 20 haughty, stubborn and presumptuous, he was deposed from his royal throne and his glory was taken from him. He was banished 21 from the society of men, his mind became like that of a beast, he had to live with the wild asses and to eat grass like oxen, and his body was drenched with the dew of heaven,

---

[h] goats' hair . . . eagles' talons: prob. rdg.; Aram. eagles' and his nails like birds'.   [i] Prob. rdg.; Aram. adds and the dwellers upon earth.   [j] Or and solving problems.   [k] Or and to solve problems.

until he came to know that the Most High God is sovereign over the kingdom of men
22 and sets up over it whom he will. But you, his son Belshazzar, did not humble your
23 heart, although you knew all this. You have set yourself up against the Lord of heaven. The vessels of his temple have been brought to your table; and you, your nobles, your concubines, and your courtesans have drunk from them. You have praised the gods of silver and gold, of bronze and iron, of wood and stone, which neither see nor hear nor know, and you have not given glory to God, in whose charge is your very breath and in
24 whose hands are all your ways. This is why that hand was sent from his very presence
25 and why it wrote this inscription. And these are the words of the writing which was in-
26 scribed: *Mene mene tekel u-pharsin.* Here is the interpretation: *mene:*[l] God has numbered the days of your kingdom and brought
27 it to an end; *tekel:*[m] you have been weighed
28 in the balance and found wanting; *u-pharsin:*[n] and your kingdom has been divided
29 and given to the Medes and Persians.' Then Belshazzar gave the order and Daniel was robed in purple and honoured with a chain of gold round his neck, and proclamation was made that he should rank as third in the kingdom.
30   That very night Belshazzar king of the
31 Chaldaeans was slain, and Darius the Mede took the kingdom, being then sixty-two years old.

Scheme to depose Daniel

6 It pleased Darius to appoint satraps over the kingdom, a hundred and twenty in num-
2 ber in charge of the whole kingdom, and over them three chief ministers, to whom the satraps should send reports so that the king's interests might not suffer; of these
3 three, Daniel was one. In the event Daniel outshone the other ministers and the satraps because of his ability, and the king had it in mind to appoint him over the whole king-
4 dom. Then the chief ministers and the satraps began to look round for some pretext to attack Daniel's administration of the king-dom, but they failed to find any malpractice on his part; for he was faithful to his trust.
5 Since they could discover no neglect of duty or malpractice, they said, 'There will be no charge to bring against this Daniel unless
6 we find one in his religion.' These chief ministers and satraps watched for an oppor-tunity to approach the king, and said to him,
7 'Long live King Darius! All we, the min-isters of the kingdom, prefects, satraps, courtiers, and viceroys, have taken counsel and agree that the king should issue a decree

and bring an ordinance into force, that who-ever within the next thirty days shall present a petition to any god or man other than the king shall be thrown into the lions' pit.
8 Now, O king, issue the ordinance and have it put in writing, so that it may be unalter-able, for the law of the Medes and Persians stands for ever.' Accordingly King Darius
9 issued the ordinance in written form.

Daniel is thrown to the lions

When Daniel learnt that this decree had
10 been issued, he went into his house. He had had windows made in his roof-chamber looking towards Jerusalem; and there he knelt down three times a day and offered prayers and praises to his God as his custom had always been. His enemies watched for
11 an opportunity to catch Daniel and found him at his prayers making supplication to his God. Then they came into the king's
12 presence and reminded him of the ordinance. 'Your majesty,' they said, 'have you not issued an ordinance that any person who, within the next thirty days, shall present a petition to any god or man other than your majesty shall be thrown into the lions' pit?' The king answered, 'Yes, it is fixed. The law of the Medes and Persians stands for ever.' So in the king's presence they said, 'Daniel,
13 one of the Jewish exiles, has ignored the ordinance issued by your majesty, and is making petition to his god three times a day.' When the king heard this, he was greatly
14 distressed. He tried to think of a way to save Daniel, and continued his efforts till sunset; then those same men watched for an oppor-
15 tunity to approach the king, and said to him, 'Your majesty must know that by the law of the Medes and Persians no ordinance or decree issued by the king may be altered.' So the king gave orders and Daniel was
16 brought and thrown into the lions' pit; but he said to Daniel, 'Your own God, whom you serve continually, will save you.' A
17 stone was brought and put over the mouth of the pit, and the king sealed it with his signet and with the signets of his nobles, so that no one might intervene to rescue Daniel.

The angel delivers Daniel

The king went back to his palace and spent
18 the night fasting; no woman was brought to him and sleep eluded him. At dawn, as
19 soon as it was light, he rose and went in fear and trembling to the pit. When the king
20 reached it, he called anxiously to Daniel, 'Daniel, servant of the living God, has your God whom you serve continually been able to save you from the lions?' Then Daniel
21 answered, 'Long live the king! My God sent
22

---

l That is numbered.   *m That is* shekel *or* weight. *three possible meanings* halves *or* divisions *or* Persians.   *n Prob. rdg.; Aram.* pheres. *There is a play on*

his angel to shut the lions' mouths so that they have done me no injury, because in his judgement I was found innocent;[o] and more-
23 over, O king, I had done you no injury.' The king was overjoyed and gave orders that Daniel should be lifted out of the pit. So Daniel was lifted out and no trace of injury was found on him, because he had put his
24 faith in his God. By order of the king Daniel's accusers were brought and thrown into the lions' pit with their wives and children, and before they reached the floor of the pit the lions were upon them and crunched them up, bones and all.

Darius issues a decree

25 Then King Darius wrote to all peoples and nations of every language throughout the whole world: 'May your prosperity increase!
26 I have issued a decree that in all my royal domains men shall fear and reverence the God of Daniel;

for he is the living God, the everlasting,
whose kingly power shall not be weakened;
  whose sovereignty shall have no end—
27 a saviour, a deliverer, a worker of signs and wonders
in heaven and on earth,
who has delivered Daniel from the power of the lions.'

28   So this Daniel prospered during the reigns of Darius and Cyrus the Persian.

Daniel's vision of the beasts

7 In the first year of Belshazzar king of Bab-

ylon, as Daniel lay on his bed, dreams and visions came into his head. Then he wrote down the dream, and here his account begins:

In my visions of the night I, Daniel, was 2 gazing intently and I saw a great sea churned up by the four winds of heaven, and four 3 huge beasts coming up out of the sea, each one different from the others. The first was 4 like a lion but had an eagle's wings. I watched until its wings were plucked off and it was lifted from the ground and made to stand on two feet like a man; it was also given the mind of a man. Then I saw another, 5 a second beast, like a bear. It was half crouching and had three ribs in its mouth, between its teeth. The command was given: 'Up, gorge yourself with flesh.' After this as I 6 gazed I saw another, a beast like a leopard with four bird's wings on its back; this creature had four heads, and it was invested with sovereign power. Next in my visions of the 7 night I saw a fourth beast, dreadful and grisly, exceedingly strong, with great iron teeth and bronze claws.[p] It crunched and devoured, and trampled underfoot all that was left. It differed from all the beasts which preceded it in having ten horns. While I was 8 considering the horns I saw another horn, a little one, springing up among them, and three of the first horns were uprooted to make room for it. And in that horn were eyes like the eyes of a man, and a mouth that spoke proud words. I kept looking, and 9 then

---

o in his judgement . . . innocent: *or* before him success was granted me.   *p* and bronze claws: *prob. rdg.*,
cp. verse 19; Aram. om.

(Dan. 7. 2)

thrones were set in place and one ancient in
years took his seat,
his robe was white as snow and the hair of
his head like cleanest wool.
Flames of fire were his throne and its wheels
blazing fire;
10 a flowing river of fire streamed out before
him.*q*
Thousands upon thousands served him
and myriads upon myriads attended his
presence.
The court sat, and the books were opened.

11   Then because of the proud words that
the horn was speaking, I went on watching
until the beast was killed and its carcass
12 destroyed: it was given to the flames. The
rest of the beasts, though deprived of their
sovereignty, were allowed to remain alive
13 for a time and a season. I was still watching
in visions of the night and I saw one like a
man coming with the clouds of heaven; he
approached the Ancient in Years and was
14 presented to him. Sovereignty and glory and
kingly power were given to him, so that all
people and nations of every language should
serve him; his sovereignty was to be an
everlasting sovereignty which should not
pass away, and his kingly power such as
should never be impaired.

Interpretation of the vision

15 My spirit within me was troubled, and, dismayed by the visions which came into my
16 head, I, Daniel, approached one of those
who stood there and inquired from him
what all this meant; and he told me the
17 interpretation. 'These great beasts, four in
number,' he said, 'are four kingdoms which
18 shall rise from the ground. But the saints*r*
of the Most High shall receive the kingly
power and shall retain it for ever, for ever
19 and ever.' Then I desired to know what the
fourth beast meant, the beast that was
different from all the others, very dreadful
with its iron teeth and bronze claws, crunch-
ing and devouring and trampling underfoot
20 all that was left. I desired also to know about
the ten horns on its head and the other horn
which sprang up and at whose coming three
of them fell—the horn that had eyes and a
mouth speaking proud words and appeared
21 larger than the others. As I still watched, that
horn was waging war with the saints and
22 overcoming them until the Ancient in Years
came. Then judgement was given in favour of
the saints of the Most High, and the time
came when the saints gained possession of
23 the kingly power. He gave me this answer:
'The fourth beast signifies a fourth kingdom
which shall appear upon earth. It shall
differ from the other kingdoms and shall

devour the whole earth, tread it down and
crush it. The ten horns signify the appear- 24
ance of ten kings in this kingdom, after
whom another king shall arise, differing
from his predecessors; and he shall bring
low three kings. He shall hurl defiance at 25
the Most High and shall wear down the
saints of the Most High. He shall plan to
alter the customary times and law; and the
saints shall be delivered into his power for
a time and times and half a time. Then the 26
court shall sit, and he shall be deprived of
his sovereignty, so that in the end it may be
destroyed and abolished. The kingly power, 27
sovereignty, and greatness of all the kingdoms under heaven shall be given to the
people of the saints of the Most High. Their
kingly power is an everlasting power and all
sovereignties shall serve them and obey them.'

Here the account ends. As for me, Daniel, 28
my thoughts dismayed me greatly and I
turned pale; and I kept these things in my
mind.

The ram and the he-goat

8
1–2
*s*In the third year of the reign of King Belshazzar, while I was in Susa the capital city
of the province of Elam, a vision appeared
to me, Daniel, similar to my former vision.
In this vision I was watching beside the
stream of the Ulai. I raised my eyes and there 3
I saw a ram with two horns standing between
me and the stream. The two horns were long,
the one longer than the other, growing up
behind. I watched the ram butting west and 4
north and south. No beasts could stand before it, no one could rescue from its power.
It did what it liked, making a display of its
strength. While I pondered this, suddenly a 5
he-goat came from the west skimming over
the whole earth without touching the ground;
it had a prominent horn between its eyes. It 6
approached the two-horned ram which I had
seen standing between me and the stream
and rushed at it with impetuous force. I saw 7
it advance on the ram, working itself into
a fury against it, then strike the ram and
break its two horns; the ram had no strength
to resist. The he-goat flung it to the ground
and trampled on it, and there was no one to
save the ram.

Then the he-goat made a great display of 8
its strength. Powerful as it was, its great
horn snapped and in its place there sprang
out towards the four quarters of heaven four
prominent horns. Out of one of them there 9
issued one small horn, which made a pro-
digious show of strength south and east and
towards the fairest of all lands. It aspired to 10
be as great as the host of heaven, and it cast
down to the earth some of the host and some
of the stars and trod them underfoot. It 11

---

q Or it.   r Or holy ones.   *s Here the Hebrew text resumes (see note at 2. 4).*

aspired to be as great as the Prince of the host, suppressed his regular offering and even
12 threw down his sanctuary. The heavenly hosts were delivered up, and it raised itself[t] impiously against the regular offering and threw true religion to the ground; in all that
13 it did it succeeded. I heard a holy one speaking and another holy one answering him, whoever he was. The one said, 'For how long will the period of this vision last? How long will the regular offering be suppressed, how long will impiety cause desolation,[u] and both the Holy Place and the fairest of all lands[v]
14 be given over to be trodden down?' The answer came, 'For two thousand three hundred evenings and mornings; then the Holy Place shall emerge victorious.'

Interpretation of the vision

15 All the while that I, Daniel, was seeing the vision, I was trying to understand it. Suddenly I saw standing before me one with the
16 semblance of a man; at the same time I heard a human voice calling to him across the bend of the Ulai, 'Gabriel, explain the vision to
17 this man.' He came up to where I was standing; I was seized with terror at his approach and threw myself on my face. But he said to me, 'Understand, O man: the vision points
18 to the time of the end.' When he spoke to me, I fell to the ground in a trance; but he grasped me and made me stand up where
19 I was. And he said, 'I shall make known to you what is to happen at the end of the
20 wrath; for there is an end to the appointed time. The two-horned ram which you saw
21 signifies the kings of Media and Persia, the he-goat is the kingdom[w] of the Greeks and the great horn on his forehead is the first
22 king. As for the horn which was snapped off and replaced by four horns: four kingdoms shall rise out of that nation, but not with power comparable to his.

23 In the last days of those kingdoms, when their sin is at its height,
a king shall appear, harsh and grim, a master of stratagem.
24 His power shall be great, he shall work havoc untold;
he shall succeed in whatever he does.
He shall work havoc among great nations and upon a holy people.
25 His mind shall be ever active,
and he shall succeed in his crafty designs;
he shall conjure up great plans
and, when they least expect it, work havoc on many.
He shall challenge even the Prince of princes
and be broken, but not by human hands.

This revelation which has been given 26 of the evenings and the mornings is true; but you must keep the vision secret, for it points to days far ahead.'

As for me, Daniel, my strength failed me 27 and I lay sick for a while. Then I rose and attended to the king's business. But I was perplexed by the revelation and no one could explain it.

Daniel's prayer for exiled Judah

In the first year of the reign of Darius son of 9 Ahasuerus (a Mede by birth, who was appointed king over the kingdom of the Chaldaeans) I, Daniel, was reading the scriptures 2 and reflecting on the seventy years which, according to the word of the LORD to the prophet Jeremiah, were to pass while Jerusalem lay in ruins. Then I turned to the Lord 3 God in earnest prayer and supplication with fasting and sackcloth and ashes. I prayed 4 to the LORD my God, making confession thus:
'Lord, thou great and terrible God who faithfully keepest the covenant with those who love thee and observe thy commandments, we have sinned, we have done what 5 was wrong and wicked; we have rebelled, we have turned our backs on thy commandments and thy decrees. We have not listened 6 to thy servants the prophets, who spoke in thy name to our kings and princes, to our forefathers and to all the people of the land. O Lord, the right is on thy side; the shame, 7 now as ever, belongs to us, the men of Judah and the citizens of Jerusalem, and to all the Israelites near and far in every land to which thou hast banished them for their treachery towards thee. O LORD, the shame falls on us 8 as on our kings, our princes and our forefathers; we have all sinned against thee. Compassion and forgiveness belong to the 9 Lord our God, though we have rebelled against him. We have not obeyed the LORD 10 our God, we have not conformed to the laws which he laid down for us through his servants the prophets. All Israel has broken 11 thy law and not obeyed thee, so that the curses set out in the law of Moses thy servant in the adjuration and the oath have rained down upon us; for we have sinned against him. He has fulfilled all that he said about 12 us and about our rulers, by bringing upon us and upon Jerusalem a calamity greater than has ever happened in all the world. It 13 was all foreshadowed in the law of Moses, this calamity which has come upon us; yet we have done nothing to propitiate the LORD our God; we have neither repented of our wrongful deeds nor remembered that thou

---

t and it raised itself: prob. rdg.; Heb. om.   u will impiety cause desolation: prob. rdg.; Heb. obscure.
v fairest of all lands: prob. rdg., cp. verse 9; Heb. host.   w Prob. rdg.; Heb. king.

14 art true to thy word. The LORD has been biding his time and has now brought this calamity upon us. In all that he has done the LORD our God has been right; yet we have not obeyed him.

15 'And now, O Lord our God who didst bring thy people out of Egypt by a strong hand, winning for thyself a name that lives on to this day, we have sinned, we have done 16 wrong. O Lord, by all thy saving deeds we beg that thy wrath and anger may depart from Jerusalem, thy city, thy holy hill; through our own sins and our fathers' guilty deeds Jerusalem and thy people have become 17 a byword among all our neighbours. And now, our God, listen to thy servant's prayer and supplication; for thy own sake, O Lord, make thy face shine upon thy desolate 18 sanctuary. Lend thy ear, O God, and hear, open thine eyes and look upon our desolation and upon the city that bears thy name; it is not by virtue of our own saving acts but by thy great mercy that we present our sup-19 plications before thee. O Lord, hear; O Lord, forgive; O Lord, listen and act; for thy own sake do not delay, O God, for thy city and thy people bear thy name.'

Gabriel's message to Daniel

20 Thus I was speaking and praying, confessing my own sin and my people Israel's sin, and presenting my supplication before the LORD 21 my God on behalf of his holy hill. While I was praying, the man Gabriel, whom I had already seen in the vision, came close to[x] me at the hour of the evening sacrifice, flying 22 swiftly.[y] He spoke clearly to me and said, 'Daniel, I have now come to enlighten your 23 understanding. As you were beginning your supplications a word went forth; this I have come to pass on to you, for you are a man greatly beloved. Consider well the word, 24 consider the vision: Seventy weeks are marked out for your people and your holy city; then rebellion shall be stopped,[z] sin brought to an end,[a] iniquity expiated, everlasting right ushered in, vision and prophecy sealed, and the Most Holy Place 25 anointed. Know then and understand: from the time that the word went forth that Jerusalem should be restored and rebuilt, seven weeks shall pass till the appearance of one anointed, a prince; then for sixty-two weeks it shall remain restored, rebuilt with streets 26 and conduits. At the critical time, after the sixty-two weeks, one who is anointed shall be removed with no one to take his part; and the horde of an invading prince shall work havoc on city and sanctuary. The end of it shall be a deluge, inevitable war with 27 all its horrors. He shall make a firm league

with the mighty[b] for one week; and, the week half spent, he shall put a stop to sacrifice and offering. And in the train of these abominations shall come an author of desolation; then, in the end, what has been decreed concerning the desolation will be poured out.'

Daniel's vision by the river Tigris

10 In the third year of Cyrus king of Persia a word was revealed to Daniel who had been given the name Belteshazzar. Though this word was true, it cost him[c] much toil to understand it; nevertheless understanding came to him in the course of the vision.

2 In those days I, Daniel, mourned for three 3 whole weeks. I refrained from all choice food; no meat or wine passed my lips, and I did not anoint myself until the three weeks 4 had gone by. On the twenty-fourth day of the first month, I found myself on the bank 5 of the great river, that is the Tigris; I looked up and saw a man clothed in linen with a belt of gold from Ophir round his waist. 6 His body gleamed like topaz, his face shone like lightning, his eyes flamed like torches, his arms and feet sparkled like a disc of bronze; and when he spoke his voice sounded 7 like the voice of a multitude. I, Daniel, alone saw the vision, while those who were near me did not see it, but great fear fell upon 8 them and they stole away, and I was left alone gazing at this great vision. But my strength left me; I became a sorry figure of 9 a man, and retained no strength. I heard the sound of his words and, when I did so, I fell 10 prone on the ground in a trance. Suddenly a hand grasped me and pulled me up on to my 11 hands and knees. He said to me, 'Daniel, man greatly beloved, attend to the words I am speaking to you and stand up where you are, for I am now sent to you.' When he 12 addressed me, I stood up trembling and he said, 'Do not be afraid, Daniel, for from the very first day that you applied your mind to understand and to mortify yourself before your God, your prayers have been heard, 13 and I have come in answer to them. But the angel prince of the kingdom of Persia resisted me for twenty-one days, and then, seeing that I had held out there, Michael, one of the chief princes, came to help me against the prince of the kingdom of Persia. And I 14 have come to explain to you what will happen to your people in days to come; for this too is a vision for those days.'

Interpretation of the vision

While he spoke to me I hung my head and 15 was struck dumb. Suddenly one like a man 16 touched my lips. Then I opened my mouth

---

x Or touched.   y flying swiftly: prob. rdg.; Heb. thoroughly wearied.   z Or restrained.   a Or sealed.
b Or many.   c him: prob. rdg.; Heb. om.

to speak and addressed him as he stood before me: 'Sir, this has pierced me to the 17 heart, and I retain no strength. How can my lord's servant presume to talk with such as my lord, since my strength has failed me and 18 no breath is left in me?' Then the figure touched me again and restored my strength. 19 He said, 'Do not be afraid, man greatly beloved; all will be well with you. Be strong, be strong.' When he had spoken to me, I recovered strength and said, 'Speak, sir, for 20 you have given me strength.' He said, 'Do you know why I have come to you? I am first going back to fight with the prince of Persia, and, as soon as I have left, the prince 21– of Greece will appear: I have no ally on my **11** 1 side to help and support me, except Michael your prince.[d] However I will tell you what 2 is written in the Book of Truth. Here and now I will tell you what is true:

'Three more kings will appear in Persia, and the fourth will far surpass all the others in wealth; and when he has extended his power through his wealth, he will rouse the whole world against the kingdom of Greece. 3 Then there will appear a warrior king. He will rule a vast kingdom and will do what 4 he chooses. But as soon as he is established, his kingdom will be shattered and split up north, south, east and west. It will not pass to his descendants, nor will any of his successors have an empire like his; his kingdom will be torn up by the roots and given to 5 others as well as to them. Then the king of the south will become strong; but another of the captains will surpass him in strength 6 and win a greater kingdom. In due course the two will enter into a friendly alliance; to redress the balance the daughter of the king of the south will be given in marriage to the king of the north, but she will not maintain her influence and their line will not last. She and her escort, her child, and also her lord and master, will all be the victims of foul 7 play. Then another shoot from the same stock as hers will appear in his father's place, will penetrate the defences of the king of the north and enter his fortress, and will 8 win a decisive victory over his people. He will take back as booty to Egypt even the images of their gods cast in metal and their precious vessels of silver and gold. Then for some years he will refrain from 9 attacking the king of the north. After that the king of the north will overrun the southern kingdom but will retreat to his own land. 10 'His sons will press on to assemble a great armed horde. One of them will sweep on and on like an irresistible flood. And after that he will press on as far as his enemy's stronghold.

The king of the south, his anger roused, will 11 march out to do battle with the king of the north who, in turn, will raise a great horde, but it will be delivered into the hands of his enemy. When this horde has been captured, 12 the victor will be elated and he will slaughter tens of thousands, yet he will not maintain his advantage. Then the king of the north 13 will once more raise a horde even greater than the last and, when the years come round, will advance with a great army and a large baggage-train. During these times many will 14 resist the king of the south, but some hotheads among your own people will rashly attempt to give substance to a vision and will come to disaster. Then the king of the 15 north will come and throw up siege-ramps and capture a fortified town, and the forces of the south will not stand up to him; even the flower of their army will not be able to hold their ground. And so his adversary will 16 do as he pleases and meet with no opposition. He will establish himself in the fairest of all lands and it will come wholly into his power. He will resolve to subjugate all the 17 dominions of the king of the south; and he will come to fair terms with him,[e] and he will give him a young woman in marriage, for the destruction of the kingdom; but she will not persist nor serve his purpose. Then 18 he will turn to the coasts and islands and take many prisoners, but a foreign commander[f] will put an end to his challenge by wearing him down;[g] thus he will throw back his challenge on to him. He will fall back 19 upon his own strongholds; there he will come to disaster and be overthrown and be seen no more.

'He will be succeeded by one who will 20 send out an officer with a royal escort to extort tribute; after a short time this king too will meet his end, yet neither openly nor in battle.

'A contemptible creature will succeed but 21 will not be given recognition as king; yet he will seize the kingdom by dissimulation and intrigue in time of peace. He will sweep 22 away all forces of opposition as he advances, and even the Prince of the Covenant will be broken. He will enter into fraudulent al- 23 liances and, although the people behind him are but few, he will rise to power and establish himself in time of peace. He will overrun 24 the richest districts of the province and succeed in doing what his fathers and forefathers failed to do, distributing spoil, booty, and property to his followers. He will lay his plans against fortresses, but only for a time.

'He will rouse himself in all his strength 25 and courage and lead a great army against

---

d Prob. rdg.; Heb. adds and as for me, in the first year of Darius the Mede.   e and he ... with him: prob. rdg.; Heb. obscure.   f Or consul or legate.   g by wearing him down: prob. rdg.; Heb. obscure.

the king of the south, but the king of the south will press the campaign against him with a very great and numerous army; yet the king of the south will not persist, for 26 traitors will lay their plots. Those who eat at his board will be his undoing; his army will be swept away, and many will fall on 27 the field of battle. The two kings will be bent on mischief and, sitting at the same table, they will lie to each other with advantage to neither. Yet there will still be an end 28 to the appointed time. Then one will return home with a long baggage-train, and with anger in his heart against the Holy Covenant; he will work his will and return to his own land.

29 'At the appointed time he will once more overrun the south, but he will not succeed 30 as he did before. Ships from the west will sail against him, and he will receive a rebuff. He will turn and vent his fury against the Holy Covenant; on his way back he will take due note of those who have forsaken it. 31 Armed forces dispatched by him will desecrate the sanctuary and the citadel and do away with the regular offering. And there they will set up "the abominable thing that 32 causes desolation". He will win over by plausible promises those who are ready to condemn the covenant, but the people who are faithful to their God will hold firm and 33 fight back. Wise leaders of the nation will give guidance to the common people; yet for a while they will fall victims to fire and 34 sword, to captivity and pillage. But these victims will not want for help, though small, even if many who join them are insincere. 35 Some of these leaders will themselves fall victims for a time so that they may be tested, refined and made shining white. Yet there will still be an end[h] to the appointed time. 36 The king will do what he chooses; he will exalt and magnify himself above every god and against the God of gods he will utter monstrous blasphemies. All will go well for him until the time of wrath ends, for what 37 is determined must be done. He will ignore his ancestral gods, and the god beloved of women; to no god will he pay heed but will 38 exalt himself above them all. Instead he will honour the god of the citadel, a god unknown to his ancestors, with gold and silver, 39 gems and costly gifts. He will garrison his strongest fortresses with aliens, the people of a foreign god. Those whom he favours he will load with honour, putting them in office over the common people and distributing land at a price.

40 'At the time of the end, he and the king of the south will make feints at one another, and the king of the north will come storming against him with chariots and cavalry and many ships. He will overrun land after land, sweeping over them like a flood, amongst 41 them the fairest of all lands, and tens of thousands shall fall victims. Yet all these lands [including Edom and Moab and the remnant of the Ammonites] will survive his attack. He will reach out to land after land, 42 and Egypt will not escape. He will gain con- 43 trol of her hidden stores of gold and silver and of all her treasures; Libyans and Cushites will follow in his train. Then rumours 44 from east and north will alarm him, and he will depart in a great rage to destroy and to exterminate many. He will pitch his royal 45 pavilion between the sea and the holy hill, the fairest of all hills; and he will meet his end with no one to help him.

At that moment Michael shall appear, **12**
  Michael the great captain,
who stands guard over your fellow-
    countrymen;
and there will be a time of distress
such as has never been
  since they became a nation till that
    moment.
But at that moment your people will be
    delivered,[i]
every one who is written in the book:
many of those who sleep in the dust of the 2
    earth will wake,
  some to everlasting life
  and some to the reproach of eternal
    abhorrence.
The wise leaders shall shine like the bright 3
    vault of heaven,
  and those who have guided the people in
    the true path
shall be like the stars for ever and ever.

But you, Daniel, keep the words secret and 4 seal the book till the time of the end. Many will be at their wits' end, and punishment will be heavy.'

Conclusion

And I, Daniel, looked and saw two others 5 standing, one on this bank of the river and the other on the opposite bank. And I said 6 to the man clothed in linen who was above the waters of the river, 'How long will it be before these portents cease?' The man 7 clothed in linen above the waters lifted to heaven his right hand and his left, and I heard him swear by him who lives for ever: 'It shall be for a time, times, and a half. When the power of the holy people ceases to be dispersed, all these things shall come to an end.' I heard but I did not understand, 8 and so I said, 'Sir, what will the issue of these things be?' He replied, 'Go your way, 9 Daniel, for the words are kept secret and sealed till the time of the end. Many shall 10

---

h Yet . . . end: prob. rdg.; Heb. has different word order.   *i Or will escape.*

purify themselves and be refined, making themselves shining white, but the wicked shall continue in wickedness and none of them shall understand; only the wise leaders 11 shall understand. From the time when the regular offering is abolished and "the abomination of desolation" is set up, there shall be an interval of one thousand two hundred and ninety days. Happy the man 12 who waits and lives to see the completion of one thousand three hundred and thirty-five days! But go your way to the end and 13 rest, and you shall arise to your destiny at the end of the age.'

THE TWELVE PROPHETS

HOSEA

(Hos. 3. 2)

1 THE WORD of the LORD which came to Hosea son of Beeri during the reigns of Uzziah, Jotham, Ahaz, and Hezekiah, kings of Judah, and during the reign of Jeroboam son of Jehoash king of Israel.

Hosea's wife and children

2 This is the beginning of the LORD's message by Hosea. He said, Go, take a wanton for your wife and get children of her wantonness; for like a wanton this land is unfaithful 3 to the LORD. So he went and took Gomer, a worthless woman;[a] and she conceived and 4 bore him a son. And the LORD said to him,

Call him Jezreel;[b] for in a little while
I will punish the line of Jehu for the blood
   shed in Jezreel
   and put an end to the kingdom of Israel.
5   On that day
I will break Israel's bow in the Vale of
   Jezreel.

She conceived again and bore a daughter, 6
and the LORD said to him,

   Call her Lo-ruhamah;[c]
for I will never again show love to Israel,
   never again forgive them.[d]

After weaning Lo-ruhamah, she conceived 8
and bore a son; and the LORD said,   9

   Call him Lo-ammi;[e]
for you are not my people,
   and I will not be your God.
The Israelites shall become countless as the 10
   sands of the sea
   which can neither be measured nor num-
    bered;
it shall no longer be said, 'They are not my
   people',
   they shall be called Sons of the Living
   God.

a a worthless woman: *or* daughter of Diblaim.   *b That is* God shall sow.   *c That is* Not loved.
d Prob. rdg.; Heb. adds (7) Then I will love Judah and will save them. I will save them not by bow or sword or weapon of war, by horses or by horsemen, but by the LORD their God.   *e That is* Not my people.

11 Then the people of Judah and of Israel shall
be reunited
and shall choose for themselves a single
head,
and they shall become masters of the
earth;
for great shall be the day of Jezreel.

An unfaithful wife

2 Then you will say to your brothers, 'You
are my people',
and to your sisters, 'You are loved.'

2   Plead my cause with your mother;
is she not my wife and I her husband?*ᶠ*
Plead with her to forswear those wanton
looks,
to banish the lovers from her bosom.
3   Or I will strip her and expose her
naked as the day she was born;
I will make her bare as the wilderness,
parched as the desert,
and leave her to die of thirst.
4   I will show no love for her children;
they are the offspring of wantonness,
5   and their mother is a wanton.
She who conceived them is shameless;
she says, 'I will go after my lovers;
they give me my food and drink,
my wool and flax, my oil and my perfumes.'
6 Therefore I will block her road with thorn-
bushes
and obstruct her path with a wall,
so that she can no longer follow her old ways.
7 When she pursues her lovers she will not
overtake them,
when she looks for them she will not find
them;
then she will say,
'I will go back to my husband again;
I was better off with him than I am now.'
8 For she does not know that it is I who gave
her
corn, new wine, and oil,
I who lavished upon her silver and gold
which they spent on the Baal.
9   Therefore I will take back
my corn at the harvest and my new wine at
the vintage,
and I will take away the wool and the flax
which I gave her to cover her naked body;
0   so I will show her up for the lewd thing
she is,
and no lover will want to steal her from
me.
ᵍ I will ravage the vines and the fig-trees,
which she says are the fee
with which her lovers have hired her,
and turn them into jungle where wild beasts
shall feed.

I will put a stop to her merrymaking,   11
her pilgrimages and new moons, her sabbaths*ʰ* and festivals.
I will punish her for the holy days   13
when she burnt sacrifices to the Baalim,
when she decked herself with earrings and
necklaces,
ran after her lovers and forgot me.
This is the very word of the LORD.

Restored to her husband

But now listen,   14
I will woo her, I will go with her into the
wilderness
and comfort her:
there I will restore her vineyards,   15
turning the Vale of Trouble into the Gate
of Hope,*ⁱ*
and there she will answer as in her youth,
when she came up out of Egypt.
On that day she shall call me 'My husband'   16
and shall no more call me 'My Baal';*ʲ*
and I will wipe from her lips the very names   17
of the Baalim;
never again shall their names be heard.
This is the very word of the LORD.*ᵏ*

'You are my people'

Then I will make a covenant on behalf of   18
Israel with the wild beasts, the birds of the
air, and the things that creep on the earth,
and I will break bow and sword and weapon
of war and sweep them off the earth, so that
all living creatures may lie down without
fear. I will betroth you to myself for ever,   19
betroth you in lawful wedlock with unfailing
devotion and love; I will betroth you to my-   20
self to have and to hold, and you shall know
the LORD. At that time I will give answer,   21
says the LORD, I will answer for the heavens
and they will answer for the earth, and the   22
earth will answer for the corn, the new wine,
and the oil, and they will answer for Jezreel.
Israel shall be my new sowing in the land,   23
and I will show love to Lo-ruhamah and say
to Lo-ammi, 'You are my people', and he
will say, 'Thou art my God.'

Hosea buys back his wife

The LORD said to me,   **3**
Go again and love a woman
loved by another man, an adulteress,
and love her as I, the LORD, love the Israelites
although they resort to other gods
and love the raisin-cakes offered to their
idols.
So I got her back*ˡ* for fifteen pieces of silver,   2

f is she . . . husband?: *or* for she is no longer my wife nor I her husband.   *g Verses 11 and 12 transposed.*
h Or her full moons.   *i turning . . . Hope: or* Emek-achor to Pethah-tikvah.   *j Also means* My
husband.   *k* This . . . LORD: *transposed from after* On that day *in verse 16.*   *l* got her back: *or* bought her.

M *

a homer of barley and a measure of wine;
3 and I said to her,

Many a long day you shall live in my house
and not play the wanton,
and have no intercourse with a man, nor I
with you.

4 For the Israelites shall live many a long day
without king or prince,
without sacrifice or sacred pillar,
without image or household gods;
5 but after that they will again seek
the LORD their God and David their king,
and turn anxiously to the LORD for his
bounty in days to come.

The LORD's charge against Israel

4 Hear the word of the LORD, O Israel;
for the LORD has a charge to bring against
the people of the land:
There is no good faith or mutual trust,
no knowledge of God in the land,
2 oaths are imposed and broken, they kill and
rob;
there is nothing but adultery and licence,[m]
one deed of blood after another.
3 Therefore the land shall be dried up,
and all who live in it shall pine away,
and with them the wild beasts and the
birds of the air;
even the fish shall be swept from the sea.
4 But it is not for any man to bring a charge,
it is not for him to prove a case;
the quarrel with you, false priest, is mine.

5 Priest?[n] By day and by night you blunder on,
you and the prophet with you.
6 My people are ruined for lack of knowledge;
your own countrymen are brought to
ruin.[o]
You have rejected knowledge,
and I will reject you from serving me as
priest.
You have forgotten the teaching of God,
and I, your God, will forget your sons.

7 The more priests there are, the more they
sin against me;
their dignity I will turn into dishonour.
8 They feed on the sin of my people
and batten on their iniquity.
9 But people and priest shall be treated alike.
I will punish them for their conduct
and repay them for their deeds:
10 they shall eat but never be satisfied,
behave wantonly but their lust will never
be overtaxed,
for they have forsaken the LORD
11 to give themselves to sacred prostitution.

New wine and old steal my people's wits:[p] 12
they ask advice from a block of wood
and take their orders from a fetish;
for a spirit of wantonness has led them
astray
and in their lusts they are unfaithful to
their God.
Your men sacrifice on mountain-tops 13
and burn offerings on the hills,
under oak and poplar
and the terebinth's pleasant shade.
Therefore your daughters play the wanton
and your sons' brides commit adultery.
I will not punish your daughters for play- 14
ing the wanton
nor your sons' brides for their adultery,
because your men resort to wanton women
and sacrifice with temple-prostitutes.
A people without understanding comes to
grief;
they are a mother turned wanton. 15
Bring no guilt-offering,[q] Israel;
do not come to Gilgal, Judah,
do not go up to Beth-aven to swear by the
life of the LORD,
since Israel has run wild, wild as a heifer; 16
and will the LORD now feed this people
like lambs in a broad meadow?
Ephraim, keeping company with idols, 17
has held a drunken orgy,[r] 18
they have practised sacred prostitution,
they have preferred dishonour to glory.
The wind shall sweep them away, wrapped 19
in its wings,
and they will find their sacrifices a
delusion.

Unalterable doom

Hear this, you priests, **5**
and listen, all Israel; let the royal house mark
my words.
Sentence is passed on you;
for you have been a snare at Mizpah,
and a net spread out on Tabor.
The rebels! they have shown base in- 2
gratitude,
but I will punish them all.
I have cared for Ephraim 3
and I have not neglected Israel;
but now Ephraim has played the wanton
and Israel has defiled himself.
Their misdeeds have barred their way back 4
to their God;
for a wanton spirit is in them,
and they care nothing for the LORD.
Israel's arrogance cries out against him; 5
[s]Ephraim's guilt is his undoing,
and Judah no less is undone.

m and licence: *prob. rdg.; Heb.* they exceed.
are like those who quarrel with a priest.
people destroyed for lack of knowledge.
guilt-offering: *prob. rdg.; Heb.* Let him not be guilty.
s *Prob. rdg.; Heb.* prefixes Israel.
n the quarrel . . . Priest?: *prob. rdg.; Heb.* and your people
o My people . . . ruin: *or* Your mother (Israel) is destroyed, my
p steal . . . wits: *or* embolden my people.   q Bring no
r a drunken orgy: *prob. rdg.; Heb.* unintelligible.

6 They go with sacrifices of sheep and cattle
to seek the LORD, but do not find him.
He has withdrawn himself from them;
7 for they have been unfaithful to him,
and their sons are bastards.
Now an invader shall devour their fields.
8 Blow the trumpet in Gibeah,
the horn in Ramah,
raise the battle-cry in Beth-aven:
'Benjamin, we are with you!'
9 On the tribes of Israel I have proclaimed this
unalterable doom:
on the day of punishment Ephraim shall be
laid waste.
10 The rulers of Judah act like men who move
their neighbour's boundary;
on them will I pour out my wrath like a flood.
11 Ephraim is an oppressor trampling on
justice,
doggedly pursuing what is worthless.
12 But I am a festering sore to Ephraim,
a canker to the house of Judah.
13 So when Ephraim found that he was
sick,
Judah that he was covered with sores,
Ephraim went to Assyria,
he went in haste to the Great King;
but he has no power to cure you
or to heal your sores.
14 Yes indeed, I will be fierce as a panther to
Ephraim,
fierce as a lion to Judah—
I will maul the prey and go,
carry it off beyond hope of rescue—I, the
LORD.
15 I will go away and return to my place
until in their horror they seek me,
and look earnestly for me in their distress.

Call to repentance

6 Come, let us return to the LORD;
for he has torn us and will heal us,
he has struck us and he will bind up our
wounds;
2 after two days he will revive us,
on the third day he will restore us,
that in his presence we may live.
3 Let us humble ourselves, let us strive to know
the LORD,
whose justice dawns like morning light,[t]
and its dawning is as sure as the sunrise.
It will come to us like a shower,
like spring rains that water the earth.

Loyalty, not sacrifice

4 O Ephraim, how shall I deal with you?
How shall I deal with you, Judah?
Your loyalty to me is like the morning
mist,
like dew that vanishes early.

Therefore have I lashed you through the 5
prophets
and torn you[u] to shreds with my words;
loyalty is my desire, not sacrifice, 6
not whole-offerings but the knowledge of
God.

Corruption of Ephraim

At Admah[v] they have broken my covenant, 7
there they have played me false.
Gilead is a haunt of evildoers, 8
marked by a trail of blood;
like robbers lying in wait for a man, 9
priests are banded together
to do murder on the road to Shechem;
their deeds are outrageous.
At Israel's sanctuary I have seen a horrible 10
thing:
there Ephraim played the wanton
and Israel defiled himself.
And for you, too, Judah, comes a harvest 11
of reckoning.

When I would reverse the fortunes of my
people,
when I would heal Israel, **7**
then the guilt of Ephraim stands revealed,
and all the wickedness of Samaria;
they have not kept faith.
They are thieves, they break into houses;[w]
they are robbers, they strip people in the
street,
little thinking that I have their wickedness 2
ever in mind.
Now their misdeeds beset them
and stare me in the face.
They win over the king with their wicked- 3
ness
and princes with their treachery,
lecherous all of them, hot as an oven over 4
the fire
which the baker does not stir
after kneading the dough until it is proved.
On their king's festal day the officers 5
begin to be inflamed with wine,
and he joins in the orgies of arrogant men;
for their hearts are heated by it[x] like an oven. 6
While they are relaxed all night long
their passion slumbers,
but in the morning it flares up
like a blazing fire;
they all grow feverish, hot as an oven, 7
and devour their rulers.
King after king falls from power,
but not one of them calls upon me.
Ephraim and his aliens make a sorry mixture; 8
Ephraim has become a cake half-baked.
Foreigners fed on his strength, 9
but he was unaware;
even his grey hairs turned white,
but he was unaware.

---

t Line transposed from end of verse 5.   u Prob. rdg.; Heb. them.   v At Admah: prob. rdg.; Heb.
Like Adam.   w houses: prob. rdg.; Heb. om.
x are heated by it: prob. rdg.; Heb. draw near.

10 So Israel's arrogance cries out against
them;
but they do not return to the LORD their
God
nor seek him, in spite of it all.
11 Ephraim is a silly senseless pigeon,
now calling upon Egypt, now turning to
Assyria for help.
12 Wherever they turn, I will cast my net over
them
and will bring them down like birds on the
wing;
I will take them captive as soon as I hear
them flocking.
13 Woe betide them, for they have strayed from
me!
May disaster befall them for rebelling against
me!
I long to deliver them,
but they tell lies about me.
14 There is no sincerity in their cry to me;
for all their howling on their pallets
and gashing of themselves over corn and
new wine,
they are turning away from me.
15 Though I support them, though I give them
strength of arm,
they plot evil against me.
16 Like a bow gone slack,
they relapse into the worship of their high
god;*y*
their talk is all lies,*z*
and so their princes shall fall by the sword.

Israel sows the wind

8 Put the trumpet to your lips!
A*a* vulture hovers over the sanctuary of
the LORD:
they have broken my covenant
and rebelled against my instruction.
2 They cry to me for help:
'We know thee, God of Israel.'*b*
3 But Israel is utterly loathsome;
and therefore he shall run before the
enemy.
4 They make kings, but not by my will;
they set up officers, but without my
knowledge;
they have made themselves idols of their
silver and gold.*c*
5 Your calf-gods stink, O Samaria;
my anger flares up against them.
Long will it be before they prove innocent.
6 For what sort of a god is this bull?
It is no god,
a craftsman made it;
the calf of Samaria will be broken in
fragments.

Israel sows the wind and reaps the whirl- 7
wind;
there are no heads on the standing corn, it
yields no grain;
and, if it yielded any, strangers would
swallow it up.
Israel is now swallowed up, 8
lost among the nations,
a worthless nothing.
For, like a wild ass that has left the herd, 9
they have run to Assyria.
Ephraim has bargained for lovers;
and, because they have bargained among 10
the nations,
I will now round them up,
and then they will soon abandon
this setting up of kings and princes.
For Ephraim in his sin has multiplied 11
altars,
altars have become his sin.
Though I give him countless rules in 12
writing,
they are treated as invalid.
Though they sacrifice flesh as offerings to me 13
and eat them,
I,*d* the LORD, will not accept them.
Their guilt will be remembered
and their sins punished.
They shall go back to Egypt,
or in Assyria they shall eat unclean food.

Israel has forgotten his Maker 14
and built palaces,
Judah has multiplied walled cities;
but I will set fire to his cities,
and it shall devour his castles.

Days of punishment

Do not rejoice, Israel, do not exult like other 9
peoples;
for like a wanton you have forsaken your
God,
you have loved an idol*e*
on every threshing-floor heaped with corn.
Threshing-floor and winepress shall know 2
them no more,
new wine shall disown*f* them.
They shall not dwell in the LORD's land; 3
Ephraim shall go back to Egypt,
or in Assyria they shall eat unclean food.
They shall pour out no wine to the LORD, 4
they shall not bring their sacrifices to him;
that would be mourners' fare for them,
and all who ate it would be polluted.
For their food shall only stay their hunger;
it shall not be offered in the house of the
LORD.
What will you do for the festal day, 5
the day of the LORD's pilgrim-feast?

---

y they relapse . . . god: *prob. rdg.; Heb. obscure.*
in Egypt.   *a Prob. rdg.; Heb.* Like a.   *z Prob. rdg.; Heb. adds* that is their stammering speech
Israel.   *c Prob. rdg.; Heb. adds* so that he may be cut off.   *b* We . . . Israel: *prob. rdg.; Heb.* O my God, we know thee,
or a harlot's fee.   *f Or* fail.   *d Prob. rdg.; Heb.* he.   *e* an idol:

6 For look, they have fled from a scene of
   devastation:
   Egypt shall receive them,
   Memphis shall be their grave;
   the sands of Syrtes shall wreck them,
   weeds shall inherit their land,
   thorns shall grow in their dwellings.
7 The days of punishment are come,
   the days of vengeance are come
   when Israel shall be humbled.
   Then the prophet shall be made a fool
   and the inspired seer a madman
   by your great guilt.
8 With great enmity Ephraim lies in wait for
   God's people
   while the prophet is a fowler's trap by all
   their paths,
   a snare in the very temple of God.
9 They lead them deep into sin as at the time
   of Gibeah.
   Their guilt will be remembered and their sins
   punished.

Israel rejected by God

10 I came upon Israel like grapes in the wilderness,
   I looked on their forefathers
   with joy like the first ripe figs;
   but they resorted to Baal-peor
   and consecrated themselves to a thing of
   shame,
1 and Ephraim became as loathsome as the
   thing he loved.

Their honour shall fly away like a bird:
no childbirth, no fruitful womb, no con-
   ceiving;
2 even if they rear their children,
   I will make them childless, without posterity.
Woe to them indeed when I turn away from
   them!
3 As lion-cubs emerge only to be hunted,[g]
so must Ephraim bring out his children for
   slaughter.

Give them, O LORD—what wilt thou give 14
them?
Give them a womb that miscarries and dry
breasts.

All their wickedness was seen at Gilgal; there 15
did I hate them.
For their evil deeds I will drive them from my
house,
I will love them no more: all their princes
are in revolt.
Ephraim is struck down: 16
their root is withered, and they yield no
fruit;
if ever they give birth,
I will slay the dearest offspring of their
womb.

My God shall reject them, 17
because they have not listened to him,
and they shall become wanderers among
the nations.

God's judgement on Israel

Israel is like a rank vine **10**
ripening its fruit:
his fruit grows more and more, and more
and more his altars;
the fairer his land becomes, the fairer he
makes his sacred pillars.
They are crazy now, they are mad. 2
God himself will hack down their altars
and wreck their sacred pillars.
Well may they say, 'We have no king, 3
for we do not fear the LORD;
and what can the king do for us?'
There is nothing but talk, 4
imposing of oaths and making of treaties, all
to no purpose;
and litigation spreads like a poisonous
weed
along the furrows of the fields.
The inhabitants of Samaria tremble for the 5
calf-god of Beth-aven;
the people mourn over it[h] and its priestlings
howl,
distressed for their image, their glory,
which is carried away into exile.
It shall be carried to Assyria 6
as tribute to the Great King;
disgrace shall overtake Ephraim
and Israel shall feel the shame of their
disobedience.
Samaria and her king are swept away 7
like flotsam on the water;
the hill-shrines of Aven are wiped out, 8
the shrines where Israel sinned;
thorns and thistles grow over her altars.
So they will say to the mountains, 'Cover
us',
and to the hills, 'Fall on us.'

g As lion-cubs . . . hunted: *prob. rdg.; Heb. unintelligible.*
and his people mourn.

h the people mourn over it: *or* the high god

It is time to seek the LORD

9 Since the day of Gibeah Israel has sinned;
  there they took their stand in rebellion.
  Shall not war overtake them in Gibeah?
10 I have come against the rebels to chastise
  them,
  and the peoples shall mass against them
  in hordes for their two deeds of shame.
11 Ephraim is like a heifer broken in,
  which loves to thresh corn,
  across whose fair neck I have laid a yoke;[i]
  I have harnessed Ephraim to the pole that
  he[j] may plough,
  that Jacob may harrow his land.
12 Sow for yourselves in justice,
  and you will reap what loyalty deserves.
  Break up your fallow;
  for it is time to seek the LORD,
  seeking him till he comes and gives you just
  measure of rain.
13 You have ploughed wickedness into your
  soil,
  and the crop is mischief;
  you have eaten the fruit of treachery.

Destruction of Bethel

  Because you have trusted in your chariots,
  in the number of your warriors,
14 the tumult of war shall arise against your
  people,
  and all your fortresses shall be razed
  as Shalman razed Beth-arbel in the day of
  battle,
  dashing the mother to the ground with her
  babes.
15 So it shall be done to you, Bethel,
  because of your evil scheming;
  as sure as day dawns, the king of Israel shall
  be swept away.

God's love for Israel

11 When Israel was a boy, I loved him;
  I called my son out of Egypt;
2 but the more I called, the further they went
  from me;
  they must needs sacrifice to the Baalim
  and burn offerings before carved images.
3 It was I who taught Ephraim to walk,
  I who had taken them in my arms;
4 but they did not know that I harnessed them
  in leading-strings[k]
  and led them with bonds of love[l] —
  that I had lifted them like a little child[m] to
  my cheek,
  that I had bent down to feed them.
5 Back they shall go to Egypt,
  the Assyrian shall be their king;
  for they have refused to return to me.

The sword shall be swung over their blood- 6
  spattered altars
and put an end to their prattling priests
and devour my people in return for all their 7
  schemings,
bent on rebellion as they are.
Though they call on their high god,
even then he will not reinstate them.
How can I give you up, Ephraim, 8
how surrender you, Israel?
How can I make you like Admah
or treat you as Zeboyim?
My heart is changed within me,
my remorse kindles already.
I will not let loose my fury, 9
I will not turn round and destroy Ephraim;
for I am God and not a man,
the Holy One in your midst;
I will not come with threats[n] like a roaring 10
  lion.
No; when I roar, I who am God,
my sons shall come with speed out of the
  west.
They will come speedily, flying like birds 11
  out of Egypt,
like pigeons from Assyria,
and I will settle them in their own homes.
This is the very word of the LORD.
Ephraim besets me with treachery, 12
the house of Israel besets me with deceit;
and Judah is still restive under God,
still loyal to the idols he counts holy.
Ephraim is a shepherd whose flock is but[o] 13
  wind,
a hunter chasing the east wind all day;[p]
he makes a treaty with Assyria
and carries tribute of oil to Egypt.

Israel's past misdeeds

The LORD has a charge to bring against 2
  Judah
and is resolved to punish Jacob for his conduct;
he will requite him for his misdeeds.
Even in the womb Jacob overreached his 3
  brother,
and in manhood he strove with God.
The divine angel stood firm and held his 4
  own;[q]
Jacob wept and begged favour for himself.
Then God met him at Bethel
and there spoke with him.
The LORD the God of Hosts, the LORD is his 5
  name.

Turn back all of you by God's help; 6
practise loyalty and justice
and wait always upon your God.

---

i a yoke: *prob. rdg.*; *Heb. om.*   *j* he: *prob. rdg.*; *Heb.* Judah.   *k* leading-strings: *or* cords of leather.
l bonds of love: *or* reins of hide.   *m* I had ... child: *prob. rdg.*; *Heb.* like those who lift up a yoke.
n *Prob. rdg.*; *Heb.* adds they shall go after the LORD.   *o* is a ... but: *or* feeds on.   *p* *Prob. rdg.*; *Heb.*
adds piling up treachery and havoc.   *q* The divine ... own: *or* He stood firm against an angel, but flagged.

7 False scales are in merchants' hands,
and they love to cheat;
8 so Ephraim says,
'Surely I have become a rich man, I have
made my fortune';
but all his gains will not pay
for the guilt*r* of his sins.
9 Yet I have been the LORD your God since
your days in Egypt;
I will make you live in tents yet again, as in
the old days.

10 I spoke to the prophets,
it was I who gave vision after vision;
I spoke through the prophets in parables.
11 Was there idolatry in Gilead?
Yes: they were worthless
and sacrificed to bull-gods in Gilgal;
their altars were common as heaps of stones
beside a ploughed field.

12 Jacob fled to the land of Aram;
Israel did service to win a wife,
to win a wife he tended sheep.

13 By a prophet the LORD brought up Israel
out of Egypt
and by a prophet he was tended.

14 Ephraim has given bitter provocation;
therefore his Lord will make him answerable
for his own death
and bring down upon his own head the
blame
for all that he has done.

3 When the Ephraimites mumbled their
prayers,
God himself denounced Israel;
they were guilty of Baal-worship and died.
2 Yet now they sin more and more;
they have made themselves an image of
cast metal,
they have fashioned their silver into idols,
nothing but the work of craftsmen;
men say of them,
'Those who kiss calf-images offer human
sacrifice.'

God's care for Israel

3 Therefore they shall be like the morning
mist
or like dew that vanishes early,
like chaff blown from the threshing-floor
or smoke from a chimney.
4 But I have been the LORD your God since
your days in Egypt,
when you knew no other saviour than me,
no god but me.
5 I cared for you in the wilderness,
6 in a land of burning heat, as if you were in
pasture.

So they were filled,
and, being filled, grew proud;
and so they forgot me.
So now I will be like a panther to them, 7
I will prowl like a leopard by the wayside;
I will meet them like a she-bear robbed of 8
her cubs
and tear their ribs apart,
like a lioness I will devour them on the
spot,
I will rip them up like a wild beast.
I have destroyed you, O Israel; who is there 9
to help you?
Where now is your king that he may save 10
you,
or the rulers in all your cities
for whom you asked me,
begging for king and princes?
I gave you a king in my anger, 11
and in my fury took him away.

Judgement on Ephraim

Ephraim's guilt is tied up in a scroll, 12
his sins are kept on record.
When the pangs of his birth came over his 13
mother,
he showed himself a senseless child;
for at the proper time he could not present
himself
at the mouth of the womb.
Shall I redeem him from Sheol? 14
Shall I ransom him from death?
Oh, for your plagues, O death! Oh, for your
sting, Sheol!
I will put compassion out of my sight.
Though he flourishes among the reeds,*s* 15
an east wind shall come, a blast from the
LORD,
rising over the desert;
Ephraim's spring will fail and his fountain
run dry.
It will carry away as spoil
his whole store of costly treasures.
Samaria will become desolate because she 16
has rebelled against her God;
her babes will fall by the sword and be dashed
to the ground,
her women with child shall be ripped up.

Repentance and restoration

Return, O Israel, to the LORD your God; **14**
for you have stumbled in your evil
courses.
Come with your words ready, 2
come back to the LORD;
say to him, 'Thou dost not endure iniquity.'*t*
Accept our plea,
and we will pay our vows with cattle from
our pens.

r for the guilt: *prob. rdg.; Heb.* for me, guilt.
s among the reeds: *prob. rdg.; Heb.* between (*or* a son of)
brothers. *t* Thou ... iniquity: *or* Thou wilt surely take away iniquity.

3 Assyria shall not save us, nor will we seek
    horses to ride;
  what we have made with our own hands
  we will never again call gods;
  for in thee the fatherless find a father's love.'

4 I will heal their apostasy; of my own bounty
    will I love them;
  for my anger is turned away from them.
5 I will be as dew to Israel
  that he may flower like the lily,
  strike root like the poplar*u*
6   and put out fresh shoots,
  that he may be as fair as the olive
  and fragrant as Lebanon.

Israel shall again dwell in my*v* shadow   7
  and grow corn in abundance;
  they shall flourish like a vine
  and be famous as the wine of Lebanon.
What has Ephraim any more to do with   8
  idols?
  I have spoken and I affirm it:
  I am the pine-tree that shelters you;
  to me you owe your fruit.

Let the wise consider these things and let   9
him who considers take note; for the LORD's
ways are straight and the righteous walk in
them, while sinners stumble.

JOEL

1 The word of the LORD which came to Joel
son of Pethuel.

A mighty horde

2   Listen, you elders;
  hear me, all you who live in the land:
  has the like of this happened in all your
    days
  or in your fathers' days?
3 Tell it to your sons and they may tell theirs;
  let them pass it on from generation to
    generation.

What the locust has left the swarm eats,   4
what the swarm has left the hopper eats,
and what the hopper has left the grub eats.
Wake up, you drunkards, and lament your   5
  fate;
mourn for the fresh wine, all you wine-
  drinkers,
  because it is lost to you.
For a horde has overrun my land,   6
  mighty and past counting;
  their teeth are a lion's teeth;
  they have the fangs of a lioness.

u Prob. rdg.; Heb. like Lebanon.   *v Prob. rdg.; Heb.* its.

7   They have ruined my vines
    and left my fig-trees broken and leafless,
    they have plucked them bare
    and stripped them of their bark;
    they have left the branches white.

Cry to the LORD

8   Wail like a virgin wife in sackcloth,
    wailing over the bridegroom of her youth:
9   the drink-offering and grain-offering are
        lost
    to the house of the LORD.
    Mourn, you priests, ministers of the LORD,
10 the fields are ruined, the parched earth
        mourns;
    for the corn is ruined, the new wine is
        desperate,
    the oil has failed.
11 Despair, you husbandmen; you vinedressers,
        lament,
    because the wheat and the barley,
    the harvest of the field, is lost.
12 The vintage is desperate, and the fig-tree has
        failed;
    pomegranate, palm, and apple,
    all the trees of the country-side are
        parched,
    and none make merry over harvest.

13 Priests, put on sackcloth and beat your
        breasts;
    lament, you ministers of the altar;
    come, lie in sackcloth all night long, you
        ministers of my God;
    for grain-offering and drink-offering
    are withheld from the house of your God.
14 Proclaim a solemn fast, appoint a day of
        abstinence.
    You elders, summon all that live in the land
    to come together in the house of your God,
    and cry to the LORD:
15 Alas! the day is near,
    the day of the LORD: it comes,
    a mighty destruction from the Almighty.
16 Look! it stares us in the face;
    the house of our God has lost its food,
    lost all its joy and gladness.
17 The soil is parched,
    the dykes are dry,
    the granaries are deserted,
    the barns ruinous;
    for the rains have failed.
18 The cattle are exhausted,
    the herds of oxen distressed
    because they have no pasture;
    the flocks of sheep waste away.
19 To thee I cry, O LORD;
    for fire has devoured the open pastures
    and the flames have burnt up all the trees of
        the country-side.
20 The very cattle in the field look up to thee;
    for the water-channels are dried up,
    and fire has devoured the open pastures.

Call to repentance

    Blow the trumpet in Zion,   2
    sound the alarm upon my holy hill;
    let all that live in the land tremble,
    for the day of the LORD has come,
    surely a day of darkness and gloom is 2
        upon us,
    a day of cloud and dense fog;
    like a blackness spread over the moun-
        tains
    a mighty, countless host appears;
    their like has never been known,
    nor ever shall be in ages to come;
    their vanguard a devouring fire,   3
    their rearguard leaping flame;
    before them the land is a garden of Eden,
    behind them a wasted wilderness;
    nothing survives their march.
    On they come, like squadrons of horse,   4
    like war-horses they charge;
    bounding over the peaks they advance with 5
        the rattle of chariots,
    like flames of fire burning up the stubble,
    like a countless host in battle array.
    Before them nations tremble,   6
    every face turns pale.
    Like warriors they charge,   7
    they mount the walls like men at arms,
    each marching in line,
    no confusion in the ranks,
    none jostling his neighbour,   8
    none breaking line.

They plunge through streams without halting their advance;
9 they burst into the city, leap on to the wall,
　climb into the houses,
　entering like thieves through the windows.
10 Before them the earth shakes,
　the heavens shudder,
　sun and moon are darkened,
　and the stars forbear to shine.
11 The LORD thunders before his host;
　his is a mighty army,
　countless are those who do his bidding.
Great is the day of the LORD and terrible,
　who can endure it?
12 And yet, the LORD says, even now
　turn back to me with your whole heart,
　fast, and weep, and beat your breasts.
13 Rend your hearts and not your garments;
　turn back to the LORD your God;
　for he is gracious and compassionate,
　long-suffering and ever constant,
　always ready to repent of the threatened evil.
14 It may be he will turn back and repent
　and leave a blessing behind him,
　blessing enough for grain-offering and drink-offering
　for the LORD your God.

15 Blow the trumpet in Zion,
　proclaim a solemn fast, appoint a day of abstinence;
16 gather the people together, proclaim a solemn assembly;
　summon the elders,
　gather the children, yes, babes at the breast;
　bid the bridegroom leave his chamber
　and the bride her bower.
17 Let the priests, the ministers of the LORD,
　stand weeping between the porch and the altar
　and say, 'Spare thy people, O LORD, thy own people,
　expose them not to reproach,
　lest other nations make them a byword
　and everywhere men ask,
　"Where is their God?"'

Israel forgiven and restored

18 Then the LORD's love burned with zeal for his land,
　and he was moved with compassion for his people.
19 He answered their appeal and said,
　I will send you corn, and new wine, and oil,
　and you shall have your fill;
　I will expose you no longer
　to the reproach of other nations.

I will remove the northern peril far away 20 from you
and banish them into a land parched and waste,
　their vanguard into the eastern sea
　and their rear into the western,
and the stench shall rise from their rotting corpses
because of their proud deeds!
Earth, be not afraid, rejoice and be glad; 21
　for the LORD himself has done a proud deed.
Be not afraid, you cattle in the field; 22
　for the pastures shall be green,
　the trees shall bear fruit,
the fig and the vine yield their harvest.
O people of Zion, 23
　rejoice and be glad in the LORD your God,
who gives you good food in due measure[a]
　and sends down rain[b] as of old.
The threshing-floors shall be heaped with 24 grain,
the vats shall overflow with new wine and oil.
So I will make good the years 25
　that the swarm has eaten,
　hopper and grub and locust,
my great army which I sent against you;
　and you shall eat, you shall eat your fill 26
　and praise the name of the LORD your God
who has done wonders for you,[c]
and you shall know that I am present in 27 Israel,
that I and no other am the LORD your God;
　and my people shall not again be brought to shame.
Thereafter the day shall come 28
　when I will pour out my spirit on all mankind;
　your sons and your daughters shall prophesy,
　your old men shall dream dreams
　and your young men see visions;
I will pour out my spirit in those days 29
　even upon slaves and slave-girls.
I will show portents in the sky and on earth, 30
　blood and fire and columns of smoke;
　the sun shall be turned into darkness 31
　and the moon into blood
before the great and terrible day of the LORD comes.
Then everyone who invokes the LORD by 32 name
　shall be saved:
　for when the LORD gives the word
　there shall yet be survivors on Mount Zion
　and in Jerusalem a remnant[d]
　whom the LORD will call.[e]

---

a Or gives you a sign pointing to prosperity.　　b Prob. rdg.; Heb. adds spring rain and autumn rain.
c Prob. rdg.; Heb. adds and my people shall not again be brought to shame (cp. verse 27).　　d a remnant:
prob. rdg.; Heb. among the remnant.　　e Or when the LORD calls.

3 When that time comes, on that day
when I reverse the fortunes of Judah and
    Jerusalem,
2 I will gather all the nations together
and lead them down to the Valley of the
    LORD'S Judgement
and there bring them to judgement
on behalf of Israel, my own possession;
for they have scattered my people
throughout their own countries,
have taken each their portion of my land
3 and shared out my people by lot,
bartered a boy for a whore,
and sold a girl for wine and drunk it down.

Tyre, Sidon and Philistia

4 What are you to me, Tyre and Sidon and all
the districts of Philistia? Can you pay me
back for anything I have done? Is there anything that you can do to me? Swiftly and
speedily I will make your deeds recoil upon
5 your own heads; for you have taken my silver
and my gold and carried off my costly trea-
6 sures into your temples; you have sold the
people of Judah and Jerusalem to the Greeks,
and removed them far beyond their own fron-
7 tiers. But I will rouse them to leave the places
to which you have sold them. I will make your
8 deeds recoil upon your own heads: I will sell
your sons and your daughters to the people
of Judah, and they shall sell them to the
Sabaeans, a nation far away. The LORD has
spoken.

In the Valley of Decision

12 *f* Proclaim this amongst the nations:
Declare a holy war, call your troops to arms!
    Beat your mattocks into swords
    and your pruning-hooks into spears.*g*
Rally to each other's help, all you nations
    round about.
Let the weakling say, 'I am strong',
    and let the coward show himself brave.*h*
Let all the nations hear the call to arms
    and come to the Valley of the LORD'S
    Judgement;

let all the warriors come and draw near
    and muster there;
for there I will take my seat
    and judge all the nations round about.

Ply the sickle, for the harvest is ripe;   13
    come, tread the grapes,
for the press is full and the vats overflow;
    great is the wickedness of the nations.
The roar of multitudes, multitudes, in the   14
    Valley of Decision!
The day of the LORD is at hand
    in the Valley of Decision;
sun and moon are darkened   15
    and the stars forbear to shine.
The LORD roars from Zion   16
    and thunders from Jerusalem;
heaven and earth shudder,
    but the LORD is a refuge for his people
    and the defence of Israel.

When the LORD dwells in Zion

Thus you shall know that I am the LORD 17
    your God,
    dwelling in Zion my holy mountain;
    Jerusalem shall be holy,
and no one without the right shall pass
    through her again.
    When that day comes,   ` ˅   18
    the mountains shall run with fresh wine
    and the hills flow with milk.
All the streams of Judah shall be full of
    water,
    and a fountain shall spring from the
    LORD'S house
    and water the gorge of Shittim,
    but Egypt shall become a desert   19
    and Edom a deserted waste,
    because of the violence done to Judah
    and the innocent blood shed in her land;
    and I will spill their blood,   20-21
    the blood I have not yet spilt.
Then there shall be people living in Judah
    for ever,
in Jerusalem generation after generation;
and the LORD will dwell in Zion.

---

f The order of lines in verses 9–12 has been re-arranged in several places.   *g* Beat . . . spears: *cp. Isa. 2. 4;*
Mic. 4. 3.   *h* and let . . . brave: *prob. rdg.;* Heb. O LORD bring down thy warriors.

AMOS

(Amos. 7. 7)

1 THE WORDS OF AMOS, one of the sheep-farmers of Tekoa, which he received in visions concerning Israel during the reigns of Uzziah king of Judah and Jeroboam son of Jehoash king of Israel, two years before 2 the earthquake. He said,

> The LORD roars from Zion
> and thunders from Jerusalem;
> the shepherds' pastures are scorched
> and the top of Carmel[a] is dried up.

Damascus

3 These are the words of the LORD:

> For crime after crime of Damascus
> I will grant them no reprieve,
> because they threshed Gilead under
>   threshing-sledges spiked with iron.
4 Therefore will I send fire upon the
>   house of Hazael,
> fire that shall eat up Ben-hadad's palaces;
5 I will crush the great men of Damascus
> and wipe out those who live in the Vale of
>   Aven
> and the sceptred ruler of Beth-eden;
> the people of Aram shall be exiled to
>   Kir.
> It is the word of the LORD.

Gaza

6 These are the words of the LORD:

> For crime after crime of Gaza
> I will grant them no reprieve,

because they deported a whole band of exiles
and delivered them up to Edom.
Therefore will I send fire 7
    upon the walls of Gaza,
fire that shall consume its palaces.
I will wipe out those who live in Ash- 8
    dod
and the sceptred ruler of Ashkelon;
I will turn my hand against Ekron,
and the remnant of the Philistines shall perish.
It is the word of the Lord GOD.

Tyre

These are the words of the LORD: 9

> For crime after crime of Tyre
> I will grant them no reprieve,
> because, forgetting the ties of kinship,
> they delivered a whole band of exiles to
>   Edom.
> Therefore will I send fire upon the walls 10
>   of Tyre,
> fire that shall consume its palaces.

Edom

These are the words of the LORD: 11

> For crime after crime of Edom
> I will grant them no reprieve,
> because, sword in hand, they hunted their
>   kinsmen down,
> stifling their natural affections.
> Their anger raged unceasing,
> their fury stormed unchecked.
> Therefore will I send fire upon Teman, 12
> fire that shall consume the palaces of
>   Bozrah.

Ammon

These are the words of the LORD: 13

> For crime after crime of the Ammonites
> I will grant them no reprieve,
> because in their greed for land
> they invaded the ploughlands of Gilead.
> Therefore will I set fire to the walls of 14
>   Rabbah,
> fire that shall consume its palaces
> amid war-cries on the day of battle,
> with a whirlwind on the day of tempest;
> then their king shall be carried into 15
>   exile,
> he and his officers with him.
> It is the word of the LORD.

---

a top of Carmel: *or* choicest farmland.

MOAB

Moab

2 These are the words of the LORD:

For crime after crime of Moab
I will grant them no reprieve,
because they burnt the bones of the king of
Edom to ash.[b]

2 Therefore will I send fire upon Moab,
fire that shall consume the palaces in their
towns;
Moab shall perish in uproar,
with war-cries and the sound of trumpets,

3 and I will cut off the ruler from among
them
and kill all their officers with him.
It is the word of the LORD.

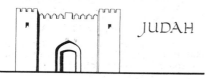

JUDAH

Judah

4 These are the words of the LORD:

For crime after crime of Judah
I will grant them no reprieve,
because they have spurned the law of the
LORD
and have not observed his decrees,
and have been led astray by the false gods
that their fathers followed.

5 Therefore will I send fire upon Judah,
fire that shall consume the palaces of
Jerusalem.

ISRAEL

Israel

6 These are the words of the LORD:

For crime after crime of Israel
I will grant them no reprieve,
because they sell the innocent for silver
and the destitute for a pair of shoes.

They grind the heads of the poor into the 7
earth
and thrust the humble out of their way.
Father and son resort to the same girl,
to the profanation of my holy name.
Men lie down beside every altar 8
on garments seized in pledge,
and in the house of their God[c] they drink
liquor
got by way of fines.

Israel's ingratitude

Yet it was I who destroyed the Amorites 9
before them,
though they were tall as cedars,
though they were sturdy as oaks,
I who destroyed their fruit above
and their roots below.
It was I who brought you up from the land 10
of Egypt,
I who led you in the wilderness forty years,
to take possession of the land of the
Amorites;
I raised up prophets from your sons, 11
Nazirites from your young men.
Was it not so indeed, you men of Israel?
says the LORD.
But you made the Nazirites drink wine, 12
and said to the prophets, 'You shall not
prophesy.'
Listen, I groan under the burden of you, 13
as a wagon creaks under a full load.
Flight shall not save the swift, 14
the strong man shall not rally his strength.
The warrior shall not save himself,
the archer shall not stand his ground; 15
the swift of foot shall not be saved,
nor the horseman escape;
on that day the bravest of warriors 16
shall be stripped of his arms and run away.
This is the very word of the LORD.

The LORD's care for Israel

Listen, Israelites, to these words that the **3**
LORD addresses to you, to the whole nation
which he brought up from Egypt:

For you alone have I cared 2
among all the nations of the world;
therefore will I punish you
for all your iniquities.
Do two men travel together 3
unless they have agreed?
Does a lion roar in the forest 4
if he has no prey?
Does a young lion growl in his den
if he has caught nothing?
Does a bird fall into a trap on the ground 5
if the striker is not set for it?
Does a trap spring from the ground
and take nothing?
If a trumpet sounds the alarm, 6
are not the people scared?

b to ash: *or* for lime.   *c Or* gods.

If disaster falls on a city,
has not the LORD been at work?[d]

7 For the Lord GOD does nothing
without giving to his servants the prophets
knowledge of his plans.

8 The lion has roared; who is not terrified?
The Lord GOD has spoken; who will not
prophesy?

Overthrow of Samaria

9 Stand upon the palaces in Ashdod
and upon the palaces of Egypt,
and proclaim aloud:
'Assemble on the hills of Samaria,
look at the tumult seething among her people
and at the oppression in her midst;
10 what do they care for honesty
who hoard in their palaces the gains of crime
and violence?'
This is the very word of the LORD.

11 Therefore these are the words of the Lord
GOD:
An enemy shall surround[e] the land;
your stronghold shall be thrown down
and your palaces sacked.

A remnant saved

12 These are the words of the LORD:
As a shepherd rescues out of the jaws of a
lion
two shin bones or the tip of an ear,
so shall the Israelites who live in Samaria be
rescued
like a corner of a couch or a chip from the leg
of a bed.[f]
13 Listen and testify against the family of
Jacob.
This is the very word of the Lord GOD, the
God of Hosts.

Israel's empty religion

14 On the day when I deal with Israel
for all their crimes,
I will most surely deal with the altars of
Bethel:
the horns of the altar shall be hacked off
and shall fall to the ground.
15 I will break down both winter-house and
summer-house;
houses of ivory shall perish,
and great houses be demolished.
This is the very word of the LORD.

4 Listen to this,
you cows of Bashan who live on the hill of
Samaria,
you who oppress the poor and crush the
destitute,
who say to your lords, 'Bring us drink':

the Lord GOD has sworn by his holiness   2
that your time is coming
when men shall carry you away on their
shields[g]
and your children in fish-baskets.
You shall each be carried straight out   3
through the breaches in the walls
and pitched on a dunghill.[h]
This is the very word of the LORD.

Come to Bethel—and rebel!   4
Come to Gilgal—and rebel the more!
Bring your sacrifices for the morning,
your tithes within three days.
Burn your thank-offering without leaven;   5
announce, proclaim your freewill offerings;
for you love to do what is proper, you men
of Israel!
This is the very word of the Lord GOD.

Failure to heed correction

It was I who kept teeth idle   6
in all your cities,
who brought famine on all your settlements;
yet you did not come back to me.
This is the very word of the LORD.

It was I who withheld the showers from you   7
while there were still three months to harvest.
I would send rain on one city
and no rain on another;
rain would fall on one field,
and another would be parched for lack of it.
From this city and that, men would stagger   8
to another
for water to drink, but would not find
enough;
yet you did not come back to me.
This is the very word of the LORD.

I blasted you with black blight and red;   9
I laid waste[i] your gardens and vineyards;
the locust devoured your fig-trees and your
olives;
yet you did not come back to me.
This is the very word of the LORD.

I sent plague upon you like the plagues of   10
Egypt;
I killed with the sword
your young men and your troops of horses.
I made your camps stink in your nostrils;
yet you did not come back to me.
This is the very word of the LORD.

I brought destruction amongst you   11
as God destroyed Sodom and Gomorrah;
you were like a brand snatched from the fire;
yet you did not come back to me.
This is the very word of the LORD.

---

d If disaster ... work?: *or* If there is evil in a city, will not the LORD act?   e shall surround: *prob. rdg.*;
Heb. and round.   f or a chip ... bed: *prob. rdg.*; *Heb.* obscure.   g *Or* baskets.   h a dunghill:
prob. rdg.; *Heb.* the Harmon.   i I laid waste: *prob. rdg.*; *Heb.* to increase.

12 Therefore, Israel, this is what I will do to you;
and, because this is what I will do to you,
    Israel, prepare to meet your God.
13 It is he who forges the thunder and creates
    the wind,
    who showers abundant rain on the earth,[j]
    who darkens the dawn with thick clouds
    and marches over the heights of the
    earth—
    his name is the LORD the God of Hosts.

Call to repentance

5 Listen to these words; I raise a dirge over
    you, O Israel:
2   She has fallen to rise no more,
    the virgin Israel,
    prostrate on her own soil, with no one to
    lift her up.

3 These are the words of the Lord GOD:
    The city that marched out to war a thou-
    sand strong
    shall have but a hundred left,
    that which marched out a hundred strong
    shall have but ten men of Israel left.

4 These are the words of the LORD to the
    people of Israel:
5 Resort to me, if you would live, not to Bethel;
    go not to Gilgal, nor pass on to Beersheba;
    for Gilgal shall be swept away
    and Bethel brought to nothing.
6 If you would live, resort to the LORD,
    or he will break out against Joseph like fire,
    fire which will devour Israel with no one
    to quench it;
8[k] he who made the Pleiades and Orion,
    who turned darkness into morning
    and darkened day into night,
    who summoned the waters of the sea
    and poured them over the earth,
9 who makes Taurus rise after Capella
    and Taurus set hard on the rising of the
    Vintager[l]—
    he who does this, his name is the LORD.[m]
7 You that turn justice upside down[n]
    and bring righteousness to the ground,
10 you that hate a man who brings the wrong-
    doer to court
    and loathe him who speaks the whole
    truth:
11 for all this, because you levy taxes on the
    poor
    and extort a tribute of grain from them,
    though you have built houses of hewn
    stone,
    you shall not live in them,
    though you have planted pleasant vine-
    yards,
    you shall not drink wine from them.

12 For I know how many your crimes are
    and how countless your sins,
    you who persecute the guiltless, hold men to
    ransom
    and thrust the destitute out of court.
13 At that time, therefore, a prudent man will
    stay quiet,
    for it will be an evil time.

14 Seek good and not evil,
    that you may live,
    that the LORD the God of Hosts may be
    firmly on your side,
    as you say he is.
15 Hate evil and love good;
    enthrone justice in the courts;
    it may be that the LORD the God of Hosts
    will be gracious to the survivors of Joseph.

A day of gloom

16 Therefore these are the words of the LORD
the God of Hosts:
    There shall be wailing in every street,
    and in all open places cries of woe.
    The farmer shall be called to mourning,
    and those skilled in the dirge to[o] wailing;
17 there shall be lamentation in every vine-
    yard;
    for I will pass through the midst of you,
    says the LORD.

18 Fools who long for the day of the LORD,
    what will the day of the LORD mean to you?
    It will be darkness, not light.
19 It will be as when a man runs from a lion,
    and a bear meets him,
    or turns into a house and leans his hand on
    the wall,
    and a snake bites him.
20 The day of the LORD is indeed darkness,
    not light,
    a day of gloom with no dawn.

God spurns Israel's sacrifices

21 I hate, I spurn your pilgrim-feasts;
    I will not delight in your sacred cere-
    monies.
22 When you present your sacrifices and offer-
    ings
    I will not accept them,
    nor look on the buffaloes of your shared-
    offerings.
23 Spare me the sound of your songs;
    I cannot endure the music of your lutes.
24 Let justice roll on like a river
    and righteousness like an ever-flowing
    stream.
25 Did you bring me sacrifices and gifts,
    you people of Israel, those forty years in the
    wilderness?

---

j who showers . . . earth: *prob. rdg.; Heb.* who tells his thoughts to mankind.   *k Verse 7 transposed to follow verse 9.*   *l* who makes . . . Vintager: *prob. rdg.; Heb.* who smiles destruction on the strong, and destruction comes on the fortified city.   *m* his . . . LORD: *transposed from end of verse 8.*   *n* upside down:
prob. rdg.; Heb. poison.   *o Prob. rdg.; Heb. places* to *before* those skilled.

26   No! but now you shall take up
     the shrine of your idol king
     and the pedestals of your images,[p]
     which you have made for yourselves,
27 and I will drive you into exile beyond
     Damascus.

   So says the LORD; the God of Hosts is his
   name.

Selfish indulgence of Zion's leaders

6   Shame on you who live at ease in Zion,
     and you, untroubled on the hill of Samaria,
     men of mark in the first of nations,
     you to whom the people of Israel resort!
2   Go, look at Calneh,
     travel on to Hamath the great,
     then go down to Gath of the Philistines—
     are you better than these kingdoms?
     Or is your[q] territory greater than theirs[r]?
3   You who thrust the evil day aside
     and make haste to establish violence.[s]
4   You who loll on beds inlaid with ivory
     and sprawl over your couches,
     feasting on lambs from the flock
     and fatted calves,
5   you who pluck the strings of the lute
   and invent musical instruments like David,
6   you who drink wine by the bowlful
     and lard yourselves with the richest of oils,
     but are not grieved at the ruin of Joseph—
7   now, therefore,
     you shall head the column of exiles;
     that will be the end of sprawling and
     revelry.

Judgement for arrogance

8 The Lord GOD has sworn by himself:

     I loathe the arrogance of Jacob,
     I loathe his palaces;
     city and all in it I will abandon to their
     fate.

9 If ten men are left in one house,
     they shall die,
10   and a man's uncle and the embalmer shall
     take him up
     to carry his body out of the house for
     burial,
   and they shall call to someone in a corner of
     the house,
   'Any more there?', and he shall answer, 'No.'
   Then he will add, 'Hush!'—
   for the name of the LORD must not be men-
     tioned.
11   For the LORD will command,
   and at the shock the great house will be
     rubble
   and the cottage matchwood.

   Can horses gallop over rocks?   12
   Can the sea be ploughed with oxen?
   Yet you have turned into venom the
     process of law
   and justice itself into poison,
   you who are jubilant over a nothing[t] and   13
     boast,
   'Have we not won power[t] by our own
     strength?'
   O Israel, I am raising a nation against you, 14
     and they shall harry your land
     from Lebo-hamath to the gorge of the
     Arabah.
   This is the very word of the LORD the God of
     Hosts.

Three visions

This was what the Lord GOD showed me: **7**
a swarm of locusts hatched out when the late
corn, which comes after the king's early crop,
was beginning to sprout. As they were de-   2
vouring the last of the herbage in the land,
I said, 'O Lord GOD, forgive; what will Jacob
be after this? He is so small.' Then the LORD 3
relented and said, 'This shall not happen.'

   This was what the Lord GOD showed me: 4
the Lord GOD was summoning a flame of
fire[u] to devour the great abyss, and to devour
all creation. I said, 'O Lord GOD, I pray thee, 5
cease; what will Jacob be after this? He is
so small.' The LORD relented and said, 'This 6
also shall not happen.'

   This was what the LORD showed me: there 7
was a man standing by a wall[v] with a plumb-
line in his hand. The LORD said to me, 'What 8
do you see, Amos?' 'A plumb-line', I
answered, and the Lord said, 'I am setting a
plumb-line to the heart of my people Israel;
never again will I pass them by. The hill- 9
shrines of Isaac shall be desolated and the
sanctuaries of Israel laid waste; I will rise,
sword in hand, against the house of Jeroboam.'

Amos and Amaziah

Amaziah, the priest of Bethel, reported to 10
Jeroboam king of Israel: 'Amos is conspiring
against you in Israel; the country cannot
tolerate what he is saying. He says, "Jero- 11
boam shall die by the sword, and Israel shall
be deported far from their native land." ' To 12
Amos himself Amaziah said, 'Be off, you
seer! Off with you to Judah! You can earn
your living and do your prophesying there.
But never prophesy again at Bethel, for this 13
is the king's sanctuary, a royal palace.' 'I am[w] 14
no prophet,' Amos replied to Amaziah, 'nor
am I a prophet's son; I am[w] a herdsman and

---

p Prob. rdg.; Heb. adds the star of your gods.   q Prob. rdg.; Heb. their.   r Prob. rdg.; Heb. yours.
s You . . . violence: or You who invoke the day of wrongdoing and bring near the sabbath of violence.
t a nothing and power: Heb. Lo-debar and Karnaim, making a word-play on the two place-names.   u a flame
of fire: prob. rdg.; Heb. to contend with fire.   v Prob. rdg.; Heb. adds of a plumb-line.   w Or was.

15 a dresser of sycomore-figs. But the LORD took me as I followed the flock and said to me, "Go and prophesy to my people Israel."
16 So now listen to the word of the LORD. You tell me I am not to prophesy against Israel or go drivelling on against the people of
17 Isaac. Now these are the words of the LORD: Your wife shall become a city strumpet[x] and your sons and daughters shall fall by the sword. Your land shall be divided up with a measuring-line, you yourself shall die in a heathen country, and Israel shall be deported far from their native land and go into exile.'

A basket of summer fruit

8 This was what the Lord GOD showed me:
2 there was a basket of summer fruit, and he said, 'What are you looking at, Amos?' I answered, 'A basket of ripe summer[y] fruit.' Then the LORD said to me, 'The time is ripe[y] for my people Israel. Never again
3 will I pass them by. In that day, says the Lord GOD, the singing women in the palace shall howl, "So many dead men, flung out everywhere! Silence!"'

Spiritual famine

4 Listen to this, you who grind the destitute
5 and plunder[z] the humble, you who say, 'When will the new moon be over so that we may sell corn? When will the sabbath be past so that we may open our wheat again, giving short measure in the bushel and taking overweight in the silver, tilting the scales
6 fraudulently, and selling the dust of the wheat; that we may buy the poor for silver
7 and the destitute for a pair of shoes?' The LORD has sworn by the pride of Jacob: I will never forget any of their doings.

8 Shall not the earth shake for this?
　　Shall not all who live on it grieve?
All earth shall surge and seethe like the Nile
　and subside like the river of Egypt.

9 On that day, says the Lord GOD,
　I will make the sun go down at noon
　and darken the earth in broad daylight.
10 I will turn your pilgrim-feasts into mourning
　and all your songs into lamentation.
　I will make you all put sackcloth round your waists
　and have all your heads shaved.
　I will make it like mourning for an only son
　and the end of it a bitter day.

11 The time is coming, says the Lord GOD,
　when I will send famine on the land,
　not hunger for bread or thirst for water,
　but for hearing the word of the LORD.

12 Men shall stagger from north to south,[a]
　they shall range from east to west,
　seeking the word of the LORD,
　but they shall not find it.
13 On that day fair maidens and young men
　shall faint from thirst;
14 all who take their oath by Ashimah, goddess of Samaria,
　all who swear, 'By the life of your god, O Dan',
　and, 'By the sacred way to Beersheba',
　shall fall to rise no more.

Judgement inescapable

9 I saw the LORD standing by the altar, and he said:
Strike the capitals so that the whole porch is shaken;
　I will smash them all into pieces[b]
　and I will kill them to the last man[c] with the sword.
　No fugitive shall escape,
　no survivor find safety;
2 if they dig down to Sheol,
　thence shall my hand take them;
　if they climb up to heaven,
　thence will I bring them down.
3 If they hide on the top of Carmel,
　there will I search out and take them;
if they conceal themselves from me in the depths of the sea,
there will I bid the sea-serpent bite them.
4 If they are herded into captivity by their enemies,
　there will I bid the sword slay them,
　and I will fix my eye on them
　for evil and not for good.

5 The Lord the GOD of Hosts,
　at whose touch the earth heaves,
　and all who dwell on it wither,[d]
　it surges like the Nile,
　and subsides like the river of Egypt,
6 who builds his stair up to the heavens
　and arches his ceiling over the earth,
　who summons the waters of the sea
　and pours them over the land—
　his name is the LORD.

7 Are not you Israelites like Cushites to me?
　says the LORD.
Did I not bring Israel up from Egypt,
　the Philistines from Caphtor, the Aramaeans from Kir?
8 Behold, I, the Lord GOD,
　have my eyes on this sinful kingdom,
　and I will wipe it off the face of the earth.

---

[x] become . . . strumpet: or be carried off as a prostitute in a raid.　　[y] ripe summer and ripe: a play on the Heb. qais (summer) and qes (end).　　[z] and plunder: prob. rdg.; Heb. to destroy.　　[a] south: prob. rdg.; Heb. west.　　[b] I will . . . pieces: prob. rdg.; Heb. I will hack them on the heads of them all.　　[c] them to the last man: or their children.　　[d] Or mourn.

A remnant restored

Yet I will not wipe out the family of Jacob
　　root and branch,
　says the LORD.
9　No; I will give my orders,
I will shake Israel to and fro through all the
　　nations
　as a sieve is shaken to and fro
　and not one pebble falls to the ground.
10　They shall die by the sword, all the sinners of
　　my people,
who say, 'Thou wilt not let disaster come
　　near us
　or overtake us.'
11　On that day I will restore
　David's fallen house;
I will repair its gaping walls and restore its
　　ruins;
　I will rebuild it as it was long ago,
12　that they may possess what is left of Edom
and all the nations who were once named
　　mine.

This is the very word of the LORD, who will
do this.

A time is coming, says the LORD,　　　　13
　when the ploughman shall follow hard on
　　the vintager,[e]
and he who treads the grapes after him who
　　sows the seed.
The mountains shall run with fresh
　　wine,
　and every hill shall wave with corn.
I will restore the fortunes of my people　14
　　Israel;
they shall rebuild deserted cities and live in
　　them,
they shall plant vineyards and drink their
　　wine,
make gardens and eat the fruit.
Once more I will plant them on their own　15
　　soil,
and they shall never again be uprooted
　from the soil I have given them.
It is the word of the LORD your God.

OBADIAH

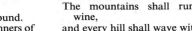

Edom's pride and downfall

1[a]　The vision of Obadiah: what the Lord GOD
　has said concerning Edom.

When a herald was sent out among the
　　nations, crying,
　'Rouse yourselves;
　let us rouse ourselves to battle against
　　Edom',
　I heard this message from the LORD:

2　Look, I make you the least of all nations,
　an object of contempt.
3　Your proud, insolent heart has led you
　　astray;
　you who haunt the crannies among the
　　rocks,
making your home on the heights,
　you say to yourself, 'Who can bring me to
　　the ground?'
4　Though you soar as high as a vulture
　and your nest is set among the stars,
　thence I will bring you down.
　This is the very word of the LORD.

5[b]　If thieves or robbers come to you by night,
　though your loss be heavy,
　they will steal only what they want;

e Or reaper.

a Verses 1–4: cp. Jer. 49. 14–16.　　*b Verses 5 and 6: cp. Jer. 49. 9, 10.*

if vintagers come to you,
will they not leave gleanings?

6 But see how Esau's treasure is ransacked,
his secret wealth hunted out!

7 All your former allies march you to the
frontier,
your confederates mislead you and bring you
low,
your own kith and kin lay a snare for your
feet,
a snare that works blindly, without wisdom.

8 And on that very day
I will destroy all the sages of Edom
and leave no wisdom on the mount of
Esau.
This is the very word of the LORD.

9 Then shall your warriors, O Teman, be so
enfeebled,
that every man shall be cut down on the
mount of Esau.

10 For the murderous violence done to your
brother Jacob
you shall be covered with shame and cut off
for ever.

11 On the day when you stood aloof,
on the day when strangers carried off his
wealth,
when foreigners trooped in by his gates
and parcelled out Jerusalem by lot,
you yourselves were of one mind with
them.

12 Do not gloat over your brother on the day
of his misfortune,
nor rejoice over Judah on his day of
ruin;
do not boast on the day of distress,

13 nor enter my people's gates on the day of
his downfall.
Do not gloat over his fall on the day of his
downfall
nor seize his treasure on the day of his downfall.

Do not wait at the cross-roads to cut off his 14
fugitives
nor betray the survivors on the day of
distress.

The LORD's dominion

For soon the day of the LORD will come on 15
all the nations:
you shall be treated as you have treated
others,
and your deeds will recoil on your own head.
The draught that you have drunk on my holy 16
mountain
all the nations shall drink continually;
they shall drink and gulp down
and shall be as though they had never
been;
but on Mount Zion there shall be those 17
that escape,
and it shall be holy,
and Jacob shall dispossess those that dispossessed them.
Then shall the house of Jacob be fire, 18
the house of Joseph flame,
and the house of Esau shall be chaff;
they shall blaze through it and consume it,
and the house of Esau shall have no
survivor.
The LORD has spoken.
Then they shall possess the Negeb, the 19
mount of Esau,
and the Shephelah of the Philistines;
they shall possess the country-side of
Ephraim and Samaria,
and Benjamin shall possess Gilead.
Exiles of Israel*c* shall possess*d* Canaan as far 20
as Zarephath,
exiles of Jerusalem*e* shall possess the cities of
the Negeb.
Those who find safety on Mount Zion 21
shall go up
to hold sway over the mount of Esau,
and dominion shall belong to the LORD.

---

c Prob. rdg.; Heb. adds this army.   *d* shall possess: *prob. rdg.; Heb.* which.   *e Prob. rdg.; Heb.*
adds who are in Sepharad.

JONAH

Jonah bound for Tarshish

1 THE WORD OF THE LORD came to
2 Jonah son of Amittai: 'Go to the great city
of Nineveh, go now and denounce it, for its
3 wickedness stares me in the face.' But Jonah
set out for Tarshish to escape from the LORD.
He went down to Joppa, where he found a
ship bound for Tarshish. He paid his fare
and went on board, meaning to travel by it
4 to Tarshish out of reach of the LORD. But
the LORD let loose a hurricane, and the sea
ran so high in the storm that the ship
5 threatened to break up. The sailors were
afraid, and each cried out to his god for help.
Then they threw things overboard to lighten
the ship. Jonah had gone down into a corner
6 of the ship and was lying sound asleep when
the captain came upon him. 'What, sound
asleep?' he said. 'Get up, and call on your
god; perhaps he will spare us a thought and
we shall not perish.'

Jonah thrown overboard

7 At last the sailors said to each other, 'Come
and let us cast lots to find out who is to blame
for this bad luck.' So they cast lots, and the
8 lot fell on Jonah. 'Now then,' they said to
him, 'what is your business? Where do you
come from? What is your country? Of what
9 nation are you?' 'I am a Hebrew,' he
answered, 'and I worship the LORD the God
of heaven, who made both sea and land.'
10 At this the sailors were even more afraid.
'What can you have done wrong?' they
asked. They already knew that he was trying to escape from the LORD, for he had told
11 them so. 'What shall we do with you,' they
asked, 'to make the sea go down?' For the
12 storm grew worse and worse. 'Take me and

throw me overboard,' he said, 'and the sea
will go down. I know it is my fault that this
great storm has struck you.' The crew rowed 13
hard to put back to land but in vain, for the
sea ran higher and higher. At last they called 14
on the LORD and said, 'O LORD, do not let
us perish at the price of this man's life; do
not charge us with the death of an innocent
man. All this, O LORD, is thy set purpose.'
Then they took Jonah and threw him over- 15
board, and the sea stopped raging. So the 16
crew were filled with the fear of the LORD
and offered sacrifice and made vows to him.
But the LORD ordained that a great fish 17
should swallow Jonah, and for three days
and three nights he remained in its belly.

Jonah's prayer

Jonah prayed to the LORD his God from the **2**
belly of the fish:

   I called to the LORD in my distress, 2
    and he answered me;
   out of the belly of Sheol I cried for help,
    and thou hast heard my cry.
   Thou didst cast me into the depths, far out 3
    at sea,
   and the flood closed round me;
all thy waves, all thy billows, passed over
   me.
I thought I was banished from thy sight 4
and should never see thy holy temple again.
   The water about me rose up to my neck; 5
   the ocean was closing over me.
   Weeds twined about my head
   in the troughs of the mountains; 6
   I was sinking into a world
   whose bars would hold me fast for ever.
But thou didst bring me up alive from the
   pit, O LORD my God.

7 As my senses failed me I remembered the
　　LORD,
　and my prayer reached thee in thy holy
　　temple.
8 Men who worship false gods may abandon
　　their loyalty,
9 but I will offer thee sacrifice with words of
　　praise;
　I will pay my vows; victory is the LORD's.

10 　Then the LORD spoke to the fish and it
　spewed Jonah out on to the dry land.

Nineveh repents

3 The word of the LORD came to Jonah a
2 second time: 'Go to the great city of Nineveh,
　go now and denounce it in the words I give
3-4 you.' Jonah obeyed at once and went to
　Nineveh. He began by going a day's journey
　into the city, a vast city, three days' journey
　across, and then proclaimed: 'In forty days
5 Nineveh shall be overthrown!' The people of
　Nineveh believed God's word. They ordered
　a public fast and put on sackcloth, high and
6 low alike. When the news reached the king
　of Nineveh he rose from his throne, stripped

off his robes of state, put on sackcloth and
sat in ashes. Then he had a proclamation 7
made in Nineveh: 'This is a decree of the
king and his nobles. No man or beast, herd
or flock, is to taste food, to graze or to drink
water. They are to clothe themselves in sack- 8
cloth and call on God with all their might.
Let every man abandon his wicked ways and
his habitual violence. It may be that God 9
will repent and turn away from his anger:
and so we shall not perish.' God saw what 10
they did, and how they abandoned their
wicked ways, and he repented and did not
bring upon them the disaster he had
threatened.

Jonah and the gourd

Jonah was greatly displeased and angry, and 4
he prayed to the LORD: 'This, O LORD, is　1 2
what I feared when I was in my own country,
and to forestall it I tried to escape to Tarshish; I knew that thou art "a god gracious
and compassionate, long-suffering and ever
constant, and always willing to repent of
the disaster".[a] And now, LORD, take my life: 3

　　　　a a god . . . disaster: cp. Exod. 34. 6.

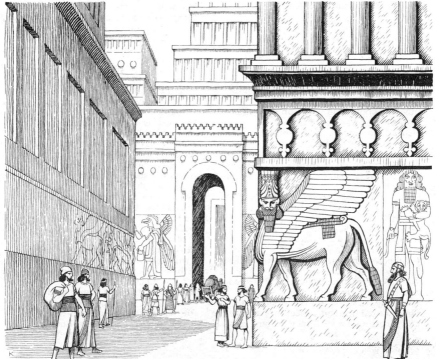

Nineveh, the capital of Assyria

4 I should be better dead than alive.' 'Are you
5 so angry?' said the LORD. Jonah went out
and sat down on the east of the city. There
he made himself a shelter and sat in its shade,
waiting to see what would happen in the city.
6 Then the LORD God ordained that a climbing gourd[b] should grow up over his head to
throw its shade over him and relieve his distress, and Jonah was grateful for the gourd.
7 But at dawn the next day God ordained that
a worm should attack the gourd, and it
8 withered; and at sunrise God ordained that
a scorching wind should blow up from the
east. The sun beat down on Jonah's head till
he grew faint. Then he prayed for death and
said, 'I should be better dead than alive.'
9 At this God said to Jonah, 'Are you so angry
over the gourd?' 'Yes,' he answered, 'mor-
10 tally angry.' The LORD said, 'You are sorry
for the gourd, though you did not have the
trouble of growing it, a plant which came
up in a night and withered in a night. And
11 should not I be sorry for the great city of
Nineveh, with its hundred and twenty thousand who cannot tell their right hand from
their left, and cattle without number?'

MICAH

1 THIS IS THE WORD of the LORD which
came to Micah of Moresheth during the
reigns of Jotham, Ahaz, and Hezekiah, kings
of Judah; which he received in visions concerning Samaria and Jerusalem.

Israel and Judah denounced

2 Listen, you peoples, all together;
attend, O earth and all who are in it,
that the Lord GOD, the Lord from his holy
temple,
may bear witness against you.
3 For look, the LORD is leaving his dwelling-
place;
down he comes and walks on the heights
of the earth.
4 Beneath him mountains dissolve
like wax before the fire,
valleys are torn open,
as when torrents pour down the hill-side—
5 and all for the crime of Jacob and the sin of
Israel.
What is the crime of Jacob? Is it not Samaria?
What is the hill-shrine of Judah? Is it not
Jerusalem?
6 So I will make Samaria
a heap of ruins in open country,
a place for planting vines;
I will pour her stones down into the valley
and lay her foundations bare.
7 All her carved figures shall be shattered,
her images burnt one and all;
I will make a waste heap of all her idols.
She amassed them out of fees for harlotry,
and a harlot's fee shall they become once
more.

Therefore I must howl and wail, 8
go naked and distraught;
I must howl like a wolf, mourn like a desert-
owl.
Her wound cannot be healed; 9
for the stroke has bitten deep into Judah,
it has fallen on the gate of my people,
upon Jerusalem itself.
Will you not weep your fill, weep your eyes 10
out in Gath?
In Beth-aphrah sprinkle yourselves with
dust;
take the road, you that dwell in Shaphir; 11
have not the people of Zaanan gone out in
shame from their city?
Beth-ezel is a place of lamentation,
she can lend you support no longer.
The people of Maroth are greatly alarmed, 12
for disaster has come down from the LORD
to the very gate of Jerusalem.
Harness the steeds to the chariot, O people 13
of Lachish,
for you first led the daughter of Zion into sin;
to you must the crimes of Israel be traced.
Let Moresheth-gath be given her dismissal. 14
Beth-achzib has[a] disappointed[b] the kings
of Israel.
And you too, O people of Mareshah, 15
I will send others to take your place;
and the glory of Israel shall hide in the cave
of Adullam.
Shave the hair from your head in mourn- 16
ing
for the children of your delight;
make yourself bald as a vulture,
for they have left you and gone into exile.

---

b a climbing gourd: *or* a castor-oil plant.

a Beth-achzib has: *prob. rdg.; Heb.* The houses of Achzib have.   b *Heb.* achzab.

Judgement for injustice

2 Shame on those who lie in bed planning evil
        and wicked deeds
    and rise at daybreak to do them,
    knowing that they have the power!
2   They covet land and take it by force;
    if they want a house they seize it;
    they rob a man of his home
    and steal every man's inheritance.

3 Therefore these are the words of the LORD:

    Listen, for this whole brood I am planning
        disaster,
        whose yoke you cannot shake from your
            necks
    and walk upright; it shall be your hour of
        disaster.

4   On that day
    they shall take up a poem about you
    and raise a lament thrice told,
    saying, 'We are utterly despoiled:
    the land of the LORD's*c* people changes
        hands.
        How shall a man have power*d*
    to restore our fields, now parcelled out*e*?'
5   Therefore there shall be no one to assign to
        you
        any portion by lot in the LORD's assembly.

6   How they rant! They may say, 'Do not
        rant';
    but this ranting is all their own,
    these insults are their*f* own invention.

The upright man's best friend

7   Can one ask, O house of Jacob,
    'Is the LORD's patience truly at an end?
    Are these his deeds?
    Does not good come of the LORD's words?
    He is the upright man's best friend.'
8   But you are no*g* people for me,
    rising up as my enemy to my*h* face,
    to strip the cloak from him that was
        safe*i*
    and take away the confidence of returning
        warriors,
9 to drive the women of my people from their
        pleasant homes
    and rob the children of my glory for ever.
10 Up and be gone; this is no resting-place for
        you,
    you that to defile yourselves would commit
        any mischief,
        mischief however cruel.

11 If anyone had gone about in a spirit of false-
    hood and lies, saying, 'I will rant to you of
    wine and strong drink', his ranting would be
    what this people like.

Promise of restoration

I will assemble you, the whole house of   12
    Jacob;
I will gather together those that are left in
    Israel.
I will herd them like sheep in a fold,
like a grazing flock which stampedes at the
    sight of a man.
So their leader breaks out before them,   13
and they all break through the gate and
    escape,
    and their king goes before them,
    and the LORD leads the way.

To the rulers of Israel

And I said: 3

Listen, you leaders of Jacob, rulers of Israel,
should you not know what is right?
    You hate good and love evil,   2
you flay men alive and tear the very flesh
    from their bones;
    you devour the flesh of my people,   3
    strip off their skin,
    splinter their bones;
    you shred them like flesh into a pot,
    like meat into a cauldron.

Then they will call to the LORD, and he will   4
    give them no answer;
when that time comes he will hide his face
    from them,
    so wicked were their deeds.

These are the words of the LORD concerning   5
the prophets who lead my people astray, who
promise prosperity in return for a morsel of
food, who proclaim a holy war against them
if they put nothing into their mouths:
Therefore night shall bring you no vision,   6
    darkness no divination;
    the sun shall go down on the prophets,
    the day itself shall be black above them.
Seers and diviners alike shall blush for   7
    shame;
    they shall all put their hands over their
        mouths,
    because there is no answer from God.

But I am full of strength,*j* of justice and   8
    power,
    to denounce his crime to Jacob
    and his sin to Israel.
Listen to this, leaders of Jacob,   9
rulers of Israel,
    you who make justice hateful
    and wrest it from its straight course,
    building Zion in bloodshed   10
    and Jerusalem in iniquity.
    Her rulers sell justice,   11
    her priests give direction in return for a bribe,

c the LORD's: *prob. rdg.*; *Heb.* my.   d have power: *prob. rdg.*; *Heb.* remove from me.   e now parcelled out: *prob. rdg.*; *Heb.* he will parcel out.   f *Prob. rdg.*; *Heb.* his.   g But . . . no: *prob. rdg.*;
Heb. But yesterday.   h my: *prob. rdg.*; *Heb. om.*   i the cloak . . . safe: *prob. rdg.*; *Heb.* mantle, cloak.
j *Prob. rdg.*; *Heb. adds* the spirit of the LORD.

her prophets take money for their divination,
and yet men rely on the LORD.
'Is not the LORD among us?' they say;
'then no disaster can befall us.'

12 Therefore, on your account
Zion shall become a ploughed field,
Jerusalem a heap of ruins,
and the temple hill rough heath.

A remnant in an age of peace

4 1k In days to come
the mountain of the LORD's house
shall be set over all other mountains,
lifted high above the hills.
Peoples shall come streaming to it,
2 and many nations shall come and say,
'Come, let us climb up on to the mountain
of the LORD,
to the house of the God of Jacob,
that he may teach us his ways
and we may walk in his paths.'
For instruction issues from Zion,
and out of Jerusalem comes the word of
the LORD;
3 he will be judge between many peoples
and arbiter among mighty nations afar.
They shall beat their swords into mattocks
and their spears into pruning-knives;
nation shall not lift sword against nation
nor ever again be trained for war,

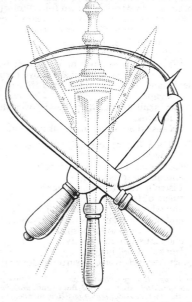

and each man shall dwell under his own 4
vine,
under his own fig-tree, undisturbed.
For the LORD of Hosts himself has spoken.

All peoples may walk, each in the name of 5
his god,
but we will walk in the name of the LORD
our God
for ever and ever.

On that day, says the LORD, 6
I will gather those who are lost;
I will assemble the exiles and I will strengthen
the weaklings.
I will preserve the lost as a remnant 7
and turn the derelict into a mighty nation.
The LORD shall be their king on Mount Zion
now and for ever.
And you, rocky bastion, hill of Zion's 8
daughter,
the promises to you shall be fulfilled;
and your former sovereignty shall come
again,
the dominion of the daughter of Jerusalem.

Purpose in Israel's captivity

Why are you now filled with alarm? 9
Have you no king?
Have you no counsellor left,
that you are seized with writhing like a
woman in labour?
Lie writhing on the ground like a woman in 10
childbirth,
O daughter of Zion;
for now you must leave the city
and camp in the open country;
and so you will come to Babylon.
There you shall be saved,
there the LORD will deliver you from your
enemies.
But now many nations are massed against you; 11
they say, 'Let her suffer outrage,
let us gloat over Zion.'
But they do not know the LORD's thoughts 12
nor understand his purpose;
for he has gathered them like sheaves to
the threshing-floor.
Start your threshing, daughter of Zion; 13
for I will make your horns of iron,
your hooves will I make of bronze,
and you shall crush many peoples.
You shall devote their ill-gotten gain to
the LORD,
their wealth to the Lord of all the earth.

A governor for Israel

Get you behind your walls, you people of 5
a walled city;
the siege is pressed home against you:
Israel's ruler shall be struck on the cheek with
a rod.

k Verses 1–3: cp. Isa. 2. 2–4.

2 But you, Bethlehem in Ephrathah,
   small as you are to be among Judah's
      clans,
out of you shall come forth a governor for
   Israel,
      one whose roots are far back in the past,
      in days gone by.
3 Therefore only so long as a woman is in
      labour
      shall he give up Israel;
   and then those that survive of his race
   shall rejoin their brethren.
4 He shall appear and be their shepherd
   in the strength of the LORD,
      in the majesty of the name of the LORD his
      God.
And they shall continue, for now his great-
      ness shall reach
   to the ends of the earth;
5 and he shall be a man of peace.

Defence against Assyria

   When the Assyrian comes into our land,
   when he tramples our castles,
we will raise against him seven men or eight
   to be shepherds and princes.
6 They shall shepherd Assyria with the
      sword
   and the land of Nimrod with bare blades;
they shall deliver us from the Assyrians
   when they come into our land,
   when they trample our frontiers.

The remnant

7 All that are left of Jacob, surrounded by
      many peoples,
   shall be like dew from the LORD,
   like copious showers on the grass,
   which do not wait for man's command
   or linger for any man's bidding.
8 All that are left of Jacob among the
      nations,
   surrounded by many peoples,
   shall be like a lion among the beasts of the
      forest,
   like a young lion loose in a flock of sheep;
   as he prowls he will trample and tear them,
   with no rescuer in sight.
9 Your hand shall be raised high over your
      foes,
   and all who hate you shall be destroyed.

10 On that day, says the LORD,
   I will destroy all your horses among you
   and make away with your chariots.
11 I will destroy the cities of your land
   and raze your fortresses.
12 I will destroy all your sorcerers,
   and there shall be no more soothsayers
      among you.

13 I will destroy your images and all the sacred
   pillars in your land;
you shall no longer bow in reverence before
   things your own hands made.
14 I will pull down the sacred poles in your
   land,
   and demolish your blood-spattered altars.
15 In anger and fury will I take vengeance
   on all nations who disobey me.

Israel denounced for her sins

Hear now what the LORD is saying: **6**
   Up, state your case to the mountains;
   let the hills hear your plea.
   Hear the LORD's case, you mountains,   2
   you everlasting pillars that bear up the
      earth;
   for the LORD has a case against his people,
   and will argue it with Israel.
   O my people, what have I done to you?   3
   Tell me how I have wearied you; answer
      me this.
   I brought you up from Egypt,   4
   I ransomed you from the land of slavery,
   I sent Moses and Aaron and Miriam to
      lead you.
   Remember, my people,   5
   what Balak king of Moab schemed against
      you,
and how Balaam son of Beor answered him;
   consider the journey[l] from Shittim to
      Gilgal,
   in order that you may know the triumph
      of the LORD.

   What shall I bring when I approach the   6
      LORD?
   How shall I stoop before God on high?
Am I to approach him with whole-offerings
      or yearling calves?
   Will the LORD accept thousands of rams   7
   or ten thousand rivers of oil?
   Shall I offer my eldest son for my own
      wrongdoing,
   my children for my own sin?

God[m] has told you what is good;   8
   and what is it that the LORD asks of you?
   Only to act justly, to love loyalty,
   to walk wisely before your God.

Hark, the LORD, the fear of whose name 9
   brings success,
   the LORD calls to the city.
Listen, O tribe of Judah and citizens in 10
   assembly,[n]
   can I overlook[o] the infamous false mea-
      sure,[p]
   the accursed short bushel?
Can I connive at false scales or a bag of light 11
   weights?

---

l consider the journey: *prob. rdg.; Heb. om.*   *m* God: *prob. rdg.; Heb. obscure.*   *n* citizens in
assembly: *prob. rdg.; Heb. unintelligible.*   *o* can I overlook: *prob. rdg.; Heb. obscure.*   *p* Prob. rdg.;
Heb. *adds* infamous treasures.

12 Your rich men are steeped in violence,
your townsmen are all liars,
and their tongues frame deceit.
13 But now I will inflict a signal punishment
on you
to lay you waste for your sins:
14 you shall eat but not be satisfied,
your food shall lie heavy on your stomach;
you shall come to labour but not bring
forth,
and even if you bear a child
I will give it to the sword;
15 you shall sow but not reap,
you shall press the olives but not use the
oil,
you shall tread the grapes but not drink
the wine.
16 You have kept the precepts of Omri;
what the house of Ahab did, you have
done;
you have followed all their ways.
So I will lay you utterly waste;
the nations shall jeer at your citizens,
and their insults you shall bear.

Disappointment turned to hope

7 Alas! I am now like the last gatherings of
summer fruit,
the last gleanings of the vintage,
when there are no grapes left to eat,
none of those early figs that I love.
2 Loyal men have vanished from the earth,
there is not one upright man.
All lie in wait to do murder,
each man drives his own kinsman like a
hunter into the net.
3 They are bent eagerly on wrongdoing,
the officer who presents the requests,[q]
the judge who gives judgement[r] for reward,
and the nobleman who harps on his
desires.
4 Thus their goodness is twisted[s] like rank
weeds
and their honesty like briars.[t]
As soon as thine eye sees, thy punishment
falls;
at that moment bewilderment seizes them.
5 Trust no neighbour, put no confidence in
your closest friend;
seal your lips even from the wife of your
bosom.
6 For son maligns father,
daughter rebels against mother,
daughter-in-law against mother-in-law,
and a man's enemies are his own household.
7 But I will look for the LORD,
I will wait for God my saviour; my God will
hear me.

O my enemies, do not exult over me; 8
I have fallen, but shall rise again;
though I dwell in darkness, the LORD is my
light.
I will bear the anger of the LORD, for I have 9
sinned against him,
until he takes up my cause and gives judgement for me,
until he brings me out into light, and I see
his justice.
Then may my enemies see and be abashed, 10
those who said to me, 'Where is he, the LORD
your God?'
Then shall they be trampled like mud in the
streets;
I shall gloat over them;
that will be a day for rebuilding your walls, 11
a day when your frontiers will be extended,
a day when men will come seeking you 12
from Assyria to Egypt
and from Egypt to the Euphrates,
from every sea and every mountain;
and the earth with its inhabitants shall be 13
waste.
This shall be the fruit of their deeds.

A prayer

Shepherd thy people with thy crook, 14
the flock that is thy very own,
that dwells by itself on the heath and in the
meadows;
let them graze in Bashan and Gilead, as in
days gone by.
Show us[u] miracles as in the days when thou 15
camest out of Egypt;
let the nations see and be taken aback for all 16
their might,
let them keep their mouths shut,
make their ears deaf,
let them lick the dust like snakes, 17
like creatures that crawl upon the ground.
Let them come trembling and fearful from
their strongholds,
let them fear thee, O LORD our God.

Who is a god like thee? Thou takest away 18
guilt,
thou passest over the sin of the remnant of
thy own people,
thou dost not let thy anger rage for ever
but delightest in love that will not change.
Once more thou wilt show us tender 19
affection
and wash out our guilt,
casting all our sins into the depths of the
sea.
Thou wilt show good faith to Jacob, 20
unchanging love to Abraham,
as thou didst swear to our fathers in days
gone by.

---

q the requests: *prob. rdg.; Heb. om.*   r who gives judgement: *prob. rdg.; Heb. om.*   s twisted:
prob. rdg.; Heb. obscure.   t their honesty like briars: *prob. rdg.; Heb. obscure.*   u *Prob. rdg.; Heb.*
I will show him.

NAHUM

1 An oracle about Nineveh: the book of the vision of Nahum the Elkoshite.

The LORD's vengeance on his enemies

2*ᵃ* The LORD is a jealous god, a god of vengeance;
    the LORD takes vengeance and is quick to anger.*ᵇ*
3 *ᶜ*In whirlwind and storm he goes on his way,
    and the clouds ̖are the dust beneath his feet.
4 He rebukes the sea and dries it up
    and makes all the streams fail.
Bashan and Carmel languish,
    and on Lebanon the young shoots wither.
5 The mountains quake before him,
    the hills heave and swell,
and the earth, the world and all that lives in it,
    are in tumult at his presence.
6 Who can stand before his wrath?
    Who can resist his fury?
His anger pours out*ᵈ* like a stream of fire,
    and the rocks melt*ᵉ* before him.
7 The LORD is a sure refuge
    for those who look to him in time of distress;
he cares for all who seek his protection

and brings them safely*ᶠ* through the sweeping flood; 8
he makes a final end of all who oppose him
and pursues his enemies into darkness.
No adversaries dare oppose him twice; 9–11
all are burnt up*ᵍ* like tangled briars.
Why do you make plots against the LORD?
He himself will make an end of you all.
From you has come forth a wicked counsellor,
plotting evil against the LORD.
The LORD takes vengeance on his adversaries,
against his enemies he directs his wrath;
with skin scorched black, they are consumed
like stubble that is parched and dry.

Israel and Judah rid of the invaders

These are the words of the LORD:

    Now I will break his yoke from your 13 necks
and snap the cords that bind you.
Image and idol will I hew down in the house 14 of your God.
    This is what the LORD has ordained for you:

---

*a Verses 2–14 are an incomplete alphabetic acrostic poem; some parts have been re-arranged accordingly.
b The rest of verse 2, The LORD takes . . . wrath, transposed to verse 11.*   *c Prob. rdg.; Heb. inserts two
lines The LORD is long-suffering and of great might, but the LORD does not sweep clean away.*   *d pours
out: or fuses or melts.*   *e Prob. rdg.; Heb. are torn down.*   *f brings them safely: prob. rdg.; Heb. om.
g all are burnt up: prob. rdg.; Heb. for until.*

never again shall your offspring be scattered;
and I will grant you burial, fickle though
you have been.

12 Has the punishment been so great?
Yes, but it has passed away and is gone.
I have afflicted you, but I will not afflict
you again.

15 See on the mountains the feet of the herald
who brings good news.
Make your pilgrimages, O Judah,
and pay your vows.
For wicked men shall never again overrun
you;
they are totally destroyed.

2 2[h] The LORD will restore the pride of Jacob and
Israel alike,
although plundering hordes have stripped
them bare
and pillaged their vines.

Nineveh's enemies triumphant

1 The battering-ram is mounted against
your bastions,
the siege is closing in.
Watch the road and brace yourselves;
put forth all your strength.
3 The shields of their warriors are gleaming
red,
their soldiers are all in scarlet;
their chariots, when the line is formed,
are like flickering[i] fire;
4 squadrons of horse advance on the city in
mad frenzy;[j]
they jostle one another in the outskirts, like
waving torches;
5 the leaders display their prowess[k]
as they dash to and fro like lightning,
rushing[l] in headlong career;
they hasten to the wall, and mantelets are
set in position.
6 The sluices of the rivers are opened, the
palace topples down;
7 the train of captives goes into exile,
their slave-girls are carried off,
moaning like doves and beating their
breasts;
8 and Nineveh has become like a pool of
water,
like the waters round her, which are ebbing
away.
'Stop! Stop!' they cry; but none turns
back.
9 Spoil is taken, spoil of silver and gold;
there is no end to the store,
treasure beyond the costliest that man can
desire.

Plundered, pillaged, stripped bare! 10
Courage melting and knees giving way,
writhing limbs, and faces drained of colour!
Where now is the lions' den, 11
the cave[m] where the lion cubs lurked,
where the lion and[n] lioness and young cubs
went unafraid,
the lion which killed to satisfy its whelps 12
and for its mate broke the neck of the kill,
mauling its prey to fill its lair,
filling its den with the mauled prey?

Fall of Nineveh

I am against you, says the LORD of Hosts, 13
I will smoke out your pride,[o]
and a sword shall devour your cubs.
I will leave you no more prey on the earth,
and the sound of your feeding[p] shall no
more be heard.

Ah! blood-stained city, steeped in deceit, 3
full of pillage, never empty of prey!
Hark to the crack of the whip, 2
the rattle of wheels and stamping of horses,
bounding chariots, chargers rearing, 3
swords gleaming, flash of spears!
The dead are past counting, their bodies
lie in heaps,
corpses innumerable, men stumbling over
corpses—
all for a wanton's monstrous wantonness, 4
fair-seeming, a mistress of sorcery,
who beguiled nations and tribes
by her wantonness and her sorceries.
I am against you, says the LORD of Hosts, 5
I will uncover your breasts to your disgrace
and expose your naked body to every
nation,
to every kingdom your shame.
I will cast loathsome filth over you, 6
I will count you obscene and treat you like
excrement.

Futile defence

Then all who see you will shrink from you 7
and say,
'Nineveh is laid waste; who will console
her?'
Where shall I look for anyone to comfort
you?
Will you fare better than No-amon?— 8
she that lay by the streams of the Nile,
surrounded by water,
whose rampart was the Nile, waters her
wall;
Cush and Egypt were her strength, and it was 9
boundless,
Put and the Libyans brought her help.

---

h Verses 1 and 2 transposed.　　i flickering: *prob. rdg.; Heb.* obscure.　　*j Prob. rdg.; Heb. adds* chariots.
k display their prowess: *or* shout their own names.　　*l Prob. rdg.; Heb.* stumbling.　　*m Prob. rdg.;*
Heb. pasture.　　*n* and: *prob. rdg.; Heb. om.　　o* your pride: *prob. rdg.; Heb.* her chariot.　　*p* your
feeding: *prob. rdg.; Heb.* your messenger.

10 She too became an exile and went into
    captivity,
  her infants too were dashed to the ground
    at every street-corner,
    her nobles were shared out by lot,
    all her great men were thrown into chains.
11 You too shall hire yourself out, flaunting
    your sex;
  you too shall seek refuge from the enemy.
12 Your fortifications are like figs when they
    ripen:
  if they are shaken, they fall into the mouth
    of the eater.
13 The troops*q* in your midst are a pack of
    women,
  the gates of your country stand open to the
    enemy,
    and fire consumes their bars.
14 Draw yourselves water for the siege,
    strengthen your fortifications;
  down into the clay, trample the mortar,
    repair the brickwork.
15 Even then the fire will consume you,
  and the sword will cut you down.*r*

Make yourselves many as the locusts,
make yourselves many as the hoppers,
a swarm which spreads out and then flies 16
  away.
You have spies as numerous as the stars
  in the sky;
your secret agents are like locusts, 17
your commanders like the hoppers
which lie dormant in the walls on a cold
  day;
but when the sun rises, they scurry off,
and no one knows where they have
  gone.
Your shepherds slumber, O king of 18
  Assyria,
your flock-masters lie down to rest;
your troops*q* are scattered over the hills,
and no one rounds them up.
Your wounds cannot be assuaged, your 19
  injury is mortal;
all who have heard of your fate clap their
  hands in joy.
Are there any whom your ceaseless cruelty
  has not borne down?

q Or people.   *r Prob. rdg.; Heb. adds* and consume you like the locust (*or* hopper).

HABAKKUK

1 An oracle which the prophet Habakkuk received in a vision.

An unanswered prayer

2 How long, O LORD, have I cried to thee,
  unanswered?
  I cry, 'Violence!', but thou dost not save.
3   Why dost thou let me see such misery,
  why countenance[a] wrongdoing?

  Devastation and violence confront me;
  strife breaks out, discord raises its head,
4   and so law grows effete;
  justice does not come forth victorious;
  for the wicked outwit the righteous,
  and so justice comes out perverted.

The mighty Chaldaeans

5   Look, you treacherous people, look:
  here is what will astonish you and stun
    you,
  for there is work afoot in your days
  which you will not believe when it is told
    you.
6   It is this: I am raising up the Chaldaeans,
  that savage and impetuous nation,
  who cross the wide tracts of the earth
  to take possession of homes not theirs.
7   Terror and awe go with them;
  their justice and judgement are of their own
    making.
8 Their horses are swifter than hunting-
    leopards,
  keener than wolves of the plain;[b]
  their cavalry wait ready, they spring
    forward,
  they come flying from afar
  like vultures swooping to devour the prey.
9 Their whole army advances, violence in their
    hearts;
  a sea of faces rolls on;
  they bring in captives countless as the sand.
10   Kings they hold in derision,
  rulers they despise;
  they despise every fortress,
  they raise siege-works and capture it.
11   Then they pass on like the wind and are
    gone;
  and dismayed are all those whose strength
    was their god.

Questioning God's methods

12   Art thou not from of old, O LORD?—
  my God, the holy, the immortal.[c]
  O LORD, it is thou who hast appointed them
    to execute judgement;
  O mighty God, thou who hast destined them
    to chastise.

thou whose eyes are too pure to look upon 13
  evil,
and who canst not countenance wrongdoing,
why dost thou countenance the treachery
  of the wicked?
Why keep silent when they devour men more
  righteous than they?
Why dost thou make men like the fish of 14
  the sea,
like gliding creatures that obey no ruler?
They haul them up with hooks, one and 15
  all,
they catch them in nets
and drag them in their trawls;
then they make merry and rejoice,
  sacrificing to their nets 16
and burning offerings[d] to their trawls;
for by these they live sumptuously
and enjoy rich fare.
Are they then to unsheathe the sword every 17
  day,
to slaughter the nations without pity?

The watch-tower

I will stand at my post, **2**
I will take up my position on the watch-
  tower,
I will watch to learn what he will say
  through me,
and what I shall reply when I am challenged.[e]

---

a Or dost thou let me see.   *b Or* evening.
we shall not die.   *d Or* incense.   *c* the immortal: *prob. original rdg.*, *altered in Heb. to*
e when I am challenged: *or* concerning my complaint.

2 Then the LORD made answer:
Write down the vision, inscribe it on tablets,
ready for a herald to carry it with speed;[f]
3 for there is still a vision for the appointed
time.
At the destined hour it will come in breathless haste,
it will not fail.
If it delays, wait for it;
for when it comes will be no time to linger.

Five woes

4 The reckless will be unsure of himself,
while the righteous man will live by being
faithful;[g]
5 as for the traitor in his over-confidence,
still less will he ride out the storm, for all
his bragging.
Though he opens his mouth as wide as
Sheol
and is insatiable as Death,
gathering in all the nations,
making all peoples his own harvest,
6 surely they will all turn upon him
with insults and abuse, and say,
'Woe betide you who heap up wealth that
is not yours[h]
and enrich yourself with goods taken in
pledge!'
7 Will not your creditors suddenly start
up,
will not all awake who would shake you
till you are empty,
and will you not fall a victim to them?
8 Because you yourself have plundered mighty[i]
nations,
all the rest of the world will plunder you,
because of bloodshed and violence done
in the land,
to the city and all its inhabitants.

9 Woe betide you who seek unjust gain for
your house,
to build your nest on a height,
to save yourself from the grasp of wicked
men!
10 Your schemes to overthrow mighty[i]
nations
will bring dishonour to your house
and put your own life in jeopardy.
11 The very stones will cry out from the
wall,
and from the timbers a beam will answer
them.

12 Woe betide you who have built a town with
bloodshed
and founded a city on fraud,

so that nations toil for a pittance, 13
and peoples weary themselves for a mere
nothing!
Is not all this the doing of the LORD of Hosts?
For the earth shall be full of the knowledge 14
of the glory of the LORD
as the waters fill the sea.

Woe betide you who make your[j] com- 15
panions drink the outpouring of your
wrath,
making them drunk, that you may watch
their naked orgies!
Drink deep draughts of shame, not of glory; 16
you too shall drink until you stagger.
The cup in the LORD's right hand is passed
to you,
and your shame will exceed[k] your glory.
The violence done to Lebanon shall sweep 17
over you,
the havoc done to its beasts shall break
your own spirit,
because of bloodshed and violence done
in the land,
to the city and all its inhabitants.

What use is an idol when its maker has 18
shaped it?—
it is only an image, a source of lies;
or when the maker trusts what he has
made?—
he is only making dumb idols.
Woe betide him who says to the wood, 19
'Wake up',
to the dead stone, 'Bestir yourself'![l]
Why, it is firmly encased in gold and silver
and has no breath in it.
But the LORD is in his holy temple; 20
let all the earth be hushed in his presence.

Prayer for mercy

A prayer of the prophet Habakkuk. **3**

O LORD, I have heard tell of thy deeds; 2
I have seen, O LORD, thy work.[m]
In the midst of the years thou didst make
thyself known,
and in thy wrath thou didst remember
mercy.

God comes from Teman, 3
the Holy One from Mount Paran;
his radiance overspreads the skies,
and his splendour fills the earth.
He rises like the dawn, 4
with twin rays starting forth at his side;
the skies are[n] the hiding-place of his
majesty,
and the everlasting[o] ways are for[p] his swift
flight.[q]

f ready . . . speed: *or* so that a man may read it easily.
Galatians 3. 11). h *Prob. rdg.; Heb. adds* till when.
k will exceed: *prob. rdg.; Heb. unintelligible.* l *Prob. rdg.; Heb. adds* he will teach. m *Prob.*
rdg.; Heb. adds in the midst of the years quicken it.
o *Or* ancient. p and . . . are for: *transposed from end of verse 6.*
with slight change, from verse 7.
g *Or* by his faithfulness (*cp. Romans 1. 17;*
i *Or* many. j *Prob. rdg.; Heb.* his.
n the skies are: *prob. rdg.; Heb.* there is.
q his swift flight: *transposed,*

5 Pestilence stalks before him,
and plague comes forth behind.
6 He stands still and shakes the earth,
he looks and makes the nations tremble;
the eternal mountains are riven,
the everlasting[r] hills subside,
7 the tents of Cushan are snatched away,[s]
the tent-curtains of Midian flutter.
8 Art thou angry with the streams?
Is thy wrath against the sea, O LORD?
When thou dost mount thy horses,
thy riding is to victory.
9 Thou dost draw thy bow from its case[t]
and charge thy quiver with shafts.
Thou cleavest the earth with rivers;
10-11 the mountains see thee and writhe with
fear.
The torrent of water rushes by,
and the deep sea thunders aloud.
The sun forgets to turn in his course,[u]
and the moon stands still at her zenith,
at the gleam of thy speeding arrows
and the glance of thy flashing spear.
12 With threats thou dost bestride the earth
and trample down the nations in anger.
13 Thou goest forth to save thy people,
thou comest to save thy anointed;
thou dost shatter the wicked man's house
from the roof down,[v]

uncovering its foundations to the bare
rock.[w]
Thou piercest their[x] chiefs with thy[y] 14
shafts,
and their leaders are torn from them by
the whirlwind,
as they open[z] their jaws
to devour their wretched victims in secret.

When thou dost tread the sea with thy 15
horses
the mighty waters boil.
I hear, and my belly quakes; 16
my lips quiver at the sound;
trembling comes over my bones,
and my feet totter in their tracks;
I sigh for the day of distress
to dawn over my assailants.
Although the fig-tree does not burgeon, 17
the vines bear no fruit,
the olive-crop fails,
the orchards yield no food,
the fold is bereft of its flock
and there are no cattle in the stalls,
yet I will exult in the LORD 18
and rejoice in the God of my deliverance.
The LORD God is my strength, 19
who makes my feet nimble as a hind's
and sets me to range the heights.

ZEPHANIAH

1 THIS IS THE WORD of the LORD which
came to Zephaniah son of Cushi, son of
Gedaliah, son of Amariah, son of Hezekiah,
in the time of Josiah son of Amon king of
Judah.

Universal devastation

2 I will sweep the earth clean of all that is on it,
says the LORD.
3 I will sweep away both man and beast,
I will sweep the birds from the air and the
fish from the sea,
and I will bring the wicked to their knees[a]
and wipe out mankind from the earth.
This is the very word of the LORD.

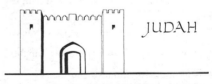

JUDAH

Judah's end

I will stretch my hand over Judah 4
and all who live in Jerusalem;
I will wipe out from this place the last
remnant of Baal
and the very name of the heathen priests,

---

r *Or* ancient.   s *are snatched away: prob. rdg.; Heb.* under wickedness.   t *Thou . . . case: prob.
rdg.; Heb.* Thy bow was quite bared.   u *The sun . . . course: prob. rdg.; Heb.* The sun raised the height
of his hands.   v *the wicked . . . down: prob. rdg.; Heb.* a head from the house of the wicked.   w *bare
rock: prob. rdg.; Heb.* neck.   x *their: prob. rdg.; Heb. om.*   y *Prob. rdg.; Heb.* his.   z *from
them . . . open: prob. rdg.; Heb.* obscure.

a *I will bring . . . knees: prob. rdg.; Heb.* the ruins with the wicked.

5 those who bow down upon the house-tops
  to worship the host of heaven
  and who swear by Milcom,
6 those who have turned their backs on the
  LORD,
  who have not sought the LORD or con-
    sulted him.

7 Silence before the Lord GOD!
  for the day of the LORD is near.
  The LORD has prepared a sacrifice
  and has hallowed his guests.
8 On the day of the LORD's sacrifice
  I will punish the royal house and its chief
    officers
  and all who ape outlandish fashions.
9 On that day
  I will punish all who dance on the temple
    terrace,
  who fill their master's[b] house with crimes of
    violence and fraud.

10 On that day, says the LORD,
  an outcry shall be heard from the Fish
    Gate,
  wailing from the second quarter of the
    city,
  a loud crash from the hills;
11 and[c] those who live in the Lower Town
  shall wail.
  For it is all over with the merchants,
  and all the dealers in silver are wiped out.

Day of wrath

12 At that time
  I will search Jerusalem with a lantern
  and punish all who sit in stupor over the
    dregs of their wine,
  who say to themselves,
  'The LORD will do nothing, good or bad.'
13 Their wealth shall be plundered,
  their houses laid waste;
  they shall build houses but not live in
    them,
  they shall plant vineyards but not drink the
    wine from them.
14 The great day of the LORD is near,
  it comes with speed;
  no runner so fast as that day,
  no raiding band so swift.[d]
15 That day is a day of wrath,
  a day of anguish and affliction,
  a day of destruction and devastation,
  a day of murk and gloom,
  a day of cloud and dense fog,
16 a day of trumpet and battle-cry
  over fortified cities and lofty battlements.
17 I will bring dire distress upon men;
  they shall walk like blind men for their sin
    against the LORD.

Their blood shall be spilt like dust
  and their bowels like dung;
  neither their silver nor their gold   18
  shall avail to save them.
On the day of the LORD's wrath, by the fire
  of his jealousy
the whole land shall be consumed;
for he will make an end, a swift end,
  of all who live in the land.

Shelter from distress

Gather together, you unruly nation, gather **2**
  together,
before you are sent far away and vanish[e] like 2
  chaff,
before the burning anger of the LORD comes
  upon you,
before the day of the LORD's anger comes
  upon you.
Seek the LORD,   3
all in the land who live humbly by his
  laws,
seek righteousness, seek a humble heart;
  it may be that you will find shelter
  in the day of the LORD's anger.
For Gaza shall be deserted,   4
Ashkelon left desolate,
  the people of Ashdod shall be driven out[f]
    at noonday
  and Ekron uprooted.

PHILISTINES

Philistia

Listen, you who live by the coast, you   5
  Kerethite settlers.
The word of the LORD is spoken against
  you;
I will subdue you,[g] land of the Philistines,
I will lay you waste and leave you without
  inhabitants,
and you, Kereth, shall be all shepherds'   6
  huts[h] and sheepfolds;
and the coastland shall belong to the sur- 7
  vivors of Judah.
  They shall pasture their flocks by the
    sea[i]
  and lie down at evening in the houses of
    Ashkelon,
  for the LORD their God will turn to them
  and restore their fortunes.

---

b Or their Lord's.   *c and: prob. rdg.; Heb. om.*
day of the LORD is bitter, there the warrior cries aloud.
f the people . . . out: or Ashdod shall be made an example.
h you . . . huts: Heb. has these words in a different order.

d no runner . . . swift: prob. rdg.; Heb. hark, the
e you are . . . vanish: prob. rdg.; Heb. obscure.
g I . . . you: prob. rdg.; Heb. Canaan.
i by the sea: prob. rdg.; Heb. upon them.

MOAB

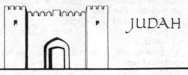

JUDAH

Moab and Ammon

8 I have heard the insults of Moab, the taunts
of Ammon,
how they have insulted my people
and encroached on their frontiers.

9 Therefore, by my life,
says the LORD of Hosts, the God of Israel,
Moab shall be like Sodom,
Ammon like Gomorrah,
a pile of weeds, a rotting heap of saltwort,
waste land for evermore.
The survivors of my people shall plunder
them,
the remnant of my nation shall possess their
land.

10 This will be retribution for their pride,
because they have insulted the people of the
LORD of Hosts and encroached upon their

11 rights. The LORD will appear against them
with all his terrors; for he will reduce to
beggary all the gods of the earth, and all the
coasts and islands of the nations will worship
him, every man in his own home.

Cush and Assyria

12 You Cushites also shall be killed
by the sword of the LORD.*j*

13 So let him stretch out his hand over the
north
and destroy Assyria,
make Nineveh desolate,
arid as the wilderness.

14 Flocks shall couch there,
and all the beasts of the wild.
Horned owl and ruffed bustard shall roost
on her capitals;
the tawny owl shall hoot in the window,
and the bustard stand in the porch.*k*

15 This is the city that exulted in fancied
security,
saying to herself, 'I am, and I alone.'
And what is she now? A waste, a haunt for
wild beasts,
at which every passer-by shall hiss and shake
his fist.

Jerusalem laid waste

3 Shame on the tyrant city, filthy and foul!
2 No warning voice did she heed, she took no
rebuke to heart,
she did not trust in the LORD or come near
to her God.

Her officers were lions roaring in her midst, 3
her rulers wolves of the plain*l*
that did not wait*m* till morning,
her prophets were reckless, no true pro- 4
phets.
Her priests profaned the sanctuary
and did violence to the law.
But the LORD in her midst is just; 5
he does no wrong;
morning by morning he gives judgement,
without fail at daybreak.*n*

I have wiped out the proud; 6
their battlements are laid in ruin.
I have made their streets a desert where
no one passes.
Their cities are laid waste, deserted, unpeopled.
In the hope that she would remember all my 7
instructions,
I said, 'Do but fear me
and take my rebuke to heart';
but they were up betimes and went about
their evil deeds.

Wait for me, therefore, says the LORD, 8
wait for the day when I stand up to accuse
you;
for mine it is to gather nations
and assemble kingdoms,
to pour out on them my indignation,
all the heat of my anger;
the whole earth shall be consumed by the
fire of my jealousy.
I will give all peoples once again pure lips, 9
that they may invoke the LORD by name
and serve him with one consent.
From beyond the rivers of Cush 10
my suppliants of the Dispersion shall bring
me tribute.

A remnant preserved

On that day, Jerusalem, 11
you shall not be put to shame for all your
deeds
by which you have rebelled against me;
for then I will rid you
of your proud and arrogant citizens,
and never again shall you flaunt your
pride
on my holy hill.
But I will leave in you a people 12
afflicted and poor.

j the sword of the LORD: prob. rdg.; Heb. my sword.
l Or evening.   *m Or carry off.*   *n Prob. rdg.; Heb. adds but the wrongdoer knows no shame.*

k Prob. rdg.; Heb. adds an unintelligible phrase.

13 The survivors in Israel shall find refuge in the
name of the LORD;
they shall no longer do wrong or speak
lies,
no words of deceit shall pass their lips;
for they shall feed and lie down
with no one to terrify them.

When the LORD reigns

14 Zion, cry out for joy;
raise the shout of triumph, Israel;
be glad, rejoice with all your heart,
daughter of Jerusalem.
15 The LORD has rid you of your adversaries,
he has swept away your foes;
the LORD is among you as king, O Israel;
never again shall you fear disaster.

16 On that day this shall be the message to
Jerusalem:
Fear not, O Zion; let not your hands fall
slack.
17 The LORD your God is in your midst,
like a warrior, to keep you safe;
he will rejoice over you and be glad;
he will show you his love once more;
he will exult over you with a shout of joy
as in days long ago.[o]

18 I will take your cries of woe[p] away from
you;
and you shall no longer endure reproach
for her.
19 When that time comes, see,
I will deal with all your oppressors.
I will rescue the lost and gather the dispersed;
I will win my people praise and renown
in all the world where once they were
despised.
20 When the time comes for me to gather
you,[q]
I will bring you home.
I will win you renown and praise
among all the peoples of the earth,
when I bring back your prosperity; and
you shall see it.
It is the LORD who speaks.

HAGGAI

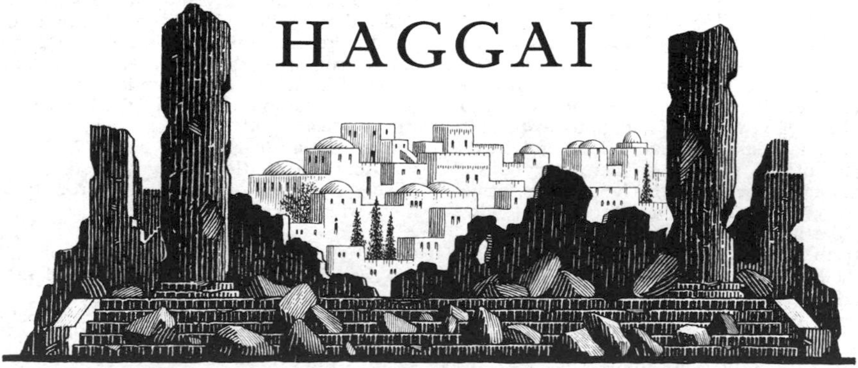

Rebuilding of the temple begins

1 IN THE SECOND YEAR of King
Darius, on the first day of the sixth month,
the word of the LORD came through the
prophet Haggai to Zerubbabel son of Shealtiel, governor of Judah, and to Joshua son
2 of Jehozadak, the high priest: These are the
words of the LORD of Hosts: This nation
says to itself that it is not yet time for the
3 house of the LORD to be rebuilt. Then this
word came through Haggai the prophet:
4 Is it a time for you to live in your own well-
roofed houses, while this house lies in ruins?
5 Now these are the words of the LORD of
6 Hosts: Consider your way of life. You have
sown much but reaped little; you eat but
never as much as you wish, you drink but
never more than you need, you are clothed
but never warm, and the labourer puts his
7 wages into a purse with a hole in it. These
are the words of the LORD of Hosts: Con-
8 sider your way of life. Go up into the hills,
fetch timber, and build a house acceptable

o as . . . ago: *prob. rdg.; Heb. obscure.* *p* cries of woe: *prob. rdg.; Heb. obscure.* *q* When . . . you: *prob. rdg.; Heb.* and in the time, my gathering you.

to me, where I can show my glory,[a] says the
9 LORD. You look for much and get little. At
the moment when you would bring home
the harvest, I blast it. Why? says the LORD
of Hosts. Because my house lies in ruins,
while each of you has a house that he can
10 run to. It is your fault that the heavens withhold their dew and the earth its produce.
11 So I have proclaimed a drought against land
and mountain, against corn, new wine, and
oil, and all that the ground yields, against
man and cattle and all the products of man's
labour.
12   Zerubbabel son of Shealtiel, Joshua son
of Jehozadak, the high priest, and the rest
of the people listened to what the LORD their
God had said and what the prophet Haggai
said when the LORD their God sent him, and
they were filled with fear because of the
13 LORD. So Haggai the LORD's messenger, as
the LORD had commissioned him, said to
the people: I am with you, says the LORD.
14 Then the LORD stirred up the spirit of
Zerubbabel son of Shealtiel, governor of
Judah, of Joshua son of Jehozadak, the high
priest, and of the rest of the people; they
came and began work on the house of
15 LORD of Hosts their God on the twenty-
fourth day of the sixth month.

The temple's future glory

2 In the second year of King Darius, on the
twenty-first day of the seventh month, these
words came from the LORD through the
2 prophet Haggai: Say to Zerubbabel son of
Shealtiel, governor of Judah, to Joshua son
of Jehozadak, the high priest, and to the
3 rest of the people: Is there anyone still
among you who saw this house in its former
glory? How does it appear to you now?
Does it not seem to you as if it were not
4 there? But now, Zerubbabel, take heart, says
the LORD; take heart, Joshua son of Jehozadak, high priest. Take heart, all you
people, says the LORD. Begin the work, for
5 I am with you, says the LORD of Hosts, and
my spirit is present among you. Have no
6 fear. For these are the words of the LORD
of Hosts: One thing more: I will shake
7 heaven and earth, sea and land, I will shake
all nations; the treasure of all nations shall
come hither, and I will fill this house with
8 glory;[b] so says the LORD of Hosts. Mine is
the silver and mine the gold, says the LORD
9 of Hosts, and the glory[b] of this latter house
shall surpass the glory[b] of the former, says

the LORD of Hosts. In this place will I grant
prosperity and peace. This is the very word
of the LORD of Hosts.

A lesson from the law

In the second year of Darius, on the twenty- 10
fourth day of the ninth month, this word
came from the LORD to the prophet Haggai:
These are the words of the LORD of Hosts: 11
Ask the priests to give their ruling: If a man 12
is carrying consecrated flesh in a fold of his
robe, and he lets the fold touch bread or
broth or wine or oil or any other kind of
food, will that also become consecrated?
And the priests answered, 'No.' So it 13
went on, But if a person defiled by contact
with a corpse touches any one of these things,
will that also become defiled? 'It will',
answered the priests. Haggai replied, So it 14
is with this people and nation and all that
they do, says the LORD; whatever offering
they make here is defiled in my sight. And 15
now look back over recent times down to
this day: before one stone was laid on another in the LORD's temple, what was your 16
plight? If a man came to a heap of corn
expecting twenty measures, he found but
ten; if he came to a wine-vat to draw fifty
measures, he found but twenty. I blasted 17
you and all your harvest with black blight
and red and with hail, and yet you had no
mind to return to me, says the LORD. Con- 18
sider, from this day onwards, from this
twenty-fourth day of the ninth month, the
day when the foundations of the temple of
the LORD are laid, consider: will the seed 19
still be diminished[c] in the barn? Will the
vine and the fig, the pomegranate and the
olive, still bear no fruit? Not so, from this
day I will bless you.

A word to Zerubbabel

On that day, the twenty-fourth day of the 20
month, the word of the LORD came to
Haggai a second time: Tell Zerubbabel, 21
governor of Judah, I will shake heaven and
earth; I will overthrow the thrones of kings, 22
break the power of heathen realms, over-
turn chariots and their riders; horses and
riders shall fall by the sword of their
comrades. On that day, says the LORD of 23
Hosts, I will take you, Zerubbabel son of
Shealtiel, my servant, and will wear you
as a signet-ring; for you it is that I have
chosen. This is the very word of the LORD
of Hosts.

---

a show my glory: *or* be honoured.   *b Or* wealth.   *c* diminish ed: *prob. rdg.; Heb. om.*

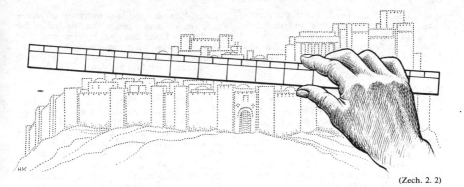

(Zech. 2. 2)

ZECHARIAH

1 IN THE EIGHTH MONTH of the second year of Darius, the word of the LORD came to the prophet Zechariah son of Berechiah, son of Iddo: The LORD was very angry with your forefathers. Say to the people, These are the words of the LORD of Hosts: Come back to me, and I will come back to you, says the LORD of Hosts. Do not be like your forefathers. They heard the prophets of old proclaim, 'These are the words of the LORD of Hosts: Turn back from your evil ways and your evil deeds.' But they did not listen or pay heed to me, says the LORD. And where are your forefathers now? And the prophets, do they live for ever? But the warnings and the decrees with which I charged my servants the prophets—did not these overtake your forefathers? Did they not then repent and say, 'The LORD of Hosts has treated us as he purposed; as our lives and as our deeds deserved, so has he treated us'?

Zechariah's vision of the horses

7 On the twenty-fourth day of the eleventh month, the month Shebat, in the second year of Darius, the word of the LORD came to the prophet Zechariah son of Berechiah, son of Iddo.

8 Last night I had a vision. I saw a man on a bay horse standing among the myrtles in a hollow; and behind him were other horses, black, dappled, and white. 'What are these, sir?' I asked, and the angel who talked with me answered, 'I will show you what they are.' Then the man standing among the myrtles said, 'They are those whom the LORD has sent to range through the world.' They reported to the angel of the LORD as he stood among the myrtles: 'We have ranged through the world; the whole world is still and at peace.' Thereupon the angel of the LORD said, 'How long, O LORD of Hosts, wilt thou withhold thy compassion from Jerusalem and the cities of Judah, upon whom thou hast vented thy wrath these seventy years?' Then the LORD spoke kind and comforting words to the angel who talked with me, and the angel said to me, Proclaim, These are the words of the LORD of Hosts: I am very jealous for Jerusalem and Zion. I am full of anger against the nations that enjoy their ease, because, while my anger was but mild, they heaped evil on evil. Therefore these are the words of the LORD: I have come back to Jerusalem with compassion, and my house shall be rebuilt in her, says the LORD of Hosts, and the measuring-line shall be stretched over Jerusalem. Proclaim once more, These are the words of the LORD of Hosts: My cities shall again overflow with good things; once again the LORD will comfort Zion, once again he will make Jerusalem the city of his choice.

The horns and the smiths

I lifted my eyes and there I saw four horns. 18 I asked the angel who talked with me what they were, and he answered, 'These are the horns which scattered Judah[a] and Jerusalem.' Then the LORD showed me four smiths. I asked what they were coming to do, and he said, 'Those horns scattered Judah and Jerusalem so completely that no

a Prob. rdg.; Heb. adds Israel.

man could lift his head. But these smiths have come to reunite them and to throw down the horns of the nations which had raised them against the land of Judah and scattered its people.'

The man with the measuring-line

2 I lifted my eyes and there I saw a man carry-
2 ing a measuring-line. I asked him where he was going, and he said, 'To measure Jerusalem and see what should be its breadth
3 and length.' Then, as the angel who talked with me was going away, another angel
4 came out to meet him and said to him, Run to the young man there and tell him that Jerusalem shall be a city without walls, so numerous shall be the men and cattle within
5 it. I will be a wall of fire round her, says the LORD, and a glory in the midst of her.

Zion, a place of blessing

6 Away, away; flee from the land of the north, says the LORD, for I will make you spread your wings like the four winds of heaven,
7 says the LORD. Away, escape, you people of Zion who live in Babylon.
8 For these are the words of the LORD of Hosts, spoken when he sent me on a glorious mission[b] to the nations who have plundered you, for whoever touches you touches the
9 apple of his eye: I raise[c] my hand against them; they shall be plunder for their own slaves. So you shall know that the LORD of
10 Hosts has sent me. Shout aloud and rejoice, daughter of Zion; I am coming, I will make my dwelling among you, says the LORD.
11 Many nations shall come over to the LORD on that day and become his people, and he will make his dwelling with you. Then you shall know that the LORD of Hosts has sent
12 me to you. The LORD will once again claim Judah as his own possession in the holy land, and make Jerusalem the city of his choice.
13 Silence, all mankind, in the presence of the LORD! For he has bestirred himself out of his holy dwelling-place.

The lamp-stand and the olive-trees

4 1[d] The angel who talked with me came back and roused me as a man is roused from sleep.
2 He asked me what I saw, and I answered, 'A lamp-stand all of gold with a bowl on it; it holds seven lamps, and there are seven
3 pipes for the lamps on top of it, with two olive-trees standing by it, one on the right
11[e] of the bowl and another on the left.' I asked him, 'What are these two olive-trees, the one on the right and the other on the left of
12 the lamp-stand?' I asked also another ques-

tion, 'What are the two sprays of olive beside the golden pipes which discharge the golden oil from their bowls?' He said, 'Do 13 you not know what these mean?' 'No, sir', I answered. 'These two', he said, 'are the two 14 consecrated with oil who attend the Lord of all the earth.'

Joshua the high priest

Then he showed me Joshua the high priest 3 standing before the angel of the LORD, with the Adversary[f] standing at his right hand to accuse him. The LORD said to the Adversary, 2 'The LORD rebuke you, Satan, the LORD rebuke you who are venting your spite on Jerusalem.[g] Is not this man a brand snatched from the fire?' Now Joshua was wearing 3 filthy clothes as he stood before the angel; and the angel turned and said to those in 4 attendance on him, 'Take off his filthy clothes.' Then he turned to him and said, 'See how I have taken away your guilt from you; I will clothe you in fine vestments'; and he added, 'Let a clean turban be put on 5 his head.' So they put a clean turban on his head and clothed him in clean garments, while the angel of the LORD stood by. Then 6 the angel of the LORD gave Joshua this solemn charge: These are the words of the 7 LORD of Hosts: If you will conform to my ways and carry out your duties, you shall administer my house and be in control of my courts, and I grant you the right to come and go amongst these in attendance here. Listen, Joshua the high priest, you and your 8 colleagues seated here before you, all you who are an omen of things to come: I will now bring my servant, the Branch. In one 9 day I will wipe away the guilt of the land. On that day, says the LORD of Hosts, you shall all of you invite one another to come and sit each under his vine and his fig-tree.

The stone with seven eyes

Here is the stone that I set before Joshua, a stone in which are seven eyes. I will reveal its meaning to you, says the LORD of Hosts. Then I asked the angel of the LORD who 4 talked with me, 'Sir, what are these?' And 5 he answered, 'Do you not know what these mean?' 'No, sir', I answered. 'These seven', he said, 'are the eyes of the LORD ranging over the whole earth.'[i]

Zerubbabel will finish the building

Then he turned and said to me, This is the 6 word of the LORD concerning Zerubbabel: Neither by force of arms nor by brute strength, but by my spirit! says the LORD of

---

b on a glorious mission: prob. rdg.; Heb. after glory. 4. 14.   e 4. 4–10 transposed to follow 3. 10. or the LORD who has chosen Jerusalem rebuke you. earth: transposed from verse 10.

c Or wave.   d 3. 1–10 transposed to follow f Heb. the Satan.   g the LORD . . . Jerusalem: h See note on 4. 11 above.   i These seven . . .

7 Hosts. How does a mountain, the greatest mountain, compare with Zerubbabel? It is no higher than a plain. He shall bring out the stone called Possession[j] while men 8 acclaim its beauty. This word came to me 9 from the LORD: Zerubbabel with his own hands laid the foundation of this house and with his own hands he shall finish it. So shall you know that the LORD of Hosts has sent 10 me to you. Who has despised the day of small things? He shall rejoice when he sees Zerubbabel holding the stone called Separation.[j]

The flying scroll

5 I looked up again and saw a flying scroll. 2 He asked me what I saw, and I answered, 'A flying scroll, twenty cubits long and ten 3 cubits wide.' This, he told me, is the curse which goes out over the whole land; for by the writing on one side every thief shall be swept clean away, and by the writing on the other every perjurer shall be swept clean 4 away. I have sent it out, the LORD of Hosts has said, and it shall enter the house of the thief and the house of the man who has perjured himself in my name; it shall stay inside that house and demolish it, timbers and stones and all.

The woman in the barrel

5 The angel who talked with me came out and said to me, 'Raise your eyes and look at this 6 thing that comes forth.' I asked what it was, and he said, 'It is a great barrel coming forth,' and he added, 'so great is their guilt 7 in all the land.' Then a round slab of lead was lifted, and a woman was sitting there 8 inside the barrel. He said, 'This is Wickedness', and he thrust her down into the barrel and rammed the leaden weight upon its 9 mouth. I looked up again and saw two women coming forth with the wind in their wings (for they had wings like a stork's), and they carried the barrel between earth and sky. 10 I asked the angel who talked with me where 11 they were taking the barrel, and he answered, 'To build a house for it[k] in the land of Shinar; when the house is ready, it[l] shall be set on the place prepared for it[k] there.'

The four chariots

6 I looked up again and saw four chariots coming out between two mountains, and the 2 mountains were made of copper.[m] The first 3 chariot had bay horses, the second black, the 4 third white, and the fourth dappled. I asked the angel who talked with me, 'Sir, what are 5 these?' He answered, 'These are the four

winds of heaven which have been attending the Lord of the whole earth, and they are now going forth. The chariot with the black 6 horses is going to the land of the north, that with the white to the far west,[n] that with the dappled to the south, and that with the roan 7 to the land of the east.'[o] They were eager to go and range over the whole earth; so he said, 'Go and range over the earth', and the chariots did so. Then he called me to look 8 and said, 'Those going to the land of the north have given my spirit rest in the land of the north.'

The man named the Branch

The word of the LORD came to me: Take 9 10 silver and gold from the exiles, from Heldai, Tobiah, Jedaiah, and[p] Josiah son of Zephaniah, who have come back from Babylon. Take it and make a crown; put the crown on 11 the head of Joshua son of Jehozadak, the high priest,[q] and say to him, These are the 12 words of the LORD of Hosts: Here is a man named the Branch; he will shoot up from the ground where he is and will build the temple of the LORD. It is he who will build 13 the temple of the LORD, he who will assume royal dignity, will be seated on his throne and govern, with a priest at his right side, and concord shall prevail between them. The crown shall be in the charge of Heldai, 14 Tobiah, Jedaiah, and Josiah son of Zephaniah, as a memorial in the temple of the LORD.

Men from far away shall come and work 15 on the building of the temple of the LORD; so shall you know that the LORD of Hosts has sent me to you. If only you will obey the LORD your God!

What the LORD requires

The word of the LORD came to Zechariah 7 in the fourth year of the reign of King Darius, on the fourth day of Kislev, the ninth month. Bethel-sharezer sent Regem- 2 melech with his men to seek the favour of the LORD. They were to say to the priests in 3 the house of the LORD of Hosts and to the prophets, 'Am I to lament and abstain in the fifth month as I have done for so many years?' Then the word of the LORD of Hosts 4 came to me: Say to all the people of the land 5 and to the priests, When you fasted and lamented in the fifth and seventh months these seventy years, was it indeed in my honour that you fasted? And when you ate 6 and drank, was it not to please yourselves? Was it not this that the LORD proclaimed 7 through the prophets of old, while Jerusalem

---

j Cp. Lev. 20. 24–26.   k Or her.   l Or she.   m Or bronze.   n to the far west: prob. rdg.;
Heb. behind them.   o to the land of the east: prob. rdg.; Heb. om.   p and: prob. rdg.; Heb. and
go on that day yourself and go to the house of . . .   q Joshua . . . priest: possibly an error for Zerubbabel
son of Shealtiel, cp. 3. 5; 4. 9.

was populous and peaceful, as were the cities round her, and the Negeb and the Shephelah?

8 The word of the LORD came to Zechariah: 9 These are the words of the LORD of Hosts: Administer true justice, show loyalty and 10 compassion to one another, do not oppress the orphan and the widow, the alien and the poor, do not contrive any evil one against 11 another. But they refused to listen, they turned their backs on me in defiance, they 12 stopped their ears and would not hear. Their hearts were adamant; they refused to accept instruction and all that the LORD of Hosts had taught them by his spirit through the prophets of old; and they suffered under the 13 anger of the LORD of Hosts. As they did not listen when I[r] called, so I did not listen when 14 they called, says the LORD of Hosts, and I drove them out among all the nations to whom they were strangers, leaving their land a waste behind them, so that no one came and went. Thus they made their pleasant land a waste.

Jerusalem restored

8 The word of the LORD of Hosts came to me: 2 These are the words of the LORD of Hosts: I have been very jealous for Zion, fiercely 3 jealous for her. Now, says the LORD, I have come back to Zion and I will dwell in Jerusalem. Jerusalem shall be called the City of Truth, and the mountain of the LORD of Hosts shall be called the Holy Mountain. 4 These are the words of the LORD of Hosts: Once again shall old men and old women sit in the streets of Jerusalem, each leaning on a stick because of their great age; 5 and the streets of the city shall be full of 6 boys and girls, playing in the streets. These are the words of the LORD of Hosts: Even if it may seem impossible[s] to the survivors of this nation on that day, will it also seem impossible to me?[t] This is the very word of 7 the LORD of Hosts. These are the words of the LORD of Hosts: See, I will rescue my people from the countries of the east and 8 the west, and bring them back to live in Jerusalem. They shall be my people, and I will be their God, in truth and justice.

Symbol of blessing

9 These are the words of the LORD of Hosts: Take courage, you who in these days hear, from the prophets who were present when the foundations were laid for the house of the LORD of Hosts, their promise that the 10 temple is to be rebuilt. Till that time there was no hiring either of man or of beast, no one could safely go about his business be-

cause of his enemies, and I set all men one against another. But now I am not the same 11 towards the survivors of this people as I was in former days, says the LORD of Hosts. For they shall sow in safety; the vine shall 12 yield its fruit and the soil its produce, the heavens shall give their dew; with all these things I will endow the survivors of this people. You, house of Judah and house of 13 Israel, have been the very symbol of a curse to all the nations; and now I will save you, and you shall become the symbol of a blessing. Courage! Do not be afraid.

Love truth and peace

For these are the words of the LORD of 14 Hosts: Whereas I resolved to ruin you because your ancestors roused me to anger, says the LORD of Hosts, and I did not relent, so in these days I have once more[u] resolved 15 to do good to Jerusalem and to the house of Judah; do not be afraid. This is what you 16 shall do: speak the truth to each other, administer true and sound justice in the city gate. Do not contrive any evil one against 17 another, and do not love perjury, for all this I hate. This is the very word of the LORD.

The word of the LORD of Hosts came to 18 me: These are the words of the LORD of 19 Hosts: The fasts of the fourth month and of the fifth, the seventh, and the tenth, shall become festivals of joy and gladness for the house of Judah. Love truth and peace.

The LORD of hosts in Jerusalem

These are the words of the LORD of Hosts: 20 Nations and dwellers in great cities shall yet come; people of one city shall come to those 21 of another and say, 'Let us go and entreat the favour of the LORD, and resort to the LORD of Hosts; and I will come too.' So 22 great nations and mighty peoples shall resort to the LORD of Hosts in Jerusalem and entreat his favour. These are the words of 23 the LORD of Hosts: In those days, when ten men from nations of every language pluck up courage, they shall pluck the robe of a Jew and say, 'We will go with you because we have heard that God is with you.'

Judah's triumph over her enemies

An oracle: the word of the LORD.   **9**

He has come to the land of Hadrach
and[v] established himself in Damascus;
for the capital city[w] of Aram is the LORD's,
as are all the tribes of Israel.
[x]Sidon has closed her frontier against 2
  Hamath,
for she is very wary.

---

r Prob. rdg.; Heb. he.   s Or wonderful.

t will . . . me?: or it will seem wonderful also to me.
u once more: or changed my mind and.   v He has come . . . and: prob. rdg.; Heb. In the land of Hadrach
he has . . .   w capital city: or chief part.   x Prob. rdg.; Heb. prefixes Tyre and.

3 Tyre has built herself a rampart;
  she has heaped up silver like dust
  and gold like mud in the streets.
4 But wait, the Lord will dispossess her
  and strike down the power of her ships,
  and the city itself will be destroyed by fire.
5 Let Ashkelon see it and be afraid;
  Gaza shall writhe in terror,
  and Ekron's hope shall be extinguished;
  kings shall vanish from Gaza,
  and Ashkelon shall be unpeopled;
6 half-breeds shall settle in Ashdod,
  and I will uproot the pride of the Philistine.
7 I will dash the blood of sacrifices from his
  mouth
  and his loathsome offerings from his
  teeth;
  and his survivors shall belong^y to our God
  and become like a clan in Judah,
  and Ekron like a Jebusite.
8 And I will post a garrison for my house
  so that no one may pass in or out,
  and no oppressor shall ever overrun them.
  [This I have lived to see with my own
  eyes.]

Zion's king

9 Rejoice, rejoice, daughter of Zion,
  shout aloud, daughter of Jerusalem;
  for see, your king is coming to you,
  his cause won, his victory gained,
  humble and mounted on an ass,
  on a foal, the young of a she-ass.
10 He shall banish chariots from Ephraim
  and war-horses from Jerusalem;
  the warrior's bow shall be banished.
  He shall speak peaceably to every nation,
  and his rule shall extend from sea to sea,
  from the River to the ends of the earth.

Zion restored

11 And as for you, by your covenant with
   me sealed in blood
   I release your prisoners from the dungeon.^z
12 (Come back to the stronghold, you prisoners
   who wait in hope.)
   Now is the day announced
   when I will grant you twofold^a reparation.
13 For my bow is strung, O Judah;
   I have laid the arrow to it, O Ephraim;
   I have roused your sons, O Zion,^b
   and made you into the sword of a warrior.
14 The LORD shall appear above them,
   and his arrow shall flash like lightning;
   the Lord GOD shall blow a blast on the
   horn
   and march with the storm-winds of the
   south.

The LORD of Hosts will be their shield; 15
they shall prevail, they shall trample on
  the sling-stones;
they shall be roaring drunk as if with wine,
brimful as a bowl, drenched like the corners
  of the altar.
So on that day the LORD their God 16
will save them, his own people, like sheep,
setting them all about his land,
like^c jewels set to sparkle in a crown.

What wealth, what beauty, is theirs: 17
corn to strengthen young men,
and new wine for maidens!
Ask of the LORD rain in the autumn, **10**
ask him for rain in the spring,
the LORD who makes the storm-clouds,
and he will give you showers of rain
and to every man grass in his field;
for the household gods make mischievous 2
  promises;
diviners see false signs,
they tell lying dreams^d
and talk raving nonsense.
Men wander about like sheep
in distress for lack of a shepherd.
My anger is turned against the shepherds, 3
and I will visit with punishment the leaders
  of the flock;
but the LORD of Hosts will visit his flock,
the house of Judah,
and make them his royal war-horses.
They shall be corner-stone and tent-peg, 4
they shall be the bow ready for battle,
and from them shall come every commander.
Together they shall be like warriors 5
who tramp the muddy ways in battle,
and they will fight because the LORD is with
  them;
they will put horsemen shamefully to rout.
And I will give strength to the house of 6
  Judah
and grant victory to^e the house of Joseph;
I will restore them, for I have pitied them,
and they shall be as though I had never
  cast them off;
for I am the LORD their God and I will
  answer them.
So Ephraim shall be like warriors, 7
glad like men cheerful with wine,
and their sons shall see and be glad;
so let their hearts exult in the LORD.
I will whistle to call them in, for I have re- 8
  deemed them;
and they shall be as many as once they
  were.
If I disperse them^f among the nations, 9
in far-off lands they will remember me
and will rear their sons and then return.

y his survivors shall belong: or he shall become kin.
equal.   b Prob. rdg.; Heb. adds against your sons, O Javan (or Greece).   c like: prob. rdg.; Heb. for.
d they . . . dreams: or dreaming women make empty promises.   e grant victory to: or expand.   f Or
scatter them like seed.   z Prob. rdg.; Heb. adds no water in it.   a Or

10 Then will I fetch them home from Egypt
and gather them in from Assyria;
I will lead them into Gilead and Lebanon
until there is no more room for them.
11 Dire distress*g* shall come upon the
Euphrates
and shall beat down its turbulent waters;
all the depths of the Nile shall run dry.
The pride of Assyria shall be brought
down,
and the sceptre of Egypt shall pass away;
12 but Israel's strength shall be in the LORD,
and they shall march proudly in his name.
This is the very word of the LORD.

11 Throw open your gates, O Lebanon,
that fire may feed on your cedars.
2 Howl, every pine-tree; for the cedars have
fallen,
mighty trees are ravaged.
Howl, every oak of Bashan;
for the impenetrable forest is laid low.
3 Hark to the howling of the shepherds,
for their rich pastures are ravaged.
Hark to the roar of the young lions,
for Jordan's dense thickets are ravaged.

The shepherd allegory

4 These were the words of the LORD my God:
5 Fatten the flock for slaughter. Those who
buy will slaughter it and incur no guilt; those
who sell will say, 'Blessed be the LORD, I am
rich!' Its shepherds will have no pity for it.
6 For I will never again pity the inhabitants of
the earth, says the LORD. I will put every man
in the power of his neighbour and his king,
and as each country is crushed I will not
rescue him from their hands.
7 So I fattened the flock for slaughter for
the dealers. I took two staves: one I called
Favour and the other Union, and so I fat-
8 tened the flock. In one month I got rid of the
three shepherds, for I had lost patience with
9 them and they had come to abhor me. Then
I said to the flock, 'I will not fatten you any
more. Any that are to die, let them die; any
that stray, let them stray; and the rest can
10 devour one another.' I took my staff called
Favour and snapped it in two, annulling the
covenant which the LORD*h* had made with
11 all nations. So it was annulled that day, and
the dealers who were watching me knew that
12 all this was the word of the LORD. I said to
them, 'If it suits you, give me my wages;
otherwise keep them.' Then they weighed
13 out my wages, thirty pieces of silver. The
LORD said to me, 'Throw it into the treasury.'
I took the thirty pieces of silver—that noble
sum at which I was valued and rejected by
them!—and threw them into the house of the
14 LORD, into the treasury. Then I snapped in

two my second staff called Union, annulling
the brotherhood between Judah and Israel.
Then the LORD said to me, Equip your- 15
self again as a shepherd, a worthless one;
for I am about to install a shepherd in the 16
land who will neither miss any that are lost
nor search for those that have gone astray
nor heal the injured nor nurse the sickly, but
will eat the flesh of the fat beasts and throw
away their broken bones.

The shepherd prophecy

Alas for the worthless shepherd who aban- 17
dons the sheep!
A sword shall fall on his arm and on his
right eye;
his arm shall be shrivelled
and his right eye blinded.
This is the very word of the LORD of Hosts: **13***i*
O sword, awake against my shepherd
and against him who works with me.
Strike the shepherd, and the sheep will be
scattered,
and I will turn my hand against the
shepherd boys.
This also is the very word of the LORD: 8
It shall happen throughout the land
that two thirds of the people shall be struck
down and die,
while one third of them shall be left there.
Then I will pass this third through the fire 9
and I will refine them as silver is refined,
and assay them as gold is assayed.
Then they will invoke me by my name,
and I myself will answer them;
I will say, 'They are my people',
and they shall say, 'The LORD is our God.'

Jerusalem, a rock

An oracle. This is the word of the LORD con- **12***i*
cerning Israel, the very word of the LORD
who stretched out the heavens and founded
the earth, and who formed the spirit of
man within him: I am making the steep 2
approaches to Jerusalem slippery for all the
nations pressing round her; and Judah will
be caught up in the siege of Jerusalem. On 3
that day, when all the nations of the earth
will be gathered against her, I will make
Jerusalem a rock too heavy for any people
to remove, and all who try to lift it shall
injure themselves. On that day, says the 4
LORD, I will strike every horse with panic
and its rider with madness; I will keep watch
over Judah, but I will strike all the horses of
the other nations with blindness. Then the 5
clans of Judah shall say to themselves, 'The
inhabitants of Jerusalem find their strength*j*
in the LORD of Hosts their God.'
On that day I will make the clans of Judah 6
like a brazier in woodland, like a torch

---

g Dire distress: *or* An enemy.   *h* the LORD: *prob. rdg.; Heb.* I.   *i* 13. 7–9 *transposed to this point.*
j The . . . strength: *prob. rdg.; Heb.* O inhabitants of Jerusalem, I am strong.

blazing among sheaves of corn. They shall devour all the nations round them, right and left, while the people of Jerusalem remain safe
7 in their city. The LORD will first set free all the families[k] of Judah, so that the glory of David's line and of the inhabitants of Jerusalem may not surpass that of Judah.
8 On that day the LORD will shield the inhabitants of Jerusalem; on that day the very weakest of them shall be like David, and the line of David like God, like the angel of the LORD going before them.
9 On that day I will set about destroying all
10 the nations that come against Jerusalem, but I will pour a spirit of pity and compassion into the line of David and the inhabitants of Jerusalem. Then

They shall look on me, on him whom they have pierced,

and shall wail over him as over an only child, and shall grieve for him bitterly as for a first-born son.
11 On that day the mourning in Jerusalem shall be as great as the mourning over
12 Hadad-rimmon in the vale of Megiddo. The land shall wail, each family by itself: the family of David by itself and its women by themselves; the family of Nathan by itself
13 and its women by themselves; the family of Levi by itself and its women by themselves; the family of Shimei by itself and its women
14 by themselves; all the remaining families by themselves and their women by themselves.

A cleansing fountain

13 On that day a fountain shall be opened for the line of David and for the inhabitants of Jerusalem, to remove all sin and impurity.
2 On that day, says the LORD of Hosts, I will erase the names of the idols from the land, and they shall be remembered no longer; I will also remove the prophets and the spirit of uncleanness from the land.
3 Thereafter, if a man continues to prophesy, his parents, his own father and mother, will say to him, 'You shall live no longer, for you have spoken falsely in the name of the LORD.' His own father and mother will pierce him through because he has pro-
4 phesied. On that day every prophet shall be ashamed of his vision when he prophesies, nor shall he wear a robe of coarse hair in
5 order to deceive. He will say, 'I am no prophet, I am a tiller of the soil who has
6 been schooled in lust from boyhood.' 'What', someone will ask, 'are these scars on your chest?' And he will answer, 'I got them in the house of my lovers.'[l]

The LORD will fight for Jerusalem

14 A day is coming for the LORD to act, and the plunder taken from you shall be shared

out while you stand by. I will gather all the
2 peoples to fight against Jerusalem; the city shall be taken, the houses plundered and the women raped. Half the city shall go into exile, but the rest of the nation in the city
3 shall not be wiped out. The LORD will come out and fight against those peoples, as in the days of his prowess on the field of battle.
4 On that day his feet will stand on the Mount of Olives, which is opposite Jerusalem to the east, and the mountain shall be cleft in two by an immense valley running east and west; half the mountain shall move northwards
5 and half southwards. The valley between the hills[m] shall be blocked, for the new valley between them will reach as far as Asal. Blocked it shall be as it was blocked by the earthquake in the time of Uzziah king of Judah, and the LORD my God will appear with all the holy ones.

The LORD will reign

6 On that day there shall be neither heat nor
7 cold nor frost. It shall be all one day, whose coming is known only to the LORD, without distinction of day or night, and at evening-time there shall be light.
8 On that day living water shall issue from Jerusalem, half flowing to the eastern sea and half to the western, in summer and winter
9 alike. Then the LORD shall become king over all the earth; on that day the LORD shall be
10 one LORD and his name the one name. The whole land shall be levelled, flat as the Arabah from Geba to Rimmon southwards; but Jerusalem shall stand high in her place, and shall be full of people from the Benjamin Gate [to the point where the former gate stood,] to the Corner Gate, and from the Tower of Hananel to the king's wine-
11 vats. Men shall live in Jerusalem, and never again shall a solemn ban be laid upon her;
12 men shall live there in peace. The LORD will strike down all the nations who warred against Jerusalem, and the plague shall be this: their flesh shall rot while they stand on their feet, their eyes shall rot in their sockets, and their tongues shall rot in their mouths.
13 On that day a great panic, sent by the LORD, shall fall on them. At the very moment when a man would encourage his comrade his hand shall be raised to strike him down.
14 Judah too shall join in the fray in Jerusalem, and the wealth of the surrounding nations will be swept away—gold and silver and
15 apparel in great abundance. And slaughter shall be the fate of horse and mule, camel and ass, the fate of every beast in those armies.

Jerusalem, centre of worship

16 All who survive of the nations which attacked

_____

k _Or_ tents.   l _Verses 7–9 transposed to follow 11. 17._   m _Prob. rdg.; Heb._ my hills.

Jerusalem shall come up year by year to worship the King, the LORD of Hosts, and to keep the pilgrim-feast of Tabernacles.
17 If any of the families of the earth do not go up to Jerusalem to worship the King, the LORD of Hosts, no rain shall fall upon
18 them. If any family of Egypt does not go up and enter the city, then the same disaster shall overtake it as that which the LORD will inflict on any nation which does not
19 go up to keep the feast. This shall be the punishment of Egypt and of any nation which does not go up to keep the feast of Tabernacles.

20 On that day, not a bell on a war-horse but shall be inscribed 'Holy to the LORD', and the pots in the house of the LORD shall be like the bowls before the altar. Every pot in
21 Jerusalem and Judah shall be holy to the LORD of Hosts, and all who sacrifice shall come and shall take some of them and boil the flesh in them. So when that time comes, no trader shall again be seen in the house of the LORD of Hosts.

MALACHI

1 An oracle. The word of the LORD to Israel through Malachi.*a*

The LORD's love for Jacob

2 I love you, says the LORD. You ask, 'How hast thou shown love to us?' Is not Esau Jacob's brother? the LORD answers. I love
3 Jacob, but I hate Esau; I have turned his mountains into a waste and his ancestral
4 home into a lodging in the wilderness. When Edom says, 'We are beaten down; let us rebuild our ruined homes', these are the words of the LORD of Hosts: If they rebuild, I will pull down. They shall be called a realm of wickedness, a people whom the LORD has
5 cursed for ever. You yourselves will see it with your own eyes; you yourselves will say, 'The LORD's greatness reaches beyond the realm of Israel.'

Unacceptable gifts

6 A son honours his father, and a slave goes in fear of his master. If I am a father, where is the honour due to me? If I am a master, where is the fear due to me? So says the LORD of Hosts to you, you priests who despise my name. You ask, 'How have we despised thy
7 name?' Because you have offered defiled food on my altar. You ask, 'How have we defiled thee?' Because you have thought that
8 the table of the LORD may be despised, that if you offer a blind victim, there is nothing wrong, and if you offer a victim lame or diseased, there is nothing wrong. If you brought such a gift to the governor, would he receive you or show you favour? says the
9 LORD of Hosts. But now, if you placate God, he may show you mercy; if you do this, will he withhold his favour from you? So the LORD of Hosts has spoken. Better far that
10 one of you should close the great door altogether, so that the light might not fall thus all in vain upon my altar! I have no pleasure in you, says the LORD of Hosts;
11 I will accept no offering from you. From furthest east to furthest west my name is great among the nations. Everywhere fragrant sacrifice and pure gifts are offered in my name; for my name is great among the nations, says the LORD of Hosts. But
12 you profane it by thinking that the table of the LORD may be defiled, and that you can offer on it food you yourselves despise. You
13 sniff at it, says the LORD of Hosts, and say, 'How irksome!' If you bring as your offering victims that are mutilated, lame, or diseased, shall I accept them from you? says the LORD. A curse on the cheat who pays
14 his vows by sacrificing a damaged victim to the Lord, though he has a sound ram in his flock! I am the great king, says the LORD of Hosts, and my name is held in awe among the nations.

Unacceptable teaching

And now, you priests, this decree is for you: **2**
2 if you will not listen to me and pay heed to the honouring of my name, says the LORD of Hosts, then I will lay a curse upon you. I will turn your blessings into a curse; yes, into a curse, because you pay no heed. I will
3 cut off your arm,*b* fling offal in your faces, the offal of your pilgrim-feasts, and I will banish you from my presence. Then you will
4 know that I have issued this decree against you: my covenant with Levi falls to the

---

a Malachi: *or* my messenger.   *b Or* posterity.

5 ground, says the LORD of Hosts. My covenant was with him: I bestowed life and prosperity on him; I laid on him the duty of reverence, he revered me and lived in awe 6 of my name. The instruction he gave was true, and no word of injustice fell from his lips; he walked in harmony with me and in uprightness, and he turned many back 7 from sin. For men hang upon the words of the priest and seek knowledge and instruction from him, because he is the mes- 8 senger of the LORD of Hosts. But you have turned away from that course; you have made many stumble with your instruction; you have set at nought the covenant with 9 the Levites, says the LORD of Hosts. So I, in my turn, have made you despicable and mean in the eyes of the people, in so far as you disregard my ways and show partiality in your instruction.

Forbidden marriages

10 Have we not all one father? Did not one God create us? Why do we violate the covenant of our forefathers by being faithless to 11 one another? Judah is faithless, and abominable things are done in Israel and in Jerusalem; Judah has violated the holiness of the LORD by loving and marrying daughters of 12 a foreign god. May the LORD banish any who do this from the dwellings of Jacob, nomads or settlers, even though they bring offerings to the LORD of Hosts.

Marriage and divorce

13 Here is another thing that you do: you weep and moan, and you drown the altar of the LORD with tears, but he still refuses to look at the offering or receive an acceptable gift 14 from you. You ask why. It is because the LORD has borne witness against you on behalf of the wife of your youth. You have been unfaithful to her, though she is your partner and your wife by solemn covenant. 15 Did not the one God make her, both flesh and spirit? And what does the one God require but godly children? Keep watch on your spirit, and do not be unfaithful to the 16 wife of your youth. If a man divorces or puts away his spouse, he overwhelms her with cruelty, says the LORD of Hosts the God of Israel. Keep watch on your spirit, and do not be unfaithful.

The LORD is coming

17 You have wearied the LORD with your talk. You ask, 'How have we wearied him?' By saying that all evildoers are good in the eyes of the LORD, that he is pleased with them, or by asking, 'Where is the God of justice?' 3 Look, I am sending my messenger[c] who will clear a path before me. Suddenly the Lord

whom you seek will come to his temple; the messenger of the covenant in whom you delight is here, here already, says the LORD of Hosts. Who can endure the day of his 2 coming? Who can stand firm when he appears? He is like a refiner's fire, like fuller's soap; he will take his seat, refining 3 and purifying;[d] he will purify the Levites and cleanse them like gold and silver, and so they shall be fit to bring offerings to the LORD. Thus the offerings of Judah and Jeru- 4 salem shall be pleasing to the LORD as they were in days of old, in years long past. I will 5 appear before you in court, prompt to testify against sorcerers, adulterers, and perjurers, against those who wrong[e] the hired labourer, the widow, and the orphan, who thrust the alien aside and have no fear of me, says the LORD of Hosts.

Defrauding God

I am the LORD, unchanging; and you, too, 6 have not ceased to be sons of Jacob. From 7 the days of your forefathers you have been wayward and have not kept my laws. If you will return to me, I will return to you, says the LORD of Hosts. You ask, 'How can we return?' May man defraud God, that you 8 defraud me? You ask, 'How have we defrauded thee?' Why, in tithes and contributions. There is a curse, a curse on you all, 9 the whole nation of you, because you defraud me. Bring the tithes into the treasury, 10 all of them; let there be food in my house. Put me to the proof, says the LORD of Hosts, and see if I do not open windows in the sky and pour a blessing on you as long as there is need. I will forbid pests to destroy the 11 produce of your soil or make your vines barren, says the LORD of Hosts. All nations 12 shall count you happy, for yours shall be a favoured land, says the LORD of Hosts.

Hard words

You have used hard words about me, says 13 the LORD, and then you ask, 'How have we spoken against thee?' You have said, 'It is 14 useless to serve God; what do we gain from the LORD of Hosts by observing his rules and behaving with deference? We ourselves 15 count the arrogant happy; it is evildoers who are successful; they have put God to the proof and come to no harm.'

The LORD's possession

Then those who feared the LORD talked 16 together, and the LORD paid heed and listened. A record was written before him of those who feared him and kept his name in mind. They shall be mine, says the LORD 17 of Hosts, my own possession against the day that I appoint, and I will spare them as a

c my messenger: Heb. Malachi.   d Prob. rdg.; Heb. adds silver.   e Prob. rdg.; Heb. adds the wages of.

18 man spares the son who serves him. You will again tell good men from bad, the servant of God from the man who does not serve him.

The triumph of the righteous

4 The day comes, glowing like a furnace; all the arrogant and the evildoers shall be chaff, and that day when it comes shall set them ablaze, says the LORD of Hosts, it shall leave 2 them neither root nor branch. But for you who fear my name, the sun of righteousness shall rise with healing in his wings, and you shall break loose like calves released from the stall. On the day that I act, you shall 3 trample down the wicked, for they will be ashes under the soles of your feet, says the LORD of Hosts.

Remember the law of Moses my servant, 4 the rules and precepts which I bade him deliver to all Israel at Horeb.

Look, I will send you the prophet Elijah 5 before the great and terrible day of the LORD comes. He will reconcile fathers to sons and 6 sons to fathers, lest I come and put the land under a ban to destroy it.

APPENDIX

MEASURES OF LENGTH

	span	cubit	rod[a]
span	1	. .	. .
cubit	2	1	. .
rod[a]	12	6	1

The 'short cubit' was traditionally the measure from the elbow to the knuckles of the closed fist; and what seems to be intended as a 'long cubit' measured a 'cubit and a hand-breadth', i.e. 7 instead of 6 hand-breadths (Ezek. 40. 5). What is meant by cubits 'according to the old standard of measurement' (2 Chr. 3. 3) is presumably this pre-exilic cubit of 7 hand-breadths. Modern estimates of the Hebrew cubit range from 12 to 25·2 inches, without allowing for varying local standards.

MEASURES OF CAPACITY

liquid measures	equivalences	dry measures
'log'	1 'log'	. .
. .	4 'log'	'kab'
. .	7½ 'log'	'omer'
'hin'	12 'log'	. .
'bath'	72 'log'	'ephah'
'kor'	720 'log'	'homer' or 'kor'

According to ancient authorities the Hebrew 'log' was of the same capacity as the Roman *sextarius*; this according to the best available evidence was equivalent to 0·99 pint of the English standard.

WEIGHTS AND COINS

	heavy (Phoenician) standard			light (Babylonian) standard		
	shekel	mina	talent	shekel	mina	talent
shekel	1	. .	. .	1	. .	. .
mina	50	1	. .	60	1	. .
talent	3,000	60	1	3,600	60	1

The 'gerah' was 1/20 of the sacred or heavy shekel and probably 1/24 of the light shekel.

The 'sacred shekel' according to tradition was identical with the heavy shekel; while the 'shekel of the standard recognized by merchants' (Gen. 23. 16) was perhaps a weight stamped with its value as distinct from one not so stamped and requiring to be weighed on the spot.

The weight and value of the shekel varied so greatly according to the district and with the passing centuries that its evaluation in modern terms is impossible. Recent discoveries suggest that it may have weighed approximately 11·5 grammes.

Coins are not mentioned before the Exile. Only the 'daric' (1 Chr. 29. 7) and the 'drachma' (Ezra 2. 69; Neh. 7. 70–72), if this is a distinct coin, are found in the Old Testament; the former is said to have been a month's pay for a soldier in the Persian army, while the latter will have been the Greek silver drachma, estimated at approximately 4·4 grammes. The 'shekel' of this period (Neh. 5. 15) as a coin was probably the Graeco-Persian *siglos* weighing 5·6 grammes.

a Hebrew literally 'reed', the length of Ezekiel's measuring-rod.

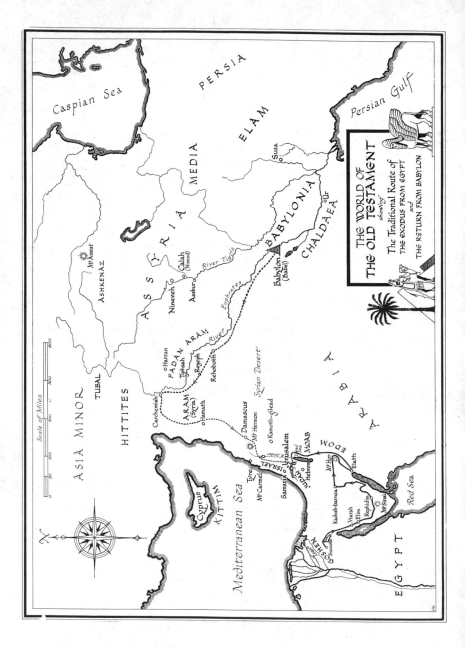

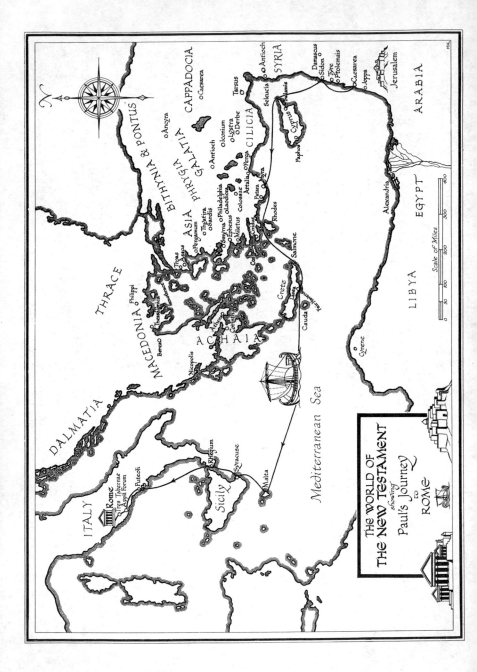

THE
NEW TESTAMENT

'Your life, what is it?' (James 4. 13–14)

HK

BETHLEHEM

THE GOSPEL ACCORDING TO
MATTHEW

Family tree of Jesus Christ

1 A TABLE of the descent of Jesus Christ, son of David, son of Abraham.

2 Abraham was the father of Isaac, Isaac of Jacob, Jacob of Judah and his brothers, 3 Judah of Perez and Zarah (their mother was Tamar), Perez of Hezron, Hezron of Ram, 4 Ram of Amminadab, Amminadab of Nah-5 shon, Nahshon of Salma, Salma of Boaz (his mother was Rahab), Boaz of Obed (his 6 mother was Ruth), Obed of Jesse; and Jesse was the father of King David.

David was the father of Solomon (his 7 mother had been the wife of Uriah), Solomon of Rehoboam, Rehoboam of Abijah, 8 Abijah of Asa, Asa of Jehoshaphat, Jehosha-9 phat of Joram, Joram of Azariah, Azariah of Jotham, Jotham of Ahaz, Ahaz of Heze-10 kiah, Hezekiah of Manasseh, Manasseh of 11 Amon, Amon of Josiah; and Josiah was the father of Jeconiah and his brothers at the time of the deportation to Babylon.

12 After the deportation Jeconiah was the father of Shealtiel, Shealtiel of Zerubbabel, 13 Zerubbabel of Abiud, Abiud of Eliakim, 14 Eliakim of Azor, Azor of Zadok, Zadok of 15 Achim, Achim of Eliud, Eliud of Eleazar, Eleazar of Matthan, Matthan of Jacob, 16 Jacob of Joseph, the husband of Mary, who gave birth to[a] Jesus called Messiah.

7 There were thus fourteen generations in all from Abraham to David, fourteen from David until the deportation to Babylon, and fourteen from the deportation until the Messiah.

Birth of Jesus Christ

This is the story of the birth of the Messiah. 18 Mary his mother was betrothed to Joseph; before their marriage she found that she was with child by the Holy Spirit. Being a man 19 of principle, and at the same time wanting to save her from exposure, Joseph desired to have the marriage contract set aside quietly. He had resolved on this, when an 20 angel of the Lord appeared to him in a dream. 'Joseph son of David,' said the angel, 'do not be afraid to take Mary home with you as your wife. It is by the Holy Spirit that she has conceived this child. She 21 will bear a son; and you shall give him the name Jesus (Saviour), for he will save his people from their sins.' All this happened 22 in order to fulfil what the Lord declared through the prophet: 'The virgin will con-23 ceive and bear a son, and he shall be called Emmanuel', a name which means 'God is with us'. Rising from sleep Joseph did as the 24 angel had directed him; he took Mary home to be his wife, but had no intercourse with 25 her until her son was born. And he named the child Jesus.

a *Some witnesses read* Joseph, to whom was betrothed Mary, a virgin, who gave birth to . . .; *one witness has* Joseph, and Joseph, to whom Mary, a virgin, was betrothed, was the father of . . .

Visitors from the east

2 Jesus was born at Bethlehem in Judaea during the reign of Herod. After his birth astrol-
2 ogers from the east arrived in Jerusalem, asking, 'Where is the child who is born to be king of the Jews?[b] We observed the rising of his star, and we have come to pay him hom-
3 age.' King Herod was greatly perturbed when he heard this; and so was the whole of
4 Jerusalem. He called a meeting of the chief priests and lawyers of the Jewish people, and put before them the question: 'Where is it
5 that the Messiah is to be born?' 'At Bethlehem in Judaea', they replied; and they referred him to the prophecy which reads:
6 'Bethlehem in the land of Judah, you are far from least in the eyes of[c] the rulers of Judah; for out of you shall come a leader to be the shepherd of my people Israel.'
7   Herod next called the astrologers to meet him in private, and ascertained from them
8 the time when the star had appeared. He then sent them on to Bethlehem, and said, 'Go and make a careful inquiry for the child. When you have found him, report to me, so that I may go myself and pay him homage.'
9   They set out at the king's bidding; and the star which they had seen at its rising went ahead of them until it stopped above the
10 place where the child lay. At the sight of the
11 star they were overjoyed. Entering the house, they saw the child with Mary his mother,

b Or Where is the king of the Jews who has just been born?   *c Or* least among.

and bowed to the ground in homage to him; then they opened their treasures and offered him gifts: gold, frankincense, and myrrh. And being warned in a dream not to go 1 back to Herod, they returned home another way.

Escape to Egypt

After they had gone, an angel of the Lord 1 appeared to Joseph in a dream, and said to him, 'Rise up, take the child and his mother and escape with them to Egypt, and stay there until I tell you; for Herod is going to search for the child to do away with him.' So Joseph rose from sleep, and taking mother 1

Frankincense

and child by night he went away with them to Egypt, and there he stayed till Herod's 1 death. This was to fulfil what the Lord had declared through the prophet: 'I called my son out of Egypt.'

When Herod saw how the astrologers had 1 tricked him he fell into a passion, and gave orders for the massacre of all children in Bethlehem and its neighbourhood, of the age of two years or less, corresponding with the time he had ascertained from the astrologers. So the words spoken through Jeremiah the 1

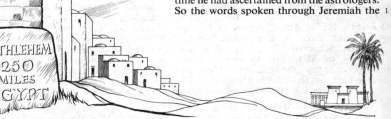

18 prophet were fulfilled: 'A voice was heard in Rama, wailing and loud laments; it was Rachel weeping for her children, and refusing all consolation, because they were no more.'

Return to Palestine

19 The time came that Herod died; and an angel of the Lord appeared in a dream to
20 Joseph in Egypt and said to him, 'Rise up, take the child and his mother, and go with them to the land of Israel, for the men who
21 threatened the child's life are dead.' So he rose, took mother and child with him, and
22 came to the land of Israel. Hearing, however, that Archelaus had succeeded his father Herod as king of Judaea, he was afraid to go there. And being warned by a dream, he withdrew to the region of Galilee;
23 there he settled in a town called Nazareth. This was to fulfil the words spoken through the prophets: 'He shall be called a Nazarene.'

John the Baptist preaches repentance

3 About that time John the Baptist appeared
2 as a preacher in the Judaean wilderness; his theme was: 'Repent; for the kingdom of
3 Heaven is upon you!' It is of him that the prophet Isaiah spoke when he said, 'A voice crying aloud in the wilderness, "Prepare a way for the Lord; clear a straight path for him."'

4   John's clothing was a rough coat of camel's hair, with a leather belt round his waist, and
5 his food was locusts and wild honey. They flocked to him from Jerusalem, from all

Judaea, and the whole Jordan valley, and 6 were baptized by him in the River Jordan, confessing their sins.

When he saw many of the Pharisees and 7 Sadducees coming for baptism he said to them: 'You vipers' brood! Who warned you to escape from the coming retribution? Then 8 prove your repentance by the fruit it bears; and do not presume to say to yourselves, 9 "We have Abraham for our father." I tell you that God can make children for Abraham out of these stones here. Already the 10 axe is laid to the roots of the trees; and every tree that fails to produce good fruit is cut down and thrown on the fire. I baptize you 11 with water, for repentance; but the one who comes after me is mightier than I. I am not fit to take off his shoes. He will baptize you with the Holy Spirit and with fire. His 12 shovel is ready in his hand and he will winnow his threshing-floor; the wheat he will gather into his granary, but he will burn the chaff on a fire that can never go out.'

Jesus is baptized

Then Jesus arrived at the Jordan from 13 Galilee, and came to John to be baptized by him. John tried to dissuade him. 'Do you 14 come to me?' he said; 'I need rather to be

HK

(Matt. 3. 12)

15 baptized by you.' Jesus replied, 'Let it be so for the present; we do well to conform in this way with all that God requires.' John
16 then allowed him to come. After baptism Jesus came up out of the water at once, and at that moment heaven opened; he saw the Spirit of God descending like a dove to
17 alight upon him; and a voice from heaven was heard saying, 'This is my Son, my Beloved,*d* on whom my favour rests.'

The temptation of Jesus

4 Jesus was then led away by the Spirit into the wilderness, to be tempted by the devil.
2   For forty days and nights he fasted, and
3 at the end of them he was famished. The tempter approached him and said, 'If you are the Son of God, tell these stones to be-
4 come bread.' Jesus answered, 'Scripture says, "Man cannot live on bread alone; he lives on every word that God utters."'
5   The devil then took him to the Holy City
6 and set him on the parapet of the temple. 'If you are the Son of God,' he said, 'throw yourself down; for Scripture says, "He will put his angels in charge of you, and they will support you in their arms, for fear you should strike
7 your foot against a stone."' Jesus answered him, 'Scripture says again, "You are not to put the Lord your God to the test."'
8   Once again, the devil took him to a very high mountain, and showed him all the
9 kingdoms of the world in their glory. 'All these', he said, 'I will give you, if you will
10 only fall down and do me homage.' But Jesus said, 'Begone, Satan! Scripture says,

"You shall do homage to the Lord your God and worship him alone."'
11   Then the devil left him; and angels appeared and waited on him.

Jesus starts work in Galilee

12 When he heard that John had been arrested,
13 Jesus withdrew to Galilee; and leaving Nazareth he went and settled at Capernaum on the Sea of Galilee, in the district of
14 Zebulun and Naphtali. This was to fulfil the passage in the prophet Isaiah which tells

of 'the land of Zebulun, the land of Naphtali, 15 the Way of the Sea, the land beyond Jordan, heathen Galilee', and says:

'The people that lived in darkness saw a 16   great light;
light dawned on the dwellers in the land of   death's dark shadow.'

From that day Jesus began to proclaim the 17 message: 'Repent; for*e* the kingdom of Heaven is upon you.'

Jesus calls four fishermen

Jesus was walking by the Sea of Galilee 18 when he saw two brothers, Simon called Peter and his brother Andrew, casting a net into the lake; for they were fishermen. Jesus 19 said to them, 'Come with me, and I will make you fishers of men.' And at once they 20 left their nets and followed him.

He went on, and saw another pair of 21 brothers, James son of Zebedee and his brother John; they were in the boat with their father Zebedee, overhauling their nets. He called them, and at once they left the boat 22 and their father, and followed him.

A wilderness

---

d Or This is my only Son.   *e* Some witnesses omit Repent; for.

Galilean fishermen

Teaching, preaching, and healing

23 He went round the whole of Galilee, teaching in the synagogues, preaching the gospel of the Kingdom, and curing whatever illness or infirmity there was among the 24 people. His fame reached the whole of Syria; and sufferers from every kind of illness, racked with pain, possessed by devils, epileptic, or paralysed, were all brought to him, and he cured them. Great crowds also 25 followed him, from Galilee and the Ten Towns,*f* from Jerusalem and Judaea, and from Transjordan.

The Sermon on the Mount

When he saw the crowds he went up the hill. **5** There he took his seat, and when his disciples had gathered round him he began to 2 address them. And this is the teaching he gave:

Who is truly blest?

'How blest are those who know their need 3
    of God;
    the kingdom of Heaven is theirs.
How blest are the sorrowful;   4
    they shall find consolation.
How blest are those of a gentle spirit;   5
    they shall have the earth for their posses
    sion.

f Greek Decapolis.

6 How blest are those who hunger and thirst
to see right prevail;[g]
they shall be satisfied.

7 How blest are those who show mercy;
mercy shall be shown to them.

8 How blest are those whose hearts are pure;
they shall see God.

9 How blest are the peacemakers;
God shall call them his sons.

10 How blest are those who have suffered
persecution for the cause of right;
the kingdom of Heaven is theirs.

11 'How blest you are, when you suffer insults
and persecution and every kind of calumny
12 for my sake. Accept it with gladness and
exultation, for you have a rich reward in
heaven; in the same way they persecuted the
prophets before you.'

Salt and light

13 'You are salt to the world. And if salt becomes tasteless, how is its saltness to be
restored? It is now good for nothing but to
be thrown away and trodden underfoot.

14 'You are light for all the world. A town
that stands on a hill cannot be hidden.

15 When a lamp is lit, it is not put under the
meal-tub, but on the lamp-stand, where it
16 gives light to everyone in the house. And
you, like the lamp, must shed light among
your fellows, so that, when they see the good
you do, they may give praise to your Father
in heaven.'

Jesus and the Law

17 'Do not suppose that I have come to abolish
the Law and the prophets; I did not come to
18 abolish, but to complete. I tell you this: so
long as heaven and earth endure, not a
letter, not a stroke, will disappear from the
Law until all that must happen has hap-
19 pened.[h] If any man therefore sets aside even
the least of the Law's demands, and teaches
others to do the same, he will have the lowest
place in the kingdom of Heaven, whereas
anyone who keeps the Law, and teaches
others so, will stand high in the kingdom of
20 Heaven. I tell you, unless you show yourselves far better men than the Pharisees and
the doctors of the law, you can never enter
the kingdom of Heaven.'

About anger and grievances

21 'You have learned that our forefathers were
told, "Do not commit murder; anyone who
commits murder must be brought to judge-
22 ment." But what I tell you is this: Anyone
who nurses anger against his brother[i] must
be brought to judgement. If he abuses his
brother he must answer for it to the court;

if he sneers at him he will have to answer for
it in the fires of hell.

'If, when you are bringing your gift to the 23
altar, you suddenly remember that your 24
brother has a grievance against you, leave
your gift where it is before the altar. First
go and make your peace with your brother,
and only then come back and offer your gift.

'If someone sues you, come to terms with 25
him promptly while you are both on your
way to court; otherwise he may hand you
over to the judge, and the judge to the constable, and you will be put in jail. I tell you, 26
once you are there you will not be let out till
you have paid the last farthing.'

About lust and adultery

'You have learned that they were told, "Do 27
not commit adultery." But what I tell you 28
is this: If a man looks on a woman with a
lustful eye, he has already committed adultery with her in his heart.

'If your right eye is your undoing, tear it 29
out and fling it away; it is better for you to
lose one part of your body than for the whole
of it to be thrown into hell. And if your right 30
hand is your undoing, cut it off and fling it
away; it is better for you to lose one part of
your body than for the whole of it to go to
hell.'

About divorce

'They were told, "A man who divorces his 31
wife must give her a note of dismissal." But 32
what I tell you is this: If a man divorces his
wife for any cause other than unchastity he
involves her in adultery; and anyone who
marries a divorced woman commits adultery.'

About oaths

'Again, you have learned that our forefathers 33
were told, "Do not break your oath", and,
"Oaths sworn to the Lord must be kept."
But what I tell you is this: You are not to 34
swear at all—not by heaven, for it is God's
throne, nor by earth, for it is his footstool, 35
nor by Jerusalem, for it is the city of the
great King, nor by your own head, because 36
you cannot turn one hair of it white or black.
Plain "Yes" or "No" is all you need to say; 37
anything beyond that comes from the devil.'

About personal wrongs

'You have learned that they were told, 38
"Eye for eye, tooth for tooth." But what I
tell you is this: Do not set yourself against
the man who wrongs you. If someone slaps
you on the right cheek, turn and offer him
your left. If a man wants to sue you for your 40
shirt, let him have your coat as well. If a 41

---

g *Or* to do what is right.
without good cause.   h *Or* before all that it stands for is achieved.   i *Some witnesses insert*

42 man in authority makes you go one mile, go with him two. Give when you are asked to give; and do not turn your back on a man who wants to borrow.'

'Love your enemies'

43 'You have learned that they were told, "Love
44 your neighbour, hate your enemy." But what I tell you is this: Love your enemies[j] and
45 pray for your persecutors;[k] only so can you be children of your heavenly Father, who makes his sun rise on good and bad alike, and sends the rain on the honest and the dis-
46 honest. If you love only those who love you, what reward can you expect? Surely the tax-
47 gatherers do as much as that. And if you greet only your brothers, what is there extra-ordinary about that? Even the heathen do as
48 much. There must be no limit to your good-ness, as your heavenly Father's goodness knows no bounds.'

Pretence and sincerity

6 'Be careful not to make a show of your religion before men; if you do, no reward awaits you in your Father's house in heaven.
2 'Thus, when you do some act of charity, do not announce it with a flourish of trum-pets, as the hypocrites do in synagogue and in the streets to win admiration from men. I tell you this: they have their reward already.
3 No; when you do some act of charity, do not let your left hand know what your right
4 is doing; your good deed must be secret, and your Father who sees what is done in secret will reward you.'[l]

About prayer

5 'Again, when you pray, do not be like the hypocrites; they love to say their prayers standing up in synagogue and at the street-corners, for everyone to see them. I tell you
6 this: they have their reward already. But when you pray, go into a room by yourself, shut the door, and pray to your Father who is there in the secret place; and your Father who sees what is secret will reward you.[l]
7 'In your prayers do not go babbling on like the heathen, who imagine that the more they say the more likely they are to be heard.
8 Do not imitate them. Your Father knows what your needs are before you ask him.
9 'This is how you should pray:

"Our Father in heaven,
thy name be hallowed;
10 thy kingdom come,
thy will be done,
on earth as in heaven.

11 Give us today our daily bread.[m]
12 Forgive us the wrong we have done,
as we have forgiven those who have wronged us.
13 And do not bring us to the test,
but save us from the evil one."[n o]

14 For if you forgive others the wrongs they have done, your heavenly Father will also
15 forgive you; but if you do not forgive others, then the wrongs you have done will not be forgiven by your Father.'

About fasting

16 'So too when you fast, do not look gloomy like the hypocrites: they make their faces unsightly so that other people may see that they are fasting. I tell you this: they have
17 their reward already. But when you fast,
18 anoint your head and wash your face, so that men may not see that you are fasting, but only your Father who is in the secret place; and your Father who sees what is secret will give you your reward.'

Cure for anxiety

19 'Do not store up for yourselves treasure on earth, where it grows rusty and moth-eaten,
20 and thieves break in to steal it. Store up treasure in heaven, where there is no moth and no rust to spoil it, no thieves to break in
21 and steal. For where your treasure is, there will your heart be also.
22 'The lamp of the body is the eye. If your eyes are sound, you will have light for your
23 whole body; if the eyes are bad, your whole body will be in darkness. If then the only light you have is darkness, the darkness is doubly dark.
24 'No servant can be the slave of two masters; for either he will hate the first and love the second, or he will be devoted to the first and think nothing of the second. You cannot serve God and Money.
25 'Therefore I bid you put away anxious thoughts about food and drink to keep you alive, and clothes to cover your body. Surely life is more than food, the body more than
26 clothes. Look at the birds of the air; they do not sow and reap and store in barns, yet your heavenly Father feeds them. You are
27 worth more than the birds! Is there a man of you who by anxious thought can add a
28 foot to his height[p]? And why be anxious about clothes? Consider how the lilies grow in the fields; they do not work, they do not
29 spin;[q] and yet, I tell you, even Solomon in all his splendour was not attired like one of

---

j Some witnesses insert bless those who curse you, do good to those who hate you. *k Some witnesses insert* and those who treat you spitefully. *l Some witnesses add* openly. *m Or* our bread for the morrow. *n Or* from evil. *o Some witnesses add* For thine is the kingdom and the power and the glory, for ever. Amen. *p Or* a day to his life. *q One witness reads* Consider the lilies: they neither card nor spin, nor labour.

30 these. But if that is how God clothes the grass in the fields, which is there today, and tomorrow is thrown on the stove, will he not all the more clothe you? How little faith
31 you have! No, do not ask anxiously, "What are we to eat? What are we to drink? What
32 shall we wear?" All these are things for the heathen to run after, not for you, because your heavenly Father knows that you need
33 them all. Set your mind on God's kingdom and his justice before everything else, and
34 all the rest will come to you as well. So do not be anxious about tomorrow; tomorrow will look after itself. Each day has troubles enough of its own.'

Judging others

7 'Pass no judgement, and you will not be
2 judged. For as you judge others, so you will yourselves be judged, and whatever measure you deal out to others will be dealt back to
3 you. Why do you look at the speck of saw-dust in your brother's eye, with never a thought for the great plank in your own?
4 Or how can you say to your brother, "Let me take the speck out of your eye", when all the time there is that plank in your
5 own? You hypocrite! First take the plank out of your own eye, and then you will see clearly to take the speck out of your brother's.
6   'Do not give dogs what is holy; do not throw your pearls to the pigs: they will only trample on them, and turn and tear you to pieces.'

Ask; seek; knock

7 'Ask, and you will receive; seek, and you will find; knock, and the door will be
8 opened. For everyone who asks receives, he who seeks finds, and to him who knocks, the door will be opened.
9   'Is there a man among you who will offer
10 his son a stone when he asks for bread, or
11 a snake when he asks for fish? If you, then, bad as you are, know how to give your children what is good for them, how much more will your heavenly Father give good things to those who ask him!
12   'Always treat others as you would like them to treat you: that is the Law and the prophets.'

The gate to life

13 'Enter by the narrow gate. The gate is wide that leads to perdition, there is plenty of room on the road,[r] and many go that way;
14 but the gate that leads to life is small and the road is narrow,[s] and those who find it are few.'

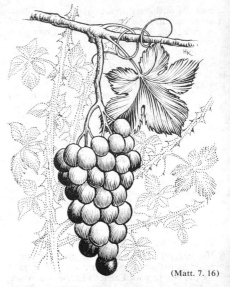

(Matt. 7. 16)

A tree and its fruit

'Beware of false prophets, men who come 15 to you dressed up as sheep while underneath they are savage wolves. You will recognize 16 them by the fruits they bear. Can grapes be picked from briars, or figs from thistles? In 17 the same way, a good tree always yields good fruit, and a poor tree bad fruit. A good tree 18 cannot bear bad fruit, or a poor tree good fruit. And when a tree does not yield good 19 fruit it is cut down and burnt. That is why 20 I say you will recognize them by their fruits.
   'Not everyone who calls me "Lord, Lord" 21 will enter the kingdom of Heaven, but only those who do the will of my heavenly Father. When that day comes, many will say to me, 22 "Lord, Lord, did we not prophesy in your name, cast out devils in your name, and in your name perform many miracles?" Then 23 I will tell them to their face, "I never knew you; out of my sight, you and your wicked ways!"'

A firm foundation

'What then of the man who hears these words 24 of mine and acts upon them? He is like a man who had the sense to build his house on rock. The rain came down, the floods rose, 25 the wind blew, and beat upon that house; but it did not fall, because its foundations were on rock. But what of the man who hears 26 these words of mine and does not act upon them? He is like a man who was foolish enough to build his house on sand. The rain 27

---

r Some witnesses read The road that leads to perdition is wide with plenty of room.   *s Some witnesses read* but the road that leads to life is small and narrow.

came down, the floods rose, the wind blew, and beat upon that house; down it fell with a great crash.'

28 When Jesus had finished this discourse the
29 people were astounded at his teaching; unlike their own teachers he taught with a note of authority.

Jesus cleanses a leper

8 After he had come down from the hill he
2 was followed by a great crowd. And now a leper[t] approached him, bowed low, and said, 'Sir, if only you will, you can cleanse
3 me.' Jesus stretched out his hand, touched him, and said, 'Indeed I will; be clean again.' And his leprosy was cured immediately.
4 Then Jesus said to him, 'Be sure you tell nobody; but go and show yourself to the priest, and make the offering laid down by Moses for your cleansing; that will certify the cure.'

The faith of a soldier

5 When he had entered Capernaum a cen-
6 turion came up to ask his help. 'Sir,' he said, 'a boy of mine lies at home paralysed and
7 racked with pain.' Jesus said, 'I will come
8 and cure him.'[u] But the centurion replied, 'Sir, who am I to have you under my roof? You need only say the word and the boy
9 will be cured. I know, for I am myself under orders, with soldiers under me. I say to one, "Go", and he goes; to another, "Come here", and he comes; and to my servant,
10 "Do this", and he does it.' Jesus heard him with astonishment, and said to the people who were following him, 'I tell you this: nowhere, even in Israel, have I found such faith.
11 'Many, I tell you, will come from east and west to feast with Abraham, Isaac, and
12 Jacob in the kingdom of Heaven. But those who were born to the kingdom will be driven out into the dark, the place of wailing and grinding of teeth.'
13 Then Jesus said to the centurion, 'Go home now; because of your faith, so let it be.' At that moment the boy recovered.

Acts of healing

14 Jesus then went to Peter's house and found
15 Peter's mother-in-law in bed with fever. So he took her by the hand; the fever left her, and she got up and waited on him.
16 When evening fell, they brought to him many who were possessed by devils; and he drove the spirits out with a word and
17 healed all who were sick, to fulfil the prophecy of Isaiah: 'He took away our illnesses and lifted our diseases from us.'[v]

The cost of discipleship

At the sight of the crowds surrounding him 18 Jesus gave word to cross to the other shore. A doctor of the law came up, and said, 19 'Master, I will follow you wherever you go.' Jesus replied, 'Foxes have their holes, the 20 birds their roosts; but the Son of Man has nowhere to lay his head.' Another man, one 21 of his disciples, said to him, 'Lord, let me go and bury my father first.' Jesus replied, 22 'Follow me, and leave the dead to bury their dead.'

Jesus calms a storm

Jesus then got into the boat, and his dis- 23 ciples followed. All at once a great storm 24 arose on the lake, till the waves were breaking right over the boat; but he went on sleeping. So they came and woke him up, 25 crying: 'Save us, Lord; we are sinking!' 'Why are you such cowards?' he said; 'how 26 little faith you have!' Then he stood up and rebuked the wind and the sea, and there was a dead calm. The men were astonished at 27 what had happened, and exclaimed, 'What sort of man is this? Even the wind and the sea obey him.'

Jesus cures two madmen

When he reached the other side, in the 28 country of the Gadarenes, he was met by two men who came out from the tombs; they were possessed by devils, and so violent that no one dared pass that way. 'You son 29 of God,' they shouted, 'what do you want with us? Have you come here to torment us before our time?' In the distance a large herd 30 of pigs was feeding; and the devils begged 31 him: 'If you drive us out, send us into that herd of pigs.' 'Begone!' he said. Then they 32 came out and went into the pigs; the whole herd rushed over the edge into the lake, and perished in the water.

The men in charge of them took to their 33 heels, and made for the town, where they told the whole story, and what had happened to the madmen. Thereupon all the 34 town came out to meet Jesus; and when they saw him they begged him to leave the district and go. So he got into the boat **9** and crossed over, and came to his own town.

Authority to forgive sins

And now some men brought him a paralysed 2 man lying on a bed. Seeing their faith Jesus said to the man, 'Take heart, my son; your sins are forgiven.' At this some of the law- 3 yers said to themselves, 'This is blasphemous talk.' Jesus knew what they were thinking, 4

---

t *The words* leper, leprosy, *as used in this translation, refer to some disfiguring skin disease which entailed ceremonial defilement. It is different from what is now called leprosy.*   u *Or* Am I to come and cure him?   v *Or* and bore the burden of our diseases.

and said, 'Why do you harbour these evil
5 thoughts? Is it easier to say, "Your sins are
forgiven", or to say, "Stand up and walk"?
6 But to convince you that the Son of Man has
the right on earth to forgive sins'—he turned
to the paralysed man—'stand up, take your
7 bed, and go home.' Thereupon the man got
8 up, and went off home. The people were
filled with awe at the sight, and praised God
for granting such authority to men.

Jesus and the tax-gatherers

9 As he passed on from there Jesus saw a man
named Matthew at his seat in the custom-
house, and said to him, 'Follow me'; and
Matthew rose and followed him.
10 When Jesus was at table in the house,
many bad characters—tax-gatherers and
others—were seated with him and his dis-
11 ciples. The Pharisees noticed this, and said
to his disciples, 'Why is it that your master
12 eats with tax-gatherers and sinners?' Jesus
heard it and said, 'It is not the healthy that
13 need a doctor, but the sick. Go and learn
what that text means, "I require mercy, not
sacrifice." I did not come to invite virtuous
people, but sinners.'

About fasting

14 Then John's disciples came to him with the
question: 'Why do we and the Pharisees fast,
15 but your disciples do not?' Jesus replied,
'Can you expect the bridegroom's friends to
go mourning while the bridegroom is with
them? The time will come when the bridegroom will be taken away from them; that
will be the time for them to fast.'

Patched clothes and old wine-skins

16 'No one sews a patch of unshrunk cloth on
to an old coat; for then the patch tears away
from the coat, and leaves a bigger hole.
17 Neither do you put new wine into old wine-
skins; if you do, the skins burst, and then the
wine runs out and the skins are spoilt. No,
you put new wine into fresh skins; then both
are preserved.'

Healing and restoration to life

18 Even as he spoke, there came a president of
the synagogue, who bowed low before him
and said, 'My daughter has just died; but
come and lay your hand on her, and she will
19 live.' Jesus rose and went with him, and so
did his disciples.
20 Then a woman who had suffered from
haemorrhages for twelve years came up
from behind, and touched the edge of his
21 cloak; for she said to herself, 'If I can only
22 touch his cloak, I shall be cured.' But Jesus
turned and saw her, and said, 'Take heart,

my daughter; your faith has cured you.'
And from that moment she recovered.
When Jesus arrived at the president's 23
house and saw the flute-players and the
general commotion, he said, 'Be off! The 24
girl is not dead: she is asleep'; and they only
laughed at him. But, when everyone had 25
been turned out, he went into the room and
took the girl by the hand, and she got up.
This story became the talk of all the country 26
round.

Sight restored to two blind men

As he passed on Jesus was followed by two 27
blind men, who cried out, 'Son of David,
have pity on us!' And when he had gone in- 28
doors they came to him. Jesus asked, 'Do
you believe that I have the power to do what
you want?' 'Yes, sir', they said. Then he 29
touched their eyes, and said, 'As you have
believed, so let it be'; and their sight was 30
restored. Jesus said to them sternly, 'See that
no one hears about this.' But as soon as they 31
had gone out they talked about him all over
the country-side.

A dumb man recovers his speech

They were on their way out when a man was 32
brought to him, who was dumb and possessed by a devil; the devil was cast out and the 33
patient recovered his speech. Filled with
amazement the onlookers said, 'Nothing like
this has ever been seen in Israel.'w

'Sheep without a shepherd'

So Jesus went round all the towns and vil- 35
lages teaching in their synagogues, announc-
ing the good news of the Kingdom, and
curing every kind of ailment and disease.
The sight of the people moved him to pity: 36
they were like sheep without a shepherd,
harassed and helpless; and he said to his 37
disciples, 'The crop is heavy, but labourers
are scarce; you must therefore beg the owner 38
to send labourers to harvest his crop.'

The twelve apostles and their mission

Then he called his twelve disciples to him 1
and gave them authority to cast out unclean
spirits and to cure every kind of ailment and
disease.
These are the names of the twelve apostles: 2
first Simon, also called Peter, and his brother
Andrew; James son of Zebedee, and his
brother John; Philip and Bartholomew, 3
Thomas and Matthew the tax-gatherer,
James son of Alphaeus, Lebbaeus,x Simon, 4
a member of the Zealot party, and Judas
Iscariot, the man who betrayed him.
These twelve Jesus sent out with the fol- 5
lowing instructions: 'Do not take the road

---

w *Some witnesses add* (34) But the Pharisees said, 'He casts out devils by the prince of devils.'   x *Some*
witnesses read Thaddaeus.

to gentile lands, and do not enter any
6 Samaritan town; but go rather to the lost
7 sheep of the house of Israel. And as you go
proclaim the message: "The kingdom of
8 Heaven is upon you." Heal the sick, raise
the dead, cleanse lepers, cast out devils. You
received without cost; give without charge.

Shekel and half-shekel

9 'Provide no gold, silver, or copper to fill
10 your purse, no pack for the road, no second
coat, no shoes, no stick; the worker earns
his keep.
11 'When you come to any town or village,
look for some worthy person in it, and make
12 your home there until you leave. Wish the
13 house peace as you enter it, so that, if it is
worthy, your peace may descend on it; if
it is not worthy, your peace can come back
14 to you. If anyone will not receive you or
listen to what you say, then as you leave
that house or that town shake the dust of it
15 off your feet. I tell you this: on the day of
judgement it will be more bearable for the
land of Sodom and Gomorrah than for that
town.'

Coming persecutions

16 'Look, I send you out like sheep among
wolves; be wary as serpents, innocent as
doves.
17 'And be on your guard, for men will hand
you over to their courts, they will flog you
18 in the synagogues, and you will be brought
before governors and kings, for my sake, to
19 testify before them and the heathen. But
when you are arrested, do not worry about
what you are to say; when the time comes,
20 the words you need will be given you; for it
is not you who will be speaking: it will be
the Spirit of your Father speaking in you.
21 'Brother will betray brother to death,
and the father his child; children will turn
against their parents and send them to their
22 death. All will hate you for your allegiance
to me; but the man who holds out to the
23 end will be saved. When you are persecuted
in one town, take refuge in another; I tell
you this: before you have gone through all
the towns of Israel the Son of Man will have
come.

'A pupil does not rank above his teacher, 24
or a servant above his master. The pupil 25
should be content to share his teacher's
lot, the servant to share his master's. If the
master has been called Beelzebub, how much
more his household!'

Freedom from fear

'So do not be afraid of them. There is nothing 26
covered up that will not be uncovered, nothing hidden that will not be made known.
What I say to you in the dark you must 27
repeat in broad daylight; what you hear
whispered you must shout from the house-
tops. Do not fear those who kill the body, 28
but cannot kill the soul. Fear him rather
who is able to destroy both soul and body
in hell.

'Are not sparrows two a penny? Yet with- 29
out your Father's leave not one of them can
fall to the ground. As for you, even the hairs 30
of your head have all been counted. So have 31
no fear; you are worth more than any number of sparrows.'

Acknowledging and disowning Jesus

'Whoever then will acknowledge me before 32
men, I will acknowledge him before my
Father in heaven; and whoever disowns me 33
before men, I will disown him before my
Father in heaven.'

Conflicting loyalties

'You must not think that I have come to 34
bring peace to the earth; I have not come to
bring peace, but a sword. I have come to set 35
a man against his father, a daughter against
her mother, a son's wife against her mother-
in-law; and a man will find his enemies 36
under his own roof.

37 'No man is worthy of me who cares more for father or mother than for me; no man is worthy of me who cares more for son or
38 daughter; no man is worthy of me who does not take up his cross and walk in my footsteps.
39 By gaining his life a man will lose it; by losing his life for my sake, he will gain it.'

About rewards

40 'To receive you is to receive me, and to receive me is to receive the One who sent
41 me. Whoever receives a prophet as a prophet will be given a prophet's reward, and whoever receives a good man because he is a good man will be given a good man's re-
42 ward. And if anyone gives so much as a cup of cold water to one of these little ones, because he is a disciple of mine, I tell you this: that man will assuredly not go unrewarded.'

11 When Jesus had finished giving his twelve disciples their instructions, he left that place and went to teach and preach in the neighbouring towns.

A message for John the Baptist

2 John, who was in prison, heard what Christ was doing, and sent his own disciples to him
3 with this message: 'Are you the one who is to come, or are we to expect some other?'
4 Jesus answered, 'Go and tell John what
5 you hear and see: the blind recover their sight, the lame walk, the lepers are made clean, the deaf hear, the dead are raised to
6 life, the poor are hearing the good news— and happy is the man who does not find me a stumbling-block.'

About John the Baptist

7 When the messengers were on their way back, Jesus began to speak to the people about John: 'What was the spectacle that drew you to the wilderness? A reed-bed
8 swept by the wind? No? Then what did you go out to see? A man dressed in silks and satins? Surely you must look in palaces for
9 that. But why did you go out? To see a prophet? Yes indeed, and far more than a
10 prophet. He is the man of whom Scripture says,

"Here is my herald, whom I send on ahead of you,
and he will prepare your way before you."

11 I tell you this: never has there appeared on earth a mother's son greater than John the Baptist, and yet the least in the kingdom of Heaven is greater than he.
12 'Ever since the coming of John the Baptist the kingdom of Heaven has been subjected

to violence and violent men[y] are seizing it.
13 For all the prophets and the Law foretold
14 things to come until John appeared, and John is the destined Elijah, if you will but
15 accept it. If you have ears, then hear.
16 'How can I describe this generation? They are like children sitting in the market-place and shouting at each other,

"We piped for you and you would not
17 dance."
"We wept and wailed, and you would not mourn."

18 For John came, neither eating nor drinking,
19 and they say, "He is possessed." The Son of Man came eating and drinking, and they say, "Look at him! a glutton and a drinker, a friend of tax-gatherers and sinners!" And yet God's wisdom is proved right by its results.'

Jesus faces unbelief

20 Then he spoke of the towns in which most of his miracles had been performed, and
21 denounced them for their impenitence. 'Alas for you, Chorazin!' he said; 'alas for you, Bethsaida! If the miracles that were performed in you had been performed in Tyre and Sidon, they would have repented long
22 ago in sackcloth and ashes. But it will be more bearable, I tell you, for Tyre and Sidon
23 on the day of judgement than for you. And as for you, Capernaum, will you be exalted to the skies? No, brought down to the depths! For if the miracles had been performed in Sodom which were performed in you,
24 Sodom would be standing to this day. But it will be more bearable, I tell you, for the land of Sodom on the day of judgement than for you.'

The Father and the Son

25 At that time Jesus spoke these words: 'I thank thee, Father, Lord of heaven and earth, for hiding these things from the learned and wise, and revealing them to the
26 simple. Yes, Father, such[z] was thy choice.
27 Everything is entrusted to me by my Father; and no one knows the Son but the Father, and no one knows the Father but the Son and those to whom the Son may choose to reveal him.

'Come to me'

28 'Come to me, all whose work is hard, whose load is heavy; and I will give you relief.
29 Bend your necks to my yoke, and learn from me, for I am gentle and humble-hearted;
30 and your souls will find relief. For my yoke is good to bear, my load is light.'

y Or has been forcing its way forward, and men of force . . . such . . .

z Or Yes, I thank thee, Father, that

About the Sabbath

12 Once about that time Jesus went through the cornfields on the Sabbath; and his disciples, feeling hungry, began to pluck
2 some ears of corn and eat them. The Pharisees noticed this, and said to him, 'Look, your disciples are doing something which is
3 forbidden on the Sabbath.' He answered, 'Have you not read what David did when
4 he and his men were hungry? He went into the House of God and ate the sacred bread, though neither he nor his men had a right to
5 eat it, but only the priests. Or have you not read in the Law that on the Sabbath the priests in the temple break the Sabbath and
6 it is not held against them? I tell you, there is something greater than the temple here.
7 If you had known what that text means, "I require mercy, not sacrifice", you would
8 not have condemned the innocent. For the Son of Man is sovereign over the Sabbath.'

A man with a withered arm

9 He went on to another place, and entered
10 their synagogue. A man was there with a withered arm, and they asked Jesus, 'Is it permitted to heal on the Sabbath?' (They
11 wanted to frame a charge against him.) But he said to them, 'Suppose you had one sheep, which fell into a ditch on the Sabbath; is there one of you who would not catch hold
12 of it and lift it out? And surely a man is worth far more than a sheep! It is therefore
13 permitted to do good on the Sabbath.' Turning to the man he said, 'Stretch out your
14 arm.' He stretched it out, and it was made sound again like the other. But the Pharisees, on leaving the synagogue, laid a plot to do away with him.

The Servant of God

15 Jesus was aware of it and withdrew. Many
16 followed, and he cured all who were ill; and he gave strict injunctions that they were not
17 to make him known. This was to fulfil Isaiah's prophecy:

18 'Here is my servant, whom I have chosen,
  my beloved, on whom my favour rests;
  I will put my Spirit upon him,
  and he will proclaim judgement among the nations.
19 He will not strive, he will not shout,
  nor will his voice be heard in the streets.
20 He will not snap off the broken reed,
  nor snuff out the smouldering wick,
  until he leads justice on to victory.
21 In him the nations shall place their hope.'

Controversy with the Pharisees

22 Then they brought him a man who was possessed; he was blind and dumb; and

Jesus cured him, restoring both speech and sight. The bystanders were all amazed, and 23 the word went round: 'Can this be the Son of David?' But when the Pharisees heard it 24 they said, 'It is only by Beelzebub prince of devils that this man drives the devils out.'

He knew what was in their minds; so he 25 said to them, 'Every kingdom divided against itself goes to ruin; and no town, no household, that is divided against itself can stand. And if it is Satan who casts out Satan, Satan 26 is divided against himself; how then can his kingdom stand? And if it is by Beelzebub 27 that I cast out devils, by whom do your own people drive them out? If this is your argument, they themselves will refute you. But 28 if it is by the Spirit of God that I drive out the devils, then be sure the kingdom of God has already come upon you.

'Or again, how can anyone break into a 29 strong man's house and make off with his goods, unless he has first tied the strong man up before ransacking the house?

'He who is not with me is against me, and 30 he who does not gather with me scatters.

'And so I tell you this: no sin, no slander, 31 is beyond forgiveness for men, except slander spoken against the Spirit, and that will not be forgiven. Any man who speaks a word 32 against the Son of Man will be forgiven; but if anyone speaks against the Holy Spirit, for him there is no forgiveness, either in this age or in the age to come.

'Either make the tree good and its fruit 33 good, or make the tree bad and its fruit bad; you can tell a tree by its fruit. You vipers' 34 brood! How can your words be good when you yourselves are evil? For the words that the mouth utters come from the overflowing of the heart. A good man produces good from 35 the store of good within himself; and an evil man from evil within produces evil.

'I tell you this: there is not a thoughtless 36 word that comes from men's lips but they will have to account for it on the day of judgement. For out of your own mouth you 37 will be acquitted; out of your own mouth you will be condemned.'

The sign of Jonah

At this some of the doctors of the law and 38 the Pharisees said, 'Master, we should like you to show us a sign.' He answered: 'It is 39 a wicked, godless generation that asks for a sign; and the only sign that will be given it is the sign of the prophet Jonah. Jonah was 40 in the sea-monster's belly for three days and three nights, and in the same way the Son of Man will be three days and three nights in the bowels of the earth. At the Judgement, 41 when this generation is on trial, the men of Nineveh will appear against it[a] and ensure

a Or will rise again together with it.

N *

its condemnation, for they repented at the preaching of Jonah; and what is here is
42 greater than Jonah. The Queen of the South will appear at the Judgement when this generation is on trial,[b] and ensure its condemnation, for she came from the ends of the earth to hear the wisdom of Solomon; and what is here is greater than Solomon.

43 'When an unclean spirit comes out of a man it wanders over the deserts seeking a
44 resting-place, and finds none. Then it says, "I will go back to the home I left." So it returns and finds the house unoccupied,
45 swept clean, and tidy. Off it goes and collects seven other spirits more wicked than itself, and they all come in and settle down; and in the end the man's plight is worse than before. That is how it will be with this wicked generation.'

Jesus's relatives

46 He was still speaking to the crowd when his mother and brothers appeared; they stood
47 outside, wanting to speak to him. Someone said, 'Your mother and your brothers are here outside; they want to speak to you.'
48 Jesus turned to the man who brought the message, and said, 'Who is my mother? Who
49 are my brothers?'; and pointing to the disciples, he said, 'Here are my mother and my
50 brothers. Whoever does the will of my heavenly Father is my brother, my sister, my mother.'

Parables

13 That same day Jesus went out and sat by the
2 lake-side, where so many people gathered round him that he had to get into a boat. He sat there, and all the people stood on the
3 shore. He spoke to them in parables, at some length.

A sower

4 He said: 'A sower went out to sow. And as he sowed, some seed fell along the footpath;
5 and the birds came and ate it up. Some seed fell on rocky ground, where it had little soil, and it sprouted quickly because it had no
6 depth of earth; but when the sun rose the young corn was scorched, and as it had no
7 root it withered away. Some seed fell among thistles; and the thistles shot up, and choked
8 the corn. And some of the seed fell into good soil, where it bore fruit, yielding a hundredfold or, it might be, sixtyfold or thirtyfold.
9 If you have ears, then hear.'

Why Jesus told parables

10 The disciples went up to him and asked, 'Why do you speak to them in parables?'
11 He replied, 'It has been granted to you to know the secrets of the kingdom of Heaven; but to those others it has not been granted.
12 For the man who has will be given more, till he has enough and to spare; and the man who has not will forfeit even what he has.
13 That is why I speak to them in parables; for they look without seeing, and listen without
14 hearing or understanding. There is a prophecy of Isaiah which is being fulfilled for them: "You may hear and hear, but you will never understand; you may look and
15 look, but you will never see. For this people's mind has become gross; their ears are dulled, and their eyes are closed. Otherwise, their eyes might see, their ears hear, and their mind understand, and then they might turn again, and I would heal them."

16 'But happy are your eyes because they see,
17 and your ears because they hear! Many prophets and saints, I tell you, desired to see what you now see, yet never saw it; to hear what you hear, yet never heard it.'

The parable of the sower explained

18 'You then, may hear the parable of the
19 sower. When a man hears the word that tells of the Kingdom but fails to understand it, the evil one comes and carries off what has been sown in his heart. There you have the
20 seed sown along the footpath. The seed sown on rocky ground stands for the man who, on hearing the word, accepts it at once

---

b Or At the Judgement the Queen of the South will be raised to life together with this generation.

21 with joy; but as it strikes no root in him he has no staying-power, and when there is trouble or persecution on account of the 22 word he falls away at once. The seed sown among thistles represents the man who hears the word, but worldly cares and the false glamour of wealth choke it, and it proves 23 barren. But the seed that fell into good soil is the man who hears the word and understands it, who accordingly bears fruit, and yields a hundredfold or, it may be, sixtyfold or thirtyfold.'

Wheat and darnel

24 Here is another parable that he put before them: 'The kingdom of Heaven is like this. 25 A man sowed his field with good seed; but while everyone was asleep his enemy came, sowed darnel among the wheat, and made 26 off. When the corn sprouted and began to fill out, the darnel could be seen among it. 27 The farmer's men went to their master and said, "Sir, was it not good seed that you sowed in your field? Then where has the 28 darnel come from?" "This is an enemy's doing", he replied. "Well then," they said, 29 "shall we go and gather the darnel?" "No," he answered; "in gathering it you might 30 pull up the wheat at the same time. Let them both grow together till harvest; and at harvest-time I will tell the reapers, 'Gather the darnel first, and tie it in bundles for burning; then collect the wheat into my barn.' " '

A mustard-seed

31 And this is another parable that he put before them: 'The kingdom of Heaven is like a mustard-seed, which a man took and 32 sowed in his field. As a seed, mustard is smaller than any other; but when it has grown it is bigger than any garden-plant; it becomes a tree, big enough for the birds to come and roost among its branches.'

Yeast

33 He told them also this parable: 'The kingdom of Heaven is like yeast, which a woman took and mixed with half a hundredweight of flour till it was all leavened.'

Jesus's way of teaching

34 In all this teaching to the crowds Jesus spoke in parables; in fact he never spoke to them 35 without a parable. This was to fulfil the prophecy of Isaiah:[c]

'I will open my mouth in parables;
I will utter things kept secret since the world was made.'

The wheat and darnel parable explained

He then dismissed the people, and went into 36 the house, where his disciples came to him and said, 'Explain to us the parable of the darnel in the field.' And this was his answer: 37 'The sower of the good seed is the Son of Man. The field is the world; the good seed 38 stands for the children of the Kingdom, the darnel for the children of the evil one. The 39 enemy who sowed the darnel is the devil. The harvest is the end of time. The reapers are angels. As the darnel, then, is gathered 40 up and burnt, so at the end of time the Son 41 of Man will send out his angels, who will gather out of his kingdom whatever makes men stumble, and all whose deeds are evil, and these will be thrown into the blazing 42 furnace, the place of wailing and grinding of teeth. And then the righteous will shine as 43 brightly as the sun in the kingdom of their Father. If you have ears, then hear.'

Buried treasure

'The kingdom of Heaven is like treasure 44 lying buried in a field. The man who found it, buried it again; and for sheer joy went and sold everything he had, and bought that field.'

The finest pearl

'Here is another picture of the kingdom of 45 Heaven. A merchant looking out for fine pearls found one of very special value; so 46 he went and sold everything he had, and bought it.'

A net full of fish

'Again the kingdom of Heaven is like a net 47 let down into the sea, where fish of every kind were caught in it. When it was full, it 48 was dragged ashore. Then the men sat down and collected the good fish into pails and threw the worthless away. That is how it will 49 be at the end of time. The angels will go forth, and they will separate the wicked from the good, and throw them into the 50 blazing furnace, the place of wailing and grinding of teeth.

'Have you understood all this?' he asked; 51 and they answered, 'Yes.' He said to them, 52 'When, therefore, a teacher of the law has become a learner in the kingdom of Heaven, he is like a householder who can produce from his store both the new and the old.'

Unbelief in Nazareth

When he had finished these parables Jesus 53 left that place, and came to his home 54 town, where he taught the people in their synagogue. In amazement they asked, 'Where does he get this wisdom from, and these miraculous powers? Is he not the 55

---

c Some witnesses omit of Isaiah.

carpenter's son? Is not his mother called Mary, his brothers James, Joseph, Simon, 56 and Judas? And are not all his sisters here with us? Where then has he got all this 57 from?' So they fell foul of him, and this led him to say, 'A prophet will always be held in honour, except in his home town, and in his 58 own family.' And he did not work many miracles there: such was their want of faith.

Disturbing news for Herod

14 It was at that time that reports about Jesus 2 reached the ears of Prince Herod. 'This is John the Baptist,' he said to his attendants; 'John has been raised to life, and that is why these miraculous powers are at work in him.'

The death of John the Baptist

3 Now Herod had arrested John, put him in chains, and thrown him into prison, on account of Herodias, his brother Philip's 4 wife; for John had told him: 'You have no 5 right to her.' Herod would have liked to put him to death, but he was afraid of the people, in whose eyes John was a prophet. 6 But at his birthday celebrations the daughter of Herodias danced before the guests, and 7 Herod was so delighted that he took an oath to give her anything she cared to ask. 8 Prompted by her mother, she said, 'Give me here on a dish the head of John the Baptist.' 9 The king was distressed when he heard it; but out of regard for his oath and for his guests, he ordered the request to be granted, and had John beheaded in prison. The head 10 was brought in on a dish and given to the girl; and she carried it to her mother. Then 12 John's disciples came and took away the body, and buried it; and they went and told Jesus.

Feeding five thousand

When he heard what had happened Jesus 13 withdrew privately by boat to a lonely place; but people heard of it, and came after him in crowds by land from the towns. When he 14 came ashore, he saw a great crowd; his heart went out to them, and he cured those of them who were sick. When it grew late the 15 disciples came up to him and said, 'This is a lonely place, and the day has gone; send the people off to the villages to buy themselves food.' He answered, 'There is no need 16 for them to go; give them something to eat yourselves.' 'All we have here', they said, 'is 17 five loaves and two fishes.' 'Let me have 18 them', he replied. So he told the people to 19 sit down on the grass; then, taking the five loaves and the two fishes, he looked up to heaven, said the blessing, broke the loaves, and gave them to the disciples; and the disciples gave them to the people. They all ate 20 to their hearts' content; and the scraps left over, which they picked up, were enough to fill twelve great baskets. Some five thousand 21 men shared in this meal, to say nothing of women and children.

Jesus walks on the water

22 Then he made the disciples embark and go on ahead to the other side, while he sent the
23 people away; after doing that, he went up the hill-side to pray alone. It grew late, and
24 he was there by himself. The boat was already some furlongs from the shore,*d* battling with
25 a head-wind and a rough sea. Between three and six in the morning he came to them,
26 walking over the lake. When the disciples saw him walking on the lake they were so shaken that they cried out in terror: 'It is a
27 ghost!' But at once he spoke to them: 'Take heart! It is I; do not be afraid.'
28 Peter called to him: 'Lord, if it is you, tell
29 me to come to you over the water.' 'Come', said Jesus. Peter stepped down from the boat, and walked over the water towards
30 Jesus. But when he saw the strength of the gale he was seized with fear; and beginning
31 to sink, he cried, 'Save me, Lord.' Jesus at once reached out and caught hold of him, and said, 'Why did you hesitate? How little
32 faith you have!' They then climbed into the
33 boat; and the wind dropped. And the men in the boat fell at his feet, exclaiming, 'Truly you are the Son of God.'

Jesus heals in Gennesaret

34 So they finished the crossing and came to
35 land at Gennesaret. There Jesus was recognized by the people of the place, who sent out word to all the country round. And all
36 who were ill were brought to him, and he was begged to allow them simply to touch the edge of his cloak. And everyone who touched it was completely cured.

About traditions

15 Then Jesus was approached by a group of Pharisees and lawyers from Jerusalem, with
2 the question: 'Why do your disciples break the ancient tradition? They do not wash their
3 hands before meals.' He answered them: 'And what of you? Why do you break God's commandment in the interest of your tradi-
4 tion? For God said, "Honour your father and mother", and, "The man who curses his
5 father or mother must suffer death." But you say, "If a man says to his father or mother, 'Anything of mine which might have been used for your benefit is set apart for
6 God', then he must not honour his father or his mother." You have made God's law null and void out of respect for your tradi-
7 tion. What hypocrisy! Isaiah was right when
8 he prophesied about you: "This people pays me lip-service, but their heart is far from
9 me; their worship of me is in vain, for they teach as doctrines the commandments of men."'
10 He called the crowd and said to them,

'Listen to me, and understand this: a man 11 is not defiled by what goes into his mouth, but by what comes out of it.'

What defiles a man

Then the disciples came to him and said, 12 'Do you know that the Pharisees have taken great offence at what you have been saying?' His answer was: 'Any plant that is not of 13 my heavenly Father's planting will be rooted up. Leave them alone; they are blind guides,*e* 14 and if one blind man guides another they will both fall into the ditch.'

Then Peter said, 'Tell us what that parable 15 means.' Jesus answered, 'Are you still as dull 16 as the rest? Do you not see that whatever goes 17 in by the mouth passes into the stomach and so is discharged into the drain? But what 18 comes out of the mouth has its origins in the heart; and that is what defiles a man. Wicked 19 thoughts, murder, adultery, fornication, theft, perjury, slander—these all proceed from the heart; and these are the things that 20 defile a man; but to eat without first washing his hands, that cannot defile him.'

A woman's faith

Jesus then left that place and withdrew to 21 the region of Tyre and Sidon. And a Canaan- 22 ite woman from those parts came crying out, 'Sir! have pity on me, Son of David; my daughter is tormented by a devil.' But 23 he said not a word in reply. His disciples came and urged him: 'Send her away; see how she comes shouting after us.' Jesus re- 24 plied, 'I was sent to the lost sheep of the house of Israel, and to them alone.' But the 25 woman came and fell at his feet and cried, 'Help me, sir.' To this Jesus replied, 'It is 26 not right to take the children's bread and throw it to the dogs.' 'True, sir,' she an- 27 swered; 'and yet the dogs eat the scraps that fall from their masters' table.' Hearing this 28 Jesus replied, 'Woman, what faith you have! Be it as you wish!' And from that moment her daughter was restored to health.

After leaving that region Jesus took the 29 road by the Sea of Galilee and went up to the hills. When he was seated there, crowds 30 flocked to him, bringing with them the lame, blind, dumb, and crippled, and many other sufferers; they threw them down at his feet, and he healed them. Great was the amaze- 31 ment of the people when they saw the dumb speaking, the crippled strong, the lame walking, and sight restored to the blind; and they gave praise to the God of Israel.

Feeding four thousand

Jesus called his disciples and said to them, 32 'I feel sorry for all these people; they have been with me now for three days and have

---

d Some witnesses read already well out on the water.　　　*e Some witnesses insert* of blind men.

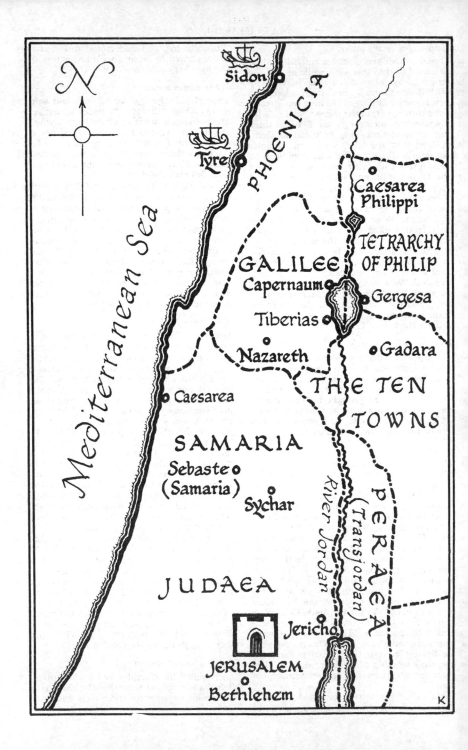

nothing to eat. I do not want to send them away unfed; they might turn faint on the 33 way.' The disciples replied, 'Where in this lonely place can we find bread enough to 34 feed such a crowd?' 'How many loaves have you?' Jesus asked. 'Seven,' they replied; 35 'and there are a few small fishes.' So he ordered the people to sit down on the 36 ground; then he took the seven loaves and the fishes, and after giving thanks to God he broke them and gave to the disciples, and 37 the disciples gave to the people. They all ate to their hearts' content; and the scraps left over, which they picked up, were enough to 38 fill seven baskets. Four thousand men shared in this meal, to say nothing of women and 39 children. He then dismissed the crowds, got into a boat, and went to the neighbourhood of Magadan.

Demand for a sign

16 The Pharisees and Sadducees came, and to test him they asked him to show them a sign 2 4 from heaven. His answer was:ᶠ 'It is a wicked generation that asks for a sign; and the only sign that will be given it is the sign of Jonah.' So he went off and left them.

A warning to the disciples

5 In crossing to the other side the disciples 6 had forgotten to take bread with them. So, when Jesus said to them, 'Beware, be on your guard against the leaven of the Pha- 7 risees and Sadducees', they began to say among themselves, 'It is because we have 8 brought no bread!' Knowing what was in their minds, Jesus said to them: 'Why do you talk about bringing no bread? Where 9 is your faith? Do you not understand even yet? Do you not remember the five loaves for the five thousand, and how many basket- 10 fuls you picked up? Or the seven loaves for the four thousand, and how many basket- 11 fuls you picked up? How can you fail to see that I was not speaking about bread? Be on your guard, I said, against the leaven of 12 the Pharisees and Sadducees.' Then they understood: they were to be on their guard, not against baker's leaven, but against the teaching of the Pharisees and Sadducees.

Peter's confession of faith

13 When he came to the territory of Caesarea Philippi, Jesus asked his disciples, 'Who do 14 men say that the Son of Man isᵍ?' They answered, 'Some say John the Baptist, others Elijah, others Jeremiah, or one of the 15 prophets.' 'And you,' he asked, 'who do you 16 say I am?' Simon Peter answered: 'You are

the Messiah, the Son of the living God.' Then Jesus said: 'Simon son of Jonah, you 17 are favoured indeed! You did not learn that from mortal man; it was revealed to you by my heavenly Father. And I say this 18 to you: You are Peter, the Rock; and on this rock I will build my church, and the powers of death shall never conquer it.ʰ I will give 19 you the keys of the kingdom of Heaven; what you forbid on earth shall be forbidden in heaven, and what you allow on earth shall be allowed in heaven.' He then gave his 20 disciples strict orders not to tell anyone that he was the Messiah.

Jesus speaks of his death

From that time Jesus began to make it clear 21 to his disciples that he had to go to Jeru- salem, and there to suffer much from the elders, chief priests, and doctors of the law; to be put to death and to be raised again on the third day. At this Peter took him by the 22 arm and began to rebuke him: 'Heaven for- bid!' he said. 'No, Lord, this shall never happen to you.' Then Jesus turned and said 23 to Peter, 'Away with you, Satan; you are a stumbling-block to me. You think as men think, not as God thinks.'

On following Jesus

Jesus then said to his disciples, 'If anyone 24 wishes to be a follower of mine, he must leave self behind; he must take up his cross and come with me. Whoever cares for his 25 own safety is lost; but if a man will let him- self be lost for my sake, he will find his true self. What will a man gain by winning the 26 whole world, at the cost of his true self? Or what can he give that will buy that self back? For the Son of Man is to come in the glory 27 of his Father with his angels, and then he will give each man the due reward for what he has done. I tell you this: there are some 28 of those standing here who will not taste death before they have seen the Son of Man coming in his kingdom.'

Jesus is transfigured

Six days later Jesus took Peter, James, and **17** John the brother of James, and led them up a high mountain where they were alone; and 2 in their presence he was transfigured; his face shone like the sun, and his clothes be- came white as the light. And they saw Moses 3 and Elijah appear, conversing with him. Then Peter spoke: 'Lord,' he said, 'how good 4 it is that we are here! If you wish it, I will make three shelters here, one for you, one for Moses, and one for Elijah.' While he 5

ᶠ Some witnesses here insert 'In the evening you say, "It will be fine weather, for the sky is red"; (3) and in the morning you say, "It will be stormy today; the sky is red and lowering." You know how to interpret the appear- ance of the sky; can you not interpret the signs of the times?'   ᵍ Some witnesses read that I, the Son of Man, am.   ʰ Or the gates of death shall never close upon it.

A city by the Sea of Galilee

was still speaking, a bright cloud suddenly overshadowed them, and a voice called from the cloud: 'This is my Son, my Beloved,[i] on whom my favour rests; listen to him.' 6 At the sound of the voice the disciples fell 7 on their faces in terror. Jesus then came up to them, touched them, and said, 'Stand up; 8 do not be afraid.' And when they raised their eyes they saw no one, but only Jesus.

More about John the Baptist

9 On their way down the mountain, Jesus enjoined them not to tell anyone of the vision until the Son of Man had been raised from 10 the dead. The disciples put a question to him: 'Why then do our teachers say that 11 Elijah must come first?' He replied, 'Yes, Elijah will come and set everything right. 12 But I tell you that Elijah has already come, and they failed to recognize him, and worked their will upon him; and in the same way the Son of Man is to suffer at their hands.' 13 Then the disciples understood that he meant John the Baptist.

Jesus heals an epileptic boy

14 When they returned to the crowd, a man came up to Jesus, fell on his knees before 15 him, and said, 'Have pity, sir, on my son: he is an epileptic and has bad fits, and he keeps falling about, often into the fire, often 16 into water. I brought him to your disciples, 17 but they could not cure him.' Jesus answered, 'What an unbelieving and perverse generation! How long shall I be with you? How

long must I endure you? Bring him here to me.' Jesus then spoke sternly to the boy; the 18 devil left him, and from that moment he was cured.

The power of faith

Afterwards the disciples came to Jesus and 19 asked him privately, 'Why could not we cast it out?' He answered, 'Your faith is too 20 small. I tell you this: if you have faith no bigger even than a mustard-seed, you will say to this mountain, "Move from here to there!", and it will move; nothing will prove impossible for you.'[j]

Jesus again speaks of his death

They were going about together in Galilee 22 when Jesus said to them, 'The Son of Man is to be given up into the power of men, and 23 they will kill him; then on the third day he will be raised again.' And they were filled with grief.

Paying a tax

On their arrival at Capernaum the collectors 24 of the temple-tax came up to Peter and asked, 'Does your master not pay temple-tax?' 'He 25 does', said Peter. When he went indoors Jesus forestalled him by asking, 'What do you think about this, Simon? From whom do earthly monarchs collect tax or toll? From their own people, or from aliens?' 'From aliens', said Peter. 'Why then,' said 26 Jesus, 'their own people are exempt! But as 27 we do not want to cause offence, go and cast

---

i Or This is my only Son.   *j Some witnesses add* (21) But there is no means of casting out this sort but prayer and fasting.

a line in the lake; take the first fish that comes to the hook, open its mouth, and you will find a silver coin; take that and pay it in; it will meet the tax for us both.'

A lesson from a child

18 At that time the disciples came to Jesus and asked, 'Who is the greatest in the kingdom 2 of Heaven?' He called a child, set him in 3 front of them, and said, 'I tell you this: unless you turn round and become like children, you will never enter the kingdom 4 of Heaven. Let a man humble himself till he is like this child, and he will be the greatest 5 in the kingdom of Heaven. Whoever receives 6 one such child in my name receives me. But if a man is a cause of stumbling to one of these little ones who have faith in me, it would be better for him to have a millstone hung round his neck and be drowned in the 7 depths of the sea. Alas for the world that such causes of stumbling arise! Come they must, but woe betide the man through whom they come!

8 'If your hand or your foot is your un-doing, cut it off and fling it away; it is better for you to enter into life maimed or lame, than to keep two hands or two feet and be 9 thrown into the eternal fire. If it is your eye that is your undoing, tear it out and fling it away; it is better to enter into life with one eye than to keep both eyes and be thrown into the fires of hell.

10 'Never despise one of these little ones; I tell you, they have their guardian angels in heaven, who look continually on the face of my heavenly Father.'[k]

The sheep that strayed

12 'What do you think? Suppose a man has a hundred sheep. If one of them strays, does he not leave the other ninety-nine on the hillside and go in search of the one that 13 strayed? And if he should find it, I tell you this: he is more delighted over that sheep than over the ninety-nine that never strayed. 14 In the same way, it is not your heavenly Father's will that one of these little ones should be lost.'

On settling grievances

15 'If your brother commits a sin,[l] go and take the matter up with him, strictly between yourselves, and if he listens to you, you have 16 won your brother over. If he will not listen, take one or two others with you, so that all facts may be duly established on 17 the evidence of two or three witnesses. If he refuses to listen to them, report the mat-ter to the congregation; and if he will not listen even to the congregation, you must

then treat him as you would a pagan or a tax-gatherer.

'I tell you this: whatever you forbid on 18 earth shall be forbidden in heaven, and what-ever you allow on earth shall be allowed in heaven.'

About prayer

'Again I tell you this: if two of you agree on 19 earth about any request you have to make, that request will be granted by my heavenly Father. For where two or three have met to- 20 gether in my name, I am there among them.'

About forgiveness

Then Peter came up and asked him, 'Lord, 21 how often am I to forgive my brother if he goes on wronging me? As many as seven times?' Jesus replied, 'I do not say seven 22 times; I say seventy times seven.'[m]

'The kingdom of Heaven, therefore, 23 should be thought of in this way: There was once a king who decided to settle accounts with the men who served him. At 24 the outset there appeared before him a man whose debt ran into millions.[n] Since he had 25 no means of paying, his master ordered him to be sold to meet the debt, with his wife, his children, and everything he had. The man 26 fell prostrate at his master's feet. "Be patient with me," he said, "and I will pay in full"; and the master was so moved with pity that 27 he let the man go and remitted the debt. But 28 no sooner had the man gone out than he met a fellow-servant who owed him a few pounds;[o] and catching hold of him he grip-ped him by the throat and said, "Pay me what you owe." The man fell at his fellow- 29 servant's feet, and begged him, "Be patient with me, and I will pay you"; but he refused, 30 and had him jailed until he should pay the debt. The other servants were deeply dis- 31 tressed when they saw what had happened, and they went to their master and told him the whole story. He accordingly sent for the 32 man. "You scoundrel!" he said to him; "I remitted the whole of your debt when you appealed to me; were you not bound to 33 show your fellow-servant the same pity as I showed you?" And so angry was the master 34 that he condemned the man to torture until he should pay the debt in full. And that is 35 how my heavenly Father will deal with you, unless you each forgive your brother from your hearts.'

About marriage and divorce

When Jesus had finished this discourse he **19** left Galilee and came into the region of Judaea across Jordan. Great crowds fol- 2 lowed him, and he healed them there.

---

k Some witnesses add (11) For the Son of Man came to save the lost.
m Or seventy-seven times.   *n Literally* who owed 10,000 talents.
l Some witnesses insert against you.
o Literally owed him 100 denarii.

3 Some Pharisees came and tested him by asking, 'Is it lawful for a man to divorce his
4 wife on any and every ground?'[p] He asked in return, 'Have you never read that the Creator made them from the beginning male
5 and female?'; and he added, 'For this reason a man shall leave his father and mother, and be made one with his wife; and the two shall
6 become one flesh. It follows that they are no longer two individuals: they are one flesh. What God has joined together, man
7 must not separate.' 'Why then,' they objected, 'did Moses lay it down that a man might divorce his wife by note of dismissal?'
8 He answered, 'It was because your minds were closed that Moses gave you permission to divorce your wives; but it was not like
9 that when all began. I tell you, if a man divorces his wife for any cause other than unchastity, and marries another, he commits adultery.'[q]
10 The disciples said to him, 'If that is the position with husband and wife, it is better
11 not to marry.' To this he replied, 'That is something which not everyone can accept, but only those for whom God has appointed
12 it. For while some are incapable of marriage because they were born so, or were made so by men, there are others who have themselves renounced marriage for the sake of the kingdom of Heaven. Let those accept it who can.'

Jesus welcomes children

13 They brought children for him to lay his hands on them with prayer. The disciples
14 rebuked them, but Jesus said to them, 'Let the children come to me; do not try to stop them; for the kingdom of Heaven belongs
15 to such as these.' And he laid his hands on the children, and went his way.

A rich man's question

16 And now a man came up and asked him, 'Master, what good must I do to gain
17 eternal life?' 'Good?' said Jesus. 'Why do you ask me about that? One alone is good. But if you wish to enter into life, keep the
18 commandments.' 'Which commandments?' he asked. Jesus answered, 'Do not murder; do not commit adultery; do not steal; do
19 not give false evidence; honour your father and mother; and love your neighbour as
20 yourself.' The young man answered, 'I have kept all these. Where do I still fall short?'
21 Jesus said to him, 'If you wish to go the whole way, go, sell your possessions, and give to the poor, and then you will have riches in
22 heaven; and come, follow me.' When the young man heard this, he went away with

a heavy heart; for he was a man of great wealth.
Jesus said to his disciples, 'I tell you this: 23 a rich man will find it hard to enter the kingdom of Heaven. I repeat, it is easier for a 24 camel to pass through the eye of a needle than for a rich man to enter the kingdom of God.' The disciples were amazed to hear 25 this. 'Then who can be saved?' they asked. Jesus looked at them, and said, 'For men 26 this is impossible; but everything is possible for God.'

About rewards

At this Peter said, 'We here have left every- 27 thing to become your followers. What will there be for us?' Jesus replied, 'I tell you this: 28 in the world that is to be, when the Son of Man is seated on his throne in heavenly splendour, you my followers will have thrones of your own, where you will sit as judges of the twelve tribes of Israel. And 29 anyone who has left brothers or sisters, father, mother, or children, land or houses for the sake of my name will be repaid many times over, and gain eternal life. But many 30 who are first will be last, and the last first.'

Labourers in the vineyard

'The kingdom of Heaven is like this. There 20 was once a landowner who went out early one morning to hire labourers for his vineyard; and after agreeing to pay them the 2

A denarius (see Matt. 20. 2 and footnote)

usual day's wage[r] he sent them off to work. Going out three hours later he saw some 3 more men standing idle in the market-place. "Go and join the others in the vineyard," he 4 said, "and I will pay you a fair wage"; so off they went. At midday he went out again, and 5 at three in the afternoon, and made the same arrangement as before. An hour before sun- 6 set he went out and found another group standing there; so he said to them, "Why are you standing about like this all day with nothing to do?" "Because no one has hired 7 us", they replied; so he told them, "Go and join the others in the vineyard." When even- 8 ing fell, the owner of the vineyard said to his steward, "Call the labourers and give them their pay, beginning with those who came 9 last and ending with the first." Those who had started work an hour before sunset came forward, and were paid the full day's wage.ˢ 10 When it was the turn of the men who had come first, they expected something extra, but were paid the same amount as the others. 11 As they took it, they grumbled at their 12 employer: "These late-comers have done only one hour's work, yet you have put them on a level with us, who have sweated the whole 13 day long in the blazing sun!" The owner turned to one of them and said, "My friend, I am not being unfair to you. You agreed on the usual wage for the day,ᵗ did you not? 14 Take your pay and go home. I choose to pay 15 the last man the same as you. Surely I am free to do what I like with my own money. 16 Why be jealous because I am kind?" Thus will the last be first, and the first last.'

Jesus again speaks of his death

17 Jesus was journeying towards Jerusalem, and on the way he took the Twelve aside, 18 and said to them, 'We are now going to Jerusalem, and the Son of Man will be given up to the chief priests and the doctors of the 19 law; they will condemn him to death and hand him over to the foreign power, to be mocked and flogged and crucified, and on the third day he will be raised to life again.'

True greatness

20 The mother of Zebedee's sons then came before him, with her sons. She bowed low 21 and begged a favour. 'What is it you wish?' asked Jesus. 'I want you', she said, 'to give orders that in your kingdom my two sons here may sit next to you, one at your right, 22 and the other at your left.' Jesus turned to the brothers and said, 'You do not understand what you are asking. Can you drink the cup that I am to drink?' 'We can', they 23 replied. Then he said to them, 'You shall indeed share my cup; but to sit at my right or left is not for me to grant; it is for those to whom it has already been assigned by my Father.'

24 When the other ten heard this, they were 25 indignant with the two brothers. So Jesus called them to him and said, 'You know that in the world, rulers lord it over their subjects, and their great men make them feel 26 the weight of authority; but it shall not be so with you. Among you, whoever wants to 27 be great must be your servant, and whoever wants to be first must be the willing slave of 28 all—like the Son of Man; he did not come to be served, but to serve, and to give up his life as a ransom for many.'

Sight restored to two blind men

29 As they were leaving Jericho he was fol- 30 lowed by a great crowd of people. At the roadside sat two blind men. When they heard it said that Jesus was passing they shouted, 'Have pity on us, Son of David.' The people 31 told them sharply to be quiet. But they shouted all the more, 'Sir, have pity on us; have pity on us, Son of David.' Jesus stopped 32 and called the men. 'What do you want me to do for you?' he asked. 'Sir,' they answered, 33 'we want our sight.' Jesus was deeply moved, 34 and touched their eyes. At once their sight came back, and they followed him.

Jesus rides into Jerusalem

They were now nearing Jerusalem; and when **21** they reached Bethphage at the Mount of Olives, Jesus sent two disciples with these 2 instructions: 'Go to the village opposite, where you will at once find a donkey tethered with her foal beside her; untie them, and bring them to me. If anyone speaks to you, 3 say, "Our Master needs them"; and he will let you take them at once.'ᵘ This was to ful- 4 fil the prophecy which says, 'Tell the daugh- 5 ter of Zion, "Here is your king, who comes to you in gentleness, riding on an ass, riding on the foal of a beast of burden."'

The disciples went and did as Jesus had 6 directed, and brought the donkey and her 7 foal; they laid their cloaks on them and Jesus mounted. Crowds of people carpeted 8 the road with their cloaks, and some cut branches from the trees to spread in his path. Then the crowd that went ahead and the 9 others that came behind raised the shout: 'Hosanna to the Son of David! Blessings on him who comes in the name of the Lord! Hosanna in the heavens!'

When he entered Jerusalem the whole city 10 went wild with excitement. 'Who is this?' people asked, and the crowd replied, 'This 11 is the prophet Jesus, from Nazareth in Galilee.'

Jesus drives traders from the temple

Jesus then went into the temple and drove 12 out all who were buying and selling in the temple precincts; he upset the tables of the money-changers and the seats of the dealers in pigeons; and said to them, 'Scripture says, 13 "My house shall be called a house of prayer"; but you are making it a robbers' cave.'

Applause and opposition in the temple

In the temple blind men and cripples came 14 to him, and he healed them. The chief priests 15 and doctors of the law saw the wonderful things he did, and heard the boys in the temple shouting, 'Hosanna to the Son of

---

ˢ *Literally* one denarius each.   ᵗ *Literally* You agreed on a denarius.   ᵘ *Or* "Our Master needs them and will send them back straight away."

16 David!', and they asked him indignantly, 'Do you hear what they are saying?' Jesus answered, 'I do; have you never read that text, "Thou hast made children and babes
17 at the breast sound aloud thy praise"?' Then he left them and went out of the city to Bethany, where he spent the night.

A lesson from a fig-tree

18 Next morning on his way to the city he felt
19 hungry; and seeing a fig-tree at the roadside he went up to it, but found nothing on it but leaves. He said to the tree, 'You shall never bear fruit any more!'; and the tree withered
20 away at once. The disciples were amazed at the sight. 'How is it', they asked, 'that the
21 tree has withered so suddenly?' Jesus answered them, 'I tell you this: if only you have faith and have no doubts, you will do what has been done to the fig-tree; and more than that, you need only say to this mountain, "Be lifted from your place and hurled into the sea", and what you say will be done.
22 And whatever you pray for in faith you will receive.'

About the authority of Jesus

23 He entered the temple, and the chief priests and elders of the nation came to him with the question: 'By what authority are you acting like this? Who gave you this auth-
24 ority?' Jesus replied, 'I have a question to ask you too; answer it, and I will tell you by
25 what authority I act. The baptism of John: was it from God, or from men?' This set them arguing among themselves: 'If we say, "from God", he will say, "Then why did you not believe him?" But if we say,
26 "from men", we are afraid of the people, for they all take John for a prophet.' So they
27 answered, 'We do not know.' And Jesus said: 'Then neither will I tell you by what authority I act.'

Two sons and their father

'But what do you think about this? A man
28 had two sons. He went to the first, and said, "My boy, go and work today in the vine-
29 yard." "I will, sir", the boy replied; but he
30 never went. The father came to the second and said the same. "I will not", he replied, but afterwards he changed his mind and
31 went. Which of these two did as his father wished?' 'The second', they said. Then Jesus answered, 'I tell you this: tax-gatherers and prostitutes are entering the kingdom of God ahead of you. For when John came to
32 show you the right way to live, you did not believe him, but the tax-gatherers and prostitutes did; and even when you had seen that, you did not change your minds and believe him.'

HK.

Tenants in a vineyard

33 'Listen to another parable. There was a land-owner who planted a vineyard: he put a wall round it, hewed out a winepress, and built a watch-tower; then he let it out to vine-
34 growers and went abroad. When the vintage season approached, he sent his servants to the tenants to collect the produce due to
35 him. But they took his servants and thrashed one, killed another, and stoned a third.
36 Again, he sent other servants, this time a larger number; and they did the same to
37 them. At last he sent to them his son. "They
38 will respect my son", he said. But when they saw the son the tenants said to one another, "This is the heir; come on, let us kill him,
39 and get his inheritance." And they took him, flung him out of the vineyard, and killed
40 him. When the owner of the vineyard comes, how do you think he will deal with those
41 tenants?' 'He will bring those bad men to a bad end', they answered, 'and hand the vine-yard over to other tenants, who will let him have his share of the crop when the season
42 comes.' Then Jesus said to them, 'Have you never read in the scriptures: "The stone which the builders rejected has become the main corner-stone. This is the Lord's doing,
43 and it is wonderful in our eyes"? Therefore, I tell you, the kingdom of God will be taken away from you, and given to a nation that yields the proper fruit.'*v*
45 When the chief priests and Pharisees heard his parables, they saw that he was referring
46 to them; they wanted to arrest him, but they were afraid of the people, who looked on Jesus as a prophet.

A wedding-feast

2 Then Jesus spoke to them again in parables:
2 'The kingdom of Heaven is like this. There was a king who prepared a feast for his son's
3 wedding; but when he sent his servants to summon the guests he had invited, they
4 would not come. He sent others again, telling them to say to the guests, "See now! I have prepared this feast for you. I have had my bullocks and fatted beasts slaughtered; everything is ready; come to the wedding at
5 once." But they took no notice; one went
6 off to his farm, another to his business, and the others seized the servants, attacked them
7 brutally, and killed them. The king was furi-ous; he sent troops to kill those murderers
8 and set their town on fire. Then he said to his servants, "The wedding-feast is ready; but the guests I invited did not deserve this
9 honour. Go out to the main thoroughfares, and invite everyone you can find to the
10 wedding." The servants went out into the

streets, and collected all they could find, good and bad alike. So the hall was packed with guests.
11 'When the king came in to see the com-pany at table, he observed one man who was
12 not dressed for a wedding. "My friend," said the king, "how do you come to be here with-out your wedding clothes?" He had nothing
13 to say. The king then said to his attendants, "Bind him hand and foot; turn him out into the dark, the place of wailing and grinding
14 of teeth." For though many are invited, few are chosen.'

Paying tax to the Emperor

15 Then the Pharisees went away and agreed on
16 a plan to trap him in his own words. Some of their followers were sent to him in com-pany with men of Herod's party. They said, 'Master, you are an honest man, we know; you teach in all honesty the way of life that God requires, truckling to no man, whoever
17 he may be. Give us your ruling on this: are we or are we not permitted to pay taxes to
18 the Roman Emperor?' Jesus was aware of their malicious intention and said to them, 'You hypocrites! Why are you trying to
19 catch me out? Show me the money in which the tax is paid.' They handed him a silver
20 piece. Jesus asked, 'Whose head is this, and
21 whose inscription?' 'Caesar's', they replied. He said to them, 'Then pay Caesar what is due to Caesar, and pay God what is due to
22 God.' This answer took them by surprise, and they went away and left him alone.

About resurrection

23 The same day Sadducees came to him, maintaining that there is no resurrection.
24 Their question was this: 'Master, Moses said, "If a man should die childless, his brother shall marry the widow and carry on
25 his brother's family." Now we knew of seven brothers. The first married and died, and as he was without issue his wife was left to his
26 brother. The same thing happened with the second, and the third, and so on with all
27 28 seven. Last of all the woman died. At the resurrection, then, whose wife will she be, for they had all married her?' Jesus answered:
29 'You are mistaken, because you know neither the scriptures nor the power of God. At the
30 resurrection men and women do not marry; they are like angels in heaven.
31 'But about the resurrection of the dead, have you never read what God himself said
32 to you: "I am the God of Abraham, the God of Isaac, and the God of Jacob"? He
33 is not God of the dead but of the living.' The people heard what he said, and were astoun-ded at his teaching.

v Some witnesses add (44) Any man who falls on this stone will be dashed to pieces; and if it falls on a man he will be crushed by it.

The greatest commandment

34 Hearing that he had silenced the Sadducees,
35 the Pharisees met together; and one of their
number[w] tested him with this question:
36 'Master, which is the greatest command-
37 ment in the Law?' He answered, '"Love the
Lord your God with all your heart, with all
38 your soul, with all your mind." That is the
39 greatest commandment. It comes first. The
second is like it: "Love your neighbour as
40 yourself." Everything in the Law and the
prophets hangs on these two commandments.'

About the Messiah

41 Turning to the assembled Pharisees Jesus
42 asked them, 'What is your opinion about
the Messiah? Whose son is he?' 'The son
43 of David', they replied. 'How then is it', he
asked, 'that David by inspiration calls him
44 "Lord"? For he says, "The Lord said to my
Lord, 'Sit at my right hand until I put your
45 enemies under your feet.'" If David calls
him "Lord", how can he be David's son?'
46 Not a man could say a word in reply; and
from that day forward no one dared ask him
another question.

Pride and pretence

23 Jesus then addressed the people and his
2 disciples in these words: 'The doctors of
the law and the Pharisees sit in the chair
3 of Moses; therefore do what they tell you;
pay attention to their words. But do not
follow their practice; for they say one thing
4 and do another. They make up heavy packs
and pile them on men's shoulders, but will
not raise a finger to lift the load themselves.
5 Whatever they do is done for show. They
go about with broad phylacteries[x] and with
6 large tassels on their robes; they like to
have places of honour at feasts and the chief
7 seats in synagogues, to be greeted respect-
fully in the street, and to be addressed as
"rabbi".'

Real humility

8 'But you must not be called "rabbi"; for
you have one Rabbi, and you are all bro-
9 thers. Do not call any man on earth "father";
for you have one Father, and he is in
10 heaven. Nor must you be called "teacher";
11 you have one Teacher, the Messiah. The
greatest among you must be your servant.
12 For whoever exalts himself will be humbled;
and whoever humbles himself will be exalted.'

Teachers who mislead

13 'Alas, alas for you, lawyers and Pharisees,
hypocrites that you are! You shut the door

of the kingdom of Heaven in men's faces;
you do not enter yourselves, and when
others are entering, you stop them.[y]
15 'Alas for you, lawyers and Pharisees,
hypocrites! You travel over sea and land to
win one convert; and when you have won
him you make him twice as fit for hell as
you are yourselves.
16 'Alas for you, blind guides! You say, "If
a man swears by the sanctuary, that is
nothing; but if he swears by the gold in the
sanctuary, he is bound by his oath." Blind
17 fools! Which is the more important, the gold,
or the sanctuary which sanctifies the gold?
18 Or you say, "If a man swears by the altar,
that is nothing; but if he swears by the
offering that lies on the altar, he is bound
by his oath." What blindness! Which is the
19 more important, the offering, or the altar
which sanctifies it? To swear by the altar,
20 then, is to swear both by the altar and by
whatever lies on it; to swear by the sanctuary
21 is to swear both by the sanctuary and by
him who dwells there; and to swear by
22 heaven is to swear both by the throne of
God and by him who sits upon it.'

The outside and the inside

23 'Alas for you, lawyers and Pharisees, hypocrites! You pay tithes of mint and dill and

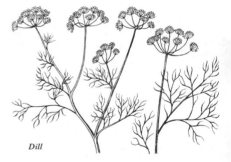

Dill

cummin; but you have overlooked the
weightier demands of the Law, justice,
mercy, and good faith. It is these you should
have practised, without neglecting the others.
24 Blind guides! You strain off a midge, yet
gulp down a camel!
25 'Alas for you, lawyers and Pharisees,
hypocrites! You clean the outside of cup
and dish, which you have filled inside by
robbery and self-indulgence! Blind Pharisee!
26 Clean the inside of the cup first; then the
outside will be clean also.
27 'Alas for you, lawyers and Pharisees,
hypocrites! You are like tombs covered with

w Some witnesses insert a lawyer.   *x See Deuteronomy 6. 8–9 and Exodus 13. 9.*   *y Some witnesses* add (14) Alas for you, lawyers and Pharisees, hypocrites! You eat up the property of widows, while you say long prayers for appearance' sake. You will receive the severest sentence.

whitewash; they look well from outside, but inside they are full of dead men's bones and
28 all kinds of filth. So it is with you: outside you look like honest men, but inside you are brim-full of hypocrisy and crime.'

A heritage of crime

29 'Alas for you, lawyers and Pharisees, hypocrites! You build up the tombs of the pro-
30 phets and embellish the monuments of the saints, and you say, "If we had been alive in our fathers' time, we should never have
31 taken part with them in the murder of the prophets." So you acknowledge that you are the sons of the men who killed the
32 prophets. Go on then, finish off what your fathers began!*z*

33 'You snakes, you vipers' brood, how can
34 you escape being condemned to hell? I send you therefore prophets, sages, and teachers; some of them you will kill and crucify, others you will flog in your synagogues and hound
35 from city to city. And so, on you will fall the guilt of all the innocent blood spilt on the ground, from innocent Abel to Zechariah son of Berachiah, whom you murdered
36 between the sanctuary and the altar. Believe me, this generation will bear the guilt of it all.

Jerusalem the doomed city

37 'O Jerusalem, Jerusalem, the city that murders the prophets and stones the messengers sent to her! How often have I longed to gather your children, as a hen gathers her brood under her wings; but you would not
38 let me. Look, look! there is your temple,
39 forsaken by God.*a b* And I tell you, you shall never see me until the time when you say, "Blessings on him who comes in the name of the Lord."'

Destruction of the temple foretold

4 Jesus was leaving the temple when his disciples came and pointed to the temple
2 buildings. He answered, 'Yes, look at it all.

---

z Or You too must come up to your fathers' standards. *witnesses add* and laid waste.

I tell you this: not one stone will be left upon another; all will be thrown down.'

Troubles and persecutions

When he was sitting on the Mount of Olives 3 the disciples came to speak to him privately. 'Tell us,' they said, 'when will this happen? And what will be the signal for your coming and the end of the age?'
    Jesus replied: 'Take care that no one mis- 4 leads you. For many will come claiming my 5 name and saying, "I am the Messiah"; and many will be misled by them. The time is 6 coming when you will hear the noise of battle near at hand and the news of battles far away; see that you are not alarmed. Such things are bound to happen; but the end is still to come. For nation will make 7 war upon nation, kingdom upon kingdom; there will be famines and earthquakes in many places. With all these things the birth- 8 pangs of the new age begin.
    'You will then be handed over for punish- 9 ment and execution; and men of all nations will hate you for your allegiance to me. Many 10 will fall from their faith; they will betray one another and hate one another. Many 11 false prophets will arise, and will mislead many; and as lawlessness spreads, men's love 12 for one another will grow cold. But the man 13 who holds out to the end will be saved. And 14 this gospel of the Kingdom will be proclaimed throughout the earth as a testimony to all nations; and then the end will come.'

'The abomination of desolation'

'So when you see "the abomination of 15 desolation", of which the prophet Daniel spoke, standing in the holy place (let the reader understand), then those who are in 16 Judaea must take to the hills. If a man is on 17 the roof, he must not come down to fetch his goods from the house; if in the field, he 18 must not turn back for his coat. Alas for 19 women with child in those days, and for those who have children at the breast! Pray 20 that it may not be winter when you have to make your escape, or Sabbath. It will be a 21 time of great distress; there has never been such a time from the beginning of the world until now, and will never be again. If that 22 time of troubles were not cut short, no living thing could survive; but for the sake of God's chosen it will be cut short.'

The coming of the Son of Man

'Then, if anyone says to you, "Look, here 23 is the Messiah", or, "There he is", do not believe it. Impostors will come claiming to 24 be messiahs or prophets, and they will produce great signs and wonders to mislead

---

a Or Look, your home is desolate.   *b Some*

even God's chosen, if such a thing were possible. See, I have forewarned you. If they tell you, "He is there in the wilderness", do not go out; or if they say, "He is there in the inner room", do not believe it. Like lightning from the east, flashing as far as the west, will be the coming of the Son of Man.

'Wherever the corpse is, there the vultures will gather.

'As soon as the distress of those days has passed, the sun will be darkened, the moon will not give her light, the stars will fall from the sky, the celestial powers will be shaken. Then will appear in heaven the sign that heralds the Son of Man. All the peoples of the world will make lamentation, and they will see the Son of Man coming on the clouds of heaven with great power and glory. With a trumpet blast he will send out his angels, and they will gather his chosen from the four winds, from the farthest bounds of heaven on every side.

'Learn a lesson from the fig-tree. When its tender shoots appear and are breaking into leaf, you know that summer is near. In the same way, when you see all these things, you may know that the end is near,^{c} at the very door. I tell you this: the present generation will live to see it all. Heaven and earth will pass away; my words will never pass away.'

No one knows the day or hour: 'keep awake'

'But about that day and hour no one knows, not even the angels in heaven, not even the Son; only the Father.

'As things were in Noah's days, so will they be when the Son of Man comes. In the days before the flood they ate and drank and married, until the day that Noah went into the ark, and they knew nothing until the flood came and swept them all away. That is how it will be when the Son of Man comes. Then there will be two men in the field; one will be taken, the other left; two women grinding at the mill; one will be taken, the other left.

'Keep awake, then; for you do not know on what day your Lord is to come. Remember, if the householder had known at what time of night the burglar was coming, he would have kept awake and not have let his house be broken into. Hold yourselves ready, therefore, because the Son of Man will come at the time you least expect him.'

The trusty servant

'Who is the trusty servant, the sensible man charged by his master to manage his household staff and issue their rations at the proper time? Happy that servant who is found at his task when his master comes! I tell you this: he will be put in charge of all his master's property. But if he is a bad servant and says to himself, "The master is a long time coming", and begins to bully the other servants and to eat and drink with his drunken friends, then the master will arrive on a day that servant does not expect, at a time he does not know, and will cut him in pieces. Thus he will find his place among the hypocrites, where there is wailing and grinding of teeth.'

Ten girls and their lamps

'When that day comes, the kingdom of Heaven will be like this. There were ten girls, who took their lamps and went out to meet the bridegroom. Five of them were foolish, and five prudent; when the foolish ones took their lamps, they took no oil with them, but the others took flasks of oil with their lamps. As the bridegroom was late in coming they all dozed off to sleep. But at midnight a cry was heard: "Here is the bridegroom! Come out to meet him." With that the girls all got up and trimmed their lamps. The foolish said to the prudent,

Lamps

"Our lamps are going out; give us some of your oil." "No," they said; "there will never be enough for all of us. You had better go to the shop and buy some for yourselves." While they were away the bridegroom arrived; those who were ready went in with him to the wedding; and the door was shut. And then the other five came back. "Sir, sir," they cried, "open the door for us." But he answered, "I declare, I do not know you." Keep awake then; for you never know the day or the hour.'

Three servants

'It is like a man going abroad, who called his servants and put his capital in their hands; to one he gave five bags of gold, to another two, to another one, each according to his capacity. Then he left the country. The man who had the five bags went at once and employed them in business, and made a profit of five bags, and the man who

c Or that he is near.

18 had the two bags made two. But the man who had been given one bag of gold went off and dug a hole in the ground, and hid
19 his master's money. A long time afterwards their master returned, and proceeded to
20 settle accounts with them. The man who had been given the five bags of gold came and produced the five he had made: "Master,"
21 he said, "you left five bags with me; look, I have made five more." "Well done, my good and trusty servant!" said the master. "You have proved trustworthy in a small way; I will now put you in charge of something big. Come and share your master's
22 delight." The man with the two bags then came and said, "Master, you left two bags with me; look, I have made two more."
23 "Well done, my good and trusty servant!" said the master. "You have proved trustworthy in a small way; I will now put you in charge of something big. Come and share
24 your master's delight." Then the man who had been given one bag came and said, "Master, I knew you to be a hard man: you reap where you have not sown, you gather
25 where you have not scattered; so I was afraid, and I went and hid your gold in the ground. Here it is—you have what belongs
26 to you." "You lazy rascal!" said the master. "You knew that I reap where I have not sown, and gather where I have not scattered?
27 Then you ought to have put my money on deposit, and on my return I should have got
28 it back with interest. Take the bag of gold from him, and give it to the one with the
29 ten bags. For the man who has will always be given more, till he has enough and to spare; and the man who has not will forfeit
30 even what he has. Fling the useless servant out into the dark, the place of wailing and grinding of teeth!" '

Judging the nations

31 'When the Son of Man comes in his glory and all the angels with him, he will sit in
32 state on his throne, with all the nations gathered before him. He will separate men into two groups, as a shepherd separates the
33 sheep from the goats, and he will place the sheep on his right hand and the goats on
34 his left. Then the king will say to those on his right hand, "You have my Father's blessing; come, enter and possess the kingdom that has been ready for you since the
35 world was made. For when I was hungry, you gave me food; when thirsty, you gave me drink; when I was a stranger you took
36 me into your home, when naked you clothed me; when I was ill you came to my help,
37 when in prison you visited me." Then the righteous will reply, "Lord, when was it that we saw you hungry and fed you, or thirsty

38 and gave you drink, a stranger and took you home, or naked and clothed you? When did
39 we see you ill or in prison, and come to visit
40 you?" And the king will answer, "I tell you this: anything you did for one of my brothers here, however humble, you did for
41 me." Then he will say to those on his left hand, "The curse is upon you; go from my sight to the eternal fire that is ready for the
42 devil and his angels. For when I was hungry you gave me nothing to eat, when thirsty
43 nothing to drink; when I was a stranger you gave me no home, when naked you did not clothe me; when I was ill and in prison you
44 did not come to my help." And they too will reply, "Lord, when was it that we saw you hungry or thirsty or a stranger or naked or ill or in prison, and did nothing for you?"
45 And he will answer, "I tell you this: anything you did not do for one of these, however
46 humble, you did not do for me." And they will go away to eternal punishment, but the righteous will enter eternal life.'

A plot to kill Jesus

26 When Jesus had finished this discourse he
2 said to his disciples, 'You know that in two days' time it will be Passover, and the Son of Man is to be handed over for crucifixion.'
3 Then the chief priests and the elders of the nation met in the palace of the High Priest, Caiaphas; and there they conferred
4 together on a scheme to have Jesus arrested
5 by some trick and put to death. 'It must not be during the festival,' they said, 'or there may be rioting among the people.'

A woman anoints Jesus

6 Jesus was at Bethany in the house of Simon
7 the leper, when a woman came to him with a small bottle of fragrant oil, very costly; and as he sat at table she began to pour it
8 over his head. The disciples were indignant when they saw it. 'Why this waste?' they
9 said; 'it could have been sold for a good sum and the money given to the poor.'
10 Jesus was aware of this, and said to them, 'Why must you make trouble for the woman?
11 It is a fine thing she has done for me. You have the poor among you always; but
12 you will not always have me. When she poured this oil on my body it was her way of preparing me for burial. I tell you this:
13 wherever in all the world this gospel is proclaimed, what she has done will be told as her memorial.'

Judas Iscariot plans to betray Jesus

14 Then one of the Twelve, the man called
15 Judas Iscariot, went to the chief priests and said, 'What will you give me to betray him to you?' They weighed him out[d] thirty silver

d Or agreed to pay him . . .

16 pieces. From that moment he began to look out for an opportunity to betray him.

Preparation for the Passover

17 On the first day of Unleavened Bread the disciples came to ask Jesus, 'Where would you like us to prepare for your Passover
18 supper?' He answered, 'Go to a certain man in the city, and tell him, "The Master says, 'My appointed time is near; I am to keep Passover with my disciples at your house.'"'
19 The disciples did as Jesus directed them and prepared for Passover.

The Last Supper

20 In the evening he sat down with the twelve
21 disciples; and during supper he said, 'I tell
22 you this: one of you will betray me.' In great distress they exclaimed one after the
23 other, 'Can you mean me, Lord?' He answered, 'One who has dipped his hand
24 into this bowl with me will betray me. The Son of Man is going the way appointed for him in the scriptures; but alas for that man by whom the Son of Man is betrayed! It would be better for that man if he had never
25 been born.' Then Judas spoke, the one who was to betray him: 'Rabbi, can you mean me?' Jesus replied, 'The words are yours.'*e*
26 During supper Jesus took bread, and having said the blessing he broke it and gave it to the disciples with the words: 'Take this
27 and eat; this is my body.' Then he took a cup, and having offered thanks to God he gave it to them with the words: 'Drink from
28 it, all of you. For this is my blood, the blood of the covenant, shed for many for the for-
29 giveness of sins. I tell you, never again shall I drink from the fruit of the vine until that day when I drink it new with you in the kingdom of my Father.'

Jesus foretells Peter's denial

30 After singing the Passover Hymn, they went
31 out to the Mount of Olives. Then Jesus said to them, 'Tonight you will all fall from your faith on my account; for it stands written: "I will strike the shepherd down and the
32 sheep of his flock will be scattered." But after I am raised again, I will go on before
33 you into Galilee.' Peter replied, 'Everyone else may fall away on your account, but I
34 never will.' Jesus said to him, 'I tell you, tonight before the cock crows you will dis-
35 own me three times.' Peter said, 'Even if I must die with you, I will never disown you.' And all the disciples said the same.

Jesus prays in Gethsemane

36 Jesus then came with his disciples to a place called Gethsemane. He said to them, 'Sit
37 here while I go over there to pray.' He took

with him Peter and the two sons of Zebedee. Anguish and dismay came over him, and 38 he said to them, 'My heart is ready to break with grief. Stop here, and stay awake with me.' He went on a little, fell on his face in 39 prayer, and said, 'My Father, if it is possible, let this cup pass me by. Yet not as I will, but as thou wilt.'

He came to the disciples and found them 40 asleep; and he said to Peter, 'What! Could none of you stay awake with me one hour? Stay awake, and pray that you may be 41 spared the test. The spirit is willing, but the flesh is weak.'

He went away a second time, and prayed: 42 'My Father, if it is not possible for this cup to pass me by without my drinking it, thy will be done.' He came again and found them 43 asleep, for their eyes were heavy. So he left 44 them and went away again; and he prayed the third time, using the same words as before.

Jesus is arrested

Then he came to the disciples and said to 45 them, 'Still sleeping? Still taking your ease? The hour has come! The Son of Man is betrayed to sinful men. Up, let us go forward; 46 the traitor is upon us.'

While he was still speaking, Judas, one 47 of the Twelve, appeared; with him was a great crowd armed with swords and cudgels, sent by the chief priests and the elders of the nation. The traitor gave them this sign: 48 'The one I kiss is your man; seize him'; and 49 stepping forward at once, he said, 'Hail, Rabbi!', and kissed him. Jesus replied, 50 'Friend, do what you are here to do.'*f* They then came forward, seized Jesus, and held him fast.

At that moment one of those with Jesus 51 reached for his sword and drew it, and he struck at the High Priest's servant and cut off his ear. But Jesus said to him, 'Put up 52 your sword. All who take the sword die by the sword. Do you suppose that I cannot 53 appeal to my Father, who would at once send to my aid more than twelve legions of angels? But how then could the scriptures be ful- 54 filled, which say that this must be?'

At the same time Jesus spoke to the crowd: 55 'Do you take me for a bandit, that you have come out with swords and cudgels to arrest me? Day after day I sat teaching in the temple, and you did not lay hands on me. But this has all happened to fulfil what the 56 prophets wrote.'

Then the disciples all deserted him and ran away.

Jesus is charged with blasphemy

Jesus was led off under arrest to the house 57 of Caiaphas the High Priest, where the

---

e Or It is as you say.　　　　　*f Or* Friend, what are you here for?

58 lawyers and elders were assembled. Peter followed him at a distance till he came to the High Priest's courtyard, and going in he sat down there among the attendants, meaning to see the end of it all.

59 The chief priests and the whole Council tried to find some allegation against Jesus on which a death-sentence could be based; 60 but they failed to find one, though many came forward with false evidence. Finally 61 two men alleged that he had said, 'I can pull down the temple of God, and rebuild it in 62 three days.' At this the High Priest rose and said to him, 'Have you no answer to the charge that these witnesses bring against 63 you?' But Jesus kept silence. The High Priest then said, 'By the living God I charge you to tell us: Are you the Messiah, the Son 64 of God?' Jesus replied, 'The words are yours.*g* But I tell you this: from now on, you will see the Son of Man seated at the right hand of God*h* and coming on the clouds of 65 heaven.' At these words the High Priest tore his robes and exclaimed, 'Blasphemy! Need we call further witnesses? You have 66 heard the blasphemy. What is your opinion?' 'He is guilty,' they answered; 'he should die.'

67 Then they spat in his face and struck him with their fists; and others said, as they beat 68 him, 'Now, Messiah, if you are a prophet, tell us who hit you.'

Peter disowns Jesus

69 Meanwhile Peter was sitting outside in the courtyard when a serving-maid accosted him and said, 'You were there too with Jesus the 70 Galilean.' Peter denied it in face of them all. 71 'I do not know what you mean', he said. He then went out to the gateway, where another girl, seeing him, said to the people there, 'This fellow was with Jesus of Nazareth.' 72 Once again he denied it, saying with an oath, 73 'I do not know the man.' Shortly afterwards the bystanders came up and said to Peter, 'Surely you are another of them; your accent 74 gives you away!' At this he broke into curses and declared with an oath: 'I do not know 75 the man.' At that moment a cock crew; and Peter remembered how Jesus had said, 'Before the cock crows you will disown me three times.' He went outside, and wept bitterly.

Jesus is handed over to the Romans

27 When morning came, the chief priests and the elders of the nation met in conference 2 to plan the death of Jesus. They then put him in chains and led him away, to hand him over to Pilate, the Roman Governor.

Judas hangs himself

When Judas the traitor saw that Jesus had 3 been condemned, he was seized with remorse, and returned the thirty silver pieces to the chief priests and elders. 'I have sinned,' 4 he said; 'I have brought an innocent man to his death.' But they said, 'What is that to us? See to that yourself.' So he threw the money 5 down in the temple and left them, and went and hanged himself.

Taking up the money, the chief priests 6 argued: 'This cannot be put into the temple fund; it is blood-money.' So after conferring 7 they used it to buy the Potter's Field, as a burial-place for foreigners. This explains the 8 name 'Blood Acre', by which that field has been known ever since; and in this way ful- 9 filment was given to the prophetic utterance of Jeremiah: 'They took*i* the thirty silver pieces, the price set on a man's head (for that was his price among the Israelites), and 10 gave the money for the potter's field, as the Lord directed me.'

Pilate questions Jesus

Jesus was now brought before the Governor; 11 and as he stood there the Governor asked him, 'Are you the king of the Jews?' 'The words are yours',*j* said Jesus; and to the 12 charges laid against him by the chief priests and elders he made no reply. Then Pilate 13 said to him, 'Do you not hear all this evidence that is brought against you?'; but he 14 still refused to answer one word, to the Governor's great astonishment.

Jesus is sentenced to death

At the festival season it was the Governor's 15 custom to release one prisoner chosen by the people. There was then in custody a man of 16 some notoriety, called Jesus*k* Bar-Abbas. When they were assembled Pilate said to 17 them, 'Which would you like me to release to you—Jesus*k* Bar-Abbas, or Jesus called Messiah?' For he knew that it was out of 18 malice that they had brought Jesus before him.

While Pilate was sitting in court a message 19 came to him from his wife: 'Have nothing to do with that innocent man; I was much troubled on his account in my dreams last night.'

Meanwhile the chief priests and elders 20 had persuaded the crowd to ask for the release of Bar-Abbas and to have Jesus put to death. So when the Governor asked, 21 'Which of the two do you wish me to release to you?', they said, 'Bar-Abbas.' 'Then what 22 am I to do with Jesus called Messiah?' asked Pilate; and with one voice they answered, 'Crucify him!' 'Why, what harm has he 23

---

g Or It is as you say.   *h Literally* of the Power. *witnesses omit* Jesus.

i Or I took.   *j Or* It is as you say.   *k Some*

done?' Pilate asked; but they shouted all the louder, 'Crucify him!'

24 Pilate could see that nothing was being gained, and a riot was starting; so he took water and washed his hands in full view of the people, saying, 'My hands are clean of this man's blood; see to that yourselves.'
25 And with one voice the people cried, 'His
26 blood be on us, and on our children.' He then released Bar-Abbas to them; but he had Jesus flogged, and handed him over to be crucified.

Soldiers jeer at Jesus

27 Pilate's soldiers then took Jesus into the Governor's headquarters, where they col-
28 lected the whole company round him. They stripped him and dressed him in a scarlet
29 mantle; and plaiting a crown of thorns placed it on his head, with a cane in his right hand. Falling on their knees before him they
30 jeered at him: 'Hail, King of the Jews!' They spat on him, and used the cane to beat him
31 about the head. When they had finished their mockery, they took off the mantle and dressed him in his own clothes.

Jesus is crucified

32 Then they led him away to be crucified. On their way out they met a man from Cyrene, Simon by name, and pressed him into service to carry his cross.
33 So they came to a place called Golgotha
34 (which means 'Place of a skull') and there he was offered a draught of wine mixed with gall; but when he had tasted it he would not drink.
35 After fastening him to the cross they divided his clothes among them by casting
36 lots, and then sat down there to keep watch.
37 Over his head was placed the inscription giving the charge: 'This is Jesus the king of the Jews.'
38 Two bandits were crucified with him, one on his right and the other on his left.
39 The passers-by hurled abuse at him: they

wagged their heads and cried, 'You would 40 pull the temple down, would you, and build it in three days? Come down from the cross and save yourself, if you are indeed the Son of God.' So too the chief priests with the 41 lawyers and elders mocked at him: 'He saved 42 others,' they said, 'but he cannot save himself. King of Israel, indeed! Let him come down now from the cross, and then we will believe him. Did he trust in God? Let God 43 rescue him, if he wants him—for he said he was God's Son.' Even the bandits who were 44 crucified with him taunted him in the same way.

The death of Jesus

From midday a darkness fell over the whole 45 land, which lasted until three in the afternoon; and about three Jesus cried aloud, 46 *'Eli, Eli, lema sabachthani?'*, which means, 'My God, my God, why hast thou forsaken me?' Some of the bystanders, on hearing 47 this, said, 'He is calling Elijah.' One of them 48 ran at once and fetched a sponge, which he soaked in sour wine, and held it to his lips on the end of a cane. But the others 49 said, 'Let us see if Elijah will come to save him.'

Jesus again gave a loud cry, and breathed 50 his last. At that moment the curtain of the 51 temple was torn in two from top to bottom. There was an earthquake, the rocks split and the graves opened, and many of God's 52 saints were raised from sleep; and coming 53 out of their graves after his resurrection they entered the Holy City, where many saw them. And when the centurion and his men who 54 were keeping watch over Jesus saw the earthquake and all that was happening, they were filled with awe, and they said, 'Truly this man was a son of God.'[1]

The burial of Jesus

A number of women were also present, 55 watching from a distance; they had followed Jesus from Galilee and waited on him. Among them were Mary of Magdala, Mary 56 the mother of James and Joseph, and the mother of the sons of Zebedee.

When evening fell, there came a man of 57 Arimathaea, Joseph by name, who was a man of means, and had himself become a disciple of Jesus. He approached Pilate, and 58 asked for the body of Jesus; and Pilate gave orders that he should have it. Joseph took 59 the body, wrapped it in a clean linen sheet, and laid it in his own unused tomb, which 60 he had cut out of the rock; he then rolled a large stone against the entrance, and went away. Mary of Magdala was there, 61 and the other Mary, sitting opposite the grave.

1 Or the Son of God.

The grave is secured

62 Next day, the morning after that Friday, the
63 chief priests and the Pharisees came in a
body to Pilate. 'Your Excellency,' they said,
'we recall how that impostor said while he
was still alive, "I am to be raised again after
64 three days." So will you give orders for the
grave to be made secure until the third day?
Otherwise his disciples may come, steal the
body, and then tell the people that he has
been raised from the dead; and the final
65 deception will be worse than the first.' 'You
may have your guard,' said Pilate; 'go and
66 make it secure as best you can.' So they went
and made the grave secure; they sealed the
stone, and left the guard in charge.

The resurrection

28 The Sabbath was over, and it was about daybreak on Sunday, when Mary of Magdala
and the other Mary came to look at the
2 grave. Suddenly there was a violent earthquake; an angel of the Lord descended from
heaven; he came to the stone and rolled it
3 away, and sat himself down on it. His face
shone like lightning; his garments were white
4 as snow. At the sight of him the guards shook
with fear and lay like the dead.
5 The angel then addressed the women:
'You', he said, 'have nothing to fear. I know
you are looking for Jesus who was crucified.
6 He is not here; he has been raised again, as
he said he would be. Come and see the place
7 where he was laid, and then go quickly and
tell his disciples: "He has been raised from
the dead and is going on before you into
Galilee; there you will see him." That is
what I had to tell you.'
8 They hurried away from the tomb in awe
and great joy, and ran to tell the disciples.

Suddenly Jesus was there in their path. He 9
gave them his greeting, and they came up
and clasped his feet, falling prostrate before
him. Then Jesus said to them, 'Do not be 10
afraid. Go and take word to my brothers
that they are to leave for Galilee. They will
see me there.'

Attempts to suppress the facts

The women had started on their way when 11
some of the guard went into the city and
reported to the chief priests everything that
had happened. After meeting with the elders 12
and conferring together, the chief priests
offered the soldiers a substantial bribe and 13
told them to say, 'His disciples came by
night and stole the body while we were
asleep.' They added, 'If this should reach 14
the Governor's ears, we will put matters
right with him and see that you do not
suffer.' So they took the money and did as 15
they were told. This story became widely
known, and is current in Jewish circles to
this day.

Jesus commissions his eleven disciples

The eleven disciples made their way to 16
Galilee, to the mountain where Jesus had
told them to meet him. When they saw him, 17
they fell prostrate before him, though some
were doubtful. Jesus then came up and spoke 18
to them. He said: 'Full authority in heaven
and on earth has been committed to me. Go 19
forth therefore and make all nations my
disciples; baptize men everywhere in the
name of the Father and the Son and the
Holy Spirit, and teach them to observe all 20
that I have commanded you. And be
assured, I am with you always, to the end
of time.'

CAPERNAUM

THE GOSPEL ACCORDING TO

MARK

John preaches repentance

1 HERE BEGINS the Gospel of Jesus Christ the Son of God.*

2 In the prophet Isaiah it stands written: 'Here is my herald whom I send on ahead of you, and he will prepare your way. A

3 voice crying aloud in the wilderness, "Prepare a way for the Lord; clear a straight

4 path for him."' And so it was that John the Baptist appeared in the wilderness proclaiming a baptism in token of repentance, for

5 the forgiveness of sins; and they flocked to him from the whole Judaean country-side and the city of Jerusalem, and were baptized by him in the River Jordan, confessing their sins.

6 John was dressed in a rough coat of camel's hair, with a leather belt round his waist, and

7 he fed on locusts and wild honey. His proclamation ran: 'After me comes one who is mightier than I. I am not fit to unfasten his

8 shoes. I have baptized you with water; he will baptize you with the Holy Spirit.'

The baptism and temptation of Jesus

9 It happened at this time that Jesus came from Nazareth in Galilee and was baptized

10 in the Jordan by John. At the moment when he came up out of the water, he saw the heavens torn open and the Spirit, like a dove,

11 descending upon him. And a voice spoke from heaven: 'Thou art my Son, my Beloved;ᵇ on thee my favour rests.'

12 Thereupon the Spirit sent him away into

13 the wilderness, and there he remained for forty days tempted by Satan. He was among the wild beasts; and the angels waited on him.

Jesus proclaims the kingdom of God

14 After John had been arrested, Jesus came into Galilee proclaiming the Gospel of God:

15 'The time has come; the kingdom of God is upon you; repent, and believe the Gospel.'

Jesus calls four fishermen

16 Jesus was walking by the Sea of Galilee when he saw Simon and his brother Andrew on the lake at work with a casting-net; for

17 they were fishermen. Jesus said to them, 'Come with me, and I will make you fishers of men.' And at once they left their nets and

18 followed him.

19 When he had gone a little further he saw James son of Zebedee and his brother John, who were in the boat overhauling their nets.

20 He called them; and, leaving their father Zebedee in the boat with the hired men, they went off to follow him.

The authority of Jesus in word and deed

21 They came to Capernaum, and on the Sabbath he went to synagogue and began to

22 teach. The people were astounded at his teaching, for, unlike the doctors of the law,

23 he taught with a note of authority. Now there was a man in the synagogue possessed

a Some witnesses omit the Son of God.

b Or Thou art my only Son.

756

24 by an unclean spirit. He shrieked: 'What do you want with us, Jesus of Nazareth? Have you*c* come to destroy us? I know who you
25 are—the Holy One of God.' Jesus rebuked him: 'Be silent', he said, 'and come out of
26 him.' And the unclean spirit threw the man into convulsions and with a loud cry left
27 him. They were all dumbfounded and began to ask one another, 'What is this? A new kind of teaching! He speaks with authority. When he gives orders, even the unclean
28 spirits submit.' The news spread rapidly, and he was soon spoken of all over the district of Galilee.

Acts of healing

29 On leaving the synagogue they went straight to the house of Simon and Andrew; and
30 James and John went with them. Simon's mother-in-law was ill in bed with fever. They
31 told him about her at once. He came forward, took her by the hand, and helped her to her feet. The fever left her and she waited upon them.
32 That evening after sunset they brought to him all who were ill or possessed by devils;
33 and the whole town was there, gathered at
34 the door. He healed many who suffered from various diseases, and drove out many devils. He would not let the devils speak, because they knew who he was.

Jesus preaches all through Galilee

35 Very early next morning he got up and went out. He went away to a lonely spot and re-
36 mained there in prayer. But Simon and his
37 companions searched him out, found him,
38 and said, 'They are all looking for you.' He answered, 'Let us move on to the country towns in the neighbourhood; I have to proclaim my message there also; that is what
39 I came out to do.' So all through Galilee he went, preaching in the synagogues and casting out the devils.

Jesus cleanses a leper

40 Once he was approached by a leper, who knelt before him begging his help. 'If only you will,' said the man, 'you can cleanse me.'
41 In warm indignation Jesus stretched out his hand,*d* touched him, and said, 'Indeed I
42 will; be clean again.' The leprosy left him
43 immediately, and he was clean. Then he
44 dismissed him with this stern warning: 'Be sure you say nothing to anybody. Go and show yourself to the priest, and make the offering laid down by Moses for your cleans-
45 ing; that will certify the cure.' But the man went out and made the whole story public; he spread it far and wide, until Jesus could no longer show himself in any town, but

stayed outside in the open country. Even so, people kept coming to him from all quarters.

Authority to forgive sins

When after some days he returned to 2 Capernaum, the news went round that he was at home; and such a crowd collected 2 that the space in front of the door was not big enough to hold them. And while he was proclaiming the message to them, a man was 3 brought who was paralysed. Four men were carrying him, but because of the crowd they 4 could not get him near. So they opened up the roof over the place where Jesus was, and when they had broken through they lowered the stretcher on which the paralysed man was lying. When Jesus saw their faith, he 5 said to the paralysed man, 'My son, your sins are forgiven.'

Now there were some lawyers sitting there 6 and they thought to themselves, 'Why does 7 the fellow talk like that? This is blasphemy! Who but God alone can forgive sins?' Jesus 8 knew in his own mind that this was what they were thinking, and said to them: 'Why do you harbour thoughts like these? Is it easier 9 to say to this paralysed man, "Your sins are forgiven", or to say, "Stand up, take your bed, and walk"? But to convince you that 10 the Son of Man has the right on earth to forgive sins'—he turned to the paralysed man—'I say to you, stand up, take your bed, 11 and go home.' And he got up, and at once 12 took his stretcher and went out in full view of them all, so that they were astounded and praised God. 'Never before', they said, 'have we seen the like.'

Jesus and the tax-gatherers

Once more he went away to the lake-side. 13 All the crowd came to him, and he taught them there. As he went along, he saw Levi 14 son of Alphaeus at his seat in the custom-house, and said to him, 'Follow me'; and Levi rose and followed him.

When Jesus was at table in his house, 15 many bad characters—tax-gatherers and others—were seated with him and his disciples; for there were many who followed him. Some doctors of the law who were 16 Pharisees noticed him eating in this bad company, and said to his disciples, 'He eats with tax-gatherers and sinners!' Jesus heard 17 it and said to them, 'It is not the healthy that need a doctor, but the sick; I did not come to invite virtuous people, but sinners.'

About fasting

Once, when John's disciples and the Pha- 18 risees were keeping a fast, some people came to him and said, 'Why is it that John's

c *Or* You have.   d *Some witnesses read* Jesus was sorry for him and stretched out his hand; *one witness has simply* He stretched out his hand.

disciples and the disciples of the Pharisees
19 are fasting, but yours are not?' Jesus said
to them, 'Can you expect the bridegroom's
friends to fast while the bridegroom is with
them? As long as they have the bridegroom
20 with them, there can be no fasting. But the
time will come when the bridegroom will be
taken away from them, and on that day they
will fast.

Patched clothes and old wine-skins

21 'No one sews a patch of unshrunk cloth on
to an old coat; if he does, the patch tears
away from it, the new from the old, and
22 leaves a bigger hole. No one puts new wine
into old wine-skins; if he does, the wine will
burst the skins, and then wine and skins are
both lost. Fresh skins for new wine!'

About the Sabbath

23 One Sabbath he was going through the cornfields; and his disciples, as they went, began
24 to pluck ears of corn. The Pharisees said to
him, 'Look, why are they doing what is
25 forbidden on the Sabbath?' He answered,
'Have you never read what David did when
he and his men were hungry and had nothing
26 to eat? He went into the House of God, in
the time of Abiathar the High Priest, and ate
the sacred bread, though no one but a priest
is allowed to eat it, and even gave it to his
men.'
27 He also said to them, 'The Sabbath was
made for the sake of man and not man for
28 the Sabbath: therefore the Son of Man is
sovereign even over the Sabbath.'

A man with a withered arm

3 On another occasion when he went to synagogue, there was a man in the congregation
2 who had a withered arm; and they were
watching to see whether Jesus would cure
him on the Sabbath, so that they could bring
3 a charge against him. He said to the man
with the withered arm, 'Come and stand
4 out here.' Then he turned to them: 'Is it
permitted to do good or to do evil on the
Sabbath, to save life or to kill?' They had
5 nothing to say; and, looking round at them
with anger and sorrow at their obstinate
stupidity, he said to the man, 'Stretch out
your arm.' He stretched it out and his arm
6 was restored. But the Pharisees, on leaving
the synagogue, began plotting against him
with the partisans of Herod to see how they
could make away with him.

A crowd by the lake

7 Jesus went away to the lake-side with his
disciples. Great numbers from Galilee,
8 Judaea and Jerusalem, Idumaea and Transjordan, and the neighbourhood of Tyre and
Sidon, heard what he was doing and came
to see him. So he told his disciples to have 9
a boat ready for him, to save him from being
crushed by the crowd. For he cured so many 10
that sick people of all kinds came crowding
in upon him to touch him. The unclean spirits 11
too, when they saw him, would fall at his
feet and cry aloud, 'You are the Son of God';
but he insisted that they should not make 12
him known.

The twelve apostles

He then went up into the hill-country and 13
called the men he wanted; and they went and
joined him. He appointed twelve as his com- 14
panions, whom he would send out to proclaim the Gospel, with a commission to drive 15
out devils. So he appointed the Twelve: to 16
Simon he gave the name Peter; then came 17
the sons of Zebedee, James and his brother
John, to whom he gave the name Boanerges,
Sons of Thunder; then Andrew and Philip 18
and Bartholomew and Matthew and Thomas
and James the son of Alphaeus and Thaddaeus and Simon, a member of the Zealot
party, and Judas Iscariot, the man who 19
betrayed him.

Controversy with the doctors of the law

He entered a house; and once more such a 20
crowd collected round them that they had
no chance to eat. When his family heard of 21
this, they set out to take charge of him; for
people were saying that he was out of his
mind.ᵉ

The doctors of the law, too, who had come 22
down from Jerusalem, said, 'He is possessed
by Beelzebub', and, 'He drives out devils by
the prince of devils.' So he called them to 23
come forward, and spoke to them in parables: 'How can Satan drive out Satan? If 24
a kingdom is divided against itself, that
kingdom cannot stand; if a household is 25
divided against itself, that house will never
stand; and if Satan is in rebellion against 26
himself, he is divided and cannot stand; and
that is the end of him.

'On the other hand, no one can break into 27
a strong man's house and make off with his
goods unless he has first tied the strong man
up; then he can ransack the house.

'I tell you this: no sin, no slander, is be- 28
yond forgiveness for men; but whoever 29
slanders the Holy Spirit can never be forgiven; he is guilty of eternal sin.' He said 30
this because they had declared that he was
possessed by an unclean spirit.

Jesus's relatives

Then his mother and his brothers arrived, 31
and remaining outside sent in a message asking him to come out to them. A crowd was 32

ᵉ Or of him. 'He is out of his mind', they said.

sitting round and word was brought to him: 'Your mother and your brothers are outside 33 asking for you.' He replied, 'Who is my 34 mother? Who are my brothers?' And looking round at those who were sitting in the circle about him he said, 'Here are my 35 mother and my brothers. Whoever does the will of God is my brother, my sister, my mother.'

Parables

4 On another occasion he began to teach by the lake-side. The crowd that gathered round him was so large that he had to get into a boat on the lake, and there he sat, with the whole crowd on the beach right down to the 2 water's edge. And he taught them many things by parables.

A sower

As he taught he said:
3 4 'Listen! A sower went out to sow. And it happened that as he sowed, some seed fell along the footpath, and the birds came and 5 ate it up. Some seed fell on rocky ground, where it had little soil, and it sprouted quickly because it had no depth of earth; 6 but when the sun rose the young corn was scorched, and as it had no root it withered 7 away. Some seed fell among thistles; and the thistles shot up and choked the corn, 8 and it yielded no crop. And some of the seed fell into good soil, where it came up and grew, and bore fruit; and the yield was thirtyfold, sixtyfold, even a hundredfold.' 9 He added, 'If you have ears to hear, then hear.'

Why Jesus told parables

10 When he was alone, the Twelve and others who were round him questioned him about 11 the parables. He replied, 'To you the secret of the kingdom of God has been given; but to those who are outside everything comes 12 by way of parables, so that (as Scripture says) they may look and look, but see nothing; they may hear and hear, but understand nothing; otherwise they might turn to God and be forgiven.'

The parable of the sower explained

13 So he said, 'You do not understand this parable? How then are you to understand any parable? The sower sows the word. 14 Those along the footpath are people in 15 whom the word is sown, but no sooner have they heard it than Satan comes and carries off the word which has been sown in them. It is the same with those who receive the 16 seed on rocky ground; as soon as they hear the word, they accept it with joy, but it 17 strikes no root in them; they have no staying-power; then, when there is trouble or persecution on account of the word, they fall away at once. Others again receive the seed 18 among thistles; they hear the word, but 19 worldly cares and the false glamour of wealth and all kinds of evil desire come in and choke the word, and it proves barren. And there are those who receive the seed in 20 good soil; they hear the word and welcome it; and they bear fruit thirtyfold, sixtyfold, or a hundredfold.'

A lesson from a lamp

He said to them, 'Do you bring in the lamp 21 to put it under the meal-tub, or under the bed? Surely it is brought to be set on the lamp-stand. For nothing is hidden unless it 22 is to be disclosed, and nothing put under cover unless it is to come into the open. If 23 you have ears to hear, then hear.'

He also said, 'Take note of what you hear; 24 the measure you give is the measure you will receive, with something more besides. For 25 the man who has will be given more, and the man who has not will forfeit even what he has.'

From sowing to harvest

He said, 'The kingdom of God is like this. 26 A man scatters seed on the land; he goes to 27 bed at night and gets up in the morning, and the seed sprouts and grows—how, he does not know. The ground produces a crop 28 by itself, first the blade, then the ear, then full-grown corn in the ear; but as soon as 29 the crop is ripe, he plies the sickle, because harvest-time has come.'

A mustard-seed

He said also, 'How shall we picture the king- 30 dom of God, or by what parable shall we describe it? It is like the mustard-seed, which 31 is smaller than any seed in the ground at its sowing. But once sown, it springs up and 32

grows taller than any other plant, and forms branches so large that the birds can settle in its shade.'

33 With many such parables he would give them his message, so far as they were able 34 to receive it. He never spoke to them except in parables; but privately to his disciples he explained everything.

Jesus calms a storm

35 That day, in the evening, he said to them, 'Let us cross over to the other side of the 36 lake.' So they left the crowd and took him with them in the boat where he had been sitting; and there were other boats accom- 37 panying him. A heavy squall came on and the waves broke over the boat until it was 38 all but swamped. Now he was in the stern asleep on a cushion; they roused him and said, 'Master, we are sinking! Do you not 39 care?' He awoke, rebuked the wind, and said to the sea, 'Hush! Be still!' The wind 40 dropped and there was a dead calm. He said to them, 'Why are you such cowards? 41 Have you no faith even now?' They were awestruck and said to one another, 'Who can this be? Even the wind and the sea obey him.'

Jesus cures a madman

5 So they came to the other side of the lake, 2 into the country of the Gerasenes. As he stepped ashore, a man possessed by an un- clean spirit came up to him from among the 3 tombs where he had his dwelling. He could no longer be controlled; even chains were 4 useless; he had often been fettered and chained up, but he had snapped his chains and broken the fetters. No one was strong 5 enough to master him. And so, unceasingly, night and day, he would cry aloud among the tombs and on the hill-sides and cut him- 6 self with stones. When he saw Jesus in the distance, he ran and flung himself down be- 7 fore him, shouting loudly, 'What do you want with me, Jesus, son of the Most High God? In God's name do not torment me.' 8 (For Jesus was already saying to him, 'Out, unclean spirit, come out of this man!') 9 Jesus asked him, 'What is your name?' 'My name is Legion,' he said, 'there are 10 so many of us.' And he begged hard that Jesus would not send them out of the country. 11 Now there happened to be a large herd 12 of pigs feeding on the hill-side, and the spirits begged him, 'Send us among the pigs 13 and let us go into them.' He gave them leave; and the unclean spirits came out and went into the pigs; and the herd, of about two thousand, rushed over the edge into the lake and were drowned.

The men in charge of them took to their 14 heels and carried the news to the town and country-side; and the people came out to see what had happened. They came to Jesus 15 and saw the madman who had been pos- sessed by the legion of devils, sitting there clothed and in his right mind; and they were afraid. The spectators told them how the 16 madman had been cured and what had happened to the pigs. Then they begged 17 Jesus to leave the district.

As he was stepping into the boat, the 18 man who had been possessed begged to go with him. Jesus would not allow it, but 19 said to him, 'Go home to your own folk and tell them what the Lord in his mercy has done for you.' The man went off and 20 spread the news in the Ten Towns*f* of all that Jesus had done for him; and they were all amazed.

Jairus's plea

As soon as Jesus had returned by boat to 21 the other shore, a great crowd once more gathered round him. While he was by the lake-side, the president of one of the syna- 22 gogues came up, Jairus by name, and, when he saw him, threw himself down at his feet and pleaded with him. 'My little daughter', 23 he said, 'is at death's door. I beg you to come and lay your hands on her to cure her and save her life.' So Jesus went with him, 24 accompanied by a great crowd which pressed upon him.

A woman healed of haemorrhages

Among them was a woman who had suf- 25 fered from haemorrhages for twelve years; and in spite of long treatment by many 26 doctors, on which she had spent all she had, there had been no improvement; on the contrary, she had grown worse. She had 27 heard what people were saying about Jesus, so she came up from behind in the crowd and touched his cloak; for she said to her- 28 self, 'If I touch even his clothes, I shall be cured.' And there and then the source of her 29 haemorrhages dried up and she knew in her- self that she was cured of her trouble. At 30 the same time Jesus, aware that power had gone out of him, turned round in the crowd and asked, 'Who touched my clothes?' His 31 disciples said to him, 'You see the crowd pressing upon you and yet you ask, "Who touched me?"' Meanwhile he was looking 32 round to see who had done it. And the 33 woman, trembling with fear when she grasped what had happened to her, came and fell at his feet and told him the whole truth. He said to her, 'My daughter, your 34 faith has cured you. Go in peace, free for ever from this trouble.'

f Greek Decapolis.

Jairus's daughter restored to life

35 While he was still speaking, a message came from the president's house, 'Your daughter is dead; why trouble the Rabbi further?'

36 But Jesus, overhearing the message as it was delivered, said to the president of the synagogue, 'Do not be afraid; only have faith.'

37 After this he allowed no one to accompany him except Peter and James and James's

38 brother John. They came to the president's house, where he found a great commotion,

39 with loud crying and wailing. So he went in and said to them, 'Why this crying and commotion? The child is not dead: she is

40 asleep'; and they only laughed at him. But after turning all the others out, he took the child's father and mother and his own companions and went in where the child was

41 lying. Then, taking hold of her hand, he said to her, '*Talitha cum*', which means,

42 'Get up, my child.' Immediately the girl got up and walked about—she was twelve years old. At that they were beside themselves

43 with amazement. He gave them strict orders to let no one hear about it, and told them to give her something to eat.

Interior of a synagogue

Unbelief in Nazareth

6 He left that place and went to his home town

2 accompanied by his disciples. When the Sabbath came he began to teach in the synagogue; and the large congregation who heard him were amazed and said, 'Where does he get it from?', and, 'What wisdom is this that has been given him?', and, 'How

3 does he work such miracles? Is not this the carpenter, the son of Mary,[g] the brother of James and Joseph and Judas and Simon? And are not his sisters here with us?' So

4 they fell foul of him. Jesus said to them, 'A prophet will always be held in honour except in his home town, and among his kinsmen

5 and family.' He could work no miracle there, except that he put his hands on a few

6 sick people and healed them; and he was taken aback by their want of faith.

Mission of the twelve apostles

On one of his teaching journeys round the

7 villages he summoned the Twelve and sent them out in pairs on a mission. He gave them

8 authority over unclean spirits, and instructed them to take nothing for the journey beyond a stick: no bread, no pack, no money in their

9 belts. They might wear sandals, but not a

10 second coat. 'When you are admitted to a house', he added, 'stay there until you leave

11 those parts. At any place where they will not receive you or listen to you, shake the dust off your feet as you leave, as a warning

12 to them.' So they set out and called publicly

for repentance. They drove out many devils, 13 and many sick people they anointed with oil and cured.

Disturbing news for Herod

Now King Herod heard of it, for the fame 14 of Jesus had spread; and people were saying,[h] 'John the Baptist has been raised to life, and that is why these miraculous powers are at work in him.' Others said, 'It is Elijah.' 15 Others again, 'He is a prophet like one of the old prophets.' But Herod, when he 16 heard of it, said, 'This is John, whom I beheaded, raised from the dead.'

The death of John the Baptist

For this same Herod had sent and arrested 17 John and put him in prison on account of his brother Philip's wife, Herodias, whom he had married. John had told Herod, 'You have no 18 right to your brother's wife.' Thus Herodias 19 nursed a grudge against him and would willingly have killed him, but she could not; for Herod went in awe of John, knowing him 20 to be a good and holy man; so he kept him in custody. He liked to listen to him, although the listening left him greatly perplexed.

Herodias found her opportunity when 21 Herod on his birthday gave a banquet to his chief officials and commanders and the leading men of Galilee. Her daughter came 22 in[i] and danced, and so delighted Herod and his guests that the king said to the girl, 'Ask what you like and I will give it you.' And he 23 swore an oath to her: 'Whatever you ask I will give you, up to half my kingdom.' She 24 went out and said to her mother, 'What shall I ask for?' She replied, 'The head of John the

g Some witnesses read Is not this the son of the carpenter and Mary . . .   *h Some witnesses read* and he said . . .
i Or A festive occasion came when Herod on his birthday gave . . . of Galilee. The daughter of Herodias came in . . .

25 Baptist.' The girl hastened back at once to the king with her request: 'I want you to give me here and now, on a dish, the head of John
26 the Baptist.' The king was greatly distressed, but out of regard for his oath and for his guests he could not bring himself to refuse
27 her. So the king sent a soldier of the guard with orders to bring John's head. The soldier went off and beheaded him in the
28 prison, brought the head on a dish, and gave it to the girl; and she gave it to her mother.
29 When John's disciples heard the news, they came and took his body away and laid it in a tomb.

Feeding five thousand

30 The apostles now rejoined Jesus and reported to him all that they had done and
31 taught. He said to them, 'Come with me, by yourselves, to some lonely place where you can rest quietly.' (For they had no leisure even to eat, so many were coming
32 and going.) Accordingly, they set off pri-
33 vately by boat for a lonely place. But many saw them leave and recognized them, and came round by land, hurrying from all the towns towards the place, and arrived there
34 first. When he came ashore, he saw a great crowd; and his heart went out to them, because they were like sheep without a shep-
35 herd; and he had much to teach them. As the day wore on, his disciples came up to him and said, 'This is a lonely place and it
36 is getting very late; send the people off to the farms and villages round about, to buy
37 themselves something to eat.' 'Give them something to eat yourselves', he answered. They replied, 'Are we to go and spend twenty pounds[j] on bread to give them a
38 meal?' 'How many loaves have you?' he asked; 'go and see.' They found out and
39 told him, 'Five, and two fishes also.' He ordered them to make the people sit down
40 in groups on the green grass, and they sat down in rows, a hundred rows of fifty each.
41 Then, taking the five loaves and the two fishes, he looked up to heaven, said the blessing, broke the loaves, and gave them to the disciples to distribute. He also divided
42 the two fishes among them. They all ate to
43 their hearts' content; and twelve great basketfuls of scraps were picked up, with what was left of the fish. Those who ate the 44 loaves numbered five thousand men.

Jesus walks on the water

As soon as it was over he made his disciples 45 embark and cross to Bethsaida ahead of him, while he himself sent the people away. After 46 taking leave of them, he went up the hillside to pray. It grew late and the boat was 47 already well out on the water, while he was alone on the land. Somewhere between 48 three and six in the morning, seeing them labouring at the oars against a head-wind, he came towards them, walking on the lake. He was going to pass them by; but when 49 they saw him walking on the lake, they thought it was a ghost and cried out; for 50 they all saw him and were terrified. But at once he spoke to them: 'Take heart! It is I; do not be afraid.' Then he climbed into the 51 boat beside them, and the wind dropped. At this they were completely dumbfounded, for they had not understood the incident of 52 the loaves; their minds were closed.

Jesus heals in Gennesaret

So they finished the crossing and came to 53 land at Gennesaret, where they made fast. When they came ashore, he was immediately 54 recognized; and the people scoured that 55 whole country-side and brought the sick on stretchers to any place where he was reported to be. Wherever he went, to farm- 56 steads, villages, or towns, they laid out the sick in the market-places and begged him to let them simply touch the edge of his cloak; and all who touched him were cured.

About traditions

A group of Pharisees, with some doctors of 7 the law who had come from Jerusalem, met him and noticed that some of his disciples 2 were eating their food with 'defiled' hands —in other words, without washing them. (For the Pharisees and the Jews in general 3 never eat without washing the hands,[k] in obedience to an old-established tradition; and on coming from the market-place they 4 never eat without first washing. And there are many other points on which they have a traditional rule to maintain, for example, washing of cups and jugs and copper bowls.) Accordingly, these Pharisees and the lawyers 5 asked him, 'Why do your disciples not conform to the ancient tradition, but eat their food with defiled hands?' He answered, 6 'Isaiah was right when he prophesied about you hypocrites in these words: "This people pays me lip-service, but their heart is far from me: their worship of me is in vain, for 7 they teach as doctrines the commandments of men." You neglect the commandment of 8

j Literally 200 denarii.   *k* Some witnesses insert with the fist; others insert frequently, or thoroughly.

God, in order to maintain the tradition of men.'

9 He also said to them, 'How well you set aside the commandment of God in order to
10 maintain[l] your tradition! Moses said, "Honour your father and your mother", and, "The man who curses his father or mother must
11 suffer death." But you hold that if a man says to his father or mother, "Anything of mine which might have been used for your benefit is Corban"' (meaning, set apart for God),
12 'he is no longer permitted to do anything
13 for his father or mother. Thus by your own tradition, handed down among you, you make God's word null and void. And many other things that you do are just like that.'

What defiles a man

14 On another occasion he called the people and said to them, 'Listen to me, all of you,
15 and understand this: nothing that goes into a man from outside can defile him; no, it is the things that come out of him that defile a man.'[m]
17 When he had left the people and gone indoors, his disciples questioned him about the
18 parable. He said to them, 'Are you as dull as the rest? Do you not see that nothing that goes from outside into a man can defile him,
19 because it does not enter into his heart but into his stomach, and so passes out into the
20 drain?' Thus he declared all foods clean. He went on, 'It is what comes out of a man that
21 defiles him. For from inside, out of a man's heart, come evil thoughts, acts of fornica-
22 tion, of theft, murder, adultery, ruthless greed, and malice; fraud, indecency, envy,
23 slander, arrogance, and folly; these evil things all come from inside, and they defile the man.'

A woman's faith

24 Then he left that place and went away into the territory of Tyre. He found a house to stay in, and he would have liked to remain
25 unrecognized, but this was impossible. Almost at once a woman whose young daughter was possessed by an unclean spirit heard
26 of him, came in, and fell at his feet. (She was a Gentile, a Phoenician of Syria by nationality.) She begged him to drive the spirit out
27 of her daughter. He said to her, 'Let the children be satisfied first; it is not fair to take the children's bread and throw it to the
28 dogs.' 'Sir,' she answered, 'even the dogs under the table eat the children's scraps.'
29 He said to her, 'For saying that, you may go home content; the unclean spirit has gone
30 out of your daughter.' And when she returned home, she found the child lying in bed; the spirit had left her.

Syrian dogs

A deaf man healed

On his return journey from Tyrian territory 31 he went by way of Sidon to the Sea of Galilee through the territory of the Ten Towns.[n]
32 They brought to him a man who was deaf and had an impediment in his speech, with the request that he would lay his hand on
33 him. He took the man aside, away from the crowd, put his fingers into his ears, spat,
34 and touched his tongue. Then, looking up to heaven, he sighed, and said to him,
35 '*Ephphatha*', which means 'Be opened.' With that his ears were opened, and at the same time the impediment was removed and he
36 spoke plainly. Jesus forbade them to tell anyone; but the more he forbade them, the
37 more they published it. Their astonishment knew no bounds: 'All that he does, he does well,' they said; 'he even makes the deaf hear and the dumb speak.'

Feeding four thousand

There was another occasion about this time **8** when a huge crowd had collected, and, as they had no food, Jesus called his disciples
2 and said to them, 'I feel sorry for all these people; they have been with me now for three
3 days and have nothing to eat. If I send them home unfed, they will turn faint on the way; some of them have come from a distance.'
4 The disciples answered, 'How can anyone provide all these people with bread in this
5 lonely place?' 'How many loaves have you?' he asked; and they answered, 'Seven.' So
6 he ordered the people to sit down on the ground; then he took the seven loaves, and, after giving thanks to God, he broke the bread and gave it to his disciples to distribute; and they served it out to the people.
7 They had also a few small fishes, which he
8 blessed and ordered them to distribute. They all ate to their hearts' content, and seven baskets were filled with the scraps that were
9 left. The people numbered about four thou-
10 sand. Then he dismissed them; and, without delay, got into the boat with his disciples and went to the district of Dalmanutha.[o]

---

l Some witnesses read establish.   *m Some witnesses here add* (16) If you have ears to hear, then hear.
n Greek Decapolis.   *o Some witnesses give* Magedan; *others give* Magdala.

Demand for a sign

11 Then the Pharisees came out and engaged
him in discussion. To test him they asked
12 him for a sign from heaven. He sighed
deeply to himself and said, 'Why does this
generation ask for a sign? I tell you this:
no sign shall be given to this generation.'
13 With that he left them, re-embarked, and
went off to the other side of the lake.

A warning to the disciples

14 Now they had forgotten to take bread with
them; they had no more than one loaf in
15 the boat. He began to warn them: 'Beware,'
he said, 'be on your guard against the leaven
of the Pharisees and the leaven of Herod.'
16 They said among themselves, 'It is because
17 we have no bread.' Knowing what was in
their minds, he asked them, 'Why do you
talk about having no bread? Have you no
inkling yet? Do you still not understand?
18 Are your minds closed? You have eyes: can
you not see? You have ears: can you not
19 hear? Have you forgotten? When I broke
the five loaves among five thousand, how
many basketfuls of scraps did you pick up?'
20 'Twelve', they said. 'And how many when
I broke the seven loaves among four thou-
21 sand?' They answered, 'Seven.' He said, 'Do
you still not understand?'

A blind man healed at Bethsaida

22 They arrived at Bethsaida. There the people
brought a blind man to Jesus and begged
23 him to touch him. He took the blind man by
the hand and led him away out of the village.
Then he spat on his eyes, laid his hands upon
him, and asked whether he could see any-
24 thing. The man's sight began to come back,
and he said, 'I see men; they look like
25 trees, but they are walking about.' Jesus laid
his hands on his eyes again; he looked
hard, and now he was cured so that he saw
26 everything clearly. Then Jesus sent him
home, saying, 'Do not tell anyone in the
village.'[p]

Peter's confession of faith

27 Jesus and his disciples set out for the villages of Caesarea Philippi. On the way he
asked his disciples, 'Who do men say I am?'
28 They answered, 'Some say John the Baptist,
others Elijah, others one of the prophets.'
29 'And you,' he asked, 'who do you say I am?'
30 Peter replied: 'You are the Messiah.' Then
he gave them strict orders not to tell anyone
31 about him; and he began to teach them that
the Son of Man had to undergo great sufferings, and to be rejected by the elders, chief
priests, and doctors of the law; to be put to

death, and to rise again three days afterwards. He spoke about it plainly. At this 32
Peter took him by the arm and began to
rebuke him. But Jesus turned round, and, 33
looking at his disciples, rebuked Peter.
'Away with you, Satan,' he said; 'you think
as men think, not as God thinks.'

On following Jesus

Then he called the people to him, as well as 34
his disciples, and said to them, 'Anyone who
wishes to be a follower of mine must leave
self behind; he must take up his cross, and
come with me. Whoever cares for his own 35
safety is lost; but if a man will let himself be
lost for my sake and for the Gospel, that
man is safe. What does a man gain by win- 36
ning the whole world at the cost of his true
self? What can he give to buy that self back? 37
If anyone is ashamed of me and mine[q] in 38
this wicked and godless age, the Son of Man
will be ashamed of him, when he comes in
the glory of his Father and of the holy
angels.'[r]

He also said, 'I tell you this: there are **9**
some of those standing here who will not
taste death before they have seen the kingdom of God already come in power.'

Jesus is transfigured

Six days later Jesus took Peter, James, and 2
John with him and led them up a high
mountain where they were alone; and in
their presence he was transfigured; his 3
clothes became dazzling white, with a white-
ness no bleacher on earth could equal. They 4
saw Elijah appear, and Moses with him, and
there they were, conversing with Jesus. Then 5
Peter spoke: 'Rabbi,' he said, 'how good it is
that we are here! Shall we make three shelters, one for you, one for Moses, and one
for Elijah?' (For he did not know what to 6
say; they were so terrified.) Then a cloud 7
appeared, casting its shadow over them, and
out of the cloud came a voice: 'This is my
Son, my Beloved;[s] listen to him.' And now 8
suddenly, when they looked around, there
was nobody to be seen but Jesus alone with
themselves.

On their way down the mountain, he 9
enjoined them not to tell anyone what they
had seen until the Son of Man had risen
from the dead. They seized upon those words, 10
and discussed among themselves what this
'rising from the dead' could mean. And they 11
put a question to him: 'Why do our teachers
say that Elijah must come first?' He replied, 12
'Yes, Elijah does come first to set everything
right. Yet how is it[t] that the scriptures say
of the Son of Man that he is to endure great

---

p *Some witnesses read* Do not go into the village.
witnesses read Father with the holy angels.
first to set everything right: then how is it . . .

q *Some witnesses read* me and my words.　　*r Some*
s *Or* This is my only Son.　　t *Or* Elijah, you say, comes

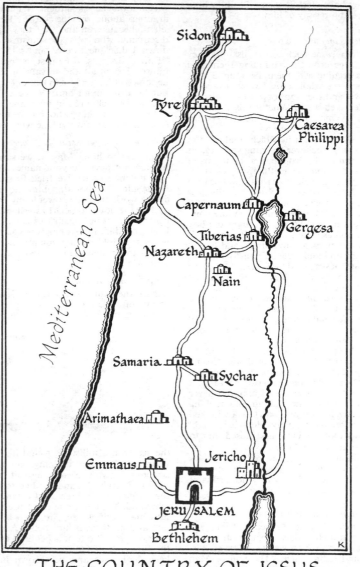

THE COUNTRY OF JESUS

sufferings and to be treated with contempt?
13 However, I tell you, Elijah has already come and they have worked their will upon him, as the scriptures say of him.'

Jesus heals an epileptic boy

14 When they came back to the disciples they saw a large crowd surrounding them and
15 lawyers arguing with them. As soon as they saw Jesus the whole crowd were overcome with awe, and they ran forward to welcome
16 him. He asked them, 'What is this argument
17 about?' A man in the crowd spoke up: 'Master, I brought my son to you. He is possessed by a spirit which makes him
18 speechless. Whenever it attacks him, it dashes him to the ground, and he foams at the mouth, grinds his teeth, and goes rigid. I asked your disciples to cast it out, but they
19 failed.' Jesus answered: 'What an unbelieving and perverse generation! How long shall I be with you? How long must I endure you?
20 Bring him to me.' So they brought the boy to him; and as soon as the spirit saw him it threw the boy into convulsions, and he fell on the ground and rolled about foaming at
21 the mouth. Jesus asked his father, 'How long has he been like this?' 'From childhood,' he
22 replied; 'often it has tried to make an end of him by throwing him into the fire or into water. But if it is at all possible for you, take
23 pity upon us and help us.' 'If it is possible!' said Jesus. 'Everything is possible to
24 who has faith.' 'I have faith,' cried the boy's father; 'help me where faith falls short.'
25 Jesus saw then that the crowd was closing in upon them, so he rebuked the unclean spirit. 'Deaf and dumb spirit,' he said, 'I command you, come out of him and never
26 go back!' After crying aloud and racking him fiercely, it came out; and the boy looked like a corpse; in fact, many said, 'He is dead.'
27 But Jesus took his hand and raised him to his feet, and he stood up.
28 Then Jesus went indoors, and his disciples asked him privately, 'Why could not we
29 cast it out?' He said, 'There is no means of casting out this sort but prayer.'*u*

Jesus again speaks of his death

30 They now left that district and made a journey through Galilee. Jesus wished it to
31 be kept secret; for he was teaching his disciples, and telling them, 'The Son of Man is now to be given up into the power of men, and they will kill him, and three days after
32 being killed, he will rise again.' But they did not understand what he said, and were afraid to ask.

A lesson from a child

33 So they came to Capernaum; and when he was indoors, he asked them, 'What were you
34 arguing about on the way?' They were silent, because on the way they had been
35 discussing who was the greatest. He sat down, called the Twelve, and said to them, 'If anyone wants to be first, he must make himself last of all and servant of all.' Then
36 he took a child, set him in front of them, and put his arm round him. 'Whoever receives
37 one of these children in my name', he said, 'receives me; and whoever receives me, receives not me but the One who sent me.'

'He who is not against us is on our side'

38 John said to him, 'Master, we saw a man driving out devils in your name, and as he was not one of us, we tried to stop him.'
39 Jesus said, 'Do not stop him; no one who does a work of divine power in my name will be able the next moment to speak evil of me.
40 For he who is not against us is on our side.
41 I tell you this: if anyone gives you a cup of water to drink because you are followers of the Messiah, that man assuredly will not go unrewarded.'

Responsibility to others

42 'As for the man who is a cause of stumbling to one of these little ones who have faith, it would be better for him to be thrown into

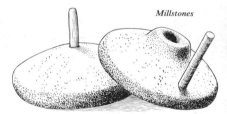
Millstones

43 the sea with a millstone round his neck. If your hand is your undoing, cut it off; it is better for you to enter into life maimed than to keep both hands and go to hell and
45 the unquenchable fire.*v* And if your foot is your undoing, cut it off; it is better to enter into life a cripple than to keep both your
47 feet and be thrown into hell.*w* And if it is your eye, tear it out; it is better to enter into the kingdom of God with one eye than to keep both eyes and be thrown into hell,
48 where the devouring worm never dies and the fire is not quenched.
49 'For everyone will be salted with fire.
50 'Salt is a good thing; but if the salt loses its saltness, what will you season it with?

u Some witnesses add and fasting. and the fire is not quenched. fire is not quenched.

v Some witnesses add (44) where the devouring worm never dies *w Some witnesses add* (46) where the devouring worm never dies and the

'Have salt in yourselves; and be[x] at peace with one another.'

About marriage and divorce

10 On leaving those parts he came into the regions of Judaea and Transjordan; and when a crowd gathered round him once again, he followed his usual practice and
2 taught them. The question was put to him:[y] 'Is it lawful for a man to divorce his wife?'
3 This was to test him. He asked in return,
4 'What did Moses command you?' They answered, 'Moses permitted a man to
5 divorce his wife by note of dismissal.' Jesus said to them, 'It was because your minds were closed that he made this rule for you;
6 but in the beginning, at the creation, God
7 made them male and female. For this reason a man shall leave his father and mother, and
8 be made one with his wife;[z] and the two shall become one flesh. It follows that they are no longer two individuals: they are one flesh.
9 What God has joined together, man must not separate.'
10 When they were indoors again the disciples questioned him about this matter;
11 he said to them, 'Whoever divorces his wife and marries another commits adultery
12 against her: so too, if she divorces her husband and marries another, she commits adultery.'

Jesus welcomes children

13 They brought children for him to touch.
14 The disciples rebuked them, but when Jesus saw this he was indignant, and said to them, 'Let the children come to me; do not try to stop them; for the kingdom of God belongs
15 to such as these. I tell you, whoever does not accept the kingdom of God like a child will
16 never enter it.' And he put his arms round them, laid his hands upon them, and blessed them.

A rich man's question

17 As he was starting out on a journey, a stranger ran up, and, kneeling before him, asked, 'Good Master, what must I do to
18 win eternal life?' Jesus said to him, 'Why do you call me good? No one is good except
19 God alone. You know the commandments: "Do not murder; do not commit adultery; do not steal; do not give false evidence; do not defraud; honour your father and
20 mother."' 'But, Master,' he replied, 'I have
21 kept all these since I was a boy.' Jesus looked straight at him; his heart warmed to him, and he said, 'One thing you lack: go, sell everything you have, and give to the poor, and you will have riches in heaven; and

22 come, follow me.' At these words his face fell and he went away with a heavy heart; for he was a man of great wealth.

Everything is possible for God

23 Jesus looked round at his disciples and said to them, 'How hard it will be for the wealthy
24 to enter the kingdom of God!' They were amazed that he should say this, but Jesus insisted, 'Children, how hard it is[a] to enter
25 the kingdom of God! It is easier for a camel to pass through the eye of a needle than for a rich man to enter the kingdom of God.'
26 They were more astonished than ever, and said to one another, 'Then who can be
27 saved?' Jesus looked at them and said, 'For men it is impossible, but not for God; everything is possible for God.'

About rewards

28 At this Peter spoke. 'We here', he said, 'have left everything to become your followers.'
29 Jesus said, 'I tell you this: there is no one who has given up home, brothers or sisters, mother, father or children, or land, for my
30 sake and for the Gospel, who will not receive in this age a hundred times as much —houses, brothers and sisters, mothers and children, and land—and persecutions besides; and in the age to come eternal life.
31 But many who are first will be last and the last first.'

Jesus again speaks of his death

32 They were on the road, going up to Jerusalem, Jesus leading the way; and the disciples were filled with awe, while those who followed behind were afraid. He took the Twelve aside and began to tell them what
33 was to happen to him. 'We are now going to Jerusalem,' he said; 'and the Son of Man will be given up to the chief priests and the doctors of the law; they will condemn him to death and hand him over to the foreign
34 power. He will be mocked and spat upon, flogged and killed; and three days afterwards, he will rise again.'

James and John ask a favour

35 James and John, the sons of Zebedee, approached him and said, 'Master, we should
36 like you to do us a favour.' 'What is it you
37 want me to do?' he asked. They answered, 'Grant us the right to sit in state with you, one at your right and the other at your left.'
38 Jesus said to them, 'You do not understand what you are asking. Can you drink the cup that I drink, or be baptized with the baptism
39 I am baptized with?' 'We can', they answered. Jesus said, 'The cup that I drink you shall

---

x Or Have the salt of fellowship and be . . .; *or* You have the salt of fellowship between you; then be . . . *y Some witnesses read* The Pharisees came forward and asked him the question . . . *z Some witnesses omit* and be made . . . wife. *a Some witnesses insert* for those who trust in riches.

Bethany

drink, and the baptism I am baptized with
40 shall be your baptism; but to sit at my right
or left is not for me to grant; it is for those
to whom it has already been assigned.'*b*
41   When the other ten heard this, they were
42 indignant with James and John. Jesus called
them to him and said, 'You know that in the
world the recognized rulers lord it over their
subjects, and their great men make them
43 feel the weight of authority. That is not the
way with you; among you, whoever wants
44 to be great must be your servant, and whoever wants to be first must be the willing
45 slave of all. For even the Son of Man did not
come to be served but to serve, and to give
up his life as a ransom for many.'

Bartimaeus recovers his sight

46 They came to Jericho; and as he was leaving
the town, with his disciples and a large crowd,
Bartimaeus son of Timaeus, a blind beggar,
47 was seated at the roadside. Hearing that it
was Jesus of Nazareth, he began to shout,
'Son of David, Jesus, have pity on me!'
48 Many of the people told him to hold his
tongue; but he shouted all the more, 'Son
49 of David, have pity on me.' Jesus stopped
and said, 'Call him'; so they called the blind
man and said, 'Take heart; stand up; he is
50 calling you.' At that he threw off his cloak,
51 sprang up, and came to Jesus. Jesus said to
him, 'What do you want me to do for you?'
'Master,' the blind man answered, 'I want my
52 sight back.' Jesus said to him, 'Go; your faith
has cured you.' And at once he recovered
his sight and followed him on the road.

Jesus rides into Jerusalem

They were now approaching Jerusalem, and **11**
when they reached Bethphage and Bethany,
at the Mount of Olives, he sent two of his
disciples with these instructions: 'Go to the 2
village opposite, and, just as you enter, you
will find tethered there a colt which no one
has yet ridden. Untie it and bring it here. If 3
anyone asks, "Why are you doing that?",
say, "Our Master*c* needs it, and will send it
back here without delay."' So they went off, 4
and found the colt tethered at a door outside in the street. They were untying it when 5
some of the bystanders asked, 'What are
you doing, untying that colt?' They answered 6
as Jesus had told them, and were then
allowed to take it. So they brought the colt 7
to Jesus and spread their cloaks on it, and
he mounted. And people carpeted the road 8
with their cloaks, while others spread brushwood which they had cut in the fields; and 9
those who went ahead and the others who
came behind shouted, 'Hosanna! Blessings
on him who comes in the name of the Lord!
Blessings on the coming kingdom of our 10
father David! Hosanna in the heavens!'

He entered Jerusalem and went into the 11
temple, where he looked at the whole scene;
but, as it was now late, he went out to
Bethany with the Twelve.

A fig-tree without fruit

On the following day, after they had left 12
Bethany, he felt hungry, and, noticing in the 13
distance a fig-tree in leaf, he went to see if

b Some witnesses add by my Father.   *c Or* Its owner.

he could find anything on it. But when he came there he found nothing but leaves; for 14 it was not the season for figs. He said to the tree, 'May no one ever again eat fruit from you!' And his disciples were listening.

Jesus drives traders from the temple

15 So they came to Jerusalem, and he went into the temple and began driving out those who bought and sold in the temple. He upset the tables of the money-changers and the seats 16 of the dealers in pigeons; and he would not allow anyone to use the temple court as a 17 thoroughfare for carrying goods. Then he began to teach them, and said, 'Does not Scripture say, "My house shall be called a house of prayer for all the nations"? But 18 you have made it a robbers' cave.' The chief priests and the doctors of the law heard of this and sought some means of making away with him; for they were afraid of him, because the whole crowd was spellbound by 19 his teaching. And when evening came he went out of the city.

A lesson from the fig-tree

20 Early next morning, as they passed by, they saw that the fig-tree had withered from the 21 roots up; and Peter, recalling what had happened, said to him, 'Rabbi, look, the fig-22 tree which you cursed has withered.' Jesus 23 answered them, 'Have faith in God. I tell you this: if anyone says to this mountain, "Be lifted from your place and hurled into the sea", and has no inward doubts, but believes that what he says is happening, it 24 will be done for him. I tell you, then, whatever you ask for in prayer, believe that you have received it and it will be yours.

25 'And when you stand praying, if you have a grievance against anyone, forgive him, so that your Father in heaven may forgive you the wrongs you have done.'[d]

About the authority of Jesus

27 They came once more to Jerusalem. And as he was walking in the temple court the chief 28 priests, lawyers, and elders came to him and said, 'By what authority are you acting like this? Who gave you authority to act in this 29 way?' Jesus said to them, 'I have a question to ask you too; and if you give me an answer, 30 I will tell you by what authority I act. The baptism of John: was it from God, or from 31 men? Answer me.' This set them arguing among themselves: 'What shall we say? If we say, "from God", he will say, "Then why 32 did you not believe him?" Shall we say, "from men"?'—but they were afraid of the people, for all held that John was in fact 33 a prophet. So they answered, 'We do not

know.' And Jesus said to them, 'Then neither will I tell you by what authority I act.'

Tenants in a vineyard

He went on to speak to them in parables: **12** 'A man planted a vineyard and put a wall round it, hewed out a winepress, and built a watch-tower; then he let it out to vine-

A vineyard watch-tower

growers and went abroad. When the season 2 came, he sent a servant to the tenants to collect from them his share of the produce. But they took him, thrashed him, and sent 3 him away empty-handed. Again, he sent them 4 another servant, whom they beat about the head and treated outrageously. So he sent 5 another, and that one they killed; and many more besides, of whom they beat some, and killed others. He had now only one left to 6 send, his own dear son.[e] In the end he sent him. "They will respect my son", he said. But the tenants said to one another, "This 7 is the heir; come on, let us kill him, and the property will be ours." So they seized him 8 and killed him, and flung his body out of the vineyard. What will the owner of the 9 vineyard do? He will come and put the tenants to death and give the vineyard to others.

'Can it be that you have never read this 10 text: "The stone which the builders rejected has become the main corner-stone. This is the Lord's doing, and it is wonderful 11 in our eyes"?'

Then they began to look for a way to 12 arrest him, for they saw that the parable was aimed at them; but they were afraid of the people, so they left him alone and went away.

Paying tax to the Emperor

A number of Pharisees and men of Herod's 13 party were sent to trap him with a question. They came and said, 'Master, you are an 14

---

d Some witnesses add (26) But if you do not forgive others, then the wrongs you have done will not be forgiven by your Father in heaven. *e Or* his only son.

honest man, we know, and truckle to no one, whoever he may be; you teach in all honesty the way of life that God requires. Are we or are we not permitted to pay taxes

15 to the Roman Emperor? Shall we pay or not?' He saw how crafty their question was, and said, 'Why are you trying to catch me out? Fetch me a silver piece, and let me look

16 at it.' They brought one, and he said to them, 'Whose head is this, and whose in-

17 scription?' 'Caesar's', they replied. Then Jesus said, 'Pay Caesar what is due to Caesar, and pay God what is due to God.' And they heard him with astonishment.

About resurrection

18 Next Sadducees came to him. (It is they who say that there is no resurrection.) Their

19 question was this: 'Master, Moses laid it down for us that if there are brothers, and one dies leaving a wife but no child, then the next should marry the widow and carry

20 on his brother's family. Now there were seven brothers. The first took a wife and

21 died without issue. Then the second married her, and he too died without issue. So did

22 the third. Eventually the seven of them died, all without issue. Finally the woman died.

23 At the resurrection, when they come back to life, whose wife will she be, since all seven

24 had married her?' Jesus said to them, 'You are mistaken, and surely this is the reason: you do not know either the scriptures or the

25 power of God. When they rise from the dead, men and women do not marry; they are like angels in heaven.

26 'But about the resurrection of the dead, have you never read in the Book of Moses, in the story of the burning bush, how God spoke to him and said, "I am the God of Abraham, the God of Isaac, and the God

27 of Jacob"? God is not God of the dead but of the living. You are greatly mistaken.'

The greatest commandment

28 Then one of the lawyers, who had been listening to these discussions and had noted how well he answered, came forward and asked him, 'Which commandment is first of all?'

29 Jesus answered, 'The first is, "Hear, O Israel:

30 the Lord our God is the only Lord; love the Lord your God with all your heart, with all your soul, with all your mind, and with

31 all your strength." The second is this: "Love your neighbour as yourself." There is no other commandment greater than these.'

32 The lawyer said to him, 'Well said, Master. You are right in saying that God is one and

33 beside him there is no other. And to love him with all your heart, all your understanding, and all your strength, and to love

your neighbour as yourself—that is far more than any burnt offerings or sacrifices.'

34 When Jesus saw how sensibly he answered, he said to him, 'You are not far from the kingdom of God.'

About the Messiah

After that nobody ventured to put any more

35 questions to him; and Jesus went on to say, as he taught in the temple, 'How can the teachers of the law maintain that the Messiah

36 is "Son of David"? David himself said, when inspired by the Holy Spirit, "The Lord said to my Lord, 'Sit at my right hand until I put your enemies under your feet.'" David him-

37 self calls him "Lord"; how can he also be David's son?'

38 There was a great crowd and they listened eagerly.f He said as he taught them, 'Beware of the doctors of the law, who love to walk up and down in long robes, receiving

39 respectful greetings in the street; and to have the chief seats in synagogues, and

40 places of honour at feasts. These are the men who eat up the property of widows, while they say long prayers for appearance' sake, and they will receive the severest sentence.'g

A poor widow's offering

41 Once he was standing opposite the temple treasury, watching as people dropped their money into the chest. Many rich people were

42 giving large sums. Presently there came a poor widow who dropped in two tiny coins, together worth a farthing. He called his

43 disciples to him. 'I tell you this,' he said: 'this poor widow has given more than any

44 of the others; for those others who have given had more than enough, but she, with less than enough, has given all that she had to live on.'

Destruction of the temple foretold

As he was leaving the temple, one of his **1.** disciples exclaimed, 'Look, Master, what huge stones! What fine buildings!' Jesus said 2 to him, 'You see these great buildings? Not one stone will be left upon another; all will be thrown down.'

Troubles and persecutions

When he was sitting on the Mount of Olives 3 facing the temple he was questioned privately by Peter, James, John, and Andrew. 'Tell 4 us,' they said, 'when will this happen? What will be the sign when the fulfilment of all this is at hand?'

Jesus began: 'Take care that no one mis- 5 leads you. Many will come claiming my 6 name, and saying, "I am he"; and many will be misled by them.

---

f Or The mass of the people listened eagerly.

g Or As for those who eat up the property of widows, while they say long prayers for appearance' sake, they will have an even sterner judgement to face.

7 'When you hear the noise of battle near at hand and the news of battles far away, do not be alarmed. Such things are bound 8 to happen; but the end is still to come. For nation will make war upon nation, kingdom upon kingdom; there will be earthquakes in many places; there will be famines. With these things the birth-pangs of the new age begin.
9 'As for you, be on your guard. You will be handed over to the courts. You will be flogged in synagogues. You will be summoned to appear before governors and kings on my account to testify in their presence. 10 But before the end the Gospel must be 11 proclaimed to all nations. So when you are arrested and taken away, do not worry beforehand about what you will say, but when the time comes say whatever is given you to say; for it is not you who will be 12 speaking, but the Holy Spirit. Brother will betray brother to death, and the father his child; children will turn against their parents 13 and send them to their death. All will hate you for your allegiance to me; but the man who holds out to the end will be saved.'

'The abomination of desolation'

14 'But when you see "the abomination of desolation" usurping a place which is not his (let the reader understand), then those who are in Judaea must take to the hills. 15 If a man is on the roof, he must not come down into the house to fetch anything out; 16 if in the field, he must not turn back for his 17 coat. Alas for women with child in those days, and for those who have children at the 18 breast! Pray that it may not come in winter. 19 For those days will bring distress such as never has been until now since the beginning of the world which God created—and will 20 never be again. If the Lord had not cut short that time of troubles, no living thing could survive. However, for the sake of his own, whom he has chosen, he has cut short the time.
21 'Then, if anyone says to you, "Look, here is the Messiah", or, "Look, there he is", do 22 not believe it. Impostors will come claiming to be messiahs or prophets, and they will produce signs and wonders to mislead God's 23 chosen, if such a thing were possible. But you be on your guard; I have forewarned you of it all.'

The coming of the Son of Man

24 'But in those days, after that distress, the sun will be darkened, the moon will not give 25 her light; the stars will come falling from the sky, the celestial powers will be shaken. 26 Then they will see the Son of Man coming in the clouds with great power and glory, and 27 he will send out the angels and gather his chosen from the four winds, from the farthest bounds of earth to the farthest bounds of heaven.
'Learn a lesson from the fig-tree. When its 28 tender shoots appear and are breaking into leaf, you know that summer is near. In the 29 same way, when you see all this happening, you may know that the end is near,[h] at the very door. I tell you this: the present genera- 30 tion will live to see it all. Heaven and earth 31 will pass away; my words will never pass away.'

No one knows the day or hour: 'be alert'

'But about that day or that hour no one 32 knows, not even the angels in heaven, not even the Son; only the Father.
'Be alert, be wakeful.[i] You do not know 33 when the moment comes. It is like a man 34 away from home: he has left his house and put his servants in charge, each with his own work to do, and he has ordered the door-keeper to stay awake. Keep awake, then, for 35 you do not know when the master of the house is coming. Evening or midnight, cock-crow or early dawn—if he comes suddenly, 36 he must not find you asleep. And what I 37 say to you, I say to everyone: Keep awake.'

A plot to kill Jesus

Now the festival of Passover and Unleavened **14** Bread was only two days off; and the chief priests and the doctors of the law were try-ing to devise some cunning plan to seize him and put him to death. 'It must not be during 2 the festival,' they said, 'or we should have rioting among the people.'

A woman anoints Jesus

Jesus was at Bethany, in the house of Simon 3 the leper. As he sat at table, a woman came in carrying a small bottle of very costly per-fume, pure oil of nard. She broke it open and poured the oil over his head. Some of those 4 present said to one another angrily, 'Why this waste? The perfume might have been 5 sold for thirty pounds[j] and the money given to the poor'; and they turned upon her with fury. But Jesus said, 'Let her alone. Why 6 must you make trouble for her? It is a fine thing she has done for me. You have the 7 poor among you always, and you can help them whenever you like; but you will not always have me. She has done what lay in 8 her power; she is beforehand with anointing my body for burial. I tell you this: wherever 9 in all the world the Gospel is proclaimed, what she has done will be told as her memorial.'

h Or that he is near.   *i Some witnesses add and pray.*   *j Literally 300 denarii; some witnesses read* more than 300 denarii.

Judas Iscariot plans to betray Jesus

10 Then Judas Iscariot, one of the Twelve, went to the chief priests to betray him to them.
11 When they heard what he had come for, they were greatly pleased, and promised him money; and he began to look for a good opportunity to betray him.

Preparation for the Passover

12 Now on the first day of Unleavened Bread, when the Passover lambs were being slaughtered, his disciples said to him, 'Where would you like us to go and prepare for your Pass-
13 over supper?' So he sent out two of his disciples with these instructions: 'Go into the city, and a man will meet you carrying a jar
14 of water. Follow him, and when he enters a house give this message to the householder: "The Master says, 'Where is the room reserved for me to eat the Passover with my
15 disciples?'" He will show you a large room upstairs, set out in readiness. Make the pre-
16 parations for us there.' Then the disciples went off, and when they came into the city they found everything just as he had told them. So they prepared for Passover.

The Last Supper

17 In the evening he came to the house with the
18 Twelve. As they sat at supper Jesus said, 'I tell you this: one of you will betray me—
19 one who is eating with me.' At this they were dismayed; and one by one they said to him,
20 'Not I, surely?' 'It is one of the Twelve,' he said, 'who is dipping into the same bowl with
21 me. The Son of Man is going the way appointed for him in the scriptures; but alas for that man by whom the Son of Man is betrayed! It would be better for that man if he had never been born.'
22   During supper he took bread, and having said the blessing he broke it and gave it to them, with the words: 'Take this; this is my
23 body.' Then he took a cup, and having offered thanks to God he gave it to them;
24 and they all drank from it. And he said, 'This is my blood, the blood of the covenant,
25 shed for many. I tell you this: never again shall I drink from the fruit of the vine until that day when I drink it new in the kingdom of God.'

k *Some witnesses add* using the same words. has been paid', 'The account is settled.'

Jesus foretells Peter's denial

After singing the Passover Hymn, they went 26 out to the Mount of Olives. And Jesus said, 27 'You will all fall from your faith; for it stands written: "I will strike the shepherd down and the sheep will be scattered." Nevertheless, 28 after I am raised again I will go on before you into Galilee.' Peter answered, 'Every- 29 one else may fall away, but I will not.' Jesus 30 said, 'I tell you this: today, this very night, before the cock crows twice, you yourself

will disown me three times.' But he insisted 31 and repeated: 'Even if I must die with you, I will never disown you.' And they all said the same.

Jesus prays in Gethsemane

When they reached a place called Geth- 32 semane, he said to his disciples, 'Sit here while I pray.' And he took Peter and James 33 and John with him. Horror and dismay came over him, and he said to them, 'My heart is 34 ready to break with grief; stop here, and stay awake.' Then he went forward a little, 35 threw himself on the ground, and prayed that, if it were possible, this hour might pass him by. 'Abba, Father,' he said, 'all things 36 are possible to thee; take this cup away from me. Yet not what I will, but what thou wilt.'

He came back and found them asleep; 37 and he said to Peter, 'Asleep, Simon? Were you not able to stay awake for one hour? Stay awake, all of you; and pray that you 38 may be spared the test. The spirit is willing, but the flesh is weak.' Once more he went 39 away and prayed.[k] On his return he found 40 them asleep again, for their eyes were heavy; and they did not know how to answer him.

The third time he came and said to them, 41 'Still sleeping? Still taking your ease? Enough![l] The hour has come. The Son of

l *The Greek is obscure; a possible meaning is* 'The money

42 Man is betrayed to sinful men. Up, let us go forward! My betrayer is upon us.'

Jesus is arrested

43 Suddenly, while he was still speaking, Judas, one of the Twelve, appeared, and with him was a crowd armed with swords and cudgels, sent by the chief priests, lawyers, and elders.
44 Now the traitor had agreed with them upon a signal: 'The one I kiss is your man; seize
45 him and get him safely away.' When he reached the spot, he stepped forward at once and said to Jesus, 'Rabbi', and kissed
46 him. Then they seized him and held him fast.
47 One of the party[m] drew his sword, and struck at the High Priest's servant, cutting
48 off his ear. Then Jesus spoke: 'Do you take me for a bandit, that you have come out
49 with swords and cudgels to arrest me? Day after day I was within your reach as I taught in the temple, and you did not lay hands on
50 me. But let the scriptures be fulfilled.' Then the disciples all deserted him and ran away.
51 Among those following was a young man with nothing on but a linen cloth. They tried
52 to seize him; but he slipped out of the linen cloth and ran away naked.

Jesus is charged with blasphemy

53 Then they led Jesus away to the High Priest's house, where the chief priests, elders, and
54 doctors of the law were all assembling. Peter followed him at a distance right into the High Priest's courtyard; and there he remained, sitting among the attendants, warming himself at the fire.
55 The chief priests and the whole Council tried to find some evidence against Jesus to warrant a death-sentence, but failed to find
56 any. Many gave false evidence against him,
57 but their statements did not tally. Some stood up and gave false evidence against him
58 to this effect: 'We heard him say, "I will pull down this temple, made with human hands, and in three days I will build another,
59 not made with hands."' But even on this point their evidence did not agree.

Then the High Priest stood up in his place 60 and questioned Jesus: 'Have you no answer to the charges that these witnesses bring against you?' But he kept silence; he made 61 no reply.
Again the High Priest questioned him: 'Are you the Messiah, the Son of the Blessed One?' Jesus said, 'I am; and you will see the 62 Son of Man seated at the right hand of God[n] and coming with the clouds of heaven.' Then 63 the High Priest tore his robes and said, 'Need we call further witnesses? You have heard 64 the blasphemy. What is your opinion?' Their judgement was unanimous: that he was guilty and should be put to death.
Some began to spit on him, blindfolded 65 him, and struck him with their fists, crying out, 'Prophesy!'[o] And the High Priest's men set upon him with blows.

Peter disowns Jesus

Meanwhile Peter was still below in the 66 courtyard. One of the High Priest's serving-maids came by and saw him there warming 67 himself. She looked into his face and said, 'You were there too, with this man from Nazareth, this Jesus.' But he denied it: 'I 68 know nothing,' he said; 'I do not understand what you mean.' Then he went outside into the porch;[p] and the maid saw him 69 there again and began to say to the by-standers, 'He is one of them'; and again he 70 denied it.
Again, a little later, the bystanders said to Peter, 'Surely you are one of them. You must be; you are a Galilean.' At this he 71 broke out into curses, and with an oath he said, 'I do not know this man you speak of.' Then the cock crew a second time; and Peter 72

m Or of the bystanders.   *n Literally of the Power.*   *o Some witnesses add Who hit you? as in Matthew and Luke.*   *p Some witnesses insert and a cock crew.*

Gethsemane

remembered how Jesus had said to him, 'Before the cock crows twice you will disown me three times.' And he burst into tears.

Jesus before Pilate

15 As soon as morning came, the chief priests, having made their plan with the elders and lawyers in full council, put Jesus in chains; then they led him away and handed him over 2 to Pilate. Pilate asked him, 'Are you the king of the Jews?' He replied, 'The words are 3 yours.'*q* And the chief priests brought many 4 charges against him. Pilate questioned him again: 'Have you nothing to say in your defence? You see how many charges they 5 are bringing against you.' But, to Pilate's astonishment, Jesus made no further reply.

Jesus is sentenced to death

6 At the festival season the Governor used to release one prisoner at the people's request. 7 As it happened, the man known as Barabbas was then in custody with the rebels who had 8 committed murder in the rising. When the crowd appeared*r* asking for the usual favour, 9 Pilate replied, 'Do you wish me to release 10 for you the king of the Jews?' For he knew it was out of malice that they had brought 11 Jesus before him. But the chief priests incited the crowd to ask him to release Barab- 12 bas rather than Jesus. Pilate spoke to them again: 'Then what shall I do with the man 13 you call king of the Jews?' They shouted 14 back, 'Crucify him!' 'Why, what harm has he done?' Pilate asked; but they shouted all 15 the louder, 'Crucify him!' So Pilate, in his desire to satisfy the mob, released Barabbas to them; and he had Jesus flogged and handed him over to be crucified.

Soldiers jeer at Jesus

16 Then the soldiers took him inside the courtyard (the Governor's headquarters*s*) and called together the whole company. They 17 dressed him in purple, and plaiting a crown of thorns, placed it on his head. Then they 18 began to salute him with, 'Hail, King of the Jews!' They beat him about the head with 19 a cane and spat upon him, and then knelt and paid mock homage to him. When they 20 had finished their mockery, they stripped him of the purple and dressed him in his own clothes.

Jesus is crucified

Then they took him out to crucify him. A 21 man called Simon, from Cyrene, the father of Alexander and Rufus, was passing by on his way in from the country, and they pressed him into service to carry his cross. They brought him to the place called 22 Golgotha, which means 'Place of a skull'. He was offered drugged wine, but he would 23 not take it. Then they fastened him to the 24 cross. They divided his clothes among them, casting lots to decide what each should have. The hour of the crucifixion was nine in 25 the morning, and the inscription giving the 26 charge against him read, 'The king of the Jews.' Two bandits were crucified with him, 27 one on his right and the other on his left.*t*

The passers-by hurled abuse at him: 'Aha!' 29 they cried, wagging their heads, 'you would pull the temple down, would you, and build it in three days? Come down from the cross 30 and save yourself!' So too the chief priests 31 and lawyers jested with one another: 'He saved others,' they said, 'but he cannot save himself. Let the Messiah, the king of Israel, 32 come down now from the cross. If we see that, we shall believe.' Even those who were crucified with him taunted him.

The death of Jesus

At midday a darkness fell over the whole 33 land, which lasted till three in the afternoon;

---

q Or It is as you say.   *r Some witnesses read* shouted.   *s Greek* praetorium.   *t Some witnesses add* (28) Thus that text of Scripture came true which says, 'He was reckoned among criminals.'

34 and at three Jesus cried aloud, '*Eli, Eli, lema sabachthani?*', which means, 'My God, my
35 God, why hast thou forsaken me?'[u] Some of the bystanders, on hearing this, said, 'Hark,
36 he is calling Elijah.' A man ran and soaked a sponge in sour wine and held it to his lips on the end of a cane. 'Let us see', he said,
37 'if Elijah will come to take him down.' Then
38 Jesus gave a loud cry and died. And the curtain of the temple was torn in two from
39 top to bottom. And when the centurion who was standing opposite him saw how he died,[v] he said, 'Truly this man was a son of God.'[w]

The burial of Jesus

40 A number of women were also present, watching from a distance. Among them were Mary of Magdala, Mary the mother of James the younger and of Joseph, and
41 Salome, who had all followed him and waited on him when he was in Galilee, and there were several others who had come up to Jerusalem with him.
42 By this time evening had come; and as it was Preparation-day (that is, the day before
43 the Sabbath), Joseph of Arimathaea, a respected member of the Council, a man who looked forward to the kingdom of God, bravely went in to Pilate and asked for the
44 body of Jesus. Pilate was surprised to hear that he was already dead; so he sent for the centurion and asked him whether it was long

since he died. And when he heard the cen- 45
turion's report, he gave Joseph leave to take the dead body. So Joseph bought a linen 46
sheet, took him down from the cross, and wrapped him in the sheet. Then he laid him in a tomb cut out of the rock, and rolled a stone against the entrance. And Mary of 47
Magdala and Mary the mother of Joseph were watching and saw where he was laid.

The resurrection

When the Sabbath was over, Mary of **16**
Magdala, Mary the mother of James, and Salome bought[x] aromatic oils intending to go and anoint him; and very early on the 2
Sunday morning, just after sunrise, they came to the tomb. They were wondering 3
among themselves who would roll away the stone for them from the entrance to the tomb, when they looked up and saw that 4
the stone, huge as it was, had been rolled back already. They went into the tomb, 5
where they saw a youth sitting on the right-hand side, wearing a white robe; and they were dumbfounded. But he said to them, 6
'Fear nothing; you are looking for Jesus of Nazareth, who was crucified. He has been raised again; he is not here; look, there is the place where they laid him. But go and 7
give this message to his disciples and Peter: "He is going on before you into Galilee; there you will see him, as he told you."' Then they went out and ran away from the 8
tomb, beside themselves with terror. They said nothing to anybody, for they were afraid.[y]

Those who saw the risen Jesus

When he had risen from the dead early on 9
Sunday morning he appeared first to Mary of Magdala, from whom he had formerly cast out seven devils. She went and carried 10
the news to his mourning and sorrowful followers, but when they were told that he 11
was alive and that she had seen him they did not believe it.
Later he appeared in a different guise to 12
two of them as they were walking, on their way into the country. These also went and 13
took the news to the others, but again no one believed them.
Afterwards while the Eleven were at table 14
he appeared to them and reproached them for their incredulity and dullness, because they had not believed those who had seen him after he was raised from the dead. Then 15
he said to them: 'Go forth to every part of

A centurion

16 the world, and proclaim the Good News to the whole creation. Those who believe it and receive baptism will find salvation; those who do not believe will be condemned.
17 Faith will bring with it these miracles: believers will cast out devils in my name and
18 speak in strange tongues; if they handle snakes or drink any deadly poison, they will come to no harm; and the sick on whom they lay their hands will recover.'
19 So after talking with them the Lord Jesus was taken up into heaven, and he took his seat at the right hand of God; but they went
20 out to make their proclamation everywhere, and the Lord worked with them and confirmed their words by the miracles that followed.

The message of eternal salvation

And they delivered all these instructions briefly to Peter and his companions. Afterwards Jesus himself sent out by them from east to west the sacred and imperishable message of eternal salvation.[z]

NAZARETH

THE GOSPEL ACCORDING TO
LUKE

Introduction

1 THE AUTHOR to Theophilus: Many writers have undertaken to draw up an account of the events that have happened
2 among us, following the traditions handed down to us by the original eyewitnesses and
3 servants of the Gospel. And so I in my turn, your Excellency, as one who has gone over the whole course of these events in detail, have decided to write a connected narrative
4 for you, so as to give you authentic knowledge about the matters of which you have been informed.

A son is promised to Zechariah

5 In the days of Herod king of Judaea there was a priest named Zechariah, of the division of the priesthood called after Abijah. His wife also was of priestly descent; her
6 name was Elizabeth. Both of them were upright and devout, blamelessly observing all the commandments and ordinances of the
7 Lord. But they had no children, for Elizabeth was barren, and both were well on in years.
8 Once, when it was the turn of his division and he was there to take part in divine ser-
9 vice, it fell to his lot, by priestly custom, to

enter the sanctuary of the Lord and offer
10 the incense; and the whole congregation was
at prayer outside. It was the hour of
11 incense-offering. There appeared to him an
angel of the Lord, standing on the right of
12 the altar of incense. At this sight, Zechariah
13 was startled, and fear overcame him. But
the angel said to him, 'Do not be afraid,
Zechariah; your prayer has been heard: your
wife Elizabeth will bear you a son, and you
14 shall name him John. Your heart will thrill
with joy and many will be glad that he was
15 born; for he will be great in the eyes of the
Lord. He shall never touch wine or strong
16 drink. From his very birth he will be filled
with the Holy Spirit; and he will bring back
17 many Israelites to the Lord their God. He
will go before him as forerunner,[a] possessed
by the spirit and power of Elijah, to reconcile father and child, to convert the rebellious to the ways of the righteous, to prepare
a people that shall be fit for the Lord.'
18 Zechariah said to the angel, 'How can I
be sure of this? I am an old man and my wife
is well on in years.'
19 The angel replied, 'I am Gabriel; I stand
in attendance upon God, and I have been
sent to speak to you and bring you this good
20 news. But now listen: you will lose your
power of speech, and remain silent until the
day when these things happen to you, because you have not believed me, though at
their proper time my words will be proved
true.'
21 Meanwhile the people were waiting for
Zechariah, surprised that he was staying so
22 long inside. When he did come out he could
not speak to them, and they realized that he

had had a vision in the sanctuary. He stood
there making signs to them, and remained
dumb.
When his period of duty was completed 23
Zechariah returned home. After this his wife 24
Elizabeth conceived, and for five months
she lived in seclusion, thinking, 'This is the 25
Lord's doing; now at last he has deigned to
take away my reproach among men.'

Mary is promised a son

In the sixth month the angel Gabriel was sent 26
from God to a town in Galilee called Nazareth, with a message for a girl betrothed to a 27
man named Joseph, a descendant of David;
the girl's name was Mary. The angel went 28
in and said to her, 'Greetings, most favoured
one! The Lord is with you.' But she was 29
deeply troubled by what he said and won-
dered what this greeting might mean. Then 30
the angel said to her, 'Do not be afraid,
Mary, for God has been gracious to you;
you shall conceive and bear a son, and you 31
shall give him the name Jesus. He will be 32
great; he will bear the title "Son of the Most
High"; the Lord God will give him the
throne of his ancestor David, and he will be 33
king over Israel[b] for ever; his reign shall
never end,[c] 'How can this be?' said Mary; 34
'I am still a virgin.' The angel answered, 'The 35
Holy Spirit will come upon you, and the
power of the Most High will overshadow
you; and for that reason the holy child to
be born will be called "Son of God".[c] More- 36
over your kinswoman Elizabeth has herself
conceived a son in her old age; and she who
is reputed barren is now in her sixth month,
for God's promises can never fail.'[d] 'Here 37 38

---

a Or In his sight he will go forth.   b Literally the house of Jacob.   c Or the child to be born will
be called holy, "Son of God".   d Some witnesses read for with God nothing will prove impossible.

The well at Nazareth

am I,' said Mary; 'I am the Lord's servant; as you have spoken, so be it.' Then the angel left her.

Mary visits Elizabeth

39 About this time Mary set out and went straight to a town in the uplands of Judah.
40 She went into Zechariah's house and greeted
41 Elizabeth. And when Elizabeth heard Mary's greeting, the baby stirred in her womb. Then
42 Elizabeth was filled with the Holy Spirit and cried aloud, 'God's blessing is on you above all women, and his blessing is on the fruit
43 of your womb. Who am I, that the mother
44 of my Lord should visit me? I tell you, when your greeting sounded in my ears, the baby
45 in my womb leapt for joy. How happy is she who has had faith that the Lord's promise would be fulfilled!'

Mary praises God for his wonderful works

46 And Mary[e] said:

'Tell out, my soul, the greatness of the Lord,
47 rejoice, rejoice, my spirit, in God my saviour;
48 so tenderly has he looked upon his servant, humble as she is.
For, from this day forth, all generations will count me blessed,
49 so wonderfully has he dealt with me, the Lord, the Mighty One.

His name is Holy;
50 his mercy sure from generation to generation toward those who fear him;
51 the deeds his own right arm has done disclose his might:
the arrogant of heart and mind he has put to rout,
52 he has brought down monarchs from their thrones,
but the humble have been lifted high.
53 The hungry he has satisfied with good things, the rich sent empty away.

54 He has ranged himself at the side of Israel his servant;
55 firm in his promise to our forefathers, he has not forgotten to show mercy to Abraham
and his children's children, for ever.'

56 Mary stayed with her about three months and then returned home.

Elizabeth's child is born, and named

57 Now the time came for Elizabeth's child to
58 be born, and she gave birth to a son. When her neighbours and relatives heard what great favour the Lord had shown her, they were
59 as delighted as she was. Then on the eighth day they came to circumcise the child; and

they were going to name him Zechariah after
60 his father. But his mother spoke up and
61 said, 'No! he is to be called John.' 'But', they said, 'there is nobody in your family
62 who has that name.' They inquired of his father by signs what he would like him to
63 be called. He asked for a writing-tablet and to the astonishment of all wrote down, 'His
64 name is John.' Immediately his lips and tongue were freed and he began to speak,
65 praising God. All the neighbours were struck with awe, and everywhere in the uplands of Judaea the whole story became
66 common talk. All who heard it were deeply impressed and said, 'What will this child become?' For indeed the hand of the Lord was upon him.[f]

Zechariah's prophecy

67 And Zechariah his father was filled with the Holy Spirit and uttered this prophecy:

68 'Praise to the God of Israel!
For he has turned to his people, saved them and set them free,
69 and has raised up a deliverer of victorious power
from the house of his servant David.

70 So he promised: age after age he proclaimed by the lips of his holy prophets,
71 that he would deliver us from our enemies, out of the hands of all who hate us;
72 that he would deal mercifully with our fathers,
calling to mind his solemn covenent.

73 Such was the oath he swore to our father Abraham,
74 to rescue us from enemy hands,
and grant us, free from fear, to worship him
75 with a holy worship, with uprightness of heart,
in his presence, our whole life long.

76 And you, my child, you shall be called Prophet of the Highest,
for you will be the Lord's forerunner, to prepare his way
77 and lead his people to salvation through knowledge of him,
by the forgiveness of their sins:
78 for in the tender compassion of our God the morning sun from heaven will rise[g] upon us,
79 to shine on those who live in darkness, under the cloud of death,
and to guide our feet into the way of peace.'

80 As the child grew up he became strong in spirit; he lived out in the wilds until the day when he appeared publicly before Israel.

e So the majority of witnesses; some read Elizabeth; the original may have had no name.   f Some witnesses
read 'What will this child become, for indeed the hand of the Lord is upon him?'   g Some witnesses read
has risen.

Mary gives birth to a son

2 In those days a decree was issued by the Emperor Augustus for a registration to be
2 made throughout the Roman world. This was the first registration of its kind; it took place when Quirinius[h] was governor of Syria.
3 For this purpose everyone made his way to
4 his own town; and so Joseph went up to Judaea from the town of Nazareth in Galilee,
5 to register at the city of David, called Bethlehem, because he was of the house of David by descent; and with him went Mary who was betrothed to him. She was expecting a
6 child, and while they were there the time
7 came for her baby to be born, and she gave birth to a son, her first-born. She wrapped him in his swaddling clothes, and laid him in a manger, because there was no room for them to lodge in the house.

The shepherds and the angels

8 Now in this same district there were shepherds out in the fields, keeping watch through
9 the night over their flock, when suddenly there stood before them an angel of the Lord, and the splendour of the Lord shone
10 round them. They were terror-stricken, but the angel said, 'Do not be afraid; I have good news for you: there is great joy coming
11 to the whole people. Today in the city of David a deliverer has been born to you—
12 the Messiah, the Lord.[i] And this is your sign: you will find a baby lying wrapped in his
13 swaddling clothes, in a manger.' All at once there was with the angel a great company of the heavenly host, singing the praises of God:

14 'Glory to God in highest heaven,
and on earth his peace for men on whom his favour rests.'[j]

15 After the angels had left them and gone into heaven the shepherds said to one another, 'Come, we must go straight to Bethlehem and see this thing that has happened, which the Lord has made known to
16 us.' So they went with all speed and found their way to Mary and Joseph; and the baby
17 was lying in the manger. When they saw him, they recounted what they had been
18 told about this child; and all who heard were astonished at what the shepherds said.
19 But Mary treasured up all these things and
20 pondered over them. Meanwhile the shepherds returned glorifying and praising God for what they had heard and seen; it had all happened as they had been told.

The child Jesus presented in the temple

21 Eight days later the time came to circumcise him, and he was given the name Jesus, the name given by the angel before he was conceived.

Then, after their purification had been 22 completed in accordance with the Law of Moses, they brought him up to Jerusalem to present him to the Lord (as prescribed in 23 the law of the Lord: 'Every first-born male shall be deemed to belong to the Lord'), and also to make the offering as stated in 24 the law: 'A pair of turtle doves or two young pigeons.'

Simeon's response

There was at that time in Jerusalem a man 25 called Simeon. This man was upright and devout, one who watched and waited for the restoration of Israel, and the Holy Spirit was upon him. It had been disclosed to him 26 by the Holy Spirit that he would not see death until he had seen the Lord's Messiah. Guided by the Spirit he came into the 27 temple; and when the parents brought in the child Jesus to do for him what was customary under the Law, he took him in his arms, 28 praised God, and said:

'This day, Master, thou givest thy servant 29
his discharge in peace;
now thy promise is fulfilled.
For I have seen with my own eyes 30
the deliverance which thou hast made ready 31
in full view of all the nations:
a light that will be a revelation to the heathen, 32
and glory to thy people Israel.'

The child's father and mother were full of 33 wonder at what was being said about him. Simeon blessed them and said to Mary his 34 mother, 'This child is destined to be a sign which men reject; and you too shall be 35 pierced to the heart. Many in Israel will stand or fall[k] because of him, and thus the secret thoughts of many will be laid bare.'

Anna's response

There was also a prophetess, Anna the 36 daughter of Phanuel, of the tribe of Asher. She was a very old woman, who had lived seven years with her husband after she was first married, and then alone as a widow to 37 the age of eighty-four.[l] She never left the temple, but worshipped day and night, fasting and praying. Coming up at that very 38 moment, she returned thanks to God; and she talked about the child to all who were looking for the liberation of Jerusalem.

Return to Nazareth

When they had done everything prescribed 39 in the law of the Lord, they returned to Galilee to their own town of Nazareth. The 40

h *Or* This was the first registration carried out while Quirinius . . .   i *Some witnesses read* to you—the Lord's Messiah.   j *Some witnesses read* and on earth his peace, his favour towards men.   k *Or* Many in Israel will fall and rise again . . .   l *Or* widow for another eighty-four years.

child grew big and strong and full of wisdom; and God's favour was upon him.

The boy Jesus in the temple

41 Now it was the practice of his parents to go to Jerusalem every year for the Passover 42 festival; and when he was twelve, they made 43 the pilgrimage as usual. When the festive season was over and they started for home, the boy Jesus stayed behind in Jerusalem. 44 His parents did not know of this; but thinking that he was with the party they journeyed on for a whole day, and only then did they begin looking for him among their 45 friends and relations. As they could not find him they returned to Jerusalem to look for 46 him; and after three days they found him sitting in the temple surrounded by the teachers, listening to them and putting 47 questions; and all who heard him were amazed at his intelligence and the answers 48 he gave. His parents were astonished to see him there, and his mother said to him, 'My son, why have you treated us like this? Your father and I have been searching for you in 49 great anxiety.' 'What made you search?' he said. 'Did you not know that I was bound 50 to be in my Father's house?' But they did 51 not understand what he meant. Then he went back with them to Nazareth, and continued to be under their authority; his mother treasured up all these things in her 52 heart. As Jesus grew up he advanced in wisdom and in favour with God and men.

John preaches and baptizes

3 In the fifteenth year of the Emperor Tiberius, when Pontius Pilate was governor of Judaea, when Herod was prince of Galilee, his brother Philip prince of Ituraea and Trachonitis, 2 and Lysanias prince of Abilene, during the high-priesthood of Annas and Caiaphas, the word of God came to John son of Zechariah 3 in the wilderness. And he went all over the Jordan valley proclaiming a baptism in token of repentance for the forgiveness of 4 sins, as it is written in the book of the prophecies of Isaiah:

'A voice crying aloud in the wilderness,
"Prepare a way for the Lord;
clear a straight path for him.
5 Every ravine shall be filled in,
and every mountain and hill levelled;
the corners shall be straightened,
and the rugged ways made smooth;
6 and all mankind shall see God's deliverance."'

7 Crowds of people came out to be baptized by him, and he said to them: 'You vipers' brood! Who warned you to escape from 8 the coming retribution? Then prove your repentance by the fruit it bears; and do not begin saying to yourselves, "We have Abraham for our father." I tell you that God can make children for Abraham out of these stones here. Already the axe is laid to the 9 roots of the trees; and every tree that fails to produce good fruit is cut down and thrown on the fire.'

The people asked him, 'Then what are 10 we to do?' He replied, 'The man with two 11 shirts must share with him who has none, and anyone who has food must do the same.' Among those who came to be baptized were 12 tax-gatherers, and they said to him, 'Master, what are we to do?' He told them, 'Exact 13 no more than the assessment.' Soldiers on 14 service also asked him, 'And what of us?' To them he said, 'No bullying; no blackmail; make do with your pay!'

The people were on the tiptoe of expectation, all wondering about John, whether 15 perhaps he was the Messiah, but he spoke 16 out and said to them all: 'I baptize you with water; but there is one to come who is mightier than I. I am not fit to unfasten his shoes. He will baptize you with the Holy Spirit and with fire. His shovel is ready in 17 his hand, to winnow his threshing-floor and gather the wheat into his granary; but he will burn the chaff on a fire that can never go out.'

Herod puts John in prison

In this and many other ways he made his 18 appeal to the people and announced the good news. But Prince Herod, when he was re- 19 buked by him over the affair of his brother's wife Herodias and for his other misdeeds, crowned them all by shutting John up in 20 prison.

The baptism of Jesus

During a general baptism of the people, when 21 Jesus too had been baptized and was praying, heaven opened and the Holy Spirit 22 descended on him in bodily form like a dove; and there came a voice from heaven, 'Thou art my Son, my Beloved;*m* on thee my favour rests.'*n*

Family tree of Jesus

When Jesus began his work he was about 23 thirty years old, the son, as people thought, of Joseph, son of Heli, son of Matthat, son 24 of Levi, son of Melchi, son of Jannai, son of Joseph, son of Mattathiah, son of Amos, 25 son of Nahum, son of Esli, son of Naggai, son of Maath, son of Mattathiah, son of 26 Semein, son of Josech, son of Joda, son of 27 Johanan, son of Rhesa, son of Zerubbabel, son of Shealtiel, son of Neri, son of Mel- 28 chi, son of Addi, son of Cosam, son of

m Or Thou art my only Son.   *n Some witnesses read* My Son art thou; this day I have begotten thee.

29 Elmadam, son of Er, son of Joshua, son of
Eliezer, son of Jorim, son of Matthat, son of
30 Levi, son of Symeon, son of Judah, son
31 of Joseph, son of Jonam, son of Eliakim, son
of Melea, son of Menna, son of Mattatha,
32 son of Nathan, son of David, son of Jesse,
son of Obed, son of Boaz, son of Sal-
33 mon, son of Nahshon, son of Amminadab,ᵒ
son of Arni,ᵖ son of Hezron, son of Perez,
34 son of Judah, son of Jacob, son of Isaac, son
of Abraham, son of Terah, son of Nahor,
35 son of Serug, son of Reu, son of Peleg, son
36 of Eber, son of Shelah, son of Cainan, son
of Arpachshad, son of Shem, son of Noah,
37 son of Lamech, son of Methuselah, son of
Enoch, son of Jared, son of Mahalaleel, son
38 of Cainan, son of Enosh, son of Seth, son of
Adam, son of God.

The temptation of Jesus

4 Full of the Holy Spirit, Jesus returned from
2 the Jordan, and for forty days was led by
the Spirit up and down the wilderness and
tempted by the devil.
All that time he had nothing to eat, and
3 at the end of it he was famished. The devil
said to him, 'If you are the Son of God, tell
4 this stone to become bread.' Jesus answered,
'Scripture says, "Man cannot live on bread
alone."'
5 Next the devil led him up and showed
him in a flash all the kingdoms of the world.
6 'All this dominion will I give to you,' he
said, 'and the glory that goes with it; for it
has been put in my hands and I can give it
7 to anyone I choose. You have only to do
homage to me and it shall all be yours.'
8 Jesus answered him, 'Scripture says, "You
shall do homage to the Lord your God and
worship him alone."'
9 The devil took him to Jerusalem and set
him on the parapet of the temple. 'If you
are the Son of God,' he said, 'throw your-
10 self down; for Scripture says, "He will give
11 his angels orders to take care of you", and
again, "They will support you in their arms
for fear you should strike your foot against
12 a stone."' Jesus answered him, 'It has been
said, "You are not to put the Lord your God
to the test."'
13 So, having come to the end of all his
temptations, the devil departed, biding his
time.

Jesus rejected at Nazareth

14 Then Jesus, armed with the power of the
Spirit, returned to Galilee, and reports about
him spread through the whole country-side.
15 He taught in their synagogues and all men
sang his praises.

So he came to Nazareth, where he had 16
been brought up, and went to synagogue on
the Sabbath day as he regularly did. He
stood up to read the lesson and was handed 17
the scroll of the prophet Isaiah. He opened
the scroll and found the passage which says,

'The spirit of the Lord is upon me because 18
he has anointed me;
he has sent me to announce good news to
the poor,
to proclaim release for prisoners and recovery of sight for the blind;
to let the broken victims go free,
to proclaim the year of the Lord's favour.' 19

He rolled up the scroll, gave it back to the 20
attendant, and sat down; and all eyes in the
synagogue were fixed on him.
He began to speak: 'Today', he said, 'in 21
your very hearing this text has come true.'ᑫ
There was a general stir of admiration; they 22
were surprised that words of such grace
should fall from his lips. 'Is not this Joseph's
son?' they asked. Then Jesus said, 'No 23
doubt you will quote the proverb to me,
"Physician, heal yourself!", and say, "We
have heard of all your doings at Capernaum;
do the same here in your own home town."
I tell you this,' he went on: 'no prophet is 24
recognized in his own country. There were 25
many widows in Israel, you may be sure, in
Elijah's time, when for three years and six
months the skies never opened, and famine
lay hard over the whole country; yet it was 26
to none of those that Elijah was sent, but
to a widow at Sarepta in the territory of
Sidon. Again, in the time of the prophet 27
Elisha there were many lepers in Israel, and
not one of them was healed, but only
Naaman, the Syrian.' At these words the 28
whole congregation were infuriated. They 29
leapt up, threw him out of the town, and took
him to the brow of the hill on which it was
built, meaning to hurl him over the edge.
But he walked straight through them all, 30
and went away.

The authority of Jesus in word and deed

Coming down to Capernaum, a town in 31
Galilee, he taught the people on the Sabbath, and they were astounded at his 32
teaching, for what he said had the note of
authority. Now there was a man in the syna- 33
gogue possessed by a devil, an unclean spirit.
He shrieked at the top of his voice, 'What do 34
you want with us, Jesus of Nazareth? Have
youʳ come to destroy us? I know who you
are—the Holy One of God.' Jesus rebuked 35
him: 'Be silent', he said, 'and come out of
him.' Then the devil, after throwing the man

ᵒ *Some witnesses add* son of Admin.   ᵖ *Some witnesses read* Aram; *Ruth 4. 19 and 1 Chronicles 2. 9*
have Ram.   ᑫ *Or* 'Today', he said, 'this text which you have just heard has come true.'   ʳ *Or*
You have.

down in front of the people, left him without
36 doing him any injury. Amazement fell on
them all and they said to one another:
'What is there in this man's words? He gives
orders to the unclean spirits with authority
37 and power, and out they go.' So the news
spread, and he was the talk of the whole
district.

Acts of healing

38 On leaving the synagogue he went to Simon's
house. Simon's mother-in-law was in the
grip of a high fever; and they asked him to
39 help her. He came and stood over her and
rebuked the fever. It left her, and she got up
at once and waited on them.
40   At sunset all who had friends suffering

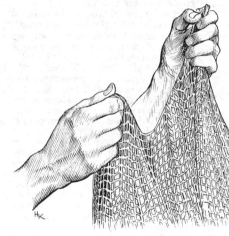

from one disease or another brought them
to him; and he laid his hands on them one
41 by one and cured them. Devils also came
out of many of them, shouting, 'You are
the Son of God.' But he rebuked them and
forbade them to speak, because they knew
that he was the Messiah.

Jesus proclaims the Gospel in Judaea

42 When day broke he went out and made his
way to a lonely spot. But the people went in
search of him, and when they came to where
he was they pressed him not to leave them.
43 But he said, 'I must give the good news of
the kingdom of God to the other towns also,
44 for that is what I was sent to do.' So he proclaimed the Gospel in the synagogues of
Judaea.[s]

Jesus calls Simon and his companions

5 One day as he stood by the Lake of Gennesaret, and the people crowded upon him

to listen to the word of God, he noticed two 2
boats lying at the water's edge; the fishermen had come ashore and were washing their
nets. He got into one of the boats, which 3
belonged to Simon, and asked him to put
out a little way from the shore; then he went
on teaching the crowds from his seat in the
boat. When he had finished speaking, he 4
said to Simon, 'Put out into deep water and
let down your nets for a catch.' Simon 5
answered, 'Master, we were hard at work
all night and caught nothing at all; but if
you say so, I will let down the nets.' They 6
did so and made a big haul of fish; and their
nets began to split. So they signalled to their 7
partners in the other boat to come and help
them. This they did, and loaded both boats
to the point of sinking. When Simon saw 8
what had happened he fell at Jesus's knees
and said, 'Go, Lord, leave me, sinner that
I am!' For he and all his companions were 9
amazed at the catch they had made; so too 10
were his partners James and John, Zebedee's

sons. 'Do not be afraid,' said Jesus to Simon;
'from now on you will be catching men.' As 11
soon as they had brought the boats to land,
they left everything and followed him.

Jesus cleanses a leper

He was once in a certain town where there 12
happened to be a man covered with leprosy;
seeing Jesus, he bowed to the ground and
begged his help. 'Sir,' he said, 'if only you
will, you can cleanse me.' Jesus stretched 13
out his hand, touched him, and said, 'Indeed I will; be clean again.' The leprosy left
him immediately. Jesus then ordered him 14
not to tell anybody. 'But go,' he said, 'show
yourself to the priest, and make the offering
laid down by Moses for your cleansing;

s Or the Jewish synagogues; *some witnesses read* the synagogues of Galilee.

15 that will certify the cure.' But the talk about him spread all the more; great crowds gathered to hear him and to be cured of their
16 ailments. And from time to time he would withdraw to lonely places for prayer.

Authority to forgive sins

17 One day he was teaching, and Pharisees and teachers of the law were sitting round. People had come from every village of Galilee and from Judaea and Jerusalem,[t] and the power of the Lord was with him to
18 heal the sick. Some men appeared carrying a paralysed man on a bed. They tried to bring him in and set him down in front of
19 Jesus, but finding no way to do so because of the crowd, they went up on to the roof and let him down through the tiling, bed and all, into the middle of the company in
20 front of Jesus. When Jesus saw their faith, he said, 'Man, your sins are forgiven you.'
21 The lawyers and the Pharisees began saying to themselves, 'Who is this fellow with his blasphemous talk? Who but God alone
22 can forgive sins?' But Jesus knew what they were thinking and answered them: 'Why
23 do you harbour thoughts like these? Is it easier to say, "Your sins are forgiven you",
24 or to say, "Stand up and walk"? But to convince you that the Son of Man has the right on earth to forgive sins'—he turned to the paralysed man—'I say to you, stand up,
25 take your bed, and go home.' And at once he rose to his feet before their eyes, took up the bed he had been lying on, and went home
26 praising God. They were all lost in amazement and praised God; filled with awe they said, 'You would never believe the things we have seen today.'

Jesus and the tax-gatherers

27 Later, when he went out, he saw a tax-gatherer, Levi by name, at his seat in the custom-house, and said to him, 'Follow me';
28 and he rose to his feet, left everything behind, and followed him.
29 Afterwards Levi held a big reception in his house for Jesus; among the guests was a
30 large party of tax-gatherers and others. The Pharisees and the lawyers of their sect complained to his disciples: 'Why do you eat

and drink', they said, 'with tax-gatherers and sinners?' Jesus answered them: 'It is 31 not the healthy that need a doctor, but the sick; I have not come to invite virtuous 32 people, but to call sinners to repentance.'

About fasting

Then they said to him, 'John's disciples are 33 much given to fasting and the practice of prayer, and so are the disciples of the Pharisees; but yours eat and drink.' Jesus replied, 34 'Can you make the bridegroom's friends fast while the bridegroom is with them? But a 35 time will come: the bridegroom will be taken away from them, and that will be the time for them to fast.'

Patched clothes and old wine-skins

He told them this parable also: 'No one 36 tears a piece from a new cloak to patch an old one; if he does, he will have made a hole in the new cloak, and the patch from the new will not match the old. Nor does any- 37 one put new wine into old wine-skins; if he does, the new wine will burst the skins, the wine will be wasted, and the skins ruined. Fresh skins for new wine! And no one after 38 39 drinking old wine wants new; for he says, "The old wine is good."'

About the Sabbath

One Sabbath he was going through the corn- **6** fields, and his disciples were plucking the ears of corn, rubbing them in their hands, and eating them. Some of the Pharisees said, 2 'Why are you doing what is forbidden on the Sabbath?' Jesus answered, 'So you have 3 not read what David did when he and his men were hungry? He went into the House 4 of God and took the sacred bread to eat and gave it to his men, though priests alone are allowed to eat it, and no one else.' He 5 also said, 'The Son of Man is sovereign even over the Sabbath.'

A man with a withered arm

On another Sabbath he had gone to syna- 6 gogue and was teaching. There happened to be a man in the congregation whose right arm was withered; and the lawyers and the 7 Pharisees were on the watch to see whether Jesus would cure him on the Sabbath, so that they could find a charge to bring against him. But he knew what was in their minds 8 and said to the man with the withered arm, 'Get up and stand out here.' So he got up and stood there. Then Jesus said to him, 9 'I put the question to you: is it permitted to do good or to do evil on the Sabbath, to save life or to destroy it?' He looked round 10 at them all and then said to the man, 'Stretch

t Some witnesses read and Pharisees and teachers of the law, who had come from every village of Galilee and from Judaea and Jerusalem, were sitting round.

out your arm.' He did so, and his arm was
11 restored. But they were beside themselves
with anger, and began to discuss among
themselves what they could do to Jesus.

The twelve apostles

12 During this time he went out one day into
the hills to pray, and spent the night in
13 prayer to God. When day broke he called
his disciples to him, and from among them
he chose twelve and named them Apostles:
14 Simon, to whom he gave the name of Peter,
and Andrew his brother, James and John,
15 Philip and Bartholomew, Matthew and
Thomas, James son of Alphaeus, and Simon
16 who was called the Zealot, Judas son of
James, and Judas Iscariot who turned traitor.

Jesus teaches and heals

17 He came down the hill with them and took
his stand on level ground. There was a large
concourse of his disciples and great numbers
of people from Jerusalem and Judaea and
from the seaboard of Tyre and Sidon, who
had come to listen to him, and to be cured
18 of their diseases. Those who were troubled
19 with unclean spirits were cured; and everyone in the crowd was trying to touch him,
because power went out from him and cured
them all.

True blessedness and its opposite

20 Then turning to his disciples he began to
speak:
'How blest are you who are in need; the
kingdom of God is yours.
21 'How blest are you who now go hungry;
your hunger shall be satisfied.
'How blest are you who weep now; you
shall laugh.
22 'How blest you are when men hate you,
when they outlaw you and insult you, and
ban your very name as infamous, because
23 of the Son of Man. On that day be glad and
dance for joy; for assuredly you have a rich
reward in heaven; in just the same way did
their fathers treat the prophets.
24 'But alas for you who are rich; you have
had your time of happiness.
25 'Alas for you who are well-fed now; you
shall go hungry.
'Alas for you who laugh now; you shall
mourn and weep.
26 'Alas for you when all speak well of you;
just so did their fathers treat the false
prophets.'

Personal wrongs

27 'But to you who hear me I say:
'Love your enemies; do good to those who
28 hate you; bless those who curse you; pray
29 for those who treat you spitefully. When a

man hits you on the cheek, offer him the other
cheek too; when a man takes your coat, let
him have your shirt as well. Give to every- 30
one who asks you; when a man takes what
is yours, do not demand it back. Treat others 31
as you would like them to treat you.
'If you love only those who love you, 32
what credit is that to you? Even sinners love
those who love them. Again, if you do good 33
only to those who do good to you, what
credit is that to you? Even sinners do as
much. And if you lend only where you expect 34
to be repaid, what credit is that to you? Even
sinners lend to each other to be repaid in
full. But you must love your enemies and 35
do good; and lend without expecting any
return;[u] and you will have a rich reward:
you will be sons of the Most High, because
he himself is kind to the ungrateful and
wicked. Be compassionate as your Father 36
is compassionate.'

Judging others

'Pass no judgement, and you will not be 37
judged; do not condemn, and you will not
be condemned; acquit, and you will be
acquitted; give, and gifts will be given you. 38
Good measure, pressed down, shaken together, and running over, will be poured
into your lap; for whatever measure you deal
out to others will be dealt to you in return.'
He also offered them a parable: 'Can one 39
blind man be guide to another? Will they
not both fall into the ditch? A pupil is not 40
superior to his teacher; but everyone, when
his training is complete, will reach his
teacher's level.
'Why do you look at the speck of sawdust 41
in your brother's eye, with never a thought
for the great plank in your own? How can 42
you say to your brother, "My dear brother,
let me take the speck out of your eye", when
you are blind to the plank in your own?
You hypocrite! First take the plank out of
your own eye, and then you will see clearly
to take the speck out of your brother's.'

A tree and its fruit

'There is no such thing as a good tree pro- 43
ducing worthless fruit, nor yet a worthless
tree producing good fruit. For each tree is 44
known by its own fruit: you do not gather
figs from thistles, and you do not pick grapes
from brambles. A good man produces good 45
from the store of good within himself; and
an evil man from evil within produces evil.
For the words that the mouth utters come
from the overflowing of the heart.'

A firm foundation

'Why do you keep calling me "Lord, Lord" 46
—and never do what I tell you? Everyone

u Or without ever giving up hope; *some witnesses read* without giving up hope of anyone.

who comes to me and hears what I say, and acts upon it—I will show you what he is
48 like. He is like a man who, in building his house, dug deep and laid the foundations on rock. When the flood came, the river burst upon that house, but could not shift
49 it, because it had been soundly built. But he who hears and does not act is like a man who built his house on the soil without foundations. As soon as the river burst upon it, the house collapsed, and fell with a great crash.'

The faith of a soldier

7 When he had finished addressing the people,
2 he went to Capernaum. A centurion there had a servant whom he valued highly; this
3 servant was ill and near to death. Hearing about Jesus, he sent some Jewish elders with the request that he would come and save
4 his servant's life. They approached Jesus and pressed their petition earnestly: 'He deserves this favour from you,' they said,
5 'for he is a friend of our nation and it is
6 he who built us our synagogue.' Jesus went with them; but when he was not far from the house, the centurion sent friends with this message: 'Do not trouble further, sir; it is not for me to have you under my roof,
7 and that is why I did not presume to approach you in person. But say the word and my
8 servant will be cured. I know, for in my position I am myself under orders, with soldiers under me. I say to one, "Go", and he goes; to another, "Come here", and he comes; and to my servant, "Do this", and
9 he does it.' When Jesus heard this, he admired the man, and, turning to the crowd that was following him, he said, 'I tell you, nowhere, even in Israel, have I found faith like this.'
10 And the messengers returned to the house and found the servant in good health.

Jesus raises a widow's son to life

1 Afterwards[v] Jesus went to a town called Nain, accompanied by his disciples and a
2 large crowd. As he approached the gate of the town he met a funeral. The dead man was the only son of his widowed mother; and many of the townspeople were there
3 with her. When the Lord saw her his heart went out to her, and he said, 'Weep no

more.' With that he stepped forward and 14 laid his hand on the bier; and the bearers halted. Then he spoke: 'Young man, rise up!' The dead man sat up and began to 15 speak; and Jesus gave him back to his mother. Deep awe fell upon them all, and 16 they praised God. 'A great prophet has arisen among us', they said, and again, 'God has shown his care for his people.' The 17 story of what he had done ran through all parts of Judaea and the whole neighbourhood.

A message for John the Baptist

John too was informed of all this by his 18 disciples. Summoning two of their number 19 he sent them to the Lord with this message: 'Are you the one who is to come, or are we to expect some other?' The messengers made 20 their way to Jesus and said, 'John the Baptist has sent us to you: he asks, "Are you the one who is to come, or are we to expect some other?"' There and then he cured many 21 sufferers from diseases, plagues, and evil spirits; and on many blind people he bestowed sight. Then he gave them his answer: 22 'Go', he said, 'and tell John what you have seen and heard: how the blind recover their sight, the lame walk, the lepers are made clean, the deaf hear, the dead are raised to life, the poor are hearing the good news— and happy is the man who does not find me 23 a stumbling-block.'

About John the Baptist

After John's messengers had left, Jesus began 24 to speak about him to the crowds: 'What was the spectacle that drew you to the wilderness? A reed-bed swept by the wind? No? Then what did you go out to see? A man 25 dressed in silks and satins? Surely you must look in palaces for grand clothes and luxury. But what did you go out to see? A prophet? 26 Yes indeed, and far more than a prophet. He is the man of whom Scripture says, 27

"Here is my herald, whom I send on ahead of you,
and he will prepare your way before you."

I tell you, there is not a mother's son greater 28 than John, and yet the least in the kingdom of God is greater than he.'
    When they heard him, all the people, in- 29 cluding the tax-gatherers, praised God, for they had accepted John's baptism; but the 30 Pharisees and lawyers, who refused his baptism, had rejected[w] God's purpose for themselves.
    'How can I describe the people of this 31 generation? What are they like? They are 32

---

v *Some witnesses read* On the next day.   w *Or* '. . . greater than he. And all the people, including the tax-gatherers, when they heard him, accepted John's baptism and acknowledged the righteous dealing of God; but the Pharisees and lawyers, by refusing his baptism, rejected . . .'

like children sitting in the market-place and shouting at each other,

"We piped for you and you would not dance."
"We wept and wailed, and you would not mourn."

33 For John the Baptist came neither eating bread nor drinking wine, and you say, "He is
34 possessed." The Son of Man came eating and drinking, and you say, "Look at him! a glutton and a drinker, a friend of tax-gatherers
35 and sinners!" And yet God's wisdom is proved right by all who are her children.'

At the house of Simon the Pharisee

36 One of the Pharisees invited him to eat with him; he went to the Pharisee's house and
37 took his place at table. A woman who was living an immoral life in the town had learned that Jesus was at table in the Pharisee's house and had brought oil of myrrh in a small flask.
38 She took her place behind him, by his feet, weeping. His feet were wetted with her tears and she wiped them with her hair, kissing them and anointing them with the myrrh.
39 When his host the Pharisee saw this he said to himself, 'If this fellow were a real prophet, he would know who this woman is that touches him, and what sort of woman she
40 is, a sinner.' Jesus took him up and said, 'Simon, I have something to say to you.'
41 'Speak on, Master', said he. 'Two men were in debt to a money-lender: one owed him five hundred silver pieces, the other fifty.
42 As neither had anything to pay with he let them both off. Now, which will love him
43 most?' Simon replied, 'I should think the one that was let off most.' 'You are right',
44 said Jesus. Then turning to the woman, he said to Simon, 'You see this woman? I came to your house: you provided no water for my feet; but this woman has made my feet wet with her tears and wiped them with her
45 hair. You gave me no kiss; but she has been
46 kissing my feet ever since I came in. You did not anoint my head with oil; but she has
47 anointed my feet with myrrh. And so, I tell you, her great love proves that her many sins have been forgiven; where little has been for-
48 given, little love is shown.' Then he said to
49 her, 'Your sins are forgiven.' The other guests began to ask themselves, 'Who is this, that he
50 can forgive sins?' But he said to the woman, 'Your faith has saved you; go in peace.'

Women who accompanied Jesus

8 After this he went journeying from town to town and village to village, proclaiming the good news of the kingdom of God. With him
2 were the Twelve and a number of women who had been set free from evil spirits and infirmities: Mary, known as Mary of Magdala, from whom seven devils had come out,

3 Joanna, the wife of Chuza a steward of Herod's, Susanna, and many others. These women provided for them out of their own resources.

The parable of a sower

4 People were now gathering in large numbers, and as they made their way to him from one
5 town after another, he said in a parable: 'A sower went out to sow his seed. And as he sowed, some seed fell along the footpath, where it was trampled on, and the birds ate
6 it up. Some seed fell on rock and, after coming up, withered for lack of moisture.
7 Some seed fell in among thistles, and the
8 thistles grew up with it and choked it. And some of the seed fell into good soil, and grew, and yielded a hundredfold.' As he said this he called out, 'If you have ears to hear, then hear.'

Why Jesus told parables

9 His disciples asked him what this parable
10 meant, and he said, 'It has been granted to you to know the secrets of the kingdom of God; but the others have only parables, so that they may look but see nothing, hear but understand nothing.

The parable of the sower explained

1 'This is what the parable means. The seed
1 is the word of God. Those along the foot-path are the men who hear it, and then the devil comes and carries off the word from their hearts for fear they should believe and
1 be saved. The seed sown on rock stands for those who receive the word with joy when they hear it, but have no root; they are believers for a while, but in the time of testing
1 they desert. That which fell among thistles

The Gergesene coast of the Sea of Galilee

represents those who hear, but their further growth is choked by cares and wealth and the pleasures of life, and they bring nothing 15 to maturity. But the seed in good soil represents those who bring a good and honest heart to the hearing of the word, hold it fast, and by their perseverance yield a harvest.'

A lesson from a lamp

16 'Nobody lights a lamp and then covers it with a basin or puts it under the bed. On the contrary, he puts it on a lamp-stand so that those who come in may see the light. 17 For there is nothing hidden that will not become public, nothing under cover that will not be made known and brought into the open.

18 'Take care, then, how you listen; for the man who has will be given more, and the man who has not will forfeit even what he thinks he has.'

Jesus's relatives

19 His mother and his brothers arrived but 20 could not get to him for the crowd. He was told, 'Your mother and brothers are standing outside, and they want to see you.' He replied, 'My mother and my brothers—they are those who hear the word of God and act upon it.'

Jesus calms a storm

22 One day he got into a boat with his disciples and said to them, 'Let us cross over to the 23 other side of the lake.' So they put out; and as they sailed along he went to sleep. Then a heavy squall struck the lake; they began to ship water and were in grave danger. 24 They went to him, and roused him, crying, 'Master, Master, we are sinking!' He awoke, and rebuked the wind and the turbulent waters. The storm subsided and all was calm. 25 'Where is your faith?' he asked. In fear and astonishment they said to one another, 'Who can this be? He gives his orders to wind and waves, and they obey him.'

Jesus cures a madman

So they landed in the country of the Ger- 26 gesenes,ˣ which is opposite Galilee. As he 27 stepped ashore he was met by a man from the town who was possessed by devils. For a long time he had neither worn clothes nor lived in a house, but stayed among the tombs. When he saw Jesus he cried out, and fell at 28 his feet shouting, 'What do you want with me, Jesus, son of the Most High God? I implore you, do not torment me.'

For Jesus was already ordering the un- 29 clean spirit to come out of the man. Many a time it had seized him, and then, for safety's sake, they would secure him with chains and fetters; but each time he broke loose, and with the devil in charge made off to the solitary places.

Jesus asked him, 'What is your name?' 30 'Legion', he replied. This was because so many devils had taken possession of him. And they begged him not to banish them to 31 the Abyss.

There happened to be a large herd of pigs 32 nearby, feeding on the hill; and the spirits begged him to let them go into these pigs. He gave them leave; the devils came out of 33 the man and went into the pigs, and the herd rushed over the edge into the lake and were drowned.

The men in charge of them saw what had 34 happened, and, taking to their heels, they carried the news to the town and country-side; and the people came out to see for 35 themselves. When they came to Jesus, and found the man from whom the devils had gone out sitting at his feet clothed and in his right mind, they were afraid. The spec- 36 tators told them how the madman had been cured. Then the whole population of the 37

ˣ *Some witnesses read* Gerasenes; *others read* Gadarenes.

Gergesene[y] district asked him to go, for they were in the grip of a great fear. So he got 38 into the boat and returned. The man from whom the devils had gone out begged leave to go with him; but Jesus sent him away: 39 'Go back home,' he said, 'and tell them everything that God has done for you.' The man went all over the town spreading the news of what Jesus had done for him.

Jairus's plea

40 When Jesus returned, the people welcomed 41 him, for they were all expecting him. Then a man appeared—Jairus was his name and he was president of the synagogue. Throwing himself down at Jesus's feet he begged 42 him to come to his house, because he had an only daughter, about twelve years old, who was dying. And while Jesus was on his way he could hardly breathe for the crowds.

A woman healed of haemorrhages

43 Among them was a woman who had suffered from haemorrhages for twelve years; 44 and[z] nobody had been able to cure her. She came up from behind and touched the edge of[a] his cloak, and at once her haemorrhage 45 stopped. Jesus said, 'Who was it that touched me?' All disclaimed it, and Peter and his companions said, 'Master, the crowds are hemming you in and pressing 46 upon you!' But Jesus said, 'Someone did touch me, for I felt that power had gone out 47 from me.' Then the woman, seeing that she was detected, came trembling and fell at his feet. Before all the people she explained why she had touched him and how she had 48 been instantly cured. He said to her, 'My daughter, your faith has cured you. Go in peace.'

Jairus's daughter restored to life

49 While he was still speaking, a man came from the president's house with the message, 'Your daughter is dead; trouble the Rabbi 50 no further.' But Jesus heard, and interposed. 'Do not be afraid,' he said; 'only show faith 51 and she will be well again.' On arrival at the house he allowed no one to go in with him except Peter, John, and James, and the 52 child's father and mother. And all were weeping and lamenting for her. He said, 'Weep no more; she is not dead: she is 53 asleep'; and they only laughed at him, well 54 knowing that she was dead. But Jesus took hold of her hand and called her: 'Get up, 55 my child.' Her spirit returned, she stood up immediately, and he told them to give 56 her something to eat. Her parents were astounded; but he forbade them to tell anyone what had happened.

The twelve apostles

He now called the Twelve together and gave 9 them power and authority to overcome all the devils and to cure diseases, and sent 2 them to proclaim the kingdom of God and to heal. 'Take nothing for the journey,' he 3 told them, 'neither stick nor pack, neither bread nor money; nor are you each to have a second coat. When you are admitted to a 4 house, stay there, and go on from there. As 5 for those who will not receive you, when you leave their town shake the dust off your feet as a warning to them.' So they set out and 6 travelled from village to village, and everywhere they told the good news and healed the sick.

Disturbing news for Herod

Now Prince Herod heard of all that was 7 happening, and did not know what to make of it; for some were saying that John had been raised from the dead, others that 8 Elijah had appeared, others again that one of the old prophets had come back to life. Herod said, 'As for John, I beheaded him 9 myself; but who is this I hear such talk about?' And he was anxious to see him.

Feeding five thousand

On their return the apostles told Jesus all 10 they had done; and he took them with him and withdrew privately to a town called Bethsaida. But the crowds found out and 11 followed him. He welcomed them, and spoke to them about the kingdom of God, and cured those who were in need of healing. When evening was drawing on, the Twelve 12 came up to him and said, 'Send these people away; then they can go into the villages and farms round about to find food and lodging; for we are in a lonely place here.' 'Give them 13 something to eat yourselves', he replied. But they said, 'All we have is five loaves and two fishes, nothing more—unless perhaps we ourselves are to go and buy provisions for all this company.' (There were about 1 five thousand men.) He said to his disciples, 'Make them sit down in groups of fifty or so.' They did so and got them all 1 seated. Then, taking the five loaves and the 1 two fishes, he looked up to heaven, said the blessing over them, broke them, and gave them to the disciples to distribute to the people. They all ate to their hearts' content; 1 and when the scraps they left were picked up, they filled twelve great baskets.

Peter's confession of faith

One day when he was praying alone in the presence of his disciples, he asked them, 'Who do the people say I am?' They

---

[y] Some witnesses read Gerasene; others read Gadarene.   [z] Some witnesses add though she had spent all she had on doctors.   [a] Some witnesses omit the edge of.

answered, 'Some say John the Baptist, others Elijah, others that one of the old pro-
20 phets has come back to life.' 'And you,' he said, 'who do you say I am?' Peter answered,
21 'God's Messiah.' Then he gave them strict
22 orders not to tell this to anyone. And he said, 'The Son of Man has to undergo great sufferings, and to be rejected by the elders, chief priests, and doctors of the law, to be put to death and to be raised again on the third day.'

On following Jesus

23 And to all he said, 'If anyone wishes to be a follower of mine, he must leave self behind; day after day he must take up his
24 cross, and come with me. Whoever cares for his own safety is lost; but if a man will let himself be lost for my sake, that man is
25 safe. What will a man gain by winning the
26 whole world, at the cost of his true self? For whoever is ashamed of me and mine,[b] the Son of Man will be ashamed of him, when he comes in his glory and the glory of the
27 Father and the holy angels. And I tell you this: there are some of those standing here who will not taste death before they have seen the kingdom of God.'

Jesus is transfigured

28 About eight days after this conversation he took Peter, John, and James with him and
29 went up into the hills to pray. And while he was praying the appearance of his face changed and his clothes became dazzling
30 white. Suddenly there were two men talking
31 with him; these were Moses and Elijah, who appeared in glory and spoke of his departure, the destiny he was to fulfil in Jerusalem.
32 Meanwhile Peter and his companions had been in a deep sleep; but when they awoke, they saw his glory and the two men who stood
33 beside him. And as these were moving away from Jesus, Peter said to him, 'Master, how good is it that we are here! Shall we make three shelters, one for you, one for Moses, and one for Elijah?'; but he spoke without
34 knowing what he was saying. The words were still on his lips, when there came a cloud which cast a shadow over them; they
35 were afraid as they entered the cloud, and from it came a voice: 'This is my Son, my
36 Chosen; listen to him.' When the voice had spoken, Jesus was seen to be alone. The disciples kept silence and at that time told nobody anything of what they had seen.

Jesus heals an epileptic boy

37 Next day when they came down from the
38 hills he was met by a large crowd. All at once there was a shout from a man in the crowd: 'Master, look at my son, I implore you, my only child. From time to time a 39 spirit seizes him, gives a sudden scream, and throws him into convulsions with foaming at the mouth, and it keeps on mauling him and will hardly let him go. I asked your 40 disciples to cast it out, but they could not.' Jesus answered, 'What an unbelieving and 41 perverse generation! How long shall I be with you and endure you all? Bring your son here.' But before the boy could reach 42 him the devil dashed him to the ground and threw him into convulsions. Jesus rebuked the unclean spirit, cured the boy, and gave him back to his father. And they 43 were all struck with awe at the majesty of God.

Jesus again speaks of his death

Amid the general wonder and admiration at all he was doing, Jesus said to his disciples, 'What I now say is for you: ponder my words. 44 The Son of Man is to be given up into the power of men.' But they did not under- 45 stand this saying; it had been hidden from them, so that they should not[c] grasp its meaning, and they were afraid to ask him about it.

A lesson from a child

A dispute arose among them: which of them 46 was the greatest? Jesus knew what was pass- 47 ing in their minds, so he took a child by the hand and stood him at his side, and said, 48 'Whoever receives this child in my name receives me; and whoever receives me receives the One who sent me. For the least among you all—he is the greatest.'

'He who is not against you is on your side'

'Master,' said John, 'we saw a man driving 49 out devils in your name, but as he is not one of us we tried to stop him.' Jesus said 50 to him, 'Do not stop him, for he who is not against you is on your side.'

A Samaritan village rejects Jesus

As the time approached when he was to be 51 taken up to heaven, he set his face resolutely towards Jerusalem, and sent messengers 52 ahead. They set out and went into a Samaritan village to make arrangements for him; but the villagers would not have him be- 53 cause he was making for Jerusalem. When 54 the disciples James and John saw this they said, 'Lord, may we call down fire from heaven to burn them up[d]?' But he turned 55 and rebuked them,[e] and they went on to 56 another village.

---

b *Some witnesses read* me and my words.
d *Some witnesses add* as Elijah did.
c *Or* it was so obscure to them that they could not . . .
e *Some witnesses insert* 'You do not know', he said, 'to what spirit you belong; (56) for the Son of Man did not come to destroy men's lives but to save them.'

The cost of discipleship

57 As they were going along the road a man said to him, 'I will follow you wherever you 58 go.' Jesus answered, 'Foxes have their holes, the birds their roosts; but the Son of Man 59 has nowhere to lay his head.' To another he said, 'Follow me', but the man replied, 'Let 60 me go and bury my father first.' Jesus said, 'Leave the dead to bury their dead; you must go and announce the kingdom of God.'

61 Yet another said, 'I will follow you, sir; but let me first say good-bye to my people at 62 home.' To him Jesus said, 'No one who sets his hand to the plough and then keeps looking back[f] is fit for the kingdom of God.'

The Lord appoints a further seventy-two

10 After this the Lord appointed a further seventy-two[g] and sent them on ahead in pairs to every town and place he was going 2 to visit himself. He said to them: 'The crop is heavy, but labourers are scarce; you must therefore beg the owner to send labourers 3 to harvest his crop. Be on your way. And look, I am sending you like lambs among 4 wolves. Carry no purse or pack, and travel barefoot. Exchange no greetings on the road. 5 When you go into a house, let your first 6 words be, "Peace to this house." If there is a man of peace there, your peace will rest upon him; if not, it will return and rest upon 7 you. Stay in that one house, sharing their food and drink; for the worker earns his pay. Do not move from house to house. 8 When you come into a town and they make you welcome, eat the food provided for 9 you; heal the sick there, and say, "The kingdom of God has come close to you." 10 When you enter a town and they do not make you welcome, go out into its streets 11 and say, "The very dust of your town that clings to our feet we wipe off to your shame. Only take note of this: the kingdom of God

has come close." I tell you, it will be more 12 bearable for Sodom on the great Day than for that town.

'Alas for you, Chorazin! Alas for you, 13 Bethsaida! If the miracles that were performed in you had been performed in Tyre and Sidon, they would have repented long ago, sitting in sackcloth and ashes. But it 14 will be more bearable for Tyre and Sidon at the Judgement than for you. And as for 15 you, Capernaum, will you be exalted to the skies? No, brought down to the depths!

'Whoever listens to you listens to me; 16 whoever rejects you rejects me. And whoever rejects me rejects the One who sent me.'

The return of the seventy-two

The seventy-two[g] came back jubilant. 'In 17 your name, Lord,' they said, 'even the devils submit to us.' He replied, 'I watched how 18 Satan fell, like lightning, out of the sky. And 19 now you see that I have given you the power to tread underfoot snakes and scorpions and

all the forces of the enemy, and nothing will ever harm you.[h] Nevertheless, what you 20 should rejoice over is not that the spirits submit to you, but that your names are enrolled in heaven.'

The Father and the Son

At that moment Jesus exulted in the Holy[i] 21 Spirit and said, 'I thank thee, Father, Lord of heaven and earth, for hiding these things from the learned and wise, and revealing them to the simple. Yes, Father, such[j] was thy choice.' Then turning to his disciples he 22 said,[k] 'Everything is entrusted to me by my Father; and no one knows who the Son is but the Father, or who the Father is but the Son, and those to whom the Son may choose to reveal him.'

Turning to his disciples in private he said, 23 'Happy the eyes that see what you are seeing! I tell you, many prophets and kings 24 wished to see what you now see, yet never saw it; to hear what you hear, yet never heard it.'

'Who is my neighbour?'

On one occasion a lawyer came forward to 25 put this test question to him: 'Master, what must I do to inherit eternal life?' Jesus said, 26

---

f *Some witnesses read* No one who looks back as he sets hand to the plough . . .   g *Some witnesses read* seventy.   h *Or* and he will have no way at all to harm you.   i *Some witnesses omit* Holy. j *Or* Yes, I thank thee, Father, that such . . .   k *Some witnesses omit* Then . . . he said.

'What is written in the Law? What is your
27 reading of it?' He replied, 'Love the Lord
your God with all your heart, with all your
soul, with all your strength, and with all
your mind; and your neighbour as your-
28 self.' 'That is the right answer,' said Jesus;
'do that and you will live.'
29 But he wanted to vindicate himself, so he
said to Jesus, 'And who is my neighbour?'
30 Jesus replied, 'A man was on his way from
Jerusalem down to Jericho when he fell in
with robbers, who stripped him, beat him,
31 and went off leaving him half dead. It so
happened that a priest was going down by
the same road; but when he saw him, he
32 went past on the other side. So too a Levite
came to the place, and when he saw him
33 went past on the other side. But a Samaritan
who was making the journey came upon
him, and when he saw him was moved to
34 pity. He went up and bandaged his wounds,
bathing them with oil and wine. Then he
lifted him on to his own beast, brought him
35 to an inn, and looked after him there. Next
day he produced two silver pieces and gave
them to the innkeeper, and said, "Look after
him; and if you spend any more, I will re-
36 pay you on my way back." Which of these
three do you think was neighbour to the
man who fell into the hands of the robbers?'
37 He answered, 'The one who showed him
kindness.' Jesus said, 'Go and do as he did.'

At the home of Martha and Mary

38 While they were on their way Jesus came to
a village where a woman named Martha
39 made him welcome in her home. She had a
sister, Mary, who seated herself at the Lord's
feet and stayed there listening to his words.
40 Now Martha was distracted by her many
tasks, so she came to him and said, 'Lord,
do you not care that my sister has left me
to get on with the work by myself? Tell her
41 to come and lend a hand.' But the Lord
answered, 'Martha, Martha, you are fretting
42 and fussing about so many things; but one
thing is necessary.*l* The part that Mary has
chosen is best; and it shall not be taken away
from her.'

About prayer

1 Once, in a certain place, Jesus was at prayer.
When he ceased, one of his disciples said,
'Lord, teach us to pray, as John taught his
2 disciples.' He answered, 'When you pray,
say,

"Father,*m* thy name be hallowed;
thy kingdom come.*n*

Give us each day our daily bread.*o*   3
And forgive us our sins,   4
for we too forgive all who have done us
wrong.
And do not bring us to the test." '*p*

Then he said to them, 'Suppose one of 5
you has a friend who comes to him in the
middle of the night and says, "My friend,
lend me three loaves, for a friend of mine 6
on a journey has turned up at my house,
and I have nothing to offer him"; and he 7
replies from inside, "Do not bother me. The
door is shut for the night; my children and
I have gone to bed; and I cannot get up and
give you what you want." I tell you that even 8
if he will not provide for him out of friendship, the very shamelessness of the request
will make him get up and give him all he
needs. And so I say to you, ask, and you 9
will receive; seek, and you will find; knock,
and the door will be opened. For every- 10
one who asks receives, he who seeks finds,
and to him who knocks, the door will be
opened.

'Is there a father among you who will 11
offer his son*q* a snake when he asks for fish,
or a scorpion when he asks for an egg? 12
If you, then, bad as you are, know how to 13
give your children what is good for them,
how much more will the heavenly Father
give the Holy Spirit*r* to those who ask
him!'

Controversy with the Jews

He was driving out a devil which was dumb; 14
and when the devil had come out, the dumb
man began to speak. The people were astonished, but some of them said, 'It is by Beelze- 15
bub prince of devils that he drives the devils
out.' Others, by way of a test, demanded of 16
him a sign from heaven. But he knew what 17
was in their minds, and said, 'Every kingdom divided against itself goes to ruin, and
a divided household falls. Equally if Satan is 18
divided against himself, how can his kingdom stand?—since, as you would have it,
I drive out the devils by Beelzebub. If it is 19
by Beelzebub that I cast out devils, by whom
do your own people drive them out? If this
is your argument, they themselves will refute you. But if it is by the finger of God 20
that I drive out the devils, then be sure the
kingdom of God has already come upon
you.

'When a strong man fully armed is on 21
guard over his castle his possessions are
safe. But when someone stronger comes 22
upon him and overpowers him, he carries

l Some witnesses read but few things are necessary, or rather, one alone; *others omit* you are fretting ... necessary.
m Some witnesses read Our Father in heaven.   *n One witness reads* thy kingdom come upon us; *some*
others have thy Holy Spirit come upon us and cleanse us; *some insert* thy will be done, on earth as in heaven.
o Or our bread for the morrow.   *p Some witnesses add* but save us from the evil one (*or* from evil).
q Some witnesses insert a stone when he asks for bread, or ...   *r Some witnesses read* a good gift;
some others read good things.

will appear against[u] them and ensure their condemnation, for she came from the ends of the earth to hear the wisdom of Solomon; and what is here is greater than Solomon. The men of Nineveh will appear at the Judge- 32 ment when this generation is on trial, and ensure[v] its condemnation, for they repented at the preaching of Jonah; and what is here is greater than Jonah.'

The lamp of the body

'No one lights a lamp and puts it in a cellar,[w] 33 but rather on the lamp-stand so that those who enter may see the light. The lamp of 34 your body is the eye. When your eyes are sound, you have light for your whole body; but when the eyes are bad, you are in darkness. See to it then that the light you have 35 is not darkness. If you have light for your 36 whole body with no trace of darkness, it will all be as bright as when a lamp flashes its rays upon you.'

The Lord denounces Pharisees and lawyers

When he had finished speaking, a Pharisee 37 invited him to a meal. He came in and sat down. The Pharisee noticed with surprise 38 that he had not begun by washing before the meal. But the Lord said to him, 'You 39 Pharisees! You clean the outside of cup and plate; but inside you there is nothing but greed and wickedness. You fools! Did not 40 he who made the outside make the inside too? But let what is in the cup[x] be given in 41 charity, and all is clean.

'Alas for you Pharisees! You pay tithes 42 of mint and rue and every garden-herb, but have no care for justice and the love of God. It is these you should have practised, without neglecting the others.[y]

'Alas for you Pharisees! You love the 43 seats of honour in synagogues, and salutations in the market-places.

'Alas, alas, you are like unmarked graves 44 over which men may walk without knowing it.'

In reply to this one of the lawyers said, 45 'Master, when you say things like this you are insulting us too.' Jesus rejoined: 'Yes, 46 you lawyers, it is no better with you! For you load men with intolerable burdens, and will not put a single finger to the load.

'Alas, you build the tombs of the pro- 47 phets whom your fathers murdered, and so 48 testify that you approve of the deeds your fathers did; they committed the murders and you provide the tombs.

'This is why the Wisdom of God said, 49 "I will send them prophets and messengers;

off the arms and armour on which the man had relied and divides the plunder.

23 'He who is not with me is against me, and he who does not gather with me scatters.[s]

24 'When an unclean spirit comes out of a man it wanders over the deserts seeking a resting-place; and if it finds none, it says,

25 "I will go back to the home I left." So it returns and finds the house[t] swept clean,

26 and tidy. Off it goes and collects seven other spirits more wicked than itself, and they all come in and settle down; and in the end the man's plight is worse than before.'

True happiness

27 While he was speaking thus, a woman in the crowd called out, 'Happy the womb that carried you and the breasts that suckled

28 you!' He rejoined, 'No, happy are those who hear the word of God and keep it.'

The sign of Jonah

29 With the crowds swarming round him he went on to say: 'This is a wicked generation. It demands a sign, and the only sign that

30 will be given it is the sign of Jonah. For just as Jonah was a sign to the Ninevites, so will

31 the Son of Man be to this generation. At the Judgement, when the men of this generation are on trial, the Queen of the South

---

s *Some witnesses add* me.   *t* *Some witnesses insert* unoccupied.   *u* *Or* will be raised to life together with . . .   *v* *Or* At the Judgement the men of Nineveh will rise again together with this generation and will ensure . . .   *w* *Some witnesses insert* or under the meal-tub.   *x* *Or* what you can afford. *y* *Some witnesses omit* It is . . . others.

and some of these they will persecute and
50 kill"; so that this generation will have to
answer for the blood of all the prophets
shed since the foundation of the world;
51 from the blood of Abel to the blood of
Zechariah who perished between the altar
and the sanctuary. I tell you, this generation
will have to answer for it all.
52   'Alas for you lawyers! You have taken
away the key of knowledge. You did not
go in yourselves, and those who were on
their way in, you stopped.'
53   After he had left the house, the lawyers and
Pharisees began to assail him fiercely and to
54 ply him with a host of questions, laying snares
to catch him with his own words.

Warning against hypocrisy

12 Meanwhile, when a crowd of many thousands had gathered, packed so close that
they were treading on one another, he began
to speak first to his disciples: 'Beware of the
leaven of the Pharisees; I mean their hypoc-
2 risy. There is nothing covered up that will
not be uncovered, nothing hidden that will
3 not be made known. You may take it, then,
that everything you have said in the dark
will be heard in broad daylight, and what
you have whispered behind closed doors will
be shouted from the house-tops.'

Freedom from fear

4 'To you who are my friends I say: Do not
fear those who kill the body and after that
5 have nothing more they can do. I will warn
you whom to fear: fear him who, after he
has killed, has authority to cast into hell.
Believe me, he is the one to fear.
6   'Are not sparrows five for twopence? And
yet not one of them is overlooked by God.
7 More than that, even the hairs of your head
have all been counted. Have no fear; you are
worth more than any number of sparrows.'

Acknowledging and disowning Christ

8 'I tell you this: everyone who acknowledges
me before men, the Son of Man will acknow-
9 ledge before the angels of God; but he who
disowns me before men will be disowned
before the angels of God.
10   'Anyone who speaks a word against the
Son of Man will receive forgiveness; but for
him who slanders the Holy Spirit there will
be no forgiveness.
11   'When you are brought before synagogues
and state authorities, do not begin worry-
ing about how you will conduct your de-
12 fence or what you will say. For when the
time comes the Holy Spirit will instruct you
what to say.'

On amassing wealth

A man in the crowd said to him, 'Master, 13
tell my brother to divide the family property
with me.' He replied, 'My good man, who 14
set me over you to judge or arbitrate?'[z]
Then he said to the people, 'Beware! Be on 15
your guard against greed of every kind, for
even when a man has more than enough,
his wealth does not give him life.' And he 16
told them this parable: 'There was a rich
man whose land yielded heavy crops. He 17
debated with himself: "What am I to do?
I have not the space to store my produce.
This is what I will do," said he: "I will pull 18
down my storehouses and build them bigger.
I will collect in them all my corn and other
goods, and then say to myself, 'Man, you 19
have plenty of good things laid by, enough
for many years: take life easy, eat, drink,
and enjoy yourself.'" But God said to him, 20
"You fool, this very night you must surrender your life; you have made your
money—who will get it now?" That is how 21
it is with the man who amasses wealth for
himself and remains a pauper in the sight
of God.'[a]

Cure for worry

'Therefore', he said to his disciples, 'I bid 22
you put away anxious thoughts about food
to keep you alive and clothes to cover your
body. Life is more than food, the body more 23
than clothes. Think of the ravens: they 24
neither sow nor reap; they have no storehouse or barn; yet God feeds them. You
are worth far more than the birds! Is there 25
a man among you who by anxious thought
can add a foot to his height[b]? If, then, you 26
cannot do even a very little thing, why are
you anxious about the rest?
'Think of the lilies: they neither spin nor 27
weave;[c] yet I tell you, even Solomon in all
his splendour was not attired like one of
these. But if that is how God clothes the 28
grass, which is growing in the field today,
and tomorrow is thrown on the stove, how
much more will he clothe you! How little
faith you have! And so you are not to set 29
your mind on food and drink; you are not
to worry. For all these are things for the 30
heathen to run after; but you have a Father
who knows that you need them. No, set 31
your mind upon his kingdom, and all the
rest will come to you as well.
'Have no fear, little flock; for your Father 32
has chosen to give you the Kingdom. Sell 33
your possessions and give in charity. Provide for yourselves purses that do not wear
out, and never-failing treasure in heaven,
where no thief can get near it, no moth

---

z Some witnesses omit or arbitrate.   *a Some witnesses omit* That . . . God; *others add at the end* When
he said this he cried out, 'If you have ears to hear, then hear.'   *b Or* a day to his life.   *c Some*
witnesses read they grow, they do not toil or spin.

34 destroy it. For where your treasure is, there will your heart be also.'

'Be ready'

35 'Be ready for action, with belts fastened and
36 lamps alight. Be like men who wait for their master's return from a wedding-party, ready to let him in the moment he arrives and
37 knocks. Happy are those servants whom the master finds on the alert when he comes. I tell you this: he will fasten his belt, seat them at table, and come and wait on them.
38 Even if it is the middle of the night or before dawn when he comes, happy they if he finds
39 them alert. And remember, if the householder had known what time the burglar was coming he would not have let his house
40 be broken into. Hold yourselves ready, then, because the Son of Man will come at the time you least expect him.'

The trusty and sensible man

41 Peter said, 'Lord, do you intend this parable
42 specially for us or is it for everyone?' The Lord said, 'Well, who is the trusty and sensible man whom his master will appoint as his steward, to manage his servants and issue
43 their rations at the proper time? Happy that servant who is found at his task when his
44 master comes! I tell you this: he will be put
45 in charge of all his master's property. But if that servant says to himself, "The master is a long time coming", and begins to bully the menservants and maids, and eat and
46 drink and get drunk; then the master will arrive on a day that servant does not expect, at a time he does not know, and will cut him in pieces. Thus he will find his place among the faithless.
47 'The servant who knew his master's wishes, yet made no attempt to carry them
48 out, will be flogged severely. But one who did not know them and earned a beating will be flogged less severely. Where a man has been given much, much will be expected of him; and the more a man has had entrusted to him the more he will be required to repay.'

Conflicting loyalties

49 'I have come to set fire to the earth, and how
50 I wish it were already kindled! I have a baptism to undergo, and what constraint
51 I am under until the ordeal is over! Do you suppose I came to establish peace on earth? No indeed, I have come to bring division.
52 For from now on, five members of a family will be divided, three against two and two
53 against three; father against son and son against father, mother against daughter and daughter against mother, mother against son's wife and son's wife against her mother-in-law.'

HK

'This fateful hour'

He also said to the people, 'When you see 54 cloud banking up in the west, you say at once, "It is going to rain", and rain it does. And when the wind is from the south, you 55 say, "There will be a heat-wave", and there is. What hypocrites you are! You know how 56 to interpret the appearance of earth and sky; how is it you cannot interpret this fateful hour?

'And why can you not judge for yourselves 57 what is the right course? When you are going 58 with your opponent to court, make an effort to settle with him while you are still on the way; otherwise he may drag you before the judge, and the judge hand you over to the constable, and the constable put you in jail. I tell you, you will not come out till 59 you have paid the last farthing.'

The need for repentance

At that very time there were some people **13** present who told him about the Galileans whose blood Pilate had mixed with their sacrifices. He answered them: 'Do you 2 imagine that, because these Galileans suffered this fate, they must have been greater sinners than anyone else in Galilee? I tell 3 you they were not; but unless you repent, you will all of you come to the same end. Or the eighteen people who were killed 4 when the tower fell on them at Siloam—do you imagine they were more guilty than all the other people living in Jerusalem? I tell 5 you they were not; but unless you repent, you will all of you come to the same end.'

The fig-tree without fruit

He told them this parable: 'A man had a 6 fig-tree growing in his vineyard; and he came looking for fruit on it, but found none. So he said to the vine-dresser, "Look here! 7 For the last three years I have come looking for fruit on this fig-tree without finding any. Cut it down. Why should it go on using up the soil?" But he replied, "Leave it, sir, this 8 one year while I dig round it and manure it.

9 And if it bears next season, well and good; if not, you shall have it down.'"

Jesus heals a crippled woman

10 One Sabbath he was teaching in a synagogue,
11 and there was a woman there possessed by a spirit that had crippled her for eighteen years. She was bent double and quite unable
12 to stand up straight. When Jesus saw her he called her and said, 'You are rid of your
13 trouble.' Then he laid his hands on her, and at once she straightened up and began to
14 praise God. But the president of the synagogue, indignant with Jesus for healing on the Sabbath, intervened and said to the congregation, 'There are six working-days: come and be cured on one of them, and not

15 on the Sabbath.' The Lord gave him his answer: 'What hypocrites you are!' he said. 'Is there a single one of you who does not loose his ox or his donkey from the manger and take it out to water on the Sabbath?
16 And here is this woman, a daughter of Abraham, who has been kept prisoner by Satan for eighteen long years: was it wrong for her to be freed from her bonds on the
17 Sabbath?' At these words all his opponents were covered with confusion, while the mass of the people were delighted at all the wonderful things he was doing.

A mustard-seed

18 'What is the kingdom of God like?' he continued. 'What shall I compare it with?
19 It is like a mustard-seed which a man took and sowed in his garden; and it grew to be a tree and the birds came to roost among its branches.'

Yeast

20 Again he said, 'The kingdom of God, what
21 shall I compare it with? It is like yeast which a woman took and mixed with half a hundredweight of flour till it was all leavened.'

The narrow door

22 He continued his journey through towns and villages, teaching as he made his way
23 towards Jerusalem. Someone asked him, 'Sir, are only a few to be saved?' His answer

was: 'Struggle to get in through the narrow 24 door; for I tell you that many will try to enter and not be able.

'When once the master of the house has 25 got up and locked the door, you may stand outside and knock, and say, "Sir, let us in!", but he will only answer, "I do not know where you come from." Then you will 26 begin to say, "We sat at table with you and

you taught in our streets." But he will re- 27 peat, "I tell you, I do not know where you come from. Out of my sight, all of you, you and your wicked ways!" There will be wail- 28 ing and grinding of teeth there, when you see Abraham, Isaac, and Jacob, and all the prophets, in the kingdom of God, and your- selves thrown out. From east and west 29 people will come, from north and south, for the feast in the kingdom of God. Yes, and 30 some who are now last will be first, and some who are first will be last.'

Jerusalem the doomed city

At that time a number of Pharisees came to 31 him and said, 'You should leave this place and go on your way; Herod is out to kill you.' He replied, 'Go and tell that fox, 32 "Listen: today and tomorrow I shall be casting out devils and working cures; on the third day I reach my goal." However, 33 I must be on my way today and tomorrow and the next day, because it is unthinkable for a prophet to meet his death anywhere but in Jerusalem.

'O Jerusalem, Jerusalem, the city that 34 murders the prophets and stones the mes- sengers sent to her! How often have I longed to gather your children, as a hen gathers her brood under her wings; but you would not let me. Look, look! there is your 35 temple, forsaken by God. And I tell you, you shall never see me until the time comes when you say, "Blessings on him who comes in the name of the Lord!"'

Jesus heals a man of dropsy

One Sabbath he went to have a meal in the **14** house of a leading Pharisee; and they were

2 watching him closely. There, in front of him,
3 was a man suffering from dropsy. Jesus asked the lawyers and the Pharisees: 'Is it permitted to cure people on the Sabbath or
4 not?' They said nothing. So he took the
5 man, cured him, and sent him away. Then he turned to them and said, 'If one of you has a donkey*d* or an ox and it falls into a well, will he hesitate to haul it up on the
6 Sabbath day?' To this they could find no reply.

Humility and hospitality

7 When he noticed how the guests were trying to secure the places of honour, he spoke to
8 them in a parable: 'When you are asked by someone to a wedding-feast, do not sit down in the place of honour. It may be that some person more distinguished than yourself
9 has been invited; and the host will come and say to you, "Give this man your seat." Then you will look foolish as you begin to take
10 the lowest place. No, when you receive an invitation, go and sit down in the lowest place, so that when your host comes he will say, "Come up higher, my friend." Then all your fellow-guests will see the respect in
11 which you are held. For everyone who exalts himself will be humbled; and whoever humbles himself will be exalted.'
12 Then he said to his host, 'When you are having a party for lunch or supper, do not invite your friends, your brothers or other relations, or your rich neighbours; they will only ask you back again and so
13 you will be repaid. But when you give a
14 party, ask the poor, the crippled, the lame, and the blind; and so find happiness. For they have no means of repaying you; but you will be repaid on the day when good men rise from the dead.'

A big dinner party

15 One of the company, after hearing all this, said to him, 'Happy the man who shall sit
16 at the feast in the kingdom of God!' Jesus answered, 'A man was giving a big dinner party and had sent out many invitations.
17 At dinner-time he sent his servant with a message for his guests, "Please come, every-
18 thing is now ready." They began one and all to excuse themselves. The first said, "I have bought a piece of land, and I must go and look over it; please accept my
19 apologies." The second said, "I have bought five yoke of oxen, and I am on my way to try them out; please accept my apologies."
20 The next said, "I have just got married and
21 for that reason I cannot come." When the servant came back he reported this to his master. The master of the house was angry and said to him, "Go out quickly into the streets and alleys of the town, and bring me in the poor, the crippled, the blind, and
22 the lame." The servant said, "Sir, your orders have been carried out and there is
23 still room." The master replied, "Go out on to the highways and along the hedgerows and make them come in; I want my
24 house to be full. I tell you that not one of those who were invited shall taste my banquet." '

The cost of discipleship

25 Once when great crowds were accompany-
26 ing him, he turned to them and said: 'If anyone comes to me and does not hate his father and mother, wife and children, brothers and sisters, even his own life, he cannot
27 be a disciple of mine. No one who does not carry his cross and come with me can be
28 a disciple of mine. Would any of you think of building a tower without first sitting down and calculating the cost, to see whether he
29 could afford to finish it? Otherwise, if he has laid its foundation and then is not able to complete it, all the onlookers will laugh
30 at him. "There is the man", they will say, "who started to build and could not finish."
31 Or what king will march to battle against another king, without first sitting down to consider whether with ten thousand men he can face an enemy coming to meet him
32 with twenty thousand? If he cannot, then,
33 long before the enemy approaches, he sends envoys, and asks for terms. So also none of you can be a disciple of mine without parting with all his possessions.
34 'Salt is a good thing; but if salt itself be-
35 comes tasteless, what will you use to season it? It is useless either on the land or on the dung-heap: it can only be thrown away. If you have ears to hear, then hear.'

The lost sheep

1 Another time, the tax-gatherers and other bad characters were all crowding in to listen
2 to him; and the Pharisees and the doctors of the law began grumbling among themselves: 'This fellow', they said, 'welcomes
3 sinners and eats with them.' He answered
4 them with this parable: 'If one of you has a hundred sheep and loses one of them, does he not leave the ninety-nine in the open pasture and go after the missing one until
5 he has found it? How delighted he is then!
6 He lifts it on to his shoulders, and home he goes to call his friends and neighbours together. "Rejoice with me!" he cries. "I have found my lost sheep." In the same way,
7 I tell you, there will be greater joy in heaven over one sinner who repents than over ninety-nine righteous people who do not need to repent.'

d Some witnesses read son.

(Luke 15. 4)

The lost silver

8 'Or again, if a woman has ten silver pieces and loses one of them, does not she light the lamp, sweep out the house, and look in every
9 corner till she has found it? And when she has, she calls her friends and neighbours together, and says, "Rejoice with me! I have
10 found the piece that I lost." In the same way, I tell you, there is joy among the angels of God over one sinner who repents.'

The lost son

11 Again he said: 'There was once a man who
12 had two sons; and the younger said to his father, "Father, give me my share of the property." So he divided his estate between
13 them. A few days later the younger son turned the whole of his share into cash and left home for a distant country, where he squan-
14 dered it in reckless living. He had spent it all, when a severe famine fell upon that
15 country and he began to feel the pinch. So he went and attached himself to one of the local landowners, who sent him on to his
16 farm to mind the pigs. He would have been glad to fill his belly with[e] the pods that the pigs were eating; and no one gave him any-
17 thing. Then he came to his senses and said, "How many of my father's paid servants have more food than they can eat, and here
18 am I, starving to death! I will set off and go to my father, and say to him, 'Father, I have sinned, against God and against you;
19 I am no longer fit to be called your son; treat
20 me as one of your paid servants.'" So he set out for his father's house. But while he

was still a long way off his father saw him, and his heart went out to him. He ran to meet him, flung his arms round him, and kissed him. The son said, "Father, I have 21 sinned, against God and against you; I am no longer fit to be called your son."[f] But 22 the father said to his servants, "Quick! fetch a robe, my best one, and put it on him; put a ring on his finger and shoes on his feet. Bring the fatted calf and kill it, and let us 23 have a feast to celebrate the day. For this 24 son of mine was dead and has come back to life; he was lost and is found." And the festivities began.

'Now the elder son was out on the farm; 25 and on his way back, as he approached the house, he heard music and dancing. He 26 called one of the servants and asked what it meant. The servant told him, "Your brother 27 has come home, and your father has killed the fatted calf because he has him back safe and sound." But he was angry and refused 28 to go in. His father came out and pleaded with him; but he retorted, "You know how 29 I have slaved for you all these years; I never once disobeyed your orders; and you never gave me so much as a kid, for a feast with my friends. But now that this son of yours 30 turns up, after running through your money with his women, you kill the fatted calf for him." "My boy," said the father, "you are 31 always with me, and everything I have is yours. How could we help celebrating this 32 happy day? Your brother here was dead and has come back to life, was lost and is found."'

---

e Some witnesses read to have his fill of ...

f Some witnesses add treat me as one of your paid servants.

A dishonest steward

16 He said to his disciples, 'There was a rich man who had a steward, and he received complaints that this man was squandering ² the property. So he sent for him, and said, "What is this that I hear? Produce your accounts, for you cannot be manager here ³ any longer." The steward said to himself, "What am I to do now that my employer is dismissing me? I am not strong enough to ⁴ dig, and too proud to beg. I know what I must do, to make sure that, when I have to leave, there will be people to give me house ⁵ and home." He summoned his master's debtors one by one. To the first he said, ⁶ "How much do you owe my master?" He replied, "A thousand gallons of olive oil."

Liquid measures

He said, "Here is your account. Sit down and make it five hundred; and be quick ⁷ about it." Then he said to another, "And you, how much do you owe?" He said, "A thousand bushels of wheat", and was told, "Take your account and make it eight ⁸ hundred." And the master applauded the dishonest steward for acting so astutely. For the worldly are more astute than the other-worldly in dealing with their own kind.

⁹ 'So I say to you, use your worldly wealth to win friends for yourselves, so that when money is a thing of the past you may be received into an eternal home.

¹⁰ 'The man who can be trusted in little things can be trusted also in great; and the man who is dishonest in little things is dis-¹¹ honest also in great things. If, then, you have not proved trustworthy with the wealth of this world, who will trust you with the ¹² wealth that is real? And if you have proved untrustworthy with what belongs to another, who will give you what is your own?

¹³ 'No servant can be the slave of two masters; for either he will hate the first and love the second, or he will be devoted to the first and think nothing of the second. You cannot serve God and Money.'

Some sayings of Jesus

¹⁴ The Pharisees, who loved money, heard all ¹⁵ this and scoffed at him. He said to them, 'You are the people who impress your fellow-men with your righteousness; but God sees through you; for what sets itself up to be admired by men is detestable in the sight of God.

¹⁶ 'Until John, it was the Law and the prophets: since then, there is the good news of the kingdom of God, and everyone forces his way in.

¹⁷ 'It is easier for heaven and earth to come to an end than for one dot or stroke of the Law to lose its force.

¹⁸ 'A man who divorces his wife and marries another commits adultery; and anyone who marries a woman divorced from her husband commits adultery.'

The rich man and Lazarus

¹⁹ 'There was once a rich man, who dressed in purple and the finest linen, and feasted in ²⁰ great magnificence every day. At his gate, covered with sores, lay a poor man named ²¹ Lazarus, who would have been glad to satisfy his hunger with the scraps from the rich man's table. Even the dogs used to come and lick his sores. One day the poor man ²² died and was carried away by the angels to be with Abraham. The rich man also died and was buried, and in Hades, where he was ²³ in torment, he looked up; and there, far away, was Abraham with Lazarus close beside him. "Abraham, my father," he called ²⁴ out, "take pity on me! Send Lazarus to dip the tip of his finger in water, to cool my tongue, for I am in agony in this fire." But ²⁵ Abraham said, "Remember, my child, that all the good things fell to you while you were alive, and all the bad to Lazarus; now he has his consolation here and it is you who are in agony. But that is not all: there is a great ²⁶ chasm fixed between us; no one from our side who wants to reach you can cross it, and none may pass from your side to us." "Then, ²⁷ father," he replied, "will you send him to my father's house, where I have five brothers, ²⁸ to warn them, so that they too may not come to this place of torment?" But Abra-²⁹ ham said, "They have Moses and the prophets; let them listen to them." "No, father ³⁰ Abraham," he replied, "but if someone from the dead visits them, they will repent." Abra-³¹ ham answered, "If they do not listen to Moses and the prophets they will pay no heed even if someone should rise from the dead."'

Responsibility to others

17 He said to his disciples, 'Causes of stumbling are bound to arise; but woe betide the man ² through whom they come. It would be better for him to be thrown into the sea with a millstone round his neck than to cause one of ³ these little ones to stumble. Keep watch on yourselves.

'If your brother wrongs you, reprove him; and if he repents, forgive him. Even if he ⁴ wrongs you seven times in a day and comes back to you seven times saying, "I am sorry", you are to forgive him.'

About faith

5 The apostles said to the Lord, 'Increase our
6 faith'; and the Lord replied, 'If you had faith no bigger even than a mustard-seed, you could say to this mulberry-tree, "Be rooted up and replanted in the sea"; and it would at once obey you.'

The right attitude of service

7 'Suppose one of you has a servant ploughing or minding sheep. When he comes back from the fields, will the master say, "Come along
8 at once and sit down"? Will he not rather say, "Prepare my supper, fasten your belt, and then wait on me while I have my meal;
9 you can have yours afterwards"? Is he grateful to the servant for carrying out his orders?
10 So with you: when you have carried out all your orders, you should say, "We are servants and deserve no credit; we have only done our duty."'

The thankful leper

11 In the course of his journey to Jerusalem he was travelling through the borderlands of
12 Samaria and Galilee. As he was entering a village he was met by ten men with leprosy.
13 They stood some way off and called out to
14 him, 'Jesus, Master, take pity on us.' When he saw them he said, 'Go and show yourselves to the priests'; and while they were
15 on their way, they were made clean. One of them, finding himself cured, turned back
16 praising God aloud. He threw himself down at Jesus's feet and thanked him. And he was
17 a Samaritan. At this Jesus said: 'Were not all ten cleansed? The other nine, where are
18 they? Could none be found to come back and give praise to God except this foreigner?'
19 And he said to the man, 'Stand up and go on your way; your faith has cured you.'

About the kingdom of God

20 The Pharisees asked him, 'When will the kingdom of God come?' He said, 'You cannot tell by observation when the kingdom of
21 God comes. There will be no saying, "Look, here it is!" or "there it is!"; for in fact the kingdom of God is among you.'[g]

The day of the Son of Man

22 He said to the disciples, 'The time will come when you will long to see one of the days of the Son of Man, but you will not see it.
23 They will say to you, "Look! There!" and "Look! Here!" Do not go running off in

pursuit. For like the lightning-flash that 24 lights up the earth from end to end, will the Son of Man be when his day comes. But 25 first he must endure much suffering and be repudiated by this generation.

'As things were in Noah's days, so will they 26 be in the days of the Son of Man. They ate 27 and drank and married, until the day that Noah went into the ark and the flood came and made an end of them all. As things were 28 in Lot's days, also: they ate and drank; they bought and sold; they planted and built; but the day that Lot went out from Sodom, 29 it rained fire and sulphur from the sky and made an end of them all—it will be like that 30 on the day when the Son of Man is revealed.

'On that day the man who is on the roof 31 and his belongings in the house must not come down to pick them up; he, too, who is in the fields must not go back. Remember 32 Lot's wife. Whoever seeks to save his life 33 will lose it; and whoever loses it will save it, and live.

'I tell you, on that night there will be two 34 men in one bed: one will be taken, the other left. There will be two women together 35 grinding corn: one will be taken, the other left.'[h] When they heard this they asked, 37 'Where, Lord?' He said, 'Where the corpse is, there the vultures will gather.'

The persistent widow

He spoke to them in a parable to show that **18** they should keep on praying and never lose heart: 'There was once a judge who cared 2 nothing for God or man, and in the same 3 town there was a widow who constantly came before him demanding justice against her opponent. For a long time he refused; but 4 in the end he said to himself, "True, I care nothing for God or man; but this widow is 5 so great a nuisance that I will see her righted before she wears me out with her persistence."' The Lord said, 'You hear what the 6 unjust judge says; and will not God vindi- 7 cate his chosen, who cry out to him day and night, while he listens patiently to them[i]? I tell you, he will vindicate them soon 8 enough. But when the Son of Man comes, will he find faith on earth?'

The Pharisee and the tax-gatherer

And here is another parable that he told. 9 It was aimed at those who were sure of their own goodness and looked down on everyone else. 'Two men went up to the temple to 10 pray, one a Pharisee and the other a taxgatherer. The Pharisee stood up and prayed 11 thus:[j] "I thank thee, O God, that I am not

g Or for in fact the kingdom of God is within you, or for in fact the kingdom of God is within your grasp, or not suddenly the kingdom of God will be among you.   h Some witnesses add (36) two men in the fields: one will be taken, the other left.   i Or delays to help them.   j Some witnesses read stood up by himself and prayed thus; others read stood up and prayed thus privately.

O*

Sycomore

like the rest of men, greedy, dishonest, adulterous; or, for that matter, like this tax-
12 gatherer. I fast twice a week; I pay tithes on
13 all that I get." But the other kept his distance and would not even raise his eyes to heaven, but beat upon his breast, saying, "O God,
14 have mercy on me, sinner that I am." It was this man, I tell you, and not the other, who went home acquitted of his sins. For every-one who exalts himself will be humbled; and whoever humbles himself will be exalted.'

Jesus welcomes children

15 They even brought babies for him to touch. When the disciples saw them they rebuked
16 them, but Jesus called for the children and said, 'Let the little ones come to me; do not try to stop them; for the kingdom of God
17 belongs to such as these. I tell you that who-ever does not accept the kingdom of God like a child will never enter it.'

A rich man's question

18 A man of the ruling class put this question to him: 'Good Master, what must I do to
19 win eternal life?' Jesus said to him, 'Why do you call me good? No one is good except
20 God alone. You know the commandments: "Do not commit adultery; do not murder; do not steal; do not give false evidence;
21 honour your father and mother."' The man answered, 'I have kept all these since I was
22 a boy.' On hearing this Jesus said, 'There is still one thing lacking: sell everything you have and distribute to the poor, and you will have riches in heaven; and come, follow me.'
23 At these words his heart sank; for he was
24 a very rich man. When Jesus saw it he said, 'How hard it is for the wealthy to enter the
25 kingdom of God! It is easier for a camel to go through the eye of a needle than for a rich man to enter the kingdom of God.'
26 Those who heard asked, 'Then who can be

saved?' He answered, 'What is impossible 27 for men is possible for God.'

Peter said, 'We here have left our belong- 28 ings to become your followers.' Jesus said, 29 'I tell you this: there is no one who has given up home, or wife, brothers, parents, or chil-dren, for the sake of the kingdom of God, who will not be repaid many times over in this 30 age, and in the age to come have eternal life.'

Jesus again speaks of his death

He took the Twelve aside and said, 'We are 31 now going up to Jerusalem; and all that was written by the prophets will come true for the Son of Man. He will be handed over to 32 the foreign power. He will be mocked, mal-treated, and spat upon. They will flog him 33 and kill him. And on the third day he will rise again.' But they understood nothing of all 34 this; they did not grasp what he was talking about; its meaning was concealed from them.

Jesus restores a blind beggar's sight

As he approached Jericho a blind man sat 35 at the roadside begging. Hearing a crowd 36 going past, he asked what was happening. They told him, 'Jesus of Nazareth is passing 37 by.' Then he shouted out, 'Jesus, Son of 38 David, have pity on me.' The people in 39 front told him to hold his tongue; but he called out all the more, 'Son of David, have pity on me.' Jesus stopped and ordered the 40 man to be brought to him. When he came up he asked him, 'What do you want me to 41 do for you?' 'Sir, I want my sight back', he answered. Jesus said to him, 'Have back 42 your sight; your faith has cured you.' He 43 recovered his sight instantly; and he fol-lowed Jesus, praising God. And all the people gave praise to God for what they had seen.

Jesus and Zacchaeus

Entering Jericho he made his way through **1** the city. There was a man there named 2 Zacchaeus; he was superintendent of taxes and very rich. He was eager to see what 3 Jesus looked like; but, being a little man, he could not see him, for the crowd. So he 4 ran on ahead and climbed a sycomore-tree

in order to see him, for he was to pass that
5 way. When Jesus came to the place, he
looked up and said, 'Zacchaeus, be quick
and come down; I must come and stay with
6 you today.' He climbed down as fast as he
7 could and welcomed him gladly. At this
there was a general murmur of disapproval.
'He has gone in', they said, 'to be the guest
8 of a sinner.' But Zacchaeus stood there and
said to the Lord, 'Here and now, sir, I give
half my possessions to charity; and if I have
cheated anyone, I am ready to repay him
9 four times over.' Jesus said to him, 'Salvation has come to this house today!—for this
10 man too is a son of Abraham, and the Son
of Man has come to seek and save what
is lost.'

Three servants

11 While they were listening to this, he went
on to tell them a parable, because he was
now close to Jerusalem and they thought
the reign of God might dawn at any moment.
12 He said, 'A man of noble birth went on a
long journey abroad, to be appointed king
13 and then return. But first he called ten of
his servants and gave them a pound each,
saying, "Trade with this while I am away."
14 His fellow-citizens hated him, and they sent
a delegation on his heels to say, "We do not
15 want this man as our king." However, back
he came as king, and sent for the servants
to whom he had given the money, to see
16 what profit each had made. The first came
and said, "Your pound, sir, has made ten
17 more." "Well done," he replied; "you are
a good servant. You have shown yourself
trustworthy in a very small matter, and you
18 shall have charge of ten cities." The second
came and said, "Your pound, sir, has made
19 five more"; and he also was told, "You too,

take charge of five cities." The third came 20
and said, "Here is your pound, sir; I kept it
put away in a handkerchief. I was afraid of 21
you, because you are a hard man: you draw
out what you never put in and reap what you
did not sow." "You rascal!" he replied; 22
"I will judge you by your own words. You
knew, did you, that I am a hard man, that
I draw out what I never put in, and reap
what I did not sow? Then why did you not 23
put my money on deposit, and I could have
claimed it with interest when I came back?"
Turning to his attendants he said, "Take the 24
pound from him and give it to the man with
ten." "But, sir," they replied, "he has ten 25
already." "I tell you," he went on, "the 26
man who has will always be given more;
but the man who has not will forfeit even
what he has. But as for those enemies of 27
mine who did not want me for their king,
bring them here and slaughter them in my
presence." '

Jesus rides into Jerusalem

With that Jesus went forward and began 28
the ascent to Jerusalem. As he approached 29
Bethphage and Bethany at the hill called
Olivet, he sent two of the disciples with these 30
instructions: 'Go to the village opposite;
as you enter it you will find tethered there
a colt which no one has yet ridden. Untie it

31 and bring it here. If anyone asks why you 32 are untying it, say, "Our Master needs it."'
32 The two went on their errand and found it 33 as he had told them; and while they were untying the colt, its owners asked, 'Why are 34 you untying that colt?' They answered, 'Our 35 Master needs it.' So they brought the colt to Jesus.

Then they threw their cloaks on the colt, 36 for Jesus to mount, and they carpeted the 37 road with them as he went on his way. And now, as he approached the descent from the Mount of Olives, the whole company of his disciples in their joy began to sing aloud the praises of God for all the great things they had seen:

38 'Blessings on him who comes as king in the name of the Lord!
Peace in heaven, glory in highest heaven!'

· 39   Some Pharisees who were in the crowd said to him, 'Master, reprimand your dis- 40 ciples.' He answered, 'I tell you, if my disciples keep silence the stones will shout aloud.'

41   When he came in sight of the city, he 42 wept over it and said, 'If only you had known, on this great day, the way that leads to peace! But no; it is hidden from your sight.
43 For a time will come upon you, when your enemies will set up siege-works against you; they will encircle you and hem you in at 44 every point; they will bring you to the ground, you and your children within your walls, and not leave you one stone standing on another, because you did not recognize God's moment when it came.'

Jesus drives traders from the temple

45 Then he went into the temple and began 46 driving out the traders, with these words: 'Scripture says, "My house shall be a house of prayer"; but you have made it a robbers' cave.'

47   Day by day he taught in the temple. And the chief priests and lawyers were bent on making an end of him, with the support of 48 the leading citizens, but found they were helpless, because the people all hung upon his words.

About the authority of Jesus

20 One day, as he was teaching the people in the temple and telling them the good news, the priests and lawyers, and the elders with 2 them, came upon him and accosted him. 'Tell us,' they said, 'by what authority you are acting like this; who gave you this 3 authority?' He answered them, 'I have a 4 question to ask you too: tell me, was the baptism of John from God or from men?' 5 This set them arguing among themselves:

'If we say, "from God", he will say, "Why did you not believe him?" And if we say, 6 "from men", the people will all stone us, for they are convinced that John was a prophet.' So they replied that they could not tell. And 7 8 Jesus said to them, 'Then neither will I tell you by what authority I act.'

Tenants in a vineyard

He went on to tell the people this parable: 9 'A man planted a vineyard, let it out to vine-growers, and went abroad for a long time. When the season came, he sent a servant to 10 the tenants to collect from them his share of the produce; but the tenants thrashed him and sent him away empty-handed. He 11 tried again and sent a second servant; but he also was thrashed, outrageously treated, and sent away empty-handed. He tried 12 once more with a third; this one too they wounded and flung out. Then the owner 13 of the vineyard said, "What am I to do? I will send my own dear son;ᵏ perhaps they will respect him." But when the tenants saw 14 him they talked it over together. "This is the heir," they said; "let us kill him so that the property may come to us." So they flung 15 him out of the vineyard and killed him. What then will the owner of the vineyard do to them? He will come and put these 16 tenants to death and let the vineyard to others.'

When they heard this, they said, 'God for-bid!' But he looked straight at them and 17 said, 'Then what does this text of Scripture mean: "The stone which the builders re-jected has become the main corner-stone"? Any man who falls on that stone will be 18 dashed to pieces; and if it falls on a man he will be crushed by it.'

Paying tax to the Emperor

The lawyers and chief priests wanted to lay 19 hands on him there and then, for they saw that this parable was aimed at them; but they were afraid of the people. So they 20 watched their opportunity and sent secret agents in the guise of honest men, to seize upon some word of his as a pretext for hand-ing him over to the authority and jurisdic-tion of the Governor. They put a question 21 to him: 'Master,' they said, 'we know that what you speak and teach is sound; you pay deference to no one, but teach in all honesty the way of life that God requires. Are we or are we not permitted to pay taxes 22 to the Roman Emperor?' He saw through 23 their trick and said, 'Show me a silver piece. 24 Whose head does it bear, and whose inscrip-tion?' 'Caesar's', they replied. 'Very well 25 then,' he said, 'pay Caesar what is due to Caesar, and pay God what is due to God.'

ᵏ Or my only son.

26 Thus their attempt to catch him out in public failed, and, astonished by his reply, they fell silent.

About resurrection

27 Then some Sadducees came forward. They are the people who deny that there is a resurrection. Their question was this:
28 'Master, Moses laid it down for us that if there are brothers, and one dies leaving a wife but no child, then the next should marry the widow and carry on his brother's
29 family. Now, there were seven brothers:
30 the first took a wife and died childless; then
31 the second married her, then the third. In this way the seven of them died leaving no
32 children. Afterwards the woman also died.
33 At the resurrection whose wife is she to be,
34 since all seven had married her?' Jesus said to them, 'The men and women of this world
35 marry; but those who have been judged worthy of a place in the other world and of the resurrection from the dead, do not
36 marry, for they are not subject to death any longer. They are like angels; they are sons of God, because they share in the resurrec-
37 tion. That the dead are raised to life again is shown by Moses himself in the story of the burning bush, when he calls the Lord, "the God of Abraham, Isaac, and Jacob".
38 God is not God of the dead but of the living; for him all are[1] alive.'
39 At this some of the lawyers said, 'Well
40 spoken, Master.' For there was no further question that they ventured to put to him.

About the Messiah

41 He said to them, 'How can they say that the
42 Messiah is son of David? For David himself says in the Book of Psalms: "The Lord said
43 to my Lord, 'Sit at my right hand until I
44 make your enemies your footstool.'" Thus David calls him "Lord"; how then can he be David's son?'

Warning against doctors of the law

45 In the hearing of all the people Jesus said to
46 his disciples: 'Beware of the doctors of the law who love to walk up and down in long robes, and have a great liking for respectful greetings in the street, the chief seats in our synagogues, and places of honour at feasts.
47 These are the men who eat up the property of widows, while they say long prayers for appearance' sake; and they will receive the severest sentence.'

A poor widow's offering

1 He looked up and saw the rich people dropping their gifts into the chest of the temple
2 treasury; and he noticed a poor widow

putting in two tiny coins. 'I tell you this,' he 3 said: 'this poor widow has given more than any of them; for those others who have given 4 had more than enough, but she, with less than enough, has given all she had to live on.'

Destruction of the temple foretold

Some people were talking about the temple 5 and the fine stones and votive offerings with which it was adorned. He said, 'These things 6 which you are gazing at—the time will come when not one stone of them will be left upon another; all will be thrown down.' 'Master,' 7 they asked, 'when will it all come about? What will be the sign when it is due to happen?'

Troubles and persecutions

He said, 'Take care that you are not misled. 8 For many will come claiming my name and saying, "I am he", and, "The Day is upon us." Do not follow them. And when you 9 hear of wars and insurrections, do not fall into a panic. These things are bound to happen first; but the end does not follow immediately.' Then he added, 'Nation will 10 make war upon nation, kingdom upon kingdom; there will be great earthquakes, 11 and famines and plagues in many places; in the sky terrors and great portents.

'But before all this happens they will set 12 upon you and persecute you. You will be brought before synagogues and put in prison; you will be haled before kings and governors for your allegiance to me. This 13 will be your opportunity to testify; so make 14 up your minds not to prepare your defence beforehand, because I myself will give you 15 power of utterance and a wisdom which no opponent will be able to resist or refute. Even your parents and brothers, your rela- 16 tions and friends, will betray you. Some of you will be put to death; and all will hate 17 you for your allegiance to me. But not a 18 hair of your head shall be lost. By standing 19 firm you will win true life for yourselves.'

Jerusalem will be trampled down

'But when you see Jerusalem encircled by 20 armies, then you may be sure that her destruction is near. Then those who are in 21 Judaea must take to the hills; those who are in the city itself must leave it, and those who are out in the country must not enter; be- 22 cause this is the time of retribution, when all that stands written is to be fulfilled. Alas for 23

---

1 Or they are all.

women who are with child in those days, or
have children at the breast! For there will be
great distress in the land and a terrible judge-
24 ment upon this people. They will fall at the
sword's point; they will be carried captive
into all countries; and Jerusalem will be
trampled down by foreigners until their day
has run its course.'

The coming of the Son of Man

25 'Portents will appear in sun, moon, and
stars. On earth nations will stand helpless,
not knowing which way to turn from the
26 roar and surge of the sea; men will faint with
terror at the thought of all that is coming
upon the world; for the celestial powers will
27 be shaken. And then they will see the Son
of Man coming on a cloud with great power
28 and glory. When all this begins to happen,
stand upright and hold your heads high,
because your liberation is near.'
29 He told them this parable: 'Look at the
30 fig-tree, or any other tree. As soon as it buds,
you can see for yourselves that summer is
31 near. In the same way, when you see all this
happening, you may know that the kingdom
of God is near.
32 'I tell you this: the present generation will
33 live to see it all. Heaven and earth will pass
away; my words will never pass away.
34 'Keep a watch on yourselves; do not let
your minds be dulled by dissipation and
drunkenness and worldly cares so that the
35 great Day closes upon you suddenly like a
trap; for that day will come on all men,
wherever they are, the whole world over.
36 Be on the alert, praying at all times for
strength to pass safely through all these
imminent troubles and to stand in the
presence of the Son of Man.'
37 His days were given to teaching in the
temple; and then he would leave the city
and spend the night on the hill called Olivet.
38 And in the early morning the people flocked
to listen to him in the temple.*m*

A plot to kill Jesus

22 Now the festival of Unleavened Bread,
2 known as Passover, was approaching, and
the chief priests and the doctors of the law
were trying to devise some means of doing
away with him; for they were afraid of the
people.

Judas Iscariot plans to betray Jesus

3 Then Satan entered into Judas Iscariot, who
4 was one of the Twelve; and Judas went to
the chief priests and officers of the temple
police to discuss ways and means of putting
5 Jesus into their power. They were greatly
pleased and undertook to pay him a sum of

money. He agreed, and began to look out 6
for an opportunity to betray him to them
without collecting a crowd.

Preparations for the Passover

Then came the day of Unleavened Bread, 7
on which the Passover victim had to be
slaughtered, and Jesus sent Peter and John 8
with these instructions: 'Go and prepare
for our Passover supper.' 'Where would you 9
like us to make the preparations?' they
asked. He replied, 'As soon as you set foot 10
in the city a man will meet you carrying a
jar of water. Follow him into the house that

he enters and give this message to the house- 11
holder: "The Master says, 'Where is the
room in which I may eat the Passover with
my disciples?'" He will show you a large 12
room upstairs all set out: make the preparations there.' They went and found every- 13
thing as he had said. So they prepared for
Passover.

The Last Supper

When the time came he took his place at 14
table, and the apostles with him; and he said 15
to them, 'How I have longed*n* to eat this
Passover with you before my death! For I 16
tell you, never again shall I*o* eat it until the
time when it finds its fulfilment in the kingdom of God.'
Then he took a cup, and after giving 1
thanks he said, 'Take this and share it among
yourselves; for I tell you, from this moment 1
I shall drink from the fruit of the vine no
more until the time when the kingdom of
God comes.' And he took bread, gave 1

*m Some witnesses here insert the passage printed on p. 834.
witnesses read For I tell you, I shall not . . .*   *n Or said to them, 'I longed . . .'   o Some*

thanks, and broke it; and he gave it to them, with the words: 'This is my body.'*p*

21 'But mark this—my betrayer is here, his
22 hand with mine on the table. For the Son of Man is going his appointed way; but alas
23 for that man by whom he is betrayed!' At this they began to ask among themselves which of them it could possibly be who was to do this thing.

A jealous dispute

24 Then a jealous dispute broke out: who
25 among them should rank highest? But he said, 'In the world, kings lord it over their subjects; and those in authority are called
26 their country's "Benefactors". Not so with you: on the contrary, the highest among you must bear himself like the youngest, the
27 chief of you like a servant. For who is greater —the one who sits at table or the servant who waits on him? Surely the one who sits at table. Yet here am I among you like a servant.

28 'You are the men who have stood firmly
29 by me in my times of trial; and now I vest in you the kingship which my Father vested
30 in me; you shall eat and drink at my table in my kingdom and sit*q* on thrones as judges of the twelve tribes of Israel.

Jesus foretells Peter's denial

31 'Simon, Simon, take heed: Satan has been
32 given leave to sift all of you like wheat; but for you I have prayed that your faith may not fail; and when you have come to yourself, you must lend strength to your brothers.'
33 'Lord,' he replied, 'I am ready to go with
34 you to prison and death.' Jesus said, 'I tell you, Peter, the cock will not crow tonight until you have three times over denied that you know me.'

Purse, pack, and sword

35 He said to them, 'When I sent you out barefoot without purse or pack, were you ever short of anything?' 'No', they answered.
36 'It is different now,' he said; 'whoever has a purse had better take it with him, and his pack too; and if he has no sword, let him sell his cloak to buy one. For Scripture says,
37 "And he was counted among the outlaws", and these words, I tell you, must find fulfilment in me; indeed, all that is written of me is being fulfilled.' 'Look, Lord,' they said,
38 'we have two swords here.' 'Enough, enough!' he replied.

Jesus prays on the Mount of Olives

39 Then he went out and made his way as usual to the Mount of Olives, accompanied
40 by the disciples. When he reached the place he said to them, 'Pray that you may be spared
41 the hour of testing.' He himself withdrew from them about a stone's throw, knelt
42 down, and began to pray: 'Father, if it be thy will, take this cup away from me. Yet not my will but thine be done.'
43 And now there appeared to him an angel
44 from heaven bringing him strength, and in anguish of spirit he prayed the more urgently; and his sweat was like clots of blood falling to the ground.*r*
45 When he rose from prayer and came to the disciples he found them asleep, worn out by
46 grief. 'Why are you sleeping?' he said. 'Rise and pray that you may be spared the test.'

Jesus is arrested

47 While he was still speaking a crowd appeared with the man called Judas, one of the Twelve, at their head. He came up to Jesus to kiss
48 him; but Jesus said, 'Judas, would you betray the Son of Man with a kiss?'

p Some witnesses add, in whole or in part, and with various arrangements, the following: 'which is given for you; do this as a memorial of me.' (20) In the same way he took the cup after supper, and said, 'This cup, poured out for you, is the new covenant sealed by my blood.' *q Or trial; and as my Father gave me the right to reign, so I give you the right to eat and to drink . . . and to sit . . . r Some witnesses omit And now . . . ground.*

The Mount of Olives

49 When his followers saw what was coming, they said, 'Lord, shall we use our swords?'
50 And one of them struck at the High Priest's
51 servant, cutting off his right ear. But Jesus answered, 'Let them have their way.' Then he touched the man's ear and healed him.*s*
52 Turning to the chief priests, the officers of the temple police, and the elders, who had come to seize him, he said, 'Do you take me for a bandit, that you have come out
53 with swords and cudgels to arrest me? Day after day, when I was in the temple with you, you kept your hands off me. But this is your moment—the hour when darkness reigns.'

Peter disowns Jesus

54 Then they arrested him and led him away. They brought him to the High Priest's house,
55 and Peter followed at a distance. They lit a fire in the middle of the courtyard and sat
56 round it, and Peter sat among them. A serving-maid who saw him sitting in the fire-light stared at him and said, 'This man was
57 with him too.' But he denied it: 'Woman,'
58 he said, 'I do not know him.' A little later someone else noticed him and said, 'You also are one of them.' But Peter said to him,
59 'No, I am not.' About an hour passed and another spoke more strongly still: 'Of course this fellow was with him. He must have been;
60 he is a Galilean.' But Peter said, 'Man, I do not know what you are talking about.' At that moment, while he was still speaking, a
61 cock crew; and the Lord turned and looked at Peter. And Peter remembered the Lord's words, 'Tonight before the cock crows you will disown me three times.'*t*

Jesus mocked and beaten

63 The men who were guarding Jesus mocked
64 at him. They beat him, they blindfolded him, and they kept asking him, 'Now,
65 prophet, who hit you? Tell us that.' And so they went on heaping insults upon him.

Jesus is charged with blasphemy

66 When day broke, the elders of the nation, chief priests, and doctors of the law assembled, and he was brought before their
67 Council. 'Tell us,' they said, 'are you the Messiah?' 'If I tell you,' he replied, 'you will
68 not believe me; and if I ask questions, you
69 will not answer. But from now on, the Son of Man will be seated at the right hand of
70 Almighty God.'*u* 'You are the Son of God, then?' they all said, and he replied, 'It is you
71 who say I am.'*v* They said, 'Need we call further witnesses? We have heard it ourselves from his own lips.'

Jesus before Pilate

With that the whole assembly rose, and they **23** brought him before Pilate. They opened the 2 case against him by saying, 'We found this man subverting our nation, opposing the payment of taxes to Caesar, and claiming to be Messiah, a king.'*w* Pilate asked him, 'Are 3 you the king of the Jews?' He replied, 'The words are yours.'*x* Pilate then said to the 4 chief priests and the crowd, 'I find no case for this man to answer.' But they insisted: 5 'His teaching is causing disaffection among the people all through Judaea. It started from Galilee and has spread as far as this city.'

Herod questions Jesus

When Pilate heard this, he asked if the man 6 was a Galilean, and on learning that he 7 belonged to Herod's jurisdiction he remitted the case to him, for Herod was also in Jerusalem at that time. When Herod saw 8 Jesus he was greatly pleased; having heard about him, he had long been wanting to see him, and had been hoping to see some miracle performed by him. He questioned 9 him at some length without getting any reply; but the chief priests and lawyers 10 appeared and pressed the case against him vigorously. Then Herod and his troops 11 treated him with contempt and ridicule, and sent him back to Pilate dressed in a gorgeous robe. That same day Herod and Pilate be- 12 came friends; till then there had been a standing feud between them.

Jesus is sentenced to death

Pilate now called together the chief priests, 13 councillors, and people, and said to them, 14 'You brought this man before me on a charge of subversion. But, as you see, I have myself examined him in your presence and found nothing in him to support your charges. No more did Herod, for he has 15 referred him back to us. Clearly he has done nothing to deserve death. I therefore pro- 16 pose to let him off with a flogging.' But*y* there 18 was a general outcry, 'Away with him! Give us Barabbas.' (This man had been put in 19 prison for a rising that had taken place in the city, and for murder.) Pilate addressed 20 them again, in his desire to release Jesus, but they shouted back, 'Crucify him, crucify 21 him!' For the third time he spoke to them: 22 'Why, what wrong has he done? I have not found him guilty of any capital offence. I will therefore let him off with a flogging.' But they insisted on their demand, shouting that Jesus should be crucified. Their shouts

---

s Or 'Let me do as much as this', *and touching the man's ear, he healed him.*   *t Some witnesses add* (62) He went outside, and wept bitterly, *as in Matthew* 26. 75.   *u Literally* of the Power of God.   *v Or* You are right, for I am.   *w Or* to be an anointed king.   *x Or* It is as you say.   *y Some witnesses* read (17) At festival time he was obliged to release one person for them; (18) and now . . .

24 prevailed and Pilate decided that they should
25 have their way. He released the man they
asked for, the man who had been put in
prison for insurrection and murder, and
gave Jesus up to their will.

Jesus is crucified

26 As they led him away to execution they
seized upon a man called Simon, from
Cyrene, on his way in from the country, put
the cross on his back, and made him walk
behind Jesus carrying it.

27   Great numbers of people followed, many
women among them, who mourned and
28 lamented over him. Jesus turned to them
and said, 'Daughters of Jerusalem, do not
weep for me; no, weep for yourselves and
29 your children. For the days are surely coming when they will say, "Happy are the barren, the wombs that never bore a child, the
30 breasts that never fed one." Then they will
start saying to the mountains, "Fall on us",
31 and to the hills, "Cover us." For if these
things are done when the wood is green,
what will happen when it is dry?'

32   There were two others with him, criminals
33 who were being led away to execution; and
when they reached the place called The
Skull, they crucified him there, and the
criminals with him, one on his right and the
34 other on his left. Jesus said, 'Father, forgive
them; they do not know what they are
doing.'*z*

They divided his clothes among them by
35 casting lots. The people stood looking on,
and their rulers jeered at him: 'He saved
others; now let him save himself, if this is
36 God's Messiah, his Chosen.' The soldiers
joined in the mockery and came forward
37 offering him their sour wine. 'If you are the
king of the Jews,' they said, 'save yourself.'
38 There was an inscription above his head
which ran: 'This is the king of the Jews.'

39   One of the criminals who hung there with
him taunted him: 'Are not you the Messiah?
40 Save yourself, and us.' But the other rebuked
him: 'Have you no fear of God? You are
41 under the same sentence as he. For us it is
plain justice; we are paying the price for our
42 misdeeds; but this man has done nothing
43 wrong.' And he said, 'Jesus, remember me
when you come to your throne.'*a* He
answered, 'I tell you this: today you shall
be with me in Paradise.'

The death of Jesus

44 By now it was about midday and a darkness
fell over the whole land, which lasted until
45 three in the afternoon; the sun's light failed.
And the curtain of the temple was torn in
46 two. Then Jesus gave a loud cry and said,

'Father, into thy hands I commit my spirit';
and with these words he died. The centurion 47
saw it all, and gave praise to God. 'Beyond
all doubt,' he said, 'this man was innocent.'

The crowd who had assembled for the 48
spectacle, when they saw what had happened, went home beating their breasts.

The burial of Jesus

His friends had all been standing at a dis- 49
tance; the women who had accompanied
him from Galilee stood with them and
watched it all.

Now there was a man called Joseph, a 50
member of the Council, a good, upright
man, who had dissented from their policy 51
and the action they had taken. He came
from the Judaean town of Arimathaea, and
he was one who looked forward to the
kingdom of God. This man now approached 52
Pilate and asked for the body of Jesus.
Taking it down from the cross, he wrapped 53
it in a linen sheet, and laid it in a tomb cut
out of the rock, in which no one had been
laid before. It was Friday, and the Sabbath 54
was about to begin.

---

z Some witnesses omit Jesus said, 'Father . . . doing.'

a Some witnesses read come in royal power.

News of the resurrection

55 The women who had accompanied him from
Galilee followed; they took note of the tomb
56 and observed how his body was laid. Then
they went home and prepared spices and
perfumes; and on the Sabbath they rested
24 in obedience to the commandment. But on
the Sunday morning very early they came
to the tomb bringing the spices they had
2 prepared. Finding that the stone had been
3 rolled away from the tomb, they went inside; but the body was not to be found.
4 While they stood utterly at a loss, all of a
sudden two men in dazzling garments were
5 at their side. They were terrified, and stood
with eyes cast down, but the men said, 'Why
search among the dead for one who lives?[b]
6 Remember what he told you while he was
7 still in Galilee, about the Son of Man: how
he must be given up into the power of sinful men and be crucified, and must rise
8 again on the third day.' Then they recalled
9 his words and, returning from the tomb,
they reported all this to the Eleven and all
the others.
10   The women were Mary of Magdala,
Joanna, and Mary the mother[c] of James,
and they, with the other women, told the
11 apostles. But the story appeared to them to
be nonsense, and they would not believe
them.[d]

The encounter on the road to Emmaus

13 That same day two of them were on their
way to a village called Emmaus, which lay
14 about seven miles from Jerusalem, and they
were talking together about all these happen-
15 ings. As they talked and discussed it with
one another, Jesus himself came up and
16 walked along with them; but something
17 kept them from seeing who it was. He asked
them, 'What is it you are debating as you
walk?' They halted, their faces full of gloom,
18 and one, called Cleopas, answered, 'Are you
the only person staying in Jerusalem not to
know[e] what has happened there in the last
19 few days?' 'What do you mean?' he said.
'All this about Jesus of Nazareth,' they
replied, 'a prophet powerful in speech and
action before God and the whole people;
20 how our chief priests and rulers handed him
over to be sentenced to death, and crucified
21 him. But we had been hoping that he was
the man to liberate Israel. What is more,
22 this is the third day since it happened, and
now some women of our company have
astounded us: they went early to the tomb,
23 but failed to find his body, and returned

with a story that they had seen a vision of
angels who told them he was alive. So some 24
of our people went to the tomb and found
things just as the women had said; but him
they did not see.'
   'How dull you are!' he answered. 'How 25
slow to believe all that the prophets said!
Was the Messiah not bound to suffer thus 26
before entering upon his glory?' Then he 27
began with Moses and all the prophets,
and explained to them the passages which
referred to himself in every part of the
scriptures.
   By this time they had reached the village 28
to which they were going, and he made as if
to continue his journey, but they pressed 29
him: 'Stay with us, for evening draws on,
and the day is almost over.' So he went in
to stay with them. And when he had sat 30
down with them at table, he took bread and
said the blessing; he broke the bread, and
offered it to them. Then their eyes were 31
opened, and they recognized him; and he
vanished from their sight. They said to one 32
another, 'Did we not feel our hearts on fire
as he talked with us on the road and explained the scriptures to us?'
   Without a moment's delay they set out 33
and returned to Jerusalem. There they found
that the Eleven and the rest of the company
had assembled, and were saying, 'It is true: 34
the Lord has risen; he has appeared to
Simon.' Then they gave their account of the 35
events of their journey and told how he had
been recognized by them at the breaking of
the bread.

Jesus appears to his disciples

As they were talking about all this, there he 36
was, standing among them.[f] Startled and 37
terrified, they thought they were seeing a
ghost. But he said, 'Why are you so per- 38
turbed? Why do questionings arise in your
minds? Look at my hands and feet. It is I 39
myself. Touch me and see; no ghost has
flesh and bones as you can see that I have.'[g]
They were still unconvinced, still wondering, 41
for it seemed too good to be true. So he
asked them, 'Have you anything here to
eat?' They offered him a piece of fish they 42
had cooked, which he took and ate before 43
their eyes.

Jesus commissions his disciples

And he said to them, 'This is what I meant 44
by saying, while I was still with you, that
everything written about me in the Law of
Moses and in the prophets and psalms was

---

b Some witnesses insert He is not here: he has been raised.   *c Or* wife, *or* daughter.   *d Some wit-*
nesses add (12) Peter, however, got up and ran to the tomb, and, peering in, saw the wrappings and nothing more;
and he went home amazed at what had happened.   *e Or* Have you been staying by yourself in Jerusalem,
that you do not know . . .   *f Some witnesses insert* And he said to them, 'Peace be with you!'   *g Some*
witnesses insert (40) After saying this he showed them his hands and feet.

45 bound to be fulfilled.' Then he opened their
46 minds to understand the scriptures. 'This',
he said, 'is what is written: that the Messiah
is to suffer death and to rise from the dead
47 on the third day, and that in his name
repentance bringing the forgiveness of sins
is to be proclaimed to all nations. Begin
48 from Jerusalem; it is you who are the wit-
49 nesses to it all. And mark this: I am sending
upon you my Father's promised gift; so

stay here in this city until you are armed
with the power from above.'

The parting at Bethany

Then he led them out as far as Bethany, and 50
blessed them with uplifted hands; and in 51
the act of blessing he parted from them.[h]
And they[i] returned to Jerusalem with great 52
joy, and spent all their time in the temple 53
praising God.

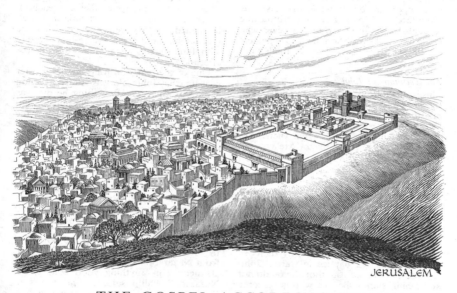

JERUSALEM

THE GOSPEL ACCORDING TO
JOHN

The Word became flesh

1 WHEN ALL THINGS began, the Word
already was.[a] The Word dwelt with God,
2 and what God was, the Word was. The
Word, then, was with God at the beginning,
3 and through him all things came to be; no
single thing was created without him. All
4 that came to be was alive with his life,[b] and
5 that life was the light of men. The light shines
on in the dark, and the darkness has never
mastered it.

There appeared a man named John, sent 6
from God; he came as a witness to testify to 7
the light, that all might become believers
through him. He was not himself the light; 8
he came to bear witness to the light. The 9
real light which enlightens every man was
even then coming into the world.[c]

He was in the world;[d] but the world, 10
though it owed its being to him, did not
recognize him. He entered his own realm, 11
and his own would not receive him. But to 12

h Some witnesses add and was carried up into heaven.   *i Some witnesses insert* worshipped him and . . .

a Or The Word was at the creation.   *b Or* no single created thing came into being without him. There was
life in him . . .   *c Or* The light was in being, light absolute, enlightening every man born into the world.
d Or The Word, then, was in the world.

all who did receive him, to those who have yielded him their allegiance, he gave the
13 right to become children of God, not born of any human stock, or by the fleshly desire of a human father, but the offspring of
14 God himself. So the Word became flesh; he came to dwell among us, and we saw his glory, such glory as befits the Father's only Son, full of grace and truth.

15 Here is John's testimony to him: he cried aloud, 'This is the man I meant when I said, "He comes after me, but takes rank before me"; for before I was born, he already was.'
16 Out of his full store we have all received
17 grace upon grace; for while the Law was given through Moses, grace and truth came
18 through Jesus Christ. No one has ever seen God; but God's only Son, he who is nearest to the Father's heart, he has made him known.[e]

The testimony of John

19 This is the testimony which John gave when the Jews of Jerusalem sent a deputation of priests and Levites to ask him who he was.
20 He confessed without reserve and avowed,
21 'I am not the Messiah.' 'What then? Are you Elijah?' 'No', he replied. 'Are you the
22 prophet we await?' He answered 'No.' 'Then who are you?' they asked. 'We must give an answer to those who sent us. What account
23 do you give of yourself?' He answered in the words of the prophet Isaiah: 'I am a voice crying aloud in the wilderness, "Make the Lord's highway straight."'
24 Some Pharisees who were in the deputa-
25 tion asked him, 'If you are not the Messiah, nor Elijah, nor the prophet, why then are
26 you baptizing?' 'I baptize in water,' John replied, 'but among you, though you do not
27 know him, stands the one who is to come after me. I am not good enough to unfasten
28 his shoes.' This took place at Bethany beyond Jordan, where John was baptizing.

The Lamb of God

29 The next day he saw Jesus coming towards him. 'Look,' he said, 'there is the Lamb of God; it is he who takes away the sin of the
30 world. This is he of whom I spoke when I said, "After me a man is coming who takes rank before me"; for before I was born, he
31 already was. I myself did not know who he was; but the very reason why I came, baptizing in water, was that he might be revealed to Israel.'
32 John testified further: 'I saw the Spirit coming down from heaven like a dove and
33 resting upon him. I did not know him, but he who sent me to baptize in water had told

me, "When you see the Spirit coming down upon someone and resting upon him, you will know that this is he who is to baptize in Holy Spirit." I saw it myself, and I have 34 borne witness. This is God's Chosen One.'[f]

The first disciples

The next day again John was standing with 35 two of his disciples when Jesus passed by. 36 John looked towards him and said, 'There is the Lamb of God.' The two disciples 37 heard him say this, and followed Jesus. When he turned and saw them following 38 him, he asked, 'What are you looking for?' They said, 'Rabbi' (which means a teacher), 'where are you staying?' 'Come and see,' 39 he replied. So they went and saw where he was staying, and spent the rest of the day with him. It was then about four in the afternoon.

One of the two who followed Jesus after 40 hearing what John said was Andrew, Simon Peter's brother. The first thing he did was 41 to find[g] his brother Simon. He said to him, 'We have found the Messiah' (which is the Hebrew for 'Christ'). He brought Simon to 42 Jesus, who looked at him and said, 'You are Simon son of John. You shall be called Cephas' (that is, Peter, the Rock).

Philip and Nathanael

The next day Jesus decided to leave for 43 Galilee. He met Philip, who, like Andrew 44 and Peter, came from Bethsaida, and said to him, 'Follow me.' Philip went to find 45 Nathanael, and told him, 'We have met the man spoken of by Moses in the Law, and by the prophets: it is Jesus son of Joseph, from Nazareth.' 'Nazareth!' Nathanael ex- 46 claimed; 'can anything good come from Nazareth?' Philip said, 'Come and see.' When Jesus saw Nathanael coming, he said, 47 'Here is an Israelite worthy of the name; there is nothing false in him.' Nathanael 48 asked him, 'How do you come to know me?' Jesus replied, 'I saw you under the fig-tree before Philip spoke to you.' 'Rabbi,' said 49 Nathanael, 'you are the Son of God; you are king of Israel.' Jesus answered, 'Is this 50 the ground of your faith, that I told you I saw you under the fig-tree? You shall see greater things than that.' Then he added, 'In 51 truth, in very truth I tell you all, you shall see heaven wide open, and God's angels ascending and descending upon the Son of Man.'

The wedding at Cana-in-Galilee

On the third day there was a wedding at **2** Cana-in-Galilee. The mother of Jesus was there, and Jesus and his disciples were 2

---

e Some witnesses read but the only one, the one nearest to the Father's heart, has made him known; *others read* but the only one, himself God, the nearest to the Father's heart, has made him known.   *f Some witnesses read* This is the Son of God.   *g Some witnesses read* In the morning he found . . .

3 guests also. The wine gave out, so Jesus's
mother said to him, 'They have no wine left.'
4 He answered, 'Your concern, mother, is not
5 mine. My hour has not yet come.' His
mother said to the servants, 'Do whatever he
6 tells you.' There were six stone water-jars
standing near, of the kind used for Jewish
rites of purification; each held from twenty
7 to thirty gallons. Jesus said to the servants,
'Fill the jars with water', and they filled
8 them to the brim. 'Now draw some off', he
ordered, 'and take it to the steward of the
9 feast'; and they did so. The steward tasted
the water now turned into wine, not knowing its source; though the servants who had
drawn the water knew. He hailed the bride-
10 groom and said, 'Everyone serves the best
wine first, and waits until the guests have
drunk freely before serving the poorer sort;
but you have kept the best wine till now.'
11   This deed at Cana-in-Galilee is the first
of the signs by which Jesus revealed his
glory and led his disciples to believe in him.

Jesus drives traders from the temple

12 After this he went down to Capernaum in
company with his mother, his brothers, and
his disciples, but they did not stay there
13 long. As it was near the time of the Jewish
14 Passover, Jesus went up to Jerusalem. There
he found in the temple the dealers in cattle,
sheep, and pigeons, and the money-changers
15 seated at their tables. Jesus made a whip of
cords and drove them out of the temple,
sheep, cattle, and all. He upset the tables of
the money-changers, scattering their coins.
16 Then he turned on the dealers in pigeons:
'Take them out,' he said; 'you must not
17 turn my Father's house into a market.' His
disciples recalled the words of Scripture,
18 'Zeal for thy house will destroy me.' The
Jews challenged Jesus: 'What sign', they
asked, 'can you show as authority for your

action?' 'Destroy this temple,' Jesus replied, 19
'and in three days I will raise it again.' They 20
said, 'It has taken forty-six years to build
this temple. Are you going to raise it again
in three days?' But the temple he was speak- 21
ing of was his body. After his resurrection 22
his disciples recalled what he had said, and
they believed the Scripture and the words
that Jesus had spoken.

Jesus knows what is in a man

While he was in Jerusalem for Passover 23
many gave their allegiance to him when they
saw the signs that he performed. But Jesus for 24
his part would not trust himself to them. He
knew men so well, all of them, that he needed 25
no evidence from others about a man, for
he himself could tell what was in a man.

Jesus and Nicodemus

There was one of the Pharisees named 3
Nicodemus, a member of the Jewish Council, who came to Jesus by night. 'Rabbi,' he 2
said, 'we know that you are a teacher sent
by God; no one could perform these signs
of yours unless God were with him.' Jesus 3
answered, 'In truth, in very truth I tell you,
unless a man has been born over again he
cannot see the kingdom of God.' 'But how 4
is it possible', said Nicodemus, 'for a man
to be born when he is old? Can he enter his
mother's womb a second time and be born?'
Jesus answered, 'In truth I tell you, no one 5
can enter the kingdom of God without
being born from water and spirit. Flesh can 6
give birth only to flesh; it is spirit that gives
birth to spirit. You ought not to be aston- 7
ished, then, when I tell you that you must be
born over again. The wind[h] blows where it 8
wills; you hear the sound of it, but you do
not know where it comes from, or where it
is going. So with everyone who is born from
spirit[h].'

h wind *and* spirit *are translations of the same Greek word, which has both meanings.*

9 Nicodemus replied, 'How is this possible?'
10 'What!' said Jesus. 'Is this famous teacher
11 of Israel ignorant of such things? In very
truth I tell you, we speak of what we know,
and testify to what we have seen, and yet
12 you all reject our testimony. If you disbelieve me when I talk to you about things
on earth, how are you to believe if I should
talk about the things of heaven?
13   'No one ever went up into heaven except
the one who came down from heaven, the
14 Son of Man whose home is in heaven.[i] This
Son of Man must be lifted up as the serpent
15 was lifted up by Moses in the wilderness, so
that everyone who has faith in him may in
him possess eternal life.'

God's love for the world

16 'God loved the world so much that he gave
his only Son, that everyone who has faith
17 in him may not die but have eternal life. It
was not to judge the world that God sent
his Son into the world, but that through him
the world might be saved.'

How men are judged

18 'The man who puts his faith in him does not
come under judgement; but the unbeliever
has already been judged in that he has not
given his allegiance to God's only Son.
19 Here lies the test: the light has come into
the world, but men preferred darkness to
20 light because their deeds were evil. Bad
men all hate the light and avoid it, for fear
21 their practices should be shown up. The
honest man comes to the light so that it
may be clearly seen that God is in all he
does.'

Jesus and John the Baptist

22 After this, Jesus went into Judaea with his
disciples, stayed there with them, and bap-
23 tized. John too was baptizing at Aenon,
near to Salim, because water was plentiful
in that region; and people were constantly
24 coming for baptism. This was before John's
imprisonment.
25   Some of John's disciples had fallen into
26 a dispute with Jews about purification; so
they came to him and said, 'Rabbi, there was
a man with you on the other side of the
Jordan, to whom you bore your witness.
Here he is, baptizing, and crowds are flock-
27 ing to him.' John's answer was: 'A man can
28 have only what God gives him. You yourselves can testify that I said, "I am not the
Messiah; I have been sent as his forerunner."
29 It is the bridegroom to whom the bride
belongs. The bridegroom's friend, who
stands by and listens to him, is overjoyed at
hearing the bridegroom's voice. This joy,

this perfect joy, is now mine. As he grows 30
greater, I must grow less.'

The heavenly and the earthly

He who comes from above is above all 31
others; he who is from the earth belongs to
the earth and uses earthly speech. He who
comes from heaven[j] bears witness to what 32
he has seen and heard, yet no one accepts
his witness. To accept his witness is to attest 33
that God speaks the truth; for he whom 34
God sent utters the words of God, so
measureless is God's gift of the Spirit. The 35
Father loves the Son and has entrusted him
with all authority. He who puts his faith in 36
the Son has hold of eternal life, but he who
disobeys the Son shall not see that life;
God's wrath rests upon him.

Jesus and a Samaritan woman

A report now reached the Pharisees: 'Jesus 4
is winning and baptizing more disciples than
John'; although, in fact, it was only the 2
disciples who were baptizing and not Jesus
himself. When Jesus learned this, he left 3
Judaea and set out once more for Galilee.
He had to pass through Samaria, and on 4 5
his way came to a Samaritan town called
Sychar, near the plot of ground which Jacob
gave to his son Joseph and the spring called 6
Jacob's well. It was about noon, and Jesus,
tired after his journey, sat down by the well.
    The disciples had gone away to the town 8
to buy food. Meanwhile a Samaritan woman 7
came to draw water. Jesus said to her, 'Give
me a drink.' The Samaritan woman said,
'What! You, a Jew, ask a drink of me, a
Samaritan woman?' (Jews and Samaritans,
it should be noted, do not use vessels in
common.[k]) Jesus answered her, 'If only you 10
knew what God gives, and who it is that is
asking you for a drink, you would have
asked him and he would have given you
living water.' 'Sir,' the woman said, 'you 11
have no bucket and this well is deep. How
can you give me "living water"? Are you a 12
greater man than Jacob our ancestor, who
gave us the well, and drank from it himself,
he and his sons, and his cattle too?' Jesus 13
said, 'Everyone who drinks this water will
be thirsty again, but whoever drinks the 14
water that I shall give him will never suffer
thirst any more. The water that I shall give
him will be an inner spring always welling
up for eternal life.' 'Sir,' said the woman, 15
'give me that water, and then I shall not be
thirsty, nor have to come all this way to
draw.'
    Jesus replied, 'Go home, call your husband 16
and come back.' She answered, 'I have no 17
husband.' 'You are right', said Jesus, 'in

---

i Some witnesses omit whose home is in heaven.   *j Some witnesses insert* is above all and . . .   *k Or*
Jews, it should be noted, are not on familiar terms with Samaritans; *some witnesses omit these words.*

18 saying that you have no husband, for, although you have had five husbands, the man with whom you are now living is not your husband; you told me the truth there.'

19 'Sir,' she replied, 'I can see that you are
20 a prophet. Our fathers worshipped on this mountain, but you Jews say that the temple where God should be worshipped is in
21 Jerusalem.' 'Believe me,' said Jesus, 'the time is coming when you will worship the Father neither on this mountain, nor in
22 Jerusalem. You Samaritans worship without knowing what you worship, while we worship what we know. It is from the Jews
23 that salvation comes. But the time approaches, indeed it is already here, when those who are real worshippers will worship the Father in spirit and in truth. Such are the worshippers whom the Father wants.
24 God is spirit, and those who worship him
25 must worship in spirit and in truth.' The woman answered, 'I know that Messiah' (that is Christ) 'is coming. When he comes
26 he will tell us everything.' Jesus said, 'I am he, I who am speaking to you now.'

27 At that moment his disciples returned, and were astonished to find him talking with a woman; but none of them said, 'What do you want?' or, 'Why are you talking with
28 her?' The woman put down her water-jar and went away to the town, where she said
29 to the people, 'Come and see a man who has told me everything I ever did. Could this be
30 the Messiah?' They came out of the town and made their way towards him.

Harvesting the crop

31 Meanwhile the disciples were urging him,
32 'Rabbi, have something to eat.' But he said, 'I have food to eat of which you know no-
33 thing.' At this the disciples said to one another, 'Can someone have brought him
34 food?' But Jesus said, 'It is meat and drink for me to do the will of him who sent me until I have finished his work.
35 'Do you not say, "Four months more and then comes harvest"? But look, I tell you, look round on the fields; they are already
36 white, ripe for harvest. The reaper is drawing his pay and gathering a crop for eternal life, so that sower and reaper may rejoice to-
37 gether. That is how the saying comes true:
38 "One sows, and another reaps." I sent you to reap a crop for which you have not toiled. Others toiled and you have come in for the harvest of their toil.'

Samaritan believers

39 Many Samaritans of that town came to believe in him because of the woman's testimony: 'He told me everything I ever
40 did.' So when these Samaritans had come to him they pressed him to stay with them;
41 and he stayed there two days. Many more became believers because of what they
42 heard from his own lips. They told the woman, 'It is no longer because of what you said that we believe, for we have heard him ourselves; and we know that this is in truth the Saviour of the world.'

An officer's son is cured

43 When the two days were over he set out
44 for Galilee; for Jesus himself declared that a prophet is without honour in his own
45 country. On his arrival in Galilee the Galileans gave him a welcome, because they had seen all that he did at the festival in Jerusalem; they had been at the festival themselves.

46 Once again he visited Cana-in-Galilee, where he had turned the water into wine. An officer in the royal service was there,
47 whose son was lying ill at Capernaum. When he heard that Jesus had come from Judaea into Galilee, he came to him and begged him to go down and cure his son, who was
48 at the point of death. Jesus said to him, 'Will none of you ever believe without seeing signs
49 and portents?' The officer pleaded with him,
50 'Sir, come down before my boy dies.' Then Jesus said, 'Return home; your son will live.' The man believed what Jesus said and
51 started for home. When he was on his way down his servants met him with the news, 'Your boy is going to live.' So he asked them
52 what time it was when he began to recover. They said, 'Yesterday at one in the afternoon
53 the fever left him.' The father noted that this was the exact time when Jesus had said to him, 'Your son will live,' and he and all his household became believers.

54 This was now the second sign which Jesus performed after coming down from Judaea into Galilee.

A cripple at the sheep-pool

5 Later on Jesus went up to Jerusalem for one of the Jewish festivals.[l] Now at the Sheep-
2 Pool in Jerusalem there is a place with five colonnades. Its name in the language of the
3 Jews is Bethesda. In these colonnades there lay a crowd of sick people, blind, lame, and paralysed.[m] Among them was a man who
5 had been crippled for thirty-eight years.
6 When Jesus saw him lying there and was aware that he had been ill a long time, he asked him, 'Do you want to recover?' 'Sir,'
7 he replied, 'I have no one to put me in the pool when the water is disturbed, but while

---

l Some witnesses read for the Jewish festival.

m Some witnesses add waiting for the disturbance of the water; some further insert (4) for from time to time an angel came down into the pool and stirred up the water. The first to plunge in after this disturbance recovered from whatever disease had afflicted him.

I am moving, someone else is in the pool
8 before me.' Jesus answered, 'Rise to your
9 feet, take up your bed and walk.' The man
recovered instantly, took up his stretcher,
and began to walk.
10   That day was a Sabbath. So the Jews said
to the man who had been cured, 'It is the
Sabbath. You are not allowed to carry your
11 bed on the Sabbath.' He answered, 'The
man who cured me said, "Take up your bed
12 and walk."' They asked him, 'Who is the
man who told you to take up your bed and
13 walk?' But the cripple who had been cured
did not know; for the place was crowded and
14 Jesus had slipped away. A little later Jesus
found him in the temple and said to him,
'Now that you are well again, leave your
sinful ways, or you may suffer something
15 worse.' The man went away and told the
Jews that it was Jesus who had cured him.

Jesus answers a charge

16 It was works of this kind done on the Sabbath that stirred the Jews to persecute Jesus.
17 He defended himself by saying, 'My Father
has never yet ceased his work, and I am
18 working too.' This made the Jews still more
determined to kill him, because he was not
only breaking the Sabbath, but, by calling
God his own Father, he claimed equality
with God.

The Father and the Son

19 To this charge Jesus replied, 'In truth, in
very truth I tell you, the Son can do nothing
by himself; he does only what he sees the
Father doing: what the Father does, the
20 Son does. For the Father loves the Son and
shows him all his works, and will show
21 greater yet, to fill you with wonder. As the
Father raises the dead and gives them life,
so the Son gives life to men, as he determines.
22 And again, the Father does not judge anyone, but has given full jurisdiction to the
23 Son; it is his will that all should pay the
same honour to the Son as to the Father.
To deny honour to the Son is to deny it to
the Father who sent him.
24   'In very truth, anyone who gives heed to
what I say and puts his trust in him who
sent me has hold of eternal life, and does
not come up for judgement, but has already
25 passed from death to life. In truth, in very
truth I tell you, a time is coming, indeed it
is already here, when the dead shall hear
the voice of the Son of God, and all who
26 hear shall come to life. For as the Father
has life-giving power in himself, so has the
Son, by the Father's gift.
27   'As Son of Man, he has also been given
28 the right to pass judgement. Do not wonder
at this, because the time is coming when all
29 who are in the grave shall hear his voice and

come out: those who have done right will
rise to life; those who have done wrong will
rise to hear their doom. I cannot act by my- 30
self; I judge as I am bidden, and my sentence
is just, because my aim is not my own will,
but the will of him who sent me.'

The testimony to Jesus

'If I testify on my own behalf, that testi- 31
mony does not hold good. There is another 32
who bears witness for me, and I know that
his testimony holds. Your messengers have 33
been to John; you have his testimony to the
truth. Not that I rely on human testimony, 34
but I remind you of it for your own salvation. John was a lamp, burning brightly, 35
and for a time you were ready to exult in his
light. But I rely on a testimony higher than 36
John's. There is enough to testify that the
Father has sent me, in the works my Father
gave me to do and to finish—the very works
I have in hand. This testimony to me was 37
given by the Father who sent me, although
you never heard his voice, or saw his form.
But his word has found no home in you, 38
for you do not believe the one whom he
sent. You study the scriptures diligently, 39

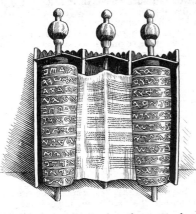

supposing that in having them you have
eternal life; yet, although their testimony
points to me, you refuse to come to me for 40
that life.
    'I do not look to men for honour. But with 41
you it is different, as I know well, for you
have no love for God in you. I have come 43
accredited by my Father, and you have no
welcome for me; if another comes self-
accredited you will welcome him. How can 44
you have faith so long as you receive honour
from one another, and care nothing for the
honour that comes from him who alone is
God? Do not imagine that I shall be your 45
accuser at the Father's tribunal. Your
accuser is Moses, the very Moses on whom

The Sea of Galilee

46 you have set your hope. If you believed Moses you would believe what I tell you, 47 for it was about me that he wrote. But if you do not believe what he wrote, how are you to believe what I say?'

Feeding five thousand

6 Some time later Jesus withdrew to the farther shore of the Sea of Galilee (or 2 Tiberias), and a large crowd of people followed who had seen the signs he performed 3 in healing the sick. Then Jesus went up the 4 hill-side and sat down with his disciples. It was near the time of Passover, the great 5 Jewish festival. Raising his eyes and seeing a large crowd coming towards him, Jesus said to Philip, 'Where are we to buy bread 6 to feed these people?' This he said to test him; Jesus himself knew what he meant to 7 do. Philip replied, 'Twenty pounds[n] would not buy enough bread for every one of them 8 to have a little.' One of his disciples, Andrew, the brother of Simon Peter, said to him, 9 'There is a boy here who has five barley loaves and two fishes; but what is that among 10 so many?' Jesus said, 'Make the people sit down.' There was plenty of grass there, so the men sat down, about five thousand of 11 them. Then Jesus took the loaves, gave thanks, and distributed them to the people as they sat there. He did the same with the fishes, and they had as much as they wanted. 12 When everyone had had enough, he said to his disciples, 'Collect the pieces left over, so 13 that nothing may be lost.' This they did, and filled twelve baskets with the pieces left uneaten of the five barley loaves. 14 When the people saw the sign Jesus had performed, the word went round, 'Surely this must be the prophet that was to come

into the world.' Jesus, aware that they meant 15 to come and seize him to proclaim him king, withdrew again to the hills by himself.

Jesus walks on the water

At nightfall his disciples went down to the 16 sea, got into their boat, and pushed off to 17 cross the water to Capernaum. Darkness had already fallen, and Jesus had not yet joined them. By now a strong wind was blowing 18 and the sea grew rough. When they had 19 rowed about three or four miles they saw Jesus walking on the sea and approaching the boat. They were terrified, but he called 20 out, 'It is I; do not be afraid.' Then they 21 were ready to take him aboard, and immediately the boat reached the land they were making for.

The food of eternal life

Next morning the crowd was standing on 22 the opposite shore. They had seen only one boat there, and Jesus, they knew, had not embarked with his disciples, who had gone away without him. Boats from Tiberias, 23 however, came ashore[o] near the place where the people had eaten the bread over which the Lord gave thanks.[p] When the people 24 saw that neither Jesus nor his disciples were any longer there, they themselves went aboard these boats and made for Capernaum in search of Jesus. They found him on the 25 other side. 'Rabbi,' they said, 'when did you come here?' Jesus replied, 'In very truth 26 I know that you have not come looking for me because you saw signs, but because you ate the bread and your hunger was satisfied. You must work, not for this perishable food, 27 but for the food that lasts, the food of eternal life.

[n] *Literally* 200 denarii.   [o] *Some witnesses read* Other boats from Tiberias came ashore . . .   [p] *Some witnesses omit* over which . . . thanks.

'This food the Son of Man will give you, for he it is upon whom God the Father has

28 set the seal of his authority.' 'Then what must we do', they asked him, 'if we are to

29 work as God would have us work?' Jesus replied, 'This is the work that God requires: believe in the one whom he has sent.'

Jesus the bread of life

30 They said, 'What sign can you give us to see, so that we may believe you? What is the

31 work you do? Our ancestors had manna to eat in the desert; as Scripture says, "He gave

32 them bread from heaven to eat."' Jesus answered, 'I tell you this: the truth is, not that Moses gave you the bread from heaven, but that my Father gives you the real bread

33 from heaven. The bread that God gives comes down*q* from heaven and brings life to

34 the world.' They said to him, 'Sir, give us

35 this bread now and always.' Jesus said to them, 'I am the bread of life. Whoever comes to me shall never be hungry, and whoever

36 believes in me shall never be thirsty. But you, as I said, do not believe although you have

37 seen.*r* All that the Father gives me will come to me, and the man who comes to me I will

38 never turn away. I have come down from heaven, not to do my own will, but the will

39 of him who sent me. It is his will that I should not lose even one of all that he has given me, but raise them all up on the last

40 day. For it is my Father's will that everyone who looks upon the Son and puts his faith in him shall possess eternal life; and I will raise him up on the last day.'

41 At this the Jews began to murmur dis-

42 approvingly because he said, 'I am the bread which came down from heaven.' They said, 'Surely this is Jesus son of Joseph; we know his father and mother. How can he now say, "I have come down from heaven"?'

43 Jesus answered, 'Stop murmuring among

44 yourselves. No man can come to me unless he is drawn by the Father who sent me; and

45 I will raise him up on the last day. It is written in the prophets: "And they shall all be taught by God." Everyone who has listened to the Father and learned from him comes to me.

46 'I do not mean that anyone has seen the Father. He who has come from God has

47 seen the Father, and he alone. In truth, in very truth I tell you, the believer possesses

48 49 eternal life. I am the bread of life. Your forefathers ate the manna in the desert and

50 they are dead. I am speaking of the bread that comes down from heaven, which a man

51 may eat, and never die. I am that living bread which has come down from heaven; if anyone eats this bread he shall live for ever. Moreover, the bread which I will give

is my own flesh; I give it for the life of the world.'

52 This led to a fierce dispute among the Jews. 'How can this man give us his flesh

53 to eat?' they said. Jesus replied, 'In truth, in very truth I tell you, unless you eat the flesh of the Son of Man and drink his blood

54 you can have no life in you. Whoever eats my flesh and drinks my blood possesses eternal life, and I will raise him up on the

55 last day. My flesh is real food; my blood

56 is real drink. Whoever eats my flesh and drinks my blood dwells continually in me

57 and I dwell in him. As the living Father sent me, and I live because of the Father, so he

58 who eats me shall live because of me. This is the bread which came down from heaven; and it is not like the bread which our fathers ate: they are dead, but whoever eats this bread shall live for ever.'

A challenge to the disciples' faith

59 This was spoken in synagogue when Jesus

60 was teaching in Capernaum. Many of his disciples on hearing it exclaimed, 'This is more than we can stomach! Why listen to

61 such talk?' Jesus was aware that his dis-ciples were murmuring about it and asked

62 them, 'Does this shock you? What if you see the Son of Man ascending to the place

63 where he was before? The spirit alone gives life; the flesh is of no avail; the words which I have spoken to you are both spirit and life.

64 And yet there are some of you who have no faith.' For Jesus knew all along who were without faith and who was to betray him.

65 So he said, 'This is why I told you that no one cán come to me unless it has been granted to him by the Father.'

66 From that time on, many of his disciples withdrew and no longer went about with

67 him. So Jesus asked the Twelve, 'Do you

68 also want to leave me?' Simon Peter answered

69 him, 'Lord, to whom shall we go? Your words are words of eternal life. We have faith, and we know that you are the Holy

70 One of God.' Jesus answered, 'Have I not chosen you, all twelve? Yet one of you is

71 a devil.' He meant Judas, son of Simon Iscariot. He it was who would betray him, and he was one of the Twelve.

A challenge from Jesus's brothers

Afterwards Jesus went about in Galilee. He **7** wished to avoid Judaea because the Jews were looking for a chance to kill him. As **2** the Jewish Feast of Tabernacles was close at hand, his brothers said to him, 'You **3** should leave this district and go into Judaea, so that your disciples there may see the great things you are doing. Surely no one can hope **4** to be in the public eye if he works in seclusion.

q Or is he who comes down . . .　　　　*r Some witnesses add me.*

If you really are doing such things as these,
5 show yourself to the world.' For even his
6 brothers had no faith in him. Jesus said to
them, 'The right time for me has not yet
7 come, but any time is right for you. The
world cannot hate you; but it hates me for
8 exposing the wickedness of its ways. Go to
the festival yourselves. I am not⁵ going up
to this festival because the right time for me
9 has not yet come.' With this answer he
stayed behind in Galilee.
10 Later, when his brothers had gone to the
festival, he went up himself, not publicly,
11 but almost in secret. The Jews were looking
for him at the festival and asking, 'Where is

A street in Jerusalem

12 he?', and there was much whispering about
him in the crowds. 'He is a good man', said
some. 'No,' said others, 'he is leading the
13 people astray.' However, no one talked
about him openly, for fear of the Jews.

At the festival

14 When the festival was already half over,
Jesus went up to the temple and began to
15 teach. The Jews were astonished: 'How is
it', they said, 'that this untrained man has
16 such learning?' Jesus replied, 'The teaching

that I give is not my own; it is the teaching
of him who sent me. Whoever has the will 17
to do the will of God shall know whether my
teaching comes from him or is merely my
own. Anyone whose teaching is merely his 18
own, aims at honour for himself. But if a
man aims at the honour of him who sent
him he is sincere, and there is nothing false
in him.

'Did not Moses give you the Law? Yet 19
you all break it. Why are you trying to kill
me?' The crowd answered, 'You are posses- 20
sed! Who wants to kill you?' Jesus replied, 21
'Once only have I done work on the Sabbath, and you are all taken aback. But con- 22
sider: Moses gave you the law of circumcision
(not that it originated with Moses but with
the patriarchs) and you circumcise on the
Sabbath. Well then, if a child is circum- 23
cised on the Sabbath to avoid breaking
the Law of Moses, why are you indignant
with me for giving health on the Sabbath
to the whole of a man's body? Do not 24
judge superficially, but be just in your
judgements.'

Reactions to Jesus in Jerusalem

At this some of the people of Jerusalem 25
began to say, 'Is not this the man they want
to put to death? And here he is, speaking 26
openly, and they have not a word to say to
him. Can it be that our rulers have actually
decided that this is the Messiah? And yet 27
we know where this man comes from, but
when the Messiah appears no one is to
know where he comes from.' Thereupon 28
Jesus cried aloud as he taught in the temple,
'No doubt you know me; no doubt you
know where I come from.ᵗ Yet I have not
come of my own accord. I was sent by the
One who truly is, and him you do not know.
I know him because I come from him and 29
he it is who sent me.' At this they tried to 30
seize him, but no one laid a hand on him
because his appointed hour had not yet
come. Yet among the people many believed 31
in him. 'When the Messiah comes,' they said,
'is it likely that he will perform more signs
than this man?'

The Pharisees overheard these mutter- 32
ings of the people about him, so the chief
priests and the Pharisees sent temple police
to arrest him. Then Jesus said, 'For a little 33
longer I shall be with you; then I am going
away to him who sent me. You will look for 34
me, but you will not find me. Where I am,
you cannot come.' So the Jews said to one 35
another, 'Where does he intend to go, that
we should not be able to find him? Will he
go to the Dispersion among the Greeks, and
teach the Greeks? What did he mean by 36
saying, "You will look for me, but you will

s Some witnesses read not yet.   *t Or* Do you know me? And do you know where I come from?

not find me. Where I am, you cannot come"?[u]

Living water

37 On the last and greatest day of the festival Jesus stood and cried aloud, 'If anyone is 38 thirsty let him come to me; whoever believes in me, let him drink.' As Scripture says, 'Streams of living water shall flow out 39 from within him.'[v] He was speaking of the Spirit which believers in him would receive later; for the Spirit had not yet been given, because Jesus had not yet been glorified.

Divided opinion

40 On hearing this some of the people said, 'This must certainly be the expected prophet.' 41 Others said, 'This is the Messiah.' Others again, 'Surely the Messiah is not to come 42 from Galilee? Does not Scripture say that the Messiah is to be of the family of David, 43 from David's village of Bethlehem?' Thus 44 he caused a split among the people. Some were for seizing him, but no one laid hands on him.

The unbelief of the rulers

45 The temple police came back to the chief priests and Pharisees, who asked, 'Why have 46 you not brought him?' 'No man', they answered, 'ever spoke as this man speaks.' 47 The Pharisees retorted, 'Have you too been 48 misled? Is there a single one of our rulers who has believed in him, or of the Pharisees? 49 As for this rabble, which cares nothing for 50 the Law, a curse is on them.' Then one of their number, Nicodemus (the man who had 51 once visited Jesus), intervened. 'Does our law', he asked them, 'permit us to pass judgement on a man unless we have first given him 52 a hearing and learned the facts?' 'Are you a Galilean too?' they retorted. 'Study the scriptures and you will find that prophets do not come from Galilee.'[w]

Jesus the light of the world

8 12 Once again Jesus addressed the people: 'I am the light of the world. No follower of mine shall wander in the dark; he shall have the 13 light of life.' The Pharisees said to him, 'You are witness in your own cause; your testi- 14 mony is not valid.' Jesus replied, 'My testimony is valid, even though I do bear witness about myself; because I know where I come from, and where I am going. You do not know either where I come from or where I 15 am going. You judge by worldly standards. 16 I pass judgement on no man, but if I do judge, my judgement is valid because it is

not I alone who judge, but I and he who sent me. In your own law it is written that 17 the testimony of two witnesses is valid. Here 18 am I, a witness in my own cause, and my other witness is the Father who sent me.' They asked, 'Where is your father?' Jesus 19 replied, 'You know neither me nor my Father; if you knew me you would know my Father as well.'

These words were spoken by Jesus in the 20 treasury as he taught in the temple. Yet no one arrested him, because his hour had not yet come.

Further questions about Jesus

Again he said to them, 'I am going away. 21 You will look for me, but you will die in your sin; where I am going you cannot come.' The Jews then said, 'Perhaps he will 22 kill himself: is that what he means when he says, "Where I am going you cannot come"?' So Jesus continued, 'You belong to this 23 world below, I to the world above. Your home is in this world, mine is not. That is 24 why I told you that you would die in your sins. If you do not believe that I am what I am, you will die in your sins.' They asked 25 him, 'Who are you?' Jesus answered, 'Why should I speak to you at all?[x] I have much 26 to say about you—and in judgement. But he who sent me speaks the truth, and what I heard from him I report to the world.'

They did not understand that he was 27 speaking to them about the Father. So 28 Jesus said to them, 'When you have lifted up the Son of Man you will know that I am what I am. I do nothing on my own authority, but in all that I say, I have been taught by my Father. He who sent me is present with 29 me, and has not left me alone; for I always do what is acceptable to him.' As he said 30 this, many put their faith in him.

God's children and the devil's children

Turning to the Jews who had believed him, 31 Jesus said, 'If you dwell within the revelation I have brought, you are indeed my disciples; you shall know the truth, and the truth will 32 set you free.' They replied, 'We are Abra- 33 ham's descendants; we have never been in slavery to any man. What do you mean by saying, "You will become free men"?' 'In 34 very truth I tell you', said Jesus, 'that everyone who commits sin is a slave. The slave 35 has no permanent standing in the household, but the son belongs to it for ever. If 36 then the Son sets you free, you will indeed be free.

'I know that you are descended from 37

u Some witnesses here insert the passage printed on p. 834.   *v Or 'If any man is thirsty let him come to me* and drink. He who believes in me, as Scripture says, streams of living water shall flow out from within him.' *w Some witnesses here insert the passage 7. 53 —8. 11, which is printed on p. 834.*   *x Or What I have told* you all along.

Abraham, but you are bent on killing me because my teaching makes no headway 38 with you. I am revealing in words what I saw in my Father's presence; and you are revealing in action what you learned from 39 your father.' They retorted, 'Abraham is our father.' 'If you were Abraham's children', Jesus replied, 'you would do as 40 Abraham did.*y* As it is, you are bent on killing me, a man who told you the truth, as I heard it from God. That is not how 41 Abraham acted. You are doing your own father's work.'

42 They said, 'We are not base-born; God is our father, and God alone.' Jesus said, 'If God were your father, you would love me, for God is the source of my being, and from 43 him I come. I have not come of my own accord; he sent me. Why do you not understand my language? It is because my revelation is beyond your grasp.

44 'Your father is the devil and you choose to carry out your father's desires. He was a murderer from the beginning, and is not rooted in the truth; there is no truth in him. When he tells a lie he is speaking his own language, for he is a liar and the father of 45 lies. But I speak the truth and therefore you 46 do not believe me. Which of you can prove me in the wrong?*z* If what I say is true, why 47 do you not believe me? He who has God for his father listens to the words of God. You are not God's children; that is why you do not listen.'

Abraham and Jesus

48 The Jews answered, 'Are we not right in saying that you are a Samaritan, and that 49 you are possessed?' 'I am not possessed,' said Jesus; 'I am honouring my Father, but 50 you dishonour me. I do not care about my own glory; there is one who does care, and 51 he is judge. In very truth I tell you, if anyone obeys my teaching he shall never know what it is to die.'

52 The Jews said, 'Now we are certain that you are possessed. Abraham is dead; the prophets are dead; and yet you say, "If anyone obeys my teaching he shall not know 53 what it is to die." Are you greater than our father Abraham, who is dead? The prophets are dead too. What do you claim to be?'

54 Jesus replied, 'If I glorify myself, that glory of mine is worthless. It is the Father who glorifies me, he of whom you say, "He 55 is our God", though you do not know him. But I know him; if I said that I did not know him I should be a liar like you. But in truth I know him and obey his word.

'Your father Abraham was overjoyed to 56 see my day; he saw it and was glad.' The 57 Jews protested, 'You are not yet fifty years old. How can you have seen Abraham?'*a* Jesus said, 'In very truth I tell you, before 58 Abraham was born, I am.'

They picked up stones to throw at him, 59 but Jesus was not to be seen; and he left the temple.*b*

Jesus gives sight to a man born blind

As he went on his way Jesus saw a man blind **9** from his birth. His disciples put the question, 2 'Rabbi, who sinned, this man or his parents? Why was he born blind?' 'It is not that this 3 man or his parents sinned,' Jesus answered; 'he was born blind so that God's power might be displayed in curing him. While 4 daylight lasts we*c* must carry on the work of him who sent me; night comes, when no one can work. While I am in the world I am the 5 light of the world.'

With these words he spat on the ground 6 and made a paste with the spittle; he spread it on the man's eyes, and said to him, 'Go 7 and wash in the pool of Siloam.' (The name means 'sent'.) The man went away and washed, and when he returned he could see.

His neighbours and those who were 8 accustomed to see him begging said, 'Is not this the man who used to sit and beg?' Others 9 said, 'Yes, this is the man.' Others again said, 'No, but it is someone like him.' The man himself said, 'I am the man.' They 10 asked him, 'How were your eyes opened?' He replied, 'The man called Jesus made a 11 paste and smeared my eyes with it, and told me to go to Siloam and wash. I went and washed, and gained my sight.' 'Where is he?' 12 they asked. He answered, 'I do not know.'

The healing investigated

The man who had been blind was brought 13 before the Pharisees. As it was a Sabbath 14 day when Jesus made the paste and opened his eyes, the Pharisees now asked him by 15 what means he had gained his sight. The man told them, 'He spread a paste on my eyes; then I washed, and now I can see.' Some of the Pharisees said, 'This fellow is 16 no man of God; he does not keep the Sabbath.' Others said, 'How could such signs come from a sinful man?' So they took different sides. Then they continued to question 17 him: 'What have you to say about him? It was your eyes he opened.' He answered, 'He is a prophet.'

The Jews would not believe that the man 18 had been blind and had gained his sight,

19 until they had summoned his parents and questioned them: 'Is this man your son? Do you say that he was born blind? How is it
20 that he can see now?' The parents replied, 'We know that he is our son, and that he
21 was born blind. But how it is that he can now see, or who opened his eyes, we do not know. Ask him; he is of age; he will speak
22 for himself.' His parents gave this answer because they were afraid of the Jews; for the Jewish authorities had already agreed that anyone who acknowledged Jesus as Messiah should be banned from the syna-
23 gogue. That is why the parents said, 'He is of age; ask him.'
24 So for the second time they summoned the man who had been blind, and said, 'Speak the truth before God. We know that
25 this fellow is a sinner.' 'Whether or not he is a sinner, I do not know', the man replied. 'All I know is this: once I was blind, now
26 I can see.' 'What did he do to you?' they
27 asked. 'How did he open your eyes?' 'I have told you already,' he retorted, 'but you took no notice. Why do you want to hear it again? Do you also want to become his
28 disciples?' Then they became abusive. 'You are that man's disciple,' they said, 'but we
29 are disciples of Moses. We know that God spoke to Moses, but as for this fellow, we do not know where he comes from.'
30 The man replied, 'What an extraordinary thing! Here is a man who has opened my eyes, yet you do not know where he comes
31 from! It is common knowledge that God does not listen to sinners; he listens to any-
32 one who is devout and obeys his will. To open the eyes of a man born blind—it is
33 unheard of since time began. If that man had not come from God he could have done
34 nothing.' 'Who are you to give us lessons,' they retorted, 'born and bred in sin as you are?' Then they expelled him from the syna-gogue.
35 Jesus heard that they had expelled him. When he found him he asked, 'Have you
36 faith in the Son of Man*d*?' The man an-swered, 'Tell me who he is, sir, that I should
37 put my faith in him.' 'You have seen him,' said Jesus; 'indeed, it is he who is speaking
38 to you.' 'Lord, I believe', he said, and bowed before him.

Blindness and judgement

39 Jesus said, 'It is for judgement that I have come into this world—to give sight to the sightless and to make blind those who see.'
40 Some Pharisees in his company asked, 'Do
41 you mean that we are blind?' 'If you were blind,' said Jesus, 'you would not be guilty, but because you say "We see", your guilt remains.'

The sheepfold

'In truth I tell you, in very truth, the man 10 who does not enter the sheepfold by the door, but climbs in some other way, is nothing but a thief or a robber. The man 2 who enters by the door is the shepherd in charge of the sheep. The door-keeper admits 3 him, and the sheep hear his voice; he calls his own sheep by name, and leads them out. When he has brought them all out, he goes 4 ahead and the sheep follow, because they know his voice. They will not follow a 5 stranger; they will run away from him, because they do not recognize the voice of strangers.'

This was a parable that Jesus told them, 6 but they did not understand what he meant by it.

Jesus the good shepherd

So Jesus spoke again: 'In truth, in very truth 7 I tell you, I am the door of the sheepfold. The sheep paid no heed to any who came 8 before me, for these were all thieves and robbers. I am the door; anyone who comes 9 into the fold through me shall be safe. He shall go in and out and shall find pasturage. 'The thief comes only to steal, to kill, to 10 destroy; I have come that men may have life, and may have it in all its fullness. I am 11 the good shepherd; the good shepherd lays down his life for the sheep. The hireling, 12 when he sees the wolf coming, abandons the sheep and runs away, because he is no shep-herd and the sheep are not his. Then the wolf harries the flock and scatters the sheep. The man runs away because he is a hireling 13 and cares nothing for the sheep.

'I am the good shepherd; I know my own 14 sheep and my sheep know me—as the Father 15 knows me and I know the Father—and I lay down my life for the sheep. But there 16 are other sheep of mine, not belonging to this fold, whom I must bring in; and they too will listen to my voice. There will then be one flock, one shepherd. The Father 17 loves me because I lay down my life, to receive it back again. No one has robbed 18 me of it; I am laying it down of my own free will. I have the right to lay it down, and I have the right to receive it back again; this charge I have received from my Father.'

These words once again caused a split 19 among the Jews. Many of them said, 'He is 20 possessed, he is raving. Why listen to him?' Others said, 'No one possessed by an evil 21 spirit could speak like this. Could an evil spirit open blind men's eyes?'

Jesus claims to be God's son

It was winter, and the festival of the Dedica- 22 tion was being held in Jerusalem. Jesus was 23

d Some witnesses read Son of God.

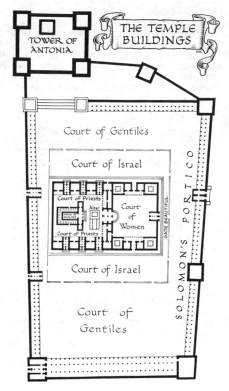

TOWER OF ANTONIA

THE TEMPLE BUILDINGS

Court of Gentiles

Court of Israel

Court of Priests
Court of Women
Altar
HOLY OF HOLIES
Court of Priests

GATE BEAUTIFUL

SOLOMON'S PORTICO

Court of Israel

Court of Gentiles

walking in the temple precincts, in Solomon's
24 Portico. The Jews gathered round him and
asked: 'How long must you keep us in
25 suspense? If you are the Messiah say so
plainly.' 'I have told you,' said Jesus, 'but
you do not believe. My deeds done in my
26 Father's name are my credentials, but because you are not sheep of my flock you
27 do not believe. My own sheep listen to my
voice; I know them and they follow me.
28 I give them eternal life and they shall never
perish; no one shall snatch them from my
29 care. My Father who has given them to me
is greater than all, and no one can snatch
30 them*e* out of the Father's care. My Father
and I are one.'
31   Once again the Jews picked up stones to
32 stone him. At this Jesus said to them, 'I have
set before you many good deeds, done by
my Father's power; for which of these
33 would you stone me?' The Jews replied, 'We
are not going to stone you for any good deed,
but for your blasphemy. You, a mere man,
34 claim to be a god.'*f* Jesus answered, 'Is it not

written in your own Law, "I said: You are
gods"? Those are called gods to whom the 35
word of God was delivered—and Scripture
cannot be set aside. Then why do you charge 36
me with blasphemy because I, consecrated
and sent into the world by the Father, said,
"I am God's son"?
   'If I am not acting as my Father would, 37
do not believe me. But if I am, accept the 38
evidence of my deeds, even if you do not believe me, so that you may recognize and know
that the Father is in me, and I in the Father.'
   This provoked them to one more attempt 39
to seize him. But he escaped from their
clutches.

Jesus is told of the death of Lazarus

Jesus withdrew again across the Jordan, to 40
the place where John had been baptizing
earlier. There he stayed, while crowds came 41
to him. They said, 'John gave us no miraculous sign, but all that he said about this man
was true.' Many came to believe in him there. 42
   There was a man named Lazarus who had 11
fallen ill. His home was at Bethany, the
village of Mary and her sister Martha. (This 2
Mary, whose brother Lazarus had fallen ill,
was the woman who anointed the Lord with
ointment and wiped his feet with her hair.)
The sisters sent a message to him: 'Sir, you 3
should know that your friend lies ill.' When 4
Jesus heard this he said, 'This illness will
not end in death; it has come for the glory
of God, to bring glory to the Son of God.'
And therefore, though he loved Martha and 5
her sister and Lazarus, after hearing of his 6
illness Jesus waited for two days in the place
where he was.
   After this, he said to his disciples, 'Let 7
us go back to Judaea.' 'Rabbi,' his disciples 8
said, 'it is not long since the Jews there were
wanting to stone you. Are you going there
again?' Jesus replied, 'Are there not twelve 9
hours of daylight? Anyone can walk in day-
time without stumbling, because he sees the
light of this world. But if he walks after 10
nightfall he stumbles, because the light fails
him.'
   After saying this he added, 'Our friend 11
Lazarus has fallen asleep, but I shall go and
wake him.' The disciples said, 'Master, if he 12
has fallen asleep he will recover.' Jesus, 13
however, had been speaking of his death,
but they thought that he meant natural sleep.
Then Jesus spoke out plainly: 'Lazarus is 14
dead. I am glad not to have been there; it 15
will be for your good and for the good of
your faith. But let us go to him.' Thomas, 16
called 'the Twin', said to his fellow-disciples,
'Let us also go, that we may die with him.'

e Some witnesses read My Father is greater than all, and that which he has given me no one can snatch . . .;
others read That which my Father has given me is greater than all, and no one can snatch it . . .   *f Or claim
to be God.*

Jesus is resurrection and life

17 On his arrival Jesus found that Lazarus had
18 already been four days in the tomb. Bethany
was just under two miles from Jerusalem,
19 and many of the people had come from the
city to Martha and Mary to condole with
20 them on their brother's death. As soon as
she heard that Jesus was on his way, Martha
went to meet him, while Mary stayed at home.
21　Martha said to Jesus, 'If you had been
here, sir, my brother would not have died.
22 Even now I know that whatever you ask of
23 God, God will grant you.' Jesus said, 'Your
24 brother will rise again.' 'I know that he will
rise again', said Martha, 'at the resurrection
25 on the last day.' Jesus said, 'I am the resurrection and I am life.*g* If a man has faith in
me, even though he die, he shall come to
26 life; and no one who is alive and has faith
27 shall ever die. Do you believe this?' 'Lord,
I do,' she answered; 'I now believe that you
are the Messiah, the Son of God who was
to come into the world.'
28　With these words she went to call her
sister Mary, and taking her aside, she said,
'The Master is here; he is asking for you.'
29 When Mary heard this she rose up quickly
30 and went to him. Jesus had not yet reached
the village, but was still at the place where
31 Martha had met him. The Jews who were
in the house condoling with Mary, when they
saw her start up and leave the house, went
after her, for they supposed that she was
going to the tomb to weep there.

Jesus weeps at the tomb

32 So Mary came to the place where Jesus was.
As soon as she caught sight of him she fell
at his feet and said, 'O sir, if you had only
been here my brother would not have died.'
33 When Jesus saw her weeping and the Jews
her companions weeping, he sighed heavily
34 and was deeply moved. 'Where have you
laid him?' he asked. They replied, 'Come
35 36 and see, sir.' Jesus wept. The Jews said,
37 'How dearly he must have loved him!' But
some of them said, 'Could not this man, who
opened the blind man's eyes, have done
something to keep Lazarus from dying?'

Lazarus is raised from the dead

38 Jesus again sighed deeply; then he went over
to the tomb. It was a cave, with a stone
39 placed against it. Jesus said, 'Take away the
stone.' Martha, the dead man's sister, said
to him, 'Sir, by now there will be a stench;
40 he has been there four days.' Jesus said,
'Did I not tell you that if you have faith you
41 will see the glory of God?' So they removed
the stone.
　Then Jesus looked upwards and said,
'Father, I thank thee; thou hast heard me.

I knew already that thou always hearest me, 42
but I spoke for the sake of the people standing round, that they might believe that thou
didst send me.'
　Then he raised his voice in a great cry: 43
'Lazarus, come forth.' The dead man came 44
out, his hands and feet swathed in linen
bands, his face wrapped in a cloth. Jesus
said, 'Loose him; let him go.'

A plot to kill Jesus

Now many of the Jews who had come to 45
visit Mary and had seen what Jesus did, put
their faith in him. But some of them went 46
off to the Pharisees and reported what he
had done.
　Thereupon the chief priests and the 47
Pharisees convened a meeting of the Council.
'What action are we taking?' they said. 'This
man is performing many signs. If we leave 48
him alone like this the whole populace
will believe in him. Then the Romans will
come and sweep away our temple and our
nation.' But one of them, Caiaphas, who 49
was High Priest that year, said, 'You know
nothing whatever; you do not use your 50
judgement; it is more to your interest that
one man should die for the people, than that
the whole nation should be destroyed.' He 51
did not say this of his own accord, but as
the High Priest in office that year, he was
prophesying that Jesus would die for the
nation—would die not for the nation alone 52
but to gather together the scattered children
of God. So from that day on they plotted 53
his death.
　Accordingly Jesus no longer went about 54
publicly in Judaea, but left that region for
the country bordering on the desert, and
came to a town called Ephraim, where he
stayed with his disciples.
　The Jewish Passover was now at hand, 55
and many people went up from the country
to Jerusalem to purify themselves before the
festival. They looked out for Jesus, and as 56
they stood in the temple they asked one
another, 'What do you think? Perhaps he is
not coming to the festival.' Now the chief 57
priests and the Pharisees had given orders
that anyone who knew where he was should
give information, so that they might arrest
him.

Mary anoints Jesus's feet

Six days before the Passover festival Jesus **12**
came to Bethany, where Lazarus lived whom
he had raised from the dead. There a supper 2
was given in his honour, at which Martha
served, and Lazarus sat among the guests
with Jesus. Then Mary brought a pound of 3
very costly perfume, pure oil of nard, and
anointed the feet of Jesus and wiped them

---

g Some witnesses omit and I am life.

Nard

with her hair, till the house was filled with
4 the fragrance. At this, Judas Iscariot, a
disciple of his—the one who was to betray
5 him—said, 'Why was this perfume not sold
for thirty pounds[h] and given to the poor?'
6 He said this, not out of any care for the poor,
but because he was a thief; he used to pilfer
the money put into the common purse,
7 which was in his charge. 'Leave her alone',
said Jesus. 'Let her keep it till the day when
8 she prepares for my burial; for you have
the poor among you always, but you will
not always have me.'[i]

A plot to kill Lazarus also

9 A great number of the Jews heard that he
was there, and came not only to see Jesus
but also Lazarus whom he had raised from
10 the dead. The chief priests then resolved to
11 do away with Lazarus as well, since on his
account many Jews were going over to
Jesus and putting their faith in him.

Jesus rides into Jerusalem

12 The next day the great body of pilgrims who
had come to the festival, hearing that Jesus
13 was on the way to Jerusalem, took palm
branches and went out to meet him, shouting, 'Hosanna! Blessings on him who comes
in the name of the Lord! God bless the king
14 of Israel!' Jesus found a donkey and mounted it, in accordance with the text of Scrip-
15 ture: 'Fear no more, daughter of Zion; see,
your king is coming, mounted on an ass's
colt.'

16 At the time his disciples did not understand this, but after Jesus had been glorified
they remembered that this had been written
about him, and that this had happened to
17 him. The people who were present when he
called Lazarus out of the tomb and raised
him from the dead told what they had seen
18 and heard. That is why the crowd went to
meet him; they had heard of this sign
19 that he had performed. The Pharisees said
to one another, 'You see you are doing no
good at all; why, all the world has gone after
him!'

Jesus sought after by Greeks

20 Among those who went up to worship at
21 the festival were some Greeks. They came
to Philip, who was from Bethsaida in Galilee, and said to him, 'Sir, we should like to
22 see Jesus.' So Philip went and told Andrew,
23 and the two of them went to tell Jesus. Then
Jesus replied: 'The hour has come for the
24 Son of Man to be glorified. In truth, in very
truth I tell you, a grain of wheat remains a
solitary grain unless it falls into the ground
and dies; but if it dies, it bears a rich harvest.
25 The man who loves himself is lost, but he
who hates himself in this world will be kept
26 safe for eternal life. If anyone serves me, he
must follow me; where I am, my servant
will be. Whoever serves me will be honoured
by my Father.'

In Jerusalem

A voice from heaven

27 'Now my soul is in turmoil, and what am I to say? Father, save me from this hour.[j] No, it was for this that I came to this hour.
28 Father, glorify thy name.' A voice sounded from heaven: 'I have glorified it, and I will
29 glorify it again.' The crowd standing by said it was thunder, while others said, 'An angel
30 has spoken to him.' Jesus replied, 'This
31 voice spoke for your sake, not mine. Now is the hour of judgement for this world; now shall the Prince of this world be driven
32 out. And I shall draw all men to myself,
33 when I am lifted up from the earth.' This he said to indicate the kind of death he was to die.
34 The people answered, 'Our Law teaches us that the Messiah continues for ever. What do you mean by saying that the Son of Man must be lifted up? What Son of Man
35 is this?' Jesus answered them: 'The light is among you still, but not for long. Go on your way while you have the light, so that darkness may not overtake you. He who journeys in the dark does not know where he
36 is going. While you have the light, trust to the light, so that you may become men of light.' After these words Jesus went away from them into hiding.

Prophecy fulfilled

37 In spite of the many signs which Jesus had performed in their presence they would not
38 believe in him, for the prophet Isaiah's utterance had to be fulfilled: 'Lord, who has believed what we reported, and to whom
39 has the Lord's power been revealed?' So it was that they could not believe, for there is
40 another saying of Isaiah's: 'He has blinded their eyes and dulled their minds, lest they should see with their eyes, and perceive with their minds, and turn to me to heal them.'
41 Isaiah said this because[k] he saw his glory and spoke about him.
42 For all that, even among those in authority a number believed in him, but would not acknowledge him on account of the Pharisees, for fear of being banned from the
43 synagogue. For they valued their reputation with men rather than the honour which comes from God.

Not to judge, but to save

44 So Jesus cried aloud: 'When a man believes in me, he believes in him who sent me rather
45 than in me; seeing me, he sees him who sent
46 me. I have come into the world as light, so that no one who has faith in me should
47 remain in darkness. But if anyone hears my words and pays no regard to them, I am not his judge; I have not come to judge the world, but to save the world. There is a
48 judge for the man who rejects me and does not accept my words; the word that I spoke
49 will be his judge on the last day. I do not speak on my own authority, but the Father who sent me has himself commanded me
50 what to say and how to speak. I know that his commands are eternal life. What the Father has said to me, therefore—that is what I speak.'

Jesus washes his disciples' feet

13 It was before the Passover festival. Jesus knew that his hour had come and he must leave this world and go to the Father. He had always loved his own who were in the world, and now he was to show the full extent of his love.
2 The devil had already put it into the mind of Judas son of Simon Iscariot to betray him. During supper, Jesus, well aware
3 that the Father had entrusted everything to him, and that he had come from God and
4 was going back to God, rose from table, laid aside his garments, and taking a towel,
5 tied it round him. Then he poured water into a basin, and began to wash his disciples' feet and to wipe them with the towel.
6 When it was Simon Peter's turn, Peter said to him, 'You, Lord, washing my feet?'
7 Jesus replied, 'You do not understand now what I am doing, but one day you will.'
8 Peter said, 'I will never let you wash my feet.' 'If I do not wash you,' Jesus replied,
9 'you are not in fellowship with me.' 'Then, Lord,' said Simon Peter, 'not my feet only; wash my hands and head as well!'
10 Jesus said, 'A man who has bathed needs no further washing;[l] he is altogether clean; and you are clean, though not every one of
11 you.' He added the words 'not every one of you' because he knew who was going to betray him.
12 After washing their feet and taking his garments again, he sat down. 'Do you understand what I have done for you?' he
13 asked. 'You call me "Master" and "Lord", and rightly so, for that is what I am. Then
14 if I, your Lord and Master, have washed your feet, you also ought to wash one another's feet. I have set you an example:
15 you are to do as I have done for you. In
16 very truth I tell you, a servant is not greater than his master, nor a messenger than the
17 one who sent him. If you know this, happy are you if you act upon it.
18 'I am not speaking about all of you; I know whom I have chosen. But there is a text of Scripture to be fulfilled: "He who eats
19 bread with me has turned against me."[m] I tell you this now, before the event, so that when

---

[j] Or . . . turmoil. Shall I say, "Father, save me from this hour"?　　[k] Some witnesses read when.　　[l] Some witnesses read needs only to wash his feet.　　[m] Literally has lifted his heel against me.

it happens you may believe that I am what I
20 am. In very truth I tell you, he who receives
any messenger of mine receives me; receiving
me, he receives the One who sent me.'

Treachery among the twelve

21 After saying this, Jesus exclaimed in deep
agitation of spirit, 'In truth, in very truth
I tell you, one of you is going to betray me.'
22 The disciples looked at one another in
bewilderment: whom could he be speaking
23 of? One of them, the disciple he loved, was
24 reclining close beside Jesus. So Simon Peter
nodded to him and said, 'Ask who it is he
25 means.' That disciple, as he reclined, leaned
back close to Jesus and asked, 'Lord, who
26 is it?' Jesus replied, 'It is the man to whom
I give this piece of bread when I have dipped
it in the dish.' Then, after dipping it in the
dish, he took it out and gave it to Judas son
27 of Simon Iscariot. As soon as Judas had
received it Satan entered him. Jesus said to
28 him, 'Do quickly what you have to do.' No
one at the table understood what he meant
29 by this. Some supposed that, as Judas was
in charge of the common purse, Jesus was
telling him to buy what was needed for the
festival, or to make some gift to the poor.
30 As soon as Judas had received the bread he
went out. It was night.

A new commandment

31 When he had gone out Jesus said, 'Now the
Son of Man is glorified, and in him God is
32 glorified. If God is glorified in him,[n] God
will also glorify him in himself; and he will
33 glorify him now. My children, for a little
longer I am with you; then you will look for
me, and, as I told the Jews, I tell you now,
34 where I am going you cannot come. I give
you a new commandment: love one another;
as I have loved you, so you are to love one
35 another. If there is this love among you, then
all will know that you are my disciples.'

Jesus foretells Peter's denial

36 Simon Peter said to him, 'Lord, where are
you going?' Jesus replied, 'Where I am going
you cannot follow me now, but one day you
37 will.' Peter said, 'Lord, why cannot I follow
you now? I will lay down my life for you.'
38 Jesus answered, 'Will you indeed lay down
your life for me? I tell you in very truth, before the cock crows you will have denied me
three times.'

Jesus the way to the Father

14 'Set your troubled hearts at rest. Trust in
2 God always; trust also in me. There are
many dwelling-places in my Father's house;
if it were not so I should have told you; for
I am going there on purpose to prepare a
place for you.[o] And if I go and prepare a 3
place for you, I shall come again and receive
you to myself, so that where I am you may
be also; and my way there is known to you.'[p] 4
Thomas said, 'Lord, we do not know where, 5
you are going, so how can we know the way?'
Jesus replied, 'I am the way; I am the truth 6
and I am life; no one comes to the Father
except by me.

'If you knew me you would know my 7
Father too.[q] From now on you do know him;
you have seen him.' Philip said to him, 8
'Lord, show us the Father and we ask no
more.' Jesus answered, 'Have I been all this 9
time with you, Philip, and you still do not
know me? Anyone who has seen me has
seen the Father. Then how can you say,
"Show us the Father"? Do you not believe 10
that I am in the Father, and the Father in
me? I am not myself the source of the words
I speak to you: it is the Father who dwells
in me doing his own work. Believe me when 11
I say that I am in the Father and the Father
in me; or else accept the evidence of the
deeds themselves. In truth, in very truth I 12
tell you, he who has faith in me will do what
I am doing; and he will do greater things still
because I am going to the Father. Indeed 13
anything you ask in my name I will do, so
that the Father may be glorified in the Son.
If you ask[r] anything in my name I will do it.' 14

The Holy Spirit promised

'If you love me you will obey my commands; 15
and I will ask the Father, and he will give 16
you another to be your Advocate, who will
be with you for ever—the Spirit of truth. 17
The world cannot receive him, because the
world neither sees nor knows him; but you
know him, because he dwells with you and
is[s] in you. I will not leave you bereft; I am 18
coming back to you. In a little while the 19
world will see me no longer, but you will
see me; because I live, you too will live; then 20
you will know that I am in my Father, and
you in me and I in you. The man who has 21
received my commands and obeys them—
he it is who loves me; and he who loves me
will be loved by my Father; and I will love
him and disclose myself to him.'

Judas asked him—the other Judas, not 22
Iscariot—'Lord, what can have happened,
that you mean to disclose yourself to us
alone and not to the world?' Jesus replied, 23
'Anyone who loves me will heed what I say;
then my Father will love him, and we will

---

n Some witnesses omit If God . . . in him.   *o Or* if it were not so, should I have told you that I am going
to prepare a place for you?   *p Some witnesses read* also. You know where I am going and you know the
way.   *q Some witnesses read* If you know me you will know my Father too.   *r Some witnesses insert* me.
s Some witnesses read shall be.

I spoke to you. Dwell in me, as I in you. No 4 branch can bear fruit by itself, but only if it remains united with the vine; no more can you bear fruit, unless you remain united with me.

'I am the vine, and you the branches. He 5 who dwells in me, as I dwell in him, bears much fruit; for apart from me you can do nothing. He who does not dwell in me is 6 thrown away like a withered branch. The withered branches are heaped together, thrown on the fire, and burnt.

'If you dwell in me, and my words dwell 7 in you, ask what you will, and you shall have it. This is my Father's glory, that you may 8 bear fruit in plenty and so be my disciples.*u* As the Father has loved me, so I have loved 9 you. Dwell in my love. If you heed my com- 10 mands, you will dwell in my love, as I have heeded my Father's commands and dwell in his love.

'I have spoken thus to you, so that my 11 joy may be in you, and your joy complete.*v* This is my commandment: love one another, 12 as I have loved you. There is no greater love 13 than this, that a man should lay down his life for his friends. You are my friends, if 14 you do what I command you. I call you 15 servants no longer; a servant does not know what his master is about. I have called you friends, because I have disclosed to you everything that I heard from my Father. You did not choose me: I chose you. I 16 appointed you to go on and bear fruit, fruit that shall last; so that the Father may give you all that you ask in my name. This is my 17 commandment to you: love one another.'

The world's hatred of Jesus

'If the world hates you, it hated me first, as 18 you know well.*w* If you belonged to the 19 world, the world would love its own; but because you do not belong to the world, because I have chosen you out of the world, for that reason the world hates you. Remem- 20 ber what I said: "A servant is not greater

come to him and make our dwelling with 24 him; but he who does not love me does not heed what I say. And the word you hear is not mine: it is the word of the Father who 25 sent me. I have told you all this while I am 26 still here with you; but your Advocate, the Holy Spirit whom the Father will send in my name, will teach you everything, and will call to mind all that I have told you.'

The parting gift of peace

27 'Peace is my parting gift to you, my own peace, such as the world cannot give. Set your troubled hearts at rest, and banish 28 your fears. You heard me say, "I am going away, and coming back to you." If you loved me you would have been glad to hear that I was going to the Father; for the Father 29 is greater than I. I have told you now, beforehand, so that when it happens you may have faith.

30 'I shall not talk much longer with you, for the Prince of this world approaches. He has 31 no rights over me; but the world must be shown that I love the Father, and do exactly as he commands; so up, let us go forward!'*t*

The vine and the branches

15 'I am the real vine, and my Father is the 2 gardener. Every barren branch of mine he cuts away; and every fruiting branch he 3 cleans, to make it more fruitful still. You have already been cleansed by the word that

---

t Or for the Prince of this world is coming, though he has nothing in common with me. But he is coming so that the world may recognize that I love the Father, and do exactly as he commands. Up, and let us go forward to meet him!   *u Some witnesses read* that you may bear fruit in plenty. Thus you will be my disciples.   *v Or* so that I may have joy in you and your joy may be complete.   *w Or* bear in mind that it hated me first.

than his master." As they persecuted me, they will persecute you; they will follow your teaching as little as they have followed mine. 21 It is on my account that they will treat you thus, because they do not know the One who sent me.

22 'If I had not come and spoken to them, they would not be guilty of sin; but now they 23 have no excuse for their sin: he who hates 24 me, hates my Father. If I had not worked among them and accomplished what no other man has done, they would not be guilty of sin; but now they have both seen 25 and hated both me and my Father.ˣ However, this text in their Law had to come trueːʸ "They hated me without reason." '

When the Holy Spirit comes

26 'But when your Advocate has come, whom I will send you from the Father—the Spirit of truth that issues from the Father—he will 27 bear witness to me. And you also are my witnesses, because you have been with me from the first.

6 'I have told you all this to guard you 2 against the breakdown of your faith. They will ban you from the synagogue; indeed, the time is coming when anyone who kills you will suppose that he is performing a 3 religious duty. They will do these things because they do not know either the Father 4 or me. I have told you all this so that when the time comes for it to happen you may remember my warning. I did not tell you this at first, because then I was with you; 5 but now I am going away to him who sent me. None of you asks me "Where are you 6 going?" Yet you are plunged into grief 7 because of what I have told you. Nevertheless I tell you the truth: it is for your good that I am leaving you. If I do not go, your Advocate will not come, whereas if I 8 go, I will send him to you. When he comes, he will confute the world, and show where 9 wrong and right and judgement lie. He will convict them of wrong, by their refusal to 10 believe in me; he will convince them that right is on my side, by showing that I go to the Father when I pass from your sight; 11 and he will convince them of divine judgement, by showing that the Prince of this world stands condemned.

12 'There is still much that I could say to you, but the burden would be too great for 13 you now. However, when he comes who is the Spirit of truth, he will guide you into all the truth; for he will not speak on his own authority, but will tell only what he hears; and he will make known to you the 14 things that are coming. He will glorify me,

for everything that he makes known to you he will draw from what is mine. All that 15 the Father has is mine, and that is why I said, "Everything that he makes known to you he will draw from what is mine." '

Grief turned to joy

'A little while, and you see me no more; 16 again a little while, and you will see me.' Some of his disciples said to one another, 17 'What does he mean by this: "A little while, and you will not see me, and again a little while, and you will see me", and by this: "Because I am going to my Father"?' So 18 they asked, 'What is this "little while" that he speaks of? We do not know what he means.'

Jesus knew that they were wanting to 19 question him, and said, 'Are you discussing what I said: "A little while, and you will not see me, and again a little while, and you will see me"? In very truth I tell you, you will 20 weep and mourn, but the world will be glad. But though you will be plunged in grief, your grief will be turned to joy. A woman 21 in labour is in pain because her time has come; but when the child is born she forgets the anguish in her joy that a man has been born into the world. So it is with you: for 22 the moment you are sad at heart; but I shall see you again, and then you will be joyful, and no one shall rob you of your joy. When 23 that day comes you will ask nothing of me. In very truth I tell you, if you ask the Father for anything in my name, he will give it you.ᶻ So far you have asked nothing in my name. 24 Ask and you will receive, that your joy may be complete.'

Parting words to the disciples

'Till now I have been using figures of speech; 25 a time is coming when I shall no longer use figures, but tell you of the Father in plain words. When that day comes you will make 26 your request in my name, and I do not say that I shall pray to the Father for you, for 27 the Father loves you himself, because you have loved me and believed that I came from God. I came from the Father and have come 28 into the world. Now I am leaving the world again and going to the Father.' His disciples 29 said, 'Why, this is plain speaking; this is no figure of speech. We are certain now that 30 you know everything, and do not need to be questioned; because of this we believe that you have come from God.'

Jesus answered, 'Do you now believe? 31 Look,ᵃ the hour is coming, has indeed 32 already come, when you are all to be scattered, each to his home, leaving me alone.

---

x Or but now they have indeed seen my work and yet have hated both me and my Father.   *y Or* let this text in their Law come true.   *z Some witnesses read* if you ask the Father for anything, he will give it you in my name.   *a Or* At the moment you believe; but look . . .

Yet I am not alone, because the Father is
33 with me. I have told you all this so that in
me you may find peace. In the world you will
have trouble. But courage! The victory is
mine; I have conquered the world.'

Jesus prays to his Father

17 After these words Jesus looked up to heaven
and said:
'Father, the hour has come. Glorify thy
2 Son, that the Son may glorify thee. For thou
hast made him sovereign over all mankind,
to give eternal life to all whom thou hast
3 given him. This is eternal life: to know thee
who alone art truly God, and Jesus Christ
whom thou hast sent.
4 'I have glorified thee on earth by completing the work which thou gavest me to do;
5 and now, Father, glorify me in thy own
presence with the glory which I had with
thee before the world began.
6 'I have made thy name known to the men
whom thou didst give me out of the world.
They were thine, thou gavest them to me,
7 and they have obeyed thy command. Now
they know that all thy gifts have come to me
8 from thee; for I have taught them all that
I learned from thee, and they have received
it: they know with certainty that I came
from thee; they have had faith to believe
that thou didst send me.
9 'I pray for them; I am not praying for
the world but for those whom thou hast
10 given me, because they belong to thee. All
that is mine is thine, and what is thine
is mine; and through them has my glory
shone.
11 'I am to stay no longer in the world, but
they are still in the world, and I am on my
way to thee. Holy Father, protect by the
power of thy name those whom thou hast
given me,[b] that they may be one, as we are
12 one. When I was with them, I protected
by the power of thy name those whom
thou hast given me,[c] and kept them safe.
Not one of them is lost except the man
who must be lost, for Scripture has to be
fulfilled.
13 'And now I am coming to thee; but while
I am still in the world I speak these words,
so that they may have my joy within them
14 in full measure. I have delivered thy word
to them, and the world hates them because
they are strangers in the world, as I am.
15 I pray thee, not to take them out of the
world, but to keep them from the evil one.
16 They are strangers in the world, as I am.
17 Consecrate them by the truth;[d] thy word is
18 truth. As thou hast sent me into the world,
19 I have sent them into the world, and for their

sake I now consecrate myself, that they too
may be consecrated by the truth.[d]
'But it is not for these alone that I pray, 20
but for those also who through their words
put their faith in me; may they all be one: 21
as thou, Father, art in me, and I in thee, so
also may they be in us, that the world may
believe that thou didst send me. The glory 22
which thou gavest me I have given to them,
that they may be one, as we are one; I in 23
them and thou in me, may they be perfectly
one. Then the world will learn that thou
didst send me, that thou didst love them as
thou didst me.
'Father, I desire that these men, who are 24
thy gift to me, may be with me where I am,
so that they may look upon my glory, which
thou hast given me because thou didst love
me before the world began. O righteous 25
Father, although the world does not know
thee, I know thee, and these men know that
thou didst send me. I made thy name known 26
to them, and will make it known, so that the
love thou hadst for me may be in them, and
I may be in them.'

Jesus gives himself up

After these words, Jesus went out with his 18
disciples, and crossed the Kedron ravine.
There was a garden there, and he and his
disciples went into it. The place was known 2
to Judas, his betrayer, because Jesus had
often met there with his disciples. So Judas 3
took a detachment of soldiers, and police
provided by the chief priests and the Pharisees, equipped with lanterns, torches, and
weapons, and made his way to the garden.
Jesus, knowing all that was coming upon 4
him, went out to them and asked, 'Who is
it you want?' 'Jesus of Nazareth', they 5
answered. Jesus said, 'I am he.' And there
stood Judas the traitor with them. When 6
he said, 'I am he', they drew back and fell
to the ground. Again Jesus asked, 'Who is 7
it you want?' 'Jesus of Nazareth', they
answered. Then Jesus said, 'I have told you 8
that I am he. If I am the man you want, let
these others go.' (This was to make good his 9
words, 'I have not lost one of those whom
thou gavest me.') Thereupon Simon Peter 10
drew the sword he was wearing and struck
at the High Priest's servant, cutting off his
right ear. (The servant's name was Malchus.)
Jesus said to Peter, 'Sheathe your sword. 11
This is the cup the Father has given me; shall
I not drink it?'

Peter disowns Jesus

The troops with their commander, and the 12
Jewish police, now arrested Jesus and

---

b Or keep in loyalty to thee those whom thou hast given me; *some witnesses read* protect them by the power of
thy name which thou hast given me.　　*c Or* kept in loyalty to thee those whom thou hast given me; *some
witnesses read* protected them by the power of thy name which thou hast given me.　　*d Or* in truth.

13 secured him. They took him first to Annas.*
Annas was father-in-law of Caiaphas, the
14 High Priest for that year*—the same Caiaphas who had advised the Jews that it
would be to their interest if one man died
15 for the whole people. Jesus was followed
by Simon Peter and another disciple. This
disciple, who was acquainted with the High
Priest, went with Jesus into the High Priest's
16 courtyard, but Peter halted at the door outside. So the other disciple, the High Priest's
acquaintance, went out again and spoke to
the woman at the door, and brought Peter
17 in. The maid on duty at the door said to
Peter, 'Are you another of this man's
18 disciples?' 'I am not', he said. The servants
and the police had made a charcoal fire,
because it was cold, and were standing round
it warming themselves. And Peter too was
standing with them, sharing the warmth.

The High Priest questions Jesus

19 The High Priest questioned Jesus about his
20 disciples and about what he taught. Jesus
replied, 'I have spoken openly to all the
world; I have always taught in synagogue
and in the temple, where all Jews congregate;
21 I have said nothing in secret. Why question
me? Ask my hearers what I told them; they
22 know what I said.' When he said this, one
of the police who was standing next to him
struck him on the face, exclaiming, 'Is that
23 the way to answer the High Priest?' Jesus
replied, 'If I spoke amiss, state it in evidence;
if I spoke well, why strike me?'
24 So Annas sent him bound to Caiaphas
the High Priest.*

Peter again disowns Jesus

25 Meanwhile Simon Peter stood warming himself. The others asked, 'Are you another of
his disciples?' But he denied it: 'I am not',
26 he said. One of the High Priest's servants, a
relation of the man whose ear Peter had cut
off, insisted, 'Did I not see you with him in
27 the garden?' Peter denied again; and just
then a cock crew.

Pilate questions Jesus

28 From Caiaphas Jesus was led into the
Governor's headquarters. It was now early
morning, and the Jews themselves stayed
outside the headquarters to avoid defilement,
so that they could eat the Passover meal.*
29 So Pilate went out to them and asked, 'What
30 charge do you bring against this man?' 'If
he were not a criminal,' they replied, 'we
should not have brought him before you.'
31 Pilate said, 'Take him away and try him by
your own law.' The Jews answered, 'We are

not allowed to put any man to death.' Thus 32
they ensured the fulfilment of the words by
which Jesus had indicated the manner of
his death.
Pilate then went back into his head- 33
quarters and summoned Jesus. 'Are you the
king of the Jews?' he asked.* Jesus said, 'Is 34
that your own idea, or have others suggested
it to you?' 'What! am I a Jew?' said Pilate. 35
'Your own nation and their chief priests
have brought you before me. What have
you done?' Jesus replied, 'My kingdom does 36
not belong to this world. If it did, my followers would be fighting to save me from
arrest by the Jews. My kingly authority
comes from elsewhere.' 'You are a king, 37
then?' said Pilate. Jesus answered, '"King"
is your word. My task is to bear witness to
the truth. For this was I born; for this I
came into the world, and all who are not
deaf to truth listen to my voice.' Pilate said, 38
'What is truth?', and with those words went
out again to the Jews. 'For my part', he said,
'I find no case against him. But you have a 39
custom that I release one prisoner for you
at Passover. Would you like me to release
the king of the Jews?' Again the clamour 40
rose: 'Not him; we want Barabbas!' (Barabbas was a bandit.)

Jesus is sentenced to death

Pilate now took Jesus and had him flogged; **19**
and the soldiers plaited a crown of thorns 2
and placed it on his head, and robed him in
a purple cloak. Then time after time they 3
came up to him, crying, 'Hail, King of the
Jews!', and struck him on the face.
Once more Pilate came out and said to 4
the Jews, 'Here he is; I am bringing him out
to let you know that I find no case against
him'; and Jesus came out, wearing the 5
crown of thorns and the purple cloak.
'Behold the Man!' said Pilate. The chief 6
priests and their henchmen saw him and
shouted, 'Crucify! crucify!' 'Take him and
crucify him yourselves,' said Pilate; 'for
my part I find no case against him.' The Jews 7
answered, 'We have a law; and by that law
he ought to die, because he has claimed to be
Son of God.'
When Pilate heard that, he was more 8
afraid than ever, and going back into his 9
headquarters he asked Jesus, 'Where have
you come from?' But Jesus gave him no
answer. 'Do you refuse to speak to me?' 10
said Pilate. 'Surely you know that I have
authority to release you, and I have authority to crucify you?' 'You would have no 11
authority at all over me', Jesus replied, 'if
it had not been granted you from above; and

---

*e See note on verse 24.   f Some witnesses give this verse after first to Annas in verse 13; others at the end of
verse 13.   g Or could share in the offerings of the Passover season.   h Or 'You are king of the Jews,
I take it', he said.*

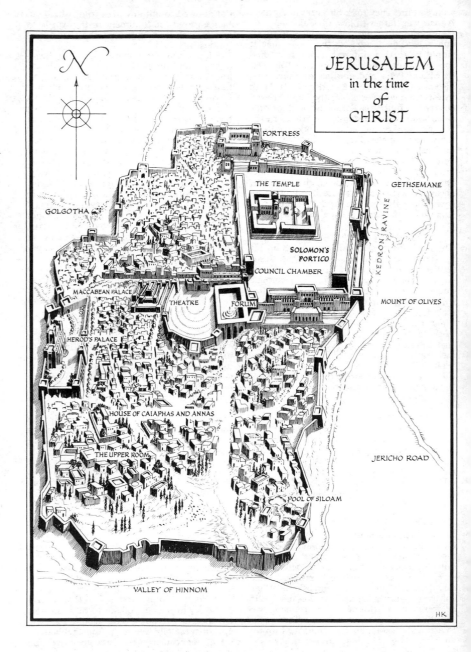

JERUSALEM
in the time
of
CHRIST

FORTRESS

GETHSEMANE

THE TEMPLE

GOLGOTHA

SOLOMON'S
PORTICO

COUNCIL CHAMBER

MACCABEAN PALACE

THEATRE

FORUM

MOUNT OF OLIVES

HEROD'S PALACE

HOUSE OF CAIAPHAS AND ANNAS

JERICHO ROAD

THE UPPER ROOM

POOL OF SILOAM

VALLEY OF HINNOM

KEDRON RAVINE

HK

therefore the deeper guilt lies with the man who handed me over to you.'

12 From that moment Pilate tried hard to release him; but the Jews kept shouting, 'If you let this man go, you are no friend to Caesar; any man who claims to be a king 13 is defying Caesar.' When Pilate heard what they were saying, he brought Jesus out and took his seat on the tribunal at the place known as 'The Pavement' ('Gabbatha' in 14 the language of the Jews). It was the eve of Passover,[i] about noon. Pilate said to the 15 Jews, 'Here is your king.' They shouted, 'Away with him! Away with him! Crucify him!' 'Crucify your king?' said Pilate. 'We have no king but Caesar', the Jews replied. 16 Then at last, to satisfy them, he handed Jesus over to be crucified.

Jesus is crucified

17 Jesus was now taken in charge and, carrying his own cross, went out to the Place of the 18 Skull, as it is called (or, in the Jews' language, 'Golgotha'), where they crucified him, and with him two others, one on the right, one on the left, and Jesus between them.

19 And Pilate wrote an inscription to be fastened to the cross; it read, 'Jesus of 20 Nazareth King of the Jews.' This inscription was read by many Jews, because the place where Jesus was crucified was not far from

i Or It was Friday in Passover.

the city, and the inscription was in Hebrew, Latin, and Greek. Then the Jewish chief 21 priests said to Pilate, 'You should not write "King of the Jews"; write, "He claimed to be king of the Jews."' Pilate replied, 'What 22 I have written, I have written.'

The soldiers, having crucified Jesus, took 23 possession of his clothes, and divided them into four parts, one for each soldier, leaving out the tunic. The tunic was seamless, woven in one piece throughout; so they said to one 24 another, 'We must not tear this; let us toss for it'; and thus the text of Scripture came true: 'They shared my garments among them, and cast lots for my clothing.'

That is what the soldiers did. But mean- 25 while near the cross where Jesus hung stood his mother, with her sister, Mary wife of Clopas, and Mary of Magdala. Jesus saw 26 his mother, with the disciple whom he loved standing beside her. He said to her, 'Mother, there is your son'; and to the disciple, 'There 27 is your mother'; and from that moment the disciple took her into his home.

The death of Jesus

After that, Jesus, aware that all had now 28 come to its appointed end, said in fulfilment of Scripture, 'I thirst.' A jar stood there full 29 of sour wine; so they soaked a sponge with

Roman soldiers

30 the wine, fixed it on a javelin,[j] and held it up to his lips. Having received the wine, he said, 'It is accomplished!' He bowed his head and gave up his spirit.[k]

Jesus's side is pierced

31 Because it was the eve of Passover,[l] the Jews were anxious that the bodies should not remain on the cross for the coming Sabbath, since that Sabbath was a day of great solemnity; so they requested Pilate to have the legs broken and the bodies taken down. 32 The soldiers accordingly came to the first of his fellow-victims and to the second, and 33 broke their legs; but when they came to Jesus, they found that he was already dead, 34 so they did not break his legs. But one of the soldiers stabbed his side with a lance, and at once there was a flow of blood and water. 35 This is vouched for by an eyewitness, whose evidence is to be trusted. He knows that he speaks the truth, so that you too may 36 believe; for this happened in fulfilment of the text of Scripture: 'No bone of his shall 37 be broken.' And another text says, 'They shall look on him whom they pierced.'

The burial of Jesus

38 After that, Pilate was approached by Joseph of Arimathaea, a disciple of Jesus, but a secret disciple for fear of the Jews, who[m] asked to be allowed to remove the body of Jesus. Pilate gave the permission; so Joseph 39 came and took the body away. He was joined by Nicodemus (the man who had first visited Jesus by night), who brought with him a mixture of myrrh and aloes, more 40 than half a hundredweight. They took the body of Jesus and wrapped it, with the spices, in strips of linen cloth according to 41 Jewish burial-customs. Now at the place where he had been crucified there was a garden, and in the garden a new tomb, not 42 yet used for burial. There, because the tomb was near at hand and it was the eve of the Jewish Sabbath, they laid Jesus.

The empty tomb

20 Early on the Sunday morning, while it was still dark, Mary of Magdala came to the tomb. She saw that the stone had been 2 moved away from the entrance, and ran to Simon Peter and the other disciple, the one whom Jesus loved. 'They have taken the Lord out of his tomb,' she cried, 'and we do 3 not know where they have laid him.' So Peter and the other set out and made their 4 way to the tomb. They were running side by side, but the other disciple outran Peter 5 and reached the tomb first. He peered in

and saw the linen wrappings lying there, but 6 did not enter. Then Simon Peter came up, following him, and he went into the tomb. 7 He saw the linen wrappings lying, and the napkin which had been over his head, not lying with the wrappings but rolled together in a place by itself. Then the dis- 8 ciple who had reached the tomb first went in too, and he saw and believed; until 9 then they had not understood the scriptures, which showed that he must rise from the dead.

Jesus appears to Mary of Magdala

10 11 So the disciples went home again; but Mary stood at the tomb outside, weeping. As she wept, she peered into the tomb; and she saw 12 two angels in white sitting there, one at the head, and one at the feet, where the body of Jesus had lain. They said to her, 'Why are 13 you weeping?' She answered, 'They have taken my Lord away, and I do not know where they have laid him.' With these words 14 she turned round and saw Jesus standing there, but did not recognize him. Jesus said 15 to her, 'Why are you weeping? Who is it you are looking for?' Thinking it was the gardener, she said, 'If it is you, sir, who removed him, tell me where you have laid him, and I will take him away.' Jesus said, 16 'Mary!' She turned to him and said, 'Rabbuni!' (which is Hebrew for 'My Master'). Jesus said, 'Do not cling to me,[n] for I have 17 not yet ascended to the Father. But go to my brothers, and tell them that I am now ascending[o] to my Father and your Father, my God and your God.' Mary of Magdala 18 went to the disciples with her news: 'I have seen the Lord!' she said, and gave them his message.

Jesus appears to his disciples

Late that Sunday evening, when the dis- 19 ciples were together behind locked doors, for fear of the Jews, Jesus came and stood among them. 'Peace be with you!' he said, and then showed them his hands and his 20 side. So when the disciples saw the Lord, they were filled with joy. Jesus repeated, 21 'Peace be with you!', and said, 'As the Father sent me, so I send you.' Then he 22 breathed on them, saying, 'Receive the Holy Spirit! If you forgive any man's sins, they 23 stand forgiven; if you pronounce them unforgiven, unforgiven they remain.'

One of the Twelve, Thomas, that is 'the 24 Twin', was not with the rest when Jesus came. So the disciples told him, 'We have 25 seen the Lord.' He said, 'Unless I see the mark of the nails on his hands, unless I put

---

j. So one witness; the others read on marjoram.   *k Or* breathed out his life.   *l Or* Because it was Friday in Passover . . .   *m Or* of Arimathaea. He was a disciple of Jesus, but had gone into hiding for fear of the Jews. He now . . .   *n Or* Touch me no more.   *o Or* I am going to ascend . . .

my finger into the place where the nails were, and my hand into his side, I will not believe it.'

Jesus and Thomas

26 A week later his disciples were again in the room, and Thomas was with them. Although the doors were locked, Jesus came and stood among them, saying, 'Peace be with you!'
27 Then he said to Thomas, 'Reach your finger here; see my hands. Reach your hand here and put it into my side. Be unbelieving no
28 longer, but believe.' Thomas said, 'My Lord
29 and my God!' Jesus said, 'Because you have seen me you have found faith. Happy are they who never saw me and yet have found faith.'

Why this book was written

30 There were indeed many other signs that Jesus performed in the presence of his disciples, which are not recorded in this book.
31 Those here written have been recorded in order that you may hold the faith*p* that Jesus is the Christ, the Son of God, and that through this faith you may possess life by his name.

Jesus appears to his disciples again

21 Some time later, Jesus showed himself to his disciples once again, by the Sea of
2 Tiberias; and in this way. Simon Peter and Thomas 'the Twin' were together with Nathanael of Cana-in-Galilee. The sons of Zebedee and two other disciples were also
3 there. Simon Peter said, 'I am going out fishing.' 'We will go with you', said the others. So they started and got into the boat. But that night they caught nothing.
4 Morning came, and there stood Jesus on the beach, but the disciples did not know
5 that it was Jesus. He called out to them, 'Friends, have you caught anything?' They
6 answered 'No.' He said, 'Shoot the net to starboard, and you will make a catch.' They did so, and found they could not haul the net aboard, there were so many fish in it.
7 Then the disciple whom Jesus loved said to Peter, 'It is the Lord!' When Simon Peter heard that, he wrapped his coat about him (for he had stripped) and plunged into the
8 sea. The rest of them came on in the boat, towing the net full of fish; for they were not far from land, only about a hundred yards.
9 When they came ashore, they saw a charcoal fire there, with fish laid on it, and
10 some bread. Jesus said, 'Bring some of your
11 catch.' Simon Peter went aboard and dragged the net to land, full of big fish, a hundred and

fifty-three of them; and yet, many as they were, the net was not torn. Jesus said, 'Come 12 and have breakfast.' None of the disciples dared to ask 'Who are you?' They knew it was the Lord. Jesus now came up, took the 13 bread, and gave it to them, and the fish in the same way.

This makes the third time that Jesus 14 appeared to his disciples after his resurrection from the dead.

Jesus and Peter

After breakfast, Jesus said to Simon Peter, 15 'Simon son of John, do you love me more than all else*q*?' 'Yes, Lord,' he answered, 'you know that I love you.' 'Then feed my lambs', he said. A second time he asked, 16 'Simon son of John, do you love me?' 'Yes, Lord, you know I love you.'*r* 'Then tend my sheep.' A third time he said, 'Simon son of 17 John, do you love me*s*?' Peter was hurt that he asked him a third time, 'Do you love me?'*t* 'Lord,' he said, 'you know everything; you know I love you.'*r* Jesus said, 'Feed my sheep.

'And further, I tell you this in very truth: 18 when you were young you fastened your belt about you and walked where you chose; but when you are old you will stretch out your arms, and a stranger will bind you fast, and carry you where you have no wish to go.' He said this to indi- 19 cate the manner of death by which Peter was to glorify God. Then he added, 'Follow me.'

Peter looked round, and saw the disciple 20 whom Jesus loved following—the one who at supper had leaned back close to him to ask the question, 'Lord, who is it that will betray you?' When he caught sight of him, 21 Peter asked, 'Lord, what will happen to him?' Jesus said, 'If it should be my will that he 22 wait until I come, what is it to you? Follow me.'

That saying of Jesus became current in 23 the brotherhood, and was taken to mean that that disciple would not die. But in fact Jesus did not say that he would not die; he only said, 'If it should be my will that he wait until I come, what is it to you?'

Testimony, written and unwritten

It is this same disciple who attests what has 24 here been written. It is in fact he who wrote it, and we know that his testimony is true.*u*

There is much else that Jesus did. If it 25 were all to be recorded in detail, I suppose the whole world could not hold the books that would be written.

---

p Some witnesses read that you may come to believe . . . your friend.   *s Or* are you my friend.   *q Or* more than they do.   *r Or* that I am *t Or* that at the third asking he should have said, 'Are you my friend?'   *u Some witnesses here insert the passage printed on p. 834.*

An incident in the temple*

53 1* And they went each to his home, and Jesus 2 to the Mount of Olives. At daybreak he appeared again in the temple, and all the people gathered round him. He had taken his seat and was engaged in teaching them 3 when the doctors of the law and the Pharisees brought in a woman caught committing adultery. 4 Making her stand out in the middle they said to him, 'Master, this woman was 5 caught in the very act of adultery. In the Law Moses has laid down that such women are to be stoned. What do you say about it?' 6 They put the question as a test, hoping to frame a charge against him. Jesus bent down and wrote with his finger on the ground. When they continued to press their question 7 he sat up straight and said, 'That one of you who is faultless shall throw the first stone.' Then once again he bent down and 8 wrote on the ground. When they heard what 9 he said, one by one they went away,*v* the eldest first; and Jesus was left alone, with the woman still standing there. Jesus again 10 sat up and*w* said to the woman, 'Where are they? Has no one condemned you?' She 11 answered, 'No one, sir.' Jesus said, 'Nor do I condemn you. You may go; do not sin again.'

* *This passage, which in the most widely received editions of the New Testament is printed in the text of John, 7. 53—8. 11, has no fixed place in our witnesses. Some of them do not contain it at all. Some place it after Luke 21. 38, others after John 7. 36, or 7. 52, or 21. 24.*

v *Some witnesses insert* convicted by their conscience. woman.

w *Some witnesses insert* seeing no one but the

PALESTINE
in the time of
CHRIST

ACTS OF THE APOSTLES

Introduction

1 IN THE FIRST PART of my work, Theophilus, I wrote of all that Jesus did
2 and taught from the beginning until the day when, after giving instructions through the Holy Spirit to the apostles whom he had
3 chosen, he was taken up to heaven. He showed himself to these men after his death, and gave ample proof that he was alive: over a period of forty days he appeared to them and taught them about the kingdom
4 of God. While he was in their company he told them not to leave Jerusalem. 'You must wait', he said, 'for the promise made by my Father, about which you have heard me
5 speak: John, as you know, baptized with water, but you will be baptized with the Holy Spirit, and within the next few days.'

Jesus is taken up to heaven

6 So, when they were all together, they asked him, 'Lord, is this the time when you are to establish once again the sovereignty of
7 Israel?' He answered, 'It is not for you to know about dates or times, which the Father
8 has set within his own control. But you will receive power when the Holy Spirit comes upon you; and you will bear witness for me in Jerusalem, and all over Judaea and Samaria, and away to the ends of the earth.'
9 When he had said this, as they watched, he was lifted up, and a cloud removed him
10 from their sight. As he was going, and as they were gazing intently into the sky, all at once there stood beside them two men in
11 white who said, 'Men of Galilee, why stand there looking up into the sky? This Jesus, who has been taken away from you up to heaven, will come in the same way as you have seen him go.'

Then they returned to Jerusalem from the 12 hill called Olivet, which is near Jerusalem, no farther than a Sabbath day's journey. Entering the city they went to the room 13 upstairs where they were lodging: Peter and John and James and Andrew, Philip and Thomas, Bartholomew and Matthew, James son of Alphaeus and Simon the Zealot, and Judas son of James. All these were con- 14 stantly at prayer together, and with them a group of women, including Mary the mother of Jesus, and his brothers.

A successor to Judas

It was during this time that Peter stood up 15 before the assembled brotherhood, about one hundred and twenty in all, and said: 'My friends, the prophecy in Scripture was 16 bound to come true, which the Holy Spirit, through the mouth of David, uttered about Judas who acted as guide to those who arrested Jesus. For he was one of our num- 17 ber and had his place in this ministry.' (This 18 Judas, be it noted, after buying a plot of land with the price of his villainy, fell forward on the ground, and burst open, so that his entrails poured out. This became 19 known to everyone in Jerusalem, and they named the property in their own language Akeldama, which means 'Blood Acre'.) 'The text I have in mind', Peter continued, 20 'is in the Book of Psalms: "Let his homestead fall desolate; let there be none to inhabit it"; and again, "Let another take over his charge." Therefore one of those 21 who bore us company all the while we had the Lord Jesus with us, coming and going, from John's ministry of baptism until the 22 day when he was taken up from us—one of those must now join us as a witness to his resurrection.'

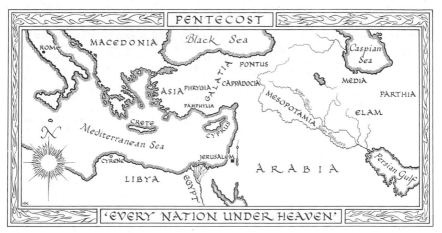

PENTECOST

'EVERY NATION UNDER HEAVEN'

23 Two names were put forward: Joseph, who was known as Barsabbas, and bore the added name of Justus; and Matthias.
24 Then they prayed and said, 'Thou, Lord, who knowest the hearts of all men, declare
25 which of these two thou hast chosen to receive this office of ministry and apostleship which Judas abandoned to go where he
26 belonged.' They drew lots and the lot fell on Matthias, who was then assigned a place among the twelve apostles.[a]

The Holy Spirit is given

2 While the day of Pentecost was running its course they were all together in one place,
2 when suddenly there came from the sky a noise like that of a strong driving wind, which filled the whole house where they
3 were sitting. And there appeared to them tongues like flames of fire, dispersed among
4 them and resting on each one. And they were all filled with the Holy Spirit and began to talk in other tongues, as the Spirit gave them power of utterance.
5 Now there were living in Jerusalem devout Jews[b] drawn from every nation under hea-
6 ven; and at this sound the crowd gathered, all bewildered because each one heard his
7 own language spoken. They were amazed and in their astonishment exclaimed, 'Why, they are all Galileans, are they not, these
8 men who are speaking? How is it then that we hear them, each of us in his own native
9 language? Parthians, Medes, Elamites; in-habitants of Mesopotamia, of Judaea and
10 Cappadocia, of Pontus and Asia, of Phrygia and Pamphylia, of Egypt and the districts of Libya around Cyrene; visitors from Rome,
11 both Jews and proselytes, Cretans and Arabs,

we hear them telling in our own tongues the great things God has done.' And they were 12 all amazed and perplexed, saying to one another, 'What can this mean?' Others said 13 contemptuously, 'They have been drinking!'

Peter explains what has happened

But Peter stood up with the Eleven, raised 14 his voice, and addressed them: 'Fellow Jews, and all you who live in Jerusalem, mark this and give me a hearing. These men are not 15 drunk, as you imagine; for it is only nine in the morning. No, this is what the prophet 16 spoke of: "God says, 'This will happen in 17 the last days: I will pour out upon everyone a portion of my spirit; and your sons and daughters shall prophesy; your young men shall see visions, and your old men shall dream dreams. Yes, I will endue even my 18 slaves, both men and women, with a portion of my spirit, and they shall prophesy. And 19 I will show portents in the sky above, and signs on the earth below—blood and fire and drifting smoke. The sun shall be turned 20 to darkness, and the moon to blood, before that great, resplendent day, the day of the Lord, shall come. And then, everyone who 21 invokes the name of the Lord shall be saved.'"

'Men of Israel, listen to me: I speak of 22 Jesus of Nazareth, a man singled out by God and made known to you through miracles, portents, and signs, which God worked among you through him, as you well know. When he had been given up to 23 you, by the deliberate will and plan of God, you used heathen men to crucify and kill him. But God raised him to life again, set- 24 ting him free from the pangs of death,

a Some witnesses read was then appointed a colleague of the eleven apostles.   *b Some witnesses read* devout men.

because it could not be that death should keep him in its grip.

25 'For David says of him:

"I foresaw that the presence of the Lord
would be with me always,
for he is at my right hand so that I may not
be shaken;
26 therefore my heart was glad and my tongue
spoke my joy;
moreover, my flesh shall dwell in hope,
27 for thou wilt not abandon my soul to death,
nor let thy loyal servant suffer corruption.
28 Thou hast shown me the ways of life,
thou wilt fill me with gladness by thy
presence."

29 'Let me tell you plainly, my friends, that the patriarch David died and was buried, 30 and his tomb is here to this very day. It is clear therefore that he spoke as a prophet, who knew that God had sworn to him that one of his own direct descendants should 31 sit on his throne; and when he said he was not abandoned to death, and his flesh never suffered corruption, he spoke with fore-knowledge of the resurrection of the Mes-32 siah. The Jesus we speak of has been raised 33 by God, as we can all bear witness. Exalted thus with[c] God's right hand, he received the Holy Spirit from the Father, as was pro-mised, and all that you now see and hear 34 flows from him. For it was not David who went up to heaven; his own words are: "The Lord said to my Lord, 'Sit at my right hand 35 until I make your enemies your footstool.'" 36 Let all Israel then accept as certain that God has made this Jesus, whom you crucified, both Lord and Messiah.'

A call to repentance

37 When they heard this they were cut to the heart, and said to Peter and the apostles,[d] 38 'Friends, what are we to do?' 'Repent,' said Peter, 'repent and be baptized, every one of you, in the name of Jesus the Messiah for the forgiveness of your sins; and you 39 will receive the gift of the Holy Spirit. For the promise is to you, and to your children, and to all who are far away, everyone whom the Lord our God may call.'

40 In these and many other words he pressed his case and pleaded with them: 'Save your-selves', he said, 'from this crooked age.' 41 Then those who accepted his word were baptized, and some three thousand were added to their number that day.

Life among the believers

42 They met constantly to hear the apostles teach, and to share the common life, to 43 break bread, and to pray. A sense of awe was everywhere, and many marvels and signs were brought about through the apostles. All whose faith had drawn them 44 together held everything in common:[e] they 45 would sell their property and possessions and make a general distribution as the need of each required. With one mind they kept 46 up their daily attendance at the temple, and, breaking bread in private houses, shared their meals with unaffected joy, as they 47 praised God and enjoyed the favour of the whole people. And day by day the Lord added to their number those whom he was saving.

Cure of a crippled man

One day at three in the afternoon, the hour 3 of prayer, Peter and John were on their way up to the temple. Now a man who had been 2 a cripple from birth used to be carried there and laid every day by the gate of the temple called 'Beautiful Gate', to beg from people as they went in. When he saw Peter and 3 John on their way into the temple he asked for charity. But Peter fixed his eyes on him, 4 as John did also, and said, 'Look at us.' Expecting a gift from them, the man was all 5 attention. And Peter said, 'I have no silver 6 or gold; but what I have I give you: in the name of Jesus Christ of Nazareth, walk.' Then he grasped him by the right hand and 7 pulled him up; and at once his feet and ankles grew strong; he sprang up, stood on 8 his feet, and started to walk. He entered the temple with them, leaping and praising God as he went. Everyone saw him walking and 9 praising God, and when they recognized 10 him as the man who used to sit begging at Beautiful Gate, they were filled with wonder and amazement at what had happened to him.

What lay behind the cure

And as he was clutching Peter and John all 11 the people came running in astonishment towards them in Solomon's Portico, as it is called. Peter saw them coming and met them 12 with these words: 'Men of Israel, why be surprised at this? Why stare at us as if we had made this man walk by some power or godliness of our own? The God of Abraham, 13 Isaac, and Jacob, the God of our fathers, has given the highest honour to his servant Jesus, whom you committed for trial and repudiated in Pilate's court—repudiated the 14 one who was holy and righteous when Pilate had decided to release him. You begged as a favour the release of a murderer, and killed 15 him who has led the way to life. But God raised him from the dead; of that we are wit-nesses. And the name of Jesus, by awakening 16

c *Or* at.　　d *Some witnesses read* the rest of the apostles.　　e *Or* All who had become believers held everything together in common.

faith, has strengthened this man, whom you see and know, and this faith has made him completely well, as you can all see for yourselves.

17 'And now, my friends, I know quite well that you acted in ignorance, and so did your 18 rulers; but this is how God fulfilled what he had foretold in the utterances of all the prophets: that his Messiah should suffer. 19 Repent then and turn to God, so that your sins may be wiped out. Then the Lord may 20 grant you a time of recovery and send you the Messiah he has already appointed, that 21 is, Jesus. He must be received into heaven until the time of universal restoration comes, of which God spoke by his holy prophets.[f] 22 Moses said, "The Lord God will raise up a prophet for you from among yourselves as he raised me;[g] you shall listen to everything 23 he says to you, and anyone who refuses to listen to that prophet must be extirpated 24 from Israel." And so said all the prophets, from Samuel onwards; with one voice they all predicted this present time. 25 'You are the heirs of the prophets; you are within the covenant which God made with your fathers, when he said to Abraham, "And in your offspring all the families on 26 earth shall find blessing." When God raised up his Servant, he sent him to you first, to bring you blessing by turning every one of you from your wicked ways.'

Peter and John called to account

4 They were still addressing the people when the chief[h] priests came upon them, together with the Controller of the Temple and the 2 Sadducees, exasperated at their teaching the people and proclaiming the resurrection from the dead—the resurrection of Jesus. 3 They were arrested and put in prison for the 4 night, as it was already evening. But many of those who had heard the message became believers. The number of men now reached about five thousand. 5 Next day the Jewish rulers, elders, and 6 doctors of the law met in Jerusalem. There were present Annas the High Priest, Caiaphas, Jonathan,[i] Alexander, and all who 7 were of the high-priestly family. They brought the apostles before the court and began the examination. 'By what power', they asked, 'or by what name have such 8 men as you done this?' Then Peter, filled with the Holy Spirit, answered, 'Rulers of 9 the people and elders, if the question put to us today is about help given to a sick man, and we are asked by what means he was 10 cured, here is the answer, for all of you and for all the people of Israel: it was by the name of Jesus Christ of Nazareth, whom you

crucified, whom God raised from the dead; it is by his name[j] that this man stands here before you fit and well. This Jesus is the 11 stone rejected by the builders which has become the keystone—and you are the builders. There is no salvation in anyone 12 else at all,[k] for there is no other name under heaven granted to men, by which we may receive salvation.'

Cautioned and discharged

Now as they observed the boldness of Peter 13 and John, and noted that they were untrained laymen, they began to wonder, then recognized them as former companions of Jesus. And when they saw the man who had 14 been cured standing with them, they had nothing to say in reply. So they ordered them 15 to leave the court, and then discussed the matter among themselves. 'What are we to 16 do with these men?' they said; 'for it is common knowledge in Jerusalem that a notable miracle has come about through them; and we cannot deny it. But to stop 17 this from spreading further among the people, we had better caution them never again to speak to anyone in this name.' They then called them in and ordered them 18 to refrain from all public speaking and teaching in the name of Jesus.

But Peter and John said to them in reply: 19 'Is it right in God's eyes for us to obey you rather than God? Judge for yourselves. We 20 cannot possibly give up speaking of things we have seen and heard.'

The court repeated the caution and dis- 21 charged them. They could not see how they were to punish them, because the people were all giving glory to God for what had happened. The man upon whom this miracle 22 of healing had been performed was over forty years old.

The church at prayer

As soon as they were discharged they 23 went back to their friends and told them everything that the chief priests and elders had said. When they heard it, they raised 24 their voices as one man and called upon God:

'Sovereign Lord, maker of heaven and earth and sea and of everything in them,

---

f *Some witnesses add* from the beginning of the world.   g *Or* like me.   h *Some witnesses omit* chief.
i *Some witnesses read* John.   j *Some witnesses insert* and no other.   k *Some witnesses omit* There is no . . . at all.

25 who by the Holy Spirit,[l] through the mouth of David thy servant, didst say,

"Why did the Gentiles rage and the peoples lay their plots in vain?

26 The kings of the earth took their stand and the rulers made common cause against the Lord and against his Messiah."

27 They did indeed make common cause in this very city against thy holy servant Jesus whom thou didst anoint as Messiah. Herod and Pontius Pilate conspired with the Gentiles and peoples of Israel to do all the things which, under thy hand and by thy decree, were foreordained. And now, O Lord, mark their threats, and enable thy servants to speak thy word with all boldness. Stretch out thy hand to heal and cause signs and wonders to be done through the name of thy holy servant Jesus.'

28
29
30

31 When they had ended their prayer, the building where they were assembled rocked, and all were filled with the Holy Spirit and spoke the word of God with boldness.

Sharing and witnessing

32 The whole body of believers was united in heart and soul. Not a man of them claimed any of his possessions as his own, but everything was held in common, while the apostles bore witness with great power to the resurrection of the Lord Jesus. They were all held in high esteem; for they had never a needy person among them, because all who had property in land or houses sold it, brought the proceeds of the sale, and laid the money at the feet of the apostles; it was then distributed to any who stood in need.

33

34

35

36 For instance, Joseph, surnamed by the apostles Barnabas (which means 'Son of Exhortation'), a Levite, by birth a Cypriot, owned an estate, which he sold; he brought the money, and laid it at the apostles' feet.

37

Ananias and Sapphira

5 But there was another man, called Ananias, with his wife Sapphira, who sold a property. With the full knowledge of his wife he kept back part of the purchase-money, and part he brought and laid at the apostles' feet. But Peter said, 'Ananias, how was it that Satan so possessed your mind that you lied to the Holy Spirit, and kept back part of the price of the land? While it remained, did it not remain yours? When it was turned into money, was it not still at your own disposal? What made you think of doing this thing? You have lied not to men but to God.' When Ananias heard these words he dropped dead; and all the others who heard were

2

3

4

5

awestruck. The younger men rose and covered his body, then carried him out and buried him.

6

About three hours passed, and then his wife came in, unaware of what had happened. Peter turned to her and said, 'Tell me, were you paid such and such a price for the land?' 'Yes,' she said, 'that was the price.' Then Peter said, 'Why did you both conspire to put the Spirit of the Lord to the test? Hark! there at the door are the footsteps of those who buried your husband; and they will carry you away.' And suddenly she dropped dead at his feet. When the young men came in, they found her dead; and they carried her out and buried her beside her husband. And a great awe fell upon the whole church, and upon all who heard of these events; and many remarkable and wonderful things took place among the people at the hands of the apostles.

7

8

9

10

11

12

Conversions and cures

They used to meet by common consent in Solomon's Portico, no one from outside their number venturing to join with them. But people in general spoke highly of them,[m] and more than that, numbers of men and women were added to their ranks as believers in the Lord.[n] In the end the sick were actually carried out into the streets and laid there on beds and stretchers, so that even the shadow of Peter might fall on one or another as he passed by; and the people from the towns round Jerusalem flocked in, bringing those who were ill or harassed by unclean spirits, and all of them were cured.

13

14

15

16

A miraculous escape from prison

Then the High Priest and his colleagues, the Sadducean party as it then was, were goaded into action by jealousy. They proceeded to arrest the apostles, and put them in official custody. But an angel of the Lord opened the prison doors during the night, brought them out, and said, 'Go, take your place in the temple and speak to the people, and tell them about this new life and all it means.' Accordingly they entered the temple at daybreak and went on with their teaching.

17

18

19

20

21

---

l *Some witnesses omit* by the Holy Spirit.
them, the common people spoke highly of them.
men and women, were added to the Lord.

m *Or* . . . Portico. Although others did not venture to join
n *Or* and an ever-increasing number of believers, both

When the High Priest arrived with his
colleagues they summoned the 'Sanhedrin',
that is, the full senate of the Israelite nation,
and sent to the jail to fetch the prisoners.
22 But the police who went to the prison failed
to find them there, so they returned and
23 reported, 'We found the jail securely locked
at every point, with the warders at their posts
by the doors, but when we opened them we
24 found no one inside.' When they heard this,
the Controller of the Temple and the chief
priests were wondering what could have
25 become of them,[o] and then a man arrived
with the report, 'Look! the men you put in
prison are there in the temple teaching the
26 people.' At that the Controller went off
with the police and fetched them, but without using force for fear of being stoned by
the people.

Before the council again

27 So they brought them and stood them before
the Council; and the High Priest began his
28 examination. 'We expressly ordered you',
he said, 'to desist from teaching in that
name; and what has happened? You have
filled Jerusalem with your teaching, and you
are trying to make us responsible for that
29 man's death.' Peter replied for himself and
the apostles: 'We must obey God rather
30 than men. The God of our fathers raised up
Jesus whom you had done to death[p] by
31 hanging him on a gibbet. He it is whom God
has exalted with his own right hand[q] as
leader and saviour, to grant Israel repent-
32 ance and forgiveness of sins. And we are
witnesses to all this, and so is the Holy
Spirit given by God to those who are
obedient to him.'
33 This touched them on the raw, and they
34 wanted to put them to death. But a member
of the Council rose to his feet, a Pharisee
called Gamaliel, a teacher of the law held
in high regard by all the people. He moved
that the men be put outside for a while.
35 Then he said, 'Men of Israel, be cautious in
36 deciding what to do with these men. Some
time ago Theudas came forward, claiming
to be somebody, and a number of men,
about four hundred, joined him. But he
was killed and his whole following was
37 broken up and disappeared. After him came
Judas the Galilean at the time of the census;
he induced some people to revolt under his
leadership, but he too perished and his
38 whole following was scattered. And so now:
keep clear of these men, I tell you; leave
them alone. For if this idea of theirs or its
execution is of human origin, it will collapse;
39 but if it is from God, you will never be able
to put them down, and you risk finding
yourselves at war with God.'
They took his advice. They sent for the 40
apostles and had them flogged; then they
ordered them to give up speaking in the
name of Jesus, and discharged them. So 41
the apostles went out from the Council
rejoicing that they had been found worthy
to suffer indignity for the sake of the Name.
And every day they went steadily on with 42
their teaching in the temple and in private
houses, telling the good news of Jesus the
Messiah.[r]

Sorting out business matters

During this period, when disciples were 6
growing in number, there was disagreement
between those of them who spoke Greek[s]
and those who spoke the language of the
Jews.[t] The former party complained that
their widows were being overlooked in the
daily distribution. So the Twelve called the 2
whole body of disciples together and said,
'It would be a grave mistake for us to neglect
the word of God in order to wait at table.
Therefore, friends, look out seven men of 3
good reputation from your number, men
full of the Spirit and of wisdom, and we
will appoint them to deal with these matters,
while we devote ourselves to prayer and to 4
the ministry of the Word.' This proposal 5
proved acceptable to the whole body. They
elected Stephen, a man full of faith and of
the Holy Spirit, Philip, Prochorus, Nicanor,
Timon, Parmenas, and Nicolas of Antioch,
a former convert to Judaism. These they 6
presented to the apostles, who prayed and
laid their hands on them.
The word of God now spread more and 7
more widely; the number of disciples in
Jerusalem went on increasing rapidly, and
very many of the priests adhered to the
Faith.

Stephen accused before the Council

Stephen, who was full of grace and power, 8
began to work great miracles and signs
among the people. But some members of 9
the synagogue called the Synagogue of
Freedmen, comprising Cyrenians and Alex-
andrians and people from Cilicia and Asia,
came forward and argued with Stephen,
but could not hold their own against the 10
inspired wisdom with which he spoke. They 11
then put up men who alleged that they had
heard him make blasphemous statements
against Moses and against God. They stir- 12
red up the people and the elders and doctors
of the law, set upon him and seized him,
and brought him before the Council. They 13

o Or wondering about them, what this could possibly mean. *p Or* . . . Jesus, and you did him to death . . .
q Or at his right hand. *r Or* the good news that the Messiah was Jesus. *s Literally* the Hellenists.
t Literally the Hebrews.

produced false witnesses who said, 'This man is for ever saying things against this
14 holy place and against the Law. For we have heard him say that Jesus of Nazareth will destroy this place and alter the customs
15 handed down to us by Moses.' And all who were sitting in the Council fixed their eyes on him, and his face appeared to them like the face of an angel.

Stephen's defence

7 Then the High Priest asked, 'Is this so?'
2 And he said, 'My brothers, fathers of this nation, listen to me. The God of glory appeared to Abraham our ancestor while he was in Mesopotamia, before he had
3 settled in Harran, and said: "Leave your country and your kinsfolk and come away
4 to a land that I will show you." Thereupon he left the land of the Chaldaeans and settled in Harran. From there, after his father's death, God led him to migrate to this land
5 where you now live. He gave him nothing in it to call his own, not one yard; but promised to give it in possession to him and his descendants after him, though he was then
6 childless. God spoke in these terms: "Abraham's descendants shall live as aliens in a foreign land, held in slavery and oppression
7 for four hundred years. And I will pass judgement", said God, "on the nation whose slaves they are; and after that they shall come out free, and worship me in this place."
8 He then gave him the covenant of circumcision, and so, after Isaac was born, he circumcised him on the eighth day; and Isaac begot Jacob, and Jacob the twelve patriarchs.
9 'The patriarchs out of jealousy sold Joseph into slavery in Egypt, but God was
10 with him and rescued him from all his troubles. He also gave him a presence and powers of mind which so commended him to Pharaoh king of Egypt, that he appointed him chief administrator for Egypt and the whole of the royal household.
11 'But famine struck all Egypt and Canaan, and caused great hardship; and our an-
12 cestors could find nothing to eat. But Jacob heard that there was food in Egypt and sent our fathers there. This was their first visit.
13 On the second visit Joseph was recognized by his brothers, and his family connections
14 were disclosed to Pharaoh. So Joseph sent an invitation to his father Jacob and all his relatives, seventy-five persons altogether;
15 and Jacob went down into Egypt. There he ended his days, as also our forefathers did.
16 Their remains were later removed to Shechem and buried in the tomb which Abraham had bought and paid for from the clan of Emmor at Shechem.

'Now as the time approached for God to
17 fulfil the promise he had made to Abraham, our nation in Egypt grew and increased in numbers. At length another king, who knew
18 nothing of Joseph, ascended the throne of Egypt. He made a crafty attack on our race,
19 and cruelly forced our ancestors to expose their children so that they should not survive. At this time Moses was born. He was
20 a fine child, and pleasing to God. For three months he was nursed in his father's house, and when he was exposed, Pharaoh's daugh-
21 ter herself adopted him and brought him up as her own son. So Moses was trained in all
22 the wisdom of the Egyptians, a powerful speaker and a man of action.

'He was approaching the age of forty,
23 when it occurred to him to look into the conditions of his fellow-countrymen the Israelites. He saw one of them being ill-
24 treated, so he went to his aid, and avenged the victim by striking down the Egyptian. He thought his fellow-countrymen would
25 understand that God was offering them deliverance through him, but they did not understand. The next day he came upon two
26 of them fighting, and tried to bring them to make up their quarrel. "My men," he said, "you are brothers; why are you ill-treating one another?" But the man who was at
27 fault pushed him away. "Who set you up as a ruler and judge over us?" he said. "Are
28 you going to kill me as you killed the Egyptian yesterday?" At this Moses fled
29 the country and settled in Midianite territory. There two sons were born to him.

'After forty years had passed, an angel
30 appeared to him in the flame of a burning bush in the desert near Mount Sinai. Moses
31 was amazed at the sight. But as he approached to look closely, the voice of the Lord was heard: "I am the God of your
32 fathers, the God of Abraham, Isaac, and Jacob." Moses was terrified and dared not look. Then the Lord said to him, "Take off
33 your shoes; the place where you are standing is holy ground. I have indeed seen how
34 my people are oppressed in Egypt and have heard their groans; and I have come down to rescue them. Up, then; let me send you to Egypt."

'This Moses, whom they had rejected with
35 the words, "Who made you ruler and judge?" —this very man was commissioned as ruler and liberator by God himself, speaking through the angel who appeared to him in the bush. It was Moses who led them out,
36 working miracles and signs in Egypt, at the Red Sea, and for forty years in the desert. It was he again who said to the Israelites,
37 "God will raise up a prophet for you from among yourselves as he raised me."[u] He it
38

u Or like me.

was who, when they were assembled there in the desert, conversed with the angel who spoke to him on Mount Sinai, and with our forefathers; he received the living utterances of God, to pass on to us.

39 'But our forefathers would not accept his leadership. They thrust him aside. They
40 wished themselves back in Egypt, and said to Aaron, "Make us gods to go before us. As for that Moses, who brought us out of Egypt, we do not know what has become of
41 him." That was when they made the bull-calf, and offered sacrifice to the idol, and held a feast in honour of the thing their
42 hands had made. But God turned away from them and gave them over to the worship of the host of heaven, as it stands written in the book of the prophets: "Did you bring me victims and offerings those forty years in the desert, you house of Israel?
43 No, you carried aloft the shrine of Moloch and the star of the god Rephan, the images which you had made for your adoration. I will banish you beyond Babylon."

44 'Our forefathers had the Tent of the Testimony in the desert, as God commanded when he told Moses to make it after the
45 pattern which he had seen. Our fathers of the next generation, with Joshua, brought it with them when they dispossessed the nations whom God drove out before them, and there it was until the time of David.
46 David found favour with God and asked to be allowed to provide a dwelling-place for
47 the God of Jacob;[v] but it was Solomon who
48 built him a house. However, the Most High does not live in houses made by men: as the
49 prophet says, "Heaven is my throne and earth my footstool. What kind of house will you build for me, says the Lord; where is
50 my resting-place? Are not all these things of my own making?"
51 'How stubborn you are, heathen still at heart and deaf to the truth! You always fight against the Holy Spirit. Like fathers,
52 like sons. Was there ever a prophet whom your fathers did not persecute? They killed those who foretold the coming of the Righteous One; and now you have betrayed him
53 and murdered him, you who received the Law as God's angels gave it to you, and yet have not kept it.'

Stephen stoned to death

54 This touched them on the raw and they
55 ground their teeth with fury. But Stephen, filled with the Holy Spirit, and gazing intently up to heaven, saw the glory of God, and Jesus standing at God's right hand.
56 'Look,' he said, 'there is a rift in the sky; I can see the Son of Man standing at God's
57 right hand!' At this they gave a great shout

and stopped their ears. Then they made one rush at him and, flinging him out of the city, 58 set about stoning him. The witnesses laid their coats at the feet of a young man named Saul. So they stoned Stephen, and as they 59 did so, he called out, 'Lord Jesus, receive my spirit.' Then he fell on his knees and cried 60 aloud, 'Lord, do not hold this sin against them', and with that he died. And Saul was 8 among those who approved of his murder.

An outbreak of persecution in Jerusalem

This was the beginning of a time of violent persecution for the church in Jerusalem; and all except the apostles were scattered over the country districts of Judaea and Samaria. Stephen was given burial by certain devout 2 men, who made a great lamentation for him. Saul, meanwhile, was harrying the church; 3 he entered house after house, seizing men and women, and sending them to prison.

Philip's mission in Samaria

As for those who had been scattered, they 4 went through the country preaching the Word. Philip came down to a city in Samaria 5 and began proclaiming the Messiah to them. The crowds, to a man, listened eagerly to 6 what Philip said, when they heard him and saw the miracles that he performed. For in 7 many cases of possession the unclean spirits came out with a loud cry; and many paralysed and crippled folk were cured; and there 8 was great joy in that city.

A man named Simon had been in the city 9 for some time, and had swept the Samaritans off their feet with his magical arts, claiming to be someone great. All of them, high and 10 low, listened eagerly to him. 'This man', they said, 'is that power of God which is called "The Great Power".' They listened 11 because they had for so long been carried away by his magic. But when they came to 12 believe Philip with his good news about the kingdom of God and the name of Jesus Christ, they were baptized, men and women alike. Even Simon himself believed, and 13 was baptized, and thereupon was constantly in Philip's company. He was carried away when he saw the powerful signs and miracles that were taking place.

The apostles in Jerusalem now heard that 14 Samaria had accepted the word of God. They sent off Peter and John, who went 15 down there and prayed for the converts, asking that they might receive the Holy Spirit. For until then the Spirit had not come 16 upon any of them. They had been baptized into the name of the Lord Jesus, that and nothing more. So Peter and John laid their 17 hands on them and they received the Holy Spirit.

v *Some witnesses read* for the house of Jacob.

18 When Simon saw that the Spirit was bestowed through the laying on of the apostles' hands, he offered them money 19 and said, 'Give me the same power too, so that when I lay my hands on anyone, he 20 will receive the Holy Spirit.' Peter replied, 'Your money go with you to damnation, because you thought God's gift was for sale! 21 You have no part nor lot in this, for you 22 are dishonest with God. Repent of this wickedness and pray the Lord to forgive 23 you for imagining such a thing. I can see that you are doomed to taste the bitter fruit 24 and wear the fetters of sin.'ʷ Simon answered, 'Pray to the Lord for me yourselves and ask that none of the things you have spoken of may fall upon me.'
25 So, after giving their testimony and speaking the word of the Lord, they took the road back to Jerusalem, bringing the good news to many Samaritan villages on the way.

Philip and an Ethiopian official

26 Then the angel of the Lord said to Philip, 'Start out and go south to the road that leads down from Jerusalem to Gaza.' (This is the 27 desert road.) So he set out and was on his way when he caught sight of an Ethiopian. This man was a eunuch, a high official of the Kandake, or Queen, of Ethiopia, in charge of all her treasure. He had been to 28 Jerusalem on a pilgrimage and was now on his way home, sitting in his carriage and 29 reading aloud the prophet Isaiah. The Spirit said to Philip, 'Go and join the carriage.' 30 When Philip ran up he heard him reading the prophet Isaiah and said, 'Do you under- 31 stand what you are reading?' He said, 'How can I understand unless someone will give me the clue?' So he asked Philip to get in and sit beside him.
32 The passage he was reading was this: 'He was led like a sheep to be slaughtered; and like a lamb that is dumb before the 33 shearer, he does not open his mouth. He has been humiliated and has no redress. Who will be able to speak of his posterity? For he is cut off from the world of living men.'
34 'Now', said the eunuch to Philip, 'tell me, please, who it is that the prophet is speaking 35 about here: himself or someone else?' Then Philip began. Starting from this passage, he 36 told him the good news of Jesus. As they were going along the road, they came to some water. 'Look,' said the eunuch, 'here is water: what is there to prevent my being 38 baptized?';ˣ and he ordered the carriage to stop. Then they both went down into the water, Philip and the eunuch; and he

baptized him. When they came up out of the 39 water the Spirit snatched Philip away, and the eunuch saw no more of him, but went happily on his way. Philip appeared at 40 Azotus, and toured the country, preaching in all the towns till he reached Caesarea.

The conversion of Saul

Meanwhile Saul was still breathing murder- 9 ous threats against the disciples of the Lord. He went to the High Priest and applied 2 for letters to the synagogues at Damascus authorizing him to arrest anyone he found, men or women, who followed the new way, and bring them to Jerusalem. While he was 3 still on the road and nearing Damascus, suddenly a light flashed from the sky all around him. He fell to the ground and heard 4 a voice saying, 'Saul, Saul, why do you persecute me?' 'Tell me, Lord,' he said, 'who 5 you are.' The voice answered, 'I am Jesus, whom you are persecuting. But get up and 6 go into the city, and you will be told what you have to do.' Meanwhile the men who 7 were travelling with him stood speechless; they heard the voice but could see no one. Saul got up from the ground, but when he 8 opened his eyes he could not see; so they led him by the hand and brought him into Damascus. He was blind for three days, and 9 took no food or drink.
There was a disciple in Damascus named 10 Ananias. He had a vision in which he heard the voice of the Lord: 'Ananias!' 'Here I am, Lord', he answered. The Lord said to 11 him, 'Go at once to Straight Street, to the house of Judas, and ask for a man from Tarsus named Saul. You will find him at prayer; he has had a vision of a man named 12 Ananias coming in and laying his hands on him to restore his sight.' Ananias answered, 13 'Lord, I have often heard about this man and all the harm he has done to thy people in Jerusalem. And he is here with authority 14 from the chief priests to arrest all who invoke thy name.' But the Lord said to him, 15 'You must go, for this man is my chosen instrument to bring my name before the nations and their kings, and before the people of Israel. I myself will show him all 16 that he must go through for my name's sake.'
So Ananias went. He entered the house, 17 laid his hands on him and said, 'Saul, my brother, the Lord Jesus, who appeared to you on your way here, has sent me to you so that you may recover your sight, and be filled with the Holy Spirit.' And immedi- 18 ately it seemed that scales fell from his eyes, and he regained his sight. Thereupon he was baptized, and afterwards he took food and 19 his strength returned.

ʷ *Literally* you are for gall of bitterness and a fetter of unrighteousness.   ˣ *Some witnesses insert* (37) Philip said, 'If you whole-heartedly believe, it is permitted.' He replied, 'I believe that Jesus Christ is the Son of God.'

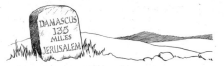

Saul proclaims Christ in Damascus

He stayed some time with the disciples in
20 Damascus. Soon he was proclaiming Jesus
publicly in the synagogues: 'This', he said,
21 'is the Son of God.' All who heard were
astounded. 'Is not this the man', they said,
'who was in Jerusalem trying to destroy
those who invoke this name? Did he not
come here for the sole purpose of arresting
them and taking them to the chief priests?'
22 But Saul grew more and more forceful, and
silenced the Jews of Damascus with his
cogent proofs that Jesus was the Messiah.

Saul in Jerusalem

23 As the days mounted up, the Jews hatched
24 a plot against his life; but their plans became known to Saul. They kept watch on
the city gates day and night so that they
25 might murder him; but his converts took
him one night and let him down by the wall,
lowering him in a basket.
26 When he reached Jerusalem he tried to
join the body of disciples there; but they were
all afraid of him, because they did not be-
27 lieve that he was really a convert. Barnabas,

however, took him by the hand and introduced him to the apostles. He described to
them how Saul had seen the Lord on his
journey, and heard his voice, and how he
had spoken out boldly in the name of Jesus
at Damascus. Saul now stayed with them, 28
moving about freely in Jerusalem. He spoke 29
out boldly and openly in the name of the
Lord, talking and debating with the Greek-
speaking Jews.ʸ But they planned to murder
him, and when the brethren learned of this 30
they escorted him to Caesarea and saw him
off to Tarsus.

Peter in Lydda and Joppa

Meanwhile the church, throughout Judaea, 31
Galilee, and Samaria, was left in peace to
build up its strength. In the fear of the Lord,
upheld by the Holy Spirit, it held on its way
and grew in numbers.
Peter was making a general tour, in the 32
course of which he went down to visit God's
people at Lydda. There he found a man 33
named Aeneas who had been bed-ridden
with paralysis for eight years. Peter said to 34
him, 'Aeneas, Jesus Christ cures you; get
up and make your bed', and immediately he
stood up. All who lived in Lydda and Sharon 35
saw him; and they turned to the Lord.
In Joppa there was a disciple named 36
Tabitha (in Greek, Dorcas, meaning a
gazelle), who filled her days with acts of
kindness and charity. At that time she fell 37
ill and died; and they washed her body and
laid it in a room upstairs. As Lydda was 38
near Joppa, the disciples, who had heard
that Peter was there, sent two men to him
with the urgent request, 'Please come over

y *Literally* the Hellenists.

(Acts 9. 25)

A city of Judaea

39 to us without delay.' Peter thereupon went off with them. When he arrived they took him upstairs to the room, where all the widows came and stood round him in tears, showing him the shirts and coats that Dorcas used to make while she was with them. 40 Peter sent them all outside, and knelt down and prayed. Then, turning towards the body, he said, 'Get up, Tabitha.' She opened her 41 eyes, saw Peter, and sat up. He gave her his hand and helped her to her feet. Then he called the members of the congregation and the widows and showed her to them alive. 42 The news spread all over Joppa, and many 43 came to believe in the Lord. Peter stayed on in Joppa for some time with one Simon, a tanner.

A divine message to Cornelius

10 At Caesarea there was a man named Cornelius, a centurion in the Italian Cohort, as 2 it was called. He was a religious man, and he and his whole family joined in the worship of God. He gave generously to help the Jewish people, and was regular in his prayers to God. One day about three in the 3 afternoon he had a vision in which he clearly saw an angel of God, who came into his room and said, 'Cornelius!' He stared at him 4 in terror. 'What is it, my lord?' he asked. The angel said, 'Your prayers and acts of charity have gone up to heaven to speak for you before God. And now send to Joppa for 5 a man named Simon, also called Peter: he 6 is lodging with another Simon, a tanner, whose house is by the sea.' So when the 7 angel who was speaking to him had gone, he summoned two of his servants and a military orderly who was a religious man, told them the whole story, and sent them 8 to Joppa.

Peter's vision

Next day, while they were still on their way 9 and approaching the city, about noon Peter went up on the roof to pray. He grew 10 hungry and wanted something to eat. While they were getting it ready, he fell into a trance. He saw a rift in the sky, and a thing 11 coming down that looked like a great sheet of sail-cloth. It was slung by the four corners, and was being lowered to the ground. In it 12 he saw creatures of every kind, whatever walks or crawls or flies. Then there was a 13 voice which said to him, 'Up, Peter, kill and eat.' But Peter said, 'No, Lord, no: I have 14 never eaten anything profane or unclean.' The voice came again a second time: 'It is 15 not for you to call profane what God counts clean.' This happened three times; and then 16 the thing was taken up again into the sky.

17 While Peter was still puzzling over the meaning of the vision he had seen, the messengers of Cornelius had been asking the way to Simon's house, and now arrived at 18 the entrance. They called out and asked if 19 Simon Peter was lodging there. But Peter was thinking over the vision, when the Spirit said to him, 'Some² men are here 20 looking for you; make haste and go downstairs. You may go with them without any 21 misgiving, for it was I who sent them.' Peter came down to the men and said, 'You are looking for me? Here I am. What brings you 22 here?' 'We are from the centurion Cornelius,' they replied, 'a good and religious man, acknowledged as such by the whole Jewish nation. He was directed by a holy angel to send for you to his house and to 23 listen to what you have to say.' So Peter asked them in and gave them a night's lodging. Next day he set out with them, accompanied by some members of the congregation at Joppa.

Peter and Cornelius

24 The day after that, he arrived at Caesarea. Cornelius was expecting them and had called together his relatives and close friends. 25 When Peter arrived, Cornelius came to meet him, and bowed to the ground in deep 26 reverence. But Peter raised him to his feet and said, 'Stand up; I am a man like anyone 27 else.' Still talking with him he went in and 28 found a large gathering. He said to them, 'I need not tell you that a Jew is forbidden by his religion to visit or associate with a man of another race; yet God has shown me clearly that I must not call any man profane 29 or unclean. That is why I came here without demur when you sent for me. May I ask what was your reason for sending?' 30 Cornelius said, 'Four days ago, just about this time, I was in the house here saying the afternoon prayers, when suddenly a man in 31 shining robes stood before me. He said: "Cornelius, your prayer has been heard and your acts of charity remembered before God. 32 Send to Joppa, then, to Simon Peter, and ask him to come. He is lodging in the house 33 of Simon the tanner, by the sea." So I sent to you there and then; it was kind of you to come. And now we are all met here before God, to hear all that the Lord has ordered you to say.'
34 Peter began: 'I now see how true it is that 35 God has no favourites, but that in every nation the man who is godfearing and does

what is right is acceptable to him. He sent 36 his word to the Israelites and gave the good news of peace through Jesus Christ, who is Lord of all. I need not tell you what hap- 37 pened lately all over the land of the Jews, starting from Galilee after the baptism proclaimed by John. You know about Jesus of 38 Nazareth, how God anointed him with the Holy Spirit and with power. He went about doing good and healing all who were oppressed by the devil, for God was with him. And 39 we can bear witness to all that he did in the Jewish country-side and in Jerusalem. He was put to death by hanging on a gibbet; but 40 God raised him to life on the third day, and allowed him to appear, not to the whole 41 people, but to witnesses whom God had chosen in advance—to us, who ate and drank with him after he rose from the dead. He 42 commanded us to proclaim him to the people, and affirm that he is the one who has been designated by God as judge of the living and the dead. It is to him that all the 43 prophets testify, declaring that everyone who trusts in him receives forgiveness of sins through his name.'

Gentile converts receive the Spirit

Peter was still speaking when the Holy 44 Spirit came upon all who were listening to the message. The believers who had come 45 with Peter, men of Jewish birth, were astonished that the gift of the Holy Spirit should have been poured out even on Gentiles. For they could hear them speaking in 46 tongues of ecstasy and acclaiming the greatness of God. Then Peter spoke: 'Is anyone 47 prepared to withhold the water for baptism from these persons, who have received the Holy Spirit just as we did ourselves?' Then 48 he ordered them to be baptized in the name of Jesus Christ. After that they asked him to stay on with them for a time.

Peter reports to the Jerusalem church

News came to the apostles and the members 11 of the church in Judaea that Gentiles too had accepted the word of God; and when 2 Peter came up to Jerusalem those who were of Jewish birth raised the question with him. 'You have been visiting men who are un- 3 circumcised,' they said, 'and sitting at table with them!' Peter began by laying before 4 them the facts as they had happened.
'I was in the city of Joppa', he said, 'at 5

---

z *One witness reads* Two; *others read* Three.

P

prayer; and while in a trance I had a vision: a thing was coming down that looked like a great sheet of sail-cloth, slung by the four corners and lowered from the sky till it 6 reached me. I looked intently to make out what was in it and I saw four-footed creatures of the earth, wild beasts, and things that 7 crawl or fly. Then I heard a voice saying to 8 me, "Up, Peter, kill and eat." But I said, "No, Lord, no: nothing profane or unclean 9 has ever entered my mouth." A voice from heaven answered a second time, "It is not for you to call profane what God counts 10 clean." This happened three times, and then they were all drawn up again into the sky. 11 At that moment three men, who had been sent to me from Caesarea, arrived at the

12 house where I was*a* staying; and the Spirit told me to go with them.*b* My six companions here came with me and we went into the 13 man's house. He told us how he had seen an angel standing in his house who said, "Send to Joppa for Simon also called Peter. 14 He will speak words that will bring salvation 15 to you and all your household." Hardly had I begun speaking, when the Holy Spirit came upon them, just as upon us at the 16 beginning. Then I recalled what the Lord had said: "John baptized with water, but you will be baptized with the Holy Spirit." 17 God gave them no less a gift than he gave us when we put our trust in the Lord Jesus Christ; then how could I possibly stand in God's way?'
18   When they heard this their doubts were silenced. They gave praise to God and said, 'This means that God has granted life-giving repentance to the Gentiles also.'

a Some witnesses read we were.
b Some witnesses add making no distinctions; *others add* without any misgiving, *as in 10. 20.*

Developments at Antioch

Meanwhile those who had been scattered 19 after the persecution that arose over Stephen made their way to Phoenicia, Cyprus, and Antioch, bringing the message to Jews only and to no others. But there were some 20 natives of Cyprus and Cyrene among them, and these, when they arrived at Antioch, began to speak to Gentiles as well, telling them the good news of the Lord Jesus. The power 21 of the Lord was with them, and a great many became believers, and turned to the Lord.

The news reached the ears of the church 22 in Jerusalem; and they sent Barnabas to Antioch. When he arrived and saw the divine 23 grace at work, he rejoiced, and encouraged them all to hold fast to the Lord with resolute hearts; for he was a good man, full of the 24 Holy Spirit and of faith. And large numbers were won over to the Lord.

He then went off to Tarsus to look for 25 Saul; and when he had found him, he 26 brought him to Antioch. For a whole year the two of them lived in fellowship with the congregation there, and gave instruction to large numbers. It was in Antioch that the disciples first got the name of Christians.

During this period some prophets came 27 down from Jerusalem to Antioch. One of 28 them, Agabus by name, was inspired to stand up and predict a severe and world-wide famine, which in fact occurred in the reign of Claudius. So the disciples agreed to make 29 a contribution, each according to his means, for the relief of their fellow-Christians in Judaea. This they did, and sent it off to the 30 elders, in the charge of Barnabas and Saul.

Herod attacks leaders of the church

It was about this time that King Herod attacked certain members of the church. He beheaded James, the brother of John, 2 and then, when he saw that the Jews approved, proceeded to arrest Peter also. This 3 happened during the festival of Unleavened Bread. Having secured him, he put him in 4

Antioch in Syria

prison under a military guard, four squads of four men each, meaning to produce him 5 in public after Passover. So Peter was kept in prison under constant watch, while the church kept praying fervently for him to God.

Peter's miraculous escape from prison

6 On the very night before Herod had planned to bring him forward, Peter was asleep between two soldiers, secured by two chains, while outside the doors sentries kept guard 7 over the prison. All at once an angel of the Lord stood there, and the cell was ablaze with light. He tapped Peter on the shoulder and woke him. 'Quick! Get up', he said, and 8 the chains fell away from his wrists. The angel then said to him, 'Do up your belt and put your sandals on.' He did so. 'Now wrap your cloak round you and follow me.' 9 He followed him out, with no idea that the angel's intervention was real: he thought it 0 was just a vision. But they passed the first guard-post, then the second, and reached the iron gate leading out into the city, which opened for them of its own accord. And so they came out and walked the length of one street; and the angel left him.

1 Then Peter came to himself. 'Now I know it is true,' he said; 'the Lord has sent his angel and rescued me from Herod's clutches and from all that the Jewish people were 2 expecting.' When he realized how things stood, he made for the house of Mary, the mother of John Mark, where a large com-3 pany was at prayer. He knocked at the outer door and a maid called Rhoda came to 4 answer it. She recognized Peter's voice and was so overjoyed that instead of opening the door she ran in and announced that Peter 5 was standing outside. 'You are crazy', they

told her; but she insisted that it was so. Then they said, 'It must be his guardian angel.'

Meanwhile Peter went on knocking, and 16 when they opened the door and saw him, they were astounded. With a movement of 17 the hand he signed to them to keep quiet, and told them how the Lord had brought him out of prison. 'Report this to James and the members of the church', he said. Then he left the house and went off elsewhere.

When morning came, there was consterna- 18 tion among the soldiers: what could have become of Peter? Herod made close search, 19 but failed to find him, so he interrogated the guards and ordered their execution.

Herod's pride and fall

Afterwards he left Judaea to reside for a time at Caesarea. He had for some time been 20 furiously angry with the people of Tyre and Sidon, who now by common agreement presented themselves at his court. There they won over Blastus the royal chamberlain, and sued for peace, because their country drew its supplies from the king's territory. So, on 21 an appointed day, attired in his royal robes and seated on the rostrum, Herod harangued them; and the populace shouted back, 'It is 22 a god speaking, not a man!' Instantly an 23 angel of the Lord struck him down, because he had usurped the honour due to God; he was eaten up with worms and died.

Meanwhile the word of God continued 24 to grow and spread.

Barnabas and Saul, their task fulfilled, 25 returned from Jerusalem,[c] taking John Mark with them.

Barnabas and Saul commissioned

There were at Antioch, in the congregation **13**

c *Some witnesses read* their task fulfilled, returned to Jerusalem; *or, as it might be rendered,* their task at Jerusalem fulfilled, returned.

there, certain prophets and teachers: Barnabas, Simeon called Niger, Lucius of Cyrene, Manaen, who had been at the court of
2 Prince Herod, and Saul. While they were keeping a fast and offering worship to the Lord, the Holy Spirit said, 'Set Barnabas and Saul apart for me, to do the work to
3 which I have called them.' Then, after further fasting and prayer, they laid their hands on them and let them go.

In Cyprus: opposition and belief

4 So these two, sent out on their mission by the Holy Spirit, came down to Seleucia, and

ANTIOCH to SELEUCIA

Seleucia   Antioch

Salamis

5 from there sailed to Cyprus. Arriving at Salamis, they declared the word of God in the Jewish synagogues. They had John with
6 them as their assistant. They went through the whole island as far as Paphos, and there they came upon a sorcerer, a Jew who posed
7 as a prophet, Bar-Jesus by name. He was in the retinue of the Governor, Sergius Paulus, an intelligent man, who had sent for Barnabas and Saul and wanted to hear the word
8 of God. This Elymas the sorcerer (so his

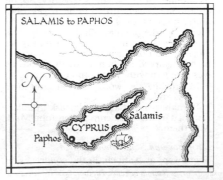

SALAMIS to PAPHOS

Salamis

CYPRUS

Paphos

name may be translated) opposed them, trying to turn the Governor away from the Faith. But Saul, also known as Paul, filled 9 with the Holy Spirit, fixed his eyes on him and said, 'You swindler, you rascal, son of 10 the devil and enemy of all goodness, will you never stop falsifying the straight ways of the Lord? Look now, the hand of the 11 Lord strikes: you shall be blind, and for a time you shall not see the sunlight.' Instantly mist and darkness came over him and he groped about for someone to lead him by the hand. When the Governor saw what had 12 happened he became a believer, deeply impressed by what he learned about the Lord.

Perga

CYPRUS

Paphos

PAPHOS to PERGA

Paul's speech at Pisidian Antioch

Leaving Paphos, Paul and his companions 1 went by sea to Perga in Pamphylia; John, however, left them and returned to Jerusalem. From Perga they continued their 1 journey as far as Pisidian Antioch. On the Sabbath they went to synagogue and took their seats; and after the readings from the 1 Law and the prophets, the officials of the synagogue sent this message to them: 'Friends, if you have anything to say to the people by way of exhortation, let us hear it.' Paul rose, made a gesture with his hand, and 1 began:

'Men of Israel and you who worship our God, listen to me! The God of this people 1 of Israel chose our fathers. When they were still living as aliens in Egypt he made them into a nation and brought them out of that country with arm outstretched. For some forty years he bore with their conduct[d] in the desert. Then in the Canaanite country 1

d Some witnesses read he sustained them.

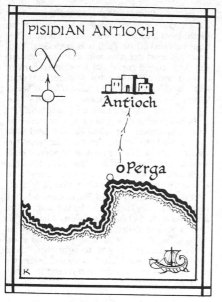

he overthrew seven nations, whose lands he
20 gave them to be their heritage for some four
hundred and fifty years, and afterwards
appointed judges for them until the time of
the prophet Samuel.
21   'Then they asked for a king and God gave
them Saul the son of Kish, a man of the tribe
of Benjamin, who reigned for forty years.
22 Then he removed him and set up David as
their king, giving him his approval in these
words: "I have found David son of Jesse to
be a man after my own heart, who will carry
23 out all my purposes." This is the man from
whose posterity God, as he promised, has
24 brought Israel a saviour, Jesus. John made
ready for his coming by proclaiming baptism
as a token of repentance to the whole people
25 of Israel. And when John was nearing the
end of his course, he said, "I am not what
you think I am. No, after me comes one
whose shoes I am not fit to unfasten."
26   'My brothers, you who come of the stock
of Abraham, and others among you who

revere our God, we are the people to whom
the message of this salvation has been sent.
The people of Jerusalem and their rulers did 27
not recognize him, or understand the words
of the prophets which are read Sabbath by
Sabbath; indeed they fulfilled them by condemning him. Though they failed to find 28
grounds for the sentence of death, they asked
Pilate to have him executed. And when they 29
had carried out all that the scriptures said
about him, they took him down from the
gibbet and laid him in a tomb. But God 30
raised him from the dead; and there was 31
a period of many days during which he
appeared to those who had come up with
him from Galilee to Jerusalem.

'They are now his witnesses before our
nation; and we are here to give you the good 32
news that God, who made the promise to
the fathers, has fulfilled it for the children*e* 33
by raising Jesus from the dead, as indeed it
stands written, in the second*f* Psalm: "You
are my son; this day I have begotten you."
Again, that he raised him from the dead, 34
never again to revert to corruption, he
declares in these words: "I will give you the
blessings promised to David, holy and sure."
This is borne out by another passage: "Thou 35
wilt not let thy loyal servant suffer corruption." As for David, when he had served the 36
purpose of God in his own generation, he
died, and was gathered to his fathers, and
suffered corruption; but the one whom God 37
raised up did not suffer corruption; and you 38
must understand, my brothers, that it is
through him that forgiveness of sins is now
being proclaimed to you. It is through him 39
that everyone who has faith is acquitted of
everything for which there was no acquittal
under the Law of Moses. Beware, then, lest 40
you bring down upon yourselves the doom
proclaimed by the prophets: "See this, you 41
scoffers, wonder, and begone; for I am doing
a deed in your days, a deed which you will
never believe when you are told of it." '

As they were leaving the synagogue they 42
were asked to come again and speak on
these subjects next Sabbath; and after the 43
congregation had dispersed, many Jews and
gentile worshippers went along with Paul
and Barnabas, who spoke to them and urged
them to hold fast to the grace of God.

Paul turns to the Gentiles

On the following Sabbath almost the whole 44
city gathered to hear the word of God.
When the Jews saw the crowds, they were 45
filled with jealous resentment, and contra-
dicted what Paul said, with violent abuse.
But Paul and Barnabas were outspoken in 46
their reply. 'It was necessary', they said,
'that the word of God should be declared

e Some witnesses read our children; *others read* us their children.   *f Some witnesses read* first.

to you first. But since you reject it and thus condemn yourselves as unworthy of eternal

47 life, we now turn to the Gentiles. For these are our instructions from the Lord: "I have appointed you to be a light for the Gentiles, and a means of salvation to earth's farthest

48 bounds."' When the Gentiles heard this, they were overjoyed and thankfully acclaimed the word of the Lord, and those who were marked out for eternal life became

49 believers. So the word of the Lord spread

50 far and wide through the region. But the Jews stirred up feeling among the women of standing who were worshippers, and among the leading men of the city; a persecution was started against Paul and Barnabas,

51 and they were expelled from the district. So they shook the dust off their feet in protest

52 against them and went to Iconium. And the converts were filled with joy and with the Holy Spirit.

At Iconium: Jewish opposition

14 At Iconium similarly they went[g] into the Jewish synagogue and spoke to such purpose that a large body both of Jews and

2 Gentiles became believers. But the unconverted Jews stirred up the Gentiles and poisoned their minds against the Chris-

3 tians. For some time Paul and Barnabas stayed on and spoke boldly and openly in reliance on the Lord; and he confirmed the message of his grace by causing signs and

4 miracles to be worked at their hands. The mass of the townspeople were divided, some siding with the Jews, others with the apostles.

5 But when a move was made by Gentiles and Jews together, with the connivance of the city authorities, to maltreat them and stone

6 them, they got wind of it and made their escape to the Lycaonian cities of Lystra and

7 Derbe and the surrounding country, where they continued to spread the good news.

At Lystra: enthusiasm and hostility

At Lystra sat a crippled man, lame from 8 birth, who had never walked in his life. This 9 man listened while Paul was speaking. Paul fixed his eyes on him and saw that he had the faith to be cured, so he said to him in 10 a loud voice, 'Stand up straight on your feet'; and he sprang up and started to walk. When the crowds saw what Paul had done, 11 they shouted, in their native Lycaonian, 'The gods have come down to us in human form.' And they called Barnabas Jupiter, and Paul 12 they called Mercury, because he was the spokesman. And the priest of Jupiter, whose 13 temple was just outside the city, brought oxen and garlands to the gates, and he and all the people were about to offer sacrifice.

But when the apostles Barnabas and Paul 14 heard of it, they tore their clothes and rushed into the crowd shouting, 'Men, what is this 15 that you are doing? We are only human beings, no less mortal than you. The good news we bring tells you to turn from these follies to the living God, who made heaven and earth and sea and everything in them. In past ages he allowed all nations to go 16 their own way; and yet he has not left you 17 without some clue to his nature, in the kindness he shows: he sends you rain from heaven and crops in their seasons, and gives you food and good cheer in plenty.'

With these words they barely managed to 18 prevent the crowd from offering sacrifice to them.

Then Jews from Antioch and Iconium 19 came on the scene and won over the crowds. They stoned Paul, and dragged him out of the city, thinking him dead. The converts 20 formed a ring round him, and he got to his feet and went into the city. Next day he left with Barnabas for Derbe.

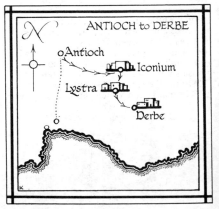

g Or At Iconium they went together . . .

The mission completed

21 After bringing the good news to that town, where they gained many converts, they returned to Lystra, then to Iconium, and then
22 to Antioch, heartening the converts and encouraging them to be true to their religion. They warned them that to enter the kingdom of God we must pass through many hard-
23 ships. They also appointed elders for them in each congregation, and with prayer and fasting committed them to the Lord in whom they had put their faith.

24 Then they passed through Pisidia and
25 came into Pamphylia. When they had given the message at Perga, they went down to
26 Attalia, and from there set sail for Antioch, where they had originally been commended to the grace of God for the task which they
27 had now completed. When they arrived and had called the congregation together, they reported all that God had done through them, and how he had thrown open the gates of
28 faith to the Gentiles. And they stayed for some time with the disciples there.

A conference at Jerusalem

5 Now certain persons who had come down from Judaea began to teach the brotherhood that those who were not circumcised in accordance with Mosaic practice could not
2 be saved. That brought them into fierce dissension and controversy with Paul and Barnabas. And so it was arranged that these two and some others from Antioch should go up to Jerusalem to see the apostles and elders about this question.

They were sent on their way by the con- 3 gregation, and travelled through Phoenicia and Samaria, telling the full story of the conversion of the Gentiles. The news caused great rejoicing among all the Christians there.

When they reached Jerusalem they were 4 welcomed by the church and the apostles and elders, and reported all that God had done through them. Then some of the 5 Pharisaic party who had become believers came forward and said, 'They must be circumcised and told to keep the Law of Moses.'

The apostles and elders held a meeting 6 to look into this matter; and, after a long 7 debate, Peter rose and addressed them. 'My friends,' he said, 'in the early days, as you yourselves know, God made his choice among you and ordained that from my lips the Gentiles should hear and believe the message of the Gospel. And God, who can 8 read men's minds, showed his approval of them by giving the Holy Spirit to them, as he did to us. He made no difference between 9 them and us; for he purified their hearts by faith. Then why do you now provoke God 10 by laying on the shoulders of these converts a yoke which neither we nor our fathers were able to bear? No, we believe that it is by the 11 grace of the Lord Jesus that we are saved, and so are they.'

At that the whole company fell silent and 12 listened to Barnabas and Paul as they told of all the signs and miracles that God had worked among the Gentiles through them.

When they had finished speaking, James 13

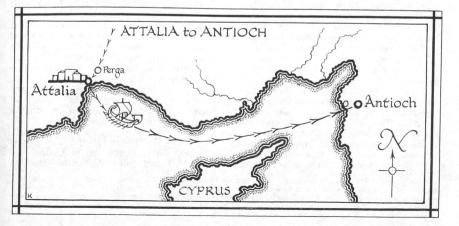

summed up: 'My friends,' he said, 'listen to
14 me. Simeon has told how it first happened
that God took notice of the Gentiles, to
choose from among them a people to bear
15 his name; and this agrees with the words of
the prophets, as Scripture has it:

16 "Thereafter I will return and rebuild the
fallen house of David;
even from its ruins I will rebuild it, and set
it up again,
17 that they may seek the Lord—all the rest of
mankind,
and the Gentiles, whom I have claimed for
my own.
Thus says the Lord, whose work it is,
18 made known long ago."

19 'My judgement therefore is that we should
impose no irksome restrictions on those of
20 the Gentiles who are turning to God, but
instruct them by letter to abstain from things
polluted by contact with idols, from fornication, from anything that has been strangled,
21 and from blood.*h* Moses, after all, has never
lacked spokesmen in every town for generations past; he is read in the synagogues
Sabbath by Sabbath.'

A letter to gentile Christians

22 Then the apostles and elders, with the
agreement of the whole church, resolved to
choose representatives and send them to
Antioch with Paul and Barnabas. They chose
two leading men in the community, Judas
23 Barsabbas and Silas, and gave them this
letter to deliver:
'We, the apostles and elders, send greetings as brothers to our brothers of gentile
24 origin in Antioch, Syria, and Cilicia. For-
asmuch as we have heard that some of our
number, without any instructions from us,
have*i* disturbed you with their talk and
25 unsettled your minds, we have resolved
unanimously to send to you our chosen
representatives with our well-beloved Barna-
26 bas and Paul, who have devoted themselves
27 to the cause of our Lord Jesus Christ. We
are therefore sending Judas and Silas, who
will themselves confirm this by word of
28 mouth. It is the decision of the Holy Spirit,
and our decision, to lay no further burden
29 upon you beyond these essentials: you are
to abstain from meat that has been offered
to idols, from blood, from anything that
has been strangled,*j* and from fornication.*k*
If you keep yourselves free from these things
you will be doing right. Farewell.'
30 So they were sent off on their journey and

Greek idols

travelled down to Antioch, where they
called the congregation together, and delivered the letter. When it was read, they 31
all rejoiced at the encouragement it brought.
Judas and Silas, who were prophets 32
themselves, said much to encourage and
strengthen the members, and, after spend- 33
ing some time there, were dismissed with
the good wishes of the brethren, to return
to those who had sent them.*l* But Paul and 35
Barnabas stayed on at Antioch, and there,
along with many others, they taught and
preached the word of the Lord.

Paul and Barnabas part company

After a while Paul said to Barnabas, 'Ought 36
we not to go back now to see how our
brothers are faring in the various towns
where we proclaimed the word of the Lord?'
Barnabas wanted to take John Mark with 37
them; but Paul judged that the man who 38
had deserted them in Pamphylia and had
not gone on to share in their work was not
the man to take with them now. The dispute 39
was so sharp that they parted company.
Barnabas took Mark with him and sailed
for Cyprus, while Paul chose Silas. He 40
started on his journey, commended by the
brothers to the grace of the Lord, and 41
travelled through Syria and Cilicia bringing
new strength to the congregations.

At Lystra: Paul meets Timothy

He went on to Derbe and to Lystra, and
there he found a disciple named Timothy,

---

h Some witnesses omit from fornication; *others omit* from anything that has been strangled; *some add* (after
blood) and to refrain from doing to others what they would not like done to themselves.   *i Some witnesses
read* have gone out and . . .   *j Some witnesses omit* from anything that has been strangled.   *k Some
witnesses omit* and from fornication; *and some add* and refrain from doing to others what you would not like done
to yourselves.   *l Some witnesses add* (34) But Silas decided to remain there.

the son of a Jewish Christian mother and
2 a Gentile father. He was well spoken of by
3 the Christians at Lystra and Iconium, and
Paul wanted to have him in his company
when he left the place. So he took him and
circumcised him, out of consideration for
the Jews who lived in those parts; for they
4 all knew that his father was a Gentile. As
they made their way from town to town
they handed on the decisions taken by the
apostles and elders in Jerusalem and en-
5 joined their observance. And so, day by
day, the congregations grew stronger in
faith and increased in numbers.

At Troas: an appeal from Macedonia

6 They travelled through the Phrygian and
Galatian region,[m] because they were prevented by the Holy Spirit from delivering
7 the message in the province of Asia; and
when they approached the Mysian border
they tried to enter Bithynia; but the Spirit
8 of Jesus would not allow them, so they
skirted[n] Mysia and reached the coast at
9 Troas. During the night a vision came to
Paul: a Macedonian stood there appealing
to him and saying, 'Come across to Mace-
10 donia and help us.' After he had seen this
vision we at once set about getting a passage
to Macedonia, concluding that God had
called us to bring them the good news.

At Philippi: the conversion of Lydia

11 So we sailed from Troas and made a straight
run to Samothrace, the next day to Nea-
12 polis, and from there to Philippi, a city of
the first rank in that district of Macedonia,
and a Roman colony. Here we stayed for
13 some days, and on the Sabbath day we went

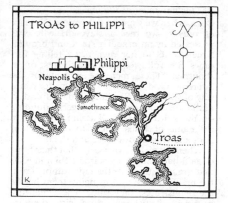

outside the city gate by the river-side, where
we thought there would be a place of prayer,[o]
and sat down and talked to the women who
had gathered there. One of them named 14
Lydia, a dealer in purple fabric from the
city of Thyatira, who was a worshipper of
God, was listening, and the Lord opened
her heart to respond to what Paul said. She 15
was baptized, and her household with her,
and then she said to us, 'If you have judged
me to be a believer in the Lord, I beg you to
come and stay in my house.' And she insisted on our going.

---

m Or through Phrygia and the Galatian region.
there was a recognized place of prayer.

n Possibly traversed.   *o Some witnesses read* where

Philippi

The fortune-teller of Philippi

16 Once, when we were on our way to the place of prayer, we met a slave-girl who was possessed by an oracular spirit and brought large profits to her owners by telling for-
17 tunes. She followed Paul and the rest of us, shouting, 'These men are servants of the Supreme God, and are declaring to you a
18 way of salvation.' She did this day after day, until Paul could bear it no longer. Rounding on the spirit he said, 'I command you in the name of Jesus Christ to come out of her', and it went out there and then.
19   When the girl's owners saw that their hope of gain had gone, they seized Paul and Silas and dragged them to the city authorities in
20 the main square; and bringing them before the magistrates, they said, 'These men are causing a disturbance in our city; they are
21 Jews; they are advocating customs which it is illegal for us Romans to adopt and fol-
22 low.' The mob joined in the attack; and the magistrates tore off the prisoners' clothes
23 and ordered them to be flogged. After giving them a severe beating they flung them into prison and ordered the jailer to keep
24 them under close guard. In view of these orders, he put them in the inner prison and secured their feet in the stocks.

Earthquake at Philippi

25 About midnight Paul and Silas, at their prayers, were singing praises to God, and
26 the other prisoners were listening, when suddenly there was such a violent earthquake that the foundations of the jail were shaken; all the doors burst open and all the
27 prisoners found their fetters unfastened. The jailer woke up to see the prison doors wide open, and assuming that the prisoners had escaped, drew his sword intending to kill

himself. But Paul shouted, 'Do yourself no 28 harm; we are all here.' The jailer called for 29 lights, rushed in and threw himself down before Paul and Silas, trembling with fear. He then escorted them out and said, 30 'Masters, what must I do to be saved?' They said, 'Put your trust in the Lord Jesus, 31 and you will be saved, you and your household.' Then they spoke the word of the 32 Lord*p* to him and to everyone in his house. At that late hour of the night he took them 33 and washed their wounds; and immediately afterwards he and his whole family were baptized. He brought them into his house, 34 set out a meal, and rejoiced with his whole household in his new-found faith in God.

When daylight came the magistrates sent 35 their officers with instructions to release the men. The jailer reported the message to 36 Paul: 'The magistrates have sent word that you are to be released. So now you may go free, and blessings on your journey.'*q* But 37 Paul said to the officers: 'They gave us a public flogging, though we are Roman citizens and have not been found guilty; they threw us into prison, and are they now to smuggle us out privately? No indeed! Let them come in person and escort us out.' The officers reported his words. The magis- 38 trates were alarmed to hear that they were Roman citizens, and came and apologized 39 to them. Then they escorted them out and requested them to go away from the city. On leaving the prison, they went 40 to Lydia's house, where they met their fellow-Christians, and spoke words of encouragement to them; then they departed.

At Thessalonica: success and opposition

They now travelled by way of Amphipolis **17** and Apollonia and came to Thessalonica,

p Some witnesses read of God.   *q Some witnesses read . . .* free and take your journey.

Thessalonica   HK

PHILIPPI
to
BEROEA

2 where there was a Jewish synagogue. Following his usual practice Paul went to their meetings; and for the next three Sabbaths he argued with them, quoting texts of Scrip-
3 ture which he expounded and applied to show that the Messiah had to suffer and rise from the dead. 'And this Jesus,' he said, 'whom I am proclaiming to you, is the
4 Messiah.' Some of them were convinced and joined Paul and Silas; so did a great number of godfearing Gentiles and a good many influential women.*r*
5 But the Jews in their jealousy recruited some low fellows from the dregs of the populace, roused the rabble, and had the city in an uproar. They mobbed Jason's house, with the intention of bringing Paul
6 and Silas before the town assembly. Failing to find them, they dragged Jason himself and some members of the congregation before the magistrates, shouting, 'The men who have made trouble all over the world
7 have now come here; and Jason has harboured them. They all flout the Emperor's laws, and assert that there is a rival king,

Jesus.' These words caused a great commo-
8 tion in the mob, which affected the magistrates also. They bound over Jason and the
9 others, and let them go.

Eager welcome at Beroea

As soon as darkness fell, the members of
10 the congregation sent Paul and Silas off to Beroea. On arrival, they made their way to the synagogue. The Jews here were more
11 civil than those at Thessalonica: they received the message with great eagerness, studying the scriptures every day to see whether it was as they said. Many of them
12 therefore became believers, and so did a fair number of Gentiles, women of standing as well as men. But when the Thessalonian
13 Jews learned that the word of God had now been proclaimed by Paul in Beroea, they came on there to stir up trouble and rouse the rabble. Thereupon the members of the
14 congregation sent Paul off at once to go down to the coast, while Silas and Timothy both stayed behind. Paul's escort brought
15 him as far as Athens, and came away with instructions for Silas and Timothy to rejoin him with all speed.

At Athens: encounter with philosophers

Now while Paul was waiting for them at
16 Athens he was exasperated to see how the city was full of idols. So he argued in the
17 synagogue with the Jews and gentile worshippers, and also in the city square every day with casual passers-by. And some of
18 the Epicurean and Stoic philosophers joined

r Some witnesses read a good many wives of leading men.

The Acropolis, Athens

issue with him. Some said, 'What can this charlatan be trying to say?'; others, 'He would appear to be a propagandist for foreign deities'—this because he was preach-
19 ing about Jesus and Resurrection. So they took him and brought him before the Court of Areopagus[s] and said, 'May we know what this new doctrine is that you pro-
20 pound? You are introducing ideas that sound strange to us, and we should like to
21 know what they mean.' (Now the Athenians in general and the foreigners there had no time for anything but talking or hearing about the latest novelty.)

22   Then Paul stood up before the Court of Areopagus[t] and said: 'Men of Athens, I see that in everything that concerns religion you
23 are uncommonly scrupulous. For as I was going round looking at the objects of your worship, I noticed among other things an altar bearing the inscription "To an Unknown God". What you worship but do not know—this is what I now proclaim.

24   'The God who created the world and everything in it, and who is Lord of heaven and earth, does not live in shrines made by
25 men. It is not because he lacks anything that he accepts service at men's hands, for he is himself the universal giver of life and breath
26 and all else. He created every race of men of one stock, to inhabit the whole earth's surface. He fixed the epochs of their history[u]
27 and the limits of their territory. They were to seek God, and, it might be, touch and find him; though indeed he is not far from
28 each one of us, for in him we live and move, in him we exist; as some of your own poets[v]
29 have said, "We are also his offspring." As God's offspring, then, we ought not to suppose that the deity is like an image in gold or silver or stone, shaped by human
30 craftsmanship and design. As for the times of ignorance, God has overlooked them; but now he commands mankind, all men
31 everywhere, to repent, because he has fixed the day on which he will have the world judged, and justly judged, by a man of his choosing; of this he has given assurance to all by raising him from the dead.'

32   When they heard about the raising of the dead, some scoffed; and others said, 'We will hear you on this subject some other
33 34 time.' And so Paul left the assembly. However, some men joined him and became believers, including Dionysius, a member of the Court of Areopagus; also a woman named Damaris, and others besides.

Working and teaching at Corinth

18 After this he left Athens and went to Corinth.
2 There he fell in with a Jew named Aquila,

BEROEA to CORINTH

Beroea

Corinth   Athens

a native of Pontus, and his wife Priscilla; he had recently arrived from Italy because Claudius had issued an edict that all Jews should leave Rome. Paul approached them and, because he was of the same trade, he 3 made his home with them, and they carried on business together; they were tent-makers. He also held discussions in the synagogue 4 Sabbath by Sabbath, trying to convince both Jews and Gentiles.

Then Silas and Timothy came down from 5 Macedonia, and Paul devoted himself entirely to preaching, affirming before the Jews that the Messiah was Jesus. But when they 6 opposed him and resorted to abuse, he shook out the skirts of his cloak and said to them, 'Your blood be on your own heads! My conscience is clear; now I shall go to the Gentiles.' With that he left, and went to the 7 house of a worshipper of God named Titius Justus, who lived next door to the synagogue. Crispus, who held office in the synagogue, 8 now became a believer in the Lord, with all

---

s Or brought him to Mars' Hill.   *t Or* in the middle of Mars' Hill.   *u Or* fixed the ordered seasons . . .
v Some witnesses read some among you.

his household; and a number of Corinthians listened and believed, and were baptized.

9 One night in a vision the Lord said to Paul, 'Have no fear: go on with your preach-
10 ing and do not be silenced, for I am with you and no one shall attempt to do you harm;[w] and there are many in this city who
11 are my people.' So he settled down for eighteen months, teaching the word of God among them.

Gallio dismisses the case against Paul

12 But when Gallio was proconsul of Achaia, the Jews set upon Paul in a body and brought
13 him into court. 'This man', they said, 'is inducing people to worship God in ways
14 that are against the law.' Paul was just about to speak when Gallio said to them, 'If it had been a question of crime or grave mis-demeanour, I should, of course, have given
15 you Jews a patient hearing, but if it is some bickering about words and names and your Jewish law, you may see to it yourselves; I have no mind to be a judge of these matters.'
16 And he had them ejected from the court.
17 Then there was a general attack on Sosthenes, who held office in the synagogue, and they gave him a beating in full view of the bench. But all this left Gallio quite unconcerned.

More journeys

18 Paul stayed on for some time, and then took leave of the brotherhood and set sail for Syria, accompanied by Priscilla and Aquila. At Cenchreae he had his hair cut off, be-
19 cause he was under a vow. When they reached Ephesus he parted from them and went himself into the synagogue, where he
20 held a discussion with the Jews. He was
21 asked to stay longer, but declined and set out from Ephesus, saying, as he took leave

of them, 'I shall come back to you if it is God's will.' On landing at Caesarea, he 22 went up and paid his respects to the church, and then went down to Antioch. After spend- 23 ing some time there, he set out again and made a journey through the Galatian country and on through Phrygia, bringing new strength to all the converts.

Apollos at Ephesus

Now there arrived at Ephesus a Jew named 24 Apollos, an Alexandrian by birth, an elo-quent man,[x] powerful in his use of the scriptures. He had been instructed in the 25 way of the Lord and was full of spiritual fervour; and in his discourses he taught accurately the facts about Jesus,[y] though he knew only John's baptism. He now began 26 to speak boldly in the synagogue, where Priscilla and Aquila heard him; they took him in hand and expounded the new way[z] to him in greater detail. Finding that he 27 wished to go across to Achaia, the brother-hood gave him their support, and wrote to the congregation there to make him wel-come. From the time of his arrival, he was very helpful to those who had by God's grace become believers; for he strenuously 28 confuted the Jews, demonstrating publicly from the scriptures that the Messiah is Jesus.

Paul's successful work at Ephesus

While Apollos was at Corinth, Paul travelled **19** through the inland regions till he came to Ephesus. There he found a number of con-verts, to whom he said, 'Did you receive the 2 Holy Spirit when you became believers?' 'No,' they replied, 'we have not even heard that there is a Holy Spirit.' He said, 'Then 3 what baptism were you given?' 'John's baptism', they answered. Paul then said, 4

---

w Or and you will not be harmed by anyone's attacks.   *x Or* a learned man.   *y Some witnesses read*
about the Lord.   *z Some witnesses read* the way of God.

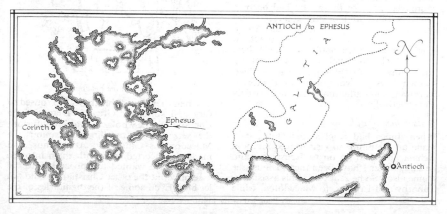

'The baptism that John gave was a baptism in token of repentance, and he told the people to put their trust in one who was to 5 come after him, that is, in Jesus.' On hearing this they were baptized into the name of the 6 Lord Jesus; and when Paul had laid his hands on them, the Holy Spirit came upon them and they spoke in tongues of ecstasy 7 and prophesied. Altogether they were about a dozen men.

8 During the next three months he attended the synagogue and, using argument and persuasion, spoke boldly and freely about 9 the kingdom of God. But when some proved obdurate and would not believe, speaking evil of the new way before the whole congregation, he left them, withdrew his converts, and continued to hold discussions 10 daily in the lecture-hall of Tyrannus. This went on for two years, with the result that the whole population of the province of Asia, both Jews and Gentiles, heard the 11 word of the Lord. And through Paul God 12 worked singular miracles: when handkerchiefs and scarves which had been in contact with his skin were carried to the sick, they were rid of their diseases and the evil spirits came out of them.

13 But some strolling Jewish exorcists tried their hand at using the name of the Lord Jesus on those possessed by evil spirits; they would say, 'I adjure you by Jesus whom 14 Paul proclaims.' There were seven sons of Sceva, a Jewish chief priest, who were using 15 this method, when the evil spirit answered back and said, 'Jesus I acknowledge, and 16 I know about Paul, but who are you?' And the man with the evil spirit flew at them, overpowered them all, and handled them with such violence that they ran out of the 17 house stripped and battered. This became known to everybody in Ephesus, whether Jew or Gentile; they were all awestruck, and the name of the Lord Jesus gained in honour. 18 Moreover many of those who had become believers came and openly confessed that 19 they had been using magical spells. And a good many of those who formerly practised magic collected their books and burnt them publicly. The total value was reckoned up and it came to fifty thousand pieces of silver. 20 In such ways the word of the Lord showed its power, spreading more and more widely and effectively.

Disturbance in Ephesus

21 When things had reached this stage, Paul made up his mind*a* to visit Macedonia and Achaia and then go on to Jerusalem; and he said, 'After I have been there, I must see 22 Rome also.' So he sent two of his assistants, Timothy and Erastus, to Macedonia, while he himself stayed some time longer in the province of Asia.

23 Now about that time, the Christian movement gave rise to a serious disturbance. 24 There was a man named Demetrius, a silversmith who made silver shrines of Diana and provided a great deal of employment for the craftsmen. He called a meeting of these 25 men and the workers in allied trades, and addressed them. 'Men,' he said, 'you know that our high standard of living depends on this industry. And you see and hear how this 26 fellow Paul with his propaganda has perverted crowds of people, not only at Ephesus but also in practically the whole of the province of Asia. He is telling them that gods made by human hands are not gods at all. There is danger for us here; it is not only 27 that our line of business will be discredited, but also that the sanctuary of the great goddess Diana will cease to command respect; and then it will not be long before she who is worshipped by all Asia and the civilized world is brought down from her divine pre-eminence.'

Diana of the Ephesians

When they heard this they were roused to 28 fury and shouted, 'Great is Diana of the Ephesians!' The whole city was in confusion; 29 they seized Paul's travelling-companions, the Macedonians Gaius and Aristarchus, and made a concerted rush with them into the theatre. Paul wanted to appear before the 30 assembly but the other Christians would not let him. Even some of the dignitaries of the 31

a Or Paul, led by the Spirit, resolved . . .

province, who were friendly towards him,
sent and urged him not to venture into the
32 theatre. Meanwhile some were shouting one
thing, some another; for the assembly was
in confusion and most of them did not know
33 what they had all come for. But some of the
crowd explained the trouble to Alexander,
whom the Jews had pushed to the front, and
he, motioning for silence, attempted to make
34 a defence before the assembly. But when
they recognized that he was a Jew, a single
cry arose from them all: for about two hours
they kept on shouting, 'Great is Diana of the
Ephesians!'
35   The town clerk, however, quieted the
crowd. 'Men of Ephesus,' he said, 'all the
world knows that our city of Ephesus is
temple-warden of the great Diana and of
that symbol of her which fell from heaven.
36 Since these facts are beyond dispute, your
proper course is to keep quiet and do nothing
37 rash. These men whom you have brought
here as culprits have committed no sacrilege
and uttered no blasphemy against our god-
38 dess. If therefore Demetrius and his craftsmen have a case against anyone, assizes are
held and there are such people as proconsuls;
let the parties bring their charges and
39 countercharges. If, on the other hand, you
have some further question to raise, it will
40 be dealt with in the statutory assembly. We
certainly run the risk of being charged with
riot for this day's work. There is no justifica-
tion for it, and if the issue is raised we shall
be unable to give any explanation of this
41 uproar.' With that he dismissed the assembly.

To Greece, Macedonia, and Troas

20 When the disturbance had ceased, Paul sent
for the disciples and, after encouraging them,
said good-bye and set out on his journey to
2 Macedonia. He travelled through those parts
of the country, often speaking words of
encouragement to the Christians there, and
3 so came into Greece. When he had spent
three months there and was on the point of
embarking for Syria, a plot was laid against
him by the Jews, so he decided to return by
4 way of Macedonia. He was accompanied by
Sopater son of Pyrrhus, from Beroea, the
Thessalonians Aristarchus and Secundus,
Gaius the Doberian[b] and Timothy, and the
5 Asians Tychicus and Trophimus. These went
6 ahead and waited for us at Troas; we ourselves set sail from Philippi after the Passover season,[c] and in five days reached them
at Troas, where we spent a week.

An all-night meeting at Troas

7 On the Saturday night, in our assembly for
the breaking of bread, Paul, who was to

leave next day, addressed them, and went
on speaking until midnight. Now there 8
were many lamps in the upper room where
we were assembled; and a youth named 9
Eutychus, who was sitting on the window-
ledge, grew more and more sleepy as Paul
went on talking. At last he was completely
overcome by sleep, fell from the third storey
to the ground, and was picked up for dead.
Paul went down, threw himself upon him, 10
seizing him in his arms, and said to them,
'Stop this commotion; there is still life in
him.' He then went upstairs, broke bread 11
and ate, and after much conversation, which
lasted until dawn, he departed. And they 12
took the boy away alive and were immensely
comforted.

Paul's farewell to the Ephesian elders

We went ahead to the ship and sailed for 13
Assos, where we were to take Paul aboard.
He had made this arrangement, as he was
going to travel by road. When he met us at 14
Assos, we took him aboard and went on to
Mitylene. Next day we sailed from there and 15
arrived opposite Chios, and on the second
day we made Samos. On the following day[d]
we reached Miletus. For Paul had decided 16
to pass by Ephesus and so avoid having to

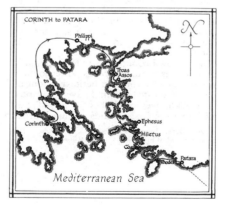

spend time in the province of Asia; he was
eager to be in Jerusalem, if he possibly could,
on the day of Pentecost. He did, however, 17
send from Miletus to Ephesus and summon
the elders of the congregation; and when 18
they joined him, he spoke as follows:
'You know how, from the day that I first
set foot in the province of Asia, for the whole
time that I was with you, I served the Lord 19
in all humility amid the sorrows and trials
that came upon me through the machinations of the Jews. You know that I kept 20

---

b Some witnesses read the Derbaean.   *c Literally* after the days of Unleavened Bread.   *d Some witnesses read . . .* Samos, and , after stopping at Trogyllium, on the following day . . .

back nothing that was for your good: I delivered the message to you; I taught you, 21 in public and in your homes; with Jews and Gentiles alike I insisted on repentance be- 22 fore God and trust in our Lord Jesus. And now, as you see, I am on my way to Jerusalem, under the constraint of the Spirit.*e* Of what will befall me there I know nothing, 23 except that in city after city the Holy Spirit assures me that imprisonment and hard- 24 ships await me. For myself, I set no store by life; I only want to finish the race, and complete the task which the Lord Jesus assigned to me, of bearing my testimony to the gospel of God's grace.

25 'One word more: I have gone about among you proclaiming the Kingdom, but now I know that none of you will see my face again. 26 That being so, I here and now declare that 27 no man's fate can be laid at my door; for I have kept back nothing; I have disclosed 28 to you the whole purpose of God. Keep watch over yourselves and over all the flock of which the Holy Spirit has given you charge, as shepherds of the church of the Lord,*f* which he won for himself by his own blood.*g* 29 I know that when I am gone, savage wolves will come in among you and will not spare 30 the flock. Even from your own body there will be men coming forward who will distort the truth to induce the disciples to break 31 away and follow them. So be on the alert; remember how for three years, night and day, I never ceased to counsel each of you, and how I wept over you.

32 'And now I commend you to God and to his gracious word, which has power to build you up and give you your heritage among all 33 who are dedicated to him. I have not wanted 34 anyone's money or clothes for myself; you all know that these hands of mine earned

enough for the needs of myself and my companions. I showed you that it is our duty 35 to help the weak in this way, by hard work, and that we should keep in mind the words of the Lord Jesus, who himself said, "Happiness lies more in giving than in receiving." '

As he finished speaking, he knelt down 36 with them all and prayed. Then there were 37 loud cries of sorrow from them all, as they folded Paul in their arms and kissed him. What distressed them most was his saying 38 that they would never see his face again. So they escorted him to his ship.

Sails set for Palestine

When we had parted from them and set sail, **21** we made a straight run and came to Cos; next day to Rhodes, and thence to Patara.*h*

There we found a ship bound for Phoenicia, 2 so we went aboard and sailed in her. We 3 came in sight of Cyprus, and leaving it to port, we continued our voyage to Syria, and put in at Tyre, for there the ship was

---

e Or under an inner compulsion.   *f Some witnesses read* of God.   *g Or, according to some witnesses,* by the blood of his Own.   *h Some witnesses add* and Myra.

Tyre

4 to unload her cargo. We went and found the disciples and stayed there a week; and they, warned by the Spirit, urged Paul to abandon his visit to Jerusalem. 5 But when our time ashore was ended, we left and continued our journey; and they and their wives and children all escorted us out of the city. We knelt down on the 6 beach and prayed, then bade each other good-bye; we went aboard, and they returned home.

Prophetic warning to Paul

7 We made the passage from Tyre and reached Ptolemais, where we greeted the brother-8 hood and spent one day with them. Next day we left and came to Caesarea. We went to the home of Philip the evangelist, who was 9 one of the Seven, and stayed with him. He had four unmarried daughters, who posses-10 sed the gift of prophecy. When we had been there several days, a prophet named Agabus 11 arrived from Judaea. He came to us, took Paul's belt, bound his own feet and hands with it, and said, 'These are the words of the Holy Spirit: Thus will the Jews in Jerusalem bind the man to whom this belt belongs, and 12 hand him over to the Gentiles.' When we heard this, we and the local people begged and implored Paul to abandon his visit 13 to Jerusalem. Then Paul gave his answer: 'Why all these tears? Why are you trying to weaken my resolution? For my part I am ready not merely to be bound but even to die at Jerusalem for the name of the 14 Lord Jesus.' So, as he would not be persuaded, we gave up and said, 'The Lord's will be done.'

15   At the end of our stay we packed our baggage and took the road up to Jerusalem. 16 Some of the disciples from Caesarea came along with us, bringing a certain Mnason of Cyprus, a Christian from the early days, 17 with whom we were to lodge. So we reached Jerusalem, where the brotherhood welcomed us gladly.

In Jerusalem: Paul and James

18 Next day Paul paid a visit to James; we were with him, and all the elders attended. 19 He greeted them, and then described in detail all that God had done among the 20 Gentiles through his ministry. When they heard this, they gave praise to God. Then they said to Paul: 'You see, brother, how many thousands of converts we have among the Jews, all of them staunch upholders of 21 the Law. Now they have been given certain information about you: it is said that you teach all the Jews in the gentile world to turn their backs on Moses, telling them to give

up circumcising their children and follow-ing our way of life. What is the position, 22 then? They are sure to hear that you have arrived. You must therefore do as we tell 23 you. We have four men here who are under a vow; take them with you and go through 24 the ritual of purification with them, paying their expenses, after which they may shave their heads. Then everyone will know that there is nothing in the stories they were told about you, but that you are a practising Jew and keep the Law yourself. As for the gentile 25 converts, we sent them our decision that they must abstain from meat that has been offered to idols, from blood, from anything that has been strangled,[i] and from forni-cation.' So Paul took the four men, and 26 next day, after going through the ritual of purification with them, he went into the temple to give notice of the date when the period of purification would end and the offering be made for each one of them.

Paul in protective custody

But just before the seven days were up, the 27 Jews from the province of Asia saw him in the temple. They stirred up the whole crowd, and seized him, shouting, 'Men of Israel, 28 help, help! This is the fellow who spreads his doctrine all over the world, attacking our people, our law, and this sanctuary. On top of all this he has brought Gentiles into the temple and profaned this holy place.' For they had previously seen Trophimus 29 the Ephesian with him in the city, and assumed that Paul had brought him into the temple.

The whole city was in a turmoil, and people 30 came running from all directions. They seized Paul and dragged him out of the temple; and at once the doors were shut. While they were clamouring for his death, 31 a report reached the officer commanding the cohort, that all Jerusalem was in an uproar. He immediately took a force of 32 soldiers with their centurions and came down on the rioters at the double. As soon as they saw the commandant and his troops, they stopped beating Paul. The commandant 33 stepped forward, arrested him, and ordered him to be shackled with two chains; he then asked who the man was and what he had been doing. Some in the crowd shouted one 34 thing, some another. As he could not get at the truth because of the hubbub, he ordered him to be taken into barracks. When Paul 35 reached the steps, he had to be carried by the soldiers because of the violence of the mob. For the whole crowd were at their heels 36 yelling, 'Kill him!'

i Some witnesses omit from anything that has been strangled.

P*

Tarsus

Paul defends himself

37 Just before Paul was taken into the barracks he said to the commandant, 'May I have a word with you?' The commandant said, 'So
38 you speak Greek, do you? Then you are not the Egyptian who started a revolt some time ago and led a force of four thousand
39 terrorists out into the wilds?' Paul replied, 'I am a Jew, a Tarsian from Cilicia, a citizen of no mean city. I ask your permission to
40 speak to the people.' When permission had been given, Paul stood on the steps and with a gesture called for the attention of the people. As soon as quiet was restored, he addressed them in the Jewish language:

22 'Brothers and fathers, give me a hearing
2 while I make my defence before you.' When they heard him speaking to them in their own language, they listened the more quietly.
3 'I am a true-born Jew,' he said, 'a native of Tarsus in Cilicia. I was brought up in this city, and as a pupil of Gamaliel I was thoroughly trained in every point of our ancestral law. I have always been ardent in
4 God's service, as you all are today. And so I began to persecute this movement to the death, arresting its followers, men and women alike, and putting them in chains.
5 For this I have as witnesses the High Priest and the whole Council of Elders. I was given letters from them to our fellow-Jews at Damascus, and had started out to bring the Christians there to Jerusalem as prisoners
6 for punishment; and this is what happened.

I was on the road and nearing Damascus, when suddenly about midday a great light flashed from the sky all around me, and I fell 7 to the ground. Then I heard a voice saying to me, "Saul, Saul, why do you persecute me?" I answered, "Tell me, Lord, who you 8 are." "I am Jesus of Nazareth," he said, "whom you are persecuting." My compan- 9 ions saw the light, but did not hear the voice that spoke to me. "What shall I do, Lord?" 10 I said, and the Lord replied, "Get up and continue your journey to Damascus; there you will be told of all the tasks that are laid upon you." As I had been blinded by the 11 brilliance of that light, my companions led me by the hand, and so I came to Damascus.

'There, a man called Ananias, a devout 12 observer of the Law and well spoken of by all the Jews of that place, came and stood 13 beside me and said, "Saul, my brother, recover your sight." Instantly I recovered my sight and saw him. He went on: "The God 14 of our fathers appointed you to know his will and to see the Righteous One and to hear his very voice, because you are to be 15 his witness before the world, and testify to what you have seen and heard. And now 16 why delay? Be baptized at once, with invocation of his name, and wash away your sins."

'After my return to Jerusalem, I was 17 praying in the temple when I fell into a trance and saw him there, speaking to me. 18 "Make haste", he said, "and leave Jerusalem without delay, for they will not accept your testimony about me." "Lord," I said, "they 19 know that I imprisoned those who believe in thee, and flogged them in every synagogue; and when the blood of Stephen thy witness 20 was shed I stood by, approving, and I looked after the clothes of those who killed 21 him." But he said to me, "Go, for I am sending you far away to the Gentiles."'

The rights of a Roman citizen

22 Up to this point they had given him a hearing; but now they began shouting, 'Down with him! A scoundrel like that is better 23 dead!' And as they were yelling and waving 24 their cloaks and flinging dust in the air, the commandant ordered him to be brought into the barracks and gave instructions to examine him by flogging, and find out what reason there was for such an outcry against 25 him. But when they tied him up for the lash,[j] Paul said to the centurion who was standing there, 'Can you legally flog a man who is a Roman citizen, and moreover has not been 26 found guilty?' When the centurion heard this, he went and reported it to the commandant. 'What do you mean to do?' he 27 said. 'This man is a Roman citizen.' The commandant came to Paul. 'Tell me, are you a Roman citizen?' he asked. 'Yes', said

The tower of the barracks

he. The commandant rejoined, 'It cost me 28 a large sum to acquire this citizenship.' Paul said, 'But it was mine by birth.' Then 29 those who were about to examine him withdrew hastily, and the commandant himself was alarmed when he realized that Paul was a Roman citizen and that he had put him in irons.

Paul before the High Priest

The following day, wishing to be quite sure 30 what charge the Jews were bringing against Paul, he released him and ordered the chief priests and the entire Council to assemble. He then took Paul down and stood him before them.

Paul fixed his eyes on the Council and **23** said, 'My brothers, I have lived all my life, and still live today, with a perfectly clear conscience before God.' At this the High 2 Priest Ananias ordered his attendants to strike him on the mouth. Paul retorted, 'God 3 will strike you, you whitewashed wall! You sit there to judge me in accordance with the Law; and then in defiance of the Law you order me to be struck!' The attendants said, 4 'Would you insult God's High Priest?' 'My brothers,' said Paul, 'I had no idea that 5 he was High Priest; Scripture, I know, says: "You must not abuse the ruler of your people."'

A division in the Council

Now Paul was well aware that one section of 6 them were Sadducees and the other Pharisees, so he called out in the Council, 'My brothers, I am a Pharisee, a Pharisee born and bred; and the true issue in this trial is our hope of the resurrection of the dead.' At these words the Pharisees and Sad- 7 ducees fell out among themselves, and the assembly was divided. (The Sadducees deny 8 that there is any resurrection, or angel, or spirit, but the Pharisees accept them.) So 9 a great uproar broke out; and some of the doctors of the law belonging to the Pharisaic party openly took sides and declared, 'We can find no fault with this man; perhaps an angel or spirit has spoken to him.' The dis- 10 sension was mounting, and the commandant was afraid that Paul would be torn in pieces, so he ordered the troops to go down, pull him out of the crowd, and bring him into the barracks.

The following night the Lord appeared to 11 him and said, 'Keep up your courage; you have affirmed the truth about me in Jerusalem, and you must do the same in Rome.'

A plot against Paul's life disclosed

When day broke, the Jews banded together 12 and took an oath not to eat or drink until

---

j Or tied him up with thongs.

13 they had killed Paul. There were more than
14 forty in this conspiracy. They came to the
chief priests and elders and said, 'We have
bound ourselves by a solemn oath not to
15 taste food until we have killed Paul. It is
now for you, acting with the Council, to
apply to the commandant to bring him down
to you, on the pretext of a closer investiga-
tion of his case; and we have arranged to do
away with him before he arrives.'
16 But the son of Paul's sister heard of the
ambush; he went to the barracks, obtained
17 entry, and reported it to Paul. Paul called
one of the centurions and said, 'Take this
young man to the commandant; he has
18 something to report.' The centurion took
him and brought him to the commandant.
'The prisoner Paul', he said, 'sent for me and
asked me to bring this young man to you;
19 he has something to tell you.' The commandant took him by the arm, drew him
aside, and asked him, 'What is it you have to
20 report?' He said, 'The Jews have made a
plan among themselves and will request you
to bring Paul down to the Council tomorrow,
on the pretext of obtaining more precise
21 information about him. Do not listen to
them; for a party more than forty strong are
lying in wait for him. They have sworn not
to eat or drink until they have done away
with him; they are now ready, and wait only
22 for your consent.' So the commandant dismissed the young man, with orders not to
let anyone know that he had given him this
information.

The case remitted to the Governor

23 Then he called a couple of his centurions
and issued these orders: 'Get ready two
hundred infantry to proceed to Caesarea,
together with seventy cavalrymen and two
hundred light-armed troops;*k* parade three
24 hours after sunset. Provide also mounts for
Paul so that he may ride through under safe
25 escort to Felix the Governor.' And he wrote
a letter to this effect:
26 'Claudius Lysias to His Excellency the
27 Governor Felix. Your Excellency: This man
was seized by the Jews and was on the point
of being murdered when I intervened with
the troops and removed him, because I dis-
28 covered that he was a Roman citizen. As
I wished to ascertain the charge on which
they were accusing him, I took him down
29 to their Council. I found that the accusation
had to do with controversial matters in their
law, but there was no charge against him
30 meriting death or imprisonment. However,
I have now been informed of an attempt to
be made on the man's life, so I am sending

him to you at once, and have also instructed
his accusers to state their case against him
before you.'*l*
31 Acting on their orders, the infantry took
Paul and brought him by night to Antipatris.
32 Next day they returned to their barracks,
leaving the cavalry to escort him the rest of
33 the way. The cavalry entered Caesarea, delivered the letter to the Governor, and
handed Paul over to him. He read the letter,
34 asked him what province he was from, and
learned that he was from Cilicia. 'I will hear
35 your case', he said, 'when your accusers
arrive.' He then ordered him to be held in
custody at his headquarters in Herod's
palace.

The case against Paul opened

Five days later the High Priest Ananias came **24**
down, accompanied by some of the elders
and an advocate named Tertullus, and they
laid an information against Paul before the
Governor. When the prisoner was called, 2
Tertullus opened the case.
'Your Excellency,' he said, 'we owe it to
you that we enjoy unbroken peace. It is due
to your provident care that, in all kinds of
ways and in all sorts of places, improvements
are being made for the good of this province.
We welcome this, sir, most gratefully. And 3 4
now, not to take up too much of your time,
I crave your indulgence for a brief statement
of our case. We have found this man to be 5
a perfect pest, a fomenter of discord among
the Jews all over the world, a ringleader of
the sect of the Nazarenes. He even made an 6
attempt to profane the temple; and then we
arrested him.'*m* If you will examine him your- 8
self you can ascertain from him the truth
of all the charges we bring.' The Jews sup- 9
ported the attack, alleging that the facts
were as he stated.

Paul's defence before Felix

Then the Governor motioned to Paul to 10
speak, and he began his reply: 'Knowing as
I do that for many years you have admin-
istered justice in this province, I make my
defence with confidence. You can ascertain 11
the facts for yourself. It is not more than
twelve days since I went up to Jerusalem on
a pilgrimage. They did not find me arguing 12
with anyone, or collecting a crowd, either
in the temple or in the synagogues or up and
down the city; and they cannot make good 13
the charges they bring against me. But this 14
much I will admit: I am a follower of the
new way (the "sect" they speak of), and it
is in that manner that I worship the God of
our fathers; for I believe all that is written

---

k Or two hundred spearmen (*the meaning of the Greek word is uncertain*).   *l Some witnesses read* '. . . before
you. Farewell.'   *m Some witnesses insert* It was our intention to try him under our law; (7) but Lysias the
commandant intervened and took him by force out of our hands, (8) ordering his accusers to come before you.

15 in the Law and the prophets, and in reliance on God I hold the hope, which my accusers too accept, that there is to be a resurrection 16 of good and wicked alike. Accordingly I, no less than they, train myself to keep at all times a clear conscience before God and man.

17 'After an absence of several years I came to bring charitable gifts to my nation and to 18 offer sacrifices. They found me in the temple ritually purified and engaged in this service. I had no crowd with me, and there was no disturbance. But some Jews from the pro-19 vince of Asia were there, and if they had any charge against me it is they who ought to 20 have been in court to state it. Failing that, it is for these persons here present to say what crime they discovered when I was 21 brought before the Council, apart from this one open assertion which I made as I stood there: "The true issue in my trial before you today is the resurrection of the dead."'

22 Then Felix, who happened to be well informed about the Christian movement, adjourned the hearing. 'When Lysias the commanding officer comes down', he said, 23 'I will go into your case.' He gave orders to the centurion to keep Paul under open arrest and not to prevent any of his friends from making themselves useful to him.

Felix leaves Paul in custody

24 Some days later Felix came with his wife Drusilla, who was a Jewess, and sending for Paul he let him talk to him about faith 25 in Christ Jesus. But when the discourse turned to questions of morals, self-control, and the coming judgement, Felix became alarmed and exclaimed, 'That will do for the present; when I find it convenient I will 26 send for you again.' At the same time he had hopes of a bribe from Paul; and for this reason he sent for him very often and talked 27 with him. When two years had passed, Felix was succeeded by Porcius Festus. Wishing to curry favour with the Jews, Felix left Paul in custody.

Paul appeals to the Emperor

5 Three days after taking up his appointment Festus went up from Caesarea to Jerusalem, 2 where the chief priests and the Jewish leaders brought before him the case against 3 Paul. They asked Festus to favour them against him, and pressed for him to be brought up to Jerusalem, for they were planning an ambush to kill him on the way. 4 Festus, however, replied, 'Paul is in safe custody at Caesarea, and I shall be leaving 5 Jerusalem shortly myself; so let your leading men come down with me, and if there is anything wrong, let them prosecute him.'

After spending eight or ten days at most 6 in Jerusalem, he went down to Caesarea, and next day he took his seat in court and ordered Paul to be brought up. When he appeared, 7 the Jews who had come down from Jerusalem stood round bringing many grave charges, which they were unable to prove. Paul's plea was: 'I have committed no 8 offence, either against the Jewish law, or against the temple, or against the Emperor.' Festus, anxious to ingratiate himself with 9 the Jews, turned to Paul and asked, 'Are you willing to go up to Jerusalem and stand trial on these charges before me there?' But Paul 10 said, 'I am now standing before the Emperor's tribunal, and that is where I must be tried. Against the Jews I have committed no offence, as you very well know. If I am 11 guilty of any capital crime, I do not ask to escape the death penalty; but if there is no substance in the charges which these men bring against me, it is not open to anyone to hand me over as a sop to them. I appeal to Caesar!' Then Festus, after conferring 12 with his advisers, replied, 'You have appealed to Caesar: to Caesar you shall go.'

Festus and Agrippa

After an interval of some days King Agrippa 13 and Bernice arrived at Caesarea on a courtesy visit to Festus. They spent several days 14 there, and during this time Festus laid Paul's case before the king. 'We have a man', he said, 'left in custody by Felix; and when I 15 was in Jerusalem the chief priests and elders of the Jews laid an information against him, demanding his condemnation. I answered 16 them, "It is not Roman practice to hand over any accused man before he is confronted with his accusers and given an opportunity of answering the charge." So when they had 17 come here with me I lost no time; the very next day I took my seat in court and ordered the man to be brought up. But when his 18 accusers rose to speak, they brought none of the charges I was expecting; they merely 19 had certain points of disagreement with him about their peculiar religion, and about someone called Jesus, a dead man whom Paul alleged to be alive. Finding myself out 20 of my depth in such discussions, I asked if he was willing to go to Jerusalem and stand his trial there on these issues. But Paul 21 appealed to be remanded in custody for His Imperial Majesty's decision, and I ordered him to be detained until I could send him to the Emperor.' Agrippa said to Festus, 'I 22 should rather like to hear the man myself.' 'Tomorrow', he answered, 'you shall hear him.'

So next day Agrippa and Bernice came in 23 full state and entered the audience-chamber accompanied by high-ranking officers and

prominent citizens; and on the orders of
24 Festus Paul was brought up. Then Festus
said, 'King Agrippa, and all you gentlemen
here present with us, you see this man: the
whole body of the Jews approached me both
in Jerusalem and here, loudly insisting that
25 he had no right to remain alive. But it was
clear to me that he had committed no capital
crime, and when he himself appealed to His
Imperial Majesty, I decided to send him.
26 But I have nothing definite about him to put
in writing for our Sovereign. Accordingly
I have brought him up before you all and
particularly before you, King Agrippa, so
that as a result of this preliminary inquiry
27 I may have something to report. There is
no sense, it seems to me, in sending on a
prisoner without indicating the charges
against him.'

Paul's defence before Agrippa

26 Agrippa said to Paul, 'You have our permission to speak for yourself.' Then Paul
stretched out his hand and began his
defence:
2 'I consider myself fortunate, King
Agrippa, that it is before you that I am to
make my defence today upon all the charges
3 brought against me by the Jews, particularly
as you are expert in all Jewish matters, both
our customs and our disputes. And therefore
I beg you to give me a patient hearing.
4 'My life from my youth up, the life I led
from the beginning among my people and
5 in Jerusalem, is familiar to all Jews. Indeed
they have known me long enough and could
testify, if they only would, that I belonged to
the strictest group in our religion: I lived as
6 a Pharisee. And it is for a hope kindled by
God's promise to our forefathers that I stand
7 in the dock today. Our twelve tribes hope to
see the fulfilment of that promise, worshipping with intense devotion day and night;
and for this very hope I am impeached, and
8 impeached by Jews, Your Majesty. Why is
it considered incredible among you that
God should raise dead men to life?
9 'I myself once thought it my duty to work
actively against the name of Jesus of Nazar-
10 eth; and I did so in Jerusalem. It was I who
imprisoned many of God's people by authority obtained from the chief priests; and when
they were condemned to death, my vote was
11 cast against them. In all the synagogues I
tried by repeated punishment to make them
renounce their faith; indeed my fury rose to
such a pitch that I extended my persecution
to foreign cities.
12 'On one such occasion I was travelling to
Damascus with authority and commission
13 from the chief priests; and as I was on my
way, Your Majesty, in the middle of the day
I saw a light from the sky, more brilliant than

the sun, shining all around me and my
travelling-companions. We all fell to the 14
ground, and then I heard a voice saying to
me in the Jewish language, "Saul, Saul, why
do you persecute me? It is hard for you, to
kicking against the goad." I said, "Tell me, 15
Lord, who you are"; and the Lord replied,
"I am Jesus, whom you are persecuting. But 16
now, rise to your feet and stand upright.
I have appeared to you for a purpose: to
appoint you my servant and witness, to testify
both to what you have seen and to what you
shall yet see of me. I will rescue you from 17
this people and from the Gentiles to whom
I am sending you. I send you to open their 18
eyes and turn them from darkness to light,
from the dominion of Satan to God, so that,
by trust in me, they may obtain forgiveness
of sins, and a place with those whom God
has made his own."
'And so, King Agrippa, I did not disobey 19
the heavenly vision. I turned first to the in- 20
habitants of Damascus, and then to Jerusalem and all the country of Judaea, and to
the Gentiles, and sounded the call to repent
and turn to God, and to prove their repentance by deeds. That is why the Jews seized 21
me in the temple and tried to do away with
me. But I had God's help, and so to this very 22
day I stand and testify to great and small
alike. I assert nothing beyond what was
foretold by the prophets and by Moses:
that the Messiah must suffer, and that he, 23
the first to rise from the dead, would announce the dawn to Israel and to the
Gentiles.'

Paul reasons with Agrippa

While Paul was thus making his defence, 24
Festus shouted at the top of his voice, 'Paul,
you are raving; too much study is driving
you mad.' 'I am not mad, Your Excellency,' 25
said Paul; 'what I am saying is sober truth.
The king is well versed in these matters, and 26
to him I can speak freely. I do not believe
that he can be unaware of any of these facts,
for this has been no hole-and-corner business. King Agrippa, do you believe the 27
prophets? I know you do.' Agrippa said to 28
Paul, 'You think it will not take much to
win me over and make a Christian of me.'
'Much or little,' said Paul, 'I wish to God 29
that not only you, but all those also who are
listening to me today, might become what
I am, apart from these chains.'
With that the king rose, and with him the 30
Governor, Bernice, and the rest of the company, and after they had withdrawn they 31
talked it over. 'This man', they said, 'is
doing nothing that deserves death or imprisonment.' Agrippa said to Festus, 'The 32
fellow could have been discharged, if he
had not appealed to the Emperor.'

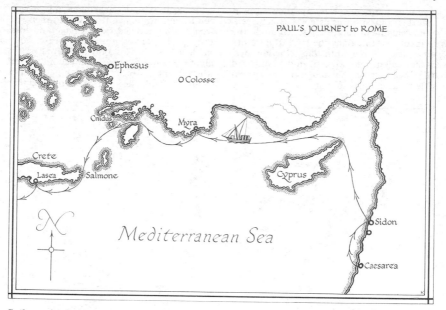

PAUL'S JOURNEY to ROME

Mediterranean Sea

Sails set for Italy

27 When it was decided that we should sail for Italy, Paul and some other prisoners were handed over to a centurion named Julius, 2 of the Augustan Cohort. We embarked in a ship of Adramyttium, bound for ports in the province of Asia, and put out to sea. In our party was Aristarchus, a Macedonian 3 from Thessalonica. Next day we landed at Sidon; and Julius very considerately allowed Paul to go to his friends to be cared for. 4 Leaving Sidon we sailed under the lee of 5 Cyprus because of the head-winds, then across the open sea off the coast of Cilicia and Pamphylia, and so reached Myra in Lycia. 6 There the centurion found an Alexandrian vessel bound for Italy and put us 7 aboard. For a good many days we made little headway, and we were hard put to it to reach Cnidus. Then, as the wind continued against us, off Salmone we began to sail under the lee of Crete, and, hugging the coast, strug- 8 gled on to a place called Fair Havens, not far from the town of Lasea.

Storm at sea

By now much time had been lost, the Fast 9 was already over, and it was risky to go on with the voyage. Paul therefore gave them this advice: 'I can see, gentlemen,' he said, 10 'that this voyage will be disastrous: it will mean grave loss, loss not only of ship and cargo but also of life.' But the centurion paid 11 more attention to the captain and to the owner of the ship than to what Paul said; and as the harbour was unsuitable for 12 wintering, the majority were in favour of putting out to sea, hoping, if they could get so far, to winter at Phoenix, a Cretan harbour exposed south-west and north-west. So when 13

Fair Havens

a southerly breeze sprang up, they thought that their purpose was as good as achieved, and, weighing anchor, they sailed along the 14 coast of Crete hugging the land. But before very long a fierce wind, the 'North-easter' as they call it, tore down from the landward 15 side. It caught the ship and, as it was impossible to keep head to wind, we had to give

said, 'You should have taken my advice, gentlemen, not to sail from Crete; then you would have avoided this damage and loss. But now I urge you not to lose heart; not a 22 single life will be lost, only the ship. For last 23 night there stood by me an angel of the God whose I am and whom I worship. "Do not 24 be afraid, Paul," he said; "it is ordained that

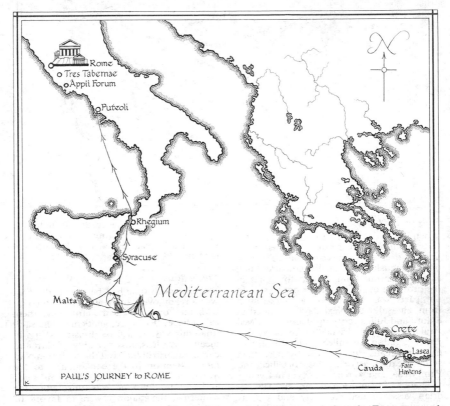

PAUL'S JOURNEY to ROME

16 way and run before it. We ran under the lee of a small island called Cauda, and with a struggle managed to get the ship's boat under 17 control. When they had hoisted it aboard, they made use of tackle and undergirded the ship. Then, because they were afraid of running on to the shallows of Syrtis, they 18 lowered the mainsail and let her drive. Next day, as we were making very heavy weather, 19 they began to lighten the ship; and on the third day they jettisoned the ship's gear with 20 their own hands. For days on end there was no sign of either sun or stars, a great storm was raging, and our last hopes of coming through alive began to fade.
21   When they had gone for a long time without food, Paul stood up among them and

you shall appear before the Emperor; and, be assured, God has granted you the lives of all who are sailing with you." So keep up 25 your courage: I trust in God that it will turn out as I have been told; though we have to 26 be cast ashore on some island.'
     The fourteenth night came and we were 27 still drifting in the Sea of Adria. In the middle of the night the sailors felt that land was getting nearer. They sounded and found 28 twenty fathoms. Sounding again after a short interval they found fifteen fathoms; and 29 fearing that we might be cast ashore on a rugged coast they dropped four anchors from the stern and prayed for daylight to come. The sailors tried to abandon ship; 30 they had already lowered the ship's boat,

pretending they were going to lay out
31 anchors from the bows, when Paul said to
the centurion and the soldiers, 'Unless these
men stay on board you can none of you come
32 off safely.' So the soldiers cut the ropes of
the boat and let her drop away.

33   Shortly before daybreak Paul urged them
all to take some food. 'For the last fourteen
days', he said, 'you have lived in suspense
and gone hungry; you have eaten nothing
34 whatever. So I beg you to have something
to eat; your lives depend on it. Remember,
35 not a hair of your heads will be lost.' With
these words, he took bread, gave thanks to
God in front of them all, broke it, and began
36 eating. Then they all plucked up courage,
37 and took food themselves. There were on
board two hundred and seventy-six of us
38 in all. When they had eaten as much as they
wanted they lightened the ship by dumping
the corn in the sea.

Shipwreck

39 When day broke they could not recognize
the land, but they noticed a bay with a sandy
beach, on which they planned, if possible,
40 to run the ship ashore. So they slipped the
anchors and let them go; at the same time
they loosened the lashings of the steering-
paddles, set the foresail to the wind, and let
41 her drive to the beach. But they found themselves caught between cross-currents and
ran the ship aground, so that the bow stuck
fast and remained immovable, while the
stern was being pounded to pieces by the
42 breakers. The soldiers thought they had
better kill the prisoners for fear that any
43 should swim away and escape; but the
centurion wanted to bring Paul safely
through and prevented them from carrying
out their plan. He gave orders that those
who could swim should jump overboard
44 first and get to land; the rest were to follow, some on planks, some on parts of the
ship. And thus it was that all came safely
to land.

Wintering in Malta

8 Once we had made our way to safety we
2 identified the island as Malta. The rough
islanders treated us with uncommon kindness: because it was cold and had started to
rain, they lit a bonfire and made us all wel-
3 come. Paul had got together an armful of
sticks and put them on the fire, when a viper,
driven out by the heat, fastened on his hand.
4 The islanders, seeing the snake hanging on
to his hand, said to one another, 'The man
must be a murderer; he may have escaped
from the sea, but divine justice has not let
5 him live.' Paul, however, shook off the snake
6 into the fire and was none the worse. They

still expected that any moment he would
swell up or drop down dead, but after waiting
a long time without seeing anything extraordinary happen to him, they changed their
minds and now said, 'He is a god.'

In the neighbourhood of that place there 7
were lands belonging to the chief magistrate
of the island, whose name was Publius. He
took us in and entertained us hospitably for
three days. It so happened that this man's 8
father was in bed suffering from recurrent
bouts of fever and dysentery. Paul visited
him and, after prayer, laid his hands upon
him and healed him; whereupon the other 9
sick people on the island came also and
were cured. They honoured us with many 10
marks of respect, and when we were leaving they put on board provision for our
needs.

Paul reaches Rome

Three months had passed when we set sail 11
in a ship which had wintered in the island;
she was the *Castor and Pollux* of Alex-
andria. We put in at Syracuse and spent 12
three days there; then we sailed round and 13
arrived at Rhegium. After one day a south
wind sprang up and we reached Puteoli in
two days. There we found fellow-Christians 14
and were invited to stay a week with them.
And so to Rome. The Christians there had 15
had news of us and came out to meet us as
far as Appii Forum and Tres Tabernae, and
when Paul saw them, he gave thanks to God
and took courage.

Discussions with the Jews

When we entered Rome Paul was allowed 16
to lodge by himself with a soldier in charge
of him. Three days later he called together 17
the local Jewish leaders; and when they
were assembled, he said to them: 'My
brothers, I, who never did anything against
our people or the customs of our forefathers,
am here as a prisoner; I was handed over to
the Romans at Jerusalem. They examined 18
me and would have liked to release me because there was no capital charge against
me; but the Jews objected, and I had no 19
option but to appeal to the Emperor; not
that I had any accusation to bring against
my own people. That is why I have asked to 20
see you and talk to you, because it is for the
sake of the hope of Israel that I am in chains,
as you see.' They replied, 'We have had no 21
communication from Judaea, nor has any
countryman of ours arrived with any report
or gossip to your discredit. We should like 22
to hear from you what your views are; all
we know about this sect is that no one has
a good word to say for it.'

So they fixed a day, and came in large 23

numbers as his guests. He dealt at length with the whole matter; he spoke urgently of the kingdom of God and sought to convince them about Jesus by appealing to the Law of Moses and the prophets. This went 24 on from dawn to dusk. Some were won over by his arguments; others remained sceptical. 25 Without reaching any agreement among themselves they began to disperse, but not before Paul had said one thing more: 'How well the Holy Spirit spoke to your fathers 26 through the prophet Isaiah when he said, "Go to this people and say: You may hear and hear, but you will never understand; you may look and look, but you will never

see. For this people's mind has become 27 gross; their ears are dulled, and their eyes are closed. Otherwise, their eyes might see, their ears hear, and their mind understand, and then they might turn again, and I would heal them." Therefore take notice that this 28 salvation of God has been sent to the Gentiles; the Gentiles will listen.'[n]

Two years in Rome

He stayed there two full years at his own 30 expense, with a welcome for all who came to him, proclaiming the kingdom of God 31 and teaching the facts about the Lord Jesus Christ quite openly and without hindrance.

THE LETTER OF PAUL TO THE
ROMANS

The Gospel of Christ

1 FROM PAUL, servant of Christ Jesus, apostle by God's call, set apart for the service of the Gospel.
2   This gospel God announced beforehand in sacred scriptures through his prophets.
3 It is about his Son: on the human level he
4 was born of David's stock, but on the level of the spirit—the Holy Spirit—he was declared Son of God by a mighty act in that he rose from the dead:[a] it is about Jesus

Christ our Lord. Through him I received 5 the privilege of a commission in his name to lead to faith and obedience men in all nations, yourselves among them, you who 6 have heard the call and belong to Jesus Christ.

Greetings and thanksgiving

I send greetings to all of you in Rome whom 7 God loves and has called to be his dedicated people. Grace and peace to you from God our Father and the Lord Jesus Christ.

---

n Some witnesses add (29) After he had spoken, the Jews went away, arguing vigorously among themselves.

a Or declared Son of God with full powers from the time when he rose from the dead.

8 Let me begin by thanking my God, through Jesus Christ, for you all, because all over the world they are telling the story 9 of your faith. God is my witness, the God to whom I offer the humble service of my spirit by preaching the gospel of his Son: God knows how continually I make men- 10 tion of you in my prayers, and am always asking that by his will I may, somehow or other, succeed at long last in coming to visit 11 you. For I long to see you; I want to bring you some spiritual gift to make you strong; 12 or rather, I want to be among you to be myself encouraged by your faith as well as you by mine.

God's way of righting wrong

13 But I should like you to know,*b* my brothers, that I have often planned to come, though so far without success, in the hope of achieving something among you, as I have in other 14 parts of the world. I am under obligation to Greek and non-Greek, to learned and 15 simple; hence my eagerness to declare the Gospel to you in Rome as well as to others. 16 For I am not ashamed of the Gospel. It is the saving power of God for everyone who has faith—the Jew first, but the Greek also 17 —because here is revealed God's way of righting wrong, a way that starts from faith and ends in faith;*c* as Scripture says, 'he shall gain life who is justified through faith'.

The godless wickedness of men

18 For we see divine retribution revealed from heaven and falling upon all the godless wickedness of men. In their wickedness they 19 are stifling the truth. For all that may be known of God by men lies plain before their eyes; indeed God himself has disclosed it 20 to them. His invisible attributes, that is to say his everlasting power and deity, have been visible, ever since the world began, to the eye of reason, in the things he has made. There is therefore no possible defence for 21 their conduct; knowing God, they have refused to honour him as God, or to render him thanks. Hence all their thinking has ended in futility, and their misguided minds 22 are plunged in darkness. They boast of their wisdom, but they have made fools of them- 23 selves, exchanging the splendour of immortal God for an image shaped like mortal man, even for images like birds, beasts, and creeping things.

God has given them up

24 For this reason God has given them up to the vileness of their own desires, and the 25 consequent degradation of their bodies, because they have bartered away the true God

for a false one,*d* and have offered reverence and worship to created things instead of to the Creator, who is blessed for ever; amen.

In consequence, I say, God has given them 26 up to shameful passions. Their women have exchanged natural intercourse for unnatural, and their men in turn, giving up natural 27 relations with women, burn with lust for one another; males behave indecently with males, and are paid in their own persons the fitting wage of such perversion.

Thus, because they have not seen fit to 28 acknowledge God, he has given them up to their own depraved reason. This leads them to break all rules of conduct. They are filled 29 with every kind of injustice, mischief, rapacity, and malice; they are one mass of envy, murder, rivalry, treachery, and malevolence; whisperers and scandal-mongers, hateful to 30 God, insolent, arrogant, and boastful; they invent new kinds of mischief, they show no loyalty to parents, no conscience, no fidelity 31 to their plighted word; they are without natural affection and without pity. They 32 know well enough the just decree of God, that those who behave like this deserve to die, and yet they do it; not only so, they actually applaud such practices.

The day of retribution

You therefore have no defence—you who 2 sit in judgement, whoever you may be—for in judging your fellow-man you condemn yourself, since you, the judge, are equally guilty. It is admitted that God's judgement 2 is rightly passed upon all who commit such crimes as these; and do you imagine—you 3 who pass judgement on the guilty while committing the same crimes yourself—do you imagine that you, any more than they, will escape the judgement of God? Or do 4 you think lightly of his wealth of kindness, of tolerance, and of patience, without recognizing that God's kindness is meant to lead you to a change of heart? In the rigid ob- 5 stinacy of your heart you are laying up for yourself a store of retribution for the day of retribution, when God's just judgement will be revealed, and he will pay every man for 6 what he has done. To those who pursue 7 glory, honour, and immortality by steady persistence in well-doing, he will give eternal life; but for those who are governed by 8 selfish ambition, who refuse obedience to the truth and take the wrong for their guide, there will be the fury of retribution. There 9 will be trouble and distress for every human being who is an evil-doer, for the Jew first and for the Greek also; and for every well- 10 doer there will be glory, honour, and peace, for the Jew first and also for the Greek.

b Some witnesses read I believe you know.
d Or the truth of God for the lie.

c Or . . . wrong. It is based on faith and addressed to faith.

How God will judge

11 12 For God has no favourites: those who have
sinned outside the pale of the Law of Moses
will perish outside its pale, and all who have
sinned under that law will be judged by the
13 law. It is not by hearing the law, but by
doing it, that men will be justified before
14 God. When Gentiles who do not possess
the law carry out its precepts by the light
of nature, then, although they have no law,
15 they are their own law, for they display the
effect of the law inscribed on their hearts.
Their conscience is called as witness, and
their own thoughts argue the case on either
16 side, against them or even for them, on the
day when God judges the secrets of human
hearts through Christ Jesus. So my gospel
declares.

17 But as for you—you may bear the name
of Jew; you rely upon the law and are proud
18 of your God; you know his will; instructed
19 by the law, you know right from wrong; you
are confident that you are the one to guide
20 the blind, to enlighten the benighted, to
train the stupid, and to teach the immature,
because in the law you see the very shape of
21 knowledge and truth. You, then, who teach
your fellow-man, do you fail to teach yourself? You proclaim, 'Do not steal'; but are
22 you yourself a thief? You say, 'Do not commit adultery'; but are you an adulterer? You
abominate false gods; but do you rob their
23 shrines? While you take pride in the law,
24 you dishonour God by breaking it. For, as
Scripture says, 'Because of you the name of
God is dishonoured among the Gentiles.'

The true Jew

25 Circumcision has value, provided you keep
the law; but if you break the law, then your
circumcision is as if it had never been.
26 Equally, if an uncircumcised man keeps the
precepts of the law, will he not count as
27 circumcised? He may be uncircumcised in
his natural state, but by fulfilling the law he
will pass judgement on you who break it,
for all your written code and your circum-
28 cision. The true Jew is not he who is such
in externals, neither is the true circumcision
29 the external mark in the flesh. The true Jew
is he who is such inwardly, and the true
circumcision is of the heart, directed not by
written precepts but by the Spirit; such a
man receives his commendation not from
men but from God.

3 Then what advantage has the Jew? What
2 is the value of circumcision? Great, in every
way. In the first place, the Jews were en-
3 trusted with the oracles of God. What if
some of them were unfaithful? Will their
faithlessness cancel the faithfulness of God?
4 Certainly not! God must be true though

every man living were a liar; for we read in
Scripture, 'When thou speakest thou shalt
be vindicated, and win the verdict when
thou art on trial.'

All under the power of sin

Another question: if our injustice serves to 5
bring out God's justice, what are we to say?
Is it unjust of God (I speak of him in human
terms) to bring retribution upon us? Cer- 6
tainly not! If God were unjust, how could
he judge the world?

Again, if the truth of God brings him all 7
the greater honour because of my falsehood,
why should I any longer be condemned as
a sinner? Why not indeed 'do evil that good 8
may come', as some libellously report me as
saying? To condemn such men as these is
surely no injustice.

What then? Are we Jews any better off?*e* 9
No, not at all!*f* For we have already drawn
up the accusation that Jews and Greeks
alike are all under the power of sin. This has 10
scriptural warrant:

'There is no just man, not one;
no one who understands, no one who seeks 11
    God.
All have swerved aside, all alike have be- 12
    come debased;
there is no one to show kindness; no, not one.

Their throat is an open grave, 13
they use their tongues for treachery,
adders' venom is on their lips,
and their mouth is full of bitter curses. 14

Their feet hasten to shed blood, 15
ruin and misery lie along their paths, 16
they are strangers to the high-road of peace, 17
and reverence for God does not enter their 18
    thoughts.'

Now all the words of the law are addressed, 19
as we know, to those who are within the
pale of the law, so that no one may have
anything to say in self-defence, but the
whole world may be exposed to the judgement of God. For (again from Scripture) 20
'no human being can be justified in the sight
of God' for having kept the law: law brings
only the consciousness of sin.

Justified by God's free grace

But now, quite independently of law, God's 21
justice has been brought to light. The Law
and the prophets both bear witness to it:
it is God's way of righting wrong, effective 22
through faith in Christ for all who have such
faith—all, without distinction. For all alike 23
have sinned, and are deprived of the divine
splendour, and all are justified by God's 24
free grace alone, through his act of liberation
in the person of Christ Jesus. For God 25
designed him to be the means of expiating

e Or Are we Jews any worse off?　　　*f Or* Not in all respects.

sin by his sacrificial death, effective through faith. God meant by this to demonstrate his justice, because in his forbearance he had 26 overlooked the sins of the past—to demonstrate his justice now in the present, showing that he is himself just and also justifies any man who puts his faith in Jesus.

27 What room then is left for human pride? It is excluded. And on what principle? The keeping of the law would not exclude it, but 28 faith does. For our argument is that a man is justified by faith quite apart from success in keeping the law.

29 Do you suppose God is the God of the Jews alone? Is he not the God of Gentiles 30 also? Certainly, of Gentiles also, if it be true that God is one. And he will therefore justify both the circumcised in virtue of their faith, and the uncircumcised through their 31 faith. Does this mean that we are using faith to undermine law? By no means: we are placing law itself on a firmer footing.

Abraham's faith

4 What, then, are we to say about Abraham, 2 our ancestor in the natural line? If Abraham was justified by anything he had done, then he has a ground for pride. But he has no such 3 ground before God; for what does Scripture say? 'Abraham put his faith in God, and that faith was counted to him as righteous- 4 ness.' Now if a man does a piece of work, his wages are not 'counted' as a favour; they 5 are paid as debt. But if without any work to his credit he simply puts his faith in him who acquits the guilty, then his faith is indeed 6 'counted as righteousness'. In the same sense David speaks of the happiness of the man whom God 'counts' as just, apart from any 7 specific acts of justice: 'Happy are they', he says, 'whose lawless deeds are forgiven, 8 whose sins are buried away; happy is the man whose sins the Lord does not count 9 against him.' Is this happiness confined to the circumcised, or is it for the uncircumcised 10 also? Consider: we say, 'Abraham's faith was counted as righteousness'; in what circumstances was it so counted? Was he circumcised at the time, or not? He was not 11 yet circumcised, but uncircumcised; and he later received the symbolic rite of circumcision as the hall-mark of the righteousness which faith had given him when he was still uncircumcised. Consequently, he is the father of all who have faith when uncircumcised, so that righteousness is 'counted' to them; 12 and at the same time he is the father of such of the circumcised as do not rely upon their circumcision alone, but also walk in the footprints of the faith which our father Abraham had while he was yet uncircumcised.

For it was not through law that Abraham, 13 or his posterity, was given the promise that the world should be his inheritance, but through the righteousness that came from faith. For if those who hold by the law, and 14 they alone, are heirs, then faith is empty and the promise goes for nothing, because law 15 can bring only retribution; but where there is no law there can be no breach of law. The promise was made on the ground of 16 faith, in order that it might be a matter of sheer grace, and that it might be valid for all Abraham's posterity, not only for those who hold by the law, but for those also who have the faith of Abraham. For he is the father of us all, as Scripture says: 'I have appointed 17 you to be father of many nations.' This promise, then, was valid before God, the God in whom he put his faith, the God who makes the dead live and summons things that are not yet in existence as if they already were. When hope seemed hopeless, his faith 18 was such that he became 'father of many nations', in agreement with the words which had been spoken to him: 'Thus shall your descendants be.' Without any weakening of 19 faith he contemplated his own body, as good as dead (for he was about a hundred years old), and the deadness of Sarah's womb, and 20 never doubted God's promise in unbelief, but, strong in faith, gave honour to God, in the 21 firm conviction of his power to do what he had promised. And that is why Abraham's 22 faith was 'counted to him as righteousness'.

Those words were written, not for Abra- 23 ham's sake alone, but for our sake too: it is 24 to be 'counted' in the same way to us who have faith in the God who raised Jesus our Lord from the dead; for he was given up to 25 death for our misdeeds, and raised to life to justify us.*g*

At peace with God

Therefore, now that we have been justified **5** through faith, let us continue at peace*h* with God through our Lord Jesus Christ, through 2 whom we have been allowed to enter the sphere of God's grace, where we now stand. Let us exult*i* in the hope of the divine splendour that is to be ours. More than this: let 3 us even exult*j* in our present sufferings, because we know that suffering trains us to endure, and endurance brings proof that 4 we have stood the test, and this proof is the ground of hope. Such a hope is no mockery, 5 because God's love has flooded our inmost heart through the Holy Spirit he has given us.

Reconciliation through Christ

For at the very time when we were still 6 powerless, then Christ died for the wicked.

g *Or* raised to life because we were now justified.
exult. j *Or* we even exult.

h *Some witnesses read* we are at peace. i *Or* We

7 Even for a just man one of us would hardly die, though perhaps for a good man one 8 might actually brave death; but Christ died for us while we were yet sinners, and that is God's own proof of his love towards us. 9 And so, since we have now been justified by Christ's sacrificial death, we shall all the more certainly be saved through him from 10 final retribution. For if, when we were God's enemies, we were reconciled to him through the death of his Son, how much more, now that we are reconciled, shall we be saved by 11 his life! But that is not all: we also exult in God through our Lord Jesus, through whom we have now been granted reconciliation.

Adam and Christ

12 Mark what follows. It was through one man that sin entered the world, and through sin death, and thus death pervaded the whole human race, inasmuch as all men have sin- 13 ned. For sin was already in the world before there was law, though in the absence of law 14 no reckoning is kept of sin. But death held sway from Adam to Moses, even over those who had not sinned as Adam did, by dis- obeying a direct command—and Adam fore- shadows the Man who was to come.

15 But God's act of grace is out of all pro- portion to Adam's wrongdoing. For if the wrongdoing of that one man brought death upon so many, its effect is vastly exceeded by the grace of God and the gift that came to so many by the grace of the one man, 16 Jesus Christ. And again, the gift of God is not to be compared in its effect with that one man's sin; for the judicial action, fol- lowing upon the one offence, issued in a verdict of condemnation, but the act of grace, following upon so many misdeeds, 17 issued in a verdict of acquittal. For if by the wrongdoing of that one man death established its reign, through a single sinner, much more shall those who receive in far greater measure God's grace, and his gift of righteousness, live and reign through the one man, Jesus Christ.

18 It follows, then, that as the issue of one misdeed was condemnation for all men, so the issue of one just act is acquittal and life 19 for all men. For as through the disobedience of the one man the many were made sinners, so through the obedience of the one man the many will be made righteous.

20 Law intruded into this process to multiply law-breaking. But where sin was thus multi- 21 plied, grace immeasurably exceeded it, in order that, as sin established its reign by way of death, so God's grace might establish its reign in righteousness, and issue in eternal life through Jesus Christ our Lord.

Dead to sin and alive to God

What are we to say, then? Shall we persist 6 in sin, so that there may be all the more grace? No, no! We died to sin: how can we 2 live in it any longer? Have you forgotten 3 that when we were baptized into union with Christ Jesus we were baptized into his death? By baptism we were buried with him, and 4 lay dead, in order that, as Christ was raised from the dead in the splendour of the Father, so also we might set our feet upon the new path of life.

For if we have become incorporate with 5 him in a death like his, we shall also be one with him in a resurrection like his. We know 6 that the man we once were has been crucified with Christ, for the destruction of the sinful self, so that we may no longer be the slaves of sin, since a dead man is no longer answer- 7 able for his sin. But if we thus died with 8 Christ, we believe that we shall also come to life with him. We know that Christ, once 9 raised from the dead, is never to die again: he is no longer under the dominion of death. For in dying as he died, he died to sin, once 10 for all, and in living as he lives, he lives to God. In the same way you must regard 11 yourselves as dead to sin and alive to God, in union with Christ Jesus.

So sin must no longer reign in your mortal 12 body, exacting obedience to the body's desires. You must no longer put its several 13 parts at sin's disposal, as implements for doing wrong. No: put yourselves at the dis- posal of God, as dead men raised to life; yield your bodies to him as implements for doing right; for sin shall no longer be your 14 master, because you are no longer under law, but under the grace of God.

Two ways of life

What then? Are we to sin, because we are 15 not under law but under grace? Of course not. You know well enough that if you put 16 yourselves at the disposal of a master, to obey him, you are slaves of the master whom you obey; and this is true whether you serve sin, with death as its result; or obedience, with righteousness as its result. But God be 17 thanked, you, who once were slaves of sin, have yielded whole-hearted obedience to the pattern of teaching to which you were made subject,*k* and, emancipated from sin, have 18 become slaves of righteousness (to use words 19 that suit your human weakness)—I mean, as you once yielded your bodies to the service of impurity and lawlessness, making for moral anarchy, so now you must yield them to the service of righteousness, making for a holy life.

When you were slaves of sin, you were 20 free from the control of righteousness; and 21

k Or which was handed on to you.

what was the gain? Nothing but what now makes you ashamed, for the end of that is 22 death. But now, freed from the commands of sin, and bound to the service of God, your gains are such as make for holiness, your 23 end is eternal life. For sin pays a wage, and the wage is death, but God gives freely, and his gift is eternal life, in union with Christ Jesus our Lord.

An illustration from marriage

7 You cannot be unaware, my friends—I am speaking to those who have some knowledge of law—that a person is subject to the law 2 so long as he is alive, and no longer. For example, a married woman is by law bound to her husband while he lives; but if her husband dies, she is discharged from the 3 obligations of the marriage-law. If, therefore, in her husband's lifetime she consorts with another man, she will incur the charge of adultery; but if her husband dies she is free of the law, and she does not commit adultery by consorting with another man. 4 So you, my friends, have died to the law by becoming identified with the body of Christ, and accordingly you have found another husband in him who rose from the dead, so 5 that we may bear fruit for God. While we lived on the level of our lower nature, the sinful passions evoked by the law worked in 6 our bodies, to bear fruit for death. But now, having died to that which held us bound, we are discharged from the law, to serve God in a new way, the way of the spirit, in contrast to the old way, the way of a written code.

Law and sin

7 What follows? Is the law identical with sin? Of course not. But except through law I should never have become acquainted with sin. For example, I should never have known what it was to covet, if the law had not said, 'Thou shalt not covet.' Through that com- 8 mandment sin found its opportunity, and produced in me all kinds of wrong desires. In the absence of law, sin is a dead thing. There was a time when, in the absence of 9 law, I was fully alive; but when the commandment came, sin sprang to life and I died. The commandment which should have 10 led to life proved in my experience to lead to death, because sin found its opportunity in 11 the commandment, seduced me, and through the commandment killed me.

Therefore the law is in itself holy, and the 12 commandment is holy and just and good. Are we to say then that this good thing was 13 the death of me? By no means. It was sin that killed me, and thereby sin exposed its true character: it used a good thing to bring about my death, and so, through the commandment, sin became more sinful than ever.

Inner conflict

We know that the law is spiritual; but I am 14 not: I am unspiritual, the purchased slave of sin. I do not even acknowledge my own 15 actions as mine, for what I do is not what I want to do, but what I detest. But if what 16 I do is against my will, it means that I agree with the law and hold it to be admirable. But 17 as things are, it is no longer I who perform the action, but sin that lodges in me. For I 18 know that nothing good lodges in me—in my unspiritual nature, I mean—for though the will to do good is there, the deed is not. The 19 good which I want to do, I fail to do; but what I do is the wrong which is against my will; and if what I do is against my will, 20 clearly it is no longer I who am the agent, but sin that has its lodging in me.

I discover this principle, then: that when 21 I want to do the right, only the wrong is

Street in a Roman city

22 within my reach. In my inmost self I delight
23 in the law of God, but I perceive that there
is in my bodily members a different law,
fighting against the law that my reason
approves and making me a prisoner under
the law[l] that is in my members, the law of
24 sin. Miserable creature that I am, who is
there to rescue me out of this body doomed
25 to death[m]? God alone, through Jesus Christ
our Lord! Thanks be to God! In a word then,
I myself, subject to God's law as a rational
being, am yet,[n] in my unspiritual nature, a
slave to the law of sin.

The conflict resolved

8 The conclusion of the matter is this: there is
no condemnation for those who are united
2 with Christ Jesus, because in Christ Jesus
the life-giving law of the Spirit has set you
3 free from the law of sin and death. What the
law could never do, because our lower nature
robbed it of all potency, God has done: by
sending his own Son in a form like that of
our own sinful nature, and as a sacrifice for
sin,[o] he has passed judgement against sin
4 within that very nature, so that the commandment of the law may find fulfilment in
us, whose conduct, no longer under the
control of our lower nature, is directed by
the Spirit.

The new life

5 Those who live on the level of our lower
6 nature have their outlook formed by it, and
that spells death; but those who live on the
level of the spirit have the spiritual outlook,
7 and that is life and peace. For the outlook
of the lower nature is enmity with God; it
is not subject to the law of God; indeed it
8 cannot be: those who live on such a level
cannot possibly please God.
9 But that is not how you live. You are on
the spiritual level, if only God's Spirit dwells
within you; and if a man does not possess
10 the Spirit of Christ, he is no Christian. But
if Christ is dwelling within you, then although the body is a dead thing because you
sinned, yet the spirit is life itself because you
11 have been justified.[p] Moreover, if the Spirit
of him who raised Jesus from the dead
dwells within you, then the God who raised
Christ Jesus from the dead will also give new
life to your mortal bodies through his
indwelling Spirit.
12 It follows, my friends, that our lower
nature has no claim upon us; we are not
13 obliged to live on that level. If you do so,
you must die. But if by the Spirit you put to
death all the base pursuits of the body, then
you will live.
For all who are moved by the Spirit of 14
God are sons of God. The Spirit you have 15
received is not a spirit of slavery leading you
back into a life of fear, but a Spirit that makes
us sons, enabling us to cry 'Abba! Father!'
In that cry the Spirit of God joins with our 16
spirit in testifying that we are God's children; and if children, then heirs. We are 17
God's heirs and Christ's fellow-heirs, if we
share his sufferings now in order to share his
splendour hereafter.

Waiting for final deliverance

For I reckon that the sufferings we now en- 18
dure bear no comparison with the splendour,
as yet unrevealed, which is in store for us.
For the created universe waits with eager 19
expectation for God's sons to be revealed.
It was made the victim of frustration, not 20
by its own choice, but because of him who
made it so;[q] yet always there was hope, be- 21
cause[r] the universe itself is to be freed from
the shackles of mortality and enter upon the
liberty and splendour of the children of God.
Up to the present, we know, the whole 22
created universe groans in all its parts as if
in the pangs of childbirth. Not only so, but 23
even we, to whom the Spirit is given as firstfruits of the harvest to come, are groaning
inwardly while we wait for God to make us
his sons and[s] set our whole body free. For 24
we have been saved, though only in hope.
Now to see is no longer to hope: why should
a man endure and wait[t] for what he already
sees? But if we hope for something we do 25
not yet see, then, in waiting for it, we show
our endurance.

The help of the Spirit

In the same way the Spirit comes to the 26
aid of our weakness. We do not even know
how we ought to pray[u] but through our
inarticulate groans the Spirit himself is
pleading for us, and God who searches our 27
inmost being knows what the Spirit means,
because he pleads for God's people in God's
own way; and in everything, as we know, he 28
co-operates for good with those who love
God[v] and are called according to his purpose. For God knew his own before ever 29
they were, and also ordained that they should
be shaped to the likeness of his Son, that he
might be the eldest among a large family of
brothers; and it is these, so fore-ordained, 30
whom he has also called. And those whom
he called he has justified, and to those

---

l Or by means of the law.   *m Or out of the body doomed to this death.*   *n Or Thus, left to myself,*
while subject . . . rational being, I am yet . . .   *o Or and to deal with sin.*   *p Or so that you may*
live rightly.   *q Or because God subjected it.*   *r Or with the hope that . . .*   *s Some witnesses*
omit make us his sons and.   *t Some witnesses read* why should a man hope . . .   *u Or what it is right*
to pray for.   *v Or and, as we know, all things work together for good for those who love God; some wit-*
nesses read and we know God himself co-operates for good with those who love God.

whom he justified he has also given his splendour.

The love of Christ

31 With all this in mind, what are we to say?
32 If God is on our side, who is against us? He did not spare his own Son, but gave him up for us all; and with this gift how can he fail
33 to lavish upon us all he has to give? Who will be the accuser of God's chosen ones?
34 It is God who pronounces acquittal; then who can condemn? It is Christ—Christ who died, and, more than that, was raised from the dead—who is at God's right hand,
35 and indeed pleads our cause.[w] Then what can separate us from the love of Christ? Can affliction or hardship? Can persecution, hunger, nakedness, peril, or the sword?
36 'We are being done to death for thy sake all day long,' as Scripture says; 'we have been
37 treated like sheep for slaughter'—and yet, in spite of all, overwhelming victory is ours
38 through him who loved us. For I am convinced that there is nothing in death or life, in the realm of spirits or superhuman powers, in the world as it is or the world as it shall
39 be, in the forces of the universe, in heights or depths—nothing in all creation that can separate us from the love of God in Christ Jesus our Lord.

The privileges of the Israelites

9 I am speaking the truth as a Christian, and my own conscience, enlightened by the
2 Holy Spirit, assures me it is no lie: in my heart there is great grief and unceasing sor-
3 row. For I could even pray to be outcast from Christ myself for the sake of my
4 brothers, my natural kinsfolk. They are Israelites: they were made God's sons; theirs is the splendour of the divine presence, theirs the covenants, the law, the temple worship,
5 and the promises. Theirs are the patriarchs, and from them, in natural descent, sprang the Messiah.[x] May God, supreme above all, be blessed for ever![y] Amen.

The true Israelites

6 It is impossible that the word of God should have proved false. For not all descendants
7 of Israel are truly Israel, nor, because they are Abraham's offspring, are they all his true children;[z] but, in the words of Scripture, 'Through the line of Isaac your des-
8 cendants shall be traced.'[a] That is to say, it is not those born in the course of nature who are children of God; it is the children born through God's promise who are

reckoned as Abraham's descendants. For 9 the promise runs: 'At the time fixed I will come, and Sarah shall have a son.'

But that is not all, for Rebekah's children 10 had one and the same father, our ancestor Isaac; and yet, in order that God's selective 11 purpose might stand, based not upon men's deeds but upon the call of God, she was told, 12 even before they were born, when they had as yet done nothing, good or ill, 'The elder shall be servant to the younger'; and that 13 accords with the text of Scripture, 'Jacob I loved and Esau I hated.'

Establishing God's justice

What shall we say to that? Is God to be 14 charged with injustice? By no means. For 15 he says to Moses, 'Where I show mercy, I will show mercy, and where I pity, I will pity.' Thus it does not depend on man's will 16 or effort, but on God's mercy. For Scrip- 17 ture says to Pharaoh, 'I have raised you up for this very purpose, to exhibit my power in my dealings with you, and to spread my fame over all the world.' Thus he not only 18 shows mercy as he chooses, but also makes men stubborn as he chooses.

You will say, 'Then why does God blame 19 a man? For who can resist his will?' Who 20 are you, sir, to answer God back? Can the pot speak to the potter and say, 'Why did you make me like this?'? Surely the potter 21 can do what he likes with the clay. Is he not free to make out of the same lump two vessels, one to be treasured, the other for common use?

But what if God, desiring to exhibit[b] his 22 retribution at work and to make his power known, tolerated very patiently those vessels which were objects of retribution due for destruction, and did so in order to make 23 known the full wealth of his splendour upon vessels which were objects of mercy, and which from the first had been prepared for this splendour?

Such vessels are we, whom he has called 24 from among Gentiles as well as Jews, as 25 it says in the Book of Hosea: 'Those who were not my people I will call My People, and the unloved nation I will call My Beloved. For in the very place where they 26 were told "you are no people of mine", they shall be called Sons of the living God.' But Isaiah makes this proclamation about 27 Israel: 'Though the Israelites be countless as the sands of the sea, only a remnant shall be saved; for the Lord's sentence on the 28 land will be summary and final'; as also he 29

---

w Or Who will be the accuser of God's chosen ones? Will it be God himself? No, he it is who pronounces acquittal. Who will be the judge to condemn? Will it be Christ—he who died, and, more than that, ... right hand? No, he it is who pleads our cause.   x Greek Christ.   y Or sprang the Messiah, supreme above all, God blessed for ever; or sprang the Messiah, who is supreme above all. Blessed be God for ever!   z Or all children of God.   a Or God's call shall be for your descendants in the line of Isaac.   b Or although he had the will to exhibit . . .

said previously, 'If the Lord of Hosts had not left us the mere germ of a nation, we should have become like Sodom, and no better than Gomorrah.'

Righteousness based on faith

30 Then what are we to say? That Gentiles, who made no effort after righteousness, nevertheless achieved it, a righteousness 31 based on faith; whereas Israel made great efforts after a law of righteousness, but never 32 attained to it. Why was this? Because their efforts were not based on faith, but (as they supposed) on deeds. They fell over the 'stone' 33 mentioned in Scripture: 'Here I lay in Zion a stone to trip over, a rock to stumble against; but he who has faith in him will not be put to shame.'

The salvation of the Gentiles

10 Brothers, my deepest desire and my prayer 2 to God is for their salvation. To their zeal for God I can testify; but it is an ill-informed 3 zeal. For they ignore God's way of righteousness, and try to set up their own, and therefore have not submitted themselves to 4 God's righteousness. For Christ ends the law and brings righteousness for everyone who has faith.[c] 5 Of legal righteousness Moses writes, 'The 6 man who does this shall gain life by it.' But the righteousness that comes by faith says, 'Do not say to yourself, "Who can go up to heaven?"' (that is to bring Christ down), 7 'or, "Who can go down to the abyss?"' (to 8 bring Christ up from the dead). But what does it say? 'The word is near you: it is upon your lips and in your heart.' This means the word of faith which we proclaim. 9 If on your lips is the confession, 'Jesus is Lord', and in your heart the faith that God raised him from the dead, then you will 10 find salvation. For the faith that leads to righteousness is in the heart, and the confession that leads to salvation is upon the lips. 11 Scripture says, 'Everyone who has faith in him will be saved from shame'—everyone: 12 there is no distinction between Jew and Greek, because the same Lord is Lord of all, and is rich enough for the need of all who 13 invoke him. For everyone, as it says again —'everyone who invokes the name of the 14 Lord will be saved'. How could they invoke one in whom they had no faith? And how could they have faith in one they had never heard of? And how hear without someone to 15 spread the news? And how could anyone spread the news without a commission to do so? And that is what Scripture affirms: 'How welcome are the feet of the messengers of good news!'

But not all have responded to the good 16 news. For Isaiah says, 'Lord, who has believed our message?' We conclude that 17 faith is awakened by the message, and the message that awakens it comes through the word of Christ.

But, I ask, can it be that they never heard 18 it? Of course they did: 'Their voice has sounded all over the earth, and their words to the bounds of the inhabited world.' But, 19 I ask again, can it be that Israel failed to recognize the message? In reply, I first cite Moses, who says, 'I will use a nation that is no nation to stir your envy, and a foolish nation to rouse your anger.' But Isaiah is 20 still more daring: 'I was found', he says, 'by those who were not looking for me; I was clearly shown to those who never asked about me'; while to Israel he says, 'All day 21 long I have stretched out my hands to an unruly and defiant people.'

God's plan for Israel

I ask then, has God rejected his people? 1 I cannot believe it! I am an Israelite myself, of the stock of Abraham, of the tribe of Benjamin. No! God has not rejected the 2 people which he acknowledged of old as his own. You know (do you not?) what Scripture says in the story of Elijah—how Elijah pleads with God against Israel: 'Lord, they 3 have killed thy prophets, they have torn down thine altars, and I alone am left, and they are seeking my life.' And what does the 4 divine voice say to him? 'I have left myself seven thousand men who have not knelt to Baal.' In just the same way at the present 5 time a 'remnant' has come into being, selected by the grace of God. But if it is by 6 grace, then it does not rest on deeds done, or grace would cease to be grace.

What follows? What Israel sought, Israel 7 has not achieved, but the selected few have achieved it. The rest were made blind to the truth, exactly as it stands written: 'God 8 brought upon them a numbness of spirit; he gave them blind eyes and deaf ears, and so it is still.' Similarly David says: 9

'May their table be a snare and a trap, both stumbling-block and retribution! May their eyes become so dim that they lose 1 their sight! Bow down their backs unceasingly!'

I now ask, did their failure mean complete downfall? Far from it! Because they offended, salvation has come to the Gentiles, to stir Israel to emulation. But if their offence means the enrichment of the world, and if their falling-off means the enrichment of the Gentiles, how much more their coming to full strength!

c Or Christ is the end of the law as a way to righteousness for everyone who has faith.

Illustration from the olive-tree

13 But I have something to say to you Gentiles. I am a missionary to the Gentiles, and as 14 such I give all honour to that ministry when I try to stir emulation in the men of my own 15 race, and so to save some of them. For if their rejection has meant the reconciliation of the world, what will their acceptance mean? Nothing less than life from the dead! 16 If the first portion of dough is consecrated, so is the whole lump. If the root is con- 17 secrated, so are the branches. But if some of the branches have been lopped off, and you, a wild olive, have been grafted in among them, and have come to share the 18 same root and sap as the olive, do not make yourself superior to the branches. If you do so, remember that it is not you who sustain the root: the root sustains you.

19 You will say, 'Branches were lopped off 20 so that I might be grafted in.' Very well: they were lopped off for lack of faith, and by faith you hold your place. Put away your 21 pride, and be on your guard; for if God did not spare the native branches, no more will 22 he spare you. Observe the kindness and the severity of God—severity to those who fell away, divine kindness to you, if only you remain within its scope; otherwise you too 23 will be cut off, whereas they, if they do not continue faithless, will be grafted in; for it is in God's power to graft them in again. 24 For if you were cut from your native wild olive and against all nature grafted into the cultivated olive, how much more readily will they, the natural olive-branches, be grafted into their native stock!

The mystery of God's mercy

25 For there is a deep truth here, my brothers, of which I want you to take account, so that you may not be complacent about your own discernment: this partial blindness has come upon Israel only until the Gentiles 26 have been admitted in full strength; when that has happened, the whole of Israel will be saved, in agreement with the text of Scripture:

'From Zion shall come the Deliverer;
he shall remove wickedness from Jacob.
27 And this is the covenant I will grant them,
when I take away their sins.'

28 In the spreading of the Gospel they are treated as God's enemies for your sake; but God's choice stands, and they are his 29 friends for the sake of the patriarchs. For the gracious gifts of God and his calling 30 are irrevocable. Just as formerly you were disobedient to God, but now have received 31 mercy in the time of their disobedience, so now, when you receive mercy, they have proved disobedient, but only in order that they too may receive mercy. For in making 32 all mankind prisoners to disobedience, God's purpose was to show mercy to all mankind.

O depth of wealth, wisdom, and knowledge 33 in God! How unsearchable his judgements, how untraceable his ways! Who knows the 34 mind of the Lord? Who has been his counsellor? Who has ever made a gift to 35 him, to receive a gift in return? Source, 36 Guide, and Goal of all that is—to him be glory for ever! Amen.

Unity and diversity in the body of Christ

Therefore, my brothers, I implore you by 12 God's mercy to offer your very selves to him: a living sacrifice, dedicated and fit for his acceptance, the worship offered by mind and heart.[d] Adapt yourselves no longer to 2 the pattern of this present world, but let your minds be remade and your whole nature thus transformed. Then you will be able to discern the will of God, and to know what is good, acceptable, and perfect.

In virtue of the gift that God in his grace 3 has given me I say to everyone among you: do not be conceited or think too highly of yourself; but think your way to a sober estimate based on the measure of faith that God has dealt to each of you. For just as in 4 a single human body there are many limbs and organs, all with different functions, so 5 all of us, united with Christ, form one body, serving individually as limbs and organs to one another.

The gifts we possess differ as they are 6 allotted to us by God's grace, and must be exercised accordingly: the gift of inspired utterance, for example, in proportion to a man's faith; or the gift of administration, 7 in administration. A teacher should employ his gift in teaching, and one who has the 8 gift of stirring speech should use it to stir his hearers. If you give to charity, give with all your heart; if you are a leader, exert yourself to lead; if you are helping others in distress, do it cheerfully.

The Christian way of life

Love in all sincerity, loathing evil and cling- 9 ing to the good. Let love for our brother- 10 hood breed warmth of mutual affection. Give pride of place to one another in esteem.

With unflagging energy, in ardour of 11 spirit, serve the Lord.[e]

Let hope keep you joyful; in trouble stand 12 firm; persist in prayer.

Contribute to the needs of God's people, 13 and practise hospitality.

---

d Or . . . acceptance, for such is the worship which you, as rational creatures, should offer.   *e Some witnesses read* meet the demands of the hour.

14   Call down blessings on your persecutors—blessings, not curses.

15   With the joyful be joyful, and mourn with the mourners.

16   Care as much about each other as about yourselves. Do not be haughty, but go about with humble folk. Do not keep thinking how wise you are.

17   Never pay back evil for evil. Let your aims
18 be such as all men count honourable. If possible, so far as it lies with you, live at
19 peace with all men. My dear friends, do not seek revenge, but leave a place for divine retribution; for there is a text which reads, 'Justice is mine, says the Lord, I will repay.'
20 But there is another text: 'If your enemy is hungry, feed him; if he is thirsty, give him a drink; by doing this you will heap live
21 coals on his head.' Do not let evil conquer you, but use good to defeat evil.

Submission to authorities

13   Every person must submit to the supreme authorities. There is no authority but by act of God, and the existing authorities are
2 instituted by him; consequently anyone who rebels against authority is resisting a divine institution, and those who so resist have themselves to thank for the punishment they
3 will receive. For government, a terror to crime, has no terrors for good behaviour. You wish to have no fear of the authorities? Then continue to do right and you will have
4 their approval, for they are God's agents working for your good. But if you are doing wrong, then you will have cause to fear them; it is not for nothing that they hold the power of the sword, for they are God's agents of punishment, for retribution on the
5 offender. That is why you are obliged to submit. It is an obligation imposed not merely by fear of retribution but by con-
6 science. That is also why you pay taxes. The authorities are in God's service and to these duties they devote their energies.

Obligations to all men

7   Discharge your obligations to all men; pay tax and toll, reverence and respect, to those to
8 whom they are due. Leave no claim outstanding against you, except that of mutual love. He who loves his neighbour has satisfied
9 every claim of the law. For the commandments, 'Thou shalt not commit adultery, thou shalt not kill, thou shalt not steal, thou shalt not covet', and any other commandment there may be, are all summed up in the one
10 rule, 'Love your neighbour as yourself.' Love cannot wrong a neighbour; therefore the whole law is summed up in love.*f*

11   In all this, remember how critical the moment is. It is time for you to wake out of

Roman workmen

sleep, for deliverance is nearer to us now than it was when first we believed. It is far on in 12 the night; day is near. Let us therefore throw off the deeds of darkness and put on our armour as soldiers of the light. Let us behave 13 with decency as befits the day: no revelling or drunkenness, no debauchery or vice, no quarrels or jealousies! Let Christ Jesus himself 14 be the armour that you wear; give no more thought to satisfying the bodily appetites.

Mutual forbearance in the church

If a man is weak in his faith you must accept **14** him without attempting to settle doubtful points. For instance, one man will have 2 faith enough to eat all kinds of food, while a weaker man eats only vegetables. The man 3 who eats must not hold in contempt the man who does not, and he who does not eat must not pass judgement on the one who does; for God has accepted him. Who are 4 you to pass judgement on someone else's servant? Whether he stands or falls is his own Master's business; and stand he will, because his Master has power to enable him to stand.

Again, this man regards one day more 5 highly than another, while that man regards all days alike. On such a point everyone should have reached conviction in his own mind. He who respects the day has the Lord 6 in mind in doing so, and he who eats meat has the Lord in mind when he eats, since he gives thanks to God; and he who abstains has the Lord in mind no less, since he too gives thanks to God.

For no one of us lives, and equally no one 7

f Or the whole law is fulfilled by love.

8 of us dies, for himself alone. If we live, we live for the Lord; and if we die, we die for the Lord. Whether therefore we live or die, 9 we belong to the Lord. This is why Christ died and came to life again, to establish his 10 lordship over dead and living. You, sir, why do you pass judgement on your brother? And you, sir, why do you hold your brother in contempt? We shall all stand before God's 11 tribunal. For Scripture says, 'As I live, says the Lord, to me every knee shall bow and 12 every tongue acknowledge God.' So, you see, each of us will have to answer for himself.

Conduct to be guided by love

13 Let us therefore cease judging one another, but rather make this simple judgement: that no obstacle or stumbling-block be 14 placed in a brother's way. I am absolutely convinced, as a Christian,[g] that nothing is impure in itself; only, if a man considers a particular thing impure, then to him it 15 is impure. If your brother is outraged by what you eat, then your conduct is no longer guided by love. Do not by your eating bring disaster to a man for whom Christ died! 16 What for you is a good thing must not be- 17 come an occasion for slanderous talk; for the kingdom of God is not eating and drink- ing, but justice, peace, and joy, inspired by 18 the Holy Spirit. He who thus shows himself a servant of Christ is acceptable to God and approved by men.

About scruples of conscience

19 Let us then pursue the things that make for 20 peace and build up the common life. Do not ruin the work of God for the sake of food. Everything is pure in itself, but anything is bad for the man who by his eating causes 21 another to fall. It is a fine thing to abstain from eating meat or drinking wine, or doing anything which causes your brother's down- 22 fall. If you have a clear conviction, apply it to yourself in the sight of God. Happy is the man who can make his decision with a clear 23 conscience![h] But a man who has doubts is guilty if he eats, because his action does not arise from his conviction, and anything which 5 does not arise from conviction is sin.[i] Those of us who have a robust conscience must accept as our own burden the tender scruples of weaker men, and not consider ourselves. 2 Each of us must consider his neighbour and think what is for his good and will build up 3 the common life. For Christ too did not con- sider himself, but might have said, in the words of Scripture, 'The reproaches of those 4 who reproached thee fell upon me.' For all the ancient scriptures were written for our

own instruction, in order that through the encouragement they give us we may maintain our hope with fortitude. And may God, the 5 source of all fortitude and all encouragement, grant that you may agree with one another after the manner of Christ Jesus, so that with 6 one mind and one voice you may praise the God and Father of our Lord Jesus Christ.

Christ came for Jew and Gentile

In a word, accept one another as Christ 7 accepted us, to the glory of God. I mean that 8 Christ became a servant of the Jewish people to maintain the truth of God by making good his promises to the patriarchs, and at the 9 same time to give the Gentiles cause to glorify God for his mercy. As Scripture says, 'Therefore I will praise thee among the Gentiles and sing hymns to thy name'; and 10 again, 'Gentiles, make merry together with his own people'; and yet again, 'All Gentiles, 11 praise the Lord; let all peoples praise him.' Once again, Isaiah says, 'There shall be the 12 Scion of Jesse, the one raised up to govern the Gentiles; on him the Gentiles shall set their hope.' And may the God of hope fill 13 you with all joy and peace by your faith in him, until, by the power of the Holy Spirit, you overflow with hope.

Paul's confidence and ambition

My friends, I have no doubt in my own mind 14 that you yourselves are quite full of goodness and equipped with knowledge of every kind, well able to give advice to one another; nevertheless I have written to refresh your 15 memory, and written somewhat boldly at times, in virtue of the gift I have from God. His grace has made me a minister of Christ 16 Jesus to the Gentiles; my priestly service is the preaching of the gospel of God, and it falls to me to offer the Gentiles to him as[j] an accept- able sacrifice, consecrated by the Holy Spirit.

Thus in the fellowship of Christ Jesus I 17 have ground for pride in the service of God. I will venture to speak of those things alone 18 in which I have been Christ's instrument to bring the Gentiles into his allegiance, by word and deed, by the force of miraculous 19 signs and by the power of the Holy Spirit. As a result I have completed the preaching of the gospel of Christ from Jerusalem as far round as Illyricum. It is my ambition to 20 bring the Gospel to places where the very name of Christ has not been heard, for I do not want to build on another man's founda- tion; but, as Scripture says, 21

'They who had no news of him shall see, and they who never heard of him shall understand.'

---

g Or on the authority of the Lord Jesus. he approves!   i See p. 884, note r. offer may be . . .

h Or who does not bring judgement upon himself by what j Or . . . of God, so that the worship which the Gentiles

Paul's immediate plans

22 That is why I have been prevented all this
23 time from coming to you. But now I have
no further scope in these parts, and I have
24 been longing for many years to visit you on
my way to Spain; for I hope to see you as
I travel through, and to be sent there with
your support after having enjoyed your
25 company for a while. But at the moment
I am on my way to Jerusalem, on an errand
26 to God's people there. For Macedonia and
Achaia have resolved to raise a common
fund for the benefit of the poor among Gód's
27 people at Jerusalem. They have resolved to
do so, and indeed they are under an obligation to them. For if the Jewish Christians
shared their spiritual treasures with the
Gentiles, the Gentiles have a clear duty to
28 contribute to their material needs. So when
I have finished this business and delivered
the proceeds under my own seal, I shall set
29 out for Spain by way of your city, and I am
sure that when I arrive I shall come to you
with a full measure of the blessing of Christ.
30 I implore you by our Lord Jesus Christ
and by the love that the Spirit inspires, be
my allies in the fight; pray to God for me
31 that I may be saved from unbelievers in
Judaea and that my errand to Jerusalem
32 may find acceptance with God's people, so
that by his will I may come to you in a happy
frame of mind and enjoy a time of rest with
33 you. The God of peace be with you all.
Amen.[k]

Personal messages

16 I commend to you Phoebe, a fellow-
Christian who holds office in the congrega-
2 tion at Cenchreae. Give her, in the fellowship
of the Lord, a welcome worthy of God's
people, and stand by her in any business in
which she may need your help, for she has
herself been a good friend to many, including
myself.
3 Give my greetings to Prisca and Aquila,
4 my fellow-workers in Christ Jesus. They
risked their necks to save my life, and not
I alone but all the gentile congregations are
5 grateful to them. Greet also the congregation
at their house.
Give my greetings to my dear friend
Epaenetus, the first convert to Christ in
6 Asia, and to Mary, who toiled hard for you.
7 Greet Andronicus and Junias[l] my fellow-
countrymen and comrades in captivity. They
are eminent among the apostles, and they
were Christians before I was.

Greetings to Ampliatus, my dear friend 8
in the fellowship of the Lord, to Urban my 9
comrade in Christ, and to my dear Stachys.
My greetings to Apelles, well proved in 10
Christ's service, to the household of Aristo-
bulus, and my countryman Herodion, and 11
to those of the household of Narcissus
who are in the Lord's fellowship. Greet 12
Tryphaena and Tryphosa, who toil in the
Lord's service, and dear Persis who has
toiled in his service so long. Give my 13
greetings to Rufus, an outstanding follower
of the Lord, and to his mother, whom I
call mother too. Greet Asyncritus, Phlegon, 14
Hermes, Patrobas, Hermas, and all friends
in their company. Greet Philologus and 15
Julia,[m] Nereus and his sister, and Olym-
pas, and all God's people associated with
them.
Greet one another with the kiss of peace. 16
All Christ's congregations send you their
greetings.
I implore you, my friends, keep your eye 17
on those who stir up quarrels and lead others
astray, contrary to the teaching you received.
Avoid such people, for such people are servants not 18
of Christ our Lord but of their own appetites,
and they seduce the minds of innocent people
with smooth and specious words. The fame 19
of your obedience has spread everywhere.
This makes me happy about you; yet I
should wish you to be experts in goodness
but simpletons in evil; and the God of 20
peace will soon crush Satan beneath your
feet. The grace of our Lord Jesus be with
you![n]
Greetings to you from my colleague 21
Timothy, and from Lucius, Jason, and
Sosipater my fellow-countrymen. (I Tertius, 22
who took this letter down, add my Christian
greetings.) Greetings also from Gaius, my 23
host and host of the whole congregation,
and from Erastus, treasurer of this city, and
our brother Quartus.[o]

Glory to God!

To him who has power to make your stand- 25
ing sure, according to the Gospel I brought
you and the proclamation of Jesus Christ,
according to the revelation of that divine
secret kept in silence for long ages but now 26
disclosed, and through prophetic scriptures
by eternal God's command made known to
all nations, to bring them to faith and
obedience—to God who alone is wise, 27
through Jesus Christ,[p] be glory for endless
ages! Amen.[q r]

---

k *See this page, note r.*   l *Or Junia; some witnesses read Julia, or Julias.*   m *Or Julias; some
witnesses read Junia, or Junias.*   n *The words* The grace . . . with you *are omitted at this point in some
witnesses; in some, these or similar words are given as verse 24, and in some others after verse 27 (see note on
verse 23).*   o *Some witnesses add* (24) The grace of our Lord Jesus Christ be with you all! Amen.   p *Some
witnesses insert* to whom.   q *Here some witnesses add* The grace of our Lord Jesus Christ be with you!
r *Some witnesses place verses 25–27 at the end of chapter 14, one other places them at the end of chapter 15, and
others omit them altogether.*

THE FIRST LETTER OF PAUL TO THE
CORINTHIANS

Thanksgiving

1 FROM PAUL, apostle of Jesus Christ at God's call and by God's will, together with 2 our colleague Sosthenes, to the congregation of God's people at Corinth, dedicated to him in Christ Jesus, claimed by him as his own, along with all men everywhere who invoke the name of our Lord Jesus Christ —their Lord as well as ours.

3 Grace and peace to you from God our Father and the Lord Jesus Christ.

4 I am always thanking God for you. I thank him for his grace given to you in Christ 5 Jesus. I thank him for all the enrichment that has come to you in Christ. You possess full knowledge and you can give full expres- 6 sion to it, because in you the evidence for the truth of Christ has found confirmation. 7 There is indeed no single gift you lack, while you wait expectantly for our Lord Jesus 8 Christ to reveal himself. He will keep you firm to the end, without reproach on the 9 Day of our Lord Jesus. It is God himself who called you to share in the life of his Son Jesus Christ our Lord; and God keeps faith.

Divisions at Corinth condemned

10 I appeal to you, my brothers, in the name of our Lord Jesus Christ: agree among yourselves, and avoid divisions; be firmly joined in unity of mind and thought. I have been 11 told, my brothers, by Chloe's people that there are quarrels among you. What I mean 12 is this: each of you is saying, 'I am Paul's man', or 'I am for Apollos'; 'I follow Cephas', or 'I am Christ's.' Surely Christ has not been 13 divided among you! Was it Paul who was crucified for you? Was it in the name of Paul that you were baptized? Thank God, 14 I never baptized one of you—except Crispus and Gaius. So no one can say you were 15 baptized in my name.—Yes, I did baptize 16 the household of Stephanas; I cannot think of anyone else. Christ did not send me to 17 baptize, but to proclaim the Gospel; and to do it without relying on the language of worldly wisdom, so that the fact of Christ on his cross might have its full weight.

God's wisdom and man's

This doctrine of the cross is sheer folly to 18 those on their way to ruin, but to us who are on the way to salvation it is the power of God. Scripture says, 'I will destroy the 19 wisdom of the wise, and bring to nothing the cleverness of the clever.' Where is your 20 wise man now, your man of learning, or your subtle debater—limited, all of them, to this passing age? God has made the wisdom of this world look foolish. As God in 21 his wisdom ordained, the world failed to find him by its wisdom, and he chose to save those who have faith by the folly of 22 the Gospel. Jews call for miracles, Greeks 23 look for wisdom; but we proclaim Christ —yes, Christ nailed to the cross; and though this is a stumbling-block to Jews and folly 24 to Greeks, yet to those who have heard his call, Jews and Greeks alike, he is the power of God and the wisdom of God.

25 Divine folly is wiser than the wisdom of man, and divine weakness stronger than 26 man's strength. My brothers, think what sort of people you are, whom God has called. Few of you are men of wisdom, by any human standard; few are powerful or highly 27 born. Yet, to shame the wise, God has chosen what the world counts folly, and to shame what is strong, God has chosen 28 what the world counts weakness. He has chosen things low and contemptible, mere nothings, to overthrow the existing order. 29 And so there is no place for human pride 30 in the presence of God. You are in Christ Jesus by God's act, for God has made him our wisdom; he is our righteousness; in 31 him we are consecrated and set free. And so (in the words of Scripture), 'If a man must boast, let him boast of the Lord.'

Nothing but Jesus Christ

2 As for me, brothers, when I came to you, I declared the attested truth of God[a] with- 2 out display of fine words or wisdom. I resolved that while I was with you I would think of nothing but Jesus Christ—Christ 3 nailed to the cross. I came before you weak, 4 nervous, and shaking with fear. The word I spoke, the gospel I proclaimed, did not sway you with subtle arguments; it carried 5 conviction by spiritual power, so that your faith might be built not upon human wisdom but upon the power of God.

Revelations by the Spirit

6 And yet I do speak words of wisdom to those who are ripe for it, not a wisdom belonging to this passing age, nor to any of its governing powers, which are declining to their end; 7 I speak God's hidden wisdom, his secret purpose framed from the very beginning to 8 bring us to our full glory. The powers that rule the world have never known it; if they had, they would not have crucified the Lord 9 of glory. But, in the words of Scripture, 'Things beyond our seeing, things beyond our hearing, things beyond our imagining, all prepared by God for those who love him', 10 these it is that God has revealed to us through the Spirit.

For the Spirit explores everything, even 11 the depths of God's own nature. Among

men, who knows what a man is but the man's own spirit within him? In the same way, only the Spirit of God knows what God is. This is the Spirit that we have 12 received from God, and not the spirit of the world, so that we may know all that God of his own grace has given us; and, because 13 we are interpreting spiritual truths to those who have the Spirit, we speak of these gifts of God in words found for us not by our human wisdom but by the Spirit. A man 14 who is unspiritual refuses what belongs to the Spirit of God; it is folly to him; he cannot grasp it, because it needs to be judged in the light of the Spirit. A man gifted with 15 the Spirit can judge the worth of everything, but is not himself subject to judgement by his fellow-men. For (in the words of Scrip- 16 ture) 'who knows the mind of the Lord? Who can advise him?' We, however, possess the mind of Christ.

All too human

For my part, my brothers, I could not speak 3 to you as I should speak to people who have the Spirit. I had to deal with you on the merely natural plane, as infants in Christ. And so I gave you milk to drink, instead of 2 solid food, for which you were not yet ready. Indeed, you are still not ready for it, for 3 you are still on the merely natural plane. Can you not see that while there is jealousy and strife among you, you are living on the purely human level of your lower nature? When one says, 'I am Paul's man', and 4 another, 'I am for Apollos', are you not all too human?

God's fellow-workers

After all, what is Apollos? What is Paul? 5 We are simply God's agents in bringing you to the faith. Each of us performed the task which the Lord allotted to him: I planted 6 the seed, and Apollos watered it; but God made it grow. Thus it is not the gardeners 7 with their planting and watering who count, but God, who makes it grow. Whether they 8 plant or water, they work as a team,[b] though each will get his own pay for his own labour. We are God's fellow-workers;[c] and you are 9 God's garden.

Or again, you are God's building. I am 10 like a skilled master-builder who by God's grace laid the foundation, and someone else is putting up the building. Let each take care how he builds. There can be no other 11 foundation beyond that which is already laid; I mean Jesus Christ himself. If anyone 12 builds on that foundation with gold, silver, and fine stone, or with wood, hay, and straw, the work that each man does will at last be 13

a *Some witnesses read* I declared God's secret purpose . . . the same.   c *Or* We are fellow-workers in God's service.

b *Or* Whether they plant or water, it is all

brought to light; the day of judgement will expose it. For that day dawns in fire, and the fire will test the worth of each man's work. 14 If a man's building stands, he will be re- 15 warded; if it burns, he will have to bear the loss; and yet he will escape with his life, as 16 one might from a fire. Surely you know that you are God's temple, where the Spirit of 17 God dwells. Anyone who destroys God's temple will himself be destroyed[d] by God, because the temple of God is holy; and that temple you are.

True wisdom

18 Make no mistake about this: if there is any- one among you who fancies himself wise— wise, I mean, by the standards of this pass- ing age—he must become a fool to gain true 19 wisdom. For the wisdom of this world is folly in God's sight. Scripture says, 'He traps 20 the wise in their own cunning', and again, 'The Lord knows that the arguments of the 21 wise are futile.' So never make mere men a cause for pride. For though everything 22 belongs to you—Paul, Apollos, and Cephas, the world, life, and death, the present and 23 the future, all of them belong to you—yet you belong to Christ, and Christ to God.

'My judge is the LORD'

4 We must be regarded as Christ's subordinates 2 and as stewards of the secrets of God. Well then, stewards are expected to show them- 3 selves trustworthy. For my part, if I am called to account by you or by any human court of judgement, it does not matter to me in the least. Why, I do not even pass 4 judgement on myself, for I have nothing on my conscience; but that does not mean I 5 stand acquitted. My judge is the Lord. So pass no premature judgement; wait until the Lord comes. For he will bring to light what darkness hides, and disclose men's inward motives; then will be the time for each to receive from God such praise as he deserves.

'Keep within the rules'

6 Into this general picture, my friends, I have brought Apollos and myself on your account, so that you may take our case as an example, and learn to 'keep within the rules', as they say, and may not be inflated with pride as 7 you patronize one and flout the other. Who makes you, my friend, so important? What do you possess that was not given you? If then you really received it all as a gift, why take the credit to yourself? 8 All of you, no doubt, have everything you could desire. You have come into your for- tune already. You have come into your kingdom—and left us out. How I wish you

had indeed won your kingdom; then you might share it with us! For it seems to me 9 God has made us apostles the most abject of mankind. We are like men condemned to death in the arena, a spectacle to the whole universe—angels as well as men. We are 10 fools for Christ's sake, while you are such sensible Christians. We are weak; you are so powerful. We are in disgrace; you are honoured. To this day we go hungry and 11 thirsty and in rags; we are roughly handled; we wander from place to place; we wear 12 ourselves out working with our own hands. They curse us, and we bless; they persecute us, and we submit to it; they slander us, and 13 we humbly make our appeal. We are treated as the scum of the earth, the dregs of humanity, to this very day.

An appeal to reason

I am not writing thus to shame you, but to 14 bring you to reason; for you are my dear children. You may have ten thousand tutors 15 in Christ, but you have only one father. For in Christ Jesus you are my offspring, and mine alone, through the preaching of the Gospel. I appeal to you therefore to follow 16 my example. That is the very reason why I 17 have sent Timothy, who is a dear son to me and a most trustworthy Christian; he will remind you of the way of life in Christ which I follow, and which I teach everywhere in all our congregations. There are certain persons 18 who are filled with self-importance because they think I am not coming to Corinth. I 19 shall come very soon, if the Lord will; and then I shall take the measure of these self- important people, not by what they say, but by what power is in them. The kingdom of 20 God is not a matter of talk, but of power. Choose, then: am I to come to you with a 21 rod in my hand, or in love and a gentle spirit?

About sexual immorality

I actually hear reports of sexual immorality **5** among you, immorality such as even pagans do not tolerate: the union of a man with his father's wife. And you can still be proud of 2 yourselves! You ought to have gone into mourning; a man who has done such a deed should have been rooted out of your com- pany. For my part, though I am absent in 3 body, I am present in spirit, and my judge- ment upon the man who did this thing is already given, as if I were indeed present: you all being assembled in the name of our 4 Lord Jesus, and I with you in spirit, with the power of our Lord Jesus over us, this man is 5 to be consigned to Satan for the destruction of the body, so that his spirit may be saved on the Day of the Lord.

---

d Some witnesses read is himself destroyed.

Discipline within the fellowship

6 Your self-satisfaction ill becomes you. Have you never heard the saying, 'A little leaven
7 leavens all the dough'? The old leaven of corruption is working among you. Purge it out, and then you will be bread of a new baking. As Christians you are unleavened Passover bread; for indeed our Passover has begun; the sacrifice is offered—Christ
8 himself. So we who observe the festival must not use the old leaven, the leaven of corruption and wickedness, but only the unleavened bread which is sincerity and truth.
9 In my letter I wrote that you must have
10 nothing to do with loose livers. I was not, of course, referring to pagans who lead loose lives or are grabbers and swindlers or idolaters. To avoid them you would have to get
11 out of the world altogether. I now write that you must have nothing to do with any so-called Christian who leads a loose life, or is grasping, or idolatrous, a slanderer, a drunkard, or a swindler. You should not even
12 eat with any such person. What business of
13 mine is it to judge outsiders? God is their judge. You are judges within the fellowship. Root out the evil-doer from your community.

Law-suits in pagan courts condemned

6 If one of your number has a dispute with another, has he the face to take it to pagan law-courts instead of to the community of
2 God's people? It is God's people who are to judge the world; surely you know that. And if the world is to come before you for judgement, are you incompetent to deal
3 with these trifling cases? Are you not aware that we are to judge angels? How much
4 more, mere matters of business! If therefore you have such business disputes, how can you entrust jurisdiction to outsiders, men who count for nothing in our community?
5 I write this to shame you. Can it be that there is not a single wise man among you able to give a decision in a brother-Christian's
6 cause? Must brother go to law with brother
7 —and before unbelievers? Indeed, you already fall below your standard in going to law with one another at all. Why not rather suffer injury? Why not rather let yourself be
8 robbed? So far from this, you actually injure and rob—injure and rob your brothers!
9 Surely you know that the unjust will never come into possession of the kingdom of God. Make no mistake: no fornicator or idolater, none who are guilty either of adultery or of
10 homosexual perversion, no thieves or grabbers or drunkards or slanderers or swindlers,
11 will possess the kingdom of God. Such were some of you. But you have been through

the purifying waters; you have been dedicated to God and justified through the name of the Lord Jesus and the Spirit of our God.

Lust and fornication

'I am free to do anything', you say. Yes, but 12 not everything is for my good. No doubt I am free to do anything, but I for one will not let anything make free with me. 'Food 13 is for the belly and the belly for food', you say. True; and one day God will put an end to both. But it is not true that the body is for lust; it is for the Lord—and the Lord for the body. God not only raised our Lord 14 from the dead; he will also raise us by his power. Do you not know that your bodies 15 are limbs and organs of Christ? Shall I then take from Christ his bodily parts and make them over to a harlot? Never! You surely 16 know that anyone who links himself with a harlot becomes physically one with her (for Scripture says, 'The pair shall become one flesh'); but he who links himself with Christ 17 is one with him, spiritually. Shun fornication. 18 Every other sin that a man can commit is outside the body; but the fornicator sins against his own body. Do you not know that 19 your body is a shrine of the indwelling Holy Spirit, and the Spirit is God's gift to you? You do not belong to yourselves; you were 20 bought at a price. Then honour God in your body.

About marital relationships

And now for the matters you wrote about. 7
It is a good thing for a man to have nothing to do with women;[e] but because there 2 is so much immorality, let each man have his own wife and each woman her own husband. The husband must give the wife 3 what is due to her, and the wife equally must give the husband his due. The wife 4 cannot claim her body as her own; it is her husband's. Equally, the husband cannot claim his body as his own; it is his wife's. Do not deny yourselves to one another, 5 except when you agree upon a temporary abstinence in order to devote yourselves to prayer; afterwards you may come together again; otherwise, for lack of self-control, you may be tempted by Satan.
All this I say by way of concession, not 6 command. I should like you all to be as I 7 am myself; but everyone has the gift God has granted him, one this gift and another that.
To the unmarried and to widows I say 8 this: it is a good thing if they stay as I am myself; but if they cannot control themselves, they should marry. Better be married 9 than burn with vain desire.

e Or You say, 'It is a good thing . . . women'; . . .

About divorce

10 To the married I give this ruling, which is not mine but the Lord's: a wife must not
11 separate herself from her husband; if she does, she must either remain unmarried or be reconciled to her husband; and the husband must not divorce his wife.

Marriage between Christians and pagans

12 To the rest I say this, as my own word, not as the Lord's: if a Christian has a heathen wife, and she is willing to live with him, he
13 must not divorce her; and a woman who has a heathen husband willing to live with
14 her must not divorce her husband. For the heathen husband now belongs to God through his Christian wife, and the heathen wife through her Christian husband. Otherwise your children would not belong to God,
15 whereas in fact they do. If on the other hand the heathen partner wishes for a separation, let him have it. In such cases the Christian husband or wife is under no compulsion; but God's call is a call to live in peace.
16 Think of it: as a wife you may be your husband's salvation; as a husband you may be your wife's salvation.

Remain as you were called

17 However that may be, each one must order his life according to the gift the Lord has granted him and his condition when God called him. That is what I teach in all our
18 congregations. Was a man called with the marks of circumcision on him? Let him not remove them. Was he uncircumcised when he was called? Let him not be circumcised.
19 Circumcision or uncircumcision is neither here nor there; what matters is to keep
20 God's commands. Every man should remain in the condition in which he was
21 called. Were you a slave when you were called? Do not let that trouble you; but if a chance of liberty should come, take it.*f*
22 For the man who as a slave received the call to be a Christian is the Lord's freedman, and, equally, the free man who received the
23 call is a slave in the service of Christ. You were bought at a price; do not become
24 slaves of men. Thus each one, my friends, is to remain before God in the condition in which he received his call.

Celibacy and marriage

25 On the question of celibacy, I have no instructions from the Lord, but I give my judgement as one who by God's mercy is fit to be trusted.
26 It is my opinion, then, that in a time of stress like the present this is the best way for a man to live—it is best for a man to be as he is. Are you bound in marriage? Do not
27 seek a dissolution. Has your marriage been dissolved? Do not seek a wife. If, however,
28 you do marry, there is nothing wrong in it; and if a virgin marries, she has done no wrong. But those who marry will have pain and grief in this bodily life, and my aim is to spare you.

What I mean, my friends, is this. The time
29 we live in will not last long. While it lasts, married men should be as if they had no
30 wives; mourners should be as if they had nothing to grieve them, the joyful as if they did not rejoice; buyers must not count on keeping what they buy, nor those who use the
31 world's wealth on using it to the full. For the whole frame of this world is passing away.

I want you to be free from anxious care.
32 The unmarried man cares for the Lord's business; his aim is to please the Lord. But
33 the married man cares for worldly things; his aim is to please his wife; and he has a divided
34 mind. The unmarried or celibate woman cares*g* for the Lord's business; her aim is to be dedicated to him in body as in spirit; but the married woman cares for worldly things; her aim is to please her husband.

In saying this I have no wish to keep you
35 on a tight rein. I am thinking simply of your own good, of what is seemly, and of your freedom to wait upon the Lord without distraction.

But if a man has a partner in celibacy*h*
36 and feels that he is not behaving properly towards her, if, that is, his instincts are too strong for him,*i* and something must be done, he may do as he pleases; there is nothing wrong in it; let them marry.*j* But
37 if a man is steadfast in his purpose, being under no compulsion, and has complete control of his own choice; and if he has decided in his own mind to preserve his partner*k* in her virginity, he will do well. Thus, he who marries his partner*l* does well,
38 and he who does not will do better.

A wife is bound to her husband as long
39 as he lives. But if the husband die, she is free to marry whom she will, provided the marriage is within the Lord's fellowship. But she is better off as she is; that is my
40 opinion, and I believe that I too have the Spirit of God.

Christians in a pagan society

Now about food consecrated to heathen 8 deities.

Of course we all 'have knowledge', as you

---

f Or but even if a chance of liberty should come, choose rather to make good use of your servitude.   *g Some witnesses read* . . . his wife. And there is a difference between the wife and the virgin. The unmarried woman cares . . .   *h Or* a virgin daughter (*or* ward).   *i Or* if she is ripe for marriage.   *j Or* let the girl and her lover marry.   *k Or* his daughter.   *l Or* gives his daughter in marriage.

say. This 'knowledge' breeds conceit; it is
2 love that builds. If anyone fancies that he
knows, he knows nothing yet, in the true
3 sense of knowing. But if a man loves,[m] he
is acknowledged by God.[n]
4   Well then, about eating this consecrated
food: of course, as you say, 'a false god has
no existence in the real world. There is no
5 god but one.' For indeed, if there be so-
called gods, whether in heaven or on earth
—as indeed there are many 'gods' and many
6 'lords'—yet for us there is one God, the
Father, from whom all being comes, towards whom we move; and there is one
Lord, Jesus Christ, through whom all things
came to be, and we through him.

The Greek gods Chronos and Apollo

7   But not everyone knows this. There are
some who have been so accustomed to
idolatry[o] that even now they eat this food
with a sense of its heathen consecration, and
their conscience, being weak, is polluted by
8 the eating. Certainly food will not bring us
into God's presence: if we do not eat, we
are none the worse, and if we eat, we are
9 none the better. But be careful that this
liberty of yours does not become a pitfall
10 for the weak. If a weak character sees you
sitting down to a meal in a heathen temple
—you, who 'have knowledge'—will not his
conscience be emboldened to eat food con-
11 secrated to the heathen deity? This 'knowledge' of yours is utter disaster to the weak,
12 the brother for whom Christ died. In thus
sinning against your brothers and wounding
their conscience,[p] you sin against Christ.
13 And therefore, if food be the downfall of my
brother, I will never eat meat any more, for I
will not be the cause of my brother's downfall.

Rights and duties of an apostle

9 Am I not a free man? Am I not an apostle?
Did I not see Jesus our Lord? Are not you

my own handiwork, in the Lord? If others 2
do not accept me as an apostle, you at least
are bound to do so, for you are yourselves
the very seal of my apostolate, in the Lord.
   To those who put me in the dock this is 3
my answer: Have I no right to eat and drink? 4
Have I no right to take a Christian wife 5
about with me, like the rest of the apostles
and the Lord's brothers, and Cephas? Or 6
are Barnabas and I alone bound to work for
our living? Did you ever hear of a man 7
serving in the army at his own expense? or
planting a vineyard without eating the fruit
of it? or tending a flock without using its
milk? Do not suppose I rely on these human 8
analogies, for the law says the same; in the 9
Law of Moses we read, 'You shall not muzzle
a threshing ox.' Do you suppose God's
concern is with oxen? Or is the reference 10
clearly to ourselves? Of course it refers to
us, in the sense that the ploughman should
plough and the thresher thresh in the hope
of getting some of the produce. If we have 11
sown a spiritual crop for you, is it too much
to expect from you a material harvest? If 12
you allow others these rights, have not we
a stronger claim?
   But I have availed myself of no such right.
On the contrary, I put up with all that comes
my way rather than offer any hindrance to
the gospel of Christ. You know (do you not?) 13
that those who perform the temple service
eat the temple offerings, and those who wait
upon the altar claim their share of the
sacrifice. In the same way the Lord gave 14
instructions that those who preach the
Gospel should earn their living by the Gospel.
But I have never taken advantage of any 15
such right, nor do I intend to claim it in
this letter. I had rather die! No one shall
make my boast an empty boast. Even if I 16
preach the Gospel, I can claim no credit for
it; I cannot help myself; it would be misery
to me not to preach. If I did it of my own 17
choice, I should be earning my pay; but
since I do it apart from my own choice,
I am simply discharging a trust.[q] Then what 18
is my pay? The satisfaction of preaching
the Gospel without expense to anyone; in
other words, of waiving the rights which my
preaching gives me.

How Paul proclaims the Gospel

I am a free man and own no master; but 19
I have made myself every man's servant, to
win over as many as possible. To Jews I 20
became like a Jew, to win Jews; as they are
subject to the Law of Moses, I put myself
under that law to win them, although I am
not myself subject to it. To win Gentiles, 21

m Some witnesses read loves God.   *n Or* he is recognized.   *o Some witnesses read* in whom the
consciousness of the false god is so persistent . . .   *p Some witnesses insert* weak as it is.   *q Or* If I
do it willingly I am earning my pay; if I did it unwillingly I should still have a trust laid upon me.

who are outside the Law, I made myself like one of them, although I am not in truth outside God's law, being under the law of
2 Christ. To the weak I became weak, to win the weak. Indeed, I have become everything in turn to men of every sort, so that in one
3 way or another I may save some. All this I do for the sake of the Gospel, to bear my part in proclaiming it.

Illustrations from the world of sport

4 You know (do you not?) that at the sports all the runners run the race, though only one
5 wins the prize. Like them, run to win! But every athlete goes into strict training. They do it to win a fading wreath; we, a wreath

6 that never fades. For my part, I run with a clear goal before me; I am like a boxer who
7 does not beat the air; I bruise my own body and make it know its master, for fear that after preaching to others I should find myself rejected.

Illustrations from history

1 You should understand, my brothers, that our ancestors were all under the pillar of cloud, and all of them passed through the
2 Red Sea; and so they all received baptism into the fellowship of Moses in cloud and
3 sea. They all ate the same supernatural food,
4 and all drank the same supernatural drink; I mean, they all drank from the supernatural rock that accompanied their travels—and
5 that rock was Christ. And yet, most of them were not accepted by God, for the desert was strewn with their corpses.

6 These events happened as symbols to warn us not to set our desires on evil things,
7 as they did. Do not be idolaters, like some of them; as Scripture has it, 'the people sat
8 down to feast and rose up to revel'. Let us not commit fornication, as some of them did—and twenty-three thousand died in one
9 day. Let us not put the power of the Lord[r] to the test, as some of them did—and were
10 destroyed by serpents. Do not grumble against God, as some of them did—and were destroyed by the Destroyer.

11 All these things that happened to them were symbolic, and were recorded for our benefit as a warning. For upon us the ful-
12 filment of the ages has come. If you feel

sure that you are standing firm, beware! You may fall. So far you have faced no trial 13 beyond what man can bear. God keeps faith, and he will not allow you to be tested above your powers, but when the test comes he will at the same time provide a way out, by enabling you to sustain it.

Questions of conscience

So then, dear friends, shun idolatry. I speak 14 15 to you as men of sense. Form your own judgement on what I say. When we bless 16 'the cup of blessing', is it not a means of sharing in the blood of Christ? When we break the bread, is it not a means of sharing in the body of Christ? Because there is one 17 loaf, we, many as we are, are one body;[s] for it is one loaf of which we all partake.

Look at the Jewish people. Are not those 18 who partake in the sacrificial meal sharers in the altar? What do I imply by this? that an 19 idol is anything but an idol? or food offered to it anything more than food? No; but the 20 sacrifices the heathen offer are offered (in the words of Scripture) 'to demons and to that which is not God'; and I will not have you become partners with demons. You 21 cannot drink the cup of the Lord and the cup of demons. You cannot partake of the Lord's table and the table of demons. Can we defy the Lord? Are we stronger 22 than he?

'We are free to do anything', you say. Yes, 23 but is everything good for us? 'We are free to do anything', but does everything help the building of the community? Each of 24 you must regard, not his own interests, but the other man's.

You may eat anything sold in the meat- 25 market without raising questions of con- science; for the earth is the Lord's and 26 everything in it.

If an unbeliever invites you to a meal and 27 you care to go, eat whatever is put before you, without raising questions of con- science. But if somebody says to you, 'This 28 food has been offered in sacrifice', then, out of consideration for him, and for con- science' sake, do not eat it—not your 29 conscience, I mean, but the other man's.

'What?' you say, 'is my freedom to be called in question by another man's con- science? If I partake with thankfulness, why 30 am I blamed for eating food over which I have said grace?' Well, whether you eat or 31 drink, or whatever you are doing, do all for the honour of God: give no offence to Jews, 32 or Greeks, or to the church of God. For my 33 part I always try to meet everyone half-way, regarding not my own good but the good of the many, so that they may be saved. Follow **11** my example as I follow Christ's.

r Some witnesses read of Christ.   *s Or* For we, many as we are, are one loaf, one body.

Men and women in the church

2 I commend you for always keeping me in mind, and maintaining the tradition I
3 handed on to you. But I wish you to understand that, while every man has Christ for his Head, woman's head is man,*t* as Christ's
4 Head is God. A man who keeps his head covered when he prays or prophesies brings
5 shame on his head; a woman, on the contrary, brings shame on her head if she prays or prophesies bare-headed; it is as bad as
6 if her head were shaved. If a woman is not to wear a veil she might as well have her hair cut off; but if it is a disgrace for her to be cropped and shaved, then she should
7 wear a veil. A man has no need to cover his head, because man is the image of God, and the mirror of his glory, whereas woman
8 reflects the glory of man.*u* For man did not originally spring from woman, but woman
9 was made out of man; and man was not created for woman's sake, but woman for
10 the sake of man; and therefore it is woman's duty to have a sign of authority*v* on her head,
11 out of regard for the angels.*w* And yet, in Christ's fellowship woman is as essential to
12 man as man to woman. If woman was made out of man, it is through woman that man now comes to be; and God is the source of all.
13   Judge for yourselves: is it fitting for a
14 woman to pray to God bare-headed? Does not Nature herself teach you that while
15 flowing locks disgrace a man, they are a woman's glory? For her locks were given for covering.
16   However, if you insist on arguing, let me tell you, there is no such custom among us, or in any of the congregations of God's people.

The Lord's Supper

17 In giving you these injunctions I must mention a practice which I cannot commend: your meetings tend to do more harm than
18 good. To begin with, I am told that when you meet as a congregation you fall into sharply divided groups; and I believe there
19 is some truth in it (for dissensions are necessary if only to show which of your members
20 are sound). The result is that when you meet as a congregation, it is impossible for you
21 to eat the Lord's Supper, because each of you is in such a hurry to eat his own, and while one goes hungry another has too much
22 to drink. Have you no homes of your own to eat and drink in? Or are you so contemptuous of the church of God that you shame its poorer members? What am I to say? Can I commend you? On this point, certainly not!

For the tradition which I handed on to 23 you came to me from the Lord himself: that the Lord Jesus, on the night of his arrest, took bread and, after giving thanks to God, 24 broke it and said: 'This is my body, which is for you; do this as a memorial of me.' In 25 the same way, he took the cup after supper, and said: 'This cup is the new covenant sealed by my blood. Whenever you drink it, do this as a memorial of me.' For every time 26 you eat this bread and drink the cup, you proclaim the death of the Lord, until he comes.

It follows that anyone who eats the bread 27 or drinks the cup of the Lord unworthily will be guilty of desecrating the body and blood of the Lord. A man must test himself 28 before eating his share of the bread and drinking from the cup. For he who eats and 29 drinks eats and drinks judgement on himself if he does not discern the Body. That is 30 why many of you are feeble and sick, and a number have died. But if we examined 31 ourselves, we should not thus fall under judgement. When, however, we do fall under 32 the Lord's judgement, he is disciplining us, to save us from being condemned with the rest of the world.

Therefore, my brothers, when you meet 33 for a meal, wait for one another. If you are hungry, eat at home, so that in meeting 34 together you may not fall under judgement. The other matters I will arrange when I come.

About gifts of the Spirit

About gifts of the Spirit, there are some things of which I do not wish you to remain ignorant.

You know how, in the days when you were still pagan, you were swept off to those dumb heathen gods, however you happened to be led.*x* For this reason I must impress upon you that no one who says 'A curse on Jesus!' can be speaking under the influence of the Spirit of God. And no one can say 'Jesus is Lord!' except under the influence of the Holy Spirit.

There are varieties of gifts, but the same Spirit. There are varieties of service, but the same Lord. There are many forms of work, but all of them, in all men, are the work of the same God. In each of us the Spirit is manifested in one particular way, for some useful purpose. One man, through the Spirit, has the gift of wise speech, while another, by the power of the same Spirit, can put the deepest knowledge into words. Another, by the same Spirit, is granted faith; another, by the one Spirit, gifts of healing,

t Or a woman's head is her husband.   u Or a woman reflects her husband's glory.   v Some witnesses read to have a veil.   w Or and therefore a woman should keep her dignity on her head, for fear of the angels.   x Or . . . pagan, you would be seized by some power which drove you to those dumb heathen gods.

10 and another miraculous powers; another has the gift of prophecy, and another ability to distinguish true spirits from false; yet another has the gift of ecstatic utterance of different kinds, and another the ability to 11 interpret it. But all these gifts are the work of one and the same Spirit, distributing them separately to each individual at will.

12 For Christ is like a single body with its many limbs and organs, which, many as 13 they are, together make up one body. For indeed we were all brought into one body by baptism, in the one Spirit, whether we are Jews or Greeks, whether slaves or free men, and that one Holy Spirit was poured out for all of us to drink.

Illustration from the body

14 A body is not one single organ, but many. 15 Suppose the foot should say, 'Because I am not a hand, I do not belong to the body', it 16 does belong to the body none the less. Suppose the ear were to say, 'Because I am not an eye, I do not belong to the body', it does 17 still belong to the body. If the body were all eye, how could it hear? If the body were 18 all ear, how could it smell? But, in fact, God appointed each limb and organ to its own 19 place in the body, as he chose. If the whole were one single organ, there would not be 20 a body at all; in fact, however, there are 21 many different organs, but one body. The eye cannot say to the hand, 'I do not need you'; nor the head to the feet, 'I do not need 22 you.' Quite the contrary: those organs of the body which seem to be more frail than 23 others are indispensable, and those parts of the body which we regard as less honourable are treated with special honour. To our unseemly parts is given a more than ordinary 24 seemliness, whereas our seemly parts need no adorning. But God has combined the various parts of the body, giving special 25 honour to the humbler parts, so that there might be no sense of division in the body, but that all its organs might feel the same 26 concern for one another. If one organ suffers, they all suffer together. If one flourishes, they all rejoice together.

27 Now you are Christ's body, and each of 28 you a limb or organ of it. Within our community God has appointed, in the first place apostles, in the second place prophets, thirdly teachers; then miracle-workers, then those who have gifts of healing, or ability to help others or power to guide them, or the gift of ecstatic utterance of various kinds. 29 Are all apostles? all prophets? all teachers? 30 Do all work miracles? Have all gifts of healing? Do all speak in tongues of ecstasy? 31 Can all interpret them? The higher gifts are those you should aim at.

Love, the best way of all

And now I will show you the best way of all.

13 I may speak in tongues of men or of angels, but if I am without love, I am a sounding gong or a clanging cymbal. I may 2 have the gift of prophecy, and know every hidden truth; I may have faith strong enough to move mountains; but if I have no love, I am nothing. I may dole out all 3 I possess, or even give my body to be burnt,*y* but if I have no love, I am none the better.

Love is patient; love is kind and envies no 4 one. Love is never boastful, nor conceited, nor rude; never selfish, not quick to take 5 offence. Love keeps no score of wrongs; does not gloat over other men's sins, but 6 delights in the truth. There is nothing love 7 cannot face; there is no limit to its faith, its hope, and its endurance.

Love will never come to an end. Are there 8 prophets? their work will be over. Are there tongues of ecstasy? they will cease. Is there knowledge? it will vanish away; for 9 our knowledge and our prophecy alike are partial, and the partial vanishes when whole- 10 ness comes. When I was a child, my speech, 11 my outlook, and my thoughts were all childish. When I grew up, I had finished with childish things. Now we see only 12 puzzling reflections in a mirror, but then we shall see face to face. My knowledge now is partial; then it will be whole, like God's knowledge of me. In a word, there are three 13 things that last for ever: faith, hope, and love; but the greatest of them all is love.

Building up the community

Put love first; but there are other gifts of 14 the Spirit at which you should aim also, and above all prophecy. When a man is 2 using the language of ecstasy he is talking with God, not with men, for no man understands him; he is no doubt inspired, but he speaks mysteries. On the other hand, when 3 a man prophesies, he is talking to men, and his words have power to build; they stimulate and they encourage. The language of 4 ecstasy is good for the speaker himself, but it is prophecy that builds up a Christian community. I should be pleased for you all to 5 use the tongues of ecstasy, but better pleased for you to prophesy. The prophet is worth more than the man of ecstatic speech— unless indeed he can explain its meaning, and so help to build up the community. Suppose, my friends, that when I come to 6 you I use ecstatic language: what good shall I do you, unless what I say contains something by way of revelation, or enlightenment, or prophecy, or instruction?

Even with inanimate things that produce 7 sounds—a flute, say, or a lyre—unless their

y Some witnesses read even seek glory by self-sacrifice.

notes mark definite intervals, how can you
8 tell what tune is being played? Or again, if
the trumpet-call is not clear, who will pre-
9 pare for battle? In the same way if your
ecstatic utterance yields no precise meaning,
how can anyone tell what you are saying?
10 You will be talking into the air. How many
different kinds of sound there are, or may
be, in the world! Nothing is altogether
11 soundless. Well then, if I do not know the
meaning of the sound the speaker makes,
his words will be gibberish to me, and mine
12 to him. You are, I know, eager for gifts of
the Spirit; then aspire above all to excel in
those which build up the church.

13   I say, then, that the man who falls into
ecstatic utterance should pray for the ability
14 to interpret. If I use such language in my
prayer, the Spirit in me prays, but my
15 intellect lies fallow. What then? I will pray
as I am inspired to pray, but I will also pray
intelligently. I will sing hymns as I am
inspired to sing, but I will sing intelligently
16 too. Suppose you are praising God in the
language of inspiration: how will the plain
man who is present be able to say 'Amen'
to your thanksgiving, when he does not
17 know what you are saying? Your prayer of
thanksgiving may be all that could be
desired, but it is no help to the other man.
18 Thank God, I am more gifted in ecstatic
19 utterance than any of you,[z] but in the congregation I would rather speak five intelligible words, for the benefit of others as
well as myself, than thousands of words in
the language of ecstasy.

Appeal for order

20 Do not be childish, my friends. Be as innocent of evil as babes, but at least be grown-
21 up in your thinking. We read in the Law:
'I will speak to this nation through men of
strange tongues, and by the lips of foreigners;
and even so they will not heed me, says the
22 Lord.' Clearly then these 'strange tongues'
are not intended as a sign for believers, but
for unbelievers, whereas prophecy is designed
not for unbelievers but for those who hold
23 the faith. So if the whole congregation is
assembled and all are using the 'strange
tongues' of ecstasy, and some uninstructed
persons or unbelievers should enter, will
24 they not think you are mad? But if all are
uttering prophecies, the visitor, when he
enters, hears from everyone something that
searches his conscience and brings convic-
25 tion, and the secrets of his heart are laid
bare. So he will fall down and worship God,
crying, 'God is certainly among you!'

To sum up, my friends: when you meet 26
for worship, each of you contributes a hymn,
some instruction, a revelation, an ecstatic
utterance, or the interpretation of such an
utterance. All of these must aim at one
thing: to build up the church. If it is a matter 27
of ecstatic utterance, only two should speak,
or at most three, one at a time, and someone
must interpret. If there is no interpreter, 28
the speaker had better not address the meeting at all, but speak to himself and to God.
Of the prophets, two or three may speak, 29
while the rest exercise their judgement upon
what is said. If someone else, sitting in his 30
place, receives a revelation, let the first
speaker stop. You can all prophesy, one at 31
a time, so that the whole congregation may
receive instruction and encouragement. It 32
is for prophets to control prophetic inspiration, for the God who inspires them is not 33
a God of disorder but of peace.

As in all congregations of God's people,
women[a] should not address the meeting. 34
They have no licence to speak, but should
keep their place as the law directs. If there 35
is something they want to know, they can
ask their own husbands at home. It is a
shocking thing that a woman should address
the congregation.

Paul's authority

Did the word of God originate with you? 36
Or are you the only people to whom it came?
If anyone claims to be inspired or a prophet, 37
let him recognize that what I write has the
Lord's authority. If he does not acknowledge 38
this, God does not acknowledge him.[b]
In short, my friends, be eager to prophesy; 39
do not forbid ecstatic utterance; but let all 40
be done decently and in order.

The resurrection of Christ

And now, my brothers, I must remind you 1
of the gospel that I preached to you; the
gospel which you received, on which you
have taken your stand, and which is now 2
bringing you salvation. Do you still hold
fast the Gospel as I preached it to you? If
not, your conversion was in vain.[c]

First and foremost, I handed on to you 3
the facts which had been imparted to me:
that Christ died for our sins, in accordance
with the scriptures; that he was buried; that 4
he was raised to life on the third day, according to the scriptures; and that he appeared
to Cephas, and afterwards to the Twelve.
Then he appeared to over five hundred of 6
our brothers at once, most of whom are
still alive, though some have died. Then he 7

---

z *Or . . . man. I say the thanksgiving; I use ecstatic speech more than any of you.*   a *Or of peace, as in
all communities of God's people. Women . . .*   b *Some witnesses read* If he refuses to recognize this, let
him refuse!   c *Or* Do you remember the terms in which I preached the Gospel to you?—for I assume you
did not accept it thoughtlessly.

appeared to James, and afterwards to all the apostles.

8 In the end he appeared even to me. It 9 was like an abnormal birth; I had persecuted the church of God and am therefore inferior to all other apostles—indeed not fit to be 10 called an apostle. However, by God's grace I am what I am, nor has his grace been given to me in vain; on the contrary, in my labours I have outdone them all—not I, indeed, but the grace of God working with me. 11 But what matter, I or they? This is what we all proclaim, and this is what you believed.

The resurrection of believers

12 Now if this is what we proclaim, that Christ was raised from the dead, how can some of you say there is no resurrection of the dead? 13 If there be no resurrection, then Christ was 14 not raised; and if Christ was not raised, then our gospel is null and void, and so is your 15 faith; and we turn out to be lying witnesses for God, because we bore witness that he raised Christ to life, whereas, if the dead are 16 not raised, he did not raise him. For if the dead are not raised, it follows that Christ 17 was not raised; and if Christ was not raised, your faith has nothing in it and you are still 18 in your old state of sin. It follows also that those who have died within Christ's fellow- 19 ship are utterly lost. If it is for this life only that Christ has given us hope,[d] we of all men are most to be pitied.

20 But the truth is, Christ was raised to life —the firstfruits of the harvest of the dead. 21 For since it was a man who brought death into the world, a man also brought resur- 22 rection of the dead. As in Adam all men die, 23 so in Christ all will be brought to life; but each in his own proper place: Christ the firstfruits, and afterwards, at his coming, 24 those who belong to Christ. Then comes the end, when he delivers up the kingdom to God the Father, after abolishing every kind 25 of domination, authority, and power. For he is destined to reign until God has put all 26 enemies under his feet; and the last enemy 27 to be abolished is death.[e] Scripture says, 'He has put all things in subjection under his feet.' But in saying 'all things', it clearly means to exclude God who subordinates 28 them; and when all things are thus subject to him, then the Son himself will also be made subordinate to God who made all things subject to him, and thus God will be all in all.

29 Again, there are those who receive baptism on behalf of the dead. Why should they do this? If the dead are not raised to life at all, what do they mean by being baptized on their behalf?

And we ourselves—why do we face these 30 dangers hour by hour? Every day I die: 31 I swear it by my pride in you, my brothers —for in Christ Jesus our Lord I am proud of you. If, as the saying is, I 'fought wild 32 beasts' at Ephesus, what have I gained by it?[f] If the dead are never raised to life, 'let us eat and drink, for tomorrow we die'.

Make no mistake: 'Bad company is the 33 ruin of a good character.' Come back to a 34 sober and upright life and leave your sinful ways. There are some who know nothing of God; to your shame I say it.

Animal body, spiritual body

But, you may ask, how are the dead raised? 35 In what kind of body? How foolish! The 36 seed you sow does not come to life unless it has first died; and what you sow is not the 37 body that shall be, but a naked grain, per- haps of wheat, or of some other kind; and 38 God clothes it with the body of his choice, each seed with its own particular body. All 39 flesh is not the same flesh: there is flesh of men, flesh of beasts, of birds, and of fishes —all different. There are heavenly bodies 40 and earthly bodies; and the splendour of the heavenly bodies is one thing, the splen- dour of the earthly, another. The sun has 41 a splendour of its own, the moon another splendour, and the stars another, for star differs from star in brightness. So it is with 42 the resurrection of the dead. What is sown in the earth as a perishable thing is raised imperishable. Sown in humiliation, it is 43 raised in glory; sown in weakness, it is raised in power; sown as an animal body, it is 44 raised as a spiritual body.

If there is such a thing as an animal body, there is also a spiritual body. It is in this 45 sense that Scripture says, 'The first man, Adam, became an animate being', whereas the last Adam has become a life-giving spirit. Observe, the spiritual does not come first; 46 the animal body comes first, and then the spiritual. The first man was made 'of the 47 dust of the earth': the second man is from heaven. The man made of dust is the pattern 48 of all men of dust, and the heavenly man is the pattern of all the heavenly. As we have 49 worn the likeness of the man made of dust, so we shall wear the likeness of the heavenly man.

'O Death, where is your victory?'

What I mean, my brothers, is this: flesh and 50 blood can never possess the kingdom of God,

---

d Or If it is only an uncertain hope that our life in Christ has given us . . .   e Or Then at the end, when . . . power (for he . . . feet), the last enemy, death, will be abolished.   f Or If, as men do, I had fought wild beasts at Ephesus, what good would it be to me? or If I had been in no better case than one fighting beasts in the arena at Ephesus, what good would it be to me?

and the perishable cannot possess immor-
51 tality. Listen! I will unfold a mystery: we
shall not all die, but we shall all be changed
52 in a flash, in the twinkling of an eye, at the
last trumpet-call. For the trumpet will
sound, and the dead will rise immortal, and
53 we shall be changed. This perishable being
must be clothed with the imperishable, and
what is mortal must be clothed with im-
54 mortality. And when*g* our mortality has
been clothed with immortality, then the
saying of Scripture will come true: 'Death is
55 swallowed up; victory is won!' 'O Death,
where is your victory? O Death, where is
56 your sting?' The sting of death is sin, and
57 sin gains its power from the law; but, God
be praised, he gives us the victory through
our Lord Jesus Christ.
58   Therefore, my beloved brothers, stand
firm and immovable, and work for the Lord
always, work without limit, since you know
that in the Lord your labour cannot be
lost.

A gift for Christians in Jerusalem

16 And now about the collection in aid of
God's people: you should follow my direc-
2 tions to our congregations in Galatia. Every
Sunday each of you is to put aside and keep
by him a sum in proportion to his gains, so
that there may be no collecting when I come.
3 When I arrive, I will give letters of introduction to persons approved by you, and
send them to carry your gift to Jerusalem.
4 If it should seem worth while for me to go
as well, they shall go with me.

Paul's plans

5 I shall come to Corinth after passing through
Macedonia—for I am travelling by way of
6 Macedonia—and I may stay with you, perhaps even for the whole winter, and then
you can help me on my way wherever I go
7 next. I do not want this to be a flying visit;

I hope to spend some time with you, if the
Lord permits. But I shall remain at Ephesus 8
until Whitsuntide, for a great opportunity 9
has opened for effective work, and there is
much opposition.
    If Timothy comes, see that you put him 10
at his ease; for it is the Lord's work that he
is engaged upon, as I am myself; so no one 11
must slight him. Send him happily on his
way to join me, since I am waiting for him
with our friends. As for our friend Apollos, 12
I urged him strongly to go to Corinth with
the others, but he was quite determined not
to go*h* at present; he will go when opportunity
offers.
    Be alert; stand firm in the faith; be valiant 13
and strong. Let all you do be done in love. 14

A request and greetings

I have a request to make of you, my brothers. 15
You know that the Stephanas family were
the first converts in Achaia, and have laid
themselves out to serve God's people. I wish 16
you to give their due position to such persons,
and indeed to everyone who labours hard at
our common task. It is a great pleasure to me 17
that Stephanas, Fortunatus, and Achaicus
have arrived, because they have done what
you had no chance to do; they have relieved 18
my mind—and no doubt yours too. Such
men deserve recognition.
    Greetings from the congregations in Asia. 19
Many greetings in the Lord from Aquila and
Prisca and the congregation at their house.
Greetings from all the brothers. Greet one 20
another with the kiss of peace.
    This greeting is in my own hand—PAUL. 21
    If anyone does not love the Lord, let him 22
be outcast.
    Marana tha—Come, O Lord!
    The grace of the Lord Jesus Christ be 23
with you.
    My love to you all in Christ Jesus. Amen. 24

g Some witnesses insert our perishable nature has been clothed with the imperishable, and . . .   *h Or but
it was by no means the will of God that he should go . . .*

THE SECOND LETTER OF PAUL TO THE
CORINTHIANS

Divine consolation

1 FROM PAUL, apostle of Christ Jesus by God's will, and our colleague Timothy, to the congregation of God's people at Corinth, together with all who are dedicated to him throughout the whole of Achaia.

2 Grace and peace to you from God our Father and the Lord Jesus Christ.

3 Praise be to the God and Father of our Lord Jesus Christ, the all-merciful Father, the God whose consolation never fails us!

4 He comforts us in all our troubles, so that we in turn may be able to comfort others in any trouble of theirs and to share with them the consolation we ourselves receive from

5 God. As Christ's cup of suffering overflows, and we suffer with him, so also through

6 Christ our consolation overflows. If distress be our lot, it is the price we pay for your consolation, for your salvation; if our lot be consolation, it is to help us to bring you comfort, and strength to face with fortitude

7 the same sufferings we now endure. And our hope for you is firmly grounded;[a] for we know that if you have part in the suffering, you have part also in the divine consolation.

8 In saying this, we should like you to know, dear friends, how serious was the trouble that came upon us in the province of Asia. The burden of it was far too heavy for us to bear, so heavy that we even despaired of life.

9 Indeed, we felt in our hearts that we had received a death-sentence. This was meant to teach us not to place reliance on ourselves,

10 but on God who raises the dead. From such mortal peril God delivered us; and he will deliver us again,[b] he on whom our hope is

11 fixed. Yes, he will continue to deliver us, if you will co-operate by praying for us. Then, with so many people praying for our deliverance, there will be many to give thanks on our behalf for the gracious favour God has shown towards us.

The one thing we are proud of

12 There is one thing we are proud of: our conscience assures us that in our dealings with our fellow-men, and above all in our dealings with you, our conduct has been governed by a devout and godly sincerity,[c] by the grace of God and not by worldly wisdom. There is nothing in our letters to 13 you but what you can read for yourselves, and understand too. Partial as your present 14 knowledge of us is, you will I hope come to understand fully that you have as much reason to be proud of us, as we of you, on the Day of our Lord Jesus.

It was because I felt so confident about all 15 this that I had intended to come first of all to you[d] and give you the benefit of a double visit: I meant to visit you on my way to 16 Macedonia, and after leaving Macedonia, to return to you, and you would then send me on my way to Judaea. That was my in- 17 tention; did I lightly change my mind?[e] Or do I, when I frame my plans, frame them as a worldly man might, so that it should rest with me to say 'yes' and 'yes', or 'no' and 'no'? As God is true, the language in 18 which we address you is not an ambiguous blend of Yes and No. The Son of God, 19 Christ Jesus, proclaimed among you by us (by Silvanus and Timothy, I mean, as well as myself), was never a blend of Yes and No. With him it was, and is, Yes. He is 20 the Yes pronounced upon God's promises, every one of them. That is why, when we give glory to God, it is through Christ Jesus that we say 'Amen'. And if you and we 21 belong to Christ, guaranteed as his and anointed, it is all God's doing; it is God also 22 who has set his seal upon us, and as a pledge of what is to come has given the Spirit to dwell in our hearts.

I appeal to God to witness what I am going 23 to say; I stake my life upon it: it was out of consideration for you that I did not after all come to Corinth. Do not think we are 24 dictating the terms of your faith; your hold on the faith is secure enough. We are working with you for your own happiness. So I **2** made up my mind that my next visit to you must not be another painful one. If I cause 2 pain to you, who is left to cheer me up, except you, whom I have offended? This is 3 precisely the point I made in my letter: I did not want, I said, to come and be made miserable by the very people who ought to

---

a Some witnesses give these clauses If distress . . . firmly grounded *in different sequence.*   *b Some witnesses read* and he still delivers us.   *c Some witnesses read* by sincere and godly singleness of mind.   *d Or* had originally intended to come to you . . .   *e Or* In forming this intention, did I act irresponsibly?

have made me happy; and I had sufficient confidence in you all to know that for me to 4 be happy is for all of you to be happy. That letter I sent you came out of great distress and anxiety; how many tears I shed as I wrote it! But I never meant to cause you pain; I wanted you rather to know the love, the more than ordinary love, that I have for you.

Forgiveness and restoration

5 Any injury that has been done, has not been done to me; to some extent, not to labour 6 the point, it has been done to you all. The penalty on which the general meeting has agreed has met the offence well enough. 7 Something very different is called for now: you must forgive the offender and put heart into him; the man's sorrow must not be 8 made so severe as to overwhelm him. I urge you therefore to assure him of your love for 9 him by a formal act. I wrote, I may say, to see how you stood the test, whether you fully 10 accepted my authority. But anyone who has your forgiveness has mine too; and when I speak of forgiving (so far as there is anything for me to forgive), I mean that as the representative of Christ I have forgiven 11 him for your sake.*f* For Satan must not be allowed to get the better of us; we know his wiles all too well.

In Christ's triumphal procession

12 Then when I came to Troas, where I was to preach the gospel of Christ, and where an opening awaited me for the Lord's work, 13 I still found no relief of mind, for my colleague Titus was not there to meet me; so I took leave of the people there and went 14 off to Macedonia. But thanks be to God, who continually leads us about, captives in Christ's triumphal procession, and everywhere uses us to reveal and spread abroad the fragrance of the knowledge of himself! 15 We are indeed the incense offered by Christ to God, both for those who are on the way to salvation, and for those who are on the 16 way to perdition: to the latter it is a deadly fume that kills, to the former a vital fragrance that brings life. Who is equal to such a 17 calling? At least we do not go hawking the word of God about, as so many do; when we declare the word we do it in sincerity, as from God and in God's sight, as members of Christ.

The old covenant and the new

3 Are we beginning all over again to produce our credentials? Do we, like some people,

need letters of introduction to you, or from you? No, you are all the letter we need, a 2 letter written on our heart; any man can see it for what it is and read it for himself. And as for you, it is plain that you are a 3 letter that has come from Christ, given to us to deliver: a letter written not with ink but with the Spirit of the living God, written not on stone tablets but on the pages of the human heart.

It is in full reliance upon God, through 4 Christ, that we make such claims. There is no question of our being qualified in ourselves: we cannot claim anything as our own. The qualification we have comes from God; it is he who has qualified us to dispense his 6 new covenant—a covenant expressed not in a written document, but in a spiritual bond; for the written law condemns to death, but the Spirit gives life.

The law, then, engraved letter by letter 7 upon stone, dispensed death, and yet it was inaugurated with divine splendour. That splendour, though it was soon to fade, made the face of Moses so bright that the Israelites could not gaze steadily at him. But if so, 8 must not even greater splendour rest upon the divine dispensation of the Spirit? If 9 splendour accompanied the dispensation under which we are condemned, how much richer in splendour must that one be under which we are acquitted! Indeed, the splen- 1 dour that once was is now no splendour at all; it is outshone by a splendour greater still. For if that which was soon to fade 1 had its moment of splendour, how much greater is the splendour of that which endures!

With such a hope as this we speak out 1 boldly; it is not for us to do as Moses did: 1 he put a veil over his face to keep the Israelites from gazing on that fading splendour until it was gone. But in any case their 1 minds had been made insensitive, for that same veil is there to this very day when the lesson is read from the old covenant; and it is never lifted, because only in Christ is the old covenant abrogated.*g* But to this 1 very day, every time the Law of Moses is read, a veil lies over the minds of the hearers. However, as Scripture says of Moses, 'when- 1 ever he turns to the Lord the veil is removed'.*h* Now the Lord of whom this passage speaks is the Spirit; and where the Spirit of the Lord is, there is liberty. And because for us there is no veil over the face, we all reflect as in a mirror the splendour of the Lord; thus we are transfigured into his likeness, from splendour to splendour; such is the influence of the Lord who is Spirit.

f Or that I have forgiven him for your sake, in the presence of Christ.   *g Or* in Christ is it abolished.
h Or as Scripture says, when one turns to the Lord the veil is removed.

Open declaration of truth

4 Seeing then that we have been entrusted with this commission, which we owe entirely 2 to God's mercy, we never lose heart. We have renounced the deeds that men hide for very shame; we neither practise cunning nor distort the word of God; only by declaring the truth openly do we recommend ourselves, and then it is to the common conscience of 3 our fellow-men and in the sight of God. And if indeed our gospel be found veiled, the only people who find it so are those on the 4 way to perdition. Their unbelieving minds are so blinded by the god of this passing age, that the gospel of the glory of Christ, who is the very image of God, cannot dawn upon 5 them and bring them light. It is not ourselves that we proclaim; we proclaim Christ Jesus as Lord, and ourselves as your servants, for 6 Jesus' sake. For the same God who said, 'Out of darkness let light shine', has caused his light to shine within us, to give the light of revelation—the revelation of the glory of God in the face of Jesus Christ.

Treasure in earthenware pots

7 We are no better than pots of earthenware to contain this treasure, and this proves that such transcendent power does not come 8 from us, but is God's alone. Hard-pressed on every side, we are never hemmed in; bewildered, we are never at our wits' end; 9 hunted, we are never abandoned to our fate; struck down, we are not left to die. Wherever we go we carry death with us in our body, the death that Jesus died, that in this body also life may reveal itself, the life that Jesus lives. For continually, while still alive, we are being surrendered into the hands of death, for Jesus' sake, so that the life of Jesus also may be revealed in this mortal body of ours. 12 Thus death is at work in us, and life in you.

But Scripture says, 'I believed, and therefore I spoke out', and we too, in the same spirit of faith, believe and therefore speak 14 out; for we know that he who raised the Lord Jesus to life will with Jesus raise us too, and bring us to his presence, and you with us. Indeed, it is for your sake that all things are ordered, so that, as the abounding grace of God is shared by more and more, the greater may be the chorus of thanksgiving that ascends to the glory of God.

Outward decay, inward renewal

No wonder we do not lose heart! Though our outward humanity is in decay, yet day by day we are inwardly renewed. Our troubles are slight and short-lived; and their outcome an eternal glory which outweighs them far. Meanwhile our eyes are fixed, not

on the things that are seen, but on the things that are unseen: for what is seen passes away; what is unseen is eternal. For we 5 know that if the earthly frame that houses us today should be demolished, we possess a building which God has provided—a house not made by human hands, eternal, and in heaven. In this present body we do indeed 2 groan; we yearn to have our heavenly habitation put on over this one—in the hope 3 that, being thus clothed, we shall not find ourselves naked. We groan indeed, we who 4 are enclosed within this earthly frame; we are oppressed because we do not want to have the old body stripped off. Rather our desire is to have the new body put on over it, so that our mortal part may be absorbed into life immortal. God himself has shaped 5 us for this very end; and as a pledge of it he has given us the Spirit.

Serving the unseen Lord

Therefore we never cease to be confident. 6 We know that so long as we are at home in the body we are exiles from the Lord; faith 7 is our guide, we do not see him.[i] We are 8 confident, I repeat, and would rather leave our home in the body and go to live with the Lord. We therefore make it our ambition, 9 wherever we are, here or there, to be acceptable to him. For we must all have our lives 10 laid open before the tribunal of Christ, where each must receive what is due to him for his conduct in the body, good or bad.

A new world

With this fear of the Lord before our eyes 11 we address our appeal to men. To God our lives lie open, as I hope they also lie open to you in your heart of hearts. This is not 12 another attempt to recommend ourselves to you: we are rather giving you a chance to show yourselves proud of us; then you will have something to say to those whose pride is all in outward show and not in inward worth. It may be we are beside ourselves, 13 but it is for God; if we are in our right mind, it is for you. For the love of Christ leaves us 14 no choice, when once we have reached the conclusion that one man died for all and therefore all mankind has died. His purpose 15 in dying for all was that men, while still in life, should cease to live for themselves, and should live for him who for their sake died and was raised to life. With us therefore 16 worldly standards have ceased to count in our estimate of any man; even if once they counted in our understanding of Christ, they do so now no longer. When anyone is united to 17 Christ, there is a new world;[j] the old order has gone, and a new order has already begun.[k]

i Or faith is our guide and not the things we see.   *j Or* a new act of creation.   *k Or* When anyone is united to Christ he is a new creature: his old life is over; a new life has already begun.

Be reconciled to God!

18 From first to last this has been the work of God. He has reconciled us men to himself through Christ, and he has enlisted us in 19 this service of reconciliation. What I mean is, that God was in Christ reconciling the world to himself,[l] no longer holding men's misdeeds against them, and that he has entrusted us with the message of reconciliation. 20 We come therefore as Christ's ambassadors. It is as if God were appealing to you through us: in Christ's name, we implore you, be 21 reconciled to God! Christ was innocent of sin, and yet for our sake God made him one with the sinfulness of men,[m] so that in him we might be made one with the goodness of 6 God himself. Sharing in God's work, we urge this appeal upon you: you have received the grace of God; do not let it go for 2 nothing. God's own words are:

'In the hour of my favour I gave heed to you; on the day of deliverance I came to your aid.'

The hour of favour has now come; now, I say, has the day of deliverance dawned.

The apostle's sufferings

3 In order that our service may not be brought into discredit, we avoid giving offence in 4 anything. As God's servants, we try to recommend ourselves in all circumstances by our steadfast endurance: in distress, hard- 5 ships, and dire straits; flogged, imprisoned, mobbed; overworked, sleepless, starving, 6 We recommend ourselves by the innocence of our behaviour, our grasp of truth, our patience and kindliness; by gifts of the Holy 7 Spirit, by sincere love, by declaring the truth, by the power of God. We wield the weapons of righteousness in right hand and left. 8 Honour and dishonour, praise and blame, are alike our lot: we are the impostors who 9 speak the truth, the unknown men whom all men know; dying we still live on; disciplined 10 by suffering, we are not done to death; in our sorrows we have always cause for joy; poor ourselves, we bring wealth to many; penniless, we own the world. 11 Men of Corinth, we have spoken very frankly to you; we have opened our heart 12 wide to you all. On our part there is no constraint; any constraint there may be is 13 in yourselves. In fair exchange then (may a father speak so to his children?) open wide your hearts to us.

Call to consecration

14 Do not unite yourselves with unbelievers; they are no fit mates for you. What has righteousness to do with wickedness? Can 15 light consort with darkness? Can Christ agree with Belial, or a believer join hands with an unbeliever? Can there be a compact between the temple of God and the idols of the heathen? And the temple of the living God is what we are. God's own words are: 'I will live and move about among them; I will be their God, and they shall be my people.' And therefore, 'come away and leave them, separate yourselves, says the Lord; touch nothing unclean. Then I will accept you, says the Lord, the Ruler of all being; I will be a father to you, and you shall be my sons and daughters.' Such are the promises that have been made to us, dear friends. Let us therefore cleanse ourselves from all that can defile flesh or spirit, and in the fear of God complete our consecration.

A quarrel healed

Do make a place for us in your hearts! We have wronged no one, ruined no one, taken advantage of no one. I do not want to blame you. Why, as I have told you before, the place you have in our heart is such that, come death, come life, we meet it together. I am perfectly frank with you. I have great pride in you. In all our many troubles my cup is full of consolation, and overflows with joy.

Even when we reached Macedonia there was still no relief for this poor body of ours; instead, there was trouble at every turn, quarrels all round us, forebodings in our heart. But God, who brings comfort to the downcast, has comforted us by the arrival of Titus, and not merely by his arrival, but by his being so greatly comforted about you. He has told us how you long for me, how sorry you are, and how eager to take my side; and that has made me happier still.

Even if I did wound you by the letter I sent, I do not now regret it. I may have been sorry for it when I saw that the letter had caused you pain, even if only for a time; but now I am happy, not that your feelings were wounded but that the wound led to a change of heart. You bore the smart as God would have you bear it, and so you are no losers by what we did. For the wound which is borne in God's way brings a change of heart too salutary to regret; but the hurt which is borne in the world's way brings death. You bore your hurt in God's way, and see what its results have been! It made you take the matter seriously and vindicate yourselves. How angered you were, how apprehensive! How your longing for me awoke, yes, and your devotion and your eagerness to see justice done! At every point you have cleared yourselves of blame in this trouble. And so, although I did send you that letter,

---

l Or God was reconciling the world to himself by Christ.   *m Or* and yet God made him a sin-offering for us.

it was not the offender or his victim that most concerned me. My aim in writing was to help to make plain to you, in the sight of 3 God, how truly you are devoted to us. That is why we have been so encouraged.

The mission of Titus

But besides being encouraged ourselves we have also been delighted beyond everything by seeing how happy Titus is: you have all helped to set his mind completely at rest. 4 Anything I may have said to him to show my pride in you has been justified. Every word we ever addressed to you bore the mark of truth; and the same holds of the proud boast we made in the presence of Titus: that 5 also has proved true. His heart warms all the more to you as he recalls how ready you all were to do what he asked, meeting 6 him as you did in fear and trembling. How happy I am now to have complete confidence in you!

About giving to fellow-Christians

8 We must tell you, friends, about the grace of generosity which God has imparted to[n] 2 our congregations in Macedonia. The troubles they have been through have tried them hard, yet in all this they have been so exuberantly happy that from the depths of their poverty they have shown themselves 3 lavishly open-handed. Going to the limit of their resources, as I can testify, and even 4 beyond that limit, they begged us most insistently, and on their own initiative, to be allowed to share in this generous service 5 to their fellow-Christians. And their giving surpassed our expectations; for they gave their very selves, offering them in the first instance to the Lord, but also, under God, 6 to us. The upshot is that we have asked Titus, who began it all, to visit you and bring this work of generosity also to completion. 7 You are so rich in everything—in faith, speech, knowledge, and zeal of every kind, as well as in the loving regard you have for us[o]—surely you should show yourselves 8 equally lavish in this generous service! This is not meant as an order; by telling you how keen others are I am putting your love to 9 the test. For you know how generous our Lord Jesus Christ has been: he was rich, yet for your sake he became poor, so that through his poverty you might become rich.

Here is my considered opinion on the matter. What I ask you to do is in your own interests. You made a good beginning last year both in the work you did and in your willingness to undertake it. Now I want you to go on and finish it: be as eager to complete the scheme as you were to adopt it, and give

according to your means. Provided there is 12 an eager desire to give, God accepts what a man has; he does not ask for what he has not. There is no question of relieving others 13 at the cost of hardship to yourselves; it is 14 a question of equality. At the moment your surplus meets their need, but one day your need may be met from their surplus. The aim is equality; as Scripture has it, 'The man 15 who got much had no more than enough, and the man who got little did not go short.'

A delegation to Corinth

I thank God that he has made Titus as keen 16 on your behalf as we are! For Titus not only 17 welcomed our request; he is so eager that by his own desire he is now leaving to come to you. With him we are sending one of 18 our company whose reputation is high among our congregations everywhere for his services to the Gospel. Moreover they 19 have duly appointed him to travel with us and help in this beneficent work, by which we do honour to the Lord himself and show our own eagerness to serve. We want to 20 guard against any criticism of our handling of this generous gift; for our aims are en- 21 tirely honourable, not only in the Lord's eyes, but also in the eyes of men.

With these men we are sending another 22 of our company whose enthusiasm we have had many opportunities of testing, and who is now all the more earnest because of the great confidence he has in you. If there is 23 any question about Titus, he is my partner and my associate in dealings with you; as for the others, they are delegates of our con- gregations, an honour to Christ.[p] Then give 24 them clear expression of your love and justify our pride in you; justify it to them, and through them to the congregations.

An incentive to giving

About the provision of aid for God's people, 9 it is superfluous for me to write to you. I know how eager you are to help; I speak 2 of it with pride to the Macedonians: I tell them that Achaia had everything ready last year; and most of them have been fired by your zeal. My purpose in sending these 3 friends is to ensure that what we have said about you in this matter should not prove to be an empty boast. By that I mean, I want you to be prepared, as I told them you were; for if I bring with me men from Macedonia 4 and they find you are not prepared, what a disgrace it will be to us, let alone to you, after all the confidence we have shown! I have accordingly thought it necessary to 5 ask these friends to go on ahead to Corinth, to see that your promised bounty is in order

---

n Or how gracious God has been to . . .
which we have kindled in your hearts.   o Some witnesses read the love we have for you, or the love
p Or they are . . . congregations; they reflect Christ.

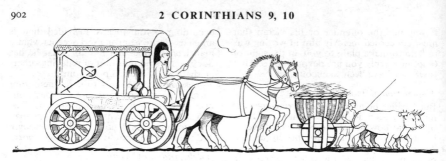

Transport in the first century

before I come; it will then be awaiting me as a bounty indeed, and not as an extortion.

God's care for the generous

6 Remember: sparse sowing, sparse reaping; sow bountifully, and you will reap bounti-
7 fully. Each person should give as he has decided for himself; there should be no reluctance, no sense of compulsion; God
8 loves a cheerful giver. And it is in God's power to provide you richly with every good gift; thus you will have ample means in yourselves to meet each and every situation, with enough and to spare for every good
9 cause. Scripture says of such a man: 'He has lavished his gifts on the needy, his benevo-
10 lence stands fast for ever.' Now he who provides seed for sowing and bread for food will provide the seed for you to sow; he will multiply it and swell the harvest of your
11 benevolence, and you will always be rich enough to be generous. Through our action such generosity will issue in thanksgiving to
12 God, for as a piece of willing service this is not only a contribution towards the needs of God's people; more than that, it over-
13 flows in a flood of thanksgiving to God. For through the proof which this affords, many will give honour to God when they see how humbly you obey him and how faithfully you confess the gospel of Christ; and will thank him for your liberal contribution to
14 their need and to the general good. And as they join in prayer on your behalf, their hearts will go out to you because of the richness of the grace which God has im-
15 parted to you. Thanks be to God for his gift beyond words!

Paul's weakness and strength

10 But I, Paul, appeal to you by the gentleness and magnanimity of Christ—I, so feeble (you say) when I am face to face with you,
2 so brave when I am away. Spare me, I beg you, the necessity of such bravery when I

come, for I reckon I could put on as bold a face as you please against those who charge us with moral weakness. Weak men we may be, but it is not as such that we fight our battles. The weapons we wield are not merely human,*q* but divinely potent to demolish strongholds; we demolish sophistries and all that rears its proud head against the knowledge of God; we compel every human thought to surrender in obedience to Christ; and we are prepared to punish all rebellion when once you have put yourselves in our hands.

The apostle's authority

Look facts in the face.*r* Someone is convinced, is he, that he belongs to Christ? Let him think again, and reflect that we belong to Christ as much as he does. Indeed, if I am somewhat over-boastful about our authority—an authority given by the Lord to build you up, not pull you down—I shall make my boast good. So you must not think of me as one who scares you by the letters he writes. 'His letters', so it is said, 'are weighty and powerful; but when he appears he has no presence, and as a speaker he is beneath contempt.' People who talk in that way should reckon with this: when I come, my actions will show the same man as my letters showed in my absence.

The apostle's discretion

We should not dare to class ourselves or compare ourselves with any of those who put forward their own claims. What fools they are to measure themselves by themselves, to find in themselves their own standard of comparison!*s* With us there will be no attempt to boast beyond our proper sphere; and our sphere is determined by the limit God laid down for us, which permitted us to come as far as Corinth. We are not overstretching our commission, as we should be if it did not extend to you, for we

---

q Or charge us with worldly standards. We live, no doubt, in the world; but it is not on that level that we fight our battles. The weapons we wield are not those of the world . . .   *r Or* You are looking only at what catches the eye.
s Some witnesses read On the contrary we measure ourselves by ourselves, by our own standard of comparison.

15 were the first to reach Corinth in preaching the gospel of Christ. And we do not boast of work done where others have laboured, work beyond our proper sphere. Our hope is rather that, as your faith grows, we may attain a position among you greater than ever before, but still within the limits of our 16 sphere. Then we can carry the Gospel to lands that lie beyond you, never priding ourselves on work already done in another man's 17 sphere. If a man must boast, let him boast of 18 the Lord. Not the man who recommends himself, but the man whom the Lord recommends—he and he alone is to be accepted.

Sham-apostles

11 I wish you would bear with me in a little of 2 my folly; please do bear with me. I am jealous for you, with a divine jealousy; for I betrothed you to Christ, thinking to present you as a chaste virgin to her true and only 3 husband. But as the serpent in his cunning seduced Eve, I am afraid that your thoughts may be corrupted and you may lose your[t] 4 single-hearted devotion to Christ. For if someone comes who proclaims another Jesus, not the Jesus whom we proclaimed, or if you then receive a spirit different from the Spirit already given to you, or a gospel different from the gospel you have already accepted, you manage to put up with that 5 well enough. Have I in any way come short of those superlative apostles? I think not. 6 I may be no speaker, but knowledge I have; at all times we have made known to you the full truth.

7 Or was this my offence, that I made no charge for preaching the gospel of God, 8 lowering myself to help in raising you? It is true that I took toll of other congregations, accepting[u] support from them to serve you. 9 Then, while I was with you, if I ran short I sponged on no one; anything I needed was fully met by our friends who came from Macedonia; I made it a rule, as I always shall, 10 never to be a burden to you. As surely as the truth of Christ is in me, I will preserve my pride in this matter throughout Achaia, and 11 nothing shall stop me. Why? Is it that I do not love you? God knows I do.

12 And I shall go on doing as I am doing now, to cut the ground from under those who would seize any chance to put their vaunted 13 apostleship on the same level as ours. Such men are sham-apostles, crooked in all their practices, masquerading as apostles of 14 Christ. There is nothing surprising about that; Satan himself masquerades as an angel 15 of light. It is therefore a simple thing for his agents to masquerade as agents of good. But they will meet the end their deeds deserve.

Paul's ground for boasting

I repeat: let no one take me for a fool; but 16 if you must, then give me the privilege of a fool, and let me have my little boast like others. I am not speaking here as a Christian, 17 but like a fool, if it comes to bragging. So 18 many people brag of their earthly distinctions that I shall do so too. How gladly you 19 bear with fools, being yourselves so wise! If a man tyrannizes over you, exploits you, 20 gets you in his clutches, puts on airs, and hits you in the face, you put up with it. And we, 21 you say, have been weak! I admit the reproach.

But if there is to be bravado (and here I speak as a fool), I can indulge in it too. Are 22 they Hebrews? So am I. Israelites? So am I. Abraham's descendants? So am I. Are they 23 servants of Christ? I am mad to speak like this, but I can outdo them. More overworked than they, scourged more severely, more often imprisoned, many a time face to face with death. Five times the Jews have given me 24 the thirty-nine strokes; three times I have 25 been beaten with rods; once I was stoned; three times I have been shipwrecked, and for twenty-four hours I was adrift on the open sea. I have been constantly on the road; I have 26 met dangers from rivers, dangers from robbers, dangers from my fellow-countrymen, dangers from foreigners, dangers in towns, dangers in the country, dangers at sea, dangers from false friends. I have toiled and 27 drudged, I have often gone without sleep; hungry and thirsty, I have often gone fasting; and I have suffered from cold and exposure.

Apart from these external things,[v] there 28 is the responsibility that weighs on me every day, my anxious concern for all our congregations. If anyone is weak, do I not share 29 his weakness? If anyone is made to stumble, does my heart not blaze with indignation? If boasting there must be, I will boast of the 30 things that show up my weakness. The God 31 and Father of the Lord Jesus (blessed be his name for ever!) knows that what I say is true. When I was in Damascus, the com- 32 missioner of King Aretas kept the city under observation so as to have me arrested; and 33 I was let down in a basket, through a window in the wall, and so escaped his clutches.

Paul's visions and revelations

I am obliged to boast. It does no good; but 12 I shall go on to tell of visions and revelations granted by the Lord. I know a Christian 2 man who fourteen years ago (whether in the body or out of it, I do not know—God knows) was caught up as far as the third heaven. And I know that this same man 3 (whether in the body or out of it, I do not

---

t Some witnesses insert purity and . . .   *u Or* Did I take toll of other congregations by accepting . . .?
v Or Apart from things which I omit.

4 know—God knows) was caught up into paradise, and heard words so secret that
5 human lips may not repeat them. About such a man as that I am ready to boast; but I will not boast on my own account, except of my
6 weaknesses. If I should choose to boast, it would not be the boast of a fool, for I should be speaking the truth. But I refrain, because I should not like anyone to form an estimate of me which goes beyond the evidence of
7 his own eyes and ears. And so, to keep me from being unduly elated by the magnificence of such revelations, I was given[w] a sharp physical pain[x] which came as Satan's messenger to bruise me; this was to save me
8 from being unduly elated. Three times I
9 begged the Lord to rid me of it, but his answer was: 'My grace is all you need; power comes to its full strength in weakness.' I shall therefore prefer to find my joy and pride in the very things that are my weakness; and then the power of Christ
10 will come and rest upon me. Hence I am well content, for Christ's sake, with weakness, contempt, persecution, hardship, and frustration; for when I am weak, then I am strong.

The marks of a true apostle

11 I am being very foolish, but it was you who drove me to it; my credentials should have come from you. In no respect did I fall short of these superlative apostles, even if I am
12 a nobody. The marks of a true apostle were

there, in the work I did among you, which called for such constant fortitude, and was attended by signs, marvels, and miracles.
13 Is there anything in which you were treated worse than the other congregations—except this, that I never sponged upon you? How unfair of me! I crave forgiveness.

Paul's aim in his coming visit

14 Here am I preparing to pay you a third visit; and I am not going to sponge upon you. It is you I want, not your money; parents should make provision for their children, not children for their parents. As for me,
15 I will gladly spend what I have for you— yes, and spend myself to the limit. If I love you overmuch, am I to be loved the less?
16 But, granted that I did not prove a burden to you, still I was unscrupulous enough, you
17 say, to use a trick to catch you. Who, of the men I have sent to you, was used by me to
18 defraud you? I begged Titus to visit you, and I sent our friend with him. Did Titus defraud you? Have we not both been guided by the same Spirit, and followed the same course?

19 Perhaps you think that all this time we have been addressing our defence to you. No; we are speaking in God's sight, and as Christian men. Our whole aim, my own
20 dear people, is to build you up. I fear that when I come I may perhaps find you different from what I wish you to be, and that you may find me also different from what

w *Some witnesses read* . . . ears, and because of the magnificence of the revelations themselves. Therefore to keep me from being unduly elated I was given . . .   x *Or* a painful wound to my pride (*literally* a stake, *or* thorn, for the flesh).

Ships of the period

you wish. I fear I may find quarrelling and jealousy, angry tempers and personal rivalries, backbiting and gossip, arrogance and

21 general disorder. I am afraid that, when I come again, my God may humiliate me in your presence, that I may have tears to shed over many of those who have sinned in the past and have not repented of their unclean lives, their fornication and sensuality.

A warning

13 This will be my third visit to you; and all facts must be established by the evidence of

2 two or three witnesses. To those who have sinned in the past, and to everyone else, I repeat the warning I gave before; I gave it in person on my second visit, and I give it now in absence. It is that when I come this

3 time, I will show no leniency. Then you will have the proof you seek of the Christ who speaks through me, the Christ who, far from being weak with you, makes his power felt

4 among you. True, he died on the cross in weakness, but he lives by the power of God; and we who share his weakness shall by the power of God live with him in your service.

Self-examination

5 Examine yourselves: are you living the life of faith? Put yourselves to the test. Surely you recognize that Jesus Christ is among you?—unless of course you prove unequal

6 to the test. I hope you will come to see that

7 we are not unequal to it. Our prayer to God is that you may do no wrong; we are not concerned to be vindicated ourselves; we want you to do what is right, even if we

8 should seem to be discredited. For we have no power to act against the truth, but only

9 for it. We are well content to be weak at any time if only you are strong. Indeed, my whole prayer is that all may be put right

10 with you. My purpose in writing this letter before I come, is to spare myself, when I come, any sharp exercise of authority— authority which the Lord gave me for building up and not for pulling down.

Farewell and greetings

11 And now, my friends, farewell. Mend your ways; take our appeal to heart; agree with one another; live in peace; and the God of

12 love and peace will be with you. Greet one

another with the kiss of peace. All God's 13 people send you greetings.

The grace of the Lord Jesus Christ, and 14 the love of God, and fellowship in the Holy Spirit, be with you all.

A Corinthian column

THE LETTER OF PAUL TO THE
GALATIANS

1 FROM PAUL, an apostle, not by human appointment or human commission, but by commission from Jesus Christ and from God the Father who raised him from the dead. 2 I and the group of friends now with me send greetings to the Christian congregations of Galatia.

3 Grace and peace to you from God the 4 Father and our Lord Jesus Christ,*a* who sacrificed himself for our sins, to rescue us out of this present age of wickedness, as our 5 God and Father willed; to whom be glory for ever and ever. Amen.

Paul defends the gospel of Christ

6 I am astonished to find you turning so quickly away from him who called you by 7 grace,*b* and following a different gospel. Not that it is in fact another gospel; only there are persons who unsettle your minds by 8 trying to distort the gospel of Christ. But if anyone, if we ourselves or an angel from heaven, should preach a gospel at variance with the gospel we preached to you, he shall 9 be held outcast. I now repeat what I have said before: if anyone preaches a gospel at variance with the gospel which you received, let him be outcast!

10 Does my language now sound as if I were canvassing for men's support? Whose support do I want but God's alone? Do you think I am currying favour with men? If I still sought men's favour, I should be no servant of Christ.

11 I must make it clear to you, my friends, that the gospel you heard me preach is no 12 human invention. I did not take it over from any man; no man taught it me; I received it through a revelation of Jesus Christ.

Paul defends his apostleship

You have heard what my manner of life 13 was when I was still a practising Jew: how savagely I persecuted the church of God, and tried to destroy it; and how in the 14 practice of our national religion I was outstripping many of my Jewish contemporaries in my boundless devotion to the traditions of my ancestors. But then in his good pleasure 15 God, who had set me apart from birth and called me through his grace, chose to reveal 16 his Son to me and through me, in order that I might proclaim him among the Gentiles. When that happened, without consulting any human being, without going up to Jerusalem 17 to see those who were apostles before me, I went off at once to Arabia, and afterwards returned to Damascus.

Three years later I did go up to Jeru- 18 salem to get to know Cephas. I stayed with him for a fortnight, without seeing any other 19 of the apostles, except*c* James the Lord's brother. What I write is plain truth; before 20 God I am not lying.

Next I went to the regions of Syria and 21 Cilicia, and remained unknown by sight*d* to 22 Christ's congregations in Judaea. They only 23 heard it said, 'Our former persecutor is preaching the good news of the faith which once he tried to destroy'; and they praised 24 God for me.

Dispute and agreement in Jerusalem

Next, fourteen years later, I went again*e* to **2** Jerusalem with Barnabas, taking Titus with us. I went up because it had been revealed 2 by God that I should do so. I laid before them—but at a private interview with the men of repute—the gospel which I am

---

a Some witnesses read God our Father and the Lord Jesus Christ. who called you by grace, *or* from him who called you by grace of Christ. unknown personally. *e Some witnesses omit* again.   *b Some witnesses read* from Christ   *c Or* but only.   *d Or*

accustomed to preach to the Gentiles, to make sure that the race I had run, and was 3 running, should not be run in vain. Yet even my companion Titus, Greek though he is, 4 was not compelled to be circumcised. That course was urged only as a concession to certain[f] sham-Christians, interlopers who had stolen in to spy upon the liberty we enjoy in the fellowship of Christ Jesus. These 5 men wanted to bring us into bondage, but not for one moment did I yield to their dictation; I was determined that the full truth of the Gospel should be maintained for you.[g]

6 But as for the men of high reputation (not that their importance matters to me: God does not recognize these personal distinctions)—these men of repute, I say, did not 7 prolong the consultation,[h] but on the contrary acknowledged that I had been entrusted with the Gospel for Gentiles as surely as Peter had been entrusted with the Gospel for 8 Jews. For God whose action made Peter an apostle to the Jews, also made me an apostle to the Gentiles.

9 Recognizing, then, the favour thus bestowed upon me, those reputed pillars of our society, James, Cephas, and John, accepted Barnabas and myself as partners, and shook hands upon it, agreeing that we should go to 10 the Gentiles while they went to the Jews. All they asked was that we should keep their poor in mind, which was the very thing I made[i] it my business to do.

Paul at odds with Peter

11 But when Cephas came to Antioch, I opposed him to his face, because he was 12 clearly in the wrong. For until certain persons[j] came from James he was taking his meals with gentile Christians; but when they[k] came he drew back and began to hold aloof, because he was afraid of the advocates of 13 circumcision. The other Jewish Christians showed the same lack of principle; even Barnabas was carried away and played false 14 like the rest. But when I saw that their conduct did not square with[l] the truth of the Gospel, I said to Cephas, before the whole congregation, 'If you, a Jew born and bred, live like a Gentile, and not like a Jew, how can you insist that Gentiles must live like Jews?'

Jews, like Gentiles, saved by faith

15 We ourselves are Jews by birth, not Gentiles 16 and sinners. But we know that no man is

ever justified by doing what the law demands, but only through faith in Christ Jesus; so we too have put our faith in Jesus Christ, in order that we might be justified through this faith, and not through deeds dictated by law; for by such deeds, Scripture says, no mortal man shall be justified.

If now, in seeking to be justified in Christ, 17 we ourselves no less than the Gentiles turn out to be sinners against the law,[m] does that mean that Christ is an abettor of sin? No, never! No, if I start building up again a 18 system which I have pulled down, then it is that I show myself up as a transgressor of the law. For through the law I died to law 19 —to live for God. I have been crucified with 20 Christ: the life I now live is not my life, but the life which Christ lives in me; and my present bodily life is lived by faith in the Son of God, who loved me and gave himself up for me. I will not nullify the grace of 21 God; if righteousness comes by law, then Christ died for nothing.

Appeal to experience

You stupid Galatians! You must have been 3 bewitched—you before whose eyes Jesus Christ was openly displayed upon his cross! Answer me one question: did you receive 2 the Spirit by keeping the law or by believing the gospel message[n]? Can it be that you are 3 so stupid? You started with the spiritual; do you now look to the material to make you perfect? Have all your great experiences 4 been in vain—if vain indeed they should be? I ask then: when God gives you the Spirit 5 and works miracles among you, why is this? Is it because you keep the law, or is it because you have faith in the gospel message? Look at Abraham: he put his faith in God, 6 and that faith was counted to him as righteousness.

Appeal to Scripture

You may take it, then, that it is the men of 7 faith who are Abraham's sons. And Scrip- 8 ture, foreseeing that God would justify the Gentiles through faith, declared the Gospel to Abraham beforehand: 'In you all nations shall find blessing.' Thus it is the men of 9 faith who share the blessing with faithful Abraham.

On the other hand those who rely on 10 obedience to the law are under a curse; for Scripture says, 'A curse is on all who do not persevere in doing everything that is written in the Book of the Law.' It is evident that 11

---

f Or The question was later raised because of certain . . . even . . . is, was under no absolute compulsion to be circumcised, but for the sake of certain . . . of Christ Jesus, with the intention of bringing us into bondage, I yielded to their demand for the moment, to ensure that gospel truth should not be prevented from reaching you.   g Or, following the reading of some witnesses, Yet even . . . is, was under no absolute compulsion to be circumcised, but for the sake of certain . . . of Christ Jesus, with the intention of bringing us into bondage, I yielded to their demand for the moment, to ensure that gospel truth should not be prevented from reaching you.   h Or gave me no further instructions.   i Or had made, or have made.   j Some witnesses read a certain person.   k Some witnesses read he.   l Or I saw that they were not making progress towards . . .   m Or no less than the Gentiles have accepted the position of sinners against the law.   n Or by the message of faith, or or by hearing and believing.

no one is ever justified before God in terms of law; because we read, 'he shall gain life who
12 is justified through faith'. Now law is not at all a matter of having faith: we read, 'he who does this shall gain life by what he does'.
13 Christ bought us freedom from the curse of the law by becoming for our sake an accursed thing; for Scripture says, 'A curse is on everyone who is hanged on a gibbet.'
14 And the purpose of it all was that the blessing of Abraham should in Jesus Christ be extended to the Gentiles, so that we might receive the promised Spirit through faith.

Illustration from ordinary life

15 My brothers, let me give you an illustration. Even in ordinary life, when a man's will and testament has been duly executed, no one
16 else can set it aside or add a codicil. Now the promises were pronounced to Abraham and to his 'issue'. It does not say 'issues' in the plural, but in the singular, 'and to your issue'; and the 'issue' intended is Christ.
17 What I am saying is this: a testament, or covenant, had already been validated by God; it cannot be invalidated, and its promises rendered ineffective, by a law made
18 four hundred and thirty years later. If the inheritance is by legal right, then it is not by promise; but it was by promise that God bestowed it as a free gift on Abraham.

From law to faith

19 Then what of the law? It was added to make wrongdoing a legal offence.*º* It was a temporary measure pending the arrival of the 'issue' to whom the promise was made. It was promulgated through angels, and there
20 was an intermediary; but an intermediary is not needed for one party acting alone, and God is one.
21 Does the law, then, contradict the promises? No, never! If a law had been given which had power to bestow life, then indeed righteousness would have come from keep-
22 ing the law. But Scripture has declared the whole world to be prisoners in subjection to sin, so that faith in Jesus Christ may be the ground on which the promised blessing is given, and given to those who have such faith.
23 Before this faith came, we were close prisoners in the custody of law, pending the
24 revelation of faith. Thus the law was a kind of tutor in charge of us until Christ should come,*º* when we should be justified
25 through faith; and now that faith has come, the tutor's charge is at an end.

For through faith you are all sons of God 26 in union with Christ Jesus. Baptized into 27 union with him, you have all put on Christ as a garment. There is no such thing as Jew 28 and Greek, slave and freeman, male and female; for you are all one person in Christ Jesus. But if you thus belong to Christ, you 29 are the 'issue' of Abraham, and so heirs by promise.
This is what I mean: so long as the heir **4** is a minor, he is no better off than a slave, even though the whole estate is his; he is 2 under guardians and trustees until the date fixed by his father. And so it was with us. 3 During our minority we were slaves to the elemental spirits of the universe,*q* but when 4 the term was completed, God sent his own Son, born of a woman, born under the law, to purchase freedom for the subjects of the 5 law, in order that we might attain the status of sons.
To prove that you are sons, God has sent 6 into our hearts the Spirit of his Son, crying 'Abba! Father!' You are therefore no longer 7 a slave but a son, and if a son, then also by God's own act an heir.
Formerly, when you did not acknowledge 8 God, you were the slaves of beings which in their nature are no gods.*r* But now that you 9 do acknowledge God—or rather, now that he has acknowledged you—how can you turn back to the mean and beggarly spirits of the elements?*s* Why do you propose to enter their service all over again? You keep 10 special days and months and seasons and years. You make me fear that all the pains 11 I spent on you may prove to be labour lost.

A personal plea

Put yourselves in my place, my brothers, 12 I beg you, for I have put myself in yours. It is not that you did me any wrong. As you 13 know, it was bodily illness that originally*t* led to my bringing you the Gospel, and you 14 resisted any temptation to show scorn or disgust at the state of my poor body;*u* you welcomed me as if I were an angel of God, as you might have welcomed Christ Jesus himself. Have you forgotten how happy you 15 thought yourselves in having me with you? I can say this for you: you would have torn out your very eyes, and given them to me, had that been possible! And have I now made 16 myself your enemy by being frank with you?
The persons I have referred to are envious 17 of you, but not with an honest envy:*v* what they really want is to bar the door to you so that you may come to envy*w* them. It is 18

---

o Or added because of offences.　　*p Or* a kind of tutor to conduct us to Christ.　　*q Or* the elements of the natural world, *or* elementary ideas belonging to this world.　　*r Or* were slaves to 'gods' which in reality do not exist.　　*s See note on 4. 3.*　　*t Or* formerly, *or* on the first of my two visits.　　*u Or* you showed neither scorn nor disgust at the trial my poor body was enduring.　　*v Or* paying court to you, but not with honest intentions.　　*w Or* pay court to.

always a fine thing to deserve an honest
envy[x]—always, and not only when I am
19 present with you, dear children. For my
children you are, and I am in travail with
you over again until you take the shape of
20 Christ. I wish I could be with you now; then
I could modify my tone;[y] as it is, I am at
my wits' end about you.

Illustration from Scripture

21 Tell me now, you who are so anxious to be
under law, will you not listen to what the
22 Law says? It is written there that Abraham
had two sons, one by his slave and the other
23 by his free-born wife. The slave-woman's
son was born in the course of nature, the
24 free woman's through God's promise. This
is an allegory. The two women stand for two
covenants. The one bearing children into
slavery is the covenant that comes from
25 Mount Sinai: that is Hagar. Sinai is a mountain in Arabia and it represents the Jerusalem
of today, for she and her children are in
26 slavery. But the heavenly Jerusalem is the
27 free woman; she is our mother. For Scripture says, 'Rejoice, O barren woman who
never bore child; break into a shout of joy,
you who never knew a mother's pangs; for
the deserted wife shall have more children
than she who lives with the husband.'
28 And you, my brothers, like Isaac, are
29 children of God's promise. But just as in
those days the natural-born son persecuted
30 the spiritual son, so it is today. But what does
Scripture say? 'Drive out the slave-woman
and her son, for the son of the slave shall
not share the inheritance with the free
31 woman's son.' You see, then, my brothers,
we are no slave-woman's children; our
5 mother is the free woman. Christ set us free,
to be free men.[z] Stand firm, then, and refuse
to be tied to the yoke of slavery again.

Either law or Christ

Mark my words: I, Paul, say to you that if 2
you receive circumcision Christ will do you
no good at all. Once again, you can take it 3
from me that every man who receives circumcision is under obligation to keep the entire
law. When you seek to be justified by way of 4
law, your relation with Christ is completely
severed: you have fallen out of the domain
of God's grace. For to us, our hope of attain- 5
ing that righteousness which we eagerly
await is the work of the Spirit through faith.
If we are in union with Christ Jesus circum- 6
cision makes no difference at all, nor does
the want of it; the only thing that counts is
faith active in love.[a]
You were running well; who was it hin- 7
dered you from following the truth? What- 8
ever persuasion he used, it did not come
from God who is calling you; 'a little leaven', 9
remember, 'leavens all the dough'. United 10
with you in the Lord, I am confident that
you will not take the wrong view; but the
man who is unsettling your minds, whoever
he may be, must bear God's judgement. And 11
I, my friends, if I am still advocating circumcision, why is it I am still persecuted? In that
case, my preaching of the cross is a stumbling-
block no more. As for these agitators, they 12
had better go the whole way and make
eunuchs of themselves!

The work of the Spirit

You, my friends, were called to be free men; 13
only do not turn your freedom into licence
for your lower nature, but be servants to
one another in love. For the whole law can 14
be summed up in a single commandment:
'Love your neighbour as yourself.' But if 15
you go on fighting one another, tooth and
nail, all you can expect is mutual destruction.

x Or to be honourably wooed.   *y Or now, and could exchange words with you.*   *z Or What Christ has done is to set us free.*   *a Or inspired by love.*

Oxen under a yoke

16 I mean this: if you are guided by the Spirit you will not fulfil the desires of your lower 17 nature. That nature sets its desires against the Spirit, while the Spirit fights against it. They are in conflict with one another so 18 that what you will to do you cannot do. But if you are led by the Spirit, you are not under law.

19 Anyone can see the kind of behaviour that belongs to the lower nature: fornica- 20 tion, impurity, and indecency; idolatry and sorcery; quarrels, a contentious temper, envy, fits of rage, selfish ambitions, dis- 21 sensions, party intrigues, and jealousies; drinking bouts, orgies, and the like. I warn you, as I warned you before, that those who behave in such ways will never inherit the kingdom of God.

22 But the harvest of the Spirit is love, joy, peace, patience, kindness, goodness, fidelity, 23 gentleness, and self-control. There is no law 24 dealing with such things as these. And those who belong to Christ Jesus have crucified the lower nature with its passions and desires. 25 If the Spirit is the source of our life, let the Spirit also direct our course.

Fulfilling the law of Christ

26 We must not be conceited, challenging one another to rivalry, jealous of one another. 6 If a man should do something wrong, my brothers, on a sudden impulse,*b* you who are endowed with the Spirit must set him right again very gently. Look to yourself, each 2 one of you: you may be tempted too. Help one another to carry these heavy loads, and in this way you will fulfil the law of Christ.

3 For if a man imagines himself to be some-body, when he is nothing, he is deluding 4 himself. Each man should examine his own conduct for himself; then he can measure his achievement by comparing himself with himself and not with anyone else. For every- 5 one has his own proper burden to bear.

When anyone is under instruction in the 6 faith, he should give his teacher a share of all good things he has.

Make no mistake about this: God is not 7 to be fooled; a man reaps what he sows. If 8 he sows seed in the field of his lower nature, he will reap from it a harvest of corruption, but if he sows in the field of the Spirit, the Spirit will bring him a harvest of eternal life. So let us never tire of doing good, for if we do 9 not slacken our efforts we shall in due time reap our harvest. Therefore, as opportunity 10 offers, let us work for the good of all, especially members of the household of the faith.

Paul's one boast

You see these big letters? I am now writing 11 to you in my own hand. It is all those who 12 want to make a fair outward and bodily show who are trying to force circumcision upon you; their sole object is to escape persecution for the cross of Christ. For even 13 those who do receive circumcision are not thoroughgoing observers of the law; they only want you to be circumcised in order to boast of your having submitted to that out-ward rite. But God forbid that I should 14 boast of anything but the cross of our Lord Jesus Christ, through which*c* the world is crucified to me and I to the world! Circum- 15 cision is nothing; uncircumcision is nothing; the only thing that counts is new creation! Whoever they are who take this principle for 16 their guide, peace and mercy be upon them, and upon the whole Israel of God!

In future let no one make trouble for me, 17 for I bear the marks of Jesus branded on my body.

The grace of our Lord Jesus Christ be 18 with your spirit, my brothers. Amen.

b Or If a man is caught doing something wrong, my brothers, . . .   *c Or* whom.

THE LETTER OF PAUL TO THE

EPHESIANS

Spiritual blessings in Christ

1 FROM PAUL, apostle of Christ Jesus, commissioned by the will of God, to God's people at Ephesus,[a] believers incorporate in Christ Jesus.

2 Grace to you and peace from God our Father and the Lord Jesus Christ.

3 Praise be to the God and Father of our Lord Jesus Christ, who has bestowed on us in Christ every spiritual blessing in the 4 heavenly realms. In Christ he chose us before the world was founded, to be dedicated, to be without blemish in his sight, to be full of 5 love; and he[b] destined us—such was his will and pleasure—to be accepted as his sons 6 through Jesus Christ, in order that the glory of his gracious gift, so graciously bestowed on us in his Beloved, might redound to his 7 praise. For in Christ our release is secured and our sins are forgiven through the shedding of his blood. Therein lies the richness 8 of God's free grace lavished upon us, im- 9 parting full wisdom and insight. He has made known to us his hidden purpose— such was his will and pleasure determined 10 beforehand in Christ—to be put into effect when the time was ripe: namely, that the universe, all in heaven and on earth, might be brought into a unity in Christ.

The pledge of our heritage

1 In Christ indeed we have been given our share in the heritage, as was decreed in his design whose purpose is everywhere at work. 2 For it was his will that we, who were the first to set our hope on Christ,[c] should cause 3 his glory to be praised. And you too, when you had heard the message of the truth, the good news of your salvation, and had believed it, became incorporate in Christ and received the seal of the promised Holy Spirit; and that Spirit is the pledge that we 14 shall enter upon our heritage, when God has redeemed what is his own, to his praise and glory.

Prayer for spiritual illumination

Because of all this, now that I have heard of 15 the faith you have in the Lord Jesus and of the love you bear towards all God's people, I never cease to give thanks for you when 16 I mention you in my prayers. I pray that 17 the God of our Lord Jesus Christ, the all-glorious Father, may give you the spiritual powers of wisdom and vision, by which there comes the knowledge of him. I pray 18 that your inward eyes may be illumined, so that you may know what is the hope to which he calls you, what the wealth and glory of the share he offers you among his people in their heritage, and how vast the 19 resources of his power open to us who trust in him. They are measured by his strength and the might which he exerted in Christ 20 when he raised him from the dead, when he enthroned him at his right hand in the heavenly realms, far above all government and 21 authority, all power and dominion, and any title of sovereignty that can be named, not only in this age but in the age to come. He 22 put everything in subjection beneath his feet, and appointed him as supreme head to the church, which is his body and as 23 such holds within it the fullness of him who himself receives the entire fullness of God.[d]

a Some witnesses omit at Ephesus.   b Or . . . sight. In his love he . . .   c Or who already enjoyed the hope of Christ, or whose expectation and hope are in Christ.   d Or as supreme head to the church, which is his body and as such holds within it the fullness of him who fills the universe in all its parts; or as supreme head to the church which is his body, and to be all that he himself is who fills the universe in all its parts.

From death to life

2 Time was when you were dead in your sins
2 and wickedness, when you followed the evil
ways of this present age, when you obeyed
the commander of the spiritual powers of
the air, the spirit now at work among God's
3 rebel subjects. We too were once of their
number: we all lived our lives in sensuality,
and obeyed the promptings of our own instincts and notions. In our natural condition
we, like the rest, lay under the dreadful
4 judgement of God. But God, rich in mercy,
5 for the great love he bore us, brought us to
life with Christ even when we were dead in
our sins; it is by his grace you are saved.
6 And in union with Christ Jesus he raised us
up and enthroned us with him in the heavenly
7 realms, so that he might display in the ages
to come how immense are the resources of
his grace, and how great his kindness to us
8 in Christ Jesus. For it is by his grace you are
saved, through trusting him; it is not your
9 own doing. It is God's gift, not a reward for
work done. There is nothing for anyone
10 to boast of. For we are God's handiwork,
created in Christ Jesus to devote ourselves
to the good deeds for which God has
designed us.

Two made one in Christ

11 Remember then your former condition: you,
Gentiles as you are outwardly,*e* you, 'the
uncircumcised' so called by those who are
called 'the circumcised' (but only with refer-
12 ence to an outward rite)—you were at that
time separate from Christ, strangers to the
community of Israel, outside God's covenants and the promise that goes with them.
Your world was a world without hope and
13 without God. But now in union with Christ
Jesus you who once were far off have been
brought near through the shedding of
14 Christ's blood. For he is himself our peace.
Gentiles and Jews, he has made the two one,
and in his own body of flesh and blood has
broken down the enmity which stood like
15 a dividing wall between them; for he annulled the law with its rules and regulations,
so as to create out of the two a single new
humanity in himself, thereby making peace.
16 This was his purpose, to reconcile the two
in a single body to God through the cross,
on which he killed the enmity.*f*
17 So he came and proclaimed the good news:
peace to you who were far off, and peace to
18 those who were near by; for through him we
both alike have access to the Father in the
19 one Spirit. Thus you are no longer aliens in
a foreign land, but fellow-citizens with God's
20 people, members of God's household. You

are built upon the foundation laid by the
apostles and prophets, and Christ Jesus
himself is the foundation-stone.*g* In him the 21
whole building*h* is bonded together and grows
into a holy temple in the Lord. In him you 22
too are being built with all the rest into a
spiritual dwelling for God.

The unfathomable riches of Christ

With this in mind I make my prayer, I, Paul, **3**
who in the cause of you Gentiles am now
the prisoner of Christ Jesus—for surely you 2
have heard how God has assigned the gift
of his grace to me for your benefit. It was by 3
a revelation that his secret was made known
to me. I have already written a brief account
of this, and by reading it you may perceive 4
that I understand the secret of Christ. In 5
former generations this was not disclosed
to the human race; but now it has been
revealed by inspiration to his dedicated
apostles and prophets, that through the 6
Gospel the Gentiles are joint heirs with the
Jews, part of the same body, sharers together in the promise made in Christ Jesus.
Such is the gospel of which I was made a 7
minister, by God's gift, bestowed unmerited
on me in the working of his power. To me, 8
who am less than the least of all God's
people, he has granted of his grace the
privilege of proclaiming to the Gentiles the
good news of the unfathomable riches of
Christ, and of bringing to light how this 9
hidden purpose was to be put into effect. It
was hidden for long ages in God the creator
of the universe, in order that now, through 10
the church, the wisdom of God in all its
varied forms might be made known to the
rulers and authorities in the realms of
heaven. This is in accord with this age-long 11
purpose, which he achieved in Christ Jesus
our Lord. In him we have access to God with 12
freedom, in the confidence born of trust in
him. I beg you, then, not to lose heart over 13
my sufferings for you; indeed, they are your
glory.

The love of Christ

With this in mind, then, I kneel in prayer 14
to the Father, from whom every family*i* in 15
heaven and on earth takes its name, that out 16
of the treasures of his glory he may grant
you strength and power through his Spirit
in your inner being, that through faith 17
Christ may dwell in your hearts in love.
With deep roots and firm foundations, may 18
you be strong to grasp, with all God's
people, what is the breadth and length and
height and depth of the love of Christ, and 19
to know it, though it is beyond knowledge.

e Or by birth.   *f Or . . . cross. Thus in his own person he put the enmity to death.*   *g Or built
upon the foundation of the apostles and prophets, and Christ Jesus himself is the keystone.*   *h Or every
structure.*   *i Or his whole family.*

So may you attain to fullness of being, the fullness of God himself.[j]

20 Now to him who is able to do immeasurably more than all we can ask or conceive, 21 by the power which is at work among us, to him be glory in the church and in Christ Jesus from generation to generation evermore! Amen.

The unity of the body

4 I entreat you, then—I, a prisoner for the Lord's sake: as God has called you, live up 2 to your calling. Be humble always and gentle, and patient too. Be forbearing with 3 one another and charitable. Spare no effort to make fast with bonds of peace the unity 4 which the Spirit gives. There is one body and one Spirit, as there is also one hope held out 5 in God's call to you; one Lord, one faith, one 6 baptism; one God and Father of all, who is over all and through all and in all.

7 But each of us has been given his gift, his 8 due portion of Christ's bounty. Therefore Scripture says:

'He ascended into the heights
with captives in his train;
he gave gifts to men.'

9 Now, the word 'ascended' implies that he also descended to the lowest level, down to 10 the very earth.[k] He who descended is no other than he who ascended far above all heavens, so that he might fill the universe. 11 And these were his gifts: some to be apostles, some prophets, some evangelists, some 12 pastors and teachers, to equip God's people for work in his service, to the building up of 13 the body of Christ. So shall we all at last attain to the unity inherent in our faith and our knowledge of the Son of God—to mature manhood, measured by nothing less than 14 the full stature of Christ. We are no longer to be children, tossed by the waves and whirled about by every fresh gust of teaching, dupes of crafty rogues and their deceit- 15 ful schemes. No, let us speak the truth in love; so shall we fully grow up into Christ. 16 He is the head, and on him the whole body depends. Bonded and knit together by every constituent joint, the whole frame grows through the due activity of each part, and builds itself up in love.

Be made new in mind and spirit

17 This then is my word to you, and I urge it upon you in the Lord's name. Give up living like pagans with their good-for-nothing 18 notions. Their wits are beclouded, they are strangers to the life that is in God, because ignorance prevails among them and their 19 minds have grown hard as stone. Dead to all feeling, they have abandoned themselves to

vice, and stop at nothing to satisfy their foul desires. But that is not how you learned 20 Christ. For were you not told of him, were 21 you not as Christians taught the truth as it is in Jesus?—that, leaving your former way 22 of life, you must lay aside that old human nature which, deluded by its lusts, is sinking towards death. You must be made new in 23 mind and spirit, and put on the new nature 24 of God's creating, which shows itself in the just and devout life called for by the truth.

Then throw off falsehood; speak the truth 25 to each other, for all of us are the parts of one body.

If you are angry, do not let anger lead you 26 into sin; do not let sunset find you still nursing it; leave no loop-hole for the devil. 27 The thief must give up stealing, and instead 28 work hard and honestly with his own hands, so that he may have something to share with the needy.

No bad language must pass your lips, but 29 only what is good and helpful to the occasion, so that it brings a blessing to those who hear it. And do not grieve the Holy Spirit of 30 God, for that Spirit is the seal with which you were marked for the day of our final liberation. Have done with spite and pas- 31 sion, all angry shouting and cursing, and bad feeling of every kind. Be generous to one another, tender- 32 hearted, forgiving one another as God in Christ forgave you.

In a word, as God's dear children, try to 5 be like him, and live in love as Christ loved 2 you, and gave himself up on your behalf as an offering and sacrifice whose fragrance is pleasing to God.

Fornication and indecency of any kind, 3 or ruthless greed, must not be so much as mentioned among you, as befits the people of God. No coarse, stupid, or flippant talk; 4 these things are out of place; you should rather be thanking God. For be very sure 5 of this: no one given to fornication or indecency, or the greed which makes an idol of gain, has any share in the kingdom of Christ and of God.

Daylight and darkness

Let no one deceive you with shallow argu- 6 ments; it is for all these things that God's dreadful judgement is coming upon his rebel subjects. Have no part or lot with them. 7 For though you were once all darkness, now 8 as Christians you are light. Live like men who are at home in daylight, for where light 9 is, there all goodness springs up, all justice and truth. Try to find out what would please 10 the Lord; take no part in the barren deeds 11 of darkness, but show them up for what they

---

j Or the fullness which God requires.   *k Or descended to the regions beneath the earth.*

Greek home life

12 are. The things they do in secret it would be
13 shameful even to mention. But everything, when once the light has shown it up, is illuminated, and everything thus illumined is
14 all light. And so the hymn says:

> 'Awake, sleeper,
> rise from the dead,
> and Christ will shine upon you.'

15 Be most careful then how you conduct yourselves: like sensible men, not like
16 simpletons. Use the present opportunity to
17 the full, for these are evil days. So do not be fools, but try to understand what the will
18 of the Lord is. Do not give way to drunkenness and the dissipation that goes with it,
19 but let the Holy Spirit fill you: speak to one another in psalms, hymns, and[1] songs; sing and make music in your hearts to the Lord;
20 and in the name of our Lord Jesus Christ give thanks every day for everything to our God and Father.

To wives and husbands

21 Be subject to one another out of reverence for Christ.
22 Wives, be subject to your husbands as to
23 the Lord; for the man is the head of the woman, just as Christ also is the head of the church. Christ is, indeed, the Saviour of
24 the body; but just as the church is subject to Christ, so must women be to their husbands in everything.
25 Husbands, love your wives, as Christ also loved the church and gave himself up for it,
26 to consecrate it, cleansing it by water and
27 word, so that he might present the church to himself all glorious, with no stain or wrinkle or anything of the sort, but holy and without
28 blemish. In the same way men also are bound to love their wives, as they love their own bodies. In loving his wife a man loves him-
29 self. For no one ever hated his own body: on the contrary, he provides and cares for it; and that is how Christ treats the church,
30 because it is his body, of which we are living

parts. Thus it is that (in the words of Scrip- 31
ture) 'a man shall leave his father and mother and shall be joined to his wife, and the two shall become one flesh'. It is a great truth 32
that is hidden here. I for my part refer it to Christ and to the church, but it applies also 33
individually: each of you must love his wife as his very self; and the woman must see to it that she pays her husband all respect.

To children and parents

Children, obey your parents, for it is right **6**
that you should. 'Honour your father and 2
mother' is the first commandment with a promise attached, in the words: 'that it may 3
be well with you and that you may live long in the land'.

You fathers, again, must not goad your 4
children to resentment, but give them the instruction, and the correction, which belong to a Christian upbringing.

To slaves and masters

Slaves, obey your earthly masters with fear 5
and trembling, single-mindedly, as serving Christ. Do not offer merely the outward 6
show of service, to curry favour with men, but, as slaves of Christ, do whole-heartedly the will of God. Give the cheerful service of 7
those who serve the Lord, not men. For you 8
know that whatever good each man may do, slave or free, will be repaid him by the Lord.

You masters, also, must do the same by 9
them. Give up using threats; remember you both have the same Master in heaven, and he has no favourites.

The armour which God provides

Finally then, find your strength in the Lord, 10
in his mighty power. Put on all the armour 11
which God provides, so that you may be able to stand firm against the devices of the devil. For our fight is not against human 12
foes, but against cosmic powers, against the authorities and potentates of this dark world, against the superhuman forces of

1 Some witnesses insert spiritual, *as in Colossians 3. 16.*

13 evil in the heavens. Therefore, take up God's armour; then you will be able to stand your ground when things are at their worst, to complete every task and still to stand.
14 Stand firm, I say. Fasten on the belt of truth;
15 for coat of mail put on integrity; let the shoes on your feet be the gospel of peace, to
16 give you firm footing; and, with all these, take up the great shield of faith, with which you will be able to quench all the flaming
17 arrows of the evil one. Take salvation for helmet; for sword, take that which the Spirit gives you—the words that come from God.
18 Give yourselves wholly to prayer and entreaty; pray on every occasion in the power of the Spirit. To this end keep watch and persevere, always interceding for all God's
19 people; and pray for me, that I may be granted the right words when I open my mouth, and may boldly and freely make known his hidden purpose, for which I am 20 an ambassador—in chains. Pray that I may speak of it boldly, as it is my duty to speak.

A personal note

You will want to know about my affairs, 21 and how I am; Tychicus will give you all the news. He is our dear brother and trustworthy helper in the Lord's work. I am sending him 22 to you on purpose to let you know all about us, and to put fresh heart into you.

Peace to the brotherhood and love, with 23 faith, from God the Father and the Lord Jesus Christ. God's grace be with all who 24 love our Lord Jesus Christ, grace and immortality.*m*

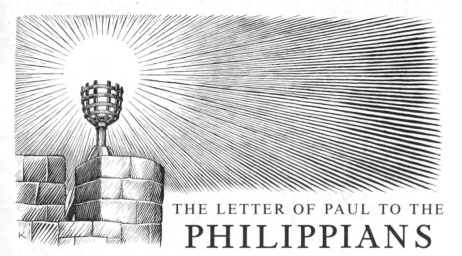

THE LETTER OF PAUL TO THE
PHILIPPIANS

1 FROM PAUL and Timothy, servants of Christ Jesus, to all those of God's people, incorporate in Christ Jesus, who live at Philippi, including their bishops and deacons.
2 Grace to you and peace from God our Father and the Lord Jesus Christ.

Thanksgiving and prayer

3 I thank my God whenever I think of you;
4 and when I pray for you all, my prayers are
5 always joyful, because of the part you have taken in the work of the Gospel from the
6 first day until now. Of one thing I am certain: the One who started the good work in you will bring it to completion by the Day of Christ Jesus. It is indeed only right that I 7 should feel like this about you all, because you hold me in such affection, and because, when I lie in prison or appear in the dock to vouch for the truth of the Gospel, you all share in the privilege that is mine.*a* God 8 knows how I long for you all, with the deep yearning of Christ Jesus himself. And this 9 is my prayer, that your love may grow ever richer and richer in knowledge and insight of every kind, and may thus bring you the 10

m Or who love . . . Christ with love imperishable.

a Or I am justified in taking this view about you all, because I hold you in closest union, as those who, when I lie . . . of the Gospel, all share in the privilege that is mine.

gift of true discrimination.[b] Then on the Day of Christ you will be flawless and without
11 blame, reaping the full harvest of righteousness that comes through Jesus Christ, to the glory and praise of God.

Paul's imprisonment and its results

12 Friends, I want you to understand that the work of the Gospel has been helped on, rather than hindered, by this business of
13 mine. My imprisonment in Christ's cause has become common knowledge to all at headquarters[c] here, and indeed among the
14 public at large; and it has given confidence to most of our fellow-Christians to speak the word of God fearlessly and with extraordinary courage.
15 Some, indeed, proclaim Christ in a jealous and quarrelsome spirit; others proclaim him
16 in true goodwill, and these are moved by love for me; they know that it is to defend
17 the Gospel that I am where I am. But the others, moved by personal rivalry, present Christ from mixed motives, meaning to stir up fresh trouble for me as I lie in prison.[d]
18 What does it matter? One way or another, in pretence or sincerity, Christ is set forth, and for that I rejoice.

A difficult choice

19 Yes, and rejoice I will, knowing well that the issue of it all will be my deliverance, because you are praying for me and the Spirit
20 of Jesus Christ is given me for support.[e] For, as I passionately hope, I shall have no cause to be ashamed, but shall speak so boldly that now as always the greatness of Christ will shine out clearly in my person, whether
21 through my life or through my death. For
22 to me life is Christ, and death gain; but what if my living on in the body may serve some good purpose? Which then am I to choose?
23 I cannot tell. I am torn two ways: what I should like is to depart and be with Christ;
24 that is better by far; but for your sake there is greater need for me to stay on in the body.
25 This indeed I know for certain: I shall stay, and stand by you all to help you forward and
26 to add joy to your faith, so that when I am with you again, your pride in me may be unbounded in Christ Jesus.

Standing firm

27 Only, let your conduct be worthy of the gospel of Christ, so that whether I come and see you for myself or hear about you from a distance, I may know that you are standing firm, one in spirit, one in mind, contending

as one man for the gospel faith, meeting 28 your opponents without so much as a tremor. This is a sure sign to them that their doom is sealed, but a sign of your salvation, and one afforded by God himself; for you 29 have been granted the privilege not only of believing in Christ but also of suffering for him. You and I are engaged in the same con- 30 test; you saw me in it once, and, as you hear, I am in it still.

The example of Christ in becoming man

If then our common life in Christ yields any- 2 thing to stir the heart, any loving consolation, any sharing of the Spirit, any warmth of affection or compassion, fill up my cup 2 of happiness by thinking and feeling alike, with the same love for one another, the same turn of mind, and a common care for unity. There must be no room for rivalry and per- 3 sonal vanity among you, but you must humbly reckon others better than yourselves. Look to each other's interest and 4 not merely to your own.

Let your bearing towards one another 5 arise out of your life in Christ Jesus.[f] For 6 the divine nature was his from the first; yet he did not think to snatch at equality with God,[g] but made himself nothing, assuming 7 the nature of a slave. Bearing the human likeness, revealed in human shape, he hum- 8 bled himself, and in obedience accepted even death—death on a cross. Therefore God 9 raised him to the heights and bestowed on him the name above all names, that at the 10 name of Jesus every knee should bow—in heaven, on earth, and in the depths—and 11 every tongue confess, 'Jesus Christ is Lord', to the glory of God the Father.

Children of God

So you too, my friends, must be obedient, 12 as always; even more, now that I am away, than when I was with you. You must work out your own salvation in fear and trembling; for it is God who works in you, inspiring 13 both the will and the deed, for his own chosen purpose.

Do all you have to do without complaint 14 or wrangling. Show yourselves guileless and 15 above reproach, faultless children of God in a warped and crooked generation, in which you shine[h] like stars in a dark world[i] and 16 proffer the word of life.[j] Thus you will be my pride on the Day of Christ, proof that I did not run my race in vain, or work in vain. But if my life-blood is to crown that 17 sacrifice which is the offering up of your faith,

---

b Or may teach you by experience what things are most worth while.   *c Or* to all the imperial guard, *or to* all at the Residency (*Greek* Praetorium).   *d Or* meaning to make use of my imprisonment to stir up fresh trouble.   *e Or* supplies me with all I need.   *f Or* Have that bearing towards one another which was also found in Christ Jesus.   *g Or* yet he did not prize his equality with God.   *h Or* . . . generation. Shine out among them . . .   *i Or* in the firmament.   *j Or* as the very principle of its life.

I am glad of it, and I share my gladness with you all. Rejoice, you no less than I, and let us share our joy. 18

Timothy and Epaphroditus

I hope (under the Lord Jesus) to send Timothy to you soon; it will cheer me to hear news of you. There is no one else here who sees things as I do, and takes[k] a genuine interest in your concerns; they are all bent on their own ends, not on the cause of Christ Jesus. But Timothy's record is known to you: you know that he has been at my side in the service of the Gospel like a son working under his father. Timothy, then, I hope to send as soon as ever I can see how things are going with me; and I am confident, under the Lord, that I shall myself be coming before long. 19 20 21 22 23 24

I feel also I must send our brother Epaphroditus, my fellow-worker and comrade, whom you commissioned to minister to my needs. He has been missing all of you sadly, and has been distressed that you heard he was ill. (He was indeed dangerously ill, but God was merciful to him, and merciful no less to me, to spare me sorrow upon sorrow.) For this reason I am all the more eager to send him, to give you the happiness of seeing him again, and to relieve my sorrow. Welcome him then in the fellowship of the Lord with whole-hearted delight. You should honour men like him; in Christ's cause he came near to death, risking his life to render me the service you could not give. 25 26 27 28 29 30

And now, friends, farewell; I wish you joy in the Lord. 3

A personal confession

To repeat what I have written to you before is no trouble to me, and it is a safeguard for you. Beware of those dogs and their malpractices. Beware of those who insist on mutilation—'circumcision' I will not call it; we are the circumcised, we whose worship is spiritual,[l] whose pride is in Christ Jesus, and who put no confidence in anything external. Not that I am without grounds myself even for confidence of that kind. If anyone thinks to base his claims on externals, I could make a stronger case for myself: circumcised on my eighth day, Israelite by race, of the tribe of Benjamin, a Hebrew born and bred;[m] in my attitude to the law, a Pharisee; in pious zeal, a persecutor of the church; in legal rectitude, faultless. But all such assets I have written off because of Christ. I would say more: I count everything sheer loss, because all is far outweighed by the gain of knowing Christ Jesus my Lord, for whose sake I did in fact lose everything. I count it so much garbage,[n] for the sake of gaining Christ and finding myself incorporate in him, with no righteousness of my own, no legal rectitude, but the righteousness which comes[o] from faith in Christ, given by God in response to faith. All I care for is to know Christ, to experience the power of his resurrection, and to share his sufferings, in growing conformity with his death, if only I may finally arrive at the resurrection from the dead. 2 3 4 5 6 7 8 9 10 11

It is not to be thought that I have already achieved all this. I have not yet reached perfection, but I press on, hoping to take hold of that for which Christ once took hold of me. My friends, I do not reckon myself to have got hold of it yet. All I can say is this: forgetting what is behind me, and reaching out for that which lies ahead, I press towards the goal to win the prize which is God's call to the life above, in Christ Jesus. 12 13 14

Let us then keep to this way of thinking, those of us who are mature. If there is any point on which you think differently, this also God will make plain to you. Only let our conduct be consistent with the level we have already reached. 15 16

Citizens of heaven

Agree together, my friends, to follow my example. You have us for a model; watch those whose way of life conforms to it. For, as I have often told you, and now tell you with tears in my eyes, there are many whose way of life makes them enemies of the cross of Christ. They are heading for destruction, appetite is their god, and they glory in their shame. Their minds are set on earthly things. We, by contrast, are citizens of heaven, and from heaven we expect our deliverer to come, the Lord Jesus Christ. He will transfigure the body belonging to our humble state, and give it a form like that of his own resplendent body, by the very power which enables him to make all things subject to himself. Therefore, my friends, beloved friends whom I long for, my joy, my crown, stand thus firm in the Lord, my beloved! 17 18 19 20 21 4

I beg Euodia, and I beg Syntyche, to agree together in the Lord's fellowship. Yes, and you too, my loyal comrade, I ask you to help these women, who shared my struggles in the cause of the Gospel, with Clement and my other fellow-workers, whose[p] names are in the roll of the living. 2 3

---

k Or no one else here like him, who takes . . . read who worship by the Spirit of God.   l Some witnesses read who worship God in the spirit; others read who worship by the Spirit of God.   m Or a Hebrew-speaking Jew of a Hebrew-speaking family.
n Or dung.   o Or and in him finding that, though I have no righteousness of my own, no legal rectitude, I have the righteousness which comes . . .   p Some witnesses read my fellow-workers, and the others whose . . .

The peace of God

4 Farewell; I wish you all joy in the Lord. I will say it again: all joy be yours.

5 Let your magnanimity be manifest to all.

6 The Lord is near; have no anxiety, but in everything make your requests known to God in prayer and petition with thanks-7 giving. Then the peace of God, which is beyond our utmost understanding,*q* will keep guard over your hearts and your thoughts, in Christ Jesus.

8 And now, my friends, all that is true, all that is noble, all that is just and pure, all that is lovable and gracious,*r* whatever is excellent and admirable—fill all your thoughts with these things.

9 The lessons I taught you, the tradition I have passed on, all that you heard me say or saw me do, put into practice; and the God of peace will be with you.

Giving and receiving

10 It is a great joy to me, in the Lord, that after so long your care for me has now blossomed afresh. You did care about me before for that matter; it was opportunity that you 11 lacked. Not that I am alluding to want, for I have learned to find resources in myself 12 whatever my circumstances. I know what it is to be brought low, and I know what it is to have plenty. I have been very thoroughly initiated into the human lot with all its ups and downs—fullness and hunger, plenty and want. I have strength for anything through 13 him who gives me power. But it was kind of 14 you to share the burden of my troubles.

15 As you know yourselves, Philippians, in the early days of my mission, when I set out from Macedonia, you alone of all our congregations were my partners in payments and receipts; for even at Thessalonica you con-16 tributed to my needs, not once but twice over. Do not think I set my heart upon the gift; 17 all I care for is the profit accruing to you. However, here I give you my receipt for 18 everything—for more than everything; I am paid in full, now that I have received from Epaphroditus what you sent. It is a fragrant offering, an acceptable sacrifice, pleasing to God. And my God will supply all your wants 19 out of the magnificence of his riches in Christ Jesus. To our God and Father be glory for 20 endless ages! Amen.

Final greetings

Give my greetings, in the fellowship of 21 Christ Jesus, to each one of God's people. The brothers who are now with me send their greetings to you, and so do all God's people 22 here, particularly those who belong to the imperial establishment.

The grace of our Lord Jesus Christ be with 23 your spirit.

q Or of far more worth than human reasoning.   *r Or of good repute.*

THE LETTER
OF PAUL TO THE
COLOSSIANS

you may bear fruit in active goodness of every kind, and grow in the knowledge of God. May he strengthen you, in his glorious 11 might, with ample power to meet whatever comes with fortitude, patience, and joy; and 12 to give thanks[c] to the Father who has made you fit to share the heritage of God's people in the realm of light.

The supremacy of the Son of God

He rescued us from the domain of darkness 13 and brought us away into the kingdom of his dear Son, in whom our release is secured 14 and our sins forgiven. He is the image of the 15 ·invisible God; his is the primacy over[d] all created things. In him everything in heaven 16 and on earth was created, not only things visible but also the invisible orders of thrones, sovereignties, authorities, and powers: the whole universe has been created through him and for him. And he exists before every- 17 thing, and all things are held together in him. He is, moreover, the head of the body, the 18 church. He is its origin, the first to return from the dead, to be in all things alone supreme. For in him the complete being of 19 God, by God's own choice, came to dwell. Through him God chose to reconcile the 20 whole universe to himself, making peace through the shedding of his blood upon the cross—to reconcile all things, whether on earth or in heaven, through him alone.

Reconciliation by Christ's death

Formerly you were yourselves estranged 21 from God; you were his enemies in heart and mind, and your deeds were evil. But now by 22 Christ's death in his body of flesh and blood God has reconciled you to himself, so that he may present you before himself as dedicated men, without blemish and innocent in his sight. Only you must continue in your 23 faith, firm on your foundations, never to be dislodged from the hope offered in the gospel which you heard. This is the gospel which has been proclaimed in the whole creation under heaven; and I, Paul, have become its minister.

Disclosing God's secret

It is now my happiness to suffer for you. 24 This is my way of helping to complete, in

1 FROM PAUL, apostle of Christ Jesus commissioned by the will of God, and our 2 colleague Timothy, to God's people at Colossae, brothers in the faith, incorporate in Christ.

Grace to you and peace from God our Father.

Thanksgiving and prayer

3 In all our prayers to God, the Father of our Lord Jesus Christ, we thank him for you, 4 because we have heard of the faith you hold in Christ Jesus, and the love you bear to- 5 wards all God's people. Both spring from the hope stored up for you in heaven—that hope of which you learned when the mes- 6 sage of the true Gospel first came to you. In the same way it is coming to men the whole world over; everywhere it is growing and bearing fruit as it does among you, and has done since the day when you heard of the graciousness of God and recognized it 7 for what in truth it is. You were taught this by Epaphras, our dear fellow-servant, a trusted worker for Christ on our[a] behalf, 8 and it is he who has brought us the news of your God-given love.[b]

9 For this reason, ever since the day we heard of it, we have not ceased to pray for you. We ask God that you may receive from him all wisdom and spiritual understanding 10 for full insight into his will, so that your manner of life may be worthy of the Lord and entirely pleasing to him. We pray that

a *Some witnesses read* your. b *Or* your love within the fellowship of the Spirit. c *Or* with fortitude and patience, and to give joyful thanks . . . d *Or* image of the invisible God, born before . . .

my poor human flesh, the full tale of Christ's afflictions still to be endured, for the sake 25 of his body which is the church. I became its servant by virtue of the task assigned to me by God for your benefit: to deliver his mes- 26 sage in full; to announce the secret hidden for long ages and through many genera- 27 tions, but now disclosed to God's people, to whom it was his will to make it known—to make known how rich and glorious it is among all nations. The secret is this: Christ in*e* you, the hope of a glory to come.

28   He it is whom we proclaim. We admonish everyone without distinction, we instruct everyone in all the ways of wisdom, so as to present each one of you as a mature member 29 of Christ's body. To this end I am toiling strenuously with all the energy and power **2** of Christ at work in me. For I want you to know how strenuous are my exertions for you and the Laodiceans and all who have 2 never set eyes on me. I want them to con- tinue in good heart and in the unity of love, and to come to the full wealth of conviction which understanding brings, and grasp God's 3 secret. That secret is Christ himself; in him lie hidden all God's treasures of wisdom and 4 knowledge. I tell you this to save you from being talked*f* into error by specious argu- 5 ments. For though absent in body, I am with you in spirit, and rejoice to see your orderly array and the firm front which your faith in Christ presents.

Complete in Christ

6 Therefore, since Jesus was delivered to you as Christ and Lord, live your lives in union 7 with him. Be rooted in him; be built in him; be consolidated in the faith you were taught;*g* let your hearts overflow with thankfulness. 8 Be on your guard; do not let your minds be captured by hollow and delusive specula- tions, based on traditions of man-made teaching and centred on the elemental spirits of the universe*h* and not on Christ.

9   For it is in Christ that the complete being 10 of the Godhead dwells embodied,*i* and in him you have been brought to completion. Every power and authority in the universe 11 is subject to him as Head. In him also you were circumcised, not in a physical sense, but by being divested of the lower nature; 12 this is Christ's way of circumcision. For in baptism*j* you were buried with him, in baptism also you were raised to life with him through your faith in the active power of 13 God who raised him from the dead. And although you were dead because of your sins

and because you were morally uncircum- cised, he has made you alive with Christ. For he has forgiven us all our sins; he has 14 cancelled the bond which pledged us to the decrees of the law. It stood against us, but he has set it aside, nailing it to the cross. On 15 that cross he discarded the cosmic powers and authorities like a garment; he made a public spectacle of them and led them*k* as captives in his triumphal procession.

Warning against self-mortification

Allow no one therefore to take you to task 16 about what you eat or drink, or over the observance of festival, new moon, or sab- bath. These are no more than a shadow of 17 what was to come; the solid reality is Christ's. You are not to be disqualified by the decision 18 of people who go in for self-mortification and angel-worship, and try to enter into some vision of their own. Such people, bursting with the futile conceit of worldly minds, lose hold upon the Head; yet it is 19 from the Head that the whole body, with all its joints and ligaments, receives its supplies, and thus knit together grows according to God's design.

Did you not die with Christ and pass 20 beyond reach of the elemental spirits of the universe*l*? Then why behave as though you were still living the life of the world? Why let people dictate to you: 'Do not handle 21 this, do not taste that, do not touch the other'—all of them things that must perish 22 as soon as they are used? That is to follow merely human injunctions and teaching. True, it has an air of wisdom, with its forced 23 piety, its self-mortification, and its severity to the body; but it is of no use at all in combating sensuality.

The old life and the new

Were you not raised to life with Christ? **3** Then aspire to the realm above, where Christ is, seated at the right hand of God, and let your thoughts dwell on that higher 2 realm, not on this earthly life. I repeat, you 3 died; and now your life lies hidden with Christ in God. When Christ, who is our life, 4 is manifested, then you too will be mani- fested with him in glory.

Then put to death those parts of you 5 which belong to the earth—fornication, in- decency, lust, foul cravings, and the ruthless greed which is nothing less than idolatry. Because of these, God's dreadful judgement 6 is impending; and in the life you once lived 7 these are the ways you yourselves followed.

e Or among.   *f Or* What I mean is this: no one must talk you ...   *g Or* by your faith, as you were taught.   *h Or* the elements of the natural world, *or* elementary ideas belonging to this world.   *i Or* corporately.   *j Or* ... nature, in the very circumcision of Christ himself; for in baptism ...   *k Or* he stripped himself of his physical body, and thereby boldly made a spectacle of the cosmic powers and authorities, and led them ...; *or* he despoiled the cosmic powers and authorities, and boldly made a spectacle of them, lead- ing them ...   *l Or* the elements of the natural world, *or* elementary ideas belonging to this world.

8 But now you must yourselves lay aside all anger, passion, malice, cursing, filthy talk 9 —have done with them! Stop lying to one another, now that you have discarded the 10 old nature with its deeds and have put on the new nature, which is being constantly renewed in the image of its Creator and 11 brought to know God. There is no question here of Greek and Jew, circumcised and uncircumcised, barbarian, Scythian, slave and freeman; but Christ is all, and is in all.

12 Then put on the garments that suit God's chosen people, his own, his beloved: compassion, kindness, humility, gentleness, pa-13 tience. Be forbearing with one another, and forgiving, where any of you has cause for complaint: you must forgive as the Lord 14 forgave you. To crown all, there must be love, to bind all together and complete the 5 whole. Let Christ's peace be arbiter in your hearts; to this peace you were called as members of a single body. And be filled 6 with gratitude. Let the message of Christ dwell among you in all its richness. Instruct and admonish each other with the utmost wisdom. Sing thankfully in your hearts to God,*m* with psalms and hymns and spiritual 7 songs. Whatever you are doing, whether you speak or act, do everything in the name of the Lord Jesus, giving thanks to God the Father through him.

Personal relationships

8 Wives, be subject to your husbands; that is 9 your Christian duty. Husbands, love your 10 wives and do not be harsh with them. Children, obey your parents in everything, for that is pleasing to God and is the Christian 1 way. Fathers, do not exasperate your chil-2 dren, for fear they grow disheartened. Slaves, give entire obedience to your earthly masters, not merely with an outward show of service, to curry favour with men, but with single-mindedness, out of reverence for the Lord. 3 Whatever you are doing, put your whole heart into it, as if you were doing it for the 4 Lord and not for men, knowing that there is a Master who will give you your heritage as a reward for your service. Christ is the 5 Master whose slaves you must be. Dishonesty will be requited, and he has no 1 favourites. Masters, be just and fair to your slaves, knowing that you too have a Master in heaven.

Persevere in prayer, with mind awake and 2 thankful heart; and include a prayer for us, 3 that God may give us an opening for preaching, to tell the secret of Christ; that indeed is why I am now in prison. Pray that I may 4 make the secret plain, as it is my duty to do.

Behave wisely towards those outside your 5 own number; use the present opportunity to the full. Let your conversation be always 6 gracious, and never insipid; study how best to talk with each person you meet.

Final greetings

You will hear all about my affairs from 7 Tychicus, our dear brother and trustworthy helper and fellow-servant in the Lord's work. I am sending him to you on purpose 8 to let you know all about us and to put fresh heart into you. With him comes Onesimus, 9 our trustworthy and dear brother, who is one of yourselves. They will tell you all the news here.

Aristarchus, Christ's captive like myself, 10 sends his greetings; so does Mark, the cousin of Barnabas (you have had instructions about him; if he comes, make him welcome), and Jesus Justus. Of the Jewish Christians, 11 these are the only ones who work with me for the kingdom of God, and they have been a great comfort to me. Greetings from 12 Epaphras, servant of Christ, who is one of yourselves. He prays hard for you all the time, that you may stand fast, ripe in conviction*n* and wholly devoted to doing God's will. For I can vouch for him, that he works 13 tirelessly for you and the people at Laodicea and Hierapolis. Greetings to you from our 14 dear friend Luke, the doctor, and from Demas. Give our greetings to the brothers 15 at Laodicea, and Nympha and the congregation at her house.*o* And when this letter is 16 read among you, see that it is also read to the congregation at Laodicea, and that you in return read the one from Laodicea. This 17 special word to Archippus: 'Attend to the duty entrusted to you in the Lord's service, and discharge it to the full.'

This greeting is in my own hand—PAUL. 18 Remember I am in prison. God's grace be with you.

m Some witnesses read the Lord.   *n Or* stand fast, mature and complete . . .   *o Some witnesses read* Nymphas and the congregation at his house.

THESSALONIANS

1 FROM PAUL, Silvanus, and Timothy to the congregation of Thessalonians who belong to God the Father and the Lord Jesus Christ.

Grace to you and peace.

The Gospel at Thessalonica

2 We always thank God for you all, and men-
3 tion you in our prayers continually. We call to mind, before our God and Father, how your faith has shown itself in action, your love in labour, and your hope of our Lord
4 Jesus Christ in fortitude. We are certain, brothers beloved by God, that he has chosen
5 you and that*a* when we brought you the Gospel, we brought it not in mere words but in the power of the Holy Spirit, and with strong conviction, as you know well. That is the kind of men we were at Thessalonica, and it was for your sake.

6 And you, in your turn, followed the example set by us and by the Lord; the welcome you gave the message meant grave suffering for you, yet you rejoiced in the Holy Spirit;
7 thus you have become a model for all
8 believers in Macedonia and in Achaia. From Thessalonica the word of the Lord rang out; and not in Macedonia and Achaia alone, but everywhere your faith in God has reached men's ears. No words of ours are
9 needed, for they themselves spread the news of our visit to you and its effect: how you turned from idols, to be servants of the living
10 and true God, and to wait expectantly for the appearance from heaven of his Son Jesus, whom he raised from the dead, Jesus our deliverer from the terrors of judgement to come.

The apostle's example

2 You know for yourselves, brothers, that our
2 visit to you was not fruitless. Far from it; after all the injury and outrage which to your knowledge we had suffered at Philippi, we declared the gospel of God to you frankly and fearlessly, by the help of our God. A
3 hard struggle it was. Indeed, the appeal we make never springs from error or base
4 motive; there is no attempt to deceive; but God has approved us as fit to be entrusted with the Gospel, and on those terms we speak. We do not curry favour with men;

we seek only the favour of God, who is continually testing our hearts. Our words 5 have never been flattering words, as you have cause to know; nor, as God is our witness, have they ever been a cloak for greed. We have never sought honour from 6 men, from you or from anyone else, although as Christ's own envoys we might have made our weight felt; but we were as gentle with 7 you as a nurse caring fondly for her children. With such yearning love we chose to impart 8 to you not only the gospel of God but our very selves, so dear had you become to us. Remember, brothers, how we toiled and 9 drudged. We worked for a living night and day, rather than be a burden to anyone, while we proclaimed before you the good news of God.

We call you to witness, yes and God him- 10 self, how devout and just and blameless was our behaviour towards you who are believers. As you well know, we dealt with you 11 one by one, as a father deals with his children, appealing to you by encouragement, as well as by solemn injunctions, to live lives 12 worthy of the God who calls you into his kingdom and glory.

The Thessalonians' sufferings

This is why we thank God continually, 13 because when we handed on God's message, you received it, not as the word of men, but as what it truly is, the very word of God at*b* work in you who hold the faith. You have 14 fared like the congregations in Judaea, God's people in Christ Jesus. You have been treated by your countrymen as they are treated by the Jews, who killed the Lord Jesus and the 15 prophets*c* and drove us out, the Jews who are heedless of God's will and enemies of their fellow-men, hindering us from speak- 16 ing to the Gentiles to lead them to salvation. All this time they have been making up the full measure of their guilt, and now retribution has overtaken them for good and all.*d*

Paul's concern for them

My friends, when for a short spell you were 1⁷ lost to us—lost to sight, not to our hearts— we were exceedingly anxious to see you again. So we did propose to come to Thes- 1 salonica—I, Paul, more than once—but

---

a Or . . . chosen you, because . . .   *b Or word of God who is at . . .*   *c Some witnesses read their*
own prophets.   *d Or now at last retribution has overtaken them.*

9 Satan thwarted us. For after all, what hope or joy or crown of pride is there for us, what indeed but you, when we stand before our 10 Lord Jesus at his coming? It is you who are indeed our glory and our joy.

3 So when we could bear it no longer, we 2 decided to remain alone at Athens, and sent Timothy, our brother and God's fellow-worker[e] in the service of the gospel of Christ, to encourage you to stand firm for the faith 3 and, under all these hardships, not to be shaken;[f] for you know that this is our 4 appointed lot. When we were with you we warned you that we were bound to suffer hardship; and so it has turned out, as you 5 know. And thus it was that when I could bear it no longer, I sent to find out about your faith, fearing that the tempter might have tempted you and my labour might be lost.

Timothy brings good news

6 But now Timothy has just arrived from Thessalonica, bringing good news of your faith and love. He tells us that you always think kindly of us, and are as anxious to see 7 us as we are to see you. And so in all our difficulties and hardships your faith re-8 assures us about you. It is the breath of life 9 to us that you stand firm in the Lord. What thanks can we return to God for you? What thanks for all the joy you have brought us, 10 making us rejoice before our God while we pray most earnestly night and day to be allowed to see you again and to mend your faith where it falls short?

11 May our God and Father himself, and our Lord Jesus, bring us direct to you; 12 and may the Lord make your love mount and overflow towards one another and to-13 wards all, as our love does towards you. May he make your hearts firm, so that you may stand before our God and Father holy and faultless when our Lord Jesus comes with all those who are his own.

Call to holiness

And now, my friends, we have one thing to beg and pray of you, by our fellowship with the Lord Jesus. We passed on to you the tradition of the way we must live to please God; you are indeed already following it, but we beg you to do so yet more thoroughly.

For you know what orders we gave you, in the name of the Lord Jesus. This is the will of God, that you should be holy: you must abstain from fornication; each one of you must learn to gain mastery over his body, to hallow and honour it, not giving way to lust like the pagans who are ignorant

of God; and no man must do his brother 6 wrong in this matter,[g] or invade his rights, because, as we told you before with all emphasis, the Lord punishes all such of-fences. For God called us to holiness, not to 7 impurity. Anyone therefore who flouts these 8 rules is flouting, not man, but God who bestows upon you his Holy Spirit.

About love for our brotherhood you need 9 no words of mine, for you are yourselves taught by God to love one another, and you 10 are in fact practising this rule of love to-wards all your fellow-Christians throughout Macedonia. Yet we appeal to you, brothers, to do better still. Let it be your ambition to 11 keep calm and look after your own business, and to work with your hands, as we ordered you, so that you may command the respect 12 of those outside your own number, and at the same time may never be in want.

About death and resurrection

We wish you not to remain in ignorance, 13 brothers, about those who sleep in death; you should not grieve like the rest of men, who have no hope. We believe that Jesus 14 died and rose again; and so it will be for those who died as Christians; God will bring them to life with Jesus.[h]

For this we tell you as the Lord's word: 15 we who are left alive until the Lord comes shall not forestall those who have died; because at the word of command, at the 16 sound of the archangel's voice and God's trumpet-call, the Lord himself will descend from heaven; first the Christian dead will rise, then we who are left alive shall join 17 them, caught up in clouds to meet the Lord in the air. Thus we shall always be with the Lord. Console one another, then, with these 18 words.

The Day of the Lord

About dates and times, my friends, we need **5** not write to you, for you know perfectly well 2 that the Day of the Lord comes like a thief in the night. While they are talking of peace 3 and security, all at once calamity is upon them, sudden as the pangs that come upon a woman with child; and there will be no escape. But you, my friends, are not in the 4 dark, that the day should overtake you like a thief.[i] You are all children of light, children 5 of day. We do not belong to night or dark-ness, and we must not sleep like the rest, but 6 keep awake and sober. Sleepers sleep at 7 night, and drunkards are drunk at night, but we, who belong to daylight, must keep 8 sober, armed with faith and love for coat of mail, and the hope of salvation for helmet.

---

e *Or* and fellow-worker for God; *one witness has simply* and fellow-worker.   f *Or* beguiled away.
g *Or* must overreach his brother in his business (*or* in lawsuits).   h *Or* will bring them in company with
Jesus.   i *Some witnesses read* thieves.

9 For God has not destined us to the terrors of judgement, but to the full attainment of salvation through our Lord Jesus Christ. 10 He died for us so that we, awake or asleep, 11 might live in company with him. Therefore hearten one another, fortify one another—as indeed you do.

Final instructions and greetings

12 We beg you, brothers, to acknowledge those who are working so hard among you, and in the Lord's fellowship are your leaders and 13 counsellors. Hold them in the highest possible esteem and affection for the work they do.

You must live at peace among yourselves. 14 And we would urge you, brothers, to admonish the careless, encourage the fainthearted, support the weak, and to be very patient with them all.

15 See to it that no one pays back wrong for wrong, but always aim at doing the best you can for each other and for all men.

16 Be always joyful; pray continually; 18 give thanks whatever happens; for this is what God in Christ wills for you.

19 Do not stifle inspiration, and do not de-21 spise prophetic utterances, but bring them all to the test and then keep what is good in 22 them and avoid the bad of whatever kind.*j*

23 May God himself, the God of peace, make you holy in every part, and keep you sound in spirit, soul, and body, without fault when 24 our Lord Jesus Christ comes. He who calls you is to be trusted; he will do it.

25 Brothers, pray for us also.

26 Greet all our brothers with the kiss of peace.

27 I adjure you by the Lord to have this letter read to the whole brotherhood.

28 The grace of our Lord Jesus Christ be with you!

THE SECOND LETTER OF PAUL TO THE
THESSALONIANS

1 FROM PAUL, Silvanus, and Timothy to the congregation of Thessalonians who belong to God our Father and the Lord Jesus Christ. 2 Grace to you and peace from God the Father and the Lord Jesus Christ.

Thanksgiving for steadfastness under trials

3 Our thanks are always due to God for you, brothers. It is right that we should thank him, because your faith increases mightily, and the love you have, each for all and all 4 for each, grows ever greater. Indeed we boast about you ourselves among the congregations of God's people, because your faith remains so steadfast under all your persecutions, and all the troubles you en-5 dure. See how this brings out the justice of God's judgement. It will prove you worthy of the kingdom of God, for which indeed you are suffering.

Judgement Day

6 It is surely just that God should balance the account by sending trouble to those who 7 trouble you, and relief to you who are troubled, and to us as well, when our Lord Jesus Christ is revealed from heaven with his mighty angels in blazing fire. Then he 8 will do justice upon those who refuse to acknowledge God and upon those who will not obey*a* the gospel of our Lord Jesus. They 9 will suffer the punishment of eternal ruin, cut off from the presence of the Lord and the splendour of his might, when on that 10 great Day he comes to be glorified among his own and adored among all believers; for you did indeed believe the testimony we brought you.

With this in mind we pray for you always, 11 that our God may count you worthy of his calling, and mightily bring to fulfilment every good purpose and every act inspired by faith, so that the name of our Lord Jesus 12 may be glorified in you, and you in him, according to the grace of our God and the Lord Jesus Christ.

About the coming of our Lord

2 And now, brothers, about the coming of our Lord Jesus Christ and his gathering of us to himself: I beg you, do not suddenly 2

---

j Or . . . utterances. Put everything to the test; keep hold of what is good and avoid every kind of evil.

a Or justice upon those who refuse . . . and will not obey . . .

lose your heads or alarm yourselves, whether at some oracular utterance, or pronouncement, or some letter purporting to come from us, alleging that the Day of the Lord 3 is already here. Let no one deceive you in any way whatever. That day cannot come before the final rebellion against God, when wickedness will be revealed in human form, 4 the man doomed to perdition. He is the Enemy. He rises in his pride against every god, so called, every object of men's worship, and even takes his seat in the temple of God claiming to be a god himself.

5 You cannot but remember that I told you 6 this while I was still with you; you must now be aware of the restraining hand which ensures that he shall be revealed only at the 7 proper time. For already the secret power of wickedness is at work, secret only for the present until the Restrainer disappears from 8 the scene. And then he will be revealed, that wicked man whom the Lord Jesus will destroy with the breath of his mouth, and annihilate by the radiance of his coming. 9 But the coming of that wicked man is the work of Satan. It will be attended by all the powerful signs and miracles of the Lie, and all the deception that sinfulness can impose on those doomed to destruction. Destroyed they shall be, because they did not open their minds to love of the truth, so as to 11 find salvation. Therefore God puts them under a delusion, which works upon them 12 to believe the lie, so that they may all be brought to judgement, all who do not believe the truth but make sinfulness their deliberate choice.

Stand firm

But we are bound to thank God always for you, brothers beloved by the Lord, because from the beginning of time God chose you[b] to find salvation in the Spirit that consecrates 14 you, and in the truth that you believe. It was for this that he called you through the gospel we brought, so that you might possess for your own the splendour of our Lord Jesus Christ.

Stand firm, then, brothers, and hold fast to the traditions which you have learned from us by word or by letter. And may our Lord Jesus Christ himself and God our Father, who has shown us such love, and in his grace has given us such unfailing encouragement and such bright hopes, still

encourage and fortify you in every good deed and word!

A request for prayer

And now, brothers, pray for us, that the 3 word of the Lord may have everywhere the swift and glorious course that it has had among you, and that we may be rescued 2 from wrong-headed and wicked men; for it is not all who have faith. But the Lord is to 3 be trusted, and he will fortify you and guard you from the evil one. We feel perfect con- 4 fidence about you, in the Lord, that you are doing and will continue to do what we order. May the Lord direct your hearts towards 5 God's love and the steadfastness of Christ!

Earn your own living

These are our orders to you, brothers, in the 6 name of our Lord Jesus Christ: hold aloof from every Christian brother who falls into idle habits, and does not follow the tradition you received from us. You know yourselves 7 how you ought to copy our example: we were no idlers among you; we did not accept 8 board and lodging from anyone without paying for it; we toiled and drudged, we worked for a living night and day, rather than be a burden to any of you—not because 9 we have not the right to maintenance, but to set an example for you to imitate. For even 10 during our stay with you we laid down the rule: the man who will not work shall not eat. We mention this because we hear that 11 some of your number are idling their time away, minding everybody's business but their own. To all such we give these orders, 12 and we appeal to them in the name of the Lord Jesus Christ to work quietly for their living.

A word of warning

But you, my friends, must never tire of doing 13 right. If anyone disobeys our instructions 14 given by letter, mark him well, and have no dealings with him until he is ashamed of himself. I do not mean treat him as an enemy, 15 but give him friendly advice, as one of the family. May the Lord of peace himself give 16 you peace at all times and in all ways.[c] The Lord be with you all.

The greeting is in my own hand, signed 17 with my name, PAUL; this authenticates all my letters; this is how I write. The grace[d] 18 of our Lord Jesus Christ be with you all.

b Some witnesses read because God chose you as his firstfruits . . . wherever you may be.   d Or . . . letters. My message is this: the grace . . .   c Some witnesses read at all times,

THE FIRST LETTER OF PAUL TO

TIMOTHY

1 FROM PAUL, apostle of Christ Jesus by command of God our Saviour and Christ
2 Jesus our hope, to Timothy his true-born son in the faith.

Grace, mercy, and peace to you from God the Father and Christ Jesus our Lord.

The law and its purpose

3 When I was starting for Macedonia, I urged you to stay on at Ephesus. You were to command certain persons to give up teach-
4 ing erroneous doctrines and studying those interminable myths and genealogies, which issue in mere speculation and cannot make known God's plan for us, which works through faith.*a*
5 The aim and object of this command is the love which springs from a clean heart, from a good conscience, and from faith that
6 is genuine. Through falling short of these, some people have gone astray into a wilder-
7 ness of words. They set out to be teachers of the moral law, without understanding either the words they use or the subjects about which they are so dogmatic.
8 We all know that the law is an excellent
9 thing, provided we treat it as law, recognizing that it is not aimed at good citizens, but at the lawless and unruly, the impious and sinful, the irreligious and worldly; at parri-
10 cides and matricides, murderers and fornicators, perverts, kidnappers, liars, perjurers —in fact all whose behaviour flouts the
11 wholesome teaching which conforms with the gospel entrusted to me, the gospel which tells of the glory of God in his eternal felicity.

Paul's gratitude to Christ

12 I thank him who has made me equal to the task, Christ Jesus our Lord; I thank him for judging me worthy of this trust and appoint-
13 ing me to his service—although in the past I had met him with abuse and persecution and outrage. But because I acted ignorantly
14 in unbelief I was dealt with mercifully; the grace of our Lord was lavished upon me, with the faith and love which are ours in Christ Jesus.
15 Here are words you may trust, words that merit full acceptance: 'Christ Jesus came into the world to save sinners'; and
16 among them I stand first. But I was mercifully dealt with for this very purpose, that Jesus Christ might find in me the first

occasion for displaying all his patience, and that I might be typical of all who were in future to have faith in him and gain eternal life. Now to the King of all worlds, immortal, 17 invisible, the only God, be honour and glory for ever and ever! Amen.

A personal word to Timothy

This charge, son Timothy, I lay upon you, 18 following that prophetic utterance which first pointed you out to me. So fight gal- 19 lantly, armed with faith and a good conscience. It was through spurning conscience that certain persons made shipwreck of their faith, among them Hymenaeus and Alex- 20 ander, whom I consigned to Satan, in the hope that through this discipline they might learn not to be blasphemous.

The prayers of the church

First of all, then, I urge that petitions, **2** prayers, intercessions, and thanksgivings be 2 offered for all men; for sovereigns and all in high office, that we may lead a tranquil and quiet life in full observance of religion and high standards of morality. Such prayer is 3 right, and approved by God our Saviour, whose will it is that all men should find 4 salvation and come to know the truth. For 5 there is one God, and also one mediator between God and men, Christ Jesus, himself man, who sacrificed himself to win free- 6 dom for all mankind, so providing, at the fitting time, proof of the divine purpose; of 7 this I was appointed herald and apostle (this is no lie, but the truth), to instruct the nations in the true faith.

It is my desire, therefore, that everywhere 8 prayers be said by the men of the congregation, who shall lift up their hands with a pure intention, excluding angry or quarrelsome thoughts. Women again must dress in be- 9 coming manner, modestly and soberly, not with elaborate hair-styles, not decked out with gold or pearls, or expensive clothes, but with good deeds, as befits women who 10 claim to be religious. A woman must be a 11 learner, listening quietly and with due submission. I do not permit a woman to be a 12 teacher, nor must woman domineer over man; she should be quiet. For Adam was created first, and Eve afterwards; and it was 13 not Adam who was deceived; it was the woman who, yielding to deception, fell into

a Or cannot promote the faithful discharge of God's stewardship.

15 sin. Yet she will be saved through mother-hood[b]—if only women continue in faith,[c] love, and holiness, with a sober mind.

Character of a church leader

3 There is a popular saying:[d] 'To aspire to
2 leadership is an honourable ambition.' Our leader, therefore, or bishop, must be above reproach, faithful to his one wife,[e] sober, temperate, courteous, hospitable, and a good
3 teacher; he must not be given to drink, or a brawler, but of a forbearing disposition, avoiding quarrels, and no lover of money.
4 He must be one who manages his own household well and wins obedience from his children, and a man of the highest principles.
5 If a man does not know how to control his own family, how can he look after a congre-
6 gation of God's people? He must not be a convert newly baptized, for fear the sin of conceit should bring upon him a judgement
7 contrived by the devil.[f] He must moreover have a good reputation with the non-Christian public, so that he may not be exposed to scandal and get caught in the devil's snare.

Character of a deacon

8 Deacons, likewise, must be men of high principle, not indulging in double talk, given neither to excessive drinking nor to money-
9 grubbing. They must be men who combine a clear conscience with a firm hold on the
10 deep truths of our faith. No less than bishops, they must first undergo a scrutiny, and if there is no mark against them, they may
11 serve. Their wives,[g] equally, must be women of high principle, who will not talk scandal,
12 sober and trustworthy in every way. A deacon must be faithful to his one wife,[e] and good at managing his children and his
13 own household. For deacons with a good record of service may claim a high standing and the right to speak openly on matters of the Christian faith.

The mystery of our religion

4 I am hoping to come to you before long,
5 but I write this in case I am delayed, to let you know how men ought to conduct themselves in God's household, that is, the church of the living God, the pillar and bulwark of
6 the truth. And great beyond all question is the mystery of our religion:

'He who was manifested in the body,
vindicated in the spirit,
seen by angels;

who was proclaimed among the nations,
believed in throughout the world,
glorified in high heaven.'

How to counter subversive doctrines

The Spirit says expressly that in after times 4 some will desert from the faith and give their minds to subversive doctrines inspired by devils, through the specious falsehoods 2 of men whose own conscience is branded with the devil's sign. They forbid marriage 3 and inculcate abstinence from certain foods, though God created them to be enjoyed with thanksgiving by believers who have inward knowledge of the truth. For everything that 4 God created is good, and nothing is to be rejected when it is taken with thanksgiving, since it is hallowed by God's own word and 5 by prayer.

Limitless benefits of religion

By offering such advice as this to the brother-6 hood you will prove a good servant of Christ Jesus, bred in the precepts of our faith and of the sound instruction which you have followed. Have nothing to do with those 7 godless myths, fit only for old women. Keep yourself in training for the practice of reli-gion. The training of the body does bring 8 limited benefit, but the benefits of religion are without limit, since it holds promise not only for this life but for the life to come. Here are words you may trust, words that 9 merit full acceptance: 'With this before us 10 we labour and struggle,[h] because[i] we have set our hope on the living God, who is the Saviour of all men'—the Saviour, above all, of believers.

A further word for Timothy

Pass on these orders and these teachings. 11 Let no one slight you because you are young, 12 but make yourself an example to believers in speech and behaviour, in love, fidelity, and purity. Until I arrive devote your atten-13 tion to the public reading of the scriptures, to exhortation, and to teaching. Do not 14 neglect the spiritual endowment you possess, which was given you, under the guidance of prophecy, through the laying on of the hands of the elders as a body.[j]

Make these matters your business and 15 your absorbing interest, so that your pro-gress may be plain to all. Persevere in them, 16 keeping close watch on yourself and your teaching; by doing so you will further the salvation of yourself and your hearers.

b Or saved through the Birth of the Child, or brought safely through childbirth.   c Or if only husband and wife continue in mutual fidelity . . .   d Some witnesses read Here are words you may trust, which keep interpreters attach to the end of the preceding paragraph.   e Or married to one wife, or married only once. f Or the judgement once passed on the devil.   g Or . . . serve. Deaconesses . . .   h Some witnesses read suffer reproach.   i Or since 'It holds promise . . . to come.' These are words . . . acceptance. For this is the aim of all our labour and struggle, since . . .   j Or through your ordination as an elder.

5 Never be harsh with an elder; appeal to him as if he were your father. Treat the
2 younger men as brothers, the older women as mothers, and the younger as your sisters, in all purity.

Providing for dependent relatives

3 The status of widow is to be granted only to widows who are such in the full sense.
4 But if a widow has children or grandchildren, then they should learn as their first duty to show loyalty to the family and to repay what they owe to their parents and grandparents;
5 for this God approves. A widow, however, in the full sense, one who is alone in the world, has all her hope set on God, and regularly attends the meetings for prayer
6 and worship night and day. But a widow given over to self-indulgence is as good as
7 dead. Add these orders to the rest, so that
8 the widows may be above reproach. But if anyone does not make provision for his relations, and especially for members of his own household, he has denied the faith and is worse than an unbeliever.
9 A widow should not be put on the roll under sixty years of age. She must have been
10 faithful in marriage to one man, and must produce evidence of good deeds performed, showing whether she has had the care of children, or given hospitality, or washed the feet of God's people, or supported those in distress—in short, whether she has taken every opportunity of doing good.
11 Younger widows may not be placed on the roll. For when their passions draw them
12 away from Christ, they hanker after marriage and stand condemned for breaking
13 their troth with him. Moreover, in going round from house to house they learn to be idle, and worse than idle, gossips and busybodies, speaking of things better left un-
14 spoken. It is my wish, therefore, that young widows shall marry again, have children, and preside over a home; then they will give
15 no opponent occasion for slander. For there have in fact been some who have taken the wrong turning and gone to the devil.
16 If a Christian man or woman has widows in the family, he must support them himself;[k] the congregation must be relieved of the burden, so that it may be free to support those who are widows in the full sense of the term.

Pastoral responsibility

17 Elders who do well as leaders should be reckoned worthy of a double stipend, in particular those who labour at preaching
18 and teaching. For Scripture says, 'You shall not muzzle a threshing ox'; and besides, 'the worker earns his pay'.

Do not entertain a charge against an elder 19 unless it is supported by two or three witnesses. Those who commit sins you must 20 expose publicly, to put fear into the others. Before God and Christ Jesus and the angels 21 who are his chosen, I solemnly charge you, maintain these rules, and never pre-judge the issue, but act with strict impartiality. Do not be over-hasty in laying on hands in 22 ordination,[l] or you may find yourself responsible for other people's misdeeds; keep your own hands clean.

Stop drinking nothing but water; take 23 a little wine for your digestion, for your frequent ailments.

While there are people whose offences are 24 so obvious that they run before them into court, there are others whose offences have not yet overtaken them. Similarly, good 25 deeds are obvious, or even if they are not, they cannot be concealed for ever.

All who wear the yoke of slavery must **6** count their own masters worthy of all respect, so that the name of God and the Christian teaching are not brought into disrepute. If the masters are believers, the 2 slaves must not respect them any less for being their Christian brothers. Quite the contrary; they must be all the better servants because those who receive the benefit of their service are one with them in faith and love.

Snares to be avoided

This is what you are to teach and preach. If 3 anyone is teaching otherwise, and will not give his mind to wholesome precepts—I mean those of our Lord Jesus Christ—and to good religious teaching, I call him a 4 pompous ignoramus. He is morbidly keen on mere verbal questions and quibbles, which give rise to jealousy, quarrelling, slander, base suspicions, and endless wran- 5 gles: all typical of men who have let their reasoning powers become atrophied and have lost grip of the truth. They think religion should yield dividends; and of 6 course religion does yield high dividends, but only to the man whose resources are within him. We brought nothing into the 7 world; for that matter we cannot take anything with us when we leave, but if we have 8 food and covering we may rest content. Those who want to be rich fall into tempta- 9 tions and snares and many foolish harmful desires which plunge men into ruin and perdition. The love of money is the root of 10 all evil things, and there are some who in reaching for it have wandered from the faith and spiked themselves on many thorny griefs.

---

k Some witnesses read If a Christian woman has widows in her family, she must support them herself.   *l Or* in restoring an offender by the laying on of hands.

The great race of faith

11 But you, man of God, must shun all this, and pursue justice, piety, fidelity, love, fortitude, 12 and gentleness. Run the great race of faith and take hold of eternal life. For to this you were called; and you confessed your 13 faith nobly before many witnesses. Now in the presence of God, who gives life to all things, and of Jesus Christ, who himself made the same noble confession and gave his testimony to it before Pontius Pilate, 14 I charge you to obey your orders irreproachably and without fault until our Lord Jesus 15 Christ appears. That appearance God will bring to pass in his own good time—God who in eternal felicity alone holds sway. 16 He is King of kings and Lord of lords; he alone possesses immortality, dwelling in unapproachable light. No man has ever seen or ever can see him. To him be honour and might for ever! Amen.

A word to the rich

Instruct those who are rich in this world's 17 goods not to be proud, and not to fix their hopes on so uncertain a thing as money, but upon God, who endows us richly with all things to enjoy. Tell them to do good and 18 to grow rich in noble actions, to be ready to give away and to share, and so acquire a 19 treasure which will form a good foundation for the future. Thus they will grasp the life which is life indeed.

Conclusion

Timothy, keep safe that which has been 20 entrusted to you. Turn a deaf ear to empty and worldly chatter, and the contradictions of so-called 'knowledge', for many who 21 lay claim to it have shot far wide of the faith.

Grace be with you all!

THE SECOND LETTER OF PAUL TO

TIMOTHY

1 FROM PAUL, apostle of Jesus Christ by the will of God, whose promise of life is ful- 2 filled in Christ Jesus, to Timothy his dear son.

Grace, mercy, and peace to you from God the Father and our Lord Jesus Christ.

Thanksgiving

3 I thank God—whom I, like my forefathers, worship with a pure intention— when I mention you in my prayers; this I 4 do constantly night and day. And when I remember the tears you shed, I long to see you again to make my happiness complete. 5 I am reminded of the sincerity of your faith, a faith which was alive in Lois your grandmother and Eunice your mother before you, and which, I am confident, lives in you also.

A word of encouragement

6 That is why I now remind you to stir into flame the gift of God which is within you 7 through the laying on of my hands. For the spirit that God gave us is no craven spirit, but one to inspire strength, love, and self- 8 discipline. So never be ashamed of your testimony to our Lord, nor of me his prisoner,

but take your share of suffering for the sake of the Gospel, in the strength that comes from God. It is he who brought us salvation 9 and called us to a dedicated life, not for any merit of ours but of his own purpose and his own grace, which was granted to us in Christ Jesus from all eternity, but has now at 10 length been brought fully into view by the appearance on earth of our Saviour Jesus Christ. For he has broken the power of death and brought life and immortality to light through the Gospel.

Paul's plight

Of this Gospel I, by his appointment, am 11 herald, apostle, and teacher. That is the 12 reason for my present plight; but I am not ashamed of it, because I know who it is in whom[a] I have trusted, and am confident of his power to keep safe what he has put into my charge,[b] until the great Day. Keep 13 before you an outline of the sound teaching which[c] you heard from me, living by the faith and love which are ours in Christ Jesus. Guard the treasure put into our charge, with 14 the help of the Holy Spirit dwelling within us.

As you know, everyone in the province of 15 Asia deserted me, including Phygelus and

a *Or* I know the one whom . . .   b *Or* what I have put into his charge.   c *Or* Keep before you as a model of sound teaching that which . . .

16 Hermogenes. But may the Lord's mercy rest on the house of Onesiphorus! He has often relieved me in my troubles. He was not 17 ashamed to visit a prisoner, but took pains to search me out when he came to Rome, 18 and found me. I pray that the Lord may grant him to find mercy from the Lord on the great Day. The many services he rendered at Ephesus you know better than I could tell you.

Facing hardship

2 Now therefore, my son, take strength from the grace of God which is ours in Christ

2 Jesus. You heard my teaching in the presence of many witnesses; put that teaching into the charge of men you can trust, such men as will be competent to teach others.
3 Take your share of hardship, like a good 4 soldier of Christ Jesus. A soldier on active service will not let himself be involved in civilian affairs; he must be wholly at his 5 commanding officer's disposal. Again, no athlete can win a prize unless he has kept the 6 rules. The farmer who gives his labour has 7 first claim on the crop. Reflect on what I say, for the Lord will help you to full understanding.
8 Remember Jesus Christ, risen from the dead, born of David's line. This is the theme 9 of my gospel, in whose service I am exposed to hardship, even to the point of being shut up like a common criminal; but the word of 10 God is not shut up. And I endure it all for the sake of God's chosen ones, with this end in view, that they too may attain the glorious and eternal salvation which is in Christ Jesus.
11 Here are words you may trust:

'If we died with him, we shall live with him;
12 if we endure, we shall reign with him.
If we deny him, he will deny us.
13 If we are faithless, he keeps faith,
for he cannot deny himself.'

A firm foundation

Go on reminding people of this, and charge 14 them solemnly before God to stop disputing about mere words; it does no good, and is the ruin of those who listen. Try hard to 15 show yourself worthy of God's approval, as a labourer who need not be ashamed; be straightforward in your proclamation of the truth. Avoid empty and worldly chatter; 16 those who indulge in it will stray further and further into godless courses, and the infec- 17 tion of their teaching will spread like a gangrene. Such are Hymenaeus and Phile- tus; they have shot wide of the truth in 18 saying that our resurrection has already taken place, and are upsetting people's faith. But God has laid a foundation, and it stands 19 firm, with this inscription: 'The Lord knows his own', and, 'Everyone who takes the Lord's name upon his lips must forsake wickedness.' Now in any great house there 20

are not only utensils of gold and silver, but also others of wood or earthenware; the former are valued, the latter held cheap. To 21 be among those which are valued and dedi- cated, a thing of use to the Master of the house, a man must cleanse himself from all those evil things;[d] then he will be fit for any honourable purpose.
Turn from the wayward impulses of youth, 22 and pursue justice, integrity, love, and peace with all who invoke the Lord in singleness of mind. Have nothing to do with foolish 2: and ignorant speculations. You know they breed quarrels, and the servant of the Lord 24 must not be quarrelsome, but kindly to- wards all. He should be a good teacher, tolerant, and gentle when discipline is 2: needed for the refractory. The Lord may grant them a change of heart and show them the truth, and thus they may come to their 2

d Or must separate himself from these persons.

senses and escape from the devil's snare, in which they have been caught and held at his will.*

A time of troubles

3 You must face the fact: the final age of this
2 world is to be a time of troubles. Men will love nothing but money and self; they will be arrogant, boastful, and abusive; with no respect for parents, no gratitude, no piety,
3 no natural affection; they will be implacable in their hatreds, scandal-mongers, intemperate and fierce, strangers to all goodness,
4 traitors, adventurers, swollen with self-importance. They will be men who put
5 pleasure in the place of God, men who preserve the outward form of religion, but are a standing denial of its reality. Keep clear
6 of men like these. They are the sort that insinuate themselves into private houses and there get miserable women into their clutches, women burdened with a sinful past, and led
7 on by all kinds of desires, who are always wanting to be taught, but are incapable
8 of reaching a knowledge of the truth. As Jannes and Jambres defied Moses, so these men defy the truth; they have lost the power to reason, and they cannot pass the tests of
9 faith. But their successes will be short-lived,

for, like those opponents of Moses, they will come to be recognized by everyone for the fools they are.

Steadfastness under persecution

But you, my son, have followed, step by 10 step, my teaching and my manner of life, my resolution, my faith, patience, and spirit of love, and my fortitude under persecutions 11 and sufferings—all that I went through at Antioch, at Iconium, at Lystra, all the persecutions I endured; and the Lord rescued me out of them all. Yes, persecution will 12 come to all who want to live a godly life as Christians, whereas wicked men and char- 13 latans will make progress from bad to worse, deceiving and deceived. But for your part, 14 stand by the truths you have learned and are assured of. Remember from whom you learned them; remember that from early 15 childhood you have been familiar with the sacred writings which have power to make you wise and lead you to salvation through faith in Christ Jesus. Every inspired scripture 16 has its use for teaching the truth and refuting error, or for reformation of manners and discipline in right living, so that the man 17 who belongs to God may be efficient and equipped for good work of every kind.

e Or escape from the devil's snare, caught now by God and made subject to his will.

In an ancient library (2 Tim. 4. 13)

Proclaim the message, press it home

4 Before God, and before Christ Jesus who is to judge men living and dead, I charge you solemnly by his coming appearance and his 2 reign, proclaim the message, press it home on all occasions,*f* convenient or inconvenient, use argument, reproof, and appeal, with all the patience that the work of teaching 3 requires. For the time will come when they will not stand wholesome teaching, but will follow their own fancy and gather a crowd 4 of teachers to tickle their ears. They will stop their ears to the truth and turn to mythology. 5 But you yourself must keep calm and sane at all times; face hardship, work to spread the Gospel, and do all the duties of your calling.

Nearing the end

6 As for me, already my life is being poured out on the altar, and the hour for my de- 7 parture is upon me. I have run the great race, I have finished the course, I have kept faith. 8 And now the prize awaits me, the garland of righteousness which the Lord, the all-just Judge, will award me on that great Day; and it is not for me alone, but for all who have set their hearts on his coming appearance.

Personal requests

9 10 Do your best to join me soon; for Demas has deserted me because his heart was set on this world; he has gone to Thessalonica, Crescens to Galatia,*g* Titus to Dalmatia; 11 I have no one with me but Luke. Pick up Mark and bring him with you, for I find

him a useful assistant. Tychicus I have sent 12 to Ephesus. When you come, bring the cloak 13 I left with Carpus at Troas, and the books, above all my notebooks.

'The Lord stood by me'

Alexander the copper-smith did me a great 14 deal of harm. Retribution will fall upon him from the Lord. You had better be on your 15 guard against him too, for he violently opposed everything I said. At the first hear- 16 ing of my case no one came into court to support me; they all left me in the lurch; I pray that it may not be held against them. But the Lord stood by me and lent me 17 strength, so that I might be his instrument in making the full proclamation of the Gospel for the whole pagan world to hear; and thus I was rescued out of the lion's jaws. And the Lord will rescue me from every 18 attempt to do me harm, and keep me safe until his heavenly reign begins.*h* Glory to him for ever and ever! Amen.

Final greetings

Greetings to Prisca and Aquila, and the 19 household of Onesiphorus.

Erastus stayed behind at Corinth, and I 20 left Trophimus ill at Miletus. Do try to get 21 here before winter.

Greetings from Eubulus, Pudens, Linus, and Claudia, and from all the brotherhood here.

The Lord be with your spirit. Grace be 22 with you all!

THE LETTER OF PAUL TO
TITUS

1 FROM PAUL, servant of God and apostle of Jesus Christ, marked as such by faith and knowledge and hope—the faith of God's chosen people, knowledge of the truth as 2 our religion has it, and the hope of eternal life.*a* Yes, it is eternal life that God, who 3 cannot lie, promised long ages ago, and now in his own good time he has openly declared himself in the proclamation which was entrusted to me by ordinance of God our Saviour.

4 To Titus, my true-born son in the faith which we share, grace and peace from

God our Father and Christ Jesus our Saviour.

Character of an elder

My intention in leaving you behind in 5 Crete was that you should set in order what was left over, and in particular should institute elders in each town. In doing so, observe the tests I prescribed: is he a man 6 of unimpeachable character, faithful to his one wife,*b* the father of children who are believers, who are under no imputation of loose living, and are not out of control?

---

f Or be on duty at all times. *g Or* Gaul; *some witnesses read* Gallia. *h Or* from all that evil can do, and bring me safely into his heavenly kingdom.

a Or apostle of Jesus Christ, to bring God's chosen people to faith and to a knowledge of the truth as our religion has it, with its hope for eternal life. *b See note on 1 Timothy 3. 2.*

7 For as God's steward a bishop must be a man of unimpeachable character. He must not be overbearing or short-tempered; he must be no drinker, no brawler, no money-grubber, but hospitable, right-minded, temperate, just, devout, and self-controlled.

8

9 He must adhere to the true doctrine, so that he may be well able both to move his hearers with wholesome teaching and to confute objectors.

Call for discipline

10 There are all too many, especially among Jewish converts, who are out of all control; they talk wildly and lead men's minds astray.

11 Such men must be curbed, because they are ruining whole families by teaching things they should not, and all for sordid gain.

12 It was a Cretan prophet, one of their own countrymen, who said, 'Cretans were always

13 liars, vicious brutes, lazy gluttons'—and he told the truth! All the more reason why you should pull them up sharply, so that they

14 may come to a sane belief, instead of lending their ears to Jewish myths and commandments of merely human origin, the work of men who turn their backs upon the truth.

15 To the pure all things are pure; but nothing is pure to the tainted minds of disbelievers, tainted alike in reason and

16 conscience. They profess to acknowledge God, but deny him by their actions. Their detestable obstinacy disqualifies them for any good work.

Older men and women

2 For your own part, what you say must be

2 in keeping with wholesome doctrine. Let the older men know that they should be sober, high-principled, and temperate, sound

3 in faith, in love, and in endurance. The older women, similarly, should be reverent in their bearing, not scandal-mongers or slaves to strong drink; they must set a high standard,

4 and school the younger women to be loving

5 wives and mothers, temperate, chaste, and kind, busy at home, respecting the authority of their own husbands. Thus the Gospel will not be brought into disrepute.

Younger men

6 Urge the younger men, similarly, to be

7 temperate in all things, and set them a good example yourself. In your teaching, you

8 must show integrity and high principle, and use wholesome speech to which none can take exception. This will shame any opponent, when he finds not a word to say to our discredit.

Slaves

Tell slaves to respect their masters' authority 9 in everything, and to comply with their demands without answering back; not to 10 pilfer, but to show themselves strictly honest and trustworthy; for in all such ways they will add lustre to the doctrine of God our Saviour.

The happy fulfilment of our hope

For the grace of God has dawned upon the 11 world with healing for all mankind; and by 12 it we are disciplined to renounce godless ways and worldly desires, and to live a life of temperance, honesty, and godliness in the present age, looking forward to the 13 happy fulfilment of our hope when the splendour of our great God and Saviour[c] Christ Jesus will appear. He it is who sacri- 14 ficed himself for us, to set us free from all wickedness and to make us a pure people marked out for his own, eager to do good.

These, then, are your themes; urge them 15 and argue them. And speak with authority: let no one slight you.

Practical directions

Remind them to be submissive to the govern- 3 ment and the authorities, to obey them, and to be ready for any honourable form of work;[d] to slander no one, not to pick 2 quarrels, to show forbearance and a consistently gentle disposition towards all men.

For at one time we ourselves in our folly 3 and obstinacy were all astray. We were slaves to passions and pleasures of every kind. Our days were passed in malice and envy; we were odious ourselves and we hated one another. But when the kindness 4 and generosity of God our Saviour dawned upon the world, then, not for any good deeds 5 of our own, but because he was merciful, he saved us through the water of rebirth and the renewing power of[e] the Holy Spirit. For 6 he sent down the Spirit upon us plentifully through Jesus Christ our Saviour, so that, 7 justified by his grace, we might in hope become heirs to eternal life. These are words 8 you may trust.

Such are the points I should wish you to insist on. Those who have come to believe in God should see that they engage in honourable occupations, which are not only honourable in themselves, but also useful to their fellow-men.[f] But steer clear of 9 foolish speculations, genealogies, quarrels, and controversies over the Law; they are unprofitable and pointless.

A heretic should be warned once, and 10 once again; after that, have done with him,

---

c *Or* of the great God and our Saviour . . .   d *Or* ready always to do good.   e *Or* the water of rebirth and of renewal by . . .   f *Or* should make it their business to practise virtue. These precepts are good in themselves and useful to society.

11 recognizing that a man of that sort has a distorted mind and stands self-condemned in his sin.

Final note and greeting

12 When I send Artemas to you, or Tychicus, make haste to join me at Nicopolis, for that is where I have determined to spend the 13 winter. Do your utmost to help Zenas the lawyer and Apollos on their travels, and see that they are not short of anything. And 14 our own people must be taught to engage in honest employment to produce the necessities of life; they must not be unproductive.

All who are with me send you greetings. 15 My greetings to those who are our friends in truth.*g* Grace be with you all!

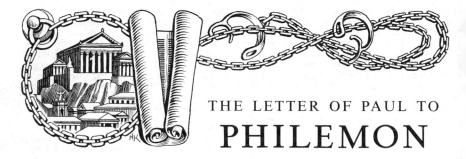

THE LETTER OF PAUL TO
PHILEMON

Slave into brother

1 FROM PAUL, a prisoner of Christ Jesus, and our colleague Timothy, to Philemon our 2 dear friend and fellow-worker, and Apphia our sister, and Archippus our comrade-in-arms, and the congregation at your house. 3 Grace to you and peace from God our Father and the Lord Jesus Christ.

4 I thank my God always when I mention 5 you in my prayers, for I hear of your love and faith towards the Lord Jesus and to- 6 wards all God's people. My prayer is that your fellowship with us in our common faith may deepen the understanding of all the blessings that our union with Christ 7 brings us.*a* For I am delighted and encouraged by your love; through you, my brother, God's people have been much refreshed.

8 Accordingly, although in Christ I might 9 make bold to point out your duty, yet, because of that same love, I would rather appeal to you. Yes, I, Paul, ambassador as I am of Christ Jesus—and now his prisoner 10 —appeal to you about my child, whose father I have become in this prison. 11 I mean Onesimus, once so little use to you, but now useful indeed, both to you 12 and to me. I am sending him back to you, and in doing so I am sending a part of my- 13 self. I should have liked to keep him with

me, to look after me as you would wish, here in prison for the Gospel. But I would 14 rather do nothing without your consent, so that your kindness may be a matter not of compulsion, but of your own free will. For perhaps this is why you lost him for a 15 time, that you might have him back for good, no longer as a slave, but as more than a 16 slave—as a dear brother, very dear indeed to me and how much dearer to you, both as man and as Christian.

If, then, you count me partner in the 17 faith, welcome him as you would welcome me. And if he has done you any wrong or is 18 in your debt, put that down to my account. Here is my signature, PAUL; I undertake to 19 repay—not to mention that you owe your very self to me as well. Now brother, as a 20 Christian, be generous with me, and relieve my anxiety; we are both in Christ!

I write to you confident that you will meet 21 my wishes; I know that you will in fact do better than I ask. And one thing more: have 22 a room ready for me, for I hope that, in answer to your prayers, God will grant me to you.

Epaphras, Christ's captive like myself, 23 sends you greetings. So do Mark, Aristar- 24 chus, Demas, and Luke, my fellow-workers. The grace of the Lord Jesus Christ be 25 with your spirit!

g Or our friends in the faith.

a Or that bring us to Christ.

A LETTER TO
HEBREWS

The Son of God

1 WHEN IN former times God spoke to our forefathers, he spoke in fragmentary and varied fashion through the prophets. 2 But in this the final age he has spoken to us in the Son whom he has made heir to the whole universe, and through whom he 3 created all orders of existence: the Son who is the effulgence of God's splendour and the stamp of God's very being, and sustains^a the universe by his word of power. When he had brought about the purgation of sins, he took his seat at the right hand of Majesty 4 on high, raised as far above the angels, as the title he has inherited is superior to theirs.

5 For God never said to any angel, 'Thou art my Son; today I have begotten thee', or again, 'I will be father to him, and he 6 shall be my son.' Again, when he presents the first-born to the world, he says, 'Let all 7 the angels of God pay him homage.' Of the angels he says,

'He who makes his angels winds,
and his ministers a fiery flame';

8 but of the Son,

'Thy throne, O God, is for ever and ever,
and the sceptre^b of justice is the sceptre of his
kingdom.
9 Thou hast loved right and hated wrong;
therefore, O God, thy God^c has set thee
above thy fellows,
by anointing with the oil of exultation.'

10 And again,

'By thee, Lord, were earth's foundations laid
of old,
and the heavens are the work of thy hands.
11 They shall pass away, but thou endurest;
like clothes they shall all grow old;
12 thou shalt fold them up like a cloak;
yes, they shall be changed like any garment.
But thou art the same, and thy years shall
have no end.'

To which of the angels has he ever said, 13 'Sit at my right hand until I make thy enemies thy footstool'? What are they all 14 but ministrant spirits, sent out to serve, for the sake of those who are to inherit salvation?

Thus we are bound to pay all the more **2** heed to what we have been told, for fear of drifting from our course. For if the word 2 spoken through angels had such force that any transgression or disobedience met with due retribution, what escape can there be 3 for us if we ignore a deliverance so great? For this deliverance was first announced through the lips of the Lord himself; those who heard him confirmed it to us, and 4 God added his testimony by signs, by miracles, by manifold works of power, and by distributing the gifts of the Holy Spirit at his own will.

The son of man

For it is not to angels that he has subjected 5 the world to come, which is our theme. But 6 there is somewhere a solemn assurance which runs:

'What is man, that thou rememberest him,
or the son of man, that thou hast regard to
him?
Thou didst make him for a short while lower 7
than the angels;
thou didst crown him with glory and honour;
thou didst put all things in subjection be- 8
neath his feet.'

For in subjecting all things to him, he left nothing that is not subject. But in fact we do not yet see all things in subjection to man. In Jesus, however, we do see one who^d for 9 a short while was made lower than the angels, crowned now with glory and honour because he suffered death, so that, by God's gracious will, in tasting death he should stand^e for us all.

---

a Or bears along. *b Or* God is thy throne for ever and ever, and thy sceptre . . . *c Or* therefore
God who is thy God . . . *d Or* in subjection to him. But we see Jesus, who . . . *e Some witnesses*
read so that apart from God he should taste death . . .

Christ and his brother-men

10 It was clearly fitting that God for whom and through whom all things exist should, in bringing many sons to glory, make the leader who delivers them perfect through sufferings.
11 For a consecrating priest and those whom he consecrates are all of one stock; and that is why the Son does not shrink from calling
12 men his brothers, when he says, 'I will proclaim thy name to my brothers; in full
13 assembly I will sing thy praise'; and again, 'I will keep my trust fixed on him'; and again, 'Here am I, and the children whom
14 God has given me.' The children of a family share the same flesh and blood; and so he too shared ours, so that through death he might break the power of him who had death at his command, that is, the devil;
15 and might liberate those who, through fear of death, had all their lifetime been in servi-
16 tude. It is not angels, mark you, that he takes
17 to himself, but the sons of Abraham. And therefore he had to be made like these brothers of his in every way, so that he might be merciful and faithful as their high priest before God, to expiate the sins of the people.
18 For since he himself has passed through the test of suffering, he is able to help those who are meeting their test now.

Jesus and Moses

3 Therefore, brothers in the family of God, who share a heavenly calling, think of the Apostle and High Priest of the religion we
2 profess,*f* who was faithful to God who appointed him. Moses also was faithful in
3 God's household; and Jesus, of whom I speak, has been deemed worthy of greater honour than Moses, as the founder of a house enjoys more honour than his house-
4 hold. For every house has its founder; and
5 the founder of all is God. Moses, then, was faithful as a servitor in God's whole household; his task was to bear witness to the
6 words that God would speak; but Christ is faithful as a son, set over his household. And we are that household of his, if only we are fearless and keep our hope high.

God's promised rest

7 'Today', therefore, as the Holy Spirit says—

'Today if you hear his voice,
8 do not grow stubborn as in those days of rebellion,
at that time of testing in the desert,
9 where your forefathers tried me and tested me,
and saw*g* the things I did for forty years.

And so, I was indignant with that generation and I said, Their hearts are for ever astray; they would not discern my ways;
as I vowed in my anger, they shall never enter my rest.'

See to it, brothers, that no one among you has the wicked, faithless heart of a deserter from the living God; but day by day, while that word 'Today' still sounds in your ears, encourage one another, so that no one of you is made stubborn by the wiles of sin. For we have become Christ's part-ners*h* if only we keep our original confidence firm to the end.

When Scripture says, 'Today if you hear his voice, do not grow stubborn as in those days of rebellion', who, I ask, were those who heard and rebelled? All those, surely, whom Moses had led out of Egypt. And with whom was God indignant for forty years? With those, surely, who had sinned, whose bodies lay where they fell in the desert. And to whom did he vow that they should not enter his rest, if not to those who had refused to believe? We perceive that it was unbelief which prevented their entering.

Therefore we must have before us the fear that while the promise of entering his rest remains open, one or another among you should be found to have missed his chance. For indeed we have heard the good news, as they did. But in them the message they heard did no good, because it met with no faith in those who heard it. It is we, we who have become believers, who enter the rest referred to in the words, 'As I vowed in my anger, they shall never enter my rest.' Yet God's work has been finished ever since the world was created; for does not Scripture somewhere speak thus of the seventh day: 'God rested from all his work on the seventh day'?—and once again in the passage above we read, 'They shall never enter my rest.' The fact remains that someone must enter it, and since those who first heard the good news failed to enter through unbelief, God fixes another day. Speaking through the lips of David after many long years, he uses the words already quoted: 'Today if you hear his voice, do not grow stubborn.' If Joshua had given them rest, God would not thus have spoken of another day after that. Therefore, a sabbath rest still awaits the people of God; for anyone who enters God's rest, rests from his own work as God did from his. Let us then make every effort to enter that rest, so that no one may fall by following this evil example of unbelief.

For the word of God is alive and active.

---

f Or of him whom we confess as God's Envoy and High Priest.   *g Or* though they saw . . .   *h Or* have been given a share in Christ.

It cuts more keenly than any two-edged sword, piercing as far as the place where life and spirit, joints and marrow, divide. It sifts the purposes and thoughts of the 13 heart. There is nothing in creation that can hide from him; everything lies naked and exposed to the eyes of the One with whom we have to reckon.

A great high priest

14 Since therefore we have a great high priest who has passed through the heavens, Jesus the Son of God, let us hold fast to the 15 religion we profess. For ours is not a high priest unable to sympathize with our weaknesses, but one who, because of his likeness to us, has been tested every way,[i] only 16 without sin. Let us therefore boldly approach the throne of our gracious God, where we may receive mercy and in his grace find timely help.

Christ and Melchizedek

5 For every high priest is taken from among men and appointed their representative before God, to offer gifts and sacrifices for sins. 2 He is able to bear patiently with the ignorant and erring, since he too is beset by weakness; 3 and because of this he is bound to make sin-offerings for himself no less than for the 4 people. And nobody arrogates the honour to himself: he is called by God, as indeed 5 Aaron was. So it is with Christ: he did not confer upon himself the glory of becoming high priest; it was granted by God, who said to him, 'Thou art my Son; today I have be-6 gotten thee'; as also in another place he says, 'Thou art a priest for ever, in the succession 7 of Melchizedek.' In the days of his earthly life he offered up prayers and petitions, with loud cries and tears, to God who was able to deliver him from the grave. Because of his humble submission his prayer was heard: 8 son though he was, he learned obedience in 9 the school of suffering, and, once perfected, became the source of eternal salvation for 10 all who obey him, named by God high priest in the succession of Melchizedek.

11 About Melchizedek we have much to say, much that is difficult to explain, now that 12 you have grown so dull of hearing. For indeed, though by this time you ought to be teachers, you need someone to teach you the ABC of God's oracles over again; it has come to this, that you need milk instead of 13 solid food. Anyone who lives on milk, being an infant, does not know[j] what is right. 14 But grown men can take solid food; their perceptions are trained by long use to discriminate between good and evil.

Warning and encouragement

Let us then stop discussing the rudiments of 6 Christianity. We ought not to be laying over again the foundations of faith in God and of repentance from the deadness of our former ways, by instruction[k] about cleansing 2 rites and the laying-on-of-hands, about the resurrection of the dead and eternal judgement. Instead, let us advance towards maturity; and so we shall, if God permits. 3

For when men have once been enlightened, 4 when they have had a taste of the heavenly gift and a share in the Holy Spirit, when they have 5 experienced the goodness of God's word and the spiritual energies of the age to come, and 6 after all this have fallen away, it is impossible to bring them again to repentance; for with their own hands they are crucifying[l] the Son of God and making mock of his death. When 7 the earth drinks in the rain that falls upon it from time to time, and yields a useful crop to those for whom it is cultivated, it is receiving its share of blessing from God; but if it bears 8 thorns and thistles, it is worthless and God's curse hangs over it; the end of that is burning. But although we speak as we do, we are con-9 vinced that you, my friends, are in the better case, and this makes for your salvation. For 10 God would not be so unjust as to forget all that you did for love of his name, when you rendered service to his people, as you still do. But we long for every one of you to show the 11 same eager concern, until your hope is finally realized. We want you not to become lazy, 12 but to imitate those who, through faith and patience, are inheriting the promises.

The hope set before us

When God made his promise to Abraham, 13 he swore by himself, because he had no one greater to swear by: 'I vow that I will bless 14 you abundantly and multiply your descendants.' Thus it was that Abraham, after 15 patient waiting, attained the promise. Men 16 swear by a greater than themselves, and the oath provides a confirmation to end all dispute; and so God, desiring to show even 17 more clearly to the heirs of his promise how unchanging was his purpose, guaranteed it by oath. Here, then, are two irrevocable acts 18 in which God could not possibly play us false, to give powerful encouragement to us, who have claimed his protection by grasping[m] the hope set before us. That hope we 19 hold. It is like an anchor for our lives, an anchor safe and sure. It enters in through the veil, where Jesus has entered on our behalf 20 as forerunner, having become a high priest for ever in the succession of Melchizedek.

i Or who has been tested every way, as we are.   *j Or* is incompetent to speak of . . .   *k Or, according to some witnesses,* laying the foundations over again: repentance from the deadness of our former ways and faith in God, instruction . . .   *l Or* crucifying again.   *m Or* to give to us, who have claimed his protection, a powerful incentive to grasp . . .

Melchizedek and Abraham

7 This Melchizedek, king of Salem, priest of God Most High, met Abraham returning from the rout of the kings and blessed him;
2 and Abraham gave him a tithe of everything as his portion. His name, in the first place, means 'king of righteousness'; next he is
3 king of Salem, that is, 'king of peace'. He has no father, no mother, no lineage; his years have no beginning, his life no end. He is like the Son of God: he remains a priest for all time.
4   Consider now how great he must be for Abraham the patriarch to give him a tithe
5 of the finest of the spoil. The descendants of Levi who take the priestly office are commanded by the Law to tithe the people, that is, their kinsmen, although they too are
6 descendants of Abraham. But Melchizedek, though he does not trace his descent from them, has tithed Abraham himself, and given his blessing to the man who received the
7 promises; and beyond all dispute the lesser
8 is always blessed by the greater. Again, in the one instance tithes are received by men who must die; but in the other, by one whom
9 Scripture affirms to be alive. It might even be said that Levi, who receives tithes, has
10 himself been tithed through Abraham; for he was still in his ancestor's loins when Melchizedek met him.

Limitations of the Levitical priesthood

11 Now if perfection had been attainable through the Levitical priesthood (for it is on this basis that the people were given the Law), what further need would there have been to speak of another priest arising, in the succession of Melchizedek, instead of
12 the succession of Aaron? For a change of
13 priesthood must mean a change of law. And the one here spoken of belongs to a different tribe, no member of which has ever had any-
14 thing to do with the altar. For it is very evident that our Lord is sprung from Judah, a tribe to which Moses made no reference in speaking of priests.
15   The argument becomes still clearer, if the new priest who arises is one like Melchizedek,
16 owing his priesthood not to a system of earth-bound rules but to the power of a life
17 that cannot be destroyed. For here is the testimony: 'Thou art a priest for ever, in
18 the succession of Melchizedek.' The earlier rules are cancelled as impotent and useless,
19 since the Law brought nothing to perfection; and a better hope is introduced, through which we draw near to God.
20   How great a difference it makes that an
21 oath was sworn! There was no oath sworn when those others were made priests; but for this priest an oath was sworn, as Scripture says of him: 'The Lord has sworn and

will not go back on his word, "Thou art a priest for ever."' How far superior must 22 the covenant also be of which Jesus is the guarantor! Those other priests are appointed 23 in numerous succession, because they are prevented by death from continuing in office; but the priesthood which Jesus holds 24 is perpetual, because he remains for ever. That is why he is also able to save absolutely 25 those who approach God through him; he is always living to plead on their behalf.

Jesus fits our condition

Such a high priest does indeed fit our condition—devout, guileless, undefiled, separated from sinners, raised high above the heavens. He has no need to offer sacrifices 27 daily, as the high priests do, first for his own sins and then for those of the people; for this he did once and for all when he offered up himself. The high priests made by the 28 Law are men in all their frailty; but the priest appointed by the words of the oath which supersedes the Law is the Son, made perfect now for ever.

The two covenants

Now this is my main point: just such a high **8** priest we have, and he has taken his seat at

High priest of the Levitical priesthood

the right hand of the throne of Majesty in
2 the heavens, a ministrant in the real sanctuary, the tent pitched by the Lord and not by
3 man. Every high priest is appointed to offer gifts and sacrifices; hence, this one too must
4 have[n] something to offer. Now if he had been on earth, he would not even have been a priest, since there are already priests who offer the gifts which the Law prescribes,
5 though this they minister in a sanctuary which is only a copy and shadow of the heavenly. This is implied when Moses, about to erect the tent, is instructed by God: 'See to it that you make everything according to the pat-
6 tern shown you on the mountain.' But in fact the ministry which has fallen to Jesus is as far superior to theirs as are the covenant he mediates and the promises upon which it is legally secured.

7 Had that first covenant been faultless, there would have been no need to look for a
8 second in its place. But God, finding fault with them, says, 'The days are coming, says the Lord, when I will conclude a new covenant with the house of Israel and the house
9 of Judah. It will not be like the covenant I made with their forefathers when I took them by the hand to lead them out of Egypt; because they did not abide by the terms of that covenant, and I abandoned them, says
10 the Lord. For the covenant I will make with the house of Israel after those days, says the Lord, is this: I will set my laws in their understanding and write them on their hearts; and I will be their God, and they
11 shall be my people. And they shall not teach one another, saying to brother and fellow-citizen,[o] "Know the Lord!" For all
12 of them, high and low, shall know me; I will be merciful to their wicked deeds, and I will
13 remember their sins no more.' By speaking of a new covenant, he has pronounced the first one old; and anything that is growing old and ageing will shortly disappear.

The first covenant

9 The first covenant indeed had its ordinances of divine service and its sanctuary, but a
2 material sanctuary. For a tent was prepared —the first tent—in which was the lamp-stand, and the table with the bread of the Presence;
3 this is called the Holy Place. Beyond the second curtain was the tent called the Most
4 Holy Place. Here was a golden altar of incense, and the ark of the covenant plated all over with gold, in which were a golden jar containing the manna, and Aaron's staff which once budded, and the tablets of the
5 covenant; and above it the cherubim of God's glory, overshadowing the place of expiation. On these we cannot now enlarge.

Under this arrangement, the priests are 6 always entering the first tent in the discharge of their duties; but the second is entered only 7 once a year, and by the high priest alone, and even then he must take with him the blood which he offers on his own behalf and for the people's sins of ignorance. By this the 8 Holy Spirit signifies that so long as the earlier tent still stands, the way into the sanctuary remains unrevealed. All this is symbolic, 9 pointing to the present time. The offerings and sacrifices there prescribed cannot give the worshipper inward perfection. It is only 10 a matter of food and drink and various rites of cleansing—outward ordinances in force until the time of reformation.

The new covenant

But now Christ has come, high priest of 11 good things already in being.[p] The tent of his priesthood is a greater and more perfect one, not made by men's hands, that is, not belonging to this created world; the blood 12 of his sacrifice is his own blood, not the blood of goats and calves; and thus he has

entered the sanctuary once and for all and secured an eternal deliverance. For if the 13 blood of goats and bulls and the sprinkled ashes of a heifer have power to hallow those who have been defiled and restore their external purity, how much greater is the 14 power of the blood of Christ; he offered himself without blemish to God, a spiritual and eternal sacrifice; and his blood will cleanse our conscience from the deadness of our former ways and fit us for the service of the living God.

And therefore he is the mediator of a new 15 covenant, or testament, under which, now that there has been a death to bring deliverance from sins committed under the former covenant, those whom God has called may receive the promise of the eternal inheritance. For where there is a testament it is necessary 16

n Or must have had.　　o Some witnesses read brother and neighbour.　　p Some witnesses read good things which were (or are) to be.

for the death of the testator to be estab-
17 lished. A testament is operative only after
a death: it cannot possibly have force while
18 the testator is alive. Thus we find that the
former covenant itself was not inaugurated
19 without blood. For when, as the Law
directed, Moses had recited all the commandments to the people, he took the blood
of the calves, with water, scarlet wool, and
marjoram, and sprinkled the law-book itself
20 and all the people, saying, 'This is the blood
of the covenant which God has enjoined
21 upon you.' In the same way he also sprinkled
the tent and all the vessels of divine service
22 with blood. Indeed, according to the Law,
it might almost be said, everything is cleansed
by blood and without the shedding of blood
there is no forgiveness.

The once-and-for-all sacrifice of Christ

23 If, then, these sacrifices cleanse the copies
of heavenly things, those heavenly things
themselves require better sacrifices to cleanse
24 them. For Christ has entered, not that
sanctuary made by men's hands which is
only a symbol of the reality, but heaven itself, to appear now before God on our be-
25 half. Nor is he there to offer himself again

and again, as the high priest enters the
sanctuary year by year with blood not his
26 own. If that were so, he would have had to
suffer many times since the world was made.
But as it is, he has appeared once and for
all at the climax of history to abolish sin
27 by the sacrifice of himself. And as it is the
lot of men to die once, and after death comes
28 judgement, so Christ was offered once to
bear the burden of men's sins,[q] and will
appear a second time, sin done away, to
bring salvation to those who are watching
for him.

The new covenant replaces the old

10 For the law contains but a shadow, and no
true image,[r] of the good things which were
to come; it provides for the same sacrifices
year after year, and with these it can never
bring the worshippers to perfection for all
2 time.[s] If it could, these sacrifices would surely

have ceased to be offered, because the worshippers, cleansed once for all, would no
longer have any sense of sin. But instead, 3
in these sacrifices year after year sins are
brought to mind, because sins can never 4
be removed by the blood of bulls and
goats.

That is why, at his coming into the world, 5
he says:

'Sacrifice and offering thou didst not desire,
but thou hast prepared a body for me.
Whole-offerings and sin-offerings thou didst 6
not delight in.
Then I said, "Here am I: as it is written of 7
me in the scroll,
I have come, O God, to do thy will." '

First he says, 'Sacrifices and offerings, whole- 8
offerings and sin-offerings, thou didst not
desire nor delight in'—although the Law
prescribes them—and then he says, 'I have 9
come to do thy will.' He thus annuls the
former to establish the latter. And it is by 10
the will of God that we have been consecrated, through the offering of the body
of Jesus Christ once and for all.

Every priest stands performing his service 11
daily and offering time after time the same
sacrifices, which can never remove sins. But 12
Christ offered for all time one sacrifice for
sins, and took his seat at the right hand of
God, where he waits henceforth until his 13
enemies are made his footstool. For by one 14
offering he has perfected for all time those
who are thus consecrated. Here we have also 15
the testimony of the Holy Spirit: he first
says, 'This is the covenant which I will make 16
with them after those days, says the Lord:
I will set my laws in their hearts and write
them on their understanding'; then he adds,
'and their sins and wicked deeds I will 17
remember no more at all.' And where these 18
have been forgiven, there are offerings for
sin no longer.

Encouragement and warning

So now, my friends, the blood of Jesus 19
makes us free to enter boldly into the sanctuary by the new, living way which he has 20
opened for us through the curtain, the way
of his flesh.[t] We have, moreover, a great 21
priest set over the household of God; so 22
let us make our approach in sincerity of
heart and full assurance of faith, our guilty
hearts sprinkled clean, our bodies washed
with pure water. Let us be firm and un- 23
swerving in the confession of our hope, for
the Giver of the promise may be trusted.
We ought to see how each of us may best 24
arouse others to love and active goodness,
not staying away from our meetings, as 25

---

q Or to remove men's sins.   r One witness reads a shadow and likeness . . .   s Or bring to perfection the worshippers who come continually.   t Or through the curtain of his flesh.

some do, but rather encouraging one another, all the more because you see the Day drawing near.

26 For if we wilfully persist in sin after receiving the knowledge of the truth, no sacrifice
27 for sins remains: only a terrifying expectation of judgement and a fierce fire which
28 will consume God's enemies. If a man disregards the Law of Moses, he is put to death without pity on the evidence of two or three
29 witnesses. Think how much more severe a penalty that man will deserve who has trampled under foot the Son of God, profaned the blood of the covenant by which

he was consecrated, and affronted God's
30 gracious Spirit! For we know who it is that has said, 'Justice is mine: I will repay'; and
31 again, 'The Lord will judge his people.' It is a terrible thing to fall into the hands of the living God.

The need for endurance

32 Remember the days gone by, when, newly enlightened, you met the challenge of great
33 sufferings and held firm. Some of you were abused and tormented to make a public show, while others stood loyally by those
34 who were so treated. For indeed you shared the sufferings of the prisoners, and you cheerfully accepted the seizure of your possessions, knowing that you possessed something
35 better and more lasting. Do not then throw away your confidence, for it carries a great
36 reward. You need endurance, if you are to do God's will and win what he has promised.
37 For 'soon, very soon' (in the words of Scripture), 'he who is to come will come; he will
38 not delay; and by faith my righteous servant shall find life; but if a man shrinks back,
39 I take no pleasure in him.' But we are not among those who shrink back and are lost; we have the faith to make life our own.

Men of faith through the ages

11 And what is faith? Faith gives substance[u] to our hopes, and makes us certain of realities we do not see.
2 It is for their faith that the men of old stand on record.
3 By faith we perceive that the universe was fashioned by the word of God, so that the visible came forth from the invisible.
4 By faith Abel offered a sacrifice greater than Cain's, and through faith his goodness was attested, for his offerings had God's approval; and through faith he continued to speak after his death.
5 By faith Enoch was carried away to another life without passing through death; he was not to be found, because God had taken him. For it is the testimony of Scripture that before he was taken he had pleased
6 God, and without faith it is impossible to please him; for anyone who comes to God must believe that he exists and that he rewards those who search for him.
7 By faith Noah, divinely warned about the unseen future, took good heed and built an ark to save his household. Through his faith he put the whole world in the wrong, and made good his own claim to the righteousness which comes of faith.
8 By faith Abraham obeyed the call to go out to a land destined for himself and his heirs, and left home without knowing where
9 he was to go. By faith he settled as an alien in the land promised him, living in tents, as did Isaac and Jacob, who were heirs to the
10 same promise. For he was looking forward to the city with firm foundations, whose architect and builder is God.
11 By faith even Sarah herself received strength to conceive, though she was past the age, because she judged that he who had pro-
12 mised would keep faith; and therefore from one man, and one as good as dead, there sprang descendants numerous as the stars or as the countless grains of sand on the sea-shore.
13 All these persons died in faith. They were not yet in possession of the things promised, but had seen them far ahead and hailed them, and confessed themselves no more than
14 strangers or passing travellers on earth. Those who use such language show plainly that they
15 are looking for a country of their own. If their hearts had been in the country they had left, they could have found opportunity to
16 return. Instead, we find them longing for a better country—I mean, the heavenly one. That is why God is not ashamed to be called their God; for he has a city ready for them.
17 By faith Abraham, when the test came, offered up Isaac: he had received the promises, and yet he was on the point of offering

u Or assurance.

18 his only son, of whom he had been told, 'Through the line of Isaac your descendants 19 shall be traced.'ᵛ For he reckoned that God had power even to raise from the dead— and from the dead, he did, in a sense, receive him back.

20 By faith Isaac blessed Jacob and Esau and 21 spoke of things to come. By faith Jacob, as he was dying, blessed each of Joseph's sons, and worshipped God, leaning on the top of 22 his staff. By faith Joseph, at the end of his life, spoke of the departure of Israel from Egypt, and instructed them what to do with his bones.

23 By faith, when Moses was born, his parents hid him for three months, because they saw what a fine child he was; they were 24 not afraid of the king's edict. By faith Moses, when he grew up, refused to be called the 25 son of Pharaoh's daughter, preferring to suffer hardship with the people of God rather than enjoy the transient pleasures of 26 sin. He considered the stigma that rests on God's Anointed greater wealth than the treasures of Egypt, for his eyes were fixed 27 upon the coming day of recompense. By faith he left Egypt, and not because he feared the king's anger; for he was resolute, as one who saw the invisible God.

28 By faith he celebrated the Passover and sprinkled the blood, so that the destroying angel might not touch the first-born of 29 Israel. By faith they crossed the Red Sea as though it were dry land, whereas the Egyptians, when they attempted the crossing, were drowned.

30 By faith the walls of Jericho fell down after they had been encircled on seven successive 31 days. By faith the prostitute Rahab escaped the doom of the unbelievers, because she had given the spies a kindly welcome.

32 Need I say more? Time is too short for me to tell the stories of Gideon, Barak, Samson, and Jephthah, of David and Samuel and 33 prophets. Through faith they overthrew kingdoms, established justice, saw God's promises fulfilled. They muzzled ravening lions, 34 quenched the fury of fire, escaped death by the sword. Their weakness was turned to strength, they grew powerful in war, they 35 put foreign armies to rout. Women received back their dead raised to life. Others were tortured to death, disdaining release, to win 36 a better resurrection. Others, again, had to face jeers and flogging, even fetters and 37 prison bars. They were stoned,ʷ they were sawn in two, they were put to the sword, they went about dressed in skins of sheep or goats, in poverty, distress, and misery. 38 They were too good for a world like this.

They were refugees in deserts and on the hills, hiding in caves and holes in the ground. These also, one and all, are commemorated 39 for their faith; and yet they did not enter upon the promised inheritance, because, 40 with us in mind, God had made a better plan, that only in company with us should they reach their perfection.

With eyes fixed on Jesus

And what of ourselves? With all these wit- **12** nesses to faith around us like a cloud, we must throw off every encumbrance, every sin to which we cling,ˣ and run with resolution the race for which we are entered, our eyes 2 fixed on Jesus, on whom faith depends from start to finish: Jesus who, for the sake of the joy that lay ahead of him,ʸ endured the cross, making light of its disgrace, and has taken his seat at the right hand of the throne of God.

The discipline of sons

Think of him who submitted to such opposi- 3 tion from sinners: that will help you not to lose heart and grow faint. In your struggle 4 against sin, you have not yet resisted to the point of shedding your blood. You have for- 5 gotten the text of Scripture which addresses you as sons and appeals to you in these words:

'My son, do not think lightly of the Lord's discipline,
nor lose heart when he corrects you;
for the Lord disciplines those whom he loves; 6
he lays the rod on every son whom he acknowledges.'

You must endure it as discipline: God is 7 treating you as sons. Can anyone be a son, who is not disciplined by his father? If you 8 escape the discipline in which all sons share, you must be bastards and no true sons. Again, we paid due respect to the earthly 9 fathers who disciplined us; should we not submit even more readily to our spiritual Father, and so attain life? They disciplined 10 us for this short life according to their lights; but he does so for our true welfare, so that we may share his holiness. Discipline, 11 no doubt, is never pleasant; at the time it seems painful; but in the end it yields for those who have been trained by it the peaceful harvest of an honest life. Come, then, 12 stiffen your drooping arms and shaking knees, and keep your steps from wavering. 13 Then the disabled limb will not be put out of joint, but regain its former powers.

The man who sold his birthright

Aim at peace with all men, and a holy life, for 14 without that no one will see the Lord. Look 15

---

v Or God's call shall be for your descendants in the line of Isaac.   *w Some witnesses insert* they were put to the question.   *x Or* every clinging sin; *one witness reads* the sin which all too readily distracts us. *y Or* who, in place of the joy that was open to him, . . .

to it that there is no one among you who forfeits the grace of God, no bitter, noxious weed
16 growing up to poison the whole, no immoral person, no one worldly-minded like Esau. He
17 sold his birthright for a single meal, and you know that although he wanted afterwards to claim the blessing, he was rejected; though he begged for it to the point of tears, he found no way open for second thoughts.

Sinai and Zion

18 Remember where you stand: not before the palpable, blazing fire of Sinai, with the dark-
19 ness, gloom, and whirlwind, the trumpet-blast and the oracular voice, which they
20 heard, and begged to hear no more; for they could not bear the command, 'If even an animal touches the mountain, it must be
21 stoned.' So appalling was the sight, that Moses said, 'I shudder with fear.'
22 No, you stand before Mount Zion and the city of the living God, heavenly Jeru-
23 salem, before myriads of angels, the full concourse and assembly of the first-born citizens of heaven, and God the judge of all, and the spirits of good men made perfect,
24 and Jesus the mediator of a new covenant, whose sprinkled blood has better things to
25 tell than the blood of Abel. See that you do not refuse to hear the voice that speaks. Those who refused to hear the oracle speaking on earth found no escape; still less shall we escape if we refuse to hear the One who
26 speaks from heaven. Then indeed his voice shook the earth, but now he has promised, 'Yet once again I will shake not earth alone,
27 but the heavens also.' The words 'once again'—and only once—imply that the shaking of these created things means their removal, and then what is not shaken will
28 remain. The kingdom we are given is unshakable; let us therefore give thanks to God, and so worship him as he would be
29 worshipped, with reverence and awe; for our God is a devouring fire.

Directions for Christian living

3 Never cease to love your fellow-Christians.
2   Remember to show hospitality. There are some who, by so doing, have entertained angels without knowing it.
3   Remember those in prison as if you were there with them; and those who are being maltreated, for you like them are still in the world.
4   Marriage is honourable; let us all keep it so, and the marriage-bond inviolate; for God's judgement will fall on fornicators and adulterers.
5   Do not live for money; be content with what you have; for God himself has said, 'I
6 will never leave you or desert you'; and so we

can take courage and say, 'The Lord is my helper, I will not fear; what can man do to me?'
7   Remember your leaders, those who first spoke God's message to you; and reflecting upon the outcome of their life and work, follow the example of their faith.
8   Jesus Christ is the same yesterday, today, and for ever. So do not be swept off your
9 course by all sorts of outlandish teachings; it is good that our souls should gain their strength from the grace of God, and not from scruples about what we eat, which have never done any good to those who were governed by them.
10   Our altar is one from which[z] the priests of
11 the sacred tent have no right to eat. As you know, those animals whose blood is brought as a sin-offering by the high priest into the sanctuary, have their bodies burnt outside
12 the camp, and therefore Jesus also suffered outside the gate, to consecrate the people by
13 his own blood. Let us then go to him outside the camp, bearing the stigma that he bore.
14 For here we have no permanent home, but we are seekers after the city which is to come.
15 Through Jesus, then, let us continually offer up to God the sacrifice of praise, that is, the tribute of lips which acknowledge his name,
16 and never forget to show kindness and to share what you have with others; for such are the sacrifices which God approves.
17   Obey your leaders and defer to them; for they are tireless in their concern for you, as men who must render an account. Let it be a happy task for them, and not pain and grief, for that would bring you no advantage.
18   Pray for us; for we are convinced that our conscience is clear; our one desire is always
19 to do what is right. All the more earnestly I ask for your prayers, that I may be restored to you the sooner.

A prayer

20 May the God of peace, who brought up from the dead our Lord Jesus, the great Shepherd of the sheep, by the blood of the
21 eternal covenant, make you perfect in all goodness so that you may do his will; and may he make of us what he would have us be through Jesus Christ, to whom be glory for ever and ever! Amen.

A personal note

22 I beg you, brothers, bear with this exhorta-
23 tion; for it is after all a short letter. I have news for you: our friend Timothy has been released; and if he comes in time he will be with me when I see you.
24   Greet all your leaders and all God's people. Greetings to you from our Italian friends.
25   God's grace be with you all!

---

z Or one like that from which . . .

A LETTER OF
JAMES

1 FROM JAMES, a servant of God and the Lord Jesus Christ.

Greetings to the Twelve Tribes dispersed throughout the world.

Wisdom and faith

2 My brothers, whenever you have to face trials of many kinds, count yourselves su- 3 premely happy, in the knowledge that such 4 testing of your faith breeds fortitude, and if you give fortitude full play you will go on to complete a balanced character that 5 will fall short in nothing. If any of you falls short in wisdom, he should ask God for it and it will be given him, for God is a generous giver who neither refuses nor reproaches 6 anyone. But he must ask in faith, without a doubt in his mind; for the doubter is like 7 a heaving sea ruffled by the wind. A man of that kind must not expect the Lord to give 8 him anything; he is double-minded, and never can keep[a] a steady course.

Poverty and wealth

9 The brother in humble circumstances may 10 well be proud that God lifts him up; and the wealthy brother must find his pride in being brought low. For the rich man will 11 disappear like the flower of the field; once the sun is up with its scorching heat the flower withers, its petals fall, and what was lovely to look at is lost for ever. So shall the rich man wither away as he goes about his business.

Trial and temptation

12 Happy the man who remains steadfast under trial, for having passed that test he will receive for his prize the gift of life promised 13 to those who love God. No one under trial or temptation should say, 'I am being temp-ted by God'; for God is untouched by evil,[b] and does not himself tempt anyone. Tempta- 14 tion arises when a man is enticed and lured away by his own lust; then lust conceives, 15 and gives birth to sin; and sin full-grown breeds death.

Make no mistake, my friends. All good 16 giving, every perfect gift, comes[c] from above, from the Father of the lights of heaven. With him there is no variation, no play of passing shadows.[d] Of his set purpose, by 18 declaring the truth, he gave us birth to be a kind of firstfruits of his creatures.

Hearing and doing

Of that you may be certain, my friends. But 19 each of you must be quick to listen, slow to speak, and slow to be angry. For a man's 20 anger cannot promote the justice of God. Away then with all that is sordid, and the 21 malice that hurries to excess, and quietly accept the message planted in your hearts, which can bring you salvation.

Only be sure that you act on the message 22 and do not merely listen; for that would be to mislead yourselves. A man who listens 23 to the message but never acts upon it is like one who looks in a mirror at the face nature gave him. He glances at himself and goes 24 away, and at once forgets what he looked like. But the man who looks closely into the 25 perfect law, the law that makes us free, and who lives in its company, does not forget what he hears, but acts upon it; and that is the man who by acting will find happiness.

True religion

A man may think he is religious, but if he 26 has no control over his tongue, he is deceiving himself; that man's religion is futile. The kind of religion which is without stain 27

---

a Or anything; a double-minded man never keeps . . . *b Or* God cannot be tempted by evil. *c Or* All giving is good, and every perfect gift comes . . . *d Some witnesses read* no variation, or shadow caused by change.

or fault in the sight of God our Father is this: to go to the help of orphans and widows in their distress and keep oneself untarnished by the world.

About snobbery

2 My brothers, believing as you do in our Lord Jesus Christ, who reigns in glory, you
2 must never show snobbery. For instance, two visitors may enter your place of worship, one a well-dressed man with gold rings, and the other a poor man in shabby clothes.
3 Suppose you pay special attention to the well-dressed man and say to him, 'Please take this seat', while to the poor man you say, 'You can stand; or you may sit here*e* on
4 the floor by my footstool', do you not see that you are inconsistent and judge by false standards?
5 Listen, my friends. Has not God chosen those who are poor in the eyes of the world to be rich in faith and to inherit the kingdom he has promised to those who love him?
6 And yet you have insulted the poor man. Moreover, are not the rich your oppressors?
7 Is it not they who drag you into court and pour contempt on the honoured name by which God has claimed you?
8 If, however, you are observing the sovereign law laid down in Scripture, 'Love your
9 neighbour as yourself', that is excellent. But if you show snobbery, you are committing a sin and you stand convicted by that law
10 as transgressors. For if a man keeps the whole law apart from one single point, he
11 is guilty of breaking all of it. For the One who said, 'Thou shalt not commit adultery', said also, 'Thou shalt not commit murder.' You may not be an adulterer, but if you commit murder you are a law-breaker all
12 the same. Always speak and act as men who
13 are to be judged under a law of freedom. In that judgement there will be no mercy for the man who has shown no mercy. Mercy triumphs over judgement.

The evidence of faith

14 My brothers, what use is it for a man to say he has faith when he does nothing to show
15 it? Can that faith save him? Suppose a brother or a sister is in rags with not enough food
16 for the day, and one of you says, 'Good luck to you, keep yourselves warm, and have plenty to eat', but does nothing to supply their bodily needs, what is the good of that?
17 So with faith; if it does not lead to action, it is in itself a lifeless thing.
18 But someone may object: 'Here is one who claims to have faith and another who points to his deeds.' To which I reply: 'Prove to me that this faith you speak of is real

though not accompanied by deeds, and by my deeds I will prove to you my faith.' You 19 have faith enough to believe that there is one God. Excellent! The devils have faith like that, and it makes them tremble. But 20 can you not see, you quibbler, that faith divorced from deeds is barren? Was it not 21 by his action, in offering his son Isaac upon the altar, that our father Abraham was justified? Surely you can see that faith was 22 at work in his actions, and that by these actions the integrity of his faith was fully proved. Here was fulfilment of the words of 23 Scripture: 'Abraham put his faith in God, and that faith was counted to him as righteousness'; and elsewhere he is called 'God's friend'. You see then that a man is 24 justified by deeds and not by faith in itself. The same is true of the prostitute Rahab 25 also. Was not she justified by her action in welcoming the messengers into her house and sending them away by a different route? As the body is dead when there is no breath 26 left in it, so faith divorced from deeds is lifeless as a corpse.

The tongue, an intractable evil

My brothers, not many of you should be- **3** come teachers, for you may be certain that we who teach shall ourselves be judged with greater strictness. All of us often go wrong; 2 the man who never says a wrong thing is a perfect character, able to bridle his whole being. If we put bits into horses' mouths to 3

make them obey our will, we can direct their whole body. Or think of ships: large they 4 may be, yet even when driven by strong gales they can be directed by a tiny rudder on whatever course the helmsman chooses. So 5 with the tongue. It is a small member but it can make huge claims.*f*

What an immense stack of timber*g* can 6 be set ablaze by the tiniest spark! And the tongue is in effect a fire. It represents among

---

e Some witnesses read Stand where you are or sit here . . .; *others read* Stand where you are or sit . . .   *f Or* it is a great boaster.   *g Or* What a huge forest . . .

our members the world with all its wickedness; it pollutes our whole being; it keeps the wheel of our existence red-hot, and its
7 flames are fed by hell. Beasts and birds of every kind, creatures that crawl on the ground or swim in the sea, can be subdued
8 and have been subdued by mankind; but no man can subdue the tongue. It is an intractable evil, charged with deadly venom.
9 We use it to sing the praises of our Lord and Father, and we use it to invoke curses upon our fellow-men who are made in God's
10 likeness. Out of the same mouth come praises and curses. My brothers, this should not be
11 so. Does a fountain gush with both fresh and brackish water from the same opening?
12 Can a fig-tree, my brothers, yield olives, or a vine figs? No more does salt water yield fresh.

Earthly and heavenly wisdom contrasted

13 Who among you is wise or clever? Let his right conduct give practical proof of it, with
14 the modesty that comes of wisdom. But if you are harbouring bitter jealousy and selfish ambition in your hearts, consider whether your claims are not false, and a defiance of
15 the truth. This is not the wisdom that comes from above; it is earth-bound, sensual,
16 demonic. For with jealousy and ambition
17 come disorder and evil of every kind. But the wisdom from above is in the first place pure; and then peace-loving, considerate, and open to reason; it is straightforward and sincere, rich in mercy and in the kindly deeds
18 that are its fruit. True justice is the harvest reaped by peacemakers from seeds sown in a spirit of peace.

About envious desires

4 What causes conflicts and quarrels among you? Do they not spring from the aggressive-
2 ness of your bodily desires? You want something which you cannot have, and so you are bent on murder; you are envious, and cannot attain your ambition, and so you quarrel and fight. You do not get what you
3 want, because you do not pray for it. Or,

if you do, your requests are not granted because you pray from wrong motives, to spend what you get on your pleasures. You 4 false, unfaithful creatures! Have you never learned that love of the world is enmity to God? Whoever chooses to be the world's friend makes himself God's enemy. Or do 5 you suppose that Scripture has no meaning when it says that the spirit which God implanted in man turns towards envious desires? And yet the grace he gives is 6 stronger. Thus Scripture says, 'God opposes the arrogant and gives grace to the humble.' Be submissive then to God. Stand up to the 7 devil and he will turn and run. Come close 8 to God, and he will come close to you. Sinners, make your hands clean; you who are double-minded, see that your motives are pure. Be sorrowful, mourn and weep. Turn 9 your laughter into mourning and your gaiety into gloom. Humble yourselves before God 10 and he will lift you high.

About judging your neighbour

Brothers, you must never disparage one 11 another. He who disparages a brother or passes judgement on his brother disparages the law and judges the law. But if you judge the law, you are not keeping it but sitting in judgement upon it. There is only one law- 12 giver and judge, the One who is able to save life and destroy it. So who are you to judge your neighbour?

About planning without God's guidance

A word with you, you who say, 'Today or 13 tomorrow we will go off to such and such a town and spend a year there trading and making money.' Yet you have no idea what 14 tomorrow will bring. Your life, what is it? You are no more than a mist, seen for a little while and then dispersing. What you ought 15 to say is: 'If it be the Lord's will, we shall live to do this or that.' But instead, you boast 16 and brag, and all such boasting is wrong. Well then, the man who knows the good he 17 ought to do and does not do it is a sinner.

Eastern traders

A word to the wealthy

5 Next a word to you who have great possessions. Weep and wail over the miserable fate
2 descending on you. Your riches have rotted;
3 your fine clothes are moth-eaten; your silver
and gold have rusted away, and their very
rust will be evidence against you and consume your flesh like fire. You have piled up
4 wealth in an age that is near its close. The
wages you never paid to the men who mowed
your fields are loud against you, and the outcry of the reapers has reached the ears of
5 the Lord of Hosts. You have lived on earth
in wanton luxury, fattening yourselves like
cattle—and the day for slaughter has come.
6 You have condemned the innocent and
murdered him; he offers no resistance.

Be patient and stout-hearted

7 Be patient, my brothers, until the Lord
comes. The farmer looking for the precious
crop his land may yield can only wait in
patience, until the autumn and spring rains
8 have fallen. You too must be patient and
stout-hearted, for the coming of the Lord
9 is near. My brothers, do not blame your
troubles on one another, or you will fall
under judgement; and there stands the
10 Judge, at the door. If you want a pattern of
patience under ill-treatment, take the prophets who spoke in the name of the Lord;
11 remember: 'We count those happy who stood
firm.' You have all heard how Job stood
firm, and you have seen how the Lord treated

him in the end. For the Lord is full of pity
and compassion.

The power of prayer

Above all things, my brothers, do not use 12
oaths, whether 'by heaven' or 'by earth' or
by anything else. When you say yes or no,
let it be plain 'Yes' or 'No', for fear that you
expose yourselves to judgement.

Is anyone among you in trouble? He 13
should turn to prayer. Is anyone in good
heart? He should sing praises. Is one of you 14
ill? He should send for the elders of the congregation to pray over him and anoint him
with oil in the name of the Lord. The prayer 15
offered in faith will save the sick man, the
Lord will raise him from his bed, and any
sins he may have committed will be forgiven. Therefore confess your sins to one 16
another, and pray for one another, and then
you will be healed. A good man's prayer is
powerful and effective. Elijah was a man 17
with human frailties like our own; and when
he prayed earnestly that there should be no
rain, not a drop fell on the land for three years
and a half; then he prayed again, and down 18
came the rain and the land bore crops once
more.

My brothers, if one of your number 19
should stray from the truth and another
succeed in bringing him back, be sure of 20
this: any man who brings a sinner back from
his crooked ways will be rescuing his soul
from death and cancelling innumerable sins.

THE FIRST LETTER OF
PETER

A living hope for a time of trial

1 FROM PETER, apostle of Jesus Christ, to those of God's scattered people who lodge for a while in Pontus, Galatia, Cappadocia, 2 Asia, and Bithynia—chosen of old in the purpose of God the Father, hallowed to his service by the Spirit, and consecrated with the sprinkled blood of Jesus Christ.

Grace and peace to you in fullest measure.

3 Praise be to the God and Father of our Lord Jesus Christ, who in his great mercy gave us new birth into a living hope by the resurrection of Jesus Christ from the dead! 4 The inheritance to which we are born is one that nothing can destroy or spoil or wither. 5 It is kept for you in heaven, and you, because you put your faith in God, are under the protection of his power until salvation comes—the salvation which is even now in readiness and will be revealed at the end of time. 6 This is cause for great joy, even though now you smart for a little while, if need be, 7 under trials of many kinds. Even gold passes through the assayer's fire, and more precious than perishable gold is faith which has stood the test. These trials come so that your faith may prove itself worthy of all praise, glory, and honour when Jesus Christ is revealed.

The theme the prophets pondered

8 You have not seen him, yet you love him; and trusting in him now without seeing him, you are transported with a joy too great for 9 words, while you reap the harvest of your 10 faith, that is, salvation for your souls. This salvation was the theme which the prophets pondered and explored, those who pro-

phesied about the grace of God awaiting you. They tried to find out what was the 11 time,[a] and what the circumstances, to which the spirit of Christ in them pointed, fore-telling the sufferings in store for Christ and the splendours to follow; and it was dis- 12 closed to them that the matter they treated of was not for their time but for yours. And now it has been openly announced to you through preachers who brought you the Gospel in the power of the Holy Spirit sent from heaven. These are things that angels long to see into.

A call to holy living

You must therefore be mentally stripped 13 for action, perfectly self-controlled. Fix your hopes on the gift of grace which is to be yours when Jesus Christ is revealed. As obedient 14 children, do not let your characters be shaped any longer by the desires you cherished in your days of ignorance. The One who called 15 you is holy; like him, be holy in all your be-haviour, because Scripture says, 'You shall 16 be holy, for I am holy.'

If you say 'our Father' to the One who 17 judges every man impartially on the record of his deeds, you must stand in awe of him while you live out your time on earth. Well 18 you know that it was no perishable stuff, like gold or silver, that bought your freedom from the empty folly of your traditional ways. The price was paid in precious blood, as it 19 were of a lamb without mark or blemish—the blood of Christ. Predestined before the 20 foundation of the world, he was made mani-fest in this last period of time for your sake. Through him you have come to trust in God 21

a Or who was the person . . .

948

who raised him from the dead and gave him glory, and so your faith and hope are fixed on God.

Born anew

22 Now that by obedience to the truth you have purified your souls until you feel sincere affection towards your brother Christians, love one another whole-heartedly with all 23 your strength. You have been born anew, not of mortal parentage but of immortal, through the living and enduring word of 24 God.[b] For (as Scripture says)

'All mortals are like grass;
all their splendour like the flower of the field;
the grass withers, the flower falls;
25 but the word of the Lord endures for ever-more.'

And this 'word' is the word of the Gospel preached to you.

Spiritual appetites

2 Then away with all malice and deceit, away with all pretence and jealousy and recrimina-2 tion of every kind! Like the new-born infants you are, you must crave for pure milk (spiritual milk, I mean), so that you may 3 thrive upon it to your souls' health. Surely you have tasted that the Lord is good.

A spiritual temple; a holy priesthood

4 So come to him, our living Stone—the stone rejected by men but choice and precious in 5 the sight of God. Come, and let yourselves be built, as living stones, into a spiritual temple; become a holy priesthood,[c] to offer spiritual sacrifices acceptable to God through 6 Jesus Christ. For it stands written:

'I lay in Zion a choice corner-stone of great worth.
The man who has faith in it will not be put to shame.'

7 The great worth of which it speaks is for you who have faith. For those who have no faith, the stone which the builders rejected has 8 become not only the corner-stone,[d] but also 'a stone to trip over, a rock to stumble against'. They fall when they disbelieve the Word. Such was their appointed lot!

9 But you are a chosen race, a royal priest-hood, a dedicated nation, and a people claimed by God for his own, to proclaim the triumphs of him who has called you out 10 of darkness into his marvellous light. You are now the people of God, who once were not his people; outside his mercy once, you have now received his mercy.

Christian behaviour

Dear friends, I beg you, as aliens in a foreign 11 land, to abstain from the lusts of the flesh which are at war with the soul. Let all your 12 behaviour be such as even pagans can recog-nize as good, and then, whereas they malign you as criminals now, they will come to see for themselves that you live good lives, and will give glory to God on the day when he comes to hold assize.

Submit yourselves to every human institu- 13 tion for the sake of the Lord, whether to the sovereign as supreme, or to the governor as 14 his deputy for the punishment of criminals and the commendation of those who do right. For it is the will of God that by your good 15 conduct you should put ignorance and stupidity to silence.

Live as free men; not however as though 16 your freedom were there to provide a screen for wrongdoing, but as slaves in God's service. Give due honour to everyone: love 17 to the brotherhood, reverence to God, honour to the sovereign.

To servants

Servants, accept the authority of your 18 masters with all due submission, not only when they are kind and considerate, but even when they are perverse. For it is a fine[e] thing 19 if a man endure the pain of undeserved suffer-ing because God is in his thoughts. What 20 credit is there in fortitude when you have done wrong and are beaten for it? But when you have behaved well and suffer for it, your fortitude is a fine thing[f] in the sight of God. To that you were called, because Christ 21 suffered[g] on your behalf, and thereby left you an example; it is for you to follow in his steps. He committed no sin, he was con- 22 victed of no falsehood; when he was abused 23 he did not retort with abuse, when he suf-fered he uttered no threats, but committed his cause to the One who judges justly. In 24 his own person he carried our sins to[h] the gibbet, so that we might cease to live for sin and begin to live for righteousness. By his wounds you have been healed. You were 25 straying like sheep, but now you have turned towards the Shepherd and Guardian of your souls.

To wives

In the same way you women must accept the **3** authority of your husbands, so that if there are any of them who disbelieve the Gospel they may be won over, without a word being 2 said, by observing the chaste and reverent behaviour of their wives. Your beauty should 3 reside, not in outward adornment—the

---

b Or through the word of the living and enduring God. *c Or* a spiritual temple for the holy work of priesthood. *d Or* the apex of the building. *e Or* creditable. *f Or* is creditable. *g Some witnesses read* died. *h Or* on.

braiding of the hair, or jewellery, or dress—
4 but in the inmost centre of your being, with
its imperishable ornament, a gentle, quiet
spirit, which is of high value in the sight of
5 God. Thus it was among God's people in
days of old: the women who fixed their hopes
on him adorned themselves by submission
6 to their husbands. Such was Sarah, who
obeyed Abraham and called him 'my master'.
Her children you have now become, if you
do good and show no fear.

To husbands

7 In the same way, you husbands must conduct your married life with understanding:
pay honour to the woman's body, not only
because it is weaker, but also because you
share together in the grace of God which
gives you life. Then your prayers will not
be hindered.

About personal wrongs

8 To sum up: be one in thought and feeling,
all of you; be full of brotherly affection,
9 kindly and humble-minded. Do not repay
wrong with wrong, or abuse with abuse; on
the contrary, retaliate with blessing, for a
blessing is the inheritance to which you
yourselves have been called.

10 'Whoever loves life and would see good days
must restrain his tongue from evil
and his lips from deceit;
11 must turn from wrong and do good,
seek peace and pursue it.
12 For the Lord's eyes are turned towards the
righteous,
his ears are open to their prayers;
but the Lord's face is set against wrongdoers.'

13 Who is going to do you wrong if you are
14 devoted to what is good? And yet if you
should suffer for your virtues, you may count
yourselves happy. Have no fear of them:[i]
15 do not be perturbed, but hold the Lord
Christ in reverence in your hearts.[j] Be
always ready with your defence whenever
you are called to account for the hope that
is in you, but make that defence with modesty
16 and respect. Keep your conscience clear, so
that when you are abused, those who malign
your Christian conduct may be put to shame.
17 It is better to suffer for well-doing, if such
should be the will of God, than for doing
18 wrong. For Christ also died[k] for our sins[l]
once and for all. He, the just, suffered for the
unjust, to bring us to God.

Significance of baptism

In the body he was put to death; in the
19 spirit he was brought to life. And in the

spirit he went and made his proclamation
to the imprisoned spirits. They had refused 20
obedience long ago, while God waited patiently in the days of Noah and the building
of the ark, and in the ark a few persons,
eight in all, were brought to safety through
the water. This water prefigured the water 21
of baptism through which you are now
brought to safety. Baptism is not the washing
away of bodily pollution, but the appeal
made to God by a good conscience; and it
brings salvation through the resurrection of
Jesus Christ, who entered heaven after re- 22
ceiving the submission of angelic authorities
and powers, and is now at the right hand
of God.

Changed lives

Remembering that Christ endured bodily **4**
suffering, you must arm yourselves with a
temper of mind like his. When a man has
thus endured bodily suffering he has finished
with sin, and for the rest of his days on earth 2
he may live, not for the things that men
desire, but for what God wills. You had 3
time enough in the past to do all the things
that men want to do in the pagan world.
Then you lived in licence and debauchery,
drunkenness, revelry, and tippling, and the
forbidden worship of idols. Now, when you 4
no longer plunge with them into all this
reckless dissipation, they cannot understand
it, and they vilify you accordingly; but they 5
shall answer for it to him who stands ready
to pass judgement on the living and the dead.
Why was the Gospel preached to those who 6
are dead? In order that, although in the body
they received the sentence common to men,
they might in the spirit be alive with the life
of God.

Serving one another

The end of all things is upon us, so you must 7
lead an ordered and sober life, given to
prayer. Above all, keep your love for one 8
another at full strength, because love cancels
innumerable sins. Be hospitable to one an- 9
other without complaining. Whatever gift 10
each of you may have received, use it in
service to one another, like good stewards
dispensing the grace of God in its varied
forms. Are you a speaker? Speak as if you 11
uttered oracles of God. Do you give service?
Give it as in the strength which God supplies. In all things so act that the glory may
be God's through Jesus Christ; to him belong
glory and power for ever and ever. Amen.

Encouragement in time of persecution

My dear friends, do not be bewildered by 12
the fiery ordeal that is upon you, as though

---

i Or Do not fear what they fear.   *j Or* hold Christ in reverence in your hearts, as Lord.   *k Some*
witnesses read suffered.   *l Some witnesses read* for sins; *others read* for sins on our behalf.

that flock of God whose shepherds you are, and do it, not under compulsion, but of your own free will, as God would have it; not for gain but out of sheer devotion; not 3 tyrannizing over those who are allotted to your care, but setting an example to the flock. And then, when the Head Shepherd 4 appears, you will receive for your own the unfading garland of glory.

To younger men

In the same way you younger men must be 5 subordinate to your elders. Indeed, all of you should wrap yourselves in the garment of humility towards each other, because God sets his face against the arrogant but favours the humble. Humble yourselves then under 6 God's mighty hand, and he will lift you up in due time. Cast all your cares on him, for 7 you are his charge.

Awake! be on the alert!

Awake! be on the alert! Your enemy the 8 devil, like a roaring lion, prowls round looking for someone to devour. Stand up 9 to him, firm in faith, and remember that your brother Christians are going through the same kinds of suffering while they are in the world. And the God of all grace, who 10 called you into his eternal glory in Christ, will himself, after your brief suffering, restore, establish, and strengthen you on a firm foundation. He holds dominion for ever 11 and ever. Amen.

Final greetings

I write you this brief appeal through Silvanus, 12 our trusty brother as I hold him, adding my testimony that this is the true grace of God. In this stand fast.

Greetings from her who dwells in Babylon, 13 chosen by God like you, and from my son Mark. Greet one another with the kiss of 14 love.

Peace to you all who belong to Christ!

13 it were something extraordinary. It gives you a share in Christ's sufferings, and that is cause for joy; and when his glory is revealed, 14 your joy will be triumphant. If Christ's name is flung in your teeth as an insult, count yourselves happy, because then that glorious Spirit which is the Spirit of God is 15 resting upon you. If you suffer, it must not be for murder, theft, or sorcery,^m nor for 16 infringing the rights of others. But if anyone suffers as a Christian, he should feel it no disgrace, but confess that name to the honour of God.

17 The time has come for the judgement to begin; it is beginning with God's own household. And if it is starting with you, how will it end for those who refuse to obey the gospel 18 of God? It is hard enough for the righteous to be saved; what then will become of the 19 impious and sinful? So even those who suffer, if it be according to God's will, should commit their souls to him—by doing good; their Maker will not fail them.

To elders

5 And now I appeal to the elders of your community, as a fellow-elder and a witness of Christ's sufferings, and also a partaker 2 in the splendour that is to be revealed. Tend

m Or other crime.

THE SECOND LETTER OF
PETER

1 FROM SIMEON PETER, servant and apostle of Jesus Christ, to those who through the justice of our God and Saviour Jesus Christ share our faith and enjoy equal privilege with ourselves.
2 Grace and peace be yours in fullest measure, through the knowledge of God and Jesus our Lord.

Life and true religion

3 His divine power has bestowed on us everything that makes for life and true religion, enabling us to know the One who called us
4 by his own splendour and might. Through this might and splendour he has given us his promises, great beyond all price, and through them you may escape the corruption with which lust has infected the world, and come to share in the very being of God.
5 With all this in view, you should try your hardest to supplement your faith with virtue,
6 virtue with knowledge, knowledge with self-control, self-control with fortitude, fortitude
7 with piety, piety with brotherly kindness, and brotherly kindness with love.

Gifts worth possessing

8 These are gifts which, if you possess and foster them, will keep you from being either useless or barren in the knowledge of our
9 Lord Jesus Christ. The man who lacks them is short-sighted and blind; he has forgotten how he was cleansed from his former sins.
10 All the more then, my friends, exert yourselves to clinch God's choice and calling of you. If you behave so, you will never come
11 to grief. Thus you will be afforded full and free admission into the eternal kingdom of our Lord and Saviour Jesus Christ.

The message of the prophets confirmed

12 And so I will not hesitate to remind you of this again and again, although you know it and are well grounded in the truth that has
13 already reached you. Yet I think it right to keep refreshing your memory so long as I
14 still lodge in this body. I know that very soon I must leave it; indeed our Lord Jesus Christ
15 has told me so.[a] But I will see to it that after I am gone you will have means of remembering these things at all times.
16 It was not on tales artfully spun that we relied when we told you of the power of our Lord Jesus Christ and his coming; we saw

him with our own eyes in majesty, when at 17 the hands of God the Father he was invested with honour and glory, and there came to him from the sublime Presence a voice which said: 'This is my Son, my Beloved,[b] on whom my favour rests.' This voice from heaven 18 we ourselves heard; when it came, we were with him on the sacred mountain.

All this only confirms for us the message 19 of the prophets,[c] to which you will do well to attend, because it is like a lamp shining in a murky place, until the day breaks and the morning star rises to illuminate your minds.

False prophets, false teachers

But first note this: no one can interpret any 20 prophecy of Scripture by himself. For it was 21 not through any human whim that men prophesied of old; men they were, but, impelled by the Holy Spirit, they spoke the words of God.

But Israel had false prophets as well as **2** true; and you likewise will have false teachers among you. They will import disastrous heresies, disowning the very Master who bought them, and bringing swift disaster on their own heads. They will gain many adher- 2 ents to their dissolute practices, through whom the true way will be brought into disrepute. In their greed for money they will trade on 3 your credulity with sheer fabrications.

God's judgements in the past

But the judgement long decreed for them has not been idle; perdition waits for them with unsleeping eyes. God did not spare the angels 4 who sinned, but consigned them to the dark pits of hell,[d] where they are reserved for judgement. He did not spare the world of 5 old (except for Noah, preacher of righteousness, whom he preserved with seven others), but brought the deluge upon that world of godless men. The cities of Sodom and 6 Gomorrah God burned to ashes, and condemned them to total destruction, making them an object-lesson for godless men in future days. But he rescued Lot, who was a 7 good man, shocked by the dissolute habits of the lawless society in which he lived; day 8 after day every sight, every sound, of their evil courses tortured that good man's heart. Thus the Lord is well able to rescue the 9 godly out of trials, and to reserve the wicked under punishment until the day of judgement.

a Or I must leave it, as our Lord Jesus Christ told me. *b Or* This is my only Son. *c Or* And in the message of the prophets we have something still more certain. *d Some witnesses read* consigned them to darkness and chains in hell.

Character and destiny of false teachers

10 Above all he will punish those who follow their abominable lusts. They flout authority; reckless and headstrong, they are not afraid 11 to insult celestial beings, whereas angels, for all their superior strength and might, employ no insults in seeking judgement against them before the Lord.

12 These men are like brute beasts, born in the course of nature to be caught and killed. They pour abuse upon things they do not understand; like the beasts they will perish, 13 suffering hurt for the hurt they have inflicted. To carouse in broad daylight is their idea of pleasure; while they sit with you at table they are an ugly blot on your company, because they revel in their own deceptions.*e*

14 They have eyes for nothing but women, eyes never at rest from sin. They lure the unstable to their ruin; past masters in mercenary greed, God's curse is on them! 15 They have abandoned the straight road and lost their way. They have followed in the steps of Balaam son of Beor, who consented 16 to take pay for doing wrong, but had his offence brought home to him when the dumb beast spoke with a human voice and put a stop to the prophet's madness.

17 These men are springs that give no water, mists driven by a storm; the place reserved 18 for them is blackest darkness. They utter big, empty words, and make of sensual lusts and debauchery a bait to catch those who have barely begun to escape from their 19 heathen environment. They promise them freedom, but are themselves slaves of corruption; for a man is the slave of whatever 20 has mastered him. They had once escaped the world's defilements through the knowledge of our Lord and Saviour Jesus Christ; yet if they have entangled themselves in these all over again, and are mastered by them, their plight in the end is worse than 21 before. How much better never to have known the right way, than, having known it, to turn back and abandon the sacred com-22 mandments delivered to them! The proverb has proved true: 'The dog returns to its own vomit', and, 'The sow after a wash rolls in the mud again.'

Why the Lord delays his return

3 This is now my second letter to you, my friends. In both of them I have been recalling to you what you already know, to rouse you 2 to honest thought. Remember the predictions made by God's own prophets, and the commands given by the Lord and Saviour through your apostles. 3 Note this first: in the last days there will come men who scoff at religion and live self-indulgent lives, and they will say: 'Where 4 now is the promise of his coming? Our fathers have been laid to their rest, but still everything continues exactly as it has always been since the world began.'

In taking this view they lose sight of the 5 fact*f* that there were heavens and earth long ago, created by God's word out of water and with water; and by water that first world was 6 destroyed, the water of the deluge. And the 7 present heavens and earth, again by God's word, have been kept in store for burning; they are being reserved until the day of judgement when the godless will be destroyed.

And here is one point, my friends, which 8 you must not lose sight of: with the Lord one day is like a thousand years and a thousand years like one day. It is not that the Lord is 9 slow in fulfilling his promise, as some suppose, but that he is very patient with you, because it is not his will for any to be lost, but for all to come to repentance.

The Day of the Lord

But the Day of the Lord will come; it will 10 come, unexpected as a thief. On that day the heavens will disappear with a great rushing sound, the elements will disintegrate in flames, and the earth with all that is in it will be laid bare.*g*

Since the whole universe is to break up 11 in this way, think what sort of people you ought to be, what devout and dedicated lives you should live! Look eagerly for the coming 12 of the Day of God and work to hasten it on; that day will set the heavens ablaze until they fall apart, and will melt the elements in flames. But we have his promise, and look 13 forward to new heavens and a new earth, the home of justice.

Final words

With this to look forward to, do your utmost 14 to be found at peace with him, unblemished and above reproach in his sight. Bear in mind 15 that our Lord's patience with us is our salvation, as Paul, our friend and brother, said when he wrote to you with his inspired wisdom. And 16 so he does in all his other letters, wherever he speaks of this subject, though they contain some obscure passages, which the ignorant and unstable misinterpret to their own ruin, as they do the other scriptures.*h*

But you, my friends, are forewarned. 17 Take care, then, not to let these unprincipled men seduce you with their errors; do not lose your own safe foothold. But grow in 18 the grace and in the knowledge of our Lord and Saviour Jesus Christ.*i* To him be glory now and for all eternity!

---

e Some witnesses read in their love-feasts.   *f Or* They choose to overlook the fact . . .   *g Some witnesses read* will be burnt up.   *h Or* his other writings.   *i Or* But grow up, by the grace of our Lord and Saviour Jesus Christ, and by knowing him.

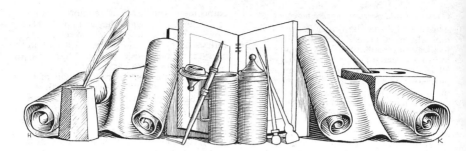

JOHN

The word of life

1 IT WAS THERE from the beginning; we have heard it; we have seen it with our own eyes; we looked upon it, and felt it with our own hands; and it is of this we tell. Our theme ² is the word of life. This life was made visible; we have seen it and bear our testimony; we here declare to you the eternal life which dwelt with the Father and was made visible ³ to us. What we have seen and heard we declare to you, so that you and we together may share in a common life, that life which we share with the Father and his Son Jesus ⁴ Christ. And we write this in order that the joy of us all may be complete.

God is light

⁵ Here is the message we heard from him and pass on to you: that God is light, and in him ⁶ there is no darkness at all. If we claim to be sharing in his life while we walk in the dark, ⁷ our words and our lives are a lie; but if we walk in the light as he himself is in the light, then we share together a common life, and we are being cleansed from every sin by the blood of Jesus his Son.

Sin and forgiveness

⁸ If we claim to be sinless, we are self-deceived ⁹ and strangers to the truth. If we confess our sins, he is just, and may be trusted to forgive our sins and cleanse us from every kind of ¹⁰ wrong; but if we say we have committed no sin, we make him out to be a liar, and then his word has no place in us.

2 My children, in writing thus to you my purpose is that you should not commit sin. But should anyone commit a sin, we have one to plead our cause*a* with the Father, ² Jesus Christ, and he is just. He is himself the remedy for the defilement of our sins, not our sins only but the sins of all the world.

Knowing Christ and living in him

Here is the test by which we can make sure ³ that we know him: do we keep his commands? The man who says, 'I know him', ⁴ while he disobeys his commands, is a liar and a stranger to the truth; but in the man ⁵ who is obedient to his word, the divine love has indeed come to its perfection.

Here is the test by which we can make sure that we are in him: whoever claims to ⁶ be dwelling in him, binds himself to live as Christ himself lived. Dear friends, I give you ⁷ no new command. It is the old command which you always had before you; the old command is the message which you heard at the beginning. And yet again it is a new ⁸ command that I am giving you—new in the sense that the darkness is passing and the real light already shines. Christ has made this true, and it is true in your own experience.

A man may say, 'I am in the light'; but if ⁹ he hates his brother, he is still in the dark. Only the man who loves his brother dwells ¹⁰ in light: there is nothing to make him stumble. But one who hates his brother is ¹¹ in darkness; he walks in the dark and has no idea where he is going, because the darkness has made him blind.

Children; fathers; young men

I write to you, my children, because your sins ¹² have been forgiven for his sake.*b*

I write to you, fathers, because you know ¹³ him who is and has been from the beginning.*c*

I write to you, young men, because you have mastered the evil one.

---

a Literally we have an advocate . . .   *b Or* forgiven, since you bear his name.   *c Or* him whom we have known from the beginning.

To you, children, I have written because you know the Father.

4 To you, fathers, I have written because you know him who is and has been from the beginning.[d] To you, young men, I have written because you are strong; God's word remains in you, and you have mastered the evil one.

The world, or the Father's love

15 Do not set your hearts on the godless world or anything in it. Anyone who loves the world is a stranger to the Father's love.

16 Everything the world affords, all that panders to the appetites or entices the eyes, all the glamour of its life, springs not from the

17 Father but from the godless world. And that world is passing away with all its allurements, but he who does God's will stands for evermore.

False teachers and the true

18 My children, this is the last hour! You were told that Antichrist was to come, and now many antichrists have appeared; which proves to us that this is indeed the last hour.

19 They went out from our company, but never really belonged to us; if they had, they would have stayed with us. They went out, so that it might be clear that not all in our company truly belong to it.[e]

20 You, no less than they, are among the initiated;[f] this is the gift of the Holy One,

21 and by it you all have knowledge.[g] It is not because you are ignorant of the truth that I have written to you, but because you know it, and because lies, one and all, are alien to the truth.

22 Who is the liar? Who but he that denies that Jesus is the Christ? He is Antichrist, for

23 he denies both the Father and the Son: to deny the Son is to be without the Father; to acknowledge the Son is to have the Father

24 too. You therefore must keep in your hearts that which you heard at the beginning; if what you heard then still dwells in you, you will yourselves dwell in the Son and also in

25 the Father. And this is the promise that he himself gave us, the promise of eternal life.

26 So much for those who would mislead you.

27 But as for you, the initiation[h] which you received from him stays with you; you need no other teacher, but learn all you need to know from his initiation, which is real and no illusion. As he taught you, then, dwell in him.

Children of God

28 Even now, my children, dwell in him, so that when he appears we may be confident

and unashamed before him at his coming.

29 If you know that he is righteous, you must recognize that every man who does right is

3 his child. How great is the love that the Father has shown to us! We were called God's children, and such we are;[i] and the reason why the godless world does not recognize us is that it has not known him. Here and

2 now, dear friends, we are God's children; what we shall be has not yet been disclosed, but we know that when it is disclosed[j] we shall be like him,[k] because we shall see him

3 as he is. Everyone who has this hope before him purifies himself, as Christ is pure.

4 To commit sin is to break God's law: sin,

5 in fact, is lawlessness. Christ appeared, as you know, to do away with sins, and there

6 is no sin in him. No man therefore who dwells in him is a sinner; the sinner has not seen him and does not know him.

Two parents, two ways of life

7 My children, do not be misled: it is the man who does right who is righteous, as God is

8 righteous; the man who sins is a child of the devil, for the devil has been a sinner from the first; and the Son of God appeared for the very purpose of undoing the devil's work.

9 A child of God does not commit sin, because the divine seed remains in him; he cannot be a sinner, because he is God's

10 child. That is the distinction between the children of God and the children of the devil: no one who does not do right is God's child, nor is anyone who does not

11 love his brother. For the message you have heard from the beginning is this: that we should love one another; unlike Cain, who

12 was a child of the evil one and murdered his brother. And why did he murder him? Because his own actions were wrong, and his brother's were right.

Loving like Christ

13 My brothers, do not be surprised if the world

14 hates you. We for our part have crossed over from death to life; this we know, because we love our brothers. The man who does not love is still in the realm of death,

15 for everyone who hates his brother is a murderer, and no murderer, as you know,

16 has eternal life dwelling within him. It is by this that we know what love is: that Christ laid down his life for us. And we in our turn are bound to lay down our lives for

17 our brothers. But if a man has enough to live on, and yet when he sees his brother in need shuts up his heart against him, how can it be said that the divine love[l] dwells in him?

---

d Or him whom we have known from the beginning.   *e Or* that none of them truly belong to us.   *f Literally* have an anointing *(Greek* chrism).   *g Some witnesses read* you have all knowledge.   *h Literally* the anointing.   *i Or* We are called children of God! Not only called, we really are his children.   *j Or* when he appears.   *k Or* we are God's children, though he has not yet appeared; what we shall be we know, for when he does appear we shall be like him.   *l Or* that love for God . . .

Conscience and the commands of Christ

18 My children, love must not be a matter of words or talk; it must be genuine, and show 19 itself in action. This is how we may know that we belong to the realm of truth, and 20 convince ourselves in his sight that even if our conscience condemns us, God is greater than our conscience *m* and knows all.

21   Dear friends, if our conscience does not condemn us, then we can approach God 22 with confidence, and obtain from him whatever we ask, because we are keeping his commands and doing what he approves. 23 This is his command: to give our allegiance to his Son Jesus Christ and love one another 24 as he commanded. When we keep his commands we dwell in him and he dwells in us. And this is how we can make sure that he dwells within us: we know it from the Spirit he has given us.

How to distinguish truth from error

4 But do not trust any and every spirit, my friends; test the spirits, to see whether they are from God, for among those who have gone out into the world there are many 2 prophets falsely inspired. This is how we may recognize the Spirit of God: every spirit which acknowledges that Jesus Christ has 3 come in the flesh is from God, and every spirit which does not thus acknowledge Jesus is not from God. This is what is meant by 'Antichrist'; *n* you have been told that he was to come, and here he is, in the world already!

4   But you, my children, are of God's family, and you have the mastery over these false prophets, because he who inspires you is greater than he who inspires the godless 5 world. They are of that world, and so therefore is their teaching; that is why the world 6 listens to them. But we belong to God, and a man who knows God listens to us, while he who does not belong to God refuses us a hearing. That is how we distinguish the spirit of truth from the spirit of error.

The love God has for us

7 Dear friends, let us love one another, because love is from God. Everyone who loves 8 is a child of God and knows God, but the unloving know nothing of God. For God is 9 love; and his love was disclosed to us in this, that he sent his only Son into the world to 10 bring us life. The love I speak of is not our love for God, but the love he showed to us in sending his Son as the remedy for the 11 defilement of our sins. If God thus loved us, dear friends, we in turn are bound to love 12 one another. Though God has never been

seen by any man, God himself dwells in us if we love one another; his love is brought to perfection within us.

Here is the proof that we dwell in him 13 and he dwells in us: he has imparted his Spirit to us. Moreover, we have seen for 14 ourselves, and we attest, that the Father sent the Son to be the saviour of the world, and if a man acknowledges that Jesus is the 15 Son of God, God dwells in him and he dwells in God. Thus we have come to know 16 and believe the love which God has for us.

When love is brought to perfection

God is love; he who dwells in love is dwelling in God, and God in him. This is for us the 17 perfection of love, to have confidence on the day of judgement, and this we can have, because even in this world we are as he is. There is no room for fear in love; perfect 18 love banishes fear. For fear brings with it the pains of judgement, and anyone who is afraid has not attained to love in its perfection. We love because he loved us first. But 19 if a man says, 'I love God', while hating his brother, he is a liar. If he does not love the brother whom he has seen, it cannot be that he loves God whom he has not seen. And 20 indeed this command comes to us from Christ himself: that he who loves God must also love his brother.

Victory over the world

Everyone who believes that Jesus is the 5 Christ is a child of God, and to love the parent means to love his child; it follows 2 that when we love God and obey his commands we love his children too. For to 3 love God is to keep his commands; and they are not burdensome, because every child of 4 God is victor over the godless world. The victory that defeats the world is our faith, for who is victor over the world but he who 5 believes that Jesus is the Son of God?

Divine witness

This is he who came with water and blood: 6 Jesus Christ. He came, not by water alone, but by water and blood; and there is the Spirit to bear witness, because the Spirit is truth. For there are three witnesses, the 7 Spirit, the water, and the blood, and these three are in agreement. We accept human 9 testimony, but surely divine testimony is stronger, and this threefold testimony is indeed that of God himself, the witness he has borne to his Son. He who believes in the 1 Son of God has this testimony in his own heart, but he who disbelieves God, makes him out to be a liar, by refusing to accept

11 God's own witness to his Son. The witness is this: that God has given us eternal life, 12 and that this life is found in his Son. He who possesses the Son has life indeed; he who does not possess the Son of God has not that life.

Summing up

13 This letter is to assure you that you have eternal life. It is addressed to those who give their allegiance to the Son of God.

14 We can approach God with confidence for this reason: if we make requests which 15 accord with his will he listens to us; and if we know that our requests are heard, we know also that the things we ask for are ours.

16 If a man sees his brother committing a sin which is not a deadly sin, he should pray to God for him, and he will grant him life—that is, when men are not guilty of deadly sin. There is such a thing as deadly sin, and I do not suggest that he should pray about that; but although all wrongdoing is sin, 17 not all sin is deadly sin.

18 We know that no child of God is a sinner; it is the Son of God who keeps him safe, and the evil one cannot touch him.

19 We know that we are of God's family, while the whole godless world lies in the power of the evil one.

20 We know that the Son of God has come and given us understanding to know him who is real; indeed we are in him who is real, since we are in his Son Jesus Christ. This is the true God, this is eternal life. My 21 children, be on the watch against false gods.

THE SECOND LETTER OF
JOHN

Truth and love

1 THE ELDER to the Lady chosen by God, and her children, whom I love in truth—and not I alone but all who know the truth 2 —for the sake of the truth that dwells among us and will be with us for ever.

3 Grace, mercy, and peace shall be with us from God the Father and from Jesus Christ the Son of the Father, in truth and love.

4 I was delighted to find that some of your children are living by the truth, as we were 5 commanded by the Father. And now I have a request to make of you. Do not think I am giving a new command; I am recalling the one we have had before us from the begin-6 ning: let us love one another. And love means following the commands of God. This is the command which was given you from the beginning, to be your rule of life.

7 Many deceivers have gone out into the world, who do not acknowledge Jesus Christ as coming in the flesh. These are the persons described as the Antichrist, the arch-deceiver. Beware of them, so that you may 8 not lose all that we worked for, but receive your reward in full.

9 Anyone who runs ahead too far, and does not stand by the doctrine of the Christ, is without God; he who stands by that doctrine possesses both the Father and the Son. If 10 anyone comes to you who does not bring this doctrine, do not welcome him into your house or give him a greeting; for anyone 11 who gives him a greeting is an accomplice in his wicked deeds.

12 I have much to write to you, but I do not care to put it down in black and white. But I hope to visit you and talk with you face to face, so that our joy may be complete. The 13 children of your Sister, chosen by God, send their greetings.

THE THIRD LETTER OF
JOHN

Loyalty and discord in the church

1 THE ELDER to dear Gaius, whom I love in truth.

2 My dear Gaius, I pray that you may enjoy good health, and that all may go well with you, as I know it goes well with your 3 soul. I was delighted when friends came and told me how true you have been; indeed 4 you are true in your whole life. Nothing gives me greater joy than to hear that my children are living by the truth.

5 My dear friend, you show a fine loyalty in everything that you do for these our fellow-Christians, strangers though they are 6 to you. They have spoken of your kindness before the congregation here. Please help them on their journey in a manner worthy 7 of the God we serve. It was on Christ's work that they went out; and they would accept 8 nothing from pagans. We are bound to support such men, and so play our part in spreading the truth.

I sent a letter to the congregation, but 9 Diotrephes, their would-be leader,[a] will have nothing to do with us. If I come, I will bring 10 up the things he is doing. He lays baseless and spiteful charges against us; not satisfied with that, he refuses to receive our friends, and he interferes with those who would do so, and tries to expel them from the congregation.

My dear friend, do not imitate bad ex- 11 amples, but good ones. The well-doer is a child of God; the evil-doer has never seen God.

Demetrius gets a good testimonial from 12 everybody—yes, and from the truth itself. I add my testimony, and you know that my testimony is true.

I have much to write to you, but I do not 13 care to set it down with pen and ink. I hope 14 to see you very soon, and we will talk face to face. Peace be with you. Our friends send their greetings. Greet our friends one by one.

A LETTER OF
JUDE

1 FROM JUDE, servant of Jesus Christ and brother of James, to those whom God has called, who live in the love of God the Father and in the safe keeping of Jesus Christ.

2 Mercy, peace, and love be yours in fullest measure.

Urgent appeal to defend the faith

3 My friends, I was fully engaged in writing to you about our salvation—which is yours no less than ours—when it became urgently necessary to write at once and appeal to you to join the struggle in defence of the faith, the faith which God entrusted to his people 4 once and for all. It is in danger from certain persons who have wormed their way in, the very men whom Scripture long ago marked down for the doom they have incurred. They are the enemies of religion; they pervert the

free favour of our God into licentiousness, disowning Jesus Christ, our only Master and Lord.[a]

A reminder from history

You already know it all, but let me remind 5 you how the Lord,[b] having once delivered the people of Israel out of Egypt, next time destroyed those who were guilty of unbelief. Remember too the angels, how some of 6 them were not content to keep the dominion given to them but abandoned their proper home; and God has reserved them for judgement on the great Day, bound beneath the darkness in everlasting chains. Remember 7 Sodom and Gomorrah and the neighbouring towns; like the angels, they committed fornication and followed unnatural lusts; and they paid the penalty in eternal fire, an example for all to see.

a Or who enjoys being their leader.

a Or disowning our one and only Master, and Jesus Christ our Lord. b Some witnesses read Jesus (which might be understood as Joshua).

Character and destiny of false teachers

8 So too with these men today. Their dreams lead them to defile the body, to flout author-
9 ity, and to insult celestial beings. In contrast, when the archangel Michael was in debate with the devil, disputing the possession of Moses's body, he did not presume to con-demn him in insulting words,[c] but said, 'May the Lord rebuke you!'
10 But these men pour abuse upon things they do not understand; the things they do understand, by instinct like brute beasts,
11 prove their undoing. Alas for them! They have gone the way of Cain; they have plunged into Balaam's error for pay; they have rebelled like Korah, and they share his doom.
12 These men are a blot on your love-feasts, where they eat and drink without reverence. They are shepherds who take care only of themselves. They are clouds carried away by the wind without giving rain, trees that in season bear no fruit, dead twice over and
13 pulled up by the roots. They are fierce waves of the sea, foaming shameful deeds; they are stars that have wandered from their course, and the place for ever reserved for them is blackest darkness.
14 It was to them that Enoch, the seventh in descent from Adam, directed his prophecy when he said: 'I saw the Lord come with his
15 myriads of angels, to bring all men to judge-ment and to convict all the godless of all the godless deeds they had committed, and of all the defiant words which godless sinners had spoken against him.'

They are a set of grumblers and mal- 16 contents. They follow their lusts. Big words come rolling from their lips, and they court favour to gain their ends. But you, my 17 friends, should remember the predictions made by the apostles of our Lord Jesus Christ. This was the warning they gave you: 18 'In the final age there will be men who pour scorn on religion, and follow their own godless lusts.'

Fortify yourselves

These men draw a line between spiritual and 19 unspiritual persons, although they are them-selves[d] wholly unspiritual. But you, my 20 friends, must fortify yourselves in your most sacred faith. Continue to pray in the power of the Holy Spirit. Keep yourselves in the 21 love of God, and look forward to the day when our Lord Jesus Christ in his mercy will give eternal life.

Some doubters need pity

There are some doubting souls who need 22 your pity;[e] snatch them from the flames and 23 save them.[f] There are others for whom your pity must be mixed with fear; hate the very clothing that is contaminated with sensuality.

Glory to God!

Now to the One who can keep you from fall- 24 ing and set you in the presence of his glory, jubilant and above reproach, to the only 25 God our Saviour, be glory and majesty, might and authority, through Jesus Christ our Lord, before all time, now, and for evermore. Amen.

c Or to charge him with blasphemy.　　　*d Or* These men create divisions; they are . . . 　　*e Some wit-nesses read* There are some who raise disputes; these you should refute.　　*f So one witness; the rest read* some you should snatch from the flames and save.

Patmos   HK

THE REVELATION
OF JOHN

1 THIS IS the revelation given by God to Jesus Christ. It was given to him so that he might show his servants what must shortly happen. He made it known by sending his 2 angel to his servant John, who, in telling all that he saw, has borne witness to the word of God and to the testimony of Jesus Christ.*a*

3 Happy is the man who reads, and happy those who listen to the words of this prophecy and heed what is written in it. For the hour of fulfilment is near.

Greetings to the seven churches

4 John to the seven churches in the province of Asia.

Grace be to you and peace, from him who is and who was and who is to come, from the 5 seven spirits before his throne, and from Jesus Christ, the faithful witness, the first-born from the dead and ruler of the kings of the earth.

To him who loves us and freed us from 6 our sins with his life's blood, who made of us a royal house, to serve as the priests of his God and Father—to him be glory and dominion for ever and ever! Amen.

Behold, he is coming with the clouds! 7 Every eye shall see him, and among them those who pierced him; and all the peoples of the world shall lament in remorse. So it shall be. Amen.

'I am the Alpha and the Omega', says the 8 Lord God, who is and who was and who is to come, the sovereign Lord of all.

A vision of Christ

I, John, your brother, who share with you 9 in the suffering and the sovereignty and the endurance which is ours in Jesus—I was on the island called Patmos because I had preached God's word and borne my testimony to Jesus. It was on the Lord's day, and 10 I was caught up by the Spirit; and behind me I heard a loud voice, like the sound of a trumpet, which said to me, 'Write down 11 what you see on a scroll and send it to the seven churches: to Ephesus, Smyrna, Pergamum, Thyatira, Sardis, Philadelphia, and Laodicea.' I turned to see whose voice it was 12 that spoke to me; and when I turned I saw seven standing lamps of gold, and among the 13 lamps one like a son of man, robed down to

a Or has borne his testimony to the word of God and to Jesus Christ.

his feet, with a golden girdle round his breast.
14 The hair of his head was white as snow-white
15 wool, and his eyes flamed like fire; his feet
gleamed like burnished brass refined in a
furnace, and his voice was like the sound of
16 rushing waters. In his right hand he held
seven stars, and out of his mouth came a
sharp two-edged sword; and his face shone
like the sun in full strength.
17   When I saw him, I fell at his feet as though
dead. But he laid his right hand upon me and
said, 'Do not be afraid. I am the first and the
18 last, and I am the living one; for I was dead
and now I am alive for evermore, and I hold
the keys of Death and Death's domain.
19 Write down therefore what you have seen,
what is now, and what will be hereafter.
20   'Here is the secret meaning of the seven
stars which you saw in my right hand, and
of the seven lamps of gold: the seven stars
are the angels of the seven churches, and the
seven lamps are the seven churches.'

A message to Ephesus

2 'To the angel of the church at Ephesus write:
   ' "These are the words of the One who
holds the seven stars in his right hand and
2 walks among the seven lamps of gold: I
know all your ways, your toil and your
fortitude. I know you cannot endure evil
men; you have put to the proof those who
claim to be apostles but are not, and have
3 found them false. Fortitude you have; you
have borne up in my cause and never flagged.
4 But I have this against you: you have lost
5 your early love. Think from what a height
you have fallen; repent, and do as you once
did. Otherwise, if you do not repent, I shall
come to you and remove your lamp from its
6 place. Yet you have this in your favour: you
hate the practices of the Nicolaitans, as I do.
7 Hear, you who have ears to hear, what the
Spirit says to the churches! To him who is victorious I will give the right to eat from the tree
of life that stands in the Garden of God." '

A message to Smyrna

8 'To the angel of the church at Smyrna write:
   ' "These are the words of the First and
the Last, who was dead and came to life
9 again: I know how hard pressed you are,
and poor—and yet you are rich; I know how
you are slandered by those who claim to be
Jews but are not—they are Satan's syna-
10 gogue. Do not be afraid of the suffering to
come. The Devil will throw some of you
into prison, to put you to the test; and for
ten days you will suffer cruelly. Only be
faithful till death, and I will give you the
11 crown of life. Hear, you who have ears to
hear, what the Spirit says to the churches!
He who is victorious cannot be harmed by
the second death." '

A message to Pergamum

'To the angel of the church at Pergamum 12
write:
   ' "These are the words of the One who
has the sharp two-edged sword: I know 13
where you live; it is the place where Satan
has his throne. And yet you are holding fast
to my cause. You did not deny your faith in
me even at the time when Antipas, my faithful witness, was killed in your city, the home
of Satan. But I have a few matters to bring 14
against you: you have in Pergamum some
that hold to the teaching of Balaam, who
taught Balak to put temptation in the way
of the Israelites. He encouraged them to eat
food sacrificed to idols and to commit fornication, and in the same way you also have 15
some who hold the doctrine of the Nicolaitans. So repent! If you do not, I shall 16
come to you soon and make war upon them
with the sword that comes out of my mouth.
Hear, you who have ears to hear, what the 17
Spirit says to the churches! To him who is
victorious I will give some of the hidden
manna; I will give him also a white stone,
and on the stone will be written a new name,
known to none but him that receives it." '

THE SEVEN CHURCHES
of ASIA
○Pergamum
   ○Thyatira
      ○Sardis
○Smyrna ○Philadelphia
○Ephesus ○Laodicea
Patmos○
ℵ

A message to Thyatira

'To the angel of the church at Thyatira 18
write:
   ' "These are the words of the Son of God,
whose eyes flame like fire and whose feet
gleam like burnished brass: I know all your 19
ways, your love and faithfulness, your good
service and your fortitude; and of late you
have done even better than at first. Yet I 20
have this against you: you tolerate that
Jezebel, the woman who claims to be a
prophetess, who by her teaching lures my
servants into fornication and into eating

21 food sacrificed to idols. I have given her time to repent, but she refuses to repent of
22 her fornication. So I will throw her on to a bed of pain,[b] and plunge her lovers into terrible suffering, unless they forswear what
23 she is doing; and her children I will strike dead. This will teach all the churches that I am the searcher of men's hearts and thoughts, and that I will reward each one
24 of you according to his deeds. And now I speak to you others in Thyatira, who do not accept this teaching and have had no experience of what they like to call the deep secrets of Satan; on you I will impose no further
25 burden. Only hold fast to what you have,
26 until I come. To him who is victorious, to him who perseveres in doing my will to the end, I will give authority over the nations—
27 that same authority which I received from my Father—and he shall rule them with an iron rod, smashing them to bits like earthen-
28 ware; and I will give him also the star of
29 dawn. Hear, you who have ears to hear, what the Spirit says to the churches!"'

A message to Sardis

3 'To the angel of the church at Sardis write: ' "These are the words of the One who holds the seven spirits of God, the seven stars: I know all your ways; that though you have a name for being alive, you are dead.
2 Wake up, and put some strength into what is left, which must otherwise die! For I have not found any work of yours completed in
3 the eyes of my God. So remember the teaching you received; observe it, and repent. If you do not wake up, I shall come upon you like a thief, and you will not know the
4 moment of my coming. Yet you have a few persons in Sardis who have not polluted their clothing. They shall walk with me in
5 white, for so they deserve. He who is victorious shall thus be robed all in white; his name I will never strike off the roll of the living, for in the presence of my Father and his angels I will acknowledge him as mine.
6 Hear, you who have ears to hear, what the Spirit says to the churches!"'

A message to Philadelphia

7 'To the angel of the church at Philadelphia write: ' "These are the words of the holy one, the true one, who holds the key of David; when he opens none may shut, when he
8 shuts none may open: I know all your ways; and look, I have set before you an open door, which no one can shut. Your strength, I know, is small, yet you have observed my commands and have not disowned my name.
9 So this is what I will do: I will make those of Satan's synagogue, who claim to be Jews but are lying frauds, come and fall down at your feet; and they shall know that you are
10 my beloved people. Because you have kept my command and stood fast, I will also keep you from the ordeal that is to fall upon the
11 whole world and test its inhabitants. I am coming soon; hold fast what you have, and let no one rob you of your crown. He who is
12 victorious—I will make him a pillar in the temple of my God; he shall never leave it. And I will write the name of my God upon him, and the name of the city of my God, that new Jerusalem which is coming down out of heaven from my God, and my own
13 new name. Hear, you who have ears to hear, what the Spirit says to the churches!"'

A message to Laodicea

14 'To the angel of the church at Laodicea write: ' "These are the words of the Amen, the faithful and true witness, the prime source of all God's creation: I know all your ways;
15 you are neither hot nor cold. How I wish
16 you were either hot or cold! But because you are lukewarm, neither hot nor cold, I will
17 spit you out of my mouth. You say, 'How rich I am! And how well I have done! I have everything I want.' In fact, though you do not know it, you are the most pitiful
18 wretch, poor, blind, and naked. So I advise you to buy from me gold refined in the fire, to make you truly rich, and white clothes to put on to hide the shame of your nakedness, and ointment for your eyes so that you may
19 see. All whom I love I reprove and discipline. Be on your mettle therefore and repent.
20 Here I stand knocking at the door; if anyone hears my voice and opens the door, I will come in and sit down to supper with him
21 and he with me. To him who is victorious I will grant a place on my throne, as I myself was victorious and sat down with my
22 Father on his throne. Hear, you who have ears to hear, what the Spirit says to the churches!"'

A vision of a throne in heaven

4 After this I looked, and there before my eyes was a door opened in heaven; and the voice that I had first heard speaking to me like a trumpet said, 'Come up here, and I will show you what must happen hereafter.' At
2 once I was caught up by the Spirit. There in heaven stood a throne, and on the throne
3 sat one whose appearance was like the gleam of jasper and cornelian; and round the throne was a rainbow, bright as an emerald.
4 In a circle about this throne were twenty-four other thrones, and on them sat twenty-four elders, robed in white and wearing
5 crowns of gold. From the throne went out flashes of lightning and peals of thunder.

b One witness reads into a furnace.

Burning before the throne were seven flam-
6 ing torches, the seven spirits of God, and
in front of it stretched what seemed a sea of
glass, like a sheet of ice.

In the centre, round the throne itself, were
four living creatures, covered with eyes, in
7 front and behind. The first creature was like
a lion, the second like an ox, the third had
a human face, the fourth was like an eagle
8 in flight. The four living creatures, each of
them with six wings, had eyes all over, inside
and out; and by day and by night without
a pause they sang:

'Holy, holy, holy is God the sovereign
Lord of all, who was, and is, and is to
come!'

9 As often as the living creatures give glory
and honour and thanks to the One who sits
on the throne, who lives for ever and ever,
10 the twenty-four elders fall down before the
One who sits on the throne and worship him
who lives for ever and ever; and as they lay
their crowns before the throne they cry:

11 'Thou art worthy, O Lord our God, to
receive glory and honour and power, because thou didst create all things; by thy
will they were created, and have their
being!'

The Lamb receives a sealed scroll

5 Then I saw in the right hand of the One who
sat on the throne a scroll, with writing inside
and out, and it was sealed up with seven
2 seals. And I saw a mighty angel proclaiming
in a loud voice, 'Who is worthy to open the
3 scroll and to break its seals?' There was no
one in heaven or on earth or under the earth
able to open the scroll or to look inside it.
4 I was in tears because no one was found who
was worthy to open the scroll or to look in-
5 side it. But one of the elders said to me: 'Do
not weep; for the Lion from the tribe of
Judah, the Scion of David, has won the right
to open the scroll and break its seven seals.'
6 Then I saw standing in the very middle of
the throne, inside the circle of living creatures
and the circle of elders,[c] a Lamb with the
marks of slaughter upon him. He had seven
horns and seven eyes, the eyes which are
the seven spirits of God sent out over all the
7 world. And the Lamb went up and took
the scroll from the right hand of the One
8 who sat on the throne. When he took it, the
four living creatures and the twenty-four
elders fell down before the Lamb. Each of
the elders had a harp, and they held golden
bowls full of incense, the prayers of God's
9 people, and they were singing a new song:

'Thou art worthy to take the scroll and
to break its seals, for thou wast slain and

by thy blood didst purchase for God men
of every tribe and language, people and
nation; thou hast made of them a royal 10
house, to serve our God as priests; and
they shall reign upon earth.'

Then as I looked I heard the voices of 11
countless angels. These were all round the
throne and the living creatures and the
elders. Myriads upon myriads there were,
thousands upon thousands, and they cried 12
aloud:

'Worthy is the Lamb, the Lamb that was
slain, to receive all power and wealth,
wisdom and might, honour and glory and
praise!'

Then I heard every created thing in heaven 13
and on earth and under the earth and in the
sea, all that is in them, crying:

'Praise and honour, glory and might, to
him who sits on the throne and to the
Lamb for ever and ever!'

And the four living creatures said, 'Amen', 14
and the elders fell down and worshipped.

The breaking of the six seals

Then I watched as the Lamb broke the first 6
of the seven seals; and I heard one of the
four living creatures say in a voice like
thunder, 'Come!' And there before my eyes 2
was a white horse, and its rider held a bow.
He was given a crown, and he rode forth,
conquering and to conquer.

When the Lamb broke the second seal, 3
I heard the second creature say, 'Come!'
And out came another horse, all red. To its 4
rider was given power to take peace from
the earth and make men slaughter one
another; and he was given a great sword.

When he broke the third seal, I heard the 5
third creature say, 'Come!' And there, as
I looked, was a black horse; and its rider
held in his hand a pair of scales. And I 6
heard what sounded like a voice from the
midst of the living creatures, which said,
'A whole day's wage for a quart of flour, a
whole day's wage for three quarts of barley-
meal! But spare the olive and the vine.'

When he broke the fourth seal, I heard 7
the voice of the fourth creature say, 'Come!'
And there, as I looked, was another horse, 8
sickly pale; and its rider's name was Death,
and Hades came close behind. To him was
given power over a quarter of the earth, with
the right to kill by sword and by famine, by
pestilence and wild beasts.

When he broke the fifth seal, I saw under- 9
neath[d] the altar the souls of those who had
been slaughtered for God's word and for
the testimony they bore. They gave a great 10
cry: 'How long, sovereign Lord, holy and

c *Or* standing between the throne, with the four living creatures, and the elders . . .   d *Or* at the foot of . . .

true, must it be before thou wilt vindicate us and avenge our blood on the inhabitants 11 of the earth?' Each of them was given a white robe; and they were told to rest a little while longer, until the tally should be complete of all their brothers in Christ's service who were to be killed as they had been.

12   Then I watched as he broke the sixth seal. And there was a violent earthquake; the sun turned black as a funeral pall and the moon 13 all red as blood; the stars in the sky fell to the earth, like figs shaken down by a gale; 14 the sky vanished, as a scroll is rolled up, and every mountain and island was moved 15 from its place. Then the kings of the earth, magnates and marshals, the rich and the powerful, and all men, slave or free, hid themselves in caves and mountain crags; 16 and they called out to the mountains and the crags, 'Fall on us and hide us from the face of the One who sits on the throne and from 17 the vengeance of the Lamb.' For the great day of their vengeance has come, and who will be able to stand?

Israel's hundred and forty-four thousand

7 After this I saw four angels stationed at the four corners of the earth, holding back the four winds so that no wind should blow on 2 sea or land or on any tree. Then I saw another angel rising out of the east, carrying the seal of the living God; and he called aloud to the four angels who had been given 3 the power to ravage land and sea: 'Do no damage to sea or land or trees until we have set the seal of our God upon the foreheads 4 of his servants.' And I heard the number of those who had received the seal. From all the tribes of Israel there were a hundred 5 and forty-four thousand: twelve thousand from the tribe of Judah, twelve thousand from the tribe of Reuben, twelve thou- 6 sand from the tribe of Gad, twelve thousand from the tribe of Asher, twelve thousand from the tribe of Naphtali, twelve thou- 7 sand from the tribe of Manasseh, twelve thousand from the tribe of Simeon, twelve thousand from the tribe of Levi, twelve thou- 8 sand from the tribe of Issachar, twelve thousand from the tribe of Zebulun, twelve thousand from the tribe of Joseph, and twelve thousand from the tribe of Benjamin.

A vast throng no one could count

9 After this I looked and saw a vast throng, which no one could count, from every nation, of all tribes, peoples, and languages, standing in front of the throne and before the Lamb. They were robed in white and 10 had palms in their hands, and they shouted together:

'Victory to our God who sits on the throne, and to the Lamb!'

And all the angels stood round the throne 11 and the elders and the four living creatures, and they fell on their faces before the throne and worshipped God, crying: 12

'Amen! Praise and glory and wisdom, thanksgiving and honour, power and might, be to our God for ever and ever! Amen.'

Then one of the elders turned to me and 13 said, 'These men that are robed in white— who are they and from where do they come?' But I answered, 'My lord, you know, not I.' 14 Then he said to me, 'These are the men who have passed through the great ordeal; they have washed their robes and made them white in the blood of the Lamb. That is why 15 they stand before the throne of God and minister to him day and night in his temple; and he who sits on the throne will dwell with them. They shall never again feel hunger or 16 thirst, the sun shall not beat on them nor any scorching heat, because the Lamb who 17 is at the heart of the throne will be their shepherd and will guide them to the springs of the water of life; and God will wipe all tears from their eyes.'

The breaking of the seventh seal

Now when the Lamb broke the seventh seal, 8 there was silence in heaven for what seemed half an hour. Then I looked, and the seven 2 angels that stand in the presence of God were given seven trumpets.

Then another angel came and stood at 3 the altar, holding a golden censer; and he was given a great quantity of incense to offer with the prayers of all God's people upon the golden altar in front of the throne. And 4 from the angel's hand the smoke of the incense went up before God with the prayers of his people. Then the angel took the censer, 5 filled it from the altar fire, and threw it down upon the earth; and there were peals of thunder, lightning, and an earthquake.

The first four trumpets blown

Then the seven angels that held the seven 6 trumpets prepared to blow them.

The first blew his trumpet; and there came 7 hail and fire mingled with blood, and this was hurled upon the earth. A third of the earth was burnt, a third of the trees were burnt, all the green grass was burnt.

8 The second angel blew his trumpet; and what looked like a great blazing mountain was hurled into the sea. A third of the sea 9 was turned to blood, a third of the living creatures in it died, and a third of the ships on it foundered.

10 The third angel blew his trumpet; and a great star shot from the sky, flaming like a torch; and it fell on a third of the 11 rivers and springs. The name of the star was Wormwood; and a third of the water turned to wormwood, and men in great numbers died of the water because it had been poisoned.

12 The fourth angel blew his trumpet; and a third part of the sun was struck, a third of the moon, and a third of the stars, so that the third part went dark and a third of the light of the day failed, and of the night.

13 Then I looked, and I heard an eagle calling with a loud cry as it flew in mid-heaven: 'Woe, woe, woe to the inhabitants of the earth when the trumpets sound which the three last angels must now blow!'

The fifth trumpet; the first woe

9 Then the fifth angel blew his trumpet; and I saw a star that had fallen from heaven to earth, and the star was given the key of the 2 shaft of the abyss. With this he opened the shaft of the abyss; and from the shaft smoke rose like smoke from a great furnace, and the sun and the air were darkened by the 3 smoke from the shaft. Then over the earth, out of the smoke, came locusts, and they were given the powers that earthly scorpions 4 have. They were told to do no injury to the grass or to any plant or tree, but only to those men who had not received the seal of 5 God on their foreheads. These they were allowed to torment for five months, with torment like a scorpion's sting; but they 6 were not to kill them. During that time these men will seek death, but they will not find it; they will long to die, but death will elude them.

7 In appearance the locusts were like horses equipped for battle. On their heads were what looked like golden crowns; their faces 8 were like human faces and their hair like women's hair; they had teeth like lions' 9 teeth, and wore breastplates like iron; the sound of their wings was like the noise of 10 horses and chariots rushing to battle; they had tails like scorpions, with stings in them, and in their tails lay their power to plague 11 mankind for five months. They had for their king the angel of the abyss, whose name, in Hebrew, is Abaddon, and in Greek, Apollyon, or the Destroyer.

12 The first woe has now passed. But there are still two more to come.

The sixth trumpet; the second woe

The sixth angel then blew his trumpet; and 13 I heard a voice coming from between the horns of the golden altar that stood in the presence of God. It said to the sixth angel, 14 who held the trumpet: 'Release the four angels held bound at the great river Euphrates!' So the four angels were let 15 loose, to kill a third of mankind. They had been held ready for this moment, for this very year and month, day and hour. And their squadrons of cavalry, whose 16 count I heard, numbered two hundred million.

This was how I saw the horses and their 17 riders in my vision: They wore breastplates, fiery red, blue, and sulphur-yellow; the horses had heads like lions' heads, and out of their mouths came fire, smoke, and sulphur. By these three plagues, that is, by the 18 fire, the smoke, and the sulphur that came from their mouths, a third of mankind was killed. The power of the horses lay in their 19 mouths, and in their tails also; for their tails were like snakes, with heads, and with them too they dealt injuries.

The rest of mankind who survived these 20 plagues still did not abjure the gods their hands had fashioned, nor cease their worship of devils and of idols made from gold, silver, bronze, stone, and wood, which cannot see or hear or walk. Nor did they repent 21 of their murders, their sorcery, their fornication, or their robberies.

The angel with a scroll

Then I saw another mighty angel coming 10 down from heaven. He was wrapped in cloud, with the rainbow round his head; his face shone like the sun and his legs were like pillars of fire. In his hand he held a little 2 scroll unrolled. His right foot he planted on the sea, and his left on the land. Then he gave 3 a great shout, like the roar of a lion; and when he shouted, the seven thunders spoke. I was about to write down what the seven 4 thunders had said; but I heard a voice from heaven saying, 'Seal up what the seven thunders have said; do not write it down.' Then the angel that I saw standing on the 5 sea and the land raised his right hand to heaven and swore by him who lives for ever 6 and ever, who created heaven and earth and the sea and everything in them: 'There shall be no more delay; but when the time comes 7 for the seventh angel to sound his trumpet, the hidden purpose of God will have been fulfilled, as he promised to his servants the prophets.'

Then the voice which I heard from heaven 8 was speaking to me again, and it said, 'Go and take the open scroll in the hand of the angel that stands on the sea and the land.'

9 So I went to the angel and asked him to give me the little scroll. He said to me, 'Take it, and eat it. It will turn your stomach sour, although in your mouth it will taste
10 sweet as honey.' So I took the little scroll from the angel's hand and ate it, and in my mouth it did taste sweet as honey; but when I swallowed it my stomach turned sour.
11 Then they said to me, 'Once again you must utter prophecies over peoples and nations and languages and many kings.'

The temple and the two witnesses

11 I was given a long cane, a kind of measuring-rod, and told: 'Now go and measure the temple of God, the altar, and the number of
2 the worshippers. But have nothing to do with the outer court of the temple; do not measure that; for it has been given over to the Gentiles, and they will trample the Holy
3 City underfoot for forty-two months. And I have two witnesses, whom I will appoint to prophesy, dressed in sackcloth, all through
4 those twelve hundred and sixty days.' These are the two olive-trees and the two lamps that stand in the presence of the Lord of the
5 earth. If anyone seeks to do them harm, fire pours from their mouths and consumes their enemies; and thus shall the man die who
6 seeks to do them harm. These two have the power to shut up the sky, so that no rain may fall during the time of their prophesying; and they have the power to turn water to blood and to strike the earth at will with
7 every kind of plague. But when they have completed their testimony, the beast that comes up from the abyss will wage war upon
8 them and will defeat and kill them. Their corpses will lie in the street of the great city, whose name in allegory is Sodom, or Egypt,
9 where also their Lord was crucified. For three days and a half men from every people and tribe, of every language and nation, gaze upon their corpses and refuse them
10 burial. All men on earth gloat over them, make merry, and exchange presents; for these two prophets were a torment to the
11 whole earth. But at the end of the three days and a half the breath of life from God came into them; and they stood up on their feet
12 to the terror of all who saw it. Then a loud voice was heard speaking to them from heaven, which said, 'Come up here!' And they went up to heaven in a cloud, in full
13 view of their enemies. At that same moment there was a violent earthquake, and a tenth of the city fell. Seven thousand people were killed in the earthquake; the rest in terror did homage to the God of heaven.
14 The second woe has now passed. But the third is soon to come.

The seventh trumpet; the third woe announced

Then the seventh angel blew his trumpet; and 15 voices were heard in heaven shouting:

> 'The sovereignty of the world has passed to our Lord and his Christ, and he shall reign for ever and ever!'

And the twenty-four elders, seated on their 16 thrones before God, fell on their faces and worshipped God, saying: 17

> 'We give thee thanks, O Lord God, sovereign over all, who art and who wast, because thou hast taken thy great power into thy hands and entered upon thy reign. The nations raged, but thy day of 18 retribution has come. Now is the time for the dead to be judged; now is the time for recompense to thy servants the prophets, to thy dedicated people, and all who honour thy name, both great and small, the time to destroy those who destroy the earth.'

Then God's temple in heaven was laid 19 open, and within the temple was seen the ark of his covenant. There came flashes of lightning and peals of thunder, an earthquake, and a storm of hail.

Enmity between the dragon and the woman

Next appeared a great portent in heaven, a **12** woman robed with the sun, beneath her feet the moon, and on her head a crown of twelve stars. She was pregnant, and in the anguish 2 of her labour she cried out to be delivered. Then a second portent appeared in heaven: 3 a great red dragon with seven heads and ten horns; on his heads were seven diadems, and with his tail he swept down a third of 4 the stars in the sky and flung them to the earth. The dragon stood in front of the woman who was about to give birth, so that when her child was born he might devour it. She gave birth to a male child, 5 who is destined to rule all nations with an iron rod. But her child was snatched up to God and his throne; and the woman herself 6 fled into the wilds, where she had a place prepared for her by God, there to be sustained for twelve hundred and sixty days.

War in heaven; the dragon overthrown

Then war broke out in heaven. Michael and 7 his angels waged war upon the dragon. The dragon and his angels fought, but they had 8 not the strength to win, and no foothold was left them in heaven. So the great dragon was 9 thrown down, that serpent of old that led the whole world astray, whose name is Satan, or the Devil—thrown down to the earth, and his angels with him.

Then I heard a voice in heaven proclaim- 10 ing aloud: 'This is the hour of victory for our God, the hour of his sovereignty and power, when his Christ comes to his rightful rule! For the accuser of our brothers is overthrown, who day and night accused them before our God. By the sacrifice of the Lamb they have conquered him, and by the testimony which they uttered;*e* for they did not hold their lives too dear to lay them down. Rejoice then, you heavens and you that dwell in them! But woe to you, earth and sea, for the Devil has come down to you in great fury, knowing that his time is short!'

The dragon wages war on earth

When the dragon found that he had been thrown down to the earth, he went in pursuit of the woman who had given birth to the male child. But the woman was given two great eagle's wings, to fly to the place in the wilds where for three years and a half she was to be sustained, out of reach of the serpent. From his mouth the serpent spewed a flood of water after the woman to sweep her away with its spate. But the earth came to her rescue and opened its mouth and swallowed the river which the dragon spewed from his mouth. At this the dragon grew furious with the woman, and went off to wage war on the rest of her offspring, that is, on those who keep God's commandments and maintain their testimony to Jesus. He took his stand on the sea-shore.

A beast out of the sea

Then*f* out of the sea I saw a beast rising. It had ten horns and seven heads. On its horns were ten diadems, and on each head a blasphemous name. The beast I saw was like a leopard, but its feet were like a bear's and its mouth like a lion's mouth. The dragon conferred upon it his power and rule, and great authority. One of its heads appeared to have received a death-blow; but the mortal wound was healed. The whole world went after the beast in wondering admiration. Men worshipped the dragon because he had conferred his authority upon the beast; they worshipped the beast also, and chanted, 'Who is like the Beast? Who can fight against it?'

The beast was allowed to mouth bombast and blasphemy, and was given the right to reign for forty-two months. It opened its mouth in blasphemy against God, reviling his name and his heavenly dwelling.*g* It was also allowed to wage war on God's people and to defeat them, and was granted*h* authority over every tribe and people, language and nation. All on earth will worship it, except those whose names the Lamb that was slain

keeps in his roll of the living, written there since the world was made.

Hear, you who have ears to hear! Whoever is to be made prisoner, a prisoner he shall be. Whoever takes the sword to kill, by the sword he is bound to be killed. This is where the fortitude and faithfulness of God's people have their place.

A beast out of the earth

Then I saw another beast, which came up out of the earth; it had two horns like a lamb's, but spoke like a dragon. It wielded all the authority of the first beast in its presence, and made the earth and its inhabitants worship this first beast, whose mortal wound had been healed. It worked great miracles, even making fire come down from heaven to earth before men's eyes. By the miracles it was allowed to perform in the presence of the beast it deluded the inhabitants of the earth, and made them erect an image in honour of the beast that had been wounded by the sword and yet lived. It was allowed to give breath to the image of the beast, so that it could speak, and could cause all who would not worship the image to be put to death. Moreover, it caused everyone, great and small, rich and poor, slave and free, to be branded with a mark on his right hand or forehead, and no one was allowed to buy or sell unless he bore this beast's mark, either name or number. (Here is the key; and anyone who has intelligence may work out the number of the beast. The number represents a man's name, and the numerical value of its letters is six hundred and sixty-six.)

A new song; a ransomed people

Then I looked, and on Mount Zion stood the Lamb, and with him were a hundred and forty-four thousand who had his name and the name of his Father written on their foreheads. I heard a sound from heaven like the noise of rushing water and the deep roar of thunder; it was the sound of harpers playing on their harps. There before the throne, and the four living creatures and the elders, they were singing a new song. That song no one could learn except the hundred and forty-four thousand, who alone from the whole world had been ransomed. These are men who did not defile themselves with women, for they have kept themselves chaste, and they follow the Lamb wherever he goes. They have been ransomed as the firstfruits of humanity for God and the Lamb. No lie was found in their lips; they are faultless.

---

e Or the word of God to which they bore witness.
stood by the sea-shore and . . .   *g Some witnesses read* reviling his name and his dwelling-place, that is, those
that live in heaven.   *h Some witnesses read* It was granted . . . (*omitting the words* was also . . . them, and).
f Some witnesses read . . . testimony to Jesus. Then I

An angel with the eternal Gospel

6 Then I saw an angel flying in mid-heaven, with an eternal gospel to proclaim to those on earth, to every nation and tribe, language 7 and people. He cried in a loud voice, 'Fear God and pay him homage; for the hour of his judgement has come! Worship him who made heaven and earth, the sea and the water-springs!'

A second angel

8 Then another angel, a second, followed, and he cried, 'Fallen, fallen is Babylon the great, she who has made all nations drink the fierce wine of[i] her fornication!'

A third angel

9 Yet a third angel followed, crying out loud, 'Whoever worships the beast and its image and receives its mark on his forehead or 10 hand, he shall drink the wine of God's wrath, poured undiluted into the cup of his vengeance. He shall be tormented in sulphurous flames before the holy angels and before the 11 Lamb. The smoke of their torment will rise for ever and ever, and there will be no respite day or night for those who worship the beast and its image or receive the mark of its name.' 12 This is where the fortitude of God's people has its place—in keeping God's commands and remaining loyal to Jesus.

Happy are those who die in the faith

13 Moreover, I heard a voice from heaven, saying, 'Write this: "Happy are the dead who die in the faith of Christ! Henceforth",[j] says the Spirit,[k] "they may rest from their labours; for they take with them the record of their deeds."'

The harvest of the earth

14 Then as I looked there appeared a white cloud, and on the cloud sat one like a son of man. He had on his head a crown of gold 15 and in his hand a sharp sickle. Another angel came out of the temple and called in a loud voice to him who sat on the cloud: 'Stretch out your sickle and reap; for harvest-time has come, and earth's crop is over-ripe.' 16 So he who sat on the cloud put his sickle to the earth and its harvest was reaped. 17 Then another angel came out of the heavenly temple, and he also had a sharp 18 sickle. Then from the altar came yet another, the angel who has authority over fire, and he shouted to the one with the sharp sickle: 'Stretch out your sickle, and gather in earth's grape-harvest, for its clusters are 19 ripe.' So the angel put his sickle to the earth and gathered in its grapes, and threw them into the great winepress of God's wrath. The 20 winepress was trodden outside the city, and for two hundred miles around blood flowed from the press to the height of the horses' bridles.

The seven last plagues announced

15 Then I saw another great and astonishing portent in heaven: seven angels with seven plagues, the last plagues of all, for with them the wrath of God is consummated.

2 I saw what appeared to be a sea of glass shot with fire, and beside the sea of glass, holding the harps which God had given them, were those who had won the victory over the beast and its image and the number of its name.

3 They were singing the song of Moses, the servant of God, and the song of the Lamb, as they chanted:

'Great and marvellous are thy deeds, O Lord God, sovereign over all; just and true are thy ways, thou king of the ages.[l] 4 Who shall not revere thee, Lord, and do homage to thy name? For thou alone art holy. All nations shall come and worship in thy presence, for thy just dealings stand revealed.'

5 After this, as I looked, the sanctuary of the heavenly Tent of Testimony was thrown 6 open, and out of it came the seven angels with the seven plagues. They were robed in fine linen, clean and shining, and had golden 7 girdles round their breasts. Then one of the four living creatures gave the seven angels seven golden bowls full of the wrath of God 8 who lives for ever and ever; and the sanctuary was filled with smoke from the glory of God and his power, so that no one could enter it until the seven plagues of the seven angels were completed.

16 Then from the sanctuary I heard a loud voice, and it said to the seven angels, 'Go and pour out the seven bowls of God's wrath on the earth.'

The outpouring of the bowls of wrath

So the first angel went and poured his bowl 2 on the earth; and foul malignant sores appeared on those men that wore the mark of the beast and worshipped its image.

i Or drink the wine of God's wrath upon . . . dead who henceforth die in the faith of Christ!" "Yes," says the Spirit . . . the nations.

j Or Assuredly.

k Some witnesses read ". . . the

l Some witnesses read king of

3 The second angel poured his bowl on the sea, and it turned to blood like the blood from a corpse; and every living thing in the sea died.

4 The third angel poured his bowl on the rivers and springs, and they turned to blood.

5 Then I heard the angel of the waters say, 'Just art thou in these thy judgements, thou 6 Holy One who art and wast; for they shed the blood of thy people and of thy prophets, and thou hast given them blood to drink. 7 They have their deserts!' And I heard the altar cry, 'Yes, Lord God, sovereign over all, true and just are thy judgements!'

8 The fourth angel poured his bowl on the sun; and it was allowed to burn men with its 9 flames. They were fearfully burned; but they only cursed the name of God who had the power to inflict such plagues, and they refused to repent or do him homage.

10 The fifth angel poured his bowl on the throne of the beast; and its kingdom was plunged in darkness. Men gnawed their 11 tongues in agony, but they only cursed the God of heaven for their sores and pains, and would not repent of what they had done.

12 The sixth angel poured his bowl on the great river Euphrates; and its water was dried up, to prepare the way for the kings from the east. 13 Then I saw coming from the mouth of the dragon, the mouth of the beast, and the mouth of the false prophet, three foul spirits 14 like frogs. These spirits were devils, with power to work miracles. They were sent out to muster all the kings of the world for the great day of battle of God the sovereign 15 Lord. ('That is the day when I come like a thief! Happy the man who stays awake and keeps on his clothes, so that he will not have to go naked and ashamed for all to see!') 16 So they assembled the kings at the place called in Hebrew Armageddon.

17 Then the seventh angel poured his bowl on the air; and out of the sanctuary came a loud voice from the throne, which said, 18 'It is over!' And there followed flashes of lightning and peals of thunder, and a violent earthquake, like none before it in human 19 history, so violent it was. The great city was split in three; the cities of the world fell in ruin; and God did not forget Babylon the great, but made her drink the cup which was filled with the fierce wine of his vengeance. 20 Every island vanished; there was not a 21 mountain to be seen. Huge hailstones, weighing perhaps a hundredweight, fell on men from the sky; and they cursed God for the plague of hail, because that plague was so severe.

The great whore

Then one of the seven angels that held the 17 seven bowls came and spoke to me and said, 'Come, and I will show you the judgement on the great whore, enthroned above the ocean. The kings of the earth have com- 2 mitted fornication with her, and on the wine of her fornication men all over the world have made themselves drunk.' In the Spirit 3 he carried me away into the wilds, and there I saw a woman mounted on a scarlet beast which was covered with blasphemous names and had seven heads and ten horns. The 4 woman was clothed in purple and scarlet and bedizened with gold and jewels and pearls. In her hand she held a gold cup, full of obscenities and the foulness of her fornication; and written on her forehead was a 5 name with a secret meaning: 'Babylon the great, the mother of whores and of every obscenity on earth.' The woman, I saw, was 6 drunk with the blood of God's people and with the blood of those who had borne their testimony to Jesus.

As I looked at her I was greatly astonished. But the angel said to me, 'Why are you so 7 astonished? I will tell you the secret of the woman and of the beast she rides, with the seven heads and the ten horns. The beast 8 you have seen is he who once was alive, and is alive no longer, but has yet to ascend out of the abyss before going to perdition. Those on earth whose names have not been inscribed in the roll of the living ever since the world was made will all be astonished to see the beast; for he once was alive, and is alive no longer, and has still to appear.

A clue to interpret the vision

'But here is the clue for those who can inter- 9 pret it. The seven heads are seven hills on which the woman sits. They represent also 10 seven kings,[m] of whom five have already fallen, one is now reigning, and the other has yet to come; and when he does come he is only to last for a little while. As for the 11 beast that once was alive and is alive no longer, he is an eighth—and yet he is one of the seven, and he is going to perdition. The 12 ten horns you saw are ten kings who have not yet begun to reign, but who for one hour are to share with the beast the exercise of royal authority; for they have but a single 13 purpose among them and will confer their power and authority upon the beast. They 14 will wage war upon the Lamb, but the Lamb will defeat them, for he is Lord of lords and King of kings, and his victory will be shared by his followers, called and chosen and faithful.'[n]

Then he said to me, 'The ocean you saw, 15

---

m Or emperors.   *n Or . . .* kings, and his followers are faithful men, called and selected for service.

where the great whore sat, is an ocean of peoples and populations, nations and lan-
16 guages. As for the ten horns you saw, they together with the beast will come to hate the whore; they will strip her naked and leave her desolate, they will batten on her flesh
17 and burn her to ashes. For God has put it into their heads to carry out his purpose, by making common cause and conferring their sovereignty upon the beast until all that
18 God has spoken is fulfilled. The woman you saw is the great city that holds sway over the kings of the earth.'

The fall of Babylon

18 After this I saw another angel coming down from heaven; he came with great authority and the earth was lit up with his splendour.
2 Then in a mighty voice he proclaimed, 'Fallen, fallen is Babylon the great! She has become a dwelling for demons, a haunt

Earth mourns, heaven exults

The kings of the earth who committed 9 fornication with her and wallowed in her luxury will weep and wail over her, as they see the smoke of her conflagration. They will 10 stand at a distance, for horror at her torment, and will say, 'Alas, alas for the great city, the mighty city of Babylon! In a single hour your doom has struck!'

The merchants of the earth also will weep 11 and mourn for her, because no one any longer buys their cargoes, cargoes of gold 12 and silver, jewels and pearls, cloths of purple and scarlet, silks and fine linens; all kinds of scented woods, ivories, and every sort of thing made of costly woods, bronze, iron, or marble; cinnamon and spice, incense, 13 perfumes and frankincense; wine, oil, flour and wheat, sheep and cattle, horses, chariots, slaves, and the lives of men. 'The fruit you 14 longed for', they will say, 'is gone from you; all the glitter and the glamour are lost, never to be yours again!' The traders in all these 15 wares, who gained their wealth from her, will stand at a distance for horror at her

HK

for every unclean spirit, for every vile and
3 loathsome bird. For all nations have drunk deep of*⁰* the fierce wine of her fornication; the kings of the earth have committed fornication with her, and merchants the world over have grown rich on her bloated wealth.'
4 Then I heard another voice from heaven that said: 'Come out of her, my people, lest you take part in her sins and share in her
5 plagues. For her sins are piled high as heaven, and God has not forgotten her
6 crimes. Pay her back in her own coin, repay her twice over for her deeds! Double for her the strength of the potion she mixed!
7 Mete out grief and torment to match her voluptuous pomp! She says in her heart, "I am a queen on my throne! No mourning
8 for me, no widow's weeds!" Because of this her plagues shall strike her in a single day —pestilence, bereavement, famine, and burn- ing—for mighty is the Lord God who has pronounced her doom!'

(Rev. 18. 12)

torment, weeping and mourning and saying, 16 'Alas, alas for the great city, that was clothed in fine linen and purple and scarlet, bedizened with gold and jewels and pearls! Alas that in one hour so much wealth should 17 be laid waste!'

Then all the sea-captains and voyagers, the sailors and those who traded by sea, stood at a distance and cried out as they 18 saw the smoke of her conflagration: 'Was there ever a city like the great city?' They 19

o Other witnesses read have been ruined by . . .

threw dust on their heads, weeping and mourning and saying, 'Alas, alas for the great city, where all who had ships at sea grew rich on her wealth! Alas that in a single hour she should be laid waste!'

But let heaven exult over her; exult, apostles and prophets and people of God; for in the judgement against her he has vindicated your cause!

Then a mighty angel took up a stone like a great millstone and hurled it into the sea and said, 'Thus shall Babylon, the great city, be sent hurtling down, never to be seen again! No more shall the sound of harpers and minstrels, of flute-players and trumpeters, be heard in you; no more shall craftsmen of any trade be found in you; no more shall the sound of the mill be heard in you; no more shall the light of the lamp be seen in you; no more shall the voice of the bride and bridegroom be heard in you! Your traders were once the merchant princes of the world, and with your sorcery you deceived all the nations.'

For the blood of the prophets and of God's people was found in her, the blood of all who had been done to death on earth.

The Lamb's wedding-day

After this I heard what sounded like the roar of a vast throng in heaven; and they were shouting:

'Alleluia! Victory and glory and power belong to our God, for true and just are his judgements! He has condemned the great whore who corrupted the earth with her fornication, and has avenged upon her the blood of his servants.'

Then once more they shouted:

'Alleluia! The smoke goes up from her for ever and ever!'

And the twenty-four elders and the four living creatures fell down and worshipped God as he sat on the throne, and they too cried:

'Amen! Alleluia!'

Then a voice came from the throne which said: 'Praise our God, all you his servants, you that fear him, both great and small!'

Again I heard what sounded like a vast crowd, like the noise of rushing water and deep roars of thunder, and they cried:

'Alleluia! The Lord our God, sovereign over all, has entered on his reign! Exult and shout for joy and do him homage, for the wedding-day of the Lamb has come! His bride has made herself ready, and for her dress she has been given fine linen, clean and shining.'

(Now the fine linen signifies the righteous deeds of God's people.)

Then the angel said to me, 'Write this: "Happy are those who are invited to the wedding-supper of the Lamb!"' And he added, 'These are the very words of God.' At this I fell at his feet to worship him. But he said to me, 'No, not that! I am but a fellow-servant with you and your brothers who bear their testimony to Jesus. It is God you must worship. Those who bear testimony to Jesus are inspired like the prophets.'[p]

The Rider on a white horse

Then I saw heaven wide open, and there before me was a white horse; and its rider's name was Faithful and True, for he is just in judgement and just in war. His eyes flamed like fire, and on his head were many diadems. Written upon him was a name known to none but himself, and he was robed in a garment drenched in blood.[q] He was called the Word of God, and the armies of heaven followed him on white horses, clothed in fine linen, clean and shining. From his mouth there went a sharp sword with which to smite the nations; for he it is who shall rule them with an iron rod, and tread the winepress of the wrath and retribution of God the sovereign Lord. And on his robe and on his thigh there was written the name: 'King of kings and Lord of lords.'

Then I saw an angel standing in the sun, and he cried aloud to all the birds flying in mid-heaven: 'Come and gather for God's great supper, to eat the flesh of kings and commanders and fighting men, the flesh of horses and their riders, the flesh of all men, slave and free, great and small!' Then I saw the beast and the kings of the earth and their armies mustered to do battle with the Rider and his army. The beast was taken prisoner, and so was the false prophet who had worked miracles in its presence and deluded those that had received the mark of the beast and worshipped its image. The two of them were thrown alive into the lake of fire with its sulphurous flames. The rest were killed by the sword which went out of the Rider's mouth; and all the birds gorged themselves on their flesh.

The dragon chained

Then I saw an angel coming down from heaven with the key of the abyss and a great chain in his hands. He seized the dragon,

p Or . . . *worship. For testimony to Jesus is the spirit that inspires prophets.*   *q Some witnesses read* spattered with blood.

that serpent of old, the Devil or Satan, and
3 chained him up for a thousand years; he
threw him into the abyss, shutting and sealing it over him, so that he might seduce the
nations no more till the thousand years were
over. After that he must be let loose for a
short while.

Christ's thousand-year reign

4 Then I saw thrones, and upon them sat those
to whom judgement was committed. I could
see the souls of those who had been beheaded
for the sake of God's word and their testimony to Jesus, those who had not worshipped the beast and its image or received
its mark on forehead or hand. These came
to life again and reigned with Christ for a
5 thousand years, though the rest of the dead
did not come to life until the thousand years
were over. This is the first resurrection.
6 Happy indeed, and one of God's own people,
is the man who shares in this first resurrection! Upon such the second death has no
claim; but they shall be priests of God and
of Christ, and shall reign with him for the
thousand years.

Final overthrow of the Devil

7 When the thousand years are over, Satan
8 will be let loose from his dungeon; and he
will come out to seduce the nations in the
four quarters of the earth and to muster
them for battle, yes, the hosts of Gog and
Magog, countless as the sands of the sea.
9 So they marched over the breadth of the
land and laid siege to the camp of God's
people and the city that he loves. But fire
came down on them from heaven and con-
10 sumed them; and the Devil, their seducer,
was flung into the lake of fire and sulphur,
where the beast and the false prophet had
been flung, there to be tormented day and
night for ever.

The Day of Judgement

11 Then I saw a great white throne, and the
One who sat upon it; from his presence earth
and heaven vanished away, and no place
12 was left for them. I could see the dead, great
and small, standing before the throne; and
books were opened. Then another book was
opened, the roll of the living. From what was
written in these books the dead were judged
13 upon the record of their deeds. The sea gave
up its dead, and Death and Hades gave up
the dead in their keeping; they were judged,
14 each man on the record of his deeds. Then
Death and Hades were flung into the lake
of fire. This lake of fire is the second death;
15 and into it were flung any whose names were
not to be found in the roll of the living.

A new heaven and a new earth

Then I saw a new heaven and a new earth, 2
for the first heaven and the first earth had
vanished, and there was no longer any sea.
I saw the holy city, new Jerusalem, coming 2
down out of heaven from God, made ready
like a bride adorned for her husband. I 3
heard a loud voice proclaiming from the
throne: 'Now at last God has his dwelling
among men! He will dwell among them and
they shall be his people, and God himself
will be with them.*r* He will wipe every tear 4
from their eyes; there shall be an end to
death, and to mourning and crying and pain;
for the old order has passed away!'
Then he who sat on the throne said, 5
'Behold! I am making all things new!' (And
he said to me, 'Write this down; for these
words are trustworthy and true. Indeed they 6
are already fulfilled.') 'I am the Alpha and
the Omega, the beginning and the end. A
draught from the water-springs of life will
be my free gift to the thirsty. All this is the 7
victor's heritage; and I will be his God and
he shall be my son. But as for the cowardly, 8
the faithless, and the vile, murderers, fornicators, sorcerers, idolaters, and liars of every
kind, their lot will be the second death, in
the lake that burns with sulphurous flames.'

The new Jerusalem

Then one of the seven angels that held the 9
seven bowls full of the seven last plagues
came and spoke to me and said, 'Come, and
I will show you the bride, the wife of the
Lamb.' So in the Spirit he carried me away 10
to a great high mountain, and showed me
the holy city of Jerusalem coming down out
of heaven from God. It shone with the glory 11
of God; it had the radiance of some price-
less jewel, like a jasper, clear as crystal. It 12
had a great high wall, with twelve gates, at
which were twelve angels; and on the gates
were inscribed the names of the twelve tribes
of Israel. There were three gates to the east, 13
three to the north, three to the south, and
three to the west. The city wall had twelve 14
foundation-stones, and on them were the
names of the twelve apostles of the Lamb.
The angel who spoke with me carried a 15
gold measuring-rod, to measure the city, its
wall, and its gates. The city was built as a 16
square, and was as wide as it was long. It
measured by his rod twelve thousand furlongs, its length and breadth and height
being equal. Its wall was one hundred and 17
forty-four cubits high, that is, by human
measurements, which the angel was using.
The wall was built of jasper, while the city 18
itself was of pure gold, bright as clear glass.
The foundations of the city wall were 19

r *Some witnesses read* God-with-them shall himself be their God (*see Isaiah 7. 14; 8. 8*).

adorned with jewels of every kind, the first of the foundation-stones being jasper, the second lapis lazuli, the third chalcedony, the fourth emerald, the fifth sardonyx, the sixth cornelian, the seventh chrysolite, the eighth beryl, the ninth topaz, the tenth chrysoprase, the eleventh turquoise, and the twelfth amethyst. The twelve gates were twelve pearls, each gate being made from a single pearl. The streets of the city were of pure gold, like translucent glass.

Light and life

I saw no temple in the city; for its temple was the sovereign Lord God and the Lamb. And the city had no need of sun or moon to shine upon it; for the glory of God gave it light, and its lamp was the Lamb. By its light shall the nations walk, and the kings of the earth shall bring into it all their splendour. The gates of the city shall never be shut by day —and there will be no night. The wealth and splendour of the nations shall be brought into it; but nothing unclean shall enter, nor anyone whose ways are false or foul, but only those who are inscribed in the Lamb's roll of the living.

Then he showed me the river of the water of life, sparkling like crystal, flowing from the throne of God and of the Lamb down the middle of the city's street. On either side of the river stood a tree of life, which yields twelve crops of fruit, one for each month of the year; the leaves of the trees serve for the healing of the nations. Every accursed thing shall disappear. The throne of God and of the Lamb will be there, and his servants shall worship him; they shall see him face to face, and bear his name on their foreheads. There shall be no more night, nor will they need the light of lamp or sun, for the Lord God will give them light; and they shall reign for evermore.

Jesus promises to return

Then he said to me, 'These words are trustworthy and true. The Lord God who inspires the prophets has sent his angel to show his servants what must shortly happen. And, remember, I am coming soon!'

Happy is the man who heeds the words of prophecy contained in this book! It is I, 8 John, who heard and saw these things. And when I had heard and seen them, I fell in worship at the feet of the angel who had shown them to me. But he said to me, 'No, 9 not that! I am but a fellow-servant with you and your brothers the prophets and those who heed the words of this book. It is God you must worship.' Then he told me, 'Do 10 not seal up the words of prophecy in this book, for the hour of fulfilment is near. Meanwhile, let the evil-doer go on doing 11 evil and the filthy-minded wallow in his filth, but let the good man persevere in his goodness and the dedicated man be true to his dedication.'

'Yes, I am coming soon, and bringing my 12 recompense with me, to requite everyone according to his deeds! I am the Alpha and 13 the Omega, the first and the last, the beginning and the end.'

Happy are those who wash their robes 14 clean! They will have the right to the tree of life and will enter by the gates of the city. Outside are dogs, sorcerers and fornicators, 15 murderers and idolaters, and all who love and practise deceit.

'I, Jesus, have sent my angel to you with 16 this testimony for the churches. I am the scion and offspring of David, the bright star of dawn.'

'Come!' say the Spirit and the bride. 17 'Come!' let each hearer reply.

Come forward, you who are thirsty; accept the water of life, a free gift to all who desire it.

A final word of warning

For my part, I give this warning to everyone 18 who is listening to the words of prophecy in this book: should anyone add to them, God will add to him the plagues described in this book; should anyone take away from 19 the words in this book of prophecy, God will take away from him his share in the tree of life and the Holy City, described in this book.

He who gives this testimony speaks: 'Yes, 20 I am coming soon!'

Amen. Come, Lord Jesus!

The grace of the Lord Jesus be with 21 you all.[s]

---

s Some witnesses read with all; others read with all God's people; others read with God's people; some add Amen.

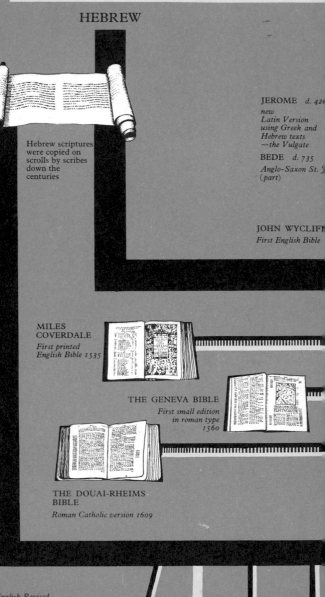

HOW OUR BIBLE

TRANSLATIONS OF THE BIBLE

3rd CENTURY B.C.
Greek

2nd CENTURY A.D.
Latin
Syriac

3rd CENTURY
Coptic

4th CENTURY
Ethiopic
Gothic
Georgian

5th CENTURY
Armenian

6th CENTURY
Nubian

7th CENTURY
Arabic

8th CENTURY
Anglo-Saxon

9th CENTURY
German
Slavonic
Frankish

12th CENTURY
French

13th CENTURY
Spanish
Italian
Dutch
Polish
Icelandic

14th CENTURY
English
Persian
Czech
Danish

15th CENTURY
THE INVENTION OF PRINTING
in Europe increased book
production, and the Renaissance
stimulated further translation.
Gutenberg Bible printed *c.* 1455

16th CENTURY
The roman letter form, developed
as a type-face, gradually replaced
the use of 'black-letter' and made
it possible to produce books
smaller in size yet easier to read.
After years of opposition the
Bible in English was set up in
churches to the joy of the people

19th CENTURY
The Industrial Revolution enabled
book production to meet the
advance of popular education.
1804 The British and Foreign
Bible Society was founded to
encourage the wider circulation
of the Scriptures. During this
century of the pioneer
missionaries translations
increased to more than 500

20th CENTURY
Through the Bible Societies
Scriptures now go out into all
the world in over 1400 languages

HEBREW

Hebrew scriptures
were copied on
scrolls by scribes
down the
centuries

JEROME *d. 420*
new
Latin Version
using Greek and
Hebrew texts
—the Vulgate

BEDE *d. 735*
Anglo-Saxon St. J
(part)

JOHN WYCLIF
First English Bible

MILES
COVERDALE
First printed
English Bible 1535

THE GENEVA BIBLE
First small edition
in roman type
1560

THE DOUAI-RHEIMS
BIBLE
Roman Catholic version 1609

English Revised
Version 1881-5

Revised Standard
Version 1952

Jerusalem Bible 1956

MODERN TRANSLATIONS

Holy
Bible